Major Characters in American Fiction

General Editors: Jack Salzman and
Pamela Wilkinson

with Lucile Bruce, Janet Dean, Cybele Merrick,
and the staff of the
Columbia University Center for
American Culture Studies

A HENRY HOLT REFERENCE BOOK

Henry Holt and Company
New York

A Henry Holt Reference Book
Henry Holt and Company, Inc.
Publishers since 1866
115 West 18th Street
New York, New York 10011

Library of Congress Cataloging-in-Publication Data
Major characters in American fiction / general editors, Jack Salzman
and Pamela Wilkinson; with Lucile Bruce, Janet Dean, Cybele
Merrick, and the staff of the Columbia University Center for
American Culture Studies.
        p.   cm.
Includes index.
1. Characters and characteristics in literature—Dictionaries.
    2. American fiction—Dictionaries.   I. Salzman, Jack.
            II. Wilkinson, Pamela.
    PS374.C43M35   1994
    813.009′27′03—dc20   94-11460
                                    CIP

ISBN 0-8050-3060-3

First Edition—1994

Designed by Paula R. Szafranski

Printed in the United States of America
All first editions are printed on acid-free paper.∞
    1   3   5   7   9   10   8   6   4   2

Contents

Introduction

In 1988 Jason Schulman, then head of a book-packaging company called Blue Cliff Editions, approached me with an idea for a reference work. He knew that the Center for American Culture Studies at Columbia University had produced a number of important reference works in the area of American cultural studies, and he was interested in having us undertake yet another work. The idea was simple and intriguing: we would commission a number of scholars, from Columbia and elsewhere, to write "biographies" of the most important characters in American fiction. Like many simple—and intriguing—ideas, this one proved to be more complex than it first appeared.

Two obvious questions needed to be answered at the outset: Who were the most important characters in American fiction? Could a scholar who had invested a part of her or his academic career in interpreting a writer's life and art write character biographies that would avoid the critical morass that is such a fundamental part of academic writing? As we struggled with these questions, trying to determine what kind of book would be of greatest general use, it became clear that the volume should not focus exclusively—as originally suggested—on characters like Captain Ahab, Hester Prynne, Jay Gatsby, and Holden Caulfield; we were convinced that a book that centered only on such well-known characters, given their familiarity to scholars and general readers alike, would be of limited value. Our decision, then, was to think of those books and characters who were of most interest to us—figures in American literature who had significance for the collective staff of the Center for American Culture studies.

As a consequence, this volume includes entries on not only the most canonized of figures, but a large number of characters who may never make their way into the canon or school curriculum. It also includes more fictional characters imagined by so called minority writers than does any volume we know.

Our concern throughout has been selecting the important characters, not particular works of fiction, which helps explain why, for example, works such as Herman Melville's *Confidence Man,* Gilbert Sorentino's *Steelwork,* Paul Goodman's *Empire City,* and William March's *Company K* are not represented here; the structures of these novels simply do not result in the development of a character whose life might readily be retold. In cases where characters appear in more than one work, for example, in the novels of William Faulkner, J. D. Salinger, and Louise Erdrich, we had to make choices about how to represent those characters in the most cogent and comprehensible fashion.

Choices, of course, are endemic to a work like this one, and are always subject to disagreement. We hardly expect unanimous agreement on the selection of characters included in this volume; nor do we expect everyone to concur with our decision not to include more characters from works of short fiction than we have. Conspicuously absent from this book are characters from American plays, which we refrained from including because they are numerous and various enough to merit a volume of their own.

Less debatable, I hope, will be my resolve to have the entire work completed by the staff of the Center for American Culture Studies. I wanted the character biographies

Introduction

to be as objective and enjoyable to read as they possibly could be; this volume, after all, is meant to serve as both reference book and a work to be browsed through for pleasure. I could think of no better way of accomplishing this than to ask the staff of the Center to take on the project. As always, they have done a remarkable job. I am grateful to all the contributors, and especially to those who share title page credit with me. In every sense imaginable, this volume could not have been completed without them; this is even more so in the case of my coeditor, Pamela Wilkinson.

Some people at Columbia deserve recognition for their support both of the Center and of this project: Joy Hayton, Martin Meisel, Victoria Prince, and Joe Ridgely have always been most helpful, as was the late Ward Dennis. My thanks for their many kindnesses over the years. At Henry Holt, Ken Wright and Mary Kay Linge have been patient and encouraging. Above all, however, I want to offer special thanks to Rebecca and Phoebe, both of whom came into being as this volume was struggling to have its own birth. They have brought with them a light and joy that I had not imagined possible.

Jack Salzman

A

Abel. *House Made of Dawn.* N. Scott Momaday. 1966.

Abel, a Navajo-Tanoan, is a product of the Native American diaspora. In his effort to forge an identity, he must grapple with the conflicting pressures of his heritage and his modern needs and desires.

The novel opens with a short prologue in which the quiet yet resilient Abel, smeared with ceremonial ashes, participates in a traditional race to promote better hunting and a more fruitful harvest, a race that his grandfather, Francisco, competed in and won many years ago. The narrative then moves back seven years to the Tanoan reservation, Walatowa Cañon de San Diego, where a drunk Abel returns after World War II.

At the behest of the local Christian clergyman, Father Olguin, Abel gets employment chopping wood for Angela Grace Saint John, an attractive, affluent blonde who is renting a local house while her husband remains in Los Angeles. Although Abel remains dispassionate toward her, Angela is attracted by his vitality and identifies him with the mythic images of the bear and badger. Abel is plagued by his inarticulateness and cannot reconcile himself to the traditions of his people. He is unable to compose his own creation story, an exercise that would signify his ability to fully embrace his Navajo-Tanoan heritage.

Several days before Abel and Angela consummate their relationship, the reservation celebrates the annual Feast of Santiago, a christianized native holiday. The celebration includes a competition in which the winner is given license to flay someone of his own choosing. This year the victor, an albino Tanoan named Juan Reyes Fragua, selects Abel. Four days later, Abel, feeling defeated and ostracized after the flogging, stabs the albino to death when the two meet in a bar. He shows little remorse over the incident.

After Abel serves a seven-year prison sentence for murder, a relocation officer places him in Los Angeles where he works in a factory with his Navajo roommate, Ben Benally. Accompanied by Benally, Abel attends the Holiness Pan-Indian Rescue Mission where the Pastor and Priest of the Sun, John "Big Bluff" Tosamah, presides. Basing his sermon on the Book of John, Tosamah wishes to resurrect the sanctity of language that he believes contemporary Anglo culture has undermined, and in his sermon he encourages his Native American congregation to take pride in their heritage. Soon after, however, Tosamah derides Abel for his failure to adjust to present-day conditions.

Indeed, Abel has fallen into a pattern of binge drinking that causes him to lose his job. He is also harassed by Martinez, a Chicano policeman who one day beats him

until he requires hospitalization. While in the hospital, Abel is visited by Angela who tells him about her young son Peter. With an intuitive understanding of native lore, Angela says she has frequently told Peter the story of a young Indian brave, born of a bear and a maiden, who became a great leader and saved his people. She always thought of Abel when she told this story, and her revelation infuses Abel with a restored sense of cultural identity.

Following his hospital stay, Abel returns to the reservation in time to carry on the tradition of his dying grandfather. The novel concludes with the same scene with which it began: Abel, running in a ceremonial race against the powers of evil and death, chants the opening words of the Navajo creation story, "House made of dawn."

Ackerman, Noah. *The Young Lions.* Irwin Shaw. 1948.

Noah Ackerman had never paid much attention to his Jewish heritage because of his father's hypocrisy. Until his dying day, Noah's father fervently espoused all the Hebraic beliefs while at the same time consistently breaking all their laws in his deeds. An alcoholic, he beat his wife and left Noah, his only son, destitute.

After moving to New York City, Noah meets Roger, the first friend he has ever had. Roger finds him a job at the public library and even offers to share his apartment with him. For the first time in his life, Noah feels he has found happiness, but then he confesses to Roger that he wishes he had a girlfriend. Roger immediately throws a party at their apartment, where Noah meets a young Brooklyn woman named Hope Plowman. The two fall in love, and Noah spends many long nights on the subway commuting between Hope's apartment in Brooklyn and his own on the Upper West Side.

Noah and Hope marry after a long-drawn-out battle with Hope's parents, who disapprove of Noah's religion. Soon afterward, America enters World War II. After initially failing his physical because of scars on his lung tissue, Noah, swept up in the national enthusiasm and eager to join, passes a second physical and enlists in the infantry.

In basic training in Florida, Noah is brutally victimized by the other soldiers, and a sadistic drill sergeant harasses him to the point of physical and mental breakdown. When ten dollars is stolen from his footlocker, he posts a sign demanding to know the culprit so that he may exact satisfaction. The ten largest men in the division not only confess but taunt him to do something about it, and Noah arranges to fight them one at a time over a period of five weeks.

After almost constant hospitalization and dozens of near permanent injuries, Noah is able to win his last fight. When the other soldiers still fail to show him the respect he has earned, he goes AWOL. He is captured, and while no charges are pressed because of the extenuating circumstances of his desertion, he is forced to return to his old platoon. Much to Noah's surprise, the men who once bullied him now show admiration for his strength and courage.

Noah becomes a leader of his company after they arrive in Europe for combat. When they are cut off and surrounded by Nazis in an abandoned farmhouse, he guides them to safety. His company is also the first to discover a deserted Nazi concentration camp. Overwhelmed by the horrors he sees, Noah gets permission from his commanding officer to hold Jewish services in remembrance of the victims of the camp, despite numerous protests from his own company. He is shot by CHRISTIAN DIESTL, a lingering German sniper, and dies attempting to reconcile his religious beliefs.

Adams, Alice. *Alice Adams*. Booth Tarkington. 1921.

Alice Adams, twenty-two years old and a "right pretty girl," is outwardly confident and composed. Nevertheless, she continually struggles against the rising fear that life has already passed her by and that, thwarted in her attempts to make a happy and successful marriage, she will be forced to become a working girl. Throughout the novel, the specter of Frincke's Business College haunts Alice, symbolizing for her the potential failure of all her aspirations.

Alice first appears, characteristically, in front of a mirror where she is practicing the repertory of gestures and expressions that she believes give her a memorable vivacity. This affectation is Alice's response to her greatest regret of all—that her parents are not wealthy and respected members of local society. Although Alice genuinely loves her father and chastises her mother for criticizing Mr. Adams's ability to provide for his family, she believes that it is her father's disregard for money and status that has made her life so different from how she had imagined it would be. For although Alice had an early success with the young men of the town, she has recently been condemned as "pushy" by the local matrons and their daughters, who now respond to her with polite lack of interest. Following the example of their women, the local men, too, have condemned Alice to a life that she sees as crippled by the misfortune of her birth. Yet Alice is nothing if not resourceful, and, repeatedly spurned at the few dances to which she is invited, she falls back on the courageous and pitiful act she has often rehearsed to prevent others from seeing her rejection and her disappointment.

Alice is potentially rescued from a bitter and disap-

pointed middle age by the arrival in town of Arthur Russell, a charming and eligible veteran. She suddenly finds everything she has longed for within her grasp and sets out to make herself as attractive as possible to this innocent spectator. As their relationship progresses, Alice falls in love with Russell and for the first time begins to question her need to deceive and impress by hiding her real self beneath a veil of artifice and affectation. The more intimate she and Russell become, the more she becomes helplessly caught up in the lies she has told. She feels incapable of establishing the truth and terrified that someone will reveal her dishonesty.

Yet Alice is finally forced to confront her lies and acknowledge the family she has desperately tried to conceal. Russell learns that Alice's brother Walter has absconded with money stolen from his employer and that Alice's father is not the tycoon she has described. Faced with Russell's sudden detachment, Alice determines to stand by her family, finally realizing that this bond is more important than the social status she has been seeking. As the novel ends, Alice stands in front of Frincke's Business College, but this time, far from being shaken by the life it symbolizes, she resolutely accepts that this is the way she must take.

Adams, Nick. *In Our Time*. Ernest Hemingway. 1925.

Nick Adams is the quiet man whose life experiences are fragmentarily traced in this collection of short stories. The stories, interspersed with short, raw portrayals of battle and destruction, describe the traumatic, often violent episodes that shape Nick from his boyhood in the Michigan woods to his return from World War I. Nick is wounded in the war, but it is his psychological wounds from the war and from violent events throughout his life that seem to need the most healing.

"Indian Camp," in which Nick is a boy, relates one such scarring incident. His father, a country doctor, takes Nick with him when he goes to the neighboring Indian camp to deliver a breech baby. The labor has been long and painful, and the mother screams in agony when Nick and his father enter her shanty. On the bunk above lies her husband, who has injured his foot. Nick's father operates on the woman without using anesthetic, all the while explaining to Nick what he is doing so that his son will learn from the experience. But when they complete the procedure, they see that the father, perhaps unable to bear the sound of his wife's cries, has cut his own throat.

In "The Battler," Nick, now a young man, meets a prizefighter-turned-hobo whose mangled face and missing ear at first seem shocking. The hobo and his traveling companion, a black man named Bugs, befriend Nick and offer him a share of their makeshift meal. But while they are eating the fighter suddenly becomes antagonistic toward the young man and dares him to fight. As the man approaches Nick menacingly, Bugs knocks his friend unconscious. Afterward, he explains to a bewildered Nick that he must do this whenever his friend, made crazy by too many beatings, becomes violent.

In "The End of Something," Nick, feeling "as though everything was gone to hell inside," sullenly ends his relationship with his fiancée while they are on a fishing trip together. A companion story, "The Three-Day Blow," describes Nick's feelings of sorrow and loneliness as he is getting drunk with a friend shortly thereafter. His friend assures him that ending the affair was all for the best, but Nick can't help feeling that "it was all gone now." "Cross-Country Snow" finds Nick in happier times, skiing with a friend in Switzerland and then drinking wine in an alpine inn. But even as he cherishes this time in his life, he also realizes that it is passing, that no matter how they might wish to relive this experience, "there isn't any good in promising."

Finally, in "Big Two-Hearted River," Nick goes on a solitary fishing trip that seems intended to help him begin to heal his inner wounds. After a ride in the baggage car of a passing train, Nick finds himself at the remains of a burned-out and deserted town where even the grasshoppers have grown black with soot. He hikes away from the town along the river, feeling satisfied as he crosses the fire line and begins to wade through ankle-high ferns.

When he stops to make camp, Nick takes quiet pleasure in pitching his tent, building a fire, and opening cans to make a meal. Making coffee the way his friend Hopkins insisted it must be made, Nick momentarily fears the memories that begin to return. But he knows he is tired and can "choke it."

The next morning Nick methodically catches grasshoppers and packs a lunch to take fishing. He catches two large trout, sometimes becoming weak with the excitement of the chase, and cleans them by the river. He considers wading into the swamp where he knows he can hook big trout, but he feels fishing there in the shadows would somehow be "tragic." Instead, he heads back to his camp, satisfied and at peace with himself, knowing that "there were plenty of days coming when he could fish the swamp."

Adare, Karl. *The Beet Queen.* Louise Erdrich. 1987.

Karl Adare leads a relatively peaceful life until the age of fourteen. His mother, Adelaide, is the mistress of a wealthy Kansas farmer, Mr. Ober, who is Karl's father. Mr. Ober provides everything for them, but when he dies in a grain-loading accident, Adelaide and her two children must leave their home, which was in the father's name. Money runs out quickly, and when a third child is born, Adelaide becomes desperate. The day they are evicted from their apartment, Karl persuades Adelaide to take them to the town fair, called The Orphans' Picnic. There, "The Great Omar, Aeronaught Extraordinaire," is performing stunts and giving airplane rides. Adelaide gets into the

plane and flies off with Omar, leaving her three children behind forever. A mysterious man takes the newborn boy, leaving Karl and his sister, MARY ADARE, alone.

Karl and Mary take a train to Argus, North Dakota, where Adelaide's sister, Fritzie, runs a butcher shop. They leap from the train together and walk through the town, but Karl stops to smell a blossoming tree. A vicious dog leaps out at him, and both children panic and run. Mary runs toward Aunt Fritzie's, but Karl leaps back onto the boxcar. Starving and confused, Karl is comforted by a man named Giles. They lie sleeping in the boxcar; when Karl turns toward him, Giles responds sexually. Giles refuses to reciprocate, however, when Karl says, "I love you," and Karl leaps out into the night.

Injured by his fall from the boxcar, Karl lies helpless until a silent Indian woman named FLEUR PILLAGER, an itinerant peddler, rescues him. After curing him of pneumonia and carrying him on her cart for some distance, Fleur leaves Karl with the nuns at a church. Eventually they send him to a seminary, where he studies sacred texts and also has encounters with "thin hard hoboes who had slept in the bushes."

After graduating from the seminary, Karl embarks on his hapless career as a traveling salesman while his varied sexual life flourishes. At a farmers' convention in Minneapolis, he seduces Wallace Pfef, a shy virgin. Afterward, a strange inspiration causes Karl to bounce on the bed, attempting a somersault. He falls off the bed, injuring his back, and spends a period in the hospital with Wallace as his only visitor. In his pain he admits to Wallace that his sister lives in Argus, which is also Wallace's town.

Once he recovers, Karl goes to Argus and spends two weeks living with Wallace. He goes to Fritzie's butcher shop looking for his sister but instead finds CELESTINE JAMES, Mary's closest friend. Without a word to Wallace, Karl moves in with Celestine, and they have a passionate but short-lived affair. Celestine grows tired of Karl quickly and throws him out. After Celestine bears Karl's child, WALLACETTE DARLENE "DOT" ADARE, she agrees to marry Karl but makes him promise to leave them alone.

When Dot turns fourteen, Celestine agrees to a meeting of the three of them. Although Dot is openly hostile toward Karl and hits him on the head with a can of oysters, he remembers their meeting as a "moment of sweetness." Later in his life, during a period of despair and indecision, Karl thinks of this moment. He immediately drives to Argus to find Wallace and Dot; in his absence they have developed an awkward relationship, just like an average father and daughter.

Adare, Mary. *The Beet Queen.* Louise Erdrich. 1987.

Mary Adare is a stubborn, plain girl who becomes the manager of a butcher shop. Although Mary is neither charming nor attractive, her determination and practical nature give her a certain advantage over her seductive brother, KARL ADARE, and her stylish cousin, Sita Kozka. After resolving never to seek romance, Mary settles down to running the butcher shop and, to a great extent, the private life of her friend, CELESTINE JAMES.

Mary insists on her ordinariness, but her childhood is full of extraordinary events. Her mother Adelaide is the mistress of a wealthy Kansas farmer, Mr. Ober, who leaves them both destitute when he dies. Out of desperation, Adelaide flies off with "The Great Omar, Aeronaught Extraordinaire," at a town fair. Mary is eventually left holding Adelaide's newborn boy and unwillingly gives him up to a man who never brings him back. Mary and Karl take a train to Argus, North Dakota, where Adelaide's sister Fritzie runs a butcher shop. When they arrive in Argus, Karl pauses to smell a blossoming tree and is attacked by a dog. Karl leaps back onto the boxcar, and Mary finds her way to Fritzie's shop alone.

Fritzie and her husband Pete welcome Mary but immediately start a rivalry between her and their daughter Sita. They put Mary in Sita's room, at first relegating Sita to a cot, and give Mary half of Sita's dresses. The competition between them intensifies when Mary "steals" Sita's best friend Celestine. Mary also usurps Sita's position as most-sought-after girl at their Catholic school, St. Catherine's. After the novelty of her newness wears off, Mary inadvertently performs a miracle. On a freezing winter day she goes down a slide headfirst and smashes her face on a sheet of ice covering the playground. The ice cracks into a marvelous form: the face of Christ, perfectly etched on the surface. Mary becomes a heroine for several months, and the incident is "included in catechism textbooks throughout the Midwest as the Manifestation at Argus." Mary is essentially unmoved by the miracle and never reveals the fact that she recognizes the face as that of her brother Karl.

Although she is skeptical about the miracle, Mary's attitudes become increasingly superstitious and mystical as she grows older. She experiments with various cards and magical bones in an effort to divine the future. Mary predicts a romantic future for Celestine's brother Russell in a single, brief attempt at seduction, but he is unimpressed and resists her suggestion. Mary has surprising luck, however, with winning the rather hard heart of WALLACETTE DARLENE "DOT" ADARE, Celestine's daughter with Karl.

Just as she had enraged Sita by stealing Celestine, Mary infuriates Celestine by becoming her daughter's closest confidante. Mary demands inclusion in every aspect of Dot's life, while Celestine and Wallace Pfef, a sort of godfather, make obvious efforts to get her out of the way. As Dot grows older, she rejects the attentions of all three. But in spite of Dot's rejection, Mary, like the others, persists in making clumsy gestures of affection toward her, battling to be first in her heart.

Adare, Wallacette Darlene "Dot." *Love Medicine; The Beet Queen.* Louise Erdrich. 1984; 1987.

Wallacette Darlene Adare, nicknamed "Dot," receives constant attention not only from her mother, CELESTINE JAMES, but also from her aunt, MARY ADARE, and from Wallace Pfef, who was present at her unusual birth.

Celestine gave birth to Wallacette on Wallace's couch, and she named the baby after him. Soon afterward the baby's aunt Mary nicknames her Dot, and only Wallace continues to call the baby by her formal name.

Known as a demanding baby, Dot grows fat and greedy, and by the time she enters first grade, she is as big as most children twice her age. Dot dominates the class, making more enemies than friends. One boy whom Dot likes has the misfortune of being in a Christmas play with her. When he refuses to cooperate with her during the performance, she hits him on the head, ruining his costume and knocking him flat.

Dot finds an ally in her aunt Mary, who resembles her in many unfortunate ways. When Dot has a disagreement with her teacher, Mrs. Shumway, Mary promptly drives to school and intimidates the teacher into giving Dot free reign. Children are afraid to come to Dot's birthday parties because Mary directs their games with militaristic enthusiasm. When Mary goes to live with Celestine while her store is being renovated, she stays awake with Dot, whispering and laughing. Celestine is infuriated by her constant intrusions and goes to great lengths to exclude Mary from Dot's life.

Even without Mary, Dot has no lack of adoring adults. Her father Karl sends her presents, although she hit him on the head with a can of oysters at one of their first meetings. Wallace Pfef organizes the greatest possible demonstration of his love for Dot. The Beet Festival is ostensibly a celebration of the success of the new sugar beet industry in Argus, for which Wallace is largely responsible. Wallace's real intention, however, is to give Dot the pleasure of being crowned Beet Queen. He rigs the election to be sure that Dot will have this boost to her ego, which Wallace sees as essential to her well-being.

Newly decked out in boots, a tight miniskirt, and thick makeup, Dot feels ridiculous wearing such formal attire on the day of the festival. News that the election was secretly rigged reaches her ears while she is riding on the float toward the platform where she is to be crowned. A short while later she finds Wallace perched above a vat of water, the target for dunking in a carnival game. Dot, an excellent athlete with expert aim, expresses her anger by successfully pitching him into the vat. Then, just as she is about to be crowned, she bolts across the field and climbs into a skywriting plane. She asks the pilot's help in a "publicity stunt" and has him write all ten letters of her "whole long awful name" above the festival-goers' heads. By the time she returns, the grandstand has been vacated and the area emptied of people. Only her mother remains waiting, radiant with maternal love. At the close of *The Beet Queen*, Dot is lying at home in bed, listening to sounds of an approaching storm; she imagines her mother lying, as she is, awake and expectant, in the next room.

Dot herself becomes a mother in *Love Medicine*. Although she and the kind outlaw Gerry Nanapush have a baby, Shawn, Dot has no compunction about threatening the life of Albertine Kashpaw, who she wrongly suspects of flirting with Gerry. Still, Dot resigns herself to raising Shawn alone and seeing Gerry only when he can either escape from jail or make his way back into the country.

Addams, Frankie. *The Member of the Wedding.* Carson McCullers. 1950.

In the summer of her twelfth year, Frankie Addams hovers between childhood and adulthood and feels suspended, isolated, and afraid. Her mother died long ago in childbirth, her father no longer allows her to sleep in his bed at night, and her tomcat has run away; moreover, Frankie refuses to play with Barney MacKean because he has done "something strange" with her, and she longs for her best friend who has moved away.

Excluded from the other girls' clubs and cliques, Frankie feels that she is not a member of anything. She spends a great deal of time sitting at the kitchen table, whiling away the long, hot hours with her cousin John Henry and the family housekeeper, Berenice Sadie Brown. She sometimes feels like crying for no apparent reason; at other times, to relieve the tightness in her chest, the tomboyish Frankie behaves frantically and compulsively and ends up feeling silly and awkward.

When her brother Jarvis and his fiancée visit the Addamses prior to their marriage, Frankie, as Berenice puts it, falls in love with the idea of a wedding. Enchanted by the young couple, whom she sees as "the we of me," she decides to live with them after their wedding. Ignoring Berenice's warnings, she insists that she and the newlyweds will live lives of constant adventure and travel.

On the day before the wedding, as a gesture of farewell to her town, Frankie wanders about "telling the wedding" to a series of strangers with whom she now feels a strong connection. That afternoon she, Berenice, and John Henry discuss lost love and the separateness of people until they are so sad that they begin to cry. Later that afternoon Frankie has a date with a red-haired soldier; when he makes a pass at her, she knocks him unconscious.

The next day, following the wedding, Frankie becomes hysterical when the newlyweds leave without her. Inconsolable, she decides to run away, but after hours of wandering about in the dark, she is so overcome by loneliness that she yields passively when apprehended and taken home.

When we last see Frankie, she is thirteen, and everything has changed. John Henry has died suddenly of meningitis, the family home has been sold, the Addamses are moving in with relatives, and Berenice has given notice. Frankie now reads poetry and conducts tea parties with her new best friend, and she is excited about moving. John Henry's death is like a dream to her, and she does not seem to notice that in the process of growing up she has left Berenice behind.

Adverse, Anthony. *Anthony Adverse.* Hervey Allen. 1933.

Anthony Adverse, an orphan striving to make his way in the world, is the young hero of this historical romance. With alternating success and failure, Anthony works to achieve financial success, domestic bliss, and Christian self-knowledge amid a tangled panorama of mercantile capitalism, bureaucratic machination, Catholic ritual, and European imperialism.

Anthony is the son of a dashing Irishman in the French royal guard and the adulterous wife of Don Luis, an evil nobleman with French, Tuscan, and Spanish titles. Don Luis, whose acute gout has kept him from consummating his marriage with his child bride, is under no illusions about the paternity of young Anthony. A few hours after birth, Anthony is left at a Tuscan convent. His father has died in a duel with Don Luis, and his mother has been left to die in the Alps. Raised a virtual prisoner in the Italian convent, Anthony finally runs away and follows a pretty girl named Florence to nearby Livorno. Florence's father persuades the convent officials to apprentice Anthony to a trade, and he remains in this Tuscan port.

Miraculously and without his knowledge, Anthony is working at the trading house of his own grandfather, a nostalgic Scotsman who immediately recognizes the resemblance between the boy and the young bride Don Luis led away. Anthony matures and falls in love with a pretty girl named Angela. The Scotsman names the oblivious Anthony his heir.

When Napoleon invades Italy, all the Scotsman's business ceases, and Anthony sails to Cuba to collect a few last substantial debts for his benefactor. The debts are with a large slave-trading concern, and Anthony enters into a complex scheme to both collect his grandfather's debt and secure power for one of Cuba's ruling factions. He meets an attractive young woman named Dolores and spends the next three years as a slave kidnapper in Africa. Anthony collects and exports slaves to Cuban markets, and he makes millions. His nefarious dealings end, however, when he gets malaria and a priest who has befriended him is crucified by a neighboring witch doctor.

Abandoning Africa, Anthony heads to Italy and then Paris, where he becomes involved in a complicated scheme to import Mexican currency into war-torn Europe. Anthony next goes to New Orleans to engineer the American side of the Parisian scheme, and he becomes even richer. He builds his own slave-worked plantation and discovers and marries the long-lost Florence, who doesn't mind that he has a son in Europe by Angela. When Florence and his young daughter die in a fire, Anthony leaves New Orleans and heads into the American wilderness. He lives alone with his faithful African hound until he is captured by Indians who are then captured by Spain's colonial government in the American Southwest. In Santa Fe he meets Don Luis, who recognizes Anthony and, before dying of a heart attack at the shock, sentences him to prison in Mexico.

On the march to Mexico and while in prison, Anthony gradually comes to realize his Christian potential. He cares for lepers, acquires a saintly aura, and then accidentally meets Dolores again when she is on a philanthropic visit to the prison. Anthony and Dolores eventually have two daughters and live happily on the remote recesses of her hacienda until Anthony accidentally kills himself while cutting down a tree.

Ah Sing, Wittman. *Tripmaster Monkey: His Fake Book.* Maxine Hong Kingston. 1987.

Wittman Ah Sing, a young Chinese-American, has lived since his graduation from Berkeley in a dingy apartment in San Francisco and considers suicide daily. Possessing far more imagination than is required for his job as a salesman in a department store, Wittman spends his nights writing Beat-influenced poetry and surrealistic plays. When he is fired from his job, he sets off on an odyssey seeking kindred spirits to help him produce his epic masterpiece, *A Pear Garden in the West.*

When the novel begins, Wittman is working in a toy department well stocked with plastic guns. Protesting the Vietnam War, he tries to dissuade mothers from buying war toys and games for their children. Wittman's supervisor interrupts him and sends him downstairs to the stockroom, where he discovers a scruffy man hiding, relaxing, and smoking a joint. The man gives him spiritual counsel and identifies himself as a former Yale Younger Poet. Later in the afternoon Wittman accompanies his supervisor to a Mattel Toy conference where retailers hear the news about the company and watch films on the latest toys. The shameless stupidity of this gathering eliminates the last remnants of Wittman's patience with his job. When he returns to the store, he arranges the dolls in obscene positions, resulting in his termination.

Released from his job and feeling "a kind of bad freedom," Wittman takes a bus to Oakland for a party. On the way, a Chinese-American girl, Judy Louis, tries to engage the uncooperative Wittman in conversation. While she innocently discusses the social life of Japanese- and Chinese-Americans, he notices that she has suddenly been transformed into a blue boar with impressive tusks.

Wittman arrives at the home of Sunny and Lance Ka-

miyama, old friends from Berkeley who were recently married. The high point of the party for Wittman is an impromptu poetry recitation by a girl who introduces herself afterward as Tana De Weese. Wittman dramatically whispers his appreciation into her ear, then disappears mysteriously. Wittman later acts out a portion of his play for the last remaining guests, and then Tana takes him home. When he agrees that they will not be bound to each other, Tana and Wittman make love.

The next day they wander through the city and meet Gabe, a fellow draft protester and self-proclaimed minister, who promptly performs a marriage ceremony for them. Wittman then takes Tana to meet his mother, Ruby Long Legs, and his numerous aunts, all of whom were show girls. He discovers that his parents have abandoned his grandmother PoPo and decides to find her.

After spending the following day at the unemployment agency, Wittman searches through the city and conveniently bumps into an "old fut," who turns out to be PoPo's new husband. The old man is affiliated with the Family Association and promises to lend Wittman their hall so that he can produce his play. Wittman immediately calls everyone he has met and offers them parts in *A Pear Garden in the West.* Everyone accepts.

Wittman closes his extravagant epic with a long, improvised monologue criticizing American culture, and particularly American racism. After the performances, the players and the audience participate in a lavish wedding celebration for Tana and Wittman. By putting on the play, Wittman draws together the peculiar characters he has met in the course of the novel and fulfills his promises to them.

Ahab, Captain. *Moby Dick; or, The Whale.* Herman Melville. 1851.

Captain Ahab is the mad, monomaniacal antihero of this nineteenth-century epic of American whaling. A man of exceptional strength, intelligence, and feeling, Ahab is nevertheless consumed by his desire for vengeance. In bending his charismatic energies to a single, irrational purpose—the killing of Moby Dick, the fabled white whale—he destroys himself, his ship, the *Pequod,* and her crew.

Ahab, whose fearful reputation precedes him, remains in his cabin until the ship is well out to sea. When he finally steps forth, he presents a formidable appearance, with his craggy features, his stricken but indomitable countenance, and his ivory leg. An ugly white scar runs from the middle of his brow, down his neck, and (it is rumored) the length of his entire body. Assembling the men on the quarterdeck, he delivers a stirring speech about the white whale and nails a gold doubloon—the prize for the first sailor to sight him—to the mast. By the time he is finished, Ahab has exacted from each crew member a pledge to hunt down and kill Moby Dick.

As the *Pequod* continues on her ill-fated way, ISHMAEL,

the novel's narrator, describes the transformation that took place in Ahab during his previous voyage when, with a stroke of his sicklelike jaw, Moby Dick ripped off his leg. As he lay in a feverish delirium, Ahab's "torn body and gashed soul bled into one another; and so interfusing, made him mad." He emerged from his cabin several months later, an outwardly calm yet inwardly demented man.

The extent of Ahab's obsession with Moby Dick becomes startlingly apparent when the *Pequod* sights her first whale and prepares for the hunt. Five Asian men who have been hiding in the hold leap onto the deck. They are the crew of Ahab's personal whaleboat, brought aboard for the sole purpose of killing Moby Dick. Though he rarely speaks, it soon becomes clear that their turbaned leader, Fedallah, has a strange, symbiotic hold on Ahab; during the long nights he often sits silently regarding the old man as he restlessly paces the deck.

The closer Ahab draws to his quarry, the blinder he becomes to the ill omens that thrust themselves into the *Pequod*'s path. During a terrible thunderstorm, the ship's masts catch fire and the quadrant breaks; but Ahab continues undeterred, flaunting his pride, cursing the gods, and, in an especially maniacal moment, baptizing his harpoon *in nomine diaboli*—in the name of the devil.

Just before Ahab sights Moby Dick, Fedallah prophesies death for them both: "I shall go before thee thy pilot," he says, though "hemp alone can kill thee." Ahab misinterprets the latter as a testament to his own unshakable strength and presses on.

At the same time, and despite the quickening of his madness, Ahab is still capable of humane, almost tender exchanges. In a rare moment of compassion, he gazes into the eyes of his first mate, STARBUCK, and remembers the young wife and child they have each left behind. Ahab also takes under his wing the young Pip, an African-American boy who went mad when he was temporarily abandoned on the open sea. As soon as Ahab senses the whale is near, however, he is conscious of neither the safety of the crew as a whole nor the special needs of Pip, his faithful companion. He also turns a deaf ear to pleas from the captain of another ship, the *Rachel*, requesting the *Pequod*'s assistance in searching for a missing whaleboat whose crew includes the captain's son.

Ahab's sighting of Moby Dick from his perch two-thirds of the way up the mast marks the beginning of a grueling three-day chase, which he pursues in spite of Starbuck's pleas, Fedallah's death, and repeated injuries to his own person. At last, in a final act of malice, Moby Dick overturns all three whaleboats and heads straight for the *Pequod*. "I spit my last breath at thee," Ahab cries as he hurls his last harpoon. The barb sinks into Moby Dick's flesh; at the last moment, however, the lines, which are made of hemp, become wrapped around Ahab's neck, and he is jerked "voicelessly" out of the boat. As Ahab and his crew perish in the whirlpool created by the sinking ship, the white whale swims effortlessly away.

Airman, Noel. *Marjorie Morningstar*. Herman Wouk. 1955.

Noel Airman is a handsome and brilliant young composer and lyricist who, at the age of twenty-eight, has already had several hit songs and seems well on his way toward a lucrative career. He is also well-known for his frequent and brief affairs with the women in and around the theater community. His life is irrevocably changed, however, when he meets and falls in love with young MARJORIE MORNINGSTAR.

Noel's family does not share in the adulation accorded him in the theater. His father, a prominent judge, his mother, and his younger brother all seem, to varying degrees, disappointed or bemused by Noel's career. The chief reason for this may well be that Noel has changed his name from its original Saul Ehrmann and has dropped out of the study of philosophy and law, which especially angers his father. This rupture and the fact that one arm is crippled due to Erb's palsy constitute the only discernible difficulties in Noel's life.

Noel encounters Marjorie Morningstar at South Wind, a summer resort where he is the theatrical director. He responds warmly to her during their first meetings and is impressed by the speed with which she learns various aspects of mounting a theatrical production. Although they are attracted to each other, their relationship does not become sexual for quite some time. Ultimately they develop an on-again, off-again pattern, with Noel precipitating many of the breakups. During one period when Noel and Marjorie are close, he goes to her parents' house, as do his own parents, for a seder. Noel, who is atheistic, generally finds such rites and rituals absurd but this time during the ceremony, which is conducted in Hebrew, he is deeply moved. In fact, the seder prompts a religious crisis in Noel that develops into a more generalized intellectual inquiry.

Marjorie, who is frightened by Noel's physical appearance as he becomes more involved in his intellectual awakening, finally meets him at a restaurant, and he tries to explain his new theory—that all motivation is the desire for a "hit." Having explained this, he plunges into work on his new play, *Princess Jones*. Unfortunately, once written and produced on Broadway, the play is a colossal flop, and Noel becomes despondent.

Noel's despair and disillusionment are only exacerbated by his relationship with Marjorie, which has become burdensome. Finally, he once again breaks off with her, explaining that he is going to France to resume his study of philosophy. Nearly a year later, when Marjorie arrives in Paris intending to marry Noel, she finds him living with an expatriate German woman. Even though he proposes, something he has always been opposed to doing, she refuses and returns to New York.

Shortly after her return Marjorie meets and becomes engaged to Dr. Milton Schwartz. Noel, who had frequently teased Marjorie that she belonged in the suburbs as a Mrs. Schwartz, arrives, somewhat chastened and seedy-looking, in time to attend her wedding. Following this, Noel moves to Hollywood where he resumes his career in entertainment with marginal success and marries the German woman with whom he had lived in Paris.

Aker, Mark. "Beyond the Glass Mountain." Wallace Stegner. 1940.

Mark Aker, the story's middle-aged protagonist, pays a visit to his best friend from college, Mel Cottam, in their old college town of Iowa City. Mark and Mel graduated seventeen years ago; Mark, a former Rhodes scholar, now teaches science at Yale, and Mel runs his father's business in Iowa City. Though they were constant companions and soulmates in college, the two men have not seen each other in years. After telephoning Mel, Mark makes his way to his friend's house and prepares to feel nostalgic.

Walking across the campus, Mark looks around. Moved by odd compulsions, he finds himself reciting the names of university buildings as he crosses the main quadrangle. The smells of the old eating shack where he and Mel had stopped almost every morning, the sound of locusts buzzing on the hill, the sight of the tennis courts and field house—these things remind Mark of what he and Mel had once been. He reflects that since those days he has lost his ability to enjoy himself completely.

Mel and his wife Tamsen greet Mark when he arrives at their door. Mark is dismayed to see that Mel and Tamsen have been drinking; Mel's thickening voice and whiskey breath make him feel slightly ill. He senses that Mel has a need and is reaching out but cannot do so openly. In Mel's two phone calls to him over the past ten years, Mark heard the same loneliness and neediness in his friend's voice.

Mark and Mel talk casually, trying to keep up a playful facade. Tamsen's presence, coupled with their own fears of intimacy, make it impossible for them to talk freely. When she leaves the room to pour drinks, Mark imagines what he would like to say to Mel: that he has heard about Tamsen's continuing affair with a golf pro, that he wishes he had warned Mel about her deceptive nature, that he thinks Mel should leave her now before she completely destroys him, and that Mel is slipping away, hiding behind alcohol and a comedy-routine front. But Mark knows people don't say things like that, and he feels the distance between them even more acutely.

Tamsen returns, and more small talk follows. Mark wants to reminisce with Mel about the good old times, but he cannot speak of them. Mark rises to leave; he must catch a train. Saying good-bye to Tamsen, he wonders if he sees a look of triumph in her eyes or if he is only imagining it. Mel walks Mark to the corner where they shake hands before parting. With a tightening throat, Mark begins to extend himself to his friend. "If there's ever a time I can . . ." he says, but he stops short, unable to continue. Looking at Mel's face, he sees pained, intent, sad eyes and a flicker of derision on his lips.

Albert "Mister." *The Color Purple.* Alice Walker. 1982.

Longing all the while for the woman his father refused to let him marry, Albert becomes an abusive husband in two destructive marriages to other women. He desperately pursues SHUG AVERY, an elegant blues singer while continuing to brutalize his wife CELIE. When Shug and Celie become lovers, Albert is forced to reevaluate his behavior. In doing so, he realizes that his often selfish actions reverberate in the lives of others.

Albert fell in love with Shug when they were adolescents, and they were unable to part, although Albert's father considered her a tramp. He forced Albert to marry a classmate, Annie Julia, but the marriage did not put an end to his affair with Shug. Albert spent most of his time with her, and Annie Julia had to chase him around town in order to beg for grocery money for her and the children. When Annie Julia was murdered by her lover, Shug went on a singing tour, and Albert was left to look for another woman to clean the house and care for the children.

During the time in which the novel takes place, Albert notices Celie's sister NETTIE in church, and after several visits he requests permission to marry her. The girl's stepfather refuses to let her go and offers Celie instead. Albert deliberates for several months and then accepts the offer. Not long after the marriage, Nettie comes to stay at Albert's house to comfort Celie. Albert showers Nettie with compliments, but when she refuses to give in to his advances, he drags her into the woods and attempts to rape her. Nettie manages to fight him off, but as revenge he vows that the sisters will never hear from each other again. From that time on he intercepts all of Nettie's letters to Celie.

When Shug falls ill, Albert brings her home so that Celie can nurse her back to health. Celie watches in astonishment as Shug orders Albert to give up his drinking and pipe-smoking, and sit quietly by her bed. She allows Celie to bathe and feed her, however, and the two gradually become friends. Shug insists that Albert stop beating Celie; eventually the women leave together for Shug's mansion in Memphis.

Albert undergoes a drastic transformation while Shug and Celie are away. Apparently withering under a curse laid on him by Celie, he cowers in bed, unable to move. His son Harpo returns home to comfort him and convinces him to send Nettie's letters back to her sister. Once free of his burden of guilt, Albert begins to develop a new awareness of the world, which his family describes as his effort to "git religion."

When Celie returns to their hometown, she finds a reformed Albert. He listens with interest and sympathy to the details of Nettie's letters. Celie teaches him to sew, and they muse over Shug together. He asks Celie to marry him again, this time "in spirit as well as in the flesh." Although Celie refuses, Albert remains an integral part of Celie's extended family.

Alden, Bessie. *An International Episode.* Henry James. 1878.

Bessie Alden is a wealthy young American woman who has firmly set ideas about what the English are like and a vaguer sense of what she wants from them.

Bessie is the younger sister of Mrs. Westgate, wife of J. L. Westgate, a wealthy New Yorker. Bessie is asked to help her sister entertain two Englishmen at their summer home in Newport: Neither Lord Lambeth nor Percy Beaumont has had any experience with American life. Beaumont, the older of the two, has come on business and has brought Lambeth along for company. He cautions Lambeth, who is a bit of a womanizer, not to flirt. Lambeth laughs, but Beaumont is serious. He says an unmarried American girl is a dangerous item; if Lambeth is not careful, one of them may try to "land" him. Lambeth has been warned.

The two men are charmed by Newport and by the attention of their two lovely hosts. But while the older Beaumont is borne down upon by the safely married Mrs. Westgate, Lambeth finds himself whisked away by Bessie, who is fascinated by Lord Lambeth. She has spent a great deal of time reading English novels, and she would like to enter into the vision of English life she has gained from her reading. Now she is encountering the genuine article: Lambeth is the first Englishman she has ever met. "I'm sorry I'm not a better specimen," Lambeth says with a laugh. "You must remember you're only a beginning," says Bessie.

Bessie questions Beaumont about the Lambeth lineage. She is delighted to learn that when his father dies, Lambeth will become Duke of Bayswater. Beaumont is outraged. "Depend upon it," he tells Lambeth, "that girl means to have a go at you." But Lambeth, whose attitude toward his peerage is nonchalant, assures Beaumont that she has asked him the very same questions. Nevertheless, Beaumont writes to Lambeth's mother, who calls the two men back to England on the pretense that Lambeth's father is ill. Lambeth leaves regretfully, telling Bessie that if she ever goes to England, he must be the first person she contacts.

The following May, Bessie and her sister sail for England. Bessie casually mentions how nice it will be to call on Lord Lambeth. Her sister sadly assures her that once on his native turf, Lambeth will have quite forgotten them.

The two sisters stay at Jones's Hotel in London. Bessie once again suggests they get in touch with Lambeth. Mrs. Westgate gets annoyed. "Are you in love with him?" she asks. "Not that I know of," Bessie says. Mrs. Westgate persists until Bessie is blushing and walking anxiously about the room. That is all Mrs. Westgate can get out of her, but she agrees to write to Lord Lambeth.

The two sisters decide to spend the day at Hyde Park observing British society on a summer afternoon. Bessie is exhilarated as all her preconceptions of London come to life before her. While she watches silently, a rider dismounts and comes toward her. "Fancy your being here!" he says. It is Lambeth. With her imagination already in flight, he looks more splendid to Bessie than anyone she has ever seen.

Lambeth seems hurt that Bessie hasn't contacted him before. But soon he is reminiscing about the happy days at Newport and planning to take Bessie around London. He adds that he would like her to meet his family. Mrs. Westgate tells Bessie that if there is really no danger of her being in love with him, she would like to frighten his family with the idea that a mere American girl has captured his affections. Bessie is appalled by the idea and horrified to think that Lambeth's family would be against her.

Bessie and Lambeth visit the Tower of London, where Bessie asks questions about its history that Lambeth cannot answer. "You can't honestly expect people to know as awfully much as you," Lambeth says. "I should expect you to know a great deal more," Bessie returns. Somehow, Lambeth does not quite match her image of an English noble. "You're so disappointing, you know," Bessie says with a smile. Lambeth says that is the worst thing she could possibly say. "No," she replies, "it's not so bad as to say that I had expected nothing of you."

Bessie continues to see London, sometimes with Lambeth, sometimes without him. She tells herself that he is wonderfully kind but that she is not in love with him, yet at times he still strikes her with wonder. Lambeth, for his part, calls on Bessie every day. In spite of Beaumont's warnings and his family's growing dread, he fears that Bessie is not really interested in him.

Then Lambeth's mother and sister agree to pay a visit. Mrs. Westgate feels a sense of triumph in having caught these aristocratic birds. But Bessie admonishes her, saying that however much she likes Lambeth, she does not like him enough to make trouble for him with his family. The visit of the Duchess of Bayswater affords Mrs. Westgate an opportunity to display her American wit. Bessie feels pained at being "inspected" by Lambeth's people, however, and afterward seems deep in thought. The next day Mrs. Westgate sees Lambeth outside the hotel, and he has a sad air about him. Going upstairs she learns that Bessie has refused him. She is not sorry to hear this, but she regrets that the Duchess of Bayswater will think she has succeeded in scaring them away. But Bessie seems to regret nothing.

Alden, Roberta. *An American Tragedy.* Theodore Dreiser. 1925.

Roberta Alden, the shy but self-sufficient daughter of poor farmers, dreams of a "newer and greater life," of a time when she won't feel socially inferior in the presence of most men. However, her first priority is simply to work and supplement her parents' meager income. She moves to nearby Lycurgus, New York, to live with her Methodist friend Grace Marr and work in the shirt-and-collar factory run by Samuel Griffiths and his son.

Roberta's floor supervisor is CLYDE GRIFFITHS, the handsome nephew of Samuel Griffiths, who is alienated from the rest of the family because of his poor social and economic background. Though she likes Clyde, Roberta is well aware of the community's social stratification that divides their respective positions.

On a trip to Crum Lake with Grace, Roberta is surprised to encounter Clyde, about whom she had just been thinking. They row together, and a relationship develops. Grace soon becomes concerned about Roberta's morals. Roberta, resenting Grace's interference, moves into her own room in another house. One cold night Clyde storms away when Roberta refuses to let him come in, and Roberta, caring deeply for him and also believing that he represents a way out of her restricted life, is terrified at the thought of losing him. Eventually she relents; they become sexually intimate, and Roberta becomes pregnant.

By this time Clyde begins to break engagements regularly since he has begun to admire a wealthy young woman named Sondra Finchley. Roberta begins to suspect his excuses and his growing disregard for her, and so her pregnancy becomes a source of panic. She cannot go home to her loving religious family in disgrace. She tells Clyde of her pregnancy, and with his assistance she tries to terminate it with medication and a trip to a hypocritical country doctor who refuses to perform an illegal abortion. Roberta now insists that Clyde marry her, either in secret or after they have moved, but Clyde, fearful of losing his hold on Sondra and the high society of Lycurgus, equivocates and says he must remain where he is for now in order to save money.

When Clyde tells Roberta to go to her parents and prepare clothes for their marriage while he continues working, she complies. Clyde has no intention of marrying or even visiting her, however, and Roberta, sensing this after some weeks, writes him a letter giving him one day to either come and get her or suffer exposure upon her immediate return to Lycurgus. Clyde calls and tells her to meet him on a train, and they will take a brief trip before their assumed marriage. They travel to a remote lake. Roberta is somewhat happy even if, as she knows, Clyde does not love her and their marriage is only for the eight months necessary for her to get on her feet in another city. At least her immediate disgrace will be prevented.

Once on the lake, Roberta notices that Clyde has a tormented look on his face. Although she does not know it, he has plotted this trip to kill her. She gets up in the boat to move down and comfort him, but he strikes out at her. Clyde then gets up, perhaps to assist her, but when the boat capsizes, he ignores her calls for help, and eventually she drowns.

Allagash, Tad. *Bright Lights, Big City.* Jay McInerney. 1984.

Tad Allagash personifies narcissism, instant gratification, and reckless self-destruction. Perpetually charming, unceasingly witty, Tad is a tour guide to good times for the NARRATOR, whose wife has recently left him and whose mother has recently died. Together they prowl the nightclubs and bars of contemporary New York. Tad's goal is to be "wherever there are dances to be danced, drugs to be hoovered, women to be Allagashed."

Whenever the narrator is feeling down, Tad dreams up some excitement to distract his friend in the form of mischief, drugs, and women. For instance, when the narrator loses his job, partly as a result of their carousing, Tad plots revenge on his friend's boss. The two of them sneak into her office at night and release a ferret there. Tad normally abandons the narrator just as the effects of the evening's drugs are wearing off, often leaving his friend trapped in conversation with a trendy but uninteresting woman or at a glamorous but uninteresting place. At these moments the narrator realizes he has not had as much fun as Tad said he would have. But even though he is uncomfortable with the meaningless existence he leads, he continues to carouse with Tad.

The one truly good thing Tad does for the narrator is introduce him to his cousin Vicky. A philosophy student at Princeton, Vicky helps the narrator see an alternative to the destructive life he is leading. At the novel's end, it is Tad who is left at a party as the narrator begins to try to put the pieces of his broken life together again.

Allen, Elisa. "The Chrysanthemums." John Steinbeck. 1938.

Slender, vigorous, thirty-five-year-old Elisa Allen is the troubled, repressed figure in this sensual short story. On a typically cold, quiet, gray December Saturday in California's Salinas Valley, while working in her flower garden trimming chrysanthemums, Elisa has an experience that upsets her seeming complacency by altering her regularly simplistic life and arousing a desire to escape its confinements.

Crouching over her stalks, her hair stuffed in a hat that covers her eyes and wearing an oversized masculine farming apron filled with tools, Elisa exchanges a few words with her husband Henry, who praises her planting talent and her new chrysanthemum crops. Excited over the recent sale of his steers, Henry suggests that the two celebrate by going to town later that afternoon for a nice dinner and a movie.

After Elisa delightedly accepts the invitation for dinner, Henry leaves, and she continues to work methodically in her garden. She is interrupted by the approach of an old covered wagon advertising household fix-it services on the side of its canvas; the wagon, drawn by a horse and burro, is driven by a large grizzly-looking man. The rugged man stops to ask Elisa for directions, and she notices his large, strong physique, graying hair and beard, dark, brooding eyes, and rough hands. She attempts to direct the stranger, but he draws her into conversation and quickly tries to sell her his professional services, which she refuses with equal quickness. Dejected and weary from having no work and from having gotten lost, the stranger successfully persists in his efforts to win Elisa's favor, with the hope of fixing something for her. When he shows an interest in her chrysanthemums, Elisa's once nonresponsive tone grows immediately cheerful, and she proudly admits that she raises the largest stalks in the valley.

Taking advantage of Elisa's eagerness to talk about her chrysanthemums, the stranger asks if he might have some seeds to take to a woman down the road who also has a passion for the flower. Elisa invites the stranger into the yard while she zealously prepares a flower pot with seeds and excitedly explains how to care for the chrysanthemums once they take root. Kneeling on the ground as she does so, Elisa's obscured femininity is partially exposed when she removes her hat and gloves. As she and the stranger share a conversation about the splendor of the night, she reaches out in a passionate motion to grab his legs, but instead her hand falls limp and she cowers on the ground.

Softened by the fleeting sensuality of this episode, Elisa allows him to fix some of her old cooking pans. She watches admiringly as he works, and she expresses a curiosity and envy for the stranger's nomadic life. But the stranger immediately quells her romantic notions by telling her that it is no life for a woman. After the stranger leaves, Elisa, her sensuality newly awakened, stares at her clean, naked body in the mirror and then carefully dresses in her comeliest clothing to wait for her husband. Henry is pleasantly shocked to find Elisa looking beautiful and possessing a new confidence.

Heading to town for their evening, Elisa notices the chrysanthemums that she had given to the stranger tossed on the road; his interest in Elisa and her wild flowers was feigned after all. When they pass the wagon later on, Elisa faces her husband to avoid seeing the stranger. She asks Henry if they might have wine with their meal. Henry is also surprised by Elisa's behavior when she asks him to explain what happens at the fights, which she imagines to be bloody and violent. In a discouraging tone, Henry tells

Elisa that he will take her to a fight if she really wants to go, but he is sure she will not enjoy it. She sinks down into the seat, her strengthened identity and sexuality lost. As she feebly mutters that having wine at dinner will be sufficient, she hides her face and weeps.

Allerton, Abigail. *Capital City.* Mari Sandoz. 1939.

Left a widow after her husband was killed in World War I, Abigail Allerton, already the author of a number of novels, accepts a teaching position at the State University of Kanewa. Despite the pervading conservative attitude of the city of Franklin, Kanewa, where she encounters a number of difficulties because of her gender and her liberal beliefs, Abigail lives in relative happiness in her new environment. She decides that it would be a fitting subject for her next novel.

Her best friend in Franklin is an intellectual named HAMM RUFE whose left-wing views have similarly alienated him from the socially elite class into which he had been born. While avoiding any kind of romantic involvement, she and Hamm spend much time together, bemoaning the reactionary attitudes of Franklin toward the growing labor movement that Hamm is helping to organize.

Abigail finishes her novel, *Anteroom for Kingmakers*, which tells the story of the happenings of a hotel in a capital city of a southwestern state much like Kanewa. Suddenly in the literary spotlight, Abigail finds herself an instant celebrity among the aristocracy of Franklin, none of whom have yet read her novel. She is invited to numerous luncheons and dinner parties, most of which she declines, and she is heralded by the voices of the community as Franklin's most beloved daughter.

Her fame quickly becomes infamy, however, when her influential book becomes widely available to the inhabitants of Franklin. Her insightful yet brutally accurate novel is labeled "communist" by the powers of Franklin as well as a number of respected faculty members at the university. The local papers call for Abigail's resignation, believing that her scandalous novel has become a public embarrassment to the people of Franklin. Unable to withstand the fierce public pressure, Abigail resigns her position at the university, much to Hamm's disappointment.

Abigail harbors a growing attraction for Hamm and begins working with him on the gubernatorial campaign of labor sympathizer Carl Halzer. She becomes disheartened when an ex-lover of Hamm's, a beautiful young woman named Stephani, arrives from out of state to aid in the campaign. As Halzer's campaign gains momentum, due in no small part to Abigail's efforts, she begins to give up hope of winning Hamm's affections.

After Halzer wins the election, however, Abigail is stunned when the candidate, who had been having a secret affair with Stephani, leaves Franklin with the young woman. Abigail goes to console Hamm, realizing that the two of them are once again alone in the city amid a sea of conservative values and attitudes.

Alpine, Frank. *The Assistant.* Bernard Malamud. 1957.

Frank Alpine is a young Italian-American who appears one day on the streets of a Brooklyn neighborhood. Orphaned by his mother soon after his birth and abandoned by his father when he was five, Frank was raised in orphans' homes and tough foster families in and around San Francisco. He is dark-bearded and tall, with melancholy eyes and a nose made permanently crooked by a badly set break. Most important, the intelligent but impatient Frank feels that he is destined for something greater than most people achieve. Disgusted with his lack of conventional success, he opts to pursue a criminal life in New York.

Frank hooks up with Ward Minogue, the ne'er-do-well son of a policeman who has disowned him. While robbing a grocery store—and in spite of Frank's objections—Ward smashes the grocer over the head with a gun. During the robbery, Frank takes pity on the man and gets him a drink of water. Later remorseful that the grocer, MORRIS BOBER, was hurt, Frank, whose criminal identity is unknown to Morris, helps carry crates of milk into the store to stock the shelves. When Morris discovers that the hungry and homeless Frank has been pilfering milk and bread from his storefront each morning, he takes pity on the young man. Frank persuades Morris to let him clerk for room, board, and a little pay, telling him that he is grateful for the opportunity to learn the business. The storekeeper agrees over the objections of his wife Ida who does not trust the Italian stranger.

Frank works for Morris to soothe his conscience and to prove to himself that he can finally settle down in one place. Morris's business is failing, however, and he warns Frank about the oppressive responsibility of running the store. Because he is hopelessly attracted to Morris's pretty and lonely twenty-three-year-old daughter, HELEN BOBER, Frank remains. He seems to attract more business for Morris and works hard, although his mind is usually on Helen and not on business.

Frank is not completely reformed, however. Despite a guilty conscience, he cannot control his urge to pocket change now and then from the register. He keeps careful track of the sum he steals, planning to pay it back someday. In addition, Frank's obsession with Helen continues, and he even spies on her when she is in the bathroom. Determined to get closer to her, he follows her to the library, where he finally engages her in a conversation about books. Though Helen is resistant because Frank is not Jewish and because he does not seem to aspire to anything greater than clerking in a grocery, she slowly falls in love with him.

Frank becomes interested in the Jews as a people, questioning Morris and reading about them at the library. He fluctuates between disgust at his dreary life in the store and his desire to be near Helen. He finally wins her over by telling her that he plans to attend college and make something of himself, and he insists that she keep a volume of Shakespeare he had given her. She still refuses to consummate their relationship because she is not altogether certain that she loves him. Frank, although frustrated, admires her ideals.

When business takes a turn for the worse, Frank starts slipping his savings back into the register. After he has depleted his funds, however, he is caught pocketing a dollar, and Morris asks him to leave. Later that night Frank meets Helen in the park and rescues her from Ward Minogue, who has attacked her. Feeling that she is now forever out of reach because Morris has fired him, Frank pressures her into having sex with him. She recoils from him in disgust, and Frank is filled with self-hatred and remorse.

Frank haunts Morris's store and twice saves the elderly grocer's life: once from gas fumes when Morris forgets to light the heater, and once from a fire Morris himself attempted to start. Both times, while Morris is recovering, Frank returns to the store to keep it going, feeling that he is indebted to the grocer and needs to be absolved for what he did to Helen. Because he is convinced that Frank is working only in order to steal, Morris leaves his sickbed to banish him from the store. Soon after, the old grocer contracts pneumonia and dies. Frank takes over the store and pays Ida an inordinately high rent, which he earns by working nights at a place called the Coffee Pot so that Helen can go to college.

Eventually Frank decides to turn the store into a restaurant in order to raise its income. He has himself circumcised and becomes a Jew, thereby taking the ultimate step in creating a new life for himself.

Altschuler, Edgar. *World's Fair.* E. L. Doctorow. 1986.

Edgar Altschuler recalls the Bronx in the late 1930s as a place of wonder where he discovered the complexities of life, and he does so with an innocence that is both charmingly naive and, with the adult Edgar's sure narrative voice, knowingly structured.

Beginning with his earliest memories as an infant, Edgar narrates his life. He lives in a private house on Eastburn Avenue with his mother, father, older brother Donald, and his maternal grandmother. Edgar is aware early on that his parents are of opposing natures. His mother is a vigilant and authoritative homemaker while his father, part owner of a music store in Manhattan, is a politically liberal, self-styled free spirit. Edgar enjoys the position of younger brother for the wisdom Donald is able to pass along to him. His grandmother teaches him much about traditional Jewish ways. She is the only person in the house who maintains the Jewish rituals; only after she dies does his mother begin to practice them.

Meanwhile, anti-Semitic feelings are growing as Hitler gains power in Europe. Edgar finds swastikas on the garage doors and becomes aware that the boundaries of his safe existence are illusory. His social life expands when he begins school, makes new friends, and gains more independence. That summer his family is forced to move to the upstairs apartment when the house is sold to a family of German Jews who behave condescendingly to the Altschulers, second-generation Russian Jewish immigrants.

One summer Edgar's appendix bursts, and he almost dies. He is hospitalized for months; afterward, he convalesces at his aunt and uncle's manor in Pelham. He likes their very comfortable life but misses the intensity of his own home life. Edgar's father must move his store and soon loses it because of the disruption of the move, which has been compounded by his own bad business practices.

Meanwhile, the World's Fair has come to New York, but because of his illness and the tensions in the family, Edgar is unable to go. The family then moves again, out of their private house and into an apartment. At the library one day, Edgar learns of a contest to describe the typical American boy, sponsored by the World's Fair Corporation. On the way home that day, he is threatened for being Jewish. He lies about his heritage and is disturbed by his own cowardice. The essay he later writes does not use himself as the model but rather the boy he would like to be.

Meg, Edgar's friend from school, takes Edgar with her to the World's Fair because her mother works there and can get them in free. Edgar is awestruck by the spectacle of the fair. That September he receives an Honorable Mention in the contest, and the entire family goes to the fair together. This time Edgar notices the flaws of the park more, and his father makes a point of explaining the propagandist nature of the exhibits and the exclusion of certain races from the items in the time capsule.

Still, Edgar identifies with the future that the fair, and specifically the time capsule, symbolizes. Back home he creates his own time capsule, incorporating many remembrances of his own life. At the last moment he retrieves a book, *Ventriloquism Self-Taught*, from the capsule. After burying the capsule, he begins to try to learn how to throw his voice.

Amar. *The Spider's House.* Paul Bowles. 1955.

Amar is a Moroccan boy living in Fez who is caught in his country's struggle for independence from the French in 1954. He is a descendant of the Prophet Mohammed, and he dreams of saving his people from the French. While pious and aware of being gifted, Amar has never attended school or kept a job, although when he does find employment with a potter, he is extremely diligent and skillful. Torn between his father's devout old Moslem world and the modern promise of new possibilities, Amar finds himself increasingly alone and directionless. He works his tedious job merely to save enough money to buy a pair of shoes.

As he wanders through the tense city of Fez, Amar is confused by the sudden alteration of its daily life. He wishes the hostile French would leave, but unlike his militantly nationalistic peers in the Istiqlal, he believes that victory must be won by pious Moslems guided by Allah, not by rigid obedience to political parties. Accused by his father and employer of behaving like a naive boy, Amar feels guilty for still being immersed in the pleasures of his childhood; and as the moral clarity of his former existence disappears, he becomes increasingly sensitive to the passing of time.

One hot morning, Amar decides to create some excitement instead of going to work. He and his friend Mohammed rent bicycles and ride to a lake. Because Amar resents Mohammed for his wealth, his smug willingness to follow the Istiqlal's orders, and his propensity for analyzing the weakness of the Moroccan people, he picks a fight with him and rides away. On the way home he is caught in the orchard of Moulay Ali, a nationalist leader, who invites him into his house and introduces him to a group of eager young nationalists.

After leaving Ali's house, Amar discovers that no buses are going to his quarter. He wanders into a traveling fair and meets Benani, an older boy sent by Moulay Ali to find out what Amar knows and how secretive he is. Amar goes home and the next day wanders about the violent city. Harassed by French police, he retires to a French café just outside the city walls where he meets two Americans, JOHN STENHAM and POLLY "LEE" BURROUGHS. Although Amar is shocked at Lee's brazen clothes and smoking, he strikes up a conversation with John. Fighting suddenly erupts outside between nationalists and the French police, and John and Lee take Amar back to their hotel; they protect him from the French by claiming that he is their servant.

When the hotel is forced to close, John decides to go to the mountains where devout Moslems are observing an annual feast the Istiqlal have prohibited in the city. Amar, outraged at the restriction, goes with John and Lee. Although Amar finds John's attempts to understand the subtleties of Moslem belief inadequate, he considers him a sincere friend and protector.

After leaving the feast, Amar, finding he has no place to go, ends up at the house of Moulay Ali, who accuses him of working for the French. Although Amar defends himself by daring to criticize Ali's ignoble distrust, Ali later tricks him into acting as a decoy so that he can escape from the French who have surrounded his house. Amar is clever enough to escape, but he feels utterly lonely and insignificant. He finally agrees with his father's appraisal of politics as a world of lies. In better understanding the world, Amar more clearly sees its futility.

Returning to John's hotel, Amar feels secure and happy that Allah has reunited him with this stranger who he believes is destined to take care of him. Since John and

Lee, now lovers, are about to depart for Casablanca, Amar asks for a ride to Meknés, the city to which his family has escaped. John tells Amar that he cannot take him along and asks him to step out of the car. Not understanding this final abandonment, Amar runs after the car, believing that it must stop; when he reaches a curve in the road, he finds that John and Lee have disappeared.

Amerigo (Prince). *The Golden Bowl.* Henry James. 1909.

A young aristocrat from a corrupt Roman family, Prince Amerigo finds an enthusiastic reception among an indulgent circle of American expatriates in London. The Prince speaks perfect colloquial English and with his cleverness and beauty makes an easy amusement of flirting. However, he has the misfortune of falling in love with CHARLOTTE STANT, an American who grew up in Florence. A marriage between them is impossible—neither has enough money to continue living on the grand scale each sees as necessary. Charlotte breaks off the affair by leaving for America, and the Prince devotes his time to new social prospects in London.

FANNY ASSINGHAM, an older woman who wants to help the Prince, introduces him to MAGGIE VERVER, the daughter of an American millionaire. The Prince has never lowered himself to actively pursue a woman as he does Maggie. He devotes six months of his life to courting her energetically before the wedding date is fixed. As their marriage approaches, the Prince finds himself feeling grave and unsettled. When he turns to Fanny one evening for comfort, he discovers that Charlotte has returned to London and will be arriving shortly at Fanny's home. During her brief visit, Charlotte and the Prince spend a few tense moments alone, and she asks him to help her find a wedding gift for Maggie.

In spite of the Prince's desire to avoid it, the "hunt" for the wedding gift does take place. Guilt and longing plague the Prince on this excursion, and he expresses the hope that Charlotte will soon marry as well. His anxiety about his upcoming marriage flares up again when Charlotte finds, in a small Bloomsbury shop, the gift she thinks appropriate for Maggie. It is a golden bowl; she thinks it is exquisite, and only the Prince sees its flaw: a minute crack under the gold veneer. He regards the flaw as an omen that threatens his marriage and his happiness, and insists that Charlotte leave the object.

When the Prince and Maggie are vacationing in Paris after the wedding, he receives a letter from Charlotte explaining that Maggie's father, a widower, has asked her to marry him. He advises her to accept the proposal. Even after Mr. Verver marries Charlotte, she and the Prince remain closely allied. When Maggie gives birth to a son, it serves only to strengthen the bond between the Prince and Charlotte. Maggie restrains herself from showing how desperately she loves the Prince, and he is therefore free to continue his illicit romance with Charlotte.

By a terrible coincidence Maggie wanders into the same Bloomsbury shop visited by the Prince and his lover and purchases the golden bowl that had fascinated Charlotte. The shop owner recalls for her the conversation he overheard between the lovers, confirming Maggie's suspicions about their ongoing affair. Maggie invites Fanny Assingham over to hear the story, and the Prince enters at the moment when Fanny, angered by the news, smashes the bowl on the floor. When the older woman leaves, Maggie speaks to him with uncharacteristic anger and directness, and the Prince confesses to his illicit affair.

After this incident, the Prince begins to look forward to the time he will be truly alone with his wife. When he and Maggie receive word that the Ververs will soon be leaving, the Prince conceals his emotions, as does Charlotte. The former lovers also assist each other in denying any unhappiness they might feel. At the close of the novel, during the first moments of authentic solitude with his wife, the Prince embraces her with a few words that suggest his commitment to her is finally complete.

Ames, Harry. *The Man Who Cried I Am.* John A. Williams. 1967.

A celebrated black writer, Harry Ames leaves the United States to seek artistic and personal freedom. Although Europe welcomes this expatriate black writer and his white wife, Harry is destroyed by a hatred of blacks that apparently knows no national boundaries.

Like many intellectuals, Harry has flirted with communism in his search for a philosophy that can recognize and overcome the oppression faced by African Americans. Although never a member of the party, Harry is dogged by his affiliation with it throughout his life while being confronted simultaneously with simple racism.

When he receives word that he has been granted a prestigious fellowship which will allow him to live in Europe for a year, Harry and his wife Charlotte make plans to depart. As Harry gleefully tells his friend MAX REDDICK, also a writer, this is the recognition he has longed for, the kind of honor white writers normally receive. Deliberately insensitive to Max's lack of commercial success, Harry gloats over the award. Harry's sense that he has "made it" is frustrated, however, when the fellowship is withdrawn. Harry and Max suspect that it is Harry's marriage to a white woman that has disqualified him, although no official statement to that effect is made. Harry's publisher gives him a large enough advance on his next book to allow him to go to Europe as planned, but Harry is still bitter. He will never return to the United States.

In Europe, Harry practices his craft in an environment more congenial to black artists. Competition within the ever-growing group of expatriate black writers is fierce, however. One young writer, Marion Dawes, attacks Harry in print and tells him to his face that the attack is nothing personal but is the natural act of a "son" killing his literary "father." Although Harry denies that he is any kind of a father to Dawes, he recognizes that he does have a certain stature among black writers.

Art is not Harry's only concern. He has several extra-marital affairs and forms a long alliance with a French woman, Michelle. Harry also witnesses the breakup of Europe's colonial empires. His attitude toward emerging African nations is ambivalent, however, especially when he sees that, in addition to many honest and hardworking African leaders, there exists a class of opportunists seemingly little better than Europeans. One of these men, Jaja Enzkwu, shamelessly propositions almost every white woman he meets.

It is Enzkwu who reveals to Harry the existence of Alliance Blanc, a coalition of nations devoted to continuing the organized exploitation of blacks worldwide. When Enzkwu is murdered for this knowledge, Harry becomes the only one who knows about Alliance Blanc and about the King Alfred plan orchestrated by the United States to deport American blacks if race relations deteriorate. Knowing that possessing this information has doomed him, and perhaps wanting to doom his friend and rival Max Reddick, Harry delivers a document from Enzkwu to his lover Michelle, instructing her to give it to Max if he is murdered. Michelle gives Max the sealed package just days after the funeral of Harry Ames.

Amory, Philip. *The Lamplighter*. Maria Susanna Cummins. 1854.

Philip Amory, a man haunted by tragedy, seems fated to wander in an elusive search for happiness. Eventually, however, he does find contentment, thanks to his daughter, GERTY FLINT.

Philip's father died when he was a child, and his mother married Mr. Graham, father of Emily Graham. Mr. Graham is strict and disapproves of the intimacy between his stepson and Emily. One day, enraged to find the two together, Graham accuses Philip of embezzlement, and Emily faints. To revive her, Philip throws on her face what he thinks is cologne; the liquid is acid, however, and Emily is blinded. Philip is horrified, and the incident affects him for the rest of his life.

Unable to face the Grahams, Philip flees to South America. En route, he meets Lucy Grey, whose father, the ship's captain, has died, leaving her defenseless. Out of pity, Philip marries her and they have a child, Gerty. When he is stricken with malaria in another city, his absence convinces Lucy that he has abandoned her. Philip's friend Ben Grant takes Lucy and Gerty to Boston. Some years later, after Ben and Lucy have died, Gerty is left in the care of Ben's cruel wife, Nan Grant.

Philip wanders the globe and makes a fortune in the California gold rush. While there, he meets Nan Grant's corrupt son who tells him where and how to find Gerty. Philip tracks her down, finally spotting her on a steamboat cruising up the Hudson. Under the name of Mr. Philips, he befriends Gerty, who is traveling with Emily. When the ship wrecks and a fire engulfs it, Philip saves a woman he thinks is Gerty, although he ends up rescuing Isabel Clinton instead. Ultimately, he writes his entire life story for Gerty, pleading with her not to hate her father for his supposed abandonment of her. Gerty, in fact, loves him and restores him to Emily, who has been pining for him all those years. In the end, he is reconciled with Emily's father and marries Emily.

Amy. "Old Mortality." Katherine Anne Porter. 1939.

Remembered as the most beautiful woman in the entire family, Amy is an awe-inspiring figure to her niece MIRANDA. Even though she died long before Miranda was born, Amy still exerts influence in Miranda's large southern family and in Miranda's imagination.

Amy is legendary not only for her dark-haired beauty but for her willfulness and coquetry. In life, men flocked around her; she made and broke two marriage engagements for her own whimsical reasons. Still, she was beloved by her cousin Gabriel, who was finally able to win her, but not for long.

Miranda knows the story of her long-dead aunt almost by heart. Annoyed more than amused by her clumsy cousin's attentions, Amy consistently rebuffs Gabriel. Coming on the heels of the two broken engagements, her behavior is shocking but completely in character. Amy is not deliberately cruel, but she is impatient—with Gabriel, with herself, and even with life. Amy, who is tubercular, is given to telling her mother that she is "not long for this world." Her tendency to ride hard and dance every dance at every ball only weakens her.

One night at a costume ball, Amy is becomingly—and scantily—dressed as a milkmaid. While Gabriel seethes, incensed by all the attention she is receiving from other men, Amy dances gaily. When Raymond, her former fiancé, arrives, Amy greets him familiarly, dances with him, then joins him alone outside. Gabriel, believing that Raymond has kissed Amy, challenges Raymond to a duel. The incident ends when Amy's brother Harry shoots the unarmed Raymond.

For this breach of etiquette Harry must flee to Mexico. When Amy, feverish the morning after the ball, learns that Gabriel and her brother have ridden off, she has her horse saddled and rides after them to bid Harry farewell. A few weeks later, after an extended relapse, Amy agrees to marry Gabriel. Amy's acceptance is halfhearted at best. Gabriel is too happy to notice his fiancée's indifference, but Amy confesses to her mother that she does not really love her cousin. She is only marrying him, she claims, because he won't go away.

A honeymoon in New Orleans during which Gabriel

treats Amy like a fragile princess has a tragic ending. Amy's tuberculosis worsens, causing a hemorrhage and necessitating a nurse's care. One night, either deliberately or accidentally, Amy takes an overdose of her medication. The death comes just six weeks after her marriage. Although this bright life is snuffed out, Amy lives on in the memories of relatives, among whom she is celebrated as a headstrong beauty for years to come.

Anderson, Charley. *U.S.A. (The 42nd Parallel; Nineteen Nineteen; The Big Money).* John Dos Passos. 1930; 1932; 1936.

Simple, honest, inarticulate, and corruptible, Charley Anderson represents the fate of the American worker when he moves into the world of finance capitalism. Growing up in a Fargo hotel, Charley leaves home as a teenager to work for his brother Jim as a mechanic in Minneapolis. Wanting to see the world, he becomes an itinerant mechanic in Chicago, St. Louis, Louisville, and New Orleans. When World War I begins, he joins the ambulance service and goes to New York and to France.

Four years later, Charley, now a decorated aviator, rides home from France with Paul Johnson and EVELINE HUTCHINS. In New York he meets and falls for a young socialite, Doris Humphries, who is impressed with his aviation heroics.

Back in Minneapolis, Charley lives the life of a returned soldier. He spends most of his time quarreling with Jim and his family and resenting questions about his combat experiences. After his mother dies, Charley breaks with his brother over what to do with Charley's share of her estate: Jim wants to invest it in his Ford dealership, while Charley wants to use it to start an airplane-engine company with his friend Joe Askew. Charley abandons his share of the legacy and flees to New York.

When Joe falls seriously ill, Charley must take care of himself. After living off the Johnsons for a while, he grudgingly takes a job as a mechanic and then as an automobile salesman, but he gambles away most of his money. He tries to see Doris, but she is put off by his seedy clothing and coarse manners. Bored, he has an affair with Eveline.

Finally, Joe shows up, and the airplane-engine business begins to move forward. They attract some big investors, and Charley becomes chief mechanic of the company, at a salary of $250 per week.

When Charley next resurfaces, he has been living with Joe's family, and he announces that it is "the first time I've had my overalls off in a year." The business is moving along well. A friend of Doris's family counsels him to start buying stock in the company, and he soon begins to show signs of prosperity.

On a promotional trip to Washington, D.C., Charley makes some connections in the legislature; altogether unintentionally, he is an effective promoter of his own financial interests. With the money that is not tied up in the market, he buys a new set of clothes and a Packard, and moves into his own apartment, complete with a Japanese valet.

When Doris returns from a trip abroad, they have an affair, and Charley is convinced that they will soon marry. But she throws him over for an English gentleman, and in his reckless despair he agrees to quit his job and sign on with a manufacturer in Detroit who has long been trying to enlist his services.

He marries Gladys Wheatley, the daughter of a Detroit financier, has two children, and begins a life of suburban comfort. But he and Gladys cannot get along, and he turns his attention back to the market. One day, while testing a plane, he crashes, killing a longtime friend and mechanical assistant. Recuperating from his own injuries in Florida, he meets MARGO DOWLING. Back in New York to head off a financial debacle, he loses $400,000 and gets caught in bed with a chorus girl. Gladys divorces him, and he loses his position in the company.

Thereafter, Charley becomes a heavy-drinking, high-rolling stock investor. He rousts about New York and Florida with Margo, profits by some inside information from one of his Washington connections, and drinks more and more. One night he wrecks his car at a grade crossing, and after virtually everyone he has ever known has had a chance to get as much money out of him as possible, he dies of peritonitis.

Anderson, Clem. *Clem Anderson.* R. V. Cassill. 1961.

Clem Anderson, a famous writer, was born and raised in the midwestern town of Boda. He draws upon his early years in his successful volume of poetry, *The Throne of Oedipus*, which focuses on his conflicting relationships with two girls, one a "nice" girl and one the town "tramp."

The narrator, a college English professor named Dick Hartsell, meets Clem during their college years when Clem is living the life of the bohemian poet with a vengeance. He drinks to excess, has promiscuous sex, is unkempt, and is consumed with the task of writing poetry. During these years Clem surprises everyone by falling in love with the demure and conventional Sheila.

Clem serves in the army during World War II, distinguishing himself as a soldier but suffering a nervous breakdown after he kills a German soldier. When he recovers, he returns to America, marries Sheila, has two children, and enters into the most productive and peaceful years of his life. While living in Acapulco, New York, and Paris, he produces steadily, writing a volume of poetry, *Angel at Noon*, a novel, and a play, *Death and the Devil*, based on an affair he had during the war.

After their return from Paris, things begin to go downhill for the Andersons. Clem, unable to get his play produced, begins to drink more heavily than ever and has a series of brief affairs. By 1953 he has divorced Sheila. He marries a stripper, Cindy Hunt, who soon dies in childbirth along with their baby. Thereafter Clem's behavior becomes increasingly frenetic, and although he speaks frequently of the great poem he is writing, he produces nothing. It seems to Dick Hartsell that Clem is now living out his poetic visions rather than writing them down.

In 1956, Clem is found dead with one of his girlfriends in her apartment. The woman had apparently turned on her gas stove in order to kill both herself and Clem, and Clem had apparently been too drunk to stop her. He dies, a testament to the lives of the many hard-drinking and self-destructive American writers of his time.

Anderson, Nonnie. *Strange Fruit*. Lillian Smith. 1944.

Nonnie Anderson, a genteel and loving young woman, and her sister Bess occupy the house they have inherited from their mother. At the outset of the novel, Nonnie, who is known to family and friends as Non, has recently returned from completing her education at Spelman College, a fact that earns her prestige from some quarters and scorn from others. Because she is a black woman, there are few jobs open to her—despite her education—in Maxwell, Georgia, after World War I. She has taken a job caring for Boysie Brown, a white boy who is retarded and requires constant care. In addition to her nursing and domestic work with the Browns, Nonnie also resumes her lifelong affair with TRACY DEEN, the son of Dr. Tut Deen, one of Maxwell's leading white citizens.

Ever since her early teens, when Tracy was approximately twenty, Non has been unswervingly in love with him, ignoring the racial barrier that would have prevented most interracial couples from a continuing romance. Nonnie's idealistic love brooks no interference, including her sister's trying to break them up. She becomes pregnant soon after her return, and while she is happy about the child because it was conceived in love, her sister argues strongly against the pregnancy. Non remains steadfast in her desire to bear the child, however, and decides to tell Tracy the good news.

When Tracy learns of the pregnancy, he is not pleased because he has been recently pressured into an engagement with Dottie Pusey, a white girl who has long had a crush on him and with whom he has carried on a desultory affair for more than seven years. When Nonnie learns of Tracy's impending marriage, she is deeply hurt but is unshaken in her resolve to bear her child. She and Tracy continue to have regular trysts, but these turn sour when Tracy arrives one night in a very drunken state and assails her with her worthlessness because she is black. He follows this with a beating and rape. Although he is later contrite, this behavior marks the point at which Non's idealism begins to erode. Her transformation is completed when she learns from Tracy that he has hired the grotesque Big Henry—a mentally slow black man who has been his servant and friend since childhood—to marry Nonnie,

although he assures her that he will kill Henry if he ever tries to touch her.

Meanwhile, Nonnie's brother Ed, who has returned to Maxwell in order to persuade Non to leave the town to go to New York with him, accidentally hears Henry bragging about the deal he and Tracy struck. After punching Henry, Ed leaves the bar he is in, resolving to kill Tracy himself. Later that same night, Ed does kill Tracy. After telling Bess and Nonnie what he has done, he makes his escape from Maxwell with the aid of Dr. Sam Perry, the Andersons' friend since childhood.

In the aftermath of Tracy's murder, Nonnie retreats into a world of silence where she grieves for Tracy and the loss she has sustained. Bess redoubles her efforts to persuade Non to abort the fetus. However, as Bess tells Dr. Perry, and as she knows herself, Tracy's death makes it all the more important for Non to have her child in spite of any social consequences. On the day of Tracy's funeral, Non is at work at the Browns', and at Mrs. Brown's request she brings a bouquet of flowers to the Deen home, in recognition of the family's loss.

Andrews, George. *Mama Day*. Gloria Naylor. 1988.

George Andrews, who knows neither his father nor his mother, a prostitute in Harlem, spends his childhood and adolescence under the tutelage of the indomitable Mrs. Jackson at the Wallace P. Andrews Shelter for Boys on Staten Island. She instills in him a sense of self-reliance and the necessity of living only in the present. With no family and no past, George learns he has to make his own future.

George puts himself through Columbia University by working at the New York City Hilton. He studies math and receives a degree in engineering. Unlike his business partner, Bruce Stein, George has little imaginative capacity; still, his technical abilities suffice to implement all of Bruce's ideas.

George is not a superstitious person; yet when OPHELIA "COCOA" DAY comes to his office for a job interview after unknowingly eating lunch near him at a local coffee shop, he has a nervous feeling that he cannot fathom. He almost succeeds in forgetting her and their confrontational meeting, but then he receives her letter thanking him for the interview. The job goes to another person, but he remembers his peculiar reaction to her as he attempts to wash the yellow powder from the letter off his hands. Without any conscious forethought he recommends her to a client looking for an account manager.

George and Cocoa's first dinner together is hardly pleasant. They find each other boring, strong-willed, and limited in their views; nonetheless, George asks if he can show Cocoa the many facets of his city. Throughout the fall they spend Saturday mornings traveling to all the boroughs and small neighborhoods, and gradually they fall in love. Because they are both stubborn and fearful of intimacy, their courtship continues to be tumultuous. But just when his relationship with Cocoa has gotten as bad as it can, she asks him to marry her.

George enjoys professional football, and even after his marriage he continues to take his two-week vacation in January so that he can see all the playoffs and the Super Bowl. After several years, however, he finally takes a vacation with Cocoa, accompanying her on a summer visit to her former home on the island of Willow Springs. Although Cocoa's neighbors think little of George, her grandmother Abigail and great aunt MIRANDA DAY (Mama Day) hold him in high regard. The men of the island gain respect for George when he beats the local con artist and distiller of bootleg alcohol at poker. But when George, a teetotaler, drinks some of the concoction, he has to be carried back to Abigail's house.

George's math and engineering background, as well as his unwavering self-reliance and predilection to focus on only the present, contrast with the more mystical and supernatural attitudes of the islanders. When Cocoa falls prey to a mysterious and deadly illness, George cannot fathom that it may be the result of the dark workings of a jealous woman. When a severe hurricane strikes the island and takes out the one bridge to the mainland, George can think only that he must help fix the bridge in order to get Cocoa to a hospital. He cannot understand when Mama Day, a conjuring woman of great power, tells him that to save Cocoa he must believe in the supernatural. He suffers from a congenital heart condition and is dangerously fatigued by his work on the bridge. Finally, desperately frightened by Cocoa's steady deterioration, George tries to work with Mama Day. But at the critical moment in their conjuring effort he falters, and his weak heart bursts under the physical and mental strain. As Mama Day well knows, however, in death there is life: His demise miraculously restores Cocoa's health.

Andrews, John. *Three Soldiers.* John Dos Passos. 1921.

John Andrews is an aspiring classical composer, fresh out of Harvard, who has enlisted in the infantry during World War I.

In training camp John gets his first taste of the army's methodically brutal suppression of individuality. The work is mind-numbing, and the drilling is incessant. He forms a friendship with CHRIS CHRISFIELD, an Indiana farm boy, but this does little to alleviate his loneliness. Lying awake at night, he speculates about the others: Did they have dreams like his? Or were they raised only to fight? John knows that Chris has many of the same feelings, but Chris takes out his frustrations on people. John takes on the role of the soothing friend, calming Chris's passion with gentle talk.

Overseas, their regiment is thrown into the battle of the Argonne. Pausing to contemplate frogs swimming in a roadside puddle, John is wounded by a stray shell. While semidelirious in a hospital, he has a magnificent vision of the Queen of Sheba proceeding with her entourage. Music for the scene begins to well up in his imagination. After a week of rest, a new resolve sweeps over him: He will begin to live again. But a crucial bit of self-knowledge also comes to light: He had gone to war because he did not have the strength to live. All his life he had been weak and a coward.

The war ends, and John gets special duty to study music at the Sorbonne. He becomes acquainted with a sophisticated group of people and eventually meets Genevieve, the daughter of a wealthy family devoted to music. She believes in his talent and encourages his art and affection. All of this is abruptly wrenched from his grasp. On a day excursion with Genevieve some miles outside Paris, John is accosted by the military police; having forgotten his papers, he cannot produce them when the MPs demand them. The officers assume he is a deserter, arrest and beat him, and commit him to a labor camp without a trial.

John makes a daring escape from the camp. While traveling in civilian clothes, he meets up with Chris who has also just deserted. Chris confesses that he had to flee because he murdered an officer.

After some adventures, John finally arrives at Genevieve's country house. When she finds out that he has deserted, she leaves him to return to Paris. He hides in a small village inn and feverishly works to finish the music inspired by the Queen of Sheba. Just before its completion, the military police arrive. The novel ends with his abandoned, unfinished score blowing away in the wind.

Andrews, Polly. *The Group.* Mary McCarthy. 1954.

Polly Andrews is the most reserved member in her clique of seven Vassar College students, class of 1933, who share a dormitory suite. Despite her taciturn personality, she is an enterprising young woman who majors in chemistry and tries to enter the medical profession upon graduation from college. Passionate by nature, Polly is leery of entering into the world of sexual relationships, which she fears will become too important if she seeks to satisfy her desires.

The Andrewses are an exceptionally discreet family with a very distinguished background of well-connected, wealthy men and women who are well born enough to sit for portraits painted by the famous John Singer Sargent. They are considered eccentric both because they seem unruffled by the fact that they lost their fortune in the Depression, thereby foiling Polly's wish to study medicine, and because there is a history of mental illness in the family. The tendency causes Polly to hesitate to have children for fear that they will be afflicted with some form of insanity.

Polly's brand of her family's penchant for originality is manifested in her habit of making friends with what her

Vassar buddies consider colorless people: They are usually much older, and she is overly generous to them. But Polly's personality, placid as it is, is in tune with those of her odd friends; she does not long for a more fashionable life-style despite the group's insistence that she spice up the flavor of her own existence.

Polly makes an exception to her tendency to date when she meets a very successful thirty-year-old editor, Gus LeRoy, at a party given by one of the married members of the group, KAY LEILAND STRONG. Polly and Gus, married but separated from his wife, and the father of a son, become lovers. The quality of their relationship is marred, however, because Gus has problems with his psychotherapy treatments, and his ability to decide to divorce his wife in order to marry Polly is seriously hindered. Finally, after almost a year, Polly can no longer tolerate the fact that a psychologist and a wife stand between her and her lover, and she suggests that Gus return to his wife and son.

Immediately following her split with Gus, Polly's parents announce their amicable divorce on the grounds of Mr. Andrews's manic-depressive tendencies, which had at one time warranted his being institutionalized. Polly's father moves into her bachelorette apartment. Experiencing financial difficulties due to her father's innocently spendthrift habits, Polly begins selling her blood at the medical center where she works as a technician to support herself and her father. She is reprimanded for endangering her health by giving blood too often by a kindly doctor, Jim Ridgely, who promptly falls in love and proposes to her.

Polly's group of friends had long hoped that she would meet an upstanding young doctor through her work and are thrilled for her when they hear of her engagement. They warn her that she should not let her father live with her and her husband-to-be because his presence would undermine the young couple's nascent love. Jim is also an extremely generous person, however, and has no qualms about sharing a home with his future father-in-law. The young couple marries, settles down, and proves to be very compatible, in contrast to the shaky marriages and unfortunate divorces of the group's other members. At the novel's close, Polly has a baby girl.

Andrews, Sara. *Dark Princess, a Romance.* W. E. B. Du Bois. 1928.

Sara Andrews is among Chicago's shrewdest politicians in the 1920s. Although a fiercely independent and ambitious woman, Sara can rise to power only through her alliances with men. She masterminds the careers of two successful African-American politicians, SAMUEL SCOTT and MATTHEW TOWNS, but suffers the consequences of her limited control over their actions.

Sara was born in Indiana, the daughter of an African-American woman, the chambermaid in a local hotel, and a white German cook. Her parents divorce and her mother dies when she is still a girl, but she manages to finish high school and attend business college. A small, trim, striking woman, Sara is always impeccably dressed and invariably attracts attention. Men never attempt to flirt with her more than once, however, because she scares them off immediately with her abrupt, businesslike manner. After graduation from college, she works as a stenographer in a dry goods store at a salary considered "fabulous" for a woman. In 1922 she leaves the small Indiana town and moves to Chicago where she becomes secretary to the Honorable Sammy Scott.

Sammy is a politician who found a place in the Chicago political "machine" and learned to manipulate it for the benefit of "black Chicago." He hires Sara because she radiates intelligence and capability, and because she can easily "pass" for white. After fighting off Sammy's advances, she sets about transforming his business into a highly efficient and profitable organization. Once Sammy has come to rely on her judgment, however, Sara makes an unusual suggestion. She has carefully watched the trial and conviction of Matthew Towns, a highly educated and intelligent young man who was sent to jail because he would not reveal the name of a criminal friend. With such a determined and courageous young man added to their team, Sara believes Sammy could win an election to Congress. Through her efforts, Matthew is released, and Sammy hires him.

Sara grows to admire hardworking Matthew, sees the potential for success in him, and accepts his proposal of marriage. Their union takes place with the understanding that they do not love each other because, as Sara explains to him, she sees nothing in so-called love. After marrying Matthew, Sara begins living on a grand scale, using some of her savings to purchase a large house and to furnish it elegantly. She gets Matthew elected to the state legislature by using her talent for campaigning and a fair amount of bribery. This era culminates when Sara gives an elegant dinner for a select group of powerful figures in Chicago politics and secures Matthew's nomination for Congress.

Just before the announcement of his nomination is to be made, however, Matthew refuses the position, walks through the astonished and outraged group, and leaves the house with an unknown woman. After this fiasco and the failure of all her well-laid plans, Sara travels to New York City. She stays at the Plaza Hotel, attends plays and concerts, and visits museums. After New York she moves on to Atlantic City, Boston, Newport, and other cities. When she finally returns to Chicago, Sammy is there to meet her.

He has had a windfall, bought an ostentatious mansion and a luxury car, and now feels prepared to propose to Sara. She considers the offer doubtfully since Sammy is middle-aged and no longer so handsome, but finally she acknowledges that they need each other. Matthew later comes to her home to offer an apology, but she simply slams the door in his face. He tries again to apologize in court on the day of the divorce, but before he is able to finish, Sammy and Sara leave together.

Sara's second marriage is a demonstration of her resilience and persistent determination. She has always faced difficulty by hardening herself and boldly moving forward. With her marriage to Sammy, Sara forms a more appropriate partnership with a man who, unlike her former husband, values wealth, power, and security to the utmost.

Andrews, Todd. *The Floating Opera.* John Barth. 1956.

Todd Andrews, a Maryland lawyer, learns as a young man that he has a heart condition that may kill him any day. He concludes that there is no reason for living. He narrates the events of a day in 1937 when he woke up and decided to kill himself, and in so doing he brings the other stages of his life into view. In his highly self-conscious narration he asks his readers to imagine that they are spectators on the river's bank, watching the story of his life pass by like the showboat in his town called *The Floating Opera.*

In 1919 while serving in World War I, Todd learns about his heart condition from an army doctor. During the battle of the Argonne, he spends hours in a mud hole with a German soldier. Without any language but mutually terrified by death, they share a moment of deep human intimacy. They smile, communicate by sign language, and become friends. When the battle ends, Todd is afraid to leave him, so he drives his bayonet into the German's throat and hears a sound he can never forget.

When he returns from the war, he goes to Johns Hopkins to take the prelaw curriculum. As a college man he adopts the self-conscious mask of a roué. One night while visiting a bordello, he encounters Betty June Gunter, the woman with whom he had his first sexual encounter when he was seventeen, and requests her as his prostitute. He tries to apologize to her for the fact that when they first had sex he burst into laughter upon looking at himself in the mirror. Enraged, she tries to kill him with a broken bottle. The incident puts an end to his life as a roué, and he adopts the second mask of a contemplative saint.

While acting the saint and attending law school, he meets and becomes friends with a socialist, Harrison Mack. After law school, Todd's father, Thomas Andrews, kills himself when his assets are destroyed by the stock market crash. Todd writes an enormous, never-to-be-completed manuscript inquiring into his father's death. He stops playing the saint and adopts his third mask, that of a cynic. After he takes over his father's practice, Todd meets Harrison Mack again, this time with his wife Jane. Harrison and Jane decide that Jane should sleep with Todd, and she seduces him. Todd tells them what he imagines

they want to hear: that he loves her and is a virgin. Later, offending them deeply, he reveals that he lied to them and falsely hints that he routinely exacts sex from black women in exchange for legal services.

The finest money of Todd's legal career is won in a complicated battle over Harrison Mack's father's many wills. The old man used his wills to threaten his family, and he accumulated more and more wills as he became progressively more insane. Seventeen wills were in existence at his death, but only the last one he wrote while still sane was legally binding. Todd champions a will that leaves everything to Harrison Mack on the condition that Harrison not support communism; if he refuses, he will receive his father's bottled and collected feces, and the estate of $3 million will go to his mother. Although Harrison has long since given up political radicalism, the mother's attorney proves that Harrison gave money to the anti-fascist resistance in Spain, and Harrison loses the hearing. Todd then has a flash of insight: If Harrison does not receive the feces, the conditions of the will are unfulfilled, and he must therefore receive the money. He demonstrates in court that the mother's maid discarded the feces and wins Harrison's estate for him.

One night when he is impotent with Jane, Todd's mask of cynicism falls away. He decides that the solution to his life's problem is suicide. He is amused later that morning when he hears two old men in the hotel where he lives arguing whether there are any consolations for old age. He makes fun of the one, Haecker, who believes wisdom justifies the pains of old age.

That day, Jane decides to leave him. Todd takes their daughter to *The Floating Opera* showboat to see a poor rendition of Hamlet's soliloquy "To Be or Not to Be" booed off the stage and replaced by a minstrel show. He tries to blow up the showboat but fails. He returns home to find that Haecker has killed himself. Todd decides not to kill himself and writes in his inquiry that logically there is no reason for living or for suicide either.

Angstrom, Harry "Rabbit." *Rabbit, Run; Rabbit Redux; Rabbit Is Rich; Rabbit at Rest.* John Updike. 1960; 1971; 1981; 1990.

Harry "Rabbit" Angstrom is a white American male who tries all through his life to reconcile self-centeredness with a faith in the ultimate rightness of authorities. His greatest problems, however, arise out of his own duties as an authority figure in his family and in society. Harry's saving grace is his ability to rationalize these conflicts or ignore them altogether.

Harry is a former high school basketball star. His story begins in the town of Brewer, Pennsylvania, where he works demonstrating kitchen gadgets. To Harry's dismay, his wife JANICE SPRINGER ANGSTROM spends her days drinking and watching television while she cares for their child Nelson in their claustrophobic apartment in Mt.

Judge, a Brewer suburb. One day, almost mechanically, Harry flees. Dreaming of Delaware's rich DuPont women, he drives in a vague southerly direction. After his return to Mt. Judge, he meets and moves in with Ruth Leonard, a sometime prostitute.

Harry eventually senses animosity coming from Ruth, who sees that he has a low opinion of her. When Harry learns that Janice is going into labor with their second child, he runs repentantly to the hospital. He is proud of her upon her return home, but when Janice refuses to have sex with him, Harry runs to Ruth again. Alone, Janice gets drunk and accidentally drowns the baby. At the funeral, Harry publicly blames Janice for the death. He runs into the nearby woods and then to Ruth's. When he gets there, Ruth implicates him in the baby's death, calling him "Mr. Death himself." Then she tells him that she is pregnant and asks him to divorce his wife and marry her. Again, Harry runs away.

Ten years later, in the summer of 1969, Harry is working with his father at the Verity Press and living with Janice and Nelson in the new subdivision of Penn Villas. Harry proudly sports an American flag decal on the rear window of his car and has a patriotic attitude about the Vietnam War. His American dream is disrupted, however, when his father tells him of rumors that Janice is cheating on him. When Harry discovers that she is indeed having an affair with Charlie Stavros, a coworker at her father's Toyota dealership, Janice defies him, but Harry acquiesces, telling her to have the affair if she wants it. Janice moves in with Stavros and takes the car.

One night in a bar, Harry meets Jill Pendleton, a young white runaway from a wealthy Connecticut home, and Hubert "Skeeter" Johnson, a radical black Vietnam veteran who is wanted on drug charges. To the dismay of Harry's racist neighbors, the two strangers move in with him and Nelson. Eventually two neighbors confront Harry and warn him of the consequences of his behavior. Harry's house is burned down one night, and Jill is killed in the blaze. Harry drops Skeeter off on a country road, and he and Janice reconcile.

Another ten years pass, and Harry becomes rich working at Springer Motors with Charlie Stavros. His interest in Janice has waned. He longs for sex with Cindy Murkett, an attractive married woman whose house has a sunken living room. This peace is fractured when Nelson drops out of college and returns home with a friend, Melanie. Against Harry's objections, Nelson goes to work and begins making bizarre trades.

Harry believes his son is irresponsible; indeed, when Nelson impregnates and then marries Pru Lubell, this further convinces Harry of it. Nelson and Pru move in with the Angstroms and Bessie Springer, Janice's mother. At home Nelson often presumes to sit in Harry's cherished Barcalounger. Harry and Janice soon embark on a tropical vacation with their friends, including the Murketts. They

decide to swap partners, but Harry does not get to sleep with Cindy. The next afternoon Bessie Springer asks them to return immediately because Nelson has deserted Pru. Harry and Janice return to their own house, which does not have a sunken living room but rather a step down into the den.

By late 1988, Harry is spending his winters with Janice at their condominium in Valhalla Village in Deleon, Florida. In his mid-fifties, he is tired, fat, and convinced that he is going to die soon. Nelson, who now directs Springer Motors, visits with Pru and their two children, and Harry notices that he is irritable and nervous. Nelson also mysteriously fails to return one night after borrowing his parents' Toyota. Meanwhile, Harry entertains the children. He is sunfishing with his nine-year-old granddaughter Judy when they capsize and he suffers a heart attack.

Back in Pennsylvania, Harry undergoes heart surgery and learns from his mistress, Themla Harrison, that Nelson is a cocaine addict and an embezzler. Nelson enters a rehabilitation program, but the Toyota Motor Corporation terminates the franchise and demands restitution. Harry is reluctant to go along with Janice's plan to sell their house and move back into the old Springer home with Nelson's family. Meanwhile, one night while Nelson and Janice are away, Harry and Pru have sex. When the brief affair is exposed, Harry drives south, as he did thirty years earlier, but this time he continues to Florida.

Harry lives a melancholy existence in Florida, filling up the time by walking around the less plasticized neighborhoods in this land of death. Despite advice from doctors, Harry cannot refrain from eating unhealthy foods. During a game of basketball, Harry suffers another attack. He lies once again in the hospital, perhaps near death.

Angstrom, Janice Springer. *Rabbit, Run; Rabbit Redux; Rabbit Is Rich; Rabbit at Rest.* John Updike. 1960; 1971; 1981; 1990.

Janice Springer Angstrom, the wife of HARRY "RABBIT" ANGSTROM, is a woman whose apparent stupidity and lack of originality mask a latent streak of assertiveness. Despite the trials she endures with her selfish husband, Janice clumsily holds on to her own interests and identity.

Janice and Rabbit met when he was a high school senior and a basketball star and she was a freshman working at a department store in Brewer, Pennsylvania. As a young wife, Janice has one son, Nelson, and is expecting another child. While Harry works, Janice cares for Nelson, and drinks and smokes in front of the television. One night Harry abandons his family after he and Janice have a fight. When Janice goes into labor, Harry leaves his mistress and goes to the hospital to be with his wife. In her drugged state after the delivery, Janice is affectionate and forgiving, but the next day she finds Harry's repentance boring. After returning home, Janice is unwilling to make love, and Harry flees. A drunk Janice accidentally drowns the baby.

At the funeral Harry coarsely alludes to her "killing" the baby and runs into the woods.

Ten years later Janice has grown more independent, both mentally and economically. She now works at Springer Motors, founded by her father, and is having an affair with Charlie Stavros, a coworker. When Harry finds out and confronts her, she is at once apologetic about her actions and emphatic about her needs, and is frustrated to find Harry basically indifferent. Although Janice tells her husband that she is going to break off the affair, she instead leaves a note for Harry and moves in with Charlie.

Janice learns through her friend Peggy that Harry is sharing the house with a runaway white girl and a black radical, raising eyebrows in their all-white neighborhood. Janice asks Harry for a divorce and custody of Nelson, whom she fears is being corrupted in this unorthodox ménage. Although apart for a time, Janice and Harry reunite after Janice's affair sours and racists bomb the Angstrom home.

By the end of the 1970s, Janice and Harry are enjoying prosperity. Janice's father has died, leaving Harry in control of Springer Motors, and Janice spends her days playing tennis and drinking with friends at the Flying Eagle Country Club. She and Harry share the Springer house with Janice's mother Bessie. When their son Nelson drops out of college and returns home with a girl, Melanie, Janice and Harry disagree over whether he should be allowed to work for the company, which would require the dismissal of Charlie Stavros. Janice and Bessie align against Harry, and after Nelson's true girlfriend, Pru Lubell, arrives pregnant, the two young people marry and move into the already cramped Springer/Angstrom household. Janice and Harry then agree to get their own house.

In 1988, Janice and Harry are living half the year at their Florida condominium. Bessie died seven years earlier, so Janice has complete title to the company, which is now run by Nelson. Janice finds out, however, that Nelson is a cocaine addict and that he has embezzled thousands of dollars from the business. She hires an accountant, and when the scale of the theft is discovered, she tells Nelson that he must enter a rehabilitation program or face possible legal action.

Janice, newly self-assertive, enrolls in real estate classes, which she was inspired to take after seeing the film *Working Girl*. Unfortunately, however, the Toyota Motor Corporation terminates their franchise and demands restitution of the embezzled money. Janice considers selling their house, a deal that would also provide her with a sale and a commission. Harry, as co-owner, refuses to agree.

Janice is shocked to learn from Pru that she has had a one-night stand with Harry. Janice telephones him; in response, Harry, instead of driving to see her at the old Springer house, drives to the condominium in Florida. Janice refuses to call or talk to him, but when Harry has his second heart attack, she and Nelson fly to Florida.

Apley, George William. *The Late George Apley*. John P. Marquand. 1937.

George William Apley was born in 1866 into a wealthy, established Boston family. Snobbish and conservative, a staunch defender of the privileged class, Apley is nevertheless a man of strict principles who struggles throughout his life with private, mostly unarticulated doubts about the imperatives of his tradition.

Apley receives a well-tutored and disciplined upbringing designed to prepare him to take his place among upper-class Boston society. In the middle of his senior year at Harvard, he commits one of the few improprieties of his life: He becomes infatuated with Mary Monahan, a young woman from South Boston. His father soon puts an end to the affair, however, deeming it unsuitable because Mary is a member of a lower class. Upon graduating from college, Apley is sent to Europe for the summer; he returns ready to take on the responsibilities of his social position. He attends Harvard Law School and works summers as a laborer at the family cotton mill. It has been decided that he has no head for business, so his inheritance is put in trust. A position is found for him in a law firm specializing in real estate management, and he eventually becomes a partner.

Although he is clearly not in love, Apley marries Catherine Bosworth, a young woman from a good family whom he has known since childhood. The couple has a son, John, and a daughter, Eleanor. Apley spends the passing years quietly and punctiliously fulfilling the familial and social responsibilities expected of him. But he is increasingly troubled by the changes he sees taking place in American society and culture in general and by the rebelliousness of his own children as they grow into adults. He is bitterly disappointed by his son's lack of respect for the family tradition, which becomes apparent after the young man's service in World War I; he is shocked when his daughter espouses the ideas of Freud. Apley then becomes active in conservative municipal politics, alienating several important Boston businessmen in the process.

Ever the proper Bostonian, Apley nevertheless appears to mellow somewhat as he ages, in response to private disappointments, public difficulties, and an increasing feeling of futility in the face of change. Outraged at first when his son marries a divorcée, Apley becomes quite fond of her in the end. He makes the mistake of starting a campaign against a powerful, corrupt Irish politician and as a result is lured to a hotel room and arrested in a frame-up. At first he intends to go through with a public trial despite the damage to his reputation, but he is contacted by the love of his youth, Mary Monahan, who as it happens is related to the politician in question. George meets with the Irishman, decides that he likes him, hires the policemen who arrested him to be watchmen at the

Apley Mills, and thereafter begins to withdraw from public life. Keeping his conservative principles intact, he manages to take a tolerant stand with regard to certain issues of the day: He is actively anti-Prohibition and argues in support of such literary innovators as Ernest Hemingway and D. H. Lawrence.

Apley is shrewd enough to get out of the stock market before the crash of 1929, but he falls ill shortly thereafter and his health begins to fail. He becomes increasingly introspective during this time, acknowledging in a letter to his son that the obligation of convention has caused him unhappiness even as he recognizes its necessity. Apley spends his last months enjoying the company of his grandson and arranging his affairs, making sure in particular that his son will tactfully give assistance to Mary Monahan should she require it. Apley dies in December 1933, two weeks after his son returns to take his place in Boston society.

Appalachee Red. *Appalachee Red.* Raymond Andrews. 1978.

Appalachee Red is the son of Little Bit Thompson by her white employer, John Morgan, who forced her to become his lover while her husband, Big Man, was serving time on a chain gang. Little Bit gives birth to a red-skinned baby in a house given to her by Morgan, and she sends the baby to Chicago with a sister before Big Man returns. They then sell the house to Sam Wallace, who opens a café there.

In 1945 the "red" baby, now grown, returns, although no one knows who he is. Big, mean-looking, and silent, he takes a room above Sam's Café and also dares to take Baby Sweet as his mistress. Baby Sweet had been the mistress of the brutally racist Sheriff Clyde "Boots" White, who had murdered Big Man Thompson and driven Little Bit insane. The sheriff instinctively fears the stranger and relinquishes Baby Sweet to him.

Soon called Appalachee Red for his light-skinned red color, the stranger strikes fear in everyone's hearts, especially when his presence has a mysteriously debilitating effect on Sam, who dies, leaving the café to Red. Red opens a drinking and gambling club, protected by Boots in return for bribes and political support.

Over time, rumors and fears about Appalachee Red abate somewhat, but no one comes close to him, not even Baby Sweet, whom he treats kindly and to whom he shows passion but not affection. Red is also kind to Blue Thompson, son of Big Man and Little Bit. Although the half-brothers meet only twice, Red hires Blue to work at the café and later pays his way through college.

Red grows wealthy, inspiring the admiration of the black community and the indignation of the white when he rides his black chauffeur-driven Cadillac through town every Sunday morning to Morgan Hill, where he watches his father's house. This ritual attracts the attention of John

Morgan's daughter Roxanne, who becomes sexually obsessed with Red.

When Blue, now a Freedom Marcher, returns home upon the death of Little Bit, Appalachee Red reveals to him his history and his true identity. Accepted by neither blacks nor whites, Red became a loner, intent on achieving his aims at all costs. After deserting the army, he returned to the house where he had been born to claim his due. Yet when Blue returns, bringing his civil rights perspective with him, Red knows he must leave.

The next day at Little Bit's funeral, Roxanne ends up driving away with her half-brother in the black Cadillac. That night Red kills Boots, thus exacting the full measure of his vengeance before leaving town.

Arbuton, Miles. *A Chance Acquaintance.* William Dean Howells. 1873.

Miles Arbuton, a Bostonian gentleman who has a chance encounter with a provincial American girl named KITTY ELLISON, assumes the cultural sophistication and superiority of his European counterparts and, despite his self-perception as a just and equitable man, suffers from severe social prejudice. He considered entering the ministry, but the thought of "persons of low extraction" entering heaven was so distasteful to him that he abandoned his religious calling.

On a return trip from Niagara Falls to Boston via Quebec, Arbuton encounters the Ellisons, a family from the Midwest, traveling with their niece Kitty. He considers the Ellisons boorish and provincial and avoids their company. When Kitty mistakenly clutches his arm aboard the ship, Arbuton's sense of propriety is so rigid that he feels he must apologize for their physical contact. He continues to interact with the Ellisons out of social obligation but finds himself increasingly drawn to the forthright and earnest Kitty.

Upon their arrival in Quebec, Arbuton offers to help the Ellisons find accommodations. He finds an excuse to stay in the same lodgings and pay frequent visits to Mrs. Ellison, who is nursing a twisted ankle, and her niece. Arbuton and Kitty take frequent walks, becoming better acquainted with Quebec and with each other. On an expedition to Montgomery, Arbuton saves Kitty from a vicious dog by throwing himself between her and the attacking animal. Propriety then dictates that he apologize to the dog's owner, a kindly old man, and offer him his torn coat. Kitty is impressed by his gentlemanly behavior, and he becomes increasingly protective and possessive of her. Soon even the proprietor of the inn mistakes them for newlyweds. So infatuated is Arbuton with Kitty that he decides to ask for her hand in marriage, despite the difference in their social standing.

Just after Arbuton confesses his unconditional love for Kitty, he encounters two female acquaintances from Boston. Suddenly embarrassed by her obviously inferior station, he not only avoids introducing Kitty but abandons her in order to escort the women home. Upon returning to his erstwhile fiancée, Arbuton claims that he was waiting to introduce her at a time when she could make her best impression. Kitty rightly accuses him of being ashamed to acknowledge her because of her country travel clothes. When Kitty rejects his proposal despite his protestations of love, Arbuton is left to confront the severity of his social prejudice and the true rudeness of his own behavior toward the woman he loves.

Archbald, Jenny Blair. *The Sheltered Life*. Ellen Glasgow. 1932.

This story recounts the life of the shallow ingenue JENNY BLAIR ARCHBALD through childhood and into young adulthood when she falls passionately in love with GEORGE BIRDSONG, an older married man. Jenny Blair lives in Virginia with her widowed mother, her two aunts, and her grandfather General Archbald. Spirited and impulsive, she wants a life different from that of the other women in her family, but she is never able to follow through on any of her plans to escape to the exciting North.

As a child Jenny Blair likes roller-skating much more than reading the books assigned by her mother. She also looks forward to her visits to the home of George and Eva Birdsong, close friends of her family. Jenny Blair idolizes Eva, but it is with her husband George that Jenny makes a special alliance. One day while roller-skating in an unsavory part of town called the Bottom, she falls and hurts her head. She is taken to the home of Memoria, a black woman who does the Archbalds' laundry. There, coincidentally, she meets George Birdsong, who explains that she shouldn't mention her adventure to anyone because it would worry her mother. Jenny Blair, thrilled by George's romantic, roguish air, treasures their secret.

Though generous and considerate, Jenny Blair is often thoughtless. She attends to Eva when she falls mysteriously ill, and then while Eva is undergoing a potentially fatal operation, she flirts with George, who is pacing in the hospital courtyard. They talk, and he teases her before leaving her with a romantic kiss. Although George later pretends that nothing happened, Jenny Blair falls in love with him. After Eva gets out of the hospital, Jenny gives her presents and keeps her company, but continues to nurse a secret passion for George.

Jenny Blair has been trying to decide what to do with her life, but after that afternoon at the hospital, her plans to go to New York with her friend Bena dwindle. She stops refusing her mother's plans to give her a debutante ball and resigns herself to the search for a husband; however, even this effort is hampered by her love for George.

Jenny Blair is tortured whenever she sees George, for he doesn't seem to remember that he once kissed her. Confronting him before her summer vacation in the coun-

try, she asks if he remembers that afternoon at the hospital. He does, but he reminds her that he is much older than she and admonishes her to forget about him. She goes away with her family and briefly romances a boy her own age. But at the summer's end, Jenny Blair returns home and is captivated by George once more.

As the novel progresses, Jenny Blair spends more and more time with Eva, who seems to be having a mental breakdown. Although she vows never to do anything that would hurt Eva, Jenny Blair's resolve weakens, and she remains unable to overcome her attraction to George. And George finds her equally difficult to resist.

One evening Jenny Blair comes upon George sitting alone on the porch. They converse awkwardly, for George seems cruelly preoccupied with Eva's health. When he turns to go, the anguished Jenny Blair breaks down and confesses her jealous devotion. No sooner does George take her in his arms, however, than Eva appears in the doorway. He thrusts Jenny Blair from him and at his wife's command disappears into the shadowy interior of the house. Abandoned and confused, Jenny Blair races down to the garden, where her childhood nightmares rise up to meet her. Amid the clatter of ancient voices she hears a large crashing sound: George has been shot. Jenny Blair stumbles into the library to find him sprawled lifeless in his chair, with Eva sitting pale and waxlike nearby. The novel ends with Jenny Blair hysterically proclaiming her innocence: "I didn't mean anything," she cries, flinging herself into her grandfather's arms. "I didn't mean anything in the world."

Archer, Isabel. *The Portrait of a Lady*. Henry James. 1881.

The adventures of Isabel Archer, the novel's questing, imaginative heroine, begin when Isabel travels to England to visit her aunt Lydia Touchett, her wealthy uncle Daniel, and her cousin Ralph at Gardencourt, their country estate. Isabel's parents are dead, and there is nothing in particular to keep her in her native Albany, New York. She arrives in England with high hopes and noble goals: to see life, to choose her own path, to be as happy as possible, and "to know." But over the next six years Isabel's life follows a path to knowledge that she could not have predicted when she departed from America as a vivacious and curious young woman.

In England, Isabel instantly charms her acquaintances, who are refreshed by her perceptive mind and her talent for verbal self-expression. Lord Warburton, Ralph's friend, a kind and immensely wealthy English nobleman, falls in love with Isabel and asks her to marry him. She refuses, insisting that in marrying him she would be trying to escape her fate. Nor is it Isabel's fate to marry CASPAR GOODWOOD, the grim, energetic young Bostonian who courted Isabel in Albany and travels to Europe only to have his proposal rejected by her for the second time.

When MADAME SERENA MERLE, a friend of Mrs. Touchett's, visits Gardencourt, she and Isabel become close friends. While impressed by this older woman's insights and talents, Isabel is nevertheless vaguely puzzled when Madame Merle avoids talking about her personal history. After Madame Merle departs from Gardencourt, Daniel Touchett dies as the result of a long illness. His will names Isabel as a major heir; at the age of twenty-two she is the stunned recipient of approximately £70,000.

Soon after, Madame Merle invites Isabel to meet an old acquaintance of hers—GILBERT OSMOND, a bachelor who lives in Florence, Italy. While vacationing in Florence with Aunt Lydia, Isabel meets Osmond, and a courtship begins between them. Overwhelmed by what she sees as Osmond's originality, his exquisite taste, and his shrewd powers of observation, she eventually accepts his proposal of marriage. Her friends, relatives, and rejected suitors are universally dismayed by Isabel's decision. When Ralph tells her that she is making a mistake and calls Osmond a "sterile dilettante," Isabel vehemently defends Osmond for the very qualities that others criticize: his lack of title, property, position, reputation, and money. Osmond, she believes, is simply a man "and not a proprietor."

Isabel marries Osmond and moves to Rome, where she resides with her husband and his meek, innocent teenage daughter Pansy. The marriage is unhappy, and it is not long before Isabel begins to realize the extent of her misjudgment. Nevertheless, remaining true to her sense of loyalty, Isabel stays with Osmond and works very hard to conceal her unhappiness.

Now a stepmother, she becomes an important presence in the life of Pansy, whom Osmond does his best to keep as if she were an object in one of his collections. Pansy, eligible for marriage, falls in love with Edward Rosier, a sincere youth with little money who is totally devoted to the sweet, obedient girl. Isabel, who is no longer her vital, opinionated self but instead prone to long silences and much observation, declines to involve herself in Pansy's courtship. She refuses to help Rosier and, moreover, against her husband's self-interested urgings, refrains from encouraging the wealthy Lord Warburton to propose to Pansy.

One day Isabel catches a glimpse of Osmond and Madame Merle together in the parlor, posed in an unusually relaxed, familiar fashion. The image haunts her; in the novel's most famous chapter, she sits by the fireplace and reflects at great length on her situation, concluding, among other things, that her husband actually hates her. Indeed, when Warburton does not pursue Pansy, Osmond blames Isabel and assumes she is working against him. Soon after, Isabel receives a letter from Aunt Lydia informing her that Ralph is dying. Isabel, who adores Ralph, wishes to go to England, but Osmond strongly opposes her.

While deliberating over the painful decision she must make, Isabel receives a visit from Osmond's sister, the Countess Gemini, who tells her the true history of Osmond's relationship with Madame Merle. Armed with the knowledge that Osmond and Madame Merle were once lovers, that Madame Merle is secretly the true mother of Pansy, and that her own marriage to Osmond has been the design of an infinitely calculating older woman, Isabel departs for England against the wishes of her husband. Before leaving Rome, she visits the frail and brokenhearted Pansy in the convent where Osmond has sent her, and she promises Pansy that she will return. At the convent she encounters Madame Merle, who adds to Isabel's knowledge by telling her something she never suspected: Years ago it was Ralph, not Isabel's uncle, who arranged for Isabel's vast inheritance.

In England, sitting beside her cousin's deathbed, Isabel passionately and tearfully expresses her love for Ralph and tells him she now believes Osmond married her only because she was rich. After Ralph dies, Isabel lingers at Gardencourt, wondering whether she should return to Rome, to Osmond, to her miserable marriage, or whether she should break her promise to Pansy and remain in England. Deep in thought, she is interrupted by Caspar Goodwood, who urges her to leave Osmond and stay with him. Goodwood takes Isabel in his arms and kisses her passionately. Filled for the first time with the powerful sensation of what it is to be loved and desired, she breaks away from him and runs across the Gardencourt lawn.

This is the last time Isabel appears in the novel. In a brief concluding chapter, her friend Henrietta Stackpole informs a dumbfounded Caspar Goodwood that Isabel departed that morning for Rome.

Archer, Lew. *The Moving Target.* Ross MacDonald. 1948.

Narrator Lew Archer is a cynical private detective whose already battered moral sense is turned inside out as he makes his way blindly through the Sampson case, which he calls "the wildest mess I'd ever seen or heard of."

The story begins when Archer visits Mrs. Sampson, the wife of a Texas millionaire who has disappeared. Archer, whose own wife is divorcing him because "she didn't like the company I kept," is sickened by Mrs. Sampson, who says she wants her marriage to last so that she can outlive her rich husband. Archer has a slightly kinder response to Sampson's daughter Miranda and to young Alan Taggert, who pilots Sampson's private plane and has a hard time keeping Miranda at bay. Taggert, who flew planes in World War II, seems arrogant but trustworthy. Miranda seems hysterical, but she is still young.

Archer's kindest feelings are for Albert Graves, the man who put him onto the Sampsons in the first place. He had known him when Graves was an idealistic young district attorney. Since then, Graves's idealism has worn away, and he has been working as a lawyer for the rich. But there is one idealistic spark left: Graves clearly loves Miranda. Archer pities Graves, knowing that an older man won't be able to compete with Taggert. Then Archer remembers that Graves is only a few years older than he is.

Archer learns that Sampson was last seen in Los Angeles with an aging actress named Fay Estabrook. Archer picks Fay up at a bar, and they slowly fall into an alcoholic stupor. Archer glances up at the mirror behind the bar and decides that if he saw his own face on a stranger, he wouldn't trust it. He grows disgusted with himself and with Fay, who is not giving him any leads. He takes her home and looks around her house while she sleeps. The phone rings. It is a woman named Betty at the Wild Piano bar. Just then a man named Troy enters. He says he is Fay's husband and throws Archer out. Archer goes to the Wild Piano where a woman named Betty Fraley is singing "The Psychosomatic Blues." Archer pretends to be a fan of hers. He begins a round of questioning that collapses when she realizes he has never heard any of her records. Betty calls Puddler, the bouncer. The next thing Archer knows, Taggert is pulling Puddler away and dragging Archer from the alley.

Archer and Taggert drive back to Fay's house and find evidence that Sampson has been kidnapped. The next day Mrs. Sampson receives a letter asking for a $100,000 ransom. Miranda now begins flirting with Archer, who responds by giving her "a filial kiss." He is torn between desire for Miranda and cynical detachment. He feels even sorrier for Graves. Then another letter arrives, telling them to leave the money on the highway that night. Graves drops off the money while Archer waits. A gun goes off and a car speeds away. Archer rushes up to find a man lying dead in a black limousine with an empty money bag next to him. Archer follows after, fights with Puddler, and kills him. He has been feeling death in the air for the last few days—and now he feels more confused than ever.

The next morning Archer goes to the Sampson house and hears from one of the servants that Taggert has some of Betty Fraley's records. Archer finds nothing in Taggert's room, but he remembers seeing Taggert throwing something in the ocean a few days earlier. Archer dives down and finds a black disk. He confronts Taggert, realizing it was he who kidnapped Sampson. Taggert is genial. He denies everything, then pulls a gun. Suddenly Graves appears and shoots Taggert dead. Archer is grateful but realizes that Graves is an excellent shot and could have simply wounded Taggert. Now they've lost the key to the whole case. When Miranda hears that Taggert is dead, she embraces Graves and says that she will marry him now. Archer realizes why Graves killed Taggert.

With the dim hope of still finding Sampson alive, Archer searches for Betty Fraley and finds her in a suburban house being tortured by Fay Estabrook and Troy. Archer learns that Betty was their partner in crime until she fell in love with Taggert. Betty and Taggert had decided to kidnap Sampson with the help of Betty's hated brother—the dead man in the black limousine. Archer rescues Betty and demands she take him to Sampson. She says Sampson is in an abandoned building by the sea. Archer calls Graves, telling him to get there as soon as possible with doctors and the police. Archer arrives to find nobody there at all. He enters and is immediately knocked unconscious.

When he awakens, Graves is standing over him, apparently having rescued him. Graves says Sampson is dead. Archer cannot figure out who the killer could be, but when he calls the police and asks why they never arrived, they say Graves never called them. Archer realizes that Graves killed Sampson for the money—he and Miranda were married that afternoon. Archer goes to Humphreys, the D.A., and expresses bitterness that Graves could have done something like this. Humphreys says it wasn't for money; Graves was a good man who worked hard all his life until suddenly everything went sour and lost its meaning. Graves struck out blindly and killed a man, then found he could kill again. Graves is miserable and has just confessed. Archer, who has continually seen shrewdness and evil in the wrong places, finds he is as blind as anyone else.

Archer, Newland. *The Age of Innocence.* Edith Wharton. 1920.

When Newland Archer, a contemplative young dilettante and member of elite New York society, sees the unconventional COUNTESS ELLEN OLENSKA at the opera, he is intrigued. Listening to stories by his acquaintances, he learns that Ellen, the unhappy black sheep of her family, recently abandoned her wealthy Polish husband and returned home to New York. Newland wonders why he should be concerned with Ellen's fate, especially since he has just announced his engagement to MAY WELLAND, Ellen's cousin. But after meeting Ellen, he finds himself increasingly reflective, silently critical of the social constructs of which he is a part and which his fiancée unthinkingly endorses. More and more preoccupied with Ellen, he visits her at her home and sends her a dozen yellow roses without a card.

Soon after, a partner at the law firm where Newland is employed tells him that Ellen Olenska is suing her husband for divorce. Informing Newland that the whole family is against Ellen's action, the partner gives him Ellen's papers and letters and tells him to handle the case. He visits Ellen, who vehemently expresses her desire to be free and wipe out her past. Newland admits that their society is narrow and unjust, but nevertheless he counsels her to remain married, and she finally agrees.

Failing to answer an urgent note from Ellen because he is confused about his feelings toward her, Newland tries to convince May that they should marry sooner than planned. When he sees Ellen again, he is shocked to learn that her husband wants to take her back. In an emotional confrontation, Newland tells Ellen that she is the woman he would have married if it had been possible. Ellen, who feels the same strong attraction to him, points out the irony in Newland's confession: He is also the man who made it impossible for them to be together because he prevented her from suing for divorce. Returning home that night, Newland receives a telegram from May accepting his proposal for an early spring wedding.

Now married but not very happily, Newland is the only family member who believes Ellen should not return to her husband. When Newland hears that Ellen went to Boston to answer a mysterious telegram, he travels there to find her. In Boston he meets Monsieur Rivière, a messenger from Ellen's husband who has come to persuade her to return to him. Speaking privately to Newland, Monsieur Rivière expresses his firm belief that Ellen should not return to her husband. Newland begins to imagine leaving May for Ellen. Ellen says it is impossible; they cannot act to destroy the lives of their loved ones.

Thirty years later Newland is a widower with three happy children. Though his days have been filled decently and completely, he knows he has missed "the flower of life." When his energetic son Dallas telephones to invite him to travel to Paris, Newland accepts. Once there, Dallas insists that they visit the Countess Olenska, whom he has heard about but never met. Newland goes with his son to her house but decides at the last minute not to go in. He sits on a bench and gazes up at the Countess's balcony, trying to imagine the scene. "It's more real to me here than if I went up," he finds himself saying, and after a long time, when he sees the manservant close the balcony shutters, Newland walks back alone to his hotel.

Archie, Howard. *The Song of the Lark.* Willa Cather. 1915.

Howard Archie, a physician in the small town of Moonstone, Colorado, becomes the admiring guardian of a gifted singer. Partly to avoid a home life made cheerless by a dour and stingy wife, Archie promotes the musical talent of THEA KRONBORG, the sixth child of the town's Methodist minister.

Archie's romanticism colors his attitudes toward his work and his personal relationships. In medical school he took the ideals of the profession very seriously, but he married Belle White for sentimental reasons: She was considered the most beautiful girl in their small Michigan town and had set her sights on Archie. When Archie meets Thea some years later, his wife has lost her charm. "Dry and withered," Belle also wants no children. The community believes that the doctor gravitates toward Thea because he longs for a daughter.

Archie treats Thea for pneumonia when she is eleven, and a friendship develops between them. Thea goes to Archie's office frequently and sometimes accompanies him on visits. He often stops to hear her practice the piano,

which she does with passionate devotion. As she enters adolescence, Thea reveals to Archie her dreams of developing her talent and studying music in Germany. Archie also treats Thea's admirer, Ray Kennedy, when he is badly injured in a railroad accident. Ray leaves Thea his entire savings of $600 and instructs Archie on how she is to spend it. Ray wants Thea to spend a winter in Chicago studying with the finest musicians. Archie convinces Thea's parents to allow her to go and takes her to Chicago himself.

When Thea returns from Chicago the following summer, she again turns to Archie for support. Thea's siblings resent the special treatment she receives, but Archie encourages her because her enthusiasm allays his own doubts about his purpose in life. A year later, after Thea has spent another winter studying in Chicago, she contacts him and requests that he meet her immediately in New York. Archie, who has never been to that city, departs instantly. Thea explains to him that she has become involved with FRED OTTENBURG, a very perceptive and generous young businessman, but she cannot marry him because he is unable to obtain a divorce from his first wife. Rather than borrow money from Fred, who is quite willing to lend it, Thea asks Dr. Archie to fund a trip to Germany where she plans to study. Archie happily lends her the money, and she sails for Germany a few days later.

During the next ten years while Thea is achieving great success in Europe, Archie's investments in the mining industry make him a very wealthy man. His wife dies, and he moves to a luxurious home in Denver where he conducts most of his business. Fred Ottenburg, to whom Thea had introduced Archie, becomes a close friend and business associate. When Thea returns to New York, Fred and Archie travel there to see her perform at the Metropolitan. When Archie first sees her on stage, he feels estranged from this compelling, dynamic woman; he can't believe it is Thea. When Archie visits Thea later at home, however, the affectionate, easy companionship between them is renewed. Archie remains in New York for some time in order to see several of Thea's brilliant performances, and his faith in her integrity and intelligence increases.

Arnold. "The Patterns of Love." William Maxwell. 1943.

Arnold, a quiet, observant man, ordinarily lives alone in town but visits the Talbot family at their country home every spring. He enjoys the lively household and the family's "patterns of love."

After being awakened by thirteen-year-old Kate Talbot's bantam rooster, Arnold joins Mrs. Talbot and George, her youngest son, for breakfast. George, who is fond of Arnold and last year slept with him in the guest room, asks Arnold if he misses him. Arnold replies that he does and tells George that there was no one to talk to and no one to watch him shave. Mrs. Talbot, slightly possessive of George, changes the subject by telling Arnold that Kate will be going to a house party that afternoon and needs to have her hair done. Arnold says he plans to take *Anna Karenina* to the nearby "little house," a small structure on the property that Mrs. Talbot had built after reading *A Room of One's Own.*

Sitting in the little house, Arnold hears George arguing with Duncan, his older brother. Eventually, the boys appear at the window and ask Arnold for permission to enter. Once inside, they immediately begin to argue again until Satan, the family's Great Dane, appears at the door. They let Satan enter, and things become very noisy until Mr. Talbot comes along and orders the boys and the dog to leave Arnold in peace. As the boys leave, Arnold notices the way Duncan helps George jump out of the window and George accepts his brother's assistance. Arnold decides that their hostility has two faces, one being the face of love.

Arnold has always been impressed by the proliferation of animal life at the Talbots'. In addition to the bantam roosters and the Great Dane, the family also has cats, rabbits, chickens, and two new bantam ducklings. Resting in his room, Arnold compares his own well-ordered life in town without children or pets to the Talbots' life in the country.

The next morning Mr. Talbot is upset because Kate's bantam hen is missing from its nest. Arnold observes that the whole family feels Kate's loss; what affects one of them affects them all. Later that afternoon, Mrs. Talbot discovers that one of the bantam ducklings is also missing from its cage. The family finds the duckling with Kate, much to their relief.

The Talbots, including Satan, take Arnold to the train. At the last minute Mrs. Talbot, perceiving Arnold's loneliness, offers him some radishes, but he refuses. As he gets out of the car, George and Duncan are arguing, but they are finally persuaded to say good-bye to him. Arnold watches the station wagon drive away and listens in vain for the sound of the wood thrush, which he often heard from the Talbots' little house.

Arrowsmith, Martin. *Arrowsmith.* Sinclair Lewis. 1925.

When he begins studying medicine at the University of Winnemac, Martin Arrowsmith, a pale, ascetic twenty-one-year-old, is considered "romantic-looking" by the university's coeds. However, at this early stage of his career, Martin is preoccupied with the opposing demands of practical medicine and scientific research. These divergent paths are symbolized by two characters: the learned and benign Professor Edward Edwards, head of the department of chemistry, and the enigmatic MAX GOTTLIEB, professor of bacteriology, who is dedicated to an isolated and seemingly futile attempt to synthesize antitoxin. Martin alternately vilifies and idolizes each man as he vacillates between the ideals of high-minded asceticism and pragmatism, unable, as always, to choose the path that will give him the greatest fulfillment and satisfaction.

As his education draws to a close, Martin embroils himself in another contradiction, this time with LEORA TOZER and Madeline Fox, the two women to whom he is engaged. The prosaic Leora triumphs over Madeline, whose energetic pursuit of literature and refinement Martin had admired. Shortly thereafter Martin and Leora are married.

Following an argument with Gottlieb, now his mentor, Martin abandons research and decides to become a small-town doctor. He and Leora move to Wheatsylvania, North Dakota, Leora's hometown. But Martin finds that the local inhabitants do not share his enthusiastic and enlightened approach to medicine, and after a few successes and a series of near disasters, he leaves his practice and moves on to tackle the problems of public health in Nautilus, Iowa. There he falls under the supervision of the local hero, Dr. Almus Pickerbaugh, and Pickerbaugh's young daughter Orchid. Just as he had embraced the cause of practical medicine, so Martin now pursues public health education with fervor.

Yet once again Martin is forced to give up this position under a hail of public accusation and misunderstanding, and it is not until he arrives in New York and begins work as a medical researcher at the prestigious McGurk Institute that he finds his true vocation. At McGurk, Martin begins his most productive research and painstakingly discovers "the phage," a potential cure for epidemics and plagues.

The final test of both Martin's newfound resolve and his recent discovery comes when he is sent to the island of St. Hubert where a plague is raging. Once again he finds himself caught between opposing ideals: on one side the practical and humane impulse to distribute his phage liberally, and on the other the single-minded scientific approach that would allow him to use the inhabitants of the island as guinea pigs in his experiments. Martin faces another conflict when he meets and finds himself attracted to Joyce Lanyon, a member of the world of high society that he has so fervently condemned. His dilemma is tragically resolved with the death of Leora, and Martin immerses himself in a new project: to find a cure for the plague that is ravaging St. Hubert.

On his return to New York, Martin tries to lose himself in his research but becomes increasingly attracted to Joyce and is soon enmeshed in her wealthy, seductive life-style. Finally realizing that he must make a choice, he ultimately leaves Joyce and their young child to pursue his lonely research with the taciturn Terry Wickett in an isolated cabin far from the city. As the novel ends, Martin is on the verge of his greatest discovery, made possible by his realization that if he is to pursue his research with the dedication it demands, he must bow to no other god.

Ashford, Nancy. *Magnificent Obsession.* Lloyd C. Douglas. 1929.

Nancy Ashford, the superintendent of Brightwood Hospital, is a strong and understanding woman who acts as a guide and counsel to young doctors, a confidante to the nurses, and an assistant to DR. WAYNE HUDSON, an eminent brain surgeon.

As a young woman, Nancy married a promising brain surgeon, a protégé of Dr. Hudson's, but early in the marriage her husband became ill and died. Shortly afterward Nancy joined the staff of Dr. Hudson's experimental hospital as an operating nurse, but she quickly assumed many of the administrative responsibilities burdening the brilliant man. In time her decisions came to represent his opinions, and she acquired a quiet but unmistakable authority at Brightwood.

Because of her compassion, Nancy never excites any jealousy despite her unmistakable influence over Dr. Hudson. Patients and staff turn to her for comfort and advice. Nancy is a somewhat incongruous figure, with her masculine restraint, young, feminine face, and hair that turned white when her husband died.

Nancy's extreme reserve prevents her from revealing her love for Dr. Hudson. Their working relationship is very close: He confides every indecision and difficulty to her. Nancy is also aware of his having contributed, secretly and with mysterious motives, to certain private charities. Although Dr. Hudson has reciprocal romantic feelings for her, they refuse to acknowledge their affection. They cannot marry because Joyce, Dr. Hudson's daughter from his first marriage, would not allow her father to marry a woman whom she considers "only a nurse." When Dr. Hudson informs Nancy that he will marry a college friend of Joyce's, it requires all her strength to congratulate him. Although she assures Dr. Hudson that she is "all right," Nancy knows that nothing will ever be "all right" again.

No one at Brightwood Hospital guesses the depth of Nancy's sorrow when Dr. Hudson drowns in the lake near his country estate. He might have been saved if the oxygen inhalator, which he normally kept at his home, had been immediately available. By a terrible coincidence, the inhalator was across the lake, saving the life of BOBBY MERRICK, a young profligate who, drunk and alone in his sailboat, was knocked unconscious into the water by the jibbing boom. Bobby is sent to Brightwood Hospital to recover from pneumonia and head injuries.

After the accident, Nancy ministers to Bobby. When he demands an explanation of what happened and why he is receiving such peculiar treatment, Nancy assures him that it is none of his concern. Later, when Bobby overhears the story, he suggests to Nancy that he could make a financial settlement with the Hudson family. Extremely offended by this proposal, Nancy responds that there is only one way of justifying his existence. Nancy encourages

him to follow in Dr. Hudson's footsteps and make use of the talent he has already shown to become a brain surgeon.

Nancy's continuing faith and support enable Bobby to follow this course by enrolling in the Michigan State University medical school. Bobby deciphers an encoded diary left by Dr. Hudson, and together he and Nancy read the incredible story of his religious conversion, which explains the acts of charity that puzzled Nancy. When Bobby also begins undertaking such generous enterprises, Nancy is able to assist him. She remains Bobby's closest friend and an extremely important figure in the hospital.

Ashley, Brett. *The Sun Also Rises.* Ernest Hemingway. 1926.

Lady Brett Ashley is a thirty-four-year-old Englishwoman living an aimless, frustrated, hedonistic life in Paris in the early 1920s. Deeply unhappy, she seeks fitful solace in the arms of countless men.

Brett acquired her title during World War I by marriage to Lord Ashley after her first lover died of dysentery. As the novel opens, however, she is in the process of getting a divorce in order to marry Mike Campbell, a Scotsman. Much of Brett's frustration comes from the fact that the man she purports to love most, JAKE BARNES, is impotent as the result of a war injury. While she loves Jake and wants to be with him, she cannot reconcile herself to a life of celibacy and engages in one empty sexual encounter after another.

Brett is not a victim, however. She consistently takes the upper hand in her relationships, whether with Jake, Mike, the American writer ROBERT COHN, or the matador Pedro Romero. Her hair is cut short like a boy's, and she wears a man's hat. But rather than being liberating, her sexual aggressiveness, like Jake's impotence, leads only to a painful anxiety.

Brett first appears in a Paris club in the company of a group of gay men, and she is constantly surrounded by members of café society such as Count Mippipopolous, a Greek nobleman with an inordinate love of champagne. She often visits Jake late at night at his apartment but rejects his proposal that they live together because she couldn't bear staying with him and sleeping with other men.

Brett goes to San Sebastian with Cohn, and they have an affair. After leaving Cohn, she meets her fiancé, and the couple rejoins Cohn, Jake, and Bill Gorton in Pamplona for the fiesta of San Fermin. During the fiesta Brett is fascinated by the violent spectacle of the bullfight and is enormously attracted to Pedro Romero, a brilliant nineteen-year-old matador. With Jake's tacit approval she seduces the young man, much to the disgust of the innkeeper Montoya and the other Spaniards who believe Romero will lose his competitive edge and become corrupted.

Coinciding with the end of the fiesta, Brett's affair catalyzes the dissolution of the group of Americans. Mike realizes (as he has suspected all along) that he means no more to Brett than any of her other lovers. Cohn is enraged over her affair with the matador and seeks to "rescue" Brett by battering Romero to a pulp. Brett angrily turns on Cohn, however, and he dissolves into a state of remorse. His face completely bruised, Romero dedicates the final bullfight of the fiesta to Brett, who travels to Madrid with him after the fiesta. Not long after, she deserts him, refusing to become "one of these bitches that ruin children." Brett cables Jake to join her, and when he arrives, she announces that she is going back to Mike: "He's so damned nice and so awful. He's my sort of thing." The novel ends as Brett and Jake ride through Madrid in a taxi, their love as necessary and as impossible as ever.

Ashton, Julia. *Bid Me to Live*. H.D. (Hilda Doolittle). 1960.

Julia Ashton, an American expatriate, lives in London at the start of World War I. Although the war rages on for several years, it is the prolonged bombardment of London in 1917 that serves as the setting for much of the action of this autobiographical novel. Julia, an accomplished though little-known poet, has suffered the stillbirth of her first child and has been cautioned to avoid a second pregnancy. Although Julia has recuperated from the physical trauma, she still suffers emotional pain. The fact that her husband Rafe has to go to war exacerbates her fears and loneliness.

Before Rafe Ashton leaves, it appears that the couple are loving and close despite the loss they have shared. After he has been away for a time, however, Julia gradually begins to realize that she has lost interest in her husband. She nonetheless continues to write him frequently, keeping her tone light enough to sustain him while he is gone. As she acknowledges late in the novel, she deliberately avoids mentioning upsetting news such as the fevers that plague the city in order not to upset Rafe unduly. When Rafe returns after a time and Julia's interest has waned, she recognizes Rafe's interest in Bella Carter, a performer who has come to live with Julia, and agrees to the couple's liaison. Julia even goes so far as to let them use her bed for their tryst. Eventually, however, she blames Rafe for betraying her, forgetting or ignoring that it was she who had lost interest first.

One of the reasons for Julia's diminished interest in her husband is her growing interest in Frederico, a fictional stand-in for D. H. Lawrence, with whom Julia shares hours of passionate conversation about the nature of art, writing, and the problems inherent in dealing with matters of nature and the spirit. She admires Rico's knowledge and his genius, although she doesn't agree with his assumptions about a rigid separation of the sexes. For Julia, being an artist represents a blending of the male and the female; Rico maintains that the male is man-as-man, the

female woman-as-woman when either is an artist. This debate, unresolved in the novel, fuels Julia's interest in her own writing. She sets out to translate some Greek poetry, all the while searching for a way to focus on the words themselves, making them—more than the project of translation—her final focus.

As a part of her resolution to escape the consequences of war, Julia decides to accept an invitation to Cornwall, and it is here that she arduously struggles with her poetry and translation while composing frequent letters to Rico, whom, she has decided, she will not see anymore. The failure of her relationship with Rafe and the loss of their child form a continuous backdrop to Julia's struggles with her writing and with her desire to continue living despite her loneliness and artistic isolation. At the end of the novel, following an extended discussion of Vincent van Gogh and his commitment to his art, Julia resolves to continue writing, for she has come to an understanding of herself as an artist at last.

Assingham, Fanny. *The Golden Bowl*. Henry James. 1909.

Fanny Assingham, an American living in London, falls in love with an impoverished Roman prince. Because she is married and much older than PRINCE AMERIGO, she can do nothing more than contrive to keep him within her social circle. By arranging a marriage between the prince and a close friend, MAGGIE VERVER, she succeeds, but when the Prince fails to live up to her expectations, Fanny comes to regret her interference and becomes convinced that she has perpetrated a terrible crime.

Fanny is a very public figure in a circle of people who are much concerned with following forms, and she is bound to act in covert ways. She is praised as the first American woman among these aristocratic Londoners to have married an Englishman. Although a marriage between an American and an Englishman is no longer regarded as unusual, the younger generation views Fanny as having made such marriages possible. She has two significant misfortunes to bear: poverty and childlessness in middle age. As the prince notes, however, one clearly dominates her rather simpleminded and frail husband, Colonel Robert Assingham, whom she refers to as Bob.

As the novel opens, Prince Amerigo pays a visit to Fanny a few days before his marriage to Maggie Verver, the daughter of an American millionaire. The prince is in a panic about the new life he is to begin, but he and Fanny are able to comfort each other with the assurance that the marriage was brilliantly conceived and will be elegantly carried out. It is, they believe, the wisest solution to the prince's financial problems. While they are drinking their tea, Fanny casually mentions that CHARLOTTE STANT, an old school friend of Maggie's, has arrived in London and will be coming shortly to stay with the Assinghams. In her characteristically light manner, Fanny comments that Charlotte's appearance is a "complication." The prince had a love affair with Charlotte; because both were poor, they had no hope of marrying. In a later conversation with Colonel Assingham, Fanny declares her intention to "back" Charlotte and implies that this will involve finding her a husband.

The success of this well-intentioned endeavor implicates Fanny further in the unfolding domestic tragedy. She allows Charlotte to move to Portland Place, the home of Maggie's widowed father, while the prince and his wife are on vacation. Knowing nothing of her affair with Prince Amerigo, ADAM VERVER becomes convinced that he will please Maggie by marrying her friend Charlotte. After the marriage takes place, Fanny observes unhappily that Charlotte and the prince are continuing their affair. Her suspicion and despair increase when she sees how Maggie is suffering, but she considers it her solemn duty to lie when the young woman requests the truth about them.

When concrete evidence of the prince's liaison with Charlotte does appear, Fanny's impulse is to destroy it. The object is a golden bowl that Charlotte and the prince had seen together in a Bloomsbury antique shop and that Maggie happens upon later and purchases. The shop owner relates his earlier visitor's conversation to Maggie, confirming her suspicions of their ongoing affair. Fanny smashes the bowl on the floor just as the prince walks in and discovers that he has been exposed.

While Maggie undergoes the ordeal of convincing her beloved father to leave for America with his wife, Fanny remains her only confidante and support. During the course of the novel, Fanny has seen each of the other protagonists as virtuous and worthy of assistance, but her deepest loyalties remain with Maggie, who emerges clearly as the heroine. Fanny endures tremendous guilt as a result of the two marriages, which she sees as her responsibility, and regretfully watches Maggie lose her moral innocence. By the book's end, however, it is clear that she possesses the courage to remain involved in her friends' lives until this painful era in their history comes to an end.

Atencio, Ephanie. *The Woman Who Owned the Shadows.* Paula Gunn Allen. 1983.

Of Guadelupe Indian and Hispanic origin, Ephanie Atencio struggles to understand the history of her people and to recover a lost sense of self.

As a child, Ephanie is arrogant and adventurous, always imagining new games and exploring the desert surrounding her town. Elena, her playmate and constant companion, perpetually lags a little behind Ephanie and waits for her to take the first step in any new endeavor. When they reach adolescence, Ephanie and Elena remain intimate friends and gradually become lovers. Elena becomes frightened, however, and asks a sister at their Catholic school about their "hugging and giggling." After warning her against this behavior, the sister promptly tells Elena's mother. The friends are forbidden to see each other, and

Ephanie is cruelly launched into a new phase of life.

Even before this separation, Ephanie's childhood exuberance had given way to a more ladylike, subdued, and conventional standard of behavior. A very diligent student, she goes to college, where she studies literature. She becomes deeply involved in the civil rights movement and leaves school temporarily, outraged at the injustices she perceives. She eventually marries and has two children, Ben and Agnes, but the marriage dissolves and Ephanie enters a period of deep depression. Stephan, an older man whom she has known since childhood, moves in with Ephanie and does his best to comfort and help her. Although Ephanie seems to need Stephan's care and thinks of him as *hermano*, brother, he is constantly suppressing a desire to ask him to leave. When Stephan finally leaves of his own accord, Ephanie drives to San Francisco where she begins a new life.

Her children soon join her, and Ephanie finds much to interest her. Agnes and Ben draw her into the community at the Inter-Tribal House, a gathering place for American Indians where the children participate in traditional dances. Ephanie also joins a therapy group, and although extremely cautious with her words there, she is able to share the hope of the other group members. One of them, a woman named Teresa, invites Ephanie to her home, insisting she must do a psychic reading. Ephanie is impressed by the reading, and Teresa agrees to teach her what she knows about witchcraft. Teresa tries to dissuade Ephanie from entering into a second equally destructive marriage, this time with a Japanese-American man. Ephanie, however, feels her passivity dooms her to marriage; she has no strength to resist.

Before the marriage with Thomas collapses, Ephanie gives birth to twins. One infant dies, sending Ephanie into another terrible depression. She attempts suicide, but after cutting the rope away from her own throat and saving herself from death by hanging, Ephanie speaks to her absent grandmother and assures her that she will be all right.

After her brush with death, Ephanie begins researching her history. In studying Native American history and myths, she recovers the memory that is crucial to her well-being. Ephanie remembers a day in her childhood when Stephan enticed her into jumping over a gully; she fell, breaking her ribs and puncturing a lung. The accident created a rift in Ephanie's life: The bold child abruptly became a passive and overly cautious adult. Once Ephanie remembers the accident and its effects, she feels united with the child she had been and with that child's destiny. With her personal history restored and her knowledge of Native American traditions, Ephanie reenters the world with youthful strength.

Athénaïse. "Athénaïse." Kate Chopin. 1897.

To excuse her willful behavior, people often say that Athénaïse will eventually mature and discover what she really wants. But this beautiful, independent heroine will surely not acquire this knowledge through philosophic introspection: It will have to come in a flash of inspiration.

After only two months of marriage, Athénaïse leaves her devoted husband Cazeau and flees to the home of her parents. Her parents cannot understand why she left Cazeau, for he has committed none of the reprehensible acts typical of an undesirable husband. She tells them she doesn't hate her husband, she only resents being tied to a man all the time. Exasperated, they ask why she married him in the first place. Because it is customary for a young woman to do so, she replies. Only Montéclin, Athénaïse's brother, is sympathetic to her plight. He doesn't like Cazeau and is disappointed that his beloved sister has no grounds for divorce. Cazeau soon comes to reclaim Athénaïse. Patient and loving, he leads Athénaïse to realize that she has no recourse against the grand institution of marriage. Furious in her defeat, Athénaïse returns to her conjugal home.

Knowing she can never untie the Gordian knot of marriage, Athénaïse soon vows to sever it, this time enlisting the help of Montéclin, whom she considers a kind and chivalrous brother. Montéclin smuggles Athénaïse to New Orleans where she hides at the boardinghouse of a Creole black woman, Madame Sylvie. As the weeks pass, Athénaïse becomes bored and lonely, even homesick; she befriends a fellow boarder, Monsieur Gouvernail. Athénaïse confides to Gouvernail how much she misses Montéclin, and he suspects she misses Cazeau also, without realizing it. This troubles Gouvernail, for he is falling in love with Athénaïse, although he realizes he is no more than a surrogate brother to her. He can do only so much to alleviate her loneliness.

Athénaïse becomes increasingly languorous, and Madame Sylvie, who is much wiser, counsels her. After their lengthy interview, Athénaïse is stunned, then filled with rapturous wonder. She feels utterly transformed. Feeling sudden anger at Montéclin for abetting her separation from Cazeau, she resolves to return to her husband and immediately writes her family and husband of her intentions. Athénaïse is pregnant.

In a mood of happy anticipation, Athénaïse, with scarcely a farewell to Gouvernail, leaves New Orleans and is welcomed home by her husband. Cazeau kisses her fervently, and for the first time Athénaïse returns his fervor. But their mutual passion is arrested as they hear from the servants' quarters the wail of a newborn baby.

Atkins, Cora. *Plains Song: For Female Voices.* Wright Morris. 1980.

The novel opens in the early twentieth century with a woman identified only as Cora, who marries Emerson Atkins more from lack of choice than from a desire to be married. She does not wish to end up like her spinster aunt but is also reluctant to leave her gentle, doting father. An unusual-looking girl, Cora is tall, thin, pale, somber, and pragmatic. Although she enjoys doing chores and has enough practical education to make a good farm wife, she knows that most men prefer plump and spoiled women. Emerson, a slow, patient, quiet man establishing his farm on a government homestead in Wisconsin, makes Cora's acquaintance on his trip back to Ohio for supplies. Recognizing Cora's values as a helpmate, he proposes marriage. Overwhelmed at the idea of settling west of the Missouri, Cora nonetheless feels no particular aversion to Emerson and agrees to marry him.

The married couple immediately begin their trip west together, but Emerson calmly waits for the proper time and place to consummate the marriage. Cora despises the very thought of intercourse, however, and bites her knuckle to the bone in silence on their first conjugal night. She requires medical attention, and Emerson tells the doctor she was bit by a horse, establishing a tacit precedent for their married life. They will maintain a formal, physical distance from each other and divide their chores as if they were work partners. Cora and Emerson spend their first years together setting up their new house and farm, and they have a daughter, (Beulah) Madge, as a result of their one night together. Cora is a stern, pragmatic mother with no time or inclination for affection; she is too busy working in the hen house, among other chores, to play with the child.

Emerson's brother Orion and his hillbilly wife Belle live nearby. When Belle dies giving birth to her second daughter, Cora cares for her children as well. Although Cora thought Belle was wild and reckless, she is surprised to find she misses her. Cora and Emerson have two more daughters, and Cora believes the family is cursed to have only female children. Belle and Orion's eldest daughter, the feisty SHARON ROSE (ATKINS), and Madge grow up as inseparable friends.

The hen house earns a moderate income, which Emerson considers Cora's personal allowance. Cora spends her money on floor tiling, a piano for the house, and seed for a lawn but never buys anything for herself. As the girls grow older, this angers Sharon Rose, who finds Cora a pitiful martyr. Madge, a plump farm girl destined to follow in her mother's footsteps, does not question Cora's ways. When Madge inevitably marries, Sharon Rose is angered at her complacency and insults her; Cora takes Sharon into the house and raps her hand with a hairbrush. When Sharon decides to leave and pursue music in college, Cora is unable to understand her desire for independence and a different way of life.

Cora continues in her sullen ways, and because she cannot stand to travel or be in a foreign environment, Sharon must return to the farm to visit the family. When Emerson dies, the aging Cora has difficulty caring for herself but refuses to leave her farm. Her chores bring meaning to her life. After Cora passes away, it is the liberated Sharon Rose who is most deeply affected by her absence. The older woman's determined complacency haunts Sharon for the rest of her life.

Atkins, Sharon Rose. *Plains Song: For Female Voices.* Wright Morris. 1980.

Sharon Rose is the first daughter born to Belle and Orion Atkins. She is a curious and pleasant baby, and her aunt CORA ATKINS fears for the influence wild Belle will have on the child. Redneck Belle is more childish than motherly, although she is much more affectionate to Sharon and Cora's daughter, (Beulah) Madge, than is pragmatic and somber Cora. When Belle dies giving birth to her second daughter, Fayrene, Cora takes Sharon and the baby as her own children. Sharon and Madge grow up together as inseparable sister-friends and shun Fayrene as if they hold her responsible for Belle's death. A remarkably inquisitive child, Sharon questions the values of her midwestern upbringing and finally rejects the role typically assigned to females in the traditional farming community of her youth.

Madge takes an interest in finding a husband, whereas Sharon Rose gets a short, manly haircut and enrolls in college. Outraged when she learns that Madge is engaged, Sharon yells for all to hear, "Does he want a wife or a housemaid?" Cora reprimands her by smacking her palms with a hairbrush, an incident that Sharon never forgets. She feels contempt for the self-denial and complacency of farmers' wives; she cannot understand how Cora could live such a pitiful life or why Madge hoped to emulate it. Sharon moves to Lincoln to study music at the university, and there she meets other young women desiring education and independent lives. Still, she feels homesick at times and somewhat envious of the security of farm and family life. She turns down an invitation to spend the summer in England with her wealthy friend Lillian Baumann, choosing instead to visit Madge, who is now a mother herself. Sharon feels intimidated upon seeing Cora again.

When Blanche, Madge's eldest daughter, enters adolescence, Sharon realizes that Blanche is the image of Cora and has a similar disposition. Hoping to encourage Blanche's self-worth, Sharon enrolls her in a special creative school in the city. Blanche likes school and enjoys Sharon's company, but her new environment has little effect. Sharon suggests that the girl return home, where she is happy to resume her former life of farm chores and caring for others, much to Sharon's dismay.

Finding it difficult to distance herself entirely, Sharon visits the farm intermittently. She has had several close friendships with various women, and although it is never stated, it is implied that Sharon is a lesbian. As an older woman she visits the family and is surprised to learn that she has been a role model for some of the many females in the family who see her as liberated; Sharon actually feels confused and lonely. Upon returning to her hotel, she is invited to stay with Alexandra Selkirk, the guest speaker at a feminist convention, whom she had met in the airport. Although she finds Alexandra moody and dramatic, Sharon joins her, and the novel closes with them rising from bed to watch the sunrise.

Atreides, Paul. *Dune.* Frank Herbert. 1965.

Paul Atreides, heir to Duke Leto of Caladan, a powerful force in Imperial politics, has been schooled since birth in the arts of battle, hand-to-hand combat, mind control, clairvoyance, and telepathy. As the son of a duke and a leader of a matriarchal spiritual movement, Paul is destined to rule, but not before he has triumphed in a terrible struggle with his enemies, the Harkonnens.

For eighty-five years the Harkonnens have controlled the desert planet Arrakis and mined its geriatric spice, melange, which prolongs life and youth, and is the most valued substance in the universe. Now the Padishah emperor, ruler of a universe, in concert with the Landsraad, a federation of united planets, and the Spacing Guild, controller of all commerce and space travel, has decreed that House Atreides will assume the operation of Arrakis. Many consider this proposition highly suspect. Why would the emperor oust the Harkonnens from the richest fiefdom in the galaxy and turn it over to Duke Leto? The delicate preparations for the move to Arrakis must be carried out by Paul's trusted teachers and the duke's right-hand men, Gurney Halleck, Thufir Hawat, and Duncan Idaho.

Within a few days of arriving on Arrakis, House Atreides is attacked by the Harkonnens, who have retained troops and weapons on the planet. Duke Leto dies as a result of a traitorous plot within his own ranks. The Harkonnens kidnap the wife of the trusted Atreides family physician, Doctor Yueh, but Yueh is able to help Paul and his mother, Lady Jessica, escape in an ornithopter packed with basic supplies for desert survival.

After surviving a major storm in the desert, Paul and Jessica set down in order to avoid detection by Harkonnen patrollers who believe that the pair has perished in the storm. They travel stealthily by foot dressed in stillsuits, moisture-reclaiming garments that must be worn to survive in the open desert. Paul and his mother meet a group of Fremen, natives of Arrakis, who at first would like to kill the pair. With a combination of fighting skill, voice, and mind control, Paul and Jessica convince the Fremen that, at least temporarily, they are worth more alive than dead.

Paul and Jessica accompany the Fremen to an underground dwelling, one of a vast network on Arrakis. Paul, with his gift of prescience, sees a possible future where, with the aid of the Fremen masses, he regains the power of House Atreides and becomes the powerful messianic figure Muad'Dib. Soon after this vision Paul assumes the name Muad'Dib, after a kangaroo mouse who can survive well in the open desert.

For many years Paul and his mother Jessica live in hiding among the Fremen. Paul marries Chani, a Fremen, and gradually assumes a position of leadership among the people. The Fremen also accept Jessica as their Reverend Mother because of her Bene Gesserit training in the mysteries of mind control and future sight. Paul learns to ride the fearful giant sandworms whose metabolic processes produce the spice melange. Once he has mastered the worm, Paul is ready to confront his true destiny.

Since the murder of Duke Leto, the Harkonnens have continued to rule and exploit Arrakis under the auspices of the emperor. After years of secret planning, Paul and the Fremen, during one of the emperor's visits to Arrakis, start a tremendous storm on the planet's surface utilizing the atomic weapons of House Atreides. Under cover of the storm Paul and the Fremen attack and subdue the Imperial and Harkonnen forces. Paul fights a duel, or kanly, in hand-to-hand combat with his cousin, the Harkonnen Feyd-Rautha. After killing Feyd-Rautha, Paul reveals to the emperor that he is now in control of the empire because he has the power to destroy the entire spice-mining operation on Arrakis. No one challenges Paul because universal addiction to the melange has made such destruction impossible to withstand. Paul banishes the emperor to the prison planet Salusa Secundus and takes the emperor's Bene Gesserit–trained daughter Irulan as his wife. At the close of the novel, Paul Atreides has achieved his destiny of ultimate rulership.

Avery, Shug. *The Color Purple.* Alice Walker. 1982.

A beautiful and passionate blues singer, Shug Avery liberates her lover CELIE from a life of miserable obedience and physical abuse. The affair between Shug and Celie's husband ALBERT is notorious in their rural southern town. When Shug falls ill, only Albert is sympathetic. He takes her home so that Celie can nurse her back to health, and Shug, in turn, becomes Celie's protector.

Shug arrives elegantly dressed at Albert's house and sneers contemptuously at Celie. Her hostility wears off quickly, however, when she realizes that Celie has no interest in competing for Albert's affection. Celie tenderly bathes Shug and coaxes her into eating. Shug feels strong enough to sing again while Celie is lovingly combing her hair, and she tells her that the song is "something you help scratch out my head."

Against Albert's wishes, Shug insists after her recuperation that Celie come to her first concert, where she sings the melancholy tune she calls "Miss Celie's Song." Shug's allegiance shifts decisively to Celie's side when the young wife tells Shug that Albert beats her; indeed, after she makes Albert stop the beatings, she soon finds that she no longer wants a romantic relationship with him.

Shug eventually leaves Celie and Albert to go on tour as a singer. The trip is enormously successful; she meets other famous blues singers and buys herself fancy clothes, a car, and a mansion in Memphis. When Shug returns to Celie and Albert, she brings her decidedly ordinary new husband, Grady. He immediately begins eyeing Squeek, a family friend, while Shug devotes her attention to Celie. When Albert and Grady are away on a trip, Celie tells Shug the story of her repeated rapes by her stepfather. Shug embraces Celie to comfort her, and they make love.

Shug's confidence serves as a model for Celie, and she becomes more demanding. When Shug and Celie discover that Albert has been hiding the letters that Celie's sister Nettie has been sending to her, Celie is murderously angry and decides to leave him. Shug takes Celie to her luxurious mansion in Memphis. Because Shug continues to travel, both women lead increasingly independent lives. Celie amuses herself by sewing pants for Shug, and when others begin to request them, it becomes a thriving business. Shug continues to be a great success as a singer.

Shug and Celie are estranged from each other for a short time. Celie inherits a house and returns to their hometown to fix it up. In the meanwhile, Shug falls in love with Germaine, a young flute player in her band. She travels with Germaine and visits her grown children, who were raised by their grandparents. Although passionate, the affair does not last long. Germaine enrolls in college, and Shug returns to Celie.

In the final scenes of the novel, Celie welcomes Shug into her house, and Shug is once again at the center of their extended family. The configurations of the group have been radically altered, however. The firm allegiance between Shug and Celie has given them independence from Albert, and together they command a new respect from him and from the community as a whole.

Aylmer. "The Birthmark." Nathaniel Hawthorne. 1846.

Aylmer, a brilliant scientist, has unlocked many of nature's secrets while working in his laboratory. He has long been haunted, however, by the fact that he could neither create life as nature could nor sustain it indefinitely. Frustrated, he abandoned this urge to create long ago, but the existence on Georgiana's cheek of a small red birthmark in the shape of a human hand reawakens his desire to manipulate the wonders of nature.

Georgiana has always had the tiny birthmark, which some of her ardent admirers have labeled the most charming element of her beauty. Aylmer had scarcely noticed the mark during his courtship of Georgiana, but after they were married, it grew more prominent in his mind. The mark takes on a fearful aspect for Aylmer, intruding even into his dreams; Georgiana informs him that during a nightmare he cried out that the blemish must be removed lest she die.

Seeing the hold the mark has on Aylmer's imagination,

Georgiana asks her husband to remove it so that he may love her without reservation. With the help of his faithful, animal-like servant Aminadab, Aylmer prepares for the spot's removal. While Georgiana sits in a sumptuously furnished antechamber, Aylmer works in his laboratory. He periodically emerges to dazzle her with some scientific wonder: a seed that bursts into vibrant bloom, then dies; a photographic device; a potion that can prolong life or induce death. When Georgiana asks if he plans to use a bleaching liquid on her birthmark, he mysteriously answers that the remedy for her blemish must penetrate deeper.

Aylmer retreats to his laboratory once more, unaware that Georgiana, feeling restless and somewhat uncomfortable, has followed him and is shocked by what she finds. The laboratory walls are naked, but the room is filled with strange devices emitting frightening noises. Aylmer himself is deathly pale and in deep concentration. Georgiana's entry breaks his concentration, and he angrily accuses her of mistrusting him. Georgiana firmly but lovingly insists that she know exactly how serious the operation will be. Death threatens, he tells her, because the tiny hand has somehow gotten a grip on her soul.

Aylmer administers a potion to Georgiana, which she drinks willingly. While she sleeps, the mark grows fainter until it is barely perceptible. Awakening, Georgiana looks at her face in a mirror, smiles sadly, then tells Aylmer that she is dying. As Aminadab chuckles at his master's misguided pursuit of perfection, Georgiana dies. Aylmer is left in the presence of perfect beauty and death.

B

Babbitt, George Follansbee. *Babbitt.* Sinclair Lewis. 1922.

George Follansbee Babbitt, a prosperous realtor and prominent citizen of Zenith, a small town in the Midwest, is to all appearances a devoted, if unromantic, husband. Yet Babbitt in truth is racked with doubts and insecurities. Dismayed by the thought that he has never done a single thing he really wanted to do, he nurses an overwhelming desire to rebel. In a secret recurring dream he imagines he is visited by a "fairy child," a beautiful young woman who can see the gallant youth behind Babbitt's middle-aged appearance. When the illusions that pervade his well-made life begin to crumble, Babbitt attempts to make this dream a reality.

The novel opens in Babbitt's Dutch Colonial house in Floral Heights, a residential area of Zenith, where Babbitt lives with his wife Myra and their two children, Verona and Ted. Babbitt's life-style is a monument to the romance of the new age: His house is a veritable shrine to a god of modern appliances, his office is his "pirate ship," and his car is "his poetry and tragedy, love and heroism." He is an outspoken proponent of the virtues of domesticity, education, commercialism, and the mentality of small-town America. Babbitt's almost religious commitment to the Wheels of Progress propels him through a series of successful, if modest, reforms, and he slowly rises through the ranks of solid citizens to become one of the foremost men of Zenith.

Yet Babbitt's sense of difference from his peers remains, and in moments of inactivity the fairy child returns to remind him of what he has given up. The balance between Babbitt's two lives is suddenly upset by the news that his closest friend, Paul Riesling, one of Zenith's model citizens, has shot his wife, Zilla. Babbitt is especially shaken because in Paul, a manufacturer and wholesaler of prepared-paper roofing whom Babbitt had always suspected possessed great artistic talent, Babbitt had recognized his own secret life.

After Paul's imprisonment, Babbitt abandons his hard-won sense of propriety and position. Searching for the elusive fairy child, he embarks on a series of extramarital affairs. In his quest for the other man he thinks he can be, Babbitt takes his first vacation alone since his marriage, but after two weeks of disillusioned self-examination, he returns to Zenith to resume the life he realizes he cannot escape.

Yet once back in Zenith, Babbitt finds that he cannot keep to the choice he has made. His wife and children leave on vacation, and in a haze of whiskey and cigarettes, Babbitt, realizing that he is no longer leading the sane, diligent, and unimpassioned life he has always advocated, joins the town's wild set. As he slips into a relationship with the unconventional Tanis Judique, Babbitt finds himself increasingly disillusioned with the comforts and rewards that life in Zenith has to offer. In his stubborn resolution to cling to this rejection of his old values, Babbitt refuses membership in the prestigious Good Citizens' League and stands, unsure and alone, between his old life—which is gradually disintegrating—and the new life he is no longer sure he wants.

Babbitt's dilemma is resolved by his wife's near fatal case of appendicitis. When she recovers, Babbitt finds himself drifting back into intimacy with her and into the security of his former respectable life. As the novel ends, Babbitt is welcomed into the Good Citizens' League and regains his self-respect, his placidity, and the affection of his friends. His spirit of rebellion is still alive, however. In a rare moment of understanding with his son, Babbitt accepts the course his own life has taken but urges Ted not to be tamed by Zenith and to "tell 'em to go to the Devil!"

Baby Suggs. *Beloved.* Toni Morrison. 1987.

Baby Suggs is a broken old woman with a deep heart and a gift for prophecy. The Garners, owners of the Kentucky farm Sweet Home, bought her from the rice and tobacco plantations of Carolina along with her youngest and only remaining son Halle. While in Carolina, Baby Suggs broke her hip and now walks with a bad limp. Old and crushed by slavery, she works in the house at Sweet Home, where the Garners never think to ask her name and just call her Jenny because that was the name on the bill of sale.

By the time Baby Suggs has Halle, her eighth child, she has stopped trying to love her children or their fathers. Her first seven children were sold, traded, or lost in card games before Baby Suggs had a chance to watch them grow; however, they let her keep Halle. He watches her use both hands to lift her leg out of bed each morning and knows the pain that standing causes her hip. The Garners allow him to rent himself out to other farms in order to pay for Baby Suggs's freedom. Halle wants to give his mother the chance to sit down; this, Baby Suggs explains, is the first time anyone has done something for her. Still, she doubts that Halle's effort is worth an old woman's freedom. Once "payment" has been arranged, Mr. Garner himself takes Baby Suggs to Cincinnati and delivers her to the home of abolitionists, the Bodwins.

The Bodwins allow Baby Suggs to live in a house they own just outside the city, at 124 Bluestone Road. They also help her get work as a cobbler and arrange for her to take in wash. Under Baby Suggs, 124 becomes a cheerful place and something of a way station. She fixes the house so that it no longer has a back door and puts the kitchen inside. She knows that slavery has worn her body beyond any physical help she can offer to others and feels that she has only her love left to give.

In the summers Baby Suggs goes to the Clearing and offers the black people her heart. Asserting that she is too ignorant to preach, she simply calls them to her. Baby Suggs accepts no title, but the people put a "holy" after her name.

When Baby Suggs's grandchildren arrive at 124 followed by her daughter-in-law SETHE, Baby Suggs begins to hope that Halle will manage to run away from Sweet Home as well. Not wanting to thank God too early, she tries to suppress this hope. Nevertheless, she cannot quell her expectations of happiness when Stamp Paid picks two buckets of blackberries and thereby provides an excuse for a dinner to become a party for the whole community. The following day while hoeing in her garden, Baby Suggs can smell her neighbors' disapproval and envy, and senses an impending evil as well.

The new master of Sweet Home and several others come to take Sethe and her children back to Kentucky. Baby Suggs knows then what she had heretofore been able only to sense—that disaster will strike her home. To keep her children from slavery, Sethe kills one of her daughters and tries to kill the others. After Sethe is taken to prison, Baby Suggs despairs, stops going to the Clearing, and withdraws from the community. Wanting to think of something harmless, she goes to bed. She focuses on colors. When she dies, she has gotten as far as lavender.

Bailey, Tom. *Story of a Bad Boy.* Thomas Bailey Aldrich. 1930.

The narrator and hero of this autobiographical novel, Thomas Bailey, has been sent at a very early age from his home in New Orleans to be educated in the North. Bailey stays with his grandfather, Captain Nutter, a firm but softhearted old man with whom he will spend the greater part of his childhood. After some typical and not-so-typical childhood adventures, Thomas matures into a thoughtful young man.

In the small town of Rivermouth in which Captain Nutter resides, Bailey soon makes a number of friends by joining a secret boys' society known to its members as the Rivermouth Centipedes. Through an elaborate army ranking system, Bailey, despite being a relatively new arrival, is soon promoted to the rank of major. His rank is especially significant because it allows him to command others on the battlefield during the many snowball fights the Centipedes have with other boys from the south side of town. Like the military forces on which they model themselves, the Rivermouth Centipedes defend their snow fort on top of Slatter's Hill.

On his first Fourth of July at Rivermouth, Bailey learns of the town tradition of the community's boys starting an enormous bonfire in the center of town. Rather than asking his grandfather for permission to go and running the risk of his refusal, Thomas sneaks out of his bedroom that night. After making the bonfire, he and his friends decide to go joyriding in a wagon they steal from an unpopular old man. They are soon discovered, however, and are forced to flee, with Thomas barely escaping to his bedroom in time. The next morning Thomas learns that the maid, Abigail, discovered the rope that he used to escape the house hanging out of his bedroom window.

Abigail, much to Thomas's relief, keeps the secret to herself.

While wooing a young girl named Nelly Glentworth at school, Thomas spends time with his friends reconstructing a rickety boat they call the *Dolphin*. They decide at the end of the summer that it is ready for its maiden voyage. A storm overtakes them, however, capsizing the boat and drowning one of the boys.

Thomas's relationship with Nelly blossoms into a full-fledged romance, and he finds himself hopelessly in love. But tragic news soon arrives to disrupt his happiness: Thomas's father has died in New Orleans. Overwhelmed with grief, Thomas hastily leaves Rivermouth to visit his mother in the South, where the two attend to the details of his father's funeral.

After doing his best to console his mother, Thomas, with her encouragement, decides to return to his grandfather in Rivermouth and the life he has built there.

Balcom, Editha. "Editha." William Dean Howells. 1905.

Editha Balcom is a young woman living in upstate New York at the time of the Spanish-American War; her primary virtues are her red hair and her blue eyes. She is a frivolous person with a predilection for war, which she reads about in the newspapers. Instead of thinking critically about its destructive aspects, she flings herself into a romantic fantasy in which she will be a self-denying belle seeing her man off as he heads for glory at the front.

Editha's beau, George Gearson, was raised by a pacifist mother and is instinctively opposed to war. Despite his intelligence and wit, he is vulnerable to Editha's charms and to his own sense of loyalty to his country. Editha tells George that the impending war is a noble one to be waged for freedom and that he must be willing to give up his life—as she would her man—for the sake of their country. George wavers until Editha presses the point by implying that she will be unable to continue seeing him unless he fulfills his duty by enlisting.

During an impromptu meeting, George is elected captain by his peers in town. After signing up for the draft along with the rest of the boys, he goes to Editha's home. He says that he will honor the "holy war ordained by the pocket Providence that blesses butchery." Editha is very excited at the prospect of fulfilling her destiny as a proud and noble woman waiting for her man to return from battle. After Editha promises to see his mother if anything happens to him, George leaves for the front.

Almost immediately Editha receives news of George's death. She enters into the appropriate period of mourning, during which she falls prey to a mysterious illness and at one point seems close to dying. But she soon recovers her health and obeys her deceased lover's last wish by traveling with her father to western Iowa to visit Mrs. Gearson. At first George's invalid mother does not recognize Editha, but then she identifies her as the girl who wrote the silly letters glorifying her son as a hero and who caused him to go to war in the first place.

Uncomprehending at first, Editha realizes by the end of her visit that she is being treated with scathing contempt. She returns home to contemplate Mrs. Gearson's anger. Could Editha be blamed for anything that happened? Has she not comported herself nobly and righteously, in the manner called for by the most fervent newspaper editorials? After time passes, Editha is finally able to reconcile her love for George with his mother's foul words to her. Editha concludes that Mrs. Gearson was being vulgar. With this epiphany she is able to continue living her untroubled, idealized life.

Ballinger, Drew. *Deliverance.* James Dickey. 1970.

Drew Ballinger, one of four friends who take an ill-fated canoeing trip in backwoods Georgia, is a decent, quiet man who is devoted to his family and enthusiastic about his job as a sales supervisor for a soft-drink company. He is well liked by his fellow adventurers: sportsman LEWIS MEDLOCK, the cynical BOBBY TRIPPE, and ED GENTRY, the narrator. Drew voices his worry about the danger of the trip for someone like himself who knows little about rivers or woods but finally agrees to go if he can bring along his guitar.

Drew and his friends take a Friday off from work and drive to Oree, where they stop to get information at the local gas station. The man who works there is decidedly hostile until he catches a glimpse of Drew's old Martin guitar. He tells his son, an albino with a deformed eye, to bring out his banjo, and the two play a duet that leaves Drew ecstatic—he has never played better in his life. Before starting down the river, he takes the country boy's name and address, intending to return someday.

Drew is awkward at first on the river, but after passing through a set of rapids, he is surprised to find he is enjoying himself. On the second day Ed and Bobby go ashore to rest when the other canoe is lagging far behind. When their boat catches up, Drew and Lewis hear Bobby screaming. They land and circle through the woods, Lewis armed with bow and arrows and Drew carrying a canoe paddle as a weapon. Two men with a gun have tied Ed to a tree and are raping Bobby. Lewis shoots one of them in the back, but the other makes his escape.

The four men then debate what should be done with the body. Drew is horrified when Lewis argues that they should bury the corpse and keep the killing a secret because the authorities in that part of the state would be unlikely to consider it justifiable homicide. Drew passionately opposes this line of action, but the others want to avoid legal proceedings. He helps them bury the body deep in the woods, still trying to convince them to change their minds.

The friends, feeling completely isolated from one another, return to the canoes. Without speaking, Drew and Ed maneuver down the river into a gorge with sheer cliffs on either side. As night begins to fall, they enter a series of difficult rapids. Without warning Drew is shot in the back of the head by an unseen sniper. He slumps over, capsizes the canoe, and disappears in the white water. He is found the next day by the others, who decide to dispose of his body because the bullet wound would be impossible to explain. Ed weights his friend's corpse down with rocks, says that Drew was the only decent and sane one among them, and then sinks him in the river.

Banastre, Hortensia Reedmuller. *Southern Discomfort.* Rita Mae Brown. 1982.

Hortensia Reedmuller Banastre, a married woman with two children, is a solid member of the post-Reconstruction southern aristocracy. Although she cultivates friendships with artists and insists on riding her horse as hard as any man, Hortensia knows that she can push the rigid boundaries of her small world only so far. She can protest her husband's involvement with a low-class hooker, but she may not leave him for this indiscretion. She does not have to pretend to love the husband for whom she feels no passion, but she must submit to his infrequent sexual demands on her. The rules of the social world she inhabits demand that Hortensia serve as an attentive mother to her sons Paris and Edward, and as a faithful wife to her husband.

Driven by love, however, Hortensia breaks the rules. They no longer matter to Hortensia when fifteen-year-old Hercules Jinks, the son of one of segregated Montgomery's most respected black families, starts delivering wood to the Banastre home. Intelligent and strong, Hercules has an interest in architecture that Hortensia feeds by lending him some books on the subject. By the time he has finished all the architecture titles in Hortensia's extensive library, the two have become lovers. When Hercules goes to Chicago to try a boxing career, Hortensia follows him, and they share a brief, beautiful time away from the prying eyes of Montgomery.

Eventually, Hercules is able to rent a cottage in a poor section of town where they can meet. Hortensia visits Hercules undetected until he is killed while pulling his father out of the way of a moving train. The prostitute who owns the cottage brings Hortensia the news of Hercules's death but tells no one of the society woman's involvement with the black teenager.

Distraught, Hortensia reveals the truth to her mother, who is surprisingly understanding. More concerned that Hortensia's happiness was so short-lived than aghast over her lover's skin color, Mrs. Reedmuller sends Hortensia north to recuperate. She gives birth to a child in Chicago, the same city where she and Hercules shared so much joy.

The child, Catherine, grows up in Hortensia's home believing one of the servants is her mother.

All goes well until Paris, Hortensia's vindictive and cruel younger son, figures out the truth about Catherine. He threatens to expose Hortensia unless she allows him to have sex with her. Ever fearful that Paris will break his promise, Hortensia submits to the act. When he tries to rape Hortensia a few months later, Catherine comes to her rescue. As Paris tries to choke Catherine, knowing that Hortensia loves her more than she does him, Hortensia shoots Paris dead.

Because he owes a debt to Hercules's father, the sheriff promises to attribute Paris's death to a gun-cleaning accident. Hortensia finally tells Catherine that she is her mother.

Bandello, Cesare Rico. *Little Caesar.* W. R. Burnett. 1929.

Rico, a small, dark Italian hood, experiences his own version of the great American success story as he climbs from rags to riches in the Chicago underworld of the 1920s. Rico's cold, businesslike style of murder and mayhem brings him wealth and respect from his peers, but his ruthlessness ultimately makes him the number one enemy of the police, who hunt him down furiously. Rico has only one friend in the world, Ramón Otero, who idolizes and takes care of him. But in the end even Otero can't save his boss from death at the hands of the police.

Rico first distinguishes himself from the other hoods in Sam Vettori's gang by killing an off-duty police captain during a speakeasy holdup. The other gang members, including Vettori, are alarmed at the violence. Sam tries to bring Rico in line with his mild policies, but Rico scoffs and instead insists that his hard-line methods are the most effective. Unwilling to risk a comfortable living for larger gains, Sam eventually steps down. Rico becomes a feared and respected member of the Chicago criminal community and even gains the support of the "Big Boy," the man in charge of organized crime for the entire region.

But the "old Man," or the chief of police, is infuriated at the death of an officer. The police hound Rico, following him everywhere and threatening him with dire consequences if he does not confess to the murder. Rico scoffs, too busy enjoying his newfound wealth to be concerned. He moves into a new apartment, buys flashy clothes, acquires the girlfriend of a defeated rival, and even survives an assassination attempt. But Rico's empire comes crashing down around him when an arrested gang member betrays him to the police, and he is forced to go underground.

Humiliated, Rico leaves Chicago for Youngstown, Ohio, his birthplace. Keeping his identity and his reputation a secret, he is reduced to working for small-time thugs. Rico is able to remain incognito for a time, but he eventually divulges his identity in order to start a new gang in Youngstown. A jealous rival betrays him, and the police descend. After a chase through the streets, Rico is shot to death in an alley. Rico's last words reflect his surprise at not fulfilling what he had thought was his destiny: "Is this the end of Rico?"

Bandini, Arturo. *Ask the Dust.* John Fante. 1939.

Arturo Bandini, a young writer living in extreme poverty in the Bunker Hill section of Los Angeles, manages to write and publish a novel about his experiences.

Arturo arrives in Los Angeles from his parents' home in Colorado, moves into Mrs. Hargraves's boardinghouse, and proceeds to write letters to his mother announcing the great success of his short stories. He has in fact had one story, "The Little Dog Laughed," published in a journal. Everyone in the boardinghouse is encouraged to read the story, and Arturo turns to it perpetually in his despair. Since he makes no effort to get a job, the money from the story diminishes quickly, and Arturo is reduced to a diet of oranges. He finally types a long, desperate letter to his editor, which is accepted as a short story. When the check for this story arrives, Arturo spends a day buying suits, shoes, and stationery, and then is astonished to find the money almost gone only a few days later.

Arturo goes to drink coffee at a bar near his house called the Columbia Buffet. He notices that the waitress, Camilla Lopez, a Mexican woman of about twenty, is practically perfect except for her tattered huaraches. As she approaches his table, he flirtatiously insults her shoes. She glares at him, infuriated, but when he returns to the bar the next day, she is obviously pleased.

They drive to the beach together in Camilla's convertible, and after playing in the water, lie down together on the sand. Camilla expects Arturo to make love to her, and when he is unable, she treats him with contempt. He sends poetry and then a marriage proposal to Camilla, but she is unresponsive.

One night a woman, Vera Rivken, knocks on Arturo's door and insists on telling him a series of strange stories. Arturo decides that if he slept with Vera, he might be more confident with Camilla. He visits Vera in Long Beach and allows her to seduce him. Afterward he is seized by guilt, which he exorcises by writing a novel about Vera.

Camilla appears one day and asks Arturo to look at some short stories written by her lover, Sammy Wiggins. They visit Sammy together, but he is hostile toward Camilla. Camilla goes through a period of madness and heavy marijuana smoking and is committed to an institution from which she eventually escapes. She returns to Arturo, who finally shows some genuine kindness toward her. They buy a dog and drive to Laguna Beach, where Arturo rents a house. When he returns from picking up his belongings in Los Angeles, she has already left. Arturo pursues her to Sammy's house in the Mojave Desert, but Camilla is gone. Signing a copy of his book, "To Camilla,"

Arturo drives into the desert and flings the book out the window. Having performed this ceremonial good-bye, Arturo returns to Los Angeles.

Banks, Margaret. *The Lime Twig.* John Hawkes. 1961.

Margaret Banks is a devoted wife and landlady who becomes a victim of kidnapping, brutal assault, and ultimately murder, in connection with the involvement of her husband MICHAEL (BANKS) in the theft of a racehorse named Rock Castle. Innocent and unsuspecting, she finds herself helpless to combat the enormous forces of evil that exist around her.

Lonely without her husband, Margaret takes a trip to the racetrack at Aldington to visit him. On the train she meets a strange woman named Dora and Dora's friend Larry. Margaret finds herself going with Dora to meet a woman named Sybilline, who later seduces her husband, and Dora's young daughter Monica. They end up in a hotel room near the racetrack, where the trapped Margaret discovers that the innocent excursion has actually been a kidnapping.

The abductors remove her clothes and burn them, along with all her other belongings. They put a white hospital robe on her and lock her in the hotel room with Monica, with whom the confused Margaret plays cards. Later on, when one of her kidnappers dozes after receiving a morphine injection from his colleague, Margaret dresses in some garish clothing she finds in a trunk downstairs and goes out to the racetrack. She is caught again, and this time she is stripped, bound, and beaten. When she awakens later, she is terrified, but she momentarily forgets about herself when Monica wakes up screaming from a nightmare. She comforts Monica, and in return the young girl tries to help her escape but can't undo the ropes that bind her. When one of the abductors finally cuts the ropes, Margaret thinks she is being freed. In cutting the ropes, however, he deliberately slashes her wrists, and she is killed.

Banks, Michael. *The Lime Twig.* John Hawkes. 1961.

In this expressionistic novel, Michael Banks is a mild-mannered, middle-class English landlord whose desire to own a racehorse results in his death as well as those of his wife and at least three other people.

Michael and one of his tenants named Hencher steal the racehorse Rock Castle from a barge. The horse had been owned by an elderly woman, Lady Harvey-Harrow, who forgot that she had it. Hencher introduces Michael to a devious and dangerous gang of criminals who assist in the theft. The first casualty occurs when Hencher, attempting to remove the horse, gets stuck in the stall and the animal kicks him to death.

Michael, claiming to be the owner of Rock Castle, goes to the track at Aldington to register for an important race, the Golden Bowl; however, a power struggle ensues, the terms of which are never fully disclosed. In the men's room at the track, three men called "eunuchs" approach Michael and order him to find Sybilline, a strange woman, at the racetrack Pavilion. Unbeknownst to Michael, these three men are part of the gang that has also kidnapped and beaten his wife MARGARET (BANKS). When Michael goes to meet Sybilline, he is intrigued by her, but she quickly disappears. Meanwhile, Margaret appears at a distance, wearing clothes that are not hers, but Michael cannot contact her. Later on, after a member of the gang has been stabbed to death in the steam room, the gang members take Michael with them to a party at an Italian restaurant called Spumoni's. There he dances with Sybilline and falls in love with her.

Sybilline, who was told to seduce Michael by the very same gang with whom he stole Rock Castle, sleeps with Michael the night before the big race. Then they go to a party at the home of "the widow." She, too, seduces Michael. Michael falls asleep; when he wakes up, he hears a shot outside his window and sees that an old man has killed a little girl. A constable comes by, and the constable and the old man brutally beat Michael.

When the day of the big race finally arrives, Michael has been through such a frenzy of murder, rape, and seduction, all in connection with Rock Castle, that he decides to end it all, both for himself and for the gang. In the middle of the race he runs onto the racetrack in front of the oncoming horses. Tripping up Rock Castle and thus destroying the gang's chance of victory, Michael is crushed and killed.

Barkley, Catherine. *A Farewell to Arms.* Ernest Hemingway. 1929.

Catherine Barkley is an English nurse serving in Italy during World War I. She was engaged to her childhood sweetheart for eight years when the war broke out, and he was literally blown to pieces in a brutal battle on the Somme. She had dreamed of his being wounded, perhaps by a saber cut, and her tending to him in the hospital, but the horrifying manner of his death destroyed her romantic illusions and made her realize the terrifying nature of war.

As the novel opens Catherine meets FREDERIC HENRY, an American volunteer in the ambulance corps of the Italian army. Though immediately attracted to him, she resists his advances for a time because she is unwilling to fall in love with another soldier who could be taken from her by the war.

Frederic has been sent to a hospital in Milan to recover from injuries sustained in a mortar attack. Catherine transfers to Milan to be near him, and they fall in love. She visits him at night in the hospital and brings him crackers and vermouth. After an operation on his knee, he is released, and they soon move in together. They plan to get married and in fact consider themselves married

from the first day she arrived at the hospital. Catherine's insecurity still remains, and she constantly asks Frederic if he really loves her. By this time he does, but despite his assurances, she is terrified of losing him. She has visions of either herself or Frederic being killed and lying dead in the rain.

At the end of the summer Frederic returns to the front, and Catherine discovers that she is pregnant. They vow to be faithful to each other and to meet again when Frederic can get another leave. On their last day together they buy a good regulation pistol for Frederic so he can defend himself. They spend their last night in a hotel, which at first makes Catherine feel cheap, but Frederic reassures her. After Frederic leaves, Catherine makes arrangements to have the child on her own.

Frederic deserts from the army after almost being killed by the Italian militia in the confusion of the retreat from Caporetto. He rejoins Catherine in Milan, and they plan to flee to Switzerland to escape the war. They stay for a few days at a hotel in Stresa and finally sneak across the Swiss border at night by rowing a small boat across the lake. For the remainder of the winter and Catherine's pregnancy they stay in a small cabin in the mountains near Montreux; they are very happy. When it comes time for Catherine to give birth, however, there are complications. She tries to be brave, although she fears she will die. Both Frederic and Catherine had wanted a girl; she gives birth to a boy. Frederic sees the child and tells Catherine he is fine, but a few minutes after he leaves her room, a nurse tells Frederic the child is stillborn. He does not have a chance to tell Catherine. Shortly after the birth, she hemorrhages as a result of her cesarean operation and dies without regaining consciousness.

Barnard, Charlotte. *Pembroke.* Mary Wilkins Freeman. 1894.

The beautiful young Charlotte Barnard is weeks away from marriage as this nineteenth-century novel begins. One evening her father, Cephas Barnard, discusses politics with Charlotte's fiancé, hot-tempered Barnabas Thayer. This conversation soon escalates into a fierce argument, culminating in Barnabas's storming out of the house and vowing never to return. Shocked and frightened, Charlotte follows Barnabas outside, calling his name, but the young man will not even look back. As news of the broken engagement quickly spreads through the small village of Pembroke, Charlotte mournfully sets her wedding clothes aside. She resigns herself to being a spinster.

When Barnabas's mother, DEBORAH THAYER, hears of her son's stubbornness, she immediately seeks to effect a compromise; however, both Barnabas and Cephas are unyielding. Deborah banishes her son from her home as an indication of her shame for his lack of filial respect. Throughout the disagreement and continuing through Barnabas's banishment, Charlotte and Barnabas rarely encounter each other, although they are neighbors. The villagers assume that Charlotte will forget Barnabas eventually and will settle down with someone else. Their opinion changes when Charlotte sends the college-educated and richest youth in town, Thomas Payne, away from her parlor; she insists that she will never marry anyone but Barnabas.

Charlotte is able to build a friendship with the shamed Rebecca Thayer, who became pregnant out of wedlock. Their friendship is scorned by the gossipers who view it as Charlotte's ploy to remain near Barnabas, although this is not the case. Charlotte genuinely cares for the sickly woman who could have been her sister-in-law. Finally, things take a turn when Charlotte's Aunt Sylvia, long thought to be a chronic spinster, is suddenly rescued from the poorhouse by the man she has loved all her life. Barnabas is stunned to see Charlotte's fine wedding dress adorning the newly wed older woman. Chagrined once again but too proud to acknowledge it, Barnabas vows to replace the expensive material.

When Charlotte discovers the package of fine material, she immediately goes to Barnabas and informs him that she cannot accept any gift from him, ever. Charlotte is every bit as proud and stubborn as her former lover. Brokenhearted once again, she returns home. Following this, they have little further contact; when Barnabas's mother dies suddenly, however, Charlotte is there to comfort the grief-stricken husband and son.

Upon hearing later of Barnabas's own serious illness, Charlotte hastens to his aid. She is fully prepared to disregard her parents' outrage and the impropriety of living with and attending a young man to whom she is not wed. It is now ten years since the original engagement ended, and Barnabas is thrilled when he realizes that Charlotte has come to him. Their bubble bursts when church officials arrive, warning Charlotte of the public consequences should she continue this sinful behavior. Realizing that Charlotte has placed herself in jeopardy, Barnabas demands that she return to her frantic parents. But this time Barnabas swallows his pride and painfully hobbles toward her home. When he arrives at the Barnard homestead, Barnabas seems to have regained some of his old dignity. As the novel concludes, Charlotte embraces her lover, who has finally returned.

Barnes, Jake. *The Sun Also Rises*. Ernest Hemingway. 1926.

Jake Barnes is an American journalist working in Paris in the early 1920s. As a result of injuries suffered fighting on the Italian front in World War I, he is impotent. Though his condition is never directly stated, his awareness of his loss underlies all of his actions. In a literal sense, Jake is forced to find a way of living in a world forever robbed of any chance for romantic fulfillment.

Unlike his wealthy friend ROBERT COHN, Jake does not indulge in self-pity. Instead, he makes a virtue of a certain quiet resilience. But he is not unfeeling: When he is alone at night, he gives in to his grief. His reserved, hard-boiled manner is reflected in the spare, austere style of his narration.

Working in Paris as a reporter, Jake is very much a part of café society and spends his nights drifting from one club to another. He is deeply in love with BRETT ASHLEY, but of course their love cannot be consummated. He proposes that they live together, but she refuses, saying it would only make matters worse.

To get away from Paris, Jake goes on a trip to Spain with Cohn and Bill Gorton. Bill and Jake manage to get away for a week to go trout fishing in the mountains, a tranquil interlude before they rejoin Cohn, Brett, and her fiancé Mike Campbell for the fiesta of San Fermin in Pamplona.

Jake has been to the fiesta several times before, and Montoya the innkeeper knows him well. He respects Jake and dubs him a bullfighting aficionado, although he is embarrassed by Jake's friends who are only slightly better behaved than the busloads of tourists from Biarritz. The innkeeper introduces Jake to Pedro Romero, a young matador fighting in Pamplona for the first time. Brett is entranced by Romero and seduces him with Jake's tacit consent. After this, Montoya no longer speaks to Jake; he believes Jake has conspired to corrupt Romero.

Montoya is not the only one disturbed by Jake's involvement in the affair. Cohn, jealous of the matador and unwilling to accept the fact that his own liaison with Brett meant nothing, accosts Jake in a bar, accuses him of being a pimp, and knocks him unconscious. Later, Cohn is filled with remorse, and Jake wearily accepts his apology.

After the fiesta, Jake travels back to France with Bill and Mike, but he soon leaves them and drifts back to Spain. He passes several days alone in San Sebastian, doing nothing but swimming and hanging around the hotel lounge. Here he receives a telegram from Brett asking him to meet her in Madrid. She has left Romero and is quite upset. He joins her. The novel ends with the two of them together, drawn by their love for each other but held apart by the impossibility of its fulfillment.

Barnes, Solon. *The Bulwark*. Theodore Dreiser. 1946.

Born into a Quaker family in the late nineteenth century in Maine, Solon Barnes is a quiet and respectful son. He is close to his mother, Hannah, and admiring of his father, Rufus, a farmer and merchant who teaches Solon the practical aspects of his work. His father's lessons prove useful in Solon's later banking career.

When Solon is ten, his family moves to Dukla, Pennsylvania, where his father is to look after the affairs of his wealthy widowed sister. Solon and his sister Cynthia attend the Quaker Friends' school at Dukla, where Solon notices that the students wear finer dress and carry themselves with a reserved air far different from that of his former mates in Maine. Solon admires and befriends Benecia Wallin, the shy daughter of Justus Wallin, a well-to-do Quaker who is an important figure in the Philadelphia banking community. Benecia is in turn attracted to Solon, but they both realize that Solon will not be attending the same school as Benecia in the fall.

When Justus Wallin invites the Barneses to his home one day, he notes young Solon's keen, inquiring mind. Also aware of Rufus's growing reputation in the area for honesty and industry, Justus asks Rufus and his son to represent his bank in the Dukla area. Rufus agrees, and Justus, who learns of Solon's affection for his daughter and who is also concerned by his lack of a male heir, later offers Solon a position at the bank in Philadelphia.

Solon displays interest and efficiency in the banking field, and the following summer he and Benecia are married. With a house in Dukla from which Solon commutes, the couple is well respected as honest and prosperous. Over the years they have five children: Isobel, Orville, Etta, Dorothea, and Stewart. Meanwhile, Solon is promoted to a higher position, but in prospering, his Quaker-trained conscience is unsure where industry becomes greed.

Solon also finds that as the world changes it is hard to make his children hew to the ethic of simplicity and self-restraint under which he himself was raised. For example, when Etta, a dreamy romantic who likes French novels, insists on going to the secular, progressive University of Wisconsin, Solon refuses, only to see her run away to Madison and Greenwich Village, where she becomes the lover of a painter who eventually leaves her. Stewart, a fun-loving sensualist with an affinity for burlesque and risqué magazines, gets in trouble with friends from boarding school when a girlfriend of one of them is accidentally poisoned and abandoned to die. Stewart, ashamed at his irresponsibility, kills himself in jail, putting Solon's respectable family in the headlines.

This event and Benecia's death from grief soon after awaken Solon to the consequences of insisting on a rigid moral standard for children exposed to a world far different from the one in which he was raised. His self-examination also leads him to resign from the Philadelphia bank, which has degenerated into a corrupt dispenser of bad loans under the new management. Solon is inspired by nature, the love of his daughter Etta (who returns to care for him), and the *Journal* of Quaker John Woolman to feel a reaffirmed sense of love and unity in the universe. Long recognized as a bulwark of the community, he is now seen as a bulwark of the faith.

Barrett, Will. *The Last Gentleman; The Second Coming.* Walker Percy. 1966; 1980.

Will Barrett lives in a New York YMCA and works as a night janitor at Macy's. A chance meeting with Mr. Vaught, an old acquaintance of his parents, changes his life. He becomes the companion of Mr. Vaught's son Jamie, who suffers from leukemia. Jamie and Will go to college together, along with Mr. Vaught's daughter Kitty, with whom Will falls in love.

Suffering from a sudden fit of amnesia, Will becomes disoriented one day and ends up wandering aimlessly. Finally, his memory returns and he pursues Jamie, who has run away from college. Will is reunited with his sick friend just in time to help him die a bit more comfortably. Jamie's death seems to shock Will into normality.

Years later Will seems an exceptionally successful and fortunate person. As a top lawyer married to a wealthy heiress, he enjoys the good life of a rich Manhattanite. However, well before the regular age for retirement, he resigns his position and moves to a resort town in North Carolina. Shortly after the move his wife dies, and six months later he finds himself in a devastating psychological and spiritual crisis.

The first outward sign of this crisis is a fainting spell on the golf course, but soon there are other indications that something is deeply wrong with Will. He begins to see life as farcical and senseless, and on more than one occasion contemplates suicide. He is also troubled by a disturbing memory that begins to take over his consciousness.

The repressed memory is shrouded in the dark recesses of his consciousness, and Will struggles to bring it to light. The event occurred during a boyhood hunting excursion with his father. While ostensibly shooting at birds, his father wounded both himself and his son. Will returns repeatedly to the haunting memory. He imagines interrogating his father about his intentions and motives. Although his father survived the serious self-inflicted wound, he committed suicide shortly thereafter. Will slowly comes to see that his father had intended to kill himself as well as his son on the hunting trip. The motive was a strange sense of compassion, for the elder Barrett wished to spare his son the agony of a meaningless and alienated existence.

Like his father, Will finds life utterly unbearable. He is ready to concede that his father may well have been right, that there may be no God, that life may be nothing but a farce and suicide the most reasonable of responses. He faults his father for not making any attempt to find an alternative to suicide. Determined not to make the same error, Will devises an empirical test in which God can prove his existence and thereby make sense of what appears to be chaos. He descends deep into the bowels of a mountain cave to wait for an unambiguous sign from God, a sign that will save his life, for if there is no divine intervention, he plans to die in the cave.

Will does not get the clear sign that he seeks. Instead, an agonizing toothache aborts his great religious experience. The pain becomes so severe that he must leave the cave. He can't decide whether his ailment is a sign from God or merely a banal human frailty.

On exiting the cave Will becomes lost and falls through a small opening. He finds himself in a greenhouse built into the side of the mountain ridge. A young woman, Allison Huger, has lived there since her recent escape from a mental hospital. Will and Allison fall in love. Through their relationship they begin to heal the profound psychological afflictions they both suffer.

They decide to marry. Will returns to practicing law in the resort town of Linwood. After his experience in the cave and his relationship with Allison, the debilitating existential malaise dissipates rapidly. God has finally revealed himself in the love that human beings have for one another.

Bart, Lily. *The House of Mirth.* Edith Wharton. 1905.

Lily Bart is the luminous heroine of this tragic turn-of-the-century novel. Inhabiting a social world in which appearances count for everything, Lily inherits her mother's innate delicacy and decorum as well as her dread of dinginess and dissolution; in conversation as in dress, she exhibits an exquisite yet artful beauty. However, expensive tastes require an equivalent income, a task for which Lily is unprepared.

Verging on thirty, Lily must from the beginning of the novel confront the end of her glorious reign as the most beautiful and charming unmarried woman in "society." Setting her sights on the socially inept but fabulously wealthy Percy Gryce, she seems destined for success. But through her weakness for gambling, her betrayal by her friend Bertha Dorset, and her impulsive attentions to the more attractive, if poorer, LAWRENCE SELDEN, Lily lets Gryce slip through her fingers.

She soon feels the repercussions of her failed suit. Having been orphaned by parents who had hidden their poverty beneath a veneer of high social standing, she must survive on a small income and the good graces of her aunt, Mrs. Peniston, with whom she lives. Finding herself increasingly in debt, Lily allows Gus Trenor, the husband of her close friend, to use her money to speculate in the stock market. When he later wants repayment in the form of sexual favors, she is shocked. She knows she must pay Gus back in full to retain her dignity, but she has no means with which to earn the money. In the meanwhile, Gus has lured Lily to his house under false pretenses, and gossip about her "loose" character begins to circulate. Even Selden, who has fallen passionately in love with Lily, withdraws.

Unable to absolve her debt to Gus, Lily flees to the Riviera where she becomes the toast of the European aristocracy. Here she ends her friendship with Bertha Dorset, who, attempting to cover up her own marital infidelities,

falsely accuses Lily of seducing her husband George. When Lily returns to New York, she finds herself further ostracized from society.

Thus begins the severest stage of Lily's collapse. Disinherited by moralistic Aunt Peniston, who was already appalled by Lily's penchant for gambling before learning of her supposed affair with Bertha's husband, Lily becomes a kind of social sponsor to first one, then another, marginal but wealthy aspirant to high society. All renounce her as soon as they get "in" with more firmly established social elites.

Lily ends up working, rather incompetently, in a hat shop. In a chance meeting, a wealthy former suitor, SIMON ROSEDALE, urges her to blackmail Bertha Dorset with some love letters the latter had written to Selden some time back. When she is laid off and forced to wander the cheerless streets, the thought of Bertha's letters again crosses Lily's mind. Suddenly resolving to act, she sets out for the Dorset home. En route she spies Selden's house and impulsively enters. Selden, believing the rumors about Gus, treats her kindly but remains remote. Lily realizes the strength of her love for him as well as its hopelessness and surreptitiously tosses Bertha's letters into the fire.

Lily then runs into Nettie Struther, an impoverished secretary she had helped in happier days. Nettie still worships Lily and brings her home to meet her baby, who captivates her. Back in her shabby boardinghouse, Lily arranges her accounts, writes a check covering her debt to Gus Trenor, and takes a heavy dose of chloral, the sleeping potion to which she has become addicted. As she sinks into a drugged sleep, she imagines that Nettie's child lies sleeping in her arms. She wakes once in terror but falls back to sleep when the hallucinatory child reappears. Divested of all her material appurtenances, Lily dies quietly alone.

Bartleby. "Bartleby, the Scrivener: A Story of Wall Street." Herman Melville. 1853.

Bartleby's story is told by a Wall Street lawyer—a prudent, unambitious, complacent man of about sixty years—who has recently been appointed the Mastery in Chancery of New York City. The influx of new business forces the lawyer to hire a new scrivener, a sort of human machine whose job it is to copy tediously dull legal documents. Bartleby—pallid, neat, and forlorn—appears one day like a foundling, is hired, and does impeccably precise work.

After several days the lawyer asks Bartleby to help in the proofreading of a document. For the first time, in a cold yet firm voice, Bartleby utters his famous denial: "I would prefer not to." Irritated yet captivated by such a blatant rejection of duty, the lawyer begins to observe Bartleby's behavior. He never eats dinner; he never seems to leave the office; he sits constantly at his desk, in catatonic reverie, staring at the brick wall opposite his window. Bartleby, it seems, is alone in the world.

Although frustrated by Bartleby's passive resistance to authority, the lawyer decides to treat his scrivener with sympathy, not scorn, but all of his attempts at reason and charity are thwarted by Bartleby's persistent denial. The lawyer finally resolves to dismiss Bartleby, but the scrivener, who has now ceased even to copy documents, prefers not to leave the premises. The lawyer's colleagues begin to take notice of the vestigial employee, and their gossip jeopardizes his professional reputation. The only solution, the lawyer concludes, is to move from the office himself.

The new tenant of the office seeks out the lawyer and complains that the ghostlike scrivener continues to haunt the building. Fearful of his reputation and feeling the pangs of charitable responsibility, the lawyer returns to his old premises to reason with and even threaten his stubborn ex-employee. But again Bartleby refuses to budge. The new tenant calls in the police, and Bartleby, the vagrant who would not wander, is taken to jail.

Suffering tremendous guilt, the lawyer visits Bartleby in the Tombs, but the scrivener shuns him. Bartleby, it seems, refuses to take meals and now spends his time staring at the walls of the prison. Finally, the lawyer returns to the jail and finds an emaciated Bartleby lying by a wall, dead.

Although Bartleby reveals nothing about his personal history, the lawyer later hears a highly uncertain rumor that his late employee had been a subordinate clerk in the dead letter office in Washington, D.C.—a place where the best-intentioned missives of charity and love end up in the ash heap of wrongly addressed letters. Bartleby— at once everyman and no man—remains an unopened mystery.

Bascomb, Asa. "The World of Apples." John Cheever. 1973.

Asa Bascomb, a celebrated poet living in Italy, is not on a quest for something tangible, although he would like to win a Nobel Prize. Rather, his search is for meaning and the knowledge that what he has created will endure.

Bascomb should be satisfied. Throughout his long career he has received the kind of acclaim from critics, governments, and the public that few poets enjoy. Unlike the four poets of his generation whom he most admired, he is still alive and still working. Fans of his best-selling collection of poetry, *The World of Apples*, flock to his small villa outside Rome to ask for his autograph. Still, Bascomb is afraid. An elderly man, he realizes that he is approaching death, although he has little desire to commit suicide or drink himself to death as each of his four admired poets had. He obsesses about the natural memory loss that accompanies aging, even going as far as devising mental puzzles designed to convince himself that he is as sharp

as ever. One day Bascomb must drag himself out of a warm bed to look up Lord Byron's first name in an encyclopedia because he cannot remember it on his own.

When he goes on a drive with an admirer, Bascomb witnesses a seemingly innocuous sight that plunges him into depression. Going into the woods to relieve himself, he stumbles across a couple making love. The incident jars him, driving out of his mind thoughts of the cathedrals he had visited with his fans and inspiring instead a fixation on sex. He tries to cure his obsession by having sex with his housekeeper, but still he feels unsettled and pursued by obscene thoughts.

He interrupts his daily routine of poetry writing and begins writing pornography instead. Stories and poems follow, and finally the greatest indignity: He starts writing dirty limericks. Disgusted, he burns what he has written, but his thoughts of sensuality still plague him. When he thinks of rail travel, he imagines couples copulating in the sleeping cars; when he attends a recital in Rome, he fantasizes in vivid detail of undressing the soprano and having his way with her.

A look at the work of Juvenal and Petronius convinces Bascomb that their pornography contains none of the wickedness evident in his own work. He wonders what has changed about the world in those centuries, crowding out beauty from his mind and replacing it with pornography, and what about him has been lost. He realizes that his dirty works are devoid of anxiety and love, the two emotions he connects with his family, especially his dead wife Amelia.

When his housekeeper mentions a place of pilgrimage that cleanses all who visit it from sin, Bascomb decides to visit the site. The trip gives him pleasure even though he is caught in a rainstorm and confronts what seems to be a hostile dog. When he realizes that the dog is just frightened and that the world seems cleansed by the storm, a feeling of peace comes over him. He makes his offering and returns home the next morning to begin writing his last poem, a meditation on "the inalienable dignity of light and air."

Bascombe, Frank. *The Sportswriter.* Richard Ford. 1986.

When Frank Bascombe, the philosophizing narrator, was young, he wrote a highly acclaimed collection of short stories that established him as a powerful writer. Yet after this early success, Frank developed chronic writer's block, so he abandoned fiction and became a sportswriter. Sport provides him with a series of metaphors and lessons for understanding life, and again and again he returns to the world of sport to make sense of his own experience, especially the death of his son Ralph and the subsequent breakup of his marriage. Frank responds to the present with an ironic detachment that counters his too-passionate involvement in the past, and his narration of the novel's events, which focus on one week in his life, is characterized by a dispassionate, almost objective tone. Underlying this lack of passion, however, is a profound regret at his inability both to write and to come to terms with his grief.

The novel opens with Frank's annual meeting with his ex-wife at their son Ralph's grave to mark the anniversary of his death. This meeting causes Frank to reflect again on the past and on his marriage to his unnamed ex-wife, from whom he grew estranged after Ralph's death and with whom he became increasingly unable to communicate. In a characteristic moment, Frank weighs this past against the promise of a future with his new girlfriend, Vicki Acrenault, and an interview in Detroit with Herb Wallagher, an ex-football player who is now confined to a wheelchair. This day is, he feels, both an anniversary and a new beginning. The past offers him the man he was, while Vicki offers him security and love, and Herb Wallagher is a lesson in how to deal with regret and unfulfilled potential. Yet in spite of the hopeful prospects the day holds, Frank implicitly wants to retrieve the past, and as he feels himself drawing nearer to his ex-wife, his strongest hope for the future seems to be that he can return to the way things were.

As if to confirm this feeling, the trip to Detroit that was to resolve Frank's regret becomes a series of disappointments. Herb Wallagher, formerly an inspiration to his team, is now married and training to become a lawyer, and has turned out to be a bitter and violent man. Far from overcoming his personal tragedy, he has let it overwhelm him. Frank leaves him feeling disillusioned and bleak. His relationship with Vicki, too, is more complicated than he had thought; he realizes he is jealous of her ex-husband, and she is jealous of his ex-wife. He begins to acknowledge that Vicki is slipping away from him, yet he will not make any moves to win her back. This seems to result partly from the diffidence with which he views his life as a divorced man and partly from his attachment to his former wife. After an Easter lunch with Vicki and her family, Frank leaves knowing that his relationship with Vicki is over. He expresses no regret about this, and Vicki fades unnoticeably from his narrative.

The detachment that seems to keep Frank at one remove from the episodes he is narrating is penetrated only by his feelings about the past and by one event in the present. This event is the suicide of Walter Luckett, a member of the divorced men's club to which Frank belongs. Frank is reluctant even to consider Walter a friend, but Walter insists on confiding in him, telling him about an affair he has had with another man. Walter's final gesture of confidence in Frank is to address his suicide note to him. Frank's first response to this, when he is questioned by the police, is one of annoyance that he should be involved in another man's sorrow. Yet this annoyance breaks through his customary diffidence, and as he grows to feel

more responsible toward Walter, he becomes more passionately involved in the present.

At the novel's close, Frank, sensing that the "simpler truth of the athlete" for which he is searching might be found away from the scene of his regrets, gives up his job as a sportswriter. Although he speculates about a possible reconciliation with his ex-wife, he seems finally satisfied with the present and the world of concrete events. The constant analysis that has typified his narrative gives way at the end of the book to a simple description of his surroundings and an acceptance of the way things are, independent of the past or future.

Baxter, Jody. *The Yearling.* Marjorie Kinnan Rawlings. 1939.

A lonely twelve-year-old boy with an affinity for rambling, Jody Baxter knows no other life than the one he lives on a harsh, subsistence-level farm. He is the only surviving child of PENNY (BAXTER), a Confederate Army veteran, and his wife ORA (BAXTER), and lives with them on Baxter Island, a cultivated area in the vast Florida pine barrens.

A typical boy, Jody allows his jobs, hoeing the corn and chopping the wood, to wait while he builds a fluttermill in a stream. Since his only friend is a strange and imaginative disabled boy, Fodder-wing Forrester, Jody longs for a pet to ease his lonely existence. Finally, over the protests of his mother, who is concerned that a pet would take precious food from their meager supply, he is allowed to have a fawn, which he names Flag. He nurtures the fawn, sneaks it into the house to sleep beside him, worries about it, attempts to train it, and loves it with unswerving devotion.

In the months that follow, Jody encounters death when he takes Flag to see Fodder-wing, only to discover that the boy has died. He sees death in another guise when a terrible autumn storm causes a plague that devastates the animal population in the wild. Flag becomes a constant companion when Jody works on the farm, hunts with his father, or rambles through the woods.

With the coming of spring, Flag, a yearling now, begins to tamper with the Baxters' food supply, thereby threatening their survival. When Flag tramples the tobacco, a cash crop for trading, Jody restores the planting. When he spills the dried peas, Jody picks up every one. But when the deer eats the corn seedlings for the second time, both Penny and Ora insist that he must be shot. Penny, too disabled with rheumatism to leave his bed, orders Jody to shoot his pet. When Jody will not, his mother takes the gun and wounds the deer with a bad shot. Jody follows the frightened and bleeding animal, finally killing it to end its suffering. Following that, he decides to run away from home with the vague notion of traveling to Boston. He grows steadily more hungry with each passing day until he eats grass in an attempt to fill his empty stomach.

At last he returns home, having narrowly survived his confrontation with starvation. He realizes that he can endure the loss of his pet, that with his father crippled he must accept some of the responsibility for procuring food, and that he is no longer a "yearling" himself but a responsible member of the family with a life of hard work and suffering but also of opportunity before him.

Baxter, Ora. *The Yearling.* Marjorie Kinnan Rawlings. 1939.

Ora Baxter is a hardworking backwoods wife and mother. Large-framed, she is twice the size of her husband PENNY (BAXTER), who chose her to share a life of hardship in the Florida pine barrens just after the Civil War. After burying a succession of babies in tiny plots on the Baxter property, Ora gave birth to JODY (BAXTER) when she was nearly past childbearing age. While she loves her twelve-year-old son, she does not pamper him because she wants him to become accustomed at an early age to a lifetime of hard work.

Ora's life is both lonely and difficult. Isolated on the Baxter farm, she dislikes her only neighbors and journeys to the nearest town only twice a year. Wise in home remedies, she knows the treatment for any disease and is masterful in the frugal arts of patching, turning, quilting, and mending. Though water is far away and washing is difficult, she insists on cleanliness and neatness in the tiny cabin. Her days are a monotonous round of chores, mostly dealing with the storage and preparation of rations. When a bear kills her brood sow or steals a calf, or when a dreadful week-long storm devastates crops and causes a plague in the animal world, she sees these disasters only in terms of the food she will not have to put on the Baxter table. She knows that "old starvation" could visit the Baxters if the crops fail or the hunting is poor. Because of this, she denies her lonely son his request for a pet fawn; however, she eventually concedes to his wishes.

When accused of being a hard woman, Ora replies, "Being hard is the only way I can stand it." Her survival instinct allows her to bear not only the loss of her children but also the loss of her husband as a provider when he suffers a ruptured hernia. When Penny becomes bedridden, she shoulders more and more of the responsibilities of the farm.

Jody's fawn, now a yearling, tramples the tobacco and spills the peas, and Ora helps her son build a high fence to corral the deer. But when the fence proves ineffective and the yearling eats the corn seedling twice, she realizes the fawn must be killed. Since Penny is bedridden and Jody refuses to shoot his pet, she takes the gun. A poor shot, she wounds the fawn, and Jody is forced to finish the killing, which he does before running away. When Jody returns much later, it is to find his mother attempting to plant the fields for a third time, working hard to fend off starvation and keep the Baxters alive through another year.

Baxter, Penny. *The Yearling.* Marjorie Kinnan Rawlings. 1939.

The son of a poor, fundamentalist preacher, Ezra "Penny" Baxter knew only work from the time he could toddle. When he reached adulthood he was so poorly nourished that he was no bigger than a "penny piece," and thus earned his nickname. A hardworking farmer in his fifties, Penny takes his wife ORA (BAXTER) and his only surviving child JODY (BAXTER) to a scrappy farm in the Florida scrub because he is drawn to its peace.

Penny is a poor but resourceful man who feels a real affinity for nature, but he believes that you "kill or go hungry." He goes after Old Slewfoot, a murderous bear who kills his brood sow and later a calf, and fights the animal with great bravery. But when his neighbors devise a plan to poison the wolves that threaten to overrun their farms, he refuses to comply because he feels poisoning isn't natural.

A shrewd though fiercely honest trader, Penny is generous with the little money he has and with his labor. He trades a precious hide for the fabric his wife desires so she can have a Christmas dress. And when Jody goes rambling instead of hoeing corn, it is Penny who does the work for him. Unlike his wife Ora, he believes the boy should have the opportunity to frolic and savor his childhood. When Jody begs for a pet fawn, Penny gives in, going against his wife's more practical refusal.

Penny knows that death in various forms lurks in the wilderness that surrounds their tiny clearing. On a trip to retrieve pigs stolen by his irascible neighbors, the Forresters, he is bitten by a rattlesnake and nearly dies. When a week-long September storm devastates his crops just at harvest and causes a plague in the wild, he knows that finding food for the coming winter will be difficult.

In early spring Penny becomes crippled with rheumatism but hobbles out to do the necessary planting, only to rupture his hernia when attempting to remove a tree stump. This injury leaves him a semi-invalid who in his own opinion is "not worth shooting." When Jody's beloved fawn, a yearling now, begins to eat seedlings and destroys the Baxters' food supply, Penny knows that though it will break Jody's heart, the deer must be shot. Too disabled to do the job himself, he orders Jody to kill the deer. When the boy refuses, Ora takes the gun and wounds the deer with a bad shot. Jody kills the frightened and bleeding animal to end its suffering, then runs away from home. When Jody returns, having met "old starvation," Penny rejoices knowing that his son has matured and is capable of facing life in these unforgiving and harsh surroundings.

Bayliss, George. *Marching! Marching!* Clara Weatherwax. 1935.

The owner of an enormous lumber mill, George Bayliss controls all of the local activity in the small community in which he lives. Bayliss enjoys this position because of the economic importance his mill represents. Throughout his career at the mill, he employs numerous ruthless and immoral methods to ensure his hold over the community, as well as the financial well-being of his company.

Too miserly to waste money on safety mechanisms, Bayliss forces his workers to labor under dangerous conditions for meager wages. Rather than pay compensation to the widow of one of the lumberjacks killed on the job at his mill, he forces her to give sexual favors in return for meager reparations. He then compels her son, as soon as he is old enough, to work at the mill as a kind of management spy under his employ.

It is through this spy, a young lumberman named Peter, that Bayliss becomes aware of rumors of possible union activities. He orders Peter to discover the leader of this labor movement. Peter finds the upstart—an immigrant named Mario—but only after being brutally beaten by him. When the youth warns of the unrest in the mill, Bayliss responds to the possible uprising with his typical strong-arm tactics.

Things come to a head when another lumberjack is killed in an accident at the mill and Bayliss refuses, once again, to pay any kind of compensation to the widow. This last injustice by the mill owner turns out to be the catalyst for a large union organizational meeting, which Bayliss learns about through his usual network of informants. In an effort to destroy any chance of a possible strike before it begins, he hires a gang of thugs to beat the union organizer Mario savagely.

Bayliss's strategy ultimately backfires, however, when, at the instigation of his coworker JOSEPH STRONG, Mario becomes a martyr-like hero for the unhappy lumberers, and they walk out of the mill on strike a few days later. A furious Bayliss is forced to close the mill, but he employs a number of his typically ruthless tactics to ensure that the lumberers' strike is short-lived. He is able to buy off several local police officers, and local hoodlums serve as strike breakers to help subdue the picketing workers. He portrays the strikers as subversive communists to the media, and after employing scab workers, he is able to reopen the mill on a part-time basis.

When even this is not enough to break down the solidarity of the striking workers, Bayliss, after stumbling down a flight of stairs during a demonstration, claims that he was pushed by the two union leaders and has them imprisoned for attempted murder. With the local justice system, like everything else in town, under the firm control of the lumber king, Bayliss has no trouble getting the two labor leaders imprisoned indefinitely.

Once again, however, Bayliss finds that his strong-arm tactics have backfired. Shortly after the imprisonment of lower-echelon union organizers, the striking workers stage a parade through the town in a show of strength. As the mill owner watches the picketing workers, he won-

ders to himself what it will take to finally disrupt their solidarity.

Bayoux, Carter. *Her First American.* Lore Segal. 1985.

Carter Bayoux, a brilliant but disillusioned black writer, struggles bravely with private and political issues. The novel follows Carter's romance with ILKA WEISNIX, a young Jewish refugee from Vienna, who adores Carter and is willing to withstand the pressures of racism for the sake of their friendship.

When he meets Ilka in a bar in Nevada, Carter seems a self-assured, "weighty" man. In his public incarnation he is the center of a large group of progressive New York artists and intellectuals. He impresses Ilka's erudite cousin Fishgoppel with anecdotes from his years in Europe where he met James Joyce and Gertrude Stein.

With elegant and commanding language, Carter is able to organize people, rouse them against oppression, or seduce them. He is a master of "protocol," an art he practices professionally as the United Nations correspondent for the *Harlem Herald*. He persuades a reluctant guard to admit him backstage at Carnegie Hall. At a fine restaurant he introduces Ilka to a famous painter, William Rauschenquist. When Carter interviews a popular gospel singer, he turns the conversation into a sophisticated social critique. He takes Ilka to see his ex-wife Ebony perform a skit that mocks white stereotypes of blacks.

Carter and Ilka spend their summer in a house in Connecticut, which they share with a white couple and two other interracial couples. Carter acts as spokesman and mediator, coolly observing the uncomfortable debate over the white couple's crusade to adopt a black baby. He privately explains the argument to Ilka by telling her stories that illuminate American social injustice with humor, bitterness, and accuracy.

Even on their first disastrous outing Carter exposes his weaker side. Arriving at the wedding reception of an old girlfriend, Carter neglects Ilka and begins to drink. In a drunken rage he shouts at the well-meaning bridegroom, sending him into tears. Like the rest of the company, Ilka is astonished but eventually forgives him. Even the bridegroom, Philip, persists in visiting Carter at his hotel to listen to stories and ask for advice.

Carter periodically withdraws into his hotel room, draws the shades, and begins drinking. He sends the bellhop across the street for more liquor and calls Ilka at work to beg her to bring him a meal. He annoys the hotel switchboard by perpetually asking for the time of day. Carter admonishes himself to "snap out of it" and "reestablish protocol," but his drinking bouts regularly end with him in the hospital.

Ilka finally leaves Carter when she recognizes that no one will be able to rescue him from his alcoholism. After Carter moves to the West Coast, Ilka receives distressing news about him from his new girlfriend, a childish blonde she calls the "Californian Specimen." After several months she calls Ilka, weeping; Carter has died after another period of heavy drinking. Ilka attends a memorial service, during which Carter's graduate students read his work and reminisce about his escapades.

Beal, General Ira "Bus." *Guard of Honor.* James Gould Cozzens. 1948.

After a distinguished period of service during World War II, General Ira "Bus" Beal, the youngest two-star general in the Air Force, has been assigned to a training installation in Alabama. There he will gain administrative experience for what all predict will be a long and illustrious military career.

As he approaches the base in Alabama, General Beal is almost killed along with LIEUTENANT COLONEL BENNY CARRICKER, CAPTAIN NATHANIEL HICKS, and a couple of other officers when their plane almost collides with a B-17 that started to land without receiving permission from the control tower. As soon as their plane touches down, Carricker, Beal's copilot and old friend, knocks the lead pilot of the B-17 unconscious. As it turns out, the B-17 had been piloted by a group of black aviators taking part in an official experiment to integrate the Air Force, and Beal has no choice but to place Carricker, who served with him overseas, under arrest.

The next morning Beal learns that Colonel Woody Woodman, a long-term acquaintance with whom he had argued bitterly the night before, committed suicide by shooting himself in the head sometime after their encounter. In order to relieve the stress that Carricker's actions have placed on him and the guilt that he feels over Colonel Woodman's death, Beal takes a plane out for a short flight without notifying anyone of his destination. When he returns, he finds General Joseph Josephson Nichols, a supervisor from Washington, waiting for him at the base. Although his right-hand man, Colonel Norman Ross, tried to cover for him in his absence, Beal is aware of a vague disapproval on the part of the visiting general.

A variety of problems then arise that Beal must handle under the watchful eye of General Nichols. When Beal resists pressing charges against his friend Carricker, the black pilots organize a protest. No sooner is their mini-rebellion quelled by Beal than several of their paratroopers, engaged in simulated war games, drown in a nearby lake. The men had not been instructed, as is customary when parachuting near any body of water, to wear life preservers; and the "crash-boat," a craft that should have been standing by in case of emergency, had been inoperative that day.

Beal organizes an investigation of the incident in order to find out who was responsible for allowing the pilots to go on the mission without taking the necessary precautions. It soon becomes apparent that the blame lies with the aged and slightly senile Colonel Pop Mowbray, who serves directly under Beal with Colonel Ross. Beal cannot bring himself to condemn Mowbray, who was taught to fly by Wilbur Wright himself, and although he seems committed to following up on the details of the investigation, he devotes his efforts primarily to protecting the reputation of the Air Force. Beal is saved from taking responsibility for the accident by the appearance of Mr. Botwinick, Colonel Mowbray's clerk, who informs him that he had "accidentally" burned a file that would have incriminated Mowbray. With no hard evidence against Mowbray, the questions surrounding the case will remain unanswered; in time, Beal reasons, the incident will be forgotten.

Before leaving the base, General Nichols congratulates Beal on his handling of this delicate situation. Beal and Ross watch Nichols's plane take off with a mixture of satisfaction and relief. Beal's one remaining concern is Mowbray. He asks Ross to "pick up" after the old man: "It isn't really much, it isn't really often; but watch it, will you?" The two men are interrupted by the sound of a horn, and they turn to find Mrs. Beal hailing them from a car. Before leaving to join his wife, Beal pauses and watches the general's plane disappear into the night sky; the sound of its engines fades, and its lights become indistinguishable, "no more than stars among the innumerable stars."

Beaucaire, Monsieur. *Monsieur Beaucaire.* Booth Tarkington. 1900.

In this turn-of-the-century novella, a young Frenchman playing cards in his room with an English gentleman, the Duke of Winterset, catches the duke cheating. He threatens to expose the duke to society as a cheat unless he is introduced that evening as a friend and gentleman in Bath, the fashionable English city where the story takes place. The duke resists violently because he knows that, although well groomed and handsome, his accuser is not a gentleman and is in fact the discharged barber of a French nobleman. The duke protests that the men of Bath society will recognize the barber, Monsieur Beaucaire, as the host of their own recent gambling expeditions. Removing his wig and mustache, Beaucaire holds sway over the duke with his threat.

Beaucaire greets Bath society that very evening on the arm of the duke. He is an immediate success, most especially with Lady Mary Carlisle, the chief object of every gentleman's desire. At this first meeting Beaucaire, who is introduced as Monsieur Chateaurien, secures a token of her affection, a red rose. As further proof of his success he bests two young Englishmen in separate duels, proving himself of noble lineage to Bath society.

One evening, having secured the highest regards of Lady Mary, Beaucaire is granted the honor of escorting her carriage home from a fete. On the road they are overtaken by a band of masked men who attack Beaucaire, calling out "Barber! Barber!" He fights valiantly, distinguishing himself as true nobility in the eyes of Lady Mary and especially one of her party, Mr. Molyneux. He is almost taken until his own servants, who were riding at a distance so as not to disturb his amours with Lady Mary, arrive to vanquish the masked men.

Wounded, he is about to be placed into Lady Mary's carriage when the Duke of Winterset arrives and shows himself as one of the masked men. Covering up his own culpability, he exposes Beaucaire to Lady Mary and her party as a lower-class citizen, a former barber. When Beaucaire is unable to counter the charge, Lady Mary, horrified by having been courted by a peasant, leaves him by the side of the road. Beaucaire assures them that he will see them in a week's time in the Assembly Room, the meeting place of Bath society.

One week later Lady Mary arrives at the Assembly Room on the arm of the Duke of Winterset who has, with the banishment of Beaucaire, asserted a strong claim as Lady Mary's companion. There is a large crowd due to the arrival in Bath of Count de Beaujolais, a French prince, who is accompanied by the French ambassador of Louis XV. Feeling faint from the crush, Lady Mary retires to a side room where she discovers the outcast Beaucaire playing cards with Mr. Molyneux. She offers Beaucaire a chance to slip away without embarrassment before she calls the guards to have him removed; Molyneux tries to protest. Meanwhile Winterset and several gentlemen, having learned that Beaucaire has gained entrance to the Assembly Room, arrive to remove him. Molyneux finally makes himself heard and introduces Beaucaire as a prince of France. Winterset shouts his disbelief. The Count of Beaujolais is summoned and greets Beaucaire—in reality the Prince de Valois—as a brother and friend. It is revealed that Valois had previously angered the king of France by refusing the king's request to marry a lady who loved him dearly. Valois had been hiding out in England as Beaucaire, waiting for the king's wrath to abate.

The company is aghast at their own rough treatment of the prince. Beaucaire/Valois exposes Winterset for the cheat and villain he is. Lady Mary apologizes—but too late. Monsieur Beaucaire has decided to return to France to marry the one woman who never would have rejected him.

Beauchamp, Lucas. *Intruder in the Dust.* William Faulkner. 1948.

Lucas Beauchamp, a black man with partial white ancestry, incenses the white population of Yoknapatawpha County by refusing to imitate the traditionally servile manner of blacks in the South. He wears a meticulous black suit, pale felt hat, and a watch chain and toothpick of gold. He becomes known in the area as "the

Negro . . . who said 'sir' and 'mister' to you if you were white, but who you knew was thinking neither."

Beauchamp's description comes largely from Charles "Chick" Mallison, a white adolescent who meets the notorious black man while hunting rabbit on the property of Carothers Edmonds, a wealthy white landowner. Chick falls into an icy creek and emerges drenched to find Beauchamp standing on the bank. Beauchamp virtually commands the boy to come to his home and dry off. On the way Chick remembers that his guide is a descendant of Edmonds's great-grandfather and that he has been granted a house and ten acres in perpetuity.

Beauchamp's black skin and "white" demeanor fascinate and disturb Chick. Chick accepts a seat by Beauchamp's fire, and more reluctantly, partakes of the dinner that Molly Beauchamp has prepared for her husband. Later, Chick offers them all the money that he has, seventy cents. As soon as he holds it out, he realizes that he has made a terrible mistake. Beauchamp refuses the change, not scornfully but with an air on noncomprehension. Overcome by rage—the same helpless rage that the local whites experience when dealing with this "uppity" black man—Chick drops the coins. Beauchamp orders two black boys to return them to their owner.

This short time with Beauchamp proves to be a transforming experience for Chick. He grows more and more distrustful of the validity of the social customs upon which he has been raised. Four years after the creek incident, Beauchamp is arrested for the murder of Vincent Gowrie, a white citizen of the county's notoriously violent and clannish district, Beat Four. The townspeople are quick to solve the crime as a punishment for Beauchamp's lifelong disrespect of his white superiors. While Beauchamp sits in a cell, a crowd comes to the jail and threatens a lynching. Beauchamp singles out Chick, who is against the lynching, and tells him to get his uncle, GAVIN STEVENS, the county attorney.

The first meeting between Beauchamp and Stevens ends unsatisfactorily; the attorney does not believe in his client's innocence and urges Beauchamp to plead guilty to manslaughter. But Beauchamp later meets with Chick and offers to pay him to dig up Gowrie's body. Beauchamp hopes to prove that the gun used for the murder was not his own.

Despite misgivings, Chick steals into the burial ground with Aleck Sander, a black hired hand, and Eunice Habersham, an old white spinster who was raised with Beauchamp's wife. In Gowrie's grave they find the body of Jake Montgomery, a timber buyer from a neighboring county. This discovery, relayed back to the sheriff and Stevens, prompts a series of revelations that absolve Beauchamp.

After Beauchamp's release, they bring the real murderer (Gowrie's brother Crawford) to justice. The mob outside the jail breaks up, and the townspeople, many still resentful of Beauchamp but now unable to harm him, slowly return to their everyday lives.

Bech, Henry. *Bech: A Book; Bech Is Back*. John Updike. 1965; 1975.

Jewish novelist Henry Bech, the protagonist of two collections of short stories, is nearly fifty years old and has thinning curly hair and a "melancholy Jewish nose." Bech's first novel was a great success for which he still receives much critical acclaim. He also wrote a more "surreal" and "existential," even "anarchist," work, as well as a collection of essays and articles. His most recent novel took five years to complete and received little recognition. He is said to be working on a new novel entitled *Think Big*, but he has reached an impasse in his literary and personal life.

Despite Bech's initial literary success, he is neither wealthy nor personally satisfied. He received few of the royalties from his first novel and has lived the past twenty years in a dingy apartment on the Upper West Side of New York City. In order to make money, Bech occasionally contributes to such magazines as *Commentary* and *Esquire*, and is reduced to lecturing at universities and conferences around the world.

When Bech is enlisted by the U.S. government to lecture in Eastern Europe, he finds himself in a series of short-lived, unsatisfying relationships with an embassy wife in Prague, a chanteuse in Rumania, and a Mongolian sculptress in Kazakstan. At one point Bech thinks he has found his mate in Vera Glavanakova, a tall, blond, self-assured Bulgarian poetess. After having cocktails together the two exchange writings but nothing more.

During the fifteen years after the publication of his first novel, Bech has sustained relationships with two sisters, Norma and Bea. Norma is older, more seductive, and childless. Bea is younger, plumper, and more practical. She is recently divorced and has twin daughters and a son. When Bech experiments with marijuana with the two sisters and one of his former college students, he and Bea find themselves romantically involved. Bech has, in effect, taken "pot luck" with the sisters and leaves Norma for the younger, more conventional Bea. Soon, however, he begins to feel restless with Bea; he finds her suburban life-style stifling and has difficulty reconciling her double role as lover and mother. On a trip to a girls' school in Virginia, Bech is overwhelmed by an impending sense of death. After having a brief affair with a Jewish assistant professor, he returns to New York and leaves Bea.

Bachelor Bech then has a fling with a woman who becomes the model for a character in his next novel; but he finds little satisfaction in the life of a swinger. At the end of the first collection, Bech finds himself being honored for his literary achievement among other literary legends he thought dead. He imagines his mother's proud face in the crowd and is left wondering "What next?"

The second collection commences with Bech's marriage to Bea and the publication of his long-awaited novel *Think Big*. He moves to upstate New York to live with Bea and her children, and derives a certain satisfaction from their suburban life-style. He enjoys playing catch with Bea's son and sitting down to meals with the family. He also feels somewhat stifled, however, by Bea's "old money" background and misses his New York apartment and the freedom of bachelorhood. Bea pressures him to resume his writing for his own well-being as well as for the financial survival of the family.

Bech writes with renewed vigor, and the book is finally published with great success. He can hardly go out in public without being recognized and approached for autographs. When Bea takes a vicarious pleasure in his success and assumes partial credit for getting him started, Bech begins to feel stifled by her self-satisfied, domineering manner. One evening when Norma stops by, Bech commits adultery with her and soon afterward divorces Bea.

The last story finds Bech back in the New York artist scene at a photographer friend's party. Before leaving with a female mud wrestler he meets at the party, Bech thinks "treyf," meaning unclean in Yiddish.

Bedford, Sarah Tait "Sallie." *So Red the Rose*. Stark Young. 1934.

Sarah Tait Bedford courageously faces a series of trials in this novel about the effects of the Civil War on Mississippi planter society. The second wife of wealthy planter Malcolm Bedford, Sarah lives on Malcolm's lovely Mississippi plantation, Portobello.

As the novel opens, Sallie, originally from Alabama, has been married to Malcolm for twenty-three years. Although she is subject to twinges of jealousy over her husband's first wife, whom she knows he loved, she feels secure in his love for her. This fact, along with her own deep love for Malcolm, enables her to overcome her jealousy as well as to tolerate Malcolm's tendency to drink to excess. Indeed, throughout the Civil War, Sallie finds the strength to tolerate many trials and tribulations.

Sallie's primary concern throughout the novel is the absence of her husband and her son Duncan, both of whom enlist in the Confederate Army after the Civil War begins. Although anxiety about their welfare underlies all of Sallie's thoughts, she must attend to a large household, and her numerous duties help her to remain relatively calm. In addition to her two small daughters, Sallie cares for five-year-old Middleton, the child of her husband's dead sister, and Julia Valette Somerville, the child of a dead friend and Duncan's unofficial fiancée. Furthermore, two of Sallie's siblings live at Portobello—her senile brother, Henry Fairfax, and her lovable sister, Rosa Tait. Then, too, Portobello is frequently visited by the redoubtable Mary Cherry, an aging and crotchety spinster whom Sallie tolerates because of Mary's essentially kind and loyal nature. Finally, there are the slaves, whom Sallie sees as inferior, childlike, shiftless beings that she must rule strictly.

Sallie is kept busy by her many responsibilities until Malcolm is sent home after the fall of Vicksburg. Learning that Malcolm has contracted diphtheria and that the doctor can do nothing for him, Sallie sends the children and guests away and nurses her husband as he slowly dies, raving about the fall of Vicksburg and the incompetence of General Pemberton.

As the Union Army approaches Portobello, Sallie is disgusted by her slaves' desertion, but she continues on alone, plowing the Portobello fields, warding off marauding soldiers, and reducing the family's expenditures to a level she would once have considered disgraceful. But the strain of the hard wartime years eventually tells on her, and she begins to visit the mortally wounded to give them messages to give to her loved ones who have died.

Sallie finds her courage rewarded when Duncan returns home at the novel's close. Knowing that she has lost much to the fall of the Confederacy, she is nevertheless able to take comfort in Duncan's promise that he and his new bride, Julia Valette, will never again leave her side.

Behrman, S. *The Octopus.* Frank Norris. 1901.

S. Behrman, the local agent of the Pacific and Southwest Railroad, represents more than the railroad's financial interests; he embodies the voracious, ruthless forces of the politico-financial complex—involving governments, markets, and industries all over the world—that strangles the farmers and ranchers in the San Joaquin Valley. Fat, hairy, sneering, Behrman is a caricature of a melodramatic villain: He is a convenient viaduct for a nameless force that devours the farmers, a force larger than the railroad itself.

While Behrman seems to be on hand for every major event in the novel, he never really sets those events in motion. It is Behrman who, when rancher MAGNUS DERRICK seeks to remove his new plows from a train, insists that they be rerouted through San Francisco, according to regulations. It is he who announces to the ranchers that land which they had been promised at two dollars and fifty cents an acre would be sold for more than ten times that amount, and to the hops-farmer Dyke that the railroad is trebling the cost of carrying his grain. He accompanies the posse who capture Dyke when the latter defiantly robs a train, and he is with the team of deputies that comes finally to displace Magnus Derrick from his house. But he remains aloof from the scuffle with Dyke and from the gun battle with the farmers.

Behrman's status as mere representative becomes more apparent toward the end of the novel. The poet PRESLEY, roused to socialistic ardor after a gun battle between the U.S. marshals and the ranchers, hurls a pipe bomb through Behrman's window. The room is destroyed, but the rail-road agent is miraculously unharmed. Like the railroad itself, Behrman seems impervious to any efforts at opposition.

Finally, Behrman gains control of Magnus Derrick's ranch, Rancho de Los Muertos, which he has long coveted, and humiliates Derrick. Prosperous and proprietary, he is surveying the loading of a shipment of his wheat destined for India when he trips and falls into the ship's hold. Wheat begins pouring in, drowning his cries for help and stifling his gasps for air.

Bellefleur, Germaine. *Bellefleur.* Joyce Carol Oates. 1980.

Germaine Bellefleur is the youngest child of LEAH (BELLEFLEUR) and her husband GIDEON (BELLEFLEUR). By the time Leah and Gideon were married a year, they were the parents of a set of twins; however, it is six more years before Leah becomes pregnant again. The pregnancy is long and difficult, and terminates, after more than ten months, in Germaine's shocking birth. The infant's maternal grandmother immediately notices that the child is a monstrosity: protruding from her body is the torso and genitalia of an infant male. The grandmother quickly cuts the male body parts away from Germaine and sutures the infant. Leah is immediately taken with her new infant, who suckles greedily and almost immediately begins to grow prodigiously.

Soon after Germaine's birth it becomes apparent that she possesses psychic powers beyond those of most of the other Bellefleurs. Leah, for her part, becomes slavishly attached to the infant and brings her along when she travels about the state in an effort to rebuild the failing Bellefleur fortune. In fact, the impulse itself is credited to Germaine whom Leah imagines has begun to instruct her in the campaign to recoup the losses of the past.

As Germaine gets older, she repeatedly demonstrates that she is able to foresee events, especially disastrous ones. In one case she cries hysterically about a fire, and within hours her young cousin is assaulted in an outbuilding on the estate, which is then set on fire, causing the death of her attacker. Numerous such instances lead Leah, in particular, to pay close attention to the young child's moods and mannerisms. On the day of her great-great-grandmother's one hundredth birthday party, Germaine is quite edgy, and Leah is sure that the day will turn out disastrously. And indeed it does: The area suffers one of its worst rainstorms ever, leading to many deaths and a great deal of destruction.

When she overhears a lengthy and bitter quarrel between her parents who have long since realized that their marriage is a failure, Germaine is horribly upset. She is too young to understand fully her parents' words, but their tone is clear enough. From this point on Germaine's physical and mental development slows and her psychic powers seem to abate.

As is the case every year, there is a large party planned for Germaine's fourth birthday. Germaine, who dearly loves her father, begs to be allowed to have a ride in his plane for her birthday. After much persistence Gideon finally relents and takes his oddly edgy daughter for a flight. Embittered and drunk, Gideon decides at the last minute that he has had enough of life. With Germaine in the passenger seat, he crashes the plane into Bellefleur Manor, destroying it and the family in one stroke.

Bellefleur, Gideon. *Bellefleur.* Joyce Carol Oates. 1980.

Gideon Bellefleur is the hard-living, hard-drinking scion of Bellefleur Manor whose recklessness and sensuality render him a dashing and romantic but dangerously destructive figure.

Having had a wild youth, Gideon is astonished to find himself, at nearly twenty-five, in love with his beautiful cousin LEAH BELLEFLEUR. After a brief courtship they marry and settle down in the manor. From the start their relationship is dominated by their relentless physical passion for each other; nevertheless, they are surprised when Leah swiftly becomes pregnant and delivers a set of twins.

Eventually Gideon's wild streak begins to reassert itself with a vengeance, and he resumes his bachelor ways, frequently taking risks that suggest a self-destructive nature. When Leah becomes pregnant again, Gideon realizes that he has lost touch with his wife, who no longer seems to obey him. Soon after the birth of their daughter GERMAINE (BELLEFLEUR), Gideon begins an affair with Garnet, a local girl. The two fall in love, and Garnet eventually bears him a daughter, though he does not officially acknowledge his paternity.

While Leah is busy rebuilding the family fortune, Gideon increases his efforts to decrease it by engaging in high-stakes poker games, wild horse races, and automobile and airplane stunts. During a horse race, on which all the Bellefleurs place secret bets, Gideon's wild behavior leads to tragedy. Though the family profits financially from the race, only the death of Gideon's best friend enables the final outcome. Gideon is guilt-ridden and all the more driven to dangerous actions.

After a disastrous poker game, Gideon and his brother return to the manor with Goldie, a young half-Indian girl whom they "won" in the game. Both men rape the girl, and Gideon eventually develops an obsession for her. He and his young nephew Garth come to bitter blows over the girl, but Garth elopes with her, thus taking the matter out of Gideon's hands.

Gideon acquires a new mistress and is amazed when Leah brings Cassandra, his and Garnet's daughter, into the family, insisting that she will adopt the child and raise it as a Bellefleur. The child is soon abducted and killed by the legendary Noir Vulture, prompting an angry hunting campaign. Gideon, who leads the hunt, is nearly killed when the party stumbles on a group of dwarves. One of them, wounded during the fight, returns to the manor with the hunting party and becomes Leah's personal servant.

When his interests turn to flying, Gideon takes up with yet another mistress, the mysterious Mrs. Rach, who is also a pilot. As the years pass, Gideon reappraises his life, acknowledges his sexual appetites, and attempts to come to terms with the failure of his marriage. Unable to hold his drinking and recklessness in check, however, Gideon commits suicide on Germaine's fourth birthday by plunging his plane into the manor, destroying it and the entire family, which has gathered there for a birthday party.

Bellefleur, Leah. *Bellefleur.* Joyce Carol Oates. 1980.

Leah Bellefleur is the aggressive, ambitious, and conniving co-heir to the vast Bellefleur holdings. From her early youth, spent living in the shadow of her relatives' wealth, Leah has been self-sufficient and scornful of her kin. This changes when she is won over by her cousin GIDEON BELLEFLEUR's ardent pursuit of her, which culminates in his deliberate crushing of her pet spider. Shortly after this event, Leah agrees to marry Gideon and moves into the family estate, the huge and crumbling Bellefleur Manor, home to several generations of the reputedly cursed Bellefleurs.

Shortly after her marriage, Leah is astonished to find that she is pregnant; the surprise grows when she delivers twins, a son and a daughter. Despite her pride in her accomplishment, Leah becomes frustrated by her inability to conceive again. The relationship between Leah and Gideon remains quite passionate, and their apparent infertility puzzles both of them. Finally, though, six years after the twins are born, Leah becomes pregnant again. When the child is born, Leah's mother, who assisted in the long delivery, takes the child and immediately surgically removes a male twin who projects from the girl's abdomen.

Leah becomes inordinately attached to her new daughter, who is named GERMAINE (BELLEFLEUR) after an ancestor. In accordance with what seem to be the wishes of her new child, she vows to renew the family's income and holdings, and soon embarks on an ambitious campaign that takes her traveling across the state. She always brings her youngest daughter along as a kind of talisman.

Leah is also involved in a number of odd, if not supernatural, events that occur in and around the manor. When Gideon and his hunting companions find a midget, Leah names him Nightshade, and he becomes her devoted servant and actually seems to grow slowly in stature. Leah also manages to have her great-uncle released from prison where he has served a lengthy term for the murders of ten men. Soon after his release, the supposedly mild-mannered innocent repeats his act, killing many of the fruit pickers working on the estate.

Leah is increasingly beset by difficulties, including Gideon's extramarital affairs and many dangerous exploits in fast cars, and she gradually withdraws from her role as the operative head of the family. She also becomes concerned about Germaine, who seems to be growing detached from the family and losing her ability to foresee critical events. The matter is brought to a head on the day of Germaine's lavish fourth birthday party, which ends in tragedy when the drunken Gideon plunges his plane into the manor, destroying it and the entire family in the process.

Bellerophon. *Chimera.* John Barth. 1972.

On the eve of his fortieth birthday, Bellerophon, king of Lycia, lies in bed with his wife Philonoe. Reading the life story of another Greek hero, Perseus, has made him feel inadequate, and Philonoe is trying to console him. She tells her husband that he has reached the point in life where a prosperous kingdom and happy family should bring him enough satisfaction. But Bellerophon still longs for immortality, and the discussion with his wife prompts a retelling of his youthful adventures, focusing on aspects of daily life never found in traditional Greek mythology.

Bellerophon experienced a childhood marked by mystery. He and his twin brother, Deliades, are officially the sons of Glaucus, king of Corinth. But the king suspects others—most notably Poseidon, god of the sea, and Polyeidus, a teacher and soothsayer—of Bellerophon's paternity. Although the citizens of Corinth are divided over this issue, Bellerophon has no doubt that Glaucus favors Deliades. As he grows older, he comes to realize that Glaucus plans to make Deliades the successor to the throne.

During his adolescence, Bellerophon rebels in ways typical of a young man. One day at a festival he takes an aphrodisiac and goes off in the brush to make love with Sibyl, the daughter of Polyeidus. During the chariot race, the horses become attracted to the scent of the aphrodisiac and crash through the side gates to get at it. Both Glaucus and Deliades are killed in this accident. Fearing the citizens will think it a plot on his part, Polyeidus advises Bellerophon to leave Corinth temporarily.

Bellerophon escapes to Tiryns, where Proteus and Anteia are king and queen. When Anteia, an ambitious woman who is dissatisfied with her husband, tries to seduce Bellerophon, he refuses her out of concern for his reputation. Proteus then asks him to kill Perseus, the hero who beheaded Medusa, a hideous monster whose face turned all who saw it into stone. When asked why he wants Perseus dead, Proteus cites the famous oracle: that Perseus would kill his grandfather. Knowing that this has already been done and that Proteus is in no way related to Perseus, Bellerophon feels compelled to refuse this directive as well.

Because Bellerophon is so uncooperative, Proteus sends him to Iobates, king of Lycia and father of Anteia, with a sealed letter stating that Bellerophon should be put to death for his violation of the queen of Tiryns. When Iobates sees that his other daughter, Philonoe, is falling in love with Bellerophon, he is reluctant to carry out the execution himself. Instead, he challenges Bellerophon to attempt other treacherous tasks. With the help of Pegasus, a beautiful winged horse, Bellerophon easily manages to defeat the Carian pirates and the Amazons, both of whom threaten the security of Lycia.

Dismayed that Bellerophon has survived the battles, Iobates sends his guest off to kill Chimera, a monster with the head of a lion, the body of a goat, and the tail of a snake. Spewing fire, Chimera lives in a cave and is supposedly invincible. On the advice of Polyeidus, Bellerophon lances his spear with a chunk of lead and shoves it down Chimera's throat. When Chimera breathes, the fire melts the lead into her stomach and she dies. Realizing that Bellerophon must have the gods on his side, Iobates makes Bellerophon his heir and offers him Philonoe's hand in marriage.

Years later, when his fame is fading, Bellerophon attempts another heroic feat. He tries to fly into heaven on Pegasus, but Zeus, king of the gods, sends a gadfly to sting Pegasus. The novella ends with a remembrance of Bellerophon toppling off the horse and falling back to earth, an image that best represents Bellerophon's futile longing for immortality.

Bellew, Clare Kendry. *Passing.* Nella Larsen. 1929.

Although she chose to take advantage of her light skin and "pass for white," the cold and "catlike" Clare Kendry Bellew finds her choice burdensome and stifling.

As a child Clare had endured the wrath of her alcoholic and mean-spirited white father. He died when she was only fifteen; soon after his death, Clare's white relatives appeared and took her away from the black neighborhood in which she had grown up. Because of her light skin and her aunts' uneasiness about acknowledging a black relative, Clare decided to cross the color line. Without revealing her heritage, she married businessman John Bellew, and they had a daughter.

Years later, Clare is dissatisfied with the results of her choice. She enjoys the middle-class comforts that marriage to a successful businessman affords in the 1920s, but she longs for the companionship of other blacks. When she happens upon IRENE REDFIELD in the dining room of an exclusive Chicago hotel, she tries to reestablish her relationship with this childhood acquaintance and fellow black woman. Irene seems only slightly interested in befriending Clare but agrees to go to Clare's home and meet her husband. The meeting is a disaster as John, believing that both the light-skinned Irene and his wife are white, launches into a harsh condemnation of the race to which his wife and her guest actually belong. He even calls his wife "Nig" because, he says, she has grown darker since they were married.

The next day Clare sends Irene a note of apology, but Irene never answers. Two years later, while visiting New York City, Clare writes to Irene, again asking for her friendship. Although Irene is ambivalent, she finds Clare as beguiling as she is beautiful. The two establish a somewhat tense relationship; its uneasiness increases when Irene begins to suspect that Clare has seduced her husband Brian.

Clare is careless in her frequent visits to Harlem to visit Irene and expresses little fear that her husband will discover her true heritage. When asked by Irene if she knows what she would do if John found out, Clare only flashes a mysterious smile and says, "Yes."

John does find out: When he runs into Irene one day downtown and sees the obviously black friend she has been shopping with, he realizes that Irene is black and surmises that his wife must be black as well. One evening he bursts into a party that Clare and the Redfields are attending and angrily and tearfully accuses Clare of deceiving him. Irene rushes to the enigmatically smiling Clare, and just as she lays her hand on Clare's arm, Clare throws herself out an open window and falls to the snow-covered ground below. The stunned guests' horror at her death is augmented by their uncertainty over whether Clare killed herself or was murdered by Irene.

Beloved. *Beloved.* Toni Morrison. 1987.

Beloved is the restless spirit of a dead child who haunts the life of her mother, SETHE. The third child of Sethe and Halle born on the Garners' Kentucky plantation, Sweet Home, Beloved has not even begun to crawl or eat solid food when, in 1855, Sethe saves her from slavery by putting her and her brothers on the underground railroad. When their heroic mother joins them some days later at the home of their freed paternal grandmother, BABY SUGGS, at 124 Bluestone Road in the outskirts of Cincinnati, the baby has just begun to crawl.

The master of Sweet Home, accompanied by a slave catcher and the sheriff, comes to take Sethe, Beloved, the newborn Denver, and the two boys back to Kentucky. Sethe sees them approach and snatches up her children. Terrified, she herds all of them into a woodshed behind the house. To save Beloved from a life of slavery, Sethe cuts her throat with a handsaw. Sethe also tries to kill the three other children but fails.

Of her child's burial, Sethe remembers only the preacher's first two words: "Dearly Beloved." When she gets out of prison three years later, Sethe prostitutes herself to a stonemason in return for a rose-colored headstone with one word, "Beloved," cut into it. The baby's spirit begins to haunt 124 Bluestone Road that same day. A child's handprints suddenly appear in the cake; the dog, Here Boy, is lifted into the air and thrown against a wall; the

house shakes and shivers, and drives the two brothers away. When the last of the Sweet Home men, PAUL D GARNER, turns up one afternoon and tries to enter 124 with Sethe, he is bathed in a pool of red light. Sethe explains that the light emanates from her dead daughter and indicates sadness, not evil. Paul D steps through the light unscathed, though moments later the house trembles, pitches, and hurls a table at him. He fights with the house, throwing furniture and breaking windows until the house quiets and the spirit of the dead girl leaves.

Shortly thereafter, Sethe, Paul D, and Denver come upon a mysterious young woman sitting in the front yard; her name, she tells them, is Beloved. She looks about nineteen years old, although her hands and feet are soft and without lines, like a baby's. She wears new clothes, and her shoes have not been worn. At first Beloved sleeps almost continuously and even wets the bed. She seems to wake only when Sethe's other daughter, Denver, offers her sweets. Even more than sweet food, however, Beloved likes to follow Sethe and listen to her stories.

At times Beloved remembers existence among the dead. She recalls sitting in a cramped position with a dead man lying on top of her. To return to Sethe, Beloved explains, she had to cross a long, dark bridge. But that is all she can recall of her journey.

Beloved and Paul D become competitors for Sethe's attention. Paul D wonders when Beloved will leave and harasses her with questions. Beloved drives Paul D from Sethe's bed and then from the house itself. Once Paul D begins to sleep in the woodshed, Beloved goes to him and forces him to have sex with her.

Paul D leaves 124, and Sethe at last realizes the identity of her guest. Beloved and Sethe become concerned only with each other. Beloved wants all of her mother's attention, and Sethe feels compelled to explain why she killed her. When the townswomen come to exorcise Beloved from 124, she and Sethe appear together at the door. When the women look again, Beloved has disappeared.

Benedict, Jordan "Bick." *Giant.* Edna Ferber. 1952.

When Bick Benedict travels from his native Texas to Virginia to buy a racehorse, he returns with the horse and also with a wife, LESLIE LYNNTON BENEDICT. Bick, who claims to have been born virtually on horseback, is co-owner with his sister Luz of Reata, a three-million-acre ranch on which over five hundred thousand head of cattle graze. To him, Texas isn't "a geography, but a history, a whole world," and it is clearly his world. When he arrives home with his new bride, he leaves her alone in the palatial fifty-room Big House while he goes on roundup. He makes it clear to her that the ranch comes first in all things and that his goal in life is to develop a flea- and heat-resistant strain of Kashmir Bull, a task he is willing to spend twenty years to complete.

While Bick loves Leslie, he does little to ameliorate her

problems with his domineering spinster sister Luz, the "madama" of Reata, who makes no secret of her dislike for and jealousy of Bick's wife. When trouble develops, it subsides only when Luz is killed in a bizarre riding accident. Although he grieves, her death allows Bick to pay more attention to Leslie.

Leslie becomes pregnant and has a son, Jordan, followed the next year by a daughter, Luz. The relationship between Bick and Leslie seems solid, but difficulties continually arise. Leslie is appalled by the treatment of the Mexican workers on Reata. She becomes angry when Bick forbids her to go into the town where the workers live or to interfere in their lives. Bick is a decent husband but can also be a harsh man whose attitude toward the starving "wetbacks" seems inhumane. Leslie's anger grows when she discovers that he routinely tells the Mexican employees how to vote.

Bick has difficulty expressing his strong love for his wife. When she returns to Virginia, ostensibly for a visit but with some thoughts of remaining there, he realizes how empty his life is without her and travels to meet her. When she warns him that she can't be ruled by him, he tells her to come home and that he "likes a little vinegar with his greens."

Bick is disappointed in his son Jordy, who prefers medicine to ranching, but prides himself on the cattle ranching expertise of his daughter, "a real Benedict." When oil is discovered on land near Reata by JETT RINK, his longtime adversary and former employee, Bick steadfastly refuses to enter into the "oil game." He declares it all right for others but insists he wants no part of it, preferring to remain what he has always been: a cattle rancher.

Bick remains an enormously wealthy cattle rancher but suffers the vicissitudes of weather and climate in his attempt to breed superior cattle. He gradually changes with the times. He softens his attitude toward the Mexican laborers and gives them better working conditions, schools, and hospitals. He develops a benevolent attitude toward his son, who marries a Mexican woman. Yet Bick continues to resist change in other areas: He rejects modern comforts, will not move into town, and refuses to give over his land to oil wells.

Benedict, Leslie Lynnton. *Giant*. Edna Ferber. 1952.

Leslie Lynnton Benedict, the daughter of a Virginia physician, surprises everyone by her whirlwind courtship and quick marriage to JORDAN "BICK" BENEDICT, a wealthy Texas cattle rancher.

Leslie, who had been a "bluestocking" back home in Virginia in the era between the world wars, is immediately amazed by Texas. As she and her new husband arrive at Reata, in their private rail car, she is stunned by the vast space of the three-million-acre ranch, the fifty-room Big House, and the handsome Mexican vaqueros. But much about her new home appalls her. The Big House, which

seems like a hotel, is under the imperious command of Bick's spinster sister Luz, who makes it clear that she detests Leslie as an interloper. In her jealousy Luz puts Leslie and Bick in separate bedrooms and announces that she, not her sister-in-law, will be the "madama" of Reata.

Leslie soon realizes that the Mexican workers live in abject poverty, to which her husband seems indifferent. Soon after, a rude ranch hand named JETT RINK scares her by his inappropriate attention. The other ranch wives invite her to a barbecue, where they horrify Leslie by enthusiastically devouring the brains from a slowly cooked calf head.

Leslie is made to feel unwelcome by Luz and is ignored by her busy husband, but things change dramatically when Luz is killed in a riding accident. Although Bick grieves for his sister, Leslie realizes that now she can assume her proper role at Reata. Her position is assured when she realizes she is pregnant. She gives birth to a son, Jordan, and soon after to a daughter, Luz.

Leslie loves Bick but finds it hard to accept many of his attitudes. She is appalled by conditions in the Mexican town and by the sad lives of the migrant workers, and she is ashamed of her husband's callous attitude toward the "wetbacks" who cross the Rio Grande illegally. Her anger and frustration increase when Bick orders her to keep away from the Mexicans. After two years of feeling out of place, Leslie returns to Virginia, ostensibly for a visit but in reality to decide if she wants to continue living in Texas and with Bick.

During her respite, Leslie finds that she does love Bick and grows to appreciate him more for the hardworking, dedicated man that he is. When he comes to Virginia to see her, she tells him that she can't be ruled by him, but she does return with him to Texas.

As the years pass, Leslie becomes more and more a Texan. She gives her enthusiastic approval when her son rejects cattle ranching for the life of a physician, but she also proudly watches her daughter develop into a dedicated rancher. She grows to appreciate her friends for their kindness and openness. She even becomes accustomed to the Texas heat, noise, and dust.

To Leslie's satisfaction, Bick improves conditions for the Mexican laborers at Reata. When the oil boom rages around the state, Leslie comes to approve of Bick's steadfast determination to remain a cattle rancher. She finally understands her husband and the other Texans who possess great wealth and are exuberant in their excess. After twenty-five years, she concedes that she is completely at home in Texas.

Beniger, Thomas. *The Violated*. Vance Bourjaily. 1958.

An asthmatic and sickly child, Tom lived through his older sister Ellen's heartbreaks and first dates. His vicarious life ended, however, when his stepfather decided to disobey the doctor's orders and encouraged Tom to start walking around the house.

As a freshman at Roper Preparatory School, Tom plays on the football team. At Roper he meets Guy Cinturon, a rebellious young Mexican who is assigned to room with Tom because of his fluency in Spanish. Because he is brash and arrogant, neither Tom nor his classmates have much patience for Guy despite his spectacular athletic ability. When a number of teammates gang up on Guy, however, Tom comes to his defense, and the two become fast friends.

Still a virgin by his senior year, Tom goes on a date with a local girl named Ruby. The two fall in love, and Ruby becomes pregnant with his child. When a panicked Tom turns to Guy for help, Guy manages to convince him that the pregnancy is a false alarm. The unsuspecting Tom forgoes any further communication with Ruby, for whom Guy has secretly arranged an abortion. Shortly after this episode, Tom graduates and attends Washburn College, where he and Guy continue to play football and where they meet and befriend another teammate, EDWARD BISSLE. When World War II breaks out, Tom joins the military and is stationed in London, where he meets an Englishwoman named Lala, whom he marries. She moves with him to the United States after the war, and Tom returns to Washburn to finish his education. He and Lala live in extreme poverty, their condition worsened by a number of miscarriages Lala suffers after repeated attempts to have children.

When Tom gets a job as a writer for a popular television game show, he makes enough money to send Lala back to London to see her parents. Much to his disappointment, the show he writes for is canceled, leaving him without a job or the means to meet Lala in London as he had promised. His frustration increases when he receives word that she is pregnant.

After a brief period of unemployment, during which he has an affair with one of his sister's friends, Tom is able to borrow enough money to pay for his wife's return to the United States. She gives birth to a baby girl shortly thereafter. Tom, in the depths of poverty, takes Lala and his daughter to live rent-free in a cabin owned by a friend on Long Island.

Tom is still barely able to provide for his family. Unable to buy groceries to feed them, he sneaks out one night to steal a cabbage from the fields. His drunken friend Eddie mistakes him for one of the migrant workers and shoots him in the chest. Tom dies, leaving behind a grieving widow and daughter.

Benway (Dr.). *Naked Lunch.* William Seward Burroughs. 1959.

By turns maniacal and ingratiating, Dr. Benway is a horrifying presence in this surreal novel. Although it seems clear that Dr. Benway is not fit to practice medicine, he manages to secure positions of power in Freeland and Interzone, countries of indeterminate size and location, originating in the drug-induced hallucinations of the narrator, WILLIAM LEE. Benway, like all the characters who people the universe of the novel, is an addict. His addiction is not for drugs or sex, however, but for control. According to his philosophy, torture is unnecessary because it is sometimes inefficient; more useful is the art of Total Demoralization, or T.D. Through clever manipulation of the needs of the subjects under his control, Benway can bring about T.D., thereby convincing his victims that their victimization is entirely necessary. As a practitioner of mind control and unnecessary surgery, Benway is the perfect bureaucrat in the oppressive police state of Interzone as well as in the seemingly benign welfare state of Freeland.

Experimenting with drugs in order to find an efficient means of mind control, Benway is able to discover those substances that will induce schizophrenia and "give the highest yield of automatic obedience." Sexual humiliation, abuse of psychotherapy, hypnosis, and identity manipulation are all part of Benway's arsenal of weapons to ensure the spread of T.D. Benway displays with pride the victims of his twisted experiments while he recounts the story of becoming a doctor on board a smuggler's ship after being arrested for bungling an operation.

That operation—actually botched, Benway claims, by his baboon assistant, Violet—was only one in a series of bizarre surgical procedures. In one instance, Dr. Benway conducts an operation in a bathroom. After an incision is made in the patient's chest, Benway massages the unfortunate woman's heart with a plunger rinsed out in the toilet bowl. The patient dies as Benway boasts of having once removed a ruptured appendix with a tin can and a uterine tumor with his teeth. Viewing surgery as an artistic exercise in which the patient's well-being is incidental, Benway is unconcerned if his patients die or if, as sometimes happens, they have their gold fillings stolen by the anesthetist.

Agents of the Nationalist Party suspect the doctor of being a western agent, communist, black magician, or French Jew, and although they stalk him, they cannot defeat the man. He continues to work toward his goal of reducing the human body to a mass of Undifferentiated Tissue which can be controlled by a bureaucracy. When last seen, Dr. Benway is serving in the Ministry of Mental Hygiene and Prophylaxis, where, through subtle hints and humiliating tests, he exercises an insidious yet effective control over the population of Freeland.

Beragon, Montgomery "Monty." *Mildred Pierce.* James M. Cain. 1941.

An attractive and polished man, Montgomery Beragon, known to his friends as "Monty," represents a world that has been denied MILDRED PIERCE. Monty enters Mildred's life when he walks into a diner where she is working. He is initially attracted to Mildred by her voluptuous legs and takes her away to his beach house for the day. This purely physical attraction is returned by Mildred, who hopes for nothing more from a relationship with someone so far removed from her own concerns. Yet the mutual physical attraction develops into a more established relationship, one that answers to two individual needs yet offers no real compatibility. Monty, who is a loafer at heart and has never worked both because of his wealth and his natural inclination, is content to take what he is given, just as he is content in all other parts of his life.

As Mildred's success increases, Monty becomes more and more a part of her life and an essential element in her family, bringing Mildred closer to her arrogant and snobbish daughter VEDA PIERCE. Unlike his relationship with Mildred, Monty's relationship with Veda is based on a real compatibility and a mutual understanding that undercuts any sense of respect. Veda and Monty are two of a kind—ambitious, cruel, and self-serving—and they recognize their common characteristics. Monty marries Mildred but excludes his new wife from the life he comes to share more and more with her daughter.

Monty falls into increasingly bad habits, relying on Mildred for money yet refusing to act as her husband in even the most limited way. Mildred's response is to dominate him and to treat him with no respect. In this way their marriage enters a downward spiral that is broken only when Monty leaves.

When he next enters Mildred's life, Monty's fortunes have taken a turn for the worse, and he is trying to sell his family home. Mildred, having grown increasingly distant from Veda, sees Monty as the way to Veda's heart, and using her new fortune, she buys both Monty and Veda the Beragon home. Monty, unable or unwilling to work, recognizes the nature of this arrangement and is content to be a part of it, but the subsequent peace is fragile and short-lived. Monty and Veda quickly work their way through Mildred's resources, crowning their selfish partnership with an illicit affair. When Mildred finally learns of this, she throws them both out, realizing at last that Monty is not the symbol of what she cannot give Veda but of Veda's low-life equal.

Bergson, Alexandra. *O Pioneers!* Willa Cather. 1913.

Alexandra Bergson, the eldest daughter of Swedish immigrant farmers, is a pioneer whose dedication to the land and indomitable will make her the heroine of the Nebraska Divide. Sympathetic but strong, Alexandra is an appealing and important figure who is affected but never conquered by life's adversities.

After Alexandra's father dies, she takes over the management of the family farm and homestead and binds herself to the land. When hard times fall, Alexandra is distinguished from her neighbors and her bitter brothers, Oscar and Lou, by her tenacity. Although others are losing their farms to drought and crop failure and are threatened by the hardships of life on the Divide, Alexandra's dauntless manner and faith in the land prevail. Saddened to see Carl Linstrum, her closest childhood friend, and his family driven off the Divide, she is not discouraged but rather encouraged to invest in more land, over her brother's objections.

When Oscar and Lou marry, the land is divided equally between them and Alexandra. Alexandra's farm eventually flourishes to be the richest, most distinct on the Divide. Her success allows her to send her youngest brother, Emil, to college; but her prosperity and independence alienate Oscar and Lou.

In her unique relationship to the land, Alexandra sacrifices human intimacy. With Emil and Carl Linstrum gone, and estranged from Oscar and Lou, Alexandra's only remaining confidante on the Divide is Marie Tovesky, her younger Bohemian neighbor. Out of kindness and to quell her own incipient feelings of emptiness, Alexandra invites Ivar, a crazy old Norwegian neighbor, into her home. While Alexandra takes pleasure in counseling Marie, Ivar, and her other elderly neighbors, she gives most of her energy to pioneering as she approaches her fortieth year.

Later, Emil returns from college, and Carl Linstrum returns for a visit en route to Alaska. Alexandra and Carl renew and strengthen their friendship during long walks and nostalgic talks. Oscar and Lou, highly contemptuous of Carl because they think he is a loafer, fear his marrying Alexandra to procure the land, which they believe rightfully belongs to them as much as to Alexandra. Unable to endure the criticisms of Alexandra's petty brothers, Carl leaves for the West.

After Emil and Carl have departed, Alexandra again experiences feelings of desertion and loneliness. A year later Emil returns. He and Marie Tovesky consummate their love for each other, only to suffer a brutal and tragic death when Frank, Marie's hot-tempered and jealous husband, opens fire on them in the orchard.

Soon after Emil's death, Alexandra grows keenly conscious of an emptiness and despair. Suffering physical weariness for the first time and longing to be free, she experiences, more frequently and vividly than ever before, her single childhood fantasy of being lifted up and carried away by someone very strong. Bolstered by this dream, Alexandra decides to visit Frank in jail. Understanding his burden, Alexandra forgives and determines to help free him.

At the end of the novel, Alexandra reunites with Carl Linstrum. She confesses her need for his companionship and, deciding to marry, they pledge a platonic rather than passionate love for each other.

Berlin, Paul. *Going After Cacciato.* Tim O'Brien. 1977.

The product of a middle-class, midwestern upbringing,

Paul Berlin, an Everyman in his early twenties, is unprepared for the brutality he encounters during his year-long tour of Vietnam. The complexity and illogicality of this war without front lines or set rules of combat deeply disturb Berlin's conscience. The real time of the novel spans the roughly six hours Berlin stands guard at an observation post by the South China Sea. Interwoven with Berlin's nighttime meditations at the guard post, the novel offers two juxtaposed narratives—one a recollection of actual wartime events as Berlin recalls them, the other a fantastic adventure, purely imagined, whereby he attempts to gain some measure of control over his fears.

Berlin recalls his company's attempted capture of a seventeen-year-old deserter, Cacciato, who had previously announced his flight on foot to Paris. Using this actual event as a springboard for the imagination, he proceeds to envision his outfit's pursuit of the runaway across the Asian continent, through Vietnam, Laos, Burma, India, Afghanistan, Iran, and Turkey, into Europe, culminating in the company's arrival in Paris in the spring of 1969. Along the way, the handful of soldiers experience many adventures. In Vietnam they encounter a teenage girl named Sarkin Aung Wan, who accompanies the men on their journey and with whom Berlin becomes romantically involved. Later they come face-to-face with the enemy after having dropped into the dreaded Viet Cong tunnel network. In Afghanistan the company enjoys the hospitality of a small town mayor, while in New Delhi they engage in a good bit of rest and recreation. In Iran, however, the group witnesses an execution and then is arrested on two separate occasions.

Up to this point in Berlin's imagination there has been no questioning of the feasibility of the trek, but with his intervening memories of actual combat comes the possibility that the fantasy posse could fail. Berlin imagines that the company is imprisoned in Tehran, beaten into a confession of abandoning the war and crossing into sovereign territory, and finally threatened with death. But he imagines being rescued by none other than Cacciato himself, who breaks them out of prison, allowing for a spectacular escape. The group finally reaches Paris and combs the city in pursuit of Cacciato.

Meanwhile, Berlin and Sarkin have contemplated renting an apartment together in Paris. Then Berlin hesitates, questioning the wisdom of such an arrangement. Sarkin attempts to persuade him to abandon his unit and remain with her in Paris since that is not only what he really desires but is also the moral thing to do. Berlin parries her argument by citing not only his responsibility to his men and country but his own fear of desertion.

Ultimately, Berlin fantasizes, the company hunts down Cacciato and prepares to ambush him in his apartment in Paris. Berlin panics, wets himself, and fires wildly, permitting Cacciato to escape. This episode concludes the fantasy narrative and fades into his memory of the actual attempt to capture Cacciato when he lost control of his bladder and fired prematurely. The novel ends as the memory jars Berlin back into the realities of war.

Berman, Daniel. *Therefore Be Bold*. Herbert Gold. 1960.

Dan Berman is the novel's narrator, who, now older and wiser, looks back on himself as a high school student and tells the story of his coming of age.

As an intelligent, romantic, Jewish teenager, Dan was preoccupied with poetry and girls. He and his best friends Juicer Montague and Tom Moss spent their time going to school, debating philosophical subjects, discussing great authors such as Thomas Wolfe and James Branch Cabell, and talking and dreaming of love. When Dan confessed his love for Eva Masters, he surprised his friends; they thought that he, like the rest of them, was devoted to the young harpist Lucille Lake. One afternoon Dan and Eva visited alone in the newspaper office. At the end of their mundane but significant conversation, Eva slipped into Dan's coat, and he offered to walk her home.

Dan and Eva had an understanding after their first meeting, although they hardly spoke, but Dan, in a moment of fear, fled to the safety of his male friends. He, Juicer, and Tom went to the state park on a camping trip. Among the pine needles they talked into the night about life and young women. They felt, the narrator remembers, very large and important. After the trip, Dan returned to civilization knowing that Eva would be waiting for him.

At the next snowfall Dan and Eva took a walk together. They kissed and both confessed they wished the night would never end. They were happy and felt they had many things in common. But when Eva's parents expressed their disapproval of Dan—whom they called a "bad influence"—and told Eva not to associate with him, the young man was troubled. Defying them, Eva steadfastly insisted she would continue to see him, telling her parents she felt "humanly bonded" to him. Eva's father, Euclid Masters, a bigoted, narrow-minded but clever businessman, was disturbed by his daughter's sentiments. Eva and Dan continued to take romantic walks together, and Euclid Masters continued to disapprove.

Bending under her father's pressure, Eva abandoned Dan for a short time and dated Chuck Hastings, an empty-headed philosophical fellow who seemed to her to be rugged and experienced. Dan, in pain over losing Eva, went on one date with a girl who meant nothing to him. Dejected, distraught, and confused about why Euclid Masters would hate him, he had an argument with his parents and vehemently attacked them, yelling, "I hate you all!" Later, accompanied by his friends, Dan visited a prostitute on the other side of town. Each young man lost his virginity, and they rode home on the bus together without speaking much.

Soon after, Dan was visited by Red Masters, Eva's smart

and precocious younger brother. Red told him that Eva wanted him back. At a meeting at the drugstore, Eva told Dan that she was finished with Chuck Hastings, and they were reunited. One night Dan and Eva were visiting in her kitchen when Mr. and Mrs. Masters came home. Stating his opinion once and for all, Mr. Masters warned Dan not to see his daughter. Mr. Masters was cryptic when Dan asked why, but Mrs. Masters let slip the truth: They hated Dan because he was Jewish.

Faced with this blatant anti-Semitism, Dan did not know how to respond. Eva urged him to say something, to explode, to strike out at her father in some epic way, but Dan remained calm and quiet, amazed at Euclid Masters's ability to summon hate and laughter in the same breath, and overwhelmed by the face of evil in front of him. Eva mistakenly interpreted his lack of outrage as cowardice, and this scene in the Masters' kitchen, though never acknowledged as such by Dan or Eva, ultimately ended their relationship.

Years later the older and wiser Dan Berman reflects on why their lives unfolded as they did. Unable to find any answers, he concludes by urging the reader to "be bold for the children of everyone [and] look well! It will improve our judging tomorrow."

Bernice. "Bernice Bobs Her Hair." F. Scott Fitzgerald. 1920.

Bernice is probably in her upper teens, beautiful, intelligent, wealthy, and an absolute failure when it comes to socializing. One day in September she leaves her small hometown, Eau Claire, to visit her cousin Marjorie Harkin in Tarleton, a city in southern Georgia. Although not as wealthy as Bernice, Marjorie is socially much more vigorous and adept. The two cousins do not take to each other immediately, and although they do experience an intervening period of companionship and goodwill, Bernice's visit ends with unexpected and disastrous results.

To the dismay of her young host, Bernice proves virtually leprous when it comes to men. She bores them with small talk, dances poorly, and wears ugly dresses. Marjorie complains to her mother that she has made attempts to bring these problems to her cousin's attention, but in vain: Bernice always responds by seeming either annoyed or oblivious. Bernice overhears the conversation and confronts Marjorie the next day: She will go home early, she claims, if she is not treated with respect. But when Marjorie urges her to leave, Bernice bursts into tears.

Willing at last to improve her social skills, Bernice begs Marjorie to teach her the ways of the world. She becomes her cousin's protégé and at the next dance appears transformed. Bernice dances smoothly, wears an exceedingly fashionable dress, is impeccably groomed, and manages to engage in scintillating conversations with the most awkward of males. She thrills everyone with statements such as "I'm thinking of bobbing my hair" and even wins over

one of Marjorie's beaus, a handsome Yale man named Warren, whose affection for Marjorie knew no bounds until he encountered the new Bernice.

It is not long before Marjorie realizes that she has created a monster. Warren had bored her, but now that she is threatened by the loss of her status as the reigning social queen, he suddenly seems like a prize. In front of all of their friends, Marjorie taunts the unwitting Bernice into following through on her professed desire for bobbed hair, a symbol of the independent, even scandalous, female. Bernice gets her hair bobbed and is immediately sorry. Without her long flowing locks, she looks much less attractive. Even worse, she remembers that she has promised to attend a dance given in her honor by an older socialite who hates bobbed hair.

Realizing she has been set up, Bernice decides to leave town in order to hide her shame. She packs her bags and composes a note to her aunt explaining why she has left early. Then she has an idea. She sneaks into Marjorie's room with a pair of scissors and, without disturbing her sleep, clips off her cousin's long ponytails. On her way to the train, Bernice throws the ponytails onto Warren's front porch and anticipates with glee the shock Marjorie—and Warren—will experience upon waking.

Berry, Winslow. *The Hotel New Hampshire.* John Irving. 1981.

Winslow "Win" Berry is a father of five who takes his family on a bizarre odyssey of hotel entrepreneurship. The novel opens in the middle of Win's telling his children the countlessly retold story of how he met his wife and bought a bear in the summer of 1939.

Mary Bates and Win are childhood friends who fell in love while working for the summer at the Arbuthnot-by-the-Sea, a resort hotel in Maine. The resort featured State o' Maine, a trickless bear owned by a Viennese Jew with a limp and an unpronounceable name, who for the sake of convenience was called Freud. Win bought the bear and his motorcycle from Freud, who had decided—after allowing State o' Maine to maul a "Nazi" guest—to return to German-occupied Vienna. After marrying Mary, Win toured hotels with his "bear act," attended Harvard, and began teaching at the Dairy School in New Hampshire.

The Berrys sell their home in order to buy the Thompson Female Seminary School, which is to become the first Hotel New Hampshire. The family moves into the "hotel," which, though renovated, retains certain odd characteristics such as inappropriate bathroom fixtures and an intercom/P.A. system.

When Win's father, "Coach" Bob, dies of a heart attack, the grieving family sells their hotel to a circus act in order to move to Vienna, where they have been invited by the aging, blind Freud to help run a hotel along with his new seeing-eye bear Susie, who is actually a rape survivor in a bear suit. On their way to Vienna, Mary and their six-year-old partially deaf son Egg are killed when their plane crashes in the ocean.

In Vienna, the second Hotel New Hampshire is inhabited by prostitutes who mother Win's children and radicals who are plotting an attempt to blow up the State Opera House. The radicals' plan is thwarted when the leader is squeezed to death by the novel's narrator, John Berry, who has been lifting weights ever since his sister Franny was gang-raped. Meanwhile, Freud is killed when he detonates a bomb-rigged car. Win is blinded by flying glass, and the Opera House saviors return to the United States where Lily, Win's youngest daughter and a dwarf, writes an account of the hotel family, which is turned into a movie with Franny playing herself. The family becomes very wealthy with Lily as a writer, Franny a movie star, and Frank a successful agent.

After Lily commits suicide by jumping out of a hotel window, the family buys the Arbuthnot-by-the-Sea so that their blind father can have a third Hotel New Hampshire. They renovate the resort as a home for anyone in the family to use and maintain the pretense, for the father's benefit, that theirs is an extremely successful first-class hotel. John marries Susie the bear, who moves into the hotel and runs a rape crisis center whose clients are thought by Win to be hotel guests. The clients are inadvertently counseled by Win, who treats them as important guests in need of a restful stay at a quality hotel.

Bess. *Porgy.* DuBose Heyward. 1925.

Bess is a dissolute young woman living on the fringes of Catfish Row, a turn-of-the-century black ghetto in Charleston, South Carolina. Bess, whose forays into self-destruction have included alcoholism, drug addiction, and a willing enslavement to her brutal lover Crown, begins to see the possibility of a very different kind of life for herself when she is taken in by PORGY, a crippled beggar.

The chain of events leading Bess to Porgy begins with a crap game in Catfish Row during which Crown murders another player. Crown flees Charleston, confident that none of the black inhabitants of Catfish Row will turn him over to the "white folks." Several weeks later Bess comes to the Row in search of Crown. Intoxicated and hungry, she is given a meal by Maria, owner of a cook shop in the Row. Bess has heard of Porgy, a legless beggar who gets around by means of a goat and a small cart. After Maria points out Porgy's door, Bess enters.

Within weeks Bess has set up housekeeping with Porgy. While Porgy is out begging, she cleans and cooks. None of the other women in the quarters is willing to associate with the disreputable Bess. Undisturbed, she disdains their company and devotes herself to Porgy. She decides to give up alcohol and heroin.

But Bess's resolution to remain clean of drugs is broken when one of her old pushers shows up. Before anyone is aware, she has bought two packs of dope. Later that eve-

ning she overhears one of the women making disparaging remarks about her, and in a drug-crazed fit she attacks the woman. The police arrive and take her to the station house. Bess is sentenced to jail for ten days or until she identifies her dealer. When she returns from jail, she suffers from a fever for a week. During her illness, Porgy nurses her and sends money to a conjure woman, whom he asks to heal Bess. Though neither the money nor Porgy's request ever reach the conjuror, Bess recovers.

When a baby is orphaned by a hurricane that blows through Charleston, Bess and Porgy adopt the child, thus creating a family. The two adults and the baby live happily until Bess encounters Crown in the woods during a picnic. She spends the day with him, and when it is time to leave, Crown tells her that she may remain with Porgy until cotton season. At that time, Crown warns, he will come for her. Unable to resist her former lover, she acquiesces.

When Porgy learns of the pact, he asks Bess if she intends to accompany Crown. She responds that she does, but as cotton season approaches, she implores Porgy to save her. Crown appears for Bess one night, but she is spared from leaving with him. The next morning the police find Crown stabbed to death. It is believed that Porgy committed the deed and removed the body with the help of an accomplice, but no evidence or witness can be located to support the charge. Porgy is ordered to appear at the coroner's inquest to identify the body.

When a buzzard lands on the roof over his apartment door, Porgy fears that Crown's spirit has returned to curse him. He flees the police when they come to take him to the inquest. For his flight, he is charged with contempt of court and jailed for five days. In Porgy's absence, Bess, unable to endure the waiting and loneliness, is lured off by a group of men. When Porgy returns, his baby is in the arms of a neighbor woman and Bess has gone, apparently to return no more.

Bicek, Bruno "Lefty." *Never Come Morning.* Nelson Algren. 1941.

Bruno "Lefty" Bicek is a young Polish-American growing up on Chicago's North Side. An only child, he lives with his ailing mother, who is unable to control him. He takes to the streets at a young age and is often in trouble with the law. Bruno dreams of becoming the heavyweight champion of the world.

As the story begins, Bruno and his friends Casey Benkowski and "The Finger" Idzikowski rob a roadhouse so that they can afford haircuts from Bonifacy the barber. Bonifacy, in return for their patronage, agrees to buy baseball uniforms for them and pull some strings for Bruno, who wishes to engage in a legitimate boxing match at the City Garden Center. The holdup is a violent one. Bruno struggles with the coin-filled slot machine that he has torn from the wall and then punches the owner of the roadhouse as he runs after his property.

Bruno exercises cruel force over the person he loves the most, his longtime girlfriend Steffi Rostenkowski. After robbing the roadhouse, he goes to Steffi's apartment and rapes her as she struggles to preserve her virginity. He regrets his brutality afterward and takes Steffi to a carnival in an attempt to compensate for his violence. After the carnival, however, he gets her drunk and takes her to a deserted warehouse in order to have sex with her again. When his fellow teammates, Catfoot and Kodadek, find him and Steffi together, Bruno is unable to protect her from their advances. Attempting to prove his manhood by acting as if Steffi means nothing to him, he stands by and allows Catfoot, Kodadek, and others to rape her. While more and more young men gather to participate in the gang rape, Bruno finally lashes out against a Greek youth and kicks him to death.

Bruno is arrested later for allegedly murdering a bum in an alley, although no mention is made of the murder that Bruno did commit. Tenczara, the police chief, mistrusts Bruno, but when the bum that Bruno allegedly killed turns up alive, he is released.

Bruno gets a job as a guard at a whorehouse, where Steffi is now employed. Steffi is sleeping regularly with Bonifacy the barber but still shows her undying love for Bruno. Bruno's cruel treatment of Steffi as well as his prison term have caused the barber to turn against him: Bruno will fight at the City Garden with Casey as his manager, but Bonifacy will not profit at all from the fight. Hence, Bonifacy attempts to foil Bruno's chances of victory by using Steffi as a tool; he tries to make her seduce Bruno and get him drunk the night before the boxing match. Steffi's love for Bruno makes it impossible for her to follow the barber's orders. Bruno and Steffi express their affection for each other in Steffi's room before Kodadek and Catfoot burst in and start a brawl to prevent Bruno from winning the boxing match. Bruno drives them away, wins the match, and temporarily realizes his dream of becoming a champion boxer.

The thrill of victory is cut short, however, when Tenczara appears and demands that Bruno accept responsibility for murdering the Greek youth on the night of Steffi's gang rape. Having achieved his only true goal, Bruno accepts his fate and allows himself to be taken into police custody.

Billy. *Billy Bathgate.* E. L. Doctorow. 1989.

Raised on the mean streets of the Depression-era Bronx, fifteen-year-old Billy of Bathgate Avenue recounts the manner in which he becomes a full-fledged member of the Dutch Schultz gang. The narrative begins with Dutch's amusement at a juggling exhibition Billy undertakes near one of the gang's beer drops. After being referred to by the gangland leader as a "capable boy," Billy aspires to ingratiate himself further with Dutch. He enters the mobster's headquarters and impresses Dutch's financial genius, "Abbadabba" Berman, with his audacity. Berman gives Billy his first job with the gang, the pickup of extortion money from a candy store owner in Harlem. And despite the constraints imposed on his mob ventures by government pressure, Dutch nonetheless quickly initiates Billy into his illegal activities.

In preparation for Dutch's impending trial on racketeering charges, the gang travels to Onondaga, New York, where Dutch engages in public relations ploys aimed at improving his image. The gang is instructed to spread goodwill by being on its best behavior and liberally spending money throughout the community. During this period, Billy, the dutiful, Sunday school–attending youth, helps lend an air of legitimacy to the mobsters' activities.

Just days before the trial, Dutch astounds Billy by first converting to Catholicism in a ceremony attended by Lucky Luciano and then by brutally murdering a business associate involved in Schultz's restaurant extortion racket. The latter action results in a broken nose for Billy when it is decided that the gang needs an alibi for the large bloodstain on the Onondaga Hotel carpet. During the trial itself, Billy is ordered to travel to Saratoga with Drew Preston, who had been the girlfriend of Dutch's partner Bo Weinberg before Dutch had him killed and appropriated her for himself. Once in Saratoga, Billy and Drew have a romantic interlude. Any possibility for an extended affair is quashed by Billy's realization that Dutch has decided to kill Drew. With great skill Billy conspires to have Drew's husband spirit her out of the country.

Dutch is ultimately found innocent, and when the gang returns to New York City, Billy rejoins it. When New York Attorney General Thomas Dewey resolves to step up the pressure on Schultz with an imminent indictment on tax evasion charges, Billy is ordered to shadow Dewey in preparation for an assassination attempt. Lucky Luciano takes umbrage at Schultz's brazen behavior, and, finally, all members of the Dutch Schultz gang, minus a very lucky Billy, are gunned down in a New Jersey restaurant.

Dutch clings to life for a full day, and Billy visits him in the hospital and transcribes his fallen leader's ramblings. After returning to his mother's Bronx apartment, Billy is apprehended by Lucky Luciano's agents, then questioned by the Godfather himself as to the location of Schultz's presumed hidden fortune. After his release, Billy is inspired to study his transcript of Dutch's dying words. The decoded mutterings lead him to an abandoned warehouse where Billy discovers millions of hidden dollars, a legacy that allows him to fashion a hugely successful business career. In conclusion, he relates that one day, sometime after Dutch's death, a baby was mysteriously delivered to his mother's apartment. As it turns out, the child is the product of his brief liaison with Drew.

Birdsong, George. *The Sheltered Life.* Ellen Glasgow. 1932.

George Birdsong is a handsome, roguish older man, the husband of the elegant but fading Eva Birdsong and young JENNY BLAIR ARCHBALD's secret suitor in this novel of triangular love. Though George appears devoted to his wife, their marriage cannot withstand the test of time. An unfaithful husband, he also abandons a promising career in law for a life of drink and debauchery.

At the novel's opening, George and Eva have been married for several years. Eva appears to ignore George's failings, while George, filled with remorse and self-hatred, tries again and again to reform. He repeatedly turns his attention to other women, however, ever fearful that Eva might find out about his romantic misadventures.

When Eva falls ill, George devotes his attentions exclusively to her. He stays by her side all the way to the hospital where Eva is to have a potentially fatal operation. While George anxiously awaits the outcome, Jenny Blair Archbald, a family friend, arrives. The young Jenny has a crush on George, who teases her playfully at first and then succumbs to her ingenuous ardor. They kiss in the hospital courtyard. To George, this incident is the measure of a passing flirtation, but Jenny sees the kiss as a sign of an enduring, illicit love.

Eva miraculously survives the operation, although she never fully regains her health and soon begins to behave oddly. George remains devoted to her but is increasingly tempted by Jenny Blair's petulant charm. The strain of their marriage begins to show, and both George and Eva seem to age more rapidly. George takes Eva to the country to rest but must return to the city to take care of business. While his wife is away, George returns to his old, irresponsible habits and kisses Jenny when she comes to see him.

Returning from the country in better health, Eva throws herself into cleaning up the neglected house. George seems pleased to have her back but frets about her health and sanity, and conscientiously endeavors to persuade her to rest more.

Although he feels responsible for his wife's illness, George is unable to free himself from Jenny's allure and the memory of his lost youth. One evening George, retiring to the porch with his evening cocktail, encounters Jenny. They converse awkwardly; George speaks only of Eva as Jenny waits in a mute agony of love. He turns to go, and she blurts out her jealous despair. George, warmed and surprised by this confession, takes her in his arms. Just at that moment Eva appears on the doorstep. Although his wife shows no emotion, George is stricken with horror at her discovery of his infidelity. He drops his arms and backs quickly away. When Eva says tonelessly, "I want you," George follows her in abject silence. The couple disappears into the shadows of the house. Moments later Jenny hears a crashing sound. She rushes to the library and finds George dead in his Windsor chair and Eva gazing numbly out the window. George's gun lies a few feet from her petticoat, as though it had fallen unheeded to the floor.

Birnam, Don. *The Lost Weekend.* Charles Jackson. 1944.

Don Birnam does little to escape the cycle of addiction that has grown to encompass his entire existence. A bingeing alcoholic, Don drinks, dreams, and wallows in self-pity for six days while his brother Wick is away from the apartment the two share.

Although thirty-six years old, Don is supported by his younger brother. Don has always been the dreamer in the family, and now, well into adulthood, he has been around the world and calls himself a writer, although he has produced little. He believes he has promise but blames others for his failings. Success eludes him, he feels, because his father left his mother or because his fraternity kicked him out when he developed too strong a crush on one of his fellow Greeks. Seldom does he consider that his problems may be of his own making; he calls the therapist who tried to get him to admit responsibility "the foolish psychiatrist."

The lost weekend begins when Don declines to go with his girlfriend Helen and his brother to the opera. He would rather rest, he tells Wick, to be ready for the trip to the country they plan to take together. Once Wick is gone, Don takes the money he left for the cleaning lady and heads for a bar, where he gazes at himself in the mirror and plots out the brilliant novel he will write. By the time he has finished drinking, the planned novel seems not so brilliant. Nothing Don writes could be as brilliant as what he dreams, so, he reasons, why stop drinking and start writing at all?

Eluding his brother when he returns with a car to go to the country, Don is able to devote himself to serious drinking. Scenes from the past are replayed as he drains glass after glass, bottle after bottle. In a Greenwich Village nightclub he takes a woman's purse because it seems so easy. He is stopped and thrown out before he gets very far.

When his money runs out, Don decides to pawn his typewriter. Finding the first few pawnshops closed, he continues uptown, sure that Second Avenue is littered with such establishments. His stumbling stupor is broken when he is told that all the shops are closed for Yom Kippur. Only then does he realize he has walked over three miles.

Don stumbles home, but there he falls down the stairs and is knocked unconscious. His bleary eyes open to the vision of beds filled with men in various stages of drunkenness and delirium tremens. Attempting to disregard the knowing smirks of the ward nurse, he checks out of the hospital, ready to drink again.

At home with another bottle, Don tries to ignore the ringing phone. He knows it is either Wick or Helen checking up on him even though they know what his condition must be. Helen eventually has the porter admit her to the apartment, and she persuades him to go home with her. In bed after a hot bath, he suffers a horrifying hallucination of a bat attacking a mouse that has climbed out of a hole in the bedroom wall. Although his primary reaction is terror, Don also feels fellowship with the tiny rodent.

The next morning, sober and alone in Helen's apartment except for the cleaning lady, he plots his course of action. He can find neither money nor alcohol anywhere around, so he steals Helen's leopard jacket and pawns it for five dollars. As he puts the cash in his pocket, he discovers some money he thought he had lost. Ecstatic, he heads for a liquor store, then takes home the bottles that will see him through a few more drunken days.

Bissle, Edward. *The Violated.* Vance Bourjaily. 1958.

The only son of a Long Island contractor, Edward Bissle has grown up regarding his mother as an alcoholic and a tramp, and his father as a cheat. The real role model for Eddie in his formative years is his grandfather, who passes on to him his one great and overwhelming passion: football. Eddie learns to play with the same reckless abandon that his grandfather did. While always short for his age, he becomes muscular by the time he is fifteen and plays with a kind of fearless intensity that intimidates his opponents.

By the time he attends Washburn College, Eddie has won a football scholarship and is driving a new green convertible that his father bought him as a high school graduation present. He possesses no social skills whatsoever, however, and soon becomes an outcast. While he is respected by members of the freshman football team, he is merely a short, sullen, muscle-bound freshman to the rest of the school.

Eddie's only two friends at Washburn are members of the football team: THOMAS BENIGER, an introverted, thoughtful classics major, and Guy Cinturon, a Mexican star receiver who tolerates Eddie out of respect for Tom. While Tom and Guy never invite Eddie along with them when they visit women's colleges on weekends, they nonetheless include him in enough of their activities that Eddie is never far from them during his first three years at Washburn.

Eddie's senior year is interrupted by the outbreak of World War II, and despite his academic qualifications, he enlists in the general infantry. His determination and recklessness allow him to thrive in the army, and he is soon promoted to the rank of sergeant. When the war ends, Eddie is fully prepared to remain in the military until he learns that he can do so only as a private due to the abundance of officers after the war.

After leaving the army, Eddie starts a farm out on Long Island and takes occasional trips into New York City, where he has a hotel room in which he maintains an affair with Tom's married sister Ellen. While growing distant from Tom, who unlike Eddie and Guy completed his last year at Washburn, Eddie develops a close relationship with

Guy, now a slick New York entrepreneur. The two engage in a number of profitable business ventures and investments. Guy also begins to share a few of his numerous girlfriends with Eddie, whose previous experience with women has been limited.

Eddie soon learns that Tom has not been sharing his and Guy's financial success. When Tom's new wife Lala gives birth to their daughter, Eddie gives them a small cabin on the edge of his farm where they can live for free. Driving home extremely drunk one night from an encounter with Ellen, Eddie spies someone stealing cabbage from his fields. Thinking it is one of the migrant workers, he shoots the thief—who turns out to be none other than his friend Tom.

While cleared of any legal consequences, Eddie cannot bear the overwhelming guilt he feels for the murder of his friend. After drinking a bottle of whiskey one night, he shoots himself in the head.

Bjornstam, Miles. *Main Street.* Sinclair Lewis. 1920.

Miles Bjornstam, nicknamed the Red Swede because of his fiery red mustache, is the town rebel in Gopher Prairie, Minnesota. Although Bjornstam does become relatively conventional for the few years that he is married, his attempts to conform to the conventions of what he considers a petty and hypocritical small-town society weaken when his wife and son die of typhoid.

Miles, who calls himself the town badman, is the only Democrat in Gopher Prairie. An atheist whom the town considers slightly insane, Miles reads such social historians as Thorstein Veblen and advocates revolutionary social changes. When World War I breaks out, he criticizes the war effort and claims that workingmen are forced to fight against one another for the benefit of industrial capitalists in order to preserve a "democracy of death." He complains that the dollar has replaced God and undermined human decency, and he enjoys a bitter delight at shocking the town with his proletarian philosophy.

Miles lives in Swede Hollow, a slum on the outskirts of Gopher Prairie. He supports himself by acting as the town handyman and by periodically spending summers horse trading in Montana. His life changes radically when he meets Bea Sorenson, who has left her family's farm to work as a maid in Gopher Prairie. Miles and Bea marry, and he takes a job as an engineer at Jackson Elder's planing mill. He also starts a dairy business that thrives. A shocked town witnesses the Red Swede actually acting in a friendly, respectable manner toward people he had previously treated with scorn.

Eventually Bea and Miles have a son named Olaf who is such a beautiful baby that, much to the chagrin of the townspeople, he wins the Best Baby prize during the first child-welfare week in Gopher Prairie. Despite Miles's upstanding behavior, he is still disliked and viewed as the town pariah. The only person in town who deigns to visit the Bjornstams is CAROL KENNICOTT for whom Bea had worked as a maid before her marriage. Like Miles, Carol is disgusted with the lack of culture and social conscience in Gopher Prairie.

The Bjornstams' domestic bliss is interrupted when Olaf and Bea come down with typhoid due to a contaminated water supply. Faced with this tragedy, the town rallies and sends representatives to the Bjornstams' house bearing food, magazines, and novels. Furious, Miles sends them away with the admonition that their friendly gestures are far too late. Despite the conscientious care provided by Carol and her husband, Dr. Will Kennicott, Miles's wife and son both die of the disease.

The town, angered by Miles's rebuff, blames the deaths on the widower and claims that he neglected his family due to a drinking problem. The loss devastates the Red Swede. He sells his dairy and moves to a farm in northern Alberta in order to live as far from human contact as possible.

Black Boy. "The Night's for Cryin'." Chester Himes. 1937.

Black Boy, the story's explosive central character, slams his drink on the bar with an irritated bang, silencing a fat, light-skinned black man who is in the middle of telling a story. Black Boy, whose skin is dark and who does not like "yellow niggers," waits in the bar for Marie, his woman, to take her to the Regis Hotel where she works as a maid. When a stoop-shouldered black man whispers something in Black Boy's ear, Black Boy sloshes his drink all over the bar, gets up fast, and makes his way out of the crowded room.

Out on the New York City street, Black Boy looks around desperately until he sees Marie stepping into the green sedan of a "yellow nigger." The sedan pulls away; Black Boy hails a cab and tells the driver to follow it. The cab driver, a dark-skinned black man, speeds uptown, recklessly doing whatever it takes to catch the other car. When they arrive at the Regis, the sedan stops, and Marie gets out. Black Boy runs after her; she tries to escape from him, but he catches her and beats her on the sidewalk as she pleads with him not to kill her.

The driver of the green sedan cannot bear to watch Black Boy kick Marie. At first he is indecisive; an instant later, when he realizes that this is where he works as a bellhop and that the whites will take his side against Black Boy, the driver commands Black Boy to stop. Black Boy, turning toward him, claims Marie is his woman and tells the driver to keep out of it. When two white men appear in the hotel doorway, the driver boldly steps forward and punches Black Boy in the face. Enraged, Black Boy pulls a knife and stabs him to death. As he runs from the scene of the crime, Marie cries out that the driver had "pulled a gun on Black Boy." Black Boy hears this and laughs, satisfied that she is still his.

Three shots ring out. Black Boy stops running and holds both hands up in the air. The police take him to prison and beat him; eventually he is sentenced to the electric chair. Waiting on death row, Black Boy seems neither worried nor grim during his final days. He knows that Marie is still his, "heart, body, and soul," and the knowledge makes him laugh freely, kidding the other condemned men and the guards and telling tall tales about himself and Marie. When Marie visits, she brings him fried chicken and kisses him; his lovemaking talk can be heard across death row. But at night when the corridors are empty and the cells are dark, Black Boy huddles in the corner of his cell, thinking of Marie and crying softly.

Black, Harry. *Last Exit to Brooklyn.* Hubert Selby, Jr. 1963.

Harry Black is described as the worst of the thousand workers in the Brooklyn plant where he is employed. Harry is thirty-three years old, unhappily married, and, more upsetting for him, the father of an infant son. Partly because of his problems at home and partly because of his insecurity, Harry is fairly active in his union and is eventually appointed shop steward; in this capacity he spends most of his time goofing off or preparing for an impending strike.

When the strike finally occurs, Harry is inordinately proud to find himself appointed to "be in charge" of strike headquarters. Accordingly, he prepares signs and takes attendance as the strikers appear each morning. The excitement soon pales, so Harry takes to ordering large amounts of beer to keep himself and the other men entertained. As more and more people learn of the free beer and food, these orders increase in size and frequency; along with this increase, Harry's sense of his own importance, derived from his newfound purchasing power, becomes inflated.

Some of the local toughs seem to befriend Harry, bringing him into contact with a part of the world he knew nothing about prior to the strike. These men, most of them petty thieves, use Harry as a source of beer, food, and money, and mock him both behind his back and to his face. They introduce him to Ginger, a drag queen, whose exotic appearance and physical strength both captivate and appall Harry. He becomes interested in finding out about people like Ginger. He finds a nightclub called Mary's where he can meet even more drag queens. Soon he becomes infatuated with Regina, who in a thrilling moment for Harry introduces him to sex with another man. Despite his excitement and pleasure, this activity also spurs Harry to an even greater contempt for his wife, toward whom he becomes increasingly vicious and physically abusive. As long as he has money, he is considered an attractive, if potentially dangerous date by Regina and the other patrons of Mary's. Finally, Harry reaches out to Alberta, another drag queen, and he becomes quite dependent on her.

Meanwhile, the strike has dragged on, and it has taken a great toll on the financial and domestic situations of most of the men. But for Harry, who is ignorant of the fact that both the company and the union plan to dump him as part of the eventual settlement, the strike remains a tremendous boon. When it comes to an end and Harry's ready money supply vanishes, Alberta rejects his advances. She mocks his desire, and Harry slips into a fairly deep depression. After his calls have been ignored, he returns to Mary's but is rejected there as well. Then, in a misguided moment of desperation, Harry sexually molests a young boy, who breaks away from him and runs to a local bar. The men find Harry sobbing in the vacant lot where he had committed the assault, and without further ado they gang up on him and beat him senseless. As Harry's story ends, he sinks, near death, to the ground, cursing God whom he blames for his sorrow and mistakes.

Blackburn, Theodore. "Of This Time, of That Place." Lionel Trilling. 1943.

Theodore Blackburn is a charismatic student at fictional Dwight College located in New England. Blackburn, a senior, attends a class taught by JOSEPH HOWE, a young instructor who also happens to be a poet. Blackburn's presence serves as a contrast to another one of Howe's students, FERDINAND TERTAN, a kind but awkward and extremely out-of-place freshman.

Theodore Blackburn is very popular on campus. He serves as vice president of the Student Council, manager of the debate team, and secretary of the school's literary society. The dean thinks Blackburn is a fine, if somewhat overly ambitious, young man. Despite the fact that he is a social science major, Blackburn wants to take Howe's advanced course on the Romantic poets; he believes that he has more than enough intelligence to handle the course's requirements. Howe has reason to doubt Blackburn's ability and interest. The senior had audited another one of his courses and didn't attend the lecture after the first day. By persistence, however, Blackburn gains admission to the class.

Howe has other problems to contend with: He becomes convinced that another student, Tertan, is insane. He reports the matter to the dean, who promises that some sort of action will be taken. Tertan, unaware of Howe's suspicions, asks the instructor to recommend him for a position on the board of the college's literary society. Howe consents; later, Blackburn uses this information against him.

Blackburn fails the midterm examination for Howe's class. When he complains to the instructor, Howe allows him to take a makeup test, and the second time around, Howe gives Blackburn a C−, not because the student improved but because he feels intimidated by Blackburn's

bullying tactics. Blackburn again complains about the low mark. He tells Howe that if he does not raise the grade, he will report the instructor to the administration, promising that the dean will not take kindly to the idea that Howe recommended a known lunatic to an important position in the campus literary society. Howe refuses to let Blackburn intimidate him anymore. He changes the grade to an *F*. Blackburn becomes hysterical, and he begs Howe not to fail him. He whines that his future will be ruined if he fails the Romantics course. Unimpressed by Blackburn's melodramatics, Howe tells the senior that the only way he can avoid failure is to drastically improve his work. Blackburn whimpers and leaves his office.

Howe now believes Blackburn to be insane as well, but he does not report him to the dean. Thus, at the end of the school year, the highly intelligent but socially inept Tertan must face an indefinite time under psychiatric observation, while Blackburn looks forward to a lucrative and highly successful future.

Blackford, Judith. *Weeds.* Edith Summers Kelley. 1972.

Judith Blackford is a robust child with an artist's eye for the blossoming life around her. She has a keen intellect and a propensity for sketching that set her apart from the surrounding dull-witted Kentuckians. But her school, run by a prematurely aged spinster, provides little education and no opportunity for escaping the grinding poverty in the community.

The young Judith is something of a phenomenon in the county: attractive, vivacious, in love with life, quick-witted, and perceptive. Only her joy-filled and humorous uncle Jabez shares these qualities. She is regarded with suspicion and hostility by the neighboring girls, a distrust that foreshadows the damaging gossip that will plague her throughout her life.

Judith is wooed by the handsome and honest Jerry Blackford, whom she casually marries. Their marriage begins in innocence, and they experience some prosperity. Judith works beside him in the fields and is able to raise chickens and draw as well. For a time they are happy and content with each other; however, with the onset of pregnancy and the birth of her first child, Judith starts to loathe her life and to feel chained to the house and to Jerry. She begins to reevaluate her staid husband, and recognizing how dull and tiresome her life has become, she cannot help feeling isolated, bored by her neighbors, and unenthused at the prospect of keeping house. Only occasional visits from Uncle Jabez punctuate the monotony of her daily routine.

When World War I begins, Jerry is tempted to enlist, but knowing how desperate Judith's situation would be if he left, he decides to stay by her. Judith is amazed at the depth of passion that springs up in the community for the distant enemy. At a revival meeting one day, she is strongly attracted to the preacher, who follows her home and makes love to her in a field. They begin trysting in a berry patch, and the county gossips once more about Judith's wildness.

Fortunately, the trusting Jerry fails to discover the liaison; it ends quickly, with Judith despising the somewhat haughty and patronizing preacher and laughing at his condemnation of her "temptress" ways. When she discovers that she is pregnant, however, the odious prospect of childbirth fills her with dread. She jumps on the mule and rides wildly for hours on the county roads in the vain hope of inducing an abortion. When this fails to work, she experiments with a knitting needle, then tries to drown herself in a pond. Finally, after drinking the most noxious of herbal brews, she becomes so sick that the child is aborted.

Judith, determined to be the master of her own body, directs at Jerry her cold fury at the grinding conditions of her life. One night when he comes home drunk and cannot be roused from a chair, she hits him over the head with a frying pan; he leaps up and repeatedly smashes her head against the wall, then flees into the night.

Judith makes herself a cot to sleep in, and the couple live in an uneasy truce through the winter. Then she discovers that Jerry has begun an affair with the wife of a neighbor. She is enraged but accepts her rage as unjust. When their smallest child catches the flu, she and Jerry must endure a week-long vigil by her bed. The child miraculously recovers, and Jerry and Judith hug each other in relief, thereby breaking the barriers between them. As the novel closes, Judith has only learned to accept her fate; she does not love Jerry. Indeed, when she hears the next day that Uncle Jabez has died, she realizes that this quick-witted, contemplative man was the only person she really loved. With his death, anything that might have sustained her in this harsh, empty life has likewise disappeared.

Blackwood, Mary Katherine "Merricat." *We Have Always Lived in the Castle.* Shirley Jackson. 1962.

The eighteen-year-old narrator, Mary Katherine Blackwood, or "Merricat," as she is called by her beloved older sister Constance, lives with Constance and their old uncle Julian in the decaying Blackwood mansion. The rest of the Blackwood family, including Merricat's parents, were mysteriously poisoned six years before. Constance was suspected and tried for the murders at that time, and although she was acquitted, the stigma of murder still hangs about her and makes the rest of the Blackwood family outcasts in their community. As the story unfolds, Merricat is revealed as the poisoner of the family; she relishes being an outcast, and her greatest wish is to keep Constance to herself in their own private world.

Merricat lives largely in her own imagination. She turns a simple shopping trip in town into an expedition filled with terror, imagining that she can kill people with her thoughts and dreams. Merricat's imagination is both ethe-

real and demonic, but with it she pictures an ideal world in which she and Constance can live happily. Any intrusions into this ideal vision give rise to intense hatred and thoughts of murder and destruction.

In the six years since the poisonings, Merricat's life has matched her happiest fantasies. Because Uncle Julian is completely ineffectual, Merricat's only companion has been Constance, whose treatment of her is like that of an indulgent parent: She caters to her whims, laughs at her caprices, and lets her run wild within the small orbit in which she is decidedly happy.

But the outer world slowly begins to encroach on the Blackwoods. First, two neighborhood busybodies—Helen Clark and Lucille Wright—come to visit, urging Constance to forget the wounds of the past and to emerge from isolation. Although Constance joins Merricat in laughing at the two women, they touch a chord in her. For the first time Merricat senses a restlessness in her sister and resolves that she will not allow things to change.

But with the arrival of Cousin Charles, a crass man in his early thirties, change seems inevitable. He and Merricat immediately become antagonists. Charles tells Constance that the strange arrangements in the Blackwood mansion have gone on too long. At first Merricat tries to wish her cousin away; eventually she asks him to leave. He refuses, boasting of his alliance with Constance and saying that it is perhaps Merricat who will not be at home there in a little while.

But Charles underestimates the bond between the two sisters. Sensing that what Charles really wants is the house, Merricat sets it on fire. When the townspeople arrive, all of their old suspicions about the Blackwoods return, and instead of helping, they watch the house burn.

During the fire, in which Uncle Julian burns to death, Merricat and Constance flee to the woods to escape the angry townspeople. When they return, they begin to set up house in the remaining shell of the mansion. Merricat loves the adventure of the enterprise, and Constance, now recognizing Charles's greedy motives, seems resigned to her fate. When Charles returns and begs Constance to talk to him, she and Merricat hide in the ruins. Having seen through Charles, Constance also sees how much Merricat needs her and how much she and Merricat are bound together.

The two sisters live on among the ruins. The townspeople, perhaps feeling guilty over their passivity during the fire, gradually try to make contact with them. They send food and clothing, and the two sisters are both grateful and amused. Wary but accepting, the townspeople regard them as two odd creatures who might be witches but who are probably simply harmless eccentrics, fading quietly into old maidenhood. Constance is happy with her lot, but Merricat is elated. "Oh, Constance," she says, "I told you you would like it on the moon."

Blaine, Amory. *This Side of Paradise.* F. Scott Fitzgerald. 1920.

Auburn-haired and green-eyed, Amory Blaine spends his youth as a traveling companion for his extravagant mother Beatrice. On the way to Italy when he is thirteen, he has an emergency appendectomy, and Beatrice suffers a nervous breakdown. Amory is sent to spend the next two years with his aunt and uncle in Minneapolis. He then rejoins Beatrice in Lake Geneva and convinces her to send him away to boarding school; she decides on St. Regis in Connecticut. Before setting off for New England, Amory goes to New York to visit Monsignor Darcy, one of Beatrice's suitors before she married his father for his blue-blood background. Over lunch and countless cigarettes, the jovial prelate and the intent young man form a lifelong attachment.

At St. Regis, Amory is considered arrogant and is unpopular with both students and faculty. After two painful years, however, prep school manages to rid him of his conceit and lay down more conventional planking for the "fundamental Amory." Still, when the time comes to choose a college, Amory favors Princeton purely for its country club allure.

At Princeton, Amory writes for the *Daily Princetonian*, performs in a musical comedy, and reads widely if not discriminately. He takes an immediate liking to the brothers Kerry and Burne Holiday and also befriends Thomas P. D'Invilliers, a writer of impassioned, flowery poetry. Over vacation Amory visits Minneapolis, where he falls in love with Isabelle Borge. He maintains an intermittent correspondence with her from Princeton, writing her rapturous thirty-page missives even though he finds her letters aggravatingly unsentimental. They reunite on the crest of Amory's young egotism; she rushes into his open arms, and they kiss. Moments later, however, she finds him a strain on her nerves. Their relationship fails, and Amory wonders if he is temperamentally unsuited for romance.

Amory's dreams of undergraduate success fade as he fails mathematics in the fall of his junior year. He is removed from the *Princetonian* board and ruins his chances for Senior Council. His father dies quietly, and due to some unfortunate investments, Beatrice and Amory must limit their extravagance. Amory consults the monsignor and tells him about the destruction of his "egotistic highways." Monsignor answers that now he has a clean start and is ready to embark on "the education of a personage."

During Amory's final days at Princeton, Burne Holiday turns to radicalism, leading a movement to reform Princeton's social system. Amory admires Burne's ardent brilliance, but he realizes the limitations of his dogmatism.

After Amory's mother passes away and he returns from war duty, he takes an apartment in New York City with Tom D'Invilliers and Alec Connage, another classmate from Princeton. Amory takes a job at an advertising agency and meets Alec's sister, Rosalind Connage, a debutante with beautiful blond hair. The two fall madly in love, but Amory still has Rosalind's other suitors to compete with, most notably Dawson Ryder who is wealthy and sure of success. Rosalind parts tearfully from Amory, the only man she has ever loved, knowing she would be miserable if she had to live in relative poverty with him. Heartbroken, Amory goes on a drinking spree for three weeks until Prohibition forces him to stop. Sober, Amory engages his roommate Tom in endless discussions on politics, novelists, and poetry. Although Amory wants to write, he believes too much in the responsibilities of authorship to start just yet.

When his bachelor household in New York falls apart, Amory sets off to find Monsignor Darcy in Washington. On the way he stops in Maryland and meets Eleanor Savage, an impetuous and intelligent young woman with glittering green eyes. She and Amory are drawn to each other as they recite poetry together during a violent rainstorm. Amory stays with her for a month until she recklessly sends her horse over a cliff, narrowly escaping the same fate herself. Amory is shocked, and when she tells him of a crazy streak she inherited from her mother, his love wanes.

Amory never does visit the monsignor; instead, he runs into Alec Connage in Atlantic City. There he sacrifices his reputation and takes the blame for Alec, who was illegally entertaining an underage woman in his hotel room. On the same page as the newspaper account of his disgrace, Amory reads Rosalind and Dawson Ryder's wedding announcement. Later the same week he receives news of the monsignor's death. Bereft of love, heroes, and wise counsel, Amory becomes thoroughly disillusioned. On a walk back to Princeton he is offered a ride by a large, wealthy man with goggles. Amory ardently argues socialism against the man's capitalism, but when he discovers that the man is the father of one of his classmates who was killed in the war, they are able to disagree without wishing each other ill.

At the end, Amory's romantic disillusion has given him a sense of duty, a love of life, and a rediscovery of old ambitions. But, he concedes, thinking of Rosalind and what he has lost, it is all a poor substitute at best.

Blake, Henry. *Blake, or the Huts of America.* Martin Delany. 1859.

Born free in Cuba, only to be kidnapped and sold into bondage, Henry Blake eventually makes his way back to his native land. Once there, he sets about putting his dream of a black revolution into action.

At the novel's beginning, Blake returns to the Mississippi plantation that had been his home for twenty years. Blake had been on a voyage on his master's behalf, and his wife Maggie, left behind with their son, had been sold in his absence because she resisted her master's sexual advances. Acting quickly, Blake disregards the advice of

Maggie's parents and flees the plantation after providing for his son's safe passage to Canada.

Dressed as a groom, Blake travels unmolested throughout the South. Although he has some run-ins with dogs who are trained to hunt escaped slaves, whites believe his story that he is searching for his master's horse. Blacks are quite eager to welcome him to their homes, and he reveals to them his plans for the blacks to revolt and seize their freedom.

After visiting every slave state except Kentucky, where Blake feels the slaves are reluctant to fight for freedom because their bondage is relatively mild, Blake goes back to his master's plantation. He is able to help a whole group of slaves escape, including his in-laws, by pretending that a light-skinned slave escaping with them is their master. The group reaches Canada safely, but Blake still longs for his wife, who is now the slave of an American woman living in Cuba with her Cuban husband.

Blake manages to ship to Cuba as a seaman on an American vessel. While on board he hears several American planters who are resettling in Cuba discuss their plan of making the island part of the United States. Blake, however, has plans to make the island a free country, not another slave state.

Able to purchase his wife thanks to a Cuban law that requires a master to sell a slave when that slave offers a fair market price, Blake makes his way to Havana where he visits the respected black poet PLACIDO. He reveals that he is Placido's cousin Henrico Blacus—Henry Blake being an anglicization of the name. Placido is ecstatic at the return of his cousin and is fascinated by Blake's story of how he had been kidnapped and sold into slavery twenty years before.

Reunited with his cousin and parents, Blake then sends for his son and in-laws. Although his family is now complete, his real dream remains unfulfilled. Placido agrees to help Blake in his designs for a black revolution in the Americas. They decide to start the revolutionary activity in Cuba. Placido introduces Blake to the island's most influential free blacks and most freedom-hungry slaves. An Army of Emancipation is formed, with Blake as general-in-chief.

As the leader, Blake emphasizes the need for the blacks to be united. Pure black, mulatto, quadroon, octoroon—all must work together because if anyone is denied rights, they are all as good as enslaved. He also urges them to reject the perverted Christianity of their masters and read and interpret the Bible themselves. Their spirits aroused, the island's blacks seem poised on the brink of revolution by the end of the narrative.

Blake, Nathaniel "Nat." *Little Men.* Louisa May Alcott. 1871.

Nathaniel Blake joins twelve other "little men," most of whom are orphans or children struggling with a handi-

cap, at Plumfield, an idyllic school for children. He arrives at Plumfield with a recommendation from Theodore Laurence, a friend of the Bhaers, who own and run the school. Mr. Laurence found the boy hiding in a cellar, sick and mourning his dead father.

Nat spent most of his first twelve years traveling with his father, a street musician, and Nicolo, the other band member. He earned his keep by playing violin in the band, and music is his greatest joy in life. As a result of his father's beatings, however, the child is meek and frail, despite his rough life, and after his father's death, he is utterly alone.

When he arrives at Plumfield, Nat is immediately welcomed by the rowdy crew of boys, offered medicine for his cough, and promised the use of Mr. Bhaer's old violin. Inspired by the kindness shown him, Nat expresses his thanks that evening by playing a beautiful melody on the instrument.

The following day is Sunday, and Nat is left in the company of Tommy Bangs, the liveliest boy in the school, who shows him the Plumfield gardens and the farm, with animals belonging to each of the children. Tommy owns two hens and agrees to share the profits of his little egg business if Nat will hunt for the eggs. His engagement at T. Bangs and Co. is an important step in Nat's acceptance at the school. Tommy Bangs becomes his "patron," and the twins Daisy and Demi, his friends and protectors. Nat has never had formal schooling and is ashamed of his ignorance, but with private instruction from one of the older boys, he makes steady progress with his education.

Nat has only one flaw that causes the Bhaers any concern—his tendency to lie—and they go to great lengths to cure him of it. Mr. Bhaer establishes the rule that if Nat tells a lie, his punishment will be to strike Mr. Bhaer's hands with a rod. Nat remains on guard against his habit until Emil, a rather hot-headed boy, threatens to "thrash" whoever ran over the best corn in his garden, and Nat is afraid to confess. When an eyewitness proves that he is responsible, Nat is forced to strike the professor's hand twelve times. Breaking down in tears after this ordeal, Nat promises never to lie again.

An incident involving T. Bangs and Co. causes the Plumfield population to doubt Nat's truthfulness once again. Tommy has been saving the profits from their egg business in order to reach the five-dollar mark when he will be allowed to spend it. Mrs. Bhaer finally gives him the fifth dollar in exchange for four dozen eggs, and Tommy runs to the barn to show Nat the money. When the two are called away to look at a snake someone has found, Tommy quickly hides the money in the winnowing machine. When he returns, it is gone. Nat was the only one who saw him hide it, and the boys are absolutely convinced that he is the thief. It is also general knowledge that Nat has been saving to buy a violin. For several miserable days Nat continues to insist that he is innocent, but the others exclude him. Only Daisy, his little girlfriend, defends him, until his friend Dan claims to have taken the money. The real culprit, a greedy boy named Jack, eventually confesses, and Nat remains especially devoted to Dan for protecting him. Once Nat is cleared of suspicion, he is instantly welcomed back into the group.

The novel ends on Thanksgiving, which is celebrated at Plumfield with an evening of amusing performances by the students, including a play, a poetry reading, a gymnastics demonstration, and Nat's own contribution, a violin solo composed by Mr. Laurence. Mrs. Bhaer proudly notes Nat's talent and the progress he has made since his arrival at the school. Mr. Laurence, also much impressed, promises to take the boy after two more years at Plumfield and launch him properly in his career as a musician.

Blake, Rachel Colbert. *Sapphira and the Slave Girl.* Willa Cather. 1940.

Thirty-seven-year-old Rachel Colbert Blake is the unselfish and uncomplaining daughter of slave owner SAPPHIRA COLBERT. Most of Rachel's time is taken up by the care of her two young daughters, Mary and Betty, and by innumerable acts of charity for all and sundry. She is conspicuously aware of and solicitous toward her mother's slaves, although she rigidly disapproves of slave ownership.

Rachel's life had once been one of grandeur and excitement. At the age of fifteen she met the thirty-year-old congressman Michael Blake. He was instantly smitten by her even though she was not generally considered beautiful. They soon married, and the young Rachel quickly learned how to manage a large household and to provide a seemingly endless round of dinners for an illustrious company of politicians and other Washington, D.C., notables. They had four children; one died in infancy, but their son Robert and daughters Mary and Betty flourished under Rachel's care.

Although they were not wealthy, the Blakes spent prodigious amounts of money on their entertainment, and Rachel was frequently worried about finances, despite her vigorous efforts to economize. Then suddenly her husband and son contracted yellow fever and died. Rachel's worst fears were realized when she discovered that Michael had let his life insurance lapse. Nothing was left for her except the furniture and clothes. Her father, Henry, paid off the remaining creditors and brought his prostrate daughter back to the Mill.

Rachel has gradually acclimated herself to her changed fortunes and become the unselfish mainstay of those less fortunate. In one particularly bold instance she assists her mother's slave, NANCY TILL, to escape via the Underground Railroad. Soon afterward Sapphira severs relations

with her daughter in retribution for the blow to her dignity incurred by Nancy's escape.

Rachel does not attempt to dissuade her mother but merely continues ministering to those who need her help. In the fall of 1857, however, her two daughters are stricken with diphtheria during the usual yearly epidemic; the youngest, Betty, dies after a few days. The news of her granddaughter's death softens the sickly Sapphira's heart, and she requests that Rachel and Mary move in with her. As the winter of 1858 deepens, mother and daughter reach a rapport they had not previously attained, and Sapphira takes great delight in her granddaughter's company. But illness eventually takes its toll, and despite her best efforts, Rachel can do no more than ease her mother's discomfort. Before the winter ends, Sapphira dies, leaving Rachel the care of the house, her father, and the slaves, who are manumitted immediately by the grieving family. Rachel remains in the area during the Civil War and the postwar reconstruction, living the same unselfish life she had led prior to the personal and national tragedies.

Bleilip. "Bloodshed." Cynthia Ozick. 1976.

When he takes a bus from New York City to the rural Orthodox Jewish village where his cousin Toby resides with her husband Yussel and four young sons, Bleilip is disappointed. His former Brooklyn College classmate has given up her aspirations to be the first female president of the United States in order to raise a family.

Hostile toward the Hasidic community, Bleilip is embittered because he feels that Yussel and the little religious village have destroyed his cousin's dreams. He resents the community's emphasis on male spiritual education at the expense of the needs of women and its boast of eleven-hour school days for children. He is especially opposed to the system's use of the rebbe as a mediator between humanity and divinity.

One afternoon Bleilip mockingly accepts Yussel's invitation to that evening's religious service. After the men perform the various rites, the rebbe stands and speaks to the group. Without warning he sharply addresses Bleilip. The rebbe's tone is accusatory, and Bleilip, his antagonism fed by this unexpected confrontation, answers sometimes defensively, sometimes with intimidation. When the rebbe asks Bleilip what he thinks the Hasidim are all about, Bleilip begins relaying several examples of miraculous legends he had heard. He evades answering when the rebbe asks if he expects to see such magic today.

The rebbe then demands that Bleilip empty his pockets. Bleilip hesitates, but when the rebbe presses him more harshly, he tosses a toy gun onto the table. The formerly skeptical Bleilip is stunned that the rebbe forced him to remove the contents of his pocket as if he had known what it held. From the expression on Yussel's face, Bleilip gathers that this procedure was well out of the ordinary.

The rebbe dismisses the others, and for a moment it

appears that his interrogation of Bleilip is finally over. Then he demands that Bleilip empty the other pocket. This time Bleilip pulls out a real gun. Yussel, alone with Bleilip and the rebbe, is flustered and infuriated at this revelation. When Yussel becomes nearly hysterical, the rebbe dismisses him as well.

Now alone with the rebbe, Bleilip is both excited and afraid. When the rebbe claims to detect a bad odor from the real gun, Bleilip confesses that he once used it to kill a pigeon. Still confrontational, Bleilip accuses the Hasidim of being capable of murder if it is part of a sacrificial rite. Unperturbed and sensing Bleilip's defensiveness, the rebbe asks him if he is the kind of nonbeliever who sometimes believes in the religion he condemns. Bleilip hesitates, then says yes, and the rebbe returns the guns.

Blue, Angela. The *"Genius."* Theodore Dreiser. 1915.

Angela Blue from Blackwood, Wisconsin, is attractive and passionate, but her passion is subdued under a regime of conventional morality. She is tired of teaching and watching her sisters get married.

One day on a trip to a friend's house in Alexandria, Illinois, Angela is introduced to EUGENE WITLA, a handsome but shy aspiring illustrator who has moved to Chicago. Angela is taken by his ambitious, artistic nature, and the two arrange to meet on Angela's next trip to Chicago. When she does visit, she notices and admires Eugene's "vivid interest in life." Angela, thinking of Eugene as a possible husband, holds to the doctrine of "one life and one love." When Eugene eventually asks for her hand in marriage, she first consults her parents and then agrees.

Nearly two years pass before they marry, as Eugene moves to New York in an attempt to get a better job and save money. He pays a visit to Blackwood when Angela writes him that either they marry or she kills herself.

After they marry in Buffalo, Angela and Eugene move into a rented studio in New York. Angela admires some of Eugene's friends, but others strike her as condescending. Nevertheless, she is pleased with Eugene's growing success as a newspaper illustrator, and the two share a happy trip to Paris where Angela looks after the artist's every need. Angela is now more confident and self-assured than when she first arrived in New York.

When Eugene has a nervous breakdown, Angela goes home to Blackwood while he attempts to recover. When she returns, she finds that Eugene has been having an affair. Eugene has grown tired of her conventionality. Things improve when Eugene appears to restrain his passions while he climbs the ladder of success in the publishing field. Angela plays the role of the loving wife, and the two socialize constantly in high-society circles. To secure her hold on Eugene, Angela allows herself to get pregnant.

One night Angela discovers Eugene and eighteen-year-old Suzanne Dale in a loving posture. She informs him in a rage that she is pregnant, but Eugene boldly counters with indifference, claiming that it is either a lie or a trap. Eugene then struggles to hold on to Suzanne in the face of fierce opposition from Angela and Suzanne's mother. When Angela, who has a weak heart and a small frame, goes into labor, a repentant Eugene attends her at the hospital, but she dies giving birth.

Bobbit, Miss Lily Jane. "Children on Their Birthdays." Truman Capote. 1949.

Miss Lily Jane Bobbit, the ten-year-old heroine, exhibits uncanny sophistication and poise for a girl her age. Shockingly, Miss Bobbit sports both an adult coiffure and makeup, and she is unabashed by boys and discussions of the devil. Although she is a curiosity to those who first meet her, Miss Bobbit is also level-headed, just, and honest.

As the story opens, the neighborhood children are celebrating Billy Bob's birthday. They are all eating tutti-frutti on the front porch and hoping that something unusual will happen when a young girl in a fancy dress, accompanied by her rather bedraggled mother, sashays up to them. In a voice both childlike and sophisticated, she introduces herself as Miss Lily Jane Bobbit from Memphis. The boys giggle nervously, whereupon she pronounces them mere country children. Departing for Mrs. Sawyer's house across the street where she and her mother have recently taken rooms, Miss Bobbit announces as an afterthought that her mother has a speech impediment, so she always speaks for her. As soon as she disappears, the girls razz her and the older boys, especially Billy Bob and Preacher Star, are quiet, intrigued. The boys soon walk to the edge of the yard to watch as Miss Bobbit, who has brought her Victrola into the Sawyer yard, gracefully dances.

The boys don't see Miss Bobbit again for some time, but every day Preacher joins Billy Bob in his yard, and they linger there together, hoping to catch a glimpse of her. But Miss Bobbit never pays any heed to either of them. Every day she sits on her porch, dressed to the nines, embroidering, styling her hair, or reading the dictionary, always friendly in a formal way. Billy Bob and Preacher can't find the courage to approach her.

One day while they are horsing around in the yard, Billy Bob and Preacher spy a chubby black girl carrying a pail of berries up the street. They taunt her, then spill her berries and shove her down. Outraged, Miss Bobbit rushes across the street, wagging her finger like a schoolmarm and chastising them for not protecting a lady, which all gentlemen were put on this earth to do. Miss Bobbit instantly befriends the girl, and the boys are ashamed, although they continue to vie for her attentions.

One day Manny Fox's show comes to town, featuring an amateur contest in addition to a fan dancer without a fan. Really a huckster, Manny Fox promises to get young boys jobs on fruit ships for a fee of only $150, and he promises the winner of the amateur contest a Hollywood screen test. Miss Bobbit enters, performing a tap dance and a bawdy song, belting out, "If you don't like my peaches, stay away from my can, o-ho o-ho!" Miss Bobbit concludes her song with a flash of her blue lace underwear and is the winner of the contest. But Manny Fox skips town, leaving many boys short $150, and Miss Bobbit without her Hollywood screen test.

Miss Bobbit responds by organizing the Manny Fox Hangman's Club, writing over three hundred flyers and dispatching them to sheriff's offices throughout the South. As a result, Manny Fox is caught and forced to pay reparations to the boys he fleeced. Miss Bobbit earns the Good Deed Merit Award from the Sunbeam Girls of America, but she does not approve of the organization or the award. A good deed, she declares, is really something you do because you want something in return.

Miss Bobbit proposes to the boys who recouped their money that they invest it in something worthwhile—her. She wants them to pool their money and send her to Hollywood, for which she will repay them with ten percent of her life's earnings. Initially reluctant to part with their money, the boys ultimately cannot resist the request of the charming Miss Bobbit.

On the day she is to leave for Hollywood, Miss Bobbit is dressed in white as if she were going to communion. Billy Bob and Preacher pick armfuls of roses to bring across the street to her, while she is consumed with emotion by their approach. Running toward them with her arms outstretched, she is blind to the disaster that Billy Bob and Preacher see coming. Miss Bobbit, oblivious to their warning shouts, is run over by the six o'clock bus.

Bober, Helen. *The Assistant.* Bernard Malamud. 1957.

Helen Bober is the attractive, blue-eyed daughter of MORRIS (BOBER), a poor Jewish grocer in Brooklyn, and his wife Ida. Helen has both economic and romantic aspirations that she struggles to attain.

Helen dreams of someday studying at New York University full time but has been able to afford to take only a few night classes in literature. She feels that a college education is the key to escape from the stifling, hopeless life of labor that her father has led. To help her poor family make ends meet, she gives her father most of her earnings from her job at Levenspiel's Louisville Panties and Bras.

Ida worries about Helen, feeling that, at twenty-three, she should soon be married. She constantly asks Helen why she has been avoiding Nat Pearl, an ambitious and handsome law school student whom Helen had dated the previous summer. Helen continues to be cold toward Nat because although she built dreams of love on his attentions, she soon realized that his interest in her was purely physical. She has pangs of guilt over losing her virginity to him and wants to avoid yielding to him again, for she suspects that he feels she is too poor and uneducated for

him. She keeps her distance, although Nat presses her for an explanation of her sudden withdrawal from him.

Meanwhile a stranger, FRANK ALPINE, has begun working in her father's store. Unknown to anyone, Frank was one of the thieves who held up Morris Bober's grocery store some months earlier. Ida has a natural mistrust of Frank, partly because of his Italian-American background and partly because he constantly keeps his eyes on Helen. Helen shares her mother's suspicions of the *goy* but at the same time finds herself attracted to him. Frank follows her to the library, and they begin meeting there and walking home together, sometimes stopping in the park to talk. She recommends novels to him, for she begins to believe that, like herself, he has greater aspirations and desires a college education. After Frank insists that she keep a book he bought her, against her better judgment, she begins to return his romantic interest in her. Still, she remains unsure of her feelings and resists consummating her relationship with him.

When the suspicious Ida sees them kissing on a park bench one day, she is distraught. To appease her mother, Helen agrees to go out with Nat Pearl one night. She calls Frank in the store to tell him she will meet him in the park afterward. She arrives late, unaware that Frank had been fired earlier that afternoon by Morris who caught him stealing from the cash register. While she is waiting for Frank, a man attacks her, and then Frank appears and rescues her. She is joyful and relieved and tells him that she had come to the park to tell him that she loves him. Nevertheless, she resists his persistent and increasingly violent advances. Urged on by the whiskey he has been drinking, Frank ignores her protests and tries to force her to have sex. Helen recoils from him in disgust.

Helen curses herself for imagining that Frank was something he could never be. When her father falls ill and Frank returns to run the store, Helen refuses to acknowledge his presence except to thank him for helping the family. Soon after, her father dies, and Helen begins seeing Nat Pearl again. But Frank manages to run into her outside the library, and before she can express her contempt, he tells her he wants to pay for her college education. Though she declines, she is moved by his offer. One day she looks at his haggard form at the grocery counter and realizes the depth of his repentance and love. He again offers to pay for her education, and to make him happy she tells him that she will consider it.

One night Nat Pearl and Helen have an argument in the hallway, and it is overheard by Frank. Pearl insults Helen, and she smacks him before running up the stairs. The novel ends on this note, with a dedicated Frank converting to Judaism and planning to turn the store into a restaurant.

Bober, Morris. *The Assistant.* Bernard Malamud. 1957.

Morris Bober is a fifty-five-year-old grocer who has worked sixteen hours a day in the same store on Eastern

Parkway in Brooklyn for more than twenty years. He lives above his grocery in a drab five-room flat with his wife Ida and his twenty-three-year-old daughter, HELEN (BOBER). He came to America after having escaped from the czar's army, but he does not imagine himself a free man; the store confines him, and he often feels that it will be his grave. Scrupulously honest and gentle-hearted, Morris barely manages to eke out a living and has nothing to show for his years of toil. Worse yet, instead of providing Helen with the college education for which she yearns, he must take her meager paycheck from her in order to make ends meet. Broken from years of labor, Morris laments his lost youth and mourns the loss of his son Ephraim who died many years ago.

One day two men with handkerchiefs over their faces enter Morris's store. Angered that the grocer has little money to surrender, one of the thieves smashes him over the head with a gun, despite the objections of the second thief. The compassionate thief, FRANK ALPINE, who gives Morris a drink of water, is a stranger to the neighborhood. Morris does not recognize the young man when he later returns to the store to help Morris, who is still weak from the blow, drag in the milk crates in the morning.

Morris listens to Frank Alpine's sad life story, and despite Ida's objections, he lets the young man assist him as a clerk in the store in return for room and board and a tiny stipend. He does not suspect that Frank is stealing from his register; in fact, business in the store flourishes with Frank working there. Later on a neighboring merchant, Karp, informs him that his business has been improving because the owner of the new grocery store nearby has fallen ill. In the past Morris had found it nearly impossible to compete with the new store. Karp also tells him that the new store will soon be taken over and that Morris should sell out while he can because the takeover will put him out of business. Soon afterward Morris catches Frank stealing from the register and asks him to leave.

Morris wearily climbs into bed for a nap but forgets to light the heater. His tenant, Nick Fuso, and Frank smell the gas fumes, break down Morris's door, and save his life. Frank, who is in love with Helen, returns to run the store while Morris is ill. It occurs to Morris that Frank was one of the thieves that held him up, and as soon as he can, he crawls out of bed to ask Frank to leave once more.

Business dwindles to almost nothing, and Morris, thoroughly worn out, resolves to put his store up for auction at a loss. Alone one evening he is startled by a bony man who offers his services as an arsonist. Morris is tempted by the insurance money but nevertheless chases the man from his store. Later, however, he tries to set fire to the store when no one else is home. His clothes catch fire, and once again Frank saves his life.

Bitter over his fate, Morris wishes that Karp's liquor store would burn down, but he is immediately ashamed of his thoughts. Ward Minogue, the thief who clubbed Morris, breaks into the liquor store and sets fire to it. Soon after, Karp makes a generous offer to buy Morris's grocery to relocate his business, and for the first time Morris accepts, feeling at ease with the world. Although it is April, it snows, and Morris feels a sudden urge to shovel the sidewalk, to breathe free for the first time since his youth. Despite Ida's protests, he rushes outside without a coat. He dies of pneumonia three days later.

Bogen, Heshalle ''Harry.'' *I Can Get It for You Wholesale.* Jerome Weidman. 1937.

Heshalle ''Harry'' Bogen is the shrewd, con-man narrator of this tale of New York's seamy rag trade. Harry was born and raised in the Bronx, where he still lives with his widowed mother. A self-centered dynamo, he relentlessly pursues his personal passions of money, fast women, and blintzes. The one person to break through Harry's egoism is his mother, whom he loves and respects. One of Harry's greatest pleasures is to spoil the woman, and he buys her fancy new clothes and furniture so she can impress her friends.

Harry's story centers on his grandiose plan to make a fortune in New York City's Garment District. The first stage of his scheme involves inciting the district's shipping clerks to strike. Harry hires one of his friends to act as his mouthpiece and convinces the clerks to walk out. The strike appears to be heading for success as the clerks effectively shut down the garment industry and have the owners on the verge of agreeing to their demands.

Then Harry undermines the very strike he created. He approaches the company owners with a proposal to deliver the dresses at prices lower than the ones demanded by the shipping clerks. He puts thousands of shipping clerks out of work and gains a monopoly on the dress delivery business.

Since he owns the only dress delivery business in town, business booms for Harry. Meanwhile, his mother continues to try to set him up with a ''nice'' girl. One evening Harry arrives home and is introduced to Betty Rivkin. Even though Betty is not particularly attractive, Harry is strangely drawn to her. The two go upstate together for a weekend. Harry has the opportunity to sleep with Betty, but a strange feeling stops him at the last minute, and he simply drives back to the city.

When other entrepreneurs begin to open competing delivery businesses, Harry decides to open his own design house. He sells out his half of the business to his partner and convinces the top salesman and the hottest designer in town to join him. The three form Apex Modes Inc. The fledgling business begins to make its mark on the New York fashion scene, and the company's shows are huge successes. The company is soon ready to produce expensive evening gowns to compete with the older, established firms.

Betty eventually drops out of Harry's life altogether, and he discovers a new challenge in Martha Mills, a Broadway starlet. Putting all his energies into bedding Martha, Harry spends months wining and dining her and buying her expensive presents. With each of her rejections he becomes more determined to possess her. His gifts to Martha become more and more extravagant, and he starts using the company's money to finance his pursuit.

Before he knows it, Harry has spent almost all of the company's available cash. When he can't make good on his debts, the creditors take him to court. At the bankruptcy trial, Harry throws the blame on his partner, who winds up having to pay the fines and serve a jail sentence.

Harry's business folds, but he doesn't mind. He has managed to stash away a sizable savings that will allow him to live comfortably until his next business deal takes off. And more important to him, he has at last convinced Martha to sleep with him.

Bok, Yakov. *The Fixer.* Bernard Malamud. 1966.

Yakov Bok is a poor Jewish handyman in early-twentieth-century Russia. Although he disdains any involvement in politics, Yakov finds his indifference overcome when he is arrested for a crime he did not commit.

Partly out of restlessness and partly out of a desire to "educate" himself, Yakov decides to leave the rural shtetl in which he lives and travel to Kiev. Shmuel, his father-in-law, warns Yakov of anti-Semitism in Kiev, but the handyman shrugs it off, as he does all political matters. Politics, he feels, is useless unless one is an activist. Yakov heads for Kiev on a bony horse, with little more than a few morsels and his bag of tools. En route to Kiev he is shaken by an encounter with an anti-Semite who does not recognize his Jewish identity. Once in Kiev, Yakov settles in the Jewish quarter.

One day Yakov comes across a wealthy man passed out in the snowy street. After reviving the man, Nikolai Lebedev, Yakov escorts him home, where he is warmly thanked and invited back by Lebedev's daughter. When Yakov returns the next day and gives a false, non-Jewish name, Lebedev asks if he, being a handyman, would like to renovate a four-room flat upstairs that he owns. Yakov agrees to the job, impresses Lebedev with his work, and becomes friendly with the daughter. Lebedev is so pleased that he asks Yakov to take over the task of supervising a brickyard he owns—situated in a district forbidden to Jews. Yakov accepts, but not without trepidation.

Once in the brickyard, Yakov antagonizes several of the workers who steal bricks during the night, the kind of activity Yakov is there to prevent. Despite this difficulty and Yakov's fear that his religion will be discovered, his life is pleasant. He reads, walks around Kiev, and enjoys his newfound wealth.

When a local Gentile youth is found murdered and drained of blood, Yakov is abruptly arrested for the crime. Yakov finds out later that Proshko, one of the thieves, had discovered Yakov's identity and avenged himself by turning in the watchman. Bibikov, a sympathetic investigator, informs Yakov that the boy was actually murdered by the mother's boyfriends, they and the mother being part of a gang of criminals. Meanwhile, Yakov is thrown into the brutal Kiev Prison and held for over two years, trapped by a web of lies and a cruel prison administration. Eventually Bibikov's sympathies are discovered by the authorities. He is put in the cell next to Yakov's, where he hangs himself.

In the face of brutality and pressure to confess to a crime he didn't commit, Yakov discovers within himself a deep vein of moral strength. He refuses to confess even if it means possible freedom and responds to his tormentors with a mixture of defiance and resistance to provocation. With his trial finally approaching, Yakov is aware that he is a public figure who does enjoy sympathy from some parts of the population, at least from those who are aware of his case. On the way to his trial, Yakov, once apathetic, realizes that no man is truly "nonpolitical," especially if he is a Jew. He sees that history intersects with every life.

Bokonon. *Cat's Cradle.* Kurt Vonnegut, Jr. 1963.

Bokonon, the philosopher and theologian, was born Lionel Boyd Johnson in 1891, as a British subject on the island of Tobago. An insatiable appetite for adventure took him to London, where he attended college; to Europe, where he was a soldier in World War I; to Rhode Island, where he worked on an estate; and to India, where he became a follower of Mohandas Gandhi. After being deported from India by the British government, he set sail again and eventually landed in Port au Prince, Haiti, which was occupied by U.S. Marines. Earl McCabe, a Marine deserter, offered Johnson $500 for transportation to Miami, and they set sail together.

A gale blew them ashore on the impoverished and over-populated island of San Lorenzo. The island was in anarchy, its people were being exploited by Castle Sugar, Inc., and the Catholic Church provided no comfort to the desperate and diseased people. San Lorenzo was ripe for a political, economic, and religious revolution, and Johnson and McCabe, full of Utopian ideals, were destined to be its leaders.

Since Castle Sugar had never made a profit on the island, it withdrew without a fight. McCabe soon began designing a new economic and political system, and Johnson, whose name is pronounced Bokonon in the San Lorenzan dialect, designed a new religion. According to *The Books of Bokonon*, one of the central tenets of the religion is to "live by the *foma* [harmless untruths] that make you brave and kind and healthy and happy." Its most important ritual, *boko-maru*, occurs when two practitioners rub the soles of their feet together. Bokonon wrote a series of several hundred poems, or calypsos, celebrating the history and explaining the principles of Bokononism.

Eventually, McCabe and Johnson agree to outlaw the religion because they believe a religion sanctioned by the government lacks fervor. The people are told that anyone caught practicing the religion will die on a torture instrument called "the hook."

When McCabe finally dies, his majordomo, "Papa" Monzano, succeeds him in political control of the island. One of Monzano's associates has invented a crystal called ice-nine, which raises the melting point of water that it comes into contact with over 100 degrees. Through a sequence of bizarre events, the ice-nine gets into the island waters and freezes all of the world's seas. Any human being who touches ice-nine freezes into a statue. Bokonon tells his followers that they were misled by the false prophet Bokonon and that since God is trying to kill them, they should commit suicide—which they do, en masse. One of the few survivors of this catastrophe is JOHN, the novel's narrator. Bokonon himself does not die, and as the novel closes, John finds Bokonon, who has just completed the final ironic pages of his magnum opus, *The Books of Bokonon*, in which he says: "If I were a younger man, I would write a history of human stupidity; and I would climb to the top of Mount McCabe and lie down on my back with my history for a pillow; and I would take from the ground some of the blue-white poison that makes statues of men; and I would make a statue of myself, lying on my back, grinning horribly, and thumbing my nose at You Know Who."

Bolling, John Bickerson "Binx." *The Moviegoer.* Walker Percy. 1961.

Narrator John Bickerson Bolling is called "Jack" by his friends and "Binx" by his very wealthy New Orleans family. Binx lives in the suburban town of Gentilly, manages a branch office of his uncle's brokerage firm, and lunches weekly with the charming, domineering matriarch of the Bolling family, Aunt Emily. All the while he is consumed by what he calls his "vertical search," an existential quest for something meaningful that he can't quite name.

Binx is a moviegoer, drawn to the celluloid images that free him momentarily from the monotony of his daily life. Determined to help him find his place in the world, Aunt Emily issues a command: At the end of the week, on his thirtieth birthday, Binx is to report to her with a decision about what he would like to do with his life.

Aunt Emily is also worried about beautiful, strange KATE CUTRER, her chronically depressed, drug- and alcohol-addicted stepdaughter who lives with Emily and Emily's husband Jules. Emily senses that Binx is the only one who can get through to Kate, and she enlists his help.

As he talks to the young woman, Binx learns the extent of her problems.

The moviegoer has his own strange relationship with experiences in the external world; for example, when talking to his superficial cousin Nell, he is struck by an overwhelming impression that the people around him are dead. And when his uncle tells him that he must attend a conference in Chicago during Mardi Gras, he is distressed, not because he will miss the carnival but because he cannot bear being in an unfamiliar place. To distract himself from these feelings, Binx makes a habit of becoming infatuated with his pretty young secretaries. He is particularly charmed by his current secretary, Sharon Kincaid, and he invents extra work so that he can spend more time near her.

When Kate tells Binx that she is ready to stop seeing her psychiatrist, he knows she is headed for an emotional fall. Wanting badly to help her, he half-seriously proposes marriage, but Kate brushes him off. Soon after, Binx invites Sharon to the beach. On the way they are involved in a minor hit-and-run accident. While tending the injury he has received, he reveals the scar of a wound he suffered in the war, a physical manifestation of the psychological damage he has undergone.

Binx takes Sharon to the summer cottage where his mother, who remarried after the death of Binx's father, is staying with her family. Of his six younger half-brothers and -sisters, Binx is particularly taken with Lonnie, a precocious young philosopher who is ill and confined to a wheelchair. Lonnie is also a moviegoer, and Binx takes him and Sharon to a matinee.

When he returns to Gentilly, Binx learns that Kate has attempted suicide. Although she took only a few pills and claims that she could never actually kill herself, Binx knows she is suffering greatly. Kate suddenly decides she will accompany Binx to Chicago, and she convinces him that they must take the train immediately. She leaves without telling her stepmother where she is going.

On the train Kate continues to take pills, then awkwardly seduces Binx. They do not stay in Chicago long: Aunt Emily, alarmed at Kate's sudden disappearance, tracks the pair down and demands that they return at once. Binx arrives in Gentilly and, not knowing what else to do, phones Sharon. Her roommate answers and informs him that Miss Kincaid is engaged to be married. He replies that he, too, is soon to be married—to Kate Cutrer.

That evening Kate agrees to marry Binx, but she warns him that it may be a long time before she recovers from her mental illness. Binx realizes that the only thing he can do with his life is help other people and allow himself to be helped by them. He decides to enter medical school in the fall.

An epilogue to the novel finishes Binx's story. The scene is one year later, shortly before Lonnie's death. Binx comforts his other siblings, who are waiting for their parents, then turns to Kate, now his wife, and asks her to run an errand for him. She is terrified but listens quietly to his careful instructions as he hands her a flower to hold while she is on the bus. With Binx's love and support, Kate may find the courage to face the difficult path ahead of her. Binx, too, finds an end to his restless search—in love.

Bolt, Cameron. *Glass People.* Gail Godwin. 1972.

Cameron Bolt, a cold and ambitious district attorney, is the epitome of the self-made man. For Cameron, happiness comes with domestic cleanliness and order: cooking, cleaning, dressing—all are rituals he executes to perfection. He has chosen every piece of furniture, every stitch of drapery in the California home he shares with his wife FRANCESCA (BOLT). But his most prized decoration is Francesca herself.

Cameron has noticed a significant transformation in his wife. Though extraordinarily beautiful, Francesca has lost her radiance, her charm. Cameron, supremely confident of his powers of perception, organizes a change for her—a visit to her mother, Kate, now living on the East Coast. While Francesca is away, Cameron adheres strictly to the details of his routine and ponders his future. His election to the position of attorney general is practically assured. When Francesca calls to say that she has missed her return flight, Cameron knows she is lying but decides to play along with her. In life as in politics, he knows that he will get what he wants. All he has to do is wait. Francesca telephones the next day from a hotel in New York where she is staying with a lover, Mike. Cameron suspects the truth but says nothing; instead he offers to send her a bank draft to cover her expenses.

A reporter, Jerry Freeman, comes to interview Cameron at his office. Jerry arrives out of breath, yet Cameron suggests a brisk walk, claiming that it enables him to clear his head. He expounds on the art of politics, the only field that challenges his energies to the fullest. Cameron has been called an "extremist-conservative" by the press—a label that seems to him reductive and imprecise. Cameron, harkening back to Plato, considers himself a Conservator, a guardian of living forms. Jerry is captivated by Cameron's inscrutability and formidable control; no longer able to think for himself, he sinks exhausted into a chair as Cameron energetically orders their lunch.

Cameron next appears in New York where his wife has fallen ill. His arrival seems miraculous (he had not been summoned), yet it reflects his perfectly honed instincts. Francesca wants to leave him but knows—and shows—that he is needed. He feels that he alone can preserve her loveliness. After Francesca recovers, he takes her shopping. She models a rare and expensive gown, and her physical beauty moves him to tears.

Francesca, now pregnant with Mike's child, returns with Cameron to California. Out of respect for her confinement, Cameron moves formally into the study. This new form of marriage suits him perfectly. He knows that Francesca will blossom under his care, and he has been relieved of the pressure of physical intimacy. In every sense he has won.

Bolt, Francesca. *Glass People.* Gail Godwin. 1972.

Francesca Bolt, the young wife of CAMERON (BOLT), embodies the emptiness and futility of wealthy American womanhood. Her exquisite looks prove to be her only resource as she struggles vainly to overcome her dependence on her husband and his money.

The novel opens with Francesca moving listlessly about her California home, tastefully decorated and meticulously maintained by her husband. As she ponders her beauty and her idleness, Francesca recalls her childhood and adolescence—days of silk and skin creams, parties and lighthearted companionship spent with Kate, her mother and only friend, now living on the East Coast. Francesca wonders vaguely what went wrong. Seeking to escape her boredom and her loneliness, Francesca writes to Kate, whose letters have grown shorter, more mysterious, reticent, and sporadic. Cameron arranges for her to return to the East for a visit.

Francesca arrives to find a new Kate; since the death of her second husband, she has been forced to give up the riches she once cherished. Living in a backwoods cabin with Ware Smith, the ebullient, ruddy-cheeked owner of a natural foods store, Kate is no longer the witty raconteur of days past. She has become dowdy and shapeless, a homebody anticipating a second child. Francesca spends most of her vacation alone and leaves more disheartened and confused than ever.

At the airport Francesca meets Mike, a traveling salesman. They are instantly attracted to each other. Mike reawakens Francesca's dreams of passion, fulfillment, and independence. They drive into New York City together and find a hotel. The one Mike chooses is cheap and shabby, and he leaves her after a few days.

While awaiting his return, Francesca decides to leave Cameron and look for a job. She soon discovers that she has no skills. Rejected by an employment agency, she answers an ad for an amanuensis. "M. Evans," her new employer, is an eccentric whose "project" consists of collecting and typing all the "desirable traits" of fictional and real-life characters. Instead of being paid a wage (for M. has lost her checkbook), Francesca ends up buying groceries for M., paying her bills, and cleaning her apartment.

When Francesca returns to the hotel, she hears the woman next door vomiting in the bathroom. Mike calls to tell her he won't be able to see her until the following weekend. Francesca suddenly realizes that her relationship with Mike is not a great love but merely a tawdry affair. Unable to cope with this brutal truth and feeling feverish, she crawls into bed. Voices and figures from the past crowd around her as she slips in and out of consciousness. As if from a great distance, she hears the telephone ring. It is Cameron, calling from the lobby of her hotel.

The novel closes with Francesca languishing once more in her California home. Cameron has restored her to sanity and opulence. Now content to be dressed, waited on, and paraded about, Francesca greedily consumes one of Cameron's gourmet meals as she awaits the birth of Mike's child.

Bolt, Molly. *Rubyfruit Jungle.* Rita Mae Brown. 1973.

Scrappy and opinionated, Molly Bolt grows up in the mid-1950s in Coffee Hollow, a rural town outside York, Pennsylvania. Her parents are poor, and Molly finds out at age seven that she is actually adopted, having been born the bastard daughter of a local woman. In part because of her background, Molly always feels like an outsider. In school she breaks the rules, selling peeks at a boy's penis, tricking a classmate into eating rabbit manure mixed with raisins, and punching the local rich girl when she informs Molly that as a woman she can't be a doctor. When her mother tries to punish her for this act, Molly promptly locks her in the cellar.

Molly decides that she is never going to get married, a notion that surprises all her friends. But in sixth grade she changes her mind after falling in love with fellow student Leota B. Bisland. Molly and Leota kiss in the woods after school, and Molly excitedly proposes marriage. Later she sleeps over at Leota's house and has her first lesbian experience.

The relationship ends abruptly, however, when Molly's family moves to Fort Lauderdale, Florida, in search of greater economic opportunity. Placed in a strange new environment, Molly decides that if she can make her new classmates laugh, she will fit in and be accepted. Although she manages to fit in, she still feels alienated by her sexuality. When she is in the eighth grade, Molly loses her virginity to her cousin Leroy, and the experience makes her realize that she is indeed different.

In high school she goes out with two of her friends one night and sees the principal and the dean of women on an illicit date. Molly uses this knowledge to get elected student council president. She also seduces her friend Carolyn Simpson, the head cheerleader.

Molly enrolls at the University of Florida at Gainesville, the only school that offers her a scholarship, and has an affair with her wealthy roommate. When the deans find out, she loses her scholarship and is expelled from the school. With only fourteen dollars and sixty-one cents in her pocket she hitchhikes to New York where she hopes to be accepted for what she is. She spends the first few nights sleeping in an abandoned car, but within a week she gets a cheap apartment and a job serving ice cream and hamburgers in a silly costume.

Molly meets a tall beautiful woman at her job who introduces her to a rich, socialite lesbian scene. She is now

intent on a career in film and convinces New York University to give her a full scholarship to film school. Molly attends film school at night and works at a publishing company during the day. Ever the prankster, she fills the desk of an annoying coworker with dog excrement. Molly also works on a book with a forty-one-year-old female classics professor, Polina Bellantoni, whom she soon seduces. But the woman is obsessed with playing out sexual fantasies involving men, and Molly soon becomes more interested in her sixteen-year-old daughter.

Molly eventually returns to Coffee Hollow to see all the people with whom she grew up. Her friends are all married, living the same lives that their parents lived, and they understand her even less than they did when they were young. Soon after her trip Molly sneaks out of New York with the university's film equipment and returns to Florida to shoot her final film project. She does a simple documentary-style piece on her mother, which makes her appreciate her mother's life and brings the two closer. After the film's showing, she graduates summa cum laude and is a member of Phi Beta Kappa. Following graduation, however, while her male classmates land big directing jobs, Molly only receives offers to be a secretary or to work in an office; the novel ends with her vowing to continue to fight for her place in the world.

Bon, Charles. *Absalom, Absalom!* William Faulkner. 1936.

Desperately seeking recognition from a father who rejects him for his partial black ancestry, Charles Bon is a doomed figure. Fifty years after his death, QUENTIN COMPSON and a Harvard roommate, Shreve McCannon, piece together this story of miscegenation, denial, and racial hysteria.

Charles is born in the nineteenth-century West Indies to THOMAS SUTPEN (of West Virginia and later Mississippi) and the daughter of a Haitian sugar planter. Sutpen, who is socially ambitious, abandons his family when he realizes that his wife has black ancestors. Growing up pampered in New Orleans, Charles does not know exactly why his father is absent, but he does sense that his mother is preparing him for some type of retributive action.

As a young man, Charles takes an octoroon mistress who bears him a son, Charles Etienne de Saint Valery. Freed from working by his mother's money, the elder Charles leads the idle but restless life of a New Orleans aristocrat—or so Quentin and Shreve imagine. They also surmise that a lawyer who administered Charles's money was scheming to blackmail Sutpen, who had become one of the wealthiest farmers in Jefferson, Mississippi.

Perhaps under the direction of this lawyer, Charles enrolls in the University of Mississippi, where he is introduced to Henry Sutpen, his half-brother. They become good friends. Charles visits the Sutpen farm and has a romance with Henry's sister JUDITH (SUTPEN). Thomas suspects Charles is his son and confirms this suspicion on his next trip to New Orleans. Sutpen reveals to Henry, but not to Judith, that Charles is their half-brother, but Henry does not want to believe it. He and Charles leave to fight in the Civil War.

Quentin and Shreve suppose that at some point during the war Charles and Henry debated the propriety of Charles's courtship of Judith. During a battle, Charles saves Henry, who begs to be left to die so that he will never know whether the marriage takes place. Later in the war Sutpen, now a colonel, visits the regiment and tells Henry that Charles is part black.

Charles seems undisturbed when Henry tells him that he is black, but he cannot forgive Sutpen, who has never spoken to him personally, nor has he acknowledged his paternity or apologized for abandoning Charles's mother. This slight seals Charles's determination to marry Judith. Henry, more disturbed by miscegenation than incest, begs Charles to reconsider. Charles challenges Henry to kill him. Henry refuses until they reach the farm. There he shoots Charles and deposits the body at Judith's feet.

Bone, Tristram. *A Long Day's Dying.* Frederick Buechner. 1950.

Tristram Bone's outstanding feature is his incredible obesity, which makes him quite inept, he realizes, at being a lover. Yet his immensity enhances his dignity, giving him the gravity of a Roman senator or a cardinal. Although Tristram's demeanor and life-style are serious and intellectual, he is clever enough to recognize the value of the ridiculous, and he enjoys acting silly with his pet monkey on occasion. Since Tristram lives alone with his housekeeper, his monkey is more like a child or close friend than a pet.

As a suitor of Elizabeth Poor, Tristram has a rival in his close friend George Motley. George and Elizabeth visit her son Leander at his college one weekend, during which George jealously suspects that Elizabeth had sex with Leander's teacher, Paul Steitler. Loyal to Tristram and envious of his innocent complacency, George confirms his suspicion.

Although Tristram receives this disturbing intelligence with equanimity and skepticism, and is reluctant to interrogate Elizabeth, he nevertheless asks her to explain her relationship to Paul. Elizabeth, refusing to admit that she slept with Paul, rashly claims that Paul seduced her son. Tristram is puzzled and saddened by the news of Leander's involvement in a homosexual relationship, but characteristically he strives for a thoughtful and accurate—if elaborately metaphorical—assessment of the situation: He compares Paul to a trained acrobat urging a less sophisticated one to perform a dangerous leap without a safety net. He then apologizes for having hurt Elizabeth, and with his plea for mutual kindness he seems to acknowledge that their courtship can no longer be maintained.

Despite his polished eloquence and the inertia of his passive and lethargic habits, Tristram feels rashly impelled to search out the facts by questioning Paul. He asks the teacher to meet him in New York's Cloisters and confronts him with Elizabeth's accusation. Although Paul recognizes some truth in the claim that he loves Leander, he informs Tristram that Elizabeth is mistaken. Tristram is primarily concerned with protecting Leander's innocence, and he discourages Paul from mentioning the accusation to the boy.

Tristram writes to Elizabeth of the reassuring results of his interview. He realizes that the situation has become more harmful than he expected, however, when he receives a telegram from Elizabeth's ancient and kind mother Maroo who is coming all the way from the South to visit her distraught daughter. For the first time Tristram loses hope that the intrigue can be resolved; his despair is heightened when he meets Maroo at the train station and discovers that she has developed a severe cough during her trip.

Once he delivers Maroo safely to Elizabeth, Tristram dispels his despair by a conviction in his ability to see the situation clearly and objectively. He feels that he has reached the lowest possible point and is confident that he will rise above any further entanglements. As if to confirm his newfound serenity, he symbolically confronts danger by running the dull side of a straight razor across his throat. But his monkey, who has been watching, suddenly takes up the blade and accidentally cuts its own throat in imitation of his master's action.

The following day, when Tristram visits the dying Maroo, he babbles to her about the monkey's death and his own pathetic life. Tragically, as Maroo herself is fading, he concedes that "everything now will be different."

Bonham, Daisy. "Daisy." Joyce Carol Oates. 1977.

A strange and intimate relationship exists between Francis Bonham, an aging and eccentric poet, and Daisy, his eccentric daughter. The story, written largely in flashbacks, opens in a Massachusetts seaside town where Francis has rented a suite in an old hotel. Other guests notice how attentive he is to his daughter, how he treats her as if they were lovers or as if Daisy were a small child of six or seven. But it is soon revealed that Daisy is a very unusual, brilliant woman of thirty-six.

A child prodigy, Daisy drew, played the piano, and recited Francis's poetry at the age of three. At six she put on a puppet show for which she alone created the puppets, costumes, and stage. Too precocious to get along with children her own age, Daisy had no playmates other than her father. She and Francis shared a multitude of secrets, mimicking others and parodying the stupidity of those with less genius.

When her mother died, Daisy began to have violent and frightening tantrums, throwing and breaking things around the house, even tearing up her own paintings. At fourteen she began to refuse to eat, bathe, or leave the house. Francis thought she was just being stubborn, a trait the two shared, but her behavior forced him to stop writing poetry in order to care for her for two years.

Daisy's behavior continued to worsen. One winter night she ran out after her father with no coat and only slippers on her feet. It took three men to contain her, and Francis was forced to place her in a mental hospital where she was drugged and subjected to electroshock treatments. Only when a badly administered spinal tap left her partly paralyzed was he able to get her out of the institution.

Francis brought Daisy to a series of resorts and sea towns along the East Coast to recuperate. In the Massachusetts town they now visit, they take hikes by the sea and draw caricatures of the other guests. Francis is still amazed and delighted by Daisy, although he is sometimes frightened by the way she can guess who is about to call on the phone and by the conversations she reports having with her dead mother. They have established rituals for their life together, without which Daisy gets too upset. At the story's end Daisy is frustrated because she cannot get a drawing exactly right. Francis worries that she'll go down to the sea and hurt herself, and he urges her to go instead to her room to sleep. Later, when she wakes, their strange equilibrium has again been established.

Bonham, Joe. *Johnny Got His Gun*. Dalton Trumbo. 1939.

Joe Bonham is a once-contented young man whose life is completely destroyed when he is drafted into the army and then wounded in action in France during World War I. Before unwillingly becoming a soldier, the narrator is employed in the night shipping department of a bakery in Los Angeles and is very happily courting Karen, a young woman whom he plans to marry when he returns from his stint in the service. But all of his plans are thwarted when he is caught in shellfire and dives into a dugout where a high explosive shell blows up every chance he has to enjoy a self-determined, meaningful existence.

Following the explosion that blows Joe Bonham's face off but miraculously fails to damage his spine or his jugular vein, he remembers nothing, as he slips in and out of consciousness, until he realizes that he is deaf. As his grasp on reality improves with the passage of time, he also slowly discovers, amid excruciating physical and emotional anguish, that his ears, mouth, nose, jaw, tongue, and teeth have been destroyed. His gaping wound of a face is covered with a cloth mask so that only his relatively unmutilated forehead is visible.

Joe is fed and breathes through tubes; in addition, his legs and arms have been amputated, reducing his body to a stump of agonized flesh. Joe is so horrendously disfigured that one of the nurses assigned to care for him is sickened by the sight of him. Although he desperately wants to be dead, he is so helpless that he cannot even commit suicide. He has no choice but to remain imprisoned in his destroyed body with only his isolated and tortured consciousness intact.

In an effort to retain his sanity in his limited world, Joe begins to assign tasks to himself. He challenges himself by trying to set up his own calendar, attempting to determine when the sun will rise by painstakingly gauging changes in temperature that he can detect on what little skin remains undamaged on his body. Having achieved this feat, he notes how many visits the nurses make to his bed during the course of a twenty-four-hour period, and he successfully and excitedly establishes a calendar that at least connects him to the world through time.

Years pass, and then one day Joe comes up with the notion of tapping his head up and down on his pillow in imitation of the dot and dash system of Morse code in order to communicate with people. For a long time his attendants do not know what his head jerks mean. When an extremely kind and sympathetic nurse fills in for his usual daytime nurse, who is taking time off for the Christmas holidays, she traces the letters that spell "Merry Christmas" on his chest. Nodding his head to inform her that he understands her communication, Joe finally manages to inform the outside world that his mind has not been impaired despite the extreme mutilation of his body. The nurse fetches a man who understands Morse code, but Joe Bonham cannot be provided with what he really desires: to be liberated from his bed and his body. The novel ends with the anguished and furious invalid relentlessly tapping out his helplessness and his outrage at the existence of war.

Bowen, Lina Ridgely. *Indian Summer*. William Dean Howells. 1886.

Lina Ridgely Bowen, an elegant widow, is first regarded, through the eyes of Theodore Colville, as somewhat worthy of derision, a superficial yet delightful woman of fashion. Having first met Theodore in Florence fifteen years before, Lina has returned to the banks of the Arno with her prepubescent daughter Effie after the death of her husband, a midwestern politician. Although she had greatly admired Theodore years before, she kept her ardor hidden in deference to his clearly misguided fascination with the beautiful and flamboyant woman with whom she had then been traveling. Seeing him once again on the Ponte Vecchio rekindles those feelings.

Now one of Florence's most eminent foreign ladies, Lina, never dreaming that she could be eclipsed by a pretty face twice, invites Theodore to a party and introduces him to Imogene Graham, her beautiful young traveling companion. When Imogene begins taking Theodore's flirtations seriously and he begins flattering himself over his reawakened youthfulness, Lina discreetly—and somewhat angrily—withdraws into the background.

In order to appear liberal to Theodore, Lina consents to attend a rather raucous ball and even permits Imogene to dance. But while Theodore and Imogene linger over their dancing, Effie becomes ill and must be whisked home. The young lovers do not return until late.

Lina is enraged. She intimates to Imogene that Theodore has been trifling with her affections and urges him to leave Florence immediately in order to avert an unwise betrothal. When her plans miscarry and they become engaged, Lina again withdraws into the background for a time. A carriage accident changes everyone's expectations. Theodore is injured, and Lina takes it upon herself to nurse him back to health.

When Theodore recovers, Lina tells him that his engagement has been broken. Theodore now declares his love for her. She says it is too late for them to marry but then relents, not because of her own love but because Effie needs a father figure. Punctilious to the end, Lina remains incapable of performing an action in which her own interests come first.

Bowers, Bowie A. *Thieves Like Us.* Edward Anderson. 1974.

At the age of twenty-seven, Bowie A. Bowers has spent the last third of his life in an Oklahoma prison. Convicted of killing a storekeeper in a robbery attempt, he was given the death penalty; when this is later commuted to a life sentence, Bowie—already superstitious—believes he has "nine lives" to live. But his superstitions ultimately prove false when his plan to escape from prison with his two friends Chicamaw and T-Dub leads him to the girl with whom he falls in love and for whom he tries to abandon his dangerous life of crime.

A model prisoner, Bowie plays on the prison baseball team and gets along well with the warden, whom he genuinely likes. When he escapes, Bowie secretly plans to give himself up after he, Chicamaw, and T-Dub rob a bank. He figures he can send the money to his mother and that the warden will go easy on him and let him out for good in a few years. T-Dub and Chicamaw, whose plans are less beneficent, admire Bowie's proficiency as a criminal but are slightly amused by the cracked innocence of this superstitious country boy.

The three men seek refuge at the home of Chicamaw's cousin, Dee Mobley, who owns a small gas station. Dee's wife has run away, leaving only his daughter Keechie, a mysterious girl in her early twenties who seems never to have been away from the gas station. Chicamaw and T-Dub say that Keechie is stuck-up, but Bowie feels differently.

In Zelton, Texas, Bowie and his friends rob a bank and make off with a much greater haul than they had expected—nearly $22,000 apiece. Bowie realizes he won't be turning himself in to the warden after all. He buys some new clothes and goes out on the town, but when a hotel porter asks him if he's looking for a nice lady friend for the night, Bowie brushes him off. He is thinking instead about Keechie Mobley and wondering what she would look like all dressed up in finery. He buys her a wristwatch with six diamonds on the band. Then he asks himself what a girl like Keechie would want with a thief like him.

The three men part temporarily; T-Dub goes to Houston, and Bowie and Chicamaw drive to Dallas in separate cars. But Bowie gets into an accident on the way. Chicamaw, who is behind him, stops his car and tries to rescue Bowie and the money. Police cars and ambulances arrive, and there is chaotic gunplay as Chicamaw pushes Bowie into his car and speeds off—in the direction of Dee Mobley's gas station.

Chicamaw leaves Bowie in Keechie's care, and in the few days they spend together, Bowie and Keechie fall in love. Bowie finds in Keechie a perfect match. She seems to have lived a long time, yet she is strangely innocent and unworldly. Bowie's screwy superstitious thoughts vanish when Keechie is in the room, and he knows he would stay in that room forever if it were not for the pressure to meet up again with Chicamaw and T-Dub. Then one day Bowie reads in a newspaper that a cop was killed at the scene of his accident. Knowing they are in danger, he and Keechie hit the road.

Bowie and Keechie attempt to make a home for themselves in various motel rooms, cheap apartments, and boardinghouses. When Bowie takes a paternal liking to a young boy at a motor court, Keechie says that maybe he would like to have a child, but he vehemently denies it. A few months later Keechie gets sick, and Bowie is afraid she is going to die. He begs her to leave him behind, but she says that if she lost him, she would have nowhere to go. Finally they learn that Keechie is pregnant and must remain in bed. Bowie resolves to stay by her always, but when he learns that Chicamaw has been arrested and taken to a brutal work camp, he knows he must rescue him. Keechie protests, but Bowie remains loyal to his old friends.

The rescue mission is successful enough to get Chicamaw a few miles down the road, but when Chicamaw insults Keechie, Bowie throws him out of the car and wonders why he ever left Keechie's side. He wants to get back to her as fast as he can, and for the first time in his life he prays, wanting only to be at her bedside when she wakes up.

Bowie makes it back to their motel room, where he gently greets Keechie and assures her he will never leave her. As he goes into the kitchen to get her a strawberry soda, he hears a voice saying "Don't let a move out of you." "Cat with seven lives," Bowie thinks, and he draws his gun. It is too late. A group of policemen open fire on Bowie and Keechie, killing them both.

Bowman, R. J. "Death of a Travelling Salesman." Eudora Welty. 1936.

R. J. Bowman is back on the road selling shoes after a severe bout with the flu. It's a winter day but the sun is high and hot, and Bowman is lost and feeling angry and helpless. As he drives along he starts to reflect on his fourteen years as a traveling shoe salesman in Mississippi. Bowman never missed a day of work until the recent illness that took him off the road. Now he finds himself questioning everything he has gained. Despite his success at moving up the ladder, making more money and staying in better and better hotels, he feels as if his life is tinged with loneliness and emptiness.

Driving along, Bowman finally has to admit that he has lost his way, but he is afraid to stop and ask for directions. He comes to the end of a wooded road and realizes that the road drops into a ditch and that he won't be able to stop the car in time. He slows down just enough to grab his bags and get out of the car before it goes over, then turns around and walks back to a house on a hill.

Bowman is greeted at the house by a reserved old woman. He explains his predicament, and the woman replies that Sonny will be back soon to help him. Assuming that Sonny is the woman's boy, Bowman settles down to wait for his return, but he begins to feel something strange. He is struck by an inexplicable desire to express to the woman somehow that he has felt real loneliness for the first time in his life and to communicate to her his longing to experience a connection with another person. Still, he remains silent, unable to speak.

The afternoon grows long. At last Sonny comes home, and the woman tells him about Bowman's car. Sonny confidently assures Bowman that with the help of his mule he'll have the car out of the ditch in no time. Once again Bowman and the woman wait. This time Bowman feels a desire to embrace the woman, thinking that as he looks at her she is growing "old and shapeless."

They wait a long time, and it gets dark before Sonny returns. Understanding that he will have to return to the car and to the dark, Bowman suddenly senses a warmth and unity in the house that he cannot share, although he would desperately like to do so. He tells the two that he is still recovering from being sick and cannot go back to his car, that he must stay.

Sonny goes to a neighbor's to get "fire," a burning torch to get their own fire going, despite Bowman's offer of matches. Bowman and the woman again wait in the dark until Sonny returns, and the woman sets about preparing supper. It is not until the meal is ready and the woman smiles at the two men, inviting them to eat, that Bowman sees from the youth and light in her face that she is not Sonny's mother at all; she is in fact quite young and must

be Sonny's wife. Sonny tells him that she's pregnant. Bowman is overwhelmed by this sudden transformation of the scene. What he had thought was mysterious and "remote" about the house is really only the usual privacy of a couple, "the ancient communication between two people." In a flash of comprehension he sees the mundane meaning of the place, not anything strange or wonderful, not anything that relates to the deep need and emptiness in his own life.

After dinner Bowman lies down on the floor before the fire to sleep, but he cannot calm his turbulent emotions or stop thinking about the unborn child and wishing it were his. He gets up, leaving money for all the couple has done for him, and retreats into the dark to find his car.

Boyce, Selina. *Brown Girl, Brownstones.* Paule Marshall. 1959.

Selina Boyce is the youngest child of two Barbadian immigrants, Silla and Deighton Boyce. During the course of the novel Selina struggles to forge her identity against the confusing backdrop of Brooklyn before, during, and immediately after World War II. The combined forces of racism in society and her mother's ruthless pursuit of the American dream of home ownership disgust Selina, but they cannot thwart her in her determination to achieve an education and independence.

The Boyce family lives in a brownstone rented from a white family that has left the Fulton Street area in Brooklyn, perhaps in flight from the "dark sea" of Barbadian immigrants. As Silla notes in heated discussions with both family and friends, however, many of these immigrants have already managed to purchase their homes, and she plans to join their ranks.

After word arrives from Barbados that Deighton has inherited land from his sister, Silla plans to use the land as leverage to buy her brownstone. Selina, appalled at her mother's plan, informs her father that Silla is going to sell his land. Deighton does not believe his daughter, and for a time the matter is dropped.

As Deighton continues his desultory study of accounting through a correspondence course, Silla leaves her job as a domestic worker for a more lucrative position in a defense plant. Concerned about her parents, Selina turns to Miss Thompson, an African American from the South. Miss Thompson helps Selina grapple with the oddities of the adult world and at the same time educates her about racism in the United States.

In the meantime, Silla, through forgery and deception, manages to convince Deighton's sister in Barbados that he wants to sell the land to use the money. Accordingly, a money order in excess of $900 arrives. But Deighton manages to cash it and spend it all before Silla can find a way to stop him. As a result of this shopping trip, an amazed Selina becomes the happy, if uneasy, recipient of several fine dresses and a new coat.

Silla vows revenge when she finds out what Deighton has done. Additionally, as word of Deighton's folly spreads through the Barbadian community, he is completely shunned. Shortly afterward he is injured in an accident and is hospitalized. Following his return home—and much to Selina's horror—Deighton becomes involved in a new religion and withdraws completely from his family.

Silla gets her revenge when she turns Deighton in as an illegal alien. He is deported to Barbados but dies, either by accident or suicide, within sight of the Barbadian coast. Selina's grief solidifies her rage against her mother, who by now has managed to purchase her brownstone with the aid of a loan shark.

The next few years witness Selina's entrance into college. She becomes romantically involved with a sometime artist, Clive Springer, who is an apathetic veteran of the war. This relationship crumbles once Selina rejects Clive in favor of her own independence. The novel ends as Selina, after one last argument with Silla, leaves her mother's home in order to establish herself in her own life and career.

Boyer, J. *The Coquette;* or, *The Life and Letters of Eliza Wharton.* Hannah Foster. 1797.

J. Boyer is one of two suitors competing for the hand of the coquettish ELIZA WHARTON. Set in New England in the late eighteenth century and epistolary in form, this sentimental novel tells the tragic story of Eliza's inability to choose between the two men and of her subsequent fall from grace, which leads ultimately to her untimely death.

Boyer is a serious young cleric who meets the vivacious Eliza when she is visiting relations after the death of her fiancé, a dispassionate clergyman who was chosen by Eliza's family to be her betrothed. He is immediately entranced by her and determines to win her love and her hand in marriage. Elated to be free from what would have been a miserable marriage to Mr. Haly but wary of entering into the stifling existence she would lead as a cleric's wife, Eliza hesitates. Frustrated but nevertheless undaunted, Boyer leaves for several months of religious instruction, after first securing Eliza's promise to write to him while he is away.

In the meantime, Boyer's rival, the roguish MAJOR PETER SANFORD, has begun courting Eliza. Secretly in financial straits, Sanford knows that he will not marry her because she does not possess the fortune he desires, yet he is driven by the challenge Boyer presents and pursues Eliza fervently.

When Boyer returns, he presses Eliza for an answer to his proposal. Determined to please her family and friends, who approve of Boyer, she resolves to accept his offer. But when Eliza meets with Sanford to inform him of her decision, Boyer discovers the two and believes that he has

been betrayed by Eliza's coquetry. Refusing to hear her side of the story, he storms away and then ends their relationship with a letter condemning her behavior.

Boyer's actions have a devastating effect on Eliza. She becomes despondent and her health fails. Several months later she writes to him begging his forgiveness. Boyer responds with a cruelly condescending letter delineating her faults and informing her of his engagement to another woman. In a state of deep despair, Eliza then succumbs to the seductions of Sanford, who has by this time married a wealthy woman and returned to town. When it becomes obvious that Eliza is carrying Sanford's child, she takes up residence in Danvers, Massachusetts; there, after a stillbirth, she dies alone, still repenting her hesitation concerning Boyer and her subsequent fall from virtue.

Bradley, James ''Brad.'' ''Duel with the Clock.'' Junius Edwards. 1967.

James Bradley, known primarily as Brad, faces the horror of witnessing a sudden death. He and his army buddy Walter, who is a medic, sneak away from their barracks in order to get some heroin. It has been determined that this is the day Brad will graduate from smoking heroin to shooting it into his veins. But Walt takes the first dose and overdoses; he dies almost instantly in front of the stunned eighteen-year-old Brad. As soon as he can manage it, Brad runs back to his barracks, where he sits frantically warding off the escalating craving for the drug and the panic he feels at the suddenness and finality of Walt's death.

All Brad can think of at first is the odd lack of comfort in all his years of church-going. Then his thoughts angrily turn to Walter who as a medic should have known better than to overdose; on the other hand, Brad reasons that Walt, and death itself, spared him the same pain—for it was belatedly decided that Walt would go first. This realization brings him little relief, however; he still wants some heroin.

After a while another soldier comes in and sees Brad sprawled dejectedly across his bunk. This soldier, Doc, notes Brad's condition and suggests that the young man accompany him up the hill where there is a house of prostitution that services the soldiers when they have their weekend or evening passes. Brad is in no mood for a sexual encounter, and he abruptly shrugs off the invitation, claiming that he is ill. This works, and the soldier goes off, presumably to visit the prostitutes. But Brad is not left alone: Sergeant Eaton appears and immediately approaches him.

Sergeant Eaton is not one of Brad's favorites, but as a superior officer he must be treated with a measure of respect and deference. Eaton offers to issue him a pass for the evening, but Brad declines the offer, again citing his sickness. Eaton is not that readily dissuaded; he moves closer to Brad, and, touching his thigh, invites him back to his room. Eaton first offers food and then drinks, but

Brad knows that Eaton is actually pursuing him sexually; he refuses outright to have anything to do with the sergeant. Eventually, after Brad's anger becomes overt, Eaton warns him to be careful and again insists that he take a pass for the evening or go to the dispensary. Brad allows the sergeant to leave a pass on the pillow but does not respond any further.

After Eaton leaves, Brad is even more dejected than before; his body is increasingly racked with withdrawal pains, but his mind remains focused on Walt's death. He realizes that he must not go out of the barracks that evening, for the body remains undiscovered as yet, and if an investigation follows, Brad now has at least two witnesses who can acknowledge that he was not out that night—that he was in fact ill.

Meanwhile, as Brad lies on his bunk, the pass itself becomes a source of great temptation, and it seems to grow before his eyes, becoming bigger and whiter with each passing moment. Finally, overcome by the temptation to seek some heroin and escape, Brad seizes the pass and crumples it up in his fist before allowing it to fall to the floor. As the story ends, Brad remains on his bunk, the pass momentarily forgotten, as he sobs violently, alone.

Brainard, Erastus. *The Cliff-Dwellers.* Henry B. Fuller. 1893.

Erastus Brainard, owner of the Underground National Bank, is a powerful figure in late-nineteenth-century Chicago. A gruff man with few friends or social acquaintances, Brainard makes his presence felt by whatever means are at his disposal.

Brainard is interested in social climbing and is indifferent to domestic affairs; his time is occupied with his many business concerns throughout the Midwest. His empire was not built on honest foundations, however. As a young man he was associated with a railroad and later made shrewd deals in the streetcar field. He is widely suspected of having manipulated city councils and state legislatures in order to further his schemes. A man believed to have served time in prison, Erastus Brainard is not hesitant to take advantage of widows and other gullible investors.

Although he is indifferent to his family, he does take a simpleminded position on family matters that come to his attention. For example, when he learns that his younger son Marcus wants to be an artist, he refuses to allow any artistic schooling and essentially banishes him from the family. When his daughter Mary marries a shiftless swindler named Russell Vibert, he is unyielding in his opposition, even going as far as barring Mary and her new baby from the Brainard house when Vibert deserts her.

Brainard's grim and businesslike facade is not entirely impregnable, however. When his older son Burt marries a secretary, Cornelia McNabb, Brainard is cowed by Cornelia's utter lack of fear of him. Eventually he softens his position toward Mary and allows her to move back home, although he stipulates that the baby must be kept out of his sight. But reconciliation cannot be achieved with Marcus, who takes to drink and bad company. One night Marcus, drunk and enraged at his father, returns home and stabs Brainard, who dies the next day.

Brand, Ethan. "Ethan Brand." Nathaniel Hawthorne. 1852.

The bizarre and mysterious Ethan Brand is given to the contemplation of intense and complicated metaphysical questions. While carrying out the duties of his profession of lime-burning by stoking a huge kiln that burns marble until it is metamorphosed into lime, Ethan spends hours probing his mind.

Ethan's originally sympathetic and humanitarian concern with the hearts and souls of his fellow human beings leads him to be interested in the guilt and sorrow that plague his neighbors and himself. In his effort to explore the deepest recesses of the human heart, his intellect performs amazing feats of insight that surpass even the sophistication achieved by the most erudite philosophers and scholars. Although he initially prays that he will be thwarted in his effort to discover the Unpardonable Sin, he becomes increasingly obsessed with his conviction that somewhere, lodged in the heart of some malicious malefactor, absolute evil lies waiting for him to uncover its wicked head. As he travels in search of the ultimate sin, he becomes more and more ruthless because his heart is unable to keep pace with the incredible power of his intellect.

Finally, Ethan's heart withers completely and is destroyed, and nothing stands in the way of his manipulating people like puppets in order to force them into performing horrific deeds that he studies with a fiendish alacrity. After eighteen years of increasingly demented cruelty, he succeeds in discovering the Unpardonable Sin in himself and, his goal reached, he returns to the site of his original conception of his quest, the limekiln.

In his absence Ethan's kiln had been taken over by a strong, hardworking man named Bartram and his sensitive son. The boy is frightened one evening by the sound of the bitter, scornful laugh of a slightly insane man who approaches the limekiln and informs the uneasy father and son that he is Ethan Brand, a man who is legendary in the community. Amazed at the sight and strange behavior of Ethan, Bartram dispatches his son to the village tavern to inform the customers there of the return of the man who is said to have conversed with Satan himself.

A small group of derelict men who have nothing better to do than loiter around the pub appear and greet Ethan, but he castigates them, calling them brutes whose unsavory characters are little better than his own. The silly spectacle of an old dog chasing his own tail temporarily relieves some of the tension in the gathering crowd until

Ethan, concluding that the dog's futile efforts are somehow analogous to his own useless life, lets loose another of his awful, disillusioned laughs. Terrified by the sound, the company disperses for the night, leaving the weird man alone with his diabolical thoughts. When Bartram and Joe awaken the following morning and check the fire in the limekiln, they find that Ethan has committed suicide by throwing himself into the blaze. All that remains of him is his skeleton, which has been converted into lime and houses the shape of a human heart, which Bartram speculates must have been made not of flesh and blood but of hard, unyielding marble.

Bras-Coupé. *The Grandissimes.* George Washington Cable. 1879.

Bras-Coupé is a prince of the Jaloff Nation of Africa before his tragic abduction into slavery. Bras-Coupé's name, which means "Arm-Cut-Off," refers to the maiming of his spear-throwing arm. Though Bras-Coupé does adapt to plantation life temporarily to become the most valuable slave on Don José Martinez's Louisiana estate, the fetters of slavery rankle his indomitable spirit.

Having survived the atrocities of passage across the Atlantic on the slave ship *Egalité*, Bras-Coupé is initially pleased by his reception at Don José Martinez's plantation, La Renaissance. He receives what he considers the gifts of clean clothes and a whitewashed log cabin that is more impressive than his palace in Africa had been. But when the foreman of the plantation escorts him into the fields and places a hoe in his hands, Bras-Coupé goes wild, killing the foreman and wounding several Congo field hands. Breaking into a run for freedom, he is shot by the overseer of the plantation. According to legend, the bullet hit his forehead but, finding no vulnerable spot, shot back out of the hole through which it had entered. Finally, Bras-Coupé is subdued and chained. When Don José confronts him concerning this incident, he is so impressed with the African prince's dignified gaze and courageous strength that he decides not to punish him. Instead, Don José arranges for an interpreter who speaks Bras-Coupé's language to endeavor to pacify him so that he will agree to serve in some capacity at La Renaissance.

Upon the arrival of the translator, Palmyre la Philosophe, a gorgeous octoroon voodoo woman whose spirit is as invincible as Bras-Coupé's own, he becomes immediately entranced and acquiesces to almost every demand expected of a slave. He agrees to become an overseer of slaves on the condition that he be allowed to marry Palmyre la Philosophe after six months of service, despite her unwillingness to enter into such a union. Bras-Coupé performs so well as a driver of slaves that he is promoted to the position of gamekeeper long before his period of probation has ended. On the appointed day he is married to Palmyre. At the wedding reception, Bras-Coupé becomes inebriated and strikes Don José when his demand for more wine is not honored. Before fleeing to the swamp to escape death, which is the *Code Noir* punishment for a slave who raises his hand against his master, Bras-Coupé pronounces a voodoo malediction against La Renaissance.

The curse causes devastation throughout the plantation: Worms devour the indigo crop in a single night; the slave population is decimated by fever; and Don José himself eventually succumbs to the voodoo plague. While Don José is on his deathbed, the Spanish police finally capture Bras-Coupé and proceed to cut off his ears, sever the tendons behind his knees, and whip him. Having been transported back to La Renaissance, he awaits death with silent dignity. Meanwhile, Don José dies, asking with his last breath that Bras-Coupé forgive him for the abuse he has suffered at his hands. Noble until the end, Bras-Coupé lifts the curse he had placed on La Renaissance. With an ecstatic smile and an upward gaze, he utters a final, hopeful phrase—"To Africa"—and dies.

Brave Orchid. *The Woman Warrior: Memoirs of a Girlhood Among Ghosts.* Maxine Hong Kingston. 1976.

Brave Orchid fled to America from China during the Communist Revolution. She had gone to medical school during the era of Sun Yat-sen and become a doctor in a small village where the killing of female babies, as in all of China, was routine. In America, however, Brave Orchid does not have the necessary schooling to be a surgeon and must settle for working in her husband's laundry and looking after their children.

Although Brave Orchid never complains explicitly about being underemployed, the stories she tells her daughter, the novel's unnamed narrator, convey that she is torn between traditional Chinese views of the female in society and the career opportunities that are opening up for women in post–World War II America.

The most harrowing of Brave Orchid's stories concerns an aunt who committed adultery while her husband was working in America, at the "Gold Mountain," to pay for her passage from China. According to Brave Orchid, her sister-in-law got pregnant in 1924 and refused to reveal her lover. As punishment for upsetting the social standards of their small village, the family home was ransacked and the animals were killed the night this aunt gave birth. She was found the next day in a well, having drowned her baby and committed suicide. Brave Orchid's American daughters detest this story because it suggests that a Chinese woman will be responsible for all transgressions and pay the hardest price. The narrator in particular does not want to become a "ghost" like her aunt, who is never mentioned by Brave Orchid's husband.

Not all of Brave Orchid's stories suggest that a proper Chinese girl should be passive and accepting of her subservient role. One of the narrator's favorite tales is a legend about a Chinese girl who leaves her family and village to become a warrior. She learns the martial arts, starts an army, and fights to avenge her plundered village.

As her children are getting older, Brave Orchid begins to question her role as a quiet, obedient woman. She pays for Moon Orchid, a sister she hasn't seen in thirty years, to move to America. The two then pursue Moon Orchid's husband, who has become a successful doctor in Los Angeles and married a pretty nurse. Moon Orchid's husband does not want his American life disrupted but agrees to support Moon Orchid and her daughter.

Brave Orchid's daily life continues to be consumed by the strenuous demands of the laundry and the attitudes of her Chinese customers. She urges her daughters to marry and lets their suitors work in the laundry. Her daughters insist, however, that they do not feel compelled to marry in order to gain respect and a place in the world. The youngest, in particular, lets it be known that she will not allow herself to become trapped in a traditional Chinese marriage. Though shocked by her daughter's outburst, Brave Orchid realizes that she has experienced similar doubts, and resolves not to stand in the way of her children's American opportunities.

Breckinridge, Myra. *Myra Breckinridge.* Gore Vidal. 1968.

Myra Breckinridge is the physically attractive and sexually perverted narrator of this novel. Claiming to entertain a life's dream of vindicating women by liberating them from the bondage of the overbearing phallus, Myra is convinced that her larger-than-life stature will enable her to completely revamp the balance of power between the sexes. She believes she may thereby rescue the world from the total annihilation that threatens the self-destructive human race.

A film buff since she was a child, Myra is thrilled to move to Hollywood from New York City on the supposed death of her homosexual husband, Myron Breckinridge. On her arrival in California, Myra looks up her husband's uncle, Buck Loner, who made his fame as a cowboy singer and actor and is in the process of making his fortune by running the Academy of Drama and Modeling, which is located just outside Hollywood on land that Buck and Myron's mother Gertrude inherited from their father. Myra approaches Buck to demand that he grant her Myron's rightful share of the estate. Averse to giving up any portion of his fortune to Myra, Buck hires lawyers who attempt to prove that Myra and Myron were never legally married.

Having been offered a job at the academy by her uncle-in-law who wants her safely nearby, Myra embarks on a career as a teacher of posture and empathy. She revels in her new position because it affords her access to good-looking young men whom she would like to humiliate and tame through both mental and physical abuse. In the class-

room Myra brutally insults her students, who masochistically flock to her lectures.

The climax of Myra's career at the academy occurs when she successfully completes her tyrannical assault on Rusty Godowsky, an extremely handsome young man. In her role as a dedicated but perverted gender vigilante, Myra hopes to destroy the cocky Rusty's aggressive masculinity. Having hoodwinked Rusty's girlfriend, Mary-Ann Pringle, into thinking that she is an ally, Myra launches her campaign against Rusty by insulting his performance in posture class. Myra painstakingly continues to terrorize the young man until his male superiority complex is finally broken. Because he believes Myra has connections that will help him become a movie star, Rusty agrees to allow Myra to subject him to a bizarre medical examination. Having performed a series of degrading violations of privacy on the aspiring actor, Myra culminates the sadistic session by brutally raping Rusty with a huge dildo she has strapped to her waist.

Adding insult to Rusty's injury, Myra entices Mary-Ann into a close friendship that ends in marriage when the young woman discovers that Myra is in fact Myron Breckinridge, a man who, through the use of hormones, has been living as a woman. Reciprocating Mary-Ann's love, she decides to adopt the gender identity of the male once again, and Myra/Myron Breckinridge settles down to a quiet life with Mary-Ann in the San Fernando Valley where he makes his living as a screenwriter for ABC, practices Christian Science, and works for Planned Parenthood.

Breedlove, Cholly. *The Bluest Eye.* Toni Morrison. 1970.

Cholly Breedlove is PECOLA BREEDLOVE's father and rapist in this novel of African-American life set in Ohio. Cruel, tortured, and violent, he represents the far-reaching and degrading legacy of slave culture in the United States.

Left at four days old on a junk heap in rural Georgia by his mentally impaired mother, Cholly is raised by his great-aunt Jimmy. He goes to school for six years and then works as a shop boy in a local feed and grain store until his aunt dies. At the banquet after her funeral, Cholly has his first sexual encounter with a girl named Darlene. Two white men interrupt the lovers, aim guns and flashlights at Cholly's buttocks, and threaten to shoot him if he stops. Powerless as a black adolescent, Cholly directs his anger not at the white men but at Darlene instead.

Alone after his aunt's death and fearing Darlene because she knows of his humiliation, Cholly makes his way to the city of Macon with the hope of finding Samson Fuller, the man his aunt had suspected of being his father. He discovers Fuller in an alley playing craps but, suddenly terrified, cannot force his mouth to shape words. Fuller assumes that Cholly is his son by another woman and, yelling, forces him away.

For years Cholly is continually on the move. Young and attractive, he has no responsibilities but also nothing permanent. He then meets, marries, and has two children with PAULINE WILLIAMS (BREEDLOVE). The abrupt end to the variety in his life that marriage and a family bring also kills the freedom of his imagination. He takes refuge in alcohol and begins the violent fights with his wife that will characterize the rest of his life.

On a spring day, Cholly comes drunkenly into the kitchen where his eleven-year-old daughter Pecola stands washing dishes. Seeing her bent, defeated shoulders and her lifted foot scratching her bare calf, he recalls his first meeting with his wife. Unlike the happiness that he could bring Pauline and other women when he was young, he realizes that he is now unable to help his daughter. Despondent and drunk, he reaches to caress the girl and offers her the only kind of intimacy he knows: sex. He rapes her, impregnates her, and, ultimately, destroys her sanity. Cholly dies in a workhouse, a miserable, broken man.

Breedlove, Pauline Williams. *The Bluest Eye.* Toni Morrison. 1970.

Pauline Breedlove, the mother of PECOLA (BREEDLOVE) is the ninth of eleven children born to Ada and Fowler Williams in rural Alabama at the turn of the century. At the age of two a rusty nail impaled Pauline's foot, leaving her with a twisted limb. For the rest of her life Pauline believes her foot to be a deformity which no one can see past.

After the beginning of World War I, Pauline moves with her family to a town in Kentucky where, having finished with schooling after only four years, she has the opportunity to indulge her love of ordering and arranging the family home. One hot summer day CHOLLY BREEDLOVE comes upon her dreamily leaning against a fence and kneels to tickle her injured foot. Throughout the courtship that ensues, Pauline feels that Cholly alone considers her foot an endearing quality.

Once married, the naive, country-bred Pauline moves north with Cholly to urban Lorain, Ohio, where she finds it difficult to adjust to the ways of northerners. She relies on Cholly as her only human contact, and in time he comes to resent her dependence. They begin to argue as she stumbles in her attempts to assimilate. Learning of these ever more frequent battles, one of the white women for whom Pauline works as a maid attempts to "help" her by withholding Pauline's wages until she agrees to leave Cholly.

Yet Pauline sticks by her husband, and when she becomes pregnant with her first child, Sammy, her marriage grows more peaceful. She returns to her own housework, and Cholly is once again attentive. Pauline also begins to go to movies and there falls victim to the ideals of romantic love and physical beauty depicted on the screen. She sits contentedly in a theater eating candy and trying to look like Jean Harlow. When one of her front teeth falls out, she becomes despondent and eventually ceases to care about her life, her marriage, and, in time, her family.

Pauline Breedlove goes back to work when Sammy and her second child, Pecola, are still young. She becomes a cold, intimidating woman, so much so that even her children call her "Mrs. Breedlove." She no longer loses herself in dreams and romantic fantasies but instead works to support her children and husband. Emotionally she depends on her family, particularly during her violent fights with Cholly, to distinguish her monotonous days from one another. Also, these brutal quarrels with an alcoholic husband help her maintain the sense that she is a responsible Christian woman implementing God's will by punishing a sinning man.

Pauline's work in the homes of white folks fulfills her desire for order and control. She elevates these homes—with their thick shag carpets muffling the sound of her injured walk and their families' cute, blond children—over her own home and black family. In these homes, for the first time in her life, Pauline Breedlove receives a nickname: Polly.

Breedlove, Pecola. *The Bluest Eye.* Toni Morrison. 1970.

Pecola Breedlove is an eleven-year-old black girl who yearns for her share of the adoration adults and children alike pay to "pretty" white girls. She believes that if she had the blue eyes of "cute" white children, the misery of her life would miraculously disappear. The boys and girls in her school would no longer jeer at her ugliness; her parents would stop their ritualized, brutal fights. Each night, therefore, she fervently prays to God for the blue eyes that would transform her world.

With her brother Sammy and her parents, PAULINE WILLIAMS (BREEDLOVE) and CHOLLY (BREEDLOVE), Pecola lives in the two poorly furnished front rooms of an abandoned storefront in Lorain, Ohio. Three prostitutes, the bane of the town's stiff-backed Christian women's existence, live and work in the apartment above them. Pecola visits the prostitutes often, running their errands and listening attentively to their stories. Because they do not despise her, she loves them.

When Pecola's alcoholic father Cholly burns the Breedloves' home and once again beats his wife, the state places Pecola in the home of schoolmates Claudia and Frieda MacTeer and their family. Pecola's rapturous preoccupation with blue eyes becomes markedly apparent during her stay. In particular, she takes every opportunity to drink milk from the MacTeers' Shirley Temple glass. While living with the MacTeers, Pecola has her first period and is told that she can now have babies.

Claudia and Frieda remain friends with Pecola even after she returns home. They defend her from the attacks of the schoolboys who circle her chanting malicious taunts, and together the three girls stand up against the "cute" Maureen Peal when she, too, turns on Pecola. They are with Pecola when her mother rejects her for the little white girl of her employers. Claudia and Frieda cannot help Pecola overcome her feelings of profound ugliness, however.

On a Saturday afternoon in the spring, as Pecola washes dishes, Cholly returns drunk to their storefront apartment. With alcohol-induced clarity, he recognizes his inability to alleviate the pain of Pecola's hopeless life. In a twisted effort to offer her the only expressions of love and tenderness he knows, Cholly rapes his daughter. Later, pregnant with her father's child, Pecola turns to the town charlatan, Soaphead Church, and asks him to grant her wish for blue eyes. When he realizes his inability to help, Soaphead Church decides to tell Pecola that her wish will be granted. She believes him and sees in her mirrored reflection the bluest eyes. Her child is stillborn, and Pecola is now insane.

Breen, Bill. "The Man in the Brooks Brothers Shirt." Mary McCarthy. 1941.

Bill Breen, a forty-one-year-old steel industry executive and a resident of Cleveland, orders custom-made Brooks Brothers shirts by the dozen. He is a bland-looking, graying man with a nasal Midwest accent and political views that coincide with his conservative attire. Having earned a B.A. in chemistry in 1917 at a state university, he wanted to teach science on the high school level and perhaps pursue an M.A., but his plans were foiled when he was drafted to serve in the cavalry of the U.S. Army. Cherishing his period of service as one of the highlights of his lifetime, Bill orders Brooks Brothers shirts with an emblem in the shape of the number two that signifies his membership in an officer's club comprised of his best war buddies.

After a brilliant and decorated career as an army captain, Bill returned to the United States and took advantage of newfound connections to join a steel company where he first worked as a metallurgist and then, thanks to his amiability and charisma, as the chief purchasing agent and vice-president of the company. He devoted his evenings to handball at the local athletic club. Having nearly married a worldly Vassar graduate named Eleanor, he finally marries a more conservative woman named Leonie, with whom he has two sons and a daughter. A frequent traveler due to his executive duties, Bill learns to pass the long hours spent on trains by befriending interesting-looking people who are willing to provide entertainment in the form of recounting their life stories. In the case of the story's unnamed PROTAGONIST, a more elaborate species of interaction is achieved.

Having jokingly introduced himself as a lowly traveling salesman in approaching the attractive young woman, Bill finds that his ruse is successful and convinces her to join him for highballs in his private berth. Cocktails lead to lunch and eventually dinner as they continue to converse, and he finds himself divulging political views that he hides even from his wife, despite the fact that he disapproves of the liberal politics of his more Bohemian companion. Having plied the young woman with cocktails, Bill proceeds to seduce her in his preferred manner, which includes the accompaniment of various four-letter words and a barrage of blows to her buttocks at the height of his passion. The following morning Bill succeeds in assuaging the woman's guilt and humiliation for another day of conversation and sexual intercourse, fantasizing about their future together. But although he has succeeded in extracting an appreciation and disrupting her plans to remarry a man she had met in New York, the woman nevertheless detrains in Sacramento. When they see each other on a couple of subsequent occasions, it is clear that their brief sexual liaison has been terminated, although his memories of this glorious encounter continue to sustain his fantasy life.

Brent, Robert. *Susan Lenox: Her Fall and Rise.* David Graham Phillips. 1917.

Robert Brent, an enigmatic New York playwright, is the only man to offer SUSAN LENOX an opportunity for genuine emancipation. He does not demand marriage, sex, or dependence but desires only to nourish Susan's dramatic talents, for he is convinced that she can become a great actress.

By the time Susan arrives in New York, Brent is well established there as a moody genius. He is the rival of her current lover, RODERICK SPENSER, and the better talent in the theater scene. Immaculately attired and possessing exquisite taste, Brent frequents fashionable restaurants and is always surrounded by lively theater people. One evening when he sees Susan at a nearby table, he stares at her unabashedly. When they meet by chance at a theatrical agent's office a few months later, he invites her matter-of-factly to his Park Avenue home. His very presence provokes an aesthetic awakening in Susan, who evaluates her living conditions anew as a result of their meeting. Life with Spenser, Susan concludes, is squalid. Preaching the virtues of individual will and judgment as well as arduous training (he is a success story himself), Brent engages Susan at a good salary as an actress in his plays and even gives a theatrical break to her by-then-estranged lover Spenser who is failing professionally. Although Brent works obsessively with Susan, he dismisses any suggestions of an amorous relationship with great impatience.

When Brent leaves abruptly for Europe, Susan panics and presumes he has dropped the acting project. She becomes the companion of Freddie Palmer, a pimp and slum ganglord, now turned respectable. The two travel first class to Paris where they meet Brent who introduces them to his friends and guides them on matters of taste. Brent and Susan fall in love, although they conceal it from each other with mutual "Parisian" restraint. Enraged with jealousy, Freddie pressures Susan to marry him. Brent, who is critical of the forces within capitalism that force women into dependence, persists in his vision of Susan as a great actress. He refuses to think of her as a mere companion to a rich ruffian and contrives to have her resume her dramatic training.

Brent leaves for New York and arranges for Susan to follow. He is murdered by Freddie's underworld hitmen before she is able to join him. He has willed all his money to Susan. She becomes a brilliant actress, working "as a living incarnation of Brent," whose artistic genius and social conscience she adopts as her own.

Brewton, Colonel James. *The Sea of Grass.* Conrad Richter. 1936.

Uncle Jim Brewton is full of what his nephew HAL calls "that lusty pioneer blood." The "sea" of the novel's title is really the arid Texas range where, before settlers came and the open land of the Southwest was parcelled and fenced, Uncle Jim owned a ranch as big as Massachusetts and Connecticut combined. Uncle Jim, or Colonel Brewton as he is deferentially called by everyone in the neighborhood of Salt Fork, Texas, is a godlike figure at the beginning of Hal's story, a titan who not only holds sway over ranch, cowboys, and cattle but also controls the judicial system and much of the economy of Salt Fork. He seemingly controls the destiny of individuals, too, and arranges to marry LUTIE CAMERON (BREWTON), a beautiful St. Louis woman who is impossibly out of place in the rancher's vast, empty beef empire. He spends his days in the saddle, managing the ranch, and returns at night to Lutie, Lutie's dinner table, her dinner guests, and eventually their three children, Jimmy, Brock, and Sarah Beth.

Uncle Jim's established domestic life is far from secure, however. Waves of settlers, small homesteaders from places like Missouri, steadily encroach. These newcomers are championed by Salt Fork's handsome district attorney, Brice Chamberlin, but universally hated by the cattlemen. To Uncle Jim "the nesters" are a pitiful bunch, too late or too afraid to be real pioneers in an unpeopled wilderness. They are condemned to the cowboy's epitome of degradation, a life of scratching the dirt. But they are the enemy as well; after a few years of good weather, the nesters' fences begin to be seen around Salt Fork and the Brewtons' ranch.

When Lutie leaves him, Uncle Jim withdraws. He continues to work and to struggle against the nesters, but something of his life is gone the moment she, defiant and possibly adulterous, abandons what she has come to consider a form of death: the stultifying boredom and loneliness of a woman's life on the ranch. The children grow up without their mother and barely heeded by their father; Brock grows into a rebellious prodigal and looks more and more like Brice Chamberlin than Brewton. Brock ultimately becomes an outlaw, and Uncle Jim, braving bul-

lets when the sheriff's deputies will not, is the one who subdues the renegade once and for all. Brock, however, is killed.

Lutie returns at last, as silent about her motivation for coming back as she is about her years away. Approaching old age, she and Uncle Jim contentedly sit in their home, gazing out at Brock's tombstone, upon which he orders to be carved that he, James B. Brewton, was Brock's father.

Brewton, Lutie Cameron. *The Sea of Grass.* Conrad Richter. 1936.

Lutie Cameron Brewton's mysterious story, full of suggestion and rumor, is sketchily told by HAL, her husband's nephew. When Hal's narrative begins, Lutie Cameron of St. Louis, Missouri, arrives at a tiny outpost on the "sea of grass," the town of Salt Fork on the edge of the gigantic Texas range. She has come to marry COLONEL JAMES BREWTON, one of the area's biggest cattlemen, owner of the Cross B ranch. Upon arriving in Salt Fork, Lutie sees three strange sights: a murderer who has just been lynched, a rundown encampment of settlers or "nesters," and a trial at which two employees of her future husband are acquitted of a homesteader's murder. She has landed in the middle of an intense struggle between the Southwest's cattlemen, who are determined to keep the range open for grazing, and the inevitable influx of Midwestern settlers, who are determined to homestead and fence their parcels. She has also landed in the middle of nowhere, and when she becomes Mrs. Brewton, she is cooped up in a ranch house surrounded by hundreds of square miles of a burned, brown wasteland.

Lutie does her best to make a happy life for herself on the range. She has the house decorated, she entertains when and whomever she can, and she nightly greets her husband, a taciturn but charismatic giant, when he returns from a day in the saddle. She bears three children, Jimmy, Brock, and Sarah Beth. Eventually she leaves.

Rumor suggests an adulterous assignation with Brice Chamberlin, Salt Fork's handsome district attorney and her husband's chief enemy in the struggle against nesters. In fact, as Brock grows up, he looks a good deal like Brice and little like Colonel Brewton. But Chamberlin doesn't leave Salt Fork when Lutie does; she goes alone to Denver and then to a thousand possible locations and a thousand possible destinies. Hal goes after her for the colonel but cannot find her.

Fifteen years pass before Lutie returns. Her son Brock has become an outlaw; just as she comes back to Salt Fork, he is hunted by a party of deputies and killed by Colonel Brewton. Curiously, she stays with Brewton. It is as if Brock's death had purged her, her husband, or the "sea of grass" of some evil force. But about her mysterious absence—where she was, how she lived, or under what circumstances she returned to the ranch—Lutie never utters a word.

Brice, Stephen. *The Crisis.* Winston Churchill. 1901.

Stephen Brice is a figure of hope for the United States as the nation moves closer to the Civil War. The novel begins with the hero's arrival in St. Louis, Missouri. Although not financially independent, Stephen comes from an aristocratic Boston family. His grandfather had made money in the India trade and once served as ambassador to France. While Stephen does not inherit the family fortune, he does inherit the typical conservative outlook of the New England upper class. He remains stiff and somber until he meets Abraham Lincoln, who inspires him to embrace the abolitionist cause.

Stephen goes to St. Louis to study law with the ardent Judge Silas Whipple, a friend of his deceased father. It is the judge who first introduces Stephen to the anti-slavery movement. At first he distrusts the judge's liberal political stance. Unlike Stephen, Whipple is self-made, eccentric, and somewhat radical. The judge believes that Stephen has natural virtues that have been warped by a society which values property over human happiness.

The judge sends Stephen to meet with Abraham Lincoln so that the young man will be convinced to accept the abolition of slavery as the right and proper course for the nation. Stephen has an almost spiritual experience in his meeting with Lincoln. The judge notices the transformation; the young attorney appears to have been born again in the West. It pleases Whipple how readily Stephen now accepts the abolitionist cause.

Stephen's other concern in St. Louis is his romance with Virginia Carvel, daughter of prominent slave owner Colonel Comyn Carvel. Stephen's competition for her hand materializes in the form of Eliphalet Hooper, the colonel's clerk. Like Stephen, Hooper is from the North, but he is a self-made man and not of aristocratic bearing.

When the Civil War begins, Stephen leaves to fight for the Union. He fights heroically in battle and gets promoted to the rank of major. During the war Stephen meets such important military figures as Ulysses S. Grant and William Sherman. While he is away, Hooper, who now trades on the black market, makes advances on Virginia, which she refuses. Judge Whipple takes ill and dies. The war ends in 1865, and once again Stephen stands face-to-face with Abraham Lincoln, but this time he has Virginia at his side. The two—one from the North, one from the South—plan to marry, as Lincoln hopes that the divided nation itself can reunite.

Bridge, India. *Mr. Bridge; Mrs. Bridge.* Evan S. Connell, Jr. 1969; 1959.

India Bridge, who always felt vaguely that her exotic name did not fit her, is a wife and mother in Kansas City in the era between the two world wars.

India falls in love with and marries Walter Bridge, who becomes a prominent attorney. They have three children: Ruth, who is rebellious; Carolyn, who is more like her mother; and Douglas, whom India is never able to understand. She raises her children with little help from her husband, who is always working, and with the firm conviction that they should be known above all for their manners and socially correct behavior. India teaches them never to use guest towels, to differentiate between a lady, such as herself, and a woman, such as a servant. She gives each girl a girdle on her fourteenth birthday, sees to it that they carry a purse, and decides when her son should begin wearing a hat.

Since she has a cook, a cleaning woman, and a laundress, India's days are filled with the activities of her children and her home. She worries about having tasteful Christmas decorations, attends the correct church, and is a member of the Mission Country Club. She does charity work for the Auxiliary and gives food to the poor at Christmas.

As her children grow older, India's life becomes emptier and more perplexing. Ruth, her eldest daughter, proves to be difficult and leaves her mother mystified when she dresses inappropriately, dates strange men, stays out until dawn, and makes love to her boyfriends on the family sofa. Douglas troubles her with his schoolboy pranks and complete disregard for church, table manners, dress codes, and proper decorum. Only Carolyn remains true to the virtues India has tried to instill in her children.

Although her life is as full as the lives of her friends, India feels "oppressed by the sense that she is waiting." She tries to learn Spanish from records. She follows a vocabulary-building course and takes painting lessons, but with no household obligations and her children nearly grown, her days seem long and monotonous, each one passing exactly like the one before.

The routine of India's life is disrupted when her friend, Grace Barron, a woman as bored as she, suddenly commits suicide. Then a lengthy tour of Europe that she has planned with her husband is cut short by the onset of World War II. She returns home with the conviction that "the world is reeling." Her private world finally crumbles when her husband dies suddenly at his desk one winter afternoon, leaving her to go through the proper motions of grieving and widowhood.

With her husband dead and Douglas away in the army, India realizes that she now weeps more often, that she has lived her entire life for and through her family, and that nothing remains of the time but photo albums. She spends long hours with them in her quiet empty home, reliving happier moments.

Bridge, Walter. *Mr. Bridge; Mrs. Bridge.* Evan S. Connell, Jr. 1969; 1959.

Walter Bridge is an attorney who lives in Kansas City with his wife India (Bridge), and their three children: Ruth, Carolyn, and Douglas. Tall, redheaded, and dignified, Walter has risen from poverty to become the patri-arch of a prominent family in the fashionable Mission Hills district. He belongs to the correct club; he is a member of the correct church, though he seldom attends; and he keeps his conservative stocks and bonds in the correct bank. He loves his wife but is never able to tell her "how deeply he feels her presence." He loves his three children but leaves their rearing to India, interfering only to settle disputes or answer questions regarding science, money, or the use of the car. He works long hours, but because he feels that his life is cut in half "like a melon" and the two halves can never be joined, he seldom brings his work home with him.

Astute and energetic, Walter Bridge is a man of decided attitudes. He keeps a pistol from his service in World War I under his mattress. He has no fondness for Roosevelt, labor unions, communists, people who commit suicide, or progressive educators. Opposed to panhandlers and beggars, he even refuses to be intimidated by a holdup man. His racist attitudes offend two of his three children. He dislikes African Americans and believes they are in a plot to upset the social stability so important to his happiness. Only Harriet, the Bridge's black cook, gets his admiration.

Walter is as staunchly conservative in morals as he is in politics. Horrified when he is erotically aroused by the sight of his sunbathing daughter, he is equally appalled when his legal secretary of twenty-five years, Julia, suddenly declares her love for him. Through all his adult years he remains a faithful husband; his wife is able to count the years of their marriage by the extravagant gifts she receives from him: an ermine coat, a Lincoln, a trip to Europe, and jewelry. He also tries to be a good father. Because he works such long hours, he has little time for his children but occasionally makes an effort to see each one alone and follow his or her progress.

As the children grow older and begin to leave home, Walter has the feeling that the years are "falling over like ducks in a shooting gallery." He takes his wife on a grand tour of Europe but spends much of his time feeling awkward, bored by India's enthusiasm for art galleries and anxious to return to Kansas City. When the Germans invade Poland, their trip is cut short, and they return home.

As a father, Walter Bridge always felt that his children should be "neat, polite, truthful, modest, and adequately educated." They prove to be somewhat disappointing. Ruth, his favorite but the one who always shocks him with her rebellious behavior, becomes part of the Bohemian counter-culture of Greenwich Village, New York. Carolyn begins college but leaves to marry, and Douglas, in the face of impending war, prefers to enlist in the army rather than attend college.

Walter sums up his life one Christmas in church when he realizes that he has been content and even happy at times but "has never known joy." He has always kept his heart condition a secret and dies suddenly at his desk one winter afternoon while speaking into his Dictaphone.

Bridges, Harold "Hal." *The Track of the Cat.* Walter Van Tilburg Clark. 1949.

At nineteen, Harold Bridges is the youngest in a family of six living on a ranch in Virginia sometime during the nineteenth century. He is a kind and considerate son, hard-working, compassionate, calm, and steady. He is in love with Gwen Williams, a girl from a neighboring ranch, and would like to marry her. At the time of the story, Gwen has come for a visit, in part to convince the Bridges that she would be a worthy bride for Harold. The family's reaction to her is mixed. Harold finds himself in veiled competition with his older brother Curt, who is selfish and impetuous, and would like Gwen for his own.

While there is never any question that Gwen prefers Harold, there is some doubt as to which of the sons will inherit the ranch, and Curt would like to prove himself more worthy. To do so, he decides to hunt down a panther that has been killing the Bridges' cattle. At first Harold resists the challenge, preferring to let Curt have his way. Curt goes out in blizzard conditions in order to stalk the panther, who is fabled to be as big as a horse. He takes with him his brother Arthur, the family dreamer, who has already had premonitions about the cat; Harold stays behind with the rest of the family.

When Arthur is killed by the panther, Curt brings the body home and amid the ensuing grief insinuates that, had Harold come, the death would not have occurred. After Curt sets out again, the family tries to come to terms with Arthur's death. Harold builds a coffin and, with Gwen, helps Mrs. Bridges take care of the corpse. Harold must also mediate between Gwen and Mr. Bridges, who has never liked her and thinks her presence has somehow contributed to Arthur's death.

When Curt fails to return after a number of days, Mrs. Bridges convinces Harold to go out looking for him. Curt, meanwhile, has been struggling against the blizzard and has lost his way. He ends up close to home but not close enough. He is hysterical with fear of the cat that he believes is chasing him and falls off a cliff. When Harold finds Curt's body, he sees a prowling cat as well and summarily kills it. He returns home saddened by the deaths of his siblings but somewhat secure in the feeling that he will be able to marry Gwen Williams and preside over the Bridges' ranch.

Brill, Joseph. *The Cannibal Galaxy.* Cynthia Ozick. 1983.

Joseph Brill, the pedantic principal of the Edmond Fleg Primary School, is one of nine children born in Paris to parents of Eastern European background.

While Brill is a youth at the Sorbonne, Rabbi Pult proclaims, "You will be a teacher." Shortly thereafter, World War II begins, and he is taken in by the nuns. They hide him in the cellar of the convent, which is full of books. There, Brill satisfies his voracious appetite for knowledge by reading countless books. He uncovers work written by one Edmond Fleg and finds himself whiling away the days thinking about Fleg and his work. Who was this Fleg? Was he Christian or Jewish?

While hiding in the cellar, Brill declares to himself that if he survives the war, he will fulfill Rabbi Pult's wish: He will become a teacher. When the war ends, he moves briefly to Paris and then sets out for the United States; once there, he settles in the Midwest and finds a wealthy benefactress who is willing to donate money to found a school. He names the school the Edmond Fleg Primary School and institutes the dual curriculum, which combines the classics of the European and Jewish traditions.

As time passes, Brill comes to expect nothing of himself and still less of his teachers and students. As the principal, he presides with contempt for everyone—until he meets Hester Lilt. When the renowned philosopher brings her daughter Beulah to Brill's school, she reawakens his long-dormant intellectual curiosity. Obsessed with winning Hester's approval, he calls her frequently on the telephone, although she gives him no more than token attention. By the conventional measurements of Brill's school, Beulah is a failure, but Hester refuses to accept this evaluation of her daughter, whom she insists is an original. Brill pities Hester's delusion and wonders how such a brilliant woman could have such a lackluster child.

After a candid debate with Hester concerning Beulah's intelligence, Brill commits an impulsive act: In midsemester he replaces Beulah's severe and demanding teacher with a gentle young teacher who lets the students doodle in class. He hopes this change will aid the shy Beulah, but it seems to have no effect on her and only enrages the parents. Beulah graduates inconspicuously, considered unexceptional by her peers and teachers. Hester has been assigned a post in Paris and upon Beulah's graduation, mother and daughter leave for Europe.

Meanwhile, Brill, an aging bachelor, marries his feisty secretary Iris. He is proud of his tall, young wife, although she lacks education and grace. Iris has a child, Albert, from her first marriage. Brill is initially eager to adopt the role of father to Albert but then becomes more tentative as he realizes that Albert is not exceptionally gifted.

Brill and Iris soon produce Naphtali. During her pregnancy, Brill was plagued by doubts about the intelligence of the unborn child; at one point he even hoped for a miscarriage. Naphtali proves to be a clever child, however; he excels under the school's regimen, and even Brill's rigorous demands on his son are satisfied.

One night Brill sees Beulah Lilt on television being touted as one of the most respected and articulate artists of her generation. During an interview, Beulah is asked about her midwestern education, and she scoffs: "I don't think you could exactly call it an education." Brill follows Beulah's career much as he had followed Hester's. Beulah, however, soars to heights her mother never reached. He sees her on a magazine cover, naming her "The Artist of the Year."

Meanwhile, despite Brill's wishes for him to go to the Sorbonne, Naphtali opts for Miami University instead, majoring in business administration. The irony of Naphtali's and Beulah's careers in relation to the Edmond Fleg School's assessment of their abilities does not escape Brill. He questions the educational system he has established. Before retiring, he creates the Joseph Brill Ad Astra Award to be given to the graduate with the most creative potential regardless of class standing.

Broder, Herman. *Enemies.* Isaac Bashevis Singer. 1972.

Herman Broder, a Jewish refugee from Nazi Germany, lives a cautious, cloistered existence in New York in the early 1950s. Herman's nightmares about the past and his dread of the future are exacerbated by his precarious romantic entanglements.

Herman's entire family was killed in the Holocaust. He survived only because Yadwiga, a family servant, had hidden him in a hayloft. When Herman learned after the war that his wife and children had been shot by the Nazis, he married Yadwiga and took her to America. They now live in a small apartment in the Coney Island section of Brooklyn. Yadwiga is completely ignorant of American life; by urging her not to talk to strangers or to answer the telephone, Herman keeps her in the dark. He tells her he is a bookseller who must frequently leave the city on business trips. Actually, his meager income comes from a job writing sermons for Rabbi Lampert, a fraudulent Manhattan rabbi.

When Herman claims to be away on business, he is actually visiting his mistress Masha, a refugee from a concentration camp who lives with her mother in the Bronx. Masha is a high-strung, passionate woman, jealous even of Herman's past lovers, although she has had scores of lovers herself. Herman is sexually obsessed with Masha and fascinated by the twists and turns of her mind. But when she and her mother argue about God's existence, Herman merely sits in the kitchen, idly perusing the Yiddish newspaper. It is while doing so that he accidentally comes upon his own name in a "Personals" column. Yaroslaver, the uncle of Herman's dead wife Tamara, is looking for Herman.

Herman visits Yaroslaver, and the old man greets him saying he has joyous news. Tamara is not dead after all. She is alive and in America. In fact, she is in the next room. Tamara enters. "I didn't know you were alive,"

Herman says. "That's something you never knew," says Tamara. Besides, she says, she is not alive, not really. Herman understands. He, too, feels like one of the dead. Tamara asks Herman about his present life, and he tells her. Two dead people needn't have any secrets from each other.

Meanwhile, Yadwiga is becoming more interested in Judaism. She decides she wants to convert and have Herman's child. Although he has no desire to bring another child into the world, Herman goes to bed with her. Then he leaves for a week in the Adirondacks with Masha, who tells Herman she is pregnant and wants to have the child. She wants to marry Herman in a Jewish ceremony so the child won't be a bastard; Herman, she says, can visit Yadwiga once a week. At first Herman rejects this outlandish plan, but he relents after Masha threatens to have an abortion and never speak to him again.

Herman marries Masha despite the fact that it makes him a polygamist. Then, while spending the night in Brooklyn, he gets a call saying Masha is ill. He rushes to the Bronx and learns that she has been hemorrhaging but will recover and that she is not pregnant after all. A few days later he returns to Brooklyn and learns that Yadwiga is pregnant. In the midst of this chaos, Tamara shows up at his door. She is gentle and kind toward Yadwiga and laughs off Yadwiga's suggestion that she and Herman remarry. She asks Herman how long he thinks he can continue shuttling back and forth between Brooklyn and the Bronx.

The answer comes a few weeks later when Herman and Masha attend a party at Rabbi Lampert's. A guest who has seen Herman with both Yadwiga and Tamara reveals the truth. After arguing with Masha, Herman gets sick and rushes out into the night. With nowhere to turn he calls Tamara, who invites him to her apartment. She tells him that his life is out of control and if he will let her, she will take over, provided he agrees to do whatever she tells him. Exhausted, Herman agrees.

For the next few months Herman achieves a sort of balance. Tamara gets him a job in her uncle's bookstore. She instructs him to look after Yadwiga during her pregnancy. On Passover she, Yadwiga, and Herman have a seder together. Yet Herman can't forget Masha. When she calls in the late spring saying that she is going away forever and wants him to join her, he rushes to her side. But he arrives in the Bronx to find that things are worse than ever. The apartment has been robbed, and Masha's mother is seriously ill. The next day Masha's mother dies, and Masha suggests that she and Herman commit suicide together. Herman agrees, and Masha gets a bottle of pills. Before they take them, she asks Herman if he has been unfaithful with anyone except Yadwiga. He admits he slept with Tamara, but only once. Masha laughs and admits that she slept with her husband a few months ago to get him to finalize their divorce. Suddenly Herman decides he does not want to go through with the suicide. He does

not want to go through with anything anymore. When he sees that Masha can't be talked out of killing herself, he says good-bye and leaves, not for Yadwiga or Tamara but for points unknown.

Brooke, John "Demi." *Little Men.* Louisa May Alcott. 1871.

Like the other "little men" of this novel, John Brooke, an imaginative, frail, and reclusive child, is sent to board at Plumfield, a school for children run by his aunt and uncle, Mrs. and Mr. Bhaer. The boys at Plumfield sometimes affectionately refer to John as "the deacon" because he is so moral and so fond of preaching, but he is usually called "Demi," short for "Demijohn," because his father is also named John.

Demi's parents hope that Plumfield will toughen him up and foster his more practical side, and he surprises them by adapting quickly to life at the school. On visits home he amuses them with such uncharacteristic behavior as slamming doors, stomping around the house in his heavy new boots, and exclaiming, "By George." His twin sister Daisy, who accompanied him to Plumfield, remains as feminine as she was at home. She enjoys cooking, sewing, and caring for her dolls, and she avoids playing with the boys. The others laugh at Demi for boldly declaring his love for his sister, but the friendship between the twins remains strong. In spite of his bookishness and unmanly behavior, the boys come to respect Demi and value his affection.

When a new boy, NATHANIEL "NAT" BLAKE, arrives at Plumfield, Demi welcomes him warmly and proudly introduces his sister. On the following evening Demi visits Nat before bedtime, and they discuss a picture of Christ, belonging to Demi, that hangs at the foot of Nat's bed. Nat asks Demi to tell him the story of Christ's life, and when Mrs. Bhaer peers in, she is deeply moved by the tableau. As his friendship with Nat develops, Demi takes great pleasure in reading to him and explaining his favorite books, including *Robinson Crusoe* and *Arabian Nights*, which are new to Nat. Demi and Nat form a threesome with Tommy Bangs, who adds a livelier element to their play.

DAN, a homeless boy of fourteen who is the opposite in character to the obedient Demi, comes to Plumfield briefly but is banished when he causes a fire in the house. When he returns a month later and decides to remain in order to improve himself, Dan turns to Demi for encouragement. Sitting beneath the willow tree, where the boys often go to discuss important matters, Demi explains the "play" he uses to protect his soul. He thinks of his mind as a room and his soul as a winged creature that lives there. The room is lined with shelves and drawers where he can keep his good thoughts and ideas, and lock up the bad ones. Every Sunday, Demi "puts the room in order," and speaks with the spirit living there. Dan, who is usually scornful of innocent games, is very impressed with this "play," and asks if Demi will help him organize his "room" in this way. Demi happily agrees, and Dan promises to tell him stories about his adventures in exchange.

After Demi's father becomes ill and dies, he tries to set aside childish ways and help his mother and sister. Mrs. Bhaer assigns him small jobs around the house, and Demi dutifully brings his earnings to his mother. Although he has never liked mathematics, Demi now tells the Bhaers that he wishes to be a bookkeeper like his father, and he makes a renewed effort in this area. Mrs. Bhaer comes to think of him as her most promising student and predicts that he will do something "good and great in the best sense of the word."

Brown, Elvira Dutton "Vyry." *Jubilee*. Margaret Walker. 1966.

Elvira Dutton Brown, known as Vyry, begins her remarkable life as a slave on the Dutton plantation in Georgia. As the unacknowledged daughter of the plantation's owner, Vyry receives scorn and harsh treatment from Dutton's wife, Missy Salina, but Vyry nonetheless manages to endure, suffering as a mere toddler through the death of her mother and the subsequent deaths, departures, and beatings comprising the horrid routine of her adolescence. By the time she is in her late teens, Vyry strongly aspires to freedom, going as far as asking if she can be freed to marry Randall Ware, a free black man who runs his own blacksmith shop. Because he likes her cooking, Dutton refuses Vyry's request but allows her to marry Ware by "jumping the broom" like other slaves. After her marriage, officiated by Brother Ezekiel, another slave, Vyry continues to work in the Dutton kitchen, and she bears two children, a boy, Jim, and then a girl, Minna. Soon afterward, disaster strikes the plantation as the Civil War erupts.

Mr. Dutton, who had had political aspirations, has an accident and lingers near death for quite some time. Following his funeral, Vyry hopes that his offer of freedom for her in his will will happen, but Salina Dutton makes no indication that Vyry is to be freed. Eventually Vyry's white half-brother goes off to war. He is wounded in the battle at Chickamauga, and after being brought home by his manservant, he, too, dies. The war slowly changes everything at the Dutton plantation, and Vyry, although she wants to leave, remains, hoping that Randall, who had gone to fight for the Union Army, will return.

Vyry gradually comes to assume most of the operation of the estate, especially after Salina is attacked by Union soldiers and also dies. This leaves Vyry saddled with the care of Miss Lillian, her half-sister, as well as her two children, since Lillian has become mentally deranged after the deaths of her parents, brother, and husband. Soon after Salina's death, Vyry is attacked, but a stranger, Innis Brown, arrives just in time to save her.

Innis Brown, a former slave, remains on the plantation

with Vyry and eventually manages to convince her to marry him and homestead elsewhere. Despite her misgivings, she realizes that Randall is probably dead, since word had come that he was quite ill, and she agrees to marry Innis. After Miss Lillian has been settled with some relatives, Vyry, Innis, and her two children move away from the plantation. Their first home, the site of the birth of Vyry's third child, Harry, is lost when a severe flood destroys much of their property. The Browns move on, spurred by Vyry's courage and determination, but they meet disaster again when their second home, a beautiful house they designed and built, is burned by a Ku Klux Klan raiding party. This coupled with a severe miscarriage reduces the indomitable Vyry to a mere shadow of her former self, and she forbids Innis to rebuild.

They move one more time, and Vyry's determination to succeed emerges intact as she forces herself to meet and greet what she hopes will be her new neighbors. Among these people she encounters racism and bigotry, but she is finally accepted into the community. The Browns are quite happy in their new home, and Innis and Vyry once again begin farming and raising crops and livestock; in addition, Vyry turns her attention and ambition to her children, whom she hopes will one day be educated. Her hopes are realized for Jim, who is sent to school after his father, Randall Ware, arrives to claim him. The novel ends with Vyry happily looking forward to the birth of her fourth child and to a peaceful future for her and the rest of the family.

Brown, Jacob "Jake." *Home to Harlem*. Claude McKay. 1928.

Jacob Brown, known as "Jake," a carefree, energetic young man, flourishes in the decadent world of Harlem in the 1920s. Eager to fight in World War I, Jake enlists, but his black company is held at Brest, hauling lumber to build huts. Disappointed, Jake deserts military service and eventually crosses to London where he works at the docks until the armistice. When race riots break out in London's East End, Jake becomes desperately homesick and gets a job as a stoker on a freighter bound for New York City.

Jake arrives in New York wearing a handsome English suit and carrying fifty-nine dollars in his pocket. Almost as soon as he enters a cabaret, his eyes light on a beautiful girl. They bicker flirtatiously, and Jake gallantly agrees to pay her fifty dollars, all the money he has, for a good time. They spend a memorable evening drinking, dancing, and making love. The next morning Jake discovers that she has made him a "little gift": She has returned the fifty dollars to his pocket with an affectionate note.

Although Jake longs to see her the next evening, he discovers that he has neither her name nor her address. He continues to go to the bar where he met her, but she never appears again, and he ends up spending most of his time with his friend ZEDDY PLUMMER drinking in various saloons and cabarets.

The voluptuous cabaret singer Congo Rose is immediately attracted to Jake and asks him to be her lover. Jake moves into her apartment, but refusing to be a "sweetman" entirely supported by his mistress, he gets work at the docks. Jake finds himself wishing for the woman he had met on the first night since there is little passion between him and Congo Rose. She begins to have a regular visitor, and when she refuses Jake's advances one day, he slaps her. Jake now feels guilty and miserable, but he overhears Rose bragging to her friend about how powerful the slap was and how it proved to her that Jake was a man. She protests while Jake packs his bags, but he explains that he does not like to hit women.

After the episode with Congo Rose, Jake feels the need to leave Harlem for a while. He takes a job as a cook on a train. There he meets RAYMOND, a sensitive, educated man from Haiti who was forced to leave school when his father was jailed for political reasons. Although they are opposites in many ways (Ray prefers to read a book rather than go out drinking), the two become close friends. When Jake becomes ill and is confined to bed, Ray and his girlfriend Agatha care for him. Jake eventually moves into an apartment in Ray's building.

Not long afterward, however, Ray decides to leave Harlem. After his departure, Jake goes to a club called the Sheba Palace and spots the girl he had met on the first night. They leave before her escort gets back from the men's room, and during their long walk, Jake learns her name—Felice. After several romantic weeks together, they run into Felice's old lover, who turns out to be Jake's friend Zeddy. After a violent confrontation between them, Jake and Felice decide to move to Chicago together. Zeddy later apologizes and effects a reconciliation with Jake. But to Jake the move to Chicago still sounds appealing; he dances all night with Felice, and they take an early morning train to the Windy City.

Brown, Young Goodman. "Young Goodman Brown." Nathaniel Hawthorne. 1846.

Young Goodman Brown is a naive young man whose Puritan family has deep roots in his seventeenth-century New England community. During the course of the story, he makes a journey into the woods that challenges his faith and his preconceptions about his community.

As the story opens, Goodman Brown leaves his pretty wife Faith to journey into the forest on a mysterious errand. As he does so, he vows that after this night he will remain by her side forever. On the road into the woods he keeps his appointment with a grave companion, an older man who bears a striking resemblance to Goodman Brown but his air is far more worldly than the younger traveler's. Goodman Brown is reluctant to go deeper into the forest, but the older man convinces him to walk on, telling him that Goodman Brown's father and grandfather had also walked the path with him.

In a short time they see ahead of them on the path a figure whom Goodman Brown recognizes as Goody Cloyse, the pious woman who taught him catechism when he was a boy. Not wanting to be questioned about his errand, the young man hides in the woods while his friend intercepts the woman. To his surprise he sees that Goody Cloyse and his friend are acquainted. He listens in shock as their conversation runs to witchcraft and deviltry, and to the young man who will be taken into communion at the evening's meeting. When Goodman Brown turns his eyes away in astonishment, the old woman disappears from view. Dumbfounded, he rejoins his companion.

After walking a short way, Goodman Brown resolves that he will not go a step farther into the woods and sits down on a stump to rest, happy that he will be able to meet his minister and good Deacon Gookin with a clear conscience in the morning. But he is not seated long when the minister and the deacon ride by on horseback, and Goodman Brown overhears them discussing the demonic meeting they are about to attend in which, it is said, a young woman will be taken into communion. Faint and sick at heart at what he hears, Goodman Brown bolsters himself with the memory of his wife Faith, the only person he feels can save him from the devil. At that moment he hears the sound of many voices, several of which he recognizes as belonging to members of his church. Among them he hears his own wife's lamentations. As he cries out her name, a scream emits from the forest, and Faith's pink ribbon flutters down from the sky.

Mad with despair, Goodman Brown tears into the forest until he reaches a rock with a shape not unlike a pulpit. He is compelled toward a figure who looks like his own dead father, while a veiled young woman is led to stand beside him. The dark figure at the pulpit tells the pair that the people whom they have revered as the holiest of their community stand around them, the wickedest of sinners and devil worshipers all. Goodman Brown sees that it is his wife who stands beside him, and she in turn recognizes her husband, just as the fiend tells them that "evil is the nature of all mankind." At the moment they are being baptized by the dark figure, Goodman Brown calls out to Faith to look up to heaven and resist the demon. But he cannot tell whether she heeds his warning, for in the next instant he is alone in the damp, quiet forest.

The next morning Goodman Brown awakens a changed man. It is with dread that he lives the rest of his life, as he shrinks from his minister and congregation, and often from Faith, with horror and disgust. Although he and Faith are succeeded by many generations, he dies a grim, hopeless old man.

Brunner, Eddie. *Butterfield 8.* John O'Hara. 1935.

Eddie Brunner was born in California and educated at Stanford, where he was well liked. A talented cartoonist with a fondness for certain phonograph records, Eddie fell easily into a comfortable life of honest laziness. Yet this easy life changes drastically when Eddie's father suddenly dies and the family fortune is lost in the Depression. Eddie finds himself in New York, desperate for money and eager to take any job that will pay him enough to eat. So begins his quest to establish security for himself.

Eddie first appears in the novel when GLORIA WANDROUS arrives at his apartment, wearing only a mink coat that she has stolen from WESTON LIGETT, a married man, after she spent her first night with him. With characteristic practicality, Eddie helps Gloria out of her immediate dilemma with a change of clothes and urges her to return the coat. Eddie's close and supportive friendship with Gloria is based on the platonic nature of their relationship. Although Eddie is attracted to Gloria, he realizes that if he allows himself to give in to this attraction, he will become just another one of the men who have slept with her. This sexual tension makes Eddie feel extremely protective toward this woman who is more than capable of looking after herself. Eddie is continually surprised by the intensity of his emotion for her, which he realizes is far different from the objective ambivalence that characterizes most of his relationships.

It is Gloria's ability to draw him out of this ambivalence that fascinates Eddie. Throughout the novel Eddie has a relationship with Norma Day, a woman who is exactly like every other woman he has ever loved. He is caught between the comfort of the familiar and the excitement of the unknown, represented by Gloria.

The tension between them increases, and Eddie realizes that he could easily fall in love with Gloria and risk losing both their friendship and his own self-respect. One evening when he finds himself torn between his feelings for Gloria and his criticism of everything she seems to stand for, Gloria admits that she loves him. For a moment Eddie is faced with making what he knows will be a crucial decision, but he is rescued by the ringing of the telephone. When he returns, the moment has gone, and he realizes that he is in love with Norma and will marry her.

Eddie considers this moment a stroke of luck and believes the intervention of something beyond his understanding has been the most important event of his life. The incident marks his increasing detachment from Gloria as he finally determines to face the issues and responsibilities he always meant to take up when he was older. As the novel ends, Eddie has rediscovered the security and stability of his former life.

Bruno, Giovanni. *The Origin of the Brunists.* Robert Coover. 1966.

Born the son of a poor mine worker, Giovanni Bruno is destined for a strange type of greatness. Mildly retarded, Bruno was something of an outcast in the fractional Italian community of the small mining town of West Condon. While alive, his parents ignored him; upon their death,

Bruno, a young boy, was left with only his indifferent sister to look after him.

As soon as Bruno was old enough, he, like all the young men of West Condon, went to work in the mine, the economic center of the town. Almost universally disliked by the other miners because of his lack of comprehension, Bruno once again became an outcast, despite the fact that his large size and ability to follow orders unquestioningly made him an outstanding worker.

Bruno's life and the course of life in West Condon change forever when an explosion is set off in the mine. He is trapped along with over a hundred other miners inside the many miles of tunnels that lie far beneath the surface of the earth. After wandering the tunnels for days, Bruno, who is shunned by the other trapped miners, has a vision of a white bird flying past him within the depths of the mine. Finally fainting from hunger and exhaustion, Bruno utters his last words to a nearby miner in an attempt to relate his vision; he is dismissed as a crazed ranter by the other doomed workers.

Days later the residents of West Condon are finally able to enter the mines and bring out the corpses of the miners who were suffocated or burned inside. Miraculously, Bruno is found separated from the other miners—comatose but still alive. He is immediately transported to a hospital in a nearby city and quickly becomes a national celebrity. He serves as a potent symbol of the strength and determination of the small mining town. Bruno proves the doctors at the hospital wrong when, despite their predictions, he comes out of his coma with no additional damage to his already impaired brain.

Much to the disapproval of the other Italian miners, who are dismayed that such a dimwitted man should represent their community, Bruno's return is a town holiday. He is shocked to see all the townspeople who had scorned him celebrating his return. A self-proclaimed prophet named Eleanor, who had been on the verge of being run out of town by the disapproving townspeople before the accident at the mine, proclaims Bruno a new messiah.

The townspeople are so thrilled by this symbol of survival of the catastrophe that devastated their town that the new religion of Brunism, founded by Eleanor, begins to spread. At weekly meetings of the Brunists, Bruno recounts his vision of the white bird. Despite widespread mockery outside West Condon, the religion's popularity grows.

Bruno's death at one of the group's meetings does nothing to lessen the popularity of the religion. When an autopsy reveals that it was caused by a blood clot on the brain, he is proclaimed a martyr by his followers.

Brush, George Marvin. *Heaven's My Destination.* Thornton Wilder. 1934.

George Marvin Brush is a young textbook salesman who experiences a profound religious conversion while a sophomore in college. As part of his Christian faith, he believes in Gandhi's tenets of nonviolence, in voluntary poverty, and in *ahimsa*, the principle of doing good to someone who does you wrong. Unfortunately, he is so serious and dogmatic in his beliefs that he alienates many people he meets on his travels.

Among George's dogmatic beliefs is his disapproval of banks. He withdraws all his money, explaining to the bank president that he thinks earning interest is wrong and keeping money in a bank is a sign of fear and lack of faith. Thinking George insane, the president has him jailed, but he is released after he tells his story to the judge.

George harbors terrible guilt for a sin he committed with a young woman, a sin he tries desperately to right. Stranded at a Kansas City farm during a storm one night, he had sex with one of the farmer's daughters and then wandered away, distraught, the next morning. Since that day, George has tried in vain to find the house again so that he can marry the girl. This secret shame prevents him from seeking work as a preacher, even though he often finds himself preaching about his beliefs.

In his travels around the northern Midwest, George has made several friends, who take the place of his faraway family. Still, he never really feels comfortable with them, and after his religious conversion, he feels even less so. At Queenie's boarding house in Kansas City, his friends Louis, Bat, and Herb like nothing better than to drink and play cards. They've struck an uneasy truce with George, who is tolerated only if he stays away from the topics of religion and morals.

On one particular visit George arrives at Queenie's feeling slightly ill. His friends give him a new "medicine" designed to combat the flu, but it turns out to be only alcohol. Oddly, once he knows he has been given liquor, George decides to have some more and try the experience of intoxication. He leads his friends on a spree around the city, climbing on monuments and running through movie theater lobbies.

The next day, emboldened by the success of the liquor venture, the men play another trick on George. They invite him to the home of Mrs. Crofut and her daughters for Sunday dinner. George is charmed by the plethora of lovely young women, all around sixteen, obviously not all Mrs. Crofut's offspring. After dinner George accompanies the young ladies to the movies. They each kiss George good night after the show and beg him to come again for a visit. On the way back to Queenie's, Herb reveals that Mrs. Crofut's "home" is actually a brothel. Although angry, George refuses to fight over the incident. The men, fed up with his priggish attitudes, throw him to the ground and beat and kick him senseless. He is taken to the hospital where he tries to understand why he always makes people hate him.

After this episode, George decides to find the farmer's daughter. He hires a private investigator, who discovers her whereabouts and her name, Roberta. George goes to the restaurant where Roberta works. She dismisses his advances several times, but his persistence finally wears her down. A few weeks later Roberta agrees to marry George. They set up a house together, and after George's friend Herb passes away, they assume the care of Herb's five-year-old daughter Elizabeth.

Within a short time it becomes clear that George and Roberta are ill suited to each other. When George sets out on a long business trip, Roberta moves back to her parents' farm with Elizabeth. George is crestfallen. On his own after the breakup, George loses his faith. He becomes ill and is confined to a hospital bed for weeks. Queenie comes to visit and brings with her a spoon, sent as a present for George from her old friend Father Pasziewski, now passed away, who always prayed for George. After receiving this gift, George recovers and resumes his work selling textbooks. Reports are soon heard throughout his region of a young man doing good works and exhorting others to live a clean life.

Brydon, Spencer. "The Jolly Corner." Henry James. 1908.

Spencer Brydon, a fifty-six-year-old native New Yorker, has just returned to his home after spending more than three decades living in Europe. Spencer owns a house on what he calls "the jolly corner." This multistory town house has been in the Brydon family for years; now totally empty, it is awaiting the renovation that Spencer has finally decided to pursue. When the story opens, Spencer is walking through the house with his old friend Alice Staverton. Alice, a single middle-aged woman who lives modestly and never wastes words, recently told Spencer that he had neglected "a real gift" for years. This statement makes Spencer think that if he had stayed at home in New York all these years, he would have become something different and perhaps discovered his latent genius.

Walking through the empty house, Alice and Spencer cryptically discuss what Spencer might have been. Alice admits that she does not think Spencer is as good as he could have been, although her positive feelings toward him remain unchanged. Spencer expresses his determination to see his other self, and Alice mysteriously tells him that she has seen this being twice in a dream. When Spencer asks her what he was like, she will not say.

Returning frequently—sometimes twice a day—to the jolly corner house by himself, Spencer walks through the place from attic to cellar in order to wander, linger, and listen. The familiar social rooms set him at ease, but the extensively subdivided rear, with its abundance of servants' rooms, nooks, and corners, makes him uncomfortable.

One night Spencer sees a closed inner door at the rear of the house; he stares, startled, and contemplates whether or not he is hallucinating. Afraid of what he might find behind the closed door, Spencer finally leaves. Downstairs, he is frightened to see another door now open that he was certain he left closed. Judging from the evidence, Spencer believes he is in the presence of an occult force. He encounters a dense, dark, spectral figure of a man of his own stature. The figure's face is covered by its own raised hands. Spencer gapes in horror at what he believes is his other self. When the figure drops its hands, he sees that the face is not his but that of a stranger.

Alice and the cleaning woman find Spencer lying on the floor beyond the vestibule where he had fallen unconscious after seeing the specter. After waking up, he is sure that Alice has literally brought him back to life. Alice kisses and holds him; Spencer pleads for her to "keep" him. Alice confesses to him that prior to his arrival she knew that Spencer would inevitably see the specter. She had encountered the figure again in a dream early that morning. The figure was not a horror to her, and she accepted him. Spencer, who first insists that the ghost he has seen is not himself, listens to Alice's impressions of the worn, unhappy, pitiable ghost to whom "things have happened." When she mentions the ghost's wounded right hand and his poor eyesight, Spencer winces; he, too, has a damaged right hand and deteriorating sight. Spencer's final remark is that although the ghost had "a million a year," it did not have Alice Staverton. Alice, to the last, is certain that Spencer Brydon and the ghostly figure are not the same man.

Buchan, Lacy. *The Fathers.* Allen Tate. 1938.

Lacy Buchan is an upstanding, ingenuous young man whose pleasant life is disrupted by familial strife and the horrific events of the Civil War. Growing up on a farm called Pleasant Hill in northern Virginia, Lacy is sixteen years old when the war breaks out and cannot initially figure out whether he supports the Union or the Confederacy. His beloved father, a member of Virginia's southern aristocracy, uncharacteristically disapproves of secession. The tragedies caused in Lacy's life by the war are accompanied by a severe romantic disappointment when Jane Posey, the woman he loves, becomes an impossible candidate for marriage. Becoming increasingly disillusioned with both his personal life and the tempestuous state of the nation, Lacy finally joins the Confederate Army with an indifference as to whether or not he survives the war.

Recounting his experiences during the era of the Civil War as an unmarried sixty-five-year-old man, Lacy is the fourth of four children born to old-fashioned parents who are determined to raise their son in the antebellum tradition of southern chivalry. Lacy's mother died when he was fifteen years old. Soon afterward he fell in love with Jane, the younger sister of his brother-in-law GEORGE POSEY, whom Lacy idolizes. This romantic attraction never subsides, but the young man's amorous inten-

tions are frustrated by Jane's engagement to Lacy's older brother Semmes. When a slave named Yellow Jim, who is the Poseys' half-brother and Jane's childhood nurse, assaults her in her bedroom, she is so upset by the attack that she retracts her intention to marry Semmes and enters a convent. Semmes murders Yellow Jim in retaliation, and George in turn murders Lacy's brother to revenge his half-brother's death.

Lacy vacillates between allegiance to his father and his hero worship of George, who sympathizes with the Confederate cause and uses his vast wealth to smuggle supplies to the cotton states' army. Eventually, however, Lacy decides to join the southern army and enters its ranks as a private in the Seventeenth Virginia Brigade under the command of General Longstreet. Accompanied by George, Lacy locates his brigade and joins the ranks, but this initial involvement in the war effort is interrupted when George shoots an officer in the face, thus terminating his short-lived membership in the Confederate Army. Lacy returns with George to Pleasant Hill to pay respects to Mr. Buchan, but the old man has been killed by the Yankees for refusing to leave his land. When George proposes that Lacy accompany him to Georgetown, the young man refuses, despite his devotion to his brother-in-law; he decides to return to the army instead. He manages to survive the war and eventually attends the Columbian Medical College to prepare himself to confront civilian life as a doctor in the postbellum United States.

Buchanan, Daisy. *The Great Gatsby.* F. Scott Fitzgerald. 1925.

Daisy Buchanan, the novel's heroine, exudes helplessness, poignancy, and charm. From the novel's beginning, Daisy, with her whispery voice and careless, slightly jaded gaiety, bewitches the narrator, NICK CARRAWAY. Seemingly oblivious to her husband Tom's surliness and unfaithfulness, Daisy languishes, drinking cocktails and whiling away the summer evenings in their lavish house on Long Island Sound.

Daisy once loved a young soldier, JAY GATSBY. Wealthy, beautiful, and popular, she was the belle of Louisville. She and Gatsby would linger for hours on the front steps of her parents' home. When Gatsby left for Europe, Daisy waited for him; she stopped going to parties and had a falling out with her parents. After a while her high spirits returned, and several months later she married Tom Buchanan. The day before her wedding she received a letter from Gatsby, whereupon she collapsed, drunk and weeping, in her room.

Daisy is stunned when, five years later, she discovers that Jay Gatsby and Nick's neighbor, the famous host of sumptuous, all-night parties, are one and the same. Nick invites her to tea at his house, where Gatsby is waiting anxiously. When she sees Gatsby, Daisy almost swoons.

After a few painfully awkward moments, Nick manages to leave them alone. It soon seems as though their five-year separation had never occurred. They are completely absorbed in each other. The weeks pass. Gatsby's brilliantly lit lawn goes dark; he dismisses his servants so that he and Daisy can spend the days alone in the mansion he built for her.

But their happiness is short-lived. Daisy invites Gatsby to her house, and their attraction to each other becomes startlingly clear to Tom. He and Gatsby argue. Gatsby insists that Daisy tell Tom she never loved him, but she refuses, claiming that she cannot rewrite the past. What is important, she says, near tears, is that she loves Gatsby now.

As Daisy and Gatsby are driving back to Long Island, Tom's mistress Myrtle runs into the middle of the road and is instantly killed by Gatsby's car. Daisy is driving. When Tom finds out about the accident, he rushes home. Nick spies Tom and Daisy through the kitchen window. They are talking earnestly, intimately. Suddenly Nick knows that Daisy will never leave Tom. Gatsby waits all night, yet she does not signal him from the window as she had promised, nor does she call the following day.

It is unclear whether or not Daisy is present when Tom speaks with George Wilson, Myrtle's husband, who avenges his wife's death by shooting Gatsby, who he believes was driving the car. Daisy's absence from Gatsby's funeral is conspicuous and predictable, a reminder that she, like her wealthy husband, can afford to be heartless and cowardly.

Buck. *The Call of the Wild.* Jack London. 1903.

Buck, the legendary wolf dog, heroically struggles to survive and flourish in the primitive Yukon during the gold rush. The tale begins when Buck is stolen from an estate in the Santa Clara Valley where he has comfortably ruled every domain. Proud, intelligent, strong, and spirited, this part St. Bernard and part Scotch shepherd dog has never faced any kind of hardship. His first encounter with cruelty offends his pride but does not break his spirit. He quickly learns the law of the club, a lesson he incorporates into his survival techniques, a combination of patience and ruthlessness.

Buck is bought by French Canadian mail carriers who try to make him into a sled dog. When he observes a friendly Newfoundland being ripped apart by another dog while a ring of huskies wait to complete the kill, he realizes that only the strongest and smartest survive. From the other dogs in the traces, Buck gleans his duties faster than any dog his owners have ever seen. He adapts to almost unbearable conditions of cold and exhaustion by turning to his primitive instincts. Discarding civilized traits that make survival impossible, Buck calls on the deeply buried memories of his species.

His natural leadership soon makes him the enemy of Spitz, the seasoned lead dog, and both owners understand that these two will eventually fight for mastery of the team. After many covert attacks, that day finally arrives, and Buck's superior intelligence allows him to vanquish the more experienced Spitz. Now under Buck's leadership, the team sets distance and speed records. Without an opportunity for rest, Buck and team are turned over to new owners who treat the dogs decently if not affectionately, and they continue their brutal work pace. When they have driven more than twenty-five hundred miles of frozen tracks, the dogs, in dire need of rest, are sold to some incompetent Americans.

Through neglect and stupidity, these owners destroy the entire team except Buck, who is saved by a man named John Thornton. Recuperating under Thornton's loving care, Buck in turn performs heroic feats of courage and strength in devotion to this man. After twice saving Thornton's life and then upholding his reputation by hauling a thousand-pound sled one hundred yards to win a bet, Buck becomes the most respected and feared dog in the North.

With the winnings from the bet, Thornton and his partners venture into the wildest and remotest areas of the North in search of legendary lodes of gold. Accompanying his beloved master and yet free to roam, Buck is the happiest he has ever been. Still, he is drawn deeper and deeper into the forest by a mysterious call, and only his overpowering loyalty to Thornton draws him back to camp. After stalking and killing a large moose, Buck returns to find the camp deserted, the men and dogs killed by Indians. In a rage, he chases and slays the invaders. Free now to follow the call of the wild, Buck joins and ultimately leads a pack of wolves. He lives on in the legends of the Indians who call him the Evil Spirit and in the young cubs of the pack who exhibit his markings.

Buck, Billy. *The Red Pony.* John Steinbeck. 1937.

Billy Buck, known as the finest horseman in the area, is a ranch hand for Carl Tiflin. When Carl buys a pony at a sheriff's auction for his young son JODY TIFLIN, Billy, who calls himself "half horse," teaches Jody all about the care and handling of horses. Jody looks up to him with great admiration and respect. In Jody's eyes, Billy Buck can do no wrong.

Carl has promised Jody that he will be allowed to ride the pony Gabilan after the Thanksgiving holiday. Winter brings rain, and Gabilan is cooped up in the stable for weeks. One day the rain lets up, and Jody tells Billy Buck he will leave Gabilan in the corral while he is at school. Billy agrees, telling Jody he is sure it won't start to rain again; even if it does, he says, it won't be dangerous for Gabilan. Billy is twice wrong: It does rain, and by the end of the afternoon they realize that Gabilan has come down with a severe cold. Billy knows he has suddenly become fallible in the little boy's eyes, and this is worse for him than losing the horse.

Gabilan's condition worsens despite Billy's promises that he will bring the pony back to health. Finally, in order not be wrong a third time, he must admit to Jody that Gabilan has strangles. He still tries to convince the boy that he can take care of the pony, but the horse eventually dies. Jody is overcome with grief, and it is Billy Buck, even more than Jody's father, who truly understands.

Billy's encouragement prompts Carl Tiflin to offer another pony to Jody. This time Jody must work off the five dollars it will cost to breed the Tiflins' mare Nellie with a neighbor's stallion. Billy again takes charge of the situation, telling Jody how long he will have to wait for the foal, speculating on its color, and promising to deliver a good colt to the boy. When Jody asks him, remembering Gabilan, if he'll let anything happen to this one, Billy Buck feels guilty and embarrassed. When Nellie's pregnancy begins to show, Billy teaches Jody how to care for her. Jody is anxious for the foal to arrive and checks constantly on Nellie's condition, making sure that Billy will call him when she is ready to deliver the foal. Billy becomes irritated at Jody's worrying, feeling insulted that his capability is being questioned.

Billy calls Jody down to the barn to help when Nellie is about to deliver. As Billy prepares to help the mare, he discovers that the foal is turned the wrong way. He knows that Nellie will not be able to deliver unless the foal is turned around, and if the foal can't be turned, it should be sacrificed to save the mare. Determined to keep his promise to Jody, Billy desperately smashes a hammer into the mare's head, knocking her to the ground, and rips into her with his knife. He pulls the foal out of its sac and lays it down in front of Jody, screaming at the boy to get hot water to clean it off. Although killing a good mare this way is abhorrent to a horseman like Billy Buck, it was more important to him not to disappoint the boy a second time.

Budd, Billy. *Billy Budd, Sailor* (An Inside Narrative). Herman Melville. 1924.

Combining brute strength with gracious beauty, Billy Budd epitomizes the ideal of the "handsome sailor." With an adolescent, almost feminine complexion that makes him appear younger than his twenty-one years, this illiterate foundling remains ignorant of the cunning ways of sophisticated society. His innocence and vitality make him resemble a noble savage, but his perfection has a flaw: When challenged by uproar or danger, his usually melodious voice locks into a paralytic stutter.

It is the summer of 1797. Britain is at war with France and has recently suffered a devastating mutiny of its naval fleet. Billy has been serving on the crew of the English merchantman *The Rights-of-Man*, now on its homeward voyage. Before his arrival, the crew had been querulous and fractious, but the presence of the angelic, handsome sailor serves as a harmonious influence on them. Unfor-

tunately, Billy is provoked into beating his irascibly jealous shipmate Red Whiskers. Soon after this incident, Billy is impressed into duty for the English navy by the lieutenant of the outward-bound man-of-war, the HMS *Bellipotent*. While departing the freedom of the merchant ship for the servitude of the warship, Billy utters an unintentionally ironic farewell, "Good-bye to you, old *Rights-of-Man!*"

The captain of the *Bellipotent* is the Honorable EDWARD FAIRFAX VERE, a forty-year-old bachelor who is both a contemplative aristocrat and a rigid authoritarian. Thirty-five-year-old JOHN CLAGGART serves as the ship's icily intellectual master-at-arms. Despite his flawless service, Billy finds himself getting into trouble for minor infractions of the ship's rules. The Old Dansker, the ship's wrinkled, mystical oracle, announces to Billy that "Jemmy Legs"—the crew's unflattering nickname for Claggart—is "down" on him, yet the unsuspecting Billy continues to believe that he is a favorite of the master-at-arms.

One day a sailor surreptitiously sent by Claggart hints to Billy that there is a plan for mutiny afoot. Billy stutters a rebuke but innocently fails to inform Captain Vere of the incident. This failure to talk soon allows Claggart to charge Billy with the conspiracy. Vere, still more suspicious of Claggart than of Billy yet mindful of the recent insurrections in the British fleet, calls Billy into his quarters to face the charge. At the critical moment, Billy's stutter prevents him from speaking in self-defense. Instead, he instinctively strikes Claggart on the forehead and kills him.

Vere almost instantly decides Billy's fate and holds a trial on the deck of the *Bellipotent*. Although by martial law Billy is guilty and Claggart innocent, by any higher law the truth is the reverse. Still fearful of mutiny, Vere insists on the authority of the naval code, and just one and a half hours after the incident, Billy is sentenced to hang.

At four o'clock the next morning, just before being hoisted up the mainmast, Billy utters his haunting last words: "God bless Captain Vere." With one voice the gathered crew echoes this prayerlike farewell. Then Billy is hanged and buried at sea.

His story lives on, however, as history and myth among the sailors. Chips off the mast from which he was hanged circulate like relics from Christ's cross. And his tale, although largely revised and distorted, becomes a popular sailor's ballad.

Buddy. "A Christmas Memory." Truman Capote. 1946.

Buddy is the seven-year-old narrator of this short story of an unusual and deeply felt friendship. He shares his life with a distant cousin, a woman of sixty, who lives with Buddy and his family. In spite of her stooped shoulders and the lines on her face, Buddy's friend has the heart of a child, and the two play together and undertake various projects while they conspire to avoid the other, more dour members of the family.

It is late November, and Buddy's friend insists, as she does every year, that it is time for the two of them to make fruitcake. The friends begin the yearly ritual by journeying into a neighbor's yard to harvest pecans, which they carry home in a baby carriage once used to ferry Buddy. They shell the nuts until they have a large pile, enough for thirty cakes.

Next they count out the change they have either earned or collected from reluctant adults. Their change is just enough to pay for the supplies they need, including a pint of whiskey to be purchased illegally from a local Native American. Once made, the fruitcakes are sent to people the two friends like and admire. Among them are President Roosevelt, two Baptist missionaries who had voyaged to Borneo, and the Native American, Mr. Haha Jones, who donated his whiskey in return for a cake. In celebration of their accomplishment, Buddy and his friend drink the remaining whiskey. They dance and sing merrily but are stopped by the adults, who scold Buddy's friend for giving him alcohol.

Buddy is soon to be sent away to military school, but before he goes he and his friend enjoy a final Christmas together. They chop down a fir tree and drag it home, then spend several days making decorations for it. Together they buy the family dog, Queenie, a rawhide bone and impatiently await Christmas day. They fall asleep together on Christmas Eve, having confided that they have given each other homemade kites. The other gifts Buddy receives are disappointing in comparison to the kite, which he loves almost as much as he loves his friend.

Buddy and his friend spend an idyllic afternoon flying their kites, one so lovely that his friend assures him she could "leave the world with today in my eyes." After Buddy has left, she writes to him faithfully, telling him when Queenie dies and sending him the best of her fruitcakes every year. When she does leave the world, Buddy knows of her departure even before his family informs him of it; he feels that somehow a connection is broken to a special place inside him. He spends the sad December morning walking across campus, looking upward and scanning the skies for a pair of lost kites.

Bull. *Wind from an Enemy Sky.* D'Arcy McNickle. 1978.

Bull, chief of the Little Elk Indians, witnesses the tragic destruction of his culture in the hands of thoughtless white officials. As the novel opens, Bull, accompanied by his grandson Antoine, looks on in pained disbelief at a recently constructed dam and exclaims that it has "killed the water." Angered, fearful, yet powerless, he shoots at the dam—an act that of course alters nothing.

Shortly thereafter an aged man arrives at Bull's camp. It is Henry Jim, elder brother of Bull, who was once chief but who left his people thirty years before to become an agriculturalist with the white men. At his departure, according to traditional practice, his younger brother was

named leader. Having experienced a change of heart, Henry Jim has returned to urge his people to "bring back our medicine, our power," to go to the white man and demand that their medicine bundle, long missing, be returned. Bull retreats to be alone and contemplate the situation.

While he is gone, Pock Face, one of the tribe's young men, takes Bull's gun and goes to the dam, where he shoots at a white man surveying it. The shooting kills Jimmie Cooke, nephew of ADAM PELL, the engineer who built the dam. The local Indian Agency holds Bull accountable until the culprit is found. But Toby Rafferty, superintendent of the Little Elk Indian Agency, eventually agrees to let Bull and his men leave. Rafferty's decision angers a local physician, Doc Edwards, who maintains that "if not for [Bull], more Indian land would be in white ownership." Rafferty and Bull make arrangements for Bull to return to the agency for further questioning. When Bull returns, the slain man's parents and Pell are there. Bull explains the circumstances behind the murder. Much to their own surprise, Pell and the Cookes find Bull a respectable and compelling figure and believe that he is innocent of the crime. They are proven correct almost immediately when Pock Face enters and confesses.

Once the murder has been cleared up, attention turns again to recouping the lost sacred medicine bundle, traditionally explained as a gift from the great Thunderbird. Thunderbird, Bull says, changed himself into a feather, fathered a child, Feather Boy, and offered the mother a feather bundle that was to keep the culture intact. Pell, who has had a longstanding interest in Indians, feels he can be of help in locating the feather bundle because he works as curator at a major New York City museum.

Pell does locate the lost object but finds that years of neglect in museum storage have left it mice-eaten and decayed beyond repair. In retribution for this and for his role in constructing the dam—which he now, in agreement with the Indians, regards as a disruption of the universe— he decides to offer the Little Elk people his most prized possession, an ancient Incan relic. Told they are to receive "a gift," Bull and his men arrive at the agency expecting the return of the medicine bundle.

Ignoring Rafferty's warning that sacred symbols cannot be substituted and that knowledge of the feather bundle's loss will completely devastate the Little Elk, Pell proceeds with an explanation of the condition of the bundle and offers Bull the Incan idol. Shocked and agonized, Bull picks up his gun and shoots Rafferty and Pell. In turn, their Indian interpreter shoots Bull. Off in the distance, Two-Sleeps, the tribal sage, approaches on horseback singing the tribal death song.

Bumppo, Nathaniel "Natty." *The Leatherstocking Tales (The Pioneers; The Last of the Mohicans; The Prairie; The Pathfinder; The Deerslayer).* James Fenimore Cooper. 1823; 1826; 1827; 1840; 1841.

Known as Hawkeye, Pathfinder, Deerslayer, and la Longue Carabine, Nathaniel "Natty" Bumppo is the uniquely American hero of *The Leatherstocking Tales*, a collection of five novels. Together with his rifle "killdeer" and his Indian companion CHINGACHGOOK, Natty inhabits the American wilderness, a bold personification of Yankee virtues.

Natty was born on the East Coast and raised for the most part by the dwindling Delaware Indian tribe in the area now known as New York State. Accidents of parentage and upbringing have combined in Natty the superior wilderness skills of the Native Americans along with an unlettered pietism that is marked by naive sincerity and a reverence for both nature and humankind. Natty's character and abilities receive their first test during the French and Indian War when Natty's lifelong struggle against the "Mingos," or Iroquois, has its beginning. He crosses the threshold of maturity when he first sheds human blood, mortally wounding an Iroquois who dubs him "Hawkeye" for his deadly aim. Natty then acts to protect two white women, Judith and Hetty Hutter, but is himself captured by the Iroquois. Judith, Hetty, and Chingachgook all try to secure his release, which is eventually effected by the arrival of a company of British soldiers. Judith, a beauty of little moral mien, is chastened by Natty's righteousness, although Natty, with his knack for judging human nature, cannot return the love that Judith offers.

Subsequently, Natty's protection of the Hutter sisters is recalled in his efforts to guide the Monro sisters, Cora and Alice, through the forest to the safety of a British fort. Cora and Alice are captured by hostile Indians, and Natty participates repeatedly in woodland skirmishes on their behalf. Dressed in a medicine man's bear costume, Natty finally infiltrates the enemy camp. In one last mad pursuit, however, both Cora and Chingachgook's young son are killed. Haunted by this memory, Natty heads west toward Lake Ontario, where he serves as a scout for a small outpost of British troops.

Although by now advanced to middle age, Natty is persuaded by his friend Sergeant Dunham to consider marrying the sergeant's comely young daughter Mabel. Natty's concern and love for Mabel grow quickly as the violence and treachery of the frontier erupt. Sergeant Dunham is killed and Mabel herself besieged in a blockhouse until Natty saves her. His is not the only gallantry, however, and his marriage suit is rejected in favor of another. Disappointed, Natty returns to the woods.

In the years that follow, Natty's allegiance shifts from Britain to the newly united American states. The frontier disappears around him. As Natty ages, the laws of nature seem usurped everywhere by the laws of property and government. After the death of Chingachgook, Natty heads west again. He walks alone across North America

to the Pacific. On the long walk back, Natty has one last taste of warfare: White squatters and pioneers have edged their way onto the midwestern prairie, and Natty finds himself in the ranks against a group of squatters and a band of Sioux. Over eighty years old, Natty is taken in by a tribe of Pawnee when the frontier's fragile peace returns. His last word, uttered as he faces west, is "Here!"

Bunch, Byron. *Light in August.* William Faulkner. 1932.

Byron Bunch is a conscientious, mild-mannered blue-collar worker who is also a loner by nature. His social life is so limited that he works overtime alone at his job at a planing mill on Saturday afternoons for lack of more stimulating outside interests. His mundane, methodical life is interrupted when LENA GROVE, an unmarried pregnant woman, shows up at the mill one Saturday afternoon in search of Lucas Burch, the father of her child, who has jilted her. Although initially unconscious of the fact, Byron immediately falls in love with her; he undertakes to provide for both Lena and then her newborn son, and they become the focus of his previously empty life.

Byron lives alone in a boardinghouse room in Jefferson, Mississippi, and has a single friend, GAIL HIGHTOWER, an ex-minister who is even more detached from the social life of the town than Byron. The only variation in Byron's habitual schedule of working, sleeping, and eating occurs on Saturday evening when he changes into an inexpensive serge suit and rides thirty miles on his mule to a country church to spend Sunday directing a choir in an all-day service. On Monday morning Byron invariably arrives promptly at the planing mill in his coveralls for another uneventful week of all work and no play. The traditional scenario of falling in love and raising a family does not occur to him, and he seems to be perfectly content with his monotonous life-style.

When Byron meets Lena, his life changes dramatically. Upon learning that Lena is both husbandless and unprovided for, he offers to let her spend the night in his room. He then arranges for her to stay in an abandoned cabin. Ironically, the cabin has just been deserted by her delinquent ex-lover, Lucas Burch, whose adoption of an alias, Joe Brown, suggests his shady character.

When Lena's time comes, Byron solicits the aid of Hightower, who successfully delivers her healthy baby boy. All the while, Byron sleeps in a tent near Lena's cabin and keeps a watchful eye on his vulnerable but naively contented charge. Thanks to his new preoccupation, Byron is a changed man; he gains an unprecedented confidence that is exhibited in a less fumbling manner of speaking and a more assured, deliberate carriage.

Although Byron has succeeded in figuring out that Brown is the father of Lena's child, he refrains from informing her of his whereabouts because Brown, soon to be implicated in the brutal murder of the middle-aged spinster JOANNA BURDEN, is residing in a cell at the local jailhouse. When the real murderer, JOE CHRISTMAS, is caught, Byron arranges with the sheriff for Joe Brown to be brought to Lena's cabin and forced to acknowledge their child. But Brown once again eludes his responsibility by escaping through the window of Lena's cabin. Byron pursues Brown, and although he knows that Brown is the stronger of the two, attempts to beat him up, only to find himself soundly pummelled. When Lena decides to take to the road again, ostensibly to continue her search for Brown, Byron decides to quit his job and accompany her. Although Lena consistently rebuffs his romantic advances, he remains doggedly loyal in his support of the young mother and child.

Bundren, Addie. *As I Lay Dying*. William Faulkner. 1930.

Addie Bundren, one of the novel's fifteen narrators, is the strong-willed woman who prompts the most vivid responses in other characters. A mother of five, she has a markedly different relationship with each of her four sons and her daughter.

As a young woman, Addie works as a schoolteacher. Because she distrusts the intangibility of words, she makes it a habit to whip her pupils. True communication, she believes, involves strong emotions, often best aroused by violence and sometimes resulting in the letting of blood.

Addie notices a strange, vulturelike man, ANSE BUNDREN, lingering at the school. He proposes to her during their first conversation. Unaccountably, she marries him, but she never feels touched by him. He speaks of "love," but he does not stir strong emotions in her. Upon the birth of their first son, Cash, Addie experiences what it really means to love someone. Afterward she has less patience for her husband's talk about love. She sees the word as an invention by people who have never really experienced love.

After the birth of her second son, DARL (BUNDREN), Addie begins an affair with Whitfield, a local preacher. She loves the son she has by him, JEWEL (BUNDREN), most of all and expresses this by beating him more than the others.

Addie has two more children, DEWEY DELL (BUNDREN) and Vardaman. A few years later, bedridden, she realizes that she is dying. She elicits from her husband a promise that he will have her buried with her own relatives in the town of Jefferson, Mississippi. Dewey Dell, her only daughter, fans her, while Cash busily makes her coffin outside the window, much to the frustration of Jewel who is outraged that the family is treating her illness as a lost cause. Despite this tension, Cash nevertheless shows her every board as he prepares it for the coffin, and she watches carefully.

Just before their mother's death, Darl persuades Jewel to leave with him on a trip for lumber. In Jewel's absence,

Addie sends the doctor out of the room, fixes her eyes on Vardaman, and dies.

Bundren, Anse. *As I Lay Dying*. William Faulkner. 1930.

Anse Bundren, a lazy and bumbling farmer, takes as his personal motto, "I wouldn't be beholden," although he's constantly indebted to others. He tells everyone that a rare disease makes him ill if he sweats.

Anse first notices ADDIE (BUNDREN) passing by the school where she teaches. He begins going four miles out of his way in order to see and be seen by her. The first time they speak, Addie asks if he is married, and he replies, "That's what I come to see you about." An ill-matched pair, they nevertheless marry and have two sons, Cash and DARL (BUNDREN), within a short period of time.

During the early years of the marriage, Addie realizes that she has no real emotional bond with her husband and takes a local preacher, Whitfield, as her lover. This affair results in the birth of another son, JEWEL (BUNDREN). She later gives birth to a daughter, DEWEY DELL (BUNDREN), and a third son, Vardaman, both fathered by Anse.

Anse reacts to Addie's imminent death with typical ineptitude. When the doctor comes, Anse points out that he did not call and therefore will not pay for any treatment. The funeral is held the day after Addie dies, and neighbors advise Anse not to go to Jefferson, where his wife has requested burial, because all the bridges in the area are down. Contrary to common sense, Anse insists he must immediately meet this obligation to Addie.

Darl and Jewel are delayed in returning home to bury their mother because their wagon, loaded with lumber, gets stuck in the mud. Thus, it is not until three days after Addie's death that the boys are able to carry the coffin down the steep hill to the wagon. They set off with Anse and the other siblings but discover that their neighbors have informed them correctly about the bridges. On the second day of the journey, Anse, Dewey Dell, and Vardaman walk across a nearly submerged bridge while Darl, Jewel, and Cash try to ford the river. They make progress until a log upsets the cart, breaking Cash's leg. The accident also drowns the mules. Without consulting his sons, Anse trades the money Cash had saved for a record player plus Jewel's horse for a new team of mules.

On the fifth day of the journey, the Bundrens stop in Mottson, where they buy cement to set Cash's leg. The marshal, horrified by the odor of the decomposing body, tells Anse that he cannot stay in the town, but Anse insists that he has a right to park his wagon on a public street. That night they stay with a family named Gillespie, and in an unsuccessful attempt to end the absurd and macabre journey, Darl sets fire to the barn where they have stored Addie's coffin.

On the last day of the journey, the Bundrens arrive in

Jefferson. Anse has forgotten to bring a spade, and he borrows two from a woman in a house where music from a gramophone can be heard. The family buries Addie, and afterward the men from the Jackson insane asylum, aided by Jewel and Dewey Dell, take Darl away. The family then goes back to town, and Anse spends a long time returning the spade. He later takes the ten dollars the pregnant Dewey Dell had intended to use for an abortion and buys himself a set of false teeth. That evening, wearing his new teeth and with his hair slicked down, Anse returns again to the house where he borrowed the spades. The next morning, after a night in a hotel, Anse introduces his children to the woman with the gramophone, his new wife.

Bundren, Darl. *As I Lay Dying;* "Uncle Willy." William Faulkner. 1930; 1935.

Darl Bundren is the mentally troubled second son of ADDIE (BUNDREN) and ANSE BUNDREN. Darl's inability to cope with the world seems to stem, paradoxically and tragically, from his ability to understand it and see its hypocrisy more clearly than others.

Darl has been disturbed for some time, perhaps since returning from the war, and the law has threatened to remove him from the family. People are suspicious of Darl because he looks at them as though he could see inside them. He does, in fact, know things about people: He knows that his sister DEWEY DELL (BUNDREN) is pregnant even though she never told him "in words"; he also knows that Anse is not the father of JEWEL (BUNDREN), his brother, and that his mother, Addie, cares more about Jewel than the rest of her children. Darl thinks about Jewel all the time and is obsessed with Jewel's more intimate relationship with their mother. He imagines their relationship mirrored in Jewel's treatment of his horse and recalls the strange way that his brother is erotically sadistic and violent with the animal. Later, Darl voices his feelings when he says, "Jewel's mother is a horse."

Darl and Jewel leave in order to haul a load of wood for the three dollars they will earn; Darl purposely takes Jewel along with him even though he knows Addie will die and Jewel will miss a final good-bye with her. While they are loading, he senses that Addie has died and tells Jewel so in a cruelly taunting manner. Finishing the job and returning home to bury their mother takes several days because their wagon gets stuck, and they must get a new wheel.

Three days after Addie's death, the family loads the coffin onto the wagon in order to take it to Jefferson, Mississippi, where she demanded her body be buried. The river has risen quite high because of recent rains; nevertheless, the family tries to take the wagon across. With his brother Cash, Darl rides in the wagon while Jewel rides his horse. The others walk across the footbridge. The wagon is upset by a large log, the mules are drowned,

the coffin falls out, and Cash's leg is broken. It is Jewel who retrieves the coffin. After a number of days the Bundrens set Cash's leg with cement, which they have to crack off when the foot ultimately becomes gangrenous.

On the eighth day of the journey, the corpse smells horribly, and Darl is offended by the absurdity and indignity of the trip to town. When the coffin is lying in a barn owned by the Gillespies, people who shelter the Bundrens for the night, Darl sets the barn on fire in order to burn the coffin. Jewel again "rescues" Addie's body. Their brother Vardaman sees Darl burn the barn and tells Dewey Dell. When Mr. Gillespie finds out that Darl set fire to his barn, the Bundrens must commit Darl to a mental institution or risk being sued by Gillespie.

While the family is finally burying Addie in town, two men from the state asylum come to the cemetery to take Darl away. Both Dewey Dell and Jewel jump on Darl, Dewey Dell "scratching and clawing at him like a wild cat" and Jewel insisting, "Kill the son of a bitch." Now completely insane, Darl talks about himself in the third person, asking himself why he is laughing. He pointedly recalls having seen, while in the war, the image of a woman and a pig copulating, an image that highlights the absurdity of life. As the novel closes, Darl is locked in a room in Jackson, looking out and foaming, "Yes yes yes yes yes yes yes yes."

Bundren, Dewey Dell. *As I Lay Dying; The Sound and the Fury.* William Faulkner. 1930; 1929.

Dewey Dell Bundren is the seventeen-year-old daughter of ADDIE (BUNDREN) and ANSE BUNDREN. While Addie is dying and the rest of the family plans the burial trip to Jefferson, Mississippi, Dewey Dell is absorbed by her own pregnancy. She wants to use the trip as an excuse to go to town for an abortion.

Dewey Dell has been moving a fan back and forth across her mother's face for ten days. While she nurses Addie, she thinks about her lover, Lafe, and the first time they made love: They were picking cotton along a row, and she promised that if her sack were full by the time she got to the end of the row, she would submit to him. But Lafe outsmarted her, putting all of his cotton into her sack, and Dewey Dell made good her promise. Dewey Dell's brother DARL (BUNDREN) knows that she is pregnant and that she is eagerly waiting for their mother to die. Still, when Addie does finally die, Dewey Dell throws herself across her mother's body until her father Anse makes her leave the body to cook dinner. The doctor arrives, and Dewey Dell thinks about how he could help her if she told him about her plight.

Three days later, after the funeral and after Darl and Jewel have returned from hauling lumber, the family sets off for Jefferson. Dewey Dell carries a parcel she tells her father contains cakes but that actually contains clothes that she will wear to the drugstore. The journey is difficult because bridges have been washed out by recent rains. On the second day of the journey, Anse, Dewey Dell, and her brother Vardaman walk across a nearly submerged bridge while her brothers JEWEL (BUNDREN), Darl, and Cash try to ford the river. They are making progress until a log upsets the cart, drowning the mules and breaking Cash's leg.

On the fifth night, in an unsuccessful attempt to end the absurd and macabre journey, Darl sets fire to a barn where Addie's coffin has been stored. When Vardaman tells Dewey Dell that he saw Darl's action, she swears him to secrecy. Nevertheless, the owner of the barn discovers Darl's identity. Cash suspects that it was Dewey Dell who told, presumably because Darl knows Dewey Dell is pregnant.

On the sixth and last day of the journey, the family finally buries Addie. Two men from the state mental institution come to the cemetery to take Darl away because the barn owner has threatened to sue the Bundrens if he is not put away. Dewey Dell and Jewel are quick to help them bind Darl.

Later, Dewey Dell, who put on her town clothes earlier in the day, enters a drugstore at lunch time in order to obtain an abortion. The clerk, Skeet MacGowan, tells her that he is the doctor but that he expects more payment than she can offer him in money. She agrees to meet him at ten o'clock. That night he gives her talcum powder in tablets and obtains his "payment" in the form of sexual assault. She soon realizes that she has been tricked.

When Anse finds out that Dewey Dell has ten dollars, he takes it from her, despite her pleas that it is not hers, and buys himself some false teeth. With these he goes courting and returns to the family with a squat little woman, the new Mrs. Bundren.

Bundren, Jewel. *As I Lay Dying*. William Faulkner. 1930.

Jewel Bundren is the illegitimate son of ADDIE BUN-DREN and her lover Reverend Whitfield. Although he does not know the secret of his parentage, Jewel is aware of a special relationship with his mother, who is presumed to love him more than the rest of her children since she whips him more than the others. He reciprocates with very intense feelings of love and violence toward her. It is his dedication to the memory of his mother that finally gets her dead body to the town of Jefferson, Mississippi, where she had wanted to be buried.

At the beginning of the novel, Jewel is furious with his father ANSE (BUNDREN) and the rest of the family for acting as though nothing can be done to prevent Addie's death. In an act of denial of this fact, Jewel agrees to accompany his brother DARL (BUNDREN) on a job hauling wood. Darl, who has an uncanny gift of perception, knows intuitively when Addie dies and goads Jewel into a fury with this knowledge. Unfortunately, their wagon becomes

stuck in a rut, and the brothers must spend the night with strangers and then get another wheel. The entire family is not united until two days after Addie's death, and then they set off with the body for Jefferson, forty miles away.

All of the family rides in the wagon with the body except Jewel, who rides the horse he bought with money he earned by working nights plowing a field. The river has risen quite high because of recent rains; nevertheless, the brothers Cash, Darl, and Jewel try to take the wagon across, while the others walk on the footbridge. The wagon is upset by a large log, the mules are drowned, the coffin falls out, and Cash's leg is broken. But Jewel retrieves the coffin, and the ill-fated journey continues.

On the eighth day of the journey, the decomposing corpse begins to reek. Darl, offended by the absurdity and indignity of the journey to town, sets fire to the barn in which the coffin lies while the family is staying with strangers for the night. Again, Jewel "rescues" his mother's coffin, thus fulfilling Addie's prophecy that Jewel would go through fire and water for her.

The next day, as the family arrives in town, Jewel overhears some people on the road making comments about the horrible smell of the wagon. He is livid, and Darl has to restrain him and force him to apologize. Later that day, when they are finally burying Addie, two men come to the cemetery to take Darl to a mental institution for his "insane" act of burning the barn. Both Jewel and his sister DEWEY DELL (BUNDREN) attack Darl as he is dragged away. Soon after, Anse goes to town and returns with a squat little woman, whom he introduces to his children as the new Mrs. Bundren.

Burden, Jack. *All the King's Men*. Robert Penn Warren. 1946.

The cynical narrator, Jack Burden, is an aide to ruthless populist Louisiana governor WILLIE STARK. Jack grows up on the Gulf Coast among the elite families of Burden's Landing. His parents separate when he is young, and as a succession of stepfathers come and go, a prominent neighbor, Judge Montague Irwin, acts as his mentor. Adam and Anne Stanton, the children of the governor of the state, are Jack's best friends. In his college years he and Anne have a passionate but unconsummated summer romance. Anne refuses to marry him, sensing that Jack's purposelessness and cynicism are more than the familiar symptoms of adolescence. Indeed, in his twenties Jack grows into a directionless, even solipsistic, young man, deeply alienated from his family and friends. He is given to periods of what he calls "the Great Sleep" in which he shuts his life down and slumbers.

After flunking out of law school, Jack finds work at a metropolitan newspaper, the *Chronicle*. In 1922 he meets the idealistic young treasurer of Mason County, Willie Stark, and is involved over the years in Willie's transformation into a bare-knuckled rabble-rouser. Yet Jack cannot transform himself; his hard-boiled exterior conceals only an equally hard-boiled interior. He pursues a Ph.D. in American history but abandons his dissertation when he finds he cannot grasp his subject, a paternal great-uncle named Cass Mastern. Mastern guiltily drove himself to an early death after an adulterous affair caused both a suicide and the separation of a slave couple. Mastern's guilty conscience is incomprehensible to Jack, who feels that life's events are unconnected. Returning to newspaper work, Jack marries the lovely Lois Seager but abandons her, too, after realizing he must relate to her as more than simply a sexual partner.

Soon after Burden leaves the *Chronicle* during the 1930 gubernatorial campaign, Willie Stark, the victorious candidate, puts him on his personal payroll. Jack works on everything from drafting legislation to helping Willie browbeat legislators, but he considers himself a hired hand. To the surprise of the people of Burden's Landing, he honestly supports Willie's mission to serve the people at the expense of the elite. And he seems hardly troubled by Willie's strong-arm methods.

By Willie's second term, Jack has grown so distant from the world of his youth that when Willie requests that he dredge up something incriminating about Judge Irwin, he hesitates only because he thinks nothing will be found. After months of probing, though, he turns up evidence that Irwin, while serving as state attorney general more than twenty years earlier, had accepted bribes from a corporation and that then-Governor Stanton had covered up the crime.

Burden relates his discovery to Anne and Adam Stanton. Adam, now a noted surgeon, had declined the directorship of a state hospital project, refusing to associate himself with Stark's political machine. Upon learning of his own father's corrupt actions, he grudgingly reverses his position. Jack's revelation has another, unintended consequence. Anne, long fascinated by the charismatic Stark and now learning her world is no less tainted than his, becomes Willie's lover. Even though Jack's own romance with Anne had ended nearly twenty years before, he is shattered when he learns of the affair. He finds solace in a sort of determinism he calls the "Great Twitch." Neither Anne nor anyone can be called to account, he reasons, for life is nothing but biology.

Jack continues to work for Stark, and late in the summer of 1937 "the Boss" directs him to use whatever he has found on Irwin to blackmail the judge for political purposes. Anxious to confront Irwin and confirm the bribery charge, Jack proceeds. The judge, in turn, commits suicide—without revealing that he was Jack's real father. Burden soon learns from his distraught mother that he has, in effect, caused his father's death.

It takes a second cataclysm to move Jack toward a more complete understanding of his place in the world. Late in November 1937, Adam is told a lie: that he was named

hospital director only because Anne is Stark's mistress. He assassinates Stark in the state capitol building and is killed by a bodyguard. Jack witnesses the deaths and is numbed by them. When he learns from Willie's secretary, Sadie Burke, that she and Lieutenant Governor Tiny Duffy had provoked Adam into killing Willie, Jack still cannot act. Only later, after encounters with Willie's widow and his grieving bodyguard give him a new sense of Willie's peculiar greatness, can he become a better judge of both himself and other people.

As Jack ends his narrative, he is married to Anne Stanton and caring for Ellis Burden, the man the world knew as his father, now an ailing and shabby religious fanatic. Anne and Jack plan to live in Judge Irwin's residence in Burden's Landing only until Ellis Burden dies, and Jack finishes the book he is writing about Cass Mastern, a man who no longer seems quite so unfathomable.

Burden, Jimmy. *My Ántonia.* Willa Cather. 1918.

Jimmy Burden, the story's narrator, arrives at his grandparents' farm in Nebraska, having left Virginia after the death of his parents. Jimmy rides out from the train buried in hay with the fifteen-year-old Bohemian girl ANTONIA SHIMERDA. Jimmy and Antonia begin their lifelong friendship when the boy teaches the older girl to speak English. The two spend countless hours together exploring the countryside and absorbing the stories of the local people. On one adventure Jim miraculously and accidentally kills a giant rattler and finally wins the approval and respect he has been craving from Antonia.

While Antonia lives with her destitute family on a struggling farm, Jimmy lives in relative comfort with his grandparents and their farmhands Otto and Jake, who teach the boy farm work and entertain him with stories of their adventures. During the first winter, a despairing one for the Shimerda family, Mr. Shimerda commits suicide because he is unable to adapt to the demanding farm life. After the death of Antonia's father, Jimmy and Antonia grow apart; she joins her brother in the fields, and Jimmy continues with school.

Soon thereafter the Burdens move into the town of Black Hawk as farm work becomes too strenuous for Jimmy's aging grandparents. Worried about Antonia's increasingly coarse manners, Grandma Burden finds work for her as a housekeeper for their next-door neighbors, the Harlings. Jim then spends all his free time in the Harling kitchen, playing with their children and conversing with Antonia.

As Jim progresses in school he is encouraged to set his sights on a university education. The sensitive boy increasingly becomes a loner, spending more and more time with his books. He observes the tension between hired girls like Antonia and the wealthier town boys, who are attracted to the girls but would never marry them. Jim, too, is secretly infatuated with Antonia and her friends.

Finding the town girls his own age insipid and dull, Jim sneaks off to the dances to enjoy the earthy charm and vivacity of Antonia and LENA LINGARD. When his disapproving grandparents discover his clandestine trips, he abandons the dances and buries himself still further in his schoolwork. Before leaving town to attend the university in Lincoln, Jim helps Antonia by staying at the Cutters', her employers, in her stead. Believing him to be Antonia, Wick Cutter sneaks in and tries to kiss the sleeping Jim. Jim's sense of shame and humiliation far outweigh the pain of the broken nose caused by Wick's clumsy attempt.

At the university, Jimmy meets Gaston Cleric, an enthusiastic young professor who inspires him in a study of the classics. Yet he nearly forgets the importance of his studies when Lena Lingard seeks him out. A seductive woman and a successful dressmaker, Lena says she would like to be Jim's first girlfriend; they dine out and visit the theater together. Eventually, Gaston Cleric urges Jim to follow him to Harvard and continue his work. Although Jim is afraid of disappointing Lena by leaving, she tells him quite directly that she never had any intention of marrying him. Jim takes Gaston's advice and, after completing his law degree, settles in the East.

Jim returns to Black Hawk twenty years later to find Antonia—now a mother of ten children—living on a moderately successful farm outside the town limits. In the company of her large and boisterous family, Jim and Antonia reminisce and renew their friendship. Although Antonia's face shows signs of her hard life, her spirit remains unbroken, and Jim's affection for her is unchanged. They promise to see each other regularly in years to come, and Jim leaves feeling reconnected to the land where he grew up.

Burden, Joanna. *Light in August.* William Faulkner. 1932.

Joanna Burden, an ostracized, middle-aged descendant of northern abolitionists, lives alone in a large old house outside the town of Jefferson, Mississippi. The inhabitants of Jefferson have long borne a grudge against the Burden family for their sympathetic treatment of black people. Joanna's grandfather and brother have been murdered by an ex-Confederate soldier and slaveholder outraged at the Burdens' encouragement of black men voting shortly after the Civil War. Joanna follows in the footsteps of her family's dedication to the rights of black people by advising the administrations of a dozen black colleges and schools concerning the conduct of their financial and even religious activities. In addition, Joanna's house is open to black women from miles around who come to her doorstep for solace and support. When a man named JOE CHRISTMAS, who claims to have some black blood, moves into a cabin on the premises of Joanna's estate, she begins to cook meals for him and eventually has an affair with him that culminates in destruction.

When Joe Christmas first enters Joanna Burden's bedroom with the intention of raping her, he is surprised to find that, instead of resisting him, she seems to welcome his violent advances. In contrast to her upstanding philanthropic zeal, Joanna possesses a perverse tendency toward nymphomania that she exercises imaginatively with her newfound lover. In order to spice up their sex life, Joanna hides in closets or even outside in the shrubbery, either dressed in rags or naked, panting in anticipation of her lover's brutal physicality. After two years of this strange affair, Joanna announces to Joe that she is pregnant and proposes that they marry. But she mistakes the symptoms of menopause for those of pregnancy, and Joe, disgusted by this sign of impending old age, abruptly ends the affair.

Joanna's interest in Joe does not cease, however, when they stop having sex. Having offered to let Joe take over her work with the black schools in order to provide meaning in his life, she then proposes that he take advantage of her connections in order to attend college. But he only scoffs at this proposal. Eventually, Joanna develops a religious devotion and insists that Joe pray with her for forgiveness for their transgressions, a request that infuriates him. Joanna's emotional state becomes so depressed that she muses out loud to Joe that it might be better if they were both dead.

Although Joe has begun to hate Joanna, he is obsessed with thoughts of her and cannot bring himself to leave town even though he feels that if he does not, something awful will happen. Unable to stand his malaise any longer, he takes his razor and ascends to Joanna's bedroom, where she is sitting propped up in her bed with an old-fashioned revolver in her hand. There are two bullets in the revolver, one for Joe and one for her, but the first bullet fails to discharge, giving Joe the opportunity to slit her throat. Because of her reclusive life-style, it might have been months before her bloody body was discovered had not a passerby spotted smoke coming from the house. He rushes upstairs to rescue her body from the fire consuming the last remnants of the Burdens in Jefferson, Mississippi.

Burroughs, Polly "Lee." *The Spider's House.* Paul Bowles. 1955.

Polly "Lee" Burroughs is a young American woman touring Morocco in 1954 during its war for independence from the French. Originally in Fez to enjoy its ancient wonders, Lee finds herself increasingly involved with and dependent on another American, the writer JOHN STENHAM, as the political situation worsens. Although Lee dislikes John's politics and resents his romantic advances, she eventually finds herself attracted to him.

Lee is an independent and impulsive woman who enjoys the thrill of discovering Morocco's exotic beauties on her own. Although she knows little about their culture and history, Lee feels that the Moroccan people should "advance." Unlike John, who wants the Moroccans to resist modernization, Lee believes that the country's poor peasants would welcome the influx of modern European conveniences and that they must and will accept Western philosophy, technology, and culture. This facile confidence comes from a mind not used to profound thought or conjecture but to carefully organizing and presenting those thoughts that are most clearly and precisely developed.

Yet despite her evolutionary idealism, Lee is less patronizing and more compassionate than John, who believes that all Moroccans are basically the same. While trapped in a café during a violent skirmish between nationalist marchers and French police, Lee and John meet AMAR, a Moroccan boy. Lee insists that they shield Amar from the French police outside, who would probably arrest him. Over John's protests, she prevails in a plan to take the appreciative boy to their hotel under the guise of a servant.

Having spent an adventurous day with John, Lee leaves Fez the next day without warning, and after traveling to various sites, returns just as suddenly. This gives John the impression that she must be crazy not to be afraid to travel alone. Lee's daring recklessness is tinged, however, by a naive assurance in her privileged status: She doesn't seem to understand that the impending war might prevent her from traveling about as she pleases. When the escalating war forces Lee to leave her hotel, she is indeed petulant and indignant, and is angry at John for his unchivalrous indifference to her predicament as an unaccompanied American woman. She had previously declined his romantic advances, finding him both clumsy and calculating, and resents feeling dependent on him now for her safety.

She reluctantly agrees to go with John and Amar to the mountains to observe an annual Moslem feast. While watching the communal rites to which she is a complete outsider, Lee feels for the first time an awareness of her insignificance in the universe, a fear that she "doesn't matter." She soon feels, also for the first time, that her Moroccan journey has been a failure. For unknown reasons, but perhaps as a result of her newfound need to be desired and appreciated, Lee suddenly develops an affection for John. Once physically repelled by him, she inexplicably finds herself attracted to him, and they become lovers.

The novel ends as Lee and John, having returned to the hotel in Fez, are about to leave for the city of Meknès. When Amar unexpectedly appears at the hotel, they offer him a ride, although John insists that the boy leave the car before they reach Meknès. Lee fears that Amar will be hurt if the French catch him in the city, but the Americans' abandonment of Amar suggests that, now safe with each other, they no longer have to concern themselves with the plight of this lonely Moroccan boy.

The Bus Driver. "Defeat." Kay Boyle. 1941.

The story's protagonist, an unnamed French soldier identified only as "the bus driver," is a disillusioned World War II veteran whose belief in the integrity of his fellow citizens is crushed by his horrendous experiences as a soldier. Having escaped a prison camp near Rennes, he and a war buddy borrow bikes and begin to make their way back to their homes, taking back roads by day and speeding along the main road in the concealing darkness. As dawn is breaking on the second day of their journey, they spot a woman in an abandoned schoolhouse and approach her to ask for civilian clothing and sustenance, which she agrees to provide. Impressed by the woman's self-confident, even defiant manner, the bus driver remarks that, although the dispirited and incompetent French army has recently been forced to surrender to invading German troops, France will remain undefeated for as long as its women remain courageous and loyal to the noble spirit of the country. As his journey progresses, however, the bus driver's faith in French women is undermined by a betrayal that ironically takes place on July 14, Bastille Day.

Unlike the majority of the war veterans returning from action, the bus driver silently returns to his job driving a mail bus. He does not divulge his experiences in the military, except once, to a pair of traveling salesmen with whom he drinks wine at the Café Central. After having described his escape from prison and his encounter with the impressive woman, the bus driver continues his tale of traveling by bicycle with his companion. Although he and his buddy had just risked their lives in defense of their beleaguered country, the protagonist was disappointed and annoyed when their appeals for food and lodging, which they were willing to pay for, were sometimes rebuffed because of people's disgust with the military and their fear that the Germans would punish them for harboring soldiers. On Bastille Day, the third day of their sojourn, a bicycle tire developed a leak, and they were forced to seek the assistance of the owner of a garage. Generous to an extreme, the man not only fixed the tire but invited the two veterans to join him for dinner and drinks in celebration of the national holiday.

Noticing a group of German soldiers erecting a dance platform and stringing up colored lights in preparation for a dance they intended to have with local French women, the bus driver was reminded of tracts that had been dropped from German airplanes that admonished Frenchmen to construct their coffins and invited Frenchwomen to prepare their party dresses in anticipation of the Bastille Day festivities. The bus driver remarked that the Germans were wasting their time because he was sure that his esteemed female French counterparts would not deign to carouse with the enemy. Upon retiring for the evening in one of the garage owner's rooms, he peered out the window to check on the progress of the fete preparations. Below, a crowd of curious townspeople were loitering among the soldiers, who were still anxiously awaiting the arrival of the women. A band was playing waltzes, and a long table was spread with a sumptuous feast. Amused at what he considered the ludicrous faith of the German soldiers, who actually believed that they would soon be dancing with willing French *filles*, the bus driver was amazed and disgusted when the women began to arrive to enjoy the hospitality of the enemy that had so recently defeated them.

When the bus driver has finished telling the traveling salesmen his tale, he is so upset by his own narrative that there are tears of outrage and agony in his eyes.

Butler, Aileen. *The Financier; The Titan; The Stoic.* Theodore Dreiser. 1912; 1914; 1947.

Aileen Butler is the daughter of Edward Malia Butler, a prominent figure in late-nineteenth-century Philadelphia. Aggressive, attractive, and vain, Aileen's life is a long odyssey of wealth, love, and bitter frustration.

As a young girl, Aileen attends St. Agatha's convent school in Philadelphia. She is conscious of the various degrees of social status enjoyed by her classmates. Although her father, who made a fortune out of the city's garbage franchise, is wealthy, he belongs to a newer set of entrepreneurs who lack the tradition, manners, and refinements of the city's older elite. Nevertheless, Aileen has a good home with a loving family and plenty of attention.

One night Aileen and her parents attend a lavish party at the home of FRANK COWPERWOOD, a rising star in the Philadelphia financial scene who does substantial business with her father and his associates. Stunningly dressed and indisputably beautiful, Aileen is showered with compliments by Cowperwood. Aileen is more compassionate and less conventional than Cowperwood's wife Lillian, and the two soon begin to have clandestine meetings that evolve into an affair.

Aileen's father receives an anonymous note informing him of his daughter's dalliance with the financier. Infuriated, the protective, loving, and conservative patriarch vainly attempts to have Aileen shuffled off to Europe and out of harm's way. When Aileen stubbornly refuses to leave, Butler hires a detective to assist him in capturing the two transgressors together. When Butler catches them at a house of assignation, Aileen remains defiant. Butler conspires to ruin Cowperwood and succeeds in doing so during a financial panic. Aileen can only look on and sympathize as Frank fails and is imprisoned for his part in an embezzlement scheme that has come to light. Aileen patiently awaits his release and pays passionate visits to him in jail.

Upon Frank's release, he and Aileen marry and travel together to Chicago, hoping to make a new fortune and aspiring to break into society despite their past. Frank discovers, however, that Aileen is a social handicap. She is intellectually weak and too showy. Aileen sees Frank begin to drift away spiritually, although the two maintain a facade of conventional domesticity. Soon Aileen becomes embittered over Frank's affairs and nearly kills one of his lovers in a fit of hysteria. In retaliation, she spends time with Polk Lynde, a young playboy who escorts her into the Chicago demimonde. Nevertheless, Aileen sees Lynde's shallowness and is also pained by Frank's indifference to her infidelity. She cannot get over Frank, but she also cannot see why she is not good enough for him. Aileen moves into a new mansion that Frank has built in New York, where she lapses into a life of drinking and dissipation. Frank tells Aileen that he no longer loves her, and she attempts suicide.

Aileen becomes a tenacious but peripheral wife. She is lonely, yet determined never to divorce him. Moreover, on a trip to Europe, she discovers that a young man who shows interest in her was hired by Cowperwood to entertain her, thereby leaving him free to pursue his own alliances. Aileen decides to have nothing to do with Frank anymore and retreats to the lonely New York mansion. When Frank dies, Aileen dismisses his lawyer and hires another one. Cowperwood's estate is tied up and dissolved in years of litigation.

Butler, Joe. "My Old Man." Ernest Hemingway. 1923.

Growing up around racetracks, following his father around Europe from one stint as a jockey to another, Joe Butler learns to be exceedingly fond of horses, the sport of racing, and all of its accoutrements.

Joe fondly refers to his father as "my old man" and very happily forgoes school and a more traditional family life in order to accompany his parent to the world's racetracks and cafés. Because his father is not naturally as thin as befits a professional jockey, he and Joe begin every day by jogging together along country roads. Joe notices his father's fellow jockeys do not need to work as hard to maintain their svelte figures, but his esteem does not falter and in fact thrives on the fact that his father is conscientious and hardworking. Nothing is more desirable to Joe than watching the horses line up at the post and then fly around the racetrack under the expert supervision of their mounts. But Joe's father becomes disillusioned with the quality of horse racing in Italy and quits that particular circuit in order to pursue greener pastures and faster horses in Paris.

Joe and his father settle down outside the city where the boy happily explores the beautiful forest and lake with other children. His father, however, failing to contract as many jobs, takes to hanging around cafés, and Joe, who is often taken along, notices that he is steadily putting on weight. They still go to the tracks on occasion, and Joe witnesses his father cavorting with the working jockeys.

One day George Gardner, a fellow jockey, slips Joe's father a tip as to who will win the race in which he is riding a magnificent yellow horse named Kzar. Kzar is favored in the odds and apparently fails to win only because George holds him back in order to cater to the cheaters betting on Kircubbin, the horse slated behind the scenes to win. Joe is disillusioned when he realizes that horse racing is a corrupt business, and his father, who wins a bundle on Kircubbin, is not immune to this shady aspect of the sport.

Using the proceeds of this fixed race, Joe's father buys a fine bay named Gilford, who is adept at jumping. Joe and his father tend to the horse's needs together and begin to race him. In Gilford's first steeplechase, they place third. Joe is thrilled; he expects a grand future for them all. But the second steeplechase proves less successful; Joe's father is thrown off Gilford's back and then crushed under the huge frame of his steed's body. Having broken his leg, Gilford is mercifully shot, and Joe's father dies as a result of his injuries. Already jaded, Joe overhears several of his father's cronies muttering that the dead jockey deserved his fate because of the dubious manner in which he conducted his career.

Butler, Rhett. *Gone with the Wind.* Margaret Mitchell. 1936.

Rhett Butler scorns the Confederate cause, an attitude that makes him quite unpopular with his fellow Southerners, who are preparing to fight the War of Secession. The black sheep of his reputable Charleston family, Rhett has fallen out of favor and is no longer "received" in his hometown. His most serious transgressions were against military and social conventions: He was expelled from West Point and subsequently disgraced an unmarried Charleston girl by refusing to marry her after a public but unchaperoned buggy ride. A debonair, self-interested realist, Rhett meets his challenge when he falls in love with the haughty, proud, and beautiful SCARLETT O'HARA.

Arriving at a barbecue at Twelve Oaks, the Wilkes family plantation in Georgia, Rhett is instantly captivated by Scarlett. He estranges himself from the Southern gentlemen at the gathering by mocking their war ambitions. Aware of the North's superior military and industrial strength, he sees little hope for Southern success in a war of secession. Later, while resting unseen in the Wilkeses' mansion, he witnesses Scarlett declare her love to the gentlemanly ASHLEY WILKES in what she thinks is a private encounter.

During the Civil War, Rhett becomes a highly successful blockade runner and, by war's end, has amassed a considerable fortune. While doing this, Rhett also periodically encounters Scarlett. He is attracted to her and amused by her machinations with other men. Rhett watches her marry Charles Hamilton because she is piqued over Ashley's marriage to MELANIE HAMILTON (WILKES). Following Charles's death, Scarlett appeals to Rhett for money in order to save Tara, her family plantation, but he refuses. Scarlett then marries another man whom she does not love, Frank Kennedy, because he has the money she needs.

Eventually Frank Kennedy dies in a Ku Klux Klan raid on a black shantytown conducted to avenge an attack on Scarlett. Rhett rescues Ashley and the other men but is too late to save Frank. Although Scarlett is only recently widowed, Rhett decides that he cannot wait forever to catch her between husbands, so he proposes. She scoffs initially but agrees to marry Rhett after he assures her that he will make her one of the richest women in Atlanta.

At first the marriage works well. The couple enjoys a splendid honeymoon, marred only by Scarlett's frequent nightmares, and they return to Atlanta to construct the city's most ostentatious home. They gradually widen their circle of acquaintances to include carpetbaggers and other Northerners who have stayed in the postwar South. They eventually have a child, Bonnie, who becomes the focus of Rhett's existence. The marriage deteriorates, however, because Scarlett still believes herself in love with Ashley. When Bonnie is killed after being thrown from the pony that her father gave her, Rhett is distraught. This tragedy, combined with his worsening relations with his wife, makes him turn to drink.

After Ashley's wife Melanie dies, Rhett recognizes the futility of his love for Scarlett and decides to free her to pursue Ashley. Scarlett realizes that she has been mistaken: She has loved Rhett, not Ashley, all along. But Rhett, drunk and embittered, turns a deaf ear to her entreaties. Refusing to live the lie that their marriage has become, he steadfastly announces he is leaving her and delivers the final, shattering words: "I wish I could care what you do or where you go, but I can't. . . . My dear, I don't give a damn."

Butterwick, Lige. "A Tooth for Paul Revere." Stephen Vincent Benét. 1937.

According to the story's unnamed narrator, Lige Butterwick was a peace-loving, hardworking man who worked a farm some eight miles from Lexington, Massachusetts, and quite comfortably supported his spouse and their five children. Singularly uninterested in the rising tensions between King George and the Sons of Liberty, he was nevertheless confronted by the conflict when a severe toothache forced him to make the journey into Lexington in order to seek the services of a barber. But when the barber saw the size of the inflamed molar and meditated on the huge gap that would result upon its extraction, he suggested that Lige travel to Boston to find Paul Revere, who was an expert in making artificial silver teeth. Although he was originally shocked by the newfangled notion of artificial teeth, Lige finally agreed to contact Paul Revere.

In Boston, Lige was startled by the British warships in the harbor and the city's generally tense and explosive atmosphere. Ignorant of the volatile situation, he offended a group of political activists in a tavern and was soundly beaten and thrown out of the establishment. While searching for Paul Revere's shop, he naively approached a group of British soldiers to ask about the silversmith's whereabouts. He was chased, and was saved from their wrath only by hiding in a filthy old tar barrel. When he did find the animated and ingenious Paul Revere, the latter informed him that his tooth was too inflamed to be repaired and that if he returned the following morning, the dental work could be accomplished. He then showed Lige a beautiful but strange little box that he claimed was filled with gunpowder, battles, and the birth of a new nation—in short, the box housed the American Revolution itself. Paul Revere supplied Lige with a box of liniment to ease his aching tooth, and they parted for the night.

Later that evening Lige discovered that he had mistakenly taken Revere's strange little box, which did in fact seem to house something living and dangerous. Putting his ear close to the box, he heard the sounds of war. At first he was frightened, but then he started thinking about the silversmith's political fervor. Lige himself felt more like an independent New Englander than an Englishman. His revolutionary consciousness aroused, Lige broke open the box and let loose the American Revolution, in which he served as a Minuteman.

C

Cabot, Mary. *The Gate's Ajar.* Elizabeth Stuart Phelps. 1869.

Mary Cabot, a serious-minded young New Englander, faces a profound spiritual crisis. From the beginning of the novel when she learns of her brother Roy's death on a Civil War battlefield, Mary calls into question the premises on which she has based her life. She shares a sense of injustice suffered by anyone who must endure great loss, but she is particularly angry at her own fate, for now, while still a young woman, she has no parents and no siblings. At first extremely disconsolate, she refuses the condolences offered by neighbors and friends. Roy's funeral passes in a blur, and only later can she recall some details from the first traumatic days after his death. Mary's spiritual and moral journey begins only after she rediscovers an old journal and begins recording her thoughts and feelings as she slowly emerges from grief.

When Deacon Quirk arrives to discuss Mary's spiritual condition, his interference angers her, and she withdraws from the religious community. Her withdrawal continues until the arrival of her maternal aunt, Winifred Forceythe, and the latter's young daughter, Faith. Mrs. Forceythe has also known grief, and she still mourns for her deceased husband. Winifred seeks to console Mary by discussing the nature of the afterlife. Mary soon decides that her aunt's attitude toward life after death is both generous and unorthodox. Winifred succeeds in persuading Mary to attend religious services conducted by a Dr. Bland, but Mary remains more interested in her aunt's view of things. Eventually, when Winifred prepares to return to her own home, Mary begs her to remain and suggests that they set up a household together. Although a little reluctant, Winifred agrees, and soon the two women share both their home and duties as Sunday school teachers.

As teachers they must discuss theological matters, and Winifred's unusual opinions become a matter of public record when a young student of hers claims that Winifred told her that she would certainly have a piano in heaven. Winifred's belief that one will have what one most truly desires upon arrival in the heavenly kingdom pleases Mary, who imagines that she and Roy will reunite upon her death. When Dr. Bland and others in the community castigate Winifred for espousing these views, Mary proves herself a strong ally, and the officials soon back down from their extreme opposition.

Mary undergoes an emotional and spiritual rebirth as the seasons change from winter to spring; by summertime she is deeply involved in new activities and neglects her journal for a time. The writing eventually resumes, and Mary notes that Winifred has begun making secret trips that take up a full day's journey. She soon learns that her aunt suffers from breast cancer. Despite her grief and fear, Mary prepares to make her aunt as comfortable as possible. Winifred lingers for several months, but her deathbed is a peaceful scene, for she looks forward to her reunion with her late husband and trusts that Mary will be a more than adequate guardian for the soon-to-be-orphaned Faith. Upon Winifred's death, Mary resolves to care for Faith as if she were her own, and with the aid of her faithful servant, Phoebe, she sets out to finish rearing the child.

Cain, Georgie. *Blueschild Baby.* George Cain. 1970.

Georgie Cain, the central character in this autobiographical work, is a twenty-three-year-old drug addict whose search for identity takes him through street life and prison before he is able to embark on a promising college career.

Georgie's story begins in the late 1960s in New York City, where he roams the streets in search of his friends. He has just been released from a Texas prison and is in search of drugs. He ends up in the house of an old friend named Sun, and after getting high and avoiding questions about his past, he decides to leave with him.

Georgie and Sun walk through Harlem, their old neighborhood, where Sun buys drugs from a woman. When rival drug dealers arrive, however, Sun passes the drugs to Georgie and leaves, and Georgie is chased by the men until he finds refuge in a taxi heading downtown. When he returns later to Sun's apartment, he finds out that Sun has been arrested. The police raid Sun's building, and Georgie is forced to stash the drugs behind a chimney. When he is questioned by the police, he lies about his past and they release him.

After exhausting himself in New York, Georgie decides to visit his parents in Newark, New Jersey. He is surprised to see the violence brought on by the race riots there. When he steps off the bus into a parade of angry white faces, he recalls his experiences of moving into this community years ago. He breaks through the crowd and makes it to his parents' house, where he meets his daughter, a "halfbreed" named Sabrina, for the first time. She is the offspring of a relationship with an Italian-American woman named Nicole. He also learns that his parole officer has been looking for him and suddenly decides to go back to New York City.

While in the city Georgie meets a friend who is also a junkie and is carrying a stolen trunk. Georgie allows this friend to store the trunk in his room. He eventually opens the trunk, discovers that it has money in it, and decides to steal it. At a loss as to where to take the trunk, he goes to Nicole's apartment and decides to stay for a while.

When Georgie moves in with Nicole, he feels he must remain high on drugs in order to cope with his growing disgust of her. One night while he is roaming the streets, he runs into his childhood sweetheart Nandy and instantly sees what he has been missing: a strong black woman. Out of desperation and love for her, he decides to change everything about himself, to "overhaul his mind."

But even though he sees how little she has to offer him, Georgie is still unable to leave Nicole and grows increasingly despondent. One morning while Nicole is away, Chris, a sixteen-year-old friend of Nicole's, offers to prepare breakfast for Georgie. They begin dancing, pressed close together. Georgie begins to kiss her and eventually rapes her while his daughter looks on with horror. Realizing what he has done, he rushes out of the apartment.

In Harlem, Georgie finds Nandy, confesses that he is a drug addict, and begs her to help him recover. She agrees to stay with him in his room until he is clean. While experiencing the painful symptoms of withdrawal, Georgie dreams of the past—of his grandmother who died in a fire, of his troubled childhood, of his alienation in an all-white prep school, of his guilt at being ashamed of his family and his hatred of white people and himself. At the same time he comes to understand that no one is responsible for an addiction but the addict himself—a realization that, paradoxically, sets him free.

Calhoun, Rutherford. *Middle Passage.* Charles Johnson. 1990.

Rutherford Calhoun grows up in slavery on the farm of a widowed and childless minister in Illinois. The minister raises Rutherford and his older brother as his own and educates them far better than most of the whites in the area. Rutherford is intelligent but mischievous, the opposite of his sober brother who greatly admires their master. In the months before his death, the minister becomes increasingly mystical: He renounces materialism and promises to free his slaves. On his deathbed he leaves the distribution of his property to Rutherford's brother. Excited that they will be financially secure as well as free, Rutherford is shocked when his brother, influenced by the minister's piety, decides to give the many workers on the farm an equal share in the estate.

Angered at the pittance he receives, Rutherford, at twenty-two, travels to New Orleans and quickly spends his inheritance in bars, brothels, and gambling establishments. He becomes a thief to support his habits and soon finds himself dodging the police and creditors on a daily basis. Isadora Bailey, a prim schoolteacher from Boston, falls in love with him and unsuccessfully begs him to reform. Unbeknownst to Rutherford, Isadora offers to pay off his main creditor, Papa, if Papa can force Rutherford to the altar. Papa, a Creole with shady connections to the underworld, tells Rutherford that he must marry or risk death at the hands of Santos, a burly thug.

Determined to remain single, Rutherford stows away on a rickety ship, the *Republic*, which turns out to be a slaver heading for Africa. Captain Falcon, an eccentric dwarf, takes pity on him and lets him work assisting the ship's cook. Sensing that Rutherford is bright, Falcon—who would rather spend his time reading philosophy and working on his sea journal—asks him to spy on the crew, whom the captain suspects of being mutinous. Rutherford discovers that the crew is indeed planning a rebellion. By the time they pick up the blacks in Africa, however, Rutherford agrees with the first mate, Cringle, that Falcon has gone mad. Rutherford must feign loyalty to both sides in order to save himself.

The black captives on board are Allmuseri, known for their strength and magical powers. Falcon has also captured their god, which he keeps stored in a box at the bottom of the ship. With the help of this god, during the ensuing struggle between Falcon and his crew, the Allmuseri manage to break free and take control of the ship. Before he dies, Falcon has Rutherford promise to inform others of these extraordinary events by finishing the sea journal. The Allmuseri do not kill all the crew members because they need help guiding the ship back to Africa. The old ship continues to decay, however, and they make little progress toward any land. In the weeks that follow, many die from illness and starvation. Rutherford retains enough strength to care for an Allmuseri girl, Baleka, who has been orphaned. The people on the ship eventually must resort to cannibalism.

During a storm, the *Republic* finally sinks. Miraculously, a ship manages to rescue Baleka and Rutherford, who is now near death from exhaustion. When he regains consciousness some days later, Rutherford is surprised to learn that Papa, Santos, and Isadora are on board. Rutherford fears for his life until he learns that Papa plans to marry Isadora in a shipboard ceremony. Papa wants a respectable mother for his children, which Rutherford now understands because he feels like a father to Baleka.

Through Falcon's journal, Rutherford has learned that Papa held a partial interest in the *Republic* even though he knew it ran slave missions. Realizing that Rutherford plans to blackmail him with this information, Papa orders Santos to seize the journal. But Santos, a descendant of the Allmuseri, turns his wrath on Papa instead. The novel closes with Rutherford and Isadora in each other's arms, planning their future with Baleka and children of their own.

Calixta. "At the 'Cadian Ball"; "The Storm." Kate Chopin. 1894; 1898.

Lively, voluptuous Calixta intrigues the men of her small Acadian prairie community. Her kinky flaxen hair, rich contralto voice, languid blue eyes, and vibrant personality tantalize these men, but none more than the lumpish but adoring Bobinôt and the bourgeois but passionate ALCÉE LABALLIÈRE.

"At the 'Cadian Ball" opens with Bobinôt deliberating on whether or not to go to the ball. He knows that the unattainable Calixta will be there but despairs of ever winning her attentions. Longingly, Bobinôt recalls an incident the previous year when Calixta, accused by a friend of behaving improperly on a clandestine trip to Assumption, cursed roundly in Acadian French and slapped the young woman, an action Bobinôt attributes to her part-Cuban blood. He decides not to attend the ball, but then he learns that Alcée Laballière, his rival for the affections of Calixta, will be there.

At the ball, Calixta, although not elegantly dressed, charms the guests with her animation, abandon, and wit, and is soon drawn into the shadows by Alcée. Remembering their rendezvous in Assumption, they flirt and caress each other, but they are soon interrupted by Clarisse who comes to reclaim Alcée. Although Alcée is infatuated

with Calixta, he has deep affection for the cool, proper, and beautiful Clarisse, and they depart together, ignoring Calixta. Resigned to defeat, Calixta tells Bobinôt, who has appeared at her side, that she will marry him.

In "The Storm," five years later, Calixta is intently sewing at home while Bobinôt and their son Bibi are in town. She does not notice a rapidly approaching cyclone until it is almost upon her. Quickly sealing the house, she is surprised when Alcée arrives seeking sanctuary from the storm. He respectfully asks to wait out the storm in her gallery; she insists he come inside. Calixta worries about Bibi's safety, and Alcée offers soothing reassurance. Her fear of a lightning bolt flashing nearby sends her into his embrace. She attempts to free herself, but Alcée's passion has been reignited by her palpitating body. Alcée reminds her again of their tryst in Assumption, where they were both delirious with unconsummated passion, until Alcée left, fearing he would dishonor the sensuous but virginal Calixta. But now, feeling free from the constraints of honor, they submit to their mutual desire and make love with abandon, unaware of the cyclone outside. When the storm subsides, Alcée and Calixta dare not linger in their satiety. He departs, beaming at her adoringly as she laughs warmly. Alcée goes home to write to Clarisse, who is vacationing with their children in Biloxi, and Calixta is soon joined by Bobinôt and Bibi, who safely weathered the storm and have brought a gift of shrimp, much to her relief and delight.

Calvin, Dr. Susan. *I, Robot.* Isaac Asimov. 1950.

Dr. Susan Calvin is born in the year 1982, the same year that her future employer, U.S. Robot and Mechanical Men, Inc., is founded. At the age of twenty, Dr. Calvin attends a seminar taught by the founder, Dr. Alfred Lanning, at Columbia University. He demonstrates to the class the use of the first mobile verbal robot. Described by an unnamed interviewer as a cold and passionless woman, Susan Calvin decides to make robots the focus of her life's work since she believes that mechanical man is essentially more decent than the organic variety. She graduates from Columbia in 2003 with a B.A. In 2008 she obtains her Ph.D. and becomes U.S. Robot's and, indeed, the world's first robopsychologist.

An important official at U.S. Robot, she assigns Gregory Powell and Michael Donovan, the corporation's two troubleshooters, to Mercury, to a satellite orbiting the sun, and finally to an asteroid to test and repair defects in newly designed robot models. Dr. Calvin herself has to deactivate Herbie, a mind-reading robot created accidentally on the assembly line. Since Herbie can read minds, it tells humans exactly what they want to hear. Alfred Lanning, for instance, asks Herbie to identify the flaw on the assembly line that made Herbie telepathic. Herbie refuses to respond because the answer would damage Lanning's ego. Dr. Calvin points out to Herbie the paradox of the situation: To answer the query would hurt Lanning and not to answer would also hurt him. Herbie, unable to reconcile Calvin's logic, drives itself insane and shuts down in order not to violate the First Law of Robotics, which states that no robot may cause harm to a human.

Dr. Calvin has to travel from Earth for the first time to locate Nestor, a robot trying to escape the Hyper Base space station because it believes itself superior to man. It has sneaked onto a spacecraft containing sixty-two robots physically identical to itself. Dr. Calvin finds Nestor by playing a trick with infrared light. She is able to deduce that Stephen Byerley, the first coordinator of the world government, is in fact a robot.

Having foreseen a time when machines would stand between the human race and its own destruction and having worked to see robots control the world economy, Dr. Susan Calvin peacefully dies at the age of eighty-two.

Campbell (Sheriff). "The Sheriff's Children." Charles W. Chesnutt. 1889.

Sheriff Campbell of Branson County, North Carolina, the story's central character, is a man of exceptional wealth, education, and social standing in his community. A faithful and dutiful man, he seems to have clear knowledge of his duty as sheriff and protector of justice until a situation arises one night that tests his notion of duty and dramatizes the evils inherent in a racist society.

The Sheriff is at home eating dinner with his daughter Polly when a black man arrives with significant news: A lynch mob is on its way to the jail to lynch the mulatto man being held prisoner for the murder of old Captain Walker, a former Confederate officer. Despite Polly's protests, Sheriff Campbell goes immediately to the jail to prevent the lynching.

When the lynchers arrive at the jail, Sheriff Campbell confronts them authoritatively, saying he will not surrender the jail. The mob leaders insist that the prisoner is sure to hang anyway; they want to do something to teach the "niggers" their place in Branson County. The Sheriff steadfastly refuses to argue with them, and he closes the door to the jail. Inside, the prisoner, trembling with fear, insists that he is innocent. Sheriff Campbell unshackles him and, ordering him to step away from the window, tells him he must defend himself if his protector is shot.

As the mob withdraws, a single shot is fired at the jail. Sheriff Campbell fires twice in response, then reaches for his second pistol. But his other weapon is gone. He turns around slowly, only to find himself face-to-face with the prisoner, who points the pistol directly at him. The prisoner intends to escape, and to save himself he must kill Sheriff Campbell. The Sheriff is shocked and amazed that this man would kill the person to whom he owes his life. The prisoner reveals, however, that he "owes his life" to Sheriff Campbell more than the Sheriff suspects. He is Tom, the son of Cicely, Sheriff Campbell's former slave,

and of Sheriff Campbell himself. Years ago Sheriff Campbell had sold Cicely and their child to a speculator; now the Sheriff's son has returned to face his father.

Tom bitterly points out that Sheriff Campbell has no right to ask anything as a father, for he never fulfilled any fatherly role toward his son. Sheriff Campbell replies that Tom is free now that the war is over, but Tom scorns the notion of this so-called freedom. Offering the Sheriff a way out, Tom asks that he let him escape and call no attention to the incident until morning. Sheriff Campbell hesitates, considering his dilemma. Tom raises his gun to shoot, but just then Polly appears and shoots from behind. She hits Tom's right arm; the gun falls from his hand, he collapses, and Sheriff Campbell immediately puts him back into his cell. Wrapping his arm in a cloth, the Sheriff plans to call a doctor in the morning.

Back at home, the Sheriff thinks late into the night. Changed by his face-to-face encounter with death as well as with his own past sins, he realizes that he owes some duty to his son. He no longer doubts Tom's innocence and resolves to uncover the truth about the murder of Captain Taylor. After securing Tom's acquittal, he plans to make every effort to help him, thereby atoning for his own sin toward his son, his society, and God.

But Sheriff Campbell has no opportunity to fulfill these well-intentioned plans. Arriving at the jail the next morning, he finds Tom lying on the floor, absolutely still. Rattling the door, the Sheriff receives no response. When he enters the cell, Sheriff Campbell discovers that Tom had torn the bandage from his arm and bled to death during the night.

Cameron, Ben. *The Clansman: A Historical Romance of the Ku Klux Klan.* Thomas Dixon, Jr. 1905.

Ben Cameron, a nineteen-year-old colonel of the Confederate Army, lies in a makeshift hospital in Washington, D.C., at the end of the Civil War. He is befriended by Union sympathizer ELSIE STONEMAN, a volunteer nurse and the daughter of AUSTIN STONEMAN, the most powerful congressman in Washington. Ben has been falsely accused and sentenced to death for unlawful acts during the war; Elsie uses her influence to arrange a meeting between Ben's mother and President Lincoln, and at the meeting Mrs. Cameron persuades the president to pardon her son.

Ben recovers from his wounds, leaves the hospital, and attempts to convince Elsie that they were meant to be together. Elsie has doubts and tells Ben that their politics and their families are just too different. And indeed they are: Elsie's father is a liberal reformer determined to take land and power away from Southern whites to give to freed blacks. Nevertheless, it does not take Ben long to win Elsie over.

When Ben moves back to his hometown of Piedmont, South Carolina, he is quickly followed by Elsie, her brother Phil, and their ailing father, who has been told to seek warmer climates to regain his health. Back in his own environment and confronted by the new Reconstruction governments, Ben reveals a side of his personality that Elsie has not seen before: In one incident Ben sees a newly appointed "Negro" soldier patrolling the streets and tells him to move, but when the soldier does not obey, Ben hits him over the head with a block of wood. He is arrested for this, but Phil later tricks the jailers into releasing him.

As the tension between blacks and whites mounts, and the power and control of the Southern whites continue to slip, Ben begins to organize people and call them to secret meetings. At this time in the narrative, Ben's true identity is revealed: He is the Grand Dragon of the South Carolina Ku Klux Klan.

Ben and the Klan begin to mobilize their forces following the suicides of a mother and daughter who had been attacked by several blacks. The Klan murders one of the attackers. In the meantime, Elsie's father receives a note from the Klan threatening to run him out of town. As the force behind the "Negro" takeover in Piedmont, Stoneman is Ben's archenemy. Elsie implores Ben to give up his role in the Klan. When he refuses, she leaves him and claims they will never see each other again.

Soon after, Phil shoots and kills a black man. Ben is arrested for the murder and sentenced to death. Phil, thinking that his father will get him released from jail immediately, secretly trades places with Ben. But Stoneman is not found quickly enough, and the plans for execution proceed. Ben and the Klan finally intercede and rescue Phil. Ben is the hero, and in the end he not only remains a force in the Klan but has regained the undying love of Elsie as well.

Canaan, Ari Ben. *Exodus.* Leon Uris. 1958.

Ari Ben Canaan is one of the heroic leaders of a post–World War II Zionist organization. A man of courage and intelligence, he devotes his life to the creation of the Israeli nation.

Growing up in a Middle East settlement, Ari early on became accustomed to hard work. Like other settler children, he worked outdoors helping to reclaim land and at the same time learned to fight prejudice and persecution. When he was fifteen, Ari joined the Haganah, the secret Army of Self-Defense. The girl he loved, Dafna, also joined. At twenty-two, Ari and two other young men were picked to lead a group of people, including Dafna, to start a kibbutz in a strategically important area. In a brutal ambush at the kibbutz, Dafna was killed.

As the novel opens, Ari and his organization are working to smuggle Jews into Palestine. Their base is a detention camp at Caraolos, Cyprus, for those waiting to be allowed by the British officials to enter Palestine. Vacationing on Cyprus is the American nurse KITTY FREMONT, whom Ari meets through the reporter Mark Parker, an old friend of Kitty's. Ari asks Kitty if she would be interested in being

a nurse and acting as a courier for the movement. On a visit to the camp, Kitty agrees to work for the movement if KAREN HANSEN (CLEMENT), a girl who reminds Kitty of her dead daughter, can stay with her.

Soon after Kitty's arrival, the organization begins to prepare for an important mission. The plan is to allow a ship filled with smuggled children to be stopped in the harbor by the British in order to create an international media event. All goes according to plan. The ship is stopped in the harbor by the British; negotiations begin under widespread media attention. The smugglers threaten to blow up the ship if they are not allowed passage, and the children stage a hunger strike. The ship is finally allowed to pass to Palestine. Kitty soon follows the settlers.

Ari offers to help Kitty get established in her new home. They travel together to Jerusalem and to Gan Dafna, the settlement where Karen is living. Ari and Kitty eventually become attracted to each other, but Kitty, frightened of falling in love, pulls away when they grow intimate. A confused Ari leaves town the next morning.

Soon after, Ari is badly injured trying to free his uncle from prison, and he sends for Kitty. She rushes to his side and removes a bullet from his leg while they are in hiding from the British. As he is recovering, Kitty tells him that she is leaving him and Palestine behind to return to America with Karen. At the last minute, however, Kitty decides to stay.

Ari works at various assignments and continues to fight doggedly for the Israeli nation. When he meets Kitty again, they discover that Karen has been murdered during a raid by a band of Arabs. In their sorrow, Kitty and Ari turn to each other for comfort and support. Each needs the other desperately. As the novel closes, they are united not only by their memories of Karen—still painfully fresh—but by plans to marry in celebration of their new-found love.

Carella, Stephen. *Cop Hater.* Ed McBain. 1956.

Steve Carella, a detective in a large city police department of the 1950s, is called along with his partner Hank Bush to the scene of a routine homicide during an unprecedented heat wave. They discover that the victim, Mike Reardon, was one of their colleagues, an 87th Precinct detective. Carella, a large, powerful man who has been hardened to crime but never to "staring death in the face," vows to find the killer whom he assumes is a cop hater with a grudge against the detective. The shooting of a second 87th Precinct detective a few nights later only strengthens his resolve. In both cases the crime involved a .45 revolver.

Carella and Bush go to a local bar to investigate a man named Frank Clarke, who owns a .45. They later make use of an informer to track down a heroin addict named Dizz Ordiz, an ex-con who had a grudge against Reardon.

Carella locates Ordiz in the city's brothel district but discovers that he is innocent.

A reporter, Savage, writes for one of the city tabloids and suspects that the cop killings are the work of teenage gangs. He begins to interfere in the investigation process, enraging Carella and also causing the nonfatal shooting of a rookie cop.

Carella and Bush think they have a lead on the murderer when, during a routine lineup, they find David Broncken, who has been shooting out streetlights with a .45. Their elation fades, however, when Broncken's heel print fails to match the one left by the murderer at the scene of the shooting.

One night a mystery man waits for and shoots Hank Bush with a .45 as he returns home from work. Bush dies but not before a fight in which he shoots his assailant in the shoulder. Carella pays a visit to Alice Bush, Hank's sensual and seductive wife, who seems to be having difficulty playing the part of a grieving widow. She becomes rattled when Carella suggests the murders may stem from personal motives. As he rethinks the three murders, Carella realizes the motive must go deeper than the shields the detectives wore. He explains the theory to Savage "off the record," only to discover the next day that Savage has printed the story with personal information including the name of Carella's fiancée, Teddy Franklin. After reading the story in the paper, the murderer goes to Teddy's apartment and waits for Carella. Teddy manages to warn Carella as he approaches her door, and he arrests Paul Mercer, the cop killer.

Carella knows, however, that Mercer is not the person he really wants. Mercer confesses that he killed the three detectives for Alice Bush who wanted her husband dead and who had the other men killed merely to establish a convincing motive. Before the terrible heat wave breaks, Carella sees Alice condemned to death in the electric chair. On a happier note, he soon marries Teddy Franklin, a woman who knows and understands the difficult life of a big-city cop.

Carlisle, Jim. "Daughter." Erskine Caldwell. 1935.

Jim Carlisle, a black southern sharecropper who is jailed for killing his eight-year-old child, finds that his case arouses some sympathy in his town due to the circumstances surrounding the incident. He killed his daughter Clara because for a whole month she had been complaining of hunger; one morning, when the girl woke up and once again told her father she was hungry, he found that he could not bear listening to her anymore, so he simply picked up his shotgun and shot her.

Jim has been a sharecropper for Colonel Henry Maxwell for the past nine or ten years. Earlier in the month, Maxwell came and took Jim's portion of the crop as well as the shares normally due him, saying that Jim was responsible for the death of one of the colonel's mules. Jim

claimed that he did not kill the mule but that it had dropped dead in the barn at a time when he was not even around.

On the morning of the killing, a worker passing by on his way to the big house to feed the mules takes word to Colonel Maxwell, who in turn phones the sheriff. Jim is arrested, put in jail, and left alone in his cell while the sheriff goes home to eat breakfast. Jim paces the floor and adjusts his hastily donned clothes. He tries to get a drink of water, but the sheriff forgot to fill the water pail. The prisoner then goes to the window and looks at the men who, having learned of the tragedy, are beginning to gather outside the jail. He realizes that he recognizes everyone there and wonders how they heard the news so rapidly. The sheriff returns with a meal that his wife prepared for Jim, but the prisoner refuses to eat and says that he is not hungry but his daughter is. The sheriff becomes nervous and backs out of the cell, advising Jim not to get careless.

The crowd continues to gather, pressing close to the window where the prisoner can be seen. As the sheriff watches uneasily from outside, Jim looks out through the bars of his cell and begins to answer the questions posed to him by the townsfolk, who are obviously interested in hearing his side of the story. When Jim explains that he killed his daughter because she was hungry, a couple of people admonish him for not having come to them for help. He replies that it would not have been right to ask his neighbors for food because he had been working all year and would have made enough for his family to eat if Colonel Maxwell had not taken it all away.

The area outside the jail is soon filled with men and boys. The sheriff becomes increasingly nervous about the size and noise of the crowd and periodically interrupts the discussion by telling Jim to calm down. It is clear that the sentiments of the townspeople are with Jim; some express their resentment toward the colonel. One man drives off and returns with a crowbar, then someone suggests that they pry open the bars of Jim's cell. As the crowd approaches the jail door, the sheriff tells Jim to take it easy, then turns around and walks quickly toward his house.

Carlyle. "Fever." Raymond Carver. 1983.

This story depicts a traumatic period in the life of Carlyle and his family. As the story opens, Carlyle, a high school art instructor, is trying to find a suitable babysitter for his two young children, Keith and Sarah. The school year is about to begin, and he is forced to hire help because his wife left for California and seems to have no intention of returning. In desperation, Carlyle hires Debbie, whom he refers to as "the fat girl."

Although it seems that things will be fine, when Carlyle returns from work he finds the children outside playing with a huge dog. Inside, Debbie is smoking cigarettes, drinking beer, and cavorting with several teenage boys while music blares from the stereo. Losing his temper, Carlyle fires Debbie and throws her and her friends out of his home. Then, after cleaning up the children, feeding them, and settling them in bed, Carlyle tries to figure out what to do.

He calls Carol, a secretary at the school with whom he is having an affair, to solicit advice, for she, too, is a single parent. They decide that things will work out by the weekend when she'll help him find suitable help. Eileen, Carlyle's estranged wife, calls and says that her lover, Richard, has set up a babysitter/housekeeper for him through his mother. This prospective employee, Mrs. Jim Webster, arrives the next day and seems to get on well with the children immediately. Carlyle, more relaxed than he has been in months, gradually comes to depend on Mrs. Webster.

Carlyle begins slowly to assess the dissolution of his marriage. His wife's intermittent phone calls, wherein she discusses such issues as karma, convince him that she is losing her mind. In general, the children seem not to mind her absence very much, and with Mrs. Webster's help, their life soon falls into a routine.

Carlyle is surprised to be stricken with a fever one morning midway through the semester. After calling in sick, he avails himself of Mrs. Webster's tender loving care and spends most of the day in bed, somewhat delirious.

When he awakens, Mrs. Webster informs him that she and her husband are leaving the area and that she cannot work for him anymore. This news and a sudden phone call from Eileen, who urges him to record his feelings about having a fever as did the French author Colette, prompts a resurgence of emotion in Carlyle. Without intending to do so, he sits down and tells Mrs. Webster the story of his marriage, beginning after the children's birth and then returning to the dawning of his and Eileen's love. Mrs. Webster silences the children who sit noiselessly while their father talks on and on. Carlyle continues to talk even after Mr. Webster has joined them, until the story is over. Mrs. Webster tells him that he will be all right, as will his wife, once they have gotten through the rough patch. As the elderly couple departs in their dilapidated truck, Carlyle waves to them, and as he does so, he realizes it is true that this phase of his life will pass and that he will go on in spite of the loss and the changes he has encountered.

Carmichael, Margaret. *The Keepers of the House.* Shirley Ann Grau. 1964.

Margaret Carmichael, this novel's proud and lonely protagonist, seems destined for a life of poverty and isolation. An outcast in her own community, Margaret must draw her strength from the life and power of the land itself. Her story, narrated by her lover's granddaughter, ABIGAIL HOWLAND MASON, is one of quiet resilience in a hostile world.

The illegitimate daughter of a white man and a black woman, Margaret is abandoned by her mother at the age of eight. Her great-grandmother raises her amid a bevy of children in the poverty-ridden backwoods of the deep South.

From the first, Margaret is left to her own resources. She sleeps during the day in order to avoid the crush of other bodies and spends the nights wandering alone through the woods and swamplands. She feels at home and at peace there. Her adolescence slips by in a haze of loneliness and unanswered questions. Who was her father? Why did her mother leave her? Why do her features show no trace of white blood?

When her great-grandmother dies, Margaret feels no sorrow, no sense of loss. The community crowds into the house for the wake. Disturbed by the noise and uncomfortable in the presence of so many strangers, Margaret retreats to the night outside. Suddenly, her great-grandmother's ghost appears and claims her as flesh and blood.

When the winter floods come, Margaret goes with her relatives to seek higher, dry ground. She does not sleep with her relatives in their makeshift shack; instead, she stays by herself in the hollows of trees, tending fires during the night to keep herself warm.

The years pass. One day, as she is washing clothes by the creek, Margaret looks up to find WILLIAM HOWLAND standing before her. She refuses to lower her eyes, to defer to him as a black woman would before a white man. They simply regard each other in silence. Margaret knows he is the man she has been waiting for all these years.

Soon after, Margaret walks for two days to get to the Howland farm. She is shown by the housekeeper to a servant's room, which, though shabby by white standards, seems luxurious to Margaret. She and Will do not communicate much, and yet their understanding of each other grows. Margaret teaches herself to sew, and weeks later when she has made herself a nightgown, she goes to Will's room.

She and Will live happily together for thirty years. They marry in secret. When their children are old enough to go to school, Margaret sends them north, where they will be considered white. She never communicates with them again.

When Will dies, Margaret returns to the black community at the edge of the swamp. She inherits money and property from Will but no longer wants to live without his companionship. Four years later she hears a voice calling her into the wintry night. She gets up from her rocker and walks out into the woods, past the creek to the crumbling brick baptistry where she drowns herself in a bottomless pool, half-frozen and muddied with leaves.

Carol. "O Yes." Tillie Olsen. 1956.

At the start of the story, Carol, a white teenage girl, sits wonderingly in the church where her best friend Parialee Philips, a black girl known as Parry, is about to be baptized. As the service begins, Carol already feels estranged by the unusual environment; she is unused to people openly expressing their deepest feelings, and she desperately tries to sort out the words as the choir sings. Carol even thinks that it would be best if she could record the sounds and unravel them later. As the service continues, the religious ardor mounts; the congregants and choir join together, lifting their voices in prayerful song. Carol looks about her and sees that various people are becoming more frenzied; finally, one old woman begins to shake and writhe in her seat. Induced by the elderly woman's thrashing, more and more people join in the exuberant release of pent-up emotions until, overcome by the spectacle, Carol nearly faints.

Once outside the church, she is attended by her mother and by Parry's mother, Ava, and is told to take deep breaths to compose herself. Although Carol lies to Ava, the truth is that she was simply terrified by behavior that seemed more than out of control. It is at this point Ava undertakes to explain to the young girl that the expressiveness she had witnessed was the result of the release of long-pent emotions. Ava tells her that these people rely on their religion as a way to withstand their everyday lives, but Carol is too shaken to take this in completely. Later that day, when she has begun to feel better, her parents and elder sister confer over what is to be done with Carol. Her father, somewhat unnerved that the nature of the service wasn't explained until after the fact, suggests that she'll be herself soon. Her older sister interjects that this isn't likely since the social pressures Carol and Parry face at school will soon force them to cease their close relationship. Although her mother protests that that isn't the case, her daughter is able to provide telling examples that prove her argument. At this the father cuts short the conversation, stating that his wife now looks as if she is about to pass out. At the same time he points out that Carol and Parry, and other children, are happily playing together outside.

Soon, though, things begins to change, at first in small ways and then more dramatically. The friendship between the girls wanes as Parry becomes more interested in boys and music and in her own crowd, and Carol becomes more involved in schoolwork. As her sister had foretold, the schoolteachers at Horace Mann do assiduously separate students, using race as the first criterion.

Later in the school year Carol becomes ill with the mumps and has to remain at home. Reluctantly and meanly, the teachers send homework via Parry. Parry arrives, dumps off the books and papers, and after a few succinct remarks, swiftly departs, officially ending the friendship. Later on, while in a restless sleep, Carol awakens and hears a spiritual on the radio. Screaming for the music to be shut off, she rushes down to her mother. Carol sobs out that she has never gotten the church experience

out of her mind, and she asks her mother why they behave that way. Trying to soothe her daughter, the mother attempts to explain the nature of life and its unaccountable emotional and physical hardships. At the same time she honestly tells Carol that she had better immerse herself in life rather than keep herself aloof and alone, despite the pain and heartache that inevitably follow human entanglements, with or without the additional barrier of racial difference.

Carraway, Nick. *The Great Gatsby.* F. Scott Fitzgerald. 1925.

Nick Carraway, the novel's young narrator, is the quintessential observer. People are immediately drawn to him, for he seems earnest and trustworthy, and is, above all, a good listener. In his encounters with JAY GATSBY and his circle, Nick paints a haunting portrait of the glamour and decadence of life in the roaring twenties.

The son of a prominent midwestern family, Nick journeys to New York in order to escape a souring romance. He embarks on a career as a Wall Street bondsman and rents a small house in West Egg, Long Island.

A man of modest means and aspirations, Nick becomes intrigued by the opulent life-style of Gatsby, his next-door neighbor. Before calling on Gatsby, Nick visits DAISY BUCHANAN, a distant cousin. Nick finds Daisy bewitching but does not care for her arrogant and self-centered husband Tom. Before the evening's end, he finds himself reluctantly privy to Tom and Daisy's marital problems. When Nick returns home, he sees Gatsby standing alone in the shadows of his magnificent lawn. He thinks of introducing himself, but Gatsby seems to have vanished into the night.

Later that summer, Nick receives an invitation to one of Gatsby's parties. He tries not to look awkward as he wanders aimlessly among the guests. He suddenly catches sight of Jordan Baker, a woman friend of Daisy's, and is relieved to see a familiar face. Together they drift through the dancing, drinking multitudes. When Nick finally meets his host, he is surprised at, and charmed by, Gatsby's awkwardness.

Soon afterward Gatsby drives Nick into New York for lunch. Gatsby shows him some souvenirs—war medals and a picture—and Nick becomes convinced that Gatsby's romantic tales about his past are true. In a crowded basement restaurant, Gatsby introduces Nick to Mr. Wolfsheim, a business associate. Nick sees Mr. Wolfsheim as a pathetic and shady character, and his suspicions of Gatsby are again aroused.

When Nick meets Jordan later that day, he learns of Gatsby's long and secret love for Daisy. Gatsby's concerns seem increasingly unimportant, however, as Nick begins to notice Jordan. They walk arm in arm through the city streets. Nick pauses at the entrance to Central Park and, seduced by Jordan's lithe and cynical beauty, turns to kiss her.

Gatsby is waiting for Nick when he comes home. Irritated by his neighbor's intrusion, Nick rebuffs him, then grudgingly agrees to arrange a meeting between him and Daisy. As he watches them fall in love, Nick comes to respect Gatsby above the others.

After an accident in which Tom's mistress is killed by Gatsby's car, Nick goes to Tom and Daisy's house. He finds out that Daisy was the driver, not Gatsby as he had originally suspected. Knowing that Daisy will not leave Tom, Nick pities Gatsby, whom he discovers waiting anxiously outside.

When Gatsby is shot and killed by the dead woman's vengeful husband, Nick withdraws from Daisy, Tom, and Jordan. They are a part of a careless and cowardly world; he can neither respect nor love them. But he holds an abiding sympathy for Gatsby. Ever the pragmatist, Nick could not share in Gatsby's illusions, but in the briefest of summer moments, he had succumbed to the magic of Gatsby's dreams.

Carricker, Lieutenant Colonel Benny. *Guard of Honor.* James Gould Cozzens. 1948.

Although temporarily grounded, Lieutenant Colonel Benny Carricker is perhaps the greatest fighter pilot in the history of the U.S. Army's Air Forces. Carricker proved himself with acts of unequaled bravery and flying skill in the Pacific in the early years of World War II and was awarded the Distinguished Service Medal. The victim of a burn accident, he is forced to spend some time stateside receiving numerous skin grafts.

In an effort to exploit Carricker's flying abilities, the War Department orders him to return to an Air Force training base in Alabama, where he will instruct new pilots. Although he is disappointed at being taken away from combat, Carricker brightens when he learns that he will be serving under his former squadron leader, GENERAL IRA "BUS" BEAL.

On his flight to the base, Carricker is almost killed along with General Beal, CAPTAIN NATHANIEL HICKS, and a couple of other officers when a B-17 lands without having secured permission from the control tower. Although he is able to avoid hitting the plane, which has landed directly in front of him, Carricker is unable to refrain from confronting the pilots of the B-17. Much to his surprise, they are a group of African-American aviators who have been sent to the base as part of an Army experiment in integrating the U.S. Air Forces. Carricker immediately demands to know who the lead pilot is, and when the man steps forward, he beats him brutally until restrained by MP officers.

General Beal places his hot-tempered subordinate under arrest. Carricker sullenly locks himself in his room with a local prostitute and a bottle of rum and goes on a binge that lasts the next forty-eight hours. When he is summoned by Beal for a preliminary hearing the next morning, Carricker, still intoxicated and barely able to stand, alienates his superior officers still further by failing to appear. That night, to make matters worse, he goes out flying, drunk, in a high-powered attack plane.

The next day the gravity of his situation finally dawns on Carricker. On the advice of another officer, he visits the hospital where the black pilot, whose nose he had broken, is convalescing. Swallowing his considerable pride, Carricker publicly apologizes to him before going on to General Beal's office to make amends. There, he waits for Beal for an entire day in an effort to show his desire to rectify the situation.

When the General finally arrives, Carricker, feigning repentance, convinces him not to press charges. Saved from yet another scrape by his sterling military record, he is free to return once more to his brash and arrogant ways.

Carroll (Madam). *For the Major.* Constance Woolson. 1883.

The daughter of a minister, Madam Carroll was married at a very early age to an abusive husband. When her husband got into a barroom brawl one night and killed a man in cold blood, he was forced to flee town and took with him their young son Julian. Madam Carroll received news later that the two of them were drowned while trying to escape down the river.

With no money, Madam Carroll moved eastward, trying to make ends meet by giving private tutoring sessions as she went along. After ten years of living in this manner of poverty and despair, she meets Major Carroll. Determined to marry the Major and relieve her economic hardship, she tells him that she is twenty-two years old when in reality she is thirty-five, and she also keeps her previous marriage a secret from him. She succeeds in winning the Major, who marries her and takes her back to his mansion in the small mountain town of Far Edgerley. The two have a son, Scar.

Madam Carroll devotes her life to the Major, whose health begins to fail in his advancing age. He comes to depend on her and spends each week resting up for his rare appearance in town, where he is regarded as a kind of local hero. When the Major's daughter from a previous marriage, SARA CARROLL, returns from school in the East, she is dismayed to see how indispensable Madam Carroll has become to her father. But the rivalry that develops between Madam Carroll and Sara for the Major's attention is short-lived, for Sara soon realizes she will never be able to compete with her new stepmother.

Soon after Sara arrives, Madam Carroll is shocked to find one day that her son Julian, who she had thought died long ago, has arrived in Far Edgerley. While pleased to be reunited with her son, a musician who has taken the name Louis Dupont, Madam Carroll is nonetheless frightened about the effect the knowledge of her true age and previous marriage will have on the Major's unstable health.

Madam Carroll's predicament gets more complicated when her son, after a brief absence from Far Edgerley, returns and falls seriously ill. Unable to care for both the Major and Dupont simultaneously, and aware of her stepdaughter's boundless desire to do anything directly or indirectly to help her father, Madam Carroll confesses her secret to her. Knowing that her stepmother must not show an inordinate amount of concern for the musician in order to avoid scandal, and wanting to ensure her own father's well-being, Sara agrees to care for Dupont.

As she cares for the Major, Madam Carroll adds to Sara's misery by perpetuating rumors of her involvement with her son. When the Major suffers a stroke that erases his entire memory, he is finally completely dependent on Madam Carroll, much to Sara's dismay. As the novel closes, Madam Carroll is the only person with whom the Major has any kind of emotional bond.

Carroll, Sara. *For the Major.* Constance Woolson. 1883.

The only daughter of Major Carroll by his first marriage, Sara Carroll was away at school when her father remarried. Fiercely attached to her father, Sara looked on the new marriage and her new stepbrother Scar with apprehension. She soon develops a rapport with her new family, but her tolerance is fueled by her desire to do whatever is necessary to please her father.

When Sara returns from school to her father's mansion in the small mountain town of Far Edgerley, a rivalry with her stepmother develops. The Major, who is recovering from a serious illness he suffered in the fall, requires almost constant care and has grown to depend on his doting new wife. Sara senses that her father, although always affectionate, views her visits with annoyance. As Sara's trips into her father's chambers become less frequent, her stepmother, (MADAM) CARROLL, becomes virtually the only liaison the Major has with the outside world. Always careful to maintain the Major's elevated status among the townspeople, Madam Carroll spends the week preparing him for his only outing, a weekly trip to the town church.

Sara sinks into a depression, causing her to behave coldly toward the townspeople. When a stranger, a musician by the name of Louis Dupont, arrives in town, she remains unimpressed in spite of the fact that his musical talents soon make him a local celebrity. As soon as Dupont leaves, Sara notices an immediate change in her stepmother. She becomes withdrawn, and much to Sara's horror, begins to neglect her duties to Major Carroll. Unable to bear her secret any longer, Madam Carroll finally confesses to Sara that Dupont is her son from an earlier marriage she has kept hidden from the Major. Knowing the Major's fragile condition, Madam Carroll impresses upon Sara the importance of keeping him unaware of her secret.

Soon after Dupont returns to Far Edgerley, he becomes severely ill. Sara gives the young man the constant attention he requires so that Madam Carroll can tend to the Major. Rumors linking her and Dupont romantically begin to spread around town; Sara bears the disgrace valiantly out of love for her father.

Yet as she nurses the stricken Dupont, Sara does begin to develop an affection for him. Only when the Major has a slight stroke does she leave Dupont's bedside. The Major survives his stroke, but his memory has completely left him. He has no knowledge of his family or past life, and can only perform the most rudimentary of functions. To Sara's dismay, her father is finally completely dependent on her stepmother for his survival.

Upon returning to Dupont for solace, Sara finds that he has passed away in her absence. Filled with sorrow, she returns home, where she finds strength in the knowledge of the sacrifices she has made for the Major.

Carson, Edward "Pimples." *The Wayward Bus.* John Steinbeck. 1947.

Edward Carson is the quintessential frustrated adolescent. Known as Pimples, he works as the assistant mechanic at an isolated roadside garage in Rebel Corners, California. Pimples expects and encourages unfriendly behavior from others and is surprised when his boss, JUAN CHICOY, begins treating him with respect and even fondness.

Along with running the garage at Rebel Corners, Juan Chicoy regularly drives a bus filled with passengers across the San Ysidro River to San Juan, where travelers can make connections to other cities in California or Mexico. At the opening of the novel, Pimples wakes up early to help Juan fix the bus, which he calls "Sweetheart." Pimples is a heavy sleeper, especially during his frequent periods of depression, and he is rarely alert. On this morning when Juan barks at Pimples to wake up, Pimples shakes himself and makes an unusual effort to follow directions and be helpful.

As they work, Juan and Pimples discuss the Pritchards, a family from Boston that has stayed overnight to wait until the bus is fixed. During the course of their amiable conversation, Pimples decides to make a request. He asks that Juan not call him Pimples. When he was in grade school, Pimples explains, the children used to call him "Kit" after his distant relative, Kit Carson. Juan doesn't react to this statement, but when he tells Pimples to go get some coffee, he addresses him as "Kit." Pimples is breathless with joy, although it is apparent that Juan must make a considerable effort to switch the names.

Happily following Juan's order, Pimples goes to the diner, sits on one of the stools, and asks Juan's wife Alice for coffee and a slice of coconut cake. Alice gives him the piece of cake but advises him to cut back on "all that sweet stuff." Protesting that he needs "food energy," Pimples eats the cake and dumps several teaspoons of sugar in his coffee.

Pimples later helps Juan unload pies that have arrived on a bus from San Ysidro. A strikingly beautiful woman, Camille Oaks, gets off the bus. Pimples looks helplessly at Juan, who suggests that he take the day off and ride the bus to San Juan where she is certainly going. Occupying a seat that affords him a good view of the back of Camille's head, Pimples suffers a painful longing as he admires her. When they stop at a store by the San Ysidro River, he offers to buy Camille a soda, and while she drinks it, he tells her about his plans to study radar. Camille looks at him with a fixed smile and at the first possible moment retreats with Norma, her new friend, to the ladies room.

It becomes clear as the trip goes on that Pimples has very little hope of winning Camille's heart. He begins to reconsider Norma, the waitress at Rebel Corners, who seems to have undergone a transformation since she began talking with Camille. If he is unable to win the goddess Camille, Pimples thinks, he might still have some hope with Norma. When the bus gets stuck in the mud, Camille leaves her seat, and Pimples sits down next to Norma. With no warning, he expresses his sudden romantic interest in her. When it appears that this has been well received, Pimples makes a pass at Norma, causing her to leap up, shrieking, and run to Camille. Pimples feels sick with disappointment until Juan kindly asks him to "take charge" and help get the bus out of its rut and moving toward San Juan again.

Carter, Nick. "Scylla, the Sea Robber." Frederick Van Rensellaer Dey. 1905.

Having just returned from seven months abroad solving a mystery in Japan, famous detective Nick Carter is immediately confronted with a new challenging mystery. Nick is informed by the chief inspector of the New York City Police Department of a rash of acts of piracy in New York Harbor committed by a gang of beautiful women lead by the enigmatic Scylla, the Queen of the Sirens.

Nick immediately interviews a sea captain named Buttle who had the latest encounter with Scylla. While alone in his cabin one night, Buttle relates to Carter, a voluptuous woman wearing a mask mysteriously appeared, telling him to empty out the ship's safe and other valuables into the ocean. When the woman then disappeared off the side of the ship, Buttle goes on to explain, he jumped off after her, only to be amazed to find a dozen other women swimming around the side of the boat. Buttle was then taken by the sea robbers through a tunnel and into a secret hideaway where he was fed and entertained by the twelve women and their leader. After promising not to tell anyone of his adventure, Captain Buttle was returned to his ship.

When the captain goes on to tell the amazed Carter that Scylla promised to return to him that night, the de-

tective asks the captain if he can accompany him back to his ship and hide in his cabin so that he may catch a glimpse of the elusive siren. Captain Buttle, enamored with the beautiful sea robber, flatly refuses. After meeting privately with the inspector, Carter arranges to have the captain detained by the police in order to allow Carter, cleverly disguised as the captain, to take his place aboard the ship.

After waiting in the captain's quarters until midnight, Carter is finally visited by the mysterious woman, who takes him to the secret hideaway. After being carefully interrogated by Scylla as to the activities that day, Carter is shocked to learn that the clever woman has known all along that he is the world-famous detective. Because he is bound by his duty to uphold the law, Carter is unable to promise that he will not attempt to bring the sea robbers to justice. Left with no other choice but to kill him, the women take him to a buoy floating in the harbor, tie him up with four hundred pounds of weights, and throw him off the side to drown.

Carter is saved when one of the sea robbers, who has fallen in love with him, swims down and unties the weights. The detective escapes and returns to the secret hideout later that day with the inspector and a band of officers to bring Scylla and her cohorts to justice.

Carteret (Major). *The Marrow of Tradition.* Charles W. Chesnutt. 1901.

An embittered and frustrated ex-Confederate soldier, Major Carteret has lost his family mansion and money in the Civil War and is the last male of his family line. Although he has regained his wealth and position through his marriage to Olivia Merkell, he is determined to wrench control of the South from the recently freed and franchised blacks who are enjoying the hiatus of Reconstruction.

Together with Captain McBane, an ex-slave overseer who has accumulated wealth through dealing in convict labor, and General Belmont, a lawyer and former slave owner, Carteret plots to end black domination of the political scene in his hometown, Wellington, and in the rest of the South. The three use Carteret's newspaper to incite hatred and discontent in the region. The murder of an elderly white woman enables the conspirators to goad the populace of Wellington into an angry mob that comes close to lynching an innocent black man. When it becomes apparent that the murder was committed by a white man, the mob reluctantly disperses.

Still determined to stir up violence against the blacks of Wellington and those whites who support equal rights, Major Carteret and his cohorts plan a riot. Led by Captain McBane, the vicious mob attacks any blacks found roaming the streets of Wellington. Helpless men, women, and children flee the town for the surrounding woods. The black-controlled newspaper and hospital are torched, while black and white members of the city government are forced to resign and leave town. By the time the mob has burned the hospital and massacred a group of black men who have dared to resist, the inciters of the riot realize that they have unleashed a force which has grown beyond their power to control. Ironically, Carteret's attempt to reason with the group is misinterpreted as a signal for additional violence.

Realizing the hopelessness of curbing the violence, Carteret returns home where he learns that his young son Dodie is dangerously ill. To his dismay all of the five or six white doctors of Wellington have been incapacitated by the riot. Consequently, Carteret is forced to go to DR. WILLIAM MILLER, the black doctor whose services he has previously refused because of his race.

After Dr. Miller refuses to come at the behest of a messenger, Carteret himself goes to ask the doctor's help. Reminding Carteret of his earlier refusal of his medical aid, Miller dramatically reveals that his own young son has been killed by a stray bullet during the rioting, and he again denies aid to Dodie. In desperation, Mrs. Carteret flies to the Miller home to plead her child's case.

Torn between his rage and his Hippocratic duty, Miller agrees to do whatever his wife, who is grieving over her dead child, bids him to do. In the end Mrs. Miller agrees to send her husband—not because Mrs. Carteret has finally acknowledged her as the half-sister she is or because she has promised to give her half of their father's estate but because, she says, she wants the Carterets to know that a noble spirit which can do good in the face of injustice exists in her home. As the novel closes, Dr. Miller rushes away with Mrs. Carteret to do what he can for Dodie. Mrs. Carteret faints under the stress of her emotions, and as Major Carteret receives her at the door of their home, he tells Dr. Miller that Dodie is, "thank God," still alive.

Cartwheel, Vera. *Miss MacIntosh, My Darling.* Marguerite Young. 1965.

Vera Cartwheel is the narrator of this experimental novel depicting the precariousness of consciousness and the perils of isolation. As Vera's inner life unfolds, the reader becomes acquainted with the peculiar set of characters whom Vera has experienced as "family": her bedridden, opium-addicted mother; Mr. Spitzer, an old friend; and, most important, her former governess, Miss MacIntosh.

Miss MacIntosh, Vera's childhood caretaker, vanished one day, leaving Vera with an aching and seemingly permanent sense of loss. When the novel opens, Vera, a young and lonely transient, is on a bus heading across America toward Miss MacIntosh's midwestern birthplace. She has been traveling around without ever keeping to one place or job for very long. During the ride to What Cheer, Iowa, Vera's mind flashes back to her childhood.

Vera had grown up the daughter of a rich, widowed opium addict, Catherine Cartwheel, in a huge, isolated house on a New England beach. Catherine would lie in bed and inhabit a world of fantasy peopled by dead celebrities and sperm whales. As Catherine was unable to care for Vera and often forgot that her daughter existed, a family friend hired Miss MacIntosh to raise her. Vera, too, was accustomed to inhabiting her own world of dreams, which Miss MacIntosh then sought ardently to dispel. From seven to fourteen Vera had been told to live only in the present reality, but she often lapsed and rebelled against Miss MacIntosh's stern grip on "things as they are."

In the month before Miss MacIntosh vanished, Vera discovered her secrets: She was completely hairless and had only one breast. Once Vera discovered these facts, she forced Miss MacIntosh to talk about her past. Their relationship changed greatly, and Miss MacIntosh began to slip away from Vera. One morning Miss MacIntosh vanished from the beach, leaving all her clothing and paraphernalia on the sand.

Shortly after Miss MacIntosh's disappearance and possible death Vera begins the wandering that eventually leads her to a lonely midwestern town. Vera stays in a strange old hotel in a room with a sign that says FIRE ESCAPE. The walls are thin, and she hears the fights and nightmares of her neighbors. In this town Vera befriends a waitress and marries a deaf man. We follow her internal life, which seems to have become one with the people and place around her. The line between Vera and others and the line between dream and reality vanish in What Cheer, Iowa—itself a vanishing point between Vera's childhood and her present.

Carvel, Colonel Comyn. *The Crisis.* Winston Churchill. 1901.

Colonel Comyn Carvel, the epitome of the Southern gentleman, is a prominent slave owner in St. Louis, Missouri. Colonel Carvel has a high standing in the community. His argument against freeing the slaves, logical but morally vacuous, helps convince the novel's hero, STEPHEN BRICE, to join the abolitionist struggle.

Despite his stand on the slavery issue—he refers to slaves as "a low breed that ain't fit for freedom"—the colonel is a man of some principles. He once shot a man who tried to buy his influence. He is also a good friend of the abolitionist JUDGE SILAS WHIPPLE, Stephen's mentor, even though he disagrees with his friend's radical politics.

The colonel and the judge argue frequently. Judge Whipple takes the position that it is immoral for a person to hold another in bondage, and he comments that most slave owners are more concerned with their own material goods than with the spiritual needs of slaves. The colonel counters with the argument that the South's economic foundation would collapse if slavery were made illegal. The colonel's economic theories make sense, but they also contain a great deal of prejudice; he believes that blacks lack self-control, and therefore the education necessary to mold them into good citizens would take centuries.

The Civil War breaks out shortly, leaving the colonel with a huge dilemma on his hands. His daughter Virginia has been promised in marriage to Stephen, who has become a soldier in the Union Army. He is gravely disappointed by the fact that Stephen will not join the Confederate cause but decides not to break his word to the younger man and allows him to remain engaged to his daughter.

Carvel sacrifices everything for the Confederacy, including his business and his life, but he continues to be honorable in his own way. Despite division over the war, his loyalty to old friends never wavers. When Judge Whipple lies dying on the other side of the battle front, Carvel risks charges of spying for the Confederacy by sneaking to the North to see his friend one last time.

Carvel dies before the end of the war, but his legacy lives on in his daughter. Virginia possesses much of his honor and dignity and brings those qualities to her marriage with Stephen as North and South attempt to reunite after the bitter conflict.

Carvel, Richard. *Richard Carvel.* Winston Churchill. 1899.

Presented as the memoirs of an eighteenth-century Maryland gentleman, this historical novel takes its narrator-hero through a long and stirring career. Born in Annapolis to a wealthy colonial family, Richard Carvel begins his tale by introducing the figures who will play the largest roles in his life: his grandfather, who becomes his guardian after the early deaths of his parents; his tutor, Mr. Allen; a visiting nobleman, Lory Comyn; his unscrupulous Uncle Grafton; and his lifelong ladylove, Dorothy Manners. The heir apparent to Carvel Hall and its large and prosperous estates, Richard lives the life of a young blade until Mr. Allen and Uncle Grafton, hoping to gain control of the property, have him kidnapped and thrown aboard a slave ship bound for the West Indies. The slaver is sunk by a vessel commanded by John Paul, who rescues Richard and transports him to Scotland. There Richard persuades John Paul to accompany him to London where he expects to find business agents of his grandfather who will return him to Annapolis and give John Paul command of one of the family ships.

In London, Richard learns that Dorothy Manners and her parents have settled in the capital because her father hopes to marry her off to the rich but repugnant Duke of Chartersea. Dorothy, the toast of the town, has so far resisted this plan; together with Lord Comyn, she introduces Richard to the world of fashion and power. He becomes intimate with such figures as Horace Walpole and Charles James Fox, the great statesman sympathetic to the North American colonies. He manages to foil the marriage plot engineered by Dorothy's father, but his own suit is delayed when he learns that he has been cheated out of his Maryland estates by Uncle Grafton, and he is forced to return to America.

When the Revolutionary War breaks out, Richard enlists in the navy to serve under his old friend, now Captain John Paul Jones. He is badly wounded in the great sea battle that makes Jones an American naval hero. Taken secretly to London, he is nursed by Dorothy Manners, who at last consents to wed him and escapes with him back to America. With his Maryland estates restored, he looks forward to a long and prosperous life with Dorothy in the now independent nation.

Carver, Betsy. *A Summons to Memphis.* Peter Taylor. 1986.

Betsy Carver, the sister of the novel's narrator, is an unmarried woman in late middle age whose life has been thwarted by her inability to detach herself from her father.

Betsy was born in Nashville in 1911. Her father is a prominent attorney, her mother a lovely woman of the best Nashville stock; both have high hopes for Betsy and her siblings to attain the prominence in Nashville life that they themselves have achieved. Betsy is a vivacious and athletic girl, a witty conversationalist, and a popular figure among the smart high school set. When it is time for her make the circuit of debutante balls and coming-out parties, she succeeds handsomely. Betsy finds herself being wooed by a young man named Wyant Brawley—a most eligible suitor descended from two of Nashville's most distinguished families. Wyant plans to go to medical school, and Betsy plans to wait for him to finish his schooling and then marry him.

But when Betsy is twenty, something happens that drastically alters the course of her life. Her father's partner, Lewis Shackelford, gambles with her father's money and with the stock of his business. Shackelford loses, plunging himself and all those associated with him into financial ruin. Betsy's father, a man of strong will and character, refuses to be daunted by this loss. He resolves to move his family to Memphis. The move is a success for Betsy's father, but it proves fatal to the rest of the family. Once they have moved to Memphis, they find it impossible to get their lives back together.

Wyant still wants to marry Betsy. He helps her family with their move, visits frequently, and invites Betsy to come and stay with his family in Nashville. But Betsy's father grows suspicious of Wyant; it is as though he has grown suspicious of everything and everyone associated with Nashville. He begins to treat Wyant coldly, and the young man, sensitive to this sudden rebuke, dares to question him on the matter. Betsy's father says that he has reasons not to trust Wyant although he won't say what they are. Betsy goes to speak with her father. He speaks warmly and kindly about Wyant at first but then begins to show her what is wrong with Wyant's character. Betsy's father is a wonderfully handsome and charming man, and he is an excellent lawyer. His physical attributes and his proficiency at argument win Betsy over, and she breaks off her engagement with Wyant.

In the next year, Betsy's younger sister Josephine similarly breaks up with a young man, generated by her father's disapproval. And now the two sisters begin to live a life in Memphis unlike anything they could have planned for themselves. Betsy begins to drink a great deal, to attend parties and functions at the Memphis Junior League, to become an outgoing, gossipy figure, something of a joke and something of a terror on the Memphis social scene.

Betsy and Josephine eventually go into business together, establishing a successful real estate firm and moving out from under their father's roof into their own separate, well-maintained houses. Betsy becomes an outlandish dresser. It seems that the closer she gets to middle age, the more she feels the need to dress as a young girl, to wear clothing that almost parodies her present condition; it is as if she is playing a strange charade of her life for her father's benefit.

All goes smoothly until, many years later and after her mother has died, Betsy's father begins to court younger women, women almost the same age as Betsy. It is clear that the old man wants to marry again, and this is something Betsy and Josephine cannot abide. The two women, now in late middle age, actually go out and spy on their octogenarian father and the young women he is courting. Their father's remarriage would present the ultimate rejection of the lives they have been living for his benefit. For better or worse, the old man's attempts to remarry do not work out. In fact, he ends up being rejected by a much younger woman. Betsy, seeing how miserable the old man is, decides that he needs her and her sister more than ever. She abandons her wild clothing for a more practical housedress. Josephine feels the same way. The two aging women will close up their individual houses and move back in with their father.

Carwin, Francis. *Wieland, or The Transformation: An American Tale.* Charles Brockden Brown. 1798.

The mysterious and frightful events in the novel revolve around the actions and talents of Francis Carwin, an intelligent but strange-looking man who has traveled extensively in Europe and the United States. In his memoirs Carwin discusses his early life as the son of a farmer in rural Pennsylvania; while still in his teens, he discovers that he possesses a rare ability to mimic other voices and animal sounds and to project these voices at will. Carwin's ventriloquism, called biloquism in both his memoirs and in the novel, improves as he assiduously practices and hones his craft. He moves to Philadelphia where he lives with his widowed aunt and pursues an independent course of study. After her death, which leaves him destitute, Car-

win meets the wealthy and weird Mr. Ludloe, an Irishman. Ludloe takes Carwin under his wing and pays for their passage to Ireland, where Carwin resides with the Ludloes and continues to study literature and philosophy.

On a trip to Spain, which results in Carwin's conversion to Catholicism, he meets PLEYEL and the two become somewhat friendly. When Pleyel returns to the United States, he resumes his friendship with THEODORE WIELAND and CLARA WIELAND. Eventually, Carwin himself arrives and befriends the Wielands. Shortly after Carwin's arrival, a series of apparently supernatural events occur. Chief among these events are the repeated and unaccountable voices that the Wielands and Pleyel begin to hear. These voices, a device of subterfuge used by Carwin to conceal his ongoing affair with Judith, Clara's servant, indirectly contribute to Theodore Wieland's developing madness, for the latter has long had a propensity toward belief in the supernatural and a susceptibility to proofs of its existence. Carwin's ventriloquism and mimicry directly lead to the disruption of a romance between Pleyel and Clara, as Pleyel overhears what he takes to be a conversation between Carwin and Clara. The contents of the conversation, later shown to be Carwin's fabrication, shock Pleyel into a total rejection of Clara.

In an effort to stop Carwin's interference, Clara agrees to meet him late one evening at her home. She arrives to find a note from him and the gruesome spectacle of the body of Catharine Wieland, her sister-in-law. It is soon revealed that the entire Wieland family, with the exception of Wieland himself, has also been murdered. Suspicion is immediately cast on Carwin, but the distraught Clara collapses and falls seriously ill before she can act on her suspicions. When she recovers, she learns that Wieland himself had committed the crimes and is currently in prison for life. As she prepares to depart for Europe, she returns home to destroy her diary. Here she again encounters Carwin, who explains his unintentional role in Wieland's actions. They are interrupted when the escaped Wieland arrives, intending to kill Clara as yet one more sacrifice. Wieland is stopped when Carwin projects his voices and explains that the divine order has been rescinded, and Wieland learns the true folly of his beliefs and actions.

Cary, Olivia Blanchard. *Comedy: American Style.* Jessie Redmon Fauset. 1933.

From early childhood, Olivia Blanchard Cary is unable to experience the joy of human relationships. Marred by racial prejudice as a little girl, Olivia resents her father, Lee Blanchard, for having made her "colored" and looks with incomprehension on her parents' happiness. She becomes a single-minded woman, obsessed with a desire to enter the white world, to be a member of the white ruling class.

Two events lead directly to the formation of Olivia's

obsession. The first takes place one winter when she is very small. She accidentally hits a girl with a snowball, and the child calls her a "nasty little nigger." Although the children playing nearby have been aware that pale-skinned Olivia has a dark father, it has never occurred to them to classify her this way. From then on, the children set her apart and exclude her.

About a month later, after her father has died of pneumonia and she has moved with her mother to a new town, the second event occurs. A young schoolteacher who does not know her name calls her the "little Italian girl." She realizes that people in the new town do not know she is African American. Olivia later tells her disappointed mother that if others think she is white, she'd "better be white."

When Olivia is seventeen, her mother Janet decides to move to nearby Cambridge, Massachusetts, where for two years she has been taking courses at Harvard. A generous professor helps Janet purchase a house, which she sets up as a boardinghouse for black students. Determined to marry into a better class, Olivia begins dating a boardinghouse resident, a light-skinned African-American medical student named Christopher Cary.

Her mother's remarriage to a man named Ralph Blake and the birth of their twins finally cause Olivia to marry Chris Cary. The Blakes have almost the same coloring as herself and Christopher, so Olivia assumes that her two children will be as white as the twins. Her first two children, TERESA (CARY) and Christopher, are in fact fair enough to "pass." To her disappointment, however, both children share Dr. Cary's pride in his African heritage and, like him, grow to resent his obsession with "passing." The third child, OLIVER (CARY), is an exquisite, talented, and charming little boy. Olivia treats him with reflexive cruelty, however, because he has the dark bronze coloring of her father.

Olivia's prejudice plays an increasingly destructive role in her children's lives. Her daughter Teresa plans for two years to elope with a dark-skinned engineering student, knowing that Olivia would never approve of the marriage. Olivia manages to intercept them on the day of the elopement, and Teresa is plagued with regret years afterward. Her son Oliver, after years of enduring her humiliations and struggling to understand her coldness toward him, comes across a letter clearly expressing her racism. Not long afterward, he kills himself.

Soon after his son Christopher marries an African-American woman named PHEBE GRANT, Dr. Cary falls ill and the family loses its entire fortune. When the Carys move into the Grant home, Olivia is uncooperative and hostile toward Mrs. Grant, who is dark-skinned. After Phebe and Olivia argue, Dr. Cary finally expresses his anger toward his wife and her prejudice. Packing her bags and picking up her secret savings in New York, Olivia then travels to southern France.

When breaking up her daughter's first engagement, Olivia had arranged one more to her liking by promising the suitor a handsome allowance. Teresa lives unhappily with her French husband in Toulouse, where Olivia now seeks refuge. But because the allowance was never delivered, the husband denies Olivia entrance to their house. She retreats to Paris, where she lives in solitude in increasingly dingy hotels. At the book's close, Olivia, finally rejected by her family, feels for the first time pangs of longing for human affection.

Cary, Oliver. *Comedy: American Style.* Jessie Redmon Fauset. 1933.

Oliver Cary is a beautiful and gifted child for whom life and art are sources of deep joy. Of the three Cary children, all diligent and serious, Oliver is the only one who attains brilliance. Because of his mother's unspoken dislike for him, however, he never develops self-esteem, and his life ends in tragedy.

Before Oliver's birth, his mother, OLIVIA (BLANCHARD CARY), a fair-skinned African American, plans to take him to England where they will live for five years and she can mold him to think, speak, and act as a member of the white race. His birth is a difficult one for Olivia. She cannot nurse, and a month goes by before she sees him. Olivia is enraged to find that Oliver has her father's coloring—bronze skin and black hair. As soon as he is old enough to be out of his mother's sight, Oliver is sent away and spends most of his first ten years with his two sets of grandparents.

Not surprisingly, young Oliver never quite understands where he belongs. Of the three houses among which he divides his time, Oliver most loves the Philadelphia home of his grandparents, Aaron and Rebecca Cary. They love him deeply, indulge and protect him, teach him pride in his history, and encourage him to strive for excellence. The home of his maternal grandparents, Janet and Ralph Blake, is more lively and fun. There, he romps with his uncle David and aunt Janet, who are twins only two years older than Oliver's sister TERESA (CARY). Oliver is fascinated by his father's West Philadelphia house, but he feels least at home there; he is always conscious of his mother's mysterious disdain. When her white friends are present, she avoids acknowledging that he is her son. She does not even respond when Oliver sees her on the street one day and runs toward her, calling. When he is older, Olivia makes Oliver act as butler for her fancy lunches until his older brother puts a stop to this humiliating deception.

In spite of Olivia's cruelty, Oliver manages to find endless beauty in life as well as hope for the future. He loves music, practices the piano religiously, and plans to become a composer. As his friend Marise, a dancer, tells him, everyone expects him to do "something great." Another source of joy for Oliver is the deep-seated affection of his sister Teresa whom he adores. She promises him that once she is married, he will come to live with her. Oliver places all of his faith in Teresa and the fulfillment of this dream.

However, when Teresa's first engagement fails, she goes to France, marries a French professor, and settles in Toulouse. While his father is on a business trip and Olivia is in Europe, Oliver comes across a letter from his mother that frankly describes her racist hatred of her son. If it were not for him, "the millstone around our necks," the entire family could "pass" for white. Deeply saddened by this discovery, he writes to Teresa and asks if he may come to live with her.

Oliver waits anxiously for his sister's reply, which arrives on the day both parents are due home. The letter explains that Teresa's husband, who does not know that she is African American, is also a racist. Oliver, with his "telltale color," would reveal the secret; she cannot allow him to come. His brother Christopher hears a pistol shot and runs upstairs to find Oliver dead, a strange smile frozen on his face.

Cary, Teresa. *Comedy: American Style.* Jessie Redmon Fauset. 1933.

Teresa Cary, the oldest child of a prosperous African-American family in Philadelphia, feels doomed to lead an unhappy life. As an adolescent, Teresa recognizes that she lacks the courage to disobey her mother, although she knows that her obedience can only bring misery. With the help of her fiancé Henry Bates, Teresa is able to glimpse, for a brief period, the satisfying life that might have been possible for her were she not under her mother's control.

Teresa's father, a physician named Christopher Cary, and her mother OLIVIA (BLANCHARD CARY), are both Africans Americans of mixed heritage whose fair coloring would allow them to "pass" for white if they wished. Dr. Cary is proud of his African ancestry, participates actively in the black community life, and relates stories to his children of the "heroes of the race." However, Olivia's obsession has been to enter the white world and be a member of that race, which she regards as superior. She is determined that her children marry white, and the fair-skinned Teresa senses that she will be forced to do so. While her brother Christopher feels comfortable among people of all colors, Teresa is at ease only among African Americans and hates the secrecy and deceit of "passing."

In her late teens, Teresa regretfully leaves her close friends in Philadelphia to attend an exclusive New Hampshire boarding school, Christie's Academy, which her mother has selected. She does well there but makes no close friends until another black girl arrives. Alicia Barrett, the daughter of a Chicago judge, is the first girl to whom Teresa reveals the truth of her heritage. By keeping Alicia's race a secret from her mother, Teresa is able to spend the summer at the Barretts' home in Chicago. There she meets Alicia's brother, Alexander Barrett, and his close friend, Henry Bates, an engineering student at the Massachusetts

Institute of Technology. By the end of the summer she has fallen in love with Henry.

Finding Henry a loving, carefree, and reckless young man, Teresa feels certain that her new home will not have the stifling atmosphere of her mother's house. Because of Henry's dark skin, however, she is careful to keep their engagement a secret from Olivia. She promises her youngest brother OLIVER (CARY), whom Olivia has mistreated because of his dark coloring, that he can live with them after they marry. Teresa spends two happy years at Smith College, waiting for Henry to graduate, after which they plan to elope.

At the conclusion of these two years, Teresa travels to Boston for Henry's graduation and stays at the home of her maternal grandparents, the Blakes. Just as she and Henry are about to board their train, Olivia shows up unexpectedly at the station. When Henry explains that they are to be married, Olivia rejects the idea out of hand: Henry is not white. Teresa, desperately trying to effect a reconciliation, suggests to Henry that they could easily pass for Mexican. Shocked that she would even propose spending a life "passing," Henry leaves, and Teresa never hears from him again.

Teresa spends the ensuing months sick with unhappiness and refuses to return to school in the fall. She begins tutoring some of her brother's college friends in French, and he encourages her to go to France to earn a degree. Olivia accompanies her to Toulouse where she is to study. After Teresa hears that Henry has married a Hispanic woman, she allows a young French professor, Aristide Pailleron, to court her. Olivia secures the marriage by promising Aristide that Dr. Cary will send a regular allowance.

With her husband, Teresa experiences none of the passion she felt for Henry or even any real companionship, and finds herself utterly alone except for her sympathetic maid. Still hoping to bring Oliver to live with her, Teresa tries questioning Aristide about Africans and African Americans, and finds that he is a shameless racist. After receiving her letter saying that it is impossible for him to live there, Oliver kills himself. Teresa settles into her "colorless, bleak, and futile" life in Toulouse, keeping alive only the smallest hope that Chris will come someday and take her home. Looking back on the course of events, it seems absurd and tragic to Teresa that her life has taken this course, determined by her mother's ambitions.

Cassard, Maurice. *Dirty Eddie.* Ludwig Bemelmans. 1947.

Maurice Cassard is a Frenchman working as a Hollywood writer during the booming 1940s. The cynical Maurice spends more time pursuing a starlet than writing, but an idea he has for a movie starring a pig is a big hit. When the finished picture is flawed, Maurice is not surprised at how quickly he falls out of favor with the studio that once catered to his every whim.

Maurice is paid $2,500 a week by Olympia Studios to work on the script of a film titled *Will You Marry Me?* His bosses do not know, however, that he has yet to read the script. One evening he goes to the home of the film's producer, Vanya Vashvily, to tell him the plot is worthless. All talk of the film is forgotten when Maurice meets Vanya's protégé Belinda. The married Maurice takes Belinda to a restaurant on the pier at Santa Monica, where he attempts to seduce her, but Belinda is not impressed. After five hours of martinis he is in no shape to drive his lavender convertible, so Belinda enlists the help of an Air Force second lieutenant. Belinda and the officer stop to dance at a nightclub on the way home, leaving the sleeping Maurice in the car. He wakes and watches them, then calls Vanya to tell him he will redo *Will You Marry Me?* for Belinda.

At a party celebrating the liberation of Paris, Maurice meets Ludlow Mumma, a writer who has recently arrived at Olympia in order to collaborate with Maurice on the film. Ludlow is dazzled by all of the attention and money heaped on him by the head of Olympia, Moses Fable. The canny Maurice tells Ludlow to enjoy the fat years while they last but warns him that the day will come when the studio will realize that expensive writers are bad investments.

Belinda marries the second lieutenant and leaves town for a few months but returns to Hollywood after his sudden death. Maurice sees her driving one day and follows her to the restaurant on the pier. Belinda still refuses to go out with him even though he tells her his wife doesn't care. He suddenly realizes that she came to the restaurant because it reminds her of her husband, and he promises to never speak of romance to her again. Soon after, Maurice tells Ludlow that he and his wife are getting an amicable divorce.

When Vanya's servant Nightwine quits, Maurice hires him, but he is chagrined to discover that the servant is a former thief and prospective writer, who forces Maurice to read his script at gunpoint. When Maurice picks up the wrong script, he finally reads *Will You Marry Me?*

While driving one weekend, Maurice and Belinda hit a small black pig. Belinda insists on taking it to a vet, and Maurice reluctantly pays the owner, Farmer Weatherbeat, for the pig. Maurice is irritated by the expense and nuisance, but in the middle of the night he gets an idea. He tells Belinda to keep the pig a secret, and in the morning he goes to see Weatherbeat and requests a meeting with all of the men working on the film.

Making up the plot as he paces, Maurice changes the setting and includes a new character—a little black pig. With Weatherbeat acting as his owner, the pig, Dirty Eddie, goes to work on the film. He is so good that the other actors persuade Weatherbeat that Dirty Eddie should make more than $40 a week. When the farmer requests $5,000 a week, Vanya has a fit, and Dirty Eddie refuses to work until they renegotiate his contract. Unable

to find a suitable new pig, the studio awards Dirty Eddie a new seven-year contract.

Soon thereafter Belinda finally accepts Maurice's marriage proposal. Their wedding night is interrupted by a phone call from an angry Moses telling Maurice he'll never work again. Moses has just viewed the completed film and discovered that the pig shrinks as the film progresses. They had shot the ending first, and Dirty Eddie gained weight during his two-month walkout. Having anticipated this, Maurice has a farewell luncheon with Ludlow and Vanya at Romanoff's, a snooty restaurant where anyone who is "in" goes to be seen. They are snubbed by everyone there. Maurice concocts a story that will allow Ludlow to leave town with dignity. But as he is leaving his hotel, Ludlow receives a call. Audiences at a sneak preview loved the film, and Moses wants to offer him a contract and double his salary. His agent will meet him at Romanoff's to discuss it.

Castelli, Tommy. "The Prison." Bernard Malamud. 1950.

Twenty-nine-year-old Tommy Castelli is the bored and reticent owner of a candy store on Prince Street in Greenwich Village, New York. When he was young, Tommy dreamed of getting out of his neighborhood, escaping poverty, and making something of his life. But now, after entering into an arranged marriage with his paranoid and sometimes hysterical wife Rosa, he sees that everything "fouled up against him" before he could escape. He feels caught, trapped by all of his old mistakes, and unable to break out of the pattern into which he has fallen.

Tommy's routine never varies. He works all day and evening, sleeps one hour at lunch, sleeps all day on Tuesdays when the store is closed, and goes to the movies alone on Tuesday nights. In the past he had attempted to make some extra money, first with a punchboard and then with a slot machine that he installed in the candy store. With the punchboard, he made fifty-five dollars and hid it in the cellar without telling Rosa. The slot machine, however, was destroyed by Rosa's protective father after Rosa discovered it and screamed wildly. Now Tommy only curses Rosa, the store, and his entire unhappy life.

On one of his boring days, a ten-year-old girl comes to the store to buy tissue paper. Though he does not know her name, he has seen her many times because she comes every week, always on Mondays, to buy the same thing. Going into the back of the store to get the paper, Tommy happens to look up at the mirror that Rosa put there to catch shoplifters. In the mirror he sees a small hand reach for two chocolate bars. When the girl innocently emerges to wait for him, Tommy knows she has stolen the candy. He remembers his youth and thinks he should warn the girl and urge her to do something before she fouls up her life. But he says nothing, and after she pays for the tissue paper, the girl runs out with the stolen chocolate bars.

During the following week Tommy cannot stop thinking about the girl, and his desire to speak to her grows stronger. But when she returns, she steals again, and again he is tongue-tied. He blames himself for being afraid and decides to slip her a hint. The next Monday morning he puts two chocolate bars out where he knows she will take them. Inside one of the wrappers he hides a note that reads, "Don't do this anymore or you will suffer your whole life."

Tommy waits all morning for the girl, but she does not come. He gets depressed and feels terribly hurt. At lunchtime Rosa comes down to relieve him temporarily, and Tommy goes upstairs for his nap. Lying on his bed, he thinks about life. He reflects that we never get what we want, and no matter how hard we try, we cannot get beyond our mistakes; we can never see the sky outside or the ocean, he thinks, because we are in a prison.

Returning to the store, Tommy finds that Rosa has caught the girl stealing the candy bars he left for her. Rosa shakes the girl and screams at her; Tommy, suddenly tense, hits his wife and tells her he lets the girl take the candy. The girl's mother enters, sees what has happened, and socks her daughter across the ear. As the girl is dragged out of the store, she turns around and sticks out her tongue at Tommy.

Castillo, Cesar. *The Mambo Kings Play Songs of Love.* Oscar Hijuelos. 1989.

This recreation of the lives and times of 1940s musicians Cesar and Nestor Castillo takes the nostalgic perspective of Cesar, who sits through the night in a room in the Hotel Splendour recalling the past and drinking himself to death.

As a child in Cuba, Cesar hated and feared his strict, stern father and his occupation—farming. At sixteen, with a natural musical talent and an ego bolstered by his adoring mother, he joined a wandering band of musicians as a singer and trumpet player. In this capacity he attracted the attention of renowned bandleader Julian Garcia, who took him on as a singer and embraced him as a son.

Cesar married Garcia's daughter Luisa, but because he was strikingly handsome and insatiably lusty, he did not remain faithful to her, and before long the marriage dissolved. Throughout his life Cesar felt twinges of guilt and sadness about Luisa and their daughter Mariela, but as usual he ignored his feelings and contented himself with occasionally sending gifts to his daughter.

In 1949, Cesar and his brother moved to New York where they lived with relatives on La Salle Street. It was the era of the mambo, and the Castillo brothers soon formed a band, the Mambo Kings. Workers by day, they became stars at night in the big dance halls, cutting several records and achieving the height of their fame when Desi Arnaz invited them to appear on the *I Love Lucy* show.

While Nestor was virtually incapacitated by depression, Cesar lived like a bull. He thrived on the boisterous atmosphere of dance halls and nightclubs, where he enjoyed food, alcohol, and women with equal gusto. As he recalls this happiest time of his life, the fondest of his many sexual memories are of Vanna Vane, who appeared on the cover of the Mambo Kings' first album and was Cesar's steadiest lover.

Cesar's glory days came to an end, however, when Nestor was killed in a car wreck. Although Cesar played with other bands for a time, he found that without his brother and counterpart, he had lost his enthusiasm for music. Happiness returned briefly when he bought into the Club Havana, but after his partner began using the club to sell drugs, Cesar sold out.

Toward the end of his life, Cesar worked as a superintendent in the building where he lived with Nestor's widow Delores and his adoring nephew Eugenio. He was comforted by an affair with a younger woman, but eventually she became disgusted by his decrepit body and left him.

Virtually all of Cesar's bodily functions are failing due to a lifetime of overindulgence. Rather than control his habits, Cesar has come to the Hotel Splendour with a record player and a stack of Mambo Kings albums to relive the days and ways of his youth, and to die.

Casy, Jim. *The Grapes of Wrath.* John Steinbeck. 1939.

Jim Casy, who holds on to philosophical ideals about social justice, stepped down from being the local preacher when he could no longer face his own hypocrisy. For some time he had been sleeping with the young women whose souls he was supposed to be saving. Sitting alone for a long time, Casy realized that "the spirit" was strong in him but that it was not the kind of spirit usually associated with a preacher. Deciding that there is no sin and no virtue—"There's just stuff people do"—Casy, whose love for others is sometimes overwhelming, begins a kind of secular search, an investigation into what it is to be human.

Sitting on a fence and drinking from a flask of liquor, Casy meets TOM JOAD who is heading home after serving four years in prison. Telling the story of his decision to turn away from preaching, Casy walks with Tom, the sturdy eldest son of the Joad family. When they arrive at the Joads' abandoned house, Casy and Tom are dismayed to learn that the encroachment of large agricultural interests has driven farm families everywhere off their land. He and Tom find the rest of the Joad family, and when the Joads invite Casy to leave Oklahoma and travel with them to California, Casy agrees.

On the road, Casy is often silent. When Tom asks what is on his mind, Casy begins to talk about what he has noticed—that it seems the whole country is moving west. Casy perceives a restlessness in the air that people don't yet understand; he believes a significant change will come from the exodus of farmers into a strange new world.

Much later he tells Tom he has been listening closely to people along the way. They are beating their wings like a bird against a window—bursting to escape. Tom listens with wide eyes as Casy describes the underpaid, malnourished, unrespected work force as being pushed to a breaking point.

Indeed, soon after Casy makes these predictions, a fight breaks out when a deputy tries to arrest an innocent man. Tom kicks the deputy, who fires a shot. The deputy's bullet destroys the hand of a woman who is standing nearby. Casy tells Tom to run and hide, and Tom obeys. When the authorities come, Casy turns himself in and tells them to take care of the woman whose hand has been shot. The police load Casy into their squad car. Sitting proudly between two officers, the rebel Casy has a curious look of conquest on his face as they drive him away.

Several weeks later Tom Joad again finds Casy by chance. Casy has led a labor uprising at the farm where the Joads stop to work. Casy, camping with a few other outlaws in a tent outside the grounds, explains to Tom that when the management offered them only two and a half cents per box for picking fruit, he and his friends protested and went on strike. He asks Tom to spread the word among workers at the farm, all of whom are being paid five cents per box but do not realize that their wage will be cut in half as soon as the strike is broken. Before Tom leaves, however, a group of strikebreakers find Casy's tent. Casy tries to tell them they have no idea what they're doing, that they are contributing to the starvation of children, but one of the men murders Casy by clubbing him on the head. Avenging Casy's death, Tom kills the murderer and flees.

Although Casy's life is over, his work is not. Later, when Tom Joad must leave his family because of the crime he committed, Casy's words inspire him to join the long and difficult fight for social justice.

Caudill, Boone. *The Big Sky.* A. B. Guthrie. 1947.

Boone Caudill is the quintessential mountain man, a savage, uncivilized hunter who braves the unexplored American West and lives his life without a roof over his head. He is rude, little prone to conversation, proud, and brutal to women, and he lives outside the normal laws and ways of civilization. As a hunter, explorer, laborer, and husband of an Indian squaw, Boone confronts many dangers during his uprooted, sometimes perilous years in the wilderness and ultimately sees his way of life disintegrate as the West is settled.

In 1830, Boone, age seventeen, leaves his parents and his town in Appalachia, where the law is after him for beating up a man. Traveling west, he meets Jim Deakins, another vagabond. When Boone and Jim temporarily separate, Boone gets into a fight with a stranger who steals his rifle. Boone is arrested and brought to trial. His characteristic inarticulateness lands him in jail until Jim re-

turns. Jim helps Boone escape from jail, and the two men steal horses and head for the open country.

Boone and Jim get jobs working as boatmen on the French riverboat *Mandan*, which is run by an ambitious captain named Jourdonnais and manned by his French-speaking crew. There they meet Dick Summers, the boat's hunter, who teaches them how to hunt buffalos and other animals. The crew faces much adversity during its expedition up the Missouri River and is continually threatened by the presence of the Blackfoot Indians. Jourdonnais remains confident because he and his men have kidnapped a bargaining chip: Teal Eye, the twelve-year-old daughter of the Blackfoot chief Heavy Otter. Boone takes a liking to the beautiful Teal Eye but is separated from her when the crew is ambushed by the Blackfoot and she mysteriously disappears.

Seven years later, Boone and Jim team up with Dick Summers and Predevil, a friendly Blackfoot, in a hunt for beaver pelts. Boone continues his long quest to find Teal Eye, who is now a grown woman. At a rowdy Western-style trading session, Boone gets into a fight over his Blackfoot sympathies and stabs a man to death in front of a crowd of onlookers.

Continuing north, Boone steals a prized horse from the Sioux camp so he can have something to trade for Teal Eye when he finds her. He and his partners finally reach Blackfoot country—only to find that most of the tribe, struck by a smallpox epidemic, has been reduced to a pile of rotting corpses. They press onward and finally find the Blackfoot survivors. Red Horn, Teal Eye's brother, is the new chief, and he grudgingly accepts Boone's marriage proposal. Boone weds the shy and quiet squaw of his dreams and begins to live as an Indian.

Five years later, after Boone has settled completely into the Blackfoot ways, Jim Deakins visits and tells him of a lucrative expedition to chart a trail west. Despite having just learned that Teal Eye is pregnant, Boone takes the job and abruptly leaves her behind. The expedition proves extremely treacherous because of heavy snows and hostile Indians. One explorer is killed; another eats his corpse. Boone survives by killing and eating a mountain goat. When Jim is shot by Indians, Boone nurses him back to health.

Spring comes, and Boone returns to his Blackfoot camp, where Teal Eye has given birth to a son who was born blind. Boone wants to kill the child, but Teal Eye will not let him. In his anger he imagines that he is not the real father, despite every indication that Teal Eye is eternally faithful. He lays a plot to see if Jim Deakins might be the father. Boone pretends to leave and corners Jim with Teal Eye in a tepee at night. They embrace as friends; furious, Boone immediately barges in and kills his best friend. He abandons his wife and child and heads back to civilization.

A reflective Boone retraces the steps of his life. He visits the town where he was put on trial but is disappointed to learn that the men he hoped to hunt down and kill have since died. He returns to his hometown, where he feels bored and hemmed in. He persistently seduces a local girl, but when she begs him to marry her, he leaves town. He visits Dick Summers, who has now abandoned the mountain life, gotten married, and become a farmer. Disgusted with civilization yet unable to continue forever in the shrinking wilderness of the West, Boone wanders off into the darkness.

Caulfield, Adam. *The Last Hurrah.* Edwin O'Connor. 1956.

Adam Caulfield is the young, idealistic, and confused nephew of a ruthless Irish-American politician. When Adam's uncle, Mayor FRANK SKEFFINGTON, invites him to join in the campaign for the mayor's reelection, Adam feels ambivalent about the opportunity. He would like to observe the campaign and become better acquainted with his uncle, his only connection to his dead parents, but worries that his young wife Maeve will not be happy about his spending time with Skeffington. Maeve's father has indoctrinated her to hate Skeffington and his political tactics. But while Adam knows that some describe his uncle as a corrupt crook, he also knows that to many Skeffington is an effective politician and a great man. He becomes determined to find out which of these descriptions is closer to the truth, to discover what kind of man his uncle really is.

Without telling Maeve, Adam goes with Skeffington to a funeral. He is shocked to find that the atmosphere in the funeral parlor is that of a political rally rather than a somber ceremony. When Adam accuses his uncle of political opportunism, Skeffington responds that the real reason for the rally and the crowd of supporters is to keep the dead man's widow from learning how few people really want to pay their respects to her husband. Politics, he explains to Adam, is of great importance to the city's Irish community because it provides not only opportunity for the ambitious but also aid for the unlucky.

Watching Skeffington at a myriad of political and social functions, Caulfield comes to appreciate the mayor's ability to flatter, make promises to, and placate his constituents. And as he comes to know his uncle better, Adam grows to like him more. One night, after taking Adam to a series of dinners and political rallies, Skeffington visits Adam's house and sits down to talk with Maeve. Adam watches happily as his uncle tells Maeve sentimental stories about her deceased mother, and he begins to believe that his uncle is not only a skilled politician but also a compassionate man. Although Skeffington does many "corrupt" things as mayor, Adam reasons, he does them for the good of others.

Since the newspaper for which he works is staunchly opposed to Mayor Skeffington, Adam is glad that his job as a comic-strip writer is not connected with city politics.

But he neglects his work as he gets more and more involved in the excitement of the approaching election. On election night Adam goes to Skeffington's headquarters and is as surprised as his uncle when Skeffington loses the election by a wide margin.

After the election, Skeffington has a heart attack, and Adam takes charge of his household. Seeing all the people who wish Skeffington well while he is sick and then mourn him when he dies, Adam is more mystified about how his uncle lost the election. He feels as if he has been lucky to see the "last hurrah" of his uncle and the era he represented. He realizes, too, that during the campaign he had been more than the mayor's observer, he also had been his friend.

Caulfield, Holden. *The Catcher in the Rye.* J. D. Salinger. 1951.

Holden Caulfield, the sardonic young narrator, is a figure of youth at war with experience. Wise beyond his years, Holden stands on the cusp of adulthood and sees a society that is cruel, alienating, and filled with "phonies." He protests by failing out of prep school and leaving his dorm in the middle of the night. Too afraid to confront his parents with his failure, he spends three days wandering through the hotels, bars, and parks of Manhattan.

Holden's adventure begins with his last day at Pencey Prep where he is failing four of five subjects in spite of his obvious intelligence. After saying good-bye to his well-meaning history teacher, Holden returns to his dormitory. Soon after, Stradlater, Holden's good-looking but boorish roommate, returns from a date with Jane Gallagher, a friend of Holden's. Holden flies into a rage at Stradlater's hint that he "gave her the time," and the ensuing fight leaves Holden's face bloodied. Depressed, he decides to leave for New York even though he is not expected home for three days.

In New York, Holden checks into a hotel where, after a lonely trip to a bar on the East Side, he accepts the elevator man's offer of a prostitute. But when the prostitute arrives, Holden only wants to talk with her. Angry, she takes her money and leaves, then returns with the elevator man and demands more money. When Holden protests, the elevator man hits him.

The next morning Holden calls Sally Hayes, a girl he has dated before, and arranges to meet her. Their date is going tolerably well when Holden confesses his feelings of being "fed up" and then, on a whim, asks Sally if she would like to live with him in a cabin in the woods. Sally insists that the idea is ludicrous, and Holden insults her. He is instantly sorry, but Sally walks away, hurt.

Deeply depressed now, Holden gets drunk and begins to cry. After a frigid walk in the park that sobers him somewhat, he decides to go to his parents' house to wake his sister PHOEBE (CAULFIELD). Ten-year-old Phoebe is also very wise for her age, and when Holden tells her he failed at school because he didn't like it, she counsels him in her own way. They speak of their brother Allie, whose death from leukemia caused the thirteen-year-old Holden to have a breakdown. Holden confesses to Phoebe that his dream is to be "a catcher in the rye"—a protector who stands by a cliff in a field and catches the playing children who stray too near the edge. Sitting on the edge of his sister's bed, he cries.

When their parents return, Holden slips away and goes to see Mr. Antolini, a former teacher who has always been understanding. When the teacher invites him to spend the night, an exhausted Holden accepts the offer and falls asleep but awakes some time later to find the older man stroking his hair. Alarmed and confused, Holden leaves to spend the rest of the night in the train station.

The next day he determines that he will run away to the West, and he sends Phoebe a note instructing her to meet him at the Metropolitan Museum of Art so that he can say good-bye. When she arrives, she insists that she is going with him. Holden tells her she can't, then soothes her hurt feelings by suggesting a trip to the zoo. There, Phoebe rides the carousel. As he watches his sister riding the carousel, Holden is afraid; he realizes, however, that it would be wrong to try to keep her from all danger. Rain begins to fall, but Holden continues to watch his sister, and he feels suddenly, inexplicably happy.

In the final chapter of the novel, Holden reveals that he has been telling his story from a hospital, where he sees a psychoanalyst who asks him if he will "apply himself" when he returns to school in the fall. Holden does not know the answer to that question, but he does know that he misses everyone he ever met, even the elevator man in the hotel.

Caulfield, Phoebe. *The Catcher in the Rye.* J. D. Salinger. 1951.

Phoebe Caulfield is the precocious younger sister of the troubled protagonist HOLDEN CAULFIELD. Affectionate, innocent, and wise beyond her ten years, Phoebe helps to rescue Holden as he struggles to negotiate his adolescence in what he sees as a world of "phonies."

Phoebe's brother, who narrates the book, introduces her by insisting "You never saw a little kid so pretty and smart in your whole life." Holden loves his sister as much as he does his brother Allie, who died of leukemia as a child. When Holden flunks out of prep school (in spite of his intelligence) and begins to wander in New York, it is Phoebe whom he longs to call. He hesitates, however, because he knows that his parents will answer the phone, and he doesn't want them to know that he left school before the end of the term.

Finally, after a disastrous encounter with a prostitute, a meaningless date, and a drunken walk in the park, the despondent Holden steals into his parents' house at night so that he can visit Phoebe. She awakes instantly, delighted

to see her brother. They talk of her role in the school play and of the movie she saw that day, and she bubbles over with joy at having her brother at home. When she discovers, however, that he has flunked out of Pencey, his third prep school, she is disappointed. He tells her that he didn't like the school, but Phoebe points out that he hasn't liked anything in recent years. When she asks him what he would like to be, Holden confesses his dream of being "a catcher in the rye," a guardian who would stand on the edge of a cliff protecting the children playing in the field nearby from falling off.

Phoebe and Holden are interrupted by the return of their parents who have been at a party. Holden hides, and Phoebe explains the smell of Holden's cigarette by telling her mother that she had been smoking. After her mother has left the room, Phoebe gives Holden her Christmas money so that he will have enough for food and a place to stay. Overcome, Holden cries, and Phoebe quietly comforts him.

After presenting his sister with his favorite hat, Holden leaves. The next day he leaves a message at her school, explaining that he has decided to run away to the West and asking her to meet him at the Metropolitan Museum of Art so that he can say good-bye. Phoebe arrives with a suitcase and insists that she will go with him.

Holden scolds her, and Phoebe starts to cry. Angry, she refuses to speak as they walk together to the zoo. She continues her silence until they reach the carousel where she wonders shyly if she is too old to ride. Holden buys her a ticket and she boards. After one ride she tells her brother she has forgiven him, and he buys her a handful of tickets. As Holden watches his sister on the carousel, his depression seems to dissolve, and he feels suddenly happy.

For all his personal despondency, Holden seems to be preparing to face the adult world. It is clear that he is buoyed in part by his love for his sister and her love for him.

Cavan, Edward. *Faithful Are the Wounds.* May Sarton. 1955.

Edward Cavan, a passionately political, middle-aged Harvard English professor, commits suicide, leaving his family and friends to wonder how they misunderstood him and to try to find meaning in his death.

When Edward's sister Isabel is notified of the suicide, she leaves her safe bourgeois home and conservative husband, a surgeon, to go to Cambridge, Massachusetts, for the funeral. On the plane she remembers their childhood in Iowa and Edward's endless battles with their rigid father. She thinks of Edward as a sensitive, neurotic, and angry young man who cut himself off from his family when they did not conform to his political principles. Most painful to Isabel is the fact that Edward never forgave her for not telling him, when he was studying at Oxford, that their mother was dying of cancer, although it was their mother's wish that he be spared the pain of her decline.

At Harvard, Edward's close friends remember him as a maverick professor: a brilliant, calmly analytical teacher of modern poetry on the one hand and, on the other, an intensely committed, radical political activist. His protégé, a graduate student named George Hastings, admired Edward's intellect and convictions but felt frustrated when the professor rebuffed him for not being able to relate to his experiences during the Spanish Civil War and the Czechoslovakian communist invasion.

Ira Goldberg, a respected colleague, also felt the bite of Edward's hard-edged political principles. When Ira refused to sign a petition protesting the firing of a professor in Nebraska for his suspected communist beliefs, Edward told him that they would no longer be friends. Edward also cut off his old friend Damon Phillips for not being radical enough in his socialist convictions. His only friends at the time of his suicide were Grace Kimlock, a radical elderly woman who attended ACLU meetings with Edward, and Orlando Fosca, an older professor who combatted Italian fascism.

When Isabel meets the members of Edward's circle at Harvard and reminisces with them about her brother, she shares their anger and guilt at not having understood him. This is a time of healing, but they continue to wish they had made some gesture to let Edward know that he was loved. They realize that Edward was desperately seeking communion and connection with others but because he set abstract principles before personal affections, he was haunted by loneliness and anguish. Before Isabel returns home, she goes to Edward's apartment where she senses the absence of companionship and intimacy in his life, and understands that his political activities were an attempt to achieve solidarity with the world.

The novel closes with Damon being brought before the House Committee for Un-American Activities, five years after Edward's death. Damon bravely refuses to inform on any of his friends or colleagues. He asserts before the committee that Edward was right in his belief that intellectuals must not take refuge in the ivory tower of the university but must be politically and socially engaged. Ira Goldberg, Grace Kimlock, and George Hastings, now a professor, support Damon's stand, having learned from Edward's life and untimely death the importance of both personal and political involvement.

Celie. *The Color Purple.* Alice Walker. 1982.

Celie, the novel's heroine, is born into a life of poverty and degradation. Trapped in a rural town, forcibly separated from her sister, and married as a teenager to a man who beats and abuses her, Celie seems doomed to spend her life buried in the role of housewife and stepmother to a family she can barely tolerate. But she courageously perseveres, and when she falls in love with SHUG AVERY,

her husband's mistress, she awakens to a wealth of inner resources that enable her to forge, against terrible odds, a will and destiny of her own.

The novel is constructed entirely of letters, most of which are Celie's letters to God. When her stepfather, whom she believes is her father, rapes her, he forbids her to tell anyone except God. During her first pregnancy, Pa takes Celie out of school although she is as eager to learn as her brilliant sister NETTIE. Pa removes both her children, and Celie quietly assumes she will never see them again.

Without Celie's protection, Nettie is in danger of the same abuse. Celie offers herself to Pa in place of Nettie and is eventually married off to Nettie's unattractive suitor ALBERT, referred to as Mister by Celie, who only wants someone to take care of his four children. To comfort herself about the marriage, Celie plans to bring Nettie along. Nettie does spend some time in their house to escape Pa, but Albert is no less threatening. When Nettie finally leaves, Albert attempts to rape her and then vows to intercept all her letters to Celie. Nettie eventually finds refuge with the couple that has adopted Celie's missing children.

Without Nettie, Celie's only comfort is her dreams of Shug Avery, the elegant but unpredictable and demanding blues singer. Before her marriage Celie had heard rumors of the affair between Shug and Albert, but she nevertheless doted on a glamorous photograph of Shug. When Shug falls ill, Albert brings her home so that Celie can nurse her back to health.

Shug's initial hostility toward Celie wears off quickly when she realizes that Celie has no interest in competing for Albert's attentions. Celie bathes Shug, combs her hair, and coaxes her into eating, and soon her romantic feelings toward Shug intensify. When Shug is well enough to sing again, she demands that Celie come to her concert, which is against Albert's wishes, and devotes a song to her. When Celie later confesses to Shug that Albert beats her, Shug insists that he stop.

Shug leaves for several months on a singing tour and returns with a new husband, Grady, in whom she evidently lacks interest. When Grady and Albert are away on a trip together, Celie reveals the story of her repeated rapes. Moved by her words, Shug embraces Celie, and they make love. For the first time Celie experiences lovemaking as a response to her own desires.

Soon after, Shug discovers the numerous letters from Nettie that Albert had been hiding. Together, Shug and Celie read the astonishing story of Nettie's life as a missionary in Africa. Murderously angry at Albert, Celie finally finds the courage to leave him and moves into Shug's mansion in Memphis, Tennessee. While living in Memphis, Celie amuses herself by sewing pants for Shug, and when others begin to request similar pairs, she turns this domestic talent into a thriving business. Celie returns to her hometown when Pa dies, to take over the house and store he has left her.

Returning home, Celie finds a reformed Albert who chats quietly with her while they sew. The novel closes when Celie is reunited not only with Shug but with Nettie, who arrives suddenly from Africa, bringing Celie's grown children.

Cereno, Don Benito. "Benito Cereno." Herman Melville. 1855.

Don Benito Cereno, captain of the *San Dominick*, is victimized by the cargo of slaves aboard his ship. Although he eventually escapes his predicament, Don Benito is haunted by the trauma he undergoes.

Appearing at first as a reserved, gentlemanly young Spaniard, Cereno evinces a moodiness that baffles AMASA DELANO, captain of the American ship *Bachelor's Delight*, and a visitor to the *San Dominick*. Delano is confused by Cereno's capricious behavior, but Cereno is obliged to keep up a front, for the ship is actually controlled by the slaves who had earlier revolted, killing most of the crew. Operating on instructions from Babo, an armed slave, Cereno is forced to conceal his predicament from the American captain. For fear of discovery, Cereno allows breaches of conduct on the part of the slaves to go unpunished. Cereno's behavior is so strange that Delano fears the Spaniard is either plotting his murder or is simply too emotionally weak to captain a vessel.

As far as Delano can see, Cereno is dutifully attended by Babo. Babo's seemingly solicitous concern for Cereno is actually a sign of the slaves' efforts to keep Cereno constantly under guard. Even when Babo insists on shaving the unwilling Cereno—cutting him in the process—Captain Delano does not detect in Cereno's shaking body and fearful eyes a plea for help.

At Babo's silent urging, Cereno reluctantly questions Delano about his cargo and crew. Under the control of the wily Babo, Cereno can neither reveal his plight to Delano nor warn him of the very real danger to *Bachelor's Delight* and Delano himself. Over lunch in his cabin, Cereno watches anxiously as Babo stands behind Delano while they dine, ready to kill the American should Cereno make a false move. After the meal Cereno declines to go up on deck with Delano immediately.

Once Babo allows him to go on deck, Cereno joins Delano to bid him farewell. Declining to return the favor of Delano's visit by taking coffee on *Bachelor's Delight*, Cereno grasps his new friend's hand and utters a fervent prayer that God protect him. As soon as the boat bearing Delano begins to pull away, Cereno jumps overboard into the small vessel. Delano grabs Cereno, whom he fears is trying to kill him, until Babo's leap into the boat and attempt on Cereno's life prove that Babo is the potential murderer and Cereno has been the victim all along.

Now liberated, Cereno wishes only to be taken to *Bach-elor's Delight*, but Delano sends his own sailors to crush the rebellion on board *San Dominick*. At a later tribunal in Lima, the entire story of the slaves' rebellion is revealed. Finally freed from the nightmarish events on board, Cereno is nonetheless gravely psychologically wounded by the episode and plagued by a sense of darkness. Three months after the trial and Babo's execution, Benito Cereno dies.

Cevathas, Sonny. *Afterlife*. Paul Monette. 1990.

Sonny Cevathas, a young man in his twenties, has completed a year of mourning for his dead lover Ellsworth Downs. As a member of a "widow's circle" along with STEVEN SHAW and LORENZO DELGADO "DELL" ESPINOZA, Sonny has been working through the grief and anxiety incumbent upon those who have lost lovers to AIDS.

Ellsworth had been Sonny's longest and most serious emotional involvement; the two met after Sonny had spent much of his youth on the move. Sonny left his family's home at the age of seventeen after being caught having sex with his uncle. Sonny's father, who adored his youngest son, rejected him utterly when he found him with his brother-in-law; for his part, Sonny was almost glad to escape the confines of his Greek-American family. Even after leaving his parents' home, he continued to be drawn to older, married men.

After a series of relationships, some lasting as long as a year, Sonny found himself in New York, where he encountered Ellsworth, the son of a wealthy toy manufacturer. The two moved to California, where Sonny had once lived with a woman named Romy who introduced him to New Age thinking and theories of reincarnation. Like many others, Ellsworth was enamored of Sonny's well-toned body, but he also enjoyed delving into metaphysical mysteries with him.

Unlike the other "widows," Sonny refuses to take an antibody test and does not know whether he has been exposed to HIV, the AIDS-related virus. When he begins a relationship with wealthy Sean Pfeiffer, it appears the older man will provide the economic security that Sonny has lacked since he was thrown out of his home by Ellsworth's family following Ellsworth's death. Sonny occupies the guest room at his friend Steven's house while he awaits the outcome of his relationship with Sean. The day after noticing a "crimson welt" on Sonny's arm, however, Sean rejects him. This symptom of the HIV virus frightens Sonny, and he retreats quickly into denial.

Spurned by Sean on Thanksgiving Day, Sonny returns to Steven's house to share a dinner with several others from the devastated homosexual community. One of the guests introduces him to Salou, a channeler who—the friend claims—will help Sonny discover his destiny. Two sessions later, after Salou tells him that he is not homosexual and that he should leave California, Sonny decides to depart. He takes with him the stray dog he has befriended at Steven's house and the false hope that, after three years of being "straight," he will have beaten the HIV virus.

Chambers, Frank. *The Postman Always Rings Twice.* James M. Cain. 1934.

Frank Chambers is an amoral young tramp whose steamy love affair with a married woman plunges him into a macabre comedy of errors.

Making his way toward Los Angeles, Frank stops at a roadside restaurant to con the owner out of a free meal. The con fails, but the owner, Nick, offers Frank a job as a handyman and introduces him to his wife CORA PAPA-DAKIS. Frank is instantly attracted to Cora's smoldering sexuality. He finds her dark hair and shapely body entic-ing, but more than that, he is drawn by her smell. Within a day of their first meeting, Frank has initiated an affair with the unhappily married young woman.

His common sense clouded by the love and passion he feels for Cora, Frank agrees that they should kill Nick so the two of them can be together. Their plan backfires, however, and they succeed only in wounding Nick. They then call for an ambulance and concoct a story for the police. Nick, suffering from a concussion, does not con-tradict them. Frightened by their narrow escape, Frank and Cora decide to run away together rather than attempt to murder Nick again.

Frank, a vagabond of long-standing, sets off down the highway with his lover. After several hours of walking, Cora decides that she cannot stand life on the road. Hitch-ing a ride, Frank continues on to San Bernardino while Cora returns to the Greek's restaurant. Some time later Frank runs into Nick, who is fully recovered from his accident. When Nick offers him his job back, Frank, de-spite his love of wandering, jumps at the chance to be with Cora again.

When Nick begins pressuring Cora to have a child, Frank brings up the subject of murder once again. They decide to kill Nick by staging a car accident on their return from a festival. Nick is killed, but Frank himself is wounded when the car rolls over him. Cora is charged with murder when Sackett, the district attorney, discovers that Nick has a $10,000 life insurance policy on himself. Sackett convinces Frank to sign a complaint of attempted murder against Cora in order to prove his own innocence. Cora is given a six-month suspended sentence when the lawyer Frank hires pleads her guilty of murder.

Now free of Nick, Frank and Cora return to the res-taurant, but when Frank has a brief affair while Cora is called home for her mother's funeral, their happiness seems in jeopardy. Cora threatens to turn Frank over to the D.A., pointing out that she cannot be tried a second time. Frank toys with the idea of murdering Cora, but when she tells him she is pregnant and could never turn him in, the two decide to marry.

On their honeymoon at the beach, Cora overexerts her-self while swimming. Afraid that she might be having a miscarriage, Frank rushes her to the car. Speeding toward the hospital, they have an accident and Cora dies. Con-victed for Cora's murder, Frank sits on death row, writing his story and wondering if Cora, in that split second before her death, thought that he meant to kill her.

Chance. *Being There.* Jerzy Kosinski. 1970.

Chance is a middle-aged man who has spent his life working as the gardener at an old man's Manhattan estate. Chance, who does not know who his parents are or where he came from, has never stepped outside the house or the enclosed garden walls. His consciousness has been shaped by watching television—which, in addition to eating, sleeping, and gardening, has always been his principal occupation. But one day after the old man dies and lawyers evict him from the estate, Chance is thrown headfirst into the "real world" when he is hit by a limousine and brought home by its passenger, Mrs. Benjamin Rand, wife of the chairman of the board of the First American Financial Corporation, to recover from the accident.

When Chance tells Mrs. Rand, known as "EE," that he is "Chance the Gardener," she misunderstands and calls him "Chauncey Gardiner." At home EE introduces Chance to her husband, who is very ill. Mr. Rand im-mediately assumes that Chance—a handsome, well-dressed, seemingly focused, seemingly experienced man of few words—is a businessman. When the President of the United States visits Rand at home, Rand invites Chance to join them. During this meeting Chance's comments about the garden in which he worked are taken as astute analyses of business conditions. The President is also im-pressed, and when he mentions "Chauncey Gardiner" in his speech to the Financial Institute, Chance is instantly thrust into the national spotlight. But all along he remains totally unaware of what is happening around him and watches television whenever he can. When major news-papers contact him, he declines to be interviewed, saying he does not read.

Chance and EE attend a United Nations reception where he is introduced to several important diplomats, including Ambassador Skrapinov of the Soviet Union. When Skrapinov speaks Russian to him, Chance, who knows he is being filmed by television cameras, raises his eyebrows and laughs because he has never been addressed in a foreign language before. Delighted, Skrapinov is sure from this reaction that Chance does indeed speak Russian.

Later, at a private party, a gay man approaches Chance and invites him to join him upstairs. Chance tells the man that he would like to watch. Upstairs, the man masturbates in front of Chance, who watches without comprehending. That night Chance also tells EE that he likes to watch; the lovesick EE, surprised but willing to oblige, mastur-bates on his bed as light emanates from the television set. Afterward she tells Chance that she feels very free with him. She sleeps, and Chance watches TV until he dozes off.

In the meantime, the President of the United States and Ambassador Skrapinov have separately and secretly ordered extensive investigations into Chance's background. Their staffs can find nothing—no evidence of his birth, family, property, or credit history. Eight other foreign powers have put Chance on their spy priority lists, but no one has been able to discover anything about him. The President's assistant assures him the investigation will continue around the clock.

At another social gathering, Chance pushes his way through the crowded room and steps into the garden, where he is alone. Around him, the beautiful garden lies still. Not a single thought enters Chance's brain, and peace fills his chest.

Chancellor, Olive. *The Bostonians.* Henry James. 1886.

Olive Chancellor is a strong-willed woman who devotes her life to campaigning for women's suffrage in post–Civil War America. Her struggle hinges on the fate of a young woman, VERENA TARRANT, whose love for a conservative Southerner eventually foils Olive's plans.

A fanatical feminist, Olive avoids the distraction of pleasures and devotes herself entirely to the cause. She is repressed, humorless, and self-controlled. When challenged, she often gives way to a kind of hysterical hatred. As her young protégé Verena observes, meeting Olive gives one the idea of what Judgment Day might be like.

Olive's deep passions are never explained. Upon discovering the beautiful Verena at a suffragette meeting, she decides she must harness the young woman's immense talent for public speaking to the cause. Like Verena, she is unaware that their attraction is at least partly sexual, although Olive also takes a maternal interest in the younger, unschooled woman.

Olive yearns for fame and recognition. She becomes Verena's manager and sets about educating her and improving her rhetorical skills. Unlike Verena, with whom she shares a heartfelt desire for women's rights, Olive's ideological zeal is portrayed as only a thin patina covering a more fundamental hatred for men. This hatred soon finds a target in her cousin BASIL RANSOM, a Southerner who is also attracted to Verena. Her jealous stewardship of the girl pits her against him as he falls in love and repeatedly pierces her defenses in his efforts to woo Verena.

With Verena's apprenticeship nearing an end, Olive's victory over Ransom seems assured. In what will be a public coup for women's suffrage, Olive arranges for Verena to speak before a large gathering of Boston's elite. Just as Verena is about to go onstage, however, Ransom appears and persuades her to forfeit the engagement in order to elope with him. Although desperate with anguish, Olive realizes the folly of trying to hold on to Verena by

recalling past pledges and obligations, and she is able to relinquish the young woman without reproach. As the novel closes, Olive, ever the ardent suffragette, goes onstage to address the audience and confront the wreckage of her hopes and dreams.

Chapman, Catherine Lewis. *The Women on the Porch.* Caroline Gordon. 1944.

When Catherine Lewis Chapman discovers that her husband is carrying on an affair with another woman, she reacts with a pride born of her Virginia family heritage. Writing her husband a curt note, she takes their car and their dog and leaves their Manhattan apartment for the Virginia hills. The Lewis family has owned a plantation in Virginia for generations; now she returns to her ancestral home, Swan Quarter, where her aging female relatives still live.

As she slowly recovers from her shock, Catherine begins to enjoy the simple, earthy pleasures of country living, and she resolves to remain at Swan Quarter and breed horses. This resolve is strengthened when, after some initial resistance on her part, she enters into an affair with a neighbor, Tom Manigault.

Life at Swan Quarter is not as idyllic as it first seemed, however. For one thing, although she overcomes her initial concern about the age difference between her and Tom (she is thirty-five, he twenty), Catherine soon realizes that Tom's intense love-hate relationship with his mother constitutes an obsession that will always prevent him from being a satisfactory mate for her.

Then, too, the thwarted lives of Swan Quarter's inhabitants begin to make her family home seem like a prison of sadness. Her grandmother has become increasingly senile, and after a stroke her mind remains fixed on the Civil War days of her youth. Her spinster aunt Willy leads a depressing and difficult existence as the sole caretaker of the old lady and the manager of the failing Swan Quarter farm. Cousin Daphne, who had been abandoned on her wedding night, wanders about collecting mushrooms, and Maria, the black house servant, nurses her sorrow and bitterness over the imprisonment of her favorite son.

The tragedies of these women's lives and previous tragedies lived out at Swan Quarter impart a spectral atmosphere to the old plantation, and Catherine begins to feel that the air is swarming with ghosts. The only hopeful note for the family is that Willy has raised a promising stallion whom she and her trainer, Mr. Shannon, take to a horse show with the idea that if the horse performs well, he may become a valuable source of income as well as an object of beauty and delight for Willy.

When Catherine's husband Jim eventually comes for her, she bluntly informs him of her affair with Tom. He tries to strangle her but recovers himself and stumbles off into the woods. The next morning the couple meet and talk in a calm, civil manner. They are interrupted by Willy's return from the horse show and the news that although the horse had won first place in the show, he died by electrocution in a bizarre accident. At this point Catherine's husband tells her that they must leave Swan Quarter.

Charles. *Chilly Scenes of Winter.* Ann Beattie. 1976.

Charles is obsessed with his former lover Laura, who has returned to her husband. Charles's memories of Laura sustain him through this particularly bleak winter during which his mother becomes increasingly unstable. Although Charles is extremely passive in most situations, he is powerfully determined to get Laura back.

The novel opens when Charles's younger sister Susan is on Christmas vacation from college. Susan visits him in the house he inherited from his grandmother, which is also frequently occupied by SAM MCGUIRE, Charles's best friend. While Susan is visiting, they receive a phone call from their mother Clara, saying she has an intense pain in her side. Charles and Susan drive the short distance to her house and rescue Clara from the bathtub where she often sits to ease her imaginary pains. They follow her ambulance to the hospital and make sure she is given proper attention.

As they drive back to the hospital the next morning, Charles reminisces about his father who died when he was young. He cannot help making comparisons between his father, who was imaginative and playful, and Pete, his stepfather. Pete is awkward, cruel, full of self-pity, and has trouble communicating with Charles and Susan. Charles still feels somewhat sorry for him since Clara is insane and was only recently released from the psychiatric ward at the time of this relapse. But Pete harasses Charles regularly with drunken phone calls, and it is clear that he avoids spending more time with Charles and Susan than is necessary.

Susan leaves with Mark, her boyfriend from college, and Charles returns to work at his dull government desk job where he glumly considers asking out the dumpy typist Betty, a friend of Laura's. This thought has the effect of making Charles even more determined to get Laura back. He saw Laura once, briefly, after his mother was admitted to the hospital and since then has only had the courage to drive by the A-frame house where she lives with her husband Jim. Sam teases Charles about his fixation on Laura, encouraging him to find someone new. Not only does Charles tolerate Sam's prodding but when Sam loses his job, he invites him to move into the house. Although Sam's presence is comforting, Charles continues to think obsessively about Laura.

One evening after work Charles invites Betty, who obviously likes him, for dinner. It is a hopelessly uncomfortable situation since Charles cannot make himself appear interested in anything Betty says. As Charles is driving Betty home, she casually mentions that she had dinner with Laura at her apartment a couple of nights before. Laura, she tells him, has left her husband again and is sharing an apartment with a woman. Charles spends the following day in a panic, wondering why she has not called him. When Charles finally reaches Laura, he insists upon seeing her and bursts out with "I love you!"

Charles arrives at Laura's apartment, but she makes it clear that she is not ready to jump into a love affair. After a short, unsatisfying visit, she asks Charles to leave, promising to make him dinner the next night. When he arrives, Charles asks Laura to make, instead of dinner, a special dessert she always made, with chocolate and oranges. As she cooks, she wonders out loud why she returned to her husband. Before the dessert is finished, she walks over to Charles's chair and sits in his lap, admitting that he has won her back. Charles kisses Laura's hair and tells her that this is a story with a happy ending.

Charles, Nick. *The Thin Man.* Dashiell Hammett. 1932.

Nick Charles is the wisecracking, cocktail-swilling former detective who reluctantly becomes involved in a murder case while visiting New York City during the Christmas holidays in 1932. Nick has been happily married to the irrepressible NORA (CHARLES) for the last seven years and is the proud owner of a Schnauzer terrier named Asta. Six years earlier he had quit the Trans-American Detective Agency in New York and moved to San Francisco to "look after" the business interests Nora had inherited from her father; when he visits his hometown, however, few people believe his claim that he is no longer a practicing detective.

One evening while waiting in a speakeasy for Nora to finish her Christmas shopping, Nick is approached by Dorothy Wynant, the estranged daughter of an eccentric inventor who had hired the detective many years before. She asks him if he knows the whereabouts of her father, Clyde Wynant, who is the "thin man" of the novel's title; Nick can only suggest that she contact Wynant's lawyer, Herbert Macaulay. Macaulay, whose life Nick had saved when they were fellow soldiers in World War I, phones him the following day and arranges a meeting. The lawyer suspects that Nick is working for Wynant's ex-wife Mimi Jorgensen; he claims that he has not seen his client since October although he regularly arranges for sums of money to be forwarded to him through Wynant's secretary and mistress Julia Wolf.

While recuperating from his usual hangover the next morning, Nick reads in the newspaper that Julia has been found murdered and that the police are looking for the inventor. From this moment on, the former detective struggles in vain to remain uninvolved in the case. He receives phone calls and visits from various members of the eccentric Wynant family, including Mimi with whom he apparently had been sexually involved many years before. Nora takes pity on the daughter, Dorothy, and tries to persuade Nick to return to his former profession and investigate the murder. He refuses, even after a newspaper article erroneously announces that he is working on the case.

Nick wakes in the middle of the night to find a man with a gun standing by his bed. It is Shep Morelli, a petty criminal and drug addict who was a friend of the deceased. Morelli is convinced that he is being framed for murder; when the police arrive at the Charleses' hotel suite, he thinks that the former detective is responsible. Nick quickly knocks Nora unconscious to get her out of harm's way, then is shot by Morelli as the police break down the door. As it turns out, he is only grazed by the bullet, but both the wound and the hostile attitude of the authorities serve to stimulate his interest in the case.

Nick begins to sort out the various lies, false clues, and deceptions on the part of the numerous characters involved in the mystery. The man who identified Julia's body, a shadowy character named Arthur Nunheim, is found murdered, apparently because he knew too much about the first crime. The police are somewhat suspicious of Nick because of his past involvement with Mimi, but Wynant is still missing and therefore considered the prime suspect. They are even more convinced of the inventor's guilt when Macaulay tells them that he has seen his client in town and Mimi claims that her ex-husband visited her in order to see his children and to give her some stock market securities.

The authorities view the case as solved when they discover a belt engraved with the initials of one of Wynant's enemies among the remains of a decomposing corpse in the basement of the inventor's workshop. Nick, however, guesses that the body is that of Wynant himself; the lawyer, Macaulay, killed his client and used his power of attorney to steal what remained of the man's estate with the help of Julia Wolf, who soon became a liability. Nunheim was killed as well because he attempted to blackmail Macaulay. Nick's reputation as a detective is vindicated when Mimi admits to the police that the lawyer persuaded her to lie about seeing her ex-husband in exchange for the stocks and bonds. Macaulay is arrested, and Nick is more than happy to be done with the case.

Charles, Nora. *The Thin Man.* Dashiell Hammett. 1932.

Imperturbable twenty-six-year-old Nora Charles is a perfect companion and drinking partner for her husband, the wisecracking former detective NICK CHARLES. In 1927, one year after Nora and Nick were married, her father died and left a substantial inheritance. Nick then quit his job at the Trans-American Detective Agency in New York, and the couple moved to San Francisco. With their Schnauzer terrier Asta in tow, Nick and Nora Charles return to Manhattan in December 1932 purportedly because Nick dislikes spending the holidays with his in-laws in California. During their visit Nick reluctantly becomes embroiled in a murder mystery, and Nora encourages him

to return, at least temporarily, to his former profession.

Nick had worked on a case many years before involving an eccentric inventor named Clyde Wynant; the detective remembered him as the thinnest man he had ever met. Wynant's daughter Dorothy introduces herself to Nick while he is waiting in a speakeasy for Nora to finish her Christmas shopping. The young woman is trying to locate her father, and Nick suggests that she call Wynant's lawyer, Herbert Macaulay. After the inventor's secretary is found murdered the next day, Nora tries unsuccessfully to get her husband interested in the crime and then wakes him up in the middle of the night to ask him whether he ever thinks of resuming his work as a detective. Nick, however, strongly resists the idea of getting involved in the case.

In the next few days Nick is contacted by various members of the Wynant family, their acquaintances, and the police, none of whom believe him when he says he is no longer a detective. Even the newspapers announce that he is in New York to investigate the murder. Early one morning while Nick is asleep, Nora is forced at gunpoint to let a shady character into their hotel room; the man believes he is being framed for the murder and gets angry when Nick says he is not involved in the case. Nora is more curious and excited by the situation than frightened. When the police arrive without notice, Nick knocks Nora unconscious to get her out of the line of fire. She soon regains her senses and at first is simply disappointed that she wasn't able to watch the fight; but when she finds out that a bullet grazed her husband a few inches below his heart, she promptly suggests that they return home.

But Nick is now interested in solving the murder. Nora accepts his change in attitude without criticism. She amuses herself in the following days by playing close attention to the developments in the case, asking endless questions, pouring drinks, going to parties, and thoroughly enjoying the varied and often rough-mannered company her husband keeps. After Nick finally figures out that the lawyer Macaulay killed both Wynant and his secretary in order to get his hands on the inventor's money, Nora questions her husband relentlessly about the details of the murders and is very dissatisfied with the various loose ends and the lack of definite proofs with which the case was concluded.

Chastain, DL. *Vineland.* Thomas Pynchon. 1990.

During the late 1960s, Darryl Louise Chastain was the best friend of FRENESI GATES, a student activist who eventually became a tool of the federal government and set up the murder of a prominent student leader. Now, in 1984, DL relates the story of Frenesi's act of betrayal and collaboration to Frenesi's sixteen-year-old daughter Prairie, who has been sheltered from this truth throughout her life.

During her own teen years, DL came to a realization

about herself that determined her future and prepared her for the narrative role she assumes in the novel. As a youth growing up on an American military base in Japan, DL was told by her mother that every wife is necessarily subjected to abuse, as evidenced by her mother's own bruises. DL was subsequently discovered by a martial arts master, and while developing Ninja-like skills, she reached the conclusion that her body belonged to herself. DL is distinguished from Frenesi, another daughter of the sixties, by the strength of her feminism. Whereas Frenesi compromises her youthful ideals and collaborates with the government, DL, portrayed most vividly in black leather atop a powerful motorcycle, maintains an adversarial stance toward authority.

DL's martial arts master selected her as his student not only because he recognized her physical gifts but also because he sensed her inability to be wholly rational under extreme pressure. He trains her, not to fight in the error-free world of the Ninja and the Samurai but rather in the human world where the distinction between good and evil, oneself and one's enemy, is not always clear and where one's teachers are always to some extent corrupt. DL is thus especially well suited to teach Prairie the dark truth of her own past. While she admits that the student movement ultimately became indistinguishable from the institutional hypocrisy it wanted to reveal and protest, she also appreciates the danger of this truth. Because DL is her teacher, hope remains that Prairie will not become disillusioned, but rather, like DL, wise and forever rebellious.

Chavez, Pearl. *Duel in the Sun.* Niven Busch. 1944.

In the opening of this tale of lawless passion, Pearl Chavez appears as a figure of mystery, a wild and beautiful girl who constantly rides the plains alone, oblivious to impropriety or danger and pursuing mysterious purposes. Most of the novel is a sustained flashback that uncovers the mystery of Pearl.

The daughter of a southern man and a mestizo (part American Indian, part European) woman, Pearl had arrived in the West orphaned and penniless at the age of twelve to be taken in by her father's cousin, wife to the wealthy and powerful rancher Senator McCanles. She fell in love with one of the McCanles sons, Lewt, a handsome and daring but spoiled and shiftless young man. When Pearl came of age, the two carried on an affair, but Lewt refused to commit himself to marriage with his mixed-breed poor relation. In an effort to separate Pearl and Lewt, Mrs. McCanles brought Pearl out socially, and an enterprising ranch foreman fell in love with her and proposed marriage. Although she did not love the man, Pearl accepted, knowing that Lewt would never marry her and eager, after so many years of being an outsider to the McCanles family and to her community, to have a family and a place of her own.

Just prior to Pearl's marriage, however, Lewt murdered her intended husband in a barroom fight. At this point Pearl renounced her search for a conventional life and gave herself over entirely to Lewt, who as a wanted man was on the run from the law. It is in order to be with fugitive Lewt that Pearl rides the plains alone.

Lewt turns to a life of crime, and eventually he and his partner enlist Pearl's aid in a train robbery, after which Lewt and Pearl are captured and jailed. When the McCanles clan breaks into the jail to rescue them, Pearl refuses to accompany Lewt for fear of slowing him down. She remains in jail, awaiting death by hanging.

Another of the McCanles brothers, Jesse, is a lawyer, and although he disapproves of Pearl, he offers to defend her. She warns him not to get involved with her, explaining that she will always do whatever Lewt tells her to do whenever he tells her to do it. But Jesse insists on defending her and soon falls in love with her—so deeply that he goes against his principles and collaborates in a patent lie that gets Pearl acquitted.

After the trial Pearl and Jesse plan to marry, but Pearl gets a message from Lewt and rides off to meet him. When Jesse discovers this, he rides after her with the intention of killing them both, but when Pearl locates her former lover, she looks one last time into his eyes and inhabits for one last time that "position in the country of the mind . . . that Lewt and Pearl have never left, in which they lived and conducted all business that really mattered to them." Then she pulls the trigger of her gun and kills him. Thereafter she and Jesse marry and set out together to stake a claim in Oklahoma and start their lives anew.

Chesser, Ellen. *The Time of Man.* Elizabeth Madox Roberts. 1926.

Ellen Chesser's is the central consciousness of this novel, which takes as its subject her growth into adulthood, her search for identity and for moral and physical strength, and her enduring closeness to and respect for nature.

Ellen's parents are migrant farmers who travel through Kentucky in search of a better situation. At fourteen years of age, Ellen is a sturdy girl who helps her father earn a living on the farm. She not only works the land but feels pleasure and wonder at its mysterious processes.

As she grows older, Ellen sees herself becoming a woman. She yearns for more privacy than their small house can provide and begins to take interest in the young men who live nearby. She knows that her clothes are old and faded, but tells herself that she possesses an unrecognized beauty. Although she feels oppressed at times by her tedious, lonely, and purposeless life, she is also able to experience the thrill of simply being alive and connected to the earth.

When Ellen is eighteen, she meets her first romantic interest, Jonas Prather. One day Jonas confesses to Ellen that a married woman has had his child. Instead of rejecting him, Ellen comforts him; Jonas, in turn, appreciates her compassion and pledges his faith. When Jonas takes a farming job far away, he promises Ellen that he will return to marry her. Time passes without any news from him, and Ellen finally learns that he has married another woman. Filled with deep loss, anger, and hatred, she has thoughts of killing both Jonas and herself, but endures.

The Chessers move to a new farm where Jasper Kent, a powerful young farmer, helps Ellen with the field work and trusts her to store his money. They develop a close romantic friendship; Ellen has the feeling that she is one with him. When Jasper is accused of burning down a barn and is forced to flee, Ellen alone has faith that he will return. He finally does, and they marry and move away to their own house.

Although Ellen's life with Jasper is difficult, she remains dedicated to him. She endures various trials: Jasper's soiled reputation, her poverty and responsibility in raising five children, Jasper's adultery, and his suspecting her of committing adultery. They are brought together again by the death of a young son whom Jasper originally thought was not his.

The novel ends several years later when Jasper is accused of burning down another barn and several men severely whip him for his supposed crime. Ellen refuses to let Jasper leave the country without her. As her parents did long ago, Ellen and her husband gather the children and their belongings into a wagon and head out in search of a better life.

Chicoy, Juan. *The Wayward Bus.* John Steinbeck. 1947.
Juan Chicoy, the owner of a roadside garage, contemplates fleeing to Mexico in order to escape his dreary existence with his alcoholic wife Alice. The son of an Irish mother and a Mexican father, Juan had grown up in Mexico but moved to the United States in order to earn more money. During the time described in the novel, Juan, estranged from his wife and tempted by the amorous advances of a young female customer, confronts the emotional consequences of his deep indifference to life.

In addition to the garage where he works, Juan owns a diner presided over by Alice. Alice has grown bitter and hostile from years of hard work at this isolated junction in Rebel Corners, California, but she remains desperately in love with her husband. Juan exerts a powerful control over her and is able to handle her drinking bouts and periods of hysteria with a calm, even humorous attitude.

One day when Juan's bus breaks down on a scheduled trip to San Juan, the Pritchards, a family from Boston, must stay overnight at Rebel Corners. Juan allows the Pritchards to sleep in the bed he normally shares with Alice, and she is infuriated. In the morning Alice explodes in anger at Norma, an innocent waitress, while Juan goes promptly to the garage to fix the bus before serving the Pritchards breakfast in the diner. Mildred Pritchard, a

young college radical, is obviously fascinated by Juan, and they exchange significant glances.

Juan takes the two employees with him on the bus to San Juan so that Alice can be alone to drink herself into a state of contentment. Along with the Pritchards, several other passengers ride with Juan to the edge of the San Ysidro River. The Breeds, who own a roadside store there, have been watching the heavy rain and are concerned about the rickety bridge Juan usually takes. They suggest that he avoid the bridge and instead take an old back road that goes around the river bend. Juan asks the passengers if they want to risk taking the bridge, and they vote for the old road.

As the bus, "Sweetheart," creeps along the narrow, muddy road in the rain, Juan begins wondering if he wants to return to Rebel Corners and Alice. Only laziness keeps him there, he thinks; now would be the perfect time to flee. Juan makes a bargain with Our Lady of Guadalupe, his mother's chosen saint, represented by a small statue sitting on the dashboard. If the bus gets stuck, Juan will travel onward to Mexico, but if it reaches San Juan without incident, he will return to Alice. Juan becomes desperately impatient for the saint's answer and purposely spins the wheels into the mud, getting the bus firmly stuck.

Juan tells the passengers that he is going to get a tow truck and call a taxi, but instead he wanders along the road until he comes upon an abandoned house. He curls up in the barn and goes to sleep. He is awakened by Mildred Pritchard, who slyly explains that she has been walking about abandoning the bus, but he has changed his mind. He will go back, get the bus out of the mud, and after San Juan, drive home to Alice. Before Juan leaves the barn, however, he makes love to Mildred, and, holding hands, they walk back along the road toward the bus.

Childs, Jadine. *Tar Baby.* Toni Morrison. 1981.
Jadine Childs struggles for authenticity in both black and white worlds. A black woman born in Philadelphia and orphaned at the age of twelve, she attended the Sorbonne because she believed her opportunities both in and out of school would be greater in Europe than in the United States. Jadine becomes a successful model, a "face" on French fashion magazines. Despite her success, she continually argues with herself, her relatives, and her lover, SON, all of whom fear that Jadine has abandoned her culture and with it a particular concept of womanhood.

After her parents' deaths, Jadine lived with or received support from her aunt and uncle, Ondine and Sydney, the domestic servants of Valerian Street, the wealthy owner of a candy company who helped finance part of her education. Now, at twenty-five, with a degree in art history and a modeling career, Jadine knows it is time for her to care for her adoptive parents. When uncertainties arise with Ryk, a German man in Paris who wants to marry her, Jadine finds an excuse to spend two or three months with her aunt and uncle at the Street retirement home in the Caribbean. On the island she plays her role as daughter to her childless aunt and uncle, and social secretary and companion to MARGARET STREET, Valerian's unhappy wife. She also acts as audience and mediator for the Streets, who constantly bait one another.

Deeper conflicts develop when Son, a black American outlaw and exile, finds his way into the Streets' mansion. Valerian infuriates Jadine's aunt and uncle when he invites Son, who had hidden in and around the house for several days before being discovered, to take the guest room. Jadine, although frightened by Son's vulgarity and brutality, is soon seduced by him. During Christmas dinner when the family tensions finally explode, Jadine turns to Son for comfort, and together they secretly plot an escape to New York City.

In New York, Jadine and Son spend several blissful months together. Their rapture begins to wane when Jadine accompanies Son on a visit to Eloe, his hometown in southern Florida. Jadine regards the poverty-stricken village as primitive and pathetic, a stronghold of ignorance and misguided puritanism. But Son prizes the sense of fraternity among its inhabitants. When Jadine insists on returning to New York and to her work as a model, Son remains in Eloe several days longer than he had planned.

After this divisive incident, the differences between them become increasingly apparent. Jadine insists that Son attend college, prepare to do something with his life, and stop romanticizing the isolation of Eloe. Son regards her demands as evidence of her submission to white culture and to capitalist attitudes instead of to him. After their arguments escalate into physical violence, Jadine leaves New York without an explanation. She returns briefly to the Street mansion in the Caribbean but refuses her aunt's demands that she stay and take care of her aging relatives. Instead, Jadine flies to Paris to start afresh, leaving behind the fantasies of safety she had shared with Son.

Chillingworth, Roger. *The Scarlet Letter.* Nathaniel Hawthorne. 1850.

Roger Chillingworth is the cold and cuckolded husband of HESTER PRYNNE. As calculating as Hester is passionate, Chillingworth is determined to avenge his pride by discovering the identity of his wife's lover and to punish the man in his own way. So blinded is he by his single-minded spirit of revenge that he is unaware the truth he so eagerly seeks will lead to his undoing.

Chillingworth first appears in Boston on the day of Hester's trial for adultery. Having sent his young wife ahead of him to settle in New England, the elderly scholar was shipwrecked and captured by Indians. After two years he makes his way to Boston, appearing at the edge of the crowd congregated to hear Hester's sentence. Hester rec-

ognizes the humpbacked man with horror but keeps her silence. She refuses to reveal the name of her partner in sin; after her sentence is imposed—she will wear the embroidered scarlet letter on her bosom for as long as she lives—she and her infant are led back to their prison cell. She is soon visited by her husband, who has posed as a doctor willing to examine the prisoner and her young daughter PEARL (PRYNNE). In his interview with his wife, the man calling himself Chillingworth exhorts her to reveal to him the name of his cuckolder. She refuses but is persuaded to swear that she also will never reveal her husband's identity. Before leaving the cell, Chillingworth vows to discover the man himself.

Chillingworth settles in town and establishes himself as a physician. He also becomes acquainted with ARTHUR DIMMESDALE, the town's revered young minister (and the father of Hester's child), whose health has been in decline. Chillingworth, Hester, and Dimmesdale meet at a conference with the governor over Hester's fitness as a mother to young Pearl. With Dimmesdale's help, Hester convinces the governor to leave Pearl in her custody and departs, but not before noticing that Chillingworth has become more sinister-looking since their last meeting.

When Dimmesdale's health continues to fail, Chillingworth suggests that they live together so that he may better treat the minister's illness. Attracted by Chillingworth's intelligence and concern, Dimmesdale accepts. Chillingworth scrutinizes his patient carefully, growing more diabolical in his determination to discover what secrets burn in the minister's heart, but Dimmesdale does not give in to the doctor's urgings to unburden his soul. One afternoon when the minister is asleep, Chillingworth pulls back his patient's vestment; what he sees is not revealed, but the old man is at once horrified and exalted by the sight.

Meanwhile, Hester, disturbed by her lover's failing health, resolves to warn him of Chillingworth's identity and his evil intent. The two agree to take passage on a ship to England and to raise Pearl in a new community. On the eve of their departure, Dimmesdale delivers his final sermon. While he does, Chillingworth is in conference with the commander of the vessel that is to sail to England. Moments later the seafarer informs Hester that the doctor has taken passage on the same vessel.

The sermon seems to have drained from the ailing minister the last of his vitality. He weakly mounts the public pillory, and Chillingworth follows. As Dimmesdale proclaims his sin to the townspeople, tearing his clothes to reveal his breast, Chillingworth sinks to his knees, muttering "Thou hast escaped me!" again and again. Having unburdened himself at last, Dimmesdale collapses and dies.

After Dimmesdale's death, Chillingworth becomes despondent and withered. Within a year he, too, dies, leaving Pearl properties in the New World and in England that make her the richest heiress of her day.

Chinaski, Henry "Hank." *Post Office; Factotum; Women; Ham on Rye; Barfly* (movie); *Hollywood.* Charles Bukowski. 1971; 1975; 1978; 1982; 1987; 1989.

Henry "Hank" Chinaski seeks nobility in the ignoble, grace in the disgraceful, and courage in the cowardly. He follows an inverted system of values throughout his episodic adventures—good is bad and bad is good, and all a person must do to prove his worth is bear life's tremendous pain in a stiff-lipped fashion, albeit drunk beyond repair.

Hank's first memory is of being under a table at his family home in Germany in 1922. He feels comfortable there, safe from the family battles that rage around him. His grandmother Emily's favorite phrase is "I will bury all of you"; Hank does not doubt that she will.

By the time the family moves to Los Angeles, Hank's grandfather Leonard has separated from Emily and been excommunicated by the rest of the family. Hank considers his grandfather the most beautiful man ever, standing tall and straight with pure white hair and shining blue eyes. On the ride home in the family's Model T, however, not a word is said about Leonard. Later Hank's father ruefully describes Leonard as sweet when he is drunk but the "meanest man in the world" when he is sober.

Henry, Sr., is Hank's arch-foe. Ashamed of being poor, he burns with rage at the world for standing in the way of his ascension to the riches he feels he deserves. When he loses his job as a milkman, Hank says, he pretends to drive to work every day anyway. He sends Hank to a school mostly populated by rich kids so that he, Henry, Sr., will feel rich. Katherine, Hank's mother, keeps a low profile, avoiding her husband's frequent rages and other conflicts that might arise. Although sympathetic to Hank, she insists that "the father is always right." When Henry forces Hank to mow the lawn every week so that no more than three blades stick up over the others, Katherine does not interfere with the beatings that ensue.

Hank follows his mother's method of nonresistance to the family despot for most of his childhood until he reaches his mid-teens. Withstanding the frequent beatings, he takes courage in the fact that he never cries out in pain. As Hank gradually realizes that he has grown to be as large as his father, he feels less and less intimidated until finally he loses his fear altogether. On the day of his last beating, Henry, Sr., goes through his furious routine, unbuttoning and pulling down Hank's pants in the bathroom and slamming a strap against his buttocks again and again. Hank doesn't cry; he smiles. His father tries to continue but is soon overwhelmed with frustration and exhaustion. Hank smiles and asks for more. His father storms out of the room, defeated.

One day, while horsing around with his friend Baldy, Hank discovers the remarkable anesthetizing power of alcohol. Baldy doesn't seem to think much of the liquid, but Hank is overcome with a strange feeling of well-being. He

wonders why no one ever told him about it. "With this, life was great, a man was perfect, nothing could touch him."

By the time Hank reaches college, he is serious about being a writer. He discovered this talent in elementary school when his description of the president's speech, which he did not attend, far outshone the dull recountings of other students who had actually been there. From this experience Hank concluded that his talents lay not only in writing but in producing "beautiful lies." When it becomes clear that a professor at the City College of Los Angeles is enamored of his writing and of him, Hank decides that he is tired of school and sick of talking about writing. His teacher tries to convince him to stay, but he drops out and embarks on a life of drunken, bruising adventure, seeking to find many stories to tell that are, if not beautiful, at least true.

Chingachgook. *The Leatherstocking Tales (The Pioneers; The Last of the Mohicans; The Prairie; The Pathfinder; The Deerslayer).* James Fenimore Cooper. 1823; 1826; 1827; 1840; 1841.

Chingachgook, NATTY BUMPPO's stalwart companion, is a proud member of a threatened and dwindling race. Chingachgook is also known as "le Gros Serpent," "Indian John," and "the Sagamore." And he has the sad distinction of being the last of the Mohicans.

Born during the early years of the eighteenth century, Chingachgook reaches maturity during an epoch of fitful conflict between Britain and France. In Chingachgook's native forests, the European dispute is pursued by soldiers, American woodsmen, and variously allied native tribes. His Delaware nation allies itself with Britain and is opposed by its long-standing enemy, the French-allied Iroquois, or "Mingos," as this inveterate foe is styled by Chingachgook and Natty Bumppo.

Chingachgook's induction into the vagaries of battle comes in the early 1740s on the waters and shores of Lake Otsego in what would later become New York State. He arranges a rendezvous with Natty (or Hawkeye, as he is soon dubbed) so that the two can recover Chingachgook's betrothed, Wah-ta!-Wah, who has been kidnapped by the Mingos for absorption into their tribe. Chingachgook's purpose is momentarily sidetracked, however, by the necessities of Hawkeye's acquaintances, Harry March, Thomas Hutter, and Hutter's two daughters: dimwitted Hetty and wild and attractive Judith. Through a sequence of ambuscades, ransoms, scalpings, and sorties, Chingachgook assists Hawkeye and regains his lover.

Wah-ta!-Wah soon bears Chingachgook's son, Uncas, and although Wah-ta!-Wah does not survive, Uncas grows to manhood under the tutelage of Chingachgook and Hawkeye. Together the three continue to pursue the Mingos, until 1757 when they are enlisted to protect the daughters of a besieged British officer. Chingachgook notices that Uncas's head has been turned by Cora, the darker

Chipping (Mr.)

complected of the two women, but so has the head of an enemy chief. The two women are captured and rescued, captured and rescued, and finally recaptured, all in their chaotic passage through the American woods. When they are at last again within reach of Chingachgook and his companions, Cora and Uncas are killed in battle, leaving Chingachgook alone, feeling like "a blazed pine in a clearing of the pale-faces."

Grieving, Chingachgook continues to aid his friend Hawkeye in his scouting missions and his repeated protection of vulnerable white women in the woods. After the war for American independence, the two settle for a time near Otsego. The region is settled by then, however, and the septuagenarian Chingachgook finds himself further alienated by the settlers' legislated hunting seasons and the property disputes they worry about officiously, with full disregard for the claims of any native tribe. Finally, in 1793 and in the midst of a forest fire, with thunder clouds impending, the depressed Chingachgook dies. One of his arms points resolutely west as his lips utter the self-praise of a warrior, a chieftain, and a whole tribe who are passed on to their reward.

Chipping (Mr.) *Goodbye, Mr. Chips; To You, Mr. Chips.* James Hilton. 1935; 1938.

The schoolmaster Mr. Chipping is affectionately known to his students and colleagues as "Mr. Chips." Drawn from the reminiscences of Chips as an old man, the novel traces his career from his arrival at Brookfield, an English boarding school for boys, until his death there some seventy years later.

At age twenty-two, Chips is a nervous young man known for having discipline problems at his previous job. Trying to compensate for this mistake, he begins his Brookfield career on a strict note and is determined to be respected at the cost of being liked.

Mr. Chips teaches his courses, Greek and Latin, year after year with the same lesson plan. His lectures are interspersed with the same jokes, although these improve over the years and he becomes famous for them. He also has an enormous capacity for remembering the names and faces of the boys at the school and anecdotes about each one. As generations pass, he is able to tell the boys stories about their fathers and grandfathers. Every year he carefully studies the photographs in the directory for incoming students—a habit that persists long after his retirement from teaching. He makes a point of having all the new boys over for tea and getting to know them. He then fondly recounts stories about them with his housekeeper, Mrs. Wickett.

Although not a dynamic teacher or an administrative genius, Chips becomes a part of the tradition at Brookfield. At one point in his career, when he is in his early sixties, Chips has a row with the new headmaster, Ralston, an ambitious and efficient man whom Chips dislikes. Ralston considers Chips a disgrace, both for his outdated teaching methods, which he refuses to change, and for his notoriously tattered gown, which Ralston considers slovenly. When Ralston tries to force Chips's retirement, generations of Brookfield graduates and the entire student body rise up in arms.

Although Chips is considered a bachelor by most of the students and faculty, that is not in fact the case. He had a short-lived, extremely happy marriage from 1896 to 1898. He met his wife, Katherine Bridges, while they were hiking during the summer holidays. He was forty-eight, and she was twenty-five. He saw her first as the epitome of the New Woman, a concept he abhorred in theory, and her confident, independent behavior and obvious intelligence alarmed him. She considered him old and stodgy, set in his ways and incapable of changing. Within a week they were passionately in love and married before the fall term. Katherine gave Chips new life and energy, and he respected and adored her. She died in childbirth two years after they met, and although she had been loved, she was soon forgotten by most of the school. Chips keeps her alive in his memory, however, and rarely makes a decision without asking himself what Katherine would have thought. Chips is in his nineties when he dies, fondly remembering her face and those of hundreds of Brookfield boys.

Chita. *Chita: A Memory of Last Island.* Lafcadio Hearn. 1889.

Chita appears almost miraculously in a Creole community on a coastal Louisiana island. Mysterious and graceful but unsure of her past, Chita becomes the adopted child of a local family.

In the wake of a hurricane that devastates L'Ile Derniere (Last Island), the small child is pulled from the still-violent waters of the Gulf of Mexico by a big-hearted fisherman named Feliu Viosca. Though Feliu's heroic efforts save the child from immediate death, it is only through the painstaking efforts of Feliu's wife Carmen that the little girl is gradually nursed back to health.

Unable to determine the girl's identity, let alone locate any of her living relatives, Feliu and Carmen Viosca take her into their modest home. The child reminds the Vioscas of their own daughter Conchita who died at an early age some years before. In memory of her, they call the adopted child "Chita."

Not long after the hurricane, a lugger full of mainland officials and soldiers arrives at the island and moors at the Vioscas' wharf. The officials are part of an expedition that is trying to locate the bodies of those lost in the storm. Pleasantly surprised at hearing of the young girl's rescue, the captain of the expedition requests an interview.

Chita is brought out and spoken to in several different languages—English, French, Spanish, Italian, German— but with no sign of her understanding. Then a sailor

140

named Laroussel is called forward. Speaking to the girl in a Creole dialect, Laroussel learns that Chita's real name is Lili and her nickname Zouzoune. But for some reason Lili cannot remember her surname. Unable to do much with this new information, the captain decides to leave the girl with the Vioscas for the time being and to search for her true relatives elsewhere.

Long considered dead, Zouzoune's real father, Julien La Brierre, turns up six months later on the streets of New Orleans. He visits his own grave and feels a strong sense of being an unwelcome guest, an intruder among the living. Nonetheless, he goes about his work as a doctor, thinking that Zouzoune perished along with her mother in the hurricane.

Meanwhile, Chita has been growing accustomed to life with the Vioscas. She learns Spanish and the ways of the island. Carmen and Feliu, having become dearly attached to the child, dread her possible identification. Chita possesses a natural elegance, a perceptive intelligence, and a general sensitivity to life. After initially being afraid of the sea, she gradually learns to love it and grows strong and healthy swimming in its waters.

Back in New Orleans, there is an outbreak of malaria, and Julien grows weak from overwork and exhaustion. Still, when he receives a message from a friend requesting an emergency housecall, Julien cannot refuse. As it turns out, the patient lives on the same small island as Chita and the Vioscas. To travel there takes many hours, and by the time Julien arrives, the patient is already dead. Julien soon finds himself assaulted with malarial symptoms. Noticing his fever, the Vioscas offer him a room and bed to rest himself.

Julien's fever worsens. When he finally encounters Chita, who comes into his room to offer him food and water, he is so sick and feverish that, although he strongly suspects it, he is never certain that she is his lost daughter. Chita, for her part, does not seem to recognize her father, who soon succumbs to the malaria, never to taste the pleasure of reunion.

Chrisfield, Chris. *Three Soldiers*. John Dos Passos. 1921.

Chris Chrisfield, one of the three young men after whom the novel is titled, is the embodiment of murderous rage. A loyal friend and competent soldier, Chris has one bizarre and dangerous characteristic: his habit of focusing his anger on arbitrarily chosen victims.

Chris first reveals himself to another enlisted man, JOHN ANDREWS, while they are in infantry training camp for World War I. A "non com" named Anderson has been bothering Chris during drill, and Chris tells Andrews that he wants to kill another soldier. He once lost all control, he says, and nearly slashed a stranger to death over a game of cards.

When their regiment ships overseas, Chris and Andrews become best friends. Andrews is continually on the watch

for Chris's temper, particularly in bars where virtually anything can ignite his friend's rage.

One day in the fall of 1918, the Americans are advancing through wooded French countryside, and Chris is on his first patrol, tense and alert, ready for action. A low-hanging branch knocks his helmet off, and he is seized by terror. His anger has once again taken hold. Chris becomes intractable, reacting with violence to any teasing from all but Andrews, who draws him off each time.

In another incident Anderson catches Chris sleeping on guard. Chris threatens him and almost gets court-martialed. In the end his punishment is light, but Chris vows to Andrews: "Ah'm going to shoot that bastard."

During his second battle, Chris gets separated from his unit in the woods. While wandering alone, he comes across a wounded man propped against a tree. It is Anderson, who, delirious, begs him for water. Chris begins to walk away. Anderson staggers to his feet and threatens him. Chris pulls the pin on first one and then a second grenade and throws them both at Anderson. He then walks quickly away.

That same day, Andrews is wounded, and he and Chris are separated. The next time they meet, the war is over. Chris is a corporal headed for Coblenz, and Andrews is headed for Paris. At their brief meeting Chris confesses the murder to Andrews.

Their final meeting occurs six months later. At this point they are both deserters hiding out in Paris. Chris, suspecting that someone knew of his crime, has had to run away. He finally exits from the story with half of all the cash Andrews has, to seek a new hiding place.

Christian, Candy. *Candy*. Terry Southern and Mason Hoffenberg. 1958.

Candy Christian, a young Wisconsin girl of college age, is a quintessentially innocent virgin and at the same time marvelously attractive. In a series of loosely connected episodes, she searches for a sort of truth, whether intellectual or philosophical or spiritual, and while she searches, a number of ostensible guides take advantage of her.

The first who tries to take advantage of Candy is Professor Mephesto, an old and learned man who teaches a college course entitled Contemporary Ethics, which is in fact a forum for his personal views. The professor gives Candy an A+ for her paper on "Contemporary Human Love" and is enthralled with her thesis: to give of oneself fully is not just a duty but a privilege. He invites her to his office and makes a clumsy attempt at sexual advances. Candy hardly notices, however, because she is so taken with the authoritative professor and with the high grade he has given her.

Next, Candy is almost ravished by the family gardener, Emmanuel, who hardly speaks English. She is attracted to

Emmanuel and considers running off with him, but fate intervenes when her overprotective father, Sidney Christian, discovers the tryst and breaks it up violently. There are intimations that Sidney is saving Candy for himself, but in any case, in the altercation with the gardener, Sidney ends up with a trowel through his skull and must be rushed off to Racine County Municipal Hospital. Candy goes with her father and is met by two relatives, Uncle Jack, a staid and boring individual, and Aunt Livia, who is, in 1950s parlance, a "swinger." Aunt Livia is obsessed with Candy's virginal beauty and makes many lewd remarks that are embarrassing to all. Candy is invited to join Livia and Jack at a hotel named Halfway House where Livia makes more lewd remarks. From here the story spins out to encompass a couple of perverse doctors who have their way with Candy and a bizarre hospital room orgy that leaves Uncle Jack in Sidney's bed. Amid the confusion, Sidney leaves the hospital and disappears.

From here Candy links up with a hunchbacked homosexual mute who doesn't know what to make of her but upon whom she takes great pity. She is then led to a strange religious cult called the Cracker Foundation by its spiritual leader, Peter Uspy, who rescues her from the perils of Greenwich Village in New York. Uspy, a rather twisted ascetic, convinces Candy to undertake spiritual training which requires that she not have an orgasm while having sex with him. Candy masters these new techniques and eventually flies to Tibet for further study. She somehow finds herself having sex with Buddha, who turns out to be none other than Sidney, her missing father.

Christmas, Joe. *Light in August.* William Faulkner. 1932.

Joe Christmas, an orphan who suspects that he may have some black blood, receives his bizarre name upon arriving as an infant on the doorstep of an orphanage for white children, an institution that remains his home until the matron discovers the secret of his mixed ancestry. Although Joe usually passes as a white person, his obsessive suspicions concerning the composition of his blood are indirectly responsible for ruining his life and for the violent manner in which he dies.

When the secret of Joe's blood is divulged by a dietician at the orphanage, the matron of the institution places him in the home of the McEacherns, a childless couple who farm for a living. Mr. McEachern, a pious, brutal man, unsuccessfully attempts to discipline Joe by beating him and depriving him of food. Their conflict culminates in Mr. McEachern's apparent death when he follows Joe to a dance he attends with his girlfriend Bobbie, a waitress and prostitute who is some fifteen years the boy's senior. Furious that his foster father would dare to humiliate him with moral castigations in front of everyone, Joe bashes him over the head with a chair and flees.

Fifteen years later, Joe arrives in Jefferson, Mississippi, after having wandered from Oklahoma to Mexico to Chicago, holding down jobs as a laborer, prospector, gambler, and soldier. Penniless, he finally finds employment at a planing mill where he works shoveling sawdust.

Joe begins living in an abandoned cabin that stands on the estate of JOANNA BURDEN, a middle-aged white woman. A descendant of northern abolitionists, she supports the civil rights of black people, which has made her notorious in town. Joanna soon becomes aware of Joe's mixed blood and begins to cook meals for him, and the two become involved in a tempestuous romantic affair.

As their relationship intensifies, Joe begins to believe that Joanna's nymphomania is somehow corrupting him. She insists on spicing up their sex life by hiding naked in closets or in torn clothes in the shrubbery surrounding the house, waiting for Joe to come and ravish her. She offers to let him take over her business of advising the administrators of a dozen black schools and colleges concerning financial and religious matters, but he refuses, preferring to work at the planing mill and to supplement his salary there by selling whiskey. He also refuses her offer to send him to a black college to study law and rejects her offer of marriage.

The affair persists for two years, and then Joanna mistakes menopause for pregnancy. Upon discovering the truth, Joe is disgusted by this sign of her impending old age and breaks off their physical relationship. One night Joanna sends for Joe. He finds her in bed with an antique revolver loaded with two bullets: one for him and one for her. When the first bullet fails to discharge, Joe retaliates by slitting her throat with the razor blade he has brought with him.

Joe is finally caught by the police and taken to trial. He escapes on his way to the jury room and runs to the house of the ex-minister, GAIL HIGHTOWER, in an effort to hide from his pursuers. Percy Grimm, a racist vigilante, discovers him there and brutally murders him, castrating him for daring to enter a white woman's bedroom.

Citrine, Charles. *Humboldt's Gift.* Saul Bellow. 1973.

Charles "Charlie" Citrine is an intellectual, Pulitzer Prize–winning author, and the novel's narrator. The novel begins just as Charlie's career is beginning to plummet from its high commercial success. Although he gradually loses his fortune and his girlfriend, he finds a measure of inner peace through meditating on the life and death of his friend FLEISCHER VON HUMBOLDT.

Charlie gains access to the literary world when he is a young Fuller Brush salesman by writing a letter to and instigating a friendship with the highly acclaimed Humboldt, whose powerful ballads had moved him deeply. The two share in the Greenwich Village literary scene until Humboldt receives a position as Writer-in-Residence at

Princeton University and helps Charlie get a one-year position there. At Princeton, Charlie and Humboldt grow closer, spending evenings together drinking and developing wild screenplay plots—including one that features a cannibalistic Italian named Caldofreddo. They initiate a "blood-brotherhood" friendship symbolized by their exchanging signed blank checks with each other.

Unfortunately, the friendship falls apart. Humboldt becomes a paranoid manic depressive, accusing Charlie of betraying him when he is eventually committed to Bellevue. His sense of this betrayal coincides with Charlie's achievement of fame and fortune with a Broadway hit, *Von Trenck*. Humboldt pickets Charlie's show and cashes his check for almost $7,000.

Charlie admits that his Broadway show is shallow and that he had little to do with what caused its success. He is deeply hurt by Humboldt's cashing the check, however, and the dissolution of the friendship combined with the death of his girlfriend in a plane crash cause him to become deeply depressed. The last time Charlie sees Humboldt, his old friend looks poverty-stricken and near death. Charlie is not surprised to hear, soon after, that Humboldt has died from a heart attack.

After his success with *Von Trenck*, Charlie's life seems charmed. He writes several highly respected biographies and marries an attractive woman, Denise, who tries to separate him from his lower-class friends and initiate him into high society. The two eventually divorce, and Denise is awarded his entire fortune.

Soon after this decision is handed down, Charlie heads to Europe with his new girlfriend Renata. Before leaving the country, they stop in New York to pick up a bequest Humboldt had left him. The bequest includes a sane letter of apology for treating Charlie unjustly and a plot for what Humboldt saw as a great screenplay, but Charlie thinks it is as foolish as any they developed on drunken evenings at Princeton.

Renata, tired of waiting for him to offer her the security of marriage, leaves Charlie in Europe. When his money runs out, he moves into a cheap rooming house with Renata's son and reads "anthroposophical" tracts about the immortality of the soul, reincarnation, and the possibility of accessing divine knowledge through sleep. Contemplating these mystical concepts and musing about his relationship with the brilliant but troubled Humboldt, Charlie feels extraordinarily fulfilled, content, and peaceful.

One day Cantabile, a Mafia-linked friend, shows up to inform Charlie that a movie called *Caldofreddo* is receiving worldwide acclaim, and he could make a fortune by proving its makers stole the idea from him and Humboldt. More to help Humboldt's uncle, who is languishing in a nursing home in Coney Island, than himself, Charlie demands and wins a settlement of $80,000. Charlie and the

uncle have Humboldt and his mother's bodies moved from the pauper's graveyard in which they were buried to a quiet family plot. Soon after they find crocuses blooming near the graves.

Claffey, Ira. *Andersonville.* McKinley Kantor. 1955.

Ira Claffey is a Southern plantation owner, staunch Confederate, and principal character in this novel that details the horrors of the South's enormous prison camp built at Anderson, Georgia.

Claffey loses all three of his sons in the war and is left with his daughter Lucy (Claffey), his wife Veronica, who is slowly retreating into a madness caused by grief, and a few faithful slaves. Although he considers himself a kind master who treats his slaves as children, Claffey is shocked at the idea of abolition. When the Confederate leaders decide to build a prison camp on the edge of his land, he hesitates and unwillingly sends conscripted slaves to help erect the huge stockade.

While his loyalty to the Confederate cause does not waver, Claffey is appalled and offended by Andersonville, where over thirty thousand prisoners are crammed together in an open stockade with no shelter other than what they themselves can erect. Without sanitation, the creek running through the stockade soon becomes a swamp of human excrement. The Claffeys are forced to burn smudge pots and make cologne masks to endure the stench, which worsens as prisoners begin to die in huge numbers from malaria, dysentery, and scurvy caused by their diet of corn pone and contaminated water. Veronica, completely detached and in a state of self-induced starvation, seems to have a ghoulish fondness for the odor, which she associates with her dead children.

Ira watches Andersonville and gradually begins to realize that he must do something about the atrocity. He and a local minister, Cato Dillard, amass a huge amount of vegetables and clothing and take it to the camp, only to be turned away and branded Yankee sympathizers. Personal tragedy strikes Ira when Veronica, in a demented attempt to reach her dead children, escapes the house and wanders toward the "smell." He discovers her almost drowned in the fetid swamp near the stockade.

Following the death of his wife, Claffey decides to make the dangerous trip to Richmond in an attempt to speak with someone in command who can do something to alleviate the prisoners' suffering. He gets only to northern Georgia before the train he is riding is taken by Union soldiers. He returns home on foot, convinced that the Confederate cause is in shambles. Only the marriage of his daughter Lucy to Harrell "Harry" Elkins, a doctor at the Andersonville camp, creates happiness in the bleak autumn of the end of the war.

After the surrender, Ira frees his slaves and reluctantly sees some of them leave the plantation to attempt to make their future in the destroyed South. He thinks they may have a future brighter than his, brighter even than that of the baby his daughter Lucy is carrying. With the prisoners gone, he wanders around the ghostly desolate stockade of Andersonville, which even the birds shun, thinking back on this place that was the sight of such a great tragedy in the nation's history.

Claffey, Lucy. *Andersonville.* McKinley Kantor. 1955.

Lucy Claffey, a strong, passionate Southern woman, attempts to lead a normal life amid the calamities of the Civil War and the atrocities of a nearby prison camp. The daughter of IRA (CLAFFEY), a Georgia plantation owner, and his wife Veronica, Lucy was engaged to a Confederate soldier who died in an early campaign in the war. To add to her grief, her three older brothers all go to war and are killed, leaving Lucy the only survivor of the eight children her mother bore. Burdened by the tragedy of her dead children, Veronica Claffey retreats into madness, leaving Lucy to run the plantation, aid the sick, manage the slaves, and somehow overcome her own bitter sorrow.

With the aid of her sympathetic father, young Lucy tries to cope with the war and with the horrors of Andersonville, the prison camp that has been built next to the Claffey property. When HARRELL "HARRY" ELKINS, an army surgeon and friend of her brother Sutherland, comes to visit, she feels drawn to him and is troubled by her romantic dreams in which he plays a part.

Harry leaves to go to another camp, and Lucy grows desperate, burdened as she is with the care of her mother, who believes she is caring for her dead children who are in chests in a bedroom. Far more horrible, however, is the atrocity of Andersonville. By summer the stockade holds over thirty thousand Yankee soldiers, without shelter, sanitation, or adequate food. The stench from the stockade fills the Claffey home, and the noise creates a constant monotonous din. When gangs within the stockade fight, the Claffeys cannot ignore the uproar and subsequent hangings. Appalled by the terrible suffering, Lucy tells her father she wants to damn God for allowing such misery. Her problems become acute when her mother escapes from the house and nearly drowns in the swamp of human excrement outside the prison stockade. When Veronica dies soon after, Lucy feels both relieved and guilty.

Through the spring and summer, Lucy and Harry Elkins have maintained a valued correspondence. When Harry succeeds in being transferred to Andersonville as a prison surgeon, Lucy asks him to live at the Claffey home, and he agrees. Lucy is overjoyed, but months go by and Harry, driven to desperation by the insurmountable job he has undertaken, never attempts to begin a romance. Finally, when they are alone one evening, Lucy resolves to be forward and seduces him. He returns her affection, and soon her fantasy of being married to Harry becomes a reality.

The defeat of the Confederacy means a change in Lucy's way of life. She watches her father free their slaves and knows that life will never be the same, but Lucy, who is pregnant, feels the hope that peace brings and is confident that she and Harry can create a happy life together after having endured so much misery.

Claggart, John. *Billy Budd, Sailor* (An Inside Narrative). Herman Melville. 1924.

John Claggart, the master-at-arms of the warship *Bellipotent*, possesses an instinct for evil that manifests itself as "a peculiar ferreting genius." A shapely man with silken curls and delicate hands, Claggart evolves an intense yet mysterious hatred for the handsome sailor BILLY BUDD and contrives to ruin him. Ironically, his efforts lead not only to Billy's execution but to his own death.

In his capacity as a maritime chief of police, Claggart is an unpopular figure with the crew, who call him "Jemmy Legs" behind his back. His past remains obscure, but it is rumored that he may have been some kind of villain or thief. He began his navy career in the lowliest of positions but was able to rise rapidly through the ranks by evincing a superior intelligence, austerity, and patriotism.

Aside from the ship's captain, EDWARD FAIRFAX VERE, Claggart is perhaps the only person capable of appreciating the "moral phenomenon" presented by Billy Budd's innocence and personal beauty. However, unlike Vere, who is fond of Billy, Claggart regards the young sailor with envy and loathing—emotions he keeps hidden beneath a veneer of ironic politeness.

Claggart's antipathy toward Billy initially takes the form of carefully engineered minor infractions—the improper stowage of his belongings, for instance, or an apparent oversight in the keeping of his hammock. One day as Claggart is passing through the mess, the ship lurches, and Billy spills the contents of his soup bowl in his path. Claggart, who is about to pass on, suddenly notices Billy and gives him a sharp rap on the buttocks with his rattan. "Handsomely done, my lad!" he exclaims melodiously before stepping over the greasy liquid and continuing on his way. No sooner does Claggart turn his back, however, than his features dissolve into a strange, distorted expression, and he venomously chastises another sailor who has inadvertently caught his eye.

Each time he sees Billy, Claggart's enmity toward him increases. When gazing unobserved at the young man, his eyes seem to be tinged, at first, with melancholy and yearning—as though he might be capable of loving Billy were it not for the "elemental evil" within him. Then his expression hardens; his fierce hatred emerges, and red sparks flash from his eyes.

Claggart arranges for an afterguardsman to prompt Billy, who was impressed into service on the *Bellipotent*, to mutiny. When this attempt proves unsuccessful, he approaches Captain Vere. He reminds his superior officer of the navy's recent difficulties with mutineers and accuses Billy of being "a dangerous man." Vere, vaguely repelled by Claggart and suspicious of any charges against the congenial young sailor, decides to meet with the two men privately in his cabin.

When Billy arrives, Vere asks Claggart to tell him why he has been summoned. Claggart strides purposefully forward and, standing a short distance from Billy, repeats his accusations. As Billy, who suffers from a speech impediment, struggles to respond, Claggart holds him transfixed with a serpentlike gaze. In the seemingly endless moment of their confrontation, Claggart undergoes a strange metamorphosis: His violet eyes, once "lights of human intelligence," grow muddied and protrude inhumanly like "the alien eyes of certain uncatalogued creatures of the deep." Finally, the innocent Billy, unable to find his voice, strikes out with his powerful forearm. Claggart falls, gasps, and dies.

Clare, Bernard. *Bernard Clare.* James T. Farrell. 1946.

Bernard Clare, twenty-one, arrives in New York from Chicago. He rooms at a flophouse and spends his days reading and writing at the Forty-second Street library where he daydreams of beautiful women and literary success. A letter comes from his angry father, disowning Bernard for leaving home and advising him to find a job and forget the literary life. Bernard dismisses his family, with its drinking and show of religiosity, as the epitome of hopelessness.

Bernard follows closely the murder trial of anarchists Sacco and Vanzetti. The case inflames his working-class sympathies and embitters him against the middle and upper classes. He meets another young aspiring writer, Al Jackson. Although Bernard strongly rejects Al's hedonistic view of life, the two become friends.

Bernard finds a job selling advertising in Queens. An instant success, he is suddenly flush with money and free time. One day in the park he meets a woman with a child. She smiles at him, and when he spots her on Eighth Street a few days later, she greets him. After some conversation, Bernard invites her to his room, and they have sex. For the next four months Eva Stone, who is seven years older than Bernard and married, becomes the center of Bernard's life. She loves Bernard but cannot leave her husband Sid because he supports her son and her aged parents. When Sid catches the lovers together in bed, a violent scene ensues, and Eva must break off her affair with Bernard.

On his own again, Bernard becomes increasingly embittered and turns to alcohol. In the book's final scene, he makes a spectacle of himself at a party of middle-class friends whose values he insults before passing out in his own vomit. The book ends with a note to Eva telling of his return to Chicago to begin afresh and thanking her for the self-confidence she has given him.

Clark, Sappho. *Contending Forces.* Pauline E. Hopkins. 1900.

When the mystery that surrounds Sappho Clark is revealed, the novel's beautiful heroine learns that it would have been less complicated not to have concealed the details of her painful past. Happiness is eventually restored, however, as Sappho is reunited with her true love, WILL SMITH, despite the attempt by JOHN P. LANGLEY to have her as his own.

A boarder in the Boston home of Mrs. Smith, Sappho works as a freelance stenographer. She has decorated the room she occupies in a charming manner and always leaves the door open for Dora, Mrs. Smith's daughter. The two share tea and secrets, but Sappho is silent about most aspects of her past. She will say little more than that she was born in New Orleans and raised by black nuns. Despite her penchant for secrecy, Sappho becomes loving friends with Dora and begins to feel part of the Smith family.

With her beauty, southern manners, and aura of secrecy, Sappho becomes an object of interest in Boston's black community. In particular, she draws the attention of Will Smith, Dora's studious brother, and John P. Langley, Dora's fiancé, a rising young Boston lawyer. Sappho is flattered by Will's regard but troubled by the interest of her friend's fiancé. Not only does she feel guilty that she has inadvertently aroused John's passion but she is also put off by his overly smooth manner. She does not want John for herself, but neither does she want Dora to marry him.

At a fair organized by church-going members of the black community, Sappho is sought out by Will. As the two sit in a secluded area together, Will hints at his interest in her. The pair is interrupted by John, who tells Will that his mother wants him. Left alone with John, Sappho is approached by a beautiful little boy, Alphonse, the servant of a fortune-teller who is entertaining at the fair. Alphonse gives Sappho a favorable message from the fortune-teller. Sappho feels little happiness, however, because John insists on telling her of his interest in her, and she is finally forced to reject him.

News reaches Boston of the lynching in the South of a black rape suspect, and Sappho is among the concerned participants in a hastily called meeting. When white politicians and John P. Langley insist on a conciliatory attitude, a man in the audience asks to take the floor. He tells the moving story of a dishonored black woman, raped by a wealthy white man years before in New Orleans, and of her death while giving birth in a convent. Sappho faints on hearing the tale.

A few days later, on Easter Sunday, Will finally asks Sappho to marry him. After debating with herself a while, Sappho, deeply in love, consents. Will and Sappho agree to wait until the next morning to tell his family. That evening, however, her joy is shattered. John barges into her room while she is alone in the house and tells her that he knows she is the abused southern woman in the story whose death had been reported to protect her from her rapist. Telling her that Will would never marry a non-virgin, John offers to take care of her. Sappho sobs that she will marry no one but Will. When it becomes clear that John intends to take her as his mistress, not his wife, Sappho dismisses him. That night she packs a few things and leaves.

Sappho goes to the home of the fortune-teller, who is her aunt, and takes Alphonse, the son she had never before acknowledged. They travel to New Orleans where she is again assisted by black nuns. With their help, she is able to secure a position as governess to the daughters of a wealthy elderly black man. In time, he asks her to marry him.

Three years pass, and one day when Sappho is visiting Alphonse in the church-run orphanage where he is staying, she is met by Will. As he embraces her, she finally realizes that his love is too strong to be diminished by the crime that was committed against her. Since she had not accepted her employer's offer of marriage, she is free to marry the man she thought could not accept her.

Clavering, Lee. *Black Oxen.* Gertrude Atherton. 1923.

A drama critic and young dilettante in the 1920s, Lee Clavering has a scathing wit and formidable intellect that make him feared and respected by the members of the elite New York social circles he inhabits. Because he has a daily column in the New York *Times*, Clavering spends the greater part of his life at opening nights at the theater, cocktail parties, and other refined activities sponsored by members of his class.

At one of these events, opening night of a play he is reviewing for his column, Clavering sees a beautiful blond woman sitting a few rows in front of him. Knowing virtually every member of the social circle that typically frequents such events, Clavering is immediately taken with the mysterious stranger. His curiosity increases when an old friend, Mr. Dinwiddie, claims that the woman is the exact image of another New York society woman, MARY OGDEN, a belle who had charmed his generation some twenty years earlier before marrying an Austrian count.

After following the mysterious woman home to her apartment one night, Clavering is invited inside for a drink. She explains to him that she is a distant cousin of Mary Ogden and is in New York to settle some of her relative's business affairs. After being invited to a dinner the following night, Clavering leaves, still having lingering doubts about the explanation of her identity.

As Clavering continues to woo the beautiful young woman in the ensuing weeks, Mr. Dinwiddie continues his quiet investigation as to Mary's identity. After learning that Mary Ogden has no such cousin, he warns her that the alias she has invented for herself will not stand up to

the scrutiny of New York society. In the meantime, Clavering, fully aware that the woman has a great secret she is not revealing to him, has fallen hopelessly in love. He proposes to the young woman, who tells him that she will reveal her secret to him in a week's time, and if he still wishes to marry her afterward, she will consent.

Clavering spends the week overwhelmed with curiosity as to what her secret could be and vows to marry her no matter what. When the night arrives, however, he is shocked when she reveals to him that she is, in fact, Mary Ogden herself. Her youthful physical features are the result of an operation she had in Vienna that reverses the effect of aging. Thus, while looking no more than thirty, she is in reality close to sixty years old.

Stunned by this revelation, Clavering still wants to marry Mary, despite the notoriety and the resentment she receives from the other society women when she reveals her identity. They plan to marry in two months' time in Vienna, after Clavering finishes a play he is writing in New York.

After finishing his play, however, Clavering is dismayed to learn that an old Austrian lover of Mary's has arrived in New York for a visit. Clavering takes Mary to a retreat in the country with friends of theirs to keep her away but finds one morning that she has returned to the city. Fearing the worst, Clavering follows her, and after forcing his way into her house, learns that Mary plans to return to Austria with her old lover. He is overwhelmed with grief until Mary gently explains to him the vanity and arrogance that caused her to seek a husband half her age, as well as the fact that while his life would forever be in New York, hers is in Austria. Realizing the truth in her words, Clavering leaves, never to see Mary Ogden again.

Clay. *Less Than Zero.* Bret Easton Ellis. 1985.

Clay, a world-weary eighteen-year-old, tells the story of his contemporaries: bored, rich, self-destructive adolescents living in Los Angeles in the 1980s. The novel documents the sad, lost, and erratic lives of a group of jaded young adults who live for drugs, worship the sun and rock music, and frequent Los Angeles's most expensive and talked-about spots.

Clay returns to Los Angeles during Christmas break after having completed his first term in a New Hampshire college. In his description of his four weeks at home with his high school buddies and girlfriend, he paints a disturbingly unpleasant portrait of the vacuous, valueless lifestyle that surrounds him. All of Clay's friends and even his family live superficial, high-priced lives filled with alcohol, drugs, sex, and flashy cars. Although Clay's four months on the East Coast have given him some distance from this life-style and although he attempts to tell his story with a certain objectivity, Clay himself is representative of a world where meaningful communication and intimacy do not exist and where individuals' goals and dreams are conspicuously absent. His detached and laconic style of narration expresses not only his contempt for those he describes but also the futility and ruin of his own life.

Arriving in Los Angeles, Clay is greeted by Blair, his high school girlfriend. Clay shows little emotion for Blair, but she passionately and enthusiastically welcomes him home, tells him he looks pale, and invites him to her Christmas party that evening. At the party, Clay's friend Trent also notes that Clay looks pale and suggests he try going to a tanning salon; by the end of the evening Clay is convinced that a tan is what he needs.

This first evening sets the precedent for Clay's vacation as he moves languidly through the L.A. nightlife of clubs, parties, and after-hours restaurants. He spends much of his time looking for his mysteriously elusive drug dealer and the rest of the time snorting cocaine until his nose bleeds. The sense of time in the novel becomes increasingly distorted as Clay falls deeper into an abyss of meaningless thrills. Endless evenings of partying and cheap sexual encounters blur into wasted days spent sleeping off his drug highs, watching music videos, and smoking cigarettes.

While in Los Angeles, Clay visits a psychiatrist, who spends more time talking about his sports car, his two beach houses, and his feeble attempts to write a screenplay than he does about Clay's problems. Irritated by his self-absorbed doctor but unable to get his attention, Clay decides to make up bizarre sexual fantasies. Later, frustrated to the point of tears, Clay rebuffs his therapist over the phone and tells him he will not see him anymore.

As the novel closes, Clay's sense of hopelessness and helplessness is reflected in a series of violent dreams and images, and in his blank stares down long, empty roads and into the city's fluorescent lights. While watching a religious program on television, he waits expectantly but vainly to feel some change within him, and when he does not, decides to snort more cocaine. His increasingly terse narration and his frequent flashbacks of past vacations spent in Palm Springs with his family reflect Clay's troubled state. Yet his callous and indifferent nature tragically prevents him from changing his life, and after confessing to Blair that caring is too painful, he leaves Los Angeles with the final image of "people, teenagers [his] own age, looking up from the asphalt and being blinded by the sun."

Clay, Robert. *Soldiers of Fortune.* Richard Harding Davis. 1897.

Robert Clay is the novel's tanned, broad-shouldered, confident hero. His father, a mercenary, died when Clay was a child, and finding that he had to support himself at a young age, Clay embarked on an adventurous career. After beginning work as a mercenary—a "soldier of fortune"—he developed a talent as an engineer and became involved in military, mining, and construction projects around the world.

Now an adult, Clay is hired to investigate a possible mining site in the South American country of Olancho. He sails along the coast and decides that a large amount of iron ore can be extracted if certain large engineering projects are undertaken. He sends a letter to Mr. Langham, his employer in New York, and six months later the Valencia Mining Company is formed. Clay, whose abilities are legendary, is hired to construct railroads and piers and to look after the native and imported workers.

After construction is under way, Mr. Langham's son Teddy arrives in Olancho to oversee his father's interests. Observing that Clay is proceeding efficiently, Teddy announces that his father and two sisters will spend the winter there. Clay is excited because a year earlier he had met the elder sister, Alice Langham, whom he has long been worshiping from afar. Clay and his friend MacWilliams construct a bungalow for the family. He eagerly looks forward to Alice Langham's enjoying a home in which he has invested so much energy for her benefit.

When the Langhams arrive, Clay enthusiastically shows them around Valencia and the mining sites. When he boldly expresses his admiration for Alice, however, she remains somewhat detached, claiming that their friendship must be held on social rather than personal grounds. Clay is also taken aback and depressed when Alice belittles all he has achieved in his active, physical career. When he is with her, he feels uncharacteristically humiliated and inadequate.

In sharp contrast to Alice, Hope Langham, her younger sister, takes a sincere and hearty interest in Clay and his occupations. When Alice prevents Hope from attending a state dinner on the grounds that she has not yet "come out," Clay finally sees that Alice can only operate within narrow conventions and rules. Clay returns from the dinner to see Hope, and from this point on, they are spiritually united.

Meanwhile, Clay is occupied with trying to prevent a coup against President Alvarez of Olancho, a man friendly to American interests but also tolerant of a corrupt wife who steals from the national treasury. If a coup succeeds, Clay is informed, the revolutionaries will confiscate the mines and drive the Americans out. Clay succeeds in forming an alliance of miners and loyal soldiers, and together they put down the coup attempt after a brief battle. Hope involves herself in the strife and saves Clay, MacWilliams, and Teddy from certain death. Then she and Clay openly express their mutual love and agree to marry. After the restoration of order they steam toward New York dreaming of an adventurous life together.

Clayton, Cicero. "A Matter of Principle." Charles W. Chesnutt. 1899.

Cicero Clayton, a member of the Blue Vein Society, finds himself uncomfortably bound by his principles concerning race. Mr. and Mrs. Clayton and their daughter Alice are prominent members of the society, a group of Negroes organized shortly after the Civil War whose chief requirement for eligibility was skin fair enough to show blue veins. The Claytons are stalwart supporters of this restriction, and they are determined that Alice find her husband among those represented by the society.

In an effort to broaden the field of selection, Alice is sent to spend several weeks in Washington, D.C., where society of the kind the Claytons approve abounds. While there, Alice meets a number of young men, among them a congressman who becomes attracted to her. She returns home, and the Claytons are delighted when a letter arrives from young Congressman Brown informing them that he will be in town on business and expressing his desire to see Alice again. That Congressman Brown's intentions portend more than a mere acquaintance is evident to the Claytons. To the dismay of her parents, however, Alice cannot remember Brown's physical features and, consequently, the Claytons are not certain that the prospective betrothed is light-skinned enough.

When a family friend who had attended college with Brown informs them that the young man has near-white skin and straight hair similar to a Spaniard or a Portuguese, their fears are eased. The friend notes parenthetically that there had been two Browns at college, and one of them had quite African features. Alice is sure that the Mr. Brown with whom she danced in Washington had Caucasian features. The Claytons immediately wire Brown, inviting him to stay with them during his visit. They also plan several elaborate social gatherings to which they invite the crème de la crème of the Blue Vein Society.

On the day of Brown's expected arrival, Mr. Clayton and Jack, a poor relation who resides with the Claytons and who has had romantic designs on Alice, go to the train station to meet Brown. The two are chagrined when they arrive to find a stout black man of decidedly Negroid features waiting patiently next to luggage clearly marked with Brown's name. Convinced that Alice has been mistaken and that they have invited the second Mr. Brown mentioned by their friend, Mr. Clayton sends Jack to verify his suspicions. Jack returns with the news that the dark man is indeed Mr. Brown of Washington, D.C.

Jack and Mr. Clayton concoct a note to Mr. Brown, explaining that Alice has contracted diphtheria and that they are unable to entertain him as promised. A doctor is bribed to post a quarantine sign on the home, and all the social events planned in Mr. Brown's honor are canceled. Alice is forced to remain at home. Finally, the Claytons breathe a collective sigh of relief, happy that they have successfully avoided a social calamity.

Later, while reading the newspaper, Mr. Clayton learns that the congressman had traveled to Groveland in the company of a Negro minister who from the description provided by the newspaper is the man he saw in the depot. He realizes that he mistook the bishop for the congress-man, and it is apparent that he was aided in this misconception by the deliberate help of Jack. Alice's chief rival spends the next few days entertaining the congressman and eventually marries him, while Alice is left to contemplate marriage to her socially inferior cousin Jack.

Clayton, Edward. *Dred, a Tale of the Great Dismal Swamp.* Harriet Beecher Stowe. 1856.

Although he is the heir of a prominent Southern family, Edward Clayton becomes a staunch proponent of the anti-slavery cause. Always reform-minded, Clayton is finally moved to oppose slavery when he experiences love and bears witness to injustice and indifference.

A very eligible bachelor, Clayton becomes captivated by the coquettish NINA GORDON. Clayton is not the only man with whom the seventeen-year-old plantation owner has been friendly, but realizing his fine qualities, she chooses him over all others. Clayton's sister Anne expresses reservations about the match because Nina is flighty. But Clayton is in love and able to see the kind and generous heart that beats beneath Nina's frivolous exterior. They do not formally become engaged, but agreement exists between them that a marriage will surely take place.

During an extended visit to Canema, Nina's plantation, Clayton demonstrates the kind of faithfulness and support that causes Nina to love him. When HARRY GORDON, Nina's slave and half-brother, asks Nina to protect his wife Lisette from the sexual advances of Nina's lascivious brother Tom, Clayton intervenes. He advances Nina the money to buy Lisette from the Creole woman who owns her, ruining Tom's plans to purchase Lisette for his personal use.

Clayton renders even greater service to Nina and to the anti-slavery cause when he argues a court case for his beloved. Clayton, who along with Anne imagines his role as a planter to be more like that of a teacher than a master, is incensed when he hears of the mistreatment of Nina's mammy, Aunt Milly. Nina had allowed Milly's time to be hired by a neighboring farmer in order to earn money for Canema. Milly's employer severely wounded her in a drunken rage, and Nina pressed charges.

Clayton exerts all his talent as a skillful lawyer and eloquent public speaker to win a conviction of the man; however, the decision is reversed on appeal. Clayton's own father, Judge Clayton, sits on the case and finds that since slaves are property, they can be treated in any way their masters desire. Offended by such laws, Clayton resigns from the bar and undertakes a career as an anti-slavery speaker.

Awakened to religion after Nina's conversion and certain after her death from cholera that Christianity and slavery are incompatible, Clayton hopes to win support from the Church. It becomes clear, however, that the ministry is more concerned with preserving order than pursuing justice. Only one minister, Father Dickson, dares to side with Clayton, and when he is threatened for his outspokenness by a group of ruffians led by Tom Gordon, Clayton saves him.

Later, Clayton is himself beaten senseless by Tom but is rescued by Harry Gordon and DRED VESEY, an escaped slave who makes his home in the Great Dismal Swamp. Harry, now a fugitive with his wife, assists in speeding Clayton's recovery. While he is healing, Clayton spends time talking with the many fugitive slaves who live in the swamp. His attention is drawn to the powerful, visionary Dred. Clayton tries to persuade Dred that if it is God's will that slavery end, only God, not men, may strike a physical blow to end it.

Dred is killed before he can lead his slave rebellion, but Clayton does his best, in his own way, to weaken the institution of slavery. He provides money for the escape northward of the swamp's inhabitants. Realizing that he can no longer live in the unfree South, Clayton moves his entire plantation to Canada, where he frees his slaves. He organizes a community where the relationship between white and black is one of equality rather than absolute power on one side and absolute subservience on the other.

Clement, Karen Hansen. *Exodus.* Leon Uris. 1958.

Karen Hansen Clement is a gentle young Jewish woman whose life is radically changed by the rise of the Nazis in Germany. When she is eight years old, Karen is separated from her family and spends her life in exile. Still, her identity as a Jew is the core of her existence and the factor that draws her to Palestine, the setting for the novel.

When the Nazi threat became too great to ignore, Karen's father put her on a train to Denmark, sent the rest of the family to France, and went into hiding. In Denmark, Karen was taken in by a Christian family and raised as their own daughter. After the war, determined to find her father, Karen moves to a series of displaced persons camps in Sweden, Belgium, and France. In southern France she learns that her father is probably alive and resolves to go to Palestine where she believes he may be living.

Karen takes passage on a ship that is making an illegal run to Palestine, but the vessel is captured, and those aboard are held in a detention camp on Cyprus. Here Karen meets the American nurse KITTY FREMONT. Kitty is drawn to Karen because of the girl's striking resemblance to her own daughter who died tragically along with Kitty's husband when she was still in America. Karen becomes very close to Kitty and to an angry and withdrawn young Auschwitz survivor named Dov. Karen is persistent in trying to draw the boy out of his shell, and they soon become friends. When Dov, an expert forger, finds out that he and Karen are not included in a group to be smuggled into Palestine, he is angry and refuses to create the papers that the Zionist smugglers need. At last ARI BEN CANAAN, the leader of the Zionists, agrees to let them join the group.

The smugglers have planned to allow the ship, the *Exodus*, to be stopped in the harbor in order to create a media event that will force the British to grant them passage. When the ship is halted, those on board announce that they are carrying dynamite and will blow themselves up. Negotiations continue, and the children go on a hunger strike. The ship is finally allowed to sail, and its passengers arrive in Palestine. Karen makes her new home in the settlement Gan Dafna.

Karen's father is eventually found. Kitty accompanies Karen to Tel Aviv where her father is said to be alive but very sick. But when Karen goes to his side, she discovers that the man's war experience has left him deranged; he doesn't even recognize his daughter.

The news about Karen's father travels to Gan Dafna, and Dov decides to leave so that Karen will go with Kitty to America where she can start a new life. When she becomes convinced that Dov does not want to see her anymore, Karen sadly agrees to leave. By now Dov has been arrested by the British, and Karen must visit him in an Acre jail to say good-bye.

But Karen and Kitty's departure is delayed by a raid on Acre in which Dov escapes. Ari Ben Canaan has been injured, and Kitty must remove a bullet from his leg. After returning to Gan Dafna, Kitty, influenced by her love for Ari, decides not to leave. She and Karen remain in Palestine, and Kitty begins training Karen to be a nurse. Dov returns to Gan Dafna to apologize and confess his love for Karen, and she in turn admits that she loves him.

After Israel's War of Liberation, Karen goes into the army to continue her nurse's training. She is stationed at a hospital in a region called the Sharon, where she is able to see both Kitty and Dov often. Dov finishes his studies and is offered a chance to go to America for more schooling. He wants to marry Karen and take her with him. After they make plans, Dov must return to his post, but he promises to see her soon at a holiday celebration with the Ben Canaan family. Before that happens, however, Karen is killed during an Arab raid. As the novel ends, Dov, Kitty, and Ari mourn her death.

Clovis, Cletus James. *The Bushwhacked Piano.* Thomas McGuane. 1971.

Cletus James Clovis, a con man and a drifter, uses dreams of celebrity to stave off his encroaching despair. He watches television obsessively and becomes as hysterical and insistent as a TV commercial. NICHOLAS PAYNE, his business partner, looks upon Clovis with admiration as a member of a flourishing American underground of "artful dodgers" and anarchists.

Clovis's arrogance, which would seem inconsistent with his character, comes from having conquered his problem with obesity. He weighed 480 pounds when, along with two enormously fat friends, he decided to take a vow to lose all of his excess weight. His friends went on crash diets they invented, while Clovis dieted under the supervision of a doctor. The episode ends sadly: Both of his fat friends die. Clovis manages to lose the excess weight, but because he reduces too quickly, he also loses one leg to gangrene.

Before losing his leg, Clovis was a sign painter of terrifying, surreal billboards. After the operation he uses his surprisingly extensive knowledge of bats to develop a get-rich-quick scheme. Bats eat mosquitoes, which are a nuisance and carry dangerous diseases. So Clovis decides to build towers that will conveniently house bats so they will perform their bug-eating services for the owners of the buildings. The hitch is that Clovis has no way of ensuring that the bats, once released, will ever return to the tower. The prospective client is not likely to know this, however, and Clovis is a very convincing salesman for his "pest control structures." He manages to gather crowds to listen to speeches about the angelic bats doing their part for the common good.

Nicholas Payne, a rebellious and sometimes insane young man, is instantly won over to Clovis's side when they meet in a Detroit bar. Clovis is attracted by Payne's "youthful power" and later writes to him, promising a high salary if he will be foreman for the new "Batworks." When Clovis receives Payne's letter accepting the offer, he immediately begins driving his motor home west to Livingston, Montana, where Payne is experimenting in the rodeo business. In Livingston, the partners camp out near Bangtail Creek and plan the "Bat Tower" enterprise. They soon obtain a contract for a "Batrium," as Clovis calls the small version of the Bat Tower, but Payne must build it alone. Clovis is in the hospital again, this time for the amputation of a gangrenous arm.

When they finally have a contract for a full-scale Bat Tower in Key West, Florida, Clovis must again turn over the responsibility to Payne and a local contractor named Digo Fama. This time, hospitalized for a heart condition, Clovis begs Payne to join him there. At first Payne is unmoved by Clovis's frightened pleas, but he finally agrees to be admitted and undergo the hemorrhoid operation he has been deferring. The doctor insists that Clovis's ailment is merely psychosomatic, and he is never treated, while Payne undergoes an excruciating operation.

Clovis and his partner are both released in time for the opening celebration of the Bat Tower. But when he is given a turn at the microphone, Payne bluntly tells the crowd, "You've been fleeced!" In fact, the bats simply fly off and disappear when they are let out of their cage. By the time Clovis reaches the microphone, the failure of the scheme is already apparent, and he can only gasp that his heart is on the "fritz." He then collapses and dies on the podium, as if by force of will, leaving Payne to face charges of fraud. Payne is the solitary mourner at Clovis's funeral, and although he is genuinely sorry, he also feels relieved to be liberated from Clovis's tenacious immorality.

Coates, Abner. *The Just and the Unjust.* James Gould Cozzens. 1942.

Abner Coates is a third-generation small-town lawyer. In the course of the novel, Abner, a mild, methodical man, must make private and professional choices that will forever alter his ordered existence.

Still a bachelor at thirty-one, Abner lives at home with his sick father and serves as the assistant district attorney in the small New England town of Childerstown. When the novel opens, he is nervously preparing for his first murder trial, at which he will assist the very capable district attorney, Martin "Marty" Bunting. The two defendants are accused of kidnapping and murdering a dope addict. Expecting the defendants to be sentenced to death, Marty delegates much of the responsibility for the case to Abner.

On the evening of the first day of the trial, Abner attends a barge party with his girlfriend Bonnie. Many people have urged him to marry, but he and Bonnie cannot agree on the subject. A distant cousin of Abner's, Bonnie has lived in the Coates household for several years. She supports her mother on her salary as a high school secretary. Irritated by Abner's assumption that she will quit her job and marry him, Bonnie is cool and reserved at the party. Later that evening, Abner receives a phone call. There has been a traffic accident: One driver was killed; the other is being held in custody.

The next day Abner ably questions the state's star witness. Marty later tells him that the surviving driver from the night before, Hamilton Mason, is the son of a friend of the local party chairman, Jesse Gearhart. Abner greatly dislikes Jesse, who uses his considerable influence in the elections and resents his interest in the Mason case. Seeing his reaction, Marty becomes angry and tells Abner that he is making a serious mistake. Marty will soon be leaving and wants Abner to take over his position.

Although he has always assumed that he would succeed Marty, Abner is ambivalent about running for D.A. But when he meets Jesse, he can't seem to voice his feelings. Abner ends up suggesting that Jesse find someone else. Leaving his office, Abner realizes that he has done exactly what he didn't want to do—change his life.

Abner soon decides to quit his job. He goes to see Bonnie but doesn't know how to tell her about his change in plans without appearing to qualify his marriage proposal.

Later that evening Abner is called away by Marty. A teacher at the local high school has been charged with photographing and touching female students. Abner knows that the charges will mean trouble for the high school principal, Mr. Rawle, and he hopes Rawle will lose his job so that Bonnie, in turn, will lose hers.

As the trial wears on, Abner begins to question his choice of professions; but when Jesse again asks him to run for D.A., he agrees, provided he can make his own appointments. Jesse concurs.

Abner gets a marriage license and takes it to Bonnie that evening. She agrees to complete it only after Abner agrees to trust her and tell her things. He tells her about running for D.A., and Bonnie says she'll quit her job if they don't need the money. As she is filling out the application, Abner gets scared, but when he thinks about the two major commitments he has made, he realizes that his loss of freedom will be outweighed by more important and long-lasting gains.

Abner has examined each aspect of the murder trial closely, and so he is surprised when the jury votes to convict the defendants of murder in the second degree. Observing Marty's fury at this decision, Abner believes he has a better temperament to be the D.A.

Abner returns home and tells his father about his plans. He is still troubled by his career decision, but the wise judge reminds him of the fact that it is just a job. Every day people go to their jobs and come home to their families. Impossible though it might seem, this order keeps the world running. All they are asking of Abner, his father tells him, is the impossible.

Coffin, Adam. *Daddy Was a Number Runner*. Louise Meriwether. 1970.

Adam Coffin, a number runner in Harlem in 1934, is the father of FRANCIE (COFFIN), the novel's twelve-year-old narrator. Coffin is a big, handsome man who is fond of his doting daughter and stern with his two sons, Sterling and James Junior. He has the reputation of being an honest runner, and he feels important in the social life of the ghetto where everyone dreams of escaping poverty by winning at the illegal gambling game.

Coffin has difficulty providing for his family but obstinately refuses to ask for government relief or to allow his wife to work. He had been a cook in the navy during World War I, a janitor in Brooklyn, and a house painter when the family moved to Harlem, but now he earns his money illegally. Every now and then he makes extra cash by playing the piano at weekend parties. After one such weekend for which he accepted most of his payment in food, his wife Henrietta fights with him until he agrees to let her find a job doing housework in the Bronx.

One day Coffin is arrested but is let off because the police could not find his number slips. He then begins to put all of his commission as a runner back into the numbers, at which point his wife insists on asking for government relief. He responds with great anger and storms out of the house. When he returns, he appears to have swallowed his pride, but his daughter notices that some of his spirit seems to have gone out of him; he rather listlessly urges his children to be proud of their heritage as descendants of Yoruba, an African princess.

Things go from bad to worse. He begins working as a janitor in their building in exchange for a reduction of their rent, but he is cut off from government relief because

he does not report the job. His son Junior is then arrested for a murder committed by the street gang he runs with, and Coffin has to borrow $150 in order to pay for a defense lawyer. Junior is acquitted, but the family continues to struggle with its debts. Coffin works for a while for the WPA cleaning out sewers, but he gets pneumonia, loses the job, and cannot get back on relief. This time his wife doesn't even ask him before taking on more day work.

Coffin stops collecting the numbers and starts hanging out on street corners and playing poker through the night. He argues constantly with his wife and finally stops coming home at all. Thereafter, when his daughter goes to look for him, she usually finds him playing poker at the house of a widow named Mrs. Mackey. It takes Francie a while to understand that her father is living with the woman; when she figures it out, she is angry and accuses him of having forgotten he is one of Yoruba's children. He tries to pretend that nothing has happened, but the rift between them cannot be healed. When they meet briefly some weeks later, Francie is cold and distant. Half a block down the street, she turns and watches him walk away. He does not seem as big as he used to be.

Coffin, Francie. *Daddy Was a Number Runner*. Louise Meriwether. 1970.

Francie Coffin, the narrator, is a twelve-year-old girl struggling to understand what it means to grow up black and female in Harlem during the Depression.

Francie lives in a rat-infested tenement with her parents and two brothers, James Junior and Sterling. She adores her father ADAM (COFFIN) and is proud of his special status in the ghetto as a number runner. Mr. Coffin has difficulty supporting his family, however, and throughout the novel Francie is witness to a perpetual fight between her parents over money. As time passes, the family only gets poorer. Mr. Coffin begins to play his commission back into the numbers and stays out all night playing poker; he increasingly resents his wife's efforts to feed and clothe the children by doing housework and asking for government relief.

Francie's best friend is thirteen-year-old SUKIE MACEO, who is generous at times but has a habit of beating up Francie when in a bad mood. Every now and then the two girls go to a section of the park frequented by bums, where they earn some extra money by allowing the men to look at their genitals. Francie also receives money from a white man who follows her to the movies when she is alone and feels her. In the same manner, she obtains extra soup bones from the butcher and free rolls from the baker. Throughout the novel Francie struggles to understand her own sexuality with very little help from her elders. She is confused when she starts menstruating, ashamed by her own reaction when the man at the movies puts his hand inside her, and terrified when a neighborhood boy almost rapes her.

As time passes, Francie witnesses the slow breakdown of her parents' marriage and the family structure as a whole under the pressures of poverty and racism. After various crises, including being arrested for murder, her brother Junior leaves home; her father eventually leaves as well. Francie gradually begins to assert herself and to insist on maintaining the integrity of her own body. She angers Sukie by refusing to go to the park where the men are, and shortly after realizing that her father is living with another woman, she stands up to her friend for the first time by punching her in the nose. After this, the two girls decide that they are too old to fight like children.

Francie's relationship with her father disintegrates once she understands that he has abandoned the family. When they meet, he pretends that nothing has changed, but Francie is cold and distant, commenting to herself as he walks away that he does not seem as big as he used to. At the novel's end, Francie and Sukie are sitting on the stoop trying not to cry when Sterling comes along and asks why they are upset. Francie explains that she does not want to live there anymore and that Sukie is afraid she will become a prostitute like her older sister China Doll. Sterling tells the girls to move over, sits down between them on the steps, and pronounces judgment on the whole mess with a curse. After a moment of silence, Francie repeats the word.

Cohen, Harry. "The Jewbird." Bernard Malamud. 1963.

Harry Cohen, a frozen foods salesman, lives in a top-floor apartment on First Avenue near the East River in lower Manhattan with his wife Edie and ten-year-old son Maurie. The family usually spends August away, but after two weeks in Kingston, New York, Harry's aging mother fell ill; Harry dutifully packed his family and returned to the steamy city. One August evening, a black bird flies in his window and lands next to his lamb chop, and Harry's troubles begin.

In his typically angry and accusatory tone, Harry demands that this odd bird declare its business. When the bird claims that it is a Jewbird named Schwartz running from the anti-Semites, Harry laughs. His cruelty is tempered by Edie's kindness and Maurie's delight at having a new friend. Harry agrees to let the bird have some food and stay awhile as long as it remains out on the balcony. One night he even brings home a bird feeder filled with dried corn. When the bird tells him it cannot eat such things because of its poor digestion, Harry berates it for becoming too comfortable with the family's generosity and reminds it of its migratory lot in life.

In September, Edie implores Harry, who has been threatening to oust the bird, to let Schwartz stay until Maurie adjusts to going back to school. Schwartz takes on full responsibility for Maurie's performance in school. In spite of his enmity toward Schwartz, Harry is pleased with Maurie's progress and begins to cultivate hopes of getting the boy into an Ivy League school. But when the bird evaluates Maurie realistically as a good boy scout but no scholar, he loses his patience.

As time goes on, Harry becomes obsessed with getting rid of Schwartz. He abuses him for smelling like fish and for being cross-eyed. He starts reading about bird migration and then declares open war on Schwartz when Schwartz refuses to leave. Harry takes to mixing water and cat food with the herring slices in Schwartz's food dish and blowing up and popping paper bags outside the birdhouse while Schwartz is asleep. Finally, he brings home a full-grown cat, which he claims is a gift for Maurie.

Harry's frustration mounts when he sees that these strategies only succeed in making the bird's life miserable rather than making it flee. The day after Harry's mother dies in her flat in the Bronx, Maurie comes home with a zero on his arithmetic test. Harry decides to blame all his troubles on the jewbird. So after Edie takes Maurie to his violin lesson, Harry openly attacks the bird, chasing it onto the balcony with a broom, grabbing it by the legs, and whirling it around his head. Schwartz tries to fight back by catching Harry's nose in his beak but succeeds only in provoking Harry to his full capacity of violence. He swings the bird around again and then flings it, along with the bird feeder, off the balcony into the night.

Harry tells Edie and Maurie that Schwartz just flew away after a fight, but when springtime comes, Maurie finds the dead bird near the river with its eyes plucked out.

Cohn, Robert. *The Sun Also Rises.* Ernest Hemingway. 1926.

Robert Cohn doggedly pursues his compatriots as they drift aimlessly from the Paris bars to the Spanish bullfights of the early 1920s. Although generous at heart and often appealingly naive, Cohn consistently alienates his companions with showy displays of wealth and bravado. His arrogance masks a deep insecurity that soon becomes apparent as he tries vainly to secure the love of Lady BRETT ASHLEY, who loses interest in him after their brief affair.

A member of one of the richest and oldest Jewish families in New York, Cohn attended Princeton University and became middle-weight boxing champion there (although he disliked the sport) in order to counteract the prejudice he was subjected to as a Jew at an Ivy League university. Upon graduation he married and within five years was the father of three. His wife left him just before he decided to leave her. Divorced, he fell in with the literary set in California, was taken in hand by a woman named Frances, and drifted to Europe after the failure of a literary journal he had bankrolled. Settling in Paris, he wrote a bad but successful novel and at the age of thirty-four has just returned from a book tour in New York.

Cohn is a bored, frustrated man who longs for the sort of intensely romantic adventures he reads about in books. He decides he doesn't care for Paris and tries to persuade his "tennis friend" JAKE BARNES to go to South America with him. Jake rejects Cohn's suggestion, but Lady Brett Ashley takes pity on him and invites him to San Sebastian, thus effectively ending Cohn's relationship with Frances. Unfortunately, Cohn, who is quite insecure, takes his affair with Brett far more seriously than circumstances warrant.

When Jake and his friend Bill take a trip to Spain to attend the fiesta of San Fermin in Pamplona, Cohn decides to meet them in Bayonne. His smug hints about his affair with Brett annoy Jake, and neither Jake nor Bill is displeased when Cohn decides to meet Brett and her fiancé Mike Campbell rather than go fishing with them in the hills.

By the time Jake and Bill rejoin the others, Cohn's self-pity and petulant assertiveness have made him a source of annoyance to all concerned. His morose insecurity makes him incapable of appreciating the violent energy of the fiesta, and he foolishly remarks that the "bullfights might be boring." Typically, Cohn cannot handle his liquor and falls asleep before anyone else. The others begin to resent his seriousness, and there is more than a hint of anti-Semitism in their feelings.

Although it is obvious that Brett has no strong attachment to him, Cohn lacks the will to leave her or to put the affair behind him. Mike (who realizes that Brett does not love *him*, either) finally loses his temper, telling Cohn he isn't wanted and should leave. They almost fight, but Jake intercedes.

Shortly afterward, Brett seduces Pedro Romero, a brilliant young bullfighter, and her attraction to a man who is in every way his opposite proves too much for Cohn to endure. In a misdirected rage, he attacks Jake and Mike in a bar before proceeding to Brett's room where he batters Pedro but cannot overcome him. Like a storybook hero, Cohn tries to "rescue" Brett, but she refuses to go. Filled with remorse, he breaks down and cries. He attempts to apologize to Romero, who responds by hitting him in the face. Having ruined his friendship with both Jake and Brett, Cohn leaves Pamplona, presumably to return to Frances. By this time, however, none of the others are overly concerned with his fate.

Colbert, Sapphira Dodderidge. *Sapphira and the Slave Girl.* Willa Cather. 1940.

From the beginning of her life, Sapphira Dodderidge, the daughter of a privileged slave-owning family, was known for both her beauty and her temperament. She was quite proud of her mother's English birth and heritage, and when she married the staid Henry Colbert and left city life for the rural setting of their mill, she shocked her family and friends. The marriage was successful, however,

and the couple had three daughters, only one of whom, RACHEL COLBERT BLAKE, remained nearby to attend her mother and her mother's slaves. Sapphira, ill with dropsy, has become more cantankerous than usual and for some less than obvious reason has begun to turn on NANCY TILL, the young slave who had been the older woman's obvious favorite. Although the other slaves have conjectured that Sapphira is jealous of Nancy's affections for Mr. Colbert and that she suspects there may be some reciprocation, there is no proof that anything untoward has transpired. Nonetheless, Sapphira, from her wheelchair, dominates and unsettles the young girl.

Although hardly cruel, Sapphira does concoct a plan to undermine Nancy and to set her in her place once again. Accordingly, she invites her husband's nephew, the roguish Martin Colbert, for a prolonged stay. This young man is known already for his disregard of propriety, and it seems certain that Sapphira desires, although she never says so, that Martin despoil her slave girl. Because she rarely goes out, the young man's flattery and companionship come to mean a great deal to Sapphira, and the visit is lengthy. Meanwhile, Sapphira's health slowly begins to worsen, and she requires more direct attention. She is highly respected for her ability to uncomplainingly withstand the pain, but her personal slaves and her family know all too well what a blow the illness is to her pride and dignity. To keep an eye on Nancy, Sapphira has her sleep on a pallet outside her bedroom door; unfortunately for Nancy, who has been assigned to Martin's chamber as a maid, her position here also allows him access to her. Things finally escalate to the point where Nancy, with Rachel Colbert Blake's assistance, runs off on the Underground Railroad. This event, a severe indignity in Sapphira's eyes, forces her to cut off relations with Rachel, who stoically understands her mother's motivations.

Prior to Nancy's departure, Sapphira makes what will be her last annual Easter journey to visit with her sisters in Winchester. This time Nancy is brought along as Sapphira's companion in order that she may learn some good town manners. Despite what others think, this is not a reversal of affections: Sapphira had been toying with the idea of selling Nancy off to rid herself of the problem. Upon her return to the mill, Sapphira joins the rest of the household in tending to Jezebel, the oldest slave on the plantation who, at the age of at least ninety-five, has reached her final illness. When she dies, Sapphira orders an elaborate funeral and requests that Jezebel's far-flung relatives be assembled from other plantations in order that the funeral be appropriately successful. It is, and it is also the last major event that Sapphira plans.

As the winter of 1858 settles in, a severe diphtheria epidemic strikes, and one of Rachel's daughters dies from the disease. This moves Sapphira to pity and rekindles her maternal affection for her own daughter, and she invites Rachel to share the mill house, knowing, as she says to her astonished and petrified husband, that the coming winter will be her last. Soon after, now confined to bed almost the entire day each day, Sapphira enjoys the casual conversation she has with her young granddaughter, and she and Rachel manage to overcome some of their mutual reserve. Sapphira is found dead in her chair, in the parlor she had so lovingly decorated with objects inherited from her parents. Although she could have rung for assistance as the final pains struck, the family and servants all took it as a measure of her dignity that she preferred to face her end alone.

Coleman, Gaillard "Gay." *Imperial City.* Elmer Rice. 1937.

Gaillard Coleman, or "Gay," as he is called, is an openminded bourgeois and the moral center of this Depressionera novel about the confusions and cruelties of New York City in the age of Big Capital. Gay's cross to bear is the Coleman name itself. Born to Gregory Coleman, a banker, Gay is stuck in one of New York's most affluent and powerful dynasties. Fortunately for him, it is his brother Christopher who has the responsibility of directing the family fortune and sitting on several interlocking boards of directors. The other Colemans are free to dally in whatever interests them; Gay devotes himself to progressive politics, while the others indulge in their passions for alcohol and New York's "fast" life.

Gay rejects the world of privilege with all its trappings when he does not marry the woman whom family and high society have tacitly agreed he should. Nor does he remain in the insular world of affluent drawing rooms. Instead, he brushes shoulders with immigrants, artists, radicals, laborers, and literati. A Columbia University professor, he lives in a Morningside Heights bachelor apartment and teaches "social legislation."

Gay falls in love with Judy Brookes, the daughter of a former professor. Judy, who must tend to her ailing father more frequently than her courting professor, is but one of Gay's many interesting students. Another disaffected bourgeois, the son of New York's department store king, gravitates toward Gay; at one point, Gay saves the boy from suicide. Other students who have been expelled for protesting the capitalist interests encroaching upon the university's board of trustees have Gay's sympathy as well. He is forced to resign when his wheeling and dealing brother Christopher, himself a trustee, threatens to cause a scandal over Gay's affair with Judy.

Gay then becomes a progressive candidate for Manhattan borough president. When his campaign fails, he throws some of the family fortune into starting a nonprofit research bureau, one that investigates social and political issues and employs the students he has befriended. His bureau's first major interest involves the arbitration of a dispute between the Interborough Light and Power Company and the strike-ready Federated Union of Electrical Workers. As always, the Coleman family is involved. Christopher also happens to be on the board of the power company, and he and Gay are again at odds. Furthermore, in the midst of the heightening conflict, Gay's playboy brother Greg shoots and kills a famous actor whom he supposed was the former lover of his showgirl wife. Scandal erupts. Then, while the jury deciding Greg Coleman's fate deliberates and while Judy's father lays dying in a hospital bed, New York City's lights go out, snuffed by a wildcat strike. Gay and New York are left in the dark, in the tangled empire of celebrities and prostitutes, accidents and abortions, poverty, riot, blackmail, and murder.

Colville, Theodore. *Indian Summer.* William Dean Howells. 1951.

Forty-one years old, bearded, and a little bit paunchy, Theodore Colville arrives in Florence from his long-time home of Des Vaches, Indiana. He has been forced out of the editorship of a local newspaper and plans to reawaken his long-dormant interest in Italian architecture. As Florence had been the site of his life's sole love affair, he also seems hopeful of stimulating again some sort of boyish romantic ardor.

The first person Theodore meets is an old friend, LINA RIDGELY BOWEN. The widow of a senator, Lina is now residing in Florence with her prepubescent daughter Effie and a young protégée named Imogene Graham. Fifteen years before, Theodore had fallen in love with Lina's friend and traveling companion Jenny, who has since become Mrs. Milbury. He had carried the memory of her rejection of him back home to Indiana.

Charming them all, Theodore is taken up by the three women. Imogene gets the bulk of his attention, however, less because of his attachment to her than because of his flirtation with youthfulness itself. At one party he humiliates himself by attempting a complicated dance with her that he has not performed for many years.

Undaunted, he continues trying to arouse Imogene's interest, encouraging her enthusiastic chattering about literature and art because they flatter an odd kind of vanity within him. One evening when Imogene and Theodore spend too long dancing at a somewhat libertine festival, Lina abandons them to attend to Effie, who is sick in bed.

The next time Imogene sees Theodore, she intimates that he has been trifling with her affections. Outraged despite the essential justice of the charge, Theodore accuses Lina of interference. He agrees with her suggestion that he leave Florence at once, but because of a bank holiday he must stay through the weekend. This brief interval is long enough for Imogene to write a turgid letter of apology to him. Still planning to leave, Theodore spends his last day walking in the Boboli Gardens, where he runs into Imogene herself. They emerge after a lengthy conversation, apparently engaged.

For the next few weeks Theodore attends all the nocturnal frolics of the youth of Florence with Imogene and finds himself napping on the succeeding days. Clearly the lovers like to take things at different paces. Theodore is becoming more and more aware of the mistake he has made but feels he cannot disgrace Imogene by terminating their engagement.

Salvation comes in the form of a highway accident. As the family carriage is turning out of control toward a cliff, Theodore reaches first to help Lina, leaving the spurned Imogene to the care of an admiring young curate. Only Theodore is injured in the ensuing crash. Imogene's mother comes to take her daughter away, and Lina nurses the invalid. Awakening to find himself cared for by the only one who has truly loved him, Theodore proposes; he finally gains Lina's acceptance through the mediation of Effie. The happy family remains in Italy.

Compson, Benjamin "Benjy." *The Sound and the Fury; The Mansion.* William Faulkner. 1929; 1959.

Benjamin Compson, the youngest son of a once-aristocratic family in Jefferson, Mississippi, has been retarded since birth. To him, past and present are indistinguishable, and his rendering of the Compson household is frequently bewildering although emotionally perceptive. The novel's other, more conventional narratives serve to augment Benjy's jarring associations and observations, and taken along with later clues, they suggest a chronology for Benjy's life.

Mrs. Compson, a spoiled, complaining woman, originally names her youngest son Maury, after her brother, but changes the name to Benjamin when she realizes that he is retarded. Throughout Benjy's life she refers to him, even when he is present, as God's judgment on her.

An unquenchable love for his older sister, CANDACE "CADDY" (COMPSON), dominates Benjy's impaired consciousness. During childhood Caddy loves and tends to him as no other member of the family. She alone can stop his inexplicable bellowing, and she protects him from JASON (COMPSON), their malicious brother.

Benjy cannot bear to be separated from Caddy or to witness her involvement with others. When she goes to school, he waits at the gate leading to the pasture until her return. When she begins entertaining boyfriends on the swing, he howls uncontrollably until she focuses all attention on him. According to Benjy, Caddy smells like trees, but as she grows older, her use of perfume and contact with her many male admirers increasingly changes her presence for him. He becomes extremely disturbed, for example, when Caddy comes home after having slept with a man for the first time.

Over the years, supervision of Benjy is often delegated to the black household servants, especially Versh, T.P., and Luster—two sons and a grandson of the cook, DILSEY GIBSON. On the day of Caddy's wedding, for instance,

T.P. has instructions to keep Benjy far from the house. But the two of them find liquor, get drunk, and make a scene.

After Caddy has left Jefferson with her husband, Benjy continues to whimper at the pasture gate. Girls often pass on their way to school, and their presence reminds him of his missing sister. Once, when the gate has not been locked properly, he runs out and grabs one of the girls. Because the neighbors believe that Benjy wanted to rape her, Jason has his younger brother castrated so that he will no longer be a menace to the community.

By Benjy's thirty-third birthday, the Compsons have sold the pasture, and it has been converted into a golf course. Benjy spends as much time as Luster will let him at the fence, listening for the golfers to cry "caddie." Upon hearing his sister's name, he begins bellowing. The servants calm him by handing him an old slipper of Caddy's or by letting him stare into an open fire.

The only clue to Benjy's fate is mentioned later. The inhabitants of Jefferson speak of an "idiot" who was committed to an institution in 1933 and who returned and burned down the old family home.

Compson, Candace "Caddy." *The Sound and the Fury; The Mansion.* William Faulkner. 1929; 1959.

Candace "Caddy" Compson is the troubled center of her three brothers' lives. QUENTIN (COMPSON) and the retarded BENJAMIN "BENJY" (COMPSON) share an unquenchable, protective love for her, while the hatred of JASON (COMPSON) for her is uncontainable. But her brothers' visions of her, as stifling as they are, cannot wholly prevent Caddy from shaping a life of her own.

During her childhood in Jefferson, Mississippi, Caddy shows great affection for Benjy. She carries him from place to place and has him sleep in her bed when he is scared or upset. As a precocious teenager, she still appeases him whenever she can. She stops wearing perfume, for example, when she realizes that he misses her natural, tree-like smell. It also upsets Benjy terribly when she sits in the family swing with a boy. Benjy eventually becomes the first to realize that she has slept with a man. He bellows and tries to push his now "unclean" sister into the bathroom.

Caddy's older brother Quentin is horrified by her loss of virginity. A morbid young man who is alternately protective and perversely desirous of his sister, he wants Caddy to either commit suicide with him or tell their father that they have committed incest. She refuses to do either.

When Caddy becomes pregnant, she is not sure of the father. In order to avoid a scandal, she goes with her mother to French Lick, Indiana, to find a husband. She dutifully marries businessman Sydney Herbert Head, but when the girl, Quentin, is born, Sydney realizes that he is not the father. He throws Caddy and the child out of his house. Caddy flees town but later sends Quentin back to Jefferson to live in the Compson home. Mr. Compson agrees to raise Quentin on the condition that Caddy never see her. Mrs. Compson further decrees that Caddy's name should never be spoken in their house again.

After her father's death, Caddy secretly moves back to Jefferson for a time. Throughout Quentin's childhood she makes arrangements with Jason to see her daughter and to provide money for Quentin's necessities. But Jason, who blames his sister for having sabotaged his bank career and for having ruined the family name, steals the money in order to use it for his own get-rich schemes.

Ostracized by her family, Caddy seeks to make a life for herself by marrying and divorcing powerful men in Hollywood and, later, in Paris.

Compson, Jason. *The Sound and the Fury; The Mansion.* William Faulkner. 1929; 1959.

Jason Compson appears in a number of Faulkner's novels and short stories. As a child in Jefferson, Mississippi, his general ill-will prevents him from earning the trust and affection of his brothers, QUENTIN (COMPSON) and BENJAMIN "BENJY" (COMPSON), and of his sister, CANDACE "CADDY" (COMPSON). But the children's selfish mother, Caroline, regards Jason as the only one of her children who has anything in common with her.

When Jason is a teenager, Sydney Herbert Head, Caddy's husband, promises him a future position at the town bank. Unfortunately for Jason, before he can finish school, Sydney discovers that Caddy's baby has been fathered by another man. Sydney banishes Caddy and her daughter Quentin from town. For the rest of his life, while he works as a mean-spirited clerk in a country store, Jason blames his sister for this lost opportunity.

Caroline will not allow Caddy's name to be uttered in the house, but shortly before his death, Mr. Compson allows Quentin to return to Jefferson on the condition that Caddy will not be allowed to see her. After Mr. Compson, long an alcoholic, finally dies, Jason becomes the head of the household and discovers that his father did little to check the downward spiral of the family finances.

Quentin is a constant reminder to Jason of the family's dwindling honor. He routinely abuses her verbally. Contrary to his father's wishes, however, he does allow Caddy to see her daughter. On the day of his father's funeral, for example, Jason collects $100 from Caddy even though her visit amounts to watching Jason gallop by her carriage with Quentin in his arms. For the rest of Quentin's childhood Jason continues to charge his sister for time with her child. In addition, he secretly cashes the checks that Caddy periodically sends for Quentin's support.

Once he gains power of attorney over his mother's property, Jason quietly takes her investments out of the general store. He buys himself a car with this money and then invests the family's savings in the stock market, which fails. Jason even considers selling Quentin to Caddy for $1,000.

Jason's unrelenting animosity succeeds in warping his niece's life. Just as his mother once had him follow Caddy as an adolescent, Jason begins to follow the teenaged Quentin to keep her from staining the family name in the same way. When Jason sees her with a man from a traveling show, he chases the car. The two trick him easily, however, by letting the air out of his tires.

The next day Jason discovers that Quentin has broken into his room, stolen the thousands of dollars that he had been hiding in his closet, and fled. Assuming that she has left with the man from the show, he races to the show's next destination, but they are not there. In order to temper his fury, Jason tries to believe that it was not the girl who outsmarted him but the man with whom she ran away.

Jason's circumstances after this incident remain obscure. It is subsequently revealed that after his mother's death he not only sold the Compson property but finally succeeded in ridding himself of the responsibility of Benjy's upkeep by committing him to an institution.

Compson, Quentin. *The Sound and the Fury; Absalom, Absalom!* William Faulkner. 1929; 1936.

Quentin Compson, the eldest son of a declining southern family, is a narrator and character in a number of Faulkner's short stories. A moody and contemplative young man, Quentin is obsessed with the passage of time, southern history, and the honor and purity of his sister CANDACE "CADDY" (COMPSON). These obsessions drive him to an early suicide.

The Compsons live in Jefferson, Mississippi, where, by 1910, their aristocratic position has almost entirely eroded. Although Quentin is aware of the contradictions and cruelties of southern history, he also fears the pace of modern life. He begins to associate the southern ideal with the purity of Caddy. When she loses her virginity at an early age, he wants her to commit suicide with him at once. She refuses and also refuses to tell her father that they've committed incest. Quentin does tell their father this lie, but he doesn't believe him. Quentin's fascination with his sister's virginity emanates in part from his own virginity.

Quentin confronts Dalton Ames, Caddy's first lover. He demands that Ames leave town before sundown because he has destroyed his sister's honor. Ames believes all women are bitches. He hands Quentin a gun with which to shoot him, but Quentin faints.

With hopes that Quentin can redeem their flagging fortunes, the Compsons sell a pasture so that Quentin can go to Harvard. His college roommate is a young Canadian, Shreve, and the two pass the time by piecing together all the family stories that Quentin has heard from his father and from Rosa Coldfield, a spinster who talked about THOMAS SUTPEN and his family. At Rosa's request, Quentin once drove to the old Sutpen house in an attempt to uncover the tragic secrets of Sutpen's children, Henry and

JUDITH (SUTPEN), and their connection to Judith's fiancé and stepbrother CHARLES BON. On June 2, 1910, Quentin skips chapel and his classes. He carefully shatters the crystal of his watch and twists the hands off its face. He puts on his best suit and then wanders around Cambridge where he purchases two six-pound weights. He takes a trolley to an outlying town, and there he notices a little Italian girl following him. He walks through the strange town trying to find her family. The girl's brother appears and accuses him of kidnapping her. A sheriff arrests Quentin, but a few Harvard friends happen by and win his release for a small fine. When one of the men begins to boast of his sexual exploits, Quentin becomes enraged, and they have a fistfight. During the fight, Quentin imagines the revenge he has never taken on Dalton Ames.

Quentin returns to his dormitory. His day-long contemplation of time, coupled with the purchase of the weights, clearly suggest that he plans to eradicate his consciousness of the Compson failures by committing suicide.

Concepción, María. "María Concepción." Katherine Anne Porter. 1930.

María Concepción, a Mexican-Indian woman, is the eighteen-year-old bride of Juan Villegas. Villegas works for an American architect named Givens on a dig near their village. María is expecting her first child and is very contented with her life, but when she discovers Juan betraying her with the young beekeeper María Rosa, her life changes.

The sight of her husband in the embrace of another woman has a chilling effect on María. She merely goes about her work, raising and selling fowl to the men on the dig, with a cool automation. Juan and María Rosa go off to fight together in a war, and when María Concepción's newborn baby dies shortly afterward, she does not weep. All the while, hatred for María Rosa is welling up in her.

Juan and María Rosa are gone for a year, during which time María Concepción continues to work hard and attends church with a renewed passion. She becomes gaunt and withdrawn, and rarely talks to her fellow villagers. Only when Juan and a now very pregnant María Rosa return to the village does María Concepción seem to come to life.

Juan must be bailed out of jail by his employer because he has deserted the army. Givens warns him that María Concepción will not take kindly to his recent behavior, but Juan brushes him off, insisting he can control his wife. However, when he returns to their home and beats her to show his superiority, María Concepción resists fiercely. She then leaves home, intending to take her fowls to the market. Suddenly erupting with sadness and anger, she breaks down along the way.

When she returns home sometime later, she is holding a large, bloodied knife. Juan first thinks the weapon is intended for him, but he soon understands what has happened. He promises to protect María Concepción from the authorities. It is not long before the gendarmes arrive to question them, and they take Juan and María to the home of María Rosa. Juan lies to create an alibi for his wife, and María answers the gendarmes as she has been instructed by her husband. The villagers, who have always had sympathy for María Concepción, now support her story, and she and Juan are released. Before she leaves the dead woman's house, María Concepción picks up a wriggling bundle left in a corner. She takes the newborn son of Juan and María Rosa home with her, and as she prepares to feed the child, a feeling of peace and utter happiness comes over her.

Congreve, Katharine. *The Catherine Wheel.* Jean Stafford. 1951.

Katharine Congreve is the aristocratic mistress of Congreve House, an idyllic summer home. For many years she has provided the Shipley children with an escape from their dreary winters in Boston. While their parents, John and Maeve, are taking their yearly trip abroad, Harriet, Honor, and ANDREW SHIPLEY join Cousin Katharine in the port town of Hawthorne. In Katharine's presence it becomes an enchanted world, a beatific landscape enlivened by parties and genteel, comical conversation with the neighbors.

Congreve House was left to Katharine by her father, a gentleman scholar whom she thinks of admiringly as "the Humanist." Her childhood and adolescence were difficult despite the privileges of wealth and education. Her parents' marriage was troubled, and Katharine chose to devote herself almost exclusively to her father. When Katharine's orphaned cousin Maeve Maxwell arrived, however, Mr. Congreve obviously favored her. Although they grew up as sisters, attending school together and traveling through Europe, Katharine hid a deep resentment of Maeve.

The rivalry increased in adolescence since the girls had a tendency to be attracted to the same boys. Katharine was essentially unmoved by anyone until at seventeen she met John Shipley, a young architect. He brought her flowers devotedly, in exchange for her readings from classical literature. One day while kneeling before the statue of Minerva in the garden at Congreve House, Katharine vowed to marry him. John did not meet Maeve until the evening of her birthday party when everything seemed to emphasize her already astonishing beauty. The party culminated in a fireworks display, and Katharine looked over at Maeve and John by the light of rockets and pinwheels, to see them holding hands. As the last Catherine wheel faded, she realized that John would never choose her.

John and Maeve cheerfully regarded Katharine as their matchmaker, assuming that the three would form a lifelong alliance. Still aching with jealousy, Katharine managed to play this game, even accompanying the Shipleys on their honeymoon. To make matters worse, Mr. Congreve died shortly before the marriage, leaving Katharine alone with her secret.

After nearly twenty years of marriage, John Shipley has begun to have doubts. He begs Katharine to run away with him to a distant island, and in a moment of weakness she agrees. Katharine struggles with the terrible implications of her assent but finally comes to the conclusion that she already has what she wanted: John desires her more than Maeve. Secure in this knowledge, she prefers to remain in her peaceful, invulnerable position at Congreve House. After writing John a letter expressing her unwillingness to leave, Katharine orders a tombstone for herself. The image depicting her suggests a martyr, but her "halo" is a Catherine wheel.

On the last day of the summer, Katharine gives an extravagant party that is to end with a fireworks display. She tells several of her guests that she has never been happier in her life. An impressive show of fireworks is set off before a large crowd, but the last one, a Catherine wheel, will not light. Charles Smithwick, who has been lighting them, sets his hair on fire trying to light the Catherine wheel. Katharine runs toward him in a panic, and her dress catches fire, seriously burning her. On her deathbed Katharine requests that Andrew Shipley, her favorite of the children, burn the diary that documents her ill-fated romance with his father.

Connie. "Where Are You Going, Where Have You Been?" Joyce Carol Oates. 1966.

At fifteen years of age the egotistical and attractive Connie is going through a phase of boy-craziness and obsession with her physical appearance. Telling her parents that she is going to the movies at a shopping mall near her home, Connie surreptitiously joins her best friend Nancy Pettinger on flirtatious sprees at a drive-in restaurant that is a favorite hangout of older teenagers. During the course of one evening at the restaurant, a dark-haired young man with scraggly, unkempt hair catches her eye, wags his finger at her, and claims that he is going to "get" her. Connie thinks nothing of this passing incident that will ultimately put both her virginity and her life in danger.

One Sunday afternoon Connie displays her haughty lack of interest in her relationship with her family, which she considers provincial, by refusing to accompany them to a barbecue at her aunt's house. Having washed her beautiful long hair, she takes advantage of the family's absence by languishing in the sun, enjoying the physical sensation of her slowly drying hair, and daydreaming about the young man she had flirted with at the drive-in the previous evening. When the sun's heat becomes too intense, Connie goes into the house where she throws herself down on her bed and listens to her favorite radio

station. The fast-paced tunes, with screaming vocals and a jazzy commentary from the disk jockey, Bobby King, stir Connie's imagination, and she loses herself in languid and sensual fantasies that center around the rise and fall of her bosom as she breathes in the warm summer air.

Connie's reveries are interrupted when she suddenly hears a car approaching the house on her family's driveway. Rushing to a window, she spots an unfamiliar convertible that is bizarrely painted in a bright gold hue with weird messages such as DONE BY A CRAZY WOMAN DRIVER, a quip that covers a smashed fender. Characteristically, Connie's first reaction is to speculate whether she is physically presentable and alluring. Two males are seated in the car, and Connie vaguely recognizes the driver as the shaggy black-haired man who had wagged his finger at her and pronounced his intention to "get" her. The driver of the jalopy introduces the silent passenger in the car as Ellie Oscar. His name is Arnold Friend, and his intention is to befriend Connie immediately, he claims, and he suggests that they begin their relationship with a ride in his jaunty car. Connie is intrigued with her bold visitor; she approves of his hard, muscular body and appreciates the way he is dressed, in tight jeans stuffed into scuffed-up boots. But her initial interest is replaced by alarm when she realizes that Arnold Friend is not as young as he first appeared to be. Her fear multiplies as Arnold begins to recount a litany of vital statistics concerning herself, her family, and her friends—knowledge that he could only have attained by carefully researching her background. As his entreaties that she join him for a jaunt in the car become more aggressive, his initially friendly and controlled facade breaks down. He begins to stagger drunkenly and to allude to the sexual favors he intends to demand from Connie when she becomes his lover. She starts to panic and threatens to call the police, but Arnold insists that if she does not comply with his requests, he will see to it that her family suffers the consequences. Locked in a state of utter terror, Connie gets into the car, shedding her fear and volition, and entering into a trance-like state of overwhelming emptiness.

Conroy, Frank. *Stop-Time.* Frank Conroy. 1967.

Frank Conroy is a desperately lonely youth whose life is continually uprooted by his unsteady family situation. Frank's father lives in and out of rest homes for continual nervous breakdowns and dies of cancer when Frank is twelve. After his death, Frank's Danish mother, Dagmar, takes up with a man named Jean, a ne'er-do-well, fallen New Orleans aristocrat. Frank spends three years at a boarding school in Pennsylvania and then moves with his sister Alison, Dagmar, and Jean to Florida where Jean plans for them to live in deserted developments. This is the first of many moves for Frank, who tries repeatedly to escape from the anger, boredom, and disapproval that plague his childhood and adolescence.

In Florida, Frank befriends Tobey, a country boy, and has one last good year before getting into trouble becomes his way of life. When the family fails to find work in Florida, they return to the Northeast. Jean and Dagmar get jobs as weekend wardens at a Connecticut state institution, and Frank is forced to sleep alone in the cabin and spend endless hours doing nothing. He finds solace in the institution's library and begins to read voraciously. Soon the family moves back to Florida, where Frank, who now has a northern accent and a large vocabulary, is an oddity in school. When two Chinese expert yo-yoers come to town from California, Frank finds his calling. He delves into the magical world of the yo-yo and wins the Grand Prize Black Beauty Diamond Yo-Yo at the town championships.

Life in Florida ends again, however, and Frank begins an unsuccessful career at Stuyvesant High School in Manhattan. He pitches pennies on the streets before school, is always late, and although he is intelligent, he fails most of his classes because he doesn't do the work. During the summer he sells fruit on the street with Jean and learns to pay off policemen to keep his selling space.

Dagmar gives birth to Frank's half-sister Jessica and takes the baby to Denmark for a while. During their absence, Jean picks up a suicidal crazy woman, Nell Smith, who moves into the apartment. Fed up with Nell, Jean, and his own life, Frank runs away, determined to return to Florida. He gets tired by the time he reaches Wilmington, Delaware, and finally returns home because of his unconditional love for Jessica.

Back in New York, Frank gets a job as a lab assistant in an electroplating company. As usual, he stirs up noise and trouble, always goofing off and playing games with Bunsen burners, tubes, and water propellants. When he accidentally squirts his boss in the chest, Frank gets fired; the boss eventually rehires him after he makes an "about-face" in his behavior by coming to work when he isn't being paid and by voluntarily organizing the old packing room. Around this time he loses his virginity with a Belgian girl he meets in the dark at a movie theater.

Frank is seventeen when his mother sends him to an international high school in Elsinore, Denmark. He falls for a beautiful Swedish girl from a conservative small town, but when she falls in love with him, he deserts her. He improves as a student, and during his senior year he is accepted to Haverford College. Frank begins college with the hope of erasing his past and starting with a clean slate.

In England ten years later, Frank writes the epilogue to these memoirs. His life has not improved; his loneliness has not left him. Driving about ninety miles per hour, he tries to kill himself by skidding into a fountain. He survives the crash, however, and can only laugh at the irony of his luck.

Constant, Malachi. *The Sirens of Titan.* Kurt Vonnegut, Jr. 1959.

Malachi Constant is the world's richest man in this existential science fiction novel. He is the chairman of the board of Magnum Opus, an enormous conglomerate founded by his father through a series of accidents. The dumb luck that made his father a billionaire has continued for Constant; for some reason his business affairs prosper despite his total indifference to his own financial matters.

One day Constant travels from his Beverly Hills home to the Newport, Rhode Island, mansion of WINSTON NILES RUMFOORD, a world-famous entrepreneur who materializes on Earth only occasionally. Rumfoord's wife BEATRICE (RUMFOORD) summoned Constant at the request of her husband and against her own wishes. Rumfoord himself, after having traveled through a phenomenon known as a "chrono-synclastic infundibula" in his spaceship, has acquired the ability to see the future. Rumfoord has summoned Constant to inform him of his important destiny.

Rumfoord tells Constant that he will travel to Mars with his wife Beatrice, who will be the mother of Constant's child, Chrono. He will then voyage to Mercury, back to Earth, and ultimately end up on Titan, a moon of Saturn. Disturbed, Constant goes back to Hollywood and takes steps to see that Rumfoord's prophecy is not carried out. He sends obscene letters to Beatrice and sells all his stock in a company of his that owned a private spaceship. He throws a fifty-seven-day party in an attempt to make himself physically unfit for a mission to Mars.

Eventually, however, Constant's uncanny business luck changes, and he is left penniless. With nothing left for him on Earth, he is recruited by the Army of Mars as a lieutenant-colonel. On the ride up to Mars, he is forbidden to enter a secret room that contains, he is told, the most beautiful woman in the universe. Constant sneaks in one night and rapes the woman, only to find the next morning that it was Beatrice Rumfoord.

On Mars, Constant has most of his memory removed and has a small antenna inserted in the back of his neck by which pain is inflicted whenever he fails to behave properly. Under the antenna's control, Constant executes a man who turns out to be his best friend Stony. He does not completely forget images of his past and is driven by the vague knowledge that somewhere on Mars he has a wife and a son. After eight years he is able to desert the army and make his way to the only city on Mars, Phoebe, where he tracks down Chrono. After Chrono behaves utterly indifferently toward him, he finds Beatrice, who like himself is able to remember very little of their previous life.

Constant is captured by Rumfoord, the mastermind behind the Army of Mars, and sent to Mercury while the army embarks on an ill-fated invasion of Earth. When the invasion fails completely, Rumfoord creates a new religion called God the Utterly Indifferent, which soon has a following of over three billion people.

When Constant is brought back to Earth, he is hated by Rumfoord's Church of God the Utterly Indifferent. Rumfoord exiles Constant, Beatrice, and Chrono to Titan. On Titan, Constant learns from Rumfoord, who appears out of the chrono-synclastic infundibulum, how the Trafalmadorians have manipulated human history. After Rumfoord disappears, Constant and Beatrice live together on Titan until they die within twenty-four hours of each other, at the age of seventy-four. Constant had realized a year before Beatrice's death that the purpose of life is to love anyone who is available to be loved. Upon her death, while wandering grief-stricken across Titan, Constant meets Salo, who returns him to Earth where he dies of exposure. Just before his death he envisions his friend Stony appearing in a golden spaceship to take him to paradise with Beatrice.

Continental Op, The. *The Continental Op*. Dashiell Hammett. 1923.

The Continental Op, a detective, narrates seven tales of intrigue in an unsentimental, police-blotter style punctuated by wry epigrams about the human capacity for vice. After fifteen years with the Continental Detective Agency, he expects deception from everyone, including clients.

The Op mentions that he is thirty-five, a World War I veteran, balding, and slightly fat, but he states little else about himself. He keeps his name secret and never encounters family, friends, or lovers in the course of a typical day. His character is implied by the way he approaches criminal cases.

The Op works according to a pattern. He is generally called in on a case, shown some clues, and given a fabricated version of the events leading to a crime. In one case, for example, a handsome young poet hires the Op to find his beautiful girlfriend, who has cashed a large check from the poet's family account and then disappeared. The Op doubts the poet immediately, and through contacts in the San Francisco underworld, coupled with steady surveillance, he discovers that the poet and the girlfriend have been working together to extort money from the poet's wealthier relatives.

Like other Hammett heroes, the Op prides himself on a ruthless determination to get the job done, although it remains unclear exactly what motivates him to continue in this dangerous line of work. He deals frequently with those led astray by alcohol and narcotics, but he himself is no crusader for temperance (he often begins the day's work with a hangover). Nor does he have an unusually high respect for the law or the revelation of truth. In one case, for instance, he lets two armed robbers and an accomplice escape justice because their arrest might reveal an affair that the client's wife once had.

Many of the Op's cases involve beautiful but deadly women. According to the narrator, such women have the power to make cowardly men into reckless thugs and to turn the most upstanding ones away from respectable society. Occasionally the Op suggests that he's experienced bad luck with women. Once, observing the way a henchman has blindly followed some harlot's wishes, he notes: "In his place, I might have believed her myself—all of us have fallen for that sort of thing at one time or another." This is as close as he comes to admitting that romance has ever entered his life; it may also be a pledge that it will never besmirch it again.

The Op's tone is one of deep cynicism formed by immersion in a relentlessly corrupt world. His guiding code, his underlying motivation, is as much a mystery at the end of a case as it is at the beginning. The Op seems intent on suggesting that he doesn't have to explain his behavior to anyone. On the other hand, he is the quintessential company man, available at any hour to investigate a break in his current case.

Converse, John. *Dog Soldiers*. Robert Stone. 1987.

John Converse is a journalist operating out of Saigon during the Vietnam War in the early 1970s who decides to involve himself in heroin trafficking for excitement. After purchasing three kilograms of the drug from a young, well-connected hustler named Charmian, Converse convinces an old acquaintance in the Merchant Marines, RAY HICKS, to move the dope back to the States for him. Hicks agrees to deliver the drug package to John's wife Marge, and everything appears to be running smoothly from John's perspective.

Shortly after Hicks has allegedly delivered the heroin, Converse returns home to Berkeley, California, and discovers that his plan has gone dreadfully amiss. Not only are Marge and Ray nowhere to be found, but John's father-in-law, Elmer Bender, informs him that he is being sought by a federal agent named Antheil. The agent's functionaries, the psychotic Danskin and Smitty, ultimately apprehend Converse and, after torturing him, set out with their captive to find Marge, Hicks, and the heroin.

Antheil tracks Marge and Hicks to the mountains of New Mexico, and Danskin, Smitty, and Converse drive off in pursuit. After several terrifying days, the trio catches up with Antheil, who informs his men they have no more than one day to retrieve the drugs before Antheil will be forced to request local police involvement.

After a frustrating hike up to the mountain retreat where Marge and Hicks have taken refuge, Danskin, Smitty, and Converse eventually reach a ledge from which they can communicate with Hicks. Converse is persuaded to coerce his wife into turning over the heroin, and Marge, fed up and clearly coming unglued, begins her trek down the mountainside with the drugs. When the entire group reaches Antheil and his crooked Mexican friend Angel at the base of the mountain, they find that Hicks has substituted sand for the heroin. Just as retribution is about to be exacted on the Converses, John manages to save Marge's life, and the pair retreat to the safety of Hicks's fortifications. Hicks, having already killed Danskin and Smitty, has himself been wounded in the arm. Nonetheless, he insists on continuing to pin down Antheil and Angel while John and Marge make their getaway. They agree that in the morning Hicks will sneak away and meet the Converses on the railroad tracks in the New Mexican desert. John and Marge manage to escape just ahead of Antheil and Angel after discovering Hicks's dead body on the side of the tracks.

Conway, Hugh. *Lost Horizon.* James Hilton. 1933.

Hugh Conway is an extremely talented and successful man in the British foreign service who searches for a sane way to live his life during World War I and its aftermath. Handsome, athletic, and intelligent, Conway excels in virtually all of his endeavors and is consequently the object of much hero worship. By the age of thirty-seven he has traveled much of the Eastern world, learned many languages, and lived for several years in China. Although his job with the British Consular Service appears glamorous and exciting, he suffers from malaise and has never formed satisfying emotional attachments with any person or place.

In May 1931 when Conway and three companions are being evacuated from Baskul, they are kidnapped by an unknown airline pilot and taken to the mountains of Tibet. The plane crash-lands on the side of the mountain, and the pilot is mortally wounded in the disaster. The four surviving passengers are greeted by a strange entourage that emerges from a passage in the mountain and escorts them to the beautiful hidden valley of Shangri-la. The policy at the monastery of Shangri-la, where the four travelers are housed, is to treat guests with as much courtesy as possible without revealing too much information about what their futures might entail. For Conway, this is a blessed relief from his past, which demanded constant plans and projections, allowing for little enjoyment of the present moment. For the first time in his life he finds himself at peace in a setting that allows for reflection, contemplation, and appreciation of the classics that have somehow made their way to the valley's libraries.

Conway becomes friends with Chang, the monk who originally greeted the four travelers, and with Father Perrault, the High Lama, who explains to him the mysterious slowing of the age process that takes place within the valley. He also falls in love with a beautiful Manchurian princess, Lo-Tsen, a pupil at the monastery who looks eighteen but, according to Chang, is sixty-five. In addition

he maintains a strong regard for Charles Mallinson, one of his fellow survivors of the plane crash. While Mallinson worships Conway, he is frustrated by his companion's contentment and wishes to escape Shangri-la with his help.

Conway and the High Lama meet frequently and enjoy an inspiring mutual respect. At the end of their last meeting, Perrault tells Conway that he has awaited his arrival for a long time. Having designated the newcomer as his successor, the Lama abruptly dies. Conway is profoundly honored by his appointment and feels uncannily competent as the new leader of the kingdom of Shangri-la. Shortly after assuming the role of High Lama, he meets Mallinson, who informs him that he and Lo-Tsen intend to escape and want him to join them. Conway desperately tries to convince them to abandon their plans to flee, but finding that his entreaties are ineffectual, he decides in a passionate moment to accompany the only two people in his life he has been able to love. The result of the exodus is the tragic death of both Mallinson and Lo-Tsen. Conway himself falls victim to a serious illness and suffers from amnesia. Convalescing in a hospital in China, he is ultimately able to remember what happened and returns to Tibet to try to find the hidden valley of Shangri-la. The results of his quest are unknown.

Cooke, Ebenezer "Eben." *The Sot-Weed Factor.* John Barth. 1960.

Ebenezer "Eben" Cooke and his twin sister Anna were born at Malden, the family tobacco plantation in Maryland. But shortly after their mother's death, they moved to England. For many years they studied under a tutor known then as Burlingame, a brilliant and charismatic young man with a mysterious past. When their father, Andrew, began to suspect that Burlingame was falling in love with Anna, he banished the teacher from their home.

As the novel opens, Burlingame, a great master of disguise, renews contact with the twins after a long absence. Anna finally tells Eben that she has been in love with the tutor for a long time. Given their father's attitude, this admission troubles Eben, but Burlingame himself repeatedly asserts an idea that Eben finds far more disturbing: He thinks that Anna is subconsciously in love with Eben. At first Eben dismisses this illicit notion. He thinks it reveals less about Anna than it does about their former tutor, whom Eben has long suspected of unconventional erotic interests.

Eben remains extraordinarily indecisive about his life until he falls in love with Joan Toast, a prostitute who frequents his neighborhood tavern. One night, instead of undressing her, he proclaims his eternal love; she thinks he is joking at her expense and demands payment for her wasted time. Word of the ensuing quarrel reaches Andrew, who commands Eben to depart for Malden. Despite his embarrassment, Eben at last discovers his vocation: He will translate his unrequited love into great poetry. Before the trip to America, he meets with a man he believes to be Lord Baltimore, the titular leader of Maryland, and outlines his epic poem (to be called the "Marylandiad") extolling the brave people who had settled this part of the New World. Eben becomes the first poet laureate of Maryland.

Eben has great difficulty even reaching America. Many dangerous people think that the laureate is a front man for Lord Baltimore, a Catholic suspected of masterminding a Papist plot to convert the largely Protestant colonies. For safety's sake, the poet switches identities with his valet during the voyage across the sea. This role change exposes Eben to a multitude of indignities: He barely escapes countless sexual propositions; he cannot conspicuously write verse; and he must play servant to the valet, who eventually loses the Malden estate through reckless shipboard gambling. When he isn't walking the plank or salvaging his virginity, Eben imagines his vindication in the Maryland courts, which he assumes have been modeled on the impeccable standards of English law.

Eben wants to write an epic in the spirit of Virgil, but once in Maryland, he finds little that is heroic. Instead of toiling industriously to build a new land, the white people seem most interested in fast money and brothels, and the Native Americans, under the spell of opium, are plotting to rid the area of all English-speaking people. Burlingame appears now and then to add to the confusion. First he admits that he is bisexual and has long been in love with the twins. Then the former tutor discovers that he is actually the long-lost son of a Native American chief. After preventing what would have been a bloody rebellion, Burlingame adopts the Native American life-style and disappears from Eben's life. Meanwhile, Anna, distraught over Eben's and Burlingame's absences, has traveled to America and become a squaw to another Native American man who turns out to be Burlingame's half-brother.

The novel concludes with a hearing at Malden under the supervision of an English official. Based on evidence brought forth by Anna, Andrew, and the syphilitic Joan Toast, Eben regains the estate. Eben marries Joan, and although she dies soon after the birth of their child, Eben lives a long life and gains a measure of fame for his satiric poem about Maryland, which he renames the "Sot-Weed Factor."

Cooper, Dolly Hawkins. *Daughter of the Hills.* Myra Page. 1950.

The strong-willed Dolly Hawkins Cooper struggles against almost overwhelming adversities so that her children will be able to escape the confines of the small prejudicial Tennessee mining town in which they live. Set at the turn of the century, the novel begins when Dolly Hawkins meets John Cooper, a stranger from Kentucky. From the time she was a child, Dolly had been warned by her mother never to put her trust in any man, and she resists falling in love with the admiring stranger. But while she is determined not to give in to her love for John, he is just as determined to win her. After a battle of wills, she surrenders, and they marry.

Dolly is a resolute, self-sufficient woman who has learned much from life at the mines. Her younger brother Clyde and her uncle Harry are both miners, as was her father and one of her older brothers who was killed in a mine collapse. As a child, Dolly had fearlessly tried to hitch rides in the mine cars before she learned of the dangers of the shafts. When she was older, she waited anxiously with her mother to hear the mine whistle, which signified that their men would come home unhurt.

Dolly has two sons and a daughter. The couple prefers to sacrifice so that their sons can stay in school and never go into the mine. When John is injured in a mine collapse, Dolly takes in washing so that they will at least be able to eat, but she continues forbidding her older son to help out by going into the mine.

After a long depression, John finally finds the will to live and begins to use a new wooden leg. But he works too hard felling trees with Dolly, and the strain on his heart proves fatal. The novel ends after John's death, as Dolly's son helps his mother to understand that although John is dead, there is a future for her. As the story closes, Dolly's son promises that although he must now go and work in the mines, he will eventually return to his education.

Cooper, Minnie. "Dry September." William Faulkner. 1931.

Miss Minnie Cooper is an aging white woman who claims that she had been attacked by a black man. The incident is the subject of hot debate at a white barbershop in Jefferson, Mississippi, where the men indignantly discuss the matter. For the most part, the allegation is treated with a fierce certainty: Most of the men are already convinced that Will Mayes was the culprit. All agree except for one barber who insists that such a deed would be totally out of character for Will. Without specific details, however, the men decide to act on their opinion and leave hastily in search of Will. The dissenting barber joins them in the hopes of warning the black man.

Meanwhile, Minnie continues her normal round of daily activities. She appears in mid-morning, sits on the porch of her home, and rocks back and forth until the heat of the day becomes intolerable. She then retreats inside where she naps for a while. Eventually she dons one of her regular new summer dresses and travels downtown to window-shop or attend a film. When she was younger, Minnie was attractive and fairly popular, and had garnered the attention of several men. Her childhood female companions matured, married, and bore children who called her "Aunty." This pleased Minnie for a time, but she eventually asked that these children, once they matured, address her as "Cousin." The years continued to pass Minnie by, and at the time of the story, when Minnie has almost reached forty, she has been without male companionship for many years. The last man she was seen with was a bank clerk who usually smelled of whiskey and who contributed to the decline of her reputation. He, too, moved out of town, and Minnie was left alone with her elderly mother, who no longer leaves her room, and an elderly aunt, who runs the household.

After alleging that she had been attacked and despite the town's awareness that her unmarried state may have led to an overactive imagination, Minnie acts as if it is an ordinary day. She goes into town to see a movie in the company of friends who long to hear the details of the attack as soon as she has had time to recover from the shock. Once at the theater, she feels unusually strange, and as the movie begins, she has trouble suppressing a laugh. Before long the laughter develops into hysteria, and she is escorted out of the theater into a cab and brought home. She calms down somewhat but soon is laughing hysterically once more. This prompts her attendants to wonder lasciviously if her story is true.

But it is too late for Will Mayes. When Minnie arrives downtown, it is noted that there are no blacks visible anywhere. This is because the black community already knows that Will has been seized, taken out of town in handcuffs, and lynched. The barber who attempted to help him was unable to do so; overcome with nausea and disgust, he leaped from the car and walked back to town. The lynchers passed him on their way home from the murder but did not acknowledge a man they considered a traitor to his race. The story ends as one of the lynchers tiredly wipes the sweat off his brow and gazes out into the hot dark night. He is unconcerned, as he had been all along, with Miss Minnie Cooper's welfare or with the veracity of her claim.

Copeland, Brownfield. *The Third Life of Grange Copeland.* Alice Walker. 1970.

Brownfield Copeland, the son of GRANGE (COPELAND), was left alone early in childhood to fend for himself while his father worked in the cotton fields and his mother dug worms to sell as fish bait to gentlemen in town. At the age of four Brownfield was responsible for feeding the pigs and collecting firewood near his decaying gray home in Green County, Georgia. He was eventually sent to the fields to pick cotton with other children. His most vivid memories are those of his father and the strange and fearful way in which he reacted to the landowner, Mr. Shipley.

Brownfield fears his father but adores the gentle, kind manner of his mother. As the love in their marriage is gradually transformed by violence, drunkenness, and poverty, his mother begins to change. When she gives birth to a child who is not her husband's, Brownfield resents his half-brother. He is often left in charge of him, and the

child disturbs his pleasant daydreams. Angry and hurt, Brownfield blames his father for the change in his mother.

After his mother's suicide, Brownfield, feeling more alone than ever, leaves his parents' home and refuses Mr. Shipley's offer to remain and work for him. His aim is to head north and make a new life for himself. After weeks of wandering, he stumbles upon Josie's Dew Drop Inn. He begins work there and soon becomes Josie's lover. Josie takes good care of him, but two years later he remains annoyed that he still feels he has no life to call his own.

At the Dew Drop Inn, Brownfield meets MEM (COPELAND), a sweet and proper girl who reminds him of his mother. She teaches him to read the alphabet and some simple phrases, and they fall in love. They marry and move to a plantation where they plan to stay just long enough to save enough money to go to the North.

By the time their eldest daughter Daphne is five years old and is sent to the fields to work, their dreams of living a free and independent life are shattered. Their increasing indebtedness depresses Brownfield, who turns, as his father had, to violence and drunkenness. The fact that he cannot provide for his wife and family makes him resent their existence. He blames his actions on the whites that have oppressed him, feeling that their acts of oppression somehow make him less responsible for his own.

Brownfield's father, Grange, returns from the North a new man. Brownfield resents Grange's charitable visits to his family. Mem, desperate and alone with Brownfield one morning, points a shotgun at her husband's head and demands that he change his ways. For three years the Copelands live in a comfortable apartment in town where Brownfield works in a frozen pie factory. He is angry because he actually enjoys the work. Brownfield has sworn to avenge himself on Mem. Ill, fatigued, and pregnant again, Mem is soon unable to pay their bills. They lose the apartment and move to an old barn.

On Christmas Eve of that year, Brownfield, in a drunken stupor, shoots and kills his wife on the steps of their home as she is returning from work. Brownfield's explanation for murdering his wife is that she had become too skinny; she was a constant reminder of his failure to provide for his family. Mem's greatest weakness, Brownfield thinks, was her ability to forgive.

While in prison Brownfield reflects angrily on his daughter Ruth, now living with Grange, the same man who had abandoned him as a child. He swears to take her from him one day. While on parole Brownfield accosts Grange, who chastises him for blaming all the troubles in his life on the whites who have treated him badly. He cries to his son, "We are guilty . . . and need to admit it." Brownfield refuses.

Brownfield's obsession is to take Ruth from her grandfather, not because he loves her but because he doesn't want his father to have her. He is awarded custody by a crooked judge, but Brownfield's bitter life ends when

Grange appears, gun in hand, in front of the court. He kills his son there and then—a sacrifice that will cost him his own life.

Copeland, Grange. *The Third Life of Grange Copeland.* Alice Walker. 1970.

Grange Copeland is a black tenant farmer in the South in the 1920s. In his struggle to build a sense of self-worth, Grange learns to accept responsibility for the choices he has made in his life.

At the novel's beginning, the thirty-five-year-old Grange is a restless and bitter man. The unremitting poverty of the Copeland family has left him hopeless and distressed. He is unable to provide for his wife and children. To escape from this tragic reality, Grange turns to drink and domestic violence. He has an affair with Josie, owner of the Dew Drop Inn, his Saturday evening haunt. His wife Margaret, once a humble, kind, and dedicated woman, is soon broken and vengeful. Three weeks after Grange abandons his family for what he assumes will be a life of freedom in the North, Margaret poisons herself, leaving their son BROWNFIELD, now a young man, alone in the world.

In New York City, Grange must beg and steal in order to survive. Suffering from hunger, he hides in the trees in Central Park. Initially touched by the warmth of the reunion that he witnesses between a pregnant white woman and her lover, Grange soon notices the situation growing tense and serious. The man offers the woman a great deal of money, which she allows to fall indifferently to the ground. After the woman leaves, Grange greedily gathers the dollars. Feeling pity for the woman, he decides to offer her half the money. As he approaches her, she becomes proud and haughty, obviously disgusted at the thought of speaking with such an unkempt, foul-smelling man as Grange. They argue, and the woman, attempting to distance herself from Grange, falls into the icy pond. Grange tries to help her, but she lets go of his hand, murmuring, "Nigger." Having learned that he is not even worthy enough to save the life of a white person, Grange becomes crazed with hatred for all whites. He decides to return to the South where with some luck he will be able to hide from them forever.

Two weeks after he arrives in Georgia, Grange marries Josie. He knows that he will be able to persuade her to sell her business and buy a farm outside of town. Sadly, Grange learns that his son Brownfield, once a tenant farmer, has also fallen victim to the same cycle of poverty, violence, and drunkenness that has been his own lot. Feeling pity for his son's family, Grange visits them often and brings them food and clothing. One Christmas Eve, Brownfield, in a drunken stupor, brutally murders his wife. Grange, heartbroken and feeling guilty, refuses to allow the youngest of Brownfield's daughters, Ruth, to be taken away to the North with her older sisters. He raises Ruth in a manner he wishes he had raised his own son.

Grange's mission is to prepare Ruth for a life of hardship and suffering. Ruth tends to see the good in people, but Grange attempts to convince her of the evils of the white population. Not surprisingly, he remains skeptical of those participating in the growing Civil Rights movement. When Brownfield is released from prison, the judge rules that Ruth is to be returned to him. This idea is so painful to Grange that he shoots his son to death in the courtroom. He and Ruth escape to their farm, where Grange had promised Ruth she would always be safe. While Ruth is lying quietly in the playhouse Grange had built for her, the police search the woods near their home. Sitting crouched in prayer, Grange is found and killed.

Copeland, Mem. *The Third Life of Grange Copeland.* Alice Walker. 1970.

Mem is a quiet, plump young woman at the novel's opening. Although she lives in a room over Josie's bar, she is able to avoid the noise and havoc by taking leisurely walks in the woods near Josie's home. Mem's mother is long dead; her father, a northern preacher, sends her money to attend a teacher's college in Atlanta. She is an educated, well-spoken girl whose proper gait causes some, including BROWNFIELD COPELAND, to criticize her for thinking herself above others.

As time passes, Brownfield grows to care deeply for Mem; she is for him a symbol of purity and grace. Mem expresses her fondness for the illiterate Brownfield by teaching him the alphabet and simple phrases. One evening they declare their love for each other in a passionate embrace. Brownfield promises to take care of Mem forever, and she believes him. They marry and move to a plantation where they plan to work for two years until they can save enough money to go to the North.

Their early years of marriage are happy, passionate ones in which they seek refuge in each other from the burdens of daily life. It is not until their oldest daughter Daphne is five and sent to the fields to spray the cotton that they realize their dreams of a free and independent life are shattered. Because her intelligence hurts his pride, Brownfield forces Mem to leave her job as a teacher, and she takes a position as a domestic. Brownfield begins to criticize Mem's refined speech; the criticism turns to regular beatings and unjust accusations of infidelity. Mem changes, as Brownfield's own mother had, into a haggard, serious woman, sad and thin and toothless.

Despite these changes, Mem remains hardworking and determined. She saves her pennies in an attempt to be able someday to provide her children with a better life. Suffering great pain, Mem gives birth to Ruth, the third of her surviving children, on a Saturday evening while Brownfield, too drunk to fetch the midwife, sleeps indifferently in the corner of the room.

Some months later Mem regains her strength as well as her courage. Finding Brownfield in a drunken stupor, she puts a shotgun to his head and threatens to kill him if he so much as attempts to thwart her efforts. The family lives for three years in a comfortable four-room apartment in town, but then Mem, ill, fatigued, and pregnant again, fails to pay the rent and heat for the apartment. Brownfield refuses to help, and they are forced to move.

Dragged back into a life of misery, the family lives in a sad and broken old barn at which Mem, after years of moving from one shack to another, refuses to plant flowers. Brownfield, having returned to his old ways, grows to hate his wife and the children. Late one Christmas Eve, Mem, returning from work, is shot by her husband on the steps of their home. The children remain huddled by their mother, who lies motionless among the peppermint sticks and oranges that had dropped from her arms. Gazing at her dying mother, Ruth notices the holes in her shoes; they had been stuffed with newspaper to fight the cold of winter.

Corde, Albert. *The Dean's December.* Saul Bellow. 1982.

Albert Corde is a beleaguered university administrator in Chicago. When the mother of his wife Minna, a defector to the United States, suffers a catastrophic stroke, Corde must accompany Minna to Bucharest, Romania. Unable to offer his wife practical assistance in the alien and hostile country, he is forced to spend the closing weeks of December in his mother-in-law's apartment.

While Minna copes first with the problems of visiting her mother in the rigidly administered hospital and then with the arrangements for her funeral, Corde broods over the controversies he has left back home. Foremost among Corde's concerns is the furor he has unwittingly aroused by the publication of a series of articles on the state of Chicago. Charged with intense fury, obscure imagery, and esoteric philosophical allusions, Corde's series has infuriated every quarter of Chicago's populace. Having had no intentions of arousing such ire, Corde ponders his motives for writing the articles and wonders at the indignation of Chicagoans.

Corde has also been courting controversy in another arena. He muses over his involvement in the trial of a black man, who along with a prostitute is accused of murdering a white student. In his capacity as dean, Corde has become active in the case, prompting the college to post a reward for information concerning the murder. Ironically, Corde's radical nephew is at the forefront of the groups who charge the dean with racism, while the media uses the occasion to retaliate against the administrator for his criticism of them in his *Harper's* articles.

While Corde conducts these mental trips back to Chicago, he is called upon to aid Minna as she attempts to circumvent the vindictive communist regime that will allow her to visit her dying mother only once. His visit to the American embassy serves only to aggravate the colonel in charge of the hospital, while the intervention of his childhood friend Dewey Spangler, now a famous and influential columnist, comes only after the woman has died.

A long conversation with Spangler and more introspection lead Corde to believe that his motives for writing his bitter diatribes about Chicago were more personal and more incendiary than he had originally thought. He acknowledges that after returning from Paris, where he had been a journalist, to Chicago, where he became a professor and then a dean, he found himself disillusioned with the academic world. When his hopes in academia were disappointed, Corde now realizes, he then went out to investigate the city. Thwarted in that arena as well, he resorted to the attacks on the modern urban scene that became the *Harper's* study. The same motives have led him to involve himself and the school in the murder trial.

By the time Corde arrives at these self-realizations, his mother-in-law has been buried and his wife has become ill. He arrives home to discover that the jury has found the accused man guilty of murder and that the long, reacquainting session he had with his journalist friend has been converted into a column. After reading the piece, he concludes that, coupled with his *Harper's* articles, it has sealed his fate as a dean, despite the fact that the college came off rather nicely with the trial. Not long after, Corde reveals to his wife that he has resigned his position as dean.

Corleone, Don Vito. *The Godfather.* Mario Puzo. 1969.

Don Vito Corleone, known as "the Godfather," leads the most powerful Mafia "family" in New York. Originally from Sicily, Corleone leaves his peasant village at the age of twelve in order to escape death at the hands of the local hoods who killed his father. He travels to New York City where he marries and sets up house in a tenement apartment near the grocery store where he works.

Corleone's career as a Mafia man begins early: He joins a group of neighborhood truck hijackers and later decides to kill Fanucci, a petty mafioso who tries to extort a share of the hijackers' profits. Following Fanucci's murder, Corleone becomes a man of respect in his community. His influence slowly extends as people increasingly come to him for help, and he pays off scores of politicians, judges, bankers, and policemen in an effort to bypass all existing civic and legal systems. His power depends on two things: his skillful ability to reason with any opponent, and the vast network of men—great and small—who remain interminably in his debt. But as Corleone grows older, a new generation of Mafia men, including his own sons, brings a different set of rules and ideas to the Mafia empire. The Don struggles to uphold peace and maintain order between rival Mafia families.

In 1946, the Don is tremendously powerful but also

vulnerable. Virgil Sollozzo, a large-scale Sicilian narcotics dealer, asks the Don for help in setting up a heroin operation with the Tattaglia family, one of New York's five Mafia families. When Don Vito refuses, Sollozzo has him gunned down, hoping to eliminate this formidable opponent to the immensely profitable drug business and to join forces with Sonny Corleone, the Don's hot-tempered oldest son and heir. But the Don, although critically wounded, survives the hit and is hospitalized.

Sonny, furious over his father's attempted murder, organizes a war against Sollozzo and the Tattaglias that soon costs him his own life. MICHAEL CORLEONE—the Don's intelligent, level-headed youngest son and favorite child—joins the war, murders Sollozzo in retaliation, and flees to Sicily, where he goes into hiding. Grieved by the terrible explosion of violence, Don Vito Corleone, who is still convalescing, calls for a national meeting of all Mafia families and sues for peace.

At the meeting, Mafia heads from the western United States urge the Don to help the narcotics business with his web of connections. They convince him that the business will ultimately be safer if the families can regulate it. Don Vito respects these men and finally agrees, but only after gaining assurance that Michael will be allowed to return from Sicily unharmed.

Now an old man, Corleone takes on the two tasks of eradicating any evidence linking Michael to Sollozzo's murder and planning his family's eventual move to Las Vegas. He ignores the encroachments of other New York families on his gambling and union operations. After Michael returns, Corleone hands the empire over to him and retires.

He spends his final months at home, with his grandchildren, tending to his house and garden. One afternoon he suffers a heart attack and dies in Michael's arms, leaving his son to avenge Sonny's death and the indignations suffered by the Corleone family during the so-called peace.

Corleone, Michael. *The Godfather.* Mario Puzo. 1969.

In 1946, Michael Corleone, youngest son of the Mafia "godfather" DON VITO CORLEONE, returns home from serving as a Marine in World War II—against his father's will. At his sister Connie's lavish wedding, he sits apart from his family with his Anglo-American girlfriend Kay Adams, whom he met before the war while he was a student at Dartmouth College. Michael is trying to maintain a distance from the family business of organized crime, but by the end of this novel Michael has succeeded his father as the head of a vast criminal empire.

Michael was not raised to be a gangster. By keeping him out of the family business, Don Vito hoped to lead his smartest son toward politics or legitimate business. But when his father is gunned down by a rival family in retaliation for refusing to support a newly formed Mafia

heroin operation, Michael takes a more active role in the family.

In the midst of the ensuing Mafia war—begun by Michael's oldest brother Sonny in retaliation for his father's shooting—Michael saves his father from a second attempt on his life. Arriving at the hospital long past visiting hours, he discovers that the police and family bodyguards have been ordered out of the hospital by the corrupt Captain McCluskey. Michael challenges McCluskey and receives a shattering blow to the head, but he maintains his composure long enough to ensure that reinforcements are brought in to guard his father.

As a result of this incident, Michael realizes that his father is still in mortal danger. When Sollozzo, the head of the heroin operation, requests a meeting with him to negotiate an end to the war, Michael volunteers to execute Sollozzo and his bodyguard, Captain McCluskey. Clemenza and Tessio, the *caporegimes*, or captains, of his father's organization, and Tom Hagen, the family counselor, devise a plan to hide a gun in the bathroom of the public restaurant where the meeting is to take place. Michael kills both men in a burst of gunfire and gets away. That night he is smuggled on board a merchant ship to relative safety in Sicily.

After a long stretch of inactivity in Sicily, under the protection of his father's old friends Don Tommasino and Dr. Taza, Michael meets a beautiful young peasant girl, Apollonia. He is struck by what the Sicilians call the "thunderbolt," a consuming, possessive love. Apollonia is natural, virginal, and passionate, a woman quite unlike the familiar and conservative Kay Adams whom Michael left behind in America. After a few weeks of courtship, he and Apollonia marry. Their ecstatic union is cut short when their Alfa Romeo explodes, killing Apollonia in a blast meant for Michael. The loss devastates Michael, for whom the potential for love and purity is now lost forever.

While Michael is spending three years in Sicily, his father and Tom Hagen arrange for a convicted murderer to confess to the killings of Sollozzo and McCluskey. When Michael returns home, he is free of the threat of prosecution. In order to ensure Michael's safety, Don Vito has made peace among all the Mafia families of the United States and has agreed to use his legal influence to help the heroin trade. Forging this peace is the last major act of the Don's career. He goes into semi-retirement and allows Michael to act as head of the family.

Once settled at home, Michael reunites with Kay Adams. After their wedding, they move to the compound, Don Corleone's fortresslike property on Long Island where he lives with his family and bodyguards. Michael's main concern is to shift family operations from New York to Las Vegas, an open town in the late 1940s and early 1950s due to legalized gambling. Working with the Don's advice, Michael readies the family for the move to Las Vegas.

Just before the final move, Don Vito dies of a heart attack. Now alone, Michael activates a long-planned vengeance against the enemies of the Corleone family. Targets include his sister Connie's husband, Carlo Rizzi, who set up Sonny to be executed during the war. In one master stroke, Michael orders the executions not only of Rizzi but also of Fabrizio, the man who murdered Apollonia; Phillip Tattaglia, the head of the rival Tattaglia family; and Tessio, his father's trusted *caporegime* who has been working simultaneously for a rival family.

In front of the entire family, Michael's sister Connie accuses him of murdering her husband. He tries to convince Kay that he is innocent, but in a moment of clarity she sees Michael for who he is: the new Don, leader of a Mafia family. The novel ends with Kay praying for the soul of Michael Corleone.

Cornplow, Hazel. *The Prodigal Parents.* Sinclair Lewis. 1938.

Married to WILLIAM "FRED" CORNPLOW, Hazel Cornplow is content with her role as the wife of one of the leading merchants of Sachem Falls and mother of the handsome HOWARD (CORNPLOW) and the elegant SARA (CORNPLOW). Yet as Fred grows to realize that the independence he has so strongly desired is not what he thought, so Hazel undergoes a subtle change in terms of her own independence.

At the beginning of the novel, Hazel is very much the keeper of Fred's home, providing for him the warmth and domesticity he needs. In the early part of the novel she appears always on the point of sleep or recently awakened, providing a sounding board for Fred's complaints. She embodies for Fred the virtues of sweetness, tranquility, and comfort, and as the embodiment of these virtues, she rarely speaks except to confirm Fred's sense of his values and priorities. While Hazel is Fred's surest ally, she never openly takes part in his confrontations with their children and is content for him to lead the way. She only breaks this comfortable silence when Fred's searching threatens to upset her material well-being, and her complaints stand feebly in the way of Fred's drive for freedom.

Hazel begins to find her own freedom on their trip to Europe. As the boat pulls away from the shore, she bitterly regrets leaving her family and home, and feels frightened at the prospect of what lies before them. As Fred comes to see how different Europe is, Hazel finds everything disconcertingly familiar and understands implicitly how this world works. She refuses to be daunted by the superior claims of Europe and the Europeans she meets, and indeed it is her newfound love of this continent that keeps them abroad long after Fred has admitted to himself that travel is not the kind of freedom he had anticipated. When Howard's wife Annabel comes to beg the Cornplows to return home and rescue Howard from the alcoholism into which he has sunk, Hazel decides to stay in France with Annabel.

Together they go to Paris, where Hazel tests her fledgling independence.

Hazel returns to Sachem Falls unexpectedly while Fred and Howard are on a camping trip in the Canadian wilderness. Using her new initiative, she hires an Indian to take her upriver on a boat to find them. As the two of them arrive at the campsite, Fred and Howard see only two Indians approaching through the dark. It is a mark of how much Hazel has changed that the earlier warm, comforting presence could now be seen as potentially threatening. As the novel ends, Hazel has taken over Fred's role of adventurer and plans new voyages with an enthusiasm and vigor that bears little resemblance to her previous languor as a devoted wife.

Cornplow, Howard. *The Prodigal Parents.* Sinclair Lewis. 1938.

Howard Cornplow, the only son of WILLIAM "FRED" (CORNPLOW) and HAZEL (CORNPLOW), is as unintelligent as he is good-looking; he has "a face handsome as a magazine cover and stupid as a domesticated carp." As a junior at Truxon College, Howard has the reputation of a good-humored athlete who knows nothing of Plato or calculus. Although he is kind and well intentioned, he lacks any foresight or perception and so is easily manipulated by others and swayed by his love of a life of leisure. For Howard, the present is carefree and secure. He knows his father will supply him with the funds his life-style demands while assuring him of a comfortable future in the family business, which Howard assumes he will inherit. The son of a successful father, he is a directionless and rather weak young man.

It is Howard's complacency and lack of independence that frustrate his father, Fred. Life seems simple and straightforward to Howard; he is always full of unrealistic plans for making easy money and is unable to see that these plans might not bear fruit. He is also sure that in difficult times his father will bail him out. This confidence in an undefined yet certain future wealth bodes ill for him until, early in the novel, he makes two decisions that seem to set him on the road to independence. The first is his marriage to Annabel Staybridge, who is much his intellectual superior and marries him with her eyes open. The second is his decision to abandon his hopes of entering his father's business and instead start a real estate company. Howard's hopes of success are unrealistically high, but with an intelligent and realistic wife and an ambitious business partner, it seems that he might succeed.

Yet Howard's laziness and aversion to hard work wreak havoc on his marriage and career. The aimless drinking of his college days becomes a hardened attempt to escape from the failure of his business and the demands of his pregnant wife. With his parents' departure for Europe, Howard falls in with a bad crowd and drinks up his remaining capital. Without the support and demands of his father, he risks spoiling his own life and that of his wife and child. Finally, Annabel rushes to Europe to find Fred and Hazel, and she begs them to come home and rescue their son. Leaving Hazel and Annabel in Europe, Fred returns to Sachem Falls and finds Howard in a drunken stupor.

In this state, Howard is incapable of resisting his father and allows his cronies to be banished, his house to be cleaned, and himself to be taken camping in the wilderness of Canada. Here, away from the pressures of family and small-town life, Howard begins to discover that he has real strengths and ambitions. For the first time he begins to analyze his prospects and think seriously about what the future holds for him. This introspection creates a new ambition in Howard, one he feels is not forced on him by his father. As the novel ends, he begins to realize the virtues of hard work and responsibility. Annabel stays in Europe, but Howard is now prepared to earn the love that he had previously taken for granted, in the same way that he will earn the respect of his family and town.

Cornplow, Sara. *The Prodigal Parents.* Sinclair Lewis. 1938.

Sara Cornplow, the only daughter of WILLIAM "FRED" (CORNPLOW) and HAZEL (CORNPLOW), is intolerant and scornful, reveling in the admiration and awe her regal bearing inspires in her parents and using her cleverness to deflate what she sees as her parents' naive enthusiasms. Although she is much more intelligent and perceptive than her brother HOWARD (CORNPLOW), she shares his sense of birthright, feeling that her parents owe her everything she wants. Like Howard she is not quite sure of what it is she wants but is willing to let her parents pay the price of the mistakes she makes on the way to discovering it.

As the book opens, Sara enters into a venture that appears to be designed to aggravate and infuriate her father, Fred. Through Howard she meets the radical agitator Eugene Silga and falls in love with him and, consequently, his politics. While Eugene clearly seems to be using her, Sara uses her father to provide the communist newspaper edited by Eugene with examples of the ridiculous opinions of bourgeois capitalists. When the paper collapses and Eugene abandons her, Sara accepts her father's help, taking his money and advice without a word of thanks. Seemingly relieved that she can now go back to the tennis clubs she loves without the interference of Eugene's politics, Sara begins a new career as an interior designer, again demanding that Fred give her the financial help she needs.

This career has a more tangible effect on her family's life than her brief spell as a radical newspaper editor. Dismissing her parents' taste as lower class, she redecorates their house, alienating them from their own home. As her success grows, so does her sense of infallibility. She counters Fred's yearning for adventure with an insidious

attack on his sanity. Using Fred's desire to be closer to her, she lures him to New York where she takes him to see a psychiatrist. Sara's threat to Fred's freedom is a real one: She is intelligent enough to make him feel both foolish and guilty about his desires, and she commands the respect and attention of all the people Fred is trying desperately to escape.

Although Sara tries to prevent her parents from going, they finally leave for Europe. On her own for the first time, Sara embraces the life she has always seemed to despise by marrying Walter Lindbeck, a friend of her father. She moves into this new life with an ease and assurance born from her feeling that she has finally come home. Of all the Cornplows, Sara remains the least affected by Fred's attempt to free himself from the dependence of his children. However, as Fred tries to save Howard from alcoholism and despair, Sara expresses her concern with an unusual gentleness and an apology—the first she has made in her life.

Cornplow, William "Fred." *The Prodigal Parents.* Sinclair Lewis. 1938.

William "Fred" Cornplow works as the district agent for Triumph and Houndtooth automobiles in the Sachem Falls area, and lives in respectable bourgeois prosperity with his wife HAZEL (CORNPLOW) and children HOWARD (CORNPLOW) and SARA (CORNPLOW). However, the Cornplow family is riven by intergenerational conflict, and Sachem Falls provides only the comforts of respectability and a modest celebrity. Fred yearns to escape the tyranny of his children and of his career, and dreams of the "crazy" freedom that could be his if only he had the courage to grasp it.

Early in the novel, Fred bemoans the fact that his adult children are still dependent on him, yet faced with their pleas for help, he always relents. The novel opens with an accident in which Howard's car is ruined, and in a pattern that becomes familiar, Fred's initial burst of severity is tempered by his pride in his son and his willingness to believe his feeble excuses. When his daughter Sara takes up with Eugene Silga, a radical agitator, and taunts her father by quoting his bourgeois capitalist views in the communist paper she edits, Fred cannot hide his annoyance. Yet when the paper is threatened by police and angry creditors, he steps in to save Eugene and Sara. While he acknowledges his children's lack of gratitude, Fred cannot stop himself from responding to their demands.

But the "padded servitude" of this world finally becomes too much. Disillusioned with his work and unwilling to sacrifice his search for freedom on the altar of his family, he takes his wife Hazel away on a surprise trip to a remote area where he hopes Sara and Howard will not be able to find them. Away from their children and the materialistic comfort of their own home, Hazel and

Fred discover how much they enjoy a simpler life. They also discover how much they like each other, and Fred begins to reflect on the happiness his marriage has brought him. Yet this idyll is spoiled by the arrival of Sara and Howard, who drag their reluctant parents back to the world of their responsibilities.

After this small adventure, Fred's restlessness and his troubles grow. He feels misunderstood by everyone except his new daughter-in-law, Annabel, and even Hazel begins to listen to Sara's claims that Fred's yearning for travel and freedom are the products of a disturbed and overworked mind. Sara lures her father to New York where she takes him to see a psychiatrist, and it is this encounter that precipitates Fred's final escape. He rushes back to Sachem Falls and tells Hazel to pack, and soon they are on a boat to Europe.

On this journey Fred discovers that both he and Hazel are not the people he had assumed. Away from his hometown, Fred loses his desire for company and begins to spend time on his own. He finds Europe strange and incomprehensible, and realizes it is only in Sachem Falls that he is the solid, outgoing Fred Cornplow who is known and trusted by everyone. As he watches Hazel take on Europe, Fred begins to feel more and more isolated in a world that doesn't need him.

He is rescued from this isolation by the arrival of Annabel, who has come to beg Fred to return home to rescue Howard who is drinking heavily. Fred at once feels his old self returning and is forced to admit that he is as dependent on his children as they are on him: He really does want them to need him. He returns to Sachem Falls to find that Howard is on the verge of destroying his few small achievements. In an effort to set Howard on the right track, Fred takes him to the wilderness of Canada. Here, for the first time, he lets Howard enjoy himself without placing demands on him and consequently realizes that he has always expected Howard to show the same driving ambition that he had when he was young. On their return to Sachem Falls, Fred realizes that the freedom he had been seeking was not escape from the physical circumstances of his life but from the expectations he had placed on it.

Corregidora, Ursa. *Corregidora*. Gayl Jones. 1975.

Ursa Corregidora is a mixed-race blues singer whose painful life is hopelessly intertwined with her family history. Corregidora was the name of the man who was both Ursa's great-grandfather and her grandfather, a slave owner in Brazil. Ursa's great-grandmother and grandmother escaped from forced prostitution by running away to Louisiana, where Ursa's mother was born. Ursa's grandmother tells her the story of all the Corregidora women except Ursa's mother and tells her to "make generations" to bear witness to the history of abuse associated with the family name.

This charge to have children becomes possible for Ursa a few months later when she marries Mutt Thomas. Ursa meets Mutt while she is singing at Happy's Café. Unlike other men who make sexual advances toward her during her break between sets, Mutt just wants to talk. They eventually get to know each other better, and they fall in love and are soon married. Mutt is jealous and wants Ursa to end her singing career, but she refuses. His temper gets shorter, and he begins to drink heavily. Sexual problems between Mutt and Ursa become an arena for battles of will and power.

As Mutt gets more and more jealous, and more volatile, his personality begins to change. He is sometimes very cold and sometimes extremely aggressive; watching other men watch Ursa sing, he frequently causes public scenes. One night he is thrown out of Happy's Café for his behavior, and after waiting outside for Ursa, who is pregnant, he throws her down a flight of stairs.

The fall causes a miscarriage that leads to a subsequent hysterectomy. Tadpole McCormick, the owner of Happy's Café, lets Ursa stay with him after she is released from the hospital. Tadpole has been attracted to Ursa for some time and is happy to take care of her. Ursa refuses to see her husband.

Ursa goes to stay with her friend Cat across the road for a few days until she discovers that Cat and Cat's fourteen-year-old friend Jeffy are sexually involved. Disgusted, she goes back to Tadpole's. Soon after, she divorces Mutt and marries Tadpole. She continues to sing at Happy's Café and gets a job singing one night a week at the Spider, another club.

Ursa's relationship with Tadpole is also troubled. She has problems having sex and finds she is sometimes so tense that she is unable to have intercourse at all. Powerless to help her, Tadpole begins to feel rejected by her. He hires a very young woman to sing on the night that Ursa sings at the Spider, and one night Ursa comes home from her show and finds Tadpole and the young singer in bed.

Ursa is furious and leaves. She obtains full-time work at the Spider and divorces Tadpole. Now Ursa refuses to become sexually involved with anyone, and she makes it clear to the owner of the Spider that he should not make sexual advances if he wants her to work there. For a long time Ursa passes her time wrapped up in her music and her family stories.

Finally, Ursa's mother tells Ursa the history of her stormy relationship with Ursa's father, an African-American named Martin. They were married after discovering that she had become pregnant by him. Their relationship had been intensely sexual; once they were married, however, he came to hate her, and when he began to beat her, she left him. Soon after this revelation, Mutt comes into the Spider. Carrying with her the knowledge of her heritage, Ursa leaves with him. Together they try to resolve their relationship, the complicated weave of love, sex, violence, and history.

Correspondent. "The Open Boat." Stephen Crane. 1897.

On a wide and terrifying ocean, in a small two-oar dinghy after a shipwreck, four men—a correspondent, an injured captain, an oiler, and a cook—fight to stay afloat amid the huge waves that toss them around brutally. As they stare with fright at the violent sea, the correspondent wonders why he's there. But while he endures the struggle for survival, he confronts his own mortality and learns that human beings are insignificant to the powerful, indifferent forces of nature.

Although the cook insists that on-land "houses of refuge" are staffed by teams of rescuers, the correspondent is sure they are not. While he and the oiler take turns rowing the dinghy, trying with all their might to move toward land, the correspondent feels a certain comradeship develop between the men on the boat; although he never speaks of it, he knows this is "the best experience of his life." When they sight dry land in the distance and see a house of refuge, the correspondent miraculously finds four dry cigars in his pocket. Someone produces dry matches, and they all puff on the cigars as they approach the land.

When no one emerges from the house of refuge, the men decide to attempt to get the dinghy through the violent breaking waves that create a barrier between them and the shoreline. Knowing this maneuver will be life-threatening and wanting their families to be informed if they die, the men briefly exchange addresses and admonitions. But their attempt to cross the waves fails, and they move back out to sea. As night falls, they spot people on shore, but the people seem to think the dinghy is a fishing boat and make no effort to rescue them.

In the black of night, the correspondent rows while the others sleep; he wishes someone was awake so he could have company. He hears the sound of a shark fin moving in the water. The shark goes away, and the correspondent suddenly remembers a verse about a soldier who lay dying in Algiers and who knew he would never see his native land again. Now the correspondent can visualize the soldier clearly, and he feels deep sympathy for him. When the captain sits up in the bow and says something about the shark, the correspondent realizes someone has been awake all along.

At dawn, the captain says they should try to swim ashore. The correspondent sees the tall wind tower on the land and interprets it as a symbol of the serenity of nature amid the struggles of the individual. As he swims, he can see the captain, the oiler, and the cook around him. He ceases to make progress when a strong current catches

him, and he anticipates his own drowning. The captain, who has held on to the boat and is ahead of the correspondent, calls him to the dinghy. As the correspondent nears the dinghy, a huge wave flings him over the boat and beyond it, and he lands in waist-high water. A man comes running along the shore, strips off his clothes, enters the water, and rescues them all except the oiler who lies face down in the shallow surf. The correspondent collapses on the sand, and while some of the villagers bring food and blankets for the men, others carry the oiler's body away. As the story closes, the correspondent and his companions hear the great ocean roar and feel they can now be its interpreters.

Coulter, Nathan. *Nathan Coulter.* Wendell Berry. 1960.

This coming-of-age novel, set in Kentucky tobacco country, focuses on the early life of Nathan Coulter, the young protagonist and narrator. Nathan is the younger son of a tobacco grower who lives on a farm adjacent to one that has been in the Coulter family for several generations. As the novel begins, he and his older brother Tom, usually referred to as Brother, are forced to spend a good deal of time being quiet in deference to their mother's ill health. Her health has steadily deteriorated since her younger son's birth; before long she is forced to remain in bed all day, and eventually she dies. Nathan and Brother are brought to their grandparents' farm where they stay for the duration of the novel as their father struggles to hold on to his farm and his sanity.

The boys extend their relationship with their uncle Burley, who lives with his parents most of the time. Burley occasionally gets drunk and has had his difficulties with his parents, but by and large he is a good role model for inquisitive Nathan, who seems closer to him than does Brother. The boys slowly emerge from preadolescence, and Nathan, as he recognizes the ties that have bound his family to their land, develops a special relationship with the land and nature around him. He greatly admires and respects his grandfather, who teaches, through his example, the value of good, hard, steady labor.

As Nathan and Brother grow older, their strong sibling bond gradually weakens. Brother drifts away from Nathan; their relationship is finally severed, at least for a time, when Brother and their father come to blows while arduously cutting tobacco plants. The father, having goaded his sons into competing with him in the swiftness and accuracy of their work, is relentless in his teasing. Brother finally attacks him, and the two have to be separated by Burley. That evening Brother, despite his grandparents' pleas, leaves the family fold. Nathan is left alone to deal with his elders and the many lessons they want to impart.

In Brother's absence, Nathan spends more time with Uncle Burley, fishing and hunting. From Burley, Nathan learns not only timeless techniques but also how to respect nature. With Burley's help, Nathan improves his skills as a farmer. His lessons are not lost on Brother, who now works on a nearby farm. In an apparent truce with his father, Brother eventually returns to the family and joins them once a month for Sunday dinner.

Tobacco season ends, and Nathan's grandfather begins talking about his own death. As the story concludes, Nathan, who has been sent to see that the elderly man gets home safely, is with Grandpa as he collapses and dies on the land he loved so much. Nathan, bewildered in spite of his preparation for this event, picks the old man up off the ground and carries him back to his home.

Courtney, Iris. *Because It Is Bitter, and Because It Is My Heart.* Joyce Carol Oates. 1990.

Iris Courtney is a young white girl living in rural Hammond, New York, in the 1950s, who matures under the stress of her parents' dissolving marriage and her mother's declining health. At the outset of the novel, the Courtneys dote on Iris as proof of an ideal relationship. However, the couple's decision to defer having more children, to preserve Persia Courtney's buxom figure, signals their inherent selfishness. This quality becomes increasingly apparent to young Iris as she watches her father sacrifice their well-being to his compulsive gambling. The family eventually must leave their house and relocate to an inferior neighborhood, a process that will be repeated as Duke Courtney loses more and more money at the racetrack. Each move brings the family closer and closer to that section of town inhabited by poor whites and blacks. These neighbors, Iris learns from her father, are contemptible.

Iris herself feels differently about the neighbors. In fact, as she matures sexually, she finds herself increasingly attracted to several black boys, particularly, VERLYN RAYBURN "JINX" FAIRCHILD, a local high school basketball star. Iris and Jinx soon share an ugly secret that remains with them for the rest of their lives. One evening, after the Courtneys' divorce and while Persia is pursuing her new career as a "hostess" at a local bar, Iris is chased by Red Garlock, a possibly retarded but definitively disgusting racist teenager who delights in sexually taunting young girls. Fearful of Garlock's taunts, Iris retreats to a local store where Jinx works. Jinx insists on walking her home, and when Garlock continues to hurl racial and sexual epithets at the couple, the boys begin to fight. Jinx kills Red and dumps his body in a river. While the murder will never be officially solved and the case becomes yet another blur in an uncaring town's history, Jinx and Iris are irrevocably changed by the fight, the death, and their mutual attraction.

Meanwhile, mindful of the need to keep her secret, Iris continues her studies in high school. She becomes more and more aware of her mother's devastating alcoholism, although she believes that her mother could, if she wished, gain control over her drinking and smoking. Iris remains in need of a strong parent figure, for she knows Persia has essentially given up on life. After several years of witnessing Persia's deterioration, during which Iris more or less drops out of school in favor of working at the local library, Iris continues to fantasize about Jinx. She rarely sees him in private but is at least able to see him by attending all of his basketball games. Finally, after Persia's death, Iris returns to school and then enrolls in Syracuse University, where she studies art history under Dr. Byron Savage.

Iris grows close to the Savage family and eventually becomes engaged to Dr. Savage's son Alan. She returns to Hammond for a visit, hoping to close a chapter in her life, and gets sexually assaulted by a group of black youths. This event does not alter her love for Jinx, however, which is never fulfilled or abandoned. Her fiancé, shocked at the assault, encourages her recovery. At the conclusion of the novel, Iris becomes Mrs. Savage.

Coverdale, Miles. *The Blithedale Romance.* Nathaniel Hawthorne. 1852.

Although his decision to live in the utopian community of Blithedale seems to have been made lightly, Miles Coverdale comes to realize that his tenure there was the most important phase of his life. Coverdale, a poet given to observation and contemplation, does little to act but is acted upon by a group of remarkable people.

Arriving at Blithedale one wintry afternoon after seeing Boston society off in style the night before, Coverdale is more excited at the prospect of finally meeting the famous women's rights advocate ZENOBIA than he is by the idea of laboring on a farm. Zenobia, beautiful, self-possessed, and rich, is everything he had imagined and the most striking evidence that woman is every bit the equal of man. No sooner has Coverdale taken his place at the supper table, ready to enjoy hearty food and Zenobia's conversation, than the party is interrupted by a knock. In bursts HOLLINGSWORTH, making his first appearance at Blithedale, along with a slight young woman, Priscilla, whom a strange old man, Mr. Moodie, had urged Hollingsworth to take to Blithedale.

Like everyone else at Blithedale, Coverdale works hard on the farm, but he devotes time as well to observing the community's residents. He pays particular attention to Hollingsworth, Zenobia, and Priscilla. Coverdale wonders at Priscilla's devotion to Zenobia, whom she had never seen before arriving at Blithedale, and of Zenobia's admiration for Hollingsworth. Coverdale recognizes that Hollingsworth has force and determination, but his singleminded devotion to prison reform renders him somewhat tiresome company.

Seeking solitude, one day Coverdale walks in the woods surrounding Blithedale and is accosted by a rude man who asks where he can find Zenobia. Put off by the stranger's insinuating manner, Coverdale mentions the location of one of Zenobia's haunts, then goes on his way. Later, sitting in one of his favorite trees, Coverdale sees Zenobia in animated conversation with the man, Professor Westervelt. He can hear few of the obviously angry words but is able to discern that Zenobia and Westervelt have some connection, perhaps an intimate one.

Soon after, Hollingsworth tries to enlist Coverdale in his prison reform plans. When Coverdale, skeptical of philanthropy, refuses to get involved, Hollingsworth tells him that they cannot be friends if Coverdale does not support him. Hurt by the withdrawal of Hollingsworth's friendship and sensible to a coolness toward him on the part of Zenobia and Priscilla, Coverdale decides to leave Blithedale for a time.

Back in Boston, Coverdale continues his habit of observation. On looking out his window one day he sees Zenobia and Westervelt in the next house. Rather than manifest shame when Zenobia sees him spying on her and pulls the curtain, Coverdale boldly pays a visit the next day. He speaks with Zenobia, who can barely conceal her disdain for him. He also sees Priscilla, whose beauty, it seems, blooms more fully in the city than in the country. The visit is interrupted when Westervelt arrives to take the women to a show.

A few days later Coverdale goes to see a performance by a medium, the mysterious Veiled Lady. During the performance, conducted by the oily Westervelt, the Veiled Lady removes her covering and reveals herself to be Priscilla. Hollingsworth, also in the audience, releases her from the thrall of Westervelt and takes her from the stage.

Eventually returning to Blithedale, Coverdale encounters a heartbroken Zenobia, whom Hollingsworth has rejected in favor of Priscilla. Coverdale does what little he can to help the distraught woman, but later that night, on finding her handkerchief on the shore of a pond, he fears she may have killed herself. Dragging the pond with Hollingsworth's help, Coverdale sees the lovely Zenobia once more, but she is now stiff and lifeless.

Years later Coverdale pays a visit to Priscilla and Hollingsworth. He finds his former friend bent and frail, weighted down by the thought that he caused Zenobia's death. Coverdale takes a perverse pleasure in mocking Hollingsworth for his failure to obtain prison reform, but, as he confesses, Hollingsworth is not the only one who failed to carry out his dreams. He himself did nothing to try to win Priscilla, with whom he was in love while at Blithedale.

Cow. "Cow." Ben Field. 1935.

Cow is a Jewish Marxist who works on a country farm one summer and changes the lives of its inhabitants. An enormous man, he is sent by a New York agency to help finish the haying on Dan Smith's farm. When Gnat, the ill-tempered little foreman, first sets eyes on the man, he

tells the narrator, a hired hand named Mose, that he does not think the new help will last long because he is nothing but a cow. The man apparently overhears him and introduces himself by the nickname "Cow."

Cow, whose real name is not mentioned in the story, was born in Russia and immigrated to America with his family when he was five years old. He first lived in Passaic, New Jersey, where his father worked in the handkerchief business. Cow attended public school for ten years; then, inspired by the writings of Jack London, he ran away to sea. He worked in a quartz mine in South America during World War I, spent a year tramping through the Andes, and was a strong man with a circus in the United States. A married man, Cow claims to be a carpenter by trade and says that he has decided to try farming because he wants to study farm conditions in preparation for the revolution.

During his first few days on the farm, Cow reveals himself to be tireless, energetic, and good-natured. He is clumsy at first with each new chore but very quickly becomes more competent at them than the other workers. Every night before going to bed, he washes his clothes and then walks two miles to mail the letters he is constantly writing. One morning Cow and Mose come across Gnat and the owner's wife having sex. Cow is indignant when he learns that the impotent Smith knows about the affair but does nothing. A couple of days later Cow physically accosts the farmer, holds him up in the air, calls him a stinkbug, and then tells him that he is living a lie and must change his ways. Instead of firing the hired man, Smith begins to read Cow's pamphlets and listen to his political arguments.

One day Cow tells Mose that he encountered Smith's wife wearing her nightgown in the kitchen, and he brags, somewhat suspiciously, about the discipline that enabled him to send her back to bed. Moments later Gnat starts a fight with the much larger man, screaming that he saw him in the kitchen with the woman the night before. Cow, furious, jumps from the mow to the barn floor and is gored by a pitchfork lying in the hay. Mose visits the injured man's bedside. Before dying, Cow admits that he himself is a bug, too, with no discipline. The next day Cow's pregnant wife and her father take the corpse back to the city with them. Mose, who is a writer, decides to return to the city as well. Both he and Smith realize that they will never be the same after having known the man who called himself Cow.

Cowardly Lion. *The Wonderful Wizard of Oz.* L. Frank Baum. 1900.

The Cowardly Lion is the gentlest and most courageous of DOROTHY's incongruous traveling companions. He bounds with a terrible roar from the dark forest in which he lives, knocking over the SCARECROW, trying to scratch the TIN WOODMAN, and threatening to bite the little dog Toto. But the Lion cowers and bursts into tears when Dorothy, a sweet little girl from Kansas who has been blown to the strange land of Oz by a cyclone, roundly reproaches him with a slap on the nose.

Despite this inauspicious beginning, the Lion soon becomes friends with the travelers and accompanies them to Oz. He admits that he is really a coward, and determined to ask the WIZARD OF OZ for some courage, he sets off with them down the yellow brick road.

The group soon comes to a ditch so huge that there seems to be no way to continue their travels. But the Lion bravely says he will leap the ditch and carry each member of the party over on his back. After getting beyond this obstacle and several others, the travelers find themselves in a field of poppies that causes Dorothy, Toto, and the Cowardly Lion to become very sleepy. Not being made of flesh and blood, the Tin Woodman and the Scarecrow do not feel drowsy and are able to carry Dorothy and Toto to safety. The Lion is too heavy for them to carry, however, so they build a cart and then enlist the help of thousands of field mice to pull him out.

At long last the travelers arrive in the Emerald City, and each of them has a separate audience with the Wizard Oz. To the Lion, the Wizard appears as a fierce Ball of Fire. In a low, quiet voice, Oz tells the Lion what he had told his friends: None of their requests will be granted until they kill the Wicked Witch of the West.

The travelers set off to do just that, but the Witch sees them coming and sends her band of Winged Monkeys after them. The Monkeys destroy the Woodman and the Scarecrow, and take Dorothy, Toto, and the Lion to their mistress's castle. She tries to tame the Lion for her fiendish uses, but he resists. Before long, Dorothy kills the Witch by throwing water on her, and they escape. They repair their two friends and return to the Emerald City to tell Oz the good news.

They soon discover that Oz has no magical powers, but he is willing to do what he can to help. He gives the Cowardly Lion a drink, no doubt alcoholic, that fills him with courage. The only one Oz is unsuccessful in helping is Dorothy, for nothing but magic can return her to Kansas.

The four friends (plus Toto) set off on another adventure, this time to the country of the Quadlings where Glinda, the Good Witch of the South, resides. Their path takes them into a dark forest where all the animals fear for their lives because of a huge, spiderlike monster that has been devouring them like flies. The Lion agrees to kill the monster in exchange for the job of ruler of the forest. He accomplishes his part of the deal by pouncing on the monster in its sleep. In the end, after Dorothy is safely returned to Kansas with the help of Glinda, the Lion becomes King of the Beasts in a forest paradise.

Cowperwood, Frank. *The Financier; The Titan; The Stoic.* Theodore Dreiser. 1912; 1914; 1947.

Frank Cowperwood, the subject of Theodore Dreiser's "Trilogy of Desire," is a man whose obsession is power and whose motto is "I satisfy myself." Shrewd, ruthless, and yet sensitive to beauty, Cowperwood gets what he wants only to yearn in later life for the one thing his money cannot recapture: youth.

Early in his life Cowperwood realizes that only the strong succeed and that the masses are comprised of timid, ignorant fools hamstrung by a moral system created by hypocrites. Fascinated by his father's work as a bank teller, Cowperwood sees that money is the one thing that can bring power and control over others. This conviction is soon recognized by his first employers, and before long he is well versed in the nuances of the Philadelphia Stock Exchange. However, Cowperwood sees that those who control capital are in a position vastly superior to that of small-fry like himself who scramble around the floor of the exchange.

Cowperwood goes into the note-brokerage business in an attempt to rise in the system, and he also develops an interest in street-railway stocks. He now has a wife, Lillian, a house, two children, and his own seat on both the Philadelphia and New York exchanges. He invests in street railways with Edward Malia Butler, a powerful local figure who has an attractive, energetic daughter, AILEEN (BUTLER). Aileen catches Cowperwood's fancy, and the two begin a passionate affair. Butler eventually learns of this, however, and he develops a bitter, secret antagonism toward Cowperwood.

When a financial panic arises following the Chicago fire of 1871, Cowperwood, with several large debts, is in a precarious position. Butler arranges a citywide blockade of credit to Cowperwood, who fails as a result. Cowperwood is also found to have participated in an illegal scheme involving the exploitation of city funds, and he is jailed for over a year.

Frank and Aileen leave for Chicago, where Frank is determined to make a new start. Frank cultivates financial alliances with the aim of gaining control over the expanding city's promising gas franchises. He profits in this area, calling attention to his financial prowess but also antagonizing members of the city's older financial element. Cowperwood, true to his nature, is unintimidated, and so he begins working on a new street-railway scheme. He makes inroads with the help of cronies and corrupt politicians and also succeeds in satisfying himself in his personal life, despite the deterioration of his marriage. Frank becomes involved in numerous affairs, and Aileen moves to a mansion in New York where she sinks into a life of dissipation and drink.

A powerful figure in Chicago, Hosmer Hand, discovers that Cowperwood has been enjoying his wife's intimate attentions. He enlists other figures, already opposed to the upstart, in a plan to forestall Cowperwood's voracious acquisition of street-railway franchises. Cowperwood is defeated in the City Council in an attempt to get a fifty-year franchise.

Cowperwood then wistfully turns his attention to London and to Berenice Fleming, a woman some forty years younger with whom he has fallen in love. Now aging, he tries to gain control of the London underground system. He begins to make progress in forming connections with British financiers, but his efforts are only half-hearted. He now yearns more than ever for Berenice, beauty, art, and, above all, youth. His will to power has become mechanical; he already has all he wants. Before succeeding in his London scheme, Cowperwood dies of a kidney disease, and his massive estate is eroded in a welter of legal battles.

Crabb, Jack. *Little Big Man.* Thomas Berger. 1964.

In 1852, ten-year-old Jack Crabb, the narrator of this story, is adopted by a band of northern Cheyenne Indians. After living with them for six years, he is haunted by the fact that, as he says, "I am a white man and never forgot it." In his subsequent history, leading up to the Battle of the Little Big Horn in 1876, he is caught between the white and red man's worlds. Among Indians he gropes toward a spiritual meaning, and among whites he feels immersed in confusion.

Jack loses his white family when his father gives whiskey to some visiting Cheyenne who then drunkenly murder him. Jack and his older sister Caroline are forced to go to the Indian camp, but Caroline soon escapes, leaving him alone. OLD LODGE SKINS, the chief, adopts Jack, and all the Indians accept him—except Younger Bear, a powerful boy who bullies Jack because he is white and small of stature. They become enemies when Jack humiliates Younger Bear by surprising him with boxing techniques and bloodying the Indian's nose.

Jack becomes a warrior and is named Little Big Man when, at fifteen, he kills a Crow warrior and saves Younger Bear's life. A year later Jack is captured in a skirmish with the U.S. Cavalry and is sent back to Missouri where he is adopted by the Reverend Pendrake and his beautiful young wife. But Jack is distressed when he spies Mrs. Pendrake committing adultery, and he runs away.

Jack next joins the gold rush in Colorado. In Denver he becomes a prosperous storekeeper, marries, and has a son. His partners cheat him, however, and after his wife and child are abducted by the Cheyenne, Jack falls into despair and starts to drink. He meets Caroline again, reforms himself, and the two of them go into business as muleteers. After another fight with the Cheyenne, Jack decides to rejoin them. He takes an Indian wife and fathers a child. A year later Custer's Seventh Cavalry massacres his new family in a raid against the Cheyenne on Washita Creek, and Jack returns once more to white life. He becomes a card shark and befriends Wild Bill Hickok. In 1876, on a quest for gold in the Black Hills, Jack joins Custer's expedition against the Sioux. He witnesses the Last Stand of Wounded Knee and is its lone survivor, saved by Younger Bear in repayment of the old debt. In the final

scene, Old Lodge Skins takes Jack to the summit of a high mountain. The chief sings his death song, gives thanks to the "Everywhere Spirit," and beseeches It to guard the life of his only surviving son.

Crane, Helga. *Quicksand.* Nella Larsen. 1928.

The beautiful and restless Helga Crane travels from a southern college town to New York City, to Copenhagen, and finally to the South again in a fruitless quest to find a place where she can feel comfortable and achieve a true sense of identity.

As the novel opens, Helga sits in a room on the campus of Naxos, a black college in the South, where she is on the faculty. At first excited by the opportunity that a career at Naxos represented, after two years of teaching Helga has grown disenchanted with what she feels is a stifling environment. She resolves to leave Naxos, abandon her fiancé and fellow teacher James, and go to Chicago where she plans to borrow money from her uncle Peter to finance a new start in life.

When Helga meets with the principal, Dr. Anderson, to tender her resignation, he reawakens in her a desire for service that almost persuades her to stay. When Dr. Anderson tells her, however, that her dignity distinguishes her, dignity that he believes she inherited from a good family, Helga rankles. Angrily, she tells him that she was born in a Chicago slum of a white immigrant mother and a black gambler father who deserted them both.

The exchange with Dr. Anderson causes Helga to remember her childhood. When Helga was six, her mother had married a prosperous white businessman with children from a previous marriage. Her mother died when Helga was fifteen, and it was only with the assistance of Uncle Peter, her mother's brother, that she received a decent education.

Helga finally breaks her engagement to James and leaves for Chicago. Despite the help he gave her years ago, she is nervous about seeing Uncle Peter again. When she finally reaches his home, she is rebuffed by her uncle's new wife and leaves without the loan that she had been depending on.

After weeks of searching, Helga finds a job as a traveling companion and secretary for a woman who lectures to black women's clubs. They travel to New York City, and Helga feels welcome in Harlem. She attends parties with the black elite and makes friends with Anne Grey, a relative of her employer. She quickly becomes dissatisfied with her life, however; the parties and amusements seem frivolous. A chance meeting with Dr. Anderson convinces Helga of the emptiness of her existence. Just as she is despairing, she receives a letter from her uncle with a check for $5,000 and the advice that she visit her aunt Katrina in Copenhagen.

In Denmark, Helga finds a new sense of freedom. She becomes a popular party guest and attracts the attention of everyone around her, especially Axel Olsen, a painter. He becomes fascinated with her, but Helga soon tires of being regarded as an exotic creature. She turns down his offer of marriage and returns to New York where Anne is about to be married to Dr. Anderson.

In New York City, Helga feels her friendship with the newlywed Anne growing cold and gradually realizes that she is attracted to Dr. Anderson. After Helga and Dr. Anderson kiss at a party, she toys with the idea of pursuing an affair with him, but when he tells her later that he was drunk when he kissed her, she is crushed.

Weeks later, depressed and angry, Helga storms out of her apartment in a violent tantrum. She stumbles to a storefront church to find shelter and seems to undergo a religious conversion. In the church she meets the Reverend Mr. Pleasant Green, and after sleeping with him she decides to marry him and travel with him to Alabama.

Life as the wife of a minister in a poor town is to Helga as stifling as teaching at Naxos and as purposeless as socializing in Harlem. Her body weakened by the births of four children in rapid succession and her mind numbed by oppressive rural poverty, Helga dreams of escape. But her dreams are only that, for as the novel closes, she is about to give birth to her fifth child.

Crane, Ichabod. *The Legend of Sleepy Hollow.* Washington Irving. 1820.

Ichabod Crane, a lanky, avaricious schoolmaster, resides in the drowsy, dreamy glen of Sleepy Hollow on the majestic Hudson River. Sleepy Hollow is a town under the influence of ghost stories and superstitions, the most famous of which recounts the legend of a Hessian trooper in search of the head he lost in battle during the Revolutionary War.

Ichabod commands a bizarre presence in this town. He is exceedingly tall, with narrow shoulders and a small head but huge feet, ears, and nose. Yet his slender physique belies his voracious appetite: For the always-hungry Ichabod, the flora and fauna of Sleepy Hollow are so much raw material for a feast. Although he does not spare the rod with his schoolhouse charges, he nevertheless charms the local lasses with his odd mixture of awkward grace and wit. A spellbound fan of Cotton Mather's book on witchcraft, Ichabod often whiles away the days by swapping ghost stories with old Dutch wives.

Ichabod is smitten with plump, rosy-cheeked Katrina, the flirtatious eighteen-year-old daughter of farmer Baltus Van Tassel. He plans to woo the country coquette and head west with her. One evening the hopeful schoolmaster dresses to the nines, borrows the sorry old horse Gunpowder from his neighbor, and heads to a sumptuous banquet thrown by Van Tassel. Also in attendance is Brom Van Brunt, a burly, roistering blade with broad shoulders, curly hair, and an arrogant disposition. Nicknamed Brom

Bones, this frolicking good fellow rivals Ichabod for Katrina's affections.

The partygoers' attention soon turns to ghost stories. Brom Bones boasts of having almost beaten the Headless Horseman in a horse race, only to have the Hessian trooper disappear at the finish line. As the party breaks up, Katrina spurns Ichabod's latest amorous advances. Under the spell of unrequited love as well as the power of local myths, Ichabod heads home along the same path on which many of the ghostly episodes allegedly occurred. Whistling nervously, Ichabod hears an insistent stomping following him. A stranger, a headless horseman with a head resting on the pommel of his saddle, pursues Ichabod, hurls his head—actually a pumpkin—at the schoolmaster's skull, and flees into the darkness.

Ichabod fails to show up at his schoolhouse the next day, and the old wives of the town collectively conclude that he has been carried away by the Headless Horseman. But since he was no one's husband and owed no one money, he is quickly forgotten. Actually, Ichabod leaves Sleepy Hollow because he fears both the Goblin and further rejection from Katrina. He goes on to study law and becomes a journalist and politician, and eventually a court justice. Meanwhile, Brom Bones, now married to Katrina, laughs a bit too knowingly every time the story of Ichabod and the pumpkin is mentioned.

Cravat, Sabra Venable. *Cimarron.* Edna Ferber. 1930.

Sabra Venable is a pretty girl from a Wichita, Kansas, family with very rigid social standards. Anxious to escape her constricting family life, she marries YANCEY CRAVAT, a dashing young lawyer and newspaper publisher with a mysterious past. As she grows to womanhood, helping to tame the western town where she settles with Yancey, Sabra gains a sense of herself as a strong woman.

Sabra and Yancey have a son and then, against the wishes of Sabra's mother, leave for Osage, a town in the newly settled Oklahoma Territory. Sabra is thrilled to be leaving Wichita, but on the rough journey to her new home she is shocked and dismayed at the coarseness and lawlessness of the territory. Learning that her husband is well known to the uncultured people she meets along the way only adds to her discomfort.

Sabra begins to learn to run a household and care for her child. Realizing that she is not the "little fool" that her husband endearingly calls her, Sabra begins to see that men, and especially her husband, are often wrong-headed and irresolute. Whereas her husband dreams of building a new society in the new land, Sabra works to reproduce the values and rules of Wichita in Osage, Oklahoma.

Through the women's clubs she founds and the society pages she writes for her husband's newspaper, Sabra and the women of Osage slowly change the town from a lawless, dangerous outpost where every man wears a gun to a genteel town governed by the laws of middle-class aesthetics and propriety. When her restless husband leaves town, Sabra takes over the job of running the newspaper. She learns to write and to use the newspaper as a means of furthering her views on moral and social matters in Osage. Yancey returns after five years, only to disappear again almost immediately. His wandering and returning become commonplace, and Sabra resolves to accept his nomadism as part of his nature.

But Sabra refuses to accept her husband's and her son's arguments that the Indians who live in the territory are good people. She steadfastly believes that they are worthless and dirty, little better than animals. Her dogmatism causes her to break with her son Cim, now grown. Cim determines to make his home with the Indians; Yancey resumes his wandering; and Sabra finds herself alone.

Her alienation from her family forces Sabra to recognize her strength as a woman and as an individual. In time she becomes a U.S. senator. She espouses her husband's ideas about the strong women who helped settle America and eventually becomes an advocate for the rights of the Indians. When she encounters her dying husband after years of not seeing him, Sabra forgives him for leaving her so many times. She understands it was his dreaminess and wandering that made her become conscious of her own desires and talents.

Cravat, Yancey. *Cimarron.* Edna Ferber. 1930.

Yancey Cravat is a tall, handsome lawyer and newspaper publisher with a mysterious past who shows up in Wichita, Kansas, and wins the hand of SABRA VENABLE (CRAVAT), the daughter of a prosperous society family. Fired by a fierce desire to uphold truth and a system of justice, Yancey founds a newspaper in Osage, a town in the Oklahoma Territory. The paper's first story is an investigation into the murder of the town's first newspaperman. Yancey's idealism, his gunfighting ability, and his familiarity with the ways of the territory enable him to survive and establish a successful publication. In the course of his adventurous life, he becomes a popular symbol of the untamed but noble spirit of the American frontier and is nicknamed "Cimarron" after the Indian territory in Oklahoma he helped settle.

Yancey uses his newspaper to write editorials advocating the causes of the Indians, displaced and crowded on reservations; the cowboys, without jobs or purpose because their land has been fenced in by settlers; and the prostitutes, honest women who earned their living by providing comfort to lonely men. Sabra disagrees with his support of each of these groups. In fact, most of the townspeople disagree with Yancey's views although they respect him for his high values and dramatic style. He is often urged to run for public office but feels he could not be part of the very government and society that he now battles.

Yancey constantly resists his wife's efforts to gentrify the new territory and to recreate Wichita society in Osage. Incurably restless, he leaves Osage for long periods of time, usually with no explanation. Sabra manages the household and business while he is gone and uses the newspaper to further the causes he had so violently opposed.

After an absence of five years, Yancey returns to Osage just in time to defend a prostitute whom his wife was trying to have imprisoned. Soon after, he again disappears. His second return coincides with the discovery of oil on the Osage Indian reservation, and he supports the Indians in their new position of power and wealth.

Yancey disappears a third time, and after many years some people believe he may be dead. He appears on an oil field, however, and miraculously saves the lives of many people by catching a can of nitroglycerine that shoots up into the air. But he is mortally wounded in the attempt. His wife happens to be at the site of her husband's last heroic deed, and she comforts the dying man and forgives him for the times he abandoned his family.

Some time after Yancey's death, a statue is commissioned to show the spirit of the Oklahoma pioneer. The statue shows Yancey Cravat, the man who exemplified the spirit of the untamed Cimarron, leading an Indian.

Craven, Charles. *The Yemassee: A Romance of Carolina.* William Gilmore Simms. 1835.

Charles Craven, who assumes the alias of Captain Gabriel Harrison until the conclusion of this historical novel, is a cavalier of Charles Stuart II and the Governor and Lord Palatine of seventeenth-century Carolina. In anticipation of a rebellion on the part of the Yemassee and other neighboring Indian nations against the British colonists in the Atlantic coast frontier district known as Beaufort, Craven assumes his alias and goes to that region to mobilize the populace. A man of boundless energy, he also takes this opportunity to woo his future wife, Bess Matthews, the attractive and pure daughter of a stern old Puritan minister. A classic romantic hero, Craven wins both the war against the Yemassee and the favor of his beloved, who agrees to marry him and settle down in Charleston, the seat of government.

When Craven arrives in the Beaufort region, the colonists exhibit a marked inability to defend themselves. Lulled by years of peaceful coexistence with the Yemassee, many of the settlers are skeptical about the possibility of an Indian uprising. They refuse to heed Craven's exhortations to take refuge in the abandoned block house that had been built originally as a garrison station. Having combed the area and alerted everyone, Craven undertakes the task of spying on the Yemassee in order to anticipate their martial strategies. Stealing through the forest to the town of Pocota-ligo, the capital of the Yemassee nation, he hides behind a thicket on a small hill overlooking the altars of Battle-Manneyto, the Yemassee God of War. Gathered below are representatives of many Indian nations who are engaged in traditional rites of battle; also present is a group of pirates who have brought guns and ammunition from a rival Spanish settlement in St. Augustine.

As Craven surveys this intimidating scene, an Irish settler named Teddy Macnamara is dragged in by a hunting party that intends to torture him to death as an offering to Battle-Manneyto. He watches with courageous composure until the victim temporarily escapes from his torturers and flees, pursued by a band of warriors brandishing clubs, in the direction of Craven's hideout. Just as Macnamara reaches the tree behind which Craven is concealed, the Indians overtake the Irishman and beat him to death. Detected, Craven stabs a Seratee chief in self-defense and is immediately seized by a multitude of warriors. The prophet of the Yemassee nation, Enoree-Mattee, restrains them; he reminds them that their god Manneyto insists that only one English victim should be sacrificed before the nation sings the battle song, and he tells them that Craven must therefore be reserved for the postwar sacrifice. Craven is imprisoned in a small log cell with two Indian sentries and has nothing to do but contemplate the gruesome death that awaits him.

At least one Yemassee has compassion for Craven, whose noble countenance reminds her of her beloved dead son. This bereaved mother, the wife of Chief Sanutee, eventually recognizes Craven, despite his disguise, as a man she had once met in Charleston and who had been kind to her father. Using a traditional Indian method, she charms the guards to sleep and liberates Craven, who races back to the block house. On the way he joins a troop of armed colonists and assumes command over them. When they finally reach the block house, it is in flames; the settlers trapped inside are saved only through Craven's timely intervention. Craven then saves his beloved Bess from the dangerous grip of a Spanish pirate who has kidnapped her. Finally, having routed the Yemassee from Beaufort, he returns to a besieged Charleston and organizes troops that annihilate the Indians, whose insurrections had heretofore been successful. Having almost single-handedly saved all of Carolina, Craven divulges his true identity to an amazed Bess, who almost faints at the thought of marrying such a worthy gentleman and courtier.

Craven, Colin. *The Secret Garden.* Frances Hodgson Burnett. 1962.

Colin Craven, a young recluse, emerges from his lifelong invalidism when his new friend, MARY LENNOX, brings him into the private world of her walled-in garden. Colin's father, Archibald Craven, unable to forgive Colin when his lovely mother died after childbirth, travels frequently to forget his sorrows. Isolated in the gloomy Misselthwaite Manor, Colin remains a miserable little tyrant until Mary discovers him and he becomes determined to regain his health and joy in life.

When Mary's parents die in a cholera epidemic, she is brought from her home in India to the Yorkshire estate of her uncle, Mr. Craven. The children are kept apart from each other, and when Mary hears Colin crying in the night, her maid quickly supplies the excuse that it is only the wind "wuthering" around the house. One rainy day Mary decides to explore the mansion with its hundred locked rooms, and she finds the source of the crying: a pale, thin boy in a somber bedchamber.

Mary begins telling Colin of India, the garden, and of her friend, DICKON SOWERBY, a Yorkshire boy who charms the moor animals. It is the first time Colin has taken an interest in others, and he demands that Mary come to see him every day. Mary privately compares him to an Indian prince, a "young rajah," because of the way he rudely orders the servants around. The servants cannot understand the harmony between the two cousins and finally attribute it to their equally nasty tempers. When Colin throws one of his tantrums and insists that he will either die or be a hunchback like his father, Mary harshly informs him that he only says that to make people sorry for him. She later examines his back, and finding no hint of a lump, she convinces Colin to get out of bed and go into the garden.

Colin orders the head gardener to keep everyone away from a certain area of the grounds, with the explanation that because of his illness, he hates to be seen. Colin, Mary, and Dickon are therefore able to keep their walled garden a secret. The garden had been a favorite of Colin's mother and was locked up ten years before when she died. Colin enters the garden in a wheelchair. One day the surly old gardener, Ben Weatherstaff, discovers them; never having seen Colin before, Ben asks him how a cripple is able to come into the garden. Proudly and with great resolve, Colin stands up. Once he has found the strength to stand, he becomes determined to get well.

Each day the three children meet in the garden to tend the flowers and watch the progress of spring. Colin discovers a mysterious force he calls "magic" that enables him to walk a little further every day. Dickon's mother, Susan Sowerby, provides the children with eggs, potatoes, and fresh rolls, thus allowing Colin to refuse food in the house and keep his recovery a secret so that he can surprise his father.

After Mr. Craven returns from his trip, he strolls through the garden one day and hears children's voices. The next moment Colin bursts through the door of the garden, triumphant after having won a race with Mary. Craven does not even recognize his transformed child. After Colin tells his father the story of the garden, they return side by side to the mansion and its astonished occupants.

Crawford, Janie Mae. *Their Eyes Were Watching God.* Zora Neale Hurston. 1937.

As a wistful teenager, Janie Mae Crawford dreams of an ideal marriage that is as beautiful, mysterious, and exciting as the blossoming of a pear tree in early spring. She is therefore disappointed when her grandmother informs her that she is to be wed to Logan Killicks, an unappealing old farmer with a large plot of land. Janie resists but must eventually succumb to her grandmother's materialistic values and marry "Mist' Killicks." On Killicks's farm, Janie is forced to work long and hard, but she is depressed less by the physical labor than by being trapped in a loveless marriage. When a stylishly dressed JOE "JODY" STARKS promises her a happier life, Janie runs away from Killicks and the farm forever.

Jody marries Janie immediately and takes her to Eatonville, a newly formed all-black township. Ambitious and confident, he immediately buys land and begins building the town's first store, and the townspeople elect him their first mayor. But Janie is uncomfortable with the awe her husband receives from the townspeople and with her own role as the mayor's wife. Jody is jealous and possessive, and won't allow Janie to participate in the tale-telling sessions the villagers hold on the store's front porch. He keeps her working in the store and, knowing that men find her attractive, forces her to cover her beautiful long hair with a kerchief. Once again Janie finds herself trapped in an unhappy marriage.

After several years Janie resigns herself to a public life as the submissive wife of a rich and powerful man, and she resolves to keep private her existence as a lonely and unhappy woman. But when Jody insults her in front of some of the townspeople, she strikes back with a reference to his impotence. Jody is deeply humiliated. Soon his health begins to fail, and after a final confrontation with Janie, he dies. Janie upholds a public image as the grieving wife but inside feels joy at the thought of beginning a new, independent existence. She spends her time minding the store and discouraging the advances of the many suitors who seek her hand.

After some time spent enjoying her autonomy as a widow, Janie is surprised to find herself falling in love with one of her suitors. Several years her junior, VERGIBLE "TEA CAKE" WOODS is a fun-loving man who teaches Janie to fish and play checkers. Janie creates a scandal in town when she leaves Eatonville to marry the penniless young man. Together they move to "de Muck," as the swampy Florida Everglades are known, where Tea Cake picks vegetables with other itinerant workers. Hating to be separated from Tea Cake for even a day, Janie dons overalls and joins him the fields. They enjoy working side by side, and although they sometimes fight bitterly, their love for

each other endures and grows. The other workers are drawn to the happy couple, and the porch of their shack becomes the community gathering place when work is done.

The couple's happy life is shaken, however, when a hurricane hits the Everglades. The two are trapped in a house for a time and are then forced to make their way out into the flooded fields. In deep water Tea Cake saves Janie from a rabid dog and is bitten by the creature. As the flooding subsides, Tea Cake's wound heals, but he soon develops a serious fever. Desperate to save him, Janie leaves his side to procure medicine; when she returns, a delirious Tea Cake accuses her of infidelity. His fever raging, he aims a pistol at her. Knowing that she has no choice but to save herself, Janie shoots him in self-defense.

Acquitted of murder by a white judge and jury, Janie sadly returns to Eatonville, wearing her overalls instead of the fancy blue dress in which she had left. But although she misses Tea Cake, Janie feels at peace as she tells her story to Phoeby, for she knows that she has at last learned to live for herself. As her story ends, Janie settles, replete with happy memories of Tea Cake, into a new life.

Crawford, Sonny. *The Last Picture Show.* Larry McMurtry. 1966.

Together with his best friend Duane, Sonny Crawford, a naive sixteen-year-old, faces life in the dusty little Texas town of Thalia. In the early 1950s, this north-central Texas town is the scene of Sonny's coming of age. Instead of living at home, Sonny and Duane board at a rooming house. Duane works as a "roughneck" on a local oil drilling crew, and Sonny delivers butane to outlying farms and ranches. Their lives center around the poolhall run by Sam the Lion, who functions as a surrogate father for the boys, and Duane's hopeless pursuit of Jacy Farrow, the richest girl in Thalia.

The novel opens on the Saturday morning after football season ends, as Sonny waits for Duane to arrive at the poolhall so they can make arrangements for their Saturday night date. Once Duane arrives, the two have breakfast, decide who gets first dibs on the truck they share for necking purposes, and separate. That night Sonny breaks up with Charlene, an unattractive girl who often rebuffs his sexual advances.

For Sonny, however, the beginning of basketball season brings an unexpected twist to his life. One day Coach Popper, a fat, chauvinistic clod of a man, asks Sonny to drive his wife to Olney to see her doctor. The drive proves eventful when Ruth Popper, ignored and dominated by her husband, makes timid advances toward Sonny, who is unsure how to respond. Several weeks later when Mrs. Popper makes another, more aggressive move at a county-wide dance held at the Legion Hall, Sonny kisses her and makes plans to meet her at her home.

Although overwhelmed with guilt and fear during their

first rendezvous, the couple soon allows their friendship to develop into an affair. Sonny manages at least three visits per week to the Popper home during basketball practice. But as Sonny's relationship with Ruth blossoms, Duane's involvement with Jacy deteriorates into a one-sided concern.

After attending a nude swim party hosted by some Wichita Falls country club pals, Jacy decides that she prefers that crowd to Duane and makes plans to break up with him by the end of the school year. When Duane learns of the nude swim party, he decides to cure his depression by going with Sonny to Matamoros, Mexico. But the boys are completely disillusioned by their trip and return to Thalia after one night in Mexico with memories of overpriced pornography and pregnant prostitutes. On their return they learn that Sam the Lion has died and left his poolhall to Sonny and Billy, a retarded boy who liked to sweep.

Sonny takes up residence over the poolhall to take care of Billy as Sam had done, but two weeks later he joins his fellow seniors on a trip to San Francisco. In San Francisco, Jacy allows Duane to take her virginity. Their relationship is never stable, however, and at the end of the school year, Jacy does break up with him. Devastated, Duane decides to go to Midland to work as a roughneck. After quitting his delivery job, Sonny has more time to spend with Ruth, and his summer progresses nicely until Jacy, bored while waiting for the college semester to begin, decides to date him.

Jacy's youthful beauty soon defeats any hold Ruth might have on him, and Sonny deserts the older woman. While the two old friends are out drinking one Saturday night, Duane accuses Sonny of moving in on his girlfriend. The two get into a fight that results in a serious eye injury for Sonny. Although the fight mends their friendship, Sonny loses most of the sight in his eye and must wear a patch.

Flattered by being at the center of the fight and pleased at the romance of being involved with a one-eyed man, Jacy convinces Sonny that they should get married, and the two make plans to elope. Aware that her parents will come after her and impede the marriage, Jacy leaves a detailed note about their plans. The couple manages to get married before the Farrows overtake them, and then Jacy and her father head back to Thalia in one car, while Sonny and her mother drive Jacy's car back. Tired and vaguely disappointed, Sonny is surprised when Mrs. Farrow seduces him.

The coming of fall brings little to Sonny's life. Jacy leaves for Dallas to await the opening of school. The movie theater that Sam the Lion had owned goes bankrupt. Sonny makes a futile attempt to explain to Billy that there will be no more picture shows. One morning Billy gets killed when he puts on two of Sonny's patches and sweeps his way down the street into the path of a cattle truck.

Billy's death stuns and frightens Sonny so badly that he seeks refuge with Ruth, whom he has not had the courage to face since their breakup. Ruth delivers a ferocious tirade, reminding Sonny of his ruthless abandonment and callous disregard. Only after her barrage, when Sonny grabs her hand, does Ruth's anger subside. As the novel ends, she mutters words of comfort to Sonny.

Cree, Lucius. *The Velvet Horn.* Andrew Lytle. 1957.
Lucius Cree is the son of Julia Cropleigh and her cousin Joe Cree, and he lives in an unnamed state in the rural South after the Civil War. When Lucius's father, Joe Cree, is killed by a falling tree during a lumbering operation, he leaves behind an unexpected, mysterious legacy that Lucius must solve in order to reach adulthood.

Lucius and his uncle, Jack Cropleigh, go up to the Peaks of Laurel, the hills above the Cree farm, to "witch" a well (i.e., to locate hidden springs by running a forked stick along the ground). On the peaks they run into trouble when Othel Rutter, a disturbed young man, tries to shoot them to keep them from digging the well. He is protecting the land owned by the richest man in town, Pete Legrand.

Lucius and Jack also meet up with the rest of the Rutter clan, including the lithe young Ada Belle. Although the class difference between them makes a formal statement impossible, Lucius and Ada Belle begin a relationship.

Sol Leatherbury, the boss of the timbermen, arrives on the peak to give Lucius the news of his father's death. On the return trip to the Cree farm, Lucius ponders the mystery of how his father, an expert timberman, could have let a tree fall on him. He feels that he has failed his father by going away with Uncle Jack to witch the well. Lucius knew that the farm and timber business were deeply in debt to his aunt Amelie, and he imagines that with his help his father would have kept on trying.

At the funeral Pete Legrand offers to help Lucius hold on to the farm and the timber business by covering his loans to Amelie. Lucius is mystified by this offer of help from a man who everyone assumes is solely interested in profit. Legrand insists that he owes a debt of gratitude to Lucius's dead father for treating him with respect after the war.

Lucius becomes the head of the timber operation. He eventually earns the workers' respect by firing men, hired by Legrand, who are not hardworking or capable. His debt to Legrand continues to nag at him. When he visits his mother at the farm, he finds the man a frequent visitor and his mother no longer in mourning. Lucius finally decides to ask for an extension from Aunt Amelie so that he can remove the farm from the influence of Legrand.

He rushes to town to meet his aunt and is shocked when she offers him the unencumbered deed to all the timber land that his father had mortgaged. She explains that Joe Cree believed himself responsible for her husband Duncan's death during the war, and so mortgaged away his future in order to repay his debt to her. Lucius returns exultant to the farm but is more confused than ever about the true reasons for his father's apparent suicide.

In the meantime, Lucius's mother has summoned Legrand. She is terrified that Amelie will tell Lucius that Legrand is his father: He and Julia had spent one youthful night together before she married her cousin Joe. When Legrand tries to convince her to tell the boy the truth, Julia turns on him with an even deeper and more awful secret, known to no one but the dead Joe Cree: Legrand is not the father of Lucius. It was her own brother Duncan who, in a fit of jealous rage at losing his beloved sister to Cousin Joe, forced himself on her. This is the secret that drove Joe Cree to throw himself beneath a falling tree.

Instead of revealing the truth, Legrand tells Lucius that he is his father. For Lucius the story serves as an explanation for Joe Cree's death. He recoils and heads up to the peak to find comfort from Ada Belle. When he discovers that her mother is about to marry her off to another man, he realizes that his love for her goes beyond physical passion. She tells him that she is pregnant with their child; that night they run away to the next county to marry.

After their marriage, the young people go to Uncle Jack for help. He councils that acceptance on both sides will be hard won; Lucius is now a bastard and Ada Belle an outcast from her family. Jack assembles the two groups at the Cree farm. When Lucius begins to speak, Othel Rutter, Ada Belle's disturbed brother, misunderstands his intention and thinks he is refusing to marry Ada Belle. He raises his gun and, in the ensuing melee, shoots and kills Jack Cropleigh. Lucius is left to make peace with his mother, Legrand, and his new wife's family. For his fortune he'll work the timber—like the man he had always thought of as his father, Joe Cree.

Cresswell, Mary Taylor. *The Quest of the Silver Fleece.* W. E. B. Du Bois. 1911.

New England–born Mary Taylor Cresswell is a central character through whom the wealthy southern cotton planters and northern entrepreneurs of Wall Street come together in the southern county of Tooms. After being educated at Wellesley, Mary is sent by her brother John ostensibly to teach in Miss Sarah Smith's School for black children, but in actuality to gather information about the cotton industry.

Although she approves of black education in the abstract, Mary is disappointed by the reality of teaching black children in the swamps of Alabama. She feels particularly plagued by ZORA, the daughter of the local conjure woman. The black girl's independent demeanor, her innocence, and her absolute honesty often leave the New Englander nonplussed. Zora's relationship with Bles Alwyn, a promising young male student at the school, seems ill-advised to Mary. Despite her displeasure with

the school, Mary manages to send her brother an account of Tooms that entices him to make a trip south.

John's communication with the Cresswells, the wealthiest cotton-growing family in the county, enables Mary to enter a social arena more to her liking. Because of John's visit, Mary meets Harry Cresswell, son of Colonel Cresswell. The subsequent business dealings between the Cresswells and the Taylors allow the northerner and his business associates to corner the cotton market while returning the southerners to their former state of wealth. By the following Easter the Taylor siblings marry Harry and Helen, the Cresswell son and daughter, in a double wedding.

Two years later, Mary finds herself in Washington, D.C., with her husband, the congressman. Poised to direct her spouse's political career, Mary finds her New England work ethic thwarted by Harry's pursuit of the life of leisure he had led on his father's plantation. Desiring meaningful activity, she joins the Civic Club and begins to work diligently for the passage of a child-labor law, without knowing that it directly opposes her husband's business dealings in Tooms. When her husband learns of her activities, he demands that she cease her involvement in the Civic Club; having learned that she is pregnant, Mary is only too willing to withdraw her services.

The Cresswells' baby is born "less than dead," and after a six-month illness Mary returns to her Washington home. Having lost her youthful beauty, she decides to work for her husband's appointment as ambassador to France. Her efforts are defeated, however, when she is schooled by the politically savvy Mrs. Vanderpool, who has designs on the position for her own husband. When Mary masterminds an art show displaying the artwork of southerners, Mrs. Vanderpool tricks her into accepting the work of a black woman, who wins the first prize and refuses to withdraw from the competition at Mary's request. With his wife accused of trying to incite the "Negro question," Cresswell has no chance of attaining the ambassadorship.

The same night that Mary learns of Mrs. Vanderpool's trickery, she follows her husband to the Willard Hotel and discovers him drinking, gambling, and fraternizing with socially unacceptable women; she promptly faints. When she awakens, her husband informs her that they will no longer reside together and that he is sending her to his father in Tooms.

When Mary arrives in Tooms, she learns that much has changed. Political control has shifted: white mill workers, imported from the North, wield the political clout that the black sharecroppers of the South have always been prevented from acquiring. Zora has turned her swamp into a community area complete with a hospital, nursery school, and farmland that is tilled by local blacks who have become tenants.

Mary watches as her father-in-law appeals to the prejudices of the new power brokers and sets off a wave of racial violence that results in the lynchings of two blacks. Three months later, the now guilt-ridden Colonel reveals the contents of his will. In addition to bequeathing the bulk of his money and his plantation to Miss Smith's School, he leaves Mary a substantial sum in return for her having put up with his son Harry. With this inheritance, Mary decides to pay the mortgage on the school and then flees abroad so as never to return to Harry or America.

Crewe, Sara. *A Little Princess.* Frances Hodgson Burnett. 1905.

As the book begins, the imaginative, sweet-natured heroine, Sara Crewe, is being driven in a hansom through the foggy streets of Victorian London with her doting father, Captain Ralph Crewe. Captain Crewe is taking her from their home in India to a boarding school run by the cold-hearted and worldly headmistress, Miss Minchin, and her foolish sister, Miss Amelia. Before returning to service in India, Sara's father installs her in the seminary as a special parlor boarder with her own French maid and buys a wardrobe fit for a princess both for the child and for her new doll, Emily.

Although flattered and pampered by all concerned during the next few years, Sara is a generous and clever child who manages to remain unspoiled by her treatment. A gifted storyteller, she is fond of entertaining her fellow pupils with games of make-believe; in particular she befriends the less fortunate and least popular of the school's society. As a result, she is soon being referred to as Princess Sara by friends and enemies alike.

On her eleventh birthday, Sara's life changes forever. She is informed that her father has died of brain fever, after having allowed an old school friend to invest and subsequently lose all of his money in a scheme involving diamond mines. The ruthless Miss Minchin, who had always carried a grudge against Sara because of her cleverness, turns the now-penniless orphan into the school drudge and requires that Sara earn her room and board by tutoring the younger students, running errands, and helping the abusive cook and understaff of the seminary. Sara, who becomes more gaunt and shabby with each passing day, is eschewed by her former classmates, with the exception of the temperamental young Lottie and the kindly but slow-witted Ermengarde. She is made to live in the attic next to the scullery maid, Becky, who becomes a friend and companion during this adversity.

Sara sustains herself through the hardest times by pretending she is really a princess disguised in rags, by befriending the resident rat, Melchisedec, and by taking a spectator's interest in the doings of an ailing gentleman who moves in next door. One evening, after having been sent out on errands all day in the foulest weather and deprived of supper due to the cook's spiteful caprice, Sara is caught by Miss Minchin while hosting a small party in her attic with Ermengarde and Becky. Severely disciplined

by the headmistress, she falls asleep cold and hungry, with the knowledge that she will receive no food at all the following day. She awakes in the middle of the night to find the attic adorned with comfortable furniture, beautiful objects, and a hot meal on a small table in front of a warming fire in the grate.

Sara is convinced that it is "Magic" itself that has come to her aid. What she does not yet know is that the invalid next door is her benefactor. The gentleman, whose name is Mr. Carrisford, is in reality Captain Crewe's old friend. Distraught by his inability to locate Crewe's little daughter and return to her the fortune that had not in fact been lost in the diamond mines, Carrisford has taken pity on the waif who lives next door and never imagines that she is the child he seeks.

Sara greatly exasperates Miss Minchin and puzzles the rest of the seminary during the next few weeks by looking increasingly contented and well fed: Day after day the "Magic" has been providing her with more comforts and luxuries. One evening Sara finds Mr. Carrisford's pet monkey scratching at the window of her attic. When she returns the animal to the man the next morning, he amuses himself by asking her about her life, thereby discovering her true identity. Despite the efforts of the discomfited Miss Minchin to convince the young heiress to return to the seminary, Sara remains with her new guardian, who thereafter takes great pleasure in treating her like a little princess.

Croft, Sergeant Sam. *The Naked and the Dead.* Norman Mailer. 1948.

Sam Croft is the staff sergeant of a reconnaissance platoon taking part in an army invasion of the fictional Japanese island of Anopopei during World War II. Croft's limitless desire for control of himself, his men, and his environment is often expressed in brutal and perverse behavior. Brought up on ranching, hunting, and corralling on the dusty Texan plains, he knows no laws but his own. His only ideal is his zeal for mastery, which manifests itself in the blind assertion of his will.

Restless when out of combat, Croft releases his tension by bullying the soldiers in his platoon, whose anxiety, fear, and exhaustion disgust him. Despite the fear he experiences for a moment in the foxhole when the Japanese soldiers come charging across the river, he revels in combat. The combination of conquering his own fear and killing the enemy enlarges his ego and satisfies his hunger for power. Any measure of compassion he may feel must be squashed before it can result in an act. When he leaves the outpost with Red Valsen, a Montana miner turned soldier, and Gallagher, a bigoted Irishman from Boston, to pick up rations and the men happen upon some resting Japanese soldiers, Croft indulges in gratuitous play with the only one who survives their attack. After having relaxed the Japanese prisoner with Gallagher's chocolate and cigarettes, Croft elicits a smile and tears of joy from his prey and then shoots him in the forehead.

Croft accepts the fear and hatred of the men in his platoon. Valsen rebels against Croft's amoral, radical totalitarianism with an impotent defiance. Both men fiercely guard themselves from human relationships, but whereas Valsen lives out a kind of passive nihilism, Croft actively seeks to conquer his social and natural environment. When LIEUTENANT ROBERT HEARN is unexpectedly assigned to his platoon, Croft is furious, knowing that the discipline and command of the platoon that he has built up over the months will go to pot under the inexperienced officer. Hearn's attempts to befriend his subordinates irritate Croft's sense of military ethics. The only man on the platoon Croft likes is Julio Martinez, a small Mexican sergeant adept at scouting, whom Croft affectionately calls "Japbait." In his turn, Martinez is unquestioningly loyal to Croft. At a crucial stage in the platoon's advance beyond Japanese commander Toyaku's front line, Martinez is sent out to scout the mountain pass for Japanese. Croft asks him not to tell Hearn that he discovered two encampments and that the Japanese will be expecting them because Martinez was forced to kill one of the guards.

For Croft, Mount Anaka, the highest peak on Anopopei, represents everything he must know and conquer. It is a measure of his own immortality, and he resolves to climb it whether it becomes necessary for the campaign or not. The men are morally and physically fatigued and in no way prepared for the perilous cliffs. They are clearly ready to rebel. When Roth, one of the newer and weakest soldiers, finds an injured bird, Croft reacts to the men's show of compassion by crushing it in his bare hands. At that moment the company, led by Valsen, is on the verge of a revolt against Croft and his despotic command when Hearn interferes to prevent a showdown. Croft is soon free to pursue his insane quest because Hearn, who had wanted to turn back, is shot by the Japanese as he leads them through what Martinez had said was unguarded terrain.

While making his way up the mountain, Croft steps on a nest of hornets that pursue him and the remaining men like an avalanche of fire. As the platoon turns and flees back down the mountain, Croft thinks, in "a last fragment of his ambition," of regrouping them at the bottom. However, he knows that the exhausted men will not be able to attempt the climb again. Afterward, he experiences a moment of relief; and as the novel draws to a close, the reader learns that "for that afternoon at least," Croft "was rested by the unadmitted knowledge that he had found a limit to his hunger."

Cross, Damon. *The Outsider*. Richard Wright. 1953.

Damon Cross is beset by difficulties resulting from a broken marriage as well as from his affair with a young girl who has become pregnant. A subway accident initially offers him the chance to run away from his problems, but as the novel progresses it becomes clear that changed circumstances and a new identity can do nothing to temper the violence with which he lives.

Although Cross and Gladys had been happily married for a time, the rapid arrival of three sons and mounting financial pressures soon lead Cross to conspire irrationally against his wife. Repeatedly and with no explanation he begins to strike her violently after he arrives home, until she finally throws him out. Meanwhile, Cross's mother chronically details his inadequacies. Cross seeks solace in an extramarital affair with a younger woman, Dot, until he finds out that she is only sixteen.

Knowing that he will be presumed dead from the subway accident, Cross decides to leave Chicago. He takes with him the money he had borrowed to forestall Gladys, who plans to take legal action against him. But before leaving, he spends some time in a flophouse, which allows him the opportunity to witness his own funeral; while there, however, he kills a coworker in order to prevent being exposed as a survivor, not the victim, of the subway accident.

Fleeing the murder, Cross takes a train to New York. While still on the train, he encounters a porter, Bob Hunter, and a New York district attorney, Ely Houston. In conversation with these men he uses the name Addison Jordan. After his arrival in New York, however, he painstakingly researches a new identity, Lionel Lane, and burns the draft board building to prevent his ruse from being discovered. Despite frequent brushes with racism, Cross manages to set himself up in New York, where he befriends Bob and his wife Sarah. As it turns out, Bob is a member of the Communist Party and an illegal alien who had fled his homeland in order to avoid imprisonment for Party activities.

It is at the Hunters' apartment that a skeptical Cross meets Gil and Eva Blount, a white couple from Greenwich Village who are also involved with the Party. Gil proposes that Cross move in with them in order to frustrate their racist landlord. Within a matter of days, a violent fight erupts between Gil and the landlord, and Cross, who has sexual if not romantic designs on Eva, takes advantage of the fight to kill both men. The investigation that follows brings Ely Houston and Party officials to the scene. One of the officials, Jack Hilton, realizes that Cross had in fact killed the combatants and plans to use the information to force Cross into an allegiance to the Party. Cross figures out that Jack knows of his guilt, and he kills him, too.

After the third murder is discovered, the police and Party officials question Cross, but he steadfastly refuses to give in to their pressures. Ely Houston eventually realizes that Cross is guilty of the murders, but he lacks concrete proof. He does manage to bring Gladys and her boys from Chicago to identify Cross, and he informs Cross that his mother died of shock upon hearing that her son was still living. When Eva learns of Cross's duplicity, she feels deeply shocked and betrayed, and jumps out of an apartment window to her death. The novel closes with the murder of Cross by the Party members: They did not know how else to stop him.

Cross, Selena. *Peyton Place.* Grace Metalious. 1956.

Selena Cross is a strong-willed, beautiful, and determined woman in this novel of small-town intrigue. The daughter of an itinerant woodsman who is more often drunk than not, Selena fights against despair and self-pity, swearing to escape the life that has left her mother an abused drudge.

Practical and mature beyond her years, Selena accepts pity from no one. She, her younger brother Joey, and her mother Nellie live with her abusive and alcoholic stepfather Lucas in one of the shacks that line the edge of Peyton Place. An outcast because of her family's poverty, Selena is best friends with ALLISON MACKENZIE, the sensitive, idealistic daughter of Constance Mackenzie, whom Selena idolizes because of her beauty, poise, and independence.

As her eighth-grade year passes, Selena begins to work her way toward the life-style for which she yearns. She acquires an after-school job in Constance's Thrifty Apparel Shoppe and begins to go steady with Ted Carter, whom she plans to marry after high school. Darkly beautiful and sultry, Selena is physically mature, and she is constantly threatened by her stepfather's sexual advances.

Two years later Selena finds herself pregnant by her stepfather. Although she loves Ted and knows that he loves her, she knows the price that girls who "get into trouble" must pay, and she is unwilling to hurt him. She goes to Doc Swain and asks for his help. At first he refuses to abort the child, but when he learns that Lucas is the father, he secretly performs the operation. He also forces Lucas to sign a document admitting his guilt and then orders him to leave Peyton Place, never to return.

The years following Lucas's departure are eventful. Nellie, consumed by her knowledge of Selena's abortion and Lucas's culpability, hangs herself. Selena's older stepbrother Paul returns to Peyton Place with his wife and makes a home for the teenage Selena and Joey. By the time Selena graduates from high school, a house with indoor plumbing and a fireplace has replaced the shack once occupied by the Cross family. Now alone, Selena lives happily with Joey while she and Ted prepare for their future. However, Lucas, who has joined the Navy, returns to threaten this utopian existence and attempts to molest Selena. Determined not to become pregnant by him again, she bludgeons him to death and with Joey's help buries the body in the sheep pen.

When Lucas's murder is discovered later that spring, Selena is put on trial. Although she admits to killing Lucas, Selena offers no other statement. Her silence is the debt she is willing to pay to Doc Swain for the illegal abortion

he performed years ago. Defended by Peter Drake, a young lawyer new to Peyton Place, Selena must face her trial without Ted, who abandons her.

Selena's trial lasts only a day. After several days of agonizing soul-searching, Doc Swain decides that only he can help the young woman. After he reveals Lucas's incest, Selena's pregnancy, and the subsequent abortion, the court rules Lucas's death a justifiable homicide and finds Selena not guilty.

Selena returns to the Thrifty Apparel Shoppe. As the novel draws to an end, she is observed carrying on friendly conversations with the lawyer Peter Drake, and the busybodies of Peyton Place foresee a wedding.

Croy, Kate. *The Wings of the Dove.* Henry James. 1902.

Kate Croy, a twenty-five-year-old London socialite, is implicated in the death of MILDRED "MILLY" THEALE, her intimate friend. Although Kate is a thoughtful and perceptive woman, her actions are often motivated by ambition and greed. Kate's grotesque betrayal of Milly is the result of her scheme, with the help of her lover MERTON DENSHER, to inherit a portion of Milly's enormous fortune.

At the opening of the novel, Kate chooses to leave her imperfect and unglamorous family to live with Mrs. Maud Lowder, her more favorably situated aunt. When Kate's mother dies, the Croys' already disintegrating family structure collapses completely. Kate's sister Marian made the shameful blunder of marrying a clergyman who later died, leaving her with several small children and very little money. Lionel Croy, Kate's father, committed a terrible, unnamed crime when she was a child and since then has lived in exile and relative poverty. Upon her mother's death, Aunt Maud gives Kate an ultimatum: She will take her in and admit her to the elite circle of London's Lancaster Gate, but Kate must never see or communicate with her father, whose unspeakable crime Maud cannot forgive. During a brief visit with Lionel Croy, Kate offers to take his side against Aunt Maud, but he advises her to accept the proposal.

Kate sacrifices more than her father when she agrees to ally herself with Maud Lowder. Aunt Maud quickly assumes responsibility for Kate's future and chooses Lord Mark, a colorless English nobleman, as a suitor for her. Inconveniently, Kate falls in love with Merton Densher, a handsome journalist who matches her in intelligence, unconventionality, and sophistication. Aunt Maud firmly opposes Densher's suit because of his poverty. Densher, who fails to see the advantage of enslavement to Aunt Maud, encourages Kate to liberate herself. She refuses, but they are nevertheless secretly engaged before Densher leaves London to complete a journalistic assignment in America.

During Densher's absence an eccentric American heiress, Milly Theale, arrives at Lancaster Gate with her companion, SUSAN SHEPHERD STRINGHAM. Kate, along with London society in general, is thoroughly enchanted by

Milly, who possesses the compelling innocence and gentle beauty of a dove. Milly singles Kate out for friendship and tells her of the astonishing series of tragic illnesses in her family that have left Milly completely alone. Meanwhile, Kate has been exchanging letters with Densher in America and learns that he had met Milly in New York before her departure for Europe.

When it emerges that Milly is stricken with a fatal disease, Kate becomes a conspirator, along with Aunt Maud, Susan Stringham, and Densher, to entice Milly into a romance—perhaps even a marriage—with Densher. The result would be, they assume, that Milly would leave her immense fortune to him, enabling him to marry Kate. Their plot gains momentum when Milly's illness worsens and the entire party moves from London to Venice, where Milly has rented a palace. When she and her aunt return to London, Kate demands that Densher remain in Venice to court Milly. Densher agrees on the condition that Kate "come to him" as proof of her commitment, and Kate does so.

The flaw in their scheme turns out to be the apparently harmless Lord Mark who, having proposed on separate occasions to Milly and Kate and been rejected by both women, goes to Venice with the purpose of telling Milly that Kate and Densher are engaged. When Densher fails to deny Lord Mark's assertion, Milly becomes severely ill and dies. After Densher returns to London, Kate gradually realizes that Densher had fallen in love with Milly. Her memory, she tells him, is his love; he can have no other, and so a marriage between them is impossible. Milly does will her fortune to Densher, leaving him free to marry Kate, but the novel closes with Kate's ambiguous and unpromising assertion that they will never be together as they were.

Crunch, Abbie. *The Narrows.* Ann Petry. 1953.

Abbie Crunch occupies the unenviable position of a black woman forced to conform to notions of aristocratic gentility while living in the black section of Monmouth, Connecticut, in the early 1950s. While Abbie was married to the Major, her life was happy and tranquil; she was content to absorb his world view unquestioningly, and seldom if ever asserted herself. After his sudden death following a stroke, Abbie's world is turned upside down. In her grief she completely forgets about her son, LINCOLN "LINK" WILLIAMS, whom she and the Major had adopted. It isn't until three months later that Abbie's closest friend, FRANCES K. "F.K." JACKSON, is able to bring Abbie back to reality, whereupon the grief-stricken widow resumes as best she can the raising of her son. Abbie requires a good deal of help, however, most of which is supplied by the steadfast F.K.

The other major force in her son's life, the saloon owner Bill Hod, is a source of great discomfort for Abbie. His associations with illegal businesses, drinking, card playing,

and prostitution lead her to try to keep her son away from him. But since Link spent the three months after the Major's death with Bill Hod, the older man remains a powerful force in the boy's life. Finally, with F.K.'s kindly intervention, Abbie agrees to let Link work for him. This situation continues even after Link graduates from college and returns from his stint in the Navy. Despite her misgivings, Abbie mostly keeps her opinions about Bill Hod to herself, although Link knows very well how she feels.

After the Major's death, Abbie began renting her upstairs apartment to the courtly Malcolm Powther, a butler, and his family. She begins to spend a great deal of time with J.C., one of the Powther children. It is at J.C.'s prompting that Abbie discovers Link in bed with a white woman, Camilo Sheffield. In a fury Abbie throws the woman out of her house, and Link follows after her.

Link, consumed with anger at Abbie, remains apart from her and spends most of his time with Bill Hod and his cronies. When Link eventually breaks off the relationship, Camilo has him arrested for attempted rape, and shortly thereafter he is murdered by her husband.

Once again F.K. comes to Abbie's aid, offering solace and seeing to Link's funeral arrangements. As the novel ends, F.K. proposes that the two live together since they have lost everything else. Despite her love for her best friend, Abbie is not yet ready for such a move. While it is clear that the two women will remain close, Abbie has also realized her feelings of tenderness toward J. C. Powther. In order to alleviate her loneliness and sorrow, she seems to take on the role of grandmother to the young boy.

Cudlipp, Ernest. *Men and Brethren.* James Gould Cozzens. 1936.

Ernest Cudlipp is an Episcopal minister in the parish of the Holy Innocents, New York City. He presides over an eccentric parish that includes an adulterous Park Avenue wife needing an abortion and an addle-brained missionary who has returned from years in Alaska to take on an assistantship in an urban setting. On the verge of poverty and ecclesiastical censure, Cudlipp manages nevertheless to help everyone who crosses his path in the two days that comprise the novel's events.

Geraldine Binney, a frustrated young wife, carries sleeping pills in her purse after she learns that she is pregnant with her lover's child. Ever resourceful and unmoved by the usual Episcopalian notion of the sacredness of fetal life, Cudlipp arranges an abortion to prevent her suicide. The same day, Alice Breen, the wife of his friend Lee, hints at divorce and flirts with Cudlipp over dinner. Cudlipp blankly reiterates his celibacy to Alice and privately reviews the motives for his own misogyny. Doctor Lamb, the vicar, also shows up in Ernest's parlor, along with Wilber Quinn, the socialist-youth assistant priest, and Mr. Johnston, the chapel's organist. The group sings hymns at the piano into the early morning, while Ernest takes calls from Carl Willever, a homosexual who has been asked abruptly to leave the Holy Order of the Trinity, and Lulu Merrick, an alcoholic idling in a New Jersey boarding-house, who appears at the chapel demanding a new life. Cudlipp sends them all to sleep in various rooms of the vicarage.

Complaining all the while about the burden of extra guests, Lily, Cudlipp's irascible housekeeper, brings cold coffee and rolls the next morning. Well before noon Ernest learns that Lulu leaped off the ferry to New Jersey and died. In the meantime, Geraldine's abortion is successful, and Carl Willever remains unrepentant. Episcopalianism, Carl sneers, is much less potent than Roman Catholicism. At lunch Alice tells Cudlipp that he is being used by this crowd of needy people, but Cudlipp insists that he can dismiss them at will. Exhausted by all these events, he takes a moment to read Mr. Johnston's proposed sermon on the miracle of the draft of fishes, a particularly hilarious piece of writing by a man who has lived among Eskimos for twenty-five years and who approaches theology with the thick skin of a whaler. Heartened by Johnston's sincerity, Cudlipp is finally able to conclude that "the hungry shall be filled."

Culver, Jack. *The Long March.* William Styron. 1952.

Jack Culver, a young lawyer from New York City, has been called away from his family to a military base in the South at the beginning of the Korean War. A veteran of World War II and now a lieutenant in the Marine Reserves, Culver never thought he would be so close to active duty again. During a forced march around the camp, he ponders the absurdity of military life.

The novel opens in the aftermath of an accident. During a practice session at the base, two old mortar shells have misfired and hit the mess hall, killing eight young men and wounding many others. Mangled bodies lie among the wreckage, food, and metal dining utensils. Culver witnesses this horrific scene, and the carnage sickens him. He retires to his bunk and thinks about his wife, his young daughter, and their pleasant life in Greenwich Village. He would like them to move closer to him, but accommodations in the nearby town are inadequate.

Colonel Templeton, a mysterious and terse man, commands the base. When he hears about the disaster, he shows no emotion. Instead, he simply procures an extra doctor and chaplain for the survivors. Templeton is the opposite of Captain Mannix, a passionate and outspoken soldier. Like Culver, Mannix is a reserve who never expected to be back in uniform, but unlike Culver, Mannix often expresses his contempt for the Marines by challenging Templeton's authority.

The night before the accident Templeton had announced a mandatory thirty-six-mile overnight march through the swamps surrounding the base. When the ac-

cident occurs, he makes clear to his subordinates that the march will go on as planned. Mannix points out that the men of his company are largely reserves and should not be subjected to such a grueling hike without gradual conditioning. Templeton counters that there should be no distinction between a regular Marine and a reserve; all must be prepared to meet the aggressor in combat. Culver, a witness to this argument, likens Templeton's quiet rage to that of a shackled slave.

The march begins promptly after sundown. Mannix, aggravated by a nail lodged in his boot, barks unceasingly at his men, promising extra duties to anyone who drops out of the hike. This annoys Culver, but he knows that he and Mannix are really troubled by the same thing: the absurdity of what they are doing. At the same time they have partly internalized the Marines mentality and would rather do anything than not finish the march.

At first the hike goes along at a rapid pace. During the breaks, Culver sees that Mannix's foot wound is getting worse. Templeton also notices, and he offers Mannix a ride back to the base. The offer infuriates Mannix, and he refuses. By the middle of the night most of the men have dropped out. When a truck passes by to relieve the Headquarters and Service Company, Mannix makes a wild attempt to prevent his men from dropping out. At this point Templeton orders Mannix to desist, and he goes berserk. He curses Templeton. Templeton responds by reaching for his pistol and telling Mannix that, upon completion of the march, he will be court-martialed for gross insubordination and then sent to Korea.

Culver and Mannix manage to finish the march, stumbling into camp around noon. At the end of the novel they are both recuperating in their quarters. Culver lies on his cot, weary of the senseless pain inflicted the previous day and saddened that Mannix will be thrown into another war.

Cummings, Edward Estlin. *The Enormous Room.* e. e. cummings. 1922.

Edward Estlin Cummings works in a volunteer ambulance corps in France at the beginning of World War I. He spends time with the Frenchmen in his unit, although he and his close friend, B., are often censured by the American commander of their company for spending so much time with the "dirty French." When French officials arrest B. for writing letters found treasonous by the censor, the commander tells them that Cummings, as B.'s best friend, was probably involved in the crime.

When Cummings is taken into custody, he impresses his interrogators with his command of the French language and his desire to become better acquainted with French people and culture. His professions of loyalty to France assure his examiners that he is not a traitor like his friend. Although he realizes that he will be spared the fate of his friend if he says that he hates the Germans, Cummings refuses to respond with a straightforward "yes." The inquisitors therefore regretfully tell him that he cannot go free.

Finding out that Cummings is an American, some of the residents of the prison at Mace direct him to his friend B. Cummings learns from B., who arrived a few days before, that the camp is a detention center where suspected spies are held before being judged. B. confesses to Cummings that he prefers prison to service in the ambulance corps. Cummings is surprised that his friend is happy to be in prison, but he shares B.'s relief at getting away from their commanding officer.

Cummings goes through the daily routine of "La Ferté": prison meals, walks in the courtyard, and time locked in "the enormous room" where all the men live. The camp is a world unto itself, with disgruntled prisoners, their wives and prostitutes, and unfeeling guards for whom service at the detention camp is a respite from front-line duty. By the end of his first day of internment, Cummings agrees with B. that their prison is "the finest place on earth."

Fascinated with his fellow inmates, Cummings makes many friends and tries to find out what each man has been incarcerated for. The stories of these people, accused of spying because they wrote letters criticizing France or who had once been anarchists or communists or simply did not speak French, make Cummings disgusted with the French government. He does not understand how a government can take men away from their homes and families for such petty reasons.

Time loses its significance for Cummings as he passes the days not knowing how long his sentence will be. The daily routine is interrupted occasionally by the arrival of new prisoners and the appearances of the examining commission that decides their fate.

After six months at the detention camp, Cummings is finally released through the efforts of the U.S. Embassy. He leaves with memories of the good people whom he met at "La Ferté" and anger toward the government that put them there.

Cummings, General Edward. *The Naked and the Dead.* Norman Mailer. 1948.

Major General Edward Cummings, commander of 6,000 American troops on the fictional Japanese island of Anopopei, is a pathologically ambitious man. If SERGEANT SAM CROFT seems to crave domination by instinct, General Cummings, self-aware and introspective, is his intellectual counterpart; both men are obsessed with a desire for omnipotence, which their positions in the military fulfill to varying degrees.

A brilliant tactician, Cummings has planned his rise to greatness like a battle campaign. He views his military career as a step toward control of the postwar political arena. In one of many conversations with his subordinate LIEUTENANT ROBERT HEARN, Cummings outlines his vision of a future society in which the military maintains order by intimidation and force. When Hearn points out the enormous anxiety such a system would generate, Cummings calmly asserts that anxiety is the natural state for twentieth-century man, thereby revealing his indifference to human suffering.

Cummings's intellectual isolation prompts him to seek out Hearn, in whom he thinks he recognizes a similar aptitude for manipulation. Hearn, for his part, is fascinated by Cummings's character, which he studies but cannot fully fathom. Hearn gradually comes to understand the General as a man virtually consumed by his lust for power, who turns his inner emptiness to advantage by assuming roles—the General, the Professor, the Statesman, the Philosopher—that reflect his ambitions for the future.

Yet Cummings is not without his contradictions. On one occasion the General, normally controlled, purposeful, and objective, reveals to Hearn a surprising streak of self-pity. A rather extreme outburst, along with what Hearn half-disbelievingly interprets as a sexual overture, turns Cummings's relationship with his subordinate officer into a perverse game of psychological manipulation. Cummings, exposed and vulnerable, cannot rest until he finally succeeds in humiliating Hearn by issuing a senseless, petty command. He throws a cigarette at Hearn's feet and orders him to pick it up from the floor. Hearn, intimidated and fearful, obeys.

The military command that Cummings directs on the island eventually succeeds. But the General soon learns that the Japanese succumbed due to hunger, exhaustion, and lack of supplies; his meticulously planned invasion had little to do with their surrender of Anopopei. Thinking ahead to future campaigns, Cummings estimates that the current war would probably not afford him the time or the opportunity to amass the absolute power he craves. He has gained nothing. Even the men directly under his command refuse to submit to him entirely. Forced to scale down his ambitions, Cummings resigns himself to a postwar career in the State Department.

Cutrer, Kate. *The Moviegoer.* Walker Percy. 1961.

Beautiful, troubled Kate Cutrer is the charge of narrator JOHN BICKERSON "BINX" BOLLING. A member of a wealthy New Orleans family ruled over by her loving and strong-willed stepmother Emily, Kate has suffered for a number of years from the "long nightmare" of recurrent depression. Her condition has worsened in recent months, and her father and stepmother rightly suspect that she is addicted to drugs and alcohol. For this reason Emily recruits help from her nephew Binx who has emotional problems of his own but is the only person Kate has been able to respond to in recent weeks.

Kate confesses to Binx that she cannot marry Walter, her well-meaning but insensitive fiancé, and that her depression is now deeper than it has ever been before. In fact, she confides, the happiest times she remembers are the moments following the car accident that claimed the life of her first fiancé. She feels most comfortable, she tells Binx, when she is close to death.

Binx is able to read the changes in Kate's mood with uncanny accuracy, and when she tells him she does not need to see her psychiatrist anymore, he knows her confidence is only temporary and that disaster is imminent. As they talk, he half-seriously asks her to marry him, but she becomes unsettled and brushes him off. When Binx returns from a weekend at his mother's summer cottage, he learns that Kate has attempted suicide.

Kate's family is visibly shaken by the incident, although she insists that she never really intended to die and only took enough barbiturates to put herself "off dead center." She carefully explains her feelings to Binx and then suddenly decides that she will accompany him on a business trip to Chicago during the New Orleans Carnival festivities. Although Binx has airline tickets for the next day, she insists that they take a train that evening, and she slips out of the house without telling her stepmother of her plans.

On the train to Chicago, Kate repeatedly excuses herself, and Binx knows that she is taking pills in the lavatory. In her sleeper Kate awkwardly propositions Binx, who just as awkwardly accepts. The two spend an uncomfortable night together. In Chicago, both are saddened when they visit Binx's old war buddy, a man who has dedicated himself to a suburban, upper-middle-class way of life. Back at their hotel, they receive a message from Emily. She is furious and demands that they both return immediately.

In New Orleans, after his aunt Emily has lectured Binx soundly, the two agree that they will marry. Kate warns that her road to recovery will be a long one and that Binx will have to help her every step of the way. Her terror of everything is crippling, she says, and she needs someone who will dispel her fears of the outside world. Binx quietly promises to do just that.

In an epilogue to the novel, set one year later, it is unclear whether Kate will eventually recover. Married to Binx, who is now in medical school, she is still unsure of herself. But when Binx asks her to run an errand alone, she nervously listens to his careful instructions, then slowly makes her way out into the world.

Cynthie (Miss). "Miss Cynthie." Rudolph Fisher. 1933.

Miss Cynthie has spent nearly all of her seventy years in a small town in the South. A visit to her grandson in the North challenges her ideas about morality.

It has long been Miss Cynthie's ambition to travel north to New York to visit her grandson, David Tappen, whom she reared from his early childhood. One of her tasks on this visit is to find out what exactly it is that her grandson

does that enables him to send money home, for even on his last visit to the South he was reticent about his profession. When she arrives in New York City, Miss Cynthie is astounded by the politeness of the redcap who calls her madam, something that had never happened to her before. She immediately begins telling him about her trip and about her grandson and her pride in him. She hopes, she says, that he is some kind of doctor or a minister or, at the very least, an undertaker. All she really wants to know is whether or not he earns his living honestly and in a Christian manner.

When David arrives to pick her up, Miss Cynthie is impressed with the newness of his car, and she greatly enjoys the smooth ride uptown and along Central Park West. Her enjoyment gives way to genuine happiness as they approach and travel through Harlem, which she recognizes right away from things she has heard. They arrive at David's apartment building, and Miss Cynthie is impressed by the apartment's size and furnishings. She also approves of David's wife Ruth. Again, Miss Cynthie asks David to tell her what he does, but he puts her off by saying that she has to wait until the following night. While Miss Cynthie is in her room freshening up, the couple can hear her singing an old song, one that she had taught David when he was quite small.

The next night they travel to a theater where Miss Cynthie is appalled to find a talking film in progress. Although she heartily disapproves of this, the devil's medium, she takes her place in a special box seat, and the party is joined by two men who are introduced as David's managers. The film gives way to a revue that features black performers reenacting cotton-picking scenes while singing and dancing. At this point David and Ruth excuse themselves, and Miss Cynthie grows more and more appalled as the dance numbers become progressively more energetic and the costumes, in her opinion, more lewd. Her outrage is sharpened when David appears onstage and begins to sing, and Ruth joins him, scantily clad and dancing wildly, at least in Miss Cynthie's opinion. This revelation saddens the old woman, who reasons that she has completely failed to educate her grandson and that he has become a complete sinner. She is unimpressed by his and Ruth's stunning success, nor does the prospect of another stint on Broadway and a European tour for the show interest her. Her attitude changes at the end of the show, however, when David tap-dances while he sings the very song she had sung in happiness the night before. At the end of the number, which has softened Miss Cynthie's attitude quite a bit, she notes that the audience was childlike in its pleasure, and she decides that David is childlike in his as well. Her approval is assured when David, at the conclusion of his song, publicly acknowledges her as his teacher and most significant influence. The story ends with a happy, if bemused, Miss Cynthie basking in the shared glory of her grandson's rising star.

Cypress. *Sassafrass, Cypress & Indigo.* Ntozake Shange. 1982.

Cypress, one of the three daughters of Hilda Effrania, has always loved to dance. From her childhood on, dance has been her passion, and her interest in it takes her all over the country. At fifteen she travels to New York to begin her study of dance under the tutelage of her aunt Effie; her particular interest is in achieving the expressiveness of the black woman's body.

After training for a time, Cypress joins a dance troupe, The Kushites Returned, which focuses on ancient Egyptian dance and movement. For a time this troupe pleases her, and she is selected to travel on the road as the only permanent female member of the company. Her interest eventually wanes, however, and she settles in San Francisco where she deals cocaine to support herself and a household filled with dancers, musicians, and other artists. It is to this place that her sister SASSAFRASS journeys following a disruption of her relationship with her lover.

Cypress soon feels the call of dancing again, and she returns to practicing and then to New York. There, she joins up with Celine and Ixchall, two women who have formed an all-female dance company, the Azure Bosom, and who live in a virtually all-female community. For Cypress the access to all of these women is thrilling, and before long she becomes romantically and sexually involved with Idrina, one of the dancers. The relationship goes well for a while, until Cypress learns that Idrina's lover, Laura, is due to return to New York. The knowledge that she will be summarily dropped abruptly dissolves Cypress's interest in dance as well as in the com-munity of women, and she spends several weeks on a drinking binge. While in a bar, she hears music that she recognizes, and it turns out to be that of Leroy Mc-Cullough, a saxophonist with whom Sassafrass had had a brief affair in San Francisco. That same night Leroy brings her to his home after she passes out in his arms, and the two become lovers; before long they are living together, and Cypress returns with renewed energy to dancing.

At the same time, Leroy's career begins to take off, and he is offered the opportunity to travel to Europe on an extended tour. Since the trip includes a recording contract with a French company, the couple agrees that it cannot be rejected. Accordingly, Leroy departs for Europe, and then Cypress begins to realize how much her joyous experience of New York depended on the presence of Leroy and his music. She continues to work at her dancing, however, and shortly before Leroy's return she is invited to join a company that will travel throughout the South, performing for Civil Rights groups in places hardest hit by the violence that has led to church bombings and other acts of "retribution." When Leroy calls shortly before Cypress is scheduled to leave, he begs her to wait, cautioning her against the dangers she will encounter as part of that troupe. He wants to marry her, he says, and he wants their wedding to take place at the Charleston, North Carolina, home of her mother, Hilda Effrania. At the end of the novel, Cypress has returned to her mother's home, where she will marry Leroy and assist in the birth of Sassafrass's first child.

D

Dadier, Rick. *The Blackboard Jungle.* Evan Hunter. 1953.

After serving in World War II, Rick Dadier graduates from college. With his pregnant wife Anne to support, he is thrilled to be hired at North Manual Trades, a vocational school for boys with a reputation as one of the worst in the New York City system. Rick's idealism is threatened on the first day when he meets many of his cynical colleagues and when he saves Lois Hammond, another new teacher, from an attempted rape. Since the student rapist is turned over to the police, Rick's students, led by GREGORY MILLER and Artie West, give him the silent treatment in class. Later, he and fellow teacher Josh Edwards are severely beaten by seven boys.

Although discouraged, Rick perseveres, convinced that he will ultimately be able to reach the students in his five difficult classes. He realizes that they are limited, that most have IQs below 80. Altercations with West and Miller, who call him "Daddy-oh," are constant. Complications occur when Josh Edwards quits his job and when Lois Hammond tries to seduce Rick—an act he finds tempting because of the forced celibacy during his wife's advanced pregnancy. Although he refuses Lois, anonymous notes telling of his affair are mailed to Anne.

At one point Rick gives a lesson on the impropriety of

using racial and ethnic slurs, only to discover he has been reported to the office for using such slurs in class. Blaming Miller, he endures many observations and a sharp reprimand from his department chairman and principal. As a less overt reprisal, he is assigned to direct the Christmas assembly.

Rick throws himself into the assembly wholeheartedly and even gains the help of Miller, who lends valuable assistance to the project but continues to lead the misbehavior in class. Two days before the assembly, Rick teaches an impromptu lesson on the story, "The Fifty-First Dragon," which he considers a breakthrough. For the first time he feels like a teacher. His happiness is short-lived, however, because that same day Anne gives birth to a stillborn son. The assembly goes on without him.

After the Christmas holiday, Rick returns to room 206 and finds that his one great lesson has been forgotten, and although the boys are aware of his personal tragedy, they do not even attempt to modify their classroom behavior. When he becomes involved in a fight with West over possession of a knife, Rick realizes he is fighting for his life and is certain all the boys will turn against him. He is surprised when Miller comes to his aid. Soon afterward he finds out that it was West, not Miller, who was his chief antagonist and who sent the notes to Anne.

Rick survives the fight with the understanding that it is only one small victory in his attempt to teach at North Manual Trades. In the end he is confident that with Miller and some of the others on his side, he will prevail and will be accepted as a teacher.

Daily, Lincoln Agrippa "Banjo." *Banjo: A Story Without a Plot.* Claude McKay. 1929.

Lincoln Agrippa Daily, an African American called "Banjo" for the instrument he plays, arrives in Marseilles, France, after serving in World War I. He soon recognizes that Europe, like America, offers few opportunities to a person of color; he therefore resolves to form a jazz band and just enjoy himself.

Unlike his friend Ray, a well-educated man from Harlem, Banjo tries not to dwell on the universal plight of blacks. Ray reads Tolstoy and has a deeper understanding of the role money plays in his race's oppression. But Banjo's comic response to life is better suited to life in the "Ditch," the seedy and sometimes violent entertainment sector of Marseilles. Banjo knows that one must have either power or cunning to get by in the white man's world. Since he doesn't have the former, he relies on the latter.

Banjo soon falls in with the beach boys, a group of expatriate black musicians who live off the ships that come to port. Banjo and the beach boys live day by day, working at odd jobs on ships, panhandling the tourists, and drinking the night away. Occasionally some leave to pursue real jobs, but one by one they return, lured back by their dream of playing music for a living. They try to get gigs all over Marseilles, but only the African Bar allows them to play regularly. Between songs and bottles of wine, the beach boys talk about being black and argue strategies for improving their situation. Nights are their happiest times, except when occasionally disrupted by a jealous lover or an episode with the police.

When Banjo falls sick with a kidney ailment, his friends rush him to the hospital, only to be told that Banjo will not be admitted without an official identity card. The boys go to the consulate, and after meeting some resistance, they finally shame the official into providing approval for Banjo's admittance to the hospital. After his illness, Banjo accepts provisions from the consulate with the understanding that he will take the next available ship to the United States. But at the last minute he decides to stay in the Ditch. He tells his friends that he has been traveling too long to settle down. When the boys question why Marseilles is any better than America, Banjo reveals that in America he witnessed the lynching of his younger brother.

Banjo and the beach boys find steadier jobs on a Caribbean ship that has docked for maintenance. The owner is so pleased with their work that he hires them as crew for his next trip to the West Indies. He even offers them a month's wages in advance. No one is surprised when Banjo accepts the captain's offer. Everyone assumes he will spend all of his advance pay on his last night in Marseilles. Instead, Banjo tells Ray that he plans to run off with the money; to protect himself, he has registered under a false name.

Dan. "Helen, I Love You." James T. Farrell. 1930.

Dan is an imaginative young protagonist who, having recently moved to a new neighborhood, is extremely concerned with his reputation among the other children in the area. He is especially anxious that he not be considered a sissy, a particularly wretched insult, in the boy's opinion. Already amorous at his tender age, Dan is obsessed with unrequited love for Helen Scanlan, a curly red-haired girl who had once held his hand but had recently scorned his attentions.

The previous summer Dan had earned half a dollar by delivering bills to various mailboxes in town. Afterward he and Helen rode together in the back of a grocery wagon. Dan blissfully held Helen's hand and happily spent his money on her. That evening, when Dan's parents scolded him for recklessly throwing his money away, he became extremely upset and began crying and cursing in the parlor. Somewhat later in the evening, Helen came to visit, but Dan thoughtlessly responded to her arrival by saying that her presence on his front steps meant nothing to him. From that time on, Helen has ignored him, and he rues the day he acted so foolishly as to alienate her.

When Dick Buckford, a pushy boy who lives in the neighborhood, begins pestering Dan in front of Helen's house and threatening to pick a fight, Dan silently hopes that they will not come to blows. If he loses, he will be humiliated in front of Helen. But Dan holds his ground in order not to appear the coward, and when Dick calls him names, he counters with his own insults. As their verbal battle wages on, Dan begins to daydream that he is successfully beating up Dick while an admiring crowd, including Helen, watches his heroic deeds. He also recalls other episodes in his relationship with Helen, such as the day he gave her a hat emblazoned with the Cracker Jack logo. Dan felt wonderful all day because she had deigned to wear his gift. His pleasant memories are interrupted by the recurring fear that Dick will beat him up and humiliate him in front of his peers. He will be ostracized by them and called a sissy. But Dick finally abandons the idea of a fight and leaves Dan alone to ponder his lovesick predicament.

Once left alone, Dan congratulates himself for not backing down when faced with Dick's insults. After sitting for a few moments on an iron fence, he decides to take a stroll and walks down to Fifty-eighth Street to buy some candy, which he wishes he had the opportunity to share with his beloved Helen. Feeling very lonely and melancholy, he walks to Washington Park and continues to daydream, this time about how he would have shown Dick who was boss had the latter actually had the courage to pick a fight with him. Helen would have witnessed his combative skills, cheered for him, and expressed her neverending love for him. In another scenario, Dan imagines that Helen is kidnapped and he saves the day by throwing a rock at the evil kidnapper, who is rendered unconscious by the blow. Dan goes so far as to imagine his picture in the newspaper with an account of his role in foiling the kidnapping. As the day's light begins to wane, Dan becomes frightened and decides that he should go home for dinner. He wishes ruefully that Helen were with him so that he could act brave, assuage her fears, and protect her from harm.

Dan. *Little Men.* Louisa May Alcott. 1871.

Dan, a homeless boy of fourteen, is taken to Plumfield, a school for children, by his younger friend, NATHANIEL "NAT" BLAKE. Nat, who had also been on the street only a few weeks before, hopes that the Bhaers, who run the school, will accept Dan as a student as well. During their first brief interview, Mrs. Bhaer fears that Dan, a slouching and sullen boy, is a "bad specimen." In spite of their concerns, the Bhaers decide to try the risky experiment of taking the boy in.

Although Nat insisted that Dan had been kind to him when they were both homeless, Dan makes no effort to show the Bhaers any appreciation or to be gentle toward the other boys. At first he is disciplined for minor infractions, such as fighting and teasing the farm animals. A

more serious incident, however, causes Dan to be banished from Plumfield.

Late one evening, after they are supposed to be in bed, Dan invites Nat and another adventurous boy, Tommy Bangs, to his room. A bottle of beer and a cigar that Dan had stashed away are brought out for the occasion, and Dan teaches his innocent friends how to play poker. When the nurse nearly discovers them, the boys disperse frantically, and Tommy tosses the burning cigar under his bed. His room is soon blazing, and two boys are injured before the fire is extinguished. The following morning, after he learns what has happened, Mr. Bhaer decides to send Dan to Mr. Page's school some distance away. If he behaves well there, they tell him, he will be allowed to return to the Bhaers' school. Dan merely sneers at this possibility; his pride prevents him from showing any regret or begging for another chance.

Mrs. Bhaer has grown attached to Dan in spite of his troublemaking. She has observed certain qualities in him that convince her of his potential goodness: He has a special understanding of animals and a careful, playful manner with her baby son Teddy. When the Bhaers receive a letter saying that Dan has run away from Mr. Page's, they wait anxiously for him to reappear.

One night more than a month later, Mrs. Bhaer discovers him sleeping outside the house; Dan claims he only wanted a glimpse of her and Teddy, but she coaxes him into the house. A stone has fallen on his foot and broken it, and he now has difficulty walking. As he waits, bedridden, for the foot to heal, Dan becomes determined to stay at Plumfield. He is deeply affected by the Bhaers' generosity this time and needs the love that Mrs. Bhaer is so willing to offer him.

While staying at Mr. Page's, Dan became acquainted with Mr. Hyde who taught him a great deal about wildlife. When they learn of his interest, the other boys bring Dan all types of odd gifts from the fields and gardens around the school: bugs, crabs, frogs, and butterflies. Mrs. Bhaer allows him to use a large cabinet that has many drawers where he can organize a miniature natural history museum. After Dan is well and active again, he is involved in an event that disrupts Plumfield for some time. Some money belonging to Tommy Bangs is stolen, and after a long, anxious period, Dan returns the money and confesses to the crime. Dan, whom the others exile for his misdeed, saves another boy, Jack Ford, from a dangerous fall out of a tree. Immediately afterward Jack disappears, leaving behind a note saying that he had taken the money; Dan was only protecting Jack and his friend Nat, also a suspect. The boys are impressed with this selfless act, and as a peace offering they pool their money to buy him a microscope.

There are still moments when Dan's wildness threatens to overwhelm him, and he must constantly find ways of occupying himself productively so that he is not tempted to run away. He receives permission from Mrs. Bhaer to drive to town regularly to run errands, and Mr. Bhaer gives him the job of chopping firewood. When even these tasks are not enough to occupy Dan, he secretly works at taming a young colt belonging to a friend of the Bhaers. They are pleased with his bravery and perseverance when they see how well he has broken the colt. At Thanksgiving, Dan is rewarded with a visit from Mr. Hyde, who wants the boy to accompany him on a voyage to South America the following year. The delighted Bhaers agree, knowing that Dan will be a faithful and enthusiastic assistant.

Dance, Nichol. *Ninety-two in the Shade.* Thomas McGuane. 1972.

Nichol Dance, a hard-drinking and violent man, is one of the best fishing-boat captains or guides in Key West, Florida. He learns this art from his friend, Faron Carter, a methodical man who catches a respectable number of fish each day. Dance, on the other hand, is unpredictable: Some days he brings in an astonishing amount, but other times he catches nothing at all. When a talented young fisherman, THOMAS SKELTON, decides he wants to enter the business, Dance makes several violent attempts to scare him off.

Most people in Key West know the crucial facts about Dance and have reason to distrust him. He was born in Center, Indiana, in 1930, where he remained and eventually inherited the town hardware store. Dance spent most of the first six months of ownership drinking and hunting with his friends, until his sister tried to sue him for the small portion of inheritance money still left. Holding on to some of the money, Dance drove to Kentucky and bought a tavern.

A year later Dance got involved in an argument with a man named George Washington whose job was exercising horses. Washington waited until the bar closed and then beat Dance nearly to death with a tire iron. Four months later Washington appeared again and threatened to shoot him, but Dance had his gun ready and killed him. Dance pleaded self-defense, and as soon as the trial ended, he left town with the intention of driving toward the sea to "start over." In Key West his damaged car caught fire and burned with all his belongings inside. He didn't lose his gun, however, because he carried it on his person.

Dance worked at various odd jobs in Key West, including helping Faron Carter, until he was able to buy a skiff and become a guide himself. Haunted by thoughts of the man he murdered, he considered suicide. After a terrible marriage that lasted only fifty-seven days, Dance began drinking heavily again.

Dance first meets Thomas Skelton when Carter and Skelton find his boat drifting in a tidal creek, with Dance lying unconscious inside it. When Dance comes to and recognizes the newcomer Skelton, he shoots the revolver, emphasizing his threat to stay off the water. When they return to the dock, Dance assaults Roy, the dockmaster, in a fit of rage.

Dance later plays a trick on Skelton, allowing him to borrow his skiff for a day of guiding, then evacuating the customers when the young man's back is turned. Skelton is terrified that they have drowned or somehow gotten lost. After Skelton gets his revenge by setting Dance's skiff on fire, the conflict escalates. Dance vows to kill Skelton if he tries to become a guide in Key West or in any nearby port town. In spite of this threat, Skelton has a new skiff built and prepared while Dance must content himself with an old boat and a beaten-up engine.

To help him, Carter arranges for the Chamber of Commerce to buy a day's guiding from Dance. It is to be used as a prize for a pie-eating contest they have organized as one of the group's "touristic activities." Olie Slatt, a miner from Montana, wins the contest, but by the time he has recovered from eating so much pie, Dance is booked for sixteen days and sends him to Carter instead. Carter, who is also booked, passes Slatt on to Skelton.

Dance arrives at the dock shortly after Skelton has left with Slatt in his new skiff. The worn-out engine on Dance's boat refuses to start, and Carter offers the use of his skiff. Although Carter, along with virtually everyone else in Key West, knows of Dance's threat to Skelton, he does not believe that Dance will carry it out; instead, he thinks Dance intends to kill himself. Taking Carter's skiff, Dance motors out to Snipe Point where Skelton is looking for bonefish. He climbs into Skelton's boat and shoots him in the chest. Dance then hands the gun to Olie Slatt, who, thinking at first of simply shooting Dance, decides instead to kill him by beating him over the head with it.

Daquin, Mimi. *Flight.* Walter White. 1926.

Mimi is a young woman forced by circumstances to radically alter her life. She is of Creole descent and was raised by her father Jean to believe in herself and her own ability. It is her uncompromising sense of justice and determination to live her life the way she sees fit that forces her to continually leave her native community and people.

Mimi is raised in the genteel tradition of New Orleans Creole aristocracy. Among the upper-class Creoles, petty gossip, criticism, and class-conscious behavior mirror the prejudices of the white community. Jean, raised in Louisiana, finds the life-style disturbing. His second wife, Mary, has no reservations, however, and becomes a central figure in the community.

Mimi makes friends with a young woman named Hilda and through her is introduced to Carl, a tempestuous, moody, wild youth who fancies himself a writer and unfit for "ordinary" work. Mimi falls in love with him despite her loyalties to Hilda, who is also smitten by this brooding character. Mimi and Carl declare their love for each other the night Jean dies.

Jean's death devastates Mimi. When Aunt Sophie,

Jean's sister, asks her to come to New York, Mimi resolves to stay in New Orleans in order to be with Carl.

Mimi soon learns that she is pregnant. Unfortunately, Carl proves himself to be as weak as Jean had predicted. He suggests an abortion, and Mimi, disgusted, refuses to marry him. Determined to raise the child herself, Mimi sets out for Philadelphia where she bears the child and adopts the life-style of a self-supporting "widow."

Mimi and little Jean are forced to live on the meager earnings her sewing provides and the charity of the elderly couple they board with. Mimi realizes that she can never provide adequately for her son. She decides to place him in a Catholic home where he can pass as white and thus receive better treatment.

Mimi travels to her aunt Sophie's in Harlem. She enters the cosmopolitan city with an open mind, only to discover the same lurking gossip and maliciousness as in New Orleans. When a Harlem paper publishes an account of her fatherless child, Mimi flees downtown in order to spare her aunt embarrassment.

Mimi's light complexion and French accent allow her to enter the white-dominated world of fashion. She becomes a seamstress at an exclusive shop called Francine's where she becomes friends with a woman named Sylvia. From her new friend Mimi learns of the plight of the Jewish people.

Mimi stays at Francine's, saving money for her and Jean's future. Because of her skill and enthusiasm, she soon becomes Madame Francine's star employee. She begins accompanying Madame Francine to Paris where she meets and marries Jimmie, a white man who, like the other peripheral white characters in the novel, turns out to be miserable and bigoted. Mimi eventually decides that she is no longer satisfied with the trappings of wealth and that she must return to her true community, to the world of "song and joy," and to her son.

Darling, Christian. "The Eighty-Yard Run." Irwin Shaw. 1950.

Christian Darling stands alone on his college's football field while remembering his exhilarating eighty-yard run in a practice and meditating on the course of the fifteen years that followed. At thirty-five, Darling recalls the run and the brief meeting afterward with Louise, his girlfriend at the time, as the high point of his life.

With exquisite clarity, Darling is able to recount the moments of the eighty-yard run as if they occurred in slow motion. After catching the ball, he picks up speed, breathing easily, smiles, and listens to the sound of his cleats behind him. As he runs, he achieves a visionary catharsis and is released from the perpetual confusion of his existence. Darling walks off the field knowing that this moment has altered his life. Louise is waiting in her car when he leaves the stadium. She kisses him, and he feels sure that, for the first time, Louise "means it."

For the next two years Darling is moved from the second team to the first and plays every Saturday. The experience is never what he had hoped it would be, but the recognition he receives is nevertheless gratifying; he is regarded as an "important figure." After college he marries Louise, and they move to New York City where her father provides him with a lucrative job in his ink-manufacturing company. On Darling's ample salary the couple enjoys the theater, galleries, and speakeasies of New York. Darling has several insignificant, casual affairs but feels perfectly secure about Louise's love for him, which is apparently very strong.

In 1929 the Depression ruins the ink-manufacturing company, Louise's father commits suicide, and Darling loses his job. He begins drinking and refuses to be comforted by Louise. The couple moves downtown, but he continues drinking. Accepting increasing responsibilities on the job while paying the bills at home, Louise works at a fashion magazine. As time goes on, she becomes part of a glamorous, sophisticated society of writers, painters, and poets, a suspicious, alien world to Darling. After finally admitting to himself that he feels threatened and overshadowed by this mysterious world, Darling tries to find a job.

Although he goes through the motions of working at selling cars and real estate, Darling never achieves success and never earns very much money. Meanwhile, Louise, becoming even more involved in her fashionable circles, receives a promotion to assistant editor. She tries persistently to include her husband, but he refuses to cultivate any genuine interest. Darling considers it sufficient that he go where Louise pleases and that he make enough to pay for his own liquor. He drifts on in this manner until he is offered a job as a tailor's representative, traveling from college to college. It pays relatively well, and although he desperately hopes Louise will ask him to remain in New York, he correctly predicts that she will advise him to take the job.

Darling, now thirty-five, travels to the college he attended when he first met Louise and stands on the field where he made his remarkable eighty-yard run. There must have been a moment, he thinks, when he could have taken Louise's hand and moved with her into the complex world she discovered. Somehow he never learned the skills that would have enabled him to do that. Fighting back tears, Darling again runs the eighty yards he ran at age twenty. As he reaches the goal line, he notices with embarrassment a boy and a girl watching him curiously. He tells them that he had once played on this field.

Darrow, George. *The Reef.* Edith Wharton. 1912.

George Darrow, an ordinarily confident and smooth young diplomat, struggles to find the proper way to court the aristocratic ANNA SUMMERS LEATH. Twice, Darrow loses his patience, and although his interest in Anna never wavers, he becomes involved with women whose feelings are easier to interpret and who are less cautious with their company. Darrow's womanizing proclivities continue to threaten his relationship with Anna even after they marry, and his desperate diplomatic maneuvers fail to heal the breach that has opened up between them.

Darrow meets Anna when she is still Anna Summers, the daughter of a sophisticated, wealthy, and excessively proper family residing on West Fifty-fifth Street in New York City. Undeniably a product of this rarified atmosphere, Anna is extremely reserved and proud, and Darrow has great difficulty reading her intentions. He grows impatient and lapses into a light flirtation with a more adventurous member of Anna's circle, Kitty Mayne, and his relations with Anna are eventually broken off.

During the ensuing years, Darrow's unpredictable emotions settle as he develops his career as a diplomat. Twelve years later, after Anna has married Fraser Leath and been widowed, they meet again at a dinner at the American embassy in London. He is still enchanted by Anna, and her friendly reception gives him hope that their friendship might be renewed.

Their subsequent meetings continue to raise his hopes, although Darrow notes with disappointment that Anna has not lost her protective reserve. When he receives a second curt letter delaying his long-awaited visit to her French country house, Givre, he feels defeated and miserable. Darrow is waiting at the dock, debating whether he should make the crossing from England to France despite Anna's rejection, when a distressed young woman explains to him that she has lost her trunk and requests his help. He remembers her vaguely from Mrs. Murrett's, a house where he often dined when he was pursuing a certain Lady Crispin. He decides to accompany the woman, Sophy Viner, who is alone and without much money, to Paris where she has friends. Both lonely and in need of comfort, Darrow and Sophy are reluctant to part. The days in Paris begin innocently as he takes his delighted young companion to the theater, a rare treat for her. When the conversation between them loses its charm, Darrow gives way to his passionate impulses, and the lighthearted holiday becomes an affair.

Darrow's story picks up five months later when the temporary estrangement between him and Anna Leath has ended and, harmoniously united at Givre, they are planning their wedding and the first years of married life. After a few days of paradisiacal peace, the situation begins to disintegrate. Darrow meets Anna's nine-year-old daughter Effie, who has been away, and is shocked when Sophy Viner is introduced as her governess. He is reduced to desperation when it emerges that Owen Leath, Anna's impetuous stepson, intends to marry Sophy and that Anna has promised to support his decision.

At first Darrow tries to conceal everything, admitting only to having known Sophy slightly at Mrs. Murrett's. In a series of clandestine conversations he attempts to persuade Sophy that the marriage would be unwise. Sophy eventually tells him that because she still loves Darrow, she cannot marry Owen. Meanwhile, Owen, who happens to observe their private meetings, becomes suspicious. Sophy suddenly declares her intention to leave Givre for a few days. Anna questions Darrow, who now confesses to having seen her in Paris, but it is Sophy who breaks down under interrogation, revealing the fact of their affair. Sophy departs, and Anna dismisses Darrow from the house in great sorrow.

Several days later Darrow leaves his post in London and pursues Anna to Paris, where she surrenders to his arguments that they should return to Givre together, at least to keep Owen from suspecting the reason Sophy has refused him. Despite his sense of the past as a "huge looming darkness," Darrow is able to act with composure and persuade the insecure Anna that she will someday understand why they must not give each other up. Darrow is successful in convincing her, but his past misjudgments have a powerful lingering effect on his wife's feelings toward him.

Dave. "The Man Who Was Almost a Man." Richard Wright. 1961.

Dave, the story's protagonist, hungers for the abilities and freedom of adulthood. Most particularly this desire is manifested in his longing to purchase a gun. For most of the summer he has worked at Mr. Hawkins's farm, routinely proffering his income to his mother as a contribution to the family's maintenance. After keeping this routine for quite a while, Dave stops in at the local store and talks to the proprietor about buying a gun. He borrows the proprietor's Sears catalog and dreamily returns home, where his parents query him about the catalog.

Rather than blurting out his intentions, Dave informs his parents that the catalog is Joe's and that he is just borrowing it. After eating rapidly, he decides to tell his mother about his desire for a gun. At first she is skeptical, insisting that there is no reason for him to buy a gun, but Dave is resourceful and convinces her that it is a good idea by telling her it would really be his father's gun and that there should be one in the house. His mother gives him the money to purchase an old gun directly from Joe, without having to wait for delivery from Sears.

The next day Dave eagerly acquires the gun, which is loaded, leaves the store, and heads for the Hawkins farm. Walking behind Jenny, Mr. Hawkins's mule, he plows two whole rows before stopping and pulling out his gun to admire it. The impulse to fire is overwhelming, and when the gun does go off, Dave feels as though his arm has been severed from his body. As if this shock were not enough, Dave is horrified to discover that Jenny has taken off across the field. When he catches up with the mule, he realizes she has been shot.

While the mule continues to bleed and nothing he does

can stanch the flow of blood, Dave realizes that he is going to be in a great deal of trouble. Finally, Jenny dies, and Dave buries his gun. Later that day, as the mule is being buried, Dave's parents arrive and begin to question him about what happened. None of the adults really believe the quite improbable lie Dave concocted to explain the hole in Jenny's side. Dave's father eventually forces him to admit that he shot the mule, but Dave lies about the gun, insisting that he threw it in the creek.

It is decided that Dave will retrieve the gun the next day and begin to pay off the cost of the mule (fifty dollars), by giving Mr. Hawkins the two dollars he will get for selling the gun back. That night Dave figures that at two dollars a month it will take him two years to pay for the dead mule, and he will have no gun. Rather than face this predicament, Dave gets up and goes to dig up his treasured gun. Thinking that he is a great shooter, he fires it off, using all the remaining bullets. He then decides that he needs to be a man and that this is not possible if he continues living at home. As the story ends, Dave hops a passing train bound for an unknown place.

David. *Giovanni's Room.* James Baldwin. 1956.

David is a young blond American expatriate living in France. As the novel opens, he is alone in a house in southern France where he has fled after the failure of two major relationships.

David, who is somewhere in his twenties, first came to Europe to avoid the unhappiness caused by his home life. Following the death of his mother, he was raised by his father's unmarried sister and a father who was only occasionally attentive to his son's needs. Emphasizing that his son would grow to be a "man," the two fight frequently about how David should be reared. In response David becomes increasingly rebellious, and he is nearly killed when he is involved in a drunk-driving accident. While he is recovering, David and his father attempt a reconciliation, but they cannot overcome their differences.

When father and son fail to come to terms with each other, David moves to France. Once in Paris, he becomes emotionally and sexually involved with Giovanni, a "dark" Italian who has come to Paris to escape a stultifying life in a small village where he had been married and fathered a child that died soon after birth. David and Giovanni spend the spring and summer together, living most of the time in the small room of the novel's title. Their relationship during this period is characterized by long philosophical conversations about love, life, nationalities, and sexuality. David is also encouraged to confront and deal with the many doubts he has about his own sexual identity and his emotional fears and anxieties. While David spends his time with Giovanni, he becomes a habitué of Paris's homosexual community even though he knows his girlfriend, Hella Lincoln, will soon return from Spain where she has "gone to look at men." Hella

finally does return, and David abruptly leaves Giovanni, who is heartbroken and quickly begins to live and act like a vagrant.

David resumes his relationship with Hella, and the two begin to contemplate marriage; soon after this decision, they accidentally meet Giovanni and his friend Jacques. David learns of Giovanni's depression and anger, and without Hella's knowledge he returns to spend a night with his former lover.

Once she becomes aware of David's bisexuality, Hella decides not to continue their relationship. At the same time, Giovanni, in despair, murders his former employer, a homosexual who was the scion of one of France's aristocratic families. Although it is unclear as to whether the murder was premeditated or accidental, Giovanni flees; he is soon captured, tried, convicted, and sentenced to death.

David leaves Paris with Hella in a final attempt to rekindle their affair, but the get-together quickly sours. She leaves him alone in the room in which the novel begins. Here David spends the night leading to the day of Giovanni's execution. Staring at his image in the mirror, he reminisces about his father, his aunt, Hella, and Giovanni, and contemplates his eventual return to the United States.

David. "Tell Me a Riddle." Tillie Olsen. 1961.

David has been married to Eva for forty-seven years. Both Russian immigrants, he and Eva raised six children—Hannah, Paul, Vivi, Clara, Sammy, and Lennie—through intense poverty and hardship. David now longs for freedom from the responsibility of a large household and tries to convince his wife to move to the Haven, his lodge's cooperative for the elderly. Eva is adamantly opposed.

David cannot stop pestering Eva. He follows her around the house as she does her chores, pointing out to her all the ways in which living at the Haven would be easier for her. He claims he is going to sell the house without her consent. When their son Paul suggests that Eva see a doctor about her sudden listlessness, David cannot resist adding that free medical care would be included at the Haven. He then uses the doctor's prescription for a careful diet and a little fun in life as further enticement for a place where meals and activity are provided.

When David invites some of their children for dinner, one daughter insists on taking Eva back to Connecticut with her so that her husband Phil, a physician, can examine her. The gall bladder surgery that Phil orders for Eva reveals she is dying of cancer. David is overcome, unable to bear the thought of Eva having to live the rest of her life with such sickness. He keeps the news from her for the sake of her peace of mind and is determined not to take her home again to all the "old associations." The future terrifies him now, and although Eva begs him to take her home, David insists on traveling around the country to visit each of their children. For David, to go back home is to go to death.

David takes Eva to Los Angeles for sun and rest before continuing on to Lennie's in San Francisco. He goes with her to the beach and to visit old friends, and tries to get her interested in activity, but Eva grows more and more withdrawn. When David finally agrees to ask the doctor's permission to return home, an infection keeps Eva bedridden for a while and renders her too weak to travel even after it passes. Eva sleeps in a rented hospital bed, and at night husband and wife hold hands across the gap between their beds.

When another infection strikes, the doctor tells David to bring Eva to the hospital. She often babbles incoherently from fever. David is heartbroken by the anger he hears in Eva's muttering and singing. He cannot bear how she has changed and wishes a quick death for her.

It saddens David that now, while dying, Eva has nothing to say of him or the children and their long life together. He feels abandoned, remembering her as a girl who sang of freedom and truth. Suddenly the torrent of sorrow he has hidden his whole life rushes over him, and he grieves for the pain he and his people have suffered. As Eva waits to die, David goes to sleep holding her hand and weeping in agony for all he has lost.

Davies, Arthur. *The Ox-bow Incident.* Walter Van Tilburg Clark. 1940.

Arthur Davies, a store owner in the small western town of Bridger's Wells, staunchly abides by his humanitarian principles but is powerless to prevent violence and bloodshed.

When Larry Kinkaid, a rancher, is murdered, the citizens of Bridger's Wells suspect cattle rustlers since news of missing cattle accompanies the news of Kinkaid's death. A small posse forms to find and lynch the murderers. Davies is among the first to protest, but while he argues that the rustlers might outnumber such a small group, more townspeople volunteer. Davies tries to stall them as he sends Art Croft, the book's narrator, and a younger man to talk to the local judge, who would deem the posse's intent illegal and prevent the lynching. The judge first attempts to placate the mob by urging the men to allow his deputy to arrest the rustlers. When he realizes the posse's insistence, however, he condones the search but orders that the rustlers be returned alive. The searchers swear a brief oath and depart.

A terrible snowstorm plagues the men throughout their journey and impedes their progress. When Croft is shot in an unfortunate encounter with a stagecoach, Davies is the first to tend to his wound and assure him that it is not serious. He tries to persuade Croft to return home, arguing that food and rest would be better for him than continued traveling through bad weather. Despite Davies's support by other posse members, Croft refuses to turn back.

When the posse discovers the rustlers, Davies again protests the opinion of the majority. The vigilantes plan to hang the three rustlers: Juan Martinez, a Mexican; Alva Harwick, a mildly insane older man; and Donald Martin, a younger man. Arguing that the individuals are innocent until proven guilty, Davies demands a fair trial, and he almost comes to blows with MAJOR TETLEY, the posse leader. It is decided that the men will be hanged the day after their final requests are granted. Juan Martinez wants to make a confession, and Martin wants a letter delivered to his wife. Having been entrusted with this letter by Martin, Davies shows it to the other men, thus incurring Martin's anger. Davies first protests that he was trying to prove Martin's innocence, and then he simply promises to mail the letter. When Martin tries to take the letter back, Davies reminds him of its beauty and compassion and encourages him to mail it; Martin concedes.

On the morning of the execution, Davies tries but fails to stop it. When Martin squirms too much in the noose, Tetley orders him shot. After returning to Bridger's Wells, Davies remains distraught for several days over the senselessness of the execution. He reveals to Croft that Martin declared his innocence in his final letter, and although Croft calms Davies somewhat, his guilt and misery resurface when he learns of the suicides of both the elder Tetley and Tetley's son Gerald. The insensitivity of humankind reduces him to tears; he is put to bed and does not reappear in the novel.

Davies, Elmer. "Nigger Jeff." Theodore Dreiser. 1899.

Elmer Davies is a reporter for a midwestern newspaper who comes to the small town of Pleasant Valley to report on a lynching. He learns that a local African American, Jeff Ingalls, has been accused of assaulting Ada Whitaker, the nineteen-year-old-daughter of a wealthy farmer; the community is about to seek retribution. Davies considers Ingalls's crime abominable but is wary at the prospect of a lynching, especially one he may have to witness.

Upon arriving in Pleasant Valley, Davies discovers that Ingalls has been picked up by Sheriff Mathews and is being escorted back to prison for the trial. A local mob has gathered under the leadership of Jake Whitaker, the victim's father, who is unwilling to wait for legal recourse.

Davies tries to observe the confrontation between the sheriff and the mob with the impartial eye of a reporter. The crowd, he notices, is more curious than courageous and will likely back down. Ingalls, meanwhile, cowers like a frightened animal. Davies remains detached enough to notice the beauty of the countryside despite the rumblings in the potentially violent crowd. The mob eventually acquiesces and disbands, and Davies makes arrangements to wire the story back to his newspaper.

Later that evening the mob returns with more solemn determination; Davies recalls how Ingalls had cowered before it earlier in the day, and he is suddenly struck by the horror of the situation. Nevertheless, he has a job to do, and he moves into the center of the crowd in order to get a better view of Ingalls. Ingalls, crouched low and foaming at the mouth, finally collapses, unconscious. Davies makes a note of his movements and the colors and mood of the atmosphere, the better to enhance his story. He feels a mixture of fascination and dread at Ingalls's fate; the mob sets upon him and drags his partially mangled body to the site of the hanging. Davies watches from a distance as Ingalls, hoisted into the air, thrashes about and finally hangs still.

Davies looks out at the peaceful surroundings and feels a sense of relief. He decides to wait until morning to report the story and to spend the day gathering additional information. He goes to Ingalls's home where he finds the man's sister tending the house. The girl tells Davies that her brother had returned to say good-bye to his family before he was caught by the police. She directs him to a back room where the body is being kept. As Davies examines the corpse, he hears an eerie whimpering sound and turns to see Ingalls's mother sobbing in the corner. Davies is suddenly struck by the reality of the human suffering he is witnessing and flees from the sight. Then, remembering his duties as a reporter, he hopes to convey the pathos of the situation through his art and enthusiastically exclaims, "I'll get it all in!"

Davis, Ben. "The Web of Circumstance." Charles W. Chesnutt. 1899.

Set during the years following the Civil War, this story opens as Ben Davis, a hardworking blacksmith, shoes Colonel Thornton's horse. Ben admires a handsome whip belonging to the white man, and after the colonel leaves, several black men who were present during the exchange chide him for attempting to be uppity.

Ben responds by arguing that colored people never had a chance before the war to own anything. Now, however, the only thing preventing them from obtaining things like the colonel's whip is their own lack of thrift. Colored people, he argues, will only gain respect once they stop lining the white man's pocket and acquire property. These remarks are overheard by several white men who approach the shop as Ben concludes.

Before long Ben is being tried for the theft of the colonel's whip, which has been found hidden in his shop. Ben's open admiration of the whip and his theories concerning black advancement and property complete the circumstantial evidence that convicts him. The halfhearted defense of his lawyer speeds him to prison even though the demeanor of Ben's assistant, Tom, suggests that Ben has been framed.

After five years in the penitentiary, Ben returns to find his previously happy family disintegrated and dispersed. His neat, well-kept house has been sold to meet the mortgage. His daughter became a drunkard and drowned while under the influence. His son was recently lynched for killing a white man. And his wife has taken up with his former assistant and lost her reputation as a decent woman.

Years of hard labor and cruel treatment have transformed Ben into a brute, and the destruction of his family renders him hateful and vengeful. The wronged man resolves to slay the source of his troubles, Colonel Thornton, and he goes to the colonel's home prepared to carry out his resolve. While waiting for the colonel to arrive home, he falls asleep in some bushes and is awakened by a young white child whose loving ministrations dissolve Ben's desire for vengeance. When the child wanders away, Ben gets up to flee from the colonel's land. Just as he bounds away, the colonel rounds a bend in the drive and sees a savage-looking man whom he does not recognize seemingly running toward his young daughter with a club in his hand. The colonel shoots Ben, completing the web of circumstance that has been the blacksmith's downfall.

Davis, Rhea. *The Death of Jim Loney.* James Welch. 1979.

As the companion of JIM LONEY, Rhea Davis provides the novel's protagonist with consolation, love, and security—elements absent from Jim's thirty-five years. Life with Jim in the otherwise bleak environment of Harlem, Montana, allows Rhea to escape the confines of her former existence, and although she and Jim must part in the end, her world has been enriched by his presence.

An attractive, well-educated blond, Rhea grew up in Dallas and attended Southern Methodist University, where she received a master's degree in religious studies. She became engaged to a cosmopolitan Jewish lawyer but broke off the engagement because of her discomfort with southern ways and ambitious southern men. Seeking to establish a new life, she fled Texas and went to Harlem, where she began teaching school. One day while selling tickets for a high school football game, she encounters Loney, whom she had heard about earlier and knew was a former high school basketball champ.

At first Rhea is attracted to Loney by his darkness. Over time, however, she comes to know the real man behind the facade of exoticism she had painted. She realizes his drinking is not a passing crisis but a path to his downfall and decides to break him of it and get his life in order. Yet Rhea feels overshadowed when Kate, Loney's assertive, ambitious, and striking sister, writes Loney, urging him to join her in Washington, D.C., and to embark on a new course in life, far removed from the downward spiral he has commenced. When Jim does not respond to Kate's letters, Kate attempts to enlist Rhea's help by writing her and asking that she encourage Jim to consider the idea before Kate's anticipated visit, after which she intends to bring Jim back east with her. A battle for Jim's life begins between the two women who might otherwise be friends.

Rhea tries to persuade Jim to move to Seattle with her

at the end of the school year. She hopes that by relocating he can begin a new life and escape the haunting visions that have plagued him in Harlem. Jim offers Rhea some hope by sharing his fleeting recollections of his experience in Seattle following military service, but in the end he declines Rhea's offer. For Jim, leaving would mean severing his minimal ties to his past.

Jim's decision not to join Rhea ends the possibility that they will share their lives together and marks a turning point in the direction Jim's life will take. Feeling lost and confused, Rhea resolves to return to Texas. On the evening before she is to leave, Loney arrives at her door. He has killed his friend Pretty Weasel in a tragic hunting accident and confesses that after a frustrating encounter with his father that day, he fired his gun at a window of the man's home and probably hit him. At first Rhea thinks he is lying. They hold each other, and she declares her love for him. The next morning the two say their final good-byes. Jim flees to Mission Canyon, where he and Rhea had vacationed during better times, and is shot by the police.

Davison, Helena. *The Group.* Mary McCarthy. 1954.

Helena Davison is an intelligent and talented young woman from Cleveland, Ohio, whose droll sense of humor and multifaceted personality cause seven other Vassar graduates, class of 1933, to value her friendship and consider her their beloved mascot. The only child of a vivacious and socially active Canadian mother and a Scottish father who made his fortune in the steel industry, Helena is, unlike the majority of her companions, oblivious to class snobbery. The only heterosexual in the group who does not marry, Helena is eventually envied by various members whose troubled married lives make her independence appear favorable in comparison.

As a child growing up in Cleveland, Helena is provided with excellent training in a myriad of activities and disciplines including tennis, golf, lacrosse, skiing, figure skating, sailing, leather tooling, pottery, bird watching, dancing, drawing, chess, chemistry, geology, and even printing. In the field of music she is a proficient singer and plays the violin, piano, flute, and trumpet. According to KAY LEILAND STRONG, one of her ex-roommates, Helena has so many attributes and potential careers that she doesn't know which one to pursue most actively. Having attended boarding school in New England, she then graduates from Vassar; her keen wit and finely tuned writing style land her a position as author of the Class Notes appearing in the college's *Alumnae Magazine.* Upon graduation Helena's plan to teach piano and art at an experimental nursery school in Cleveland is foiled by her father, who insists that women of her social class should not waste their time performing such ordinary public services. In addition, he feels that his daughter looked worn out at Vassar's commencement ceremonies and that she should therefore repair to Europe for a rest.

A short, slight young woman with a boyish build, Helena is manifestly uninterested in romance and love. Her friend Kay insists that she is a neuter in the manner of a mule and will therefore never marry. Although she is privy to the mechanics of sex at an early age, Helena herself admits that she has no interest in passion; she considers sex a joke in which she declines to participate. Having returned to the United States and spent some time back at home in Cleveland with her family, she eventually moves to New York City, where she lives alone and contentedly in a pleasant studio apartment on West Eleventh Street.

When the divorced Kay falls to her death from the twentieth story of the Vassar Club, Helena and her mother, who is visiting, join the old clique of Vassar friends to make the funeral arrangements. Helena contacts Kay's parents who, because they have become estranged from their daughter, grant her permission to act in their stead at the funeral parlor. The mourners lay the deceased's body in Helena's studio until all the arrangements have been completed, and then the devastated group attends the moving Episcopalian funeral service that concludes the novel.

Day, Clarence. *Life with Father; Life with Mother.* Clarence Day. 1920; 1936.

Clarence Day is the imperious but tender-hearted New York businessman who as a young man during the Civil War joins the Seventh Regiment but never actually engages in combat. Following the war he purchases a seat on the New York Stock Exchange and with his friend Fisher Johnson opens a very successful firm on Wall Street—thus establishing himself financially at the age of twenty-five. When he has amassed enough money, Clarence travels across the Atlantic to spend a holiday in Europe. On the ship he meets his future wife, VINNIE STOCKWELL (DAY), whom he marries after a three-year courtship. Now a family man, Clarence conducts the affairs of his household with blustering vigor, guaranteeing that his family never experience a moment of boredom or monotony.

Clarence and Vinnie set up a household in a Madison Avenue brownstone with a coachman, cook, and waitress, and they build a summer house on a farm near Harrison, New York. They produce four redheaded boys, whom they raise with the help of nannies. An extremely conventional man who wants his family to conform to the conservative mores of the late nineteenth century, Clarence has extremely high expectations for his sons and provides an excellent example of the integrity that befits the model man. Insisting that his sons should be well rounded, he provides them with instruction in music and foreign languages and sends them to the best possible boarding schools and colleges. Clarence directs the lives of his wife and sons with a noisy gusto that they accept as his way of showing affection for them. Despite his frequent temper tantrums and egotistical insistence on domination, Clarence is a jolly, well-liked man whose foibles are forgiven because they are sufficiently offset by his charms.

When not seeking his fortune on Wall Street, Clarence amuses himself by horseback riding, playing piano and billiards, and spending time with his friends at his club. Bursting with virile energy, he abhors illness and is convinced that most maladies are the figments of weak imaginations. He is shocked and enraged when his toe is injured in an equestrian accident, as he had heretofore considered himself indestructible, and is insulted by this challenge to his supposed perfection. Although Clarence is willing to spend money to buy his clothes from a chic and expensive shop in London, he is thrifty at home and spends an enormous amount of energy hollering about how wasteful Vinnie is and trying to moderate her spending.

In keeping with his conservative personality, Clarence resists change. For years he refuses to purchase a telephone; he finally breaks down and buys one but is annoyed by its ringing and impatient with how it operates. When the peace of his Madison Avenue home is disturbed by the new streetcars, which replace the old horsecars of which he approves, Clarence takes the drastic step of moving. He scorns his wife's suggestion that they move to an apartment, considering it beneath him, and stubbornly purchases a house on Sixty-eighth Street, where he lives with her until his death at almost eighty years of age.

Day, Miranda "Mama Day." *Mama Day.* Gloria Naylor. 1988.

Miranda Day, called Mama Day, lives across the street from her sister Abigail on the coastal island of Willow Springs. The other residents of the small island respect Mama Day, a conjure woman, for her wisdom and power. Even after she has turned ninety, they still visit her in her silver trailer.

Mama Day is a descendant of the nearly mythical Sapphira Wade, who in 1823 mysteriously caused her white husband and former owner, Bascombe Wade, to will the whole of the island to his slaves. Although the large house he built in the West Woods belongs to the Days, along with some 5,000 acres of the island, the house now has certain mystical associations and only Mama Day goes near it. She cares for the "other place" and interacts with the spirits of her relatives still present there. At the other place she grows the herbs and mixes the potions and remedies that she needs. Thus, when the young neighbors Bernice and Ambush Duvall cannot have a baby, they come to Mama Day. After exhausting all other options and curing Bernice of the ovarian cysts that she contracted from fertility drugs, Mama Day takes her to the other place and performs a mysterious rite. Bernice conceives soon after.

Each morning Miranda watches the *Phil Donahue Show.* She wants to learn about the people who live near her great-niece, OPHELIA "COCOA" DAY, in New York.

Mama Day and Abigail raised Ophelia, and the two still love her as their "Baby Girl." Abigail nurtured and cuddled Ophelia, whereas Mama Day took a peach switch to her if she thought she needed it. Still, Mama Day is very protective of Ophelia, sometimes more than Ophelia would like.

When Ophelia and her husband GEORGE ANDREWS visit Willow Springs in late August 1985, Mama Day senses death. Although she now walks with her father's old cane, she knows that it is not her death. In fact, she has already decided to live until the next century so that she can see Ophelia's children. Mama Day has enough energy and strength to exhaust George thoroughly when he first takes on a condescending tone with her.

Mama Day knows that a severe hurricane is coming but does not anticipate her neighbor Ruby's poisoning of Ophelia. Ruby thinks that Ophelia wants to seduce her repellent husband, Junior Lee, and disregards Mama Day's greater power. When Mama Day discovers what Ruby has done to Cocoa, she causes lightning to destroy Ruby's house and seriously burn its owner. Nevertheless, Mama Day knows that she needs George's help or George's life to save Ophelia. She tells George that he must believe in supernatural forces in order to keep Ophelia alive, but when George tries to follow Miranda's instructions, he dies of heart failure. His spirit stays in Willow Springs, however, in the West Woods near Mama Day's other place.

Day, Ophelia "Cocoa." *Mama Day.* Gloria Naylor. 1988.

Ophelia Day, one of the novel's three first-person narrators, is called "Cocoa" by her acquaintances in the island community of Willow Springs and "Baby Girl" by her grandmother Abigail Day and her powerful great-aunt MIRANDA "MAMA" DAY. Cocoa is one of the last living members of the Day family and the only surviving Day of her generation. A willful woman with a tenacious spirit and a fiery tongue, the thin and pale-skinned Cocoa is an important member of Willow Springs, where the history of her ancestors has acquired mythical stature.

Cocoa attends a two-year business college in Atlanta, then works in New York City for seven years as the office manager of Omega Home Insurance. When the company folds, she interviews with GEORGE ANDREWS of the engineering firm Andrews & Stein; he does not offer her the job as office manager but remembers her well enough to recommend her to one of his clients.

Cocoa and George, both strong-willed and self-reliant, are an unlikely pair. Nonetheless, George undertakes to educate Cocoa by showing her the many distinct neighborhoods and small, quiet enjoyments of New York, and she eventually falls in love with him. After a stormy beginning, Cocoa asks George to marry her. Several weeks later, while in New Orleans for the Super Bowl, she and

George call Willow Springs to tell Abigail and Miranda that they have married.

Once married, Cocoa stops working and pursues a bachelor's degree in history at New York University. She continues to visit Willow Springs for the last two weeks of August, as she has each summer since first leaving. When they have been married for four years, George finally accompanies Cocoa to the island. Cocoa is less nervous about introducing George to her great-aunt and grandmother than she is about what the other residents of Willow Springs will think of him. Unable to dispel her tensions and insecurities before a large party her grandmother has arranged for them, Cocoa fights with George. Their argument escalates until she throws a vase at him, cutting open his head. During the party George and Cocoa sit as far away from each other as possible. The lascivious Junior Lee, sensing the palpable animosity between Cocoa and her husband, attempts to seduce Cocoa. She refuses to have anything to do with him, but he chases her; when his jealous wife Ruby catches Junior Lee in the chase, she claims that Cocoa lured him.

Shortly thereafter, when George and Cocoa are still not talking to each other, Cocoa goes to Ruby to have her hair braided. Ruby, a conjure woman of some stature, works poisons into Cocoa's head. Her concoctions cause Cocoa to hallucinate; when she looks in the mirror, she feels that wormlike bugs are eating her from the inside. Mama Day can cut Cocoa's hair, but in order to stop Cocoa's body from decaying, George must believe in mystical forces. George cannot believe, however, and only his sudden death releases Cocoa from her torturous decline.

Three years later Cocoa, now living in Charleston, South Carolina, marries and has the first of her two boys. She lives nearer to Willow Springs and often returns there. Every time she visits, she goes out to the West Woods to talk with George.

Day, Vinnie Stockwell. *Life with Father; Life with Mother.* Clarence Day. 1920; 1936.

Vinnie Stockwell Day is an energetic and feisty New York high-society woman. Reared in Painesville, Ohio, in the middle of the nineteenth century, Vinnie leaves her hometown and moves to Manhattan to attend Miss Haines' School in Gramercy Park. By the time she is twenty years old, she has entertained several suitors and received a total of six marriage proposals. But the man who eventually steals her heart is the wealthy CLARENCE DAY, whom she marries after three years of courtship.

After a few years of marriage, Vinnie and Clarence move to Madison Avenue with their retinue of a cook, a waitress, a coachman, and nannies who help take care of their four sons. Although Vinnie does not work, she busies herself with domestic matters and leads an active social life. But most of her energy is devoted to her boisterous

but lovable husband, whose headstrong opinions and imperious ways create a series of household adventures.

While Vinnie holds fine men in very high regard and believes that males belong to a privileged class, she also asserts that women have certain rights and prerogatives that men must honor. One such right, according to Vinnie, is that every woman is entitled to receive an engagement ring as a token of her future husband's esteem—a duty Clarence fails to perform, thereby throwing a bone of contention into their marriage. Although Clarence gives Vinnie any number of elegant rings, Vinnie is simply not satisfied because, beautiful as they are, they are not engagement rings per se.

One day Vinnie learns from Clarence's mother that he had given his first fiancée an engagement ring, which she returned after they decided to cancel the wedding. Vinnie is livid and insists that Clarence hand over the ring; he does. Although the ring is paltry compared to the others she has received from him, she accepts it—and then purloins Clarence's pearl studs and takes them and the ring to Tiffany's where she has them combined in a new setting. Often devious in her efforts to outwit Clarence to get her way, Vinnie once again successfully circumvents his miserly tendencies.

After considerable coaxing, Vinnie convinces her husband to give her money to accompany some friends on a trip to Egypt. When she returns, she has money left over, which she hides from Clarence and uses until it runs out. After enjoying the freedom that these funds afforded her, she becomes fascinated with the idea of an allowance, which some of her younger, more liberated friends are urging her to demand. She finally convinces Clarence to give her a set amount of money each month, which she claims will cover household expenses and the charitable donations she occasionally proffers. But after the allowance routine is established, Vinnie refuses to pay household expenses, preferring instead to hoard the money and increase her nest egg.

Despite their financial altercations, Vinnie and Clarence are a loving couple and enjoy a long and happy life together. Clarence dies when he is almost eighty years old. Afterward, Vinnie moves to a new apartment that she remodels to suit her tastes. She thoroughly enjoys showing off her new place until her death, due to angina pectoris, at the age of seventy-six.

de Bellegarde, Valentin. *The American.* Henry James. 1877.

Valentin de Bellegarde is an idealistic young nobleman: Spontaneous, amicable, and ever the gallant, he stands in contrast to the stuffy urbanity of his mother, Madame de Bellegarde, and his older brother, Urbain de Bellegarde. Although he is an aristocrat, Valentin is penniless and will remain so, for his genteel family would never allow him to sully his hands in the pedestrian world of commerce.

He has nothing to do but amuse himself, and his dilettantism contrasts markedly with the enterprising self-reliance of his newfound American friend CHRISTOPHER NEWMAN.

Valentin and Newman develop a friendship when Newman becomes a frequent visitor to the Bellegarde household, where he is wooing Valentin's sister, the widow CLAIRE DE CINTRÉ. Though opposites, Valentin and Newman are quick to appreciate each other. Valentin commends Newman for his resourcefulness and ambition—for the fact that Newman has made his own place in the world—while he laments the dominance of his mother and the fact that his place in the world has been made for him. As an American, Newman has been able to make a success of himself, while the only pursuit open to a French nobleman such as Valentin is that of pleasure. Newman, for his part, idealizes Valentin as the epitome of French tradition and romance.

With Valentin, Newman discusses his suit for the hand of Claire de Cintré, and Valentin explains the resistance to such a match that Newman, a commoner, is sure to meet from the patrician Bellegardes. But when Newman declares his unbounded appreciation of Claire, Valentin decides that this appreciation alone qualifies Newman as a match for his sister: All men of taste, he effuses, are created equal. Thus Valentin resolves to plead Newman's case to his mother and brother.

Influenced by the prospect of bringing Newman's fortune into the family, the Bellegardes reluctantly permit the courtship. But when Claire de Cintré actually agrees to marry Newman, the haughty Bellegardes ultimately cannot tolerate the idea of a lowly commoner—even one of vast wealth—marrying into their family. They force Claire to terminate the engagement, and she, recognizing that it will never be her fate as a Bellegarde to marry happily, enters a Carmelite nunnery.

In the meantime, Newman has introduced Valentin to Noémie Nioche, a young painter whom Newman has commissioned to make copies of selected Louvre masterpieces. Valentin is quick to discern that Mademoiselle Nioche's artistic profession is but a ruse; her true ambition is for social prominence. He sees her for the mercenary coquette that she is, but he is nonetheless intrigued by her. Although Noémie is common in her ambition, she is, Valentin decides, rare in her determination and guile. Newman tries to talk Valentin out of his fascination with the woman, but Valentin disregards his pleas. He is ultimately governed not by reason but by his romantic nature. This proves to be his downfall, for he is soon mortally wounded in a duel to defend Mademoiselle Nioche's questionable honor.

On his deathbed, Valentin apologizes to Newman for the travesty that the ancient house of Bellegarde has now become. He tells Newman that he suspects a horrible family secret, which only the Bellegarde housekeeper, Mrs.

Bread, fully knows. If Newman will only beseech Mrs. Bread, in Valentin's name, to reveal the secret, then Newman will have the means to blackmail the Bellegardes into permitting his marriage to Claire de Cintré. With his dying breath, Valentin promises that this secret will avenge his friend Newman. Valentin dies, never fully knowing the ghastly Bellegarde secret nor what use Newman finally makes of it.

de Cintré, Claire. *The American.* Henry James. 1877.

Claire de Cintré is the dutiful daughter of an aristocratic French family, the Bellegardes. Her character is a mixture of cleverness and circumspection, gaiety and gravity, genteel sophistication and humble sweetness. Early in the tale her tragic fate is sealed when she agrees to be courted by a good-natured and enterprising American, CHRISTOPHER NEWMAN.

Newman has recently arrived in Paris where he reveals to his confidante, Mrs. Tristram, that he wants to acquire a wife who will be the ultimate trophy of his remarkably prosperous life. Mrs. Tristram introduces him to Claire, whom Newman soon decides is the woman he wants to marry. She resists his suit, however, for she has already suffered through one brief but unhappy marriage: As a very young woman she was forced by her indomitable mother, Madame de Bellegarde, into a loveless match with the elderly Comte de Cintré, who died not long after they were married. After the death of the Comte, Claire de Cintré made a solemn promise to her mother to do anything that was asked of her—anything, that is, but submit to another arranged marriage.

But Newman soon wins Claire's affections, and she demurely consents to a lengthy courtship, after which she will reconsider his proposal. Her mother and her brother, Urbain de Bellegarde, intrigued solely by the prospect of bringing Newman's fortune into the family, reluctantly agree to the courtship. When Claire actually agrees to marry Newman, however, the Bellegardes recant their consent, realizing that they could never abide the idea of a lowly commoner marrying into their family. They insist that Claire break off the engagement, and she complies. Distraught, Newman appeals her decision, but she explains that she must obey her mother unquestioningly. Her obedience is founded both in her adherence to French custom, which holds that the good of the family supersedes individual preference, and in her fear of her tyrannical mother. Although she still wants to marry Newman, she is simply not capable of the defiance that such a marriage would require.

Realizing that it will never be her lot to marry happily, Claire resigns herself to becoming a Carmelite nun, which will, she believes, gain her peace and safety from a world that deals cruel fate even to the innocent. She joins the austere order of the Carmelites. In the meantime, Newman's allies, VALENTIN DE BELLEGARDE, Claire's friendly and unpretentious brother, and Mrs. Bread, the kindly Bellegarde housekeeper, provide Newman with a terrible secret about the Bellegardes: Several years earlier Madame de Bellegarde did away with her husband by withholding his medication. Armed with this information, Newman endeavors to blackmail the Bellegardes into permitting the marriage, but they will not relent. A bitter and disillusioned Newman decides to visit the house of the Carmelites where Claire has taken her final vows to become Sister Veronica. Meditating outside the convent walls, Newman finally accepts that she is irrevocably lost to him. His hopeless yearning for her disappears and with it his vengeful anger toward the Bellegardes. Claire is cloistered for life, but her fate endures as testament to a tragic collision between enterprising American idealism and rigid old-world gentility.

De la Vega y Arillaga, Don Vincente. "The Pearls of Loreto." Gertrude Atherton. 1902.

This tale, set in Spanish California, is the tragic love story of Don Vincente de la Vega y Arillaga and Ysabel Herrera, the most beautiful woman in the Californias. The story begins at a horse race where Don Vincente—a handsome, mysterious native of Los Angeles—sits with his host, General Castro, a prominent citizen of Monterey. When challenged by Guido Cabañares, a hot-headed Montereno, Don Vincente races his champion black horse against Cabañares and wins. The victory brings Don Vincente fame throughout the city. After the race, on the way into town, Don Vincente and Ysabel see and are instantly attracted to each other.

That night at a dance, Don Vincente hovers in a corridor, watching the beautiful Ysabel. He emerges from the darkness and, taking her into his arms, begins to dance with her, telling her he wants her for a wife. At the end of the dance, Ysabel is surrounded by suitors who resent Don Vincente's intrusion. Cabañares publicly tells Don Vincente that Ysabel will wed no man who does not bring her a lapful of pearls.

Disconcerted and disillusioned, Don Vincente at first cannot believe this materialistic request. But Ysabel confirms that it is true. When the music begins again, Don Vincente boldly waltzes Ysabel through an open door into a bedroom and makes her promise that she will marry him no matter how he gets the pearls. She swears. Returning to his room, he takes out a letter from his friend which reveals that not long ago Indian divers discovered a rich bed of pearls in the ocean and brought the pearls to the Mission of Loreto. According to the letter, the pearls now adorn a statue of the Most Sacred Lady of Loreto, the Virgin Mary.

Determined to win Ysabel, Don Vincente travels a great distance to the Mission of Loreto. Late that night he goes to the chapel with an open sack. Jumping up on the altar, he severs the strands of pearls with his knife. The priest

enters; he sees Don Vincente and curses him, but before he can complete his malediction, Don Vincente stabs and kills him.

Don Vincente returns to Ysabel and drops the pearls into her lap. Ysabel is stunned. A man of honor, he tells her the truth about how he acquired the pearls. Ysabel is overwhelmed that he should kill his "immortal soul" for her, and she says she will go to hell with him. They plan to escape from Monterey that night.

Another costume ball is under way, and when Ysabel arrives adorned with the pearls, a gasp of awe fills the room. Inspired by Don Vincente, Ysabel dances as never before. The people go wild, shouting their approval and flinging handfuls of gold at her feet. Suddenly, a cloaked friar points accusingly at Don Vincente. He reveals that Don Vincente has robbed the church, stripped the Virgin statue, and killed the priest. Don Vincente admits this is true; Ysabel runs to his side, exclaiming that he did it for her. General Castro demands that the people of Monterey offer their hospitality instead of their blood, but outside they rise up and approach the house, seeking revenge on Don Vincente. Don Vincente sweeps Ysabel into his arms and dashes across the room.

Don Vincente and Ysabel reach the ocean and call out for the boatman, whom they have arranged to meet on the shore. The boatman does not answer, and dense fog prevents the lovers from seeing the rocks. Don Vincente says they must swim, but before they can get away, he is shot by the approaching mob. Ysabel drags the dying Don Vincente to the edge of the rocks. She hurls herself into the water, carrying him with her. The waves toss them up, grind them against the rocks, and bury them.

de Paris, Jocko. *End as a Man*. Calder Willingham. 1947.

The only son of General Arthur de Paris, one of the most successful and esteemed graduates of the Southern Military Academy, Jocko follows in his father's footsteps by attending the academy after high school. With his father annually bestowing large gifts on the academy, including a new wing of the boys' freshman dormitory, the young cadet soon feels himself above the institution's strict rules.

When Jocko is beaten by an upperclassman named Gatt as part of a cruel hazing ritual for incoming freshmen, he pays a visit to the commanding officer at the academy, his father's best friend, the retired General Haughton. He outlines the extent of his abuse at the hands of Gatt. Jocko is shocked when the general tells him in no uncertain terms that he, like all the other incoming freshmen, must endure this tradition, for it serves as part of the conditioning that will allow him to end four years there "as a man."

Bitter, Jocko is able to survive his freshman year but vows to exact revenge on the oppressive Gatt. In the first week of classes his sophomore year, Jocko gets drunk one night and passes out in a bar. When he wakes up, he is surprised to find that he has been taken home by a fresh-man named Robert Marquales. The next morning Jocko is so hung over that he fails to make roll call in time and is unable to clean his room for the daily inspection. When he is brought before General Haughton, the arrogant young man makes veiled threats to have his father with-hold some of the endowment that he annually lavishes upon the academy. The furious general informs him that he is on probation for the remainder of his stay at the academy and will be expelled for his next infraction, how-ever minor.

After a friendship develops between Marquales and Jocko, an opportunity for revenge presents itself when Gatt invites him to a friendly poker game with a few other academy upperclassmen. Jocko develops an elaborate cheating system and brings Marquales to the game; the group initially protests the freshman's presence but finally allows him to play. Jocko and Marquales then proceed to cheat Gatt out of ninety dollars.

When Gatt confronts Marquales the next day and asks him to return his money, Marquales, following careful instructions, refers him to Jocko. Feigning submission to Gatt's demands, Jocko writes Gatt a check for ninety dol-lars. When signing the check, however, Jocko, normally right-handed, signs it with his left hand so that the sig-nature looks fake, and afterward he informs the admin-istration that his checkbook has been stolen.

But Jocko's plan is foiled when General Haughton learns of their exploit and summons him to his office. There, the unrepentant young man is expelled from the academy once and for all.

Dead, Macon "Milkman." *Song of Solomon.* Toni Mor-rison. 1977.

The life story of Macon Dead, nicknamed "Milkman," from birth to middle age is told in this powerful novel of violence and memory. Estranged from his family, Milkman sets out to search for gold, only to discover the truth about his heritage from strangers. He returns home eager to embrace those he has neglected but finds that in some cases he is too late.

The only son of Ruth and Macon Dead, Milkman ac-quired his nickname when his mother was found still nurs-ing him four years after his birth. His brooding father is a successful real estate developer who has little to do with his family or his sister, Pilate, who makes and sells wine. Milkman is drawn to his mysterious aunt, and he and his best friend Guitar spend happy days with Pilate, her daughter Reba, and her granddaughter Hagar. But when Macon finds out, he forbids Milkman to see Pilate again.

Working at his father's office, Milkman falls into a relationship with his cousin Hagar and drifts through the next few years. One night Macon hits Ruth, and Milkman starts a fight with him. Macon tells Milkman afterward that Ruth and her father had been incestuously close. Dis-turbed by this story, Milkman begins to question his re-lationships with everyone and ends up breaking off his relationship with Hagar.

Milkman grows increasingly bored and restless as time goes by. One day, while talking with Macon, Milkman mentions a green sack Pilate has hung up in her house. This detail suddenly animates Macon, who tells Milkman of a youthful episode in which he killed a man in Pilate's presence. Pilate refused to let Macon take the man's gold, but she and the gold later disappeared. Macon believes the gold is in the green sack, and he urges Milkman to steal it.

Enlisting the help of his friend Guitar, Milkman at-tempts to steal Pilate's "gold." They are arrested and dis-cover that the bag contains only bones. Pilate, who has secured their release, admits that the bones belong to the man Macon killed in the cave.

Obsessed now with unearthing the lost gold, Milkman sets out for Pennsylvania. After talking to people who had once known his family, he finally finds the cave in which the murder took place, but it is empty. Now believing that Pilate has hidden the gold, he sets out for Virginia.

After several encounters with the inhabitants of a small Virginia town, Milkman loses interest in the gold and begins to learn about his family's origins. He feels ashamed of his carelessness toward his parents and Hagar. He suddenly realizes that the song the town children sing contains the names of his grandparents. From Susan Byrd, a former neighbor of the family, he hears that his grand-father was the son of Solomon, who one day flew out of the fields and back to Africa. He tried to take his son but dropped him. Milkman's grandmother's parents found and raised the boy, whose real name was Jake.

Heading for home, Milkman realizes that the only people who value him are those for whom he has done nothing: Pilate and Ruth. He rushes home, but when he goes to tell Pilate of his revelation, she breaks a bottle over his head. The grief-stricken Hagar has died in his absence.

Milkman and Pilate journey back to Virginia to bury the sack of bones, which, Milkman has discovered, belong to Pilate's father, not to the man Macon had killed. Guitar, bound by a pact with a secret society called the Seven Days to avenge the death of all murdered blacks, is de-termined to kill Milkman in retribution for the death of Hagar, for which he blames him. Aiming for Milkman, Guitar shoots Pilate instead. Milkman holds her and sings to her as she dies. He then leaps at Guitar, realizing that "if you surrendered to the air, you could ride it."

Deadwood Dick. *Deadwood Dick, the Prince of the Road.* Edward J. Wheeler. 1877.

The black-clad Deadwood Dick is a mysterious Wild West bandit in this late-nineteenth-century dime novel se-ries set in and around the California territories being mined during the gold rush. Throughout the series of popular novels, Deadwood Dick defies his enemies and disregards the law as he ingeniously leads his band of nomad followers. Actually an orphan who has spent his life trying to escape from the clutches of his abusive uncle, he does not reveal his true identity until the end of the first book in the series.

When we first see Deadwood Dick, he comes upon a poster announcing a $500 reward for the "notorious young desperado Deadwood Dick," signed by Hugh Vansevere. Laughing loudly, Deadwood Dick rides off to find Vansevere, whom he does not know. Deadwood Dick discovers Vansevere on the street in the town of Deadwood, shoots him instantly, and departs.

Soon after, a youth named Ned Harris watches a card game between Harry Redburn and a dishonest gambler. Harris exposes the gambler, and when he does, Redburn, following the laws of the town, kills the gambler. Chaos erupts in the saloon, and Harris and Redburn, now friends, leave the place together. With the help of Calamity Jane, Harris and Redburn escape from Deadwood and make their way to Harris's log cabin in the woods. Harris's melancholy sister Anita lives in the cabin, and Harris, in order to protect her, tells Redburn that if he falls in love with Anita, he must not express it to her. Leaving Redburn with Anita, Harris goes off to take care of some unspecified business.

Ned Harris, as we learn at the conclusion of the story, is Deadwood Dick. After leaving Redburn, he encounters his enemies: his evil uncle Alexander Filmore and Filmore's blood-hungry son. The Filmores, who hired Hugh Vansevere to find Deadwood Dick, have come west to take matters into their own hands. Riding aboard a stagecoach that Deadwood Dick surrounds and holds up, the Filmores shoot Deadwood Dick. He falls clutching his breast, but suddenly scores of masked men emerge from the woods to save him. A bitter exchange follows between Dick and the elder Filmore; the bandits then tie up the Filmores and ride away with their leader.

Out of his bandit costume, Ned Harris runs into FEAR-LESS FRANK in Deadwood. When the two old enemies meet, Harris challenges Fearless Frank to a duel, and Fearless Frank shoots him. Thinking Harris is dead and feeling some remorse, Fearless Frank and his companion, Alice Terry, continue on to Deadwood.

In the meantime, gold miners have overrun the formerly peaceful valley where Redburn and Anita are living. One day Deadwood Dick rides into the valley, and Redburn and Anita give him shelter. Redburn, who has taken control of matters in Ned Harris's absence, begins to like this strange masked man whom he believes to be a gentleman in disguise.

After dinner one night, Redburn, Anita, and Alice's father "Nix" are singing together. The music makes Deadwood Dick recall memories of old times, and he lets out

a deep sigh before returning to his men. Later, Deadwood Dick is captured by the Filmores and almost killed. After being saved by Calamity Jane and Fearless Frank, he orders his men to bring the Filmores and two nooses to the cabin. At the cabin he reveals that he is indeed Ned Harris, Anita's brother. He tells the story of his origins and his struggle with the Filmores. When Deadwood Dick asks Alice Terry to marry him, she refuses, confessing her love for Redburn. Calamity Jane also refuses his proposal and says they can only be friends, not mates. And so Deadwood Dick submits to being single for the rest of his life and takes to the hills again. Grim and uncommunicative, he continues to roam the West with his gang, performing feats of unequaled daring wherever he goes.

Deane, Ferdinand "Fer." *Strike!* Mary Heaton Vorse. 1930.

Ferdinand "Fer" Deane is the northern labor organizer who, somewhat unwillingly, leads a group of workers in a long, harrowing strike against a southern textile mill. The strike, which ultimately requires Fer's martyrdom for its success, is only one step in a larger plan to gain a foothold for the unionization of all southern textile workers.

The town's angry middle class believes that the fabric of their society will unravel if a strike transpires, and Fer becomes the target of their fear and hostility. Fer recognizes that they mistakenly identify him and not the conditions of life at the mill as the source of the strike. While neither a weak nor a compromising leader, he often wishes aloud that he could return to the North (or at least go fishing for a few weeks) to escape the adversity and threats of violence. The most he can do is preach nonviolence to the workers, which he does continually, knowing that if a single worker throws a brick or fires a gun, the authorities will descend on them.

When the National Guard is brought into town to quell the strike, Fer, foreseeing total and bloody warfare, argues for complete nonconfrontation and orders the striking women to fraternize with the National Guard. His plan succeeds; under the influence of the women, the guardsmen cease to be allied fully with the oppressive Armed Forces, and finally, the town's leaders ask for their removal. After the Guard leaves, however, the local police no longer have reason to restrain themselves. They continue with the looting and dynamiting of strike headquarters and the night attacks on sympathizing households. When workers are eventually thrown out of already overpriced company houses, the police enforce these evictions, and Fer must organize a "tent city" to house the strikers.

Finally, what Fer has feared most comes to pass. One night when a police patrol approaches the tent city, the strikers guarding its perimeter open fire and kill the sheriff. Blood has been shed, and the strikers are responsible. The townspeople destroy the tent city and with flaming torches in hand begin a manhunt for strikers through the woods. Fer and eight other strike leaders are found and tried for murder. Fer predicts the verdict: Along with three others he is convicted on conspiracy and murder charges and sentenced to twenty years in prison.

After his sentencing, Fer is released on bail. During his trial the strikers continued to organize and plan for a walkout at the main mill, and now they ask him to speak at their rally at the mill gates. He does, knowing that he is risking his life—but also knowing that he must speak if the union is to succeed. His appearance provokes a police riot that results in his death and the deaths of five other workers. At their trial the police are excused for doing their duty.

Fer and the others are buried by a crowd of determined workers whose ideals have been tempered through injustice and violence. In their final eulogies they purge Fer of his human frailties and turn him into a fearless martyr, a symbol of the unstoppable unionization of the South.

Deckard, Richard ''Rick.'' *Do Androids Dream of Electric Sheep?* Philip K. Dick. 1968.

Rick Deckard, an average citizen of a futuristic dystopia, strives to accumulate visible material wealth so he can impress the neighbors and keep his wife Iran happy. Nevertheless, he worries continually that his values clash with the teachings of Mercerism, the predominant religion of the twenty-first century. In Mercerism, human and animal life are held in the highest regard, and empathy is believed to be what distinguishes humans from their manufactured counterparts, the androids. Although Rick makes his living as a bounty hunter by destroying androids, he sometimes wonders whether they, too, are not deserving of his empathy.

Rick has lost enthusiasm for his work, but when he receives his latest assignment—to hunt and "retire" six androids of the Nexus-6 line that have escaped from Mars—he accepts it, anticipating the monetary reward. He will be paid $1,000 per android, and he knows that this money will enable him to replace the cheap electric sheep on his rooftop at home (a poor man's status symbol) with a real, living animal, a highly prized commodity.

When Rick meets the android Rachael Rosen, his cynical indifference toward androids gradually leaves him, and he begins to fall in love. Rachael, the latest creation of Eldon Rosen and his Rosen Association, is one of the most vividly human androids ever invented. Programmed to believe that she is Eldon's niece and assistant, Rachael does not even know she is an android. When Rick determines, after testings, that she is indeed an android, he tells her the truth. She is saddened by the news, and Rick—an empathetic human—feels sad with her. She promises to help him find the escaped androids, knowing that she will best understand their psychology.

The first three androids are relatively easy to retire because once they are found, they submit, lacking the human will to live. The last three, including the ringleader Roy Baty, are more difficult to find, and once found, cling more tenaciously to life. They have hidden themselves in an apartment building in the desecrated suburbs of San Francisco.

Deckard finally destroys all of his android quarry, but not without realizing that he loves Rachael and feels sorry for the others. With his reward money he buys a very expensive goat, which dies almost immediately. Now with little money to show for his trouble and love for an android whose life span is predetermined to be two years, he has a newfound respect for the tenets of Mercerism and for all life, mechanical and otherwise.

Deen, Tracy. *Strange Fruit.* Lillian Smith. 1944.

Tracy Deen, the only son of Alma and Dr. Tut Deen, has returned to his racially divided hometown after a stint in the military during World War I. Although now in his mid-twenties, Tracy, a spoiled and privileged white southern gentleman, has as yet shown little interest in establishing himself independently of his parents. Almost as soon as he returns to Maxwell from the military he resumes his secret affair with his black lover, the refined and gentle NONNIE ANDERSON, who lives with her sister Bess in a house in Maxwell's Colored Town.

Soon after the resumption of the affair, Non becomes pregnant and decides to keep the child. Tracy, who has been under increasing pressure from his family to make a respectable match, becomes engaged to Dottie Pusey, a white woman. Under the tutelage of the Reverend Dunwoodie, he also becomes a member of his parents' church during its revival meetings. Tracy professes his acceptance of the church publicly during a service shortly after his engagement is announced.

At the same time that he becomes engaged, Tracy begins to negotiate with his father on the matter of a future profession. Dr. Deen, who had been forced to abandon and then sell his family's farm, hopes that his son will take an interest in buying the farm back and in making it operate profitably. For a time at least, Tracy seems to agree with this idea, although he makes no firm commitment.

Meanwhile, with attention to matters of morality honed by his conversion, Tracy decides to renounce his affair with Non. Because he loves Nonnie in his own way and doesn't want to abandon her entirely, he decides, on the advice of Reverend Dunwoodie, to buy her off. With $300 borrowed from his mother, Tracy concocts a plan to marry Nonnie off to Big Henry, his companion since childhood. Henry, who occupies a small cabin on the Deens' property, has spent his entire life obeying Tracy's commands, so he is willing to take the $100 and the pretty wife that Tracy is offering in order to please his white friend.

In a muddled effort to overcome the temptation that he feels Nonnie's sexuality and blackness represent, Tracy beats and rapes his pregnant lover. He then offers her $200 to marry Henry, assuring her that he will kill Henry if he tries to have sex with her once they are married.

Tracy's plans are thwarted, however, when Henry brags about the deal they made in the presence of Nonnie's brother Ed. Enraged by the callousness of his sister's former lover, Ed kills Tracy. Henry, innocent but careless, is lynched by the whites of the town for the murder.

Delano, Captain Amasa. "Benito Cereno." Herman Melville. 1855.

Amasa Delano, a naive and complacent American, is captain of the *Bachelor's Delight*, a trader lying at anchor off the coast of Chile, one hazy morning in 1799. In this story based on an actual occurrence, Captain Delano boards the *San Dominick*, a Spanish slave ship, which he perceives yawing haphazardly nearby. By steadfastly turning a blind eye to the strange events that unfold, he unwittingly jeopardizes his own life as well as that of the *San Dominick*'s captain, DON BENITO CERENO.

Upon his arrival aboard the *San Dominick*, Captain Delano is greeted by Don Benito, who seems oddly listless and bedraggled in comparison to his attendant, a small black man named Babo. Captain Delano notices that the ship is in a sad state of disrepair; in the throng that gathers about him, the blacks greatly outnumber the whites, while a group of six blacks sit some eight feet above the crowd, polishing their hatchets by clashing them menacingly together. Captain Delano attributes this disarray to the marked absence of superior officers and registers with no small degree of satisfaction the contrast presented by Babo's solicitous attentions to his "master."

Captain Delano inquires politely after the *San Dominick*'s circumstances. When Don Benito responds with a garbled account of the ship encountering a gale off Cape Horn and a subsequent outbreak of scurvy, Captain Delano forbears criticizing the Spaniard's seamanship. Instead, he thinks compassionately of the vessel's obvious need for supplies. Don Benito frequently falters in his conversation and must be propped up by Babo, who never leaves his side. Suddenly, one of the blacks on the deck strikes one of the white sailors on the head with a knife—an act so lacking in discipline that Captain Delano cannot refrain from thinking, "I know no sadder sight than a commander who has little of command but the name."

As the day wears on, Captain Delano begins to grow irritated with Babo's habit of conferring in whispers with Don Benito; what had initially seemed a charming attachment on the part of the black now strikes the American as overly familiar. Also, one of the few Spanish sailors remaining appears to be glancing significantly in Captain Delano's direction. Waiting for the boat from the *Bachelor's Delight* to return, Captain Delano begins to wonder uneasily whether Don Benito and the blacks were contemplating some sort of foul play. But blacks are "too stupid," he thinks: "Yes, this is a strange craft; a strange history, too, and strange folks on board. But—nothing more."

When the supplies arrive, Captain Delano commands the blacks, who have eagerly crowded around, to step back. At this the hatchet polishers rise, and Don Benito utters a cry. Captain Delano—again suspecting the Spaniard—almost jumps into his boat, but the crowd immediately desists. Babo then accompanies Don Benito down to the cabin for a shave. Watching Babo, razor in hand, meticulously shave his quaking "master"—Don Benito almost faints when, at one point, Babo draws blood—Captain Delano asks himself, bemused, what the purpose of this ritual might be.

Captain Delano departs at last. As his boat is pulling out, Don Benito springs over the side of the *San Dominick* and lands at his feet. "This plotting pirate means murder!" Captain Delano exclaims. Babo, dagger in hand, also leaps into the boat. Captain Delano manages to disarm him, and holding Babo down on one side and Don Benito on the other, begins madly rowing away. But Babo draws a second knife out of his robe and lunges forward. At that moment Captain Delano sees that Babo's target is not himself but Don Benito, and the fact that the blacks have actually mutinied finally becomes clear. Captain Delano fells Babo with a blow and "with infinite pity" releases Don Benito.

Several days later Captain Delano embarks on a voyage with Don Benito to Lima, where the mutineers are to be tried. The two converse warmly about their impressions of that fateful day—Captain Delano ruefully admitting that he had misjudged his fellow officer, and Don Benito praising Captain Delano's forthright demeanor. Although his spirits have temporarily revived, Don Benito is unable to recover his health and predicts that his own death is near. At this the good-natured Delano is both astonished and pained. He begs his friend to banish his forebodings. After all, he cries, "You are saved!"

Demetrius. *The Robe.* Lloyd C. Douglas. 1942.

Demetrius, the loyal Corinthian slave of MARCELLUS GALLIO, plays a central role in the unfolding of this religious narrative. Born and bred in a cultivated Greek home where he studied the classics and became a great athlete, Demetrius is a young man of exceptional promise. However, the invasion of Corinth by Roman legions radically alters the course of his life. Demetrius's father is put to death, and the rest of the family is enslaved. Demetrius himself is taken to Rome where a Roman senator purchases him as a gift for his son. When his new young master, Marcellus, becomes the commander at the Roman fort at Minoa, Demetrius accompanies him.

During their tenure in Palestine, the soldiers in the garrison at Minoa are ordered to go to Jerusalem to keep the peace throughout the Jewish Passover. On the road into the ancient city, Demetrius has an encounter that affects him deeply and permanently. There is a sudden stirring in the crowd entering the city, and he is curious to see what all the commotion is about. When he reaches the center of the excitement, he sees a simply clad man sitting on a donkey, surrounded by a circle of men who are attempting to clear a way for him through the crowd. The man appears to be resignedly sad, and he surveys the enormous crowd with silent compassion.

The eyes of the stranger come to rest on Demetrius, who instantly feels himself held in an invisible grip. He senses in those eyes a sacred power, one that obliterates all the pain of afflicting circumstances no matter how grave or terrible. The experience overwhelms Demetrius, and he breaks down in tears.

Later, Demetrius is horrified to learn that this singular person, Jesus of Nazareth, has been condemned to death and that his master is charged with carrying out the execution. Demetrius goes to the site of the crucifixion and finds Marcellus callously rolling dice for the executed Galilean's robe. Marcellus wins the robe and orders Demetrius to take charge of it. Demetrius does so gladly, in the hopes that he will be allowed to keep the garment. The thought of owning something that the great man wore comforts him.

That evening at a drunken banquet given by Pilate, Marcellus is pressed by the unruly crowd to put on the robe. The experience is so humiliating for the proud young commander that he orders Demetrius to burn the garment immediately. The slave disobeys his master for the first time by keeping the robe. Later that evening he aborts an attempt to escape to freedom because he feels his master is intensely depressed and in need of his aid. Demetrius does everything within his power to help Marcellus out of his agonizing psychological state, but to no avail.

Before accompanying Marcellus to Greece, Demetrius turns down an offer from his master's father to travel with Marcellus as a free man, for he believes that any alteration in the status of their relationship may be detrimental to his master's recovery. While in Greece, Marcellus becomes suicidal. When he looks for a dagger in his slave's baggage, he finds the robe Demetrius has hidden there. Seizing it, he is miraculously healed of his psychological affliction.

During their stay in Greece, Demetrius falls in love with a Greek woman. When a Roman Tribune makes lewd advances toward her, Demetrius intervenes and beats the Tribune unconscious. Fleeing Greece, he seeks refuge in Jerusalem where he meets the followers of Jesus, learns of the resurrection, and converts to Christianity.

When Demetrius attempts to return to Rome, he is critically wounded by cavalrymen. On the verge of certain death, he is miraculously restored to health by the supernatural healing powers of Peter, a disciple of Jesus.

In order to heal Demetrius, Peter has promised Christ that Demetrius will carry the Christian message of Jesus to his own countrymen and testify to the miraculous healing. Demetrius is last seen preparing to fulfill this promise, to return to Greece and begin his ministry.

Denis. *A Sign for Cain.* Grace Lumpkin. 1935.

Denis returns to his home in the southern town of Jefferson to care for his ailing mother and improve life for the poor and oppressed. Nancy, his overworked mother, is the most devoted black servant of a prominent white family, the Gaults. Immediately after arriving, Denis begins the dangerous work of organizing a union for the farm workers.

In the North, Denis had worked in a mill where the union organizers circulated Marxist literature and educated him in communist thought. In Jefferson, where the majority is against this type of reform, Denis proceeds to disseminate information and rally support with extreme caution. Many of the black workers fear the consequences of making new demands on their employers. However, Denis does find a number of people, both black and white, willing to fight for reforms. Among them are BILL DUNCAN, a newspaper editor; Lee Foster, an overseer on the Gault plantation; and Ficents, a worker on the plantation.

The first achievement of the new organization is modest but significant. Denis, Lee Foster, and several others from the Gault plantation visit Colonel Gault and formally request that the workers and sharecroppers be provided with sufficient supplies. Colonel Gault consents. Several days later the sheriff, who has heard that Denis is "causing trouble," warns Colonel Gault that Denis will be in danger if he continues his activities. Although the Colonel angrily dismisses the sheriff, he in turn advises Denis that his activities can only bring harm to him and his "comrades."

Denis continues to distribute pamphlets and attend meetings. Returning home after dark from a meeting, he and two friends, Ficents and Ed Clarke, see a car stopped in the middle of the road and a white shape lying in the grass nearby. Concerned, they debate whether to stop to see if someone needs help. Not wishing to risk the danger of being seen out at night, they proceed home.

When the murdered body of Evelyn Gardner, a relative of the Gaults, is later discovered in the road, the sheriff seizes this as an excuse to arrest Denis and Ficents as suspects. The sheriff learns that an ignorant girl, Mary Sellers, had seen them on the road that evening; he bribes her into testifying that she saw Denis rape and murder the woman. Denis's friends, who know that there is no evidence to support this accusation, work frantically to protect him and try to ensure a fair trial. Bill Duncan manages to quell an ensuing lynch mob and arranges for northern lawyers to defend Denis and Ficents. Nevertheless, these friends cannot protect the prisoners from the sheriff, who beats them senselessly—leaving Denis unconscious and inducing Ficents to sign a statement confessing to the murder.

Before the trial even begins, JIM GAULT, Evelyn Gardner's nephew and the real murderer, succumbs to the browbeating of his drunk cohorts, enters the jail, and shoots both suspects to death. The novel closes with a meeting of workers organizing a massive funeral and protest in memory of Denis and Ficents.

Densher, Merton. *The Wings of the Dove*. Henry James. 1902.

Merton Densher, an attractive and ambitious young journalist, extinguishes the very romance he wishes to sustain. Densher believes he is being faithful to his lover, KATE CROY, by participating in a scheme to deceive MILDRED "MILLY" THEALE, an American heiress. Although their plot is successful, Densher cannot set aside his guilt or the unexpected depth of feeling he has for Milly.

Growing up on the continent, where his father worked as a chaplain, Densher was educated at Swiss schools and at a German university. By his own choice he returned to Britain to study at his father's college in Cambridge. From there he moved to London and began his career as a newspaper journalist. Densher meets Kate in a London gallery at a party of artistic foreigners. Although they have an unusually long and engaged conversation, Densher makes no arrangement to meet Kate again. Their next encounter takes place by chance on the Underground Railway several months later. Despite opposition from Kate's guardian, her aunt Maud Lowder, they meet regularly for long walks. Aunt Maud considers Densher too poor for Kate and has chosen Lord Mark, an English nobleman, to be Kate's suitor. Kate's value, Densher comes to believe, is in her unconventionality, and it is for her "differences" that he wishes to marry her. They make extravagant pledges to each other and are secretly engaged before Densher leaves for America on a journalistic assignment.

Densher's tour of America, which extends across the entire country, includes a stay in New York City, where he is entertained for several days by Milly Theale. A series of illnesses in her family has left young Milly alone and enormously rich; now she plans to leave New York and travel to Europe. Densher is not particularly struck by Milly, but he begins receiving enthusiastic praise of her in Kate's letters. Milly and her companion, SUSAN SHEPHERD STRINGHAM, have been welcomed into Maud Lowder's circle at Lancaster Gate in London and have become intimate friends. After he returns to London, Densher realizes that Milly is falling in love with him. But while the rest of London society is captivated by Milly, Densher cannot understand their fascination with this pale, odd little person.

Kate, secure in both Milly's faith and Densher's love, conceives of a brilliant plan when she learns that Milly is stricken with a fatal illness. If Densher can court and perhaps marry Milly for the rest of her brief life, he will inherit her ample fortune, with which he could then marry Kate. Densher pleads with Kate to accept him as he is, but her refusal forces him to comply with her plan. The party moves in August from London to Venice, where Milly has rented a palace. When Kate and Maud Lowder return to London, Densher stays behind with orders from Kate to court Milly. He agrees to stay on the condition that Kate "come to him" as proof of her commitment. Comforting himself with the memory of his first night with Kate, Densher diligently but mechanically visits Milly at the palace every day.

The courtship proceeds smoothly until Densher is suddenly denied entrance to the palace. When he catches a glimpse of Lord Mark, Kate's supposed suitor, Densher suspects the horrible reason. After several agonizing days of solitude, Densher receives a visit from Milly's companion, Susan Stringham, who explains that Lord Mark has informed Milly that Densher is engaged to Kate and that the news is literally killing her. Densher knows that if he denies the engagement, he can save her; he feels, however, that such a statement would be binding, and he would erase his hope of marrying Kate. Milly receives Densher at the palace one final time and dismisses him from Venice. In order to endure the journey back to London, Densher must think of Milly as already dead. She dies soon after he returns to London.

An unhappy strain settles on Densher and Kate, who no longer enjoy each other's company. When a letter arrives announcing that Milly has left her fortune to Densher, he begs Kate to help him renounce it and says he can marry her only if she accepts him as he is, without the money. Kate also has a condition: that he swear he is not in love with Milly's memory. But Densher cannot meet this condition, and their relationship is now changed forever—regardless of whether they marry.

Derrick, Magnus. *The Octopus*. Frank Norris. 1901.

Proud, domineering Magnus Derrick rules the ominously named Rancho de Los Muertos, the largest ranch in the area of California's San Joaquin Valley. Derrick's story is emblematic of the struggle of the ranchers against the sprawling, politically powerful railroad. Despite his strength of character and his vast fields of wheat, Magnus feels the crushing tentacle of the Pacific and Southwestern Railroad as severely as the rest of the ranchers.

When one of the other ranchers proposes a corrupt scheme to "buy" a sympathetic state railroad commission in order to ensure a protectionist policy, Magnus is initially reluctant, disdaining to sully his honorable name with a corrupt undertaking. But realizing that he cannot help but benefit from the scheme if it succeeds, the same sense of honor prompts him to back the other ranchers, and they succeed in installing one of Magnus's own sons, the lawyer Lyman Derrick, in a pivotal post on the commission. Lyman ultimately fails to support the ranchers, however, thus betraying his own father.

Meanwhile, the railroad has been angling for portions of the ranchers' lands to which it holds a dubious title. The ranchers, knowing now that they cannot defeat the railroad in court, determine to fight for what they consider their land, and once again Magnus lends his moral authority to their cause. But word of his part in the corrupt election of the railroad commission gets out, and his moral reputation is jeopardized. It is wondered whether the ranchers are earnest, honest men who want only to raise their wheat in peace or whether they are scheming politicians, as base as the system they oppose. To protect the positive public image of his brethren, Magnus submits to blackmail by a local journalist, a henchman of the Pacific and Southwestern Railroad. Inevitably, the battle for the land becomes violent. Magnus encourages dialogue, but shots are fired, and his other son, Harran, and several ranchers end up dead. Bankrupt and broken in spirit, Magnus prepares to give up the battle.

But more indignities await him. During a public hearing on behalf of the ranchers, his part in the election is disclosed, and he flees the lectern in disgrace. By the novel's end, he has become a half-senseless old man, obsequiously accepting a menial job from S. BEHRMAN, the local agent of the railroad.

Devil-Bug. *The Quaker City; or, The Monks of Monk-Hall.* George Lippard. 1844.

A one-eyed twisted monstrosity of a man, Devil-Bug is the key figure in the convoluted plot of this Gothic protest novel. Born in a brothel, he has known no life but that of underground Philadelphia, a morally vile world of sexual and social crime.

As the novel opens in the year 1842, Devil-Bug is acting as general factotum of Monk-Hall, a private club where outwardly respectable citizens can safely indulge in all the vices they publicly denounce. A fantastic old mansion with underground levels, Monk-Hall provides its members with resources for sexual affairs, drinking, gambling, and even murder. At present Devil-Bug is aiding a prominent "Monk," Gus Lorrimer, a wealthy roué who specializes in the deflowering of young upper-class women.

Gus's prey for the evening is Mary Arlington, whose scruples he has overcome by promising her a clandestine marriage in the precincts of Monk-Hall. The fake service, set up by Devil-Bug, is halted by a guest whom a boastful Gus has invited to watch his evil scheme. The horrified guest, known to Gus only as Byrnewood, recognizes that the intended "bride" is his sister. Gus is only momentarily balked; he has Byrnewood held captive by Devil-Bug and proceeds to rape Mary, who loses her mind after his violent assault. Throughout the rest of the novel Byrnewood pursues Gus, although his vengeance is delayed by the continued assaults of Devil-Bug. Only after Byrnewood's final escape from Monk-Hall does he waylay the fleeing Gus and shoot him dead.

This is but one of the many horrific episodes in which Devil-Bug is the agent who promotes not only sexual crime but also moral corruption in the worlds of such Philadelphians as the merchant prince, the society matron, and the clergyman. Yet if he is a victimizer, Devil-Bug is also a victim of his own tragic past. Years before, he had given shelter in Monk-Hall to a young woman who had fled her home after delivering an illegitimate child. While in Monk-Hall she was impregnated by Devil-Bug and had returned to the outside world to bear their daughter. By a convoluted plot twist, this daughter now stands to gain a fortune, but only if her true parentage remains unknown. In his only decent action in the book, Devil-Bug arranges his own death in the pit of Monk-Hall, just as a finally aroused police force closes in to storm the old den of vice.

Devon, Christie. *Work.* Louisa May Alcott. 1873.

Christie Devon is orphaned at a very early age and sent to live with her aunt and uncaring Uncle Enos. Desiring to escape her uncle's authority, Christie leaves home at the age of eighteen and sets out to make her own way in the world.

After taking a room at a local boardinghouse, Christie, who initially wanted a position as a governess, finds she is only qualified for a job as a maid. She moves in with the Stuart family, where the tyrannical rule of Mrs. Stuart makes life almost unbearable for her. Her only consolation is a friendship she develops with a matronly black servant named Hepsey.

Christie is finally fired from the Stuarts' household when a candle she was using for reading is accidentally overturned and the attic catches fire. Filled with remorse, she returns to the boardinghouse, and one of the lodgers suggests that she audition for a local theater troupe. Christie gets a small part in a local production and stays with the theater for three years. Her roles become increasingly prominent, and she is on the verge of stardom when a light falls from a rafter and severely injures her.

Afraid that her life in the theater had been making her a ruthlessly ambitious woman, Christie looks upon the accident as a blessing in disguise and decides not to return to the theater after her recovery. In any case, she feels that she is now finally refined enough to get the governess job she had initially desired. Working for the Carroll family, Christie attracts the attentions of a Mr. Fletcher, who finally asks for her hand in marriage. Sensing a condescending tone in Fletcher's voice and hesitant to surrender the freedom and independence she has earned, Christie declines.

After a short, unsuccessful stint as a seamstress, Christie is unable to find work and falls into a deep depression. She is on the verge of drowning herself when Rachel, an old friend from the seamstress shop, finds her and tells her of a family that will take her in.

Christie stays with the Wilkens family for a time, helping the ebullient Mrs. Wilkens take care of her six children. She eventually befriends and falls in love with David Sterling, a neighboring young man who is friendly and sensitive but withdrawn. David's mother hints at a reason for his behavior when she tells Christie that David is recovering from a very traumatic experience about which he is unable to speak.

Mr. Fletcher arrives unexpectedly soon afterward and again asks Christie to marry him. Despite her uncertainty about David's feelings for her, Christie once again declines. Her faith in David is soon rewarded when his sister, whose disappearance was the source of his anxiety, returns to their family. David confesses his love to Christie, and the two are married.

When the Civil War breaks out, Christie follows David to work as a nurse in a Yankee hospital. He is killed during the last months of the war in an attempt to avenge the slaughter of a family of slaves by Confederate soldiers. After a period of mourning, Christie returns to the Wilkenses, where she finds comfort once again in the independence and freedom she derives from her work.

Diana, Reverend Hubert. "The Man Who Saw Through Heaven." Wilbur Daniel Steele. 1925.

When Reverend Hubert Diana and his wife visit Boston one week before they are scheduled to set sail for their mission to Africa, the story's narrator tries to entertain them. A stern, mirthless man, Reverend Diana is a firm believer in what the narrator calls "old-time religion," and he retains a strict, puritanical vision of God and man. Possessing no social graces, the Reverend and his wife have spent most of their marriage faithfully traveling through distant lands, converting as many heathens as possible to Christianity.

As the narrator soon discovers, such a couple is difficult to keep occupied by the usual methods of entertainment. When the Reverend is taken to the observatory, however, he becomes fascinated by the theological implications of a lecture given by Krum, an astronomer. Krum explains to the bewildered Reverend that the galaxy is only a small speck within the infinite boundaries of the universe and that we are no more than a tiny ring on the finger of the galaxy. When Mrs. Diana and the narrator grow tired of the observatory, the enthralled Reverend encourages them to go home, and they leave. The Reverend stays with Krum, who is flattered by the attention, to discuss matters of the cosmos.

The next day Reverend Diana embarks on the ocean liner to Africa a changed man. One morning, much to the horror of his wife, he preaches stark naked to a group of passengers on the ship's top deck. At the first port of call in Algiers, the Reverend abandons his wife and wanders the countryside to preach his new astro-religion to all who will listen. After failing to convert anyone, he decides to venture through the African continent alone to spread his new brand of religion to the natives.

Much to Reverend Diana's disappointment, the inhabitants of the small villages in Africa are no more receptive to his teachings than the Algerians had been. Undaunted, the Reverend travels from village to village, leaving in his wake strange mud models of the planet and solar system. Much later, haggard, worn, and feverish from his exposure to the jungle, he finally arrives in a village called Tara. The inhabitants of Tara, who think the Reverend is a very queer man, give him the name "Father Witch." The Reverend, now totally defeated, uses his last ounces of energy to erect a mud statue of himself. When the mud idol is finished, he wanders out of the village. A half-mile into the jungle, he dies a martyr to a religion that had no followers. If not for the efforts of Mrs. Diana and the narrator to find the Reverend after his disappearance from Algiers, the story of Hubert Diana would have been lost forever.

Didymus (Father). "Lions, Harts, Leaping Does." J. F. Powers. 1944.

An elderly friar residing in a monastery, Father Didymus continually analyzes his motivations, hoping to maintain the spirit of his vows. When he becomes annoyed with Titus, his plodding, simple-minded companion, for his ability to better withstand the severe cold, he chides himself for manifesting vanity. Fearing that the spiritual value of his work may have been vitiated, he wonders if he is wrong to choose the teaching of geometry out of personal preference. He purposely stubs his toe because he has attempted to ward off the cold by wearing woolen socks, but then immediately charges himself with exhibitionism. Even his vows of poverty, chastity, and obedience mean little now that they have become such habits as to require no spiritual effort.

Didymus reasons that physical adherence to the vows "did not promise perfection"; rather, "it was the spirit of the vows which opened the way and revealed to the soul . . . the means of salvation." When his ninety-two-year-old brother Seraphin, who is also a priest, writes asking Didymus to visit him in St. Louis, the friar sees an opportunity for significant self-sacrifice. Since he has not seen his brother in twenty-five years and he would be forgoing human love in order to "fully tend to his creator," Didymus refuses his brother's invitation without giving any explanation. This decision pleases him.

Then he receives a telegram from St. Louis informing

him that his brother has died. Later that night he falls ill during vespers and is thereafter confined to a wheelchair. As the days and nights pass, Didymus finds himself in a dilemma. He wants to get well and walk again. However, if he was being punished for glorying too much in his refusal to visit Seraphin, to pray for healing would be to ignore "the divine point." Consequently, his illness might be fraught with meaning, requiring not routine pious exercises but "faith such as saints and martyrs had." But the friar is unwilling to "see the greatest significance in his affliction." Instead, he simply prays to get well.

After his spiritual crisis, Didymus sits in his chair and watches a canary that Titus has brought to keep him company. Over the following days he watches the canary lose its vivacity. Finally, when the bird clings to the side of the cage and peers imploringly at him, the friar uses the last of his strength to drag his body from the wheelchair and open the canary's cage. This symbolic action leads Didymus to realize that he has spent his entire life "tied down, caged," always lukewarm, "neglecting the source." Now fully understanding that the life lies "in the highest attachment only," Didymus is able to pray. As he finishes his prayer, the canary flies through the open window. Didymus attempts to lose himself in the sight of God, fails, and realizes that he must look inside himself to find God manifested. With that the dying priest closes his eyes on the snow falling outside his window.

Diestl, Christian. *The Young Lions.* Irwin Shaw. 1948.

Tired of his aimless life as an Austrian ski instructor, Christian Diestl, a former communist, becomes an ardent fascist. Although dark-skinned, he has other "Aryan" features and soon comes to believe in Adolf Hitler's desire to place all other races under German rule. During his years in the army, Christian witnesses the decline of the Nazi war machine. He also realizes the disparity between the official rhetoric and his own struggle to survive during the chaos of World War II.

Christian, a sergeant, is first stationed in Paris where he serves under the cold and ruthless Lieutenant Hardenburg. Christian resents his superior officer; although they have been ordered to take photographs for Nazi propaganda, Hardenburg spends more time in the Parisian brothels. Frustrated, Christian longs to experience combat where he can sharpen his skills as a leader. When Hardenburg orders Christian to deliver a gift to his wife Gretchen in Berlin, Christian exacts revenge on the lieutenant by having an affair with her.

Upon his return to Paris, Christian learns that he and Hardenburg must relocate to Africa. In Africa, Christian and the other Germans suffer not only from enemy attacks but also from heat exhaustion, lack of water, and malaria. When faced with a hopeless battle against superior forces, Hardenburg sacrifices most of his company in order to delay the Allied advances while he and Christian escape on a motorcycle.

Christian tries to relieve the intense guilt he feels at abandoning his comrades by convincing himself that their deaths are justified by Hitler's ultimate goals. During the motorcycle ride across the African desert, he comes to admire Hardenburg's robotlike strength and apparent lack of human empathy—qualities that make him a perfect German soldier. Just after they meet up with another German division, they are struck by a British mortar shell. Christian suffers only minor injuries; the lieutenant loses his entire face. Visiting Hardenburg in the hospital, Christian is struck by his stoicism in the face of this horrible disfigurement. After a time Hardenburg asks him to smuggle in a bayonet so that he can commit suicide, but the only instrument Christian is able to procure is a blunt pocket knife, which he duly delivers.

When he returns to combat, Christian finds himself transformed into the kind of soldier Hardenburg had once been. His bravery soon earns him a furlough, and he immediately travels to Berlin to see Gretchen Hardenburg. He is dismayed to find that she barely remembers him. She tells him offhandedly that Hardenburg is dead and admits that she had asked him not to come home because she couldn't bear to look at him. Christian takes a photograph that Hardenburg had taken of himself after the accident and sent to Gretchen, and leaves.

As the German army continues to lose battles and to retreat from the Allies, Christian meets Lieutenant Brandt, an old army friend, who convinces him to desert. He goes AWOL and hides with Brandt, Brandt's fiancée Simone, and Simone's friend Françoise in Paris where many are anxiously awaiting liberation by the Americans. Christian has a passionate affair with Françoise but becomes enraged when she mocks the thousand-year empire Hitler had once planned to create. Although he no longer believes in a German victory, Christian visits the local Gestapo and has Brandt, Simone, and Françoise arrested as traitors.

Now completely lost and sure of nothing but the absurdity of his existence, Christian gains access to a German concentration camp during a prisoner rebellion. Realizing that he is on the losing side, he dons a prisoner uniform and helps the Nazi victims execute the Germans who once ran the camp. Then he perches in a tree to await the arrival of the invading troops. He manages to kill NOAH ACKERMAN and a few other American soldiers before being shot himself.

Dimmesdale, Arthur. *The Scarlet Letter.* Nathaniel Hawthorne. 1850.

A young Puritan minister looked upon by his parishioners in seventeenth-century Boston as a moral leader, Arthur Dimmesdale carries with him a secret burden of guilt, for he is the father of HESTER PRYNNE's illegitimate child. He watches silently as his lover patiently endures her punishment, wearing the scarlet letter *A* that brands her an adulteress. Ultimately, however, Hester's public penance is less torturous than the private pain that Dimmesdale conceals.

Dimmesdale enters the novel at the scene of Hester Prynne's trial at the town pillory. Exhorted by a fellow clergyman, he begs Hester to reveal the father of the infant she holds in her arms. Hester refuses and is escorted back to her prison cell as Dimmesdale wonders at her strength and generosity.

When Hester's term of imprisonment comes to an end, she establishes herself in an abandoned cottage at the edge of town, befriending the sick and poor and providing for herself and her daughter Pearl by doing needlework for the townspeople. Arthur Dimmesdale, meanwhile, has been declining. The young minister grows sickly and pale, and accepts the proffered medical aid of ROGER CHILLINGWORTH who becomes his constant companion. The mysterious doctor, a stranger to the townspeople, is actually Hester's husband who has been missing for two years. On the day of the trial, the elderly scholar had persuaded Hester to swear she wouldn't reveal his identity, vowing at the same time to find the man who had cuckolded him.

Chillingworth's scholarly demeanor and apparent concern attract Dimmesdale, and when the doctor suggests that they live together, the minister agrees. One afternoon when Dimmesdale is asleep in a chair, the doctor pushes aside his patient's vestment; what he sees there is not revealed, but it puts a look of joy mixed with horror on the old man's face.

One night in May, Dimmesdale and Hester meet accidentally in the center of town. As they stand on the pillory, Pearl asks him if he will stand in the same spot with them the following day. He replies that he will stand with them on Judgment Day. Just then the three see an immense letter *A* lighting up the sky.

Soon after, Hester, disturbed by Dimmesdale's failing health, resolves to reveal Chillingworth's identity and to warn the minister of his intentions. She and Pearl meet with Dimmesdale one afternoon in the woods near town, and she convinces him that they must escape the community and take passage to England where they can begin a new life together. They agree to leave with little Pearl in three days.

Walking out of the woods, Dimmesdale seems to be a changed man. He meets several of his parishioners on his way and must strain to resist the impulse to be blasphemous and insulting. When he returns home, he dismisses Chillingworth and begins writing his final sermon with renewed energy. He delivers the sermon for the new governor on the eve of his departure, but doing so seems to have robbed him of his last bit of vitality. Supported by Hester and Pearl, he climbs the pillory and stands before the townspeople. Gathering all his remaining strength, the young minister declares that he has sinned, and ripping

away his vestment, he reveals what some spectators claim is a letter engraved on his chest. He acknowledges Pearl and Hester, praises God's mercy, and dies, leaving his parishioners to wonder at what they have seen.

Dinsmore, Elsie. *Elsie Dinsmore.* Martha Finley. 1868.

From her young girlhood, Elsie Dinsmore is stalwart in her devotion to Christian beliefs and practices. Even as a child she is remarkable for her beauty and goodness, and for finding ways to instruct her elders in appropriate social interaction and prayer.

Born the only daughter of an extremely wealthy young woman, Elsie is soon orphaned by her mother's death. Elsie's father had been forced to separate from his young wife due to his family's objection to the union. Having sojourned in Europe for nearly nine years, Horace Dinsmore eventually returns to the southern plantation where his father and stepmother are rearing Elsie.

Upon her father's return, the young girl is overcome with love and fear, and spends many anxious hours worrying about whether or not he really loves her. The two form a close bond and spend many hours together studying and reading the Bible. As Elsie grows, so does her beauty and her wealth, and by the time she is nearly twenty, she is worth over $3 million. After establishing herself as a capable mistress of a large plantation left to her by her mother, Elsie becomes engaged to marry the much older Edward Travilla, a lifelong friend of Horace's. Despite the disparity in their ages, Horace approves of the match, and the two are wed. Soon after, the couple departs for Italy with Horace and his relatives. Much to their sorrow and concern, the Civil War erupts and prevents their return for five years. During this period Elsie gives birth to the first three of her eight children, and the bond between her and her husband continues to deepen.

When they finally return to the United States, Elsie and her family seek to rebuild her home plantation, Roselands, while living at Ion, the plantation of Edward Travilla's family. When Edward dies after a sudden illness, nearly all of Elsie's family and friends suffer for her loss. Elsie bears her grief with Christian fortitude and embarks on the task of raising her family without her husband. As was the case before her husband's death, the children's education, both religious and secular, is of primary concern to Elsie; she sends her sons to college while training her daughters at home in the domestic arts.

Elsie eventually becomes a grandmother and continues to nurture those within her family and beyond. Throughout the remainder of her long life she is looked upon as a rare exemplar of faith and love.

Diver, Dr. Richard "Dick." *Tender Is the Night.* F. Scott Fitzgerald. 1933.

Dr. Richard "Dick" Diver is a man of extraordinary personal charm, capable of inspiring an unquestioning devotion in virtually every person he meets. When he is first spotted in the French Riviera by the budding young actress ROSEMARY HOYT, Dick is at the height of his powers; brilliant, vital, and charismatic, he is renowned for his skills as a psychiatrist as well as for the parties he hosts with his beautiful but fragile wife, the heiress NICOLE WARREN DIVER. It soon becomes clear, however, that he will be unable to sustain this image of personal and material success.

The novel is the story of Dick Diver's decline as he struggles with increasing futility to recapture the excitement and wonder of youth. As the novel opens, Dick appears to be entertaining Abe North, the McKiscos, and other members of the American expatriate set by raking the gravel on the beach near Rosemary's hotel. Rosemary is struck by his presence: His fine looks, bright clothing, and manner—a combination of gravity and gaiety—give the impression of good-humored strength, kindness, and sophistication. Yet the effort that his performance is costing him is already apparent. Later in the day he finds Rosemary asleep on the beach, and he tells her that it is half-past one—"not a bad time, not one of the worst times of the day."

Rosemary begins to spend more time with the Divers and their children Topsy and Lanier, and she falls madly in love with Dick. Although flattered by her amorous advances, he continues to remind her of the difference in their ages and of the fact that he is still in love with Nicole. When they meet again in Paris, however, Dick finds himself increasingly attracted to her and eventually succumbs to her charms. One day Rosemary finds a dead body in her hotel room; she summons Dick, who manages to get the body into the hallway and contact the authorities without involving her. Following him back to his suite, she stumbles on a disturbing scene: Nicole muttering incoherently and weeping and swaying in front of the bathtub, and Dick telling her firmly over and over, to "control yourself."

After this revelation about the Divers' marriage, Dick's personal history unfolds. By the time he was twenty-six, he had left his home in Buffalo, New York, obtained a degree in psychology, and worked with Sigmund Freud in Vienna. He was sent to Zurich, Switzerland, during World War I, where he continued his research and published his first book. It was during this period—"a favorite, a heroic period"—that he met Nicole Warren, then eighteen years old and a patient at the psychiatric clinic run by his friend Dr. Franz Gregorovius. Nicole began a correspondence with him; a romance blossomed between them, and over her family's objections, Dick became Nicole's husband and physician.

Dick initially feared that the vast wealth of his wife's family would compromise his independence and tried to keep his distance from it. However, as the years pass and his second book remains unwritten, he is forced to use Nicole's income to buy into a partnership with Franz in a clinic for wealthy patients. At first this return to psychiatry seems to offer him a refuge from the midlife crisis that his brief but unconsummated affair with Rosemary portended; but he begins to drink more heavily and to lose self-control. He soon finds himself falling in love with every pretty woman that he sees—and Nicole has a breakdown. She tries to kill the family by steering their car off a mountain road. Dick, deeply shaken, decides that he needs a vacation from her and goes to Munich for a month.

Dick returns to the United States to attend his father's funeral and then heads to Rome. There, he meets Rosemary, now a famous movie actress, and they briefly resume their affair. This time, however, they are both disappointed. Dick then gets into a scrap with and gets beaten up by the Italian police, and he must ask his wealthy sister-in-law, Baby Warren, to bail him out of jail. When Franz asks him to resign from the clinic, he does so with relief; weary and dissipated, he can no longer continue in the heroic role that his wife, friends, and colleagues had demanded of him.

As the novel closes, the reader learns that Dick returned to New York and set up practice in one small town after another, continuing to get into scrapes either with women or with the law. Nicole hears from him occasionally and prefers to remain optimistic: "Perhaps, so she liked to think, his career was biding its time."

Diver, Nicole Warren. *Tender Is the Night.* F. Scott Fitzgerald. 1933.

When Nicole Warren was eleven, her mother died, leaving her with her wealthy father and her manipulative older sister, Baby Warren. After making her his constant companion, Nicole's father had sex with her. He eventually placed her in a boarding school; when Baby noticed that Nicole seemed unstable, he submitted her to psychological treatment. Finally, he engaged a U.S. cruiser to run the wartime German blockade and brought his daughter to Switzerland for the best psychiatric care.

By chance, Nicole and her nurse meet a visiting U.S. Army doctor, the very attractive DR. RICHARD "DICK" DIVER. Nicole, still unbalanced and under constant supervision at the clinic, begins to write disjointed letters to the unsuspecting young doctor. He replies and observes during the course of the next eight months that her letters become more and more coherent. At the war's end Nicole again meets her correspondent; for the most part she has regained her health, and she has fallen in love with Dick.

Although Nicole's doctors think that Dick and his letters have been good for her, they advise him to dissuade the beautiful heiress from any thought of a relationship with him. In addition, Nicole's sister plans to bring her back to Chicago, where Baby has decided she will induce a young psychologist to marry and care for Nicole. When Nicole and Dick again meet in the Swiss mountains where they are on a holiday, their love and infatuation for each other make marriage inevitable, albeit much objected to by Baby and Nicole's doctors.

With her husband-doctor and their two children, Nicole takes up life as a wealthy American with a home on the Riviera. To all appearances the quiet and pretty Nicole and her handsome and successful husband are an icon of domestic perfection, an image essential to and maintained by all of their friends and especially by Dick. When Nicole suffers two breakdowns, one right after the other, caused in part by Dick's encouraging response to a young Hollywood actress's crush, they return to Switzerland and a sanatorium. In part to afford Nicole even more care, Dick finally swallows enough of the guilt he felt toward the Warren fortune to underwrite and become a partner in a clinic. Yet Nicole's condition grows even more acute. At her worst, she nearly kills herself and her whole family by grabbing the steering wheel and trying to aim their car down a hillside.

Nicole slowly recovers as she gains more and more emotional and practical autonomy from Dick and the ideal he had set for the two of them. Dick seems to go through his own decline in order that Nicole can become self-reliant. Freeing herself at last from Dick's paternal but now also confining shelter, Nicole has an affair with a longtime friend and admirer, the mercenary soldier Tommy Barban. Nicole eventually leaves Dick and marries Tommy, but she still keeps in contact with her former husband. Dick returns to New York to set up a medical practice and sends her a postcard from time to time.

Dobrejcak, John "Dobie." *Out of This Furnace.* Thomas Bell. 1941.

Dobie Dobrejcak is a member of the third generation of Slovak immigrants whose struggles are chronicled in this saga of life in the steel mills of Pennsylvania. It is Dobie and his generation who finally achieve unionization in the 1930s.

Dobie is the oldest of four children born to Mary and MIKE DOBREJCAK; he is eleven when his father dies in a mill explosion. He helps his widowed mother by collecting scrap metal, bottles, and rags, selling them for pennies. Later he becomes a newspaper boy. At thirteen he gets a job working in a glass factory. He keeps the job a month into the school year, and when he finally returns to school, he is very far behind, unable to catch up and distraught over being labeled a foreigner or "hunky." He produces some false papers claiming that he is sixteen and leaves school permanently to learn a trade as an apprentice in an electric shop at the mill. He completes his apprenticeship four years later, the same year his mother dies of consumption.

Following his mother's death, he goes to live with his aunt. He isn't there long, however, before he decides to move to Detroit, where he goes from one car plant job to another, buying fancy clothes, watching burlesque shows, enjoying the life of a young bachelor. Five years later he returns to Braddock, Pennsylvania, and resumes his job in the electric shop.

The Depression soon hits. The mills grow quieter and quieter, and Dobie, now thirty years old, finds only two days of work a month. He falls in love and marries, and he and his new wife, Julie, move into a small house with Dobie's grandfather, GEORGE DZEDO KRACHA, as their boarder.

Meanwhile, Dobie becomes involved in the labor movement. When the Amalgamated Association of the A.F.L. (American Federation of Labor) holds a meeting in a neighboring town, Dobie attends and then helps to gather men in Braddock to start a union. The meetings catch on; Dobie is elected secretary of their branch. Soon he and the other union men in Braddock begin to have doubts about the leadership of the Amalgamated Association in Pittsburgh and the representative they sent to Braddock. The representative eventually leaves, and Dobie and the others find themselves in charge. They meet with the steel company executives to request recognition of the union and a contract for the workers covering wages, hours, vacations, and seniority. Nothing is granted to them. The workers are ready to strike, but the Amalgamated Association votes against it.

Disillusioned with the A.F.L., Dobie and two other union leaders decide to try another tactic: They run for office in the company-sanctioned union. They are elected and immediately start negotiating, but, again, little comes of their efforts. Things begin to change, however, once the C.I.O. (Congress of Industrial Organizations) and its Steel Workers Organizing Committee are formed.

Dobie travels to Pittsburgh several times a week to talk to, and work with, the Labor Board. He is subpoenaed by the board to testify in Washington, D.C., about the mill. Despite the fact that the steel company does not give him time off and threatens to fire him if he goes, Dobie makes the trip to Washington.

After another hearing in Washington, the corporation relents and agrees to sign a contract with the C.I.O. The novel leaves Dobie contemplating the arrival of his first child, content and proud in the knowledge that he has played a role in securing a better future for the next generation of Slovak steelworkers.

Dobrejcak, Mike. *Out of This Furnace.* Thomas Bell. 1941.

Mike Dobrejcak is a second-generation immigrant in this novel chronicling the lives of three generations of Slovak workers. After arriving in the United States at the age of fifteen, Mike boards with Dorta and Joe Dubik and goes to work in the steel mill furnaces of Braddock, Pennsylvania, where he suffers through back-breaking twelve-hour days, attends English class for foreigners, and eventually becomes an American citizen.

In his twenty-seventh year, Mike wakes one summer Sunday morning to find Mary, the daughter of GEORGE DZEDO KRACHA, visiting with Dorta in the kitchen. Although he has known her for years, he is suddenly smitten by her beauty. Mary has a job looking after the boy of an "American family," and she lives with them in a big brick house that has a bathroom, electricity, and steam heat. Mike dreams about the day when he and Mary will move up in the world and live in such splendor.

Mike and Mary get married in the spring, less than a year after they began dating. In March their first child, JOHN "DOBIE" (DOBREJCAK), is born. The new family lives in a small two-room apartment off an alleyway. Work in the mills slows down in the fall and stays slow throughout the winter and spring; another baby arrives in November, and although Mike is able to find more work, he and Mary are still very much in debt. Even though Mike dislikes the idea, they move to a larger apartment, and Mary takes in six boarders to make extra money. They have their third child. Jobs continue to come and go unpredictably, and Mike must repeatedly defer his dream of a better life for himself and his family.

Despite the warnings of her doctor, Mary becomes pregnant with their fourth child. Well into her pregnancy, she faints, and the doctor informs Mike that she must work less and take better care of herself. They give up their six boarders and move to a smaller apartment. Their living arrangements are more bearable, but money is now even tighter than before. Mike's anger over the discrimination against Slovak workers and the futility of any Slovak trying to get a decent position or salary intensifies. In the presidential elections of 1912, he votes for Eugene Debs on the Socialist ticket, despite the fact that it could have cost him his job. Two years later this philosophical man, having dreamed of a better life for his family and fellow workers, dies in an explosion at the mill.

Doc. *Cannery Row.* John Steinbeck. 1945.

Doc is the owner and proprietor of the Western Biological Laboratory. Although he makes his living killing and preserving sea life for use in scientific experiments, Doc has a soft heart, and everyone in his impoverished little community is indebted to him in one way or another. His laboratory, in which he nourishes his passions for fine music and cold beer, is a haven for the troubled and downhearted of Cannery Row.

Doc has been trained as a scientist, but his demeanor is hardly that of the cool detached researcher. He is passionate when angry, and gentle when touched by those in need. Among those who turn to Doc for understanding is Frankie, a young boy whose abusive home life has left him withdrawn and frightened. Frankie's clumsiness makes him a hazard around the laboratory, but Doc continues to welcome him and he wins the boy's undying love. Doc also has the devotion of MACK, the ringleader of a group of ambitionless men who occupy an unused building they call the Palace Flophouse and Grill. Mack is a smooth-talking chiseler with a taste for liquor, but he often means well.

When he decides to throw a surprise party for his good friend Doc, Mack wants to raise money by going to work with his boys. Doc is always wary of Mack and his schemes, but he eventually agrees to have the boys help him fill an order for several hundred frogs. As the boys go off to start their hunt, Doc begins a long drive to La Jolla where he plans to collect small octopi.

At La Jolla, Doc works steadily through the low-tide hours. As the tide begins to return, he comes upon the body of a young girl trapped in the rocks, and the scene disturbs him greatly. After telling a local about the body, he returns home, tired and upset, only to find his laboratory in chaos. The party Mack planned had disintegrated into a brawl and had broken up before the guest of honor arrived. The revelers have left behind broken windows, spilled specimen jars, and extensively damaged equipment. Doc's anger explodes, and he hits Mack, bloodying his face. His rage soon subsides, however, and after listening to Mack's tearful apologies, he sighs and sets about cleaning and securing a bank loan to pay for the repairs.

Aided by his own brand of philosophy, Doc completely forgives Mack and the boys; nevertheless, they and the rest of Cannery Row feel they must make it up to him by throwing another party—one he will be able to attend. Fortunately, Doc learns about the celebration in time to lock away anything breakable, and this time the celebration is a huge success. All the citizens of Cannery Row turn out, and Doc is showered with carefully chosen gifts. Although this party, too, ends in a brawl, all the guests enjoy themselves thoroughly, most especially the guest of honor.

The Doctor. "The White Horses of Vienna." Kay Boyle. 1946.

Set high in the Alps during the 1930s, just prior to the annexation of Austria by Germany, this story tells of a doctor who injures his leg one night while climbing the mountain. He decides to send to Vienna for a student-doctor to tend patients while his leg mends. When the student-doctor arrives, the doctor's wife is shocked that he is Jewish. The doctor, who has spent years in Siberia as a prisoner of war, is unmoved by his wife's prejudices and greets young Dr. Heine amiably.

Dr. Heine joins the household and proves to be not only agreeable to the older doctor's methods of caring for his patients but also a genuinely good man. The wife's prejudice against the young man does not subside, and when she listens to him tell her two sons of the royal white horses of Vienna, she fumes at what she imagines to be evidence of his inherited mercenary affinities.

Dr. Heine relates how a maharaja had seen the royal horses perform their statuesque dances, bowing in homage "to the empty, canopied loge," formerly the seat of royalty. An extremely wealthy man, the maharaja had requested that the state sell him one of the Lippizaners to take back to his homeland. Charging an exorbitant fee, the Viennese state agreed to sell one of the horses. All the while that Dr. Heine is telling the story, the doctor's wife thinks to herself that of course this Jewish doctor would be moved by money. But the point of his tale proves to have nothing to do with money after all.

Although arrangements were made for the horse's rider to accompany him, no provisions were made for the animal's groom to go along. The groom loved the horse and had always given it special care. When the time arrived for the horse to be transported, he was found to have a deep cut over one of his hooves. The Viennese state promised to medicate the animal and send him to the maharaja in a few weeks. Several weeks later the animal was found to have a second similar wound; this time the horse's blood had become poisoned, and he had to be destroyed. Not until the groom committed suicide after the Lippizaner had been killed did anyone realize that he had inflicted the wounds because of his great love for the animal.

Just as the young doctor finishes his story, the family's dinner is interrupted by a group of pro-Nazi Heimwehr who have come up the mountain to quell a swastika burning. They want the doctor to show them the fastest route up, but he smilingly explains that he has a bad leg. When Dr. Heine and the doctor's wife reiterate that the doctor cannot move, the leader of the Heimwehr says that the doctor will have to move if he is wanted at the Rathaus again. The leader subtly lets the group know that he suspects the doctor of being responsible for such incidents as the swastika burning. When the men leave, Dr. Heine is very disturbed and complains that everything is concerned with politics. He compliments the doctor for making his puppets, "keeping the artistic thing uppermost." As he quietly works on the wings of a cloth grasshopper, the doctor explains that when he was in prison they played cards but that now there was something to do.

Later that evening when the doctor puts on a puppet show, a hobby for which he is known around the village, it becomes apparent that his craft is no mere diversion. The show consists of two characters, a grasshopper and a clown. The grasshopper is very beautiful and graceful, and when he sees it dance, Dr. Heine compares it to the Lippizaners of Vienna. The clown, on the other hand, is small and graceless, and carries a huge sword and a bunch of flowers that he says he is going to place on his own grave. For no apparent reason the wise grasshopper is always referred to as "Leader" while the ridiculous clown is called "Chancellor." The Chancellor is obviously the fool of the piece, and the doctor's family, along with their guests, including the Burgermeister, laugh at his stupidity and clumsiness.

Several weeks later the Heimwehr come and inform the doctor that he is wanted at the Rathaus again. His wife wakes her sons and tells them that their father is about to be taken to prison and that they are not to cry. Dr. Heine rushes from the house as the doctor is taken away on a stretcher and asks him what he can do for him. The doctor says he can throw him peaches and chocolate from the street, for his wife's hands shake and cause her aim to be off. Dr. Heine promises to remember and thinks of the Lippizaners, "the relics of pride, the still unbroken vestiges of beauty bending their knees to the empty loge of royalty where there was no royalty anymore."

Dodsworth, Samuel. *Dodsworth*. Sinclair Lewis. 1929.

Samuel Dodsworth is a subtle and complex rendering of an American stereotype. A Yale graduate and football star, he becomes a pioneer in the developing automotive industry, a loving father to his two children, and a devoted husband to his lovely and sparkling, but childlike, passionless, and domineering wife. Living in the midwestern town of Zenith, Dodsworth leads a pleasant, moderate existence, playing golf and poker with his friends but also enjoying Proust and Beethoven. At the age of fifty, however, Dodsworth's life is changed in such a way as to force him to look beneath its surface.

When Dodsworth's company is bought out by a larger one, he embarks on a tour of the world with his wife Fran. As soon as they begin their travels, Fran begins to belittle Dodsworth for his lack of sophistication, and she turns her attentions toward a series of younger European men. As Dodsworth tags along behind Fran, who makes impressive social conquests wherever they go, he begins to feel increasingly lost and unsure of himself. Although he is capable of intense aesthetic responses to some aspects of European culture and geography, Fran half-convinces Dodsworth that he, and America in general, are too materialistic and too work-oriented, and altogether ignorant of the finer elements in life. He feels increasingly that Fran's values, ambitions, and acquaintances are supercilious.

Confused and disoriented by Fran and Europe, and uncomfortable with his position as retiree, at one point Dodsworth leaves Fran in Europe and returns briefly to America. Back in Zenith, however, he feels alienated from and unwanted by his two grown children and his former friends. The only thing that gives meaning to his life is Fran, whom he has always thought of as "the most exquisite child in the world." But when he returns to Europe, he discovers that she has taken a young Frenchman as a lover, and when Dodsworth whisks her away to Berlin, she only falls in love with a young German.

Deeply depressed, Dodsworth leaves Fran with her new

lover and wanders about Europe alone. When he meets Edith Cortright, an unpretentious, attractive widow who appreciates him for what he is, his life takes on new meaning as he begins to regain confidence in himself. His newfound security is threatened when, on impulse, he leaves Edith and rushes protectively to Fran's side when her German lover abandons her. He discovers that Fran has not changed, however, and he announces his desire for a divorce in order to return to Edith, whom he plans to take back to the United States and with whom he will begin a career designing recreational vehicles.

Nevertheless, Dodsworth remains haunted by the vision of Fran as a frightened and bewildered child whom he feels he has deserted; indeed, although a sympathetic figure, Dodsworth appears by the novel's end to have been partially responsible for Fran's indifference.

Donatello. *The Marble Faun: Or, the Romance of Monte Beni.* Nathaniel Hawthorne. 1860.

Perhaps the most striking thing about Donatello is that he resembles a statue of the Faun of the Praxiteles. In fact, legend has it that the young man, the current Count of Monte Beni, is descended from the mythical beast. This legend is never proven, however, because he will never reveal his ears, which, according to the myth, should be covered with fur.

The Italian Donatello becomes the close friend of three foreign artists who are living in Rome. His companions in wandering through the Eternal City are Kenyon, an American sculptor; HILDA, a copyist from the same country; and MIRIAM, a mysterious painter. Donatello has a particular interest in Miriam. Although their temperaments—hers moody and secretive, his playful and flighty—are opposed, Donatello is unabashedly attracted to Miriam. He constantly expresses his love and loyalty for her, but she seems annoyed at his almost doglike devotion.

One evening the four friends, in the company of a larger group, go rambling among the hills and ruins of Rome. Donatello and Miriam are left alone to gaze over the edge of a steep precipice. Just then a menacing man who had been following Miriam for some time appears. Donatello sees fear in Miriam's face, then a silent plea in her eyes. In a flash he seizes the man and flings him over the cliff to his death.

At first this secret seems to unite Donatello and Miriam. For the first time she confesses a love for him, and the two believe they can overcome the shared guilt of the murderous act. Remorse steals over Donatello, however, stifling his formerly lively spirit. Kenyon notices the change the very next day when he meets Miriam and Donatello at the Church of the Capuchins. Donatello's dread only increases when the group sees the dead man's body laid out in the church, dressed in the garb of a monk.

Although Miriam loves Donatello, she realizes that the guilt-ridden young man can never be happy in her presence. She bids him to go back to his country home but promises that a single word from him will restore her to his arms. Donatello returns home, with Kenyon arriving for a visit some months later. Kenyon notices that Donatello still seems melancholy, but it is a melancholia tinged with a depth of feeling and understanding that the young Italian had never before manifested. Seeking solace, Donatello visits many religious shrines.

Unbeknownst to his friend, Kenyon has arranged an opportunity for Donatello to meet Miriam once again. He sees her and, overcome with love, speaks her name. She rushes to him, and the two are reunited. They share but a short time together, though, for Donatello is arrested for the murder he committed. Although Donatello is irrevocably stained with blood, the experience has in fact been an education, curing him of his faunlike manner and teaching him true knowledge of good and evil.

Dorman, Darius. *Honest John Vane.* J. W. De Forest. 1875.

Darius Dorman is an unscrupulous behind-the-scenes political leader who is so consistently dirty and frantic that his detractors call him the "scorched monkey." Growing up in the small New England town of Slowburgh, Darius Dorman lacked the physical attributes necessary to pursue his life's ambition of a career as an elected official. However, he still plays an active role as an informal party boss, handpicking aspiring politicians he feels will be accepted by the general public and then helping package them to make them suitable for election. Once elected, these people would owe considerable favors to this conniving politico.

When Representative James Bummer is forced to resign due to charges of scandal, Dorman searches for another worthy candidate. He decides on JOHN VANE, a local refrigerator manufacturer, believing that the well-meaning but not overly bright Vane will be easily manipulated. He dubs him "Honest John Vane" for purposes of the election, and Vane is indeed a simple and honest man.

At the party caucus, Dorman, having carefully rehearsed with Vane what to do beforehand, shouts out his nomination for Vane as party candidate. Vane, who is known throughout Slowburgh as a slow but honest businessman, is immensely popular in the wake of the scandal left behind by Bummer and easily wins the nomination. After a carefully managed campaign in the general election, Vane wins by a landslide.

Planning to capitalize on his investment, Dorman follows Vane to Washington where he works as a lobbyist. There he meets Simon Sharp, a manipulative, mercenary representative who introduces him to a money-making scheme involving interstate highways that will be funded by the federal government if a certain bill passes Congress.

Dorman, after convincing Sharp of his ability to enlist Vane's help, is cut in for a percentage of the profits.

He and Sharp travel to Vane's office where Dorman tactfully explains the operation, all the while reminding Vane of his debt to him for his election. The indignant Vane throws them out. Dorman tries to convince Sharp that Vane will change his mind once he grows accustomed to the widespread corruption that plagues Congress. As Dorman predicted, a few months later a changed Vane listens carefully to their proposal and finally gives his assent.

All goes well for Dorman until an investigation is launched in the House concerning his operation, which is quickly growing into a scandal. While apprehensive at first, Dorman contacts Vane once again and tries to convince him to head the investigation himself. Believing it to be the only way to save their careers, Vane once again agrees.

Dorman is shocked, however, when Vane at the last moment declines to head the committee, claiming that it might represent a conflict of interest. Vane is able to separate himself from the entire operation while at the same time implicating Dorman. Although never formally charged, Dorman is forced to leave Washington, and he must once again start his political mountain climbing from the bottom.

Dormer, Nicholas. *The Tragic Muse.* Henry James. 1890.

Nicholas Dormer, a rising young politician, struggles with "two men" within him. One wants only to oblige his family and fulfill his obligations to them by pursuing a political career. The second desires to be "on the side of beauty," devoting himself to painting. With the help of his enigmatic and prophetic friend Gabriel Nash, Nick finds the courage to follow the more difficult path, that of becoming an artist.

The Dormers are titled English nobility, aristocrats who are much concerned with upholding family traditions. Nick attends the boarding school his father, Sir Nicholas Dormer, also attended, and continues his education at Oxford. While Percival, Nick's older brother, inherits their father's estate, Nick is expected to inherit his profession and become a Member of Parliament. Although Sir Nicholas dies young, he lives long enough to see his son Nick's first success in politics. He wins the seat for Crockhurst, in the process proving himself as a speaker of great talent. On his deathbed his father imparts to Nick his ideas on the "highest national questions," laying before him the work he expects his son to carry out in his political career. In spite of the fact that Nick loses his seat soon after his father's death, Nick's mother, Lady Agnes Dormer, and the other members of the family still push Nick to fulfill his father's expectations and achieve his goals in government.

The family sees in Nick's moodiness and tendency toward reverie proof that he is thinking over his father's final words to him, but a conversation early in the novel with his sister Biddy, suggests that his mind is occupied with something else. Nick has a genuine talent for painting and has kept a studio in London even while acting as a Member of Parliament. While walking with Biddy in a Paris gallery, he not only demonstrates a thorough knowledge of art and a deep sensitivity to its power, but he also expresses regret at not having made a serious commitment to artistic endeavor. Moments later a chance meeting with Gabriel Nash, Nick's old friend from Oxford, awakens a hope that he might reconsider this choice. Nash openly criticizes Nick's choice of pursuing politics and has himself written an important work of fiction; Nash is therefore squarely on "the side of beauty." Nick feels determined to hold on to Nash's friendship as if this odd, witty, thoroughly unconventional genius might give him the courage to change.

Unfortunately, a position has just opened up in a district called Harsh, and Nick's cousin, Julia Dallow, offers to finance his campaign and support Nick if elected. After overcoming his doubts and agreeing to run, Nick becomes caught up in the excitement and pressure of the campaign. A potential romance with the austere, striking Julia blossoms when Nick wins the race to represent Harsh. He is soon engaged to Julia, although she is thoroughly political and has neither understanding nor patience for art. For Julia's sake and for his family, Nick manages to perform the dull and undignified tasks required of a parliamentary member.

On one occasion, however, he persuades Julia to allow him to shirk his political obligations in order to spend two weeks alone, painting in his London studio. Gabriel Nash pays him a visit there and, immensely impressed by the work he sees, offers to bring MIRIAM ROOTH, a gifted young actress, to sit for a portrait. This magnificent, spirited woman has the effect of drawing out Nick's "sleeping" talents and instincts, opening him up to new joy and inspiration in his work. Later, when they are admiring the results of the second sitting, Julia appears at the door and is shocked by the scene: an unknown woman lounging casually and familiarly in the studio, with Nick hanging affectionately over the back of her chair. Several hours later when Nick visits her to explain, Julia breaks off their engagement. She "hates" art, Julia explains simply, while it is the only thing Nick wants. It is clear to her they must part.

Soon afterward Nick resigns his post as the Member for Harsh, at once throwing away a fortune promised him by Mr. Carteret, a former supporter of his father, and causing Lady Agnes enormous unhappiness. He then forces himself to remain in London and work conscientiously, when he might avoid shame by going abroad. In his solitary struggle to refine his work, Nick is comforted by a romantic friendship with Miriam Rooth, who has become famous, and by the continued support of his sister Biddy, now studying sculpture. Even Julia Dallow eventually expresses her acceptance of Nick's courageous decision by allowing him to paint her portrait. Nick's future is left unclear, but he remains firm in his decision, and if Gabriel Nash is correct, his life will be pleasant and his painting a success.

Dorn, Erik. *Erik Dorn.* Ben Hecht. 1921.

Erik Dorn, a thirty-five-year-old Chicago newspaperman, is virtually devoid of human emotions. Completely cynical and detached, he is utterly without convictions, beliefs, or ideals, and he experiences only the vaguest flickerings of feeling. A brilliant writer and speaker, Dorn astounds his associates with his felicitous phrasings, but he does not mean what he says or writes; indeed, as he knows, he speaks well only because he has nothing at all to say. Dorn believes he can see through appearances to the tawdry and hypocritical motivations of people and nations, and so he remains coolly aloof from the news events he reports, the national crises he witnesses, and the women who love him.

As the narrative opens, Dorn is a successful and respected newspaperman living with his aging father and adoring wife Anna. He has virtually hypnotized Anna with repeated, ritualistic expressions of passion and devotion, and as a result of his ardent lies, she has become so thoroughly absorbed by him that she has lost all sense of herself. Meanwhile, he cares for her only insofar as she is a reflection of himself and an audience for the exercise of his remarkable vocabulary.

Then Dorn meets and falls in love with Rachel Laskin, an artist with a personality much like his own. He is uncharacteristically loath to hurt his wife Anna but ends up abandoning her. While Rachel initially seems to elicit new depths of emotion from Dorn, he falls out of love with her almost immediately; she is, finally, only another reflection of himself and another sounding board for his scintillating verbiage. Realizing how Dorn feels, Rachel leaves him, in spite of the fact that she loves him desperately. At this point Dorn senses that he has returned to the nothingness in which he had existed before meeting Rachel, but he does not grieve deeply or long.

After Rachel leaves, Dorn seeks an opportunity to go to Berlin to report on the turmoil in Germany after World War I. In Europe as in America, he views political machinations and social upheaval with cynical indifference. His final report on postwar events in Germany is the most brilliant piece of writing he has produced, but as always it betrays no beliefs or convictions on Dorn's part.

Arriving back in the United States, Dorn attempts to return to Anna. She has broken free of the vacuum of his personality, however, and has divorced him and become engaged to another man. Dorn thereupon looks up Rachel,

and at the end of the novel he is hoping to see her again—not because he loves her but because she may provide him with a fleeting sensation of life.

Dorothy. *The Wonderful Wizard of Oz.* L. Frank Baum. 1900.

When a cyclone picks up young Dorothy's one-room house, taking her and her dog Toto with it, she is transported from bleak Kansas to the brilliant Land of Oz. Dorothy's house falls on the Wicked Witch of the East, killing the woman feared by the diminutive, peace-loving Munchkins. Coming out of her house, Dorothy is met by three Munchkins and an old woman, who is the Good Witch of the North. The Witch of the North kisses Dorothy's forehead, leaving a silver mark that protects the girl from harm, and gives Dorothy the silver shoes of the late Witch of the East. When Dorothy asks to return to Kansas, she is told that the only one who can help her go home is the all-powerful WIZARD OF OZ.

The good witch sends Dorothy down the yellow brick road to the City of Emeralds, where Oz resides. The young girl soon meets her first companion, a SCARECROW, who agrees to travel with her in hopes that Oz will give him a brain. As they continue along the yellow brick road, Dorothy explains to him that she wants to leave this beautiful country and return to her native Kansas because "there is no place like home."

The following day they meet a TIN WOODMAN, who joins them in hopes that Oz will give him a heart. Next they encounter the COWARDLY LION, who, after frightening them all and being chastised by Dorothy, admits to being a coward. He goes along, hoping to receive courage. On their travels Dorothy's three companions protect her from many dangers, and when at last Dorothy arrives in the Emerald City and has an audience with the Wizard, she is disappointed to learn that she must kill the Wicked Witch of the West before he will grant her and her friends' wishes. Nevertheless, Dorothy and her friends set off for Winkieland where the Witch lives.

When the Wicked Witch sees them coming, she tries various methods to stop them, at last sending her band of Winged Monkies to capture them. The monkies destroy the Tin Woodman and the Scarecrow, but they take Dorothy, Toto, and the Lion back to the Witch's palace. After some time in captivity, Dorothy gets angry at the Witch and tosses a bucket of water on her, causing her to melt. Dorothy, Toto, and the Lion leave the castle, find and repair their friends, and with the help of the now friendly Winged Monkies, return to the Emerald City.

Unhappily, Dorothy soon discovers that Oz is a fake; he is not a wizard but simply a man. He sincerely wants to help her return to Kansas, however, and he offers to take her there by balloon. Unfortunately, the balloon slips up into the sky before Dorothy can board. Forced to find another means of returning to her beloved home, she sets off to see Glinda, the Good Witch of the South. Her friends help her battle fighting trees and vicious Hammerheads to arrive in the land of the Quadlings, where Glinda the Good Witch presides. Glinda tells Dorothy she has had the power to return home all along: It is in her silver shoes. After saying her good-byes, Dorothy clutches Toto and, tapping her heels together, swiftly returns home to Kansas.

Dorset, Louisa. "Venus, Cupid, Folly and Time." Peter Taylor. 1969.

Miss Louisa Dorset shares her life with her brother Alfred. The Dorsets, an elderly and decidedly odd couple, dwell on West Vesey Place, the respectable part of the town of Chatham. They have lived in the house ever since the deaths of their parents many years before. At the time of the story, in the early 1930s, the Dorsets have been reduced to a form of poverty that requires they remove the third floor of their home as well as its south wing to lower the taxes they can barely afford. Despite their clinging to a distant splendor, the Dorsets survive on a meager income generated by the sale of the paper flowers Louisa makes and of ill-tasting figs raised by Alfred in their backyard.

Louisa, in particular, annoys the males in the area as she insists on being seen in her nightclothes, something most of the men and boys are unaccustomed to seeing. In addition, both the Dorsets are known to appear in public wearing their nightclothes underneath their regular garments. Louisa sometimes also wanders the house nude and while performing such duties as vacuuming and flower arranging. All these habits contribute to her already strange reputation. The town is also aware of the fact that Louisa, who is over sixty years old, still dyes her hair jet black, and does it badly. But it is the annual party for twelve- and thirteen-year-olds that is truly responsible for the reputation the Dorsets built and cultivated, however unknowingly.

Each year the couple opens their home to a group of local children chosen through Louisa's ability to "know" quality people when she sees them. Louisa and Alfred fondly tease each other, conduct a tour of their home, and dance for the entertainment of their guests during these annual parties. They also participate in a set conversation during which Louisa describes the splendid life-styles of her parents and their generation, and lovingly recalls the past in general.

One night some of the children decide to play a joke on the odd couple. Ned and Emily Merriwether decide to invite the local paper boy to the party. Tom passes himself off as Ned, who sneaks into the crowd later at the Dorsets' doorway. As the party gets under way, Tom begins kissing Emily, who sits passively under his caresses. Eventually the elderly couple note the behavior and seem to condone it, smiling and grinning back and forth at each other. Finally, for reasons he cannot comprehend but that probably stem from his awareness of Louisa and Alfred's per-

missive attitude, Ned shouts out that Emily and Tom are brother and sister.

Needless to say, the Dorsets are completely stunned by this, and in the madcap pursuit that follows, Ned is able to call the Merriwethers while Tom makes his escape. When the Merriwethers arrive, the Dorsets, unable to really understand what has happened, vanish into their room upstairs. The Merriwether children are sent off to boarding school. Meanwhile, Louisa and her brother retire from the party-giving routine and die after living the last years of their lives as recluses.

Dorsinville, Vanise. *Continental Drift.* Russell Banks. 1985.

The victim of a life of poverty in her Haitian village of Allanche, Vanise Dorsinville resolves to journey to the United States with her nephew Claude and infant son. Vanise, fearing harsh reprisals for her nephew's "crime"— pilfering a ham from a wrecked delivery truck—pays what little money she possesses to be transported to Florida but is instead shipped to North Caicos Island, six hundred miles from her ultimate destination.

Once here, the trio encounters George McKissick, a hard-drinking farmer who, in return for food, shelter, and an assurance not to turn them over to the authorities, demands the right to sleep with Vanise. There is, however, a former employee who is currently at odds with McKissick, and in retaliation for perceived injustices, the former employee procures passage for the family on a boat headed for the Bahamas. The journey proves a dreadful one as the three are held in the ship's foul steerage for the duration of the trip. Vanise is repeatedly raped by the boat's captain, his mate, and three other passengers. Finally, Claude himself falls victim and is brutally sodomized.

Once in the Bahamas, the Dorsinvilles travel to Elizabeth Town, where Vanise is sold into prostitution by Jimmy Grabow. Her mental state deteriorating rapidly, Vanise refuses to flee Grabow. Claude does, however, and finds employment doing odd jobs on another part of the island. After managing to earn enough money to secure their passage to America, a hardened Claude returns to Elizabeth Town, kills Grabow, and flees with Vanise and her baby.

Ultimately, the trio is retrieved from a Haitian mambo ritual by novice immigrant smuggler ROBERT RAYMOND "Bob" DUBOIS and his more experienced first mate Tyrone. In all, fifteen Haitians pay for transportation to Miami. Just off the coast of Hollywood, Florida, however, Dubois's boat is sighted by the Coast Guard. A panicky Tyrone makes the passengers leap overboard while a hysterical Bob looks on with horror. The only survivor of this tragedy is Vanise, who somehow struggles to shore and is eventually spotted by passing Haitians and taken to her brother's home in the Little Haiti section of Miami.

Vanise, horribly traumatized, falls into a stupor and insists on attending a ritual ceremony presided over by Ghede, a god with powers over death.

Afterward, Vanise is visited by Bob Dubois. He asks forgiveness and attempts to hand over the money he had been paid to transport the Haitians. But Vanise turns away from Dubois, adamant in her refusal "to remove the sign of his shame."

Douglas, Charlotte Amelia Havemeyer Bogart. *A Book of Common Prayer.* Joan Didion. 1977.

Charlotte Douglas is an eccentric woman who abandons her second husband in San Francisco and attempts to escape from haunting memories that threaten to undermine her sanity. Having moved to Boca Grande in Central America, Charlotte installs herself in the Caribe Hotel where she becomes known for strange behavior that she takes no pains to disguise. She is as oblivious to public opinion as she is to the dictates of conventional conduct. When the precarious political balance of Boca Grande's government threatens to erupt into a dangerous civil war, Charlotte irrationally refuses to flee from the violence despite repeated warnings and entreaties from her newfound friends, who finally leave her to her fate amid the impending chaos.

Born and raised in California, Charlotte attended Berkeley for two years before she ran off to New York with Warren Bogart, an untenured professor to whom she was married for five years and who is the father of her daughter Marin. Charlotte's second marriage to Leonard Douglas, a famous civil rights lawyer, was interrupted when a group of FBI agents visited their house to inform her that her daughter Marin had lied to her about being on a skiing trip and is actually in hiding after having participated in a terrorist bombing of the Transamerica Building and the hijacking of a P.S.A. L-1011 airplane. Dazed by this revelation, Charlotte leaves Leonard and decides, without explaining her motives, to travel around the United States with her first husband for a few months. Once Warren's alcoholic binges turn violent, however, she leaves him, too. Pregnant by Leonard, Charlotte eventually checks into a clinic in New Orleans. She gives birth to a hydrocephalic baby who dies two weeks later in Merida. After weathering this additional tragedy, Charlotte moves to Boca Grande where she tries to repress the additional emotional horror that threatens to rob her of her already precarious sanity.

Having settled into her hotel room in the Caribe, Charlotte proceeds to fill her days with bizarre hobbies such as frequenting Boca Grande's airport without apparent motivation, writing "Letters from Central America" to *The New Yorker* in which she inaccurately describes the customs and landscape of the country, and devising an elaborate scheme to organize an annual film festival in Boca Grande with the intention of boosting the nation's economy through increased tourism. During a serious cholera epidemic, Charlotte volunteers her labor and spends thirty-four consecutive hours administering inoculations against the dread disease. In the same philanthropic vein, Charlotte volunteers her services full-time at a birth control clinic where she advocates the diaphragm as the most effective means of family planning. She begins to have an affair with Gerardo Strasser-Mendana, the son of her best friend, GRACE TABOR STRASSER-MENDANA, whose family is prominent in Boca Grande's complex and volatile government. When Gerardo and Grace flee the country on the eve of a civil war, Charlotte irrationally refuses to take exile and is shot to death and deposited on the lawn of the American embassy, thus ending the disturbed and bizarre life of a sensitive and abused woman.

Douglass, Cato Caldwell. *!Click Song.* John A. Williams. 1982.

A talented black novelist, Cato Caldwell Douglass achieves critical and commercial success but struggles against prejudice. Cato is assaulted by racism in his personal and professional life, and haunted by a recurring nightmare. What's more, he is plagued by the not-so-friendly rivalry of Paul Cummings, a white fellow writer and friend.

Cato and Paul meet soon after World War II when they are pursuing college degrees with the help of the G.I. Bill. Paul seems to cast himself as Cato's teacher while simultaneously congratulating himself for, and feeling uneasy about, his friendship with a black man. Cato must cope with a crumbling marriage and a circle of insecure, often insensitive and competitive literary friends of which Paul is a part. When he realizes that New York City is stifling him, Cato decides to go abroad.

While living in Barcelona and longing for female companionship, Cato meets Monica Jones, a Spanish prostitute of partly African origin. He invites the poverty-stricken young woman to move into his house with her son but warns her that he will return to the United States when his first novel, which is slated for publication, is released. Monica accepts this arrangement, and when she discovers after a few months that she is pregnant, she and her son leave Cato without saying good-bye.

Returning to the United States, Cato falls into his old crowd and tries to maintain a relationship with Glenn, the child from his ruined marriage. As his relationship with Paul grows increasingly strained, Cato begins wondering if they are friends or merely rivals. He realizes that the publishing industry breeds rivalry between writers. He learns as well, during a brief affair with agent Sandra Queensbury, that Hollywood is not the only town with casting couches.

Despite the depressing realities of the publishing industry, Cato remains enthusiastic about his writing. He attends a session of Middlebury College's Bread Loaf writing workshop, and although he spends little time honing his craft, he does come away from his summer in Vermont with something of value. He meets Allis Greenberg, a poet who has been told that she has little talent. The two eventually marry and have a child together.

Returning to New York City, Cato lands what promises to be an exciting project. He is asked to write and host a television series on the black experience. He travels the country with a small crew, sampling the ideas and attitudes of black Americans. After a shootout with racist rednecks on the southern leg of the journey, the group charters a plane to go to Africa and film there.

When in California, Cato tried to look up Paul's father and failed. Now back in New York, he learns that Paul lied about his past, his name—Kaminsky—and his Jewishness. To much fanfare, Paul publishes a novel that grapples with his self-hatred. Cato feels wounded by the lies and more than a little angry that Paul is so acclaimed when blacks, many of whom are better writers, have trouble being published.

Books by blacks fall from favor, and Cato must get a job teaching at a state university. By day he deals with ill-prepared students and indifferent administrators; by night he battles dreams in which he is pursued or forced to play pool with God. Cato is cheered when he receives word from Monica that she is happily married and that their son, Alejo Cato Donoso, is a celebrated poet. Glenn, now also a writer, travels to Europe where he meets Alejo and arranges for him to visit his father. Expectation turns to sadness, however, when Alejo and his girlfriend disappear mysteriously.

Cato decides to change publishers because the company with which he has a contract will not promote his books. Soon after, he learns that Paul has committed suicide. With the rivalry he never wanted now ended in a way he could never have anticipated, Cato contemplates the different meanings of the word *success*.

Dowling, Margo. *U.S.A. (The Big Money)*. John Dos Passos. 1936.

Margo Dowling's rise to stardom is an archetypal and theatrical rags-to-riches tale. Abandoned by her widower alcoholic father, she is raised in Queens, Brooklyn, and Manhattan by her stepmother Agnes. Margo spends her early childhood attending convent school and working in a bakery with Agnes. But she is ruthlessly ambitious, and when Agnes starts living with Frank Mandeville, a vaudeville actor, Margo goes on the stage as a child actress.

One night the dissolute Frank rapes her. After this, Margo hates her home and starts spending time with Tony Garrido, a handsome Cuban who also aspires to the stage. They marry and move to Havana when she is sixteen; Margo hates the restrictions of Cuban wifehood, however, and after giving birth to a blind child who subsequently

dies, she flees back to New York with the aid of an enraptured consulate clerk.

Living with Agnes and Frank again, Margo becomes a chorus girl for Florenz Ziegfeld and is courted by Ted Whittlesea, a Yale halfback. At the end of the theatrical season she and a friend go with Ted and another Yale student to Florida for a promised two weeks on a yacht. The event sours when they encounter down-and-out, drug-addicted Tony Garrido in a Jacksonville speakeasy. Margo takes him in, but he and a bellhop lover rob her and run away, leaving her with nothing but fifteen cents and a diamond ring.

At this low ebb Margo meets CHARLEY ANDERSON in a diner. He takes her to Miami, then continues seeing her and supports her financially when they get back to New York. To supplement the money she gets from Charley, Margo takes a job modeling and just before she returns to Florida with Charley, she meets Sam Margolies, an aspiring photographer and filmmaker. Charley is then mortally injured in a car crash, and while he lies in bed, Margo wheedles his last few thousand dollars from him.

When these resources start to run out, she and the now twice-widowed Agnes set out for California, with a sworn-to-reform Tony Garrido chauffeuring them in the car Margo got from Charley. Margo, Agnes, and Tony spend three years in California, moving from one cheap bungalow to another, before Margo has her first break in film. She meets Sam Margolies at a party, and he immediately signs her on to appear in his next picture opposite film star Rodney Cathcart. Tony, whose sexual debauchery and drug addiction have become increasingly embarrassing to Margo, is conveniently killed in a fight.

Sam convinces Margo to marry him. Soon after, Rodney sexually assaults her in Sam's house. Nevertheless, the three become inseparable companions, and all go on to stardom. When Margo is last seen in the novel, she is at a flamboyant New York party with Sam and Rodney, and it is being rumored that her career is at an end because she has no voice for talking pictures.

Drake, Temple. *Sanctuary; Requiem for a Nun; The Town*. William Faulkner. 1931; 1951; 1957.

Temple Drake, an undergraduate at the University of Mississippi in Oxford, is the victim of sexual violence. The repercussions of this abuse are explored when the story of her tragic life continues in *Requiem for a Nun*, the sequel to *Sanctuary*.

The errant daughter of a judge, Temple is on probation at the university for sneaking out of her dormitory to go out with boys from town who, unlike students, own cars. But Temple's privileged and protected life is rudely interrupted when she agrees to a date with a young "gentleman" graduate from the University of Virginia, GOWAN STEVENS. They have not been driving long when the drunken Gowan crashes his car near the remotely situated

Old Frenchman's Place, a dilapidated mansion that is home to bootlegger Lee Goodwin.

When Gowan passes out after doing some more drinking, Temple is left at the mercy of the men who have gathered at the house. Harassed and repeatedly sexually threatened, Temple begs the assistance of Ruby Lamar, an ex-prostitute from Memphis who is the mother of Lee Goodwin's child and the only other woman at Old Frenchman's Place. When the men's advances become more aggressive, Ruby hides Temple in a corncrib and stays with her until morning. That same morning Gowan, ashamed of his mistreatment of Temple, sneaks away from Old Frenchman's Place and pays a man with a car to pick up Temple and deliver her to the university. The driver never arrives.

Shortly thereafter a man named POPEYE VITELLI finds Temple in the corncrib and shoots Tommy, a dimwitted man who is trying to protect her. Impotent yet diabolically sexual, Popeye then proceeds to rape Temple with a corncob. Treating Temple as if she were his personal property, Popeye transports her to a house of prostitution in Memphis where he keeps her locked up for his bizarre sexual needs. Unable to ravage her himself, he brings in a man named Alabama Red to have sexual intercourse with Temple while he watches.

In order to assuage her terror and pain, Temple starts drinking heavily and eventually loses her grip on reality. She even begins to call Popeye "Daddy." Gowan's uncle, the lawyer GAVIN STEVENS, locates her and tries to convince her to testify against Popeye in a case in which Lee Goodwin is being tried for the murder of Tommy, but she remains loyal to Popeye. Later, Temple rents a hotel room for herself and Red so they can have sex without Popeye's knowledge. Popeye finds them, murders Red for his audacity, then flees.

Temple's final perverse act causes Lee's death at the hands of an outraged mob of vigilantes. At Lee Goodwin's trial she testifies that it was Lee who murdered Tommy. Temple probably perjures herself in this way at the instigation of her father who wants to cover up Temple's rape and forced prostitution. After Temple's testimony, a lynch mob hauls Lee out of jail and burns him to death. When last seen in *Sanctuary*, Temple is with her father in the Luxembourg Gardens, yawning and checking on her appearance in a compact mirror.

Requiem for a Nun continues recounting the lives of Temple and Gowan. Eight years have passed since the events in *Sanctuary*, and during this time Gowan has tried to provide what reparations he can by marrying Temple. Together they have had a son and a daughter. Tragedy continues to stalk her, however. Temple and Gowan's daughter is smothered to death in her crib by her nanny, Nancy Monnigoe, a former prostitute and drug user.

The night before Nancy is to be hanged for first-degree murder, her lawyer, Gavin Stevens, convinces Temple to accompany him to the governor's mansion in order to request that he mitigate Nancy's sentence. In the presence of the governor and Gavin, and with Gowan concealed in the room, Temple reveals evidence that she had heretofore kept secret. Temple tells the men that she has been on the verge of running off with Alabama Red's brother Pete who has been threatening to blackmail her with letters she had written to Red at the height of their affair. Nancy killed Temple's child in the misguided belief that the tragedy would draw Temple closer to her husband Gowan, forcing her to stay with him.

Although Nancy's sentence is not altered as a result of Temple's confession, her honesty does serve to open the Stevenses' eyes to the fact that the repercussions of evil cannot be avoided through hypocrisy. The novel concludes with Nancy assuring Temple that salvation is achieved through suffering and faith in the mercy of God.

Drew, Nancy. *The Mystery at the Moss-Covered Mansion.* Carolyn Keene. 1941.

Stirred by suffering, misery, and injustice wherever she sees it, Nancy Drew is the teenaged, slender, titian-haired sleuth who solves mysteries in and around the fictional town of River Heights. A modest amateur who refuses all but the most sentimental rewards, Nancy always avoids referring to her achievements. Most of the Nancy Drew Mystery Stories stem from the criminal cases of her renowned father, lawyer Carson Drew, who knows his only child to be clever, sensible, and talented. Her best friends, George Fayne, a brave young woman, and Bess Marvin, George's plump yet plucky cousin, assist Nancy, as does Nancy's college beau Ned Nickerson, who is always careful not to curtail her independence and insatiable curiosity.

In this story, Nancy, George, and Bess discover an overgrown Revolutionary War–era home deep in the woods near the fictional southern town of Ashley. While helping Mr. Drew locate the missing heiress June Campbell, who stands to inherit a $52,000 estate, they come upon the mansion from which emanate supernatural moanings, unearthly screams, and gunshots. Usually calm in the face of danger, even Nancy's courage ebbs, yet she tenaciously returns again and again to the grounds to ferret out the mystery. Nancy begins to make connections between various suspects: Ramo, a local gypsy; Madame Cully, a vicious fortune-teller; Venus, Madame Cully's beautiful veiled daughter; Mrs. Labelle, the heiress's former nanny; Jules Raynad, a renowned portrait artist who paints Nancy in oils; and a scruffy red-haired man who seems to inhabit the mansion.

When Venus impersonates June and tricks Mr. Drew into unwittingly handing over to her the $52,000 in cash, Nancy not only must recover the rightful heiress's fortune but must salvage her own father's professional reputation as well. Nancy rightly suspects that Ramo and the fortune-teller are siblings working in cahoots, and they have forced

Venus, a talented mime, into their plot. Working with a clue that Nancy discovers in Venus's room, Nancy and Mr. Drew bravely set out by plane in the midst of a bad storm to find the real June at her last-known address, only to crash-land near the mansion. Nancy manages to leave the wreck and pull fuselage off the survivors before she succumbs to head injuries. When she regains consciousness, she finds herself inside the iron-barred mansion. Not knowing whether to expect friend or foe, she escapes into its confines and begins to realize wild animals may be kept there, a fact that would explain bizarre noises and shots. She wonders about the identity of a beautiful woman whom she spies arriving at the place, apparently a guest of its red-haired inhabitant.

Chatting with Raynad, her portraitist, Nancy discovers that he is an old friend of the missing June and that June's adventurer father had befriended many prominent artists before his death. Nancy returns to the forest with her chums and learns that Ramo is burying much of the stolen inheritance in tin cans and secret cabinets in and around the moss-covered grounds. She arranges for state troopers to arrest Ramo and the fortune-teller when they come for the loot.

Nancy finally uncovers the mystery when she decides to enter the house, and a leopard, escaped from its cellar, nearly devours her. The red-haired man, who saves her from Bola's jaws, turns out to be the famous wild-life painter Karl Karter, who keeps and paints jungle beasts inside the mansion's walls. His latest subject, the newly arrived young woman, is none other than June the heiress! Nancy salvages her father's reputation, restores the estate to its rightful owner, and in consequence even manages to save the frail Mrs. Labelle from her genteel poverty and broken health. In this case as always, she accepts no reward for her efforts.

Driscoll, Bill. "The Ransom of Red Chief." O. Henry. 1910.

Bill Driscoll is a man who, along with his erudite, well-spoken partner Sam, decides to commit a kidnapping in the sleepy Alabama town of Summit. Sam and Bill need $2,000 more to pull off a fraudulent town-lot scheme in Illinois, so they decide to kidnap the ten-year-old son of Ebenezer Dorset, a mortgage financier. The seemingly solid plan turns out to be Bill's undoing.

The trouble begins immediately when Sam and Bill try to entice the boy with candy and he throws a piece of brick at Bill, catching him in the eye. With some effort the men get the boy to a nearby cave where he becomes most enthusiastic about the adventure of camping out. Sam leaves Bill in charge of the boy while he pursues the ransom scheme. The boy begins to drive Bill crazy with his incessant chatter, unanswerable questions, and violent games.

First they play Indian, with the boy as Red Chief and

Bill as Old Hank, the Trapper. When Red Chief makes a most realistic attempt to scalp Old Hank, Sam is horrified by his cohort's shrieks of terror and realizes that Bill's spirit is already broken. When the boy drops a red-hot boiled potato down Bill's back and then smashes it with his foot, Bill talks Sam into reducing the ransom to $1,500; he points out that he has stood by Sam through earthquakes, fire and flood, tornadoes, poker games, and police raids without ever losing his nerve, but the boy is too much for him.

While Sam delivers the ransom note, Bill and the boy play Black Scout; in this game Bill is the horse, and is ridden ninety miles by the Black Scout and fed imaginary oats in the form of sand. With this game Bill finally cracks; he takes the boy down the mountain and kicks him toward Summit, then limps back to the cave, covered in bruises and cuts. He explains to Sam in his typically malapropic speech that he has tried to be faithful to his and Sam's "articles of depredation" but that the boy pushed him too far. At this point Bill's rose-pink features are suffused by peace and contentment, but when he turns and sees that the boy has followed him back to the cave, he seems on the brink of insanity.

Sam assures Bill that the kidnapping scheme will be completed by midnight and leaves Bill playing the Russian in a Japanese war. However, where Sam expects to receive $1,500, he instead receives a note from Ebenezer Dorset saying that he will take his son back if he is paid $250. That night, at Bill's pleading, the two crooks take the boy home and give his father the money. Then Bill takes off running, and although it is dark and Bill is fat, it is a good mile and a half out of Summit before Sam catches up with him.

Driscoll, Thomas à Beckett. *Pudd'nhead Wilson.* Samuel L. Clemens (Mark Twain). 1894.

Apparently the heir of a wealthy family, Tom Driscoll is actually Valet de Chambre, the ninety-seven-percent white son of the slave Roxana. Fearing what will become of him if he grows up black and knowing he can easily "pass" for white, she exchanges him in his infancy for her master's infant, Thomas à Driscoll. The slave child grows up coddled and petted, while the actual heir to one of the greatest fortunes in Dawson's Landing, Missouri, grows up as his slave, forced to bear his unwitting usurper's orders, taunts, and abuses.

Cowardly and vicious, Tom returns from college with a taste for gambling that his uncle and guardian, Judge Driscoll, detests. Having once been temporarily disinherited because of his bad habits, he realizes he can no longer go to his uncle to settle his debts. He takes to stealing, disguised as a woman.

The mystery generated by the unsolved thefts excites comment but nothing to match the arrival of Italian noblemen twins Luigi and Angelo Cappello. At a political rally Tom makes the mistake of insulting the brothers. Luigi responds by kicking Tom's rear end, sending him sailing over the heads of a crowd of onlookers. The cowardly Tom takes his case to court rather than fight a duel. This dishonorable behavior causes him to fall out of his aristocratic uncle's good graces once again.

To make matters worse for Tom, the now-free Roxana has returned in poverty after several years away, asking that he support his former nursemaid. When he refuses, she says she has damaging information about him that she could communicate to Judge Driscoll. Frightened that she knows of his new gambling debts, Tom complies with her wishes. She soon reveals the secret of his ancestry, and he becomes furtive and sheepish, imagining that everyone he passes can tell that he is actually black.

Unable to sell an exquisite dagger he has stolen from the twins, and bereft of his other booty (by some hidden hand on board a steamship), Tom must quickly find some way to repay his insistent creditors. His loving mother volunteers to allow herself to be sold back into slavery, with the understanding that Tom will find a lenient master and that he will buy her back as soon as he can afford to.

Instead, the scurrilous youth sells her "down the river." When she escapes and confronts him, he is desperate to buy her back immediately and conceives a plan of robbing his uncle. Judge Driscoll wakes in the middle of the robbery, and Tom stabs him with the stolen dagger. Smug and confident that he has escaped detection, Tom attends the trial of Angelo and Luigi and their hapless defense by DAVID "PUDD'NHEAD" WILSON, an eccentric fingerprint-collecting lawyer. Visiting David during a recess in the proceedings in order to gloat, Tom smudges a glass with his fingerprint. David immediately recognizes the print as that on the murder weapon and pronounces in court the next day that Tom is the murderer of Judge Driscoll. More shocking is the revelation, based on fingerprints taken during his and the real Tom's infancy, that Tom is in fact Roxana's child and thus a slave. At the end of the novel, Tom's true name and status are restored to him, and although found guilty of murder, he is sold down the river to settle debts to his master's estate.

Drouet, Charles. *Sister Carrie*. Theodore Dreiser. 1900.

Charles Drouet is a handsome young traveling salesman. He is also a "masher," intent on wooing "susceptible young women" with his manner and dress. Well-versed in the techniques of flattery and persuasion, Drouet is a man whose main concern in life is pleasure.

When Drouet notices a young, innocent-looking woman one Friday on a train heading into the city of Chicago, he takes the opportunity to display his charm and urbanity for her benefit. He asks her name and address, gives her his business card, and promises to visit her on Monday.

The girl is CAROLINE "CARRIE" MEEBER; Drouet does not go to visit her as promised, but he does run into her on the street a few days later. She is depressed because she is ill, has had to quit her job, and may have to return to her hometown in Wisconsin. Drouet talks her into accepting money for clothes, knowing that this is an issue to which the poorly clad girl must be sensitive. Lunches escalate into shopping and the theater. Drouet all the while exploits the young girl's reluctance both to go back to Wisconsin and to return to her sister Minnie's dingy flat where she has been living. He soon rents her a room, ostensibly so that Carrie can keep her new clothes out of sight of Minnie and her somber, frugal husband Hanson.

As their relationship intensifies, Drouet resists Carrie's urgings that they marry. Yet when Drouet witnesses the favorable reaction of his friend GEORGE HURSTWOOD to Carrie, he realizes he has a prize. Nonetheless, the damage has already been done. Carrie feels increasingly attracted to Hurstwood, a wealthy saloon manager, and while Drouet is away on business they meet constantly and confess their love for each other. When Drouet returns, he mentions marriage, but he is still insincere and indifferent to her feelings. Carrie realizes this when Drouet fails to appreciate her enthusiasm for winning a role in a money-raising "theatrical" put on by his Elks lodge.

When he sees the play, Drouet is immensely affected by the power of Carrie's dramatic performance, but true to his nature, he fails to grasp the meaning of what Carrie's character says about love being the only true criterion for a relationship. Afterward he is aglow with pride in Carrie; Carrie remains engrossed in Hurstwood.

The morning after Carrie's play, Drouet, having forgotten some bills, returns to the flat moments after leaving for work. Somewhat perplexed to find Carrie gone, he nonetheless proceeds to flirt with the chambermaid. When she offhandedly inquires after Hurstwood, Drouet discovers that Hurstwood had visited Carrie nearly every day while he was out of town. That night he confronts Carrie and informs her that Hurstwood is married. Carrie decides to leave, but Drouet charitably convinces her to stay through the month and says that he will leave instead. Still confident and casual, Drouet inwardly believes that he will be able to rekindle their romance. When he does return one day, Carrie is out looking for work. After waiting in vain, he stares wistfully at a picture of her before leaving and says, "You didn't do me right, Cad."

Years later Drouet shows up at Carrie's dressing room door on Broadway in New York, where she has ended up after scandalously eloping with Hurstwood. He tries to bring up the past, but Carrie insists there is no time. Before leaving he tells Carrie that Hurstwood stole money from his employer when the two of them left Chicago. At the close of the novel, Drouet is in New York's Imperial Hotel where he and a friend happily look forward to a night out with "a couple of girls."

Dubin, William. *Dubin's Lives.* Bernard Malamud. 1977.

After a short and failed career as a lawyer, William Dubin finds that he feels dissatisfied with his life. Although he has a family, Dubin's detachment from his wife, daughter, and stepson creates a void in him that he attempts to fill by writing biographies.

When the novel begins, Dubin, having just been commissioned to write a biography of D. H. Lawrence, becomes distracted by Fanny, a beautiful young house cleaner hired by his wife. With his children grown up and moved away, and his wife at work, Dubin and Fanny have the house to themselves each day, and Dubin finds himself drawn to the aura of sexuality that the young housekeeper exudes. The two finally consummate the attraction they both feel and maintain the affair for the next few months. When a disagreement arises from Dubin's refusal to make love to her in the bed he shares with his wife, Fanny moves to New York.

Dubin is unable to forget Fanny, however, and after meeting with her on a business trip to New York, he takes her with him on a vacation to Venice. Much to Dubin's disappointment, Fanny becomes ill and spends most of her time in the hotel room. Dubin is horrified when he returns to the hotel after an afternoon of sightseeing to find her on the floor making love to a gondolier who had followed her up to the room.

A devastated Dubin returns home but is unable to concentrate on his biography of Lawrence. He begins an affair with the wife of his best friend to overcome the agony of the loss of Fanny, whose letters he stoically refuses to answer. Dubin sinks into a deep depression that he is unable to shake even with help from his wife Kitty.

When he receives word from Fanny that she has returned to New York City, Dubin cannot resist seeing her once again. Despite his intentions, their affair resumes immediately. Dubin is once again consumed by thoughts of Fanny; he ignores his wife, with whom he becomes impotent, and brings Fanny to stay in a barn outside their house so that he can see her more often. However, when Dubin forces Fanny to hide from his wife, who makes a surprise visit to the barn, she breaks off their relationship.

Dubin's life once again deteriorates, but despite the emptiness of their marriage, he and Kitty find themselves too set in their ways for divorce. Fanny moves to a neighboring town to live on a farm with her new boyfriend, and Dubin continues to see her platonically on occasion. Dubin suffers lasting effects from their affair, however, the most disturbing of which is his inability to achieve an erection from any kind of stimulation but Fanny's presence. After kissing his lover good-bye, the story ends with Dubin rushing home, trying to save his semi-erection for his wife.

Dubois, Robert Raymond. *Continental Drift.* Russell Banks. 1985.

Robert Raymond Dubois is a man whose frustration with his own life and background lead him to take a series of shortcuts to the good life. Through a fateful series of events, after becoming involved with a host of shady characters and dealings, he falls short of his goal and unwittingly cuts short his own life.

A man of plain appearance and common desires, Bob was raised in a working-class New England town with working-class values and friends. He and those with whom he associates lead lackluster lives sheltered from the dangers of the fast living of more urbanized environments and devoid of contact with cultures and "races" other than their own.

Bob is married, but he doesn't have the will to resist temptation and feels little regret for his adulterous relationships, which give him a sense of self-worth. Beyond these affairs, Bob is bored with his day-to-day existence and longs for freedom from such concerns as making money for his family.

He has a nagging fear of living the kind of meaningless lives his parents lived, and he especially fears that his children will be stuck in the same rut. To fulfill his desire to seek a better life, he decides to accept his brother's offer to work for him managing his liquor store in Florida. His brother Eddie lives life in the fast lane and has gained his material success through illicit dealings with powerful and shady persons. Bob's wife has little respect for Eddie, but she nevertheless agrees to pick up and move to Florida where, it is presumed, they can quickly can start a new life.

A short time after the move, Bob experiences a passion for the daughter of an old man who works in the store he manages. Marguerite is black, and although Bob has followed the dictates of his heart and admitted that he's in love with her, he has trouble shedding the prejudices he has acquired from his isolated and racist upbringing. The issue of race becomes more complicated for Bob when he encounters two black men who try to rob the liquor store. Bob somehow manages to save himself but fatally shoots one of them.

Meanwhile, Bob's wife has given birth to the son he has always wanted. Bob was with his new lover when his wife went into labor, and his subsequent feelings of guilt cause him to end the relationship with Marguerite soon afterward.

Eddie soon falls into financial trouble and loses the liquor store. Bob is left without a job, and in an attempt to get himself out of the ensuing financial muddle, he takes out a loan from an old friend who earns his living selling drugs. The friend, who is himself in financial straits, suggests that Bob might be able to make money quickly by transporting Haitian immigrants to America. Bob agrees to the scheme.

Unfortunately, the boat transporting the Haitians is spotted by the Coast Guard. Bob's Jamaican partner in the scheme becomes nervous and fires his guns, causing the frightened Haitians to jump overboard. None can swim, and the majority drown. Drugs are found on the boat, and Bob's two accomplices are later apprehended.

Catapulted into trouble, Bob and his wife decide to flee and return to their New Hampshire town. They are also convinced that the money Bob received from the Haitians is blood money. Bob feels that he could redeem himself for all his past transgressions if he could somehow return the money to the Haitian community. He searches for the lone survivor of the boat accident, but she refuses the money. A group of thugs demand the money, but Bob doesn't feel they should be the ones to take it. The thugs stab him and Bob dies, a victim of his own desire for a better life.

Dudley, Bruce. *Dark Laughter.* Sherwood Anderson. 1925.

Bruce Dudley, a newspaper writer, leaves his home in Chicago and adopts a new identity. He drops his real name, John Stockton, and when he returns to his hometown, Old Harbor, Indiana, no one recognizes him. While working in a wheel factory there, he contemplates his failed marriage and dreams of finding another woman.

Bruce once lived in a fashionable studio apartment in Chicago with his wife Bernice, also a journalist. Bernice was aggressive and independent, with a separate set of friends. Bruce felt uneasy among these sophisticated painters, musicians, and writers, and while he was establishing a respectable position at the paper, his wife seemed to be achieving greater recognition as a writer. Bruce regarded Bernice's friends as superficial, however, and her writing amateurish and indelicate. Bernice could sense his scorn and felt it when he wore a strange, fixed grin. One night during dinner, when Bruce was grinning this way, Bernice left the table. After sitting in darkness for a few hours, Bruce got his hat and left the house.

Traveling slowly south, Bruce arrives at Old Harbor and takes a job at a factory painting wheels. While working he clarifies his thoughts about Bernice and contrasts them with vivid memories of his mother, whom he adored. She died when Bruce was young, and he remembers her as unfailingly loving and very fragile. The chattering of Sponge Martine, a coworker, sometimes interrupts Bruce's thoughts. Sponge is a cocky, tough old man who goes on delirious weekly drinking binges with his "old woman." Sponge first points out that the factory owner's wife, ALINE ALDRIDGE GREY, frequently watches Bruce from her car.

When Aline places an ad in the paper for a gardener, Bruce sees this as an invitation for romance. He quits his job at the factory before going to the Grey house. Aline offers him the job and a small room. They spend hours in the garden together. Bruce admires her artistic hands as she explains how to care for flowers. Even the servants recognize the attraction between them, and Aline's husband, FRED (GREY), grows suspicious. Aline and Bruce make love one afternoon while Fred is away, and then Bruce disappears for several months.

During this period, Bruce spends much of his time lounging in his hotel room, working only intermittently. He finally decides that Aline must leave Fred, as he had left Bernice; he believes a marriage cannot withstand one partner's dissatisfaction. Bruce goes to Aline's house and finds her extremely glad to see him because she is pregnant with his child. After Aline gives Fred a matter-of-fact explanation, she and Bruce walk slowly away. As they go, Bruce feels oddly distracted and realizes that finding the "right woman" is only a part of the dilemma. He still needs to find his life's work.

Dudley, Constantia. *Ormond.* Charles Brockden Brown. 1799.

At the age of sixteen, living in early republican Philadelphia with her father, Constantia Dudley has acquired a classical and scientific education far surpassing the usual schooling of women in the eighteenth century. She is guided by rational principles in all of her undertakings and as a consequence rejects a number of marriage proposals either on the grounds of her youth or the suitor's intellectual incompatibility.

Constantia's comfortable existence with her father is shattered when he is financially ruined by a trusted associate and she is forced to take charge of the family's situation. With her father embittered and increasingly prone to drink, she must steer them through a period of abject poverty and an epidemic of yellow fever by gaining employment as a seamstress. During this period, Constantia has a chance encounter in the street with Ormond, the man who cheated her father. In her subsequent meeting with the man responsible for their poverty, Constantia precipitates a change in Ormond's ideas regarding women. Ormond previously considered women intellectually inferior beings and therefore beneath his concern, but having at last encountered a woman who is his intellectual equal, he determines to possess her. After Constantia's intercession on behalf of his mistress not only fails to sway him but more firmly cements his desire for Constantia, Ormond breaks off his liaison with his present mistress, who commits suicide.

Ormond then begins to visit Constantia regularly at her home. He confesses his love for her and attempts to convince her to become his new mistress since marriage to any woman is abhorrent to him, but Constantia's rational principles prevent her from acceding. During this time Ormond helps restore the sight of Constantia's father, who had previously gone blind. Once his sight returns, Constantia's father revives his former passion for painting and, clearly divining Ormond's intentions toward his daughter, determines to go to Europe with Constantia to take up painting in earnest while affording her further educational opportunities. Ormond becomes aware of their plans by listening to their conversation from a secret room adjoining their house, and seeing this development as an obstacle to his possession of Constantia, he arranges to have her father murdered.

Shortly after her father's death, Constantia encounters her friend, the book's narrator, whom she has not seen in years. To put aside her grief and begin anew, she determines to accompany her friend to England. Upon discovering her intention to leave, Ormond traps Constantia in their former house in New York, now vacant, and attempts to rape her. Constantia stabs him to death in self-defense. The novel closes with Constantia with her friend in England pursuing her passion for knowledge and reason.

Dudley, Esther. *Esther.* Henry Adams. 1884.

Esther Dudley, a woman coming of age in New York City in the late nineteenth century, disapproves of the social conventions that derive from religion. Although her beauty attracts many suitors, Esther's outspoken agnosticism also earns her the scorn of the society in which she moves.

The daughter of an aged, free-thinking lawyer, Esther has managed to retain her autonomy from suitors by devoting her energy to the care of her ailing father. For years Mr. Dudley has jealously protected his only child from prospective lovers, but eventually, knowing that he hasn't long to live, he begins to worry that Esther will turn into an old maid. He allows her more time away from him, with the hope that she will meet an eligible man.

Known for her artistic talent, Esther is recruited by George Strong, a cousin and sometime suitor, to paint a mural at a nearby church. As a scientist well versed in the theory of evolution, Strong is even more skeptical of religion than Esther, but he wants to help his old Harvard friend, the new minister Stephen Hazard, finish the renovation of the church as soon as possible. Under the tutelage of Wharton, a famous muralist and interior designer, Esther's painting skills blossom. She also enjoys hearing these three highly educated men argue about topics ranging from science to art to religion. At first Esther feels comfortable sitting at her easel, coolly weighing the relative merits of the various philosophies being discussed around her. But gradually she realizes she is falling in love with the handsome and zealous Hazard, the man least suited to her own worldview.

After Mr. Dudley dies, Esther grows more attached to Hazard and eventually accepts his offer of marriage. They try to keep the engagement secret, but their obvious affection for each other soon becomes the source of local gossip. Hazard's parishioners vehemently disapprove of Esther; they fail to see how a minister could even consider friendship with a woman so disrespectful of religion. When Esther realizes that her views could damage Hazard's career, she attempts to learn more about Christianity. But the more she reads, the more she realizes that no book will give her the faith required to be a proper minister's wife. Instead of convincing her to submit to Hazard's religion, the reading prompts Esther to become even more critical of marriage in general. To Esther, organized religion and marriage are institutions that restrict the freedom of women. She decides to forgo allegiance to either.

Esther breaks her engagement to Hazard and flees to Niagara Falls. Hazard pursues her, pressing her to explain her rejection of him. Determined to preserve her autonomy, Esther says she is not rejecting him but the religion he serves and the domestic bondage to which she would be relegated. Strong, seeing his chance, also asks for Esther's hand, but she rejects him as well, and the story ends with her declaration that she has loved only Hazard.

Dudley, Quintus Cincinnatus Lovell. *A Woman of Means.* Peter Taylor. 1950.

Quint, as Quintus Cincinnatus Lovell Dudley is known, has lived alone with his father Gerald since Quint's birth and the death of his mother. They live in a series of boardinghouses while Gerald Dudley ekes out a meager living as a hardware salesman. Quint generally spends his summers under the care of his maternal grandmother and in the company of his cousins. He enjoys these summers in the country but frequently causes fights between his father, who wishes him to be reared as a city boy, and Grandmother Lovell, who wishes Quint to be as familiar with the farm and nature as his mother had been.

Shortly after Quint turns ten, his father announces that he is finally going to marry the wealthy divorcee Anna Barnes Lauterbach. Father and son relocate to New Orleans to Anna's sumptuous home, Casa Anna. Although overwhelmed by the house and by the fact that he is about to go to his eighth school, Quint immediately falls in love with his new stepmother and before long is calling her "Mother." At the same time, Gerald Dudley develops an emotional attachment to his stepdaughters, Laura and Bess Lauterbach, two independently wealthy teenagers who lead a life more or less apart from parental control.

Quint admires his new sisters, and over the course of the next few years, he gradually comes to appreciate their high-spiritedness. As he settles in, he realizes that for the first time he will be able to attend the same school, this time The Country Day School, for more than one year. Meanwhile, Gerald Dudley is promoted through the ranks of his company and before too long achieves the rank of president. This development roughly coincides with the fact that the girls have gone north to attend school and are thus less available to Gerald. The company's owner dies unexpectedly, and Gerald is placed under more stress than usual. But Gerald is soon dismissed, because of the former owner's negligence, and his marriage takes a turn for the worse.

Quint, who senses that something bad is happening, notices the separation developing between his parents. He also notices that his stepsisters have less and less time for Gerald, even on their brief visits home. As tensions persist in the Dudley household, Gerald plans for the resumption of their boardinghouse life-style and insists that neither he nor his son will subsist on Anna's charity.

As Anna tells the perplexed Quint, she had married Gerald in the hopes of having a son, while he had married her because she had money. Anna has come to love Gerald and is puzzled that he cannot see things her way. As the time for their departure draws nearer, Anna collapses and informs Gerald that she is pregnant. But Gerald swiftly realizes that she is not pregnant: She is suffering a breakdown. Quint spends a great deal of time with Anna, and he notices the rapid decline in her mental capacity. Guilty about a second failed marriage and mourning the loss of Quint, Anna breaks down irrevocably. On the day Lucky Lindbergh arrives in France after his historic flight, Quint weeps bitterly while Laura and Bess coldheartedly make plans for Anna's removal to a sanitarium and for the dismantling and sale of Casa Anna and its contents.

Duffy, Jack. *The Foundry.* Albert Halper. 1934.

Jack Duffy, nicknamed "Lieutenant," is the most junior of the three partners who run the Fort Dearborn Electrotype Foundry, where he is in charge of all outgoing curved printing plates. A small, wiry man in his early forties, Jack is celebrated for his off-color jokes and oratorical flights of fancy; a number of the workers have begun to speak in the same eccentric fashion, called "the Duffy vernacular." Having inherited his share of the business from his father, Jack does his job without much enthusiasm and dislikes his partners, the hardworking MAX'L STEUBEN and Ezekiel Cranly, a weak and ill-tempered former clerk. He has developed an easygoing, good-natured, but superficial rapport with the workers, who secretly despise him for being a weak boss.

Jack is bitterly unhappy at home and is cruel to his wife because she cannot bear him a child. He constantly pursues extramarital affairs and has a habit of accosting female workers at the foundry. In the fall of 1928, however, the three partners become interested in the stock market, and Jack temporarily stops fighting with his wife in order to obtain some of her money to invest in stocks. Shortly thereafter he meets a married woman, Mrs. Edith Hill, at the movies. The shy young Edith, whose husband is in the Southwest dying from tuberculosis, is so different from Jack's previous lovers that he rapidly falls in love with her.

Throughout the fall and spring of 1929, Jack gradually becomes less witty and caustic at work. Happily preoccupied with his newfound romance, he pays little attention to the developing conflict between workers and bosses at the foundry. Jack merely acts as an overseer while Max'l engages in a power struggle with the union and eventually makes embarrassing concessions after the workers sabotage the foundry's newest machinery.

In the summer Jack is elated when he is able to send his wife to a resort and spend his vacation with Edith instead. He becomes seriously depressed, however, when he learns that Edith's husband is actually recovering during his stay in the sanatorium that Jack himself has helped finance. In the fall, Jack, preoccupied with worries about the improving health of Edith's husband, pays little heed to his partners' growing obsession with the status of their investment in the stock market, even after he suffers some losses. He begins to drink heavily when he learns that Edith's husband is indeed making a full recovery.

On Tuesday, October 29, Jack's world falls apart. He loses all of his money in the crash and Edith's husband returns home. A few evenings later Jack stays late at the foundry even though he is due to appear at the annual show meant to boost the morale of the workers. Edith arrives at his office to say an awkward and bitter goodbye. After she departs, he goes to the privy and, leaving a sardonic note for the foundry workers, shoots himself in the head.

Duncan, Bill. *A Sign for Cain.* Grace Lumpkin. 1935.

Bill Duncan is the editor of a popular newspaper in the corrupt southern town of Jefferson. Although related to a prominent family, the Gaults, and respected by the white aristocracy, he works fiercely to bring about justice for the town's workers, black and white. When two of the Gaults' black workers are framed for murder, Bill leads the fight to prove their innocence, thereby effecting a final break with the Gaults and the ideals they uphold.

Bill's father, William Duncan, an extended relative of the Gault family, performs a heroic deed that unites the families from the time of Bill's childhood. Colonel Gault, an orator and politician, was engaged in a heated debate with his rival, Judson Gardner. When Gardner drew a gun and attempted to fire at Gault, Bill's father stepped between them, thus preventing the tragedy. A happier connection between the Duncans and the Gaults was an adolescent romance Bill had with CAROLINE GAULT, the Colonel's daughter.

As the story begins, Bill and Caroline are both in their late twenties and have taken very different courses in life. Bill has inherited his father's position as editor of the Jefferson *Record.* His devotion to the paper leaves little room for other pursuits, and he lives a relatively sequestered life in a boardinghouse. Caroline has moved to New York where she has a career as a successful novelist. When the Colonel becomes ill with throat cancer, Caroline returns to Jefferson to care for him, and after a brief interval her romance with Bill resumes.

Initially, Bill and Caroline seem to share a concern with

improving the lives of the poor in Jefferson. Bill publishes editorials decrying lynchings and other forms of violence against blacks. Well versed in communist thought, he dreams of a revolution in which blacks and whites would band together and defeat the racist aristocracy. The paper serves as a connection with northern communist sympathizers who provide support and information. Secretly, Bill begins organizing a farm workers' union with the help of DENIS, a black farm worker; Lee Foster, a white overseer; and the staff of the Jefferson *Record*.

Bill believes that social change can occur only through the efforts of an entire community, while Caroline insists on the importance of individual effort. Bill claims that such individualism is the earmark of the upper class to which she belongs. When Caroline's wealthy Aunt Evelyn is murdered and Denis and Ficents, another union farm worker, are framed, it becomes apparent that Caroline's talk about social change is a pretense. She refuses to risk the interests of her own family to protect Denis, although she knows her brother JIM (GAULT) committed the murder. Bill does not know that Jim Gault is the murderer, but he remains convinced that his friends Denis and Ficents are innocent.

Bill knows that lawyers from the South would be happy to use Denis and Ficents as scapegoats. Bill also realizes that this duo had been visibly linked to the unpopular communist efforts at reform taking place in Jefferson. Because they have already aggravated a number of powerful townspeople—including the sheriff—in their concerted effort to unionize farm workers, Bill fears that a trial would be disastrous for these black men. Arousing the anger of the conservative townspeople, Bill summons lawyers from the North, hoping that they will ensure a fair trial. He helps suppress a lynch mob, but he cannot prevent Jim Gault from entering the jail. Pretending to avenge the honor of his family, Jim shoots the two suspects dead before the trial. In despair, Bill nevertheless continues to support the friends and family of Denis and Ficents by arranging for their safety. He advises Selah, Ficents' girlfriend, to "go on hating and learn to fight."

Duncan, Sissie Peterson Joplin. *Sissie.* John A. Williams. 1963.

As she lies on her deathbed awaiting the arrival of the children she has not seen for years, Sissie Peterson Joplin Duncan remembers the events that brought her to this point. A black woman who has faced many obstacles, Sissie has always been strong, but her very strength has adversely influenced the lives of the people around her.

Early in the century Sissie traveled from the southern farm that had been her home to a small city in New York state. Riding in the Jim Crow car of a train, she met Arthur, a young college student working as a porter. The two carried on an affair that continued intermittently even after she met and married the would-be singer Big

Ralph Joplin. Sissie loved Ralph, but she could not withstand the attractions of the confident upwardly mobile Arthur even though she knew that the promises he made her were empty.

Sissie's hard work to keep her family warm and fed, her fights with Big Ralph, and their dingy flat in a poor section of town had all taken a toll on her sense of self-worth. She felt that only by rekindling her affair with Arthur could she remove herself, if only briefly, from the hopelessness of her situation. Although she knew the child she was carrying was her husband's, Sissie planned to tell Arthur it was his in the hope that he would take her away with him. Her plans went awry, however, when Big Ralph stabbed her in the throat after she returned home late one night from visiting her lover. The physical wound was slight, but Sissie's anger over this action ran deep.

After Big Ralph's release from prison, where he served time for the attack, he begged Sissie to return to him and their son RALPH (JOPLIN), which she did. Big Ralph promised to treat IRIS JOPLIN (STAPLETON), whom Sissie had never told him was really his daughter, as if she were his own child. Feeling guilty for allowing her husband to believe this lie, Sissie became distant toward Iris. She was domineering and demanding with her son Ralph; all her love and dreams were lavished on her younger son Robbie. After the death of another child, Mary Ellen, Big Ralph deserted Sissie.

Forced to work even harder to support the family, Sissie felt trapped. Alcohol and sex seemed to be the only things that gave her pleasure. Resentful of Sissie's domination and her affinity for drink and male companionship, her children kept their distance. They left home early: Ralph for service in World War II, and Iris as the wife of a career soldier. A second marriage, to Oliver Duncan, eventually gave Sissie the financial security she desired, but she was still not satisfied. Ralph's success as a playwright and Iris's as a jazz singer meant little, and she was haunted by Robbie's death in the Korean War.

Finally, at the end of her life, she longs to speak to the two children she has pushed away for so long. She exacts from Ralph the admission that he loves her despite her treatment of him. However, even though she tells Iris that she is indeed her father's child, Sissie dies without the satisfaction of hearing Iris say that she loves her.

Dunn, Theresa. *Looking for Mr. Goodbar.* Judith Rossner. 1975.

Based on a true story, this novel follows its heroine, Theresa Dunn, as she struggles to come to terms with her sexuality in the 1960s while living alone in New York City. Troubled by an unhappy childhood, an unresponsive family, and a terror of intimacy, Theresa blindly accepts the degradation of meaningless sexual experience.

Theresa is raised in a conservative Irish-Catholic family in the Bronx. At four she is stricken with polio and is briefly paralyzed. She recovers, but her illness has made her a withdrawn, inactive child. When Theresa's older brother Thomas is killed in an army accident, her mother goes into a deep depression and her father stays longer at work. Preoccupied, they do not notice that Theresa's spine has curved until it is too late to correct the defect with minor surgery. Her eleventh year is spent in a body cast.

When Theresa is seventeen, her older sister Katherine confesses to her that she has had an abortion. Theresa is moved but is also vaguely disturbed by her feelings of mistrust toward her superficial sister. Theresa begins classes at City College and meets Martin Engle, a cynical and manipulative English professor and part-time poet. Engle admires Theresa's writing, and she becomes devoted to him. When they begin to meet privately, Engle tells her only half-jokingly that he will help her become a better writer by "raising your threshold of pain." Theresa takes a position as his assistant and begins a four-year affair with the married professor, who is alternately tender and cruel to her. He gradually loses interest, and shortly before Theresa's graduation he ends the relationship.

Devastated, Theresa becomes physically ill and is unable to eat until the threat of hospitalization forces her recovery. Katherine suggests that Theresa spend the summer with her and her new husband Brooks on Fire Island. There she is introduced to drugs and to Katherine's unorthodox life-style. In the fall, Theresa accepts a teaching position at a grade school in Manhattan and moves into an apartment below her sister and brother-in-law. She enjoys teaching and spends her free time decorating her apartment.

When Katherine tells Theresa that she plans to have a second abortion and to leave Brooks, Theresa becomes depressed. She moves into a new apartment and begins frequenting neighborhood bars and bringing strange men back to her apartment. Feeling she is leading a double life, she continues to teach and keeps her promiscuity hidden from her colleagues and family.

In a bar Theresa meets Tony Lopanto, a gruff, unintelligent parking garage attendant. Tony is a good lover but unpredictable and abusive. While having an affair with Tony, Theresa meets James Morrisey, a lawyer who is kind and attentive but whom Theresa finds sexually uninteresting. She resists his advances, preferring the degradation of anonymous sex to the prospect of an intimate relationship. In spite of her sardonic cruelty, James falls in love with Theresa and proposes marriage. Theresa feels trapped, unwilling to marry James but also unwilling to end their relationship.

On New Year's Day, 1970, having made the decision to begin seeing a psychiatrist, Theresa feels she is starting a new life. She cleans her apartment thoroughly and thinks seriously about her relationship with James and about returning to teaching after the Christmas break. But in the evening she becomes restless. At a neighborhood pub,

Mr. Goodbar, she meets a man named Gary and invites him home. When she asks him to leave after they have had intercourse, Gary becomes violent. He attacks her, suffocates her with a pillow, rapes her, and smashes a lamp over her head. The next morning he has sex with her corpse.

Dunyazade. *Chimera.* John Barth. 1972.

Dunyazade is a young woman who lives under the rule of King Shahryar and Shah Zaman, two brothers who have killed their adulterous wives. To ensure that they are never fooled again, the brothers announce that henceforth each of them will rape a virgin every night and execute her the following morning. Dunyazade joins forces with her older sister Scheherazade to stop this senseless violence.

Dunyazade spends her nights at the foot of Shahryar's bed where Scheherazade tells her story and then makes love to the king. Shahryar has reportedly decapitated more than nine hundred girls, but Scheherazade has been spared because she is such an artful lover and storyteller. The king always wants to hear the end of her story the next day, but the story never ends; it simply links to another segment. Shahryar, taken in by the lyrical Scheherazade, appears blind to the fact that her tales are not original. In truth, she depends on a magical source: Every night the sisters conjure up a genie to receive the next day's narrative. This genie, a creature from the twentieth century, provides them with contemporary versions of *The Thousand and One Nights.* All goes smoothly until one night the genie runs out of stories. He tells Dunyazade and Scheherazade that they are on their own.

Fortunately for the sisters, the king and his brother decide to remarry. Shahryar will have Scheherazade, and Zaman will wed Dunyazade. Although Dunyazade is still a virgin, her experience at the foot of the king's bed convinces everyone that she will be as great a lover and storyteller as her sister. But the sisters do not intend to become meek wives in a harem. In fact, they want revenge for all the girls who have been killed; before the double wedding, they make plans to castrate the grooms.

On the night that the wedding would be consummated, Dunyazade meets briefly with Scheherazade, who slips her a razor. Dunyazade has gone off on the pretext of learning some erotic secret. She returns and tells Zaman that she must tie him up for the thrill of his life. Once this is done, she makes clear her disgust for him and prepares to take revenge. Zaman makes a final request: that Dunyazade listen to one of his stories and then decide whether he should live or die.

In his story Zaman reveals that although he could not openly defy his brother, he has never complied with the king's decree. Instead of killing the virgins, he has sent them to live on a remote island with the intention of returning them to the kingdom one day. Although Dunyazade at first doubts this account, Zaman eventually convinces her that he would be a kind husband. But Dunyazade is still concerned about her sister, who is supposedly carrying out the murderous plan in another bedchamber. Zaman relieves Dunyazade of this worry as well. He tells her that the king already knew about the plot, is well guarded, and will not punish Scheherazade because he truly loves her.

Dupin, C. Auguste. "The Murders in the Rue Morgue"; "The Mystery of Marie Rogêt"; "The Purloined Letter." Edgar Allan Poe. 1841; 1842; 1845.

C. Auguste Dupin, a masterful sleuth, was raised in a once wealthy and reputable Parisian family that lost its fortune under mysterious circumstances, and he is forced to subsist on an income that permits him few luxuries beyond the books that he insists on buying and reading voraciously. In the course of his literary perambulations, Dupin meets a fellow bookworm at an obscure library in Montmartre. The two men become companions then housemates, renting a remote Gothic mansion in the Faubourg St.-Germain. Possessed of a creative and analytical mind, Dupin proceeds to amaze his friend, who is never named, by performing astute feats of criminal investigation that invariably result in a solution to the ghastly mysteries under their scrutiny.

In "The Murders on the Rue Morgue," a newspaper alerts the two reclusive friends to the bizarre and brutal murder of a woman named Madame L'Espanaye and her daughter who lived on the Rue Morgue. The men are both characteristically fascinated by the disaster and follow the story carefully in the newspaper. The details of the case center around the conundrum of a locked room. Neighbors heard the murder being perpetrated, but when rescue was attempted, the victims were found to have been murdered in a room tightly locked from the *inside*. In addition, the scene of the crime displayed no trace of the criminal despite the fact that the two victims' neighbors had heard the voices of a Frenchman and another man. Intrigued by the case, Dupin and his companion obtain permission to enter the home of the deceased in order to examine the premises. Dupin finds a spring mechanism that opens and closes one of the windows. This window, he reasons, was the murderer's means of entering and leaving, although an unnatural agility would have been required to use this difficult route.

The facts of a frightfully brutal murder and a miraculously agile murderer eventually lead Dupin to the solution that the murderer was an ourang-outang. Through an advertisement in the newspaper announcing the capture of the escaped beast, Dupin lures the owner to his home where the distraught man confesses the fact that his pet committed the ghastly murders while he looked on helplessly.

In "The Mystery of Marie Rogêt," Dupin is also in-

trigued by the murder of Marie Rogêt, a beautiful young woman whose corpse was found floating in the Seine. Once again the newspapers provide obscure clues that allow the crafty Dupin to solve the case. Having demolished the speculations of a number of editors, the sleuth accuses the murdered woman's former suitor, who wanted to extricate himself from their relationship.

Both this case and the case of the Rue Morgue murders excite the approbation of the public and the attention of the Prefect of the Parisian Police. As a result, the Prefect begs Dupin's assistance in the mystery of "The Purloined Letter." In this case, an acquaintance of Dupin's named Minister D— has stolen a letter from the royal boudoir by replacing it with a replica for the purpose of blackmail. Having failed to find the letter after a painstaking search of the minister's home, the Prefect approaches Dupin with his problem. Through identification with his opponent, Dupin is able to find the letter by dropping in to visit the minister and spying a tattered edge in a cheap letter folder carelessly tacked to a wall. Dupin realizes that this must be the letter in question, slyly placed in the most obvious, rather than least evident, location. On a return visit to the minister's rooms, Dupin replaces the letter with a replica while his host is distracted by a disturbance that Dupin has staged in the street. Awestruck, the Prefect of Police awards Dupin the 50,000 francs reward, thus cementing Dupin's reputation as an ace sleuth in the precincts of Paris.

Durand, Jesse. *Vanishing Rooms.* Melvin Dixon. 1991.

Jesse Durand is a young African-American dancer. As the novel begins, his world has been shattered by the vicious bias attack that resulted in the death of his white lover, Jon-Michael Barthé, nicknamed "Metro." The death and its brutality wrench Jesse from the complacency of their relationship, which had begun in college and continued after they moved to New York.

In the aftermath of the murder, Jesse turns to RUELLA MCPHEE, whom he nicknames "Rooms." She is able to help him for a brief time, but their relationship becomes too much for Jesse once she reveals that she has fallen in love with him. Even though Jesse moves out of Ruella's apartment, she continues to assist him as he recovers from the shock, and she pressures the police to find Metro's killers.

Jesse, driven to despair by his grief and by a measure of guilt, begins to reexamine his relationship with Metro. With the assistance of a cynical older man whom he meets in a bathhouse, Jesse begins to see the relationship in terms of its latent racism. Ultimately, Jesse develops an anger against Metro that he is barely able to control. He recalls, against his will, a time during sex when Metro called him a "nigger." Associated with this, he remembers instances from his childhood that inculcated in him and in his young brother the racism rampant in the United States during the 1950s. A particularly disturbing memory is associated with the death of his grandmother and the racism he, his brother, and his mother endured when they traveled to the South for the funeral services. Nonetheless, Jesse still bitterly misses his lover and nearly precipitates his own death by searching the dangerous terrains that were the site of Metro's murder.

Once again Ruella intervenes. She goes to an abandoned warehouse, the scene of Jesse and Metro's last encounter, where she finds Jesse exhausted and covered in splinters and bits of glass. She saves him from his own self-destructive impulses, and despite Ruella's resentment at the failure of their sexual relationship, the two manage to audition for and be accepted by the dance company they wanted to join.

By this time, due to the guilt-ridden confession of the youngest of the attackers, Metro's murderers have been arrested, and they are soon sent to various prisons. One day while visiting Ruella's brother in jail, Jesse notices one of the murderers, and his hysterical outburst inadvertently leads to a revenge rape on the one who had actually tried to prevent Metro's murder.

Jesse is better able to deal with his grief when he meets another dancer, this time a black man, in whom he becomes interested. The two cautiously begin a relationship against a backdrop of Ruella's jealousy and Jesse's burgeoning interest in choreography. As the novel ends, Jesse has been given a chance to choreograph his first dance, which focuses on a relationship between two men. His assiduous research into the movements of the male body and his careful work with his dancers lead to a tremendously successful debut. He and Ruella have managed to heal the rift between them, and each embarks on a new life with a new partner and an established career in dance.

Durgin, Thomas Jefferson "Jeff." *The Landlord at Lion's Head.* William Dean Howells. 1897.

Thomas Jefferson Durgin is the amoral young man who dreams of becoming the landlord of Lion's Head, a nineteenth-century country inn. Spoiled and indulged as a child, Jeff develops into a man without a conscience who is convinced that it is useless for one to attempt to do right or wrong. According to Jeff, whether or not a man acts with moral intentions is irrelevant, and there is no God waiting to reward good behavior. Living a life based on this theory, Jeff does what pleases him, with little or no regard for moral considerations.

When the family farm no longer produces a living for the Durgin family, Mrs. Durgin decides to turn the place,

located near a scenic mountain, into a summer lodge called Lion's Head. She is encouraged in this idea when, one summer, a young painter from Boston lodges in her home for several weeks and offers to place ads for her in the Boston papers.

When the painter returns to Lion's Head five years later, he finds the Durgins running a thriving business. Mrs. Durgin, now prosperous, wants to send Jeff to Harvard and does so in the fall. Jeff's freshman year at Harvard is unsuccessful. Arrested for vandalism and drunkenness, Jeff is suspended from college and spends his first year working his way to Europe on a ship. While he is away, he spends a great deal of time observing the inns of Europe and decides that eventually he wants to be the landlord of Lion's Head.

When Jeff informs his mother that he would prefer to stay on at Lion's Head, Mrs. Durgin is adamant about his returning to Harvard. He does return, but before doing so, he proposes to Cynthia Whitwell, his companion from childhood, and she accepts. Jeff returns to Harvard where his poor reputation and low social standing do not improve.

During his remaining university years, Jeff, although marked as a socially unacceptable "jay," attempts to enter "society" at Harvard and succeeds on a small scale. His lack of standing in society attracts Bessie Lynde, a young socialite known for her daring. Proud and vengeful, Jeff knows Bessie is simultaneously fascinated and repelled by him. After allowing the flirtation to go on for several months, Jeff proposes to Bessie, who accepts. Within days, however, he breaks the engagement and takes a train to Lion's Head to inform Cynthia of his unfaithfulness.

Lion's Head has grown even more, and Jeff's desire to become the landlord has intensified. Once informed of Jeff's infidelity, Cynthia breaks the engagement. Jeff, who has remained at Harvard at Cynthia's insistence, discontinues his studies. From this point, fate moves rapidly in Jeff's favor. His older brother Jackson and his mother die in quick succession, leaving him in charge of Lion's Head. Now able to run it in the European fashion as he has always wanted to do, Jeff hires Cynthia, her brother, and their father as caretakers of the lodge, and he goes to Europe.

While Jeff is in Europe, Lion's Head burns. He is now free to build the inn in the style he deems correct. The insurance company investigation yields no problems. Jeff returns from Europe with a new wife and begins work on the new Lion's Head. Within several years the lodge is again thriving, and Jeff's theory appears to have been validated in every respect.

E

The Earl of Dorincourt. *Little Lord Fauntleroy.* Frances Hodgson Burnett. 1928.

The Earl of Dorincourt experiences a profound change of character as he develops a relationship with his grandson CEDRIC "CEDDIE" ERROL. The Earl's youngest son, also named Cedric, was his favorite, and it plagued him that the only son he liked was the least likely to succeed him as Earl. When the Earl learned that Errol had fallen in love with and married a young American woman, the Earl was furious and disinherited his son. A few years later Errol died, leaving a wife and a small boy. The Earl made no effort to communicate with or help Errol's widow until, with the death of his two other sons, young Cedric became his only heir. He then summoned Cedric to England.

The Earl still hates Errol's wife, and although he allows Mrs. Cedric Errol to accompany her son, he insists that she live in a cottage a few miles from Dorincourt Castle. Because the Earl has a low opinion of Americans in general and his daughter-in-law in particular, he is certain that his grandson will be a disappointment and that Cedric, for his part, will hate him. At his first meeting with Cedric, however, the Earl is surprised to see that the boy clearly intends to love him and has no knowledge of his grandfather's bad reputation. In addition, the Earl cannot help but be proud of such a handsome, athletic, and intelligent grandson.

For the first time in his life, the Earl has something to concentrate on besides his own pleasure and pain. He begins to think less about his gout and more about the joy Cedric brings to his life. At first it amuses him to discover that Cedric assumes he is generous and kindhearted. As he becomes more attached to the boy, the Earl wants to live up to this good reputation. When Cedric informs the Earl of the poverty-stricken conditions plaguing the tenants on his property, the Earl responds immediately although he has heard the same complaints for years and had previously done nothing.

It troubles the Earl that Cedric clearly loves his mother more than anyone else, and he cannot help but be jealous. The more he sees of Mrs. Errol in church and the more he hears of her from Cedric and others, the more convinced he becomes that she is worthy of such affection. But his antipathy remains intact.

One day a woman claiming to be the widow of the Earl's first son and the mother of the true heir presents herself to the Earl. When his grandson's inheritance is threatened, the Earl clearly realizes his love for Cedric. He also notes the contrast between the new woman's greed and dishonest manipulations and the generosity and moral character of Cedric's mother. Finally abandoning his unfounded hate for Mrs. Errol, the Earl seeks her counsel. As it turns out, the new woman is an impostor, and when her dishonesty is confirmed, the Earl warmly invites Mrs. Errol to live at the castle.

Eastlake, Elinor "Lakey." *The Group.* Mary McCarthy. 1954.

Elinor Eastlake is a rich, beautiful, and extremely intelligent Vassar College graduate of the class of 1933. A member of a clique of eight young women who roomed together in the dormitory system at Vassar, Elinor, whose nickname is "Lakey" because she comes from Lake Forest, Illinois, is considered the brightest and most beautiful of the group, so much so that her friends are often in awe of her. As the members of the clique grow older, Lakey's friends are shocked to discover some of her proclivities that, despite their intimacy, had escaped them during their undergraduate careers.

The last time the group sees Elinor Eastlake before she leaves for an extended stay in Europe is at the wedding of KAY LEILAND STRONG to Harald Petersen, a match approved by none of the group. After Lakey's departure the group hears from her only on important occasions such as when one of them bears a child, but for the most part she is, characteristically, the most aloof of the group. In Paris she studies art history in pursuit of an advanced degree and begins hobnobbing with famous art critics and European nobility; news of these activities both impresses and intimidates her college friends.

Upon her return from Europe some seven years after Kay's wedding, Lakey's friends assemble on a New York City pier to surprise her by meeting her ship. Lakey appears to be thrilled to see them and insists that they lunch together after dropping her many bags off at the hotel where she and her traveling companion, a baroness from Germany whom she introduces as Maria, have reservations.

Noticing that Maria calls Lakey "darling" and seems rather jealous of the intrusion of her many friends, the group deduces that the ravishing Lakey is a lesbian. As the weeks go by, the baroness becomes friendlier with the group and they in turn relax, but they are never entirely comfortable with the idea that Maria and Lakey are lovers.

When their friend Kay Strong Petersen dies by falling out of a twentieth-story window, the group attends the funeral in a state of shock. After the heart-wrenching service, the deceased Kay's abusive ex-husband asks Lakey to give him a lift to the cemetery, and she begrudgingly agrees to accommodate him. When he attempts to make a pass at Lakey in the car and attacks Kay's integrity, Lakey craftily takes her revenge on him on behalf of Kay and all mistreated women by refusing to tell him whether or not she and his ex-wife were ever involved in a relationship. His curiosity and jealous anger is so piqued that he insists on being let out of the car. The group, meanwhile, bolstered by their friendship, inters its unfortunate friend.

Eden, Martin. *Martin Eden.* Jack London. 1908.

Martin Eden begins life in poverty and spends most of his teenage years working, chiefly as a sailor. This lends him a rather uncouth appearance that belies his keen intelligence, sense of beauty, and desire to improve his mind. These qualities as well as Martin's creativity and determination are eventually borne out as he struggles to become a writer.

At twenty, Martin meets RUTH MORSE, who is three years his senior and about to earn her bachelor's degree. Ruth takes a great interest in Martin, and he eagerly responds to her attentions. Influenced by his attraction for her and aware that she is far better educated, he begins to study at the local libraries whenever possible. When his money runs out, he sets off to sea again for eight months and is able to earn enough to support himself during a few months of study.

Ruth informs Martin that he needs to work on his grammar in order to progress to where he should be, and Martin agrees that she should correct his grammatical errors at all times. He slowly but surely begins to acquire a good deal of knowledge and starts to envision a career as a writer. The most important thing to Martin at this point, however, is that he knows he is in love with Ruth.

His love for her fuels his desire for education and provides him with inspiration for his earliest writings, which include a series of poems. After he convinces her to marry him, they begin a long engagement during which Martin plans to prove himself as a writer. He tells Ruth that this will take him two years. Martin writes several pieces and is amazed by the speed with which he has ideas. He soon learns, though, that his work is not well received by editors. When his money runs out, he begins to lose faith in his dreams.

A disillusioned Martin contemplates abandoning writing, but after a brief stint as a laundryman, he decides to rededicate himself to his art. Once again his efforts are in vain, and he descends to a level of poverty that forces him to pawn his only suit. Finally, Martin's work is rewarded when a story is accepted and he receives five dollars. This is the beginning of a great period of financial success, during which one story after another is published. But the happy phase comes to an end when Martin's stories cease

selling, and Ruth berates him for the uncommercial love poems he has begun writing.

During his period of relative prosperity, Martin slowly became more politicized. He frequently argued about politics in the presence of Ruth's father. This tendency is accelerated when Martin befriends Russ Brissenden, a writer who is impassioned both politically and artistically but who suffers from a lingering and ultimately fatal illness. Russ offers Martin friendship and encouragement but also attempts to dissuade him from maintaining his relationship with Ruth. Martin remains firm, but eventually his political activities come to the attention of the Morses, who are opposed more than ever to their daughter's liaison. Finally, Ruth unceremoniously severs the relationship.

Fueled by the posthumous publication of Russ's work, Martin's career as a writer takes off, and he sells everything he ever wrote. However, he stops writing new material. After buying a house for his landlady and expanding his brother-in-law's business, Martin gets his revenge on Ruth. He rejects her effort—based mostly on his newfound fame—to reconcile with him. Following this, and in despair about writing and the profession, Martin boards a ship to leave. Almost immediately, in a defiant but private gesture, he commits suicide by jumping overboard.

Edny, Clithero. *Edgar Huntly*; or, *Memoirs of a Sleep-walker.* Charles Brockden Brown. 1799.

Clithero Edny is a man who, despite intelligence and youthful promise, is by the end of the novel a murderous psychotic feared by the people who once loved him. His descent into insanity is swift and tragic.

While Clithero was growing up on his parents' farm in Ireland, there was nothing to suggest that his destiny would be such a bleak one. In fact, when Euphemia Lorimer, the wealthy owner of the land on which his parents toiled, meets the young man and offers to provide for his education, all concerned are sure his future will be bright. But Clithero's growing involvement in the Lorimer family and his love for Euphemia contribute to his mental imbalance.

Euphemia treats Clithero as a son and makes him steward of her home and vast property holdings. Honored to be given such responsibility and affection, Clithero performs his service faithfully. When he falls in love with Clarice, the illegitimate daughter of Euphemia's wastrel brother Arthur Wiatte, Clithero resolves to leave Euphemia's employ. He fears that his patroness will think it audacious of him to want to marry the young lady, whom Euphemia has taken into her home after her mother's death and her father's abandonment. Euphemia banishes Clithero's fears by blessing the relationship.

Clithero is happy and believes that he and Clarice will be luckier in love than Euphemia was in her youth. Euphemia had hoped to marry Sarsefield, a poor surgeon, but her evil twin brother Wiatte frustrated Euphemia's plans by forcing her to marry Mr. Lorimer, who died soon after, and by driving Sarsefield out of the country. Years later Wiatte, after turning to a life of crime, was believed to have been killed at sea.

But Sarsefield reappears and claims that he still loves Euphemia; at the same time, Wiatte resurfaces and attacks Clithero in a dark alley. Clithero kills Wiatte in self-defense but is immediately remorseful and anxious because Euphemia has always believed her destiny was tied to that of her twin brother. Clithero determines to kill Euphemia in her sleep rather than allow her to learn of Wiatte's death and thus die of grief. He is foiled in this attempt but confesses to her that her brother is dead. Euphemia faints, and Clithero, believing her to be dead, flees.

Clithero travels to Pennsylvania where he finds work as a common laborer. A neighbor, EDGAR HUNTLY, intrigued by Clithero's grave manner and his sleepwalking, and suspecting that Clithero was involved in the death of his fiancée's brother, questions Clithero. Clithero relates his tale but denies involvement in the death of Edgar's friend. He seeks neither pity nor help from Edgar; instead, he resolves to hide in one of the many labyrinthine caves in the area's rugged wilderness and commit suicide.

Days after his flight into the wilderness, Clithero is brought back to civilization. He has broken his suicidal vows and suffered life-threatening wounds at the hands of marauding Indians. He is saved by the medical skill of Sarsefield, now the husband of Euphemia.

Although his body recovers fully, Clithero's mind is still troubled. When Edgar tells him that Euphemia is still alive, is living in New York, and is married to Sarsefield, Clithero exclaims that he will make sure that she dies, and he bolts away to murder her. He does not complete the task. Sarsefield, warned by Edgar of Clithero's plans, has the insane man seized and put on a boat bound for Pennsylvania. As he attempts to swim to shore, Clithero jumps overboard and drowns. The now pregnant Euphemia, although untouched by Clithero's knife, is so shaken when she inadvertently learns the murderous designs of the man she once loved as a son that she miscarries.

Edwards, Foxhall "Fox." *You Can't Go Home Again.* Thomas Wolfe. 1934.

Although he is a respected and successful editor, Foxhall "Fox" Edwards nurtures a particular trend of pessimism that colors everything he encounters in life. Even GEORGE WEBBER, for whom Fox becomes a good friend as well as an excellent editor, is led to end his professional relationship with the man when his spirit of fatalism becomes too pronounced.

George first meets Fox when his agent sells his manuscript to Fox's publishing company, James Rodney & Co.

Something of a legend in the publishing industry, Fox recognizes in George's first novel the mark of an undisciplined genius. A bit brusque in manner but eminently principled, Fox befriends George and becomes something of a second spiritual father to the younger man. Fox welcomes the relationship; not only does he respect George's talent but, as the father of five daughters, he has always wanted a son.

During George's darkest period—while living in the slum of Red Hook, Brooklyn, during the early years of the Depression—Fox is George's anchor. After abandoning the "literary lions" who feast on the flesh of young writers, and leaving his married lover ESTHER JACK, George turns to Fox for spiritual comfort, and Fox does not turn away. Despite his eccentricities, or perhaps because of them, Fox is supportive of those who see themselves as different. Fox's fourteen-year-old daughter Ruth also comes to him after a narrow-minded teacher gives her English essays poor grades. Fox counsels Ruth to disregard the teachings of "academics" who are blind to creativity.

Even people whom he does not know are the focus of Fox's concerned scrutiny. Fox combs the papers every morning and evening, reading about the tragedies and disappointments of those far removed from his own home in Turtle Bay. Perhaps because George is living in Brooklyn, Fox is particularly absorbed by the account of a man who plunged from the window of a downtown Brooklyn hotel. Fox speculates on the life of this possible suicide, imagining that the moment his body splattered on the busy sidewalk was the only time he removed himself from the monotony and pointlessness of life in the modern city.

For all the compassion he possesses, Fox himself is the victim, George recognizes, of a curious fatalism, one that contains within it some hope but is, in the final analysis, pessimistic. With an acknowledgment of the literary and personal enrichment Fox has given him, George severs his professional relationship with Fox because of the fundamental, and seemingly insurmountable, difference in their philosophies.

Effingham, Edward. *Home As Found.* James Fenimore Cooper. 1838.

Mr. Edward Effingham stands as a pillar of stability, integrity, and propriety amid the crowded, democratic world of James Fenimore Cooper's novel of manners. More than all other characters in the book, Effingham maintains a healthy connection with the land, neither feeling that working with the earth is beneath him nor abusing the land and its occupants by engaging in speculation. Mr. Effingham wishes justice in all things regardless of the opinion of the majority.

The story opens with the arrival of Mr. Effingham, accompanied by his beautiful and intelligent daughter EVE (EFFINGHAM) and his cynical mercantile brother JOHN

(EFFINGHAM) in New York City after a stay of eight years abroad. The Effinghams, eager to renew old acquaintances and to acclimate themselves to American society, seek the diversions of the Manhattan elite and spend time at dinners, drawing room parties, and balls.

While in New York, Mr. Effingham demonstrates his gentle wit and his somewhat grudging love for his native America after living for a decade at the courts of Europe. As a host or guest, he is at all times gracious and polite, regardless of the social station of the individual before him. At one point, during a dinner at his home, Mr. Effingham honors the warm-hearted and brave Captain Truck who, while coarse and unsophisticated, has won the respect of Effingham and his family.

After a devastating fire, Mr. Effingham insists that his family and guests leave the city and go to his country estate in rural Templeton, New York. Effingham is distressed to see the changes that have occurred since he last resided in Templeton and blames the current passion for land and town speculation for creating a society in flux where something becomes ancient if it has stood for twelve months.

He returns to a town that has forgotten his existence because his family has been away for so long. When he attempts to assert his rights as an owner of substantial property in the region, he finds himself resented and ridiculed by the townspeople. This tension climaxes in a dispute over a stretch of land that had been used as a picnic ground by the townsfolk in the Effinghams' absence. While Effingham does not begrudge the public use of the property, he vehemently denies that it is public property. The townsfolk claim that the property has been held by the public for all of common memory.

Mr. Effingham's land agent, Aristabulus Bragg, fears a lynch mob will result from Effingham's unyielding attitude, but Effingham refuses to accept a tyranny of the masses, holds firm, and reclaims his right. After settling himself on his estates, he joyfully gives his daughter's hand to the mysterious but honorable Paul Powis, and sees his niece and ward married to a kindhearted English baronet.

Effingham, Eve. *Home As Found.* James Fenimore Cooper. 1838.

Eve Effingham represents the refined and cultured young American gentlewoman of Jacksonian America. She has the unfailing ability to reconcile her love of her native country with the absurdities of its people and the deleterious effects of the "tyranny of the masses." Her constant restraint and objectivity allow her to escape the prejudices and pretensions of her social class and nationality. This presence of mind also allows her to marry for love instead of the desire for improved social standing.

The novel opens in New York City. Eve, her upright father EDWARD EFFINGHAM and her often cynical uncle JOHN (EFFINGHAM) have recently completed a dangerous

and arduous voyage from Europe after eight years on that continent. The Effinghams, happy for diversion after so long a voyage, join in the social activities of the Manhattan elite. Soon after settling in to their town house, the Effinghams host a dinner to celebrate their homecoming.

At this dinner and at the various social functions the Effinghams attend afterward, Eve begins to form a picture of her fellow Americans that, according to her discussions with her cousin Grace Van Cortlandt, is not entirely favorable. First, Eve objects to the behavior of the otherwise intelligent American women because they denigrate their own culture as barbaric and remain slavishly attentive to what they perceive as more sophisticated styles from Paris and London. Second, Eve disapproves of those who are captivated by Sir George Templemore—an English baronet who became a guest of the Effinghams—simply because he has a title.

After a short stay in New York, the Effinghams move to their country house in Templeton, New York. Eve, always the agent of moderation, constantly seeks to reconcile the opinions of the Europeans and the Americans in the party who incessantly debate the subject of whose continent possesses the greatest natural beauty. While in Templeton, Eve, reunited with her close friend Paul Powis, becomes the subject of vicious gossip because she also refuses to believe that just because people have political power, they have a right to be consulted in all things. A love between Eve and Paul, a mysterious but very well bred young man, quickly develops. Yet Paul has a secret with which he would not endanger the reputation of a wife, and so he remains aloof. He resolves this conflict by confessing his illegitimate birth to John Effingham. Paul is exonerated and asks Eve to marry him, and the novel ends shortly after their marriage.

Effingham, John. *Home As Found.* James Fenimore Cooper. 1838.

John Effingham, a gentleman in Jacksonian America, demonstrates how speculation and the pursuit of "mere wealth" can affect an otherwise kindhearted man. Although always scrupulously polite in all social circles, Effingham is a pessimistic cynic, and after a lengthy stay abroad he views the shortcomings of his fellow Americans with less and less charity. Their asinine behavior soon becomes the target of his caustic sense of humor. Yet there lurks beneath this jaundiced exterior an upright and warmhearted man who genuinely seeks the betterment of those who have gained his trust.

The narrative opens as the Effingham party settles in to its New York City town house. The group consists of John, a wealthy land speculator; his brother EDWARD (EFFINGHAM), an even wealthier landowner; Edward's beautiful, self-possessed daughter EVE (EFFINGHAM); the English baronet Sir George Templemore; and the leader of their recent voyage, Captain Truck. Eager to entertain their guests and renew lapsed friendships, the Effinghams seek the diversions of polite Manhattan society. After a touching scene where Edward, John, and Eve honor the rustic but kindly and brave Captain Truck, the party begins a circuit of dinners, drawing room dates, and balls.

During these functions, John remains aloof, somewhat disgusted and amused by the childishly insistent attempts of the American socialites to obtain a flattering comparison with European society. After observing the attention paid to Sir George simply because of his English title, John endeavors to pass off Captain Truck as a famed English ecclesiastic. Captain Truck becomes immediately revered by the Manhattan literati, and John's opinions of his fellow Americans are reinforced.

In an effort to explain the American obsession with land speculation, John takes Sir George to the Exchange. There, farms, towns, and entire counties are bought and sold through the use of practices that even John, whose fortune rests in the trade, finds highly distasteful.

The party moves to Edward's country estate in rural Templeton, New York. While on this journey the mischievous John contrives that the party dismount and go the last few miles on foot. This hike allows them to see Templeton's beauties firsthand and also reunites the party with the enigmatic Paul Powis, who has been awaiting their arrival.

John and Paul have personal business to discuss concerning a packet of papers left by their mutual acquaintance, the dying Mr. Monday. The papers describe the illicit affair between Mr. Monday's mother and a gold-digging Englishman. The episode leads to Paul confessing his illegitimate origins and life as a ward and naval officer. Paul also reveals his love for Eve. John wholeheartedly approves of the match and adopts Paul in order to silence any gossip about the union. The story ends after the joyous wedding of Eve and Paul.

Eisen, Sam. *The Old Bunch.* Meyer Levin. 1937.

Sam Eisen fights to retain his values in this account of a group of Jewish youths coming to maturity in Chicago in the 1920s. The story begins with the group's graduation from high school; after the ceremony, the male members of the group, including Sam, form a club called the Big 10, which is designed to provide intellectual stimulation and professional support to its members. The manner in which each of the young men participates in this club foreshadows his later direction in life, and Sam's independent and idealistic tendencies are announced when he quits the Big 10 on the grounds that the club has renounced its original intellectual purposes in favor of merely social ones. Sam's idealism is confirmed shortly thereafter when he is expelled from Illinois University because he has refused, on principle, to join the campus R.O.T.C.

However, after he has passed the bar, become a lawyer, and married Lil Klein, Sam compromises his idealism. Sam had initially spurned Lil because of her nonintellectual nature, but she eventually manages to attract him and then becomes pregnant by him. After they marry, Sam becomes a tool of Lil's wealthy and corrupt father, himself a tool of Chicago's mob-controlled mayor. Sam initially justifies his participation in mob politics by telling himself that working with the strong party will enable him to learn the tricks of the political trade, and he manages to keep his own ward fairly clean. As Al Capone's influence on civic affairs grows increasingly violent and overt, however, Sam becomes disgusted with himself for the part he has played in the corruption of Chicago.

At the same time, Sam becomes increasingly repulsed by his expedience-minded wife, who has gained dominance over him due to her father's political, professional, and financial support. Lil consistently nags him to renounce every idealistic impulse that stirs him. A recurring point of contention is Sam's continued fondness for and support of his old friend Dave Plotkin, who has been unsuccessful as a lawyer and whom Lil therefore despises.

Sam and Lil attend a party at which Lil's friends have organized a modern version of the seder that makes a mockery of the venerable Jewish ritual. When Lil enters delightedly into the mock ritual, Sam walks out of the party just as he had walked out of the Big 10 meeting years ago. He and Lil separate, and although they briefly reunite, Sam divorces Lil when she argues with him about his refusal to take a case he considers immoral. He breaks off all contact with her, their two children, and his father-in-law.

At this point Sam begins to be true to his own ideals of justice and to his leftist leanings. He becomes a powerful and successful lawyer and enters into an affair with a fellow employee. By the novel's end it is clear that he has achieved true independence from "the old bunch" and its other members' less high-minded concerns.

Eitel, Charles Francis. *The Deer Park.* Norman Mailer. 1955.

Charles Francis Eitel, a brilliant director exiled to the California town of Desert D'or, has been the subject of a congressional hearing on subversion. Having been blacklisted by Hollywood and shunned by his friends and colleagues in the film industry, Eitel retreats to the tiny resort village and its parties filled with gossip columnists, socialites, and other visiting revelers.

At one party Eitel meets Sergius O'Shaugnessy, the novel's narrator. O'Shaugnessy is a heavily decorated young pilot who has retreated to Desert D'or to recover from emotional scars inflicted by a brutal war. The two quickly become close friends. Also in Desert D'or for a time is Herman Teppis, a powerful movie mogul and one of Eitel's biggest enemies in Hollywood. Teppis hates Eitel but is taken with O'Shaugnessy, and knowing the two are best friends, he invites both of them to a party.

At the party, one of the most extravagant of the season, Eitel causes a stir when he arrives with Elena Esposito, a former dancer and the mistress of Carlyle "Collie" Munshin, an ambitious producer. Munshin is Teppis's son-in-law, but he is on fairly good terms with Eitel. Eitel sticks by Elena as a favor to Munshin who is trying to find an easy way out of what has become a sticky extramarital affair with her. But in the course of the evening, Eitel becomes more and more intrigued by the striking young woman, and the two become lovers. As it happens, O'Shaugnessy also finds love at Teppis's party when he meets the actress LULU MEYERS, Eitel's ex-wife.

Invigorated by a new love affair, Eitel turns with renewed enthusiasm to a project he has been considering, a film script about a man who makes a fortune with a television program in which he hears the problems of others and offers bits of superficial advice. Convinced that it will be his masterpiece, Eitel has Munshin read what he has of the script, knowing that the producer will stop at nothing to make a profit from his talent. Munshin is enthusiastic about the project but suggests that the main character be a former priest. The two decide to collaborate: Eitel will finish writing the script, and Munshin, whose reputation in Hollywood is as yet unsullied, will sell it to Teppis as his own.

In the meantime, the relationship between Eitel and Elena flags. Eitel feels he should end the relationship but doesn't want to interrupt his writing with a painful parting. Marion O'Faye, the son of a well-known socialite and the proprietor of a local call-girl establishment, arranges a date for him with Bobby, a divorcée turned prostitute. Bobby's miserable existence as a single parent depresses Eitel, as does her willingness to love him for $500.

Finally, Elena leaves Munshin for Marion O'Faye. She lives with O'Faye for several days, considering suicide. O'Faye encourages her depression and even urges her to end her life. Elena eventually decides to leave, but she has a car accident on the way to the airport. Hearing that Elena is in the hospital, Eitel decides that he must marry her. He goes to her and proposes, and they are wed in Elena's hospital room.

At the novel's end, Eitel returns to Hollywood. Having compromised his principles in a deal with Teppis and the congressional committee, he resumes making movies, but his new works are bland, blatantly commercial comedies. Although he remains married to Elena and the two have had a child, he secretly begins a loveless affair with Lulu. Cynical and jaded, Eitel accepts that the compromises he has made have been the inevitable ones. As he contemplates his life, he acknowledges the end of his "over-extended youth" and the death of his artistic desires.

Elizabeth. "A Spinster's Tale." Peter Taylor. 1940.

Elizabeth is the first-person narrator of this story set in the luxurious and masculine world of the turn-of-the-century South. From the outset of the story, when she is only thirteen years old, Elizabeth is frightened by the regular appearance of the drunken Mr. Speed, who passes by her father's mansion several times a week. She has observed Mr. Speed many times, and his appearances become related in her young mind to her mother's illness and death following the stillbirth of her last child. For Elizabeth, who is left more or less alone to cope with the loss of her mother, Mr. Speed's drunkenness is disturbingly associated with her brother's habitual insobriety.

In the course of the story, Elizabeth constantly notes that she is surrounded by men. She observes the ways they talk to each other, noting that Father and Brother talk to each other and argue in a way that makes no sense to her. The young girl finds their thinking obtuse and their manner bestial, especially when alcohol has heightened their inability to curb their boorishness and boisterous manner. She also worries increasingly that Mr. Speed will somehow invade the sanctity of their home. Elizabeth feels that the connection between Mr. Speed's drinking and Brother's will render the latter as frightening as the former within a matter of years. Eventually she notes that even Father, in the months following his widowhood, has begun to consume more than his usual "one drink" on Saturdays when his bachelor brothers, a doctor and a colonel, come for their weekly visit.

Elizabeth's notions of masculinity become associated with physicality and heavy drinking. One night she sits up and waits for Brother to come home. When he does come in, drunk as usual, Elizabeth tries to talk to him and insists that they spend more time together. Even though he is drunk, Brother responds to his younger sister's loneliness, and although she is repulsed by the cheap whiskey smell of his breath, Elizabeth is grateful for his attention. The next day Brother returns home early, and the siblings begin a game of chess. Mr. Speed soon appears and loses his hat in a gust of wind. When Brother rushes outside to help him retrieve it, Elizabeth watches from the house, fascinated by Brother's ease with the drunk.

Soon after Mr. Speed's appearance and Brother's assistance, Elizabeth is further ostracized when Brother's friends, the Benton boys, come to the house to invite them for a ride in their family's horseless carriage. Although attracted by the idea of such a ride, Father declines the invitation for her, and she remains behind when Brother, the uncles, and the Benton boys depart in the fabulous machine. At this point Elizabeth learns that Mr. Speed has a spinster sister who ostensibly takes care of him and his household. His reappearance has frightened her to tears again, but her greatest fear is that he will actually come to the house. One day, several months after the males have their car ride, Mr. Speed does appear at the door, driven there by a sudden and fierce downpour. Elizabeth, alone with her upstairs maid Lucy, is frightened by the knock on the door and immediately telephones the police. When Mr. Speed hears the phone call, he turns to leave, cursing the young girl as he goes. Drunker than Elizabeth has ever seen him, he stumbles and falls, and is knocked unconscious. Because of her fear and loathing, Elizabeth does nothing to help him; she simply waits for the police to come and remove him. As it turns out, Elizabeth never sees Mr. Speed again, although she will always recognize him in her brother's masculinity and in his drinking behavior.

Elkins, Harrell "Harry." *Andersonville.* McKinley Kantor. 1955.

Harrell "Harry" Elkins, a young Confederate soldier and surgeon, finds himself struggling against enormous odds as he attempts to alleviate the appalling human suffering in this historical novel.

Elkins, who was reared by a doctor who mistreated him, grew up with a sympathetic heart and a desire to aid the sick. Following his medical studies he enlists in the Confederate Army during the Civil War and relocates to a plantation near the site of the Andersonville prison. Harry feels sympathy for Veronica and IRA CLAFFEY, the owners of the plantation, because they have lost three sons to the war. He finds himself drawn to LUCY CLAFFEY, who, faced with her mother's growing madness, is attempting to manage the plantation house and its slaves by herself.

Because of his kind nature, Harry is overwhelmed by Andersonville, where over 30,000 men are crammed inside the stockade, deprived of shelter and clothing, given only corn pone to eat and unsanitary water to drink. While the hospital located outside the stockade gives shelter to the sick and dying, it is nearly as bad as the prison itself. Harry valiantly attempts to alleviate the suffering of the morbidly ill men in his care, but with the Confederate cause floundering, he does not even have the most basic supplies at his disposal. He steals vinegar and cauliflower, which he attempts to use to counteract the scurvy that is killing so many. Gradually, he has nothing but water to use as treatment for the most grave illnesses and injuries. As the situation worsens, Harry writes a long detailed report to the Confederate high command, listing the problems in the camp and explaining the simple measures needed to make the camp more habitable and humane. His report falls on deaf ears, and in despair, he burns it in a candle in the Claffey parlor.

As Harry labors long hours at the prison, he grows wan and skeletal, and his romance with Lucy founders. Although he lives at the Claffey plantation, he is seldom able to leave his post except to sleep. Even at home he cannot forget the prison. Because of its proximity, the stench and the din from the stockade are always present.

At last, one evening when they are alone, Lucy decides she must act and makes a brave attempt to seduce Harry. He realizes that there is a place for love even in a world that seems filled with nothing but misery, and the two are soon married.

As the war draws to a close, the situation at Andersonville worsens. The prisoners who are able to walk are transferred to another camp, leaving 15,000 severely ill soldiers in need of medical care. When the surrender comes, Harry is relieved even though the Confederacy has fallen. He knows Lucy is pregnant and is assured that the two of them can begin life now that the horror of the war is behind them.

Ellis, Charles. *The Garies and Their Friends.* Frank J. Webb. 1857.

Although he faces the same obstacles that other African Americans do, Charles Ellis manages, through perseverance and industry, to find happiness. His unwillingness to be defeated by the prejudice surrounding him sets him apart from his friend CLARENCE GARIE, JR., who, despite wealth and advantage, dies a broken man.

Charlie's childhood in a lower-middle-class Philadelphia family is fairly carefree. He is content to spend most of his time attending school, where he is a fine young scholar, playing with his friend Kinch, and annoying his sister Caddy. A local white woman is so impressed with Charlie that she asks that he be allowed to go into service to her. Although he objects, Charlie is sent to work for Mrs. Thomas, but he manages to make himself so much of a nuisance that he is soon let go.

Now free to engage in boyish pursuits, Charlie gets underfoot when Caddy is readying a home for the arrival of the Garies, a southern family relocating to Philadelphia. As he tries to back away from his sister, whom he had annoyed in some trivial way, he falls down a flight of stairs and breaks his arm. It takes a long time for Charlie to recover, but visits from Kinch and Clarence Garie, Jr., help to break up the monotony of convalescence. When Mrs. Bird, a woman who had admired Charlie's intelligence, proposes that he spend time with her in the country, he jumps at the chance.

Romping in the country sunshine does wonders for Charlie. Once Mrs. Bird's white servants understand that Charlie is a guest, not a serving boy, the child begins to enjoy himself. However, his idyll is soon interrupted by tragedy. Word arrives that his father has been seriously injured in an anti-black riot, and Charlie must return home.

In Philadelphia, Charlie discovers that his father is a physical and mental wreck. He also learns that Clarence Garie and his sister Emily were orphaned in the rioting. These discoveries sober Charlie, who resolves to work to support his family. After coping with the prejudice of employers who appreciate his intelligence but are either unwilling or afraid to hire blacks, Charlie finds a position as an apprentice.

A few years later Charlie is a prosperous young man, engaged to be married to Emily Garie. After their wedding, Clarence Garie comes to their home. Unlike his equally light-skinned sister, Clarence chose to attempt to pass for white. He was banished from the home of his white fiancée when the truth about his race was revealed, and he is now near death. When Clarence dies, Charlie, victimized by racism but not defeated by it, begins a new life as a married man.

Ellis, Lillie. *Pink and White Tyranny.* Harriet Beecher Stowe. 1871.

Lillie Ellis, a pampered socialite, meets her future husband, JOHN SEYMOUR, a wealthy and idealistic businessman from the old New England aristocracy. Although she does not love John, Lillie marries him for his money, his social position, and his willingness to submit to her childlike beauty and charm.

Lillie has always been taught that she needs only to look pretty, and she has an undeveloped intellect and moral sense. Yet she is no fool: She knows precisely how to cajole her normally prudent but lovestruck husband into doing anything she wants. Living in rural Springdale, Lillie needs constant attention and novel stimulations. She has the house redecorated in the French style, spends the summer in Newport, and invites her "shoddy aristocracy" friends to a spectacular and unprecedented party—all of which sends John into moral and financial difficulties.

While visiting her friends in New York, Lillie encounters an old romantic interest, the handsome and newly wealthy Harry Endicott. Lillie once encouraged Harry's attentions but cruelly scorned him because he was poor. Now Harry tries to avenge himself by snubbing Lillie and courting her friend Rose. Tormented by this unaccustomed denial, Lillie makes passionate advances toward Harry, who rejects her and lectures her about the duty and dignity of marriage.

Under Harry's blunt chastisement, Lillie becomes momentarily disenchanted with her frivolous life and returns to John. Yet when she gives birth to a daughter, she is unwilling to nurse the child or to pay it much attention. Instead, she sees little Lillie as a rival for the attentions she has always strived to obtain.

Lillie must face reality when John's business fails and he can no longer afford her extravagant life-style. She proclaims that she should never have married John, who won't stoop to cheating in order to remain solvent. Then when their finances improve, Lillie contents herself with the role of the patient martyr.

After the birth of her third child, Lillie becomes chronically ill. As she grows physically weaker, she begins to realize that she has led a selfish and empty life. She finally admits to John that he deserved a better wife and that she regrets her worldly past. The novel ends with Lillie's death and with John's remembrance of her through their daughter, a "sacred and saintly" Lillie.

Ellis, Louisa. "A New England Nun." Mary Wilkins Freeman. 1900.

As she waits for her fiancé to return from a long absence, Louisa Ellis lives in a state of nunlike serenity. At the opening of the story, Louisa sits sewing peacefully, and after setting her work neatly aside, she makes herself a dainty meal of tea and cakes. When her fiancé Joe Dagget finally arrives, this small disruption of daily routine seems almost catastrophic in Louisa's world.

Louisa and Joe were engaged fifteen years before. A docile girl, Louisa accepted her mother's advice and consented to marry Joe, although he was her first and only lover. After the engagement, Joe was determined to earn some money. Leaving for Australia, he assured Louisa that his absence would not be long. Fourteen years later, he returns to find that Louisa had remained faithful, secure in the knowledge that Joe would someday marry her.

During Joe's absence, however, Louisa had steadily worked her way into a pattern of life that required perfect solitude. After her mother and brother died, she was alone except for Ceasar, a spiritless old dog. Louisa is left to polish her windows, sew, arrange her bureau drawers, and perform other quiet, orderly tasks, which she does with enthusiasm.

Anticipating her marriage, Louisa envisions "terrible" disorder and confusion: Ceasar will be let off his chain, her cherished possessions will not look the same in Joe's big house, and Joe and his domineering mother will laugh at her "old maid" ways. Louisa patiently continues to sew her wedding dress and endure daily visits from Joe, whose loud voice echoes through the house. She will not be the one, Louisa thinks, to break the engagement when he has worked and waited so long for her.

A week before her wedding day, Louisa takes a walk by moonlight and, hearing voices close by, ducks into the shadows until the people pass. She recognizes Joe's voice and that of Lily Dyer, a lovely young woman who often comes to take care of his mother. From the conversation Louisa gathers that on the previous day Joe and Lily had confessed to being in love with each other. Although both are resigned to Joe's upcoming marriage to Louisa, Lily declares she will never marry another man.

The next day Louisa carries out her usual household tasks but does not work on her wedding dress. When Joe arrives, she diplomatically inquires about his feelings, hinting that it might be wiser to call off the marriage. Without mentioning Lily Dyer, Louisa is able to ascribe her hesitation to the fact that she has lived alone too long and fears change. Joe concedes that although he is still perfectly willing to marry her, it is probably better this way.

Ellison, Kitty. *A Chance Acquaintance.* William Dean Howells. 1873.

Kitty Ellison, the orphaned daughter of a Kansas free-statesman, grows up in the care of her uncle, Jack Ellison, a doctor and an active abolitionist. When the Ellisons move from the slave state of Virginia to Erie Creek, New York, where Dr. Ellison takes part in the Underground Railroad, Kitty learns the value of racial equality and comes to idealize Boston, Massachusetts, the hub of abolitionist activity. Despite her provincial upbringing, she has an active imagination and a thirst for adventure, and when presented with an opportunity to travel, she eagerly seizes it to broaden her knowledge and experience.

When invited to visit Niagara Falls with her relatives, Colonel and Mrs. Ellison from Milwaukee, Kitty happily accepts. The novel begins on the return trip to New York via Quebec and Boston. On board a ship for Quebec, Kitty and her relatives meet MILES ARBUTON, a fellow traveler from Boston. Miles is a society man from the East who looks with condescension upon the provincial midwestern Ellison family. When Kitty mistakenly clutches his arm on deck, he feels a social obligation to apologize. She is immediately put off by his air of superiority; he is hardly the magnanimous and socially conscious Bostonian of her uncle's description. Despite his social reservations, however, Miles is intrigued by Kitty's natural integrity and openness to experience. The two become acquainted, and when the ship docks in Quebec, Arbuton offers to help the Ellisons find accommodations.

During their stay, Kitty's affection for Mr. Arbuton grows, although she senses a social rift between them. When they go for walks through the streets of Quebec, he seems to judge her taste in the arts and her choice of friends in America. Later, on an expedition to Montgomery, Arbuton saves Kitty from a dog that is about to attack her, then apologizes to the owner and offers him his torn coat. After this incident, Kitty has a new admiration for Arbuton, and he becomes increasingly possessive and protective of her. Kitty happily accepts his attention, and Mrs. Ellison secretly hopes for a match. But when Arbuton finally offers his hand, Kitty is overcome with doubt. She considers herself unworthy of a man of such high social standing, and she believes the differences in their backgrounds are irreconcilable.

Kitty's doubts are confirmed when Arbuton encounters two female acquaintances from Boston on one of their outings. He not only neglects to introduce Kitty but also abandons her in order to escort the ladies home. He later tries to justify his actions by claiming he wanted to wait until Kitty could make her best impression. Kitty realizes that Arbuton was ashamed to acknowledge her while she was wearing her travel clothes. Knowing this, she declines to marry him, despite his protestations of sincerity. For all of his social skills, Arbuton comes to see that he, and not Kitty, has been rude.

Before leaving for New York, Kitty encounters the man with the dog, who has found some letters to Arbuton in his coat pocket. She deliberately neglects this opportunity to rekindle her romance with Arbuton by passing the letters on to her uncle. She returns to New York without regret but with a keener sense of social awareness gained from her travel experience.

Emily. "I Stand Here Ironing." Tillie Olsen. 1962.

The unnamed narrator is an overworked mother of five children who reviews the difficult upbringing of her first child, Emily, as she irons clothes in her family's home. Deserted by her first husband when she was nineteen and Emily was only eight months old, mother and daughter were the victims of extreme poverty during the pre-WPA era of the Great Depression. Although the narrator cares for Emily and endeavors to provide her with the secure and loving environment that children need to grow up into contented and confident adults, the tribulations of single parenting and financial crises take their toll on Emily. Yet, as she reminisces, the narrator concludes that she did her best to be a good mother.

Having left a farewell note to the effect that he can no longer tolerate the impoverished family life that they share, Emily's father deserts wife and daughter without making any provisions for their welfare. In order to hold down a job, the narrator is forced to leave her daughter with a neighbor who is not sufficiently attentive to the baby's needs. Sensing the inadequacy of this arrangement, the narrator takes a job as a waitress at night, but her finances eventually become so strained that she is forced to send Emily off to live with her ex-husband's family. When she is finally able to send for her daughter to live with her, she has changed substantially from a beautiful baby to a thin, nervous two-year-old. The narrator then sends Emily first to a very poorly run nursery school where she is subjected to unsympathetic teachers and abusive fellow students and then back to her in-laws. Only when she remarries is she able to retrieve her daughter.

When the narrator bears her second child, Susan, Emily is extremely ill with measles and is not allowed to go near them due to fear of contagion. Emotionally distraught, she does not recover properly from the illness, becomes emaciated, and begins to suffer from nightmares. She is eventually sent to a convalescent institution for eight months where she is wretchedly unhappy and does not regain her strength. Emily grows up a shy and lonely child, jealous of her pretty, charming sister. Despite her unhappiness she is consistently stoic and uncomplaining.

Emily's mother is convinced that, despite her trials, her daughter will discover her niche in the world and build a meaningful life. From out of the unhappiness and pain of her youth, Emily has somehow developed a keen sense of humor which she utilizes as a performing comedian. With this talent, her blossoming beauty, and other positive qualities that she has managed to salvage in her personality, the narrator trusts that her daughter will successfully make her way in life.

Engelhardt, Albert. "Double Birthday." Willa Cather. 1929.

Albert Engelhardt, a handsome and contented but relatively unsuccessful middle-aged man, lives in Pittsburgh and supports himself by working at a desk job in the county clerk's office. He and his uncle, DR. ALBERT ENGELHARDT, a retired doctor of medicine, share December 1 as their birthday. They also share a modest house in a rather shabby part of town on the south side. They manage to keep up the house by renting out the ground floor to an elderly glass engraver and his wife. When Albert and his uncle forgo their habitual evening pastimes to celebrate their birthdays, a cherished friendship with a beautiful and well-to-do childhood pal is renewed, much to their mutual satisfaction.

Albert's father was a wealthy Civil War veteran whose vast fortune was squandered by his five sons after his death. Albert used his part of the inheritance to spend three years in Rome and on trips to New York City to take in the opera. Far from regretting his present penury, however, Albert remembers with pleasure his interesting and amusing past. He would not trade his memories for the wealth and present security of a family life. At home at night with his uncle, Albert amuses the old man by skillfully playing the piano after enjoying a dinner prepared by their tenants. When the elder Albert retires for the evening, his nephew sits down to a good book in front of the fire. Surrounded by such memorabilia as files of the *Yellow Book*, volumes by Oscar Wilde, and a portfolio containing Aubrey Beardsley drawings dating from his more bohemian days, Albert is at peace with past and present.

Having met the distinguished Judge Hammersley of Pittsburgh by accident on the street, Albert proceeds to request that the judge give him some wine to treat his uncle Albert on their birthday. Although the judge is critical of Albert's unproductive career, he agrees to supply the wine and invites him to come to pick it up at his home on Squirrel Hill. When Albert visits the judge to fetch the promised wine, Marjorie Parmenter, the judge's elegant widowed daughter, meets him at the door and expresses her delight in seeing Albert, with whom she had once spent a summer in Rome. They enjoy reminiscing about such pleasurable times as when they fantasized about running off to Russia together. Pleased with their interview, Marjorie silently vows to see more of Albert, and he contemplates her beauty and charm. Albert momentarily regrets his lowly station in life, which he thinks prevents him from socializing with attractive and accomplished women like his old friend.

When December 1 finally arrives and Albert and his uncle are preparing to celebrate their "double birthday," Marjorie Parmenter suddenly appears with yet another bottle of champagne and a bouquet of beautiful roses. She compliments Dr. Engelhardt on his distinguished career and personality, and after a moment's hesitation, agrees to grace their dinner table. Albert observes that Marjorie knows just how to flatter the old man. The dinner is a great success. Albert, too, is affected by Marjorie's champagne toast to their continuing friendship. She says that she prefers the two Alberts to anyone she knows and vows to become a frequent visitor. Thanks to his winning romantic and artistic temperament, Albert's lackluster career has come to seem bohemian rather than unfortunate.

Engelhardt, Dr. Albert. "Double Birthday." Willa Cather. 1929.

Dr. Albert Engelhardt, an eighty-year-old retired doctor, lives a quiet, carefully regulated life on the south side of Pittsburgh. The doctor shares a small house in a relatively rundown part of town with his middle-aged nephew, also named ALBERT ENGELHARDT. Although Dr. Engelhardt had once enjoyed an active and contented life-style, his happiness is marred by the memory of a crushing disappointment he suffered at the end of his medical career.

Dr. Engelhardt's uneventful, almost reclusive existence following his retirement contrasts sharply with his image of himself as a younger man who, although a confirmed bachelor, prided himself on his taste in women and his way with them. When explaining how he sustained a prominent scar that runs along his throat, the doctor denies the rumor that he hurt himself while wandering drunk in a garden and claims instead that he received it at the hands of a jealous husband. In addition, he suggests to his nephews that his big, pendulous nose is the sure sign of a sensual personality. His romantic disposition makes him all the more susceptible to the disappointment he experiences in conjunction with a young woman whom he had taken under his wing.

Professionally, Dr. Engelhardt takes particular interest in the throat and enjoys the patronage of a number of accomplished singers. His popularity is due in part to his laxness concerning the payment of fees, especially when artists give him autographed photographs of themselves. One day when the doctor is taking his daily constitutional before reporting to the office, he hears a magnificent soprano voice emanating from the Allegheny High School. He approaches the singer, an extremely naive, German-accented junior named Marguerite Thiesinger. She charms the Doctor, who offers to send her to New York City to embark on a singing career. Although flattered, Marguerite refuses the offer in favor of finishing high school and singing in a local church choir. The doctor attends the church services that Marguerite participates in and tries to generate ambition in the young woman, but she persists in her indifference to the idea of a brilliant performance career. Upon graduating from high school, she abruptly elopes with an insurance agent and moves to Chicago.

Some three years following her elopement, Marguerite suddenly appears in Dr. Engelhardt's office and professes her desire to take him up on his offer to invest in her career. She explains that her husband is now perfectly amenable to the idea of her making as much money as possible out of her voice. The doctor proceeds to introduce his young charge to the proper professionals and teachers in New York, and with exquisite excitement he watches Marguerite as she brightens the music scene in the city with her impressive voice and successful career. After two years of continuing musical triumph in which the doctor participates happily and vicariously, he receives a letter in which she complains of a swelling that turns out to be a malignant growth. She dies within a year at the age of twenty-six, and the doctor, devastated by the loss, loses interest in his career and retires.

English, Julian. *Appointment in Samarra.* John O'Hara. 1934.

Handsome, well-born Julian English is refined, aware, instinctively gallant but impatient with what he sees as the crudeness of the people around him. His impulse to reveal the insufferable complacency and stupidity behind the veil of social behavior is tempered only by his good manners.

The novel opens with Julian at the very center of polite society in Gibbsville, Pennsylvania. It is just after midnight on Christmas Eve at the Lantenengo Country Club dance. Julian sits in the smoking room, the inner sanctum of this prestigious club, surrounded by other members of the elite "Lantenengo Street Crowd": the spenders, drinkers, and socially secure. Julian and his wife Caroline seem to epitomize the group's values, and both are liked and admired. Yet even within this set, Julian has a sense of his own social and intellectual superiority and feels distant from those around him. As the evening wears on, he focuses his frustration on the figure of Harry Reilly.

Julian suddenly realizes that he abhors Reilly, whose only claims to social status are his mysteriously acquired fortune and his talent as a social climber. Julian longs to insult and embarrass the man and to show him that he will always be an outsider, but he is momentarily restrained by the thought that he is financially indebted to Reilly and that any insult will be interpreted as jealousy. Nevertheless, as attention is turned to the dance, a shock wave runs through the club: Julian English has just thrown a highball in Harry Reilly's face.

Julian wakes the next morning and remembers the night before with horror. He regrets the social difficulties of his impulsive act and the embarrassment it will cause his wife, but he feels no remorse for what he did to Reilly and justifies his bad behavior by recalling Reilly's "fat, cheap,

gross Irish face." The incident releases in Julian all the egotism, superiority, and self-pity that he has so long repressed. As his tendency to articulate these feelings through bad behavior increases, his standing within society diminishes and his relationship with Caroline quickly disintegrates. Christmas Day continues, and Julian desperately seeks an ally but finds that through this one act he has insulted the entire community upon which his status has rested.

Caught between his disgust for everything Gibbsville stands for and the realization that he owes his standing, reputation, and even his self-esteem to this world, Julian repeatedly attempts to make amends, then regrets this impulse and falls deeper into his dilemma. As the novel progresses, Julian realizes that his sense of self-worth cannot protect him from the attack of his former friends, who now feel licensed to express their long-held dislike of him. His business, too, is failing, and Julian has cut himself off from any source of financial support. In a final attempt to set things right, he goes to apologize to Reilly, but Reilly is too busy to see him. Julian mistakes Reilly's response for a rebuff and, alone and deserted by Caroline, his only ally, he sits in his car with a bottle of whiskey and a pack of cigarettes, turns the engine on, and waits to die.

Errol, Cedric "Ceddie." *Little Lord Fauntleroy.* Frances Hodgson Burnett. 1928.

Cedric "Ceddie" Errol, the novel's title character, is a boy who experiences the kind of change in status about which most children can only dream. Until the age of seven he lives happily with his mother, Mrs. Cedric Errol, in their humble house in New York City. He plays with the other children on the block and is good friends with the grocer, Mr. Hobbs, and the bootblack, Dick. Handsome and athletic, Ceddie likes to use big words and discuss politics. He has known no unhappiness other than the death of his father, and surrounded by love, he is loving in return.

When Ceddie is seven years old, a lawyer, Mr. Havisham, arrives from England to inform him that he is the only remaining descendant of the Earl of Dorincourt. Although his grandfather, the Earl, had disowned his father for marrying an American, Ceddie is now being summoned to take up his proper position in society. Ceddie is uncertain as to how to feel about this, for he has heard nothing from his mother about the situation and knows only that Mr. Hobbs dislikes earls and other royalty. However, when Mr. Havisham gives him money to do whatever he likes, he begins to appreciate his good fortune. He immediately gives his mother's friends money to pay their rent and buy food, and he spends the rest on other generous projects.

On the trip to England, Mrs. Errol tells Ceddie nothing about the long-standing hatred his grandfather has borne for her or the reason she will not be able to live in the same house with him. When he meets his grandfather for the first time, he assumes that the Earl is a good and generous man. The Earl is so astounded by Ceddie's clear intention to love him that he forgets his usual ill-humor. As the days pass, the Earl becomes proud of the boy's intelligence, frankness, and natural good looks. Ceddie is adored by all who meet him.

When Ceddie learns about the poverty-stricken conditions of the people who live on his grandfather's property, he assumes that the Earl is not aware of the situation. The Earl has been decidedly ungenerous all his life, but as he grows fonder of his grandson, he becomes unwilling to let him know his true character and immediately grants his requests for aid to the poor tenants. Thus the young boy's impression that his grandfather is the most generous man on earth is constantly reinforced. The people realize that Ceddie is behind all these positive changes, and they love him and look forward to having him as the next earl.

Ceddie's wealth and stature are threatened when, out of the blue, a woman arrives claiming to be the widow of the Earl's oldest son and the mother of the true heir. The Earl is heartbroken to think that Ceddie will not succeed him, but Ceddie assures him that even if he is not the next earl, he will always be the Earl's little boy. The woman is discredited, however, and Ceddie's position is secured.

Escobar, Isidro. *Isidro.* Mary Austin. 1905.

Isidro Escobar is a twenty-year-old Mexican who travels to the Mission of San Carlos in Monterey, California, in order to become a priest. A courteous and chivalrous young man who upholds the honor of his ancient family, Isidro undertakes to enter the priesthood only to keep a promise his father made to Saint Francis in return for marrying a nun. But before taking his orders, Isidro becomes involved in several dangerous and romantic adventures that forestall his vocation and eventually convince him that the priesthood is not his true calling.

On the road to Monterey, Isidro encounters some sheep that once belonged to Mariano, a Portuguese man who was recently killed by Juan Ruiz, his disgruntled shepherd of mysterious origin. Shortly before his death, Mariano told Juan Ruiz that he had known Juan Ruiz's mother, implying that he might be his father. Isidro decides to adopt the sheep and become a shepherd himself. While traveling with the sheep, Isidro encounters a young boy with a sharp tongue—aptly named El Zarzo, the Briar— who insists on accompanying him to Monterey; Isidro reluctantly complies.

El Zarzo is allowed to stay at the mission as Isidro's servant and pupil in Christianity, despite the annoyance of the mission fathers. When Isidro hears talk blaming the mission fathers for holding their Indian neophytes in captivity, he uses El Zarzo as an audience to help him define his thoughts. One of these escaped neophytes, an Indian named Mascado, believes that Isidro has taken El Zarzo

away from him. Angrily seeking revenge, he tells the authorities that Isidro killed Juan Ruiz, who is missing, and Isidro is promptly arrested.

Father Saavedra, who knows that Ruiz is alive, finds him and gets a written confession from him. Saavedra thus succeeds in releasing Isidro from prison, but not before Mascado kidnaps El Zarzo—actually a young woman, Jacinta—and takes her into the woods where he intends to make her his "bride." When Isidro learns that El Zarzo is a girl, he is thrown into a state of confusion. Knowing that he will be dishonored for keeping a mistress disguised as a boy, he fears Father Saavedra's disdain and his father's fury.

Isidro finds Mascado, fights him, and rescues Jacinta. To save her reputation, he takes Jacinta to San Antonio and marries her. He does not ask her consent, for he believes she wouldn't know what's good for her anyway. Without consummating the marriage, Isidro immediately abandons the insulted Jacinta in order to query El Zarzo's adopted father, Peter Lebecque, about her background. Lebecque tells Isidro that Jacinta is actually the lost daughter of the *comandante* of Monterey, who has recently hired a man to search for her.

On his way back to the mission, Isidro is captured by Mascado, who along with a group of disgruntled Indians has been raiding the mission's cattle. Mascado brings Isidro to their forest camp where Isidro honors his word not to attempt to escape. When Jacinta and Mascado's mother Marta arrive at the camp in search of him, Isidro apologizes to Jacinta for stranding her in San Antonio and for not returning sooner.

Their reunion is tragically disrupted by a forest fire that the *comandante* rashly starts in order to rout the renegade Indians. Isidro and Jacinta escape, but Mascado and Marta are killed. Isidro feels for the first time what he lacked in not having a wife: someone to comfort and to protect from danger. He tells Jacinta he is overjoyed to have her as his wife, and he renounces his vow to the Church.

Back at the mission, Isidro explains to Father Saavedra that facing danger and death have made him want to live as a man, not as a priest. He realizes that he does not possess the selfless spirit necessary to become a priest; he wants a life of simple pleasures and labor, with a wife, children, and a home. Moreover, his experience with Jacinta and Mascado has convinced him that the priests are treating the Indians unjustly. Isidro and Jacinta leave together for Mexico, where Isidro enjoys a successful political career and the young couple rejoice in the birth of their first child.

Esmé. "For Esmé—with Love and Squalor." J. D. Salinger. 1953.

Esmé, about thirteen years old, walks into the civilian tearoom in Devonshire with her five-year-old brother

Charlie and their governess, Miss Megley. She smiles radiantly at the American soldier, referred to as SERGEANT X in the story, who is sitting alone and watching them. With her soaking wet blond hair, her tartan dress, and her matter-of-fact manner, she strides up to the stranger's table and declares that she thought Americans despised tea. A frank and careful communication ensues between the lonely American and this precocious young English girl.

Having agreed to join him, Esmé sits with poise on the edge of her chair. Esmé says she recognizes the sergeant as the man who had been in the church at her choir practice just moments before. When he replies that she has a very fine voice, she nods in agreement, declaring she will become a professional singer of jazz on radio in order to make a lot of money.

Ignoring the signals from her governess to leave the man alone, Esmé, in her ingenuous manner, remarks that the sergeant seems quite intelligent for an American and that he has a sensitive face. After asking whether he's deeply in love with his wife, Esmé explains that she's not usually so gregarious but he seemed to be rather lonely and she is currently training herself to be more compassionate because her aunt says she's a terribly cold person. She has lived with her aunt since the death of her mother, who was an intelligent, sensuous, and passionate extrovert. Charles, her five-year-old brother who has just joined them, misses their extremely gifted father, who was slain in North Africa. Her experiences in the war—the loss of both her parents and the assumption of responsibility for her brother—have forced her into premature adulthood.

Inquiring into his profession before the war, Esmé finds out that Sergeant X wants to be a professional short story writer. When Sergeant X asks her if her large chronographic-looking wristwatch was her father's, she self-consciously responds that he had given it to her purely as a memento just before she and Charles were evacuated, presumably from North Africa. But Esmé is more interested in returning to the subject of writing and asks Sergeant X if he would write a story exclusively for her—not a childish and silly story, though, because she prefers stories about squalor.

Charles has left the table in a huff, and Esmé regretfully tells Sergeant X that she must leave also. She thought that he might like her company because she is very precocious for her age. Moments after leaving the tearoom she returns with Charles, who wants to kiss Sergeant X good-bye. She reminds him to write her that squalid story and hopes he will return with all his faculties intact.

In the letter that Sergeant X receives a year later, Esmé thinks of their extremely pleasant half-hour together on April 30, 1944, and hopes that D-Day will end the war. As a lucky talisman, she encloses her father's wristwatch, which, she adds, is waterproof, shockproof, and can record walking velocity. By the time he receives this letter,

he has suffered a nervous breakdown; the memory of his day with Esmé and the kindness communicated to him through her intelligent and sensitive letter offer him hope of once again becoming whole. Six years later Sergeant X learns that Esmé will be getting married, and holding to his promise, he writes a story for her with love and squalor.

Espinoza, Lorenzo Delgado "Dell." *Afterlife.* Paul Monette. 1990.

Lorenzo Delgado Espinoza, known to his American friends as "Dell," is a landscape artist who founded his own company in the Los Angeles area after leaving Mexico as a young man. Like his friends STEVEN SHAW and SONNY CEVATHAS, Dell is attempting to piece together a life in the aftermath of the death, due to complications caused by the AIDS virus, of his lover, the historian and gay rights activist Marcus Flint.

The year that has passed since Marcus's death has been one of despair and loneliness for Dell as well as for his younger sister Linda, who shared his love for Marcus and who helped care for the dying man. In fact, Linda had married Marcus shortly before his death in order to prevent his family from throwing Dell out of his apartment.

From the novel's beginning Dell is obsessed with the rantings of an evangelist, Mother Evangeline, who thanks God for bringing the AIDS virus to earth in order to destroy homosexuals, the "sinners." He acts on this obsession by making a prank call in which he claims falsely that he has dumped AIDS-infected blood into a reservoir. Although this causes a brief panic, it does not satisfy Dell's rage.

Dell becomes increasingly angry at both AIDS and Mother Evangeline. After a second reservoir prank, Dell decides to vent his spleen only on specific targets—the professed enemies of the gay community. He dresses as a ghoul on Halloween and goes to Mother Evangeline's "Family Church of the Eternal Light." Once alone, he sprinkles turkey blood all over the files, computers, and typewriters before stealing the evangelist's subscription lists. This deed does give him some satisfaction, but it also leads the police to conclude that the prank calls and vandalism at the church were the work of the same individual. Linda manages to convince Steven Shaw to take Dell in until the pressure is off. Dell seems to comply with Steven's and Linda's wishes and stays indoors most of the time. By Thanksgiving, however, he has decided that one thing more must be done about Mother Evangeline.

Dell tells Steven that he is returning to Mexico, where he has long been a local legend for his financial success in the United States as well as for his ongoing devotion to his mother and sisters. Instead, however, he trades in his truck for a gun and returns to Mother Evangeline's church. After listening to the evangelist for a while, he draws the gun and shoots her in the face; then, almost as if not sure he wants to, he puts the gun to his head and kills himself.

Esteban. *The Bridge of San Luis Rey.* Thornton Wilder. 1927.

Esteban, an inhabitant of early-eighteenth-century Lima, dies in the collapse of the finest rope bridge in Peru. This tragic event kindles the curiosity of the novel's unnamed narrator, who retraces the path of Esteban's life in search of a divine justification for this seemingly accidental death.

Esteban and his twin brother Manuel were orphans raised at the Convent of Santa María de las Rosas in Lima. The twins were well treated by the abbess, Madre María del Pilar. As they grew older, they took on various clerical duties by working at the sacristies in town polishing brass, trimming hedges, and assisting the priests. The brothers were not suited for the ecclesiastical life, however, and eventually they became scribes.

Esteban and Manuel were virtually inseparable. Their mutual love was so profound that everything beyond it seemed strange and hostile, and their need for each other was so great that it produced miracles. They even spoke a secret language that no one else was able to understand.

The brothers' harmonious life together was disturbed when Manuel fell in love with Señora Camila Perichole, an actress known as the Perichole. Camila, unaware of Manuel's love for her, was having an affair with an unnamed nobleman when she employed Manuel as a scribe to write her love letters.

Late one night the Perichole came to the brothers' room to request a special letter from Manuel. Esteban, suddenly realizing his brother's congeniality with the actress, was overcome by misery at being excluded from what he saw as the lovers' paradise. Manuel, in turn, experienced a terrifying vision in which he recognized that all attachments in the world, even to the Perichole, were mere shadows compared to the twins' mutual attachment, and he swore to dissociate himself from the woman in every way.

After an accident in which he wounded his knee, Manuel was confined to bed, where he fell into a delirium brought on by the excruciating pain. Esteban, following the doctor's orders, changed the bandages on Manuel's knee once every hour. This process was so painful for Manuel that every time it approached, he begged Esteban to spare him. As the delirium grew worse, Manuel, in his rage and pain, accused Esteban of coming between him and the Perichole. When a lucid interval allowed Manuel a respite, he denied that he felt any ill-will toward his brother and swore by a crucifix that only the excruciating pain made him utter the curses.

Despite Esteban's conscientious efforts, Manuel died. Esteban, shocked at this great loss, fell into an extended daze. Half-demented, he grew taciturn and became alienated from society. Madre María del Pilar, alarmed at seeing Esteban in this condition, resolved to bring about Esteban's recovery. She requested the assistance of Captain Alvarado, a seaman who in the past had gained Esteban's respect.

Hoping that a hardy sea voyage would cure his limitless grief, Captain Alvarado offered Esteban a position on his ship. On the morning he was supposed to leave, however, Esteban attempted suicide. His death was averted through the chance intervention of the captain, who then redoubled his efforts at employing Esteban by giving him advance wages.

Esteban decided to use his advance pay to purchase a present for Madre María del Pilar, who had been so kind to him. On his way to town for this purpose, accompanied by strangers UNCLE PIO and DOÑA MARÍA MARQUESA DE MONTEMAYOR, he was suddenly killed in the collapse of the Bridge of San Luis Rey.

Eva. "Tell Me a Riddle." Tillie Olsen. 1961.

Eva, a septuagenarian Russian immigrant and the mother of six children, experiences solitude for the first time in her life. She has spent most of her life caring for others, but feeling the inevitable approach of death, she wants to enjoy the quiet and emptiness of a house without children.

But DAVID, her husband of forty-seven years, has other plans. He tries to persuade Eva to move into a cooperative living community for the aged so that he will not have to take care of the big, empty house anymore. Eva bitterly resents David for never having stayed home with the children so she could go out. As he continues to press her to move, Eva begins to relive the old hurts and angers of her years of toil.

One night after a dinner party with some of the children, their daughter Hannah decides to bring Eva with her to Connecticut where her husband, a doctor, can examine her. It is determined that her gall bladder must be removed, and surgery reveals that Eva has cancer. For a time after the surgery Eva enjoys being with Hannah in Connecticut. No one has told her about the cancer, and its partial removal relieves her feelings of illness. But soon she begins asking David to take her home. The religious rituals that Hannah performs, such as the lighting of the Friday night prayer candles, unnerve Eva because she has renounced Judaism, which she feels stifles women and forces them into subservience.

But rather than take her home, David takes Eva to Ohio to see their daughter Vivi and her new baby. Eva becomes frightened and withdrawn. She doesn't know how to express that she wants to journey onward to something else, to experience her own needs and solitude. The feel of her grandchild in her arms calls up unbearable associations, and she avoids the baby as much as possible.

Next, David insists on going on to Los Angeles where he thinks the sun and warmth will be good for Eva. Eva's condition worsens, and she becomes more and more withdrawn. She keeps her hearing aid turned down so the noises and voices won't invade the silence she so desperately needs. She retreats into her memories of Russia, of wars, of prison, and of the Holocaust.

Eva begs David to bring her home, but when he finally agrees to ask the doctor's permission, she develops an infection and must remain in a rented hospital bed in their Los Angeles apartment. The illness causes Eva to vomit constantly, and she must be fed intravenously. She becomes incoherent and begins singing the songs of her youth, songs of freedom and belief. As she nears death, Eva's body is ravaged by pain, but in her mind she is transported to a time in her childhood when she first heard music, at a wedding in the village where she was born.

Evans, Miss Amelia. *Ballad of the Sad Cafe.* Carson McCullers. 1951.

Miss Amelia Evans is a cross-eyed, big-boned woman who owns a store, operates a still, is a skilled carpenter and holistic healer, and loves to sue her fellow townspeople. The richest person in a sad, dreary little town somewhere in the South, Amelia is also a solitary woman who cares nothing for men until the arrival of a hunchbacked dwarf, Cousin Lymon, who changes her and her sleepy hometown forever.

One evening in April, Lymon appears as if from nowhere and claims to be Miss Amelia's kin. Although everyone expects this strange character to be immediately booted from the property, Amelia uncharacteristically offers him liquor, food, and a place to sleep. Then, after two days of mysterious silence during which rumors fly that Amelia has murdered Lymon, the store reopens as a cafe where whiskey and crackers are served. The hunchback establishes a fast and intimate connection with everyone who comes in, while Miss Amelia hangs back, looking at Lymon "lonesomely" like a lover.

Over the next four years Amelia and Lymon become inseparable. Amelia begins to temper her adversarial nature, litigating less and singing to herself more. She is in love with Lymon and quite protective of him, although there is no sexual intimacy between them. Amelia confides in the curious hunchback stories of her life that she has never told anyone else—except the dreadful one about her ten-day marriage to Marvin Macy, an evil character who is now in jail.

One day Marvin's brother receives a letter that Marvin has been released. When Marvin shows up on the dusty main road, the town is filled with tense anticipation as everyone waits for Marvin and Amelia to face each other. Lymon, perhaps understanding that Marvin is the only person who might be stronger than Amelia, tries desperately to win the convict over, switching his attentions and loyalties from Amelia to her most hated enemy. But

Marvin ignores the dwarf, calls him names, and even hits him once.

Amelia seems powerless to stand up to Marvin. Although it causes her intense emotional pain, she does nothing to stop Lymon's obsequious attentions to Marvin or to protect Lymon from Marvin's beratement. She closes the cafe, and her behavior becomes erratic and confused, as if she cannot decide which way to turn. Even when Marvin moves into the store with her and Lymon, Amelia does not protest.

Some months later Amelia and Marvin at last decide to have the fight for which the town has been hoping. Each spends a day resting to store up strength. Marvin is a considerable opponent, but Amelia is the stronger of the two and is about to overpower her former husband when Lymon jumps on her back and pulls her away, allowing Marvin the victory.

Defeated more emotionally than physically, Amelia sits stunned in her office recovering from the bout. Marvin and Lymon deface and loot the cafe before disappearing from the town. Amelia initially waits for Lymon to return to her but eventually breaks down when it becomes obvious that she has been abandoned. She stops taking care of herself, and after three years of waiting for Cousin Lymon's return, she has the store boarded up and only appears as a ghostlike face in a second-floor window.

Everett, Walter "Win" Jr. *Libra.* Don DeLillo. 1988.

In this fictional account of events surrounding President John F. Kennedy's assassination, Walter "Win" Everett, Jr., a fifty-one-year-old former CIA operative, finds himself in "semi-retirement" due to his maverick behavior in scheming to oust Fidel Castro from power. Since falling victim to "motivational exhaustion," Everett has been assigned by the agency to teach at Texas Women's University. He cannot overcome his obsession with Cuba, however, and thus calls a meeting of two of his anti-Castro cronies, Laurence Parmenter and T. J. Mackey. He tells them their movement needs to be revived because Kennedy is moving toward what Everett believes is a settling of differences with the hated Cuban communist.

Everett says that if they want to ensure a successful invasion of the island, they will need an electrifying event, something of the magnitude of an attempt on the life of the President of the United States that points clearly to Cuban involvement. He proposes a fake assassination attempt on Kennedy, something to pin on Castro so as to get the United States riled and primed for action. Everett has in mind a complex plan for faking the involvement of the Cuban government, to script a person out of "ordinary pocket litter" and leave a trail pointing to Cuban agents. In conjunction with his plot, Everett begins creating the layers of paperwork that will point to a Cuban conspiracy. This "pocket litter" will make investigators believe that

Kennedy wanted Castro dead and that Castro decided to retaliate.

Everett, Parmenter, and Mackey ultimately settle on LEE HARVEY OSWALD as their "hit man." Everett sets to work creating a false trail that will tie Oswald to the Cuban Intelligence Directorate. The idea is to create coincidences so bizarre that they must be believed. Unbeknownst to Everett, however, Mackey has decided to take the plan one step further and actually have Kennedy murdered. Everett has a premonition that something like this may happen, but because he is unwilling to take the necessary measures to ensure that it does not, the plan slips out of his control. He loses contact with Mackey and eventually gives up on his plan, believing his own men to have failed him. Mackey, however, is now operating on his own.

After Kennedy's assassination, Everett continues his academic career, ultimately becoming assistant to the president of Ross State College. But in May 1965 he is found dead, ostensibly of a heart attack, in a motel room outside Alpine, Texas.

Everhard, Avis. *The Iron Heel.* Jack London. 1907.

Avis Everhard moves from a bourgeois life in her father's house to the violent world of a socialist revolutionary. The career of her husband, ERNEST EVERHARD, a socialist leader, unfolds through her eyes during a time (1912–20) of violent worker repression by the capitalist class.

Avis's radicalization begins at her first meeting with Ernest. Her father, who has seen him preaching socialism on the streets, invites him to their home to dine with some clergymen friends. In a debate over metaphysics Ernest asserts the worth of observation based on scientific socialism over speculative philosophy. Impressed, Avis reads a book of his that explicates the work of Karl Marx. At a second meeting she accuses him of fomenting class hatred. He answers by calling her home, her clothing, her whole life-style "bloody," bought with dividends from the mills where workers are regularly maimed by unsafe machinery and defrauded of compensation. Angry, she challenges him to prove it. She then sets out on an investigation that opens her eyes to the injustice and misery of the worker's life.

Converted, Avis marries Ernest. He becomes a prominent spokesman for the cause and is offered the post of U.S. Labor Commissioner. He refuses the offer, which he considers a bribe proffered by the heads of the great business trusts, a group known as the "Oligarchy."

Meanwhile, Avis's father loses his job, home, and investments due to his association with Ernest. The Oligarchy, having bought out the U.S. government, next makes a series of moves: It closes the socialist press; uses federal troops to crush organized labor; and reduces the Democratic Party to impotence. The desperate workers respond by electing the socialists to Congress, with Ernest at their head. Avis accompanies Ernest to Washington where, after a short period, all the socialist members of Congress are imprisoned for life. Avis, too, is thrown into jail but is released after six months.

From underground, the socialists build a resistance network. In her hideout in the Sonoma Hills of California, Avis becomes a link in the network's chain, and she learns to alter her habits of speech and gesture so that she is able to assume a new identity. Ernest escapes and joins her. He has cosmetic surgery, and together they join the Oligarchy's organization as moles. A mass revolt is planned, but the Oligarchy, through its agents provocateurs, instigates its untimely outbreak in Chicago and murders the city's proletariat en masse. Avis witnesses three days of street fighting. Her memoir breaks off mid-sentence with Ernest already dead and her and the remaining leaders awaiting the next day and the beginning of the second revolt.

Everhard, Ernest. *The Iron Heel.* Jack London. 1907.

Ernest Everhard is the ideal socialist revolutionary hero. Intelligent, learned, and full of unstinting devotion to the cause, his virtues are contrasted in the novel with the muddled blindness of the middle class, the contradictory thinking of the clergy, and the power-mad bestiality of the capitalist class. His career unfolds during a period (1912–20) when the capitalists have undertaken a class war against the masses.

The narrative follows the form of a memoir by the hero's widow, AVIS EVERHARD, who meets and falls in love with him at her father's house. Avis's father heard Ernest preaching socialism in the street and invited him to dine with members of the clergy. Ernest debates them, asserting that metaphysics has no basis in the real world; unlike objective science, its premises are rooted in subjective consciousness, and the falseness of its method shows in the ministers' ignorance of what is going on around them—the plight of the workers.

At a second meeting with Avis and one of the ministers, Ernest goads them into action. They take up the investigation of the case of a worker maimed on the job and defrauded of compensation by the company-corrupted courts, and the ministers are converted.

As a prominent socialist author, Ernest is invited to speak at a lecture society composed of the local magnates. Using Marxist arguments, he vilifies their class. They have mismanaged society, he maintains, and power will be taken from them. Next, Ernest is offered the U.S. Labor Commissioner's post. He refuses it, considering it a bribe, and predicts some sort of violent repression in the works planned by the heads of the national business trusts known as the "Oligarchy."

When Ernest marries Avis, her father is defrauded of home, job, and investments due to his association with a radical. Nationally the Oligarchy makes a series of moves: They close the socialist press, use the army to break a national machinists' strike, destroy the middle-class capitalists, break up the Hearst empire (pro labor), and, finally, effectively reduce the Democratic Party to impotence. In the political vacuum, the workers elect the socialists to Congress, with Ernest as their leader. The Oligarchy imprisons them all. From jail they direct preparations for a mass revolt. Ernest escapes jail, has cosmetic surgery, and becomes a mole within the Oligarchy's organization. The novel's final chapter recounts the failure of the revolt on the streets of Chicago, where its untimely outbreak, orchestrated by the agents provocateurs of the Oligarchy, ends in a universal slaughter of the working class.

Here the memoir breaks off, as if the author has suffered violence. A footnote adds that nothing is known of when or where Ernest was captured and executed.

Exely, Frederick "Ex." *A Fan's Notes.* Frederick Exely. 1968.

Frederick Exely is the name of both the main character and the author, who claims that although many of the events in the story are the same as those in his own life, the character Frederick Exely and the author are not one and the same.

"Ex," as the main character is known to his friends, recalls throughout the book the events that contributed to his state of quiet desperation. He is divorced and has two sons whom he has not seen in many years. He recently began to teach high school English in a small backward town in upstate New York. Because his reputation as an alcoholic preceded him, Ex had to make a deal with the principal that he would not drink while living and working in the town. But Ex makes up for his abstinence by driving fifty miles every weekend to his hometown of Watertown, where he drinks himself into oblivion and watches the New York Giants football game in his favorite bar.

At the book's opening, Ex has a nervous breakdown in the bar before the game begins and is taken to Watertown Hospital where the doctor recognizes him as the son of the beloved townsman Earl Exely. When he was young, Earl Exely had an opportunity to be a football great; Ex reflects a great deal on why his father never developed his talent. Ex resents having to spend his life in the shadow of his father's reputation as an athlete and local hero. He is unable to reconcile the contradiction between his father's actions and his reputation: His father drinks too much and has a violent tendency that leads him into weekly barroom brawls, yet he is loved by the town.

Ex recalls his young adulthood. He went to Hobart College for a year until, after suffering a broken heart, he transferred to the University of Southern California. At USC he was part of a social group of outsiders who were unable to conform to the USC norm. But Ex could not overcome his fascination with the football player and cheerleader social scene that dominated the university. He became obsessed with the star USC player Frank Gifford, an All-American who later went on to play for the Giants.

After college Ex tried to obtain a high-paying advertising job by faking a resume. At first he went on many interviews, but then he slid into a depression in which he fantasized about finding the perfect woman and building a perfect life with her. Ex grew more and more depressed until he was finally committed to a mental hospital by his mother. Although he hoped that he would be cured by the doctors, he did not feel any different when he left.

Ex traveled from New York to Chicago and then to Florida. He hoped to fulfill his fantasy of finding a perfect job and woman, but every time he found something close, he ruined it. He got fired from high-paying jobs because of his drunkenness, and when he found the women of his dreams he became impotent. In his last fiasco, Ex was at work on a novel. He had a beautiful rich wife who loved him and had just given birth to triplet sons. Hating himself, Ex was overcome with anxiety and deserted her.

At the novel's end, it seems as though Ex is settled in his schoolteacher life upstate, but there is no reason to believe that he will not ruin this situation as he has all the others. He compares his plight to that of America: Just as America cannot cope with the ugly unwanted parts of itself and pretends they do not exist, so are its individual citizens unable to find the strength to overcome their emotional defects.

F

Fairchild, Verlyn Rayburn "Jinx." *Because It Is Bitter, and Because It Is My Heart.* Joyce Carol Oates. 1990.

Verlyn Rayburn Fairchild, known to his friends and most of his family as "Jinx," is the second son of Minnie and Woodrow Fairchild, who live in Lowertown, the black section of town in Hammond, New York, in the

1950s. Spirited and physically attractive in his own right, Jinx is raised in the shadow of his older brother Sugar Boy whose natural ease and grace earn him general admiration. In addition to being influenced by his brother, Jinx is reared with an iron hand by his mother Minnie, a practical nurse for a rich white doctor, and by his father who is many years older than Minnie. In his early teens Jinx displays talent as an athlete, and he quickly becomes a favorite among the teenage girls. His admirers include IRIS COURTNEY, a younger white girl. Jinx finds Iris somewhat attractive but spends too much time concentrating on basketball to notice her. Soon he comes to be known as the "Iceman" because of his coolness in the face of pressure while on the court.

One evening in 1956, Jinx and Iris share a devastating experience. A distraught Iris arrives at Jinx's job as he is leaving. When he asks what is wrong, she points to "Little Red" Garlock, a local white teenager who stands some distance away taunting her with sexual insults. Jinx offers to escort her home, and along the way Garlock continues to assail them. Before long a brutal confrontation erupts between the two, and Jinx ends up murdering Garlock. He throws the body in the river and sends the shocked Iris home. In response to Iris's complicity, Jinx develops a complicated emotional connection to her, built on his guilt and desire.

His parents convince Jinx not to confess his crime. To repress the memory of the killing and to keep his feelings for Iris at bay, Jinx sharpens his athletic skills. As he nears the end of high school, he is his coach's favorite and a superior student. At a crucial juncture during his final tournament, however, he breaks his ankle, seemingly deliberately and in such a way as to preclude a career in basketball. Only Iris understands the guilt that provokes him to arrange this accident.

After a period of many years, Jinx and Iris meet again. Wizened by his brother's gruesome death in a drug-related dispute and awakened, after his marriage, to the fact that relationships do not endure, Jinx refuses to have sex with Iris. Dissatisfied with his marriage and looking for financial security, Jinx decides to join the army. Before he enlists, he has his photo taken and sends it to Iris as a token of what will never be.

Faith. "The Long-Distance Runner." Grace Paley. 1971.

Faith begins jogging in her early forties so that she can travel through the New York neighborhoods and revisit the seascapes with which she grew up. Urban renewal has since changed the area, and she wants to explore the environment before her own waning strength makes it impossible for her to get around.

Donning silk shorts and a white undershirt, Faith begins to train and tone her rather flabby body in the spring in the countryside of Connecticut. When summer arrives, she feels sufficiently confident of the strength in her legs and the development of her lung capacity, and she ventures into the suburbs where she can be scrutinized by passersby. Then, bidding farewell to her two nearly adult sons and asking her folksy friend Mrs. Raftery to keep an eye on them, she takes the subway to Brighton Beach, the landscape of her childhood.

Faith jogs the mile and a half from the beach to her old neighborhood and is confronted, not by a crowd of Jewish people who had once inhabited the area, but by hundreds of blacks who feel free to comment on the imperfections of her blubbery body. Pausing to chat with a group of jiving and rambunctious youths, Faith tells them that she grew up in the area, and they in turn inform her that a certain Mrs. Luddy now occupies the apartment her family had once rented. Cynthia, a young Girl Scout, offers to take Faith to visit her old home, and after protesting that she is not properly dressed for a visit and cannot bear to reminisce about her parents in the very apartment they used to inhabit, she accepts the girl's offer and is escorted to the building where she spent her childhood.

Having entered the building, Faith suddenly gets spooked by the neighborhood and the notion that she might be accosted. Not knowing what else to do, she seeks refuge in her old home. She is admitted into the apartment and meets the cantankerous but kindly Mrs. Luddy, her young son Donald, and three baby girls that Mrs. Luddy tends to. Still fearful of the neighborhood and sentimental about being in the rooms she grew up in, Faith is reluctant to leave the apartment and so ends up living with the Luddys for three weeks. She helps care for the babies and becomes exceedingly fond of the lovable, precocious Donald, whom she tutors in reading and generally dotes on.

One morning Mrs. Luddy abruptly wakes Faith and declares that it is time for her to go home to her own sons. Faith follows her hostess's injunction despite the fact that she loves the company of both Donald and his mother. Having left them, she runs along Ocean Parkway and notices that in the three weeks she has been in Mrs. Luddy's apartment, jogging has become a popular sport. At home, Faith finds that her lover Jack has returned, learns from her sons that their father has sent a letter from Chile, and observes that her household has remained generally unchanged. When she tries to describe her adventures in her old neighborhood, no one can really understand the significance of her eccentric sojourn into the past.

Farange, Maisie. *What Maisie Knew.* Henry James. 1897.

Maisie Farange, the young heroine of this novel of innocence and experience, spends her childhood shuttling back and forth between her divorced parents, Beale and Ida Farange. It is her fate to witness much more than she can immediately understand but also understand much more than perhaps any little girl should.

According to the terms of the Faranges' divorce settlement, Maisie is to spend six months of the year with each parent. During her tenure with Beale Farange, Maisie is bombarded with accusations and insults directed against her mother in Mr. Farange's effort to alienate her from her mother and to make her the unwitting courier of his spite. Ida Farange makes the same selfish use of her daughter. But the six-year-old Maisie soon grows wise to this scheme, and she vows to feign ignorance for the sake of peace. This noble effort only wins Maisie the contempt of her parents for her apparent stupidity.

Maisie's domestic predicament is further complicated when her father becomes enamored of and marries Maisie's former governess, the beautiful Miss Overmore, who is henceforth known to the child as Mrs. Beale, while her mother marries the dashing young Sir Claude. The only stable influence in Maisie's life is her new governess, Mrs. Wix, who has been retained by Maisie's mother.

The elderly Mrs. Wix is uneducated and prone to dogmatic moralizing. Nevertheless, governess and child form a sympathetic bond. Maisie marvels that Mrs. Wix is more maternal than either her natural mother or her stepmother. Mrs. Wix, loyal to Maisie's mother, expresses freely to her young charge her moral condemnation of Mrs. Beale, while at the same time both Maisie and Mrs. Wix grow extremely fond of Maisie's stepfather, the affable and charismatic Sir Claude. Sir Claude returns the affection of his spirited and perceptive stepdaughter, and the two become constant companions.

All too soon the new marriages become unstable. Maisie and Mrs. Wix dream of escaping this domestic morass with Sir Claude to form their own little family, but Sir Claude is too afraid of Maisie's tempestuous mother ever to effect such a move. Maisie is eventually enticed by her father into living with him and Mrs. Beale. She agrees to this but does not realize until it is too late that this move cannot include Mrs. Beale's nemesis, Mrs. Wix. Maisie's natural parents become increasingly absent from her life, while Sir Claude, drawn by his love for Maisie, becomes a frequent visitor to Mrs. Beale's household.

Thus brought together by Maisie, Sir Claude and Mrs. Beale fall in love. In the meantime, Maisie's natural parents, who are both divorcing their spouses, abandon her so that they can pursue their respective affairs. Ida relinquishes her custody of Maisie to Sir Claude, who reengages the services of Mrs. Wix, to Maisie's delight.

But the happy little trio of Maisie, Sir Claude, and Mrs. Wix will soon be joined by Mrs. Beale, whom Mrs. Wix continues to denounce as a self-serving temptress. Sir Claude explains to Maisie that she must choose to live either with him and Mrs. Beale or with Mrs. Wix. While Mrs. Wix decries the immorality of the impending liaison

between Sir Claude and Mrs. Beale, Maisie deliberates. Although Maisie's lovable nature has not been corrupted by the sordidness of her domestic situation, she has been rendered wise beyond her years. She understands the choice she must make.

After an ugly confrontation between Mrs. Wix and Mrs. Beale, Maisie chooses to live with Mrs. Wix, the only adult who has ever loved her unconditionally and reliably. As they depart together, Mrs. Wix remarks in disgust that Sir Claude has now gone to Mrs. Beale. Maisie responds simply that she, of course, already knows this, leaving Mrs. Wix to marvel over just how much Maisie knows.

Farquhar, Peyton. "An Occurrence at Owl Creek Bridge." Ambrose Bierce. 1891.

A civilian who jeopardizes his life for the Confederate cause, Peyton Farquhar awaits his execution at the beginning of this macabre story.

Wrists bound, eyes unbandaged, Farquhar stands on a railroad bridge surrounded by Union soldiers. Farquhar is about to be hanged for the crime of attempting to destroy the very bridge on which he stands. As the soldiers prepare for the execution, Farquhar tries with difficulty to think not of his death but of his wife and children. The ticking of his watch distracts him.

When a soldier steps off the plank beneath Farquhar's feet, the condemned man drops down and plunges into the water below the bridge. He regains consciousness, which he had lost when the noose first tightened around his throat. The sensation of pain and movement is quickly succeeded by the return of the faculty of thought, and he begins to struggle against death. He frees the cord from his wrists and then the noose from his neck, all the while sinking more deeply into Owl Creek. His senses seem to come alive in the water; he sees, hears, and feels more vividly than he ever had before.

When Farquhar rises to the surface, he is met by shots fired by soldiers on the bank and the bridge. A deep breath and a deep dive move him farther downstream. The Union soldiers even try a cannon shot to stop the prisoner's escape, but he hurls himself from the stream and into the safety of the forest.

Urged on by the thought of seeing his family again, Farquhar continues. The wilderness seems both familiar and uncannily foreign to him. The trees are black and looming, hedging him in; even the constellations of the stars seem strange and menacing. Unearthly sounds and whispers emanate from the forest on either side of his path, confusing him.

Soon the pain in his body becomes almost unbearable. His tongue, neck, and eyes have swollen. The faint path beneath his feet disappears entirely. Moments later, it seems, he stands before the gates of his home again. His wife rushes out eagerly to meet him, her arms open and welcoming. But as she approaches, a heavy blow strikes his back, and he is blinded by light, then plunged again into darkness.

The story closes with an image of Farquhar's lifeless body hanging from the bridge, twisting slowly in the breeze.

Farrago, Captain John. *Modern Chivalry.* H. H. Brackenridge. 1846.

Despite his extensive academic education, John Farrago decides that he has little knowledge of his "real world," late-eighteenth-century America. Much like the ancient knights-errant, Farrago, a member of his town's militia, takes his trusty manservant, TEAGUE O'REGAN, and sets off on a journey across Pennsylvania to discover the world he has been missing.

They do not journey far before stumbling upon a local election where a lowly weaver is on the verge of being elected to the state legislature. Horrified that such an important position should go to a common laborer, Captain Farrago dissuades the weaver from serving. No sooner is he finished than Captain Farrago's uneducated squire, Teague, decides that he himself will run for office. The captain explains the refined and academic nature of holding public office and is able to dissuade Teague before traveling onward.

A little farther along in their journey, Captain Farrago is irritated when Teague is again almost taken from him, this time by a member of the Society for Philosophers, who, seeing a rare bird that Teague has taken along with him, thinks him a genius. Captain Farrago, after explaining the awesome duties of a philosopher to Teague, is again able to convince the affable but dimwitted servant to remain at his side and continue on their journey.

While stopping at an inn a few days later, Captain Farrago must continue his struggle to keep Teague under his employ when an encounter with a clergyman makes Teague decide that now he must pursue a career in the church. In the course of his stay, the captain develops an attraction for a young woman, whom he courts. But the young woman is already promised to another suitor who promptly challenges the captain to a duel. After writing a note to his challenger, explaining frankly that he has no desire to shoot him or be shot at, Farrago takes Teague and flees.

Very shortly afterward, the two of them arrive in Philadelphia—at that time the nation's capital; Teague disappears here. Remembering his servant's previous ambitions, Captain Farrago visits a local political rally, a Society of Philosophers meeting, and the local churches, all to no avail. He finally discovers Teague at the theater where he has joined a local acting troupe. Teague later returns to Captain Farrago after being fired for making a pass at the manager's daughter.

The captain finally decides that he should help to further his servant's ambitions, and he hires private tutors and dance instructors. In the hopes of making Teague a

gentleman, Captain Farrago also helps by teaching him about decorum and refinement. After a meeting with the President of the United States, the Captain is able to secure a position for Teague as revenue collector.

As soon as Teague and Farrago arrive in the appointed district, however, a mob, angry at the new whiskey tax imposed by the government, carries Teague off for tarring and feathering. Government troops arrive too late, and they arrest Captain Farrago on suspicion of aiding in the mini-rebellion. After impressing his innocence upon the arresting officers, Captain Farrago is released to return home alone, now educated in the ways of the world.

Farragut, Ezekiel. *Falconer.* John Cheever. 1977.

A drug addict convicted of killing his brother, former professor Ezekiel Farragut spends most of the time span of this novel in a New York state jail. Although confined, Farragut, as everyone calls him, wanders outside the walls of Falconer Correctional Facility in his mind.

Falconer is a prison, but its social life is as active as that which Farragut left behind in his home of Southwick, Connecticut. The men who live and work in Farragut's small corner of the prison—Tiny the guard, and the inmates (the Cuckold, Chicken Number Two, the Stone, and the Mad Dog Killer)—become Farragut's new neighbors as they suffer through the banalities of bad food, prison lawyers, and venereal disease tests.

Farragut has been confined only a short time when he meets Jody, a young man serving a long sentence for kidnapping and robbery. After a month their friendship becomes a sexual relationship, and Farragut finds himself falling in love. Although he tries to convince Jody and himself that the affection he feels for the younger man is paternal, Farragut's dependence on Jody grows stronger, and Jody's eventual escape leaves a gap in Farragut's life that he neither anticipated nor wishes to acknowledge.

Although Farragut clearly loves Jody, a homosexual relationship inspires in him two other deeply uncomfortable responses: the fear of narcissism and the fear of death. The women Farragut had so restlessly pursued charmed him with their mysteriousness. No matter how well he thought he knew his wife or his mistresses, they remained unfathomable. Love of a man, Farragut imagines, may simply be love of what is familiar: himself. He also believes that no matter how much pleasure it gives him to love Jody, doing so somehow courts death and is as "unnatural as the rites and procedures in a funeral parlor."

Thoughts of death and decline occupy Farragut's mind much of the time in the form of memories of his family. For most of Farragut's childhood his parents had been rich, and the family wore its affluence in the graceful manner of old, wealthy families. When the family fortunes disintegrated, Farragut's mother tried a number of schemes to earn money while her husband tried to cover his depression with an air of shabby gentility. When his father threatened suicide, Farragut did his best to protect the man, although it was difficult to love him.

Before he was imprisoned, Farragut flirted with his own death, abusing heroin and alcohol. Addiction provided him with a sweet form of escape even as it poisoned his body, harmed his teaching career, and strained his marriage. The addiction also led to the murder that landed him in prison, since without the drugs Farragut could not control his emotions. When his brother screamed at him that their father did not love Farragut and had tried to persuade his mother to have an abortion when she was pregnant with him, Farragut allowed the release of all the anger and resentment he had felt toward his father and brother, and he struck his brother over the head with a fireplace iron.

One man's death brought Farragut to prison, and, ironically, it is another man's death that provides the means for his escape. When a fellow inmate dies, Farragut takes the man's place in his body bag and is carried out of the walls of Falconer. The novel ends as Farragut boards a bus headed into town, elated by his first taste of freedom.

Father. *Ragtime.* E. L. Doctorow. 1974.

Although Father is never referred to by a proper name in the novel, he is an amateur explorer known throughout the world for daring and adventurous missions. A retired army officer with combat experience in the Philippines, where he fought against the Moro guerrillas during the Spanish-American War, Father nonetheless claims that his most valorous feat took place not on a distant mountain peak or battlefield but in downtown New York City. In J. Pierpont Morgan's priceless library on Thirty-sixth Street, Father acts as the mediator between city officials and a highly skilled, murderous terrorist group. The library has been mined and wired with bombs; Father seeks to assuage the wounded sensibilities of the terrorists, who feel that the rights of their leader, COALHOUSE WALKER, JR., have been usurped as a result of racism.

Father is a careful, industrious, and sober man whose flag manufacturing firm and fireworks company provide a very comfortable existence for his son, The LITTLE BOY, and wife. The success of his marriage is due in part to his extended absences when he engages in conquering natural wonders. During his involvement in Commander Robert Perry's expedition to the North Pole, his wife discovers a newborn infant buried in the garden of their house in New Rochelle, New York. Upon identifying the child's errant mother, a domestic servant named Sarah, Mother decides to take in both mother and child. Meanwhile, Father returns from the Arctic a changed man. His health has suffered substantially during the expedition, and his position of authority in his family has been undermined by his lengthy absence. Nevertheless, he is able to rise to the challenge of the Coalhouse Walker, Jr., saga shortly after his return.

Walker is driven to violence when his car is vandalized and Sarah, his fiancée, is murdered in a misguided attempt to help him. He has organized a band of vigilantes and taken over J. Pierpont Morgan's library when Father is called in to act as a mediator. Father is amazed to find that one of the six members of Walker's group is his own brother-in-law, known in the novel as MOTHER'S YOUNGER BROTHER. The young man is sympathetic to Walker's wounded honor and is well versed in the art of bomb-making, thanks to his experience as a designer of fireworks at Father's firm. With the help of fellow mediator Booker T. Washington, Father successfully convinces Walker to modify his demands and surrender to the authorities, and the library is saved.

Father is last seen on board the sinking *Lusitania* en route to Europe where he is to impart to the United States' allies in World War II the advanced ballistic information that his errant brother-in-law had discovered.

Fathers, Sam. "The Bear." William Faulkner. 1950.

Sam Fathers is a sage and noble woodsman whose spiritual life is integrally connected with the Mississippi wilderness, where he chooses to live in a humble shack. The son of a legendary Chickasaw chief, Ikkemotubbe, and a quadroon, Sam is sold by his father to Lucius Quintus Carothers McCaslin, a wealthy plantation owner. Sam and his mother are eventually granted freedom, but Sam continues to associate with the McCaslins. As an old man, Sam takes the youngest, ISAAC "IKE" McCASLIN, under his wing with the idea of teaching the boy about the spiritual power of nature and the ethics of hunting. Sam foresees that technological progress will one day destroy the Edenic life of the backwoods.

The most notable attraction of the wilderness is a towering bear named Old Ben, whose tracks reveal a mangled, two-toed foot deformed by a trap. Nevertheless, Old Ben manages to consistently elude the hunters. Sam has successfully tracked the bear but has refrained from killing him. To Sam, the bear symbolizes the grandeur of nature.

Sam trains and traps with an enormous mongrel dog called Lion. Although Sam loves the bear more than his fellow human beings, he also senses that one day Lion will hold Old Ben at bay while the hunters kill him. The fated day arrives, and BOON HOGGANBECK, a shoddy hunter, is given the opportunity to destroy the cornered bear. He buries a knife deep into the bear's fur while Lion hugs the bear with the wildness of embracing lovers.

The momentous occasion proves too much for Sam, who falls to the ground and experiences something like a stroke. A doctor later diagnoses the condition as mere exhaustion, but Sam dies shortly thereafter. At his request Sam is buried beneath a platform that houses a sacred Chickasaw artifact. True to his predictions, it isn't long before a lumber company buys and strips the land.

Fawcett, Ralph. *The Mountain Lion.* Jean Stafford. 1947.

The rebellious Ralph Fawcett, the only male in his home, is reared with his three sisters Molly, Rachel, and Leah by their widowed mother. Ralph and Molly are both scornful of their snobbish, prim mother and older sisters. The two of them band together in order to defy and provoke the rest of the family. Growing up, both are small and sickly, and neither is very popular at school. Later they spend time at their uncle's ranch where Ralph grows healthy and confident and the two become distant.

Ralph and Molly enjoy Grandpa Kenyon's visits. A rugged, elderly man, he owns several ranches, and his company provides a welcome change to the overbearing rectitude of Mrs. Fawcett and her two older daughters. When he dies during one of his yearly visits, Ralph and Molly are devastated. At his funeral, they meet their uncle Claude for the first time. Ralph follows Uncle Claude around while he is there, and Claude invites both children to his ranch in the summer. At first the overprotective Mrs. Fawcett refuses to let them go, but after she discovers that a widow and her daughter reside there as well, she finally agrees. It will be their first trip alone.

Even though Ralph and Molly are very close, they fight often. This fighting intensifies when they arrive at the ranch. Both are scared of learning to ride horses. Ralph gradually learns to ride and starts to spend a great deal of time with his uncle Claude. Although he has a few embarrassing moments on horseback, he eventually adjusts. Under the influence of his uncle, Ralph stops wearing his glasses and begins to fill out.

After their first visit, they return to the ranch each summer, and it becomes a part of their lives. Ralph is still somewhat eccentric, but he enjoys masculine pursuits such as hunting. He grows away from Molly, who has changed little over time. When Mrs. Fawcett decides to take Leah and Rachel on a year-long trip around the world, she sends Molly and Ralph to stay at the ranch.

One day while he and Uncle Claude are hunting, they spot a mountain lion. They spend the whole season trying to find and kill the big cat. Ralph wants very badly to be the one to kill it as proof of his manhood. Finally, Ralph and Uncle Claude find the mountain lion. They fire their rifles at the same time, but when they examine the dead cat, they find only one bullet. Moments later they find Molly's lifeless body nearby—she was killed accidentally by one of their bullets. Ralph goes into shock, feeling that he is to blame even though he was not aware that Molly was even in the area.

Fay, Felix. *Moon-Calf.* Floyd Dell. 1957.

Felix Fay is the youngest child in a family of four, and as the baby of the family, he receives a special kind of attention. His mother reads him marvelous stories of adventure, and when he is not lost in this world, Felix imagines and playacts his own fantastic tales. Before the age of four Felix discovers he can read by himself, and the excited family prepares to send him to school in the upcoming fall. Only after an ordeal in which he beats up the town bully who had been harassing him does school become tolerable for Felix. He discovers the town library and tricks the librarian into lending him books for adult readers. After a fire destroys the Fays' house, he overhears a boy telling a tall tale about him: that he rushed back into the burning house to rescue his precious books. Felix is secretly proud of the story.

Although Felix is not close to his family or very social at school, he develops a few intimate friends and becomes attracted to utopian ideals. The Fay family moves into a house owned by an elderly man who has a granddaughter, Rose. One day Rose discovers Felix reading in the attic, and they go outside together. In the woods near their house, Rose puts on an impromptu dramatic performance, using lines she learned from her mother who was an actress. Felix is enchanted by her; however, after Rose and Felix spend the night in the woods together, Rose is sent away by her grandfather. Felix betrays her inexplicably by not going to the last meeting they had arranged before her departure.

When the family moves to a nearby town called Vickley, Felix falls under the spell of a young man named Stephen Frazer. Like Felix, Stephen is widely read and passionately interested in changing the world. Stephen is the first to nudge Felix away from utopianism and toward a more practical form of socialist political thinking. The friendship fades when Felix leaves school to work in a candy factory where he falls in love with Margaret, a mocking, witty, and beautiful girl of seventeen. Both friendships, with Margaret and Stephen, are broken off abruptly when Felix's parents separate, and he must move away from Vickley.

In Port Royal, living with his brother Ed and his wife Alice, Felix begins a new life. He experiences a phase of intense creativity, and Helen Raymond, the town librarian, takes an interest in his poetry and helps him get it published. Felix soon redirects his interests, however, and after a stint at a candy factory, takes a job at the Port Royal *News.*

With his talent for writing and his critical eye, Felix does quite well at the *News.* One aspect of his job is to visit law firms and question lawyers for interesting material. At the office of the lawyer James Bassett, Felix meets Joyce Tennant, whom he mistakes for a stenographer. When Felix visits her house, however, he discovers that she is Bassett's niece and was in his office that day only to "see what it was like." Joyce, a rebellious girl who was recently expelled from Oberlin College, becomes Felix's first lover. They conceal their romance in a little cabin on an island belonging to her uncle.

When Felix loses his job at the *News* because the romance has been distracting him, he goes to his friend Tom's farm to write a novel. During this time Felix and Joyce see each other once a week, but they become increasingly estranged. Upon his return to Port Royal, he discovers that Joyce has decided to marry her other suitor, a more sensible (and wealthier) young man. Joyce comforts Felix by telling him that he has outgrown both her and Port Royal and needs to move on. Mastering his despair, Felix decides that she is right, and he looks forward to beginning again in Chicago.

Fearless Frank. *Deadwood Dick, the Prince of the Road.* Edward J. Wheeler. 1877.

At the beginning of the first book in this nineteenth-century dime novel series, the buckskin-clad Fearless Frank is the youngest member of a wagon train heading west for "gold country." Fearless Frank's history remains unknown until the first book's melodramatic conclusion when we learn about his long separation from his love, Anita Harris, sister of the lawless masked rider DEAD-WOOD DICK.

After riding silently all afternoon, the men of the wagon train suddenly hear low, faint cries coming from a thicket. Fearless Frank bravely insists on investigating. When the callous leader of the train refuses to wait for him, Frank goes anyway and is left behind. In the thicket Fearless Frank discovers a young woman stripped to the waist and tied to a stake, her back covered with bleeding welts. He leaps forward to rescue her and sees Sitting Bull, the sadistic Sioux Indian Chief. After some negotiations, Sitting Bull agrees to free the girl. When she regains consciousness, Fearless Frank learns that her name is Alice Terry and that she came west to meet her father in the Black Hills. Frank and Alice start out together for the town of Deadwood.

On their way to Deadwood they search for Alice's father but are unable to find him. Then one day Fearless Frank encounters Ned Harris (who, when disguised, is actually Deadwood Dick). From their darkening expressions it is clear these men are old enemies who must now settle their conflict in a duel. Acknowledging that Harris hates him because of a wrong he did to Harris and his kin, Fearless Frank asks whether an unnamed woman is still alive. Harris replies that she is but that her life is a blank and she grieves terribly. Fearless Frank asks to see her, but Harris refuses to allow it. In the duel, Fearless Frank shoots Harris. After kneeling remorsefully beside the body, Fearless Frank continues toward Deadwood with Alice.

Fearless Frank and Alice arrive in a bustling valley where Harry Redburn and his partner General Nix are mining gold. When Redburn mentions the name "Anita," Fearless Frank gasps and asks to see her. Redburn refuses, sensing something strange about Fearless Frank's reaction, but he allows Alice Terry to stay in the log cabin with

him, Nix, and Anita. Alice is overjoyed to find Nix, who is her long-lost father. One night she reveals that Ned Harris, Anita's brother, was killed in a duel by Fearless Frank. Anita faints, and when she recovers, she vows to punish Fearless Frank herself.

Fearless Frank sits on the rocks and thinks deeply about his life. He has seen Anita around the cabin, and now he longs to settle down with her. His thoughts are interrupted by Calamity Jane, who orders him to help her save Deadwood Dick from the men who are about to murder him. Following Deadwood Dick's rescue, everyone meets at the cabin and all untold stories are revealed. Fearless Frank, whose real name is Justin McKenzie, had married Anita, but because of his lust for gold, he lied about their marriage in order to inherit the wealth of his next of kin, an evil fur trader who ordered him to swear that Anita was not his wife. When the fur trader discovered the truth, he wrote McKenzie out of his will, and McKenzie found himself poor and without his true love. Now, in the presence of Anita and all the others, he acknowledges her as his lawfully wedded wife. Admitting that he misunderstood the situation, Deadwood Dick—who is truly Ned Harris and was not killed in the duel—happily approves of McKenzie's reunion with his sister. Anita and McKenzie embrace and are remarried in Deadwood.

Federner, Anna. *Three Lives.* Gertrude Stein. 1909.

Anna Federner is a domestic servant who emigrates as a young woman from Germany to the town of Bridgepoint in the southern United States. Anna's reigning characteristics—her "goodness"—are her strict old-world sense of propriety and her reckless devotion to her friends and employers. Her selfless generosity ultimately causes her demise.

Anna's first employer in Bridgepoint is Mary Wadsmith, a timid, lazy woman burdened with the upbringing of her dead brother's two children, Edgar and Jane Wadsmith. In the course of the six years that Anna works for Miss Mary, Anna's health progressively deteriorates due to her self-imposed regimen of labor and worry. Although Anna resists Miss Mary's attempts to convince her to take better care of herself, she finally agrees to see Dr. Shonjen, who performs an operation from which she recovers with patient docility. But as soon as her convalescence is completed, she reverts back to compulsive work and ill health.

When young Jane Wadsmith marries Mr. Goldthwaite and sets up her own household, Miss Mary decides to make her home with her newlywed niece. Although guilt-ridden at the prospect of abandoning Miss Mary, Anna terminates her service for fear that she will not be able to run the new Mrs. Goldthwaite's household in her accustomed domineering fashion. Anna is then engaged as Dr. Shonjen's housekeeper. The doctor's mischievous, merry ways delight Anna by giving her constant opportunities to scold him, an activity that appeals to her self-righteous sense of propriety; and Shonjen, in turn, enjoys the scoldings of his persnickety employee.

During this period Anna habitually spends her free time with her best friend Julia Lehntman who is ambiguously described as the romantic element in Anna's life. Mrs. Lehntman shocks Anna by devoting her energies to midwifery, helping young girls in trouble by taking them into her house and supporting them until they can return to their homes unburdened of their disgrace. Despite her prudery, Anna often exhausts her own savings by providing Mrs. Lehntman with funds. But Anna cannot countenance Mrs. Lehntman's actions when she adopts the baby boy of one of her secret charges. Anna stops visiting Julia and begins to devote her energies to Mrs. Drehten, one of Dr. Shonjen's patients.

In contrast to Anna and Mrs. Lehntman's "sacred" friendship, there is no "fever" in the relationship between Anna and Mrs. Drehten. But Anna finds solace for the wound caused by her breach with Mrs. Lehntman by devoting herself to the sickly Mrs. Drehten's seven children and alcoholic husband. Eventually, unable to stay away from the only romance she has ever experienced, she renews her relations with Mrs. Lehntman and helps her buy and renovate a larger home in which to conduct her business. Shortly thereafter Mrs. Lehntman begins working with a mysterious doctor, a possible abortionist, and once again Anna breaks off relations. The romance, too, has ended, because Anna has found a new person upon whom to lavish her attentions, Miss Mathilda.

Miss Mathilda is Anna's last employer, and with her Anna is happier than she has ever been. But this relationship shares the fate of all her attachments when Miss Mathilda moves out of Bridgepoint. The victim of one separation too many, a broken Anna decides to abandon the role of domestic servant. She takes in boarders for whom she slaves as relentlessly as ever. Working herself to the threshold of death's door, she once again agrees to an operation from which she does not awaken.

Feiler, Clarence. "The Gonzaga Manuscripts." Saul Bellow. 1956.

Clarence Feiler is obsessed with the works of Spanish poet Manuel Gonzaga. When he travels to Madrid, Clarence learns that numerous poems of the Spanish master remain in the hands of Gonzaga's mistress. His curiosity about these poems, which Gonzaga gave to his mistress before his death in the Spanish Revolution, lead him into a long and complicated search for the missing Gonzaga manuscripts. Ultimately, Clarence discovers not the literature he has so idealistically sought but the Spaniards' powerful anti-American sentiments and their negative perceptions of the American people.

Arriving in Madrid, Clarence pays a visit to Guzmán el Nido, who was Gonzaga's comrade-in-arms in the Moroccan War and his literary executor. Surprisingly, el Nido shares none of Clarence's enthusiasm for Gonzaga's work. When Clarence expresses his desire to find the missing manuscripts, el Nido refuses to reveal their whereabouts. Changing the subject, he invites Clarence to a dinner party to take place a few nights later.

That evening, while eating at his boardinghouse, Clarence gets into a heated argument with a young red-haired woman about American culture, political philosophy, and the atomic bomb. Frustrated and angry, he returns to his bedroom and vows to find the manuscripts and leave Spain as soon as possible. The next day he visits Miss Ungar, an attractive young woman, to get currency exchanged on the black market. Clarence is intrigued by Miss Ungar, and he invites her to dinner. Over their meal he explains to her his mission regarding the Gonzaga manuscripts. He is surprised when Miss Ungar warns him that his attempts will be resisted by the Spanish people. Returning that night, Clarence finds his room has been searched by local police. Furious, he complains to the owner; the owner makes empty apologies and asks him, gently but suspiciously, why the police are trailing him.

Clarence attends el Nido's dinner party and listens as el Nido and his friends make mildly insulting remarks about America. Still determined to learn where Gonzaga's poems are, Clarence represses his temper. Finally, el Nido tells him that the manuscripts are in fact love letters that Gonzaga wrote to a countess who, like Gonzaga, also died in the revolution. El Nido gives Clarence the address of his cousin, Don Luis Polvo, who might be of some assistance to him. Clarence writes to Polvo who lives by himself in the town of Alaciá, and Polvo writes back, inviting Clarence to visit. Believing that the elusive Gonzaga manuscripts are now within his grasp, Clarence packs his bags. He plans to exit the country as soon as he retrieves Gonzaga's work from Polvo.

When he arrives in Alaciá, however, Clarence must first endure an extended tour of Polvo's village and listen while Polvo gives a detailed account of the village's history. Frustrated and impatient, Clarence tries to get Polvo to give him information about the manuscripts, but to no avail. Polvo eventually reveals that he owns a large share of a uranium mine. Clarence is horrified to learn that Polvo, thinking that Americans are primarily concerned with the development of atomic warfare, believed Clarence had contacted him to buy uranium. Polvo knows nothing about Manuel Gonzaga.

Devastated, Clarence returns to his hotel in Madrid. He is no closer to attaining the Gonzaga manuscripts now than when he first arrived.

Fidelman, Arthur. *Pictures of Fidelman: An Exhibition.* Bernard Malamud. 1958.

This picaresque novel sketches six periods in Arthur Fidelman's life and work. Fidelman travels to Italy to prepare a study of Giotto with the financial support of his older sister Bessie, who raised him from the age of ten.

When Fidelman first arrives in Rome, Susskind, a Jewish refugee, accosts him because he recognizes Fidelman as a fellow Jew. The irrepressible beggar follows him through the city, demanding that Fidelman accept some responsibility for him by giving him his extra suit. When Susskind steals Fidelman's first chapter on Giotto, Fidelman searches relentlessly for the thief, delaying his departure for Florence. Unable to continue work without his first chapter, he decides to relinquish his suit in the hope of retrieving his manuscript. He finds that Susskind has destroyed it, but in a burst of insight, he gratefully offers Susskind the suit and turns from research to art.

Remaining in Rome, Fidelman shares a rundown apartment with another artist, Annamarie Oliovino, with whom he falls instantly in love. Although she treats him with contempt and carelessness, he tries to win her approval by painting her portrait. Annamarie is so moved by the portrait that she seduces him, only to cast him from her bed when he ejaculates prematurely. After this episode she further harasses and degrades Fidelman until, in desperation and unable to work, he dresses up as a priest to paint a self-portrait. When Annamarie sees Fidelman as a priest, she throws herself at his feet, begs forgiveness, and requests penance. Fidelman as father confessor pronounces that her penance is to sleep with him, which she does on the condition that he remain in costume.

When Fidelman botches an attempt to pickpocket a tourist, he finds himself a captive slave in a Milano whorehouse where he cleans toilets and gambles away his wages. The padrone, Angelo, and his lover Scarpio devise a plan to steal Titian's "Venus of Urbino" from a local museum by replacing it with a forgery that they force Fidelman to paint. After much difficulty Fidelman finishes a stunning reproduction. In the midst of stealing the original, he knocks Scarpio unconscious and proudly rows across the lake with his own copy.

Years after arriving in Italy, the now impoverished Fidelman lives in Florence painting and carving madonnas to sell to tourists. He attempts his greatest work, "Mother and Child," struggling for years to recreate his mother's face from a snapshot taken in his childhood. He finally paints the face of his lover, the prostitute Esmerelda, who supports and keeps house for him. Ludovico, her former pimp and a self-proclaimed art expert, recognizes the genius of Fidelman's masterwork when it is completed and hopes to profit by it. Yet on Ludovico's suggestion, Fidelman tampers with the finished product and ruins the painting. In the morning, realizing what he has done, he destroys the painting and stabs himself in the stomach.

Next, Fidelman travels throughout Italy as a sculptor, charging ten lire for a view of the square holes he digs. A stranger, mocking Fidelman, knocks him over the head, and he dreams of Susskind as a Christ figure to whom he acts as a Judas betrayer. In this dreamlike state he also visits his sister for the last time before her death, emerging to bid her good-bye from a cave in her basement where he has been painting for years.

Finally, in Venice, middle-aged Fidelman is reduced to carrying people on his back across flooded streets for money. He begins an affair with an older married woman but becomes the lover of her husband Beppo. A glassblower by trade, Beppo seduces Fidelman, tells him to destroy his derivative art, and teaches him his own craft. Fidelman's love for Beppo exceeds any he has previously known. Taking Beppo's advice, he approaches glassblowing with the same fervor as painting, and although Beppo ridicules his pretension, he succeeds in producing one great work in glass. When Beppo's wife pleads with Fidelman to leave because he is destroying her family, Fidelman agrees and finally returns to the United States, where he continues his work as a glassblower and enjoys affairs with both men and women.

Finch, Atticus. *To Kill a Mockingbird.* Harper Lee. 1960.

Atticus Finch, a small-town lawyer, stands out as one of the most admirable fathers in American literature. Selected to defend a black man charged with the rape of a white woman in an insular southern town, Atticus must counter the hypocrisy, bigotry, and violence that erupts with compassion, integrity, and wisdom. As a father, Atticus preserves his children's faith in the American justice system and humankind as they encounter the cynical attitudes of neighbors and relatives.

Set during the early Depression years in the town of Maycomb, Alabama, the novel revolves around the accusation and subsequent trial of Tom Robinson, a decent, family-oriented black man charged with the rape of Mayella Ewell. Ewell is the daughter of Bob Ewell, a white man who spends his relief check on alcohol, forcing his motherless children to scrounge for food in the town dump. Appointed by the court to defend Robinson, Atticus determines to truly defend him. Keenly aware that he and his family will face verbal and physical abuse and that he will most likely lose the case, Atticus views Robinson's trial as the once-in-a-lifetime case that will prove his integrity as a lawyer to himself and to his children, JEAN LOUISE "SCOUT" (FINCH) and JEM (FINCH).

Once the townsfolk learn of Atticus's sincere intentions regarding Robinson, the Finch family begins to suffer the repercussions of "Maycomb's usual disease." Scout, Atticus's eight-year-old tomboy, defends her father against the charge of being a "nigger lover" as her classmates repeat comments that they have overheard from adults at home. Admonished by Atticus to "fight with [her] head" rather than her fists, Scout must do what she has never done in her life—walk away from a fight and passively bear the appellation "Coward!" Atticus's sister, Alexandra, declares that Atticus will be the "ruination" of the family.

In the carnival atmosphere that pervades Maycomb on the day of the Robinson trial, Atticus proves beyond all reasonable doubt that the defendant is innocent of all charges against him. The attorney first establishes that Mayella was savagely beaten by someone who led with his left hand; that her father, although ambidextrous, is mostly left-handed; and that Robinson's left hand is a shriveled, useless stump due to a childhood accident. Having shown Robinson physically incapable of delivering the blows that Mayella suffered, Atticus further reveals the true sequence of events that had been played out in the Ewell home on the day of the alleged rape.

Through the testimony of nineteen-year-old Mayella, Atticus exposes the tragic story of poverty, ignorance, and longing. With no mother to guide her and no friends to console her, Mayella, trapped in filth and squalor, leads a wretchedly lonely life. Emblematic of the young woman's sorrowful existence is the bewildering presence of a row of slop jars containing lovely red geraniums in the otherwise filthy, rodent-infested front yard that the Ewells call home.

Seeking to alleviate her misery, she chose the most unacceptable path for a southern white woman: "She tempted a Negro." The code that mattered little to her before she acted, Atticus argues in his closing statement, "came crashing down on her afterwards." Mayella's own guilt and her father's violent anger at her actions have their day in court. Atticus pleads with the all-white jury to put aside its prejudices and acquit Robinson, whose only crime has been to feel sorry for a white woman. Yet, in the face of the defendant's obvious innocence, the jury returns a guilty verdict.

The Ewells' white complexion temporarily erases the class prejudice of the jury. Their victory proves transitory, however. Having recognized the Ewells' privileged position over a black man, Maycomb perfunctorily returns them to their "white trash" status and takes no more notice of them.

Meanwhile, the convicted Tom Robinson, lacking faith or hope in an appeal to a higher court, attempts a reckless escape from prison and is mercilessly gunned down by the guards.

Finally, making good on his threat to avenge himself against Atticus, Bob Ewell stalks Jem and Scout as they return from a Halloween carnival. A mysterious benefactor saves the children but not before Ewell gives Scout some bumps and bruises and breaks Jem's left arm. Later, Heck Tate, the sheriff, finds Ewell lying dead from a stab wound. After a long discussion, during much of which Atticus mistakenly believes that Jem killed Ewell, he learns that Boo Radley, the eccentric recluse from next door, came to the children's rescue, making sure that Ewell would never again hurt anyone. In deference to Boo's extraordinary shyness, Sheriff Tate convinces Atticus to

agree to an altered version of the night's events: that Ewell accidentally fell on his own knife while trying to commit murder. Atticus thanks Boo for saving his children's lives. Scout returns her rescuer to his home while Atticus prepares to spend the night beside Jem's bed.

Finch, Jean Louise "Scout." *To Kill a Mockingbird.* Harper Lee. 1960.

Jean Louise "Scout" Finch, the tomboy narrator of this novel, paints a lively and disturbing portrait of small-town America in her story of a murder trial in a southern town. Narrating retrospectively from adulthood, Jean Louise reanimates the village of her childhood during the early Depression years. She combines the insight and irony of age with the naivete and honesty of childhood to provide delightful, often poignant vignettes of the characters who people Maycomb County, Alabama.

Spanning several years, the novel opens the summer before Scout enters the first grade with the arrival of Dill, the imaginative and precocious nephew of a neighboring woman. It is this "pocket Merlin" who first interests Scout and her ten-year-old brother JEM (FINCH) in attempting to lure from his home Boo Radley, the mysterious recluse who lives down the street from the Finches. Their imaginations fed by the myths of Boo's ghoulish appearance and behavior—he is said to be six and a half feet tall with bloodstained hands and yellow rotten teeth, and to live on a diet of raw squirrels and cats—Scout, Dill, and Jem spend long summer days scheming to get a look at the hermit.

Eventually Scout begins school with Miss Caroline, a brand-new teacher who dislikes the fact that Scout has been taught to read and write by her lawyer father ATTICUS (FINCH) and the Finch cook, Calpurnia. Each day after school the children dash past the Radley house mindful of all they have heard. As Scout's first year of school draws to an end, she makes a discovery. Hidden in the knothole of an oak tree that fronts the Radley homestead, the first grader spies two sticks of Wrigley's Double-Mint Chewing Gum. These findings prove the first in a succession of items that appear in the old tree: Indianhead pennies, twine, soap dolls, a spelling medal, a pocket watch. Unbeknownst to Scout and her brother, they have had their first encounter with Boo Radley. It is not to be their last.

Events of the adult world interrupt the children's romantic exploits with Boo. Atticus is appointed to defend Tom Robinson, a black man accused of raping Mayella Ewell, a nineteen-year-old white woman. Atticus believes Robinson is innocent and determines to defend him as he would a white man. This decision results in mean-spirited reactions from the residents of Maycomb County. Honor-bound, Scout defends her father against charges of being a "nigger lover" and finds herself ordered by Atticus to fight with her mind rather than with her fists. He explains that in the months ahead he and they will be fighting their friends and neighbors. Yet, regardless of the outcome, they must not hold grudges or become bitter.

When the trial date arrives, Maycomb's response to the situation escalates from mere name-calling to near violence. The night before the trial is to begin, Robinson, who has been held outside Maycomb during the intervening months, is returned to the county jail. Warned that a group of farmers from the backwoods of the county intends to remove Robinson and lynch him, Atticus prepares to spend the night on the jailhouse steps to protect the accused man. As expected, the Old Saram bunch, bolstered by moonshine, descend on the jail after sending the sheriff on a "snipe hunt."

Alarmed by Atticus's mid-evening departure from home, the Finch children and Dill pursue him downtown and watch secretly as the lynch mob arrives. As Atticus attempts to dissuade the group of men, led by Mr. Cunningham, a farmer for whom he has performed legal work, Scout dashes from her hiding place. Bewildered by the congregation's unenthusiastic response to her arrival, the eight-year-old attempts to normalize matters by addressing Cunningham. Slowly, confronted by Scout's earnest and naive efforts at conciliation, the mob dissolves and leaves Atticus to thank God for his daughter's innocence.

On the day of the Robinson trial, all of Maycomb County makes its way to the courthouse square, arriving in buckboard wagons, on horseback, and on foot, carrying cold biscuits and fried chicken. The three young comrades, too, join the throng at the trial and sit in the balcony among the black citizens.

The children watch as Atticus shows not only that Robinson did not deliver, indeed could not, the awful beating that Mayella suffered but also that Robinson committed no rape. In fact, the shrewd lawyer proves that the desperately lonely girl "tempted" Robinson and was savagely beaten by her father when he surprised her in the act. Encouraged by Atticus's legal acumen and Robinson's obvious innocence, the youngsters are shocked when the jury convicts Robinson despite the undeniable evidence.

Court adjourns and Maycomb returns to its daily routines. But Mayella's father, Bob Ewell, tries to seek revenge on Atticus by attacking Scout and Jem as they return from a Halloween carnival. Bruising Scout and breaking Jem's left arm, Ewell is prevented from fatally harming the children by a mysterious man. Scout and the others soon realize that Ewell has been stabbed to death by none other than Arthur "Boo" Radley. Heck Tate, the sheriff, and Atticus agree that Boo's extraordinary shyness exempts him from public disclosure. As Scout later explains to Atticus, it would be "like shootin' a mockingbird" to bring Boo under the cruel public eye. The sheriff deems Ewell's death accidental by his own hand. Fulfilling a long-desired

wish, Scout, with a display of southern charm, takes Boo's arm and walks him home.

Finch, Jem. *To Kill a Mockingbird.* Harper Lee. 1960.

Jem Finch passes from childhood to manhood during his father's most difficult legal case. Together with his younger sister, JEAN LOUISE "SCOUT" (FINCH), and their summertime companion, Dill Harris, he witnesses the hypocrisy that overtakes his hometown when a black man is accused of raping a young white woman. Throughout the ordeal, Jem must combat the bitterness, disillusionment, and cynicism that threaten to defeat him.

Spanning the early years of the Depression, the novel opens with the exploits of Jem, Scout, and Dill, who spend their summer days plotting ways to entice Arthur "Boo" Radley, the neighborhood recluse, out of his home. So enchanted are the children with the myths that surround Boo that they create dramas based on what they know of his life, and eventually they attempt to catch a glimpse of him. ATTICUS FINCH's new case interrupts their siege against Boo's privacy.

Jem's father, Atticus, has been appointed to defend Tom Robinson, a black man accused of raping Mayella Ewell, a white woman. The months that precede the Robinson trial bring Jem harsh abuse from neighbors and friends who are angered by Atticus's determination to defend Robinson as he would any white client. In the face of "Maycomb's usual disease," Jem begins to realize the horror of racial prejudice and the resulting hypocrisy.

Although he observes the angry mob his father faces down the night before the trial, Jem's belief in his father and the American justice system prevails throughout the proceedings. As Atticus shows that Robinson neither raped nor beat Mayella Ewell, Jem becomes convinced that an acquittal of the black man will be forthcoming. Instead, he is shocked to learn that Robinson's innocence plays no role in the trial. The color of Robinson's skin separates him from justice. The members of the all-white jury sympathize with the Ewells and convict Robinson despite incontrovertible evidence of his innocence.

After the trial Jem struggles to understand the events that have altered his faith in the people of his hometown and in the justice system. Robinson's subsequent escape attempt and resulting death only serve to complicate Jem's struggles with the issue. After an intense conversation with Atticus, during which the lawyer enumerates the positive aspects of Robinson's trial, Jem manages to regain some sense of hope in people and institutional fairness.

In the meantime, although given the satisfaction of Robinson's conviction, Bob Ewell has been returned to the status of "po' white trash" by Maycomb's finest and swears to avenge himself on Atticus. He seeks to do so on Halloween night by stalking Jem and Scout as they return from a Halloween carnival. He brutally breaks Jem's arm and renders him unconscious, but Scout escapes and finds help.

As the affair unfolds, the sheriff discovers Ewell lying dead from a stab wound. After some conversation, he and Atticus agree that the town recluse, Boo Radley, rescued the children but that his heroism must be kept a secret for his own peace of mind. Scout witnesses all these events and comments that Jem, who remains unconscious throughout the proceedings, will be upset that he has missed what will turn out to be his only opportunity to see Boo Radley. Atticus takes up a vigil next to Jem's bed, and the novel closes with Scout's observation that Atticus would be next to Jem all night and "he would be there when he waked up in the morning."

Finchley, Sondra. *An American Tragedy.* Theodore Dreiser. 1925.

Sondra Finchley, smart, vain, and attractive, is the daughter of a wealthy manufacturer in the town of Lycurgus, New York. Part of a new, fast social set, Sondra is a friend of Bella Griffiths, whose father, Samuel, owns a large shirt and collar factory. On a visit to the Griffiths', Sondra sees CLYDE GRIFFITHS, a poor cousin from the West who is working at the factory. Mrs. Griffiths explains that Clyde has not had many "advantages" and that they are giving him a chance to improve his life. Sondra notices Clyde's striking good looks and feels it is unfortunate that his social position is so low.

One day while out driving, Sondra calls to Clyde on the sidewalk, thinking he is Gilbert Griffiths, Samuel's brutally snobbish son who looks almost exactly like Clyde and with whom Sondra is temperamentally at odds. Sondra realizes her mistake but then asks Clyde if he wants a ride anyway. Since Clyde betrays an obsequious, ingenuous affection for her, Sondra sees that she can easily manipulate him. In order to spite Gilbert, who resents Clyde's presence in their family and in the town, Sondra decides to invite Clyde to a dance. Soon Sondra actually finds herself admiring Clyde, but because of his social position she cannot manifest her admiration publicly.

Since Clyde was at this dance, others assume that it is acceptable to invite him to their own functions. After all, he is a Griffiths. Sondra thus decides that being with Clyde will not be such a problem socially, and she advises him to be a little more restrained than he has been. After a while Clyde is so frequently a member of the social set that she is able to "seek him out" more openly. Clyde initially appeals to Sondra's vanity, but eventually she falls in love with him.

As summer approaches, Sondra alludes to inviting Clyde to her family's wealthy lake resort area and even makes veiled suggestions of an elopement in October when she will be of age to marry. When Clyde arrives in the community to stay with another wealthy family, however, Sondra's mother, who is concerned about Clyde's real status, warns Sondra that after this vacation there must be no more intimate contact between the two. Sondra informs Clyde of her mother's feelings, and Clyde proposes that they run away at once. In response Sondra virtually promises Clyde that they will elope in the fall.

Unbeknownst to Sondra, however, ROBERTA ALDEN, a lower-class factory worker whom Clyde had been seeing since before his relationship with Sondra began, is pregnant by Clyde. Roberta threatens to expose Clyde if he does not marry her, and since Clyde does not want to lose Sondra and her social world with all its delights, he lures Roberta to a remote lake in order to kill her. At the last minute Clyde finds himself unable to follow through on his murderous intentions, but the boat accidentally overturns and Clyde, at once fearful and relieved, passively watches her drown.

A few days after the murder, Clyde is hunted down and arrested. Sondra's name is left out of the papers by an agreement between the lawyers, but "Miss X" and her mother and sister nonetheless retreat to Maine. Sondra has no more contact with Clyde other than sending a note to him on death row saying that she can't understand why he did what he did but that she feels sympathy for him and wishes him freedom and happiness.

Finkle, Leo. "The Magic Barrel." Bernard Malamud. 1953.

Leo Finkle is a young, studious rabbinical student from Cleveland, Ohio, studying at the Yeshiva University in New York City. In anticipation of his ordination in a few months, Leo is confronted with the bothersome prospect of finding a wife since married rabbis have a better chance of obtaining a position in a congregation than do single rabbis. Because he has spent the past six years doing little but studying, his social life is virtually nonexistent, and he is not acquainted with eligible single women. After agonizing over the advisability of doing so, Leo finally breaks down and decides to consult PINYE SALZMAN, an experienced marriage broker from the Bronx.

When the thin, dingy matchmaker arrives at Leo's dark rooming house apartment, he eagerly produces a number of worn cards representing prospective brides. But none of the prospects appeal to Leo, and he sends Salzman away in despair. Leo's relationship with the matchmaker worsens when Salzman returns and convinces him to meet with a schoolteacher who turns out to be much too old.

During the weeks following the unsuccessful rendezvous with the teacher, Leo's health begins to fail, and he becomes so depressed and disillusioned with his life that he considers dropping out of school. When Salzman finally drops by Leo's apartment again, he ignores Leo's protestations that he is no longer interested in utilizing the services of a marriage broker and gives him a packet of pictures of young unmarried women. Leo refuses to look at the pictures, but he does vow to undertake a more active social life. As time passes, his health improves, and he is able to maintain his old routine. But his efforts to socialize are relatively ineffectual, and his dilemma remains unsolved.

One day, in desperation, Leo opens the manila envelope containing the photographs and is delighted to find that one of the faces appeals to him. Its subtly evil expression intrigues him, and he feels that he might be able to help the young woman who appears to have suffered from experiences that she somehow regrets. Excited by this discovery of emotion in himself, he rushes off to find Pinye Salzman. When the matchmaker hears Leo's choice, he groans and insists that the photograph was inadvertently placed in the envelope and that the woman is far too wild and shameless to make a suitable wife for a rabbi. But Leo will not take no for an answer and finally persuades Salzman to divulge the woman's name and identity.

When Leo learns that the woman's name is Stella and that she is Salzman's own daughter, he suspects that the matchmaker may have secretly orchestrated the entire affair. But this possibility does not dissuade him, and the story ends abruptly when Stella and Leo meet, and the latter is deeply moved by the troubled innocence reflected in her eyes.

Finn, Huckleberry "Huck." *The Adventures of Tom Sawyer; The Adventures of Huckleberry Finn.* Samuel L. Clemens (Mark Twain). 1876; 1884.

Huckleberry Finn is a boy attempting to escape the constraints of a stifling society. He samples the various social environments of the antebellum Mississippi River basin and ultimately rejects them all in favor of the unencumbered, "uncivilized" life he shares with the slave JIM out on the water.

Having helped TOM SAWYER discover $12,000 in a cave, Huck finds himself a wealthy foster child being "sivilized" by the benign Widow Douglas and her strict sister, Miss Watson. He is uninterested in his friend Tom's romantic adventures and Miss Watson's tales of heaven and hell but finds "sivilized" life acceptable enough. When his father, the ne'er-do-well Pap Finn, gets word of his son's fortune, he attempts to take custody, finally resorting to kidnapping. Locked away in a cabin, the adaptable Huck nevertheless begins to enjoy life with his father.

When his father's drunkenness becomes too menacing, however, Huck decides he must leave. Elaborately feigning his own murder, Huck escapes to Jackson's Island, where he meets Jim, Miss Watson's slave, who is also an escapee. Together they build a raft to journey down the river to safety.

While floating toward the Ohio River and freedom for Jim, they come upon a floating house, where Jim finds a corpse, and a foundering riverboat, whose passengers are murderous robbers. Huck makes brief sorties to the shore, lying when necessary in order to get directions and in-

formation from the people he meets, but most of his time is spent resting naked under the stars with Jim, away from all the complications of society. Huck wavers between his socially imposed belief that he should turn Jim in and his innate understanding that Jim is a human being who deserves his caring and loyalty.

One night during a dense fog, Huck and Jim are separated. Huck eventually makes his way back to the raft while Jim is sleeping. The next morning Huck tricks Jim into believing for a time that he had dreamed the whole incident. Huck feels guilty that he has misled a man who truly cares for him, especially when he realizes that because of the trick they have missed the Ohio River and are traveling deeper into slave territory.

While Jim remains hidden on the raft, Huck has adventures in the towns along the river. He lives briefly with the Grangerfords, a family whose apparent gentility is belied by its senseless and bloody feuding with the Shepardsons, a neighboring family. Almost killed in the subsequent battle that he inadvertently touches off, Huck then takes up with a pair of confidence men, the King and the Duke. He participates in swindling people at a camp revival meeting and the performance of a bogus play called *The Royal Nonesuch* but thwarts the unscrupulous pair in their attempt to rob two sisters of their inheritance.

However, Huck is powerless to stop the two from capturing Jim and collecting the reward money. While Jim is imprisoned on the farm of Tom Sawyer's Aunt Sally, Huck must decide whether to regard Jim as a friend in need of assistance or as property to be returned to its rightful owner. Rejecting social codes, although still haunted by them, he determines to free Jim from his imprisonment. Despite the unexpected appearance of Tom and the unnecessarily complicated escape plot he concocts, Jim is freed. Jim is soon recaptured, however, because he stays to attend to the bullet wound Tom received during the episode.

Tom finally reveals that Jim has already been freed by the dying Miss Watson and that the whole enterprise has been superfluous. Jim reveals to Huck that the body he found in the floating house was Pap Finn. Now released from the possibility of exploitation by his father, Huck resolves to free himself of societal constraints as well and head for the unsettled territories of the American West.

Firman, Father John. "The Valiant Woman." J. F. Powers. 1947.

Father John Firman, the story's main character, realizes that the situation between him and his housekeeper has developed into an all-too-recognizable relationship. What is more, Father Firman can do nothing to alter the matter.

One night after having one of his fellow priests over for dinner, Father Firman contemplates the position that his housekeeper, Mrs. Stoner, has assumed in his life. Mrs. Stoner had taken an active part in the evening's conversation and uttered a wifely sigh of relief when the visiting father departed. During the deadly game of cards that the two engage in nightly, Father Firman recalls Mrs. Stoner's faults, with strikingly conjugal overtones.

Dominating the rectory, Mrs. Stoner cleans excessively, snoops into parishioners' records, prevents Father Firman from smoking, hides his books, chooses his friends, and attends morning Mass religiously. And Father Firman hates her complaints, such as having given him "the best years of her life." Most disconcerting of all to the priest is the housekeeper's residing in the guest room rather than in the back room where a person of her station should be located.

As he gets ready for bed, Father Firman admits to himself for the one and only time that Mrs. Stoner has become more his wife than his housekeeper. He finally recognizes that although he silently bemoans his predicament, he is not prepared to dismiss Mrs. Stoner; it is the only option he has to alter their relationship.

Fisher, Leon. *Union Square.* Albert Halper. 1933.

Leon Fisher is an idealistic artist and dedicated Communist Party member living in New York City at the beginning of the Great Depression. Leon, who was once a very promising student at an art school, works as a photograph retoucher by day and paints at night.

One October day in 1931, Leon quits his job in order to devote all of his energies to painting posters for the Communist Party. He then visits his friend JASON WHEELER, an embittered alcoholic who was formerly a celebrated young poet and active Party member. The jaded and disillusioned writer habitually makes fun of Leon's political beliefs and they argue frequently, but Leon cares for his friend, worries about him when he is ill, and pays his bills for him when he needs help. That same evening Leon attends a meeting and is introduced to Helen Jackson, an activist from New Orleans who moves into Jason's building with several fellow comrades. When the virginal Leon falls in love with Helen, his friends neglect to tell him, in order to spare his feelings, that Helen is the mistress of the brutish Jose Morales.

Leon is friendly with Celia Chapman, the eighteen-year-old daughter of his landlady, but appears oblivious to the fact that she is madly in love with him. He asks her to pose for him, finishes the portrait in a week, and submits it for inclusion in an exhibition in Philadelphia. Leon visits Helen frequently in the following weeks, cleaning and fixing up her apartment for her. On Christmas Day he finds out that his painting of Celia has been accepted by the Pennsylvania National Academy. He rushes to tell Helen, who agrees to go out to dinner with him and offers to pose in the nude for him someday. It is not until New Year's that Leon guiltily realizes he has not told Celia about the picture.

One day Leon finds Jason lying unconscious in his apartment; the writer has been taking dope. Worried about his friend, Leon persuades him to attend a political meeting a few days later. Afterward they go to a proletarian poetry reading, where Jason angers the crowd by criticizing the poems, claiming that they are irrelevant to the working class and that there are no first-rate proletarian artists in the country. But he praises Leon for devoting his energies to making fiery posters for the Party that can be used in demonstrations and marches.

Leon is in fact working hard at preparing placards for an upcoming demonstration in Union Square; his funds are running low, however, and he must ask for his job back at the engraving house. At a meeting the day before the big event, he is brave enough to speak up and make a useful suggestion, and later receives a kiss from Helen as a reward. He cries with happiness on his way home, meets Celia, and is extremely abrupt and cruel to her when she notices his tears and expresses concern for him. Unbeknownst to Leon, Celia has been saving her money to fix a broken front tooth so that her smile may be more attractive to him.

Leon actively participates at the demonstration in Union Square; he feels proud and exalted by the experience and runs to tell Helen and Jason about it. Jason had left his apartment earlier to watch the demonstration and had carelessly thrown a cigarette butt in the basement on his way out. By the time Leon arrives, the building is on fire. He rushes upstairs, knocks on Helen's door to give the alarm, only to discover her stark naked, climbing out of bed with Jose. The building empties, and Leon stands there for a few moments facing the full misery of his lonely life. He then exits through a back door and runs home, sobbing, leaving Jason and Helen to believe that he has perished in the fire. As the novel ends, Leon is lying on his bed staring at the ceiling in pain and despair, without knowing that Celia is eagerly waiting downstairs to show him her new tooth.

Fisher, Matthew (Max Disher). *Black No More.* George S. Schuyler. 1931.

Matthew Fisher, the protagonist in this satire of an America in which blacks can transform themselves into Caucasians, begins the story as Max Disher, a black man in Harlem. He and a close friend, Bunny Brown, desire light-skinned women, but they continually reject them because of their darker hue. One day, after having been rebuffed by a captivating white woman from Atlanta, Max reads of the discovery of a new technique whereby blacks can be outwardly transformed into Caucasians. Max, fresh from the sting of rejection, is first in line for the radical skin-changing powers of Dr. Junius Crookman, a black scientist. After the change, none of Max's old friends recognize him. As the world's first "whitened" man, he sells his story to the papers and uses the money to go to Atlanta to seek his heart's desire.

Meanwhile, thousands more are being "whitened." Dr. Crookman sees huge profits as the black population flocks to his national chain of sanatoriums, Black No More Inc. In Atlanta, Max, now Matthew Fisher, searches for the girl and a job but finds neither. Hoping to advance in the world, Matt presents himself to the Reverend Henry Givens, leader of the Knights of Nordica, a militant white group. Matt tells Givens that he is an anthropologist from New York City who shares Givens's concern that Dr. Crookman's sanatoriums are a grave threat to racial integrity. Using his intimate knowledge of racism, Matt masterfully manipulates racial fears and quickly becomes the wealthy second-in-command of the Knights of Nordica. He soon discovers that the woman he's been searching for is Reverend Givens's daughter Helen, and they marry.

Two years after Dr. Crookman began his treatments, there are few people left with brown skin. Bunny, now whitened, joins Matt at the Knights, and they gain more power and money. But the whitening process is not genetically transferable; as a result, when Helen becomes pregnant, Matt is terrified that he will be discovered. To his relief, Helen miscarries.

The Knights, now a national political power, ally themselves with the Anglo-Saxon Association and sponsor Reverend Givens as their Democratic candidate for President of the United States. Their central campaign issue is lineage checks, which they insist must take place to prevent interracial marriage. They amass statistics to support their position, but the plan backfires because they discover that most people, including their candidates, are tainted with "Negro blood." The Republicans steal the report. Helen, pregnant again, gives birth on election day to a brown baby; headlines reveal the Democrats' tainted lineage, and the Republicans win a landslide victory.

Matt boldly admits to Helen that he was brown-skinned, and she loves him anyway. Matt, Helen, Bunny, and the Reverend and Mrs. Givens escape by plane to Mexico with plenty of money. In the States, an article by Dr. Crookman declares "whitened" persons to be more fair-skinned than hereditary Caucasians. This starts an anti-white bias that brings darker skin into vogue.

Fitzgerald, Ann. *The Bushwhacked Piano.* Thomas McGuane. 1971.

Ann Fitzgerald, a spoiled young woman who fancies herself an artist, tries to defer the responsibilities of adulthood while deciding whether or not to rebel against her parents' values. The two options available to Ann are represented by two lovers who are opposed in their beliefs and life-styles. Safe in her parents' home, Ann dabbles in photography and poetry while she contemplates the merits and disadvantages of the men who are pursuing her.

Ann's parents stand for the conservative ideals that have led them to financial success in the Detroit automobile business. They also manage to hold a marriage together

in spite of their loathing for each other. Although Ann, at twenty-one, is understandably skeptical of their way of life, she is accustomed to luxury. She is therefore willing to take an interest in her parents' candidate for a husband, George Russell, if only because the move from their ostentatious home to his would be relatively smooth. George, an associate of Mr. Fitzgerald's, is on his way to becoming an executive at General Motors. He is already quite comfortable financially and has paid for the publication of a volume of Ann's poetry.

While Ann is in the midst of a passionate affair with a rebel named NICHOLAS PAYNE, George tries to persuade her to go to Europe with him. As a "trial run," Ann goes to a hotel with George and finds that she compares unfavorably with Payne as a lover. She overcomes her doubts, however, in order to take advantage of George's offer. The trip runs smoothly according to George's meticulous plans, but his snobbery embarrasses Ann and makes her long for Payne. When they return, Ann finds that Payne has sorely missed her, and they rent a house together for a week.

Ann soon tires of Payne, who is abrasive and unpredictable, and periodically returns to George. When she is out with George one evening, Payne breaks into the Fitzgeralds' house and threatens her mother with a rifle. After this, Ann is forbidden to see him, and the family moves to their ranch in Livingston, Montana. Here Ann takes refuge in her room or makes excursions to photograph the dramatic landscape around the ranch. Payne is on her mind most of the day, as her feelings vacillate wildly between anger and desire.

When Payne turns up in Livingston for a short stint as a bronco rider in the local rodeo, Ann sees him in a particularly impressive performance. Shortly afterward her parents give way to her prompting, and Payne is able to move in as a house guest. Mr. and Mrs. Fitzgerald are both desperate to reestablish their hold on Ann, who now announces that she is leaving them to live with Payne. Mrs. Fitzgerald offers her daughter a half-interest in her profitable "wig bank" (a service that disinfects and stores wigs) if she will stay, but Ann refuses.

However, as soon as she has said good-bye to her parents and is riding down the road in Payne's green Hudson Hornet, Ann feels like a "hoor." Almost immediately their adventure begins to look like a mistake, and Ann casts about for a way to end it. Payne's friend and business associate CLETUS JAMES CLOVIS is in the hospital for heart trouble, and she persuades Payne to admit himself as well for the hemorrhoid operation he has been postponing. While Payne is there, Ann spends her time as the center of attention at a local bar. After the operation, Payne is at his least appealing, and Ann leaves him a note saying, "This is it."

Having exorcised any leftover fascination with Payne, Ann promptly calls George to say that she will marry him. Just before flying to Detroit to meet him, she wires her parents for money and indulges in a celebratory shopping spree. At the book's end, Ann and George are running toward each other at the Detroit airport, and it is apparent that Ann has returned with relief to her parents' world.

Flagg, Mason. *Set This House on Fire.* William Styron. 1959.

Handsome, sophisticated, and manipulative, Mason Flagg is both attractive and repulsive to PETER LEVERETT and Cass Kinsolving, two men who draw close to him and whose lives he attempts to control. Through his outrageously selfish behavior, Mason misjudges the extent to which he can control the hatred and loathing he seems consciously to arouse, and he precipitates the events leading to his own death.

Mason enters the novel as a prep school friend of Peter Leverett. He is the son of a famous father who despises him and an alcoholic mother who adores him, and he has arrived at the school after having been expelled from several others. Even at this young age, Mason describes his life with a series of lies and exaggerations, impressing his friends with a sophistication and sexual experience that are completely of his own making. In a foreshadowing of later events, Mason rapes the thirteen-year-old daughter of an oysterman and is threatened with death by her enraged father. Although he is disgusted by his son's behavior, Mason's father impassively rescues him, and Mason is expelled from school. He shows no remorse for what he has done once the immediate danger has passed, and is only afraid that his mother will be upset that he has again spoiled his chances of going to Princeton.

Peter and Mason meet again some years later in New York, where Mason, still obsessed with sex, is living a glamorously hedonistic life. He treats Peter to a week of indulgence in New York by introducing him to an artistic, bohemian crowd and providing him with more sexual partners than he had ever dreamed of. Mason seems to make all things possible and presides over his circle of friends with a generous, if manipulative, largesse. His aura of success is augmented by his tales of a war spent fighting in Yugoslavia and a wound gained in the process, and by his theories about sexual liberation. Yet underneath this heroic and flamboyant libertinism, Mason's life is sordid. He mistreats his adoring wife by theorizing about his infidelities and becoming violent when she questions him. Furthermore, his tales of fighting in Yugoslavia turn out to have come from books. In spite of his protestations and claims of living life to the fullest, Mason seems aware of the hollowness of his life, and he desperately tries to defend his deceptions and infidelities. Although it becomes clear that Mason is trying to hide or to escape from something, he never reveals precisely what lies behind his carefully constructed mask.

Mason next appears in his villa in Sambuca, Italy, again surrounded by a hedonistic, glamorous group of people. His life seems even more openly sordid and violent. His girlfriend shows signs of bruising, and Mason, now a full-blown alcoholic, is constantly enraged with everyone around him. As Mason's anger increases, he turns on two people in particular: Cass Kinsolving, an impoverished and alcoholic artist, and Francesca, a young Italian girl who works at the villa. On the night of his death, Mason, with demonic genius, humiliates Cass in front of the other guests and Cass's wife and children. Peter attempts to stop him, but Mason enjoys asserting his power over the dejected Cass if only to make his friends laugh. His humiliation of Francesca is even more disturbing: He continually makes advances, which she spurns, and threatens to rape her if she does not give in. As his anger becomes uncontrollable, Mason's moods swing wildly, and as the night progresses, he moves nearer to the rape he has threatened and to violent action against Peter or Cass. When Francesca is found raped and fatally injured, and Mason's body is discovered at the foot of a cliff, it is assumed that he has raped her and killed himself in a fit of remorse.

Yet remorse is not an emotion Mason was capable of feeling, and when Peter and Cass meet several years later to unravel the events of that night, Cass reveals that it was he who murdered Mason, both to avenge the rape of Francesca and to free himself from Mason's diabolical influence. Far from helping to explain the character of Mason Flagg, these revelations only complicate an already complex character. As Peter and Cass tell their stories and compare the man they each knew, the character of Mason grows more and more enigmatic. It seems that Mason, at once fascinating and repellent, has come to symbolize the baser and more uncontrollable elements of the people whose lives he entered.

Fleming, Henry. *The Red Badge of Courage.* Stephen Crane. 1895.

Henry Fleming is an infantry private in the Union Army of the Potomac during the Civil War. He enlists enthusiastically, filled with a desire to prove himself in defense of the Union and impatient to go into battle. Henry's courage and pride are eventually challenged, however, when his romantic ideals of war are shattered by his contact with its brutal realities.

After days of marching and countermarching, delayed advances and unexplained withdrawals, the youth finally comes under fire. At first he reacts mechanically, caught up in the rhythm of load, fire, and reload. His brigade repulses a charge, and he is for a time elated. A few minutes later, however, the enemy counterattacks and he flees in terror, certain the entire army is in full retreat and the battle lost. Once safely in the rear, he hears an officer saying the line has held, and he is overcome with shame.

Filled with self-pity, he wanders farther and farther from the front lines, seeking solace in nature. Yet even in the quietest, most secluded part of the forest he finds a soldier's rotting corpse. Fleeing from this horrible sight, he realizes from the ever-growing roar of the distant battle that the engagement he had fled was a mere skirmish. He joins a column of wounded, stumbling toward the rear, and befriends a tattered soldier, but he avoids him when the man asks where he has been wounded. Among the crowd of injured, Henry longs for a wound, a little "red badge of courage." He suddenly meets his friend Jim Conklin, who has been badly injured. Henry tries to help his friend, but Jim runs madly across the field, pursued by Henry and the tattered soldier. It is only when they catch up to him that Henry realizes Jim is dying.

After Jim's death the tattered soldier and Henry continue on, and the youth soon learns that the tattered soldier is more gravely wounded than he seemed. When the injured man persists in questioning Henry about his "wound," the youth is once again filled with shame and deserts the tattered soldier, leaving him wandering helplessly in a field.

Disgusted with himself, Henry wants to return to the fighting and either redeem himself or die, but he has no rifle and is afraid. In the midst of his internal debate, a group of fleeing soldiers come racing down the road toward him. Henry attempts to stop one to ask what has happened, but the soldier is mad with fear and beats him aside, wounding him in the head with the butt of his rifle. Stumbling and dazed, Henry is assisted by a cheerful soldier who leads him back to his regiment. His comrades are glad to see him alive, and he does not tell them how he received his wound.

The combat continues the next day. The brigade fights well, but Henry's pride is stung when he hears a general refer to them as "a bunch of mule drivers." Because its members are considered expendable, Henry's brigade is placed at the front of the coming attack. Facing almost certain death, the men continue to fight well. When the standard-bearer is shot, Henry seizes the flag. He helps to rally the men, and the brigade charges, scattering their enemy. Despite their local success, however, they are given the order to retreat at the end of the day. As the regiment trudges back over the ground it had won, Henry reflects on his experiences in combat. While he still feels guilty for having run and especially for having deserted the tattered soldier, he accepts his weaknesses as part of his experience. He believes he will be a better man for them. Most important, he realizes he has faced death and survived.

Fletcher, Phillip. *Work.* Louisa May Alcott. 1873.

The son of very wealthy parents, Phillip Fletcher enjoyed his privileged childhood in a small mansion in New England. However, when he was thirteen, his parents were both stricken with disease and died. Along with the small fortune he had inherited, the young Fletcher was sent to live with his aunt and her husband.

Overwhelmed with grief at the loss of his parents, Fletcher becomes very ill and spends the rest of his youth bedridden at his aunt's house. It is not until his twenty-third birthday that he is able to stand or walk for any length of time. Fletcher is sullen and bitter for having been robbed of his youth, and his misery is increased when his aunt gives birth to a pair of twins, whom he always refers to as "the brats."

Because of the lure of his fortune, Fletcher becomes the object of much desire among the eligible young ladies of the town. He overhears a number of women discussing him after church one day and is dismayed to hear them conclude his fortune would only be worthwhile if he died shortly after they were married. Withdrawn and sullen, he spends most of his time taking long walks by himself on the beach to avoid his aunt and her family, and cursing his fortune, which he would gladly trade for a single friend.

Fletcher's life changes dramatically when his aunt hires a governess named CHRISTIE DEVON to take care of her twins. Although Fletcher first treats her as nothing more than a shadow, Christie's warmth and friendliness soon have an effect on the cautious young man. They begin to take long walks together, and he spends most of his time with her and the children. Through Christie he begins to recapture his lost youth.

Although Fletcher discovers that Christie had previously been employed as an actress—a disreputable profession, according to the views of his society—he decides nevertheless to propose marriage. He tells her that he is willing to overlook her tarnished past and goes on to point out the sizable fortune into which she will be marrying. Much to his great surprise, Christie politely declines. She leaves Fletcher's family a few days later.

Fletcher is crushed and spends the next two years cursing his own arrogance and insensitivity. He finally convinces himself that his life will be forever miserable unless he can find Christie and win her heart. He tracks her for months and finally finds her working as a maid to a large family farther north.

Fletcher tries to impress upon Christie the difference the past few years have made and what a change her rejection of him brought. While Christie admits that she sees in him a new maturity and sense of humility, she once again rejects his offer of marriage. Thus spurned, Fletcher finds himself unable to return to his aunt's home. When the Civil War breaks out, he immediately enlists, wholeheartedly embracing military life as an escape from his personal sorrow. When he is shot by Confederate bullets, his last vision as he lays dying in a hospital is that of Christie looking down at him.

Flinders, Margaret "Maggie." *The Unpossessed.* Tess Slesinger. 1934.

Margaret Flinders, a 1930s wife and working woman, is torn between her two domestic and professional worlds. Defined by the men in her life, Maggie struggles against their domination but also wants to be recognized as a feminine woman. When her husband persuades her to abort a pregnancy, Maggie painfully realizes that she will leave nothing behind her when she dies.

A college-educated intellectual, Maggie lives in Greenwich Village with her dour husband Miles, who plans to start a socialist magazine with old college friends. Maggie alternately loves and hates her husband, and communication between them is almost nonexistent. Maggie is more interested in a peaceful life than in the far-flung socialist causes they pursue, but she knows better than to voice her feelings to Miles for fear of losing him.

On their way to a meeting about the magazine, Miles broods silently. Frustrated by his behavior, Maggie turns for attention to their host, the licentious Jeffrey Blake, cofounder of the magazine and Miles's old friend. By flirting with her, Jeffrey makes Maggie feel alive. While Miles and Jeffrey's wife talk on the other side of the door, Maggie and Jeffrey embrace in the kitchen.

Maggie finds her brief tryst with Jeff disappointing. She feels that she has been unfaithful not only to Miles but to herself. Realizing that she still loves Miles, she returns to the party hoping that he will show his love for her. But the brooding Miles is oblivious to what has occurred between his wife and his friend.

As the meeting continues, Maggie sits in the background feeling aloof and unfulfilled. Reflecting on her situation, she feels that her independence has resulted in an empty lap, with no needlework or children to satisfy her. Abruptly, Maggie splits the meeting's tense silence when she spits out "God damn it." When the discussion is revived, the leader of the group says that women are defined by their wombs. Courageously, Maggie counters him, saying that men are scared of what they do not have. Miles is at once frightened by and drawn to Maggie. She seems beautiful and radiant. Shaken, Miles realizes that he has fallen in love with her again.

Understanding Miles's bewilderment and reluctance to get too close to her, Maggie is cautious. She knows that she must temper her ecstasy to a level that he can handle or risk losing him. Joyous to discover that she is pregnant, Maggie stays home one evening from a magazine meeting to take a bath. When Miles suggests staying home himself so that they can make love, Maggie persuades him to go. She knows that she and the magazine make each other possible, and she doesn't want to upset the precarious peace that has recently come into their lives. Alone in her bath, Maggie counts the months until the baby will be born.

The Flinders attend a Hunger March party at which the magazine founders plan to present their manifesto of the publication to backers. Hosted by an upper-class matron who is having an affair with Jeffrey, the party is attended by society snobs who are only interested in seeing who else is there. Glowing in her pregnancy, Maggie feels that she finally sees people as they really are. Miles is irritated when Maggie admits that she doesn't understand the magazine's cause, because he knows there is some truth in what she says. But nothing can change Maggie's secret pride and happiness. The baby is something that belongs, for now, only to her.

Miles is distressed when one of the magazine founders denounces their cause, and he later tells Maggie that they cannot bring a child into this world because a baby will make them hostages to daily life and force them to give up their intellectual activities. Maggie offhandedly agrees to an abortion, but she resents Miles for it. On their ride home from the hospital they are again two separate, lonely people.

Flint, Gerty. *The Lamplighter.* Maria Susanna Cummins. 1854.

Gerty Flint, the novel's saintly and self-sacrificing heroine, was born in Rio de Janeiro and is the daughter of Lucy Grey and PHILIP AMORY. When Amory becomes sick in another city and is unable to return, Lucy assumes that he has abandoned the family. Gerty and her mother go to Boston to live with Amory's friend Ben Grant. Ben and Lucy die, leaving Gerty in the care of Nan Grant, Ben's cruel wife. Nan tells Gerty nothing of her parentage and raises her to think herself ugly and worthless.

When Gerty is eight years old, Trueman Flint, the lamplighter on her block, gives her a kitten. But the cruel Nan discovers the pet and tortures it to death by plunging it in boiling water. Gerty, enraged, throws a piece of wood at Nan, and Nan evicts her from the house. Trueman Flint finds her and takes her to live with him.

At her "Uncle True's" house, Gerty meets the kindly Mrs. Sullivan, her father, Mr. Cooper, and her curly-headed, congenial son Willie Sullivan. Willie and Gerty become close friends, although Willie works at an apothecary shop and can only visit on weekends. Some years later, when Uncle True has a paralytic stroke, Gerty cares for him tenderly. When he dies, she goes to live with Emily Graham, the blind, angelic daughter of the wealthy Mr. Graham. Emily tries to teach Gerty to overcome her most serious flaw—her bad temper. Gerty finds it difficult to live with the Grahams' critical and unkind housekeeper, Mrs. Ellis, but she restrains her temper and proves to be the superior woman.

Willie leaves for India to make his fortune, but he and Gerty keep up a loving and regular correspondence. When Gerty is eighteen, she asserts her independence from Emily's self-centered father, who demands that Gerty accompany the family on a trip to the South. Gerty refuses because she sees it as her duty to live with Willie's ill mother and senile grandfather, Mr. Cooper. She gets a job as a teacher's assistant and cares for the two older people until their deaths. She then returns to the Grahams to be Emily's companion.

While in the South, Mr. Graham marries the Widow Holbrook, a sister-in-law of Mr. Clinton, Willie's employer. She and her two nieces, Isabel Clinton and Kitty Ray, come to live with the Graham household. These showy, "valueless" women disrupt the Grahams' domesticity. Resentful of Emily and Gerty's obvious moral superiority, they effectively banish them from all of the house except Emily's bedroom.

To escape the household tension, Emily and Gerty move to Boston, where they spend "a blissful and improving winter." Early the following summer Gerty and Emily accompany their friend Dr. Jeremy and his wife on a boat trip up the Hudson to fashionable Saratoga Springs. En route they meet a handsome, white-haired stranger who takes an unaccountably keen interest in Gerty. In Saratoga, Gerty sees Willie in the company of Isabel and hears the distressing rumor that the two are engaged. Gerty despairs, for she had always fantasized about marrying Willie herself. On the boat trip back down the Hudson, the boat catches fire and the stranger rescues Emily and Isabel, whose safety Gerty ensures before rescuing herself. The tall stranger turns out to be none other than Gerty's father, Philip Amory, and he is restored to her and to his beloved Emily, whom he had tragically and mistakenly blinded when she was sixteen. Willie denies any interest whatsoever in Isabel, asking whether "such a woman could bless and adorn a fireside." He values Gerty for her selflessness and sincerity, and as the novel closes, the two marry and keep a happy home.

Flood, Nora. *Nightwood.* Djuna Barnes. 1936.

Nora Flood, an eccentric bohemian, has a New York salon that attracts beggars, radicals, circus performers, black magic practitioners, and artists. In contrast to her colorful guests, Nora appears to have a reliable and steady nature. But her fascination with degraded and sometimes evil people leads to her involvement with ROBIN VOTE, a woman whose depravity ultimately causes Nora's demise.

A patron of the Denckman circus even when she is not actively involved in its production, Nora is watching one of their performances in New York in 1923 when she notices that the circus animals are reacting oddly to the boyish-looking woman in the next seat. When a lioness begins to pay frighteningly aggressive attention to the woman, Nora grabs her by the hand and escorts her out of the tent. The charismatic stranger introduces herself as Robin Vote, and they immediately embark on an intense and distressing love affair.

The lovers stay in Nora's large estate until midwinter and then move to a Paris apartment of Robin's choosing.

Nora pays the rent and becomes aware that Robin expects her to provide a stable home and emotional environment. Once they are moved in, Robin begins to traipse around the city and indulge in drunken binges. For a while Nora follows Robin around in order to protect her from the catastrophes that she naturally courts, but this well-intentioned chaperoning proves too painful in the long run. Waiting at home during interminable nights, Nora lies in her bed in the fetal position, unable to cry despite her despair. The demanding and jealous Robin insists that Nora be completely isolated from other people; Nora is allowed no visitors or mail. This nightmarish norm is sometimes interrupted by affectionate episodes, but Nora descends increasingly into despondency. Exasperated, Robin takes on a new lover, Jenny Petheridge, a wealthy middle-aged widow with whom she sails back to New York.

Nora never recovers from the broken heart caused by Robin's flight. In an attempt to understand her ex-lover's behavior, she seeks Robin's previous drinking and sexual partners in the bars and cafés of Marseilles, Tangiers, and Naples. She continues to write unanswered letters to Robin in the United States until she can no longer bear their separation and makes the passage across the Atlantic.

When Nora arrives, she discovers that Robin has continued her aimless wandering and unconventional behavior. At the close of the novel, Nora finds Robin frolicking with a frightened dog in the estate chapel. Robin has positioned herself on all fours as if desiring intercourse with the animal.

Follet, Jay. *A Death in the Family.* James Agee. 1957.

Jay Follet is a thirty-six-year-old family man who enjoys a contented relationship with his wife MARY and two young children, Catherine and RUFUS (FOLLET). A businessman in Knoxville, Tennessee, Jay supports his family economically and provides a secure and loving environment both in his own home and in the household of his parents. This happiness is no antidote to adversity, and Jay's idyllic life is tragically interrupted by a sudden accident that leaves his entire family dazed with sorrow.

Jay demonstrates his devotion to his children in myriad ways: singing lullabies when they have trouble sleeping, taking them to movies, and going on excursions to the countryside surrounding Knoxville. On one trip the family visits Jay's great-grandmother. Although her memory is failing at the age of one hundred and four, she recognizes Jay and his family with great pleasure and pride, and Jay feels an intense sense of familial continuity. Jay's love for his family is reciprocated in a variety of touching ways. His son Rufus, in particular, anxiously stations himself in front of one of the windows of their home each afternoon in order to catch the first possible glimpse of his father when he returns home from work.

A reformed alcoholic, Jay has learned to forgo the excitement of intoxication in favor of domestic tranquility. However, his brother Ralph is still a slave to the bottle; one night he makes a drunken call to Jay to inform him that their father is dangerously ill with a chronic heart condition. Although he is not sure whether Ralph is over-reacting, Jay decides that he cannot take the chance of doubting his brother's word and decides to make the trip by car to a neighboring town where his parents live. Jay insists that his wife stay in bed, but she ignores his re-monstrances and he agrees to let her make him breakfast before he leaves. Then, touched by her loving diligence and concerned that she will not be able to fall back asleep, Jay makes her a cup of hot milk before going to his car.

Upon arriving at his parents' house, Jay discovers that his brother has in fact exaggerated the severity of their father's condition. Since there is no real crisis, he decides to wait until his return home to explain the situation to his wife in person.

A very fast driver by habit, Jay is racing home, hoping to arrive in time for dinner, when the cotter pin that holds the steering column of his car falls out. As his automobile crashes, he bangs his chin on the steering wheel, is in-stantly killed by a brain concussion, and is thrown from the car. In death he is unblemished except for a small cut on his chin and a small bruise on his lip. His wife and other members of his family believe that Jay's ghost visits his house on the night of his death, advancing up the stairs to take a final look at his beloved children, and leaving only when Mary has assured him that she will continue to love and care for them in his absence.

Follet, Mary. *A Death in the Family.* James Agee. 1957.

Mary Follet is an extremely devout Catholic convert whose faith is put to the test by the sudden and tragic death of her husband JAY in a car accident. Transformed overnight from a contented wife and mother to a belea-guered widow with two young children, Catherine and RUFUS (FOLLET), Mary attempts to reconcile the death of her husband with the promise of love and mercy central to her adopted Christian faith. Ultimately, she finds the strength to face the tragedy that threatens her spiritual and emotional well-being, and she vows that for the sake of her children she will carry out her responsibilities de-spite her intense grief.

The rare beauty of the quality of love that exists be-tween Mary and Jay Follet is exemplified by their last interaction with each other just hours before his fatal crash. After Jay is awakened by a phone call from his brother announcing the imminent death of their father due to heart disease, Jay decides that the dangerous news warrants his immediate departure to visit his father's sick bed. Although it is the middle of the night, Mary insists on getting up with her husband in order to prepare a nice breakfast for him before he goes on the road. Jay is touched by his wife's solicitation and makes her a cup of hot milk

so that she will find it easier to fall back asleep after he leaves. After a tender farewell, Mary returns to bed.

After she puts the children to bed the following evening, Mary receives a call from a man who informs her that her husband has met with a serious automobile accident and asks her to send her brother Walter to the scene of the mishap. Too shocked to inquire about the exact nature of her husband's condition, Mary is forced to wait in agony until Walter returns with the news that Jay is dead as a result of a head injury. As the news of her beloved hus-band's death begins to sink in, Mary chastises herself for thinking that her brother might have used the story of the dysfunctional steering mechanism to cover up the possi-bility that Jay, a reformed alcoholic, lost control of his car due to intoxication. In an effort to survive the shock of the tragic news, Mary surrounds herself with family and plies herself with whiskey in the hope that she can mo-mentarily escape her misery through sleep. As the family bands together against their grief, a bizarre and profound presence visits them, and Mary is convinced it is Jay's worried spirit coming to check up on his wife and children. Having assured this spirit that he has nothing to fear, that she will continue to care for his family, Mary finally goes to bed, only to meet another tribulation in the form of an uncharacteristic and unwonted inability to pray. She begs God's forgiveness for the lapse of her faith.

The following morning Mary is confronted with the task of explaining to her two bewildered young children that their father will no longer share their lives. Then, following a few days of emotional collapse, Mary gathers together her mental resources to face the funeral. Her grief is intensified by the fact that Father Jackson, the priest conducting the burial of her husband, refuses to recite certain funeral passages that are reserved for confirmed Catholics because Jay was never baptized. Mary survives the formal ordeal of burying her husband, and her faith ultimately remains intact as she comes to terms with God's inexplicable designs, which include the trial of accepting her husband's death as part of a larger celestial plan of cosmic grace.

Follet, Rufus. *A Death in the Family.* James Agee. 1957.

Rufus Follet is the ingenuous and confused six-year-old boy whose cozy family life is gravely disrupted when his father, JAY (FOLLET), is killed in a car accident. A pre-cocious youngster whose simple life in Knoxville, Tennes-see, is dominated by his relationships with his devoted parents and his little sister Catherine, Rufus finds that his point of view is colored by his admiration for the worldly older boys in his school and especially for his father. He stations himself in front of one of the windows of their house every day to catch the first glimpse of him when he returns from work. When his father's life is brutally ter-minated by an automobile accident, the shock is so severe that Rufus is almost unable to fathom the reality of the tragedy.

From the first, Rufus and his father demonstrate an exceptional affinity for each other. While Rufus is still sleeping in a crib, Jay attends tirelessly to his every need. Then when a teary-eyed Rufus cries out for his father one evening, Jay stations himself beside Rufus's crib for a full hour and comforts him by singing songs and lighting matches in dark corners of the room in order to assure the boy that nothing dangerous is lurking there. Rufus loves to attend movies with his father and experiences a heightened state of contentment as, on their way back home in the dark, he and his father sit down on a rock in a special private spot in a vacant lot near their house. They silently enjoy each other's company while gazing at the stars, both fully aware that their happiness comes from the presence of the other. Rufus is well aware that his father is proud of him and is eager to live up to his parents' image of him as a smart and well-behaved son.

When Rufus's distraught mother and Aunt Hannah inform him and his sister that their father has been killed, the gravity of the news does not immediately sink in. Instead, he is disappointed that he does not have to attend school that day because he is anxious to bask in the attention he is sure to attract when his schoolmates learn that his father is dead. Unable to resist the urge to brag about his status as "half an orphan," Rufus sneaks out of the house and intercepts a group of children on their way to school and proceeds to show off by recounting to them the details of his father's accident. As he begins to comprehend that his father is actually dead and might be watching his son from heaven, Rufus feels guilty. He thinks that his father, who had always discouraged any form of boasting, might disapprove of his having broadcast the story of his death in order to feel special. Upon his return to his home, Rufus stealthily examines his father's favorite chair, sniffing at its upholstery with the hope of activating vivid memories of his father by recalling the wonderful way he used to smell.

When Rufus contemplates the figure of his father for the last time in an open coffin, he marvels at the poise and beauty of his dead features and the unparalleled indifference of his expression. At the book's end he realizes that his father has been swallowed up by the immutable finality of death that allows no return to the land of the living.

Fools Crow (White Man's Dog). *Fools Crow.* James Welch. 1986.

Fools Crow was not always fortunate. Although he is eighteen years old, the other members of his tribe of Blackfeet still call him "White Man's Dog," since as a small child he had been devoted to a white man, a "Napikwan," who visited the camp and told stories. The leaders of the tribe, including his father, view the young, untried man

as small, unexceptional, and unlucky; the young women, with the exception of his father's youngest wife, don't look at White Man's Dog.

When the arrogant son of an important chief, Fast Horse, asks the reputed horse raider Yellow Kidney if White Man's Dog can accompany them on a raid against the Crow, White Man's Dog fears that his own ill-luck will lead to an inglorious death. The powerful medicine man Mik-api helps to excise the bad spirits from White Man's Dog and strengthens the link between the young man and the wolverine, his totem animal.

The Blackfeet raid is a success for White Man's Dog, whose level-headed actions result in the taking of many horses. But Yellow Kidney and Fast Horse meet a different fate. When a mutilated Yellow Kidney finally returns to the tribe months later, he reports that Fast Horse had lost his head and alerted the Crow warriors. The tribe and White Man's Dog now understand why Fast Horse has seemed withdrawn ever since he returned from the raid. As White Man's Dog's luck and status in the tribe begin to ascend, that of his former friend Fast Horse rapidly declines. It is White Man's Dog who wins the greatest honor when the Blackfeet exact their revenge from the Crow chief responsible for Yellow Kidney's torture. Shot once, the Crow leave White Man's Dog for dead, but he rises and kills their chief. For this, White Man's Dog earns the new name, "Fools Crow."

Yellow Kidney gives his daughter Red Paint to Fools Crow, who has nurtured a secret passion for her since his return from the horse raid. In taking a bride, however, Fools Crow must also take on the role of hunter and protector for his wife's family. Remembering Mik-api, the medicine man, and all the help the spirits provided in his time of need, Fools Crow becomes his companion and apprentice, and the tribe comes to rely on him not only as a brave warrior but as a healer and a wise voice in their councils.

Important to the Blackfeet in all these ways, Fools Crow is ever in demand as the Napikwans, bringing smallpox as well as alcohol, move farther and farther into the land that they had themselves allotted to the Blackfeet. Fools Crow and the chiefs of the tribe must decide whether they should fight the enemy, turn over their weapons and become farmers in the arid lands designated by the invaders, or flee farther north and west. Outlaws like the disgraced Fast Horse, who raid and kill the white farmers and traders, force the moment of crisis on all the Blackfeet. But Fools Crow, gazing at a Pikuni camp that has been decimated by the whites, sees the inevitable futility of the Native Americans' effort to resist invasion.

Forrester, Gene. *A Separate Peace.* John Knowles. 1960.

Gene Forrester, the middle-aged narrator, is still haunted by events that occurred in his sixteenth year. In the early 1940s, at a New Hampshire boys' school not quite insulated from the war that was raging in Europe, Gene and his best friend PHINEAS contended with forces that propelled them from innocence into the world of experience.

The story begins during summer session at Devon, a school that has already seen some of its graduates trundled off to fight in World War II. Roommates and best pals Gene and Phineas are only sixteen, still too caught up in the outrageous adventures of youth to be concerned with a distant war. Their daily summer ritual consists of jumping out of a perilously high tree into the river below, a feat dreamed up by the adventurous and physically adept Phineas. Gene admires his friend Finny's athletic prowess and the silver tongue with which he wriggles out of all confrontations with Devon faculty. But after failing an exam because of one of his friend's many unauthorized escapades, Gene becomes convinced that Finny is jealous of his academic achievement and is out to ruin his chances of being first in the class. The next time they are at the tree, Gene, in a moment of blind fury, jostles the branch on which his friend stands and Finny falls to the riverbank.

The accident shatters Finny's leg and puts an end to his participation in sports. Overwhelmed by guilt, Gene visits Finny and tries to tell him that he was responsible for the fall, but Finny refuses to accept Gene's explanation for the accident. When he returns to Devon later in the fall, he insists on training Gene to be the great athlete he himself will never be. Finny sets his sights for Gene on the 1944 Olympics, and when Gene tells him the games might be canceled because of the war, Finny responds with his theory that the war is merely an illusion devised by world leaders who want more control of their subjects. For his part, Gene plays along, silently resolving "to become a part of Phineas."

The war eventually begins to infiltrate the peaceful Devon campus. Gene and Finny are both surprised to learn that their friend Elwin "Leper" Lepellier, an introverted nature lover, has enlisted, in the hope of joining the ski troops. In an effort to counter the somber atmosphere created by recruiting efforts and troop trains running near the campus, Finny engineers a winter carnival. But before the festivities are over, Gene receives a telegram from Leper saying that he has "escaped" and needs his friend's help.

Gene reaches Leper's home and discovers that the young recruit left the army after a mental breakdown. Leper tells Gene that he knows what actually caused Finny's accident, then begins detailing his own emotional collapse. Unable to listen, Gene tears away. Back at school, he flatly tells Finny what happened to their friend. Later, when Finny sees Leper lurking in the bushes on campus, he admits to Gene that the war is indeed very real.

Soon after, Brinker, the class politician, forces Finny and Gene to attend a mock inquisition into the events leading to Finny's accident. When someone suggests that Leper knows what happened, there is a campus search,

and he is brought in to testify. Leper indicates that Gene caused the fall, and Finny, upset, rushes from the room and falls down a flight of stairs, once again breaking his leg. The next day, in the infirmary, Finny confronts and then tearfully forgives Gene for his part in the fall. Then, while his leg is being set, Phineas dies of heart failure.

Soon after graduation, Gene enlists in the navy, but the war ends before he sees any fighting. In fact, he reflects many years later, his war ended before he ever put on a uniform, for he fought a war of his own and killed his own enemy as a schoolboy.

Forrester, Marian. *A Lost Lady.* Willa Cather. 1923.

Marian Forrester enters the novel as a ministering angel to the injured young NIEL HERBERT. Through his eyes we see a beautiful and vivacious woman, a member of the railroad aristocracy, who eschews social pretensions to bring a plate of home-baked cookies to a group of local boys. Marian's peculiar charm is her apparent devotion to any man within her range; thus, no man—adolescent boy or elder statesman—can resist her.

At first Marian and her husband, Captain Forrester, live in Sweet Water only in the summer, but as Captain Forrester's health fails, they begin to spend increasing amounts of time in the isolated small town. During their first winter in Sweet Water, Marian throws a dinner party for some visiting railroad tycoons. Niel is, as ever, smitten by her and watches her jealously as she flirts with Frank Ellinger, a notorious womanizer from Denver. The older Captain Forrester retires and is propped up on a narrow iron cot in order to ease his sore back, while Marian takes a last brandy with Mr. Ellinger. One of the locals later sees the pair making love in a secluded area after a sleigh ride arranged for this purpose. Marian's obvious sexual contentment and their intimate and casual interaction indicate that the affair is one of long standing.

As the winter wears on, isolation begins to take its toll on Marian. Niel notices her deterioration during their regular games of whist. She frequently appears desolate and lonely, and seems to miss the social excitement of Denver and Colorado Springs. She assuages her desperation with secret drinking. But she never complains, and continues to serve her husband with the profound solicitude that Niel has always admired.

Niel's image of her is soon shattered when he accidentally overhears the sounds of lovemaking coming from her room during one of her husband's business trips. She is with Frank Ellinger, whose surprise visit to town coincides all too neatly with Captain Forrester's absence. The captain then returns with the news that the Forresters are bankrupt. Marian takes the news stoically, and when the captain falls victim to another stroke, she becomes his tireless nurse. The couple goes into decline and is forced to remain in Sweet Water for both health and financial reasons.

Marian, feeling that men of the old school are out of touch with new realities, turns over some of the family assets to the disreputable Ivy Peters, as members of the aristocracy go bankrupt all around them. Although she continues to flirt with Niel and still retains much of her old charm, hard luck and hard spirits corrode her beauty. She continues to carry on her affair by correspondence and permits Ivy Peters's advances as she continues to care for her slowly dying husband. When Frank Ellinger announces his plans to marry a younger woman, Mrs. Forrester calls him in a rage from Niel's office, but Niel cuts the wire when she becomes hysterical. Niel is not able to protect her from the jealous gossip of the local women, who take over her house under the guise of helping her until Niel steps in to protect her from their maliciousness.

When the captain finally dies, Marian tries to recreate the glory days of the railroad tycoons, but there is no one left to appreciate her talents. Always in need of an audience, she invites a group of Niel's contemporaries to an elaborate dinner party, yet even her best efforts cannot turn these boors into witty gentleman.

News of Marian comes to Niel after he has left Sweet Water: She had traveled to Brazil and married a wealthy Englishman; however, she never forgot her first husband, and had flowers delivered to his grave every year until her own death.

Fox, Alvin. *The Old Bunch.* Meyer Levin. 1937.

In this sprawling narrative about a group of Jewish youths growing up in Chicago, Alvin Fox occupies the position of rebel without a cause. Highly intelligent and radical, Alvin dabbles in a variety of daring intellectual and spiritual milieus but fails to discover the direction and purpose necessary to fulfill any of his designs.

After graduation from college, Alvin delights his parents when he announces his plans to become a rabbi. On a post-graduation trip to Europe with his friend JOE FREEDMAN, he becomes sidetracked, however. In Paris he and Joe become acquainted with Aaron Polansky, a learned Jew who, they discover, has become a convert to Catholicism. Alvin enters eagerly into the study and discussion of neo-Catholicism with Polansky and his friends, and he also marries Eunice, a Christian.

After returning to America and going to work for his father, a manufacturer of folding chairs, Alvin is disturbed by the news of Arab uprisings against the Jews in Palestine. Feeling a traitor to his race, he renounces his Catholic leanings and begins to feel guilty about having married Eunice. Alvin and Eunice remain married, but Alvin retains a permanent sense of separation from his wife.

As his father begins to become mentally unhinged by the disastrous effects of the Great Depression on the family business, Alvin takes on more and more responsibility in running the factory. Given that Alvin has strong communist sympathies and that he had begun life as an "arty

wastrel," as he puts it, he recognizes the irony in the fact that he has become the responsible, reliable, conservative member of the family. Thinking of himself as "one of those damned Jews with creative propensities but lacking specific talent," he resigns himself to the lack of fulfillment in his marriage and in his career and works steadily to run the factory and support his relatives through the Depression. He maintains his intellectual interests with readings in communist ideology and Gestalt psychology, but derives equal satisfaction from designing modernist chrome chairs that eventually achieve moderate success on the market.

Alvin becomes increasingly depressed by the waste of his cleverness and originality. Although he tries to enter into an affair with a married woman, he finds that he cannot even become interested in sex, and his depression worsens when his father becomes insane and is institutionalized. At the end of the novel, when he and Eunice attend Jewish Day at the Chicago World's Fair, he is disgusted by his own people and by the Jewish rituals that had once inspired him. Feeling the sickness of the whole world inside him, Alvin decides that the answer to the Jewish question is for the entire race to disappear over time. He makes his contribution to that goal by deciding to let the Christian Eunice have the child she has been wanting.

Fox, Mardou. *The Subterraneans.* Jack Kerouac. 1958.

Mardou Fox is the beautiful young black woman at the center of this beat generation novel. Mardou survives on the fringes of a group of young artists and intellectuals living in San Francisco during the 1950s. At the beginning of the novel, Mardou is still recovering from a rocky relationship with one of the subterraneans. Unemployed and seeing a therapist, she spends much of her time roaming around to bars and parties with the subterraneans, often ending up in bed with one or another of this incestuous group.

Enter LEO PERCEPIED, a minor literary celebrity who becomes obsessed with Mardou after meeting her one night outside a bar. At first Mardou barely acknowledges Leo, but she ends up in bed with him after a typical night of bar-hopping with the subterraneans. The following morning Mardou, wanting him to stay but sensing his fear of commitment, allows Leo to rush off.

After a few days Mardou runs into Leo at a friend's apartment, and they spend the day together cuddling in a chair as she tells him her story. Young and naive when she began hanging out with the subterraneans, Mardou spent most of her time smoking marijuana and partying with the group. After a couple of bad trips and a steadily increasing feeling of paranoia, she finally broke down one night at the apartment of Ross Wallenstein, one of the main subterraneans. Rushing out of his apartment naked after a night of sex, Mardou found herself in a deserted alleyway. She had to calm down and collect her wits before getting the courage to knock on a neighboring woman's door to beg for some clothes and money. She eventually wandered home, where her sisters, sensing that she was on the edge, urged her to seek therapy, which she does while continuing to hang out with the group.

It soon becomes apparent that Leo has difficulty dividing his time between his writing and Mardou. Mardou can sense a lingering racist doubt in him as to the feasibility of their relationship. She continues to endure his jealousy and insensitivity, however, even to the point of missing sessions with her therapist, in an attempt to hold on to him.

The break inevitably comes. Late one night Mardou is snubbed by Leo, who abandons her in a cab without any money so that he can go to another party. She arrives home only to encounter Yuri, Leo's rival for her affections. She unenthusiastically goes to bed with him. At the end of the book, she insists on breaking up with Leo and declaring her need for independence.

Fox, Stephen. *The Foxes of Harrow.* Frank Yerby. 1946.

Stephen Fox was born in Ireland and taken to the United States at the age of four. Although he spent some time in the North, the majority of his young adulthood was spent as a successful riverboat gambler on the Mississippi River where his Parisian education in gambling, lovemaking, and the French language stood him in good stead. After losing badly at cards, however, Stephen is put ashore with nothing other than the clothes on his back and a huge pearl concealed in his boot. He is eventually picked up by a passing pig barge, captained by another Irishman, Mike Farrel. Despite wide differences in their ages and deportment, the two become friends. Farrel's barge brings Stephen to New Orleans, where he has vowed to establish himself and become a wealthy plantation owner.

After a few days of roaming the city's cheap, filthy hotels, Stephen decides to prepare himself for his new career by gambling his way to fortune. One night while walking alone, he hears cries for help. He sees a man who has been mugged and stripped of most of his clothes. This man, Andre Le Blanc, is the scion of one of the city's oldest Creole families; as a result of Stephen's helpfulness, these two become friends. Through Le Blanc, Stephen is introduced to New Orleans society and soon sees, from afar, the famous Arceneaux sisters. Stephen decides impulsively that he will marry Odalie, the lesser accessible of these two rich, remote beauties.

As Stephen's fortunes accrue, he takes possession of a huge tract of riverfront land fifteen miles north of the city. Here he commences building the region's largest and finest mansion. The estate, called Harrow, is completed within a few years, and Stephen is ready to pursue his marriage plans.

Awed by the size and beauty of the estate and captivated by Fox's confident pursuit, Odalie finally becomes mistress of Harrow. Despite Stephen's affections, however, she remains frigid, and the marriage is not a success. Within a few years the Foxes do have a son and heir, Etienne, but they are barely speaking to each other. Stephen becomes the lover of Desiree, a beautiful quadroon, and he establishes a house for her in New Orleans. Odalie, under the tutelage of the voodoo-practicing slave Tante Caleen, seduces Stephen and becomes pregnant. During the pregnancy, Odalie learns of Stephen's liaison with Desiree, and she once again rejects him. Soon after, she delivers a stillborn daughter and dies.

For the next several years the plantation continues to grow despite Stephen's guilt and sorrow. He decides to marry again; this marriage, to Odalie's sister Aurore, is successful, for she has loved him since their first meeting. The couple has one child, a daughter.

The Civil War breaks out, and Stephen and Etienne are captured by Union troops. Eventually they are freed by Inch, formerly Etienne's personal slave and now, under Reconstruction, the commissioner in New Orleans. As the novel ends, father and son return together to rebuild their ravaged estate.

Foyle, Kitty. *Kitty Foyle.* Christopher Morley. 1939.

Kitty Foyle, the novel's narrator, is a "working-class gal from Philly" who comes of age during the boom and bust of the twenties and thirties. Kitty is an early example of a feminist: Repeatedly offered the chance to be taken care of, she stubbornly insists on independence and self-sufficiency. Her descriptions of the rough-and-tumble world of a working girl show how, on the one hand, she is determined to identify her personal needs and desires, while on the other hand, she appraises the many people in her life—the men, the black woman servant who dotes on her father, the immigrants who run the speakeasies—in terms of their class and race.

Growing up in Philadelphia in a small Scottish-Irish family, Kitty is schooled in the ways of the world by her father, an independent but mildly disabled man who was once groundskeeper of the cricket fields of Philadelphia high society. From him Kitty acquires a hard sense and honesty, an openness about sexuality, and a flair for embroidering stories.

When her mother dies, Kitty is sent to live with relatives in rural Illinois. Here she matures in an environment of prosperity and staid regularity. She begins to see herself as a smart, urbane young woman who longs for adventure. One day Wyn, a wealthy scion, visits her father to chat about cricket, and seeing her, he falls madly in love. He is a shy, sheltered, sincere, upper-class young man. Though she, too, has fallen for him, Kitty has a clear-eyed view of his weaknesses; from the start her scrappiness and good sense are offset by Wyn's nobility and softness.

Inspired by his relationship with Kitty, Wyn seeks to

escape the world of banking he is expected to enter and tries to start a New Yorker–style magazine. Kitty signs on as his secretary. The business soon flounders, however, and Kitty realizes that Wyn's family, comprised strictly of Philadelphia blue bloods, simply will not permit him to marry her. She flees to Chicago, losing herself in the working world until Wyn shows up and, for the second time, proposes marriage. They return to Philadelphia just as Kitty's father is dying.

After a short, idyllic spell with Wyn, Kitty again terminates their affair and goes to New York to recover. Here she begins working for Delphine Detaille, a Frenchwoman who owns and runs a blossoming perfume business. For fulfillment, Kitty turns to the world of advertising where she succeeds as a knowing and slightly cynical manipulator of women's fears and desires.

Wyn appears yet again. This time Kitty's romance with him is cut short by his unwilling engagement to a Philadelphia socialite, and Kitty, now pregnant by him, must have an abortion. She survives the ordeal with her self-respect intact and reaffirms her emotional and economic independence. Indeed, she never blames Wyn for what has happened. As she sees it, whereas she has escaped her working-class surroundings and succeeded through hard work and determination, Wyn has failed to follow his own path by succumbing to the desires of his family.

Free of Wyn at last, Kitty takes a vacation from work and meets Mark, a Jewish doctor. She admires his straightforwardness and charity, but her appreciation of him is poisoned by her nascent anti-Semitism as well as a reluctance to give up her independence. At the novel's end, it is uncertain whether or not Kitty will stay with Mark; what is clear is that he, unlike Wyn, is a grown-up whom she must confront on equal terms.

Frado. *Our Nig; or, Sketches from the Life of a Free Black.* Harriet E. Wilson. 1859.

The child of a white mother and a black father, Frado enters a hostile world the moment she is born. Her mother, who married Frado's father in order to escape starvation, resolves to rid herself of her child after the father's death and thus escape the stigma of having a mulatto daughter. The five-year-old Frado is abandoned at the home of a well-to-do white New England family, the Bellmonts.

Out of a mixture of pity and practicality, the Bellmonts decide to take the child into their home, and she becomes the one-person household staff and part-time field hand for Mr. and Mrs. Bellmont, their children Jane, Mary, and Jack, and Mr. Bellmont's sister, Aunt Abby. Any deviation from Mrs. Bellmont's exacting routine or complaint from Frado elicits stern words and harsh physical abuse from the woman. Mr. Bellmont, although critical of his wife's treatment of the little girl, declines to interfere.

After a year, Frado, dubbed "our Nig" by the family, is allowed to go to school with Mary on the condition that her chores at home not be neglected. Although initially the white children ridicule her, all except Mary grow to love Frado, who has developed a sense of humor despite the adversity she has faced. Frado finds friends in Jack and Jane, who in contrast to their mother's and sister's poor treatment of her, and their father's virtual indifference, try to shield her from harm and even give her a pet dog, Fido.

Judging Frado's education complete after three years of schooling, Mrs. Bellmont withdraws the nine-year-old from school so that she can devote all her time to serving the family. When Mrs. Bellmont's treatment of her becomes more and more abusive, Frado runs away, but Jack finds her with Fido's help and persuades her to return. Jack's older brother James, who has been visiting the family, tries to console Frado, but her sorrow leads her to question why God chose to make her black and allowed her to be victimized by so many people.

The few joys in Frado's life disappear when Jack and Jane leave home; only Aunt Abby remains to protect her from Mrs. Bellmont's and Mary's wrath. Aunt Abby and James, who returns home to recuperate from an illness, try to secure better treatment for Frado, who is herself suffering the effects of physical abuse and malnutrition. Despite her other chores, Frado helps nurse James, and he gives her religious instruction, against his mother's wishes. Her spirit rallies, but Frado's body grows so weak that she is unable to stand. Her sickness precipitates a particularly cruel beating by Mrs. Bellmont.

Cursing her condition, Frado doubts whether God cares for her, and after James's death she mourns his loss and perceives her own unfitness for heaven. She turns for advice to Aunt Abby, who offers her guidance as James had. Frado decides to stay with the family until she is eighteen.

When she is finally free from Mrs. Bellmont, the frail Frado languishes in county-run rest homes for three years until she recovers sufficiently to work again. She moves to Massachusetts where she works as a seamstress and devotes her spare time to reading and Christian study. She meets and falls in love with Samuel, a man who travels the area giving lectures on his experiences as a slave and a fugitive. After a brief courtship, they marry and have a child. Eventually revealing that he had never in fact been a slave but had lectured only to make money, Samuel deserts his family. Frado, in poor health, is once again left to fend for herself.

Frances. "The Girls in Their Summer Dresses." Irwin Shaw. 1950.

On a Sunday stroll down Fifth Avenue, Michael and Frances, a married couple, walk toward Washington Square after deciding to spend the entire day together away from friends and family.

Frances begins to plan the day, then realizes that Michael is not paying her the least bit of attention. Instead, his gaze is drawn toward a beautiful young woman. When her husband remarks on the woman's attractiveness, Frances displays her anger. To make up for his faux pas, Michael apologizes and declares himself happily married. Because she does not want to spoil their day together, Frances consciously returns to her former carefree mood.

Later, however, over a brandy, the two talk honestly about Michael's habit of watching other women and commenting on their looks to Frances. Michael admits that he has a proclivity for girl-watching. Moreover, he confesses that one of the things he likes best about New York is "the battalions of women."

When Frances tags his habit as adolescent, Michael argues that even in middle age he still enjoys looking at women. Frances finally charges Michael with looking at other women as though he wished he were free to pursue them. Michael denies this, but Frances continues to push, telling her husband that eventually he is going to leave her. Again, Michael denies his wife's accusations. In the face of her earnest appeals, however, he admits that she is correct. Hurt but resolved, Frances requests that from now on Michael refrain from bringing her attention to each woman he finds attractive.

Having reached this agreement, the couple forgo their Sunday together and decide to drive to the country with friends.

Frances. "Wunderkind." Carson McCullers. 1936.

Frances, a fifteen-year-old pianist, must live with the burden of having once been a *Wunderkind*, or child prodigy. For the last four months, Frances has been having trouble with her music. As she waits for her lesson to begin, she thinks back on what has happened. Since she was twelve years old, Frances has studied piano with Mr. Bilderbach, a kind, middle-aged man of German descent who teaches music in Cincinnati. When Frances first came to Mr. Bilderbach, she impressed him by playing the whole Second Hungarian Rhapsody from memory. He had told her then that there was more to playing music than mere cleverness, more than mere mechanics. Still, he had pronounced her a *Wunderkind*, and the two of them had gone on to devote their energy to bringing out what she surely had in her.

Throughout junior high school Frances practiced every day for three hours, five hours, or more. She met twice a week with Mr. Bilderbach for lessons, after school on Tuesdays and on Saturday afternoons. Sometimes after the Saturday lesson she would stay for dinner with Mr. Bilderbach and his wife, then spend the night and take the streetcar home in the morning. When she was thirteen, it dawned on her that Mr. Bilderbach and his wife had no children. They were affectionate toward her and concerned about her in ways her parents were not. When Mr. Bilderbach learned that Frances was going to borrow her cousin's dress to wear for junior high graduation, for instance, he personally went downtown with her and selected materials, and his wife made a new dress especially for her.

During this time Frances's only friend her own age is a boy named Heime Israelsky, a violinist who has been playing since age four. Heime studied with Mr. Bilderbach's good friend Mr. Lafkowitz, and the two old teachers would sometimes play music together and then listen proudly as their two *Wunderkinder*, Frances and Heime, played a duet.

With trepidation, Frances remembers the concert she and Heime played together. It wasn't until months afterward that she realized it had not been a success for her. While the newspapers praised Heime to the skies, Frances was criticized for her coldness, her lack of emotion. Frances can blame this partly on the fact that the piece they played was more favorable to the violin than the piano, but the question of why the concert failed still gnaws at her and haunts her dreams. She tells herself that as she grows older she will get better, yet in the last four months she has felt less connected with her playing than ever before; the notes have been coming out with a dead intonation.

As Frances waits, she notices a copy of the *Musical Courier*, with a picture of Heime on page one. Heime went to New York where he ate at the Russian Tea Room and prepared for a recital at Carnegie Hall. It is a silly picture of Heime, yet seeing it makes Frances want to cry. She has felt that way a lot recently, finding herself on the verge of tears for no good reason. She thinks that perhaps it is adolescence but wonders why she can't express the longing she feels through her playing.

The lesson begins. Mr. Bilderbach is, as always, gentle, sweet, and paternal. "Today I expect something from you," he says. He asks her to play a Beethoven sonata, the first Beethoven sonata she ever learned. The piece is technically not a problem. Mr. Bilderbach wants her to concentrate on the emotion. Frances concentrates but expresses no emotion. It is as if her hands are separate from the music that is within her. She finishes, and Mr. Bilderbach looks at her with a thoughtful expression. "No," he says simply.

"I can't help it," says Frances. Mr. Bilderbach smiles. Then, in the kind of voice he would use with a child, he asks her to play "The Harmonious Blacksmith," one of the first things they ever worked on together. "So strongly you used to play it," he says, "like a real blacksmith's daughter. You see, I know you so well—as if you were my own girl. I know what you have—I've heard you play so many things so beautifully. You used to—"

Mr. Bilderbach stops, as if confused by his own speech. "Make it simple and happy," he says. Frances begins to play, but she cannot stop looking at Mr. Bilderbach, watching hopefully and expectantly. Frances wants desperately to fulfill his hopes, but her heart feels dead. She looks down at the piano and sees her tears falling on the white keys. "I can't," she whispers. "I don't know why, but I just can't—can't anymore." She grabs her music, her coat and mittens, and her schoolbooks, and runs from the room—quickly, so that Mr. Bilderbach will not have the chance to say anything. She stumbles down the steps into the wintry twilight and rushes in the wrong direction down the busy street where other children are playing games in the cold afternoon.

Françon, Dominique. *The Fountainhead.* Ayn Rand. 1952.

Dominique Françon, the novel's female protagonist, is a beautiful, cold woman who overcomes her fear of the world through her relationship with HOWARD ROARK. The daughter of leading architect Guy Françon, Dominique has a troublesome relationship with her father, whom she terrifies. Ruthlessly independent, she follows a peculiar moral code of her own, allowing her scorn of insincerity and pretense to keep a barrier between herself and the world. She graduates from college, after which she writes a column on home decoration for a vulgar daily paper, *The Banner*, owned and run by Gail Wynand. In this column she sometimes pans her father's buildings, disgracing and infuriating him, although he recognizes her superior understanding of architecture. Many men fall in love with her—among them Peter Keating, a rising architect in her father's firm—but all find her thoroughly unresponsive.

When Dominique is twenty-five, she spends the summer at her father's house in Connecticut, near his granite quarry. One day she visits the quarry and is captivated by a tall, red-haired worker. Unable to forget him, she contrives to have him come to her house at night. He realizes her obsession and enjoys resisting her until one night he makes violent love to her. When he leaves the quarry suddenly, she is devastated. He has filled her with a passion she has never known before.

Dominique returns to the city and sees a brilliant architectural drawing in the paper by a man named Howard Roark. She meets Roark at a cocktail party and recognizes him as the man from the quarry, although they betray no signs of recognition. Dominique is terrified of this man's genius and uncompromising drive for excellence that stand apart from all she has known and despised in the world. She determines to ruin him while secretly hoping that he cannot be ruined. Publicly, she goes on a social and journalistic campaign against him; privately, they are lovers, with him feeling the sting of her vicious efforts while enjoying the challenge to overcome them.

Dominique poses for a statue to be placed in the center of a temple Roark is building. When Roark becomes involved in a lawsuit as a result of the building, Dominique publicly defends him and loses her job at *The Banner*. He loses, but while he is unscarred, she is devastated. She realizes she must learn to face her horror of the world before she can be worthy of Roark. Thus, she commits herself to enduring all that she despises, marrying first Peter Keating and then Gail Wynand. After years of separation, Dominique and Roark are brought together through Wynand, who recognizes Roark's genius. Dominique observes the intimate friendship between the two men, accepts the love of both, and waits for Roark. When he requests her help, she obeys. Wynand chooses to betray Roark in order to save his business, leaving Dominique and Roark to each other, a publicly united couple.

Frazer (Mr.). "The Gambler, the Nun, and the Radio." Ernest Hemingway. 1933.

Mr. Frazer is a patient in an isolated Montana hospital who numbs his physical pain and emotional despair by listening to the radio. If he listens to various programs in his private room, Frazer can safely maintain an interest in the outside world without confronting it. The few real human encounters he has during the course of the story convince him of the necessity of the anesthetic of radio to ease the inevitable pains of human existence.

Frazer's hospital stay, the original cause of which is never explained, is prolonged by a strange accident. The doctor, pointing out to Frazer a pair of pheasants on the lawn outside, upsets a lamp, and its iron base hits Frazer on the head, knocking him unconscious. He recovers enough, nevertheless, to act as interpreter for a Mexican named Cayetano who has been injured in a shooting. As the police stand by, Frazer attempts with patience and humor to convince Cayetano to name the man who shot him. But the Mexican considers it dishonorable to denounce one's assailant and refuses to help the police. Following the interview, Frazer does not see Cayetano for some time; each day he waits for Sister Cecilia, a nun, to bring news of the injured man.

Three Mexicans visiting Cayetano stop in Frazer's room; he offers them drinks and engages them in conversation. He learns that Cayetano is a gambler and the only good guitar player in town. On their next visit with Frazer, the Mexicans bring beer in spite of the insistence of one man that alcohol, like religion, is an "opium of the people." By this time Frazer's emotional state has deteriorated, and he begins to take imaginary journeys at night to the sources of the various radio programs he hears. When Sister Cecilia visits, however, Frazer is able to listen patiently to her dreams of becoming a saint. He also sees Cayetano, whose health is much improved, and is again impressed by his humility and stoicism.

Frazer remains passive during these encounters, fighting the temptation to think or feel. During the third visit from the three Mexicans, however, Frazer becomes lost in his own thoughts. Listening to the Mexicans play ridiculous songs, he contemplates the metaphor of religion as an "opium." In his mind he compiles his own list of opiates, including ambition, education, faith in government, and bread. Confronting the Mexican whose statement spawned his introspection, Frazer argues that all the opiates of the people are actually good. The two men conclude that they do not understand each other, and Frazer dismisses the Mexicans. As they leave, Frazer anticipates turning on his radio and returning to the anesthetized state that it guarantees.

Freedman, Joe. *The Old Bunch.* Meyer Levin. 1937.

Joe Freedman is the only artist in this account of a group of Jewish youths coming of age in Chicago in the 1920s and 1930s. As such, he is particularly sensitive and vulnerable to the difficulties encountered by his generation.

One of these difficulties is parental expectations. Joe's father owns a flophouse, and like his friends' parents, Joe's parents are eager for him to rise to a position of respectability and material comfort. Joe's girlfriend Sylvia holds similar expectations; she exerts heavy pressure on Joe to eschew idealism in favor of material forms of success. Due to these pressures, Joe majors in architecture rather than art at Illinois University.

However, on a post-graduation trip to Europe, Joe is inexorably drawn to sculpture. After returning to America, he is frequently forced to channel his artistic impulses into purely profit-making ventures such as designing car hood ornaments. Nevertheless, he becomes increasingly dedicated to sculpture and eventually ends his relationship with Sylvia, recognizing that she will be happier with his friend MITCH WILNER, a young doctor with a promising career in medical research.

Joe wins a Guggenheim Fellowship that enables him to spend a year in Paris. In Europe, Joe is plagued by a sense of spiritual emptiness that prevents him from being able to create, but a visit to Palestine has an inspiring effect on him. Whereas the other members of "the old bunch" achieve only passing sensations of continuity with their heritage, Joe enjoys a deep sense of connection with his people as he works on the sculpture of a heroic Zionist pioneer.

Back in America, the Great Depression has begun, and Joe cannot sell his pieces or acquire commissions. Still haunted by his love for Sylvia, who has married Mitch, he moves to New York for a time, but finding only meaningless commercial work, he returns to Chicago.

At this point Joe's situation begins to improve. When his father dies, Joe feels that he has finally become a man, and when he encounters the now pregnant Sylvia, he realizes that he has always been in love with love rather than with her. Joe now understands that his creativity has always been hindered by two ideals instilled in him from childhood: romantic love and financial security. Renouncing these, Joe feels that he can finally create.

Meanwhile, he has been commissioned to create sculptures for the Chicago World's Fair, one of which is a colossal figure of Moloch for Jewish Day at the fair. Working on this figure gives Joe the same sense of satisfaction he had experienced with his Zionist sculpture, and on Jewish Day he is once again deeply moved by the beauty of his people and their heritage. As the novel ends, Joe has been taken on by one of the new federally funded arts projects, and he is ready to use this opportunity to create a monument not only to Jewish Americans but to the American mystique in itself.

Freedman, Oscar "Ozzie." "The Conversion of the Jews." Philip Roth. 1959.

Oscar Freedman is a questioning, rambunctious thirteen-year-old whose rebellious behavior has often gotten him in trouble at his Hebrew school. As the story opens, Ozzie has once again found himself in hot water, this time for asking Rabbi Binder why, if God was powerful enough to create the universe, he couldn't also have impregnated Mary without intercourse.

Oscar's mother is coming for a third conference with the rabbi on Wednesday after Hebrew school. During that afternoon's free discussion period, Rabbi Binder forces Ozzie to speak; Ozzie complies by demanding to know why God can't "make anything He wants to make." Then, feeling particularly victimized by the rabbi and also by the fact that his mother slapped him when she heard the story the night before, he accuses Binder of not knowing anything about God. The rabbi slaps Ozzie hard enough to make his nose bleed, and Ozzie, cursing at Binder, runs as fast as he can to the roof of the synagogue.

Once on the roof, with everyone staring up at him, Ozzie is surprised to feel a certain peacefulness and power. Rabbi Binder begs him desperately to come down, but Ozzie doesn't comply; when the old janitor calls the fire department and engines rush onto the scene with a great clamor, Ozzie suddenly realizes that what for him was an attempt to get away from Binder is being interpreted as a threat of suicide. He begins to play with the firemen, running from corner to corner of the roof and forcing them to rush after him with their huge yellow net. Ozzie's friends soon begin shouting to him to jump, sounding a strange counterpoint to Rabbi Binder's pleas for Ozzie to come down safely.

Mrs. Freedman arrives for her appointment with the rabbi; when she sees her son on the roof and hears the childish shouts of "Jump!" she begs him not to be a martyr. The sound of her voice compels Ozzie to action. He demands that everyone kneel, and in a strange kind of catechism, he makes them all admit that God is capable of anything, that he "can make a child without intercourse." He ends his sermon by telling his mother, "You should never hit anybody about God." The story closes with Ozzie jumping safely into the net.

Fremont, Kitty. *Exodus.* Leon Uris. 1958.

Kitty Fremont, an American woman drawn to Palestine after the deaths of her husband and young daughter, hopes that work will help her recover from her loss. She becomes a nurse and takes a job at an orphanage on Salonika. When her work there is finished, she vacations on Cyprus, where, through an old friend, she meets ARI BEN CANAAN, an agent working undercover for a Zionist organization that helps Jews enter Palestine. Ari asks Kitty to work as a nurse and courier in a detention camp for Jews in the town of Caraolos. Kitty is reluctant at first, but touched by Ari's dedication, she agrees to visit the camp. At the camp she sees KAREN HANSEN CLEMENT, a young girl who bears an uncanny resemblance to her dead daughter, and she resolves to do all she can to help the Zionists with their cause.

The organization has secretly planned to have a ship filled with children stopped by the British outside of Palestine in order to create a media event that will force the authorities to allow them passage. Kitty is concerned when Karen begs to accompany the other children on the ship. The older woman knows the trip will be dangerous, but because she cannot tell Karen of the secret plan to have the ship stopped in the harbor, she must watch as the young girl leaves with the others.

The plan goes according to schedule, and the ship, the *Exodus*, is held. When the British refuse passage, the smugglers threaten to blow up the ship, and the children begin a hunger strike. The authorities finally allow the ship to pass, and Karen and the others are admitted to Palestine. Concerned about the young girl who has become a surrogate daughter, Kitty decides to follow them.

In Palestine, Ari Ben Canaan drives Kitty to Jerusalem, and she soon begins work as the head nurse at Gan Dafna, the settlement where Karen is living. Kitty runs the clinic and hospital with strict efficiency, but she is very warm with the children. She and Karen grow still closer, and Kitty begins to train Karen to be a nurse. Kitty sees Ari occasionally, but he is often away on business. When she and Ari go away together for a few days, they find they are strongly attracted to each other. But Kitty becomes frightened of their intimacy, and she suddenly withdraws. Ari checks out of the hotel the next morning without saying good-bye.

Kitty decides to leave for America and asks Karen, now a young woman, to go with her. But when Ari is severely wounded after breaking out of prison with a terrorist group, Kitty postpones her trip and rushes to his side. She removes a bullet from his leg, but once she knows that he is out of danger, she decides to leave again and still does not allow herself to love him.

When a group of new nurses need to be trained, Kitty puts off her travel plans again to help. Finally, on the eve of her planned departure, Kitty decides to stay at Gan Dafna after all and to continue her work there.

Kitty eventually becomes very important to the Jewish cause and even learns Hebrew, but after several years she decides once again to leave Israel. Soon after, at a holiday celebration to which both Kitty and Ari are invited, the two learn of Karen's death in an Arab raid on a kibbutz. Ari and Kitty turn to each other for comfort. Then, on his knees, Ari asks for Kitty's hand in marriage. She agrees, and at the novel's close they are planning their life together.

French, Carl. *Sent for You Yesterday.* John Edgar Wideman. 1983.

Carl French, black and an only child, grows up in Homewood, a Philadelphia neighborhood, during the 1930s. Carl and his friends, BROTHER TATE and LUCY TATE, spend a great deal of time together. Brother's albinism initially repels Carl, but later he fancies that he can see right through his friend's pale skin, and this perception inspires a closeness and a feeling of protectiveness that will characterize their lifelong friendship. The boys develop a dangerous game of standing as near as possible to speeding railroad trains, and this draws them even closer. Meanwhile, Carl finds himself increasingly attracted to the maturing Lucy.

One day Lucy shows Carl a piece of a skull that she found cleaning up after a murder in a bar. The horror of this souvenir of Albert Wilkes, his father's best friend, and Lucy's physical attractiveness drive Carl to distraction, and before he really knows what is happening, the youngsters begin making love. During the act, Carl fears he might urinate and embarrass himself in front of Lucy. For the next several years Carl longs to repeat the experience, especially as he grows to understand how his body works. Finally, after three years of waiting, he and Lucy make love again; this time both enjoy it a great deal.

Although Carl wants nothing more than to remain in Homewood, he is drafted at the beginning of World War II. Throughout the war Carl retains his affection for Lucy and Brother, and he anticipates returning to a normal life. The images and horrors of the war plague him long after his return home, however, and in particular he recalls the macabre task of plowing the bodies of dead G.I.s off a cliff and into the sea.

When Carl returns to Homewood, he and Lucy make love for the third time and reach a tacit agreement that they are a couple, although they do not marry. Brother, in the meantime, fathers a son, Junebug, who dies in a horrible accidental fire in 1946. Carl steadfastly stays by his grief-stricken friend, who abandons both his music and speech in response to the boy's death. Carl eventually introduces Brother to drawing, which seems to help although he remains mute.

Carl confides only in Lucy about his frustrations with the racism he encountered during the war that plagues him during his G.I. Bill–funded studies at the university. When Brother kills himself in 1962 on the train tracks where he and Carl once played as boys, Carl assiduously tries to communicate to his nephew, Doot French, the feeling of life in Homewood and of Brother's importance to that past.

French, Mary. *U.S.A. (The Big Money).* John Dos Passos. 1936.

As a little girl growing up in the mining town of Trinidad, Colorado, Mary French is torn between her constantly battling parents. Her father is a doctor with socialist leanings who insists on treating immigrant mining families at little or no charge instead of attending to the prosperous clientele of his wife's choosing. At the instigation of Mary's mother, the family moves to Colorado Springs where Mary gets a better education and (to the regret of her anti-Semitic mother) becomes best friends with Ada Cohn.

By the end of Mary's junior year at Vassar, her parents are divorced. After a brief time working at Hull House in Chicago, Mary returns to Denver to help her father with office work. He dies from overwork during a flu epidemic, and resolving to stay in Chicago rather than finish college, she leaves Colorado—and her mother—forever.

In Chicago, Mary works at Hull House and takes up with the philandering labor leader G. H. Barrow. Soon tiring of social work, however, she leaves Chicago to work in a diner in Cleveland and then goes to Pittsburgh where she writes for one of the major newspapers.

One of Mary's newspaper stories is a feature about labor organizers involved in a steel industry strike. Under the tutelage of Gus Moscowski, a young organizer, she becomes devotedly sympathetic toward the striking workers. When the newspaper rejects her piece, she starts writing for the union.

After seeing Gus get arrested, Mary is ready to leave Pittsburgh; she goes to Washington, D.C., as G. H. Barrow's secretary, gets pregnant, has an abortion, and goes to live with her old friend Ada Cohn in New York.

Through working for the Ladies' Garment Workers' Union, Mary meets the fugitive communist Ben Compton. She hides him in Ada's apartment (Ada is away), and they have a love affair until his emotional volatility leads them to quarrel.

After Ben leaves her, Mary flees to Boston to support Sacco and Vanzetti. Passionate in her efforts to vindicate the innocent anarchists, she works tirelessly, obtaining money from her estranged but now wealthy mother in Colorado Springs. Finally, she gets arrested and clubbed by policemen at a rally, and wins the esteem of communist leader Don Stevens. When they return to New York, they live together until he is called away to Russia on "party business."

When he returns, Mary learns he has married an attractive young English communist in Moscow. Angry and bitter, she mopes around for a while until Ada coaxes her

to attend a party at the home of her friend EVELINE HUTCHINS. There she meets G. H. Barrow again and finds that she now despises his cynicism. She also sees such glitzy people as the actress MARGO DOWLING. Revolted, Mary returns to her Party work. When she learns the next day that Eveline has committed suicide, it only serves to confirm her belief that all life is hollow unless one works for the revolution.

Frome, Ethan. *Ethan Frome.* Edith Wharton. 1911.

Ethan Frome is a man in his fifties who looks much older. Bent and taciturn, he has suffered heavily on the austere landscape of his farm in Starkfield, Massachusetts. After years of mind-numbing labor, Ethan unexpectedly encounters beauty and excitement in the person of MATTIE SILVER, his wife's impoverished cousin, but the hope she instills in him is extinguished by a brutally ironic twist of fate.

As a youth Ethan had left his family farm to study his great love, science, in Worcester, and once he went as far as Florida for a brief engineering job. But the illness of his parents called him home, and he never escaped again. He married ZENOBIA "ZEENA" PIERCE (FROME), a distant cousin who nursed his mother, because he was lonely and fearful. Shortly thereafter he settled into back-breaking farm work.

Ethan's circumstances brighten considerably with the arrival of Mattie, who comes to help with the housework when Zeena begins to suffer a host of presumably imagined ailments. On their long walks together, he shares with her what little he knows about the beauty of the countryside, trying to communicate the sense of wonder he has always felt about the earth and the sky and the distant constellations. He feels that in Mattie he has at last found a kindred spirit, and the young woman secretly falls in love with him.

Although unsure of Mattie's feelings and terribly shy about his own, Ethan becomes jealous of the attention Mattie gets from the village youths. Walking her home one night after a dance, he begins to reveal his affection for her. The episode causes Zeena to increase her already strong resentment of her cousin.

When Zeena goes away overnight for medical attention, Ethan comes even closer to revealing his love by kissing a piece of muslin Mattie is sewing. But Zeena's return puts an end to the fledgling romance. She announces that she needs better care than Mattie can provide and that Mattie can no longer be supported by the household. Heartbroken, Ethan comes close to fleeing with Mattie, going so far as to write Zeena a farewell letter; but he realizes that not only can he not abandon his ailing wife, he does not have enough money to start a new life with Mattie in the West.

On his way with Mattie to the station for her departure, Ethan convinces her to go sledding with him. After one transporting flight down the hill, he kisses her ardently and knows he can never leave her. Hoping to perish in a moment of bliss and to flee forever a world in which they do not feel they belong, Ethan and Mattie descend the hill again, steering toward the menacing elm below.

But the lovers are not destroyed. Instead, Mattie is horribly maimed and is brought back to the house where Zeena, her stronghold reaffirmed, can act as a nurse to her now helpless cousin. Ethan remains in the shut-away house with the two women. The reader is left to imagine his horror and despair as the once sweet and beautiful Mattie takes on both the outer and inner characteristics of Zeena until the two women seem finally to have become interchangeable.

Frome, Zenobia Pierce "Zeena." *Ethan Frome.* Edith Wharton. 1911.

The least communicative of this novel's taciturn characters, Zenobia "Zeena" Frome, née Pierce, is both a shrew and an emblem of the strength and endurance of the people of Starkfield, Massachusetts.

Seven years older than ETHAN FROME, Zeena had originally come to stay with him to nurse his ailing mother and had then become his wife because, as she says, he "couldn't do no less than" marry her. She soon reveals, however, that she is sicklier than Ethan's own mother had been, a victim of a host of unnamed and presumably half-imagined "troubles" and "complications." Shortly after the marriage, Zeena begins to torment her husband with nagging, moaning, and badgering, and with the debts she incurs by buying one patent medicine after another.

After her impoverished but bright and cheerful young cousin MATTIE SILVER comes to live with the Fromes, Zeena becomes more reserved. If she is aware of the growing affection between Mattie and Ethan, she says nothing explicit about it, but she drives her young helper hard in the house and complains about her inefficient household work.

One morning Zeena announces her intention of going to a neighboring town overnight to see a special physician from Springfield. When she returns, ever jealous of Mattie, she informs Ethan that her condition is more serious than even she had imagined and that she must have a real hired girl to do the housework for her. In fact, a girl has already been contracted and will arrive the next afternoon. This means Mattie must leave and somehow find other employment to support herself. Whether Zeena has concocted this story in order to rid her household of Mattie is unclear, but once she sees that her plans are to be carried out, she energetically torments the unfortunate Mattie about various missing or broken items.

However, when Mattie is paralyzed in a sledding accident, Zeena becomes more sympathetic. Knowing that her injured cousin must now stay with her and Ethan, she assumes the duties of caring for her and for the household.

By the end of the novel, much to Ethan's horror, the once lovely Mattie has become a carbon copy of Zeena, nagging and whining in a plaintive, reedy voice.

Frowenfeld, Joseph. *The Grandissimes.* George Washington Cable. 1879.

Joseph Frowenfeld is the lens through which George Washington Cable portrays New Orleans Creole society. Although American born, Frowenfeld is consistently referred to as an immigrant because he is a northerner of German descent who is not always sympathetic to the Creole way of life.

Frowenfeld moves to New Orleans with his family in 1803, the year Napoleon ceded Louisiana to the United States. Almost immediately the entire family falls victim to a fever that Joseph alone survives. Upon recovering, one of his first excursions is to the graves of his family. At the cemetery he meets HONORÉ GRANDISSIME, the director of a mercantile house and the chief financial advisor of his Creole family's plantation empire. Shortly thereafter, Frowenfeld, who has decided to open an apothecary shop, is surprised to learn that the landlord of the building in which he intends to house his store is owned by Honoré's elder half-brother HONORÉ GRANDISSIME, f.m.c. ("free man of color"). Both brothers attempt to befriend Frowenfeld, but the social and ethnic structure of Creole society limits Frowenfeld's contact with Honoré f.m.c. Frowenfeld and the younger Honoré form a friendship despite profound differences in their cultural and political points of view.

The political atmosphere in New Orleans in 1803 is explosive; Frowenfeld has no sympathy for the outrage of such Creole families as the Grandissimes, whose wealth is threatened by Congress's reticence to honor land titles authorized by the previous governments of France and Spain. The younger Honoré eventually becomes a kind of disciple to Frowenfeld, who condemns the plantation system.

Frowenfeld involves himself further in the Grandissimes' affairs when he convinces two members of the family to call off a scheduled duel. A substantial faction of the Grandissime family, under the leadership of Honoré's uncle Agricola Fusilier, destroys Frowenfeld's apothecary shop and are only deterred from burning it to the ground by the arrival of the new governor's police. Undaunted, Frowenfeld opens a new store, once again in the Creole quarter.

Despite his aversion to certain aspects of his Creole milieu, Frowenfeld falls in love with Clotilde Nancanou, whose mother Aurora is a De Grapion, the traditional rival family of the Grandissimes. With Clotilde's financial backing, Frowenfeld's new business thrives. The novel concludes with an account of Frowenfeld's courtship of Clotilde and the younger Honoré's proposal of marriage to Aurora. Having gained social acceptance through his friendship with Honoré and romantic satisfaction through his relationship with Clotilde, Frowenfeld achieves success at last as the northern entrepreneur whose commercial skills will replace the plantation system of the Old South.

Fry, Tony. *Tales of the South Pacific.* James A. Michener. 1946.

Tony Fry is the guiding spirit behind this collection of stories and vignettes. Although Tony appears as a central character in only five of the tales, it is his brand of happy-go-lucky élan that invests the book with its appealing humanism.

Tony Fry is a lieutenant in the naval reserve who is serving under Admiral Kester in the Pacific theater of operations during 1941–43, crucial years in which the American forces turned the tide of the war against the Japanese. His assignments are never routine; for instance, he is put in charge of building an airstrip on Norfolk Island, a former penal colony and the present abode of the descendants of Fletcher Christian and the Bounty mutineers. The only viable location for the airstrip would require cutting down an avenue of Norfolk Island's distinctive pine trees planted by past generations of the inbred Bounty folk. Tony personally cannot make the decision to cut down the pines, and when they are being cut, he actually keeps the spirit of mutiny alive in the islanders by helping them blow up a bulldozer, although admittedly a useless one.

Tony has a sensitivity for the Pacific Islanders and their culture which the American forces cannot possibly have en masse. He also exhibits an irreverence for military discipline and a flare for bending the rules. He is never without a supply of liquor, even when posted to listen on the barren island of Tulagi for the faint radio signals of a spy behind enemy lines. In fact, he uses an old navy plane to supply his friends with Christmas spirits. He undermines the authority of more traditional officers and is considered good luck by the enlisted men who take him on occasional PT boat cruises.

Tony's erratic enthusiasms and obsessions reach their climax when he falls in love with Latouche De Becque, the beautiful "Frenchman's daughter," as she is called by her admirers. Tony is unlike other Americans in the book whose prudery and racism make it impossible for them to conceive of interracial marriages; he happily marries Latouche in a Buddhist ceremony.

But even Tony cannot counter the devastating effects of the war with love. When the allies attack the Japanese-held island of Kuralei, he is assigned to be beachmaster, managing the arrival and organization of troops and supplies on one of the beachheads. After his beach is secure, Tony is killed in a surprise attack from the Kuralei cliffs.

Fulton, Jesse. "The Happiest Man on Earth." Albert Maltz. 1938.

Jesse Fulton makes desperate attempts to support his family during the Great Depression. Although he has worked as a linotypist, the economic recession adversely affects this business, and he must rely on the meager proceeds he receives through a governmental relief program. Driven half mad by his inability to make ends meet, he walks from Kansas City, Missouri, all the way to Tulsa, Oklahoma, where his brother-in-law Tom Brackett lives, in the hope of using his relative's connections to find gainful employment.

The poverty brought about by the Depression has left its mark on the Fultons. Jesse's little boy has deformed legs, the result of rickets stemming from an inadequate diet. Jesse also notices with dismay that his wife Ella, once a beautiful young woman, has lost her looks at the age of twenty-nine. Jesse himself is so changed by poor food and despair that his brother-in-law does not recognize him when they meet after five years of separation. Although furious at Tom's undisguised amazement at the extent to which he has deteriorated, Jesse must rely on his good graces in order to get a job.

Although Tom is looking for new employees, he refuses to consider his brother-in-law for a job because of the danger involved in the line of work. Jesse knows that Tom dispatches trucks carrying nitroglycerin, which is so combustible that it can be transported only at night along special roads in custom-made trucks with rubber cushioning. When Jesse insists that he is willing to assume the risk, Tom counters with the news that Egbert, the man who had told Jesse that Tom was hiring, had been blown to bits the previous night. The explosion was so fierce that it destroyed the bridge on which the fatal accident took place; not one piece of the dead man's body survived the blaze.

Jesse continues to insist that he can no longer face his family or hold his head up in public; he simply will not take no for an answer. They wrangle for quite some time, until Jesse becomes so agitated that tears come to his eyes as he pleads with his brother-in-law. When Tom insists that Jesse must buck up and recover his hope in the future, Jesse maintains that it is too late to rely on hope and that he must somehow attempt to make up for his past failures for the sake of his family. He refuses to accept Tom's suggestion that his failure is not personal but the result of hard times.

Jesse's persistent arguments finally convince Tom to offer him a job as a driver. Ironically, having accepted a job that very seriously jeopardizes his life, Jesse sheds tears of elation and whispers, "I am the happiest man in the world."

Furness, Howard. *The Groves of Academe.* Mary McCarthy. 1952.

Howard Furness, a teacher at a small Pennsylvania college, shifts his loyalties during the course of a political struggle among the faculty over the position of HENRY

MULCAHY, an instructor in Furness's department. A cynic who apparently believes in nothing, Furness conveniently associates himself with the faction in power, adopting the stance that involves the least emotional and professional risk.

Furness heads the literature department at Jocelyn College, a small "progressive" school. A specialist in modern fiction, he is known at Jocelyn for his Proust-Joyce-Mann course. Henry Mulcahy, an expert in the same period, comes to the college and takes up the responsibility of teaching the same course in alternate years. The course serves as a buffer between the two men, who greatly dislike one another. Mulcahy has some terrible habits, however: He fails to turn in grades, neglects to return students' work, and misses conferences and tutorials. Furness becomes increasingly impatient with him. As department head he is forced to act as a mediator between Mulcahy and the student council, the bursar, the registrar, and the school newspaper.

When Mulcahy receives notice that his contract may not be renewed, he plots to undermine the reputation and authority of the college president, Maynard Hoar. Mulcahy spreads the rumor that he is not being punished for bad teaching but because the president has learned of his membership in the Communist Party. Furness knows that Mulcahy has no connections to the Party and speaks against him at a faculty meeting. But the other teachers are convinced that Mulcahy is a martyr and the president, a turncoat liberal. Even a furious look from DOMNA REJNEV, with whom he is half in love, only makes Furness more resolved to stand his ground. Mulcahy has also gained widespread sympathy by telling another lie, that he has a dying wife who has been upset by the questioning of his professional status.

Because the department cannot reach the unanimous decision necessary for dismissal, Mulcahy's contract is renewed. Furness is wooed by a disciple of Mulcahy's named Ellison and consents to support the two in their campaign for election to the committee in charge of organizing a poetry conference at Jocelyn. Although Furness knows that Mulcahy is a liar, he finds himself spending time at the Mulcahy home, which has become a "center of literary and artistic pronouncements" ever since Mulcahy criticized the president. Because he adores shifts of fashion, Furness takes delight in the reversal of fortune that has brought Mulcahy into power.

The poetry conference proceeds smoothly enough until a "proletarian poet," Vincent Keogh, approaches Mulcahy at a reception and reminds him of their good old days in the John Reed Club. Furness hustles Keogh out of bed the following morning and escorts him to President Hoar's office. Keogh confesses that he had once been assigned to recruit Mulcahy to the Communist Party but had been unsuccessful. During the final confrontation between Mulcahy and President Hoar, Furness is busy en-

tertaining a group of visiting poets. In the end, Hoar, who has just renewed Mulcahy's contract, is forced to resign over outrage that he had been harassing Mulcahy without cause. Furness emerges from the battle unscathed, having judiciously shifted his position each time a reversal of fortune occurred.

Fuselli, Dan. *Three Soldiers.* John Dos Passos. 1921.

Dan Fuselli is a young man from the urban working class who has faith in the army as an organization where ambition pays off. At the time he goes to fight in World War I, he has only one other aspiration—to remain faithful to Mabe, his fiancée back in San Francisco.

In 1917, Fuselli is an army private in a company of medics about to be shipped to France. He sets out to realize his primary purpose, promotion through the army ranks, by continually volunteering for extra duty. The corporal in his squad is consumptive, and Fuselli hopes that the man will be incapacitated enough to be discharged so that he can take over the position. By the time the company is in transit on a troopship overseas, Fuselli has become the first sergeant's favorite. On board ship, however, Fuselli begins to have some doubts: The steerage where the troops are quartered is a reeking, claustrophobic hole. "They had no right to treat a feller like that," he thinks.

Billeted in France, Fuselli's doubts begin to deepen. After witnessing a scene in which a veteran breaks down in public, he experiences real fear. Also, his first promotion to private first class finally comes through. He meets a woman, Yvonne, in the village near where his regiment is quartered. She takes him as her lover and sneaks him nightly past her aged mother to her bedroom.

When Fuselli's consumptive corporal is finally ordered to take sick leave, the sergeant gives him a temporary corporalship. In the flush of his success, Fuselli takes the sergeant to Yvonne's to celebrate. A few weeks later when he goes to Yvonne's for a midnight tryst, he hears her signal, and from out of the darkness next to him, the sergeant steps up to the door. Fuselli has been replaced. Returning to the barracks that night, he meets the sick corporal who has just returned from leave; the next day Fuselli is back to private first class.

When the company receives orders to head for the front, Fuselli begins to reflect on his situation. That very day he has heard of a job opening for an optical goods clerk at the camp. It is the job he did as a civilian. He puts in for it, and the hour his company entrains for the front, he is called out of the ranks and assigned to the clerkship.

The novel's last glimpse of Fuselli takes place one year later. The war is over. He is in a labor battalion doing kitchen work for an officers' mess in Paris—his punishment for having contracted gonorrhea. Mabe has married another man, and his ambitions have deserted him completely.

G

Gallagher, Tommy. *Tommy Gallagher's Crusade.* James T. Farrell. 1939.

Dull-witted and cowardly, Tommy Gallagher becomes an active participant in racial hatred and the resulting violence that filters into the United States during Hitler's actions against German Jews. After hearing the views of Father Moylan, a Catholic priest turned white supremacist demagogue, Tommy convinces himself that his poor station in life results from Jewish control of capital and media in the United States.

Although the Depression continues, Tommy's two brothers and his father have managed to remain employed throughout. Tommy, on the other hand, has lost job after job. Father Moylan and his organization, the Association for Christian Freedom, have supplied him with a scapegoat for his own failures. He forgoes his quest for employment, refusing any help from his brothers and his father, and sells *Christian Justice*, the group's newspaper. As the group's activities become increasingly violent, Tommy imagines himself performing feats of heroism, ridding America of the communists and the Jews.

Meanwhile, Tommy's family has become frustrated with his attitudes and his behavior. Evening after evening they attempt to persuade him to disavow Father Moylan and seek employment. Tommy becomes increasingly resentful, accusing his family of succumbing to "eagle-beaks" who control the country. The harder his family pushes him to relent, the closer Tommy moves to Father Moylan's camp.

As the activities of the white supremacists increase around the country and the city, Tommy and other young men involved in the Association for Christian Freedom become violent. Initially, the unemployed men inflate their egos and bolster their self-esteem by harassing isolated individuals with apparently Semitic features. But as the communist and Jewish communities begin to organize in response to the increased violence, the hooligans disrupt street-corner meetings and pick fights. Encouraged by the success of these encounters and the publicity received by several men who are arrested and treated lightly by the authorities, Tommy and his friends plan to use strong-arm tactics to disrupt another meeting.

At this encounter the gang is surprised by the number of people present and their determination not to be intimidated. The five or six men find themselves outnumbered and outfought. They suffer numerous injuries and eventually must flee the scene. For several days Tommy hides at home, embarrassed to be seen in public with a horrible black eye. His entire family has lost patience with him

and demands that he quit his activities. When they threaten to stop supporting him, he storms out of the house in a rage.

He spends several hours roaming the city. As he rides the subway, he observes other people together and realizes how very alone and lonely he is. He skulks back home, crawls into bed, and does not respond to his brother's taunt that he does not even have the guts to sleep in the park.

Gallio, Marcellus. *The Robe.* Lloyd C. Douglas. 1942.

Marcellus Gallio, the novel's hero, is the son of a gallant and intrepid Roman tribune. Hot-headed and cocksure, he burst into laughter during the reading of a panegyric full of unwarranted praise for the pompous Prince Gaius, the emperor's heir apparent. As the novel opens, Gallio learns the consequences of this indiscretion: He has been given command of a Roman fort in remote Palestine, an assignment that amounts to virtual exile from the Roman court.

The fort at Minoa is notorious for its unruly ranks. True to their reputation, the soldiers are initially hostile to their new commander, but with his strong leadership, Marcellus is able to win their respect. Soon after his arrival the garrison is called to Jerusalem to keep the peace during the Jewish Passover. The assignment marks the beginning of Marcellus's conversion to Christianity.

In Jerusalem, Marcellus and his loyal Corinthian slave DEMETRIUS witness the trial of Jesus of Nazareth. When a guilty verdict is handed down, Marcellus is ordered by the procurator, Pilate, to carry out the execution of Jesus. Uncomfortable with his participation in the crucifixion, Marcellus distracts himself by drinking. Intoxicated, he callously rolls dice for the robe of the crucified martyr and comes away from the gambling table with his prize, a torn and bloodstained garment.

That evening at a banquet held by Pilate, the inebriated crowd shouts for Marcellus to don the garment. He reluctantly puts on the robe, but as he does so, he is momentarily paralyzed, struck by an overwhelming feeling of dread. He then orders the robe to be destroyed, and for several months after this, he is profoundly depressed.

Marcellus goes to Greece in an attempt to recover from his depression, but to no avail. Desperate, he decides to take his own life. While searching through Demetrius's baggage for a dagger, Marcellus discovers the robe. The slave, recognizing the garment's sacred power, hid it after his master had ordered it destroyed. Marcellus is horrified to see the object that had engendered his unbearable depression, but when he seizes the robe, his despair vanishes and he feels a sudden peace and well-being.

Struck by the miraculous experience, Marcellus decides to return to Palestine in order to learn more about the man who wore the robe. As he travels through the countryside, he is deeply moved by the humility, charity, and faith of the people who had known Jesus. Still, he remains skeptical when he hears the stories of the great miracles Jesus performed and of his resurrection from the dead.

However, when he witnesses the stoning of Saint Stephen, Marcellus is converted to Christianity. Looking into the dying Stephen's eyes, Marcellus is certain that it is Jesus who escorts the martyr into God's kingdom. The tribune's faith in Christ is now unshakable, and he begins to spread the message to others.

Marcellus is eventually led to proclaim his faith to Emperor Caligula, even though it is clear that doing so will result in his execution. Finding an inner strength in his faith, the young tribune faces his impending execution with a calm resignation. The novel ends with Marcellus looking joyfully toward the day when he will be united with Christ in paradise.

Galt, Thomas "Skinner." *The End of My Life.* Vance Bourjaily. 1947.

Thomas "Skinner" Galt exerts a powerful influence over other people, drawing disparate characters together through his compelling and wide-ranging intelligence. Yet he always remains detached and disaffected, and is convinced that, as much as there are elements of other people in himself, there is little of himself in any of his companions. This distance from others is increased by his tendency to subject his fellows to relentless and piercing analysis— analysis that he is afraid to turn on himself.

For Skinner, people and events are interesting only until they have joined "the category of things known." He recognizes that this highly rational approach to the world is ultimately destructive but maintains that he would rather destroy what he cares for through rationality than allow his irrational emotions to render him vulnerable.

When the novel opens, Skinner is leaving his New York home and his girlfriend Cindy to join the armed forces in Europe as an ambulance driver. Although he claims that he would like both to be a war hero and to rush headlong into marriage with Cindy, he is not capable of sustaining the necessary ideologies of love and war. His decision to join the allies is an attempt to escape from life at college; his feelings for Cindy have grown suddenly because his time with her is limited. Skinner admits that he is prompted to love and to fight only by curiosity and escapism.

Once he arrives in North Africa, Skinner quickly establishes a friendship with three other Americans, again becoming the center of a group. He maintains his characteristic detachment by realizing that the group spirit he has so easily established will not survive the group's separation. In much the same way, his early interest in North Africa threatens to be destroyed by his quick assimilation and understanding of this unknown continent. Yet Africa also shakes Skinner's intellectual arrogance, and for the first time he humbly realizes that he is confronted with something that will always remain unknowable.

After this moment Skinner grows increasingly disaffected with his relationship with Cindy. Their relationship had been characterized from the beginning by Skinner's simultaneous detachment and involvement, admitting that he loved Cindy yet realizing that "they were only words, but they came surely and sounded well." As Skinner becomes increasingly disillusioned, he responds to Cindy's letters by mocking her love for him, deriding his former feelings, and confessing his recent infidelities. Willfully cut off from any human contact, Skinner finally turns his cruel analysis on himself. As he cares less and less, he argues that suicide would be the final intellectual proof of his detachment and that this decision requires no courage but only an understanding of how meaningless life is.

Yet Skinner is prevented from suicide by a sentry. He never sees this chance as a reprieve, only discovering that suicide is merely an emotional and therefore an inferior choice. From this point on, Skinner is infected by a melancholia that deprives his thoughts and actions of any meaning. In a final act of betrayal, he takes a young American nurse on a date and tries to impress her by showing her the front. She is killed by a stray bullet, and Skinner is court-martialed and imprisoned. He receives a visit from Cindy and brutally turns her away, welcoming only the listlessness that his cell offers.

Gant, Benjamin Harrison. *Look Homeward, Angel.* Thomas Wolfe. 1929.

Ben Gant, whose twin brother Grover dies at age twelve from tuberculosis, is most remembered in this novel for his frequent expression of disbelief: "Oh for God's sake! Listen to this, won't you!" Highly critical of his family's behavior, he exudes a silent cynicism, captured in his brooding, scowling face. Ben is also a sickly person; he never engages in self-pity, but his often gloomy nature and listless movements reflect a continuing awareness of his fragile health. Although he has an occasional outburst, expressing contempt for his parents' stinginess and selfishness, Ben remains a very placid figure and is known by his family as the "quiet one."

As he becomes partially self-sufficient from his earnings as a newspaper boy, Ben manages to separate himself from most of his family, save for his little brother, EUGENE (GANT). Although he socializes frequently with his coworkers and other people around town, Ben remains a shadowy figure. Yet he is not withdrawn from everyone. The lack of any meaningful communication between Ben and his father, and the sensitivity he lacks in most dealings with his mother are compensated for in his affection for and protection of Eugene.

Despite his aloofness from most family members, Ben shares many of his father's and siblings' traits. Like some of his brothers, he attracts and is attracted to large, older women. He has several affairs with the women who lodge in his mother's boardinghouse, one whose daughter is Ben's age. Although he drinks on occasion and smokes habitually, Ben does not slip into the drunken and degenerate life-styles of his father and his oldest brother Steve. He uses his energy for hard, honest work that gives him a strong sense of pride and financial independence.

Denied admission to the armed services because he has weak lungs, Ben stays on at the newspaper in Altamont, his home in North Carolina, while taking an advertising course at night school. His increasing despondency encourages him to wander through the South selling space for advertisements to small-town merchants. He secures a job on a newspaper in a small tobacco town but returns home for Christmas and other occasions. On one of those occasions his health gradually worsens and keeps him at home. He dies from pneumonia at age twenty-six in the fall of 1918.

Gant, Eliza Pentland. *Look Homeward, Angel.* Thomas Wolfe. 1929.

Eliza Gant, wife of W. O. GANT and mother of the Gant children, sacrifices little of her own life to tend to the needs of her large family. To compensate for her own impoverished upbringing by her father, Major Thomas Pentland, Eliza is an avaricious and miserly adult. She seeks financial success at the expense of her children, demanding that they start work at an early age in order to become self-sufficient. She rarely gives them money without lecturing them, and although she claims to be teaching them the "value of a dollar," her motives are self-aggrandizing.

When Eliza meets W. O. Gant, she is working as a teacher and book publishing agent, using her savings to buy land in areas surrounding Altamont, North Carolina, where she later settles with Gant. Throughout their life together Eliza shamefacedly endures Gant's constant drunkenness, occasional invectives, and sometimes good humor and affection. Yet domestic commotion and familial demands pose no threat to her business aspirations.

Eliza bears ten children, only seven of whom live. With the birth of her last child, EUGENE (GANT), comes an intense desire to give her money-making schemes top priority. When Eugene is four years old, she takes him and his

siblings to the St. Louis Fair where she opens a boardinghouse. While there, Grover, one of Eliza's twin sons, dies of typhoid, and this forces her to return to Altamont.

When Eugene is old enough to work and sufficiently care for himself, Eliza buys and operates Dixieland, a boardinghouse that quickly occupies all of her time. The proximity of Dixieland to the Gant house allows Eliza to keep a motherly hold on Eugene: She makes him sleep in the same bed with her until he is nine years old and won't allow him to have his baby curls cut.

During her first winter at Dixieland, Eliza suffers severe attacks of rheumatism and other ailments. She takes several trips to the warmer climate of Florida, primarily in an effort to improve her health but always with an eye for valuable real estate. Her business interests and personal concerns are always more interesting to her than any of the interests or illnesses of others. Even when Eliza's health is perfect, she complains about every minor ache and pain. She is infamous for her reaction to others' sickness as something that is "all in the imagination."

After her son BENJAMIN HARRISON (GANT) dies of pneumonia and Eugene graduates from college and prepares to leave for graduate school, Eliza dedicates herself entirely to her financial acquisitions. Although she still runs Dixieland even in her sixties, she relinquishes the daily management to a housemaid. Her husband's imminent death after a lengthy battle with cancer gives her control over all his property, on which she quickly capitalizes. As his condition worsens, she talks incessantly of real estate.

Gant, Eugene. *Look Homeward, Angel.* Thomas Wolfe. 1929.

Eugene Gant is the hero of this novel, which records his growth and maturation from birth to the age of nineteen when he graduates from college and prepares to leave for graduate school. As a result of his excessive sensitivity and introspection, his growing fascination with literature, and his budding genius, Eugene is an isolated, contemplative figure who seeks fulfillment from life in his dreams and imagination.

As the baby of his family, Eugene suffers from the control of his parents and the jealousy and ridicule of his siblings. His mother, ELIZA (PENTLAND GANT), breast-feeds him until age three, makes him sleep with her until age nine, and prevents him from cutting his baby curls. Paradoxically, when Eugene is eight, Eliza attempts to foster a business sense in him by sending him out to sell subscriptions to the *Saturday Evening Post* and, later, to distribute advertisements for her boardinghouse, Dixieland.

Eugene's father W. O. GANT, has nurtured his reflective nature by reading Shakespeare and poetry to him at an early age. But when he later recognizes his son's intelligence and academic success, he hopes and plans for Eugene to become a lawyer, statesman, or politician. Eugene's affinity for escapist literature never ceases, however; it provides diversion from his mother's business operations and sets him apart from the extroverted personalities of his father and most of his siblings.

During his formative years, Eugene is forced to move frequently from his father's house to his mother's boardinghouse a few miles away. During summers and afternoons when Eugene is not accompanying his father to the movie house, he is in the library devouring books. Identifying with the fictional heroes, he imagines himself in exalted, triumphant roles.

When he is twelve, Eugene wins an essay contest that admits him to a private boys' school. Eugene feels uncomfortable with his contemporaries at the school because he has an awkward physique, a brooding temperament, and a superior intellect. He studies and excels in Greek, Latin, English literature, and poetry, and at fifteen he knows every major lyric in the English language. Admiring Shakespeare, Eugene writes an essay on the playwright that wins him a medal; he plays Prince Hal in a Shakespeare festival; he copies Ben Jonson's words, "My Shakespeare, rise!" onto his wall.

Although Eugene interacts socially during this time, he tends to be somewhat withdrawn. He gets a job as a paper carrier and befriends many of the other paperboys, but the job appeals to him mostly as an activity that he can perform alone. Increasingly sensitive to sights and smells, he especially likes having the early morning route because it leaves him free to observe and contemplate nature in the dawning hours of the day.

Margaret Leonard, the proprietor's wife and a teacher at the private school, inspires Eugene's love for poetry and nurtures his imagination. She wants him to attend Harvard, Vanderbilt, or even Oxford. Eugene's father, anxious to make Eugene a famous, wealthy politician, insists that he attend the state university and sends him off before he is sixteen years old.

A lanky six-feet-three-inches tall when he enters college, Eugene is at once a social outcast and a social attraction. His unusual appearance, introverted tendencies, and ignorance of campus life attract the mockery of his colleagues. Knowing that others single him out because of his looks or strange habits, Eugene glorifies his own uniqueness. He indulges in and romanticizes a life of seclusion. Academically, Eugene is passionate about the subjects he likes and lazy about the ones he does not. He continues to seek fulfillment and mind expansion through literature. Despite his initial antisocial tendencies, he joins every academic and social fraternity and acquires the position of managing editor of the college paper. He is eventually known, at least by name, to everyone he passes. Throughout college Eugene has many acquaintances but no one he can call his best friend.

Eugene's first intimate relationship with someone other than his brother BENJAMIN HARRISON (GANT) is a summer romance with Laura James, a boarder in his mother's house. Eugene, sixteen years old, falls in love with twenty-one-year-old Laura, and their love is consummated one afternoon during a picnic in the hills of Altamont. Soon after, Laura returns to her home in Virginia and sends Eugene a letter telling him that she is engaged to be married. Suffering from heartbreak and haunted by the constant memory of Laura, Eugene later goes to Richmond on a desperate, obsessive search for her, but they are never reunited.

At the end of his college career, Eugene's brother Ben, with whom he has had the closest and most meaningful relationship, dies of pneumonia. While Eugene was growing up, Ben was always the most encouraging and caring member of the family. The powerful effect of Ben's death on Eugene marks Eugene's desire to sever all family ties and influences his decision to attend Harvard graduate school. At the end of the novel, before Eugene leaves for Harvard, he imagines seeing Ben's ghost in the town square. From a dialogue with the ghost, Eugene derives the final inspiration to indulge his imaginative talents through the advanced study of literature and to fulfill his dreams by leaving home.

Gant, W. O. *Look Homeward, Angel.* Thomas Wolfe. 1929.

W. O. Gant, husband of ELIZA PENTLAND (GANT) and father of the Gant children, is the liveliest member of the Gant family. He has an abundance of energy, a large but lean physique, and a tremendous physical and emotional appetite that is never satiated. From his father he learns the craft of stonecutting and the spirit of wanderlust. Through his travels, experiences, and work he searches fervently for meaning and stability in life.

Gant moves from his childhood home in Baltimore to Sydney, North Carolina, where he opens a stonecutting shop and marries Cynthia. After Cynthia's sudden death from tuberculosis, he sinks into despair. Attempting to alleviate feelings of emptiness and loss, he drinks heavily. Gant's drinking causes his eventual deterioration, leading him near the fate he fears.

After enduring this period of depression, Gant journeys to Altamont, North Carolina, where he opens another stonecutting shop. He places before the door an imported Italian marble angel—a statue that both pleases and mocks him with a beauty more delicate than anything he has the skill to create. Gant meets, courts, and marries Eliza Pentland, and proudly builds the house where they will raise their large family. For Gant, this house is an extension of himself, but for Eliza it is a piece of property from which she can eventually profit. Gant enjoys wealth and abundance in any form, but he despises his wife's overweening interest in accumulating property. He denounces all of her real estate pursuits because he believes that property taxes rob him of his money.

Gant quickly establishes a reputation among the townspeople of Altamont because of his bimonthly frenzies in which he drinks, frequents prostitutes, and rants maniacally. Upon hearing that Eliza is pregnant with Eugene, their last child, Gant hurls insults at his wife. He constantly bemoans the paucity of funds, although his pocket is rarely empty. Bearing the brunt of Gant's unpredictable outbursts and unable to endure the abuse, Eliza sends Gant off to a sanitarium to be treated for alcoholism. Gant returns from treatment essentially unchanged, still restless and tormented by a lack of fulfillment. In an effort to find inner peace, he travels to California at the age of fifty-six.

Despite his wildness, Gant can be a warm and generous father. Although such affection is inconsistent, his children are inspired by his love of life. When Eliza moves out to open a boardinghouse a few miles away, he becomes dependent on his daughter Helen for care and sympathy. Gant frequents Eliza's boardinghouse and entertains the boarders with stories of his experiences, telling and retelling them as if they were legends. As he grows older, Gant's need for excitement increases. He becomes a desperate old lecher who pursues the middle-aged women staying at his wife's boardinghouse but fails to seduce the black cook.

When Gant is diagnosed as having prostate cancer, he becomes self-pitying. He cries out to God and curses everyone in sight for his misfortune. Jealous of his wife's health and her indifference to his illness, he gets insanely drunk and feigns death. Frequent trips for radiation treatments cause his vigor and resilience to decline. As he weakens, the shadow of his impending death darkens the lives of his family. Despite Helen's tender care, Gant continues to deteriorate. He dies while his wife and his other children argue over their future inheritance.

Gantry, Elmer. *Elmer Gantry*. Sinclair Lewis. 1927.

Elmer Gantry is an ambitious and amoral revivalist minister who manipulates the religious sentiments of his parishioners in order to further his own career. Born in Paris, Kansas, Elmer begins his adulthood by earning a reputation for carousing and for heroics on his college football team. Although the tall, husky, and good-looking young man is renowned in his college community, the fact is that, with the exception of his roommate, no one actually likes him. Under the auspices of his roommate, he is coached in the ways of the unregenerate, and the two young men openly scoff at religion and religious people. As it turns out, though, Elmer, swayed by an ex-athlete turned preacher, is convinced that he has had a genuine religious experience. This severs the relationship with his

roommate and sends Elmer off on a new career path: He decides to become a minister.

Shortly after his graduation from Terwillinger College, Elmer begins to study at the Mizpah Theological Seminary. Despite reservations on the part of several faculty members, Elmer learns enough after two years to be assigned to his first ministry. Here he becomes sexually interested in the daughter of one of the deacons, and before long it is revealed that the couple has been intimate. Since this conduct is unbecoming to one in Elmer's station, he is punished by expulsion from the seminary; however, he dupes the girl and her former admirer into a situation that allows him to break off the engagement sanctimoniously.

Once Elmer has been ejected from the Baptist ministry, he takes up a career as a shoe salesman; as with other careers that he flirts with, he imagines himself capable of scaling the heights of the profession, but it is not particularly lucrative. He eventually meets Sharon Falconer, a self-styled evangelical revivalist, and smitten with her, he assiduously plots to become her confidant. Before long Elmer becomes her lover as well as her assistant, earning a fairly handsome fee all the while. Elmer's greed mounts, and he conspires to manage Sharon and her business; for a time this works well as the meetings they lead garner more and more attention. Unfortunately for Elmer, disaster strikes, and Miss Falconer and many others are killed when their floating revival tent burns during a large meeting. Dauntlessly and with his habitual eagerness, Elmer takes up a new trade, this time with a woman who preaches what is called "New Thought." He is soon caught stealing, however, and is fired.

Elmer's greatest triumph comes, as he sees it, when he decides to return to the ministry, this time as a Methodist since their churches are both larger and richer. After talking his way into church membership, Elmer receives his first congregation. It is here that he meets and marries his wife, whom he does not love but who has the necessary attributes to facilitate his rise to at least a bishopric. After a successful stint as minister, Elmer begins a rapid climb from one church to the next, with each succeeding parish growing in wealth and importance.

Finally, after several years, Elmer becomes pastor of the Wellsprings Church in Zenith. Here he enlarges the congregation, garnering attention by engineering raids on illicit drinking establishments, arresting prostitutes, and exposing rival ministers for their heresies. All the while his attention is firmly riveted on his career, and his meteoric rise is accomplished by a careful distinction between what he does and what he preaches. As the novel ends, Elmer, having just brushed off a potential adultery scandal with the aid of a lawyer and the church, is given a nationally prominent position in a "purity" league and moves once again to a larger church. Despite their knowledge of his behavior, Elmer's congregation loudly and enthusiastically claps and cheers for their triumphant soldier against the wages of sin.

Garner, Paul D. *Beloved.* Toni Morrison. 1987.

Paul D Garner is the last remaining male, former slave of the Sweet Home plantation. Plagued by horrible memories, he struggles to come to terms with the scars he bears from the experience of slavery.

Although he had never left Sweet Home, Paul D tries to escape one night with other slaves. Caught, restrained with a spiked iron collar, and silenced with a bit in his mouth, Paul D is then sold by his master. He attempts to kill his new owner and lands in a nightmarish prison for blacks in Alfred, Georgia. Along with the forty-five other black men to whom he is chained, Paul D breaks rocks with a sledgehammer during the day and sleeps in a box buried in the earth at night.

Paul D finds that when he is alone, he cannot control a trembling in his limbs. In order to preserve himself, he learns to shut off his feelings. He conditions himself to love only small things so that it won't hurt as much when a white person takes them away.

A spring flood threatens to drown the men in their underground boxes, but they manage to swim out through the mud. Paul D's chain gang takes refuge with a band of sick and dying Cherokee. Confused by the wideness of the world, Paul D finally asks how he can get north. The Cherokee tell him to follow the tree flowers. He makes his way as far as the colored section of Wilmington, Delaware, where he knocks on the back door of a weaver woman's cabin. She opens her door to him, gives him food and shelter, and loves him. Eighteen months later his former owners, the Northpoint Bank and Railroad Company, track him down and purchase him. He runs away to join a colored regiment, but when the Union Army refuses to allow black soldiers to carry arms, the Northpoint Bank again finds Paul D. He is sold by the bank to the South, where he first sorts the dead on the battlefields, and then to a smelting factory in Selma, Alabama. When the war ends he heads north and begins his seven years of wandering.

While at Sweet Home, Paul D had selected a tree he named "Brother" as his only friend. Now free, he still believes himself incapable of spending long periods of time with others. Women, however, find Paul D to be the type of man they can cry in front of, and their emotions, no matter how suppressed, come out in his presence. In 1873, Paul D arrives at the home of another former Sweet Home slave, SETHE, and she responds in the expected way. Paul D, along with the other male slaves at Sweet Home, had lusted after Sethe when she was the only black woman on the plantation. Now, eighteen years later, he and Sethe become lovers.

Sethe asks Paul D into her home but does not warn him that the spirit of her dead daughter also occupies the house. A red light bathes Paul D when he enters, and moments later he and the house have a pitched battle. Paul D succeeds in driving the spirit from the house, but like Sethe, he does not comprehend that the mysterious woman calling herself BELOVED, who inexplicably appears in front of the house a short time later, is actually Sethe's dead daughter reincarnated. When Paul D and Beloved become competitors for Sethe's attention, it is Beloved who drives Paul D first from Sethe's bed and then from the house entirely. She finally has him sleeping in the woodshed behind the house and forces him to have sex with her.

Paul D eventually leaves Sethe and takes up residence in the unheated basement of a church with only a bottle of liquor for company. When Beloved disappears, he returns to help Sethe recover from the trauma of her child's ghostly return and subsequent disappearance.

Garie, Jr., Clarence. *The Garies and Their Friends.* Frank J. Webb. 1857.

Clarence Garie, Jr. is haunted by racism and touched by tragedy. The child of a racially mixed marriage, Clarence discovers that antebellum northern prejudice can be just as murderous as the southern variety.

Clarence's father is a white man who owns his mulatto wife. Despite Mr. Garie's ownership of his wife, son, and daughter Emily, he is a kind husband and father who will do anything for his family. He agrees to move north to Philadelphia where his family can be free, and the Garies become close friends with the Ellises, an industrious lower-middle-class black family. Despite the differences in their social station, Clarence and young CHARLES ELLIS become playmates.

By moving north the family has escaped slavery, but prejudice is rampant even in the city of brotherly love. The Garies' new neighbor, the corrupt lawyer George Stevens, nicknamed "Slippery Stevens," plans to capitalize on the hostility toward blacks for his personal gain. He incites a mob to attack the Garie home and murder Mr. Garie. While Clarence huddles in a woodshed with his sister and mother, the mob ransacks their new house. Sick from fear and shock, Mrs. Garie gives birth prematurely, and both mother and child die.

Now orphaned, Clarence and Emily go to live in the home of Mr. Walters, a wealthy black businessman. When Mr. Garie's will cannot be found, George Stevens reveals that he is distantly related to the man he had killed and demands that Garie's considerable estate be turned over to him. He settles only a small sum on Clarence and his sister.

The grief-stricken Clarence must make a choice about his future. His father's lawyer proposes to the white-appearing boy that he go to an exclusive boarding school where no one will know his true heritage. Although Mr. Walters knows the dangers and the feeling of shame a black person passing for white will encounter, he acknowledges the obstacles facing blacks and reluctantly advises Clarence to take the chance. The boy goes off to be educated at Sudbury.

A few years later Clarence has grown into a strikingly handsome young man and is engaged to be married. He reveals to an older woman friend, the one who knows his secret, that he has told his white fiancée nothing. Clarence hates committing this sin of omission, but he fears even more that the young lady, whom he calls Birdie, will reject him if he reveals the truth to her. The burden of his guilty conscience is weakening Clarence. He is agitated and feverish, and his friend tells him that the only way he will be able to live with himself is to unburden his heart to Birdie and hope that she will stay true to him.

Planning to tell all, Clarence goes to New York to see her. When she tells him about a nightmare in which he is covered with black spots and then reads to him, her voice indicating her incredulity, a newspaper article about a white man marrying a quadroon, his fear returns. He keeps quiet and allows the wedding plans to continue. An unexpected visit from one of Birdie's former suitors—the son of Slippery George—results in the truth being revealed.

Thoroughly crushed, Clarence hovers on the edge of insanity and sickness. He eventually makes his way back to his sister, recently married to Charles Ellis. Emily never tried to pass for white, but she does not condemn him for his decision; rather, she tries to nurse him back to health. Knowing he is near death, Clarence dictates to Emily a letter to Birdie requesting that she come and see him, but when a still-loving Birdie arrives, Clarence is already dead.

Garp, T. S. *The World According to Garp.* John Irving. 1976.

T. S. Garp, the novel's protagonist, struggles to find his identity in a world of women. His mother Jenny Fields is an eccentric, highly individualistic nurse who becomes a leading figure in the women's movement of the 1970s. Jenny is surrounded by adoring and needy women, and has little time to spend with her son. Garp embarks on a career as a writer but is overshadowed by the publication of his mother's autobiography, *A Sexual Suspect*, which becomes a controversial best-seller. Only when Garp becomes a father does he find a real purpose and a sense of identity.

Garp was born of the union between his mother and the man she was nursing, a paralyzed, brain-damaged war veteran known as Technical Sergeant Garp. Jenny Fields did not want a husband, so she availed herself of the wounded man before his impending death in order to have a child on her own. Garp spends his childhood at Steering, a New England preparatory school for boys, where Jenny

is the nurse. He eventually enrolls in Steering, where he becomes an excellent wrestler and receives his first encouragement to write. He also gets his ear bitten off by a local dog named Bonkers, but by the end of his stay at Steering, he manages to return the favor by consuming the dog's ear.

Upon graduation from Steering, Garp spends a year in Vienna with his mother, both of them pursuing writing seriously. Jenny is able to complete her autobiography in which she tells about her life as a woman independent of men, and Garp completes his first successful short story, "The Pension Grillparzer," about a family who goes around testing the hotels of Europe for a ratings guide. Garp uses this short story to propose marriage to his lifelong friend Helen Holm, stating it is proof of his successful future as a writer. They marry on Garp's return from Europe.

Garp and his wife are supported by his mother, who, having written a best-seller, has become a *cause célèbre*. Garp continues to write and act as a househusband, while Helen obtains a higher degree and becomes a professor. Garp cherishes his two sons, Duncan and Walt, sometimes to a fault. Despite his efforts to protect them from life's random dangers, however, Walt is killed in a car crash involving the whole family and Duncan loses an eye. Since the crash was an indirect result of marital strife, the Garp family is left in ruins. They go to recuperate at Jenny's mansion, a retreat for women.

Jenny is soon assassinated for her feminist activities, and Garp becomes one of the executors of her estate, along with his friend Roberta, a transsexual former professional football player who had acted as a bodyguard for Jenny. The mansion continues to serve as a retreat for women in need until Garp is assassinated by a radical feminist while teaching wrestling in his new job at Steering Academy. He leaves behind him several novels and his short story, "The Pension Grillparzer," which he sadly acknowledges was his best work. But his son Duncan, who goes on to become a respected painter and photographer, is Garp's real success.

Garth, Priscilla "Sip." *The Silent Partner.* Elizabeth Stuart Phelps. 1871.

Priscilla Garth, known as "Sip," is an impoverished mill worker in her late teens. Sip works twelve or more hours a day before going home to take care of her deaf and mute sister Catty. PERLEY KELSO, a young woman who has inherited a share of the Hayle and Kelso mills located in the town of Five Falls, becomes involved in the lives of the workers and soon strikes up an unorthodox friendship with Sip. Perley usually visits the Garth home, but she eventually invites both sisters to her formal parties.

Sip's life consists of steady and exhausting labor lightened only by the time she devotes at home to her handicapped sister, who is physically grotesque. When Catty is sad, Sip coaxes her back into a better mood by challenging her to endure a hardship or to cease a particular behavior, "for love's sake." Sip relates this request through an intricate finger-spelling system that the sisters use to communicate. The sisters share a small stone house that, like the mills, retains heat in summer and cold in winter. Despite their hardships, they achieve some contentment, especially on play day, which Sip has christened the "Lord's day." The generous-hearted Sip frequently abandons her own plans in order to remain with Catty, but she also recognizes Dirk Burdock's attentions.

Sip soon realizes that Catty is going blind. Working in the cotton mills as a child has ruined the skin on her hands, and now, because she rubbed them on her face, her eyes have been affected as well. Sip tells Perley that she doesn't have the courage to tell her sister that she will face even more hardship. One day during a horrendous downpour, Sip is called away from the stone house. The now blind Catty, feeling water flooding the house, leaves in search of her sister. She wanders onto a weakened bridge and dies when it collapses. Dirk covers Sip's eyes just in time to prevent her from seeing Catty's death.

Sip grieves but tries to remain positive. Since the silence they had always shared remains, Sip reasons that Catty somehow remains, and before long Sip, now in her early twenties, becomes an increasingly well-known street preacher. She reaches out to the workers with a practical brand of Christianity, stressing an awareness of life's hardships and dismissal of rhetoric and false promises.

Gates, Frenesi. *Vineland.* Thomas Pynchon. 1990.

Frenesi Gates embodies the contradictions of the student movement of the 1960s. On one hand, she is a student activist: As the main cameraperson for 24fps, a guerilla movie outfit whose name is short for "24 frames per second," she documents the student movement's battle with the government and believes in the moral truth of her actions. But on the other hand, her attraction to figures of authority leads her to become romantically involved with the federal agent Brock Vond, whom she has been assigned to film. After gaining access to her footage, Brock convinces her to spy on, and then participate in the murder of, a prominent student leader.

Running away from her past, Frenesi starts a new life, marrying amateur rock guitarist and house painter Zoyd Wheeler and giving birth to a daughter, Prairie. But unable to escape the hold that Brock has on her, she soon leaves Zoyd. In a program for its informants, the federal government relocates her to a Sunbelt city, supports her financially, and keeps her whereabouts hidden from family and friends. The Witness Protection Program has a particular appeal to Frenesi because, although she is haunted by the infant daughter she left behind, it allows her to live completely and securely in the present, without her past or the consequences of her actions in the future.

However, with federal budget cuts in the 1980s, Frenesi is suddenly dropped from the Witness Protection Program and is forced once again to go above ground with her new husband Fletcher and their son Justin. Returning to Vineland for a Gates family reunion, she confronts her now teenage daughter. The novel's final scenes suggest not only that Frenesi, child of the 1960s, has failed to overcome her desire for authority but also that this desire has been passed on to Prairie, representative of the new generation. The freedom that mother and daughter possess at the novel's end is the consequence not of their self-reliance but rather, ironically, of President Reagan's budget cuts, which have emasculated the government, making it unable to satisfy or manipulate the desire for authority.

Gatsby, Jay. *The Great Gatsby.* F. Scott Fitzgerald. 1925.

Handsome, elusive, and wistful, Jay Gatsby is one of the most haunting characters in American fiction. His jaunty, extravagant manner, worn thin but never destroyed by his love for an unattainable woman, expresses the hopes and fears of the Lost Generation of the 1920s.

Gatsby is the legendary owner of a sumptuous mansion in West Egg, Long Island. His parties are unequaled in their extravagance. His house and magnificent gardens are brilliantly lit, and the narrator, NICK CARRAWAY, describes the endless flow of food, drink, and guests; but Gatsby himself remains obscured by the gossip surrounding his quick rise to fame and fortune.

When Nick finally meets his famous neighbor at one of Gatsby's parties, he mistakes him for one of the guests. But Gatsby's radiant smile sets Nick at ease immediately. Gatsby then asks Nick's girlfriend Jordan to come with him to the library, where he confides an astonishing secret that Nick later reveals: Gatsby is in love with DAISY BUCHANAN, the now married belle of Nick's hometown.

Gatsby's tale gradually unfolds. Born James Gatz to a poor midwestern family, he dreamed of adventures on the high seas. One day, walking by the shore of Lake Superior, he saw a yacht about to drop anchor. The yacht's owner, Dan Cody, took him on, and Gatsby's new life and identity began.

After Cody's death, Gatsby joined the army and met Daisy while on furlough. They fell deeply in love, but their time together was cut short when Gatsby was sent overseas. A few years later Gatsby learned of Daisy's marriage to Tom Buchanan. Believing himself the great love of Daisy's life, Gatsby set about amassing his fortune as a bootlegger. He built his mansion across the bay from where she lived, and since then he has spent his nights staring with unremitting yearning at the green light that gleams from the dock of her house on the opposite shore.

Gatsby finally contrives to meet Daisy at a tea party at Nick's. After the initial shock of recognition, they are lovingly absorbed in each other again. Soon, the lights grow dim in Gatsby's garden, the guests vanish, and serving staff and caterers are dismissed as Gatsby devotes his energies to spending time alone with Daisy. One hot summer day Daisy invites Gatsby, along with Nick and Jordan, to her house. Their affair, well known to their mutual friends, suddenly becomes apparent to Daisy's philandering husband Tom. In order to curb the mounting tension between Gatsby and Tom, Daisy suggests a drive to New York City, where a confrontation ensues. So obsessive has Gatsby's dream of Daisy become, he cannot bear to think of her ever having loved Tom.

As Gatsby's car is heading back to West Egg, with Daisy at the wheel, Myrtle, Tom's mistress, runs out into the road and is killed. Gatsby tells Nick that he is responsible for the accident. After hiding the dented car, Gatsby returns to Daisy's house. He stands outside, watching the light to her room, waiting to rush in and help her should Tom become violent. Daisy never signals him, but Gatsby, heading home at last in the early morning hours, refuses to give up hope.

The next day Nick comes to see Gatsby, who finally tells him the truth about his decidedly unglamorous, poverty-stricken childhood. Gatsby is waiting nervously for Daisy to call. Later that day Nick returns to find his body floating in the marble pool; Myrtle's deranged husband George lies dead nearby.

Gatsby's funeral is meager and dour. Only Nick will remember him as he was: young, effervescent, clinging fast to a garish future while dreaming of an irretrievable past.

Gault, Caroline. *A Sign for Cain.* Grace Lumpkin. 1935.

Caroline Gault, an idealistic young novelist, is the only member of her family who leaves her hometown of Jefferson. The daughter of an aging southern politician who is dying of cancer, she returns to Jefferson and becomes embroiled in turbulent issues of race, poverty, and crime.

Caroline leaves Jefferson for New York City, where she becomes a successful novelist. Her novels draw extensively on her personal experience, fitting the romance genre perfectly. By the time she returns to Jefferson in her late twenties, she has been married and divorced twice. Although her family and friends discuss her books with some disapproval, they read them avidly. One of her most devoted fans is the otherwise serious-minded editor of the Jefferson *Record*, BILL DUNCAN, with whom she had had an adolescent romance. Bill brings a professional colleague, Muriel Browdie, to greet Caroline at the train station upon her return to Jefferson. Even no-nonsense Muriel has been impressed by Caroline's problematic romance novels and praises the author for her work; she notes they are delightful, yet real and complete.

Caroline occupies an uncomfortable position at home. She acts as a mediator between her two brothers: JIM (GAULT), an impulsive alcoholic, and Charles, a minister. Caroline's father, whose health is rapidly declining, also

demands constant attention. Nevertheless, Caroline has the energy to carry on an intense friendship with Bill.

Both Caroline and Bill express utopian visions and an interest in helping the underprivileged of Jefferson. Bill, an ardent socialist, insists that social change can come about only through the efforts of an entire community. He understands the inequalities between southern blacks and whites, and works to build unions to protect the interests of the underclass. Caroline accuses him of seeing only misery and tries to point out to him, as she does in her novels, the beauty of life. Strangely, as Caroline tries to impress Bill with her commitment to social reform, their heated debates spark a new romance between them.

Caroline believes that individual efforts can have greater effect than the community solidarity that Bill speaks about, and to prove her point, she visits two women in an effort to help them. One, Selah, a young black girl, is "bound out" and must work without pay until she is eighteen. The Browdies, the racist family she works for, often beat her. Caroline also visits Mary Sellers, an extremely poor white girl who works as a prostitute while still living in her father's house. Caroline has little success with either project. Selah cannot trust her, and although Mary craves her company, Caroline cannot bring herself to remain with Mary for very long.

Bill soon has reason to say that Caroline's veneration of individualism betrays her ties to the upper classes. Her brother Jim murders his aunt Evelyn in a drunken fit of anger and leaves her body by the side of the road. Two black farm workers from the Gault plantation are quickly arrested and framed for the murder. Although Jim confesses the murder to her, Caroline refuses to do anything to prevent the conviction of the two workers. Instead, she decides to save her brother by safeguarding this information from the authorities. When she discovers that Bill has called in northern lawyers and made every effort to protect the suspects, Caroline tells him their ideals are too different for their relationship to continue. After Jim shoots the suspects to death, however, she desperately begs his forgiveness. Refusing her appeal, Bill asks harshly, "Where is all your honesty and truth?"

Gault, Jim. *A Sign for Cain.* Grace Lumpkin. 1935.

Jim Gault is the decadent son of a declining patrician family. Colonel Gault, Jim's father, had always taken great pride in managing his former slave plantation wisely showing compassion toward the black laborers and sharecroppers. When the Colonel passes the management of the business to Jim, it loses money steadily, and there is increasing unrest among the workers.

Jim clearly has no aptitude for running the plantation, and his failure makes him hostile and evasive. The self-proclaimed "black sheep" of the family, he seeks solace in drinking. Jim finds himself scrambling every week to secure enough money for alcohol, and he deprives the farm workers of essential supplies in order to fund his own pleasures.

Jim's well-to-do aunt Evelyn consents to lend him small sums of money regularly, and her stepson Jud shares with him his substantial allowance. A falling-out occurs between Evelyn and Jim when she discovers that he spends most of his "allowance" on his long-term black mistress Maria, whom he visits frequently in nearby Junction City. Although Jim had been forewarned and forbidden by his father to "take up" with any "colored mistress," he becomes enchanted with his prized possession. Jim pays for Maria's apartment and buys her extravagant clothing. She, in turn, makes him feel "large and magnificent." They provide a specific reciprocal security for each other. Although Evelyn is by no means puritanical and lives quite luxuriously herself, she sternly refuses all Jim's requests for money once she learns about his black mistress.

A particularly ugly exchange occurs when Jim rudely intrudes on a private discussion between Evelyn and a suitor, the school principal Allen Broadwater. Having just found out that his father is ill with cancer, Jim wanted Evelyn to donate money for his treatment. Because he is drunk and inarticulate, Evelyn angrily orders him to leave.

Jim's brother Charles, a minister, manages to placate Evelyn. When he explains the nature of the Colonel's illness, Evelyn agrees to ask Jim's forgiveness and hopes to end the feud with her brothers. She arrives at the Gault house, and everything appears to be going smoothly until Jim heartlessly announces Evelyn's intention to marry Allen Broadwater. The Colonel, infuriated that Evelyn should marry such an "upstart," ends the meeting abruptly.

Jim's attempts to reverse his mistake are equally disastrous, and his alcoholism worsens. One night while drunk, Jim threatens Evelyn as she drives home. When she responds only with a stiff smile, Jim bashes her head open with a rock and leaves her dead by the side of the road.

Many suspect Jim of the murder, but two black men, rumored to be union organizers, are taken into custody, arrested, and beaten until they "confess." Shortly before the trial, the judge's son gets Jim drunk and convinces him that any real man would protect the honor of his family by shooting the men who allegedly raped and murdered his aunt. Jim enters the jail and shoots DENIS and Ficents, the two suspects, winning the respect of the reactionary majority and becoming a hero to the whites.

Gayheart, Lucy. *Lucy Gayheart*. Willa Cather. 1935.

Lucy Gayheart lives out the first eighteen years of her life in the relatively small town of Haverford on the Platte River in the Midwest. Here she is loved by virtually everyone and is well known for her special affinity for music. Because of her love of music and her talent for playing the piano, Lucy, with her father's encouragement, leaves her hometown for Chicago, where she pursues an education in music and supports herself by giving lessons. This changes one day when she auditions for the position of practice accompanist to Clement Sebastian, the internationally famous, Chicago-born baritone.

Lucy and Sebastian strike up a close friendship that centers for a while solely on their work. The middle-aged artist is already married, although quite unhappily, but eventually Lucy falls deeply in love with him. He returns her affection, and they develop a relationship that, though passionate, does not go further than fervid kisses, long walks, and late dinners.

After several months, Lucy is forced to fulfill a promise given to Harry Gordon, Haverford's richest son, who had been assured of her company at the opera every night for a week upon arriving in Chicago. Although reluctant and filled with longing for Sebastian, who is then on tour, Lucy agrees to the arduous schedule of an opera a day, in addition to dinners and walks. But Lucy gradually tires of Harry, and she is shocked when in his stumbling manner he proposes marriage for that very spring. Because of his insistence, Lucy lies, allowing him to believe that not only did she love another but that the relationship had been consummated. At this news the young man storms out of the elegant restaurant and leaves Lucy to fend for herself.

She soon hears from her sister that Harry hastily married a wealthy heiress and brought her back to Haverford, where his banking business is centered. The news does not disturb Lucy since by now Sebastian has returned and plans are under way for the remainder of the spring. Lucy eventually learns that he wants her to study hard all summer so that she can join him in New York for the winter season, then accompany him to Europe. Amazed at her fortune, she resolves to study hard and spends hours in his studio while he tours Europe.

Lucy's idyllic world is abruptly shattered when she reads of Sebastian's sudden death by drowning during a storm on Lake Como. Devastated, she leaves Chicago and returns to Haverford, where she endures her elder sister's jealous moodiness and her father's affection. She must also endure the town's inquisitive eyes as people seek to understand what happened between her and Harry. Wanting to inform him of her lie and of her grief, Lucy assiduously seeks an opportunity to speak with Harry in private. But for various reasons this meeting does not occur.

With the healing of time, Lucy begins to come around to life; she takes great comfort in private hours in the orchard on the family farm, and she starts playing the piano again. A real turning point comes when Lucy is inspired by a traveling opera company whose soprano moves her to rekindle her own commitment to the arts. She arranges to return to Chicago in early spring. This information slips out in an argument with her sister Pauline, who resents Lucy's favor, and Lucy storms out of the house to go skating. What she doesn't know is that her childhood skating spot has been radically altered by a shift in the riverbed. She encounters Harry, who swiftly insults her, refusing her a lift to the skating site. Soon after she gets on the ice, it cracks and collapses, and Lucy drowns when her skate is caught on a submerged tree.

Gaylord, Marcia. *A Modern Instance.* William Dean Howells. 1881.

Marcia Gaylord enters the narrative as the brightest and loveliest young woman of Equity, Maine, devoted to her father, Squire Gaylord, and to the editor of the town newspaper, BARTLEY HUBBARD. She is so in love with Bartley that when he leaves her house one night, she kneels down and kisses the doorknob he has just touched. Marcia agrees to marry Bartley, then breaks the engagement when she learns he has been flirting with a local strumpet. She soon regrets her rash actions and follows him when he leaves town in order to beg him to take her back. They marry and move to Boston.

Thanks to Marcia's thrift, the young couple is able to support themselves while Bartley finds employment. Marcia gains sympathy and acceptance from her father but refuses his financial support, while Bartley sells one story after another to the Boston papers.

Combined with the vanity and quick temper of her husband, Marcia's rashness makes her particularly prone to quarrels. Bartley cannot talk to an attractive young woman without Marcia's jealousy rising, and she cannot rebuke him without his hurling at her the most hurtful insults he can imagine. A pattern of combat, insult, and forgiveness develops and pervades their marriage.

A year into the marriage, Marcia gives birth to a daughter, whom Bartley magnanimously offers to name Flavia after Marcia's father, Flavius. But the gesture fails to prevent the deterioration of their marriage. One night when he refuses to accompany her on a visit to Equity, Marcia goes so far as to lock him out. When he returns, drunk, in the arms of their friend Ben Halleck, she becomes convinced that he is grievously ill, and she can scarcely be dissuaded from sending for a doctor. The moralistic Halleck, who has long admired Marcia, begins to adore and pity her, and to despise Bartley.

Due to Bartley's long stays at the newspaper and at the local beer gardens, Marcia begins to spend more time with the Halleck family and especially with Ben. Out of love and pity for Marcia, Ben controls the urge to break his friendship with Bartley and even consents to lend him money. But on the night of Bartley and Marcia's last fight, Ben realizes he must conquer his love for her, and he flees to Uruguay.

Her dearest friend gone, Marcia then discovers that Bartley, too, has disappeared. For years she refuses to acknowledge that her husband has simply abandoned her, insisting that he must be in an amnesiac daze somewhere. Finally, hearing of her situation, Ben returns from South America to marry her, but she still cares for her husband. When Ben receives information that Bartley is in Indiana seeking to have his marriage annulled, he and Squire Gaylord persuade Marcia to contest the ruling and file for divorce herself. They go to Indiana to prove him a perjurer, but Marcia refuses to have him jailed. She returns to live in Equity with her ailing father. Years later, after she is widowed, she is still sought after by Ben, now a minister who wonders whether or not it would be morally right to marry her.

Gellert, Edward. "What Every Boy Should Know." William Maxwell. 1977.

Edward Gellert, a naive and curious young boy, lives in a middle-class neighborhood with his parents and sister Virginia. Although beset with myriad questions about sexuality and marriage, he keeps his queries to himself for fear of shocking his elders or being questioned about his secrets. He consults a book, *What Every Boy Should Know,* hoping that it will enlighten him, but the volume proves to be filled with useless knowledge, and he must search for more valuable sources of information on his own.

Edward's hobbies include playing with his chemistry set, constructing a ball of tin foil, and organizing his stamp and coin collections. When he reaches the age of twelve, his father decides that he should hold down a job in order to learn the value of money. Planning to buy a new bicycle with the proceeds of his labors, Edward lands a job as a paperboy at the Draperville *Evening Star* and reports to the press every day after school in order to pick up newspapers. At first he delivers to houses in a particularly squalid section of town. The impoverished condition of Edward's clients poses a problem because they don't always pay him the weekly fee that he collects on Saturdays. He must submit the newspaper's percentage of the sum regardless of how much money he actually takes in. The job poses another problem: The linotype machines are temperamental and often break down so that he must wait to get his papers, which means that sometimes after completing his route he does not get home until after seven o'clock in the evening. He and his fellow paperboys eventually get so fed up with this inconvenience that they go on strike. But the strike is short-lived, and nothing changes as a result of their absence from the job.

When the strike is over, Edward makes a bargain with God that he will give up all his vices if the management at the newspaper agrees to give him back his route. They rehire him on the condition that he never strike again. Edward eventually acquires a larger route in a more pleasant neighborhood, and he can finally afford the bicycle of his dreams. Accompanied by his father, he goes to the bank to withdraw his savings and then chooses a beautiful Blue Racer at Kohler's bicycle shop in town. Extremely proud of his purchase, he only grudgingly lets his friends ride it. Misfortune strikes when Edward breaks company policy by leaving his bike on the curb while he races inside to deliver the paper's percentage of the week's proceeds. While he is inside, a man inadvertently runs over and mutilates his bike. The man apologizes but does not offer to repair or replace it. Witnesses provide the driver's name, and Edward and his father visit him, but he denies committing the crime. Edward realizes that his only alternative is to borrow money from his father to have the bike repaired. At the close of the story, he bemoans the condition of his shiny Blue Rider and remains unreconciled to the dashing of his dreams.

Gentry, Ed. *Deliverance.* James Dickey. 1970.

Narrator Ed Gentry is one of four men who take a harrowing three-day canoe trip through backwoods Georgia in September. The vice-president and graphics director for a moderately successful advertising studio, Ed thinks of himself as steady, somewhat mediocre, and primarily interested in getting through life as comfortably and easily as possible. He is married to Martha, a down-to-earth former surgical nurse, with whom he has one child, Dean. Ed loves his family but takes them for granted, admitting to himself that one of his motives for going away on the trip is to be delivered from the normalcy his wife represents.

Ed's best friend is LEWIS MEDLOCK, the adventurous survivalist who organized the trip and who shares with him an interest in archery. Ed claims not to have much use for Lewis's rather extreme individualist ideas but is looking forward to the excursion as a way of shaking off a general feeling of malaise; Ed's other friends who go on the trip, DREW BALLINGER and BOBBY TRIPPE, are less enthusiastic.

The first day passes without major mishap, but on the second day Ed and Bobby, far ahead of the second canoe, pull over to shore to stretch their limbs. Suddenly two men step out of the woods, one armed with a shotgun. These men, believing their victims to be alone, tie Ed to a tree and rape Bobby. Just as they turn their attention to Ed, Lewis arrives on the scene and shoots one of them through the chest with an arrow. The other man flees. The four friends then debate what to do with the body. Lewis argues that he will probably face homicide charges if they report the incident; Drew passionately disagrees. Ed, somewhat against his conscience, sides with Lewis. The men finally decide to bury the body in the forest and conceal the event from the authorities.

Ed and the others proceed down the river, but their feeling of easy camaraderie has vanished; each man feels isolated. While braving a particularly rough series of rapids, Drew is shot in the head by an unseen gunman, and both canoes capsize. Ed manages to keep hold of his bow and arrows, and is swept downstream through a rocky section of the river. He, Lewis, and Bobby manage to make it to shore, but Lewis's upper thigh is painfully broken.

Ed, realizing that they are still a target for the man who shot Drew, finds that their survival depends on him. After a terrifying climb up the sheer cliff in the middle of the night, Ed ambushes the gunman, injuring himself with one of his own arrows in the process. Ed ties rocks to the man's corpse, causing it to sink to the bottom of the river, and later conceals Drew's body in the same way so that the police will believe he died in a drowning accident.

Ed manages, mostly singlehandedly, to complete the dangerous and difficult journey downstream. He, Lewis, and Bobby are received with some suspicion, but Ed coaches the other two in the lies they tell the authorities. They are eventually allowed to leave for home, changed forever by their experiences on the river.

George. "The Killers." Ernest Hemingway. 1927.

George is the unsuspecting owner of a lunchroom beset by two killers. As George stands behind the counter talking to his friend NICK ADAMS, two men enter and order dinner. When they discover that dinner is not yet being served, the two similarly dressed strangers, who call one another Al and Max, begin to joke in a menacing way. George responds politely to his strange customers, although he is certain that they are up to no good. They become belligerent and are not appeased by being served their food.

The stranger called Max begins to bait George, asking him what he's looking at and what he means by it. Confused, George laughs, but the strangers don't find anything funny. They order Nick, whom they address as "bright boy," to go behind the counter with George. They then tell George to have the cook, the only other person in the restaurant, come out of the kitchen.

Finally the strangers tell George what they are doing. They have been sent to kill Ole Andreson, a Swede who often comes to the restaurant for dinner. In answer to their inquiries about the man, George will only say that Andreson sometimes eats there, and he usually shows up by six o'clock. The killers won't tell George why they want to kill Andreson, and after a short time George realizes it is best not to ask.

Andreson hasn't arrived by 7:15, and Al and Max decide to leave. Although the cook cautions him against getting involved, George sends Nick to warn the Swede of the plot against his life. Nick returns after only a few minutes to tell George that the Swede knows about the contract on his life and doesn't plan to do anything about it. As far as George is concerned, he's done all he can. He advises Nick not to think about the man's impending murder.

George. "Spring Evening." James T. Farrell. 1937.

George and a friend, Jack, take a walk through a 1930s suburb of Chicago. As they stroll along, the former high school pals talk about their past lives, their hopes for the future, and their unfulfilled desires. George, now twenty-four, has worked for four years in a cramped, noisy office in the Loop, the main business district in downtown Chicago. While acknowledging that his salary of forty-five dollars a week is higher than most of his contemporaries, he dislikes the work and dreads going to the office every morning.

George dreams of striking it rich by meeting a wealthy woman, betting on the ponies, or winning a dance marathon. He and Jack amuse themselves by talking about all the wonderful things they would do if they were "bigshots." George worries about his health, thinking that he smokes too much and doesn't get enough exercise. He imagines how much healthier and happier he would be if he could live in the country, and he envisions an idyllic existence "close to Nature," if he ever gets a break in his luck.

George discusses women in a ribald and confident manner. Secretly, however, he worries that he may be sterile. He professes to yearn for a life-style whereby he could be with a different woman every night of the week, but he also admits to himself that he would like to settle down and marry a decent girl. George loves Clara Eldridge, whom he met at his senior prom. One lovely spring evening some years before, while walking her home from a date and feeling happily romantic, he had asked her if she loved him. He was rejected but still dreams of becoming worthy enough—or rich enough—to get her back.

Toward the end of their walk, George and Jack sit in a park smoking cigarettes and wistfully watch a couple pass by. They decide to go to Twenty-second Street and pay for prostitutes, but when they count their money, they discover that they do not have enough. George reluctantly thinks of having to go to work the next morning and begins to feel tired. The two friends walk back, share a chocolate malted milk at a crowded chain drugstore, and exchange racing tips before parting. George goes home, thinking of Clara and wishing he were "up in the bucks."

Georgette. *Last Exit to Brooklyn.* Hubert Selby, Jr. 1957.

Georgette, a tall and flamboyant drag queen, is hopelessly in love with Vinnie, a petty criminal and the nominal leader of a group of young men of a similar background. For much of the time Vinnie uses Georgette for easy sex or, even more commonly, for drugs and drink.

From the beginning of Georgette's story, her forlorn situation is clear. She is the butt of a knife-tossing game between Vinnie and Harry, another member of the group. The knife, purposely thrown at Georgette, becomes embedded in her leg. Although Georgette is in pain, Vinnie refuses to drive her to a hospital and takes her home

instead. There, she is coddled by her mother and abused by her heterosexual brother Arthur.

Despite Vinnie's habitual coldness and cruelty, Georgette's feeling for him intensifies rather than abates. During the week or so that she must stay bedridden, Arthur constantly abuses her, scorning her for her sexual orientation and for her outrageous dress and demeanor. More particularly, she is allowed no visitors and must face the time and pain without her usual escape of benzedrine, other drugs, and gin. Eventually, when she is feeling somewhat better, Georgette sneaks to a friend's house where a party is under way.

At this party Georgette maintains almost complete control over the atmosphere and conversation. While jazz music plays in the background, she holds court until Vinnie and his pals arrive. Once the other men appear, Georgette and the drag queens flirt and openly contend for their attention. The steady supply of drugs and alcohol keeps things moving until the party is interrupted by the arrival of the hugely pregnant Mary, who announces that she is in labor. This event threatens the stability of the party, and even more so when her water breaks and labor starts in earnest. Because the men are far more interested in their party than in the woman's plight, Mary is summarily hastened out of the apartment, put in a cab, and sent to the hospital. Meanwhile, Georgette gropes for a way to make the evening work, with herself as the center of attention. She wants everyone there to realize that she isn't just any queen, she is "the queen." In this effort she locates a book and begins reading what turns out to be Edgar Allan Poe's poem, "The Raven."

While Georgette reads this poem of irrevocably lost love, she continues her ardent pursuit of Vinnie, hoping that he will be attentive to her and perceiving glimmers of love in the way he looks at and listens to her. Vinnie, for his part, muses to himself that it is too bad Georgette is homosexual; given that, he decides she is a nice guy. This is close enough for Georgette, who senses this softening in Vinnie's attitude toward her. As the night continues, however, sexual pairings take place, and Georgette grows ever more anxious about her chances with Vinnie.

Finally, at Harry's prompting, Vinnie retires to the bedroom, along with Harry, to have sex with another one of the drag queens. While he is gone, Georgette, in an effort to maintain her spirits, injects morphine on top of the benzedrine, marijuana, and alcohol she has already consumed. The combination makes her extremely high, and when Vinnie and Harry are done, she is as attentive as she can be. She begins to have sex with Harry, whom she mistakes for Vinnie. Upon recognizing her lover as Harry, she retreats into her own mind, dancing through the room to ballet music. As the story ends, Georgette, still quite high and now desperate with longing, wonders about her love and her life, which she hopes—against hope—wasn't merely a waste.

Gerard, Brother Francis. *A Canticle for Leibowitz.* Walter M. Miller, Jr. 1960.

Brother Francis Gerard is the unsophisticated young man who, some years before the opening of this futuristic novel, escaped from the warlock of his shepherding tribe in the Utah Territory and joined the Albertine Order of Leibowitz at its desert monastery. By the time of Brother Francis's arrival, the monks of the abbey have spent six centuries striving to preserve the knowledge of the pre-nuclear holocaust age from the attacks of those who blame the intellectuals of the late twentieth century for the near destruction of the earth. None of the monks, including Brother Francis, understand much of the information that they save.

While on the first of his seven lenten vocational vigils and fasts in the desert, an ageless wanderer, Benjamin, marks a stone for the nearly starved Brother Francis to use as the keystone in the roof of his shelter. When Brother Francis tries to pry the stone from the ground, he discovers the remains of a twentieth-century fallout shelter. Although he fearfully imagines a "fallout" as some kind of fire-breathing monster and cannot figure what a shelter for such a beast would be, he does recognize the importance of the name "Leibowitz" that appears on some of the documents found in the outer chamber.

When Brother Francis first reports his findings to the priests and monks of the Abbey, they assume that the desert sun and the weeks without food and water have caused him to hallucinate. However, when the other novices learn of the sacred artifacts that Brother Francis has discovered, including a quick shopping list and a blueprint of a complicated transistorized circuit design, they give his story many romantic flourishes. Abbot Arkos, who worries that the fanciful stories that have risen to embellish Brother Francis's discoveries will hinder rather than help the order's effort to have New Rome canonize its founder, sends Brother Francis back to the desert and decides not to allow him to take his vows.

Seven years later, after the uproar over Brother Francis's discoveries has settled and the canonization of Leibowitz seems likely, the abbot allows Francis to take his vows and begin work as a copyist. To help relieve the monotony of hours of uninterrupted copying, Brother Francis asks if he may take on the pet project of making an Illuminated Copy of the Leibowitz blueprint. Using gold leaf and a bleached sheep skin, Brother Francis spends fifteen years crafting a beautiful facsimile of the utterly incomprehensible transistor circuit.

When New Rome finally agrees to canonize Leibowitz, the abbot sends Brother Francis to New Rome, and he suggests that the Illuminated Copy be offered as a gift to the pope. During his long and dangerous journey, however, three cannibalistic mutants ambush him. They agree to let him go but take his artistic rendering of the blueprint. The pope gives him gold to try to buy his work back, but Brother Francis is killed by hungry mutants before he has a chance to do so.

Gereth, Adela. *The Spoils of Poynton.* Henry James. 1897.

Adela Gereth, a feisty widow, falls victim to both the custom of her country and her own obstinacy. After the death of her husband, Mrs. Gereth must, in accordance with English laws of primogeniture, surrender proprietorship of her husband's estate, Poynton, to her son OWEN (GERETH), and spend her remaining days at Ricks, a modest dower house. But Mrs. Gereth will not abide by this unjust custom, and she stubbornly fights to retain Poynton. Her tenacity has a tragic outcome for both herself and her loyal young friend, FLEDA VETCH.

Having dedicated her entire married life to making Poynton an aesthetic showplace, through prudent use of her husband's income, Mrs. Gereth considers the estate a part of her identity. Much more than an assemblage of the finest in furniture and artifacts from around the world, the "spoils" of Poynton are the very record of Mrs. Gereth's adult life. Mrs. Gereth shares her reverence of Poynton with Fleda Vetch, who, although she has never had such splendid possessions, has an innate sense of taste. Sure that Fleda, her fellow aesthete, would allow her to keep nominal proprietorship of Poynton, Mrs. Gereth schemes to have Fleda marry Owen.

But Owen admires the beautiful but tasteless Mona Brigstock, and he asks her to marry him. Motivated by avarice rather than appreciation, Mona covets Poynton simply because it will be rightfully hers as Owen's wife. Mrs. Gereth knows the marriage of Owen and Mona would result in her permanent exile from Poynton, so she freely expresses her contempt for Mona, while Fleda, who secretly loves the vacuous but charming Owen, privately grieves over the engagement. The helpless Owen begs Fleda to plead his case to Mrs. Gereth. Loving him as she does, Fleda cannot deny Owen's request, so she convinces Mrs. Gereth to move to Ricks.

Mrs. Gereth does move to Ricks, but she takes with her all the "spoils" of Poynton, leaving Owen and Mona a shell of a house. The philistine Mona, realizing that Poynton has been effectively snatched from her grasp, delays her marriage to Owen until he can find the courage to take back the "spoils" from his mother. Mona's postponement is Mrs. Gereth's opportunity: If Mrs. Gereth can withhold the "spoils" long enough, then perhaps Mona and Owen will never marry.

Lacking the courage to confront either Mona or his mother, Owen turns increasingly to Fleda for emotional sustenance, growing more openly fond of her. Mrs. Gereth shrewdly suspects Fleda's love for Owen; however, she does not yet suspect that Owen is also falling in love with Fleda. Mrs. Gereth entreats Fleda to openly declare her love to Owen, knowing that her insipid son will be easily captivated by Fleda's loving sensitivity. But Fleda, bound by her sense of honor, will not openly declare her love for a man who is still technically engaged.

Mrs. Gereth continues to retain the "spoils" until it seems as though the marriage of Owen and Mona will never occur. Confident of her victory over Mona, and sure that her son will soon marry Fleda, Mrs. Gereth restores all the sumptuous artifacts and furniture to Poynton. Meanwhile Fleda, increasingly sure of Owen's feelings for her, reveals her true feelings to Owen, who promises to terminate his engagement to Mona. Mona has learned of the restoration of Poynton, however, so she seduces Owen, and they elope.

With Poynton now lost to both of them forever, Mrs. Gereth and Fleda resign themselves to living together at Ricks. This dower house, although somewhat spartan, has a simple charm, and Fleda earnestly declares her hope that she and Mrs. Gereth can find modest happiness there. Fleda soon receives a letter from Owen, who is on an extended honeymoon, requesting that Fleda journey to Poynton to select an artifact for a keepsake, as both an indirect apology and a token of his esteem. Fleda decides to do so, but she arrives only to see Poynton, the victim of accident and negligence, burn to the ground.

Gereth, Owen. *The Spoils of Poynton.* Henry James. 1897.

Owen Gereth is a weak-willed young man who is haplessly torn between three very different yet equally resolute women. The insipid Owen is not an adept governor of his fate in the domestic realm, so his future will be determined by the maneuverings of ADELA (GERETH), his obstinate, recently widowed mother; Mona Brigstock, his beautiful and mercenary fiancée; and FLEDA VETCH, his plain but devoted and sensitive friend.

At the outset of the story, Owen expects to take legal proprietorship of Poynton, the family estate. In keeping with English custom, Owen will then install his mother in a humble dower house, Ricks. Mrs. Gereth has invested much energy into making Poynton a showplace, however, and she cannot placidly relinquish it. Owen, who has the option of legal recourse, cannot bring himself to file a suit against his own mother even though he continues to want what is legally his. Thus, mother and son are deadlocked.

The tension between Owen and Mrs. Gereth is exacerbated by Owen's engagement to Mona Brigstock, a beautiful woman of vulgar tastes. Mrs. Gereth would much prefer that her son marry Fleda Vetch, a penniless young woman who nonetheless has innate good taste and is sympathetic to Mrs. Gereth's awkward position. If Owen were to marry her, then surely the fair-minded Fleda would allow Mrs. Gereth to retain at least a nominal proprietorship of her beloved Poynton.

Owen entreats the diplomatic Fleda to convince his mother to leave Poynton. In love with Owen, she selflessly

agrees to help him. Although stubborn, Mrs. Gereth finally relents and moves to Ricks, but she takes the entire contents of Poynton with her. Owen is crushed when Mona, realizing that Poynton has been effectually snatched from her hands, delays her marriage to Owen until he can muster the courage to retrieve the "spoils" of Poynton from his mother. Mrs. Gereth only becomes more adamantly entrenched in her stance, knowing that if she retains the "spoils" long enough, the engagement will dissolve altogether.

The weak-willed Owen is now utterly distraught, for neither his mother nor Mona will relent, and he is incapable of coercing either of them. He turns to Fleda for sympathy and companionship, and when he confesses to her that his feelings for Mona have changed, she senses that Owen is falling in love with her. The closest that the inexpressive Owen ever comes to a declaration of love, however, is an appeal to Fleda to "save" him.

The engagement of Owen and Mona becomes increasingly protracted until both Fleda and Mrs. Gereth are convinced that the marriage will not take place. Fleda finally reveals a glimmer of her affection to Owen, and thus fortified, he goes at Fleda's behest to terminate his engagement to Mona. Mrs. Gereth, now certain that Fleda and Owen will be married, returns all of the "spoils" to Poynton. But Mona, learning of the restoration of Poynton, seduces Owen, who easily falls victim to her feminine wiles, and they marry on the spot.

Owen, as a meager reparation for his cowardly betrayal of Fleda, asks her to select for herself one of Poynton's treasures as a token of his esteem. When Owen and Mona are on an extended vacation, she goes to Poynton to choose from its treasures, arriving in time to see Poynton consumed by an accidental fire.

Gerhardt, Jennie. *Jennie Gerhardt.* Theodore Dreiser. 1911.

Jennie Gerhardt is the attractive, naturally sympathetic eighteen-year-old daughter of poor German immigrants in Columbus, Ohio.

When Jennie and her mother obtain work at a fancy hotel near the state capital that is patronized by important political and social figures, she gradually becomes acquainted with Senator George Brander. He in turn notices her beauty and feels sorry for her family's condition.

Brander begins to fondle Jennie when she brings him his laundry. He also gives her presents and provides money for the destitute Gerhardt clan. One day when Jennie's brother Bass is arrested for stealing coal from the railroad for their home, she runs to Brander for money to get him out of jail. Brander arranges his release, and in gratitude Jennie sleeps with him. Brander promises to marry her later, but she is soon confronted with the twin facts of her pregnancy and his sudden death from heart failure.

Jennie gives birth to a daughter and moves with her to

Cleveland, where she is hired as a maid in the upper-class lodging house of Mrs. Bracebridge. Here Jennie sees another social sphere apart from her own, one of cultured manners, tastes, and fashion. One wealthy young man who is occasionally in town on business, LESTER KANE, the son of a wealthy carriage manufacturer, strikes her with his magnetic charm. He is insistent and presumptuous when, having noticed her, he declares, "You belong to me." Jennie finds herself powerless to resist him despite her efforts to adhere to conventional morality.

When Jennie's father is seriously injured at his job, Jennie remembers offers of money that Lester made. She takes his money, and he asks her to come to New York with him. She agrees and begins a long masquerade as Lester Kane's "wife." Eventually Jennie moves to Chicago, where Lester later comes to oversee the construction of a building for his father's company, in which he occupies a prominent position. Lester equivocates on the question of marriage since he is being pressured by his family to leave Jennie for someone more socially suitable. When he finds out that she already has a child, it gives him an excuse to remain distant about marriage. Jennie feels the shame of her past constantly intruding into the present.

Jennie and Lester live a false but comfortable married life in a wealthy neighborhood, but in time the newspapers and social gossip expose the truth. Furthermore, unknown to Jennie, Lester is faced with the choice of either leaving her or losing his inheritance when his father dies soon after the exposure of their relationship.

On a trip to Europe, Jennie notices Lester's intellectual and social affinity with a long-time friend he encounters, the wealthy, widowed Letty Pace Gerald. On her return to Chicago, Jennie is told by a lawyer sent by Lester's brother what Lester stands to lose, and she tells Lester she is leaving. She finds that he is more upset at his brother than sad about the end of their affair.

Jennie settles with her daughter Vesta in a country cottage, only to see the child die of typhoid. She learns of Lester's marriage to Letty Gerald in the papers. One day, years later, she is called to Lester's deathbed, where he confesses to her that she is the only woman he ever really loved. She attends his funeral, feeling at once a part of and apart from the scene of Lester's coffin and the wealthy mourners.

Gibson, Dick (Marshall Maine). *The Dick Gibson Show.* Stanley Elkin. 1970.

Dick Gibson is a radio personality who hosts numerous programs on stations across the country from the Depression through the late 1960s. Gibson's real name, which he goes by in the beginning of the novel, is Marshall Maine. Known as Marshall Maine in the small New England town where he hosts a show at the start of his career, he eventually changes his name to Dick Gibson because he likes its crisp, anonymous, all-American quality.

Dick's search for new names and new radio shows is part of his deeper search for an identity. With each new show he attempts to develop a fresh personality. His visits to his family in Pittsburgh seem only to contribute to his identity crisis, for Dick's parents and younger brother behave like actors, avoiding exposure by constantly acting out clichéd roles. Dick himself has only a vague idea of who they really are.

On a train headed east from Des Moines, Dick meets Miriam Desebour, a nurse at a convalescent home. Although he is perfectly healthy, he goes with her to a nursing home in Morristown, New Jersey, and lets her take care of him. For a while Dick lives as an invalid and is pampered by Miriam. When he learns she is having an affair with another patient, he goes home to Pittsburgh and then returns to radio, reading commercials and public service announcements.

In 1943, Dick is called up by five draft boards because of his multitude of personae. He eventually gets a show on armed forces radio, but he is unhappy with the show's blandness. Dick finally demonstrates character when he interrupts an insipid song by shouting "Bullshit!" repeatedly into the microphone.

After the war, Dick hosts a talk show on WHCN in Hartford, Connecticut. One night on the show he meets the renowned psychologist Dr. Edmond Behr-Bleibtreau, who instantly becomes his nemesis. Behr-Bleibtreau exerts a mysterious power over the minds of the other guests on the panel, and he manipulates them into telling deeply personal stories about themselves.

The evil psychologist tries to make Dick publicly humiliate himself as well, and Dick becomes obsessed with eluding him. But his efforts are unnecessary: Behr-Bleibtreau has no power over Dick Gibson because Dick's personality is as unreal as his name. He has no embarrassing story to tell. The lack of identity that has plagued him his entire life is ultimately what saves Dick Gibson.

Gibson, Dilsey. *The Sound and the Fury;* "That Evening Sun." William Faulkner. 1929; 1931.

Dilsey Gibson has worked most of her life as a cook for the Compsons, a once-aristocratic family in Jefferson, Mississippi. Overworked and underappreciated by her white employers, she nevertheless endures as one who is motivated by generosity and common sense. She struggles to maintain order in a household rife with pettiness, hypocrisy, and cruelty.

On Easter, April 8, 1928, Dilsey is looking forward to attending church with her daughter Frony and grandson Luster, but they cannot go until Dilsey makes breakfast for the Compsons. Because Luster has stayed out late and overslept, she finds that she must do more than cook. She collects kindling, lights the fire, and tries to anticipate the complaints of Mrs. Compson, who constantly interrupts her work in the kitchen. She locates Luster, has him dress

BENJAMIN "BENJY" COMPSON, the adult, retarded son, and bring him downstairs. Besides CANDACE "CADDY" COMPSON, who fled the family years before, Dilsey is the only member of the household who genuinely cares for Benjy. She knows Benjy cannot endure any deviation in his daily routine, so she orders the resentful Luster to see that Benjy remains pacified during his feeding.

Mrs. Compson and JASON (COMPSON), her son, come down for breakfast. Jason, the head of the family, asks the whereabouts of Quentin, his teenage niece. Dilsey, who dislikes Jason's constant hounding of the girl, pleads with him to let her sleep in. But Jason goes back upstairs and finds Quentin's door locked. When she doesn't answer, Mrs. Compson gets hysterical. Mrs. Compson imagines that her granddaughter has committed suicide like her namesake, QUENTIN COMPSON. While Dilsey tries to calm Mrs. Compson, Jason realizes that Quentin is not in her room at all. He runs back to his own room and discovers that she has stolen thousands of dollars. Knowing that she has run off with her current boyfriend, a man from a traveling show, he rushes out of the house to pursue them.

Dilsey and Luster bring Benjy to the Negro church. Some of Dilsey's friends disapprove of her bringing a white man, even a retarded one, to worship with them. Dilsey says that God doesn't care whether Benjy is bright or not. An emotional preacher gets Dilsey thinking about her many years with the Compsons. On the way home she begins to cry. When Frony asks her what's wrong, she can only say, "I seed the beginning, en now I sees de endin."

Giles (Billy Bocksfuss). *Giles Goat-Boy.* John Barth. 1966.

From infancy, Giles Goat-Boy lives with a herd of goats with whom he fully identifies. It is not until he is in his early teens that Giles, then known as Billy Bocksfuss, realizes some of the essential differences between himself and the goats. This awakening, along with an encounter with a beautiful woman whom he dubs Lady Creamhair, sparks in Giles a quest for full humanity. As the novel unfolds, he comes to realize that he is at the center of an allegorical account of the tumult facing a society as it readjusts after a cataclysmic war and awaits what amounts to a Second Coming.

While a young boy, Giles is tended by Max Spielman, a former professor. Despite Max's love and attention, Giles, once awakened by Lady Creamhair, decides that he wants to be a man. Accordingly, Max tutors Giles for seven years; at the end of this tutorial period, Giles decides that he is the awaited Grand Tutor. In order to assert this status, Giles and Max journey from the farm to the main campus of New Tammany College, which is divided into feuding factions, East and West. Not surprisingly, the Goat-Boy's assertion that he is the Grand Tutor meets with significant resistance. Giles eventually learns that WES-

CAC, the computer that runs the campus, once had a project called GILES—Grand-tutorial Ideal, Laboratory Eugenical Specimen. Armed with this knowledge and assuming that he is correct in his belief, Giles descends into the belly of WESCAC, a process necessary to the proclamation of a Grand Tutor.

In response to the seven tasks he receives from the computer, Giles begins to progress toward becoming the Grand Tutor; however, another man, Harold Bray, works against him and easily subverts his efforts. After his exposure to WESCAC's challenges, Giles learns that Lady Creamhair is his mother and that she was impregnated by WESCAC when she was a virgin and gave birth to Giles and his twin sister Anastasia. This knowledge serves as proof for Giles that he is definitely that long-awaited Grand Tutor. Meanwhile, in order to maintain his position, Bray manages to manipulate events so that Giles ends up serving time in Detention. There he again meets Max, who has been incarcerated on a murder charge. Under the harsh conditions of the Detention Center, Giles discovers that a paradox forms the essence of WESCAC's teachings or rule. After hearing of Giles's new understanding, Bray assumes that the younger man has accepted that it is Bray, not Giles, who is the Grand Tutor, and he pardons him.

For his part, Giles, armed by his newfound appreciation of WESCAC's functioning, reinterprets the seven tasks he had originally received from WESCAC. Finally, even Bray calls him the true "GILES." The two men once again enter the computer's belly; as before, Giles and Bray emerge only to have Bray turn the crowds against Giles. On his third visit through WESCAC's challenges, Giles is accompanied by his sister Anastasia; this time they emerge, and Giles has attained true wisdom. It has been revealed that he and Anastasia are not siblings. They have intercourse that results in her pregnancy. Although certain that he is the Grand Tutor, Giles is incapable of finding a believing audience; Max, who is innocent of the murder to which he confessed, is publicly executed in the authorities' effort to maintain control over the university's restive student body. At the end of the novel, Giles is thirty-three years old, and he and Anastasia have two children. She and their longtime friend Peter Greene remain Giles's only apostles.

Gilley, Gerald. *A New Life.* Bernard Malamud. 1961.

Gerald Gilley exemplifies the rigid intellectual structure against which the two main characters, PAULINE GILLEY and SY LEVIN, rebel. As the head of composition in the English department at Cascadia College, located in a small northwestern town, Gilley's primary concern is that he eventually succeed as head of the entire department.

Although his relationship with his wife Pauline seems relatively happy from the outside, their inability to have children is a source of major stress. Their decision to adopt two children seems to be working only moderately well.

Gerald is significantly older than Pauline, and she does not meet his expectations of her as a faculty wife. He feels that her inability to entertain properly is detrimental to his career.

Gerald is exceedingly pleasant and accommodating to Sy Levin, whom he hired to replace the English instructor Leo Duffy, a "radical" who was forced to leave Cascadia as the result of some unpleasant business. Gerald hired Levin hoping that he would be malleable, and he does many favors for him in the department, such as giving him a big office and putting him in charge of the textbook committee. He also offers to take him fishing and golfing frequently. When Levin refuses these friendly overtures, Gerald is at a loss as to how to respond.

Gerald has been allowing students to switch out of Levin's class into the class of an easier grader. When Levin questions this and other underhanded activities that go on in the department, Gerald tells him not to make waves his first year and warns him of the fate of Leo Duffy.

The most important thing for Gerald is that he be liked by everybody, especially in the upcoming election for department head. He spends the majority of his time politicking, trying to get people to pledge their vote to him and promising in return to work on the changes each person desires.

Although Gerald is unaware that Pauline and Levin are having an affair, he comes to realize that Levin dislikes him. The greatest insult to Gerald comes when Levin, despite all Gerald has done for him, decides to run against him for head of the department. When Levin gets involved in the politics of the event, he discovers why Gerald hated Duffy: Pauline and Duffy had an affair, and Gerald took a photograph of the two of them swimming together naked. Gerald showed the photograph to all his colleagues in power in order to get Duffy fired. Levin considers Gerald despicable because of this act.

When Pauline tells Gerald that she is going to marry Levin, Gerald announces it publicly in the department, with the result that he soundly wins the election. Then he begs Pauline not to leave him and threatens not to let her have the children. He also insists to Levin that he loves Pauline in his way and understands her more than Levin ever could. His last act is to take a photograph of the couple as they drive out of town.

Gilley, Pauline. *A New Life*. Bernard Malamud. 1961.

Pauline Gilley is an unhappily married woman who seeks "a new life" by leaving her husband for another man. The wife of GERALD (GILLEY), director of composition in the English department of Cascadia, a small northwestern college, she feels unsuccessful and dissatisfied with her role as a faculty wife. She does not have the social skills to entertain adequately, and Gerald feels that she is partly responsible for his not moving up in the department. After years of being unable to have children,

she and Gerald finally made the commitment to adopt, and the addition of two children to their already strained marriage makes Pauline feel even more inadequate.

Pauline has been unfaithful to Gerald. Her lover was Leo Duffy, a "radical" who was fired in disgrace from the college ostensibly for his political insubordination. The primary reason, however, was that Gerald produced a photograph of Pauline and Duffy swimming together naked. The scandal was cause enough for Duffy's expulsion. When Gerald and Pauline are attempting to keep their marriage together, Pauline asks if she can choose Duffy's replacement. She selects SY LEVIN, whose picture somehow reminds her of Duffy.

Pauline falls in love with Levin not long after his arrival. Their attraction takes a while to develop, but once it does, they become obsessed with each other. While Gerald is out at meetings, Pauline hires a babysitter and sneaks over to Levin's apartment. Although they realize they are in love, the terror of being discovered becomes too stressful for them to maintain their relationship. Pauline is particularly frightened when she learns that through her oversight the children were left alone in the house. When she again becomes faithful to Gerald, Levin makes no objection.

Pauline cannot hide her discontent, feeling that she could have been more successful had she not gotten married when she was so young to someone so much older. Levin, like Duffy, represents the possibility of a new life for her, and she is torn between the responsibility and the love she thinks she feels for Gilley and the hope of doing something satisfying with her own life.

Her decision is sudden. She notifies Levin that she is ready to marry him; in the meantime, however, he has become involved in the race against Gilley for department head. Levin has also found out about Duffy and feels for the first time that he might have a chance of success at work, so he agrees to marry her. When Pauline tells her husband, Gilley publicizes their affair and Levin loses the election.

Pauline insists on taking the children with her, but Gerald objects and begs her to stay with him. As she and Levin are about to drive away from the town, she announces that she is pregnant. For both of them the pregnancy means a chance to start life over.

Gilmore, Gary. *The Executioner's Song.* Norman Mailer. 1979.

Through letters, court and police transcripts, and the reminiscences of those who knew him, this "factual account . . . [written] as if it were a novel" tells the "true life story" of convicted murderer Gary Gilmore. Gary's cousin Brenda remembers him as a bright, creative, and caring child; his twenty-year-old lover Nicole Barrett depicts him as an alternately gentle and terrifying man, seemingly well-read, obsessively in love. In tracing Gary's emotional development as a child of abuse and neglect through an adolescence and adulthood spent largely in reform schools and prison, the novel poses an increasingly compelling, yet ultimately unanswerable question: Was Gary born a murderer, or did society make him one?

The facts of Gary's story are straightforward. After serving thirteen years of a twenty-two-year sentence, he is paroled from jail and goes to live in the Mormon stronghold of Orem, Utah, where he becomes involved with Nicole. After a string of jobs and a number of disappointments, Gary goes out one night to hold up a gas station. He secures the cash and ruthlessly executes the attendant. He repeats the crime the following night, murdering a motel desk clerk, who also happens to be a Mormon.

After he is caught and brought to trial, Gary is convicted of first-degree murder and sentenced to death. Although no one on death row in America has been executed for ten years, Gary decides to forgo all stays of execution, and he requests that he be shot by firing squad.

Gary's reasons for committing the murders are suggested and hypothesized but never made absolutely clear. At first his cold rage seems to result from a terrible childhood, the dramatic impact on his mind of the prison-administered drug Prolixin, and his failure to adapt to his new life outside of prison.

However, other, more subtle explanations are also offered. Perhaps Gary killed the two Mormons out of revenge: The Mormon church refused to help his mother pay back taxes on his childhood home, and the family eventually lost the house to the state. Then again, it is conceivable that Gary was simply lost, out of place, in Orem—a Mormon paradise where all roads end in desert. The inhabitants of this town present a life of kitschy, doe-eyed innocence, while Gary's is the coarse, unstable, and crisis-ridden experience of a member of the unskilled poor.

Like his motives for cold-blooded murder, Gary's insistence on his own execution is of an extremely complex and mysterious origin. His father was the illegitimate son of the escape artist Harry Houdini, and the book suggests that he may have coveted a starring role in the media circus created by the idea of his execution. He also shows a distinct penchant for control and manipulation in his reactions to his lawyers, the warden, the reporters, his family, and the worldwide audience.

On the other hand, his press statements seem to indicate sincere repentance. His letters to Nicole suggest that this sincerity might stem from sexual guilt—that his demand for death might signify a subconscious flight from his own pedophilia.

While waiting on death row, Gary forms a suicide pact—to overdose on sleeping pills—with Nicole. Neither succeeds. But even this circumstance proves troubling and ambiguous. Did Gary really intend to die with Nicole, or did he simply want her dead so that no one else could have her? His letters to her refer obsessively to other men with whom Gary imagines she is sleeping. Gary was certainly familiar enough with dosages to know that his share would not prove fatal to a person of his body weight but might kill someone lighter and smaller. Also, Gary did not take his pills at midnight, as they had agreed, but six hours later—perhaps to be found in time.

Then again, Gary tries to end his life one more time before his sentence is finally carried out. On January 17, 1976, he is brought to an old cannery, hooded, tied loosely to an old chair, and shot by a squad of four men. He bleeds profusely before dying, some twenty seconds after the shots have been fired.

The Girl. *The Girl.* Meridel LeSueur. 1978.

This young female protagonist and narrator is approximately twenty years old when she arrives at the German Village, a speakeasy in St. Paul, Minnesota. From the start, The Girl is flabbergasted by the bawdiness of the speakeasy and its environs. She is befriended by Clara, a prostitute and sometime waitress; Belle, the proprietor of the Village; and Amelia, a seemingly shattered woman who has lost all six of her children. While poverty itself is not new to The Girl, whose father had been buried with public funds, the element of crime is quite frightening to her. However, she is immensely attracted to Butch Hinkley, one of the men who hang around the German Village, and responds when he makes advances toward her.

Following her father's death, The Girl returns to St. Paul, where she and Butch decide to marry. It is unclear whether they enact a legal ceremony, but the relationship is consummated, painfully for The Girl, in a dingy hotel room for which she had to pay. Meanwhile, Butch, under the direction of Ganz, a gang leader, and along with Hoinck, Belle's husband of thirty years, is planning a robbery. It will be their biggest crime yet, and they are nervous but excited. The Girl uneasily agrees to become involved by driving one of the escape cars on the day of the bank robbery.

After this is settled, The Girl is offered twenty-five dollars by Ganz, who wants to sleep with her. When he arrives at the hotel, he is with Mr. Hone, his lawyer, and the two men tell her that the money was too high. They make her jump for a ten-dollar bill but then grab her, beat her senseless, and rape her. The Girl accepts this brutality as part of her lot as a woman. Ironically, this event causes great anger in Butch, who later beats her for her infidelity.

Among the other developments as the day of the planned robbery approaches are the discoveries that The Girl is pregnant from her first experience with Butch and that Clara is seriously ill. Butch is angered by the pregnancy and eventually brings The Girl to an old woman abortionist, but The Girl flees after he leaves. Finally, after an anguished final night, the day of the robbery arrives. The Girl, driving the getaway car, is the calmest of the lot. Once in the bank, though, Ganz mercilessly shoots

Hoinck in the back; in response, Butch shoots Ganz and is then shot himself as the dying man retaliates while falling to the floor. Butch manages to get to the car, and the couple takes off. Although The Girl does the best she can to help him, Butch dies by morning, and she is forced to leave his body by a cornfield in Iowa.

The Girl sneaks back to St. Paul and stealthily makes her way to Belle's. Here, the women convince The Girl not to abort her baby, and she makes her home with them. The Girl eventually tries to get on relief herself but is given no more than a bureaucratic run-around. The women finally relocate to an abandoned warehouse, and they form a community united against economic oppression. The Girl had been rescued from the relief maternity home by Amelia, who turns out to be active in the Worker's Alliance. This group opposes discriminatory relief practices and plans a demonstration to insist on equitable distribution of food and vitamins. On the day of the planned demonstration, as The Girl realizes she is in labor, Clara dies. At the end of the novel, The Girl washes her friend's body, and with the women who remained behind, she dresses her and lays her out. By the time the demonstrators return, elated at the turnout, the delivery is close. Amelia positions herself as midwife, and with a circle of women watching, The Girl's daughter, Clara, is born.

Gladney, Jack. *White Noise.* Don DeLillo. 1985.

Jack Gladney, chairman of the Hitler Studies department of a small college in middle America, struggles with a constant fear of death. He roves the campus in an academic gown and dark glasses, hoping to hide the fact that he cannot speak German. With his fourth wife Babette, Jack rears four outspoken and precocious children who constantly badger their parents about everything from nutrition to cosmic randomness.

For no apparent reason Jack begins waking up in the middle of the night with "death-sweats." Death hovers over everything he does, a great nebulous cloud, and he tries to block it out by filling his mind with the gibberish of American culture: grocery commodities, television, tabloid journalism, intentionally obfuscating political or scientific language, and academic interpretations of culture.

One day this nebulous threat becomes material in the form of a black cloud of "Nyodene D," an insecticide by-product, that forces the Gladney family and the rest of the town to evacuate while Mylex-suited men monitor the "airborne toxic event." During the event Jack is exposed to the toxin for a brief period. This brief exposure implants in him a kind of time-released death; he now carries his death inside of him, in the form of a "nebulous mass" that has appeared in his body—the black billowing cloud internalized.

Meanwhile, Jack learns from one of his daughters that Babette has been taking a strange saucer-shaped pill. Babette initially denies this but finally confesses that she has

answered an advertisement in a tabloid that promised a cure for "fear of death," and in return for sexual favors granted to a project supervisor, she has become the guinea pig in the development of an inhibitor for the sector of the brain that dreads mortality.

Jack is now equally obsessed with finding out the identity of his wife's lover and with obtaining a supply of the pill Dylar. Acting on the theory that plots are a defiance of death, he embarks on an elaborate scheme to find and eradicate the man involved. He finally learns that the man, Willie Mink, has been dismissed from the project for unorthodox research methods.

Jack locates Mink at the motel where he has liaisons with Babette. Mink is a pathetic parrot of television shows, throwing gobs of Dylar into his mouth like popcorn. Jack shoots him, but in staging the act to look like a suicide, he is also shot by the wounded Mink. Finally, Jack actually saves Mink by taking him to a hospital run by German-speaking nuns. The nuns, in whose pure faith Jack had hoped to find a kind of salvation by proxy, believe in nothing, and Jack is left to confront his fears alone.

Glass, Buddy. *Raise High the Roof Beam, Carpenters; Seymour: An Introduction.* J. D. Salinger. 1963; 1963.

Buddy Glass is beginning his twelfth year as a writer-in-residence at a women's two-year college in upstate New York in 1959. Raised in Manhattan, he now lives alone, "catless," on the less accessible side of a mountain. His home is small, unwinterized, and without electricity or a phone. Buddy's literary output to date consists of one novel and a collection of short stories.

Born in 1919 to the vaudevillians Les and Bessie Glass, Buddy is the second of the seven Glass children. Throughout his life he views his older brother SEYMOUR (GLASS) as the most morally and intellectually incorruptible person ever to have lived. Along with Seymour and his other siblings, Buddy spent years of his childhood as a panelist on the coast-to-coast radio quiz show "It's a Wise Child." Buddy explains that his mastery of baseball trivia at the age of two led to his participation on the show. From an early age he was also secure in the knowledge that he would be a superlative writer.

Buddy follows Seymour to Columbia University, where the more self-conscious Buddy strives to fit in with his classmates. When Buddy does not finish college, he feels that he cannot compete with Seymour even though both are voracious and eclectic readers. Buddy knows many languages, Eastern as well as Western, and is considered an authority on Eastern cultures and religions by his colleagues at the college, although he teaches English literature and writing. When still alive, Seymour had expressed concern that Buddy valued Seymour's opinion of his stories more than his own.

When the United States becomes involved in World War II, Buddy volunteers for the Army Infantry. In the spring of 1942, after thirteen weeks of basic training, he finds himself in an army hospital in Georgia with pleurisy. Of the war-scattered Glass family, only Buddy makes it to New York City for Seymour's wedding. When the wedding guests leave the church after vainly waiting for Seymour's arrival, Buddy unwittingly jumps into a limousine with the bride's maid of honor and several others. Buddy tries to hide the fact that he is the absent groom's brother, but the maid of honor exposes his secret. He ends up bringing the whole group to his and Seymour's apartment on the Upper East Side.

When Seymour kills himself while on vacation in Florida, Buddy brings his remains back to New York. He also comes into possession of three years' worth of Seymour's poems. After twelve years of threats from his various family members to do something with Seymour's stories, Buddy now plans to have them published.

Glass, Frances "Franny." *Franny and Zooey.* J. D. Salinger. 1961.

Born in 1934, Frances "Franny" Glass is the youngest of the seven extraordinary Glass children. The members of the Glass family began their careers in life appearing on the radio program "It's A Wise Child," a show designed to exhibit the intellectual sophistication of its panelists. While in college, Franny suffers an acute spiritual and psychological crisis in her search for a person possessing true wisdom. Fearing that she herself, an emerging actress, may be tripping toward egomania, she has a breakdown. She recuperates with the unlikely help of her brother ZACHERY MARTIN "ZOOEY" (GLASS).

Franny and Zooey had their schooling directed by the two eldest Glass children. BUDDY (GLASS) and the prodigious SEYMOUR (GLASS) believed that Franny and Zooey would benefit from a non-traditional education. They taught Franny and Zooey various metaphysical and theological points of view in order to provide a context for the two youngest Glasses to consider the problem of "Being."

This unique start leaves Franny with peculiar yearnings—for wisdom and beauty rather than success or popularity, the values esteemed by her fellow college students and her academic boyfriend Lane. With standards derived from world-renowned holy men and prophets, Franny cannot help but see her contemporaries' concerns as self-centered and conformist. She fears, however, that she herself does not have the courage to be undistinguished and wishes to meet someone who does not consider the acquisition of knowledge an end in itself.

Although she has made an impressive start as an actress both in summer stock and in student plays at her college, Franny quits the theater because she fears the growth of her own ego. While lunching at a fashionable restaurant with the self-absorbed Lane, she breaks out in a cold sweat and then faints in the ladies' room.

One source of her breakdown is a small green book of Seymour's that Franny has secreted in her handbag called *The Way of the Pilgrim.* In it a sweet lame pilgrim learns to chant the "Jesus prayer" incessantly in order to achieve a state of perfect union with Jesus Christ. Franny is enormously attracted to this prayer and has begun practicing it. This practice and the feelings of self-doubt it raises have brought on her agitated state of mind.

After collapsing, Franny returns to her family's apartment on the Upper East Side of Manhattan. She lies under a pale blue afghan on the couch, silently reciting the "Jesus prayer." Her brother Zooey lectures her on her use of the Jesus prayer, accusing her of seeking spiritual escapism instead of Christ-Consciousness, the "true" result of the prayer. Feeling battered and unable to respond, she puts her head down on the couch and sobs.

Soon Franny gets a phone call from Buddy, her favorite brother, and she sits on her parents' bed, smoking and talking to him. Franny keeps insisting, however, that Buddy must have a terrible cold or that they have a bad connection because his voice sounds so strange. They are talking about Zooey and how he uses his cigar as a ballast to keep his feet on the ground when Franny suddenly realizes that it is actually Zooey on the phone.

Although she calls off their game, Franny does manage to continue talking on the phone with Zooey. Together they grope toward a memory of their dead brother Seymour who has remained a central figure in the family even though he is no longer alive. Franny remembers an instance when Seymour asked her to be funny for the "Fat Lady," an audience they used to imagine when they did a radio show as children. When Zooey reminds her that everyone is Seymour's Fat Lady, Franny is filled with joy. She sits cradling the phone for a long time, even after he has hung up. Then Franny turns down the covers and falls into a quiet slumber.

Glass, Seymour. "A Perfect Day for Bananafish"; *Raise High the Roof Beam, Carpenters; Seymour: An Introduction.* J. D. Salinger. 1953; 1963; 1963.

Seymour Glass, poet and mystic, strives to answer the essential questions of Being. His brother BUDDY (GLASS) would write that, more often than not, Seymour "talked with the classical conception . . . of a mukta, a ringding enlightened man, a God-Knower."

Seymour is the eldest child of Les and Bessie Glass, retired vaudevillians living in New York City. Seymour, and each of his brothers and sisters after him, is a featured guest on the coast-to-coast radio program "It's A Wise Child." Under the pseudonym "Billy Black," Seymour appears on the show for six years, during which he changes the format from a children's quiz show to that of a round-table discussion. At times unapproachably quiet, Seymour has nonetheless mastered language to such an extent that when he does talk—and he is perfectly capable of performing monologues that last for hours—his listeners' entertainment is assured.

Seymour firmly establishes his voracious reading when, as a preteen, he carries three library cards. When a particular subject catches his interest, Seymour would sooner forgo his few hours of nightly sleep than interrupt his learning. At fifteen he is an undergraduate at Columbia University; by twenty-one he is teaching in the English department. His taste in poetry runs to the Eastern tradition more than to the works of Western poets. For his own verse he prefers the stark haiku or sometimes a double haiku, which he writes in either English, Japanese, Italian, or German. Seymour feels that his poems have in them something that would affront Western readers or possibly appear as elitist, and he declines to publish them.

At the outbreak of the involvement of the United States in World War II, Seymour registers for the draft and by 1942 is a corporal in the Air Corps at a B-17 base in California. In May of that year he returns to New York City for his wedding to Muriel Fedder. Although he misses the two rehearsals, Seymour does arrive in time for the ceremony itself. Nevertheless, as he tries to explain to Muriel on the day of their wedding, he feels too happy to go through with the ceremony. He does not go to the church. Hours after the aborted ceremony, he and Muriel elope.

Not long after, Seymour is sent to fight in Germany. Although the events that befall him in the war remain somewhat murky, Seymour clearly is unhinged by them: He tries to kill himself and spends time in an army psychiatric hospital. After his return to the States, the still-fragile Seymour and Muriel, whom he now calls "Miss Spiritual Tramp of 1948," vacation in Florida. There, while Muriel is in their hotel room reading a magazine article called "Sex Is Fun—or Hell" and talking with her mother by phone, Seymour spends time on the beach with young Sybil Carpenter. They soon wade into the water, where Seymour tells Sybil about the "very tragic life" of the "bananafish" who swim into a banana hole, eat too many bananas, and can't get out of the hole again—"Can't fit through the door." Seymour then kisses the arch of Sybil's foot, returns to his room, and, after first looking at the sleeping Muriel, fires a bullet through his right temple.

Glass, Zachery Martin "Zooey." *Franny and Zooey.* J. D. Salinger. 1961.

Zachery Martin "Zooey" Glass is an actor encumbered with more metaphysical issues than he can handle. His honesty, artistic merit, and unwavering standards of behavior leave most of the world reeling and Zooey himself with an ulcer. He has grown tired of having to generate a moral consciousness in the minds of other people.

Zooey was the sixth of the seven Glass children to appear on the coast-to-coast radio talk show "It's A Wise

Child." For the audience who followed the show throughout its full run, from 1927 to 1943, Zooey was second only to his oldest brother SEYMOUR (GLASS) in listener appeal. Of all the Glass children Zooey was subjected to the most extensive battery of tests and interviews aimed at discovering the source of his prodigious intellect.

When Zooey's story opens he is about to settle down in the bathtub with a four-year-old letter from his brother BUDDY (GLASS). Along with his younger sister FRANCES ("FRANNY" GLASS), who is presently suffering a nervous breakdown on the Glass family sofa, Zooey received his early education from his older brothers Buddy and Seymour. The two younger children were schooled in the great religious and mystical thinkers, including Lao-tze, the Buddha, and Jesus, before they learned to read. Both are haunted by the remnants of this early thinking.

While Zooey reads and smokes a cigar in the tub, he is paid an irksome although characteristic visit by his mother Bessie, who is overcome with worry about Franny. Zooey is poring over Buddy's old letter for a ghostly trace of Seymour, who committed suicide seven years earlier but remains the emotional and spiritual center of the family.

Following his morning ablutions, where he assiduously avoids his near-flawless face in the bathroom mirror, Zooey ventures out to the family's overstuffed living room sofa to see Franny. Unfortunately, his lack of sympathy for the failings of others make him a less than ideal person to help her. He can't keep himself from challenging her motives for breaking down and her choice of the family couch as the stage for her theatrics.

After reducing Franny to tears in a matter of minutes, Zooey retires to Seymour and Buddy's old bedroom. He studies the memorabilia left behind by his dead and absent brothers: a huge board of quotations from the world's great works of literature and a stack of shirt cardboards Seymour used as a diary. He finally picks up his brother's phone, which is still paid for every month and listed under Seymour's name in the phone book, and with his handkerchief over his mouth to disguise his voice, he calls Franny and pretends to be Buddy. They chat briefly about Franny's condition until Zooey reveals himself.

Although Franny is angry at the trick, she agrees to stay on the line, and Zooey keeps talking, trying to comfort her and guide her through her spiritual crisis in his gruff and unforgiving manner. He exhorts Franny to return to their chosen profession—acting—and to do it for God, if necessary, with all the best parts of herself. As he is trying to help Franny, Zooey has an epiphany about Seymour.

As a child, Zooey had once refused to shine his shoes before appearing on "It's A Wise Child" because, he insisted, the audience was comprised of morons. Seymour asked him to do it for the "Fat Lady," whom Zooey had imagined sitting in a wicker chair, suffering from cancer, in front of a blaring radio. As Franny reveals that she developed an almost identical fantasy when Seymour asked her to be funny for the Fat Lady, Zooey senses that he is finally reaching his sister. For his big finish he reminds Franny that "there isn't anyone anywhere who isn't Seymour's Fat Lady" and that the Fat Lady "is Christ himself, buddy."

Glendinning, Pierre. *Pierre; or The Ambiguities.* Herman Melville. 1852.

Pierre Glendinning's story opens on a sentimental note with the promise of romance and happiness. The innocent, naive, nineteen-year-old Pierre is the devoted son of the affluent, vain, well-preserved widow Mary Glendinning. They reside at Saddle-Meadows, the patriarchal homestead of Pierre's late grandfather, a Revolutionary War hero. Pierre takes great pride and comfort in the conventions of the traditional aristocratic society of his forefathers. He eagerly anticipates his marriage to the lovely Lucy Tartan, a blond-haired, blue-eyed seventeen-year-old of transcendent beauty.

But Pierre's joy rapidly plunges into despair. His undoing begins with his confession to Lucy that he is bewitched by a mysterious face he has seen at a recent event for charity. It is the face of the sad-eyed, dark-haired, olive-skinned Isabel Banford. Later, Pierre receives a note from this same Isabel, a winsome plea for help from an outcast of the world who is, in fact, Pierre's illegitimate sister. This disclosure shakes Pierre's unquestioned faith in the sanctity of his father. Believing he has gained a new insight into darkness, Pierre challenges his own belief in the moral and traditional world of Saddle-Meadows and pledges to embark on an uncompromising quest for Truth.

Driven equally by the Christian duty to suffer the sins of the father and by an unacknowledged sexual desire for his mysterious half-sister, Pierre hastens into the woods to visit Isabel in her cottage. There, she relates her mournful story and casts a mesmeric spell of lust, guilt, and love on her brother. Pierre soon confronts a Hamlet-like dilemma: Caught between opposing desires for Isabel and Lucy, he ponders and broods in inactivity. Finally, he impulsively resolves to assume the role of the self-sacrificing savior of Isabel. His plan is to pretend to be married to her and to move to New York. He hastily spurns Lucy and his mother, but with disastrous consequence: Mary disowns her rebellious son, and he will soon be penniless.

Isabel and Pierre go to New York to seek help from his cousin and dear childhood friend Glendinning Stanly. But Glen, as he is called, has recently returned from Europe a foppish dandy and refuses to help the "newlyweds." Desperate for money, Pierre decides to resume his former career as a writer. He and Isabel take up residence in the seedy "Church of the Apostles," once a noble church and now a home to lawyers and starving artists. Here Pierre undertakes work on a huge philosophical treatise devoted to the "higher Truth." While still without a publisher for his book, Pierre receives news that his mother has died and has left the family fortune to Glen.

Meanwhile, Lucy, whom Glen has been courting, resolves to return to her true love. Posing as Pierre's cousin, she arrives in New York to assume the role of angelic savior of Isabel and her former fiancé. But Pierre's mental health has degenerated to the brink of madness; he is beyond salvation.

A short while later, Glen and Lucy's brother arrive in New York to save the wayward Lucy. In a fit of madness and jealous revenge, Pierre shoots and kills Glen. While he is in prison, Lucy dies of grief. Finally, desperate and despondent, Pierre, together with Isabel, ingests a fatal dose of poison. His naively impulsive attempt to undermine tradition and discover Truth thus ends in unenlightened destruction.

Glick, Sammy. *What Makes Sammy Run?* Budd Schulberg. 1941.

Sammy Glick has one salient characteristic: ruthless ambition. A self-made man, he is constantly running, looking ahead to the next phase of his career while forgetting those he steps on as soon as they can no longer help him.

The narrator, Al Mannheim, is a writer who becomes obsessed with finding out "what makes Sammy run." Al first meets Sammy while working as a theater critic for a New York newspaper. Sammy quickly beats Al at his own game, rising from office runner to featured columnist before he is eighteen, without an education or even a flair for writing. Sammy plagiarizes and falsifies for the sake of getting himself noticed. Al watches in disbelief as Sammy continues to rise, stealing a radio script from Julian Blumberg, an unknown writer who comes to him for help. Sammy sells the script to Hollywood and then heads west.

Al goes to Hollywood, too, and while he struggles to become a screenwriter, he watches Sammy push his way into producing movies through milking and manipulating others. Al tries to stand up to Sammy on moral questions, but Sammy has no morals. Everything rolls off his back. Sammy lies to and abandons his girl from home, cheats his own ghostwriter, and sabotages a noble attempt to create a screenwriters' union. Despite his outrage, Al Mannheim's success stems from his connections to Sammy who has become one of the most powerful producers in town.

Pushed past the breaking point, Al returns to New York to be a journalist again. But curiosity propels him to probe further into the question of what makes Sammy run. He researches Sammy's miserable childhood on the Lower East Side and meets Sammy's Orthodox Jewish mother and brother. The father died of grief years earlier over Sammy's errant ways. Al decides that Sammy's behavior is a reaction to the desperate poverty of tenement life and to what young Sammy believed was a dogmatic and oppressive religion.

Al gives in to Sammy's request that he return to Hollywood. He watches as Sammy destroys the career of the longtime studio head Sidney Fineman. Sammy drives the executive to resignation and suicide, and then takes the powerful job for himself.

Sammy finally meets his match in a woman. While Al is falling in love with a boyish screenwriter, Kit Sargent, Sammy woos and marries Laurette Harrington, the beautiful and sophisticated daughter of a wealthy studio trustee. He enjoys her snobbish abuse during the courtship but is devastated when she abandons him for another man on their wedding night. They cannot divorce because of the scandal it would cause. Sammy, for once, feels trapped and powerless.

The narrator draws a lesson from Sammy's remarkable rise: that we Americans pay for our success with loneliness and fear, making "individualism the most frightening ism of all."

Goering, Christina. *Two Serious Ladies.* Jane Bowles. 1943.

Christina Goering's struggle for a place is thwarted by her uncompromising sensibilities and the harsh realities of 1930s America in this sardonic novel. Christina, a woman with a mystical bent, is caught between the independent existence made possible by her fortune and her conflict-ridden relations with men and women. Housing and financially supporting the demanding Lucy Gamelon and the whiny Arnold (an aspiring suitor), Christina engages in a tentative exploration of larger society that brings to a head the gap between her quirky inner life and the world around her.

Born into a wealthy industrialist family, Christina exhibits her religious proclivities early. Wrapping her sister's friend Mary in burlap and then packing her in mud, Christina performs a play baptism with a seriousness that alarms her companions. Later, after she is left with the family house, Christina enjoys the companionship of the first woman who seems to appreciate her peculiarities, Lucy Gamelon. Lucy, however, is intent on dominating the domestic side of Christina's life; not only does she move in with Christina, but she deeply resents Christina's budding relationship with Arnold, whom she had met at a party.

Christina allows Arnold to woo her despite her own decided indifference to him, and the childish Arnold goes so far as to move in with her and Lucy. However, when she is visiting Arnold's family one night, Christina finds herself both attracted to and repelled by Arnold's cranky father Edgar. The lively old man decides, in turn, to leave his wife and move into the Goering household. All this crowding and abuse of her easy generosity becomes too much for Christina; resolute on having an adventure, she embarks on a train trip to reassert her freedom.

Christina makes friends easily in a bar at the end of her journey. One of them, a down-on-his-luck barfly named Andy, has her move in with him and tries to interest her in a business deal. Christina rejects Andy because of his lack of self-assertiveness and despondency and takes up a desperate relationship with Ben, an abusive highroller. She fends off Ben's sexual advances, finding herself put off by his abusive behavior, but she is attracted by the decisiveness of his crass machismo. Finally, sitting at a restaurant with an old friend, Mrs. Copperfield, who has gone through a similar period of change and adventure, Christina regards her life in weary terms, unable to determine if her saintliness is to come from heroism or degradation.

Gold, Bruce. *Good as Gold.* Joseph Heller. 1976.

Bruce Gold is lean, tense, and dark. At forty-eight, this professor of literature at a Brooklyn College and author of both fiction and nonfiction books is widely regarded as a top intellectual. But his most notable talent is his propensity for "doublespeak," his remarkable ability to stand simultaneously on two opposing sides of an issue in order to realize his political ends.

The son of Russian Jewish immigrants, Gold was raised in Coney Island, where his mother died when he was in high school. He is married to a perfect if boring wife, Belle. He despises his family: His father Julius constantly belittles him, and his stepmother Gussie says "Another screw has come loose" every time a new article by Gold comes out. Gold's large and heavy brother Sid constantly baits him in order to ridicule him in front of his family. His sisters, Rose, Esther, Ida, Muriel, and Joannie, idolize him for his fame, but not one has read any of his books. Still, Gold dines frequently with his family.

Gold's ability to manipulate language has enabled him to hide his lack of genuine commitment to any cause. This careful diplomacy is reflected in his recent review of the book by the President of the United States. The ambivalent review meets with the admiration of the President, whose aide, Ralph Newsome, a friend of Gold's from Columbia University's graduate school, encourages Gold to seek a position in Washington. Gold is amenable, particularly when Ralph also encourages him to seduce the lovely and tall Andrea Biddle Connor who holds a doctorate in home economics. Gold believes a connection with Andrea would immeasurably further his chances for advancement; her height and Anglo-American looks would make him appear taller and less Jewish. Ralph is even more encouraging after Gold prints three articles: "Every Change Is for the Worse," "Education and Truth, or Truth in Education," and "Nothing Succeeds as Planned." These are hailed by Ralph and the President because they seem to authorize the President's total incompetence. As reward, Gold receives an appointment to a presidential commission on education, which accomplishes nothing. When he tells a reporter he does not know what has been accomplished, the entire political world begins a similar policy of candor, proudly declaiming its incompetence.

Gold's mind is "boggled," but he accepts the honors he receives because he craves power and money. For these reasons he also silently suffers the violent bigotry of Andrea's father, who he assumes will soon be his father-in-law although he has not yet informed Belle of this prospective change. "Invite a Jew to the White House (and you make him your slave)": Gold finds examples of this maxim in his own fawning, that of his old acquaintance Maxwell Lieberman, and most virulently in the example of Henry Kissinger. He keeps a file of clippings on Kissinger, whom he detests yet unconsciously envies. Kissinger's hypocrisy as well as the continuing omnipresence of bigotry and injustice lead him to another maxim: "We are not a society. We are not worth our salt."

An affair with Linda Book, his daughter's teacher, renders Gold's life increasingly complicated, and between juggling jobs and women and suffering humiliation and belittlement from everyone, he has a heart attack. He is in the hospital for ten days, yet no one misses him. What's more, Ralph Newsome admits that if he and Bruce had lived in Nazi Germany, he would not have hidden Gold. While at the Embassy Ball, Gold learns that his brother Sid has died. Simultaneously resentful and proud of being Jewish, he returns to Brooklyn and rejects the President's offer of the job of Secretary of State.

Gold, Herman. *Jews Without Money*. Michael Gold. 1930.

Herman Gold, the father of MICHAEL (GOLD), the narrator of this autobiographical novel, is a Rumanian Jewish immigrant who is a house painter by trade. Although Herman has a lively, full-blooded temperament, the frustrations and setbacks he encounters trying to support his wife, sons, and daughter on the Lower East Side of New York City break his spirit. When he arrived in New York, he became a partner with his cousin Sam Kravitz who owns a factory that manufactures the cotton ends that fasten suspenders to trouser buttons. At the close of the novel he has been reduced to peddling bananas on street corners. He considers his immigration to the United States his life's most monumental error.

Having established himself at the suspender factory, Herman Gold heeds the advice of a matchmaker who suggests that it is time he marry and introduces him to his future wife, KATIE (GOLD). He decides to marry her because she is kind and hardworking. When he returns from a week-long honeymoon to Niagara Falls, he finds that the suspender factory has vanished. He finally locates his cousin Sam, who has hoodwinked Herman in his absence by procuring from a lawyer a paper proving com-

plete ownership of the business. Jobless and without legal recourse, Herman then turns to a career as a house painter.

Herman is famous in his neighborhood for his extraordinary expertise as a storyteller. Every evening a large group of Jewish peddlers, clothing workers, and house painters gather at the Golds' apartment to listen to his tales and to play poker and pinochle. Although largely uneducated, this group of friends also shares a great passion for drama and spends many evenings together at the theater. But this relatively pleasant life-style is eventually interrupted by a calamity from which Herman never completely recovers.

Although Herman suffers from periodic nausea and dizziness due to lead poisoning obtained from paint fumes, he thrives at his job and ultimately becomes a foreman. At this point in his life he joins the Baruch Goldfarb Lodge, a Democratic club whose members are pledged to provide one another with financial support. He plans to move his family to Borough Park, Brooklyn, into a house that he has agreed to buy from his boss, Zechariah Cohen. But once again Herman's luck fails him, and he seriously injures his feet when a scaffold collapses on the job. For a few months the Baruch Goldfarb Lodge pays an illness benefit of eight dollars per week. But when they cease to provide money, Katie and their son Michael are forced to go to work.

After a year-long period of recuperation, Herman returns to the painting profession only to find that he cannot work any longer due to a newly developed case of acrophobia, and he then spends months moping around the house. His wife becomes too depressed to continue working at a Broadway café after their daughter Esther is hit and killed by a delivery truck, so Herman attempts to find a decent job, but he is unsuccessful. Finally, despite excruciating humiliation, he rents a pushcart and begins to peddle bananas. A broken man, he drags his way through life, cursing the trap of poverty that has ensnared him.

Gold, Katie. *Jews Without Money*. Michael Gold. 1930.

Katie Gold, raised in a poor Jewish family in Hungary, is sent by her parents to the United States in the hopes that she will be able to earn enough money to send for the rest of the family. But Katie's American dream becomes a nightmare as the tribulations of ghetto life on the Lower East Side of New York City rob her of her youthful energy and optimism. By the end of the novel, Katie is so battered by the brutality of the slums that she can do little more than sit in a chair by the window and read her prayer book.

After arriving in the United States, Katie works in a restaurant for five dollars a month. A matchmaker eventually introduces Katie to HERMAN GOLD, a young Rumanian immigrant whose prospects at this juncture in his life are quite promising. Herman and Katie marry and raise a family. A woman of unbounded generosity, Katie mothers the entire neighborhood in which they live, acting as midwife, nurse, and peacemaker. When Lower East Side families are evicted from their apartments because they are unable to make rent payments, Katie dons her old shawl and solicits money door-to-door on their behalf. An eminently practical woman, she organizes a rent strike when their landlord, Mr. Zunzer, refuses to repair the antiquated plumbing in their building. Where there is trouble, there is Katie Gold and competence.

Katie is an extremely down-to-earth woman who proudly calls herself a workhorse. She thinks that her husband's gift of a diamond ring is a frivolous waste of money and uses it as collateral at the pawn shop when economic crises occur. She insists that shoes are simply the unnecessary trappings of vanity and often walks barefoot in the streets. When her husband Herman becomes incapacitated and unable to work, she assumes the financial burden of the family and lands a job as a chef's assistant in a posh Broadway café. Her fellow employees begin to call her "Momma" in honor of her brusque, nurturing personality. Her energy is unflagging, and her good spirits remain undaunted.

But even Katie Gold has an Achilles heel. Among the many outlets of emotional energy she maintains, she is passionately fond of her children, Esther and MICHAEL (GOLD). When Esther is struck and killed by a delivery truck while gathering wood in the snowy streets for their stove, Katie cannot countenance the grief she experiences. She is forced to quit her job, and Herman reassumes the chore of supporting the family by peddling bananas in the street. Katie never recovers from the shock of her daughter's violent death. Unconsoled until her own death, she spends her days sitting, weeping, and praying.

Gold, Michael. *Jews Without Money.* Michael Gold. 1930.

In this autobiographical novel, Michael Gold describes his impoverished childhood at the turn of the century in the Lower East Side of New York City. Gold's neighborhood is a red-light district peopled with prostitutes, pimps, gamblers, bums, and thugs. Whereas many of his friends become gangsters, Gold manages to transcend the vicissitudes of the ghetto. At the close of his personal narrative, he praises the efficacy of the workers' revolution, which he credits as the vehicle that enables him to escape from the nightmarish environment of his youth.

Michael's parents, HERMAN (GOLD) and KATIE (GOLD), Jewish immigrants from Eastern Europe, desperately want him to become a doctor. But the struggle to survive in the Lower East Side makes their dream impossible despite the fact that he is a precocious student. Michael is given his first book to read by Harry the Pimp, who acts as a role model to the young boys of the neighborhood because he is one of the few available examples of American affluence. Michael and his friends are soon roaming the streets in violent territorial gangs. The leader of Michael's gang, a boy named Nigger, instigates such mischievous activities as stealing perilous rides on streetcars, stealing apples from pushcarts, and throwing dead cats into the shops of infuriated storekeepers. The boys swim in the East River among dead dogs and the stench of ordure. As they grow older, these relatively innocent pastimes are replaced with increasingly violent activities.

Despite the tough and ugly environment, Michael retains a righteous sensitivity. He is horrified by the concept that God, who is supposed to be benevolent, could possibly have made bedbugs. He steals sugar from home to feed to Ganuf, an abused livery stable horse in his neighborhood. When Ganuf dies despite his loving care, Gold questions the legitimacy of a God who could allow such a tragic event to occur. All his life he regrets tormenting his little sister Esther, who is killed when she is run over by a delivery truck while gathering wood in the streets for their stove. When his aunt Lena is threatened with rape by a local gangster, Louis One Eye, Michael risks his life by yelling to neighbors to come to the rescue despite Louis's menacing threats.

Young Michael is attacked in an Italian section of town by eight boys who beat him with sticks and call him a "Christ-killer." When he recovers from this traumatic physical and emotional assault, he asks his spiritual and educational mentor, Reb Samuel, if the Messiah would resemble Buffalo Bill and have the capacity to annihilate the enemies of the Jews. He is disappointed when Reb Samuel assures him that the Messiah would be young and would only use love to conquer the world. Raised on the power principle of the streets—violence—Gold wants a savior who can pack a punch.

When his father, who is a painter, becomes incapacitated after falling from scaffolding, Michael begins to peddle newspapers. His mother takes a job at a café, but Esther's death renders her incapable of working. At the age of twelve, Michael defies his parents' will in order to help support his family; he quits school to get a job in a factory that manufactures incandescent gas mantles. Like his father before him, who had been poisoned by the toxic emissions of paint, Michael is poisoned by the air in the factory, and his health begins to suffer. When his mother forces him to get a different job, he does so and then drifts from job to job. He feels doomed to reside in what his father refers to as "poverty's trap" and is so unhappy that he seriously contemplates suicide throughout his adolescence. But then one fated day he hears a soapbox orator describing the workers' revolution, and he discovers the vehicle for the hope that existence is worthwhile because the quality of the lives of the poor is worth fighting for.

Golightly, Holly. *Breakfast at Tiffany's.* Truman Capote. 1958.

Holly Golightly is both a mercenary beauty cashing in on the lust of rich men and an idealistic romantic running from her past. Burdened by a bad case of angst—which she calls "the mean reds"—and longing for a home, Holly nevertheless emerges as a woman who refuses to succumb to the demons that haunt her.

After a failed attempt at an acting career, the frivolous Holly has come to live in an apartment on Manhattan's Upper East Side along with her cat, Cat, a stray with whom she shares a noncommittal relationship. Always on the run from her creditors, Holly makes her living entertaining men and passing Mafia tips. Although she is frank to the point of brazenness about the intimate details of her life, Holly becomes elusive when asked to reveal more information about herself than she is willing to give. Only with the novel's narrator, a writer with whom she establishes a friendship based on his resemblance to her brother Fred, does Holly let down her guard. The two grow closer, although they see each other infrequently, and celebrate the publication of his first story that Christmas.

In May, Holly receives a surprise visit from Doc, the man who married her when she was a fourteen-year-old orphan living in Tulip, Texas. Unwillingly reminded of her past, Holly gently refuses to return with him to the South. Soon after, Holly suffers a nervous breakdown when she learns of her brother Fred's death in World War II.

During the fall, Holly learns that her brief affair with José, her roommate Mag's boyfriend, has resulted in pregnancy. José moves in with Holly—who had been living alone after Mag had run off with her other boyfriend—and the two plan to relocate to Rio de Janeiro. Holly's hope of finding a home is upset, however, when she is arrested for her involvement in organized crime. While in custody, Holly suffers a miscarriage, and José, appalled by Holly's publicized arrest, leaves to protect his reputation.

Facing criminal charges, Holly decides to use her ticket to Rio to escape. Soliciting the assistance of the narrator, who is in love with her, Holly flees to the airport. As part of her bid for independence, she stops the car on the drive to the airport and abandons Cat. Almost immediately, Holly realizes that she has lost the one thing she could associate with a home. Nevertheless, she boards a plane and cuts the last of her ties to the past.

Goodwin, Morton. *The Circuit Rider.* Edward Eggleston. 1874.

Morton Goodwin is involved in a struggle not only with the forces of evil in the world but with the forces of evil inside himself. At the novel's start he is a robust young atheist more interested in winning a corn-shucking contest than in religion or a higher calling. But Mort undergoes a transformation through the course of the book, in part because of the influence of his friend Hezekiah "Kike" Lumsden and in part out of love for Kike's cousin Patty Lumsden.

Mort is first introduced as the winner of a corn-shucking contest held by the Hissawachee community. The community regularly holds quilting bees, shucking contests, and the like, where one group competes against another to fulfill the larger tasks required by individual families. This not only gets barns built and clothing made but provides an opportunity for the older folks to get together and chat, while the younger people are further introduced in a kissing game. Mort is apparently in love with Patty Lumsden, the daughter of Captain Lumsden, a powerful landowner and strict atheist. Captain Lumsden tolerates Mort's advances toward his daughter, despite Mort's poor and ignoble family background, because of his own atheism.

Conflict arises when the Captain has a terrible disagreement with Mort's friend Kike over some Lumsden family land. Captain Lumsden, knowing the land would rightfully go to Kike Lumsden once he comes of age, tries to sell it. Kike vows to kill the Captain but is instead converted to Methodism by a traveling preacher, a "circuit rider." Mort alienates the Captain by siding with Kike. When it becomes clear that he will not be allowed to marry Patty, he leaves town in search of adventure. He becomes involved with criminals, loses his money in gambling, and arrives at a desperately nihilistic moment, from which he is rescued by Kike's teachings. Mort decides that he, too, will be a circuit rider, and he devotes his efforts to neutralizing the notorious Micajah Harp gang that terrorizes the locals.

As the novel concludes, Mort mourns the death of his friend Kike, who has succumbed to malnutrition and exhaustion brought on by self-abnegation. Patty Lumsden is thrown out of the house by her father when she is converted to Methodism. She and Mort are happily married, and Mort pursues his preaching on the Jenkensville Circuit.

Goodwood, Caspar. *The Portrait of a Lady.* Henry James. 1881.

Caspar Goodwood, ISABEL ARCHER's most sincere suitor, is a Bostonian and the son of a well-known proprietor of cotton mills in Massachusetts. A strong, square-jawed young man who is full of energy but always grim and serious, Goodwood's central ambition is to marry the vibrant Isabel whom he has been courting. When Isabel rejects his first marriage proposal, he follows her to England and sends a letter to her at Gardencourt, her aunt and uncle's estate, requesting permission to visit her.

Isabel fails to answer his letter, and an irritated Goodwood learns from their mutual friend Henrietta Stackpole, a lady journalist, that Isabel is staying in a hotel in London. When they meet, she stubbornly maintains that she will not marry him; she values her liberty. Goodwood, who has never been afraid of having a freely moving wife and recognizes that single women are decidedly unfree in their society, tells Isabel that he wants to marry her precisely in order to give her that liberty. Their points of view seem irreconcilable, and when Isabel asks him to leave, Goodwood agrees to do so, but only temporarily.

Much later, back in Boston, Goodwood learns that Isabel plans to marry GILBERT OSMOND. He immediately travels to Florence to see her; extremely upset, he wants to hear the sound of her voice and learn if the news of her engagement is true. More important, because he believed her months ago when she said she would never marry anyone, he seeks some explanation as to why she is going to go through with the marriage. Isabel offers no explanation; again, Goodwood leaves disappointed.

One year passes; Isabel is now married to Osmond, and Goodwood takes a trip to Europe. In Florence, he is visited by Henrietta Stackpole, who suggests that he visit Isabel at the Osmonds' Roman villa. Goodwood cannot help sensing that something is wrong with Isabel's marriage, and that this young woman—whom he still loves—is profoundly unhappy. He takes the train to Rome with Henrietta and eventually calls on Isabel at her home.

While in Rome, Goodwood sees Isabel regularly and meets Osmond but fails to penetrate the essence of Isabel's situation. One day Isabel asks him to escort her sickly cousin Ralph Touchett, who has been staying in Rome, back to England. By this time Goodwood has figured out that Isabel only pretends to be happy; he knows she wants him to leave Rome because she thinks he is watching her. He confesses to Isabel, who now seems so unlike her former self, that he is going to England only because she asked him to, and he asks what she has made of her life. Goodwood bravely and honestly says that he loves her now as he has never loved her before. When he asks Isabel if he may pity her, she cryptically replies that he might give a thought to it every once in a while.

On the trip from Rome to England, Ralph Touchett asks Goodwood to do everything he can for Isabel—everything, that is, that she will let him. Ralph dies; Goodwood attends the funeral and fixes his unrelenting gaze on Isabel. A few days later he approaches Isabel on the lawn at Gardencourt where she sits alone, deep in thought. With renewed vigor he urges her not to return to her evil husband. Indeed, Goodwood understand Isabel's predicament: Having violated Osmond's wishes by coming to see Ralph in England, she must now decide whether or not to return to Rome where she knows her life will be more difficult than ever. Goodwood insists that she should stay with him; he loves her and wants to save her. Passionately asserting that she is not alone and can turn to him, he takes Isabel in his arms and kisses her. She breaks away and runs across the lawn to the Gardencourt mansion.

Two days later Goodwood knocks at Henrietta Stackpole's door in London, looking for Isabel. Henrietta tells Goodwood that Isabel departed that morning for Rome. He stammers, looks down, and turns away, but when Henrietta grabs his wrist and says, "Just you wait," Caspar Goodwood looks up at her again.

Gordon, Harry. *Dred, a Tale of the Great Dismal Swamp.* Harriet Beecher Stowe. 1856.

Although the son of a wealthy landowner, Harry Gordon has the legal status of a slave. Born to his father's slave mistress, Harry becomes the property of his half-white sister NINA (GORDON). For many years Harry remains loyal to his family and its plantation, but his brotherly love for Nina ensures his loyalty even when his life and marriage are threatened by her evil brother Tom.

As the bastard son of Colonel Gordon, Harry has more opportunities than the other slaves at Canema, the Gordon plantation. He receives as fine an education as his half-brother Tom until he is a teenager. In fact, because education is a rare commodity for blacks, Harry applies himself with more seriousness to his studies. On his deathbed Colonel Gordon does not free Harry but rather exacts from him the promise that he will see to the smooth running of the plantation, which has been willed to Nina.

Harry treasures his position, but it is a difficult one. He finds that he must use the money he has been saving to purchase his own freedom in order to keep Canema solvent. Loyalty to his half-sister keeps Harry willing to make this sacrifice, but with the reappearance of Tom Gordon, who has been away from home for several years, he begins to regret this decision. Tom enjoys ordering Harry around and makes clear his intentions of buying Harry's wife Lisette, who belongs to a Creole woman. Nina and her lover, EDWARD CLAYTON, intervene to spare Lisette the fate of becoming Tom's mistress.

Aware that his marriage vows are meaningless as long as he remains a slave, Harry nevertheless feels reluctant to leave Canema because of his promise to his father and his love for his sister. DRED VESEY, an escaped slave who makes his home in the Great Dismal Swamp, offers Harry and Lisette the opportunity to join the growing community of free blacks there, but Harry cannot leave Nina alone on the plantation with Tom.

A court case begins to change Harry's mind. Aunt Milly, a slave of Nina's who hires out her time, suffers at the hands of a temporary master. With Clayton as her attorney, Nina presses charges against the man. Thanks to Clayton's eloquence, the man is found guilty of assault, but the decision is reversed on appeal. Edward Clayton's own father, Judge Clayton, renders the decision that slaves are property, not people, and can thus be treated in any way their masters see fit. When he hears this ruling, Harry realizes the full injustice of his position. A few weeks later, after Nina dies of cholera, Harry strikes Tom Gordon, his new master, and flees to the Swamp with Lisette.

While in the Swamp, Harry communicates with Clayton by letter. He asks Clayton to learn the fate of his sister Cora, who had married her owner, been freed by him, and moved to Ohio with their two children. Taken back into slavery on her husband's death, Cora had become the property of Tom Gordon. Clayton learns that Cora killed her children rather than see them become slaves. He informs Harry of his sister's desperate act and of her willingness to follow her children and husband into death.

Although bitter, Harry still eschews violence. However, he does want a freedom more secure than what he enjoys in the Swamp. With the help of Clayton, whose antislavery sentiments are becoming more pronounced, he devises a plan for a mass escape. The plan becomes a reality after Dred dies trying to save an escaping slave. Harry and Lisette make their way to New York and eventually to Canada, where Clayton has settled with the men and women who were once his slaves and are now his neighbors.

Gordon, Lee. *Lonely Crusade.* Chester Himes. 1947.

At the outset, Lee Gordon, a black native Californian, has recently accepted a job as a union organizer. This job, his first steady employment in years, offers the promise of a new lease on life, for until now Lee has depended on his wife Ruth's employment. As he begins the new job, Lee is warned against the Communist Party, which he is told will attempt to lure him by using either a black man or a white woman to get his attention.

Despite the warning, Lee is gradually embroiled in the tensions generated by the opposing interests of the party, the union, and the management of the plant to be unionized. These difficulties are augmented by the ubiquitous face of racism, which Lee confronts on several levels. Many of the couples in the novel are interracial couples, and soon Lee himself becomes involved in an affair with Jackie Forks, a white woman who works for both the Communist Party and for Mr. Foster, the owner of the Cornstock Plant. Lee's innate fear of the consequences of sexual involvement with a white woman, as well as the fact that the affair rapidly contributes to the deterioration of his marriage, complicates his life. To make matters worse, he becomes drawn further into the web of intrigue surrounding the union's activities.

While Lee's affair with Jackie develops, there is a corresponding escalation in the union's efforts. Mr. Foster begins to offer bribes to both union and Party figures in the hopes that he can undermine the efforts of both factions. At one point Lee becomes the innocent victim of the system when he is beaten by the sheriff's deputies, who are actually Foster's agents, while his companion Luther, a black Party member, escapes the beating by confessing to taking a bribe when he had not. Lee suspects that Luther is the traitor; then he decides, after being further manipulated, that Lester McKinley, who had just quit his job with Foster, was the informer. After a confrontation with McKinley, Lee is more convinced than ever that the latter was the culprit, but he is hamstrung by his inability to report a fellow black man to white authorities. Eventually, Lee himself is suspected of bribe-taking and betrayal, and Jackie is denounced by the Party.

Meanwhile, the affair with Jackie continues, and she becomes pregnant, although Lee is not informed. Lee moves out of his home, abandoning Ruth, but he soon leaves Jackie after a quarrel. The novel's pace accelerates as Lee innocently becomes involved in the brutal murder of one of the deputies who had beaten him earlier. He is arrested, but the union provides an alibi for him on the condition that he organize the union in the six days remaining before the vote to adopt the union is held.

Despite several factors against him, Lee assiduously works for the union cause until the day of the vote when, under a new warrant for his arrest, Lee is hidden by union officials as a rally begins. The police presence is strong and hostile. When the workers begin their march, they are attacked. Lee, at great personal risk, swiftly decides to take his fate into his own hands as he leaps from the van in which he is hidden to pick up the fallen banner and lead the workers on their march.

Gordon, Nina. *Dred, a Tale of the Great Dismal Swamp.* Harriet Beecher Stowe. 1856.

In the course of this novel, the coquettish heiress Nina Gordon is transformed into a Christian. Upon the death of her father, Colonel Gordon, Nina became the sole owner of Canema, her father's plantation. The Colonel, knowing that his son Tom was a gambler, drunkard, and fornicator, entrusted the property to his childish but kind-hearted daughter. Nina's overseer and confidante is HARRY GORDON, a slave who is, unbeknownst to Nina, her half-brother. Nina's extravagant ways contribute to Canema's debt, but thanks to Harry's expert management, the plantation runs smoothly.

Nina returns to Canema after a period in a New York finishing school where she learned little more than how to dance, embroider, and flirt. Because of her coquettish ways, she must face the prospect of two of her suitors visiting Canema at the same time. Frederic Carson, a member of New York society, and EDWARD CLAYTON, the son of an old, wealthy southern family, have both accepted Nina's invitation to visit. Nina quickly realizes that she is strongly attracted to the serious and steady Clayton.

Clayton's speedy intervention in a difficult situation endears him to her. Nina's brother Tom returns to Canema after a long absence and makes sexual advances toward Harry's wife Lisette. Clayton provides Nina with the money to purchase Lisette from her present owner, thereby thwarting Tom's plans to buy the lovely young woman.

A few weeks after this initial visit, Clayton returns to Canema with his sister Anne. Nina is nervous about meeting Anne, who is even more serious than her brother. Anne proves a good influence, however, inspiring Nina to temper her enthusiasm with good judgment. Nina exercises her newfound judiciousness when she provides financial and spiritual assistance to a pair of orphaned poor white children and their faithful servant, Old Tiff.

Nina wants to deepen her religious feeling but finds it difficult to do so because it seems that the very people who call themselves Christians mistreat slaves and deny them religious instruction. Only through talking with Aunt Milly, her mammy, is Nina able to encounter true faith. Milly has suffered greatly from slavery—all her children but one have been sold away from her, and she was once brutally beaten by a man who hired her—but she is not bitter. She loves God, and she is able to forgive even the man who wounded her. Nina, with Clayton's assistance, has taken the man to court, but Milly thinks such action is too vengeful for a Christian to undertake.

Her religious spirit awakened, Nina continues to read the Bible to Old Tiff and the two children in his care. Eventually she experiences conversion and puts her trust in God's power. This new faith serves her well when cholera strikes the plantation. Nina remains calm, and her cool management of the crisis lessens the impact of the many deaths that result. As the plague wanes, Nina realizes that she has been infected. She dies, but with the faith of a Christian.

Gottenberg, Abraham. *Minds.* David Black. 1982.

Large, bearded, and forbidding, Abraham Gottenberg is the patriarch and founder of the Gottenberg Clinic for the treatment of mental disorders, which he built with his two sons on a deserted farm outside of Galilee, Nebraska, in 1909. The novel chronicles Abraham's rise to wealth and prominence, from his humble beginnings as a doctor to Galilee's poverty-ridden settlers, through his early, intuitive attempts at listening to patients with "odd" problems, to the construction of the psychiatric clinic that continues to prosper long after he has died.

Arriving in Galilee with his wife Rosa and their infant sons Jacob and Hermann, Abraham sets himself up as a doctor in three rooms at the back of a printer's shop—quarters as cramped as those he had left behind in New York City. The people in the area are poor, suspicious of strangers, and resistant to change, but he doggedly treats the few cases that come his way. One day Fritz Lorenz, a druggist who, prior to Abraham's arrival, had been making his living as a quack doctor selling patent medicines and home remedies, sends his son to fetch Abraham with the false claim that he is sick. The men gather around as Abraham approaches the shed where Lorenz is supposed to be resting; upon entering, he is attacked by a large and vicious dog. He recovers his wits in time to strangle the beast to death with his bare hands.

From this point on, Abraham's business flourishes. As he sets about treating his patients, however, he becomes increasingly interested in the psychological symptoms they display—in their idiosyncratic habits, delusions, and fan-

tasies. At night he fills ledger upon ledger with anecdotes about his visits to the patients and their families. He becomes known throughout the area as the "Talking Doctor" and wakes one day to find that "he'd become obsessed with oddness."

When Abraham's meticulous notes and late-night musings continue to present him with more questions than answers, he decides to lock his ledgers away and concentrate more fully on his routine medical practice. One night he sees Helen Blankenship, a young woman whom he has known since infancy, running naked on all fours through the neighborhood. He begins visiting her regularly in the afternoons, until her parents forbid him to return, claiming that such behavior is "not proper." Shortly afterward Helen hurls herself through a glass window and dies. Abraham sits down to write a detailed account of her story, his first case history.

Psychology soon becomes Abraham's ruling passion. He wades through stacks of journals searching for cures but remains frustrated with medical theories and explanations. Then, in the fall of 1909, he travels to Worcester, Massachusetts, to attend a series of lectures given by Sigmund Freud, and he returns to Galilee a changed man. Having forgotten in his excitement to send a wire announcing the time of his arrival, Abraham runs all the way home, wakes his sons—now young men—and drives them to an abandoned farm: the site of the new psychiatric clinic they will help him build.

Although his sons both end up following in his footsteps, Abraham sustains problematic relationships with them throughout his life. When Jacob, the elder and more imaginative of the two, comes of age, Abraham insists on giving him his watch, even though Jacob makes it clear that he has no intention of going to medical school. A few years later Jacob informs his father that he has changed his mind, whereupon Abraham, who had earlier claimed to need his help with the clinic, tells him he has "no conviction, no character." As he ages, Abraham purports to be deaf in order to ignore his younger son Hermann, who disapproves of Jacob's methods of treatment, and speaks officiously not only of his own plans for expanding the facilities but of the clinic's administrative problems. On his deathbed, before making him director of the clinic, Abraham shrewdly extracts from Hermann a promise not to interfere with his older brother's methods. He then sends for Jacob, to whom he gives his blessings. Abraham dies suddenly, with his eyes rolled up "as though he were astonished by something he'd just seen on the ceiling."

Gottlieb, Max. *Arrowsmith.* Sinclair Lewis. 1925.

Max Gottlieb, professor of bacteriology and a medical researcher, is a vicious assailant of slackness, lies, and pomposity. A gifted researcher who through his work becomes one of the great philanthropists, Gottlieb is an idealist who hates "more than the devil or starvation" men who rush into publication unprepared. In his own field he functions with absolute certainty and confidence, but he is unable to cope with the political and social demands of his profession.

Born in Saxony in 1850, Gottlieb spent his youth doing medical research in Germany, where he embarked on his lifelong quest to discover an artificial antitoxin. He fled the persecution of the Junker regime and moved with his wife and family to the United States, a country he believed could never become militaristic or anti-Semitic. Even at this early stage, Gottlieb is fated to be continually misunderstood and unappreciated in a world whose heroes are "building bridges . . . and selling miles of calico and cigars."

When the novel opens, Gottlieb is a professor of bacteriology in the medical school of the University of Winnemac, where he pursues his research with lonely devotion. Gottlieb is pessimistically philanthropic: Although determined to discover an end to great epidemics, he nevertheless speculates that if science conquers all plagues, the world will become overcrowded and a famine-driven scramble for existence will destroy all beauty, ease, and wisdom. Mocked and feared by students and faculty, Gottlieb discovers in the scholar MARTIN ARROWSMITH a similar commitment to scientific research, but he compulsively alienates his young protégé and only ally.

Still more misunderstandings plague Gottlieb's career. He is eventually forced to leave the university and sacrifice his ideals by accepting a job at a pharmaceutical company, whose commercialized and materialistic directors attempt to use his research for financial gain. Gottlieb is easily manipulated by clever, money-grabbing strategists but clings to his determined idealism. He is rescued from this environment by a job in the renowned McGurk Institute, a research center that Gottlieb feels complements his own aims and ambitions. He is joined at the institute by Martin Arrowsmith, and it is under his rigorous and high-minded tutelage that Arrowsmith finds a remedy for plague.

Gottlieb has been sidetracked from this pursuit, however. Believing that at last he can establish an institute truly devoted to science, he accepts the position of director of McGurk. He struggles to impose his ideals on the institute and battles hard against the demons of public opinion and financial considerations, both of which finally overwhelm him. As the novel ends, Gottlieb, left only with his daughter Miriam, has rejected all that America stands for and is unable to deal with the ideology of the new world he finds himself in. As he sits blank-eyed, unable even to remember the language of this new world, Gottlieb retreats further and further into the past and sinks slowly toward his death.

The Governess. *The Turn of the Screw.* Henry James. 1898.

One Christmas Eve in England, a group of holiday celebrants regale each other with tales of the supernatural. All agree that the involvement of a child in such a tale makes it all the more horrifying, adding another turn of the screw. One reveler, Douglas, promises to return in a few days with a manuscript, his own recording of a horrifying tale told by his sister's late governess, telling of her experience long ago with the supernatural while serving as governess to two small children. Douglas assures his interlocutors that the macabre tale will reveal the governess was in love, and with whom, but not in any literal way. He returns in a few days with the manuscript and thus begins the eerie tale.

At the opening of Douglas's tale, the youngest daughter of a poor country parson answers an advertisement for a governess. She meets with her prospective patron, a bachelor with cavalier charm, who informs her that he is the guardian of his nephew and niece, Miles and Flora, and that he has installed them at Bly, his country estate. The sole condition of her employment is that she never trouble him. The new governess takes special pride in knowing that she can fulfill her employer's deepest wish.

Arriving at Bly, the Governess is instantly captivated by the angelic eight-year-old Flora and shortly thereafter by the charming ten-year-old Miles, who has been expelled from boarding school for mysterious reasons. The Governess ponders how to continue Miles's studies, then concludes it is she who is being educated; in the company of these two children, she is learning for the first time how to be amused and amusing.

One afternoon while the children are napping, the Governess strolls about the grounds and fantasizes about encountering a handsome man. Glancing up at a crenelated tower of Bly, she suddenly sees a strange man boldly staring at her. The Governess later describes this stranger to the housekeeper, the prosaic Mrs. Grose, who identifies him as Peter Quint, former valet to the master. However, declares Mrs. Grose, Peter Quint died shortly after leaving the master's employ. The Governess concludes that this horrible apparition is after the children, and she resolves to shield them.

Soon thereafter the Governess is playing with Flora by the lake when she spies a ghastly woman in black amid the foliage on the opposite shore. After the Governess's description, Mrs. Grose identifies this woman as Miss Jessel, a former governess, who is now also dead. Mrs. Grose implies that Miss Jessel had once been a lady but that Quint had done with her; indeed, he had done with them all whatever he wished. The Governess despairs of successfully protecting the children from these two sinister apparitions, but she nevertheless vows to try.

The Governess encounters the evil Quint and the ghastly Miss Jessel on several more occasions. Mrs. Grose always believes the Governess's horrifying accounts, but she has never actually seen these apparitions herself, and neither have Miles and Flora, apparently. In her growing anxiety, the Governess begins to suspect that the children's innocence is feigned, that they are in secret collusion with the two sinister ghosts, and she interprets what may simply be childish antics as evidence of this collusion. Frantic, the Governess finally decides to go against her employer's wishes by writing to him, but she never receives a reply.

Although it is never clear if she is actually haunted or suffering from hysterical delusions, the Governess is now crazed with fear. Ranting, she accuses little Flora of conspiring with Miss Jessel and terrifies the child into illness. She then takes her last stand against Quint. Crushing Miles to her chest, she screams her reprobation at Quint, thus exorcising him, only to discover that Miles, terrified, has died in her arms.

Gramby, Lillian. *Country Place.* Ann Petry. 1947.
Lillian Gramby, the wife of the wealthiest man in Lennox, Connecticut, is the ambitious and conniving mother of GLORIA "GLORY" ROANE. Although she has scored a coup by marrying Mearns Gramby against the wishes of his elderly mother, Lillian remains unhappy. A virtual prisoner in her mansion and despised by her household staff, Lillian detests Mearns's mother, the grande dame of the town. Lillian actually begins plotting the murder of the old woman when she realizes that her mother-in-law will likely live ten years. Lillian's rotten moods are exacerbated when her daughter, who has lost interest in her husband, comes to her for advice. Lillian swiftly and rudely rejects her daughter's overtures and concentrates instead on her own misery.

Because her marriage, which she thought would bring her ease and social significance, turns out poorly, Lillian has a brief affair with Ed Barrell. Unfortunately for her, this affair comes to light, and Mrs. Gramby, although she doesn't wish to hurt her son, informs him of his wife's infidelity. He leaves the mansion for a few days in order to determine his course of action. While Lillian knows there is no love between her and Mrs. Gramby, she seeks the older woman's company to ease her fears on the night of a vicious storm. In the hours she spends with Mearns's mother, she becomes increasingly agitated by the woman's very existence. Lillian covets the necklace and ring that the older woman wears in a ritualistic salute to her long-dead husband, and she also senses a new level of hostility in the house. She resolves to kill the old woman, who is diabetic, by removing her insulin kit and substituting a box of chocolates, which she knows will prove irresistible.

On the servants' day off, Lillian takes the insulin and syringe, hoping that the old woman will poison herself and die. Mrs. Gramby does devour a lot of the candy, and when she realizes that she is getting sick, she seeks her insulin only to find it gone. But a servant arrives and alerts the doctor, who manages to save her life, although she remains ill for some time. The authorities easily discover Lillian's role in this "accident."

After Mrs. Gramby recovers sufficiently, she travels downtown and changes her will to ensure that there will be no inheritance for Lillian. On her way out of the courthouse with Ed Barrell, who is helping her walk, Mrs. Gramby stumbles and falls down the steps, taking him with her. They both die there on the steps.

At the reading of the will, Lillian learns that Mrs. Gramby has bequeathed money and property to her servants but nothing to her daughter-in-law. When Lillian turns on her husband in anger, Mearns quietly reveals that he assisted in his mother's revision of her will. At this Lillian erupts in an hysterical outburst, claiming that she will take the issue to court and break the will on the basis of the old woman's senility and disease. It is an idle threat, however, since all present know of her role in precipitating Mrs. Gramby's death; Lillian only reveals herself to be a shameless schemer. She has no hope of restoring her name in the town, which has already begun to redefine itself in the absence of Mrs. Gramby, that pillar of society.

Grandissime, Honoré f.m.c. *The Grandissimes.* George Washington Cable. 1879.
This novel recounts the history of a powerful New Orleans Creole family, focusing on the careers of two half-brothers who share the name Honoré Grandissime. The eldest of the two Honorés, who is often identified by the initials f.m.c.—free man of color—is an outcast in his family due to his racial status; a quadroon, he is considered an insult to the Grandissimes' ethnic integrity, which in 1804 is a delicate issue in the Creole community. Although his younger brother HONORÉ (GRANDISSIME), who is the patriarch of the family, eventually overcomes his prejudice and invites his half-brother to become his partner in the mercantile house that manages the family's plantation-generated wealth, Honoré f.m.c. never gains the social and familial esteem to which he is entitled.

As children, the two Honorés live as equals in Paris, where they are sent to be educated in old-world fashion. Upon the death of their father, the younger Honoré inherits the vast landholdings of the Grandissime empire. Honoré f.m.c., although not ignored in the will, inherits money, which does not carry with it the prestige of land ownership. The elder Honoré invests his capital in real estate and becomes a very wealthy rentier. This wealth does not make him an upstanding or well-respected citizen, however. The social equality with his younger brother that he had enjoyed as a youth in Europe evaporates in New Orleans where racial strife is endemic.

All of Honoré f.m.c.'s aspirations are thwarted by the racism of Creole society. His true love—the beautiful Palmyre la Philosophe, who is a voudou and, like the elder Honoré, a free quadroon—refuses to return his affections because she is obsessed with the highly unlikely prospect of marrying the more prestigious Honoré. Becoming increasingly lovesick, Honoré f.m.c. is restrained by his half-brother from committing suicide by throwing himself into the Mississippi flood waters. The younger Honoré's conscience is finally piqued by his family's ill-treatment of his brother. When he offers him a partnership in his mercantile house and changes its name to the Grandissime Brothers, their uncle, the fanatically racist Agricola Fusilier, proposes to form a family contingency whose goal is to lynch the elder Honoré. Agricola's plan is thwarted when Honoré f.m.c. stabs and kills him for insulting and striking him.

Honoré f.m.c. walks unmolested away from the scene of the stabbing. Accompanied by Palmyre la Philosophe, who also had designs on Agricola's life, he boards a brig bound for the Bordeaux region of France, thereby escaping his family's wrath. Although Palmyre is now convinced that the younger Honoré will never marry her, she resolutely continues to rebuff Honoré f.m.c.'s love proposals. Having stipulated in his will that Palmyre should receive $50,000 annually from the proceeds of his rented properties, Honoré Grandissime, f.m.c., commits suicide by drowning in the Atlantic Ocean. His motive is ostensibly the agony of unrequited love, but the tragedy of his social and familial ostracization lurks as a concomitant cause of his death.

Grandissime, Honoré. *The Grandissimes.* George Washington Cable. 1879.

Honoré Grandissime is the elegant young patriarch of his New Orleans Creole family. Although his family places their financial interests in Honoré's hands, they are horrified by his progressive opinions concerning the civil rights of blacks and are resistant to his involvement with the new Yankee governor who assumes control of Louisiana in 1803—the year Napoleon cedes that region to the United States. Although Honoré is a model Creole gentleman—handsome, refined, respected, and wealthy—he is haunted by the thought that his privilege is founded in part on his culture's racist transgressions.

Anticipating the vast political and economic changes that occur when the United States assumes control of Louisiana, Honoré mortifies his family by becoming a merchant rather than holding public office as his forebears had. In addition to his business interests, Honoré manages the extensive real estate interests of the Grandissimes, which are now threatened by Congress's reluctance to honor the plantation titles that had been authorized by the previous governments of France and Spain. Honoré avoids financial disaster by selling some of the plantation titles despite his fear that, if validated by Congress, his relatives will denounce him for depriving them of their prestige as landowners.

Honoré further scandalizes his family when he invites his elder quadroon brother HONORÉ (GRANDISSIME F.M.C. ["free man of color"]), the son of his father's mistress, to join him as a partner in his mercantile house and offers

to change the name of the business to the Grandissime Brothers. Although this public recognition of kinship with his elder brother is honorably motivated, it also serves a practical purpose: Honoré f.m.c. is a wealthy rentier whose capital can save the mercantile house regardless of the fate of the land titles. Honoré's attempt to legitimize his elder brother is foiled when Honoré f.m.c. commits suicide due to the unrequited love he bears for the octoroon voudou Palmyre la Philosophe, who is herself in love with the younger Honoré.

Various members of Honoré's family are also initially displeased when he falls in love with Aurora Nancanou, a member of the De Grapion family, the great rival clan of the Grandissimes. Aurora and her daughter Clotilde, destitute throughout the majority of the novel, regain their fortune when the younger Honoré restores their wealth; he does so because he can no longer ignore the likelihood that his uncle Agricola Fusilier, who killed Aurora's husband in a duel, had obtained the lucrative plantation dishonorably.

Honoré's conscience is activated in part by what he describes as the fruits of the tree of "our dead father's mistakes." Once again, however, the beneficent act of conscience appears to serve a selfish purpose, namely, to advance Honoré's love interest. Although his grandfather had killed Aurora's in a duel, his father Numa Grandissime had made Agricola promise, against his will, that he would foster the match between Aurora and Honoré. The novel ends with Honoré's proposal of marriage to Aurora who, although she persists in refusing, lets him hold her in his arms.

The Grandmother. "A Good Man Is Hard to Find." Flannery O'Connor. 1955.

As the story opens, the grandmother and her family, which consists of her son Bailey, his wife, and their three children, are embarking on a trip to Florida. Knowing how Bailey would protest, she hides from him the basket containing her cat, whom she fears could not get along without her for three days.

The grandmother sits in the backseat between the two older children and talks incessantly during the trip. She chatters on about the changing times, the current paucity of moral values, and an escaped criminal called The Misfit, who is said to be roaming Florida.

As they travel on, the old woman recalls a plantation she is sure is in the vicinity that she visited as a young lady. When she invents a legend about the house, the children become excited. They goad their father into taking the dirt road their grandmother says leads to the old plantation.

On the road, which looks as if it has not been traveled in months, there is no sign of the house. After some time the grandmother has the embarrassing thought that the house she is thinking of might be in a different state. The thought startles her so that she upsets her cat's basket. The cat jumps onto the back of Bailey's neck, causing him to lose control of the car.

When the car comes to rest after rolling into a gulch, no one is seriously hurt, but the grandmother says she has been injured so that she might delay Bailey's wrath. Within a few minutes a car arrives and three men get out, one of them holding a gun. The grandmother recognizes the leader of the three as The Misfit and says so loudly, much to her son's consternation.

Because he has been recognized, The Misfit has his men take the rest of the family aside. Shots ring out in the forest. All the while the grandmother continues babbling to the convict, insisting that she knows he is "a good man . . . from nice people," one who wouldn't shoot a lady. The Misfit responds to the grandmother with a quiet, steady voice, telling her that he doesn't remember ever being bad, although he knows he has done something terribly wrong. Desperate, the grandmother tells the convict to pray, for Jesus will help him; the convict agrees that Jesus might help him but says that praying is unnecessary because he needs no help.

As they talk, the grandmother becomes more and more frightened. Dizzy with terror, she reaches out for the man. As she does, he shoots her through the chest. When his cohorts return, The Misfit tells them she might have been a good woman if somebody had been there "to shoot her every minute of her life."

Grant, Phebe. *Comedy: American Style.* Jessie Redmon Fauset. 1933.

Fragile and feminine Phebe Grant draws on a hidden reserve of courage when she faces the problematic issue of her racial heritage. Phebe, who has gold hair, blue eyes, and fair skin, chooses to identify herself as an African American because her mother was African American. A deeply-rooted sense of allegiance to her people and her family sustains Phebe through crises until she is eventually able to establish a secure home.

Phebe's early childhood is spent in extreme poverty until her mother finds steady work as a seamstress. As a child, she boldly and openly identifies herself as African American in a not-always-accepting world. She wears a locket containing a picture of her dark-skinned mother, and her closest friend, Marise Davies, is a charming dark-brown girl.

Nicholas Campbell, one of Phebe's childhood playmates, becomes her boyfriend and remains faithful to her through adolescence. He is a handsome, romantic young man who studies medicine, and Phebe is determined to marry him. While she is waiting, Phebe works in an elegant dress shop to help her mother pay off the house. While Phebe's career is proceeding well, Nicholas begins to have trouble in school. A professor objects to his seeing a "white girl" and is about to fail him for it. Because he is confused about his love for Phebe anyway, Nicholas uses the incident as an excuse to end their relationship.

For several months Phebe isolates herself as she tries to recover from the shock of the sudden separation. When she finally starts to go out again, she spends much of her time with a wealthy white aristocrat, Llewellyn Nash, who once visited the dress shop with his cousin. Because of the obvious class difference, Phebe assumes he will never take her seriously and is speechless when he asks her to marry him. She immediately explains that she is "colored"; Nash agrees that a marriage, in that case, would be unthinkable. When Nash disappears without a trace, Phebe is proud of feeling unhurt. She begins to date the brother of an old friend, the young doctor Christopher Cary.

Although she is not in love with Christopher as she was with Nicholas, Phebe approves of his vision of married life and accepts his proposal. Shortly before the marriage, Christopher comes to Phebe in desperation, explaining that the Carys, like so many families during the Great Depression, have lost their entire fortune. Phebe generously suggests that the Carys move into her home, and her married life commences under these uncomfortable, cramped conditions. Christopher's father is sick and depressed, and his mother is spoiled and refuses to live peacefully with Phebe's mother. Phebe is overworked, and her patience gradually drains away. When she receives a passionate letter from Nicholas, who is now married, Phebe rushes to New York to see him and withholds the true reason for her trip from her family.

Moments before she and Nicholas are to meet secretly at a hotel, Phebe recounts the experiences that led to this moment. A vivid image of her husband's tired, shabby figure haunts her. Thinking of his loyalty to her and of Nicholas's deceptions, she suddenly becomes disgusted with what she is about to do and rushes away from the hotel. When she returns home, her husband and family greet her warmly and explain that, after an argument with Christopher, her troublesome mother-in-law has left. The household is transformed: Christopher's father begins to get well, and everyone's hope for his medical practice revives. Phebe has chosen the more difficult path for herself, but her integrity has brought her closer to establishing the strong, fulfilling family life she desires.

The Gray Champion. "The Gray Champion." Nathaniel Hawthorne. 1835.

The Gray Champion is a venerable patriarch who stands in defense of the American people against British tyranny. He appears in the streets of Boston one afternoon in April 1689. The governor of the colony, Sir Edmund Andros, has amassed his councillors and the Governor's Guard and begun a march through the city; the townspeople have assembled in King-street and are preparing themselves for a possibly violent confrontation with the troops of the Crown. As the soldiers draw near, an ancient man steps into the middle of the street between the two factions.

The old man has a long gray beard and wears the dress that was the fashion among Puritans at least fifty years before. He carries a heavy sword and walks at first with the help of a staff. The man proceeds down the street toward the troops, turning at one point to the crowd of colonials with a gesture of both encouragement and warning. He walks with such dignity and authority that the townspeople excitedly speculate on his identity and wonder why they do not recognize him. As he draws closer to the soldiers, he appears to gain strength and begins to march with the step of a younger man.

When he is twenty yards from the governor's troops, the Gray Champion pauses, holds his staff in front of him, and orders the soldiers to stand. The old man's commanding presence causes the Guard to stop short; the governor and his councillors ride forward to discover the reason for the halt and, still mounted on their horses, surround the gray-bearded figure. He stands thoroughly unintimidated and unmoved as the governor's men alternately threaten and laughingly insult him. Sir Edmund Andros then asks him if he is mad, to interfere with the progress of King James's governor. The old man calmly answers that in the past he has stayed the march of a king himself and explains that he has appeared once again on earth in response to the cry of an oppressed people. He then announces that James, unbeknownst to the colonials, has been deposed and that by the next day the governor himself will be in prison.

The townspeople, thrilled by the words of their champion, confront the soldiers without fear. Andros, cowed either by the mien of the venerable old man or by the attitude of the crowd, orders a retreat. The Gray Champion disappears in the excitement that follows this victory of the colonials over their oppressors, and a few individuals claim to have seen his spectral figure fade before their eyes. The men of that generation watch for his reappearance in vain, but it is rumored that he walks again in King-street eighty years later.

Grebe, George. "Looking for Mr. Green." Saul Bellow. 1951.

Rescued from unemployment and abject poverty by a job provided by the city of Chicago during the Great Depression, George Grebe is charged with the responsibility of delivering relief checks to needy recipients who are too infirm to pick them up. Grebe braves the extremely cold weather, searching through a black neighborhood in the city where people hesitate to provide him with information concerning the whereabouts of various individuals, both because they are wary of strangers generally and specifically suspicious of Caucasians. Despite the difficulty of his job, Grebe is determined to successfully locate the relief recipients, and he even works overtime in his attempt to find a particularly elusive crippled man named Tulliver Green.

Having been summoned by city officials to report to work at the relief office, George Grebe checks in with a young man named Mr. Raynor who questions him about his former employment, which includes selling shoes and window shades and teaching classical languages at St. Olaf's College. After Raynor warns Grebe that he must be stubborn and persistent in his effort to locate his assigned relief recipients, the latter takes to the streets and begins his search for Tulliver Green. Following Raynor's recommendation, Grebe tries to locate Green by questioning shopkeepers in the neighborhood, the janitor of the building in which Green is thought to live, and other residents, but everyone proves unwilling or unable to provide him with information. After a conscientious effort to locate Green, Grebe decides that he can spend no more time trying to find the cripple and moves on to the next check.

After listening to a tirade delivered by Winston Field, the next recipient, concerning the unfortunate plight of black people, Grebe gives the lonely and talkative old man his check and once again walks the streets of the depressingly rundown neighborhood. Although it is six o'clock and he is technically finished for the day and free to go home, he is obsessed with the desire to locate Tulliver Green and decides to resume his efforts on his own time. As he passes the deserted schools, dirty vacant lots, and condemned apartment houses, he ruminates on the tragedy of poverty and wonders how people can tolerate such squalid lives. Returning to the building in which Green supposedly lives, he is told by a man on the second floor that it is possible Green lives downstairs. When he descends, Grebe finds only an exit into a yard where there is a ramshackle bungalow with a mailbox bearing the name "Green." Triumphant, Grebe rings the doorbell and is eventually greeted by a naked, drunken woman who begins to abuse him verbally. When she demands that he give her the check, he temporarily demurs but eventually gives in because he is afraid to enter the house. Despite his ultimate failure to actually locate Tulliver Green, George Grebe experiences an odd elation as he contemplates the mere possibility that his search could be successful.

Green, Dexter. "Winter Dreams." F. Scott Fitzgerald. 1926.

Dexter Green begins working at age fourteen as a golf caddie. He is a daydreaming boy, imagining himself playing golf with the wealthy T. A. Hedrick and living as a rich man. One day the eleven-year-old Judy Jones appears on the green. Dexter immediately senses that a romance with her would be a contest of wills, and he quits his job to avoid being her caddie.

Years later, grown wealthy from his own laundry business, Dexter fulfills his childhood vision and plays golf with T. A. Hedrick, but the dull reality falls far short of the dream. Suddenly Mr. Hedrick is struck by a golf ball hit by Judy. She comes over, unrepentant, spontaneous, and beautiful, and is immediately the center of attention. Dexter's old vision of golf with Mr. Hedrick is supplanted by the diaphanous vision of Judy, who becomes the central driving force in his life.

Dexter and Judy begin to date, but the romance is difficult at best. Judy is unprincipled, capricious, and involved with a whole string of interested men. Dexter finally leaves her. He develops a romance with the solid and considerate Irene and gradually begins to forget Judy. But once he and Irene are engaged, Judy, on little more than a whim, successfully pulls him away from his fiancée. Having destroyed the engagement, she then drops Dexter.

A number of years pass. Dexter, a successful Wall Street businessman, often reflects on his affair with Judy. He holds no bitterness; in fact, he barely recalls Judy's betrayals, although her beauty is always on his mind. He gives no thought to the hurt he inflicted on Irene.

He then meets Devlin, a man from his hometown who knows of Judy's current marriage. Devlin talks about her in a casual way that shows he doesn't share Dexter's vision of her. According to Devlin, Judy's beauty has faded; she has become a doting mother whose husband drinks and is unfaithful to her.

After Devlin leaves, Dexter lies down on his office sofa and looks out at the sun setting on the New York City skyline. He thought he had nothing else to lose, but now he realizes he has just lost something more: his dreams. He remembers scattered images of Judy that had touched his senses, and for the first time in many years tears stream down his face—not for her, but for himself. Realizing he can never revisit the "country of youth . . . where his dreams had flourished," Dexter knows that something in him has disappeared forever.

Green, Philip. *Gentleman's Agreement.* Laura Z. Hobson. 1947.

Philip Green is a reporter looking for the story of his career. He moves to New York from California with his mother and his young son in order to work for *Smith's Weekly Magazine.* The editor, John Minify, made him an irresistible offer: a five-article series with an audience of three million readers. Philip jumped at the offer, and after procuring the sublease of an apartment from an editor assigned overseas, he moved his little family to the East Coast.

The series that Philip is assigned to cover is about anti-Semitism. He is faced with the question of how to make it interesting and eye-catching, different from all the other statistical breakdowns and composite sketches that have graced the pages of the other New York papers.

Shortly after his arrival, Philip is invited to John Min-

ify's luxury apartment for cocktails and a chance to meet Minify's family. He is initially put off by the wealth of his surroundings and the association with the upper classes. Philip, a hard-nosed reporter unaccustomed to penthouse suites, feels uncomfortable. He is introduced to Minify's wife Jessie and his niece Kathy Lacey, whom he automatically perceives as part of the establishment and cannot resist passing judgment on her remote, cultivated ways. Despite his disapproval, he finds himself drawn to her and her beauty.

The evening leads to dinner at a restaurant, drinks, and probing conversation. Philip feels lonely; his wife Betty died seven years earlier, leaving him alone with his one-year-old son. He filled the gap in his life through his devotion to his work, making himself into the best, most conscientious reporter he knew how to be. Through his drive and perseverance, he landed this assignment and a chance at a new life.

Philip is determined to make his articles fresh and exciting, and to show Kathy "what reporting is all about." He thinks about the stories he was most proud of. All of his successes turned on his becoming an integral part of a community, a "miner or an Okie," living their experience and telling the story, rather than reporting as an objective observer. The idea suddenly occurs to him, in the midst of this pondering, that in order to really explore anti-Semitism he must experience it firsthand. Hence, he must become a Jew.

The story unfolds as Philip enters the world with this new Jewish identity. He soon finds people responding differently toward him. Aware of his presence when they refer to a Jewish stereotype, they are embarrassed by their racist remarks. He becomes hyper-aware of every comment and whispered slur. Newly politicized, he forces individuals and establishments to answer to their own rhetoric and racism. The most explosive incident occurs when Philip makes reservations at an exclusive lodge. He asks the manager if they have a policy of accepting all religious faiths. The management gets nervous and tells him they have no more vacancies. Philip then goes to the lodge and once again he is given a room, only to have it canceled when he asks about the issue of faiths. Philip attacks the manager and leaves in a rage.

All of Philip's relationships bear the burden of his new politicization and identity. His relationship with Kathy, in particular, becomes strained and filled with tension unforeseen by either of them. Kathy is forced to come to terms with her own identity when she must accept the notion that she is engaged to a "Jewish" man. When she refuses to become actively vocal about injustice, despite her internal opinions, and Philip feels betrayed by her desire for a "comfortable" life, the two decide to part ways. Once the article is published, however, and Philip returns to the world of the gentile, both come to accept their judgments of each other. Kathy realizes that she doesn't "speak her mind," and Philip comes to accept the fact that he is too demanding. Ultimately, the two are reunited.

Greener, Faye. *The Day of the Locust.* Nathanael West. 1939.

Faye Greener is a seventeen-year-old would-be actress who claims that she will commit suicide if she does not become a star in the film industry. Faye's ambitions are so exaggerated that she refuses to date men who are not rich or who cannot advance her career, unless they are "criminally handsome." She leaves a trail of suitors in her wake as she selfishly pursues her aspirations, taking advantage of each one's generosity for as long as it serves her purposes. It is Faye's good fortune that she is never held accountable for her mercenary behavior. Rather, like a cork on a rough sea, she floats blithely through waters that would sink even the strongest ships.

At the beginning of the novel, Faye lives with her father, a veteran of the vaudeville and burlesque circuit, in an apartment building called the San Bernardino Arms. There she meets TOD HACKETT, the protagonist of the novel, who is an artist. In his masterpiece-in-progress, "The Burning of Los Angeles," Tod includes a representation of Faye that accurately portrays her unthinking free spirit: She is naked and grinning enigmatically as she flees from a mob that is in the process of torching the city. Although Tod immediately falls in love with Faye, he is rebuffed because he does not measure up to her romantic and economic expectations. She does, however, accept his assistance in nursing her ailing father Harry Greener. When her father dies, Faye embarks on a short career as a prostitute in order to pay for the funeral expenses, despite the fact that Tod volunteers to foot the bill. Faye does manage to land bit parts in various films; for example, she plays the role of a dancing girl in a film that depicts an American drummer's escapades in a rich Damascus merchant's seraglio. In this film she delivers a single line with little dramatic success.

For most of the novel Faye supports herself by sponging off an admirer, HOMER SIMPSON, whom she rewards with callous verbal abuse. A maladjusted, nervous midwesterner who migrates to California for his health, Homer enters into what he and Faye call a business agreement. He provides room, board, and clothes for her in exchange for her promise that when she becomes a star, she will pay him back for his hospitality. Their relationship is strictly platonic, and while living with Homer she maintains a sexual liaison with Earle Shoop, a tall, handsome cowboy from Arizona who makes a meager living working horse operas. Faye eventually convinces Homer to let Earle and his Mexican friend Miguel live in the garage. Her cruel treatment of Homer culminates in an incident that causes him literally to lose his sanity. Homer walks in on Faye and Miguel while they are having sexual intercourse

in his home. The next morning Faye packs her belongings and moves out of Homer's house, presumably to find another male victim upon whom she can heartlessly exercise her wiles.

Greenwood, Esther. *The Bell Jar.* Sylvia Plath. 1963.

Esther Greenwood is a sensitive and intelligent young woman growing up in the oppressive milieu of 1950s America. She wants to see the world, to write poetry, and to be an accomplished and independent person but feels great pressure to marry and become a mother and housewife. The conflict between her desire for self-fulfillment and the demands of the conventional world eventually drive her insane. She becomes increasingly depressed and incapable of dealing with people, and gradually descends into a suicidal mood. Esther feels as though she is trapped beneath a bell jar where the thick glass separates her from the clean air of normalcy, and she can only breathe the odors of her own despair.

At the opening of the novel, Esther, a college student, receives an award from *Ladies' Day*, a fashion magazine, for her high grades and writing ability. The magazine brings Esther and ten other young women to New York for a month, where they are showered with cosmetics and treated to accommodations and fine meals. In New York, Esther first realizes that her efforts to prove herself may be futile. The falsehood of the fashion world disturbs her, and while the other young women enjoy flings with the men of the city, Esther languishes in bed, unable to convince herself that she should get out.

Conformity beckons from home in Boston in the form of Buddy Willard, a young medical student whom Esther has known and admired from afar for years. Buddy has recently become enamored of Esther, but as Buddy's passions rise, Esther's decline. She sees in him the hypocrisy of the average man and the average way of life, and hates him for it. While Buddy yearns for a future of marriage and children, Esther can only see him as a means of losing her virginity, which she sees as a millstone around her neck. She feels pressure from both her mother and Buddy's parents to marry, but she doesn't want to give up her artistic goals.

Esther returns from New York to find that she has been rejected by a writing teacher with whom she had intended to study. Devastated, she spends the summer with her mother and gradually loses interest in everyday life. Esther stops washing, sleeping, and dressing in anything but pajamas. Worst of all, she finds that she can no longer read or write, and soon she becomes swept up in a search for a painless means of suicide. Her mother is sympathetic but inept, and because her father died when she was nine, Esther has no one else to help her. Esther swallows fifty sleeping pills, but she is discovered, rescued, and then placed in a state institution. Her doctor, unsympathetic to her plight, attempts to cure her with shock therapy, which only traumatizes her more.

Finally, when all seems lost, Esther begins treatment with a caring woman named Dr. Nolan. She still receives shock therapy but in a more benign form, and the new doctor has a wisdom upon which she can usefully draw. Esther also reunites with an old friend named Joan who has also been admitted, and they both benefit from this companionship. At the novel's end Esther awaits an interview with the hospital administrators who will assess her readiness to leave the hospital and return to college. Esther is hopeful at this moment that she has escaped the confines of her bell jar but wonders if it will ever return to seal her back into emotional despair.

Grendel. *Grendel.* John Gardner. 1971.

Grendel, the narrator, is the nihilistic monster who terrorizes Hrothgar's kingdom in this revision of the Beowulf legend. Grendel lives with his mother in a cave; his mother seems to have forgotten how to speak. She is the only creature who loves him, but she can never answer his questions. As a child, Grendel plays alone, explores his environment, and eventually finds his way outside of the cave.

One day while climbing a tree, Grendel catches his foot in a crack and wounds himself. Unable to climb down, he cries for his mother, but she doesn't come. A nearby bull spies Grendel and charges but is not able to knock him out of the tree to gore him. In dire pain, Grendel suddenly realizes that the world is nothing but a meaningless, brutal place. The bull eventually leaves and Grendel falls asleep, only to be awakened by a group of men. Frightened that they can't figure out what he is, the men shoot arrows at him. Just when he thinks he will die, his mother appears, charges down from the cliff, and saves him.

Curious about humans after his run-in with them, Grendel begins to spy on the people and their activities. He watches Hrothgar, their king, grow very powerful through bloody wars, truces, and tributes. Grendel is amazed when a bard, the Shaper, arrives at Hrothgar's court. He knows that the Shaper's stories about Hrothgar's exploits are untrue, but he is enthralled by the beauty of the Shaper's songs. At the same time, Grendel begins to feel evil and be ashamed of himself for his habit of eating stray humans.

Shortly thereafter, Grendel meets a dragon sitting on a huge hoard of treasure. The dragon's knowledge of everything, even Grendel's thoughts, terrifies and fascinates him. The dragon assures Grendel that the Shaper knows nothing about true, total reality. Urging Grendel to continue his bloody forages into the human settlements, the dragon casts a spell so that no weapon can cut him.

Grendel's new invulnerability only makes him feel more alone. He begins raiding Hrothgar's halls regularly, for he enjoys the violence and bloodshed and dislikes Hrothgar. When a would-be hero, Unferth, tracks him to his lair, Grendel is amused. He teases and torments Unferth, and rather than killing him, allows him to live on with the knowledge of his impotence.

Grendel continues his vigil over Hrothgar and his house. Then the king marries a young woman named Wealtheow whose innocent beauty makes Grendel feel more and more ashamed of himself. Jealous and lonely, Grendel invades the meadhall and bursts into Wealtheow's bedroom, planning to kill her. When none of the other humans makes a move to protect her, however, he decides that it would be meaningless to murder Wealtheow; he releases her, and leaves.

A group of strangers arrives one day from another land. They have heard about Grendel and have come to fight him themselves. Excited and a little afraid, Grendel prepares himself to face this new challenge. He bursts again into the meadhall, intending to devour both the foreigners and Hrothgar's people. But just as Grendel begins another bloodbath, the leader of the strangers seizes his arm with a steely grip. The stranger breaks the spell of Grendel's invulnerability with a bizarre incantation and rips off the monster's arm. Although Grendel manages to escape, in his terror and confusion he falls over a cliff to his death.

Grey, Aline Aldridge. *Dark Laughter.* Sherwood Anderson. 1925.

Aline Aldridge spends a privileged childhood and adolescence in Chicago, and in her early twenties is already engaged to be married. Her fiancé, Teddy Copeland, leaves to fight in World War I and dies of a virus in a European army camp. After the war is over, Aline's father hires a fashionable painter, Joe Walker, to do a portrait of her dead brother. Aline becomes friendly with Joe and his wife Esther, and they persuade her to spend a year in Paris with them studying art.

Joe and Esther are members of a circle of intellectuals and artists living in Paris. Aline is taken to elegant parties and learns to emulate Esther, who plays the part of the charming American woman abroad. One night at the apartment of a successful journalist, Rose Frank, Aline has two significant encounters. First, she notices a dark, quiet man, apparently Rose's lover, who fascinates her. She never speaks to him, however, and leaves instead with a former soldier, FRED GREY. After drinking several brandies, Fred and Aline take an all-night ride in a carriage. They feel a strange, feverish attraction to each other, and by the end of the night, Fred has asked Aline to marry him. The pressure from Rose, Esther, and other members of their circle makes Aline feel that she cannot refuse. Aline and Fred are married in Paris.

After another month in Paris, Aline moves to Old Harbor, Indiana, where Fred has recently inherited a wheel factory from his father. Aline is obviously bored and rest-less in Old Harbor, and Fred, hoping to keep her satisfied, indulges her whims. She wants children but is unable to conceive, and attributes this problem to the vast emotional distance between herself and Fred. Their estrangement increases when Fred becomes more involved in the man-agement of the factory. Aline has absolutely no interest in anything that concerns her husband.

One day when Aline is picking Fred up after work, she notices a worker emerging from the factory. He bears a remarkable resemblance to the quiet man she had seen in Rose Frank's apartment. A silent exchange occurs between them, and Aline becomes determined to speak to him. She places an ad for a gardener, and as she suspected, the man applies for the job. BRUCE DUDLEY begins working for the Greys and living in their spare room. Aline and Bruce spend hours together in the garden, discussing the plants and admiring each other. When Fred is away one after-noon, they make love, and Aline feels transformed by the experience.

Bruce disappears for several months after this incident, and although she remains obsessed with her lover, Aline is able to act affectionately toward Fred. When she an-nounces her pregnancy to Fred, however, her reticence arouses his suspicion. Bruce eventually returns, and Aline weeps with relief and joy. She decides without hesita-tion to leave with him, although as she walks away from the house, she thinks somewhat regretfully of Fred sitting alone.

Grey, Fred. *Dark Laughter.* Sherwood Anderson. 1925.

Deeply disturbed by his experiences in World War I, Fred is content to immerse himself in the task of run-ning his wheel factory in the small town of Old Harbor, Indiana.

Fred's father and grandfather were also businessmen in Old Harbor, and Fred's life is relatively sheltered until he is drafted. During the war Fred is shocked by the de-meaning deaths he sees, and once becomes so hysterical that he shoots a man without ever knowing whose side he is on. After the armistice, Fred remains in Paris for a year studying art and hobnobbing with sophisticated art-ists and writers.

One night Fred finds himself at a party in the apartment of Rose Frank, a successful American journalist. He leaves the party with a young woman named ALINE ALDRIDGE (GREY). Fred drinks several brandies to extinguish memo-ries of the war, and he and Alice spend the night riding through Paris in a carriage. By morning Fred has asked her to marry him, hoping to forget Europe forever by marrying an American girl and bringing her back to In-diana. Immediately after they are married in Paris, Fred returns to Indiana to see his dying father.

Fred inherits the wheel factory and is able to give Aline

a luxurious life. They find, however, that the intimacy they felt on the night in Paris was illusory. Aline becomes colder and more distant as Fred becomes increasingly involved in the managing of the factory. During dinner Aline re-mains silent while Fred chatters nervously about matters she considers banal. Every night before they retire they pause a moment and Fred asks timidly, "Shall I come to you tonight?" Aline usually refuses.

Tension between them increases when Aline hires hand-some, young BRUCE DUDLEY to work in their garden. Although there is no actual evidence that they are having an affair, Fred must restrain himself from questioning her or asking her to dismiss Bruce. One spring day Fred is to march in a veterans' parade, and Aline refuses to go. When he returns from the celebration, Aline is strangely affec-tionate. They make love more passionately than they ever have, and from this time on, Aline seems happier and more responsive to Fred. She eventually announces that she is pregnant.

Fred wonders vaguely about the fact that the gardener disappeared the day Aline underwent this change. His suspicions are heightened by the reserved way in which she tells him of her pregnancy. Aline and Bruce finally confront Fred: The baby is not Fred's, and the lovers are prepared to leave. Fred allows them to depart by a path through the woods, but after a few minutes chases them with a revolver, intending to kill Bruce. They have man-aged to move quickly, however, and Fred is unable to find them. He sits by a river and weeps, then returns home, half-expecting Aline to appear and apologize. Alone, he practices saying the excuse he will use when he is forced to explain to his business associates: "She has gone to Chicago."

Grierson, Emily. "A Rose for Emily." William Faulkner. 1930.

Emily Grierson is an elusive, eccentric member of a once rich and influential family. Living alone in a decaying old house in a seedy section of a small southern town, Emily is never seen in public and relies on an old black manservant named Tobe, the only human being who inter-acts with her, to do her shopping and cooking. Besides this servant, no one has been admitted into her home for a decade.

Emily is a legendary figure in a community that has assumed responsibility for her in a number of discreet ways. When her father dies and leaves her penniless in 1894, the mayor, Colonel Sartoris of Civil War fame, de-cided to remit her taxes for the duration of her life. Well aware that she would refuse any proffered charity, he pretends that her father had at one point lent the town money. When subsequent, less chivalrous generations of aldermen attempt to collect taxes from her, she refuses to comply with their requests, recommending that they consult with the deceased Colonel Sartoris concerning the matter. The people in the town are perversely pleased that her inheritance is meager because the Griersons always acted as if they thought they were better than other people. In her fallen financial situation, they can allow themselves the luxury of pitying "poor Emily."

When the town commissions a construction company to pave the sidewalks, a large, boisterous Yankee named Homer Barron comes to town as the foreman for the project. Shortly thereafter Homer begins courting Emily, and they are seen on Sunday afternoons taking drives in the country in a hired car. At first the town is happy for Emily, but they return to pitying her when they decide that a Yankee day laborer is socially her inferior. As the courtship progresses, the community begins to be uncomfortable with the couple's public display of affection. They vacillate in their opinions, sometimes sure that they will eventually marry and at other times skeptical of the legitimacy of Homer's intentions. When Emily buys arsenic from a local druggist, rumor has it that she intends to kill herself due to love-sick grief. But she surprises the gossipers when she purchases a complete suit of men's clothing and a silver toilet set engraved with the initials H.B. The affair ends when Homer Barron suddenly and mysteriously disappears and is never heard from again.

A few days later several of Emily's neighbors complain to local authorities about a horrendous smell coming from Emily's house. To avoid insulting her by openly confronting her about the problem, a small group of men sneak around her home during the night and sprinkle lime around the house and its outbuildings. The smell subsequently goes away, and the incident is generally forgotten. After the disappearance of her suitor, Emily becomes even more reclusive and only opens her house to the young women who seek her services as a teacher of china-painting. When she is found dead, the entire town attends her funeral, both out of respect for her legendary status and out of curiosity to see the interior of her mysterious house. Following the funeral, a group of townspeople break into a dusty, locked bedroom where they find the rotting body of Homer Barron. On the pillow next to his body they perceive a slight indentation and a strand of gray hair that matches that of the murderess, Emily Grierson.

Griffiths, Clyde. *An American Tragedy.* Theodore Dreiser. 1925.

As the novel opens, Clyde Griffiths appears as a teenager in the company of his shabbily dressed family, singing hymns on the forsaken corner of a Kansas City street. Always thinking how he might better himself materially and enjoy clothes, girls, and a more stimulating life-style as other boys do, Clyde first finds a job at a soda fountain and then at the Green-Davidson Hotel. He begins to socialize with the other bellboys, a jaded set of adolescent wanderers who enjoy brothels, drinking, and the company of uninhibited lower-class girls. Hortense Briggs, a shallow, manipulative, but—to Clyde—dazzlingly pretty girl, captures his affections. This phase of Clyde's life comes to an abrupt end when, on a group outing, the driver of their car kills a little girl, and Clyde flees the site of the accident.

Unable to return to Kansas City, Clyde spends three years wandering through various cities until he ends up working as a bellhop at the Union League Club in Chicago. One day he hears that his rich uncle, Samuel Griffiths, is in town; he introduces himself and secures a position at Griffiths's shirt and collar factory in Lycurgus, New York, working in the basement shrinking room.

Because he is considered socially inferior, Clyde is rarely invited to the Griffiths' grand home. His first few months in Lycurgus are lonely and unhappy, until he becomes secretly involved with ROBERTA ALDEN, a soft-spoken daughter of poor farmers, whom he supervises. One day he encounters SONDRA FINCHLEY, the attractive, vain daughter of another wealthy Lycurgus manufacturer; and Clyde, smitten by her glamorous and coquettish ways, contrives other chance meetings. As Sondra leads him into the social whirl, Clyde grows more and more indifferent toward Roberta.

Winning Sondra's heart at last, Clyde finds himself on the brink of material and social success. Roberta's disastrous news—that she is pregnant by him—thrusts him into a dilemma: Could he marry Roberta when doing so would mean giving up Sondra and all of his dreams? Yet if he did not marry her, their relations might become known, and he would be ruined. His desperation increases with each passing day until he comes across a newspaper account of the mysterious drowning of a vacationing young couple. Knowing she cannot swim, he lures Roberta to a remote lake, planning to drown her, make it appear that he drowned, too, and escape back to the area where the Finchleys spend their summers.

On the lake, Clyde, realizing the significance of his actions, is paralyzed with guilt and fear. When Roberta notices his stricken expression and leans over to soothe him, he strikes out, hitting her inadvertently with his camera and capsizing the boat. An expert swimmer, he treads water as she drowns, screaming.

Since he has been inept in obscuring his identity, his movements, and his connection with Roberta, he is arrested some days later and eventually convicted. After months of agonized waiting and several frenzied appeals, Clyde, still confused as to the extent of his criminal responsibility and still yearning for that gilded world of pleasure and beauty that Sondra symbolizes, prepares for his execution. He publishes a parting statement, warning other young men to beware of their wayward passions. He tells his mother he has found peace. But to the end he is haunted by secret doubts and goes with a weak and fearful heart to meet his death in the electric chair.

Grimes, Elizabeth. *Go Tell It on the Mountain.* James Baldwin. 1953.

Elizabeth Grimes left the South to be with the young man she wished to marry. Although the couple had planned a quick marriage, there were considerable obstacles in establishing a secure economic foothold in the North. Elizabeth's boyfriend Richard has tried unsuccessfully to get a good job so the two can marry; meanwhile, Elizabeth lives with an older female relative who doesn't monitor her activities.

After about a year in New York, Elizabeth realizes that she is pregnant. Although she wants to tell Richard and is at once frightened and pleased, she decides to wait a little longer. In the meantime, Richard is arrested for a robbery he did not commit. He is swept up with a group of black youths who did rob the store as they waited on the subway platform. The four are taken to the police station where Richard is severely beaten despite his protestations of innocence. He remains in the jail for a time, and Elizabeth visits him; seeing his pain and torment, she is unable to tell him of her pregnancy. Soon after this, Richard is released on bail and returns to his rooming house where he commits suicide.

Elizabeth enters the world of single-parenting soon after Richard's death, going to work to support their child JOHN (GRIMES). She eventually befriends a coworker, Florence Grimes, and begins to develop a social life. She meets GABRIEL GRIMES, Florence's younger brother, who has just emigrated to the North, and with his assurance that he will love and protect her son as though he were his own, the two marry. Their life together is difficult, and Gabriel's income is barely enough to keep them afloat. The Grimes family, as it grows, becomes more and more involved in the community surrounding their church, the Temple of the Fire Baptized. Elizabeth is able to draw some satisfaction from the relationships she forms among these people. For the most part she devotes her efforts to keeping an eternally filthy house clean and enlists the aid of her two oldest sons, John and Roy, to keep the Grimes home in order.

When Roy is stabbed, and especially when Roy's anger erupts against Gabriel, Elizabeth bears the brunt as Gabriel strikes her in anger. At that evening's church service, while her son John moves toward his "salvation" in a dramatic scene of spiritual ecstasy, Elizabeth recalls her sins and their punishments. When she hears John's cry as he falls on the "threshing floor," Elizabeth is reminded of the day of his birth and recognizes the cry as a chance for him to be born again and to escape the sinfulness of his parents.

Grimes, Gabriel. *Go Tell It on the Mountain.* James Baldwin. 1953.

Gabriel Grimes becomes an ominous figure of power and authority. Born in the South, the last child of a former slave, Gabriel alternately leads a life of preaching and dissolution. His knowledge of a gang rape that occurred during his childhood has a profound impact on his life. The sixteen-year-old victim of that attack, Deborah, becomes the sign of the community's sin and despair. She is ostracized by most of the town, but FLORENCE GRIMES, Gabriel's older sister, befriends her.

When Florence, incapable of withstanding the stultifying life imposed on blacks in the South, eventually decides to leave Gabriel and their dying mother and head north to New York, Deborah steps in to help Gabriel. After his mother's death, Gabriel becomes deeply religious and begins a career as a preacher. He and Deborah marry and become pivotal figures in their religious community. Shortly after the marriage, however, Gabriel enters into an affair with a young girl who works as a domestic for a white family. The affair lasts only nine days, but it produces an illegitimate child. Gabriel tells his lover, Esther, that he cannot leave his wife, and he steals the money that Deborah has saved and gives it to Esther so she can leave town. But Esther dies shortly after the birth of her son, Royal, and he is brought to his grandparents' house. Over the course of the next twenty years Royal matures as Deborah declines. Finally, Royal dies in a violent barroom fight in Chicago, and Deborah, before her own death, tells Gabriel that she knew all along that Royal was his son. She insists that she would have raised Royal as her own had Gabriel acknowledged him.

After Deborah's death, Gabriel travels to New York where he reunites with his sister Florence and meets her friend ELIZABETH GRIMES, who is already the mother of an illegitimate son, John. Gabriel agrees to love and cherish both Elizabeth and her child, and the two marry. Despite Gabriel's expression of love for John, he tends to be abusive and even cruel, and clearly favors his second son, Roy, who bears a resemblance to the first Royal. Gabriel remains religious, at least superficially, but inculcates hatred in his sons. Although he serves as a deacon of the church, he must work long hours in a factory to support his continually growing family.

At the conclusion of the novel, following John's "awakening" in a dramatic scene that leaves the boy thrashing and speaking in tongues, Gabriel stands aloof. He does not wish to see the bastard become one of the saved while his favorite, Roy, remains unregenerate.

Grimes, John. *Go Tell It on the Mountain.* James Baldwin. 1953.

John Grimes is a boy in his early teens, the eldest child of a black family living in Harlem. The two-day span of the novel shows John at a crossroads. He feels at once drawn to the secular world around him, both inside and beyond Harlem, and bound to the social conventions of the community of his church. His stepfather, GABRIEL GRIMES, serves as deacon of the church, the Temple of the Fire Baptized. John's relationship with his stepfather causes much of the tension John feels as he wrestles with himself over the two worlds that beckon. John cannot make sense of his stepfather's behavior because he doesn't know the facts of his own parentage. Gabriel Grimes, in an apparent act of charity, married ELIZABETH (GRIMES) after she had borne John out of wedlock. Gabriel and Elizabeth have several children after their marriage, and although Gabriel insists he loves his stepson, he clearly favors his own children.

John and his brother Roy are never prepared for their Sunday school lesson and thus repeatedly incur the wrath of their father, who toils all week in a factory since his duties as deacon bring no remuneration. At the beginning of the novel, John cannot answer a question posed by Brother Elisha, the seventeen-year-old nephew of the pastor. John pays more attention to the sound of Elisha's voice and to the way he moves than to the theology under discussion. John's failure to answer the question generates an increased anxiety about his fitness to belong in the church's community of Saints.

John completes his daily chores and, against his father's advice, leaves Harlem, walks through Central Park and down Fifth Avenue, and eventually stops to see a movie on Broadway with the money his mother gave him on his birthday. When he returns home, still early for that evening's service, he finds that his brother Roy has been stabbed in a fight but is not seriously injured. This fight spurs a disruption within the Grimes family that results in physical violence between the parents.

After the fight, the Grimeses go to the Saturday night prayer meeting. There is great emotional pressure on John, who now bears even more of his father's wrath for not having been the one stabbed. In addition, John struggles with guilt over the lust he feels and the temptations that sway him.

John arrives at the basement church early, in time to clean up before the service. He wrestles sensually with Elisha, evoking both the play of boys and the fury of fighting men. The wrestling ends amicably before the rest of the Saints arrive. During the service that follows, the hatred Gabriel feels toward his stepson grows as he realizes that John rather than Roy will be the one to accept salvation.

After Elisha sings, John falls on the "threshing floor." Moved by the passionate sounds and the enthusiasm of the rest of the Saints, he soon finds himself speaking in tongues and envisioning the river of baptism and the multitudes of the saved. The congregation celebrates John's acceptance. Although his mother reveals her pleasure at the event, Gabriel remains unmoved by John's salvation. The novel ends with John's plea that Elisha bear witness, regardless of what happens later, that John has been "there," that he is saved.

Grove, Lena. *Light in August.* William Faulkner. 1932.

Although Lena Grove is an orphaned, unmarried, and pregnant young woman, she remains unruffled throughout her search for Lucas Burch, the father of her child. She is motivated to walk and hitchhike from Doane's Mill, Alabama, to Jefferson, Mississippi, where, she has been told, he is employed at a planing mill. Thanks to her childlike innocence and the charity of strangers, Lena successfully delivers a baby boy and manages to survive without a husband, money, or any plan to generate an income. She simply trusts that God will see to it that she is reunited with her ex-lover.

Immediately upon her arrival in Jefferson, Lena goes to the planing mill, hoping to find her ex-lover at work despite the fact that it is a Saturday and the mill is closed. She is greeted there by BYRON BUNCH, a kind, docile man who works alone at the mill on Saturdays for lack of any engaging personal concerns. Bunch immediately but unconsciously falls in love with Lena. After conversing for a while, Bunch realizes that Lucas Burch had been temporarily employed as a sawdust shoveler at the mill under the alias Joe Brown.

Bunch does not disclose that he knows the whereabouts of Brown; instead, he escorts Lena into town and installs her in his own boardinghouse room until he can determine how to proceed in this delicate situation. In the meantime, Brown has been interned in the local jailhouse for his peripheral involvement in the brutal murder of JOANNA BURDEN, an eccentric middle-aged woman whose house was also torched. Bunch eventually tells Lena that Brown is out of town on a business trip and artfully shelters her from gossip concerning the murder.

Fearless or unaware of her future, the unflappable Lena settles down in the small cabin that Brown and his murderous friend JOE CHRISTMAS have recently vacated. As she patiently awaits her ex-lover's return, Lena passively accepts Bunch's financial support. Shortly after the delivery of her baby, Bunch arranges with the local sheriff for Brown, who has since been proven innocent of the murder and the arson, to be forcibly delivered to Lena's doorstep so that he will not be able to avoid accepting his responsibilities as a father. The cagey Brown escapes this fate, however, by jumping out of a window and running away.

During this incident, Lena remains unmoved. She simply decides that she will take to the road again in order to search for Brown. Although she continues to rebuff the dogged Burch's romantic advances, she does allow him to escort her and her baby boy on their seemingly aimless journey.

H

Hackett, Tod. *The Day of the Locust.* Nathanael West. 1939.

Tod Hackett, an artist and set and costume designer for National Films in Hollywood, is youthful but already disillusioned. A graduate of the Yale School of Fine Arts, Hackett is a newcomer in Hollywood and is able to analyze the city's social milieu with an outsider's rueful objectivity. According to Tod, California is filled with people who moved to the state because they thought, consciously or unconsciously, that it was the perfect place to die. His goal as an artist is to capture the atmosphere of Hollywood in a painting titled "The Burning of Los Angeles." Hackett's painting depicts a mob of people, their faces modeled on those of real Los Angeles denizens, dancing and singing with joyous hysterical abandon in the red light that emanates from the burning city they themselves have torched.

When Tod sees FAYE GREENER, a would-be actress and dancer, in the hall of the Moorish-style San Bernardino Arms, he decides to move into the building to be near her. Although Tod courts Faye and even helps her nurse her father, an ex-vaudeville performer who is on his deathbed, she refuses to accept his advances because he is neither wealthy nor good-looking and cannot further her career. Tod becomes even more frustrated when Faye takes a job as a prostitute to pay for her father's funeral but will not even let him sleep with her as a paying customer. In his desperation, Tod fantasizes about brutally raping her in order to crush her indifferent self-sufficiency.

Tod often uses Faye as the subject of his paintings and drawings. His sadistic feelings toward her are reflected in "The Burning of Los Angeles" where she is depicted naked in the foreground, running away from the pillaging mob with a weird grin on her face; a woman in the crowd is in the process of throwing a rock at her in an effort to prevent her flight. Although Faye's presence torments Tod, his efforts to stop himself from chasing her are unsuccessful. He begins to wonder if he is using Faye to torment himself in order to overcome the unhealthy apathy he might share with the people in his painting who resort to violence in order to overcome their morbid boredom.

During the course of one of Tod's pursuits of Faye, he wanders by the set of *Waterloo*, a motion picture in which he thinks Faye is playing a bit part. In a large field just to the side of the set, Tod spies a pile of used sets and props that he mentally calls a "dream dump," as he thinks of the dreams of glamour and wealth inevitably lost by the disillusioned people in his painting. Tod is sufficiently sensitive to the plight of people whose dreams end up in the "dream dump" to befriend one of Faye's more successful suitors, the midwesterner HOMER SIMPSON. To Tod, Simpson is the epitome of the man who has moved to California to perish.

Faye moves in with Homer for a short time, and she takes advantage of his selfless hospitality and rewards his generosity with catty verbal abuse. When Faye eventually moves out, Homer suffers a severe mental breakdown. Intending to return home to Wayneville, Iowa, he endangers his life by trying to walk through an unruly crowd of movie fans while carrying suitcases filled with his possessions. The crowd has massed at Kahn's Persian Palace Theatre in order to catch a glimpse of the celebrities who are attending a premiere there. Tod risks his life in an attempt to extricate Homer from the seething mob and is injured in the process. He is rescued by a police officer who offers to drive him home. In the police car Tod's sanity snaps, and the novel ends with him laughing hysterically as he imitates the squeal of the siren.

Hal. *The Sea of Grass.* Conrad Richter. 1937.

Hal narrates this novel set in the vast Texas cattle country sometime after the invention of barbed wire. A nostalgic young man, Hal longs for the past glories of the open range that once surrounded his guardians, his uncle, COLONEL JAMES BREWTON, and Brewton's wife, LUTIE CAMERON (BREWTON).

As a boy Hal believes that all evil in the world comes from the East in general, and Missouri in particular. From Missouri have come the homesteaders, the "nesters," who endlessly settle, divide, and fence the cattlemen's range. From Missouri has also come Lutie Cameron, Uncle Jim's bride who, Hal thinks, is the reason he is being sent away to boarding school in Missouri.

Hal meets Lutie at the train station in the dusty town of Salt Fork and inducts her into the life of the Southwest by walking her past scenes of violence and squalor on the way to the courthouse. Uncle Jim, an influential figure in town, is busy intimidating a jury and a judge in the trial convened against two of his cowboys for murdering a nester.

Hal adores his uncle, who embodies the energy and grandeur of the cattle country, and heartily deplores the nesters and their champion, Brice Chamberlin, the Salt Fork district attorney. But Hal cannot hate Lutie, an improbable rancher's wife; she is talkative, violet-scented, and eager to entertain anyone and everyone, even a childish student.

Hal attends college and medical school in the East but spends many vacations at the Cross B Ranch. His early memories glow with Lutie and his vigorous uncle, but later memories are sadder, full of hatred for the encroaching nesters and missing the warmth and light of Lutie who, suffering from loneliness, eventually abandons the ranch, her husband, and their three children. Uncle Jim sends Hal after Lutie, but he does not find her.

After medical school, Hal returns to Salt Fork to take over the practice of the town's old doctor. Called to attend a wounded deputy in the next county, Hal comes upon a scene that could never lend itself to nostalgia. Deputies have surrounded an outlaw, Brock Brewton, Lutie's son, who has grown up to look much more like Brice Chamberlin, Uncle Jim's enemy, than Uncle Jim himself. Uncle Jim arrives and rides up to the cabin where Brock remains holed up. Hal ministers to Brock's wound as he dies. The novel closes with Lutie's return. She reunites with Uncle Jim but remains silent about her activities during the intervening years.

Halescy, Edwin. *The New Yorkers.* Hortense Calisher. 1959.

Born in Czechoslovakia after his mother was raped by an anonymous stranger, Edwin Halescy emigrated with his mother and his two aunts to the United States when he was very young. He was raised in New York City during the Depression, and the family's extreme poverty frequently forced Edwin to steal in order to survive.

Walking home from school one day, Edwin meets a young girl, RUTH MANNIX, whose mother committed suicide when she was very young. She takes Edwin back to her mansion and introduces him to her brother DAVID (MANNIX) and their father, the eminent Judge SIMON MANNIX.

Edwin quickly becomes a close friend of the family, endearing himself both to David and the Judge, who is generous enough to rent out a nearby apartment for Edwin's mother and aunts. Impressed with the boy's ambition and intelligence, the Judge takes young Edwin under his wing as a kind of protégé and ultimately pays for Edwin's first-year tuition at Harvard Law School.

The Judge is so impressed with Edwin, in fact, that he offers to make him his personal secretary when he decides to return to public life midway through Edwin's stay at Harvard. Edwin, seeing this as a chance to further his own political ambitions, quickly agrees and transfers to Columbia to finish law school in New York.

It is during his last year of school at Columbia that Edwin begins to hear rumors about Judge Simon Mannix, whose reputation Edwin had previously believed to be beyond reproach. He learns that the death of the Judge's wife, Miriam, had taken place under suspicious circumstances. After further investigation and questioning of various local officials, Edwin discovers that it is commonly believed the Judge murdered his wife.

Armed with this new piece of information, Edwin launches a subtle campaign to blackmail Judge Mannix. With mock innocence he begins to question the Judge about the circumstances surrounding his wife's death. He tests his power over the Judge when he publishes an article written by the Judge in his own name; the Judge is fully aware of Edwin's plagiarism but says nothing. Edwin's arrogance continues to grow until, at a party where the Judge originally intended to announce his return to politics, Edwin gets very drunk and rapes the Judge's daughter, Ruth.

The Judge quickly dismisses Edwin from his employ but does his best to cover up the rape in order to maintain what is left of his increasingly tarnished reputation. Edwin, however, continues to plagiarize freely from the Judge's writings as his own law career flourishes. He sees the Judge once more, an old, crippled man, at the wedding of his daughter Ruth a year later.

Hall, Ruth. *Ruth Hall.* Fannie Fern. 1855.

Born into a solidly middle-class family, Ruth Hall endures hardship at the hands of her unloving father, who sends her to a boarding school where she is teased for her seriousness. While her schoolmates sneak out to meet their boyfriends, Ruth hones her skills as a writer. Any thoughts of a career evaporate, however, when she marries Harry Hall, with whom she can invest all her feelings of love and be loved in return. After her father's coldness and her sibling Hyacinth's unbrotherly disdain, Harry proves a worthy companion.

In the early months of their marriage, Ruth and Harry live with the young man's parents. Old Dr. Hall and his wife are nosy, sharp-tongued, and disapproving of Ruth. When their meddling becomes too much for the young couple, Harry buys a country home where they can express their love without self-consciousness. They soon have a daughter, Daisy, and Ruth spends her time keeping house and roaming the fields with her child.

Joy turns to sorrow when little Daisy becomes sick. Dr. Hall wastes precious time in coming to see the child, and she dies of the croup. Ruth is crushed, but life continues. Eight years later, while Ruth and Harry are vacationing on the sea with their two other daughters, Katy and Nettie, Harry becomes ill. Old Dr. Hall and his wife arrive just in time for the doctor to tell his son that he will surely die. His will to live shaken by his father's brutal honesty, Harry dies while his wife looks on.

The spiteful Halls refuse offers by Harry's business acquaintances to help Ruth, who has been left destitute because of her husband's bad business ventures. Dr. Hall and Ruth's father allot the grieving widow and her children only a pittance on which to live. Ruth is forced to take lodgings in a poor section of town and supports her daughters on meager fare. Attempts to find work sewing and teaching fail, and Ruth despairs.

Ruth remembers her love of writing and wonders whether she might make some money with the newspapers. She applies to her brother Hyacinth, a newspaper editor, but he scorns her. Determined to feed her children somehow, Ruth remains undaunted and eventually begins to publish stories under the name "Floy." To cut expenses, she reluctantly agrees to allow Nettie to stay with the Halls.

Ruth's reputation as a columnist grows, and she begins to write exclusively and at a much higher rate for one paper. She also signs a deal to have Floy's articles published in a book. Financial success proves the best revenge for Ruth, who retrieves Nettie from her parents-in-law's home, invests in bank shares, and buys a house in the country where she lives with her children and continues to write successfully.

Hall, Willie "Littleman." *The Lynchers*. John Edgar Wideman. 1973.

Willie "Littleman" Hall is a severely crippled, angry young black man who engineers a plot to strike back against racism. His proposed plan is thwarted, however, when two of his co-conspirators realize it is as violent and unjust an act as racism itself.

Because of his severely deformed legs, Littleman has sat on the sidelines for most of his life. He has formed a circle of friends who respect him for his fiercely held opinions about race and racism, but for the most part he is unable to find a place for himself. Eventually his anger finds expression in a methodical plan that involves three of his friends including a schoolteacher, THOMAS WILKERSON. He decides that the city must be taught a lesson on the black community's anger about and resistance to racism. Littleman convinces his friends that they should murder a black prostitute who is under the authority of a white policeman, frame the officer for the murder, and then publicly kill him as revenge.

Before the plan can come to fruition, Littleman is severely beaten when he is accosted by several policemen during a public harangue on the steps of Woodrow Wilson Junior High School. The police, ignoring his handicap, decide that his cane is a dangerous weapon, and this suffices as justification for the treatment he suffers. His friends encounter great difficulty in locating him, but they finally find him in the hospital, and at his insistence they decide to continue with their plan.

During his hospitalization, Littleman recalls an affair he had with Angela Rowena Taylor, a woman he met one night at the beach, where she thought he was about to kill himself. The two decided to live together, and despite the meager opportunities available to him, Littleman was able for a time to support her while she simply lay in bed

all day waiting for his return. The loss of this relationship and his ongoing anger serve to fuel his desire for the successful completion of his master plan.

Because he realizes that he can no longer participate, Littleman recruits a young orderly named Anthony, who he hopes will be an adequate replacement as the fourth member of the lynching party. He educates Anthony in subversion while continuing to manipulate his other friends toward the actual crime.

Despite Littleman's mastery of persuasive techniques, the plan begins to unravel as two of the group's members begin to question the legitimacy of the entire project. Littleman continues to apply pressure on the group, and the initial stages of the plan go fairly smoothly. Littleman's anger also begins to mount, however, and at a crucial juncture he begins shouting at Anthony about his beating and its significance in the racist environment he wanted to rebel against. The tirade causes the nurse to come into his room and sedate him. Even though he has a concealed razor blade, available either to attack or to commit suicide, Littleman allows the nurse to sedate him. Unbeknownst to Littleman, the plan is sabotaged by Wilkerson and another member of the group. At the novel's end it is uncertain whether Littleman knows of the fate of his plan of revenge.

Halloway, Charles. *Something Wicked This Way Comes*. Ray Bradbury. 1962.

When a fantastic and evil carnival comes to town, the middle-aged Charles Halloway must find courage within himself that he never knew he had. Charles is a mild-mannered library janitor whose ambitions died long ago. He still has dreams, but he never shares them with his thirteen-year-old son WILL (HALLOWAY), from whom he is emotionally distant. At fifty-four, Charles feels more like a grandfather than a father to Will; content to sweep the mazelike floors of the library and pore over its dusty books, he remains an enigmatic figure to his wife and son.

When Will and his best friend JIM NIGHTSHADE run off to investigate the mysterious carnival that has just arrived in town, Charles, too, is drawn to it, but he feels he is too old to be affected by a dusty, harmless carnival and does not want to be a burden to the boys. His outlook changes, however, when Will and Jim eventually confide in him that the charms of the carnival are actually quite monstrous. Charles somehow discovers that the carnival has the ability to promise people what they want most—be it love, youth, or wisdom—and then instead of granting their wishes, to change them into carnival freaks. The boys tell Charles they have had a series of threatening encounters with Mr. Dark, the proprietor of the carnival, who they insist is certain Will and Jim know too much and is trying to capture them for his freak show.

Charles's love of old library books proves valuable in deciphering the carnival conundrum. He discovers that a carnival with the same name—Cooper and Dark's Pandemonium Shadow Show—has been visiting the area for decades. He surmises that the carnival has been recruiting new victims with empty and deadly promises for centuries. As Charles is telling the boys of the carnival's history, Mr. Dark comes calling. The carnival proprietor finds him and Will hidden in the library stacks, and he crushes Charles's right hand when he tries to save them.

Charles is wounded, but when the Witch, one of Mr. Dark's freaks, tries to kill him, he retaliates with a powerful weapon: Charles begins to giggle at the image of a carnival freak hovering over him. The Witch draws back and finally retreats; in this way Charles discovers that the one thing the freaks cannot endure is laughter. Empowered with this knowledge, Charles runs off to save Will and Jim. He successfully breaks Mr. Dark's spell over the boys, but when Jim is released, he heads for the merry-go-round—a carnival attraction that can make its riders younger or older, depending on which way it turns. As Will tries to pull Jim off the carousel, Charles kills Mr. Dark, who has been turned into a small boy with the aid of the merry-go-round.

With Mr. Dark dead, the carnival begins to fall apart. The rides crumble, and freaks flee in every direction. Charles pulls his son away from the body of Jim, who has fallen from the carousel. Realizing that only love and celebration can defeat the death and despair the carnival represents, Charles and Will laugh, dance, and sing. Jim miraculously revives. The three race back to town together, and Charles's love of life and of his son is renewed.

Halloway, Will. *Something Wicked This Way Comes.* Ray Bradbury. 1962.

Thirteen-year-old Will Halloway, ripe for adventure, investigates a carnival with his best friend and next-door neighbor JIM NIGHTSHADE. When the adventure turns deadly, Will finds a hero in an unlikely source: his father CHARLES (HALLOWAY). The appearance in town of a traveling lightning rod salesman seems to foretell strange happenings. When the salesman warns Jim that lightning will strike his house, Will must convince his carefree friend that they need to at least protect Jim's mother from burning to death in the coming storm. Will's caution serves him well over the next few days.

That night the boys explore the dark streets of their town and find a flyer for a carnival. Cooger and Dark's Pandemonium Shadow Show is in town. Visiting the carnival grounds in the dark, Will and Jim are dazzled when the carnival train pulls in. The whole show has a sinister air, and Will feels his skin crawl and the hair rise on the back of his neck.

In the next morning's daylight the carnival doesn't seem quite so ominous, although Will warns their teacher, Miss Foley, not to go into the hall of mirrors. Later that day when Jim disappears from Will's side, Will finds his friend in the hall of mirrors, staring into their depths as if searching for something. Jim, attracted and repulsed by what he has seen, begs his friend not to desert him. It is Will's first indication that Jim may be slipping away from him. That same evening they discover the carnival's mysterious merry-go-round that can make its riders older or younger depending on the direction it turns. The gleam in Jim's eyes serves as a warning to Will that his friend wants to ride the attraction and grow older.

While examining the ride, the boys first meet the Illustrated Man, Mr. Dark. The tattoo-covered owner of the carnival is a menacing figure who doesn't want curious boys snooping around. Mr. Dark sends the boys away but not before they see the co-owner of the carnival, Mr. Cooger, changed into a boy their age after riding the merry-go-round. They later find Mr. Cooger masquerading as Miss Foley's nephew.

Later that night both boys are in their respective homes when they awaken simultaneously, sensing danger. Will's quick thinking keeps the Dust Witch, one of the freaks in Mr. Dark's carnival, from destroying Jim's house. Now that the Witch knows where the boys live, however, they are no longer safe from Mr. Dark. Will tries to kill the Witch on his own with his bow and arrow but succeeds only in annoying her.

When Jim and Will are finally captured by Mr. Dark, they are saved by Charles Halloway. Will loves his father despite his being middle-aged and unsure of himself. In the crisis Charles rises to the occasion, convincing his son that the carnival is powerful because it plays on people's fear of death and pretends to offer them their fondest wishes.

In the end, Will must pull his friend off the spinning carousel, and Jim is killed in the fall. Charles shows his son that they must laugh, sing, and dance, not mourn. Skeptical, Will joins his father in what seems to him a pointless and cruel display, but in a few moments Jim revives. Laughing, the three return to town, Will having grown closer to his father through their shared adventure.

Hamilton, Berry. *The Sport of the Gods.* Paul Laurence Dunbar. 1902.

Berry Hamilton has been Maurice Oakley's butler for twenty years. He lives with his family in a cottage in the yard of the Oakleys' mansion in a small southern town. Berry is one of the many slaves who had not gone to the North after the emancipation and instead went to work for a white man. He has worked faithfully over the years and managed to save some money from his modest earnings. His son Joe, daughter Kitty, and wife Fannie have all managed to live quite well on Berry's earnings and have been helped along by free room and board. Berry is a trusted member of the Oakleys' staff and, indeed, almost a member of the family when the novel begins.

One day it is discovered that $986 is missing from a

dresser drawer, and a similar amount has been deposited in Berry's bank account. The stolen money was to have been used by Maurice's younger brother Frank on his trip to Europe. Frank leaves for Europe anyway and, supported by Maurice, tries to establish a career as a painter in Paris. As the discoverer of the stolen money, Frank is the only one who might have exonerated Berry.

Berry is instantly accused of the theft and thrown in jail. His family is turned out of their little home. Berry, who maintains his innocence throughout, cannot understand how years of faithful and honest service could warrant such ill treatment from the Oakley family. Even after arriving in jail, he continues to believe that some terrible mistake has been made that will soon be rectified. In the meanwhile, Joe, Kitty, and Fannie are forced to take the family savings and find another dwelling. They are refused work by all the townspeople because of their association with the crime and are harassed so severely that they decide to go to New York to start over again.

Years later Berry is released from prison when Frank Oakley returns from Paris and confesses that he lost the stolen money while gambling. Berry's simultaneous bank deposit was a coincidence and was comprised solely of Berry's earnings. Berry goes to New York and finds that Fannie has remarried, Kitty has become a full-time singer, and Joe, an alcoholic and a murderer. When Fannie's husband dies, she returns to Berry, and the two of them go back to the little cottage in the Oakleys' yard where they will be allowed to live out the rest of their days in peace—without again falling prey to "the sport of the gods."

Hammer, Mike. *I, the Jury.* Mickey Spillane. 1947.

Mike Hammer, the tough and determined hero of many of Spillane's mystery novels, is the very model of the hard-bitten, hard-boiled detective figure popular in American fiction. In this first novel, Hammer's relentless way of pursuing justice reveals that although he has no illusions about others, he retains his personal ideals against all odds. To enact these ideals, he becomes more vigilante than private eye.

Upon the murder of his best friend, Jack Williams, Hammer swears vengeance. He challenges the policeman assigned to the case to a race: Whoever finds the murderer first will mete out justice as he sees fit. Hammer makes it clear to the policeman that he holds an eye-for-an-eye view of justice: His friend was shot in the stomach, so Hammer will do the same to the murderer.

Hammer begins his investigation by checking up on the guests at a party held by Williams the night before the murder: Myrna Devlin, Williams's fiancée and an ex-junkie; George Kalecki, a former bootlegger supposedly turned legitimate; Hal Kines, a medical student; the Bellemy twins, Mary and Esther, wealthy social-ites; and Charlotte Manning, a beautiful and prominent psychologist.

As he investigates these suspects, leads and motives proliferate. Hammer initially suspects that a drug operation mentioned by Myrna Devlin is somehow involved in Williams's murder, but instead he uncovers a prostitution racket run by Kalecki and Kines. These two men are killed, however, before Hammer can get to the bottom of things.

Meanwhile, the Bellemy twins offer no leads or motives, but since Mary Bellemy is an attractive nymphomaniac, Hammer enjoys "questioning" her anyway. This excites the jealousy of Hammer's secretary Velda; Hammer explains to the reader that Velda always reacts angrily to his liaisons, and although he finds Velda distractingly attractive, he does not want to mix business with romance. At one point, however, he does admit that Velda would probably have snared him in the end if it weren't for the fact that he has fallen in love with—and proposed to—the lovely Charlotte Manning.

Throughout his investigation of the seamy Los Angeles underworld, women throw themselves at Hammer while men fall back in awe and fear of this World War I veteran who brings his overseas battle experience to bear on his war against crime in America. Hammer has a reputation, and he is eager to support and extend it by knocking together as many criminal heads as he possibly can.

At the end of the novel, Hammer discovers that his beloved Charlotte Manning is the murderer not only of Williams but of four other people as well. He confronts her with his evidence and then, ignoring her attempt to seduce him, shoots her in the stomach. Dying, she asks, "How could you?" Hammer answers, "It was easy," and washes his hands of this case in which he has been not only judge and jury but also the executioner.

Hand, Laurel McKelva. *The Optimist's Daughter.* Eudora Welty. 1969.

In this autobiographical novel, Laurel McKelva Hand returns to the South from Chicago to be with her father, Judge McKelva, when he sees an eye specialist. A Mississippi native, Judge McKelva travels to New Orleans when he begins having trouble with his eye, and he is immediately admitted to a hospital to undergo surgery. Laurel and Fay, her father's second wife, a selfish woman known to Laurel and the people of Mount Salus, Mississippi, as "poor white trash," alternate in a bedside vigil while the Judge is kept inert after his surgery. As the days go by, Laurel realizes that her father appears to be patiently awaiting death, offering no fight whatsoever. On her birthday Fay attempts to violently shake the Judge into life but is prevented from doing so by the nurses. That very night the Judge dies.

Laurel and Fay return with the Judge's body to Mount

Salus and are met by Laurel's "bridesmaids," the six women who had been her attendants at her wedding, and the undertaker. Arrangements are made for the funeral to be held, and Laurel is taken home by the bridesmaids to a house full of the Judge's old friends.

Early the next morning Judge McKelva's body is brought home for viewing. To Laurel's dismay, not only family friends and acquaintances but town characters make appearances in the McKelva parlor. Although her father had been a public figure, Laurel is appalled that he must be exposed in this way and wants desperately to protect him. However, her desire to have the coffin remain closed is overruled by Fay. Laurel is further horrified when Fay's crude and uncouth family arrives from Madrid, Texas. To the delight of her family and Laurel's complete consternation, Fay creates a scene by collapsing in a vociferous contortion of grief. Laurel's unhappiness is complete when her father is buried in a new plot near the interstate, far from his first wife and Laurel's mother. After the funeral, Fay decides to return with her family to Texas for a while, and she voices her desire that Laurel be gone when she returns.

Laurel spends the next several days grieving, a process that extends from her current loss to the deaths of her husband and her mother. She goes through her father's desk and finds little there to console her. Searching through her mother's desk proves to be more profitable. There she discovers the letters that her father had written her mother over the years. The letters and other memorabilia conjure memories of Laurel's childhood, summers spent at her grandmother's home in West Virginia, her mother's long illness, her own courtship and wedding, and her young husband's death during the war. The remembrance of her lost love finally leads to a release of her pent-up tears, and after a long cry she falls asleep in her parents' bedroom.

The next morning Laurel burns all of her mother's letters and prepares to leave for the train station. Her attention is drawn to the kitchen, where she searches in the cupboard and finds a breadboard made by her husband for her mother. When she realizes that Fay has used the board to crack walnuts, she is furious. At this moment Fay returns from Texas, and Laurel finally allows her resentment of Fay as an interloper in her life to surface. The two confront each other, and Laurel attempts to make Fay understand the damage she has done to the memory of her loved ones. Seeing that Fay has neither the passion nor the imagination to appreciate the past, Laurel is driven to attacking her with the breadboard. She does not strike Fay, suddenly realizing that her memory of the past is impervious to material changes. The fact that the memory is vulnerable means that it lives. Consoled by this thought, Laurel is able to leave the damaged breadboard and her childhood home behind forever with no fear of ever forgetting them or the loved ones they represent.

Hankshaw, Sissy. *Even Cowgirls Get the Blues.* Tom Robbins. 1976.

Sissy Hankshaw leaves home after spending an unhappy childhood in Richmond, Virginia, as an outcast with a physical deformity—her monstrously oversized thumbs—without which she would have been a virtually perfect beauty. But Sissy turns her thumbs into an asset: Developing an ardent love for hitchhiking, she hitches her way out of Richmond and into a series of adventures and encounters with life.

Soon after her departure from home, Sissy meets the Countess, a wealthy but slimy New York–based male entrepreneur who markets female deodorant spray. Sissy becomes his favorite model. Through him she meets Julian Gitche, a Mexican artist, and the two enter into a brief and relatively unsexual affair. Sissy leaves, drawn again to the road, but finds herself suddenly lonely and unhappy. When Julian expresses his love for her, she returns to New York, marries him, and temporarily sacrifices her hitchhiking career.

Several months later the Countess offers Sissy a job filming a commercial with a flock of whooping cranes at the Rubber Rose Ranch, which the Countess owns but which has been taken over by feminist rebel Bonanza Jellybean and her cowgirl associates. Arriving at the Rubber Rose Ranch, Sissy meets Bonanza Jellybean, who speaks of her efforts to make every girl free to realize her fantasies and who warns Sissy about the dangers of love and marriage. Sissy and Jellybean become lovers. Upon leaving the ranch, she meets the Chink, a legendary Chinese spiritualist and hermit.

Sissy returns to Julian but falls into a deep depression. In a psychiatric hospital she tells her kind and mellow therapist, Dr. Robbins, the story of her encounter with the Chink, from whom she received a spiritual and sexual education. As a result she is changed: She now has new notions about the cosmos, human civilization, and freedom. Dr. Robbins, exhilarated by her story and convinced of Sissy's mental health, orders her release from the hospital. Once home, however, Sissy grows pale and feels increasingly lost and dissatisfied with life.

One day Sissy hears about the disappearance of the last remaining flock of whooping cranes. She knows the cowgirls are responsible, and she longs to return to the Rubber Rose Ranch. When the Countess makes a disparaging remark about the cowgirls, Sissy attacks him with her thumbs, causing him to be hospitalized. A warrant is issued for her arrest, so she flees New York and goes to Richmond where she seeks the help of a plastic surgeon and begins procedures to alter the size of her thumbs. The series of operations is not completed, however, because she hears on the national news that the whooping cranes have been discovered at the Rubber Rose Ranch.

By the time Sissy reaches the ranch, a showdown has begun between the cowgirls and federal authorities. The

FBI has surrounded the ranch with armed agents as, stubborn and fearless, Jellybean and the other cowgirls refuse to return the cranes to the masculine world that has been so harmful to them. Sissy, upon learning that the cowgirls are feeding the cranes peyote, becomes confused and goes to consult the Chink. The Chink, amused that the cranes—"birds of poetry"—are at the center of the conflict between the cowgirls and the government, suggests that poetry and magic are the only forces that can redeem society.

Sissy returns to the ranch to witness Jellybean's assassination by a federal agent. When the Chink tries to respond to the gunshot, he is wounded, and the confrontation ends with the cranes flying off toward Texas. After the cowgirls mourn Jellybean, Sissy is offered a job as ranch overseer, which she accepts. The Chink comes to the ranch to convalesce; Sissy nurses him, and they conceive a child. When he is well, the Chink leaves Sissy and the ranch to continue his spiritual quest, and Sissy—with cowgirl Delores del Ruby, her new lover—remains at the ranch to fulfill her cowgirl dream.

Hansa, Beret. *Giants in the Earth.* O. E. Rölvaag. 1927.
Beret Hansa is the wife of the novel's courageous hero, PER HANSA. Beret herself is no heroine; rather, she represents the unsung casualties of the American frontier and its settlement. The great plains, conquered and peopled by hardy pioneers and immigrants, seem to her a limitless desolation fit only for the damned and the dead.

Beret was born in a small Norwegian village. She fell in love with Per Hansa, a daring young fisherman, had one child out of wedlock, married against her parents' wishes, and had two more children. When Per Hansa conceived the idea of emigrating to America, Beret dutifully packed her great-grandfather's chest and followed him. She was not dazzled by the America they reached, but Per Hansa, full of grandiose dreams and a thirst for adventure, pushed westward, finally leading his family—Beret pregnant with a fourth child—out to the vast, empty Dakota Territory.

In the tiny settlement of four Norwegian homesteads, Beret feels lonely, isolated, and forsaken. Although the settlement requires the back-breaking labor of all its members and thus leaves little time for reflection, Beret has a growing sense of doom. The plains are lifeless. Their homestead has an Indian burial site and an accompanying air of heathenism and death. She sees her children growing up uncivilized and imagines her husband, a resourceful and successful sodbuster, drifting to corruption and sin. What seems to others a new land of Canaan, of promise, becomes for Beret the wilderness in which the damned must wander, full of unspeakable fears and lingering guilt.

After a very difficult delivery, which Beret is surprised to have survived, her fourth child is born. She is horrified when Per Hansa christens him Peder Victorious, a name she considers a blasphemy of unholy pride. Beret becomes cynical and pessimistic. Other settlers pass by, going, she supposes, to their hopeless ends in the barren waste; in one covered wagon lies a shackled woman, driven mad by the loss of her son. The summer brings a swarm of locusts, which to Beret is yet another sign, a biblical plague, that indicates the apocalypse is coming. Beret herself goes mad.

Years of madness pass. Relief comes only when a minister, pioneering like other Norwegians, comes to the settlement and gives holy communion before a makeshift altar in the Hansa household, Beret's great chest. Beret gains serenity in religion, believing she will survive the frontier by living a holy life free of sin. Once alone in despair and then in insanity, Beret is alone now in her faith. She is alone all the more when Per Hansa dies. At the end of the novel Beret remains solitary, backward-looking, a symbol of the New World's price, not its promise.

Hansa, Per. *Giants in the Earth.* O. E. Rölvaag. 1927.
Per Hansa is the hero of this epic novel of Norwegian-American sodbusting. Marked by the title's allusion to the Genesis verse, "There were giants in the earth in those days," Per Hansa stands as an embattled colossus of the American frontier, wresting his own manifest destiny from the harsh realities of the great plains.

When the novel opens, Hansa is leading his family in their diminutive wagon train: two oxen, two rickety wagons, and a cow. Born to the rough life of a Norwegian fishing village, he has abandoned the dangers of the sea for those of the New World. Moved by the love he has for two individuals, Hans Olsa, a massive, benevolent friend, and BERET (HANSA), his young wife and the mother of his three children, Hansa has followed the urgings of the former and all but quelled the fears of the latter in their journey. He leads his family west to Canada, to Minnesota, and finally, in the spring of 1873, to a settlement of just four homesteads on Spring Creek in the Dakota Territory.

With visions of prosperity before him, Hansa constructs his sod house—one room for the family and one for the livestock—and plants his first crop. Through strength, fortitude, and canniness, he makes a new life for himself and his family. He is confident in the face of poverty and hardship, and he names his fourth child, born the first Christmas on the plains, Peder Victorious.

The two greatest tests the plains offer are the maddening, lonely boredom of the Dakota winter and the ravaging horror of locust swarms in summer. Hansa is more than equal to both tests, and yet year by year his grand dreams for the future outstrip his occasional triumphs and steady, back-breaking labor. His progress is checked by worry; his wife, fragile and homesick, drifts to an intermittent madness that he is powerless to dispel. He fears for his children, the youngest in particular, and is worn and bent, prematurely aged by his wife's illness.

Although the Spring Creek settlement prospers and the Dakota frontier is gradually tamed, Per Hansa is ultimately a tragic hero, a sacrificial victim given up to the success and the mettle of the sodbusters. Near the end of the novel, his lifelong friend, Hans Olsa, lies on his deathbed asking for a minister. His wife Beret, her madness tamed by determined religiosity, calls upon Per to satisfy his friend's last wish. And Per Hansa, knowing full well the impossibility of the attempt, sets out on skis through the Dakota winter and is found dead when the spring thaw comes.

Harding, Anne "Nan." *Little Men.* Louisa May Alcott. 1871.

Anne Harding, known to her friends as "Naughty Nan," rivals the boys at the Plumfield Academy with her bravery and ceaseless energy. Rather than making her quiet and mournful, the death of her mother has caused Nan to "run wild." Finding that he can no longer control her, her father consults with Mrs. Bhaer, the mistress of Plumfield, and decides to enroll her there. Mrs. Bhaer is fond of adventurous children, having been one herself, and hopes that Nan will influence Daisy, her only female student, who is timid and shy. Daisy is skeptical when she hears that Nan will be staying at Plumfield, but the boys, especially Tommy Bangs, the school "scapegrace," rejoice.

Nan stirs up the school from the moment she arrives by immediately accepting a challenge to prove her bravery. She claims that nothing can make her cry, and a pampered boy called Stuffy decides to test her claim. First, Stuffy dares her to pick up a nettle and then demands that she bang her head against the barn wall. Nan performs these feats without a whimper. Daisy, who is very concerned about Nan's blistered hand and bruised head, pours out the story to Mr. Bhaer, and Stuffy is reprimanded.

With this incident barely over, Nan causes another scene by disappearing one evening. She is discovered hauling her luggage, which had arrived late at the station, down the long road to Plumfield. When Nan vanishes for the second time, however, her tale ends unhappily. She and the rest of the older children are setting off to pick huckleberries one morning when Mrs. Bhaer's five-year-old son Rob overhears and begs to go along. After some debate, Mrs. Bhaer consents, and Nan takes the child into her care for the afternoon. When she grows tired of picking berries, Nan suggests that they hide in a cave she discovered, eat their lunches, and wait for the others to find them. Once darkness falls and no one has come, Rob pleads to go home. Nan is marvelously confident as they wander in the woods trying to find the road. Eventually they are too exhausted to go farther, and Mrs. Bhaer finds them later that night, asleep under a tree. The next day Nan must submit to the curious punishment of spending

the day tethered to the living room couch. After this ordeal Nan solemnly vows never to be "naughty" again.

Nan grows more careful about running off, but she remains as bold and impatient as ever, always fighting for her right to participate in the boys' games. The Bhaers see her aggression as an indication that Nan is destined to have a career and "something to live for." After observing the sense of importance Nan gets from tending to the children's cuts and bruises, they give her a medicinal herb garden and encourage her to become a doctor. Mrs. Bhaer, commenting to a friend on Nan's success at the school, reveals how she has helped Daisy learn to participate in the boys' games. The novel closes with the idea that Nan's wild energy is now being turned toward shaping plans for adulthood.

Hardy, Frank and Joe. *The Tower Treasure.* Franklin W. Dixon. 1927.

Successfully solving over fifty cases in the Original Hardy Boys Mystery Series and roughly the same number in the later Hardy Boys Casefiles Series, Frank and Joe Hardy remain literature's two most enduring teenage investigators. When not aiding their famous father Fenton Hardy on his latest detective case or uncovering local crimes of their own, the dark-haired Frank and his blond younger brother Joe attend high school in the small town of Bayport where they live with their mother and aunt Gertrude.

In *The Tower Treasure*, Frank and Joe accidentally stumble across an international gang of jewel thieves who have hidden a cache of priceless jewels somewhere in an abandoned tower on the outskirts of Bayport. With the aid of their ever-faithful friend Chet Morton, Frank and Joe try to locate the hidden treasure in Bayport while their father attempts to infiltrate the gang of smugglers from New York City. When Fenton and the FBI are able to capture the jewel thieves, who refuse to reveal the location of their hidden treasure, it is up to the Hardy Boys to locate the missing jewels. After setting a trap for a mysterious tower inhabitant, the Hardy Boys nab the last member of the gang of thieves, who reveals the location of the tower treasure. With the reward money for finding the jewels, the boys set up a crime lab in their barn.

The Hardy Boys Casefile Series, an update of the Hardy Boys series, adds a number of new mysteries. In *Dead on Target*, Joe's girlfriend Iola Morton is killed when a terrorist bomb intended for the Hardy Boys explodes in their car. As they try to infiltrate the terrorist network, they learn that Iola's murderer, an international killer known as "The Assassin," has further plans to kill presidential candidate and election front-runner Phillip Walker. In *Evil Inc.*, Frank and Joe travel to Paris where they stumble upon a gang of Panamanian gunrunners. Forced to go undercover to infiltrate the gang, Frank and Joe disguise themselves as a pair of punk rockers. Their investigation leads them to a giant corporation of killers whose business is terrorism.

The Hardy Boys Casefiles Series represents a marked departure from the Original series, with adventures becoming more complex as they take a decidedly contemporary turn. Nevertheless, the Hardy Boys continue to solve case after case with their characteristic mixture of wit, intelligence, and aplomb.

Harkless, John. *The Gentleman from Indiana.* Booth Tarkington. 1899.

John Harkless, the enigmatic protagonist, causes a stir among the inhabitants of Plattville when he revives the failed newspaper of this small Indiana town. A successful businessman, Harkless is idealistic yet shrewd; and despite his public success, political influence, and spotless reputation, he feels unworthy of praise. He leads a lonely, reclusive life until he falls in love and must stand up for his political belief in the face of violence and hardship.

Harkless's first move on arriving in Plattville is to hire Mr. Fisbee, an eccentric professor who, after a long series of financial mishaps, has lost his career and family and taken to drink. A seemingly unlikely candidate, Fisbee soon proves to be a most valuable reporter as well as a good friend. Harkless also prevents a corrupt politician, Rod McCune, from running for reelection by threatening to expose his criminal activities.

One day at a lecture Harkless meets HELEN SHERWOOD. Extremely romantic at heart, he discovers that Helen is the embodiment of a woman he has dreamed about all his life. He falls in love with her at the town fair, but she rejects his professions of love that same evening. Distraught, he runs into a summer night storm and is abducted by McCune's dubious band of supporters, the "Whitecaps."

When Harkless is discovered missing, the town forms a posse the following day, and a bloody battle ensues. It is later revealed that one of the seriously injured men is Harkless beneath the bandages. The critically injured Harkless has little will to live because of Helen's rejection, but the arrival of his best friend from college days, Tom Meredith, aids in his recovery.

In the meantime, Fisbee's "nephew," H. Fisbee, comes to Plattville to assume temporary control of the *Herald*. H. Fisbee turns the paper into a daily, and his coverage of potential oil deposits in Plattville causes the town to boom. Harkless is extremely pleased with H. Fisbee's work and, while still in recuperation, plans to give him the paper. But when McCune returns to town with intentions of running for Congress, H. Fisbee gives the appearance of collusion because he disobeys Harkless's instructions to print the documents that will incriminate McCune.

Outraged, Harkless recovers his strength and returns to Plattville to find that there is no danger of McCune returning to politics because H. Fisbee has secretly nominated Harkless as the congressional candidate with overwhelming support. Harkless then discovers that H. Fisbee is actually Helen Sherwood, Fisbee's daughter who was raised by relatives when Fisbee fell to ruin. Helen ran the paper out of gratitude for what Harkless did for her father and a desire to prove her feminine worth in a man's world. Helen finally admits her love for Harkless, who has gained a new appreciation for Plattville and looks forward to representing the town in Congress as "the gentleman from Louisiana."

Harney, Lucius. *Summer.* Edith Wharton. 1917.

Intelligent and talented but weak-willed, Lucius Harney is a young architect caught up in a complicated love affair with CHARITY ROYALL. He is struck by her beauty when he sees her working in the town library, where he plans to research the area's older homes. His appreciation of the library's rare books stands in contrast to Charity's ignorance of their value. When Lucius's aunt, the head librarian, hears about the neglected condition of the books, she wants to fire Charity, but Lucius persuades her to reconsider. This kindness marks the beginning of Lucius's relationship with her.

Lucius and Charity spend more time together; she helps him with his research while he assists a builder assigned to the library building's renovation. They talk a great deal, and Charity is awed by Lucius's knowledge and sophistication. He then rents a buggy from Charity's guardian, Mr. Royall, and begins taking his meals with them. But Mr. Royall becomes envious of the time Lucius spends with Charity and terminates their arrangement about the buggy and the meals. Lucius then leaves for a stay in another town, and he and Charity have an uncomfortable parting. He sends her a note, though, offering his friendship and asking her to meet him, and they quietly reunite.

They celebrate a romantic Fourth of July together in a nearby town, rowing on the lake, seeing a moving picture, and eating dinner at a small café. That evening during a fireworks show, Lucius kisses Charity passionately, and she responds. But the evening ends badly, for they run into a drunken Mr. Royall, who becomes furious and swears loudly.

Hurt by this encounter, Charity decides to leave town for the mountains. Lucius finds out and takes her to an abandoned house nearby to talk. Charity tells Lucius about an episode in which a drunken Mr. Royall made sexual overtures toward her, and Lucius becomes indignant. Feeling protective of her and carried away with his passion, he kisses her ardently. They then begin to meet secretly in the abandoned house.

But Lucius has another life, one in which he is already engaged to a rich, sophisticated young woman named Annabel Balch. He can't seem to break off his relationship with her, nor can he give up Charity. He doesn't say anything about the other engagement, but Charity realizes how much stands between them when she sees him sitting next to Annabel, whispering in her ear.

That night Mr. Royall finds Lucius and Charity together. Charity is defiant, but Lucius is visibly shaken when Mr. Royall asks him if he plans to marry Charity. Lucius reluctantly agrees. After Lucius leaves town, ostensibly to arrange their marriage, Charity hears a rumor that he is indeed engaged to Annabel Balch. When Charity tells Lucius that she doesn't want to force him into marriage, he thanks her for her understanding and promises to return to marry her. However, locked in a situation with no honorable solution, Lucius takes the first opportunity to flee the consequences of his actions. He thus abandons Charity, and his passion for her falls prey to the demands of his other "social" life.

Harper, Duncan. *The Voice at the Back Door.* Elizabeth Spencer. 1956.

As the novel opens, Duncan Harper, a small-town grocery store owner, is paid a visit by the sheriff, Travis Brevard, who is about to die. Travis asks Harper to take over as sheriff after he is gone. Brevard reminds Duncan of his past as a high school and college football hero and how the whole county idolized him in his youth. The legacy of Duncan Harper's days as a football star follow him throughout the novel, creating the expectation of future greatness—an expectation that goes unmet and leads, perversely, to his early death.

Even before Duncan has been appointed temporary sheriff he sets in motion inevitable changes in Winfield County. One night at home with his wife Tinker and his two best friends, Jimmy Tallant and Kerney Woolbright, Duncan outlines his ideas: He wants to stop both the sale of illegal liquor and the unequal treatment of the Negro population. This is Mississippi in the mid 1950s, and Duncan's early years as a golden boy have given him an unrealistic sense of what is possible. Jimmy Tallant is the immensely popular local bootlegger with a roadhouse out on the highway. Tinker predicts, and rightly, that this move toward politics will ruin their friendship.

Once he is appointed temporary sheriff, Duncan closes down the Tallant liquor operation. Although liquor is the staple form of recreation and Tallant's roadhouse is the county hangout, Duncan steadfastly pursues his ideals. He believes that alcohol has caused too many accidents and created an unsafe situation in the county, and he wants to uphold the law even though he himself has broken it in the past.

Duncan also knows that if he wants to be elected sheriff he has to keep his ideas about equality for Negroes to himself. However, his opponents find a way to draw him out. One night a local Negro, Beckwith Dozer, appears at the back door of Harper's house and asks for protective custody. Dozer claims that he was in a fight with Bud Grantham, Jimmy Tallant's partner. He and Duncan wait together for the inevitable violence. Sometime after midnight Tallant and a group of men pretend to storm the jail, but instead they take a picture of Duncan protecting Dozer. This picture surfaces a few weeks later in a Negro paper from Chicago, lauding Duncan as a champion of Negroes. The article, written by Dozer, turns out to be a setup by Grantham and Tallant to expose Duncan's sympathy for blacks in order to keep him from winning the race for sheriff.

After this sham is exposed, Tallant and Grantham are approached by a liquor and gambling syndicate from New Orleans that wants to go into business with them. The syndicate wants to put money into Willard Follansbee's campaign, the former deputy running against Duncan for sheriff. Tallant refuses and is accidentally shot and badly wounded by one of the men from the syndicate. They pass the word that Tallant was seen arguing with Dozer.

When Dozer finds out that he is the prime suspect in the Tallant shooting, he hides out in the next county. Although Tallant insists that Dozer didn't shoot him, public sentiment turns against Duncan for not bringing Dozer in. When Tallant refuses to reveal who actually did shoot him, Duncan is forced to investigate the crime. He and Kerney Woolbright find out what actually happened from the boy who did the shooting.

On the morning of the rally for candidates running for office, Duncan waits for a telegram that will confirm his findings. He needs this information to clear himself before his neighbors, who are still angry about his refusal to bring Dozer in. The telegram is delivered to Kerney Woolbright, who reads it without telling Duncan. A few minutes later, in front of the entire county, Kerney Woolbright disassociates his candidacy from Duncan's, withdrawing his endorsement for county sheriff because of Duncan's desire for equal rights and his protection of Negro citizens.

After hearing this speech, Duncan realizes that there will be trouble when he speaks, and he decides to take Tinker and the kids home. There, he finds a message that Beck Dozer is waiting for him behind a local grocery store. He and Tinker go to meet Beck, who wants to be driven into town to face the locals now that his innocence has been proven. Duncan insists on taking him into protective custody in the next county for his own safety.

As they leave the grocery store they are harassed by two white men. One leans down close to the tire as they pull away. On the highway they discover that they are being followed by an angry crowd from the rally who heard a rumor that Duncan Harper was protecting Beck Dozer again. Driving very fast to elude the mob, Duncan feels the tire blow out as the steering wheel jumps in his hand. The car sails and tumbles through the air. Tinker and Dozer are hurt but not badly; Duncan Harper is dead.

Harrington. *The Power of Sympathy*; Or, *The Triumph of Nature*. William Hill Brown. 1789.

Harrington, a young man of colonial New England gentry, is the victim of an ill-fated love affair in what is widely considered the first American novel. Sensitive and romantic, he falls in love with pretty young Harriot and intends to marry her. But a friend makes it known that their relationship is more than connubial love: Harrington and Harriot are actually brother and sister. The news drives Harriot to an early death and ultimately leads Harrington to commit suicide.

The doomed lovers' story is told by a series of letters, most of them written by Harrington and several high-minded friends. When he first becomes attracted to Harriot, an orphan employed as a companion to a disagreeable widow, Harrington admits to his friend that he would never marry a young lady of such low social standing. He intends instead to take her as a mistress. But a look of virtue in Harriot's eyes causes him to abandon his plan of seduction, and he resolves to marry her. When his father discourages the union, Harrington plans a secret wedding.

Harrington's friends, meanwhile, offer moralistic advice. His friend Worthy, his sister Myra (to whom Worthy is engaged), and her friend Mrs. Holmes correspond with one another and exchange opinions on such issues as female education and politics. They also trade several grim tales of seduction, which they advance as moral lessons to naive young lovers. The didactic tone of their correspondence contrasts sharply with that of the romantic Harrington who dismisses his friends' "dull sermons." Harrington also differs from the other letter writers in his understanding of class relations. Mrs. Holmes sneeringly describes an acquaintance who has assumed a higher rank in life than her own breeding can support; Harrington, on the other hand, is appalled when a young woman is scorned for being a mechanic's daughter, and he longs for the day when there are no such class distinctions among Americans.

Harrington's love for Harriot continues to grow, so much so that when she accompanies the widow to Rhode Island, he is beside himself with longing for her. In the meantime, however, the couple's alarming history comes to light. Mrs. Holmes cryptically warns Myra that she must stop her brother from marrying Harriot. When Harrington remains determined, Mrs. Holmes discloses a long-held secret: Harriot, who was taken in as an infant by Mrs. Holmes's mother-in-law, is the illegitimate daughter of Harrington's father, the product of a seduction as disreputable as any in the tales told among his friends.

An anonymous note to Harrington acquaints him with the horrifying news, while Myra tells Harriot. Unable to withstand her grief and shame, Harriot becomes weaker and weaker, and soon dies. Distraught, Harrington writes several letters to his friend Worthy threatening suicide and begging Worthy to come to him. Worthy's lofty response—urging him to act sensibly—does nothing to dissuade him. Convinced that he will be with Harriot in the next world, Harrington shoots himself. Worthy arrives too late to save his friend, and he and the others mourn the loss of the two innocent lovers who seemed bound by the power of sympathy.

Harris, Joan. "Torch Song." John Cheever. 1947.

Men who are down on their luck and near death hold a certain fascination for Joan Harris. Always calm and placid, Joan seems to be a sort of foolish benefactress who takes into her home men who take advantage of her. As the story progresses, however, the truth about this perpetually black-clad woman emerges.

Joan arrives in New York City in the mid-1930s, the same time that Jack Lorey, a man from the same town in Ohio, moves east. For a while Jack and Joan see a great deal of each other, but Jack loses contact with his friend when the two of them begin to move in different crowds. Sometimes their paths do cross. Joan will be with a different man each time—always one who is shabby, somewhat pathetic, and abusive. One man, who claims he is a Swedish count, forces Joan to procure morphine to satisfy his habit. Joan's social status falls considerably as she deals with pushers, has an abortion, and even moves into a cheap hotel with the count when he tries to leave her. She seems determined to share his misfortune.

Strangely, Joan seems unaffected by this and other tawdry episodes. When she and Jack occasionally run into each other, he is always impressed with her beauty, apparent innocence, and good nature. Each time Jack visits Joan in her walk-up apartment in Greenwich Village there is a different man's name written above hers on the mailbox and a different man—a German refugee, an obnoxious American, a doctor with a wife and children on Riverside Drive—living in her apartment. Jack is concerned about Joan but impressed that she is so unshakable. Even when she is forced to move out of the neighborhood because she is suspected of being a prostitute, Joan displays no anger or shame. Jack has the feeling, however, that someone has just died when he goes to her apartment. He thinks of her as "The Widow."

For a few years around the time of World War II Joan and Jack lose contact; but when Jack, twice-divorced and down on his luck, is forced to live in a series of cheap hotels, Joan finds him. She appears like an angel of mercy, bearing Scotch and cigarettes. Although Jack apologizes for the shabby surroundings, Joan takes pleasure in the filth and squalor of the home of a man she never visited when he was married, working, and well-off. He questions her about the men who had lived with her. They are all dead. As Jack screams at her to get out because he is still young and strong and is not dying, Joan calmly collects her things. Wearing her black dress, she leaves him but promises, oblivious to his curses, that she will return after work to take care of him as she has so many others.

Harris, Tom. "The Hitch-hikers." Eudora Welty. 1941.

Driving toward Memphis one night, Tom Harris, a thirty-one-year-old salesman, picks up two hitchhikers: one a talkative guitar player, and the other a silent, uncommunicative man. As they drive toward the small town of Dulcie, Harris and the guitar player talk pleasantly about a variety of topics. Along the way Harris buys the two dinner and, once in Dulcie, arranges a place for them to sleep. It surprises Harris when a young boy runs into the hotel to say that the two men have attempted to steal his car and that one has dangerously injured the other by cracking him over the head with a beer bottle.

Harris returns to find the garrulous guitar player slumped over the front seat of his car, gushing blood. He drives him to the hospital and learns from the doctor that the man's condition will not be known for a while. In the meantime, the authorities place the second vagabond, Sobby, under arrest. Harris checks into his hotel again and calls up a woman friend who has invited him to a party.

He attends the party, hoping that word of the violence has not reached those in attendance. For a while the incident remains at bay, but a phone call alerts the guests to the occurrence, and a report of the wounded man's death turns the event into a story that Harris must tell. When Harris telephones the hospital, he discovers that the man has not died—his condition remains the same. Harris eventually leaves the party and returns to his hotel room. He cannot sleep, so he muses about how his life on the road involves him in so many incidents and lives that are not his own. He hears a woman whistling outside his window. This young woman had been at the party and remembered him from his early days as a salesman. He takes her to a joint for a Coke. She tells him that she was crazy about him the first time she met him and remains so. He thanks her for her sentiment and puts her in a taxi.

He telephones the hospital the next morning and learns that the guitar player has finally died and that Sobby has been charged with murder. Sobby blandly confesses that he met the dead man two weeks earlier and that the man was uppity. He also maintains that it was the guitar player who had attempted to steal Harris's car.

Several hours later Harris has his car serviced at a filling station and prepares to return to the road.

Harris, Will. *If We Must Die.* Junius Edwards. 1963.

Will Harris is a black Korean War veteran who has returned to his bigoted hometown in the Deep South. At the time of the novel, Will has been home for approximately two years. During this time he has completed his recovery from a serious injury suffered when he was shot during an enemy assault in Korea. Will lives with his mother, an indomitable woman who takes great pride in her son's accomplishments and efforts. Most of the two years since he has been home have been filled with an arduous study of U.S. and state history and constitutional law. At his mother's request, Will plans to do the impossible: He intends to register to vote.

While Will is waiting to be called in to register, several white men swiftly register within minutes. Among these registrants is a recent émigré who barely speaks English but who smilingly tells a reporter how proud he is to be like every other American. A stoic witness to this blatant discrimination, Will continues to wait. Finally he is called into the office, where he is forced to endure ridicule, humiliation, and psychological torture before he is rejected on a technicality that results from the white clerks' cruelty and bigotry.

When Will arrives at work that afternoon, he is called into the supervisor's office. The time off promised to workers who wanted to register to vote does not apply not to "boys," black workers such as Will and his friend Flip, but to the "others," the white men Will saw while he waited. Will is informed in no uncertain terms that he is fired and that as a reprimand for his attempt to move beyond his "place," he will not work again in the town.

When he returns home, his mother urges him to stay optimistic. She insists that he will soon find a job; in the meantime, she reminds him that he should visit his fiancée Mary. Deeply in love, the young couple spends a romantic if anxious evening together, and by the time Will leaves at midnight, they have planned to leave town after he tries once more to get a local job. As Will walks home, he is interrupted by a sudden, violent attack. Before he can adequately defend himself, he is knocked out, bound, and gagged.

When Will regains consciousness, he hears three men plotting his fate. His terror mounts, and a steady stream of punches continues as Will is trapped in the backseat of a car with Luke who revels in torturing him. Finally, Will's captors agree to leave him alive but to cut off his penis as a warning to the town's black population. Although they beat him severely once they reach the woods, none of the rednecks is capable of the dismemberment they had laughed about while planning Will's fate. Sensing their indecision, Will seizes his chance and flees through the woods, dragging himself from tree to tree. He rigs a tourniquet to stanch the flow of blood from his hands and wrist where he was cut while protecting himself. He collapses by the side of the road, and an old deaf black man appears, sees Will, and attempts to help him. Although conscious, Will is too weak to speak and thus unable to warn his benefactor to leave the tourniquet alone. As the novel ends, Will lies on the flatbed of his rescuer's truck, watching the sunrise as he slowly bleeds to death.

Harron, Dalton "Diddy." *Death Kit.* Susan Sontag. 1967.

Dalton Harron is the novel's mild-mannered thirty-three-year-old protagonist. Nicknamed "Diddy," he comes from an affluent middle-class family and was raised in part by a nurse named Mary. He has one brother, Paul, a famous pianist. Diddy was educated at Dartmouth College, where he pursued a premed degree. He abandoned his plan to become a doctor, married, and moved with his wife Joan to New York City where he took a job with Watkins & Company, a firm that makes microscopes equipped with built-in cameras. Diddy's marriage failed, but his life remains otherwise unchanged and is relatively devoid of purpose or meaning. The restless years of the 1960s, punctuated by nightly television reports chronicling fatalities in Vietnam, seem to reflect rather than inspire Diddy's own anomie. Deeply depressed by his troubled milieu, Diddy attempts suicide by drug overdose but succeeds only in losing a substantial amount of weight and suffering the indignity of having his stomach pumped.

When Watkins & Company sends Diddy on a business trip to upstate New York, he finds himself in a train compartment with an odd collection of people, including a blind young woman named Hester and her aunt, with whom he engages in conversation. The progress of the ultramodern train, the *Privateer*, is obstructed by debris in the middle of a tunnel, and he and his fellow passengers wait impatiently for the train to proceed on its journey. Diddy, at least as he remembers it, leaves the train, advances along the tracks, and ends up bludgeoning a workman to death in front of the train. Back on the *Privateer*, Diddy proceeds to make love in a lavatory to the willing blind woman, who later claims that he never left the compartment at all and is therefore innocent of the supposed murder.

A confused Diddy spends a week meeting with Watkins & Company executives and visiting Hester in the hospital, where she undergoes an unsuccessful corneal transplant. The newspaper reports the death of a workman at the site where the *Privateer* had stopped to clear the tracks, but the report claims the death was the result of an accident. Diddy stays on in upstate New York after his business responsibilities are fulfilled in order to spend more time with Hester, and eventually he decides to quit his job. Quite abruptly, he proposes to Hester, who agrees to marry him, and when her convalescence is over, it is Diddy rather than her aunt who chaperones her when she leaves the hospital.

Back in New York City, Diddy and Hester develop a bizarre symbiotic relationship that proves mutually destructive. Diddy is fascinated by Hester's blindness, the result of her mother's having attacked her with lye. He is also captivated by her victimization, with which he empathizes on the one hand, and connects with his own guilt, depression, and paranoid fears on the other. Ultimately

unable to shake off his presumed memory of the violent incident on the train tracks, Diddy finally takes Hester back to the tunnel to reenact the supposed murder of the train workman. Encountering a man who looks oddly like his previous victim, Diddy murders this workman in the same manner, beating him to death with a crowbar. Having carried the dazed Hester away from the scene of the crime, Diddy sets off to explore the tunnel, which opens into a cavernous series of crypts; the bodies of countless Americans are stacked, partially preserved both in and out of coffins. At the book's end Diddy is unsure where his life has ended and his surreal death has begun.

Harry. "The Snows of Kilimanjaro." Ernest Hemingway. 1938.

Harry is a middle-aged professional writer on holiday in Africa with his wife Helen. Accompanied by a group of Africans, the two of them are enjoying a safari, indulging their mutual penchant for hunting. But the safari is ruined when Harry scratches his knee on a thorn while attempting to photograph waterbuck and does not properly attend to the cleanliness of the wound. The resulting infection proves to be life-threatening.

This was not the first attempt to establish a permanent relationship for either Harry or Helen. Helen was a widow, and both of them had had a series of lovers. Harry has a history of becoming attached to rich women, and Helen is the richest of them all. At the same time, he is impatient with the rich, whom he thinks are frivolous hedonists. Although Helen's wealth affords them the luxury of this exotic holiday, it is a bone of contention between them. They bicker about the possibility that money has somehow compromised Harry's talent by spoiling him and softening his resolve to write. Harry's regret concerning his career as an artist comes home with a vengeance when he smells the foul breath of death, the stench that is being emitted from his gangrenous rotting leg. He castigates both himself and his wife, ruing the fact that he had procrastinated and thereby missed his chance to write down all the stories his life had generated. If he dies, his stories will follow him to the grave.

Stranded due to the breakdown of their truck, Harry, Helen, and the Africans camp out in the veld, surrounded by zebras, hyenas, antelopes, and the vultures that are attracted by the smell of Harry's leg. Helen, who is repressing the gravity of the situation, keeps assuring her skeptical husband that the long overdue rescue plane will arrive the next day. Although the gangrene is so advanced that Harry is not experiencing any pain, he is apparently mentally affected by his injury. His mood shifts wildly, and he alternates between telling his wife that he loves her and castigating love, which he claims is no more valuable than a dungheap. He engages in extensive revelries, synopses of the numerous stories that he never got around to writing: the snow that covered the tracks of the army deserter in the Gauertal; the young male half wit who murdered an old man for attempting to steal some hay from a barn; the wounded World War I officer who begged his fellow soldiers to shoot him to put him out of his misery; and Harry's life in Paris. He periodically senses death approaching, cloaked in the shape of a bird or hyena, or resting its head near his feet on the bed. Ignoring his wife's denials, he insists that his life is worthless and that the only thing he didn't lose along the way was his curiosity. Convinced that he will not survive the night, he tries to do some writing but is soon exhausted and forced to retire.

The narrative of the story then skips to the following morning. The Africans have built large bonfires to try to advertise their location. A plane eventually lands successfully, picks up Harry, and begins to fly him to the nearest medical facilities. This story, which is in fact Harry's dream or delirious vision, concludes with Harry's parting glimpse of the incredibly white snow shining in the sun on the top of Mount Kilimanjaro. The narrative shifts once again to the real world where a hyena, crying with an almost human voice, awakens Helen. Sensing something strange in the tent, Helen becomes hysterical when she realizes that Harry is dead.

Hartman, Reverend Curtis. "The Strength of God" (*Winesburg, Ohio*). Sherwood Anderson. 1919.

The docile and ingenuous Reverend Curtis Hartman struggles to maintain the moral purity of his thoughts while besieged with flaming sexual fantasies. Happily married to the daughter of an underwear manufacturer from Cleveland, the Reverend is horrified by the intrusion of lascivious thoughts concerning one of his neighbors, KATE SWIFT, whom he had accidentally spied lying in her room smoking a cigarette with an enticing absence of clothing and a snowy white throat. Once introduced to this provocative vision from the bell tower of his Presbyterian church, he cannot resist taking subsequent surreptitious peeks at her through a small hole that he cuts in a stained-glass window. The guilt that he experiences in conjunction with his Peeping Tom behavior threatens to undermine his mental health and his devotion to the service of God.

At the age of forty, Reverend Hartman enjoys the esteem of the town of Winesburg, Ohio, due to his decade of service as an unpretentious and refined minister. By nature reticent and shy, he experiences considerable nervous tension while preparing and delivering the two sermons that he is expected to provide for the weekly services of his congregation, and he is wont to ascend to the bell tower of the church every Sunday morning to ask God to grant him the strength to preach his word with adequate power and conviction. Despite his devotion to God, the Reverend worries at times about the quality of his religious convictions. Perhaps, he thinks, he lacks the ardent flame

of spirituality that characterizes those who are truly called to spread the word of God.

Despite Reverend Hartman's desperate efforts to repress his awakened carnal drives, he becomes obsessed with the thought of Kate Swift and begins to entertain the blasphemous notion that God is somehow responsible for tempting him with sensual iniquities against his will. All his life he has striven to follow the narrow path of moral and physical righteousness. In addition, he begins to resent his wife to the point of almost despising her because she is embarrassed by passion and has consequently cheated him out of an active and fulfilling sex life. Despite repeated efforts to quell the allure of his transgressive fantasies, the minister finds it impossible to resume his former innocent frame of mind.

Having failed in fending off his newborn carnality, the Reverend finally decides to plunge into the sensuous folds of his fantasies about the schoolteacher, and he proceeds to ascend to the bell tower despite bitter winter weather. He is well aware that he is risking his health in choosing to wait in the tower for the appearance of the secret object of his desire. As the hours pass, the minister develops a life-threatening fever that shakes his body but not his resolve. When Kate Swift finally appears, she throws herself naked onto her bed and, distraught and crying, begins to pray fervently. Convinced that his dark and sensual night of the soul was sent to him from heaven, Reverend Hartman rediscovers his passion for God in the shape of her strong female physique, whose praying countenance reminds him of his own spiritual convictions.

Hartshorn, Priss. *The Group.* Mary McCarthy. 1954.

Priss Hartshorn is the relatively dull but well-intentioned member of the clique of eight young Vassar graduates, class of 1933. Although the group is fond of Priss, they call her the group "grind" or the student who studies diligently but receives very little fulfillment despite her efforts. Sharing a large dormitory suite with the group enables Priss to become intimate with her friends. She keeps track of them after graduation and is reunited with them on several occasions throughout her young adulthood. After she completes her undergraduate degree in economics, Priss looks forward to a job in the Consumer Division of the National Recovery Administration of the Depression era and to marrying Sloan Crockett, a handsome, ambitious young pediatrician.

The daughter of a broad-minded Vassar trustee and granddaughter of a reform mayor in New York, Priss is a small, meticulous young woman who carries on the family's liberal tradition by solemnly contemplating political and economic issues. When, at the close of the novel, KAY LEILAND STRONG, one of the members of the group, falls to her death from a twentieth-story window of the Vassar Club, Priss blames the tragedy on the Depression rather than on her friend's personal problems.

Priss's liberal approach to such political and economic topics annoys her more conservative husband and causes him to call her "Little Captain Boycott." Any deviation from his point of view bothers Sloan, and as Mrs. Crockett, Priss seems increasingly devoid of her own opinions. Having had three miscarriages due to a retroverted uterus, Priss quits her present job at the League of Women's Shoppers to spend the first five months of her fourth pregnancy in bed in the hope that she will have a healthy baby. The precaution proves successful, and after a protracted labor lasting twenty-two hours, Priss gives birth to a bouncing baby boy, Stephen, named in honor of the first Christian martyr.

The ambitious young Dr. Crockett possesses a number of newfangled notions concerning proper child care practices, and he inflicts his professional prescriptions on both baby and mother. Convinced that the bottle is an old-fashioned fad and that breast-feeding introduces important immunities into babies' bodies, Sloan insists that Priss breast-feed Stephen despite the fact that Stephen screams for an average of ten hours a day—both because her milk supply is insufficient and because the child's father insists that babies should be fed at intervals of four hours regardless of their tearful demands to the contrary. In addition, Sloan insists that to hold a crying child is to spoil it and invite further attention-getting misbehavior, so Stephen is only touched at mealtime unless a nurse takes pity on him and surreptitiously picks him up to soothe him.

Priss tries to be the perfect mother, but she is afraid of her child and, pitying his apparent discomfort, begins to doubt the efficacy of her husband's regime. She worries that she is being used by him to advertise his avant-garde pediatric theories. When she fails to toilet-train her child, who at the age of two and a half still wears diapers and produces smelly messes that embarrass and disgust her, Sloan blames her for not adhering more strictly to his prescribed child-rearing notions. Finally, exasperated by the rigidity of her husband's recipe for the perfect child, she attributes her son's unruly refusal to use the toilet as his malicious way of punishing her for the inhumane treatment and neglect that she inflicted on him through her passivity.

Haskins, Timothy. "Under the Lion's Paw." Hamlin Garland. 1891.

Timothy Haskins is a displaced farmer in this tale of midwestern life in the 1890s. Originally from Canada, Timothy and his wife Nettie have successfully worked the fertile lands of the plains states. They have recently been driven from their farm in Kansas, which was overrun by grasshoppers. Seeking an opportunity for work, they arrive in the small town of Rock River, Wisconsin, where they meet a generous farmer, Stephen Council, and his wife. The Councils house the Haskins temporarily and help Mr. Haskins and his son find work. Council tells Haskins about a farm in the area that has recently been vacated; however, he warns the newcomer about Jim Butler, a land speculator who has bought out much of the property in the area in order to sell or rent it at a profit.

Haskins, eager to start a new home in Wisconsin, agrees to see Butler. Council, who is more experienced in business matters, negotiates a deal with Jim Butler whereby the Haskins agree to rent and work the land for three years with the option to buy. Grateful for the opportunity to better their situation, the Haskins labor day and night to make the farm a success.

After three years, the absentee landlord, Jim Butler, returns to find fertile land, a neat garden, a well-filled barn, and a stocked pigpen. Haskins proudly shows off the land and discusses the hundreds of dollars he has invested in improving the house and grounds. Butler listens knowingly and asks Haskins whether he is interested in buying the farm. Haskins offers to pay Butler the $2,500 he had originally asked or maybe even $3,000. Now that the farm is so productive, Butler says, it has at least doubled in value; the new asking price is $5,500.

Butler's extortionist tactics outrage Haskins. After working beyond human capacity for three years to make a home for himself and his family, Haskins does not like being cheated. Ordinarily a hardworking and mild-mannered man, Haskins grabs a nearby pitchfork and threatens Butler, crying, "You'll never rob another man, damn ye!" As he moves to strike Butler, however, Haskins looks up and sees his two-year-old daughter playing happily in the grass. He drops the pitchfork to the ground and agrees to sign a deed and mortgage for the land.

Hasleman, Paul. "Silent Snow, Secret Snow." Conrad Aiken. 1950.

Paul Hasleman is a twelve-year-old boy caught in the grip of his own imagination. As the story unfolds, the world he creates in his psyche becomes more and more dominant until at last it obliterates the reality from which he longs to escape.

Paul's imaginary world is born one day when he awakes to find that the morning's usual sounds seem muffled. The postman's steps can usually be heard as he rounds the corner onto Paul's street, but on this morning they are not audible until he is already at the first house. As he lies in bed, Paul imagines that there is a thick blanket of snow on the ground, and he is excited by the promise of silence, peace, and sleep that it represents. When he goes to the window, however, he is surprised to see that the streets are bare and that there is no sign of snow.

Still, Paul begins to have a sense of snow falling all the time. His delusion is so vivid that each morning the postman's steps seem less distinct. Paul listens for the postman every day and discerns that he gets closer and closer to Paul's house before his footsteps are audible. Although Paul continues to go to the window only to see bare cobblestones below, he feels that the snow is growing heavier with each passing moment and is gradually muffling the world outside.

As his delusion continues, Paul finds he has trouble reconciling his world of silent snow with the reality of daily life. Determined to keep the snow secret, he makes an effort to respond to his parents' questions and to continue to do his schoolwork, going through the perfunctory motions of day-to-day life as best he can. He spends each day watching the world through a wall of falling snow, sometimes taking pride in his ability to see the blackboard through the flurry and to hear the school bell when it is muffled by the storm. Despite his best efforts, his parents and teacher begin to notice that he is constantly distracted.

Paul continues to take great pleasure in his snowy world and the peace and comfort it provides, yet he still feels he must keep his private world a secret even if it means causing others pain. His worried parents consult a doctor who examines him one evening. The doctor finds nothing wrong with the boy physically, and Paul insists he feels fine. But when the doctor begins to question him about his thoughts, Paul feels threatened. He thinks of the snow that will greet him in his room, snow with a voice that promises to tell him a story and that encourages him to banish the adults in the house. When the doctor presses him, Paul at last blurts out that he has been thinking about snow. Then, as the adults stare at him, he excuses himself and retreats to his room.

Beautiful waves of snow engulf him there, and he feels comforted by the laughing voice he hears. When his mother enters and clutches him, he cries out "I hate you!" The words seem to exorcise all remnants of the concrete world from Paul's life, and in the next moment he is swallowed up by the comforting snow.

Hawkins, Laura. *The Gilded Age.* Samuel L. Clemens (Mark Twain) and Charles Dudley Warner. 1873.

Born to the Van Brunt family, young Laura Hawkins is rescued by the westward-moving Hawkins family when her parents are presumed to have been killed in a steamboat explosion. She is raised by the Hawkinses and takes on some of the rhetorical flourish and optimistic vision of her stepfather and his friend, the unscrupulous businessman Beriah Sellers.

The most beautiful and intelligent young woman of Hawkeye, Missouri, Laura is as voracious for romantic conquest as Colonel Sellers is for financial speculation. With each romantic novel she reads, she further resents the limitations of her own conditions. During the Civil War she runs off with and marries a swashbuckling southern officer named Colonel Selby. A few months later he abandons her, informing her that he has long had a real wife, and she returns to Hawkeye in disgrace.

Laura's fortunes rise when Senator Dilworthy, the pious and ethical representative of an adjacent state, invites her

to Washington, D.C., to help him promote his programs among members of Congress. In the capital, Laura's charms are refined. Amid rumors of her great wealth and land possession, she becomes the most popular young woman of Washington society.

As a behind-the-scenes operative for Dilworthy, Laura flirts, cajoles, and ultimately blackmails her way into control of various influential congressmen and lobbyists. With Machiavellian efficiency, she manipulates hardened and corrupt bureaucrats into supporting Dilworthy's land grant bill that involves land owned by Laura's own family.

At the height of her glory, however, Laura's nemesis Colonel Selby reappears. He is now a distinguished southern gentleman seeking reparation for the Federal Army's destruction of his cotton crop. All of Laura's energies immediately center on him. She first determines to destroy him, but he charms his way back into her heart with ease. Rumors of their affair circulate throughout the capital city.

When Selby plans a trip to Europe with his family instead of with Laura, she once again feels betrayed. She trails him to a New York hotel, calls him down to the lobby, and shoots him dead.

Languishing unrepentant in a New York prison, she awaits her trial with resignation. She is acquitted partly because of Colonel Beriah Sellers's testimony regarding her mental state.

With no means of support and no prospects for marriage, Laura sets out on a lecture tour. When that proves disastrous, her spirit is crushed, and with nothing more to live for, she dies a broken woman.

Hawley, Ethan Allen. *The Winter of Our Discontent.* John Steinbeck. 1962.

Ethan Allen Hawley, the heir of a lost fortune and a descendant of one of the oldest families in New Baytown, Long Island, has been reduced to working as a grocery clerk in the block that his family used to own. In his present circumstances he can only dream of the former grandeur and romance of a grandfather who, as owner and captain of whaling ships, had amassed the family fortune.

Early in the novel, Ethan finds his family discontented with their social and economic standing. His wife Mary and his children, Allen and Ellen, chide him about his lowly position in the face of the family's former status in New Baytown. When the discontent of his family takes the form of bitter denunciations of his lack of ambition, Ethan must devise a plan to appease their frustration.

Mr. Baker, the town banker and a member of another old New Baytown family, offers Ethan a route to financial success in the form of an inside tip on some New Baytown real estate. On the surface, Ethan hesitates to invest because he is afraid to use money inherited by his wife, but actually he is revolted by the conniving and moral compromise he must make in order to become economically successful. But because of his family's continued entreaties, he sacrifices his sense of integrity and fair play.

Within several months Ethan sets in motion a series of events designed to make his fortune. Among his plans is a plot to gain ownership of the grocery store where he works. He calls the Immigration Bureau and informs the authorities of his suspicions that his boss, Alfio Marullo, entered the country illegally. While this drama plays itself out, Ethan begins work on acquiring the capital he will need to run the grocery store once he owns it. Ethan plans to rob the bank across the alley from the store.

Once he has decided to enter the world he considers money-grubbing, self-interested, and materialistic, Ethan proves himself a shrewd and merciless high-stakes player. Through Baker he learns that a childhood friend, Danny Taylor, now a drunkard, owns land that certain investors would like to acquire as a site for an airport. Ethan secretly gives Danny several thousand dollars to be used ostensibly for alcohol abuse treatment. Both Danny and Ethan know that the money, which has been given in cash, will result in something other than Danny's rehabilitation.

During the Fourth of July weekend, Ethan carries out his plans. He has perfected the scheme for robbing the bank, which due to the holiday weekend has a large amount of cash on hand. He also learns that Marullo will be deported, leaving the way for him to purchase the store. With this information in hand, Ethan walks out of the store to rob the bank. Just as he does so, he is hailed by a young man whom he recognizes as the investigator from the immigration office, and he is forced to abandon the attempt. Ironically, a subsequent conversation with the young man reveals that the deported Marullo has decided to give the grocery store to Ethan for the honesty he has displayed while working for him.

Possessed of this startling news, Ethan leaves for the holiday weekend with his wife. They are summoned home during the middle of their trip to celebrate their son's attaining Honorable Mention in a national essay contest. The Hawleys find themselves inundated with good tidings. In the midst of these celebrations, the last of Ethan's schemes climaxes. Danny, owner of the choice piece of real estate, has drunk himself to death and left a promissory note giving Ethan control of the land.

Although each of his machinations has proved profitable, Ethan is discontented and filled with remorse. He cannot take pleasure in his gains, and while he notes the look of admiration Mr. Baker gives him when the banker realizes that Ethan has outwitted him in obtaining Danny's land, he does not feel triumphant, only guilt-ridden. The final blow comes through his children. He arrives home late one night to find an official from the board that had read the essay Allen had entered. The man informs him that Allen plagiarized his entire essay. Based on the information he gathers from the conversation, Ethan realizes that it was his daughter Ellen who turned Allen in.

When his son is not concerned with his crime but only with Ellen's betrayal, Ethan is deeply hurt. The boy's rationalization that "everybody does it" and his suggestion that his father, too, is corrupt convince Ethan of the immorality of his recent machinations. He leaves home and heads to the old whaling dock where he used to go with his grandfather. From there he walks into the ocean and prepares to slit his wrists with razor blades. As he reaches into his pocket for the blades, he feels a translucent stone, a talisman to him and his daughter. The touch of the stone reminds him that the future would be lost if he dies before he can pass the stone on to Ellen, who could rekindle the light of integrity and self-respect in the Hawley family. He will not die before he can return the talisman to its new owner.

Hayman, Philip. *Summer in Williamsburg*. Daniel Fuchs. 1934.

Philip Hayman, twenty years old, lives with his middle-aged parents in Williamsburg, a largely Jewish neighborhood in Brooklyn, New York, in the 1920s. The novel opens at the beginning of summer with the suicide of the local butcher in Philip's apartment building. This drastic action confounds the neighbors. The butcher had always appeared cheerful, and he leaves behind a beautiful wife and two small children. Equally bewildered, Philip consults Miller, an old scholar and miser, for a solution to this mystery. Miller tells Philip that the reason for anyone's actions can best be explained by that person's relationship to money. At first Philip resists this idea, but as the summer wears on, he comes to see that the decisions of those around him (which often turn out to be mistakes) usually have an economic motivation.

The shabby apartment houses of Williamsburg shelter many desperate people, several of whom vie for influence over Philip. Harry, Philip's older brother, has begun working for their uncle NICHOLAS PAPRAVEL, a gangster who hopes to establish a busing monopoly. Harry is estranged from their father, who disapproves of such dishonest work. Philip feels torn between his father, who earns a meager but honest living as a grocer, and Harry, who is enjoying the material comforts that their parents could never provide.

The expensive tastes of Philip's longtime girlfriend Tessie also make Philip long for wealth. When a successful garment salesman emerges as a rival for Tessie's affections, he quickly wins the young woman over with his promise of financial security. Within a short time Tessie marries the salesman. Only Cohen, an unattractive and lonely ne'er-do-well in the building, seems unconcerned with money. Cohen fancies himself an intellectual, and he tells Philip that the matters of the mind are the only important things in life. Philip finds this refreshing but has his doubts about Cohen's philosophies, which change every week.

With hopes to control the transportation of tourists

from the city to upstate New York, Papravel brings his gang, including Harry, to the Catskills. Harry writes Philip and entreats him to take advantage of the opportunities that Papravel provides. Depressed over Tessie's marriage, Philip agrees to visit, and while he is in the Catskills, Harry plays up the seductive aspects of resort life: liquor, money, and beautiful, available women. Philip, however, senses the ruthless violence that supports all this, and after a few weeks he returns to his parents' home.

Much happens in Williamsburg while Philip is away. Miller dies and leaves his family fighting over the inheritance; Cohen tries to commit suicide. Philip must also contend with the renewed attentions of Tessie, who now realizes that she married for the wrong reasons. She sends letters to the Hayman household and invites Philip to her apartment, all at great risk to her marriage.

Harry enjoys the fast life-style in the Catskills until a man dies as a result of a botched strike operation, whereupon Harry moves to Chicago and settles for less money in exchange for an honest living at a tie factory. This decision pleases Philip, but he wonders how Harry will handle being a part of the working class again. Philip himself has once again felt the brunt of his social standing in the loss of a girlfriend whose parents disapproved of him.

Near the end of summer, the butcher's wife jumps off the bridge with her two children. Cohen, having failed as a writer, a lover, and even as a political activist, becomes even more depressed. One night Philip tries to cheer Cohen's spirits with some wine. Cohen gets so drunk that Philip must undress him and put him to bed. When a fire breaks out in the apartment house that night, Philip tries to rescue the inebriated Cohen, but his friend, wary of ridicule, will not run outside without being dressed. Philip's family survives, but Cohen dies from the fumes.

Autumn finds Philip more experienced but still undetermined about his future. The novel ends with Philip's acceptance of the importance of money and his hopes of emulating Harry's discovery of honest but profitable work.

Haze, Charlotte Becker. *Lolita.* Vladimir Nabokov. 1955.

Charlotte Haze, née Becker, an unfortunate woman in her middle thirties, provides a striking contrast to her beautiful twelve-year-old daughter DOLORES "LOLITA" HAZE. Although not unattractive, Charlotte looks like a watered-down version of Marlene Dietrich: Her face is squarish, her forehead shiny, and her eyebrows plucked.

Charlotte lived with her first husband in the midwestern town of Pisky. Mr. Haze, who was twenty years her senior, died leaving Charlotte alone with the willful Lolita (her other child, a boy born two years after Lolita, died in 1939). In 1945, Charlotte and Lolita moved to the town of Ramsdale and took up residence in the home of Char-

lotte's deceased mother-in-law. During her two years in Ramsdale, Charlotte worked for her church and tried to meet the mothers of Lolita's more socially worthy classmates and became, according to the narrator HUMBERT HUMBERT, an acceptable but not prominent member of the town.

In the summer of 1947, Charlotte offers lodging to Humbert Humbert, who takes it only because he finds her young daughter sexually attractive. For her part, Charlotte finds her European lodger desirable; Lolita is an unappreciated rival. Charlotte decides to send the star-struck Lolita to summer camp, and after several less than subtle candlelit dinners, writes a letter declaring her love for Humbert. He accepts her marriage proposal in order to remain near Lolita.

Charlotte and Humbert marry hastily yet properly, and Charlotte, much impressed by her new husband's inherited income, improves their household and makes plans for their future. Her unwavering belief in the tenets of her church intimidate Humbert, and her firmly middle-class tastes evoke only condescension. Humbert finds his wife's insatiable jealousy a cause for some amusement. Charlotte wants to know every detail of her new husband's past romantic involvements but never realizes that her true competition is her preadolescent daughter. She views Lolita as an ill-behaved child whom she would prefer to be away from home. When she informs Humbert that Lolita will go directly from her summer camp to a boarding school and never again live with them in Ramsdale, Humbert becomes frantic and considers murdering his wife.

After fifty days of marriage, Charlotte succumbs to her possessive desire to know more about her husband and breaks into the table drawer in which Humbert keeps his diary. Reading it, she learns of his lust for her daughter as well as his disdain for her. In a frenzy, she confronts Humbert with her discovery. She then quickly writes a letter warning the child and another telling Humbert her thoughts for their future. Running from the house to deposit these letters in a mailbox, Charlotte is struck and killed by a neighbor's car, leaving Humbert Humbert free to possess Lolita.

Haze, Dolores "Lolita." *Lolita.* Vladimir Nabokov. 1955.

Dolores "Lolita" Haze, a nubile adolescent girl, has lived with her widowed mother in the New England town of Ramsdale for two years. Known at school by the more formal name Dolores, Lolita is an average student with minor discipline problems. She has friends among her classmates, but these friends are not always of the social standing that her mother would like. At twelve years of age, Lolita still resists taking showers, reads comic books voraciously, and relentlessly engages her mother, CHARLOTTE (BECKER HAZE), in adolescent arguments. But despite these childlike tendencies, Lolita has entered puberty; she develops a sudden crush on the Hazes' thirty-seven-year-old lodger and the book's narrator HUMBERT HUMBERT.

For Humbert, whose sexual desires are limited to "nymphets" between the ages of nine and fourteen, Lolita is the primary object of his insuppressible lust. Lolita also fantasizes about Humbert, but both she and Humbert are thwarted by Charlotte Haze's own love for her lodger. When summer comes, Charlotte sends Lolita to camp and proposes marriage to Humbert; Humbert accepts in order to gain uninterrupted access to Lolita.

Lolita is not called back from camp for the hasty wedding. Distracted by the activities at camp, she seems unaffected by the union. Once married, Charlotte declares that Lolita, whom she considers a rather homely and unimpressive child, should never again live at home: She will go from summer camps to boarding schools until she is in college. This plan for Lolita's life suddenly alters when Charlotte reads Humbert's diary and discovers his mocking disregard for his wife and his infatuation with her young child. However, as Charlotte rushes to mail a letter warning Lolita of Humbert, a car strikes and kills her.

Now Lolita's legal guardian, Humbert collects his fantasy child from camp and takes her to a remote inn, The Enchanted Hunters. At dinner he gives her a sleeping pill so that she will be unconscious when he molests her. The pill turns out to be a placebo, and Lolita sleeps only fitfully. In the morning, however, Lolita tells Humbert that each day for the past month she and another camper have had sex with the camp mistress's son. Lolita thinks sex is a game kids play and shows surprise when Humbert claims never to have heard of it.

Still in pain after having had sex with an adult, twelve-year-old Lolita is taken on a wandering cross-country drive by her new father. Humbert ensures Lolita's silence with threats of a life in an orphan's home or a juvenile center or with a cruel aunt. In addition, they develop a pecuniary system wherein Humbert pays Lolita for sexual favors. After approximately a year of driving, they settle in the town of Beardsley.

Lolita enters the Beardsley School and becomes involved in the school play. She tries to gain some independence from jealous Humbert and also begins a secret relationship with Clare Quilty, a young male playwright. When the conditions at their home reach an unbearable level of tension, Lolita and Humbert embark on their second cross-country drive. This time Lolita maps the route, thus allowing Quilty to follow them and steal moments with her.

Lolita and then Humbert fall ill in Elphinstone, Colorado. While Humbert recovers at his hotel, she escapes with Quilty. Humbert cannot discover the identity of Lolita's secret lover, and she remains lost to him for four years. Lolita finally sends a letter to Humbert asking him for money. She explains that since leaving Quilty she has

married Richard Schiller, whom she met while working at a diner. Now pregnant and poverty-stricken, she has made an unglamorous home in a rural area where her husband can hardly find work.

Hazel. "Gorilla, My Love." Toni Cade Bambara. 1972.

Hazel is a smart, angry child attuned to injustice and willing to go to any lengths to correct a moral outrage. In this cautionary tale, Hazel is faced for the first time with an injustice she is powerless to change: her favorite uncle's betrayal of his promise to marry her when she grows up.

As the tale opens, Hazel is with her uncle Hunca Bubba and her brother Baby Jason in a truck her grandfather is driving. Hazel, a natural leader, navigates for them all, giving directions to her grandfather from a map on her knee. Meanwhile, Hunca Bubba is passing around a picture of his new fiancée. In the picture behind the fiancée there is a movie theater; this triggers Hazel's memory of a riot she once created.

Hazel narrates this adventure. She, Baby Jason, and her other brother, Big Brood, are enticed into a movie house by the title, *Gorilla, My Love*, on the marquee. They soon find out they have been swindled: The film turns out to be a Christian passion play, and this angers an already rambunctious audience.

At first Hazel's response is to daydream. She mockingly invents a crucifixion scene featuring Big Brood as Christ, with her whole family shouting for him to come down and stop his foolishness. But as the crowd in the movie house grows more rowdy, Hazel realizes that daydreaming will not change the fact that she has been swindled. She decides to defy the monstrously fat matron who keeps the peace in the movie house, and she starts the crowd in a chant to get their money back.

Hazel goes so far as to lead a charge against this injustice by marching to the manager's booth. She confronts him, then discovers that neither the audience nor her brothers have followed her. When the manager is not impressed by the appearance of a lone scrappy child, Hazel takes his matches, lights a fire in the lobby, and leaves before anyone notices her.

When Hazel returns home, her act of righteous fury is debated by the family. After she argues her case with eloquence, her parents come to see Hazel's point of view. They decide not to punish her and are proud that she has such a deep sense of right and wrong.

After this flashback, Hazel's attention returns to the car. She asks her uncle in cold fury if he remembers the promise he had made some time ago that he would marry her. Hunca Bubba suddenly realizes she is deeply hurt by his engagement; that she sees it as a betrayal like the one that occurred in the theater.

The grandfather tries to quiet her with an unconvincing, sophistic argument. He says that the man who made the promise was young and inexperienced, and if the family would call Hunca Bubba by his proper name, Jefferson Winston Vale, his old promises would no longer apply. To Hazel, this argument is as much of a lie as calling a Jesus movie *Gorilla, My Love*. She bursts into tears at the injustice of a world run by adults who ceaselessly lie and deceive, who hold out promises that turn out to be empty.

Head (Mr.) "The Artificial Nigger." Flannery O'Connor. 1948.

Mr. Head is a fierce old man who fancies himself a wise and experienced teacher for young people. He is especially eager to prove this wisdom to his ten-year-old grandson NELSON, an illegitimate boy he has raised alone since the deaths of his wife and daughter. Mr. Head has little tolerance for Nelson's sharp tongue and know-it-all attitude, particularly the boy's claim that he is "from the city" simply because he was born in Atlanta. Accordingly, Mr. Head has devised a plan to rid Nelson once and for all of his unfounded pride and contempt for his grandfather: He will take Nelson to Atlanta for a day, and both the strange sights of the city and Mr. Head's leadership will overwhelm the boy and put him in his place.

On the train to Atlanta, Mr. Head takes care to point out a black family to Nelson, who has never seen a black person in his life, and thereby quickly establishes his own worldliness and superiority. But insurmountable changes have been made in Atlanta in the fifteen years since Mr. Head's last trip to the city. He is soon disoriented by the noise and teeming pedestrians, and in order to keep the train station in view at all times, he leads Nelson around and around in a huge circle.

Nelson soon begins to complain that the old man doesn't know his way. Desperate to maintain control over the situation, Mr. Head takes a new turn into a different part of town. It is not long before the two are lost in the poor black section of the city. Mr. Head, who is unabashedly prejudiced, refuses to ask a black person for directions, but when Nelson does, Mr. Head listens to the advice of an old black woman to take a trolley car back. He decides that if they just follow the trolley tracks, they will eventually come into the station. Not long after, however, Nelson decides he is too tired to continue; he sits down and falls asleep on the sidewalk.

Mr. Head looks at the sleeping boy and feels that he will teach the impudent Nelson a lesson. He walks off across the street and hides himself in an alley so that when Nelson wakes up alone, he will finally be scared enough to make him realize his dependence on Mr. Head. But when the boy awakens, his disorientation and terror are so great that he runs and collides with an elderly woman, who screams that Nelson has broken her ankle and that she is going to have the police take care of "this boy's daddy."

Mr. Head hangs back from the scene, not wanting to acknowledge the extent of his inability to control what is going on. Nelson suddenly sees him and runs to him. Mr. Head is terrified that the police are going to cart him away, and he denies any connection with Nelson, walking stiffly past the horrified looks of the gathered crowd.

He soon steals a look behind him to see Nelson following a good distance behind, staring at his grandfather with an icy glare. Mr. Head is so ashamed of his behavior that he tries to make it up to Nelson by suggesting they go for a soda. When Nelson doesn't respond, Mr. Head feels the impact of his grandson's hate and begins to imagine an old age bereft of respect and love.

The two eventually wander into a wealthier, white section of town, and Mr. Head asks directions back to the train. He already feels more hopeful, and his dignity begins to return. As they continue on toward the train stop, they pass a mansion with a small plaster figure of a black man on the lawn, and Mr. Head tells Nelson it is an "artificial nigger." Grandfather and grandson stop before the spectacle and stare at this strange symbol of the wealthy white person's ability to shrink and contain a black person. Somehow the image of control renews Nelson's respect, and they return to the country with the hierarchy between them properly restored.

Hearn, Lieutenant Robert. *The Naked and the Dead.* Norman Mailer. 1948.

Second Lieutenant Robert Hearn is an idealist who struggles ineffectually to be heroic while fighting in World War II. Before joining the service, Hearn tried to rebel against affluent Chicago society by espousing liberal ideas and falling in with communist literati, who soon rejected him as a quixotic bourgeois. Now, burdened by guilt and skepticism, he is unable to impose his will or take command with the passion and confidence expressed by his fellow officers, GENERAL EDWARD CUMMINGS and SERGEANT SAM CROFT.

Hearn struggles with the guilt he feels about his officer's privileges and his wealthy background throughout the American campaign against the Japanese on the island of Anopopei. General Cummings, who has adopted Hearn as his confidant and protégé, is the initial repository for his resentment, awe, and envy. If the General had not chosen him as his aide, Hearn would have been in combat—a situation he would have welcomed. The relative monotony of life at the headquarters enables the General to whittle away at Hearn's weak liberalism during their intellectual discussions and to manipulate him in petty but significant ways.

General Cummings makes various attempts to convert Hearn to his own system of ethics, based on the accumulation of power and the inducement of fear. For example, the General assigns Hearn the task of building an officers' recreation tent. The enlisted men, charged with the drudgery of carrying out the assignment, grow hostile;

Hearn finds himself disgusted by their laziness and contemptuous of their lack of education. He gradually realizes that the General gave him the assignment to prove to him that he could not rid himself of the prejudices of his class.

Hearn's relationship with Cummings, which had previously been only intellectually combative, turns deeply antagonistic after a late-night encounter during which Cummings seems to make a sexual overture to Hearn. Hearn is unable to sufficiently mask his revulsion for his superior officer, and Cummings, aware that he has made himself vulnerable, grows to despise him. Hearn tries to maintain his integrity with silent defiance. However, the General eventually succeeds in humiliating him by tossing a cigarette at his feet and ordering him to pick it up. In a gesture symbolic of his subjugation, Hearn complies.

Throughout the novel, Hearn wrestles with his ideals and with his distaste for the military; but when he is transferred to a post as troop commander of the reconnaissance platoon headed by Sergeant Croft, he, too, acquires a taste for power. He fails to lead the men assigned to him effectively, and they resent his attempts to ingratiate himself with them. Croft, sensing Hearn's weakness, initiates an unspoken struggle with him for control of the platoon.

While approaching a pass on Mount Anaka, Hearn's patrol mission encounters a Japanese ambush. Hearn, who has never been in combat before, is suddenly paralyzed with terror. Pulling himself together with great effort, he orders the men to retreat. That evening while he is trying to decide on a further course of action, he realizes that the patrol has little chance of surviving if attacked; nevertheless, he would rather press ahead than return and face Cummings empty-handed. The realization that he would consider risking the lives of nine men in order to win Cummings's approval shocks Hearn but does not dissuade him from attempting the advance.

In continuing to ponder his situation, Hearn experiences another revelation: He enjoys the power he wields. He had always associated the desire for control with the totalitarian impulse in people like Cummings, but he found it in himself. Hearn resolves to turn back and resign his commission. Croft refuses to give in, however, and persuades Sergeant Martinez, the scout, to make the false report that the way ahead is clear. Hearn no longer has an excuse to retreat. The next morning Hearn, rested and eager, leads the platoon forward. He is shot and killed the moment they reach the pass.

Hector. *The Warriors.* Sol Yurick. 1965.

Hector is a member of a New York street gang called the Coney Island Dominators in this gritty urban novel of the 1960s. Within the gang, he is known as an "uncle," the second in command to the gang's leader, or "father," Arnold. Tough and extremely good-looking, Hector follows a system of ethics based solely on loyalty to the gang.

In his world of poverty and desperation, no other morality exists.

The novel opens as the gang travels to Van Cortland Park in the Bronx on July 4 to attend an unprecedented meeting of all New York's gangs. The meeting has been called by a charismatic figure named Ismael, leader of the largest gang in the city, the Delancey Thrones. Like the other gang members there, Hector is immediately impressed by Ismael's powerful presence and by his vision of a unified system of gangs.

Hector agrees that the gangs in the city will never achieve anything unless they unite. But as he listens to the speech and cheers along with the rest of the crowd, a scuffle breaks out, and soon the police arrive to break up the melee. As soon as Hector and the other gang members hear the sirens, they conclude that Ismael has set them up; they beat a hasty retreat while gunfire rains down on them.

As the Dominators are leaving, Arnold pauses to look at Ismael, now a bloody corpse on the ground. He is immediately jumped by vengeful members of the Thrones and cut off from the rest of his gang. Hector, the "uncle," must take over as the "father" and lead the gang safely home. He puts in a desperate call to a social worker the gang knows, and they wait for an hour to be picked up. When the social worker fails to appear, they take the subway, only to be forced back to the surface because of repairs being made on the track.

Hector sets out with his "family" through enemy gang territory. They immediately run into the leader of the Borinquen Blazers, Jesus Mendez. Hector chats with Jesus, and the two seem to be on good terms until Jesus's girlfriend decides to alleviate her boredom by instigating a fight. She criticizes Jesus, who then tells Hector his gang may not pass without taking off their Dominator pins. Hector, considering this a point of pride, refuses.

As the Dominators walk nervously through the streets, waiting for sniper fire or an outright attack, they are followed by one of the Blazers, who, egged on by Jesus's girlfriend, will not let the matter of the insignia drop. Hector decides to capture the girlfriend as a hostage and thereby ensure their safe passage. The gang succeeds in their plan; once beyond the Blazer perimeter, they gang-rape the young woman and leave her behind. Having passed beyond the track work, they return to the subway at Ninety-sixth Street, only to encounter the police. Because one of them is carrying a knife, they separate and flee.

Hector and two henchmen, Lunkface and Bimbo, head down Riverside Drive. Lunkface wants to remove his pin to avoid more trouble, but Hector insists that he leave it on, partly because of gang ethics and partly to show that he is in command of the "family." Continuing their journey, they meet a middle-aged nurse, sitting on a bench. She makes sexual overtures toward Hector; at the urging of Lunkface and against his own inclinations, Hector takes her into the park, where the gang attempts to rape her. The nurse screams for help, and they run away but are immediately apprehended by the police, who happen to be nearby.

As the woman tearfully explains that she was assaulted by the young men, the police rough up the gang members. Hector claims that she gave them "the come on"; the police punch him in the face, knocking loose a tooth. It seems that the police, smelling liquor on the woman's breath, would not normally be sympathetic to her complaints, but it's a bad night for gang members.

Hector and his compatriots are taken off to jail, and this is the last that is heard of them. At the novel's end one of the other gang members arrives home safely, and for the first time the reader is introduced to living conditions that may have shaped Hector's attitudes and behavior: a tiny, filthy apartment; a mother engaging openly in sexual intercourse with her boyfriend; a baby languishing, unattended, in a crib.

Henderson, Eugene. *Henderson the Rain King.* Saul Bellow. 1959.

Eugene Henderson, a millionaire's son and a man of strong passions and appetites, tells the story of how he came to travel to Africa. An enormous man, violent in hate and love, Henderson is an alcoholic in the process of destroying his second marriage. An inner voice drives him, saying, "I want, I want, I want," but Henderson never knows quite what he wants. When the woman who cooks for his family dies in their kitchen, he pins a note on her that says "Do not disturb" and flees to Africa with his friend Charlie and Charlie's wife. Once there, however, he sets out on his own into the wilderness, along with a hired sidekick named Romilayu.

The first tribe they meet are the Arnewi, a gentle group of people who love their cattle like their own children. They are heartbroken because a plague of frogs is clogging their water reservoir, but it is forbidden for the Arnewi to harm the frogs in any way, so their cattle are dying.

Henderson extravagantly promises to get rid of the frogs with gunpowder. He feels that by doing this for the Arnewi he can make up for all the disorder and violence he has caused in his life. He becomes wildly excited by his mission and is touched by the great trust the Arnewi have in him. He makes the gunpowder charge too strong, however, and blows through the wall of the reservoir, with the result that all the water is lost. Henderson is horribly upset; he sees his mistake a symbol of his extravagant, destructive passion. He ruins everything because he overdoes everything. He leaves with Romilayu in despair.

The next tribe that the two meet, the Wariri, are, in contrast to the Arnewi, a suspicious and somewhat hostile people. When Henderson comes upon them, they disarm him and take him into custody. He believes he is going to be killed, but instead they take him to a ceremony to bring

rain. They ask him to lift a heavy statue of a goddess; when he does, the rain comes, and he is proclaimed the Rain King. The Wariri begin to treat him with great respect, but he does not completely trust them.

He becomes close friends with the king of the tribe, who has many enemies among his people. Henderson admires the steadiness and simplicity of the king's nature and fears for the man's life. He tries to warn the king, who listens to him with equanimity but refuses to worry.

The king must kill a certain lion in order to prove his legitimacy, but when he tries, the lion kills him because someone has frayed the rope of the trap. It seems to Henderson that the king knew this would happen and accepted it. Henderson escapes the tribe, taking with him a lion cub who is said by the Wariri to carry the king's soul, and returns to America, where at last he can feel at peace.

Henry, Frederic. *A Farewell to Arms.* Ernest Hemingway. 1929.

Frederic Henry, an American volunteer ambulance driver for the Italian army during World War I, is a reticent, matter-of-fact, and jaded young man. In the midst of the war's horrors, Frederic cultivates a pleasant life of camaraderie and drink. Only after falling unexpectedly in love with CATHERINE BARKLEY does he abandon his cynical attitudes—until she dies, suddenly and tragically, and his hopes are extinguished for good.

Frederic meets Catherine, a British nurse, while serving on the Alpine front. They have an affair, but neither of them wishes to become emotionally involved. After his leg is severely injured in a bombardment, however, Frederic goes to Milan to recover from his wounds; Catherine transfers to the hospital there in order to be near him, and they soon realize they have fallen in love.

Until his operation, Frederic remains confined to bed, but within a short time he can leave the hospital on crutches. He and Catherine pass an idyllic summer together. They think of getting married, but the formalities are too complicated under Italian law. They spend the summer in cafés and at the races, but when autumn comes, Frederic receives orders to return to the front. At the same time Catherine discovers she is three months pregnant. They plan to meet again when Frederic gets his next leave; Catherine will make arrangements to have the baby on her own.

Frederic rejoins his unit just in time for the debacle of the Italian attack on Caporetto. The weather turns wet and cold, and as much as he disliked the war before his injury, Frederic now comes to hate it. The general violence and waste, and the hypocrisy and corruption of the Italian forces, infuriate him. In view of the daily atrocities of modern war, the rhetoric of patriotism comes to disgust him.

Although not involved in the actual fighting, Frederic's unit must retreat after the German breakthrough at Caporetto. Because of torrential rain, Frederic's truck sinks into a sea of mud. He and his friends start walking. In the confusion of the route, their little group gets fired upon by both Germans and Italians, and several are killed. Italian militia capture the survivors and kill any officers they find separated from their troops. Suspected of being a spy because of his foreign accent, Frederic narrowly escapes execution by leaping into a river.

Once in the clear, he decides to desert and flees to Milan, where he rejoins Catherine. They plan an escape to Switzerland and stay briefly in Stresa with Count Greffi, a ninety-four-year-old diplomat Frederic had met on a previous trip to the area. The lovers flee Italy by rowing across the lake to Switzerland in the dead of night.

Frederic and Catherine spend another idyllic period in Switzerland, living in a small cabin in the woods. But when the time comes for Catherine to give birth, she experiences complications and dies in labor; the child is stillborn. Frederic forces his way into Catherine's room after she is dead, but once inside, he feels nothing. The novel ends as he leaves and walks back to his hotel in the rain.

Henry, Velma. *The Salt Eaters.* Toni Cade Bambara. 1980.

Velma Henry, an organizer and activist, is driven to attempt suicide when her close-knit community splinters. She is able to hold the opposing groups together until events in her personal life begin to exert additional pressure. MINNIE RANSOM, a healer, visits her in the hospital, but Velma resists her efforts.

During the course of Minnie's visit, Velma remembers scenes from her childhood up through her years of political struggle. There were only rare moments when others cared for Velma and attended to her needs. She recalls when pneumonia threatened her and she was watched over by her closest relatives, M'Dear Sophie and Daddy Dolphy. Her godmother, the psychic Sophie Heywood, sensed Velma's talents even at her birth and noticed moments when Velma was transfixed by something others could not see. Velma had visions of her ancestors, whom she calls the "mud mothers." They are witchlike cave dwellers with a supernatural strength that Velma possesses in some measure.

As an adult, Velma works with ferocious energy for a variety of political causes. She is particularly fervent about antinuclear activism. Her town, Claybourne, Georgia, is the location of a plant called Transchemical, and the damage to the environment, as well as to the health of the workers, is apparent. Velma and her closest friends belong to an organization called The Academy of the 7 Arts, which serves as the headquarters for Claybourne's political activists and its spiritual instructors. The differences between the two factions increase in the late 1970s, and Velma is the only one with the ability to negotiate.

A combination of factors leads to Velma's attempted

suicide. Her responsibilities at the academy are vast and include bookkeeping, supervising, fund-raising, and organizing conferences and seminars. Velma finally leaves when she is offered a job at Transchemical. Obie, the father of their child, protests, arguing that Velma cannot be a proper mother to Lil James if she takes the job, which would take her out of town frequently. Velma points out that Obie was the first to break the trust between them by having affairs. After her suicide attempt, however, Velma's friends see the cause as her despair over the split in the community centered at the academy.

Minnie Ransom brings her followers, called The Master's Mind, to the Southwest Community Infirmary to perform a healing on Velma. Everyone is aware of Velma's resistance; even Sophie Heywood gives up and leaves the circle. Minnie repeatedly demands to know if Velma is ready to shoulder the burden of health. Finally, after running through memories of her entire life, Velma responds to the healers, getting up from the stool where she has been hunched and beginning to dance. Velma knows that the challenges facing her are greater than the ones she has seen. The entire town experiences a strange jolt at the moment Velma chooses to be whole once more.

Henshawe, Myra. *My Mortal Enemy.* Willa Cather. 1926.

This novel, set in the early twentieth century, presents Myra Henshawe at two moments in her life: as a middle-aged woman living comfortably in New York City and as an embittered old woman, dying in a run-down hotel on the West Coast. The rest of her story is filled in by the narrator, Nellie, a young woman from Myra's hometown of Parthia, Illinois.

Although she has known about Myra for as long as she can remember, Nellie first meets her when she is invited to spend the Christmas holidays with the Henshawes. For years Myra and her runaway marriage were the most interesting topics of conversation, indeed the only interesting things to talk about, in Parthia. An orphan raised by her rich old uncle, Myra had once had everything: the most beautiful clothes, the most beautiful jewels, and a fine riding horse. She gave up all of this to marry Oswald Henshawe, a railroad worker. But Myra's marriage did not bring her happiness.

In middle age Myra has become rather extravagant, although her only real extravagance, Nellie observes, is that she cares about so many people so much. Oswald complains that she is always helping some love affair along while going to great lengths to preserve the romance of her own marriage. Even so, there is a sense that for Myra love is not enough. The afternoon before Nellie is to leave, she witnesses a heated argument between Myra and Oswald over a mysterious key. What is so shocking about the argument is not what is said but Myra's profound certainty that her husband and her marriage have failed her.

It is ten years before Nellie sees the Henshawes again. When she runs into them on the West Coast, Oswald has lost his job with the railroad and with it their Madison Avenue apartment and all that was associated with their life in New York. Myra, too frail to leave her bed, reflects on her life and her marriage. She tells Nellie that she and her husband have been the best of friends and the worst of enemies, that they have virtually destroyed each other. Defeated by love, she attempts to reclaim all that she has given up for it: her Catholic faith, her fortune, and her happiness.

Myra is drawn in her final days to a quiet headland on the Pacific Ocean where she imagines she can see the first dawn. It is there that she chooses to die rather than in her husband's home, alone with her mortal enemy.

Herbert, Melanctha. *Three Lives*. Gertrude Stein. 1901.

The story of Melanctha Herbert takes place in the black community of Bridgepoint and opens with an account of Melanctha's devotion to her then best friend, Rose Johnson, who has recently married Sam Johnson, a steamer deckhand. Melanctha delivers Rose's first baby and tends to both mother and child in her own home until she finds it necessary to leave them for a few days. Abruptly, the unnamed child dies due to Rose's selfish negligence. Rose moves back home, and she and Sam quickly forget the loss of their child. But Melanctha's perceptions of this are not so simple. She is afflicted with a sensitivity that engenders melancholia and suicidal impulses.

Although Melanctha desires a quiet, calm life like that of her mother, she is irresistibly drawn to the brutality of her biological father, James Herbert. Awakened in part by her father's lascivious accusations concerning her burgeoning womanhood, Melanctha begins to experience the power of her sexuality, which she explores by "straying" to railroad yards, docks, and construction sites. She keeps enough distance from the workmen there to avoid attaining "the knowledge" that she both fears and desires.

As the story progresses, Melanctha's past relationships unfold. At the age of sixteen, some years before meeting Rose, Melanctha had been intimate with Jane Harden, an alcoholic who was expelled from a black college for bad conduct. Jane became Melanctha's guide on the tour of "the ways that lead to wisdom." She introduced Melanctha to a higher economic level of men, mostly businessmen and commercial travelers. By the time Melanctha was eighteen years old, Jane ceased to play the role of teacher, and Melanctha became the more dominant of the two. Their relationship did not survive this shift in power, and Melanctha began again to wander alone. However, she found no satisfaction with the men she met because none of them seemed capable of exciting the fleeting vision of wisdom that eluded her.

When Melanctha's mother takes ill, Melanctha, with the help of a serious young black doctor named Jefferson Campbell, tends to her needs until her death. Dr. Campbell also treats Jane Harden, who has descended into a dangerous alcoholic state since the deterioration of her friendship with Melanctha. Melanctha falls in love with Jeff, but he is initially dissuaded from returning her affection by Jane's abusive descriptions of Melanctha, whom she feels has deserted her. After a lengthy courtship, Melanctha succeeds in convincing Jeff that she has a good mind, which Jeff considers a prerequisite to marriage. But by the time Melanctha has both validated her intellect and educated Jeff in the ways in which sexuality can exist within the realm of respectability, she herself has lost interest in the romance. For her, the relationship has become a tedious repetition of misgivings and miscommunications, and Melanctha wanders once more, alone.

Melanctha resumes her relationship with Rose after Jeff has disappeared from the scene. Rose's neediness comes as a relief to Melanctha, who, without Jeff, needs an outlet for her frustrated energies. When Melanctha begins dating Jem Richards, a dashing man-about-town who is involved with horse racing, the self-righteous Rose disapproves. Ultimately, the Johnsons forbid Melanctha entry into their house, despite her past kindnesses to them. When Jem's luck in betting at the tracks abandons him, he in turn abandons Melanctha, saying he would never consider marrying when in financial trouble.

Deeply depressed, Melanctha considers suicide, although she never goes through with the act. The story ends abruptly after Jem and Rose's disappearance from her life. A recurring fever causes doctors to send her to a hospital for consumptives, where she dies.

Herbert, Niel. *A Lost Lady*. Willa Cather. 1923.

Niel Herbert, the novel's protagonist, observes the decline of the pioneer spirit through the parallel decline of MARIAN FORRESTER and her husband Daniel. As an orphan who is raised by his uncle, Judge Pommeroy, Niel is both part and outside of the frontier aristocracy. He first meets the mysterious and compelling Marian when he breaks his arm while playing with some Sweet Water boys at the Forrester place. Niel immediately develops a crush on Mrs. Forrester, who is unlike any woman he has ever seen. Her grace, charm, and self-possession mesmerize the young boy as well as men of all generations.

As Captain Forrester's health declines and the couple begins to spend more time in Sweet Water, Niel becomes a frequent house guest. His love of literature is only one of the refinements that set him apart from his contemporaries in the town. When he is invited as an escort to a Forrester dinner party, Niel can hardly take his eyes off Marian, yet he is equally impressed by Captain Forrester's strength and dignity. He finds that he admires their relationship as well as each of them individually.

Soon after the party, Niel innocently delivers flowers to Mrs. Forrester while her husband is away on business. When he hears the sounds of lovemaking emanating from her bedroom window, he is crushed and disillusioned by her betrayal of her heroic husband and of his own romantic image of her. His despair deepens when he learns that the Forresters have lost their fortune. Before leaving for Boston to study architecture, Niel visits them one last time, and they toast him with their traditional toast, "Happy days."

After two years in the East, Niel returns a sophisticated young man. He learns that the Forresters have been forced to lease some of their property to Ivy Peters, a disreputable young lawyer. Niel is distressed to observe that Mrs. Forrester permits Ivy's forwardness. While visiting the Captain, Niel also learns that she is still carrying on her affair with Frank Ellinger. He watches poverty and loneliness erode Mrs. Forrester's charm as she struggles to maintain her buoyancy and comes to depend increasingly on alcohol. He visits less frequently as Marian's reputation begins to deteriorate. When Frank Ellinger marries a young woman who had been entertained at the Forrester home, Niel prevents Mrs. Forrester from humiliating herself and completely ruining her reputation by calling him on the phone.

When Captain Forrester has his last stroke, Niel, delaying his return to Boston, eventually intercedes to prevent the total degradation of the Forrester home by the townswomen, who have always resented the beautiful Mrs. Forrester. Niel moves in with them to nurse the Captain and assist Marian with the heavier chores. After the Captain finally dies, a frustrated Niel tries to convince Marian that she is drinking too much and feeding gossip through her unseemly relationship with Ivy Peters. Marian invites him to help her with a dinner party, and he looks on sadly as the other young men respond to her efforts at elegance with incomprehension and apathy, for they are unable to appreciate her sophistication. Depressed by the whole spectacle, Niel begins to plan his return to Boston.

Niel cements his plans when he sees Ivy Peters put his arms around his beloved Marian; he resents her as much for this indiscretion as for her unquenchable thirst for life. After this second betrayal of his romantic notions, he never returns to the Forrester home. Niel hears about Mrs. Forrester from time to time, and years later he learns that she married a wealthy Englishman and died in Brazil.

Herf, Jimmy. *Manhattan Transfer*. John Dos Passos. 1925.

While most of his fellow characters make their sometimes rough way up from obscurity to fame and fortune, Jimmy Herf carries the banner for those few who through disinclination, failure of nerve, or simple bad luck find themselves disinherited by Manhattan, the new metrop-

olis. His sympathies are with the infamous and the marginal: with bootleggers and vagabonds; with Bud Korpenning, who hides in New York after killing his sadistic stepfather, only to end up friendless, jobless, and hurling himself from a bridge; with Joe Harland, Jimmy's uncle, once known as the "wizard of Wall Street" but now a ruined rummy; with Stan Emery, the ne'er-do-well son of New York's most prominent attorney, who spends his family's money as though he were burning trash.

As a small boy, Jimmy arrives in New York with his mother on Independence Day. A beautiful, wealthy divorcée with unstable nerves, Lily Herf takes Jimmy to live at a fashionable hotel where he tries to satisfy his voracious curiosity about the world by spending endless hours reading the encyclopedia and occasionally venturing to the corner candy store.

When Lily Herf dies of a stroke, Jimmy goes to live with the Merivales, his rich relatives on Riverside Drive. The relatives want him to go into business, but Jimmy soon realizes that he loathes everything about the life they lead. Instead, he becomes a reporter and falls in with a crowd of bohemian stage people, including the beautiful actress ELLEN THATCHER.

Jimmy works for several years as a reporter but is impatient at being always on the fringes of events rather than participating in them. During World War I both he and Ellen work for the publicity department of the Red Cross; their old friendship becomes a love affair for him and a benign convenience for her. They return from Europe married and with a child.

Unable to find work, Jimmy is supported by his wife for a time, and he becomes more and more aimless. He finally gets a job writing features for the New York *Times*, but once again he feels like a "parasite on the drama of life." He envies his friend, the swashbuckling bootlegger Congo Jake, for his freedom, but once Congo has become prosperous and respectable, Jimmy realizes they have no more to say to each other.

Ultimately Ellen leaves Jimmy. He quits his job and wanders aimlessly around the city for a while, seeing and bearing witness to strange and shocking events. Wandering has been, in fact, his primary occupation since childhood: As a boy he had walked from his relatives' home on Riverside Drive all the way to the Bronx, and one night some ten years later he walks home from Canarsie to his Manhattan apartment in a heavy rain. Not the parasite he deems himself, he is nevertheless peripheral—sublimely so. When last seen, he is hitching a ride out of New York, still aimless, a sort of confused and holy vagabond.

Hertzfeld, Kurt. *Never Call Retreat*. Joseph Freeman. 1943.

The German playwright and poet Kurt Hertzfeld is a good-natured, charismatic intellectual who devotes his life to socialist politics with ardor but without fanaticism. A gentle soul who takes personal responsibility for the world's problems, he is ever willing to sacrifice his life for the cause and holds on to his beliefs even though he is betrayed by his comrades.

Born in a Rhineland village, Kurt has a difficult and poverty-stricken childhood in Germany after World War I. He wanders through Europe as a young man, observing social conditions in Switzerland, Italy, and Spain. He later works in factories to support himself while taking economics courses at the university, then becomes a journalist for a socialist newspaper in Berlin and begins writing plays and poems. Kurt meets Hans Bayer, a popular socialist leader who becomes the young man's mentor and friend, and becomes involved in international party politics. In the mid-1930s, Hans sends Kurt for a year to Vienna, where he lives with the family of PAUL AUGUST HEINRICH SCHUMAN, an Austrian professor of the history of civilization. During this time he lectures and attends public activities for the cause, all the while watching with fear as the Nazis grow more powerful in his homeland.

Kurt, Hans, and Schuman's wife Peggy then go to Spain to fight in the Civil War. Peggy is killed, and Kurt and Hans are arrested and sent to a German concentration camp, where eventually Paul is also sent. Life in the camp is brutal. In addition to the atrocities committed by the Nazi guards, Kurt must contend with quarrels between prisoners holding different political viewpoints. He is a talented mediator in these disputes, primarily because he is constitutionally incapable of bitterness or antagonism; but his peacekeeping role in the end is not appreciated by Hans, who is the leader of a secret organization that communicates with activists on the outside. Kurt angers his comrades by arguing that men's hearts as well as their political institutions must change in order for the revolution to be successful. He is also resented when he says that the best way for a poet to serve the cause is to write good poetry, not doggerel propaganda.

As time passes, the conflict between Hans and Kurt becomes critical. Kurt sacrifices himself on a number of occasions for his friend; he is whipped and sent to solitary confinement for infractions he has not committed. Following an abortive escape attempt, Kurt challenges Hans to take responsibility for a prisoner's death. In return, Hans causes Kurt to be ostracized by the other prisoners by publicly questioning his loyalty and spreading lies about his activities. Even kindhearted Paul Schuman is afraid to be openly friendly with him. Kurt feels utterly spiritless, lost, and alone but refuses to betray his principles despite further persecution by the Nazis. During a long stay in solitary, Kurt writes a poem, probably intended as a rebuke to Hans, that treats both his private anguish and his earnest belief in the ultimate victory of his vision. The Nazis believe the poem is a message in code, however, and they investigate; Hans repudiates the poet, but both are sentenced to die. On August 31, 1939, Kurt is executed after giving a speech about love and hope to his fellow prisoners.

Herz, Paul. *Letting Go.* Philip Roth. 1962.

While a graduate student in English at the University of Iowa, Paul Herz falls deeply in love with Libby, a frail young woman who, much to the consternation of his family, does not share his Jewish heritage. Despite their religious differences and against the pleas of his family, Paul and Libby are married by a justice of the peace after a rabbi refuses to perform the service for a couple of different religions.

Paul and Libby live in relative happiness in the initial weeks after their marriage. They are extremely poor; Paul is finishing his dissertation, a novel. Their brief period of marital bliss comes to a halt when Libby becomes pregnant. Knowing that he cannot support a child financially, Paul finds an illegal abortionist. He then coerces Libby into having an abortion, which leaves her unable to bear children again.

After graduating, Paul moves with Libby to Chicago where his friend GABE WALLACH has secured a teaching position for him at the University of Chicago. But the outspoken young author soon begins to alienate some of the older faculty members. As his position at the university becomes increasingly tenuous, Paul's marriage starts to deteriorate. Libby has been forced to quit her job in the dean's office because of her failing health, and she becomes restless and bitter about her inability to bear children. Returning home to New York City for a brief vacation, Paul tells his favorite uncle that he has made a mistake in marrying Libby and now wants to leave her.

When Paul returns to Chicago, Gabe tells him of a pregnant student who wants to put her baby up for adoption. Paul tries to convince the increasingly neurotic Libby to adopt the unwanted baby, while Gabe arranges the transaction. After much argument and emotional strain, the baby, Rachel, is delivered to Paul and Libby.

Life thereafter gets noticeably better. The excitement of their new infant gradually lifts Libby out of her seemingly terminal depression, and Paul, fed up with the petty politicking that takes place among the faculty members in his department at the university, resigns in order to teach high school English. His friendship with Gabe also improves, and Gabe often babysits when Paul and Libby go out.

One evening Paul and Libby return and are horrified to learn that Gabe has kidnapped their daughter and is in the process of trying to get the mother to sign over the adoption papers to him. After failing in his attempt, Gabe returns Rachel and goes overseas. Paul learns years later that Gabe has found a teaching position in Italy. He tracks down the address of his friend and, as a token of his forgiveness, mails him an invitation to Rachel's fifth birthday party.

Herzog, Moses Elkanah. *Herzog.* Saul Bellow. 1964.

Moses Elkanah Herzog began life near Valleyfield, Quebec, where his parents emigrated from the Soviet Union in 1913. Throughout the novel, as Herzog undergoes an intellectual and moral crisis, he is haunted by his past and relives traumatic childhood experiences such as his father's funeral and the sexual assault he suffered. As a form of therapy he writes "mental letters"—some on paper—to a host of people, from Heidegger and Nietzsche to Dwight D. Eisenhower.

Herzog concerns himself as much with his earlier life as with the present repercussions of his marriage to, and divorce from, Madeleine Pontritter. Madeleine is Herzog's second wife and the mother of their daughter June; his first wife, Daisy, is the mother of Herzog's son Marco. Herzog's life includes an eclectic assortment of other women as well. He met Wanda, a French woman, in Poland; he left Sono, who was Japanese, for Madeleine; and, most recently, he became involved with Ramona Donsell, who is from Buenos Aires.

Herzog is preoccupied with the pain he suffers because Madeleine has left him for Valentine Gersbach, a man Herzog considered his best friend. A pseudointellectual with hot eyes and flaming copper hair, Valentine is also married, but his wife Phoebe, who knew about the affair long before Herzog, pretends not to know in order to preserve her marriage. Herzog first learns of the affair through his true best friend Lucas Asphalter, a zoologist at the Chicago university at which Herzog once taught. Asphalter has heard of the affair through his girlfriend Geraldine Portnoy who babysat for June.

Obsessed with the idea that June is being mistreated by Madeleine and Valentine, Herzog flies from New York, where he lives, to Chicago. While in Chicago, Herzog visits his stepmother Tante Taube and steals a loaded pistol and some czarist rubles that belonged to his late father Jonah. A year before Jonah's death he had drawn the gun on Herzog and threatened to disinherit and to shoot him.

At Madeleine's Harper Avenue home, Herzog spies on Valentine giving June a bath and must confess to himself that Valentine is tender and kind with her. Nonetheless, he is determined to gain custody. But his visitation with her ends disastrously when he and his daughter are involved in a car accident, and Herzog, having passed out, awakens to find the police examining the gun and the rubles. Herzog is humiliated when Madeleine comes to pick up June at the police station where he is being held for questioning.

Bailed out by his brother Will, Herzog leaves Chicago for the rundown summer house in Ludeyville, Massachusetts, which he bought with his inheritance. There, he sorts

through Madeleine's maternity clothes and confronts the memories they evoke. He tries desperately to find a tangible way to prove his love to June. Will, convinced that Herzog is losing his sanity, soon comes to visit. Herzog fights back tears when his kind brother tries to convince him to seek psychiatric help. He refuses to see a professional and instead takes steps to begin healing himself. He asks Will to take him to town for supplies and invites his lover Ramona, who has called from a nearby town, to dinner. At the novel's close, Herzog is picking flowers and making dinner preparations. It is unclear whether he will be able to recover and live in the present, but he does take an important step toward recovery: He resolves to stop writing mental letters.

Hickock, Dick. *In Cold Blood.* Truman Capote. 1966.

Dick Hickock, mastermind of the robbery in this novel based on a true account of the murder of the Herbert Clutter family, can be an exceptionally personable young man. But his winning smile masks the disturbed personality of a ruthless and arrogant killer.

Dick first appears in the narrative a few hours before the murder, as he picks up his former cellmate PERRY EDWARD SMITH outside a restaurant in Olathe, Kansas. A jaunty, good-looking fellow, Dick has a charming smile and a way with people. Newly paroled from prison, twice married, and the father of three children, he is living with his parents and brother and working as a mechanic. But Dick's reunion with his old friend has a grisly purpose: The car is stocked with fishing tackle, a knife, a flashlight, and a twelve-gauge shotgun.

As they are driving toward Holcomb, Kansas, Dick reveals his plan to Perry. While in prison he heard about a wealthy farmer, Herbert Clutter, who keeps a safe full of cash in his home. Dick has a map of the house; they will steal everything and leave no witnesses.

The Clutter farm is quiet and dark. The robbers search the house and, finding nothing, ascend the stairs to rouse Herbert Clutter from his bed. He tells them he has no safe. Perry believes him; Dick, embarrassed at his mistake, pretends not to. They lock Herbert Clutter in the upstairs bathroom along with his wife, teenage daughter, and son. One by one the family members are taken out, tied up, and shot.

A few days later Dick and Perry meet in Kansas City where Dick cashes enough phony checks to get them to Mexico. They become drifters, selling off stolen goods and staying in cheap boardinghouses as they wind their way down to Acapulco. Dick secretly scorns Perry's dreamy preoccupation with deep-sea diving and buried treasures. A drinker and womanizer, he is nonetheless the more "pragmatic" of the two; when their money runs low, it is Dick who insists on returning to Kansas.

After a second spree of check-cashing in Kansas City, Dick and Perry continue drifting through Florida, Texas, and Nevada. They grow impatient with each other and quarrel frequently. In Las Vegas, Dick considers abandoning Perry and working the casinos. So engrossed is he in these contemplations, he does not notice a patrol car pulling up alongside.

Arrested, Dick tries to stick to the story he and Perry had prepared but finally breaks down under the detectives' relentless questioning. He confesses to being in the Clutter house; however, he attributes all the killings to Perry.

Awaiting his trial in the Garden City jail, Dick seems affable and unperturbed. Secretly, though, he is hard at work assembling a "shiv" of wood and hard wire—a weapon used like an ice pick for stabbing prison guards between the shoulder blades. The sheriff confiscates the weapon before he has time to use it.

Sentenced to death by hanging, Dick spends five years on death row. His father has died, believing in his innocence; his mother still visits him faithfully. He works hard at reversing his sentence: "I'm no goddamn killer," he writes in endless letters of appeal. On April 14, 1965, Dick shakes hands with those responsible for his conviction, and with a parting all-American grin, coolly mounts the steps to the scaffold.

Hicks, Annie Eliza. *Such Was the Season.* Clarence Major. 1987.

As her story begins, Annie Eliza Hicks, the elderly and worldly narrator, welcomes DR. ADAM "JUNEBOY" NORTH, her nephew, on his first visit south in many years. While proud of her nephew's accomplishments as a sickle cell anemia researcher, she is also wary of his northern ways and manners. Annie Eliza, who lives in the Atlanta home that her husband Bibb bought in 1947, has lived most of her long life in and around the city. She is the proud mother of two sons, one of whom, Reverend Jeremiah Hicks, is an eloquent preacher. The other son, DeSoto Hicks, is a police officer. She also displays a great deal of pride in her complicated ancestry: Her mother, Eva Mae Obscure, an African American, was thought by many to possess strange and awesome powers, while her father, Olaudah Equiano Sommers, was of mixed Caucasian and Cherokee heritage.

In the course of Juneboy's brief visit, Annie learns that her daughter-in-law Renee, Jeremiah's wife, has decided to run for office. Against opposition from Atlanta's political hierarchy, she plans to oppose the incumbent state senator, Dale Cooper, in the upcoming fall elections. Her platform, which has been developed with the aid of Clarence Toussaint L'Ouverture Butler, is a strange one. It stresses the existence of what Renee calls the Greenhouse Tomato Conspiracy, wherein fruits and vegetables are purchased at low prices in Mississippi and Florida and sold as homegrown at a much higher price in Georgia. Annie Eliza finds the platform bizarre, but as events continue, it turns out that there is such a conspiracy.

As Renee's campaign escalates, Annie Eliza learns of the mysterious illness of Senator Cooper. Cooper's longtime friend, Cherokee Jimmy, asserts that Cooper was taken ill while visiting a secret male lover. Annie Eliza begins to ask questions, interviewing the mayor and various politicians. She gradually pieces together a tale of deception and sordid business dealings that lead back to her son, the Reverend. While she is shocked when Cherokee Jimmy's suicide publicly exposes his homosexuality, she is more disturbed by the ultimate revelation that her son was involved in the conspiracy his own wife sought to expose for her political gain.

Jeremiah and Senator Cooper are arrested for the conspiracy, even though by this time Cooper is seriously ill with a relatively rare form of sickle cell anemia. Meanwhile, Juneboy returns to his life in the North, having learned a wealth of family history from Annie Eliza that enables him to start life anew. Annie Eliza settles down to await her son's conspiracy trial and the outcome of the fall elections, for which Renee continues to campaign. While she feels that her time will soon come and her pain grows, Annie Eliza only hopes that these new troubles will not be any worse than those she has already faced.

Hicks, Captain Nathaniel. *Guard of Honor.* James Gould Cozzens. 1948.

With the coming of World War II, Nathaniel Hicks, a successful magazine editor, is forced to leave his wife and two children to travel to Alabama where he has accepted a captain's commission with the Special Services branch of the U.S. Air Force. His first assignment is to do a story on the new types of aircraft the Air Force is employing against the Japanese. Although he doubts the story will be of interest to the general public, Hicks is nonetheless pleased because the assignment will allow him to travel to New York where he has numerous contacts in the magazine industry and where his wife and children remain.

While flying to an Air Force base in Alabama, Hicks discovers another possible story. He, LIEUTENANT COLONEL BENNY CARRICKER, GENERAL IRA "BUS" BEAL, Second Lieutenant Amanda Turck, and a couple of other officers are almost killed when a B-17, flown by and carrying a group of African-American pilots, lands in front of their plane without first receiving permission from the control tower. In a fit of temper, Colonel Carricker, a famous fighter pilot and the copilot of Hicks's plane, attacks Willis, the lead pilot of the B-17.

As Hicks investigates the story, he meets a black reporter named James who has come to the base to do a story on the unprecedented black bomber division. However, James is quickly escorted off the base by MP officers. While supposedly gathering information for his propaganda article, Hicks continues to follow the plight of the black pilots. These pilots become enraged when they learn that the base commander, General Beal, has decided not to press charges against Colonel Carricker, who had put Willis in the hospital with a broken nose.

Hicks, now resented by other white officers for his sympathies with the black pilots, continues to follow the story of their attempt to exact justice. When Hicks is apprehended during a protest staged by the black pilots at the Officer's Club—which they are prohibited from entering—he is informed by General Beal that his assignment, and consequently his trip to New York to see his family, has been canceled.

With the protest by the black pilots crushed before it ever began, Hicks bemoans his failure to Amanda Turck. After drinking for most of the night, Hicks invites the attractive lieutenant up to his hotel room, where they make love. Late that night he receives a call from General Beal saying that he has been put back on assignment and that a staff car will arrive at his hotel in half an hour. Stunned, Hicks dresses and goes to meet the staff car that will take him to the plane.

Hicks, Ray. *Dog Soldiers.* Robert Stone. 1987.

A merchant marine and reader of Nietzsche stationed in Saigon during the Vietnam War, Ray Hicks is turned into a drug smuggler by his friend JOHN CONVERSE. A journalist, Converse convinces Hicks to smuggle three kilos of heroin out of Vietnam and into the United States where he is to deliver the drugs to Marge Converse in Berkeley, California. Initially reluctant, Hicks ultimately agrees to run the drugs.

After successfully smuggling the heroin into the United States, Hicks discovers that Marge, a drug addict, is unprepared for his arrival. Before he is able to respond one way or another, however, two ex-cons in the employ of a corrupt federal agent named Antheil are spotted by Hicks outside the Converse house. As these two criminals, Danskin and Smitty, attempt to break into the house and take the heroin, they are surprised by Hicks who beats them both before fleeing with Marge and the dope into the hills of Los Angeles. Once there, Hicks retrieves an automatic rifle he had hidden before sailing off for Vietnam.

Unsure of exactly what steps he should take next, Hicks ultimately decides to unload the drugs in Los Angeles, hoping a big-time Hollywood wheeler-dealer named Eddie Peace will be able to move the dope for them. After attempting to intimidate Hicks, Peace appears at Hicks and Marge's hotel room with a rich, thrill-seeking couple Peace believes can be taken for a financial ride. After shooting himself up, Peace can only look on in horror as Hicks plunges a needle into the arm of one of the prospective clients, thereby inducing an overdose.

Afterward, Hicks and Marge drive into the mountains of New Mexico to a remote, 1960s counter-culture retreat to which Hicks had once belonged. Once there, Hicks is warmly greeted by Dieter, the aging hippie Hicks had once

looked to for spiritual guidance. Their reunion is short-lived, however, as Hicks and Marge are tracked down by Antheil's heavies who have taken John Converse hostage. Marge insists on turning the heroin over, but Hicks, understanding there is no deal to be made with these men, double-crosses Antheil by replacing the heroin with sand before turning the package over to Marge for delivery. With no time to waste, Hicks maneuvers down the mountain and positions himself where he can observe Antheil. When the agent discovers he has been tricked, Hicks opens fire, killing Smitty and forcing the others to take cover. In the confusion, Marge and John escape and take refuge with Hicks, who has since been shot in the arm by Danskin. Hicks insists on holding on to the heroin, but he directs the Converses to take his jeep and make their escape while he continues to engage Antheil and Angel until he can get away himself and meet John and Marge on the railroad tracks in the New Mexico desert.

After a short shoot-out, Hicks makes his way back up to Dieter. After helping Hicks treat his wound, Dieter takes possession of the heroin and refuses to give it back. Hicks attempts to give chase but cannot due to his weakened state. When it appears that Dieter might make off with the drugs, Hicks shoots him dead and begins his journey to the railroad tracks. The gunshot wound, lacking the necessary medical treatment, begins to sap Hicks's strength. Through an extraordinary effort of will, however, he is able to walk for several miles before finally succumbing. Hicks dies on the railroad tracks before he is reached, first by John and Marge and then by Antheil and Angel, who retrieve the drugs.

Hightower, Gail. *Light in August.* William Faulkner. 1932.

Gail Hightower, an obese recluse and widower, lives a lonely and embittered life because his youthful prospects as a Presbyterian minister have been dashed by his eccentric behavior and his wife's scandalous reaction to his neglect of their relationship. The source of Hightower's pathological life-style is his obsession with the image of his grandfather, who was shot off his horse in the Civil War. Stories conflict as to whether he was shot while galloping gallantly down the streets of Jefferson, Mississippi, in his Confederate uniform or while stealing chickens from a hen house. Every evening at dusk Hightower sits by his study window, performing a vigil wherein he recreates the image of his grandfather on his galloping horse thundering through the streets in pursuit of vainglorious adventures.

As a young seminarian, Hightower pulls strings in order to be placed in the Presbyterian church in Jefferson, Mississippi, so that he can live close to the scene of his grandfather's military escapades. From the beginning of his ministry, Hightower shows an inability to focus on preaching the word of God due to his obsession with his grandfather's career. He raves from the pulpit about religion, the Confederate cavalry, General Grant, and his grand-father's colorful death in the same breath. Presumably he is equally distracted because his neglected wife has been slipping off to Memphis where she is conducting illicit affairs while pretending to be visiting family.

Within a year of the young couple's installation in their house in Jefferson, the expression of Hightower's wife becomes detached and wooden, and her emotional un-happiness finally culminates in her screaming hysterically at him during one of his sermons while she is seated in the congregation. She is institutionalized for a brief time and then returns home and behaves in a manner befitting a minister's wife. Her reform is short-lived, however. She resumes her Memphis excursions and then one day is found dead outside a Memphis hotel, having either jumped or been pushed out of a window. She had been registered as the wife of a man who was found drunk at the scene of the crime.

Hightower's religious community is enraged by this calamity, and they demand his resignation from the pulpit. After considerable pressure he agrees to step down.

Hightower subsequently refuses to move away from Jefferson, despite the fact that members of the K.K.K. drag him into the woods, tie him to a tree, and beat him until he loses consciousness. But Hightower is more stubborn than the town is brutal, and he successfully clings to his decision to remain, a fact that the town ultimately accepts, though grudgingly. Although Hightower puts up a sign in his front yard that offers his services as an art instructor, greeting card illustrator, and photograph developer, no one commissions his services, and he is forced to live on a meager inheritance, half of which he donates to a Memphis institution that supports delinquent girls.

Although Hightower is generally cut off from the community, on two occasions he delivers babies when the doctor cannot be fetched in time. One of these infants is the child of LENA GROVE, a young unmarried woman whom his friend BYRON BUNCH has taken under his wing.

Hightower's despair persists unabated throughout the novel and culminates when the murderer JOE CHRISTMAS, who runs into Hightower's house to seek refuge from a vigilante mob, is brutally castrated in front of him. High-tower tries to stop the murder by providing Christmas with an alibi, claiming that Christmas was at his house on the night of the murder; this futile effort only leads to disappointment and suffering, which have characterized his life.

Hilda. *The Marble Faun: Or, the Romance of Monte Beni.* Nathaniel Hawthorne. 1860.

A gifted copyist and a true daughter of the Puritans, Hilda practices her art in Rome. Her home in a medieval tower known as the Shrine of the Virgin is an apt symbol for Hilda herself—a lofty tribute to matchless purity. As the occupant of the furthest reaches of this tower, Hilda

is charged with tending the eternal flame that must burn in its window. The doves that make the window their home seem appropriate companions for the pristine young woman. However, evil soon threatens to soil Hilda's snowy whiteness.

One evening while exploring the hills and ruins of Rome with a group of young people, including her friends MIRIAM, DONATELLO, and Kenyon, Hilda witnesses a scene that will forever haunt her. Miriam and her admirer Donatello had hung back from the larger group to gaze over the edge of a precipice. Hilda tells Kenyon, who is in love with her, that she wants to go back and speak to Miriam. Just as Hilda opens the door of the tiny courtyard where Miriam has remained, she sees Donatello fling a man into the chasm on Miriam's silent urging. Horrified over the death of this man, a mysterious figure who had been menacing Miriam for weeks, Hilda withdraws without making her presence known to her friend.

The next day Hilda forgoes meeting her friends. Miriam, concerned, goes to the Shrine of the Virgin. Hilda forbids Miriam to even touch her and condemns her for her part in the murder she witnessed. Hilda laments the loss of Miriam's friendship but regrets even more the burden of guilt she now feels. As she tells her former friend, there is no one with whom she can share this terrible secret. Rejecting Miriam's suggestion that she confide in the sculptor Kenyon, Hilda collapses, grief-stricken, in the corner of her studio.

Soon after, Miriam disappears, and Donatello departs for his home in the country, with Kenyon following for a visit. Hilda is utterly alone in her grief. She tries to continue working, to make the copies of the works of the Italian masters for which she is so renowned, but all the pictures seem empty, all her talent crushed.

Unable to carry the knowledge she has hidden any longer, Hilda, although a Protestant, goes to confession. She feels some relief in telling her story to the priest but is shaken when he tells her that the rules of confession do not apply to her because she is a heretic. She begs him not to reveal the story of Miriam and Donatello's crime to the authorities. He seems to relent but urges her to join the Catholic Church, which she refuses to do. When concluding her meeting with the priest, Hilda is observed by Kenyon, who has returned to Rome. He fears for her faith but is happy to learn that she plans to remain a Protestant.

The next day Hilda suddenly remembers the existence of a package that Miriam had asked her long ago to deliver to a house in Rome on a certain date. Hilda delivers the package and then disappears. Kenyon now fears for her safety, especially when the eternal flame goes out, but Hilda reappears during carnival. She had been detained by the authorities on suspicion that she was somehow involved in the crime she had witnessed. The lonely girl soon agrees to give her hand to Kenyon, and the two marry and return to America.

Hinckley, Joe. "The Little Wife." William March. 1935.

Joe Hinckley is an unassuming man who makes a living as a traveling salesman and a home with his adored wife Bessie in Mobile, Alabama.

One hot June, while he is in Montgomery on business, Joe returns from a meeting to find a telegram waiting at his hotel. His mother-in-law, Mrs. Thompkins, has sent word that Bessie delivered their child—a boy—and that the doctors don't expect her to live for more than a few hours. Although Mrs. Thompkins will wire again if there are new developments, he should nevertheless come home immediately.

While waiting for the train to Mobile, Joe still fails to grasp the full import of the telegram. He rationalizes that the doctors don't know for certain that Bessie will die. It pains him to realize that the urgent telegram lay waiting for him at the hotel while he was off laughing and telling smutty jokes with a buyer. The train finally comes, but Joe is barely seated when hailed by a porter who received a telegram for Mr. J. G. Hinckley as the train was pulling out of the station. Fearing the worst, Joe doesn't respond, then reluctantly accepts the telegram, deciding it must be notification of a canceled business appointment. Clutching the unopened telegram, Joe walks to the rear of the train, where he begins to feel sick. Without opening it, he defiantly shreds the telegram and flings it from the end of the train. As he watches the fragments flutter away, Joe feels relieved, even glad.

Returning to his seat, Joe banters with the conductor, then strikes up a conversation with two giggling girls whom he admonishes to get a good education. They laugh at his fatherliness, so Joe tells them he has in fact just become a father. Feeling increasingly convivial, Joe invites an elderly woman to join their conversation, which quickly becomes a monologue. He animatedly tells the story of how he and Bessie met, then describes in detail their married life, even going into the finer points of Bessie's housekeeping abilities. His monologue becomes rapid, even feverish, marked by the emphatic refrain that he has the best little wife in the world. Finally sensing his audience is bored, Joe approaches an elderly couple with an offer of conversation and promptly launches into the same manic soliloquy.

Mrs. Thompkins, dressed in black, meets Joe at the Mobile train station. Astounded by his smiling, excited expression, she immediately asks if he received her second telegram. Joe instantly realizes that he has been deceiving himself and that he has been trying to keep Bessie alive by talking about her. He immediately breaks down, and Mrs. Thompkins admonishes him not to give in: He should take this like a man.

Hippolyte. *The Benefactor.* Susan Sontag. 1963.

Hippolyte, the son of a prosperous French industrialist, spends a lifetime reflecting on his dreams and attempting to merge the world of these dreams with that of his real life. The result is an unusual and erratic existence that resembles a dream. At times Hippolyte's sanity is questionable, but he argues that he made a rational but unconventional choice to be a completely "self-elected" man.

Hippolyte's childhood and youth are unremarkable except for the death of his mother when he is five. He grows up in a large provincial city and moves to the capital (presumably Paris, although he refrains from naming it) to attend the university. After three years of academic experimentation, Hippolyte abandons his formal studies for more adventurous methods of learning, such as foreign travel. The publication of a philosophical article gains him admission to the salon of a wealthy Bohemian woman, Frau Anders, and he spends much of his time there. Soon after embarking on this "period of inquiry," Hippolyte has the first of a series of dreams that transform him. Like the others, this first dream, the "dream of the two rooms," deals with forms of enslavement and the inability to act and is pervaded by a sense of shame. Each of the dreams repeats itself with variations for a certain period, until Hippolyte dreams an entirely new dream.

From the beginning, Hippolyte regards his dreams not as keys to his psyche but rather as models and motives for action. His dreams dictate all his important actions and are the source of his decisions. He seduces the middle-aged hostess of his favorite salon, Frau Anders, because she plays an erotic role in his "dream of the unconventional party." Hippolyte eventually teaches her to play the roles of characters in his dreams. He allows the dreams to determine the bizarre course of the affair. They leave the capital city secretly, settle for the winter on an island, and then move to an Arab city. There, Hippolyte sells her to a merchant whom he believes will fulfill her exotic fantasies.

Once liberated from Frau Anders, Hippolyte resumes his life in the capital and makes increasing efforts to free himself from his bothersome everyday "personality," which clashes with his dreams. Unwilling to take time from his personal meditations for any demanding occupation, Hippolyte decides on a brief career as an actor. Because he craves no great success and is supported by his father, Hippolyte is content acting in a string of odd films. He believes film is an analogue for dream because of the camera's freedom with space and time.

In his personal life, Hippolyte maintains a friendship with JEAN-JACQUES, an eccentric writer, and has an affair with Monique, a political activist. The unexpected return of Frau Anders, now divorced, marks the end of this affair. Hippolyte has no intention of renewing their old romance and even tries to murder Frau Anders by setting fire to her house, but the indestructible woman manages to escape and continues to harass him.

When Frau Anders begins to insist that Hippolyte marry her, he responds by choosing a wife from his native province. His married years are Hippolyte's happiest, but unfortunately his wife dies, young and childless, of leukemia. Hippolyte spends six years in solitude and mourning, occupying the large, nearly empty house he had outfitted for Frau Anders after his return. At this point Hippolyte's story takes a strange turn, bringing his sanity into question. A second Frau Anders appears, this one still beautiful and imperious, and orders Hippolyte out of the house, and he gets a small apartment elsewhere in the capital. He finds peace here and ceases to dream.

Looking back on his life from this serene, dreamless refuge, Hippolyte confesses that he experienced a period of delusion during which the line between dream and reality blurred and became indistinguishable. His preoccupation with himself comes to an end with the cessation of his dreams, and he devotes himself to helping others. Hippolyte's narrative trails off quietly, ending with the image of himself in his bare, isolated room.

Hirsch, Meyer. *Haunch Paunch and Jowl.* Samuel Ornitz. 1923.

The son of a poor Jewish family on Ludlow Street, Meyer Hirsch joins a juvenile gang, which he soon teaches to extort protection money from local merchants. Meyer's specialty is cunning: He hatches schemes while others do the legwork. He also propounds his opinions on Jews and society to the adults around him, including his uncle Philip, a Talmudic intellectual, and Barney Finn, an impassioned, idealistic Irishman who wants to make the world a better place. Although Meyer comes of age with a bar mitzvah, he prefers gang warfare and brothels to the rituals of the Jewish religion.

At the insistence of Uncle Philip, Meyer goes to City College to become a lawyer. He begins spending time at the courts and learns by observation how to manipulate the justice system. He meets Maxie Freund, another cagey young law student. During this time Meyer also begins to have affairs with women. Esther, an idealistic young teacher, is his unrequited love; Gretel, a local servant girl, satisfies his sexual urges. In order to pay for school, Meyer joins some of his friends in a singing quartet. They lead the high life, singing and performing in the clubs of Greenwich Village at night while attending law school or medical school by day. Meanwhile, Uncle Philip, in his new and ruthless manufacturing career, amasses wealth by exploiting immigrant labor.

Meyer and Maxie, a shrewd and calculated pair, open a law practice. They join the Democratic Party and begin organizing a political power base on the Lower East Side. As a lawyer and favor broker, Meyer quickly finds himself a local political boss. He manages new immigrants, police, and local merchant associations to further his ends, using his old gang buddies to do the work. Meyer takes Gretel in as his servant. In his new role, Meyer cleans up the brothel district for purely political reasons. He also or-

ganizes the fledgling union movement among garment workers into a potent force that shuts down all the big factories except his uncle's. As he wallows in corruption, he enjoys publicity as an upstanding friend of the people. Due to his increasing girth, the Socialists dub him "Haunch Paunch and Jowl." Only Esther, with her belief in higher ideals, troubles him. He still craves her but continues to find solace in Gretel.

By now Meyer, his mother, and the hugely wealthy Uncle Philip have moved to the Upper West Side. His old friends become either successful doctors or join the entertainment business. Still pulling strings downtown, Meyer fully enjoys the benefits of his position uptown. Uncle Philip manages to marry into an elite society of German Jews; he urges Meyer to drop Gretel and do the same. After their conversation, a depressed Meyer visits an Irish prostitute on the Lower East Side. While he is there, the madam of the brothel approaches him about a statutory rape case involving a local girl and a prominent millionaire. Meyer blackmails the millionaire with this information, and he in turn pressures the governor to award Meyer a judgeship. On the bench, Meyer continues to gain weight, and yielding to pressure from his mother and Gretel, who threaten a law suit, he finally marries Gretel. The scandal of taking a maid as his bride finishes him politically, and they live plumply ever after on the Upper West Side.

Hobbes, Paul. *Go.* John Clellon Holmes. 1988.

Paul Hobbes is the most reserved member of a clique of bohemians in New York City. Modeled after the central figures of the "Beat Generation," Paul's friends prowl the city every night, attending wild parties and experimenting with marijuana. Paul, whose marriage is already difficult, gets drawn into the circle, despite increasing concern about its effect on his relationship with his wife Kathryn.

When Hobbes was sixteen, his parents separated, and he moved to Westchester with his mother who worked in a real estate office. After high school Paul was admitted to Columbia University, and he takes the train into the city every morning to attend classes. On the train Paul meets Kathryn, who is two years older and already working full-time at an export firm. Both feel alienated in their elitist, gossipy town, and form an uneasy opposing alliance. A tempestuous romance leads to their decision to marry, although it is against the wishes of Paul's parents.

The marriage takes place shortly before Paul is drafted and stationed in San Diego. Kathryn follows him there, where she lives in an inexpensive room and works in a department store. Paul and Kathryn are able to spend only a few ecstatic weekends together, while the rest of their lives seems chaotic and nightmarish. The pattern of intimacy and loneliness continues when Paul is stationed outside New York and Kathryn has a room in the city. When

Paul is finally discharged from military service, both are unprepared for the demands of a steady relationship.

Paul returns to Columbia to finish his studies while Kathryn continues to work. In one of his philosophy classes, Paul meets Liza Adler, an aggressive, brilliant woman who initiates a friendship with him. As their competitive, intellectual relationship develops, Paul's marriage pales in comparison, and he begins to fall in love with Liza. When Liza has a breakdown and leaves school, Paul writes long, elaborate letters that she rarely answers. He continues to write to her after leaving Columbia and beginning his career as a professional writer.

Through a friend who works in publishing, Arthur Ketcham, Paul meets David Stofsky and Gene Pasternak, and they become his links to the "Beat" group. After spending the day isolated, working on his novel, Paul grows restless and often finds himself wandering down to Times Square where Pasternak and his friends are usually drinking in some dingy, hip bar. Paul persuades Kathryn to come to their parties, at which the main attraction is smoking "tea," as marijuana is called. Both Paul and Kathryn become involved in brief affairs: Kathryn with Pasternak, and Paul with a woman named Estelle. They are able to accept each other's transgressions, but when Kathryn finds the collection of letters addressed to Liza, she is deeply hurt and, at first, determined to leave him. Although they remain together, Paul and Kathryn are quietly miserable and unable to forget the trouble.

Paul's sense of hopelessness increases when the novel he has been working on for years is rejected by his publishing company. Their circle of friends is also shaken by crises: Stofsky is arrested for possession of stolen goods, and another friend, Agatson, is killed in a strange subway accident. The group gathers in a bar in Hoboken, New Jersey, to mourn Agatson's death, and Paul suddenly feels the emptiness of their way of life. Paul and Kathryn leave the bar together, clinging to each other. They hold each other tightly on the ferry ride back to New York, both looking intently at the skyline, trying to discern their own home.

Hobbs, Roy. *The Natural*. Bernard Malamud. 1952.

As a young man, Roy Hobbs hopes to play baseball for the Chicago Cubs. Roy is awkward and naive but fiercely ambitious. He wants, he tells the mysterious dark-haired lady who catches his eye on the train, to be the best in the game. To prove his determination to the lady, Roy accepts a stopover pitching challenge from Walter "the Whammer" Wambold, the American League batting champion, and soundly trounces the professional. During the challenge, however, Roy's catcher, Sam, takes a pitch in the chest and later dies. Grieving, Roy accepts the dark-haired lady's invitation to her hotel room in Chicago. Roy doesn't realize that she is a murderess who has been roaming the country, claiming as her victims promising young

athletes. As Roy enters the room, she draws a gun and shoots him with a silver bullet.

Due to a difficult recovery, Roy's career does not resume until he is thirty-four. Still, he manages to secure a contract with the New York Knights, who are impressed by Roy's powerful hitting ability using Wonderboy, his homemade bat. The Knights' only other real talent is Bump Bailey, a wisecracking practical joker. Bailey is involved with MEMO PARIS, a stunning redhead who, in a case of mistaken identity engineered by Bump, crawls into bed beside Roy one night. Memo is mortified at her mistake and refuses to speak to Roy, who desires her desperately.

In spite of his remarkable talent and his ability to pack the Knights' stadium, Roy is turned down for a raise by the team owner, Judge Goodwill Banner. To make matters worse, he continues to be rebuffed by Memo even after Bump's death in a freak ballpark accident. She comes around temporarily when Roy's fans show their appreciation with a "Roy Hobbs Day" at the stadium. Roy takes Memo for a drive in the new Mercedes he receives. As the evening progresses, Memo becomes upset by Roy's advances and insists on driving the car with the headlights out. They hit something, and Roy insists he saw a boy in the road just before impact, but Memo refuses to investigate the possibility.

Soon after, Roy suffers a slump. His teammates and fans begin to worry when their ace does not hit well in game after game, and Roy himself becomes deeply depressed. Finally, in an important game, Roy turns in the batting box to see a woman standing up in the stands, wearing a striking red dress. She gives him the inspiration to hit a home run. Her name, he discovers, is Iris Lemon, and although she is not as attractive as Memo, Roy is drawn to her. They make love, but he is disgusted when she tells him that she is a grandmother at thirty-three, and he doesn't read the letter she later sends him.

Roy eventually regains his ambition. As the team leader, he rouses the players into raucous celebrations after their increasing victories. His appetite for success is rivaled only by his appetite for food; he begins to devour huge quantities without ever feeling satisfied. At a party thrown by Memo before a pennant race game, Roy eats so much that he must be rushed to the hospital to have his stomach pumped.

On the eve of the game, the Judge approaches Roy and offers him money to throw the game. Pressured by Memo, who insists she cannot marry him if he is poor, Roy accepts. Doing his best not to get a hit in the game, Roy fouls a ball that strikes Iris, who was standing in the bleachers. Roy runs to her as she is being taken to the ambulance. She whispers that he must win the game for her and for their unborn child, and Roy is overcome with love for them both. However, another powerful foul leaves Wonderboy cracked in two and useless. Using a different bat, Roy strikes out in spite of his best efforts, then strikes out again to lose the game. After the game he buries the two halves of Wonderboy on the field. He then pummels the Judge and castigates Memo for her part in the scandal. She attempts to shoot him but misses. When Roy exits the park, a boy shows him a newspaper carrying rumors of Roy's deal with the Judge and begs Roy to tell him the report is untrue. Looking at the boy, Roy breaks down and weeps.

Hobomok. *Hobomok, a Tale of Early Times.* Lydia Maria Child. 1824.

A young Indian chieftain is *Hobomok*'s eponymous hero. Set in the early 1600s, the story paints an unflattering picture of the Puritan settlers for whom Hobomok is an exemplary "noble savage." A friend of all the colonists, Hobomok is particularly attracted to Mary Conant, whose mother, the daughter of an English earl, had unwisely married a rigid Calvinist and had come with him and their child to the colony. Mary is in love with Charles Brown, a lawyer who has become disillusioned with the rugged life and the religious bickerings of the colonists. When he announces that he is still an Episcopalian and abhors the views of the dissenters, he is ordered to return to England. Some time after his departure, word comes to Mary that Charles has been lost at sea. After the death of her mother, Mary turns for solace to the lovesick Hobomok, and in defiance of the prejudices of the colony, she declares that she will become his wife.

In an Indian ritual, Hobomok and Mary wed by breaking a rod in five pieces and giving a fragment to each of the witnesses. Living in a disconsolate state because of her memories of Charles, Mary is nonetheless a good wife to Hobomok and bears him a son. Three years later, Hobomok is hunting when he is accosted by a man. It is, of course, Charles Brown, who informs the Indian that he has been held captive on the coast of Africa and only now has been able to return to claim Mary. Hobomok tells Charles of their marriage and asserts sadly that the Englishman has a prior claim and that he will divorce her. The promise is made good; Hobomok has the fragments of the rod that had sealed their marriage burned and states that, under Indian law, this act ends the union. Charles and Mary praise the unselfishness of the Indian's action and accept it; they marry and settle in the colony, after Charles promises not to quarrel over religious beliefs. Mary's son by Hobomok is sent to England to be educated, but Charles and the colonists always remember with gratitude both the noble personal sacrifice of the Indian and his services to their struggling settlement.

Hogganbeck, Boon. *The Reivers*; "The Bear." William Faulkner. 1962; 1942.

Boon Hogganbeck, the great-grandson of a Chickasaw Indian, is an enormous and somewhat simpleminded man. He will on some occasions declare that he is "at least ninety-nine one hundredths Chickasaw" and on others threaten any man who dares intimate that he might have Indian blood. He first appears as the most incompetent of a group of bear hunters and, ironically, the one who finally kills the great bear Old Ben.

Later, Boon covets and, when given the chance, steals his employer's new automobile. He convinces eleven-year-old LUCIUS PRIEST, his employer's grandson, to run off to Memphis with him. He needs the boy's company, his protection from prosecution, and his help in getting through the vast mud bogs on the road between Jefferson and Memphis.

Arriving in Memphis, Boon heads immediately for Miss Reba's brothel, home of Boon's love, a prostitute named Miss Corrie. Although he has seen her only once in six months, Boon spends as much time snarling about Corrie's other customers as he does engaging her professionally. In any case, when NED WILLIAM McCASLIN trades the stolen car for a racehorse, Boon's amorous ventures are interrupted.

On another occasion Lucius's courtly defense of Corrie's honor against a slanderous remark prompts her to forswear prostitution and to reveal her true name, Everbe. Boon is more jealous of the eleven-year-old Lucius's romantic successes than of those of a gallant railway man named Sam Caldwell and a crude, corrupt sheriff named Butch.

Although Boon plays only a peripheral role in the horse-car swap, he is legally responsible for the car. However, he is ultimately arrested for horse theft. When he is charged, he seems more pleased at having an opportunity to fight Butch than outraged at a miscarriage of justice. Finally, after the car is returned to Lucius's grandfather, the horse to its owner, and the boy to his mother, Boon settles down to marry Everbe. The novel ends with the birth of their first baby, Lucius Priest Hogganbeck.

Hohlfelder, Clara. "Her Virginia Mammy." Charles W. Chesnutt. 1899.

Clara Hohlfelder is the young dance instructor around whom this short story revolves. An orphan taken in by a German couple who had fled to the United States in 1849, Clara knows nothing of her family background. However, John Winthrop, the young man she loves, comes from a distinguished family ancestry. Although John Winthrop declares he would marry her even if he discovered that she was as black as the "Negroes" who make up her dance class, Clara remains uncomfortable with her feelings of inferiority and finds herself in a dilemma about whether or not to accept his proposal.

Particularly distraught after John's visit, Clara uses a recess in her dance class to take a respite in the ladies' dressing room. There she encounters Mrs. Harper, one of her black pupils. Yearning for sympathy, Clara takes Mrs. Harper into her confidence and explains her unhappy predicament. Clara recounts her mysterious past: A steamboat explosion had occurred up the river, and a baby girl was found floating on a piece of wreckage; she was that child, whom a German couple adopted and raised as their own.

Upon hearing the story, Mrs. Harper becomes intensely interested and asks Clara several questions. When Clara provides the name of the boat and shows the items that were found with the baby, Mrs. Harper appears even more agitated. She notices the initials "M.S." on the muslin slip that had been worn by the baby. Then Mrs. Harper explains that she had been on the ship and had known Clara's parents.

Mrs. Harper reveals Clara's family history to her. Dispelling all Clara's fears of inferiority, Mrs. Harper informs Clara that she is the daughter of one of the first families of Virginia. Although all of her family is now dead, Clara is a member of "the bluest of the blue-bloods." Finally, Mrs. Harper tells Clara that she had been her "mammy," or nursemaid.

Elated, Clara goes to John to tell him of her discovery and to accept his proposal. Mrs. Harper watches as the couple embraces, and the similarity between herself and Clara and the great emotion she shows lends credence to the idea that the two were actually mother and daughter.

Holbrook, Anna. *Yonnondio: From the Thirties.* Tillie Olsen. 1974.

Anna Holbrook, the mother in this novel of the Depression, struggles for the safety, health, and happiness of her family. Despite her determination and frugality, and her husband Jim's industriousness and willingness to relocate, their station in life hardly improves.

Like the other women in this Wyoming coal-mining town, Anna lives in fear of the blaring whistle that announces a mine accident. Jim, frustrated by back-breaking work and low wages, often vents his rage on the family. Anna can also be brutal toward the children. But when a disfigured and deranged old miner tries to throw their oldest daughter Mazie down the mine shaft, they see the extent of their degradation. They decide they must leave Wyoming in the spring.

That winter, Jim stops visiting the saloon after work, and Anna becomes even more scrupulous about the family budget. One day the dreaded whistle announces an explosion that traps a number of workers underground for five days. Although there are no deaths, Jim takes this accident as another sign to take his family away.

In April the Holbrooks drive a wagon through Nebraska to farmland in South Dakota. For a time the family thrives with the outdoor work and fresh food. In the fall, the children start school, and for the first time they are embarrassed by their ragged clothes. But Anna explains that education is the only way out of their poverty. She

hopes that by learning to read they can one day work in an office.

Jim soon realizes that tenant farming will never bring him the freedom and prosperity for which he hoped. During the winter there is no work, so he sits idle in their cabin, trying to think of ways to pay off their mounting debt. Enraged at his exploitation by the landowners, he takes it out again on Anna, who is pregnant and struggling to keep up with the housework. When the atmosphere at home becomes especially oppressive, Jim disappears for ten days.

After Anna gives birth in March, Jim decides that they should move back to their native city. Anna remembers the slaughterhouse neighborhood of her youth, and neither she nor the children want to leave the farm. But Jim is determined, so they eventually move into an unfinished two-story house with a small yard. The children continue with school. Sickened by the constant stench of meat, Anna begins to slip in and out of reality, and she starts to fall asleep in the middle of chores, which infuriates Jim who is working harder than ever in the sewers each day.

Jim is intolerant of Anna's lapses until she almost dies from a miscarriage. A contemptuous doctor uselessly advises rest, medicine, and food that the Holbrooks can't afford. Despite the efforts of others to keep her in bed, Anna soon feels compelled to resume her duties.

In the summer Jim gets a slightly better-paying job, but the heat wave keeps tempers around the Holbrook house flaring. Anna nags Mazie to help with housework, but feeling sorry for her lot as a girl, she lets her run off and play sometimes. The unfinished novel ends with the family gathered around a borrowed crystal radio set.

Holgrave. *The House of the Seven Gables.* Nathaniel Hawthorne. 1851.

A respectable and orderly young man, Holgrave has been the sole lodger in HEPZIBAH PYNCHEON's seven-gabled house for about three months. After a brief encounter with formal education, the youthful wanderer tried his hand at being a schoolmaster, a salesman, an editor, a peddler, and a dentist. While in Europe he flirted with the Utopian Fourierists and with the science of animal magnetism, called Mesmerism. Now he practices the art of the daguerreotypist. Although he has no easily fixed identity, Holgrave nevertheless possesses a strong sense of self-reliance.

Scientist, artist, and radical reformer, Holgrave exhibits the demeanor of a cool, detached observer and analyst of those around him. Early in the novel he is all intellect and no affection. Still, he is a decent sort who attempts to comfort and encourage—albeit with a half-hidden sarcasm—the histrionic Hepzibah in her moments of woe. While in the house's garden, he meets the lovely Phoebe Pyncheon, Hepzibah's distant country cousin. He shares with her his odd theory that his daguerreotypes somehow reveal the inner personality of his subjects. Although Phoebe is at first unsettled by the photographer's flights of fancy, she eventually falls under the spell of his mesmeric charm.

Yet Holgrave cannot reveal his true identity as a member of the Maule family to the young Pyncheon. The two families have been at odds since the days of the early Massachusetts settlers. The aristocratic Colonel Pyncheon had Holgrave's ancestor Matthew Maule tried and executed as a witch, and subsequently built the many-gabled house on Maule land. In return, Maule, on the scaffold, hexed the Pyncheon family with a curse of guilt. In this way Holgrave is as possessed by his past as the Pyncheons: He lives to repudiate it; they live to mourn it.

But the heroic Holgrave helps both families break free from the burden of history. At the very end of the novel, after revealing his true identity, he discloses the location of the title deed to the land and turns it over to Hepzibah and Clifford Pyncheon. He also removes the Maule's curse from the family. Finally, he repudiates his former ways as a radical reformer and dispassionate scientist to embrace the conventional domestic bliss of middle-class life with Phoebe.

Hollingsworth. *The Blithedale Romance.* Nathaniel Hawthorne. 1852.

A strong, single-minded man, Hollingsworth loses much of his emotional and physical force because he feels responsible for a woman's death. Truly passionate only about one thing—prison reform—Hollingsworth is all but indifferent to the impact his actions have on others until it is too late.

Hollingsworth does not seem the most likely candidate to join the members of Blithedale, a cooperative community just outside Boston. More used to single than cooperative efforts, Hollingsworth has been on the lecture circuit trying to drum up support for his prison reform scheme. Formerly a blacksmith who worked in grosser materials, Hollingsworth now feels that he can reform criminals by appealing to their finer sensibilities. As he confesses to MILES COVERDALE, a poet and resident of the young utopian community, he would like nothing better than to see Blithedale turned over to him and used to house lawbreakers rather than those dedicated to forming perfect communities.

Despite his dark, shaggy aspect and burly form, Hollingsworth has a sort of tenderness about him. It is this tenderness that impresses Coverdale, who is tended by Hollingsworth when he falls ill, and that inspires the love of the beautiful and wealthy ZENOBIA, a woman battling for equal rights for women. But wan, pale Priscilla, whom Hollingsworth ushers in to Blithedale one wintry evening, is the most enthralled by Hollingsworth. With little effort on his part, Hollingsworth is seemingly able to arouse in

the girl a devotion that his two more mature friends find surprising.

When their farm and house work is done, the four friends often find themselves in the woods surrounding Blithedale. A favorite spot is a place known as Eliot's Pulpit where Hollingsworth delivers impromptu sermons, enrapturing his audience. One day they debate the rights of women there, and Coverdale is surprised to hear Zenobia defending Hollingsworth's quite conservative position. To Hollingsworth, it is the man's role to be strong and resolute, with the woman remaining in a private sphere. Zenobia's declaration in support of Hollingsworth seems to add truth to the rumors that the two will marry and Zenobia will devote herself emotionally and financially to Hollingsworth's dreams of prison reform.

Hollingsworth does not have so easy a time with Coverdale, however. When Hollingsworth demands that he work with him or cease to share his friendship, Coverdale chooses not to participate in Hollingsworth's philanthropic plans. With some sadness but with the overwhelming conviction that he alone is correct, Hollingsworth dismisses Coverdale, who decides to return to Boston.

Some weeks later, while attending a Boston performance of the Veiled Lady, a supposed psychic medium who plies her trade swathed in a long white veil, Hollingsworth is surprised by a tap on the shoulder. It is Coverdale, asking the whereabouts of Zenobia and Priscilla. Hollingsworth shoos him away and turns his attention to the Veiled Lady, who has taken the stage at the behest of her manager Professor Westervelt. Moments after the performance has begun, Hollingsworth himself mounts the stage, beckoning to the Veiled Lady. She throws off her covering and reveals herself to be Priscilla. Hollingsworth leads her away.

Back at Blithedale, Hollingsworth and Priscilla confront Zenobia, and Coverdale intrudes just as the three finish talking. Hollingsworth, despite all the rumors and Zenobia's passion for him, has chosen to make Priscilla his wife. That evening, acting on Coverdale's suspicions, Hollingsworth helps Coverdale drag a nearby swamp and find Zenobia's lifeless body. Although Hollingsworth marries Priscilla, Zenobia's suicide leaves him a broken man. The last time Coverdale sees his former friend, it is Hollingsworth who must lean on the no longer frail Priscilla.

Holyoke, Horace. *Oldtown Folks.* Harriet Beecher Stowe. 1869.

Horace Holyoke is the wry and wistful narrator who chronicles his experiences of life in rural Massachusetts at the turn of the century. The novel chiefly relates Horace's early years in Oldtown, at the home of his grandparents, the Badgers, good-hearted people who care for the boy, his mother, and a host of others.

When Horace's father, a good man but an impractical scholar, dies of consumption, Horace and his mother are welcomed into his grandparents' home, a comfortable farmstead that is a center for Oldtown society, rich and poor, Indian, white, and black. A mug of cider and a plate of beans and brown bread are always ready for Sam Lawson, the village philosopher and do-nothing, or any other guest who graces the Badger doorstep.

Into this lively society come Harry and Tina Percival, two sweet, well-bred orphans. Abandoned by their father, a British soldier who has returned to England after the Revolutionary War, they lose their mother to exhaustion while traveling with her to Boston on foot. Stranded, they find their way to Oldtown and the Badgers. Harry stays on, and little Tina is adopted by Mehitable Rossiter, a kind and intelligent, though melancholy, spinster and dear friend of the Badgers.

Horace is a scholarly and reflective boy prone to waking visions. A vision of Harry Percival's mother helps Horace find the children when they first arrive in Oldtown. Because of his father's early intellectual training, Horace's speculative nature makes it difficult for him to accept faith. His visions are the closest thing he has to a spiritual life until he meets Harry Percival who is filled with the faith bestowed by his departed mother. His friendship allows Horace to enjoy a repose of spirit near to faith.

Tina, a bright, joyful little chatterbox, becomes the love of Horace's life. The three children are constant companions, with Tina always in command as the most active personality of the three. They spend hours putting on shows in Miss Mehitable's attic or lying by the stream outdoors studying and enjoying the beauty of the countryside.

Lady Lothrop, the local pastor's wife, invites the children to accompany her to Boston for Easter services in the Episcopal church. On this visit, which introduces the children to the upper reaches of Boston society, Horace meets old Madam Kittery, a dear friend of Lady Lothrop. Touched by Horace's thirst for knowledge, Mrs. Kittery promises to help him. She kindly arranges to pay for his college education, thus transforming his future with one stroke. At her home the children also meet Ellery Davenport, a charming but unscrupulous young soldier of the Revolution, destined to play a pivotal role in all their lives.

As he reaches maturity, Horace is sent with the other children to Cloudland, a tiny, beautiful town in the mountains, to live with Miss Mehitable's brother, Jonathan Rossiter, who prepares the boys for college. When Horace and Harry go off to study at Harvard, Tina returns to Oldtown and is courted by Ellery Davenport. Horace looks on with sadness when his beloved Tina eventually marries a man who, he secretly fears, is not worthy of her.

After ten years of a slowly disintegrating marriage, Ellery Davenport dies of madness, and Horace, now a successful Boston lawyer, becomes Tina's suitor. They spend their life together raising the beautiful Emily, Ellery's illegitimate daughter, in close society with Miss Mehitable

and the girl's true mother, Emily Rossiter. They pay frequent visits to Oldtown to see their remaining friends, especially Sam Lawson, the village do-nothing and wise ally of their early days.

Homos, Aristides. *A Traveler from Altruria; Through the Eye of the Needle.* William Dean Howells. 1894; 1907.

Mr. Aristides Homos, the first-person narrator of this novel, is a traveler from the fictive land of Altruria, a utopian society in the Aegean that combines the values of classical civilization and Christian socialism to form a society based on altruism or social welfare. By contrasting the "altruism" of the commonwealth of Altruria with the "egotism" of American "plutocratic" society, Homos provides a social critique of America in the 1890s.

Homos initially comes to America to observe American culture and to teach the values of his own civilization. Upon his arrival, he is hosted by Mr. Twelvemough, a writer of romances who is vacationing at a summer resort in New Hampshire. Homos interacts with the elite members of society, including a banker, a lawyer, a doctor, a minister, a professor, and various women of high society. He finds himself to be equally comfortable with the working-class members of society, and he offers to carry his own bags and helps wash his own dishes in the kitchen.

Homos's conversations with the inhabitants of the resort are predominantly on the subject of social equality. He has difficulty reconciling the model of democratic equality set forth in the Constitution of the United States and the social inequality he witnesses in actuality. The banker, Mr. Bullion, tries to explain the value of individualism in American society—the self-seeking motivation to further one's own position that is the basis of the commercial economy of America in the 1890s. Still, Homos laments the decline of agrarian communalism and warns against the dangers of a competitive market economy.

At the urging of Mrs. Makely, an American woman of leisure residing at the resort, Homos agrees to give a lecture to the local community on his native country of Altruria. In his speech Homos recounts the "evolution" of Altruria from "a commonwealth of peace and goodwill" in the early Christian republic, a land of "economic warfare" in the "Age of Accumulation," to the return of the present "commonwealth" in which people no longer live "upon" each other but "for" each other. Homos defends human nature as innately good and insists man has a natural impulse "to give and to help generously." Although the members of the community cordially praise Mr. Homos for his idealistic vision, they return nevertheless to their respective positions in the hierarchy of society.

Homos later leaves New Hampshire for New York, where he meets and falls in love with Eveleth Strange, an American woman of high society, who accepts Homos's proposal of marriage and agrees to return with him to Altruria. When she discovers, however, that she will have to abandon her fortune (for there is no need for money in Altruria) and will never to return to America, she breaks her engagement. Homos eventually convinces her to change her mind. The couple returns to Altruria to preach against the evils of social inequality.

Hooper, Father. "The Minister's Black Veil: A Parable." Nathaniel Hawthorne. 1836.

Father Hooper was a respected parson of Milford, his New England village, even before he donned his black crepe veil. What makes it all the more strange that he does so is the apparent lack of any precipitating event to cause him to cover his face. One day he arrives to give his usual Sunday sermon, and without explaining this new addition to his priestly raiment, delivers a brief and characteristically mournful sermon on "secret sin" that he believes everyone has experienced to one degree or another; he says that everyone believes he or she can hide from "the Omniscient." The sight of the veil drives this point home to his frightened audience.

Father Hooper's wife Elizabeth is at first patient and even amused by the veil. She attempts to draw him out on the subject, but his ambiguous replies offer no more specific information than did his sermon. Elizabeth begs him to remove the veil and tell her the answer to the mystery, but with an enigmatic, even wistful smile, Hooper refuses. He importunes her to bear with him and to forgo the pleasure of seeing his face. He suggests that everyone has his or her own veil of shame for sins committed, whether they wear one or not. Despite Elizabeth's tearful entreaties, Hooper states flatly that the veil will remain in place until his death. Elizabeth gives him a last, long penetrating look before bidding him "farewell."

The rest of Father Hooper's flock are more forgiving, although they are still frightened by him. The veil reminds them of their sins, and because the parson leads such an impeccable life, the fact that he chooses to hide his face makes their own faults seem all the more grave. Hooper is cut off from the normal flow of everyday social life because of the consternation the veil engenders. Far from being discouraged by the lack of human companionship, Hooper wears the veil morning, noon, and night. He continues to give the same quiet and affecting sermons as before, but with the addition of the mysterious veil, the sermons become a cause for contemplation and earnest consideration. As Father Hooper's fame spreads, his audiences grow in number, and his influence as a clergyman increases.

This continues through the years until Hooper lies on his deathbed, his face still cloaked. Those who attend to him feel sure that now is the opportunity to remove the veil and explain the sin that caused such long-lasting shame. His colleague, Reverend Clark, exhorts him to show his face and solve the mystery for them and reaches out a hand to the enfeebled dying man, who suddenly pulls his hands from beneath him and clutches the veil protectively. Clark begs to know what crime he has committed that would cause him to keep the shroud on even in these final moments. Hooper speaks his last, saying that they should not treat him differently, despite his veil, than they would treat their neighbors, for they and their neighbors are no different in the realm of sin than he. There is no human innocence: every visage is a black veil.

Hoover, Dwayne. *Breakfast of Champions.* Kurt Vonnegut, Jr. 1973.

Dwayne Hoover, a well-to-do Pontiac dealer from the American Midwest, lives alone with his dog in Fairchild Heights, a wealthy suburb of Midland City where he was born and raised by adoptive parents. His wife, also mentally unbalanced, killed herself by swallowing Drano, and his son, a homosexual piano player at the Holiday Inn cocktail lounge, no longer speaks to him. Despite his personal tragedy, Dwayne enjoys the respect of his community and is recognized as a business leader, primarily because he features himself in all his commercials.

The first signs of Hoover's insanity go unnoticed by all at Dwayne Hoover's Exit Eleven Pontiac Village except his secretly transvestite employee Henry LeSabre, who notices that Hoover is uncharacteristically ill-humored. When Dwayne goes home that evening, he takes out a pistol, shoots up his tile bathroom, and then wrecks his test-model Plymouth. Unable to recognize his hometown, he wanders in confusion before spending the night in the familiar surroundings of the Holiday Inn, in which he owns a one-third share. The next morning Dwayne forgets his dealership's Hawaiian week promotion and recoils in shock when he sees palm trees in his showroom and Henry LeSabre in a green leotard and grass skirt.

Dwayne escapes to lunch at one of his own Burger Chefs where, suffering from echolalia, he uncontrollably repeats the last word he hears. Suppressing this latest ailment, he convinces his secretary and lover Francine Pefko to make love in a nearby hotel room. When Dwayne accuses her of trying to wheedle a Kentucky Fried Chicken franchise out of him, Francine realizes that he is unbalanced and urges him to seek a new perspective from the artists at the Midland City Festival of the Arts.

Dwayne follows her advice and waits in the Holiday Inn cocktail lounge to meet one of the artists while listening to his son Bunny play the piano. When author KILGORE TROUT, a participant in the Arts Festival, finally enters, Dwayne asks him for the "message." Trout, bewildered, hands him a copy of the porn magazine containing his story. Upon speed-reading the story, Dwayne, now completely insane, believes himself to be the only non-mechanized human being on the planet. He proceeds to smash his son's face into the piano keys, bite the forefinger off Kilgore Trout's right hand, beat his lover Francine unconscious, and injure a total of nine people.

Paramedics take Dwayne to the hospital in a straitjacket. Sued by all the people he injured, Dwayne Hoover loses everything and wanders as a destitute bum along Midland City's skid row.

Hopestill. "The Wedding: Beacon Hill." Jean Stafford. 1944.

Hopestill, the young woman who marries in this story, is the niece of Miss Pride, a wealthy Bostonian who is her guardian and has taken charge of the wedding arrangements. Despite the intoxicating mood that has swept through Miss Pride's Beacon Hill home because of the upcoming event, Hopestill is clearly miserable. Observed by Sonie, a thoughtful and sympathetic narrator who is Miss Pride's household secretary, Hopestill follows through with a marriage of convenience which she regrets.

Unaware that she is being talked about and watched closely throughout the prenuptial engagements, Hopestill does not hear the dressmaker, an intuitive French woman named Mlle. Therese, remark that she is marrying a fool. Mlle. Therese guesses the truth: that Hopestill is pregnant, and she is marrying to avoid humiliation. Returning from an evening out with her fiancée, Hopestill goes upstairs and collapses on her bed in tears. Sonie hears her through the wall and pities her. Hopestill has ruined herself and can never be sure that people do not suspect the truth.

Hopestill and her fiancé Philip wanted a small wedding, but Miss Pride insisted on being lavish and inviting many people. Nevertheless, Hopestill had gotten her way on two issues. First, out of a sentimental attachment to her childhood, she had insisted on being married in the Episcopalian rather than the Unitarian church, and as she requested, her aunt had located the minister who had christened her to perform the ceremony. Second, Hopestill had refused to be given away by any relative, choosing instead an unrelated friend, Admiral Nephews, who had been her aunt's admirer. Now, marching down the aisle on the day of the wedding, Hopestill looks beautiful in her white satin gown, but there is no smile on her face. Her look, according to the narrator, is deathlike. After the ceremony Hopestill greets the well-wishers with impartial smiles, but her hand clenches her bouquet.

At the reception at Miss Pride's house, Hopestill looks ill. Toward the end of the event she beckons to Sonie and asks her to go with her upstairs. Hopestill goes to her room and pours a drink of whiskey. When Sonie joins her, Hopestill, who looks as though she has aged ten years, angrily exclaims that Philip must wait for her to return downstairs; she intends to go when she is good and ready. Hopestill confides in Sonie that she wishes she were dead and that the only accomplishment of today and of her whole life has been to transfer herself "from one martinet to another." When Sonie replies that she did not have to marry Philip, Hopestill glares at her and dismisses her from the room. As the new bride descends the stairs to rejoin her vacuous husband, Sonie can see no sign on her carefully composed face of the anger that prompted the outburst in the bedroom.

Hopewell, Hulga. "Good Country People." Flannery O'Connor. 1953.

Hulga was born with the ill-fitting name "Joy." The unwilling inhabitant of a social world where politeness is the golden rule, she chose her new name, "Hulga," by virtue of its inherent ugliness, anticipating the effect it would have on her incessantly cheery and masochistically stoic southern mother, Mrs. Hopewell. The name "Hulga" reminds Mrs. Hopewell of the "blank hull of a battleship." This is ideal for Hulga, an unattractive thirty-two-year-old woman with a doctorate in philosophy who is unmarried and thus forced to live at home.

Hulga had her leg shot off in a hunting accident when she was ten years old. She clumps around now with a prosthesis, making as much noise with the artificial limb as possible to annoy her mother and the maid, Mrs. Freeman, during their daily chats. Hulga takes little pleasure in associating with these two, nor they with her. To the two older ladies, Hulga is a pitiable creature because of her leg and her lack of beauty, and a reprehensible creature because she doesn't have the charm or the will to overcome these deficits. To Hulga, her mother and Mrs. Freeman are benighted fools who have no concept of the outside world or the world of knowledge.

One day Manley Pointer, a Bible salesman, knocks at their door. Mrs. Hopewell, answering, tells him that she doesn't need an additional Bible and that her daughter is an atheist. This gives the enterprising Mr. Pointer enough of an opening to be invited for a free dinner. While they eat, Manley plies Hulga with conversation and is undaunted by her initial reticence. She appraises him as a dullard or, as her mother says, "good country people," "the salt of the earth." But Manley is persistent, and Hulga is lonely. He points out their similarities, and Hulga is inclined to agree: They're both sober-minded and deep-thinking, and different from other people. In spite of herself, Hulga is charmed by the ingenuous attention of this country bumpkin.

Manley stops by the following day to go for a walk with Hulga. They end up in a romantic barn—exactly where Hulga had planned, in a serious round of thinking the night before, to seduce the stranger. They climb to the loft; Manley drags his suitcase full of Bibles along with him because, he says, "you can never tell when you'll need the word of God, Hulga." Showering attention on her, Manley persuades Hulga first to remove her glasses—which he pockets—and then to remove her prosthetic leg. No one has achieved such intimacy with Hulga, who is frightened and yet stimulated as well. But something is not right about Mr. Pointer's manner. Squinting, she asks for her leg back, which the salesman has shoved away.

Instead of giving the leg to her, Manley opens his suit case, revealing only two Bibles. Now that she is helpless, he places Hulga's prosthesis in his suitcase and closes it, telling her he obtained a woman's glass eye and some other items in just the same way. He informs Hulga that despite her rough appraisal of him, which was evident in her condescending attitude from the start, he has proven to be her superior. While he may indeed be "good country people," he is a lot smarter than she is and a lot smarter than all the others he has ripped off. Manley descends to the barn floor and escapes easily with his booty, leaving Hulga humiliated and possibly changed forever.

Horner, Jacob. *The End of the Road.* John Barth. 1967.

The narrator, Jacob "Jake" Horner, is twenty-eight years old in the early 1950s and does not know what to do with himself. After fixating on the most trivial decisions, he frequently sits for hours without a thought passing through his head. He calls this being "without weather," by which he means to summon up the image not of a clear blue sky but of no sky at all. Jake is most alive when he has something or someone to react against. Until then he has no steadfast opinions or beliefs of his own, but when faced with an assertion, he can come up with brilliant counterpoints that are at least facsimiles of real beliefs. When he meets Joe Morgan, however, Jake is forced to realize that his lack of values is in itself a system of belief.

After sitting all night on a bench in a train station, Jake is discovered by "the Doctor," a strange physician-psychiatrist. Fortunately, the Doctor is a specialist in odd cases and innovative treatments and runs his own "re-mobilization farm," an illegitimate but effective clinic for inpatients. After treating him, the Doctor orders Jake to take a job teaching, which he does, at Wicomico State Teachers College in Maryland. There Jake meets fellow professor Joseph Morgan and his fawning wife Rennie, and the eccentric young couple falls for him immediately. They want to test their philosophies and prescriptions for life, and Jake provides the perfect challenge because he can always see the other side of an argument.

Unfortunately, Jake falls for Rennie, and they have an affair. Rennie becomes pregnant; because her relationship with Joe has supposedly been built on absolute honesty, Rennie faces a personal crisis that Jake has difficulty understanding. When she threatens to commit suicide, Jake is faced with monumental guilt as he considers what he has done to his friend Joe and to the Morgans' marriage. Jake has trouble finding an abortionist for Rennie, but at last he is able to tell her that his physician, the Doctor from the Remobilization Farm, will do it.

Rather than take her own life, Rennie accepts this offer, but when the Doctor botches the operation, she dies anyway. Jake tells Joe immediately and waits for the consequences, but there are none. Joe lies to the authorities about Jake's involvement; clearly, the tragedy has made no one any wiser. Jake resigns from his position at the college, leaves his possessions and his apartment behind, and heads for points unknown. The last word he utters, to the taxi driver who has stopped to pick him up, is "Terminal."

Horter, Earl. *Love Among the Cannibals.* Wright Morris. 1957.

Earl Horter is one-half of a popular songwriting duo called MacGregor and Horter, the self-described "poor man's Rodgers and Hart." Earl is the lyricist, and despite his extreme cynicism about the business of making popular music, he manages to come up with catchy and romantic words to go along with the appealing piano compositions of his friend Mac. Earl's cynicism extends beyond the music business to just about everything except his search for the perfect woman and his belief that this woman, once found, will strip him of everything valuable and leave him for her next quarry. Earl believes that men and women feed on each other like cannibals.

Earl and Mac spend their days on California's Malibu beach, where Earl improves his suntan and watches the women, and Mac dreams up new topics for songs. One day a young blonde sets her towel down near them, and they strike up a conversation. Her name is Billie Harcum, she is from the Deep South, and she is not only familiar with the duo's compositions but is coincidentally an aspiring singer. Although Mac takes to her immediately, Earl, ever cynical and afraid of Mac's enthusiasm, sees Billie as a threat to the songwriting duo. But when he goes to a party with them, he becomes infatuated with another woman himself and soon loses his position of self-righteousness.

Earl falls in love with Eva Baum at first sight, despite the fact that she is twenty-three and he is forty-one years old. Eva is a curvaceous, dark-haired, lovely woman who works as a nanny for a wealthy family. She has ambitions and doesn't resist Earl's advances because she knows that she may gain something from this wealthy and successful older man. The fact that she does not bother to hide her motives both reassures and fascinates the ever-suspicious Earl. He knows she is a "cannibelle" and elects to be her cannibal. Meanwhile, Mac has decided that Billie Harcum is the one for him and that she may be a suitable addition to the musical duo.

The couples journey jointly to Mexico, ostensibly so that Earl and Mac can work on a musical having to do with cannibals and cannibelles. After much lovemaking and drinking on a beautiful beach in primitive surroundings, Billie convinces Mac to marry her, and "The Greek," as Earl affectionately calls Eva, finds a new and more useful man. Earl is left feeling stripped of his essentials, just like their abandoned car which had been stripped right down to the chassis by the locals. Despite completing a song with the line, "On the beach of love you strip down to the essentially inessential you," Earl feels hopeful about finding Eva Baum again someday, still taking care of the same kids back home.

Howe, Elena Ross. *Do with Me What You Will.* Joyce Carol Oates. 1973.

Elena Ross Howe is both strikingly beautiful and emotionally remote. When she was just seven years old, Elena was kidnapped by her father, the drunken and deranged Leo Ross, and held as a virtual prisoner for two months. As a result of this experience, Elena retreated into herself, requiring a good deal of care and attention before she would even talk again. Once she was reunited with her mother Ardis, Elena was subjected to complete domination.

Ardis forces the girl to follow in her footsteps and become a model, and then conspires to marry her off. Appearing to have no say or interest in the matter, she marries a much older attorney, MARVIN HOWE, after signing a prenuptial agreement forfeiting all future claims to his income. Between Ardis's advice, which concerns Elena's figure, and Marvin's wishes, which are not explained, it is decided that Elena will bear no children.

Elena seems happy enough in her new life; Marvin is a routinely devoted husband, and Elena seems to endure his caresses rather than take any delight in them. Her relationship with her mother has been severed because Marvin has decided that Ardis should have no influence on his wife. Elena, who occasionally watches her mother's television show, is not always certain that the woman on the television is in fact her mother. Once, when she calls, urgently needing to speak to Ardis, it is months before her mother returns the call. In the meantime, Elena begins to take adult education courses covering a wide range of topics, and she pursues them with a dogged disinterest.

One day Elena is struck by an attack of hysterics and finds herself incapable of walking any farther. At this moment JACK MORRISSEY, an attorney, appears. Knowing who she is, he endeavors to help her and drives her home.

Several months later Elena is sent to California by her husband, who plans to join her shortly; he gives her no concrete reasons for the trip, but Elena senses that there might be a threat involving one of his criminal cases. With a bodyguard around the clock, Elena remains relatively calm. When she decides abruptly to leave, she makes her way to a phone and calls Jack. Although he lives in Detroit, he agrees to meet her and flies to San Francisco the next day; the two become lovers. Elena is more thrilled by this than by anything else in her life, and her affair with Jack gradually becomes a regular part of her routine.

Jack, however, who is married and in the process of adopting a child, soon tries to force their relationship to some kind of conclusion. Finding herself incapable of change, Elena tells him to go ahead with the adoption.

As it turns out, Marvin has been secretly monitoring his wife's movements and knows all about the affair. After Elena suffers a breakdown, they move to a coastal house in Maine where Marvin hopes she will get over Jack. The move, pleasing at first, affords Elena time to think, and she finally tells Marvin that she is leaving him. She takes nothing with her but some money and goes to Detroit to ask Jack for a reconciliation. But he chooses to rebuild his ruined marriage and rebuffs her. At the novel's end, Elena, convinced that he will come to her despite his fears, grimly awaits Jack on a desolate corner of the street.

Howe, Joseph. "Of This Time, of That Place." Lionel Trilling. 1943.

Joseph Howe is a professor in this short story set at a small fictional New England college. A young instructor of twenty-six, assigned to teach composition and literature to freshmen, Howe has ambitions as a poet as well as an academic. During the course of one college year he tries to hide his poetic sensibilities from view in order to present himself as a level-headed scholar.

For Howe, the autumn term begins unpromisingly. He chances upon an article in a literary journal by a famous critic of poetry, Frederic Woolley, that attacks Howe's poetry for being too self-centered and for failing to concern itself with the general good of man. Howe believes that his colleagues will ridicule him for not having written verse that is more appropriately styled. FERDINAND R. TERTAN, an awkward young man in Howe's freshman seminar, discovers the article. Instead of vilifying his teacher, Tertan glorifies him, comparing Howe to other great professors, such as Kant, Hegel, and Nietzsche. This pleases Howe, but he can't decide what to make of Tertan and his bizarre work; his papers are comprised of nothing but tangential points built upon tangential points, all held together by an extremely florid style. During one exasperating day of class, Howe comes to the conclusion that Tertan is insane. He investigates the boy's files and discovers much about his life but nothing that explains his unusual behavior. Against his better judgment, Howe reports his suspicions to the dean, who promises to look into the matter. In Howe's mind, Tertan has ceased to be an individual and has become a cold fact.

Meanwhile, Howe is troubled by another student, THEODORE BLACKBURN, who is vice president of the Student Council and a holder of several other honors. Blackburn, a senior social sciences major, wants to take Howe's course on the romantic period. He claims to be quite an extraordinary student, but by the middle of the second semester, Howe believes otherwise. He gives Blackburn's midterm examination a failing grade. When Blackburn takes a makeup test, the grade raises only slightly. Blackburn complains and threatens that if the grade is not changed, he will report Howe to the dean. Howe does not submit to Blackburn's pressure; on the contrary, he lowers the grade to an *F*. Blackburn, begging his teacher's forgiveness, goes so far as to throw himself to his knees, but Howe, disdaining such melodramatics, remains unmoved.

Blackburn manages to graduate in spite of his failing grade, and Howe ends up standing beside him during the commencement ceremony. Blackburn plans to begin a high-paying job in business. Howe, having just been promoted to professor, is newly sensitive to the dean's proximity and makes no attempt to distance himself from Blackburn. He does glance ruefully at Tertan, however, who is sitting quietly off by himself. As Howe ponders the opposing futures of these two students, he knows that, despite his antipathy for one and sympathy for the other, he will spend his life standing next to the Blackburns of the world and abandoning the Tertans.

Howe, Marvin. *Do with Me What You Will.* Joyce Carol Oates. 1973.

When Marvin Howe first appears, he is preparing his defense of Joseph Morrissey, a man accused of premeditated murder. Marvin, a renowned young attorney, manages to win an acquittal based on temporary insanity. The son of the defendant, JACK MORRISSEY, is shocked and disturbed by Marvin's distortion and manipulation of the facts. Jack knows that his father is guilty both of the murder and of feigning mental instability. Under Marvin's tutelage, however, Jack and the entire court eventually agree that the murder was committed under the sway of imbalanced thinking. With this acquittal, Marvin begins his climb to the top of the legal profession, and before long he is called for cases all over the country. His personal wealth accumulates rapidly as he accepts houses, estates, jewels, fine clothes, and other amenities, as well as cash in remuneration for his services.

Although he has been married once before, Marvin virtually never mentions his first wife and two children. The experience was a bad one for him, and for years he resolutely refuses to entertain the possibility of a second marriage. Eventually, however, he encounters the very young and strikingly beautiful ELENA ROSS (HOWE), who under her mother's control has become a locally successful model. Marvin seeks her hand, and with her mother Ardis's assistance, their marriage is swiftly accomplished. Because he had been badly hurt by the events surrounding his first divorce, Marvin insists on a prenuptial contract in which Elena renounces all claims to his estate. He also decrees that Ardis have nothing to do with Elena; his wife will be his and his only. After these conditions are met, the couple marry, and Elena begins wearing some of the expensive clothes and jewelry that Marvin has accrued.

The Howes live in a sumptuous Detroit home, but while Elena appears to love Marvin and he looks on her with pride, their marriage is not especially warm. Marvin eventually decides that Elena needs more "polish," so she enrolls in a series of adult education courses that he knows about but does not supervise. As the years pass, Marvin's career brings him more notoriety and also some danger.

When Marvin finds out that Elena is having an affair with Jack Morrissey, he secretly investigates the liaison, which ends with Elena suffering a nervous breakdown. Out of concern for Elena's weak mental and physical health, he destroys most of the evidence he had gathered including photos of Elena and Jack together. In an effort to regroup and perhaps save the marriage, Marvin takes Elena to Maine, where he has acquired a beautiful cliffside estate. Things seem to go well for a few days, but when Marvin leaves to go out of town on business, Elena stops answering the phone although it has been Marvin's longstanding practice to call her several times a day. Upon Marvin's return, she announces that she will leave him. Marvin then spends thirty-six hours wrestling with his conscience. He has previously considered killing Jack and Elena, for he feels he has a moral right to put an end to Jack's life. But in the end he decides to leave matters in Elena's hands. He is shocked and profoundly hurt when Elena leaves, flouting his authority and refusing to take anything but a small amount of money for her immediate needs.

Howland, William. *The Keepers of the House.* Shirley Ann Grau. 1964.

William Howland lives for the land his ancestors settled and made prosper. A man of strong convictions and quiet ways, William presents a stark and resilient contrast to the hypocrisy and hatred of the surrounding white community. After the death of his young wife and his parents, William lives with his daughter Abigail on the Howland farm. Although he is considered the most eligible widower in the region, William shows no interest in society. He is content to work the land. He is not lonely, for the ghosts of his ancestors occupy the empty rooms of the large house in which he lives.

William and Abigail live in quiet understanding. In her teenage years, Abigail becomes an avid reader and decides to subscribe to the New York *Tribune*. News of the northern paper's arrival spreads through the town, and when William goes to collect his mail, the local men accuse him of treachery. But William, long indifferent to their conformist ways, just stands in the middle of the main street and laughs.

William misses Abigail when she goes away to college. He builds her a gazebo as a homecoming surprise. There, in the long summer evenings, Abigail reads to him. William does not listen to the words but concentrates instead on the familiar noises of the surrounding night.

When Abigail returns from her last year at college with the news of her impending marriage, William is jealous of her fiancé. Then, too, he begins to feel old; until now he has not noticed the passing of the years. When relatives invade the house in preparation for the wedding, William is unable to bear the loud and confusing presence of so many strangers. He retreats to an old mill and lives there until the last guest is gone.

One day in town William hears talk of a new still. He decides to play a "game" with its new owners, the Robertson family. The still operates in absolute secrecy somewhere within the nearby swamp; William claims publicly that he will find it. He has a special skiff made and sets off into the swamp. Four days later William emerges ragged yet satisfied from his successful mission, and he encounters MARGARET CARMICHAEL, a black woman living in poverty at the swamp's edges. They regard each other in silence; neither is afraid. They are at one with the land itself. William asks Margaret to come to the farm.

Soon afterward Margaret appears. She takes her own room, and she and William say little to each other. Their courtship is silent and mysterious. William waits for Margaret in his room at night. He knows that when she is ready, she will come to him.

William and Margaret live together contentedly for many years. Before the first of Margaret's five children is born, she and William drive north and marry in secret. One afternoon William is found dead, slouched over the wheel of his truck. Although ABIGAIL HOWLAND MASON, his daughter Abigail's child, inherits the farm, William's will provides Margaret with a substantial fortune.

Hoyt, Franklyn. *Good Times/Bad Times.* James Kirkwood. 1968.

Franklyn Hoyt is a sexually repressed, middle-aged, psychotic man who teaches at the elite Gilford prep school for boys in Saypool, New Hampshire. Four years after his arrival at Gilford, scandal rocked the school when a graduating senior committed suicide on the eve of commencement ceremonies after having been jilted by another of the school's seniors. Soon thereafter, Hoyt is promoted to the position of headmaster of Gilford, and he commences an all-out campaign against homosexuality in an effort to vindicate the school's reputation—a campaign he wages both on the school's campus and in his own deranged and tortured psyche. Despite his upstanding and even puritanical exterior, Hoyt is possessed with homosexual desires and, consequently, wracked with violent self-hatred.

Hoyt's repressed sexuality and psychotic aggression finally surface in his seventh year as headmaster when he falls in love with a new student, PETER KILBURN. Peter, the son of an alcoholic actor, inadvertently offends Hoyt's perverse sensibilities by arriving a day late for the school year, by dressing in a loud plaid jacket, and even by mocking the headmaster's walk when the young man thinks Hoyt is not looking. Because Hoyt is desperately trying to vindicate Gilford's image, which has been declining since the suicide, his distaste for Peter diminishes when he wins a tennis match for the school. Another scheme to improve Gilford's standing in the league of prep schools involves the annual Glee Club competition in which Peter performs Hamlet's famous "To be or not to be" soliloquy at the headmaster's insistence. As a result of these feats on behalf of the school, Hoyt becomes increasingly fond of his new charge.

Hoyt's relationship with Peter eventually develops into an unspoken love triangle when Peter befriends Jordan Legier, a glib fellow senior who suffers from a heart condition. Peter and Jordan's extraordinarily intimate but platonic relationship enrages Hoyt, and he becomes obsessively convinced that the two young men are sexually involved. When Peter sprains his back in a skiing accident, Hoyt gives him a series of alcohol "rubdowns," at least one of which is inappropriately erotic. Hearing about these massages and knowing that Hoyt's breath is tainted with alcohol, Jordan warns his terrified friend to beware of the headmaster's aggressive behavior. But given the headmaster's authoritative position, Peter is relatively powerless to defend himself.

Hoyt's powers of repression continue to erode, and he becomes uncontrollably violent when he finds Jordan and Peter asleep in bed together one morning. He slaps Peter and physically abuses Jordan to the extent that the boy suffers a heart attack and dies.

At the school's chapel that morning, the headmaster delivers an impassioned tirade against homosexuality, quoting the biblical account of Sodom and Gomorrah. Having completely lost his mental equilibrium, Hoyt is intent on forcing Peter to admit that he and Jordan were lovers, but the young man consistently refuses to confess to what is not true. Peter repeatedly tries to escape the school but is foiled by Hoyt's diligent surveillance. The boy's final attempt to flee leads to a lengthy chase through the woods across Gilford's campus and culminates in a violent scene in an abandoned boat house. Beyond all self-control by now, Hoyt corners Peter and tries to rape him, screaming wild smutty accusations as he attacks the young man. In self-defense, Peter grabs a boat hook and delivers a fatal blow to Hoyt's head.

Hoyt, Rosemary. *Tender Is the Night.* F. Scott Fitzgerald. 1933.

Rosemary Hoyt is an idealistic young actress who becomes infatuated with DR. RICHARD DIVER, a charming psychiatrist, but she is eventually disillusioned by the man and his declining abilities and social stature. Her involvement with Dick is a factor in the disintegration of his marriage to his former patient, NICOLE WARREN DIVER, a complicity Rosemary may or may not comprehend.

Almost eighteen at the beginning of the novel, Rosemary is vacationing on the French Riviera as she attempts to recover from pneumonia, which she contracted by diving repeatedly into a pool during the shooting of her first film, *Daddy's Girl*. She is very dependent on her mother, Elsie Speers, who has taught her the value of financial security and encourages her to make more decisions for herself. Rosemary first spots Dick Diver on the beach and is soon invited to one of the Divers' lavish parties. Immediately infatuated with the charismatic physician, Rosemary declares her love for Dick the very first night, but she is gently rebuffed.

The Divers accept Rosemary into their social circle, however, and at the end of the season she accompanies them to Paris where the Divers and their friends are treated to a special screening of *Daddy's Girl*. While in Paris, soon after her eighteenth birthday, Rosemary attempts to seduce Dick despite the fact that she overhears a passionate conversation between Dick and Nicole. Dick rejects her at first, explaining that he loves his wife, but later they exchange a kiss in a taxi.

One day Rosemary returns to find the body of an anonymous man in her hotel room, obviously murdered. Dick helps her avoid a potential scandal by moving the body out into the corridor. The emotionally fragile Nicole, however, becomes distraught and incoherent at the sight of the bloody bedspread, and Rosemary, horrified, perceives for the first time the nature and extent of Nicole's mental illness. Soon after, Rosemary decides to leave Paris.

When Rosemary next sees Dick, she is twenty-two years old and making a movie in Rome. In the four years that have passed since their last meeting, Rosemary has established a successful acting career and is more experienced sexually. Dick, on the other hand, is vacationing alone in order to come to terms with his sorrow about his disintegrating marriage, his failing career at the clinic where Nicole is being treated, and the recent death of his father. Rosemary and Dick finally consummate their affair, but neither is satisfied by the experience. Rosemary is pained by his gruffness and emotional distance; Dick is jealous of her flirtation with Nicotera, a young Roman. They quarrel, and although Rosemary attempts to recapture their earlier tender feelings by announcing that Nicotera means nothing to her, they part with mutual confusion and some relief.

One year later Rosemary visits the Divers on the Riviera and is disturbed by the changes she sees in Dick. He has begun to drink heavily, has been forced to resign his job at the clinic, and has lost his former ability to charm and entertain the social expatriate elite. At first she insists on seeing the "old Dick," ignoring the rumors she has heard about his dissipation, but her idealism falters as the visit wears on. She is surprised by his bitterness and embarrassed when he makes a fool of himself by attempting to show off for her when they go out in a speedboat with Nicole and some of Rosemary's friends. Rosemary and Dick briefly travel alone through Provence, but Dick feels that Rosemary has never grown up and puts her on a train

in Avignon. When Nicole, who has also taken a lover, subsequently asks Dick for a divorce, she comments that their relationship was never the same after Rosemary entered their lives.

Hsu, An-Mei. *The Joy Luck Club.* Amy Tan. 1989.

An-Mei Hsu, one of the four mothers in this novel of two Chinese-American generations, tries without success to give her American daughter the extraordinary strength she acquired growing up in China. An-Mei sees her daughter Rose watching life passively, unable to circumvent tragic events even when she sees them coming. The unusual circumstances of An-Mei's childhood taught her to act decisively according to the warnings of her acute intuition.

As a very young child, An-Mei is repeatedly reminded, by means of clever fairy tales, of the shame her mother caused the family. An-Mei is never allowed to speak of her mother, however; she is a "ghost" who is ostracized by the family and considered dead. An-Mei lives with her younger brother in the house of an affluent uncle and is cared for by Popo, her grandmother. When An-Mei is four years old, her mother returns to the house to nurse Popo who is very ill. An-Mei watches while her mother makes a traditional soup of herbs and medicines, putting into the mixture a piece of flesh from her own arm. In the course of a violent family argument, a pot of boiling soup is spilled onto An-Mei, and she is so badly burned that they are afraid she will not live. An-Mei does recover, but Popo dies. Before her mother leaves again, she tells An-Mei a fable, instructing her to carefully conceal her anger and sorrow.

Several years later, when An-Mei is nine, her mother returns, and this time An-Mei makes the decision to leave with her. Her little brother cries miserably and her uncle warns her of the disgrace, but An-Mei is still eager to see Tientsin, where her mother lives. She is a concubine or "Fourth Wife" of a wealthy rug merchant, Wu Tsing. They are welcomed to the house by Yan Chang, her mother's servant. For two weeks An-Mei blissfully explores the extravagant house, delighted by the rich furnishings. After this period, however, the other wives, who have been on vacation, return, and An-Mei is suddenly made aware of the difficulty of her mother's position. First Wife, an opium addict, is powerless in the household, while Second Wife is able to manipulate Wu Tsing, to control his money, and to bully the other concubines.

Yan Chang, An-Mei's usual playmate, relates her mother's story, explaining her extreme distrust of Second Wife. When the first three wives were unable to produce sons, Wu Tsing became restless, spending a great deal of money at teahouses in other cities. Second Wife and Wu Tsing met An-Mei's mother, a recent widow, who is extremely beautiful. Second Wife invited her to the house for dinner and a long game of mah-jongg, then insisted that she spend the night. During the night Wu Tsing raped her. Because An-Mei's mother could not accuse a rich woman like Second Wife of lying, she is forced to hide her shame by becoming Wu Tsing's third concubine.

After hearing this story, An-Mei becomes aware of her mother's terrible pain. One night An-Mei is called to her mother's room and finds the household gathered around her bed, watching the unconscious, stiffly moving figure. She dies not long afterward of an opium overdose. On the day of her mother's death, An-Mei thinks, "I learned to shout." An-Mei shows her contempt for Second Wife by crushing a necklace she had given her. She resolves not to follow her mother, concealing her feelings and remaining passive, but to "wake up" and demand justice.

Years later, after An-Mei has emigrated to America, she is frustrated to observe her mother's self-destructive passivity in her daughter Rose. Rose lacks An-Mei's *nengkan*, her powerfully motivating belief that she can do anything. When An-Mei's youngest child, Bing, is drowned, it is her *nengkan* that impels her to return to the ocean, determined to retrieve him. An-Mei is infuriated by Rose's grim acceptance of the failure of her marriage to Ted Jordan. She badgers her irritated daughter, trying to persuade her to confront Ted. An-Mei is unable to convince Rose of the necessity for decisive action, however, and the wisdom she acquired as a child remains her own.

Hubbard, Bartley. *A Modern Instance*. William Dean Howells. 1881.

Although Bartley Hubbard, the novel's protagonist, is rakish, selfish, and immoral, he is always slightly less so than other characters perceive him to be. Bartley's degeneration seems almost accidental, each step a coincidental misfortune, easily avoidable.

Bartley is the editor of the *Free Press* in Equity, Maine, but he has larger political ambitions. He studies law with the town lawyer, Squire Gaylord, and is engaged to his daughter MARCIA (GAYLORD). Marcia breaks the engagement when she learns of Bartley's flirtations with the boisterous Hannah Morrison, and Squire Gaylord banishes him for striking Hannah's young suitor. But faced with the prospect of never seeing him again, Marcia follows Bartley when he leaves town and throws herself into his arms. They marry and move to Boston without announcing their intentions to her parents.

Settling without money in Boston, Bartley and Marcia take cheap rooms, and Bartley seeks work. Postponing his ambitions of law and politics, he sells a news story to the *Chronicle*, one of the two leading Boston newspapers, and becomes a member of a men's club popular among the city's journalists. His easy affability quickly endears him to the young men of the city, and his aggressive journalistic style raises the interest of other papers.

Soon Bartley is hired as managing editor of *Events*, Boston's other leading paper. He encourages the adoption of his theory of the ideal paper, one that panders to the basest interests of the widest number of readers, with flagrant headlines about scandal and crime. As his never-resolute moral principles soften, he begins to gain weight, his corpulence becoming a symbol of the general weakening of his character.

Meanwhile, Bartley and Marcia's marriage begins to falter. Even the birth of their daughter Flavia cannot put an end to their arguments. With increasing frequency Marcia's jealousy and sensitivity to criticism make her susceptible to ungovernable rages over Bartley's flirtatiousness and vain pride. Finally, after one of their quarrels, she locks him out of their apartment. He spends the night drinking and ends up outside the home of their friend, morally-minded Ben Halleck. Halleck brings Bartley back to Marcia, but the latter's dissipation does not go unnoticed. The episode puts Bartley in a precarious position when, needing money to buy stock in his paper, he is forced to borrow it from Halleck. In the meantime, Halleck has fallen in love with Marcia, but realizing that he must squelch his love for her, he flies to Uruguay.

When the owner of *Events* discovers that Bartley has stolen a popular article from an unassuming logger acquaintance, Bartley loses his editorship, as well as the last of his friends. He squanders Halleck's money on election betting and then leaves Boston after another fight with Marcia. Remorseful, he intends to return, but when he is robbed on the train, the fate of his marriage is sealed.

Nothing is heard from Bartley for several years. Finally, Marcia receives information that Bartley is in Tecumseh, Indiana, trying to nullify their marriage. She, Halleck, Squire Gaylord, and other supporters journey to Indiana to contest what they presume to be a second marriage. Learning that Bartley has been telling people she is dead, she bursts into the courtroom, where a judge is ruling on the annulment, to sue for divorce.

Squire Gaylord denounces Bartley as a scoundrel and a perjurer. Bartley flees the town but not before justifying himself to Halleck as one who was simply trying to make the best of a bad situation: He had no plans to remarry but only wanted what was best for Marcia. The last news of him is his death in Arizona at the hands of a prominent citizen outraged by an insolent news report regarding his domestic affairs.

Hudson, Helen Brent. *Magnificent Obsession*. Lloyd C. Douglas. 1929.

Helen Brent Hudson, the widow of a renowned brain surgeon, is pursued by young ROBERT "BOBBY" MERRICK. Helen's fascination with Bobby coexists with her anger at him, and the two play a cat-and-mouse game that spans years and extends across continents.

Helen's parents were Virginians of aristocratic French origin. When orphaned as a child, she was sent to live with her father's brother, an irascible, unsuccessful lawyer.

Helen grows into an extremely compassionate young woman who is eager to protect and nurture any creature she sees as neglected or misunderstood. At college in Washington, she befriends Joyce Hudson, a troubled, rebellious girl, and encourages her to study and behave reasonably. Joyce later invites Helen to visit for the holidays at her home in Detroit. Joyce's father, DR. WAYNE HUDSON, an eminent brain surgeon at Brightwood Hospital, is deeply impressed by the transformation in Joyce's demeanor when Helen is present. The marriage that soon joins Wayne and Helen is apparently a happy arrangement among the three.

Helen insists on leaving school before graduation in order to marry Wayne, and she immediately tries to adapt to his life. She learns to respond to his moods and behave gracefully among his friends, most of whom are twice her age. The felicitous agreement among the three members of the Hudson family breaks down, however, when Wayne starts to show his loving feelings toward his wife, and Joyce becomes jealous and hostile. The situation is becoming increasingly problematic when Wayne drowns in the lake near his estate. By a disastrous coincidence, the oxygen inhalator that would have saved his life is across the lake, where Bobby Merrick, drunk and alone in his sailboat, had been knocked unconscious into the water.

Still in shock after her husband's death, Helen is visited by numerous strangers who express their sympathy and relate the same peculiar story. Wayne had given each person a loan or rescued a business at a crucial moment, while swearing the beneficiary to secrecy. Helen puzzles over these tales without understanding the motive behind her husband's generosity. She is also mystified as to how she should behave toward Joyce, who is slipping into alcoholism. She fails to prevent what proves to be a miserable marriage between Joyce and her equally irresponsible friend, Tom Masterson.

Bobby Merrick, whom Helen tries to avoid, has meanwhile undertaken to follow Wayne's example in both his career and his philosophy of life. They first meet when Helen has gotten her car stuck in a roadside ditch and Bobby comes to her aid. There is an unforgettable electricity between them, but Helen continues to distrust him. Helen travels alone to Europe and breaks off her sole friendship there, with Marion Dawson, when she finds a letter from her addressed to Bobby. While in Europe Helen finds out that her cousin Monty, to whom she has entrusted her estate, is embezzling vast amounts of money. She sold all her stock in Brightwood Hospital in order to support herself, and she becomes enraged when she finds out that Bobby purchased the stock at an inflated price for her benefit. After they meet in America and she confronts him about the stock, Helen nearly forgives him. She changes her mind, however, and returns to Europe.

Traveling in Italy one spring, Helen is badly injured in a train crash. She requires brain surgery, and Bobby, who happens to be in Paris visiting his mother, rushes to Rome to perform the operation. Although Bobby tries to conceal his identity, Helen recognizes his voice. The operation is a miraculous success. Marion Dawson travels to Rome to nurse her, and their friendship is renewed. When Helen has recovered and is about to sail from Rome, Bobby meets her at the dock, and she walks confidently into his open arms. They sail together and are married on board.

Hudson, Wayne. *Magnificent Obsession.* Lloyd C. Douglas. 1929.

Wayne Hudson diligently and unwaveringly studies to become a surgeon and at the same time nurses his ailing wife Joyce. After Joyce dies, he feels drained from her long illness and is unable to continue medical school for a time. During this period he decides to buy a marker for Joyce's grave, but when he goes to purchase a monument, he finds himself at a loss as to what the epitaph should be. The manager advises him to take a walk through the production department to see if anything appeals to him.

In a studio partitioned off from the production room, Hudson discovers a sculptor working on a fantastic angelic figure. The sculptor is Clive Randolph, a highly respected artist whose work is displayed in the most prestigious museums. Randolph asks Hudson several rather pointed questions about his life and invites him to visit that evening if he wants to know the secret that will make him the best doctor in town. Hudson dismisses the invitation but is unable to concentrate until he goes to the sculptor's home.

That evening Randolph gives Hudson a detailed account of the discoveries that enabled him to become a great sculptor. Randolph performs numerous acts of extreme generosity, which invariably result in the radical transformation of his—the beneficiary's—life. The crucial detail of the plan is that these acts must be kept secret from others or the power "leaks" in transfer. After hearing this story, Hudson leaves Randolph's house buoyed by a mystical hope and determined to carry out his own experiment in what the sculptor calls "personality projection."

Following Randolph's bizarre advice, Hudson begins seeking people who are in need of help, and he finds that the more support he offers, the more strength he feels in himself. He is now able to work with almost superhuman intensity and eventually becomes a surgeon of great renown. He assists numerous people, often rescuing them from the brink of disaster by providing money for businesses, finding jobs, and funding children's educations. The only person he seems unable to help is his own daughter Joyce who is very troubled and struggles with alcoholism. When Hudson finds HELEN BRENT (HUDSON), Joyce's college friend, capable of soothing and encouraging his daughter, he promptly marries her.

A new problem emerges, however, when Hudson begins to fall in love with Helen, and Joyce's jealousy flares up.

Before anything can be done to resolve this conflict, Hudson dies tragically, drowning in the lake near his country estate. Ironically, the oxygen inhalator that might have saved him is being used to revive ROBERT "BOBBY" MERRICK, a young profligate from a neighboring estate. Hudson leaves the secret that Randolph taught him encoded in a dairy, which is eventually deciphered and put to use by Merrick, whose life is transformed by the knowledge that he escaped death at Hudson's expense.

Huff, Walter. *Double Indemnity.* James M. Cain. 1936.

Walter Huff, the novel's first-person narrator, is an easygoing insurance man whose life is laid waste by a woman who shows him what is really in his heart.

In Hollywood on a routine policy renewal for a man named Nirdlinger, Walter meets Nirdlinger's seductive wife Phyllis. When Nirdlinger is out and Phyllis casually asks if Walter sells accident insurance, the alarmed Walter immediately decides that she wants to murder her husband. At once attracted and frightened by this idea, he knows that the best thing to do is leave and never come back. But he returns a second time; he and Phyllis become lovers, and Walter decides to help her commit the murder.

Walter tells Phyllis to leave everything to him. With Phyllis's stepdaughter Lola as witness, Walter tricks Nirdlinger into taking out a policy that pays twice as much—double indemnity—on railroad accidents. Walter feels sorry for Lola when he finds her sneaking out behind her father's back to see her boyfriend Nino, yet he feels no remorse about planning to kill her father. In fact, Walter feels hardly anything now except confidence in his plan and lust for Phyllis.

A few weeks later, Nirdlinger says he is taking a train trip to San Diego. Walter and Phyllis's complex murder plan—in which Nirdlinger is killed beforehand and Walter boards the train—runs smoothly despite minor complications. But driving home afterward, the lovers are anything but calm. They both decide it is unsafe to be seen together. When Walter gets home and lies down on his bed, he finds the whole matter has affected him. With the murder fresh in his mind, his image of himself as a cool, indifferent killer goes to pieces. Walter gets sick and cannot sleep; he decides that he hates Phyllis Nirdlinger.

The next day Walter goes to work and finds that no one thinks Nirdlinger's death was accidental. Mr. Norton, the president, thinks it was suicide, in which case the company is not liable and the two lovers will gain nothing. But Keyes, head of the claims department, has a hunch that Nirdlinger was murdered and suggests they put a close watch on Phyllis.

To relieve his tortured mind, Walter tries drink, then prayer. One night Lola comes to visit. She says she isn't seeing Nino anymore, but that isn't what she wants to talk about. She says that when her mother died, she suspected foul play, and she feels the same way now. Her mother was sick and her condition worsened considerably after a certain nurse came to care for her. Walter guesses immediately that the nurse was Phyllis. Then Keyes tells Walter they've found Phyllis's accomplice, a man named Nino. Realizing that "I had killed a man, for money and a woman. I didn't have the money and I didn't have the woman," Walter sees that there is another woman, Lola, who fills him with inner peace and sick desire. He decides that he is in love with her.

For a brief time Walter imagines that he can marry Lola and forget everything. Then Lola says that she is still in love with Nino, that she knows Nino is innocent, and that she will testify against her hated stepmother. Walter cannot bear the thought of what Phyllis will tell Lola and decides to kill Phyllis himself. He arranges to meet her up in the hills, but Phyllis gets there first and shoots him instead. Walter awakens in a hospital and learns that now Lola and Nino are suspected of killing Nirdlinger and attempting to kill him.

Walter knows Phyllis will destroy them all in time, and there is only one thing to do. He calls Keyes to his bedside and confesses everything. A feeling of great peace comes over him when he realizes he has saved Lola from further harm.

The insurance company, trying to avoid the scandal of a trial, says that if Walter signs a full confession, they will put him on a boat to the tropics. They do not say who will be on board with him: Phyllis Nirdlinger. When Walter and Phyllis meet, she jokes that now they can be married. Then she stares at the water longingly, planning to feed herself to the sharks. Walter knows this is the end of the line. "I'll go with you," he says. As the book ends, Walter is waiting for Phyllis in his cabin as the moon rises over the dark, shark-filled waters.

Hughes, Samantha "Sam." *In Country.* Bobbie Ann Mason. 1985.

Though seventeen-year-old Samantha Hughes has never been to Vietnam, she is a victim of the Vietnam War. Her father was killed in the war before she was born, her uncle Emmett may be suffering the effects of Agent Orange, and Sam is haunted by her own curiosity and confusion about the Vietnam era. In a summer that culminates in a journey from her small hometown to the Vietnam Veterans Memorial in Washington, D.C., Sam fights her own battles to understand and to come to terms with the war that left such deep wounds and scarred so many Americans.

Since her mother remarried and moved away more than a year ago, Sam has been living with Emmett in the house in which she grew up. Emmett and Sam are good friends, and they enjoy watching M*A*S*H on television and listening to music together. But lately Sam has been worried about her uncle. His mysterious skin condition is worsening, as are his chest pains and excruciating headaches.

What's more, his behavior seems more outrageous than usual. He won't look for a job and has ended his relationship with his girlfriend Anita. He has become consumed with digging a ditch alongside the house so that he can repair a crack in its foundation. Although the doctors at the V.A. hospital consider his condition minor, Sam suspects that her uncle's physical ailments—and likely his emotional troubles as well—are the result of the war. She encourages him to talk about his experience, but he resists.

Concerned but also curious, Sam joins Emmett for breakfast with his veteran friends and gleans from them what information she can about Vietnam. She likes all of the veterans and is particularly attracted to Tom, a mechanic injured in the war, whom she accompanies to a poorly attended veterans' dance. Tom is interested in Sam, but when he takes her home after the dance, he reveals that emotional scars from the war have left him impotent. Embarrassed, he stops seeing her.

After the dance, Emmett disappears. Two days later Sam's mother brings him, along with her new baby, back from her house in Lexington where Emmett had appeared one evening after a drunken spree. Sam takes the opportunity to ask her mother about the father she never knew, and after their talk her mother encourages Sam to move to Lexington and attend college. She then gives Sam money to buy a used car that Tom has offered to sell her.

Still curious about her father, Sam visits her paternal grandparents, who give her his journal from the war. Sam is appalled at what she reads. The entries at first are only brief notations, but as she reads on she finds more and more frightening reports of death and killing. Her father seems to her a heartless warmonger able to take another life without a thought. He is far different from the devoted young man described by Sam's mother and her grandparents, the man whose letters home Sam had recently read.

Confused but determined to find out for herself what Vietnam was really like, Sam runs away to the nearby swamp. She spends a frightening night there but realizes in the morning that the scenario was just that, and that she can never come close to experiencing what her father, Tom, Emmett, and others who were "in country" had lived through. Worried about her, Emmett tracks Sam down in the swamp. His fear that she was hurt prompts him to tell a story of an ambush, and he breaks down, sobbing. Sam is unable to console him.

Soon after, Emmett suggests a trip to the war memorial in Washington, D.C. Sam agrees, and they decide to take along Mamaw, her father's mother. Once there, they search for and finally find the name of Sam's father on the memorial. Touched by her grandmother's and Emmett's show of emotion, and with tears in her own eyes, Sam runs her fingers over the name. It is then that she sees her own name, Sam A. Hughes, etched in the stone near her father's. For the first time she feels some connection with the soldiers who lost their lives in Vietnam. Her scars, like Emmett's, have begun to heal.

Hull, Cora. *Reflex and Bone Structure*. Clarence Major. 1975.

Cora Hull is the central character in this experimental novel. Although a precise description of her would prove impossible, it can be gathered that she is a black actress living in Greenwich Village in New York City. The novel explores her sexual life and her struggle for fame and success on the stage and screen through a series of disconnected images and episodes, all of which end with her mysterious death.

The central story of the novel involves Cora's relationships with three men: Dale, Canada, and the first-person narrator. She is extremely independent and refuses to choose among her lovers. She moves from one to another with the same ease as a person switching channels on a television or radio. The men are extremely possessive of her, however, and are prone to fits of jealousy. As soon as one of them becomes too attached, Cora runs to one of the others, leaving him to sulk and pine for her. Although he is never actually seen engaging with Cora sexually or otherwise, the narrator comments on these activities as though he were there. He is just as prone to fits of jealousy and is especially threatened by Dale, whom he finds insincere and pretentious, and who he thinks is a bad influence on Cora. When Cora is bored with the attention of her suitors, she goes to auditions, but she never seems to land a part. Instead, she imagines herself cast in famous movies, replacing the famous white leads. Often, after a fit of passionate lovemaking, Cora retreats to the TV and, unable to find a program she likes, sees herself on the screen in these glamorous roles. Other times she simply imagines herself having the life-style of a famous actress, traveling all over the world, fighting off fans.

Cora's excessive life-style and imagination eventually catch up to her. At several points in the novel she is killed. Sometimes she is shot; at others, she is run over. Dale and Canada are both suspected because they are gun collectors, and their jealous rages are an obvious motive. But the reader is never able to determine who, in fact, is responsible. One can only conclude that somehow all the attention Cora received has eventually led to her downfall. She is likened to a starlet who chokes on too much publicity. For the men of the novel, Cora embodies a feminine ideal: She is beautiful, highly sexed, free-spirited, and unattached. But the men in her life refuse to accept her independence. She runs and runs to keep ahead of them—to "get out of herself"—and eventually runs out of breath.

Humbert, Humbert. *Lolita*. Vladimir Nabokov. 1955.

Humbert Humbert is the perverse narrator of this confessional tale. Born in Paris in 1910 to a Swiss father and a British mother, Humbert describes his early years as idyllic even though his mother was struck and killed by lightning while he looked on. His academic record—first at an English day school and later at universities in London and Paris—was, as he portrays it, nothing less than stellar.

Humbert's first teenage romance is with a thirteen-year-old girl. As he grows older, he unsuccessfully strives to repress his forbidden desire for "nymphets." For his own safety he marries, but after four miserable years, no children, and very little intimacy, his wife divorces him. Humbert then leaves Paris for the United States, where he collects an inheritance from the estate of a dead uncle.

In New York, Humbert works on his multivolume survey of French literature, and his torturous lust for nine- to fourteen-year-old girls returns. He suffers three breakdowns and spends more than a year in different sanatoriums. At the end of his last hospital stay, he sets out for a quiet summer in the New England town of Ramsdale, where he becomes the lodger of widowed CHARLOTTE BECKER HAZE.

In a complicated triangle of desire, Humbert falls in love with Mrs. Haze's thirteen-year-old daughter DOLORES "LOLITA" HAZE, Charlotte falls in love with Humbert, and young Lolita fantasizes about Humbert and becomes the victim of her mother's frustration. Several tantalizing weeks after Humbert's arrival, Mrs. Haze sends the star-struck Lolita to a summer camp and leaves a letter, proposing marriage, for her lodger. Humbert shamelessly accepts the marriage proposal in order to remain near Lolita.

Humbert's plans seem frustrated when Charlotte decides to send Lolita directly to a boarding school at the summer's end. Stunned by the prospect of living with the full-grown Charlotte rather than her nymphet daughter, Humbert considers murdering Charlotte. Charlotte, however, makes murder unnecessary. She breaks into the locked table drawer where Humbert keeps his journal and reads detailed accounts of his carnal desire for Lolita and his contempt for her. Furious, Charlotte runs out of the house to mail a warning to Lolita and is struck and killed by a neighbor's car. Humbert stays in Ramsdale only as long as it takes to bury Charlotte without raising suspicion. Then he sets out to possess Lolita.

On their first night together, Humbert slips his stepdaughter a sleeping pill. Filled with anticipation, he lays down in his bed beside her but soon discovers that the pill was a placebo and Lolita is sleeping fitfully, not soundly. The following morning Lolita, Humbert claims, seduces him. The two then set out on the first of two long, cross-country drives. In time Lolita and Humbert establish the parameters of their sexual relationship. Humbert convinces the child that if anyone learns they have intercourse, she will be sent to live either in an institution or with a tyrannical aunt. Lolita, for her part, demands financial and material recompense for her participation.

After approximately a year of circuitous driving, Humbert and Lolita settle in the town of Beardsley. Humbert cannot abide Lolita's potential involvement with boys of her own age and carefully monitors all her actions. When their situation seems to have reached a crisis, the two decide to embark on another driving tour. This time, however, Lolita demands to map the route.

The playwright Clare Quilty, with whom Lolita had begun a relationship in Beardsley, follows Humbert and Lolita throughout their tour, causing Humbert to reach new levels of desperation. When Lolita and subsequently Humbert fall ill in Elphinstone, Colorado, Quilty and Lolita escape. Unable to find any trace of the two, Humbert eventually returns to New York and enters a superficial relationship with Rita, a woman who looks young but is past the age of consent. Several years later he receives a letter from Lolita asking him for money. Lolita has married a poor man named Richard Schiller and is now pregnant. Humbert forces her to reveal the identity of the lover for whom she left him. He then tracks Quilty to his home and murders him.

Hunnicutt, Hannah. *Home from the Hill.* William Humphrey. 1958.

As Humphrey's narrative opens, Hannah Hunnicutt's body is being lowered into a grave next to those of her husband Wade and son THERON (HUNNICUTT). The gravestone marking her burial place had been erected fifteen years earlier when she buried Wade and Theron, and its inscription reads: HANNAH HUNNICUTT DEPARTED THIS LIFE MAY 28, 1939, AGED 39 YEARS. This inscription reveals the central and tragic fact of Hannah's life: that since the little happiness given to her in life was given to her by her son, when he dies she feels she has died, too. The remainder of this novel constitutes a long flashback that provides the portrait of a woman doomed by the passions of the men in her life.

Hannah had married Captain Wade Hunnicutt when she was twenty years old. Soon after becoming pregnant with Theron, she discovered that her husband was becoming famous in the community for his numerous adulterous affairs. This knowledge resulted in a permanent emotional estrangement between Helen and Wade, although she continued to treat him in a devoutly respectful fashion and even began to take a perverse pleasure in befriending his series of lovers.

Hannah directed her affections toward Theron and doted on and encouraged him in his every pursuit; indeed, she eventually realized that she had encouraged his interest in hunting too much and endangered his life by urging him to better his father in the sport. Hannah also carefully shielded Theron from the truth about his father, feeling that if he were disillusioned about his father, he would become disillusioned with her as well.

Over time, as Theron grew into a fine and respected

young man, Hannah and Wade's mutual satisfaction in their son began to draw them together. One night Hannah decided to end her long years of restraint and loneliness by going to Wade and offering herself to him. Just as she made this decision, however, she saw Wade sneaking into the house after an illicit liaison. Later that night, when Theron told her that the father of a girl he liked had refused to let him date the girl, Hannah broke her silence and explained to Theron that the man had not rejected him because of any fault in himself but rather because of Wade's reputation with women.

This night was, in a sense, the true end of Hannah's life. Her flicker of hope for love with her husband had sputtered out as soon as it had arisen, and her revelation to Theron affected him as she had always feared it would: Devastated by the truth about his father and his parents' life together, Theron turned against Hannah as well as Wade. Furthermore, Theron had already suffered from events Hannah knew nothing about, and her revelation affected him in ways that she never realized—ways that led directly to his own and his father's death. Thus, despite her stoic efforts to endure her loveless life with dignity, Hannah had been doomed from the start by her husband's inconstant nature.

Hunnicutt, Theron. *Home from the Hill.* William Humphrey. 1958.

As the novel opens, HANNAH HUNNICUTT is being buried under the gravestone she had had made for herself fifteen years earlier when her neglectful husband Wade and her beloved son Theron died. The remainder of the book constitutes a long flashback describing the accumulation of fateful ironies by which the errors of Theron's parents are visited upon their only child.

By the time Theron is born, his parents were already estranged due to Wade's adulterous behavior with other women. Hannah showered her frustrated affections on Theron, while Wade, a famous hunter, taught Theron everything he knew about hunting. Theron grew into an upstanding, forthright, well-liked if rather naive young man, but his interest in hunting became dangerous as he assayed more and more difficult feats in an attempt to compete with his father. When Theron killed a wild boar, just as his father had once done, he realized that he had been carrying on a destructive competition with his father. With this realization the competition phase of the father-son relationship was safely ended but was soon followed by deadly consequences.

Theron fell in love with Libby Halstead, and before she left for college, he made love to her—an act for which he was immediately consumed with guilt and shame. That night Hannah finally told Theron about Wade's reputation as a womanizer. This revelation devastated Theron, who now realized that his parents had always been unhappy with each other. Theron also felt that his father

was a scoundrel and that he had just proved himself to be the same.

Theron renounced hunting, avoided his parents, and fell into such a deep depression that when Libby returned from college, he rejected her without giving her the chance to tell him that she was pregnant with his child. Unbeknownst to Theron, Libby's father had informed Wade of Libby's pregnancy and asked if he would arrange for their children to marry. Wade rebuffed Mr. Halstead, and Libby married another man. When Theron heard about Libby's marriage, he married Opal, a young woman whose child Theron thought was his father's. Theron soon discovered that Opal's baby was not Wade's child and that his attempt to atone for his father by "adopting" his own brother had failed.

Theron and Opal's marriage remained unconsummated, and she soon abandoned him. Theron then discovered that he was the father of Libby's baby, and he and Libby determined to get back together again. Theron thereupon decided to mend relations with his parents and return home, but as Wade hurried to tell Hannah about their son's return, he was shot by Mr. Halstead who had come to believe that Wade was the father of Libby's child. Theron chased after Mr. Halstead, killed him, and then walked unarmed into the woods—an act which ensured his own death.

Hunter, Anson. "The Rich Boy." F. Scott Fitzgerald. 1925.

Anson Hunter is an extremely wealthy and charismatic member of one of the most deeply entrenched high-society families in New York. His pampered upbringing generates a refined but unmistakable superiority that ultimately undermines his ability to find love and happiness.

Tall and blond, Anson has been reared by extremely distinguished parents whose respectability includes shunning the more snobbish and presumptuous mannerisms of New York City's elite Gilded Age families. His social and formal education is carefully engineered to inspire self-confidence without condescension. Having earned a degree at Yale, he joins in the war movement in 1917 and is stationed in Pensacola, Florida, where he is trained as a naval pilot.

Robust, bawdy, and fun-loving, he becomes very popular in his military circle, and his friends are surprised when he tones down the raciness of his life-style in order to date Paula Legendre, a beautiful and very conservative young woman to whom he eventually becomes engaged. Their relationship begins to decline, however, when Anson arrives drunk for a date after an afternoon binge with his friends at the Yale Club in New York. This errant behavior becomes more frequent, and scarcely a day goes by when she does not smell alcohol on his breath. This tendency toward self-indulgence runs counter to Anson's otherwise strong paternal attitude, and Paula is mystified as to how to respond to this contradictory behavior.

After months of dating and courtship, Anson is sent to Europe to join the World War I military effort, and a month later his plane crashes into the North Sea. He survives the crash but contracts pneumonia from a night spent in the water before being rescued by a roving destroyer battleship. While Anson is still convalescing in the military hospital, the armistice is signed and he is sent home.

When he returns, Anson resumes his relationship with Paula, but when his drinking and carousing continue, she breaks off the engagement. With characteristic overconfidence, Anson still harbors the belief that they will eventually marry, although he makes no active effort to effect a reconciliation. In spite of the fact that he is independently wealthy, he spends long hours working as a financier on Wall Street. His evenings revolve around imbibing spirits, dancing, and playing cards at half a dozen clubs frequented by other members of his social set. He indulges in affairs with a series of women he doesn't love while holding on to the hope that Paula will one day come back to him. His love remains unrequited as Paula marries, divorces her first husband, and immediately marries another Bostonian. Anson begins to consider the possibility of marrying for companionship despite his inability to experience romantic love for anyone other than Paula. Years pass, and at the age of twenty-nine, Anson accidentally meets Paula, who is now married with children. Her evident happiness contrasts painfully with his own successful but empty existence as a bachelor whose only solace is the memory of idealized love.

Plunged into depression after this encounter, Anson is encouraged by his colleagues on Wall Street to take a long trip to recover his spirits. Before setting sail for Europe, he gets word that Paula has died in childbirth. He spends the boat trip eliciting love from a young woman in a red tam in an attempt to rekindle his old happiness.

Huntly, Edgar. *Edgar Huntly*; or, *Memoirs of a Sleepwalker*. Charles Brockden Brown. 1799.

Accustomed to a quiet life in rural Pennsylvania, Edgar Huntly is little prepared for the trials that face him following his encounter with the moody and mysterious CLITHERO EDNY. Edgar's well-intentioned but rash actions, beginning with his effort to befriend Clithero, result in numerous brushes with death and in causing grief to people he had no intention of hurting.

Edgar relates his curious tale in a letter to his fiancée Mary. One night, months after the murder of Mary's brother Waldegrave, Edgar sees Clithero, a laborer, lurking about the scene of the young man's death. A sleepwalker, Clithero repeats his nocturnal visit on another night and seems to be burying something under a tree. Edgar reasons that Clithero, recently arrived from Ireland, is somehow involved in Waldegrave's death.

When questioned by Edgar, Clithero does not acknowledge any involvement in Waldegrave's death but does relate a melancholy tale of his life in Ireland. Clithero is convinced that he caused the death of Euphemia Lorimer, his benefactress. The day after making this confession, Clithero disappears.

Edgar believes that Clithero, planning to commit suicide, has fled to one of the labyrinthine caves he frequented during his sleepwalks. He gathers some food and leaves it for the remorseful Irishman, hoping that Clithero will emerge from his despondency when he sees that someone wants to help him. The next night the curious Edgar rummages through Clithero's belongings but finds little of interest. He goes to the tree in Inglefield's yard and digs up a manuscript written by Mrs. Lorimer that Clithero had buried there. On returning to his room Edgar finds that in his absence Clithero has come and gone after discovering that Edgar has been through his belongings. Edgar returns to the cave the next day but is unable to find Clithero.

Clithero's situation is not Edgar's only concern. He wants to make a copy of Waldegrave's letters for Mary but discovers one night that they are missing. As he wonders who could have stolen them, his uncle—the guardian of Edgar and his sisters after their parents' death at the hands of Indians—enters his room and asks if Edgar has been pacing in the attic. Neither the thief nor the attic intruder is discovered. The next day, while still brooding on these new mysteries, an old friend of Waldegrave's appears and claims that the $7,500 the dead man left behind is actually his.

Preoccupied and troubled, Edgar seeks relief in a deep sleep. When he awakens, he is surrounded by darkness. He slowly comes to realize that he is in an underground cave, perhaps the same one where Clithero was hiding, and at the bottom of a deep pit. Using strenuous effort he escapes the pit but is faced with an even graver danger: a panther. He kills the beast with a tomahawk he found in the pit and then, desperate with hunger, feasts on the raw flesh of the freshly killed animal. When the wrenching pains that follow this bloody meal subside, Edgar sleeps.

It takes Edgar days to return to civilization. In his attempt to reach home, he murders five Indians who had scalped a white family and taken a young girl hostage; he braves cold, hunger, and life-threatening wounds; and he eludes the gunfire of a group of whites who mistake him for an Indian. The presence of Indian raiders not only reminds Edgar of the deaths of his parents but also arouses fears that his uncle and sisters have been murdered.

On the way home Edgar's attention is drawn to an empty house. He enters it and inside finds Waldegrave's letters; as he is examining them, a familiar figure appears. It is Sarsefield, Edgar's old tutor and second husband of Euphemia Lorimer who, contrary to Clithero's belief, is alive. Sarsefield assures Edgar that his family is still alive, and he expresses the wish that his former student look on his now wealthy friend as a benefactor.

Months later, when the excitement caused by the raid has died down, Edgar and his sisters enjoy Sarsefield's and Euphemia's generosity. Clithero, who had been captured and wounded by the Indians, has recovered. Edgar realizes that Clithero, while sleepwalking, had hidden Waldegrave's letters in the attic and that the letters had been discovered by Sarsefield. Feeling kinship with fellow sleepwalker Clithero, Edgar decides that Clithero will emerge from his ongoing depression if he knows that Euphemia still lives. A letter from Sarsefield to Edgar reveals, however, that Edgar's decision to tell the truth is a rash one. Clithero, now insane, vows to kill Euphemia, a crime he imagined he had committed long ago. He is unsuccessful, but when Euphemia inadvertently learns of his plans, she miscarries the child she was to bear for her new husband.

Hurstwood, George W. *Sister Carrie.* Theodore Dreiser. 1900.

An illicit affair causes George W. Hurstwood to fall from prosperity to poverty, and finally to end his life. Hurstwood rose from the position of barkeeper to become the manager of Fitzgerald and Moy's Saloon, a fashionable establishment in downtown Chicago where prominent businessmen and politicians socialize. A model of "upper-class" respectability, Hurstwood is deferential to those in higher orbits and amiable to those of his own level and even below, including his friend, the salesman CHARLES DROUET.

One day Drouet introduces Hurstwood to a "little peach" he met on a train, a small-town girl named CAROLINE "CARRIE" MEEBER. When the three play cards together, Hurstwood appreciates her charms. Although his attentiveness is only half-sincere, his polish and easy manner make an impression on the girl from the provinces.

However, Hurstwood is also a congenial but indifferent family man, with a sometimes surly wife, Julia, and two very ambitious, social-climbing children, George, Jr., and Jessica. His comfort in his upper-class home makes him circumspect about his behavior, but his indifference to most of his family's activities lays the groundwork for extra-familiar interests.

Drouet had once told Hurstwood that Carrie was his wife, but when Hurstwood sees him out with another woman, he shrewdly senses Drouet's weaknesses of character as an opportunity for himself. He begins to take more of an interest in Carrie, and they gradually fall in love. Hurstwood would prefer to see his comfortable existence stay that way, but when Mrs. Hurstwood learns of her husband's secret meetings with a stranger, his life rapidly reaches a crisis.

In response, Hurstwood suggests to Carrie that they run away together. She agrees, provided he promises to marry her. However, Carrie finds out from Drouet that Hurstwood is already married. Carrie consequently fails to meet him and answer his letters, and when his wife threatens immediate and scandalous divorce proceedings, Hurstwood finds his life becoming unmanageable.

One night Hurstwood, uncharacteristically drunk, goes into the back room of the saloon and finds the safe unlocked. Merely entertaining the idea of stealing, he takes out the money and then sees that the door has shut, and he does not have the combination. Scarcely thinking, he takes the money, tells Carrie a story about Drouet being in the hospital, and tricks her into boarding a train for Detroit with him. When she discovers his dishonesty, Carrie protests vehemently, but he talks her into continuing on with him with the understanding that she is free to go back.

After a bogus marriage in Montreal at Carrie's insistence, Hurstwood sends most of the money back, and the two hurry on to New York. Hurstwood cannot rely on his social connections now, and the saloon in which he invests with a drunken partner fails. Rapidly losing energy, he falls into a deep depression. He misses his days of hobnobbing in Chicago, but he can't rouse in himself the drive necessary to crash the gates of what he sees as a walled city. When he does push himself to be a scab motorman during a Brooklyn trolley strike, he is beaten and almost shot. Meanwhile, at their flat, Carrie has become repulsed by his ongoing idleness. When she gets work in a theater, she moves out, leaving him a note and twenty dollars.

Hurstwood is now a fallen man. He wanders on bitter winter nights through the city, reduced to begging, cheap beds, and park benches. Wasted in body and spirit, he gives up hope of beginning again. With the requisite fifteen cents, he checks into a Bowery lodge house, one partitioned in a way he feels is almost tailor-made for his purposes. In his little room, he stuffs the cracks and turns on the gas.

Hutchins, Eveline. *U.S.A. (The 42nd Parallel; Nineteen Nineteen; The Big Money).* John Dos Passos. 1930; 1932; 1936.

The beautiful, almond-eyed EVELINE HUTCHINS, first encountered as the museum-going companion of ELEANOR STODDARD, drifts from one love affair to another, and grows further and further apart from her old friend, until she tragically ends her life.

An unconventional and artistic daughter of a freethinking Unitarian minister, Eveline grows up in Chicago. Eveline is as interested in the artistic men that she and Eleanor encounter as she is in their artistic creations. She falls for a rogue named Dirk McArthur, but he is soon killed in an auto accident. Then she and Eleanor go to New York to design sets for a stage production by Eveline's admirer, Freddy Sergeant, but the show flops, and Eveline goes to Santa Fe with her ailing father. In Santa Fe,

Eveline has her first real love affair, with an artist named Jose O'Riely, for whom she works as a model. After she leaves Santa Fe for New York, she falls in love with a political activist named Don Stevens.

At the start of World War I, Eveline goes to Paris where Eleanor is helping JOHN WARD MOOREHOUSE, who is called Ward, with his public relations activities. The women do various kinds of Red Cross work, and Eveline has a series of brief flirtations and love affairs. Don Stevens, her New York lover, is in Europe doing peace work, and through him she meets Paul Johnson, a young private who falls for her wholeheartedly.

After the armistice she begins seeing more of Ward Moorehouse and finds herself courted by some of his political and journalistic friends. Finally she has a brief affair with Moorehouse himself—she has long admired him and envied Eleanor his attentions—but immediately regrets it. She begins to wonder what will become of her after she returns to the United States and regards marriage as her only option. Conveniently, the innocent doughboy Paul Johnson reappears, and after a brief courtship she announces that she is going to have a baby; they marry and return to New York.

Their married life is not one of mutual bliss: Paul works and cares for the baby while Eveline entertains an astonishingly wide assortment of guests: The actress MARGO DOWLING shows up at one of her parties, as does the communist MARY FRENCH (another cast-off lover of Don Stevens), the public relations executive RICHARD ELLSWORTH SAVAGE, and a variety of artists, journalists, and other partygoers. She ends up having affairs with several of these guests, most notably with Savage, the aviator Charley Anderson, and a columnist named Charles Edward Holden.

Despite its apparent exuberance, Eveline's life is growing more and more desperate. For a time Paul endures her infidelity while she endures his passivity, but eventually they separate and divorce. Eveline continues to have her parties and tries to get a little work in stage design, but she finds life "just too boring." After her last party she takes an overdose of sleeping pills.

Hutchinson, Tess. "The Lottery." Shirley Jackson. 1948.

Tess Hutchinson, an ordinary wife and mother of three, is the victim of the "lottery," a grisly ritual enacted annually by the members of her small New England town. Since their populations have increased so dramatically, most of the surrounding communities have expanded the lottery to two full days. In this small town, though, the annual date of June 27 suffices.

As has always been the local custom, Mr. Summers, the lottery conductor, arrives in the square carrying the black box that will be used for the drawing. The assembly, long used to the ritual, goes through the motions of the customary salute and murmured phrases before Mr. Summers ascertains that all required are present. At this, Tess rushes up to join her husband, Bill Hutchinson, and her children, Bill, Jr., Nancy, and little Dave. As she arrives, she gently jokes that she couldn't very well have left dirty dishes in her sink; an appreciative laugh ripples through the crowd.

Finally, it is time for the drawing of the lottery, which proceeds in alphabetical order throughout the town's population. The drawing starts with the men, who draw for their households. Amid a general anxiety, there is mumbling that some nearby towns have actually already abandoned the practice; but Old Man Warner scoffs. Attending his seventy-seventh lottery, he denies the advisability of tampering with tradition. When all the men have drawn lots, it is revealed that Bill Hutchinson has won the round. Tess immediately sets up an outcry that her husband had had insufficient time to search in the box for the exact paper he wanted. She is silenced by others who remind her that all have taken the same chance.

The next stage determines what members of a chosen household will draw. Once again Tess protests with mounting anger, and her husband tries to silence her. It's unfair, Tess asserts, that her married daughter should be counted with her husband's family rather than with the Hutchinsons, and once again she is silenced. It is determined then that the five Hutchinsons will draw again, and their papers, including Bill's, are replaced in the battered black box. The Hutchinsons approach one by one while the rest of the town looks on breathlessly. Before they begin, Tess again claims that the drawing has been unfair and that she wishes to start over.

Tess does not get her wish. Beginning with the youngest boy Dave, assisted by an older man, the lots are drawn. As the family opens their new slips of paper, they quickly reveal that none of the children has been selected. Bill reveals his slip, and then all eyes turn to Tess. Bill is told by Mr. Summers to show his wife's choice, and when he does so, the black spot on the paper is clearly visible.

With the stunned Tess standing in the middle of the square, the villagers hasten to finish the lottery ritual. Turning to the pile of stones assembled earlier, with someone providing even little Dave with ammunition, they turn on Tess. While she screams out that her lot is unfair, the villagers set upon Tess with their stones, and she reaps the rewards of this macabre lottery.

I

Ida. *Ida.* Gertrude Stein. 1941.

Ida, the novel's protagonist and title character, is characterized by an inexplicable emotional and physical lethargy. Because she is independently wealthy, she is able to spend most of her time sitting and resting, which is what she most enjoys doing. But this behavior becomes more pronounced as her life progresses, and by the conclusion of the novel, Ida has withdrawn emotionally to such a degree that she seldom leaves her home.

· The novel opens with an account of Ida's birth. Her mother does not want to bear her; shortly after her birth, Ida's parents abandon her for no apparent reason, and she lives with various relatives. As a child, Ida experiences a number of "funny things," a euphemism for vaguely sexual encounters with men. Her perceptions of these events are markedly ambivalent. Once when Ida is lost, a man pursues her and frightens her so that she begins to cry, yet later in life she feels that this was a comforting experience. On another occasion two men surprise her by jumping out from behind some trees. She tells her companions, who are also women, that they should hurry along, and she will protect them; she herself lags behind and turns toward the men, but they have disappeared. Ida feels at once attracted to and threatened by the men she encounters.

At the age of eighteen, Ida creates an imaginary twin so that if anything unusual happens, no one will know which of the two of them is responsible. Ida writes letters of praise to her twin, addressing them to "dear Ida my twin." She later renames the imaginary sister Winnie.

Ida's twin eventually begins to dominate her personality to an alarming extent. On one occasion a military officer mistakes Ida for Winnie; she feels faint and begins to doubt the value of her creation. She had remarked to her dog, Love, that since she created the twin, she retained the right to destroy it, and ultimately, in defense of her own personality, she does so.

Shortly after killing her imaginary twin, Ida begins to consider marriage. She starts engaging in obtuse conversations with various military officers and eventually marries Frank Arthur, an army officer who was once shipwrecked and had his ear frozen, and he so enjoyed the experience that he tried to duplicate it. But this marriage does not last very long. In fact, Ida marries repeatedly, showing a particular penchant for officers. Despite the disintegration of the marriages, all of her ex-husbands remain on good terms with their bizarre ex-wife.

At the close of the novel, Ida is involved with a man named Andrew, who, in direct opposition to Ida's lazy detachment, is very restless. Andrew takes many walks in order to disseminate his excess energy. In contrast, Ida's increasingly listless behavior is manifested in her reticence to engage in conversation and her tendency to dress in black. Although she continues to rest incessantly, she never seems to get the rest she needs to gratify her pathological craving for relaxation.

inBOIL. *In Watermelon Sugar.* Richard Brautigan. 1968.

The character inBOIL threatens the peaceful world of iDEATH, the commune-style town in which this experimental novel is set. In the past, iDEATH was plagued by man-eating tigers who spoke English and were kind and apologetic to their victims. At the time of the tigers, inBOIL was a resident of iDEATH. However, when all of the tigers are exterminated and the material objects representative of their tyranny are deposited in a large dump known as the Forgotten Works, inBOIL becomes restless and ornery. He is joined by other men who have become disenchanted with iDEATH.

The inhabitants of iDEATH fear and loathe inBOIL and his gang; they worry that inBOIL will, like the man-eating tigers, try to harm iDEATH in some way. One evening inBOIL and his gang arrive at iDEATH just as its inhabitants are eating dinner. InBOIL curses iDEATH and tells its inhabitants that ever since the tigers were conquered, no one has understood the true meaning of iDEATH. Telling the inhabitants that they have made a mockery of their commune, inBOIL demands that they follow him and his gang to the trout hatchery in iDEATH where he will show them exactly what iDEATH is. They follow him, worried that he will do damage to someone or something. Once in the trout hatchery, however, inBOIL and his gang take out pocket knives and cut off their own thumbs. Then, as inBOIL dances about and chants, "I am iDEATH," he and his men cut off their noses and ears, and they all bleed to death. None of the inhabitants of iDEATH attempt to stop inBOIL and his men from killing themselves. Once they are dead, the inhabitants of iDEATH remove the bodies and burn them, just as they burned the bodies of the tigers years before.

InBOIL is barely mentioned again by any of the other characters. His rebellious death, although grotesque and painful, is futile in the end because he fails to communicate the meaning of the gesture. None of the inhabitants of iDEATH understand why he killed himself in the way he did or what his death meant. Thus, his death is talked about briefly and then quickly forgotten, and the inhabitants of iDEATH continue to live peacefully.

Indigo. *Sassafrass, Cypress & Indigo.* Ntozake Shange. 1982.

Generally taciturn, Indigo, the youngest of the three sisters after whom the novel is titled, has had a special affinity with both magic and music from her earliest years. As a young girl, Indigo made her own large collection of dolls, each endowed with a special name and personality. Carrying one or more of them, Indigo roamed her neighborhood, gathering information in the form of stories and legends from older women and from the local vagabond, Uncle John Hudson.

Indigo's affection for her dolls and her openness about her ability to communicate with them eventually drives her mother Hilda Effrania to distraction. When Indigo begins to menstruate at the age of twelve, her mother informs her that it is time for her to give up her childish ways. Although her mother asks her to give the dolls away to young girls, Indigo decides that they should be preserved for the time when she and her sisters have their own daughters who will know how to treat the dolls properly. As a part of her coming-of-age, Indigo and her mother conduct a private ritual during which Hilda Effrania sings a hymn as her daughter bears the shrouded dolls, one by one, into the attic.

In the meantime, in recognition that a major change has taken place in his young friend, Uncle John has given Indigo a violin, which she learns to play in her own inimitable fashion, eschewing lessons even when her mother forbids her to play in the house. Indigo eventually attracts the attention of two young boys, Spats and Crunch, who, at once enticed and frightened by her music, decide to induct her into their society of the Junior Geechee Captains. This little troupe gradually becomes employed in working for a local club. Indigo plays her violin, and the boys prepare for and clean up after cock fights. The proprietor offers Indigo a dollar for every song she learns, and she becomes adept at copying the songs on his jukebox. It was not the role-playing to which she has turned that attracted customers, however, it was her wild and free playing, and the proprietor's girlfriend eventually chases Indigo away. Indigo is not unduly upset since she is now free to return to her own music.

Indigo soon decides to live with Aunt Haydee, a woman gifted in several aspects of herbal medicine and midwifery. Following the woman's death, she takes up residence in the old cabin and begins to take Aunt Haydee's place in the community. She continues to play her music but stays resolutely away from her mother's home in Charleston, North Carolina, for life in the cabin seems more natural to her. It is only when her oldest sister, SASSAFRASS, returns from New Orleans to give birth that Indigo leaves her cabin, joining her mother, Sassafrass, and her other sister, CYPRESS, to facilitate and celebrate the impending birth.

Isaacson, Daniel (Daniel Lewin). *The Book of Daniel.* E. L. Doctorow. 1971.

Daniel Isaacson, a graduate student at Columbia University, is a fictional character whose life mirrors that of the son of Julius and Ethel Rosenberg, communists who were executed for treason in 1953. Although Daniel expends considerable energy attempting to escape the legacy of his parents' notoriety, he finds that it is impossible to live a life not by the ghosts of his past. In addition to the task of maintaining his own mental equilibrium, Daniel is burdened with the responsibility of providing moral support for his younger sister SUSAN (ISAACSON), whose reaction to her traumatic life includes suicidal behavior.

PAUL (ISAACSON) and ROCHELLE ISAACSON, Daniel's parents, are card-carrying members of the Communist Party who attempt to raise their children according to the political principles of Lenin and Stalin. As Jewish communists they are prime targets for the House Un-American Activities Committee during the peak years of the McCarthy era. When their parents are arrested for allegedly disclosing top-secret scientific formulas to Russian communists in 1950, Daniel and his sister Susan live temporarily with two of their aunts who, because they fear being associated with their incarcerated brother, begrudgingly care for them for only five weeks. Daniel and Susan are then transported to the East Bronx Children's Welfare Shelter, a badly administered orphanage. In order to survive the gruesome conditions in the shelter, Daniel develops a hard shell and emulates the leaders of the group of orphaned boys by engaging in vicious, aggressive behavior. His most successful effort to enter the ranks of the most powerful boys in the shelter is his imitation of an autistic boy who is cruelly referred to as the Inertia Kid. Although he feels guilty when he realizes that the Inertia Kid knows he is the object of ridicule, Daniel continues this activity in order to survive. He soon begins to perform his routine when he is alone and finds it more and more difficult to terminate his performances and return to his own personality.

Finding their situation unbearable, Daniel and Susan run away from the shelter and make the dangerous journey from the East Bronx to the West Bronx, where they find their old abandoned house. Not long after, they are returned by the authorities to the shelter. Then the two children are taken in by a husband and wife who insist that Daniel and Susan attend frequent rallies on behalf of the Isaacsons, who they believe are innocent scapegoats. The children periodically visit their parents in prison until their deaths by electrocution, and eventually they are adopted by and assume the surname of Robert Lewin, the partner of the Isaacsons' lawyer and a professor of law at Boston College.

Daniel survives this disruptive upbringing more successfully than his sister. He marries; he and his wife Phyllis live on 115th Street in Manhattan with their son Paul, named after Daniel's father. Daniel's physically abusive treatment of his wife and son mars their domestic tranquility, but the family struggles to maintain the semblance of a normal life. Susan's mental health, on the other hand, is so tenuous that she is in a mental institution in Newton, Massachusetts. In an effort to elevate his sister's spirits, Daniel agrees to found the Paul and Rochelle Isaacson Foundation for Revolution, whose goal is to promote political consciousness and freedom. In addition, he interviews people who were involved in the Isaacson court case in an attempt to establish the innocence of his parents. But his efforts are in vain. When Susan dies of pneumonia, the disillusioned Daniel is the sole survivor of a family sacrificed to a political and judicial system possessed by an hysterical fear of communism.

Isaacson, Paul. *The Book of Daniel.* E. L. Doctorow. 1971.

The character of Paul Isaacson is modeled after the historical figure Julius Rosenberg, a Jewish communist from New York who was executed for treason in 1953. A passionately radical critic of the American government, Isaacson is nevertheless a political innocent: He is incapable of believing that the judicial system would miscarry justice. Faced with the charge of leaking top-secret scientific information to the Russian government, he pleads innocent and refuses to identify accomplices in the supposed crime or confess his own involvement, despite the fact that either action would mitigate the severity of his sentence. After a lengthy, grueling trial, he and his wife ROCHELLE (ISAACSON) are put to death, both victims of the nation's paranoia concerning communism during the McCarthy era.

Paul meets his wife at a Loyalist rally on Convent Street in New York City. They both attend City College until he is drafted and stationed in Washington, D.C., during World War I. Following the war they move to the West Bronx, where they raise their two children, DANIEL (ISAACSON) and SUSAN (ISAACSON). Paul makes a meager living at Isaacson Radio Sales and Repair, the shop he singlehandedly owns and manages.

Paul's political activities include selling the *Daily Worker* door to door and talking incessantly to friends and prospective customers about the injustices committed by the capitalistic economic machine. Following a concert in Peekskill, New York, by the eminent black artist Paul Robeson, Paul performs his most heroic political activity. He and a group of fellow communists charter a bus that is surrounded and attacked by an anti-communist mob threatening to overturn the bus. They are dissuaded by his appeals, but Paul suffers a broken arm as a result of his valor.

According to his son Daniel, the narrator of the novel, Paul is a tendentious man with an intense sense of self-importance and a provocative manner. When he and his wife are publicly accused by one of their closest friends, Selig Mindish, of being involved in a conspiratorial, treasonous group and are subsequently incarcerated, his confidence and self-esteem begin to crumble. He is subjected to a trial in a courtroom seething with political and racial prejudice. Although he and Rochelle agree to maintain impassive and dignified countenances, Paul's intense fear is manifested by extreme weight loss, an increasingly wan complexion, and periodic hysterical behavior.

In Daniel's imagined account of the dynamics of the crime, Paul is aware that Mindish is lying; he accuses the Isaacsons of treason in order to protect the real culprits whose escape from the country with false passports is now assured. Rochelle's discovery of Paul's knowledge of the sacrifice the two of them are making so horrifies her that she stops communicating with her husband after their third unsuccessful appeal of the case. Three years after being arrested by the FBI, Paul Isaacson precedes his wife into the death chamber, and using every ounce of his depleted strength to control his urge to scream, he is executed as a traitor.

Isaacson, Rochelle. *The Book of Daniel.* E. L. Doctorow. 1971.

The character of Rochelle Isaacson is modeled after the historical figure Ethel Rosenberg, who was executed for treason along with her husband Julius in 1953 for allegedly leaking top-secret scientific information to the Russians. The daughter of Jewish immigrants who fled from czarist Russia to escape death in the many pogroms waged against the Jewish community, Rochelle is a registered communist. A pragmatist with exceptional emotional fortitude and life-sustaining pride, Rochelle faces hostile court proceedings, three years of imprisonment, and death by electrocution with impressive impassiveness.

Rochelle falls in love with her husband-to-be, PAUL ISAACSON, at a Loyalist rally on Convent Avenue in New York City. They both attend City College; she earns a degree, but Paul is drafted into the World War I combat effort before finishing school and is stationed in Washington, D.C. After the war, the Isaacsons settle down near their radio repair shop in the West Bronx, where they live with their son DANIEL (ISAACSON) and daughter (SUSAN (ISAACSON)) until the parents' arrest in 1950.

With grim resolve, Rochelle struggles against the despair, disillusionment, and poverty that threaten to undermine her family's integrity. In the world at large, Rochelle does not expect to be rewarded for her political activism, but she wants to be part of the effort that will one day triumph over injustice and oppression. She and her husband provide their children with a rigorous and extremely progressive political and moral education, instilling in them the belief that perfection, although unattainable, is to be pursued with unflagging devotion.

Paul is accused by their good friend Selig Mindish of being involved in treasonous activities and is then arrested. Rochelle testifies before the grand jury and is subsequently incarcerated herself. More emotionally stable than her husband, she insists that they do not give their enemies the satisfaction of watching them squirm under the weight of their misfortune, and she helps support her husband as they struggle to maintain a dignified composure during the interminable trial. Rochelle clearly recognizes the political and racial prejudice that pervades the courtroom, and she has no illusions that justice will prevail.

According to the imagined account of the trial and execution provided by her son Daniel, the narrator of the novel, Rochelle is enraged when their ex-friend Mindish does not deign to look at her while delivering the testimony that will eventually cause her execution. When he finally does look at her for a split second, she confronts the eyes not of a betrayer but of a comrade who is knowingly sacrificing his life in order to protect the real conspirators—who, thanks to the arrest of the Isaacsons, were able to flee the country with false passports. With dismay, Rochelle then realizes that her husband is aware of this sacrifice and is an accomplice with Mindish for the sake of the Communist Party. According to Daniel, because of her knowledge of this betrayal, Rochelle eventually stops communicating with her husband as they await their execution at Sing-Sing Prison.

When the day of their deaths arrives, Paul is executed first because the presiding officials correctly believe that Rochelle is the stronger of the two and will therefore hold up better. Banishing the prison rabbi from the room and kissing her dear, weeping friend, the matron who has guarded her during her two-year incarceration in the death house, Rochelle meets her death with dignity and composure, and a strange smile on her lips. The prison authorities are forced to administer a double dose of electricity in order to kill Rochelle Isaacson, for her strength defies the initial throw of the switch.

Isaacson, Susan (Susan Lewin). *The Book of Daniel.* E. L. Doctorow. 1971.

Susan Isaacson is a fictionalized version of the daughter of Ethel and Julius Rosenberg, political activists who were executed for treason in 1953 during the height of the McCarthy era. As the novel opens, Susan is a patient in the Worcester State Hospital for the mentally ill, where she was admitted after having been discovered, unconscious and bleeding profusely, in a restaurant restroom where she attempted suicide by slitting her wrists. The remainder of the story chronicles the dangerous depression caused by her tragically disrupted upbringing.

When Susan was five years old, her parents, PAUL (ISAACSON) and ROCHELLE (ISAACSON), are arrested by the FBI on charges of treason for allegedly leaking top-secret scientific formulas to Russian communists. Following their parents' incarceration, Susan and her older brother DANIEL (ISAACSON) are begrudgingly taken in for five weeks by two of their aunts, who prefer not to be associated with them for fear of being implicated in the treason charges. Susan is so upset by the absence of her parents that she regresses, wetting the bed that she and her brother share. Using this and other misbehaviors as an excuse, the aunts claim they can no longer care for the children. Susan and Daniel are then taken to the East Bronx Children's Welfare Shelter, a badly administered orphanage, and are separated into the male and female sections of the institution.

In her innocence, Susan believes she is in a prison. She screams and cries at night, much to the chagrin of the resident psychologist, Mr. Guglielmi. He ultimately authorizes a breach of the rules and allows the two Isaacson children to take meals together and chat before going to bed. Nevertheless, Daniel and Susan are so upset by their environment that they run away one chilly Saturday morning and make the hazardous journey to their old, deserted home in the West Bronx. Although soon returned to the shelter, they eventually are taken in by a New Rochelle couple who accompanies them to the many demonstrations staged by sympathizers of the Isaacson case. When their parents are sentenced to death by electrocution, the Isaacson children are adopted by and assume the last name of Robert Lewin, a professor of law at Boston College, who is the partner of their parents' lawyer.

As an adult, Susan becomes politically active and is involved at Radcliffe in the antiwar movement during the 1960s. She insists that her brother Daniel join her in founding the Paul and Rochelle Isaacson Foundation for Revolution, whose goal is political consciousness-raising and active community participation in the construction of radical social policies. Less politically oriented than his sister, Daniel agrees to establish the foundation only when Susan's mental health becomes so precarious that he fears she will commit suicide.

As her mental health continues to disintegrate, Susan becomes increasingly listless and eventually stops responding to stimuli. She refuses to communicate with anyone, even Daniel. When her psychiatrist, Dr. Duberstein, suggests that she undergo electroshock therapy, her brother threatens to kill him if he submits her to this form of treatment. Susan refuses to take proper care of herself, and her physical health begins to suffer. She develops a bad case of pneumonia from which she does not recover; like her parents before her, she dies a victim of a society in which the fear of communism is both irrational and inhumane.

Ishmael. *Moby Dick*; or, *The Whale.* Herman Melville. 1851.

Ishmael, the narrator and cetologist of this nineteenth-century epic, ships aboard the *Pequod*, an American whaler, in order to see the world. A sanguine, philosophical fellow given to musing and reverie, he manages to find material for contemplation in virtually every aspect of his journey. However, while initiating the reader into the rituals of whaling, Ishmael is drawn under the influence of CAPTAIN AHAB, the ship's monomaniacal commander, and his hearty, good-natured adventure is soon eclipsed by tragedy when Ahab persists in his obsessive pursuit of Moby Dick, the fabled white whale.

Ishmael's voyage is precipitated by a melancholy, misanthropic "November" in his soul. With carpet bag in hand, he leaves the overcrowded streets of Manhattan for the port town of New Bedford, Massachusetts. Upon arriving at the Spouter Inn, a peculiarly shiplike, cheap, and rough-and-tumble establishment, Ishmael discovers that he must share a bed with another sailor. After several hours of unpleasant speculation as to who his bedfellow might be, he finally dozes off, only to be awakened by a frightful figure—a harpooner, covered with purplish tattoos, with a top-knot on the crown of his shaved head. Ishmael shrieks for the landlord, who laughingly assures him that this "cannibal," QUEEQUEG, will do him no harm.

By the following evening Ishmael has overcome his doubts and joined his bedfellow in a cozy chat and a smoke of his pipe. Queequeg enthusiastically performs a "pagan" ritual, pressing his forehead against Ishmael's and pronouncing them bosom friends. The two travel together to Nantucket and ship out on the *Pequod*. Ishmael admits to the owners of the boat that he has never been on a whaling voyage before and is accepted as a sailor with predictably poor pay. A vague anxiety creeps over him when a mad beggar, Elijah, hints mysteriously at a disastrous fate for both the ship and its charismatic but as yet unseen captain, Ahab.

Not long after the cruise begins, Ahab appears on deck and exacts from the crew a promise to assist in the hunt for the white whale, Moby Dick, to whom he has lost a leg. Despite his misgivings, Ishmael finds himself drawn, like the rest of the men, into Ahab's mad quest for vengeance.

As the cruise progresses, Ishmael finds much to interest him both in the voyage and in the natural world of the sea. Every aspect of the whaling trade offers a lesson in the exigencies of life and the proximity of death. Neither the brutality of the chase nor the whale's natural magnificence are lost on Ishmael. At the same time he cannot help but observe the ominous portents in the *Pequod*'s path as well as the conflict unfolding between Ahab and his more judicious first mate, STARBUCK, who tries to dissuade him from hunting Moby Dick.

Ishmael is greatly concerned when Queequeg succumbs to a mysterious and seemingly fatal fever midway through the voyage, and he even has a special coffin made for his burial at sea. His subsequent recovery is as sudden and inexplicable as his illness had been. It becomes increasingly clear to Ishmael that the *Pequod*'s voyage will be an ill-fated one—that Ahab's monomania has burst its confines, and he is determined to fight Moby Dick to the death, regardless of the sentiments of his crew.

As the *Pequod* plunges through the deceptively warm and welcoming Pacific, she is hailed by a passing ship, the *Rachel*, whose captain pleads with Ahab to assist him in searching for his missing son. However, when he hears that the *Rachel*'s crew had been lost in an encounter with Moby Dick, Ahab refuses to aid in the search and desperately presses on.

The *Pequod* finally sights Moby Dick, and after a grueling three-day chase, is smashed to bits by the whale. The great whirlpool created by the sinking ship swallows up Ahab and all his crew—all, that is, except Ishmael. "One did survive the wreck," he writes in a poignant epilogue to the voyage. He had replaced Ahab's lost bowman and was tossed out of the boat, thereby escaping the vortex that ensued. Queequeg's coffin, which had been used to replace the *Pequod*'s life buoy, shoots up out of the wreckage. Holding on to this talismanic remnant of his faithful friend, Ishmael floats on the surface of a quiet, enchanted sea. On the third day, he is picked up by the *Rachel*, which in combing the waters for her missing children, "only found another orphan."

J

Jack, Esther. *You Can't Go Home Again.* Thomas Wolfe. 1940.

Wife of a powerful stockbroker and member of pre-Depression-era New York's business and arts elite, Esther Jack is the lover of GEORGE WEBBER. As a noted set designer for the theater, raised in a well-to-do family, Esther is a comfortable member of a world that is alien to the southern-born, idealistic writer with whom she is having an affair.

Although she protests that she is really not that rich at all, Esther lives with her husband Frederick and daughter Alma in tasteful opulence with servants in attendance. Practically unconscious of her surroundings, Esther is more concerned with her work as a set designer than she is with her wealth. Often, as a review for one of her shows states, her sets are the best thing about a Broadway offering. Again Esther protests, but when George mockingly reads a favorable mention of her work aloud to her, Esther is proud.

Esther and George's affair has been punctuated by his complaints that the world in which she lives is inimical to his concerns as a writer. As the narrative opens, George has only recently returned from Europe, where he went with the hope that the separation from Esther would end their affair. The love they share seems too strong to keep them apart for long, however, and Esther has resumed her visits to his Greenwich Village apartment.

After much pleading on her part, Esther has persuaded George to attend a glittering party she will throw at her family's apartment. The evening features an array of people from the business and artistic community and from café society—people for whom George feels contempt. As Esther flits from guest to guest, skillfully playing the host, George broods. When only the last stragglers remain, fire engines are heard in the background, and it becomes clear that there is a blaze somewhere in the building. The partygoers evacuate, going out to the courtyard to watch the firefighters work. After the danger has passed, George and Esther return to the Jacks' living room, where Esther, giddy from all the excitement, presses George to agree with her that their love will endure.

Jackson, Frances "F.K." *The Narrows.* Ann Petry. 1953.

Frances Jackson, known as F.K., is the strong-willed but sensitive best friend of ABBIE CRUNCH. At the time of the novel's actions, F.K. has been Abbie's best friend for more than twenty years. F.K.'s life revolves chiefly around her duties as an undertaker, a profession she in-herited from her father. As a young woman, F.K. was educated at Wellesley, where she was the only black person in the student body. When the dean called her into her office to find out if F.K. would be happier elsewhere, the young woman responded by saying that happiness was irrelevant; she had been sent to school by her father in order to learn.

F.K. remembers her father, who would call her Frank, telling her that she had a "man's mind." It was his wish that she acquire a good education, so she remained at Wellesley in spite of her loneliness. When she finished college, she returned to her hometown knowing that she would never get married or have children. Since her mother had died while F.K. was in college, leaving her father alone, F.K. resolved to stay and care for him rather than go to medical school as she had planned. After her father's death she continued to run the mortuary he had established. The only relief in F.K.'s loneliness after her father's death was Abbie, whose friendship enlivened her emotional life.

F.K. eventually becomes indispensable to Abbie and her family. It is F.K. who consoles Abbie during the trauma of her husband's sudden death. She also assists Abbie in raising LINCOLN "LINK" WILLIAMS, the son Abbie and her husband had adopted. In her grief, Abbie had completely forgotten the existence of her son, and it falls upon F.K. to reunite the two by taking Link back from Bill Hod's saloon, The Last Chance, where he had been living.

Throughout the remainder of Link's childhood years, F.K. remains an essential part of the family. It is clear that F.K. possesses deep emotional feelings for Abbie and sees herself in the role of her shy friend's protector.

Whenever Abbie is faced with an unpleasant duty or there is a potential for a difficult confrontation, F.K. intervenes and performs the task herself. This includes dealing with the tough-minded Bill Hod concerning his role in Link's upbringing. Through F.K.'s negotiations, Link begins working for Hod when he is still a young boy because F.K. knew his employer at that time, a Mr. Valkill, was a pederast. F.K. also consistently encourages Abbie to be more open to the world at large.

After Link's shocking murder and his funeral, which was handled by her mortuary, F.K. experiences a grief as deep as Abbie's. She invites her bereaved friend to come to live with her, but Abbie indicates that she is not ready for such a move. At the novel's end, the two women, left only with each other's companionship, attempt to move ahead and rebuild their violently disrupted lives.

Jackson, Gideon. *Freedom Road.* Howard Fast. 1944.

Gideon Jackson is the ideal statesman. A thoughtful and intelligent man, he starts out as an illiterate freed slave and ends up a congressman and a friend of President Grant, only to be destroyed by the hostile forces of a resurgent white South.

At the book's outset, the Civil War has just ended, and Gideon, one of the thousands of Southern slaves who had fought with the Union Army, has returned to the abandoned Carwell plantation in South Carolina where his family still lives and farms.

The freedmen who are now squatters on the plantation go to Columbia to vote for the first time, and Gideon is elected a delegate to the state's Constitutional Convention. Dressed in a too-tight frock coat and a ludicrous stovepipe hat, Gideon walks to Charleston, where a whole new world opens for him. He meets educated African Americans and works long into each night, teaching himself to read.

Gideon meets a white delegate to the Convention, Stephen Holmes, a former slave owner who invites him to his home for a formal dinner. Gideon shines during the dinner conversation and leaves feeling optimistic. After his departure, though, Holmes reveals the true purpose of the dinner: to show that the convention is made up of "determined and intelligent men" like Gideon who must be kept in their place. The only way to accomplish this task, according to Holmes, is to strengthen the Ku Klux Klan.

After some time back on the plantation, Gideon tries to unite the freed slaves and poor whites by purchasing plantation land and creating individual farms. The South Carolina banks deny his loan request, so Gideon journeys to Massachusetts, where two abolitionists agree to lend him the money for the project. Gideon also arranges for schooling for all the plantation's children, black and white, and sends his son to medical school.

The years pass, and Gideon moves to Washington, D.C., where he serves in Congress. He is one of the principal people to discover that Rutherford B. Hayes was elected to the presidency through the tampering of votes. The Southern whites had made a deal to give Hayes certain states in return for ending Reconstruction. Without the protection of Union soldiers, Gideon knows that chaos and terror will reign in the South. He takes his information to the lame duck president, Grant, and begs him to do what he can to protect Reconstruction. But a weary Grant dismisses him.

Defeated, and knowing that the days of freedom and opportunity for his people are about to end, Gideon leaves Washington. Back home, the Klan starts its reign of terror. A false accusation of rape is made against three of the men of Carwell. A Klan assault forces the plantation's freedmen and poor whites to barricade themselves in the abandoned Carwell home. Gideon's people fight valiantly, but the armed Klansmen surrounding the plantation soon number almost six hundred. Finally, they drag in a howitzer. Gideon is killed by a shell, his people are destroyed, and the plantation house burns to the ground.

Jackson, Phoenix. "A Worn Path." Eudora Welty. 1980.

Phoenix Jackson struggles to preserve her own dignity as she makes a difficult journey at Christmas time. A black woman who is bent from old age, Phoenix makes her way toward the city to procure medicine for her grandson, and along the way she must contend with harsh nature, heartless people, and her own deteriorating body.

Walking through the wintry forest, Phoenix calls out to the wild animals in the brush to stay away. Her way is not easy: She must struggle up a hill, disentangle her dress from a thorn bush, and cross a creek on a tottering log. A dark figure in the field frightens her until she realizes it is only a scarecrow. Laughing at her failing sight, she moves on.

When a black dog comes at her, Phoenix is caught off guard, and topples into a ditch. She is helped out by a white man on a horse, who laughs at her for making such a treacherous journey at her age. Although she is angry at the man's condescension, she does nothing to display her rage. Instead, she secretly picks up a nickel she had seen fall from the man's pocket. After scaring off the black dog with his gun, the man jokingly points the weapon at Phoenix and asks if she is afraid. Insisting that the gun doesn't frighten her in the least, Phoenix goes on her way.

When she reaches the brightly lit city, Phoenix enters a building, where the attendant on duty loudly identifies her as "a charity case." But a nurse recognizes Phoenix and gives her a chair. The nurse asks about the condition of Phoenix's grandson who had swallowed lye some years before, but the old woman seems unable to speak. Eventually, however, she recalls why she is in this building, and apologizing for her forgetfulness, she says she has come for the soothing medicine that eases the child's pain. She tells the nurse that she and her grandson are "the only two left in the world."

When Phoenix has the medicine, the attendant offers her a few pennies. Stiffly, Phoenix asks for and receives a whole nickel. Then, carefully holding the two nickels in her hand, Phoenix tells the attendant she wants to buy a toy for her grandson. Her dignity somehow intact through all her trials, Phoenix slowly makes her way out the door.

Jadwin, Curtis. *The Pit.* Frank Norris. 1903.

Curtis Jadwin is a powerful man swept away by forces of which he is no more than an insignificant part. A wealthy and relatively cautious real estate investor who still shows the marks of his farming background, he is constantly involved in philanthropic activities. When his broker friend Samuel Gretry urges him to sink some of his wealth into wheat speculation, Jadwin insists that he does not want to make any more money. But the temptation to get involved in the fast-paced market proves a more powerful lure than the money itself, and he begins trading.

Still, Jadwin hopes, as he says, to "have some fun" with his life, and he sees marriage to his wife, LAURA DEARBORN (JADWIN), as a way to ensure that he will have it: They read together, fish together, and maintain a magnificent Lake Shore Drive mansion. But soon the Pit, as the commodities market is known, catches Jadwin in its whirl. Proving uncannily sensitive to the force of its currents, he impresses Gretry into his service and becomes bullish with a vengeance. Striking almost viciously, he makes half a million in a day.

Caught in the vortex of the wheat current, Jadwin seldom strays from the center of the Pit, and his wife begins missing him. Still having some sway with him, Laura elicits a pledge that he will cease to speculate. But then he receives the secret information that the worldwide wheat crop has been desperately poor and realizes that he already controls a sizable portion of the wheat industry himself. Jadwin resolves to corner the world market.

Once his corner is successful, however, the Pit possesses him completely. He must maintain a high market price, or else his vast holdings will become as vast a liability; to do so Jadwin must continue buying up all the wheat contracts that come through the Pit. As he describes his situation during one of his rare conversations with Laura, it is "like holding a wolf by the ears, bad to hold on, but worse to let go." And always in his mind he hears a constant din: "wheat—wheat—wheat"; he has been subsumed by an irrepressible natural force. The wheat leads him not only to abandon his marriage but to betray his best friend, Charles Cressler, driving Charles into bankruptcy and suicide.

Inevitably, Jadwin cannot corner the wheat industry much longer. A successful harvest floods the market with wheat, and he fails pathetically in his attempt to buy it all up. Ultimately, still struggling against the power of the wheat, Jadwin is defeated and bankrupt. He trudges from the Pit in a fit of nervous derangement, convalesces at home, and eventually embarks on a new life in the West with his wife.

Jadwin, Laura Dearborn. *The Pit.* Frank Norris. 1903.

Laura Jadwin, wife of commodities magnate CURTIS JADWIN, is a beautiful and brilliant woman torn between the world of art and beauty, and the world of power and wealth. Alternately devoted to her ever-absent husband and infatuated with the romantic glass-worker Sheldon Corthell, she seems unable to pledge herself to either one—or rather, she pledges herself to each, by turns.

Laura enters the narrative as a woman recently arrived in Chicago from the East who is waiting impatiently to view an opera. During the course of the opera, both Jadwin and Corthell speak intimately to her, with Corthell

proposing marriage. Nevertheless, it is Jadwin's conversation that most intrigues her, and she realizes that the modern drama of finance is "equally picturesque, equally romantic, equally passionate" to that of the opera.

A few days later, during a trip through Chicago's financial district, Laura is overwhelmed by a sudden vision of the city's energy: The metropolis seems to be a living organism. For her, the city is the nexus embodying the various forces of nature. She is deeply impressed by the men who tame those forces, warriors bent on conquest, "always cruel, always selfish, always pitiless." It is Curtis Jadwin whom she inevitably marries.

But the more involved Jadwin becomes in wheat speculation, the less time he has to spend at home. Laura knows he still loves her, but she feels she is losing her sanity as she becomes more and more inactive. Furthermore, she is tortured by the belief that Jadwin is not familiar with the many sides of her personality. Instead of truly knowing her, he is only acquainted with the character—the role she must play as his wife—not herself. Moreover, Laura cannot understand the morality of wheat speculation. She feels that if people in Europe or Asia need wheat, then Jadwin should just "give it to them."

Her emotional side, the side that cannot be expressed while playing the role of Jadwin's wife, is revealed only to Corthell, and indeed Laura learns to release it only under his tutelage. One day she is riding alone in Lincoln Park, extremely fast, and she nearly runs down a man, who coincidentally happens to be Corthell. He accompanies her home, plays the piano, and explains the mysteries of art and literature. Following their conversation, she begins dressing as Lady Macbeth and reciting lines from Shakespeare around the house. So near derangement is Laura that she is scarcely disturbed at discovering the corpse of her husband's best friend, whom Jadwin had driven to suicide.

When Jadwin fails to remember her birthday, she determines to run off with Corthell, thereby breaking convention and allowing her artistic side free rein. But when Jadwin has a nervous breakdown, she renounces her dreams of flight and nurses him back to health. She prepares to begin a new life in the West with him, believing that she has "won a victory by surrendering."

James, Celestine. *The Beet Queen.* Louise Erdrich. 1986.

Celestine James, an orphan of Chippewa origin, is a proud and private child. Statuesque and mature, Celestine is admired by Sita Kozka, a popular girl at school, and by Sita's cousin, MARY ADARE. Celestine maintains a careful distance from everyone, however, until the birth of her daughter.

Celestine lives in the town of Argus, North Dakota, where her older half-sister cares for her and her half-brother Russell. Sita, who considers Celestine her best friend, lives near the butcher shop that is run by Sita's parents. Sita's odd cousin Mary appears suddenly at the butcher shop after she is abandoned by her mother Adelaide. Celestine immediately becomes interested in Mary when she learns that Mary, too, is an orphan. Sensing that Mary is about to "steal" Celestine, Sita desperately tries to think of something to impress her. Celestine is unimpressed, however, when Sita unbuttons her blouse and shows off her breasts.

The three children are in the same class at their school, St. Catharine's, and Mary devotes all her attention to Celestine. During the winter Mary performs a "miracle." She goes down a slide, smashing headfirst onto the frozen playground and cracking the ice into a perfect image of the face of Christ. Celestine is the only one who cannot see the image that causes such excitement.

Having quit school early, Celestine takes a job at the telephone company. She later goes to work in the butcher shop Mary inherited from her aunt and uncle. Mary's brother KARL (ADARE), ordinarily a seducer of men, finds Celestine's masculine beauty intensely attractive. Karl moves into her house, and they have a passionate affair. The romance strains relations with Mary and with Russell, who moves out temporarily. After Celestine discovers that she is pregnant, she orders Karl to leave. Although they formally marry, Celestine never permits Karl to enter the house. He continues with his life as a traveling salesman.

Celestine goes into labor while she is driving to the hospital in a snowstorm. Fortunately, a neighbor, Wallace Pfef, who had himself been in love with Karl, rescues her, and she gives birth to a daughter on Wallace's couch. Celestine names the baby WALLACETTE DARLENE ADARE after him, but everyone calls the child "Dot," a nickname Mary invents.

From the beginning, Mary is Dot's closest confidante and ally. Celestine views this as a rude intrusion, an attempt to deprive her of the full privileges of motherhood. Dot, equally contemptuous of Mary and Celestine, grows into a spoiled, rebellious, greedy girl. When Wallace Pfef organizes a Beet Festival to celebrate the success of this crop in Argus, he rigs the beauty contest so that Dot will be elected Beet Queen. But when she learns what Wallace has done, Dot refuses to be crowned. Instead, she climbs into a skywriter's plane and rides with him while he writes "Queen Wallacette" in the air. When she descends, only Celestine is left waiting for her. They return to Celestine's house, and the novel ends with a rare moment of harmony and intimacy between Celestine and her daughter.

Jean-Jacques. *The Benefactor.* Susan Sontag. 1963.

Jean-Jacques, a writer, lives a divided existence with several entirely separate lives. During the daytime he occupies himself writing baroque novels, and late at night he inhabits a theatrical world of homosexual prostitutes who call themselves "madwomen of the nights." Because of Jean-Jacques's absolute commitment to writing, he feels no need to make a show of consistency in any other area.

Jean-Jacques came from a poor family, and in his early twenties he becomes a professional boxer. By the time he reaches thirty he is earning a modest living as a prostitute and thief. The novels he writes during the daytime are praised by the critics but sell only a few hundred copies. Unconcerned with his reputation, Jean-Jacques speaks freely to his friends, both of his "job," as he calls his night-time activities, and his "work," by which he means his writing.

Jean-Jacques reserves the early evening interim between these two contrasting lives for pleasures such as the opera and the salon of a wealthy Bohemian friend, Frau Anders. At this salon he meets an unusual young man named HIPPOLYTE, for whom he becomes both mentor and playmate. Hippolyte, like Jean-Jacques, leads a fractured existence, and they argue good-naturedly about strategies for juggling their various lives. In these debates, Jean-Jacques invariably emerges the victor. He criticizes Hippolyte for his excessive seriousness. For Jean-Jacques, whose "job" involves dressing up as a sailor, a tough, or a truck driver, the homosexual encounter is a dreamlike "comedy of roles." He never exerts himself to refute Hippolyte's accusation that his sexual life is insincere because it causes him no concern.

A rupture occurs in the friendship between Hippolyte and Jean-Jacques as a result of Jean-Jacques's enthusiasm for role-playing. Hippolyte's wife is dying of leukemia when he invites Jean-Jacques to visit her for the first time. It is during the Nazi occupation of France, and Jean-Jacques arrives after curfew, wearing an enemy uniform as protection. He gets so carried away playing the role of a Nazi, even pretending to kill Hippolyte, that Hippolyte finally knocks him out with a chair and carries him home. Hippolyte's wife, extremely upset by the scene, falls into a coma and dies three days later. Hippolyte refuses to see Jean-Jacques for some months after her death. When the friendship resumes, Hippolyte observes that Jean-Jacques has changed.

Having reached middle age, Jean-Jacques has been forced to give up his "nocturnal excursions" and become more respectable. He falls in love for the first time, with a young Greek theology student named Dimitri, and they live together for a time. Jean-Jacques also begins achieving literary success and receives a prestigious award. He is nevertheless unable to dispel rumors that he had collaborated with the enemy during the war, and Hippolyte gives him money to leave the capital and move south, where he can wait for the trouble to blow over.

Jean-Jacques's reputation recovers, and he returns to the capital to lead the extravagant life of a celebrated author. He is elected to the exclusive Academie, in spite of the doubts of some members regarding his political past. Jean-Jacques's supporters argue that his artistic courage and versatility merit membership in their elite circle. Early in the book Jean-Jacques was able to predict his own success because, as he tells Hippolyte proudly, he is prepared to "carry out" his character "to the extreme."

Jenkins, Dr. "The Portable Phonograph." Walter Van Tilburg Clark. 1950.

Dr. Jenkins lives in a small cell-like opening in the earth above a dry creek. The prairie landscape around him has been devastatingly scarred by bombs and tanks, which were used in a recent war. A red sunset lies on the horizon, and the air is cold, still, and vacant. Within Jenkins's tent, a small fire is glowing from four smoldering blocks of peat; the real wood, remnants of fences and timbers from long-deserted dugouts, is being saved for the days when expansive blizzards will buffet the land. Now, sitting around the fire with three guests, Jenkins, with a long matted beard and gray-white hair, carefully rewraps in a piece of burlap four leather-bound books: a volume of Shakespeare, the Bible, *Moby Dick*, and *The Divine Comedy*. He tells his guests that when he perceived what was happening in the world around him, he knew he could not save much, so he took with him what he loved.

Dr. Jenkins has just been reading *The Tempest* aloud, and now he slowly puts his books back into their niche. His three guests sit contemplatively. One comments that the doctor will "have a little soul left" when he dies; a second wishes to write, but there is no paper. The third and youngest guest, a musician who sits in a shadow away from the fire, is sick and coughs often. Finally, Jenkins grudgingly acknowledges that he knows his guests want to hear the phonograph. He goes to the back of the cell and returns with an old portable phonograph in a black case, which he places on the floor in front of them. After opening the case, Dr. Jenkins announces that because the young musician is present, he will play music on the phonograph with one of his precious steel needles rather than the usual thorn. He says he will play only one piece of music. Gershwin's "New York" is rejected by the musician, but finally they all settle on a Debussy nocturne.

The music fills the cave and overwhelms the listeners. When it is over, Dr. Jenkins removes the needle from the record to preserve it and to avoid scraping. The young musician departs without a word; the other two guests get up and start to leave, and Jenkins invites them to return in a week when he promises to have Gershwin's "New York." After they are gone, he stands in the doorway looking out over the "dome of the dead." He hears a wolf cry and the sound of a man's suppressed coughing.

Lowering his canvas door, Dr. Jenkins returns to his cave, where he quickly and quietly packs the records and the phonograph. Digging the earth away from one of his walls, he discloses a piece of board. Behind the board is a deep hole, into which the doctor places the phonograph and his bundle of books. He seals the hole again and

changes his bedding so that he can lie facing the cave entrance. He waits, watching the canvas door as if he is afraid someone is beyond it. Finally he prays, gets under his blankets, and closes his eyes. Inside the bed, next to the wall, he lays his hand on a comfortable piece of lead pipe.

Jennings, Vandyck "Van." *Herland, and with Her in Ourland.* Charlotte Perkins Gilman. 1915.

In 1915, Vandyck "Van" Jennings, the male protagonist, makes an expedition with two friends to a mystical country said to be run by women alone. Flying their airplane over the isolated little country of Herland, they see groomed forests consisting of only fruit-bearing trees, excellent roads, pinkish houses, and an orderly, clean citizenry of women.

The travelers' overview of this advanced, highly civilized society convinces them that there must be some men there, and they land and head toward town to investigate. There they are surprised to find themselves surrounded by a band of women who look calm, wise, and self-assured. They soon learn that these women are very different from their notions of women and that it is these women who have constructed this highly civilized society.

Van and his friends are chloroformed, imprisoned, stripped, and given new unisex clothing. The women provide each of the men with a teacher, an older woman who introduces him to Herland culture, history, and language. Van slowly grows to admire the society's greater decency and humanity. He also grows to love a native, Ellador, and ultimately he marries her in a triple ceremony with his two friends and their brides.

Van chafes under Ellador's indifference to sex for its own sake; she views sex only as a means of producing children. He is also frustrated with her constant use of the word *we*; her identity is far more tied with her society than it is with him. Nevertheless, their mutual love and respect grows. Van's friend Terry, however, sees his wife's sexual reticence as an insult to his male superiority; one night he breaks into her room and tries to rape her, to take what he sees as his husbandly due. She and her friends overpower him, however, and he is imprisoned, tried, and exiled. Since it is impossible for him to fly out alone, Van and Ellador accompany him.

Van and Ellador then travel about the bisexual world, observing, talking, and criticizing what they see. World War I has broken out, and Ellador is outraged at the atrocities of battle. She forces Van to concede that warlike behavior is not human nature but "man nature." Ellador is also shocked by the waste, corruption, and poverty she finds, particularly in the United States. She sees the betrayal of the promise that the New World offered to humanity as more distressing than the continuation of the more deeply ingrained injustice of the Old World. She also criticizes the women she meets since they are shallow, vain, and weak creatures, but she acknowledges that the women's movement is helping them see their own potential.

Despite Ellador's distress, the two grow to enjoy their marriage. They feel it embodies the ideal of a truly fulfilling love. They find each other good company and enjoy working and playing together. In this sense they have achieved what might be the ideal union between man and woman and, at least individually, the perfect harmony between the sexes.

Jenson, Olaf. "Big Black Good Man." Richard Wright. 1957.

Olaf Jenson is a contented sixty-year-old man who supports his wife and himself by working as a night porter at an inexpensive Copenhagen waterfront hotel. Having traveled extensively as a sailor in his youth, Olaf has settled down with his wife Karen to a contented life of work and recreation in the form of gardening and relaxing with a tasty mug of beer and a cigar. The relative calm of his everyday existence is disrupted when an immense African-American sailor named Jim arrives at the hotel and books a room for a six-day furlough. Although Olaf insists to himself that he is not prejudiced against blacks, this particular black man's stature and boisterous self-confidence unnerve the frail Danish porter, who begins to entertain murderous fantasies of avenging himself for the inferiority complex that the American inspires in him.

Having spent ten years working in New York when he was younger, Olaf is not unacquainted with American blacks. When the six-and-a-half-foot Jim enters, he thinks of pretending that the hotel is booked up for the night. But utter terror undermines his desire to turn the giant away, and Olaf shows Jim his hotel room and promises to supply him with whiskey and a prostitute to while away the evening. In addition, the cowed Dane agrees to guard $2,600 that Jim is carrying. Hypnotized by fear, Olaf witnesses six nights of Jim's enjoyment of alcohol and a prostitute and anxiously awaits his departure.

When on the sixth and final night of his stay Jim comes to the hotel office to settle his bill, Olaf's worst fears are realized as the American suddenly places one of his gargantuan hands around the Dane's throat, frightening him so much that he loses control of himself and wets his pants. Olaf's visions of death are dispelled when Jim releases him and lets out a lighthearted laugh before abruptly quitting the hotel. Devastated by shame, Olaf goes home for the night and entertains fantasies about Jim's death by drowning and subsequent ingestion by a rapacious white shark.

After a year of such fantasies, Olaf stops thinking about his black nemesis until Jim reappears at the hotel one August day. The night porter's terror is revived, and Olaf, fearing for his life, places his hands on a gun that he has hidden in the drawer of his desk. He lets go of the weapon when he realizes that Jim has visited the hotel only to deliver a set of new shirts that he has purchased for Olaf as a token of thanks for his having provided the prostitute's services the previous year. Laughing and crying hysterically in a mixture of relief and confusion, Olaf finally realizes that Jim's apparent threat to strangle him was actually an action designed to measure the porter's neck size in order to ensure that the shirts are the proper size.

Jim. *The Adventures of Huckleberry Finn.* Samuel L. Clemens (Mark Twain). 1885.

On his first appearance, Jim appears to be a bumbling, superstitious man. A slave belonging to Miss Watson, the sister of HUCKLEBERRY FINN's guardian, the Widow Douglas, Jim becomes a fugitive escaping the literal captivity of slavery and the figurative restraints of society. During his journey with Huck, Jim is revealed to be a wise and strong man, able to teach his young friend the virtues of honesty, loyalty, trust, and tenderness.

When Huck fakes his own murder to escape Miss Watson and his degenerate father, Jim, knowing Miss Watson intends to sell him, takes advantage of the confusion to escape. He meets Huck on Jackson's Island and tells him his plans to float down to the Ohio River, take a steamboat to the North, and ultimately earn enough money to buy his wife and children out of bondage. The two build a raft and embark on the journey together.

During the first part of their journey, Jim and Huck first find a floating house, then a wrecked riverboat, both of which they loot. On the riverboat, while Huck has adventures with murdering thieves, Jim remains hidden, unwilling to risk drowning or capture.

Throughout the novel, there is tension between Huck's desire for adventure and Jim's genuine anguish and real danger. During a dense fog, for instance, Huck and Jim get separated and call to each other for hours. When Huck gets back to the raft, he finds Jim sleeping and concocts a story that convinces Jim he has dreamed their whole separation. When Jim realizes he has been tricked, he feels betrayed. Huck's behavior hints at the possibility of a more serious betrayal; he has the power to turn Jim over to slave catchers. Moreover, Huck's seemingly innocent game has caused them to miss the Ohio River, thus putting Jim's freedom in jeopardy.

During Huck's on-shore adventures, Jim hides aboard the raft. His freedom is short-lived, however: Betrayed by two of Huck's crooked companions, the Duke and the Dauphin, Jim is imprisoned on a farm belonging, it turns out, to TOM SAWYER's Aunt Sally. Jim, believing himself genuinely in danger and in need of Tom's and Huck's assistance, submits to a complicated escape plot concocted by Tom. Freed by Tom and Huck and then recaptured, he is freed again when Tom reveals that Jim's owner, Miss Watson, has died and freed Jim in her will. Tom's whole escape plot was dangerous, unnecessary, and cruel, but Jim has been granted the freedom he desired and deserved.

Joad, Ma. *The Grapes of Wrath*. John Steinbeck. 1939.

The courageous and determined leader of the Joad family, Ma Joad, summons her many inner resources to keep the Joads alive, loyal to one another, and able to endure the hardships they encounter on their journey westward out of the 1930s Dust Bowl. She wisely understands that unless the family survives and a sense of community is maintained, poverty, famine, and injustice will ultimately conquer the human spirit. Accordingly, Ma does whatever is necessary to sustain the Joads during their long and trying search for a better life.

When her son TOM (JOAD) returns home after spending four years in prison, Ma greets him joyfully, relieved that he is all right and that they will not leave Oklahoma without him. Like thousands of other farm families, the Joads are being forced off their land by large agricultural interests. Later, when they are in their fully-packed truck heading for California, Ma's father, Grampa, dies. With the help of the Wilsons, another traveling family, the Joads bury Grampa in a field beside the highway. The Wilsons' car breaks down, and Tom offers to fix it while the others go ahead; Ma, knowing that the family must stick together, refuses to go along with this plan. Holding a jack handle in her hands, she forcefully tells them, "What we got lef' in the worl'? Nothin' but us." Not even her husband can argue with Ma, who becomes head of the family.

As the journey progresses, Ma continues to speak her mind. One night when Ma is in the tent with Granma and ROSE OF SHARON JOAD, her pregnant oldest daughter, a rude man disturbs them. The man tells them to leave and calls them "Okies." Ma talks back to him, and later she confesses to Tom that her own violent feelings toward the man frightened her.

At a camp, a group of children stand around hungrily watching as Ma prepares food for the Joads. Not sure of what to do but unable to turn her back on the starving children, Ma feeds her own family and then offers leftover food to the children. Later, when Rose of Sharon's husband deserts them, Ma comforts and supports her but refuses to let her feel sorry for herself. She also quiets Tom when he tells her he is afraid he will kill a deputy.

Farther down the road, Ma challenges a grocer for charging too much for food. The grocer cannot argue with Ma when she appeals to his sense of decency. That night Tom kills a man who clubbed a striking worker, and Ma makes a plan to smuggle him out of camp. At their next resting place, Ma regularly takes food to Tom, who hides in the bushes for days as the others earn money by picking cotton.

One day Ma's youngest daughter lets slip to a friend that her outlaw brother is hiding behind the camp. Ma visits Tom and tells him he must leave. Holding back tears, she says good-bye to her son and gives him seven dollars, which she has been saving secretly. After Tom goes, Ma and a neighbor act as midwives for Rose of Sharon, who gives birth to a stillborn child. Ma is saddened, but she does not rest. She moves her family into a deserted barn as a rain floods their camp. When they find a despairing man with his young son huddled in a corner of the barn, Ma tells Rose of Sharon to slip out of her clothes and wraps her in a blanket. Ma looks deeply into Rose of Sharon's eyes; when Rose of Sharon says, "Yes," Ma answers, "I knowed you would." Kissing her daughter on the forehead, Ma, who never stops believing in the existence of a life force, moves the family from the barn to a toolshed and leaves Rose of Sharon to breast-feed the emaciated man.

Joad, Rose of Sharon. *The Grapes of Wrath*. John Steinbeck. 1939.

Rose of Sharon Joad, MA JOAD's oldest daughter, heads west with her family and her husband Connie with high hopes about the future. When the journey begins, Rose of Sharon is at the beginning of her pregnancy; as it progresses, she faces extreme hardship—and learns, finally, that despite hardship, poverty, and failure, life will go on.

Glowing and whispering privately with Connie as they ride in the Joads' truck toward California, Rose of Sharon dreams of a life that is different from any she has ever known. She tells Ma of their plans: Connie will get a job in a store or a factory, she will have a doctor when the baby is born, and they will live in a house full of modern appliances. Ma tells Rose of Sharon that it isn't good for the family to break up and that she wants Rose and Connie to stay with them. Rose's eyes fill with tears as Ma tells her that although her childbirth will feel lonely and painful in their rough surroundings, she must realize the event is part of a greater whole.

At a campground where the Joads look for work, Connie tells Rose of Sharon that he would not have made the trip if he had known what it would be like. Rose of Sharon is apprehensive and worries that her husband is giving up. Days later Connie does give up, abandoning her without saying a word, and Rose of Sharon begins to grow sick and depressed. She refuses to leave camp when the family is ready to go, saying she wants to wait for Connie to return. Ma and her oldest son, TOM JOAD, comfort Rose and lead her to the truck.

A fanatical Christian woman at the government camp makes Rose of Sharon afraid that God will pass judgment on her and the Joad family, and that the child will die in her womb. But Ma insists that Rose stop thinking solely of her own plight and realize that she is one person among many. Rose of Sharon is quiet, but she continues to mope and worry. Seriously malnourished, she is unable to drink the milk she needs because the family cannot afford it. When she mentions the lack of milk to Ma, Ma comforts her by giving her a pair of earrings and piercing her ears. But Rose of Sharon's fear and anxiety return, and after Tom kills a man in a labor dispute, she lashes out at him.

Crying out in despair and self-pity, she says his deed will cause her baby to be a freak. Later, after overhearing two workers say their wages have been cut in half, she tells Tom to rest and promises to guard the cabin door lest anyone should come looking for him.

After Tom is forced to leave the family to escape prosecution, Rose of Sharon gives birth to a stillborn child. When Ma tells her the baby did not live, she covers her face and rests silently on her mattress. Outside, a tremendous rainstorm causes a flood, and the Joads are forced to find higher ground. They move into an old deserted barn where they are surprised to find a young boy huddled in a corner with his father. The boy's father is in despair and has not eaten for six days. Ma helps Rose of Sharon remove her wet clothes, and as the two women look at each other, they share the same thought. Ma moves the family into the nearby toolshed, and Rose of Sharon, naked and tired but very much alive, goes to the troubled man and offers him her breast to suckle him. Pulling him close to her and comforting him, she strokes his hair and smiles mysteriously.

Joad, Tom. *The Grapes of Wrath.* John Steinbeck. 1939.

Tom Joad, the dignified, headstrong oldest son of the Joad family, has a deep sense of justice and is not afraid to deliver retribution when a crime has been committed. Returning home after serving four years in prison for killing a man who had murdered someone else, Tom is shocked to find his family's house deserted. When he learns that the Joads have been evicted from their home and stripped of their land by large agricultural interests, Tom is deeply affected by the news and goes with the former preacher JIM CASY to his uncle's house to find them.

Tom and Casy arrive to find that the Joads are about to leave for California to find work. The family is overjoyed to see him—particularly his mother, MA JOAD, a hard-bitten woman with great strength and conviction. Tom, Casy, and the Joad family set out for California with high hopes that better times lie ahead. Tom never hesitates to go with them, even though he will break parole by crossing the Oklahoma border.

Not long into the trip, Tom's grandfather has a stroke and dies. Tom writes a note explaining the cause of death and puts the note in a bottle, which he buries with Grandpa's body. Later, when the family stops for the night at a campground, Tom, Casy, and Pa Joad talk to a ragged man who tells them about the grim situation in California. The jobs pay very little, he says, because they hire starving men who must work to survive. His wife and two children, the man reveals, died of starvation. Back inside their tent, Tom stops Pa from telling the story to Ma.

When warned by a passing field hand that dissident workers face jail and blacklisting, Tom becomes increasingly angry about the unjust politics of labor that he sees around him. After a deputy threatens him and another so-called agitator, a fight breaks out. Knowing that Tom must not be fingerprinted because he broke parole, Casy tells him to hide in the woods. The police take Casy away, and when the trouble is over, Tom's father summons him from his hiding place. Returning to the family, Tom comforts his pregnant sister, ROSE OF SHARON (JOAD), whose husband has just deserted them.

Farther down the road, the Joads come to a blockade. They do not know that the men outside are on strike for higher wages, and they accept a job picking peaches on a ranch. That night, in an effort to discover the cause of the turmoil on the road, Tom sneaks out of the camp. In the woods he is surprised to find his friend Jim Casy in a tent with a few other men. Tom learns that Casy and his fellow laborers made a stir on the ranch to protest their low wages. Casy asks Tom's help, but before Tom can do anything, several headhunters come upon Casy's tent. Casy is bludgeoned to death, and Tom murders the man who killed him. With his face badly bruised in the fight, he flees to the Joads' cabin, where he hides for a day until his family leaves the ranch.

The Joads obtain work picking cotton, and for several days Tom hides in the bushes outside camp. When Tom's little sister tells a friend about him, Ma visits Tom in the woods. They both know that Tom must leave the family. Ma worries that she will never know where he is or if he is alive, but Tom comforts her. Deeply affected by Jim Casy's philosophy and his revolutionary ideas, Tom says, "A fella ain't got a soul of his own, but on'y a piece of a big one. . . . I'll be aroun' in the dark. I'll be everywhere—wherever you look." He and Ma courageously say good-bye, and Tom sets out, following Casy's example, to stir things up in the wide and troubled world before him.

John. "By the Waters of Babylon." Stephen Vincent Benét. 1937.

This story chronicles the journey of John, son of John, to the Place of the Gods and the important discovery he makes there. Narrating his story, which is set in the distant future, John describes the life that he and his people have lived since the Great Burning.

Because his father is a priest, John has been to the Dead Places where old bones of the dead and pieces of metal are found. At a young age John is recognized as a future priest and is taught the mystical chants and spells. Yet he burns to know more. When the time comes for him to go on his journey, he wants to go to the great Dead Place where the gods are said to still be walking. He wants to travel eastward although it is forbidden to do so. After receiving several positive signs, John heads to the great Dead Place.

Having crossed the great river, John arrives in the Place of the Gods. He learns the claims are false that the ground still burns in the Great Place. He views the ruins of the high towers that the gods had once made their homes. He finds stones strewn about with writings carved on them. He finds the shattered stone image of a man who wore his hair tied back like a woman's with the letters ASHING carved on it. He remembers that the gods did not hunt but got their food from enchanted boxes and jars, and he searches for the food of the gods. John eats from the jars, and then sleeps until he is awakened by wild dogs who chase him into a dead-house.

In the dead-house John discovers that the magic has gone out of the things of the Great Place. There are lamps, yet no oil or wick. Things read "hot" and "cold," and yet they are neither. Although the magic may be gone from the objects, John still senses the spirits of the gods weighing down upon him there. He lights a fire and falls asleep.

Suddenly night is transformed into day, and John sees the Great Place as it was when the gods were alive. From the window of the dead-house he views the gods on foot and in chariots. From another window he sees the god-roads mended and alive with traffic. He feels "the pulse of the giant city, beating and beating like a man's heart." Then he sees the gods' demise. The time of the Great Burning and the Destruction is upon them. He watches the last of them die and weeps over the broken city.

Finally, John comes upon a dead god whose body has been preserved sitting in a chair overlooking the city. He knows that this god was saddened by the city's destruction. The god's spirit has not died. He then realizes that this man and all the others were humans and not gods after all.

John returns to his homeland beyond the river and tells his father of his discovery. His father warns him not to divulge the news of his journey to his people, for the gods "ate knowledge too fast." Even so, John is certain that men, not gods or demons, built the city, and he knows that people must work together to build again.

John. *Cat's Cradle.* Kurt Vonnegut, Jr. 1963.

Attempting to write a book called *The Day the World Ended,* an account of what important Americans were doing the day their nation dropped an atomic bomb on Hiroshima, John finds himself involved in a bizarre series of events that lead to a real apocalypse. An unrelated story assignment takes him through Ilium, New York, home of the late Felix Hoenikker, who worked on the development of the devastating bomb. John stops there to see if he can learn what Hoenikker and his three odd children were doing the day the bomb dropped.

In an interview with Dr. Hoenikker's boss, Dr. Breed, John learns that at the time of his death Hoenikker was toying with the idea of ice-nine, a new crystallization pattern for water that would raise its melting point to above 130 degrees. If even one crystal of ice-nine dropped in one stream, all the springs, lakes, rivers, and oceans connected to that stream would freeze, and so would all the rain that

fell. That would mean the end of the world. Breed assures John that there is no such thing, but John soon learns otherwise. Each of the Hoenikker children has a crystal of the deadly substance.

Back in his New York apartment, John picks up a supplement to the *Sunday Times* advertising a banana republic called San Lorenzo. Posing in a photograph with the island's dictator, "Papa" Monzano, is a young man identified as Major General Felix Hoenikker. It turns out that the young man, one of Dr. Hoenikker's sons, obtained his position by giving "Papa" a crystal of ice-nine.

John is able to discover more when he is assigned to do a story on San Lorenzo for a magazine. On his flight there he meets Frank's siblings, Angela and Newton Hoenikker, who are traveling to visit their brother. He also learns about the island's outlawed religion, Bokononism, which teaches that humanity is organized in teams that do God's will without knowing it. The religion, its living founder Bokonon freely confesses, is based on harmless untruths, or *foma,* and it is a great comfort to the impoverished people of San Lorenzo.

When the American travelers arrive on the island, they learn that Papa Monzano is about to die, leaving Frank in charge. Panicked at the thought of having real responsibility, Frank asks John to rule the island. When he learns that Mona, Monzano's beautiful daughter, will marry him if he accepts, John does so willingly.

Racked with pain, Monzano ingests his crystal of ice-nine, freezing himself to death. After a bizarre turn of events, his body falls into the sea, freezing it, and killing most of the people on earth in the next few days. John is one of the few survivors and lives with Mona in a shelter in the castle's basement. Mona eventually kills herself in despair over the death of her people.

As he is traveling about the island, John meets Bokonon, who is contemplating the final sentence of the religion's text, *The Books of Bokonon.* The old man hands it to John, who is now a professed Bokononist. John reads: "If I were a younger man, I would write a history of human stupidity . . . and I would take from the ground some of the blue-white poison that makes statues of men; and I would make a statue of myself, lying on my back, grinning horribly, and thumbing my nose at You Know Who."

Johns, Ray. "Mondongo." Amiri Baraka. 1990.

Confused by civilian life, Ray Johns drops out of the all-black college he attends to become a weather gunner in the U.S. Air Force. Originally from a small town in New Jersey near New York City, Johns finds himself stationed in Aquadilla, Puerto Rico, during the period described by the third-person narrator as the time of peace after the Korean War and before "Nam." The southern white boys on base refer to Johns as the "nigger snob" because he spends most of his time reading classics. He holds a position as evening librarian on the base and spends many nights after hours in the library reading, listening to music, and drinking alone. He wears dark glasses and when being social, like his friend IRV LAFFAWISS, he hangs around with quasi-intellectuals and complains.

Laffawiss, a Jew from the Lower East Side of New York, is John's closest service friend. They share a special camaraderie in that they are both discriminated against by the white, country-boy soldiers whom they call "farmhouse mother-fuckers." Beyond the circumstantial bond of being minorities, their friendship remains at the superficial level of exchanging masculine jokes about masturbation and penis size. Laffawiss feels it his duty, however, to lure Johns out of the library and into the off-base bars of Aquadilla for some "real" fun.

With great reluctance Johns eventually agrees to a night on the town. Laffawiss's true intentions for the evening are revealed when he leads Johns into the off-limits bordello area known as Mondongo. Although Johns objects at every moment, Laffawiss's enthusiasm makes him question his hesitation, and he allows his friend to arrange for a "long time" with two unattractive prostitutes. Determined to overcome his repulsion, Johns attempts to "finish" what he has started with the prostitute even though the small room affords him no privacy from Laffawiss and his partner for the evening. When the woman Johns is with claims that his time is up and prevents him from "finishing," Laffawiss refuses to pay, and they make a dangerous getaway. Although Johns's past as a track star enables him to escape, Laffawiss is apprehended by the military police. In the end, Johns also surrenders, and they are made to paint the barracks as punishment.

Johns is eventually released from the Air Force because an anonymous letter to the military brands him a communist; Laffawiss is later discharged on a hardship case. Although they renew their friendship in New York, it soon comes to an end when they are attacked on the street by a group of white men. In a scene reminiscent of their escape from Mondongo, Johns escapes, but this time Laffawiss is taken away in an ambulance. A few days later two men who claim to be Laffawiss's relatives pay Johns a visit. Johns, who was not at home, learns of the visit from his superintendent, who tells him that two men inquired about his skin color. Johns and Laffawiss never meet again.

Johnson. "Like A Winding Sheet." Ann Petry. 1946.

Johnson is a quiet, even-tempered African-American man who finds himself provoked by an accretion of racial slights into committing an act of incredible violence.

The story begins as Johnson and his wife Mae prepare to go to work. They each work night shifts at different factories, and they are just rising in the late afternoon. As Mae dresses, Johnson lingers in bed. Johnson's job involves pushing a cart around the factory all night. His legs ache from the work, and he can't seem to get enough sleep to

make them feel better. Mae jumps on the bed and laughs, looking at the outline of the sheet on Johnson's body. "You look like a huckleberry in a winding sheet," she says. Johnson listens happily to the sound of her laughter. Then Mae says he had better hurry or he will be late again. But before they leave, Mae notices it is Friday the thirteenth and only half-jokingly says she shouldn't leave the house. Johnson loves Mae too much to get angry, but it takes him fifteen minutes to persuade her to leave, and he ends up late for work.

Johnson's legs are aching before the night shift even begins. He sees the foreman—a middle-aged white woman named Mrs. Scott—and hopes she doesn't notice he is late. But as the sound of machines starts grinding in his ears, he hears her harsh voice shouting at him for his tardiness. Johnson explains that his legs were bothering him. They argue. Mrs. Scott gets angrier and exclaims that "niggers" always have excuses. Johnson says softly that she has every right to be angry and to curse him, but no right to call him a "nigger." Then something happens to his fists. They clench up as if they want to strike Mrs. Scott. The woman apologizes and starts back in fear. Johnson eyes her, and seeing the lipstick on her mouth reminds him that she is a woman. Johnson can't bring himself to hit a woman, but he'd love to hit Mrs. Scott. He would lose his job, but it would be the last time she called anybody a nigger.

As the night drags on, Johnson feels dazed. He is aware of a tension in his hands, a tension searching for a release. When the whistle finally blows, the idea of taking a crowded subway up to Harlem seems unbearable. He pauses in front of an all-night restaurant and, looking inside, sees the customers happily drinking steaming cups of coffee that are being poured from a bright urn with a blue flame beneath it. Johnson realizes that something as simple as a cup of coffee will make him feel better. He enters the restaurant.

Inside is a long line of people who have just gotten off work. Johnson waits patiently. Finally he steps up to the counter and asks for a cup of coffee. The girl behind the counter, a young white girl, looks past him, tosses her head back, and says, "No more coffee for a while." In disbelief, Johnson asks her again. He gets the same blank response. Johnson is surprised none of the men behind him are protesting. He looks at the girl and feels his hands begin to tingle. He wants to hit her so hard that she will never again refuse a man coffee because he is black. He is about to lunge for her, but his hands fall to his sides. Even now he cannot bring himself to hit a woman. He rushes out of the restaurant and does not look back—and does not see that the men who were behind him are also being turned away, as the blue flame under the urn is extinguished and the nonchalant girl behind the counter prepares to brew a fresh batch of coffee.

On the subway to Harlem, Johnson feels the tension in

his hands surging through his entire body. He is too tense to grab the overhead strap and instead rocks back and forth with the train. He arrives home to find Mae in a good mood, singing along with the radio and chewing a stick of gum. When he barely grunts a greeting, Mae tries to cheer him up by ribbing him. Johnson has always loved saying something halfway funny to his wife and then listening for the sound of her laughter. Now he doesn't hear it. Mae is standing close to him, and the tension in his body shoots up into his arms and sends his fist straight into her face. He hears the sound of flesh being struck and realizes he has hit his wife in the mouth. He is appalled, horrified, but he can't take his hands away from her face. He continues to strike her, wanting to stop but feeling as if something inside him is binding him to this act, wrapping around him like a winding sheet. The image of a winding sheet swirls in Johnson's mind as his hands reach again and again for her face.

Johnson, Avatara ''Avey.'' *Praisesong for the Widow.* Paule Marshall. 1983.

Avatara Johnson, who prefers the nickname "Avey," is an emotionally troubled sixty-four-year-old African-American woman. The mother of three grown daughters and a widow for a decade, she supports herself with her inheritance from her deceased husband (JEROME "JAY" JOHNSON) and with her full-time job as a supervisor at the State Motor Vehicle Department in Manhattan. The action of the novel takes place in the Caribbean where Avey is spending her vacation on a cruise accompanied by two companions. The tranquility of the cruise is devastatingly interrupted when Avey suddenly and inexplicably decides to leave the ship and her companions to fly back to her home in North White Plains, New York.

Although characteristically rational and well balanced, Avey begins to experience a gnawing sensation just below her stomach that is accompanied by frightening hallucinations and a strange nightmare. In the dream, Avey comes to blows with her deceased great-aunt Cuney whom she has visited on Tatem Island in the South Carolina Tidewater on her childhood summer vacations. Incapable of adequately explaining her disquiet even to herself, Avey decides, to her companions' dismay, to take the ocean liner's launch to the island of Grenada and board the first available plane back to the United States.

Having missed the daily flight out of Grenada, Avey takes a room at a resort hotel with the intention of catching the next day's flight. That night on the balcony of her room she experiences an excruciating flashback in which she relives the agonies of her marriage. Fearful that he and his family would never escape the squalor of their first apartment on Halsey Street in Brooklyn, Jerome Johnson worked two and sometimes even three jobs and took courses in order to become a certified public accountant. Although Avey's energetic and dedicated husband did be-

come both successful and financially comfortable, the romance of the marriage did not survive the strain of his efforts. Suddenly struck by the tragedy of this fact, Avey is devastated by the memory of the precious passion that they squandered in order to survive in a world where love is subsumed to financial concerns.

The following morning, the dazed and bedraggled Avey takes a walk on the beach and, losing track of time and distance, finds herself stranded far away from the hotel and faint from the intense heat of the Caribbean sun. She stumbles onto a rum pub on the beach that is run by LEBERT JOSEPH, an ancient lame man. Although initially gruff, Joseph becomes extremely sympathetic to Avey's emotional tribulations and decides to take her under his wing. He insists that she join him on the annual ceremonial excursion that he and his fellow "Out-islanders" take to their birthplace, the small island of Carriacou, and together they board a frighteningly decrepit schooner that transports them and a number of other native Carriacouans to the festivities on their island.

Although Avey becomes terrifyingly ill on the short voyage, she recovers sufficiently to witness and even participate in the ritualistic singing and dancing that takes place the following day. The activities evoke a nostalgia for the time that she spent with her aged great-aunt in South Carolina, and the entire experience proves to be both cathartic and inspiring. Having recovered her equilibrium, Avey Johnson departs by plane from her kind new friend and vows that she will renovate her deceased great-aunt's house and upon retirement will live there for part of the year in order to recover the spiritual richness that that environment always provided.

Johnson, Coffin Ed. *The Real Cool Killers; The Heat's On; Cotton Comes to Harlem.* Chester Himes. 1959; 1965; 1966.

Criminals hate them, some white cops resent them, and law-abiding citizens fear them, but all agree that Coffin Ed Johnson and his partner are the best of Harlem's police detectives. No case is too tough for them, and the mysteries that unfold in the novels featuring Coffin Ed and GRAVE DIGGER JONES are among the toughest. Although most of the criminals the two men confront are black, the two officers view the overwhelming majority of Harlemites as honest, hardworking people having a difficult time surviving in their overcrowded corner of a racist city.

Neither officer is known for his cool detachment, but Coffin Ed is even quicker to anger than his friend Jones. Because a punk once threw acid in his face, creating ugly scars that will never disappear, Coffin Ed's trigger finger is a bit itchy. At one point Coffin Ed is suspended when he shoots and kills a member of the Real Cool Moslems gang for throwing perfume in his face. Ed thinks the perfume is acid and acts before his partner can restrain him. Coffin Ed returns to the crime scene later, only to discover that his daughter Eve is being held hostage by the gang leader who has allegedly murdered a white big shot. Ed's superiors allow him to help Grave Digger rescue Eve, and Ed shoots the suspected murderer.

After Grave Digger has been mortally wounded, it is Coffin Ed's turn to work alone. Although his superiors caution Ed, who along with Grave Digger had been suspended for his involvement in the death of a pusher, to stay off the case, loyalty to his friend won't allow him to be idle. He investigates the strange case, which involves a large shipment of heroin, a dashiki-clad African, an aged drug dealer named Sister Heavenly, an overgrown albino called Pinky, and a cat-eyed woman who exudes sexuality.

After many false starts and dead-end leads, Coffin Ed is able to find Ginny, the cat-eyed woman. Resisting the urge to seduce her, he convinces her to help him crack the case. By retrieving from its hiding place a fake bag of heroin that he had planted, Coffin Ed leads a major heroin dealer to believe that he has uncovered a lost shipment of the drug. A few crosses and double-crosses later, Coffin Ed learns that the real shipment had been hidden inside five big eels that Pinky—who was unaware of their contents—threw down an incinerator. The case is closed, and Coffin Ed's fellow officers finally tell him that the report about Grave Digger dying of his wounds had been fabricated in order to achieve a speedy conclusion to the case.

Coffin Ed and Grave Digger work together once again to discover the whereabouts of a bale of cotton that has $87,000 stashed inside it. The money had been collected from Harlem families by con man Reverend Deke O'Malley in a fake "Back to Africa" enterprise and was then stolen by Colonel Robert L. Calhoun, a southerner trying to convince blacks to move "back" to the South. The two detectives discover that the bale was found by a homeless man, was then bought by Billie Belle, a dancer who wanted to use the cotton in her act, and was finally purchased by Colonel Calhoun. It turns out that the homeless man discovered the money inside, and pursuing his own dream to go to Africa, he used it to settle there in luxury, with many young wives to keep him company.

Johnson, Gertrude. *Pictures from an Institution*. Randall Jarrell. 1954.

Gertrude Johnson, an insightful but haughty novelist, accepts a one-year artist-in-residence position at Benton, a college for women. She arrives with her husband Sidney, who changes jobs every few months to follow her, and tells the charismatic Dwight Robbins, president of Benton, that they are looking forward to a quiet year away from the literary circles in Greenwich Village. Gertrude is pleased by her "friendship at first sight" with the president and soon begins teaching a creative writing class, her sole responsibility on campus. Despite this easy schedule and the admiration of her students, however, Gertrude cannot mask her contempt for the people she meets. She reveals

to the novel's narrator, an unnamed poet, that she has really come to the college to gather ideas for her next book, a satire on academic life.

Gertrude's peace at Benton lasts for all of a week. At a cocktail party she and Robbins, both drunk, argue so vehemently that their friendship never recovers. She also offends a number of other professors with her opinions. They find her cynical and narrow-minded, but she expresses her ideas with such biting sarcasm that few are able to stand up to her. One colleague later describes her novels as nothing more than a compilation of her thoughts on how bad people are. Gertrude sees good humor and friendly gestures as signs of weakness; she herself extends only the slightest courtesy to those who might be useful character models for her fiction.

Many colorful, eccentric people work at Benton, and in order to get a closer look at these specimens, Gertrude throws a dinner party for Robbins and a few professors. While she hails from the South, Gertrude is completely lacking in both southern hospitality and the art of southern cooking. As her guests pick at the paltry portions of an inedible casserole, she dominates the conversation and goes around the table making witty and scathing comments about each of them. Later that night, in bed with Sidney, she bemoans what intolerable bores her guests had all been.

During the two semesters that she teaches, Gertrude remains popular with the students despite the fact that she hates them all and hates their fiction even more. She skims their work perfunctorily and can barely pay attention to them in conference where they confide in her their heartfelt beliefs about art, writing, and life. She cares only about the possibilities for her novel-in-progress, which she comes to envision as a murder-mystery set at Benton.

At the end of the academic year, Gertrude's publisher commissions her to fly to South America in order to write a travel guide for Peru. She and Sidney say good-bye to their "friends" before leaving, and Gertrude thanks them all for making her stay at Benton such a pleasant one.

Johnson, Henry. *The Monster*. Stephen Crane. 1898.

Henry Johnson is a handsome young African American who works as a stable hand for a doctor named Trescott. Henry takes great pride in his appearance. After work he washes so thoroughly and dresses so meticulously that it is impossible to tell he has ever worked with horses in his life. He is very popular among the other blacks in his medium-sized town, and his fine appearance has won him favor among the whites. For these reasons it is all the more tragic when he is horribly disfigured in a heroic effort to save a boy from a fire.

The fire starts mysteriously in the Trescott house one Saturday evening when Mrs. Trescott and her young son Jimmie are the only ones at home. When the fire is discovered and the alarm rung, Henry is among the first on the scene. Seeing that Mrs. Trescott has escaped the flames safely, Henry dashes into the house after Jimmie. Fighting smoke and rising flame, he reaches an upstairs room and finds Jimmie on his bed. Henry wraps the boy in a blanket and carries him out of the room.

By this time flames have engulfed the stairs. Desperate for a way out, Henry rushes to a back staircase that descends to Dr. Trescott's newly constructed chemistry laboratory. Fire explodes from different corners of the room as vials of chemicals ignite, and Henry is lashed by flames and overcome by smoke. He falls unconscious, sending Jimmie spilling to the floor.

Alerted by the sirens, Dr. Trescott rushes home. He pulls Jimmie to safety and then learns that Henry is still trapped in the burning building. Before Henry can be rescued, a vial of chemicals shatters on a table above him, spilling caustic liquid on his face. When he is finally taken unconscious from the house, Henry is burned so badly that many assume he will die.

However, Dr. Trescott, grateful for what Henry did to save his son, fights to keep his employee alive. He succeeds, but his patient has suffered brain damage and is freakishly disfigured. The doctor pays a local family to care for Henry, who is shunned and feared by the neighborhood. When Henry escapes from the home and wanders through town, visiting a woman to whom he was once engaged to be married, the citizens are terrified. They appeal to the doctor for help, but short of murder, nothing can be done to protect them from the man they now call "the monster."

As the story closes, Dr. Trescott returns home from the house of an angry townsperson whose daughter has been made sick by the sight of Henry, and he finds his wife in tears. Standing before a table set for fifteen, she sobs that no one will attend her tea party. The fifteen empty teacups at the table symbolize each of the friends who have left her because of her husband's involvement in creating "the monster" now plaguing the town.

Johnson, Jerome "Jay." *Praisesong for the Widow.* Paule Marshall. 1983.

Jerome Johnson, whose nickname is "Jay," is an extremely ambitious and ultimately successful businessman. Born and raised in Leona, Kansas, Jay leaves home at the age of twelve and makes his way east via Chicago to the New York City area where, except during his stint in the army, he works and resides. Although Jay is a very loving husband and father to his three daughters, the quality of their home life is compromised by his blinding desire to succeed economically and his fear of being caught in the dangerous clutches of poverty.

Jay is a handsome black man who sports a meticulously groomed mustache and an assertive, even arrogant, countenance. His love of music is gratified by a rare record collection that he inherited from his father who had been a talent scout during the 1920s for Okeh Records. Due in part to their relatively impoverished status as a young married couple, Jay and his wife AVATARA (JOHNSON), called "Avey," spend romantic evenings dancing in their own living room. On other occasions Jay entertains his wife and daughters by singing along with records or reciting fragments of the poetry he had learned as a boy in Kansas. For the first few years of their marriage, Jay and Avey are happy together, but the quality of their domestic tranquility deteriorates drastically when the cloud of poverty affects the whole family and ultimately turns Jay into a workaholic.

When Avey is pregnant with their third child, she becomes depressed and stops attending to her personal appearance. She and Jerome are not yet ready to have another child but are too fearful of the dangers of illegal abortion to terminate the pregnancy. Forced by the pregnancy to quit her job at the State Motor Vehicle Department, Avey is stranded at home with nothing better to do than worry desperately that Jay is having an affair, despite his insistence that he is really working overtime at his job in the shipping room of a department store. The tension that her suspicions cause culminates in a fight that convinces Jay his wife's jealousy and unhappiness are really her way of reacting to the squalor that surrounds them, and he abruptly decides that his family will be ruined unless he finds a way to relieve the financial pressures that threaten them.

The once playful and cheerful Jay transforms himself into a hard-driven achiever, reading books on career management and taking courses in accountancy. The strain of holding down two and sometimes even three jobs while simultaneously pursuing his studies takes its toll on the young man, and his marriage suffers.

After many years of maintaining this grueling life-style, Jay manages to pass the exam that qualifies him to practice as a certified public accountant. But his attempts to find a job are thwarted by racism, and he is rebuffed by all prospective employers. He eventually abandons the effort to find a job and establishes his own firm, which prospers after much hard work. Finally he is able to purchase a home in the pleasant community of North White Plains. But his monumental efforts undermine his health, and he eventually dies after a series of strokes and leaves a widow who mourns the lack of passion and intimacy that characterized the majority of their married life.

Johnson, Johnny. *Beetlecreek.* William Demby. 1950.

Johnny Johnson, a young African-American boy from Pittsburgh, Pennsylvania, relocates to Beetlecreek, West Virginia, to live with his mother's brother, David Diggs. Johnny is forced to move to Beetlecreek because his father is long dead and his mother is languishing from an unspecified but apparently incurable illness that has led to her hospitalization in Pittsburgh. During the course of the novel, Johnny gradually adapts to the rural world of this small community that is divided on racial lines: The blacks live in the area near the creek, Beetlecreek, and the whites live in the more settled part of town, Ridgeville. Between these communities, but closer to the blacks, is the old May Farm, now occupied by a reclusive white man, BILL TRAPP.

Johnny first encounters Bill when he and a group of local boys are caught stealing apples from Bill's farm. Johnny, the newcomer, is the only one Bill catches. Despite Johnny's fear, the two share cider and silence until gradually a sense of camaraderie begins to develop. David, the boy's uncle, joins them, and the two men begin a friendship unique for their time and place. David's wife Mary and the rest of the black community are suspicious of this new friendship, and Mary instructs Johnny to steer clear of the old white man.

Johnny's concerns during the novel focus on his sense of estrangement; he feels as though his life in Beetlecreek is but a dream. This dream is punctuated by horror when he first joins the Nightriders, the local gang. At their clubhouse he is exposed to sex and violence, and is shocked and frightened by the boys' unselfconscious sexual activities. The ease with which they shift their attention from pornography and autoeroticism to the killing of a young bird further alienates Johnny, who, after three days of withdrawal from all of Beetlecreek, seeks Bill Trapp's company.

Because Johnny and David's friendship has rekindled the old man's desire to live, Bill decides to host a picnic for the community's children. Although the picnic itself goes well, Bill unwittingly creates trouble by mixing the races. In addition, one of the young girls rips a page from an old encyclopedia and subsequently spreads tales of Bill's collection of "dirty pictures." This culminates in a social ostracization that Johnny guiltily but readily joins.

After ignoring the gang for weeks, Johnny meets up with them again and decides to undergo an initiation rite so he can become a full-fledged member. As it turns out, Johnny's initiation task, as assigned by the leader, is to burn Bill Trapp's house. Johnny and the gang sneak up to Bill's house and douse it with gasoline before Johnny strikes the match. As the rest of the gang flees, Johnny realizes in horror that he may well be killing his best friend. As he screams the man's name, Bill appears and realizes immediately what Johnny has done. The novel ends with the fire trucks racing toward May Farm, where it will be too late to save Bill's house or to salvage their ravaged lives and friendship.

Johnson, Lutie. *The Street*. Ann Petry. 1946.

Lutie Johnson is a determined and ambitious single mother in this dramatic tale that takes place largely on and around 116th Street in Harlem. Lutie, who has just left her husband after having found him with another woman, takes a small, dark, top-floor apartment in order to gain some independence and to provide a home for her eight-year-old son Bub. While Lutie is proud of herself for being able to rent the apartment, she is also quite bitter about having worked for years as a live-in maid in Connecticut, a job she kept only so that she and her husband could make mortgage payments on a small house in Queens. In addition to his infidelity, her husband squandered most of the money she sent home and eventually lost the house after Lutie stopped sending him money altogether.

Lutie starts her new life in the ominous shadow of the building's superintendent, Mr. Jones, who develops a strong sexual desire for her. Jones's lascivious behavior continually unsettles her, especially after she notices that he has befriended her son and spends time with Bub while Lutie is working at her office job. Meanwhile, Mrs. Hedges, a neighbor who operates a brothel in her apartment, also takes an interest in Lutie and asks her if she'd like to earn extra money. Lutie declines, but she does begin to think about other ways of making money. One night she encounters Boots Smith, a musician. Smith hears her singing along with a record and tells her that she could probably become a professional. He invites her to sing with his band the next night.

Lutie performs with Smith's band; the crowd and the musicians enjoy her performance so much that she is invited to become a regular vocalist. Lutie returns home elated, already planning her and Bub's quick escape from the dirty environment of 116th Street. As she enters the building she encounters Jones, who rushes forward, consumed by lust. He is stopped from raping her only when Mrs. Hedges intervenes. This sparks even greater fury in Jones, who begins to devise a way to get to Lutie through Bub. Meanwhile, Lutie learns that she won't be paid by the band because Mr. Junto, who owns nearly everything in the neighborhood, has decided that he wants her for himself. He reasons that eventually she will have to come to him for money and that when she does, he will be able to sleep with her.

Lutie decides to stop singing for Smith's band after she realizes that there will be no salary. She redirects her energy toward gaining a civil service job. Her efforts are interrupted, however, when Bub is arrested for tampering with the mail. He has been the victim of a scheme devised by Jones, who pays Bub a few dollars a week and believes that Lutie will accept his advances once her child is out of the way.

Lutie goes to a lawyer and learns that his fee to defend Bub will be $200. Since she doesn't have anything close to that amount, she goes to Smith, who tells her that he will have the money the next night. When she returns to Smith's house, Mr. Junto is also waiting, and she is told that she can have the money if she becomes Junto's mistress. Lutie's response is swift and dramatic: She forces Junto to leave, and when Smith tries to approach her, she kills him by striking him repeatedly with a heavy candlestick. As the novel ends, Lutie heads for Chicago wondering whether or not her son, whom she cannot help now, will ever remember her.

Johnson, Margaret. *The Light in the Piazza.* Elizabeth Spencer. 1960.

Margaret Johnson, the novel's main character, is the mother of Clara, the victim of a childhood accident that left her physically unharmed but with the mental age of a ten-year-old. While vacationing in Florence, Margaret Johnson realizes her most cherished dream when Clara meets and marries a young Italian, Fabrizio.

The women meet Fabrizio on a beautiful sunny day in the Piazza della Signoria. He owns a small men's shop to which he invites his new American friends. Hesitant at first to encourage Clara's immediate infatuation, Margaret declines. Over the next few days Fabrizio is forced to make frequent appearances at all the tourist spots in Florence so that he can get to know Clara.

Margaret reasons that she should take Clara to Rome before the situation with Fabrizio progresses any further; however, little by little, she is won over to the friendship between the young people. Still, she harbors fear and guilt over the fact that she has not made Clara's situation clear to the young man. Clara is so pretty, well groomed, and sweet that, especially given the language barrier, Fabrizio has no way of recognizing that she lacks anything.

Margaret and Clara are invited to Fabrizio's home for tea. They meet his suave and handsome father, Signore Naccarelli, along with the rest of his friendly, welcoming family. After the visit Signor Naccarelli sends a profusion of lilies with suggestively elongated stamens which make it clear to Margaret that he is aware of, and approves, the direction in which Fabrizio and Clara are headed.

Margaret quickly takes Clara to Rome, which, although beautiful, is dreary and unwelcoming after Florence. Clara dutifully follows her mother from one tourist site to another, silently pining for Fabrizio. When Margaret comes upon Clara quietly weeping in a basilica of the Roman Forum, she realizes that, despite her intellectual disabilities, her daughter has become a woman. The following day they return to Florence, where Fabrizio resumes his courtship.

Margaret writes to her husband, Noel, hard at work back in Winston-Salem, North Carolina, about Clara and Fabrizio. She receives a transatlantic phone call from Noel urging her to be sensible and to protect Clara from a huge disappointment. Margaret tries to explain that she thinks Clara will be happy as an Italian wife and that no one will even notice that Clara has a problem.

Luckily for Margaret, Noel is too busy with work to come to Florence and interfere with her plans. On the appointed day, Margaret and Clara meet Signore Naccarelli and Fabrizio at the office of the priest who is to perform the wedding ceremony. Suddenly, to Margaret's

horror, Signore Naccarelli jumps to his feet and rushes Fabrizio out of the office.

That evening Signore Naccarelli comes to the hotel, and he and Margaret take a walk along the river. Signore Naccarelli explains that he cannot allow the marriage because Clara is so much older than Fabrizio, twenty-six years to Fabrizio's twenty. Margaret is immensely relieved that her secret has not been discovered. Over coffee and brandy Margaret tells Signore Naccarelli that Noel had promised Clara a $15,000 dowry. This news and the intimate evening the two older people spend, ending in a kiss, convinces Signore Naccarelli to allow the wedding to take place. Clara and Fabrizio are married just as Noel starts his journey to Florence. At the end of the story Margaret walks out into the piazza on Signore Naccarelli's arm, preparing to meet her husband and an unknown future without her daughter.

Johnson, Mattie. *One Way to Heaven.* Countee Cullen. 1932.

Mattie Johnson, a dark and lovely woman, is a heathen turned devout Christian. As the novel opens, Mattie and her aunt Mandy are attending the New Year's Eve service at Aunt Mandy's church. Stubbornly unrepentant, Mattie resists the requests of her Aunt Mandy to go to the mourners' bench and become a Christian and even fails to respond to the personal appeals of the visiting preacher from Texas. Minutes later, however, a tall, dark, one-armed young man approaches the mourners' bench, throws down a pack of playing cards and a razor, and kneels. Deeply touched by this dramatic display, Mattie goes to the bench and kneels alongside her fellow convert.

After the service, Mattie meets SAM LUCAS, the one-armed young man. Mattie asks the visiting minister, who had confiscated the cards and the knife, if she can have the items as talismans against backsliding as she begins her Christian journey.

Sam, not a true convert but a religious con artist, walks Mattie home. Intrigued by him, Mattie invites Sam to New Year's dinner. A romance quickly blossoms, and within a week of their conversion, Sam and Mattie marry.

While Mattie becomes a devout, untiring church woman, Sam begins slowly but steadily to backslide. Mattie finds it humiliating to appear at all her church functions without her husband, whose dramatic conversion has become mythical at the church. One night, desperate to get Sam back in the church, Mattie tricks him into coming. Then, in a most public manner, she reveals that she wants God to reclaim her husband. Angered at this public appeal, Sam leaves the church. At home he promises Mattie that she will never shame him in that way again because he will never again set foot in a church.

Sam begins to stay away nights, and finally Aunt Mandy reveals to Mattie that he has a mistress. Mattie prays to God for Sam's return. She even approaches Sam's mistress,

Emma May. When Sam learns that Mattie is pregnant, he comes home. Mattie's happiness is short-lived; her baby survives less than an hour. Blaming Mattie for the death, Sam leaves home again.

Her husband remains away from home for such a long period that Mattie despairs of prayer and consults a conjuror. Two nights after she sees the conjuror and one night before the spell is supposed to work, Emma May comes to tell Mattie that Sam is ill and needs her. Convinced that prayer works after all, Mattie goes to Sam and finds that he is indeed gravely ill.

The doctor's diagnosis for Sam is a fatal case of pneumonia, and Mattie tells Aunt Mandy that she could bear his death more easily if she were sure his soul would meet hers in heaven. Sam overhears Aunt Mandy explain to Mattie how one can tell whether a dying loved one will end in heaven or hell. Mattie returns to Sam's deathbed, and he tells her of the beautiful music he hears, convincing the devout young woman that her wayward husband will find a final resting place in heaven. After his death, Mattie cries but rejoices because she can tell the preacher that her husband died a saved man.

Jones, Grave Digger. *The Real Cool Killers*; *Cotton Comes to Harlem*; *The Heat's On.* Chester Himes. 1959; 1965; 1966.

One half of a pair of Harlem's toughest police detectives, Grave Digger Jones uses his wits, his muscle, his gun, and his reputation to solve crimes in the novels featuring him and his partner COFFIN ED JOHNSON. He usually works in tandem with Coffin Ed, but when Galen, a white man slumming in Harlem, is killed, Grave Digger is on his own.

Coffin Ed is suspended at the beginning of the case for shooting a member of the Real Cool Moslems youth gang who throws a liquid in his face. Before Grave Digger can stop his partner from pulling his weapon, the youth is dead. In the confusion, the gang members escape, taking with them the pot-smoking hoodlum suspected of the killing.

Harlem is turned into a police zone as cops comb the area looking for the Real Cool Moslems and the murderer. When the police determine that the gun the alleged murderer had shoots only blanks, Grave Digger goes into action trying to find out who wanted Galen dead and why. After questioning an assortment of madams, whores, pimps, junkies, and stool pigeons, Grave Digger discovers that Galen had a penchant for young black women. He would pay for their services and force them to submit not just to sex but to whippings. The father of one of his victims had tried to kill Galen with a knife earlier that night and died at the hands of the bartender in the nightspot where Galen was drinking.

When Grave Digger reports back to his superiors, who are on the street watching the progress of the neighborhood sweep, a commotion breaks out. Sheik, the leader of the Real Cool Moslems, has shot a cop and barricaded himself in a room with Coffin Ed's daughter Eve, who is the girlfriend of one of the Moslems. He demands to negotiate face-to-face with Grave Digger. Since Coffin Ed Johnson has returned to the scene, Grave Digger enlists his assistance, and together they save Eve Johnson. Galen's murder is pinned on Sheik, who is killed by Coffin Ed in the gun battle, but Ed discovers that the real murderer was Sissie, one of Galen's victims who didn't want to see other women hurt, like her friend Eve Johnson.

When a heroin caper turns bloody, Grave Digger and his partner are called upon to crack the case. Early on, however, their fatal beating of a known drug dealer gets them suspended, and they are ordered to stay home. Investigating on their own, unarmed, the two are ambushed, and Grave Digger is seriously wounded. A vengeful Coffin Ed goes to work on his own. A report of Grave Digger's death is circulated, but while his friend solves the case, he is determined to be out of danger.

Another case facing the two detectives is almost comical. Money stolen from the Reverend Deke O'Malley, who had taken it from black families in a "Back to Africa" scheme, is hidden in a bale of cotton that disappears. To Grave Digger Jones, the case is no laughing matter because hardworking families have been defrauded and innocent people murdered in the pursuit of the $87,000. Working together, Jones and Johnson crack the case, with the reluctant help of Iris O'Malley, Deke O'Malley's wife. The two cops are not able to retrieve the original $87,000—since it was taken by a homeless man who found the bale of cotton after it fell off a truck—but they coerce Colonel Robert L. Calhoun, the original thief, to replace it. Grave Digger and his friend are able to go home to their Astoria apartments knowing that Harlem families will get back their hard-earned money.

Jones, John. "Of the Coming of John." W.E.B. Du Bois. 1903.

Education brings both opportunity and tragedy to John Jones. A black man living in the post-Reconstruction South, he cannot escape white racism.

Born in Altamaha, Georgia, to former slaves, John works as a plow hand in the rice fields. The whites know him as a quiet and respectful boy, but he longs for something more than life as a manual laborer: He dreams of an education. Determined to make his way in a world larger than the one occupied by the town's other blacks, John boards a train bound for a Negro school in Johnstown. Every black person in Altamaha is at the station to bid him good-bye.

The black citizens eagerly await John's return from Johnstown, but he puts it off after he is suspended from school for the poor quality of his work. Still dreaming of completing his education, John goes off to make money, then returns to school with a newly sober attitude.

After preparatory school, college beckons, and John works studiously to fulfill his ambition. Sent to New York City with his school's singing group after graduation, John has his position as a member of a subjugated race brought home to him. He follows an attractive couple into an opera house and sits inert next to them. John enjoys the performance until an usher asks him to leave the auditorium. As John leaves he notices that he has been sitting next to a former white playmate of his, also named John. The manager lies to John about why he is being asked to leave the theater, but John understands that it is because of his race.

John decides to return home and open a Negro school in Altamaha. The dinner and church service that the town's blacks organize for him prove a dismal failure because John, enlightened by his experiences, cannot share their celebratory mood. Still, he secures permission from the Judge, the town's leading white citizen and the father of the white John, to open the school.

When word reaches the Judge that John has been teaching the black children that they have a right to equality and opportunity, he is enraged. The Judge angrily closes the school, leaving John stunned but curiously passive. While walking home John sees his sister struggling with the white John, resisting his attempt to rape her. In the same strange state in which he accepted the closing of the school, John strikes his sister's attacker with a tree limb, killing him.

Arriving home, John tells his mother that he is going north. As the story closes, John returns to the woods where his sister had been attacked to await the men who will lynch him for defending her.

Jones, Joshua "Shine." *The Walls of Jericho.* Rudolph Fisher. 1928.

Joshua "Shine" Jones lives in the Harlem of the 1920s, a community responding as creatively as possible to the racism and class strife that characterize the period. Shine cuts a heroic figure: huge, strong, a man of few words but of deep and passionate convictions. Raised in an orphanage and treated with cruelty and contempt, Shine learned early the danger of showing vulnerability and has built a self-protective wall of callousness.

In Patmore's Pool Parlor, HENRY PATMORE tries to coerce Shine into delivering bootleg liquor to Fred Merrit, an affluent African-American lawyer known in the neighborhood as a "dicky," an upper-class black. Patmore has a grudge against Merrit. Patmore knows that Shine dislikes dickies and knows that the moving company Shine works for will be moving Merrit into his new home on Court Street (in an all-white neighborhood). Shine, suspecting treachery, refuses Patmore's request.

The next day Shine and company deliver Merrit's fur-

niture, and Merrit has already received a note threatening him if he moves in. They naturally assume it is from Merrit's white neighbors since the tactic has been used before, but they move the furniture in without incident—except for the appearance of an attractive black woman, a maid, who walks by and enters a house two doors away. Weeks later Shine meets the woman, Linda Young, at a dance. Only after Shine rescues Linda from the overly aggressive Patmore does she begin to return his affection. Shine and Linda start seeing each other and soon fall in love, but Shine cannot admit his feelings. Later, the Merrits ask Linda to be their maid. Shine does not want her working for a dicky in spite of the fact that her salary and benefits would improve. They argue, and Linda decides to stop seeing him.

Not long after, Shine sustains an injury while working. He goes to the hospital to have the injury checked and learns that Linda was admitted the night before after being beaten by a man. He assumes the man was Merrit and goes to confront him. He finds Merrit devastated, in the ruins of his bombed-out home. In spite of his rage, Shine cannot harm Merrit; instead, he visits Linda. When he reveals his intention to avenge her attack, she tells him that avenging her attack is something he does for himself, not her, and only adds to the alienating wall of callousness he has built around himself. He agrees to take no action. They part with their love renewed.

At the pool hall, Shine hears Patmore boasting about how he finally got revenge on a dicky. While Patmore elaborates, Shine realizes it was Patmore who sent the threatening notes, Patmore who went to plant the explosives, and Patmore who, finding Linda alone, attacked the young woman. A vicious battle ensues in which Shine beats Patmore severely. As Shine raises his fist to strike a death blow, someone breaks the huge mirror behind the bar. The sound of the falling glass shatters Shine's rage. He lets Patmore fall to the floor and walks away.

Jones, Judy. "Winter Dreams." F. Scott Fitzgerald. 1926.

Judy Jones, a diaphanous beauty, is capricious, unprincipled, and carefree—and, for Americans in the 1920s, the very image of wealth and success.

Judy first appears in the story as an eleven-year-old ill-tempered vixen, the abusive daughter of the owner of the country club where DEXTER GREEN, the story's protagonist, works. She attacks her nurse with a golf club, and the fourteen-year-old Dexter falls in love with her. She reappears in his life six years later when she drives a golf ball into the abdomen of Dexter's stodgy golf partner. Unapologetic about the accident, she turns the injury into a joke and makes clear her belief that life is a lark.

Later, while Dexter sits on a raft in the middle of a lake, Judy, in flight from a suitor, takes a motorboat on a wild spree. She collides with the raft, introduces herself, and insists that Dexter drive the boat so she can water-ski behind it. She then invites him to her house.

That summer Judy falls in love with Dexter. Fitting him into her roster and rotating him with other young men, she demonstrates her inability to commit herself to anyone or to feel guilt over the hearts she has broken. She wants only to satisfy her passing desires and to enjoy the effects of her charm.

This charm has a number of attributes. Judy is direct; but her openness makes her seem all the more unconquerable. Her chief weapon is her inviting but humorless smile in which her lips are always curved as if ready for a kiss. But her smile, though winning, is always described as artificial; in fact, Judy is quite unhappy, prone to bouts of weeping.

After being mistreated, Dexter leaves Judy's set, grows interested in another woman, and becomes engaged to her. Judy, acting on a jealous whim, lures him back with a promise of marriage. Once Dexter's engagement is thoroughly ruined, however, she drops him permanently.

Years later Judy's situation is described to Dexter by a business associate. At twenty-seven, she is married to Lud Simms and lives in Detroit. Lud is a bad husband who drinks and runs around with a slew of women, but Judy remains a faithful wife who stays at home with her children and forgives him for his outrageous behavior. She no longer exhibits the flighty, devil-may-care attitude of her youth, and she is popular with most of the local women. To the outside observer it seems that Lud fell madly in love with Judy and that Judy probably loves him, too, but her beauty has faded; now she is little more than a nice girl with nice eyes, someone to feel sorry for.

Jones, LeRoi. *The System of Dante's Hell.* Amiri Baraka. 1963.

Author LeRoi Jones, who took the name Amiri Baraka after the publication of this autobiographical novel, is a young black man journeying through a hell structured like Dante's Inferno. In fragments and stories, LeRoi narrates the incidents, people, and places in his life. Torn between middle-class aspirations and a disdain for their falseness, he describes growing up in Newark, his years in New York City, and his subsequent experiences in the military.

As a teenager, LeRoi is known as a "smart kid" and devotes much of his time to the poetry of Eliot, Pound, and Baudelaire. He becomes extremely curious about sex and tries to experiment with girls his age. But as he matures, these sexual games grow more serious and violent. LeRoi's friends are mostly male; he goes to parties; talks loud; hangs around. One night while driving with friends, he picks up a drunken woman and begins to molest her. She resists his advances as well as those of his friends. When she starts to fight, they grow afraid and push her out of the car.

In college, LeRoi is excited by the world of literature

and by the prestige attached to higher education. But even as he enjoys a new outburst of creativity, he is consumed with disgust—at his lies, at his life, at the things that make people "important." He is attracted to and repelled by other men, and when he contemplates his homosexual experiences, he is furtive and filled with self-hatred.

After college, LeRoi joins the military. On leave from the air force, he and a friend go in to town to drink and womanize. They meet two women outside a club, and after drinks and dancing, LeRoi's friend leaves but LeRoi stays on with his new friend Peaches. Finally, when he is very drunk and tired, LeRoi tries to leave, but Peaches won't let him go. Knowing that he can't return to base without his full uniform, she steals his hat, and then she takes him home. They try to have sex, but he is incapable. After sleeping a little, LeRoi wakes up a few hours later, goes for a walk, and then returns to Peaches' place. When Peaches tells him that she likes him and wants him to stay with her, he plans to desert the air force. But while he is walking back to her house with a few groceries, he panics and decides to return to the base. On his way back, he is set upon by three men who try to rob him; he fights them off and calmly continues on his way.

Jones, Reverend Clement. *The Terrible Threes.* Ishmael Reed. 1990.

Reverend Clement Jones serves as chief of staff to President Jesse Hatch. The current administration looks back with utter contempt on Ronald Reagan's term and his peace negotiations with the Russians. Reverend Jones's party, the New Christian Majority, dominates Congress, and Jones expects his conversion bill, which will force all non-Christians to convert or leave the country, to be declared constitutional. The New Christian Majority wear "Barbie" pin-striped suits, as directed by Jones, although most do not know they are being made to emulate the image of one of Jones's heroes, Klaus Barbie. Reverend Jones believes Hitler to be a misunderstood genius who recognized the need to stem alien infiltration, but he is careful not to publicize his admiration of Nazis. President Hatch is glad to be on Jones's "team," which Jones considers God's team.

Reverend Jones has worked as a biblical scholar, an English professor, a faith healer, and a televangelist. Upon arriving in Washington, D.C., he plans to rid the city of sin. He prohibits congressmen from having affairs and disqualifies Miss Americas who have had cosmetic surgery. Marines round up those committing sins in public and send them to Sunday school. Although everyone in town has a reason to be angry with Jones, he has a way of "lubricating" his words to ease them through people's minds. Known for his modest and austere life, he is considered the spiritual leader of the country. He preaches to 250 people in his small gospel church, but thousands stand outside to listen by loudspeaker. Just as Elvis has been called a white man who could sing black music, so Reverend Jones is considered a white man who can preach like a black preacher. Jones manages to bring in millions of dollars for his church.

When a scandal nicknamed the "Terrible Threes" threatens to damage the White House, Jones appeases the press by offering them a piece of "kosher meat." He intends to distract the public with a scapegoat named Krantz, who is Jewish. Krantz once worked as a micromanager for the recently deceased Admiral Matthews, an official of the invisible government. Jones had once saved Krantz from getting hit by a car, so no one would suspect Jones of being responsible if harm came to Krantz. The Admiral, who died mysteriously, left behind some papers that incriminate the President, and Krantz is aware of this. Knowing that his life is in danger, Krantz makes a public speech and calls upon the audience to support President Hatch and Jones during these troubling times. Krantz refuses to answer press questions about the Admiral's suspicious death or accusations that Reverend Jones regularly talks to imaginary people.

When the Admiral's letter is finally published, it does little damage, for Jones has managed to ensure his position at the White House by liquidating the various officials who got in his way, including the former President and his wife. The novel ends on Christmas night, with Jones—his tactics established, his power secure—about "to lead the nation in prayer for the recovery from the terribles which have plagued the nation since Dallas, November 22, 1963."

Jones, Robert. *If He Hollers Let Him Go.* Chester Himes. 1945.

Bob Jones, a young black man who works at a World War II defense plant in Los Angeles, lives through four harrowing days in this powerful novel. As the novel opens, Bob, who has recently become a leader at the plant, awakens from a violent dream to realize that he is nearly late for work. The dream was about racism, a central aspect of his day-to-day life.

Bob is in a relationship with Alice Harrison, the daughter of an upper-middle-class black physician. Alice has great plans for Bob and assumes that he will eventually become a lawyer. There are many obstacles to this, however, not the least of which is Bob's lack of enthusiasm for such a future.

At work that day, Bob needs the assistance of another worker, and he is assigned Madge, a buxom blond who refuses to work with "niggers." Her refusal enrages Bob, who nominally outranks her. Despite his rank, however, the white bosses do not force her to do the job they assigned her. Humiliated, Bob begins to fantasize about killing the white man who defended Madge and actually follows him home and threatens him. He also begins to fantasize sexually about Madge.

Outside working hours, Madge flirts with Bob, and he becomes worked up enough to go to her house late at night, where the two engage in a violent and angry quarrel that almost culminates in rape. Bob stops himself just short of raping her because he realizes the complications that would follow his action.

As the novel progresses, Bob and Alice's relationship deteriorates. Tensions arise when the couple, out for a nice dinner, are humiliated by the arrogant white staff at one of the city's finer restaurants and are forced to sit by the kitchen and have their bill artificially padded. The problems in the relationship worsen as Bob chafes under the restraint of the elder Harrisons' notions of behavior and respectability. For the most part the Harrisons advocate the emulation of white people's attitudes and a slow evolutionary course of racial progress.

In the meantime, Alice has begun associating with upscale types, which estranges the couple even further. It is while Alice is out with her new friends that Bob goes to Madge's house. The next day, in a seemingly pleasant mood, Alice and Bob go out together. In the course of their conversation Bob is told that he is "maladjusted" because he refuses to tailor his thinking to the "actual conditions of life" as Alice sees them. Despite this, after a long discussion, Bob proposes marriage and Alice accepts.

Bob's problems at work come to a head when he is accidentally locked in a room with Madge, who quickly screams that she is being raped. This in turn leads to a violent rescue attempt that results in a severe beating for Bob at the hands of his white male coworkers. In pain, Bob flees the defense plant, but he is later arrested and taken to a police station. Although the police and judge know that his account is honest and Madge's is not, he loses his job and thus forfeits his military deferment. The novel ends with Bob's loss of job, home, and fiancée, and with the certainty that he will face death once he joins the war effort.

Jones, Seth. *Seth Jones of New Hampshire.* Edward S. Ellis. 1907.

Seth Jones is the assumed name of Eugene Northfield, the resourceful hero of this juvenile romance. Northfield disguises himself as a garrulous, uncouth woodsman and assumes his alias in order to approach the woman he loves, Mary Haverland.

The subterfuge is necessary, Northfield thinks, because Haverland may have married someone else while Northfield fought, was wounded, and survived the Revolutionary War as one of Colonel Ethan Allen's Green Mountain Boys. A jealous "friend" of Northfield's not only told Mary that her lover was dead instead of wounded but also spread the word that he was going to marry Mary when she settled with her brother and his family on the distant frontier of western New York. Northfield intends to reveal himself only when he is sure that Mary is unmarried; if married, he will nobly depart.

It is to the wilderness of New York State that "Seth Jones" turns his feet at the war's end. He soon reaches the Haverland cabin and meets Alfred Haverland, his wife, their daughter Ina, and his unmarried sister Mary. Unfortunately, before Seth can reveal himself, young Ina is kidnapped by "Injins," as Seth calls them, "pesky varmints" who burn the Haverland homestead and send all but Ina scurrying down the river to the safety of a nearby settlement.

Seth now sets off with Everard Graham, Ina's boyfriend, in pursuit of the fleeing Mohawks. Graham is a less skillful woodsman than the former army scout Seth, and he manages to push Seth off an overhang accidentally, directly into the hostile Mohawk camp. Graham escapes to join Ina's father and another woodsman scout, but Seth finds himself a captive, along with Ina, and threatened with execution. Seth manages, by eccentric bravado, to convince the Mohawks that he is insane, and their religion prohibits the murder of a maniac.

Seth and Ina resign themselves to the long forced march toward the Mohawks' base camp. Seth suspects that Graham and others are pursuing them, so he skillfully leaves a trail for them to follow. When the whites finally catch up to the Mohawk party, Seth proves essential to their success because during the war he learned to speak the Mohawk language. Seth tricks his captors, and he and Ina are rescued. Now the cat-and-mouse game is reversed: The Mohawks pursue Seth and the whites in their flight back toward safety. The dramatic chase includes trickery, ambush, espionage, and luck. In all these Seth proves to be more adept than the threatening "Injins," and he soon helps lead the whites back to safety.

Finally, in the relative comfort of the frontier settlement, Seth can let his hair dye and dishevelment slowly fade away. He gradually drops his rustic disguise and abandons his vacant expression and colorful slang for his true, genteel personality as Eugene Northfield. Mary Haverland is quickly wooed again, and the two lovers are married on the same day that Ina is wed to Everard Graham. Future bliss is assured on this impossible frontier where abject evil has one name, "Injin," and will no doubt soon be vanquished.

Jong, Lindo. *The Joy Luck Club.* Amy Tan. 1989.

Lindo Jong teaches her daughter, Waverly, the "art of invisible strength" in this novel of two Chinese-American generations. This art wins arguments and the respect of others. Lindo Jong develops this strength to escape from an unhappy marriage in China and uses it to build a new life in the United States.

When Lindo is only two years old, she is promised to the son of a family more prominent than her own. It is regarded as a fortuitous match, and throughout her childhood Lindo is reminded of her good luck in this respect. Lindo, however, has no affection for her future husband, Tyan-yu, who is a year younger, and thinks of him as a troublesome distant cousin. When a flood destroys the home of Lindo's parents, they are forced to move to the house of a relative in a distant town. Lindo, who is twelve, is left behind with Tyan-yu's family and no longer has any contact with her own.

During the first years with Tyan-yu's family, Lindo is treated as a servant. Tyan-yu's mother, Huang Taitai, is a harsh instructor, teaching Lindo all she will need to know as a competent and obedient wife. Lindo cooks Tyan-yu's meals, and washes and sews, without complaining, afraid that she would shame her own family. When Lindo is sixteen, she is married to Tyan-yu in a traditional ceremony which includes the lighting of a red candle which burns from both ends until only ash is left, thus signifying a marriage that can never be broken. During the night after the ceremony, Lindo wanders into the courtyard and sees, through a window, the matchmaker's servant guarding the burning candle. Lindo prays fervently as she looks at the candle, and Tyan-yu's end of the candle goes out. The next morning, however, the matchmaker still makes the proud announcement that her job is done, displaying the ash from the candle.

Although Lindo and Tyan-yu sleep in the same room, to Lindo's relief, Tyan-yu is too frightened to have sex. Tension in the family increases as time goes on, since Huang Taitai is impatient for grandchildren and cannot understand why Lindo does not become pregnant. Finally Lindo thinks of a plan to make Tyan-yu's family believe it was their idea to release her. One morning she wakes up weeping and howling. When Huang Taitai rushes to her side, Lindo explains that she had a terrible dream. In the dream, she says, Tyan-yu's ancestors came to their wedding ceremony and, seeing that his end of the candle had blown out, shouted that the marriage was doomed. They predicted that Tyan-yu would die if he remained in the marriage. Lindo had been unable to produce any sons because the servant girl (already pregnant) is actually a woman of imperial ancestry and Tyan-yu's "true spiritual wife." When a confession about the extinguished candle is extracted from the matchmaker's servant, Lindo is released, sent to Peking, and given enough money to go to America.

Before leaving for the United States, Lindo pays an American-raised Chinese woman to give her advice about what to say to emigration officials, how to find work, and how to become a citizen. She advises Lindo to marry a citizen or have a child. With the information given to her by this woman, Lindo is able to find an inexpensive apartment in San Francisco's Chinatown and a job in a fortune cookie factory. A friend from the factory, AN-MEI HSU, introduces Lindo to Tin Jong, who is looking for a wife. Their courtship is brief and rather comical since they speak different Chinese dialects and can barely communicate. Lindo and Tin have two sons, Winston and Vincent, and a daughter, Waverly.

Waverly learns her mother's art of "invisible strength," and when she becomes a devoted chess player, finds it useful for winning matches. She becomes a national chess champion. Lindo, however, becomes increasingly dissatisfied with her life and torments her daughter by boasting about her achievements. Waverly cannot understand why Lindo does not learn chess herself instead of feeding off her daughter's success. Lindo's subtle strength becomes destructive as she ages, and her disapproval of Waverly's choices make her a difficult opponent in her daughter's life.

Joplin, Ralph. *Sissie.* John A. Williams. 1963.

Ralph Joplin, a successful playwright, is the son of the novel's title character, SISSIE PETERSON JOPLIN DUNCAN. Although artistically and financially established, Ralph is haunted by psychological problems that he traces to his position as a black man in a prejudiced world.

As the novel opens, Ralph meets his sister, jazz singer IRIS JOPLIN STAPLETON, who has flown to New York from her home in Barcelona. Iris has jetted across the Atlantic to join Ralph, and together they will travel to California to visit their dying mother. Both Iris and Ralph have had a difficult relationship with the strong-willed Sissie. Trying to write at home while Iris and his wife Eve attend his new Broadway play, Ralph recalls the battles he has had with Sissie and with other people in his life.

Childhood memories come to Ralph in brief spurts: while he is thinking of other things or speaking to his psychiatrist. When Ralph was very young, his father, Big Ralph, tried to kill his mother. While Big Ralph was in jail and Sissie was in another part of the state with the newborn Iris, Ralph was placed in a county orphanage for a year. This period of separation from his mother, which Ralph regarded as an abandonment, would make it difficult for the two to ever love each other. Ralph also remembers seeing a rat gnaw at the baby Iris's face, and he recalls the death of Mary Ellen, another sister with whom he was very close.

Sissie and Big Ralph had reconciled for a time, but Ralph soon experienced another abandonment when his father left the family for good. Now without a father, Ralph became surly and difficult, both at school and at home with his mother. He finally felt he achieved manhood at the age of fourteen when Sissie tried to beat him with a broom, and he was strong enough to take it away from her.

An incident that occurred while he was serving in the South Pacific in World War II was to haunt Ralph. It is only years later that he can tell the story, and he relates it to his sister when he visits her home in Barcelona. A white fellow soldier, nicknamed Doughnut, took special pleasure in taunting Ralph with racial slurs. Ralph felt he could not live unless the other man died. When Dough-

nut's abuse became too much, he fought with the man and pushed him over a cliff to his death.

After the war a brief and unhappy marriage followed. Ralph also embarked on a wandering trip through Europe, during which Sherry, a young black woman from an upper-class family, sent him money. Ralph's relationship with Sherry and an affair he was to carry on with a middle-aged white woman seemed unconscious attempts to find a mother figure.

Subsequently a budding playwright working at meaningless jobs, Ralph attempted to clarify his tangled life through psychoanalysis. His relationship with his analyst, Dr. Bluman, was a tense one, however. Ralph fought the man's help, holding back the very information that would be most helpful. He refused to see the roots of his problems in childhood, ascribing everything to the difficult position he occupied as a black man in a racist society. Ralph seemed more interested in pursuing the clinic's receptionist, Eve, whom he would later marry.

When Ralph and Iris finally travel to California to see their mother for the last time, he is a good deal less judgmental than his sister. On her deathbed Sissie asks Ralph to acknowledge that she was a good mother. He calls his upbringing difficult but essentially fair and tells Sissie that, yes, he does love her. After Sissie dies, Ralph makes plans with her second husband, Oliver, for her to be brought back East, to be buried in the same cemetery where she had laid three of her five children to rest.

Joppolo, Major Victor. *A Bell for Adano.* John Hersey. 1944.

Major Victor Joppolo takes charge of the small town of Adano, Italy, following an American invasion, and instead of forcing the citizens to obey his will, he uses his time in the town to right the wrongs done by the Fascist government. Although he clearly improves Adano's standard of living, the army fails to recognize his successes and eventually punishes him for them.

Joppolo arrives in Adano shortly after the Americans have attacked it. He begins his command by locating the room that will serve as his office, and he meets Zito, his usher. Zito explains the various problems in Adano, such as the shortage of food and water. He also complains about the lack of an impressive bell; the previous bell was melted down by the Fascists. Joppolo next meets Ribaudo Giuseppe, whom he hires as an interpreter.

After several days pass, Joppolo calls all the town officials together to announce his platform. An essentially democratic man, Joppolo feels that all citizens and officials are servants of "the people," and his first major decision reflects this stance. General Marvin, one of Joppolo's superiors, has become infuriated by the presence of mule carts on the road to and from Adano. Although the carts bear food and water to the townspeople and are thus essential, Marvin sees them only as nuisances blocking traffic. After a scuffle in which a cart is destroyed and a mule is shot, General Marvin orders Major Joppolo to stop the entry of carts into Adano. Joppolo carries out the order but revokes it after appeals from the citizens.

The fishing trade in Adano had flagged before Joppolo's arrival due to excessive taxation by past governments; Joppolo revives it by placing all the Adano fishermen under the leadership of the ancient, crusty Tomasino. Tomasino is initially as suspicious of Joppolo as he is of any city head, fearing more taxation or "protection" fees, but he gradually relents as he becomes more familiar with the major's character. Joppolo's other improvements of the town show a similar desire for the good of Adano. He punishes the town's previous mayor for various infractions by ordering him to confess one crime each day. When three of Joppolo's men destroy many valuable items in the house of a wealthy older citizen during their stay there, Joppolo punishes them by ordering each soldier to maintain the house as though it were his mother's residence. In addition, Joppolo ends the black market in Adano, enacts strict sanitation laws, and, finally, brings the town a bell.

Meanwhile, Joppolo, whose wife lives in the United States, falls in love with Tina, the daughter of the fisherman Tomasino. Although his ardor cools when she asks him about the status of her boyfriend, a prisoner of war, it surges again when news of the soldier's death arrives, and it grows as the story progresses.

The news of Joppolo's admission of carts into Adano passes through various bureaucratic layers before General Marvin receives it. When he learns of the decision, he angrily orders Joppolo out of Adano. Early the next morning, as the townspeople sleep contentedly, Joppolo leaves Adano sadly, without farewells.

Jordan, Robert. *For Whom the Bell Tolls.* Ernest Hemingway. 1940.

Robert Jordan is a young university Spanish professor from Montana fighting as a partisan for the Republican forces in the Spanish Civil War. Working behind enemy lines in the mountains near Avila, he is assigned to destroy a crucial bridge with the help of local peasant guerilla bands. The mission itself is relatively easy, but because the attack must be precisely timed to coincide with a major Republican offensive, Jordan's task is not only challenging but potentially fatal.

Although Jordan is competent and committed, he encounters enormous difficulties from the very start. While his guide, the old peasant Anselmo, is loyal and eager to do whatever he can, Pablo, the guerilla leader Jordan must contact, is wavering and indecisive. A shrewd man hardened by months of guiding his small band through the mountains, Pablo realizes that the destruction of the bridge means the end of everything he has worked so hard to establish in the region. Not only will it bring him no

material gain, but whatever its success, it is likely to precipitate ruthless reprisals from the vastly superior Nationalist forces.

Soon after Jordan arrives at the cave that constitutes the guerillas' main camp, Pablo challenges him, refusing to take part in the operation. Jordan is supported, however, by Pablo's wife Pilar, a huge, strong woman who, although well aware of the risks involved in aiding Jordan, retains a loyalty to Republican ideals that Pablo has lost. Pilar assumes command of the group of nine soldiers, including Jordan, but contrary to the guerillas' code (and common sense), she and Jordan allow Pablo to live and remain in the group. As Jordan foresees, this failure to be ruthless causes difficulties later.

Among the guerillas is a young woman named Maria, who was rescued after an earlier attack on a Nationalist train. Maria's father, a Republican mayor, had been killed by the Nationalists, and she herself both beaten and raped. Pilar has helped her to recover from the emotional trauma, and in order to give the girl a chance at happiness, she prompts a romance between her and Jordan. The two need little encouragement. Realizing that he and all the guerillas might well be killed in the attack, in the two days before the assault Jordan attempts to build a relationship with Maria that will give his life purpose and significance whatever their ultimate fate. He often fantasizes about a possible future for the two of them in America or Republican Spain, but he is always aware that such dreams have little hope of fulfillment.

And of course he is right. An unlikely snowfall allows the Nationalist cavalry to track a neighboring guerilla band, led by the reliable El Sordo, that was to provide over half the manpower and equipment for the attack on the bridge. El Sordo's band is trapped on an exposed hilltop, where after a valiant defense it is eradicated by an air strike. Worse yet, Pablo, in a moment of panic, destroys Jordan's detonators the night before the attack. Although Pablo decides to rejoin the group for the assault, the task has become much more hazardous than it would otherwise have been.

Despite these difficulties, Jordan does succeed in blowing up the bridge, but half the guerillas are killed in the attack, including the old peasant Anselmo. Pablo, Pilar, and Maria manage to escape, but Jordan is crippled by a shot in the leg and must be left behind. As the novel ends, he lies on the hillside above the bridge, delirious with pain but hoping, as the trapped El Sordo did, to take at least one Nationalist with him before he dies. By this time it is clear, however, that Jordan's mission has been useless; the greatly superior Nationalist forces are more than adequately prepared to repulse the Republican attack.

Jorge. "The Pedersen Kid." William H. Gass. 1958.

In this story a series of bizarre happenings liberate Jorge, the bitter son of an alcoholic father, from his disturbing and abusive family life. Early one winter morning after a bitter blizzard, Jorge hears Big Hans yell and dashes out of the barn to see the hired hand carrying something from the crib. The object turns out to be "the Pedersen kid." By the time Jorge reaches the kitchen, Hans and Ma have stripped the nearly frozen child and are ministering to him. As he works on the child, Hans orders Jorge to wake his father so that they can obtain one of his bottles, which he keeps well hidden, to bring the Pedersen kid around. The Pedersen kid eventually regains consciousness and reveals some unwelcome news to Jorge and Hans.

The Pedersen kid describes an armed intruder, whom he has seen only from the back, wearing a green mackinaw, a black stocking cap, and yellow gloves. In his confused and weak state, he can only say Hans that the man has locked his family in the cellar. If the Pedersen family is locked in their cellar, Hans and Jorge know that they should travel the blizzard-blighted road to rescue them. Prompted by fear, Jorge argues that the child has simply been raving as a result of being nearly frozen to death. Hans, on the other hand, believes the child. Angered, Jorge forces Hans to admit that if he accepts the story, he must now act upon it. This realization gives Hans pause. The abrupt arrival of Pa settles the matter, however. Prompted by his dislike of Hans, he decides that they should go over to the Pedersens' place.

As they make their way through the snow-covered countryside, a trace on the wagon breaks. Bitterly cold and fearful of the unknown intruder, they decide to return to the farm. But Pa drops his precious bottle, and it is crushed beneath the wheels of the wagon. When Hans laughs uproariously at this, Pa retaliates by driving the wagon onward to the Pedersen place, over the objections and apologies of the now-frightened Hans. Leaving the wagon a distance from the Pedersen farm, the three men attempt to approach without being observed. They confirm that the intruder has been forced to return to the Pedersen farm when they come across his horse frozen solid in a snow drift. They hide in the barn and try to determine whether or not the intruder is in the house.

From their hiding place they can see that no smoke comes from the house. In such bitterly cold weather, "a silent chimney was an empty house." Heartened by this realization, Jorge dashes from the barn to the dining room wall and signals to Pa and Hans that the coast is clear. He is shocked when he realizes that what appeared to be a snowman was in fact the intruder, who shoots Jorge's father to death. Hans runs screaming into the woods, and Jorge goes unnoticed by the gunman.

Dazed and in shock, Jorge hides himself in the basement. Several hours later he comes up to the house proper and makes a fire. He is feeling rather cozy when his thoughts stray to the potential return of the intruder. Pan-

icked, he puts out the fire and hides. He allows his mind to form a protective coating by taking him back to his childhood days of bliss and happiness.

Hours later he awakens from these reveries. Confident that the gunman will not return, he assesses his situation. The Pedersens have frozen to death in their cellar. His father has been shot to death in the barnyard. Hans has surely frozen to death in his cowardly flight. If the intruder makes his way to their farm, Jorge's mother might also be dead. Jorge imagines that the Pedersen kid has survived, and he decides that the intruder, by killing off their families, has done them both a glorious turn. Sitting before the fire, Jorge burns up, "inside and out, with joy."

Joseph. *The Dangling Man*. Saul Bellow. 1944.

Joseph, twenty-eight years old, is a former member of the Communist Party who lives with his wife Iva in a rooming house in Chicago while waiting for his induction into the army to fight in World War II. Joseph resigned his job at the Inter-American Travel Bureau seven months ago in anticipation of his induction. However, due to the fact that he is both married and a Canadian, his induction is postponed indefinitely by a web of bureaucracy. Left with nothing to do, Joseph must sit and wait for the army to call on him.

At first Joseph enjoys his freedom, but he soon becomes increasingly frustrated with his solitude and idleness. Joseph's problem is that he is unable to adjust to a life without structure. His days are organized around the most minor of events: taking his meals, the cleaning of his room by the maid, polishing his shoes. Slowly, the dullness begins to eat away at him. He has an outburst of temper in a restaurant when a fellow Party member refuses to recognize him. He and Iva start to argue more frequently, as he resents her having to be the breadwinner.

One night Joseph and Iva go to his brother Amos's house for dinner. Joseph becomes irritable and uncomfortable when Amos, a successful stockbroker, begins questioning him about his plans for the future. Amos offers him money, which he refuses. The evening degenerates when an argument with his spoiled niece Etta ends with Joseph taking her over his knee and spanking her.

The days continue to pass, and Joseph becomes increasingly bored and irascible. Obsessed with exploring questions of human identity and freedom, he begins having vivid, violent dreams in which he must do things such as disarm live grenades. He begins having philosophical debates with himself in his diary and becomes unable to function in social situations.

Joseph has not been on good terms with the other residents of his rooming house, and matters become extremely tense when his landlady falls ill. He discovers that his irrational, drunken neighbor, Mr. Vanaker, has been stealing pairs of his socks and throwing them out the window. One night Joseph confronts Vanaker, who is unable to understand what he is being accused of doing. When Joseph gets in a fight with another tenant, he and an embarrassed Iva are asked to move out of the house.

Finally, without telling Iva, Joseph goes to the draft board and requests that he be drafted immediately. The army complies, and on his last day as a civilian, Joseph rejoices at the loss of his freedom.

Judson, Bart. *The Living Is Easy.* Dorothy West. 1948.

Bart Judson is an ambitious black businessman who makes his fortune in Boston as a fruit wholesaler specializing in expertly ripening and distributing bananas. The son of a slave, Bart inherits his mother's obsession with financial independence and begins his career as an entrepreneur at the tender age of ten, when he religiously saves the pennies he has earned shining shoes and doing miscellaneous chores at a boardinghouse where his newly freed mother works as a chef. Too busy to attend to his love life until he reaches middle age, Bart finally marries a woman twenty-three years his junior, and his heretofore simple and easygoing existence is disrupted by domestic trauma and tragedy.

Bart begins his ascent to the ownership and management of a highly successful wholesale fruit house near Faneuil Hall in Boston when he sees his first banana and decides to devote his considerable financial skills to building a kingdom in what was then a nascent trade. After years of daring yet meticulously sound buying and selling, Bart is a wealthy and highly respected man, dubbed the Black Banana King. Due in part to his pecuniary personality, Bart has been wary of women because he fears that they are interested in him only because of his money. But when the teenaged CLEO JERICHO JUDSON knocks him down on her bicycle, he forgets his phobia and is immediately love-struck. They marry without courtship or delay and move into a furnished apartment in a brownstone in the south end of Boston, an area that is deteriorating due to the increasing poverty of their neighbors. Unaware that his wife married him primarily to escape her plight as a paid companion to elderly women, Bart is willing to be patient with his new wife, who initially refuses to have sex with him and finally does so only grudgingly. Together they produce a daughter named Judy, who resembles Bart and steals his heart. Although Bart loves his frosty wife, he consistently resists her spendthrift tendencies; it is only after ten years of marriage that he gives in to her nagging request to move into a more fashionable part of town, and they rent a large, beautiful house in Roxbury.

Having undergone an intense religious conversion as a child, Bart has a spiritual personality which includes the conviction that his financial prosperity is largely due to his intimate relationship with God. But Bart's hot line to heaven is not direct enough to weather the disruption of trade due to World War I and his inability to keep abreast of newfangled business practices that undermine his cor-

ner on the market. In addition, Cleo invites her three sisters and their children to live with them, and the years of this additional monetary burden, on top of his wife's frivolous spending patterns, culminate in his financial demise. Fiscal worries affect Bart's health, and his heretofore robust body begins to deteriorate as he creeps toward sixty years of age. His business fails, despite his continued diligence, and he is forced to sell out for a meager sum that he hands over to Cleo. Informing her that his prospects in Boston are ruined, Bart leaves her with the care of his beloved daughter and declares his intention of moving to New York City to try to build another fortune in his old age.

Judson, Cleo Jericho. *The Living Is Easy.* Dorothy West. 1948.

Cleo Jericho Judson is a gorgeous, light-skinned black woman from the South who is a pathological liar and is cursed with a hardness of heart that destroys the lives of her family. At the age of fourteen, Cleo's mother decides to send her daughter north to Springfield because she fears that her tomboy proclivities might lead in adolescence to loose, "floosy" behavior. Having impressed an elderly white woman named Miss Peterson with her extreme beauty, Cleo is invited to accompany her to Springfield and act as a companion, a subservient position that she resents and longs to escape. Upon the death of Miss Peterson, Cleo is sent to Boston to keep house for another elderly woman, but she finally escapes her fate as a dependent when BART JUDSON, a rich businessman twenty-three years her senior, asks her to marry him.

Although Bart worships her and does everything in his power to make her happy, Cleo does not reciprocate his kindness and is cold both in the bedroom and in every other aspect of their life together. Cleo's alternately frosty and volatile behavior extends to their daughter Judy, whose dark skin, large flat nose, and meek demeanor annoy her ambitious mother. Greedy to an extreme, Cleo stoops to robbing her own daughter's piggy bank and lying to her husband in order to extort funds to support her extravagant tastes. Cleo's obsessive dream is to send for her three sisters and reunite them all under one roof in order to regain the familial happiness that she enjoyed as a child. Although all three of her sisters are married, she is oblivious to their domestic lives. She is hostile toward all three husbands, whom she dislikes intensely because of their poverty and their enjoyment of her sisters' affections. With this secret goal in mind, Cleo convinces Bart to rent a large house in Roxbury, a location she favors due to the almost complete absence of other black people in the neighborhood.

Having amassed enough money to pay for the train fares of her sisters, Charity, Lily, and Serena, Cleo constructs a series of lies in order to lure them to Roxbury. With Charity and Serena, Cleo uses the pretext that Lily's husband is threatening to desert her. In order to lure Lily,

Cleo implies that she is planning to leave her husband, assuming that Lily will visit in order to convince her to remain in the marriage. Cleo's scheme works perfectly, and having tricked her sisters into making the trip to Boston accompanied by their children, she manages to keep them there by withholding the funds that each of them needs in order to return to their respective homes.

The abandoned husbands eventually leave the sisters, and with the exception of Lily, who learns to like her new home, the sisters lead a miserable, dreary existence. When World War I and a series of poor business decisions ruin Bart's wholesale fruit business, the sisters are forced to get jobs, and Cleo's dream of a happy family life crumbles around her. Finally, her husband goes bankrupt and decides to move in the hopes of reestablishing himself in New York City, a city unaware of his lack of viable financial credit. Thus, despite her efforts to establish domestic tranquility and a united family, Cleo succeeds instead in destroying the lives of virtually everyone under her roof.

Julian. "Everything That Rises Must Converge." Flannery O'Connor. 1961.

Because the doctor has ordered his mother to lose twenty pounds and lower her blood pressure, cynical young Julian must take her on the bus every Wednesday night to a downtown exercise class. On the Wednesday in which the story takes place, that trip has a tragic conclusion.

A year out of college, Julian lives with his mother, a widow whose pettiness and bigotry never cease to depress him. Although they live in a shoddy southern neighborhood, she repeatedly reminds him of his wealthier origins, which are symbolized in her mind by her grandfather's plantation with two hundred slaves.

On this Wednesday night, Julian's mother is happy to find there are no blacks on the bus, and she vocalizes her relief loudly. Embarrassed and angry, Julian hides behind a newspaper and reflects on his upbringing. His mother had sacrificed greatly so that Julian could be raised properly and attend college, but in the process she attempted to instill in him her own petty values. Julian congratulates himself for having resisted her influence; he tells himself he has cut all emotional ties to his mother and her little world. Julian views his mother with hatred, imagining how he might "teach her a lesson" by making friends with some black professionals, bringing in a black doctor to treat her when she is ill, or, most shocking of all, falling in love with a black woman.

When the bus stops again, a large black woman and her young son board. To Julian's delight and his mother's horror, the woman is wearing a hat identical to the one his mother has on. Julian's mother soothes herself by playing with the boy, whom she finds "cute," and

Julian finds that this lesson has not penetrated her bigotry in the least.

When both mother and son pairs get off the bus at the same stop, Julian's mother tells Julian she wants to give the black boy a nickel. Horrified, Julian begs her not to, but she is already reaching into her purse. The black woman responds with sudden rage, swinging out her own bag and knocking Julian's mother to the ground before storming away with her son.

The incident seems to have a strange effect on Julian's mother. She is unsteady and appears not to recognize her son as he lectures her. Just after Julian tells his mother that the changes she must accept in the world won't kill her, she collapses, her face distorted by an apparent stroke. Julian rushes to her side, sobbing and calling her name, as waves of guilt and sorrow rush over him.

Jurgen. *Jurgen: A Comedy of Justice.* James Branch Cabell. 1919.

Jurgen is an inhabitant of the mythical medieval land of Poictesme. A commonplace, middle-aged pawnbroker, he is married to the voluble and shrewish Dame Lisa. His chance to free himself of her arrives unexpectedly when Jurgen comes upon a monk who has stubbed his toe on a stone and is cursing the Devil who put it in his path. Jurgen perversely praises the Devil, who appears, thanks him, and rewards him by turning Dame Lisa into a spirit who walks on the moor. Feeling that he still must try to reclaim her, Jurgen follows her image into a dark cave where he meets the centaur Nessus, who gives him a magic shirt to wear. Nessus tells him that for a year he will go on a quest—both for his wife and for the meaning of justice. Transformed into the handsome and romantic youth he once was, he sets off on the picaresque adventures—most of them amatory—that occupy the rest of the book.

Jurgen meets Guenevere, whom he courts in his new role as Duke of Logreus; he soon tires of her and moves on to Anaïtis, whose priapian rites first enthrall, then exhaust him. He meets and marries the Hamadryad Chloris, who becomes jealous of his attraction to Helen of Troy (who is also his ideal childhood sweetheart, Dorothy la Désirée). In further wanderings he goes to Hell and weds the vampire Florimel; then, seeking to understand the justice in the abduction of his wife, he ascends to Heaven as the Pope for a theological discussion with the God of his Grandmother. Here he learns of Koshchei, the supernatural being who "made things as they are," and seeks him out. Koshchei parades the beautiful women of history before him and asks, in view of their obvious attractions, if he would prefer to have Dame Lisa back.

Disillusioned by his adventures, Jurgen no longer desires to live on the high plane of romantic fantasies. Justice is an illusion: His experiences do not support the doctrine that things must somehow turn out as humans wish they would. Jurgen gives Koshchei his magic shirt, and the strange dark being vanishes. He is back in his old home again with Dame Lisa. She and his humdrum life are the known quantities, the compromises that humankind must learn to make with unattainable ideals.

K

Kaetterhenry, August. *Country People.* Ruth Suckow. 1924.

August Kaetterhenry, an Iowa farmer, drives himself relentlessly to acquire and maintain a respectable farm. A proud, quiet man whose parents emigrated from Germany in the 1880s, August remains apart from the community even when he possesses significant marks of success, such as a new house in town. August's fierce sense of commitment to his farm sustains him through a relatively isolated, Spartan life.

August's father, Caspar Kaetterhenry, had been a farm laborer in Germany and moved to Turkey Creek, Iowa, with his young wife and daughter. The family grows rapidly, and Caspar Kaetterhenry becomes notorious throughout Turkey Creek for making his wife and children work on the farm. August works on his father's farm until he is eleven, attending school infrequently. He then begins to hire himself out to work on other farms, saving money to buy his own land.

At fifteen, August moves away from home to a nearby county, Richland, to work for a wealthy, miserly farmer named Henry Baumgartner. While working in Richland, August meets two young women, also of German ancestry, Mollie and EMMA STILLE (KAETTERHENRY). They cheerfully serve food to the men who work as threshers on the farm. August's friend, Herman Klaus, begins taking Mollie to the various social events in Richland. Although August is extremely shy, he is eventually coaxed into accompanying them with Emma. August and Emma hold hands for the first time at a Fourth of July celebration, and after that they "keep company."

They are married by a country minister and move into a modest home on a farm given to them by Emma's father, Wilhelm. The first years of their marriage are the most difficult, and the oldest children are forced to work as hard as August had on his father's farm. In addition to their six children, August and Emma also support Grandma and Grandpa Stille. Emma nurses Grandma Stille during a long illness, but her death marks the end of the most strenuous years for the Kaetterhenrys.

August's sons, who are not as meticulous about money as he is, convince him that they can afford electricity, new mechanical farm equipment, and a car. With the increasing productivity of the farm, he is able to save enough to build a new house in town and retire, leaving the farm to his son Carl. August hauls material to his lot and helps build the house, but once this task has been completed, he is at a loss. Without farm work, August's health fails rapidly, although he is still relatively young. The farm, as Emma observes, has the importance of a religion for August, and he dies of a stroke when he no longer has any purpose there.

Kaetterhenry, Emma Stille. *Country People.* Ruth Suckow. 1924.

At the time she meets her future husband, AUGUST KAETTERHENRY, Emma Stille is a "giggler," whispering with her sister Mollie and flirting with the threshers who work on their father's farm. Looking at a photograph of Emma as a young woman, her grown children cannot believe that this was their reserved, sensible mother.

Like many other young unmarried women in the region, Emma teaches "country school" until she is ready to be married. She also helps her father Wilhelm by serving food to the men on the farm. Although she is playful, August admires her for being a good worker. Because August is so shy, however, it is Emma who first expresses an interest in him, arranging to sit next to him on a bobsled ride. After that, August gains confidence and invites Emma to a Fourth of July celebration. Emma and August then see each other steadily, attending country social events, until their marriage.

They are married by a country minister and move to a farm given to them by Emma's father. Their first two children, Frankie and Mary, are easy to manage, and Emma continues to help August with the farm work. When their third child, Elva, is born, Emma becomes ill and never quite recovers. She leaves the outdoor work to August and cares for the house and children. Emma's parents also move into the house, and she nurses her ailing mother during an illness that lasts five years. When

Grandma Stille dies and her children are older, some of the burden is lifted from Emma's shoulders.

August does not allow Emma to accompany him to town to buy supplies, and she is afraid to ride in the car with her sons. The only significant period of time Emma spends away from home is when she must have a gall bladder operation. She travels by train with August and her youngest daughter, Marguerite, to a clinic in Rochester, Minnesota. While at the clinic, Emma is suddenly the most important member of the family. She receives the attention of doctors and nurses shyly at first and then with increasing pleasure. Although the operation goes smoothly, the doctors advise her to be careful. But she quickly throws off her "invalid ways" and returns to her rigorous routine.

The farm is so profitable that August and Emma are able to retire fairly young. August builds a new house in town, but Emma and Marguerite are happier there than he is. Without the farm, August feels bereft, and his health fails rapidly. August dies of a stroke, and Marguerite moves away to college. Emma surprises her children by managing very well after August's death, participating in church activities and making friends among the elderly ladies of the town. Her personality, which had been smothered for so many years, is finally allowed some freedom, and she spends the last period of her life in contentment.

Kane, Lester. *Jennie Gerhardt*. Theodore Dreiser. 1911.

Lester Kane, the son of a wealthy Cincinnati carriage manufacturer, is a handsome bachelor, intelligent but confused about social and spiritual truths. Although he enjoys a comfortable, relatively carefree life in business and society, he does not accept a code of self-advancement as unthinkingly as does his brother Robert.

On a business trip to Columbus, Lester is struck by something uncommon in the manner of an attractive, shy maid at his lodging house. He senses the soft personality of this maid, JENNIE GERHARDT, and feels that she would not refuse his sexual advances. One day he grabs and kisses her, and tells her, "You belong to me." Jennie, whose family is very poor, asks Lester for financial assistance, and after helping her he proceeds to persuade her to accompany him to New York on a business trip as his "wife." Lester is noncommittal when marriage is seriously discussed, however; he knows that his family and his social world would disapprove of Jennie.

Lester eventually has Jennie move to Chicago, where he later goes to oversee a construction project for his father's carriage company. He realizes that he must be cautious, but he can't bring himself either to marry Jennie or to leave her. When he discovers that Jennie has a daughter from a previous relationship, he uses this as another reason to convince himself of the impossibility of marriage. Nevertheless, he comes to enjoy a warm home life with Jennie and Vesta, her daughter.

When Lester's sister Louise confronts him with her discovery of this unsanctioned arrangement, Lester is defiant and unapologetic. His family begins to pressure him, however, and he grows increasingly distant from them. Meanwhile, Lester and Jennie move into a house in a wealthy neighborhood as a supposedly married couple, only to find that rumors and a newspaper scandal closely follow them. Lester's father dies soon after, stipulating in his will that if Lester does not leave Jennie, he will forfeit his substantial inheritance.

True to his indecisive pride, Lester decides to leave the carriage company rather than submit to the whims of his brother Robert, who has aggressively taken control and expanded the company while at the same time reducing Lester's responsibilities in the operation. After losing money on real estate speculation, Lester and Jennie take a trip to Europe to console themselves and get away from Chicago, where they are now near-outcasts.

In Europe, Lester runs into Letty Pace Gerald, a wealthy, cultured widow whom he has known since childhood and who was always suggested to Lester by his family as a suitable wife. He sees that she exceeds Jennie in intellectual subtlety, even if not in sympathy. Jennie notices their shared qualities and mutual attraction; when she learns, upon their return to Chicago, what Lester stands to lose materially because of their relationship, she decides she should leave him. When she proposes this, Lester quietly agrees.

Letty assures Lester that leaving Jennie was for the best, and the two marry. Eventually becoming a prominent and formidable figure once again in business and society, Lester is now somewhat "soured" by his confrontation with and acquiescence to convention. When he is struck ill while on a trip to Chicago years later, he calls Jennie to his bedside and confesses to her that what he did was wrong and that she was the only woman he ever truly loved.

Kaplan, Hyman. *The Education of Hyman Kaplan*. Leonard Q. Ross. 1937.

Hyman Kaplan is the protagonist of a series of good-natured stories that follow him through the tortures of Americanization classes at the American Night Preparatory School for Adults in New York City. Hyman Kaplan's name is properly H*Y*M*A*N K*A*P*L*A*N: written in red and outlined in blue, with green stars. This is how he identifies himself in class, in his own notebooks, and in the exercises he hands in to his harried instructor, MR. PARKHILL. Kaplan is a flamboyant, assertive Jewish immigrant from eastern Europe, intent upon his subject of study, "English Americanization Civics Preparation for Naturalization."

Whereas Mr. Parkhill is worried about his pupil's academic progress, Kaplan actually has a very firm grip on the realities of "Americanized" life. The class, which centers on learning the English language, reveals Kaplan's unerring American-style logic. For him the plural of cat is Katz. Superlatives naturally run from good, to better, to "high cless," and from bad, to worse, to rotten. Asked for a noun, Kaplan provides "door." Asked for another, he declaims "another door."

A sweatshop dress-cutter by day, Kaplan's evening classes are fraught with subtler problems than low pay, no ventilation, and class inequality. In Mr. Parkhill's class the first nemesis is pronunciation; the second is Kaplan's arch rival, the prim and fairly Americanized Miss Mitnick. Huge confusions revolve around Kaplan's mispronunciations—when enamel becomes "animals," I beg your pardon becomes "a big department" and newspapers become "noose-peppers." Kaplan's Shakespeare wrote the tragedy Julius Scissor. Amid all of these confusions, Miss Mitnick is the ablest of the class to point out Kaplan's errors and in doing so inevitably incurs his wrath. Like Mr. Parkhill, Miss Mitnick cannot see through Kaplan's unconventionality to his unerring literalism and his sincere zest for the new world he has encountered.

It is useless to argue or to reason with Kaplan since logic is one of his keenest tools. How explain, for instance, that all newspapers should take a neuter pronoun when one of them is called "Harold," the *Herald Tribune*? And how interdict when Kaplan's awkward phrase, "If your eye falls on a bargain, please pick it up," is explained with placid confidence: "Mine oncle has a gless eye"?

Kaplan overflows with good intentions and perseveres with unfailing humanity. His heroes in a February speech class are, for example, the "prazidents" Judge Vashington and Abram Lincohen and a real dark horse, Jake Popper, who turns out to be a deli owner who sold on credit to needy customers and died of overwork. American history suffers horrible mangling, and the story of poor Jake Popper Kaplan ends bluntly: "An' I didn't go to de funeral," a comment meant to be some consolation.

Although Kaplan may never be advanced to Miss Higby's second-level class, Composition, Grammar, and Civics, he is the eventual victor in this book. Kaplan is an American; his very individuality assures it.

Kaplan, Suzanne. "Family Dancing." David Leavitt. 1983.

Suzanne Kaplan, recently entering her second marriage, is the protagonist of this story. Until recently Suzanne's life was that of a fairly typical housewife. She and her first husband would relocate periodically, moving through a predictable series of houses and neighborhoods; each move was an improvement over the last. They had two children, Lynette and Seth. One day when Suzanne an-

nounced her desire to move again, her then-husband Herb announced that he wanted a divorce. As the story opens, Suzanne, having shed thirty pounds, has remarried, this time to Bruce Kaplan, who along with his son and daughter was abandoned by his first wife. It is at their home that the story takes place as Suzanne makes the final preparations for the party she is throwing in Seth's honor. Her son has finally managed to graduate from prep school, a feat made possible only by extensive hard work on the boy's part and on the part of the boarding school to which Seth was sent after his learning disability was diagnosed.

Guilt-ridden over her son's long undetected disability, the failure of one marriage, the disappointment of another, the hostility of her daughter Lynette, and the nonstop riding offered by her mother, Suzanne's preparations for the party, like her thoughts and feelings, are harried, and it is only by dint of the well-staffed catering service that the pre-party process moves fairly smoothly. Once the party gets started, Suzanne almost immediately feels the need to escape. She recalls the last days of her first marriage and recognizes that her new husband is a bore; she also realizes that his children are quite hostile to her and are out of place in this situation. In addition, Suzanne has to cope with Lynette, who is fiercely critical of everything Suzanne does. This fact appears obvious when Lynette arrives at the party with her roommate John, an angular and flamboyant gay man. What Suzanne and Herb do not know is that their son Seth, the honoree of the party, is having an affair with John. In fact, as the party is barely under way, the two young men disappear into the bathhouse where they apparently make love.

As the party progresses and Lynette is held in check by John, who is angered by her rank hostility toward her mother, Herb and his new girlfriend arrive. By this time Suzanne has started drinking in order to cope, and it is helping her immeasurably. She is able to be polite to Herb and Miriam, although she feels it is necessary to continue to imbibe the martinis she barely tastes. The party is fairly successful: the food disappears since the catering, done by an extended family of black women, is excellent.

Suzanne begins to feel better and better even though she again senses, with a sinking heart, that her new marriage is a failure. The music playing encourages people to dance, and the fairly drunk Suzanne asks Herb to dance with her. With urging from Miriam, the reluctant Herb joins his former wife for a fast dance. Soon the music changes to a slow song, and Suzanne urges Herb to stay on the dance floor. As they dance, the partygoers watch. Seth is invited to dance with his parents. At this point Pearl, Suzanne's mother, and John insist that Lynette join the dancers. Very much under pressure, Lynette joins the family, and the four of them continue dancing as the remaining guests look on. Lynette sobs in the literal bosom of her family as she remembers her youth and her father's devoted attention. The family continues dancing, oblivious of the other guests.

Kashpaw, Marie Lazarre. *Love Medicine; Tracks.* Louise Erdrich. 1984; 1988.

As an adolescent with a confused Christian soul, Marie Lazarre once hoped that she did not have too much Indian blood to become a saint. By the time she has her own children, she no longer prays. Revealed to readers in *Tracks*, the third volume in a loosely connected trilogy, as the hidden daughter of the novice PAULINE PUYAT—who takes the name Sister Leopolda with her vows—and Napolean Lazarre, Marie becomes known as not just another disreputable Lazarre but as a solid and honest woman who is good to her children and to the other children that have been brought to her to raise.

Even before her fourteenth birthday, Marie decides to join the Sacred Heart Convent and become a saint. Raised in the bush, she sees the women in black who live in the town as the answer to her isolation. When she arrives at the convent she encounters Sister Leopolda. The obsessive and violent Leopolda believes that Satan has selected Marie as his special vessel, and for this reason she persecutes her mercilessly. One time the nun pins Marie on the floor half under a wood stove and pours boiling water over her back. Marie fights back: She kicks the brutal nun into the hot oven. Sister Leopolda turns, stabs Marie in the palm with a cooking fork, and knocks her unconscious with a poker.

When Marie wakes, she learns that Leopolda has told the other nuns that Marie fainted when she received the stigmata on her hand. The nuns conclude that Marie is a saint. Nevertheless, Marie leaves the convent. However, while walking down the hill away from the sisters, she is accosted by NECTOR KASHPAW, who is carrying a pair of geese he plans to sell. In what begins as a sexual assault, Marie and Nector have sex on the road in full view of the convent. Nector offers Marie the geese.

Marie marries Nector, and together they have several children and also raise the children of some of their relatives as well. Marie has plans for Nector; she knows that he is smart and that she can make something of him if she can keep him from drinking. Knowing so well the drunkenness and degradation of her own family, Marie is tireless in her effort to make the Kashpaws well respected. She sees Hector's infidelity with LULU NANAPUSH LAMARTINE as only a temporary setback to her plan. Similarly, during one of Nector's many absent nights, Marie and his twin Eli have a moment of sexual tension so intense that it awakens one of the children sleeping in the other room. But Marie does not allow the moment to be consummated, and Eli leaves. In time, Marie comes to believe that her struggle to redeem the family name has been successful. Largely through her efforts, Nector becomes the chairman of the tribe and a respected representative of the Chippewa.

On the same day that her husband decides to leave her for Lulu (he leaves a farewell note on the kitchen table), Marie takes Zelda, her daughter, to the convent to visit the despised but now dying Sister Leopolda. Marie wants to challenge the self-consciously penitent nun with the success of her secular life. Leopolda refuses to be impressed, and Marie ends by pitying her her imminent death. Returning to their home, Zelda discovers Nector's note to Marie. But Nector has changed his mind, deciding that he can't live without his wife. When Zelda returns with Nector, Marie puts the note back on the table but says nothing so that Nector will always wonder if she read it.

Toward the end of their lives, Marie and Nector move to a home for senior citizens. Discovering that the now bald and nearly blind Lulu has also moved to the home and that she and Nector have rekindled their passion, Marie considers love medicine. She asks her grandson Lipsha, a young man with some healing powers, to help her win Nector for good. Unfortunately, when she finally gets Nector to eat the turkey heart Lipsha has brought, Nector chokes and dies. At the novel's end, Marie feels that Nector's spirit visits her—the love medicine worked even between this world and the next—and having befriended Lulu, the two sit together some mornings and think of the man they both loved.

Kashpaw, Nector. *Love Medicine; Tracks.* Louise Erdrich. 1984; 1988.

As a central character in a loosely tied trilogy of Chippewa and half-Chippewa families, Nector Kashpaw is the son that Margaret "Rushes Bear" Kashpaw sends to the white school in Oklahoma; Nector's brother Eli (his twin in *Love Medicine* and many years his senior in *Tracks*) stays on the reservation and learns the way of the woods.

Even as a young boy Nector has a more calculating mind than many of the elders in his tribe. When FLEUR PILLAGER, NANAPUSH, and the Kashpaws work with one another through the winter and spring to scrape together the money they need to pay the fees on their various allotments of land (so that the government cannot give it to the ever-encroaching lumber companies), it is the young Nector who takes the money to the land office; however, when he finds that the cost has risen beyond what they had figured, he pays only for Kashpaw land.

Still, Kashpaw is an important name on the reservation, and Nector, who attributes much of his success in life to the superiority of the family, claims to be the last hereditary tribal leader. A onetime artist's model and movie extra, Nector also thinks that he should have the pick of the women on the reservation. He selects Fleur Pillager's daughter LULU NANAPUSH (LAMARTINE) as the woman he wants, but one day while carrying a pair of geese strapped to his wrists, he meets his future wife MARIE LAZARRE (KASHPAW). Nector and Marie's first sexual encounter begins with heated words and escalates to near-violence on the road near Marie's convent. During the next seventeen years of their marriage, it seems to Nector that there is not a moment of silence in which he can evaluate his choice.

A mid-life crisis, which he perceives as the moment of silence he hasn't had, comes to Nector on a summer day in 1952 when he realizes how he has aged and hardened. He escapes his feeling of despair by developing a relationship with the sensuous and much-married Lulu. For five years Nector, who has a job as a night watchman, climbs untiringly through Lulu's window every sixth night. The rest of his time he spends with Marie and their family, and is generally exhausted.

A falling-out occurs between Nector and Lulu when she hints that she may marry Beverly Lamartine, the brother of one of her former husbands and, like Nector, the father of one of her sons. In response Nector, as tribe chairman, signs an eviction notice requiring Lulu to leave the land on which she and her many sons have lived for years. Soon after signing the notice, however, Nector feels convinced that he must stay with Lulu and leave Marie. He leaves a note for Marie on the kitchen table and writes another proposing to Lulu, which he plans to deliver himself. While waiting at Lulu's home for her to return, he reconsiders and inadvertently sets Lulu's house on fire. Arriving back at his own house, he finds Marie there; his note remains on the table, although it has been moved. Nector never learns if Marie read it or not.

In his later years Nector becomes senile, an old man who yells in church because he doubts God will hear him otherwise. He and Marie enter a senior citizens' home. To Marie's horror and Nector's pleasure, they find that Lulu has also taken up residence at the home. Nector picks up with Lulu where they left off years earlier. Marie asks her grandson, Lipsha Morrisey, a healer of some power, to procure a love medicine that will ensure that Nector remains faithful. Lipsha fails to shoot the pair of geese he needs and instead gives Nector and Marie two frozen turkey hearts from the supermarket. When Nector finally tries to eat his, he chokes and dies.

Kasson, Byron. *Nigger Heaven.* Carl Van Vechten. 1926.

Byron Kasson is a proud, petulant, and foolish would-be writer. A recent graduate of the University of Pennsylvania, Byron arrives in New York to establish himself as a writer. He knows that he must earn his living in the meantime and is prepared to work. What he is not prepared for is the menial labor that proves to be the only employment available to African-American men whether or not they are college educated. But Byron is unwilling to accept help from the African-American professionals

his father has recommended, and his excessive pride ultimately results in a bitter experience.

Early in his sojourn in Harlem, Byron meets MARY LOVE, a golden brown Harlem librarian who falls passionately in love with him. After the two have known each other a short while, they become engaged. The bliss of romance does not last long, however: The relationship suffers when Mary, initially a quiet, intelligent woman, becomes jealous and possessive. To further endanger the affair, Byron fails to find a satisfactory job and becomes resentful of Mary's advice concerning employment. The two are eventually torn apart by Byron's lack of progress in the literary arena.

Byron is unjustifiably furious when he brings an idea for a short story to Mary, and she offers gentle but insightful criticism. When, after several rejections, a magazine editor agrees to read the story, he offers Byron a critique very similar to Mary's. Feeling angry and humiliated, Byron takes up with Lasca Sartoris, a notorious Harlem beauty.

Living in the lap of luxury provided by the wealthy Lasca, Byron soothes his wounded ego, but after a few decadent weeks, he is stunned when Lasca grows bored with him and sends him packing. When Mary's roommate approaches him and informs him that Mary still loves him, he savagely refuses to return to her. He continues to pursue Lasca, who has ordered her servants never to permit him to enter her apartment. Mary's visit to Byron to express her sympathy and continued love serves only to increase his sense of injury.

After Mary's visit, Byron vows to slay Lasca and the man he believes helped her dupe him. He appears one night at a cabaret frequented by Lasca with a gun concealed beneath his coat. Although Lasca does not appear at the club, the man who has apparently replaced Byron as her paramour does. But before Byron can make a move, another patron draws a gun and shoots the man. In a fit of perversity, Byron grinds his foot into the victim's face and shoots him twice. It is he whom the police arrest. As the novel closes, Byron is screaming, addressing his pleas of innocence to the absent Mary.

Kautilya, Princess of Bwodpur. *Dark Princess, a Romance.* W. E. B. Du Bois. 1928.

Kautilya, Princess of Bwodpur, emerges from a dreamlike, protected childhood to face the temptations and injustices of the world outside her country.

Born at the turn of the century, Kautilya enjoys every luxury and privilege of her royal position from earliest childhood. She is surrounded by splendid art and music, and treated with the utmost reverence. When Kautilya is twelve, a grand ceremony marks her betrothal to a young prince from Sindrabad, but he is murdered shortly afterward. Kautilya is sent with her governess to England, which she grows to love and where she becomes a "social rage."

During World War I, Kautilya runs away to serve in a Red Cross unit at the front and sees misery and suffering she could not have imagined. After the war she becomes fascinated with a young English soldier, Captain Malcolm Fortesque-Dodd, who has had his arm amputated. Just before their marriage, Kautilya overhears him talking with a woman, who strikes her as jealous. When this woman objects to his marrying a "nigger," he justifies himself by explaining that he is "mating with a throne and a fortune." Kautilya breaks off the engagement and decides instead to travel through China, Japan, Syria, Egypt, and other areas of the Middle East.

The journey provides Kautilya with many object lessons and revelations. At its conclusion, she becomes a member of an alliance of radicals from other oppressed nations engaged in fighting white imperialism. The alliance is itself prejudiced against African peoples and particularly against African Americans, whom the members regard as "slaves and half-men." In Berlin, where some of the representatives are assembling, Kautilya has a chance meeting with a young African American, MATTHEW TOWNS, who has just left medical school after being barred from continuing because of his race. She sends him home to compile a report for her on African Americans in order to determine whether they are prepared to participate in the movement. When Matthew loses contact with her, Kautilya goes to America to survey the situation herself.

On the train to Chicago, where Kautilya plans to observe a Ku Klux Klan meeting, Matthew appears again as the porter in her car. He is horrified to see her because he is involved in a plot to destroy the train and avenge the death of a friend who was lynched on another "Klan special." Matthew not only stops the train, he accepts responsibility for the potential tragedy even though the real criminal, Perigua, has died. While Matthew is in jail, Kautilya visits his mother, a devout and inspiring woman, and decides to spend seven years, the length of Matthew's sentence, doing menial labor. She works as a servant girl, a laborer in a tobacco factory, a waitress, and finally a worker at a box-making plant. During all this time she keeps watch over Matthew, who is released from prison by the Chicago politician SAMUEL SCOTT and becomes involved in the political racket himself. When Kautilya senses that he is losing his moral vision and purpose, she steps in to rescue him.

For a brief, happy period, Kautilya and Matthew live together, but when he discovers her pregnancy, she leaves abruptly without explanation. She spends the following months waiting anxiously for the baby to be born in the rural Virginia home of Matthew's mother. If it is a girl, Kautilya will have to abandon both the child and Matthew—as she explains to Matthew in a solemn moment: "Bwodpur needs not a princess, but a King." Fortunately,

a son is born, and she summons Matthew to Virginia, where they are married, and the child is crowned Maharajah of Bwodpur. Matthew praises her as the "Mother of God," and their son is heralded as "Messenger and Messiah to all the Darker Worlds."

Keefe, John "Jack." *You Know Me, Al: A Busher's Letters.* Ring Lardner. 1914.

John "Jack" Keefe, the persona created by Ring Lardner for his syndicated sports column in the *Chicago Tribune*, has few attributes beyond his prodigious talent as a baseball pitcher. As he unwittingly demonstrates in a series of letters to his friend Al, Keefe lacks intelligence, compassion, modesty, charm, grace, and virtually every other admirable or sympathetic quality.

As the letters begin, Keefe is writing to Al to explain that he has been sold to the Chicago White Sox from his bush league team in Terre Haute, Indiana. Rather than being awed and humbled by his entry into the American League of professional baseball, Keefe is cocky. He demands a $3,000-a-year salary, which by 1920s standards would be considered inordinately high. The White Sox offer to sign him on for considerably less and promise to pay him more if he proves his worth. Keefe is disgruntled but accepts the offer.

Keefe immediately gets on the wrong side of Comiskey, the team's manager, by acting stubborn and vain. A battle takes place between the two: Keefe demands a chance to prove himself, while Comiskey exacts obedience and goes about trying to break Keefe. He puts Keefe in games when his arm is sore so that his performance is impaired; otherwise, he keeps him on the bench. Outside of the games, Keefe enjoys his status as a professional ballplayer immensely. He eats extensively, buys new clothes, and takes up with a pretty blond named Violet. Instead of dwelling on these pleasures, however, Keefe rails against his treatment by Comiskey, and he soon finds himself sold back to the bush league.

Having lost everything, including Violet—who dumps him—Keefe remains undaunted. He outdoes himself in the bush league, is bought back by the White Sox, excels at his career, and takes up with a demanding woman named Florrie, whom he eventually marries. They have a child named Al, whom Keefe claims to have named after his "pal" but who is in fact named after Florrie's brother. Keefe indulges himself to such an extent in the spoils of success that he is forced to borrow money from his "pal." Al is apparently faithful in spite of Keefe's inability to fully repay the amounts that he borrows; he sends gifts and invitations to visit, but Keefe is too busy eating, drinking, smoking, and playing to take these offers seriously.

The collection ends with Keefe winning the World Series for his team and earning the admiration of his manager and teammates. He turns down another of Al's invitations in order to go on a tour of the world with an all-star team. His future looks bright, and his behavior seems in no danger of changing. The reader can only wonder how long his "pal Al" will continue to write back.

Keely, Mary Agnes. *Bridgeport Bus*. Maureen Howard. 1961.

At the age of thirty-five, gawky and eccentric Mary Agnes Keely begins a triumphant process of self-discovery. Abandoning her repressive Irish-Catholic upbringing, her tawdry small-town neighborhood, and her overbearing widowed mother, Agnes boards the bus in Bridgeport, Connecticut, and heads for a new life in New York City.

In a women's hotel in the city, Agnes meets Lydia Savaard, a prim young woman whose husband is confined to a mental institution. The two agree to share an apartment, and they settle into their own versions of domesticity: Lydia, depressed because her mother-in-law has thwarted her attempts at a divorce, comforts herself by cleaning voraciously; and Agnes, intoxicated by her new-found freedom, nourishes her creative urges by preparing lavish gourmet meals.

Agnes, who supported her mother for years by working in a zipper factory, soon finds a job as a copywriter for Wunda-Clutch, a modern fastening product meant to make the zipper obsolete. At work that she meets a commercial artist named Stanley Sarnicki. Stanley and the virginal Mary Agnes begin a happy romance and meet each Saturday, the night Lydia is away visiting her husband, for a gourmet dinner in Agnes's apartment.

Agnes makes other friends as well. An odd assortment of artists and poets begin to assemble at her apartment each Friday, drinking, philosophizing, and helping themselves to the meals that Agnes, whom they call "Ma," prepares. One of the artists, Flo, begins a work-in-progress on the linoleum floor in the kitchen. Agnes has her own artistic bent, although it is kept more private than that of her friends: She writes for hours on end, filling yellow pads with plays and stories about her mother or Lydia or Sherry Henderson, the show-girl whom Cousin Agnes befriended and admired.

Among Agnes's boisterous artist friends is a college-age poet to whom she has given money on occasion. One night, feeling sympathy for the starving artist, she brings some money to his flat, and the two have a fleeting, torrid affair. Later, when Agnes discovers she is pregnant with the poet's child, she ends her relationship with Stanley and stops going to work. Lydia and her now-released husband Henry offer to take Agnes in, but she decides instead to go back to her mother.

When she returns home, Agnes discovers that her mother is in the hospital, comatose and kept barely alive with transfusions and intravenous feedings. Sitting by the hospital bed, Agnes mutters apologies to her mother, then pours a full glass of water down her throat, choking her.

As the novel closes, Agnes is in a Catholic home for unwed mothers, anticipating the birth of her child. She is in poor health and dangerously overweight from sampling her own gourmet cooking. As she goes into labor she imagines her own death and the adoption of her child by the Savaards. But interspersed with these thoughts are her dreams of triumphantly taking her child back to New York and telling him of how his mother "burst forth upon the whole dry world."

Keith, Willie. *The Caine Mutiny*. Herman Wouk. 1951.

This World War II novel is a story of war, mutiny, and the coming of age of Ensign Willie Keith.

Spoiled and petted by his wealthy, domineering mother, Willie graduates from Princeton and amuses himself by playing piano at Manhattan clubs where his cute songs and Princetonian style of dress are well received although he lacks real musical talent. He meets and falls in love with a poor Italian singer whose stage named is May Wynn, but he lacks the nerve to introduce May to his mother, just as he lacks the wherewithal to enlist in the armed forces after his mother discourages him from doing so.

But then Willie is drafted, and with some difficulty he graduates from midshipman school. He is disappointed by his inglorious assignment to the dilapidated destroyer *Caine* and is dismayed by what he perceives as shoddy discipline among the crew. Captain de Vriess sees in Willie the makings of a fine officer, but he rides Willie hard in an effort to toughen this callow youth for combat and to bring home to him the seriousness of his responsibilities. As a lowly communications officer, Willie endures considerable hardship under de Vriess's command, and he responds to this treatment petulantly, characterizing de Vriess as an incompetent sadist.

Willie is relieved when Lieutenant COMMANDER PHILIP FRANCIS QUEEG takes over command of the *Caine*, for Queeg maintains tight discipline among the crew and treats Willie well, promoting him to morale officer and to the rank of lieutenant junior grade. However, when Queeg's strictness takes on maniacal proportions and he also proves himself to be incompetent and cowardly, Willie begins to see the wisdom of de Vriess's ways. As Queeg exhibits less and less competence and courage, Willie begins to exhibit more of both qualities.

Willie's burgeoning strength of character leads him to support the mutiny against Queeg, but when he must face a court-martial on that account, his first thought is to turn to his mother for help. At this point he also breaks off with May, largely due to his mother's disapproval of her.

The court finds Queeg incompetent, and Willie is acquitted. He then returns to the *Caine*, where he soon passes his final test of manhood: When the ship is set afire by a kamikaze plane, the new captain, Tom Keefer, abandons ship, but Willie coolly directs the crew in putting out the fire. From this episode Willie gains new self-confidence. Shortly thereafter the *Caine* is hit by mines, and this close brush with death makes him see that he truly loves May Wynn. He sets about wooing her back, and after the war ends, he returns to New York planning to become a professor of comparative literature. At the novel's close, Willie succeeds in gaining May as his wife and demands that his mother abide by his decisions.

Kelly, Mick. *The Heart Is a Lonely Hunter*. Carson McCullers. 1940.

Mick Kelly is a precocious preadolescent struggling against the confines of her family and the small southern town where she lives. Obsessed with music, she spends nights in the rich section of town, secretly sitting in the garden of a house and listening to the radio. She tries to make a violin, which she keeps in her private box under her bed. Her family is large, and her parents must rent out the extra rooms to boarders to make ends meet. One of the boarders, a deaf mute named JOHN SINGER, fascinates Mick. Despite his handicap, she thinks he knows everything about music, and she begins to pay him regular visits to talk about her dreams.

Mick has fantasies of being a famous composer. Music runs through her mind constantly—both music she has heard and music she thinks up herself. She gives up her lunch money for elementary piano lessons from an older student, and she begins to keep a notebook in which she tries to write down the music she hears in her head. Mick's visits to Singer increase since he purchases a radio to entertain his friends. She imagines her world divided into two spheres: in the outside room are school, family, and the world; in the inside room are her music and dreams. In this way she copes with the lack of privacy in her home and the restrictions placed on her creativity. Her hopes converge on Singer, whom she sees as a mentor, a man of great knowledge who understands her completely and accepts her.

As the novel progresses, Mick's family's fortune takes a turn for the worst. Her younger brother George accidentally shoots the child of a friend, and the family's finances, never very abundant, are further depleted by medical expenses. When one of Mick's older sisters develops a diseased ovary, the family loses her wages. Finally, Mick must give up her music lessons because she no longer gets lunch money.

Mick's life is further complicated by her friendship with Harry, the boy next door. Having known each other since they were children, they become close friends as they enter adolescence. Still, Mick never confides her dreams to Harry; she only listens to his. The friendship is ruptured by their first sexual experience. Guilt-ridden Harry runs away from home to find a job, leaving Mick to ponder the meaning of her sudden initiation into adulthood. She

soon falls in love with Singer and begins to follow him around obsessively.

As money becomes more pressing, Mick feels her dreams slipping away. When one of her sisters mentions a job opening at Woolworth's, Mick determines to take it, knowing she will have to quit school to work full time. In the meantime, Singer, frustrated by the demands of friends like Mick, commits suicide. At the end of the novel, Mick ponders her friend's death and wonders whether her hopes and dreams have any meaning. She feels shut out of the inside room, too tired to hear music or make plans, but she forcefully concludes that some good must come of her experience.

Kelso, Perley. *The Silent Partner*. Elizabeth Stuart Phelps. 1871.

At the age of twenty-three, Perley Kelso inherits her father's fairly large estate, which includes sumptuous homes in the city and in the mill town and her father's share in a mill company known as Hayle and Kelso. Perley has only the vaguest memories of her mother, who died when the Perley was only six, and feels a kind of freedom following her father's death. Accordingly, much to the amusement and then the dismay of Maverick Hayle, her fiancé, Perley insists on being admitted as the new partner in the mill business. Instinctively Hayle and his father oppose this idea and dismiss Perley's ambitions as a mere flight of fancy.

After being rebuffed by Maverick and his father, who hire Stephen Garrick, formerly one of the lowly mill workers, as the new partner, Perley begins to work behind the scenes at the mill. She attracts the attention of several of the impoverished mill workers when she begins frequenting their neighborhoods and establishes a library for their use. Among the workers she befriends is PRISCILLA GARTH, who goes by the name of Sip. Watching Sip and her harrowing existence as she cares for a deaf and mute sister, Perley acquires an understanding of the lives crushed by the greed of the mills. In fact, soon after she becomes involved with the workers' lives, Perley, who has by now seen more of the "real world" of the mill town than has her fiancé, she breaks off her engagement, explaining that her feelings have simply and irrevocably altered.

As Perley increasingly becomes a known and respected figure in the worker's community, she encounters the Mell family, a large and ill-kempt group whose mother lies dying of consumption and who, on the day of her death, loses her youngest son, eight-year-old Bub, to an on-the-job accident. Perley is shocked by their poverty and by their harsh attitude, particularly as espoused by Mr. Mell, toward child labor. Additionally, Perley befriends Bijah Mudge, a sixty-six-year-old nearly insane man who has found shelter at an old-age asylum after being turned away from Hayle and Kelso's mills. In a broken fashion he teaches the realities of capitalism, and Perley is a rapt and respectful pupil. She includes him in invitations to her socials, where she blends her society friends and her working friends, much to the consternation of the former.

As the novel nears its close, trouble develops at the Hayle and Kelso mills. The laborers begin to think about striking, and Maverick and his father turn to Perley for help. After Perley soothes the crowd, she angrily denounces the partners' belated reliance on her relationship with the workers. Trouble is forestalled, however, and by the end of the novel, Perley even seems, due to her steadfast insistence on social and intellectual equality, to have made some inroads against prejudice as well as against the exploitative use of women and laborers in general.

Kennicott, Carol Milford. *Main Street*. Sinclair Lewis. 1920.

Carol Milford's youthful dream is to become a champion of social reform. While she is still a student at Blodgett College in Minneapolis, Stewart Snyder, a fellow student and would-be lawyer, proposes to Carol. Although she is fond of Stewart, she declines the offer. Carol has aspirations that she thinks supersede familial responsibilities: She wants to bring culture and beauty to some unspecified, backward prairie town. Her philanthropic dream is fired in part by the fact that she has a crush on her sociology professor. But she also believes that a young woman with a college education should put it to use in order to improve society.

Upon graduating from Blodgett, Carol spends a year in Chicago studying to be a librarian. She then lands a job at the St. Paul Public Library and works there until DR. WILL KENNICOTT from Gopher Prairie, Minnesota (population 3,000), convinces Carol to marry him by appealing to her to bring art and culture to his beloved little wheat-farming town. On the train en route to her new home, Carol is frightened by the vastness of the prairie. When they have almost reached their destination, she experiences a severe case of cold feet and wonders how she had ever been persuaded to marry this stranger, Kennicott, with his thick body and heavy speech. The word *home* is anathema to her, and Gopher Prairie appears to be little more than a "frontier camp" in which her husband owns a "prosaic frame house." But she quickly reassures herself by remembering what a good man he is. Telling herself that she has read too many books and is therefore too sensitive, she vows to become fond of Gopher Prairie and to carry out her philanthropical designs.

Despite her efforts to fit into the social scene in Gopher Prairie, the conservative small-town community smothers Carol's well-meaning if naive ideals. For her it is as if the town were in a coma, so little does it respect or even recognize culture. In addition, her appreciation of the refinement that has been achieved by her husband fluctuates. She longs for the indifference of urban environments and flirts with two men whose bookish tastes remind her of the sophistication of city people. World War I rages on as Carol vacillates from respect for her husband's medical work and hope for the improvement of the town to utter rejection of the possibility that her life can continue in the presence of Will Kennicott and Gopher Prairie.

Despite a previous fear of pregnancy, Carol loves her child Hugh passionately. For a short while she gives up her reform programs to gratify her maternal instincts. But once again the word *home* raises its hoary head, and taking Hugh with her, she leaves Kennicott and domesticity to live in Washington, D.C., in order to build her own life.

Carol becomes involved with a militant suffragette network and makes her living working at the Bureau of War Risk Insurance. Kennicott visits her and admits that he has been having an affair with a friend of theirs, Maud Dyer. Not long after, Carol gets pregnant again and decides to move back to Gopher Prairie. The novel ends with her good-natured promise to Kennicott that their daughter, who remains unnamed, will realize the liberties her mother gave up for the sake of Main Street, U.S.A.

Kennicott, Dr. Will. *Main Street*. Sinclair Lewis. 1920.

Dr. Will Kennicott is a kindly country doctor who makes his home in Gopher Prairie, Minnesota. A bachelor when the novel begins, he meets CAROL MILFORD (KENNICOTT) at a dinner party when he is in St. Paul on a business trip. After a short courtship he convinces Carol to marry him and return with him to Gopher Prairie, a small wheat-farming town. Although Carol and Will never divorce, their marriage is a rocky one due to the discrepancy between his conservative rural attitudes and mannerisms and her pseudo-sophisticated sensibilities. Dr. Kennicott exemplifies the virtues and drawbacks of the life-style of stereotypical middle-class Americans on Main Streets throughout the country.

Although Will Kennicott knows that Gopher Prairie (population 3,000) does not offer as many cultural opportunities as cities like St. Paul, he is inordinately proud of the quality of life that his town offers. One of the ploys he uses to convince Carol to marry him is to appeal to her philanthropic desire to bring art and refinement to what she considers backward rural environments. Having installed his bride in his house in Gopher Prairie, he proudly introduces her to his friends and associates in the town. He is convinced that his wife will find small-town life as desirable as he does.

Dr. Kennicott is a hardworking, straightforward man with homespun tastes. From his point of view, morality is simply common sense, and hunting inspires the greatest happiness. His other hobbies include motoring and speculating in farmland, which he considers a safe investment. A generous man, he is kind to the Dutch and German farmers who are his patients; if they find it impossible to pay their bills on time, Dr. Kennicott provides health care on credit. Although Carol is impressed by her husband's professional ethics and skill, she does not share his enthusiasm for the simple way of life he offers her. When she endeavors to refine his sensibilities by reading him poetry, he listens politely but is clearly bored.

Carol's disappointment about her husband's and the town's aesthetic failings is temporarily assuaged when she and Dr. Kennicott have their first child, Hugh. Her malaise returns, however, as Hugh gets older. Desperate, she comes close to having an affair with a bookish tailor named Erik Valborg. When Will discovers the would-be lovers on a deserted country road, he does not scold Carol; he simply advises her to break off the relationship before rumors destroy her reputation. In fact, he confronts all of Carol's cries of dissatisfaction with patient dignity.

But finally, after Carol has ceased to sleep in the same room with him and he begins to feel like a stranger in his own home, Will has an affair with one of their friends, Maud Dyer. Then Carol, in a storm of frustration, decides to move with Hugh to Washington, D.C., where she supports herself and works with a militant suffragette group. On a visit to Washington, Will admits that he has been unfaithful, and they make love for the first time in years. When Carol finds out that she is pregnant, she decides to return to her husband and Gopher Prairie. In the end, the steady and patient Dr. Will Kennicott and the morality of the traditional nuclear family triumph.

Kepesh, David. *The Professor of Desire.* Philip Roth. 1977.

As he moves from happy, innocent childhood to a confused adulthood, David Kepesh, the novel's narrator, searches desperately for harmony and fulfillment through both his physical and intellectual pursuits. David suffers from the conflict between erotic desire and scholarly ambition, and his earnest but hedonistic approach to life results in increasing restlessness.

While an undergraduate at Syracuse University, David manages to achieve notoriety as both a scholar and a skirt-chaser. Working in the library, he studies and chases all types of women. Instead of working on his thesis researching Arthurian legends, David spends his fellowship year in London exploring his physical desires. Believing in sexual myths about insatiable Swedish women, he rejects his studies for an exciting relationship with two Swedes, Elisabeth and Birgitta. What originally begins as a flirtation between Elisabeth and David quickly turns— much to David's delight—into a ménage à trois involving kinky sex.

When Elisabeth attempts suicide and returns to Sweden, David looks to the sensually wild Birgitta for satisfaction. After his unsuccessful academic term ends, the two travel through Europe, and David lives out the rest of his fellowship year in unrestrained erotic adventure. Finally reaching a sexual plateau, David and Birgitta part, and

he returns to Stanford for graduate studies in literature.

David quickly finds a temporary escape from the rigors of scholarship in Helen Baird, a sexy and slightly crazy graduate student at the University of Southern California who tells him the story of her exotic past. David and Helen's three years of dating are followed by three miserable years of marriage. Dissatisfied with his personal life, David takes refuge in teaching, working sixteen-hour days, and in writing a book on romantic disillusionment in Chekhov's stories—a subject paralleling his own predicament.

Helen and David's marriage ends in a painful divorce. Soon after, David begins intensive therapy in an attempt to understand his relationship to Helen. Life following divorce brings David greater loneliness, despair, and impotence. Eventually, though, he meets Claire Ovington, a young schoolteacher whose love cures his depression and impotence and renews his physical and intellectual passion.

When they travel in Europe, David yearns for his lascivious past with Birgitta despite the comfort he receives from Claire. Tormented yet fascinated by his own insatiable nature, he finds validation of his suffering in literature. While in Prague, David visits Kafka's grave and later has a long rambling dream in which he meets the prostitute who was reputedly Kafka's lover. The dream makes David ponder the link between sexual despair and Kafka's writings, and he composes an introductory lecture on erotic desire in literary masterpieces.

Upon their return from Europe, David notices the subsided passion in his and Claire's relationship, and he struggles to devote himself to her. Only after he is visited by Helen and his father does David own up to his inability to wholly please others, including himself, and his fear that he will never change. At the end of the novel, he accepts the limits of personal happiness in an imperfect world but also acknowledges his anxiety over the future as he makes love to Claire while thinking of his aged father lying in the next room.

Kern, David. "Pigeon Feathers." John Updike. 1961.

David Kern, the fourteen-year-old protagonist of this short story, is disoriented by his family's move to Firetown. When he comes across H. G. Wells's denial of Christ's divinity in *Outline of History*, a startlingly blasphemous interpretation of the life of Jesus, David experiences a devastating crisis of faith. Even the prayers that he thought were answered now seem to be mere accidents that had nothing to do with Christ.

That evening, after dinner with his father and mother, David encounters Death in the farm outhouse. His vision shows him a long hole in the ground into which he will recede, leaving no trace of his existence behind. He scrambles out of the outhouse pursued by a hideous, dilating sun and a horde of insects. Once back in the safety of his house with his mother washing dishes and his father reading the paper by the fire, David takes down the Webster's dictionary and finds some solace in the definition it offers of the soul. At least that might remain after death.

The next day at catechism class in the Firetown church, Reverend Dobson, whom David has always liked, destroys his hope in the continuation of the soul. David asks him whether people are conscious between the time they die and the Day of Judgment. Ashamed of the difficult question and embarrassed by the looks from his fellow students, he is even more distressed when the minister replies that they are not. David, the minister adds, ought to think of Heaven as a continuing source of inspiration; as an example, he cites Abraham Lincoln, whose good deeds continue to be felt although he is long dead. However, the fact that Lincoln is not conscious of his posthumous fame, coupled with Dobson's claim that this lack of consciousness is irrelevant, horrifies and infuriates David.

Later that evening David's mother finds him poring over his grandfather's old tattered Bible. When he tells her what's wrong, she tries to console him with her radiant belief in the beauty of God's creation. But David replies with disgust that if, as she said, man created God, then there really is no God. David becomes angry and hardened against his mother's kindness and sees in his father's self-disgust a distant ally.

The school year goes by without much change, although he has lost his appetite for reading, especially mysteries and science fiction in which people die so easily. Summer comes again, and David feels oppressed by the heat and the acres of weeds and dry grass. His parents have given him a Remington .22 for his fifteenth birthday, and his grandmother encourages him to shoot the pigeons who have been fouling up her old furniture in the barn. At first averse to the idea of killing, David decides to do the job.

Alone in the dark barn, David takes aim and shoots one of the pigeons hiding in a hole in the stone wall. After his first success, he shoots many more as they fly into the hole to make their way out into the open air. Mastering the gun and commanding the barn, David feels like a beautiful avenger ridding the barn's starry sky of the filthy impudent creatures. His mother meets him outside the barn to tell him that he managed to take a chip out of the house. Slightly disgusted by her son's enjoyment of his kill, she makes him bury the pigeons past the strawberry patches.

David has never seen a bird up close. The feathers amaze him with their patterns, their usefulness, warmth, color, and softness. All this, he thinks, in each feather—and each feather intermingled with another to create a wing, a bird. David suddenly realizes that God, who took such care in creating these birds, would not have given David a temporal body without a soul that could live forever.

Kilburn, Annie. *Annie Kilburn*. William Dean Howells. 1889.

Annie Kilburn, a thirty-one-year-old independent woman, is the daughter of a judge who returns to her native New England town to institute social reform. She was raised in the small town of Hatboro, Massachusetts, and in Washington, D.C., where her father served in Congress. Upon her father's death, Annie decides to return from her eleven-year residence in Italy to do good works in the United States.

Annie is struck by the change that industrialization has made in Hatboro. The old, intellectual aristocracy led by her father Judge Kilburn and Squire Putney has been replaced by a rising middle class represented by such business moguls as Mr. Gerrish. South Hatboro has also been transformed into a resort town for the leisure class. The women of South Hatboro have undertaken a philanthropic project to raise money for the less fortunate. By organizing a theatrical presentation of Shakespeare, the residents of South Hatboro hope to raise money to form a Social Union.

Annie considers the formation of a Social Union a possible means of doing good in the community. A theatrical presentation, however, involves the social exclusion that the Social Union seeks to eliminate. Annie visits the new Unitarian minister, Mr. Peck, who was formerly married and is raising a daughter, to try to interest him in the project. He has been criticized by the more conservative merchant class for his liberal views on social equality. Mr. Peck considers the Social Union an act of philanthropy that serves little function but to ease the consciences of the privileged few. He considers social welfare degrading and even detrimental to the poor who, Peck believes, should help themselves. Annie is at first put off by Mr. Peck's stance, but then she learns that he was once poor and speaks from experience.

Annie somewhat reluctantly takes part in the theatricals, which, as Mr. Peck had predicted, serve only to accentuate the differences between classes. While Mr. Peck is off fulfilling his ministerial duties, Annie takes care of his young daughter. During one of his sermons on the corrupting influence of money, the businessman Mr. Gerrish takes personal offense and campaigns for Mr. Peck's resignation. Although he has the community's support, Mr. Peck decides to move to the small mill town of Fall River to be a schoolteacher. He will leave his daughter temporarily in the care of a couple, the Savors, who have recently lost a child.

Annie is devastated at the thought of losing Mr. Peck's daughter. She proposes to go with Mr. Peck and his daughter and even to serve as a mill hand if need be; but Mr. Peck realizes that Annie could never be satisfied with the life of a commoner and refuses. Before he can leave, though, Mr. Peck is killed in a train crash, and Annie eventually assumes the care of his daughter. Annie is also called upon to manage the $200 earned at the theatricals. She decides to fulfill Mr. Peck's intention of forming a cooperative boardinghouse in Fall River headed by the Savors. The Peck Social Union (as it is named) is established by funds raised by the people and is run by the people themselves. Annie comes to accept Mr. Peck's philosophy that people with money cannot patronize the poor, the poor must help themselves. She abandons her idealistic intentions of changing the world and is satisfied with making this slight contribution to a single community.

Kilburn, Peter. *Good Times/Bad Times.* James Kirkwood. 1968.

Peter Kilburn, in jail awaiting his trial on charges of first-degree murder, is the sensitive young narrator of this novel set in a New England prep school. Peter's father is a sporadically employed actor who became an alcoholic in response to the death of his wife. Peter has been motherless since the age of six, and the responsibility of his upbringing and education was farmed out to such individuals as his ninety-one-year-old grandfather and such institutions as a Catholic military academy and Hollywood High School, near where he and his father share an apartment. When an old friend of his father's foots the bill so that Peter can spend his senior year at a boarding school in New England, his fate as one of the victims of the perverted resident headmaster at the Gilford School in Saypool, New Hampshire, is sealed.

From his first day at Gilford, Peter is at loggerheads with the school's forbidding headmaster, FRANKLYN HOYT. He finds no solace in his dorm-mates, who collectively personify the multifarious traumas of puberty: a know-it-all, a bedwetter, a would-be actor, and a flatulent jock. Abusive interviews with Mr. Hoyt gradually progress to coercive encounters. Peter finds himself being manipulated by the headmaster into representing Gilford on the tennis team and delivering Hamlet's "To be or not to be" soliloquy in an interschool Glee Club competition. He survives the humiliation of playing Hamlet in black tights in front of an audience of adolescents with the help of a newfound friend, Jordan Legier, a wealthy but sickly boy from New Orleans who is a newcomer at the school.

Peter and Jordan quickly develop an intimate and satisfying relationship as bosom buddies. They spend evenings in endless conversation in Jordan's room or, when the harsh New Hampshire winter rages, in the warmth of Jordan's bed. Together they sneak off campus to drink in the Flame Room of the local hotel, where they befriend Fat Patti, an aging but still bubbly chanteuse. When school is temporarily closed for the Christmas holidays, Peter and Jordan take advantage of the vacation by visiting Boston and New York and generally enjoying each other's company.

But the bliss of this intimacy is threatened by Mr. Hoyt,

who enters into an odd triangle of affection with the two young men, with Peter being his obvious favorite. When Peter sprains his back skiing, Mr. Hoyt shows up late one night to give him an alcohol rubdown, ostensibly to ease the pain. When Jordan hears about the rubdown, the alcohol on Mr. Hoyt's breath, and his heavy breathing and intimate method of massage, he warns Peter to beware of the intentions of the sexually repressed headmaster. But Peter does not realize the gravity of the situation. The predicament explodes one night when Mr. Hoyt, who is rabidly homophobic despite his own obvious desire for Peter, finds the two young men innocently asleep together. The headmaster flies into a rage and becomes violent with them, and Jordan consequently suffers a heart attack and dies a few days later.

Peter's first thought in reaction to this dangerous tragedy is to escape. But the obsessive Mr. Hoyt follows him to the bus station and forces him to return to the boarding school. When he once again tries to escape, the drunken headmaster pursues him to an abandoned boat house, where Peter witnesses the complete deterioration of Mr. Hoyt's personality. Spewing smut and accusations concerning Peter's lack of moral decency, Mr. Hoyt attempts to rape him. In self-defense, Peter grabs a boat hook and delivers a fatal blow to the headmaster's head. The novel culminates with Peter awaiting his trial and writing a letter describing this nightmarish ordeal to his attorney.

Kinbote, Charles. *Pale Fire.* Vladimir Nabokov. 1962.

The true identity of the complex and mercurial Charles Kinbote, also known as Charles II, Charles Xavier Vseslav, Esq., and V Botkin, is never entirely clear. To most of the characters in his narrative, Kinbote appears as the social clod and visiting professor of literature at Wordsmith College, who has taken up temporary residence in the home of Judge Goldsworth, next door to the famous American poet John Shade. Accepting this as his identity, Kinbote is the editor and commentator of Shade's last poem, "Pale Fire," and the novel *Pale Fire*, his tenuous and often humorous attempt at literary criticism. According to this scenario, Kinbote is an arrogant, monomaniacal, self-deluding, possibly insane, homosexual, misogynist vegetarian who believes himself to be the exiled king of a small Eastern European country.

On the other hand, Charles Kinbote could actually be Charles II, deposed king of Zembla. Born on July 5, 1915, the pretender to the throne, Charles Xavier shirked his duties as both prince and king especially when those duties required him to take a woman as his wife and future queen. During his country's subsequent anti-aristocratic revolution, he narrowly escaped imprisonment by slipping through a secret passageway in his castle and fleeing across the Bera Range with the aid of his friend, the actor Odon. He then made his way to America where he happily took on the disguise of a literature professor, Charles Kinbote.

He is pursued, however, by Jack Grey, a member of the murderous "anti-Karlists" faction, who stalks him across several continents and the Atlantic Ocean. Finally arriving at Judge Goldsworth's house in New Wye, Grey attempts to assassinate Charles but fatally shoots Shade instead.

In both scenarios Charles becomes the possessive, self-proclaimed intimate friend of the not always willing Shade, who is in the process of composing his "greatest poem." To justify his role as the editor of the poem, Charles asserts that he fed Shade details of his life during their periodic evening walks together. In his foreword and commentary on "Pale Fire," Charles insists that the events of his life animate Shade's poem, thereby conferring on it the status of an epic.

Kingsblood, Neil. *Kingsblood Royal.* Sinclair Lewis. 1947.

At the outset of this novel, Neil Kingsblood is a hero returning from World War II. He has been wounded in combat and has been demobilized with the rank of captain. When he returns to his hometown of Grand Republic, Minnesota, he is ready to resume his life on the safe track it was on before the war. He returns to his young and beautiful wife Vestal and their pale, blonde, six-year-old daughter Biddy. Neil takes a job as a loan officer in a local bank, which assures him of steady advancement and a secure future, and the Kingsbloods prepare to settle into a comfortable life-style. However, a discovery about his ancestry soon shatters the complacent family life he had intended to assume.

At a family gathering held shortly after Neil's return, his father, Dr. Kenneth Kingsblood, urges him to investigate the family secret—that, as their surname indicates, they are descended from English royalty. Although skeptical, Neil decides to obey his father's seemingly eccentric wish.

After a New Year's celebration, Neil undertakes his genealogical project. Although he learns nothing about his father's side of the family, he uncovers the fact that on his mother's side he is descended from a black man, Xavier Pic. Neil is shocked by this information, for it jettisons his previous, carefully constructed notions of identity and purpose. He tries to keep this information hidden, but his ethics soon force him to seek out blacks in order to discover what he secretly comes to regard as his own nature. Along the way he meets several of Grand Republic's scorned black population, who gradually imbue him with a sense of pride in black accomplishments. Despite his completely Caucasian appearance, Neil begins to feel an overwhelming sense of identification with black people.

Neil finally feels compelled to reveal his findings to the other members of his family, and they respond with horror. Although neither Neil nor his wife is free of racist thinking, Neil responds harshly against racial oppression.

When he can no longer withstand the steady prejudice that he now sees daily, Neil publicizes the family secret at a meeting of a whites-only club.

Although Neil's act may seem brave to some, it has severe consequences for the Kingsblood clan. His father dies suddenly of a heart attack; his mother and unmarried sister become virtual recluses; and his brother Robert's wife sues for divorce on the grounds of mental cruelty and malicious deception, even though Robert immediately repudiates Neil and his testimony.

Word of Neil's status as a black spreads throughout Grand Republic, and social ostracization follows swiftly. He and Vestal are quickly dropped from their customary round of cocktail parties and are excluded from more formal social gatherings. This leads within a year to Neil's dismissal from his once-secure bank position, a demotion, and, finally, his forced resignation from the bank. In the subsequent months of increasing tension, it becomes harder and harder for Neil to find employment. In addition, neighbors in Sylvan Park, the upscale housing development in which the Kingsbloods live, steadily intensify their pressures on the family to move away.

The family's problems also intensify because Vestal's father, the wealthy and locally influential Mr. Beehouse, pressures her to get an annulment from Neil. Vestal loves her husband, however, and wants to stand by him; furthermore, as she soon reveals to Neil, they must stay together in spite of her fears about their new future because she is once again pregnant. As the novel ends, Neil and Vestal, with the aid of Neil's new friend, an African-American veteran, and a few other sympathetic blacks, attempt to defend their house against a gathering lynch mob. This results in violence, and Vestal is shot in the arm. After Neil successfully returns the gunfire, the Kingsbloods are arrested and forcibly removed from their neighborhood—which, with their departure, becomes all white once again.

Kino. *The Pearl.* John Steinbeck. 1947.

Kino, a capable, young, lithe, Indian pearl-diver, lives with Juana and their new baby, Coyotito, in a brush house on "The Gulf." Kino and his wife converse little but hear the same ancient melodies in their minds in lieu of verbal communication. Their domestic life is natural and idyllic. One morning, however, their tranquil rhythm is disturbed when a scorpion bites Coyotito. Juana sucks out the poison but declares in front of the quickly arriving neighbors that they must get the doctor. Everyone knows he will not come, so they go to him en masse. The pearls Kino has brought for payment are meager, so the Indians are turned away.

Kino and Juana proceed to the beach and paddle out in Kino's only canoe. Among Kino's first haul is an oyster that contains a huge, flawless pearl, "The Pearl of the World." News of the pearl spreads through the town to the villagers, the priest, the doctor, and the pearl buyers.

Unbeknownst to the Indians, all the buyers are agents of one man. They fix their prices and only pretend to compete with one another. Unaware, Kino declares that when the pearl is sold, he and Juana will be married in the church. He will buy a rifle, and Coyotito will go to school and learn to read and figure. He has dared to form a plan.

The doctor arrives and convinces them the baby needs further treatment. Kino cannot refuse but knows that the nausea the baby experiences after the doctor administers a pill could easily have been caused by the pill itself. He feels sure the doctor is taking advantage of him.

Thieves come at night, and Kino drives them away but is left injured. Fearing it is an evil thing that will destroy their family, Juana wants to get rid of the pearl, but Kino clings to his imagined future.

In the morning Kino and Juana, followed by a crowd, go to sell the pearl. But the agents have conspired and have offered a ridiculously low price. The song Kino now hears in his head is an evil one. He stalks off, determined to go to the capital to sell the pearl despite his fears of the unknown. Kino has defied the structure of things, and his brother, Juan Tomás, fears for him.

Kino is again attacked at night, and again Juana begs him to discard the pearl. But Kino, crafty for the first time in his life, refuses. He says he is a man and will not be cheated. They will go to the capital in the morning.

Near dawn Kino intercepts and beats Juana near the shore as she tries to throw away the pearl. As he turns for home, he is again attacked and kills a man. Knowing he will be prosecuted, Juana stops trying to reestablish their old life. They must flee, but Kino finds his boat destroyed. Turning back, he then sees Juana running from the hut with Coyotito. The hut has been torched.

They hide at his brother's house and depart in the dark of night. Kino tells Juan Tomás that he will not give up the pearl because it has become his soul. Indeed, as they go inland, Kino becomes more instinctual and animalistic. They are pursued by three trackers, one of whom has a rifle. Kino puts Juana and Coyotito in a cave and doubles back to kill the men. As Kino is about to strike, a whimper is heard. The rifleman suspects a coyote and fires into the night. Kino leaps and kills the three, then hears Juana's keening wail of death.

Kino and Juana walk back into town with Juana carrying the body of Coyotito, the top of his head blown away. At the water, Kino offers the pearl to Juana to throw, but she declines. He casts it away, and the pearl and its evil disappear.

Kirkland, John. *To Make My Bread.* Grace Lumpkin. 1932.

John Kirkland, the youngest son in a mountain family that migrates to the city to work in a textile mill, uses his hard-earned mountain sense in the deciding conflict of his life—a violent, agonizing mill strike. The strike, which destroys his family and friends and ends in disaster, leaves him a hardened, angry, and vocal opponent of free enterprise.

John's journey is a harsh one. Living off the barren land on a mountainside where they are prey to disease, carpetbaggers, and scheming land cartels, his family also contends with constant hunger and cold. Here, under his tough grandfather's hand, John learns fortitude and resilience. Through hardship he is shown the importance of community: Only the close-knit relationships between neighbors save the mountain families from starvation and the elements.

After a land cartel buys their land and then evicts them, the Kirklands, attracted by tales of wealth and prosperity, head to a nearby town to look for jobs at a textile mill. While the rest of the family works the mill's merciless hours, John is able to acquire three years of schooling.

When John is cornered by a gang of bullies and knocks their leader, the son of a mill owner, unconscious, he acquires a reputation for wildness and independence. He toys with the idea of adopting the selfish but successful outlook of his brother Basil, who is leading a Horatio Alger–like existence in town. But John's moral sensibility keeps him from taking this path, and he is pulled into the only available alternative: a life of unremitting struggle at the mill.

The conditions in the mill are terrible. Equipment regularly cuts off the hands of the workers, while unventilated rooms serve only as incubators for tuberculosis and typhoid fever. Moreover, the pay is so low that no one can afford nutritious diets, causing widespread pellagra that eventually takes the life of John's mother Emma.

After a few years John is promoted to the position of shop steward, and his coworkers, convinced that he will surely become a despot like the other stewards, begin to regard him with suspicion. John redeems himself, however, by telling the bosses that an improvement in the working conditions would increase efficiency. He is then unsuccessfully wooed by Miss Gordon, an attractive middle-class woman who, at the behest of the management, tries to recruit him as an anti-union spy.

When John recognizes that Miss Gordon is working for the management, he angrily rejects her and quits his position as manager. He then rejoins the rank and file and begins to see the viciousness of the mill owners' exploitation of them. When new machinery is installed in the mill, the majority of workers are permanently dismissed, but John is kept on. His resolve to change things slowly deepens, and during the installation of new equipment, he has time to talk about the work situation with a pro-union friend and becomes converted to the cause.

It is not long before John and the others begin organizing in earnest. When they are fired for their pro-union activities, the other workers follow them out of the mill and begin a strike. The mill owners try a number of unsuccessful tactics, including evicting everyone from their company housing, calling in the state militia, and deputizing the town's criminal elements to smash the strikers' relief store. When the strikers rally to form a picket line at the mill, John's sister Bonnie is shot and killed by deputies as she is singing a ballad. Angry and determined, the strikers carry out their plan, but they are attacked by more deputies and are eventually forced to scatter.

At Bonnie's funeral the law comes and takes her children, but John and the other mourners have finally been fully radicalized. As the book ends, they express their deep, hardened determination to carry on the struggle.

Klugman, Neil. *Goodbye, Columbus.* Philip Roth. 1959.
Narrator Neil Klugman's account of the events of the summer he fell in love with the desirable BRENDA PATIMKIN reveals an acerbic and satirical wit which is at once the mark of assuredness and his weapon and defense when this confidence is threatened.

The novel opens by the pool at the prestigious Green Lane Country Club, where Neil first meets Brenda. From the very beginning Neil is both infatuated with and condemnatory of Brenda. He romanticizes her simple elegance, seeing her as "a sailor's dream of a Polynesian maiden" among the conventional and boring club members. Yet this poise and elegance is founded on the very conventionality that Neil both despises and fears. Brenda's air of belonging reminds Neil of his own tenuous position within this rarified atmosphere, for while he mocks the pretensions of the wealthy and successful, he also admits to a certain longing for such status. Brought up in Newark and educated at Newark College, Rutgers University, Neil wields his background to debunk the pretensions of the "pug-nosed bastards from Montclair," yet he is unable to fully embrace such family eccentricities as his aunt Doris's passions for healthy eating and bourgeois respectability. He is fond of his family and humorously tolerant of their ways, but when he sees Brenda with her breasts bared floating toward him in the pool, Neil realizes that nothing is as important as this girl.

From the very first, Neil's feelings about Brenda center around what he terms a "hideous emotion"—his lust. It is this that allows him to endure his painful visits to her. Neil finally makes a proposal—that Brenda should go to the Margaret Sanger Clinic in New York and get a diaphragm. At first he is angered by her refusal, but then he is glad that, for the first time, she has disobeyed his desire. In a moment of contemplation rare in this heady summer, Neil fears his lust is conquering his reason.

Brenda finally agrees to get a diaphragm, and they go to New York. While Brenda is in the clinic, Neil enters a Catholic church and enters into an ingenious meditation: If we meet God at all, it is through carnality and acquisitiveness, yet what form does this meeting take? The noise and bustle of Fifth Avenue give Neil an answer from a

God as ironic as Neil himself: His prize will be the attainment of everything Brenda stands for.

It is at this moment that Neil gives in to his combined fear and lust, and begins to think about the future. When Brenda asks him to visit her in Boston, he thinks it is time to contemplate marriage. But Brenda has just received a letter from her mother, who has found the diaphragm, and from her father, who urges her to end her relationship. Neil believes that in some way Brenda intended her mother to find the diaphragm, and he faults her for not admitting to this. As he attempts to justify his demands, Neil realizes that he no longer loves Brenda and leaves her, thinking that she "was crying too." As the novel ends, Neil gazes at a reflection of himself and realizes that he will never understand his love for Brenda and that it will be a long time before he feels such passion again.

Knight, Alabama Beggs. *Save Me the Waltz.* Zelda Fitzgerald. 1932.
Alabama Beggs Knight is an extremely wealthy southern belle whose capricious youthful confidence is undermined by her marriage to the dashing young artist David Knight. Feeling overshadowed by the her husband's mounting fame, she struggles to build self-esteem by pursuing her own career. Initially driven by a desire to win her husband's attention and affection, Alabama finds that she must separate from him and her family in order to find herself.

As a young woman, Alabama enjoys flirting with the soldiers involved in World War I. But she eventually tires of romantic games and becomes attracted to David Knight, an aesthete of considerable personal charm. They leave the South for New York, where David soon becomes a famous painter. Alabama is identified as "one of the David Knights" and begins to feel oppressed by her husband's success.

The Knights lead a glamorous and irresponsible life of excess and adventure. Rather spontaneously they decide to set sail for France on a large ocean liner. After a terrible storm at sea in which the ship nearly goes down, Alabama suddenly sees their decadent circle of friends, nouveaux riches, as shallow and corrupt, and feels alienated from society. Her relationship with David also suffers as he becomes increasingly preoccupied with his art.

In France, Alabama falls in love with a dashing young pilot in the French air force. When David threatens to leave her, she ends the affair. In Paris she is once again dissatisfied with her existence as a society woman and views her life as insignificant. After David sleeps with a ballet dancer to get even with her for the pilot, Alabama decides to become a ballerina.

Enrolling in the studio of a Russian madame, Alabama forces herself to endure arduous physical routines that nearly kill her. She is told repeatedly that she is too old to succeed in this profession; the other ballet students wonder why, if she already has a husband and plenty of money, she is pursuing this difficult career.

What began as a device for getting attention from David slowly becomes a true devotion to dance. Only by cutting herself off from her wealthy social contacts and from her husband and child is Alabama able to make new friends among the starving young dancers at the studio. Before her career as a dancer, she found pleasure in the clever verbal sparring of the idle rich; now she enjoys the simple beauty of lilacs and the rigors of the studio. She revels in a new sense of freedom at having total mastery of her body.

Eventually, Alabama's mentor bestows a tutu upon her, signifying her achievement in dance. Soon after, Alabama is invited to Italy to perform in a troupe. She gives an accomplished performance and is offered the principal role. In the midst of her success, however, she receives a visit from her daughter, who accuses her of neglecting the family.

After the child returns to David in Paris, Alabama develops an infection in her foot. It turns gangrenous; she is hospitalized in terrible agony and for a time it appears she might lose her leg or die. In the end, she recuperates, but the injury ends her dancing career. Soon after, Alabama's father dies. At his funeral she comes to an understanding of life. Her suffering has enhanced her character and greatly increased her self-respect. She is now aware that she is more than merely Mrs. David Knight; nevertheless, she remains locked in a wifely role that limits her powers of creative expression.

Knox, Joel Harrison. *Other Voices, Other Rooms.* Truman Capote. 1948.

Delicate, fair-skinned, and pretty, Joel Harrison Knox is a boy on the brink of both manhood and despair. Living in Noon City, thirteen-year-old Joel is suspended between boyhood and manhood. With the encouragement of his epicene cousin Randolph, his tomboyish friend Idabel, and a black servant named Zoo, he overcomes both depression over his mother's death and anxiety about his sexual—and personal—identity.

As the novel opens, Joel has left his New Orleans home, where he was protected by his overly affectionate mother and, after her death, by his devoted aunt. He is to live with his father in the strange household known as Skully's Landing, about which he has heard ominous stories. When he arrives, the first person he meets is his father's slow-witted second wife Amy who is in the process of clubbing a bird to death with a poker. Later, in a window, Joel sees a strange female face that looks like Mae West's, but no one acknowledges that such a woman lives in the house.

Joel next meets his cousin Randolph (at whose window the woman had appeared), a hermit named Little Sunshine, and the servants Missouri (nicknamed "Zoo") and Jesus Fever. Zoo is considered insane, but when she is

raped by a group of white men, it becomes clear that this opinion is based on prejudice.

It is through Randolph and under the terrifying eyes of Joel's semi-catatonic father that Joel must discover himself. Randolph informs Joel that "the feeble-minded, the neurotic, the criminal, [and] the artist, have unpredictability and perverted innocence in common." The alliance Randolph creates between Joel and the novel's other marginalized characters prepares the way for Joel's dawning artistic sensibility. Randolph's talent lies in his superb imitations of movie stars, particularly Mae West.

The two cousins become close, and when Randolph confesses his longstanding infatuation with a Cuban boxer, Joel comforts him. When Joel's friend Idabel flees her ultra-conventional family, Joel leaves with her. They find themselves at a circus in Noon City, where they befriend a midget named Miss Wisteria. The three of them form a freakish love triangle, but none of the three seems able to satisfy the others' needs for love. Joel eventually returns to Skully's Landing and to Randolph.

Determined to say good-bye to the "old Joel," the hero goes with Randolph to visit Little Sunshine at an abandoned building in the middle of a swamp, a place known as the Cloud Hotel. While there he discovers his gay identity. When he and Randolph return to the Landing, he gazes toward the window in which he first saw the woman and, turning his back on "the boy he had left behind," walks without hesitation toward the beckoning face.

Kohl, Linda Snopes. *The Hamlet; The Town; The Mansion.* William Faulkner. 1940; 1957; 1959.

The watchful, conservative town of Jefferson, Mississippi, is quick to condemn both Linda Snopes and her mother, EULA VARNER SNOPES. While Eula strives to transcend their disapproval, for Linda it serves as a provocation. Linda seeks examples of injustice in Jefferson in order to battle them, until she becomes an accessory in the murder of her legal father, FLEM SNOPES, who has used his power unscrupulously to control his family and the town.

The townspeople agree that Linda has inherited only a fraction of her mother's beauty, but she still carries herself with an air of intense purpose. By the time she is in her early teens, she has several men competing for her affections. Among them is GAVIN STEVENS, the county attorney, who is twice her age and rumored to be in love with her mother. Gavin innocently claims to be merely "forming Linda's mind," and he lures her to the drugstore every week to buy her ice cream sodas and present her with volumes of poetry.

After Linda graduates as valedictorian of her class, Flem refuses to let her go to college until Eula signs away her inheritance from her grandfather, WILL VARNER. Linda visits a lawyer in Oxford, Mississippi, where she will attend the university and has him draw up a document transferring her portion of the future inheritance to Flem because she believes that a free life is more important than her grandfather's money.

Flem brings this will with him to his father-in-law's home when he finally decides, after eighteen years, to reveal to Varner that his daughter Eula is having an affair with the president of his bank, Manfred de Spain. Varner storms into his daughter's home the next morning, and that evening Eula commits suicide. Linda attends the funeral and lives with Flem at home until the Italian marble monument for her mother's grave is finally unveiled. When this ordeal is over, she boards a train for New York City, where Gavin Stevens has made arrangements for her to stay.

Linda spends the following seven years living in Greenwich Village, where she marries a sculptor named Barton Kohl. On the day of her wedding, Gavin Stevens visits, bringing a friend named McCarron. She guesses correctly that he is her real father. Along with Kohl, Linda becomes a member of the Communist Party, and the couple goes to Spain during World War II to fight the fascist forces. Kohl is killed in an airplane crash, and Linda, while driving an ambulance, has her eardrums burst by the explosion of a bomb. She returns to Jefferson and to the house once owned by Manfred de Spain, now in her father's possession.

Like the soldiers who have come home to Mississippi, Linda has changed drastically. Sleepless, driven, and solitary, she is obsessed with efforts to improve conditions for the oppressed in Jefferson. Her most courageous crusade involves plans to improve the Negro schools. Linda's efforts are met with hostility from the white townspeople and the school board, and are rejected by the principal. Racist graffiti is scrawled on the sidewalk outside the Snopes house. One of her few sympathizers is Gavin Stevens, who meets with her regularly for "lessons." He is supposedly trying to help her improve her voice, which, because of her deafness, is strange and abrasive. Linda urges Gavin to marry, which he does, in spite of his love for her.

Linda is also obsessed with an injustice within her own family. Her father's cousin, MINK SNOPES, has, thanks to Flem's cunning, spent an extra twenty years in a Mississippi prison for murder. With Gavin Stevens's help, a petition is drawn up to free Mink immediately, two years early. The pardon is granted, and once free, Mink buys a ten-dollar pistol, hitchhikes to Jefferson, enters the Snopes house, and kills Flem. Gavin Stevens is astonished to learn that, months before, Linda had ordered an expensive car as preparation for Mink's rapid departure from Jefferson. Gavin had been trying to prevent her from learning that Mink probably intended to kill Flem, but it now appears that Linda knew all along that her father would be murdered.

Before leaving Jefferson again, Linda locates the nearest relatives of Manfred de Spain, who has disappeared, and leaves them the house and property. During their final meeting, Linda tells an anguished Gavin that he is the only person she has ever loved or needed. She also leaves him an envelope full of money to give to Mink Snopes. After her departure, however, Gavin continues to insist that Linda never knew about Mink's murderous intentions, that she could not possibly have performed an action with a malevolence so characteristic of the Snopes family.

Kohler, Dale. *Roger's Version.* John Updike. 1986.

In this novel of religion and ideas, Dale Kohler is a graduate student in computer science who tries to use a computer to prove the existence of God but instead finds himself having a passionate affair with a married woman and losing his faith.

Dale had a religious upbringing in the Midwest and now studies at a respected northeastern university. He believes that contemporary science is uncovering God behind the mechanics of the universe. The creation of the universe and the evolution of human beings seem so impossible from an informed scientific perspective that it seems there must be a guiding intelligence behind them.

In order to get support for his request for a grant for his project, Dale explains his ideas to the book's narrator ROGER LAMBERT, who is the uncle of his acquaintance Verna Ekelof and a professor of theology at the university. Lambert does not agree that God can or should be proven objectively but does help him to obtain the grant.

Meanwhile, Dale has met Lambert's wife Esther at the Lamberts' Thanksgiving celebration and has begun a passionate affair with her. His guilt over the affair and his realization of the enormity—and potential heresy—of his project are making him depressed.

Dale had intended to use computer graphics to create a model of the universe and then to find the intelligence that would be the common denominator behind that model. The best he can manage, however, is to create graphics of a few objects such as a tree and a carbon molecule and to analyze them in the hope of finding a common basis. At one late-night session Dale becomes so desperate that he begins to think he sees images of Jesus' face and hand within the graphics. Lambert observes that "Dale's reasoning boils down to no more or less than a prayer, a way of making himself vulnerable to visions."

His condition worsens as Esther brings their affair to a close. Then, at a cocktail party at the Lamberts', a well-informed scientist easily crushes all his reasons for suspecting that God is behind the physical universe. By the end of the novel, Dale feels that he has lost his faith. He cannot sleep or pray; he feels sick when he tries to work on his project, and he is ready to return to Ohio. However, Lambert, who was able to regain his own faith by having an incestuous affair, is certain that Dale will regain his faith.

Kornfeld, Rabbi Isaac. "The Pagan Rabbi." Cynthia Ozick. 1966.

Rabbi Isaac Kornfeld, a prominent Jewish scholar, is the title character of this short story. As a young man Isaac attended the rabbinical seminary where he acquired a reputation as a brilliant thinker and a deeply pious man. But by the time Isaac is thirty-five and widely respected in Jewish circles, his religious beliefs have diverged radically from traditional doctrine.

At the outset of his career, Isaac marries a woman of only seventeen, already "astonishingly learned." Sheindel Kornfeld eventually gives birth to seven daughters. While his wife cares for their children, Isaac continues with his work at the seminary. He publishes several important scholarly books and is made a professor of Mishnaic history. The NARRATOR of the story, a bookseller and an old friend of Isaac's from the seminary, describes the professor's intense joy in reading all varieties of literature and criticism from Nietzsche to Thomas Mann to Hebrew scholars.

Although his academic reputation remains untouched, Isaac's private meditations take an unusual turn. At first Sheindel is charmed by what seems to be his literary imagination. Every night Isaac invents peculiar fairy tales to entertain his daughters before bedtime, and he later transcribes them. He is fascinated by nature, takes the family on strenuous excursions into the country, and hikes even farther by himself. Isaac's obsession with nature reflects his secret philosophical inquiry regarding the two types of soul: the human, or "indwelling," soul, and the free soul of plants.

Isaac comes to believe that even stones possess souls since the free-floating spirits inhabit all of nature. Divine wisdom, he asserts, is the ability to see into the self and confront one's own soul. Isaac is possessed by the desire to free his soul from his body and is convinced that others have discovered a way, that mortals coupled with free-souled dryads, mermaids, fauns, satyrs, and centaurs, thereby releasing their own human souls.

In a park called Trilham's Inlet, Isaac calls out to the free souls and is answered by a dryad called Iripomonoeia. He meets her daily and, delirious with ecstasy, they play and make love in the park. One day Iripomonoeia asks him how it feels to be without a soul. Isaac leaps weightlessly into the air, proving that his soul has in fact left his body. Although Isaac has achieved this feat, he is heartbroken since the dryad is repulsed by the sight of his soul and abandons him.

Isaac finally confronts his soul, which takes the shape of a hideous, soiled old man with a sack of tattered books. While Isaac's body cries out for Iripomonoeia, his soul stubbornly argues that the Law, expressed in the sacred books of Judaism, is superior to all of nature. The confrontation between Isaac's body and soul ends in his death.

He hangs himself from a tree in Trilham's Inlet, leaving in his pocket a letter relating the story.

Koskoosh. "The Law of Life." Jack London. 1902.

Koskoosh, an ancient former tribal chief, is the focal point of this story written at the turn of the century. As the story opens, Koskoosh's tribe is preparing to migrate toward the caribou-hunting grounds under the leadership of Koskoosh's son. It has been decided that it is time for the old man to be left behind to die, as he is no longer anything more than a liability for the rest of his community. He sits quietly with a pile of wood beside him so that he can sustain some warmth after the tribe's departure. Reconciled for the most part to his fate, Koskoosh listens as his negligent granddaughter, Sit-cum-to-ha, gathers up her belongings. He hopes that she will bring him more wood before they leave, but Koskoosh notes that she has always been unmindful and indeed disrespectful of her ancestors.

As he hears the systematic sounds of decampment, Koskoosh's anxiety grows. Just before their departure, his son comes to him and gently asks if things are well. The old man, who is inwardly fearful but outwardly stoic, replies that it is well with him and that his fate is simply that of all men. Once on his own, he touches his pile of wood, knowing that when it runs out, so will his life. He again wishes that there was more wood, but at the same time he thinks of the inexorability of life and of nature's ultimate disregard for the flesh. Koskoosh knows that the frost will soon take over his body by starting with the extremities and moving steadily inward, until he is frozen to death.

Stoking the fire one stick at a time, the old man begins to reminisce about his life; he thinks of the arrival of the missionary and the mysterious medicine box, which had brought great pleasure to his senses. He recalls the long years of severe famine, during which one in ten of his tribe, including his mother, perished. Koskoosh also recalls times of plenty when he and others, their bellies full, made war on neighboring tribes with great success. His deepest feelings are aroused, however, by the memory of Zing-ha, whose grandson married Koskoosh's wayward granddaughter. It was through Zing-ha that Koskoosh learned to hunt. His memory lights on a time when he and Zing-ha trailed an old moose that had been cut off from its herd by a pack of wolves. The wolves belligerently and persistently pursued the moose by sporadically attacking it, weakening its defenses. The two hunters tracked the whole struggle until its denouement, the bloody death of the moose.

As he thinks of the moose, Koskoosh marvels at the vividness of his memory, but he is cold again, and this time he adds two sticks to the fire, again wishing that Sit-cum-to-ha had given him more wood. As the frost strikes more deeply, Koskoosh once more envisions the shaggy coat of the old struggling moose. He begins to realize that there are wolves creeping up on him now. He can hear their breathing as they come nearer, and he thrusts a burning stick at the wild animals. They do not retreat at all. Calling to their brothers to join them, they form a patient circle around the old hunter. Finally, Koskoosh, aware that he is not going to live anyway, allows the stick to fall into the snow where it fizzles and goes out. As the story ends, the old man drops his head on his knees, thinking of the old moose he had seen killed. He wonders whether his death matters: The law of life itself is simply being reenacted.

Kracha, George Dzedo. *Out of This Furnace.* Thomas Bell. 1941.

In search of a more prosperous life, twenty-one-year-old Slovak peasant George Dzedo Kracha emigrates from Hungary to northeastern Pennsylvania in the fall of 1881. He leaves behind his wife, his mother, and a sister, and joins another sister, Francka, and her husband Andrej. Andrej works as a railroad builder; Kracha will do the same.

On the boat to America, Kracha meets and flirts with a married nineteen-year-old named Zuska. He spends all his money on a birthday party for her and consequently must walk from New York to White Haven, Pennsylvania. There he becomes the roommate (or shack mate) and best friend of Joe Dubik, another Slovak immigrant.

When he learns that his wife Elena is seriously ill after giving birth to a child who died within a month, Kracha is able to send for her. Elena arrives thin and weak, with a large, disfiguring goiter on her throat. She looks for sympathy from her husband, but Kracha is more dismayed than compassionate when he sees her. Elena's passion toward Kracha, and toward life in general, continues to dwindle, and Kracha has no patience for this. Kracha and Elena have the first of their three children (all daughters) around Thanksgiving, the same time that Dubik marries.

Meanwhile, the railroad workers are continuously moved from place to place in Pennsylvania, doing the same work and suffering the same poverty-ridden conditions. Dubik decides to give up railroading to work in the Carnegie steel mills. Francka and Andrej follow Dubik to the mills, but since Braddock, Dubik's mill, is embroiled in nasty strikes, Francka and Andrej move to Homestead. About a year later Kracha and Elena move to crowded, unpleasant Homestead as well, and Kracha begins his never-ending, unrewarding, and dangerous work at the mill.

Missing his friend Dubik and spurred on by the strikes that are now engulfing the Homestead mills, Kracha moves his family to Braddock. He works from 6:00 to 6:00— one week the night shift, one week the day shift—seven days a week. His only escape from this drudgery is in the local saloon.

One hot August day there is an explosion at the mills. Dubik is badly burned and dies two days later. Soon after Dubik's death, Kracha decides to leave mill work, and he buys a butcher shop. His new business is a success, and within a year he is fairly well-off.

One day, Zuska, the girl Kracha had met on the boat to America more than fifteen years earlier, walks into his butcher shop. A poor, recently widowed mother of two boys, Zuska has come to Braddock to stay with her sister and is searching for a new husband. Zuska and Kracha begin an affair; Elena's health grows worse, and she soon dies.

After Elena's death, Zuska informs Kracha that she is pregnant, and they marry. Meanwhile, Kracha is having serious financial trouble: He made a bad investment on some property, Elena's funeral used up most of his cash, he continues to lose customers due to his well-publicized adultery, and Zuska, as he discovers later, is stealing money from him. Soon after their wedding, Kracha is arrested for wife-beating and spends ten months in jail. At this point Zuska leaves, and Kracha never hears from her again.

Kracha loses his home and business. He boards with a family in Homestead, pays Francka to look after his daughters, and begins to work in the mills again. He moves in with his daughter Mary after her husband, MIKE DOBREJCAK, dies; while there, he is a rude and grouchy boarder. He spends his final years living with his grandson, JOHN "DOBIE" DOBREJCAK (Mary's oldest child) and Dobie's wife Julie. These last years are peaceful for Kracha, although he is not much better off financially than when he first arrived to work on the railroads fifty years earlier.

Kromer, Thomas. *Waiting for Nothing.* Tom Kromer. 1935.

Thomas Kromer, a twenty-six-year-old from Huntington, West Virginia, who finds himself unemployed and homeless during the early years of the Depression, is the narrator of this autobiographical novel.

At the beginning of the novel, Thomas is penniless and faint with hunger. He collects a heavy stick and plans to hit a well-dressed man over the head and rob him, but when given the opportunity, he cannot bring himself to do it. Thomas then stops in front of a restaurant and looks in longingly at a couple eating a delicious dinner, but he is accosted by a policeman and told to move on.

One cold and rainy night he and a number of other "stiffs" find an empty building to sleep in, but they are brutally rounded up in the middle of the night and taken to the precinct jail. The next morning he is taken to court, and without even a chance to plead his case, he is sentenced to sixty days or $100 for vagrancy.

Thomas manages to survive life "on the bum" by developing strategies for eliciting the sympathy of the more prosperous. He listens to sanctimonious preaching in the missions in order to be given an almost inedible meal and a warm place to sleep; he allows himself to be taken to bed by a homosexual in exchange for dinner and shelter; and every now and then he is befriended by other unfortunates who share what little they have with him. One day when Thomas is so hungry that he decides to stop torturing himself by asking for food and jobs that do not exist, he steals a gun from a drunk and plans to hold up a bank. When he gets to the teller's window, however, his gun gets caught in the lining of his coat pocket; he panics, runs away, and disposes of the weapon at the first opportunity.

Much of Thomas's difficult life is spent riding the rails. He struggles to survive inclement weather, hunger, hostile and abusive law enforcement officers, vicious robbers who prey on the itinerant panhandlers, religious fanatics, and lunatics. One night on the road Thomas and twenty other men are warming themselves around a fire in a garbage dump when the police arrive, search them for money, kick over their meager suppers, and order them to move on. After finding another camp, Thomas listens as his companions, whom he thinks of as walking ghosts, discuss a newspaper editorial which argued that no one would starve during the Depression.

Some time later, Thomas spends a sleepless night at a mission in a room with a thousand other men. He sees a neon sign outside flashing the words JESUS LIVES and thinks to himself that God does not exist because if he did, all of the homeless and destitute would not be spending their lives waiting for nothing. The man in the bunk next to him is dying of starvation; as the man is carried out on a stretcher, Thomas tells himself that there is no way out of this life of soup lines and railway cars, and that he, too, will probably die twenty years before his time.

Kronborg, Thea. *The Song of the Lark.* Willa Cather. 1978.

Thea Kronborg, a passionate and determined woman, struggles to perfect her art. Even in early childhood she seemed animated by an unusual force that expressed itself most clearly in her piano playing. The novel chronicles her maturation as an artist, while she analyzes her inner strength and learns to draw on it for her music.

Thea's musical sensitivity develops during her childhood in Moonstone, Colorado. She remains apart from the family, absorbed in her private concerns, quietly observing the beautiful details of life. She takes weekly piano lessons from Professor Wunsch, an inspired teacher who has been worn down by his drinking. Wunsch recognizes in Thea the natural gifts of an artist. HOWARD ARCHIE, a lonely physician, and Spanish Johnny, an unpredictable

Mexican who plays guitar for Thea, are also drawn to her special awareness.

Ray Kennedy, a simple, self-educated railroad man, adores Thea and plans to marry her when she is old enough. Ray dies in a railroad accident when Thea is seventeen, leaving her his entire savings of $600. He tells Dr. Archie, who attends him on his deathbed, that Thea is to use the money to spend a winter in Chicago studying music. Dr. Archie is able to persuade the Kronborgs to allow Thea to go, and he accompanies her to Chicago. There, Thea gets a job singing in a church choir and takes lessons from Andor Harsanyi, a sensitive and discriminating pianist. Although Thea is Harsanyi's best pupil, committed and highly gifted, he senses that they are fighting against some obstacle. One evening when Thea has dinner with the Harsanyis, she tells them about singing in the choir, and Andor insists that she sing for them. Thea's powerful, compelling voice convinces Harsanyi immediately that she must change direction and begin studying with the finest voice teacher in Chicago.

Harsanyi sends her to Madison Bowers, who instructs many famous opera singers. After twenty lessons with Bowers, Thea returns to Moonstone for the summer. There is great tension between Thea and her siblings, who are jealous of the attention she is receiving. When she departs for Chicago in the fall, she knows she will never return. During that winter she takes lessons from Bowers and works as his accompanist. Like Bowers, she finds most of his privileged students vulgar and distasteful. Only one, a young businessman named FRED OTTENBURG, interests Thea, and they become close friends. Fred recognizes Thea's enormous potential but sees that she is exhausted and depressed by her stressful life in Chicago. Thea accepts Fred's offer of a summer vacation at a friend's ranch in Panther Canyon, Arizona.

At Panther Canyon, Thea experiences a rebirth of childhood joy and energy. Meditating on the exquisite pottery left behind by cave dwellers in the canyon, she comes to a deeper understanding of her own relationship to her art. When Fred visits her after two months, he finds that Thea has been transformed into an extraordinarily beautiful and confident woman. They spend several romantic weeks at Panther Canyon, and Fred tries to persuade Thea to marry him. She agrees, until it emerges that Fred is unable to obtain a divorce from his first wife, who lives in California. Thea ends their relationship promptly by borrowing some money from Dr. Archie, and she leaves to study music in Germany.

Ten years later, after many successful performances in Europe, Thea goes to New York to sing at the Metropolitan. She wins principal parts and earns glowing reviews. Dr. Archie and Fred, now friends, travel to New York to hear Thea and are deeply impressed by her work. The romance between Fred and Thea resumes, and they are eventually married. Thea continues in her disciplined, passionate way of life, achieving even greater acclaim as a singer.

Kugelmass, Sidney. "The Kugelmass Episode." Woody Allen. 1977.

Sidney Kugelmass, a bored and frustrated professor at the City College of New York, is guided by a magician to a weekend romance with Madame Bovary.

Unhappily married for the second time, Sidney Kugelmass is increasingly depressed about the direction his middle-aged life is taking. When his psychoanalyst dismisses his requests for immediate help by explaining that he is not a magician, Kugelmass has an inspiration: A magician is exactly what he needs. He terminates his therapy and several days later receives a mysterious phone call from the Great Persky.

Kugelmass meets Persky in a dilapidated Brooklyn tenement house where Persky reveals an old Chinese cabinet. He explains that if Kugelmass climbs in, he can be projected into any novel that is enclosed with him in the cabinet. Kugelmass decides to have an affair with Emma Bovary. The Flaubert novel is thrown into the cabinet with Kugelmass, who suddenly finds himself in the Bovary bedroom, being greeted by a flirtatious Emma. They have a romantic interlude in the countryside, cut short by Kugelmass's remembering he has agreed to meet his wife in front of Bloomingdale's. He is projected back to New York, thrilled with his discovery and eager to return to the novel and his affair with Emma. What he does not realize is that he himself has started to appear as a character in *Madame Bovary* and is at that moment being read in paperback versions of the book throughout the country.

At Kugelmass's urging, the Great Persky hesitantly agrees to transport Emma to New York, and Sidney Kugelmass and Emma Bovary are transported together into the lobby of the Plaza Hotel.

After a romantic weekend of New York nightlife, Kugelmass and Emma return to Persky's apartment and attempt, unsuccessfully, to send Emma back into her novel. Kugelmass brings her back to their suite at the Plaza and spends the following week in a frenzy of phone calls to the Great Persky and visits to Emma, who grows increasingly impatient with her life in the real world. By the weekend she demands that Kugelmass get her back into the novel or marry her. Depressed, Kugelmass shows up at Persky's apartment to vent his frustrations: Madame Bovary, stashed at the Plaza, is growing fat on the food provided by room service, and another professor at City College who has identified Kugelmass as the sporadically appearing character in the Flaubert novel has threatened to turn him in. On Sunday afternoon Persky calls, certain that he has fixed his magic cabinet, and informs Sidney that he is ready to send Madame Bovary back to her book.

Kugelmass insists that he has learned his lesson and will not cheat again, but within several weeks he is back at Persky's door, asking to be thrown into the cabinet for a sexual escapade with a character from Philip Roth's *Portnoy's Complaint*. While Kugelmass is in the cabinet, there is an explosion and a shower of sparks: Persky drops dead, the magic cabinet bursts into flames, and the entire Brooklyn tenement in which it is housed burns down. Sidney Kugelmass has not been projected into the Philip Roth novel of his choice but rather into a remedial Spanish textbook. As the story closes, he is running for his life from a large and hairy irregular verb.

L

Laballière, Alcée. "At the 'Cadian Ball"; "The Storm." Kate Chopin. 1894; 1898.

Alcée Laballière runs an Acadian rice plantation where he lives with his elderly mother and her goddaughter Clarisse. Alcée is industrious and responsible but also broodingly passionate, dividing his affections between refined, beautiful Clarisse and vivacious, sensuous CALIXTA.

In "At the 'Cadian Ball," the toil-stained Alcée returns from his fields one day and impulsively grabs Clarisse and pants declarations of love. Offended, she rebuffs him.

Clarisse's demeanor toward Alcée has always been alternately cold and kind, much to his aggravation. Shortly thereafter, Alcée's rice fields are razed by a cyclone, and Clarisse attempts to console him, but he responds to her—and to the disaster—with mute sullenness. The next night, while praying by her window, Clarisse witnesses Alcée depart on horseback, and, after questioning his servant, she learns he has gone to the 'Cadian ball.

Alcée has gone to the ball to see the fiery Calixta, once the subject of scandalous whispers. They sit alone in the shadows, and as he fondles her earrings and hair, Alcée reminds Calixta of their tryst in Assumption the previous year. They flirt and caress each other, and Alcée teases Calixta about Bobinôt, her doltish but solicitous admirer. Suddenly they are interrupted by Clarisse, who has come to reclaim Alcée under the pretense of a family emergency. But Clarisse's importunities are unnecessary, for Alcée would willingly follow her anywhere. Departing with Clarisse, Alcée barely even looks back at Calixta as the fawning Bobinôt appears at her side. With dispassionate resignation, Calixta informs the delighted Bobinôt that she will marry him, while en route to the plantation Clarisse confesses her love to Alcée. As distant pistol shots signal the end of the ball, Calixta is already a fading memory for Alcée as his thoughts turn to Clarisse and their future together.

In "The Storm," five years later, Alcée is out riding when a cyclone suddenly arises. He seeks refuge at the home of Calixta, who, while Bobinôt and their son Bibi are in town shopping, has been absorbed by her sewing and has not noticed the impending storm until it is upon her. While she hastily seals the house, Alcée asks to wait out the storm in her gallery. She insists he come inside, for the storm is severe. Calixta frets over the safety of her son, and Alcée attempts to reassure her when suddenly a lightning bolt strikes a nearby chinaberry tree and sends Calixta into Alcée's arms. Calixta attempts to free herself from Alcée's embrace, but the touch of her quivering body reawakens his former infatuation and desire. Alcée recalls their long-ago rendezvous in Assumption where they kissed and caressed until he, intoxicated with desire, fled before dishonoring the passionate but virginal Calixta. But now they feel free to make love, and they revel in each other's bodies, oblivious to the storm outside. By the time the storm has passed, Alcée and Calixta are sated and dazed, yet they dare not yield to the lure of sleep. Alcée leaves, but not without a parting gaze filled with mutual delight.

To the relief and delight of Calixta, Bobinôt and Bibi soon return home with a treat of shrimp. At home that evening Alcée writes to Clarisse, who is vacationing with their children in Biloxi. He writes that he misses them, but their pleasure and health are most important to him, so she should feel free to stay another month. Clarisse is pleased by the letter, for although she is devoted to her husband, she is enjoying Biloxi society and her freedom, especially from their intimate conjugal life.

LaBas, PaPa. *Mumbo Jumbo.* Ishmael Reed. 1972.

PaPa LaBas is a voodoo priest who operates the Mumbo Jumbo Kathedral. At the outset of the novel, which traces the history of racial oppression backward from its expression in the post–World War I United States, PaPa LaBas is fifty years old and is exploring the ways in which he can broaden the appeal of his organization, which is based on ancient voodoo practices and beliefs. His efforts are assisted by his daughter Earline and by such assistants as Charlotte and her lover Berbelang.

LaBas's goals are threatened when the government tries to suppress the rapidly spreading anti-plague called Jes Grew. This germ, as it is called, spreads throughout the United States and causes people to dance energetically, move around, and feel as though they and their lives are just fine. LaBas is also opposed by the Atonists, the white colonial-minded inheritors of oppressive traditions. Their principal spokesman is HINCKLE VON VAMPTON, who edits the anti-Jes Grew tabloid, *The Benign Monster.*

While, with the aid of an assistant, LaBas attempts to recover the ancient Book of Thoth, which contains secrets derived from Osiran religious beliefs and practices of ancient Egypt, his Mumbo Jumbo Kathedral in Harlem is gradually undermined. The first desertion occurs when Berbelang leaves the organization, hoping to establish himself as an authority on the Jes Grew phenomenon. Berbelang is found murdered before he can get very far in his plan. PaPa LaBas hesitates to break the news to Charlotte, who loves Berbelang and resents his desertion. Soon she, too, is found dead. LaBas realizes that there is a conspiracy operating against him, backed by the powerful Wallflower Order, a militaristic organization dedicated to stopping the spread of Jes Grew and any expression of African-American culture or sensibility.

While LaBas deals with the murders within his organization, he feels assured that his assistant, Abdul Sufi Hamid, will be able to translate the fabled book. Hamid, who knows that secrets in the wrong hands can be dangerous, translates the book and then burns it once he actually reads what he has translated. PaPa LaBas does not know this when he discovers Hamid's body, murdered at the hands of Biff Musclewhite, a police consultant. LaBas eventually figures out that a poem found crumpled in Hamid's hand alludes to the state of Egyptian-American cotton deals, and after further decoding the poem he realizes that the manuscript he seeks is interred beneath Harlem's Cotton Club.

With his organization in disarray, LaBas tries to locate the manuscript. As it turns out, he can only find the ornate box in which the manuscript was buried. Hamid had intended to fence the box when he was murdered, as a letter later reveals, so LaBas is left without his sacred text. He must continue the Kathedral's operation without official or scriptural sanction for his practice of what is called "The Work."

After a kaleidoscopic tour through scriptural history, the novel reaches the contemporary era again, and LaBas functions as a nearly solitary figure, wandering through time. LaBas is aware from his experiences in the 1920s that the 1930s, 1940s, 1950s, and on are not the right time for him to reactivate the Kathedral, which, like the

Jes Grew phenomenon, lost strength once the text on which it depended was destroyed. As the novel concludes, PaPa LaBas heads home to Manhattan in his 1914 Locomobile to await the return of the 1920s and a true resurgence of the Jes Grew germ.

Ladd, Adam. *Rebecca of Sunnybrook Farm.* Kate Douglas Wiggin. 1903.

Adam Ladd is one of the many benefactors of the novel's child heroine REBECCA RANDALL and is himself a source of romantic intrigue for the people he encounters.

Adam's childhood was difficult and unhappy. He was poor, and his beloved mother died when he was ten. At the age of thirty he is an eligible bachelor, but although he is a handsome, successful businessman and loves children, he has no desire to marry. A look of fatigue and sadness haunts his otherwise kind face.

When Adam meets Rebecca for the first time, she and her friend Emma Jane are selling soap for some poor school friends, the Simpsons, who are trying to raise money to buy a special lamp. Adam is so attracted by the twelve-year-old Rebecca's winning nature and charming conversation as she elaborates their charitable enterprise that he buys three hundred bars of soap. The surprise literally knocks her off her stool. When he asks if she wants to know his name, Rebecca responds that he must be Mr. Aladdin from the *Arabian Nights*, and he does not correct her. At Adam's suggestion they arrange to have the lamp arrive at the Simpsons on Thanksgiving Day as a special surprise. This is the first of many examples of Adam's generosity.

Adam tells his aunt that Rebecca is the most remarkable child he has ever met. He remains in contact with his young friend, visiting her on holidays and smothering her with "useless gifts"—in his view the most enjoyable kind. He always remembers Emma Jane as well, although she did not catch his heart.

Adam becomes friends with Rebecca's boarding school teacher, Miss Maxwell, who is equally taken with her star pupil. Separately, they find themselves frustrated in their attempts to help Rebecca through the difficulties that arise in her personal situation, such as her family's poverty at Sunnybrook Farm and the illness of the aunts who support her. Together, however, they work out an arrangement in which Adam supplies the money for Miss Maxwell's enterprises, such as taking Rebecca to the sea to recover her health. Adam is also a trustee of the boarding school, and since the school is having its fiftieth anniversary, he offers to set up a student competition for the two best-written compositions, with fifty dollars as the prize. He knows that Rebecca needs the money desperately for her family's mortgage on the farm; he cannot give it to her outright but is confident she will win—which, of course, she does.

Adam finally arranges for his railroad company to buy Sunnybrook Farm's land so that Rebecca's family can become financially secure. When he attends her graduation from school, he tells her he is "glad I met the child, proud I know the girl, longing to meet the woman!" It is only when he rereads the Aladdin story in the *Arabian Nights*, however, that Adam realizes he is in love with her.

Laffawiss, Irv. "Mondongo." Amiri Baraka. 1990.

Lacking direction in civilian life, Irv Laffawiss joins the Air Force as a radio operator and is stationed in Aquadilla, Puerto Rico. Originally from a ghetto on the Lower East Side of New York City, Laffawiss is referred to as the "Groucho Bastard" by the southern soldiers because he continually imitates Groucho Marx. Extroverted and hedonistic, he spends his weekends off-base in bars and bordellos. Although he likes to read and hangs out with the quasi-intellectuals on base, he is more concerned with appeasing his body than his mind.

Laffawiss's closest service friend is RAY JOHNS, a quiet weather gunner who spends all his free time reading. Johns is the evening librarian on base and spends late nights alone listening to music, drinking, and reading in the library. An unlikely pair, they are both outcasts from the white, "country-boy" soldiers—Laffawiss because he is a Jew, and Johns because he is black. Laffawiss occasionally intrudes on Johns's haven in the library to make jokes about masturbation and penis size.

Laffawiss eventually persuades Johns to take a night on the town, but his uninhibited and seemingly naive enthusiasm makes Johns nervous. Although the bars have been officially desegregated by the military, the prejudice on base extends itself to the town. Laffawiss intends to ignore this tacit segregation, but Johns leads him into the Estrella Negra, a black bar, to prevent unnecessary trouble. After taunting a Mexican American in the bar, Laffawiss suggests that he and Johns visit "Mondongo," the off-limits area of prostitution, and Johns agrees.

Laffawiss obviously knows his way around Mondongo and is practiced in bartering for prostitutes. Against his better judgment, Johns allows Laffawiss to hire two unattractive women for a "long-time." In a small room with one bed, Laffawiss does not hesitate to make use of his prostitute in front of Johns and the other prostitute. Johns cannot do the same, however, and the woman he is with calls things off before he can finish. Laffawiss, who never intended to pay for the prostitutes' services, directs Johns in a dangerous getaway through back streets. Laffawiss is apprehended by military police, and Johns, who probably could have escaped, turns himself in. They are made to paint the barracks as punishment.

Laffawiss is eventually discharged from the Air Force on a hardship case; Johns had been discharged earlier because an anonymous letter accused him of being a communist. Although they renew their friendship in New York, it soon comes to an end when they are attacked on the street by a group of white men. In a scene entirely reminiscent of their escape from Mondongo, Johns escapes, but this time Laffawiss is taken away in an ambulance. A few days later men who claim to be Laffawiss's relatives pay Johns a visit. Johns, who was not at home, learns from his superintendent that some men had come by and inquired about his skin color. Laffawiss and Johns never meet again.

Lamar, Lancelot Andrews. *Lancelot.* Walker Percy. 1977.

Lancelot Andrews Lamar emerges from years of alcoholism when he discovers his wife's unfaithfulness. One day when looking at his six-year-old daughter Siobhan's medical records, Lancelot notices that her blood is a type that he could not possibly have fathered. After verifying this fact with a surgeon, Lancelot abruptly stops drinking and becomes painfully aware of the intrigues developing between his wife Margot and the cast of the film in which she is acting.

Lancelot and Margot live on an elegant old estate called Belle Isle, situated in the most prestigious neighborhood of their Louisiana town. Lancelot grew up at Belle Isle and attended college, where he was praised both as a scholar and an athlete, and completed a law degree. His first wife, Lucy, gave birth to a son and a daughter but died of cancer while they were still young. When Lancelot meets Margot, he is already neglecting his law practice and descending into alcoholism.

Margot, the daughter of a Texas oil magnate, is confident, slightly vulgar, and openly sexual. During the first years of their marriage, Lancelot and Margot are inseparable and very passionate. Margot is also engaged in the project of restoring Belle Isle, which enhances their enormous pleasure in living together. As time goes on, however, Lancelot drinks more heavily, watches too much television, works less, and begins to experience a debilitating apathy. Margot converts the pigeonnier, an old slave cabin that had been used as a dovecote, into a small apartment, and Lancelot moves in, leaving Margot in charge of the house.

On the day that Lancelot discovers Margot has been unfaithful, he shakes off his customary stupor, washes himself thoroughly, and becomes acutely aware of everything going on around him. He already suspects Margot of sleeping with Merlin, an actor, but he now notices her attraction to Jacoby, the director. Lancelot enlists the help of Elgin, a brilliant young black man who attends M.I.T. and serves as household help in the summer. Elgin watches the rooms at the hotel where the cast is staying and keeps a log of who enters and leaves each room during the night. His notes seem to indicate that Margot is having two affairs at once, but Lancelot is still doubtful and wants conclusive evidence.

Because the hotel owner owes Lancelot a favor, he is able to persuade the man to close the hotel, thereby forcing the cast to move into Belle Isle. Elgin sets up a complicated network of video cameras that survey their rooms. The films, which Lancelot views the next day, show Margot breaking up with Merlin and having sex with Jacoby. Lancelot's daughter is also captured in bed with two other cast members. The following night, during a dramatic hurricane, Lancelot uncaps the gas well that is under the house and fills it with methane. Drunk with methane, Lancelot makes love with Raine, one of the crew members, and afterward enters Margot's bedroom where she is sleeping with Jacoby. He slits Jacoby's throat with his grandfather's Bowie knife just before the methane causes the house to explode. Lancelot, the only one who survives, is blown through the wall and into a thicket.

After spending a year in a mental institution, Lancelot remembers the events, narrating them to an old friend from college. When he is released, Lancelot is delirious with dreams of creating a new order that will transform the world completely, one based on absolutely defined roles for men and women, and reflecting their enslavement to desire.

Lamartine, Lulu Nanapush. *Love Medicine; Tracks.* Louise Erdrich. 1984; 1988.

No one but her mother is sure who Lulu Nanapush's father is, and only Lulu herself can identify which of her many lovers are the fathers of her eight sons. A Chippewa Indian regarded by many in her community as a wild seductress, Lulu has, from birth to senior citizenship, inspired rumor.

When Lulu was seven, she had a secret playhouse where nobody could find her. One summer day she discovered the body of a man, dressed in ragged clothes, lying across the doorway of her playhouse. She watched the dead man day after day without telling anyone of her discovery. Without really thinking, she untied the old red scarf he had for a belt, and his pants fell open at the waist. She remained staring, transfixed. Lulu did not return often to her playhouse because the body began to rot and smell. Not until she was on the government bus on her way to school did she cry about the incident. After the bus ride, Lulu's tears dried, and she never wept again.

During adolescence Lulu meets NECTOR KASHPAW, the man who will remain her obsession throughout life. Through three successive marriages, Lulu makes a show of ignoring Nector while continuing to fantasize about him. Lulu claims to have married her first husband, Morissey, out of "hurt and spite," and her second, Henry Lamartine, out of fondness. Henry loves Lulu, and her unfaithfulness drives him to suicide. Immediately after the funeral, Lulu sleeps with Henry's brother, Beverly. After Beverly's departure, she is left with her many devoted sons, each of whom has a different father.

Lulu eventually becomes involved with Nector Kashpaw, who is married and also has many children. The affair continues for five years, long after the birth of her youngest son, Lyman, who is Nector's child. A falling-out occurs between Lulu and Nector when Beverly Lamartine appears suddenly, and Lulu hints that she is considering marriage to him. Nector, who is the tribe chairman, subsequently signs an eviction notice that requires Lulu to leave her house and the land she and Henry had lived on as squatters. Lulu gets her revenge by casually informing Nector that she is marrying Beverly and by announcing during a tribal meeting her determination to remain on Lamartine's land. After the meeting, Beverly Lamartine returns to Minneapolis, where he already has a wife. Lulu's house later burns down to the ground, and Lulu can sense from Nector's behavior that he is responsible. Lulu and her boys remain on the land in hastily built shacks until they are provided with a new home on better land.

Although the affair between Nector and Lulu ends after the burning, they find each other again at the senior citizens' home. There, Nector and a nearly blind Lulu make love in the laundry room of the home. When Lulu is away from the home recovering from an operation on her eyes, Nector dies. Still blind after the operation, she mourns Nector. Strangely, his wife, MARIE LAZARRE KASHPAW, volunteers to help Lulu by administering her eye drops, and the two become close friends. As Lulu regains her vision, she also acquires a second sight. She gains a psychic's awareness of others' feelings and a knowledge of the revealing details of their lives.

Lambert, Nora. *Watch and Ward.* Henry James. 1878.

At age twelve, Nora Lambert is described as ordinary in appearance and "undeniably vulgar" in action, yet possessed of "a concentrated brightness" in her eyes. Nora leaves the home she shares with her father in St. Louis to travel with him to Boston in order to clear his debts. When ROGER LAWRENCE, a wealthy Bostonian, refuses him patronage, Nora's father commits suicide, and Lawrence becomes Nor's ward, in the hope of forming her into the perfect wife. To that end, he educates her in literature, languages, and the arts.

While still under Lawrence's care, Nora receives the affections of two suitors: her cousin George Fenton and Roger's cousin, the Reverend Hubert Lawrence. Nora is happy to find a living relative in Fenton, and she remains ignorant of his interest in Roger's fortune. She is also unaware of Hubert's reputation among the ladies and considers his affection for her to be sincere.

In order to further Nora's education, Roger agrees to send her to Europe with the worldly Mrs. Keith, the recently widowed woman whom Roger had formerly courted. Nora comes out in Rome and returns to America a beautiful and refined young lady. She has shed her country frocks for the silk dresses of Paris. Learning that Roger has fallen ill, she nurses him back to health. When he sees the beautiful woman she has become, he proposes marriage to her.

This creates a dilemma for the young lady: She feels a sense of filial devotion to Roger but does not return his affections. Finally, Nora declines Roger's proposal but agrees to stay on with him as his ward. She feels betrayed, however, when she learns about Roger's self-interested intent to marry her from the start. With her long-held notion that Roger adopted her out of kindness and charity now shattered, Nora flees to New York to see her cousin, urging Roger not to follow.

In New York, however, Nora discovers that Fenton wants to marry her only to inherit Roger's fortune. She is further disillusioned when she discovers that Hubert Lawrence was engaged while he was courting her. Nora now recognizes the relative integrity and genuineness of Roger's affection for her. When Roger comes to find her in New York, she chooses to return with him as his wife.

Lambert, Roger. *Roger's Version.* John Updike. 1986.

Roger Lambert, the narrator and main character of this novel of faith and doubt, has all the trappings of a respectable professor of theology at a major northeastern university. Despite his Christian vocation, however, Lambert is troubled by impious, disreputable, and even evil thoughts and deeds.

Lambert lives with his wife Esther and son Richie in an affluent suburban neighborhood. Beneath the surface, his family life is largely a sham. He is dissatisfied with his boring life-style, Esther resents her domestic role and drinks constantly, and Richie watches television all day. Lambert's marriage is the result of an affair he had with Esther when she was a young woman in his choir. At that time he was a minister married to another woman, but he had been attracted to young women ever since he lusted after his half-sister Edna during his unhappy childhood. Lambert has also lost his faith in God and enjoys reading pornography as much as theology. He is racist in a subtle way and dislikes people in general.

Lambert is forced to deal with his imperfections when he is visited by a young man named DALE KOHLER. Dale is from the area outside Cleveland in which Lambert grew up and is now a graduate student in computer science at his university. He informs Lambert that Edna's nineteen-year-old daughter, Verna Ekelof, is now living in a nearby project with her illegitimate half-black baby Paula. Dale also tries to get Lambert to support his request for a grant for a computer project aimed at proving the existence of God.

Lambert visits Verna and is very attracted to her. He has her and Dale over for Thanksgiving and finds that Esther is as excited by Dale as he is by Verna. Esther and Dale are soon having a passionate affair, which Lambert is able to imagine in precise detail, and Lambert is coming closer and closer to having sex with Verna.

At the same time, he shows himself to be capable of positive acts. At a Grants Committee meeting he argues against Dale's proposal by saying that a provable God would be a less powerful and less personally compelling God. This is his opinion, but he phrases it in a way that he knows will cause the committee members to side against him and give Dale the grant.

Lambert gives Verna money and tries to educate her. He also puts Paula into a day-care center. When Verna becomes pregnant again, he convinces her to have an abortion, pays for it, and even goes to the clinic with her. When Verna beats Paula, Lambert takes them both to the hospital. That night he has sex with Verna. Having committed incest, adultery, and child abuse, he feels like a fallen sinner and is suddenly certain of God's existence.

Landau, Nathan. *Sophie's Choice.* William Styron. 1976.

Nathan Landau, the lover of a World War II concentration camp survivor, is intelligent and articulate but also a schizophrenic, and this illness prevents him from fulfilling his capabilities. To hide this debilitating mental illness from others, Nathan has fabricated a life for himself in which he poses as a Harvard graduate now pursuing a brilliant career as a research scientist, always on the point of revealing the discovery he is just about to make.

To most, Nathan seems very much like a brilliant scholar. He has an active mind and a comprehensive understanding of many fields; he can discourse on science and display a wide knowledge of literature, art, and music. Yet as the novel progresses, Nathan becomes increasingly less able to control his illness and resorts more and more to the drugs that seem to offer a reprieve but actually drive him further toward ruthless and uncontrollable madness.

Nathan is first introduced as SOPHIE ZAWISTOWSKA's gallant rescuer. Having survived Auschwitz, Sophie, a gentile, arrives in America still suffering from the effects of malnutrition. Nathan discovers Sophie fainting in a library in Brooklyn; he diagnoses her illness and helps her recover, falling in love with her in the process. Nathan also enables Sophie to look back on her life before Auschwitz and to rediscover her love of music, giving her records that make her forget some of the horrors she has suffered. Yet when his mood changes, Nathan can be relentlessly cruel, accusing Sophie of infidelity and, most harmfully, of saving herself at the expense of those Polish Jews who didn't survive the death camps. Just as Nathan brings all his compassion and energy to Sophie's recovery, so he uses all the resources his intelligence provides to humiliate and destroy her.

Nathan's relationship with STINGO, the narrator of the book, follows a similar though less intense pattern. Nathan's encouragement inspires Stingo to begin writing his first novel, yet he is also capable of devastating criticism. His frequent attacks on Stingo's southern heritage are at once vicious and intelligent, and while seeming almost unbearably cruel to Stingo, they lead him toward a more stringent examination of himself and his background.

Nathan becomes less able to control his moods, and the frightening nervous energy with which he attacks Sophie begins to dominate his behavior. As he exhausts the possibilities for verbal abuse, Nathan begins to attack her physically. He always returns after these fights, but as events escalate, he begins to contemplate forcing Sophie into a death pact. Finally, Nathan loses all ability to control his destructive impulses and subjects Sophie to the worst violence she has yet received from him. When he turns again on Stingo, accusing him of an affair with Sophie, and threatens to kill both of them, Sophie and Stingo run away to a peanut farm inherited by Stingo's father. Sophie returns to Nathan, however, and the two are discovered only after their double suicide.

Lane, Hondo. *Hondo.* Louis L'Amour. 1953.

A desert-tough loner, Hondo Lane has lived with the Apaches and seen more than his share of violence and death. Riding dispatch for the Army in the untamed west, the seasoned Hondo survives an Indian ambush but loses his horse. With Sam, his rugged dog and constant companion, he finds his way to an isolated homestead. Angie Lowe, a pretty pioneer woman who hasn't seen a man for some time, is there with her young son Johnny. Angie and Hondo are instantly attracted to each other, but neither acknowledges the attraction until later when the threats of the vengeful Apaches endanger both their lives.

Hondo breaks one of Angie's wild horses, pays for it, and urges her to come back to the Army post for safety. She refuses, and he departs. On his way Hondo comes across the remains of the slaughtered Company C, a troop that was sent to warn settlers but that had met with the Apaches. Unbeknownst to Hondo, Apache leader Vittoro arrives at Angie's homestead and, despite years of peaceful relations, orders a brave to kill her. Little Johnny shoots the brave, only nicking him but earning the respect of Vittoro. Vittoro makes the boy his blood brother and spares their lives. But the wounded brave, the evil Silva, is furious.

At the post Hondo fights with Ed Lowe, an ornery gambler whom he later realizes is Angie's derelict husband. Hondo, aware of the impending threat of the Apaches, decides to try to save Angie and Johnny. When Lowe sees that Hondo's horse bears his brand, he challenges him, but Hondo responds by riding off into the desert. Lowe and another gambler follow him, seeking revenge. The two men attack Hondo at dawn, but Hondo is prepared, and when a small band of Apaches launches a surprise attack at the same time, Hondo saves Lowe. Afterward, the ungrateful Lowe tries to shoot Hondo in the back, and Hondo kills him.

Vittoro returns to the homestead with several braves and insists that Angie pick one of them for a father to Johnny. Angie says her husband will return, and Vittoro grudgingly agrees to wait a bit longer. Hondo is soon caught by Silva and some other Apaches. Because he speaks their language and shows no pain, he earns their respect. For death by torture they bring him to Vittoro, who finds in Hondo's possession a tintype of Johnny that he had taken from the dead Lowe. Suspecting that Hondo is Johnny's father, Vittoro allows him to fight Silva for his life. Hondo wins and spares Silva's life, but he is wounded. Vittoro brings him to the homestead, where Angie tells him that Hondo is indeed her man.

The Apaches leave the area before the cavalry arrives but not before Silva kills Hondo's dog Sam. Angie nurses Hondo back to health, and they finally admit their love for each other. Hondo, who will stay on as the boy's father, teaches Johnny the ways of the desert. In the meantime, the cavalry chases the Apaches and kills Vittoro, but many of the Indians escape. The unsuccessful troop returns to the homestead and asks Hondo to lead them back to the post. Silva, now chief of the warring Apaches, attacks the troop. Hondo leads them to an unequivocal victory and kills the ruthless Silva in hand-to-hand combat.

Langley, John P. *Contending Forces.* Pauline E. Hopkins. 1900.

Possessed of a sharp mind and a smooth manner, John P. Langley, a black lawyer, should be satisfied, but he wants more: money, power, and, most of all, the beautiful SAP-PHO CLARK.

Having grown up in poverty, an orphan and a beggar on the streets of a southern city, John is proud of how far he has come. Now a lawyer, he enjoys growing respect in the black community of Boston and is seen by white power brokers as a well-spoken but malleable representative of black political interests. John sees himself as both hardworking and lucky, and his engagement to Dora Smith, a solid member of the black bourgeoisie, only strengthens his position.

John is a frequent visitor to the boarding house of Dora's mother, where he enjoys the company of Dora, her brother WILL (SMITH), and, when she begins living in Boston, Sappho Clark. Not averse to being attracted to one woman although engaged to another, John does little to disguise his regard for Sappho or hide his jealousy when she responds not to him but to Will. John wants her, and the ruthless part of his nature tells him he will have her.

At a fundraiser, John sees his chance to inform Sappho of his feelings. Although a fortune-teller at the fundraiser has told John that he will lose everything he has if he ruthlessly pursues what he wants, he propositions Sappho and then remains undaunted by her rejection.

When a black man is lynched in the South on suspicion of raping a white woman, the temper of the Boston black community is inflamed. A white politician meets with John and asks his support in quelling any possible unrest. Ever mindful of advancement, John addresses a meeting of Boston blacks and advises that no action be taken. His position proves unpopular, while an impromptu speaker moves the crowd with his story of the rape of a family friend by a white man who was never punished. John notices that when this story is told, Sappho faints in the audience.

John decides to have his fortune read once more by the woman who was at the fundraiser. In the waiting room of her home, he hears a familiar voice speaking to the woman. It is Sappho Clark, whom John hears calling the woman "Aunt Sally." In a flash he realizes that the fortune-teller's fair-haired assistant must be Sappho's son. He files away the information, then goes to consult with the fortune-teller. His future, as she paints it, is dark. She shows him visions of others' happiness and a final strange picture of a snowy, desolate landscape.

Putting such information from his mind, John focuses once more on winning Sappho. His plans seem thwarted when he sees Will Smith and Sappho sharing a tender moment in a park on Easter Sunday. That night he steals into Sappho's room while the rest of the house is empty. Taking a wild guess, he says that he knows she is the woman in the story—the rape victim. He taunts her, convincing her that Will cannot love her if he knows she is not a virgin. Sappho is shaken but rejects John's request that she be his mistress.

The details surrounding Sappho's subsequent departure remain a mystery to most, as does Dora Smith's reason for breaking her engagement to John. After they learn that an ancestor of John's was responsible for the disgrace of one of Mrs. Smith's ancestors, the Smith family is sure that the broken engagement is for the best. Some time after the details of this seemingly long-dead case are known, John leaves for Alaska—but first he makes a will that leaves everything to a woman living in Bermuda discovered to be his mother. John hopes to find gold in the North, but instead tragedy stalks him. One by one his prospecting party succumbs to cold and starvation, and finally John dies, lamenting the damage he has done.

Lapham, Silas. *The Rise of Silas Lapham.* William Dean Howells. 1885.

Stocky, bearded, and vigorous, Silas Lapham lives the typical life of a late-nineteenth-century American businessman. Brought up by a poor farmer in rural Vermont who found mineral paint on his property shortly before his death, Silas has exploited the paint successfully enough to become one of Boston's richest men, owner of a sprawling mansion in Back Bay. By the novel's end, however, Lapham's fortunes and his view of the business world have drastically changed.

Lapham and his family have been less than successful

in conquering Boston society. When Tom Corey, of an old established family, seeks employment in the paint business, Silas proudly takes him on and is doubly pleased to find the young man apparently falling in love with his beautiful younger daughter Irene. The Coreys, socially impeccable but only modestly rich, grudgingly invite the Laphams to a dinner party so as not to appear snobbish.

There is much brouhaha in the Lapham household over their first social event. The evening ends with the usually abstemious Silas getting drunk and boasting about his paint and his wealth all night. Although disgusted by his employer's behavior, Tom masters his mortification and declares his love to Silas's daughter. But it is the elder daughter, Penelope, he loves, not Irene; Penelope sends him off, unwilling to wound her sister, and the whole household is dismayed.

Silas, meanwhile, runs into unexpected financial troubles. A former partner, Milton K. Rogers, comes to borrow money, and since Silas's puritanical wife Persis has always been worried that Silas had mistreated Rogers, Silas lends it. He lets Rogers involve him in various ill-advised stock and real estate deals. On top of this, the market for paint is slow, and some upstarts in West Virginia are producing comparable paint for a fraction of the price. Silas has insufficient funds to pay his creditors.

He has various options to save himself, but they are all problematical. His first option is to accept a lavish offer from his employee, Tom Corey, but because of the young man's unresolved alliance with his daughter, accepting the money is impossible. Silas next considers selling his unfinished and beloved new house. Even as he ponders this, however, he carelessly leaves some embers in the fireplace, and the house burns down, uninsured. Shouldering the loss, Silas heads for New York to buy out the young West Virginia paint barons. They prove unwilling to sell but are interested in the idea of a partnership if Silas can raise the money.

Rogers is his only remaining resource. Rogers presents some Englishmen who want to buy one of the worthless properties Silas bought from him. While Silas considers the dubious moral rectitude of selling to them, Rogers offers to buy back the property to sell to the Englishmen himself, arguing that since Silas had long ago "ruined" him, he owed him this favor. Persis, who has repeatedly argued this case herself and who is already upset because of Silas's suspicious dealings with his pretty secretary, cannot help him wrestle with this dilemma.

As it turns out, Silas never has to make the decision at all because the railroad claims the land for itself. Both Rogers and Silas are ruined. Persis's suspicions prove groundless when it is revealed that the secretary is the daughter of an old army buddy who died saving Silas's life.

Ultimately, Silas's business is bought out by the West Virginia partners, and Tom, having gained Penelope's consent at last, goes to work for them. Silas returns to his home in Vermont where he will remain in the paint business on a smaller scale by selling only his old high-quality line, the Persis Brand.

Larkin, Horace. *The Mammon of Unrighteousness.* Hjalmar H. Boyeson. 1891.

Calculating and ambitious, Horace Larkin develops his political designs in the town of Torryville, New York, where he enjoys the prestige of a wealthy family and law practice. Cynical Horace sees no profit in love or ideals because they will never advance a man in the world. He marries a rich woman to increase his power and finds himself beaten at his own game.

Horace lives with his wealthy uncle Obed, founder of the local college, his idealistic brother Aleck, and Obed's adopted daughter Gertrude. Horace and Aleck practice law together and join in the small social circle of the town. When Aleck takes offense at the corrupt workings of the Republican machine, Horace declares him a fool. The party machine is a means to an end, and he intends to use it. For Horace, ethical considerations are merely polite illusions. Horace secretly becomes engaged to the local reverend's daughter, Bella Robbins. Bella adores him. Then Bella's rich cousin from New York City, Kate Van Schaak, comes for an extended visit. Horace is impressed by her social acumen and fabulous wealth; she, in turn, seems excited by his unsentimental opinions. Horace ignores Bella and entertains Kate until her country visit is over. By shady means he receives the Republican nomination and is then elected to the state senate amid rumors of bribery. Aleck abhors his brother's campaign methods, and the two split permanently. In Albany, Horace makes a name for himself in the state senate as a shrewd operator.

Then Horace breaks his engagement to Bella and goes to New York City to court Kate. She is receptive despite his lack of urban social grace. Horace and Kate wed, and Horace quickly realizes that his wife has designs of her own. She wants Horace to be a diplomat; he wants to be a rugged American politician. Their marriage is a constant power struggle. Soon Horace learns that Bella is dying, and by now he sees the damning conceit of his behavior. At Bella's death he feels pangs of remorse.

Horace persuades Kate to move to Torryville where he will launch his campaign for United States Senate. Kate offends everyone with her supercilious behavior and in so doing almost jeopardizes his political prospects. In the eleventh hour, however, she gives Horace a massive campaign contribution that he uses to buy himself into office. Then he receives a letter from the President appointing him Ambassador to Russia. Horace is flattered and accepts, only to discover that Kate's father bought the appointment. As the novel closes, Horace finds himself outmaneuvered, the pawn of his own wife.

Larsen, Wolf. *The Sea Wolf.* Jack London. 1904.

Wolf Larsen, the violent and nihilistic captain of the Alaska-bound *Ghost*, rescues drowning writer HUMPHREY VAN WEYDEN off the coast of California. Larsen has no intention of seeing Humphrey safely to land; instead, he enslaves his guest by putting him to work as a cabin boy on the ship.

The captain's erratic behavior greatly unnerves Humphrey. On the one hand, this man of high intelligence is prone to indulging in philosophical discussions with Humphrey, whom he condescendingly refers to as "Hump." But Wolf is also capable of committing extremely violent acts against those who displease him.

Wolf ultimately goes too far when, after beating three men on the ship, he provokes a mutiny. He quells the revolt but is nearly killed in the process. Later, on reaching their ultimate destination in the Bering Sea, two of the leaders of the mutiny escape. While in pursuit of these men, the *Ghost* happens upon five survivors of a shipwreck. Wolf quickly maps out fates for these people similar to the one he plotted for Humphrey. Shortly after this rescue, Wolf catches up with the mutineers, and when they attempt to board the ship, he allows them to drown.

One day while on a seal hunt, the *Ghost* encounters the *Macedonia*, a ship piloted by Wolf's brother and rival, Death Larsen. Death causes the *Ghost* to lose a day's catch, and the enraged Wolf captures several of the *Macedonia*'s hunters in retaliation. Afterward, he attacks Maud Brewster, one of the survivors, and is only prevented from ravishing her by Humphrey's forceful intervention.

In the ensuing melee Wolf is stabbed and then suffers a seizure and blindness because of a brain tumor. Humphrey and Maud escape to a desert island, but the *Ghost* is shipwrecked and Wolf, whose crew has deserted him and joined forces with Death, encounters them again. Even as he is dying, Wolf makes a futile attempt to kill Humphrey. Then, thoroughly disabled, Wolf is held prisoner by Humphrey, who succeeds in making the *Ghost* seaworthy. Ultimately, Wolf dies, defiant to the end.

Lassiter. *Riders of the Purple Sage.* Zane Grey. 1912.

Lassiter is a notorious gunslinger whose very name inspires fear in the hearts of Mormons throughout Utah. A man whose past is shrouded in mystery, Lassiter symbolizes the search for justice outside of the workings of conventional law in the Old West. Believed to be a cruel and implacable enemy of Mormon men and their society, the gunman soon reveals himself to be a defender of the poor, the helpless, and women of all creeds.

At the beginning of the novel, Lassiter rides onto a ranch owned by JANE WITHERSTEEN, the daughter of the founder of the Mormon town of Cottonwoods, and interrupts a party of men preparing to whip a young Gentile rider named Bern Venters. When Jane vouches for the honesty of the young man and explains that he is merely being punished for having befriended her, Lassiter intercedes and defies the Mormons. They are unimpressed by his interference until he coils into a distinctive stance, hand near gun, and is recognized as the infamous Lassiter, Mormon killer.

Lassiter has come to Cottonwoods in search of the grave of a woman named Milly Erne who, unbeknownst to Jane, was the gunslinger's sister. Jane, obviously struck with dread at Lassiter's questions, shows him Milly's grave but refuses to tell him the identity of the Mormon proselytizer who stole the woman from her home and husband many years before. Openly defying the wishes of her churchmen, Jane nevertheless entreats Lassiter to remain at the ranch, explaining that she intends to stay his hand against her people if at all possible. He helps her as best he can but is ultimately powerless as the long arm of the Mormon Church, directed by the sinister Elder Tull, reaches out to gradually steal or destroy everything the woman possesses.

When Bern Venters goes in search of the herd of cattle that, at the instigation of the Mormons, was rustled by a gang led by the mysterious Masked Rider, Lassiter is left with the responsibility of protecting Jane, with whom he soon falls in love. He becomes increasingly unhappy as Jane, in the name of her religion, continues to keep secret the name of the man he hunts and persists in trying to convince him to put away his gun.

When it becomes obvious that Jane has nothing left to lose but her freedom to control her own life and to choose her own husband, Lassiter rides away with her on her prized horses, setting fire to Withersteen House before departing. Out in the sage, the two meet up with Venters and his newfound love, Bess, who, although disguised for most of her life as the Masked Rider, is really Elizabeth Erne, Milly Erne's innocent daughter. At this point Lassiter reveals the fact that he is Elizabeth's uncle Jim, whereupon Jane admits that her late father was the Mormon responsible for Milly's shame. Venters and Elizabeth take the swift horses in order to ride quickly out of Utah. Jane and Lassiter, pursued by Elder Tull and his men, make their way with difficulty toward Surprise Valley, a lush, secluded spot in Deception Pass that Venters had discovered while tracking the stolen cattle. Lassiter, who had intended to take Jane into the valley and close its entrance by rolling the great rock that hovers precariously at its mouth, loses his nerve at the last moment. It is Jane who makes the decision, telling him for the first time that she loves him. At her instruction, he topples the balancing rock, causing an avalanche that crushes their pursuers and encloses the two forever in their own private Eden.

Latour, Father Jean Marie. *Death Comes for the Archbishop.* Willa Cather. 1927.

Father Jean Marie Latour, Vicar Apostolic of New Mexico and Archbishop of Santa Fe, is a young priest sent out to "win the West" for Catholicism. A pioneer, a devout priest, and a dedicated scholar, the Archbishop dies from having lived life so fully.

Born in Auvergne, France, Latour is an aristocrat from a long line of scholarly and professional men. At the outset of the novel, which chronicles nearly forty years of his life, Latour is thirty-five years old, a man of strong constitution, and full of zeal and intelligence. In 1851, accompanied by his old friend, FATHER JOSEPH VAILLANT, he sets out for Santa Fe, seat of the new diocese created by the Mexican Cession.

When the two priests first arrive in Santa Fe, they find many of the old missions in ruins, the people unguided, and the priests lax in their discipline and religious observances. Among them is Padre Martínez, a priest of somewhat suspect moral standards who retains his church because of his strong organizational skills and loyal following. Latour, fastidious and conservative, believes that strict attention to doctrine is the best means through which to establish the order and authority of the Church. Yet he is often also impressed by the simple acts of faith of his people. His sometimes cold heart is warmed by the sight of Sada, a slave girl who risks her life to pray before a statue of the Virgin Mary, and by Jacinto, his guide, who stays awake through a dark snowy evening to guard one of the secrets of the Navajo faith.

From his early years in Santa Fe, Father Latour dreams of building a cathedral. One day while riding he discovers among the green hills of New Mexico one yellow hill that he determines will be the site of his cathedral. When he brings Father Vaillant to view the site, Valliant is unimpressed. Lacking Latour's refined taste and aesthetic training, he wonders why a poor missionary bishop should care so much about a building. When the Cathedral of Santa Fe is finally completed, it is one of the most beautiful sites in all the land and, not coincidentally, Father Latour's final resting place.

Death comes for the archbishop in 1889. Preferring to remain in Santa Fe rather than return to Auvergne, Latour retires to a small farm outside the city. There, in the waning years of his life, he enjoys to the full "that period of reflection which is the happiest conclusion to a life of action," a life like the one the archbishop has led.

Laura. "Flowering Judas." Katherine Anne Porter. 1965.

Laura does not have a known past save for her apparent Roman Catholic beliefs, which belong to a world she has since left. She is a woman attempting to live only in the present, through the revolutionary struggle she has joined since becoming a sort of unofficial missionary to Mexico. Her stoicism is incomplete, however; she worries about death and blames herself for the actions she has been unable to take.

While the narrative is framed by a single evening in Laura's upper room, Laura's thoughts transcend time to encapsulate her life. While she is thinking, Braggioni, a powerful, egotistical, revolutionary leader, sings to her. He would like to seduce her, so Laura must be firm and yet subtle in her rejection night after night.

Laura is known for her virginity and for her help in the revolutionary camps. She delivers messages, borrows money from one faction to help another, and ministers to those in prison, bringing them food, cigarettes, money, and sometimes narcotics to ease the pain of imprisonment. Braggioni, for his part, cannot understand why she is there, why she is so willing to be a pawn in someone else's struggle if she is not in love with some man. He feels that one day she will find that she is not as cold as she thinks, and he wishes he could be there to counsel her.

Although she had come to this situation with romantic preconceptions and now often wishes to flee, Laura continues to teach the Indian children in a nearby town and to regard her personal fate as "nothing, except as the testimony of a mental attitude." She is overly watchful when crossing the street and still sneaks into a Roman Catholic church to say the rosary, clinging to whatever past she still has within her. Laura is haunted by love: There is a boy in the town whom she unknowingly encouraged in his romantic notions for her, and she feels for Eugenio, a prisoner in the jail, who has just committed suicide. As she sits with Braggioni, she thinks of those two and feels envy for Mrs. Braggioni, who sits in her home and weeps as long as she wants about a very real wrong Braggioni visits upon her, whereas Laura remains haunted by a love that seems to be denied her.

When Braggioni leaves, Laura wishes only to be able to sleep and forget everything. Even this is denied her, however, when she has a terrifying dream in which Eugenio blames her for his death and accuses her of betraying her humanity; she denies it, but she is afraid to sleep again.

Laurence, Theodore "Laurie." *Little Women.* Louisa May Alcott. 1868–69.

Theodore "Laurie" Laurence is a frank, precocious youngster who plays a pivotal role in the lives of the four March sisters, his neighbors. Laurie is rescued from loneliness by the inimitable JOSEPHINE "JO" MARCH. In turn, he becomes a lifelong friend and champion of the March family.

The orphaned grandson of wealthy Mr. Laurence, Laurie spends his days being tutored by a young man named John Brooke and wistfully spying on the March family through their parlor window. One day the second oldest of the four March sisters, Jo, who is naturally outgoing and friendly, decides to conquer the boy next door. After a conversation with the girl from his window, Laurie invites Jo up to his rooms. He and Jo become instant friends, and soon visits and notes fly back and forth across the hedges that separate the modest March home from the splendid Laurence mansion. Although Laurie and Jo become best pals, the young boy also becomes friendly with the three other sisters, MARGARET "MEG" (MARCH), BETH (MARCH), and AMY (MARCH), and their mother Marmee, who treats him like an adopted son. Grandfather Laurence does not escape the March circle, and he adopts the four sisters in his turn.

While the two families have been fostering friendships, the Civil War has been raging. The March girls' father has volunteered as a chaplain for the Union Army. Word comes from Washington, D.C., that the chaplain has taken ill and Marmee should come immediately. The girls are left to be watched over by Mr. Laurence while Mr. Brooke accompanies Marmee to Washington.

Laurie attempts to keep up the spirits of the March clan, but illness at home brings more grief. Beth contracts scarlet fever and after days of illness appears to be near death. The two oldest siblings, Meg and Jo, have refused to notify their mother during most of Beth's illness but agree to do so at this point. To their delighted surprise, Laurie reveals that he has already sent a telegram to Marmee, and she arrives that very night. With Marmee's return, Beth's fever breaks, and the child begins her convalescence.

At this point Laurie takes the initiative once again. Aware that Brooke loves Meg, the mischievous and romantic lad forges a letter to Meg from Brooke expressing the tutor's feelings. Meg answers and is mortified when she realizes that Laurie wrote the note. The matter is forced into the open, however, and it is decided that Brooke and Meg will be married in three years.

Four years later, it is evident that Laurie, now a gallant college man, loves Jo and will eventually express his feelings to the boyish young woman. Unwilling to accept this state of affairs, Jo decides to spend the winter in New York City working as a governess. After his graduation and Jo's return from New York, Laurie asks her to marry him. Upon being rejected by her, he goes to Europe with his grandfather.

In Europe, Laurie leads a dissolute life and revels in self-pity. Near Christmas he meets Amy in Nice and is impressed by the young woman's poise and charm. Amy, unaware of Jo's rejection and distressed by Laurie's dissipation, expresses disappointment and disdain for the young man. Grieved by Amy's assessment, Laurie sheds his affectations and indifferent demeanor and promises to become a man worthy of respect and honor. Armed with this resolve, he returns to his grandfather in London. Soon after this encounter, Beth dies back in the United States, and Laurie returns to Nice to comfort Amy.

Within several months the March family receives a letter from the pair announcing their engagement. By the time they arrive in the States later that year, they are Mr. and Mrs. Theodore Laurence. Five years later Laurie and Amy are the parents of a golden-haired baby girl named for her aunt Beth.

Lawrence, Roger. *Watch and Ward.* Henry James. 1878.

Roger Lawrence is a wealthy Bostonian bachelor in search of a wife. Outwardly a "sound and solid" man, he nevertheless suffers from an "incurable personal shyness."

At the novel's opening, Roger is courting Isabel Morton, a well-bred New England woman who has repeatedly rejected his advances. After Roger refuses patronage to Mr. Lambert, an indebted businessman, Lambert shoots himself, leaving behind his twelve-year-old daughter NORA (LAMBERT). Feeling lonely and generous, Roger offers to adopt the child.

With Nora as his ward, Roger approaches life with a new sense of purpose. He takes it upon himself to educate Nora, teaching her to read and write and studying manuals of etiquette and moral behavior. To his surprise, Roger begins to take pleasure in trying to secure Nora's happiness. Two years later he finds himself attracted to her and dreams of shaping her into his ideal wife. In order to better educate Nora, Roger seeks worldly experience. While Nora is at boarding school, Roger travels in the West Indies and South America, where he has a brief tryst with a native woman, Teresa. However, finding that he is anxious not to miss any stage in Nora's development, he hastily returns to Boston.

Roger becomes increasingly possessive of Nora, especially with regard to her interaction with other men. He has an altercation with Nora's cousin, George Fenton, whom he rightly suspects of using Nora to get to her guardian's money. Roger is also jealous of his cousin, the Reverend Hubert Lawrence, who has also taken a personal interest in Nora. Roger agrees to send Nora to Europe with a newly widowed friend, Mrs. Isabel Keith, to further her development and remove her from the potentially corrupting influence of her male suitors.

Miserable in Nora's absence, Roger falls mysteriously ill. Upon her return, Nora nurses him back to health. When he is well enough, Roger recognizes the beautiful young lady that she has become and is finally ready to propose marriage to her. But when Nora learns that Roger intended her as his wife from the start, she feels shocked and betrayed, and flees to New York to see her cousin.

Although Nora urges him not to follow, Roger is devastated by her reaction and pursues her to New York. Nora has meanwhile discovered that Fenton was only after Roger's money and that Hubert was courting her while engaged to another woman. When Roger finally finds Nora, he succeeds in convincing her of his genuine affection for her. His desires are fulfilled when she freely returns with him to Boston, not as his ward but as his wife.

Leary, Macon. *The Accidental Tourist.* Anne Tyler. 1985.

A Baltimore-based author of travel books for business people who don't like to travel, Macon has led a practical, orderly life for forty-some years. His tidy existence was drastically altered a year before when his only child, twelve-year-old Ethan, was murdered by a holdup man at a fast-food restaurant. Seeing Macon continue his routine calmly, his wife Sarah wrongly believes that he was unaffected by their son's death, and she asks him for a divorce. Macon is upset by Sarah's request, as he was by Ethan's death, but he numbly agrees to it. Since Ethan's murder, Macon has ceased to expect any good from the world. When Sarah has gone, he distracts himself by setting up household routines.

Macon's routine is disrupted when his usual kennel refuses to board his dog, Edward, because the dog bit an attendant. He takes Edward to a new kennel, the Meow-Bow Animal Hospital. The attendant there is a tall, skinny woman, MURIEL PRITCHETT, whom Edward likes immediately. She is interested in Macon, and when he returns to pick up Edward, she invites him to call her sometime. Unwilling to engage in any relationship, business or otherwise, he declines her offers to train Edward or to come to dinner.

When Macon breaks his leg stepping on a skateboard he rigged up to help carry the laundry, he moves in with his unmarried sister Rose and two divorced brothers to recuperate. Edward's behavior becomes increasingly erratic, but Macon is loath to get rid of him, for he had been Ethan's dog. He decides to enlist Muriel's help as a dog trainer. In a series of lessons she is successful at teaching Edward to heel, sit, and lie down, all while telling Macon her life story. He learns that she has raised a sickly child by herself, supporting them through a series of odd jobs. Macon admires her determination and marvels at her zest for life. Still, he remains reluctant to allow Muriel to entangle herself in his life.

Although Macon believes that he has no room in his life for anyone as unpredictable as Muriel, he begins to spend more and more time with her. He doesn't love her, but he does love the way he is when he is with her. She doesn't view him as emotionless or narrow. Eventually Macon moves in with Muriel and her son Alexander. He feels content and likes knowing that he is not responsible for them. However, when he and Edward later rescue Alexander from the taunts of his classmates, Macon realizes that he is involved in the Pritchetts' lives.

Even so, his old life tugs at him. He sees Sarah at Rose's wedding, and her presence seems very natural to him. Muriel sees Sarah, too, and she begins to worry aloud that Macon will leave her. When Macon tells Muriel that he may never be ready for marriage, she gets angry. Returning from a business trip to Canada, Macon abruptly drives back to his old house to join Sarah, although he continues to think of Muriel.

On a business flight to Paris, Macon is astonished to find Muriel on the plane. He brushes her off, explaining that he has been married to Sarah forever and he can't change; however, he agrees to go out to dinner with her in Paris.

Although Macon is tempted to invite her to explore the countryside with him, he is prevented from doing so when he injures his back. He realizes how close he had come to falling in love with Muriel again, and he doesn't answer when she knocks on his door. A few days later Sarah shows up. She sees Muriel, and although she believes Macon when he tells her that Muriel followed him, she thinks he could have stopped her.

Lying awake one night, Macon realizes that he has always just allowed events in his life to happen to him. In the morning he tells Sarah he is leaving her for Muriel. Hobbling down the sidewalk, the formerly meticulous Macon abandons his suitcase. A French boy who resembles Ethan hails a cab for him, and, imagining Ethan growing older in heaven, Macon is comforted. Seeing Muriel ahead on the sidewalk, he tells the driver to stop for her.

Leath, Anna Summers. *The Reef.* Edith Wharton. 1912.

Anna Leath spends many years searching for the "magical bridge" from her sheltered, well-regulated existence to the challenges and difficulties of life. She builds a picture of life from art and literature, and despairs that such romantic, turbulent images remain so far from her protected home. But when she finally finds herself in a situation worthy of high tragedy, she is overwhelmed by her own naiveté and loses her sustaining self-assurance.

Born Anna Summers, she grows up in an extremely proper and self-conscious household on fashionable West Fifty-fifth Street in New York City. An introspective girl, Anna feels disconnected from the orderly Summers world and isolated in her imaginary romantic realm. She marvels at the apparent certitude with which other girls make their way through this world. Anna believes that passionate love will release her from this isolation and bridge the gap between the actual world and that of her imagination. When Anna meets GEORGE DARROW, a sophisticated young diplomat, she detects all the warning signs of love and yet cannot bring herself to respond warmly in Darrow's presence. She loses courage and backs down entirely when Darrow appears to be flirting with Kitty Mayne, a more adventurous member of Anna's circle.

In the wake of this unhappy episode with George Darrow, an older man whom Anna had met in Europe, Fraser Leath, appears in New York. A widower whose residence is in rural France, Leath strikes Anna as a distinctive person whose opinions are subversive compared to those of her parents. The promise of a home in France with a husband who is a painter and collector satisfies Anna's romantic hopes. After the initial joy of arriving at Givre, Anna makes the terrible discovery that Mr. Leath's revolutionary attitudes are merely theoretical. In truth, his judgments and convictions are just as conservative as those in practice on West Fifty-fifth Street. Resigned to life in another suffocating household, Anna finds comfort only in the company of her daughter Effie and her stepson Owen, who is equally unsuited to her husband's high standards of propriety.

After a decade of marriage to Fraser Leath, Anna is widowed. By chance she encounters George Darrow at a dinner at the American embassy in London, and they arrange to meet again. Although she maintains something of her old reserve, there is a new joy and easiness in their companionship. With the rebirth of her passion for Darrow and her desire to marry him, Anna experiences the intense feeling of which she has always known she was capable. After a few unpleasant delays, Darrow finally arrives at Givre to plan the wedding, and Anna is glowing with happiness.

The atmosphere at Givre begins to change subtly when Darrow is introduced to Effie's governess, SOPHY VINER, usually a charming and outgoing woman, and becomes suddenly withdrawn. When Anna questions Darrow about her, trying to determine if it would be appropriate to leave Effie in Sophy's hands while she and Darrow are away, he is curiously evasive. He learned nothing significant about her, he claims, although he knew Sophy vaguely when she was a secretary at Mrs. Murrett's, at whose house he sometimes dined in London. Tension at Givre increases when it emerges that Owen, Anna's stepson, intends to marry Sophy, and Darrow appears to have something against the marriage. Owen claims he has seen Darrow and Sophy speaking privately several times. Anna, who has been trying to ignore her terrifying suspicions, questions Darrow further, and he confesses to having seen Sophy briefly in Paris. It is Sophy who breaks down under Anna's interrogation, revealing the affair with Darrow in Paris and asserting her love for him. Sophy leaves Givre immediately.

Anna feels she has no choice but to dismiss Darrow. The completeness of her pain confirms the sense of her inexperience and the conviction that she has previously been protected from the exigencies of life. When Darrow pursues her to Paris and she accepts him again, Anna is secretly ashamed of her dependence on him. Shortly before the marriage, Anna tries to find Sophy, thinking that if she promises Sophy she will give up Darrow, she will have no choice but to do it. Sophy has already departed for India with Mrs. Murrett, however, and Anna returns to Darrow, despite her painful doubts.

Lee. *East of Eden.* John Steinbeck. 1952.

Lee is the erudite and loving caretaker for ADAM TRASK and his twin sons, ARON (TRASK) and CALEB (TRASK). For much of the novel Lee appears in traditional Chinese garments and speaks in a stereotypical pidgin English, to conform, as he tells one friend, to the standard expectations of most Caucasian Americans. Eventually, though, as his place in the family becomes more secure, Lee reveals his ability to think clearly and well, and he shows—much to the benefit of all concerned—that he has not only mastered the English language but has a loyal and noble heart as well.

Lee, who has other names but never divulges what they are, was born the son of two Chinese citizens who arrived in America to work for a five-year term. His mother sneaked aboard the transport ship in order to be with her new husband. She masqueraded as a man for as long as she was able, but eventually her secret was discovered, shortly before Lee's birth. The lonely and sex-starved men in the work camp immediately attacked her, resulting in the onset of labor and her death after the baby's birth. Lee was raised by his father and, in a surprisingly redemptive gesture, by his mother's rapists. Although Lee was eventually able to attend college, opportunities for members of his race were quite restricted. He became a domestic and dreamed of one day opening a bookshop in San Francisco's Chinatown.

When Adam Trask arrives from the East with his new and pregnant wife, Lee is hired to tend to their household. A direct animosity develops between Lee and CATHERINE AMES TRASK, who hates her husband and his plans for their future. Soon after the birth of their twin sons, Cathy shoots Adam in the shoulder as he tries to persuade her to stay with him and their sons. She leaves, and it falls upon Lee to care for the distraught and grief-stricken Adam and the newborn boys.

As the years pass, Lee serves as a pivotal figure for the Trasks, functioning as both mother and father since for the first ten years of the boys' lives their father remains absorbed in his personal loss. It wasn't until the boys were eleven months old that, with Lee's assistance, they were finally named. Lee's stalwart devotion to the Trask family grows as Caleb and Aron mature and depend more and more on his compassionate guidance. As Adam slowly emerges from his torpor, he decides to relocate to Salinas. He rents out his large ranch, which he has neglected since his wife's departure, and Lee moves with him to continue his duties in the new household.

Although Lee knows that Cathy lives in Salinas and runs its most notorious bordello, he never volunteers the information. When the Trasks, first Adam and then Caleb, discover the secret, Lee helps them cope with their ordeal by speaking about their feelings. Throughout their lives Lee's blending of ancient Chinese wisdom and American braggadocio enables him to function as both an astute listener and a genuine problem solver. Finally, as the boys grow, Lee decides to leave the Trasks to realize his long-cherished dream of owning a bookstore, but he returns within a week. His loneliness when living without the

Trasks reveals to him that he needs to stay with what has become his family.

After Lee returns, Adam's health begins to fail as he suffers a series of strokes. When news of Aron's death in World War I comes, Adam is overwhelmed and suffers a severe stroke. Lee, fearing his friend's death, urges Adam to forgive Caleb, whom he blames for Aron's death, and to give the young man his blessing. Adam does, and the novel closes with Lee and Caleb watching by his bedside as death appears imminent.

Lee, Madeleine. *Democracy.* Henry Adams. 1880.

Madeleine Lee is a self-contained, independent, but nonetheless vulnerable woman. Madeleine, almost pruriently fascinated by democracy and government, is determined "to touch with her own hand the massive machinery of society," politics.

As the novel opens, Madeleine is a thirty-year-old widow preparing to leave New York society life and take up residence in Washington, D.C. She quickly establishes a fashionable salon, frequented by some of the most eminent politicians in Washington: lobbyists, diplomats, ambassadors, and congressmen. Madeleine's political education develops through the forum of parlor conversations typical of the times.

The most conspicuous visitor to Madeleine's drawing room is Silas P. Ratcliffe, a powerful midwestern senator and leader of his party. Ratcliffe strikes Madeleine at once as one of the least trustworthy and one of the most vital members of the Washington elite, and her urgent desire to know "whether America is right or wrong" resolves into the question of whether Ratcliffe, the "Prairie Giant from Peoria," is telling the truth when he says he believes in the people.

Madeleine had initially intended to be an almost disembodied observer in Washington, coolly evaluating the mechanism of government from a removed position. Her involvement with Ratcliffe, however, embroils her in the world of political machinations that she had hoped to control from a distance. Ratcliffe manipulates a naive president into giving him a powerful cabinet post, then manipulates Madeleine into convincing him to accept it. The nearer Madeleine comes to him, the nearer she comes to the heart of government; and what had begun as an attempt to reform his wardrobe ends as a trial of her moral integrity.

Ratcliffe finally proposes marriage to her. As she wavers, her friend, the lawyer John Carrington, communicates to her the information that Ratcliffe is a far more corrupt politician than she had imagined. She knew he had been involved in fixing elections; now she learns that he has taken huge payoffs from contractors and lobbyists. The knowledge causes her to acknowledge her own compromises and her own corruption, and in despair she flees Washington to travel in Egypt, longing, as she says, "to

live in the Great Pyramid and look out forever at the polar star!"

Lee, William. *Junky; Queer; Naked Lunch.* William Seward Burroughs. 1953; 1985; 1959.

William "Bill" Lee narrates the autobiographical novels *Junky* and *Queer* as well as the bizarre and surrealistic *Naked Lunch*. The narrator, who is referred to variously as William and Bill, is most frequently called Lee.

Lee's life is consumed by heroin and morphine addiction. The high the drugs provide, and the low that necessarily follows, become for Lee a way of life—and nearly death. Lee is first introduced to morphine, the drug from which heroin is derived, when a black marketeer asks him to sell some for him. Sampling the drug himself, Lee finds the experience both pleasurable and fearful, sending alternating waves of relaxation and terror through his body. He sells most of the morphine he has but keeps some for himself and continues to buy more to feed a quickly growing habit.

Using and dealing "junk" introduces Lee to a whole New York City subculture, to which he quickly adapts. His friends—Subway Mike, Irish, and George the Greek—teach him how to earn a living by dealing marijuana and stealing from drunks. As he starts to shoot up every day, several times a day, William begins to notice dramatic changes in himself. Heroin and morphine—buying it, keeping his supplies hidden from his user friends, and using it himself—become the central feature of his life. To support his nine-dollar-a-day habit, he does "lush work," stealing from drunks on the subway, with his friend Ray.

Eventually, after being arrested a number of times, Lee flees the United States and settles in Mexico where he continues his drug use. In Mexico City he establishes a fairly steady sexual relationship with a young man, but as he resumes taking drugs, his only physical desire is for morphine and heroin. Once again Lee attempts to give up junk, but the cure he tries—using tequila and benzedrine instead of morphine and heroin—only establishes an alcohol dependency that leads to a near-fatal case of uremic poisoning. Several cures and relapses later, Lee is still in Mexico, now off morphine and all its derivatives but experimenting with peyote and planning a trip to South America to sample another drug, Yage.

Naked Lunch, a grotesque nightmare of narcotic addiction, dehumanizing sex, disease, cannibalism, fascism, and deformations of the human body, is presented through the shifting persona of Bill Lee. The lines between Lee, who sometimes refers to himself in the third person, and the author, Burroughs, are deliberately blurred. In a work that extends the concept of addiction to those who hunger for control over other people, the story of Bill Lee reveals the naked reality of what is brutal and obscene in American society.

The novel begins with Lee in New York City disposing of his heroin paraphernalia in a Washington Square subway station, then jumping on an uptown subway train to escape a pursuing narcotics agent. With his friend Gains he travels to Chicago, New Orleans, and St. Louis, buying drugs. Lee inhabits a paranoid world in which addict-informants give each other "hot shots" of strychnine in revenge and in which suppliers always come late to make addicts feel their desperate need for drugs. Lee's paranoia gives rise to a series of fantasies in which he works for a mysterious organization called Islam Incorporated, located in Freeland, a welfare state "given over to free love and continual bathing." Here he engages the services of DR. BENWAY, head of the Reconditioning Center.

Lee imagines a series of grotesque scenarios based on his stays in detoxification wards and on his experiences in various foreign locales, especially Mexico City and Tangiers. He describes the Blackmeat Market where addicts seek out the flesh of giant black centipedes for a fix. He supplies heroin to the President by homosexual contacts, what he calls the President's "Oblique Addiction." The paranoia of the homosexual and narcotic underworlds converges in the Interzone, a horrifying place where the human form is able to dissolve into protoplasm and reform into shapes sprouting eyes, mouths, multiple rectums, and genitalia. In the Interzone, four parties contend for control: the Liquefactionists, who want to liquefy all human forms; the Divisionists, who spread their bodies like amoebae; the Senders, who broadcast their thoughts; and the Factualists, who champion human autonomy over the other three parties.

The realistic strand of the novels reappears when Lee, in New York City, escapes the two narcotic agents Hauser and O'Brien by squirting alcohol from a syringe into their eyes. Lee later travels to South America in search of sex and Yage, a hallucinogenic vine the Indians believe enables time travel. The novel ends with a disjointed series of violent incidents in South America.

Legree, Simon. *Uncle Tom's Cabin* or, *Life among the Lowly.* Harriet Beecher Stowe. 1852.

Simon Legree, the final master and murderer of the novel's title character, is an evil man but also a haunted one.

Taking after his ill-humored father rather than his Christian mother, Legree left New England for a life at sea. He returned home only once and on that visit was nearly persuaded by his mother that the life he had chosen was wrong. Sin had so penetrated his soul, however, that he resisted and, cursing her, threw his mother to the floor. Much later, after he returned to his dissolute life, he received a letter telling of her death. Enclosed with the letter was a lock of her pale blond hair, which the guilt-ridden Legree threw into a fire. But even as the flames engulfed

the lock, the memory of his mother's selfless love seemed to burn itself into his consciousness.

Years later as the prosperous owner of a southern plantation, Legree seems not to have absorbed any of the gentleness his mother labored to instill in him. He savagely beats his slaves, not caring whether they live long or die young as long as they work hard. He seems on familiar terms with his two slave foremen, Sambo and Quimbo, but instigates an active hatred between them so they will direct their frustrations toward each other rather than at him. Legree mistreats all his slaves, but Cassy, his concubine, is his special victim.

Into this scene is introduced UNCLE TOM, whom Legree has purchased in a New Orleans slave auction. Legree judges correctly that Tom's intelligence and strength will make him a good laborer, but he finds Tom's religiosity disturbing. Although Tom works as hard as any of the other slaves, his refusal to agree that Legree owns his soul as well as his body infuriates the slave owner. He has Tom beaten on more than one occasion. After one beating, Sambo brings Legree a lock of hair that Tom held in a sack hanging around his neck. Although the hair belongs to a girl whose father had owned Tom, it conjures up in Legree's mind the image of his mother's hair burning in the fire.

While Legree has been trying to break Tom, Cassy has been planning to escape with Emmeline, a woman Legree purchased to become his new mistress. Playing on Legree's superstitions, Cassy is able to convince him that the garret of the house is haunted. She and Emmeline hide there without fear of detection until the opportunity arises for them to leave the plantation grounds. When the disappearance of the two women is discovered, Legree is furious. Surmising correctly that Tom knows of their plan, he confronts the slave, then beats him to death when he refuses to betray the women.

One night soon after Tom's death, Legree sees a vision of a shroud-draped figure beckoning to him. Although it is only Cassy trying to frighten Legree in order to give the women a chance to escape the house, the man is terrified. Not just this vision but all the evil he has perpetrated begins to haunt him. Drinking more and more heavily to cloud his mind to such visions, Legree sinks into drunkenness, insanity, and finally death.

Lennox, Mary. *The Secret Garden.* Frances Hodgson Burnett. 1911.

Mary Lennox, a sour young English girl brought up in India, discovers the many secrets of a Yorkshire mansion. When Mary's parents die in a cholera epidemic, she is forgotten by everyone and spends hours in the deserted bungalow. She is finally discovered by two British military officers and taken to her uncle's estate in Yorkshire, called Misselthwaite Manor.

The dismal castle seems an appropriate place for this

spoiled, imperious girl who expects everyone to obey her without question as her Indian servant did. Her uncle, Archibald Craven, travels often to forget the death of his wife ten years before, and he leaves Mary in the care of the maids who merely feed her and allow her to do as she pleases. Finding nothing amusing in the house, Mary wanders in the many orchards and gardens. Her maid, Martha, tells her about the locked garden that had been Mrs. Craven's favorite, and Mary wonders if she can find it.

On one of her walks Mary encounters Ben Weatherstaff, an old gardener as bad-tempered as herself. Keeping Ben company is a curious robin, whom even Mary finds enchanting. Several days later Mary follows the robin, who leads her to the key of the secret garden, half-buried in the dirt. Pushing aside some vines, Mary uncovers the door and explores the garden, examining everything to see if it might still grow.

The maid, Martha, has entertained Mary with tales about her home, a cottage on the moor overflowing with fourteen children and presided over by her wise mother, Susan Sowerby. Martha's brother, DICKON (SOWERBY), spends his days on the moor, befriending the animals. Deciding to let someone else in on her secret, Mary writes to Dickon for help in revitalizing the garden. Dickon escorts her through the tangled growth, explaining how to care for each type of plant, and they arrange to meet daily to tend to them.

On a rainy day when Mary is unable to go outside, she decides to explore the house with its hundred locked rooms. Following a mysterious noise that sounds like crying, she discovers a somber room with a frail boy weeping in bed. He introduces himself as COLIN CRAVEN, Mr. Craven's son, and explains that he has been confined to bed since infancy and that if he lives, he will certainly be a hunchback like his father. Although Colin clearly has an aversion to people, he asks Mary to stay so that she can tell him stories about India and the garden.

Like Mary, Colin feels stronger and happier when he begins making daily visits to the garden. With Dickon, they plan ways to keep Colin's recovery a secret so that he can surprise his father when he returns from his latest trip. No longer sickly and "contrary," Mary pours all her newfound energy into helping Colin get well. They do exercises together and run races. Both children are rewarded when Mr. Craven comes home and Colin, to surprise him, bursts through the door of the garden into his father's arms.

Le Noir, Capitola "Cap." *The Hidden Hand: Or, Capitola the Madcap.* E.D.E.N. Southworth. 1888.

Capitola "Cap" Le Noir's father, Eugene Le Noir, is killed before her birth by his brother Gabriel, who is determined to secure for himself Eugene's fabulously wealthy estate, Hidden Hand. Cap herself narrowly escapes being murdered by Gabriel at birth. Her mother's midwife,

Nancy Grewell, saves her by telling Gabriel that the infant's stillborn twin was his brother's only heir. The living child, Cap, she claims as her own daughter.

Suspicious but temporarily convinced, Gabriel does not kill the child; instead, he engages Black Donald, an evil bandit, to sell both the midwife and Cap into slavery. Cap and Nancy manage to escape during a shipwreck and are rescued by a sailor, Herbert Grayson, and taken to New York. Nancy works there for ten years, then finally returns to Virginia and tells her story to a local landholder, Major Ira Warfield, before she dies.

Thus bereft of family and friends at the age of ten, Cap tries to find work in New York but is told that only boys will be employed. After receiving threats of sexual abuse from various men and being reduced to penury, she disguises herself as a boy and easily finds work. One day she is arrested for impersonating a male, but Major Warfield is present at the trial and identifies Cap. He makes her his ward and takes her back to Virginia to live with him.

When Gabriel Le Noir learns that his brother's heir is alive and living next door to him, he engages Black Donald to kill her. Black Donald disguises himself as a sailor with foreign goods for sale and thus gains entry to Cap's house, but he reveals his identity. Capitola bravely tries to detain him, and he falls in love with her for her pluck and bravery. She cleverly manages to evade Black Donald—who has decided to kidnap and marry her rather than kill her—by locking three of his men in a room.

The son of Gabriel Le Noir, Craven Le Noir, also falls in love with Cap, but when she rejects his proffered love, he is insulted and begins a vicious slander campaign against her. She responds by challenging him to a duel and shooting him. He gives what he thinks is a deathbed confession of her innocence, only to be humiliated by learning that she has shot him with split peas and he is not going to die after all.

Black Donald makes another attempt to abduct Cap and sneaks back into her room, but she disarms him by pretending to be glad to see him. She offers him dinner, placing his chair over a concealed trap door in her room, and drops him down into a deep pit. He survives, only to be condemned to death at his trial. Cap helps him escape on the condition that he reform himself and live an honest life.

It turns out that Cap's mother was kept prisoner in Gabriel Le Noir's home until Cap's curiosity about her neighbors caused Le Noir to confine her in an insane asylum. After Le Noir's death during the Mexican War, Capitola is finally reunited with her mother, marries Herbert Grayson, and goes to live with her family at Hidden Hand.

Lenox, John. *David Harum.* Edward Noyes Westcott. 1900.

John Lenox, a mild-mannered young man who suffers from his relatively weak financial standing, continually feels the limits drawn for him by his lack of a profession. Coming home from a two-year sojourn in Europe, during which he acquired the manners of a well-reared middle-class man in the late nineteenth century, John is relieved to be in America again and anxious to pursue a career. He is undecided, however, as to where his professional interests lie, but as his life unfolds and events happen in his favor, John finds eventual success as a small-town banker and family man.

On the ship to America, John runs into Mary Blake, an old childhood acquaintance. After several polite social encounters, John and Mary grow fond of each other but refrain from proclaiming their mutual attraction. The expected romantic conclusion to their meeting never happens, however, because the journey ends and the two must go their separate ways. After a series of unreceived letters and missed engagements, John is convinced that the nascent affair will never bear fruit, due in part to his lack of a profession. Soon after, John's father dies, leaving him with a meager inheritance and no family relations. A friend of his father's, General Wolsey, suggests that he apply for a position with David Harum, an acquaintance of his. John has little choice but to accept the offer.

David, a gregarious and down-to-earth banker in the small town of Homeville in upstate New York, hires John as his accountant. David takes John under his wing and tries to win his confidence and respect with his generosity and bits of folksy wisdom. John is tempted at first to believe the rumor that David is nothing more than an avaricious creditor and a wily horse trader, but David manages to cure John of this false impression when, one Christmas, he generously destroys the outstanding mortgage of a widow named Mrs. Cullom. Mrs. Cullom's deceased husband once paid for the young David to attend the circus, and the banker has never forgotten the favor.

Several years pass, during which John learns to manage the affairs of the bank. He moves in with David and his sister, and becomes like a son to them. But although he is satisfied with his success at the bank, John feels he cannot start a family without a more impressive financial standing. His romantic interest in one of the town's summer residents, Claricy Verjoos, comes to naught because John's professional status is below the Verjoos family requirements for a son-in-law.

David Harum senses John's predicament. On an informed tip he suggests that John invest all his savings in pork stock, and John agrees. At first the stock drops, and it looks as though he will have to sell at a loss; but there is a sudden run on pork, and John profits tremendously. Still, although finally a wealthy man, John is depressed because Claricy Verjoos became engaged to another man. John's health deteriorates, and he decides to travel to Europe to recuperate.

By sheer coincidence Mary Blake is on the very same ship. John assumes she is traveling with her husband. He corners her, expresses his regret at having lost touch with her, and confesses that his romantic feelings for her have remained. Mary, realizing that John thinks she is traveling with her husband, tells him she is not married; she is simply traveling under the name of the ticket she purchased secondhand. She expresses a similar disappointment over their aborted affair. John proposes and she accepts. They return to Homeville to enjoy a prosperous life together, and when David Harum dies, John inherits the successful bank.

Lenox, Susan. *Susan Lenox: Her Fall and Rise.* David Graham Phillips. 1917.

When Susan Lenox, illegitimate daughter of Lorella Lenox, is orphaned, her aunt Fanny takes her in. A happy and charming infant, she grows up to be a great beauty with a strong sense of individual morality; nevertheless, she must endure great difficulties and hardships before finding a secure place in the world. At sixteen, she learns of her origins from her jealous cousin Ruth. Acutely conscious of her own inferior looks, Ruth jeers at Susan's lack of social respectability. Guileless about sex and hopelessly in love with a local boy named Sam Wright, Susan leads her uncle to believe she has "disgraced" the family when she has not. Hypocritically, her family and her small hometown community conclude that "she's just like her mother," and Susan is driven out of town. As she leaves town, Susan meets RODERICK SPENSER, a journalist, who gives her money for her journey.

Susan decides that she wants to become a showboat actress. Once on board the showboat, she comes into contact with an apparently "low" set of characters, but the humanity and kindness of the theater company members contradict the rough exterior they project. A success on account of her beauty and singing talent, Susan performs a few things, and the company manager, Robert Burlingham, promises her a great theatrical future. Once grounded, however, the company disbands and Burlingham collapses from typhoid. Susan, ever loyal, and insistent that he not be condemned to the public hospital, resorts to prostitution in order to raise money for his medical bills. His death propels her to factory work and life in a slum, where she can only attempt to remain "respectable" and honest. After a year of drudgery, she and her friend Etta turn once more to prostitution. Etta meets a husband, and Susan simply saves her money.

Reunited with Roderick Spenser—ostensibly to repay him the money she lent him years back—Susan agrees to accompany him to New York where he plans to pursue a career as a playwright. Once there, Roderick quickly reveals his flaws, especially his manic possessiveness. Knowing Susan's past, he relies on her virtues and loyalty but constantly doubts her intentions. He also will not complete any plays and begins to drink.

When she finally leaves Roderick, Susan descends to

the Lower East Side slums, drinking, using opium, and working as a prostitute for the rising king of the underworld, Freddie Palmer. Again she is resurrected by improbable means: An enigmatic playwright, ROBERT BRENT, spies Susan in a restaurant and adopts her as a protégé. He pledges to turn her into a "real" actress. Capricious and remote, Brent, with whom Susan falls in love, gives her no encouragement so that when Freddie returns to offer her a life of comfort—he has arranged a respectable cover for his lucrative business—she accepts. They move abroad and live in polite society.

Now in her twenties, Susan, with her innate good taste and compelling beauty, is an immediate social success. She lends Freddie the credibility he desires. However, Brent reappears, impatient to get her back to acting and fully believing in her potential for greatness. Susan is no longer able to resist her love for Brent, but just as she is leaving Freddie, news arrives of Brent's murder in New York by thieves—Freddie's goons. Brent has left Susan all his money. Economically emancipated at last and assured by existing papers of Brent's secret love for her, Susan settles in New York, her "City of the Sun," a brilliant actress, friendless and alone.

Leonard, Bruno. *The Unpossessed.* Tess Slesinger. 1934.

Dr. Bruno Leonard is the reluctant leader of a group of friends and students planning to start a socialist magazine. The group cannot decide on the magazine's purpose, and as Bruno watches them struggle, he becomes increasingly disillusioned with the group and their cause. Finally, at a party to launch the magazine, Bruno denounces it, telling the young people to get out before they become as lost as the adults.

The respected professor of a group of college students known as the Black Sheep, Bruno had himself been a Black Sheep twelve years before on the same campus, along with his friends Miles Flinders and Jeffrey Blake. As "angry pacifists" the three of them had ignited the campus, but Bruno, because of his ethnic background, was blamed for their protests. As a German Jew, Bruno feels that he constantly wavers between two worlds: the ordinary level of life and a "subterranean Jew-level." As a consequence he sees so many sides to every issue that he is invariably unable to act. But Bruno differs from the others in more areas than ethnicity. They are interested in launching a magazine to awaken people to the plight of the working class, whereas Bruno is more interested in the "idea" than its realization.

Bruno's depression is compounded when he receives a cable from his cousin Elizabeth in Paris telling him that she may be getting married. Upset by the thought of her wedding, Bruno is typically torn by conflicting impulses: to stop her or do nothing. When Bruno sends Elizabeth a cable and she wires back that she is coming home, he is at once happy and worried about her arrival. As a result of Bruno's past advice that Elizabeth be ruthless in her relations with men, she has embarked on a series of empty relationships, always leaving the men before they leave her.

In the days before Elizabeth's arrival Bruno is consumed with work for the magazine. He frequently feels old and distanced from the students, but he is close to one, Emmett Middleton, a quiet, sad boy whose attachment to Bruno is extreme. Emmett's wealthy mother will provide much of the magazine's budget.

Bruno brings Emmett along with him to meet Elizabeth's ship. Because Emmett is around, Bruno is saved from having to speak to Elizabeth. In an effort to hurt him, Elizabeth brings up her ex-fiancé, and they discuss love. When Bruno admits that he is mystified by women, Elizabeth reminds him of all the times he urged her to play the "man's game." He admits that men prefer a woman who is weaker. When she tells him he is talking about Emmett, Bruno feels torn between the two of them.

The three return together to the Black Sheep's fundraising party, where Bruno is to deliver a speech. When he opens the envelope, he discovers that the jealous Emmett has torn his speech into tiny pieces. Meanwhile, while watching him, Elizabeth realizes she has never loved anyone but Bruno.

In a surprise move, Bruno denounces the magazine founders by saying that they have never seen a communist and do not understand the cause they supposedly support. He tells them they have become nothing but fence straddlers, and he urges the young people to abandon the cause before they become as lost as he and his friends. However, the partygoers soon become distracted, and Bruno finds himself yelling at an indifferent, fast-dispersing crowd. Only Elizabeth is watching, and as the book draws to a close, she tears herself away from the dance floor in order to run after Bruno.

Leonard, Ellie. "Home Is Where You Hang Your Childhood." Leane Zugsmith. 1937.

Ellie Leonard is the twelve-year-old girl who learns more about being an adult than she could ever have wanted to during a brief family crisis.

As the story begins, Ellie is riding home on the bus thinking about her favorite things. She is fond of her father and her only sister, six-year-old Gin. She is proud that she is now attending high school, that she can stay up until nine on weekday evenings, and that her thirteenth birthday is less than two months away. Enamored with a sixteen-year-old boy named Roy Carmody, Ellie makes a habit of getting off the bus a block early every day after school so that she can pass by his house. As she walks by on this particular day, she remembers being rendered speechless the one time he took her to a dancing class, and she is rather thankful that the boy does not make an appearance.

Shortly after Ellie arrives home, Gin's governess, Miss Purdy, enters breathlessly, asking whether Ellie's mother has returned with Gin. Mrs. Leonard, who does not live with her children and estranged husband, had convinced the governess to meet her with Gin at a department store, where they became separated. Ellie attempts to reassure Miss Purdy but silently wonders whether her mother has decided to keep her sister permanently. Waiting for her father to come home, Ellie dreamily admires the sapphire ring her mother has left as a gift, then begins to feel guilty for thinking of Roy Carmody instead of her family.

When Mr. Leonard arrives home, he is furious; Ellie is disturbed when he exclaims that his wife, being suicidal herself, has probably already killed Gin. Anxiously, Ellie suggests that the mother and child might be visiting friends in the city. They telephone all the people they know, with no success. Ellie, once again made nervous by her father's comments about the mental health of her mother, suggests that Mrs. Leonard may have asked them not to reveal her whereabouts. Mr. Leonard proceeds to take Ellie out without an umbrella into the rainy night to check at each friend's home.

While riding on the streetcar toward their first destination, they encounter Roy Carmody; he is friendly, but Ellie remains tongue-tied and finally bursts into tears. After a long evening of searching for her mother and sister, they return home cold, tired, and hungry. In the morning, a telegram arrives stating that Mrs. Leonard and Gin were at Grandmother White's in Cleveland. Ellie, relieved, attempts to be cheerful, but her father is still gloomy; while she packs a bag for his trip to Cleveland to retrieve Gin, he tells her that her mother took the six-year-old in order to get more alimony. Once the settlement is changed, she will sign a paper promising never to abduct either of the children again.

After her father leaves, Ellie goes out roller-skating and is heading automatically toward Roy Carmody's house when she suddenly remembers the previous night's encounter. Telling herself that she can never look him in the face again, she takes off her skates and walks home.

Leroy, Iola. *Iola Leroy, or Shadows Uplifted.* F.E.W. Harper. 1892.

In the waning days of the Civil War, in a Union camp in the soon-to-be-defeated South, Iola Leroy works as a nurse. The past few months of Iola's life have been marked by heartbreak and upheaval, and her future is far from certain.

The children of wealthy Southern parents, Iola and her brother Harry had lived a life of ease and privilege. Sent to a New England academy, Iola was just completing her schooling when her life was shattered by the death of her father. It was then that Iola discovered the truth about her heritage: Despite her fair skin, blue eyes, and blond hair, she was black. Her white father had married her mother Marie after freeing her from slavery, and knowing that the fact of their race would be a burden, he never told his children about their heritage. Mr. Leroy's death spelled the end of his protection and of Iola's illusions. The scheming cousin of Iola's father found an illegality in the manumission of Marie Leroy and, seizing Mr. Leroy's estate, contrived to throw Marie, Iola, and Harry into slavery. While Harry was able to escape his relative's clutches, Marie and Iola were separated and lost their freedom.

Although a series of masters tried to rape her, Iola has been rescued by the Union Army with her virginity intact. As a nurse, Iola gains the love and respect of Northern soldiers and former slaves alike. One man, Dr. Gresham, falls in love with her and asks her to marry him. Although she appreciates his attentions, she does not love him. She also feels a duty, now that she knows she is black, to work with the former slaves, and marriage to a white Northerner would frustrate that plan. Declining his offer, Iola decides instead to teach and to search for her mother and brother.

Another former slave in the camp, Robert Anderson, also hopes to search for the relatives from whom he has been separated. When he learns that the spiritual he has heard Iola sing was taught to her by her mother, he begins to suspect that Iola's mother Marie is his sister. They resolve to search together for Marie, Harry, and Robert's mother Harriet. While they send out inquiries on their missing relatives, Iola teaches and Robert starts a business in the North.

Returning to the town from which Robert had escaped years before, Iola and her supposed uncle learn from former slaves that a revival meeting will be held nearby. Because they suspect that the devoutly religious Harriet may be in attendance, they journey to the meeting, where Robert is indeed reunited with his mother. Robert returns north with Harriet, and Iola travels farther south to continue her own search.

Iola is eventually reunited with her brother, who has previously been located by Marie. Delighted to find Harry and her mother so quickly, Iola brings even more joyous news when she tells Marie about Robert and Harriet. Iola writes to Robert, and he and Harriet arrive quickly.

Reunited with her family, Iola is happy. One day she encounters another person whose image has endured in her memory: Dr. Gresham. His love for her has not diminished, but neither has Iola's resolve to serve her race. She rejects him once again. Soon another doctor, Dr. Latimer, appears to be captivated by Iola. Like Iola, Latimer is a fair-skinned black who, although he could easily "pass for white," has decided instead to live as a black man with all the hardships that entails. Iola's respect for him quickly grows into love, and they marry, determined to devote their lives to each other and to the service of their people.

Lesche, Eugene. "Rejuvenation Through Joy." Langston Hughes. 1934.

Eugene Lesche is a somewhat unscrupulous manipulator of New York's upper class. He has had a number of various careers since his birth in South Bend, Indiana: a member of a circus called "The Great Roman Chariot Races"; a model for various painters; and, largely due to the physical appeal he had for his wealthy female clientele, a successful swimming instructor. Eventually he allies himself with Sol, a man who owns a gym in Hollywood and gives Eugene a position as gigolo and swimming teacher. After becoming bored with this work, however, the two are inspired to establish a "colony" at which wealthy women will stay to improve themselves—and pay exorbitant fees to do so.

As a theme for the self-improvement program, Eugene settles on the notion of a return to the primitive. He and Sol travel to New York where Eugene looks for ways to incorporate the rhythms of Harlem jazz and blues with the rhetoric he needs to extort money from the disaffected rich. Soon he opens a six-week lecture series on various topics, a program so successful that he and Sol immediately begin to establish the Colony. Within weeks they hire a black band and a blues singer, arrange to have a mansion in Westchester redone to emphasize the primitive, and become the talk of the Fifth Avenue and Park Avenue crowds. The Colony, with its daily movement sessions featuring the sultry dance of the blues singer as backup to Eugene's inspirational "sermons," is an immediate success.

All goes well until Eugene begins to come under the sway of the wealth he is amassing. As a money-making scheme, he establishes private sessions wherein he allows the clients, mostly women, to pour out their hearts in a private audience. As Sol had warned him, this practice gives rise to great dissension among clients, chiefly in the form of jealousy. The "joyous" spirit of the Colony begins to deteriorate as the clients compete among themselves for Eugene's attention. Eugene soon realizes that the private sessions must stop, but by then the damage has been done. Several clients leave, and there is an outcry from the media about activities at the Colony.

Adding to Eugene's troubles is a growing problem in his band. The singer, who has a relationship with the drummer, becomes violently angry at her lover as he begins to stay away nights. One morning he arrives late, and when he settles down at his drums, she pulls out a gun and shoots him. Pandemonium ensues, and in the fray, some of the clients seize the gun, thinking that the singer was trying to kill Eugene. More shots ring out; Sol manages to get the gun away from the women who are fighting

over it, and by the time all settles down, it is clear that Eugene has vanished. While his disappearance elicits snide attacks from most of the media, the suggestion is also made that Eugene had the last laugh in the joke he played on the upper class: According to some, his primitivism was based on the fact that he had been passing for white.

Leslie, Hope. *Hope Leslie*. Catherine Maria Sedgwick. 1827.

Hope Leslie arrives in Massachusetts as a very young girl with her widowed mother, her younger sister Faith, an aunt, and a tutor, Master Craddock. A fervent Puritan always hindered by her family's opposition to the sect, Hope's mother is determined, after the deaths of her husband and father, to join the flock in New England. But she dies en route and in her will leaves her daughters in the care of William Fletcher, her cousin, whom she had loved and would have married had her family not interfered.

Fletcher meets the girls and their companions in Boston. Accompanied by her aunt and an Indian servant boy, Oneco, Faith is sent to the Fletcher home in Springfield. Fletcher keeps Hope and her tutor with him while he is detained in Boston. But before Fletcher, Hope, and Master Craddock arrive in Springfield, Indians attack the Fletcher home. The attack is led by Mononotto, an Indian chief whose children, Oneco and MAGAWISCA, have been servants in the Fletcher home since a brutal attack on his tribe by the colonists. In revenge, the chief murders Fletcher's wife and all but one of his children and kidnaps his son Everell and Faith Leslie. Everell escapes with the help of Magawisca, who has grown fond of the white boy during her captivity.

Some time later Everell is sent to school in England, and William Fletcher, deprived of this natural family, grows to love his adopted daughter dearly. Hope Leslie exudes charm and intelligence, although her independence often brings her into conflict with her community. When her tutor is bitten by a poisonous snake, Hope enlists the help of an old Indian woman, Nelema. Craddock recovers, but the rumor has been spread that Nelema practiced witchcraft on the dying man, and the old woman is imprisoned. Unable to see Nelema put to death, Hope secretly frees her. The incident raises Fletcher's suspicions that Hope leads too wild an existence in the wilderness of Springfield, and he arranges for her to live in Boston with the family of Governor Winthrop.

In Boston, Hope and her new friend Esther Downing meet Everell, newly returned from England. Hope suspects that something has passed between Esther and Everell, and, indeed, Esther tells her that in a moment of dire illness she once confessed her love for the boy. Although she is herself deeply in love with Everell, Hope resolves the relationship between her two friends. Meanwhile, a mysterious stranger, Sir Philip Gardiner, shows interest in Hope, but she does not return his affections.

Before her escape, Nelema had promised that Hope would see her sister Faith. Now Magawisca appears to fulfill that promise. In a secret meeting with the Indian girl, Hope learns to her dismay that Faith is married to Oneco and has embraced the Indian way of life. Determined to win her sister away from the tribe, Hope arranges a meeting. But Gardiner overhears and alerts the governor's guard. In the ensuing confrontation, the colonists capture Magawisca and Faith, and Hope is taken by Oneco.

Hope manages to escape, but the excitement has left her deathly ill. When she recovers, she is dismayed to find that Faith is despondent, longing for her Indian family, and that Magawisca has been imprisoned. With the help of Everell and of Master Craddock, Hope frees Magawisca. At the same time, Oneco rescues Faith, although in the process he is forced to take captive Jennet, the Fletchers' gossipy and mean-hearted hired woman, whom he leaves on the shore.

Meanwhile, Philip Gardiner, who is actually a fraud posing as a Puritan to escape his debtors in England, remains determined to have Hope, and he devises a plan to capture her and take her to England. However, the sailors he hires to do the job mistake Jennet for Hope, and Gardiner and his captive perish when kegs of gunpowder on the ship they board are ignited by Gardiner's distressed former lover.

Finally, Esther, who has recognized the true love that Everell and Hope have for each other, sails for England, leaving behind a letter blessing the union of her two friends. Hope and Everell are joyfully married.

Lesser, Harry. *The Tenants.* Bernard Malamud. 1971.

Harry Lesser is a thirty-six-year-old writer living in a rundown tenement on Thirty-first Street and Third Avenue in Manhattan. He has spent ten years writing his third novel. His landlord, Levenspiel, is desperately trying to get him to finish because he wants to sell the building. Harry is a fanatic about habit and order, and, more important, has no real life outside this fifth-floor room. The book he is writing is both his life and the book we are reading.

One morning Harry is bothered by the sound of a man typing in his building, which has been abandoned by all the other tenants. He is deeply distressed by the idea of another writer intruding on his space. He makes his way down the hall to discover Willie Spearmint, a black writer. After they become acquainted, Willie asks if he may store his typewriter in Harry's apartment at night. They decide to have a party to which they invite Irene, an Off-Broadway Jewish actress, and a black couple, Mary Kettlesmith and Sam Clemence. Harry soon finds himself stirred by

emotions he had long suppressed. After unsuccessfully ogling Irene, he tries to seduce Mary, who submits to his advances and then rejects him.

When Willie later asks to read his manuscript, Harry finds himself becoming irritated and distracted by Willie Spearmint's life. Impressed and moved by Willie's writing, he nevertheless advises Willie to work on his form—an act for which he receives angry rebukes about his Jewishness and his inability to understand black writing. Lesser persists in his guidance of Willie, even hiding the illegal squatter when Levenspiel, the landlord, demands to know who has camped out next door.

Soon, however, Harry is utterly depressed and unable to write. He takes to wandering in the Museum of Modern Art and the streets in his neighborhood. Levenspiel continues to offer him more and more money to move out, but Lesser will not leave until he finishes his book. He starts to suspect that his fear of finishing is a disguised fear of dying. One February evening he goes to a party with Willie and his group of black friends, and he experiences life very physically. First he has sex with Mary, and then he is verbally abused by the group. That very night he dreams about Willie's girlfriend Irene, whom he had met again at the museum, and is inspired to declare his love to her. The two writers' lives have become intertwined at this point, although the tensions produced by their differences in color persist.

When Willie confesses to Harry that he has given up writing, the tension that has been mounting between them explodes. After criticizing a section of Willie's novel, Harry reveals that he and Irene are in love and thinking of marriage. The enraged Willie smashes Harry's head against the wall. They grapple. Harry tries to free himself from Willie's grasp by stamping on the other man's naked foot. Levenspiel, the landlord, bursts into the room before Willie has a chance to throw Harry out the window. Willie grabs some clothes and rushes out of the building while Levenspiel rants at Harry for letting Willie into the building in the first place.

A few days later Harry returns to his apartment to find it turned upside down and his work of ten years burned. Although anguished by the loss, Harry diligently begins again. He defers Irene's talk of marriage and tries to forget about Willie Spearmint. One morning, however, Harry discovers some yellow paper crumpled up outside the building and knows that Willie, desperate to write, has returned. He becomes obsessed with being able to find out where Willie is in the building.

Before his encounter with Willie, Harry either has a strange dream or writes a strange episode in his novel in which two interracial marriages occur. When the two writers unexpectedly meet on the staircase, Harry tells Willie he forgives him. Willie responds that from now on the Blacks are the Chosen People, not the Jews. Distracted by Willie's angry presence, Harry cannot write. The two writers finally meet in a clearing with axes. Harry smashes Willie's bones and brains; Willie cuts off Harry's testicles.

Lester, Jeeter. *Tobacco Road.* Erskine Caldwell. 1932.

Jeeter Lester is a man of few moral values. He first appears in the story counseling Lov, the husband of his thirteen-year-old daughter Pearl, while plotting to steal Lov's turnips. The Lester family watches as Ellie Mae, another of Jeeter's daughters, whom Lov did not marry because of her unsightly harelip, flirts with Lov. Jeeter does not find anything wrong with the fact that Ellie May is seducing her brother-in-law; she uses the distraction as an opportunity to steal the turnips.

After Jeeter steals the turnips, a preacher, Sister Bessie, comes to pray with him and asks him to stop sinning. Jeeter proclaims his remorse and his faith in God while unabashedly eyeing the widowed preacher. Jeeter expresses his belief that God will make it possible for him to raise a crop this spring, although he has not been able to for the past five years.

Jeeter gladly gives his permission for Sister Bessie to marry his sixteen-year-old son Dude. He reflects on the possibility of his last remaining daughter, Ellie May, marrying. Jeeter resolves, as he has done many times since her birth, that he will take Ellie May to Augusta to have her disfiguring harelip fixed, but as he has every other time, Jeeter fails to act on his resolution.

The only real emotion that Jeeter expresses is his attachment to the land on which he lives and used to farm. Although he has no money or credit to buy the seed and fertilizer he needs to plant a crop, Jeeter refuses to leave the land that his father and grandfather before him had farmed. He remains on the farm with his wife, mother, and remaining child, coming closer and closer to starvation.

Although nine of Jeeter's twelve children left the farm to find work in the mill towns or in the city of Augusta, Jeeter will not go to work in a factory because he feels spiritually bound to the land. He hopes that his children will give him cotton seed and guano so that he can plant again. He and his wife Ada think of their children only as sources of food and money. But the older son, who earns a good salary, proclaims that he will never give anything to his worthless father.

Taking a load of blackjack to sell in Augusta is the only way Jeeter can get money for food and snuff. The wood is of poor quality and worth little money. The valuable pine seedlings that sprout on the land are killed each year when Jeeter burns the field to prepare it for the planting that does not occur, and only the worthless blackjack remains. Jeeter procrastinates about gathering, cutting, and finally taking the wood to Augusta while the family's meager food supply runs out.

Sitting on the front porch or in the field, Jeeter spends whole days thinking about the crop that he hopes to raise. He begins to feel that he will probably not be able to raise a crop, but he nonetheless sets fire to the field, as he does each year, to burn off the grass and prepare it for plowing.

It is this unreasoning attachment to the idea of growing a crop that finally means the end of Jeeter and his wife. The last time Jeeter burns the field to prepare it for plowing, the fire consumes the house and claims the sleeping Lesters as victims.

Leventhal, Asa. *The Victim.* Saul Bellow. 1947.

During his wife's long absence, Asa Leventhal comes face-to-face with the repressed fears and emotions that underlie his life as a trade paper writer in New York City. One night, isolated and lonely in his downtown apartment, he encounters an acquaintance from his past, Edward Allbee, a former trade paper writer who blames Leventhal for having lost him his job. Allbee, now derelict and rooming in the Bowery, develops an antagonistic yet symbiotic relationship with Leventhal. Although he is initially repulsed by Allbee's drinking and filthiness, Leventhal reluctantly takes him into his apartment. He becomes less and less able to extricate himself from Allbee's manipulations, and the powerlessness he feels about his own life is manifested in a perilous downward spiral of events and emotional strain.

The son of a dry goods merchant and a mother who died in an insane asylum when he was eight, Leventhal has reached his relatively secure position and marriage only after a harsh life that he feels has "disfigured" him. Spells of unemployment and working at dead-end jobs have not effaced his feeling, however, that certain things are beneath him. Even though he must stay with a family friend, Dan Harkavy, while he awaits his big break in the trade paper industry, he bears a certain pride of self.

The tension between Leventhal's pride and propriety and his insecurity about his place in society are heightened by his Jewish heritage and the subtle and not-so-subtle forms of anti-Semitism he encounters. At a party one night, Allbee, an old-time New Englander, insults Harkavy with anti-Semitic comments but also agrees to give Leventhal an interview with his boss. During the interview, Leventhal is dismissed brusquely by the boss and responds by letting him know how bland his paper really is. This gets back to Allbee, who claims he was fired because of Leventhal's insolence. The novel takes place a few years later when Allbee has hit bottom and seeks to use Leventhal to vent his spleen.

Leventhal, already made anxious by a sick nephew, is intimidated by Allbee to the point of letting him stay in his apartment. As Allbee's stay lengthens and his grip on Leventhal's moods and daily life increases, Leventhal begins to show signs of emotional distress. He is obsessed with thoughts of Allbee and also allows deep-seated fears and desires to interfere with calm thinking. His life imitates the downward spin of Allbee's life; he begins to drink, and irrationalities infest his thought patterns. He even tries, by way of reparation, to hook Allbee up with an acquaintance of his who works in the film industry.

Finally, it is Allbee who, returning to the apartment after having been thrown out for taking in a prostitute, brings the crisis to a head by attempting suicide with Leventhal's gas stove. Asleep in the apartment, Leventhal awakes just in time to save Allbee's life and his own. Allbee then disappears for several years.

In a coda to the novel, Leventhal encounters him at a Broadway show. Allbee is playing up his New England roots to the full and accompanying a famous actress. This stirs Leventhal not at all, but it is unclear whether he has resolved the tensions Allbee brought out in him or merely repressed them more thoroughly.

Leverett, Peter. *Set This House on Fire.* William Styron. 1959.

Narrator Peter Leverett describes his friendship with MASON FLAGG, a complex and disturbing character, and relates the events immediately leading up to Mason's death at his villa in Sambuca, Italy. Peter's understanding of these events is meager, yet several years after Mason's death he is still disturbed by the mystery surrounding that night.

When the novel opens, Peter, who has been in Rome for three years working for an American relief agency, is about to end this episode in his life and return to America to go to law school. Peter prides himself on being unlike the other Americans he has met in Europe, who attempt to isolate themselves from this world by living as if they had never left their country. Now a fluent speaker of Italian, he feels satisfied that he has a good understanding of the country and its people. Yet a letter from Mason, a friend from his prep school days, signals Peter's return to the life of an American abroad and an end to his simple relationship with Italy. When Mason invites Peter to his villa in Sambuca, Peter, wanting to see Italy for the last time, decides to drive there. His cosmopolitan illusions are shattered on this journey. As he drives through the Italian countryside, he is involved in a series of incidents, culminating in an accident in which a young Italian is seriously wounded, that only confirms his sense of estrangement from his adopted country. Everywhere he goes he is accused of being American, until his fluent Italian finally deserts him and, weary and upset, he finds himself venting his rage in English to blank Italian faces.

When he arrives in Sambuca, Peter has not slept for days and is distressed by the accident and by the violence of the reproaches hurled at him. He finds Mason surrounded by several American friends and a film crew, all of whom, both Italian and American, antagonize the local villagers. Mason himself seems to thrive on this antagonism, to actively induce it by manipulating the people around him. As an American and a friend from Mason's past, Peter finds himself in the unhappy position of mediator between these several antagonistic groups, grown more fraught and exhausted as tempers rise.

As the night progresses, Peter watches Mason humiliate Cass Kinsolving, an alcoholic artist dependent on Mason's largesse, and repeatedly attempt to attack Francesca, a young Italian girl working in the villa. Although he is disgusted by what he sees, Peter is unable to prevent Mason's uncontrollable anger and, through a haze of sleeplessness, watches the events leading up to Mason's death. Peter finally falls asleep, and he wakes to find that Francesca has been found raped and fatally injured and Mason's body has been discovered at the bottom of a cliff. Disgusted and disillusioned, and only guessing at how the relationship between Mason, Francesca, and Cass led to the events of the night, Peter leaves Italy.

Several years later Peter contacts Cass in an attempt to discover what really happened on the night of Mason's death. As he and Cass describe their relationship with the enigmatic Mason, Peter discloses events in his own past. Remembering Mason's obsession with sex and the erotic, his advocation of sexual liberation, and the pain his infidelities caused, Peter begins to piece together a character who is at once attractive and repulsive. In the two periods of their friendship, Peter was drawn to Mason by his glamour and the freedom his life-style seemed to offer, but he was finally repulsed by the lies, deception, and sadness that this life-style inevitably entailed. As he listens to Cass's narratives of his dependence on Mason and his humiliation at Mason's hands, Peter sees a version of his own story being told, with Mason always figuring as a Mephistopholean character, offering material rewards for the price of integrity.

At the end of the novel, Cass admits that he murdered Mason to avenge Francesca's rape and to free himself from Mason's influence, and Peter resolves his ambiguous feelings. His ethical sense, which Mason had always threatened, finally asserts itself to condemn Mason and approve Cass's action. Mason's murder seems to Peter a just retribution, and the knowledge of it allows him to bury his fears about his own involvement in Mason's manipulations. Peter's continued disturbing memories of that night seem to stem less from his friendship with Mason than from a sense of unwitting involvement in events that he ought rightly to have prevented, or at least condemned. By sanctioning Cass's action, Peter finally participates in it and frees himself at last from Mason's pernicious influence.

Levin, Henry. "The Lady of the Lake." Bernard Malamud. 1958.

Henry Levin is a romantic young Jewish man who inherits a small income that enables him to quit his job as a floor walker at Macy's in order to seek adventure and love in Europe. Determined to change his heretofore uneventful life for one with exciting new experiences, Henry establishes himself in a small hotel near the Luxembourg Gardens in Paris and changes his name to Henry R. Freeman, but he does not analyze his motivation for such a significant alteration of his identity. Although he is initially pleased with the novelty of his foreign surroundings, he soon becomes bored and determines to try his luck in Milan. Even so, an inexplicable anxiety plagues him en route to his destination. When he sees the astonishing beauty of Lake Maggiore, Henry leaves the train and installs himself in a pleasant *pensione* situated in a small village near the Stresa shore.

Henry's taste for the exotic is immediately gratified by the sights he enjoys from his room, which commands a magnificent view of a group of four islands that immediately capture his imagination. After taking day trips to a couple of the islands, he is profoundly disappointed when he discovers that the charm they exude from afar is marred by crass touristy trappings. When he complains to the *padrona* of his *pensione* about his disappointment, she assures him that Isola del Dongo is the only island that has not been contaminated by commercialism. Although Henry is initially skeptical, he finally decides to rent a rowboat to cross the lake to del Dongo. After a harrowing trip in rough water, he approaches the island and glimpses a gorgeous young woman standing with her white dress blowing seductively in the wind. Henry is tempted by this vision and determines to return to Isola del Dongo the following day. Having sneaked away from a boring tour group, Henry once again confronts the breathtakingly beautiful young woman, who surprises him by almost immediately asking him if he is Jewish, which he denies. When the young woman exhibits an interest in him and introduces herself as the Countess Isabella del Dongo, Henry's imagination runs rampant. His wildest dreams are gratified when Isabella continues to reciprocate romantic gestures and finally lures him into skinny-dipping in the lake.

As their relationship continues to ripen, Henry begins to worry about the lie he told Isabella concerning his ethnicity and is haunted by his inability to comprehend why, given the fact that he feels he does not look Jewish, she chose to ask such an incomprehensible question. Because he fears that her query was motivated by anti-Semitism, Henry cannot assuage his conscience by telling the truth. One night when Henry and Isabella are gazing at the beautiful snow-covered mountains surrounding Lake Maggiore, Isabella asks him whether he thinks the shape of the peaks resembles a Menorah or the Virgin Mary's crown. Henry first pretends he does not know the meaning of the word *Menorah* and then avers that the contour of the mountains reminds him more of the Christian than the Jewish symbol. Following this exchange, Isabella informs Henry that she lied about her identity and that she is actually a member of the della Seta family, which acts as caretakers to the royal family. She also admits to him that she is a Jewish victim of holocaust atrocities and cannot marry him if he is not also of the Jewish faith. Stammering as he attempts to reveal his Jewish identity, he reaches out to embrace her, only to find that his hesitation has undermined his purpose, and she has vanished into the mist that emanates from the lake.

Levin, Sy. *A New Life.* Bernard Malamud. 1961.

Sy Levin is a thirty-year-old college professor trying to escape a disappointing past. His initial idealism is tried when he realizes that Cascadia College, the only school out of fifty to offer him a job, is a vocational rather than a liberal arts school. Levin's liberal academic standards are the source of many of his problems at Cascadia. A rigid system at the school that stresses passing grades over quality learning is securely in place. When Levin objects to Cascadia's academic carelessness, he is immediately reminded of the sad fate of Leo Duffy, the "radical" whose position he filled. As a result, Levin is constantly torn between wanting to stand up for the educational standards he believes in and the desire to hold down a job.

Levin's two goals, in addition to keeping his job, are to find inner peace and to develop strong personal attachments. Born and raised in New York City, he is unaccustomed to the quietude and open expanses that life in a small town affords. He goes for long walks and drives, and earns a rent cut doing outdoor work for his landlady. His senses respond to the smells and the sights around him, and he feels that he is connecting with some hitherto unknown part of himself.

Levin finds, however, that loneliness is not conducive to peace. Although warned that it would be difficult to be a bachelor in such a small community, Levin was initially optimistic about his ability to make friends. He slowly realizes that the people in his department with whom he would like to be friendly do not have the time or need for him, while those whom he finds distasteful seem to want to recruit him for political reasons. His desperate desire to find a lover involves him in a brief relationship with one of his students that afterward causes him to feel guilty. His next, more serious, involvement is with Pauline Gilley, the wife of the director of composition, Gerald Gilley, whom Levin despises.

With Pauline, Levin feels for the first time in his life that he is loved. Pauline refuses to endanger her marriage, however, and eventually ends the affair. In an attempt to recuperate his emotions, Levin becomes active in departmental politics and gains enough confidence to set himself up as Gilley's competitor for the position as chairman of the department.

In addition to being ambitious, Levin is intensely curious about the fate of Leo Duffy, whose plight his colleagues often mention but refuse to fully divulge. He is shocked when he discovers that Duffy had had an affair with Pauline. He realizes how closely he has unwittingly imitated this man. To complicate matters further, just as Levin is on the brink of winning the election, Pauline returns and says she wants to marry him. They leave the town together publicly disgraced, but Levin and a pregnant Pauline have high hopes of starting over.

Levinsky, David. *The Rise of David Levinsky.* Abraham Cahan. 1917.

Once a penniless immigrant and now a self-made millionaire, David Levinsky looks back on his life and laments the spiritual bankruptcy that haunts his material success. He was born in oppressive poverty in the shtetl of Antomir in Russia. His mother is proud of her bright son and struggles so that he can put his mind to work as a talmudic scholar. When she is brutally murdered by anti-Semitic Gentiles, he enters yeshiva as a ward of the community. He excels there, befriended by the bedraggled scholar Reb Sender who warns him against losing his faith. When he eats at the home of the charitable Shiphrah Minsker, he meets her daughter Matilda—a "modern" educated girl, already married and divorced. David falls in love with her, and one night she approaches him, embraces and kisses him. To her disgust, the yeshiva boy does not know how to respond. Urging him to become educated and to cast off his old-fashioned ways, Matilda gives him money for the passage to America.

In America, David rapidly acclimates himself, dropping his religion, shaving his beard, and studying English. He struggles as a peddler. A shipmate named Gitelson, who is a tailor, persuades him to take work as a sewing machine operator. Promising himself that he will save money for college, David works diligently. One day, though, he accidentally spills milk on some goods and is humiliated by his boss. He determines to avenge this humiliation by going into business for himself, and he persuades the designer of a prominent firm to join him in this venture. At first things go roughly, but thanks to David's fierce determination, the business begins to prosper.

Although his business is flourishing, David is lonely. He meets Dora, the wife of his friend Max Margolis, and becomes a regular visitor at the Margolises' and then a boarder in their home. He and Dora gradually become closer until he confesses his love for her. She returns his feelings but is frightened by the intensity of their passion. Finally, they consummate their love. He asks her to leave Max, but Dora, stricken by remorse and a sense of her duty as a wife and mother, asks that they never see each other again.

Using non-union labor and unorthodox business practices, David prospers, moving his firm to finer quarters "uptown." He has made it—except that he is still alone and unmarried. His friends try to introduce him to women, but he finds them all unsatisfactory. At one point he encounters Matilda, now the wife of a famous Russian revolutionary. When she sees him dressed in his "capitalist" finery, she is angered and dismisses him. Finally, as he reaches forty, he decides to marry Fanny Kaplan, a traditional woman and the daughter of a wealthy businessman. Shortly before the marriage, he encounters Anna Tevkin, the young, beautiful, and intelligent daughter of a famous Hebrew poet now struggling as a rather inept real estate broker. David breaks off the engagement with Fannie and attempts to win Anna over by helping her father in business and donating to Anna's radical causes, but to no avail: She continues to rebuff him harshly.

David then attempts to reinstate his former relationships. Matilda, older and more tolerant, now accepts him cordially. He invites Gitelson, who started him on his road to success but who himself remains a poor tailor, to dinner at an expensive restaurant—an act that just serves to emphasize the social distance between them. Finally, at fifty-two, David remains lonely and sad as he reflects on his failure to find the fulfillment he once had hoped to achieve.

Levy, Arthur. *The Island Within.* Ludwig Lewisohn. 1928.

Arthur Levy is the first Levy to be born in America in this chronicle of a Jewish immigrant family. He grows up in New York City with his parents, Gertrude and JACOB LEVY, and his sister Hazel. Jacob has made his fortune in the furniture business, providing the Levy family with a comfortable home and servants. Arthur grows up feeling very safe in his neighborhood, but the specter of anti-Semitism haunts his thoughts.

After finishing high school in three years, Arthur enters Columbia and throws himself into his studies. He makes friends with a group of young Gentiles but is aware that they never invite him to their homes, as he never invites them to his. Although they don't see each other very often, he maintains a close friendship with an old Jewish pal, Joe. Arthur studies diligently and eventually enters medical school; by doing so he manages to avoid serving in World War I, and he becomes a psychiatrist.

After acquiring his degree, Arthur procures an appointment as an intern in the women's ward of a state hospital for the insane. While most of the other doctors are barely interested in their work, Arthur spends a great deal of time talking to the patients. When he discovers that some of the attendants are abusing the patients, he tries to take action by firing a nurse; however, the nurse is embroiled in an affair with one of the other doctors, and Arthur's move is dismissed. Realizing the futility of the situation, Arthur resigns—but not before he has fully outlined his reasons and warned the nurse in question that her behavior has been observed.

With the help of his father, Arthur sets up a private psychiatric practice. He soon meets and falls in love with Elizabeth Knight, a reporter who is a Protestant. When he asks her to marry him, she breaks into tears, telling him that she is pregnant. Arthur is happy, but Elizabeth feels trapped. She is a suffragist and is very uncomfortable with ideas of marriage, children, and domesticity. They are quietly married; in fact, Arthur cannot bring himself to tell his parents until a couple of months have passed.

Arthur's practice grows, and Elizabeth becomes a successful author. But Arthur soon grows tired of their active social life and yearns for some quiet time at home. One summer, after three years of marriage, Elizabeth and Arthur have their first argument. Arthur wants to buy a house in the country, but the idea of having a permanent home does not appeal to Elizabeth. They both realize that there is something missing from their marriage and decide to take a week away from each other to think their problems through. This measure produces a temporary reconciliation, but as time goes by, their marriage slowly unravels.

Arthur thinks increasingly about the complexities of being Jewish in America. Even Elizabeth seems to recoil slightly from his Jewishness. He donates some of his time to a Jewish hospital, where he finds a certain freedom in the common ground he shares with colleagues and patients alike. It is not long before Arthur makes the acquaintance of Reb Hacohen, a Hasid and distant relation. Through long discussions with this wise friend, Arthur comes to feel more at peace with himself. One night Reb asks Arthur to take part in a commission investigating the persecution of Jews in Rumania. Arthur is torn, but when Elizabeth leaves him, he eventually decides to go. She and Arthur part sadly, knowing that separation is the only answer to their problems. The novel closes as Arthur prepares for his trip to Rumania and a new beginning.

Levy, Jacob. *The Island Within.* Ludwig Lewisohn. 1928.

Jacob Levy becomes a prosperous merchant after moving to America at the turn of the twentieth century. A mischievous young boy growing up in Germany, he refuses to learn his lessons and is always staying out and following musicians. As a young man he works in a dry goods store where he gets himself in trouble with the brothers of a young Lithuanian girl he has been seeing. They come to Jacob's family with an ultimatum: Jacob's father must give them financial compensation, and Jacob must leave town forever. Jacob is more than glad to go and asks for money to get to America where he hopes that he can be free from persecution as a Jew.

Unable to speak English, Jacob arrives in New York City with a few hundred dollars. He buys a copy of a German-American newspaper and sits down in a park to look at the employment section. While he is perusing the scant opportunities, an older man arrives and, taking a seat next to him, starts talking to him in German. This man emigrated from Germany and managed to make a fortune in America; he sometimes hires immigrants to help out, especially if they are bright, German, and Jewish.

At his new job in the old man's department store, Jacob meets Nathan Goldmann. Nathan has a plan to manufacture a new kind of easy chair; he and Jacob pool their savings and get a loan from the man who hired them. They establish their own furniture business, which does very well. Jacob marries a young woman named Gertrude, whom he loves, and with her dowry, expands the business. Together, they put Europe and the Old World behind them.

Soon, Jacob and Gertrude have a son, Arthur, and a daughter, Hazel. Although they circumcise their son, they do not go to synagogue; nor do they observe many Jewish rituals. But most of their friends and associates are Jewish, and there is a sense of community even though many families anglicize their names and take pains to affirm their Americanism. Jacob's life is heavily influenced by this effort to affirm his identity as an American without denying his Jewishness.

When World War I breaks out, Jacob is pressured to cease his subscriptions to German papers and buy war bonds in order to prove his commitment to America. As Jacob grows older, he begins to feel that Jews must support one another and maintain a sense of solidarity, for they are still in exile.

When their daughter Hazel becomes engaged to a Gentile, Jacob and Gertrude panic and force her to break off the relationship. They are very relieved when she marries a young Jewish man instead. Arthur, on the other hand, marries a young Protestant woman without telling them. After they find out, they predict that the marriage won't last but are supportive nonetheless. They continue to give Arthur an allowance and are very kind to his wife Elizabeth. When Elizabeth has a son, John, they become doting grandparents.

It is to her parents that Hazel turns when she realizes that her marriage is in trouble, but Jacob forces Hazel to talk to her husband and work out their problems. Jacob and Gertrude also take care of John while Arthur and Elizabeth are trying to resolve the problems in their marriage, which proves unsuccessful in the end.

Jacob grows old, caring for his family and friends, and building his business into a rich legacy for his children. In this self-made haven, he finds refuge from the hostility of racism and outside pressure. He has always refused to pretend to be what he is not. But this negotiation is never easy, and his life is marked by continual struggle.

Lewis, Lorry. *Bottom Dogs; From Flushing to Calvary.* Edward Dahlberg. 1930; 1932.

Lorry Lewis is the illegitimate son of Lizzie Lewis, an itinerant hairdresser and abortionist. His early childhood is spent traveling from town to town with his mother until she eventually establishes a barbershop in the slums of Kansas City.

When Lorry is eleven years old, his mother begins to worry about his wild behavior and is persuaded by her lover, a tight-fisted riverboat captain, to send the boy to an orphanage in Cleveland. His life at the orphan asylum is difficult, but Lorry manages to survive until his confirmation at the age of seventeen. He looks to the strict superintendent of the orphanage as a father figure, both loving and hating him for his severity.

Once released from the orphanage, Lorry attends the local high school and obtains a night job in the American Express warehouse. He is soon fired, quits school, and works as a messenger boy at Western Union just long enough to get the train fare back to Kansas City, where he lives with his mother again and becomes a drover in the Kansas City stockyards. Dissatisfied with his life and longing to get out of Kansas City, Lorry then accepts a job as a door-to-door salesman of educational catalogs in Nebraska, but he gets stagefright at the thought of approaching potential customers and catches a train for Omaha without selling a single catalog.

Now completely penniless, Lorry roams from town to town for a while, panhandling and riding the rails. He eventually ends up in Los Angeles, where, with the help of an old friend from the orphanage, he gets a room at the YMCA and begins washing dishes in lunchrooms to earn a living. Having decided by this time that he wants to be a writer, Lorry attends "scenario school" in Los Angeles, but all of his stories are rejected by the magazines. He holds a part-time job as a clerk in a public health venereal disease clinic, is briefly attracted to vegetarianism and spiritualism, and attempts with difficulty to decipher a volume by Trotsky bought on a whim in a secondhand bookstore.

Lorry eventually decides to return to his mother in Kansas City, persuades her to sell her shop, and moves with her to Bensonhurst, New York. Here he supports Lizzie by working as an assistant shipping clerk in the downtown wharf commission-house district. After Lorry loses his job, the two move to Flushing and occupy a house opposite Calvary Cemetery. Lorry manages to eke out a living by selling newspapers in a subway station, and Lizzie contributes to the household finances by performing illegal abortions. Lorry stays away from home as much as possible because he has difficulty dealing with Lizzie's coldness to him and her constant illnesses, but he becomes more attentive when he finds out that she may need an operation. Worried about his mother and disturbed by news about the death of the superintendent of the orphanage, Lorry impulsively jumps a train bound for Cleveland to visit the asylum, his former home, only to discover that the orphanage has been abandoned. He leaves feeling empty and lost.

Lorry returns to New York and learns that his mother is in a charity ward at the hospital. When he arrives at her bedside, his mother tearfully accuses him of running away from her; he attempts to comfort her, but she becomes cold and distant. Lizzie dies on the operating table soon afterward.

In the days following the funeral, Lorry contemplates going away somewhere but is unable to decide what to do with his life. One afternoon he takes a walk in Union Square and is hit on the head while bending over to pick up a peanut off the sidewalk; he suddenly finds himself in the middle of a violent confrontation between demonstrators and the police. He extricates himself from the riot and walks away, eating the peanut and singing an old orphan-asylum hymn, vaguely thinking that for him going is easier than doing.

The Lieutenant. "An Episode of War." Stephen Crane. 1899.

An anonymous army lieutenant is the passive protagonist of this story of bodily and psychic wounding, set on one particularly harrowing day during Civil War.

As the story begins the lieutenant is preparing to divide a mass of coffee into portions to be doled out among the men in his company. He prepares for his task by spreading out his rubber blanket and drawing his sword in order to cut up the coffee. He is in the midst of his task when he suddenly cries out. The lieutenant looks at the men around him, suspecting that they were somehow involved in his injury. The men, in turn, look back at him, aghast at the sudden appearance of blood on his sleeve. All of them silently stare at the woods from which a bullet must have come and wonder how a bullet could have found its victim so surely and so suddenly.

The realization gradually sinks in for the lieutenant that he has been hit, and he begins to apprehend, as do the men watching him, that something incomprehensible has taken place. For a moment the lieutenant and the men around him gaze off into the woods nearby as though the woods can somehow explain what happened, and at the same time the lieutenant draws out his sword, even though he is incapable of efficiently holding the weapon. A few moments later, as he tries to replace the sword in its scabbard, the officer is gently assisted by other soldiers who are beginning to understand what has happened. Meanwhile, the officer realizes that he must seek help, and he makes his way slowly back through the military forces and the confusion of battle to where the medical tents have been erected.

Holding his injured arm as though it were brittle glass, the lieutenant heads for the rear. He encounters another soldier who tries to help him by tying up the injured arm in an effort to stanch the flow of blood. When the officer finally does reach medical attention, the doctor finds fault with the first aid effort. The lieutenant, suddenly nervous, wants the doctor's assurance that his arm will not be amputated, and the doctor says it won't be. As it turns out, though, amputation is necessary. The operation is apparently performed immediately on the field, and as the story ends, the lieutenant returns home where his sisters, mother, and wife all tearfully respond to the sight of the folded cloth flap that takes the place of the missing limb, while the lieutenant stoically attempts to hide his embarrassment at the women's tears.

Ligeia. "Ligeia." Edgar Allan Poe. 1838.

Beautiful, brilliant, and desirous of immortality, Ligeia is an insistent presence in this ghost story. Early in the tale the woman dies, but her spirit cannot be satisfied until it rises again.

The first thing that the narrator, Ligeia's husband, noticed about her was her beauty. Her pale skin and raven hair, coupled with a pair of unusually large eyes, fulfilled Bacon's dictum that beauty is not true beauty without some strangeness.

Ligeia brings to their marriage not only her disturbing beauty and vast wealth but also matchless intelligence. Somehow she has managed to embrace every field of learning and is without peer in every branch of knowledge. Languages, the sciences, philosophy—Ligeia is skilled in them all, becoming something of a tutor to her husband. She opens paths of knowledge for him that he had never imagined. There is not only love but gratitude in his worship of her.

After a few years of married bliss, it becomes clear to her husband that Ligeia is slowly losing her grip on this world. She fights the arrival of death with a fiery determination, but her burning desire to live fades to just a flicker within her luminous eyes.

One of Ligeia's final acts is to dictate to her husband a poem she wrote a few days before. The poem is a meditation on mortality in which Ligeia laments that life ends, inevitably, with death and that the Conqueror Worm, who gnaws the flesh of the dead, emerges as the true hero. Imploring God that the drama of her life not end in this fashion, Ligeia dies.

Or does she? Years later when the narrator, now an opium addict, marries again, the spirit of Ligeia makes itself known. The narrator's new wife, the angelic-looking Lady Rowena Trevanion of Tremaine, tells him that she feels a mysterious presence hovering over her sickbed. The narrator discounts his new wife's words as the ravings of a seriously ill woman, but one night he sees three or four drops of red liquid drip from an unknown source into her cup. Three days later she dies.

Soon Ligeia returns. As the narrator sits with the body of his newly-wed, newly-dead second wife, the body takes on a flush of life, but the color soon fades. This cycle of apparent regeneration, followed by the narrator's attempts to resuscitate his wife, and then her descent back into death, occurs many times during the long night. Finally, the shrouded body stirs and rises. She steps from the bed, lets fall her funereal wrappings, and reveals herself not as Lady Rowena but as the long-dead Ligeia, now resurrected.

Liggett, Weston. *Butterfield 8.* John O'Hara. 1935.

Weston Liggett, the married lover of GLORIA WANDROUS, is outwardly a confident and successful man. He is a former Yale athlete who married into a wealthy New England family. Yet behind this pose, Liggett maintains a precarious position in an environment he believes is above him. Financially, he is struggling: The heavy tool manufacturing business he inherited is losing money in the Depression, and Liggett barely knows enough about the field to converse intelligently with his engineers. At home he is made increasingly aware of his wife Emily's superior social position and fears that he may be considered vulgar.

Liggett's increasingly tenuous position is threatened when he meets Gloria Wandrous and, against his better judgment, invites her back to his apartment in New York, where she spends the night. When he wakes the next morning, he discovers that Gloria has gone and has taken Emily's mink coat with her. Although Liggett realizes the threat Gloria poses to everything he has achieved, he is overwhelmed by the passion she has aroused in him and remembers the previous night with conflicting emotions of pleasure, desire, and embarrassment.

In his rational moments, Liggett condemns Gloria as a common thief, a woman who would sleep with anyone, and he admires his wife's purity. Although he vilifies Gloria, he is drawn to her and desperately begins roaming the speakeasies of New York trying to find her. He finds her one evening and, after imploring her to come away with him, gets embroiled in a fight at a bar. When he returns home, he is still in love with Gloria and intends to lie to Emily.

Yet Liggett must tell someone of his dilemma, and with characteristic selfishness, he demands that Emily listen to the story of his infidelity as if it concerned another man. Then, in an attempt to recover from Gloria, to regain his self-respect and at the same time give back to Emily the respect he feels she deserves, Liggett leaves his family and moves into a hotel. His resolve is short-lived. By now obsessed with Gloria and determined to give up everything for her, he follows her onto the *City of Essex*, the boat on which she is escaping from New York. At first he hides from her; finally, he confronts her and asks her to marry him. When she refuses to spend the night with him in his cabin, Liggett is furious, but on reflection he begins to understand her reasons and to acknowledge Gloria's humanity and sensitivity to which he had been blind. As he follows her to explain his mistake, Liggett calls to Gloria, then sees her turn and fall off the deck to her death.

After Gloria dies, Liggett desperately tries to regain his former life by distancing himself from his passion for her and concealing their relationship. The independence and courage that he briefly exerted have disappeared, and he returns to being the man he was before he met Gloria Wandrous.

Lingard, Lena. *My Ántonia.* Willa Cather. 1918.

Lena Lingard, one of the hardworking "hired girls," tenaciously guards her independence by rejecting even the thought of marriage. Brought to Nebraska from Sweden as a young girl, Lena witnesses her mother's crushing servitude, and she vows never to be caught in similar circumstances. Lena helps out with the children and tends the cows on the family's struggling farm. When a local farmer's wife unjustly accuses her of indiscretion (an accusation founded solely on her husband's love-struck behavior), Lena is forced to seek work in the town of Black Hawk.

Once in Black Hawk, Lena uses her natural gift with a needle and thread to learn the dressmaking trade. Although she had worn only rags on the farm, she instinctively imitates and surpasses the style of the most fashionable women in town. She spends her free time with ANTONIA SHIMERDA and the other "hired girls," young immigrant women who send their wages home to support their family farms. When the dancing tent becomes the center of town social life, Lena and her friends dance every night with local boys and hired hands. Lena's sultry demeanor and smoldering eyes belie her innocence and reinforce her already tarnished reputation. She knows that the town boys will never marry one of the hired girls, but she doesn't care and takes her pleasure as she desires. JIMMY BURDEN, the narrator of the novel, also finds himself attracted by her sensuality, but Antonia prevents him from pursuing his interest.

When Lena moves to Lincoln to set up a dress shop of her own, she seeks out the company of Jimmy, now a college student. Although Lena habitually makes mistakes and finishes orders that are late and overpriced, the customers in Lincoln are won over by her instinctive sense of style, and so her business thrives. Lena and Jimmy dine out and attend the theater together. Without Antonia's protection, Jimmy falls prey to Lena's charms and soon joins Lena's landlord and the neighboring violin player as hopeless, love-struck suitors. While Lena is sad to see Jimmy leave Lincoln to pursue his studies at Harvard, she surprises him by stating that she never expected or desired a more permanent attachment.

At the urging of another of the successful hired girls who has left Black Hawk for greater opportunity, Lena eventually leaves Lincoln for San Francisco. There, her fashionable dress shop flourishes, and she enjoys the company of whomever she chooses. As news of her wealth reaches the small town, the citizens of Black Hawk come to regard this once poor farm girl with respect and some envy, marveling over the "bad" girl who triumphed.

Linkhorn, Dove. *A Walk on the Wild Side.* Nelson Algren. 1956.

Dove Linkhorn, the youngest son of a southern poor white family, searches for love and a sense of self-worth among the down-and-outs in the seedy red-light district of New Orleans during the early days of the Great Depression.

Dove, who is sixteen years old at the beginning of the novel, is illiterate because his father, an embittered self-proclaimed preacher, has kept him out of school in order to protest the appointment of a Catholic principal. There is no work available in his hometown of Arroyo, Texas, in the autumn of 1930, but the lonely young man is befriended by Terasina Vidavarri, the thirty-year-old Mexican owner of the local café, La Fe en Dios. He does odd jobs for her in exchange for coffee and tobacco, and she begins to teach him the alphabet. They become lovers briefly, but she throws him out in the street again when he gives his brother Byron a dollar from her cash register. The next day, angered by her continued scornful rejection, he rapes her and then, on impulse, hops a train out of town. Throughout his subsequent adventures, Dove frequently thinks about Terasina with both affection and regret.

While riding the rails, Dove meets Kitty Twist, a vagrant seventeen-year-old girl who is disguising herself as a man. They become lovers and travel to Houston, where she convinces him to rob a store; when the police arrive, however, he takes the money and leaves her behind to be arrested. Dove then catches a train to New Orleans, where his innate country savvy prevents him from being swindled by various urban predators who think he will be an easy mark. He soon finds his way to Perdido Street, the heart of the city's red-light district. In the summer of 1931, following an abortive attempt at selling coffeepots, Dove joins up with Fort Luther and Luke Luther, two hustlers with whom he engages in such schemes as selling stolen certificates for a free shampoo. Eventually tiring of these scams, Dove agrees to work for Rhino Gross, an ex-abortionist now in the business of making condoms; he soon moves on, however, after stealing his employer's money with the help of the man's wife.

Kitty Twist shows up in town after having spent a hundred days in jail, and a vicious pimp named Oliver Finnerty uses Kitty's story to coerce Dove to work for him. The young man is soon making a lot of money performing for voyeurs at Mama's, a whorehouse on Perdido Street, but he spends all of his earnings on gin. He enters into an affair with Hallie Breedlove, a prostitute with a tragic past. They live together happily for a while; she teaches him to read, and for the first time in his life he ceases to feel anguish about his ignorance. Dove wakes up one morning, however, to find her gone without a trace. He immediately goes on a bender at the local speakeasy, where he is arrested during a police raid and sent to jail. While incarcerated, the young man begins to articulate thoughts about social injustice and spends much of his time thinking about Terasina.

Upon his release from jail in April 1932, Dove returns

to the speakeasy, where he is assaulted by Achilles Schmidt, a paraplegic former circus strongman who is in love with Hallie. Schmidt is wrongly convinced that Dove knows where Hallie is living and mercilessly beats the young man's face into a pulp while onlookers do nothing. As the novel concludes, the now-blind Dove is back in Arroyo, tapping with his walking stick to find his way to Terasina's chili parlor, where he is told the light is on in an upper window.

Linwood, Clotelle. *Clotelle*; or, *the Colored Heroine.* William Wells Brown. 1867.

Although of mostly white ancestry, Clotelle Linwood, like her mixed-race mother, is legally black. Most children of slave women are destined to "follow the condition of the mother" and remain in bondage. By the end of this novel, however, Clotelle lives as a free woman who is looked on with honor and love.

Southern life offers Clotelle an uncertain future. Her mother Isabella is both the property and lover of Henry Linwood, a well-to-do Southern gentleman. Inheriting many of the features of her white father, Clotelle is nevertheless denied the freedom he and other whites take for granted. When Henry grows tired of his black mistress and marries a white woman, only the affection he feels for his daughter keeps him visiting the small house where Clotelle and Isabella live. But when his frequent absences from his own home come to the attention of Mrs. Miller, his new mother-in-law, the fragile world of the young girl and her mother comes apart. Mrs. Miller discovers Henry's second family and forces him to allow her to sell Isabella and keep Clotelle as a house servant.

Isabella could escape the slave traders, but rather than flee north, she attempts to retrieve her daughter. Captured, Isabella chooses to die by jumping from a ship into the icy waters of the Potomac rather than live as a slave. This drastic action leaves Clotelle motherless and all but fatherless since Henry allows his only child to be mistreated by the brutal Mrs. Miller. Clotelle's beauty and resemblance to Henry anger Mrs. Miller, whose daughter has borne Henry no children, and the girl suffers greatly at the hands of her vindictive mistress. By the time enough paternal feeling is aroused in Henry for him to protest his daughter's treatment, Mrs. Miller has already sold Clotelle.

Clotelle is purchased by Mr. Wilson, a minister who had owned her grandmother years before. In the minister's house Clotelle becomes close to Georgiana, the minister's Northern-educated daughter. As she blossoms into womanhood Clotelle falls in love with Jerome, a fellow slave. When Jerome receives a death sentence for striking Mr. Wilson, Clotelle exchanges clothes with him so he can escape from prison. He leaves the town dressed as a woman, vowing to be reunited with his love somehow.

As punishment for her heroic act, Clotelle gets whipped and sold out of the state. When she learns of Clotelle's treatment, the grief-stricken Georgiana ruptures a blood vessel and dies. Clotelle is again friendless but is soon offered a new chance for friendship and freedom. A young Frenchman falls in love with Clotelle at first sight and proposes a plan for her escape. True to his word, Antoine Devenant assists Clotelle and marries her once the couple reaches his native France.

But Clotelle's subsequent happiness is short-lived when Antoine dies fighting with the French forces in India. Years after his death Clotelle sees a familiar person while visiting her husband's grave. It is Jerome, who moved to Europe soon after his escape from slavery. Their love for each other is undiminished, and they decide to marry and travel on the Continent for their honeymoon.

Jerome and Clotelle pass a sleepless night in an inn in Germany, kept awake by the rantings of a delirious man in the next room. Visiting the unfortunate stranger's room the next morning, Clotelle discovers that the man is in fact no stranger but her father Henry, driven nearly insane by his guilt-ridden belief that his daughter is dead. Clotelle reveals herself to him and, happy to have a father again, forgives him.

When the Civil War breaks out, Clotelle's family returns to the United State. Henry dies in valiant service to the cause of freedom, while Clotelle works in Confederate camps assisting Union prisoners of war. At the end of the war she opens a Freedmen's School on the property where she once worked as a slave. She is dubbed by all who know her "the angel of mercy."

The Literary Critic. "The Figure in the Carpet." Henry James. 1896.

The unnamed literary critic is a young, unmarried Englishman who gets swept into a long, frustrating, and ultimately unsuccessful search to discover the authorial "intention" of a renowned contemporary writer, Hugh Vereker. The quest begins at a dinner party where the critic, who has recently written a well-received article about Vereker's works, hopes to meet the great writer in person. When the critic hears a guest at the party praising his article, his hopes rise because he believes Vereker will appreciate him for having understood his fiction. But when asked about the article, Vereker gives an ambivalent reply; when pressed, he remarks that the article is charming but that the author "doesn't see anything."

Mortified and dejected, the critic remains quiet for the rest of the dinner. On his way out, he runs into Vereker, who has just learned of his identity and wishes to explain his dismissive reaction to the article. Vereker tells the literary critic that his readers have generally failed to see what is at the heart of his work. He says there is a secret lurking behind all his writing, a figure hidden in the carpet that no one has detected. When the critic asks Vereker for a clue, Vereker impatiently answers that the clues are everywhere. Suddenly fired with ambition, the literary critic resolves to find the buried treasure at the heart of Vereker's writing. The amused Vereker is not encouraging, however, and tells the critic not to try.

Undaunted, the critic goes through all of Vereker's work but cannot find a trace of the figure in the carpet. He then tells his friend, the editor George Corvick, about Vereker's remark; Corvick decides to enter the chase and enlists the help of his fiancée Gwendolen. Soon after, the critic receives a letter from Vereker saying he regrets having given away so much in conversation. The critic immediately apologizes to Vereker for having told Corvick and his fiancée about the secret. Vereker says not to worry and adds cryptically that if a woman is involved, perhaps Corvick will have an advantage.

The search continues. The critic, increasingly bitter, watches as Corvick's and Gwendolen's enthusiasm grows. Corvick is then called away on a journey to the East; after some time he cables Gwendolen from Bombay with the news that he has found the secret. The critic and Gwendolen wait anxiously for Corvick to communicate the secret to them. Corvick finally writes that he has seen Vereker and that Vereker has confirmed his findings. Corvick remains silent about the secret and declines to reveal it to Gwendolen until they are married.

The literary critic is away from England when Corvick returns. Corvick marries Gwendolen, begins a long work on Vereker, but then is tragically killed in a coach accident. The critic immediately rushes home; once there, he looks at Corvick's work on Vereker and finds only a scrap, with no mention of the secret. Believing that Corvick might have imparted the secret to Gwendolen before he died, the critic visits the widow and presses her for a revelation. Gwendolen refuses; "I heard everything," she says, "and I mean to keep it to myself."

The critic, deeply puzzled by Gwendolen's reticence and haunted by Vereker's remark about Corvick's advantage, wonders whether only loving couples can discern the secret. He returns to Gwendolen and beseeches her to tell him; again, she adamantly refuses, and when he suggests that the secret may be nothing at all, she tells him he has insulted "the Dead." The critic subsequently develops an aversion to Vereker's work, and when Vereker's new book appears, he does not review it. Then the renowned writer unexpectedly dies.

The critic feels distraught and entirely isolated. Still obsessed with the "figure in the carpet" but now cut off from the possibility of discovering it, he grows even more disturbed when he learns that Gwendolen is about to marry Drayton Deane, the shallow and uninsightful reviewer of Vereker's last work. The critic's distress soon turns to contempt when he realizes that if Gwendolen tells Deane the secret, Deane will be too stupid either to understand it or to find joy in it. Some time later Gwendolen dies in childbirth, and the literary critic's consuming curiosity becomes whether or not Drayton Deane knows the secret.

When the critic meets Deane in a men's club and asks him about the secret, Deane does not know what he is talking about. The critic realizes that Deane is being honest: Gwendolen told him nothing. Deane believes that if the secret was important, Gwendolen would have shared it with him; the critic replies that it was important, that Gwendolen told him she had "lived on it." This upsets Deane, and the critic regrets having tampered with his memory of her. He is pleased to think, however, that Deane will share in his desire to learn the now unattainable secret, and he begins to see Deane's confusion as his single consolation—and even his revenge.

The Little Boy. *Ragtime.* E. L. Doctorow. 1974.

Born at the turn of the century into a well-to-do family, the Little Boy of this novel lives in a world peopled by such fictionalized historical characters as J. Pierpont Morgan and Harry Houdini. The boy lives with his Mother, FATHER, Grandfather, and MOTHER'S YOUNGER BROTHER in a three-story home in New Rochelle, New York. The boy's father, an amateur explorer of some repute, supports his extended family comfortably on the proceeds of his factories, which specialize in the manufacture of patriotic paraphernalia such as flags and fireworks. A highly imaginative child, the boy has a perspective of the world that is idiosyncratic and extremely colorful.

In fact, the boy possesses a knowing vision of the world that is lost on the surrounding adults. Secretly considered an odd child by his mother, the boy follows the daily newspapers and is particularly fascinated by celebrities such as the escape artist Harry Houdini. He is delighted when an automobile collides with a telephone pole near his house and the owner of the car, Houdini himself, accepts a glass of lemonade in the family's parlor. Houdini performs a few elementary magic tricks for the boy while waiting for his car to be repaired.

The boy spends a good portion of his time indulging in an intellectual life that he keeps secret from his relatives. Convinced of the mutability of life, he stares at his reflection in mirrors until he feels that he has disembodied himself and is two selves staring at each other. At times he enters so deeply into a trance that his conscious self is only recalled by some stimulus from the real world such as a loud noise. The boy explains the changeable nature of all existence to himself by assuming that the world is dissatisfied with itself, and its constant transformations are the result of an effort at self-improvement.

The child's relatively normal external existence is seriously disrupted when COALHOUSE WALKER, JR., a talented ragtime musician, begins to court Sarah, a young unmarried black woman. Sarah was taken in by the boy's softhearted mother along with the baby she had attempted to murder at birth. Walker, the father of Sarah's child, conducts a lengthy courtship during which Sarah tests his previously questionable reliability. Sarah eventually agrees to marry the musician, but the wedding never takes place because she dies, and Walker's intense grief over the loss culminates in criminal behavior. In order to avoid the ensuing barrage of reporters who plague the area surrounding the family's home, begging for comments concerning the now notorious black couple and their baby, the family relocates to a hotel in Atlantic City. There the boy joyously plays in the ocean in the company of a beautiful dark-eyed girl, the daughter of TATEH, a Jewish socialist filmmaker who poses as a European baron named Ashkenazy. Upon the death of Father on the *Lusitania*, Mother marries the filmmaker, the reconstructed family moves to California, and the novel comes abruptly to a close.

Littlepage, Cornelius ''Corny.'' *Satanstoe*. James Fenimore Cooper. 1845.

Cornelius "Corny" Littlepage, the narrator, is the only surviving child of a farming family in upstate New York. He lives in relative peace and happiness on Satanstoe, the family farm, until his father decides that at the age of fourteen his son is ready for college. Corny journeys to Princeton that fall.

Corny spends four years at Princeton and becomes learned in Latin, philosophy, art, and various other "refined" subjects. He returns to Satanstoe a gentleman and is reunited with his delighted parents. Soon after coming home, he meets and befriends a young man named GUERT TEN EYCK. The two make frequent trips to New York City, where they pass the time in a variety of aesthetic pursuits.

On one of these journeys to New York, Guert introduces Corny to a beautiful young woman named Anneke Mordaunt, a distant cousin, who is being wooed and courted by virtually every eligible young man in the area. Despite warnings from other townspeople that, with spring less than a month away, such a ride would be too dangerous, Guert takes Anneke, Corny, and a friend of Anneke's named Mary Wallace, on whom Guert has designs of his own, on a sleigh ride across the Hudson River.

Corny and his companions soon pay the price for failing to heed the warnings of others: Halfway across the Hudson, the ice begins to separate and float down the river in large chunks. The party abandons their sled and horses, which are quickly pulled under. After being separated from Guert and Mary, Corny valiantly leads Anneke to shore by hopping from one cake of ice to the next, holding her in his arms.

Soon thereafter, Corny and Guert, who was similarly able to take Mary to safety, travel with the Mordaunt family to their summer house in Albany, where they come across a company of militia heading north to fight the French. Not wanting to shirk their patriotic duty, Corny

and Guert, after delivering Anneke and her family safely to their summer house, join the company on their way to Tippicanoe.

After fighting valiantly with the French and successfully driving them back, Guert is captured by Indians. In the course of a daring rescue attempt by Corny, Guert is killed. Overwhelmed with grief at the loss of his best friend, Corny brings Guert's body to Albany for a proper burial. It is there that Corny, after the funeral of his friend, confesses his love to Anneke and asks her to marry him. Anneke agrees, and the two are wed. With his new bride, Corny returns to Satanstoe, where the two will begin their life together.

Livvie. "Livvie." Eudora Welty. 1936.

Livvie, a shy and sheltered young black woman, lives in a pleasant house with her dying husband, an old black man named Solomon who owns his own plot of land. Nine years before, when Livvie was sixteen, Solomon married her and carried her in his arms for twenty-one miles to his house in Natchez, Mississippi. Content and unquestioning, Livvie always said "Yes, sir" when Solomon asked if she was happy—even though, since she has lived there, he has given her no money, never let her venture beyond the chicken house and the well, and kept her from socializing. Now, Solomon is so old that his health has deteriorated and he is bedridden, but even though he is on the verge of death, Livvie is very much alive on this beautiful spring day.

Livvie fixes breakfast for Solomon in the morning; he does not eat it, so she eats both his breakfast and hers. Feeling spring stirring inside her and watching and listening to the distant men, women, and children working in Solomon's field, she imagines hoeing with them and, drenched with her efforts, stretching out with her cheek against the earth. But she stays inside, cooking chicken broth, and wonders what Solomon is dreaming about. She thinks he is dreaming of her, although she cannot be sure.

Soon after, Livvie is visited by Miss Baby Marie, a woman who comes to her door selling cosmetics. Miss Baby Marie shows Livvie samples from a suitcase full of bottles and jars of powder and rouge. The smell of the chinaberry flower lipstick delights and overwhelms Livvie, but she has no money to buy anything. She explains to Miss Baby Marie that Solomon keeps all the money, and Miss Baby Marie, morbidly curious, asks to see Solomon. Livvie consents, and as they stare at Solomon lying still in his bed, the two women share an unspoken secret: They know that Solomon is about to die. Miss Baby Marie departs after declining to accept Livvie's offer of eggs in exchange for the lipstick.

Walking down the Natchez Trace path, Livvie meets a man named Cash. He is carrying a guinea pig in his pocket and is wearing fancy clothes—a long green coat, bright socks, a pink satin shirt, and a plum hat with an emerald feather. He and Livvie introduce themselves and walk together. Livvie is entranced by him. When they reach Solomon's house, Livvie realizes that Cash is a transformed field hand who has probably taken Solomon's money. He tells her he's ready for Easter, and when he laughs and draws Livvie close to him, she is not afraid. She dazzles herself by kissing him, and feeling that Solomon's death is close at hand, she goes inside the house.

Solomon wakes up and sees Livvie with Cash in his room. Soon afterward, he offers his silver watch to Livvie and dies. Holding the silver watch, Livvie leaves the room with Cash. On their way out of the house, Cash picks her up and spins her around. She goes limp and drops the watch to the floor. Once outside, Cash shakes her once, and she rests silently in his arms as springtime explodes all around them.

Loftis, Helen. *Lie Down in Darkness.* William Styron. 1951.

Helen Loftis is the prideful and religiously neurotic wife and mother of a decadent southern family. Although the early years of Helen's marriage to MILTON (LOFTIS) are happy ones, the ensuing family tragedy transforms Helen into a bitter, hateful, and destructive person.

The Loftises' first daughter Maudie is born mentally retarded and physically frail. While Helen reacts to this tragedy by becoming morbidly attached to and watchful over Maudie, her husband responds by drinking more heavily. The marriage becomes strained, and the strain increases with the birth of a second child, PEYTON (LOFTIS). Helen deeply resents the fact that Milton dotes on and overindulges Peyton. In fact, Helen intuits that her husband's love for Peyton is fundamentally incestuous, and consequently she is jealous of her own daughter.

Over the years Helen becomes consumed by her attachment to Maudie, her guilt over her hatred of Peyton, and her increasingly unbending and prideful attitude toward her alcoholic husband. Her anguish expresses itself in an increasing religious fervor. When Milton eventually enters into an affair with another woman, Helen turns to her pastor, Carey Carr, with whom she shares her sorrow and bitterness. Carey counsels her to be more forgiving toward Milton and Peyton, but Helen ignores his advice, and when Maudie dies, she renounces her faith in God altogether and makes a failed suicide attempt.

Milton comes to her rescue at this point. He renounces his lover, quits drinking, and exerts every effort to heal the rift in their marriage. In gratitude to Milton, Helen attempts to repair her relationship with Peyton, who has gone away to college and who, because of Helen's hatred for her, never returns home to visit. When Peyton announces her impending marriage, Helen insists on hosting the wedding at the family home and tries very hard to make Peyton feel welcome and loved.

It is quickly revealed that Helen's show of maternal love is merely a display contrived for Milton's benefit. At the wedding a sexual pass made at Peyton by Milton unleashes all of Helen's pent-up hatred for Peyton. In a vicious verbal attack on her daughter, Helen blames Peyton for Milton's incestuous desire for her, reviling her daughter for having sexually tantalized Milton since childhood. Milton overhears this scene and immediately returns to his lover, leaving Helen alone with her self-righteous bitterness and frustration.

Soon after the wedding, Peyton commits suicide, but Helen refuses to attend her daughter's funeral until Carey Carr virtually forces her to do so. Carey also forces her to listen to Milton's pleas that they attempt to restore their marriage, but her pride prevents her from relenting, and she is left alone once again.

Loftis, Milton. *Lie Down in Darkness.* William Styron. 1951.

Milton Loftis is the well-meaning but weak-willed and self-indulgent husband and father of a decadent southern family. In the early years of his marriage to HELEN (LOFTIS), he and Helen are very happy together despite the financial hardships they endure as he struggles to become a successful lawyer. When Helen inherits a large amount of money, his wife's newfound wealth seems to undermine Milton's strength of character. Although he continues to work as a lawyer in the Tidewater, Virginia, town where they live, he never follows through on his political ambitions, and he begins to drink excessively.

Milton's problem with alcoholism is further exacerbated when his first child, Maudie, is born mentally retarded and sickly. Although Milton treats Maudie kindly and attentively, it is his second child, PEYTON (LOFTIS), who receives the full force of his fatherly love. Indeed, over the course of the novel it becomes clear that Milton's doting and overindulgent treatment of Peyton stems from an incestuous attraction to her, and it also becomes apparent that Helen's resentful attitude toward Milton and Peyton stems from her awareness of the unhealthy nature of their bond.

The Loftis family soon separates into opposing camps, with the indolent and alcoholic Milton and his favorite daughter Peyton on one side, and the increasingly bitter and neurotic Helen and her favorite daughter Maudie on the other. As Milton's and Helen's marriage becomes increasingly cold, Milton enters into an affair with the vapid but adoring Dolly. His need for Dolly grows when his beloved Peyton leaves for college and does not return home to visit.

When Maudie dies, Milton makes a determined effort to save his family. He abandons Dolly and quits drinking for almost a year, during which time his relationship with Helen improves markedly. When Peyton announces her impending marriage, Helen is so eager to please Milton that she insists Peyton be married at home.

On the day of the wedding, however, the pretense of domestic harmony falls apart. As his daughter is being given to another man, Milton is overwhelmed by the frustration of his incestuous love for her, and Helen's jealousy erupts into a vicious attack on Peyton. Milton gets drunk on this disastrous wedding day, and when he overhears Helen's attack on Peyton, he returns immediately to Dolly.

Not long after her marriage, Peyton commits suicide. When her body is returned home for burial, Milton, beside himself with grief, once again spurns Dolly and implores Helen to give him another chance. He sees that he and Helen now have only each other, and he begs her to try to make a life with him again. Helen rejects him, however, and Milton Loftis retreats through the graveyard where his daughters are buried and heads toward the nearest highway.

Loftis, Peyton. *Lie Down in Darkness.* William Styron. 1951.

Peyton Loftis's body has been shipped from New York to her hometown in the Tidewater area of Virginia to be buried. The beautiful young Peyton has committed suicide, and the bulk of the novel focuses on the elements of her family background that doomed her to madness and death.

Peyton's alcoholic father, MILTON (LOFTIS), loved her to distraction. Because his first child was born mentally retarded and sickly and his marriage was strained, Milton showered his frustrated affections on the beautiful Peyton, whom he pampered and overindulged. Because of the incestuous bond between Milton and Peyton, Peyton's mother, HELEN (LOFTIS), came to hate her. Helen's hatred intensified when Peyton and her playmates almost killed the retarded Maudie in a childish game and when, later, Peyton accidentally let Maudie fall down and hurt herself.

Peyton suffered not only from her parents' unhappy relations with each other but also because they both vented their feelings of frustration on her. Although on the surface the beautiful Peyton behaved in a lighthearted, fun-loving manner, this behavior was the mask adopted by an intelligent and sensitive young woman who suffered so deeply from family life that she became an alcoholic like her father.

Peyton was relieved to leave home for college, but when Maudie died shortly thereafter, she suffered a kind of breakdown during which she went on a sexually promiscuous drinking binge, dropped out of college, and moved to New York. In New York she met and became engaged to a young Jewish artist, Harry Miller, who exerted a stabilizing influence on her. At their wedding Milton fondled Peyton sexually, and Helen responded to this action by verbally attacking Peyton, who she believed had always sexually teased Milton.

After the wedding Peyton broke off relations with her family, except for the occasional letter to her father. She

lived in New York with her husband until he abandoned her because of her financial irresponsibility, alcoholism, and sexual promiscuity. On the last day of her life, Peyton wandered desperately through the streets of New York in an hallucinatory fog. She remembered her mother's hatred, her guilt over Maudie, and her father's sexual advances since childhood. We see that Peyton's heart has been broken and her mind deranged by her family, and when her sorrow and madness drive her to suicide on the day of the atomic bombing of Nagasaki, it only remains for her body to be returned to Tidewater.

Loney, Jim. *The Death of Jim Loney.* James Welch. 1979.

Jim Loney, a man who is a mixture of Blackfeet Indian and white, leads a destitute and solitary life, drinking and declining mentally and physically in the small town of Harlem, Montana. Although a bright man, educated at a selective mission school, and a former high school basketball champion, he has yet to achieve his potential. At age thirty-five he still clings to the emotional scars wrought by his mother, Electra Calf Looking, who abandoned him at age one, and his father, who abandoned him nine years later.

Loney's father, Ike, returned to live in Harlem after an absence of twelve years, but the two have had little contact. When Loney was younger, Ike's girlfriend Sandra, whom Loney can recall in only sketchy detail, looked after him briefly but lovingly. More recently he has been cared for by two women: his own girlfriend, RHEA DAVIS, a well-educated, blond-haired woman from Dallas who teaches school in Harlem, and his sister, Kate, an assertive, ambitious educational policymaker in Washington, D.C.

Kate has offered Loney an opportunity for a new beginning by urging him to join her in Washington. Although his life in Harlem is miserable, moving would mean severing his ties to his past, which are so fragile they have yet to be internalized. Loney is dependent on contact with the local Montana geography for a sense of connection to his personal history. He dreams about a seven-year-old boy named Amos, gesturing to an open landscape and declaring, "I live out there."

Because he is so inextricably tied to the land, Loney must decline his sister's offer. Meanwhile, Rhea attempts to convince him to move to Seattle with her at the end of the school year. Loney remains indecisive, continuing to drink and reflect on a nightly recurring vision of a slowly flying gigantic black bird, a vision he believes was sent by his mother's people but that he cannot interpret. So, too, he dwells on his need to create a past, a desire complicated by his mixed ancestry. Not fully Indian or white, he feels a lack of true identity.

Loney finally decides to leave Harlem. Soon after, he joins his childhood friend, Pretty Weasel, on a bear-hunting expedition. Momentarily disoriented, Loney accidentally shoots and kills Pretty Weasel, mistaking him for a bear. Shocked and distraught, he considers running away to Canada; instead, he runs back to Harlem where a sign at the town line ironically mocks Loney's decline by announcing that it is the home of the 1958 Class B high school basketball champs.

Looking for guidance, Loney seeks out his father at his home. Here he inquires about his mother but is told only lies. Although he hoped to find some explanation for his existence, Loney is disillusioned instead and realizes his problems are his own, not the result of his childish father. After leaving his father's home, Loney turns back and fires at the window with a gun Ike has just given him. Ike informs the local police of his son's whereabouts, and they pursue him to a nearby Mission Canyon. Loney fires on them and hits one of the policemen. Loney is then shot, and as he lies dying, he sees the vision of a dark bird climbing to a distant place.

Long, Ethel. *Beyond Desire.* Sherwood Anderson. 1932.

Ethel Long is a sophisticated twenty-nine-year-old southern woman who seeks wealth and status in the mill town of Langdon, Georgia. Educated at the University of Chicago where she attended college and library school, Ethel has gained a cultural sophistication and sense of style lacking in her small hometown. Having read literature and invested in clothing and fashion magazines, she has been courted by several men, among them a professor who tried to take advantage of her, and has culled enough experience to make her savvy in the art of love.

Upon her return to Langdon, Ethel lives with her father and his second wife Blanche. Blanche admires Ethel for her beauty and her style, and they spend a lot of time together. Blanche helps Ethel to secure a position at the local library. Ethel is soon courted by Tom Riddle, a wealthy criminal lawyer known for his shady dealings both in and out of the courtroom. A middle-aged balding man who, after taking a mistress and fathering an illegitimate child, is now divorced, Tom sees in Ethel the ideal wife for show and offers in return for marriage all the material advantages she seeks. But Ethel is attracted to RED OLIVER, a twenty-year-old, college-educated youth whom she sees as naive and idealistic. Instead of climbing the social ladder, Red has returned to work among the people at the mill in Langdon. He spends his evenings reading Marxist literature at the library, where Ethel, rightly sensing his attraction to her, spends many evenings. She realizes that she could have him if she wanted but that he would not be bold enough to make the first move.

One night during a violent thunderstorm, Ethel and Red stay at the library after closing and end up making love on a library table. Red is grateful and thinks of the possibilities for their future together. However, she has realized the impracticality of a life with this idealistic young boy and decides to accept Tom's proposal. Although Ethel feels a sense of maternal responsibility and

remorse for her actions, she nevertheless asks Red to leave. That evening she encounters Tom. He has seen her and Red enter the library but says nothing. When Ethel returns home, her father's wife, Blanche, professes her love for Ethel and tries to kiss her. Ethel rejects her advances but says nothing in order to avoid upsetting her father. The next day when she goes to Tom and accepts his proposal, they do not even touch; their relationship is "beyond desire."

Years later, after Ethel and Tom are married, she learns that Red has been killed in a labor riot in Birchfield, North Carolina. She does not attend the funeral, nor does she discuss the matter with her husband. A year later, however, during a violent thunderstorm like that of the evening she and Red were together, Ethel gets into her convertible and nearly kills herself driving in a mad frenzy. She returns to her separate bed in Tom's house early the next morning, never to discuss the matter.

Lonigan, William "Studs." *Young Lonigan: A Boyhood in Chicago Streets; The Young Manhood of Studs Lonigan; Judgment Day.* James T. Farrell. 1932; 1934; 1935.

William "Studs" Lonigan is a young man whose dreams of greatness conflict with the steady realization that his life is going nowhere, and whose sometimes fierce desires and resentments contrast with a strong sense of personal honor.

At the age of fourteen Studs, a member of an Irish Catholic family in early-twentieth-century Chicago, enjoys sneering at himself in the bathroom mirror with a cigarette hanging jauntily out of his mouth. Part of his time is spent hanging out with his neighborhood friends and indulging in sexually charged games with the local girls; the rest of his time is spent attending Catholic school and church and attempting to process his failure to observe a stringent code of behavior. Nevertheless, the Studs of the street has the finer time of it, and when he defeats a rival neighborhood tough, he becomes a local sensation among his peers. He naturally comes to resent his parents' assumption that he is a naive child who is to be spared the facts of life. His mother wants him to become a priest, while his father is more attuned to the young Studs's sensibilities.

Studs begins to feel attracted to Lucy Scanlan, an "angelic" young Catholic girl who accompanies him on pleasant excursions to the park, where one day Studs finds himself experiencing "goofy" feelings of affection—feelings he is unable to articulate. While he is at first ashamed of his "dirty" thoughts, he later determines to avoid this troublesome goofiness altogether. He focuses his attention on the Fifty-eight and Prairie Street gang, which he comes to lead. Their activities, which include messy drunken sprees, are a far cry from his dignified, innocent relations with Lucy.

A year later, World War I is impending, and Studs dreams of being a war hero, fighting for the greatest country on earth—the United States of America. However, he is inwardly afraid of death. He drops out of high school and spends most of his time in the local poolroom indulging in tough, wise-guy manhood. While Studs's job working for his father provides him with money, he does not want to paint houses for the rest of his life or be tied down to a wife. Nevertheless, he reforms for a while, working hard and staying sober. This pattern is broken when Studs participates in an ugly New Year's Eve debauch. By this time Lucy is gone forever, and Studs's main concerns involve blacks moving into the neighborhood and malcontents badmouthing the Catholic Church and the United States.

When Studs nears thirty, he feels himself growing old and is pained to think of what his life might have been. Most of his old friends are either dead or married; to him one state is about as good as the other. Studs himself continues to fear death, but a relationship with the slightly chunky but affectionate Catherine Banahan reinspires him with dreams of greatness, of constructing a good life in which he finally fulfills his "real self." He invests most of his savings in stocks, thinking of a future and a family, and although his younger brother humiliates him by beating him up and calling him a "has-been," Studs begins to find the sense of direction he has always lacked.

Studs's stocks eventually turn sour, his father's business founders, and his health fails. He still enjoys fleeting days of real happiness with Catherine and is able to acknowledge his affections openly to himself and to her. Studs cannot see how anyone could love him, but she does, and when she becomes pregnant, they are able for a time to negotiate the crisis and commit to marriage. Despite his failing health, he trudges through the rainy city looking for work and a new source of desperately needed capital for his wife and future child. Times are extremely hard for the economy and for Studs, and in a delirium brought on by pneumonia, he confronts the full dimensions of his disjointed dreams and fears.

Lonoff, Emanuel Isidore "E.I." *The Ghost Writer.* Philip Roth. 1979.

NATHAN ZUCKERMAN, an aspiring young writer, spends the night at the home of reclusive author E. I. Lonoff, an aging Jewish man whose literary works have greatly inspired him. Although Lonoff has purposely distanced himself from all forms of Jewish-American culture and tradition, Zuckerman is intrigued by him because his writing nevertheless focuses on the lives and emotions of American Jews.

E. I. Lonoff, age fifty-six, escaped as a small child from the pogroms of Russia. His parents settled in Palestine, and after they both died of typhus, Lonoff was sent to live with relatives in Brookline, Massachusetts. Through his fictional characters Lonoff examines the plight of American Jews in post–World War II America. He implies that these Jews feel guilty for having survived in America while their relatives died in European concentration camps, yet they are simultaneously distrusted and discriminated against by non-Jews in the United States.

Although it seems to Nathan Zuckerman that Lonoff has extraordinary insights into the Jewish-American mind, the aging author does not associate with other Jews in America. He lives in a secluded house in New England and is married to a Gentile woman named Hope Whittlesey. He has fathered three children, all of whom have grown up and moved away.

Lonoff continuously frustrates and infuriates his wife Hope, who constantly encourages him to be more social and to get out of the house more often. However, Lonoff tells Nathan that writing is a difficult task which requires intensive concentration and seclusion. The older that Lonoff gets and the more he works at writing, the harder it is for him to interact with others. He spends his days doing the same things over and over: He writes a sentence and then spends hours dissecting it, examining and rearranging it, before moving on to the next sentence. His life is made up of never-changing rituals; when Hope attempts to alter her husband's life-style even slightly—for example, by cooking a new dish for dinner—Lonoff complains or behaves as if he is undergoing some sort of drastic change.

Lonoff admits to Nathan that he is bored with his monotonous and secluded life-style but also acknowledges that he is incapable of accepting even the smallest change. He dreams of running off to Europe with a young, attractive woman who would take care of him and excite him sexually. This woman would replace Hope, who, after thirty-five years of marriage, no longer thrills Lonoff. Lonoff refuses to realize his own fantasies, however. He tells Nathan that he would never run away from his wife, for he appreciates her and cares for her too much to leave her. Hence, Lonoff remains, for the most part, secluded from the world outside, associating only with Hope and Amy Bellette, a young college student who admires Lonoff's writing and seems to love him as both a father figure and a romantic mate.

Hope threatens to leave Lonoff twice in the course of the novel: once at dinner and once after breakfast the next day. Nathan is shocked by Hope's tantrums, but Lonoff remains calm throughout. She tells Lonoff that she is tired of being his only link to the outside world and that his inability to accept even the most minor changes has left her exhausted and depressed. She begs him to let her go and to let Amy take her place as his companion. It is clear at the end of the novel, however, that Hope will never leave Lonoff and that Lonoff will never replace her with the younger and more enthusiastic Amy Bellette. As Nathan leaves the Lonoff house at the end of his stay, Lonoff is outside comforting the distraught Hope and begging her to come inside with him. Lonoff is used to Hope's behavior because she often throws these tantrums; they are simply regular routines that help to make up the monotonous, unchanging days of his life.

Love, Mary. *Nigger Heaven*. Carl Van Vechten. 1926.

Mary Love is an intelligent young librarian who is considered by some to be immune to the passions of the heart.

As the novel opens, Mary is a guest at a weekend party given by her wealthy acquaintance Adora Boniface. Mary finds the decadence of this very rich woman and her crowd more than she can bear, particularly when it comes to the advances of Randolph Pettijohn. She is mortified when Pettijohn asks for her hand in marriage, and she refuses despite his wealth. The one redeeming feature of the party is her introduction to BYRON KASSON, a recent college graduate who has come to New York to become a writer. Although intrigued by the young man, Mary does not meet him again until five months later when they are both guests at a dinner party.

They renew their acquaintance, and before many weeks have passed, the two are engaged. After a few weeks of blissfulness, the couple's relationship becomes troubled. Byron, who has come to New York to obtain employment while he hones his writing skills, fails to find work. Sensing his sensitivity to accepting the menial jobs that are the fare of black men, whether or not they are college-educated, Mary attempts to advise Byron. Resentful and proud, he responds with petulant fits of anger. The two lovers suffer further problems when Mary proves to be passionately jealous and possessive of Byron.

When he brings an idea for a short story to Mary, he is infuriated by her gentle but insightful criticism. After receiving several rejection slips for the story he writes, Byron and Mary are delighted by the arrival of a letter inviting the young writer to appear in a magazine editor's office. To his utter humiliation, Byron receives advice from the editor that corresponds with Mary's criticisms. This incident creates a rift in the relationship, and Byron takes up with Lasca Sartoris, a wealthy siren of notorious reputation in Harlem.

Despite Byron's desertion, Mary remains faithful and loving. Friends advise her to forget him and get on with her otherwise full and enjoyable life, but she cannot. Even after Byron has become the talk of Harlem because of his escapades with the amoral Lasca, Mary still loves him. Lasca eventually grows bored with the foolish paramour and leaves him despondent. Mary goes to him and attempts to convince him of her undying love. But for Byron, the visit only serves to heighten his sense of injury at Lasca's hands. Vowing to kill the woman and her latest lover, with whom he believes she has duped him, Byron goes to a cabaret frequented by her and her set. There he watches as another man slays Lasca's latest lover before he can. Perversely, Byron fires several shots into the dead

man and is mistakenly arrested. The novel closes with Byron confessing helplessly to Mary that he did not kill the man.

Lovejoy, Yoruba Evelyn. *The Cotillion (or One Good Bull Is Half the Herd)*. John Oliver Killens. 1971.

In this bittersweet black comedy of the 1960s, Yoruba Evelyn Lovejoy struggles to establish her own identity in the era of Black Power. The only child of Matt and Daphne Lovejoy, Yoruba grew up in Harlem, happy and secure between her father's gentle strength and common sense and her mother's domineering love and delusions of the superiority of her partly Caucasian heritage. Daphne had always tried to keep Yoruba from having any contact with the neighborhood children, but among them Yoruba found one special friend, Ernie, who moved away.

Ten years later, as the novel opens, Yoruba is an attractive young woman at odds with her mother, who is determined to raise herself and "Eve-lyn" (Daphne refuses to call her daughter "Yoruba") in social status. Daphne has decided that Yoruba must participate in the annual Cotillion of the Femmes Fatales, a group of elitist, wealthy African-American women. This year the ladies have decided to open their fete to five girls from the lower classes living in Harlem, and largely on the basis of Yoruba's beauty and her mother's groveling, Yoruba is among the chosen. Yoruba is not sure she wants to participate and is torn between her newfound awareness of her black identity and the glittering seductive pageantry of the Cotillion ball. In addition, Ernie has just come back into her life as BEN ALI LUMUMBA, an up-and-coming, semi-militant writer and intellectual. Yoruba accepts Ben as her mentor and relies on him to pilot her through the confusion she feels.

Ben understands Yoruba's dilemma and agrees, at first reluctantly, to escort her to the pre-Cotillion social event; he soon becomes fascinated with the world he encounters. Yoruba is annoyed by his enthusiasm, but he explains that there is value in all these events as a learning experience and that the Cotillion might be used to symbolize the beauty and dignity of what is African in African Americans. Ben's plan is that, instead of wearing the traditional pale pink gown and tuxedo, Yoruba and he should wear their hair natural and don the elegant robes of formal African attire. Yoruba is at first reluctant because her parents have invested a great deal of time and money in this event, and she doesn't want to cause a scene. Finally, however, she agrees.

The couple's appearance backstage at the ball nearly causes a riot. The ladies of the Femmes Fatales are about to attack the couple physically when Daphne intervenes and they escape onto the stage. The ill-advised theme of the ball is the antebellum southern plantation, and in the midst of the garish plantation decorations, Yoruba and Ben teach Daphne and the majority of the audience something of the foolishness of the Cotillion's trappings as well as the beauty and dignity inherent in all people of character, intelligence, and pride, including those of African origin.

Lovingood, Sut. *Sut Lovingood's Yarns.* George W. Garris. 1867.

Descended from a family of fools, Sut Lovingood is born for mischief; he has an unquenchable predilection for making others miserable and a talent for thinking of exotic ways to do it. When it comes time for retribution, Sut's primary physical attributes—a pair of extremely long legs—never fail to carry him out of harm's way.

Sut's stories are episodic and are related by the prankster's ethic that runs throughout. He begins by describing his father, the only person who might qualify as a challenger to Sut's foolish supremacy. When the family's horse dies, leaving them with no way to administer to their fields, Sut's father decides to take the place of the horse, not only by doing the animal's work but by acting like it as well. He takes his clothes off and asks Sut to hook him up to the plow. Then, much to the amusement of the family, he proceeds to mimic the horse's expressions, sounds, and movements. As they plow the field, the father leads Sut to a hornets' nest and investigates, just as a horse might. When the hornets, aroused and angered, chase his father, Sut watches from a safe distance, boundlessly amused.

One of Sut's favorite pastimes is the breaking up of social occasions. At a religious gathering of African-American slaves, he lets loose a passel of bees, causing some of the participants, including the parson, to throw off their clothes and run for the forest nearby. At a quilting bee, Sut ties a quilt to the hostess's horse and then wallops it with a plank to set it running wild through her house, destroying everything and forcing all the members of the household to flee. Sut's glee and satisfaction are never diminished by feelings of guilt. He is always able to rationalize his culpability: He only pulled the string on the mouth of the bag containing the hornets, or gave the horse a whack with a plank; the rest followed randomly, in circumstances beyond his control.

Nevertheless, Sut has a romantic side to his nature. He is attracted to a strapping young woman named Sicily Burns, who only returns his affections sporadically. One day Sicily, wearied by Sut's advances and more interested in another gentleman of her acquaintance, decides to cure Sut of his interest in her. She invites him to her home and offers him a series of beverages, which he compliantly drinks. When combined in his stomach, the liquids form a volcanic substance that threatens to explode through just about every bodily orifice.

Rather than embarrass himself in front of Sicily, Sut leaps on his horse and rides home as quickly as he can. Sicily gleefully calls after him, "Hole hit down, Mister Lovingood! . . . Hits a cure for puppy luv!" Sut is relieved, for the time being, of the symptoms of "puppy love"—but it is apparent that there is no cure for his demonic, mischievous nature.

Lucas, Sam. *One Way to Heaven.* Countee Cullen. 1932.

Sam Lucas is tall, dark, handsome, and a religious con artist. He has just arrived in Harlem after years of knocking about and comes upon a church ablaze with lights as it prepares to "watch in" the New Year. In need of money for food and shelter, Sam decides to run his game.

Years earlier Sam had lost an arm while hopping a freight car, and the loss of this appendage renders his act— he pretends to convert to a congregation in order to exploit the hospitality of its members—all the more pitiable. Just as the visiting evangelist is accepting new converts, Sam rises and approaches the mourners' bench. Then he dramatically tosses down a pack of playing cards and a razor. One unrepentant member of the congregation, beautiful young MATTIE JOHNSON, is so moved by this gesture that she joins Sam at the altar. The church is amazed at these conversions, and Mattie and Sam are embraced.

As the instrument of Mattie's conversion, Sam soon becomes the object of her love. In less than a week they are married, and Sam moves in with Mattie and her aunt Mandy. While Mattie becomes a devout and loyal member of the church, Sam begins a steady backslide. To appear at church functions without Sam by her side humiliates Mattie. In a desperate effort, one night she tricks Sam into attending a service with her where she publicly prays to God to reclaim her husband. Furious with embarrassment, Sam later vows to Mattie that she will never again have the opportunity to shame him. From this point the ex-shyster reverts to form.

Sam begins to stay away from home at night, acquiring a mistress named Emma May. He continues in this vein until he learns from Mattie that she is pregnant. During the pregnancy he becomes the loyal father-to-be, but when the baby boy dies within an hour of being born, he leaves home again.

Finally, Emma May comes to Mattie and informs her that Sam is gravely ill and in need of her. The doctor diagnoses the young man as having a fatal case of pneumonia, and Mattie takes him home so that she can care for him during his dying days. Sam overhears Mattie telling Aunt Mandy that she could bear her husband's death more easily if she were convinced his soul would meet hers and her baby's in heaven. The old woman explains to Mattie how she can tell whether or not a dying person will go to heaven or hell. Realizing that he is dying, Sam decides to run just one more scam.

When Mattie returns to his bedside, Sam plays out the scene he has heard Aunt Mandy describe. He dies, leaving Mattie convinced that they will meet again beyond Saint Peter's pearly gates.

Luciente. *Woman on the Edge of Time.* Marge Piercy. 1976.

Luciente is an imaginary character created by CONNIE CAMACHO RAMOS in order to escape from the horrendous environment she is forced to tolerate in a New York mental institution. An extremely self-confident woman from the year AD 2137, Luciente travels back to the twentieth century in order to establish contact with Connie. Motivated in part by a fear that the self-destructive humans of Connie's era might fail to survive and therefore preempt the future world that Luciente inhabits, she gives Connie tours of her world in an effort to ensure the safe transmission of life from the twentieth to the twenty-second century. An exemplary member of her highly regulated society, Luciente is puzzled by the haphazard, dangerous behavior she sees in twentieth-century humans.

A Wamponaug Indian who lives in Mattapoisett, Massachusetts, Luciente works as a geneticist who is actively opposed to twentieth-century genetic engineering. She does approve, however, of raising embryos in fluid receptacles in a building called the "brooder," where they bob up and down like fish. In Luciente's world, gender politics are so advanced that it is difficult to tell the men from the women. Both homosexual and heterosexual kinds of love are accepted, a freedom that Luciente exploits with pleasure. Having virtually transcended jealousy, people in her world commonly take multiple lovers; Luciente has steady relationships with two men named Bee and Jackrabbit. Luciente has made contact with several people from the past and finds that the most receptive subjects of time-traveling communication are usually women in prisons or mental institutions. Using her own culture—which recycles virtually everything—as a model, she attempts to teach these women how to be careful with the environment.

Due to her participation in a coming-of-age ritual called "naming" wherein young people travel to distant locales and demonstrate their ability to survive on their own, Luciente is well versed in wilderness survival techniques. She is thus granted the right to live independently and choose her own name, an act that signifies adulthood. When Connie temporarily escapes from the mental institution and is stranded without food while hiding from the authorities in a forest, Luciente comes to the rescue, pointing out edible plants, locating a water source, and generally offering solace and comfort. Through her imagined encounters with Luciente, Connie finds some measure of emotional support, but as she descends further into madness and becomes increasingly hardened in reaction to her inhumane treatment, Luciente's world becomes more difficult for her to visit. This time-traveler from the future eventually loses her ability to establish contact with the twentieth-century woman whom she has tried to befriend and to warn about the perils that threaten the continued existence of human life.

Lukoszaite, Ona. *The Jungle.* Upton Sinclair. 1905.

Ona Lukoszaite is the pretty sixteen-year-old daughter of a wealthy farmer in Lithuania. One day Ona meets a strong young man, JURGIS RUDKUS, at a horse fair, and he is instantly drawn to her. When Jurgis travels to see her, he finds that Ona's father has died and that her family has been forced to sell their farm. Ona's brother Jonas suggests that they all immigrate to America, where his friend Jokubas Szedvilas has supposedly "gotten rich" in Chicago's stockyards district, or Packingtown.

Once they arrive in Chicago, Ona, her cousin Marija Berczynskas, and her stepmother Teta Elzbieta go to look at a house advertised in a leaflet. Ona wants to cry out that they are being swindled by the agent but finds herself paralyzed with anxiety. She becomes excited, though, as she furnishes the house and painstakingly chooses the many small items that go into making the immigrants' first American home.

Jurgis and Ona now plan to marry, but Ona is reluctant to see much money spent on their wedding feast. However, the feast, called *veselija*, is a Lithuanian tradition, and Teta Elzbieta insists that they not abandon their cultural heritage now that they are in the New World. Ona decides that she must get work if they are to afford it, and although Jurgis opposes this, when they find out that they must also pay interest on their mortgage, the matter is settled.

Ona is hired in a sausage-wrapping room at Brown's huge packing plant after she bribes a foreman through her cousin Marija. At one point Ona forgets to ask for a trolley transfer on the way to work and must walk a long way through the mud and rain. This is the beginning of a long decline and an illness from which Ona never recovers. When she gives birth to little Antanas, she must return to work a week later out of economic necessity. Her condition rapidly deteriorates, and she is further pained that Jurgis seems unaware of her suffering. Ona wonders if he loves her less now because of all their troubles.

Ona's dream of a happy life fades, despite her best attempts to keep it alive, because of a brutal litany of misfortunes: Jurgis is injured at work; his father Antanas dies; her brother Jonas deserts them; and little Antanas drowns in a large puddle in the street. When Ona becomes pregnant again, she is often hysterical from her illness and her grief.

After a stormy winter night when she fails to come home, Ona tells Jurgis that the blizzard forced her to go home with her friend Jadvyga Marcinkus. When it happens again, Jurgis, worried, goes to Jadvyga's and finds that Ona is not there and did not go there the first time. Jurgis confronts Ona at home, and Ona confesses that her foreman forced her into prostitution under the threat of losing her job. When Jurgis hunts him down and attacks him, Ona cannot get her job back. With Jurgis in jail, Ona and the others must return to the squalid flat where they first lived. On the night when Jurgis finally returns, Ona dies giving birth to a stillborn second child in a cold, dark garret.

Lumumba, Ben Ali. *The Cotillion (or One Good Bull Is Half the Herd).* John Oliver Killens. 1972.

Ben Ali Lumumba, the novel's narrator, tells a story of intra-racism, class consciousness, the search for identity, and the discovery of a heritage in the style, idioms, and rhythms of the Harlem of the 1960s.

Born Ernest Walter Billings, Ben Ali Lumumba grew up in Harlem where he and YORUBA EVELYN LOVEJOY were close friends and confidants, in spite of the disapproval of Daphne Lovejoy, Yoruba's elitist mother. At eighteen he went to sea as a merchant marine, just as his father had before him, and his travels, reading, and natural curiosity afforded him an excellent education. He lived in Africa for several years and, after changing his name to Ben Ali Lumumba, returned home to Harlem to settle and to write poetry.

While performing his poetry one evening at a café, Ben sees Yoruba in the audience, is attracted, and decides to meet her. Yoruba finds him egotistical and phony. There is something familiar and comforting about him, however, and she allows him to walk her home. Once she pries his "slave name" out of him, she realizes that he is her beloved childhood friend. Both are overjoyed at being reunited, and they renew their friendship and find love in the midst of the confusion of Yoruba's current life. Yoruba has been chosen to participate in "the Cotillion," an annual social event held by a group of wealthy, elitist, African-American women known as the Femmes Fatales. Ben knows that the Cotillion is important to her in a certain sense, despite what Yoruba says to the contrary. He reluctantly agrees to accompany her to the pre-Cotillion social events and becomes fascinated by the world he encounters. He sees it as fertile ground for a novel and begins to participate enthusiastically; and he is accepted because he has been written up in *The New York Times* as a talented voice among African-American literati. Yoruba is distressed by his enthusiasm for such an elitist event until he explains its value as a learning experience and the way it might be used to symbolize the heritage and dignity of African Americans. Ben's plan is for him and Yoruba to wear traditional African formal attire rather than the usual gown and tuxedo to the Cotillion ball.

When Ben and Yoruba appear backstage at the ballroom, the ladies are horrified. They are about to physically attack the couple when Yoruba and her escort are introduced by the emcee. The couple escapes onto the stage, and at their appearance a stunned silence settles on the hall. A wave of applause slowly builds. As Ben and Yoruba walk from the stage, across the floor, and out the exit, the applause grows, and the couple is joined by Yoruba's parents and more than half the audience.

M

M——, Ambrose. "Lost in the Funhouse." John Barth. 1967.

Ambrose M——, the thirteen-year-old protagonist of this story, is at a turning point in his development. As the story opens, Ambrose, his parents, his brother Peter, his uncle Karl, and Magda G——, their fourteen-year-old neighbor, are driving toward Ocean City, a trip his family takes three times annually—on Memorial Day, Independence Day, and Labor Day.

This particular trip takes place on the Fourth of July. While the trip seems fairly long, over the years the family has developed several strategies, including games, to cope with the tedium of the road. By this time in his life, though, Ambrose has long since figured out the strategies behind the one that requires being the first to espy some landmark. He sometimes avails himself of the tactics he knows, but he is equally likely to ignore the game altogether.

As the trip continues, Ambrose, whose actions are continuously interrupted by the narrator's qualifications, asides, and commentaries on narration, thinks off and on about sex and about his maturation. Most of his sexual thoughts seem to center around a forbidden and barely subconscious desire for Magda. When the second landmark has been discovered, the family's anticipation accelerates, and the smell of the ocean grows stronger.

Upon their arrival, the mother gives a dollar to each of the children and warns them not to squander it hastily. She doles out these funds even though the children have brought money of their own to spend on the funhouse. Because of the World War II, Ocean City has been placed under a brownout: The city lights facing the sea are dimmed, and there are to be no fireworks, lest enemy ships shell the U.S. forces made visible in silhouette. Moreover, the family must swim in the pool because a bombed U-boat has produced an oil slick that clings to bathers. Ambrose, sensitive about his as yet undeveloped physique, shies away from swimming in front of other youths, but he manages to spend some time with Magda, who for reasons unclear to Ambrose also decides not to swim.

The children enter the funhouse and have a good deal of fun, except for Ambrose who makes his way into a restricted, indeed forgotten, area. Here, Ambrose, apparently lost, comes to grips with much about life. He fears that self-deception will be his lot and even goes so far as to lose track of himself in the reflections of the funhouse mirrors. The boy is plucky enough not to panic, however; he thinks of his embarrassing inability to control his sexual impulses and realizes that when the opportunity arose, he should not have told Magda that he loved her, although she appears not to have heard him anyway.

When Ambrose rejoins his family, it is nearly time to depart. Ambrose fantasizes about returning to Ocean City with a family and children, and he envisions himself sagely instructing his son about what a funhouse used to be. Ambrose knows the things he remembers will not be there when he returns. As the story ends, the family travels homeward, and Ambrose wonders if he will ever find happiness. He has faked emotions at so many important events. He envisions a lonely future building funhouses for others rather than traveling through a funhouse with someone he loves.

Maas, Oedipa. *The Crying of Lot 49.* Thomas Pynchon. 1966.

Oedipa Maas, a twenty-eight-year-old Young Republican housewife in Kinneret-Among-the-Pines, California, returns home from a Tupperware party to find that she has been named by the late Pierce Inverarity as executor of his will. Oedipa and Pierce, a real estate mogul, had been lovers at one time, but the affair ended, and Oedipa married Wendell "Mucho" Maas, a disk jockey for KCUF radio. Her life since has been one of isolation. When the letter comes from Metzger, the co-executor, informing Oedipa of her appointment, she leaves her herb garden and Mucho to look into Pierce's books and records. She heads south in a rented Impala and takes a room at Echo Courts in San Narciso, which had been Pierce's home and headquarters.

Throughout the novel Oedipa expresses paranoid suspicions of plots and conspiracies, and when Metzger shows up at Echo Courts, she finds him suspiciously handsome. Oedipa and Metzger play a parodic version of strip poker while being serenaded by a rock band called the Paranoids, and the night's infidelity with Metzger is the beginning of the end of Oedipa's encapsulated isolation. First with Metzger and then without him, Oedipa begins

to discover many mysterious coincidences, all centering on what she calls the "Tristero thing," the initials W.A.S.T.E., and a symbol of a muted post horn that she seems to find everywhere.

Oedipa first stumbles upon the Tristero while investigating one of Inverarity's holdings by attending a production of a Jacobean revenge play, *The Courier's Tragedy,* and hearing the word in the closing lines. During the course of the novel she discovers that the Tristero is connected to an underground mail system, which she suspects may have opposed the Thurn und Taxis postal system in Europe, attacked the Pony Express in America, produced forgeries of stamps, and served as a channel of communication for the alienated and forgotten members of California's underworld and the subculture of America.

Among those who might be involved with Tristero is Oedipa's own Mucho, who sends her a letter with a post horn symbol on the envelope and who later alienates Oedipa when he participates in an LSD study conducted by Oedipa's crazed psychiatrist, Dr. Hilarius. Oedipa encounters many bizarre participants in the Tristero system, such as John Nefastis, an apparently deluded inventor who equates the entropy of thermodynamics to the entropy of information flow by means of a metaphor he constructed himself.

Oedipa eventually has doubts regarding her own sanity and the burgeoning web of coincidences that are linked only by the word *Tristero.* She cannot decide whether she is hallucinating, paranoid, the victim of an elaborate joke or plot concocted and financed by Inverarity, or insane. Oedipa's quest for the ultimate revelation of what is behind the Tristero and Inverarity's real legacy is left unfulfilled. At the end of the novel she sits in the back of an auction room, waiting for the crying of lot 49.

McAdoo, Julius. *The Conjure Woman.* Charles W. Chesnutt. 1899.

Julius McAdoo is an ex-slave and storyteller. Born and matured to middle age in slavery, Julius remains attached to a plantation long after the Civil War is over and the plantation is in ruins. When John and Annie, a couple who move to North Carolina from the Great Lakes region, buy the plantation where Julius still lives, he attaches himself to them as a carriage driver and unofficial adviser.

In response to John's requests for advice, Julius always resorts to a folktale that is usually set in the antebellum period and deals with some aspect of slavery. Although the purpose of each of Julius's stories seems ostensibly to be personal gain, he ultimately reveals some problem with which blacks had to contend during slavery. Julius manipulates John for his own interests, but he coerces Annie into a realistic understanding of the horrific nature of slavery. The folktales center on the magic—"goopher"—performed by old conjurers, some slaves, some freed blacks. More often than not they involve the outwitting of masters by slaves.

The story of "Po' Sandy," which Julius relates in order to prevent John from tearing down an old schoolhouse for the lumber, tells the story of a slave who proves to be such a good worker that his master lends him out, like a horse, to relatives and friends. In the dialect of the plantation slave, Julius tells how Sandy loses a wife; she is sold while he is away from the plantation. Distraught by his continual mobility, Sandy complains to Tenie, his second wife and a conjure woman. To prevent Sandy's being sent to and fro, Tenie changes him into a tree. When Tenie goes to work on another plantation, Sandy is cut down and taken to the sawmill for timber. After the mistress has built a kitchen, Sandy "haints" it so that no one will set foot in it. The kitchen is eventually given over to Negroes for a school. So touched is Annie by this tale that she refuses to have her kitchen built from the old schoolhouse. Instead, she donates the building to Julius's church. The clever old man has manipulated the couple into satisfying his wishes.

Macauley, Homer. *The Human Comedy.* William Saroyan. 1943.

Fourteen-year-old Homer Macauley works part-time as a telegraph messenger boy in Ithaca, California, to help his mother support the family while his elder brother is a soldier fighting in World War II. Hardworking and sincere, Homer impresses the manager, JOSEPH SPANGLER, a man who is kind to everyone he meets, and becomes a friend to Willie Grogan, the old telegraph operator who fears being forced to retire and is often asleep or drunk when a late-night telegram comes in. Both men are pleased with Homer's speed in delivering telegrams, his drive and ambition, as well as his honesty.

On his first day on the job, Homer must deliver a telegram to a woman whose son has been killed in the war. He feels awkward as the bearer of such sad news and is made even more uncomfortable when the woman invites him into her home and treats him like her son. When he arrives home that night, Homer tells his mother his disconcerting experience with the woman whose son had died. Mrs. Macauley tells Homer that she would not react with sadness if she received a telegram announcing the death of her son Marcus because he can never really die in her heart. Contemplating what she has said, Homer realizes that his perspective on life has changed in the two days since he started working, and he tells his mother that for the first time he has begun to see the loneliness created by the war. His wise mother tells Homer that the sadness he sees is a cause of the war, not a symptom.

The next day at school, Homer decides to run in a hurdle race, which he almost misses when he is held after class by his history teacher, Miss Hicks, who lectures him about the justice she believes prevails in the world. When

he finally does start in the race, Homer is physically held back by the coach, who wants another, wealthier boy to win. Homer is surprised when the other boy, Hubert Ackley III, makes all the runners stop and wait until Homer rejoins the race. Because of his determination and Hubert's belief in justice, Homer is able to finish at the same time as Hubert.

When he has to deliver another telegram announcing the death of a young soldier, Homer asks Mr. Grogan if there is any purpose to the deaths in the war. Mr. Grogan explains that soldiers die seeking justice and moving humanity closer to the goal of universal truth. Homer is moved and expresses his desire to spend his life trying to make the world a better place by always doing what he thinks is right.

In a dream that night, Homer sees himself racing the messenger of death and trying to keep it away from Ithaca. He sobs in his sleep when he is unable to prevent Death from going to his town. By morning he has forgotten his dream, but he does talk to his mother about the growing sadness he feels. His mother explains that what he feels is pity for the evil and loneliness in the world and that he, as a good man, should try to lessen the suffering of humanity.

Upon receiving a letter from his brother Marcus, Homer declares to Mr. Grogan that he will hate the world and become coldhearted if his brother is killed. But when a telegram comes saying that Marcus Macauley has indeed been slain, Homer finds that he really cannot hate anyone for his brother's death; he must accept it and go on living. With the telegram in his hand Homer goes home to his family. His brother's best friend, Tobey George, meets Homer on the front steps and tells him to throw the telegram away. His brother is not dead, Tobey tells the boy, because he lives on in the memories of his friends and family.

MacAusland, Elizabeth "Libby." *The Group.* Mary McCarthy. 1954.

Elizabeth MacAusland, nicknamed "Libby" by her friends, is a popular blond-haired beauty from Pittsfield, Massachusetts, who becomes increasingly disliked by her eight-member clique of Vassar students. A tense but convivial young woman, Libby is president of the Circolo Italiana and is elected president of the sophomore class. However, her taste for scandal and her addiction to malicious gossip continues to try the patience of her suitemates, and they discount her more and more as the years go on.

Although Libby had been promised a full-time job at a New York City publishing house upon graduation from college, the job falls through, and her boss, the editor Augustus LeRoy, gives her a few manuscripts to assess for a meager reward of five dollars per book. Because Libby's parents are supplementing her income, she can afford to accept the arrangement and throws herself into her work with admirable enthusiasm. Even so, despite her formidable ambition and the conscientious application of her literary skills, developed at Vassar as an English major and editor-in-chief of the literary magazine, Libby loses her job. Mr. LeRoy eventually informs her that publishing is really a male profession and that, while she is a talented writer, she would be better off pursuing a career as an agent because she is too sympathetic to succeed in this hard-boiled field. When Libby hears of her dismissal, she faints. Mr. LeRoy, who thinks she has passed out from hunger, gives her eleven dollars for food and a taxi, and very kindly refers her to a relatively high-paying job as assistant to a reputable literary agent. In addition to this professional coup, she succeeds in getting one of her poems published by *Harper's* and, after only two years in New York City, her career is well under way.

Despite her busy career, Libby finds the time to enjoy picnics with the various men she dates and goes on skiing holidays at nearby resorts. On one of these excursions she meets a dashing young Norwegian baron named Nils Aslund who manages the Altan ski run. Although Libby's snobbish family criticizes Nils's profession and likens his position to that of a golf pro, she is thrilled at the prospect of his proposing to her, and when she believes that he has decided to do so, she throws a gala party. Following the party, an aroused Nils begins to fondle her and, ripping her dress from her body and pinning her down, tries to rape her. She is saved from further violation when Nils realizes she is a virgin and, therefore, as he brutally puts it, a bore. Needless to say, the relationship is terminated.

When one of the women in the Vassar group, the divorced Kay Strong Petersen, suddenly dies, Libby attends the funeral and is reunited with her estranged friends. She is now a married woman, having chosen one of her authors as a husband, but marriage seems only to have exacerbated her native crassness. Having observed that the color of the deceased's dress does not suit her, she then rudely asks if Kay's death was accidental or a suicide. The group soundly reprimands her for her constant inability to control her heartless curiosity and bluntness.

McCaskill, Angus Alexander. *Dancing at the Rascal Fair.* Ivan Doig. 1987.

A hearty Scottish immigrant who settles in northern Montana in the early 1900s, Angus McCaskill carves out a living as a sheep rancher and occasional schoolteacher.

In 1889, Angus makes the harrowing journey from Scotland to America with his best friend Rob Barclay. The two men track Rob's uncle Lucas to Gros Ventre, a small town in northern Montana. Rob and Angus aim to establish homesteads, and Lucas joins them as a partner in buying sheep. After picking out two prime homesteads, Angus and Rob build homes, fences, and barns, and begin

their sheep farming business. Despite the harshness of the first Montana winter, the sheep fare well.

Angus feels lonely and hungers for a wife. When wool and lamb prices drop, he works as the local schoolteacher, as he had in Scotland. In the fall of 1896, Angus falls in love with Anna Ramsay, the new teacher in a nearby school. They court all winter and consummate their relationship just before they part for the summer. Because Angus must tend sheep in the mountains and Anna has a job cooking for Isaac Reese's road building crew, their marriage is postponed. That summer Rob brings his pretty younger sister, Adair, over from Scotland in the hopes of marrying her to Angus. Angus angrily makes it clear that he intends to wed Anna. He pines for Anna all summer, but that fall he is devastated when Anna tells him she will marry Isaac Reese.

In his despair, Angus asks Adair to marry him and she agrees. Their marriage is hard; Angus still loves Anna, and Adair suffers through two miscarriages. Finally, in 1899, Adair gives birth to a baby boy, Varick.

Rob and Angus buy more sheep and lease grazing land from the Blackfeet reservation. One night during shearing time, Anna rests at the camp on her way to a road crew. She and Angus talk together for hours and watch the sunrise. Rob, furiously disapproving of Angus's enduring love for Anna, informs Varick of his father's extramarital desires. Varick is devastated and refuses to live or speak with his father. Angus pummels Rob for his interference, and the two become enemies.

When World War I breaks out in Europe, Varick goes off to the army. At the same time, an influenza epidemic hits Montana. Angus takes ill; Adair nurses him back to health, and he recovers to find that Anna died of the sickness. Lucas dies and leaves his share of the flock jointly to Angus, Rob, and Adair. Angus and Rob, who must tend the sheep together or forfeit, manage to function in spite of their continuing antagonism. When the war ends, Varick comes home and is reconciled with his father. But trouble sets in: Prices drop, two summers of drought deplete the flocks, and there is not enough hay for the winter, which threatens to be the worst ever. When all looks lost, Varick borrows horses from Isaac Reese and he, Angus, and Rob take sleds to the nearest railway for hay. They survive the trip and save most of their flock. The following spring, Rob drowns, Varick marries Lizabeth Reese, Anna's daughter; and Angus and Adair, who have grown closer, look forward to beginning a new season.

McCaskill, John Angus "Jick." *English Creek; Ride with Me, Mariah Montana.* Ivan Doig. 1984; 1990.

A true son of the mountains, John Angus McCaskill, known to all as "Jick," comes to manhood among the sheep and cattle ranchers of the northern Montana Rockies. Jick is a homespun antagonist who finds wonder in the small events of country life. Delivered as a memoir, his first-person narrative evokes the character of the men and women in Montana with compassion and humor.

As a lad of fourteen, Jick lives with his father, Varick, a forest ranger, and his mother, Elisabeth, in the Two Medicine National Forest near the town of Gros Ventre. He accompanies his father on a trip to count sheep on leased Forest Service land in order to see how the herds fared during the winter. On the trail they meet Stanley Meixell, an old family friend. Jick discovers that Stanley is a drunkard, but Stanley satisfies Jick's urge to learn local history with tales of the old days.

The whole family goes to Gros Ventre for the Fourth of July picnic and rodeo. Through July, Jick helps his uncle Pete harvest hay. When, at the end of August, a lightning fire in Two Medicine burns out of control, Varick is placed in charge of fighting it. It is only through following Stanley's advice, however, that Varick is able to extinguish the blaze. In the process he sees that his own plan would have led to disaster. Jick learns that years ago, Stanley was the head ranger of Two Medicine, and Varick's mentor. Stanley made a bad decision back then that unleashed the infamous 1910 forest fire, an act that Varick could never bring himself to forgive. The revelations of that summer mark Jick for the rest of his life.

Many years later, Jick's second wife has just died and his two daughters are leading their separate lives. Mariah, his younger daughter, a photo journalist, asks him to accompany her and her ex-husband Riley Wright, a reporter, on a centennial tour of Montana for a series of articles. Jick eventually agrees, and he learns about the history of the state while coming to terms with his own past.

As Jick's memories of his life unfold, he reveals that he was wounded in the Aleutians and returned to Missoula to attend forestry school, where he met his first wife. The marriage soon collapsed, and Jick married to Marcella Withrow. They had two daughters, Lexa and Mariah, and worked a sheep ranch. Marcella and Jick had planned to tour the country in a Winnebago, but Marcella was stricken with cancer and died. Now Jick tours Montana in the Winnebago with Mariah and Riley Wright, whom he doesn't like. Together they visit buffalo herds, Butte (where hundreds died in the copper mines), the Chief Joseph Battleground, and other sites. As tensions ease among the three, Riley asks Mariah to marry him again. She accepts, to Jick's dismay, and they go to tell Riley's widowed mother Leona who had been engaged to Jick's brother Alec years before.

When Leona decides to join him on their travels, she and Jick grow close. It is not long before Jick asks her to marry him, to give them both a new start on life. She proudly agrees. As the novel ends, Jick stands observing the centennial celebration in Gros Ventre. He leans his great head back and sees the centennial flags flapping in the wind, the skyline, and the ragged mountains—and Mariah snaps a picture of him, laughing.

McCaslin, Isaac "Ike." "The Bear"; "Delta Autumn." William Faulkner. 1942; 1942.

Isaac McCaslin is an idealistic and eccentric man who attempts to atone for the iniquities that resulted from the institution of slavery. Born on a plantation in the fictional county of Yoknapatawpha, Mississippi, when his father was almost seventy years old, Ike is a carpenter and an accomplished hunter and woodsman. His affinity with the wilderness harkens back to a natural philosophy related to Native American beliefs, which include the conviction that land cannot be individually owned because it has been given by God to all human beings to cherish and protect. Out of step with the acquisitive American culture that surrounds him, Isaac is forced to face the fact that a lifetime dedicated to an alternate system of ethics has been lived in vain.

At the age of ten, Ike makes his first journey to a hunting camp in the wilderness where a group of men, including several Civil War veterans, gather to shoot game. SAM FATHERS, an old man who lives alone in the wilderness and is the son of a Chickasaw chief and a black slave, decides to become Ike's mentor and immediately begins to teach the boy his version of the beliefs and practices of a noble hunter. Fathers tells the tale of a mammoth bear with a trap-injured, warped foot named Old Ben, whose destructive escapades are famous throughout the territory. During the course of his novitiate in the woods, Ike is presented with a number of chances to shoot Old Ben, but he refrains from doing so because the bear embodies the timeless grandeur of the wilderness. Old Ben is finally killed by BOON HOGGANBECK, a blithering fool incapable of appreciating the ethics of hunters like Sam Fathers, whose death soon follows.

At the age of sixteen, Ike becomes obsessed with the financial ledgers in which his family has kept track of the transactions they completed for their cotton plantation, as well as for the commissary that provided supplies for the slaves and, later, for the freed laborers who cultivated and lived on the land. To his horror, Ike discovers a history of miscegenation and incest committed by his grandfather, Carothers McCaslin. The revelation changes the course of his entire life. In a ledger entry dated June 23, 1833, Ike reads that a beautiful slave named Eunice drowned herself, and by piecing together disparate bits of information, he discovers that her act was a response to the fact that her daughter, whose father was Carothers McCaslin, had been impregnated by her own father.

Intense guilt over his grandfather's moral transgression leads Ike to refuse his inheritance of land and money. Taking up carpentry, he attempts to escape from the sins of the culture that spawned him. However, his wife, who is furious at his refusal to seize his inheritance, attempts to bribe him with sexual favors and then withdraws her love when he fails to comply with her acquisitive motives. Even more disillusioning is the fact that his nephew, Roth

Edmonds, has sired the child of one of his black relatives, yet another descendant of the incestuous relationship between Carothers McCaslin and Eunice's daughter. Sadly aware that his repudiation of his inheritance was an impotent act against the tainted morality of the South, an elderly and disenchanted Ike muses on the ethically bankrupt culture that he had vainly hoped to escape.

McCaslin, Ned William. *The Reivers.* William Faulkner. 1962.

Ned William McCaslin, a black coachman at a livery stable, is a stowaway aboard an automobile—the second automobile in Jefferson, Mississippi—that BOON HOGGANBECK and young Lucius Priest, also livery stable employees, have stolen from Lucius's grandfather. In the ensuing adventures, Ned demonstrates his cunning as he negotiates his way through the racist environment of the turn-of-the-century South.

As soon as the three arrive at their destination, a Memphis brothel, Ned vanishes, with promises to be back by the time they plan to leave. Instead he returns at two in the morning and announces that he has traded the automobile for an erratic racehorse, Coppermine, whom they rename Lightning. Amid flirtations with a gold-toothed maid, Ned assures Boon that if they can only get the horse to Parsham for a race against its nemesis, a skittish thoroughbred named Acheron, they will win back the car and a fair amount of money in addition. Ned is certain he can get Lightning, a chronic loser, to run full-tilt.

Once they reach Parsham, Ned enlists the help of some connections to house and train the horse. Using mysterious means to urge the horse into one hard run around a makeshift track, Ned lets news of the upcoming race circulate throughout the region.

At the race, Acheron wins the first heat, and the second ends in a dispute. Before the final heat, a salacious and corrupt sheriff arrests Ned and Boon for stealing the horse, but the owners of the two horses step in and insist that the competition be completed. In the final heat, Lightning wins easily.

Pressed by Lucius's uncle and the two horse owners to reveal his trade secrets, Ned shows how extensive his manipulation of events has been. Upon arriving in Memphis, he encountered a young relative, Bobo Beauchamp, who was in deep financial trouble. Since Bobo's job was caring for Lightning, he attempted to walk off with the horse to settle his debts. Ned gave Bobo's creditor the car for the horse, on the assumption that the man would be attracted to Parsham by news of the race and would venture his newly acquired car. All worked as planned, despite the arrests and the arrival of Lucius's grandfather. In a final heat, run at the request of the owners, Lightning loses by a head, and Ned, foretelling the outcome, wins $500. Ned, stage manager of the almost farcical action, is simply someone who understands how people and animals be-

have. He recognized Lightning as a fast horse who wanted only the proper bait to run (Ned used a sardine), just as he correctly gauged the behavior of Bobo's creditor, Boon, young Lucius, the sheriff, and many others.

McClellan, Everett. *Run River.* Joan Didion. 1963.

Everett McClellan, a California farmer, has spent his life trying to live up to rigid standards set by his father, who had wanted him to be a lawyer. At the beginning of the novel, Everett, driven by cumulative anger and despair, murders Ryder Channing, the former lover of Everett's dead sister and his wife's current lover. While his wife, LILY KNIGHT (MCCLELLAN), attempts to help him invent a story for the police, Everett's mind wanders over the uneven course of his life.

Following his graduation from Stanford, Everett began an affair with the young Lily Knight, with whom he soon eloped to Reno, Nevada. While their marriage was hasty, it started off well until Lily began to feel restive under the pressure of what appeared to be a competition with her sister-in-law, the younger Martha McClellan. Within two years Lily bore two children. Despite his familial responsibilities, Everett enlisted in the service at the outbreak of World War II. While he was away, Lily managed to reach an understanding with her in-laws, and although Everett did not say so, he began to dread his return home. For the first time ever, he was away from chronic concerns and pressures and actually enjoyed his stint in the army. This interlude ends when he is called home in the aftermath of his father's death. Despite his reluctance, he is granted a hardship discharge and returns to assume the responsibilities of growing hops and the expansion of his father's estate.

When Everett returns to what he thinks is a relatively stable family, he soon learns that Lily has been having an affair with Joe Templeton. Within six months of Everett's return, this affair leads to pregnancy. Despite his wounded pride and his anger, Everett helps Lily with the arrangements for a trip to an abortionist. Shortly after this, his sister's affair with Ryder Channing takes a turn for the worse when he jilts her to marry a San Francisco heiress. While Martha affects an uncaring attitude, she is irrevocably changed. When she drowns in a flood-ravaged river, it is unclear whether her death was an accident or a suicide. After finally acknowledging that Martha is dead, a fact he tried to ignore long after rescuers had stopped trying to revive her, Everett hastily buries her at the edge of the river.

After Martha's untimely death, Everett realizes that while Lily's affair with Joe Templeton may have ended, she has begun one with the notorious Ryder Channing. Still grieving over his sister's death, Everett exacts revenge for being cuckolded once again. He resolves to kill Ryder; he lures him down to the riverbank and performs the deed. At the conclusion of the novel, Everett and Lily return to the scene of the murder and effect a kind of reconciliation. Lily urges Everett to summon the police to tell them that an accident has taken place. While she awaits their arrival, Everett walks off and shoots himself dead.

McClellan, Lily Knight. *Run River.* Joan Didion. 1963.

At thirty-six, Lily Knight McClellan, EVERETT McCLELLAN's adulterous wife, has been married for almost nineteen years. Her marriage has been a tempestuous one, marked by affairs and emotional distancing. As the novel opens, Everett has just shot and killed the roguish Ryder Channing, who had been one of Lily's lovers.

Lily was raised as the pampered only child of Walter and Edith Knight. Her adulation of her father was shattered when it became clear, after his accidental death, that he had been having an affair for many years. Distressed by this information and by her mother's grief, Lily rushed into an early marriage with Everett, the son of a wealthy farmer. While she did not really love her husband, Lily became devoted to their family and adored their son Knight and daughter Julia. After the children were born, Everett joined the armed forces to serve in World War II, and he left Lily with the care of his father and much younger sister, Martha. Lily managed admirably to care for the aging Mr. McClellan, who suffered from a lingering terminal illness.

When he returned home from the war, Everett became a more ambitious farmer and increased their landholdings. At the same time, Lily became less interested in him. Eventually, she began a lengthy affair with one of their friends, Joe Templeton, whose wife Francie was an alcoholic, a fact that supposedly led to his infidelity. This affair came to a head when Lily discovered that she was pregnant. Although her relationship with Everett was severely strained, she informed him of her dilemma and of her decision to travel to San Francisco for an abortion. Everett agreed to her plan but at the same time withdrew emotionally from her. Upon returning from her stay in the city, Lily resumed her adulterous habits and took up with Ryder Channing, Martha McClellan's former lover. This affair meant little to Lily. However, following Martha's sudden drowning in the flood-engorged river, Everett became adamant about the threat posed by Ryder's affair with his wife.

The two men eventually confront each other. When Lily hears gunshots and appears at the river's edge, it is already too late. Ryder is dead. Shocked by her husband's deed, she helps him invent a story for the police. Lily and Everett appear to reach a new level of mutual understanding and regard, but while she is awaiting the arrival of the police, Lily hears yet another shot. This time Everett has taken his own life.

At the end of the novel, Lily, with her children heading off to college, is left alone. The plaintive Joe Templeton is her only companion. He still desires her and claims that he'll divorce his wife for her, an event Lily knows will never take place.

McCrae, Augustus. *Lonesome Dove: A Novel.* Larry McMurtry. 1985.

Augustus McCrae is the current co-owner of the Hat Creek Company. Gus and his partner, Woodrow Call, rode with the Texas Rangers for twenty years, helping to settle the territory west of the Rockies. Now in late middle-age, Gus and Call have set up business in the quiet Texas town of Lonesome Dove.

Gus is full of talk and life. He was born and raised in Kentucky and educated at the University of Virginia. His father had hoped that Gus would be a lawyer, and although Gus completely turned his back on conventional occupations, he retains a smattering of Latin and a love of knowledge. Living among cowhands and with his taciturn friend Call, Gus most misses good conversation. He spends much of his time in the saloon, talking with Lorena, a young whore who likes him but doesn't understand why he is so nice to her.

Jake Spoon, another former ranger, arrives in town, full of stories about the rich land in Montana. Talking to Jake, Gus realizes how boring his life has become in Lonesome Dove. He wants to go to Montana and persuades Call to begin a cattle drive north. Gus wants adventure, and he also wants to visit his old flame Clara Allen, who lives with her husband in Montana. Clara is the only woman who can out-argue him and the only woman who ever broke his heart.

The cattle drive begins. Gus looks after Lorena, who has followed along on the drive in order to be with the charming but irresponsible Jake. When Lorena gets kidnapped by Blue Duck, a vicious, murderous Indian, Gus is determined to rescue her. Call protests, saying that Gus is crazy to risk his life tracking down a whore—but he respects Gus too much to argue with him for long. Gus follows Blue Duck for several days and finally catches up with him. He rescues Lorena, now half mad with terror. Gus spends several days and nights looking after her because she is too terrified to return to the rest of the men. Lorena is unable to speak, so Gus does all the talking. By the time Lorena recovers enough to talk, she has fallen in love with him.

The great love of Gus's life has been Clara Allen. He knew her in Texas and courted her in a half-humorous manner that belied the depth of his attachment. Clara knew the truth—that Gus loved her deeply—but she also felt that no matter how much she loved him in return, the two of them were not meant to go through life together. By the time the cattle drive reaches Montana, Lorena is terrified that Gus will run back to Clara. Gus, who now feels that he loves both women, cannot decide whom to choose.

As it turns out, Gus ends up with neither woman. After

being wounded in the leg with an arrow, he learns that he has to have it amputated. When the operation doesn't remove the infection, Gus must lose the other leg. He refuses, explaining to Call that he would rather die. Call tells him that he is crazy; he must be operated on. Gus holds him off with a gun. He tells Call to bury him in a spot in Texas where he and Clara used to picnic many years before. Call agrees to transport Gus's body several thousand miles back to Texas. When Gus dies, the last thing he sees is a mist that reminds him of the morning light in the valleys of Tennessee.

McCreary, Fenian "Mac." *U.S.A. (The 42nd Parallel).* John Dos Passos. 1930.

Born in Middletown, Connecticut, to an Irish-American family, Fenian "Mac" McCreary moves to Chicago at the age of seven, upon the death of his mother. He becomes an apprentice to his uncle Timothy, a printer and a socialist, and learns his uncle's trade and alliances.

When Uncle Timothy's printing business goes bankrupt, Fenian, now seventeen, goes to work for a morally suspect salesman named Doc Bingham who claims to be president of the Truthseeker Literary Distributing Company. Fenian's new job consists of selling various pamphlets, from "Doctor Spikenard's Short Sermons" to "The Queen of the White Slaves." He and Doc Bingham travel the small towns of Michigan by train and cart for three weeks, until an irate husband chases them and Fenian is left alone on the road.

Fenian soon meets up with Ike Hall, a young itinerant socialist from Duluth, who christens him "Mac." After working for a spell in Mackinaw, the two go to Duluth, then hop a train to Winnipeg and end up working for the Canadian railway for a summer. Ike gets gonorrhea from a prostitute in Seattle, and Mac is on his own again. He works for a rancher in Oregon before moving on to San Francisco.

In San Francisco, Fenian works for a printer, fraternizes with socialists, and, during the earthquake, becomes engaged to a sales clerk named Maisie Spencer. Fred Hoff, a member of the I.W.W. (Industrial Workers of the World), convinces him to go to Goldfield, Nevada, to help publish a paper in support of striking mine workers, and Mac is torn between a desire for domesticity and his dedication to the movement. He leaves Maisie with promises to return, but even when she writes that she is pregnant, he is too deeply involved in the strike to leave.

Finally, Mac returns to San Francisco to marry Maisie. They move to San Diego, make a down payment on a bungalow, and Mac's domestic life begins. Soon he has a steady-paying job and two children. But Maisie resents Mac's lingering ties to the labor movement, and Mac feels ashamed of his defection; they quarrel constantly. When Maisie's brother lets Mac into a real estate venture, they

move to Los Angeles; Mac again takes a steady job and again feels guilty.

When Mac sends his savings to his sister to pay for his uncle Timothy's funeral, Maisie throws him out. He goes to Ciudad Juarez to see the revolution in Mexico. The Mexicans welcome him as an eminent American comrade in the movement, and he takes up with a young rebel woman named Encarnacion.

Some time later, Mac leaves Encarnacion and travels to Mexico City, where he works first as a printer and then as a bookseller. The revolution has not yet reached the capital, and many Americans and other foreigners are out to take whatever booty they can. Mac meets the American public relations giant JOHN WARD MOOREHOUSE and settles in with his new love, Concha. But the city is unsafe for Americans, and as Zapata and Villa advance, Mac returns to the north, planning to return to the United States. But when we last see him, Mac has decided instead to stay in Vera Cruz with Concha.

McCurtain, Jeff. *Trouble In July.* Erskine Caldwell. 1940.

For eleven years Jeff McCurtain has been the sheriff of Andrewjones, a small town in Julie County in the South. His political career has been characterized by his ability to turn a blind eye to any but the most minor offense committed by the white community of Julie County. When the underlying racial tension in the area erupts into confrontation, McCurtain's response is to escape by going fishing (an activity he loathes) and to leave the townspeople to take the law into their own hands. He believes his continual reelection is the result of his refusal to become involved in any controversial political incidents that might jeopardize his career.

The novel opens with an incident that demands McCurtain's involvement as an officer of the law. Sonny Clark, a young black man, has been accused of raping a white girl, Katy Barlow. The two witnesses to the rape are Katy's drunken bigoted father and Narcissa Calhoun, a local widow with a vested interest in inciting racial tension: She wants to obtain signatures for her petition to send the blacks to Africa. The local men, encouraged by Barlow's uncontrollable anger and Narcissa Calhoun's political mission, demand a lynching. However, Bob Watson, the most powerful landowner in Julie County, threatens to withdraw his considerable support if McCurtain doesn't put an end to a situation that will terrify his workforce. Caught between these opposing factions, McCurtain is desperately aware that the only way to save his career is by escaping and letting events take their course. Although he knows of Sonny Clark's innocence and realizes that the young man is being used as a scapegoat, McCurtain feels helpless, and when he is forced to choose between the young man's life and his political interests, he decides to safeguard his own future at any cost.

McCurtain's plan backfires. He locks himself in a cell in his own jailhouse, ready to claim he has been locked there by the lynching party. But when the men, led by Barlow, come to find Clark, they discover McCurtain locked in a cell with a prostitute, and they take a harmless black petty crook, Sam Brinson, as ransom. It is this incident that forces McCurtain to reevaluate the standards to which he has aspired throughout his career, for it has been his covert belief that Sam Brinson is "as companionable a fellow as you'll find in either race"—a belief that, in this racist climate, could ruin McCurtain's career. His genuine affection for Sam Brinson motivates him in a way that his responsibilities as sheriff never could. For the first time McCurtain is moved to stand by his principles at the expense of his career, and he sets out to find Brinson.

Yet McCurtain's acceptance of his moral obligations comes too late to save Sonny Clark: He is lynched as the sheriff, rendered powerless by his own cowardice and the threats of the lynching party, looks on. While McCurtain realizes he must accept responsibility for this death, he never questions the justice of what has happened. Brinson is saved, but not through McCurtain's efforts. The only thing this unjust and horrific course of events has taught the sheriff is that political life is not for him and that he should have been a farmer.

Maceo, Sukie. *Daddy Was a Number Runner.* Louise Meriwether. 1970.

Sukie Maceo, a thirteen-year-old girl living in a Harlem tenement in 1934, is the best friend and neighbor of the novel's narrator, FRANCIE COFFIN.

Sukie is the daughter of an unloving mother and an alcoholic father who dies from pneumonia after lying drunk on the stairs one night. Her sister, called China Doll by everyone in the neighborhood, works as a prostitute around the corner on 118th Street. One day Sukie and Francie are talking to China Doll when the woman's pimp, Alfred, shows up and comments that Sukie is old enough to turn a trick. China Doll threatens to kill him if he ever lays a hand on her little sister.

Sukie, who is still in elementary school because she flunked a grade twice, is both mean-tempered and generous to her friends. She has the habit of picking a fight with Francie and beating her up, often for no apparent reason. At the beginning of the novel, Sukie gets angry at Francie "on sight" one day. Francie avoids her for as long as she can but is finally cornered and thrashed about two weeks later. The following day, the two are best friends again.

Another of Sukie's habits is to steal change from her mother's purse, and she usually shares the treats she buys with Francie. She also figures out how to make money for both of them by taking her friend to the park where bums pay them nickels to drop their bloomers for them. One summer day, however, Francie angers Sukie by saying that she will no longer go to the park where the men are. Francie delays a confrontation as usual, but the following day accosts Sukie and punches her in the nose. Sukie, shocked at her friend's unprecedented aggression, refuses to continue the fight and leaves. Francie, who has just learned that her father is living with his mistress, is still angry later in the day and goes looking for Sukie. She crawls down a fire escape, looks through a window, and sees Sukie having intercourse with a man she can't identify. Sukie never discusses her sexual encounter with anyone.

That autumn China Doll is arrested after stabbing Alfred in the heart with a butcher knife. When she hears the news, Sukie tries to embrace her mother but is pushed away. Mrs. Maceo says that she thinks Sukie will come to a bad end like her sister. As the novel closes, Sukie is sitting on the stoop with her head in her hands. Francie, having just heard that China Doll pleaded self-defense and has been released, is puzzled to find Sukie crying. Sukie says that she wishes China Doll had been kept in jail forever. Francie, shocked, asks her to explain. Sukie replies that everyone, including her own mother, thinks that she is going to become a prostitute like her older sister. Her friend tries to comfort her, but Sukie concludes the conversation by saying that Francie's opinion doesn't count because she isn't an adult.

McGehee, Hugh. *So Red the Rose.* Stark Young. 1934.

Hugh McGehee is the embodiment of southern gentlemanly ideals. The proud owner of the Montrose plantation, he must endure the devastation of his family and property, and come to terms with the fact that the South he once knew has been utterly and irrevocably changed by the Civil War.

As the novel opens, Hugh is enjoying a birthday party given in his honor at Montrose on the eve of the war. Among the guests are Malcolm Bedford, the owner of Portobello, a neighboring plantation, and his family, to whom Hugh is related by marriage. As the guests discuss the election of Abraham Lincoln, it becomes apparent that no one in the McGehee family believes in the slave system. The McGehees' acquaintances feel that the family is too indulgent with their slaves because Hugh insists on such humane practices as keeping black families together and allowing miscreant slaves to be tried by their peers.

Hugh's upstanding young son Edward agrees with his father on the slavery issue, but when Mississippi secedes from the Union, his loyalty to his state and his admiration for his neighbor Jeff Davis lead him to enlist in the Confederate Army. After many anxious months, Hugh and his wife Agnes learn that their only son has been killed at the Battle of Shiloh. Agnes bravely travels to Shiloh to retrieve Edward's body, which is sorrowfully laid to rest by Hugh, Agnes, and their proud, patrician daughter Lucinda, who is devastated not only by the loss of her beloved brother but also by the death at Shiloh of the dashing young Charles Taliaferro, with whom she had been secretly in love.

As the war rages on, the Union Army advances closer and closer. Upon occupying Natchez, General W. T. Sherman visits Hugh to express his sorrow over the death of young Edward, who had been a student of his at the Louisiana Military Academy. Hugh is deeply moved by this expression of respect, but shortly after the general's visit, his home is destroyed by Sherman's marauding army. He and his family are forced to move to a small cabin on their property and to begin anew, with nothing left of their sumptuous home and furnishings except the family silver, which their loyal butler, William Veal, had hidden in the woods.

As the novel closes, Hugh is not broken in spirit, but he feels he is now an old man who has lost a great deal. He dreads the arrival of the uncultivated, uncultured carpetbaggers and scalawags, whose power is rising in the region and who represent to Hugh a loss even greater than that of his home and son: the loss of a civilized and cultured Southern way of life.

McGinnis, Mel. "What We Talk About When We Talk About Love." Raymond Carver. 1981.

He may not mean to, but Mel McGinnis turns a drunken conversation about an innocent topic into an uncomfortable exercise in this short story. As he and his wife, Terri, and their married friends, Nick and Laura, drink gin and tonic, the subject of love comes up, and Mel grabs it, forcing them to talk about love in ways that they had probably never even conceived.

The four are in Mel's house, and that fact—or, perhaps, as Nick says, the fact that he is a cardiologist—gives him the right to talk. For Mel, love is something absolute. The idea that Ed, Terri's old lover, actually loved her is ludicrous to him because Ed used to beat Terri. Terri protests that Ed's love was love of a sort, but Mel proceeds to catalog Ed's "loving" acts in an attempt to prove that what the man felt was not love.

After Terri had left Ed, Mel tells them, Ed began to threaten them both. He would leave messages at Mel's answering service and say to Mel, when he returned the calls, that he would kill him. Although Mel felt that Ed was capable of wiring a bomb or shooting him, the police could offer no assistance. Ed finally ended the problem by shooting himself in the mouth. He botched the job and took three days to die. No, Mel says, that isn't love.

Laura, married to Nick only a year and a half, claims that she knows what love is, but before she can explain, Mel refills everyone's glasses and offers a toast to love. Then he makes everyone nervous by dissecting love further: How is it that we can love, fall out of love, then fall in love again with someone new? Mel loved his first wife, he confesses, but now he loves Terri and can't imagine having loved his first wife, although he knows he did. Terri grows uneasy about the implications of what Mel is saying, and when Mel attempts to calm her, saying he loves her and Nick and Laura, somehow the meaning of the word is confused.

The story of an elderly couple he operated on, Mel says, will explain love to them. The couple was seriously injured in an automobile accident, and their chances of survival were slim. After many operations their conditions were stabilized, and husband and wife were placed in the same room. The husband was depressed, however, and not only about the accident itself. As he related to Mel, he was depressed because his bandages and the way he was placed in the room prevented him from seeing his wife. Now, Mel tells them, that is love.

As the room darkens, the four friends, now very drunk, grow quiet. When Mel announces that the last of the gin is gone, it seems that their talk of love is truly over.

McGregor, Norman "Beaut." *Marching Men.* Sherwood Anderson. 1917.

Norman McGregor is a big, homely, red-haired man, nicknamed "Beaut" by the old men of his hometown, Coal Creek, Pennsylvania. As a youth in Coal Creek, McGregor feels deep scorn for the frustrated miners who periodically strike but never manage to improve their lives. McGregor is determined to avoid the fate that faces him in the small mining town, and he dreams of escaping to the city.

In 1893, young McGregor moves to Chicago. Even in the big city his energy and confidence attract attention. Jobs are scarce, but a warehouse superintendent is impressed by McGregor. He fires six incompetent workers and hires McGregor to replace them. Incidents such as this one bolster McGregor's conviction that he is somehow superior to, and apart from, most other men. He is frustrated and confused by the chaos he perceives around him and yearns to change the condition of humanity.

After moving to Chicago, McGregor starts to read a great deal, and decides to study law. At a dance he meets Edith Carson, a thin and lonely milliner who soon falls in love with him. Edith decides to invest her life savings in McGregor. She supports him for the next few years and enables him to become a lawyer.

McGregor takes classes at the university but soon becomes disillusioned. He desires action, not meaningless talk, and he quits school, determined to study law on his own. He is obsessed with creating order out of disorder, and he wants to unite working men for a common cause, without tolerating any dissent. McGregor despises the socialist ideas that are in the air, for in socialism he sees no order or hard discipline.

The big break for McGregor comes when he is hired to represent Andrew Brown, a safecracker framed for the murder of a rich young man. With the help of Margaret Ormsby, a beautiful and privileged young woman who has a reputation for befriending neighborhood outcasts, McGregor wins the case and receives considerable publicity. After the trial he starts organizing factory men. Soon he is at the head of the "Marching Men" movement, which conducts frequent marches and drills as protests. Most of his time is devoted to this ambiguous but popular cause rather than to his law practice.

Momentarily forgetting about Edith, McGregor falls in love with Margaret Ormsby and proposes marriage. She eagerly accepts, but then McGregor realizes how much he is hurting Edith. He decides to sacrifice conjugal happiness with Margaret for what he sees as the higher good of a union with hardworking Edith. As the book ends, McGregor's Marching Men movement is spreading across the country, and he has not yet married either woman.

McGuire, Sam. *Chilly Scenes of Winter.* Ann Beattie. 1976.

Sam McGuire spends the beginning of a bleak winter mourning the loss of his dog. The dog was remarkably intelligent, seemingly clairvoyant, and almost a part of Sam's personality. She died suddenly of a heart attack, and afterward Sam begins drinking a great deal and talking perpetually of her many admirable qualities.

Sam's unusual preoccupation with his dog is a symptom of his general unhappiness. Although Sam was a devoted and brilliant student, elected a member of Phi Beta Kappa, he is working as a jacket salesman in a department store. He had planned to go to law school but is unable to pay the tuition. Sam's parents, with whom he has almost no contact, are separated and are also struggling financially. Because Sam is barely able to meet his expenses, he often drops by his friend CHARLES's house for meals and sometimes eats the leftovers while Charles is still at work. No matter what Sam does in the house, however, Charles is never angry. Sam is wry and charming, and more spirited than Charles's other acquaintances.

Charles introduces Sam to his sister Susan, who is visiting from college, and her friend Elise, a nursing student. Almost as soon as Sam walks in the door, he strikes up a typically flirtatious conversation with Elise. Charles and Susan are called away to take care of their mother, and when they return, Sam is lying naked with Elise in Charles's bed. The next day when Charles asks Sam to take Elise to his own apartment, he learns that she has already been taken to the train station. Things remain as usual between Sam and Charles; Sam appears at mealtimes, and Charles cooks or they go out. During many of their meals together, Sam teases Charles gently about Laura, his former girlfriend with whom Charles is still obsessed.

When Sam loses his job as a jacket salesman for no apparent reason, Charles invites him to move into the house. Sam hesitates at first, afraid he will get on Charles's nerves, but he eventually decides to accept the offer. Not long after Sam has moved in, they receive a phone call from Pamela Smith, an old girlfriend of Charles's, saying she is stranded several hours away, at the Clara Barton Service Area. It takes them all night to drive there and pick up Pamela, who was robbed. In the middle of the following night, Pamela goes into Sam's room and asks if he thinks it would be all right to wake Charles up and "lay" him. He says it would be better to let Charles sleep, so she instead climbs into bed with Sam. Charles wakes up, sees them together, and quietly shuts the door. Later, when Pamela has left, they discuss the incident and agree that she is unattractive.

One evening Charles brings Betty, a woman from work, home for dinner, and Sam surprises them with his new dog. It is a ridiculous-looking creature, a mixture of dachshund and cocker spaniel. Sam got the dog from a shelter because he is convinced it would have been put to death by the following morning. Sam asks Betty to think of a name for the dog, but she can't think of anything. Instead of looking for a job, Sam spends his days taking care of the dog, which learns to answer to the name "Dog."

Machine, Frankie. *The Man with the Golden Arm.* Nelson Algren. 1949.

Frankie Machine, a veteran of World War II, is an ace card dealer and morphine addict who lives on the Polish northwest side of Chicago. Frequently in and out of jail for fighting and making trouble, Frankie is haunted by his dreams of Private McGantic, a mythical soldier who carries a thirty-five-pound monkey on his back. When he takes morphine, Frankie convinces himself that he is doing so in order to soothe McGantic and his monkey. In truth, Frankie's morphine habit started during the war; he takes the drug now to ease the continuing pain of a shrapnel wound and to relieve himself of the guilt he feels for crippling his wife Sophie in a car accident he caused when he went on a drunken spree after being discharged from the army.

Frankie buys his morphine from Louie Fomorowski, a local criminal with a flashy wardrobe and a big bankroll. He hates being at Louie's mercy, but he cannot break out of the vicious cycle he is caught in. One night Frankie wins Louie's lucky coin in a card game. Taunting and teasing, Louie follows Frankie outside into the alley to retrieve it. A fight breaks out; Frankie cracks Louie across the back of the neck and accidentally kills him. Frankie's friend, Sparrow Saltskin, demolishes the evidence by throwing Louie's body into a nearby woodshed while Frankie regains consciousness. Later, when the police suspect Frankie for the murder of Louie Fomorowski, they have no evidence and can make no arrests.

Frankie, long estranged from Sophie, takes up with Molly Novotny, the pretty and pliant "girl downstairs." The former girlfriend of Drunkie John, a local bum whom she supported by seeing other men for money, Molly finally leaves this debilitating relationship after she and

Frankie fall in love. One night, feeling beaten by "the monkey," Frankie visits Molly, and she cares for him. Strengthened by her love and acceptance, he is finally able to shut out his guilt and pain, and he manages to stay clean from morphine.

But Frankie's idyllic life with Molly ends when he is arrested for stealing toasters from a local department store, and Molly subsequently goes back to Drunkie John. After he is released from prison, Frankie stays clean, but not for long. His friendship with Sparrow is ruined by a quarrel over dead Louie Fomorowski's bankroll; his relationship with Sophie has not improved; his hands begin to shake so badly that he is forced to quit dealing cards; and Molly moves out of the neighborhood. McGantic and his monkey reappear, and Frankie's morphine addiction resumes.

One bleak night Frankie calls "Piggy," Louie Fomorowski's replacement, to hook him up with a fix of morphine. Piggy, without telling him the name of the customer, pays Sparrow to make the delivery. Sparrow, despite his deep regrets, gives Frankie the shot of morphine, but soon after, the police arrive and arrest Sparrow for drug dealing. Frankie and Sparrow have been set up, and the police finally have the opening they need to arrest Frankie for the murder of Louie Fomorowski.

While the police hold Sparrow and try to coerce him into turning Frankie in, Frankie searches for Molly. He finally finds her working in a sleazy nightclub. For weeks Molly locks Frankie in her apartment to keep him out of trouble and off morphine. But soon he discovers that Drunkie John knows Molly is hiding him and is blackmailing her. Feeling tremendous pressure, Frankie returns to the old neighborhood to find out about the case against him. When he returns to Molly's, Drunkie John is there, demanding money. The police arrive and shoot Frankie in the foot as he escapes. He rides the elevated train, bleeding and sweating, and finally checks into a cheap hotel, where he hangs himself and dies.

Mack. *Cannery Row*. John Steinbeck. 1945.

The ringleader and mentor of a group of ambitionless men, Mack, a smooth-talking schemer with a taste for liquor, is one of the many colorful characters who inhabit an impoverished seaside community. He is well-meaning, however, and although his plans often go disastrously awry, they always begin with the very best of intentions.

Mack and his group of friends occupy an empty storage building known among Cannery Row residents as the Palace Flophouse and Grill. It is there, over a jug of stolen liquor, that Mack has the idea of throwing a surprise party for Doc, the kindhearted owner and operator of the Western Biological Laboratory, to whom nearly everyone in the neighborhood is indebted in one way or another. To earn the money they need for the party, Mack and the boys go to work collecting frogs for the doctor. After

gathering what supplies they can wrangle or steal, and restoring an ancient truck into working condition, the men set out.

The hunters soon find a likely-looking pool, but while they are enjoying a fireside dinner and drink, they are approached by a man who tells them they are trespassing. Ever the diplomat, Mack charms the stranger into inviting him and his friends to the frog-filled pond behind his house. By the time they begin their hunt, the stranger has been so won over that the boys leave with a jug of well-aged whiskey and the pick of a new litter of puppies, as well as several hundred frogs.

Eager to lay in supplies for the party, Mack convinces Lee Chong, the local merchant, to take a few frogs, known to be valued at five cents each, in exchange for food, whiskey, and paper decorations with which to adorn the laboratory. Unfortunately, Mack and his friends are intoxicated by their temporary wealth and soon spend all of the frogs. Worse, the party, inadvertently started before Doc returns from a specimen-collecting trip, soon degenerates into a brawl. Windows, specimen jars, and many of Doc's favorite classical records are broken in the ensuing chaos, and the frogs, positioned in the middle of the floor as a surprise to Doc, escape.

All is quiet by the time Doc returns after an emotionally exhausting trip. When he sees the damage done to his laboratory, he explodes in anger and bloodies Mack's face. Mack takes the beating humbly, then tearfully apologizes to Doc, admitting that he has botched everything he has ever attempted, including his marriage. Although Doc forgives him, Mack is woefully ashamed. He shows his face at the laboratory only when the much-loved new pup, named Darling, is sick. Doc cures the dog, and once again Mack is indebted to him.

Determined to atone for his mistakes, Mack decides to plan another party, one that Doc himself can attend. This time, however, Doc gets wind of the plan and is able to secure all of his valuable equipment before the party begins. Everyone in town attends the party, and Doc is showered with gifts, including twenty-one cats for use in biological experiments, from Mack and the boys. Unlike the first party, this one is a great success, and Doc, Mack, and the boys from the Palace Flophouse and Grill all enjoy themselves thoroughly.

McKarkle, Hannah. *The Killing Ground*. Mary Lee Settle. 1982.

Hannah McKarkle is a famous writer who returns home to discover the exact causes of her brother's death eighteen years before. When Hannah returns to her hometown of Canona, West Virginia, the ostensible reason for her visit is to be a guest speaker at a fundraiser for one of the local art galleries. Due to her intellectual abilities, her politics (which are extremely liberal), and her probing questions concerning her brother Johnny's death, Hannah incurs the wrath of Canona's elite, much as she has on previous visits.

As the novel begins, Hannah stares out the window of her hotel room on the morning of a late spring day in Canona, contemplating the colorful history of the valley where the city is situated. During the Colonial American period, her namesake, Hannah Lacey, became the first Caucasian to lay eyes on the valley of Canona. History is very important to Hannah, as she repeatedly implies, the dead continue to live on in the memories of those still alive. As she attempts to understand her brother's death, Hannah compares herself to Antigone trying to bury Polynices in the play by Sophocles. She concludes that if she can satisfy her obsession with Johnny, then his ghost will no longer haunt her.

During her time in Canona, Hannah meets several people she once knew and begins to question them. On the drive to the lecture, she sits in a Cadillac with Kitty Puss Wilson, who, while married to Hannah's cousin, slept with Johnny; Daisy, Hannah's greatest detractor; Maria, a lonely old widow; and Ann Randolph Potter, whose husband abandoned her for a hair stylist. For Hannah, these four women represent the rich and elite of the West Virginia mining city. In turn, they see Hannah as the embodiment of an existence that is totally alien to their own. Whenever Hannah returns home, one of the four calls her late at night and demands that she leave the city limits by morning. On this visit, Kitty Puss makes the call after her latest lover, Charley Bland, has committed suicide. Hannah leaves town the next day to continue her research into the death of Johnny.

She next visits her aunt by marriage, Althea Lacey Neill. Aunt Althea, resenting the writer for her appearance, explains to Hannah the various problems connected with having married into the "mighty" Neill family. Hannah then drives out to Beulah, her father's hometown, where she interviews her uncle Ephraim McKarkle and his wife, Rose Pagano McKarkle, another woman who had a brief affair with Johnny.

After her interviews are complete, Hannah thinks back to 1960, the year that Johnny was murdered, when she lived in New York City. Johnny had been accidentally killed in the drunk tank of the local jail by Jake Catlett. Hannah hopes that her search will reveal answers to what is in her mind an unsolved death.

Johnny's death is finally resolved in Hannah's mind at Aunt Althea's funeral two years later when Jake Catlett reveals that Aunt Althea had bailed him out of prison after Johnny died. Hannah no longer feels fooled by the past, and she can accept Aunt Althea's act of mercy as an appropriate memorial for the death of Johnny.

McKenney, Ruth. *My Sister Eileen.* Ruth McKenney. 1938.

Ruth McKenney is the main character in this fictionalized account of growing up in America. She narrates a series of anecdotes that follow the two McKenney sisters through childhood, adolescence, and young adulthood in Mishawaka, Indiana; Cleveland, Ohio; and New York City.

Born in 1913, Ruth is the daughter of a home appliance manufacturer. All of her comical experiences stem from the efforts of her relatives to acculturate themselves into bourgeois America. Among the requisite trappings of the upper middle class that Ruth must endure are elocution lessons, swimming instruction, French class, and a matinee series. Ruth meets each of these betterment campaigns with aplomb, and she has a knack for twisting them into farce, hoax, or scandal.

Take, for instance, the middle-class liberator of the harried McKenney parents: summer camp. Ruth and Eileen's plan to extort money from gullible distant relatives via the U.S. Mail is found out. They are bored with making unsubsidized arts and crafts, so they turn to bird walks under the leadership of the camp's sincere Bird Lover. Mystified for a few days while the other girls sight and identify birds, Ruth and Eileen eventually contribute, halting the walks periodically while they reel off bird-book descriptions of exotic varieties that the other walkers find curiously elusive. The Bird Lover is reduced to tears.

But this is only the beginning: Ruth describes her life-saving class, where she is sure the Red Cross systematically seeks to drown her; forbidden newspaper serials, addictive curiosities for a prepubescent Irish Catholic girl who doesn't understand how "Chickie" got pregnant; and later, first jobs, haywire washing machines, Georgian diamond thieves, and English scotch. Not surprisingly, given her diverse interests and taste for adventure, Ruth ends up being a journalist in New York City.

Ruth's youth is carefree. It is a world of Irish aunts, distracted parents, and neighborhood movie palaces where the world holds no evil that cannot be termed "a mixup." Whether she is battling a New York landlord or trying to shake a pack of Brazilian sailors who don't speak English, Ruth always manages to be funny.

MacKenzie, Allison. *Peyton Place.* Grace Metalious. 1956.

Allison MacKenzie's tendency to be dreamy, bookish, and reclusive makes her an outsider among the other eighth graders of Peyton Place, a cloistered New England town. Allison spends much of her time roaming the woods that surround Peyton Place and dreaming of what life would have been with the dead father whom she never knew. Her only friend is SELENA CROSS, the darkly beautiful daughter of one of the shack dwellers living outside Peyton Place.

By the time she reaches high school, Allison has become less of an outsider and more accepting of herself. She writes historical sketches for the local newspaper and has a boyfriend, Norman Page. Additionally, her world has altered somewhat. Selena now works afternoons in Constance's apparel shop while Selena's mother, Nellie, works in the MacKenzie home. Constance and Michael Rossi, the principal of the Peyton Place schools, have begun dating.

It is Allison's involvement with Norman that leads to the most startling revelation of her young life. One night Allison and Norman arrive late after an all-day picnic, and an awful scene takes place in the MacKenzie home. In a bitter rage, Constance confronts the adolescents, accusing them of fornication. Allison is horribly embarrassed by her mother's behavior and says so after Norman leaves. Her infuriated mother then delivers a hysterical diatribe on Allison, saying that she is "the bastard daughter of the biggest bastard of all!"

Allison learns that her mother was not married to her father when she became pregnant by him as a young woman. To prevent herself being "talked about" in Peyton Place, Constance, with the help of her mother, had created a fictive marriage and altered Allison's birth certificate by a year. After the death of Allison's father, Constance had moved back to Peyton Place, presenting herself as a widow with the fatherless Allison. Stunned, Allison dashes to her bedroom where she finds the body of Nellie hanging from a wooden beam in her closet. After several days in the hospital, Allison recovers from the shock.

Two years later Allison moves to New York City, where she writes short stories. One day while walking down the street in New York, she spots a newspaper headline reporting that Selena has been charged with the murder of her father Lucas. This event, along with an unfortunate sexual relationship with her agent, takes Allison back to Peyton Place, where she confronts her feelings about her mother, her hometown, and love. Finally, after much musing and self-examination, Allison makes peace with her mother. The novel closes as Allison dashes home to greet a young novelist, David Noyes, a former suitor, who has come up from New York to renew his vow of love to her.

MacLeod "Mac." *In Dubious Battle.* John Steinbeck. 1936.

MacLeod, known as "Mac," is a fanatically dedicated, skilled, and seasoned Communist Party worker who serves as mentor and comrade to the novel's protagonist, JIM NOLAN. Mac is the informal leader of a group of workers at a lodging and work center nicknamed "the Joint." When he meets the eager and idealistic Jim, he advises the young man to take "the long view" of suffering and struggle: Strikes, he says, should not be settled too quickly and easily, for adversity forces people to organize and to work together. Arriving at a settlement of fruit workers, Mac pretends to be an experienced hospital worker and delivers the baby of Lisa, the daughter of London. Since London is one of the highly regarded leaders in the community of

fruit workers, Mac immediately earns respect and prestige for his service. But Jim later learns that Mac's expertise is a fraud. He succeeded in the task out of sheer confidence and determination to use the situation to his—and the movement's—advantage.

The resourceful exploitation of people and situations in the interest of the cause is a theme that Mac continues to emphasize, sometimes to chilling effect. For instance, after the injuring of an aging worker triggers a strike, Mac coldly observes that the old man must have been "worth something after all." Mac also pretends to take a genuine interest in the prize dogs of Mr. Anderson in order to use his farmland as a camp for evicted strikers. In return, he assures Mr. Anderson that he will be protected—a promise Mac knows he will not be able to keep.

When Mr. Anderson's farm is destroyed by arsonists and the young boy who was involved in the incident is caught, Mac brutally beats him. Unrelenting at first, he is mortified at his cruelty after the boy is freed. When Jim attempts to alleviate Mac's guilt by coldly rationalizing the necessity of the violence, it is now Mac who finds this philosophy inhuman.

Shortly after this episode, however, the road is barricaded by strikebreakers armed with guns and gas, and Mac responds to the threat of violence with characteristic fanaticism. A few dead men will help the cause, he tells Jim. But he suddenly becomes reflective, remembering something a friend said about men's inability to transcend something within themselves that they hate. Anticipating an attack from the strikebreakers at dawn, Mac insists on standing and fighting, but tries to send Jim back to town. Jim refuses, chastising him for placing a personal friendship above the needs of the Party.

As Mac and Jim prepare to rouse the men, who are showing signs of abandoning the fight, they are lured outside by the false news of an injured man lying in the orchard. They dash outside, and in a sudden roar of sound and light, Jim is killed. Mac carries his faceless, bloodied corpse to a clearing, steadies it against the platform, and begins speaking to the mass of men, huddled darkly together, on comrade Jim's selfless dedication to the cause.

McLuhan, Nancy. "Welcome to the Monkey House." Kurt Vonnegut, Jr. 1968.

Nancy McLuhan is one of two Hostesses in a Federal Ethical Suicide Parlor. In the futuristic United States that Nancy inhabits, anti-aging drugs have made people immortal, resulting in incredible overpopulation. To counteract it, Suicide Hostesses like Nancy are licensed to give lethal injections to those few people, most of them old in appearance because they were already elderly when the anti-aging agent was devised, who desire it. Additionally, everyone is required to take ethical birth control pills, which deaden sensation from the waist down, thus robbing intercourse of its pleasure. The pills are deemed ethical because they stifle the desire for sex, not the ability to reproduce.

One day at work Nancy is warned by the local sheriff that the radical Billy the Poet is in the area. Billy is one of a group of people known as nothingheads—those who refuse to take their ethical birth control pills and try to win others over to their sexed way of life. Nancy, a six-foot-tall karate expert, assures the sheriff that she can take care of Billy should he come her way. By the time Nancy prepares for her next client, an elderly-looking man she has dubbed "Foxy Grandpa," the sheriff believes that Billy is making an obscene call to the Parlor from a nearby phone booth.

Nancy's client is being somewhat difficult. He cannot decide which of the meals from the Howard Johnson's next door will be his last, and he insists on telling her the story—which every schoolchild knows—of J. Edgar Nation. Nation decided to invent ethical birth control after seeing monkeys masturbating in the zoo. A bored and annoyed Nancy maintains her professional decorum only with difficulty. As sirens sound outside, signaling that the phone caller whom the sheriff believes to be Billy is being arrested nearby, Foxy Grandpa peels off his false bald spot and wrinkles, revealing himself to be Billy the Poet.

Nancy is almost a foot taller than Billy, but since he has a gun, she has no choice but to follow him out of the Parlor and into the sewer. Nancy berates the famous sexual outlaw as he leads her to his lair, but he claims that she will not be worth listening to until the ethical birth control pills wear off. Nancy is given an injection of truth serum, and although she tries to stop herself, under questioning she reveals that she is a sixty-three-year-old virgin who thinks virginity at her age is "pointless."

The next day Billy rapes the still unyielding Nancy. After the act, Billy tells her that she will one day find a lover who will make sex a pleasurable experience, unlike her deflowering. Nancy's resolve begins to weaken, and Billy gives her a book of love poetry and some "unethical" birth control pills. Left alone with her thoughts, Nancy gazes at the bottle of pills; its label reads WELCOME TO THE MONKEY HOUSE.

McMurphy, Randle Patrick. *One Flew Over the Cuckoo's Nest.* Ken Kesey. 1962.

Randle Patrick McMurphy is a brawling gambler who gets himself committed to an Oregon mental institution. Leaving a prison work farm because he "needed some new blood," McMurphy immediately stirs up the chemically sedated wards of the hospital. He gregariously introduces himself to all the patients—not just to the "Acutes," who are considered capable of recovery, but also to the "Chronics," those hopeless patients whom Chief Bromden, the narrator, refers to as the "Wheelers and Walkers and Vegetables."

Although the patients are mostly timid and unrespon-sive to McMurphy's antics, he gradually begins to affect them with his profane stories and small acts of defiance. He boasts about his gambling skills and recruits players for games of poker and blackjack. From the beginning he acts the part of the agitator, encouraging seditious thoughts among the patients and assuming the role of gang leader and troublemaker.

McMurphy's enemy in his campaign for disorder is the "Big Nurse," Miss Ratched, who runs the ward with extreme efficiency. The Chief views the Big Nurse as an all-knowing, all-seeing controller of everything that happens in the ward; her movements are precise, and her perfection makes the ward a machine dependent on her rules and authority. McMurphy views the Big Nurse in violent and sexual terms. He refers to the discussions the patients have with Miss Ratched and the ward doctor as a "pecking party" because patients are encouraged to reveal their most intimate thoughts and then made to feel ashamed and embarrassed. Calling Miss Ratched "a bitch and a buzzard and a ballcutter," he convinces the men to join him in defying her authority.

First, McMurphy tries to get the patients to join him in demanding that they be allowed to watch the World Series. When that fails, he talks of busting out of the place and going to a bar to watch the games. He proves his seriousness by trying to lift a huge water-heating control panel in the shower room, saying it is heavy enough to break the wire-enmeshed windows that keep the patients from escaping. Although he is a big and powerful man, he strains in vain but manages to convert some of the patients to his cause. The next day, during a meeting, McMurphy again calls for a vote on whether the men should be allowed to watch the World Series, an event that would break the careful schedule on the ward. The shocked staff looks on as all the patients raise their hands to support the measure. At the time the baseball game begins, the men ignore the protestations of Nurse Ratched and leave their cleaning duties to join McMurphy for a sit-down strike in front of the blank TV.

A few weeks after this first defiance of Ratched, McMurphy begins telling the men that the problem with their lives and this hospital is not this bitter woman but something larger. He tells them that he will not be used by them to challenge Ratched's authority and risk sharp retribution. In more acts of defiance, he breaks the window of the room from which she watches the ward, and leads the men on an escapade to the Oregon coast, where they steal a pleasure boat and go ocean fishing.

McMurphy eventually gives Miss Ratched the pretext for using severe means to contain his rebellion against her. When he gets into a fistfight with one of the ward attendants, Ratched has him sent to "Disturbed" and then given electric shock treatments. McMurphy returns to the ward and later has a prostitute he knows from Portland come to the hospital and spend the night with one of the patients, the shy and stuttering William "Billy" Bibbit. After Ratched humiliates Billy, the young man commits suicide.

Nurse Ratched blames McMurphy for the death, and he responds by trying to strangle her. The ward's aides pull him away from her, and he is given a lobotomy. Knowing that McMurphy would never want to live in this condition, the Chief suffocates him with a pillow, then escapes from the hospital by proving McMurphy's theory: He smashes the water-heating control panel through the window and runs free.

Macomber, Francis. "The Short Happy Life of Francis Macomber." Ernest Hemingway. 1927.

A tall, handsome, exceedingly wealthy man, Francis Macomber is on a safari in Africa led by the white hunter Robert Wilson. He has humiliated himself in front of his wife Margaret by bolting from the hunt and as a result has shown himself a coward.

As the party of three sits in the shade eating lunch, Margaret, who is also called Margot, cruelly teases her husband about the morning's fiasco before departing from the table in tears over her own humiliation. For his part, Macomber, to the irritation of Wilson, continues to talk about the embarrassing incident, repeatedly apologizing and asking the safari leader not to tell anyone of his behavior. As he lies in his cot later that night, Macomber shamefully recalls the details of the lion hunt.

His fear began, Macomber knows, when he woke up the night before the hunt to the eerie sound of a lion's roar. His uneasiness escalated as the hunt commenced, and when he saw the lion, he was almost paralyzed with fear. He shot and badly wounded the animal, who limped off to the cover of the bush. Still frightened, Macomber went so far as to suggest that they leave the suffering animal to die rather than go into the bush after it, an idea Wilson found unthinkable. When they did go after it, the lion moved to charge, and Macomber ran screaming from the bush.

Margot has not forgiven her husband for his cowardice. That night she returns to their tent after an absence of two hours, and Macomber knows she has been with the safari leader. The next morning he makes his anger apparent, but it is clear that he has no control over his wife, who continues to mock him and insists over her husband's objections that she go along to watch the day's buffalo hunt.

On this day, however, Macomber has no fear. He shoots three bull buffaloes and is thrilled that he feels only elation and not the familiar, dry-mouthed terror of the day before. Wilson congratulates Macomber, telling him that they had killed two bulls and wounded a third, which had retreated to the bush. Macomber looks back at Margaret, who is holding one of his rifles, and she watches him unhappily.

As they creep into the bush after the bull, Macomber feels no fear, only exhilaration.

Sure that the bull is dead, the hunting party is taken by surprise when it rises and charges. But Macomber remains steady, kneeling and shooting as the raging bull comes closer. Each shot just misses, and as he aims to shoot again with the huge animal almost upon him, he feels a blinding explosion in his head. Margaret, who was aiming at the bull that she feared was about to kill her husband, has shot Macomber instead.

McPhee, Ruella. *Vanishing Rooms.* Melvin Dixon. 1991.

Ruella McPhee, an aspiring dancer in New York City, becomes embroiled in the city's underworld as she works to establish her identity as a black woman and dancer.

As a child, Ruella, who is self-conscious about her blackness and insecure about her appeal as a woman, was afflicted with serious skin problems, which left her continually uncomfortable. Her pain was assuaged only by the affectionate attention of her mother and, more particularly, her brother, Phillip. Ruella believes she began to dance in order to escape the terrible pain.

Ruella is auditioning along with several others for a dance company. One day she enters a particularly successful partnering with JESSE DURAND, a young black dancer. That night she is surprised by a call from Jesse, who asks if he can stay with her. It turns out that Jesse is gay and that his white lover has just been raped and murdered by a group of teenagers. Jesse is unable to stay alone, and Ruella opens her home to him.

Before long, the two are working out together, doing stretches and practicing various dance steps. Ruella also assists Jesse with the police, and the two exert pressure on the detectives to find the killers. Soon Ruella begins to fall for Jesse. She tries to seduce him, but her attempt ends in failure, and the embarrassed Jesse leaves the apartment to wander the city. That night news comes that the killers have been apprehended.

Because of her involvement with Jesse, Ruella begins to realize that she has neglected her beloved brother, who is now serving time in an upstate prison. She visits him, and although they have not been in contact for three years, she and Phillip reestablish their relationship. She learns that he will be transferred to Rikers Island in New York and will be paroled soon after that. She promises him that he has her support and that he can live with her upon his release.

After Phillip's transfer, Ruella and Jesse visit him, and on one occasion Jesse spies one of his lover's killers among the prisoners. His angry outburst identifies the killer to Phillip and his friend Abdul, who eventually orchestrate a vicious attack on the boy—similar to the one in which the boy had participated on the streets of Greenwich Village. Ruella remains ignorant of her brother's role in the revenge attack.

Things between Jesse and Ruella cool off after he begins seeing another dancer, and she begins an affair with Abdul following his release. Ruella retains her affection for Jesse, though, and on the day of the long-awaited audition, she nearly loses her chance when she finds it hard to concentrate due to Jesse's presence and his ease in the company of his new lover. All three are accepted into the company, and Jesse attempts to interest Ruella in his new dance, which he is being given the chance to choreograph. Since the dance is about two men, Ruella has little interest and focuses instead on preparing for Phillip's release, her budding relationship with Abdul, and her own debut with the company.

On the night of her debut, Phillip and Abdul are in the audience, and Ruella dances quite well. All three are deeply moved by Jesse's dance. At the novel's end, there has been a measured rapprochement between Ruella and Jesse as each accepts the path their lives are beginning to follow.

McTeague, Mac. *McTeague.* Frank Norris. 1899.

When the enormous and brutally strong miner turned dentist realizes he may be an owner of gold rather than simply an extractor or implanter of it, Mac McTeague finds himself capable of the same mad venality as everyone around him.

Before Mac meets TRINA SIEPPE, he is content: His one companion is his febrile friend Marcus Schouler, and his one vanity is pulling the teeth of the patients in his San Francisco dental "parlors" with his hands. His only possessions are a concertina and a canary in a gilded cage. Mac dreams of owning a giant golden molar to hang outside his office, advertising his trade. But when Marcus brings his pretty young cousin Trina to Mac for some difficult dental work, the dumb giant is instantly entranced, and before completing her bridge, he has clumsily proposed to her. She ultimately yields to his animal strength.

Shortly before their wedding Trina wins $5,000 in the lottery. Mac does not immediately realize what this astronomical sum means, but Marcus does: He conceives in his jealous rage an uncontrollable enmity for his old friend, and spends the rest of the novel plotting his revenge.

Beginning with Trina's gift to Mac of the giant molar of his dreams, the marriage goes well for several years, despite Trina's increasing miserliness. When Marcus leaves to work on a ranch, however, the couple discovers that he has left instructions with political accomplices to have Mac's dental practice prohibited: It seems that he has been pulling teeth for over twelve years without a degree from an accredited dental college. This blow to

their economic stability causes Mac and Trina's relations to deteriorate severely. Mac finds work for a time making surgical instruments, but Trina has become tighter and tighter with her money, begrudging him every penny, and when he is finally laid off, she treats him mercilessly.

Sullen and angry, Mac yields one night to an offer of a few shots of whiskey. Whiskey wakes the demon in the brute, and he begins torturing his wife by pinching her and actually gnawing on her fingers. Finally he robs her of some of her savings and vanishes into the night.

When Trina refuses to take him back upon his return, Mac takes a job moving pianos for a music company and plots vengeance against his wife. Finding that she has sold his beloved concertina back to her room, he storms back to her room, beats her to death, and steals the $5,000 that she has never been able to bring herself to spend.

Taking his canary and the money, Mac heads back to his old mining camp east of San Francisco until, dogged by nameless fears, he moves farther south, one step ahead of the law. He goes prospecting with a man named Cribbens, and the two strike it rich; but before Mac can claim his share of profit, he must flee again, this time into the desert of southern California.

Lost out on the alkali flats of Death Valley, Mac is almost dying from the heat when he finds himself confronted by his ancient nemesis, Marcus Schouler. Notwithstanding their thirst, the two fight over the gold once again, and Mac beats his onetime boon companion to death. With his ebbing strength, Marcus manages to handcuff the two together, trapping the big man in the lonely desert, with no sight or sound save the faint, feeble twittering of the little bird in the gilded cage.

McVey, Hugh. *Poor White.* Sherwood Anderson. 1920.

Hugh McVey is born in a "little hole of a town" in the state of Missouri during the latter half of the nineteenth century. Hugh's father is a lazy, unemployed drunkard who frequently leaves young Hugh alone in their shack by the river. The boy's life begins to change, however, as the first sign of American industrialization, the railroad, moves through his town. Hugh begins doing odd jobs around the station and is eventually taken in by the station master and his wife, Sarah Shepard. Sarah encourages Hugh to work hard, teaches him how to read and write, and tries to rid him of the lethargic habits of his father.

Hugh lives with the Shepards until he is nineteen, all the while fighting a battle between his inclination to indolence and Sarah Shepard's expectations for his success. After the Shepards move away, Hugh, a strong but awkward young man, wanders around Missouri and the neighboring states in search of work and friendship. He remains withdrawn, meditative, and socially inept, and the people around him regard him as strange. Although he longs to make their acquaintance, he has little idea of how to communicate with others.

Out of pity, a friendly telegraph operator secures Hugh a position and lodging in Bidwell, Ohio. Determined to make something of himself, the twenty-three-year-old Hugh arrives just as the town, like so many others across the country, is changing from a rural agrarian community into an industrial city. Lonely and detached, he roams the streets and fields late at night. He starts to do simple mathematical problems in his head to relieve his boredom. Eventually these simple problems evolve into complex designs for machinery, which Hugh spends his spare time crudely sketching.

Soon, Steve Hunter, a local entrepreneur eager to ride the tide of change, convinces himself and a few others—all prominent men—that Hugh can create an apparatus that will change the town and bring millions of dollars in profits. After confronting Hugh with his plan, Steve Hunter encourages him and gives him financial support. Hugh, eager to be accepted and to leave his mark, eventually invents a piece of farm machinery. His invention singlehandedly changes the town as a factory is built, workers are brought in, and the town becomes transformed into an industrial center. The townspeople consider Hugh a genius, and his legend is only furthered by his antisocial behavior.

Hugh becomes the successful manager of a factory in Bidwell. He begins to long for female companionship and eventually asks Clara Butterworth, the daughter of one of his investors, to marry him, even though they are virtually strangers. She agrees, and they marry the same night. On the wedding night, Hugh, pained by his inability to communicate, sneaks out the window of his room. Only when Clara takes the initiative, a week later, can the marriage be consummated. But they communicate poorly, and after three years of marriage, Hugh is still unhappy.

Hugh is eventually attacked by a harness maker whose business and life have been ruined by Bidwell's modernization. After this event, Clara realizes that Hugh is less a hero remaking the world than a confused boy hurt by life, and they are able to establish a more open and intimate relationship. The attack forces Hugh to look with some ambivalence on the industrial developments he initiated, yet he cannot change what has happened. The novel closes with Clara expecting a second child and listening with Hugh to the shrill whistles of the local factories.

Madison, Little Augie. *God Sends Sunday.* Arna Bontemps. 1931.

Little Augie Madison is born in his mother's slave quarters shortly after Emancipation. Although he is born with a caul over his face—traditionally a sign of good luck—Augie is a sickly child. Small and frail, he is put to work tending livestock and grows to love the horses, on whose backs he feels huge and powerful. His mother dies when he is still very young, and he is raised by his sister Leah. At age twelve, Augie stows away on a riverboat bound for New Orleans. In that vibrant city he finds his way to the racetrack and begins working in the stables of Horace Church-Woodbine, a wealthy white thoroughbred owner.

Augie becomes a favorite of Woodbine's, and because he handles the animals well, he is soon allowed to ride in the races. In time, he becomes the leading jockey on the circuit and manages to earn money as well as a name for himself in the sporting world of New Orleans. Success transforms Little Augie's personality, however; shunning friends, he becomes an avid and abusive womanizer.

When Augie sees Florence Dessau, he falls in love with her. He soon learns, however, that Florence is Woodbine's mistress. Dejected, he decides that when the racing circuit swings to St. Louis, he will relocate, because he has heard that his sister Leah has settled there. The reunion with Leah and her four children is joyous. While Augie confesses to his sister that, despite his incredible success, he is restless and lonely, he quickly falls into the same type of sporting life he had pursued in Louisiana. But when Augie kills a man in a fight and is set free with just a slap on the wrist, guilt overwhelms him and he decides to go back to New Orleans and Florence. Although Augie feels that "home" is wherever Leah is, he does not want that place to be St. Louis.

Back in New Orleans, Augie learns that Woodbine has discarded Florence. Augie woos her, and because he is rich, Florence accepts him. When Augie moves into the house Woodbine bought her, however, the white community takes umbrage, and the two are forced to move to the outskirts of town. Augie's luck now changes. He stops winning races, loses all his money, and is abandoned by Florence, who runs off with another man. Poor and friendless, Augie hops a freight train headed west.

Twelve years later he again enters Leah's life, moving in with her and her grandson on their small farm and tending her meager livestock. He soon makes an enemy of Tisha, Leah's neighbor, by grazing his cattle on her land and then verbally abusing the woman when she complains. He avoids Tisha for a time, until he fights her man Lissus, who has been stepping out on Tisha with a young girl to whom Augie is also attracted. Augie cuts Lissus so badly in the fight that he believes he has killed him, and feeling guilty again, he takes to the road late that night.

When Augie turns back for one final look at the home he loves, he sees Tisha looming large in the moonlight, in steady pursuit. He falls, rolling into a muddy ditch, sure that when he rights himself, Tisha will be there to kill him. Angry, sad, and lonely, Augie determines to make a stand against the woman, but when he opens his eyes, she is gone. Disheartened because he has lost all his belongings in his flight, Augie continues on to the railroad crossing. Picked up by a passing truck, he goes back on the road, thinking of Woodbine and of the fast horses of long ago.

Magawisca. *Hope Leslie.* Catharine Maria Sedgwick. 1827.

Magawisca is a determined young Indian girl who challenges both Puritan notions of white supremacy and her own people's ideas of the inevitable enmity between the whites and Indians.

Magawisca's initial encounter with Puritans is a bloody one. Her tribe is attacked by colonists, and several members of her family are killed. Magawisca and her brother Oneco are taken captive and made servants in the family of William Fletcher. But in spite of the circumstances of her capture, Magawisca becomes close to the family, especially to Everell Fletcher, William's sympathetic eldest son. When she hears of her father's plans to avenge himself on the Fletcher family, Magawisca secretly meets with him to urge him to spare them.

Magawisca's father, Mononotto, is not moved by her pleas and attacks the house while Mr. Fletcher is away. He and his men kill most of the inhabitants and take Everell and the Fletchers' adopted daughter, Faith Leslie, captive. Magawisca and Oneco, who loves Faith, go with their father into the woods. But Magawisca has not submitted to her father's plan for vengeance. When he raises his arm to kill Everell, she jumps in the way. Her arm is severed by her father's tomahawk, and Everell is able to escape.

Several years later, Magawisca visits the colony. Hope Leslie, Faith's adventurous and independent sister, once rescued an old Indian woman, Nelma, who had been condemned to death by the colonist. The grateful woman swore that in repayment for her kindness, Hope would one day see her sister. Meeting with Hope in the cemetery where both of their mothers are buried, Magawisca says she will fulfill this promise. She warns the white girl that Faith has changed; now married to Oneco, she is as much an Indian as any one of the tribe and will not be willing to leave the family she has come to love. Hope is unconvinced and remains determined to return Faith to her white family.

Philip Gardiner, a fraud posing as a Puritan in order to escape his debtors in England, overhears the plans for the meeting and alerts the colony's guard. They swoop in during the meeting and capture Magawisca and Faith, while Hope is taken captive by Oneco. Magawisca is imprisoned on suspicion that she and her father encouraged Indian attacks against the Puritans. While she awaits trial, Gardiner visits her and reveals himself to be a papist who is posing as a Puritan to evade his debtors. He offers to help her escape if she will take with her his former mistress, a young girl who fell prey to Gardiner's promises of love

and followed him to the colony. The Indian girl angrily refuses and during her trial reveals Gardiner's true character to the colonists.

With the help of Hope's goodhearted tutor, Master Craddock, who poses as the Indian prisoner, Hope and Everell help Magawisca escape. Before they part, Hope and Everell beg Magawisca to return one day to live with them in the colony. But Magawisca declines, explaining sadly that the wrongs committed against her race by the white people have made this impossible. She also reminds them that Faith Leslie will never be happy unless she is returned to the bosom of her Indian family. Hope presents Magawisca with a miniature portrait of Everell by which she might remember her friends, and with a prayer that the Great Spirit be their guide, Magawisca departs forever.

Maggie. *Maggie: A Girl of the Streets.* Stephen Crane. 1893.

Maggie is a tragic victim of the unrelenting brutality of life in New York's Bowery tenements. A pretty and romantic child, she stands in sharp contrast to the filth, degradation, and violence of her environment.

As her story opens, Maggie and her two brothers struggle to survive a family life of violence and poverty. The children live in fear of their alcoholic mother, whose temper is so explosive that the children crouch in corners when she sleeps. The family is so poor that when the younger of the two boys dies, Maggie must steal a flower for his mean coffin. In this environment, Jimmie, the remaining brother, becomes a street tough and a petty criminal, but Maggie blossoms into a shy, pretty young woman and goes to work in a collar and cuff factory.

In time, Maggie is admired by Pete, a friend of Jimmie's. Pete is an uncouth, swaggering braggart, but Maggie imagines romantically that he is noble, wealthy, and powerful. Eager to impress him, she uses part of her salary to buy a decorative drapery for their slum quarters, which her mother tears down in a drunken rage.

When Pete takes Maggie out to a seedy beer hall, she continues to imagine that his manners and demeanor are elegant. She is enamored of him and accompanies him to freak shows, dime museums, and bad plays. When it becomes clear to Maggie's mother that her daughter is "ruined," she curses her loudly. Afterward, Jimmie, feeling vaguely that he should defend his sister's honor, has a bloody brawl with Pete.

Unable to return home, Maggie becomes dependent on Pete, imagining him to be a gallant rescuing her from her misery. But to her astonishment, Pete summarily leaves her for a well-dressed lady named Nell. Maggie returns home, but the jeers of her mother and the unflinching stares of her neighbors drive her away. She appeals to Pete; he dismisses her angrily.

Several months later Maggie, now a prostitute, walks the dirty streets of the Bowery. Several potential customers brush her aside, and she wanders slowly toward the river district. When she is almost to the riverbank, she notices an unsavory character, who leers and laughs at her and then follows her to the black water of the river.

Some time later, Jimmie announces to his mother that Maggie is dead. As neighbors comfort her, she sobs over her daughter's faded baby shoes, muttering, "I'll fergive her!"

Maggio, Angelo. *From Here to Eternity.* James Jones. 1951.

The feisty soldier Angelo Maggio hates the army with such fury that he risks everything to leave it. Although other enlisted men try to buck the system even as they cling to it, Maggio has no love for the institution.

One of Maggio's problems is homesickness. One of thirteen children born to Italian grocers in Brooklyn, Maggio misses his family and longs to return to his beloved Atlantic Avenue. He had willingly joined the army to escape his job as a shipping clerk in the basement of Gimbel's department store, but when he is continually assigned to menial kitchen jobs such as potato-peeling, he even longs to return to Gimbel's.

Although Maggio complains endlessly, his essentially cheerful disposition earns him the affection of his peers, especially ROBERT E. PREWITT, who also feels protective toward this slight and skinny but indomitably cocky soldier. Prewitt and Maggio often go into town on furlough together, and on one of these occasions Maggio becomes especially drunk. As a result, he and Prewitt miss curfew and are in danger of being picked up by the military police. Maggio refuses to hide from the police, however, saying he is fed up with being treated like scum. He urges Prewitt to go back to the barracks, while he furiously attacks two patrolling guards.

After being sentenced to six months' hard labor at the post stockade, Schofield Barracks, Maggio remains consistently insubordinate. He incurs the wrath of the stockade guards by his refusal to submit to their authority and earns the admiration of his peers by his ability to withstand continual beatings. After two months, Prewitt joins Maggio in the stockade, and by this time Maggio's face and body are scarred and his spirit thoroughly toughened by his ordeal. He has become a resident of the infamous but prestigious Barracks No. 2, where the most hardened and recalcitrant prisoners live, and when Prewitt also becomes a resident of Barracks No. 2, he learns of Maggio's desperate plan to get out of the army. If Maggio were to commit a serious enough offense, he would be sentenced to thirty days in "The Hole"—a particularly torturous version of solitary confinement—and if he remained in The Hole for thirty days without complaint, he would be judged insane and given a yellow dishonorable discharge. The plan is a dangerous one, for Maggio could indeed lose his mind in there, and if he succeeds, he would lose the right to vote as a U.S. citizen. But Maggio does not care, and after he attacks a guard, his plan goes into effect.

Maggio endures twenty-four days in "The Hole" as well as beatings and interrogations without ever dropping his mask of insanity. He comes out of the ordeal badly scarred but still sane and is given his discharge, whereupon his fellow prisoners applaud as he heads home to Brooklyn.

Mainz, Lena. *Three Lives.* Gertrude Stein. 1909.

Lena Mainz is a German immigrant who arrives in the United States at the age of seventeen, after being tortured throughout her transatlantic passage by sickness and intense morbid fears. For her aunt and patron, Mrs. Haydon, Lena is a find: Her passivity will enable her to be a good servant and, eventually, fall victim to one of Mrs. Haydon's favorite hobbies—matchmaking.

Mrs. Haydon procures a job for Lena with the Aldrich family, and she works for them for four years. The German cook makes sure that Lena's wages are deposited in the bank immediately, and Mrs. Haydon is pleased with Lena's performance as an American because she learns English and saves her money. She is well liked by her employers for her patient, conscientious service and for her gentle way with the Aldrich children. Typical days find Lena hard at work in the mornings, tending to domestic chores, with pleasant afternoons spent in the park watching the youngest of the children. In the park, Lena always sits with the Italian Nellie and the Irish Mary who, like Lena, spend afternoons babysitting. Although fond of Lena, Nellie and Mary like to tease her, playing off her naiveté as a recent immigrant. Far from minding being teased, Lena finds that their attentions arouse a gentle stir somewhere inside her.

Every Sunday, Lena spends her one day off with the Haydons and their three children. She is always too preoccupied, too lost in some nebulous dream world, to really focus on any form of human contact beyond a passive acquiescence to what is expected of her. Lena would prefer to do something different with her Sundays, but it literally never occurs to her that she has a choice. She is not fully aware that she is only happy around the teasing women in the park.

Having busied herself for four years trying to find the proper German husband for Lena, Mrs. Haydon decides on Herman Kreder, whose major credential is his thriftiness. Herman likes Lena as well as any woman, but he dislikes the idea of marriage, preferring to fraternize with men. His parents decide, however, that at the age of twenty-eight he should marry, and the wedding occurs.

Without a honeymoon, the new Mr. and Mrs. Kreder settle down in the house belonging to Herman's parents. Lena relies as usual on her dreamy detachment to survive yet another prescribed atmosphere. But this time her defense mechanism fails. The Kreders are stingy and unfeeling toward her. Herman, who is pleased that Lena demands nothing of him, is annoyed only by the fact that his mother attacks his wife incessantly. Wishing most of all for a life without struggle, he finally takes a house next door to his parents, but only after Lena has produced their first son. Lena withdraws from her role as mother to the extent that she begins neglecting herself and her family. She is frightened by the birth of her babies, and Herman tends to them. But she hides her fears and frustrations, or is perhaps once again not aware of them. She is always all right, so Herman does not have to think about her. Lena dies bearing her fourth child and is mourned only by her friend, the Aldrich's cook.

Malaeska. *Malaeska, The Indian Wife of the White Hunter.* Ann Stephens. 1850.

Malaeska is the beautiful Indian wife of William Danforth, a hunter and the son of a wealthy New York couple. The two have married despite social and moral codes prohibiting intermarriage between Indians and whites, and they have a son, William. Their fragile happiness is destroyed, however, when a friend of Danforth's shoots an Indian and rouses the hostility of the Indians toward the white settlers. The Indians attack the settlers, and Danforth kills, and is killed by, Malaeska's father. With his dying breath Danforth elicits from Malaeska her promise that she will go to his parents' home and learn to love the white man's God. Thus it comes about that Malaeska, bearing a letter of introduction, canoes down the Hudson to New York.

Danforth's parents are grieved at the death of their only son, and so they welcome their grandson as a replacement despite their distress over his mixed blood. They loathe Indians and will tolerate Malaeska's presence only on the condition that she never divulge she is William's mother, even to William himself. She acquiesces, but as the years go by, she finds the situation increasingly intolerable because of her naturally intense maternal feelings and her loneliness. One day Malaeska steals William away, and they spend two blissful days together in the woods, until Mr. Danforth comes and takes William away. Malaeska then moves to a shack across the river and continues an acquaintance with her son until he is grown and travels to Europe. She then returns, in loneliness, to her tribe, but they reject her for having taken away their rightful chief, William.

With nowhere else to turn, Malaeska settles near where she and her husband had lived during their brief marriage. She enjoys the friendship of a sixteen-year-old girl, Sarah Jones, until Sarah goes away to a finishing school in New York City.

By coincidence the school is next door to the Danforths' home, and Sarah meets and falls in love with William. The two return upriver for their wedding, and there William learns from Malaeska the secret of his parentage. In self-loathing and horror over having nearly destroyed Sarah's life by joining her to a husband of mixed blood, he leaps over a cliff to his death. Malaeska retreats to the tombs of her husband and father, and dies of grief.

Malánguez, Santos. *Family Installments: Memories of Growing Up Hispanic.* Edward Rivera. 1982.

Santos Malánguez narrates this autobiographical novel of an immigrant's search for identity. As he comes of age, Santos becomes increasingly estranged not only from his Puerto Rican heritage but from the immigrant community in which he had grown up in New York City.

Santos first describes the grueling and failed business ventures that led his father Gerán to leave Puerto Rico for New York. Remaining in Puerto Rico with his mother Lilia, his brother Tego, and his errant cousin Chuito, Santos lives the adventurous life of a young country boy. When the tickets arrive from New York for the family to come join their father, it becomes clear that the teenaged Chuito will be left behind. This loss stings Santos, and he never recovers the joy of his boyhood in Puerto Rico.

Santos's life in New York City is dominated by church, school, and the neighborhood surrounding his home. Educated in an Italian-and-Irish-dominated Catholic school system, Santos strongly feels the gap between his home life, which remains largely Puerto Rican, and his existence at school. He develops a passion for literature that sends him to the English program at New York's City College and spends most nights reading at home with his parents.

Gerán, a factory worker and a man of thwarted ambitions, devotes his evenings to practicing oratory from an old schoolbook and concocting "maromas," or ways to skim money off electrical bills and fool home relief inspectors. Santos's mother spends her time raising her two sons and reading a book of spiritual advice called the *Wonderland of Wisdom*. The family finally saves enough money to bring Chuito to Manhattan, where he joins the army, fights in the Korean War, and, unlike Santos, becomes a financial success.

When Santos's father becomes ill, he and Lilia decide to return to Puerto Rico. Santos remains in New York City in order to complete an advanced degree in English and finds a dingy room for himself in an SRO. Upon receiving word that his father has died, he goes to Puerto Rico for the funeral. While there he takes a brief trip to the village of his childhood, where some of his relatives remain and where all of his ancestors are buried. Gazing around him at the dilapidated huts and crumbling burial mounds, Santos wonders if he will ever return again. Then he dismisses the thought: There will be plenty of time, he says, to "brood about it on the flight back home."

Malcolm. *Malcolm.* James Purdy. 1959.

Fifteen-year-old Malcolm seems bored and unintelligent and is given to falling asleep at critical moments. He spends his days sitting on a bench near the palatial hotel where he lives, waiting for his father, who has disappeared and may or may not be dead, and for his life to begin. Malcolm, whose life is rooted in reality only in that he is running out of money, seems singularly unprepared to cope with his random and alienated existence. His only diversion is listening to the sea in his collection of seashells.

Malcolm appeals to Mr. Fox, an astrologer and "old pederast," who decides to give him a series of addresses and introductions to people who will help him experience "life." With these addresses in hand, Malcolm goes to meet Estel Blanc, an odd undertaker; Kermit Raphaelson, a painter and midget who refuses to believe in his deformity; and Lauren Raphaelson, Kermit's wife who soon leaves her small husband for "the real equipment." Later on Malcolm encounters Madame Girard, an alcoholic grande dame who collects handsome boys, and her husband, billionaire Girard Girard. A further visit takes him to the home of another eccentric couple, Eloisa Brace, a jazz singer and painter, and her husband Jerome, an ex-con. Eloisa, who is immediately attracted to Malcolm, decides to paint him, and the portrait is purchased by Madame Girard even before it is begun.

Each of the unusual people Malcolm meets seems drawn to the strange boy, but none more so than the Girards. They attempt to make Malcolm spend a month in the country with them, but he insists he cannot leave his other friends or his bench. Even when the billionaire leaves his wife to marry Lauren Raphaelson, he asks Malcolm to come with them. Madame Girard's bizarre life now becomes even more destructive when she is denied Malcolm's presence.

One evening after waiting all day at the Horticultural Garden for Girard Girard, Malcolm is picked up by Gus, a motorcyclist who takes him to the home of Melba, a famous singer. Melba decides almost immediately to marry Malcolm and sends him off with Gus to be "matured." He is taken to a tattoo palace and to Madame Rosita's Turkish Baths. Following this initiation, Malcolm and Melba are married in Chicago and have an ecstatic honeymoon in Cuba. Malcolm soon begins to lose weight and shortly afterward dies of "acute alcoholism and sexual hyperaesthesia." Madame Girard is with Malcolm when his life comes to an end, and she plans a lavish funeral.

Later, however, the undertaker and the coroner both swear that there was no body in the casket, although there had been a magnificent ceremony.

Mammy. *Gone with the Wind.* Margaret Mitchell. 1936.

Mammy, a house slave, is the vociferous and knowledgeable mainstay—nanny, nurse, governess, seamstress, and dresser—of the O'Hara family. Mammy's life of service began when she was first given charge of the infant Ellen, SCARLETT O'HARA's mother. She goes on to care for Scarlett and Scarlett's children, and her function as

nursemaid gives her daily access to the inner workings of the family's lives. Mammy never loses an occasion to assert her awareness of the traditions that must be upheld by her charges, and she constantly reprimands Scarlett for her divergence from proper etiquette. She is also watchful of Scarlett's feelings, although she is rarely granted the role of a confidante.

Mammy's devotion is limitless. When all the other slaves but one are conscripted by Union forces or flee the plantation, Mammy remains. She tends to Mrs. O'Hara in her final illness and nurses Scarlett's sisters, Suellen and Careen. Mammy constantly reminds Scarlett of the fact that ASHLEY WILKES cannot be hers once he is married to MELANIE HAMILTON (WILKES). Mammy disapproves when Scarlett rashly marries Melanie's cousin Charles Hamilton. She is angry when Scarlett lies and manipulates Frank Kennedy into becoming her second husband. Mammy's disapproval does not stop Scarlett from going through with the marriage, nor does Mammy's voice, the loudest in a chorus of disapproval, deter Scarlett from conducting business affairs in public throughout her pregnancy.

Aside from Scarlett and the O'Hara family, Mammy's chief interaction with whites in the novel occurs with RHETT BUTLER, who becomes Scarlett's third husband. From the beginning of the novel, when Rhett makes his appearance at a barbecue at the Wilkes plantation, Mammy disapproves of his entire manner. She astutely recognizes his stubborn streak, a trait she shares; she is also aware of his less than savory reputation. She is ardently opposed to the attention Rhett gives Scarlett. Eventually, despite Mammy's vociferous misgivings, Scarlett marries Rhett, who immediately seeks to gain Mammy's approval. The most telling instance of Rhett's solicitation is when he buys Mammy a red taffeta petticoat, which she initially refuses to wear because of its sinful connotations.

As the years go by, however, Mammy's heart softens toward Rhett, and she grows to appreciate his genuine love for Scarlett. On the evening Rhett and Scarlett's daughter is born, Mammy brings the good news to Rhett while wearing the petticoat purchased long before. Rhett, enormously pleased both by the birth and by the overt sign of Mammy's acceptance, shares some brandy with Mammy as they toast the new baby.

As the Butler marriage deteriorates, Mammy comes to side with Rhett who must grapple with Scarlett's rejection of him and then with his daughter Bonnie's accidental death. Rhett's violent grief following the accident moves Mammy deeply, and it is through her words that Rhett is finally vindicated.

Mancuso, Angelo. *A Confederacy of Dunces.* John Kennedy Toole. 1980.

Police officer Angelo Mancuso makes the mistake of attempting to arrest IGNATIUS JACQUES REILLY. Ignatius manages to cause disaster wherever he goes, and Angelo pays dearly for his error. Angelo withstands a series of humiliating punishments meted out by his sergeant until his luck finally changes.

Angelo is on the prowl for "suspicious characters" when he spots Ignatius standing outside the D. H. Holmes department store. Ignatius certainly merits suspicion: Enormously obese, he is wearing an odd assortment of old clothing, including a green hunting cap with earflaps, and has an unusual object hanging out of his bag. When Angelo questions him, Ignatius haughtily informs him that the object is a string for his lute. Ignatius begins bellowing at Angelo, and an angry crowd forms. An elderly man, Mr. Robichaux, shouts a defense of Ignatius, making a ridiculous remark about "communiss." Assuming that the label refers to him, Angelo drags Mr. Robichaux to the police precinct, while Ignatius bustles off with his mother, who was inside the department store.

At the police precinct, the sergeant questions Mr. Robichaux, who explains that he was only trying to defend poor Ignatius. The sergeant upbraids Angelo for bringing in "somebody's grampaw" and says he will now be exclusively responsible for arresting suspicious characters. For this task Angelo is required to go undercover, during which time he must wear a series of grotesque costumes designed to attract "bona fide" suspicious characters. After cruising for two hours in the French Quarter while wearing ballet tights and a yellow sweater, Angelo rounds the corner onto St. Ann Street, just in time to see Ignatius vomit out the window of his mother's car. They had been drinking in the Night of Joy bar, and in an attempt to get the car out of the parking space, Mrs. Reilly smashed it into a building.

When Angelo goes to the Reilly home to tell Mrs. Reilly she owes $1,000 in damages for the accident, the two have a very pleasant conversation and arrange to go bowling together. Irene Reilly becomes friendly with Angelo and his elderly aunt, Santa Battaglia. Their bowling trips and gatherings are Angelo's only comfort since his wife has a serious case of "nerves" and his status at the police force is falling steadily. Angelo tries moonlighting, hoping to find suspicious characters, but he is beaten up by three lesbians.

The sergeant is no more sympathetic when he sees Angelo wearing bandages. He accuses Angelo of having given a "phony lead" to the Night of Joy bar and sentences him to eight hours a day in the bus station restroom until he brings someone in. Sitting in the restroom all day, Angelo catches a terrible cold. He makes only one failed attempt at an arrest, but the suspect escapes with the book Ignatius had given Angelo to read in the restroom, Boethius's *The Consolation of Philosophy*.

When it becomes apparent to the sergeant that Angelo is on the verge of pneumonia or even death, he allows him to come out of the restroom. However, Angelo has only

two weeks to bring someone in, or he will be kicked off the force. Before the two weeks have elapsed, he finds himself in the middle of a crisis at the Night of Joy bar, for which Ignatius is responsible. After creating an uproar, Ignatius flees the bar, only to faint when Angelo, dressed as a wealthy fop, arrives. The bar's proprietor, Lana Lee, shows Angelo a photo of a naked woman and offers him a chance to sleep with her. Angelo promptly arrests Lana Lee for soliciting and possessing pornography. The following day, when the story makes the front page of the paper, the sergeant offers Angelo a promotion for having staged a "one-man raid" on the city's largest high school pornography racket.

Manischevitz. "Angel Levine." Bernard Malamud. 1950.

Manischevitz, a fifty-one-year-old tailor, runs a happy, successful business until a series of reversals plunges him into misery: his shop catches fire and burns to the ground, his son is killed in the war, and his daughter elopes with a lout. Following this, Manischevitz is plagued by terrible backaches and is unable to work more than an hour a day because of the pain. Worst of all, his beloved wife Fanny becomes seriously ill and must remain bedridden. The doctor says that there is little hope for her recovery.

Manischevitz tries to remain stoic, but his despair is so great that he begins to pray, asking God why this is happening to him. He begs humbly for help, imploring God to give Fanny back her health and to lessen his own pain enough to allow him to work. That night when Manischevitz is at home, he feels a strange presence in the next room. He peeks in and sees a black man sitting in his living room. The black man is dressed in a shabby suit with fraying sleeves and wears a hard derby hat on his head. Manischevitz assumes the man is a welfare worker, but the black man says that his name is Alexander Levine and that he is an angel who has come to help him in his misery.

Manischevitz is skeptical. He has never met a black Jew before, and he has certainly never met a black Jewish angel. Levine says that he is an angel on probation, but he insists that he can and will help Manischevitz, whereupon Manischevitz calls him a faker. Levine looks worried and disappointed. He says that if Manischevitz needs him, he will be in Harlem.

For the next three days Manischevitz finds he can work for four hours or more without pain. And Fanny begins to get her appetite back—things are looking up. On the fourth day, however, Fanny has a relapse and Manischevitz's pain returns. He wonders if he should have dismissed Alexander Levine.

Having decided to seek out the angel, Manischevitz wanders, confused, lost, and frightened, through Harlem at nightfall. He spies a tailor's shop and, glad to find something familiar, steps in. The old black proprietor knows no one with Levine's description, but when Manischevitz says, "He claims he is an angel," the old man nods and laughs and directs him to the Bella nightclub. Manischevitz peeks through the window of the club and sees Levine sitting at the back, looking much shabbier than before. He is wondering whether to go in when a big black woman steps up to Levine and pulls him onto the dance floor. Levine glances through the window, sees Manischevitz, and winks at him. Manischevitz goes home in despair.

Fanny's condition worsens until the doctor says she has only a day or two to live. Manischevitz goes to the synagogue to pray but soon feels that his prayers are useless. He goes home, falls asleep, and has a dream. In the dream he sees Levine standing before a faded mirror, preening small decaying wings. He wakes up and rushes back to Harlem.

By mistake Manischevitz enters a small synagogue where four black men are interpreting the Torah. Redirected to Bella's, he finds that Levine has been completely transformed: His clothes are shiny and new, and his manner is that of an uptown dandy. Manischevitz approaches him cautiously and asks leave to speak. Levine looks at him as if from out of a stupor, and when Manischevitz persists, he brushes him off bitterly. A crowd gathers, expecting violence. Although frightened, Manischevitz knows that Fanny's life depends on what he does next. "I think you are an angel from God," he tells Levine.

Levine accompanies Manischevitz to his apartment but declines to go in. From the roof of his building Manischevitz sees a dark figure in the sky, borne aloft on a pair of magnificent wings. A feather drifts down and turns white. It is snowing. Manischevitz rushes downstairs to find Fanny, vigorously mopping the floor, her health restored. "A wonderful thing, Fanny," he says happily. "There are Jews everywhere."

Mannix, David. *The New Yorkers.* Hortense Calisher. 1959.

David Mannix, the deaf son of the eminent Judge SIMON MANNIX, learned to lip-read and speak clearly through the extensive therapy insisted upon by his mother. Growing up in New York in the very brownstone his grandfather designed, he subsequently felt closer to his mother than his father. The Judge, always reticent in David's presence, seemed unable to accept his son's handicap.

David grows up in the shadow of an unhappy marriage. As a young boy he does not fully understand the estrangement between his parents, but he senses the tension between them. The Judge and his wife lead entirely separate lives and rarely see each other. David is even

more uncomfortable about his mother's frequent male guests, who pay visits at strange hours of the night.

One morning the Judge informs David and his sister RUTH (MANNIX) that their mother has shot herself to death during the night. Ruth goes into shock. A week later the Judge takes Ruth, his favorite child, on a vacation to Europe, leaving David in the care of their maid Anna.

Anna raises David almost entirely in the ensuing years. Because he blames his father for his mother's death, David keeps in contact only with Ruth. Yet, despite animosity toward both the Judge and the shallow and hypocritical world of politics that he represents, he still follows in his father's footsteps by attending Harvard Law School. But even at school he finds that he is still under his father's influence; at one point the Judge entreats one of David's classmates at Harvard to leave the school, transfer to Columbia, and become his private secretary. This is part of a larger scheme for the Judge to return to public life, which he had abandoned after the death of his wife.

Upon graduation from Harvard, David struggles to establish his own identity, ultimately finding it through a young deaf woman he meets. He quickly falls in love with her. To keep this relationship removed from his father's power, David reveals little about his lover, even to Ruth. This relationship gives him new courage to finally break from the path laid down by his father. The recent law school graduate decides to travel to Korea and aid in the war relief effort, an act he believes will be of some positive significance in the world. David's plane crashes on the way to Korea, and he dies while exulting in his newfound freedom and independence.

Mannix, Ruth. *The New Yorkers.* Hortense Calisher. 1959.

The daughter of the eminent Judge SIMON MANNIX, Ruth Mannix had always felt a vague estrangement from her mother, whom she believed favored her younger deaf brother DAVID (MANNIX). Ruth herself was her father's favorite, and he lavished gifts on her. While her father spent long hours seeking professional success and prestige, Ruth watched her mother entertain a number of different male guests, all the while sensing the subtle contempt with which she held the Judge.

Entering her mother's bedroom one night without knocking, Ruth finds her in bed with a lover. Hurt and confused, she finds the small gun hidden in the house and shoots her mother in the neck, killing her. Her father bursts into the room, and in an effort to protect his daughter, has her taken away by their maid Anna.

A week later Ruth is taken by her father on an extended vacation in Europe, to allow the stir caused by his wife's "suicide," as he explained it to the police, to settle down. Ruth never speaks directly with her father about the events surrounding her mother's death, and the excitement of her visit to Europe, where she decides to spend a year learning ballet, soon pulls her out of her initial shock.

In Europe, Ruth is finally told very delicately by her instructor (a close friend of her father's) that she lacks the talent to continue a career in ballet. Despondent, she returns home to New York where she is soon cheered up by her father, her brother David, and a number of his friends from Harvard Law School.

During this time a close friend of the family and classmate of David's, a young law student named EDWIN HALECSY, takes an interest in Ruth. A favorite of her father's, Edwin transfers from Harvard to Columbia Law School and becomes the Judge's personal secretary, to help the Judge prepare for his return to public life. Partly out of loyalty to her father, Ruth continues to see Edwin, who seems to have some strange control over the Judge for a reason not known to Ruth. In fact, Edwin suspects the Judge of being an accomplice in his wife's death. At a large dinner party thrown by the Judge to announce his return to public life, Edwin gets extremely drunk and, after taking a long walk with Ruth, rapes her and beats her brutally.

Once again doing his best to avoid scandal, the Judge sends Ruth to Europe, declining to press charges against Edwin in order to save his reputation. Ruth is still recovering from her attack by Edwin when her brother David is killed in a plane crash.

Wishing to see his only daughter married off and to gain a kind of surrogate son for himself, the Judge pressures Ruth to marry Austin, one of David's friends from Harvard Law School. Always following the wishes of her father, Ruth marries the young lawyer, whose personality proves similar to that of his father-in-law.

Mannix, Simon. *The New Yorkers.* Hortense Calisher. 1959.

Born to a wealthy New York Jewish family, Simon Mannix followed in the family tradition and attended Harvard Law School. During a long and successful career as a trial lawyer in New York, he meets his wife Mirriam and has a daughter RUTH (MANNIX) and a deaf son DAVID (MANNIX). Entering his fifties, Simon is able to call upon his considerable connections to fulfill his life's ambition of becoming a judge.

Despite his professional success, the life of Judge Simon Mannix is beset by personal problems. His relationship with Mirriam becomes increasingly strained, and they begin to live virtually separate lives, she entertaining a wide variety of younger guests (and maintaining numerous extramarital affairs), he spending most of his time on matters of business. The Judge rarely sees his son David, whom he feels his wife has turned against him.

Out of these private troubles there emerges in the Judge a boundless political ambition. Rumors of his appointment to the Supreme Court spread throughout the exclu-

sive clubs he frequents, and the Judge himself even begins considering a bid for the presidency. All of these plans are suddenly thwarted when Judge Mannix returns home late one night to see his wife shot to death by his young daughter Ruth, who had discovered her mother in the arms of one of her lovers. The Judge, wanting to protect his favorite child, pays off his wife's lover and explains to the police that his wife committed suicide.

While the reputation of the Judge is sufficient for the police to accept his story, he is forced into early retirement because of the rumors and suspicions surrounding his wife's death. He spends his time doting on his daughter, who pursues a career as a ballerina despite her obvious lack of talent. The Judge also tries to narrow the gap between himself and his son David, who follows in his father's footsteps and attends Harvard Law School.

It is when his son brings home a bright, ambitious young law student named EDWIN HALECSY that the Judge begins to reminisce about his past greatness. He starts to reconsider his decision to leave public life. After convincing Edwin to transfer to Columbia Law School and act as his personal secretary, the Judge decides to return to politics.

Edwin, already aware of the rumors surrounding the suspicious circumstances of Mirriam's death, begins a subtle blackmailing of the Judge: Essays and articles written by the Judge are circulated in Edwin's name; then, in a final act of defiance, Edwin rapes Ruth.

The Judge's health, already deteriorating rapidly, worsens when his son David is killed in a plane crash. He dismisses Edwin but is helpless to prevent him from continuing to plagiarize his legal documents. After successfully marrying off his daughter to another Harvard law student, the Judge retires for good to his mansion in New York, never again to venture into politics.

Marburg, Sonie. *Boston Adventure.* Jean Stafford. 1944.

Sonie Marburg, the novel's heroine, is an only child of poor immigrant parents eking out a living outside of Boston during the Depression. Gifted with a quick, observant eye and a powerful imagination, the child fashions for herself a vision of what life might be—a vision that enables her not just to endure but to live the life-style she has imagined for herself.

The child's inspiration first comes from her observation of LUCY PRIDE, a wealthy spinster in her sixties. Miss Pride summers each year at the resort hotel where Sonie's mother works as a chambermaid. Sonie occasionally fills in for her mother and cleans Miss Pride's room. She reverentially inspects the old woman's things and gleans clues as to what life must be like on Beacon Hill. From a distance she observes the Brahmin style—what Miss Pride wears, how Miss Pride acts, what Miss Pride says and to whom— and resolves to pattern herself after it.

Sonie's home life is disordered and deeply disturbing. She sleeps on a pallet beside her parents' bed and throughout the night hears her mother berating her father for their poverty. One night when Sonie is fifteen, she hears her father collapse into bitter, broken weeping. He deserts them the next day. When Sonie's mother gives birth to a boy, Ivan, four months later, the burden of the household's support falls on Sonie.

Over the next year Sonie's mother begins showing symptoms of insanity. She hates Ivan and abandons him to Sonie's care. Finally, due to the mother's criminal neglect, Ivan catches pneumonia and dies. Sonie appeals to Miss Pride for help in burying him. Impressed by the quality of Sonie's letter, the old woman begins to take an interest in her circumstances. Within a year Sonie is forced to commit her mother. When Miss Pride invites Sonie to live with her in Boston, Sonie agrees to go to business school to learn stenography and typing in order to help Miss Pride write her memoirs.

Sonie soon makes her debut in the circle of Miss Pride's relatives and friends, the cream of Boston society. She meets and falls in love with Philip, a doctor whom Miss Pride has chosen for her pretty, spoiled niece, Hopestill Mather. Made a plaything by the wild Hopestill, Philip begins to flirt with Sonie, who falls in love with him, much to Miss Pride's irritation. As Sonie becomes more sophisticated, she begins to be disillusioned by Miss Pride's human foibles, and a rift occurs between her and her former role model.

The tide turns, however, when Hopestill, pregnant by another man, gulls Philip into marriage. Witnessing Philip's decline and Hopestill's superficiality, Miss Pride grows increasingly anxious about the onset of old age. When she admits to Sonie her real need for her, Sonie responds with genuine warmth and affection. No longer in need of Miss Pride as a perfect example, Sonie is able to embrace her as an equal and a friend.

March, Amy. *Little Women.* Louisa May Alcott. 1868–69.

With a crown of golden curls, Amy Curtis March is the youngest of four sisters. Although selfish and affected, Amy is the most practical of the March sisters. At twelve she has already decided that she wants to be either a great artist or a wealthy gentlewoman. With her goal always in mind, Amy works to improve her talents as an artist and hone the skills she believes necessary to become a woman of society.

Set during the Civil War, the novel opens as the March family prepares for Christmas without their father, who has volunteered as a chaplain in the Union Army, and without worldly riches. Amy and her three older sisters, MARGARET "MEG" (MARCH), JOSEPHINE "JO" (MARCH), and BETH (MARCH), complain about their poverty. Amy has already begun to cultivate the favor of those whose

friendship will prove valuable, she feels. This attempt at winning the admiration of her peers results in the deepest humiliation of her young life.

Wishing to appear as generous as her friends, Amy breaks school rules by buying limes to share during recess. To Amy's dismay, a young rival alerts the instructor to her hidden contraband, and Amy is given several raps on the palm of her hand and is forced to stand before the class until recess. Amy flees to the sanctuary of home, where her mother admonishes her for disobeying the rules but is indignant at the corporal punishment. Amy never returns to the school but is thereafter taught at home with Beth.

As the months pass, several events alter the March household and place Amy in circumstances that will affect her entire life. First, the family is notified that Mr. March has become ill in Washington, D.C., and Mrs. March must go to him. While Mrs. March is away attending their father, Beth contracts scarlet fever from the children of a poor family she has been visiting regularly. To prevent her from contracting the illness, Amy is sent to stay with Aunt March, a wealthy widow for whom Jo serves as a companion. While there, Amy practices her French with the French maid and endears herself to Aunt March, who likes the child's amiable manner and ladylike ways. By the time Beth is better, Aunt March is so attached to Amy that she asks for her to take the place of Jo as her companion.

Three years later Aunt March's patronage helps Amy achieve the dream of her life. When another aunt visits Aunt March, she becomes enchanted with Amy and decides to take her to Europe as a companion to her daughters. Amy determines that in Europe she will discover whether she can be a great artist. If she cannot be great, she resolves, she will attempt to attain the remaining goal of her life.

Rome teaches Amy that she has some talent and much energy but no genius. Always practical, Amy writes home that she will marry for money, and if a wealthy young man whom she knows cares for her should ask her to marry him, she will agree.

Near Christmas, THEODORE "LAURIE" LAURENCE, the grandson of the wealthy old man with whom the March sisters had struck up a friendship years before, arrives in Nice where Amy and her party are spending the holiday season. Unknown to Amy, Laurie has expressed to Jo the love that he has had for her since childhood, but she has spurned him. He has come to Europe to assuage his pain. After several weeks of becoming reacquainted, Laurie and Amy fall in love. When word reaches Europe that Beth has died, Laurie is there to comfort Amy, and the two become engaged.

Shortly before returning home, the couple is married. With the Laurence mansion as her new home, Amy realizes her goal of becoming a gentlewoman but understands that being genteel has more to do with personal character than with wealth. Six years later, Amy is the mother of a beautiful baby girl, and Laurie has become a businessman in his grandfather's firm. As the novel closes, the Laurences join the rest of the March family for a day of apple picking.

March, Augie. *The Adventures of Augie March.* Saul Bellow. 1949.

Augie March grows up on the West Side of Chicago with no father, a passive mother, a mentally deficient brother George, an older brother Simon, and the stern and domineering Grandma Lausch, who is forever trying to make "mensches" out of Augie and Simon. The big Depression hasn't hit yet, but Augie's family is still a charity case; they have no money and must continually skimp, save, and finagle to get by. Augie, an intellectual picaresque hero in search of something to do with his life, goes where his circumstances lead him and eventually writes the story of his random adventures.

While in high school Augie becomes the personal assistant of Einhorn, a crippled real estate mogul, and learns a great deal from his employer. When the crash of 1929 hits, Einhorn's financial legacy is destroyed; all that remains is his poolroom, and Augie starts working there. After Augie graduates from high school, Einhorn takes him to a bordello, where Augie loses his virginity. He enrolls at the public college but drops out soon after and moves to Evanston, where he sells luxury items to rich suburbanites. He ends up working at a sporting goods store owned by Mr. Renling, whose wife adores Augie instantly and tries to set his life on the "right path." Mrs. Renling pays for Augie to study at the journalism school and brings him to her bridge soirees. For the first time Augie develops social ambition. He falls frantically in love with Esther Fenchel, a millionaire's daughter who spurns him but whose sister Thea is crazy about him.

When Augie discovers that the Renlings intend to adopt him, he decides to return to Chicago. There he tries to make money mostly through illegal schemes, including an intellectual book-stealing ring. Meanwhile, his brother Simon, who is now married to the very rich Charlotte Magnus and is an officer in the Magnus family business, plans to better Augie's life. Simon gives Augie a job, clothes, and a new identity, and sets him up with Charlotte's sister Lucy. When Augie helps his close friend through an illegal abortion, however, Simon, Lucy, and the entire Magnus family sever their ties with him.

Augie is working as a union organizer when Thea Fenchel tracks him down. In a brawl between union loyalists and anti-union busters, Augie gets beaten; afterward, he goes to Thea Fenchel's, and they fall into each other's arms. Directionless and in love, Augie follows Thea to Mexico so she can obtain a divorce.

In Mexico, Thea has an idea to train an American bald eagle to hunt lizards. Augie helps her, but their efforts end in disaster when he is hurt by their stampeding horse.

Depressed during his recovery, Augie takes up with a crowd of expatriate writers, poker players, and idlers while Thea hunts for snakeskins on horseback. When Stella, the beautiful wife of one of the poker players, pleads with Augie to help her leave her husband, Augie agrees, thereby pushing his now-strained relationship with Thea to its limit.

After Thea leaves him, Augie has a crisis. He has no profession, no money, and no responsibilities, and he now realizes the ugliness of his professed simplicity. Determined to reconnect with his family, he returns to America and visits his mother and brother Georgie (both in mental institutions), and makes up with Simon. Back in Chicago, he finally decides what he wants to do with his life: set up a schoolhouse, teach underprivileged children, bring his mother and Georgie to live with him, and get married. At this time the war breaks out, and his sketchy plans are deferred. One weekend while on leave from army training, he bumps into Stella in New York. They fall in love and get married. Two days later, he leaves for Europe and his ship is torpedoed. Augie is marooned in the African Sea with a crazy embryologist until the British save them.

After returning to New York, Augie follows Stella back to Europe so she can pursue her film career. He deals in surplus army goods with an Armenian lawyer, then wanders through Florence and Paris, still in search of something to live for.

March, Basil. *Their Wedding Journey; A Hazard of New Fortunes.* William Dean Howells. 1871; 1890.

Basil March, a reserved insurance agent, and his wife ISABEL (MARCH) begin a lifetime of bickering and sightseeing on their wedding trip to Niagara Falls. Having married late in life after a long engagement, Isabel wants them to appear to be a dignified married couple and admonishes her husband against any gestures that would reveal them as newlyweds. Perhaps for this reason Basil's romantic sensibilities are occupied mostly with poeticizing the landscape, while his attitudes toward Isabel are often less imaginative and generous.

The wedding journey begins on a stormy day in June, and the first stop is New York City. They proceed north by train to Niagara Falls, stopping along the way in cities such as Rochester and Buffalo, which, in their charmed state, they find delightful. As they pass each city, Basil relates to Isabel some historical anecdote. As long as he is apparently more knowledgeable than Isabel, Basil feels he has the upper hand in their genteel battle for power. Basil experiences a certain satisfaction when Isabel is too frightened to cross a rickety bridge, while Isabel has a similar feeling of triumph when she laughs at him for buying her a tasteless gift.

A truce is achieved, however, when Basil pushes the limits of Isabel's patience. In Montreal they have an argument over whether to take a one-or two-horse carriage around the mountain. Isabel insists on two horses, and when Basil refuses, she retreats to the hotel. After riding for a while with one horse, alone and remorseful, Basil suddenly sees things from Isabel's point of view. He sends an elaborate two-horse carriage to pick her up, and they take a romantic ride together. The harmony between them is sustained until they reach home in Boston, where the narrative of their wedding journey ends.

The story resumes twelve years later when Basil takes his wife and two young children, Tom and Bella, with whom he is affectionate and indulgent, back to Niagara Falls. Basil has not done as well in the insurance business as he might have hoped, and concern about money clouds the trip. Isabel discourages Basil from bringing the family to those cities that were most enjoyable on their wedding trip. Having visited Niagara Falls, the quarreling Marches head home by train.

Basil eventually quits his longtime job in the insurance business and moves to New York City to accept the editorship of a magazine, *Every Other Week*, which is run by his friend Mr. Fulkerson and financially backed by the nouveau riche Jacob Dryfoos. Settling into New York life, Basil attempts the exciting and bustling streetcars and the "L" but cannot get used to the poverty that presses its nose up against the windows of wealth. This contrast between rich and poor is augmented when he encounters Mr. Lindau, an old friend who lost a hand in the Civil War. This man—who is also a veteran of the German revolts of 1848—lives in poverty while the magazine's uncouth owner is a millionaire oil magnate. Basil helps Mr. Lindau by commissioning him to do translations for the magazine, but at a dinner party given by Mr. Dryfoos, Lindau is offended by his aggressively capitalist host and says so. Mr. Dryfoos demands that Lindau be fired; only Lindau's resignation keeps Basil from leaving as well since Basil had planned to give notice if his old friend were forced out for his socialist beliefs.

With some uneasiness Basil continues to work for the magazine. He wonders what he would have done if Mr. Lindau had not resigned of his own accord. Doubts also linger about Mr. Lindau's commitment to what Basil sees as dogmatic anticapitalist principles. Was it really necessary for Lindau to return all the money he had earned from the magazine when he resigned just because Jacob Dryfoos is a capitalist? Is Basil corrupt because he works for such a man?

Basil feels his personal moral code and moderate beliefs reaffirmed when a streetcar strike breaks out. He goes to the East Side to watch the strikers, who have had some violent altercations with the police. The crosstown streetcar that he boards to take him home to Greenwich Village comes upon a riot between strikers and police. In the melee Mr. Lindau, who had been loudly cursing the police, is clubbed by an officer. Also a casualty is Jacob Dryfoos's son Conrad, a devoutly religious young man who had been

forced by his father to work at *Every Other Week*. Innocent and naive, Conrad had hoped to calm the strikers with Christian words but is instead shot to death. The whole episode convinces Basil that radical positions—whether pro- or anticapitalist—can cause tragic events.

The death of his son so crushes Mr. Dryfoos that he offers to sell the magazine to Basil and his friend Fulkerson for a nominal sum. They take ownership just before Mr. Dryfoos and his family sail off to Paris. Sobered by his experiences in New York, Basil nevertheless continues his stewardship of the magazine.

March, Beth. *Little Women*. Louisa May Alcott. 1868–69.

Beth March is the saintly invalid sister of the less perfect March daughters. Where JOSEPHINE "JO" (MARCH) is rebellious, AMY (MARCH) is selfish, and MARGARET "MEG" (MARCH) is vain, Beth is kind, generous, and thoughtful. When the girls bicker, Beth reunites them with her gentle chiding, thereby earning her nickname, "Little Tranquility." Beth is a talented pianist who lifts her family's spirits with her soft, melodic playing while their father is away during the Civil War. Too shy to go to school, Beth is educated at home by her sisters and her mother Marmee.

When Jo befriends the boy next door, THEODORE "LAURIE" LAURENCE, the March girls meet his stodgy but kind grandfather, Mr. Laurence, who takes a liking to little Beth and induces her to practice the piano in his mansion, supposedly to keep it in tune. Although timid and bashful, Beth allows her love of music and benevolent spirit to fortify her enough to enter the stately mansion and play, much to Mr. Laurence's pleasure. When she knits him a pair of slippers, he gives her the grand piano in return. To thank him, she forgets her fear and marches into his house to kiss him on the cheek. He is delighted, for she reminds him of his long-lost granddaughter, and from then on the old man and the young girl are fast friends.

While Marmee is in Washington, D.C., tending her sick husband, Beth secretly takes on her mother's ministerial duties and visits the poor, sickly Hummel family, from whom she catches scarlet fever. Always weak, Beth never completely recovers from the illness. Her father returns from the war to find his daughter an invalid.

As the other March girls grow up, marry, and seek their fortunes, Beth never strays far from the family hearth, her wan face often shadowed by pain and sadness. At eighteen her countenance takes on a spiritual glow. Jo mistakes the change for romantic love—but Beth will never grow up and marry, and she knows that she will soon die. Jo takes Beth to the shore in hopes that the sea air will restore her health. There Beth tells Jo that she will not live long. After they return home, Beth grows increasingly angelic and spends her time making mittens, needle-books, and scrapbooks for her friends and family. Jo remains by her side until one spring morning when Beth dies peacefully in Marmee's arms.

March, Isabel. *Their Wedding Journey; A Hazard of New Fortunes.* William Dean Howells. 1871; 1890.

Isabel March and her husband BASIL MARCH make their debut as a couple on their wedding trip to Niagara Falls. They had met in Boston eight years before but subsequently broke off their engagement. At the outset of the journey, Isabel muses regretfully on the time they lost and seems glad to have finally made the decision to marry.

Isabel and Basil leave their home in Boston on a stormy day in June 1870, some weeks after their marriage. The bad weather causes a delay in their departure, but Isabel cheerfully asks her husband if he doesn't find it charming that they must wait so long. Once in New York, Isabel is unable to imagine anyone loving this city as one is able to love Boston. As they continue northward by boat and train, Basil and Isabel's happiness at being together transforms spots as ordinary as Buffalo and Rochester into enchanted cities. Basil takes a certain egotistical pride in providing poetic historical notes for Isabel, who seems ignorant of American history.

Niagara Falls is swarming with young couples, and Isabel finds their unconcealed affection offensive. She resolves not to lean her head on Basil's shoulder or make any other gestures that would reveal their identity as newlyweds. The only couple with whom they become friendly is the Ellisons, who have apparently been married for quite some time. After observing a conversation between Colonel Ellison and his wife, Isabel tells her husband that she resembles Mrs. Ellison; she, too, is amusing and illogical. Isabel exposes an irrational aspect of her personality one day after they have crossed a fragile-looking bridge to some wild islands called The Three Sisters. Although Isabel makes it over the bridge, she becomes too frightened to return; she sits down and refuses to move. When the Ellisons approach, Isabel is afraid of being seen, pulls down her veil, and marches across the bridge. Isabel does not fully recover her dignity until several days later when Basil gives her a gaudy fan; it is such a tasteless present that Isabel can only laugh at her husband. After traveling to Quebec and Montreal, they return to Boston, still delighted with each other despite a few disagreements and mishaps.

After twelve years of marriage, when Basil is forty-two and Isabel thirty-nine, they return to Niagara Falls, bringing along their two lively children, Tom and Bella. Isabel discourages Basil from bringing the family to those cities that had been most pleasurable on their wedding journey because she does not want to alter the memories. Feeling a vague sense of absence at Niagara Falls, Isabel comes to the realization that she no longer sees any brides. Basil reassures her that the young couples are still there but remain invisible to all but other newlyweds. Isabel is now

the long-married matron she had tried to portray on her wedding trip. Sitting at Niagara Falls, she wonders whether the everyday experiences of married life have vulgarized her and Basil. She breaks from this line of thought, rushes to her husband and children, and herds them onto the train, where she and Basil return to their customary petty bickering.

March, Josephine "Jo." *Little Women.* Louisa May Alcott. 1868–69.

Josephine "Jo" March, the novel's boyish heroine, is tall, dark-haired, and ungraceful. Jo cherishes the safety and comfort of the family and fights with all her might to keep the family circle unbroken. Only when she herself finds love does she realize that the marriages of her siblings do not represent a disintegration of the March clan but an expansion and strengthening of it.

As the novel opens, the Civil War is raging and Jo along with her sisters, BETH (MARCH), MARGARET "MEG" (MARCH), and AMY (MARCH), remain in their New England home with their mother Marmee while their father is away serving as a volunteer chaplain for the Union Army. In her father's absence Jo has assumed the role of the man of the house. Spunky and adventuresome, she works as companion to her wealthy widowed Aunt March. Jo's aim is to become a famous writer, and she keeps her mother and sisters amused and entertained with her romantic dramas.

Jo's first great adventure is her friendship with THEODORE "LAURIE" LAURENCE, the grandson of the wealthy old man next door. After their initial meeting, Jo captures the heart of Laurie and his grandfather, and the two families strike up a friendship that lasts for years. Laurie soon spends more time at the Marches' than in the splendid mansion that is his home.

The family friendship proves to be of practical value when word comes from Washington, D.C., that Mr. March is gravely ill and Mrs. March must go to him immediately. Jo and her sisters are left at home to be watched over by Mr. Laurence. Life becomes even graver for the March girls when Beth contracts scarlet fever. Marmee is called from her husband's side to nurse her daughter, and Beth eventually recovers. At Christmas, Mr. March returns home. To Jo's utter chagrin, it is revealed that John Brooke, Laurie's tutor, wishes to marry Meg. The wedding is set for three years later, and Jo despairs that the family circle is being torn asunder.

Four years later, time has wrought many changes in the March family: Meg and John Brooke are married and the parents of twins; Amy is traveling in Europe; Beth, who is now an invalid, remains at home; Laurie is away at college; and Jo is restless. During the intervening years, Jo has had a number of short stories and a novel published, but she wants to gain more experience of life and to avoid the avowals of love that she fears will soon be forthcoming from Laurie. She therefore decides to spend the winter in New York City working as a governess.

Upon Jo's return from New York City, her life changes drastically. When Laurie declares his love for her, Jo rejects him, and he then leaves for Europe. Beth, who has never regained her health after the bout with scarlet fever, dies. Amy and Laurie meet in Europe, comfort each other upon hearing of Beth's death, become engaged, and are married in Europe. With the death of Beth and the marriage of her younger sister and best friend, Jo feels alone and unhappy.

At this point Friedrich Bhaer, a German professor Jo met and fell in love with in New York, turns up at the March home. He and Jo declare their love for each other and are married a year later. When Aunt March dies and leaves her mansion to Jo, the Bhaers open a school for boys. Now the only writing Jo does is the stories she writes to amuse her boys. As the novel closes, Jo's school is thriving, she has two boys of her own, and the March clan is intact and stronger than ever.

March, Margaret "Meg." *Little Women.* Louisa May Alcott. 1868–69.

A sixteen-year-old beauty, Margaret "Meg" March is the eldest of four sisters. Because she is old enough to remember the time when her family was wealthy, Meg suffers more from the poverty in which the family now finds itself than do her three younger sisters. From the days of her maidenhood through her early years of marriage, Meg struggles with a desire to be a queen of society able to compete with her well-to-do young rival Sallie Gardiner. Only after many battles with vanity, pride, and envy does Meg learn the value of modesty, love in spite of poverty, and the wealth of contentment and happiness.

As the novel opens, Christmas is near and the four sisters bewail their lack of money. Meg complains of her work as the governess of four children, expressing her envy of girls who have little suppers, go to parties, drive home, read and rest. The attendance of Meg and her sister JOSEPHINE "JO" (MARCH) at a New Year's party hosted by Sallie Gardiner serves only to fuel Meg's discontent. Although she sprains an ankle and is forced to spend most of the evening in a lounge, Meg manages to receive an invitation to spend a week with Annie Moffat, a friend of Sallie's.

Meg finds herself in the splendid home of the very fashionable Moffats, and the more she sees of Annie's pretty clothes and possessions, the more she envies her and desires to be rich. Everyone takes an instant liking to Meg, and the young girl finds herself somewhat spoiled as she attends many glamorous parties during the week. But her envy of Annie's baubles and bows gets the best of her. By the final party of the week, she allows her hosts to lend her a gown and dress her like a china doll. The comments that Meg overhears that night cause her to be

ashamed of her folly and to wish she had worn her own modest attire. After a week the young adventurer returns home grateful that her experiences have cost her nothing more than discomfort.

As spring and summer pass, the attention of Meg and her sisters is drawn away from the matters of girlish trivia to the seriousness of the Civil War, which has been under way for several years. Notification that their father, who volunteered as a chaplain in the Union Army, has taken ill in Washington, D.C., requires their mother to leave the girls to be by her husband's bedside. The four sisters are left to care for one another.

While their mother is away, BETH (MARCH) contracts scarlet fever. After sending AMY (MARCH), the youngest sibling, to stay with an aunt, Meg and Jo do their best to nurse Beth. But after many long days and sleepless nights, the attending doctor fears that Beth is dying, and a telegram is sent to the girls' mother. Marmee arrives to spend more restless days beside Beth's bed. As Christmas draws near, Beth begins to recover.

On Christmas Day, Mr. March arrives to make the family circle complete. It is not long before the family recognizes a new glow in Meg's face. They discover that young John Brooke, tutor of THEODORE "LAURIE" LAURENCE, the neighbor and playmate of the March girls, is in love with Meg, and she with him. All parties agree that Meg is too young to marry and John Brooke needs time to settle into a profession that will enable him to support a wife and family. Three years later, Meg, now twenty, and John, a clerk, are married and move into their tiny cottage, Dove-cote.

Meg's life now revolves around John and her home. But even in marriage she has not lost her desire for wealth and position. Finally unable to bear her poverty, she splurges on an expensive silk dress. Realizing her mistake, she asks Sallie to buy the dress from her; she purchases an overcoat for John with the money and finally rids herself of her discontent. A year later Meg is the mother of twins, Daisy and Demi. With her mother's gentle guidance, she learns to balance children and husband, thereby creating a happy home.

Marcher, John. "The Beast in the Jungle." Henry James. 1903.

John Marcher has always felt himself destined to experience something strange, perhaps terrifying, but when it does happen, he does not even notice.

When Marcher sees May Barton at the English countryside estate of Weatherend, it has been ten years since he has spoken to her. Although they hadn't known each other very well so many years ago in Italy, Marcher is happy to see the woman. He surmises that, because she is assisting in answering visitors' questions about the stately home, May is a poor relation of the mansion's owners. They greet each other cheerfully and briefly reminisce.

Just as topics of conversation seem close to exhaustion, May startles him with a pointed but confusing question. She asks if he remembers what he had told her on a hot day off the coast of Sorrento. An embarrassed Marcher claims to remember the day but forgets what he told his companion. He wonders to himself if he made some sort of promise to her then, for its recollection would be awkward now. But no, all he told her was that he felt sure something great, even rare, would someday befall him. As his memory of the moment returns, he realizes he still believes in this premonition. He knows as well, when she asks him if he is speaking only of falling in love, that the strange, rare event cannot be that, for he has been in love before.

This conversation establishes a bond between May and Marcher. She resolves to wait and watch with him, and for the next few years they do just that. When May moves to London, after her relative dies, Marcher is able to visit her frequently. May never refuses him admission to her home and never wavers in the vigil she willingly shares with him. Marcher feels that he and May are soulmates, but he disdains the idea of marrying her. After all, if the terrible thing strikes him, a woman may watch but not participate. May, a perceptive woman, does not simply watch, however. As she reveals to him one evening, she already knows what the thing is.

Soon after that evening, May begins to grow ill. Marcher still maintains his visits but is now occasionally turned away. He becomes alarmed by the toll that age and sickness have taken on his friend's body and fears that she might die before he undergoes his ordeal. During one visit, May, while talking to an increasingly agitated Marcher, rises from her chair and approaches him, silently reaching out. But Marcher is consumed by his own concerns and does not respond to her.

The last time they meet, Marcher is jolted when May tells him that the thing has happened. Confused, and upset that he has not seen it, Marcher leaves May's home when she becomes too weak to continue the visit. She dies soon thereafter. After May's funeral, Marcher takes a trip to the East, from which he returns no more enlightened about the thing that passed him by. The truth is revealed on a visit to May's grave. When Marcher sees the face of another mourner, contorted by the grief that only the loss of true love can inspire, he crumbles. Realizing that he has lived his life as an observer and that he failed to accept real love from May and to give love in return, he flings himself facedown on her cold grave marker and cries.

Marker, Little Miss "Marky." "Little Miss Marker." Damon Runyon. 1932.

Little Miss Marker is a chubby little girl with curly golden locks and a perpetually cheerful demeanor. She doesn't say much except "Marky dance," after which she inevitably does an energetic series of dance steps that culminate with her falling on her "snoot." This doesn't seem to bother her and usually calls forth, if not applause, at least laughter from anyone watching.

"Marky," as she calls herself, first appears under the charge of a young man who is placing a bet on a horse race at a betting house on Broadway in New York City. The owner of the establishment is named Sorrowful. The young man says that he wants to place a bet on the horse Cold Cuts but needs to go to Fourteenth Street to get his money first. Since the race is about to begin, the young man offers to leave his little girl as "a marker," or collateral, so that he can place his bet even without the money.

Sorrowful lives up to his name: He is in his sixties, thin, unattractive, and wears a perpetual frown that goes along with the tales of woe he tells anyone who will listen. As he later tells his friends at the local club, he took the young man up on his offer because, although he is normally cynical in the extreme, he felt that no one could leave such a cute little girl behind. But Sorrowful was wrong. Cold Cuts loses the race, and the young man does not return.

Sorrowful's friends at the club are all hardened city dwellers with names like Regret, Wop Joey, and Guinea Mike. Despite their toughness, they are immediately taken with the little girl and her amusing dance steps. Sorrowful himself is especially enamored, the more so when Miss Marker saves his life. A mean ex-boxer named Milk Ear Willie comes into the club to shoot Sorrowful over a gambling dispute, but he puts his gun away when he sees that the cute child would be involved.

After searching halfheartedly for her father, Sorrowful gleefully sets about becoming a parent to Little Miss Marker. He rents a posh apartment, hires a nursemaid, and obtains a limousine for Miss Marker's personal use. Every night Sorrowful and the child show up at the club, and while Miss Marker enjoys herself and the music, the men exchange tips on parenting. Sorrowful becomes a mere shadow of his former self because of the little girl: He stops complaining and telling sad tales, and is even seen smiling on occasion.

All this ends when Miss Marker catches pneumonia after walking outside in the cold by herself in order to find Sorrowful at the club. The men immediately take her to the clinic, where she stays for some time without improving. The clinic is overwhelmed with flowers and get-well cards, and the men stop spending time at the club in order to be with her. One of the men suggests that a specialist, a reclusive doctor named Beerfeldt, known to work only with the very rich, be called in.

But even Doc Beerfeldt cannot save Miss Marker. She speaks her last words in response to distant strains of music: "Marky dance." As the distraught men try to cope with the death of their beloved, the young man suddenly appears and explains that he has come to collect his child, who is now heir to the fortune of a wealthy relative. But it is too late. Sorrowful, who quickly returns to his old disposition, walks out in disgust, saying that the man should pay the money he owes and never be heard from again.

Marlowe, Philip. *The Big Sleep; The Long Goodbye.* Raymond Chandler. 1939; 1953.

Philip Marlowe, a tough private investigator, encounters trouble and mystery in these two detective novels. Marlowe is a man of compassion and principle in a corrupt world. He braves deception and violence to help clients who are often the source of the problem, and he takes it all in with a wry, hard-boiled wit.

In *The Long Goodbye*, Marlowe is drawn into the troubles of Terry Lennox, a man he found passed out drunk in front of a posh club and then took home. When Lennox's wife Sylvia, the daughter of a multi-millionaire, is murdered, Lennox is a suspect. Marlowe helps him escape by driving him to Mexico, no questions asked.

When Marlowe returns, the police question him about Lennox. Marlowe refuses to talk, so the police arrest him and try to bully a confession out of him. Marlowe says nothing. He spends a few days in jail but is released when the case is quietly closed after Lennox commits suicide in Mexico and leaves a confession to his wife's murder.

Marlowe's life is quiet again until the publisher of best-selling author Roger Wade asks him to take care of the writer. Wade has a drinking problem and cannot finish his current novel. Marlowe refuses. But when Eileen Wade, the writer's beautiful wife, asks him to find Roger, who has disappeared on a binge, Marlowe agrees. Marlowe follows a few leads and eventually succeeds in bringing Roger home. He considers his job finished, but the Wades continue to call him for help. Marlowe senses a dark secret in the Wade household.

When Marlowe helps Roger out of another drinking bout, he learns that Roger was having an affair with Terry Lennox's wife Sylvia. Roger makes a weak suicide attempt, and Eileen tries to seduce Marlowe. A few weeks later, when Marlowe visits Roger for lunch, Roger begins drinking again. Disgusted, Marlowe walks down to the nearby lake; when he returns, he finds that Roger has apparently shot himself in the head. The circumstances of the suicide are suspicious, and Marlowe must clear himself as a suspect.

Marlowe investigates and discovers that Eileen had once been married to a man named Paul Marston, which Marlowe knows is an alias of Terry Lennox. The mystery begins to unravel, and Marlowe figures out that Eileen killed both her husband and Sylvia Lennox. Eileen is insane. But Marlowe does not turn Eileen in to the police because he doesn't have hard evidence; he simply lets her know that she has been discovered. Eileen kills herself with an overdose of sleeping pills, leaving behind a full confession.

Later, a Mexican man visits Marlowe with the claim that he was in the hotel when Terry Lennox killed himself. Marlowe sees through his story. Lennox faked the suicide, had plastic surgery, and dyed his hair. The Mexican is Lennox. Marlowe rejects his old friend and is finally left alone.

In *The Big Sleep*, Marlowe finds himself drawn into the complicated affairs of the wealthy Sternwood family. General Sternwood, a sick old man, has two daughters, Carmen and Vivian. He hires Marlowe to deal with Geiger, a man who claims that the mentally unstable Carmen owes him money for gambling.

Marlowe discovers that Geiger operates an illegal pornography shop. When Marlowe stakes out Geiger's house, he hears shots. He enters the house to find Geiger lying dead on the floor, and Carmen, drugged, posing for nude photos. To protect Carmen, Marlowe hustles her out of the house after a cursory search for clues. When Marlowe returns to Geiger's house, the photos and Geiger's body are both missing.

With a few lucky hunches and some quick thinking, Marlowe solves the mystery. Geiger was killed by Carmen's jealous boyfriend, who later ran his car over a railing and into the ocean. The blackmailer who found the pictures of Carmen was killed by Geiger's homosexual lover. His official work for Sternwood over, Marlowe is still curious about the disappearance of General Sternwood's son-in-law, Vivian's husband Rusty.

Marlowe suspects that Rusty has been killed. Everyone else, including the Missing Persons Bureau, thinks that Rusty ran away with another woman. Marlowe eventually rescues the woman, who is being held captive by her gangster husband, Eddie Mars. He suspects Mars of killing Rusty, but he cannot come up with a motive.

Marlowe returns to the Sternwood house, and Carmen asks him to go into the woods to practice shooting. There Carmen tries to shoot Marlowe. Fortunately, Marlowe has loaded her gun with blanks. He takes her back to the house and confronts Vivian, forcing her to admit that Carmen shot Rusty. Eddie Mars was involved to cover up the murder. Marlowe promises not to go to the police if Vivian gets psychiatric help for her sister. As the novel ends, Marlowe has solved yet another case—in his own way.

Marquales, Robert. *End as a Man.* Calder Willingham. 1947.

Although accepted to Duke University his senior year of high school, Robert Marquales decides instead to attend a southern military academy. Upon arriving at the academy, Marquales is dismayed to see his roommate Cadet Simmons, an overweight, dimwitted young man who is planning to pursue a career in the clergy but is attending the academy to please his overbearing father. When Simmons is the victim of brutal hazing by the upperclassmen, Marquales requests a room change.

Soon thereafter, Marquales, while out one weekend night on a leave, meets an upperclassman named JOCKO DE PARIS, who ends up passing out drunk in a bar in the town. Despite the protests of his friends, who have no desire to help an upperclassman, Marquales sneaks the unconscious Jocko back through the academy gates and into his dorm room.

They soon become fast friends, and Marquales is delighted when he is invited by Jocko to participate in a poker game with him and a number of other upperclassmen. He soon learns, however, that Jocko invited him along in order to cheat an old enemy of his, an upperclassman named Gatt, with an elaborate card scheme. Not wanting to lose Jocko's friendship, Marquales agrees to participate.

Gatt is cheated out of ninety dollars and demands his money back. Marquales brings Gatt to Jocko, who promptly writes him a check for the money, then privately informs Marquales that he has reported his checkbook stolen.

The next day Marquales is stunned to find he has been summoned by the commanding officer, General Haughton, who interrogates him as to the details of the poker game and its aftermath, and informs him that he will most likely be expelled for his actions. Marquales is then told to remain while General Haughton interrogates Jocko, who summarily lies about the poker game, the cheating, and his attempt to get Gatt expelled. After having the defiant Jocko forcibly removed from his office, the General then tells Marquales to wait in his room while his fate at the academy is decided.

At an assembly the next morning, Marquales learns that his inexperience has earned him probation, and although the others have been expelled, he will be allowed to remain at the academy to continue his training.

Marriott, Gordon. *The Turn of the Balance.* Brand Whitlock. 1907.

The son of a leading New York City defense attorney, Gordon Marriott has always been close to the family of wealthy broker Stephen Ward. He secretly loves their daughter ELIZABETH (WARD), but due to his long association with her family as well as a pronounced shyness on his part, he has been unable to tell her.

Soon after Elizabeth arrives home from boarding school, she comes to the young man, now a lawyer like his father, to ask a favor. Mr. Koerner, the father of her maid, was seriously injured in a work-related accident and needs a lawyer to win reparations from the railroad company for which he works. Seeing this as an opportunity to win Elizabeth's favor, Marriott gladly accepts, despite the friction he encounters from Mr. Koerner, who doesn't trust lawyers.

At a dinner party at the Ward house a few nights later, Marriott is dismayed to see Elizabeth spending most of her time with his professional rival, city prosecutor John Eades. Marriott reconciles himself to the fact that he has lost Elizabeth when he continues to see the two of them together in the ensuing weeks.

Marriott is able to win Mr. Koerner's suit against the railroad company, and the old man receives reparations of $8,000. But the payment is delayed when an appeal is granted, and he must go to the Koerner household to inform Mr. Koerner that the case must be tried all over again.

As Marriott is making preparations for the appeal, Elizabeth comes to him once more. Koerner's son Archie, she explains, has been accused of murder and faces the death penalty if Marriott cannot get him acquitted. Although overwhelmed by this point, Marriott nonetheless agrees to help because of his affection for Elizabeth.

Despite Marriott's best efforts, Archie's trial goes poorly, and he is convicted on the testimony of two of his partners. Archie is sentenced to death by electric chair, and the date for his execution is scheduled. When two additional appeals and a plea to the governor are all rejected, a frustrated Marriott watches helplessly as Archie is put to death.

Shortly after this tragedy, Marriott has the sad duty of informing Mr. Koerner that the railroad company has won their appeal. He finds out that the old man and his family are being evicted from their tiny tenement in a Brooklyn ghetto. By this time Koerner, who hadn't trusted lawyers in the first place, cannot stand the sight of Marriott in his home and angrily kicks him out.

Marriott ventures to the Ward home where, shaken from the tragic events of the past few weeks, he confesses his love to Elizabeth. His grief turns to joy when Elizabeth informs him that she returns his affection, and despite the tragedy around them, Marriott and Elizabeth are able to find happiness with each other.

Marshall, Jane. *With the Procession.* Henry B. Fuller. 1895.

Jane Marshall, the oldest and favorite daughter of Chicago millionaire David Marshall, is an intelligent, energetic young woman who wants to transform her family by moving it "into the procession" of high society. Believing they are lagging behind and wasting away, Jane urges them to plunge themselves into communal and social affairs. She throws herself fully into making the necessary improvements, challenging her father and brother RICHARD TRUESDALE (MARSHALL) to follow her lead. Jane solicits the assistance of Mrs. Granger Bates, the wealthiest and most well-known woman in the community, to help her start a charity lunchroom for working women. Mrs. Bates receives Jane coolly until she learns that Jane is the daughter of David Marshall, her old friend and former admirer. The two women become friends as Mrs. Bates shows Jane every room of her mansion and generously donates money for her cause. Mrs. Bates advises Jane on the arrangements for her sister Rosamund's debutante tea; after Rosamund has successfully entered society, Jane feels personally triumphant. Determined to orchestrate a similar success for Truesdale, she asks Mrs. Bates to help make him a floor manager at the upcoming Charity Ball. Mrs. Bates agrees, and when she invites Jane to sit with her at the ball, Jane is thrilled.

Jane goes with Mrs. Bates to the hairdresser's, the milliner's, and the dressmaker's. Watching Mrs. Bates beautify herself, Jane gains an understanding of her own imperfections and transforms herself. When Mrs. Bates wants Jane to invite her beau, Theodore Brower, to the ball, Jane finally agrees even though she knows he does not approve of society. Jane thoroughly enjoys herself at the ball, and when she arrives home afterward, she finds her father awake in his study. She tells him all about the event, expressing her regret that he had not attended. David Marshall replies that he has many other things to think about. More aggressive than ever after her social triumphs, Jane later lectures her father about his failure to contribute something lasting to the community.

When the Marshalls decide to build a new house, Jane participates in the process of designing and building. Her adamant opinions about architecture—and her persistence in communicating them—both impress and exasperate the architect. When she shows her father a drawing she has made of the future house, he seems tired and preoccupied; Jane notices that he looks unwell and seems fatigued, and she is worried about him. In the meantime, she finds her newly formed ladies' lunch club to be more trying than expected, and she works hard to mediate between members with differing points of view.

Mutual admiration between Jane and Theodore Brower grows. Jane thinks of him constantly and feels increasingly devoted to him. David Marshall falls ill, and when the family is about to move into the new house, Jane, feeling the pressure of her father's decline and growing sentimental about the past, resists the transition. Her father does dies, and Jane prepares the list of pallbearers. When Brower asks to ride in her carriage during the funeral procession, he and Jane finally acknowledge their desire to marry. Although Jane's father had been persuaded before his illness to fund a large-scale community building, in his will he revokes the plan and gives the money to Jane. Instead of accepting this inheritance for herself and Brower, Jane plans to go ahead with the building that will honor her father.

Marshall, Joanna. *There Is Confusion.* Jessie Redmon Fauset. 1924.

The determined and intelligent Joanna Marshall, a middle-class black woman living in the early 1900s, is deter-

mined to shape her own life and the lives of those around her. Methodical and ambitious, a sense of her own worth blinds her to the real difficulties she has to face. Joanna is also self-righteous and firmly believes that she is justified in manipulating her family and friends in order to achieve what is best both for them and for her. As her story unfolds, she finds herself caught in a personal struggle for social equality—one that challenges an intention she has held since childhood: "I never, never mean to let color interfere with anything I really want to do."

Joel, Joanna's father, a self-made man who has to some extent defied the limitations of his class and color, has instilled in his children a sense of ambition and worth, and of all of them, Joanna seems the most likely to succeed. Although she is not conventionally pretty or outstandingly talented, she possesses extraordinary strength and will. Joanna's ambition is to be famous, a star of the stage, and although Joel does not approve of everything this life-style entails, he admires her fixity of purpose and sees her as the inheritor of his own will to succeed.

Aware of what she has inherited from her father, Joanna believes her family's strength must not be diluted by intimate contact with anyone who is not worthy of the Marshall name. Yet people are drawn to the charismatic Marshall family—especially Peter Bye and Maggie Ellersley. As Joanna grows older, she watches Maggie become increasingly attached to her elder brother Philip, and for the first time she takes matters into her own hands. By convincing herself that Maggie couldn't really love Philip, Joanna authorizes a piece of deception that sends Maggie away from the Marshall family into the arms of the disreputable Henderson Neal. Joanna's own feelings for Peter, with whom she is falling in love, are less easy to discount, and she realizes she break away from him and her family to pursue her ambition.

Having cut herself off from Peter and separated Maggie and Philip, Joanna goes to New York. Here, away for the first time from the closed circles of Philadelphia, she encounters racism, a reality that, when viewed from the relatively privileged, sheltered environment of her home, had always seemed easily surmountable. She soon realizes that this is the great obstacle against which she will have to prove herself. Although determined not to grow disheartened, she finds herself turning more and more to Peter for the support and warmth lacking in the harsh world of New York. Peter's devotion to her never wanes despite her inability to admit she loves him. Joanna sees Peter's adoration as a temptation she must avoid if she is to succeed in professional life, for marriage would mean the end of all her aspirations. She is acutely aware of Peter's lack of ambition and direction, which she sees as incompatible with her own purpose. Peter finally takes her rebuffs to heart and leaves her. When he accidentally meets up with Maggie Ellersley, who has by now separated from her husband, the two of them quickly grow close.

Meanwhile, Joanna's career has taken off, and she seems to be within sight of realizing all her dreams. Although she does not become as famous as she had hoped, she gains some renown for her onstage interpretation of a game played by African-American children. Soon, however, she must again confront the racism and sexism she thought she had overcome; and, for the first time, she is without Peter, who is engaged to Maggie. Although she now realizes how much she loves him and admits for the first time that her earlier behavior toward Maggie had been thoughtless and self-righteous, Joanna feels she cannot tell him the truth, even though to refrain may cost her her future happiness.

Yet Peter, too, has discovered a measure of honesty. He breaks off his engagement to Maggie, who in turn realizes that she still loves Philip. Maggie marries Philip, who is dying, and discovers through this brief marriage the sense of self-worth that had always eluded her. As the novel ends, Joanna gives up her career in order to marry Peter. Relinquishing her old values of ambition and "greatness," she adopts a new creed that "calls for nothing but happiness."

Marshall, Richard Truesdale. *With the Procession.* Henry B. Fuller. 1895.

After a three-year absence, Richard Truesdale Marshall, the youngest son of Chicago businessman David Marshall, has come home. As a sophomore at Yale, Truesdale had left college and gone to Europe to pursue life at his own pace. His diverse experiences abroad—from studying philosophy in Heidelberg to dabbling in painting in Paris and to cultivating his voice in Milan—have shaped Truesdale and refined his tastes. Now, returning to his family in the United States, Truesdale must fashion a new life for himself in society while feeling, all along, that he would rather be somewhere else.

Truesdale's aunt Lydia, a sweet and well-meaning busybody, welcomes him home and says she will be happy when he gets married, settles down, and becomes a good citizen in their community. Truesdale groans at her comments, but he does not resent her efforts as a matchmaker; he realizes that her interest in him is a result of her nature and of her experience. Aunt Lydia introduces Truesdale to Bertie Patterson, a shy young woman from Madison, Wisconsin, who is spending the winter in Chicago. After chatting with Bertie at his sister's debutante tea, Truesdale decides she is quite nice and wants to know her better.

No longer interested in his old friends and determined to rebuild his social circle, Truesdale makes two new male friends: Theodore Brower, an intellectual who was "outside" of society, and Arthur Paston, a lively British businessman. Although he visits Bertie with Aunt Lydia, attends occasional social functions, and debates with Paston and Brower at the clubs in town, Truesdale has trouble

filling his time and finds the city of Chicago culturally inadequate. His ennui motivates him to move more fully into the Chicago social scene, a move that he depends on his sister JANE (MARSHALL) to help him make. With Jane's assistance Truesdale becomes a floor manager at the famous Charity Ball, where the elite community gathers once a year to dance, socialize, and scrutinize one another. At the ball Truesdale continues his ongoing flirtation with Bertie Patterson and meets a few more attractive young women—including Gladys McKenna, who later begins to annoy him with her persistent letter writing.

Truesdale agrees to paint Bertie's portrait, and she is thrilled to have the opportunity to pose. Soon afterward he has a brief affair with a working-class girl. The offense troubles his entire family, and as a result, Truesdale keeps more and more to himself. He eventually speaks to Aunt Lydia, who tells him that Bertie is about to leave Chicago and return to Madison. Later, in a heated discussion with his brother, the diligent but joyless Roger, Truesdale expresses his anger that his straitlaced mother, his "lily sisters," and his "supersensitive" father have judged him for doing something that dozens of other men have also done. He believes that the world is a very wide place and that life is to be explored as fully as possible, and he invites Roger to travel with him to Japan, even though he knows his brother is too parochial and predictable to go.

Truesdale travels to Madison and tries unsuccessfully to call on Bertie. After his father dies, he receives a card announcing Bertie's engagement. He reflects about not having a bride or a business occupation, and looking out on the city and thinking about the "human hodge-podge" he has encountered there, he resolutely decides to go to Japan. His father's will makes it possible for him to embark on this, his next voyage.

Martin, Erwin. "The Catbird Seat." James Thurber. 1943.

Erwin Martin has been head of the filing department at the F & S company for more than two decades. Inflexible and humorless, he takes great pride in the commendations of his employers, who laud his efficiency, infallibility, and abstinence. Recently, however, a problem has cropped up at work: Mrs. Ulgine Barrows.

Martin plans to rub out Mrs. Barrows. Since coming to F & S two years ago as special assistant to Mr. Fitweiler, the company president, she has threatened Martin's dominion over the filing department. Her quacking voice and braying laughter aggravate Martin, but not nearly as much as her nonsensical questions: Are you tearing up the pea patch? Are you scraping the bottom of the pickle barrel? Are you sitting in the catbird seat? Even when a coworker explains that Mrs. Barrows picked up the expressions listening to Red Barber announce Dodger games and that they have specific meanings ("tearing up the pea patch" means going on a rampage; "sitting in the catbird seat" means sitting pretty), Martin's aggravation does not abate.

Walking to Mrs. Barrows's apartment, Martin remembers that Mr. Fitweiler once labeled him infallible, and he is confident he can commit the perfect crime. If recognized en route or if she has company, he'll simply abort the murder. He stops to buy a pack of cigarettes, a red herring that, when left at the scene of the crime, will point away from Martin, famous for never having smoked or taken a drink. He arrives unseen at her apartment, and Mrs. Barrows brays a delighted welcome. Inside, she takes Martin's hat and coat, but he keeps his gloves and lights a cigarette. Mrs. Barrows is shocked but gleeful to see him smoking and asks if he'd like a drink. He would, so she goes into the kitchen to mix scotch and sodas. As Martin searches for a murder weapon, he becomes suddenly conscious of the insanity of his scheme. He abandons the killing of Mrs. Barrows on the spot and immediately hatches a different plan.

Martin confesses to Mrs. Barrows that he always drinks and smokes. Emboldened by her delighted response, he confesses a diabolical plot to bomb Mr. Fitweiler's office. Her demeanor immediately stiffens as she assumes her official mien, demanding to know if he's taking dope. Heroin, replies Martin. He'll be high on it the day he bumps off Fitweiler. Outraged, Mrs. Barrows ejects Martin from her apartment. He leaves unseen, declaring he's now sitting in the catbird seat.

The next morning Mr. Fitweiler summons Martin to his office. Mrs. Barrows, he explains, has leveled fantastic and horrifying accusations against Martin, and Mr. Fitweiler promptly consulted a psychiatrist who confirmed his suspicions: Mrs. Barrows is suffering from a persecution complex accompanied by hallucinations. Mr. Fitweiler gravely informs Martin that Mrs. Barrows will no longer be needed at F & S and then dismisses him to his duties, asking him to forget this unfortunate incident. Wearing a look of industrious concentration, Martin, ever the diligent employee, promptly returns to his post.

Martin, George. *The Town and the City.* Jack Kerouac. 1950.

George Martin is the patriarch of a large New Hampshire family. A large, outgoing man, he is capable of both excessive violence and extreme tenderness. Through the course of his life he sees the changing world swallow up his six sons and three daughters and take them away from him one by one, in both body and spirit.

At first, while all the members of his family are still together, George revels in the daily challenges of life. When his middle son PETER (MARTIN) scores the winning touchdown on a big Thanksgiving Day football game and becomes the toast of Galloway, George is there in the stands, choked up and full of pride. He feels responsible and successful, as if he has raised Peter right, so that he would score

that touchdown. Another son, Francis, does not fare as well in his father's eyes. They do not communicate, and George is confused and angered by Francis's haughty silence.

When George nears fifty, he starts to experience a new kind of restlessness. He sees his printing business fall deeper into debt, and although he realizes he may lose the business, he cannot bring himself to do anything about it. He gets the urge to forget the whole thing and just take off for Boston to play the horses. In some ways he wishes he could just jump out of his life, escape from all the responsibilities and risk everything for something new and exciting. As his debt increases, he is squeezed out of business by some greedy men, and then he begins to realize that the world is not as just as he had assumed.

George obtains employment in a downtown printing plant and starts to see himself as a failure. The family is forced to move into a smaller house. One daughter, Liz, elopes at age eighteen—an act for which George blames himself. He sees his relationship with his children disintegrating, and he begins to believe that because of his foolishness, the family is falling apart. He asks his son Peter to do well in school, as though this would reawaken the pride and happiness he had felt when Peter scored the winning touchdown.

Pleurisy and liver trouble keep George in bed for two weeks and cost him his job. He is forced to work in Meriden, Connecticut, where he lives in a rooming house, and to send most of his pay back home to Galloway. Peter drops out of school and comes home to work in Galloway; but his effort to help the family only disappoints George. Trying to understand his failure, George believes that it is part of the larger misery of life. The world is out of his control, and God has taken his children from him one by one. A trip to Chicago to see Francis, who has been hospitalized in a ward for the insane in order to evade military service, makes him realize how provincial he is. He decides to leave New Hampshire.

George, his wife, and one son, Mickey, move to Brooklyn where George gets a job working nights in a printing press. He feels more like a lonely old man than ever, and his continued distance from his children is brought home to him when he meets Francis on the street, and his son doesn't even introduce him to his friends.

George slowly sickens in Brooklyn. He becomes thin and frail, and his hands are splotched with yellow cirrhosis spots. His family learns that he is dying of cancer, but they do not tell him. Old and battered by the world, George dies in his sleep and is buried in New Hampshire as his family gathers from across the country to see him finally laid to rest.

Martin, Gilbert. *Drums Along the Mohawk.* Walter D. Edmonds. 1942.

Gilbert Martin is a member of the first generation of American pioneers, the stubborn, ambitious "little people" who are collectively the soul of the nation. Buried in the trials of day-to-day existence, Gil and his compatriots have little sense of the part they play in their country's history. Gil's horizons are limited to the land he must till, the wife he must support, and the militia duty that interferes.

Gil is what would later be called a homesteader. He stakes out and clears a small area, and builds a cabin. The novel opens when he is returning to the cabin with his new wife, MAGDELANA "LANA" BORST MARTIN. Their homestead is a desolate last outpost in the wilderness of New York's Mohawk Valley, on the tenuous edge of a frontier settled mostly by Germans. Gil races into the job of clearing and planting his land, but his valiant domesticity is interrupted by the outbreak of the American Revolutionary War. It is 1776; the British, allied with the Iroquois and inflamed by Tory colonists, raid the Mohawk Valley settlements. The Martin cabin is among the first to be burned. Gil and his wife escape downriver to the American forts and spend the rest of the war struggling for existence there—working, starving, worrying, and dreaming of an eventual return to their farm.

Gil is eventually called for militia service. A reluctant but competent soldier, he is recruited by two woodsman friends to act as a scout. His first battle is a bloody victory, and the sight of scalped neighbors, wounded leaders, and bloodied ground provoke in Gil a rigid determination to get himself and his family through the war. American troops, managed from the ridiculously out-of-touch Continental Congress, are never effectively used in the Mohawk Valley, and it is Gil and his local militia who bear the brunt of the war there. Gil farms within sight of the fort, his crops intermittently burned by enemy incursions, and he reports for militia service whenever he is called. The Americans are never successful in catching the British and Indian raiding parties that swoop down to scalp and pillage in New York's breadbasket.

In 1781, when Gil is the father of two sons and provider for a household of six, the Americans finally get their chance. Gil again becomes a scout, scouring the New York woods in the snow for a retreating company of British, Tories, and Indians. This time the militia catches its prey, and Gil helps rout the enemy with a tired, desperate vengeance in a dawn attack, which occurs simultaneously with Washington's victory against Cornwallis at Yorktown. With the war finally over, Gil can return to what is left of his farm. His family is still growing, and now the New Yorkers are moving out beyond them into the new country.

Martin, Magdelana "Lana" Borst. *Drums Along the Mohawk*. Walter D. Edmonds. 1942.

Magdelana "Lana" Borst Martin is an undistinguished, hardworking helpmate and mother undaunted by the adversities of war. With very little personal independence

and absolutely no sense of identity beyond the conventions of marriage and motherhood, Lana is buffeted by the varying fortunes of her husband and the changeful existence of a settler during the American Revolution.

Born in 1758, Lana Borst is married in the week after Independence Day, 1776, to a man she met only a handful of times. GILBERT MARTIN has purchased and begun to clear a small farm thirty miles from Lana's home, and she now follows him there. It is a wild place with a tiny, rough cabin, on the edge of the Mohawk Valley settlements. Lana works hard beside Gil in the fields and then again in the cabin, and is pregnant within two months. But Lana's life is abruptly altered in the fall when a party of Senecas allied to the British burn their home, the farm, and the rest of the small settlement. Lana and Gil just manage to escape being scalped, and while Gil goes out with the militia to chase off the raiders, Lana has a miscarriage.

For the remainder of the war Lana and Gil are virtually squatters, living in temporary homes with improvised means while they speculate about returning to their land in the future. After her miscarriage, Lana develops a morbid fear of sex and will not let Gil touch her at all. Only when Gil serves in the militia's first real campaign and is wounded in the arm do the couple unite to face the trials ahead. They find a surrogate home as hired live-ins for a widow and are able to farm, although not on their own land. Lana develops an almost daughterly relationship with the gruff Mrs. McKlennar and at last feels some security in the great stone house just across the river from the fort.

The years that follow are punctuated by enemy raids. The British, their Indian allies, and bitter Tory colonists burn and scalp their way through the rich agricultural valley. Lana bears two children in these years, suffering hunger, hard work, and constant anxiety. She is periodically evacuated to the fort, a crowded and squalid haven from which the settlers can only watch as their fields and houses are burned. During one raid she cannot get away in time and must hide with her children in the woods.

The war's last year is its worst. Fields are farmed under armed guard. Lana, the children, and everyone from Mrs. McKlennar's house are crowded into a makeshift cabin just north of the fort. The militia suffers losses; American regulars never appear. The fall of 1781 finally brings relief. Gil and his militia company rout the British in a surprise attack, and word trickles northward that General Washington has defeated the British at Yorktown. Restored to their home, now with three children, Lana and Gil can prosper as Americans.

Martin, Peter. *The Town and the City*. Jack Kerouac. 1950.

Peter Martin is the third oldest male child of Marguerite and GEORGE MARTIN. Growing up in Galloway, New Hampshire, a mill town in the middle of fields and forests,

Peter is a young and gregarious boy who is very much impressed by the small world around him. He lives in awe of his reckless brother Joe. Peter is fourteen when he first tries out for the Galloway football team. Smaller than the other players and still searching for some sort of identity, Peter can't keep up with them on the field, yet he goes to practice every day for the next two years, giving it all his effort and hoping to catch the coach's eye. He daydreams along with the other outcasts of coming off the bench at a critical moment and saving the game for his team. The coach does indeed begin to notice Peter's natural skill while the boy scrimmages with the first-string players, and suddenly Peter is a starter working out with the first stringers every day.

Peter starts to mature, gaining confidence in himself and finding an identity separate from his brothers. He becomes the star of the football team and finds himself increasingly popular with both teachers and students, especially his female classmates. At a big Thanksgiving Day game he becomes the town hero when he scores the winning touchdown as the clock winds down. Although he feels he has realized his first ambition, Peter knows there must be much more beyond them.

Peter goes off to Pine Hills prep school in Augusta, Maine, where he intends to prepare for college and work on his football skills with other high school stars from around the country. Succeeding with ease at Pine Hill, he falls in with the East Coast preppy crowd. He quickly becomes a self-assured and complacent seventeen-year-old, playing tennis with the local girls and dressing in the best *Esquire* fashions. On his return to Galloway for the summer, Peter meets Alexander Panos, a boy who interests him in books as well as notions of "beauty" and "truth," and they begin a long friendship that leads Peter to challenge and explore his notions of the world.

After the summer, full of confidence and excited by new ideas, Peter leaves for the University of Pennsylvania. He breaks his leg during a game with Columbia, and although he has to sit out the football season, he takes advantage of all that is available to him at the university. But as he sits in the train on his way home for Christmas, he realizes that nothing taught to him at the university can match the wisdom of people in rugged towns like Galloway. When Peter's father loses his job after his son's sophomore year and the family is forced to move, Peter feels changed. College seems so unreal that he quits the football team and then decides to leave school altogether. He moves back to Galloway and gets a job as a scullion on a big cargo transport ship in the Boston harbor. After many voyages, some of them dangerous, he decides to visit his younger brother Charley, who is stationed in Washington. He is happy to see his eighteen-year-old brother but feels melancholy as well.

Peter travels to New York where his family and his girlfriend from Penn, Judie Martin, are now living. With Judie he falls into a crowd of dissatisfied intellectuals, a group his father disdains. In an attempt to bridge the gap between his world and his father's, Peter invites his parents to Judie's Manhattan apartment. The meeting turns sour when the police interrupt them to tell them one of Peter's acquaintances has jumped out a window. George blames Peter for his lack of responsibility, and Judie becomes disgusted at George's old-fashioned ways.

When Peter learns that his father is dying of cancer, he abandons all his friends in Manhattan and moves back to Brooklyn to be with him. They continue to argue about the ways they see the world, the viewpoints of different generations. George eventually dies in his sleep, and the family reunites to bury him in New Hampshire. The company of his brothers and sisters does not diminish Peter's anxiety and confusion; he sets off hitchhiking, wandering alone into the shapeless and rainy night.

Marvell, Ralph. *The Custom of the Country.* Edith Wharton. 1913.

A member of the prestigious Dagonet family, Ralph Marvell has been educated to be a gentleman and an artist—to play at a profession but never to pursue business. Such undertakings are the arena of the nouveau riche, who are beginning to dominate the New York social scene with their garish wealth. Ralph decides to rescue UNDINE SPRAGG from the clutches of a newly moneyed, ostentatious, superficial class; she has come with her parents to Manhattan from the Midwest with the ambition of becoming an integral member of this set.

Ralph, a quiet young man with refined tastes and a penchant for writing, first meets Undine at a party at the magnificent Hotel Stentorian, where she and her parents are living. He recognizes that she is unread, crass, and tasteless, but he is bewitched by her youthful beauty. When he discovers that Undine is also receiving the attentions of Peter Van Degen, a married man and a notorious womanizer, Ralph resolves to marry her. Upon learning that Ralph's family name can buy her entry into the highest realms of society, Undine allows him to press his suit, and within a short period of time, the two are engaged to be married.

Ralph receives his first glimpse of Undine's inherent selfishness during their honeymoon trip to Europe. Whereas he relishes their time together, she quickly tires of him and of the quiet Italian town in which they are staying. Attributing her discontent to youthfulness and naiveté, Ralph agrees to a change of scene, and the couple journeys first to the glamorous resort of St. Moritz and later to Paris, where Undine again takes up with the Van Degen set and spends large sums of money. As Ralph becomes increasingly anxious about their finances, he discovers that, contrary to his wishes, his wife has had her engagement ring—a Dagonet family heirloom—reset; this sign of her insensitivity to his values, coupled with her refusal to curb her spending, marks the first stage of his disillusionment with Undine.

When the couple finally returns to New York, Ralph begins work at a real estate firm. The hours are long and the work taxing, especially since he has no head for business and feels unable to compete with the other members of the firm. After giving birth to their son Paul, Undine becomes increasingly irritable and distant; Ralph, although still struck by her beauty at times, finds himself repelled by her shallowness and by her utter indifference to the strain placed on him by her excessive spending. Undine eventually persuades her father to finance a trip to Paris, while Ralph remains in New York with Paul.

After Undine's departure, Ralph stays at the firm and nurses his son through a series of illnesses. He also renews his friendship with his cousin Clare, with whom he had once been in love and who is now unhappily married to Peter Van Degen. The bills from Paris continue to mount, while Undine's letters become less and less frequent until she stops writing altogether. Ralph, increasingly discouraged by Undine's silence, and strained from overwork, collapses with pneumonia.

When Ralph regains consciousness several weeks later, he discovers that Undine never answered the cable his sister had sent asking her to come home and that she was, in fact, traveling with Peter Van Degen to the Midwest in order to sue him for divorce on grounds of desertion. Although he is enraged at Undine's deception, Ralph nevertheless determines not to interfere with her relationship with Paul. Undine shows no interest in the child, however, and although she is granted custody of him, he remains with Ralph in the Marvell home.

A few years pass, and Ralph has recovered sufficiently from his disappointment over Undine to begin work on the novel he has long dreamed of writing. His friendship with Clare—who still loves him—has deepened, and he takes comfort in her companionship as well as in the companionship of his son, whom he adores. Just as he is beginning to believe that he might find happiness after all, Ralph receives word from Undine: She is planning to marry a French marquis and wants custody of Paul. As it turns out, Undine does not really want the child but needs to procure an annulment of her previous marriage, a task that requires a great deal of money.

Ralph, desperate to keep the child, raises half the sum by borrowing from his relatives and from Clare, and he goes to Elmer Moffatt, a Wall Street speculator known for his shady dealings, whom Ralph had met through Undine. Moffatt promises to double Ralph's money within a few months. As Ralph anxiously awaits the outcome of his investment, the shock of losing Paul yields to the realization that, with this last transaction, Undine would be gone from his life once and for all. He would be free to write novels and to pursue Clare, with whom he is again falling in love. A few months pass before Elmer Moffatt

reluctantly informs Ralph that the investment has fallen through. In the course of their conversation, Ralph discovers that Moffatt had not merely been an acquaintance of Undine's but had eloped with her. They were divorced after her parents caught up with them two weeks later. Stunned by this revelation of Undine's duplicity and despairing over the state of his finances and the potential loss of his son, Ralph goes home, takes out a revolver, and commits suicide by shooting himself in the head.

Marx, Nathan. "Defender of the Faith." Philip Roth. 1959.

In May 1945, Sergeant Nathan Marx has just returned from a year of combat in Europe to head a training unit at Camp Crowder, Missouri. Almost as soon as Sergeant Marx settles into his new position he is approached by Sheldon Grossbart, a nineteen-year-old Jewish trainee from New Jersey. Grossbart asks Marx to announce officially that all Jewish personnel are allowed to attend Friday night services without being accused of "goldbricking," or weasling out of work.

Resenting Grossbart's presumptuous familiarity, which is based simply on the fact that they are both Jewish, Marx at first tries to tell the trainee that no announcement is needed. But the announcement is eventually made, and Sergeant Marx follows Grossbart and his two friends, Halpern and Fishbein, to the services. Marx is surprised to see, however, that only Halpern is taking the service seriously; Grossbart and Fishbein are goofing off, playing with the sacred wine, and ignoring their prayer books.

A week later Marx learns that Grossbart's mother wrote to a congressman about the *trafe*—the non-Kosher food—served at the camp. Grossbart claims that he throws up from the food all the time and eats only what he needs to survive; Marx, however, has seen the trainee "eat like a hound at chow." In addition, he realizes that Grossbart must have written the letter himself because both of his parents speak only Yiddish. Grossbart tries to excuse the lies by saying he's only looking out for the softspoken Halpern, but Marx begins to understand that Grossbart is not only using his friends for his own good but using his religion to create an advantageous alliance with Marx.

Grossbart convinces Marx to give him, Fishbein, and Halpern a weekend pass, maintaining that his aunt in St. Louis wants to make them a belated Passover seder. But when they return from the weekend with leftover Chinese food instead of gefilte fish, the extent of Grossbart's dishonesty and scheming fills Marx with rage; he feels betrayed and used, and can no longer abide the disrespect with which Grossbart treats his friends, his superiors, and his religion.

Orders soon come that all the trainees are to be shipped out to the Pacific—all, that is, except Sheldon Grossbart, who is going to Fort Monmouth, New Jersey. Angry, Marx decides to use some of Grossbart's own string-pulling technique. He makes up a story to reverse Grossbart's orders and sends him off to the Pacific after all.

Mason, Abigail Howland. *The Keepers of the House.* Shirley Ann Grau. 1964.

Abigail Howland Mason, the novel's embittered narrator, holds fast to her family legacy of courage and independence. Married to a man she cannot respect and victimized by his political machinery, Abigail struggles alone against a hostile and potentially violent white southern community.

The novel opens with Abigail looking out on the fields of the Howland farm. She is the "keeper" of the mansion, and her ancestors, all dead, haunt the empty rooms. She thinks of her half-brother Robert, who is still alive, and of how she, in turn, will someday destroy him.

Abigail then goes back two generations to recall the story of her grandfather, WILLIAM HOWLAND, and his black mistress, MARGARET CARMICHAEL. They, and the land itself, are the most powerful forces in her life.

After returning home from college, Abigail meets John Tolliver, a poor and highly ambitious law student. Her grandfather disapproves of John but Abigail loves him, and they marry. As John's practice grows, he spends less and less time with Abigail. She feels isolated and lonely in the new house they have built for themselves. Adept at playing the role of the southern wife at teas and parties, she has acquaintances in the community but no friends.

When her grandfather dies, Abigail, John, and their children move back to the farm. In secret, Abigail visits Margaret, who has gone back to her hometown. She and Margaret understand one another, but John is a stranger to their ways.

The years pass as Abigail struggles to come to terms with John's long absences and increasingly ruthless political maneuvers. She doubts his fidelity to their marriage and to her heritage—for John, when speaking to white audiences, proclaims the inferiority of the "Negro" race.

After winning a seat in the state senate, John decides to run for governor. It is at this point that Robert, the eldest of Margaret's children, leaks the story of her marriage to William to the newspapers, and John's career is ruined. Knowing that John's political ambitions mean more to him than she does and that the white community would retaliate, Abigail stays alone to protect the Howland property. Cars appear ominously on the horizon. While the townsmen are trying to burn the barn, Abigail sets fire to their cars. She returns to the house and stands by the window, her grandfather's shotgun loaded and cocked over her shoulder. The men approach; she fires a few warning shots, and they retreat, frightened and confused.

After a call from John's political opponent, Abigail agrees not to publicize the incident and to divorce John.

She no longer cares about him—her ancestral home is her life's blood. The novel ends with Abigail waiting vengefully, phone in hand, to reveal Robert's "Negro" heritage to his new, white, and unsuspecting wife.

Mason, Alma. *The Nephew.* James Purdy. 1960.

Alma Mason, a recently retired fifth-grade teacher, is preoccupied with the fate of her soldier nephew, Cliff Mason. Alma, who never married, lives in the small town of Rainbow and is only somewhat acquainted with the townspeople. Despite the fact that she has lived in the town all her life, Alma's career, teaching out of town, kept her attention away from the town's gossip and its gossipers.

After her retirement Alma becomes a full-time Rainbow resident and lives with her brother Boyd, who has shared her home since his wife's death, and their nephew, whose parents died when he was fourteen. The boy eventually matures and at the outset of the novel has entered the army and been sent to Korea. Alma and Boyd anticipate Cliff's letters but agree that he actually says very little in them. Soon, though, the letters stop, and the Mason family is informed that Cliff is missing in action.

Alma assumes that he will return, and she decides to write a biography of Cliff in the meantime. Once she sets herself to this task, it becomes apparent that she knows little about him. Alma decides that she must meet with Professor Mannheim, one of Cliff's former teachers. To do this she enlists Boyd's aid in soliciting the help of Mrs. Barrington, Rainbow's ninety-plus-year-old doyen. From her social position Mrs. B., as she is called, can summon anyone in town to her mansion, which is just across the street from Alma's home.

A meeting is arranged, but when the professor agrees to help by giving Alma Cliff's old papers, Alma herself begins to abandon the project. She has become more involved in the daily lives of her neighbors, among them Willard Baker and his companion, Vernon Miller. Willard and Vernon eventually depart for Michigan for the summer; Alma agrees to tend to the Baker house and to forward their mail.

One night during the course of the summer, Boyd discovers smoke coming from the Baker house in a room that Alma had previously found locked. She fetches an axe, and they break open the door—only to find a raging fire and a collection of near-life-sized photographs of her nephew. Before Alma can control the flames, Boyd collapses with chest pains.

Once again Alma's inquiry into Cliff's life is resumed. While caring for Boyd during his recuperation, she again thinks of her memorial. Then a cable arrives from Washington informing her of Cliff's death. Because Boyd is still ill, she withholds the bad news from him until later. Once Alma realizes that Cliff has died, her interest in the memorial fades. She dwells on her loss and on the fact that she loved her nephew even more than she realized.

Alma's social involvement with her neighbors continues to increase, and she is genuinely saddened when Willard Baker is killed and Vernon Miller seriously injured in a collision with a drunk driver. Alma finally becomes friendly with Vernon, who had taken the photos of Cliff, and he assures her that Cliff had been a good boy. Mrs. B. reinforces Alma's reentry into the town's life when she confides her own past sorrows to Alma on Memorial Day. The novel ends with Alma and Boyd sadly resigned to the loss of their nephew but invigorated by Boyd's regained health and the strengthening of their familial bond.

Mason, Bruce. *The Big Rock Candy Mountain.* Wallace Stegner. 1943.

Bruce Mason, the younger son of HARRY "BO" (MASON) and ELSA NORGAARD MASON, is an overly sensitive boy growing up in the rootless world of his father's choosing.

Born in the first-floor suite of a North Dakota hotel that Bo and Elsa started when they got married, Bruce and his brother Chester are to go to Alaska. When the brothers come down with scarlet fever, their trip is canceled and they settle in a small Seattle logging town. Bruce is afraid of the world around him, a trait that frustrates Bo who takes out his hostility over family responsibilities by beating the child.

After Bo runs off, the boys are put into a boarding school until their mother takes them back to Minnesota to live with her father and stepmother. The boys are disappointed at Christmas when Bo, attempting to avoid high duty taxes, sends intentionally damaged presents from Saskatchewan. But for the first time in their lives they find playmates and a stable home. Within the year, however, Bo and Elsa are reconciled, and Bo convinces her to move to Canada to be with him.

In the summer of 1918, Bo, Elsa, and Bruce live on the farm, while Chet finds work in the town. Bruce is lonely; he enjoys the empty prairie and catching gophers to save the crops, but the isolation often puts him in the way of his father's quick temper. The meager and unrewarding life of farming makes Bo cruel to Elsa, and Bruce yearns for a loving home life. Bruce excels in school until a flu epidemic hits, infecting Bo, Elsa, and Bruce. They all pull through, but during the epidemic Bo has started smuggling liquor over the border. Back at the farm in the spring, Bruce feels responsible when their horse's foal is left out all night while his father was away on a "run." The foal is ruined, and although Bruce tries to nurse it back to health, it must eventually be sold for its skin.

Looking back on his childhood as the son of a smuggler, Bruce remembers only a succession of houses and the rises and declines in their style of living. He is the student of the family, and when Chet dies in the attempt to make something grand of himself, Bruce escapes to Minnesota to attend college.

Bruce visits his parents one summer at Lake Tahoe, where they now live so that Bo can run a casino, and as he drives across the country, he wonders at the notion of "home": What is it to him? That summer and fall, he watches his mother sicken and finally die of cancer. He is her comfort since Bo is unable to come to terms with her sickness. On her deathbed Elsa asks Bruce to forgive Bo for leaving her alone to die and taking up with another woman, but he cannot. After Elsa dies, Bruce almost hunts his father down to kill him but instead rebukes Bo for having been a neglectful and abusive husband and father, and deserts him in Salt Lake City. When Bo kills himself, Bruce wonders at the haphazard way that life is often lived and yet how profoundly each person leaves his or her mark on those of the next generation.

Mason, Elsa Norgaard. *The Big Rock Candy Mountain.* Wallace Stegner. 1943.

Elsa Norgaard Mason is a figure of strength and compassion as well as a loving wife to HARRY "BO" MASON and a good mother to her sons BRUCE (MASON) and Chester.

Elsa left her family in Minnesota to live with an uncle in Hardanger, North Dakota; her mother died and her father married Elsa's best friend. Overcoming her fear and suspicion of anyone different, Elsa falls in love with Bo Mason, who runs an illegal saloon in town, and despite strenuous objections from her father, they are married.

Bo wants to settle down with Elsa, but he has a wandering nature and a hunger for easy money. Elsa loses one baby girl and has two boys while Bo tries to start a hotel. But when he is arrested for selling liquor, they make plans, at Bo's prompting, to go to Alaska and cash in on the gold rush. Their trip is delayed at the last moment because of their sons' illness. To Elsa's relief, they settle in a small logging town. She objects when Bo wants to move again, and while he tries to stay put, his frustrations lead him to abuse Bruce. Elsa locks Bo out, and he runs off. Alone and unable to provide for her sons, Elsa must return home and face the scorn of her father and stepmother.

But Elsa's heart is won back the following year when Bo returns to Minnesota. He has been successful in Saskatchewan and has bought a farm. She returns with him, but within a short time he is frustrated with farming life. When a flu epidemic hits the town, he begins to smuggle liquor over the border. Although he and Elsa almost die from the flu, Bo continues to smuggle when the epidemic abates. Elsa is very unhappy because they are continually moving from place to place, unable to make friends or establish lives, but she has vowed to stay with him and keep the family together. As the moving and subterfuge continue, Elsa develops a sense of irony about the whole situation, even as she must convalesce in the mountains because of the stress of her life. But when she sees Chet determining to be as tough as his father and Bruce growing bitter over Bo's shortcomings, she grows afraid. Chet dies a failure; Bo is haunted by guilt; and Elsa continues to be his real source of strength.

After Bruce escapes to go to college in Minnesota, Elsa and Bo move from Salt Lake City to Lake Tahoe. Elsa soon discovers that she has cancer, but she suffers the pain in silence and seems to fool herself as to the inevitable end. Bruce arrives to nurse her in the summertime since Bo is unable to cope with the truth about what is happening. As the cancer spreads and it becomes obvious that she will soon die, the family moves back to Salt Lake City. Elsa, growing weaker, is understanding to the very end. When she is clearly about to die, Bo leaves to smuggle a carload of liquor, and she asks Bruce to forgive his father for leaving her alone. But Bruce, watching his mother die, cannot understand. This, too, Elsa endures. She tells him that he has been a good son, an opinion that Bruce feels ashamed to accept, and dies painfully, asking of no one in particular, "Which . . . way?"

Mason, Harry "Bo." *The Big Rock Candy Mountain.* Wallace Stegner. 1943.

Harry "Bo" Mason wishes for all of the best and is never willing to settle for anything less than everything.

In 1905, Bo is an illegal saloon owner in Hardanger, North Dakota, a small town on the plains. He was born in Rock River, Illinois, of a father who lost himself thinking up great schemes and took out his frustration by brutally beating his children. Bo leaves home young to take up a variety of trades. He excels at each but sticks to none, as a sense of independence, self-importance, and destiny pulls him away.

After six years in Hardanger, Bo is stirred again when a young woman from Minnesota comes to town to live with her uncle. He falls in love with ELSA NORGAARD (MASON) and courts her. The two are married, and although Bo promises to settle down, the hotel they attempt to start is a bust. They make plans to go to Alaska and cash in on the gold rush. Their trip is delayed when their sons, Chet and Bruce, get sick at the last moment. Bo and his family settle in a small logging town, but he soon begins to think of moving up to Saskatchewan where the land is still unsettled. Elsa wants to stay, and while Bo tries to stay put, his frustrations lead him to abuse Bruce. In the end, Bo leaves his family and heads north alone.

Bo works for a while in Saskatchewan, makes some money, builds a house on a farm, and returns to Minnesota to win Elsa's heart back. She returns with him, but although he means well, he is frustrated with the meager rewards of farming, and when a flu epidemic hits town, he begins to smuggle liquor over the border. While Bo is aware that his smuggling puts his family in danger of social ostracism and arrest, he continues to pursue his dream of

easy riches. He is resourceful and stubborn enough to fix his car in a blizzard and make it home alive, but he cannot outsmart nature: He comes down with the flu after helping a neighbor and almost dies. Soon afterward he is arrested crossing the border with a truckload of liquor at the same time that his son Chet is arrested for vandalism and robbery.

Bo moves the family to Montana to take advantage of the coming prohibition. The business is good, but Bo is determined to leave when a tightly knit crime organization tries to threaten him into working for them. Later, there is a chance for Chet to live a respectable life playing baseball in Salt Lake City, but he is unable to recover from the crushing blow of his arrest. When Chet becomes ill and dies a failure, Bo is haunted by guilt, yet he is unable to change.

Bo and Elsa move to Lake Tahoe to start again, and Bo soon becomes involved in a casino and does very well. Bruce thinks that Bo has finally managed to live on his Big Rock Candy Mountain, but when Elsa gets cancer, they return to Salt Lake where she dies a lingering death. After that, Bo slides quickly, pouring his money into a mine that never pans out. Sad and beaten, deserted by Bruce, he kills a woman who rejects him and shoots himself in a hotel lobby.

Mason, Mamie. *Pinktoes.* Chester Himes. 1962.

At thirty-nine years of age, Mamie Mason is the self-defined "Hostess with the Mostest" in Harlem. Although concerned largely with matters of food and sex, Mamie, along with most of her social acquaintances, professes to be profoundly influenced by interracial relations. Her home is frequently the scene of newsworthy—in Harlem's society pages—interracial gatherings, ostensibly to advance the cause of desegregation and racial harmony. Mamie's approach to this cause centers largely on sexual activity, however, and much of her time is occupied with keeping track of various and sundry sexual liaisons.

Mamie, who prides herself on both her faith and her ability to work within a structure determined by coincidence, manages to stimulate social upheavals and to re-orient them to her advantage. On her wedding day, Sam Banks, the groom, does not show up, and before Mamie realizes what has happened, she marries Joe Mason, who, drunk himself, has shown up at the wrong church for his own wedding. His fiancée ends up jilted, and Mamie discovers that Joe's government job proves a good way to make important social contacts.

Mamie is obsessed with the fact that one of the pillars of the community, Juanita Wright, refuses to enter her house. Juanita gained prominence when she married Wallace Wright, the "great Negro race leader." However, as is the case with every character in Mamie's world, Juanita has no compunctions about having sex with Mamie's associates. The various sexual liaisons among Mamie's friends inspire her to exact revenge on Juanita by setting up a series of rumors about Wallace Wright and his relationship with his white mistress, Peggy, one of the "pink-toes" of the title. Of course, Mamie also has several sexual relationships going, but most of her affairs are conducted with older and more prosperous white men. In each case, however, there is an element of sadism or masochism as Mamie variously whips or is whipped by her partners as a prelude to sex.

After Juanita has learned of Wallace's interracial affair, she locks him out of the house and threatens to leave him for good; this causes a backlash that endangers the success of Mamie's upcoming annual Masked Ball. She induces her friend, the Reverend Doctor Mike Riddick, to visit Peggy in order to "exorcise the devil" in her. After three days of the "exorcism," the Reverend, exhausted and spent, has decided to marry Peggy. Not willing to be left out of things, Mamie hosts the wedding reception, using it as a means to pull her social world back together. The wedding is successful enough to ensure the success of her upcoming ball.

The anxieties of recent times have led Mamie to gorge herself on various foods, including most of an eighteen-pound ham, so the month preceding the ball is one of fasting and privation for the eager hostess. The night finally arrives, and when Mamie makes her splendid entrance as queen of the interracial affair, she is accompanied by her illustrious panel of judges. It is duly noted that all four of them look peaked and bruised, the result, as they know, of a spirited *ménage à quatre* the day before the ball. As the novel ends, Mamie, blissfully installed on her throne, is asked for her solution to the "Negro problem," whereupon she replies: "More—racial—intercourse!"

Mason, Perry. *The Case of the Velvet Claws*. Erle Stanley Gardner. 1933.

The Case of the Velvet Claws sets the pattern for all the Perry Mason mysteries to come. With the help of his dedicated team, detective Paul Drake and secretary Della Street, Mason unmasks the true criminal through his tenacity and shrewd detective work.

In this first mystery, Mason, a hard-bitten yet upright lawyer, is visited by Mrs. Eva Griffin, who asks his help in keeping her name and that of prominent politician Harrison Burke from appearing in a scandal sheet known as *Spicy Bits*. The scandal in question is a holdup turned killing that she and Burke witnessed while in each other's company the evening before the story opens. The police have kept Burke's name off the witness list because of his political clout, but Frank Locke, editor and front man for *Spicy Bits*, has the information and plans to go to press.

Sensing that there is more to the story than Griffin is willing to admit, Mason begins the hunt for the person behind the intrigue at *Spicy Bits*. He finds that businessman George Belter, a figure considered above reproach, is the owner of the paper and also Eva Griffin's husband. Although Eva Griffin, really Eva Belter, has instructed Mason to bribe Frank Locke in order to hush up the story, Mason decides to threaten George Belter and Frank Locke into giving up their blackmailing tactics altogether. He swears to publicly expose the true nature of their enterprise if they don't.

While Mason is busy gathering evidence about Frank Locke's shady past, George Belter is shot to death in his study. Eva Belter calls Mason from a phone booth just after the shooting and begs him to come immediately. Before calling the police they survey the crime scene. Eva Belter insists that she heard George arguing with a man who sounded like Mason just before the shot was fired. Even though he smells a set-up, Mason decides to hang around during the preliminary investigation in order to keep the police from suspecting his client.

Doggedly fulfilling his role as lawyer turned detective, Mason carries out his own investigation of the crime. He has the gun traced and discovers that it belongs to Pete Mitchell, an associate of Harrison Burke who has conveniently disappeared. Eva Belter tells the police that she thinks she heard Mason arguing with her husband before the shooting, successfully implicating both Burke and Mason as potential suspects. To avoid the police, Mason now has to book himself into a small hotel.

It soon becomes clear, however, that Mason has more than a few tricks left up his sleeve. He invites Eva Belter to the hotel and frightens her into confessing to shooting George by producing her housekeeper, Mrs. Veitch. He makes it appear that Mrs. Veitch has already told him she heard Eva Belter and her husband arguing just before the shooting when in fact Mrs. Veitch claims to have been asleep and heard nothing. With this he is able to procure a signed confession from Eva Belter, whom he then turns over to the police.

But Mason's work is not done. Although Eva Belter is the prime suspect, he has yet to discover what actually happened. As with Eva Belter, Mason is able to trick Mrs. Veitch's daughter Norma into confessing that she covered up for her fiancé, Carl Griffin, who is George Belter's nephew. Griffin, who lived with the Belters, heard Eva shoot George and run from the house. Eva had missed: It was Griffin who actually killed George Belter in order to inherit his wealth.

Mason, Willie "White." *Linden Hills*. Gloria Naylor. 1985.

When Willie "White" Mason and his friend, Lester "Shit" Tilson, both unemployed poets, need money to purchase Christmas presents, they decide to do odd jobs in the black bourgeois neighborhood of Linden Hills. Here they take a journey that carries them to the very core of human frailty and cruelty.

As the handymen make their way through Linden Hills,

the observant Willie begins to realize that the neighborhood has fallen considerably short of the dream of its founder, Luther Nedeed, who envisioned a prosperous black neighborhood that would challenge the white establishment. Far from becoming an irritation to the white world, Linden Hills has succeeded only in mirroring the dominant culture.

Willie first glimpses beneath the facade of Linden Hills when he and Lester work as cleanup men for the wedding reception of Winston Alcott. With 665 poems stored in his memory, Willie recognizes that the lines quoted to Alcott and his bride by the best man are from a Walt Whitman poem addressed to a man. To his astonishment, Willie observes the best man, under cover of the Whitman poem, deliver a harsh and bitter farewell to the groom who, Willie correctly guesses, is the man's lover. While perplexed that Alcott weds in spite of his love for his best man, Willie is equally nonplussed that the audience appears oblivious to what is taking place before their eyes. The Alcott wedding is only the first of many tragic life stories that Willie is to witness.

While stripping wallpaper from a room in the more fashionably located home of Chester Parker, Willie overhears a group of Linden Hills residents discussing the construction of low-income housing projects. The good citizens have decided to vote with the Wayne County Citizens Alliance—the county's version of the Ku Klux Klan—on a referendum to prevent the projects.

Tupelo Drive, the most prestigious street in the neighborhood, bares new horrors to Willie. He becomes convinced that the moral deterioration of Linden Hills can be traced to the dominance of LUTHER NEDEED, a descendant of the man who founded Linden Hills in 1820 and the apparent controlling force of the area.

Laurel Dumont, a mentally unstable woman, commits suicide after Nedeed tells her that she must leave her home because her husband is divorcing her. Willie and Lester find her body and then, after speaking to the police, head home. Lester informs Willie that Nedeed has hired them to work at his place the next evening, Christmas Eve. Having observed Nedeed during the past several days and realizing that Nedeed not only witnessed but could have prevented the Dumont suicide, Willie is reluctant to accompany his friend. Although he is unable to shake his view of Nedeed as a satanic figure, he finally acquiesces and finds himself drinking brandy punch with the lord of Linden Hills on Christmas Eve.

While Willie and Lester are helping Nedeed trim his Christmas tree, Nedeed's wife Willa emerges from the basement of the house where Nedeed had imprisoned her and their son. Nedeed had suspected Willa of infidelity because their child did not resemble him. The child is now dead, and Willa carries him upstairs and confronts Nedeed. Before the startled young men can comprehend what they have witnessed, they are standing outside on the Ne-

deed porch. They run for help but are checked by a loud roar. Turning back, they see that Willa has locked up Nedeed and set the house on fire. Willie goes for help, but the residents of Linden Hills just let the house burn.

Mast, Richard. *The Pistol.* James Jones. 1958.

Private Richard Mast, nineteen, is on interior guard duty at Schofield Barracks in Hawaii when the Japanese bomb Pearl Harbor on December 7, 1941. Mast was issued a .45-caliber automatic pistol, of which he is greatly enamored, and is reluctant to return it to the army supply room at the end of his detail as he is required to do. In the confusion of the Japanese attack, he makes the bold decision to keep the pistol and risk the punishment that may result from his flagrant violation of army rules.

Mast is sent to the desolate Makapuu Point on the island of Oahu to help defend against a potential Japanese invasion. Once there, with absolutely no creature comforts and little more than grinding work assignments to occupy his time, Mast finds his spirits raised immeasurably by his possession of the gun, justifying the theft by believing there is a need to defend himself against saber-wielding Japanese. But pistols have become a rare and valued commodity among U.S. fighting men, and Mast quickly discovers, much to his chagrin, that many men at Makapuu covet the firearm every bit as much as he does. Mast therefore strikes a defensive posture and successfully wards off several attempts to steal the pistol.

The first open attempt to take the pistol comes from a big Irishman named O'Brien who tricks Mast into relinquishing the gun. Mast gets the pistol back, but shortly thereafter another assault on his peace of mind occurs when Musso, the supply room clerk to whom Mast should have returned the gun in the first place, delivers two new machine guns to Mast's company. Fortunately for Mast, Musso comes and goes without the slightest suspicion of the private's secret.

Mast manages to ward off more advances on the pistol, and by this time his obsession with the gun verges on paranoia. A corporal named Winstock pulls rank and forces Mast to turn over the pistol, insisting it should be returned to Sergeant Pender, the company's commanding officer. But when Winstock appears wearing the pistol one day, an enraged Mast steals it back. Next, Mast's squad leader, Thomas Burton, attempts to bribe Mast with an offer of $150 and a cushy assignment. But Mast insists he will need the pistol to protect himself from the imagined Samurai saber and rejects Burton's offer.

At long last Mast achieves some semblance of peace when he is selected as a member of the four-man patrol protecting the Marconi Pass. Once they have established camp, Mast believes he can finally let down his guard to some small degree. Indeed, even O'Brien, who has stubbornly refused to give up hope of owning the pistol, agrees not to pursue the weapon while on their current mission.

509

But Mast's bliss is interrupted when a G.I. named Grace simply walks into his tent and steals the pistol. Seeing no choice but to retake his prized possession by force, Mast engages Grace in a brutal, bloody fistfight. Mast emerges the winner and again regains the pistol.

Upon his return to Makapuu, Mast endures yet another "assault against his salvation" when Sergeant Paoli reports his illegal ownership of the pistol to Pender. Fearing the worst but powerless against army authority, Mast grudgingly meets with Sergeant Pender who, to his great surprise, allows him to keep the .45. This occurrence provides Mast with a surge of confidence that helps him endure even more conniving conspiracies by such adversaries as O'Brien, Winstock, Grace, and Paoli.

For all the effort Mast has put into defending his pistol, he is unprepared for the shattering blow that proves his undoing. Without warning, Musso returns to Makapuu one day to collect the pistol, having at last discovered his oversight. Mast painfully hands over the gun, overcome by the sensation that he has finally lost the means of his salvation.

Mathers, Walter. "I'm a Fool." Sherwood Anderson. 1923.

"Walter Mathers" is a pseudonym for the narrator and protagonist of this cautionary tale of missed opportunity. Walter never discloses his real name, but he does confess that the name is made up. The other lies he tells lead to the loss of a woman he would have married.

Walter got a job in Marietta, Ohio, as a "swipe," a person who takes care of racehorses—bathing, bandaging, and feeding them. He and an African American named Burt work for Harry Whitehead, a horse owner. Burt, a frustrated jockey who is not allowed to race because of his skin color, shows the narrator how to care for the horses.

Walter is very happy with his job because he enjoys being with and observing the men involved in racing and because he admires Burt a great deal. Burt knows how to drink, how to impress strangers, how to fight, and is blessed with savoir faire. Walter assimilates this information and puts it into practice during off hours. He makes good money, enough to send home and to buy himself new clothes and expensive cigars. He feels pretty good about himself and his work despite his lack of a conventional education.

On his afternoon off from a new job in Sandusky, Ohio, Walter goes to the races to experience life on the other side of the fence. He likes being a spectator as much as he likes being a swipe, especially when his eyes meet those of a girl named Lucy Wessen who sits in the stands just below Walter. Lucy is at the track with her college-educated brother Wilbur and his girlfriend, Elinor Woodbury, and when she notices Walter, she is immediately interested.

By way of introduction, Walter advises them to bet on a horse called About Ben Ahem with which he is familiar through his job. To impress Lucy, Walter lies about his connections to the horse. He says his father is a wealthy man who lives in a mansion in Marietta, Ohio, and who owns the horse and lends it out for racing purposes to a man named Bob French. Walter claims he is at the race to make sure that Mr. French is "on the square" and isn't cheating the Matherses.

The others believe his story, and they win the bets they place on About Ben Ahem. Walter becomes more and more entranced by Lucy, and by the end of the day he wants to marry her. Lucy shares his feelings, and when it is time for her to depart, they agree to correspond by mail. It is then that Walter Mathers realizes the significance of his fabrication. He will never receive the letter because there is no Walter; and because Lucy is such a fine, upright girl, he cannot confess his mistake.

Maxwell, Reverend Henry. *In His Steps.* Charles M. Sheldon. 1897.

Reverend Henry Maxwell sparks a nationwide wave of radical piety when he proposes the simple question, "What would Jesus do?", to his church congregation.

The events leading up to Reverend Maxwell's modest yet far-reaching proposal begin in the minister's study where he is wearily trying to finish his Sunday sermon. Maxwell's efforts are disturbed by a shabbily dressed man at his door who asks for help in finding a job. The minister sympathetically but swiftly rejects him, then meets the supplicant again during his church service. The man speaks at length about his woeful financial condition and the Church's lack of concern for poverty. Days later he collapses and dies at Maxwell's home.

Reverend Maxwell returns to the pulpit the following Sunday with a strong conviction that a new definition of Christian discipleship is needed. His sermon calls for his congregation to take a pledge to follow in Jesus' steps by constantly asking the question, "What would Jesus do?" The fact that a large number of people in his congregation agree to take the pledge, including many prominent citizens of Raymond, touches the minister. As the weeks pass, the resolve of these disciples causes a radical change in the town itself.

Edward Norman, editor of a local newspaper, decides to censor sensational stories of scandal, murder, and prizefights, among other things, and introduces Christian editorializing. Alexander Powers, the railroad superintendent, creates a pleasant lunchroom for his workers where they hear inspirational speakers weekly, the Reverend Maxwell being the first in the series. Never having held forth before such a rough group of working men, Maxwell is initially anxious, but his speech is favorably received and he gains satisfaction and confidence.

A new phase in Maxwell's ministry begins days later when he is asked to substitute for a revivalist who holds tent meetings in Raymond's saloon-plagued slum, the Rectangle. Faced with an audience drastically different from his own affluent church, Maxwell again feels twinges of terror, but as the angelic voice of his ever-present church soloist RACHEL WINSLOW calms the crowd, his confidence returns, and he preaches a powerful sermon. Watching the throngs stream out of the tent into the surrounding saloons, the minister realizes the true source of corruption in Raymond and vows to fight it.

Inspired by Maxwell, the town's societal leaders wage war against the saloons, but in the end, the city votes against prohibition. The following Sunday, Reverend Maxwell rebukes his congregation, many of whom seem eager to embrace his precepts and follow in the steps of Jesus. After performing a funeral at the Rectangle for a poor woman killed in election rioting, Maxwell forgoes his annual vacation to Europe and sends an impoverished family in his place.

Maxwell's particular brand of piety continues to attract a loyal following, and after a visit from an old yet impressionable seminary friend, his discipleship spreads to Chicago. Maxwell appears at his colleague's church to speak. Following an enthusiastic reception, the minister is invited to one of Chicago's largest churches, where he challenges the entire nation to become followers of Jesus. After the service, Reverend Maxwell receives a vision in which all who refuse to follow in the steps of Jesus endure a hollow existence, while those who ask "What would Jesus do?" are rewarded for their suffering with everlasting life.

May, Georgie. *Georgie May.* Maxwell Bodenheim. 1928.

Georgie May is an independent prostitute working in a small city in 1920s Tennessee. A self-respecting, honest, and strong-willed woman, she nevertheless remains caught in an economic niche that requires spineless submission and crushes her free spirit.

As the novel opens, twenty-three-year-old Georgie is having a typical day: Without a man, a dollar bill, or a place to sleep, she waits for night in order to hustle her way out of this latest dilemma. In her constant struggle against her environment, Georgie must contend with an underworld where the police are corrupt and the working class is brutal and emotionally empty.

Georgie landed in this underworld after an early liaison at the age of sixteen caused a scandal for which she was banished from her Kentucky town. Her mother, an emotionally burned-out drudge ground down by housewifery, cared nothing for her; her father, a Baptist, retreated like the rest of the community into a defensive screen of moral resentment. The women of the town condemned her while they secretly envied her freedom with men.

Georgie's self-respect springs from an insight into the motivation of others. Because she has such a knack for seeing through moral pretension, her integrity rests on the democratic conviction that "low as she is," no one is any better. Her brushes with higher society confirm this perception, revealing a world of hypocrisy and easy condemnations by soft people who know little about the realities of life.

Georgie's humanity is shown in her sisterly love for Emmy Lou, a weaker but loyal friend in the same station in life. Georgie helps Emmy Lou financially, tries unsuccessfully to keep her away from the more brutal pimps, and keeps her off cocaine. Emmy Lou eventually returns Georgie's love, hiring a lawyer for her when she goes to jail for being involved in her pimp's cocaine dealings. In Georgie's and Emmy Lou's world a caring platonic relationship is so unusual that men often assume they are lovers.

Georgie finally succumbs to the brutal realities of her environment when she becomes the mistress of a spoiled, wealthy youth. Initially only looking for sexual pleasure, the young man grows to like her because he enjoys letting her mother him. Georgie, however, falls in love for the first time. When the youth's actual mother, in the interest of propriety, tells her she must leave him and offers her a small stipend in compensation, Georgie refuses. Accepting the money would mean acquiescing to this woman's judgment of her and giving up her self-respect. Instead, she swallows a vial of poison to cheat the fate that is meted out to independent women without means in 1920s America.

Medlock, Lewis. *Deliverance.* James Dickey. 1970.

Lewis Medlock is the rugged sportsman and survivalist who persuades three of his friends to join him on a three-day canoeing trip through backwoods Georgia. A large, athletic man and a champion archer, Lewis is known for his energetic enthusiasm and has a history of trying to prove his physical and mental strength by taking chances in dangerous situations. He is a good friend of ED GENTRY, who often joins him on his adventures; he feels less close to the quiet-mannered DREW BALLINGER and the cynical BOBBY TRIPPE but convinces them to accompany Ed and him on an excursion through a region that will soon be flooded by a dam built at Aintry.

The first day of the trip is spent pleasantly enough. On the second day, at a point when Lewis's craft is lagging far behind, Ed and Bobby beach their canoe to stretch their legs. When Lewis catches up, he hears Bobby screaming in pain; he circles through the woods with his bow to where his friends are being assaulted by two vicious men. Ed is tied to a tree; one man is sodomizing Bobby while the other holds a shotgun to his head. Lewis watches, waiting, until the men turn their attention to Ed, and as they transfer possession of the gun, he shoots an arrow through one man's back, killing him. The other escapes into the woods.

The question then arises of what to do with the body.

Lewis scares and shocks his friends by arguing that they should hide it so it won't be found because he does not think the authorities in that part of the state will agree that the death was justifiable homicide. Despite their misgivings, they bury the corpse in a remote area of the woods that will soon by covered by the lake created by the dam at Aintry.

The men proceed down the river, and just as they enter into an extremely rough section of rapids, Lewis sees Drew slump over. He has been shot in the head by a sniper on the cliffs. Both canoes capsize on the rocks, and the men are swept violently downstream. By the time they reach calm water, Lewis's right thigh is severely broken. In excruciating pain, he only has strength enough to pass the responsibility for their survival to Ed, telling him to kill the man who shot Drew. Lewis stays in Bobby's care while Ed climbs the sheer cliff and proceeds to kill the man.

Lewis, lying painfully in the bottom of the canoe, is unable to do or say much, but he approves of Ed's subsequent actions. The murdered man's corpse is weighted with rocks and sunk in the river; the process is repeated when they find Drew's body because the bullet wound in his head would cause the police to ask questions.

Lewis endures the rest of the trip with difficulty, screaming in pain when they pass through rough water. He is coherent enough, however, to pay attention as Ed instructs him as to the story they should tell the police when they reach Aintry: Drew was drowned when the canoe capsized. Lewis is taken to the local hospital, and despite the severity of his broken leg and the suspicions of the authorities, he is able before long to return home, his enthusiasm tempered by the experience.

Meeber, Caroline "Carrie." *Sister Carrie.* Theodore Dreiser. 1900.

In August 1889, Caroline "Carrie" Meeber boards the afternoon train from her hometown of Columbia City, Wisconsin, to the big city of Chicago, Illinois. She is eighteen years old, a "half-equipped little knight" about to face a cosmopolitan world, of whose cunning, seductive ways she is entirely unaware. Bright and pretty but neither graceful nor intellectual, Carrie is most of all "ambitious to gain in material things."

On the train Carrie attracts the attention of CHARLES DROUET, a smooth and opportunistic salesman who wears obviously well-made clothes. At the end of their conversation Drouet gives Carrie his card and promises to look her up. But in Chicago, after living only a short time in the embarrassingly shabby apartment of her sister Minnie and Minnie's husband Hanson, Carrie abandons hope of any relation with Drouet and writes him a note to that effect.

Now a working-class girl who must support herself, Carrie takes a job in a shoe factory and is struck by the crudity of her coworkers compared with the sophistication of those with money and fine clothes. Too poor to replace her own worn-out attire or to buy a new coat, she longs for improvement, which now seems a distant possibility. Then, one afternoon downtown, Charles Drouet suddenly taps Carrie on the shoulder.

Drouet eventually rents an apartment for Carrie, buys her clothes, and the two become lovers. Carrie is not in love with Drouet, but when she meets his friend GEORGE W. HURSTWOOD, a well-off and well-connected saloon manager who seems infinitely superior to the salesman, she forms new and more significant affections. While Drouet is away on business, Carrie begins a secret affair with Hurstwood. She also receives an education on matters of wealth and social position from her friend and neighbor Mrs. Hale. One night, sitting alone in the rocking chair next to her window, Carrie recognizes the insignificance of her furnished rooms and longs for something better.

Carrie's affair with Hurstwood intensifies. Drouet returns, still unaware of their liaison, and suggests that Carrie audition for a play to be performed at his lodge. She gets the part and makes a big hit, much to the delight of Drouet and Hurstwood. Soon after the play, Drouet learns of her love affair. When he confronts her and tells her that Hurstwood is married, Carrie vehemently lashes out at him, and he leaves her alone in a state of confusion. A few days later she searches unsuccessfully for acting jobs. Discouraged and lost, she writes a letter to Hurstwood and ends their relationship.

Carrie is alone in her apartment when Hurstwood sends the urgent message that Drouet is hurt and wants to see her. The bewildered Carrie dresses rapidly and joins him in a cab. She soon finds herself on a train heading for Detroit with the fugitive Hurstwood, who in the heat of passion has deceived Carrie to get her to flee with him. At first upset by his trickery, Carrie stays with Hurstwood. Impressed by his expressions of love for her, she secretly yearns to see Montreal and New York, new horizons where he promises to take her.

In New York, Hurstwood has nothing of the social status he enjoyed in Chicago but manages to supply Carrie with the modest domestic comforts that he believes are enough for her. Carrie befriends Mrs. Vance, her attractive neighbor, who is much better dressed than she. Again she senses the staleness of her own existence; her old longings return, and she resolves to match the clothing and appearance of Mrs. Vance.

At dinner with Mr. and Mrs. Vance, Carrie meets the bright and unaffected Bob Ames, who questions the showy, money-spending tendencies of people and says, "A man doesn't need this sort of thing to be happy." Ames plants the seed of desire in Carrie to be a "good" actress, one who would gain the approval of men like Ames. Soon after, Hurstwood's business prospects fall apart. Tensions between him and Carrie increase, and they are soon sleeping in separate rooms. When they are forced to move to a smaller flat downtown, she becomes restless; thoroughly dissatisfied with her life, she decides to resume her work on the stage.

The manager of the Casino hires Carrie to work in a chorus for a low salary. She takes the stage name "Carrie Madenda," which Drouet had given her for the lodge performance in Chicago. She supports Hurstwood with her earnings, and he falls further into a state of decline. The manager eventually promotes Carrie, and when she causes a sensation in a bit part with the delivery of one line, she gets another large raise.

Carrie resents having to give Hurstwood money, especially when she sees what she could do with it herself. She finally leaves Hurstwood twenty dollars and a short note, departs for good, and moves into a flat with Lola, her friend and fellow chorus girl. Her theatrical ambitions escalate, and wonderful reviews indicate that she will continue in her rise to stardom. In the meantime, the impoverished Hurstwood commits suicide in a residence hotel in the Bowery.

Carrie, now quiet, reserved, and always in the public eye, remains unaware of Hurstwood's death. Three years later she runs into Drouet, who informs her that Hurstwood had robbed his office safe in Chicago of $10,000 before fleeing with her. Carrie now pities Hurstwood, but times have changed; due to her elevated position, it no longer seems appropriate for her to associate with Hurstwood or, for that matter, with Drouet. In her splendid rooms at the Waldorf Hotel, having obtained the material success she has always dreamed of, she still longs for something that she cannot name. As the novel closes, the omniscient narrator calls to her, "Oh, Carrie, Carrie! . . . In your rocking chair, by your window, shall you dream such happiness as you may never feel."

Merle, Madame Serena. *The Portrait of a Lady.* Henry James. 1881.

The story of Madame Serena Merle, who effectively arranges the pivotal marriage between the youthful, intelligent ISABEL ARCHER and the morbidly controlling GILBERT OSMOND, hinges on the question of why this calculating older woman should be so interested in the affairs of Osmond and Isabel. In the end, Madame Merle is exposed as Osmond's former lover; she secretly conceived a child by him—Pansy, Osmond's pure and simpleminded daughter. Wishing to conceal their extramarital affair from society, Madame Merle gave Pansy to Osmond; now, almost twenty years later, Pansy's mother is assumed by all to be Osmond's deceased wife, and Madame Merle—who maintains a strange friendship with Osmond and strives to keep their mutual promise to help each other whenever possible—has no legitimate familial ties and very little money, so she travels throughout Eu-

rope, residing for extended stays at the houses of wealthy friends.

During one of these extended visits—to Gardencourt, the English estate of her friend, Mrs. Lydia Touchett—Madame Merle first meets Isabel, Mrs. Touchett's vibrant niece. She and Isabel spend many hours together and become friends. Their intimacy has limits, however; Madame Merle avoids questions regarding her personal history, telling Isabel little more than that she was born in Brooklyn, New York, the daughter of an officer in the U.S. Navy. Before leaving Gardencourt, Madame Merle mentions Gilbert Osmond of Florence, Italy, and expresses her desire for Isabel to meet him.

After the death of Isabel's uncle, the wealthy Daniel Touchett, Madame Merle visits Mrs. Touchett in London, only to learn that Isabel has inherited a vast fortune from him. She privately tells Osmond about Isabel, stating that this young woman would fulfill his "requirements." When their courtship begins, Madame Merle fails to hide her intentions from concerned onlookers—most notably Mrs. Touchett and the Countess Gemini, Gilbert's sister, who bluntly tell her that a marriage between Isabel and Osmond would be a very bad thing.

Much later, after the marriage has taken place, Madame Merle receives a visit from Edward Rosier. He is in love with Pansy and has come to seek Madame Merle's advice. Madame Merle is sarcastic about what Rosier has to offer Pansy; he is only moderately well-off, and Madame Merle tells him that Osmond will look for a better offer for his daughter. Madame Merle immediately goes to Osmond, however, and recommends that he not reject Rosier completely; in this way Rosier will continue to seek Madame Merle's counsel in his pursuit of Pansy.

After spending several months away, Madame Merle returns to Rome and goes to see the Osmonds. She tells Isabel that she has come to "wash her hands" of the Rosier-Pansy courtship. Like Osmond, Madame Merle wants Pansy to marry Lord Warburton, an exceedingly wealthy English nobleman and an old acquaintance of Isabel. When Madame Merle returns to the Osmonds months later, she is disappointed to learn that the courtship was dropped. For the first time she insinuates to Isabel that she has had much more to do with Isabel's now miserable marriage than Isabel ever imagined, and she departs. That afternoon Osmond visits Madame Merle. With newfound compassion for Isabel, she acknowledges that Osmond is a monster and regrets the efforts she has made on his behalf. She wants to cry but cannot. Believing that Osmond has destroyed her own soul, Madame Merle realizes that she has been evil and manipulative for nothing.

Madame Merle visits Pansy at the convent where Osmond has sent her to get away from "the world" for a while. There she encounters Isabel and knows instantly that something has changed between them. Indeed, as Madame Merle guesses, Isabel now knows the history of Madame Merle's relationship with Osmond. Madame Merle further reveals that Ralph, Isabel's devoted cousin, had arranged for Isabel's inheritance. She knows Isabel is unhappy but tells her that she is more unhappy. When Isabel says she never wants to see Madame Merle again, Madame Merle announces that she will go to America.

Merrick, Robert "Bobby." *Magnificent Obsession.* Lloyd C. Douglas. 1929.

Robert "Bobby" Merrick, a young profligate, is transformed as a result of a drowning accident that nearly kills him.

Bobby was born to wealthy and irresponsible parents, Clifford and Maxine Merrick, who occupied their time with hunting, yacht racing, and traveling. His father, a heavy drinker, dies when Bobby is twelve, and Maxine, who views this occurrence with little emotion, drags him to Europe. Bobby is abandoned at a school in Versailles, where he begins to drink heavily. At seventeen he returns to the United States and is bounced out of a fancy prep school into a military academy, or as he terms it, a "ritzy reform school." At the state university in Michigan, he finally becomes involved in his studies; outside of this work, however, he is a reckless drinker and carouser, and remains so after graduation.

After leaving the university, Bobby moves in with his grandfather, Nicholas Merrick, whose estate borders on a lake outside Detroit. Nicholas, who earned the family fortune by founding the Axion car company, is as indulgent and permissive as Bobby's mother has been. One day Bobby is enjoying a sail alone on the lake and is knocked unconscious into the water by the jibbing boom. People swimming nearby haul him out, rush to the opposite side of the lake for an oxygen inhalator, and are able to restore him to consciousness.

He spends the following weeks at Brightwood Hospital in Detroit, recovering from head injuries and a case of pneumonia. He remembers nothing of the accident. Later, however, he hears an angry patient relating his own story. The oxygen inhalator that saved Bobby was the property of DR. WAYNE HUDSON, Brightwood's famous brain surgeon, whose estate was across the lake from the Merricks'. Dr. Hudson drowned as Bobby was being revived by the inhalator; he would have been saved if the inhalator had been there.

As Bobby recovers from the accident, he becomes determined to enter the university and become a brain surgeon. His grandfather and friends are shocked, and he receives most of his encouragement from Nancy Ashford, the hospital superintendent, who was a close friend of Dr. Hudson. Nancy gives him a mysteriously coded diary left by Dr. Hudson, which Bobby painstakingly deciphers. At first he is disappointed by the apparently mad tale recorded there. It describes Dr. Hudson's experience of religious conversion, explaining numerous acts of charity

that remained secret until his death. Acting on a theory revealed to him by an inspired sculptor, Dr. Hudson gained personal strength by these generous actions. Although Bobby is skeptical at first, he begins to experiment with the theory and finds that he is amply repaid for his efforts. He becomes a great success at medical school and returns to Brightwood Hospital as a promising brain surgeon.

Bobby does everything he can to help Dr. Hudson's young widow, HELEN BRENT HUDSON, despite her distrust of him. Working at a furious pace, he achieves sudden fame for inventing a surgical instrument. When his fame is at its highest, Bobby leaves Detroit to visit his mother in Paris. There he hears that Helen has been in a train accident and received severe injuries to her head. He rushes to the hospital in Rome and performs surgery to save her. Attempting to keep his identity a secret, Bobby leaves before she has fully recovered, but Helen recognizes his voice. When he returns impulsively to meet her before her departure from Rome, Helen and Bobby agree instantly to marry.

Merrill, Ned. "The Swimmer." John Cheever. 1964.

One sunny midsummer Sunday, Ned Merrill sets out to swim from a friend's house across the county to his own home. His plan is to act as if the private and public swimming pools that traverse the county are part of one stream, which he names Lucinda in honor of his wife.

The first few pools are easy to swim. Ned dives right in—he hates men who climb into pools gingerly—without protest from the owners of the pools. In fact, they welcome him, almost as if they had expected him. At the Graham house he is given a drink and makes his way through the guests at their pool party as if he were wearing a seersucker suit rather than swim trunks. The only map of the county's pools he possesses—his memory and imagination—serves him well as he deftly makes his way across familiar territory.

When he emerges from the Levys' pool, a storm rises. As he feels the sharp chill of an impending shower on his skin, he waits in the gazebo of their empty house and wonders why it is he loves such weather. After the storm clears, the air is quite cold, seeming more like fall than midsummer. He crosses the Lindleys' field, where he is surprised to find that the riding ring has been dismantled. Ned is saddened and not a little angered to find that the next pool on his mental map, the Welchers', is dry.

Humiliated by drivers when he waits for a break in the traffic in order to cross Route 424, Ned begins to feel more and more like an old fool. Yet for some reason he believes he has gone too far to go back to the Westerhazys' where he had bade his wife good-bye that morning. The Hallorans, who own the next house with a pool, tell Ned that they are sorry to hear about his "misfortunes," but Ned says he cannot recall any. He does not remember having sold the house, nor does he recall any problems with his daughters, events to which the Hallorans allude.

After this encounter, Ned suddenly feels old, thin, and weak. He crashes a party at the Biswangers' house, and although he had always felt socially superior to the nouveau riche Biswangers, the guests and even the hired help treat him rudely. At his next stop his former mistress thinks he has come to borrow money and refuses to give him a drink.

Enfeebled, he must climb, not dive, into the last pool. He barely has the energy to make his way across it, and when he pulls himself out, he is gasping for breath. He finally arrives home but finds that the garage and house are locked. He realizes, as he looks into the windows of the house he has labored so hard to reach, that his once welcoming home is empty.

Mervyn, Arthur. *Arthur Mervyn*. Charles Brockton Brown. 1799.

Arthur Mervyn is a handsome, extremely virtuous young man who leaves his father's farm at the age of eighteen to seek his fortune in the city of Philadelphia. Although his life is threatened by the devastating epidemic of yellow fever that ravages the city in the year 1793, Mervyn bravely travels around the city, performing various acts of charity that relieve the suffering of people in distress due to illness or financial insolvency.

Mervyn had expected to remain in the country to take over the husbandry of his father's farm, but he decides to abandon agriculture when his father marries a shrewish woman who intends to extort their assets and disinherit the young man. With no other prospects on the horizon, Mervyn decides to try his luck in Philadelphia where he hopes to land a position as an apprentice in a mechanical trade. Upon his arrival in the city, Mervyn finds himself in the woeful position of complete bankruptcy, with no opportunities for employment in sight. Desperate to raise money for his next meal, he approaches a sumptuous mansion where he intends to beg the owner to lend him a few cents. Suspecting that his request will elicit scorn rather than charity, however, he withdraws from the house. Just as he is leaving the mansion, he meets the owner, whose countenance invites solicitation. The stranger, Thomas Welbeck, offers to hire him as a copyist and to provide him with lodging under his own roof.

Having established himself in Welbeck's home, Mervyn begins to fantasize about the possibility of being adopted by his benefactor. He bears an uncanny resemblance to a deceased young man named Lodi, whom he assumes was Welbeck's son. He also entertains the hope that he might be considered a possible husband for Clemenza, Lodi's beautiful Italian sister who cannot speak English. Mervyn's initially positive responses to Welbeck are dashed when he learns that Clemenza has been a victim of sexual violation at the hands of Welbeck, who also seized the substantial inheritance that Lodi had willed to his abused

sister. When Welbeck's shady dealings result in his financial ruin and then death in a debtor's prison, Mervyn assumes responsibility for Clemenza, whom he attempts to save from further infamy. Although his efforts come too late to prevent the death of her illegitimate child, he is able to convince a benevolent friend to become the guardian of the unfortunate young woman.

The compassionate Mervyn also leaps to the rescue of another young woman, Eliza Hadwin, whose family is annihilated by yellow fever. Once again he is able to locate a suitable household to succor her in her distress. Although he falls in love with Eliza, he decides to postpone his avowals of affection due to her extreme youth and his own desire to explore the many opportunities that beckon to him. His resolution to take advantage of the liberties of bachelorhood is banished by the charms of Achsa Fielding, an exquisite and wealthy Jewish divorcée from Britain whose child he also embraces with unbounded joy. The novel closes with Mervyn looking forward to his union with Achsa.

Meserve, Arvay Henson. *Seraph on the Suwanee*. Zora Neale Hurston. 1948.

Arvay Henson Meserve begins her life as the sheltered and overly religious daughter of a poor Florida family. Unable to give expression to her feelings, the beautiful Arvay swamps herself with church-related work and finally becomes an object of the town's attention as she resolutely rebuffs any male who attempts to court her. This pattern is altered when the handsome JIM MESERVE arrives in town and within a matter of weeks begins an ardent courtship that culminates in their decision to marry.

The first few months of marriage are blissful, although Arvay doesn't much like the small house they live in and does not want to remain in the area for very long. However, when Arvay tells Jim she is pregnant, they postpone moving until after the child is born. This eagerly anticipated event turns out to be an unhappy occurrence when they discover that the child, Earl, is deformed. Arvay fearfully notes the odd shape of his head, the misshapen and weak hands and feet, and the tininess of his mouth. For the next several years she works assiduously on the boy, manipulating his extremities and gradually altering the shape of his skull into an approximation of the norm. While Jim is disappointed by this son, he manages to go ahead with his ambitious plans and relocates his family to Citrabelle, where he learns about growing fruit. Soon Jim is able to buy a plot of land and construct a house for Arvay, and it is here that their next two children are born.

Despite her deep love for Jim, Arvay has no notions of how he comes by his money, nor is she aware that he sees everything he does as a tribute to his wife. This comes to a head when Earl, in the throes of adolescent lust, viciously attacks the daughter of Jim's partner. While Arvay passes a fearful night, she regrets that she had fought with Jim over placing the troubled Earl in an institution. Near dawn a posse returns with Earl's body.

From this point on a slow awakening occurs in Arvay. She realizes her lack of control once again when Angeline, Jim's favorite child, elopes with her boyfriend, a Yankee, and she is furious when she later learns that Jim knew about the wedding, had consented to it and had even attended it without consulting her. Arvay is convinced that she has been shunted aside by the entire family, and she also learns from Jim that he has decided the marriage is over. He offers her an ultimatum: She has one year to think things over and must return to him on her own before that year is up. Arvay has no choice but to accept.

After several months of anger and loneliness, Arvay receives word from her sister that their mother is ill. When she returns to her hometown, Sawley, she discovers her sister in a slovenly and bitter-spirited state, and Carl, her former flame, a fat, boorish, and chronically unemployed complainer. She also finds her mother poorly cared for and quite near death. After her mother dies, Arvay is shocked to discover that her sister and brother-in-law had plundered the entire house, which had been willed to her. Arvay comes to realize that it was she who was in a large part responsible for the rift between her and her husband, and she resolves to win him back.

Before leaving for Citrabelle, Arvay burns the evil-seeming house to the ground and decides to donate the land for a park and playground. As the novel ends, she lies in her husband's arms on a shrimp boat named after her, and the couple looks forward to a bright future together.

Meserve, Jim. *Seraph on the Suwanee.* Zora Neale Hurston. 1948.

When Jim Meserve, an industrious, ambitious, and handsome stranger, arrives in Sawley, Florida, his attention is quickly drawn to the beautiful but uncertain and aloof woman who will eventually be his wife. From the first time he sees ARVAY HENSON (MESERVE), Jim resolves to marry her, despite evidence that Arvay has no interest in men. During their ardent courtship, Arvay begins to respond and finally falls deeply in love with Jim. Arvay's father willingly consents to the marriage, and the young couple elopes after Jim passionately introduces Arvay to the pleasures of making love. Jim establishes his new wife in a small house near his lumbering job but promises her that they will soon move on to bigger and better things. When Jim learns that Arvay is pregnant, he decides that they cannot move until after the child's birth. The child, Earl, is born deformed and is clearly never going to be normal; while Jim doesn't overtly punish Arvay, he shows a complete detachment from their son.

Soon after Arvay's strength returns, the couple relocates to Citrabelle, Florida, where Jim becomes involved in harvesting various fruit crops and in operating an illegal dis-

tillery. By the time Arvay is pregnant again, they are ready to move into their own home on their own land, where Jim plants several varieties of valuable fruit trees. Eventually, after the birth of their daughter and another son, Jim's life settles into the pattern he had hoped for, as his business successes continue and his overall fortunes advance. There remains a problem between Arvay and Jim, however, symbolized in part by her attachment to their eldest son, who is clearly mentally deficient. When Jim suggests that the boy be placed in an institution, Arvay angrily insists that he stay at home. This leads to tragedy, as Earl, unable to control his impulses, attacks the daughter of Jim's friend and partner. After a night spent fending off a huge posse, Earl is shot dead when he attempts to kill Jim.

Arvay's grief is limitless, and she seems to drift away from Jim and her surviving children. Finally, after enduring her lack of awareness of others around her and her inability to perceive how he loves her, Jim offers an ultimatum to his wife. He tells Arvay that while he is leaving her, he has always loved her and has struggled for her gain. He gives her one year in which to think things over, and any reconciliation will have to come from her.

Jim establishes himself as the captain of a shrimp boat, part of a fleet he had been building quietly, and Arvay returns to Sawley, where she finds her mother nearly dead and her sister living a squalid life. The death of her mother, coupled with her sister's relentless avarice, lead Arvay to the realization that it is her responsibility to work things out with Jim. She returns to Citrabelle and then travels to the coast to join him. While he is certainly glad to see her, he refrains from any overt resumption of marital relations until he sees that she has truly changed. In a shrimp boat out at sea, they confront the last barriers between them. As the novel ends, Jim and Arvay lie happily in each other's arms, facing a bright future for themselves and their surviving children.

Metzger, Irwin. *Standing Fast.* Harvey Swados. 1970.

Irwin Metzger, a mild-mannered young dentist in Buffalo, New York, is drawn into left-wing politics when his cousin Sy's friend Harry Sturm arrives to promote the "New Party."

At the time of its formation, the New Party consists of a small array of motley characters: Fred, an English professor; Vito, a painter; Big Boy, a black labor organizer; and two white organizers, NORMAN and Joe. Soon Irwin's cousin Sy and Sy's wife Bernice also move to Buffalo. At Vito's studio, Irwin meets the saucy and beautiful Carmela, one of Vito's models. He is smitten by her and pursues a romance despite the radical difference in their backgrounds: Carmela comes from a poor Catholic family, while Irwin's parents are middle-class Jews. Against his parents' wishes, Irwin and Carmela marry.

With Fred and Big Boy, Irwin canvasses for the New

Party in the black neighborhoods of Buffalo. At the same time his fledgling dentistry practice flourishes with the influx of new workers from nearby munitions factories. These moderate successes are offset by the relatively quick deterioration of his marriage. Carmela, who is not involved in the Party, begins to stray. When she does not come home for several days, Irwin tracks her to the house of a crackpot artist and orders her to return home. She appears to be grateful for his intervention, and their life together is reestablished for a time. When the Party fails to attract a large following, many of the original members move on, while Irwin stays and prospers in Buffalo. Carmela enjoys spending their money and eventually gives birth to their son Paul.

Irwin loves Paul deeply and spends hours reading to the precocious boy. Carmela, on the other hand, is not drawn to Paul's quiet intensity. Irwin and Carmela remain in touch with their friends from the Party, who have dispersed to various cities in the United States and abroad. They visit Vito, now a successful painter, in New York, before embarking on a tour to Europe and Israel, where Sy and Bernice have moved to a kibbutz. When they return to the United States, Irwin discovers that Fred, who has since become a host on a television talk show, has been charged with fraud. Irwin consoles and advises him, and indeed proves to be a supportive friend to all his old comrades. During this time, however, Irwin begins to drink more and more. He also continues to gain weight. Meanwhile, Paul is developing into a socially conscious and intensely spiritual youth. When Irwin gives him a bar mitzvah, Paul asks that the guests give their money to the Civil Rights Movement in the South rather than to him.

With his father's anxious blessing, Paul leaves to work on voter registration in the South. Carmela, disgusted by now with Irwin's alcoholism, decides to divorce him, and she moves to Manhattan to take art classes. But when Paul goes to Harlem in order to work with the poor, he is attacked in a robbery and dies from the beating. Irwin is devastated by the news. He drinks himself into a stupor before Sy, Norm, and Joe come to his aid. En route to the funeral, which Sy has arranged, Irwin sees Carmela again. She blurts out a clumsy apology: "He wouldn't have lived as he did if he hadn't been yours," she says of their son. Reunited in grief, Irwin and Carmela get into a taxi climb together and are last seen heading north to bury their son.

Meyers, Lulu. *The Deer Park.* Norman Mailer. 1955.

A beautiful, popular, and successful actress, Lulu Meyers is between films when she arrives at the California resort town of Desert D'or. Like the rest of the citizens of the town, she is given to socializing, drinking, and gambling, but she is also ambitious and allows nothing—not even love—to interfere with her career.

At a party thrown by her boss, the powerful movie tycoon Herman Teppis, Lulu meets Sergius O'Shaugnessy, a decorated war pilot, who has become friends with director CHARLES FRANCIS EITEL, Lulu's ex-husband. Sergius admires Lulu's beauty and fame, and the two fall in love. Early in their relationship, however, Sergius must make sacrifices for Lulu's career. For publicity purposes he remains in the background while Lulu strolls the village with her leading man, a homosexual named Teddy Pope.

On a whim, Sergius and Lulu cross the state line and go on a gambling spree for several days. They gamble compulsively, interrupting their play only to eat and sleep. Sergius loses most of the money he has brought with him to California, but the two continue to play obsessively. They are approached by Carlyle "Collie" Munshin, a producer who vacations in Desert D'or. Munshin offers Sergius $10,000 for the rights to his life story and goes so far as to offer him the lead role in the movie he plans to make of it. Lulu encourages Sergius to accept Munshin's offer, but she understands his decision when he refuses.

Back in Desert D'or, the couple's love for each other deepens, but both have the sense that the relationship is doomed. Lulu prepares to start shooting her next film, and for publicity's sake Sergius must trail behind her and a new leading man, a pompous minor star named Tony Tanner. After Tanner returns to Hollywood, Lulu admits to having slept with him. She leaves Sergius, ostensibly to begin working on her film.

Some time later, Herman Teppis calls Lulu into his office. He attempts to convince her that she must marry Teddy Pope, who has already confessed to Teppis that he is a homosexual, in order to boost her popularity. Hurt by Teppis's attempts to control her life, she admits that she has already married Tanner. Teppis is furious.

When the novel ends a number of years later, Lulu is considering divorcing the temperamental Tanner, now a public embarrassment who seriously jeopardizes her career. She is involved in a clandestine affair with Eitel, who has sold out his genius and resorted to directing meaningless comedies aimed at public consumption. Eitel himself is trapped in a loveless marriage, but the two remain entrenched in their superficial existences, satisfied that the sacrifices they made were inevitable.

Michael, Mattie. *The Women of Brewster Place.* Gloria Naylor. 1980.

Mattie Michael is the quiet, strong matriarch of Brewster Place. This street, literally and figuratively a dead end, houses fragmented families and individuals who are separated from the main artery of the city by a brick wall and the degradation of poverty.

Mattie, the only child of a proud Tennessee farmer, leads a protected life as a youngster. Her father is so determined that she become something special, he keeps her close to home and away from other young people. When Mattie is seduced by Butch Fuller, a young, attractive ne'er-do-well, and becomes pregnant, her father is overwhelmed by her disobedience and silence about the father of her child. He brutally beats her, and she leaves home for North Carolina to live with her friend Etta Mae Johnson.

Shortly after Mattie gives birth to her son Basil, Etta leaves for New York City, while Mattie remains in Asheville. When Basil is bitten by a rat, Mattie impetuously abandons the boardinghouse where she lives before finding another home. After roaming the streets for an entire day carrying her suitcase and Basil, Mattie resigns herself to returning home to her parents. Her reprieve comes in the form of Mrs. Eva Turner, a light-skinned, blue-eyed black woman, who offers Mattie and Basil her spare bedroom. Mattie and Basil live with Eva and her granddaughter Ciel for years.

When Eva dies and Ciel is taken away by her parents, Mattie picks up the mortgage of the old woman's house. She and Basil live there for the next twenty-five years. Mattie lives her life entirely for Basil. She fulfills his every wish without hesitation or admonition. Despite all the warnings that were offered by Eva over the years, Mattie has spoiled Basil so that he is selfish, impetuous, weak, and cowardly.

One night Basil is involved in a bar brawl and kills a man. Since there are witnesses who will testify that the death was an accident, Basil has only to appear in court. After spending several days in jail, however, Basil is afraid of the remote possibility that he will serve a prison sentence. So in spite of the fact that Mattie has pledged her home to post bail for him, Basil flees and does not show up for court. These are the events that bring Mattie to the deteriorating community of Brewster Place.

Arriving at Brewster Place as a middle-aged woman, Mattie rapidly becomes the matriarchal figure of the neighborhood. She spends the next twenty or so years offering solace and sympathy to the women of Brewster Place—women who have been treated cruelly by life and have turned to this dead-end block as a place of refuge. For her lifelong friend Etta Mae Johnson, who has used her beauty and sexuality to make her way through life, Mattie provides the sincere love and comfort that the aging woman now needs and desires. Ciel Turner, granddaughter of Miss Eva, is saved from despondency after the tragic death of her little girl when Mattie engulfs her in love. Finally, Mattie helps Kiswana Browne, a middle-class young woman attempting to reclaim her roots, establish a tenants' association. The novel closes as Mattie awakens on the day that the association has planned a block party to raise money for a lawyer. Although it is apparent that Brewster Place will not survive for many more years as a vital block, it is equally clear that the women of Brewster Place will continue their struggle to survive.

Mike. "The Biggest Thing Since Custer." William Eastlake. 1968.

Mike is a war correspondent accompanying a small helicopter party that is gathering the war dead. A young man who is unsympathetic about the war effort in Vietnam, Mike must constantly remind himself to silence his critical views concerning what he feels is the injustice and inappropriateness of the United States' involvement in the domestic affairs of Vietnam.

Mike compares the Vietnamese with Native Americans; they were attacked in order to protect settlers from the supposed threat of an enemy whose dangers were overstated by the military. Mike's disapproval of the war causes him to want to publish stories about the worst of the atrocities he witnesses in Southeast Asia, but he is warned that he must exercise discretion when writing about the war because the American public does not comprehend the vagaries of guerrilla warfare and would not be able to abide its horrors.

Descending in a helicopter on the scene of a massacre of the Alpha Company, commanded by Captain Clancy, Mike feels the scene is as awful as those participated in by General George Custer. The lieutenant in charge cautions Mike to censor his report on the battle or he will see to it that Mike's credentials are suspended.

It is evident even to a civilian that Clancy's party was annihilated because it failed to maintain control of a ridge from which it could have defended itself successfully. As he watches Army photographers take snapshots of the morbid scene, a dubious Mike is told by the lieutenant that the massacre was caused by Clancy's desire to collect as large a quantity of ears of dead Vietnamese soldiers as possible. Continuing to survey the collection of bloodied dead soldiers, Mike attempts to process the horror by silently asking himself the kind of morbidly sarcastic rhetorical questions army officials would coldly ask when trying to determine the cause of the Alpha company's massacre.

Although a few men are still alive when Mike and his military escorts arrive at the scene, they die as he continues to survey the ghastly spectacle. Each corpse has at least one bullet through the head, a precaution the Vietnamese soldiers take to ensure the deaths of their victims. In addition, many of the bodies are mutilated, by castration or in other ways. Accompanying this visual nightmare is the sound of the jungle, to Mike's ears oddly like noises used in the soundtracks of American films set in the tropics.

Mike is so upset by the horrors before him that he imagines the scene represents the death of all humanity and of the very earth that supports creatures capable of such villainy. Suddenly a shell strikes the search party's helicopter, blowing it up. The story ends abruptly as Mike is stranded within range of more shells, whose impact could add his body to the mounds of dead men surrounding him.

Miller, Cora. "Masses of Men." Erskine Caldwell. 1940.

Cora Miller is the head of her family and the one who bears the brunt of its abuse. Ironically, she is also the one who passes on the legacy of oppression to the next generation.

Cora's life was hard even prior to her husband's death. For twelve years she had worked long hours behind the counter of a local variety store while waiting to marry Hugh Miller. Hugh, a laborer with the street-railway company, had been deferring marriage to Cora until he became superintendent of construction, but after twelve years of failing to be promoted, Hugh decided, to Cora's relief, that they should marry at last.

Cora and Hugh have moved into a five-room house near Hugh's work place. Although their doorstep is in the alley where the trolleys pass, they live on a tree-lined street, and Cora likes the house. The couple has three children—Pearl, John, and Ruby—and Cora stays home to care for them. After Ruby's birth, however, Hugh gives up hope of promotion and loses interest in his home life. He falls into a pattern of coming home from work, eating his supper, and going to bed. Cora is not able to talk to her husband about things that concern her, such as the fact that her skin is becoming inexplicably darker every day and her hair is rapidly turning gray.

When their oldest child is nine, Hugh is killed in an accident at work. Not knowing what to do with his body, Cora contacts a policeman, who has the body taken away—Cora does not know where. She expects to receive a pension from the street-railway company, and when, after a month, she has not received any money, she goes to the office to ask for it. Although Hugh had worked for the company for twenty-six years, Cora is told that no one there has ever heard of him. Cora is too naive to realize she is being taken advantage of, and so, intimidated, she never returns to the streetcar company. Penniless, she and her children are reduced to scavenging for firewood and food.

On an evening when her family's situation has become desperate, Cora sells her nine-year-old daughter Pearl for a quarter to a man named Johnson, leaving her with him as she hurries to the grocery store to buy bread and pressed meat. When Cora returns, John and Ruby are asleep, and Pearl is curled up in a knot, crying. Cora stands looking at Pearl for a while, then covers her child with a coat and gets under her quilt, thinking that in the morning her children will have food.

Miller, Daisy. *Daisy Miller*. Henry James. 1878.

Beautiful, vivacious, and forthright Daisy Miller, a young American from Schenectady, New York, is touring Europe with her mother. Throughout the tour she innocently but audaciously indulges herself in the company of men, and she shocks the community of sophisticated American expatriates in Europe with her apparent lack of propriety. But to one such expatriate, FREDERICK WINTERBOURNE, she is an enigma: He cannot decide whether she is guilefully immodest or simply honest and naive.

Daisy meets Winterbourne while visiting Vevey, Switzerland. She wants Winterbourne to accompany her to visit the Chateau de Chillon, but her mother, the dyspeptic and timid Mrs. Miller, is too apathetic and uncultivated to see the need for chaperoning her daughter on such an outing. Daisy also does not see the need for a chaperone, and she declares with bold naiveté that she and Winterbourne will make the trip alone.

Meanwhile, Mrs. Costello, Winterbourne's aunt and the arbiter of their expatriate society, advises her nephew against associating with the uncultivated Millers. She declines to lower herself to meeting Daisy Miller, and she suggests that the urbane Winterbourne will make a great mistake if he becomes involved with the provincial Daisy. Daisy wants very much to meet Mrs. Costello, and when Winterbourne makes a lame excuse for his aunt's unavailability, she realizes that Mrs. Costello is snubbing her. But, undaunted, she declares that she and her mother are also exclusive, for they don't associate with some people, and some people don't associate with them, which to her untutored sensibility is virtually the same thing. Winterbourne continues to be intrigued by Daisy, and the two spend a delightful and innocent, although unchaperoned, afternoon at the Chateau de Chillon. Daisy and her mother depart for Rome, where Winterbourne will soon be joining his aunt.

Upon his arrival in Rome, Winterbourne is eager to see Daisy again, but he hears rumors that she has been keeping company with several young men. Miffed by this news, he decides to visit an old friend, Mrs. Walker, instead of seeking out Daisy. Daisy, however, is visiting with Mrs. Walker when Winterbourne arrives. Daisy and Winterbourne are pleased to be reunited, and she chides him unabashedly for not looking her up immediately. As they are chatting, Winterbourne learns that Daisy has plans to meet Mr. Giovanelli, a dashing but opportunistic Italian with whom she has been keeping regular company. Daisy simply enjoys the companionship of Mr. Giovanelli; he is, she declares unscrupulously, her intimate friend. Both Winterbourne and Mrs. Walker are shocked by the immodesty of her assertion; moreover, they are shocked that she would agree to meet this gentleman without a chaperone. Winterbourne gallantly accompanies Daisy to her rendezvous, while Mrs. Walker follows in her carriage and insists that Daisy join her immediately for the sake of propriety. Daisy refuses. Mrs. Walker and Winterbourne depart, leaving Daisy to her unchaperoned tryst. Mrs. Walker will henceforth publicly shun Daisy Miller, but Winterbourne continues to give her the benefit of the doubt.

One evening Daisy convinces Giovanelli to take her to see the Colosseum by moonlight. That such a venture is highly improper eludes the unsophisticated Daisy, but she is well aware that the Colosseum, a breeding ground for malaria, is a dangerous place to be at night. Yet, as always, Daisy does not seriously consider the consequences of her actions. While Daisy and Giovanelli consort in the shadows of the Colosseum, who should stumble upon them but Winterbourne. He decides that this is an indecent tryst, and he no longer tries to discern Daisy's innocence; he deems her unworthy of his respect. He does entreat her to leave for the sake of her health, however. Daisy perceives his loss of respect for her, to which she can only respond defiantly that she is not concerned about catching malaria.

But Daisy has caught malaria. She dies quickly but not before she sends a message to Winterbourne attesting to her innocence and to her unmet desire for his esteem.

Miller, Gregory. *The Blackboard Jungle.* Evan Hunter. 1953.

Gregory Miller, a black teenager with the body of a weight lifter and the nonchalant charm of a natural leader, is a student in an inner-city school. Miller, whose IQ of 113 puts him above the other students at North Manual Trades High School, could have attended an academic high school but chose instead one of New York City's most troubled vocational schools.

On the first day of school, Miller has a run-in with RICK DADIER, his idealistic new English teacher. Dadier sees the leadership potential in Miller and asks him to help encourage the boys in class 55-206 to behave responsibly. When Dadier stops an attempted rape, however, and sends the student perpetrator to the police, Miller uses his intelligence and popularity to organize the boys against the teacher. When Dadier has the class recite an oral grammar exercise, they do it completely wrong. When Dadier attempts a class discussion, Miller makes sure it is met by organized silence. When Dadier tries to teach, Miller monopolizes the class's attention with various jokes and antics.

Despite the fact that he is winning this contest for classroom control and provoking Dadier's anger, Miller proves that he can be helpful at times. When Dadier is assigned the huge task of putting on the Christmas assembly, Miller volunteers the assistance of a group of black student singers of which he is a member. Using his leadership potential in a positive way, he controls the rehearsals, making sure the participants follow Dadier's directions. In class, however, he continues to misbehave and makes it clear that he considers school a waste of his time.

One evening Miller stays late to help Dadier paint scenery. He explains to the teacher that he did not attend an academic institution because of his color and that professions are closed to a black man. He knows he is learning nothing at North Manual Trades, not even in the classes that should be training him as an auto mechanic. Embittered and cynical, he has learned to take the easy way in

life and says he will "drift with the tide" until something turns up.

The Christmas assembly is a success, but when Dadier returns to school after the holiday, he finds Miller as difficult as ever. The boy tells him privately that he is sorry about his personal tragedy—the birth of a stillborn son—but continues to provoke him in class. Then when a knife fight breaks out between Dadier and a student named West, Miller, realizing that Dadier is fighting for his life, comes to the aid of the teacher even though he knows it is an act that could cost him considerable social prestige. With Miller's help, Dadier subdues the boys. Miller protests when Dadier says he will take them to the principal, but then he realizes that Dadier has no choice. He shows him with a smile that he has come to accept the older man both as an authority figure and as a teacher.

Miller, Henry. *Tropic of Cancer.* Henry Miller. 1961.

In Henry Miller's semi-autobiographical novel, the narrator, Henry Miller, describes his wanderings in the decadent Paris of the 1930s. Without money and with very few scruples, Miller lives off the goodwill of others, drifting from one precarious situation to the next. Having renounced both his past connections and his hopes for the future, he leads a life of aimless and unrestrained adventure.

From his Parisian perspective, Miller looks back at his American home without a trace of longing. He depicts Paris lovingly and claims to have a mysterious, romantic attachment to places all over the globe; toward America, however, he feels "nothing at all." Of New York City, his former home, he remembers only the sense of unimportance he felt there. Miller also recalls the seven years he spent being obsessed with his wife Mona and must fight off memories of their bitter arguments, which exploded in so many familiar corners and squares of Paris. For the most part he succeeds in suppressing thoughts of his years with Mona, and knowing she has returned to New York, he feels no desire to return there.

During the first months of his solitary sojourn in Paris, Miller finds no friends and seems to subsist only on his anguished longing for Mona. He gradually builds a circle of acquaintances, many of whom are associated with an English-language newspaper. Almost all of them are willing to offer him a free meal. During one particularly fruitful period, Miller assigns his friends to a rotating schedule: Each one is to buy him dinner once a week. At one point he is sleeping with the wife of a friend from whom he is also accepting meals. The more favors he asks of his friends, Miller discovers, the better they like him.

Miller provides a catalog of his sexual experiences in Paris in explicit detail. Claiming that explicit writing is an act of religious honesty, he dedicates himself to recording "all that which is omitted in books." He remembers Germain, a noble prostitute who talked to him while soaping on the bidet, and he favorably contrasts her with Claude, another prostitute he slept with, who made him turn away when she washed herself. In Miller's opinion, modern civilization has been in decline since it lost the understanding of ecstasy: "If anyone knew what it means to read the riddle of that thing which today is called 'crack' or a 'hole,' if anyone had the least feeling of mystery about the phenomena which are labeled 'obscene,' this world would crack asunder."

When his friends' generosity finally seems exhausted, Miller adopts more extreme measures. One night he receives room and board from an earthy Russian by promising to give him English lessons. He later spends several weeks in the apartment of an eccentric Indian pearl salesman, Mr. Nanantatee, whom he privately calls Mr. Nonentity. The narrator cleans Mr. Nonentity's apartment and obeys his various peculiar orders. The extremity of his living conditions does not harden him, Miller claims, but rather serves to heighten his sensitivity and sharpen his awareness. He takes a friend of Nanantatee, a follower of Gandhi, to a brothel, and the man causes a commotion by defecating in the bidet. Some weeks later at another brothel, Miller watches the young man dance with a fat naked prostitute. He has a moment of mystical clarity in which he perceives that man causes bloodshed by searching for the miraculous, but the true miracle would be "nothing more than these two enormous turds which the faithful disciple dropped into the bidet."

After drifting this way for over two years, Miller manages to get a job at the newspaper where his friends Carl and Van Norden also work. He is perfectly contented with his proofreading assignments. He sits calmly all day and "punctuates calamities," feeling immune to the news of disease and disaster that passes through his hands. One disadvantage of the job is that Miller must remain silent or speak in monosyllables to allow his supervisor to feel superior. The result is a neurosis he calls "echolalia"; the minute he leaves the office, everything he has withheld comes streaming out uncontrollably. Miller eventually loses the position and returns without anxiety to his former uncertain existence.

When he returns to Paris, he is solicited by a homeless woman and gives her 50 francs. Later that night he meets a tall blond prostitute who says her mother is dying. He gives her 100 francs to have sex with him. After he finishes, she runs out of the room. Miller finds her purse, takes out his 100 francs and some loose change, and leaves the apartment.

Toward the end of his memoir he accepts a job as an exchange professor of English at a lycée in Dijon, and the buoyant mood he sustained in Paris vanishes in the cold, orderly world of the school. After languishing in this "penitentiary" for a semester, he receives a letter from his Carl informing him that there is a better position open at the newspaper where he had worked as a proofreader. He

leaves the school without a word to anyone. Shortly after returning to Paris, he rescues his friend Fillmore from a suffocating marriage by packing him off to America. After seeing Fillmore off, Miller is filled with a sense of peace: He surveys the Paris landscape and feels deeply grateful to be there.

Miller, Julia. *Just Above My Head.* James Baldwin. 1978.
Born to southern parents and living in Harlem, Julia Miller is "called" to God's service when she is only seven years old. As a child evangelist she exerts a subtle tyranny over her family. Her mother Florence is cowed by her presence; her father Joel is virtually emasculated. Both are brutal to Jimmy, Julia's younger brother. But Julia is also the family's chief means of support, acting as an itinerant preacher proclaiming the sins of others. When Florence becomes fatally ill, the family as a whole lacks the will to seek the proper medical attention, so accustomed are they to hearing Julia's prayer with the Lord. On her deathbed Florence finally challenges the girl, who comes to recognize her own sins of pride and hypocrisy.

Chastened and grief-stricken, Julia remains with her widowed father while Jimmy is shipped south to relatives. Her father, who lacked verve throughout his marriage and Julia's religious career, goes into further decline. Julia's refusal to continue her preaching enrages Joel, who can manage only a part-time job and nightly drunkenness. She soon becomes the despairing victim of his repeated sexual abuse. When she becomes pregnant—either by her father or by a lover she had turned to for solace—Joel beats her to within an inch of her life. Her grandmother, appearing from New Orleans, takes the convalescing fourteen-year-old to live with her and Jimmy.

Protecting, supporting, and loving her younger brother becomes Julia's sole concerns. She works as a prostitute and as a model in order to support Jimmy and return with him to New York City. Her success as a model comes just at the time America's fashion magazines first turn to African-American women.

In New York, Julia has an affair with HALL MONTANA, a slightly older friend from childhood. She, Hall, and their respective younger brothers form an ad hoc family that offers Julia a sense of belonging which she has long lacked. In search of a community, Julia leaves Hall for Africa and travels with a married diplomat she met at the United Nations. Working as an airline hostess, she stays in Abidjan for two years. Black Africa finally offers her the spirituality that has eluded her since childhood, and she returns to New York at peace with herself.

Julia buys a house in Yonkers to provide a refuge for herself and her brother Jimmy. When Jimmy's lover, ARTHUR MONTANA, Hall's younger brother, dies a tragically early death, Julia stands by, as always, to lend support. It takes Jimmy and Hall two years to deal with their grief, and they finally meet to connect their separate sorrows in the warmth and spiritual calm of Julia's abode.

Miller, Justin "Tiger." *The Origin of the Brunists.* Robert Coover. 1966.

Justin "Tiger" Miller must struggle to avoid an undistinguished adulthood after having experienced a singularly charmed childhood.

Personable and good-looking, Miller longed for fame and fortune outside the claustrophobic boundaries of the small town of West Condon and moved to New York City immediately after graduating to make a living as a newspaper reporter. Miller falls upon hard times; used to being a big fish in the small pond of his hometown, he is unprepared for the anonymity and indifference with which he is greeted in New York. Frustrated with his entry-level job and impatient to leave the mark on the world that all his well-wishers back home had convinced him he would, he becomes depressed and begins drinking. He eventually loses his job, and after wandering the country aimlessly and leading a gypsy life, he finally returns to West Condon. Only there can he enjoy the heroic status to which he feels he is entitled.

In West Condon, Miller procures a job writing for the local daily newspaper, the *Chronicle.* When the editor of the *Chronicle* confides to Miller that he is ready to retire, Miller is able to scrape enough money together to make a down payment on the paper and becomes the new editor. Finally finding something to be enthused about, Miller puts all his energy into making the *Chronicle* a first-rate newspaper. Under his new management the paper's circulation almost doubles, but it is not until the *Chronicle* recounts a controversial mine explosion that its popularity exceeds the boundaries of the small town. Miller spends sixteen hours a day by the site of the explosion, gathering information not available to the national press but available to him because of his many contacts among the townspeople.

When a mildly retarded miner named Bruno miraculously survives after being trapped underground for a week, he becomes a national hero. Much to Miller's amusement, Bruno emerges as a new messiah for the many townspeople who lost family members in the explosion. Miller writes editorials mildly jeering the zealous followers of the new "Brunist" religion that begins to spread among the inhabitants of West Condon.

A blood clot leads to Bruno's untimely death. Miller becomes concerned when he realizes that these followers of Bruno, known as "Brunists," have deemed their leader a martyr for their religion in the wake of his death. Furthermore, the number of converts to this new religion keeps increasing within and beyond West Condon. Miller finds himself and the *Chronicle* the object of attacks from the Brunist majority. When a new Brunist mayor is elected, Miller, not wanting to lose his newspaper or his home in the town he grew up in, has no choice but to convert to Brunism, the religion he had initially ridiculed.

Miller, Rudolph. "Absolution." F. Scott Fitzgerald. 1926.

Rudolph Miller is an eleven-year-old Minnesota boy enduring the pangs of conscience imposed by his Catholic upbringing. As the story opens, Rudolph meets with Father Schwartz, a desperately lonely priest. Like Rudolph, Schwartz feels oppressed by the strictures of the Church and is beginning to go mad. Not realizing this, Rudolph recounts a tale of sin that he fears will lead to his damnation.

Rudolph's tale dates from three days before the present interview. While he was in confession, the boy was asked if he ever lied; he automatically lied and said no. After he left the church, the enormity of what he had done burst upon him: He had committed a mortal sin. Then an almost certain disaster threatened: He could not take communion the next morning, and with the church closed for the night, he could not confess and purify himself.

On the way home Rudolph seeks relief from his spiritual struggles by slipping into his alternate personality, the noble Blatchford Sarnemington. Becoming Blatchford is his rebellion against authority—against his father, God, the priests, and the drab, dull world of Minnesota.

Soon, however, Rudolph's thoughts return to his moral quandary. For him Catholicism is a game of rules; his mind starts racing to find the right stratagem to avoid communion. Rudolph's metaphysics become clear at this point. God is not all-knowing: Rudolph believes there is a place in his mind where he can plan his subterfuges in secret. He finally lights on a plan to drink a glass of water in the morning. This would disqualify him from receiving communion.

When morning arrives, however, Rudolph is caught with a water glass by his father, a brutish, unsuccessful laborer, who beats him in a fit of temper and then drags him to church. In rebellion against his father, Rudolph refuses to admit his sin in confession and joins the communion ceremony with sin in his heart.

While Father Schwartz gives him communion, Rudolph is frozen with terror that the wafer will turn to poison. Swallowing it, he believes he is fallen, and as he leaves the church, the clatter of his cloven feet sound in his ears. This is the ultimate sin that led him to seek the present meeting with Father Schwartz.

At the end of his confession Rudolph feels a sense of immaculate honor. This is not religious piety; rather, he thinks of himself as a warrior, as someone who has thrown off his weakness. Drawn to glory and honor, imagining himself as a German cuirassier or a naval officer, Rudolph wants to avoid shame and achieve nobility. With his confession complete and his submission almost total, Rudolph discovers that Father Schwartz has gone insane. The priest starts to babble about the wonders of far-off places and the need for people to go "glimmering" through the night. As Father Schwartz finally collapses with a scream, the young boy flees in horror from this spectacle of an oppressed spirit.

Miller, William. *The Marrow of Tradition.* Charles W. Chesnutt. 1901.

William Miller is a light-skinned black doctor practicing medicine in the South during the era of post-Reconstruction. The intelligent, cultured grandson of a slave, Miller obtained his position in society through the determination and savvy of his father, a stevedore who made his money in the years following the Civil War. William's father gave him a professional education in hopes that "his children or grandchildren might be gentlemen in the town where their ancestors had once been slaves."

Dr. Miller recently founded a hospital and training center for nurses in Wellington, Virginia. Returning by train with supplies from the North, he meets Dr. Burns, his former professor. Dr. Burns is traveling to Wellington to perform an operation on a young child. He invites Dr. Miller to assist him. As fate would have it, the operation is to be performed on the child of his wife's "white" sister who, because of her own prejudice and shame resulting from the knowledge of her father's infidelity, has refused to acknowledge her half-sibling.

When Dr. Miller arrives at the home of MAJOR CARTERET, an ex-Confederate soldier, he is denied access to the house. Even though Dr. Burns expresses doubt as to whether he can perform the operation without Dr. Miller's aid, Major Carteret still refuses to allow him to help. Dr. Miller departs and the child recovers, for the time being, without the aid of the operation.

Unknown to Dr. Miller, Major Carteret is one of three men, calling themselves the "Big Three," who plan to end African-American participation in the political scene in Wellington and in the rest of the South. The murder of an elderly white woman enables the conspirators to goad the white populace of Wellington into forming an angry mob that comes close to lynching an innocent black man. Only when Dr. Miller appeals to old Mr. Delamere, a true Southern gentleman, does it become apparent that the murder was committed by a white man. The Big Three are forced to disperse the mob.

While Dr. Miller works to equip his Negro hospital, the Big Three continue to plot. Eventually, determined to foment violence against the Negroes of Wellington, they instigate a riot. A vicious white mob attacks any blacks found roaming the streets of the town. Helpless men, women, and children flee the town for the surrounding woods. The Negro-controlled newspaper and Dr. Miller's hospital are torched, and black and white members of the city government are forced to resign and leave town. After his hospital is burned down, Dr. Miller makes his way to town and searches for his wife and child. He arrives home to find his wife distraught and his young son dead, shot by a stray bullet.

In the midst of their grief, the Millers are interrupted by a messenger from Major Carteret asking Dr. Miller to come and attend his son. Recalling his earlier rejection, the doctor refuses. When he receives Miller's response, Major Carteret himself goes to the Miller home to request the doctor's help. The Negro doctor reminds the ex-Confederate that at one time he had disdained his medical aid and dramatically reveals the death of his own child. Major Carteret must take this bitter news to his distracted wife, who, upon hearing it, goes to Dr. Miller herself.

Mrs. Carteret, desperately trying to save her child's life, begs for the doctor's help. Miller, torn between his grief and his Hippocratic duty, promises to do whatever his wife bids him to do. Mrs. Carteret, who has never recognized that she is the half-sister of Mrs. Miller, finally acknowledges this relationship and promises to give her sibling half of their father's estate. Disdaining the monetary offer, Mrs. Miller rejects the acceptance that she has craved all her life. No amount of pleading from her white sister appears to move her. Finally, she tells her husband to go because she wants the Carterets to know that even in the face of injustice and grief, a noble spirit exists in her home. Dr. Miller rushes away with Mrs. Carteret to do what he can for the ailing child.

Milton, George. *Of Mice and Men.* John Steinbeck. 1937.

George Milton, a small and quick-witted man, is a migrant worker traveling through California with his childlike companion LENNIE SMALL, who is huge and massively strong but in need of constant attention. While Lennie's strength is a great asset on any ranch, his simpleminded lack of self-control makes him a constant burden to George.

George and Lennie grew up together in Auburn, California, and when Lennie's aunt Clara died, George took Lennie on the road with him to find work. While at first he used to play jokes on Lennie and flaunt his power over the larger man, by the time the novel opens, George is generally protective of his companion and loves him deeply, despite the frustration that caring for him entails. Although the relationship might seem one-sided, Lennie gives George the companionship and stability that is missing from the lives of the other drifters they meet. As George explains to Lennie, "Guys like us that work on ranches are the loneliest guys in the world."

Having Lennie with him permits George to dream of getting his own place, a small farm with a cow, a few pigs, and rabbits. But for all his talk of stability, George and Lennie are on the road as much as anyone else. And despite George's claims that he has an actual farm in mind ("The ol' people that owns it are flat bust an' the ol' lady needs an operation"), the pair have no more than ten dollars between them. In fact, once they settle into a new job, George is as quick to run to the whorehouse on Saturday night as any of the other hands. Nonetheless, his dream of the farm and Lennie's unwavering faith give George the illusion that things are different.

When the two drifters arrive at a new ranch, they are hired immediately. From the start there is friction between Lennie and Curley, the boss's son, who is a short-tempered lightweight boxer. Curley's natural irascibility is increased by his inability to keep his new wife from talking with the hired hands. He picks on Lennie because of his size and his obvious slowness. George manages to smooth things over, however, and the two newcomers are soon on friendly terms with most of the hands. Because of his intelligence and common sense, George has a certain affinity with Slim, the foreman who rules the bunkhouse with quiet authority.

After an initial period of suspicion, George confides his future plans to Candy, the crippled sweeper whose disability pay could be combined with George and Lennie's earnings to make a down payment on the farm. For the first time, the dream seems to be within George's grasp. But then Curley's wife makes advances on him in the barn; when he strokes her hair too roughly, she struggles. Terrified of getting in trouble, Lennie frantically attempts to quiet her and accidentally breaks her neck. Knowing he has "done a bad thing," he flees to a prearranged meeting place and waits for George.

Led by Curley, the farmhands form an armed posse. Although George and Slim both know that Lennie meant no harm, they realize that it is useless to protest. George steals a gun, slips away, and meets Lennie. He recites the story of the farm and the rabbits one last time and, his hands shaking, shoots his friend in the back of the head. After the others arrive, Slim attempts to comfort George. Although technically George and Candy could still finance the farm, it is painfully obvious that with Lennie's death no such escape is possible.

Minderbinder, Lieutenant Milo. *Catch-22.* Joseph Heller. 1961.

Stationed at a U.S. Air Force base on the small Mediterranean island of Pianosa during World War II, Lieutenant Milo Minderbinder thrives and prospers in the atmosphere of chaos and mismanagement, rising from being an anonymous pilot to being the head of an enormous black market syndicate operating on all five continents. Milo is a fervent, valiant defender of his idea of free enterprise, "the historic right of free men to pay as much as they had to for the things they needed in order to survive." While he is not necessarily callous by nature, the minute the opportunity for a deal appears, Milo becomes single-minded and ruthless.

Milo's big break comes when he is made mess officer.

Wanting to provide the officers with luxury foods of their choice rather than normal rations, Milo sets up a mysterious operation he calls "the syndicate" in which (he claims) "everybody has a share." What Milo means by this is that the resources of the base become his capital, which he uses to set up an elaborate system of trade. If anyone ever questions his actions, Milo replies that all his deals are profitable, the profit goes to the syndicate, and everybody has a share. It is therefore never in one's interest to complain.

Milo begins by trying to find an affordable source of eggs. It is a mystery to fellow serviceman JOHN YOSSARIAN, who shares more of Milo's confidence than anyone, how Milo can buy eggs in Malta for 7 cents apiece, sell them on the base for 5 cents, and still make a profit. What Yossarian later discovers is that Milo gets the eggs for a cent apiece in Sicily, sells them in Malta for 4 cents, buys them again (from himself) in Malta for 7 cents, and sells them in Pianosa for 5 cents (a 2-cent loss), all of which works out to a net profit of 4 cents an egg. By artificially driving up the price, Milo undersells everyone else.

Of course, an enterprising fellow like Milo cannot be confined to the mere business of supplying the squadron with fresh delicacies. Soon he is shipping cedars from Lebanon to Oslo sawmills to be sold as shingles on Cape Cod and shipping peas from Atlanta to Holland to pay for tulips that are sent to Geneva, where the proceeds are used to prop up the Hapsburgs. Hides from Buenos Aires are tanned in Newfoundland for shipment to Finland. Milo sells cork in New York, shoes in Toulouse, ham in Siam, nails in Wales, and tangerines in New Orleans. And of course such economic might also confers political power; Milo is given innumerable positions of authority in gratitude for his various economic miracles. Yossarian learns that Milo is the mayor of a large town in Sicily, and in Malta he is known as Major Sir Milo Minderbinder (Assistant Governor General); he is also Vice-Shah of Oran, Caliph of Baghdad, Imam of Damascus, and the Sheik of Araby.

In Milo's impressive progress there is only one misstep: In a moment of weakness he purchases the entire Egyptian cotton crop, only to find there is a cotton glut and he cannot resell his purchase. In an ingenious effort to create a new market, he begins feeding the men chocolate-covered cotton in the mess. "This stuff is better than cotton candy," he boasts, "it's made of real cotton." In the end he sells it to the U.S. government, arguing that "a strong Egyptian cotton speculating industry means a stronger America."

Milo's allegiance to free enterprise goes far beyond mere patriotism. Perhaps his ultimate coup comes when he rents his own squadron's planes and pilots to the Nazis (the Luftwaffe having no planes left), and they bomb their own base for a tidy profit. Of course, as on the earlier occasion when Milo sold all the parachutes without telling anyone, the men on the base who survive the attack are outraged. But Milo's answer remains the same as always: "Who can complain? The syndicate made a profit and (after all) everyone has a share."

Minivar, George Amberson. *The Magnificent Ambersons.* Booth Tarkington. 1918.

The Amberson "magnificence" to which George Amberson Minivar is heir began with his grandfather's fortune. It is a magnificence of money and name and soon destroys young George, the only son of the Major's only daughter, ISABEL AMBERSON MINIVAR.

At nine, George is a "princely terror" dreaded for his irascible behavior; nonetheless, he is still dressed by his doting mother in silks, ribbons, curls, and velvet. He is a leader of the toughest boys in town, whom he spends his time denouncing as "riffraff" with a snobbery that he maintains throughout his life. To them George is "King Minivar," a boy of legendary domineering arrogance.

After attending private school and an elite university back East, George returns home to live. Content to just be an Amberson, he disdains the suggestion that he practice law and occupies himself by ignoring his father, tormenting his spinster aunt Fanny, and enjoying the doting of his mother. His behavior improves somewhat when he meets Lucy Morgan, a dark-eyed beauty who steals his heart. He and Lucy are soon "almost" engaged.

George becomes upset when he hears a rumor within the family that his mother is cultivating an unsuitable friendship with Lucy's father, Eugene Morgan. A moral snob, he persists in his old-fashioned idea that things should always remain as they are, although it becomes apparent to everyone but George that times are changing. New houses, new cars, and new names are diminishing the Ambersons' stature in their midwestern town. When his father dies, George grieves only slightly since they had not interacted much in his lifetime.

George becomes enraged when his jealous aunt Fanny tells him that people all over town are talking about his mother and Eugene Morgan. He begins to see himself as a modern Hamlet, gloomily pondering the improprieties of his mother's behavior. His mood grows increasingly dark. When he realizes that open warfare against Eugene would jeopardize his relations with Lucy, whom he had been trying to coerce into marriage, George decides to end the relationship in order to preserve the good name of his family.

After his mother decides never to see Morgan again, George insists that she accompany him on a world tour. He returns home only when it becomes apparent to him that she is dying. Her death leaves him desolate and guilty, especially since he refused to allow Eugene to see Isabel on her deathbed. George's misery is compounded when his grandfather follows his mother in death and he discovers that the Amberson fortune has been depleted. Vir-

tually penniless, without even the title to his home, George is left with his aunt Fanny, a woman he never liked and whose own small income has been squandered in bad investments. They take up residence in a small apartment building, and George supports them by securing dangerous work in a nitroglycerin factory.

George's life takes an ironic turn when he is run down by a motorcar, the symbol to him of everything that is wrong with the modern world. He recovers to find Eugene Morgan at his bedside. Morgan claims to have had a vision of George's mother urging him to be kind to her dear son. George, having finally realized that he must ask Eugene for forgiveness, is at last reunited with Lucy.

Minivar, Isabel Amberson. *The Magnificent Ambersons.* Booth Tarkington. 1918.

ISABEL AMBERSON MINIVAR, a proper midwestern lady, is the daughter of the family whose fortune has made them famous. Devoted to her powerful family, the "Magnificent Ambersons," she constantly defers to her spoiled son's wants, often to the detriment of her own life.

Constantly aware of her family's stature in the community, Isabel turns down a suitor she greatly admires when he drunkenly serenades her one night, "making a clown of himself." She decides instead to marry dull and sensible Wilbur Minivar. She and Wilbur have one son, GEORGE AMBERSON (MINIVAR), and at the time of his birth, Isabel enters into a life of single-minded devotion to her child. Although most consider George an arrogant, snobbish bully, to Isabel he is an angel; she dotes on his every look and worries about him endlessly. As for the rest of her family, she prides herself on her father, Major Amberson, tolerates her spinster sister-in-law, Fanny Minivar, and ignores her husband, Wilbur.

When her son is grown and a party is given in his honor, Isabel finds herself reunited with Eugene Morgan, her former suitor, now a sober inventor who is working on the new sensation, motorcars. She dances with him, smiles at him, and convinces him once again that although she may have a touch of "the high stuff," she is "just about the finest woman in the world."

Isabel, Eugene, and Fanny soon become a constant and unusual threesome. Isabel appears to be the chaperone for Fanny and Eugene, now a widower whose daughter Lucy is much admired by Isabel's son George. But it soon becomes apparent to Fanny that she is being used, and her taciturn jealousy turns grim. When her husband begins to sicken with worry over his investments and his unsound financial affairs, Isabel accompanies him to Asheville, where he soon dies. She maintains the demeanor of a grieving widow, but it soon becomes obvious that her grief is not as abject as Fanny's genuine misery. In fact, Isabel seems to grow quite merry as the car rides and afternoons with Eugene continue.

The one obstacle to Isabel's happiness is George. Even

though he hopes to marry Lucy Morgan, George finds it difficult to like her father Eugene. When Eugene comes to call on his mother, George, stirred up by Fanny's gossip, sends his prospective father-in-law away from the house. Even though an honorable marriage was possible, Isabel agrees never to see Eugene again since it causes heartache for her "dear son." Eugene urges her to live her life as she wants, but she is too influenced by her son to see reason and writes a letter breaking off the relationship. She has spent her life worrying whether her son had dry clothes and enough to eat, and she believes she must make this final sacrifice for his happiness.

George takes his mother away to Europe. Although Isabel wants to come home, she cannot take issue with George, who insists on staying. At last she grows so ill that he has no choice but to bring her back to the city of her birth. Isabel returns a broken woman, so feeble that she must be carried from boat and train. She dies after only a few days in her own home. Eugene attempts to see her just before her death, but George will not permit him to visit.

Later, when Eugene, brokenhearted over her death, attempts to conjure up Isabel in a séance, she appears to him and urges him to be kind to George, whose financial affairs are in ruin. Aided by Isabel's spirit, George and Eugene are united at the novel's end.

Miranda. "Old Mortality." Katherine Anne Porter. 1969.

Miranda grows up nourished by the nostalgic memories of earlier generations in a traditional southern household at the turn of the century. An unusually spirited and imaginative girl, she is especially fascinated by the story of her aunt Amy, who was similar to her in character and who died very young. Against the background of this immensely powerful family myth, Miranda tries to form her own alternative visions of adulthood and womanhood.

According to Miranda's father, Harry, Aunt Amy was admired by many young men, and although engaged twice, she refused, for no apparent reason, to be married. Her second cousin, Gabriel, pursued her relentlessly for five years, during which time her health became increasingly fragile. After a very serious illness, Aunt Amy suddenly and unexpectedly agreed to marry Gabriel. She left on her honeymoon, and six weeks later the family received news of her death. Miranda is puzzled by the image of this dashing woman, whom everyone remembers as an "angel," leaving for her honeymoon with a man she does not love. Perhaps it is the legacy of this marriage that causes Miranda to constantly play the game of inventing a career for herself: airplane pilot, tightrope walker, jockey.

The images offered Miranda by her relatives become even more clouded when, at the age of ten, she meets Uncle Gabriel, who played such an important role in Aunt Amy's life. At this point Miranda and her oldest sister,

Maria, are at boarding school in New Orleans, run by very severe nuns. Saturdays are the only tolerable days for them since an uncle or a cousin usually comes to take the sisters to the racetrack. One Saturday their father visits from Texas and announces that they will go to bet on one of Uncle Gabriel's mares at the racetrack in nearby Crescent City.

Miranda, who has lately been dreaming of becoming a jockey, is enthralled by the races and literally moved to tears when Uncle Gabriel's mare wins. Afterward, however, she is astonished and disappointed on meeting Gabriel, who in no way corresponds to her romantic vision of him. A paunchy, drunken, overly emotional man, he makes no attempt to conceal the fact that his horse's victory has come in a moment of desperation. Gabriel invites Harry, whom he has not seen in many years, to bring his daughters for a visit. Almost as soon as they arrive, Miranda wishes she could escape from the shabby, cramped apartment and from the bitter remarks of Uncle Gabriel's second wife, Miss Honey. Returning that evening to the cold, orderly world of boarding school, Miranda feels cheated of her customary pleasant Saturday outing.

Eight years later Miranda is riding the train home to attend Uncle Gabriel's funeral. The impatient old lady who is sharing her car turns out to be Miranda's elderly spinster cousin, Eva. Cousin Miranda is scolded by Eva when she reveals that although she is only eighteen, she has already been married for a year after having eloped from school. As Cousin Eva proceeds to tell her version of Aunt Amy's story, Miranda feels a growing coldness toward her family. The feeling intensifies on their arrival when she senses that her father has still not forgiven her for marrying. Listening to Cousin Eva and her father exchanging their familiar stories, Miranda vows to liberate herself from her own family, from her husband's family, and from all memories that prevent her from discovering her own path in life.

Miriam. *The Marble Faun: Or, The Romance of Monte Beni.* Nathaniel Hawthorne. 1860.

In the artistic community of Rome, rumors are rife as to the true identity of the mysterious and beautiful Miriam. Everyone knows that Miriam is a strikingly beautiful painter living in Rome, but even her closest friends, HILDA, Kenyon, and DONATELLO, are unsure about her true origins. Despite this uncertainty about her past, Miriam's friends are devoted to her. Especially enamored of Miriam is Donatello, the Count of Monte Beni, who follows the young woman about with a devotion that can only be described as doglike. For her part, Miriam seems embarrassed and slightly annoyed by the innocent young man's protestations of love for her.

For some time a strange figure has been dogging Miriam's footsteps. He accosts her in the catacombs of Saint Calixtus, interrupts a joyous dance she is enjoying with

Donatello in the Borghese Grove, and somehow forces her to employ him as a model for some of her paintings. Miriam's friends think the man is only a beggar, but he is actually a figure from her past. He has the power to implicate Miriam in a crime he himself committed. Miriam begs the man to leave her alone, but he proclaims that they were united in the past and will be united henceforward.

With Donatello's help, Miriam is freed of this troubling figure's specterlike presence. One evening Miriam and Donatello are separated from a larger group that is exploring some of the city's ruins and hills. The figure appears, menacing Miriam once more. Donatello, who had once told Miriam he would gladly kill the man, grabs him and, with Miriam giving her silent approval, tosses him over a cliff to his death.

After this crime, Miriam considers herself in Donatello's debt and also realizes that she loves him. Their mutual attraction cannot overcome their shared guilt, however. Miriam releases Donatello, telling him to return to his home in the country. One word, she assures him, will restore her to his arms, for she can never give up her love for him.

Unfortunately, Hilda, who witnessed the murder, has no such sense of the all-conquering power of love. When Miriam comes to visit her, Hilda will not even allow Miriam to touch her for fear of being soiled by the same stain that has tainted the beautiful painter. Dejected, Miriam withdraws from the studio of the person who had been her closest friend.

Without her lover's knowledge, Miriam goes to live in a marble room in his country home. There she meets Kenyon, who is visiting Donatello. On Kenyon's urging she agrees to wait underneath the statue of Pope Julius the Third in Perugia for Donatello to appear. As soon as Donatello sees her, he speaks her name, and they are reunited. The statue of the Pope seems to bless the two of them.

The two lovers make the most of their time together, which proves to be short. Donatello is arrested for the murder of Miriam's tormentor, and Miriam, feeling guilty but innocent in the eyes of the law, remains free. When Kenyon and Hilda marry, Miriam gives the bride a costly bracelet. She also gives the couple her blessing. She sees the two in the Pantheon and stretches her hands to them in a gesture of both blessing and repulsion. While her friends have each other, she is now utterly alone.

Miss Lonelyhearts. *Miss Lonelyhearts.* Nathanael West. 1933.

Miss Lonelyhearts, actually the pen name for a young man, is the beleaguered and disillusioned advice columnist for the New York *Post-Dispatch*. Miss Lonelyhearts has begun his job answering letters, most of them only semiliterate, from people who sign themselves with such pseudonyms as "Sick-of-it-all" and "Desperate." These letters augment Miss Lonelyhearts's own feelings of despair. But Willie Shrike, the sadistic editor of the paper, convinces Miss Lonelyhearts that the advice column will be a useful circulation-building tactic, and the columnist continues to read and answer letter after letter.

As the novel begins, Shrike ridicules Miss Lonelyhearts by pointing at the absurdity of the optimistic yet banal advice he offers his readers. Miss Lonelyhearts advocates self-help through positive thinking but is unable to follow his own advice: The steady procession of depressing letters begins to take its toll, and Miss Lonelyhearts gradually loses his grip on his emotional life. At first he becomes hysterical, focusing much of his mental energy on his wavering faith in Christ; he subsequently develops an obsession for order, although he knows that perfect order cannot be attained.

Partly to cope with his self-doubts and doubts about the prospects of the world in general, Miss Lonelyhearts frequents a local bar, Delehanty's, where he engages in talk about the roles of literature and religion, but he is ridiculed there as well. He eventually appears at Shrike's house and goes on a date with Mary Shrike, the editor's wife. The date amounts to foreplay for the married couple since Shrike is aroused by his wife's illusion of dalliance, and Mary is aroused by her illicit flirtatious kissing and fondling of Miss Lonelyhearts. After the date, Shrike is ready for his wife, and Miss Lonelyhearts is dismissed.

Shortly thereafter, Miss Lonelyhearts meets Fay Doyle, one of the letter writers who asked for a personal meeting because her husband was crippled. Despite the fact that she is married, she and Miss Lonelyhearts almost immediately fall into bed and make love. The next day Miss Lonelyhearts awakens to find himself ill. His girlfriend Betty, a woman he had proposed to and then abandoned, arrives and begins taking care of him, urging him to resign his position at the *Post-Dispatch*. As his illness abates, Betty takes him to Monkstown, Connecticut, to the farm where she was raised. While their country interlude is pleasant, it does not alter Miss Lonelyhearts's sense of alienation and despair.

When he returns to his job, Miss Lonelyhearts masochistically immerses himself in his work. He reads a lengthy letter signed "Broad Shoulders" that is a catalog of misfortune and abuse. He then returns to Delehanty's, where Peter Doyle, the crippled husband of Fay Doyle, arrives with his own letter to Miss Lonelyhearts. After reading Doyle's story, Miss Lonelyhearts is moved and in a moment of empathy squeezes Doyle's hand. With both men feeling better, they return to Doyle's residence, hoping to achieve some reconciliation with Fay. Things go absurdly awry, however, and Peter storms out of the house, ending any chance of reconciliation.

After one more encounter with the mercilessly combative Shrike, Miss Lonelyhearts meets with Betty, who tearfully informs him that she is pregnant. He convinces her to marry him, and the couple plan their future.

When Peter Doyle arrives, Miss Lonelyhearts decides that his presence is a sign from God that he is to perform a miracle, healing Doyle. He moves toward Doyle who shouts out a warning that goes unheeded. In the ensuing scuffle, as Betty enters the building and sees the fight, Doyle's concealed gun goes off; Miss Lonelyhearts is shot, and the two men, entangled in each other's arms, fall partway down the stairs.

Mitty, Walter. "The Secret Life of Walter Mitty." James Thurber. 1942.

Knowing him only as a somewhat absentminded man, the acquaintances of Walter Mitty, including his nagging wife, don't even suspect his imaginary life. But Walter bravely navigates life's banalities and petty annoyances by resorting to private fantasies of invincible derring-do.

One day as he is driving with his wife into town, Mitty becomes the fearless commander of an eight-engined Navy hydroplane speeding into the middle of a hurricane. Undaunted, he overcomes every peril of the raging storm. But his reverie is suddenly broken by the shouts of his wife. He has been driving too fast. As she is dropped off at the hairdresser, Mrs. Mitty reminds her husband to buy overshoes and nags him for not wearing his gloves.

Slipping on his gloves, Mitty drives off to run errands while becoming a famed surgeon observing a delicate operation on a tertiary Obstreosis of the ductal tract. During the operation, the newfangled anesthetizer malfunctions, imperiling the patient. Mitty is the only one who can repair it, of course, and when dreaded Coreopsis sets in, he is asked to take over the operation. As the nurse is about to hand him a scalpel, Mitty is startled by the screams of a parking-lot attendant: He has entered through the exit lane.

Mitty repels this minor insult with yet another heroic fantasy. Now grilled by a relentless prosecutor, Mitty's testimony shocks the courtroom. As pandemonium breaks loose, his beautiful girlfriend rushes toward him on the witness stand, only to be struck ruthlessly by the prosecutor. Mitty decks the prosecutor, calling him a miserable cur, which reminds him that he has to buy dog biscuits. He thus completes his errands, easily going from vivid fantasy to mundane reality and back again.

While waiting for his wife at the hairdresser, Mitty picks up an old magazine bearing the headline CAN GERMANY CONQUER THE WORLD THROUGH THE AIR? He promptly becomes a flying ace, only to be grounded by his wife. Why is he waiting where it's hard for her to find him? Did he buy the dog biscuits? The overshoes? Why didn't he put them on in the store? Mitty replies that he didn't put the overshoes on because he was thinking. Doesn't she realize that he thinks sometimes? Exasperated, she concludes he must be coming down with something.

As he waits for his wife to run one last errand, Mitty faces a firing squad. Proud and inscrutable, he courageously stands erect, forever "Walter Mitty the Undefeated."

Moffitt, Leroy. "Shiloh." Bobbie Ann Mason. 1981.

Leroy Moffitt, a disabled Kentucky truck driver, must confront his personal history and his crumbling marriage. Because his leg has been injured, Leroy returns home to his wife after spending most of his married life on the road. Although he desperately wants to have a happy life with his wife, it becomes clear that much has changed since the early years of their marriage.

Once he returns home permanently, Leroy notices that Norma Jean sometimes seems a bit disappointed to find him there when she comes in from work. Leroy reasons that his presence reminds her of the early days of their marriage when their infant, Randy, died of crib death. Determined that they will start their marriage anew, Leroy decides to build a log house for his wife, and in spite of her protests, he writes away for blueprints.

Since Leroy's return, Norma Jean has begun an exercise regime, and as she lifts weights, she reads Leroy a list of jobs he can apply for. But he insists that he only wants to build a log cabin. When Norma Jean's domineering mother, Mabel, relates a story of an infant who died as a result of neglect, Norma Jean becomes upset. Leroy tries to comfort his wife, but he finds it difficult to talk with her, and the two fall into silence.

Norma Jean soon begins a night school course in composition, and Leroy feels even further removed from her. He turns to Mabel for advice, and she suggests the couple take a trip to Shiloh, the site of a Civil War battle. Mabel had visited it years ago on her honeymoon, one of the few trips she has ever taken. Leroy thinks the trip would be good for them and, after several rebuffs, manages to convince Norma Jean to agree to the excursion.

They pack a picnic and drive to the battlefield on a Sunday. They wander the fields for some time, talking and laughing occasionally, but when they sit down for lunch, Norma Jean tells Leroy she wants to leave him. Leroy protests that they could start all over again, but Norma Jean tells him flatly that they have already done that and "this is how it turned out." As Norma Jean walks away from him, Leroy reviews his life: his marriage, the death of his child, and the events that have led to this moment. But he realizes he is leaving out "the insides of history," that life is not as simple as a series of events and corresponding dates. He understands, sadly, that the inner workings of his marriage have escaped him.

Molineux, Robin. "My Kinsman, Major Molineux." Nathaniel Hawthorne. 1837.

Eighteen years old and eager to get his start in life, Robin Molineux journeys from the country to the city.

When he finally finds his uncle, an official in colonial Massachusetts who had promised to help the young man if he decided to leave home, Robin discovers that he has much to learn about the ways of the modern world.

When he steps off the ferry that has brought him to the city, Robin has a few pence in his pocket and no idea of how to find his uncle. He wanders the city streets inquiring of passersby whether they know Major Molineux. Everyone Robin questions either rebuffs him rudely or takes Robin's farm-fed roughness as an opportunity to ridicule him. Robin first begins to sense that something is wrong when he asks an innkeeper if he knows his uncle's home. The innkeeper is unimpressed by Robin's mention of his uncle's name; in fact, he hints that he suspects Robin is an escaped apprentice. All the guests at the inn, including a strangely featured, ill-dressed man, laugh as a confused Robin stumbles out of the public house and into the street.

A beautiful young woman seems more sympathetic. Clad in a scarlet petticoat, she peeps at the weary Robin from the half-opened door of a shabby house. She tells Robin that his uncle lives in the house but is sleeping, and beckons Robin to come inside. Before he can answer her summons, a night watchman warns him to be off. Robin sees the woman beckoning to him again from one of the upper windows of the house, but suspecting that her intentions are not pure, he ignores her.

Growing more tired and confused at every step, Robin accosts another stranger and demands to know the whereabouts of Major Molineux. The stranger, who reveals himself to be the roughly featured man, tells Robin that his uncle will appear at that very spot within an hour. Although dazed by the fact that the man's face is painted half-black and half-red, Robin resolves to wait for his uncle. While he lingers on the steps of a church, Robin's thoughts turn back to his country home. The images of his parents and siblings grow vivid in his mind as loneliness oppresses him. When he spies an open Bible inside the church, he feels even more alienated and weary.

Another stranger, this one of respectable demeanor, approaches Robin. He listens to Robin's tale of his journey to the city and fruitless search for his uncle. The man cannot tell Robin where the Major is or the meaning of the man with the painted face, but he sits down to keep Robin company. Soon an uproar is heard some distance off, and a crowd approaches. Windows on either side of the street open as their drowsy inhabitants investigate the source of the late-night cacophony. When the crowd stops, Robin sees his uncle, a tarred and feathered captive of the crowd. Uncle and nephew recognize each other, and although Robin is shocked by the sight, he joins in the crowd's laughter at Major Molineux's humiliation. Robin's voice is the loudest.

The mob finally passes, and Robin asks the stranger to direct him back to the ferry. The stranger demurs, telling Robin that he might discover he wants to remain in the city and make his way in the world without the help of his disgraced uncle.

Monk, Talbot Waller "Trick." *Wonderland.* Joyce Carol Oates. 1971.

Friendly, popular, but vaguely unsettling, Dr. Talbot "Trick" Monk is a young doctor who imposes his companionship on medical student JESSE VOGEL. Their relationship begins when Trick angers Jesse by implying that he has been involved with Jesse's fiancée, a young nurse. Jesse is outraged at Trick's intrusion into his life, but some time later he breaks off his engagement, although his fiancee denies knowing Trick, and begins a strained friendship with the unusual doctor.

When Jesse becomes engaged to Helene Cady, the daughter of one of his professors, Trick gets involved once more. After taking the couple on an unnerving tour of a laboratory in which animals are submitted to torturous experiments, Trick confesses that he has been in love with Helene for some time. Jesse reacts with anger and with an even more powerful sense that something is wrong with Trick, who wrote in his confessional letter to Jesse that he felt "drained out and soulless."

Although Jesse is uneasy, he allows Helene to talk him into accepting Trick's invitation to a restaurant for dinner. Trick takes the couple to a steak house and chatters rapidly through the meal about his forays into poetry. He excitedly reads to them a poem he had just composed, "The Madness of Crowds." Unable to make sense of the poem, Jesse laughs, and Trick takes offense. He then confesses something that reveals once and for all his ghastly pathological nature. As Jesse and Helene are cutting into their steaks, he tells them of cooking and eating part of a female corpse.

Disgusted, Helene and Jesse leave the restaurant. Trick begs them to stay, and on the street he physically attacks Jesse, then collapses on the ground. Later, after he has been taken to a hospital, Jesse and Helene learn that Trick has a heart condition.

Trick recovers but disappears from Jesse's life. It is not until many years later, after Jesse has established himself as a prominent doctor, that Trick reappears. Jesse and Helene's teenage daughter Shelly has run away from home; Jesse becomes obsessed with finding her and traces her movements around the country through the enigmatic letters she sends him. When Shelly writes that she recently met T. W. Monk at a poetry reading, Jesse rushes to New York and confronts his former friend.

Jesse finds Trick living in squalid conditions in Greenwich Village. He is now a drug-addicted poet with a minor cult following. Pallid and unhealthy looking, Trick tells Jesse that he gained popularity with a long poem on the central nervous system that was misread as a scathing antiwar poem. But Trick is distracted and incoherent, and he tells Jesse nothing about his daughter's whereabouts.

Jesse gives the poet some money and watches while Trick, muttering senselessly, falls asleep.

Monroe, James Buchannan "Jimmy." *Cast the First Stone.* Chester Himes. 1952.

In his early twenties, James "Jimmy" Monroe is beginning a prison term of at least twenty years for a robbery. As he begins to adapt to prison life, he is confronted with its organized underworld and exposed to the prison's homosexual activity.

One of the first convicts Jimmy meets is a slightly older man named Malden Streator. Amid rumors that they are lovers, Jimmy and Mal establish a platonic friendship. Although Mal is attracted to Jimmy, he suppresses his feelings, substituting what he calls a cousin's relationship for the more emotional and physical ties Jimmy eschews. Mal is eventually moved to another cellblock, and the two can communicate only occasionally by means of illegal letters or messages relayed by other convicts. Meanwhile, Jimmy refuses to continue to perform the duties assigned him as an ash hauler. He claims that the job puts additional stress on his back, which had been badly broken several years before, and soon he is reassigned to teach in the prison school. This job also fails to work out, and Jimmy is demoted to the status of pupil before being assigned to yet another position.

Through various correspondence courses, Jimmy studies writing, law, and psychology. His interest in the law emerges following a catastrophic fire in the extremely overcrowded prison in which 277 men die. Jimmy, not physically affected by the fire, becomes hysterical as he joins the firefighters, police, and fellow convicts in a melee in the prison's courtyard. After the fire, the prison administration increases the harshness of its treatment of convicts and the state legislature alters the penal code, allowing for shorter sentences and more rapid paroles.

In response to these laws, Jimmy writes to his mother, who has visited and written regularly, and to the governor, from whom he requests a pardon. The pardon is not granted immediately, but Jimmy receives assurances that his case will be considered soon. While waiting for news about his release, he joins the prison's softball league and becomes an active player, allowing others to take over his role in the illegal card games he runs within the cellblock.

After some time a new prisoner, Duke Dido, is transferred to Jimmy's dormitory. Almost immediately the two men forge a strong bond, one that includes mutual expressions of love, faithfulness, and commitment to a post-prison future together. As this relationship intensifies, Jimmy's attitude toward homosexuality is transformed, although not enough to allow a physical relationship between himself and Dido. When Dido finally expresses his desire for a physical relationship, Jimmy is disgusted and rejects him. But because so many prisoners have written letters to the warden concerning Jimmy's alleged sexual

relationship with Dido, Dido is transferred to a ward that houses gay men.

Despite the danger to his parole hearing, Jimmy declares that he and Dido must be transferred together. This happens, and Jimmy's sentence, with his "good time" taken away, is extended by several months. When he is finally given a release date, Dido despairs. Feeling he must "free" Jimmy from a bond he cannot live up to, he commits suicide on the eve of Jimmy's release.

Montag, Guy. *Fahrenheit 451.* Ray Bradbury. 1950.

This futuristic novel tells the story of Guy Montag, a fireman in a large city. In Montag's society, firemen do not put out fires; instead, they find books deemed harmful to the public, burn them and the house in which they are found, and put the owners in jail. Guy has been a fireman for ten years and likes his job very much. He lives with his wife Mildred, who spends most of her time happily popping pills and watching the television on their wall screens.

One day on his way to work, Montag meets a new neighbor, seventeen-year-old Clarisse McClellan. Clarisse's parents are forced to keep moving because they are fugitives from the law; they have a long history of owning books. Clarisse tells Montag of a time long ago when firemen put out fires instead of starting them. Montag doesn't believe her at first, but her words eventually have an effect on him. The two spend mornings and evenings together, taking long walks, until one day she disappears.

Montag and the crew of other firemen, led by Captain Beatty, the fire chief, visit the house of an Old Woman that evening, on a tip from her neighbor. When the place is doused with kerosene, the Old Woman, standing amid her books, pulls out a match. Montag watches as the rest of the firemen flee the house. He leaves as the Old Woman lights the match and puts herself and her books on fire.

Montag's wife tells him that night that Clarisse was killed in a hit-and-run accident by one of the jet cars that go speeding on the highway. Increasingly bewildered, he reaches under his pillow and feels for the treasure he has hidden there: a pair of books taken from the Old Woman. He has Mildred call in sick for him the next day, but Captain Beatty comes to visit him. He recognizes Montag's symptoms and gives him a long speech on the danger of books and the reasons for their prohibition. He concludes by saying that in cases like these he usually gives the afflicted fireman twenty-four hours to return the books he may have stolen.

Feeling he needs a teacher, Montag pays a visit to an old English professor named Faber, who has been under observation by the fire department. They talk at length, and the professor finally gives him a tiny device to stick in his ear by which they can communicate. When Montag returns to his home, he finds his wife and a number of her friends watching the wall-screen television. Enraged by their ignorance, he begins shouting poetry at them, much to the horror of Faber, who is listening in on Montag's ear device.

When Montag returns to work, to his horror the next fire alarm brings him and the other firemen to his own house. His wife Mildred, it turns out, had called them. Captain Beatty forces Montag to burn his own house and all the books he had been collecting. He then hits Montag, knocking out his ear device. When Beatty promises to trace the device to Faber, Montag burns him to death with a flamethrower. Now a fugitive, Montag flees the city, just before it is destroyed by an atomic bomb from a global war that has just broken out.

Outside the city, Montag meets a group of nomad intellectuals, each of whom has memorized a favorite book. Montag joins them, and together they make their way back toward the ashes of the city.

Montana, Arthur. *Just Above My Head.* James Baldwin. 1978.

From his earliest years in Harlem, Arthur Montana has been acclaimed for his gifted singing voice. His first venues are evangelical churches, and his first accompanist is his father, Paul. At the age of thirteen, Arthur is sexually molested by an old man, an incident that traumatizes him but also arouses his sexual curiosity. The twin passions of music and homosexuality pursue Arthur throughout his life, and he is never happier than when the two means of expression can complement each other in his day-to-day life.

As a teenager Arthur is a member of a gospel quartet, the Trumpets of Zion, a group successful enough to tour the eastern seaboard. Touring with the Trumpets, Arthur gets his first glimpse of the Deep South in the repressive days on the eve of the civil rights movement. He also gets his first taste of romance when he falls in love with Crunch, a member of the quartet. Arthur's love and his livelihood are shattered at once when Crunch and the quartet's other members are drafted, leaving the slightly younger Arthur to fend for himself. The Korean War is on, and Arthur's revered older brother HALL (MONTANA) is already overseas.

During the war years Arthur begins his solo career, a career that eventually makes him "The Soul Emperor." He tours the United States and Canada repeatedly in pursuit of success but goes to the South only when his brother and Peanut, a former member of the quartet, have returned from the service and can accompany him. There they find that the civil rights movement has provoked open hostility, and a minor incident of conflict in Atlanta leads to the abduction and, presumably, the death of Peanut. With Peanut gone, Arthur's past has been effectively erased: Crunch has been driven crazy by the war and by an inability to reconcile himself to his own homosexuality; the quartet's final member, Red, returns from Korea addicted

to heroin and disappears from view. The grieving Arthur tours Europe next and finds some solace in the bohemian ways of Paris.

It is many years before Arthur ventures south again, this time managed by his brother Hall. They see the ghost of Peanut everywhere. In Florida the two Montanas run into Jimmy, a childhood friend who eagerly becomes Arthur's accompanist, companion, and lover. With Jimmy, Arthur finally has the happiness he needs to become successful, a happiness so deep it frightens him. Thirteen years with Jimmy follow, and they include the pinnacle of Arthur's career, recognition in the United States and abroad. Sadly, these years also lead Arthur to self-destruction, quarrels, drink, and drugs. After a final lovers' spat with Jimmy, Arthur ends up in a pub in London where, drunk and alone, he falls down the stairs and is found dead in the men's room.

Montana, Hall. *Just Above My Head.* James Baldwin. 1978.

The son of a piano player, Hall Montana grows up in the churches and bars of Harlem in the early 1950s. He is groomed from youth to be responsible and to take care of his younger brother ARTHUR (MONTANA), an aspiring gospel singer. But the weight of responsibility does not rest easily on Hall's shoulders. His teenage relationships are with Sidney, a smooth-talking bartender at the Jordan's Cat, and Martha, an almost dour, self-possessed nurse at Harlem Hospital. Although Hall's mother and Martha have certain expectations, Hall is reluctant to commit himself to Martha entirely. He fights off the impulse to propose marriage to her, and then is drafted at eighteen. Disappointing to Martha but true to himself, Hall is shipped off to the horrors of the Korean War.

While in Korea, Hall is attuned to the racism in that "police action" and in the United States in general. He has a few homoerotic experiences and thinks a little bit about Martha. His primary wish is to get back to Arthur and his parents. When Hall does return, it is with the realization that he cannot continue to live in the family's home but must strike out to find a place of his own in the world. Martha has become engaged to Sidney, who, although still bartending, has had a religious conversion to the growing Nation of Islam.

Hall finds work in the advertising department of a magazine and soon comes across JULIA MILLER, his childhood acquaintance, working as a model. She becomes Hall's first mature romance. When Julia eventually leaves him, Hall plummets into a decline. His family's pressure to be responsible and to take care of his brother rouse him from his depression. His father has long hoped that Hall will learn to manage Arthur's singing career.

As his initiation, Hall accompanies Arthur on a tour of the South, which they find a tinderbox of civil rights unrest. One member of their party is abducted before they return to New York. Back in the city, Hall meets his future wife, Ruth, who finally eclipses his memories of Julia, although the latter remains a close friend. On a second trip south, Hall serves as his brother's manager. The two Montanas run into Julia's brother Jimmy, who quickly becomes Arthur's lover. The whole party—Hall, Ruth, Julia, Arthur, and Jimmy—begins years of happiness in New York; the two musicians, Arthur and Jimmy, go in and out of town in pursuit of success. Hall marries Ruth, buys a house where his brother will feel comfortable, and soon fathers a son and a daughter. His contentment is utterly destroyed, however, when news arrives that Arthur—the thirty-nine-year-old "Emperor of Soul"—has been found dead in a London pub. Aching with grief, it is two full years before Hall is able to narrate his story of growth and sorrow.

Montemayor, Doña María Marquesa de. *The Bridge of San Luis Rey.* Thornton Wilder. 1927.

Doña María Marquesa de Montemayor, an eccentric noblewoman of early-eighteenth-century Lima, was one of five travelers who, on a July midday in 1714, plunged to their deaths in the collapse of the finest bridge in all Peru. Doña María's death kindles the curiosity of the unnamed narrator who retraces the events of Doña María's life in search of her "central passion."

The daughter of a cloth merchant, Doña María led an unhappy childhood and suffered horribly under the biting persecution of her mother. Unattractive, isolated, and estranged, Doña María "lived alone and thought alone." Despite her marriage to a nobleman, which gave her the title of Marquesa, she was scorned and derided by society.

The guiding passion of Doña María's life arose from the estrangement she experienced from her own daughter, Doña Clara. It was because the Marquesa loved Clara too much and began to persecute her with a nervous attention and a fatiguing, overzealous attachment that their relationship grew strained. Unable to endure the overbearing "love" of her mother, the daughter married and moved to Spain.

Doña María Marquesa's obsession with winning back the love of her daughter through letters became the central passion, the burning flame, of her existence. She spent a week of each month scouring the streets of Lima, assiduously gathering material for her correspondence, and on the eve of the monthly mail post she poured out her sentiments in writing. The remaining three weeks of each month the Marquesa spent shut up in her bedroom, lost in a bittersweet oblivion brought on by an excessive, habitual ingestion of chicha, a South American liquor.

A few years later, on hearing the news of her daughter's pregnancy, Doña María was overcome by an entirely new scale of emotions. In order to be in a position to advise Clara, the Marquesa learned all she could on the subjects of pregnancy and childbirth by turning for guidance alternately to medical science, pagan superstition, and pious Christianity.

Finally, during a pilgrimage to the sacred shrine of Santa María de Cluxambuqua, the Marquesa discovered a letter written by her companion and servant Pepita which precipitated Doña María's recognition that the relationship she had with her daughter had been based solely on cowardice and presumed fancy on her part. The recognition hardened Doña María's resolve to change for the better.

She never had the opportunity to do so. Two days later, along with Pepita and the two strangers ESTEBAN and UNCLE PIO, Doña María Marquesa de Montemayor falls to her death while crossing the bridge of San Luis Rey.

Montgomery, Ellen. *The Wide, Wide World.* Susan Warner. 1850.

When Ellen Montgomery is ten, a doctor advises her mortally ill mother to go abroad in the hopes of stimulating her health, even though everyone involved, except Ellen, knows that hope is futile. Before leaving her little daughter forever, Mrs. Montgomery takes care to equip Ellen materially and spiritually for her approaching orphanhood. As she deems it, the necessities are a few plain and decent dresses, a writing desk, a work box, and a Bible. She consoles her daughter about losing her mother with the conviction that she has a far better, truer friend in God; she urges Ellen to turn to God with all her troubles, assuring her that he will never fail her.

Under the care of a wealthy but vain and thoughtless female acquaintance of her father's, Ellen travels to her aunt Fortune's house in Thirlwall, in upstate New York. On the boat going upriver she meets a very kind minister who gives her a book of hymns and confirms her mother's teachings. He urges Ellen to follow her Savior and be a Christian. Ellen resolves to do this, but she is severely tried by the circumstances of her new life.

In Thirlwall, Ellen receives an extremely cool welcome from her sharp-tongued and brisk aunt. As the weeks go by, the relations between the two worsen because of Ellen's inability to control her temper. One day, in a fit of passion, Ellen runs off crying and meets her kind neighbor, Alice Humphreys, who urges her to act in a more Christian manner toward her aunt. The two girls develop a close friendship, and Ellen becomes an increasingly intimate member of the Humphreys household, which is composed of Alice, her father, and her brother John, both of whom are clergymen. John undertakes Ellen's education, urging her to turn to God, subdue all her rebellious, resentful nature, and restrain her willfulness. She is particularly challenged when Alice dies, but she and John only grow closer to each other and to God during the course of this hardship.

As she grows older, various forces encourage Ellen to be less pious and more worldly. Children tease and scorn her, but she remains firm in her religious convictions. Years after her mother's death, Ellen receives a deathbed letter from her that directs her to live with relatives in Scotland. Despite her desire to remain with the Humphreys, Ellen honors her mother's last wishes and goes to live with her wealthy aunt, uncle, and grandmother. These people, cultured and educated, love everything about Ellen except what they regard as her morbid piety and her lack of interest in conventional social pleasures. They command Ellen to forget about John Humphreys and to stop her habit of daily prayer. Torn between her commitment to being obedient to them and her commitment to God, Ellen nevertheless manages to fulfill her relatives' expectations and still remain devoted to God—all without being overtly self-assertive. When she reaches maturity, she returns to America and marries John. Ellen and John settle down in a tasteful and luxurious house devoted to the love of family and God.

Montressor. "The Cask of Amontillado." Edgar Allan Poe. 1846.

Montressor, the heir to the Montressor family estate, has a serious grudge against his enemy Fortunato. As the story begins, Montressor acknowledges that he has taken all he can from Fortunato, who has injured him thousands of times. Giving Fortunato no clue concerning his hatred, he concocts a means to gain revenge while remaining undetected and unscathed; the two men meet as regularly as ever. As Montressor flatly states, it is Fortunato's weakness that he prides himself on his expertise regarding wines and their qualities. Montressor despises this weakness and plans to prey on it since he also professes and possesses a knowledge of wines.

One early evening at the height of carnival gaiety, the two men meet. Outlandishly dressed, Fortunato is already fairly intoxicated. Montressor, wearing a costume that includes a black mask, feigns delight at meeting Fortunato and immediately begins telling him of the recent but hasty wine purchase he has made. Fortunato's curiosity is piqued at the suggestion that the rare Amontillado wine may be involved, and he agrees to sample the beverage. Montressor informs Fortunato that he is en route to visit a man named Luchesi, whom Fortunato insists is ignorant of wines. Noting the interest on Fortunato's countenance, Montressor then teases him into joining him on an excursion into the family vaults, catacombs where the wine is allegedly stored. Montressor notes that Fortunato has apparently been suffering from a severe cold, and he warns the latter against the dampness of the vault, but by now Fortunato will not be swayed.

When they reach the estate, the servants have vanished, thanks to a clever ruse on Montressor's part, and only the host and guest are on the premises. They immediately seize two candles, and the men begin their descent into the catacombs. Once underground, the noticeable dampness prompts Fortunato to have a coughing fit, which Montressor eases by giving him some Medoc. This suffices to quell the attack, and the two men continue toward the Amontillado. Near the end of the bone-filled catacombs, they reach a small crypt.

Once inside this chamber, Montressor, without a word to his foe, swiftly chains the startled Fortunato to the stone. He gleefully runs his hands over the excessively damp wall and observes that this dampness is even greater than what they had felt before; meanwhile, the bewildered Fortunato begins hesitantly to ask Montressor about the Amontillado. In response, Montressor, having joked already that he was a member of the masons, produces his trowel and begins to close in the last wall of the chamber. As he does so, his victim alternatively yells, screams, laughs, and sits in silence. At one point, as the narrator has nearly finished his task, he yells along with his victim. The gruesome job is finally finished, and without ever specifying what Fortunato's crimes were, Montressor concludes the story by noting that Fortunato has not been disturbed in the fifty years that have passed since that fateful tour of the catacombs.

Moonbloom, Norman. *The Tenants of Moonbloom.* Edward Lewis Wallant. 1963.

Norman Moonbloom is the emotionally anesthetized, middle-aged manager of Moonbloom Realty, a position given to him by his brother, the proprietor of the firm, after Norman had studied and failed at half a dozen different professions. His method of coping with the dissatisfaction his life engenders is to cut himself off from all but the most superficial interaction with other people. Hoping to spare himself the pain of the strong emotions that real relationships might generate, he goes about his daily life enclosed in a kind of intellectual membrane that reduces his emotional responses to a tolerable level. During the course of his job as a landlord, however, Norman becomes involved in the lives of his tenants.

Norman's involvement with his tenants begins when he makes the rounds to collect the rent from the people living in the four decaying buildings owned by his brother. As he stops at each apartment, the occupants engage him in conversation, and he is able to see the extent to which their lives have been rendered dysfunctional: the family that escaped from Nazi Germany is tortured by the past; an impossibly ancient man who has outlived his children sits defying death in his filthy apartment; a man dying of cancer tries to maintain his dignity.

By the time he finishes his rounds, Norman has a long catalog of items that need attention. His attempts to address their complaints are curtailed, however, when he catches the flu and spends the next few days in a delirium induced by his low-grade fever. His illness marks the beginning of a profound transformation in character; instead of passively retreating from surrounding events, as has been his habit, he will try to solve the various maintenance problems in the buildings—but this is against his brother's wishes.

Upon his recovery, Norman proceeds to carry out his intentions and soon becomes involved in the various major and minor occurrences of the tenants' lives. He is present at the accidental death of one couple's child and experiences a belated sexual initiation at the hands of one of his female tenants, which serves to affirm his developing capacity for emotional involvement. Norman's transformation is complete when he experiences a symbolic rebirth while fixing the last maintenance problem on his agenda—a bulging bathroom wall that douses him with filth during his boozy, all-night effort to repair it. This constitutes a kind of epiphany for Norman, who now realizes that the inescapable point of living is experiencing life in all its painful intensity.

Moore, Archy. *The Slave*; or, *Memoirs of Archy Moore.* Richard Hildreth. 1836.

Born a slave on a Virginia plantation in the late eighteenth century, Archy Moore first relates the bitter irony of his parentage. His master, Colonel Moore, is also his father. His mother, who is the Colonel's favorite among his slave mistresses, has only a trace of African blood; in fact, her father was a member of one of the most aristocratic Virginia families. Thus Archy, white in appearance and noble in bearing, is condemned to slavery only because he carries a small portion of "tainted" blood.

As a boy Archy is made body servant to one of the Colonel's legitimate sons, James, and for a while lives happily with his kindly half-brother. But James dies early, and Archy, told by the Colonel that he must choose between being the servant of another of his sons, a sadistic young man, or working in the fields, accepts the life of a fieldhand. Under a brutal overseer, Archy is introduced to the world of the slave quarters: long hours, poor food and clothing, and frequent floggings. His only solace is finding mutual love with Cassy, another of Colonel Moore's children by a slave. Archy wants to marry her, but the Colonel, who has marked her for his own prey, forbids it. The desperate Archy flees with Cassy, marries her informally, and sets off for the North. They are quickly captured; Cassy is brutally beaten by the Colonel, and Archy is sold to a North Carolina planter.

By chance, Cassy is also sold into service on a nearby plantation, and for a while the pair is reunited by the unexpected kindness of their respective owners. This happy period, which includes the birth of a son, is short-lived. Archy's master, in debt, sells him to a new owner in South Carolina. Archy fights back against the slavery system there, aids in a slave revolt, and then manages to flee to the North, finally arriving in Boston. Here he ships out as sailor on a boat bound for France; the War of 1812 is now being fought, and Archy eventually achieves com-

mand of a British privateer. His adventures take him far abroad; free and well-to-do, he now sends agents to America to find his wife and son. The search is futile; Archy at last determines to return to America himself, find his child, and free him or die in the attempt.

Moore, Vivaldo. *Another Country.* James Baldwin. 1962.

Vivaldo Moore, a novelist of Irish-Italian heritage and RUFUS SCOTT's best friend, was raised in Brooklyn but gravitated to the art scene of Greenwich Village in his early adulthood. Vivaldo, who has more or less broken off his long-term relationship with an older woman, has recently returned to writing his novel. His attempts are not immediately successful, and he is soon distracted when he is caught up in the drama of the violent relationship between Rufus, a black man, and Leona, a white southerner. As that relationship worsens, Vivaldo's time and energy are spent preventing or patching up quarrels between the lovers. His efforts are futile, however, and Leona winds up institutionalized in the South, while Rufus commits suicide by jumping off the George Washington Bridge.

After his friend's death, Vivaldo begins a relationship with IDA SCOTT, Rufus's younger sister. Ida moves from Harlem to live with Vivaldo in a predominantly white and palpably hostile neighborhood of the Village. Their relationship, spawned in part by a mutual love for Rufus, suffers from the environment's racism as well as from their cultural assumptions about the mutual antipathy of the white and black races. Vivaldo, now working on his novel full-time, loves Ida deeply and struggles to continue the relationship.

Ida, who wants to be a professional singer, begins her career by singing with jazz musicians who had known and worked with her brother. In the course of an engagement one evening, she meets Steve Ellis, a television producer; wanting to have a relationship with her, he claims he can further her career. She begins an affair with Steve, mostly for professional reasons. In the meantime, Eric Jones, Rufus's former lover, has returned from France to appear in a Broadway play, and he and Vivaldo meet again. Drawn together by memories of Rufus and their mutual friendship with Richard and Cass Silenski, Rufus's former high school English teacher and his wife, they begin to socialize more frequently.

On an all-night binge together, Vivaldo and Eric spend the night at Eric's apartment and vow eternal love, although neither expects their sexual involvement to continue. Eric has been having an affair with Cass Silenski and is torn between his desire for Cass and for Yves, his lover who is due to arrive soon from France.

Vivaldo, whose finished novel has been accepted for publication, does not tell Ida of his liaison with Eric but instead professes his love for her and his fear of losing her. This sparks an intense and dramatic exchange between them in which they grapple with the culture's racial and sexual assumptions. In the course of their conversation, Ida reveals her ongoing affair with Steve Ellis. Despite the blow to Vivaldo's ego, Ida manages to convince him that she wants to be true to him and will strive to do so; it appears that they will be able to maintain their relationship despite the pressures that will undoubtedly escalate as each artist's career develops.

Moorehead, Edgar "Tar." *Tar: A Midwest Childhood.* Sherwood Anderson. 1926.

Edgar Moorehead is better known by his nickname "Tar," a diminutive version of his father's nickname "Tarheels." Growing up on the outskirts of various small towns in Ohio, Tar longs for the security of a permanent home. His family is poor, and they are continually on the move because his father, Dick, cannot always pay his debts. Accordingly, Tar is preoccupied with both actual and emotional domestic structures.

From his first memories, Tar has been a loner, frightened of other children. More at ease in the company of adults, he is happiest in the arms of his understanding mother, Mary. Even at a young age Tar can tell that his mother's lot is a hard one; she must care for her many children, tolerate a wastrel husband, and can rarely leave home. Tar is not entirely sure how new babies come to be, but he resents them because they take time that his mother could devote to him.

Tar's first separation from his mother occurs when as a toddler he is taken into town by a neighbor. His older sister accompanies him, but she neglects to look after him when they are left to play in the barn. Tar proceeds to eat grass in hopes of transforming himself into a farm animal, preferably a horse or a cow, because he does not want to grow into manhood. He is stung by a bee and becomes the laughingstock of his hosts. This affirms Tar's perception that his delicate mother is the only truly compassionate person in his life. He begins to resent his father, Dick, who cannot hold down a job and spends large amounts of time away from the house drinking. Dick, who loves to tell tales of his war days, sometimes takes Tar with him, but the boy hates to go because his father kisses strange women. When Tar gets older, he has a difficult time approaching women and cannot understand his father's carefree attitude.

Tar falls ill in his early childhood, but he does not remember much except that he had delirious dreams and had to be tutored at home by his mother. When he returns to school, he skips a grade because he is so far advanced. Tar spends his time watching the horses at the racetrack or swimming in the water hole with his friends until he is old enough to take over his brother's paper route. His route allows him to snoop on the townspeople, who pay him not to divulge information. A bully, Henry Fulton,

hassles him, but Tar eventually confronts Henry and, rushing at him headfirst, sends him sprawling into a flooded creek. Although this boosts his self-confidence, he still has trouble meeting the girl he fancies and settles for visiting with another girl who is fond of him. He is often invited to eat at friends' homes but goes only occasionally because his poor family cannot return the favor. Tar's childhood ends when he is about thirteen, on the day his ailing mother dies. The memories he has formed in his childhood will become the basis for the many stories he will write when he is a grown man.

Moorehouse, John Ward. *U.S.A. (The 42nd Parallel; Nineteen Nineteen; The Big Money).* John Dos Passos. 1930; 1932; 1936.

Born on the Fourth of July in America's first state, John Ward Moorehouse grows up to be a pathetic man with varied talents. Dropping out of college after his father becomes crippled, Johnny goes to work for a real estate agent. He also takes singing lessons and writes songs. His creativity soon takes a different direction, however. While working for the real estate agent, he meets a young socialite named Annabelle Strang on a train. In addition to introducing him to some wealthy but foolish real estate speculators, she seduces him, marries him, and convinces him to go by the name of J. Ward Moorehouse.

They go to Europe, and John, now called Ward, picks up some continental manners and a few business contacts. It soon becomes apparent that he was always more interested in business than in the dissolute life of the wealthy, intercontinental elite. Annabelle begins having affairs, and when they return to America, Ward leaves her. Determined to make it as a "clean-cut young executive," he moves to Pittsburgh.

Ward works for a Pittsburgh newspaper for a time but soon has an opportunity in the advertising department of a hardware manufacturing company owned by one of his Paris acquaintances. He advances to the top of the advertising department, joins a country club, and meets Gertrude Staple, daughter of a powerful industrial mogul. They marry, and with her family's millions he starts a public relations office. He establishes connections with both labor and management interests, and promotes himself as the man who can help bring the two warring parties together. In the brewing war in Europe, Ward sees a tremendous opportunity for America and for himself.

As he rises to international power, Ward's inner biography remains an enigma. He meets FENIAN "MAC" MCCREARY in Mexico, hires RICHARD ELLSWORTH SAVAGE as a secretary in Paris, and becomes the confidant and companion of ELEANOR STODDARD. His friendship with Eleanor strains his marriage, but his wife remains with him despite his affair with her friend EVELINE HUTCHINS.

Ward, a portly, jowly giant of public relations, also

plays an extensive role in postwar negotiations in Paris. Savage describes him as a "national institution," but his personal life is less successful. When Eleanor leaves him, he becomes a lonely old man with an institutionalized wife and two children who barely know him; finally, after a heart attack, Ward seems to be ceding management of his company to the opportunistic Savage.

Moran, Maggie. *Breathing Lessons.* Anne Tyler. 1988.

Maggie Moran has always felt that through small lies and timely interaction she could shape the lives of her friends and family. But as her husband tells her, sometimes it's best to stand back and leave well enough alone. The wisdom of his advice becomes clear one eventful day.

An impulsive woman, Maggie has always been a meddler. On at least one occasion her tendency to jump at the chance to involve herself in the lives of others actually yielded good results. Someone told her when she was young that Ira Moran, a fellow singer in the church choir, had been killed in an accident in boot camp. Maggie barely knew Ira, but she began to remember, after hearing the news, how attractive he was. Silent, calm, and mysterious, Ira was much more interesting, it dawned on Maggie, than her fiancé. She decided to send a sympathy note to his father. Weeks went by, but she received no reply.

Then she discovered why. Ira appeared at choir practice, and Maggie was informed that it was someone else who had died. Although chagrined, Maggie was of course happy that Ira was really alive. As time passed it became clear that the things Maggie had written in her sympathy note—that Ira was wonderful and special—were indeed true. By the time Ira and Maggie sang a duet at the wedding of Maggie's friend Serena, both of them knew that their own wedding would not be far off.

But marriage to the exasperatingly calm Ira was not without problems for Maggie. Because she is a bit accident prone, especially with their car, she feels that Ira, although loving, is always judging her. As they drive from their Baltimore home to the funeral of Serena's husband, Maggie becomes so upset that she has Ira stop the car so she can get out. She walks back to a convenience store, angrily making plans to leave Ira for good and find a better job than the one she holds as a helper in a nursing home. Just as she begins to realize that life on her own would be difficult, Ira appears, and without mentioning their spat, the two continue on their trip.

Coming back from the funeral, Maggie insists that they stop to visit their son Jesse's ex-wife and daughter. Because she had convinced the then-pregnant Fiona to marry Jesse rather than have an abortion, Maggie feels responsible for the marriage and sad about its breakup. Always convinced that she can straighten out everyone's problems, Maggie believes that she can reunite the two. She believes their breakup was all a misunderstanding; they only need to be in the same room to realize they still love each other. When

Fiona agrees to visit the Morans' house for the weekend, Maggie is ecstatic. She phones Jesse and invites him to dinner, all but telling her son that his ex-wife is ready to return to him.

Predictably, the evening is a disaster. All the evidence that Maggie had embellished and offered to Fiona as proof that Jesse still loves her is spurned by Fiona and balked at by Jesse. The final blow comes when Ira says that Jesse doesn't sleep with Fiona's old tortoise-shell soap dish, as Maggie claimed, but with a series of women. Later that night, after Jesse has gone to his apartment and Fiona has escaped to her sister's, Maggie feels foolish for having engineered this disastrous evening. Even so, Ira has trouble getting Maggie to promise not to ask Fiona if their granddaughter can live with them for a year. Feeling wistful but somehow content, Maggie goes to sleep.

More, Thomas. *Love in the Ruins.* Walker Percy. 1971.

Thomas More is a psychiatrist who tries to rescue the United States from the disastrous misuse of his own invention, the "lapsometer," which Tom "the first caliper of the soul." It measures the gap that divides a person's social self from his or her true spirit, and Tom is convinced that this division is destroying Western man.

In his early days as a doctor, Tom marries Doris, a beauty queen from Georgia, and has a daughter, Samantha. They live a pleasant, orderly life in the wealthy section of a Louisiana town called Paradise. With the help of weekly visits to the Catholic church, Tom, accompanied by Samantha, is able to control his excessive love of drinking and women. When Samantha dies at age fourteen, however, her devastated parents address their sorrow in opposite ways. While Doris chooses the spiritual path and begins to study Eastern religions, Tom turns to drink. He becomes "coarse and disorderly," and Doris leaves him after a year.

After Doris's departure, Tom continues to ease his depressions and intensify his phases of elation with alcohol. Apparently irresistible to women, he has three simultaneous affairs with women who are half his age. During this period Tom constructs the first model of his lapsometer and tries it out on various patients. Despite the supposed effectiveness of his invention, Tom himself becomes increasingly ill and wakes one Christmas morning to find his wrists slashed and bleeding. He commits himself to a mental institution and spends several happy months there. Liberated from his extreme mood swings, he is able to continue working on his invention and is accorded the unusual status of "doctor/patient."

When Tom leaves the hospital in order to continue his research, the director of the hospital regards him as an escaped patient and prevents him from applying for grants and publishing his findings. In his disappointment, Tom turns to Art Immelmann, a suspicious character who has been trying to persuade Tom to sign a contract that would permit the government to use the lapsometer indiscriminately. Art demonstrates his own discovery: The lapsometer, when adjusted in a particular way, can also treat the disease it diagnoses. Using the machine, Art stimulates the area of Tom's brain he calls the "musical-erotic," causing him to experience an overwhelming ecstasy. Tom signs the contract.

During the days that follow, chaos ensues. Art begins randomly distributing the machines, set so that they will provoke people to violent fighting or passionate love-making. In the confusion, a revolution begins, and an African-American organization called the Bantus takes over Paradise. Tom emerges reluctantly from his hiding place in an abandoned Howard Johnson's hotel, where he has been protecting his three girlfriends, to warn people of a possible disaster due to a cloud of Heavy Sodium vapor. Heavy Sodium, Tom discovered in an early investigation, can also cause a psychotic break leading to violent and unpredictable behavior. The inhabitants of Paradise refuse to heed his warnings, and subsequently the Bantus revolution succeeds.

In the post-revolution years, Tom marries Ellen Oglethorpe, one of his three girlfriends, and raises a family. Now living in a section of town called the Slave Quarters, he leads a sober and very modest life. He continues to do research on the ailments of the soul, although in Bantu-controlled society he cannot hope to achieve recognition. On the day before Christmas, he goes to confession for the first time in eleven years, returns home to have six quick drinks, and falls into bed with his wife.

Moreen, Morgan. "The Pupil." Henry James. 1892.

Morgan Moreen, a "supernaturally clever" child, is the youngest member of an eccentric family of American expatriates. Although the Moreens—the parents, two sisters, and another brother—seem to dote on Morgan, their showy affection actually disguises anxiety and suspicion.

The Moreens' strained relationship with Morgan is due in part to his serious illness. Morgan has a heart condition that has threatened his health since birth. Unfit for customary schooling, the child is placed instead in the hands of nurses and tutors. Morgan is never exposed to the structures and formulas of traditional education but nevertheless learns an astonishing amount simply by accompanying his sophisticated family in their wanderings through Europe. The result is a mind of unusual refinement and sensitivity, a temperament suited to "intellectual gymnastics," and an elegant humor.

When Morgan is eleven years old, his family hires PEMBERTON, a recent graduate of Oxford, to take charge of his education. Upon their introduction, Pemberton finds Morgan's intelligence somewhat intimidating: The child instantly throws off a series of ingenious and disarmingly frank remarks. Mrs. Moreen, looking on, informs the new tutor that his quaint sallies are the delight of the family.

Shortly after Pemberton's arrival, all responsibility for Morgan is transferred to the tutor. Rather than feeling hurt at being shunted aside, Morgan is relieved and proud. The friendship between the two flourishes. They carry on their studies as the family migrates from Nice to Venice to Paris. In each city Morgan strolls through the parks and museums with his preceptor, chatting amiably and philosophically. In contrast, Morgan is austere and distant toward his family.

The elder Moreens occupy their time with dressing up and seeing people, preferably those with a certain social standing. Because Morgan does not figure in their social strategy and because his family is secretly in serious financial straits, the boy's appearance is neglected until he resembles a homeless child. This effect of the Moreens' financial problem does not trouble Morgan, but other consequences disturb him immensely. When he begins to suspect that his parents are refusing to pay Pemberton, Morgan relates to his friend a similar incident involving Zenobie, a beloved nurse. Not only had they failed to pay her, but they accused Zenobie of lying. This incident, Morgan explains to Pemberton, is the reason he is unwilling to speak to his family.

When his parents continue to withhold Pemberton's pay, Morgan stoically encourages his friend to find a new position. Now fifteen, Morgan hopes to leave home soon and attend Oxford. After his teacher's departure, however, he experiences a relapse of his illness, loses weight, and has difficulty breathing. A desperate letter from Mrs. Moreen brings Pemberton back, and in spite of his shame, Morgan is grateful. For a brief period they relive their pleasant days in Paris together. Then a decisive financial crisis strikes the Moreens. Morgan and Pemberton return from a walk to find the apartment in disarray. Mr. and Mrs. Moreen confront Pemberton, requesting that he take Morgan away and care for him. As his parents and his tutor stand facing one another, neither willing to take on the responsibility of his care, Morgan has a heart attack and collapses. Over Morgan's body, his parents debate about whether he had wished to stay with them or not.

Moreland, Eulalia Hastings "Eula." *The Planter's Northern Bride.* Caroline Lee Hentz. 1854.

Eulalia Hastings is admired and loved by all the townsfolk and known in the small New England town of her birth as "the Village Flower." Her father, an outspoken abolitionist, has taught her that blacks are the equals of whites, but she has never been entirely convinced of it. Eula is an obedient and dutiful daughter and never voices her doubts to her father, but when the slaveholding planter RUSSELL MORELAND arrives in town with his slave, she does not resist his advances.

Moreland first spots Eula in church one Sunday while she is singing in the choir. He instantly falls in love with her voice and purity, and contrives various means to make her acquaintance. She recognizes his obvious superiority over other men yet fears her father's opposition to their union. Mr. Hastings is the editor of *The Emancipator*, a famous abolitionist journal, and he has sworn that "he would rather a daughter of his should be laid in the deepest grave of New England than be wedded to a Southern slaveholder." Nevertheless, Moreland lingers with his slave Albert in order to woo the willing Eula. At first her father will not agree to the marriage, but when Moreland nearly dies from the shock of his refusal and when Eula also falls ill, he relents and the two have a simple wedding.

They travel by steamboat to Moreland's native Georgia. Eula is impressed by her husband's masterfulness, and he is obviously adored by his slaves and family. Eula feels so much reverence for her husband that she cannot bear to call him by his first name and instead refers to him as "Moreland." Eula is an ideal wife, mistress, and mother; her gentle moral influence even succeeds in taming Effie, Moreland's willful daughter by a previous marriage.

One day Moreland's selfish, intransigent ex-wife Claudia comes to their house. Eula receives her coldly, declaring that the woman has forfeited her position as wife and mother and is henceforward excluded from "the social privileges she has wantonly abused." Effie stumbles into the confrontation, and a tug-of-war over the child ensues. Eula tells Claudia that Moreland has committed Effie to her guardianship and abjured Claudia's own maternal right. Claudia leaves, defeated.

Things go well for Eula in Georgia until the Reverend Brainard, a professed missionary to "the Negro," joins their society. Brainard is in fact an abolitionist in disguise. He convinces Moreland's slaves to revolt and provides arms for this purpose. Moreland intervenes, and the conspiracy fails.

In the North, in the company of Brainard, Vulcan, an escaped slave from Moreland's plantation, speaks out against slavery. When Moreland and Eula return to New England to visit her family, Moreland publicly confronts Vulcan, who admits that all his stories of torture on the plantation are lies. Vulcan begs to be returned to slavery, but Moreland refuses him. Eula's father, a witness to this confrontation, is so impressed by Moreland's conduct that he finally accepts him, proudly asserting, "There are few such men anywhere as Mr. Moreland." Eula is content; the two most important people in her life are finally at peace with each other. She returns to the plantation with her husband, eager to live out the life that Moreland insists she was born to assume: as a gentle but firm mistress of slaves and a devoted, grateful wife to her husband.

Moreland, Russell. *The Planter's Northern Bride.* Caroline Lee Hentz. 1854.

Russell Moreland is an aristocratic slaveholding planter from Georgia. He embodies his era's ideal of a southern gentleman: He is a kind, liberal master to his slaves, and

he surpasses all other men in looks, breeding, manners, intellect, temperament, and wealth. An ardent supporter of the plantation system, Moreland proclaims that "God has not made all men equal, though men wiser than God would have it so. Inequality is one of nature's laws."

When the story opens, Moreland is traveling in New England with his mulatto slave Albert. Moreland and Albert share a relationship similar to that of a benevolent master and a dumb, loyal puppy. When the innkeeper of the town, an abolitionist, insists that Albert eat dinner with the other guests, Albert is dumbfounded and hesitant. Moreland orders his slave to comply, although he himself is unwilling to dine under such an arrangement and leaves in a huff. Outside he encounters Nancy, a white woman who, though young, is frail and sickly from years of hard labor. Moreland contrasts her unfortunate situation with that of the luckier slave. Throughout his visit in the North, Moreland reflects on the merits of the South's slavery and becomes a spokesman for slavery in the New England village. He calmly combats the Northerners' criticisms and is bemused by their hysteria over the issue.

One day Moreland sees and falls instantly in love with EULALIA "EULA" HASTINGS (MORELAND), and eventually he weds this "Flower of the Village" and daughter of Mr. Hastings, an outspoken abolitionist and editor of *The Emancipator*. Moreland is determined to soften the abolitionist's heart and win his daughter. When he publicly debates the issue of slavery, Hastings is unable to counter his arguments; despite Moreland's triumph, when the planter requests Eulalia's hand in marriage, Hastings initially forbids it. He concedes, however, when Moreland nearly faints from the shock of Hastings's refusal. Moreland and Eulalia have a simple wedding, then travel by steamboat to Moreland's Georgian home.

The couple share several years of bliss and have a son. One day a stranger introduces himself to them as the Reverend Brainard, a missionary to the blacks. Brainard is in fact an incendiary abolitionist who gradually convinces all the slaves to revolt against Moreland, and he provides them with arms. Two slaves are arrested when they break into a bank to finance this scheme, and the jailer's wife overhears the prisoners as they discuss the details of the plot. When Moreland is told about the conspiracy, he goes to the plantation, where his commanding presence and oration subdue all but the blacksmith, Vulcan, who is beaten into submission by one of the other slaves.

Vulcan eventually escapes to the North in the company of Brainard. The two begin to speak in public against slavery. When Moreland and Eulalia travel north to visit her family, Moreland, in a fury, listens to the two speak about the tortures of slavery. Vulcan lies to the audience by giving them fictionalized accounts of the abuses he suffered. Ever the gentleman, Moreland controls his wrath, but the devoted Albert cannot bear to hear such lies about his master. Albert's emotional outburst forces Moreland to confront Brainard and Vulcan, and Moreland publicly exposes Brainard as a liar. Vulcan begs to be taken back as Moreland's slave, but the slaveholder refuses, leaving Vulcan to fend for himself. Having finally won the approval of his abolitionist father-in-law and of the northern village, Moreland then returns to the South with his wife and slave.

Morgan, Constance. *Pictures from an Institution.* Randall Jarrell. 1954.

Constance Morgan is the daughter of a professor at Benton, a small women's college in the Northeast. After her father died, she was forced to live with her grandmother. Growing up, she had very few friends her own age; she associated mostly with faculty members at Benton who were friends of her father. Constance went away to school for four years, studying to be a classical pianist; by the time she returned, her grandmother had died, leaving her entirely alone in the world. After realizing that people who major in music don't all become concert pianists, Constance, depressed and not wanting to accept the responsibilities of adulthood, returns to Benton College, where she accepts a job as the assistant to the secretary of the president.

Constance is very lonely during her first months back at Benton. She feels most comfortable around older men and women, who seem to her to represent real life. Looking for a suitable man or woman to befriend, she spends most of her first months taking long walks around the campus. After a while Constance befriends Gottfried Rosenbaum, a composer-in-residence at Benton, and his wife Irene. The affable old professor, a Jewish refugee from Austria, begins to teach Constance German and helps her with elaborate musical compositions. Constance soon begins going in and out of the Rosenbaum house as if it were her own, and she spends hours browsing through their extensive library or listening to one of their scores of records.

Constance's bliss with the Rosenbaums comes to a sudden halt, however, when GERTRUDE JOHNSON, a visiting novelist, begins to spread rumors that Constance—who, along with Dr. Rosenbaum, has become a character in Gertrude's latest novel—is having an affair with the venerable old professor. Horrified at the thought of doing anything that would bring embarrassment or shame to the couple who have shown her so much kindness, Constance confronts Gertrude on campus one day and asks her not to talk about her or Dr. Rosenbaum. But the innocent young Constance is no match for the cynical, outspoken older woman, who delivers a few scathing insults and walks away.

Much to Constance's relief, the Rosenbaums view Gertrude's insinuation with humor and beg her not to worry about the scandal that is bound to ensue. As a show of their loyalty and affection for her, Dr. Rosenbaum offers Constance a position with them as his personal secretary at the year's end when he and his wife will be returning to Europe. Given the opportunity to enjoy a few more precious years of freedom before growing up, Constance leaves Benton to join the Rosenbaums and travel abroad.

Morgan, Emma Lou. *The Blacker the Berry . . .* Wallace Thurman. 1929.

Emma Lou Morgan is a young black woman ostracized by both the African-American and Caucasian communities of her hometown due to the extremely dark hue of her skin. As a member of a family that prides itself on being the founders of the "blue vein circle" of blacks in Boise, Idaho, Emma Lou becomes brainwashed and snobbish. Although she can accept her ethnicity, she desperately wishes that her skin color were less black, for even among people of color, a lighter complexion is valued above any intrinsic personal qualities. Due to the extreme racial homogeneity in post–World War I Boise, Emma Lou is the only black student in her high school and is tortured by feelings of isolation, which she hopes to escape by attending college at the University of Southern California in Los Angeles. She finds, however, that boundaries of prejudice are rigid even in the city, and she continues to be plagued by her skin color as she tries to gain social acceptance and emotional fulfillment.

Emma Lou's initial reaction to black culture in Los Angeles is one of excitement and awe. But her aspirations to be accepted into the general milieu of African-American life on campus are thwarted both by her own refusal to mix with people with darker skin colors and a general dismissal of her social desirability by the supposedly privileged "blue vein" students. After three years as a successful student with a dismal personal life, Emma Lou decides to abandon Los Angeles for Harlem.

Once in Harlem, Emma Lou continues her search for a lighter-skinned community whose acceptance will somehow erase the stigma of her skin color. But when she is forced to seek menial employment in agencies that consistently humiliate her, she begins to doubt the wisdom of her move. Her demeaning jobs include acting as a maid to a white woman named Arline Strange, who plays the part of the "mulatto Carmen" in a melodrama purporting to depict black life in Harlem. Ironically, while Emma Lou applies bleaching face cream and lemon rinse to her face in order to appear less black, she must assist Arline in darkening her appearance to suit the role of a black Harlemite.

Hoping to assuage her loneliness, Emma Lou eventually finds a man whose color suits her and who is willing to "date" her. Alva is a hustler who prides himself on sponging money from the gullible. Emma Lou naively falls prey to his wiles; only after endless episodes of abuse is she able to break off their debilitating relationship.

Vowing to build a new life for herself, Emma Lou enrolls in courses at City College and Teacher's College, and eventually passes the Public School Teacher's exam. During this more ambitious phase of her life, she learns that one of Alva's paramours has left him with a physically and mentally impaired child. Thinking herself still in love with Alva, Emma Lou decides to move in to care for him and the child.

As she tries to work and care for both the child and Alva, who remains irresponsible and exploitative, Emma Lou experiences an epiphany. She realizes that her victimization is the result of her enslavement to the idol of the blue vein motto—"whiter and whiter every generation." This motto also lies at the root of her attraction to Alva. Steeled by this newfound self-awareness, Emma Lou is finally able to grasp the extent to which he has used her as his benefactor and nursemaid. Forcing herself to turn a deaf ear to the loud, pathetic cries of Alva Junior, she abandons Alva and, with him, her life of servitude to intraracial prejudice.

Morgan, Hank. *A Connecticut Yankee in King Arthur's Court.* Samuel L. Clemens (Mark Twain). 1889.

Knocked unconscious in the nineteenth century, Hank Morgan awakens in sixth-century England, during the reign of King Arthur. Threatened with imprisonment or execution, he recalls that a solar eclipse is imminent, and he stages it as his own work of necromancy. He humbles the court magician, Merlin, and astonishes the entire kingdom. The eclipse is the first of several supposed miracles performed by Hank. For example, in order to prove his powers greater than Merlin's, he dynamites the druid's tower. Later, with much fanfare, he restores water to a holy well.

For his services, King Arthur confers on him the honorary title of "The Boss." As Boss, Hank attempts to upgrade sixth-century life. He opens Camelot's first factory, producing everything from soap (of little use to these medieval Britons) to top hats and bicycles. He equips knights of the round table with sandwich-board signs to advertise his wares. He threads the kingdom with telephone wire, establishes a military academy, and starts the first newspaper.

Although Hank never becomes a knight, he must nevertheless prove himself through errantry. Thus, he ventures out in the company of the Lady Alisande ("Sandy," later his wife) to vanquish the ogres who have captured a number of her noble friends. When the ogres turn out to be swineherds, and the ladies, pigs, the courageous but wary Hank is relieved. Later, settling an old grudge against Sir Sagramor le Desirous, he faces all of Arthur's knights on the field of honor and puts them to flight, armed with nothing but a pair of revolvers.

For part of the novel Arthur himself accompanies Hank during his wanderings through the country. They are both disguised as commoners. When the king tries to mix with a group of farmers and reveals his utter ignorance of daily affairs, the two are mistaken for madmen and sold into slavery. Through it all, Hank is able to demonstrate to his liege some of the miseries of the life of commoners. Finally, facing execution for an attack on a slave-driver, the two are rescued by Arthur's knights, who have hastened to the spot on bicycles.

All goes well for Hank until a dispute in his stock exchange escalates into a war between the king and Sir Launcelot, the queen's lover. When Arthur dies, the Church marshals the remaining knights against The Boss. Hank, aided only by his close assistant Clarence and a few loyal progressive thinkers, takes protection in a cave surrounded by electrical wires. When the iron-clad knights attack, they are broiled silently in their armor, ghastly victims of nineteenth-century ingenuity.

After the battle, Hank's old nemesis, Merlin, casts a spell on him that puts him to sleep for another thirteen centuries. When he reawakens, he tells his strange tale to an unnamed American author.

Moriarty, Dean. *On the Road.* Jack Kerouac. 1955.

Dean Moriarty, a handsome blue-eyed drifter, captivates his friend SALVATORE PARADISE, who believes that they "understand each other on other levels of madness." For Dean, sex is the most important thing in life, and he leaves behind a trail of lovers, wives, and children as he crisscrosses America.

Born in the backseat of his parents' car, Dean spends his youth in and out of reform schools, stealing cars, and conning to survive. He goes to new York with his first wife Marylou and tells Sal that he wants to be a writer. Sal introduces him to Carlo Marx, a brooding intellectual, and the three spend long evenings discussing literature and philosophy. After working for some time as a parking lot attendant, Dean has a falling out with Marylou and leaves her to spend a year with Carlo in Denver, listening to jazz and chasing women. There Dean meets Camille, the woman who will become his second wife, and the two set off together for San Francisco.

At Christmas, Dean appears with Marylou on Sal's doorstep in New Jersey. They stay there for a while before deciding to join Sal and his friends on a road trip to New Orleans and San Francisco. Upon arriving in San Francisco, Dean disappears for a week, leaving Sal and Marylou alone in the city. When Dean returns, the three pass a few more nights bar-hopping, until Sal decides to leave for home, and they go their separate ways.

In 1949, Sal returns to San Francisco and looks up Dean, who has divorced Marylou and is now living with Camille and their child. But once again Dean and Camille are having problems, and Dean soon convinces Sal to go out on the road with him. After they are hired to drive a limousine to Chicago, Dean and Sal hitchhike back to New

York and make plans to go to Italy. However, Dean receives word that Camille has given birth to another child, and he decides to return to San Francisco to try to patch up his life with Camille.

When he reappears, this time in Denver, Dean convinces Sal and their friend Stan Shepard to come with him on a trip to Mexico. The three travel across the border, drinking, smoking marijuana, and sleeping with prostitutes as they go. One day Dean simply picks up and returns to the United States, leaving Sal and Stan to make their way back on their own.

Some time later Dean shows up once more in New York. He tells Sal that he had tried to find Marylou but wound up wandering around the country. Now tired and ravaged, he stays with Sal for a short time, then receives word from Camille that she is patiently awaiting his return. He says a final good-bye to Sal and begins to make his way to start over with Camille.

Morison, Peter "Bunny." *They Came Like Swallows.* William Maxwell. 1937.

Peter "Bunny" Morison is a shy eight-year-old boy. In the fall of 1918, Bunny's family experiences a series of crises caused by the outbreak of Spanish influenza in their Illinois town.

A melancholy and nervous child, Bunny dotes on his gentle mother Elizabeth. Needing her love desperately, he is unhappy whenever he is apart from her. The child prefers to play inside, close to his mother, rather than engage in outdoor competitive games such as baseball or marble shooting. When Elizabeth tells him she is going to have another baby, Bunny reacts with suspicion and sadness.

Unlike his brother Robert, who is popular and athletic despite having only one leg, Bunny is quiet and has few friends. Robert has little sympathy for his introverted younger brother. After saving Bunny from a beating at the hands of the neighborhood bully, he cruelly berates him for being unable to defend himself. Scared and jealous of Robert, Bunny is convinced at times that his mother loves Robert more than she loves him.

Bunny is the first member of the Morison family to come down with the Spanish flu. He starts to feel dizzy the day that his father tells him that, thanks to Germany's surrender in the European war, he does not have to go to school that day. While the family prepares to go to a local parade, Bunny becomes drained of energy. When the sick child puts his head on her lap, Elizabeth notices that he is burning with fever. Concerned, she sends him to bed.

Elizabeth's husband tells the pregnant woman to stay out of Bunny's sick room lest she come down with the disease herself. Elizabeth follows her husband's instructions until a swallow flies into Bunny's room and frightens him. Elizabeth rushes in to comfort her son, and soon afterward he recovers, perhaps strengthened by her attention.

Because she experienced complications during the births of her first two children, Elizabeth goes to Decatur to deliver her baby with the help of a specialist, James, who accompanies her. While their parents are away, Bunny and Robert stay with family, and Robert eventually falls ill. Just as he is recovering, word comes from Decatur that the baby has been born but that both Elizabeth and James are very sick. Bunny knows nothing of this until his aunt Clara tells him that his mother is dead. The boy is devastated.

Elizabeth's sister, Aunt Irene, worries about Bunny because she knows how close he was to his mother. She decides to move in with the Morisons and look after James and the children, especially Bunny, who clearly needs a maternal figure to love and to love him.

Morningstar, Marjorie. *Marjorie Morningstar.* Herman Wouk. 1955.

At seventeen, Marjorie Morningstar, naive and already strikingly beautiful, decides that she wants to be an actress, so she changes her name from Morgenstern to one she believes is more theatrical. Although born in the Bronx, Marjorie now lives with her parents and her brother Seth in a spacious apartment in the El Dorado on Central Park West in New York City. Marjorie has begun to study biology in college but decides to switch her focus to acting, something for which she has a natural talent. Her parents, who immigrated to the United States in their youth, have radically different plans for their daughter, namely, an early and successful marriage. Nonetheless, Marjorie spurns a marriage proposal from her longtime boyfriend George Drobes in order to pursue her own goals. After enrolling in acting classes at New York University and in playwriting at Columbia University, she eventually settles on Hunter College for her education.

At Hunter, Marjorie becomes involved in the school's drama productions and meets the plump but vivacious Marsha Zelenko, who slowly introduces her new friend to a broader social and cultural world. This friendship has an added attraction: Marsha's mother, who is involved in the theater, is able to introduce her daughter and her friends to theater figures. It is through Marsha's intervention that Marjorie gets a summer job in a theater camp across the lake from the notorious resort of South Wind. Once the young women arrive at the camp, Marsha immediately begins to sneak over to South Wind where, among other things, there is a large theatrical company. She eventually succeeds in bullying a petrified Marjorie into joining her, and Marjorie meets the infamous and womanizing lyricist/composer NOEL AIRMAN. She is irresistibly drawn to Noel but is too shy to confront him directly, so Marsha introduces them.

The next several years see a variety of changes: The Depression forces the Morgensterns to leave their large and well-staffed apartment, Marjorie graduates from college and begins to hunt for acting roles, and a strong but tension-filled relationship develops between her and Noel. He is approximately ten years older than Marjorie and keeps his distance, insisting that there is no need for marriage. Marjorie tries to elicit Noel's approval of her acting talent, but he is frequently unenthusiastic. The relationship begins to sour, and Noel breaks up with Marjorie. While she is still interested in acting, Marjorie gets few real job offers, and when she does, the plays seem to close. She eventually resumes her relationship with Noel, and they finally consummate their affair. At the same time, Noel is virtually ready to finish a new musical that Marjorie loves. A year later the show opens but fails miserably; simultaneously, Marjorie loses yet another acting job. She decides to work in her father's office in order to earn the money to go to Paris to convince Noel to marry her.

When Noel finally does propose, nearly a year later, Marjorie declines; she has realized the unlikelihood of happiness with him. After this, Marjorie marries a successful doctor named Milton Schwartz. Some fifteen years later, Marjorie is seen presiding over a family that consists of three children, and her ambition to act remains a thing of the past.

Morrissey, Jack. *Do with Me What You Will.* Joyce Carol Oates. 1973.

Jack Morrissey, a young and liberal-minded lawyer, is introduced to the workings of the law when he is only fifteen and his father commits a shocking murder. For Jack, this is the last in a series of events that have undermined his family ever since the birth of his younger brother Robert, who never matured enough to care for himself. It is Robert's accidental death that precipitates Jack's father's apparent insanity, which results in the murder of the man on whose property Robert's death occurred. During the legal maneuverings that follow, Jack becomes very close to his father's attorney, MARVIN HOWE, who is already gaining fame for his success with difficult cases, and Howe manages to win an acquittal on the grounds of temporary insanity. Jack has become enamored of Howe for his masculine power and authority, but eventually these feelings turn to hatred as the young boy realizes that his father was in fact guilty.

After finishing college and law school, Jack becomes involved in the civil rights movement of the mid-1960s, and he travels to the South to participate in the legal work that followed the strikes and boycotts held to end segregation. While in the South, he meets Rachel, an impassioned young woman who urges him on to greater commitment. The two activists eventually leave the South, marry, and settle in Detroit, where Jack engages in law for the Legal Aid office, and Rachel finishes her studies as a social worker. Things go well for the young couple, and they move from a dilapidated apartment to one that is more comfortable for both of them. They decide not to

have children since they both view the world as a foul place that is in need of no more new lives; after a number of years, however, they choose to adopt a child. As these plans get under way, tension develops in the marriage alongside increased pressure in Jack's professional life. He takes on an extremely difficult case that involves police entrapment of the defendant. The case is politically charged, and his efforts are chronically stymied by the collective effort of the judicial system and the prosecution. Jack loses the case.

While Jack is engaged in this defense, he encounters ELENA ROSS HOWE, who has been married to the much older Marvin for nearly ten years. Jack is instantly captivated by her beauty, and when she calls him after he has assisted her home following an apparent spell or attack, he immediately flies to California where she has been sent by her husband. The two make love, and for Jack it is the most thrilling thing he has ever done—especially since, as he says, he doesn't get caught. After Elena returns to Detroit, the couple resumes their physical relationship and gradually a sense of love develops, although they do not seem ready to make a decisive move to leave their spouses.

Meanwhile, Jack tells Elena that a decision must be made because the adoption is pending, but Elena refuses either to ask him to stop the adoption or to speak to her husband. Jack feels that the affair is over, and he and Rachel adopt a three-year-old boy. Elena suffers a nervous breakdown and relocates to Maine with her husband, who knows about the affair. She resides here for a while, and Jack remains in Detroit, attempting to adjust to the new duties of fatherhood.

The uneasy calm between Rachel and Jack is disrupted when Elena reappears. Having left her husband, Elena expects a reconciliation with Jack, but even though Rachel taunts him with her knowledge of his infidelity, Jack refuses to abandon his family. He and Rachel determine to build a future together despite their present problems.

Morse, Hazel. "Big Blonde." Dorothy Parker. 1930.

Hazel Morse is the buxom blonde protagonist in this bleak short story set in New York City. Following her widowed mother's death, Hazel supports herself by modeling in a wholesale dress shop. A contented woman who is not given to pondering the possibility of improving the quality of her life, Hazel appreciates her popularity with the men she meets on the job. After working at the dress establishment for a number of years and losing her good looks as she approaches thirty, Hazel decides that she has had her fill of dating. She marries Herbie Morse, a handsome, amusing man whose ample salary allows her to quit her job.

For the first few months of her marriage, Hazel lives happily in the uptown apartment she shares with her fun-loving husband. But soon Herbie's delight in his wife changes into disgust; previously comforting and attentive to Hazel's tearful romanticism, Herbie now becomes increasingly annoyed with his wife's histrionics and calls her a crab. At the same time, Hazel's amusement at her husband's jocular drunken behavior turns into confusion about his increasing dependence on alcohol. Frustrated with their inability to get along with each other, Herbie starts spending nights away from home. An extremely unhappy Hazel takes to the bottle in order to drown her sorrows, and her decline into alcoholism begins.

When Mrs. Martin moves into the apartment adjacent to the Morses, Hazel befriends the woman's male friends, with whom she spends evenings flirting and partying. Hazel joins the group on the frequent nights that Herbie does not come home. Eventually she becomes intimate with a married out-of-towner named Ed who enjoys a bachelorlike existence in New York City during his frequent visits. When a fed-up Herbie abandons Hazel and moves to Detroit, Hazel and Ed become lovers. Ed showers her with presents, provides her with an allowance, and eventually rents her an apartment, complete with a maid. There, despite the constraints of Prohibition, Hazel lives a lazy life-style, concerned only with getting drunk.

When Ed moves to Florida after his three-year affair with Hazel, she goes through a series of men who support her in return for sexual favors. As she increasingly becomes a slave of alcohol, the days blur together into a meaningless series of drunken nights and hung-over mornings. Horribly depressed, she contemplates suicide with more frequency. Hazel finally attempts suicide by taking Veronal, an over-the-counter sedative. The maid discovers her unconscious and rushes her to the hospital. Hazel's stomach is pumped, and she regains consciousness two days later. The story ends with Hazel toasting her maid and downing yet another glass of scotch.

Morse, Ruth. *Martin Eden.* Jack London. 1909.

Ruth Morse is a young woman from a "good family" in Oakland, California, when she first meets MARTIN EDEN, a raw and crude man who has spent most of his young life at sea and at menial jobs. For Ruth, who is three years his senior, and who is about to finish her bachelor's degree, Martin is a fascinating and dangerous figure. She is instantly attracted to him and hopes to reform his character. She encourages him to see her again, and Martin soon begins to visit her regularly. While Ruth is unaware of his growing emotional attachment to her, she is fascinated by the rate at which he improves in education and deportment under her tutelage.

As Martin grows bold enough to suggest that he loves her, the relationship takes on new tones. Although she expects trouble ahead with her middle-class parents, Ruth agrees to marry him. The two become engaged, but her parents persuade them to keep the relationship private for a time while Martin tries to establish himself. Here the first major bone of contention arises between Ruth and her would-be husband. Ruth finds that although she loves him, she cannot really say that she likes his writing, even after he has nervously read aloud to her from his work. While some of the pieces are stirring, Ruth concedes their overall aspect is one of clumsiness. She further reasons that Martin will never by able to support them on a writer's income. Despite her misgivings, she agrees to wait two years for Martin to prove himself as a writer.

During the two years of Martin's apprenticeship, Ruth spends a good deal of time socializing with other young people. It has been her mother's plan all along that Ruth should be awakened to womanhood by the attractive and intelligent Martin, but it is equally important that Ruth not err by marrying below her station. Ruth remains steadfast in her love for Martin but worries increasingly that finances will prevent the marriage. Before this can happen, however, Ruth and her family are chagrined to find that Martin has appeared on the front page of the papers as a leading socialist speaker. Outraged, the Morses immediately insist that Ruth break off her engagement. Despite the love she has professed for Martin, Ruth writes him a letter detailing the specific reasons why she must end their relationship for her family's sake. She also insists that Martin make no effort to see her since he is no longer welcome at her house. When Martin writes back, Ruth does not respond, and when he shows up at her home and asks her if she loves him, she simply shakes her head "no."

For the next several months there is no contact between them; then, after Martin has become suddenly and resoundingly famous, Ruth appears at his hotel room. She pleads with him to resume their relationship. Recognizing that Ruth has been encouraged to come by her parents, the embittered and now rich young man rejects her and reminds her that he himself has not changed. The reunion ends badly, and Martin, in silence, walks the shocked and disappointed Ruth to her home.

Mosby, Willis. *Mosby's Memoirs.* Saul Bellow. 1968.

Willis Mosby writes his memoirs in Oaxaca, Mexico. During a life spent in academia and the U.S. Foreign Service, Mosby lived through the Spanish Revolution, World War II, and the advent of East-West polarization. With an international and intellectual eye he surveys the successes of his life and recalls his controversial conservative views, but finally feels crushed by the weight of his own opinions.

Mosby sips mescal in a café and jots notes for the next chapter of his memoirs while he waits for a tour car to some Toltec ruins. He decides that he must inject some levity after the heavy chapters of intellectual evolution and outspoken positions. He recalls his life in Paris in 1947 and muses on the state of postwar Europe. He considers the sad state of mankind and bumbling politicians. When the waiter tells him when the tour will be leaving, Mosby jokingly calls himself a ruin. He remembers his meetings with famous intellectuals in Spain and France.

Then he remembers a man, Hymen Lustgarten, a Jew and ex-socialist from New Jersey who went to postwar Paris to make his fortune. Suddenly inspired, Mosby thinks he has found a comic character to lighten his memoirs. Lustgarten, incompetent yet persistent, dealt on the black market, trying various schemes to get rich, but failed when he was cheated by a German partner. Lustgarten then tried to import a Cadillac, but import regulations went into effect the day it arrived. He was so poor that he had to live in the car; when he received a generous offer for it, he crashed on his way to deliver it. Lustgarten's pretty wife Trudy left him, and he went off to Tito's Yugoslavia as a foreign VIP to witness the growth of socialism.

Mosby's thoughts turn again to his political opinions, pondering the foolish behavior of both the Right and the Left. He considers his disappointment in other conservative thinkers and recalls his forced early retirement from Princeton for his views. Mosby weighs his own memoirs against those of other famous intellectuals, and his mind wanders back to Lustgarten, who, after returning from Yugoslavia, told of his conscription into a labor brigade and the appalling conditions he endured. Years later in New York, when Mosby met him on an elevator, Lustgarten wanted to sell the story of his business success in Algeria to *Fortune* magazine.

The tour car leaves. Two Welsh women are the only other tourists. The first stop is at Tule, a small church with an ancient green cypress that inspires Mosby to ponder early man. The tour moves on to the temple ruins of Mitla, where Mosby begins to feel that he died long ago but continues to live. Recalling his affair with Lustgarten's wife, he realizes that Lustgarten was a doomed anachronism and marvels that he chose such a character to lighten his memoirs. They descend into a temple as the guide describes the life that used to animate the stones. Mosby considers how he created himself with dictums, positions, and viewpoints that built up like the huge stones of the ruins around him. Mosby feels oppressed by the weight of his own polemics and, short of breath, heads for the daylight he sees at the end of the cave.

Moseby, Kit. *The Sheltering Sky.* Paul Bowles. 1949.

Kit Moseby has two distinct lives, one before the death of her husband and the other immediately following his death. During her first life she spends twelve years of marriage accompanying her husband Port in his travels and seldom knowing a stationary existence. Presently she finds herself with Port and a mutual friend, Tanner, in North Africa, one of the few places they could get passage to by boat at the end of World War II.

A woman who is mindful of omens, Kit often feels overwhelmed and entrapped rather than aided by these signs. In her relationships with others, the consideration of omens reaches obsessive proportions. She will spend hours analyzing the meaning of minute details: a gesture, sentence, facial expression, or vocal inflection.

Of all Kit's relationships, her marriage is the most troubling one because she lives completely for her husband, and he is continually retreating from her. Taking advantage of the triangular situation at hand, Kit decides to respond to Tanner's advances in the hope of catching Port's attention. Although Port is not consciously aware of any illicit affair, he finds himself increasingly interested in renewing his relationship with his wife, and he senses that Tanner's presence is a major obstacle. Port succeeds in losing Tanner temporarily by failing to meet him in a designated city, and he and Kit find themselves alone in a remote desert town.

Port becomes seriously ill, however, and there are no medical facilities in the area. Her husband's illness paralyzes Kit, and she begins to withdraw into herself as the outside world becomes more distant. At this point Tanner shows up, and Kit spends the night with him in order to escape the painful reality of Port's illness. That same night Port dies alone, overwhelming Kit with feelings of grief and guilt.

Seeking to escape from these feelings, Kit joins a caravan in its journey across the desert. On the first night of the trip, the two caravan leaders rape her, and as the journey continues, she becomes the exclusive and willing lover of the leader, Belqassim. After arriving at Belqassim's house, she becomes part of his harem. When his visits dwindle, however, it becomes clear that he has grown tried of her.

Kit eventually escapes from Belqassim's house and finds herself a new lover, who also serves temporarily as a shield her from reality. When this lover steals her money, it is clear that she finally must face the intolerable pain she has desperately fled during the preceding months. She flies back to a major city where Tanner is waiting, and plans are made for her to return to America. At the last minute Kit changes her mind: She disappears, seemingly insane, into the crowded streets.

Moss, Big Mat. *Blood on the Forge.* William Attaway. 1941.

Big Mat Moss, the eldest of three half-brothers, has a reputation as a humorless and frightfully strong man. Big Mat is a sharecropper and locally known for his abilities as a hog butcher. He and his wife Hattie share a modest home in the rocky hills of Kentucky with his two brothers, Chinatown and MELODY (MOSS). The family's revenue derives almost exclusively from Big Mat's labors, and their situation is bleak since Mat must work off a debt he owes to Mr. Johnston, who owns the farm they live on. A few weeks earlier, the Moss brothers' mother had died while plowing, and the mule dragged her body over the rocky soil until she was virtually unrecognizable. In his rage and grief, Big Mat destroyed the mule; now he struggles to recoup the loss. When Mr. Johnston's promise of a new mule is scorned by the "riding boss," Big Mat hits him, knocks him out, and takes off with one of the farmer's mules.

Big Mat realizes that will have to leave the area because of what he has done. Ironically, his brothers had already conversed with a white man who told them of jobs available for black men up north. At midnight the three brothers board a boxcar and head north. After a torturous train ride, they arrive in Pennsylvania's steel mill area and begin to work as mill hands. Despite his separation from his beloved Kentucky and from farming as a way of life, Big Mat is gratified by the sheer physicality of the hard mill work. Unfortunately, though, word comes that Hattie has suffered a fall and for the seventh year in a row has lost their child. This only reaffirms Big Mat's belief that God is testing him with a curse.

After Hattie's miscarriage is made known, Big Mat takes up with Anna, a Mexican prostitute; she soon refuses to sleep with him, and it appears that Melody loves her. Big Mat eventually becomes incapable of communicating with either his family or his mistress. He gives up reading his Bible and devotes himself to drinking and working. While racial prejudice has been a minor issue during the time Big Mat has been working at the mill, he gradually notices that things in the town are changing. He becomes aware of the growing movement for a union that finds the workers divided, with the blacks siding with management over the union. When another black man is beaten senseless for being an informer, Big Mat begins to think about ways to get satisfaction. He is deputized by the local sheriff, who actually fears his physical power. As soon as Big Mat is deputized, earning four extra dollars each day, he returns to the shack he shares with Anna, planning to straighten things out with her. He inadvertently learns that Anna has been working as a prostitute, and infuriated and disgusted by this news, Big Mat methodically and brutally beats her senseless. Still enraged, he leaves, seeking the sheriff and hoping for orders that will permit him to behave violently.

Big Mat gets his wish when he is told that he will be the one to lead the planned raid on the union office. He is delighted with the news and sets off ready for the kill. Once in the union office Big Mat provokes heated words, which escalate into physical violence. When the deputies arrive, the office is routed, and Big Mat fights out on the street over the body of a man he had unintentionally choked to death. But this time Big Mat fares poorly. A young boy attacks him with a pickax and is amazed when his huge opponent seems unaware of his injuries until,

abruptly, he falls down. The sheriff's other deputies find Big Mat's body later, and the sheriff observes, with a faint note of regret, that black deputies from the South always seem to end up this way—even the "good" ones.

Moss, Melody. *Blood on the Forge.* William Attaway. 1941.

Melody Moss, a musically inclined dreamer, is one of three half-brothers who share the home left by their mother on a Kentucky farm owned by the white Mr. Johnston. Melody, who expresses his feelings by strumming his guitar, or "box," was renamed by his mother when he was quite young because she recognized his devotion to and use of music. Like his brothers, he was born illegitimate, but this fact seems to cause him little unrest. His soul is that of a bluesman, and Melody handles most things that come his way by turning his thoughts and feelings into songs.

The first event in his life that stymies this ability is the sudden death of his mother and the bizarre way in which her body was abused by the mule that dragged it home over the rocky hills. Although Melody's grief is as profound as his brothers', he is physically overcome at the sight of her bloodied body and of the mule hacked apart by his brother. He cannot eat for days.

When a white man comes around talking of good jobs to be had in the North, Melody and his brother Chinatown decide to ask their older brother, BIG MAT (Moss), about the idea of going there for work. As it turns out, Big Mat has had an altercation and stolen a mule, and he needs to make an escape right away. The three brothers board a boxcar and endure a rough train ride to Pennsylvania, where they become steel mill workers. The alien terrain disturbs Melody, who quickly feels his innate music fading away. Soon Melody abandons his music, convinced that he can no longer play at all. Having also injured his hand at work, he wonders how deliberate the accident had been. By the time his hand heals, the calluses that enabled him to play well have softened to the point where he cannot play anymore.

In the meantime, Big Mat has abandoned his wife in favor of a liaison with Anna, a prostitute of Mexican ancestry. Big Mat moves into a shack with Anna, leaving his brothers in the all-male bunkhouse. Although Melody respects Big Mat, he cannot help his feelings for Anna, who had rejected him when he first met her, claiming he was a "sissy." Melody does eventually have sex once with Anna and is subsequently plagued with guilt for having betrayed his brother. The relationship between Big Mat and Anna is a violent and brutal one, and Melody is continually disturbed by it, especially after the brothers decide to live together. This leads to Chinatown's involvement in a serious accident at the steel mill in which fourteen men are killed and Chinatown is permanently blinded. Melody's responsibilities are increased by Chinatown's illness, and he gradually figures out that Anna, who has tended Chinatown, is also working as a prostitute. When Big Mat learns this, he beats Anna mercilessly; Melody looks on and does nothing to stop the beating.

Big Mat is eventually killed during a street fight between strikers and anti-union "deputies." After burying his brother, Melody quits his job in the mill and heads for Pittsburgh, as so many other black men have done in the preceding months, but he dreams of returning to his Kentucky homeland.

Motes, Hazel "Haze." *Wise Blood.* Flannery O'Connor. 1952.

Hazel "Haze" Motes is a young preacher from Tennessee who tries to found his own religion, The Church Without Christ. Having yearned since childhood for proof of God's existence, Haze perversely pursues a life of cruelty and sin. He has just been released from the army when he drifts into Taulkinham, a small southern city.

After arriving in Taulkinham, Haze takes a cab to an address he has copied from a bathroom wall and spends the night there with a prostitute named Leora Watts. The next evening he meets a blind preacher, Asa Hawks, and his fifteen-year-old daughter Sabbath who are handing out religious tracts downtown. Enoch Emery, a strange, scruffy eighteen-year-old onlooker, inexplicably attaches himself to Haze, and the two follow the preacher and daughter to another section of town. There, Haze tells the preacher that he doesn't believe in Jesus; he tries to tell passersby about his Church Without Christ, but they ignore him. That evening at Leora's, Haze remembers going to a peep show as a small boy. He had punished himself afterward by wearing stones in his shoes, but to no avail: He waited and waited, and no sign came.

The next morning, despite the fact that he has no driver's license, Haze buys a car. In order to get Asa's address, he goes to find Enoch at the zoo where he works. Enoch insists on first sharing his "secret" with Haze, and Haze impatiently follows him to a museum, where Enoch shows him the shrunken, embalmed body of a man beneath a glass case. When Haze abruptly leaves, Enoch chases him, but Haze knocks him down, throws a rock at his head, and escapes.

Haze finds Asa Hawks and his daughter and follows them to a boardinghouse, where he rents a room. That night he preaches in front of movie houses about his Church Without Christ, "where the blind don't see and the lame don't walk and what's dead stays that way." He tells the people he will show them "a new jesus," but again, no one pays much attention to him.

Sabbath takes a bizarre liking to Haze, who has become obsessed with trying to see behind Asa's dark glasses. She shows him a newspaper clipping that describes Asa's act of blinding himself with quicklime to prove Jesus' re-

demption. In order to antagonize Asa, Haze decides to seduce Sabbath, to prove that he himself does not believe in sin.

One evening, as Haze is trying to preach, a man joins the audience. The stranger tells them that Haze's preaching saved him two months ago and that they, too, can join the church for a dollar. Instead of wanting to profit from the man's deception, Haze is deeply offended and drives off before the stranger can collect any money. The stranger, Hoover Shoats, follows Haze and asks him persistently about the "new Jesus." Haze angrily tells him that there isn't really any "new jesus," it's just "a way to say a thing," and he pushes him out of the car. Shoats vows to ruin him. That night Haze picks the lock on Asa's apartment and shines a match into his eyes. The two men stare at each other for a moment before the match goes out, and Haze recedes into the darkness.

Asa, his hoax discovered, leaves town the next day. That evening Shoats starts preaching near Haze with a man he calls the Prophet, who looks like Haze and wears an identical suit. The enraged Haze then goes home to find Sabbath in his bed. He decides that the time has come to move on. Enoch shows up with the shrunken body from the zoo and calls it "the new jesus"; Haze throws it against the wall and destroys it.

The next night Haze follows the Prophet and, after ordering him not to preach, demands that he take off his suit. Haze then chases the man in his car, knocks him down, runs over him, and leaves him dead on the roadside.

On his way out of town the next day, Haze is stopped by a policeman, who rolls his car off an embankment when he realizes that Haze has no license. Haze goes back to town and buys quicklime to blind himself. His landlady, Mrs. Flood, does not understand his actions, but she enjoys taking care of him. Haze refuses to eat or talk, and he begins to limp. Mrs. Flood discovers that he has rocks and broken glass in his shoes and that he sleeps wrapped in barbed wire. When she asks why, Haze tells her he isn't "clean."

Haze leaves after Mrs. Flood proposes marriage to him. The police find him lying in a ditch, and one of them hits Haze with a billy club, killing him. Not noticing that he's dead, they return him to Mrs. Flood. She also does not realize that he's dead and sits holding him, staring into his face, until everything around her goes dark, and his eyes become pinpoints of light.

Mother's Younger Brother. *Ragtime.* E. L. Doctorow. 1974.

Like all the members of his family, Mother's Younger Brother is never identified by name. On the surface he is an ordinary if lethargic and reserved man, but as the novel unfolds, Mother's Younger Brother displays a violent revolutionary streak that results in murder and arson.

Mother's Younger Brother is a lonely and detached man

whom many consider a lost soul. He works in FATHER's firm, which specializes in the manufacture of American flags and campaign paraphernalia such as banners, bunting, and fireworks. Younger Brother's only interest is in the last department, where he gratifies his penchant for explosions by designing and overseeing the detonation of fireworks. But his dedication to this pastime wanes substantially when he becomes obsessed with the notorious sex goddess Evelyn Nesbit.

Younger Brother begins following Evelyn wherever she goes. On one occasion he hides in a closet in the rooming house bedroom of anarchist Emma Goldman and watches as Goldman exhorts Evelyn to renounce the patriarchal oppression of women while treating her to a lengthy full-body massage. Witnessing this scene, Younger Brother is aroused beyond control, and he stumbles into the room, masturbating and then ejaculating onto Evelyn's naked body. Not surprisingly, the subsequent affair between Evelyn and Younger Brother is rooted primarily in sex. When their relationship ends, he drowns his sorrows by throwing himself into his work at the factory.

Younger Brother's painful experience of losing Evelyn's love seems to contribute to his decision to join the black ragtime musician COALHOUSE WALKER, JR.'s efforts to command respect in a society prejudiced against blacks. Walker's group, which calls itself the Provisional American Government, engages in various terrorist activities, including the blowing up of fire stations. Sympathetic to Walker's circumstances—his car was vandalized by firemen, and his fiancée was mortally struck down by a militia man when she tried to appeal to a politician on his behalf—Younger Brother, who is skilled in the act of bomb-making, becomes the only white member of the seven-man group.

Younger Brother joins the Provisional American Government in their takeover of J. Pierpont Morgan's priceless library, where they hold out until Fire Chief Conklin meets Walker's demands. Walker then turns himself in with the provision that his accomplices be allowed to escape. Younger Brother flees to Mexico and joins various revolutionary groups there. Although the actual circumstances surrounding his death are uncertain, it is conjectured that he was killed in a battle in Morelos about a year after his departure from the United States.

Mulcahy, Henry. *The Groves of Academe.* Mary McCarthy. 1952.

Henry Mulcahy, a professor at a small Pennsylvania college, abuses the good faith of his colleagues, who rally to support him when he receives a notice of dismissal. Henry is an anomaly at Jocelyn, a "progressive" school where most of the other instructors lack his formal training and do not share his traditional views regarding education. It is precisely his status as an outsider that enables him to take advantage of the other teachers' collective

sense of justice and facilitates a plot to reverse the decision of the college president to dismiss him.

"Hen," as his friends call him, has an honorable academic record: At forty-one, he has long since earned his doctorate (the only one in his department at Jocelyn), won prestigious fellowships, published articles, and accumulated fifteen years of teaching experience. During the era of McCarthyism, Henry's career was jeopardized by his leftist affiliations. He spent the year prior to his appointment at Jocelyn living in his mother-in-law's home in Kentucky while his wife Catharine worked in a department store. Jocelyn's president, Maynard Hoar, who has a reputation as a liberal, finally hired Henry as a visiting lecturer in humanities. The college is in financial straits, and Maynard must pay Henry from a special fund allotted for "victims of the purge in the universities." Without any assurance of tenure, Henry brings Cathy and their four young children to Jocelyn, and despite the insecurity of his position, becomes an agitator.

Immediately after receiving a letter informing him that his contract will not be renewed, Henry rushes to the office of his colleague DOMNA REJNEV. He relates to her a set of false but extremely persuasive reasons as to why the dismissal is radically unjust. He knows that because of her own family history, Domna will respond with deep sympathy to Henry's lie: Cathy, he says, is severely ill, and the news must be kept secret or the shock will kill her. As Henry's story goes, Maynard fired him knowing of the danger to Cathy and in doing so broke a verbal agreement between them that the appointment would last two years. Once he has given Domna this information, he allows the energetic young woman to organize the other faculty members for action. Although he recognizes withdrawal as the best strategy, Henry restrains himself with difficulty from directing every scene of the unfolding drama.

The result of the instructors' deliberations is a meeting between Maynard Hoar and two of Henry's advocates, including Domna Rejnev, who demand that his contract be renewed. Domna admits at dinner that evening, after some coaxing, that Maynard's account of Henry's situation differed radically from his own description. When Cathy reveals in an unfortunate slip that she already knows of Henry's dismissal, Domna leaves in a hurry, and alliances in the school shift drastically.

Two faculty members who had shown no support for Henry, HOWARD FURNESS and HERBERT ELLISON, become regular guests at the Mulcahy house and enemies of the "Domna" faction. Due to Furness's support, Henry and Herbert Ellison are elected to the committee for organizing a poetry conference at Jocelyn. They compile a long list of leftist poets. When news of their plans spreads, Herbert and Henry become notorious figures, even among the students.

Among those invited to the conference is a "proletarian poet," Vincent Keogh, who, remembering Henry from their Party days, makes a conspicuous blunder at a reception. In the president's office the following morning, Keogh confesses to Maynard that he had been assigned to recruit Henry to the Communist Party but had been unsuccessful. Henry has had no other association with the group. After Keogh calls him to relate this incident, Henry races to Maynard's office and threatens to expose him to liberal magazines and newspapers for having made this "interrogation." Maynard's reputation as a liberal would be ruined. Trapped by Henry, whose contract he has recently renewed, the president has no choice but to resign. Henry emerges from their battle victorious although he has exposed himself as a liar and as a man with questionable moral standards.

Murray, Angela. *Plum Bun.* Jessie Redmon Fauset. 1929.

Angela Murray is a young mulatto woman struggling against the constraints of color and sexual prejudice in America. Brought up in the black community of Philadelphia, Angela, determined to experience the freedom and excitement that she is sure a new life will bring, decides to cross the color line and "pass for white." In doing so she is forced to confront her culture, in which white men yield power and women are conditioned to idealize marriage and romantic love as their only means of power.

Angela's mother Mattie is, like her daughter, a mulatto, and the two have often amused themselves by passing as white. But Mattie Murray is content and will never disclaim her own people; Angela, however, regards her colored family as a burden, and she views her own lack of color as a chance to escape from what she sees as the ignominious life her parents have lived. She thanks Fate for bestowing her mother's coloring on her.

While Mattie urges her daughters to become teachers and avoid the degradation she has suffered, Angela determines to take the path that she believes will lead her to a happy and prosperous married life. After her parents die, she moves to New York—ostensibly to study as an artist—and crosses the color line.

After several months in New York, the now despondent Angela realizes that life on the other side is not without its difficulties. Then she meets and falls in love with Roger Fielding, a wealthy white man. Unsure as to how she should conduct this relationship, Angela reluctantly gives in to Roger's demands and becomes his lover, believing that he will soon marry her. Roger soon tires of the affair, however, and Angela is forced to realize that within the "privileged" society she has joined, privileges are given to women only at the discretion of men.

Even after this experience, Angela longs for marriage, which she believes will fulfill her ambitions. She turns to a fellow art student, Anthony Cross—who unbeknownst to her is passing for white as well—and swiftly falls in love. Because Anthony believes that Angela is white, he

claims that, as much as he loves her, he cannot marry her.

After this second rejection, Angela turns to her work and for the first time begins to devote herself to realizing her ambitions through her own achievements. She succeeds and wins a coveted award to study in Paris. On hearing, however, that the award has been taken away from another artist on account of her color, Angela understands that she cannot continue to live a double life. In a moment of independence and self-knowledge, she faces a roomful of reporters and acknowledges that she is black. Amid a hail of accusations from the white press, Angela leaves for Paris, determined to enjoy a new freedom.

After six months in France, Angela has finally lost what she terms the "blind optimism of youth." She is now truly independent, free from her false ideas of color and marriage. The novel ends with the unexpected reunion of Angela and Anthony, who has traveled to France to find her.

Murry, Meg. *A Wrinkle in Time; A Wind in the Door; A Swiftly Tilting Planet.* Madeleine L'Engle. 1962; 1973; 1978.

Meg Murry is a determined and ingenious girl whose intelligence and curiosity lead her to adventure. Like her five-year-old brother Charles Wallace, she doesn't really fit in at school. Although very bright, she finds it difficult to concentrate or to respect figures of authority such as the principal, Mr. Jenkins. But her parents, advanced theoretical scientists who have come to live quietly in the country and do their own research, are supportive. Meg, Charles Wallace, and their twin brothers form a close, loving family with their parents.

Meg's father has been absent for several years, working on a secret government science project in a classified location. The townspeople's speculations that he has deserted his family have made Meg's time at school even more difficult. Things begin to change for Meg when she goes with Charles Wallace to visit his very unusual new friends, Mrs. Whatsit, Mrs. Who, and Mrs. Which.

Along the way Meg and Charles Wallace meet Calvin O'Keefe, a boy to whom Meg has a special attraction. The three of them discover that Mrs. Whatsit, Mrs. Who, and Mrs. Which have come to Earth to take them to the planet Camazotz, where Mr. Murry is being held captive by the evil Echthroi's power-hungry ruler, IT, who has control of his mind.

Meg, Charles Wallace, and Calvin arrive on Camazotz and find their way to IT, who tries to take over their minds by promising they will see Mr. Murry. Charles Wallace succumbs to IT's influence and brings Meg and Calvin to Mr. Murry's cell. Although Meg manages to release him by using a pair of glasses given to her by Mrs. Who, she, Calvin, and Mr. Murry are forced to leave without Charles Wallace when they escape.

The group lands on a benevolent planet where Meg, having nearly died in the rescue attempt, is nursed back to health. After regaining her strength, she returns to Camazotz to save Charles Wallace because she is the only one who knows him well enough to rescue him from IT. She fights IT with a power available only to humans: love. When she tells Charles Wallace that she loves him, IT's power is broken, and she returns triumphantly to Earth with Charles Wallace, Calvin, and Mr. Murry in tow.

When they enter high school, Meg and Calvin begin dating. He is popular, and she is learning to cope with other people. Charles Wallace seems unhappy, however. He is regularly beaten up by the other children, and his problems are exacerbated when he becomes mysteriously ill. The illness is due to a problem with Charles Wallace's mitochondria, which Mrs. Murry has been studying. When normal scientific methods prove useless in the face of the illness, two fantastic creatures, Blajeny and Proginoskes, come to Charles Wallace's assistance.

Meg, Calvin, and Proginoskes must pass three ordeals to save the young boy's life. The first test calls for Meg to distinguish the real Mr. Jenkins, the principal of Charles Wallace's school, from two impostors. Each one speaks and tries to convince Meg that he is the real Mr. Jenkins, but Meg eventually chooses the right one.

Mr. Jenkins joins Meg, Calvin, and Proginoskes in their voyage to Metron Ariston, a planet where they can be shrunk to a size small enough to enter Charles Wallace's mitochondria. Once inside, they meet Sporos, a farandola with whom they are to work. Sporos thinks that only he and the other farae who inhabit Charles Wallace are important; he considers humans primitive. The unwillingness of the proud farae to perform their accustomed functions, to "Deepen" and sing, is causing Charles Wallace's sickness. As Meg soon discovers, however, it is not the farae who are the true villains but the evil Ecthroi, who have led them astray.

The second ordeal Meg and her friends must endure is to convince the farae to reject the deceptive advice of the Ecthroi and perform their normal functions. This is accomplished for them when the Ecthroi kidnap Mr. Jenkins—an act that leads Sporos and the other farae to resume their designated roles. In the final ordeal, which is the rescue of Mr. Jenkins, Meg and Calvin combat the Ecthroi's evil with the force of love, and although Proginoskes loses his life in the process, Charles Wallace is at last set free.

Meg and Calvin eventually marry. When Meg becomes pregnant with their first child, she becomes unable to accompany Charles Wallace on his dangerous tesseracts through time and remains in bed, connected with him mentally by "kything," a sort of psychic bond. Over the Thanksgiving holidays, Calvin leaves to attend a conference in London, while Meg and the rest of her family are joined by Calvin's cranky mother Mrs. O'Keefe. The Murrys receive a distressing phone call from the President saying that Mad Dog Branzillo, a South American dictator, is threatening world peace with nuclear weapons. Mrs. O'Keefe convinces Charles Wallace to prevent armageddon by using an ancient incantation against evil called Patrick's rune. Through "kything," Meg witnesses Charles Wallace's voyages through time. In 1865, inside the body of Matthew Maddox, Charles Wallace helps prevent the marriage between Gwen—a member of the part Native American, part Celtic tribe of seers called the People of the Wind—and Gedder, who is power-hungry and ambitious, and driven by the evil Echthroi. Instead, Gwen marries the gentle Rich, a distant cousin and therefore one of the People of the Wind. When Charles Wallace returns to the present, he finds the threat of war has vanished and that Branzillo, formerly known as "El Rabioso," is now nicknamed "El Zarco" and is a peacemaker. Meg is proud to discover that, thanks to Calvin's heritage, her unborn child is also a member of this mystical tribe, and she has a newfound respect and affection for Mrs. O'Keefe, whose rune helped save the planet.

Myron. *The Enemy Gods.* Oliver LaFarge. 1937.

Abused by a cruel stepfather on the reservation where he was born, Myron, a young Native American boy, gladly leaves his parents and culture to attend a Catholic boarding school. Given the name "Myron" by the instructors at the school, he quickly learns the English language and becomes an honor student, a model child whom the school administrators proudly display whenever a government official pays them a visit. Myron is living proof of the school's success.

Myron's life changes, however, when he must room with a young man called JACK TEASE. Jack, unlike Myron, is a rebellious student who still clings to the Navajo way of life. Jack attempts to help Myron rediscover his heritage by taking him to a venerable "medicine man" on a reservation near the school. There, the two listen to Navajo legends and stories. Myron, to whom Navajo heritage signifies abuse by his stepfather, begins to develop a respect for his culture and starts to question his own status as the favorite student among the school's instructors.

When school officials learn of Myron and Jack's illegal visits to the medicine man, they assign Jack, in their eyes a bad influence, to another room. Confused and unsure of his future, Myron decides to travel to a nearby school where an old teacher of his, Dr. Butler, has been transferred. He hopes to find the answers to some of his questions there.

Myron comes across a reservation on the way, and when his horse injures a leg, he stops at a tepee to ask for help. He finds a woman there by herself; all the men have gone out hunting. Myron, who has never had a sexual experience, ends up spending the night with the young woman and leaves in the morning with vague promises to return the next spring.

Myron finally finds Dr. Butler, but his old teacher can provide none of the answers he seeks. Butler also calls the officials from Myron's school to come pick him up. Thus betrayed, Myron returns to his school more confused than ever.

This confusion leads Myron to pursue Jack Tease's new girlfriend, Ethel. Forsaking his friendship with Jack, he uses his refined ways and "Americanized" manners to woo her away. Their affair sours once the initial passion has cooled, however, and Myron learns that he is far too "Americanized" for any of his people. Ethel soon returns to Jack, leaving Myron, neither Navajo nor white man, alone.

N

Nanapush. *Tracks.* Louise Erdrich. 1988.

Nanapush, an old Chippewa Indian, tells the story of FLEUR PILLAGER to Fleur's only daughter, LULU NANA-PUSH (LAMARTINE). Nanapush is not related to Lulu, but he gave her his name after being present at her birth; now, many years later, he gives her the story of her origins—a tale representative of the systematic violation of the Chippewa and their land by profit-hungry white men.

Nanapush was named for the mythic Chippewa who stole the first fire. A healer and hunter with some power to see the hidden, he explains that his name implies trickery and seductiveness. When he attended a Jesuit school off the reservation, he was given a white man's name; he refused to sign or utter any name among the white men because he knew that a name like his would lose its power each time a white man used it.

As a young man, Nanapush worked as a government translator. When he told his people not to put their marks on the white man's treaty, he was summarily fired. Years later, in 1912, Nanapush was only fifty but thought of himself as an old man. His family had been killed, he had buried three wives, and he had seen the destruction of the last bear, beaver, buffalo, and old birch in the land. But he had also saved the last remaining member of the powerful Pillager clan, Fleur, from consumption and starvation. Because of this, his life as tribe elder and advocate for Chippewa resistance to "white men and their dollars" becomes entwined with Fleur, the only surviving Chippewa connection to the spirits and forces of their land. Nanapush's and Fleur's lives grow even closer when his hunting apprentice, young Eli Kashpaw, comes to the old Indian for help in concocting a love medicine to use on Fleur.

Nanapush suspects that Fleur has conceived a child before she and Eli begin to live together. Nevertheless, he waits with Eli outside of Fleur's cabin as she enters labor.

Eli runs for the woods at the painful sound of Fleur's screams, but Nanapush remains to meet the young priest on his way to register the child. Alone, Nanapush thinks about his three dead wives and his dead children, and decides that because his lover, Margaret Kashpaw, can no longer bear children, he will give his name to Fleur's newborn daughter, Lulu Nanapush.

As one of the few literate members of the tribe, Nanapush recognizes that whites, in particular those who own lumber companies, have begun to buy all the land that the government had formerly "given" to the Chippewa. He is also one of the few to realize that, although the tribe might acquire quick cash for the land it sells, it will eventually become destitute. The younger Indians and those with closer ties to the white investors do not appreciate Nanapush's opinion, however. Two of them, Boy Lazarre and Clarence Morissey, abduct Margaret and Nanapush one winter night. In an attempt to punish Nanapush for his efforts to block the sale of land, Clarence and Boy humiliate Nanapush and shave Margaret's head. With the aid of NECTOR KASHPAW, Eli's young brother, the old but far from defenseless Nanapush avenges them by catching Clarence in a snare made of wire stolen from the church piano.

Nancy. "That Evening Sun." William Faulkner. 1931.

Nancy, a black washerwoman and cook, resides in Negro Hollow, the black section of Jefferson, Mississippi. At the outset of the story, told by a nine-year-old white boy named QUENTIN COMPSON, Nancy is the object of both curiosity and admiration for her ability to tote baskets on her head and simultaneously negotiate a difficult pathway. But the white children maintain a distance from this servant, partly because of their feelings of racial superiority and partly because they fear her husband Jesus, who is a razor-scarred, fierce-looking black man. Nancy also lives in fear of Jesus and spends a good deal of time with the white Compson family, cooking for them while their regular servant, DILSEY GIBSON, lies ill in her own home. This arrangement is temporary, however, because the children's mother strongly objects to her husband's catering to Nancy's fear by allowing her to sleep on a pallet in one of the children's rooms.

Trouble sets in for Nancy when she is wrongfully arrested and taken to jail. On her way there she sees Mr. Stovall, a white Baptist deacon, and yells out a question about when she'll be paid. It turns out that Stovall has slept with her three times and refused to pay. In response to her query, Stovall strikes her, knocks her down, and kicks her until she loses some teeth. At the jail, Nancy, filled with despair, tries to hang herself, but she is rescued by the jailer, who then beats and whips her for the trouble she has caused him. Nancy's oddness, attributed by most of the whites to whiskey, is due to cocaine use, the jailer reasons, because blacks don't kill themselves unless they are on that drug.

Nancy, who is pregnant, probably by Mr. Stovall, greatly fears Jesus's recriminations. She is doubly fearful after her release from jail when it appears that Jesus has left Jefferson. As Nancy's pregnancy advances, so does her fear, and she attempts to manipulate events so that she can avoid Jesus, whose presence she senses. Although people try to assure her that he is probably gone for good, she persists in believing that he is lying in wait for her. The servant Dilsey's health improves, and the Compsons no longer need Nancy to work on a daily basis. She tries to wrangle her way into the family, but Mr. Compson tells her to return to her own home. She does so only after convincing Quentin, his younger sister CANDACE "Caddy" (COMPSON), and his younger brother JASON (COMPSON) to come to her cabin.

Back at home, Nancy's fears escalate as she scrambles for ways to entertain the spoiled white children. She tells them a story, but they don't like it and tell her so; then she attempts to make them popcorn but burns the kernels to cinders. When the father arrives to take the children home, he tries to convince Nancy to go to Aunt Rachel, an elderly black woman who sometimes claims she is Jesus's mother and other times insists she is no kin to him. But Nancy is convinced that Jesus will get her, regardless of where she is, and she seems to become resigned to her fate. Since she told Jesus that her child was not his, she is certain she will know no peace. As the story ends, the white family starts walking home, and Nancy sits behind an unlocked door, stoically waiting for Jesus to come home and kill her.

Narrator. "The Author of Beltraffio." Henry James. 1885.

The narrator is a young American writer who arrives in England with a letter of introduction to the great author Mark Ambient. While visiting Ambient in his country home, the young writer gets involved in a battle of wills with Ambient's wife.

The young writer has long worshiped Ambient, whose most renowned achievement has been *Beltraffio*, a work acclaimed as a great novel of aestheticism, the ultimate statement that life must be viewed as a work of art. The young writer has been deeply affected by its philosophy. Everything and everyone he sees is understood in relation to some work of art he has studied. In his mind the world of art is the primary world; the so-called real world only provides reproductions of the artistic originals. He visits Ambient hoping to find the fountain of aesthetic thought.

He is not disappointed.

He soon learns, however, that Ambient's actual life is not a happy one. Ambient's lovely wife Beatrice is apparently a vicious opponent of aestheticism. The young writer learns with horror that Beatrice does not appreciate Ambient's work and has no great interest in his achievement. He also learns that Beatrice is highly protective of their young son Dolcino, as if she were trying to guard the boy from Ambient and his world of aesthetic thought. Beatrice listens coldly as the young writer sings her husband's praises. When he sees how unhappy he is, the young writer wonders if perhaps he can speed a reconciliation between Ambient and his wife.

Ambient's sister Gwendolen is also staying at the house, and the young writer learns from her that the rift between Ambient and Beatrice is irreparable. The young writer looks on Gwendolen with distaste; she seems to him like a vulgar flower of aestheticism, a woman who tries to parade herself as a work of art when all she really wants is a husband. He begins to see how alone Ambient is in his struggle, and he is pleased when he realizes that Ambient thinks of him as an ally.

When Dolcino becomes ill, Beatrice tends the child by herself, refusing to let Ambient see him. She fears that he will infect the little child, Ambient says sadly. The young writer consoles him, and in gratitude, Ambient gives him the proof sheets of his new book. The next afternoon Dolcino's condition worsens, and Ambient and Gwendolen go for the doctor, leaving the young writer alone with Beatrice and Dolcino. Beatrice wants nothing to do with the young writer. He realizes that she sees him as the bane of her existence, as if he were there to encourage her husband's worst tendencies. Yet he can't help appreciating the aesthetic value of her beauty. He looks at Dolcino, who seems to grow more beautiful even as he gets sicker, and sees in the boy's face a plea for him to make things better between the parents. Moreover, Dolcino's beauty seems to be evidence that Beatrice and Ambient are not opposed after all, that they are in fact two of a kind. The young writer decides to bring out the side of Beatrice that appreciates her husband. He implores her to read from Ambient's new work, and the child echoes the young writer's request. In the early evening, Beatrice takes the proof sheets from Ambient's study and disappears into Dolcino's room.

The doctor arrives that night, and the young writer assumes he will be tending Dolcino. But the next morning when the doctor is leaving, the young writer learns that Beatrice has barred him from seeing her child. He tells this to Gwendolen, who says that she peeked into the sick room in the middle of the night and saw Beatrice sitting by the bed, holding Dolcino with one hand and a copy of Ambient's new book in the other. Gwendolen says that Dolcino's condition seems worse than ever. The young writer relays all of this information to Ambient, who vows to smash down the door. But the young writer manages to calm him and to keep him walking around the garden for an hour. Then Gwendolen appears and says that now Beatrice is really scared and wants the doctor immediately. Dolcino dies before the doctor arrives.

According to Gwendolen, Beatrice did not intend to murder her child, but Ambient's new book frightened her. Beatrice began to think that by sacrificing the little boy, she would rescue him, prevent him from ever being touched by Ambient's vision. She then became terrified by what she had done and tried to save Dolcino, but it was too late. The young writer listens with horror to Gwendolen's interpretation, which seems to imply that he is a proximate cause of Dolcino's death. He makes Gwendolen swear never to tell Ambient what she has told him. Gwendolen agrees. Beatrice dies several months later. Oddly enough, the young writer learns that losing Dolcino made her a convert to Ambient's work. Before her death, Beatrice had even been seen reading *Beltraffio*.

Narrator. *Autobiography of an Ex-Colored Man.* James Weldon Johnson. 1912.

The child of a mixed-race mother and a white father, the narrator is legally black. He renounces his racial heritage, however, and "passes for white" after determining that turn-of-the-century America is a hostile, often murderous place for a black person.

Born in a Georgia town after the Civil War, the narrator lives with his mother in a small house. His earliest memories are of that home and of a distinguished white man who often visited it. After a tearful parting, the narrator and his mother leave the South, and the man his mother will later reveal is his father, and journey to Connecticut. While at school there the narrator learns that despite his fair skin and straight hair, he is not white.

Although his consciousness is radically altered by this discovery, the narrator continues to live as before, going to school, living with his mother, and playing the piano, at which he becomes very skilled. One evening, stopping at home while on the way to an after-school piano lesson, the narrator finds that the distinguished man who has figured so prominently in his childhood memories has

come to visit. A few weeks after this awkward encounter, a piano arrives, a gift from the narrator's father. Although the man promises to visit often, he never appears in their home again.

Just before he is able to realize his plans to attend a prestigious northern college, the narrator is shattered by the death of his mother. In order to earn some money, he holds a recital in his town and is able to use the proceeds to travel to the South and enroll instead at Atlanta University.

The narrator finds a bed in a boardinghouse frequented by Pullman porters and goes the next day to the university to register. On his return to the boardinghouse he discovers that all his money, $300, has been stolen from his trunk. One of the porters advises him to travel to Jacksonville, Florida, where he can easily find work and earn back the money he has lost.

Quickly finding employment in a cigar factory, the narrator settles into life in Jacksonville, encountering for the first time different classes of blacks. But when the factory closes, rather than staying in the city or returning to Atlanta University, he decides to go north, to New York.

After Jacksonville, New York City is an exciting, even dangerous place. The narrator begins to frequent illegal clubs and casinos, and lives the life of a gambler with his share of bad luck. To earn money he plays ragtime piano at one of the clubs where he is a regular. His training in classical music gives his ragtime a novel sound, and he becomes very popular. A rich patron, one of many whites who go "slumming" in black clubs, is particularly enchanted by the narrator's playing and hires him to entertain at parties. After the murder of one of the club's regular customers puts the narrator's life in danger, the millionaire white man asks the narrator to accompany him to Europe. They travel through France, England, Holland, and Germany, but the narrator begins to feel that he is wasting his talent playing ragtime music for his enigmatic benefactor. He resolves to return to the United States and, inspired by black music and culture, compose his own music.

Back in America, the narrator wanders through the South, observing the lives of blacks and whites alike. He is greatly affected by the lynching of a black man; it inspires in him a feeling of horror and outrage at the whites who commit the crime but also a more profound feeling of shame of his membership in a race that can be so treated. He decides to cross the color line and "pass for white."

Returning to New York City, the narrator establishes himself in business and soon meets and falls in love with a white woman, and asks her to be his wife. When he confesses to her the secret of his racial background, his fears that she will reject him seem to be realized, but her love for him overcomes her initial reaction of horror. As the novel closes, the narrator expresses some lingering misgivings over the life he has chosen but claims that his children will be the true beneficiaries of his decision.

Narrator. "The Black Cat." Edgar Allan Poe. 1843.

From birth the narrator is marked as one whose sympathies reached out to embrace all manner of living things. As a boy he delighted in the company of a vast array of pets provided by his doting parents. Upon maturity, he is lucky enough to fall in love with a woman whose inclinations match his own, and they spend many happy hours in the company of their favorite pets, including a dog, some rabbits and goldfish, a monkey, and a black cat named Pluto. The couple is happy for several years, but then the narrator's personality undergoes a gradual but dramatic alteration. Because of excessive drinking, the narrator becomes a violent and ill-tempered man, and he abuses the animals in his household until they all fear him.

One night, in a fit of inebriated rage, the narrator mercilessly takes a knife and gouges out one of the black cat's eyes. While he feels remorse the next day, his behavior does not change, and the cat is behaving normally and seems not to be in pain. The couple's life resumes a semblance of normalcy until once again the narrator turns against his pet. This time his actions are even more despicable: he takes Pluto, wraps a noose around his neck, and leaves him hanging from a tree. In a seemingly unrelated incident, the couple's home burns that same night; the only wall left standing bears the image of a cat with a rope around its neck. While the narrator is horrified at this image, he draws no inferences from the similarities between his behavior and the bizarre occurrence.

After the couple relocates, another cat appears that is black and missing one eye, but it has a vague white patch on its breast that gradually develops into an image of the gallows. The narrator instantly loathes the animal, but the wife adores it. Finally, unable to stand the new cat any longer, the narrator seizes an axe. As he is about to kill the animal, his wife intervenes, and the narrator plunges the axe blade into her skull. The narrator instantly plans a way to dispose of the body, and after rejecting several possibilities, determines to seal it in the cellar wall. After he does so, he realizes that the cat has vanished.

While the police are investigating the house, the narrator, observing that the house is remarkably well built, strikes a wall in the cellar with his cane. As he does so, a cry escalating to a piercing scream is heard from the wall. After a moment's shock, the police rush to the wall and tear it down. The narrator has quite literally sealed his own doom. When the wall crumbles, the rapidly decaying body of the narrator's wife is made visible, and on its head sits the furious cat.

Narrator. *A Boy's Own Story.* Edmund White. 1982.

In his account of his childhood and adolescence, the unnamed narrator explores his own struggle to come to terms with an emerging homosexual identity. Reliving key events in his life, he details the steps he took toward acceptance of his sexuality and adulthood.

The novel begins with the narrator's memory of his fifteenth year. As an adolescent, he feels inadequate because he is considered a sissy by his peers. He is imaginative and intellectual, but not athletic like other boys his age. He envies his friend Kevin who seems to possess unlimited self-confidence when he talks about sports with the narrator's father, and he wishes he had a similar assuredness around other men. The narrator and Kevin have a number of sexual encounters, but the narrator is disappointed when Kevin refuses to kiss him. All the while, trapped in an unhappy relationship with his father, the narrator dreams of living a "normal" life, although he does not wish to dissolve his secret bond with Kevin.

The narrative then shifts to the previous summer, which the narrator spent drearily with his father and stepmother. Longing for a lover to appear magically and take care of him, he spends his time reading and writing, activities that allow him to escape the unhappiness of his daily life. The tedium of his youth is interrupted when he is propositioned by a man outside a local bookstore. Although he does not have the courage to go through with the encounter, he is excited by the prospect of a sexual experience with a stranger. Soon afterward he receives a similar proposition from an inebriated man in a park, but the man fails to arrive at the planned time. They later meet by chance, and the apologetic man pays for a hustler for the narrator.

Going deeper into his memory, the narrator recalls his seventh year and his quarrels with his older sister. Shunning her company, he develops imaginary companions to take her place. When his parents later divorce, he becomes his mother's "best friend" and shares her desire for a male companion.

At age eleven, the narrator befriends Marilyn and Fred, eccentric clerks in a bookstore, both of whom, he learns some time later, are gay. His new friends arrange for a private tutor to teach the narrator German so that he can read the untranslated novels of Herman Hesse. The narrator is infatuated with his tutor and feels painfully rejected when the man misses an appointment. That summer at camp the narrator becomes fascinated with Ralph, a boy rumored to have had sex with other boys. One afternoon a counselor, Mr. Stone, makes sexual advances, but the narrator is alarmed at the adult's behavior and runs away. In the woods he meets Ralph, who persuades him to have sex.

At fifteen, still uncomfortable with his sexuality, the narrator immerses himself in the study of Buddhism because the religion calls for the "extinction of desire." Fearing that his close attachment to his mother is causing him to become a homosexual, he convinces his parents to send him to a boarding school for boys. At school he reaches a moment of self-acceptance and allows himself to fall in love with his gym teacher, Mr. Pouchet. He sends the teacher a love letter but receives no answer.

The next year the narrator becomes friends with a Latin teacher and his wife. The Scotts are alarmed by the narrator's homosexual tendencies and introduce him to a fiercely anti-gay priest, Father Burke. At a Thanksgiving dinner the narrator argues with Burke, thus cooling the Scotts' affection for him.

In the novel's final reminiscence, the narrator recalls his aversion to the music teacher, Mr. Beattie. Suspecting him of selling drugs on campus, the narrator successfully seduces the apparently heterosexual Mr. Beattie, then exposes the teacher's conduct to the headmaster, who fires the teacher. Years later the narrator regrets his actions but realizes that, for the first time in his life, he held sexual power over an adult. He feels empowered by his ability to bring pleasure to a heterosexual man and then to punish him for his heterosexuality. The narrator recognizes the event as one of the most poignant in a number of turning points on his road to self-acceptance.

Narrator. *Bright Lights, Big City.* Jay McInerney. 1984.

Not yet thirty years old, the narrator seems to have it all: a job at a prestigious New York magazine, a wife who is a model, invitations to all the right parties, and a friend who knows how to have a good time. But in the course of a week he loses everything and discovers that what he had was all surface and no substance.

The narrator is the son of well-to-do parents from Bucks County, Pennsylvania. He has spent his formative years at an Ivy League university, traveling between the East and West coasts, and in Europe. He eventually moves to Kansas where he goes to work as a journalist and seeks what he imagines will be the true American experience. He thinks he will find the inspiration to become the next Hemingway; instead, he finds Amanda, a woman who has dreamed of moving away from her degenerate mother and her home in a trailer park to embark on a glamorous life in New York City. As part of his effort to gain experience for his anticipated career as a writer, the narrator also sees merit in moving to New York, and the two of them set out for the city. He and Amanda eventually marry and settle into an apartment in Greenwich Village. She becomes a model, and as her career becomes more successful, they grow further apart. One day she calls from an assignment in Paris to tell him she will not be returning.

Some time after this phone call, the narrator is out on the town until the early hours of the morning with his hedonistic friend TAD ALLAGASH. The narrator, who has now abandoned Tad, must recover from a cocaine and alcohol hangover, find his way home from a nightclub, and then go to work in the Department of Factual Verification at a famous New York magazine. He arrives at work late, is asked to do a task that would be impossible even on a good day, and ends up getting fired a few days later when his boss discovers the factual errors he did not correct.

The narrator's firing from the magazine shatters his dream of rising in its ranks to become one of its important fiction writers. His habits become more and more destructive. He rejects the compassion of those who care about him, among them his coworker Megan, but at the same time he is beginning to realize how miserable he has become. He meets Vicky, a philosophy major from Princeton, who represents an alternative to the relentless thrill-seeking Tad had offered.

Then the narrator's brother shows up, a painful reminder of their mother's death. That tragedy had fueled his cocaine habit. Never allowing himself to grieve, the narrator buried himself in a superficial existence in order to forget. Now, unable to hide from his pain any longer, he recalls his last conversations with her and begins the process of recovery. After a final night at a party, he finds himself at the city's docks where men are unloading cargo. Longing for something of true substance, the narrator trades his sunglasses for some bread and, standing on the dock in the bright morning sun, begins to eat.

Narrator. *City of Night.* John Rechy. 1963.

The unnamed narrator was born and raised in El Paso, Texas, the youngest of a large family. His life is one of loneliness and empty relationships, and it was marked by a disturbing incident in his early childhood: He viewed a pet dog's decomposing body after it was exhumed and reburied in a deeper grave. The frightening incident led him to question authority and the meaning of life, and to alienate himself from society.

The narrator leaves El Paso and travels to New York when he is a young man. There he begins his career on the fringes of urban society, becoming a hustler who allows men to perform sexual acts with him in exchange for money or food. As the narrator becomes more skilled at hustling, he becomes disdainful of the denizens of this sexual underworld, although he continues to solicit men and their money. Eventually, when a hustler starts becoming close to him, the narrator spurns his attentions and rejects even a hint of friendship. Soon after this he tires of the New York scene and returns briefly to El Paso, where he continues to earn money as a prostitute.

The narrator then moves on again, settling this time in Los Angeles where he becomes involved with a community of drag queens, drug addicts and pushers, hustlers, and other outlaws. His relationships are kept on a superficial or professional level, although he does begin to develop a broader knowledge of the requirements of his profession. Once again, though, he tires of the routines and relocates to San Francisco.

The narrator continues to work as a hustler in San Francisco and becomes increasingly attracted to the rites and rituals of sadomasochism. Still unwilling to commit to any place or life-style, he moves once again. Chicago, the next city in which he lives, presents a similar world, one that doesn't satisfy him any more than the other cities had.

After more traveling, the narrator arrives in New Orleans just as the city is gearing up for Mardi Gras. The mood of the city is boisterous, and the bars and streets are filled and busy. The narrator frequents a bar owned by a woman named Sylvia who tolerates the comings and goings of a huge crowd of hustlers, young men, homosexual men, drag queens, and junkies. In one of the rare instances of emotional connection in the novel, the narrator is touched by Sylvia's heart-wrenching confession that she caters to these sexual "outlaws" in atonement for having rejected her son when he told her that he was homosexual. Although the narrator doesn't consider himself a homosexual because he never reciprocates in his sexual encounters, he is moved by Sylvia's evident pain.

Soon after Sylvia's confession, the narrator meets another reveler, Jeremey, and the two go to Jeremey's hotel room. The narrator is very attracted to the stranger and tells him, but not the reader, his full name. Jeremey proposes that they try to develop a permanent relationship. The narrator balks, but the couple has sex, and afterward Jeremey almost convinces him to give the relationship a try. It seems clear that it is impossible for the narrator to achieve such closeness, however, and he flees, seeking more drugs and alcohol. The narrator continues to roam the streets and bars as the city prepares for the final event of Mardi Gras, the Shrove Tuesday parades. The novel concludes with his plaintive cry, "Why can't dogs go to heaven?"

Narrator. "A Conversation with My Father." Grace Paley. 1974.

The writer-narrator attempts to write a story of the type her eighty-six-year old father will approve. Responding to her father's plea that she "write a simple story just once more . . . the kind you used to write," the narrator creates a story around the woman who has lived across the street for years.

Displeased, the father criticizes the writer for omitting details of description and background. After reviewing these real-life details, the narrator rewrites the story. This version of the tale, embellished with family history and literary allusions, leaves the heroine addicted to drugs and alone.

Rebuffing his child once again, the father charges that the narrator cannot tell a plain story. Yet he praises the last touch: "The end. The end. You were right to put that down. The end." Prodded by this compliment, the writer argues that the woman's status at the end of the story does not have to be the end. The father retorts that she lacks the ability to recognize tragedy, the absence of hope. So

struck is the writer by her father's comments that she insists on giving her invention a hopeful end. In response to this willful act, the father flatly declares that the woman will end in tragedy and wonders when the narrator will look tragedy in the face.

Narrator. *The Country of the Pointed Firs.* Sarah Orne Jewett. 1896.

In an effort to find a quiet space to write, the novel's narrator travels one summer to the coastal town of Dunnet Landing, Maine. Boarding in the home of Mrs. ALMIRY TODD, an elderly woman who grows medicinal herbs, the narrator is at first content to remain a stranger to the townspeople and her hostess. Soon, however, she finds herself initiated into the town's stories, and becomes a willing participant in the rituals of the tiny community's slow-paced but comfortable life.

Early in her visit the narrator, finding Mrs. Todd's presence in her lodgings distracting, rents the town's schoolhouse for use as a study. Her efforts to write proceed slowly, however, and she spends more time brushing away flies and feeling lonely than putting pen to paper. Only the appearance of Captain Littlepage saves her from writer's block and unwanted solitude. Although the captain is old and perhaps insane, the narrator is happy to leave her unproductive work and listen to his fascinating tales of his voyage to northern latitudes.

Mrs. Todd, warming to the narrator when she learns how attentive she has been to the eccentric captain, offers to take the narrator to visit her mother, Mrs. Blackett, who lives on Green Island, off the coast of Dunnet Landing. Visiting Mrs. Todd's mother and her brother William, the narrator finds herself drawn more and more into the lives of the townspeople. Mrs. Todd and Mrs. Blackett come to treat her as a neighbor rather than a lodger or guest, and she responds with growing concern for their well-being and an interest in the many stories they tell about Dunnet Landing inhabitants, living and dead.

The narrator's relationship with William Blackett gives her particular pleasure. William, usually quite shy with strangers, almost immediately befriends the narrator, to the pleasant surprise of Mrs. Todd and her mother. On the narrator's first visit to Green Island he takes her up a hill to gaze out over the ocean and the land. They later spend a day fishing, and although they catch no trout, their friendship is cemented as they drive through the forest. They share a pleasure in Maine's rugged natural beauty that need not be expressed in words.

The narrator's friendships with Mrs. Todd, William, and the other townspeople she meets give value to her visit, but the person whose story most interests her is not even alive at the time of her visit. The case of JOANNA TODD, a cousin of Mrs. Todd's late husband, who went to live by herself on Shell-heap Island when her fiancé broke off their engagement, fascinates the narrator. She even visits the island, imagining it as a sort of shrine to the solitary heart. While she explores the land that Joanna walked and that others have since visited, she marvels that a woman could be ashamed of facing the citizens of Dunnet Landing and hardy enough to bear the loneliness and bleakness of life on Shell-heap Island.

At summer's end the narrator leaves Dunnet Landing and the quiet fellowship she has found there to return to the busy but lonely and unfriendly city.

Narrator. "Dean of Men." Peter Taylor. 1986.

This anonymous first-person narrator is a father addressing his son Jack, with whom he does not have a close relationship. His narrative is an attempt to communicate something not only about their family history but about the nature of the male sex in general as a warning to the young man and his generation.

The narrator comes from an upper-middle-class southern family with political connections. His grandfather was briefly a U.S. senator but retired from politics after being betrayed by his protégés; he spent the rest of his bitter life tyrannizing his household and avoiding the company of men. The narrator's father, a lawyer, lost most of his money in the Depression and became reclusive after being betrayed in a business deal by a good friend.

The narrator meets his wife Marie in graduate school, and they teach at the same institution for a few years until she temporarily gives up her career to have their three children. A dozen years after graduating from a small midwestern college, the narrator returns to teach there as an assistant professor. He is relatively content even though there is some tension with his wife over academic issues. He expects to spend the rest of his life at the college. When the former chairman of the athletics department is chosen as acting president, the narrator is approached by a group of young associate professors and asked to use his personal influence with a member of the board of trustees to protest the appointment. Despite misgivings, he agrees to perform the task, and as a result, another candidate is chosen. The narrator soon regrets his action, however: The interim president exacts his revenge by denying the young professor the housing that was his due and refusing to acknowledge the validity of a letter from the previous president promising him the rank of associate. When the professors who had asked him to perform the mission in the first place promise to help and then betray him, he resigns his job.

The narrator moves on to an appointment at a large state university and struggles not to become bitter or reclusive like his father and grandfather. But his marriage has suffered severely from the ordeal, and when he secures a position as dean of men at another school, the marriage dissolves.

Shortly afterward the narrator remarries and a few years later is appointed academic dean, then president of his college. He leads a satisfied, active life. Although he has sacrificed many things, including the acquaintance of his son, he is content knowing that he has continued to "live among men," unlike his father and grandfather before him.

Narrator. "Deaths of Distant Friends." John Updike. 1987.

The first-person narrator of this story recalls a period of personal disarray in his life and remembers that while he was between marriages and preoccupied, "other people continued to live and die." Describing the lives and deaths of Len (his old golf partner), Amy Merrymount (a dignified old New Englander who had been friends with his first wife), and Canute (the family dog from his first marriage), the narrator reflects that these deaths have carried him off bit by bit and gradually erased his former self—a self living in a time of disgrace, pain, and embarrassment—from the public memory.

Len, the owner of a hardware store, died unexpectedly of a coronary. Remembering the deficiencies in his golf game, the narrator recalls Len's occasional "gorgeous putts" and describes his brightly colored golfing clothes as a sign of his high hopes for his game. Len had never spoken of the narrator's personal life, despite having spent much time with him on the golf course when he was in the middle and in the aftermath of his divorce. During their golf games, the narrator felt safe from "the entire offended social order"—the people involved in or affected by his divorce. At Len's funeral he had tried to tell Len's son that his father had been a great guy, but the words had fallen flat; Len and their friendship, he realized, contained moments of life that were too delicate to capture in words, and now they were gone.

Amy Merrymount died at the age of ninety-one. She had been a keen self-educator, a woman continually searching for "the first-rate." When the narrator and his first wife, Julia, moved to town with their young family, they became part of Miss Merrymount's tea circle. In particular, Miss Merrymount befriended Julia, and the two women grew to love each other. In the last years of the narrator's marriage, Julia had gone to Miss Merrymount's to read to her. The narrator remembers that Julia always returned from these visits looking younger and emboldened. After his divorce, the narrator attended a social engagement at which Miss Merrymount was present; she had grown extremely fragile and was almost blind. She said nothing more to him than "You have done a dreadful thing." The narrator was not displeased by her treatment of him; her judgment had been a kind of relief.

The final death that the narrator remembers is of Canute, the family's golden retriever. When the divorce was finalized, Canute resided with Julia and the children. The narrator remarried, and Julia's household seemed to him to be suffering from neglect. Julia had taken up with a new athletic boyfriend whose golf, tennis, and backpacking hobbies occupied her free time. One day the narrator's daughter brought Canute by his house. The dog seemed fat and lethargic. Learning from his daughter that Canute had been eating the neighbor's garbage, the narrator suppressed his feelings about this apparent mismanagement of the home and stood silently by as his second wife scratched the dog and talked with his daughter about dog antibiotics. A few days later Canute was found dead, his stomach bloated with garbage, far out in the marshes near Julia's house. Relishing this image, the narrator confesses that all of these deaths make him happy in a way because the "witnesses to his disgrace" are being removed and the world is growing lighter.

Narrator. "The Egg." Sherwood Anderson. 1920.

Like his father, the narrator of this story is obsessed with what he considers the upsetting existence of chickens and eggs. Having been raised on an unprofitable chicken farm near Bidwell, Ohio, the narrator claims that his relatively gloomy and pessimistic personality is the result of having witnessed the dreadful struggles that hens and roosters undergo in their unsuccessful efforts to survive. Although the narrator often ponders the question of why this dreaded object must exist in the world, he is unable to resolve this odd dilemma and continues to be haunted by the enigma of the egg.

The narrator's mother is ambitious for her complacent husband and young son; she persuades her husband to give up his position as a farmhand, sell his horse, and invest the profits in their own business, chicken farming. The narrator is so disgusted with the tragedies that befall the fowls that he daydreams about a happy life devoid of eggs, chicks, pullets, hens, or roosters. By virtue of his parents' metier, he is forced to watch the chickens fall prey to horrific diseases such as pip and cholera or, if they miraculously live, change from cute little balls of fuzz into grotesquely naked pullets that will eventually turn into full-grown birds to duplicate the sickening cycle. Equally disillusioned by human beings, he remarks that the chickens and people have in common an incurable stupidity. Although his parents spend most of their money buying chicken disease cures like Wilmer's White Wonder, their efforts at chicken farming are decidedly unsuccessful. In the end, their ineptitude, although financially disastrous, buys the young boy's freedom from the dreaded birds.

When the family abandons the farm to try restaurateuring in the nearby town of Pickleville, the narrator's father cannot resist bringing his bizarre collection of deformed dead chickens that he has preserved in bottles of alcohol. Despite the protests of his wife, who thinks that these monstrosities are morbid, he places the jars on a shelf in their restaurant. He claims that people enjoy seeing such strange and fantastic sights. The restaurant proves no more successful than the chicken farm, and the boy observes that his father's behavior begins to alter drastically when he decides that his lack of success has been due to the glum mood that he, like his son, is cursed with. According to the boy, this notion introduces ambition, a particularly American quality that will eventually cause his downfall. In an effort to drum up more business, the father attempts to entertain his customers with cheerful sallies and strange demonstrations of magical feats that one can perform with eggs. Affected by his father's changed demeanor, the boy apes his cheery mood and even smiles at their cat. But this scheme culminates in a scene that leaves a lasting impression in the boy's mind.

One night when the narrator and his mother are asleep and his father is working the night shift, an angry, piercing scream issues from the restaurant. A moment later the father furiously storms into the room with an egg in his hand and a crazy look in his eyes. Then he starts to sob and his son also begins to cry. As it turns out, his father had been laughed at by a customer when he tried unsuccessfully to insert an egg into a bottle. The sight of this distraught man cements the boy's obsessive aversion to eggs, the existence of which haunts him for the remainder of his life.

Narrator. "First Love and Other Sorrows." Harold Brodkey. 1957.

This story describes the springtime of the unnamed narrator's sixteenth year in which the arrival of spring is no longer a matter of being allowed to play outside after dinner but is instead a matter of strange stirrings and a new awareness of love and of sorrow.

Until the age of four, the narrator had lived in an opulent house overlooking the Mississippi, just south of St. Louis. On the death of his father, who had lost most of the family wealth, the narrator, his mother, and his older sister were forced to move into a more modest house in St. Louis. In the narrator's sixteenth year he becomes more aware of his mother's sorrow over her losses and of the pressures on his sister. The narrator's mother has attempted to adjust to this change gracefully but frequently bemoans their altered life-style and induces her beautiful daughter to use her looks to marry well.

The narrator also becomes painfully aware that his sister and mother seem to classify him, along with all males, as a comic figure, and he hates himself for being awkward and heavy-handed, for having to wear glasses, and for not being handsome. Although his best friend Preston disapproves of his desire to hold class office and make the track team, the narrator longs to be popular like Joel, a devastatingly handsome and sexually experienced classmate. He dreams constantly of being a success when he grows up, for he knows of no other way to be loved.

On the night when his sister expects a proposal from a wealthy man whom she does not love, the narrator is restless, plagued by the feeling that there is meaning all around him this spring, if only he were free of school, his mother, his duties and inhibitions. Wandering about his neighborhood feeling the rarity, eternality, and unhappiness of things, the narrator decides to talk to Eleanor Cullen, a classmate who has been dating Joel. Sitting with him on her porch, Eleanor tells the narrator that Joel made a pass at her on their last date and she slapped him, and now she feels miserable about herself and the world. The narrator describes his similar feelings, and the youths comfort each other, deciding that while they have been damaged by heredity, they will one day redeem themselves by doing something great. They spend the evening talking and exchanging kisses.

The narrator walks home daydreaming about Eleanor and arrives to discover that his sister has become engaged. Although he senses the distress underlying his sister's excitement, the narrator and his family members embrace during a sentimental and nostalgic moment of joy. The story ends with the narrator believing that his family will always remain close.

Narrator. "Holiday." Katherine Anne Porter. 1972.

When the narrator of this story is looking for a quiet place to spend a month-long vacation, she takes the advice of a friend and books a room with the Muëllers, a family of German immigrant farmers in Texas.

Upon her arrival at the Muëller farm one day in early spring, the narrator is at first taken aback by her hosts, an extended family of earthy, hardworking peasants. But as she gets to know the many members of the family and watches their daily activity, she finds herself feeling very much at home. Among the family members are Mother Muëller, the gruff matriarch of the family; Hatsy, the pretty younger daughter whose marriage takes place during the narrator's visit; and her sister Annetje, a young mother whose joy is to care for all the young creatures on the farm. The narrator also becomes acquainted with Father Muëller, a wealthy landowner whose peculiar interpretation of *Das Capital* puts his guest off.

But the narrator is most fascinated by Ottilie, the family's servant. Deaf, crippled, and deformed, Ottilie seems barely capable of cooking and serving the huge meals she makes for the family. Although they agree she is a good cook, the Muëllers hardly acknowledge Ottilie's presence and speak to her only to give her instructions. At family events such as Hatsy's marriage and the birth of another sister's child, Ottilie silently makes and serves huge quantities of food to the Muëllers' many guests.

One day Ottilie pulls the narrator into her dingy room off the kitchen. Gesturing wildly and seemingly trying to speak, she hands the narrator an old photograph of a pretty five-year-old girl whose blond hair and bright smile resemble that of the younger Muëllers. Turning the photo over, Ottilie shows her name written carefully on the back. The narrator is at once touched by the servant's desire to

remember the person she once was and hurt by the family's treatment of their own flesh and blood.

A devastating storm hits the area, and all the Muëllers work hard to save whatever livestock and crops they can. When the storm lifts, Mother Muëller's hard work catches up with her; she becomes ill and dies within a day. As neighbors come to pay their respects, the family's grief is vocal. Only Ottilie is quiet, as she busily prepares food and coffee for the visitors.

After the funeral procession has left the farm, the narrator retreats to her room to rest but is soon disturbed by the sound of howling. In the kitchen she finds Ottilie sobbing and wildly waving her arms in the direction the funeral procession had taken. With much struggle the narrator manages to hitch a pony to a rickety wagon and to push Ottilie aboard, hoping they might overtake the funeral train. But before they have gone very far, Ottilie begins to laugh and gurgle foolishly. Stopping the wagon, the narrator realizes that there is nothing she can do for Ottilie, that she was selfish to wish to ease her own heart by helping the crippled servant. Knowing that Ottilie is beyond the reach of any of her family members, in fact beyond any human reach, the narrator turns the wagon and returns to the farm so that the servant can start dinner.

Narrator. "I Want to Know Why." Sherwood Anderson. 1919.

The narrator is a confused adolescent whose love of horses and racing has led him to confront issues of race relations, sexuality, and the place of men and women in the world around him.

The boy, approximately fifteen years old, is intrigued by the ways in which blacks are able to accept others and, as he sees it, put them at their ease. He also envies the blacks who are able to work around racehorses, a job he would love to have. One in particular, Bildad Johnson, is an accomplished itinerant cook who follows the racing season up and down the East Coast.

The narrator and a group of friends have pooled their money and have boldly struck out from their Kentucky home to hop freight trains in the hope of attending the big race in Saratoga, New York. They have done so without their parents' knowledge or consent. Throughout the story, as the narrator discusses horses, racing, and his own self-admitted acumen when it comes to assessing horse flesh, he refers to an incident that startled him out of his childhood. Although he knows that his father would never permit him to do work considered beneath his place as a white person, he continues to aspire to some kind of career that deals with horses. At one point in the tale he relates that he was bitterly disappointed when he realized at the age of ten that he would end up too big to be a jockey. On a prankster's advice and in an effort to stunt his growth, he choked down half of one of his father's cigars. The doctor had to be called and the boy was terribly embarrassed, but he was not punished—a response that he suspects is unique to his father.

In Saratoga, on the morning of the big race, the narrator sees Jerry Tillford, a trainer, attending the horse he has trained virtually since its birth. The narrator, who claims that when he gets a lump in his throat at the sight of a particular horse, it is a winner, has that feeling as he watches the beautiful horse, Sunstreak, receiving its pre-race rubdown. As he realizes that the horse has the power and stamina to win, he looks at Jerry, and the two share the sudden knowledge of the horse's power and potential. In addition, the boy experiences a never-before-felt attraction for Jerry; he feels that he, the horse, and the trainer are the only beings in the world.

Following the race, which Sunstreak wins handily, the narrator is even more infatuated with Jerry Tillford, and he sneaks away from his friends to try to connect with Jerry for the night. He finds Jerry drunk in the company of several other men, and the boy follows them to a house of prostitution. Here he spies on the men as they flirt with bawdy women. The narrator is disgusted by the behavior he witnesses, and his unarticulated hopes are dashed when he hears Jerry stupidly bragging—taking credit for Sunstreak's performance earlier in the day. As though that weren't enough, Jerry flirts with the harshest, meanest, and most masculine-looking of the women. The boy flees as soon as he sees Jerry kissing her. That kiss destroys the boy's illusions and turns his admiration and budding love for Jerry into a loathing that includes the desire to murder him.

As he concludes his tale, the narrator is now sixteen and has yet to resolve what the source of his attraction was, nor has he figured out why he was so disappointed when Jerry turned away from what seemed a genuine bonding to cavort with a hired woman.

Narrator. "In Dreams Begin Responsibilities." Delmore Schwartz. 1935.

The young narrator remembers a powerful dream that he has just dreamed on the night before his twenty-first birthday. In the dream he sits in a theater watching a film about the night years ago when his father proposed marriage to his mother. As he watches his their evening together unfold, he is terrified and saddened that he can do nothing to stop them, alter their characters, or influence the inner workings of their marriage.

The movie begins with the narrator's father, who walks to the home of the narrator's mother to pick her up for their date. The father contemplates himself and his future; not quite sure that he wants to get married, he reassures himself by thinking of all the admirable and influential men who have had wives. When he arrives at his destination, the narrator's mother, dressed up for the night out, comes downstairs and greets him. There is a flicker in the film; the narrator is brought out of the story just long

enough to recognize the sadness he feels as he watches. The film returns to normal, and the narrator's parents depart.

The narrator observes his parents' familiar behavior: His father habitually approves or condemns the characters in a novel his mother is reading; his mother considers the pleasures of Coney Island "inferior" and will only eat dinner there and walk on the boardwalk; his father exaggerates the amount of money he made last week. The narrator begins to cry. When an old lady sitting next to him in the theater glares in his direction, he is intimidated and stops. He continues to watch as his parents stop on the boardwalk and stare absentmindedly at the ocean. Unlike his parents, the narrator is overwhelmed by the beautiful, passionate ocean and the huge glowing sun. He bursts into tears again, this time over his parents' indifference to the powerful scene before them. Unable to control himself, the narrator goes to the men's room.

When he returns to the theater, he listens as his father proposes marriage to his mother over dinner. His mother begins to cry with joy, but the narrator stands up and begins to shout to them to change their minds. "It's not too late," he says, calling out. "Nothing good will come of it." An usher hurries down the aisle and tells the narrator that unless he is quiet, he'll be evicted from the theater. The narrator is silent and closes his eyes because he can't bear to watch.

After a while the narrator glimpses the movie again. His parents, posing to have their picture taken on the boardwalk, become impatient with the photographer. When the picture is finally taken, the father's smile is a grimace and the mother's is bright and false. They later pass a fortune-teller's booth and argue about whether or not to go inside. The father finally consents and they enter the booth, but he storms out after only a few minutes and she stubbornly stays. The narrator is shocked and afraid; it feels as if a tightrope is breaking over a circus audience. He stands up and shouts out, asking why his mother refuses to go with his father. The usher seizes his arm and pulls him away, asking the narrator why a young man with his whole life ahead of him should get so hysterical over this. The narrator's dream abruptly ends as the usher drags him through the lobby of the theater.

In the end, whatever the narrator has learned from this frightening and revealing dream-movie is left ambiguously unstated. He simply wakes up on the cold and bleak winter morning of his twenty-first birthday.

Narrator. "In the Heart of the Heart of the Country." William H. Gass. 1968.

The unnamed narrator is a philosophical man whose primary subject of study is the quotidian social activities in small midwestern farming villages. Recuperating from a failed romance, he lives alone in a town called B, Indiana, with his cat, Mr. Tick, whose presence provides some comfort to him in his lovesick state. Although he is ambivalent about the quality of life and the eccentric personalities of his fellow country-dwellers, he advocates living in the heartland where one can measure one's existence against the wholesome presence of nature and maintain a sense of proportion and freedom. Despite this advocation of country life, the narrator's lovelorn condition and his wry perception of his neighbors undermine his ability to fully enjoy the fruits of the uncluttered lifestyle that rural settings have to offer.

The narrator is a poet and a teacher who has no job and regrets his subsequent insolvency. Despite his career in education, he pessimistically condemns midwesterners as an ignorant lot who are impervious to intellectual enlightenment. In place of education these small-town folk devote their passions and money to three pastimes that the narrator disparages as wastes of time: religion, sports, and politics. Part of his negative attitude is due to the hypocrisy of the townspeople, who belie their supposed devotion to religion when they ignore Christian principles and continue to wage ghastly wars, all in the name of their home team, the United States. He is disgusted by their patriotic verve, their yelling, and their vociferous celebrations of war victories.

The narrator is also critical of the townspeople's domestic political scruples, misguided in that many citizens consistently vote against policies that would actually enhance the quality of their often squalid lives. Due to the ascendancy of neighboring cities, the business sector of B has declined, causing the closing of the local Chevrolet and Frigidaire outlets, which lends a shabby aspect to the town. Displaying his historical knowledge of small-town life, the narrator laments that the once majestic houses built at the turn of the century by wealthy farmers are now deteriorating—so much so that B threatens to join many of its neighbors in becoming what the narrator calls "rural slums." Most of all he nostalgically bemoans the disappearance of people working in harmony with unsullied nature without the mediation of chemicals and monstrous machines.

Despite the litany of flaws the narrator observes in his midwestern home, he is nevertheless capable of finding beauty there. He especially admires the splendor of the harvest season with its trees bursting with fruit and its gorgeous violet skies. An avid people-watcher, he is fascinated by the local population, which includes such inexplicable figures as Billy Holsclaw, a loner who spends his time counting and recounting the number of pieces of wood and coal he collected to support his single pastime: keeping warm. Like other people in the town, Billy sparks the narrator's poetic sympathies; selfishly, the artist in him wants Billy to remain the same in the hope that one day his poetry will capture the impoverished and lonely world in which so many of the inhabitants of America's heartland live. Although disillusioned by his loveless life and

skeptical of the ability of poetry to illuminate the bittersweet vagaries of rural life, the narrator is nevertheless resolute in his aesthetic desire to capture a kind of existence that, though it may lack the amenities of so-called progress, still maintains the flavor of country simplicity and idiosyncratic diversity.

Narrator. *In Watermelon Sugar*. Richard Brautigan. 1968.

The narrator of this fantasy novel is a young male writer who lives in a strange communelike town called iDEATH. Almost everything in iDEATH is made of watermelon sugar and trout oil, and the narrator asserts that in iDEATH the sun shines a different color each day. Each person who lives in iDEATH owns a small, undecorated shack, where they occasionally go for privacy. The narrator states, however, that the members of iDEATH spend most of their time together, working, eating, and sleeping in a large group.

The narrator is somewhat removed from his surroundings. He tells his story in a cold, distant style and reveals little emotion or passion. He does not need to surround himself with other people; rather, he spends more time in his shack than anyone else does in theirs because he is writing a novel. He takes most of his meals with fellow iDEATH inhabitants but often sleeps in his own shack or in that of his lover, Pauline. The narrator is subject to nightly bouts of insomnia, and thus he frequently takes long, solitary walks in the woods surrounding the town.

The narrator's own name is the only one he refuses to reveal during the course of the novel. He explains at the start that he cannot disclose his name because it is too extraordinary. The other inhabitants of iDEATH all have names that are quite common: the narrator's best friends are Charley and Fred, his ex-lover is Margaret, and his current lover is Pauline.

In the first book of the novel, the narrator provides a careful outline of all that he plans to discuss with the reader as the book progresses. He first describes the past, a time when man-eating tigers plagued iDEATH. These tigers killed and ate his parents when he was a small child, but they spoke his language and helped him with his arithmetic. The tigers were later killed, and iDEATH became peaceful. Every material object that existed during the time of the tigers is deposited in a large dump called the "Forgotten Works."

The narrator goes on to describe Margaret, his ex-lover, whom he despises. Because she insists on exploring the Forgotten Works, she is distrusted by the other members of iDEATH. The narrator is also disgusted by Margaret's fascination with the dump, and he eventually stops speaking to her. Margaret cannot understand why the narrator no longer loves her. She makes frequent attempts at reconciliation, but when she knocks on the door of his shack, he ignores her.

In the second book of the novel, the narrator discusses INBOIL, a former resident of iDEATH who moves to the Forgotten Works, forms a rowdy gang, and becomes an alcoholic. One evening, inBOIL and his gang appear at the iDEATH dining hall and demand that everyone follow them to the town's trout hatchery. Here inBOIL and his followers cut off their own thumbs, noses, and ears, and bleed to death.

The narrator is confused by inBOIL's actions. As he and his friends are collecting the bodies to burn them, they meet Margaret, who is just returning from the Forgotten Works. Charley, a friend of the narrator and brother of the late inBOIL, informs Margaret of the gang members' deaths.

In book three, Margaret, who is deeply upset by inBOIL's death and by the narrator's refusal to speak with her, hangs herself from the branch of an apple tree. The narrator calmly witnesses her death and then informs his friend Fred. The two men share the news with Margaret's brother and with all the members of iDEATH. Margaret is buried in the traditional iDEATH manner: She is placed in a glass coffin illuminated with foxfire and buried under the river.

The narrator and the other members of iDEATH prepare for a post-funeral dance, another custom of iDEATH. The novel ends abruptly, right before the dance begins.

Narrator. *Invisible Man*. Ralph Ellison. 1947.

The narrator tells the story of his life from the brightly lit rooms he inhabits in the abandoned basement of a "whites only" building on the edge of Harlem. The "invisible man" of the title, he explains his invisibility as a factor of white people's refusal to see a bright and dynamic young black man.

The narrator tells of his grandfather's haunting declaration, spoken from his deathbed, that life is an unrelenting battle fought in quiet and insidious ways. The grandfather's assertion echoes throughout the narrator's life like a curse. The narrator hears it when he makes his high school valedictorian speech on the value of humility and again when he repeats the speech for his southern town's leading white citizens.

In this later incident, the narrator addresses the wealthy and politically influential men in the ballroom of the town's most prestigious hotel. Before he gives his speech, however, the tuxedoed, cigar-smoking, intoxicated men demand that he don boxing gloves and a blindfold and join nine other black adolescents in a boxing ring. After being pummeled in this "battle royal" by the other boys and then pushed onto an electrified rug by the white men, the narrator presents his speech. He speaks with care and great effort through bloodied and swollen lips to the generally inattentive audience. The town leaders reward him with a briefcase and a scholarship to a prestigious southern black college.

Late in the spring of the narrator's junior year, when the school's white founders and trustees visit, the college's manipulative and powerful black president, Dr. Bledsoe, asks the narrator to drive for Mr. Norton, one of the elderly white millionaires. When Mr. Norton, the self-consciously benevolent northern financier, tells him simply to drive, the still naive narrator takes him on an unforeseen odyssey through the domain of the country's impoverished black citizens. Mr. Norton's subsequent injury in a chaotic barroom brothel, which has been taken over by the inmates of a local insane asylum, prompts the narrator's expulsion from college by Dr. Bledsoe.

In a malicious effort to scuttle his ambition, Dr. Bledsoe sends the narrator to New York with sealed letters to several influential friends of the college. The narrator guilelessly accepts Bledsoe's word when he is told that these letters will help him get a summer job and that he should not open them. Once in New York and living in a men's house in Harlem, the narrator dutifully takes the letters to the addressees. Not until Mr. Emerson, the idealistic and emotionally unstable son of a businessman, shows the narrator Dr. Bledsoe's letter does the narrator perceive his predicament: The president has asked the college's trustees to lead the narrator, his former student and an embarrassment to the college, as far away from the school as possible.

Disillusioned by this revelation, far from his family, and nearly penniless in a strange northern city, the narrator takes a job in the engine room of a large paint factory. The workers' union at Liberty Paints is on the verge of a walkout, however, and its members view all newly hired blacks as scabs. Narrowly escaping from the hostile workers, the narrator returns to the basement engine room and is set upon by his elderly anti-union black foreman, who fearfully accuses him of being a part of the union. While he is defending himself from the attacks of the old man, the pressure in the furnaces builds until the plant explodes.

The narrator wakes in the factory hospital with white company doctors and nurses standing over him discussing different types of experiments to conduct on his brain. They finally settle on the administration of electric shocks. Still reeling from the voltage shot through his body and striving to determine his own identity, the amnesiac narrator is released from the hospital and dismissed from his job. Weak and sick, he collapses as he emerges from a subway station in Harlem. A kindly older black woman, Mary Rambo, takes him to her home to recover. The narrator subsequently lives as her boarder for several months.

The following winter, the narrator sees an old black couple being evicted by a white marshal and is moved to make his first political speech. Arousing his listeners to violent action, the narrator also attracts the attention of several communist activists. After his ideological training, the communists name him chief spokesperson for Harlem.

Once in Harlem and working for the communists, the narrator encounters Ras the Exhorter, a black nationalist. In time the narrator loses confidence in the communists and, having fought with Ras, doubts that the nationalists can better the lives of blacks in this country. He turns away from public action and chooses to take refuge in invisibility.

Narrator. *The Letter Left to Me.* Joseph McElroy. 1988.

The young narrator has recently begun to cope with the death of his father, who had composed a letter to his son three years before his own death. "In retrospect I am appalled by my neglect of the vistas which life has opened to me," the father wrote. The letter tells the son that his father is leaving him two things—a healthy constitution and a good education—and urges him to make the most of his abilities, to avail himself of every opportunity. At first the narrator is incapable of reading the letter, but he succeeds in committing it to memory within a few days. Without the narrator's knowledge or consent, his mother, paternal grandmother, and paternal step-grandfather decide to make a printing of the letter for distribution among their family and friends. This invasion of the narrator's privacy has far-reaching effects as the letter and its contents are disseminated in the community.

Originally educated in a Quaker school where he showed great promise, the narrator chronicles his passage into high school, using the process of the letter's progress as a guide. Gradually his schoolmates learn of the letter, and some read it. In one instance it is even used as a text for a sermon during religious services. The narrator also speculates on the events surrounding his father's final illness and death, and on the funeral services that followed. He recognizes that his father's death has left a vacuum in his life, and he meditates on the fact that his father's own father had died when he was only ten. The narrator reasons that he has already been luckier in some ways than his father had been. Even so, he comes to resent the fact that his letter has become so public.

He decides against Harvard, where his father had gone and where his father urged him to "work harder than I did," and goes instead to a small college in New England. Here, too, however, nearly three years after his father's death, the letter intrudes upon the narrator's daily life.

During his freshman year, the narrator begins to make new friends and also begins to inquire more widely into his past and probable future. In the meantime, the narrator's mother takes it upon herself to send a copy of the letter to the dean, who is impressed enough by it to print copies, write a cover letter, and place them in each student's mailbox. This event prompts a new period of self-examination by the narrator, who begins to wonder about his friends' responses to the letter and its impact on their views of him. He watches as various individuals receive the letter. Some read it, others immediately throw it away.

He finds several copies in the wastebaskets of the dorm rooms, but he also encounters students who read the letter with varying degrees of comprehension, interest, or boredom. As the novel concludes, the narrator is aware that its ultimate effect on his life may never be clear enough for him to understand.

Narrator. "The Man Who Became a Woman." Sherwood Anderson. 1923.

The rambling narrator recounts a bizarre experience he had some years ago while working as a groom or "swipe" at a racetrack in Chicago. At the time he writes the story, the narrator is a happily married man; back then he was a timid virgin who fantasized about women but could never bring himself to approach them. The experience he tells about hinges on his sexual identity—or on his mistaken sexual identity, as the case may be.

The narrator's best friend at the track was Tom Means, who has since become "a writer of some prominence." Tom often talked to the narrator about horses and writing; in fact, the narrator's memory of Tom inspired him to write this story in the first place. After Tom's departure from the track, the narrator felt lonely and lazy. He moped around and listened to other people's conversations without interacting much with anyone. His best friend was his horse, Pick-it-boy, whom he loved dearly for its purity, simplicity, and affection. Sometimes the narrator wished Pick-it-boy were a girl or that he were a girl and Pick-it-boy were a man. While he usually dreamed about women's bodies and women's lips, sometimes, after spending a day with his horse, his impulses seemed to be temporarily cured.

One dark, rainy Saturday evening, the narrator was the last one to leave the track. Idly wishing he could be someone else and not himself, he decided to go to a saloon on the outskirts of town. Inside the saloon, he imagined the miners were looking and laughing at him. He saw his reflection in the mirror and was startled when his face was not his face at all but the face of a girl. Soon a large red-haired man entered the bar with his son. When a fight broke out between the red-haired man and a troublemaker, the narrator cringed at the sight of violence and stumbled out of the saloon.

Returning to the stables, the narrator took off his wet clothes and lay down totally naked in Pick-it-boy's stall. Feeling sick at the thought of what human beings can be like, he tried to remember pleasant things from his childhood and soon fell asleep under a horse blanket. An abrupt noise woke him; two black men suddenly entered the stall and saw him. Looking at him by the light of a lantern, they apparently thought the narrator was a woman. They told him to "lie still, honey," and said they would not hurt him. The narrator was utterly speechless and realized he had become the woman in his own fantasies. He escaped from the men through a hay-feeding hole in the floor and ran for his life away from the stables.

Terrified and sure he was being followed, the narrator kept running but was unable to make a sound. He came to the slaughterhouse located just beyond the racetrack and cut himself as he stumbled over an old horse skeleton. Consumed by a deeper, blinding terror that burned the "silly nonsense" about being a girl out of him, he let out a long, loud scream and immediately felt better. While crying as he walked through an open field, he came to a haystack where a few sheep had dug a small cave for themselves. The narrator joined the sheep in their resting spot and settled down, comforted at last.

Waking up, the narrator realized he would have to go back to the racetrack to retrieve his clothes. He could not avoid walking naked across the track and into the stables, and as he predicted, the men there howled with laughter at the sight of him. Only a loyal old swipe named Burt defended the narrator, who quickly got his clothes, kissed Pick-it-boy on the nose, and ran away from the racehorse tramp life for the rest of his days.

Narrator. "No Haid Pawn." Thomas Nelson Page. 1887.

The narrator is a white southern gentleman who recalls his terrifying encounter with the ghost of "No Haid Pawn" (No Head Pond). The narrator grew up on a plantation listening to the stories of his companions, the black men and women who were his slaves. Engrossing and convincing storytellers, they instilled in him a deep belief in spirits and ghosts. In particular, they warned him of the evil ghost that inhabited the mansion and surrounding area of No Haid Pawn. According to the stories, a brutal, inhuman West Indian man had inhabited the property and committed a heinous murder there. The man had been executed for his crime, but his ghost continued to haunt No Haid Pawn—a place where the narrator, although he had explored every other area within five miles of his home, never dared to go.

The narrator's story takes place in the 1850s when he was a young man feeling a new spirit of adventure and starting to overcome the fears that had constricted him in his childhood. An avid duck hunter, he decided one day to follow a duck into the dreaded territory of No Haid Pawn. Telling no one of his intentions, he made his way with great difficulty through the thick, overgrown swamp. When he neared the mansion, he realized that the sky had grown very dark with storm clouds. Parting the bushes to peer at the pond, he heard the sound of a rattling chain and, looking up, saw a chain hanging from the beam and cross-beam where the murderer must have been executed. At this moment a huge crash of thunder gave way to torrential rain, and the narrator, with nowhere else to go, sought refuge in the gloomy mansion.

Inside he found a bedroom and waited there, terrified, for the storm to subside. But much to his chagrin, the storm grew increasingly violent, the swamp flooded over, and night fell. Filled with dread and a sense of desolation, he resigned himself to staying there overnight. After fighting against his own frightening thoughts, he finally fell asleep but was awakened during a lull in the storm by a distant yell coming from the swamp outside his window. As he looked out, a huge flash of lightning illuminated the swamp, and he saw a figure standing in the middle of a boat next to an unidentifiable mass lying in the bow.

The storm began to rage again, and the narrator soon heard the same yell—this time directly under his window. He heard a door open below and the sound of fierce oaths being spoken in half-English, half–Creole French. The ghost of No Haid Pawn was moving upstairs, dragging behind him the body of the man he had murdered. After another bolt of lightning, the giant figure, holding a long glittering knife, was standing directly in front of the narrator. At the murderer's feet was a ghastly, bloody, headless corpse.

The narrator has never been able to describe his escape from No Haid Pawn, but fortunately he did escape: That night the mansion was struck by lightning and burned to the water's edge. No Haid Pawn was gone, and as the narrator tells us, "The spot with all its awful secrets lay buried under its dark waters."

Narrator. "The Open Cage." Anzia Yezierska. 1979.

The narrator is a desperately lonely and unhappy elderly woman who lives in a rundown building in New York City along with three hundred other unfortunate boarders, each of whom occupies a single, tiny room. The boarders are plagued by an unbearable noise, a horrendous stench, and a generally unlivable environment. Because of their unhealthy, overcrowded living conditions, the residents of the building react with hostility toward one another rather than band together to lessen the misery of their plights. One particularly frustrating morning, the narrator is frightened when an unexpected visitor arrives.

The narrator begins her day intending to take a bath but discovers that the man who lives adjacent to the bathroom has hidden the stopper of the bathtub so that he is not disturbed in the morning by noise. The narrator attempts to return to her dingy room only to discover that she has locked herself out. In order to regain admission, she is forced to descend in her bathrobe to the office to get a duplicate key. Having successfully regained access to her room, she is interrupted by a tapping sound that she assumes is someone knocking on her door. The sound turns out to be a tiny bird that has flown in; extremely frightened, it is fluttering its wings. The bird hides up in the molding, but the narrator is terrified by the wildness of the bird and seeks help from a neighbor, Sadie Williams, who keeps parakeets as pets. Crooning endearments that are meant to calm the agitated bird, Sadie manages to catch it and places it in one of the cages she has stored in her own single room.

Having recovered from her initial fright, the narrator becomes fascinated with the bird and excited by the idea that fate has provided it to assuage her painful loneliness. She becomes jealous of Sadie's attentions to the bird and worries about its physical welfare. Although water and food are placed in the bird's cage, the poor creature is too frightened to eat, and Sadie informs the narrator that the bird will die if it is not immediately set free. The narrator is fearful of losing her new companion but is eventually convinced that they have no choice. The two women walk to Riverside Drive with the intention of setting the bird free.

On reaching their destination, however, the narrator grabs the cage and, hugging it tightly, once again insists that she cannot part with her beloved new pet. Sadie Williams chastises her for being selfish and childish. Impressed with the magical manner in which the bird entered her life, the narrator is shocked by Sadie's suggestion that she buy just any ordinary bird at the pet shop. Ignoring her protestations, Sadie takes the wild bird out of the cage, and it immediately makes a strong dash for freedom. Exultingly watching the bird's unfettered flight, the narrator contrasts its freedom with the prison of poverty that both she and Sadie Williams must return to at the rundown boardinghouse.

Narrator. "The Pagan Rabbi." Cynthia Ozick. 1966.

The son of a rabbi, the narrator attended the rabbinical seminary for several years before deciding that he was not meant to be "a man of the cloth." Having rejected an orthodox faith, he has nevertheless continued to seek spiritual knowledge in a longtime friendship with RABBI ISAAC KORNFELD, a renowned Jewish scholar. At the story's opening, the narrator has just received news that Isaac committed suicide by hanging himself from a tree. As he journeys to the park where Isaac's death took place, he reviews the events leading up to this moment in his life, and his past begins to unfold.

After leaving the seminary, the narrator marries Jane, a Protestant woman. To express his disapproval of the marriage, his Orthodox father declares him dead and performs all the traditional Jewish mourning ceremonies. When the narrator attends Kornfeld's wedding, Jane bluntly points out that his father, also present, refuses to speak to him. It is only a "technicality," protests the narrator; his father has a disease of the larynx and is losing his voice. And yet the narrator later confesses to Isaac that his father was right about his marriage, but for the wrong reason. Jane is never passionate toward him, and they are later divorced. The narrator also loses his father, who dies after an operation on his throat.

Following the divorce, the narrator moves to the town where Isaac and his wife Sheindel live, leaving behind his fur business and opening a bookstore. The store provides a reason for corresponding with Isaac, who has become a highly respected professor of Mishnaic history. The narrator, at Isaac's request, sends his friend many books on all topics. He is shocked when he learns that Isaac has committed suicide at the height of his fame by hanging himself from a tree. The narrator takes a subway to Trilham's Inlet to see the tree and later visits Sheindel.

Since the wedding, the narrator has had a romantic interest in Sheindel and hopes to marry her as soon as it is "seemly." When he visits her after Isaac's death, however, it is apparent that she is utterly obsessed with the memory of her husband and strangely agitated by the notebook and letter that Isaac had in his pockets when he died. She encourages her visitor to read the notebook, but he is disappointed, finding only some biblical quotes and extracts from Romantic poetry.

When the narrator returns with the notebook, Sheindel insists on reading the letter to him that describes Isaac's astonishing discoveries. Isaac had become convinced that the human soul could be free to wander. He believed that he could achieve this freedom by having a passionate romance with a free-souled dryad named Iriponoeia. As the letter explains, following the dryad's eventual rejection of him, Isaac was driven to suicide. Sheindel condemns her husband for his behavior; the narrator, however, gains a deeper respect for his friend, and he takes the story quite literally. He advises Sheindel, who is extremely distraught, to go to the park where Isaac hanged himself and to confront her husband's soul there.

Narrator. *The Painted Bird.* Jerzy Kosinski. 1979.

The narrator spends four years during World War II living in the rural parts of Eastern Europe. A boy of six at the beginning of his ordeal, he is immediately identified as a Jew or a Gypsy stray because of his dark skin and black eyes. The narrator is feared and ostracized for his appearance, and he is hounded by brutal, superstitious peasants as well as by the Nazis.

The child's father is an anti-Nazi activist before the war, and his parents are forced to go into hiding to escape the death camps. Hoping to ensure his survival, they pay a man traveling eastward to place the boy with foster parents. The man leaves him with an aged, ailing peasant woman named Marta, who dies less than two months after the child's arrival. The narrator does not understand that Marta is dead until spilled kerosene catches fire and the hut burns down with the old woman inside it.

Running from the house, the boy is captured by a farmer and sold to a witch named Olga. Because Olga's services are highly valued in the village, he is relatively safe. He is vulnerable when alone, however, and one day a group of men send him floating down the river on an inflated fish bladder. He finds refuge for a short period with a miller but escapes after he sees the man scoop out the eyes of a young plowboy who lusted after his wife. He then finds shelter with a man named Lekh, whose job it is to capture birds. Lekh's great love, a woman known as Stupid Ludmilla, lives in the woods outside the village, where she often seduces the farm workers. When Ludmilla is beaten to death by the vengeful wives of the farmers, the child fears Lekh's despair and never returns to his hut.

He remains for a short time with a carpenter and for a longer period with a blacksmith, who is relatively kind. When the blacksmith is attacked by soldiers who accuse him of helping the enemy, the narrator is turned over to the Nazis. The narrator's would-be executioner is an older, sensitive-looking soldier who allows the terrified boy to run away, shooting off his gun only to simulate the murder. After hiding for a period with a solitary farmer, the narrator is again captured by the Nazis. This time, when he is perfectly willing to submit himself to death at the hands of the polished, imposing German officer, he is turned over to the village priest. The priest in turn forces him upon a man named Garbos, who lives alone except for his murderous dog Judas.

In addition to beating the boy regularly, Garbos terrorizes him by inciting Judas against him. Only Garbos's fear of divine retribution prevents him from simply killing the child, although he considers allowing Judas to do it for him. Garbos lets the boy attend church, where he learns a vast number of prayers by heart. He mutters prayers to himself ceaselessly, thinking the practice will earn him "days of indulgence." On the important holiday of Corpus Christi he is allowed to replace one of the altar boys but is so weak that he falls when trying to lift a missal during the ceremony. The enraged peasants throw him into a pit of manure and fetid water. He crawls out of the pit and vomits; afterward he finds he can no longer speak.

After his escape from the village, the narrator finds safety with a farmer's family. He falls in love with Ewka, the farmer's strange, pale daughter, and has his first sexual experiences with her. However, when he sees Ewka performing sexual acts with a male goat, his growing belief that evil has control over the world is confirmed. After leaving Ewka's family, he hides in a village that is pillaged by Kalmuks. Soldiers of the Red Army rescue him, and he spends a happy time with them recovering from a chest injury. One soldier, Gavrila, teaches him to read. The war ends, and he is removed from the soldiers' camp and placed in a home for children displaced during the war.

When his parents come to take him to their apartment, the narrator, wanting to keep his freedom, wonders if he can refuse to go. He explores the streets every night until he is caught by the police. His parents are concerned not only about his strange behavior but also because he is too thin and does not grow. They take him for a vacation in the mountains, but the boy is injured in a ski accident and must be hospitalized. He wakes up in the sunny hospital room, and when he answers the ringing telephone, he finds he has recovered his power of speech.

Narrator. "The Real Thing." Henry James. 1893.

The thoughtful, observant narrator is an artist who makes his living illustrating serial fiction in magazines and journals. Using models, he draws a wide range of characters for a series called "Rutland Ramsay." Major and Mrs. Monarch, two authentic aristocrats, come to him desperate for work after they have lost their financial resources. Partly out of pity, the narrator agrees to hire the Monarchs as models; thus begins his encounter with "the real thing," an encounter that helps him understand the subtleties of art and of human nature.

When the Monarchs first arrive at his studio, the narrator assumes they have come to have their portraits painted, for although he survives by drawing for magazines, he aspires to paint portraits to perpetuate his fame. The Monarchs hesitate to use the word "model," but the narrator finally realizes they have come for work and hires them on a trial basis. After an agreement is reached, the narrator's top model, a freckle-faced Cockney named Miss Churm, arrives for her sitting. The Monarchs are surprised the narrator finds Miss Churm suitable for the part of a Russian princess. The narrator recognizes that the Monarchs have a very limited understanding of the alchemy involved in art and that they are too caught up in their own identities, too self-conscious, to make good models.

In the weeks that follow, the Monarchs visit the studio and pose for their portraits. When Mrs. Monarch is being drawn, Mr. Monarch comes with her and often putters about the apartment and gives the narrator helpful hints about household arrangements. When Mr. Monarch is being drawn, Mrs. Monarch stays at home; the narrator senses she wants to send a message that while he is an appropriate professional acquaintance, he is not good enough to be their equal.

The Monarchs are a stunningly attractive couple, but the narrator stays aware that even with all their perfections, he does not believe in them. They are amateur models, after all, and the "ruling passion" of the narrator's life is to detest amateurs. Moreover, he has an innate preference for the represented subject over the real one. He gradually begins to feel oppressed by their confidence that they are "the real thing" and by their unspoken opinion that he is somehow fortunate to be able to associate with them.

The narrator hires another model, a short Italian man named Oronte, who has the same mutable qualities as Miss Churm. He can tell that the Monarchs are slightly repulsed to see Oronte in the studio. By this time the narrator has submitted his first set of drawings to the magazine, the set that includes those done with the Monarchs as models. Then the narrator's best friend and most lucid critic, Jack Hawley, returns after a long trip. The narrator is happy to see him and shows him the most recent illustrations. Hawley dislikes the pictures intensely, but, uncharacteristically, he cannot specify what is wrong with them. He only says they won't do, that they are "stupid," and that the narrator should get rid of the new models.

The narrator begins to use Oronte regularly for the "Rutland Ramsay" series, but he hesitates to inform the Monarchs of this. In the meantime, he receives a pointed warning from the editors of the magazine saying that the illustrations are not what they are looking for. Realizing he cannot continue to let his career suffer merely for the Monarchs' benefit, the narrator finally informs Mr. Monarch that Oronte will replace him. Mr. Monarch skeptically asks if the narrator really considers Oronte an English gentleman; the narrator snaps back that he refuses to let the Monarchs ruin him. Three days later the Monarchs return to the studio and watch silently as the narrator draws Miss Churm and Oronte. After doing small things to improve the household, they offer to be in the narrator's service, and he agrees to pay them for about a week. After the week is over, the couple leaves, never to return.

Narrator. *Steps.* Jerzy Kosinski. 1968.

The narrator recounts episodic events, most of which take place somewhere in Eastern Europe. He seems curiously detached from the telling of these uncanny, often somber tales.

The first story is of a well-to-do traveler through a rural area who finds himself attracted to a pretty peasant girl. Claiming that simply by displaying his credit cards in shops he can have anything he desires, he shows them to the girl. The lie—which is not very far from the truth—is enough to convince the girl to accompany him to the city, where he uses the cards to buy lovely clothes for her. But perhaps the girl is not as naive as she had appeared: Aroused by the city, the narrator, and her easily obtained possessions, she displays herself before him.

In another episode, the narrator is a soldier, part of a regiment chosen to participate in the National Day parade. The rigorous training sharpens the regiment's formation but saps the strength of its members. The narrator persuades some of the men to spend the designated day not on the parade ground but in the forest. Escaping easily, they charge into the woods, then strip and fall asleep in the sun. Suddenly, the narrator hears his regiment approaching and awakens his friends. While they flee, he is frozen on the spot. When he sees the regiment's flag, he automatically salutes, then realizes with horror that he has an erection.

A brutal rape opens another story. One night in the park, the narrator and his girlfriend are attacked by a group of men who beat him and rape her. Afterward the two see a policeman, but the woman is too traumatized to report the crime. She does spend two days in a medical clinic, however. During her first night back, the narrator initiates intercourse with her before she is ready and will not treat her tenderly. He responds to her pain and confusion with the claim that the rape has changed their relationship. The woman becomes only an object to the narrator, and he encourages her drinking because it makes her more tractable. Finally, when they are at a party with his male friends, the narrator quietly encourages each one to have sex with her. When the gang rape begins, he leaves.

A recent arrival in a Western country, the narrator has been supporting himself by working on the fringes of organized crime. He is hired as a chauffeur by a man who wants him to drive with skill but apparent recklessness while he holds meetings in the car with competing underworld businessmen. A dangerous ride, the narrator's employer tells him, will trick them into not paying much attention to the details of the meetings.

The narrator is such a good driver that his employer enters him in "book-knock-off" competitions. In the contest, books are tied to the sides of randomly selected parked cars, and contestants must drive at least fifty miles an hour, knocking off as many books as possible. Skillful at handling his vehicle, the narrator easily wins many contests. One night someone steps out of a parked car as a contestant is hurtling along the course. The speeding car goes past the parked one, slamming the door and decapitating the person on the course. The games are thereafter suspended.

Narrator. "The Tell-Tale Heart." Edgar Allan Poe. 1843.

The highly excitable, unnamed narrator admits to an extremely nervous temperament but repeatedly claims that he is not insane. Although he says he loves the old man he lives with, he is severely disturbed by one of the old man's blue eyes, which is dulled by a hideous film. The narrator is convinced that it is an "Evil Eye." He becomes so obsessed with the elderly man's eye that he decides to kill him in order to rid himself of the haunting, diabolical gaze.

The narrator's senses are so acute that he describes them as being cursed with a disease that will eventually cause his undoing. He creeps surreptitiously into his elderly companion's room every night at midnight for a full week, hoping to find the vulturelike eye open. He wants to murder the old man when his eye is open because it is the eye, and not the man, that he fears and detests. On the eighth night of his murderous vigil, he slips while trimming his lantern. His would-be victim awakens and, startled, sits up. For a full hour he sits motionless while the narrator waits undetected in the pitch-black chamber. Finally, the narrator opens his lantern so that a thin streak of light shines on the wide-open Evil Eye. The narrator's pathologically sharp ears begin to register the dull, deep sound of the old man's heartbeat, which accelerates and becomes louder as his fear mounts. This infuriating sound steels the murderer's resolve. He grabs his victim, throws him on the floor, and crushes him beneath the heavy bed. After a single shout, the old man dies, and his terrifying heartbeat ceases to plague the narrator's besieged ears.

Claiming that his careful disposal of the old man's body proves his sanity, the narrator details the gruesome manner in which he dismembers the corpse, keeping it in a tub so that the blood does not stain the surfaces on which the body lies. Having chopped up the body, the murderer then dislodges three floor planks in the house and hides the body among the scantlings. This done, he carefully replaces the boards and congratulates himself on a job well done. The narrator's thoughts are interrupted by a knock at the door. He descends to find out who could be visiting in the middle of the night.

The narrator finds three policemen on his doorstep, and they inform him that a neighbor reportedly heard a shriek. Claiming that he himself emitted the yell while experiencing a nightmare and explaining that his elderly friend was out of town, he invites the gentlemen in. They search the house to no avail. Having successfully concealed his crime, the villain calmly chats with the officers about mundane and unrelated topics. As he is talking, however, he notices a strange ringing in his ears. This noise grows louder and louder until the narrator recognizes the awful heartbeat of his victim. Convinced that the policemen can also hear this "telltale heart," he confesses to the murder of his innocent companion, shouting, "Tear up the planks! here, here!—it is the beating of his hideous heart!"

Narrator. "This Morning, This Evening, So Soon." James Baldwin. 1965.

A highly successful singer and actor, the narrator achieved his fame in France where he has largely been able to avoid the prejudice he encountered as a young African American in his home state of Alabama. On the eve of his return to the United States, he discovers that he has not escaped racism, however, for it lives within him.

The narrator, his Swedish wife, and their young son Paul are about to leave for the United States where the narrator will perform in an exclusive nightclub and will probably also undertake a Hollywood film career. On the eve of his departure, the narrator has planned to spend the evening with a longtime friend, the man who directed his most successful movie. Although he looks forward to the evening out, the narrator is preoccupied with what awaits him and his family on their arrival in the States. Among other things, he recalls the bigotry he encountered on his last trip home, eight years before, on the occasion of his mother's death. Along with these haunting memories, he recollects his father's fate. The narrator fears that

his son will have to confront the racism that emotionally crippled and eventually killed the boy's grandfather. Paul's situation will be made all the more difficult because he is the product of an interracial marriage, a union still illegal in many states.

The narrator and his director friend go to a variety of places until they finally encounter a group of four young African Americans who admire the narrator and ask to buy him a drink. Soon the six are established as a group for the evening, and they sing and dance through the night. In its club-and barhopping, the party encounters an Algerian acquaintance of the narrator. This man, Boona, is a member of an ethnic group that experiences humiliations in France as routinely as do African Americans in the United States. He joins the party and is soon dancing with one of the young girls. Eventually it is revealed that some money has been stolen from one of them, and Boona is instantly accused.

The narrator knows that Boona frequently relies on theft to procure money for food, as do many other members of his ethnic group since regular employment is difficult to obtain. He intercedes and decides to question Boona himself, with the intent of giving the girl his own money in order to avoid insulting his friend. Nonetheless, like a white racist in the United States, the narrator humiliates his friend, and the evening ends on a sour note, even though the girl eventually asserts that she had probably lost the money and that she doesn't believe in Boona's guilt. All suspect that Boona probably stole the money, but the matter is dropped once the young travelers perceive Boona's humiliation.

As dawn approaches, the day of departure arrives, and the narrator, filled with uneasy anticipation, returns to his family, wakes his sleeping son, and realizes that the time has come to face the unknown.

Narrator. *Trout Fishing in America.* Richard Brautigan. 1967.

The unnamed narrator gives little direct information about himself. He reveals only that he was raised in Portland, Oregon, that he is highly knowledgeable about trout fishing, that he has a baby daughter, and that he and his daughter and a female companion are traveling about the country on a low budget. His relationship to his traveling companion is unclear, for at one point the narrator mentions that he has a pregnant wife, later he refers to "my woman," and thereafter he refers to "the woman I travel with." The narrator seems to be in his late twenties or early thirties, the time period seems to be the early or mid-1960s, and the narrator is apparently a member of the generation of young Americans known as "hippies."

Trout Fishing in America is by no means a straightforward or realistic narrative, but it is clear that the narrator and his traveling companion and child travel widely: They spend some time in San Francisco, where they meet Trout

Fishing in America Shorty, a legless wino; they travel to New York, where they go to Hotel Trout Fishing in America to visit an ex-convict and an ex-prostitute who live there. In the chapter titled "Trout Fishing on the Street of Eternity," they are visiting southern Mexico; and at one point the narrator travels to Cleveland to visit a wrecking yard that has a trout fishing stream for sale at a good price. The narrator and his family also camp in various parts of America where good trout fishing is available, and they spend a summer living in a shack in California with some friends.

This brief summary of the narrator's itinerary reflects the key themes of the novel: The narrator is traveling around America, cavorting with various socially or legally outcast characters, and, in an interesting variation on that theme, there are numerous nonsensical references to "trout fishing in America." These references clearly reflect the narrator's love of trout fishing, but it may also represent a particular aspect of American history and life for the narrator. For example, when the narrator writes a letter to Trout Fishing in America warning him or her that he or she is wanted by the FBI, "trout fishing in America" serves on one level as a metaphor for an American innocence and simplicity that the narrator feels is threatened.

It is probably unwise, however, to attempt to reduce this work to a simple or single meaning. Although the narrator at times lends serious overtones to his observations, he clearly offers his fanciful sketches in a spirit of fun—in this regard, as in others, representing the spirit of the "flower children."

Narrator. *Typee: A Peep at Polynesian Life; Omoo: A Narrative of Adventure in the South Seas.* Herman Melville. 1846; 1847.

The narrator of these two novels about life on several islands in the South Seas is an adventurous American sailor who refers to himself once as Tom, or, as the Polynesians say, "Tommo." As he describes his experiences with both the "savage" inhabitants and the missionary authorities, he proves to be a jovial and engaging raconteur.

The narrator's story begins aboard the *Dolly*, a dilapidated Nantucket whaler whose voyage, already lengthy and arduous, promises to continue indefinitely. The narrator finds himself unable to endure the ship's moldy stores, rough crew, and tyrannical captain, and decides to jump ship at the first opportunity. When the *Dolly* touches at the Marquesas Islands, he enlists the help of a dapper young seaman named Toby, and together they escape into the island's interior.

After a harrowing journey through dense thickets and steep and rocky chasms, the narrator and Toby finally arrive in a beautiful valley. But the narrator's relief turns to alarm when he discovers that its seemingly placid inhabitants are in fact the Typees, a ferocious and—it is rumored—cannibalistic tribe. He and Toby have no choice but to follow their chief to the dwelling that Marheyo, an elder tribesman, shares with Kory-Kory, his tattooed warrior son.

Contrary to the sailors' expectations, the natives appear to be exceedingly hospitable and benign, and the narrator soon settles into a pleasant routine. He suffers from a mysterious lameness, acquired during his journey to the valley, and Kory-Kory carries him daily to wash and swim in a nearby stream. But as time passes and his leg refuses to heal, the narrator has great difficulty convincing the chief to let him journey to the other side of the island. Toby is finally dispatched to procure the necessary medications; when his friend does not reappear after several days, the narrator realizes that he is not merely a guest but a captive of the Typees.

Nevertheless, he is able to enjoy the company of Fayaway, a nubile and solicitous young woman, and the friendship of many of the native men. He spends long hours wandering about the valley, observing the inhabitants in their daily occupations, and questioning Kory-Kory about everything from the making of tappa, a native cloth, to the establishment of burial grounds and feasts.

Tom's lameness vanishes for a time but eventually returns with added severity as he begins to experience a melancholy longing for home. His sense of security is badly shaken when he accidentally discovers that the contents of three mysterious bundles, which he had seen hanging in Marheyo's hut, are in fact human heads. When he hears at last that a ship has arrived in the bay, he makes his way down to the sea and, taking advantage of a moment of confusion among his captors, makes good his escape.

Aboard the *Julia*, an Australian whaler, the narrator recovers from the illness that plagued him throughout his stay with the Typees. He encounters Captain Guy, a mousy, incompetent seaman who nevertheless manages to exercise a cunning control over the crew. He also meets Dr. Long Ghost, the lanky ship's physician, with whom he becomes fast friends. It soon becomes apparent that the *Julia*, overrun by roaches, rats, and disease, is as miserable a craft as the *Dolly*, and at a stopover on the island of Tahiti, the crew refuses to continue the voyage. The narrator composes a "Round Robbin," a formal expression of the crew's grievances, with the names signed in a circle so that no one member can be charged. The crew is escorted by the French military to the village of Papeetee and placed in the "Calabooza Beretanee"—the English jail—under the care of the native Captain Bob.

In this tropical lockup, the prisoners enjoy a relaxed, vacationlike life. They use baubles and trinkets from their sea stores to bribe and befriend the islanders. As the narrator and Long Ghost roam the island, however, they discover that this once resplendent paradise has fallen into a state of decay. The residents of the island are listless and indolent. Their traditions have been debased by the misguided efforts of the Christian missionaries, who, in seeking to convert the islanders, have reduced them to poverty and contaminated them with disease.

When they are set free from the Calabooza, the narrator and Long Ghost go to work on a neighboring island as farmhands for Old Zeke, a cranky expatriate Yankee. But they soon find the work too grueling and embark instead on a journey in search of Pomaree, the Tahitian queen. On their travels through the various island communities, the two white men are warmly received, housed, and entertained. Upon arriving at the palace, however, they are afforded only a brief glimpse of the queen, who sits eating her native repast amid a careless array of porcelains and antiques—gifts of the colonizing admirals and kings. As the novel ends, the narrator ships out once again, this time on an American whaler, while his faithful friend Long Ghost opts to remain in the South Seas.

Narrator. "The Use of Force." William Carlos Williams. 1933.

The anonymous narrator is a medical doctor who makes a house call and faces the emotional consequences of having to use force in order to examine a child.

When he arrives at the house, all the doctor knows is that the family is called Olson and that their daughter is ill. The doctor is taken to the kitchen where the child is sitting fully dressed on her father's lap. The child, an attractive girl named Mathilda, acknowledges his arrival with a cold and expressionless face. He notes that she looks strong but is obviously suffering from a high fever, which the father explains has lasted for three days. The doctor is particularly concerned because within the previous month a number of diphtheria cases were discovered at the school the child attends. He asks the parents whether Mathilda has complained of a sore throat, the telltale symptom of the disease, and they say that she has not. He decides to examine the girl and tries in his best professional manner to coax her to open her mouth, but Mathilda refuses and knocks his glasses off his face when he moves his chair closer to her. The parents' admonishments only make matters worse, and the narrator begins to feel contempt for them as he increasingly admires the child's strength of will.

The physical struggle that ensues is nerve-racking, but the lurking fear of diphtheria causes the adults to persist in their attempts to get the girl to open her mouth for the doctor. He manages to insert a wooden tongue depressor between her teeth, but she reduces it to splinters and her mouth begins to bleed. It occurs to the narrator that it might be better to stop and try again later, but he has seen two children die from the disease purely out of neglect and he silently argues that early diagnosis is crucial. He also admits to himself, however, that he has lost control

of his temper and at this point actually enjoys exerting force on the hysterical child. Arguing that it is his duty to prevent Mathilda from infecting others with the contagious disease if she has it, he nevertheless experiences a powerful feeling of shame as he finally wrenches the girl's jaws open and forces a silver spoon down her throat. The child's tonsils, as he thought likely, are covered with the membrane that characterizes diphtheria.

The narrator realizes that the child has been hiding her sore throat and lying to her parents about it in order to escape being diagnosed with the dread disease. As the story ends, the tearful, furious child tries to attack him.

Narrator. "Views of My Father Weeping." Donald Barthelme. 1981.

The young narrator in this short story searches to unmask his father. While conducting his own private investigation, he is constantly bombarded with vivid, fragmentary apparitions of his father's posthumous existence.

The story opens with the narrator's stark comment that his father has been run over by the carriage of an aristocrat. The remainder of his story explains how he has gathered this information and what he eventually does with it. First, he travels to the scene of the accident. Here he learns from a little girl that the carriage looked "like an aristocrat." He imagines a conversation with the guilty aristocrat where the nobleman acknowledges his culpability and offers the young man "a purse full of money."

Interrupting his own narrative, the young man describes a scene of his father sitting in the center of a bed, weeping profusely. The young man looks on, wishing to placate his father somehow or to run away.

Back at the scene of his father's death, a man tells him that he heard two men discussing the incident in a shop. The narrator learns from one of these men that the driver could have stopped his horses if he had cared to; what's more, his father was dragged forty feet from the point at which he was struck. Finally, the narrator is informed that the driver's livery was blue and green.

As the narrative continues, the apparitions of his father become more varied. One shows him wearing a red bandanna around his face, carrying a water pistol, and crying, "Stick 'em up." Another view shows the middle-aged parent straddling an extremely large dog. In yet another scene, he pours pepper into the sugar bowl. But the scenes always return to the narrator's father weeping on the bed.

Finally, the small girl who earlier identified the coach as aristocratic comes to the narrator's room and provides him with the name of the coachman. When he hears the name Lars Bang, the narrator becomes frightened at the prospect of actually facing anyone of the staunch aristocratic world, even if the person was responsible for his father's unfortunate death. Before the wavering narrator resolves to face his father's murderer, the coachman Bang visits him and promises the orphaned narrator a full account of his father's death. He asks the young man to come to the address printed on the card he supplies.

On the advice of a friend, the narrator goes to the address located in an exclusive aristocratic neighborhood. He is carrying several bottles of expensive wine so that the watch will think he is "an honest man on an honest errand." When the narrator arrives, Bang opens and shares the wine with several other men and one young woman gathered around the pantry table. He tells his version, which characterizes the narrator's father as a madman who attacked the horses of the carriage. His attack caused the horses to rear and led to his death. Although Bang had wanted to stop, his master was so shaken and upset that he ordered him to drive on. His story finished, Bang says the narrator should be satisfied and drink another bottle of claret with them. The story ends with the dark-haired girl declaring that "Bang is an absolute bloody liar."

Narrator. "Where I'm Calling From." Raymond Carver. 1988.

Near New Year's Day, at a "drying-out facility" called Frank Martin's, the unnamed narrator confronts his devastating addiction to alcohol. This is the narrator's second time at the facility, and as he begins to understand the suffering of his fellow boarders and to review his own life, he sees that his full recovery will take pain, patience, and some luck.

Among the patients at Frank Martin's is Tiny, a good-natured electrician who seems well on the road to recovery but suffers a traumatic seizure as the result of his detoxification. Another patient at the facility is a businessman who insists he doesn't have a drinking problem although he can't remember how he got to Frank Martin's. Of all the patients, the narrator is closest to J.P., a chimney sweep whose excessive drinking put his job and his marriage in jeopardy. His hands shaking, J.P. tells the narrator how he became a chimney sweep and fell in love with his wife, and how his drinking eventually came to dominate their lives. The narrator listens intently, comforted by the sound of his friend's voice.

The narrator sympathizes with J.P., for his own marriage has crumbled under the stress of his addiction to alcohol. His wife brought him to Frank Martin's the first time, but when he returned home only to relapse into his alcoholism, she banished him from their house. The narrator then moved in with a girlfriend, the woman who later brought him back to the facility. The two had gone on a drinking binge after the woman learned she might be seriously ill. Both arrived at Frank Martin's drunk, and the narrator remembers having trouble signing the check that would admit him as his girlfriend drove away.

When J.P.'s wife Roxy arrives for a visit, the narrator is touched by her tenderness toward her husband. Suddenly he asks Roxy, who is also a chimney sweep, if she will give him a kiss for luck. She agrees, and as she and J.P. walk away hand in hand, the narrator recalls a special moment with his own wife.

As the story closes, the narrator considers calling his wife to wish her a happy New Year. He knows he will have to tell her where he is calling from, but he feels sure that when he does, he can keep his voice steady and his emotions in control.

Narrator. *Winter in the Blood.* James Welch. 1974.

The anonymous Blackfoot Indian narrator exhibits a spiritual vacancy representative of the emptiness of the land and life surrounding him on the reservation. At thirty-two, he is bereft of all that he ever really loved. His father, First Raise, died of exposure on a winter's eve ten years before en route home after a night of drinking. The half-suicidal act was in part the result of First Raise's agony over the death of his son Mose; older than the narrator by two years, Mose died at fourteen when he was struck by a car while the narrator and their father were rounding up cattle in preparation for a winter storm. The narrator carries with him the burden of both deaths, but the memory of his brother is particularly painful. Still living in the bedroom he and Mose once shared, he believes it contains "mementos of a childhood, two childhoods, two brothers, one now dead, the other servant to the memory of death."

When the novel opens, the narrator, recently beaten by a white man, is coming home to three women for whom he has little affection: his self-involved mother, Teresa; his grandmother, who was once the beautiful wife of a chief and remarried twenty-five years after he was slain; and his girlfriend Agnes. Once at home he finds that his girlfriend has left him and has taken his gun and electric razor with her. Despite his indifference toward her, the narrator decides to pursue Agnes, who has been seen in the nearby Montana town of Malta.

In Malta he befriends a man who claims he is being pursued by the FBI for theft. The man solicits the narrator to buy a used car and drive him over the Canadian border in exchange for $500 cash and the car. But before the narrator acts on this scheme, he spies Agnes and follows her into a bar. Agnes warns him away, claiming that her brother Doagie intends to attack him. Within minutes Doagie knocks him unconscious, and when he comes to, the narrator observes the arrest of the strange man he has agreed to assist.

Returning home, the narrator finds that his grandmother has passed away, forcing him to recollect with epiphanic potency the events leading up to the scene of Mose's death. Informing Yellow Calf, a local aged man, of his grandmother's death, the narrator discovers that this is the man who years earlier had rescued her from death by starvation following the inter-tribal battle that left her widowed. Moreover, the narrator realizes that Yellow Calf is his own maternal grandfather.

But the subsequent scene casts a shadow on this bright moment. In a series of events that recapitulate those leading up to the brother's death, the narrator's horse goes wild during an attempt to rescue a cow. The narrator, unable to restore order to the situation, fails symbolically to rectify the tragic events of the past. What remains is a bleak hope that "next time I'll do it right."

Narrator. "The Yellow Wallpaper." Charlotte Perkins Gilman. 1892.

The narrator is the treasured and protected wife of John, a no-nonsense doctor. She is undertaking the kind of rest cure advocated by well-known Philadelphia neurologist S. Weir Mitchell whereby women are to avoid any kind of exertion conceivable, both physical and mental, in order to overcome a mental depression. However, the so-called cure, with its insistence that women do not express themselves, think, or work, drives this woman to insanity.

The narrator's husband secures an ancestral hall for three months one summer in order for his new wife to undergo the rest cure and to free her of the responsibility of their new baby. John does not believe that there is anything seriously wrong with his wife. Her only symptom of disturbance is her tendency to hysterical excitement, and to prevent such outbursts he has forbidden her to write or think about her condition. The young wife would like to occupy a pretty downstairs room, but her husband has her occupy the nursery on the top floor. Its windows are barred to protect the children, and it is papered with flamboyantly patterned wallpaper in garish yellow. Forced to lie in bed practically all day, the narrator contemplates the wallpaper endlessly, trying to figure out its meaning. She begins to see the whorls in the pattern as bars imprisoning a woman behind the wallpaper, but she hides her vision of the imprisoned woman from John and his sister Jane because she does not want them to take her away until she has completely deciphered the wallpaper's code.

The narrator imagines the woman behind the paper coming out of the wall during the day. At the same time, the narrator begins to creep around her room, keeping the door locked because she is growing increasingly suspicious of John and his sister. On the last day of her three months' internment, the narrator tears off all the wallpaper, which by now appears to her to be "strangled heads and bulbous eyes and waddling fungus growths shriek[ing] with derision." She creeps around the room and ties a rope around herself so she can't escape. When John comes in, he faints when he sees her. Now believing that she is the woman trapped behind the paper, the narrator insists "I've got out at last in spite of you and Jane. And I've pulled off most of the paper, so you can't put me back!" She continues to creep around the room, repeatedly crawling over her unconscious husband.

Narrator. "Yellow Woman." Leslie Marmon Silko. 1974.

The narrator is a modern Native American woman whose encounter with Silva, a mysterious cattle rustler, causes her to lessen her resistance to believing in the legends of her people. Drawn to his potent sexuality and relinquishing her individuality, she stays away from her home and goes with him on a mythical sojourn.

The narrator first meets Silva on a riverbank, and they make love; the next morning, in order to find a horse, she retraces their footsteps from the night before, and when she returns, she tells him she is leaving. Silva smiles and replies, oddly enough, that she is coming with him. He calls her "Yellow Woman," the name of a mythical character in an old Indian story who goes away with a spirit for a long time and returns home with twin boys. The narrator says she is not Yellow Woman but a person with her own name from a nearby pueblo. Silva, gentle and persistent, pulls her to him. Although awakened by the feeling of his warm, damp body, she insists she does not have to go with him; she believes that what they tell in stories was only real "back in time immemorial." But when they stand up, she does follow him northward.

They arrive at a house made out of black lava rock and red mud. Inside the house Silva continues to watch the narrator closely. They eat, and the narrator, who persists in thinking that she is beyond the old legends of her ancestors, asks Silva if he has brought other women there using the same tricks. When Silva unrolls the bedroll, the narrator lies down with him. Unable to resist him, she feels his body on her and is afraid of his strength. Later, while he sleeps beside her, she is overcome by her feelings for him and kisses him on the forehead.

In the morning Silva is gone when the narrator wakes up. After eating some dried apricots, she takes a long walk and thinks of her family. Knowing that her husband, mother, son, and grandmother will manage without her, she imagines they will create a story about how she disappeared one day while walking along the river. When she returns to the lava stone house, she remembers that she meant to go home, but returning does not seem important to her anymore. Silva is there, and he asks her to go with him to Marquez to sell some meat.

On their way to Marquez, the narrator and Silva meet a white rancher who accuses Silva of rustling cattle and plans to call the state police. The narrator looks at Silva for an instant and sees an ancient, dark look in his eyes; glancing down, she catches sight of his hand on the trigger of his revolver. The narrator slaps her horse and rides off without looking back. She thinks she hears four shots fired behind her.

Much later, after riding away from the mountain, the narrator leaves the horse and walks toward home. She decides to follow the river back the way she and Silva had come. During her walk she thinks of him, and although she feels sad about leaving, she knows there was something strange about this cattle rustler. Coming to the place by the river where she first encountered him, she sees the willow leaves he had trimmed from a branch and wants to kiss him and touch him again. After telling herself that he will return one day and wait for her by the river, the narrator enters her village. At the screen door of her house, she hears the voices of her family inside. She decides to tell them that a Navajo kidnapped her; she is sorry her grandfather is not alive to hear about her adventure because he always liked the Yellow Woman stories best.

Nazerman, Sol. *The Pawnbroker*. Edward Lewis Wallant. 1961.

Sol Nazerman is a forty-five-year-old Polish Jew whose hellish experiences in a Nazi concentration camp make him feel older than his real age. A former university professor, Sol emigrates to the United States where he becomes an apprentice in a pawnshop in Harlem. After a number of years, Sol is eventually offered his own pawnshop, in reality run by a small-time mobster named Murillio. Through his pawnshop Sol earns enough to help support himself, his sister Bertha and her family (who live in Connecticut), and his girlfriend Tessie.

The novel unfolds in the month leading up to the fifteenth anniversary of the death of Sol's family in the concentration camp. In his world of trinkets and various pieces of stolen merchandise, Sol's customers and contacts come in the form of hookers, drug addicts, hoodlums, and an apprentice named Jesus Ortiz. Jesus, a young black man intent on following in the footsteps of his uncle, a successful merchant, yearns to attain Sol's financial savvy and wisdom.

As the anniversary of his family's death approaches and his elaborate defense mechanisms begin to erode, Sol is haunted by nightmares. When Murillio, in order to assert his authority over Sol, forces him to suck on the end of his gun, Sol remembers being forced by a guard to watch his wife perform fellatio on an SS officer. In a crowded subway car, Sol remembers losing his son David in the packed cattle trailer used to transport them to the concentration camp. To shield himself from these consuming memories, Sol ignores the pleas of Jesus and his nephew Morton for recognition and guidance, and fully embraces a mercenary way of life. Money, he tells Jesus, is the only constant in the universe.

However, Sol pays the price for his refusal to recognize the humanity surrounding him. After being indoctrinated into Sol's calculating values, Jesus and two of his friends attempt to rob the pawnshop on the anniversary of the death of Sol's family. Wishing for the death that was deprived him during the Holocaust, Sol is about to be shot by one of the burglars when Jesus jumps in the way of the bullet, then falls to the ground dead.

Overwhelmed with grief at the death of his assistant, Sol finally realizes the error of his ways and undergoes something of a rebirth. He phones his nephew Morton, whose pleas for guidance he had previously ignored, and tells him that he needs him. His next few dreams, he finds, are devoid of the usual horror. In a final act of redemption, Sol, now ready to meet life once again, journeys to the home of his mistress Tessie, to accompany her to the funeral of her father.

Nedeed, Luther. *Linden Hills*. Gloria Naylor. 1985.

Luther Nedeed, the fifth in an unbroken line of male heirs, controls the economic, familial, and social life of the community that his forefathers built. Linden Hills boasts a history and tradition that reaches back five generations beyond the Civil War and revolves around the Nedeed clan. A showcase of black enterprise, Linden Hills is an "ebony jewel that reflected the soul of Wayne County but reflected it black." In the mid-1980s the fifth Luther Nedeed reigns as master and guardian over the nationally acclaimed neighborhood envisioned by his ancestors. Ostensibly, Linden Hills has exceeded the Nedeeds' expectations.

Early in the novel, however, Nedeed realizes and acknowledges to himself that the neighborhood has fallen far short of his family's goal for it. Instead of proving "what black could do," Linden Hills has shown that blacks have given themselves over to the will to possess. The shining veneer of Linden Hills reflects "the bright nothing that was inside them." Nedeed finds himself ruling over a kingdom that is crumbling from the inside out, and his efforts to rescue Linden Hills only speed its disintegration.

Nedeed's own household has not escaped the malediction that plagues Linden Hills. The horrifying story taking place in Nedeed's home parallels the decline in the community. Early in the novel, Nedeed, enraged at what he convinces himself is his wife's infidelity, has locked her and her son in the basement of his home. Nedeed's charge of adultery stems from the fact that his young son does not bear the dark skin, bowlegs, and bulging eyes of the Nedeeds. Instead, he is a fair-skinned version of his maternal grandmother. Soon after this imprisonment, the child develops a fever and dies. Feeling that the mother needs time to recover from the death, Nedeed keeps the woman locked away until fate intervenes.

With Christmas Day approaching and her sanity and physical condition diminishing, Mrs. Nedeed learns the sad histories of the women who have preceded her. The fading portrait of her mother-in-law provides an object lesson of the fate that has befallen each wife. Once she has given birth to the Nedeed heir, each Mrs. Nedeed became a superfluous entity, ignored by husbands and sons alike. By Christmas Eve, Mrs. Nedeed has become insane. The same evening, Nedeed broods over his crumbling empire and admits that he is powerless to save it. To compensate for his wife's absence, he has hired Willie Mason and Lester Tilson, two young men who have been working to earn money for Christmas gifts, to help him decorate his tree.

As Mrs. Nedeed prepares to emerge from her hell, Willie and Lester help Nedeed decorate the tree upstairs in the den. At the moment that Nedeed places the last and crowning ornament atop the candle-laden fir, Mrs. Nedeed enters carrying her son's rigid body. Nedeed hustles the young men out the door and attempts to grab his wife. She locks her startled husband in a tight grip, topples the Christmas tree, and sets the house ablaze. By the time Willie and Lester rouse the neighbors to call the fire department, the house has burned to cinders. Nedeed, his wife, and child are carried from the house in one huge mass.

The Negro. "Red Leaves." William Faulkner. 1930.

This story concerns the rites and rituals that ensue after the death of an Indian chief, Issetibbeha, known to his people as "The Man." Although the entire Indian community is affected by their leader's death, none is more dramatically concerned than the dead chief's black slave, known simply as "the Negro."

The Negro, who had been captured in Guinea when he was only fourteen, has already witnessed his owner's slow death. From a secluded spot he listens as the word spreads that the chief is dying, and finally the death occurs. At this point the Negro must flee, for it is a custom that the deceased chief carry his horse, dog, and slave with him into the next world. The ritual pursuit of the runaway slave commences as two middle-aged Indians follow his trail by scent and by design, while speculating on the likelihood of a prolonged chase. These two Indians, Three Basket and Louis Berry, reflect on their people's history and traditions, thus paving the way for an account of the history of the chief's family.

As it turns out, although the Indian chiefs had intermarried with blacks, they also deliberately encouraged them to have offspring so that they could sell the slaves off to white men. This policy was arrived at after it was agreed several generations previously that blacks should not be eaten any longer and that they should be used to work the fields.

As Three Basket and Louis Berry note, the last time a chief died it was three days before the slave was caught. Needless to say, the burial cannot proceed without the slave's presence. It is also apparent that the Negro is either too dazed by his fate or is a willing actor in it, since he plans an escape route that in fact keeps him on the plantation they inhabit.

The Negro runs for hours and miles but then stops, wondering how long he can rest before the Indians following him figure out that he has doubled back and is now near the compound again. He sleeps for a while and then runs off again, faster than he had intended, but he still remains within the confines of the Indian community's land. He eventually encounters other blacks who offer him food and inform him that he must move on because it is forbidden for the dead to associate with the living. The Negro then removes his clothing and covers himself in mud, as protection from mosquitoes. He also eats ants, which he finds surprisingly salty.

Meanwhile, the Indians are becoming more concerned about the hunt. The success of the ritual depends on the willingness of the dead chief's fat son to lead the final search. At Three Basket's urging and under his direction, the new chief symbolically leads the chase for a time, but he is not especially interested in it. During this phase of the hunt, as the deceased's body begins to smell throughout the area, the Negro is bitten by a snake, and it is the sounds of his pain that finally lead his captors to him.

Now the Negro, half-crazed with exhaustion and fear, submits, as though entranced, as Three Basket informs him that he did a good job of running but it is time for the final services. They lead him back to his former master's grave site, where the body, the horse, and the dog are already waiting. The Negro asks for water but finds he cannot swallow, and the sound of his anguished breath is heard echoing in the empty water gourd as the Indians prepare to finish their ritual.

Nelson. "The Artificial Nigger." Flannery O'Connor. 1948.

Nelson is an impudent, sharp-tongued ten-year-old. The illegitimate son of a mother who died soon after bringing him from Atlanta to her father's home, Nelson has been raised by his widower grandfather, MR. HEAD, in the woods of Georgia. He likes to torture his grandfather with the claim that having been born in Atlanta means he is from there, despite the fact that he has spent almost his entire life in the country. As he and Mr. Head set out to the city for a day, Nelson reminds his grandfather that this will be the second time he has been there.

On the train to Atlanta, Nelson sits stiffly in his new suit and hat "like a miniature old man," feeling quite full of himself. When a black family enters the car and the racist Mr. Head must inform Nelson that these are black people, Nelson simultaneously experiences his own ignorance, his grandfather's wisdom, and a feeling of hatred for the black family. Some time later, when Mr. Head stops Nelson from jumping up and getting off at the wrong station, the boy begins to sense his ultimate dependence on his grandfather.

In Atlanta, however, Nelson is thrilled by the excitement of the big city, exclaiming, "This is where I come from!" When he notices that his grandfather is walking him around the center of town in a circle so as not to lose sight of the train station, Nelson angrily accuses Mr. Head of not knowing where to go. Mr. Head, embarrassed, pulls the boy in a different direction, and it is not long before they are lost in the black section of town.

Both Nelson and his grandfather are too afraid of the black people they pass to ask for directions back to the train station, although it is getting late and they are hungry and tired. Finally, Nelson catches sight of a black woman with dark eyes standing in a doorway. As he asks her how to get to the train station, he is fascinated by the woman and longs to be picked up and enveloped by her, "to feel her breath on his face." Suddenly his grandfather pulls him away, and Nelson again feels ashamed and afraid of the woman.

Nelson and Mr. Head set off along the trolley tracks, hoping this will bring them directly into the train station. In a jeering and angry tone, Nelson begins to claim that he never wanted to come to the city at all. He is exhausted and soon decides he must rest a bit before continuing any farther. He sits down on the sidewalk and in a moment is fast asleep.

Suddenly a loud bang awakens him. Disoriented and terrified, Nelson runs down the street. He rounds a corner and collides with an elderly woman, arms laden with packages and shopping bags, who begins screaming that her ankle is broken. Nelson sits motionless, dazed, on the sidewalk. After several minutes he sees Mr. Head slowly approaching and runs to him, grabbing him by the pants leg. But even more devastating than the accident itself, Mr. Head claims he has no idea who the boy is, and he walks through the crowd to continue on his way.

Nelson stares after Mr. Head for a moment, stunned by his grandfather's denial of him. Then he begins to follow some twenty feet behind the man, staring at his back. He ignores Mr. Head's attempts to reconcile and his offers of soda. They continue walking, still lost, until they finally enter a wealthier neighborhood with mansions and cultivated lawns where Mr. Head frantically asks a passerby for directions.

As Nelson's grandfather leads them on toward the train stop, they see a startling object attached to the wall surrounding a wide lawn. It is a small plaster figure of a black man, about the size of Nelson himself. Mr. Head explains the figure is an "artificial nigger," and both stare at the object as if confronted with "some monument to another's victory that brought them together in their common defeat." When at last they come to the station and the train takes them safely home, Nelson declares, "I'm glad I've went once, but I'll never go back again!"

Nettie. *The Color Purple.* Alice Walker. 1982.

Throughout the course of her adventurous life, Nettie writes devotedly to her sister CELIE. Although Nettie and Celie are cut off from each other by Celie's vengeful hus-

band ALBERT, Celie manages to discover the letters, which inspire her to abandon her destructive marriage. Nettie plays a pedagogical role in her sister's life as well as in the African town where she becomes a missionary.

As children, the sisters are allies and friends in a neglectful and brutal family. Celie is repeatedly raped and twice impregnated by their stepfather. The sisters are separated when Celie is married off to Albert, who was originally Nettie's suitor. Nettie runs away to live with Celie but must leave eventually in order to escape Albert's threatening advances. Albert follows Nettie as she leaves, drags her into the woods, and attempts to rape her. When Nettie manages to fight him off, he vows in revenge to intercept all her letters to Celie.

Nettie finds refuge with the couple who have already adopted Celie's two children. Samuel, a minister, recognizes Nettie's resemblance to their adopted children and welcomes her into the family without question. He and his wife Corrine are planning to begin their missionary work in Africa. When the other missionary is prevented from going, they invite Nettie to accompany them. She agrees, provided she can be of assistance as a schoolteacher in the village and as caretaker of the two children, Adam and Olivia.

Nettie writes to Celie about every detail of the trip, although she correctly suspects that Albert has kept his promise and that Celie never sees the letters. Life in the African village of the Olinka is extremely difficult. The villagers are usually indifferent toward the missionaries but violently resist many changes they propose. Nettie wants especially to see the obedient women and girls gain some freedom, but the Olinka refuse to send their female children to school and consider them only as potential wives. Adam and Olivia do become intimate with one Olinka girl, Tashi, and both Tashi and Adam undergo African scarification rites and are later married by Samuel.

Nettie begins to despair for the village when the Olinka land is co-opted by a rubber manufacturer in England. Claiming to own the land occupied by the Olinka, the manufacturer proceeds to destroy it, knocking down houses and plowing under crops so that rubber trees can be planted. Forced onto a barren stretch of land, the Olinka begin dying out quickly.

Enormous changes also occur within Nettie's family. Corrine falls ill, plagued by the belief that Nettie is actually her children's biological mother. Nettie manages to convince her that they are Celie's children, but Corrine dies soon afterward. Later, when the family travels to England to seek help for the Olinka, Nettie and Samuel experience the awakening of a new kind of love for each other and are soon married. They receive no help for the village, however, and after a hopeless period there, they return to the United States.

When they arrive in their hometown, they find a situation vastly different from the one they left. After discovering the hidden letters, Celie has left Albert to live with her lover, the glamorous blues singer SHUG AVERY. Their stepfather has died, leaving the house to Celie and Nettie. After the sisters' tearful reunion, Celie presides over the house and introduces Nettie to Shug and to Albert, now reformed and respectful toward both sisters.

Nevels, Gertie. *The Dollmaker*. Harriet Arnow. 1954.

Gertie Nevels is the courageous and resilient heroine of this epic novel, which tells the story of a dislocated Kentucky family during the closing years of World War II. Gertie struggles to retain her independence and heritage in the brutal and dehumanizing world of wartime Detroit.

Gertie, a big rough-hewn woman, first appears riding a mule on a rainy afternoon in rural Kentucky. Her son Amos is desperately unwell, and Gertie is determined to take him to the nearest doctor by whatever means possible. She forces her mule into the path of an oncoming car, bringing it to a halt, and before the eyes of a horrified army officer and his driver, she draws out a knife and cuts into Amos's throat to prevent him from choking. By sheer animal will and stubbornness she overwhelms the disdainful officer who consequently drives her into the local town, where Amos is saved.

Gertie's strength and resolve are drawn from her knowledge of her own world. Ignorant of the technological advances of modern society, Gertie dreams only of buying a small farm where she and her family can live independently, free from the monthly rent that must be paid with half of everything they produce. Within this small world, where most of the men are always fighting, Gertie emerges as the backbone of the community: strong, literate, generous, and determined. When her own husband, Clovis, is called for an army medical examination, Gertie is at last free to buy a farm with the money she has secretly saved during her married life. As her hopes are about to be realized, Gertie decides to devote more time to her more "foolish" aspiration: to carve the face of Christ from a piece of wood that has for years captured Gertie's imagination. Yet this vision of domestic simplicity and independence is shattered by the news that Clovis is not going to war but is staying to work in a factory in Detroit. Gertie is forced by her mother—whose vision of a vengeful and exacting God conflicts with Gertie's vision of a benign Christ—to move to Detroit, where she is to live with Clovis and their five children in a two-bedroom shack overshadowed by steel mills and coal heaps.

In this new and soulless world, Gertie battles against poverty, debt, loneliness, her own ignorance, and the prejudice of those around her. Her resistance to the life-style and values of the urban society and her failure to assimilate to its ways are marked by the gradual disintegration of her own family. Her eldest son, Reuben, returns to Kentucky, implicitly condemning Gertie for her weakness; Clytie, Enoch, and Amos enthusiastically acquiesce to the materialistic values of their new life; and Cassie, the youngest daughter, retreats further and further into her own imaginary world until she is accidentally killed by a train.

As the novel draws to a close, Gertie reluctantly realizes that, unlike Reuben and Cassie, she cannot escape. Her fears that her mother's vision of God might be true and that the poverty and steel mills of Detroit are indeed God's creation are finally confirmed. In a final and tragic act of acquiescence, she relinquishes her unique art in order to produce cheap wooden figures.

Newman, Christopher. *The American*. Henry James. 1877.

Christopher Newman is the personification of the American ideals of democracy and entrepreneurial spirit. Newman, a self-made success, has left his native America to visit Europe and to acquire a beautiful, clever wife, which he believes will result in the rags-to-riches story of his life. What he experiences in Europe, however, is a tragedy arising from the encounter between his good-natured idealism and the rigid social standards of a French patrician family, the Bellegardes.

Newman is introduced to Parisian society by Mrs. Tristram, his confidante and social mentor. Newman divulges to Mrs. Tristram his desire to marry, so she arranges for him to meet a beautiful young widow, CLAIRE DE CINTRÉ, daughter of the aristocratic house of Bellegarde. He is soon taken with the grace and sensitivity of Madame de Cintré and resolves to seek her hand in marriage.

But Claire is not amenable to the idea of marriage. Her previous marriage to an elderly nobleman, which had been arranged by her family, was unhappy, though brief. But Newman, believing that his clever persistence can surmount any obstacle, presses his suit, and Claire finally agrees to a long courtship, after which she will decide whether or not to accept his proposal. Her mother, Madame de Bellegarde, and her brother, Urbain de Bellegarde, are repulsed by Newman's lack of gentility but reluctantly agree to the courtship; their consent is rooted solely in their desire to bring Newman's fortune into the family. They tolerate Newman's suit with cool civility, but when Claire actually accepts Newman's proposal, they coerce her into breaking the engagement, for ultimately they cannot tolerate the idea of a commoner—even one of great wealth—marrying into their family. Newman appeals to Claire, but to no avail. Because she is so thoroughly under the sway of her family, she has decided that she will never remarry and will instead become a Carmelite nun.

In the meantime, however, Newman has made two allies within the Bellegarde household: the housekeeper, Mrs. Bread, and Claire's other brother, VALENTIN DE BELLEGARDE. Valentin does not share the icy reserve of Urbain and Madame de Bellegarde. He is carefree and amicable, and he quickly befriends Newman. But, tragically, Valentin is mortally wounded in a duel. On his deathbed he suggests to Newman that a terrible secret haunts the Bellegarde family. Only Mrs. Bread knows the secret that Valentin intuits; if Newman asks Mrs. Bread to reveal the secret, then he will have the means to compel the Bellegardes to permit the marriage.

Newman does learn the secret of the Bellegardes from Mrs. Bread. She tells him the sordid story of how, several years ago, Madame de Bellegarde murdered her husband by withholding his medication. Mrs. Bread reveals a note, penned by the dying Marquis de Bellegarde, that testifies to his impending death at the hands of his treacherous wife. Mrs. Bread gives the note to Newman. He confronts the Bellegardes with his newfound knowledge, and although they do not deny the charge of murder, they will not consent to the marriage of Newman and Claire. Enraged, Newman plans to reveal the Bellegarde secret to Parisian society and thereby ensure the family's ruin, but, finally, he cannot commit himself to this act of revenge.

Newman is consumed with remorse over Claire's loss and with bitterness over the perfidy of the Bellegardes; his sole pleasure is in the knowledge that his possession of the note undoubtedly terrifies the Bellegardes. He feels his entrepreneurial drive disappear, and he curses the Bellegardes for reducing him to what he believes is the most detestable of creatures—a hopeless loafer. To relieve his languor, Newman decides to visit the house of the Carmelites, where Claire de Cintré is cloistered. Gazing at the house, he realizes that she is all but buried there, that she is irretrievable. This realization frees him from the torment of his ineffectual yearning. At the same time, inspired by either Christian good will or his own innate good nature, Newman lets go of his anger toward the Bellegardes.

Resolving to leave Paris forever, Newman pays a last visit to Mrs. Tristram. He casts the infamous note into her burning fireplace and tells her of his possession of the secret—without actually revealing it—and of his former plan to use it against the Bellegardes. After hearing his story, Mrs. Tristram suggests that the Bellegardes could not be coerced by his possession of their secret: Their strength lies not in their innocence or in their cunning but in their absolute confidence in Newman's own good nature, which would ultimately not allow him to act vengefully. This insight appears to strike Newman, and he instinctively checks the fireplace for remnants of the note, but it has been completely consumed.

Newman, Lawrence. *Focus.* Arthur Miller. 1945.

Lawrence Newman is an average, unambitious racist. He does not consider his anti-Semitism a form of violence; it is virtually unconscious, a seemingly natural response to his job and environs.

The loyal employee of a large company in New York City in the 1940s, Lawrence oversees seventy-five female typists and frequently hires new ones. Throughout his term of service, Lawrence, a white Episcopalian, has adhered unquestioningly to the company's policy of not hiring "ethnics." He prides himself on having become an expert at determining a prospective employee's race, ethnicity, and religion on the basis of her appearance and comportment.

As the novel opens, Lawrence's vision seems to be failing. He has let a few women of questionable background slip into the company ranks, and his dismayed boss, Mr. Gargan, insists that he obtain a pair of glasses. Lawrence puts off getting the glasses because he senses that they will somehow be bad for him. When he finally makes the purchase, he discovers to his horror that the frames make him look like a stereotypic Jew. His nose in particular seems more aquiline with the glasses on than off.

Lawrence soon realizes that other people make the same assumption. When interviewing Gertrude Hart, a curvaceous and attractive applicant who he thinks looks too "Jewish" for the company, Lawrence is shocked to find that she holds the same opinion of him. Eventually, and despite his redoubled efforts at screening applicants, Lawrence is dismissed. After a series of demoralizing interviews, he winds up applying for a job at a company owned by a Jew and populated by Jews, Hispanics, and African Americans. His interviewer is none other than Gertrude Hart.

Gertrude is initially as rude and condescending to Lawrence as he was to her, but they are sexually attracted to each other and Gertrude is forgiving enough to hire him. Lawrence, in turn, finds that the more he likes her, the less "Jewish" she seems. After a brief but passionate romance, Lawrence marries Gertrude, who moves into the home he shares with his mother. Things go well for the couple until their neighbors organize the auspices of the "Christian Front" and begin to harass Mr. Finkelstein, a Jew who has opened a store nearby. At first Lawrence tries to ignore the conflict, but Gertrude insists that he become a member of the Front and join in the fight.

Although he sympathizes with the prejudiced view of Jews as a greedy, dirty, and unappealing people, Lawrence soon finds that he cannot abide the Christian Front's hatred of Mr. Finkelstein. Indeed, after talking to his Jewish neighbor, Lawrence sees that he is clean, polite, and noble of spirit. But the Front, resolving to cleanse the neighborhood of undesirables, physically attacks Lawrence and Mr. Finkelstein. At first Lawrence tries to persuade his attackers to get "the real Jew" and not him. When they ignore his pleas, he winds up fighting side by side with Mr. Finkelstein, and they emerge bloodied but undefeated.

A few hours later, when Lawrence goes in search of Gertrude who disappeared during the attack, he discovers that she has taken refuge in a neighbor's house and that she remains loyal to the Front and proud of her anti-Semitic credentials. Lawrence, disgusted by his wife's self-serving solution to their problems and fully cognizant of his new values, resolves to fight the anti-Semites with Mr. Finkelstein rather than keep on trying to appease them.

Newsome, Lonnie. "Kneel to the Rising Sun." Erskine Caldwell. 1935.

Lonnie Newsome is a poor white southern sharecropper who fails to find the courage to stand up to a tyrannical plantation owner. He is friends with Clem Henry, a black sharecropper and the only man in the region who dares defy the sadistic owner, Arch Gunnard. Although sympathetic to Clem and aware that they are both oppressed by the economic system of sharecropping, Lonnie cannot help allowing fear for his own safety and race loyalty to determine his actions.

One day at the filling station, Arch cuts off the tail of Lonnie's dog. The sharecropper lets Arch maim his dog without objection. Aware that Clem is watching, Lonnie is ashamed but also afraid for both their sakes that the black man will interfere. Lonnie is severely emaciated because of Arch's short rationing and was advised by Clem that morning to ask for more food, but he cannot bring himself to speak as the plantation owner walks off swinging the dog's tail.

Lonnie's wife Hatty wakes him up in the middle of the night to tell him that his father, Mark Newsome, left the house hours earlier and has not yet returned. They are particularly worried because the deaf old man was suffering considerably from lack of food. Lonnie goes out in search of his father and makes his way to Clem's house to ask for assistance. The two proceed to the big house, and they notice a commotion in Arch's pen: The hogs are fighting over Mr. Newsome's mutilated corpse. After retrieving what is left of the body, Clem insists that Lonnie wake up Gunnard.

Arch reacts to the incident by asking why they were around his house in the middle of the night. Clem angrily tells him that the old man was searching for food. As the two opponents confront each other, Lonnie becomes afraid that Arch will make good his threats to kill Clem if he steps out of line again. The white sharecropper stands by helplessly as the men begin to fight in earnest, then Clem runs for the barn and Arch goes into his house to telephone his neighbors for help. Clem asks Lonnie to help save his life by standing up for him. Without verbally agreeing, Lonnie lets Clem believe that he will speak up on his behalf and will keep Clem's hiding place in the woods a secret until the danger passes.

When Arch returns, Lonnie is intimidated and admits that he knows where Clem is hiding. Upon hearing the assembled mob talk about killing Clem, he begins to speak in his friend's defense but is cowed into silence when the crowd becomes angry at him for taking the side of a black man. Lonnie reveals Clem's location to Arch and accompanies the lynch mob through the woods. He becomes confused and for a moment thinks they are searching for his father, but as dawn nears, he is one of the first to reach the tree where Clem is hiding. He looks for a moment at Clem's face, then closes his eyes as the man's body is riddled with bullets.

Abruptly, Lonnie turns and runs out of the woods. He falls, struggles with difficulty to his knees, and stares at the rising sun. Its warmth gives him strength, and as he stands, he begins to talk to himself, trying to say things he had never articulated before. When he returns home, his wife tells him to go ask Arch Gunnard for some meat for breakfast. Lonnie says he isn't hungry.

Nightshade, Jim. *Something Wicked This Way Comes.* Ray Bradbury. 1962.

Like most thirteen-year-olds, dark-haired, green-eyed Jim Nightshade is always in trouble. But the trouble he finds is much darker than the kind most thirteen-year-olds normally face. Only through the intervention of his best friend WILL HALLOWAY and Will's father CHARLES (HALLOWAY) does Jim reach his fourteenth birthday.

The trouble begins when the carnival, Cooger and Dark's Pandemonium Shadow Show, comes to town. A lightning rod salesman also appears and gives Jim a rod to put on his roof as protection against an approaching storm. Jim, who is always looking for excitement, would actually rather see his house burn. The more level-headed Will begs Jim to accept the lightning rod, if only to keep his mom from roasting to death in the fire that would result from a lightning strike.

Although Jim loves his friend, he resents the fact that Will holds him back from dangerous fun. Will would rather take Jim to the library, where they can vicariously experience pirates' journeys and soldiers' battles, than find their own wars. Jim suspects that part of the reason Will loves the library is that his father is the janitor there.

The boys see the carnival being set up late at night and realize there is something evil about it. The mirror maze is literally a trap; the carousel will age its riders or make them younger; the sideshow freaks are all people who were bewitched by the carnival owner, the heavily tattooed Mr. Dark. Jim is enthralled, especially by the carousel. It can give him the chance to leave his boyhood behind and be just a bit older—seventeen or eighteen maybe. Attracted and repulsed by the idea of growing up, Jim is easy prey for Mr. Dark. Once Mr. Dark realizes the boys know the carnival's evil side, he must capture them. What better way than to promise Jim what he thinks he wants?

Jim is aware of his own weakness, however, and asks Will to stand by him. Together the boys evade Mr. Dark for a time, but they finally must turn to Will's father Charles for help. In the library Charles shows the boys books that document Mr. Dark's carnival and others like it. Before they can discuss how they will combat the evil that the carnival represents, Mr. Dark tracks Jim and Will to the library. The boys hide in the stacks, but when Mr. Dark convinces Jim that his mother has been killed, Jim begins to cry and betrays their hiding spot. Mr. Dark captures them, puts them in a trance, and spirits them away to the carnival.

Charles Halloway is able to break Dark's spell, but Jim runs to the carousel the moment he is freed. As the ride whirls around, Will is able to pull his friend off, but Jim is killed as he strikes the ground. Convinced by his father that love and laughter can defeat the carnival, Will joins Charles in dancing and singing as Jim lies on the ground. The celebration works: Jim regains consciousness. Restored to life and cured of his desire to grow old before his time, Jim races back to town with Will and Charles Halloway as the carnival crumbles.

Nirdlinger, Phyllis. *Double Indemnity.* James M. Cain. 1936.

Phyllis Nirdlinger is the woman in love with death. A half-crazed native of Los Angeles, she hooks the hapless WALTER HUFF in a murder plot and then drags him to his destruction.

Walter, an insurance salesman, goes to the Nirdlinger house with hopes of renewing Mr. Nirdlinger's automobile insurance. Phyllis, appearing in a pair of blue house pajamas, tells Walter that her husband isn't at home. She asks him if he would like a drink and then, very casually, asks him if he sells accident insurance. Walter is greatly attracted to Phyllis the moment he sees her, but he decides that he had better not tangle with a woman who is pricing accident insurance for her husband. Walter returns a few days later, however, and when Phyllis asks if it would be possible to take out accident insurance without her husband knowing about it, Walter takes her in his arms.

The next night Phyllis goes to Walter's house and apologizes for losing her head. Now Walter takes the helm, accusing Phyllis of planning to kill her husband. Phyllis denies everything, but Walter remains firm, saying that she is going to kill her husband and he is going to help her. Phyllis begins to cry. She says that her husband would be happier dead. She says there is something in her that loves death and that she thinks of herself as death sometimes, floating through the night in a scarlet shroud. She asks Walter if he understands what she is talking about, but he has no idea.

It will be a while before Walter understands. In the meantime, Walter tells Phyllis about an insurance policy that pays twice as much—double indemnity—for deaths in railroad accidents. Through a series of clever dealings witnessed by Phyllis's innocent stepdaughter Lola, Walter procures the accident policy without Nirdlinger knowing it but with the appearance that Nirdlinger took out the policy in secret. Soon after, Nirdlinger announces that he is planning a train trip to a college reunion.

The complex murder plan, in which Nirdlinger is killed

beforehand and Walter boards the train in his place, goes off smoothly. But driving home afterward, Phyllis raves like a lunatic, and Walter, for the first time, gets scared. He gets more scared when nobody at the insurance company believes that Nirdlinger's death was accidental. Keyes, head of the claims department, says the odds are that this was a murder, and he suggests the company keep a close watch on Phyllis.

Over the next few weeks Walter begins to crack, but Phyllis, who has other things on her mind, remains cool and distant. Unbeknownst to Walter, Phyllis is preoccupied with a small but persistent youth named Nino Sachetti, son of a doctor whom Phyllis worked for before her marriage. Phyllis had been an angel of death masquerading as a hospital nurse, and Nino's father had been ruined by his association with her. Nino, trying to get to the bottom of things, has been hanging around the Nirdlingers' house and has developed a crush on Lola.

Nino is not the only person taken with Lola. Soon after the murder, Lola visits Walter and hints at a depth of evil in Phyllis that even Walter hasn't suspected. Walter decides that Phyllis is a madwoman. At about the same time he develops a romantic interest in the innocent Lola.

Phyllis now has three flies to ensnare: Nino, Lola, and Walter. As usual, Walter makes things easy for her. Terrified of being discovered, terrified of Phyllis, terrified in general, Walter decides to strike out at the source of his fear. He phones Phyllis and tells her to meet him in the Hollywood Hills. He plans to shoot her dead, but Phyllis gets there first and beats him to it. But Walter doesn't die. Instead, he awakens in a hospital bed to learn that Lola and Nino are now suspected of killing Nirdlinger and attempting to kill him. Walter decides there is only one thing left to do. He calls Keyes to his bedside and confesses everything. Oddly enough, Walter's confession puts Phyllis where she has wanted to be all along.

The insurance company wants to prevent the scandal of a long trial. They tell Walter that if he signs a full confession, they will put him on a boat to the Tropics. They tell Phyllis the same thing. Phyllis and Walter meet on deck, and Phyllis jokes that now they can be married. She stares down at the water and says she is ready to meet the only bridegroom she has ever loved. "I'll go with you," Walter says.

A large shark begins following the ship. Phyllis says they must wait for nightfall and a bright moon—she wants to see the black fin of the shark cutting the water. As the book ends, Walter sits in his cabin as Phyllis paints her face white, wraps herself in a red shroud, and waits for the moon to come up.

Nixon, Dick. *The Public Burning.* Robert Coover. 1977.

Dick Nixon provides the point of view for this dark, satiric, post-Watergate novel about Julius and Ethel Rosenberg and the hysteria of the Cold War years. Provoked by a cast of characters that includes his wisecracking uncle Sam, The Phantom of world communism, and a National Poet Laureate named TIME, Nixon bumbles his way up to and through the Rosenbergs' execution.

Born in Yorba Linda, California, Dick spent his youth in nearby Whittier. His childhood is marked by the death of his two brothers; the combination of this tragedy and the family's Quaker past gives Dick a sense of entitlement equal to his nascent ambition, but perhaps greater than his ability. At Whittier College he warms the football team's bench, establishes his own fraternity, and indulges in amateur dramatics. His passing romantic interest in the daughter of the town police chief is succeeded by an enduring relationship with Pat, his future wife.

Dick's public service begins at the Office of Price Administration, then moves during World War II to the Pacific Theater of Operations. Returning triumphantly to Mom and Pat, he is soon launched on a political career that stretches from Congress and his apprenticeship with the House Un-American Activities Committee to the humiliation of his "Checkers Speech" and to the vice-presidency. Burdened by a perpetual five o'clock shadow and increasing flatulence, Dick falls into psychological turmoil in 1953, the year the Rosenberg "atom spies" are convicted and sentenced to die publicly in an electric chair erected in Times Square.

Although convinced of the Rosenbergs' guilt and committed to their electrocution, Dick is strangely obsessed with their past lives and with the tenuous case against them. Ethel in particular consumes his attention. He finds his mind drawn to the similarities he imagines between her life and his own: They share the same wedding anniversary, are very close in age, and both enjoyed amateur theatrical productions. Dick's reveries about Ethel and the imagined past he creates for her soon devolve into sexual fantasy, but his masturbation is interrupted by the sarcastic Uncle Sam.

On the day of the execution, Dick takes a train from Washington to New York, then continues on to Ossining to visit the Rosenbergs in prison. He hopes to convince them to confess their guilt, but his interview with Ethel soon turns into a seduction. They are interrupted, however, and Dick suddenly finds himself addressing a bloodthirsty crowd in Times Square with his pants down and "I am a scamp" lipsticked across his buttocks. With his usual rhetorical finesse, he turns the humiliation to his advantage and soon has the entire mob standing with their "pants down for God and country." The Rosenbergs are murdered; Dick withdraws from the stage and into the confusing New York extravaganza.

In the final nightmarish sequence, J. Edgar Hoover, disguised as Dick's grandmother, confronts Dick, and then Uncle Sam approaches him from behind and rapes him. Dick confesses, "I love you, Uncle Sam," at which point he is free to return to his dog Checkers, his young daughters, his lonely, strained wife, and his looming political future.

Nolan, Frances "Francie." *A Tree Grows in Brooklyn.* Betty Smith. 1943.

Frances Nolan is born and raised amid poverty and passion in the slums of Williamsburg, Brooklyn. Born to Johnny Nolan, a singing waiter and a drunk, and Katie Nolan, a practical and resilient woman who cleans tenements to support the family, Francie and her little brother Neeley must take pleasure in the more common things. She transports herself by reading and by her own imagination, and perched on the fire escape, she watches her neighbors live out their lives.

Francie first experiences the scorn the poor endure when she attends an overcrowded school staffed by poorly trained, frustrated teachers. For Frances there is the magic of reading and learning, and the pride of being American just because her parents were born in Brooklyn instead of "the old country." Francie soon moves to another school and learns that other ways of life are not beyond her reach. Aware of the life around her, she takes in the experience of becoming a woman in early 1900s New York. Soon she daydreams of becoming a writer and searching for ways to reconcile her active imagination with the reality presented by her family's daily struggle for survival.

One day Francie almost becomes the victim of a child molester. Not long afterward, Johnny dies of pneumonia—he has been sober but is finally overwhelmed by his responsibilities when Katie becomes pregnant again. Francie and Neeley are only able to finish grade school because the local saloon keeper gives them part-time work. At school Francie's teacher scolds her for writing "sordid" stories about poverty; the world's idea of beauty, she leads Francie to understand, has nothing to do with truth.

With a new baby in the family and her dreams of high school crushed when her mother decides the next year that Neeley should go instead, Francie finds work in the city. Although she does not agree with her mother, Francie develops a grudging respect and love for her tenacity. Because Francie is working, that Christmas is the first not scarred by want. The entrance of the United States into World War I brings a new job for Francie as a teletypist working the night shift; she uses this opportunity to take college summer classes, where she meets and develops a crush on Ben Blake, a high school senior with big plans for his life. The following year Francie studies to pass the Regent's exam so that she can take classes toward a college degree.

About to begin college at the University of Michigan at Ann Arbor in September, Francie arrives at an "understanding" with Ben Blake: In five years she must tell him whether she will marry him. As she prepares to leave the neighborhood she has known so well, she wonders at how the world has changed. She also marvels, as she looks out her window at a young girl reading on the fire escape and at the beautiful tree growing unnoticed out of the Brooklyn concrete, at how it stays the same.

Nolan, Jim. *In Dubious Battle.* John Steinbeck. 1936.

Jim Nolan, a purposeless and detached young drifter, attempts to lend direction to his life through Communist Party activism. Although he is given a sense of meaning and involvement at first, Jim ultimately falls prey to an all-consuming allegiance to the cause that absorbs and destroys his identity.

Jim is living in a boardinghouse when he receives a notice summoning him to an interview for admission to the Party. He explains that he wants to join in order to feel alive again. At "the Joint," a lodging and work center for Party members, Jim meets MACLEOD, "MAC," who will serve as his mentor. Jim tells Mac of his background. His father, made senseless by repeated beatings, was shot by riot police. He and the family had lived in a constant state of debilitating, futile rage. Jim could not help noticing the difference between his anger and that of the jailed activists he met while serving time for vagrancy: Their anger had meaning and purpose, for it was directed against a system. Jim also explains that he has all but ceased relationships with women for fear that he will get someone pregnant and wind up leading the tortured existence of his parents. He is willing to lead a hard, dangerous life, provided that it is in the service of a cause and that the conflict he encounters is direct and straightforward rather than insidious and gradually debilitating. Most important, he believes that people do not win battles when they are fighting alone.

After arriving in Torgas Valley with Mac and becoming absorbed in preparations for a fruit workers' strike, Jim grows increasingly dedicated, single-minded, and driven. He rarely sleeps and asks Mac for more and more responsibility. The relationship between the two men begins to change as Jim grows more autonomous and sincerely committed to the cause. Initially led and instructed by Mac, Jim is soon the one providing the older and more seasoned comrade with guidance. As strike conditions worsen and morale deteriorates, Jim reminds Mac that sometimes people struggle the hardest and fight their best when obstacles seem insurmountable.

The philosophical and idealistic Doc Burton, who helps out at the strikers' camp, begins to notice a look akin to religious fanaticism in Jim's eyes. Jim condemns Doc's references to religion as irrelevant and misguided. When the farm of Mr. Anderson, whose land had supplied the evicted strikers with a camp, is destroyed by fire, a local boy involved in the arson is caught, tied up, and brutally beaten by Mac—who afterward credits Jim as the inspiration for his relentless cruelty. When Mac begins to express remorse, Jim coldly speaks of the violence as a necessity, an "operation." As Mac had done earlier, Jim

discounts as trivial and meaningless the idea of individual suffering. Mac is startled; he finds Jim frightening and inhuman.

Yet flashes of humanity continue to break through Jim's fanatical dogmatism. Walking around in the strikers' camp, he is deeply moved by the sight of a young woman combing her hair; he sees a look in her eyes that reminds him of the eyes of the Virgin Mary, which he saw on one of his childhood visits to the Catholic church. It is a cool and an assurance, he observes, that can be derived only from being in heaven. Jim is alarmed by the peace and beauty of the countryside and finds it impossible to believe that violence is not awaiting him in it. He expresses a desire just to observe nature and reflects on how life, uninterrupted and unstructured, just works itself out.

Jim's thoughtfulness ends abruptly. He snaps back to Party rhetoric when Mac demands that he go into town in order to be protected from an onslaught of strikebreaker violence. Jim coldly refuses, accusing Mac of acting not out of concern for the cause but for friendship, a motive he deems "personal" and foolish. Attempting to unify the men, Jim suggests that he tear the bandage off his wounded shoulder and whet the men's appetite for action through the sight of blood. Then someone charges into the tent and frantically directs Jim and Mac outside, telling them that a doctor is lying injured in the orchard. Jim and Mac dash out and are confronted by a blast of fire. Jim is shot to death, his face blown away. His body is carried by Mac to a corner post of the platform where speeches are made; Mac leaps up and begins a speech on Jim's selfless dedication to the cause, with Jim's faceless, bloody corpse propped up for all to see.

Nolan, Philip. "The Man Without a Country." Edward Everett Hale. 1865.

Philip Nolan, on trial for treason in conjunction with the activities of the traitor Aaron Burr, brashly ruins his entire life by blaspheming the nascent American government. When asked by the judge at the end of his trial whether or not he wishes to establish his innocence and loyalty to his nation's government, Nolan loses his temper and says that he would prefer never to hear another word about the United States. The judge, a loyal veteran of the Revolutionary War, is so horrified by this lack of respect for the nation he had risked his life to found that he takes Nolan at his word and banishes him from the country. For the remainder of his long life Nolan is forced to live aboard navy vessels whose crews are instructed to refrain from mentioning the slightest bit of news concerning the United States. This sentence proves unbearable to the distraught Nolan, who becomes fanatically loyal to his country as a result of his exile.

Having lost his commission as a lieutenant and having been installed aboard his first government vessel, Nolan is at first obstreperous but gradually becomes timid and reserved when the frustration and despair of being denied news of his former homeland start to sink in. His presence makes the crews of his various ships nervous because they must constantly monitor their conversations to ensure that the subject of the United States never comes up in Nolan's presence. Every piece of literature or journalism that he is allowed to peruse must also be censored, and he receives novels, magazines, and newspapers that have sections cut out of them if they allude in any way to his former country. Because he is not permitted to wear the regulation army button bearing the insignia of the United States, he is given the nickname "Plain Buttons," a moniker that aptly illustrates the extent of his ostracism. He spends his days following a methodical regimen of exercise, reading and writing in his various notebooks on such subjects as history and the natural sciences. But all of his efforts to lend meaning to his existence fail to counterbalance the malaise that results from being "the man without a country."

As time goes on, Nolan becomes a legendary figure, and various myths begin to surround his name. No one who remembers him can separate fact from fiction when recounting his history. In addition, many sailors, becoming accustomed to his presence, befriend the homeless man, and he in turn takes younger men under his wing and advises and educates them. When a ship's crew is threatened by a British vessel's artillery during the War of 1812, Nolan distinguishes himself in battle and is responsible for successfully repelling the attack. The captain of the ship and other sympathetic people attempt to convince the government to pardon the now contrite Nolan, but his sentence remains unchanged and he remains at sea year after year until his health begins to fail.

Lying on his deathbed, Nolan summons Danforth, the captain of the *Levant*, who finds that Nolan has secretly decorated his room with a portrait of George Washington, an eagle, a map of the United States, and other American icons to remind him of the country that he now extravagantly reveres. Convinced that he is at death's door, Nolan begs Danforth to break the silence and give him a history of the United States during the half-century that he has been forbidden to chart the nation's progress. Taking pity on him, Danforth obliges him but neglects to mention the present crisis of the Civil War out of consideration for the old man's love of his forbidden homeland. Philip Nolan dies happily, having finally received the false but precious news of his beloved country.

Nordholm, John. "The Happiest I've Been." John Updike. 1959.

John Nordholm, a contented nineteen-year-old college sophomore from Pennsylvania, is visiting his farm home during Christmas break. John and his high school buddy, Neil Hovey, plan to drive together to Chicago, Neil's present home, where John will visit his girlfriend before the two of them return to college for the spring semester.

Although nothing extraordinary happens to John during the course of the story, he experiences a calm elation as he and his friend race along a snowy highway following a night of partying with their high school friends.

At the age of thirteen, John Nordholm's good friend Neil Hovey began to attend high school in Olinger, Pennsylvania, living with his grandparents because his father's job demanded that he travel too extensively to provide his son with a stable address. Having graduated, Neil moved to Chicago where he works, and he suffers through dental work that the army pays for in return for his promise to serve in the Korean War. John also suffers from a physical defect—a skin allergy—that constitutes one of the bonds which strengthen their relationship. The two young men are also alike in that they grew up around elderly people and have developed a humane gentleness. John supposes that married women respect this quality but that it turns off prospective girlfriends, who prefer more aggressive and brash men.

One night Neil arrives at the farm belonging to John's family, and the two friends jump into Neil's father's Chrysler, ostensibly to hit the road. Neil proposes that before embarking on the road trip they should stop by the New Year's Eve party that Larry Schuman is having a couple of days early. John agrees, and they stay at the raucous party until three o'clock in the morning. Although John remains sober, Neil becomes drunk—to the extent that he becomes jealous of John's girlfriend and in his sullenness insults John. Neil claims that his friend has good luck galore and does not understand what it is like to have none at all. Wary of Neil's bad mood, John leaves him alone to sulk, but by the time they leave the party, Neil has regained his good spirits. Having offered to give two young women a ride home from the party, John and Neil accompany them to Margaret Lentos's house where they stay until daylight, each keeping the company of one of the women. John is pleased that his companion, Margaret, trusts him sufficiently to fall asleep with her head resting on his chest.

The following morning, having finally begun their journey to Chicago, John is surprised and pleased that for the first time Neil offers to let him drive his father's car. As they speed along, Neil falls asleep with his head against the window, and John is once again pleased that someone trusts him sufficiently to fall asleep in his presence. John reviews a life that includes such pleasant features as a road trip with a good friend, a girlfriend who loves him and would marry him if he asked, and the beautiful Pennsylvania countryside on a lovely winter's day. These simple gratifications make the moment the happiest John Nordholm has ever enjoyed.

Norman "Norm." *Standing Fast.* Harvey Swados. 1970.

After graduating from college, Norman, who is usually called "Norm," travels to Mexico to pursue his studies in archaeology. There he meets the famous Communist Leon Trotsky and becomes a convert to radical politics. He returns to his home city, New York, a changed man. Newly inspired and engaged, Norm has given up his academic aspirations and is prepared to dedicate his life and career to the promotion of international socialism.

Norm's father Milton, a wealthy textile merchant, tries to persuade him to find a "real" career, but Norm agitates from a soapbox for the workers' party while Sy and Bernice, a poor young Jewish couple, pass out literature. When Sy and Bernice decide to break with the old line, Norm enthusiastically joins with them in forming a "New Party" of their own.

Norm is sent to recruit at big steel strikes and finds his way to Buffalo, New York. There he organizes among the workers at the big munitions plants. He works closely with a core of dedicated New Party members, including an English professor named Fred, a painter named Vito, and IRWIN METZGER, a young dentist. In Buffalo, Norm also meets Vera, a quiet, hardworking woman whose sister Margaret is part of the movement. Soon Sy and Bernice decide to move to Buffalo as well. Norm and Vera eventually marry, and Vera becomes pregnant. However, the Party fails to gain many followers, and Norm is drafted to fight in World War II.

While fighting throughout the islands of the South Pacific, Norm experiences the horrors of war but does not forgo his radical political principles. When the war ends, he is stationed in the Philippines, where he teaches Marxism to the local villagers and helps to organize a huge protest march among the troops lobbying to be sent home. He returns to New York City to join Vera and their young son Marlen, and he becomes a journalist and starts covering the labor movement and political events. The others who worked for the New Party have also taken different paths but continue to work for change in their own ways. Norm and Vera meet Fred, who now hosts a television talk show for intellectuals in Martha's Vineyard. As the events of the civil rights movement unfold, Norm is there to cover them. He also reports on the brief revolt against Soviet rule in Czechoslovakia and other international freedom movements.

At home in Washington, D.C., Norm's son Marlen turns out to be a sociopath who accidentally kills a girl in a car wreck and must be sent to a special school. Sy and Bernice, who went to a kibbutz in Israel and have returned to teach school in New York City, come and visit Norm and Vera for John F. Kennedy's inauguration. Secure among the Washington establishment, Norm is excited about the new breed of enlightened politicians. He finds a publisher for Joe, one of his former New Party comrades, who is trying to write a book about the evolution of the labor movement. Norm and Vera are reunited with all their old friends at the funeral of Irwin's son Paul, who had been killed while working for the poor and dispossessed in Harlem. That same day the mourners learn of President Kennedy's assassination, and Norm rushes back to Washington in order to be on hand for the arrival of Air Force One, the plane carrying the President's remains.

North, Adam "Juneboy." *Such Was the Season.* Clarence Major. 1987.

Dr. Adam North, known to his family and childhood friends as "Juneboy," is Chicago-raised and highly educated. In the course of the novel Juneboy visits his relatives in the South to research his family history and learns about his heritage in unexpected ways.

Juneboy has traveled to Atlanta, Georgia, where he has not been since childhood, to deliver a series of talks on his research into sickle-cell anemia. There he stays with his aunt, ANNIE ELIZA HICKS, and he quickly becomes close to her. Annie Eliza throws herself into the task of helping Juneboy recover his lost heritage, much of which she knows intimately. One of their first tasks is to find the grave of Juneboy's father, Scoop, a reprobate who had been divorced by his mother, Annie Eliza's sister, more than twenty-five years before. When he and Annie Eliza drive to Monroe, Georgia, they find that Scoop's grave was paved over as a parking lot for a new housing development.

Although this is a blow to Juneboy, he is able to learn a great deal about his family history from his surviving aunts, uncles, and cousins. At the same time he reveals much about his own past while talking to Annie Eliza. He recounts the story of his education and career, focusing on his years at Yale and as a researcher at Howard University, and on the story of his marriage.

Although he is currently involved with a white woman, Kirsten Steinkoenig, a teacher and researcher at Yale, Juneboy was once married and is the father of two young sons. This marriage to a woman named Margaret ended when her behavior became increasingly wild, as it had in her first marriage. Margaret deliberately taunted her first husband, provoking him with infidelities and cruelty until he was killed in a fight with one of her lovers. Although Juneboy knew of her privileged and sheltered past, and of her cruelty, he was determined to make the marriage work. When the couple's second son was born and Margaret rejected the child by shutting him up in a room, the marriage deteriorated to the point of divorce. Juneboy, although apparently very much in love with Kirsten, is leery of another marriage.

While Juneboy is in Atlanta, his family becomes embroiled in a controversy involving sex and the struggle for political power. His uncle, Reverend Jeremiah Hicks, is exposed as a key figure in a conspiracy to defraud Georgians of money by artificially inflating the prices of fruits and vegetables. Jeremiah's wife Renee ironically makes that conspiracy the platform of her race for a state senate seat that is currently occupied by one of her husband's co-conspirators. The third conspirator kills himself as the investigation proceeds, leaving a trail of speculation about his sexuality and that of the state senator, Dale Cooper, whom Juneboy diagnoses as a victim of a relatively rare form of sickle-cell anemia.

In the midst of this developing scandal, Juneboy meets long-lost relatives as well as surviving siblings of Annie Eliza's and their spouses and offspring. These relatives enable him to sustain himself in the wake of the less-than-successful talk on sickle-cell anemia that he delivers at the prestigious Emory University. As the novel concludes, Juneboy returns to Washington, D.C., where he will resume his research and meet Kirsten, who plans to fly down from New Haven to see him.

North, Theophilus. *Theophilus North*. Thornton Wilder. 1973.

In the spring of 1926, Theophilus North resigns from his position as a teacher in a boy's preparatory school, a position he has held for the four and a half years since his graduation from Yale. He feels inwardly exhausted and bereft of any sympathy for other people. Unsure of what he will do for the summer and with a vague plan of going to Canada by way of New England, Theophilus passes a sign that reads NEWPORT, 30 MILES. The sign ignites a host of pleasant memories of Newport where, eight years earlier, he had served in the navy as a member of the coast artillery defending Narragansett Bay. Theophilus decides on the spot that he will spend the summer in Newport as a tutor and reader.

Shortly after arriving in Newport, Theophilus places an advertisement in the local paper and soon finds himself cycling up and down the avenue of the Newport mansions giving lessons and readings in the summer homes of the country's richest families. He also discovers work of another sort that brings less tangible remuneration than the two dollars an hour he usually charges. The more contact he has with his wealthy clients, the more clearly Theophilus sees that their class has a peculiar set of problems. Through his cleverness, basic good will, and tremendou-

singenuity in all types of situations, he is able to extricate people from very tangled difficulties.

The first case of this sort is presented to him by Mr. Bell, a wealthy New York businessman with a summer house in Newport. Mr. Bell's daughter is about to elope with a divorced man of a lower class, and Theophilus is asked to intervene and bring the daughter to her senses. Theophilus ordinarily would have refused to insinuate himself in these kinds of affairs, but the job of one of his friends, an employee of Mr. Bell's, is at stake. Theophilus accepts the task and artfully succeeds in breaking off the elopement by eliciting the differences between the couple and having them display these differences to each other without being aware that Theophilus is orchestrating the whole scene. Once they see each other more clearly, both Miss Bell and her future husband are glad to be out of the relationship.

Throughout the summer several occasions arise in which Theophilus has an opportunity to display his resourcefulness. When one of his clients laments that her beautiful family mansion is rumored to be haunted and thus has lost all its former glory because no servants or guests will come there after dark, Theophilus creates a brilliant publicity campaign that not only reverses the negative effects of the previous rumors but also makes the house a place to which people flock. In thus effecting a complete reversal he succeeds in giving his client great pleasure.

Theophilus is also successful in restoring a youthful vigor and enthusiasm for life to a wealthy elderly gentleman whose relatives, eager for their inheritance, had convinced him that his health was rapidly deteriorating. But his final good deed in Newport is his most noteworthy; indeed, it verges on the miraculous. One night he goes to the bedside of an elderly woman in great pain whose only wish is to be allowed to die peacefully. Laying his hands on her frail body, Theophilus mysteriously grants her this wish.

When the summer ends, Theophilus leaves Newport. He plans to become a writer and record his memories of Newport for others to read.

O

O'Brien, Tim. *The Things They Carried*. Tim O'Brien. 1990.

Tim O'Brien is the narrator of this novel depicting the horrors of the Vietnam War. As the war begins, Tim is

completing his college education and graduating summa cum laude and Phi Beta Kappa. Much to his chagrin, he is drafted soon afterward, and he anxiously begins to confront his fear of war and dying.

At one point, perhaps planning to escape from the pressures on him, Tim flees north from his hometown of Worthington, Minnesota; he encounters an elderly man, Elroy Berdahl, with whom he spends almost a week. One day the two men take a fishing trip that brings the young man face-to-face with the Canadian shoreline and freedom from the draft. Although torn by the desire to flee, Tim ends up sobbing violently and deciding that he cannot run away. Assessing his decision, he remarks that as a coward, he went to the war.

The landscape and people in Vietnam produce an unreal atmosphere through which Tim and his army comrades fight and struggle to stay alive. With nearly all moral cautions discarded, the events that emerge are chilling and frightening. Tim collects both his own experiences and those of others, and these become the means through which he relates his military past as he recalls the war from a distance of twenty-two years.

Among the incidents presented is Tim's account of the time he knew he had killed a man. While the account is later denied, a fact particular to most if not all of the experiences offered, Tim recalls attempting to invent a life for the dead Vietnamese man who is partially blown up by a grenade he himself had tossed. After the death, Rat Kiley, the company medic, kindly tries to comfort the shaken narrator. In another instance Tim recalls the times he was injured. The first time, he is shot in the side and is treated quickly by the calm medic, who later goes insane and shoots himself in the foot. Tim's second wound has more serious consequences. After being shot in the buttocks, he falls into shock when the new medic, Bobby Jorgenson, freezes in his tracks and fails to adequately treat the wound. During recuperation, Tim's injury festers, becomes gangrenous, and forces him to endure an uncomfortable and at times humiliating recovery. Accordingly, he concocts a revenge plot against Jorgenson, and with the aid of another soldier, they nearly scare the medic to death while he is on watch.

In one of the present-day chapters, Tim brings his ten-year-old daughter with him on a return trip to Vietnam. She has had affecting questions about his war experiences, and he reasons that the trip, a birthday gift, will help answer some of them. But Kathleen fails to understand her father's actions as he arranges a side trip to the scene of one of the more gruesome deaths that he had witnessed. Tim ritualistically walks out into a muck-bottomed body of water and buries a hunting axe that had been owned by his friend Kiowa, who was hit by shrapnel and died while being sucked into a field filled with human excrement. This death, which was singularly disturbing for many of the soldiers, unnerved another friend of Tim's, Norman Bowker. Years after the war, after being in touch with Norman off and on, he learns from his friend's mother that Norman killed himself in the summer of 1978. For Tim, this seems to be evidence that the war, in the haunting shapes of memories and lost dreams, has yet to end, even for those fortunate enough to find their way through with the help of language and imagination.

O'Connor, Dr. Matthew. *Nightwood*. Djuna Barnes. 1937.

Dr. Matthew O'Connor is a homosexual with a penchant for embarking on wild metaphysical and philosophical tirades. Although he has not really earned an M.D., he practices medicine under the guise of being a qualified physician and takes particular pleasure in tending to gynecological patients. Bragging that he has covered half of the globe in his medical studies and drunken debaucheries, O'Connor moves to Paris to explore the bodies of the city's women and its cafés and nightlife. Attractive as a confidant, he becomes the reluctant emotional counselor to a trio of people whose lives are disrupted by sexual involvements with a bizarre, boyish-looking woman named ROBIN VOTE.

Dr. O'Connor rents a tiny room in a six-floor walk-up, where he lives in extreme squalor and dishevelment. Of an afternoon he can be found lounging on his bed amid disordered stacks of medical books, damaged surgical instruments, women's underclothing, and a bountiful collection of cosmetic supplies and perfumes. Alone at home, he habitually wears women's clothing, a wig, and makeup. This behavior is a direct expression of the doctor's deep-seated desire to live the life of a traditional housewife.

When he ventures out in public, O'Connor's diminutive, slouching figure is most often seen at the Café de la Mairie du VIème, his favorite watering hole. Holding court at this café and others, the doctor develops a reputation for delivering volatile and verbose renditions of his bizarre philosophical theories. Despite their apparent illogic, his lectures have a great influence on some of the less stable members of his audience, who desperately need his alternative vision of the world in order to deal with their own strange and upsetting lives.

But O'Connor becomes increasingly annoyed when Baron FELIX VOLKBEIN, NORA FLOOD, and Jenny Petherbridge repeatedly hound him for an explanation of the deviant behavior of Robin Vote. These three troubled lovers are sexually and emotionally involved with Robin Vote, an alcoholic with a proclivity for bestiality. The doctor goes to great lengths to characterize Robin in terms of "the night," a deviant entity that he claims overpowers her daytime personality and brings out the errant behavior. The doctor maintains that he knows the night well; he has spent a lifetime wandering debauchedly through the evening hours, and he exhibits a marked talent for haunting questionable locations at exactly the wrong time and thereby witnessing scenes most people never confront. Ultimately, impatient with the woes of the three distraught lovers, Dr. O'Connor embarks on a final tirade wherein he lists his own litany of problems and disappointments. His tirade culminates in a hysterical and drunken insistence that he be exempt from future sessions as a confidant and romantic counselor.

O'Hara, Scarlett. *Gone with the Wind.* Margaret Mitchell. 1936.

The tempestuous Scarlett O'Hara undergoes an epic journey in the South in the years before, during, and after the Civil War. A beautiful, proud, self-centered teenager, Scarlett commands the attention of several suitors and is used to holding the world in the palm of her hand. However, due to the war and her misjudgments and obsessions regarding various men, Scarlett endures physical struggles, suffering, and painful losses that test her ability to survive.

As the novel opens, Scarlett, the sixteen-year-old daughter of Gerald and Ellen O'Hara, has decided that she loves ASHLEY WILKES. Scarlett is shocked to discover that Ashley, heir to the Twelve Oaks Plantation, is betrothed, in the Wilkes family tradition, to his cousin MELANIE HAMILTON (WILKES). Piqued at this development, Scarlett hastily marries Melanie's brother, Charles Hamilton.

Meanwhile, the Civil War erupts and the men are summoned to duty. Charles contracts measles and pneumonia and dies within two months, leaving Scarlett widowed and pregnant. Shortly after the birth of her son Wade, she is sent to Atlanta to work for the Confederacy. Although she is indifferent to the Southern cause, residence in Atlanta with Melanie and her aunt Pittypat brings her nearer to Ashley.

As the war progresses and the South's fortunes decline, Scarlett redoubles her efforts to help the wounded and dying as they stream into Atlanta, despite her revulsion to sickness. Melanie becomes pregnant during Ashley's leave, and it falls upon Scarlett to care for her weaker sister-in-law. Melanie's baby is born as Atlanta is abandoned in the face of General Sherman's advancing army. It is only with the aid of RHETT BUTLER, the notorious blockade-buster and scorner of the cause, that Scarlett is able to make her escape back to Tara, her parents' plantation.

When she arrives at Tara, she finds it a shadow of its former beauty. Although it still stands, Yankee soldiers have gutted it and have taken all of the family's possessions and food. Only Pork and MAMMY, Mrs. O'Hara's black nanny, remain of Tara's slaves. Scarlett finds that her mother has recently died and her father is addlepated. Despite these horrors, Scarlett vows never to relinquish Tara, and she sets out to rebuild the plantation and to recultivate its fields.

As the war ends and the men return, the Yankee carpetbaggers levy huge taxes on Tara. After being rebuffed by Rhett Butler, Scarlett hastily woos and wins the hand of Frank Kennedy, her sister's fiancé, because he has money. Scarlett once again finds herself married to a man she does not love. The couple has one daughter, Ella Lorena, before Frank is killed in a Ku Klux Klan raid on former slaves.

Widowed again, Scarlett agrees to marry Rhett Butler, who has been in love with her for years. He promises to make her one of the wealthiest women in Atlanta. The two marry and have one daughter, Bonnie, who is the pride of Rhett's life. The marriage deteriorates, however, as Scarlett's passion for Ashley remains unabated.

After a brief trip to Europe, Rhett returns to find that Scarlett is pregnant again, but she falls during a fight at the top of the staircase in their Atlanta home and suffers a miscarriage. Soon after, their daughter Bonnie dies in a riding accident. Melanie's death, following the strain of an ill-advised pregnancy, catalyzes Scarlett's belated realization that Ashley was never really in love with her.

Despite Scarlett's protestations of love, Rhett leaves her, believing her to be still in love with Ashley. At the end of the novel, with new self-knowledge, Scarlett vows to return to Tara. Feeling certain that she can get Rhett back—there has never been a man she couldn't get—she resolves to think about it all tomorrow, at Tara: "After all, tomorrow is another day."

O'Neill, Danny. *A World I Never Made; No Star Is Lost; Father and Son; My Days of Anger; The Face of Time.* James T. Farrell. 1936; 1938; 1940; 1943; 1953.

Appearing in five novels and a series of short stories, Danny O'Neill exemplifies the Irish immigrant's experience in early twentieth-century America. The novels follow Danny through his childhood and adolescence in the Chicago slums, up to the point where he launches a writing career in order to escape poverty.

Because of his parents' financial hardship, the three-year-old Danny lives with his aunt and grandmother. Although the women of the O'Flaherty home dote on him, he grows up in fear of his disciplinarian uncle. Anxiety, traceable to the emotional stress produced by these conflicting allegiances, will plague him throughout his life.

The members of this new family, though somewhat better off than the O'Neills, constantly strive to keep afloat economically. It is a life filled with pretensions of high status, rampant alcoholism, raging drunken battles, and the misadventures of an aunt who escapes her oppression by freely sleeping with men. Such pressures fill Danny with fears, anxieties, and an early fascination with sexuality.

As he moves into adolescence, Danny becomes increasingly obsessed with morality, propriety, and the opinions of his peers. South Chicago makes for a rough-and-tumble playground, full of fights with bullies and friends and the constant attraction of living a life of crime. Meanwhile, his family's financial circumstances and his aunt Margaret's reputation as an easy woman fill Danny with shame. In spite of his superior intelligence and athletic abilities,

Danny is not accepted by his high school peers. He remains deeply influenced by his religious upbringing but begins to experience atheistic doubts. Girls become a source of failure and self-doubt, while among his friends he is regarded as a "goof" for his strange intelligence and stumbling manner. His achievements gradually become revolts against the limiting institutions of family and school.

When his biological father, Jim, a staunch unionist, dies of a stroke, Danny begins meditating on the social forces that have shaped his family. He discovers that he would not be suited for success in the business world and rejects his adopted father's authoritarian "Horatio Alger" philosophy. He resolves to go to college despite the financial hardships this entails.

In college Danny discovers literature and philosophy, and reappraises his life. He begins to see how his family's immigrant-Irish ways give them strength to withstand their situation. His hatred for their failings shifts to a condemnation of the conditions of their lives, and eventually he is able to transcend his restrictive youth and claim his share of intellectual freedom.

O'Regan, Teague. *Modern Chivalry*. H. H. Brackenridge. 1846.

A gruff and unruly Irish immigrant, TEAGUE O'REGAN serves as the faithful servant to the quixotic CAPTAIN JOHN FARRAGO. When Farrago decides to journey to see the world, the steady Teague follows along as his squire. The two men set out across the late-eighteenth-century Pennsylvania countryside.

When they stumble on an election taking place, Teague, seeing that the nomination is about to go to none other than a lowly weaver, decides that he would like to try his hand in politics. The captain dissuades the weaver from accepting the nomination and goes on to give Teague a long dissertation on the rigors of public life, finally convincing his reluctant manservant of the inappropriateness of his ambition.

A similar incident occurs later in their trek when Teague, after picking up a strange-looking bird by the roadside, meets a member of the Society of Philosophers. This "philosopher," who is impressed with Teague's find, invites him to become a member of their group. Not wanting to lose his only squire, Captain Farrago describes to Teague what would inevitably follow: Life as a philosopher would entail long hours and paltry compensation. Teague once again follows his master.

A few weeks later Teague meets a clergyman at an inn where he and the captain are lodging, and his mind becomes set on yet another profession. Once again Captain Farrago illuminates the error of this decision, pointing out the tedium and puritanical life-style of the clergy. When Teague agrees to stay, the captain instructs Teague to take his place in a duel. The enraged Teague refuses, and he and Captain Farrago flee the inn early the next morning.

As soon as they arrive in Philadelphia, Teague, yearning to be more than a servant to Captain Farrago, deserts his master to make his own life. He finds employment as an actor with a traveling theater troupe but is dismissed after he makes a pass at the company manager's daughter. He returns disheartened and penniless to Captain Farrago.

Teague is pleasantly surprised when his master, now desiring to further Teague's ambitions, hires numerous tutors and instructors in refined subjects such as art, music, and dance. Captain Farrago is able to introduce Teague to the President of the United States and secures for his former servant a position as revenue collector for a new, unpopular whiskey tax.

When Teague, now a certified government official, arrives at his district, he is carried away by an angry mob protesting the unfair excise tax. Tarred and feathered, a horrified Teague hides in a tree until he is captured as a specimen by a pair of wandering members of the Society of Philosophers.

O-lan. *The Good Earth*. Pearl S. Buck. 1931.

The plain-faced O-lan begins as a kitchen slave in a wealthy nineteenth-century Chinese household. When WANG LUNG, an illiterate farmer, buys her to be his bride, she works steadily by his side in the fields and cares for him and his aged father.

Before long O-lan delivers a son. Taking no time to recover, she rises immediately afterward to work with Wang Lung in the fields. O-lan speaks very little, but she possesses a wealth of practical knowledge and good housewifely instincts; in fact, it is largely due to her economy that she and Wang Lung are able to save enough to buy another plot of land from O-lan's former owners, who have lost much of their fortune through dissipation and neglect.

The good fortune does not last, however. O-lan delivers another boy and then a girl, but the girl is retarded and cannot learn to speak. When a famine falls over the land, O-lan's family eats first their ox, then grass, and eventually the earth itself. O-lan becomes pregnant again, but the baby is born dead.

The family journeys to a southern city, and after initial difficulty, they manage to find enough food to survive. When an insurgent mob riots and loots the palace of a rich man, O-lan secretly carries off a bag of jewels in her dress. Wang Lung has taken a cache of gold coins, and the newfound wealth soon enables them to reverse their fortune.

The family returns to its land. Wang Lung buys more land from the once-rich dynasty of the town until he has a great estate. Keeping for herself only two pearls, O-lan gives him the rest of the jewels. She soon bears twins, a boy and a girl. For a time the family is happy and at peace, but as Wang Lung prospers, he grows restless and installs a concubine in his home along with a woman named

Cuckoo, who used to be a servant in O-lan's former household. O-lan bears the presence of the concubine stoically, even giving her smitten husband the pearls to give as gifts to his new mistress, but she proudly refuses to share her kitchen with Cuckoo.

As the children grow up, they show no signs of wanting to stay on the land or become farmers. O-lan recedes into the household, performing chores but otherwise sharing little in family life. Then she is struck down by a recurrent "pain in her vitals" and lies dying for many months. Wang Lung, who now remembers his wife's fidelity and strength, fulfills her dying requests to have her second son betrothed and her eldest son properly wed. O-lan dies secure in her belief that because she has borne sons, her life has had meaning. She knows that the concubine cannot replace her, for, as she says on her deathbed, "beauty will not bear a man sons!"

Oakhurst, John. "The Outcasts of Poker Flat." Bret Harte. 1869.

This story begins as John Oakhurst, a brilliant gambler, faces a community in an uproar. The town of Poker Flat has begun wreaking its revenge on those it has deemed responsible for a recent run of bad luck. Although they have hanged two men already, the town's men agree that still more must be done. Oakhurst literally senses the likelihood of being the town's target; he is right, and he is banished from Poker Flat forever. His ability at cards has earned him this particular honor. Oakhurst is not banished alone, however; with him are a woman called "The Duchess," exiled for prostitution, another called "Mother Shipton," and Uncle Billy, the erstwhile town drunk. This motley crew turns to him for advice and leadership, whereupon he exchanges his horse for a sluggish mule ridden by The Duchess.

The party decides to head for a camp called Sandy Bar, which is a rigorous day's ride away, but they are soon halted by The Duchess, who flops out of her saddle and refuses to continue. Because of the wild beauty of their surroundings in the Sierras, they agree to make camp. The evening is spent laughing and joking, a mood enhanced by much liquor. But Oakhurst stays out of the hilarity and refuses to drink lest he lose his advantage. As he sits staring at his companions, for the first time Oakhurst is seriously oppressed by his lifelong distance from the company of others. But he rouses himself from morbidity by dusting off his clothes and readjusting his attitude and demeanor.

Oakhurst's thoughtful spell is interrupted when he hears his name being called. An old acquaintance, Tom Simpson, known as "the Innocent," and his would-be bride, Piney Woods, are eloping from Sandy Bar to Poker Flat. Oakhurst had once fleeced the boy at cards, only to privately return the money, admonishing the astonished lad to eschew gambling in the future. Oakhurst is reluctant

to accept a simpleton into their party, much less his fifteen-year-old fiancée, but the Innocent has provisions that render him highly persuasive.

The women retire to a crude hut, conveniently erected nearby, while the men slumber on the ground at the cabin's door. The first to wake, Oakhurst discovers that it is snowing and that Uncle Billy has made off with all their mounts. As if this were not enough, Oakhurst's wilderness acumen leads him to conclude ominously that a fierce storm is upon them. For a time their spirits are fairly jolly; they entertain each other, with the Innocent going so far as to regale them with his own bowdlerized account of Alexander Pope's ILIAD. But by the end of the first week of being snowed in, things are beginning to look bleak; on the tenth day Mother Shipton tells Oakhurst that she is dying. She had willfully concealed her rations and starved herself to death; at her bequest, Piney is given the food. Soon the Innocent sets out, never to be heard from again.

Finally, it is time for Oakhurst to seek aid. He unaccountably kisses The Duchess before departing. When help does come, it is too late for all; the remaining two women are found clasped together where they had fallen asleep and died. A playing card, the deuce of clubs, is found attached to one of the biggest pine trees around, and on it is inscribed the day Oakhurst's luck changed, November 23, 1850, and the day of his death, December 7, 1850. His body is found beneath the card, with a bullet hole in the heart and a derringer at its side.

Ochs, Alice. "Woolen Drawers." William March. 1945.

Alice Ochs clerks at the cigar counter of a commercial hotel in Atlanta, where she befriends traveling salesmen who, drawn by her raven hair and rosy cheeks, often linger at her counter. Well aware of her rustic allure, Alice occasionally submits to the advances of these men, in exchange for the finery in which she takes so much pride and which she otherwise could not afford. After several casual affairs, Alice feels no shame; she feels superior to any man in whom she evokes such passion and, if such a man is married, to his dowdy, unsuspecting wife. During the winter of 1907, however, Alice contracts a persistent chest cold that leads to a significant alteration in her life-style.

One inclement morning, as the recuperating Alice is about to leave for work, her roommate, Trix McAllister, insists on lending her some long underwear. Alice, proud of her own sachet-scented, ribboned, and much admired lingerie, protests the baggy, stained union suit. But Trix is adamant, so Alice consents, leaving for work with the union suit beneath her dress.

After work Alice goes on a date with traveling salesman Joe Cotton, who invites her back to his room after dinner. As a matter of course, Alice accepts. But while they are embracing, Alice suddenly remembers the homely union suit beneath her dress. She would rather die than have Joe see her in such unflattering underwear, so she feigns virtue and protests his advances. Angered, Joe accuses Alice of teasing him, but then, convinced by Alice's tearful protestations, he feels ashamed of pressuring such an innocent young woman. Alice goes home with the secret of her union suit intact, and she and Trix later share a hearty laugh over the incident.

Joe leaves Atlanta, and much to Alice's surprise, he writes her daily, commending her for renewing his faith in the goodness of womankind. They correspond regularly, and Alice eventually gives up smoking, showy clothes, and other men, all at Joe's request. In a few months Alice becomes Mrs. Joseph L. Cotton and moves with her husband to Reedyville, his boyhood home.

With her racy life behind her, Alice soon becomes a zealous member of the Reedyville church, a role that she now feels comes naturally to her. When it becomes apparent that they will never have children, Alice denies Joe sex, declaring righteously that God intended sex for procreation only. After many years of celibacy, Joe begins to pick up women and to drink while on his sales trips, but Alice, who occasionally hears of her husband's indiscretions, is not troubled by them at all; she is wholly consumed by her duties as Grand Mobilizer of the Christian Gladiators and as secretary of the Reedyville Society for the Fostering of Temperance and Eradication of Vice, much to the terror of local bootleggers and poolroom keepers.

At a regular Monday evening meeting of the temperance and vice society, the now middle-aged Alice issues a detailed report of scandalous goings-on at the Magnolia Hotel and at Mattress May's sporting house. Shocked but curious, her puritanical sisters want to know how she could have discovered these iniquities. It is her Christian duty to do so, replies Alice, declaring an innate talent for discovering sin, not unlike that of playing the piano by ear; she can simply intuit what bad women are going to do. They applaud her uncanny ability to detect and confound sinners, and roundly declare it a virtue comparable to good works or brotherly love.

Oelsligle, Kermit "Boy." *Fire Sermon.* Wright Morris. 1969.

Kermit Oelsligle, nicknamed "Boy," is an orphaned youth who leads a somewhat unconventional life. Boy lives with his uncle Floyd in California, in a trailer that is slightly too small for two people. Sent to live with his uncle, whom he had never met before his parents were killed, Boy has many adjustments to make. His life with his uncle revolves around attending school, reading letters from his beloved aunt Viola, watching people, and trying to figure out his uncle's eccentricities. Although Boy misses his family deeply, he is basically happy.

The routine of Boy's life is broken when he and Uncle Floyd receive a letter informing them that Aunt Viola has died and requesting instructions for her burial. Uncle Floyd decides that he and the boy will travel together to Aunt Viola's Nebraska home in the ancient trailer where they have been living. Three days after receiving the telegram, Floyd and Boy are on the road to Nebraska to take over Aunt Viola's house and settle her affairs.

Since Floyd is a terrible driver, Boy does much of the driving even though he is only twelve. Boy enjoys handling the slow-moving vehicle. He and Uncle Floyd pick up two hitchhikers, young hippies named Stanley and Joy who are traveling to Ohio where Stanley has a job lined up. The couple travels with them, eventually sharing some of the driving. As Uncle Floyd grows quiet, apparently ill, Boy begins to spend time listening to Joy and Stanley. He finds their stories and advice fascinating, although their unrestrained sexual activity embarrasses him.

Finally, the four of them arrive at Aunt Viola's house in Chapman, Nebraska. The house is very strange, overflowing with piles of junk. Uncle Floyd has some sort of attack in the house, and for a minute Boy is afraid that he is dead. Boy runs out to get Joy and Stanley, who are in the trailer having sex. When they return, Uncle Floyd seems to be coming around. Everyone gets comfortable in the house, but somehow a small fire starts. While Stanley, Joy, and Boy put out the fire, Uncle Floyd drives off in the car. Boy is confused, but Stanley and Joy explain that Floyd probably drove off to go away to die. Stanley, Joy, and Boy make themselves at home in Aunt Viola's house— their new home.

Ogden, George. *The Cliff-Dwellers.* Henry B. Fuller. 1893.

George Ogden is a functionary in ERASTUS BRAINARD's Underground National Bank in late-nineteenth-century Chicago. He works in an eighteen-story building, the Clifton, which is the focal point of his interaction with a wide variety of other individuals.

A newcomer to Chicago, George Ogden progresses from lamenting the loss of his native East to enjoying his position as an "interested observer" of the Chicago social world. He enjoys looking at people and classifying and dividing them. In the many ethnic groups in Chicago, Ogden calmly sees a unifying mortality.

George's sister Kittie is married to Eugene McDowell, a real estate man of dubious integrity. McDowell manages several real estate investments belonging to George and George's widowed mother. Although McDowell is not an outright thief, his handling of these assets worries George. As a man of "moderate pretensions," however, George is happy to see his sister married to a man of some importance in the community.

George becomes interested in two women: Jessie Bradley, the daughter of an indifferent couple that have moved from the city, and Abbie Brainard, the daughter of his boss. He leans toward Abbie Brainard, clearly the more socially desirable of the two. But when he hears of a vicious family dispute, he shies away from the family and ultimately from Abbie, although she is only tangentially involved. He subsequently marries Jessie Bradley, who seems to be removed from an increasingly complicated social world.

George gradually notices, however, that Jessie is actually very concerned with social contacts and expensive modifications to their rented house. Despite his reminders of their limited financial means, Jessie increasingly focuses on superficial but costly social achievements. In the meantime, George finds himself with nowhere to turn for help in sorting out his exact financial status in the face of McDowell's shady handling of his investments. To make matters worse, Jessie simultaneously becomes ill and pregnant.

Jessie gives birth, but she and the baby both die. George is then caught borrowing funds from the Underground Bank to cover his personal deficit. Seemingly at a loss as to what to do, he finally accepts his own limitations. Knowing that he is getting older and ascending no higher in Chicago society, he marries Abbie Brainard out of love and resigns himself to a "middling" but happier life.

Ogden, Mary. *Black Oxen.* Gertrude Atherton. 1923.

Mary Ogden is the most sought after and wooed woman in her small, elite circle of New York high society in the late 1800s. In order to become Countess Zattiany, Mary marries an Austrian count; her marriage soon turns sour, however, as her husband, while genial enough, spends little time at home and takes on several other lovers. Although relatively content with the wealth and luxury that accompanies her title, Mary grows lonely and begins to take on a number of lovers as well.

Mary works in a hospital at the outbreak of World War I, during which time her husband, Count Zattiany, is killed. She is still relatively young at the war's end, and her wealth and beauty attract many lovers. However, after falling deeply in love with an Austrian nobleman who leaves her to marry someone else, Mary settles down to a reclusive life. Her desirability begins to fade as her age increases, and she remains bitter about love and men in general.

When Mary learns of a new kind of operation available in Vienna that reverses the effects of aging, the allure of living her youth over again proves to be greater than she can resist. She travels to Vienna and has the operation performed, and it is a startling success. Mary then travels to New York, looking not a day over thirty, and her true identity remains unknown to the former friends and associates who are by this time well into their sixties.

After learning that her financial affairs will keep her in New York longer than she expected, Mary attends various New York society events. The beautiful young-looking blonde causes quite a stir within the small, elite circle at such functions. One night LEE CLAVERING, an eminent young drama critic, follows her home, and Mary invites him inside for a nightcap. The inquisitive young man questions Mary as to her identity, and she replies enigmatically that she is a distant cousin of Mary Ogden's and is in New York for a short time to settle some business matters of hers.

As she and Clavering continue to see each other in the ensuing weeks, Mary finds herself falling in love once again. But when Clavering finally asks her to marry him, she knows she must expose her secret. She tells him that if he still wishes to marry her after her identity is revealed, she will consent. After telling her story to Clavering, the young critic, while shaken, remains resolved to marry her, and a date is set two months away.

But Mary begins to have her doubts in the wake of the notoriety that ensues when her identity is made public. She is almost universally resented by both young and old women alike, who view her decision to marry a man half her age as vain and selfish, and she herself worries because Clavering's entire existence is centered around New York, while hers remains in Europe. When her ex-Austrian lover visits her in New York, Mary realizes her mistake in agreeing to marry Clavering, and she returns to her previous life in Austria.

Old Lodge Skins. *Little Big Man.* Thomas Berger. 1964.

Old Lodge Skins, a Cheyenne chief, is a man whose psychic and magical powers place him in conflict with civilization. Caught in the tyrannical social structure of the Old West, he is forced to choose between the roles of a buffoon aping white ways and an outlaw fleeing the hand of "civilization."

In 1852, Old Lodge Skins, accompanied by his braves, meets a wagon train in southern Wyoming. He considers himself a friend of the whites and proudly wears a medal on a chain about his neck and a black plug hat minus its lid, gifts that he received from the government for signing a treaty. The whites foolishly give the Indians whiskey, and the drunken tribesmen, literally out of their minds, first assault one another, then murder the white men, and finally rape the women. JACK CRABB, the novel's ten-year-old white narrator, is orphaned by the attack and is adopted by Old Lodge Skins, who is seeking to make reparation for the crime.

Jack first witnesses the chief's "power to make things happen" at the time the band has been without meat for some weeks. Old Lodge Skins withdraws to a sweat lodge and has a vision of antelope. He comes out, gathers the entire band together, and leads them out onto the prairie. Holding his sacred implements, he sits and chants until a lone antelope appears on the next ridge and comes down toward the chief. Behind it comes an entire herd, which the Indians proceed to corral and slaughter.

Old Lodge Skins educates Jack by recounting tales of

Cheyenne warriors, the most renowned of whom is Little Big Man, and gives Jack this name when he kills his first Crow warrior. Jack leaves the Indians for seven years. When he meets Old Lodge Skins again, the chief relates a dream full of accurate details of Jack's life in the East, where the chief has never been. He asks Jack's advice about how to respond to the U.S. Army, which wants the Cheyenne to settle on the Sand Creek reservation. Jack advises him to flee to the wilderness of northern Montana.

After another hiatus of some years, Jack meets Old Lodge Skins again and finds that the chief, who had been injured in the army's massacre of peaceful Cheyenne on Sand Creek, is now blind. Jack rejoins the band in their settlement of Washita Creek. One dawn Custer and his Seventh Cavalry attack. Jack rushes to rescue the chief and finds him unhurriedly donning his war regalia. Holding his medicine bundle aloft, Old Lodge Skins walks magically unscathed through the shooting soldiers and leads Jack to safety.

Eight years later, after Custer's Last Stand, Jack encounters Old Lodge Skins for the final time. Old Lodge Skins predicts the demise of the Cheyenne Nation. He asks Jack to accompany him on a climb to a high peak and at the summit tells Jack that there is no permanent winning or losing, that things move in a circle and life is continuous, that death is transition. He prays to the "Everywhere Spirit" and dies quietly.

Ole 'Stracted. "Ole 'Stracted." Thomas Nelson Page. 1887.

Ole 'Stracted is a poor, eccentric, old black man living alone in a shack after the Civil War. Years before he had appeared mysteriously in his present neighborhood and stayed there, working hard in the fields and saving his money. According to stories of his past, Ole 'Stracted has been "distracted" and preoccupied since he was separated from his master, wife, and son years ago in a slave trade. Seen subsequently as a harmless imbecile laboring under delusion, Ole 'Stracted devotes himself to the children of the neighborhood. They flock to him, and he tells them stories glorifying the great plantation where he lived and worked with his wife and son. Living only for the day when his master will return and reunite him with his family, Ole 'Stracted has lost touch with reality.

Ole 'Stracted's neighbors Ephraim and Polly, a poor married couple with one young son, are worried because a nearby white landowner has threatened to take away their house unless they repay their $800 debt to him in a week. Afraid that Ole 'Stracted will also be driven from his shack, Ephraim and Polly go to visit the old man and bring him some food. Arriving at Ole 'Stracted's place, they discover that he is in bed on the verge of death. When Polly offers him the shirt she has patched for him and calls him "Ole 'Stracted," the old man says for the first time that this is not his name. He is unable to remember his

real name when she asks, saying that only his master knows it.

Sure that his master will come presently, Ole 'Stracted puts on his shirt and instructs Ephraim to reach up and take down an old sock filled with money. Ole 'Stracted explains to them that he has been saving the money for forty years to give to his master, who was turned away from his land when the South lost the war. He pours $1,200 in gold into Polly's apron and says he's been so busy saving it that he hasn't had time to eat. Ole 'Stracted sadly tells Ephraim and Polly that he and his master grew up together. The dying man remains certain that his former master, who always told the truth, will return to him because he said he would.

Growing weak and tired, Ole 'Stracted dozes off. When he wakes up, he hears Polly say her husband's name—"Ephum." Electrified, Ole 'Stracted believes his master has come at last. "Ephum," we realize, is Ole 'Stracted's real name, and Ephraim is his long-lost son. Believing that his reunion is complete and the past has been restored, Ole 'Stracted dies in Ephraim's arms. Ephraim and Polly are left with his small fortune, with which they can now buy their land.

Olenska, Countess Ellen. *The Age of Innocence.* Edith Wharton. 1920.

When the mysterious and unconventional Countess Ellen Olenska abandons her wealthy Polish husband and returns to her native New York, she finds herself unprepared for the judgmental perceptions that the members of high society form of her. A black sheep among elite men and women with narrow and stringent social mores, Ellen directly confronts the conflict between an individual's freedom and the world that binds the individual—a world that does not necessarily accept what it does not understand.

Soon after her return to New York, Ellen sees NEWLAND ARCHER for the first time in many years; he is the thoughtful young lawyer who is engaged to her cousin MAY WEL-LAND. Finding in Newland a person she trusts and to whom she can speak candidly, Ellen becomes increasingly intrigued with him despite the constant attention being paid to her by a few bold men. When Ellen decides to sue her husband for divorce, Newland gives her legal advice. Ellen tries to explain her desire to be free, to wipe out the past and be a "complete American" again; Newland, although he understands her predicament, counsels her not to divorce because of the scandal that would undoubtedly ensue. Ellen reluctantly agrees to follow his advice.

Shortly afterward Ellen receives word that her husband wants her back. She has no intention of returning to him, despite her family's urgings and the tremendous material advantages that would follow. Ellen's friend, the melodramatic Marchioness Manson, visits Ellen in her New York house, which is full of avant-garde Italian art. The

Marchioness, who is emphatically in favor of Ellen's reunion with her husband, meets Newland Archer at Ellen's and tells him about the proposal made by the Count. Newland is shocked and feels that Ellen must not go to him. Privately, Newland confesses to Ellen that he loves her. Ellen is in love with Newland, but she points out that by advising her not to divorce, Newland actually prevented them from being together. Ellen tells Newland that she decided to remain married and avoid scandal for his sake and the sake of her cousin May, and not because she feared her husband's false accusations.

After Newland's marriage to May, Ellen changes. She becomes increasingly enigmatic and avoids public appearances; in particular, she avoids contact with Newland Archer. When a telegram from her husband's messenger summons her to Boston, she goes to tell the messenger she will not return to the Count. In Boston, Ellen dines with Newland, who has followed her there. Their conversations reveal that they are still heartbroken over each other. They had a glimpse of happiness, but now, because of their own choices, they are locked into living false lives. The pain for both of them is extremely difficult to endure.

Back in New York, Ellen tells Newland there can be no liaison between them. Nevertheless, she agrees to meet him secretly at the Metropolitan Museum. Newland suggests they run away together, but Ellen tells him they cannot destroy the lives of their loved ones. She agrees to go to him once, and only once, presumably to make love to him. But their love is never consummated; the next day, after a long conversation with May Welland, Ellen decides to move to Paris to live with the Marchioness Manson. Years later, when Newland Archer visits Paris, he finds himself unable to face the enigmatic Countess Ellen Olenska.

Oliver, Red. *Beyond Desire.* Sherwood Anderson. 1932.

Red Oliver, a twenty-year-old mill hand from Langdon, Georgia, is an all-American boy with red hair and freckles who plays baseball and thinks about girls. Unlike his friends who have taken prostitutes or older women as lovers, Red is somewhat shy and virtuous around women. He comes from a middle-class family; his father, the local doctor, now dead, gained a bad reputation for womanizing. Red left Georgia to be educated in the North, where he was influenced by the teachings of Karl Marx. After earning his degree, Red chose to return to work among the people at the mill in Georgia instead of pursuing the career of a "capitalist."

While working at the mill, Red spends evenings in the library reading Leftist literature and doing his own writing. He is attracted to the librarian, ETHEL LONG, a bright, attractive, thirty-year-old woman with an air of style and sophistication lacking in most of the local mill girls. She finds his idealism and his raw youth appealing, and they spend many evenings at the library talking. Red is aware,

however, that Ethel is being courted by an older, established lawyer, Tom Riddle, and expects nothing to come of his infatuation.

One evening during a violent thunderstorm, Ethel and Red remain at the library after closing and end up making love on a library table. He is grateful and even considers proposing marriage. She feels a kind of maternal responsibility and mild remorse. After their encounter she sends him away and decides to accept Tom's proposal of marriage. Red feels confused and abandoned; she used him to resolve her own feelings and then cast him aside. When Ethel goes off to live a life of luxury with Tom, Red returns to his work at the mill.

Although Red does not consider himself a communist, he finds a certain appeal in living and dying for a cause. Over the next few years he takes part in the workers' strikes at the mills in Langdon and Birchfield, North Carolina. At Birchfield he meets a mill girl, Molly Seabright, whose long, lean figure reminds him of Ethel's. Molly admires Red for what she believes are his communist principles, and he gladly responds to her attentions. When the militia is brought in during a labor riot, Red, confronted by a wealthy lawyer leading the opposition, raises his pistol above the crowd. The lawyer shoots and kills him on the spot.

Ollie Miss. *Ollie Miss.* George Henderson. 1935.

Ollie Miss, nineteen years old and African American, has lived with her lover Jule since she was sixteen. When Jule agrees to move into a house that is owned by Della Dole—Ollie's rival who has romantic designs on Jule—Ollie, always independent and enigmatic, leaves him and travels to another town where she hopes to begin her life anew. Her passion for Jule does not leave her, however.

That spring, after leaving Jule, Ollie arrives at the farm of Alex and Caroline, who hire her to plow. At first Caroline is distressed by her huge appetite, but Ollie is a hard and skillful worker who minds her own business, is loyal to Alex, and keeps her cabin clean. She continually surprises the others with her unfeminine ways: She ignores the advances of another plower, refuses the men's assistance, curses freely, and openly smokes cigarettes. This behavior infuriates the meddling Nan, another worker who builds a case for expelling Ollie from the farm. Ollie fuels Nan's suspicions when she attends a party at which she dances passionately with Willie, a young farmhand, and then allows him to walk her home. She spends the remainder of the night lying next to him on the grass by a stream.

In spite of the others' inferences, Ollie does not desire Willie. In the middle of July she takes a week's vacation to visit Jule. When Ollie arrives at Jule's house, he is not there; Della tells her that Jule spends weeks at the house of a young woman in Roba. Ollie and Della then spend the week together waiting for Jule. When he does not return, Ollie returns to the farm. Her disappointment is mild because just thinking about Jule gives her something to live for.

Late in September, Ollie attends a community church meeting every night in the hope of seeing Jule. She finally spots him on the third night, and he tells her of Della's recent death. Ollie identifies with Della's love for Jule and asks him to spend the night with her. Jule goes with Ollie to her cabin, and although he claims that he loves neither Della nor his current girlfriend, he fails to say that he loves Ollie. Trapped by a heavy rainfall, he unwillingly stays the night and leaves in the morning without indicating when or if he will return.

Ollie encounters Jule at the church meeting that night. His girlfriend Lena has tracked him down and angrily demands to know where he spent the night. When Ollie tells Lena that Jule was with her, Lena slashes her body with a razor. Ollie becomes very ill from her injury and requires constant care from Alex and the others. She claims that she is pained not by her wound but by the feeling that a part of her has died inside. Soon after, when the sheriff asks Ollie to testify against Lena, Ollie says that she has no interest in punishing her. The damage to her body and to her emotions has already been done, and nothing can cure it.

Ollie and Jule have a final conversation in which Jule pleads for her to begin with him anew. Ollie refuses, explaining that their relationship was wrong from the start; she tells Jule that she is pregnant and that she sees the baby as something to live for. Furthermore, Alex has promised to give Ollie her own land to farm. As a song rises up from the mill below, Ollie is content to know that her land will flourish under her care.

Orden, Mayor. *The Moon Is Down.* John Steinbeck. 1942.

As the leader of a sleepy and peaceful little European village, Mayor Orden has never had much trouble, nor has he had the opportunity to do noble things. At the start of this allegorical novel, when the town is invaded by an unnamed enemy, presumably the Nazis, Orden, like the rest of the townspeople, does not know how to react at first.

An unassuming, whiskery man, Mayor Orden sees himself as one of the townspeople. His manner with them is both benevolent and familiar. He respects Colonel Lanser, the head of the invaders, who is in fact rather like him in his thoughtfulness and humility. Orden also recognizes, however, that the townspeople will not give up without a fight, and he is prepared to join their efforts.

The hatred of the townspeople for their German conquerors grows steadily. They remain outwardly obedient, and the coal mine, the main object of the invasion, continues to produce, but slowly and inefficiently. At first the people express their anger only in small ways, then Alex

Morden, a young miner, refuses to work and kills an officer. At Morden's trial, Lanser urges the mayor to announce the death sentence himself, saying that his collaboration will save lives. Mayor Orden refuses, warning that the people will not give up. Lanser realizes that what Orden says is true, but nevertheless he orders Alex to be shot.

This killing consolidates the resistance of the townspeople. One man is executed for wrecking a mine car, and his brothers meet in the house of Alex's pretty young widow, Molly, before fleeing to England. The mayor and his cook, Annie, meet them, and it is revealed that Orden has been aiding the resistance all along. The boys leave, promising to send back simple weapons such as dynamite to help the town.

Meanwhile, some in the invading army are too sensitive and dislike being objects of the townspeople's hatred. One likable, romantic young man, Lieutenant Tonder, longs for personal contact and warmth. He goes to see Molly just before the resisters arrive and does not realize at first that his companions have killed her husband. She pities him somewhat, but when he returns on the heels of the resistance meeting, she hardens her heart and kills him. She then flees to the hills, aided by Mayor Orden.

The fugitives send back dynamite, complete with instructions. Colonel Lanser receives orders to stamp out its use harshly. He arrests the mayor and his friend Dr. Winter, warning that the mayor will be killed if the people use their dynamite. He knows the people will act anyway and that he will have to shoot the mayor, whom he likes, but he believes he must follow orders. Lanser asks Mayor Orden to tell his people not to light the fuses, but the mayor refuses. They hear explosions in the distance, and the mayor, reciting Plato's *Apology* with Dr. Winter, prepares to die.

Ordway, Sam. *The Ordways.* William Humphrey. 1964.

Sam Ordway lives a sedentary life until 1898 when he is thirty-three years old and his wife Agatha dies giving birth to their third child, Ned. While Sam is courting his second wife, Hester, he leaves little Ned with his neighbors, the Vinsons, a practice he continues after his second marriage whenever the family goes into town for supplies. One day shortly after his second marriage, he returns from a trip to town to find the Vinsons and little Ned gone. It takes Sam six months to realize that the Vinsons left the area because, although they already have sons and daughters, they want to keep Ned as their own child. When Sam realizes how much the Vinsons valued Ned, he feels guilty that he did not value the boy more, so he decides to spend the winter looking for him.

As Sam travels throughout Texas looking for Ned, he has numerous, often humorous adventures, all of which he undergoes with the equanimity, good nature, and sincerity that are the hallmarks of his character. More important than his colorful exploits, however, are his realizations about himself. Sam is not by nature introspective, but his travels alone make him see things about himself that he would not otherwise see. He realizes that he has been too preoccupied with the practical progress of his life to attend to his own and others' emotional needs: He was so busy seeking a second wife that he not only neglected Ned but also neglected his own grief for Agatha, and he was so eager to marry Hester for practical reasons that he neglected to make her feel wanted, welcomed, and loved.

Over the course of his long, hard winter, Sam confronts and resolves his grief for Agatha and truly falls in love with Hester. Realizing that his allegiance now lies with the children of his new wife rather than his old, he determines to continue searching for Ned only long enough to allow himself time to get home for the birth of his next child. Thus he never finds Ned.

Sam lives out his days as a devoted husband to Hester and a loving father and grandfather to his numerous children and grandchildren. With his grandson Tom, who is fascinated by the story of Ned, the seemingly unadventurous Sam relives the excitement of his travels in the West. And when Ned finally makes his appearance after the death of his adoptive father and invites the Ordway family to visit his ranch in Mexico, Sam is delighted to realize his lifelong desire to travel west again.

Orlov, Roman. *The Neon Wilderness*. Nelson Algren. 1933.

Roman Orlov, not yet thirty, spends his nights in taverns and his days sleeping in at his parents' house. One night at the Polonia Bar, the locals argue among themselves about who should have the dubious distinction of being the biggest drunk on Division Street. They decide that Roman deserves this honor, and he tells how he became such a big drinker at such an early age.

Roman grew up in a tenement crowded by his parents, a younger sister, and still younger twin siblings. Since there were only two beds in the apartment, the women slept in the bedroom, and Roman and the twins slept in the living room. Papa Orlov played the accordion in taverns all night, and being more attached to his instrument than to his wife, he was accustomed to returning home at dawn and sleeping under one of the beds until Mama left for work and the children went to school.

When Roman was thirteen, Papa began to complain that a mysterious knocking was disturbing his daytime sleep. At first no one listened to Papa; they dismissed the knocking as a drunken dream. But then Roman heard a similar sound at night. He answered the door, thinking that Papa had locked himself out, only to find an empty airshaft. Then Mama began to dream of a bloody young man lingering in the hallway outside the apartment.

Upon hearing of Mama's dream, a neighbor explained that the knocking related to the violent demise of a former tenant of the Orlov apartment. A handsome but ill-tempered young man had hanged himself in the apartment after having beaten his lover to death. The neighbor assured the Orlovs that the ghost meant no harm; he merely wanted the new residents to pray for him.

The Orlovs began to pray regularly, and the knocking stopped. Overjoyed that the ghost had been silenced, the landlord no longer charged the Orlovs rent. Papa then sold his accordion and spent his nights in bed with his wife. The Orlovs appeared to prosper. Indeed, the only bad effect of the end of the knocking was that Roman had to give up his place in the living room bed to his sister. Not being one to sleep on the floor, Roman began to sleep during the day and wander about the city bars and taverns all night.

At the end of his story, Roman relates that his widowed mother, who once thought the knocking young man was an agent of God, now considers him the devil himself, who robbed her of a good, sober son for a few years' reconciliation with a worthless husband.

Orr, George. *The Lathe of Heaven*. Ursula K. Le Guin. 1971.

George Orr, an otherwise ordinary American of the early twenty-first century, has the ability to alter reality with his dreams. George, who is passive and reserved, tries various combinations of drugs in an effort to prevent himself from dreaming. When he is caught using his friends' "Pharm Cards" to procure the drugs illegally, the authorities require George to undergo psychiatric treatment with a dream specialist named Dr. Haber.

With difficulty, George describes to Dr. Haber the first time he had an "effective" dream. When he was a teenager, his aunt Ethel, who was staying with George's family, made playful attempts to seduce him. One night George had a dream that Aunt Ethel was killed in a car accident in Los Angeles six weeks before. When George wakes up, Aunt Ethel is no longer there, and his parents remember her death, which actually occurred as a result of the dream.

After hearing this story, Dr. Haber no longer regards George as a mild neurotic with a drug habit but decides to treat him as a "severe aberration." In order to observe George asleep and help him control the dreams, Haber hooks him up to a machine called the Augmentor, which ensures that George will sleep and dream lightly or intensively, according to what the doctor requires.

Haber attempts to convince George that he should learn to use his dreams creatively and release his mental powers. George feels manipulated by the doctor and would escape from him if the law did not require him to remain in treatment. Although Haber claims he is assisting the patient, it is clear to George that the doctor is using his effective dreams to alter the world in ways he believes are helpful.

Hoping to prove that Dr. Haber is illegally invading his privacy, George asks that a lawyer, Heather Lelache, be present at one of his sessions. Heather witnesses a session during which Haber asks George to dream that the terrible overpopulation problem is no longer a source of anxiety to him. When George wakes up, there is no overpopulation problem because a plague in the late twentieth century eliminated a significant portion of the population. Both Haber and Heather accept this new reality, while sensing it was not the only one. Heather refuses to press charges against the doctor.

Haber continues to use George's dreams to change the world even more radically and to put himself in a position of great power at the center of a new international government. Before George is able to stand up to Haber, history is significantly altered, aliens land on earth, and people turn a uniform gray color. With the help of the aliens, who understand the power of dreams, George is able to recognize Haber's destructiveness and to dream effectively without him. His private dream brings back Heather, who had disappeared after one of the dreams Haber induced. Heather, now George's wife, accompanies George to the final session, where Haber instructs him to dream that he will never dream effectively again. By observation and research, Haber has learned to dream effectively himself and no longer needs George.

Haber's effective dream is a nightmare, however, and it reduces the world to chaos. This time people are aware of the shift since they are left with fragmentary memories of the previous reality. George understands what is happening and rushes to the office to interrupt Haber's dream, but as he leaves the institute, he realizes that Heather is gone. After "The Break," as the effect of Haber's dream is called, the doctor is placed in a mental institution. George gets a modest job, designing household appliances in a shop run by an alien. One day a woman resembling Heather enters the shop. The alien warmly encourages George to leave early and take her to a café.

Ortegna, Ramona. *Ramona.* Helen Hunt Jackson. 1884.

Ramona Ortegna is the illegitimate daughter of an American Indian woman and a Scottish seaman who suffers throughout her life from the prejudice engendered by the accident of her mixed parentage. As an infant she is bound over to the keeping of the woman to whom her father was betrothed but who married another man during his absence. When this woman dies, the care of the young Ramona is given to the woman's sister, Señora Moreno, who raises Ramona as her own daughter alongside her son Felipe but who never becomes capable of loving Ramona because of the stigma of her Indian parentage.

Ramona meets a young Indian man, Alessandro Assis, when he and his party of Indian sheep shearers arrive at the Moreno ranch for the spring shearing. Alessandro is asked to stay on at the ranch when the foreman is injured in a fall and Felipe is confined to bed with a fever. During his stay at the ranch, Alessandro and Ramona fall in love and determine to marry. Señora Moreno forbids Ramona to marry an Indian, and Ramona is sent off to a convent. Meanwhile, Alessandro returns to his native village to discover that his father has died and the village has been razed and disbanded by the Americans, who have purchased the land.

He returns to the Moreno estate, and he and Ramona run away together with Felipe's assistance. They are married in San Diego and build a house in the San Pasquale valley. Meanwhile, at the Moreno ranch, the dying Señora Moreno reveals to Felipe the location of a hidden cache of jewels that belonged to Ramona's mother and are Ramona's birthright but that Señora Moreno planned to give to the Catholic church. After her death, Felipe is free to try to find Ramona, whom he fears is dead.

Two years after their departure from the Moreno estate, during which time Ramona has given birth to a daughter, Alessandro and Ramona are forced off their land when it is purchased by an American. Ramona, Alessandro, and the baby move on to an Indian village. During their tenure there, the baby becomes ill and dies, after the Indian Agency's doctor refused to travel to the village to care for the child. Ramona and Alessandro move to the remote heights of the San Jacinto Mountain so that they can live out the rest of their lives unmolested by white men.

Alessandro's mental condition begins to suffer from the cumulative effects of their various tragedies, and he experiences long periods of delirium when he is not aware of his actions. During one of these periods he takes the horse of a white man, who tracks him down and kills him. The grief-stricken Ramona wanders down the mountainside, where she falls into a fever and is taken care of by the local Indians. At this point Felipe finally locates her and takes her back to the Moreno ranch, where she can now live in peace following the death of Señora Moreno. Ramona and Felipe are subsequently married and leave California for Mexico to escape the encroaching Americans.

Osmond, Gilbert. *The Portrait of a Lady.* Henry James. 1881.

In an ancient villa outside the Roman Gate of Florence, Italy, lives Gilbert Osmond, Isabel Archer's only successful suitor. Osmond, whose house is filled with tasteful art objects and comfortable furniture, is a forty-year-old, unmarried American. He has one daughter, Pansy, a teenager whom he has sent to a Roman convent for an education; he has very little money and occupies himself by occasionally painting an amateurish watercolor or collecting sketches and bibelots that suit his exquisite, particular taste. Although alluring, Osmond's taste and intelligence prove to be misleading; he is a dilettantish aesthete, a calculating, controlling man who—by his own admission—has no particular genius for anything and whose life has only affirmed his indifference to everything around him.

Osmond's courtship of Isabel Archer begins when he receives a visit from MADAME SERENA MERLE, an old friend. Madame Merle tells Osmond about Isabel and gives him the idea that he should marry her. His interest is piqued when he learns that Isabel is not only beautiful, clever, and virtuous but also very rich. He visits Isabel in Florence at the home of her aunt and later receives Isabel and Madame Merle as guests in his own villa. Making every effort to be agreeable, Osmond impresses and is impressed by Miss Archer.

Osmond begins to call frequently on Isabel. Consulting privately with Madame Merle, he expresses his interest in her but says she has one fault: She has too many ideas. When he joins Isabel for her tour of Rome, he meets several of her companions, including Lord Warburton, an English nobleman whose offer of marriage Isabel previously rejected. The idea of winning a young woman who had rejected such a suitor pleases Osmond and further increases his desire to marry her. At the end of their stay, just before Isabel is about to depart for further travels, he tells her he is in love with her. He asks her to visit Pansy in Florence, and she obliges.

Osmond marries Isabel a year later, and they reside in Rome. The differences between him and his wife quickly become apparent, and their marriage is not happy. One evening during one of Isabel's regular Thursday night socials, a young man named Edward Rosier visits the Osmonds' home. Osmond knows already from a private meeting with Madame Merle that Rosier is in love with Pansy and wants to marry her, but when Rosier declares his intentions, Osmond coldly rebuffs him, claiming that he has higher ambitions for his daughter. He eventually tells the heartsick Rosier that he is no longer welcome in their home.

When Lord Warburton—who is staying in Rome with Isabel's cousin, the ailing Ralph Touchett—arrives at the Osmonds' home and pays some attention to Pansy, Osmond begins to think that this English lord might be interested in marrying her. Insinuating that Isabel should have some influence over him, he subtly asks her to manipulate the courtship. But Warburton makes no move, and Osmond becomes agitated. He asks Isabel to write to Warburton, and when she declines, Osmond assumes that she is working against him.

When Warburton leaves Rome without proposing to Pansy, Osmond—who has continued to consult with Madame Merle about Pansy's courtship—blames Isabel and judges her harshly. He is characteristically cold and unsympathetic when Madame Merle, suddenly repentant, expresses her sadness over the changes she perceives in the once vivacious Isabel. Soon afterward he sends Pansy

back to the convent, believing she has grown "dusty and crumpled" from her contact with society.

At this point Osmond and Isabel, who have turned out to be such bitter disappointments for each other, live in a state of well-concealed mutual hatred. When Isabel receives word from England that Ralph Touchett is dying, the Osmonds' marriage reaches a crisis. Osmond, who has never liked Ralph, strongly opposes Isabel's desire to go to England to see him and expects her to obey his wishes. That day, unbeknownst to Osmond, his sister tells Isabel that Osmond and Madame Merle were once lovers and that Pansy is in fact their child. The morbid Gilbert Osmond has been profoundly deceptive, but when Isabel leaves for England and later returns to Rome to fulfill her promise to Pansy, it is clear that their life together will continue in spite of his heartless ways.

Ostrander, Avis Dobell. *The Story of Avis.* Elizabeth Stuart Phelps. 1877.

Avis Dobell is a talented and aspiring artist living in the mid-nineteenth century. From the time she is a small child in the New England university town of Harmouth, Avis is drawn to colors and their associated sensations. Because she was left motherless at an early age, Avis's "education" was sponsored by her paternal aunt, a dutiful though stern teacher who chronically despaired that Avis, who stubbornly refused to adapt herself to housekeeping, would face a dim future as a woman.

At sixteen Avis informs her father, the famous Professor Hegel Dobell, that she is going to be an artist. Although he is appalled at the effrontery of a young woman asserting such a goal, he agrees to allow her to study art for a time. Avis's passionate commitment grows as her talent emerges, and when she is twenty, she moves to Europe. There she remains for six years and becomes an ardent pupil, studying principally in Florence.

Upon her return to Harmouth at the age of twenty-six, Avis is firmly devoted to her art and has more or less decided not to marry. However, PHILIP OSTRANDER, an up-and-coming young professor whom she had fleetingly met in Italy, begins to woo her. Although she paints a portrait of him, her first completed piece since her return, Avis eventually refuses Philip's proposal of marriage; he subsequently joins the Union Army and enters the Civil War. Meanwhile, Avis continues to sketch, developing the underlying images and ideas for her first creative painting. Finally, she has a momentous vision of her subject and is ready to begin "The Sphinx." At the same time, word comes that Philip has been wounded and sent home to his mother in New Hampshire to recover. The news shocks Avis; she remains disturbed until Philip returns to Harmouth, where he recuperates at the home of one of Avis's friends. The two meet again, and under the sway of the moment, Avis agrees to marry him.

Despite her misgivings, Avis and Philip are married

within a few months. The births of a son and daughter, coupled with the duties of managing a house, force Avis to neglect her art, although she does finally complete the painting she had begun before her marriage. Shortly after their daughter's birth, Avis learns that Philip has been less than successful as a junior professor at Harmouth University and will be asked to resign. Disasters follow; Avis falls seriously ill, and while still weak, she catches Philip in an indiscretion with her nurse. Their marriage now increasingly strained, Philip decides to travel abroad. Illness strikes again during this absence, this time affecting their son, Van Dyck, who dies and is buried on the day of Philip's return. In their grief, the couple turns to each other; they decide to head south for the winter, a trip made possible by the sale of Avis's only completed painting.

While in Florida, Philip suffers a riding accident and dies. Avis, paralyzed with grief and loneliness, returns to her father, aunt, and daughter, only to find that she seems to have lost her talent: Her newest work is rejected by her former supporters. At the end of the novel, Avis, now only in her early thirties, resolves to redirect her energies so that her daughter Wait can avoid the mistakes that hampered her efforts.

Ostrander, Philip. *The Story of Avis.* Elizabeth Stuart Phelps. 1877.

Philip Ostrander is a thirtyish young man who has been trained in medicine but works as a tutor in languages. Having been abroad for a number of years, Philip returns to the United States at the time of the Civil War to take a post at the University of Harmouth in New England. Here he strikes the fancy of many of the town's young women and soon falls in love with AVIS DOBELL (OSTRANDER), an aspiring painter. Philip pursues Avis arduously but in vain, as Avis remains fiercely dedicated to her art. Rejected, the petulant Philip hastily enlists in the Union Army for a three-month stint, but he is seriously wounded before that time is up. He is sent to his mother's home in New Hampshire, but for an unspecified reason he does not wish to stay there and soon returns to Harmouth.

While recuperating Philip is nursed by Avis's friend Barbara Allen. He encounters Avis again, and she, moved by his weakness and by the love she feels for him, agrees to marry him after all. Anxious for the marriage, Philip presses Avis to set a date, and they are finally married. Philip claims that his mother is too weak to attend the wedding.

Philip tells Avis that she must continue to paint, and their marriage goes very well, at first, but Avis gradually realizes there is a side to Philip she does not know. When his mother gets sick and dies, she suspects him of having neglected her. The couple returns to their own home, where a son, Van Dyck, and a daughter, Wait, are born.

After Wait's birth, Philip's once-promising career at the university is threatened when it is revealed that he is falling short of the achievements and duties expected of him. Because he has not devoted himself singlemindedly to his departmental duties but instead has explored other academic areas, he is asked to resign from his position. Philip indignantly complies.

Avis becomes ill with diphtheria. Once again Barbara Allen is called upon for her nursing skills; unfortunately, Avis discovers them in an intimate tête-à-tête, and Barbara leaves. This incident further strains relations between Philip and Avis since she has already learned, from a former girlfriend of Philip's, that her husband is by nature both selfish and inconstant. In order to escape both the shame of his failure at the university and his wife's bitter disillusionment, Philip goes abroad again.

While he is gone, Avis returns to her painting, but her work is once again interrupted when Van Dyck falls ill,. The illness proves fatal, and Philip, unaware of what has happened, returns home on the night of the boy's funeral. The tragedy draws the grieving couple closer, and when Avis suggests that they travel south for the winter, Philip agrees. During their trip Philip vacillates between sickness and health, and between a strong support for Avis's art and a childlike dependence on her attention. For a while things seem to be going well. Philip begins to tutor again and plans to accept a new teaching position after their trip. One day he decides to take a ride and disappears alone on horseback. When he doesn't return after several hours, Avis alerts their acquaintances, and a search party is formed. They find that Philip has suffered an accident and is close to death. He expresses his love for Avis and dies cradled in her arms.

Oswald, Lee Harvey. *Libra.* Don DeLillo. 1988.

In this fictional account of the assassination of President John F. Kennedy, Lee Harvey Oswald spends most of his bitter and impoverished childhood moving around the country with his mother. They live first in the Bronx, then in New Orleans, and finally in Texas. Oswald seems to find some direction in life when he joins the Marines as a teenager in 1957. Once in the service, however, Lee becomes increasingly unhappy, and in an attempt to gain a discharge, he shoots himself in the arm. This incident, coupled with a verbal altercation with an officer, gets Oswald time in the brig where he and a cellmate, Bobby Dupard, are regularly beaten. After his release, Oswald plans to defect to the Soviet Union. A Marxist he has befriended in Atsugi, Japan, puts him in touch with a Russian agent named Braunfels who is particularly interested in the Americans' U-2 spy plane.

After a dishonorable discharge, Oswald returns briefly to his mother's home in Fort Worth, Texas, before securing passage aboard a freighter bound for Europe. Oswald crosses into the U.S.S.R. from Finland but has difficulty convincing Soviet authorities in Moscow that he is a committed Marxist looking to defect. After renouncing his American citizenship and unsuccessfully attempting suicide, Oswald is visited by KGB agent Kirilenko, to whom Lee reveals what few military secrets he actually knows. Finally convinced of Lee's sincerity, the Soviets confirm citizenship upon him and ship him off to Minsk, where he works as a metalworker.

When Francis Gary Powers is shot down during a spy mission over Russia, the Soviets use Oswald to corroborate the pilot's information concerning both the U-2 and the mission itself. Back in Minsk, Lee falls in love with and marries a young Russian named Marina, with whom he has a child. Shortly thereafter, Oswald's disillusionment with Soviet life builds to a crescendo, and he applies for repatriation, which is ultimately granted. Oswald leaves Russia with his wife and daughter after a three-year stay.

Upon his return to the United States, Oswald settles his family in Fort Worth, where he is regularly visited by both the F.B.I. and businessman George de Mohrenschildt, a participant in a plot to recruit a marksman to make a fake attempt on the life of President John F. Kennedy. This idea, hatched by a renegade CIA operative, is intended to revive the nation's interest in Cuba by leaving a trail of phony evidence leading to Fidel Castro.

Oswald, growing ever angrier and thirsting for a niche in history, moves to Dallas where he runs into his old prison pal Bobby Dupard. After purchasing a cheap mail-order rifle, Oswald recruits his friend to assist in the assassination of right-wing rabble-rouser General Edwin A. Walker. Their effort fails.

By this time Oswald has decided that he is destined to murder JFK and then seek asylum in Cuba, his latest cause. As a part of this fledgling conspiracy to kill the President, Oswald and Marina move to New Orleans where Lee opens an unauthorized branch of the Fair Play for Cuba Committee and falls under the tutelage of David Ferrie, who claims to see Oswald's fate as a product of his astrological sign, Libra. Ferrie also transports Lee to a special camp where he is able to hone his shooting skills.

After a failed attempt at procuring a travel visa to Cuba in Mexico City, Oswald returns to Dallas and accepts a job at the Texas School Book Depository on Elm Street. Increasingly estranged from Marina, Oswald is obsessed by his potential role in history. Finally, on November 22, 1963, Oswald does take his place in history by firing on the presidential motorcade from his perch in the depository. Despite hitting Kennedy in the back with his first shot, Oswald ultimately fails: Another rifleman, stationed on a grassy knoll that lines the motorcade route, scores the head shot which ultimately kills the President.

Oswald flees the depository and heads for a Dallas movie theater where he is to meet the man responsible for spiriting him out of the country. On his way to the theater, however, Lee is approached by Police Officer Tippit,

whom Oswald shoots to death. Afterward, Oswald goes inside the theater and takes a seat two rows in front of a man hired to kill him. But the Dallas police arrive before the murder can take place.

Although vilified as JFK's murderer, Oswald revels in the recognition he has secured. Two days after his arrest, Oswald, in the process of being transferred to the county prison, is shot to death in full view of the television public by Jack Ruby, who has been hired to erase the most obvious link in the successful conspiracy to assassinate John F. Kennedy.

Ottenburg, Fred. *The Song of the Lark.* Willa Cather. 1915.

Fred Ottenburg, the pampered son of a wealthy brewer, possesses an intuitive understanding of the character of the artist. Although Fred occupies an important position in his father's brewing business, he lives mostly in what he terms the "fourth dimension." This dimension, in which Fred places the life-sustaining passion for art and music, provides stability for him beside the unpredictable fluctuations of business and personal concerns.

Fred is the third son of the wealthy Chicago brewer Otto Ottenburg. His mother's favorite, Fred has always had everything he wanted. Mrs. Ottenburg, once a scandalous heiress, visits Fred regularly while he is attending Harvard, distracting him with parties and gifts. In his third year, however, he is forced to leave school after he agrees to entertain his friend Dick Brisbane's fiancée in New York. Dick's fiancée, Edith Beers, is an unusual woman— strikingly beautiful, extravagant, and rebellious. While she and Fred are driving through New York in a hansom, she tearfully explains to Fred that she has made a terrible mistake by promising to marry his friend. This has become abundantly clear in the past three days, she says, while Fred has been entertaining her. Fred and Edith leave the cab and sit for some time in a casino, where they agree to get married. The elopement takes place the following morning.

After living with his wife in Chicago for several months, Fred realizes he has made a disastrous mistake. Edith is persistently rude to his family and cruel to him. Fred begins drinking heavily. Finally, Edith accepts the offer of a luxurious house in Santa Barbara, California, that belongs to Mrs. Ottenburg. Fred is nearly liberated from her except that she will not grant him a divorce. He remains in Chicago where he lives mostly in the "fourth dimension," attending numerous concerts and socializing with the city's most admired musicians. Fred has many female friends but does not contemplate remarriage until he meets THEA KRONBORG, a young opera singer from Colorado.

Fred and Thea both take voice lessons from Madison Bowers, a famous teacher, for whom Thea is also an accompanist. Fred sees at once that Thea has enormous potential as a singer but is being worn away by her degrading and stressful life in Chicago. He offers her a summer vacation on a friend's ranch in Panther Canyon, Arizona. As Fred suspected, this retreat gives Thea new life. When he visits her after two months, Thea radiates beauty, strength, and energy. Before returning to Chicago, Fred tries to convince Thea to marry him. She agrees, but when the story of his earlier marriage emerges, Thea ends the romance abruptly by going to study music in Germany.

During the next ten years both Thea and Fred have great success; Fred becomes the head of the brewery, and Thea sings principal parts at the Metropolitan in New York. Fred meets and befriends her mentor, HOWARD ARCHIE, and visits her regularly in New York. Like Howard, Fred is deeply impressed by her talent and passion. Fred and Thea are still powerfully attracted to each other, but Thea resists him, having vowed not to become involved until he is able to obtain a divorce. Fred and Thea are eventually married, however, and he continues to support and encourage her in the pursuit of her art.

Overt, Paul. *The Lesson of the Master*. Henry James. 1888.

A writer who has already shown traces of genius in his first three novels, Paul Overt is still struggling to live up to the enormous promise that those around him claim is shown by his early works. After spending a year abroad following the publication of his fourth novel, Overt is invited to the country home of retired General Fancourt. There he is delighted to meet England's most widely read and respected novelist, HENRY ST. GEORGE, who, despite a noticeable decline in the quality of some of his later works, remains at the pinnacle of his profession.

Overt finds, however, that most of St. George's time at the Fancourt country home is spent in the company of Marian Fancourt, the General's beautiful young daughter. Immediately enamored himself of the vivacious young woman, Overt resents St. George, but his anger remains hidden beneath his respect and admiration for the famous man's writing. Overt is made doubly unhappy because he is forced to spend most of his visit in the company of St. George's shrewish and overbearing wife.

The night before he is to return to London, Overt gets his anxiously awaited opportunity to converse with the master of letters, who confesses to Paul that he has been reading the young man's novels during his stay at the Fancourts'. He goes on to tell Paul of the tremendous ability his writing reflects, and the two make plans to see each other again in London.

One week later Overt meets Marian by chance at a crowded art gallery opening in London. Overt's spirits are dampened when he learns that she is to attend the show with St. George, who soon joins them. Marian invites him to a gathering at the Fancourt mansion a week later, which St. George will be attending as well.

When Overt arrives the following week, he is thrilled to find that St. George will not be present and that he has the opportunity to speak with Marian alone over the course of the evening. A great admirer of his books, Marian tells Overt that St. George has frequently remarked to her about his great potential. He leaves that night, deeply in love with the charismatic Marian. As he walks down the street from her house, trying to hail a cab, Overt is stunned to see a cab pull up and St. George walk briskly out and into the Fancourt home.

Overt attends a dinner with St. George a few days later, where the two, in the privacy of St. George's study, have a frank discussion of the hardships to which a writer must subject himself in order to pursue his art. A wife, children, and virtually any kind of material happiness must all be forsaken, St. George argues, if a writer is truly to master his craft. When a horrified Overt, thinking of his new love, Marian, points out that St. George has a wife and three sons, the venerable master uses them as an explanation for the deterioration of his later works.

Thus inspired to subject himself to the despondency of life and to reach his own artistic potential, Overt leaves England for two years, secluding himself from the world to finish his next novel. When he returns to London, manuscript in hand, he immediately pays a visit to the Fancourt house. General Fancourt informs him that Marian is to be married to St. George, whose wife passed away the previous winter.

P

Paine, Thomas. *Citizen Tom Paine*. Howard Fast. 1943.

Tom Paine is the protagonist of Howard Fast's eponymous historical novel. As a teenager in an English town,

Tom is a staymaker like his father, and acutely aware of the sufferings of his poverty-stricken class. Having known only injustice and cruelty, he is hostile and resentful at an early age. His comportment is slovenly, and his manners are appalling. A love for drinking, which he maintains throughout his life, augments the unpleasant aspects of his character.

Paine moves to various English towns and eventually to London in the hopes of improving his situation but finds the only occupation he is fit for is that of a staymaker. He marries a young girl who dies in childbirth because he could not pay for food or help. Distraught and near despair, Paine approaches the famous Ben Franklin, who is visiting England. Franklin recognizes Paine as a potential revolutionary, in spite of his rudeness and slovenliness, and arranges for his passage to America. Thanks to a letter of recommendation from Franklin, Tom is able to find work as a tutor—only to lose his various positions because of excessive drinking.

Paine's life in America seems little different from his life in England until the publisher Aitken allows him to write for the *Pennsylvania Magazine*. Famous overnight, Paine is simultaneously appalled by the slavery in America and enthralled by revolutionaries who are fighting for freedom from England. Grasping the far-reaching implications of the struggle, he passionately supports the revolutionaries and succeeds in garnering countrywide support with the publication of a pamphlet, *Common Sense*. He travels to various encampments, explaining the cause the soldiers are fighting for and building morale with his speeches and his Crisis letters. Affectionately nicknamed "Common Sense," Paine becomes an invaluable camp aide to General Washington and others.

After the success of the revolution, Paine returns to England hoping to bring about the same results there. His pamphlet, *The Rights of Man*, is so inflammatory that he barely escapes England with his life. He goes to France just as the revolutionary movement is growing there. Sitting on the council, he joins forces with the Gerondins, who are then overridden by the Jacobins. Paine is one of few in the group who escape the guillotine.

Confused by the turn the French revolutionary movement is taking, Paine retires to a farmhouse to write *The Age of Reason*, his philosophy of religion. Finally, he is sent to the Luxembourg prison and left there, with no help from America, until the revolution ends.

Once free, Paine publishes his book and is instantly and violently condemned throughout Europe and America. Old and tired, he returns to America to die. There, he is forgotten by his friends and tormented by children and adults alike. Considered a heretic equal in power to the devil, he is shunned up to the moment of his death. Even his bones, buried in unhallowed ground, have been stolen and lost, a tragic consequence for so great a man.

Pal Joey. *Pal Joey.* John O'Hara. 1946.

Pal Joey is a nightclub singer less interested in music than in the accoutrements of success. He envies the pop-

ular crooners of his era, the 1940s, not because of their talent but because of their wealth, women, and prestige. He tries to live as though he were famous and successful, despite the obvious lack of these elements in his life. The novella consists of letters written by Pal Joey to his friend "Pal Ted," a bandleader who eventually reaches the height of popularity in the United States. Although he relates his exploits in the best possible terms, it is increasingly clear that Pal Joey is a self-deceiving and ultimately embittered loser.

In his first letter to Ted, Joey tells him that he has left Michigan for Ohio where an admirer has gotten him a job singing. Joey soon exchanges this admirer, Nan Hennessey, whom he met while on vacation in Michigan, for a wealthier woman, or "mouse," as Joey calls her. Jean Spencer is the nineteen-year-old daughter of a bank president, and Joey hopes to marry her and perhaps get into the banking business. Nan suddenly leaves town for New York, for reasons that Joey fails to explain in his letter although he does manage to recommend that Ted look her up for a proverbial "good time."

In the next letter Joey berates Ted for meeting up with Nan in New York. "Ex-pal Joey" is furious with Ted for apparently revealing to Nan the nature of his relationship with Jean Spencer. Nan has sent Jean an anonymous letter warning her about Joey, thus ruining his chances in the banking industry. He loses his job because of the scandal and is run of town by one of Jean's other, more legitimate—and stronger—suitors. Acting on the orders of Jean's father, Jerry Towle gives Joey the option of taking the 8:30 AM train to New York, or the 9:00 AM train to Chicago. Because Towle is standing over him menacingly, waiting for his decision, Joey must leave. But to "burn" Towle, he waits for the later train. By the time he gets to Chicago he has both forgiven Ted and gotten a new singing job.

In subsequent letters Joey tells of surviving a club fire, of taking advantage of another "mouse," of deceiving people with stories about his having graduated from Princeton or Dartmouth and possessing parents who lost their great wealth in the stock market crash, and of moving from job to job in a gradual decline that even he cannot conceal. By the last letter in the novella it is clear that Pal Joey's career is going nowhere. He has just blown an interview with a local columnist by bathing her in a torrent of obvious lies about his background, and he is somehow surprised that she has not fallen for his usual ploys. The last letter is one he will never send, for it is a diatribe against Ted, who has achieved the sort of success that Joey will never realize. The letter is signed "Ex-Pal Joey (Hate yr guts)."

Papadakis, Cora. *The Postman Always Rings Twice.* James M. Cain. 1934.

Cora Papadakis, a dark, sullen, sexy beauty, is lured to

Los Angeles by the promise of a career in film. She finds herself slinging hash in a café. To save herself from a hand-to-mouth existence, she marries Nick Papadakis, a blustering Greek. As the novel opens, Cora has been working faithfully with Nick in his roadside restaurant just outside Los Angeles for three years, determined "to stick by him." However, when FRANK CHAMBERS, a young vagabond, blows into the hash house one day, Cora's resolve deserts her.

In need of a handyman, Nick hires Frank for the job. Within days Cora and Frank have become lovers. Cora tells Frank about her disgust for the Greek and her desire to be free of him. In her mind only one solution seems available, and she finally convinces Frank to help her. They plan the Greek's murder and attempt to carry it out, but unforeseen events foil the plan. Nick survives with a concussion and a bad memory.

While Nick convalesces in the hospital, Cora and Frank repent their crime but not their desire for each other. Rather than try murder again, they decide to run away. They leave on foot, but less than two hours down the road Cora realizes that she cannot live the life of a vagabond, and she returns to the roadhouse. Frank continues on his way.

Several months later Frank runs into Nick, who is on the road buying supplies for the restaurant. Nick rehires the younger man and takes him home to Cora. When Cora is alone with Frank, she reveals that the Greek's accident has caused him to want children, a thought she cannot bear. The next day she and Frank murder the Greek and make the deed look like a car accident.

Frank and Cora are not so lucky this time. The police are suspicious from the beginning. When the case goes before the grand jury, Cora is shocked to learn that she alone is being charged with murder because the district attorney convinced Frank to sign a complaint against her. Even more surprising to Cora is the fact that her lawyer pleads her guilty. Enraged, she informs her lawyer that she wishes to make a statement. She reveals all that has transpired since she met Frank to the stenographer sent by her lawyer.

The next day Cora goes up for sentencing. Through a number of legal sleights of hand, Cora's lawyer manages to get Cora's murder charge lessened to manslaughter. She receives a suspended sentence and is set free. After her lawyer reveals that the man who took her statement worked for him and not the district attorney, Cora and Frank are reunited and return to the roadhouse to await the payment of the $10,000 insurance settlement that results from Nick's death.

From this point, however, events take a swift turn for the worse. Cora's mother dies back in Des Moines. When Cora returns, she and Frank are confronted by the stenographer who had taken her statement, and he attempts to blackmail the pair. Cora and Frank succeed in securing

all copies of Cora's statement from him without paying any money. But the very night of this coup, Cora learns that Frank had a brief affair in her absence and threatens to go to the district attorney with the whole story of Nick's murder. For several days the two play cat-and-mouse with each other—the one afraid of being handed over to the police, the other afraid of being murdered.

Finally, Cora discovers that she is pregnant. She and Frank call a truce and decide to get married. The day they are married, they go to the beach where Cora overexerts herself. Afraid that she is having a miscarriage, Frank gets her to the car, and as he speeds down the highway to the hospital, he causes a deadly accident. Cora is killed, and Frank writes a narrative of their story from death row, where he awaits his execution after being convicted of Cora's murder.

Papravel, Nicholas. *Summer in Williamsburg.* Daniel Fuchs. 1934.

Determined not to follow the legacy of poverty and despair left by his parents, Nicholas Papravel began devising confidence games and elaborate racketeering schemes at a very early age. The novel's villain, Papravel, intelligent and possessing a ruthless disposition, made a very profitable living in New York City and the surrounding neighborhoods during the Depression era. Much to his dismay, however, his sister, having married a poor but honest store owner, refuses to accept any of the expensive gifts he wants to lavish on her. Her eldest son Harry, as soon as he was old enough, ran away from home to secure a high-paying job in the fast-paced, dangerous world of his uncle Papravel. Her youngest son, PHILIP HAYMAN, however, resists the temptation to work for this ruthless mobster.

Papravel's latest scheme involves taking over a bus station in Williamsburg and, with the help of a powerful financial backer named Rubin, setting up a monopoly of all the bus lines in the New York City area. With his small band of hoodlums, Papravel visits the owner of the Silver Eagle Bus Lines and informs him that he is finished in Williamsburg. To prove his point, he has his men destroy the entire station, tearing apart the ticket counters and sabotaging the buses.

But the owner of the Silver Eagle Bus Lines, an elderly man named Morantz, turns out to be more defiant than Papravel had expected. When Morantz refuses to close down his Williamsburg station, Papravel, after raising more funds from the reluctant Rubin, bribes some local policemen to destroy more of the buses on account of a fictional brewery they say Morantz has hidden on the premises. Outraged, Morantz has no other choice but to hire a gang of gunmen from Detroit to protect his bus station in Williamsburg.

By this time Rubin is reluctant to spend any more money on Papravel's bus scheme. To make matters worse, one of Papravel's dim-witted henchman murders a state trooper, endangering the whole operation. Knowing that all of his power will be gone if he fails to bail out his employee, Papravel hires a big-time lawyer to save his hireling.

Papravel goes on to invent a "Bus Driver's Union," by which he is able to rouse Morantz's bus drivers into striking by setting arbitrary minimum salaries. Morantz' Silver Eagle Lines and Rubin's Empire Bus lines then engage in a fare war, driving Morantz to the point of bankruptcy.

Not only does the Williamsburg station close but the entire Eagle Bus Line collapses. Papravel, in a final coup, is able to topple Rubin as the head of Empire Bus Lines and force him into a lesser role in the company's management.

On the day of Papravel's ascension to the head of Empire Bus Lines, an elderly neighbor tearfully confesses to him her fear that he may never find happiness because he wasn't baptized at birth.

Paradise, Salvatore. *On the Road.* Jack Kerouac. 1955.

Salvatore Paradise is a World War II veteran attending college in Manhattan on the G.I. Bill. Unlike many of his contemporaries who have returned from the war with hopes of settling down to work and family life, Sal yearns to be a writer. He divorces his wife and moves in with his aunt in Paterson, New Jersey, to begin work on a novel.

In Manhattan, Sal hangs out with Carlo Marx, a brooding intellectual, and DEAN MORIARTY, a juvenile delinquent and drifter turned philosopher. The three spend long evenings discussing art and the meaning of life, listening to jazz, and wandering about the city in search of women. After Dean and Carlo travel to Texas, Sal grows restless with his writing routine and decides to follow them. He feels the need for new experiences and misses being around people "who never yawn or say a commonplace thing, but burn, burn, burn, like fabulous yellow Roman candles."

Sal takes a bus to Chicago and hitchhikes to Denver, where he meets up again with Carlo and Dean. Sal is impressed by how close the two have become, although he feels slightly left out during their all-night bull sessions. "If you keep this up," he tells them, "you'll both go crazy, but let me know what happens along the way." Next, Sal hitches a ride to San Francisco and stays with Remi Boncoeur, an old prep school friend. They find work as night watchmen at a local barracks but quickly befriend the sailors they are supposed to discipline. Shortly afterward Sal journeys to Los Angeles where he meets Terry, a young Mexican, and lives with her in a community of migrant workers for several months. When he can no longer find work, he leaves Terry and returns to the East Coast.

Arriving in Times Square during rush hour, Sal is both exhilarated and depressed as he watches "millions hustling forever for a buck among themselves, the mad dream-grabbing, taking, giving, sighing, dying, just so they could be buried in those awful cemetery cities beyond Long Island City." He stays in New York until Christmas, when Dean shows up with his wife Marylou. They soon decide to go to New Orleans with a group of Sal's old friends. After exploring the jazz scene with another old school friend, Bull Lee, the group climbs back into the car and heads to California. When he has completely run out of money, Sal heads back east.

In the spring of 1949, Sal leaves the East Coast for a third time. He stops in Denver, but he finds no one there that he remembers. Feeling lonely, he returns to San Francisco to look up Dean, and the two drive to Chicago before hitching their way back to New York. They make plans to travel to Italy, but news reaches Dean of the birth of his fourth child, and he returns to the West, leaving Sal to stay in New Jersey.

When he finally sells one of his books, Sal decides to head to Denver one more time. He stays with Dean and meets Stan Shepard, an old friend; the three head off to Mexico, where they pass the time drinking, smoking marijuana, and sleeping with prostitutes. One day Dean drives off, leaving Sal and Stan to fend for themselves.

Sal soon returns to New York and meets a woman named Laura, with whom he falls madly in love. The two are planning to move to San Francisco when Dean appears at their door. Sal is shocked by his friend's appearance: He is faded and withered, can barely talk, and stutters most of the time. Dean stays with Sal and Laura for a few days, until he receives a letter from his second wife asking him to return. Sal parts with Dean—and his old life—for the last time, before driving off to start his new life in the West with Laura.

Paris, Memo. *The Natural.* Bernard Malamud. 1952.

Memo Paris is the beautiful temptress who leads the heroic ROY HOBBS toward destruction. She is the niece of Pop Fisher, manager of the New York Knights, a baseball team that is second-rate until it is joined by the ambitious and remarkably talented Hobbs. But Hobbs's blind ambition, coupled with Memo's greed, leads, on the evening before the World Series, to the team's collapse.

When she enters the narrative, Memo is involved with the team's only other talent, Bump Bailey, who leads the league in batting. A notorious practical joker, Bump engineers a situation of mistaken identity whereby Memo crawls into bed beside Hobbs. Memo is mortified and refuses to have anything to do with Hobbs for a long time, in spite of his best efforts to win her attention. When Bump dies trying to outdo the rookie by making a spectacular catch at the outfield wall, Memo is wild with grief and becomes even colder to the well-meaning Hobbs.

When Memo comes out of mourning, she begins dating Gus Sands, a rich but unsavory bookie. Sands does his best to humiliate Hobbs in "friendly" bets, but Hobbs manages to hold his own in their dealings, and Memo finally becomes interested in him. Hobbs has been stunning the Knights fans with his outstanding batting and catching, and when they award him a new Mercedes on "Roy Hobbs Day," Memo agrees to take an evening ride with him. She becomes upset by his eager advances, however, and insists on taking the wheel and driving with the headlights off. The car hits something. Roy swears he saw a boy standing by the road just before impact, but Memo brushes him off; after Roy makes an unsuccessful search for the boy, they return to town.

Soon after their drive, Roy enters a long slump, and Memo quickly loses interest. She stops seeing him, and he takes up briefly with Iris Lemon, a devoted fan. Shortly afterward his slump ends, he leaves Iris, and Memo returns to his side.

As the season progresses, Roy becomes more and more ambitious. Unfortunately, as his desire for success grows, so does his appetite; urged on by Memo, he consumes vast quantities of food. When Memo throws a party for the team on the eve of an important game, Roy eats so much that he must be hospitalized and miss several games. He is ready to play in the deciding game of the pennant race, but on the evening before, he receives two visitors: Memo and Judge Goodwill Banner, owner of the Knights. Memo convinces Roy that she will marry him only if he has enough money to make her comfortable; the Judge tells him that he will give him the money if he throws the game. Tormented but thinking of Memo, Roy agrees to the deal.

On the day of the game, Roy tries his best not to get a hit. He fouls a ball that strikes Iris, who was standing in the stadium to cheer him on. As she is taken away in the ambulance, she tells him that she is pregnant, and Roy feels a rush of love for Iris and their unborn child. He determines to win the game, but when his lucky bat is broken with another foul, he is unable to get a hit, and the Knights lose.

After the game, Roy confronts Memo, the Judge, and Gus Sands in the empty stadium. When he physically attacks the Judge and Sands, Memo aims a gun at him and fires. The bullet misses its mark, and Memo collapses in hysterical sobs.

Parkhill (Mr.) *The Education of Hyman Kaplan.* Leonard Q. Ross. 1937.

Mr. Parkhill is employed by The American Night Preparatory School for Adults, a night school for immigrants with subjects ranging from English to civics, the ultimate aim of which is to prepare them for American citizenship. Mr. Parkhill has been employed for some time teaching the school's basic English class, and he takes his job very seriously. He considers himself a good teacher, combining an interest in what he thinks are advanced pedagogic methods with a sincere regard for his duty as the first rung

in the ladder to success that his students must be encouraged to climb.

The one cloud that appears to darken Mr. Parkhill's serene horizon and that dampens his pedagogic vanity is HYMAN KAPLAN, an immigrant from Eastern Europe. Kaplan's garish signature, written with multicolored letters and stars, becomes an agonizing affront to the instructor, whom Kaplan calls "Mr. Pockheel" in his systemic web of mispronunciations. Mr. Parkhill has never had a student who seems so thoroughly uneducable. Yet even this is not the source of Parkhill's greatest frustration. Mr. Parkhill finds himself dreading Kaplan's comments and class participation because disturbances invariably ensue: intraclass rivalries, the subversion of the planned lesson, and the diversion of the class into a morass of confusion.

Even more galling than Kaplan's bombshells of mispronunciation and twisted usage is the faint inkling Mr. Parkhill has of Kaplan's motivating logic. It is possible, Mr. Parkhill begins to suspect, that Kaplan's errors are not errors at all but are the aberrational appearances of a deeper logic, a sinister rationality, that lurks behind the student's imperturbable grin. For example, when Mr. Parkhill asks Kaplan to give a sentence using the word *pitcher*, Kaplan declaims, "Oh, how beautiful is dis picher." Mr. Parkhill lunges at Kaplan's mistake—"pitcher," not "picture"—only to be trounced by Kaplan's canny new world optimism: "In som houses is even pichers beauriful." The antonym for Parkhill's "rich" is Kaplan's "die, dead, funeral." Mr. Parkhill has met his inverse in a certain sense, but the real problem with educating Hyman Kaplan is that he will never learn enough to advance out of Mr. Parkhill's class.

Patch, Anthony. *The Beautiful and Damned.* F. Scott Fitzgerald. 1922.

A comfortable and complacent bachelor, a Harvard graduate, and the grandson of Adam Patch, a wealthy financier, Anthony Patch feels that he is destined to do something extraordinary, although he is not exactly sure what that is. In the meantime he enjoys a carefree life of socializing in New York with a couple of close friends from his college years, Maury Noble and Dick Caramel.

Dick Caramel introduces Anthony to his cousin GLORIA GILBERT (PATCH), the daughter of a wealthy celluloid manufacturer from Kansas City. Anthony, somewhat lonely, instantly recognizes Gloria's beauty and extreme self-confidence. He yearns to gain the interest of this much-sought-after twenty-two-year-old, who seems to treat most of her suitors with an air of casual indifference.

Anthony is delighted when Gloria begins to appreciate his worthiness, and although it pains him to sacrifice his dignity in order to win her, he knows that he loves her. They gradually spend more time together, and before long they are married at Adam Patch's estate. Anthony is disappointed that "Cross" Patch, as his grandfather is known, gives them only $5,000 for a wedding gift. He knows that it is because the elder Patch, a tycoon turned philanthropist and reformer, is dismayed by his grandson's lack of career plans.

Anthony and Gloria enjoy a passionate honeymoon in California, but Anthony wearies of attending to Gloria's every whim and begins to sense her consummate selfishness. Nevertheless, they do love each other, and once back East they rent a little house in the Connecticut countryside where they enjoy idyllic summer nights on the porch together.

Anthony becomes increasingly lazy, however, and only feels energized after a couple of drinks. When Adam Patch gets him a job in the bond business, Anthony is repulsed by the petty ambition and glacial pace of corporate advancement. He quits, and he and Gloria lead a frenzied life of social dissipation. One night in Connecticut, Adam Patch arrives for an unexpected visit and finds a wild party in full swing. In reaction to this episode Anthony realizes that to drift without ambition is to be drawn into trouble and that life may be more important than he has assumed. In spite of his grandson's change of heart, however, Adam Patch wills Anthony nothing when he dies some time later. Anthony, now the subject of sordid rumors, along with Gloria, in New York society, hires a lawyer to contest the will.

When the United States declares war on Germany in World War I, Anthony applies to be an officer but is denied because of his unhealthy blood pressure. Yet a few months later he is drafted and shipped to Camp Hooker in the South. As letters from Gloria become less frequent, Anthony realizes that by living only for the moment they have sacrificed the long-term health of their relationship.

While at the camp Anthony befriends Dorothy Raycroft, a local girl with a sullied reputation. When Anthony is relocated to another camp, he puts Dot up in a boardinghouse. One night they quarrel; Anthony later receives a phone call from her obliquely suggesting that she is going to kill herself. The threat turns out to be a ruse, and when he returns to camp after rushing to Dot's side, Anthony is disciplined for being late. A few days later he is jailed for drunkenness. When armistice is declared, Anthony and Gloria are happily reunited, but he quickly reverts to being a sloth. He drinks constantly and quarrels bitterly with Gloria, who is appalled by his lack of energy and direction.

On the day that the verdict on Anthony's court case is finally due, he suffers a severe breakdown. His trauma has been brought about by Dot; now living in New York, she appears at the Patch home while Gloria is out. Anthony threatens to kill her and then collapses. Anthony does recover, and because the jury has awarded him $30 million, he sails for Europe with Gloria. He leaves the country feeling vindicated in the face of those who he felt offered only scorn and punishment for his misfortunes.

Patch, Gloria Gilbert. *The Beautiful and Damned.* F. Scott Fitzgerald. 1922.

Gloria Gilbert, the daughter of a wealthy Kansas City businessman, is a selfish beauty who has always left a trail of discarded admirers behind her. While in New York with her parents, her cousin Dick Caramel introduces Gloria to his friend ANTHONY PATCH, the charming but aimless grandson of a famous ex-financier. The introduction initiates the torrid relationship that dominates the action of the novel.

At first Gloria is indifferent to Anthony. Over tea at the Plaza Hotel she makes it clear that she expects the world to perform for her benefit. One night when Gloria throws a party for herself, she and Anthony duck out and kiss. Upon their return she makes excuses to Joseph Bloeckman, a man in the film industry acquainted with her father, who manufactures celluloid. Anthony notices this and conceives a long-lasting jealous suspicion of Bloeckman.

When Anthony protests Gloria's casual attitude toward his affection, Gloria pretends not to care, and he storms out of the room. After six weeks apart they spend a blissful day together. It becomes clear to both that their attraction is mutual and certain, and they marry. During a long honeymoon in California, Gloria and Anthony enjoy wine, shopping, leisure, and friends. Yet Gloria tests Anthony's patience with her constant demands, and, on her part, the young bride notices that her husband can be cowardly but also strangely reckless.

Gloria and Anthony rent a house in Connecticut on a trying day when Gloria, who insists that she be allowed to drive, promptly runs the car into a fire hydrant. On another occasion Gloria insists that they return home early from the beach club, but Anthony, inebriated and enjoying their friends, is unwilling to leave. Frustrated at her selfishness, he violently attacks her on the train platform in front of strangers. He then feels remorseful, noticing suddenly something pathetic in the scene: For the first time Gloria, tearful and disheveled in her new dress and holding a broken parasol, does not have things her own way.

The two waste their time in drink and profligate spending, in both the country and the city where they winter. By now Gloria's self-centeredness has been transformed into indifference concerning the consequences of their behavior. When Anthony quits a Wall Street job arranged by his grandfather, Gloria wants to scold him but is suddenly moved by his utter spiritlessness. Adam Patch, Anthony's wealthy grandfather, dies, and much to their disappointment, he leaves Anthony out of his will because of his lack of ambition and self-control. To make matters worse, a friend of Gloria's informs the pair that they are the subject of scandalous rumors in New York social circles. Gloria begins to sense that Anthony is indifferent to her, and she recognizes in her own conflicting emotions a certain hatred for him.

With the onset of World War I, Anthony is drafted and sent to camp in the South; Gloria misses him despite their recent troubles and hopes that the army will give him some sense of discipline. She is generally uninterested in the men she meets while he is away and begins to feel stronger and less needy. Her happier mood is interrupted, however, when Anthony returns to his drunken lethargy soon after their reunion, and as her twenty-ninth birthday approaches, Gloria wonders if her beauty has morally corrupted her. Bloeckman gets her a screen test for a movie role, roll, but she is considered too old for the part. She and Anthony move far uptown, and although Anthony drinks constantly, Gloria spends much of her time simply reading and walking.

Anthony has been contesting his grandfather's will in court. He suffers a breakdown on the day the verdict is due but soon recovers. The court awards him $30 million. He and Gloria decide to sail for Europe, leaving their disaffected lives behind.

Patimkin, Brenda. *Goodbye, Columbus.* Philip Roth. 1959.

Brenda Patimkin is the beautiful and sexy, if myopic, girlfriend of NEIL KLUGMAN. She comes from a wealthy Jewish family that has been able, through the success of Patimkin Sink, to move from Newark to the affluent area of Short Hills. Brenda's father is devoted to her, and she is grateful for everything he has given her and loves him for his generosity. Her relationship with her mother is far more problematic. She is disparaging about her mother's attitude toward money, claiming that "she still thinks we live in Newark," and she interprets her mother's distance from her as jealousy.

Brenda first meets Neil by the pool at the prestigious Green Lane Country Club when she casually asks him to hold her glasses while she dives. To Neil, she is elegantly simple and stands out among the other members of the club like "a sailor's dream of a Polynesian maiden." She is also an accomplished sportswoman: a graceful diver, a determined golfer, and a competitive tennis player. Brenda is above all confident of her status and her looks; she acknowledges that she was pretty before her nose job but is prettier now, and she has no qualms about admitting to the expense and vanity of such an operation. She doesn't fully understand Neil's nervous sarcasm or his rudeness, but she knows that she can silence him by offering a kiss and win him by offering her body.

Both Brenda's poise and her unquestioning nature are the mark of an uncomplicated character. She asks Neil few questions, and when she ask him if he loves her, she seems to be prompted by a rather detached curiosity, claiming that she will still sleep with him regardless of his answer. Brenda's composure is rarely ruffled, and even her lovemaking seems pragmatic and uncomplicated. In the early stages of their relationship, Brenda is truly passionate only once, and this passion is aroused by her family in a fit of anger at her mother's lack of concern. Brenda demands that Neil make love to her on an old sofa in an unused room in her parents' house. From that moment on her relationship with Neil becomes an implicit act of defiance and a rejection of everything she feels her parents stand for.

As their relationship progresses during this one summer, Brenda is forced out of her rather detached complacency. When Neil asks her to go to the Margaret Sanger Clinic in New York to get a diaphragm, Brenda is at first horrified by the thought of making what she considers an adult decision. But she changes her mind, and the new diaphragm, previously a strange and frightening object, instantly becomes a further mark of her poise and confidence. Although she claims that she loves Neil, Brenda seems strangely unmoved by this love, and much as she had given herself easily and without complication, she now adapts to this new seriousness.

Yet when Neil comes to visit her at Radcliffe, Brenda's poise has finally been shaken by her mother's discovery of the diaphragm, which Brenda had left at home. She angrily rejects Neil's "psychoanalytic" interpretation that she left the diaphragm where her mother would easily find it, but she cannot offer another explanation for her carelessness. She acquiesces to her father's covert suggestion that she should end the relationship by refusing to answer Neil's accusations. She returns to her parents and, because of the choice she has made, blames Neil for his lack of understanding.

Patmore, Henry. *The Walls of Jericho.* Rudolph Fisher. 1928.

Henry Patmore owns Patmore's Pool Parlor, a gathering place for men in the Harlem of the 1920s. As the novel begins, Patmore's customers discuss the possibility of a race riot. An African American has bought a home on all-white Court Street, and the black community expects, as has happened before, that the Caucasian residents will use violence to dissuade the newcomer from settling there.

The buyer is Fred Merrit, a lawyer Patmore knows well. Merrit once cost Patmore $10,000 in a legal suit. Patmore notices JOSHUA "SHINE" JONES drinking at the bar, attempts to engage him in conversation, and, when that fails, attempts to coerce him. He knows that Shine manages the moving company that will handle Merrit's move. Patmore knows, too, that Shine dislikes "dickties" (affluent African Americans in Harlem slang) and offers him $10 to deliver, along with Merrit's furniture, a half-case of Patmore's bootleg liquor. He claims he does not hold a grudge and only wants to get Merrit as a customer, but Shine refuses.

At the annual costume dance, Patmore sees a beautiful woman named Linda Young. He introduces himself and claims that as one of the judges of the costume competition, he has already judged hers one of the best. Shine, who had seen Linda weeks before while moving Merrit's belongings, also introduces himself and tries to warn her about Patmore. She brushes Shine off, but later, when she learns there is no costume competition and Patmore aggressively offers her twenty-five dollars for sex, it is Shine who comes to her rescue while Patmore beats a hasty retreat.

Shine and Linda fall in love, but Shine, afraid of being vulnerable, cannot tell her he loves her. They argue and stop seeing each other when Shine objects to Linda's work as a maid in the Merrit household. Two weeks later Shine learns that Linda was admitted to the hospital after being beaten by a man. He assumes the attacker was Merrit and goes to confront him. He finds Merrit sitting alone in the bombed-out ruin of his home. Shine then visits Linda in the hospital to tell her of the bombing and vows to avenge her attack. She tells him that the revenge he seeks is merely the facade of the street tough he hides behind and uses to fend her off. When he realizes that she is right, he agrees to take no retaliation. He can finally tell her he loves her.

He leaves her and goes to Patmore's. There he overhears Patmore boasting about how he has finally gotten revenge on a dickty who thought to outsmart him, how he so thoroughly outsmarted the dickty and everyone else that his act is being blamed on race hatred, and how the evidence is clear for all to see over on Court Street. Shine begins to realize that it was Patmore who sent the notes threatening Merrit, Patmore who went to plant the explosives, and Patmore who, finding Linda alone, attacked her. When Shine confronts him, Patmore pulls a gun, and a vicious battle ensues in which Patmore is severely beaten. Shine is about to deal Patmore a death blow when someone shatters the huge mirror behind the bar. The sound of the falling glass breaks through Shine's rage, and he lets Patmore fall to the floor.

Paul. *Christ in Concrete.* Pietro di Donato. 1937.

Paul is the twelve-year-old son of devout Italian immigrants in Pietro di Donato's semi-autobiographical novel. Eldest of eight children, Paul lives in a New York tenement during the late 1920s. His father, Geremio, a master bricklayer and construction foreman, is killed on Good Friday when the supports of a building collapse and bury him under the rubble. When his pregnant mother, Annunziata, almost commits suicide after her husband's funeral, Paul promises her that he will take on the role of father of the family. He retrieves his father's trowel, goes in search of work as a bricklayer, and is given a chance to learn the job by kindhearted Vincenz Nazone, a friend who manages to convince the bosses to hire the boy.

During the first heartbreaking, difficult week, the sensitive twelve-year-old works alongside his self-appointed godfather. He eagerly awaits payday but is shocked when the bosses give him only five dollars for the week. Paul is mistreated and taken advantage of because he is underage,

but he is nevertheless expected to keep up with the adults on the job. Soon he is suffering from extreme physical fatigue and nervous exhaustion; when he is again given only a few dollars on the next payday, the distraught child goes home and sobs himself to sleep in his mother's arms. Paul awakens in the middle of the night screaming hysterically. A doctor says he has developed a strained heart, and the boy quits working and spends the next few weeks recuperating.

Some time later a man who had known Geremio offers Paul a job that pays normal wages. He learns his trade quickly and, despite a perpetually aching body, is proud of the fact that he is able to support his family. As time passes, he grows stronger and develops an interest in women. Paul, now fifteen years old, begins work on a skyscraper downtown and soon distinguishes himself by winning a contest for the best bricklayer on the job. Now a full-fledged journeyman, he manages to keep his job when the crash of 1929 threatens the building industry.

Paul's life is changed forever, however, when Nazone is accidentally pushed to his death off a scaffolding by one of the skyscraper's overseers. The devastated young man comes to the conclusion that the conditions of the workers are unfair and that the boss is their enemy. He continues to work on the job but becomes taciturn, refuses to go to Mass, and loses his belief in the existence of God. When he crushes his mother's crucifix because she will not listen to his new beliefs, she assaults him and proclaims that he is dead to her. He leaves the tenement flat and walks in the streets for a time. When he returns home to make peace with his mother, he finds that she has forgiven him but has had an attack of some sort and is dying, blessing him with her last breath.

Paul. "Paul's Case." Willa Cather. 1905.

Paul, the story's hero, is a troubled youngster who longs to escape from his dreary world in Pittsburgh, Pennsylvania. A trial to his teachers and a puzzle to his family, Paul eventually takes a dramatic step to rescue himself from what he feels is a humdrum existence.

As the story opens, Paul is being castigated by a circle of teachers. His attitude toward them and to the charges of misbehavior being levied against him is symbolized in the flippant red carnation he wears and the strange smile he continues to sport. When at last he is dismissed, he tears from school toward his haven, Pittsburgh's Carnegie Hall, where he spends evenings working as an usher. Paul loves the atmosphere at the famous music hall and revels in the symphonies he hears there, although he has no particular affinity for music. In the same way, he loves to be around the theater where his friend Charley Edwards works even though he has no aspirations to act. Paul simply feels that it is only in the music hall and the theater that he is actually alive.

The rest of Paul's world pales in comparison to the

exciting world of performance. He lives in a middle-class neighborhood on a street where all the houses are the and all the people aspire to the same middle-class goals. Indeed, Paul's father holds as a model for his son one of the young men in the neighborhood, a clerk who married a brittle school mistress and began an unexciting career in the shipping business.

When news of Paul's misbehavior in school reaches his father, the boy is taken out of school, put to work in an office, and forbidden to frequent the music hall or theater. The punishment moves Paul to live out a dream he has rehearsed many times before. He steals a large amount of money from the office where he works and boards a train to New York.

After buying a lavish new wardrobe, Paul checks into the Waldorf Hotel and makes sure that fresh flowers decorate his room. He spends more than a week dining in style, attending the theater, and going to concerts. Finally, on the eighth day after his arrival, he finds that his wrong-doing is detailed in his hometown newspaper. According to the paper, his father is headed to New York to find him.

Feeling that going back to his tepid life would be worse than a lifetime in prison, Paul eyes the revolver he has brought along with him for a day such as this. But he does not use the gun; instead, he takes a ferry to Newark, then hails a cab and asks the driver to follow the railway tracks. Well into the country, he dismisses the cab and walks until he reaches a hillside where the tracks run some twenty feet below. Sure that he has lived the life he was meant to live, Paul waits for an approaching train and jumps.

Paul, Melissa. *The Chinaberry Tree.* Jessie Redmon Fauset. 1931.

Melissa Paul is the niece of SARAH STRANGE, whom she calls "Aunt Sal"; her mother Judy had left Sal's town years before under mysterious circumstances. Like her mother, Melissa is lively and flirtatious; unlike her, she has a strong feeling for the conventional and plans to avoid the type of men she has seen in her mother's life by marrying a doctor or lawyer instead. Melissa's sense of her own propriety is founded on her birth: Although poor, she is at least legitimate, unlike her cousin LAURENTINE STRANGE. However, by returning to the scene of her mother's mysterious past, Melissa unknowingly confronts and threatens her own sense of identity and importance.

Melissa leaves her home in Philadelphia and arrives at Aunt Sal's house, and instantly she feels "the inherited mantle of her mother's hardness slipping away from her own slender shoulders." The calm domesticity of Sal's household provides for Melissa a homely past that comes to supplant the irregularity of her life with her mother. She soon has a large circle of friends and grows proud of her achievements, especially when compared with the friendless isolation into which Laurentine is forced by her illegitimacy. When Asshur Lane proposes to her, Melissa

does not accept even though she acknowledges she might love him; Asshur is kind and loyal but does not offer Melissa the social possibilities she desires. However, at eighteen, with one proposal already, Melissa is content that everything is going her way. Asshur leaves for the South after making Melissa promise him that she will be "good" in his absence.

Melissa soon makes friends with a new and more elite circle and through them meets Malory Forten, who seems to her everything she desires in a husband. They fall in love but keep their feelings secret so that few people suspect what is happening. This secret is imposed on them by Laurentine, who resents the effect Melissa is having on her life and unwittingly causes a potential tragedy. It soon becomes clear that Melissa is the child of her mother Judy's affair with Malory's father. Without knowing the reason, Melissa begins to dream that her marriage to Malory will never take place. This dream becomes prophetic when Malory learns of their real relationship and heartlessly abandons her.

Melissa suffers a long illness after this, an illness that reveals to her the foolishness of her expectations. Asshur returns to her, and when confronted by his loyalty and strength, she admits Malory's weakness and her own blindness. As the novel ends, Melissa is forced to acknowledge that her sense of superiority was founded on a lie and that she must now establish her identity in her own right.

Payne, Nicholas. *The Bushwhacked Piano.* Thomas McGuane. 1971.

The demonic Nicholas Payne, who is destined to inherit his father's successful Detroit law practice, chooses instead to pursue his own strange and mysterious goals. A set of jumbled but passionately upheld ideals and beliefs guide Payne along a course that sometimes loses its logic—even for him.

Payne's childhood memories begin with the vision of himself destroying the neighbor's piano with a rifle, and continue in a straight line to "lunacy." At the conclusion of a series of disturbing, disconnected flashes of adolescent memory, he recalls the humiliating experience of being put in a straitjacket and hospitalized. He recovers sufficiently to attend school, but his life is always punctuated by periods of insanity. They often cause him to disappear, travel cross-country, and live in secrecy. At twenty-five, Payne is still living with his parents and has no job or any ambition regarding his personal future, although he has some idealistic notions about the global future. Payne sees himself as a romantic villain whose motto is *Non Serviam* and whose coat of arms shows a "snake dragging its heels."

Through adolescence and into his twenties, Payne has one consistent relationship: his liaison with a young woman named ANN FITZGERALD. Although passionate and intense, the romance between them is not always harmonious. Ann periodically drops Payne for a young General Motors executive named George Russell. One evening when Ann is out with George, Payne, who has been drinking to comfort himself, breaks into her parents' house and threatens Mrs. Fitzgerald with a rifle. Because the Fitzgeralds do not want their name in the paper, the police are never called, and Payne simply goes home. The following day Payne argues with his father, who, tired of supporting his idle son, issues an ultimatum: Payne must either leave home or help fix the breakwater in the river in order to prevent the destruction of the family's property. Payne leaves and eventually drives his green Hudson Hornet toward Livingston, Montana, where the Fitzgeralds have taken refuge at their ranch.

In Livingston, Payne meets with his friend CLETUS JAMES CLOVIS, an eccentric whose dream is to build towers to house bats, which eat disease-carrying mosquitoes. Clovis hires Payne as foreman for the "Batworks," and they camp out together while they develop their scheme. As a way of capturing Ann's attention, Payne also gets involved with the local rodeo and practices to become a bronco rider. The Fitzgeralds are present at Payne's first, astonishingly good bronco performance. Ann is so impressed that she defends Payne against her parents when he later appears at their house, where he is even allowed to stay as a guest.

Unfortunately, Payne continues to be hostile toward the Fitzgerald parents. They encourage their homicidal hired man, Wayne Codd, to give Payne what he "ought to have." The incompetent Codd gives Payne a blow to the head, which hospitalizes but does not kill him. After a meeting with Payne's lawyer, the Fitzgeralds release Ann to accompany Payne when he travels south on a mission to collect a truckload of fifteen hundred bats for Clovis's first full-scale Bat Tower.

Soon after they depart, Payne detects Ann's regret. By the time they arrive in Key West, the future location of the Bat Tower, Clovis is in the hospital for a heart condition; sparked by Clovis's plea for Payne's company, Ann does her best to convince Payne, who has been deferring a much-needed hemorrhoid operation, to join him there. The operation is performed by an incompetent doctor, and Payne is in considerable discomfort afterward. While he is recovering from this humiliating experience, Ann becomes thoroughly disenchanted with him and leaves a simple message before her final departure: "This is it."

Payne is released from the hospital for the dedication of the Bat Tower. During his turn at the microphone, he flatly tells the audience that they have been cheated. The bats fly off and disappear as soon as they are let out of their cage, dramatically confirming Payne's statement. In the face of the failure of his scheme, Clovis collapses on the podium and dies. Payne must later go to court in Clovis's stead to defend himself against a charge of fraud.

He is cleared in exchange for participating in a dramatization of the case on a TV show, *Night Court*. When the trial is over, he travels north with no particular goal in mind. Alone on the beach one evening, he concludes that his experiences have completed or "rendered" him, and he feels content, "at one with things."

Peace, Eva. *Sula.* Toni Morrison. 1973.

Abandoned by her husband with three young children to care for, Eva Peace, the grandmother of SULA MAY PEACE, is desperate for a means of survival. During a bitter winter in the hill area outside of Medallion, Ohio, the African-American community where the story takes place, she drops off her three children at a neighbor's house and leaves town. Three years later she returns, missing a leg but with plenty of money. She retrieves her children and sets about making a place for herself in the community.

Eva loves men and always has plenty around her. She manages to make her one leg attractive by wearing hose and a pretty slipper. She spends the majority of her time in her upstairs room receiving her callers and playing checkers. Her daughter Hannah takes care of her as well as the many people Eva welcomes into the house: a drunk named Tar Baby, three small boys, all of whom she names Dewey, and plenty of newlyweds.

Eva's son Plum returns from the war emotionally and psychologically scarred. He is perfectly pleasant but has no ambition. All he wants is peace and comfort. Breaking a habit of years, Eva leaves her room and makes her way to Plum's room in the basement. She holds him tight and rocks him. Then she covers his body with kerosene, lights him on fire, and makes her way back upstairs to the sound of his screams.

Some time later, Hannah asks Eva if she ever loved them, and Eva is furious at the question. Hannah asks why she burned Plum, and Eva tells her that he wanted to crawl back into her womb, and she did not have room for him anymore. When by a freak accident Hannah catches fire, Eva throws herself out of her window in an attempt to reach Hannah and put out the flames. Hannah dies almost instantly, but Eva lives for another thirty-seven years, each day cursing Willy Fields, the orderly in the hospital who saved her life by drawing attention to her bleeding body when the rest of the staff remained preoccupied with the horror of Hannah's charred remains.

Eva is still living in her house when Sula returns after being away for ten years. Within minutes they are fighting over who is going to be the authority of the house. Sula wins by spitefully having Eva moved to an old-age home. Knowing that Eva was a little addled but not senile enough to be put away, the townspeople are furious. When Sula dies, Eva refuses to attend the funeral.

Many years later Eva is visited by Nel Wright, Sula's best friend. Although Eva's mind wanders in many ways, she has gained a startling clarity concerning incidents about which she had previously known nothing, such as Sula's accidental drowning of Chicken Little, a neighborhood boy. Her knowledge and intuition are terrifying to Nel, especially when Eva reveals that Plum is her source of information. Eva outlives her whole family, retaining in her old age the authority and presence she gained as a young woman.

Peace, Sula May. *Sula.* Toni Morrison. 1973.

Sula May Peace is the granddaughter of EVA PEACE, one of the mainstays of the black community living in the hilly area around the small town of Medallion, Ohio, known as the Bottom. Two major events in her childhood form Sula's world view. She overhears her mother Hannah say that while she loves Sula, she does not like her. Then when she is playing with a small boy, Chicken Little, swinging him around like an airplane, she lets go of his hands, and he sails into the water and drowns. These experiences shatter her faith in other people and in herself. She develops a belief that she is the only person in the world who counts. Because of this barrier between herself and others, she is able to feel nothing but curiosity when she sees her mother burn to death.

Sula has one close friend, Nel Wright, who manages to break through this barrier. They meet when they are twelve and become inseparable, sharing all their activities and thoughts. Sula loves to escape from the disorder of her house to the cleanliness of Nel's. They walk through town together and give each other support when they are under the attentive gaze of the men on the streets. On one such occasion Sula is complimented by Ajax, the handsomest of the men. Years later he is the only man of whom she feels possessive, and his rejection shatters her health.

Sula's flightiness is balanced by Nel's practicality, and Nel's timidity by Sula's courage. When Nel is physically harassed by a group of Irish boys, Sula insists on a confrontation. She cuts of the tip of her finger with a knife and asks them what they supposed she could do to them if she could do that to herself. Her exhibition is effective, although Nel is more horrified than pleased. Nel comforts Sula when Chicken Little accidentally drowns. The only other person to break through Sula's barrier is Shadrack, another outcast, who sees her as a kindred soul and friend. In their two chance encounters, he is able to offer her a vision of permanency.

Sula is delighted when Nel marries Jude, a handsome, stable man. Right after, however, Sula disappears for ten years. Her boredom with the rest of the world brings her back to Medallion, where she and Nel rekindle their friendship. But when Sula assumes that she and her best friend still share everything, and sleeps with Nel's husband Jude, she puts a searing rift in their friendship. This, combined with the spiteful act of sending her grandmother to an old-age home, earns her the hatred of the community. She lives alone in her own house and sleeps with all the

men in town once and then rejects them. The whole town joins in their hatred of her, calling her a witch and keeping their children and husbands away from her. In this way her perceived wickedness has the positive effect of bringing the community together. When Sula becomes seriously ill, Nel tends to her, and having reconciled on her deathbed, she dies united in spirit with her friend.

Peck, Eli. "Eli, the Fanatic." Philip Roth. 1959.

Eli Peck, attorney, husband, imminent father, and victim of two nervous breakdowns, has been hired by the residents of posh Woodenton, a well-to-do community of Protestants and Jews, to do something about the new yeshivah, or school, for World War II displaced persons, whose strange inhabitants are making the community uneasy.

Eli goes to visit Leo Tzuref, the so-called headmaster of the yeshivah, to convince him that it's "a matter of zoning." Eli says that the law prohibits boarding schools from being set up in a residential area, but in fact he is motivated by the people's fear that the extremity of Tzuref and his children will upset the delicate balance that has been established between religions in Woodenton. The people are particularly threatened by one old man at the school who walks around town in ancient talmudic garb.

Eli is unable to reason with Tzuref, who counters any legal argument with an equally unshakable "talmudic wisdom." Tzuref doesn't see how teaching the children the Talmud constitutes a boarding school, and Eli, who feels somehow ashamed of his own position, can't bring himself to enforce the law. He decides to try to convince the townspeople to let the school stay as long as the old man exchanges his black talmudic suit for "clothing usually associated with American life in the twentieth century."

Ted, the town spokesman, is skeptical, telling Eli that he is dealing with fanatics. Eli has just as hard a time with Tzuref, who insists that the old man has nothing, literally or symbolically, except his old black suit. After fruitless arguing, and feeling caught between two unrelenting points of view, Eli rushes home and throws two of his own suits into a box, along with shirts, socks, underwear, and a hat. He deposits these on the threshold of Tzuref's house, along with a letter stipulating the town's latest demands.

The next day Eli's phone begins to ring constantly with calls from friends who have sighted the strange man from the yeshivah walking about the town in one of Eli's suits. When Eli himself sees the young rabbi coming down his street, he is consumed by a feeling that he is responsible for this new apparition, that he and the man are somehow one. He hears something at the back door and opens it to find that the old black talmudic suit has been deposited there in Eli's box. Possessed by the strange blackness and weight of the suit, Eli puts it on—the old underwear, pants, jacket, and hat. He feels weak, as if the age and meaning of the fabric were pressing down on him.

Eli works up the courage to go outside and tour the town just as the old man used to do. When his friends notice him, they assume he's having a third breakdown, but Eli manages to get all the way to the hospital, where his wife Miriam is having a baby, without being stopped. Standing before the nursery to look at his son, Eli hears the voices of worried friends and doctors around him but does not respond. They pull him away from the window to sedate him but cannot erase the effect of the old man's suit on Eli's soul.

Pedersen, Dr. Karl. *Wonderland.* Joyce Carol Oates. 1971.

Dr. Karl Pedersen, famous physician and family man, is the maniacal adoptive father of JESSE VOGEL. Literally and figuratively larger than life, Pedersen is a huge man who has made his reputation as a brilliant diagnostic doctor. He locates Jesse (then Jesse Harte) at the Niagara County Home for Boys after reading newspaper stories about the murder of the rest of the Harte family at the hands of Jesse's father. Fascinated by the boy's bizarre background and convinced that he is destined for greatness, Pedersen takes Jesse to the lavish Pedersen home in Lockport, New York.

As Jesse soon discovers, Pedersen demands a great deal of his family. Like his extraordinary new siblings, the musically gifted Friedrich and the mathematically prodigious Hilda, Jesse is required to work very hard at his studies and to report to his father each mealtime on the progress he has made. Eager to meet Dr. Pedersen's expectations, he learns to memorize whole pages of his biology and chemistry books for mealtime recital. Pedersen, confident that Jesse will follow in his footsteps and become a great doctor, begins taking the teenager to visit his famous clinic.

In time, Jesse is introduced to Dr. Pedersen's *Book of Fates*, the family scrapbook that records the remarkable achievements of Dr. Pedersen and his family. In the back of the book, in a section titled "Impersonal Fates," is Pedersen's collection of news clippings marking bizarre coincidences and macabre accidents. The final page holds an article about the massacre of Jesse's birth family.

The doctor encourages his overweight family to consume vast quantities of food. When the grossly obese Hilda must have a new dress for a mathematics competition, Pedersen subjects her to the humiliation of trying on clothes in a department store, then placates her with an ice cream sundae and a huge banana split. Later, when she breaks down at the competition, she hysterically insists that her father is trying to consume her and the rest of the family.

The consequences of Pedersen's powerful hold on each member of the family become more and more apparent. Shortly after Hilda's breakdown, Mrs. Pedersen reveals her drinking problem when she passes out, naked and smelling of whiskey, in the bathroom. Friedrich is pale and withdrawn, and Jesse begins to wonder if all of the Pedersens are actually freaks. Dr. Pedersen, insisting that "perfection is necessary," continues to monitor his children's and wife's activities closely.

Finally, shortly before Jesse is to begin studies at the University of Michigan, Mrs. Pedersen resolves that she will leave her husband. Helpless and nearly hysterical, she enlists Jesse's help, and he checks her into a hotel. Together they sit in the hotel eating huge amounts of food, while Mrs. Pedersen tells Jesse of the doctor's cruelties and his secret perversions. Each is terrified that the doctor will find them, and indeed, when Jesse goes out to get more Chinese food, he discovers when he returns that the doctor has found his wife and taken her back to Lockport, leaving behind a note disowning Jesse.

Pedlar, Dorinda Oakley. *Barren Ground.* Ellen Glasgow. 1925.

Dorinda Oakley grows up on an impoverished farm in Pedlar's Mill, Virginia. Over the years she changes from a romantic girl looking for love into a self-sufficient farmer who gains her greatest satisfaction from making her native soil profitable at last.

As a teenager, to help her debt-ridden parents, Dorinda works in the area's general store, owned by Nathan Pedlar, a plain, kind man who must endure the community's scorn for his failed experiments in progressive agriculture. Even as an immature girl, Dorinda senses Nathan's integrity, but she soon falls in love with Jason Greylock, a handsome young doctor with a cosmopolitan air. The two become engaged. Shortly before the wedding, however, Dorinda seeks shelter during a storm at Greylock's ancestral farm, Five Oaks. There, Jason's alcoholic father heartlessly informs her that Jason has decided to marry instead a wealthier woman from town. Despairing and enraged, Dorinda confronts Jason with a gun. Before he can explain the circumstances of his decision, she fires at him, but the bullet misses its mark.

Because she is pregnant, Dorinda decides she must leave on the first train the next day, regardless of its destination. She says nothing to her family and takes only a few belongings. Nathan happens to see her at the train station and provides her with a boxed lunch for what he believes is only a short trip.

New York City disappoints Dorinda with its ugliness. She lives meagerly and has trouble finding work. One day, racked with loneliness and desperation about how she will survive, she wanders into the path of a car, and the trauma causes a miscarriage. A physician takes pity on her, however, and offers her work in his office and a room in his home.

Dr. Faraday and his family become very attached to Dorinda, and Faraday's assistant, Dr. Burch, soon falls in love with her and asks her to marry him. Although she enjoys the concerts to which Burch treats her, Dorinda claims that she is through with romance. She resolves instead to learn all she can about dairy farming so that she can return to Virginia and rejuvenate her family land with the new methods.

While deliberating about accepting a farm loan from Faraday, Dorinda receives word that her father is gravely ill. She returns to Pedlar's Mill and after his death begins the process of reworking the family farm. With the loan money, she buys new equipment and animals, and relieves her inept brothers of their duties. Her mother Eudora remains on the farm, as do several of the black laborers. They all settle into a routine of hard work. Dorinda seldom leaves the farm, and Nathan, now a widower, becomes her great friend and adviser.

Dorinda's life is hardly interrupted by her mother's death. Over the years she pays off all debts and makes a success of the farm. While this pleases her, she sometimes worries that she will grow old and lonely. Still, as much as she longs for intimacy, she seems determined to show everyone that she can live without a man. Nathan periodically broaches the topic of marriage, and she resists until he lures her with the idea that as man and wife they could pool their resources to buy Five Oaks, the grandest farm in Pedlar's Mill. Dorinda agrees on the condition that their relationship remain platonic. After the marriage they buy the property from Jason, who has lost his practice and his wealth from bad investments and has plunged into alcoholism.

Several years later Nathan dies rescuing passengers after a train accident. Dorinda, who previously viewed her marriage to Nathan as one for convenience and profit, is surprised by her sense of loss, but she continues to improve the farm with Nathan's son John at her side. When it becomes known that Jason is penniless and dying, Dorinda allows the townspeople to pressure her into taking care of him. Many years have passed since he broke her heart, and although she feels little sympathy for him, she hates the thought of someone she knows dying in the poorhouse. She gives him a spare room on her family farm. As he fades away, Dorinda takes pride in her achievements and looks forward to an old age of peace and plenty.

Pedlar, Nathan. *Barren Ground.* Ellen Glasgow. 1926.

Nathan Pedlar's life is centered around Pedlar's Mill, a small community of farmers in the South. One of the sturdy men and women who work to reclaim the tired land with new farming methods, Nathan must contend with scoffing neighbors as well as with the harsh demands of nature.

Nathan and his wife Rose Emily are very happy for several years, and Rose Emily teaches Nathan to infuse his natural kindness with consideration. Rose Emily believes in Nathan's abilities and his ideas about improving the land, and she helps him on the farm and in his general store until she falls ill. Rose Emily is sick for a long time,

but she plans to get well up until the day she dies. Eventually DORINDA OAKLEY (PEDLAR), a strong-willed young woman who worked in the general store before leaving to spend two years in New York, returns to Pedlar's Mill and convinces Nathan to hire a woman to take over the tasks that his oldest daughter had assumed.

Upon Dorinda's return, Nathan finds that she shares his enthusiasm for new farming ideas and that she has obtained a large loan in New York to start a dairy farm. Nathan advises Dorinda frequently, giving her concrete ideas for improvements, and becomes accustomed to visiting her and her family often. He is kind to her family, helping out at her father's funeral and going with Dorinda's mother when she is called to testify at her son's trial for murder.

Nathan falls in love with Dorinda and asks her to marry him. She refuses at first, but he perseveres; he respects her strength and intelligence, and is a little embarrassed to ask so much of her as to love him. Nathan is willing to allow Dorinda as much freedom and independence as she wants, and eventually she agrees to the match. They have a quiet wedding, and then Nathan and his children move into Dorinda's home, Old Farm. On the night of the wedding Dorinda ends up working until midnight, and Nathan falls asleep waiting for her. But they soon settle down and are very happy together.

Nathan hires a manager for the store and goes to work on the farm. The family prospers, and they are able to purchase the adjoining farm when it comes up for sale. Nathan takes over the management of Old Farm while Dorinda works at reclaiming Five Oaks, the next adjoining farm.

Things go very well for a while, until Nathan must travel to the city in order to treat an exceedingly painful toothache. On his return trip on the train, there is an accident and people are trapped inside the burning railway cars. Nathan rushes to help pull people from the wreckage and is killed in the process. Survivors from the accident come to Nathan's funeral and take up a collection for a statue in his honor. He is revered as a hero, and people show him a respect in death that they never showed him in life. Dorinda is comforted by the thought of how happy Nathan would be if he could hear the wonderful things people say about him.

Pell, Adam. *Wind from an Enemy Sky.* D'Arcy McNickle. 1978.

Despite a long-standing interest in "making a hobby of Indians," Adam Pell—engineer, philanthropist, and museum curator—is unwittingly implicated in the thoughtless destruction of the native culture of the Little Elk Indians. Pell is the chief engineer behind a dam designed to irrigate the region of the Little Elk reservation. Unfortunately, the project will benefit the white homesteaders far more than it will the Indian inhabitants of the reservation. Intimately familiar with the local aridity and equipped with strategies for handling it, the tribes has chosen to take advantage of whatever minimal rainfall exists by farming on natural drainage basins, hill bottoms, sites the dam's waters will never reach. Yet it is not so much this but the fact that the dam has "killed the water," once free-running, that torments the Little Elk people.

Venting anger and frustration over the dam's construction, a young tribesman named Pock Face takes the gun of the tribal chief, BULL, and fires at a man surveying the dam. The slain man, Jimmie Cooke, turns out to be Pell's nephew. Thus, Pell and the slain man's parents arrive at the Little Elk Indian Agency. Pell acts as a mediator, avoiding direct accusation. He is worried that Jimmie's death will be used as an excuse to satisfy local prejudice and thus lead to the indictment of an innocent Indian.

Such concern for the Indians is consistent with Pell's past. Years ago, in New York, he befriended a Peruvian named Carlos Mendoza. Renouncing the European aspect of his Mestizo background, Mendoza led an Indian self-determination movement with much success. Pell assisted in the cause by constructing a hydroelectric plant in Peru. Having collected Indian artifacts since he was a child, he discovered in Peru that "the people who created those wonders were still with us." Over the years Pell's interest in accruing these wonders intensified, and as a museum curator he now has access to countless numbers of them. His most prized possession, however, is a small gold Incan statue of a virgin.

With newfound urgency, in part a response to such countervailing forces as the construction of the dam, the Little Elk people have requested the return of their medicine bundle, a sacred object lost in museum storage that is believed to hold the power to keep the tribal culture intact. With his museum contacts, Pell believes he can be of assistance. Moreover, he sees the recovery of the object as an opportunity to make amends for his role in constructing the dam, which he now agrees with the Indians is a disruption of the universe.

Pell does locate the medicine bundle but finds that years of neglect in museum storage have left it decayed beyond repair. Determined to make up for his implication in the demise of the Little Elk culture, he resolves to offer the Little Elk the coveted Incan statue of the virgin instead. Having heard they are to receive "a gift" and logically assuming it is the recovered medicine bundle, Bull and his men arrive at the agency with eager anticipation. But Pell ignores the warning of Toby Rafferty, superintendent of the Little Elk Indian Agency, that knowledge of the status of the medicine bundle will no doubt destroy the tribe and that "a lost world" cannot be restored "by a simple substitution of symbols." Pell informs Bull and his men of the bundle's condition and offers them the statue. Shocked and agonized, Bull takes out his gun and shoots both Pell and Rafferty. In return, the Indian interpreter

shoots Bull. Off in the distance, the tribal sage, Two-Sleeps, approaches on horseback, singing the tribal death song.

Pemberton. "The Pupil." Henry James. 1892.

Pemberton, a young Oxford-educated American, is a willing prisoner in the household of the eccentric Moreen family. When he is hired for the brilliant youngest child, MORGAN (MOREEN), Pemberton's life becomes focused on the family and on Morgan's precocious change. Even when his illusions about the "delightful" Moreen family have perished, he continues to believe in Morgan's integrity and to need his companionship.

Pemberton arrives at the Moreens' elegant villa in Nice with a recommendation from an Oxford acquaintance. Having used up his small inheritance by traveling through Europe, he resigns himself to a task he regards as a risky experiment: offering himself as a private tutor. To Pemberton, who has retained his innocence in spite of his travels, his new employers seem exotic and aristocratic. He is even somewhat intimidated by Morgan, his eleven-year-old pupil, and fears that the child may be more intelligent than he. Pemberton avoids bringing up the question of his remuneration; one simply doesn't speak of money with such people, he thinks. When the subject is finally broached, the Moreens are extravagantly agreeable, even suggesting that Pemberton's modest price is "positively meager."

From his intimate vantage point, Pemberton observes the Moreens and speculates on their peculiar way of life. Although they are Americans, they appear to be the height of European cosmopolitanism. The Moreens are familiar with all of Europe's most fashionable cities and move freely among them, socializing with the finest people. Pemberton and Morgan are dragged along at the rear of the party, never quite part of it.

The relationship between Morgan and his family is obviously strained, for reasons Pemberton is at first unable to discern. The older Moreens dote on Morgan, praising his genius and beauty and worrying about his heart condition. At the same time they seem to want Pemberton to take this austere and "supernaturally clever" child off their hands. Pemberton is proud to do them this service; the subtle, suggestive, and highly intellectual banter between student and teacher sustains a friendship grounded in deep mutual respect.

Pemberton's first insights into the tension between Morgan and his family occur as a result of his own difficulties with the Moreen parents. In spite of their promises regarding salary, the Moreens give Pemberton only tiny sums, and only very infrequently. Pemberton even agrees to stay free of charge, so strong is his connection to Morgan, but when Mrs. Moreen tries to borrow money from him, Pemberton finally finds a new position. By this time Morgan has openly criticized his parents' "lying and cheating"; they had similarly mistreated a nurse whom Morgan loved. Out of affection for his teacher, Morgan encourages Pemberton to leave and accepts his departure bravely.

After leaving the Moreens in Venice, Pemberton returns to Oxford, where he works tutoring a student for his college entrance exams. He sends Mrs. Moreen the amount of money she had earlier asked to borrow. Soon after, Pemberton receives a desperate letter from Mrs. Moreen, explaining that Morgan is very ill. Pemberton rushes to Paris where the family is staying in a shabby hotel and finds that he has been deceived. Although Morgan is frail, he is in no real danger. Pemberton is nevertheless persuaded to remain, and tutor and pupil return to their old ways, wandering through Paris and chattering philosophically.

One afternoon after a particularly nice walk, Pemberton and Morgan return to the Moreens' apartment to find them in a financial crisis. Mrs. Moreen hastily explains that "the change" has come; they must part with Morgan and expect Pemberton to take the boy away and care for him. During the few seconds when this question hangs in the balance, Pemberton is terrified by the look of hope and gratitude on Morgan's face. But the boy, turning pale, suddenly clutches his side, and Pemberton watches with horror as he collapses and dies. While Pemberton holds the boy's body, mumbling expressions of regret, Morgan's parents argue over whether he had wished to remain with his family or not.

Penderton, Captain Weldon. *Reflections in a Golden Eye.* Carson McCullers. 1941.

Captain Weldon Penderton is a haunted army officer who becomes obsessed with an enlisted man at a southern military post between the two world wars. The thirty-five-year-old Penderton enjoys a brilliant career in the military and is something of a savant with statistics and factual information, but he knows himself to be a coward at heart and is incapable of original thought. He is unhappily married to the handsome but dimwitted LEONORA PENDERTON and has the habit of becoming enamored with her lovers. The Pendertons' social life revolves around Major Morris Langdon and his invalid wife Alison. The Captain is aware that Langdon is his wife's lover but does not want the affair to end because he himself has become emotionally attached to the Major.

As the novel opens, Captain Penderton instructs PRIVATE L. G. "ELLGEE" WILLIAMS to clear the woods around his quarters on the outskirts of the fort. Already carrying a grudge against Williams because he takes care of Leonora's horse and once spilled coffee on an expensive suit, Penderton becomes infuriated when the soldier misunderstands his instructions and mangles the branches of a favorite oak tree. The Captain then retires to his quarters and, unaware that Williams is watching through the window, proceeds to have an argument with Leonora, who strips her clothes off and taunts her husband with her nakedness. The following afternoon Penderton goes to the stables where Williams is permanently assigned and orders the soldier to saddle Leonora's horse, Firebird, even though he has never before ridden it without his wife's permission and presence. Penderton cannot control the animal; after a wild ride through the forest, he beats the horse violently. Exhausted from his efforts, Penderton lies down in the grass and loses consciousness. He awakens to find Private Williams, completely naked, watching him. Williams, without saying a word, steps over the officer's body, takes the horse's reins, and leads the animal off into the woods. From that moment on, Penderton becomes obsessed with the soldier.

Meanwhile, the Captain is unaware that Williams has become obsessed with Leonora and has developed the habit of entering her bedroom at night to watch her as she sleeps. One evening Alison Langdon sees a figure enter the Penderton house; thinking it is her husband, she investigates, only to come face-to-face with Williams. She tries to tell Penderton that there is a man in his wife's bedroom, but he assumes it is Major Langdon and therefore pretends not to believe her in order to avoid a confrontation.

Penderton's preoccupation with Williams grows as the days pass. He develops the habit of walking each afternoon in front of the barracks where the private is quartered and is excited by the fact that the soldier does not change his routine in order to avoid him. Then late one night while suffering from insomnia, Penderton sees a shadowy figure enter his house and climb the stairs to his wife's bedroom. The officer retrieves his pistol from a drawer and follows, shooting the enlisted man twice through the chest as he squats by the sleeping Leonora's bed.

Penderton, Leonora. *Reflections in a Golden Eye.* Carson McCullers. 1941.

Leonora Penderton, a beautiful but feebleminded woman, becomes the object of a soldier's obsession at an army base in the South between the two world wars. She is married to CAPTAIN WELDON PENDERTON, an officer who has a habit of becoming enamored with his wife's lovers. For the past two years Leonora has been having an affair with Major Morris Langdon, who is unhappily married to Alison, an invalid. The daughter of a southern woman and a brigadier general from the West Coast, Leonora grew up in the army. She is a skilled horsewoman and has the reputation of being an excellent hostess at the base. She is fond of drink, cheats at cards, and manages to hide from most people the fact that she has difficulty with writing and arithmetic.

One day Leonora witnesses an argument between her husband and PRIVATE L. G. "ELLGEE" WILLIAMS. Later, in the house, the irritated Captain criticizes his wife for going barefoot, calling her a slattern. In response, Leonora proceeds to strip her clothes and taunt him with her nakedness, unaware that the soldier is watching the scene through the windows.

From that day on, Williams becomes obsessed with the Captain's wife and begins to sneak into her bedroom at night to watch her as she sleeps. Leonora is not aware of the soldier's strange behavior, nor does she realize that her husband, for reasons of his own, has become fascinated by the enlisted man. Alison Langdon sees a man leave the Penderton house early one morning and, suspicious, asks Leonora about the incident. Since Leonora feels nothing but disrespect for the wife of her lover, she pays no attention to the woman's warning.

Late one evening some months later, Captain Penderton observes a shadowy figure entering his house. He gets his pistol and follows the man into his wife's bedroom; when he discovers Williams squatting by Leonora's bed, Penderton fatally shoots the soldier. Leonora awakens at the sound of the gunshot and stares without comprehension at the bloody scene.

Penmark, Rhoda. *The Bad Seed.* William March. 1955.

Rhoda Penmark, a scrupulously neat child with polite manners, applies herself diligently to such self-imposed projects as reading books, playing piano, and crocheting. A competitive child, Rhoda is determined to be successful at everything she does. She is adored by older women, who consider her quaint and old-fashioned, but she is intensely disliked by children her own age. Her parents have always considered her an enigma and have found some of her characteristics troubling. Rhoda seems to be incapable of feeling loneliness or affection for others, although she pretends to feel such things. She also possesses an inordinate desire to acquire material belongings.

The novel begins when Rhoda is eight years old and finishing her first school term in a new town. All year she has worked hard to win the school medal for best improvement in penmanship, but by a close vote the medal is given to a small, shy boy named Claude Daigle. Rhoda felt that the medal belonged to her, and the whole morning of the school picnic she is seen demanding that Claude give it to her. Around lunchtime the teachers find Claude dead in the water, with bruises on his face and hands. The medal is gone.

Rhoda's mother, Christine Penmark, is disturbed that Rhoda seems unaffected by the boy's drowning. In the past, when Rhoda's puppy fell out a window and an elderly woman broke her neck tumbling down the stairs, Rhoda was similarly unmoved. When Rhoda is not offered a place in the school the following term, Christine recalls Rhoda's expulsion from her former school on the grounds of thievery and her unnatural lack of emotion. When questioned, Rhoda denies that she knows where the penman-

ship medal might be, but a few days later Christine finds it in Rhoda's belongings. Rhoda finally confesses to her mother that she killed Claude by hitting him on the head with the metal tips of her shoe, but she insists it was his fault because he said he would tell that she had taken the medal.

Rhoda has an unfriendly relationship with the janitor of her apartment building, Leroy Jessup, who recognizes her mean nature but feels a kind of kinship with her. He taunts her persistently about Claude's death, not realizing that she killed him, and threatens that unless she is nice to him, he will tell the police. Rhoda responds by burning him to death in his bed in the basement.

Christine, terrified of the pattern that is developing, gradually remembers her own childhood before she was adopted and realizes that she is the only remaining child of a famous murderess. She resolves to kill herself and Rhoda. Christine does die, but Rhoda is revived from the sleeping pills Christine gave her. Rhoda understood her mother's intentions, and as the novel ends she is taking better precautions with her adoring father.

Pentland, Olivia. *Early Autumn.* Louis Bromfield. 1926.

Unhappily married into a prestigious New England family, Olivia Pentland, now almost forty years old, finds herself at a moment of familial and personal crisis. She meets a handsome man who offers her an escape from her barren, demanding life with her husband Anson and his family, who rely heavily on her, but is thwarted in her desire for freedom by her commitments to her daughter Sybil and her father-in-law John.

Orphaned at eighteen, Olivia married Anson Pentland for the security he offered her. She was unaware, however, of how difficult life at Pentlands, the family estate, would be. Anson, who married her for her money and for an heir, is a weak man interested only in writing a book about his family's history. Invasive Aunt Cassie visits daily, and Olivia's insane mother-in-law requires constant care. Olivia's only consolations are John, a kind man who hides his suffering in drink, and Sybil, recently returned from school in Paris. Olivia is also refreshed by the return of Cassie's niece Sabine Callendar, whose desire to speak unpleasant truths about the family offends their stiff propriety.

Olivia has always succeeded as an outsider at Pentlands by being self-effacing and by smoothing out family troubles. But the events of this summer cause her to rebel against the family's morality. As she learns more about the Pentland family, she understands that their pettiness and false superiority arise from fear and self-deception. When Anson questions Sybil's friendship with the Irish politician Michael O'Hara, Olivia shows that she doesn't share his fear of all that is unfamiliar. She is even somewhat relieved when her chronically ill son dies, for death is a reality that even the Pentlands can't deny.

As the summer progresses, Olivia becomes liberated by a sense of peace and romance. She hopes that her daughter will marry a young man she has been dating and seems to love. Olivia spends mornings riding with O'Hara, who makes her feel desired and carefree. But despite her growing affection for O'Hara, Olivia refuses to jeopardize Sybil's chance at a happy marriage by her own behavior. She promises O'Hara that she will leave Anson as soon as Sybil is married.

At the same time Olivia begins to feel more trapped at Pentlands than ever before. Having discovered letters that reveal the current Pentlands are of bastard stock, she fears the power of their world to make the owners of Pentlands outsiders like herself. She realizes that the demise of John, who was broken by the death of her son, the family's only male heir, will increase her own burden of managing family affairs, especially when he reveals his intention to leave the inheritance to her and not to Anson. Because she fears that her inability to act on her desires may mean she really has become a Pentland, she resolves to make plans with O'Hara as soon as Sybil has eloped.

On the night of Sybil's elopement, Olivia asks Anson for a divorce, calmly explaining that their marriage has been an unhappy failure. A shocked Anson refuses to comply, and although Olivia threatens to simply run off with her lover, she feels overwhelmed at the futility of her efforts to be free.

At their final meeting, O'Hara tells Olivia that he is willing to sacrifice his political career for her. Olivia, realizing that his career is his first love and influenced by John Pentland's incredibly strong sense of self-sacrificing morality, insists that O'Hara pursue his career. Just then she sees several men carrying John Pentland, who has killed himself in a riding "accident." Olivia now feels it is impossible to run away with O'Hara: If John killed himself in order to force her to stay, he succeeded.

As she thinks of the Pentland descendants among her daughter's offspring, Olivia admits that John was right: She is one of them now. When O'Hara leaves the region for good, Olivia realizes that she will never escape. Her boring but peaceful life at Pentlands will continue if she can only keep on pretending that she feels at home.

Percepied, Leo. *The Subterraneans.* Jack Kerouac. 1958.

Leo Percepied, the main character and first-person narrator of this beat novel, is a writer living in San Francisco in 1953. The success of his first novel has made Leo a minor literary celebrity, but he is still not completely confident of his literary talents. In the course of the novel he struggles to come to terms with his creative demons while becoming involved in a brief but intense love affair.

In the first chapter of the book, Leo meets the subterraneans, an amorphous group of young artists and intellectuals who spend their time drifting to and from bars and parties, smoking marijuana, and fooling around with one another. Leo is immediately struck by Mardou Fox, a beautiful young black woman who is still getting over a rocky relationship with one of the subterraneans. He invites the entire group to smoke marijuana at the apartment of Larry O'Hara, a friend he is staying with, in an attempt to meet Mardou, but he fails to arouse her interest and she slips away as the party breaks up toward dawn.

A couple of days later Larry admits to Leo that he ran into Mardou on the street and they returned to his apartment where they cuddled and read poetry. Larry does not want a real relationship with Mardou because she is black, so he agrees to make arrangements for Leo to be present at their next meeting. This time Leo is more fortunate, and at the end of a long evening of bar-hopping he goes home with Mardou and has sex with her.

By the following morning, however, Leo has grown nervous about the implications of their night together, and he spends several days at home avoiding Mardou and trying to write. During this time he is beset by racist thoughts and by doubts about Mardou's mental stability. But the next time he runs into her at a friend's place, he is not unhappy to see her; they spend the entire day curled up in a chair as Mardou tells Leo her past. Leo, impressed by Mardou's ability to open up to him, finds himself falling in love.

Nevertheless, it soon becomes clear that Leo has difficulty with carrying on the relationship while devoting time to his writing. After one particularly drunken evening in San Francisco, Leo abandons Mardou in a cab, even though he knows she has no money to get home, so that he can go to another party. By the time he realizes how foolishly he has acted, he has lost Mardou to another man. Leo agonizes over the split for some time before sitting down to write the story of their brief affair.

Perlin, Harry. *The Old Bunch.* Meyer Levin. 1937.

This account of a group of Jewish youths coming to maturity in Chicago in the 1920s and '30s begins and ends with descriptions of Harry Perlin. The sympathetic treatment accorded this unassuming member of "the old bunch" may constitute a tribute to the one member of the group who has the ability to succeed in life but is never given the opportunity to do so.

After graduating from high school, Harry goes to college. He cannot enjoy his college experience, however, because he works so many hours to support himself, and he is actually relieved when forced to drop out due to the death of his father, a fur worker. He experiences great difficulty finding a job because of the influx of war veterans on the job market but is finally hired as a mechanic at Bienstock's garage. He is quickly promoted to manager and is able to support his family and help his younger brother Vic through college.

Perpetually on the lookout for new inventions that will make his fortune, Harry eventually gets the idea of creating an automatic garage door opener. He tries for several years to sell his idea to manufacturers, one of whom suggests that he start making door openers himself. In order to do this, Harry borrows money from the father of an old friend, Lil Klein, and sets up a small shop, hiring door-to-door salesmen to help him sell his product. Business is going well when suddenly his salesmen begin to quit, and Harry realizes that his sales manager has stolen his idea. Harry goes to a lawyer with the intention of suing but discovers that the patent he attained is inadequate and that a lawsuit is therefore not possible.

Harry is forced to dip into his mother's savings to make payments to Lil's father, and he must pick up odd mechanical jobs to make ends meet. At this point the Great Depression hits, and before long the bank forecloses on his family house and he is forced to sell his car. He eventually gets another full-time job as a garage mechanic; this not only renews his optimism but also enables him to marry Ruth Lipschultz, a schoolteacher he had met after being mistakenly arrested while observing a communist demonstration. But the good luck does not hold: Harry soon loses his job and, unable to find steady work, is reduced to living off Ruth's income.

Harry has other ideas for inventions—specifically, a dashboard emergency brake for automobiles and a car radio. At the end of the novel, as he lies awake at night worrying, he reflects on the fact that although his friends had once laughed at his car radio idea, car radios have been successfully introduced on the market. As the novel closes, Harry muses on his failure as an inventor. If he had only had the capital, he thinks, he would have shown them.

Perseus. *Chimera.* John Barth. 1972.

Perseus, a Greek king who has been deified for youthful heroism, finds himself in heaven with his longtime lover Calyxa, a temple goddess. Now at middle age, Perseus gazes at a marble mural that depicts the deeds which have made him famous. Between lovemaking, Perseus and Calyxa recount the major events of the king's past, focusing on aspects of daily life that are not found in traditional Greek mythology.

As the mural suggests, Perseus has led a dramatic life. Born to Zeus and Princess Danae of Argos, the infant Perseus and his mother were banished from their homeland when the king realized that his grandson was destined to kill him. The mother and son were lost at sea in a chest and would have drowned had Zeus not guided them near the island of Seriphos. Dictys, a fisherman who was also the brother of King Polydectes, noticed the strange vessel and rescued them. Years later, desiring to marry Danae, Polydectes sought to get rid of Perseus by tricking him into promising the head of Medusa as a wedding gift.

Polydectes assumed that Perseus would perish by Medusa, who with her snakes for hair and horrible face turned everyone who saw her into stone. But armed by the gods and looking at Medusa only in the reflection of a shield, Perseus managed to decapitate Medusa. On his way back to Seriphos, Perseus then used the lethal head to rescue Andromeda, his future wife, from a sea monster at Joppa. Finally he displayed the head at Polydectes's wedding party, turning everyone except his mother into stone.

These accomplishments have brought Perseus fame on earth and a constellation in the sky, but not contentment. In heaven with Calyxa, separated from Andromeda and out of communication with his children, he finds himself feeling a general malaise, heading for a mid-life crisis. He has tried to rejuvenate himself by touring the sites of his former triumphs, but this effort only made him look more ridiculous in his family's eyes.

Perseus finally finds in Calyxa someone interested in discussing his glorious past, but she isn't content just to listen. She constantly has her lover diverge from a reenactment of heroic feats to less stately topics. They bicker, for example, about the sexual habits of many of the gods they have known. Somehow their ramblings bring Perseus the peace of mind he has been seeking. He realizes in the end that a hardy reminiscence—which is always a creative act, as details are included and omitted in different versions—is all he really has left. As his storytelling, spoken to a captive listener with sporadic responses, demonstrates, the telling of a tale is often more invigorating than experiencing an event firsthand.

Peter. "You Were Perfectly Fine." Dorothy Parker. 1973.

At the opening of this bitterly ironic story, Peter wakes up with a fierce hangover. To his dismay he begins to learn from his girlfriend how he behaved the night before. He learns more than he wants to know.

Although she repeatedly assures him that he was "perfectly fine," Peter's girlfriend hints at some of the social damage he did during his night of drinking. For instance, after making an inappropriate pass at a well-heeled woman, he proceeded to pour clam juice down her back. But the girlfriend insists that the woman was only a "tiny bit annoyed." In fact, she tells him, most of the party actually enjoyed his antics, especially when he began singing. She mentions that some of the guests were slightly worried when he refused to stop singing an offensive ditty about a fusilier but that by and large he was quite entertaining. Peter's girlfriend goes on to tell him that he took a dislike to an older gentleman's tie, but his friends were able to take him outside before a fight could break out. When she reminds him that he then took a nasty fall on the sidewalk, Peter suddenly understands why his derriere aches.

Peter presses his girlfriend further, and she reminds him of the romantic moonlight taxi ride they took around the park. She says that he began philosophizing and that he said "such lovely, lovely things" about how he feels about her. She goes on to say that the taxi ride was the most important thing that ever happened to either of them and that she is sure they will be very happy together.

Shaken, Peter asks for a drink. As his girlfriend springs merrily from the room, he drops his head in his hands, miserable.

Peters, Lymie. *The Folded Leaf*. William Maxwell. 1945.

Lymie Peters is a sad, lonely young boy who lives in a dreary apartment in Chicago with his father. He deeply misses his mother, who died five years before, when Lymie was ten. The novel tells the story of the intimate friendship that develops between Lymie and Spud Latham, a tough new boy in school.

Before Lymie becomes friends with Spud, he is all but ignored by his classmates, for Lymie is timid in the classroom and inept on the playing field. The tensions he feels at school are compounded by an unhappy home life. Mr. Peters, Lymie's father, is a heavy drinker who does not try to understand his introverted son. A good student, Lymie often studies at the cheap restaurant near his apartment where he eats his meals, sometimes with his father but more often alone.

Lymie's friendship with Spud begins when both boys pledge a high school fraternity. Lymie is invited to pledge because of the status that his high grades will confer on the fraternity. Spud is less selfish and affected than the other boys, and Lymie admires him greatly. The two soon become inseparable.

After high school, Lymie and Spud go to the same college and room together in a boardinghouse. They make friends with Hope Davison, a smart, practical girl, and Sally Forbes, who is amusing and very attractive. Since Lymie likes to spend most of his time with Spud—they even sleep in the same bed—it is not surprising that their relationship changes when Spud and Sally fall in love.

Lymie is apparently too thin and insecure to have a girlfriend of his own, and although secretly jealous, he spends much time with Spud and Sally, and takes pride in their happiness and popularity. In befriending Sally, Lymie feels that he is placing Spud's interests above his own; however, Spud reacts negatively, and the two become estranged. A devastated Lymie tries to kill himself. The suicide attempt arouses the concern of Lymie's estranged father, who, disturbed by his son's emotional state, pays him a visit in the hospital. While he is recovering, Lymie, with a "trace of sadness in his smile," finally accepts the fact that Spud and Sally belong together and that he must make a life for himself apart from theirs.

After this resolution, Lymie gains a new and stronger sense of purpose. The novel closes with him wandering outside into the sun-lit woods and vowing that the course of events will "never rise and defeat him again."

Peters, Margot. *Laughter in the Dark*. Vladimir Nabokov. 1938.

Margot Peters is a beautiful, unscrupulous young woman who comes from a working-class family in Germany that cares very little about her. At sixteen she begins posing for artists as a model and going to dance halls. Margot's plan is to become a model and then an actress, but in the meantime she survives as a kept woman.

While working as an usherette in a Berlin cinema, Margot meets an older man named Albinus. He walks her home from work and tries to kiss her when they reach her home. She eludes him, pretending to be offended, but agrees to meet him again the next day. After toying with him, Margot allows Albinus to seduce her. He sets her up in an apartment, which she enjoys furnishing. She won't let him see the place until she is finished with it, then she writes him a letter with her address.

Albinus's relationship with Margot is discovered by his wife. When she reads Margot's letter to him, Albinus moves in with his mistress. Margot likes Albinus, but she is more interested in his money and what he can provide for her. Afraid that Albinus will tire of her and then leave, Margot wants him to marry her so that it will be harder for him to get rid of her. Eventually they move into his old apartment.

Things become complicated for Margot when a new man comes to dinner at their home. He is Axel Rex, Margot's first lover, whom she hasn't seen since he left her. Axel tries to convince her to get involved with him again, but she is unwilling to give up the comfort of her life with Albinus. Eventually she agrees to meet him secretly, and they resume their affair behind Albinus's back. Axel convinces Albinus that he is gay, and he begins to spend a great deal of time with Margot and Albinus.

Margot gets Albinus to obtain a part for her in a film, which turns out to be terrible. Seeing that she is upset, Albinus proposes a trip to cheer her up. Axel suggests that he drive for them rather than Albinus hiring a chauffeur. Albinus agrees, and the three go away. Axel and Margot continue to contrive ways to be alone together often. Finally, Albinus grows suspicious. He threatens Margot with a gun, but she convinces him that nothing has happened between her and Axel. Although he believes her, he insists that Margot leave with him immediately, without telling Axel. Desperate to keep Albinus, Margot agrees. As they are driving away, Margot chastises Albinus for his lack of faith, and they crash the car.

Albinus wakes up in the hospital, blinded for life. Margot dutifully spends almost all her time with Albinus, but she sneaks away to see Axel. Margot and Albinus go to Switzerland and set up housekeeping in an isolated chalet. Axel stays in the house with Margot and Albinus, moving very quietly so that Albinus can't tell he is there. Margot pretends to be nice to Albinus, but she and Axel make fun of him all the time. As Albinus's hearing improves, they must be more and more careful; they have several close calls, but Margot manages to convince Albinus that he is having auditory hallucinations. One day, however, Albinus's brother-in-law arrives suddenly and exposes the ruse. Back home, Albinus attacks Margot in her apartment. In their struggle Albinus is shot, and Margot runs away.

Petion, Maximilian. *Caesar's Column: A Story of the Twentieth Century.* Ignatius Donnelly. 1890.

Maximilian Petion, a wealthy New York lawyer, leads a double life in this futuristic novel. The members of his class know him, under the name Arthur Philips, as a spendthrift and drunkard, but to the members of the Brotherhood of Destruction, a secret workers' organization committed to a proletarian revolution, he is a member of the upper class who has chosen to be a leader of their organization. The desire to avenge his father, wrongly imprisoned on charges of forgery and perjury, impels Maximilian to adopt an alias and cast his lot with the working class. The decision leads eventually to a bloody revolution.

At the beginning of the novel Maximilian, disguised as a beggar, is saved from a beating at the hands of a coachman by GABRIEL WELTSTEIN, a rancher of Swiss descent visiting New York. Maximilian must in turn save Gabriel because the good samaritan dared to raise his hand against a servant of Prince Cabano, one of the city's most powerful men. Maximilian takes Gabriel to his home and, once he has removed his disguise, tells the naive visitor of how Cabano and the other wealthy members of the Council of the Oligarchy act as de facto rulers of the country.

The Brotherhood of Destruction, Maximilian tells Gabriel, is a worldwide organization with 100 million members that is plotting the overthrow of the Council of the Oligarchy. When Gabriel discovers, while secretly attending a meeting of the council, that it knows of the brotherhood's existence and plans to destroy it, Maximilian takes him to a meeting of the brotherhood and has him tell the story. The members of the brotherhood, led by Maximilian and two other men, decide to revolt.

Although Maximilian is one of the leaders of the brotherhood, he has some reservations about the impending insurrection. He has the insight to realize that revolt without reconstruction will destroy civilization but feels powerless to deflect the course of the revolution. Mistaking revenge for justice, he dreams of the opportunity to murder the man who had his father imprisoned, an opportunity that the anarchy of civil war will provide.

But Maximilian has another dream. One night he sees a beautiful and sweet-voiced woman singing in a music hall. He discovers that she is Christina Carlson, the only real source of support for a poor immigrant family. Maximilian befriends the family and finds them a pleasant home to live in outside the squalor of the slum district where they had been living. The two fall in love and marry in a double wedding with Gabriel and his fiancée Estella. The desire to protect his new family becomes as important as freeing his father from prison, and Maximilian agrees with Gabriel that they should flee the country if the revolution turns bloody.

The proletarian revolution leads to a reign of terror in which Maximilian participates, as he burns to death the man who had imprisoned his father. When the marauding mobs refuse to stop at murdering the capitalists who had oppressed them and turn on Maximilian, their former leader, he and his family and friends board an airship to escape the charred ruins of New York and head for Africa, where Gabriel and a group of other Swiss settlers live in peace.

Phelan, Francis. *Ironweed.* William Kennedy. 1983.

As a young man, Francis Phelan suffers a series of accidental misfortunes that cause him to spend the rest of his life in hiding from society and his past. When, as a young father, he attempts to pick up his baby by his diaper, the baby slips, breaks its neck, and dies. During a trolley strike in Albany, Francis hurls a rock that strikes and kills a cab driver. Francis flees his marriage and the police, losing himself in a career as a baseball player. But misfortune continues to plague him: In Chicago he kills a man who is envious of his baseball exploits. This combination of disastrous events leaves Francis a broken man, a vagrant whose past is filled with ghosts.

In 1930, Francis meets Helen Archer, another Albany native, in a bar in New York. Helen, herself a product of a life of early promise gone awry, becomes Francis's companion for nine years. Helen finds Francis to be a caring man, prone to meanness when drunk but nonetheless always concerned about her welfare.

In 1939, Francis and Helen find themselves back in Albany. Francis is again in dire straits because he has been convicted of registering to vote twenty-one times in a recent election. Francis gets a job as a grave digger in order to pay off his lawyer but works for only one day. The cemetery in which he works contains the graves of his parents and dead child, Gerald. In the first of many encounters with ghosts that take place during Francis's stay in Albany, Francis apologizes to his son through the earth for his death. He also sees the ghosts of the man he killed in the trolley strike and the man from Chicago. Francis does not grovel but rather calmly offers justification for his actions.

Francis sees his life as containing many bad decisions, but he also senses the agency of "some involuntary doom element in his life." Visiting his wife and children, Francis sees a stable, clean life that has never been and may never be his to enjoy. He makes a measure of peace with his children, but the violence that has always followed him is still present. In visiting vagrant friends in a riverside encampment, Francis breaks the back of a ruthless raider from the American Legion. Finding Helen dead from illness in her cheap hotel room, Francis hops a train, only to jump off and apparently head for the strange peace of his family's house.

Phillips, Maud Martha. *Maud Martha.* Gwendolyn Brooks. 1953.

Maud Martha, a good woman who humbly tries to make a good home, marries a young man named Paul Phillips and moves into a kitchenette apartment in New York City. Always hardworking despite depressing surroundings, Maud Martha does what she can to make their less-than-perfect apartment appealing. It soon becomes apparent that married life is also less than perfect. She and Paul go out together at times, although Paul is bored at the musicals that Maud Martha likes and does not like to go to the library at all.

When the couple receives an invitation to a ball being held by the Foxy Cats Club, both dress in their finest. Maud Martha is disappointed at the dance, however, because Paul treats her very nonchalantly, leaving her sitting for quite a while in order to dance often with a very light-skinned woman. Appearance is something of an issue between Maud Martha and Paul: Both are black, but he is lighter than she is, and both see "black" features as less beautiful.

Maud Martha becomes pregnant around this time. Her labor comes on suddenly, and before the doctor arrives she gives birth at home, with only a neighbor and her mother in attendance. Neither the two women nor Paul is very helpful to Maud Martha or to her newborn daughter Paulette.

Later, Maud Martha looks a for a job so she can buy nice things for Paulette. She finds one job as a domestic servant, but the woman for whom she works is so unbearable that Maud Martha refuses to go back after the first day. As time goes by Maud Martha focuses more on her daughter and her neighbors, and on keeping her marriage together.

Maud Martha has several unpleasant encounters with white people. One Christmas season, for example, Maud Martha takes Paulette to talk to a Santa Claus in a department store. The man seems to become deaf, paying no attention to the little girl in front of him. Maud Martha is angry, and Paulette is upset. The novel ends, however, with Maud Martha taking her daughter out for a happy stroll in the park, confident that life will get better.

Phineas "Finny". *A Separate Peace.* John Knowles. 1960.

Sincere, good-natured, and always adventurous, sixteen-year-old Phineas, called "Finny" by his friends, is known for his outstanding physical ability and his outrageous stunts. It is Finny who convinces his best friend GENE FORRESTER, the novel's narrator, to join him in a jump from a perilously high tree into the river below. The jump becomes a summertime ritual for the boys, but it leads to a crippling accident that changes both their lives.

Finny and Gene are roommates and devoted friends at Devon, a private school for boys in rural New Hampshire. Finny respects Gene's intelligence, and Gene admires Finny's athletic prowess and uncanny ability to talk his way out of his many conflicts with the Devon administration. But when one of Finny's typical escapades causes Gene to fail a crucial exam, Gene becomes convinced that Finny is jealous and out to thwart his academic career. The next time they are about to jump from the tree, Gene jostles the branch on which his friend is standing, and Finny tumbles to the riverbank, shattering his leg and ending his participation in sports forever.

While he is convalescing, Finny is visited by his guilt-ridden friend. He refuses to listen when Gene tries to tell him that he caused the crippling accident. When he returns to Devon later in the term, Finny, although hampered by crutches, has not lost his adventurous spirit. He vows to train Gene to be the athlete he himself can never be, and he begins to coach his friend for the next Olympics, in 1944. Finny refuses to consider the possibility that the Olympics will likely be canceled due to the war in Europe. In fact, he refuses to acknowledge the reality of the war, repeatedly insisting that it has been "made up" by the old men who act as world leaders.

Still, the boys cannot help but be affected by the war. Devon is the site of many recruitment programs and volunteer efforts for the cause. The boys' circle of friends is disrupted when Elwin "Leper" Lepellier, a quiet nature lover, enlists. To counter the dreary atmosphere threatening the school, Finny organizes a winter carnival that, quite predictably, turns into an uproarious party.

Finny only admits that the war is real when he sees Leper, who has left the army after suffering a mental breakdown, lurking in the bushes on campus. Soon after, Brinker, the school's student politician, arranges an elaborate inquisition into the events that left Finny crippled. Finny and Gene are forced to endure a mock trial in which Leper, found on the campus grounds, implicates Gene as the cause of Finny's fall. Upset, Finny shouts out, "I just don't care," and using his cane for support rushes from the room. Seconds later he falls down a flight of stairs.

In the infirmary, his leg broken again, Finny finally confronts his best friend. After an outburst of anger, he quiets and tearfully forgives Gene for the blind impulse that left him maimed. The two part as friends. That afternoon, when his leg is being set, bone marrow escapes into his bloodstream, and Finny dies.

Pierce, Mildred. *Mildred Pierce.* James M. Cain. 1941.

Mildred Pierce, the novel's pragmatic yet obsessive protagonist, counts as her greatest asset a determined ambition, a talent in the kitchen, and a voluptuous pair of legs that she shows off to their greatest advantage. As the novel opens, Mildred turns on her lazy and unemployed husband Bert and, sure that she can earn a living with more success, throws him out into the arms of his mistress. Faced with life on her own and two daughters to raise, Mildred begins to earn a living by making pies and tricks Bert out of the one thing she still needs from him: the family car.

Mildred soon realizes that pie making will not be enough to support her family, and she reluctantly sets out to find a job. Sensing that her arrogant and snobbish daughter VEDA (PIERCE) will despise any job her mother might have to take, Mildred refuses the only jobs for which she is qualified. She finally takes a job as a waitress in a Hollywood diner, hiding her uniform for fear of Veda's scorn. Soon Mildred begins supplying pies to the diner, and this fast-growing success is crowned by her meeting with MONTGOMERY "MONTY" BERAGON, a polo-playing socialite. Mildred is spending a day with Monty at the beach when Ray, her younger daughter, is taken fatally ill. Mildred returns before Ray dies, and after fending off the accusations of her mother-in-law, she realizes she feels a sense of relief that it was Ray and not Veda who died.

Capitalizing on the success of her pies, Mildred decides to open a restaurant, and this soon becomes a great success. Her relationship with Veda is also improving, as Monty provides the smart parties and polo matches always longed for by Veda. Mildred's feelings for Monty quickly move from awe at his wealth and background to scorn at his lack of dignity, but she stays with him for the sake of her relationship with Veda, claiming that she will do anything to stay close to her daughter. Finally, when Mildred realizes that Veda has begun to respect her wealth and Monty has begun to abuse it, she throws Monty out of the house and then dreams of fostering Veda's musical talent.

Yet Mildred's precious hold on Veda's affections is shattered when Veda, believing she is talentless, loses her interest in music and becomes involved with a young man whom she then tries to blackmail. On hearing of this, Mildred finally confronts Veda and throws her out of the house. Left to her own devices, Veda begins to make her way as a singer, and Mildred, desperate to get her back again, becomes involved with Monty. During the period of their reunion, Mildred creates a veneer of success and unity—but her inner life is collapsing. Monty and Veda are draining her resources and, unbeknownst to Mildred, having an affair. Only after divorcing Monty does Mildred realize the extent of Veda's callous deception. As the novel closes, she has found her way back to Bert and freed herself at last from her daughter's importunate ways.

Pierce, Mitchell. *dem.* William Melvin Kelley. 1967.

Mitchell Pierce is a vacuous, amoral veteran of "the last Asian war" who now lives in New York and works for an advertising firm. Accustomed to floating from one set of circumstances to the next and remaining detached from those around him, Mitchell is forced in the course of the novel to confront the presence of people in his life.

When Mitchell's colleague Goodwin, a former Marine, invites Mitchell and his wife Tam for a weekend visit, Mitchell accepts. In the car on the way to Goodwin's house, Tam and Mitchell—who are experiencing problems in their sexual relationship—argue because Mitchell failed to consult Tam about going to Goodwin's. When they arrive at Goodwin's house, Tam suggests that Mitchell doesn't love her anymore and that the romance is gone from their marriage. Mitchell does not argue.

On his way to use the bathroom, Mitchell discovers the bodies of Goodwin's wife and two children lying dead in the bedroom. Mitchell deduces that Goodwin murdered them after a fight with his wife. Deciding that Tam must not discover the corpses, Mitchell returns to Goodwin's patio without saying a word. Tam does find the dead wife and children, however, and she tells Mitchell to call the police. On their way home Tam makes Mitchell stop at a hotel, where they make love.

Mitchell and Tam hire Opal, a black nanny, to take care of their son. Opal is a wonderful nanny, but Mitchell fires her after her boyfriend calls on her at their residence. Tam gets pregnant again, and the family goes off to spend a summer at the beach.

Mitchell's relationship with his wife declines further as Mitchell begins to watch *Search for Love*, a daytime soap opera. He becomes obsessed with Nancy, a character on the show. Unable to think of anything else, Mitchell schedules his appointments around *Search for Love* and constantly fantasizes about Nancy. One night, after a fight with Tam, he leaves the apartment and rides around the city in a taxi. He catches sight of Nancy in a restaurant window and gets out of the cab to follow her home. A few nights later, on the street in front of her apartment building, he saves her from being beaten up by her soap opera co-star. Mitchell ends up in Nancy's apartment; Nancy, who is mindless and flippant, sleeps with him.

Believing he is in love with Nancy and that he must save her from her unhappy soap opera marriage, Mitchell confronts Tam and tells her he has a lover. Tam laughs at him. In the meantime, Nancy, sensing that Mitchell has grown attached to her, rejects him. Mitchell's life returns to normal until Tam gives birth to twins—one white, the other black.

The doctor tells Mitchell that the twins resulted from "superfecundation," the fertilization of two eggs within a short period of time by sperm cells from two separate intercourses. Overwhelmed, Mitchell asks Tam who fathered the black infant. She tells him it was Cooley, Opal's boyfriend. The idea of bringing the black child home and calling him their own is unthinkable to Mitchell, Tam, and Tam's mother. Tam refuses to give the child up for adoption, however, so Mitchell, following the instructions of Tam's mother, searches for Cooley to convince him to take the child. In the North Bronx he finds Opal, whom he rehires. Opal, no longer involved with Cooley, directs Mitchell to Carlyle, Cooley's friend, who takes him around the black community.

Mitchell never finds Cooley and returns home with no answer to his problems. When the white infant dies, Mitchell plans to tell the world that the black baby belongs to Opal who came to him begging for help with her illegitimate child. But Mitchell is afraid that his story will be transparent. As the novel closes, he takes a hot bath in his apartment and tries to lose himself in his fantasies.

Pierce, Veda. *Mildred Pierce.* James M. Cain. 1941.

Veda Pierce is the callous and self-serving daughter of MILDRED PIERCE. Throughout the novel she is the unresponsive object of her mother's obsessive love. Even as a young child, Veda is arrogant and haughty, and these characteristics only intensify as she grows older. Her arrogance acts as a barrier between her and her mother, and she is unmoved by both her mother's caresses and her beatings. Veda is vulnerable only to the claims of money and status, and she is moved only by music. Her snobbery and musical talent are her two passions, and she manipulates everything else, including Mildred, in pursuit of these ambitions.

Scorn dominates Veda's feeling for her mother until the day Mildred introduces her to MONTGOMERY "MONTY" BERAGON, a polo-playing socialite. Monty offers Veda the chances she has always wanted and introduces her to a world of tennis, polo, and parties from which Mildred, although married to Monty, is excluded. Veda's involvement in this world emphasizes her growing distance from Mildred, a distance that Veda is always at pains to reinforce. Veda also begins to work on her musical talent, taking lessons from Charles Hannen, a renowned piano teacher. Although Mildred finances these lessons, Veda uses them as an opportunity to distance herself further from her mother.

Yet Veda encounters a stumbling block when she auditions for Carlo Treviso, another piano teacher, and he humiliates her. Unable to bring herself to carry on, Veda turns her attention to money by attempting to blackmail the wealthy young Sam Forrester. When Mildred hears of their liaison, she tries to force Forrester to marry Veda until she realizes that it is not the man but his money that Veda is after. When Mildred sees how calculating Veda has been, she confronts her for the first time and throws her out of the house.

Left to her own devices, Veda demonstrates an indomitable, if callous, spirit. She discovers that she has a fine voice and begins to take singing lessons with the same Treviso who had previously humiliated her. Her success leads to a major advertising contract, and she is reunited with Mildred, who sacrifices her business to give Veda the life-style she wants. Yet Veda is not content with what she has earned and what Mildred can give her. While she is looking for ways to accept a more lucrative contract that would free her from Mildred, she is also having an affair with Mildred's husband Monty. One night Mildred discovers them together and turns on Veda who, cunning as always, pretends that Mildred has destroyed her voice.

For a brief time Veda seems to have grown closer to her mother, but once Mildred's divorce from Monty is finalized, Veda reveals her deceit, accepts a more lucrative contract, and leaves with Monty.

Pilar. *For Whom the Bell Tolls.* Ernest Hemingway. 1940.

Pilar is a Spanish peasant woman fighting the Nationalists as a Republican guerilla in the Spanish Civil War. She is a huge, very strong woman with "a brown face like a model for a granite monument." Her husband Pablo is the chief of a small band of guerillas who live and fight in the mountains south of Avila, near Madrid. In the early days of the war, Pablo was a brave leader, but years of living in caves in the mountains, under constant threat by enemy forces, have made him lose his nerve. While Pilar remains firmly attached to her Republican ideals, Pablo has become little more than a common bandit, stealing in order to survive but avoiding any meaningful attack on the Nationalist forces because of the incredible danger involved.

As a young woman, Pilar lived in Grenada and had affairs with several bullfighters. Eventually, however, she married Pablo and settled down in his small town in Castile. At the outset of the war, Pablo was instrumental in leading a Republican uprising in the town. He led the assault on the army barracks and personally executed the captured soldiers. He also organized the killing of the town's prominent Nationalists, although the mob got out of hand as the killing went on, and what began as an organized series of executions quickly degenerated into a massacre. While Pablo enjoyed the killings and his newfound role as military leader, Pilar felt ashamed of the cruelty involved in fighting for freedom. Three days later the fascists retook the town and began their reprisals. Pilar and Pablo fled to the hills.

As the novel begins, Pablo's band is joined by ROBERT JORDAN, an American demolitions expert sent by Republican command in Madrid to blow up a bridge in Pablo's territory. The demolition itself presents little difficulty, but the attack must be precisely timed to coincide with a major Republican offensive. Pablo is against helping Jordan because he realizes that blowing the bridge will bring no material profit but will provoke vicious Nationalist reprisals, forcing the band to flee the familiar territory they have occupied for several months and leave most of their supplies behind. He also knows that several of his small band of supporters will definitely be killed. Most of the other guerillas do not realize the necessary consequences of Jordan's mission, but Pilar does. Despite the danger, she insists that the band help Jordan with the demolition of the bridge, and in doing so she supplants Pablo as the band's leader. Contrary to the guerillas' code (and common sense), she and Jordan allow Pablo to live and remain part of the group.

This is not the first time that Pablo's band has worked with foreign experts. A comrade of Jordan's, a Russian named Kashkin, helped the group attack a train several months earlier. Although the attack on the train was successful, Kashkin was very nervous, and the guerillas have a fairly low opinion of him. In the attack they rescued a young woman named Maria, who had been beaten and raped by the Nationalists because her father was a Republican mayor. When she first joined the group, Maria was traumatized and insecure, and Pilar has helped her recover. Sensing an affinity between Maria and Jordan, Pilar encourages a romance between them, and they become lovers.

Throughout the days that Robert Jordan is with the band, Pilar provides him with support and ensures that the guerillas remain loyal to him despite overwhelming difficulties. The neighboring band, led by the reliable El Sordo, is discovered by the Nationalists and eradicated in an air strike. Worse yet, in a moment of panic Pablo destroys Jordan's detonators the night before the attack. Although he regains his nerve and joins the guerillas for the assault, they must now proceed without El Sordo's men and with jury-rigged equipment.

The bridge is blown successfully but half the guerillas die in the attempt, and Jordan is so seriously wounded that he, too, must be left behind to die. Pilar, Pablo, and Maria manage to escape on horses and head for safer territory. It is clear at this point, however, that the entire operation has been in vain, for the Republican attack is poorly organized, and the Nationalists are well prepared to deal with it, despite the loss of the bridge.

Pilgrim, Billy. *Slaughter-House Five.* Kurt Vonnegut, Jr. 1968.

Billy Pilgrim, soldier and time-traveler, is born in 1922 to a middle-class family in Ilium, New York. In 1940, Billy is forced to withdraw from optometry school when he is drafted to serve as a chaplain's assistant in the army. While in the armed forces, Billy begins to question the universally accepted linear notion of time and believes he is able to travel freely between past, present, and future. His companions—including the narrator, who knew him in the army—think their friend is "coming undone," but Billy's life experiences ultimately support his seemingly fantastical ideas.

After witnessing the Battle of the Bulge in 1944, Billy and his legion are taken as prisoners of war to Dresden and confined to a former underground shelter for pigs before slaughter, designated "slaughter-house five." While in Dresden, Billy and the other prisoners work as contract laborers in a factory that makes malt syrup for pregnant women. After witnessing the firebombing of Dresden and the American government's censorship of news of its destructive force, Billy is outraged and despairs over the war's victimization of the young and the innocent.

Upon his return to Ilium, Billy completes his degree in optometry and marries the wealthy but unattractive daughter of the founder of the optometry school. His father-in-law sets him up in a successful optometry practice, and he gains the wealth and status that his own father never had. With a house in the suburbs, a wife, two children, and a dog, Billy appears to lead a model life.

But in 1967 his life is turned upside down when martianlike aliens from the planet of Tralfamadore suddenly appear, take Billy to their planet, and put him on display at the zoo. Billy is intrigued by the Tralfamadorians' explanation of the four dimensions of time. In Tralfamadore, they explain, past, present, and future exist simultaneously; so people appear to die but in fact continue to live in the past. The notion of free will, according to the Tralfamadorians, is a fallacy that exists only on earth. While in Tralfamadore, Billy is given Montana Wildhack as a mate; she was formerly an actress on earth before her abduction to the alien planet. Montana is more attractive than Billy's wife, and she and Billy happily conceive a child.

Because of the nature of time travel, Billy is able to return to earth without any apparent passage of time. In 1968, on his way to an optometrist's convention, Billy is in a plane crash over Sugarbush Mountain in Vermont. After his release from the hospital, and because he wants to share his knowledge of time travel and his experiences in Tralfamadore, Billy starts a late-night talk show. When his daughter learns of her father's public disgrace, she tries to get medical treatment for him. Billy is temporarily hospitalized and is no longer allowed to practice optometry. Upon his release, he continues to send letters to newspapers and to speak publicly about his experiences.

A few years later, during a public address, Billy is assassinated by Paul Lazzaro, an army veteran who vowed to avenge a soldier who claimed that Billy was responsible for his death. Before the assassination, he foresees his death through time travel, but he accepts his inability to change his fate and chooses to speak anyway.

Pillager, Fleur. *Tracks.* Louise Erdrich. 1988.

Fleur Pillager is the last of the Pillagers, a Chippewa family awarded an allotment of land that included Matchimanito Lake and the surrounding forests. According to rumor on the reservation, the manito, or spirit, of the lake, has chosen Fleur as his own. By her fifteenth year, they say, Fleur had "drowned" twice; the two men who rescued her cold, stiff body from the lake on each occasion either disappeared or died mysteriously soon after saving her. As a result of these deaths, the other Chippewa recognize and fear Fleur's power and her old, deep connection to the land.

However, south of the reservation, in Argus, North Dakota, the people know nothing of Fleur's reputation. She leaves the reservation and works at Kozka Meats, where the men see her only as a woman—pretty, young, and Indian. But when she consistently beats them at their penny-ante poker games, their interest in her rises. As the stakes of the game rise and the men lose more money to Fleur, they turn violent, and three of them rape her. Fleur disappears, and a tornado levels much of the town; days later, Fleur's rapists are found frozen underneath a mountain of rubble in one of the meat lockers.

When Fleur returns to the reservation, Eli Kashpaw, the hunting apprentice of the Chippewa healer NANAPUSH, suddenly falls in love with her, and the two begin to live together. Months later, when she gives birth to LULU NAN-APUSH (LAMARTINE) with great difficulty, no one knows if the child's father is Eli, one of the rapists in Argus, or the lake manito.

When PAULINE PUYAT, a homely woman, seeks Eli's romantic attention, Fleur, secure about his affections, merely laughs. But Fleur does not anticipate that, with the help of love medicine purchased from Fleur's cousin, Pauline will arrange a sexual encounter between Eli and fourteen-year-old Sophie Morrissey. Once wronged, Fleur strikes back. She draws Sophie to her cabin and causes the girl to kneel in her yard for two days and a night. Fleur also withdraws from the unfaithful Eli.

During this time Eli tells Nanapush that he has witnessed Fleur's evening rendezvous with the lake spirits. According to Eli, Fleur leaves her bed late each night and walks to the lake. She enters the water and does not resurface. Hours later, when she finally returns to the cabin, her hair and body drip with water and plant life from the very bottom of the deep lake.

Fleur gives birth to her second child prematurely. Carrying the tiny, sickly baby and followed by Pauline, Fleur walks to where the spirits of the dead sit playing poker. Fleur gambles with them for the lives of her two children as well as for her own. Although she loses her newborn, she saves herself and Lulu. Depression overtakes her as her supernatural powers diminish; this, coupled with the Kashpaws' betrayal, leaves Fleur unable to prevent woodcutters from invading Pillager land. However, on the quiet, preternaturally still day that they arrive to remove the remaining trees from the woods around her cabin, the men of the lumber company are surprised by the effects of a sudden wind. The trees, which somehow still stand, have been sawed through at their trunks, and when the wind blows, they fall and crush the men and their tools.

Pio (Uncle). *The Bridge of San Luis Rey.* Thornton Wilder. 1927.

In the sudden and unexpected collapse of the famous rope bridge of San Luis Rey, Uncle Pio, an inhabitant of early eighteenth-century Peru, is hurled into the treacherous mountain chasm to his death. The unexpected tragedy draws the attention of a nameless narrator who, interested in finding divine justification for the accident, retraces the lives of its victims.

Uncle Pio's life was dominated by his association with the actress Camila Perichole. He first encountered her when she was a girl of only twelve, singing ballads in a café. Impressed by her every inflection, Uncle Pio decided to adopt the young child. He bought her, set her up in his house, and taught her to sing and act. Under Uncle Pio's unflagging tutelage, the Perichole, as she came to be called, developed into a graceful, potent performer.

The Perichole's rise to widespread public favor was rapid, but soon the perfection that both she and Uncle Pio demanded of her performances began to take its toll. Under the overly exacting pressure, Camila neglected her acting duties, much to the disappointment of Uncle Pio. The situation was temporarily exacerbated when Camila fell in love with the viceroy of Peru, Don Andres de Ribera, but Uncle Pio was comforted when he noticed that the relationship improved the Perichole's acting.

Over time, however, Uncle Pio and the Perichole became alienated from each other. Camila grew more impatient with the acting profession and began to refer to it as a mere pastime, claiming she wanted to be a respectable lady rather than a public performer. She decided to divorce herself from theatrical life. Despite Uncle Pio's attempt to dissuade her, she stood firm, and eventually their friendship fell apart.

Camila, having contracted a case of smallpox that marred her beauty, retired to the countryside with her son Don Jaime. Taking a sincere interest in her convalescence, Uncle Pio regained much of Camila's confidence, but the respite was short-lived. One day when Camila, despising the pockmarks on her face, uselessly attempted to mask them with excessive makeup, Uncle Pio accidentally intruded upon her privacy. Shameful and bitter, Camila drove him from her house forever.

Because he longed "as a boy of eighteen would long" to see her, Uncle Pio devised a strategy for his return. One night he hid under her bedroom window and imitated the sound of a young girl crying. When she appeared, he revealed himself and made a request: He wanted to educate Camila's son for a year in Lima. At first she refused, experiencing what she saw as the futility of a meaningless world, but she finally consented. In the end, tragedy intervened. On his way back to Lima with Don Jaime, in the company of strangers ESTEBAN and DOÑA MARIA MARQUESA DE MONTEMAYOR, Uncle Pio was killed by the collapse of the bridge of San Luis Rey.

Pitckett, Jack. "Man on a Road." Albert Maltz. 1935.

Jack Pitckett, a large, heavy-featured man of about thirty-five years of age, is a doomed miner suffering from silicosis. Pitckett comes from somewhere in the deep South and was probably raised in the mountains. At the beginning of the story, he is almost hit by the narrator's car while hitchhiking in a tunnel under a railroad bridge in Gauley, West Virginia. Standing soaked by the rain with glazed-over eyes, he is apparently unaware that the car has narrowly missed him. At first Pitckett does not hear the driver call to him, and when he is finally roused from his daze by the horn, he shows no surprise at the car's proximity. He merely steps closer and asks for a lift to a town called Weston.

Even though he is completely unnerved by the man's eerie demeanor, the narrator agrees to drive him from Gauley to Weston. During the hundred-mile trip, which takes four hours, Pitckett sits as if in a trance, often not even hearing the driver speak to him. At one point he is seized with a coughing fit that takes almost three minutes to subside. When they finally reach their destination, the driver invites Pitckett to join him for a cup of coffee and a sandwich. His face softening with gratitude, Pitckett then asks his new acquaintance to recopy a poorly written letter he wants to send to his wife.

In the letter Pitckett tells his wife that he lied when he said he could not get a job in the mines because work was scarce; the real reason is that he contracted a chronic lung disease from inhaling silica dust while drilling in the tunnel near Gauley Bridge. The supervisors at the mines nearby refused to hire any of the one hundred or so men who contracted silicosis while working on the project. The fatal illness could have been avoided if the company had installed a proper ventilation system and given the workers masks to wear. Pitckett explains to his wife that he is going away because the doctor has given him only four months to live, and he does not want to become a burden to her. He asks her never to let their son work in the mines and to tell the child when he grows up what the company did to his father. Jack concludes the letter by suggesting that his wife should find another man after a while.

Once the letter has been recopied, Pitckett warmly thanks the narrator, then slowly retreats into his sorrowful, mute absorption. They sit for a while together in the café without speaking, then Jack rises and walks out the door into the rain.

Pitkin, Lemuel. *A Cool Million.* Nathanael West. 1934.

Lemuel Pitkin, a seventeen-year-old boy from Ottsville, Vermont, goes to New York to seek his fortune in order to help his mother pay off the mortgage on their modest house. Lem's adviser is Nathan "Shagpoke" Whipple, president of the local Rat River National Bank and former President of the United States. Mr. Whipple is a great believer in America as the land of opportunity, and he

gives Lem the idea to go and make his way in the world.

On his way to New York, Lem has extremely bad luck. He gets unjustly thrown in jail in Stamford, Connecticut, where the warden orders all his teeth to be pulled. Once Lem reaches his destination, he is repeatedly beaten and abused by various thugs and con men, one of whom puts out his eye. Rather than dwelling on his many problems, however, Lem remains absurdly optimistic and passive. He never gets a chance to catch his breath and recover before somebody else comes along to trick and mistreat him.

Lem appears most active and valiant when trying to protect his childhood friend Betty Prail from the many men who abuse her, but his efforts are always in vain. He loses the job he has with a fake glass eye company when he is kidnapped by Betty's Chinese pimp. Typically resilient, Lem escapes and joins his old friend Mr. Whipple, who, after a stint in jail and a period of poverty and homelessness, is off to dig for gold in California. Betty leaves the prostitution ring in which she has been held captive and joins them.

Mr. Whipple, ever patriotic, wants to organize a new political party, the National Revolutionary Party, with the purpose of vanquishing the Jewish international bankers and the Bolshevik labor unions. Lem attends several rallies and in consequence before leaving New York is briefly kidnapped by a fat communist who mangles his hand.

By the time Lem gets to California with his friends, he has no teeth, a glass eye, and a mangled hand. The mutilation never ceases: Attempting to save Betty from being raped, he steps into a trap set by the rapist that destroys his leg; while still caught in the trap, Lem gets brutally scalped by a local Indian chief who hates all white men.

Lem is now so badly mangled that his only prospect for employment is exhibition as a carnival freak. Since the Depression is at its height, Lem feels lucky to be employed at all. His career as a human oddity does not last long, however, for Lem is soon killed by his fat communist enemy while attempting to deliver a speech on behalf of Mr. Whipple's political party.

After his death, Lem becomes an American hero, and his birthday becomes a national holiday. Schoolchildren all over the country sing "The Lemuel Pitkin Song," hailing him as a patriotic martyr rather than what he really was, a brave and naive boy with astoundingly bad luck.

Pittman, Jane. *The Autobiography of Miss Jane Pittman.* Ernest J. Gaines. 1971.

Jane Pittman recounts her long-lived struggles with slavery and freedom in the changing but still racist South. Originally named Ticey, the narrator decides to call herself "Jane" when, after the outbreak of the Civil War, she meets a young Union soldier who encourages her to reject her slave name. Deeply moved by the soldier's sincerity and concern, Jane takes his last name, Brown, for her own.

For this defiant step, Jane is brutally beaten and sent to work in the fields, but she refuses to relent.

After emancipation, Jane and a small group from the plantation set off for the North. They are ambushed by an army of white terrorists, and only Jane and a young boy named Ned, whose mother is killed in the massacre, are able to hide and survive. Almost matter-of-factly, Jane, herself no more than twelve years old, accepts the responsibility of raising Ned as her own child. At first Jane is determined to take Ned to Ohio and find her friend Mr. Brown, but as the odyssey through the Louisiana back-country seems increasingly futile, Jane agrees to settle on a plantation where Ned can attend school and she can work for wages. Because of his later activities on behalf of freed slaves, Ned's life is threatened by local Klansmen, and he decides to leave the area. Jane makes the painful but determined decision to stay where she is.

After Ned moves away, Jane marries her neighbor, Joe Pittman, and the two move to another plantation where Joe can make a better living. Jane has a series of horrifying prophetic nightmares about her husband's death, and he soon dies in circumstances very similar to those in her dreams. When Ned returns several years later, Jane is immediately concerned about losing him, too, for he has become a powerful and influential public speaker and is monitored carefully by the white community as soon as he arrives. Ned refuses to stop his work and is assassinated by Albert Cluveau, a local patroller. Jane feels particularly devastated and betrayed because she had often shared coffee with Cluveau when he was on patrol. Cluveau spends the rest of his life descending into fear, illness, and insanity, prompting many to believe that Jane has placed a curse on him. But Jane insists that there was nothing supernatural in Cluveau's fate: He was consumed by a hell that he created.

Jane moves to the nearby Samson plantation, where she joins the church and finally has a long-awaited experience of spiritual awakening. In her later years Jane's life is most strongly affected by her worshipful love for Jimmy, a local boy who grows up to participate in the civil rights movement. When a young black woman is arrested for drinking from a whites-only fountain, a protest is organized at which Jimmy is to speak. Told that they will be evicted if they participate in the developing currents of protest, Jane's friends on the plantation are torn by the desire to attend and the terror that their homes and livelihoods will be destroyed if they do. Jane, determined to fight the legacy of slavery, knows this is a chance she must take, and some of the others from the plantation dare to go with her.

As Jane had intuitively expected, Jimmy is assassinated at the protest. In the aftermath, the group of protesters encounters Mr. Samson, the plantation owner. He suggests that the group can return to his land and employment if they leave the protest quietly and behave themselves. Jane is not at all uncertain as to what is to be done. Now over a hundred years old, she walks past Mr. Samson and leads the group away and beyond him. She insists that only a part of Jimmy has died. His fight lives on, and she must continue to move forward and struggle as long as she lives.

Placido. *Blake, or the Huts of America.* Martin Delany. 1862.

A revolutionary black Cuban poet, Placido is the cousin of HENRY BLAKE, the novel's protagonist. Although somewhat overshadowed by his cousin, Placido plays an important role in organizing the blacks of his native island to end slavery.

Unlike many of Cuba's blacks, Placido is free. His talent as a poet is respected among both races, guaranteeing him an enviable social position. Despite his own nominal freedom, however, he longs to end the enslavement of all blacks. Only when the rest of his people are free, he feels, can his position be one of true liberty and equality with whites.

One day while Placido sits in his study writing, an unexpected visitor calls on him. When the visitor gives the poet his name, Placido mentions that a cousin of his, who has not been heard from by his family in twenty years, had the same name. Revealing himself to be that lost relative, Henry Blake embraces Placido. Surprised but joyous, Placido has Blake recount the adventures he has experienced in his long absence from Cuba. In addition to telling his complicated history, Blake reveals to Placido his desire that the blacks living in the Americas win their freedom. Placido, who has always expressed the dream of black freedom in his poetry, urges Blake to consider launching the plan in Cuba.

After Blake returns from voyages to the United States and Africa, Placido introduces him to the island's most influential free people of color and to slaves amenable to Blake's revolutionary designs. Placido nominates Blake as general-in-chief of the newly formed Army of Emancipation, and Placido himself becomes secretary of the Grand Council, the revolutionary government.

As the blacks begin to organize themselves, rumors circulate among the whites that a revolution is impending. Some Americans who own plantations in Cuba seize the opportunity to arouse fears that the Spanish government is not doing enough to protect the whites. In order to strengthen their position, they demand the enactment of strict codes of behavior for the blacks, both free and enslaved.

Placido falls victim to the codes. One day he enters a bookstore and the shop's owner, an American, accuses him of insubordination. Before Placido can defend himself from this unfounded charge, the bookseller attacks him. Driving Placido from the store, the man beats him and knocks him to the ground. Black witnesses to this atrocity are afraid to help Placido; whites do not even consider aiding a wounded black. Bleeding and barely able to walk,

Placido makes his way home and collapses into the arms of his friends. They are outraged, and it seems that the patience of the island's blacks is finally exhausted.

Plant, Bita. *Banana Bottom.* Claude McKay. 1933.

When Bita Plant, a young black woman, returns to her Jamaican village, Banana Bottom, she must choose either to pursue the religious missionary life for which she has been educated or return to her rich, colorful, lower-class culture.

The novel opens in Jubilee with the homecoming celebration for Bita, who has just returned from England where she has been educated in the very best schools for the past seven years under the auspices of the Reverends Malcolm and Priscilla Craig, English missionaries who live in Jubilee.

Soon afterward Bita returns to Banana Bottom for a week of Emancipation Day celebrations. She stays at her old house with her father Jordan Plant, his wife Anty Nommy, her deceased mother's sister, and her cousin Bab. After several small celebrations, Bita decides to accompany Belle Black and Yoni Legge, two Banana Bottom friends, to the tea meeting, a forbidden amusement of peasants. She is so enthralled by the celebration that she dances wildly, without inhibitions.

In Jubilee, Mrs. Craig is informed of Bita's tea meeting attendance by a gossipy midwife named Sister Phibby Patroll. When questioned about the tea meeting, Bita admits that she attended the party with her cousin and Squire Gensir, a sixty-year-old Englishman who lives among the peasants. At the mention of Squire Gensir's name, Mrs. Craig appears immediately relieved because Squire Gensir is considered a man with an honorable reputation.

The Craigs scheme to marry Bita to Herald Newton Day, a student at a theological college and the favorite to replace Reverend Craig when he retires. But Bita feels no love for Herald; she is more attracted to a young, rowdy, uneducated, and unrefined man named Hopping Dick. Before the Craigs can plan the wedding, Bita receives a telegram saying that Anty Nommy is ill, and she leaves Jubilee feeling apprehensive but relieved.

After Christmas has passed, Bita decides to attend the annual Harvest Festival, a church-oriented celebration where peasants bring gifts to church and make a love offering. While the congregation waits for Herald Newton, news reaches the church that Herald has descended into sin with a nanny goat. This incident destroys his reputation with the people of Jubilee and Banana Bottom. Meanwhile, Bita returns to Jubilee to face Mrs. Craig's opposition to Hopping Dick and soon realizes that it is time for her to leave the Craigs. Her hostility and growing resentment causes her to oppose Mrs. Craig wholeheartedly. Anty Nommy comes to Jubilee and invites Hopping Dick to the mission in order to question him about his intentions concerning Bita; and Hopping Dick admits that he could never marry a woman of Bita's station.

Bita then leaves Jubilee and returns to Banana Bottom, where she encounters many possible suitors, all of whom she rejects except for Jubban, a drayman to Jordan Plant. After the death of her father and the Reverends Malcolm and Priscilla Craig, Bita marries Jubban and lives on the land where she was born.

Pleasure Mouse. "A Visit from the Footbinder." Emily Prager. 1982.

In this short story, six-year-old Pleasure Mouse prepares for the aristocratic ceremony of female footbinding. The Chinese ritual began in the ninth century when the emperor bade a dancing girl bind her feet to resemble points of the moon sickle. Since it is the desire of all aristocratic women to be chosen as one of the emperor's concubines or, better yet, as his wife, they bind their feet to indicate their class and follow fashion. Naive to the painful process of footbinding, Pleasure Mouse sets out several days before the ceremony to inquire about the experience. She finds the tiny, silken shoes she will one day wear charming and cannot understand why no one will discuss footbinding with her.

It upsets Pleasure Mouse when the elderly palace painter, Fen Wen, whom she loves dearly, tells her that she will no longer be able to visit him in the garden once she has undergone footbinding. For the first time Pleasure Mouse realizes that this rite of passage will end life as she knows it. Tiger Mouse, Pleasure Mouse's older sister, who has successfully endured footbinding and has very desirable feet, refuses to reveal any information; no one told her what it would be like, she says, when she was Pleasure Mouse's age. Tiger Mouse considers footbinding an inevitable duty to which Pleasure Mouse must submit, like their female ancestors before them.

Although forbidden to leave the palace grounds, Pleasure Mouse escapes into the city to ask Honey Tongue, her father's concubine, to dispel the mystery of footbinding. Even though she was from the lower classes, Honey Tongue's feet were bound when she was a child. She was laughed at by her peers for striving to exceed her class, but now Honey Tongue can mock them because she is a wealthy man's courtesan whereas they are just natural-footed street merchants. Honey Tongue tells Pleasure Mouse that the two years of pain will be worth the reward of her guaranteed marriage.

Pleasure Mouse's mother, Lady Guo Guo, turns her attention from planning her own grandiose funeral arrangements to preparing for her daughter's footbinding. Lady Guo Guo has hired a woman to do the binding because she cannot bear to do it herself. Lord Guo Guo, Pleasure Mouse's absent father, suggests to Lady Guo Guo that she forgo the binding altogether and attempt to reinstate natural feet as a fashion. He suggests this more to bring guilt to the greedy mother than out of concern for his daughter; he knows that most mothers will perpetuate this crippling ritual in order to ensure desirable marriages for their daughters. Pleasure Mouse undergoes the binding, and as the bones in her feet are breaking, she experiences a visionary moment of aging in which she chooses to submit to a life dominated by ritual rather than find eternal bliss in death.

Pleyel. *Wieland; or The Transformation: An American Tale.* Charles Brockden Brown. 1798.

Pleyel occupies the position of brother-in-law, confidant, and intellectual sparring partner for THEODORE WIELAND, the novel's title character. As narrated by Theodore's sister CLARA (WIELAND), the novel treats a series of weird and fantastic happenings that irrevocably alter the lives of the Wieland and Pleyel families.

When the novel begins, Pleyel has just returned from Europe, where he has ascertained the existence of a large tract of land that by legal rights established by primogeniture should fall into Wieland's possession. When Pleyel informs his friend of his rightful ownership, he is rebuffed, for Wieland prefers his successful life in America where he already owns and occupies a fine estate bequeathed to him by his father.

Wieland's love for his house is shared by Pleyel, who lives nearby and spends a large portion of his time with Wieland in intellectual conversation while strolling the grounds of the estate. Pleyel and his friend spend hours conversing about classical literature, and they pass much of their time near a temple built by Wieland Sr. for his devotions. Wieland Sr. had seen a mysterious apparition and died of spontaneous combustion. This event is rapidly brought to mind as each of the characters in the novel experiences the sensation of hearing familiar voices while knowing that the individual speaking is not present. These events begin shortly after the arrival of FRANCIS CARWIN, an odd-looking and weirdly dressed individual. As it turns out, Pleyel made his acquaintance while traveling in Spain, and he is more than a little surprised to find Carwin in America.

After Carwin's appearance, Pleyel and the Wielands include him in their social events, and he becomes a regular guest of both Theodore and Clara Wieland. Having been informed, partly through one of the unusual voices, that the woman he loved, Theresa, Baroness de Stolberg, died in Europe, Pleyel falls in love with Clara. En route to declare his love for Clara, Pleyel overhears a "profligate" conversation between Clara and Carwin. Although he will tell only Wieland of the topic of conversation, he rejects Clara when they meet. Clara objects strenuously to his accusations, to no avail. Pleyel tells her that Carwin is an escaped murderer, which he has recently learned, and her life is imperiled by her relationship with him. At this juncture Pleyel decides to leave for Europe to escape the scenes of his amorous sufferings.

However, Wieland himself is exposed as a murderer, for in a moment of madness he kills his wife and children. After the incident, Pleyel returns to find Clara seriously ill and watches over her diligently, despite the revelation that Baroness de Stolberg is not dead and has come to America to marry him. It is eventually revealed that Carwin's ventriloquism contributed to Wieland's madness, and Wieland commits suicide. Pleyel, now married to the baroness, relocates to Boston, where his wife dies during childbirth. As the novel ends, Pleyel joins Clara in Europe, and the two are finally married.

Plummer, Zeddy. *Home to Harlem.* Claude McKay. 1973.

Zeddy Plummer, a dockworker, spends his time chasing women in Harlem's underworld. Zeddy tries to emulate the carefree ways of his friend JACOB BROWN but finds he must work harder to have as much success in romance.

After a long separation, Zeddy and Jake meet in a saloon called Uncle Doc's. Jake has just returned from Europe where he was in the army. Zeddy and Jake begin frequenting clubs together. Zeddy is particularly fond of a cabaret called The Congo because he is interested in the voluptuous singer Congo Rose. When Zeddy goes there with his friend, Congo Rose immediately begins flirting with Jake and asks him to be her "man." Although Jake moves in with Congo Rose, Zeddy seems to experience no jealousy and even helps him find a job. They work together for a few days until Jake finds out that it is a scabbing job. Jake quits after a heated argument in which Zeddy insists that blacks must do what they can to survive.

Although they no longer work together, Zeddy and Jake continue to go to saloons, parties, and cabarets. At Billy Biasse's apartment, where they often go to gamble, Zeddy has a fight with Nije Gridley, a moneylender to whom he owes a large sum. Zeddy narrowly escapes with his life. After this incident, Zeddy and Jake go more frequently to an apartment outside Harlem, on Myrtle Avenue in Brooklyn. There, a woman known as Gin-head Susy throws a nightly party and serves an unlimited quantity of gin. Both Susy and her ever-present friend Lavinia Curdy are aging and ugly, but the parties keep handsome men around.

Zeddy, who has become jealous of Jake for keeping a steady lover, moves in with Gin-head Susy. At first he finds it pleasant, since Susy feeds him and he does not have to work, but conflicts develop when Susy forbids Zeddy to go to Harlem. Zeddy misses his freedom and leaves one night against Susy's will. She later finds him at The Congo with a young woman. Zeddy returns to Susy's apartment at the end of the night and pleads with her to let him in. But she does not; he eventually picks up the suitcase that she has left sitting outside and returns to Harlem.

Zeddy continues to wander and even loses touch with

Jake, who leaves Congo Rose and gets a job on the railroad. For a while Zeddy attempts to overcome his passion for gambling and sets up a household with "a steady home-loving woman" in Yonkers. He eventually returns to Harlem, however. One night he takes an especially lovely woman, Felice, to a new cabaret, and she disappears while he is in the men's room. When he sees her again weeks later, she has already moved in with his friend Jake. Zeddy threatens him with a razor, but when Jake pulls a gun, both retreat. Just before Jake and Felice move to Chicago, Zeddy goes to their apartment and apologizes. Jake was always a good friend, Zeddy tells him, and he can stay in Harlem as long as he wants.

Pnin, Timofrey Pavlovich. *Pnin*. Vladimir Nabakov. 1953.

Timofrey Pnin, a professor of Russian literature at Waindell, a distinguished New England college, in the 1950s, has emigrated from Russia to escape persecution as a Jew. He has left behind his parents and his sweetheart, Mira Belochkin. The fate of his parents is unclear, but Mira's mother died in a German concentration camp in World War II, a memory Pnin has been fleeing from ever since. Pnin misses Russia and the people he knew there quite deeply, although he is too private an individual to say so. He has created an environment of stability for himself at Waindell, and although he has few friends, he is an object of curiosity, mirth, admiration, and many other reactions on the part of other faculty members and students.

Because of his finicky specifications for apartment living, Pnin moves frequently. At the time of the novel he moves into the home of a faculty couple named Clements, and although he finds his room drafty, he has made friends with the couple in a polite, academic fashion and decides to stay on. Pnin spends most of his time in this room, in the library, and in the classroom—the three main components of his life. He brings many books home from the library and reads them, sometimes sunning himself beneath an ultraviolet light in order to maintain his year-round tan.

Pnin enjoys his classes and particularly likes a graduate student named Betty Bliss, whom he finds unintelligent but exceedingly attractive. He would pursue Betty but for the memory of Mira and an equally powerful memory of his former wife, Liza Bogolepov, who has since become Liza Wind. Pnin recalls Liza with some bitterness because she married him in 1940 and stayed long enough for him to secure tickets for a ship to North America. Once on the ship, Liza revealed that she had made a commitment to Dr. Eric Wind, who was also on board. Not long after landing, Liza had a child named Victor that she assured Pnin was Eric's.

Victor, now a teenager, visits Pnin, and the two get along very well. Liza reveals that Victor is really Pnin's

son, and because she is leaving Eric, she demands support money from the professor. At the same time Pnin learns that he is being fired just as he is up for tenure. Enemies at the school want him replaced by another Russian expert.

The replacement professor, Vladimir Vladimovich, is an old rival whom Pnin has known and despised Vladimir most of his life. As it happens, Vladimir turns out to be the novel's narrator. Pnin leaves the school and the region in such a huff that he refuses to acknowledge his old acquaintance, choosing instead to drive off in a little station wagon filled with his belongings. As Vladimir frantically waves to him, for auld lang or because he just wants to gloat, Pnin drives by without looking and once again escapes his past.

Podkovnik, Yekl "Jake." *Yekl*. Abraham Cahan. 1896.

As Yekl Podkovnik declares, "One must not be a greenhorn in America." Coarse and selfish, the half-acculturated Yekl, who now calls himself Jake, attempts to discard Old World ties to achieve Americanization. Instead of bringing him certainty, however, his quest leads to an uncertain future that he faces with feelings of guilt and loss.

Jake, now in America three years, works as a sewing machine operator in a sweatshop on New York's Lower East Side. He is a strapping young man who parades his broken English with pride and boasts of his mastery of American culture. His crude physicality contrasts with the more refined character of his male coworkers. When Jake extols the abilities of American boxers, Bernstein, a studious coworker, derides his interest in such brutal sports and asks why he doesn't look for more "educated models." The women, on the other hand, are more susceptible to his charms, especially Fanny, a "finisher" in the shop, who has a crush on Jake.

Upset by an argument with his shopmates, Jake becomes morose. His low spirits provoke him to reminisce about his previous life in Povodye, Russia, and the wife and child he left there. He resolves to bring them to America and avoid Joe Peltner's dancing academy, where he has been spending his free time. That evening, despite his firm, newfound determination, Jake again gravitates to Joe's. He is a prized dance partner, and soon he is snared by the pert, dark-eyed Mamie, Fannie's rival for Jake's affections. Jake ends up leaving the dance hall with Mamie on one arm and Fannie on the other, and his wife and child are forgotten.

News that his father has died revives Jake's concern for his family. Overcome with guilt and nostalgia, he finally buys the tickets for their passage. The moment of reunion arrives: Jake's heart sinks at the sight of his wife Gitl and son Yossele. Bewigged, dressed in attire of "grotesque cut," Gitl reeks of steerage and the Old World. Her first word is "Yekl," the Yiddish nickname Jake has tried desperately to abandon. Gitl is stunned as well—by his beardlessness and modern dress. The gap between them is great and seemingly insurmountable.

At first they try to adjust. Jake attempts to teach "Goitie," as he now calls Gitl, to divest herself of her old habits. Their gossipy neighbor, Mrs. Kavarsky, lends her assistance, pressing upon Gitl a hat, to replace her Orthodox wig, and even a corset. Jake's coworker Bernstein, who now boards with them, encourages Gitl. Just as Jake and Gitl begin to reach some kind of understanding and mutual respect, Mamie bursts in, demanding repayment of money she lent Jake. Although she cannot understand the English conversation, Gitl senses something is wrong. Her fears are confirmed a short time later when a jealous Fanny informs Gitl that she witnessed Mamie and Jake kissing.

Mrs. Kavarsky makes Gitl into "a brand-new wife" with a new hairdo and wardrobe, but Jake is horrified; Gitl's Americanized appearance revolts him. It seems somehow improper. The confrontation disintegrates completely, with Jake calling Gitl a "scabby greenhorn." He considers himself "an American feller, a Yankee." Jake finally stomps out and goes to Mamie to declare his love for her. She offers to finance his divorce and arranges for him to stay with a relative in Philadelphia, telling him that the ticket "is as good as a marriage certificate."

Jake and Gitl meet several months later at the divorce proceedings. Gitl appears different; the "greenhorn" look is completely gone from her. After the divorce, Gitl is at first despondent, but she brightens at the prospect of her new future. She and Bernstein will open a grocery store with the settlement—funded, of course, by Mamie. As he and Mamie ride to City Hall to get married, Jake knows that he should feel elated and free; yet he cannot rid himself of the sinking feeling that he is more a victim than a victor, and each lurch of the streetcar is accompanied by a corresponding sensation in his heart.

Pontellier, Edna. *The Awakening.* Kate Chopin. 1899.

Edna Pontellier lives a sheltered life with her successful businessman husband and two young sons in the Louisiana of the 1890s. An introverted, attractive young woman, she has spent the first six years of her marriage supervising her home, caring for the children, and paying regular visits to other fashionable families in New Orleans. Though a fairly talented painter, Edna has always seen art as mainly a diversion from her wifely duties. But during a summer visit to a Creole island near New Orleans, her latent artistic impulses and erotic desires become more insistent.

Edna has always been quietly critical of her routine life as a housewife, but on Grand Isle she finally finds companions who want to hear her opinions on topics other than child-rearing and homemaking. There, Madame Ratignolle, a beautiful staple of New Orleans society, and Robert Lebrun, a charming bachelor, enjoy chatting with Edna during long walks around the beach. With the husbands usually gone during the week, they also spend many evenings playing cards, dancing, or listening to recitations by the children. Occasionally Mademoiselle Reisz, a temperamental pianist who senses Edna's passionate response to music, deigns to play for them. And one night Robert tries to teach Edna how to swim. She finds swimming easier than expected, and floating farther and farther from the shore, for a time enjoys the solitude that she rarely has in domestic life. But then the stretch of water behind her begins to frighten her, and she has a vision of death in the moonlit gulf.

Edna grows increasingly fond of Robert. One day they ferry to another island and spend the day together. They attend a Mass, and during the ceremony, she takes ill. Robert brings her to an inn where she rests until evening. The two then share an outdoor dinner and don't return to Grand Isle until nightfall. Soon after, Robert unexpectedly leaves for Mexico with the excuse of business prospects, and Edna realizes that she is deeply in love with him.

The Pontelliers return to New Orleans at the end of the summer, but Edna finds she cannot settle into her old habits. She has always received callers at her home every Tuesday, but she soon abandons this tradition for long solitary walks. To her husband's consternation, her supervision of the household becomes increasingly lax, and she shows less reserve about airing her unconventional views. Once, for example, she tells her husband that she won't attend a wedding because it "one of the most lamentable spectacles on earth."

Although she avoids most social obligations, Edna continues to keep up with Madame Ratignolle and Mademoiselle Reisz. Mademoiselle Reisz regularly receives letters from Robert, who admits that he left Grand Isle because he loved Edna and didn't want to compromise a married woman. Edna swoons when she reads of Robert's feelings, because she senses that for the first time a man is returning her sentiments with equal fervor.

While she awaits Robert's return to New Orleans, Edna takes painting lessons and soon manages to sell some of her work. Her husband spends less and less time at home and thinks it a good idea to have the children stay with their grandmother in the country. Edna feels a continual need for exciting distraction. She starts to frequent the racetrack and there meets and becomes physically attracted to Alcee Arobin, a superficial but charming man. When Mr. Pontellier goes on an extended business trip, Edna pools her inheritance and painting earnings to buy a small cottage. She moves all her belongings to the cottage and fixes it up by herself. She sometimes risks scandal by allowing men like Arobin to visit her there for tea. One day she meets Robert unexpectedly at the apartment of Mademoiselle Reisz. She is upset that he did not come see her directly upon his return. Later the same day he arrives at her cottage, and they confess their love to each other. But just as they finally kiss, a messenger arrives with news that Madame Ratignolle is giving birth. Edna must spend the night at the Ratignolles'. When she returns to the cottage, Robert has left a note saying that he'll never be able to reconcile his love with his unwillingness to violate her wedding vows.

Edna leaves for Grand Isle the next day. She has a pleasant conversation with the locals, arranges for a room, and tells everyone that she would like to take a swim before dinner. At the water's edge she takes off her bathing suit and walks naked into the surf. Enjoying the sun bearing down on her, she compares this sense of freedom to the burdens of her family life and her unconsummated love for Robert, and, overcome by emotion and weariness, she slowly disappears into the surf.

Porgy. *Porgy.* DuBose Heyward. 1925.

Porgy is a withdrawn and somewhat mysterious disabled black man who earns his bread as a beggar in the streets of Charleston, South Carolina, during the early 1900s. Porgy is a familiar sight in the Catfish Row section of Charleston; the townspeople like him and take his presence for granted, but none feel they know him well. All agree that Porgy seems to be waiting for something—living for some distant future. That future begins when news of a murder rocks the quiet section of Catfish Row and sets in motion a series of events that change Porgy's life forever.

A friendly game of crap shooting in Catfish Row is broken up when a huge stevedore named Crown murders another player. Although Porgy and several other men are witnesses to the crime, only old Peter, the wagoner, admits it to the police. Peter is taken away and jailed as a material witness. His absence forces Porgy into a more adventuresome existence.

Prior to the murder, Peter regularly picked up Porgy each morning and deposited him at the corner of King Charles Street and Meeting House Road in Charleston's financial district, where the crippled beggar would remain until the wagoner returned for him each evening. With Peter being held in prison, Porgy finds that he cannot pursue his livelihood. Out of necessity he secures a goat and fashions a cart from a packing case. Delighted with his newfound independence, Porgy drives his cart all over Charleston and realizes that he can now ply his trade wherever he desires.

Shortly after Porgy gets his cart, Bess, a heroin addict who is known to all the Row as Crown's woman, appears in the quarter. Although the other residents of the Row view her with suspicion, Porgy takes pity on Bess and offers her shelter. Soon she moves in with Porgy, and they establish a regular household together. The arrival of Bess creates a change in Porgy. His defensive exterior disappears, and instead of chasing the street children away as in earlier times, he now gives them candy. Porgy's family

is complete when he and Bess are left in charge of a baby who has been orphaned by a hurricane.

But the idyllic interlude does not last. While attending the community picnic on Kittiwar Island, Bess encounters Crown, who has been hiding on the island since the murder. Bess is unable to resist her old lover, and when Crown learns of her relations with Porgy, he tells her she may stay with the cripple only until cotton harvesting season arrives. Then, Crown says, he will come for her and take her away forever.

But when the harvesting season comes and Crown's arrival is imminent, Bess voices her desire to remain with Porgy and the baby, and Porgy promises to protect her. Several days later Crown's body is found near the black quarter. It is apparent that Porgy has killed Crown. He is helped by a close friend, Maria, to move the body, but the police can find neither evidence nor witnesses. Both the murderer and the identity of the corpse remain a mystery to the authorities. When Porgy admits that he would be able to recognize Crown, the coroner charges him to appear at the inquest to identify the body. The superstitious beggar remains stoic about the entire affair until a buzzard lands on the roof over his apartment, and Porgy believes this is a sign. He fears he has been cursed by the spirit of Crown, and his courage deserts him.

Now terrified of viewing the body of his victim, Porgy flees down the streets of Charleston in his goat cart. As pedestrians point and laugh and workmen cheer and shout, the legless beggar is finally caught by the police, who take him to the station house on the charge of contempt of court. He is not forced to identify Crown but is sentenced to five days in jail for fleeing. Upon his return to Catfish Row, Porgy finds his baby in the arms of another woman and Bess gone. After pining for Porgy, Bess gets drunk with a group of men and goes downriver to Savannah. As the novel ends, a neighbor observes to herself that Porgy has suddenly become an old man.

Porgy, Captain. *Woodcraft.* William Gilmore Simms. 1854.

Captain Porgy is an American Revolutionary commander of partisans whose fortunes become entangled in an elaborate plot by a member of the retreating British camp to transport stolen American slaves to England. Eloquent, corpulent, and fond of the finer things in life, Porgy is one of many southern plantation owners who returned from the war to discover that they had been rendered destitute by the plundering British troops. The spirit and determination with which he faces subsequent adversities reveal his true character as a southern gentleman.

While en route home from the war, Porgy and his band of partisans rescue a widow and her son from a group of men who are attempting to retrieve papers that incriminate the British plotters. One of the British agents escapes with the papers. Porgy and the widow then return to their neighboring plantation homes, where Porgy learns that the holder of the overvalued mortgage on his property is a man named M'Kewn, who is the leader of the British plot. Porgy therefore will owe him an impossibly large sum of money as soon as he wishes to collect. Porgy's plantation has been effectively gutted by the British, but his survival depends on his earning enough money to pay this debt. To this end, he and his band of partisans attempt to restore the plantation with the use of farm implements and supplies borrowed from the grateful widow.

Meanwhile, the members of the British slave-stealing conspiracy have a falling out, and the man who has escaped with the incriminating papers decides to use them to extort money from the ringleader. After the passage of several months that are consumed by the preparation of the legal case to collect Porgy's debt, the leader of the slave plot meets with his escaped subordinate to exchange the incriminating papers for a large sum of money.

By this time judgment has been rendered against Captain Porgy, and he and his band of partisans fend off the sheriff who has come to confiscate his assets. Porgy and his friends are apprised of the meeting that is currently taking place by the conspirators, and they and the sheriff arrive there just in time to confiscate the papers. The plot's leader, who knows he will be hanged for his theft of the slaves, takes his own life; Captain Porgy's debt therefore becomes null and void since the mortgage on his plantation was fraudulent. After an unsuccessful marriage proposal to the widow he rescued, Captain Porgy returns to his prosperous plantation to resume his prewar existence as a moneyed gentleman.

Porter, Jane. *Tarzan of the Apes.* Edgar Rice Burroughs. 1912.

Jane Porter is a classic damsel in distress. Beautiful and helpless, she must be rescued time and again by the noble TARZAN, who becomes her savage protector and true love.

Raised in Baltimore by her father, a doting yet nearly infantile professor, Jane sets sail on a treasure hunt on which her father has foolishly staked his career and a wealth of borrowed capital. When her father's clues unexpectedly lead to a real treasure, the Porters are cast aside by greedy mutineers. Left to die on an African coast, their small party includes Jane, Professor Porter, his secretary, and the handsome young William Clayton, who is both an eligible bachelor and an English lord. They are rescued from the various hideous deaths that the equatorial jungle holds in store for them by Tarzan, a white man raised by apes.

Jane receives a love letter from Tarzan, and soon afterward he rescues her from the clutches of a fierce ape. As she is swung through the jungle canopy in his arms, she is strangely moved by his primitivism. They kiss, and she discovers she is in love with him.

When the French navy comes to the rescue, Jane and her companions head back to America, leaving behind the heartbroken Tarzan and the treasure, which Tarzan has recovered from the mutineers and hidden away. Jane, in the cool light of reason provided by a temperate climate, is left with only a haunting memory of her jungle desire. Back in the United States, she is forced into an engagement with her father's creditor. Clayton loves her, and she feels bound to honor her father's wishes.

Tarzan, meanwhile, is making the transition from barbarism to civilization under the tutelage of a French lieutenant. As always, Tarzan arrives at an opportune moment and rescues Jane from a forest fire in Wisconsin, and by producing the treasure, he saves her from a loveless marriage. As she is carried through the Wisconsin treetops, Jane feels an echo of her old love for him, but she is disappointed that he no longer has the primitive savagery that attracted her in Africa. The differences between the adoring Clayton and the adoring Tarzan are now very few, and Jane agrees to marry Clayton, the young Lord Greystoke.

What Jane does not know is that Tarzan, although raised by apes, is the son of castaways less fortunate than the Porters: the long deceased John and Alice Clayton, Lord and Lady Greystoke. He is thus the cousin of William Clayton and the rightful Lord Greystoke. On the last page of *Tarzan of the Apes*, Tarzan chooses not to reveal his paternity, and Jane is left engaged to Clayton, although she is already regretting her betrothal.

Portnoy, Alexander. *Portnoy's Complaint.* Philip Roth. 1967.

Alexander Portnoy is a successful lawyer who finds himself imprisoned in the memories and under the influence of his childhood as a Jewish male growing up in New Jersey. As he tells his story to his therapist, Dr. Speilvogel, he finds that he can never elude the feelings of guilt and shame that have shaped his life.

Alexander's earliest memories involve his mother's "ubiquity" and his father's perennial constipation. Close to his mother, young Alexander is awed by her competence and her watchfulness, including her constant concern for Alexander's behavior and cleanliness. Alex's father, who works for a large insurance company, strikes Alex as being frustrated and self-annihilating. Schooled in perfection by his mother, he vainly wishes that he could have his father's coarseness and yet remain unashamed.

Alex's youth is filled with ritual cycles of transgression and forgiveness. When Alex misbehaves, he finds himself locked out of the house; after voicing his hatred, he invariably drops to his knees and begs forgiveness before being allowed back into the fold. Alex's most pressing moral crisis, however, involves masturbation, which he practices with vigor and variety. Competing with his constipated father for time on the toilet, young Alex finds himself unable to cease masturbating despite his fear of discovery. He cannot fathom why he continues to misbehave when his family has sacrificed so much for him; and he is at times nearly overwhelmed with shame.

When he is fourteen, Alex, who has chafed against the restrictions placed on him by his Jewish religion, announces to his father that he does not believe in God. For Alex this is not simply a question of "adolescent resentment and Oedipal rage" but rather of "integrity." Alex wants the control he feels when playing center field in softball games, when all he has to do is say "It's mine" and things take place as he determines.

As an adult, Alex becomes a lawyer and then Commissioner of Human Opportunity for the City of New York. In spite of his success, he still finds himself confused over his childhood, his sexual fanaticism, and his Jewishness. He also finds himself resistant to the idea of marriage, despite his occasional yearnings for the simple home life he so often dismisses as repressive. For example, when Alex befriends MARY JANE REED, an unintelligent ex-model nicknamed "the Monkey," he attempts to pull her out of the "perversity and wildness and lust" which he has never been able to enjoy without the accompanying burden of shame. Alex realizes that the Monkey is "uneducable," but he cannot cease his sexual fascination with her.

On a trip to Europe with the Monkey, things start to unravel for Alex. When he and the Monkey engage in sex with a Roman prostitute, a dispute arises over who initiated the perversity. In Athens the Monkey, herself tired of the wild life, threatens to jump off the hotel balcony if Alex refuses to marry her. Alex leaves and takes a flight to Israel, dreaming of a simple life as a husband and father in a quiet Jewish neighborhood back in his native New Jersey.

In Israel, Alex is concerned that he may have contracted a venereal disease from the Roman prostitute. He wonders if the Monkey killed herself. He decides to educate himself, and during his travels he encounters Naomi, a socialist who lectures him on the corrupt structure of the American system. Alex finds himself longing for a hearty life with her in the mountains and so asks her if she will bear his children. When she is taken aback, he proposes oral sex instead. Naomi criticizes Alex's "ironical" and self-deprecating nature, and after a struggle, she kicks him and tells him he should go home.

Posey, George. *The Fathers.* Allen Tate. 1938.

George Posey is a proud, extremely capable Southern gentleman who lives his life in constant motion. Characteristically impatient with the status quo, George masterfully manipulates the people and situations that surround him, while displaying a generous nature that veils his assertiveness. Motivated at all times by his desire to uphold absolutely the standards of Southern chivalry,

he eventually becomes implicated in the violence that invaes his home and his state when the Civil War begins.

Having fallen in love with Susan, the younger sister of his friends Semmes and LACY BUCHAN, George intends to announce his engagement by entering a jousting tournament designed to demonstrate the chivalrous manhood of the gentlemen of northern Virginia. Donning a mask to disguise his identity and heighten the effect of his performance, George dazzles the crowd with his impeccable display of strength and horsemanship as he lifts a series of rings from a scaffold that has been erected in the center of the field. Having dethroned John Langton, who customarily wins the contest, George is awarded the championship—an honor that entitles him to crown the woman of his choice with a wreath of laurel, designating her the Queen of Love and Beauty. George breaks with tradition and chooses a bold comic gesture instead: He drops the crown on Susan's lap.

Meanwhile, John Langton has become so incensed over George's victory that he challenges him to a duel. George accepts. But at the start of their face-off, George marks a spot on his hat that is placed on the ground at a distance. He then expertly shoots the smudge, thus displaying his extremely impressive marksmanship before punching Langton in the nose with such force that the wounded man loses consciousness. Having proven his manliness and dispensed with the threat of the duel, George returns to Susan and her family and announces his intention to marry her.

Following their marriage, George and Susan move into his home, which is filled with eccentric relatives, and eventually they have a daughter. Due to his competent business sense, George assumes control of the Buchans' plantation, thus saving the family from bankruptcy. When the Civil War breaks out, George leaves his wife and daughter with his relatives and throws himself into the war effort. Although he favors the Union over the Confederacy, George feels compelled by his loyalty to Virginia to support the cotton states, which he does by purchasing and smuggling supplies and weapons for the local army. Moreover, he temporarily buries his personal biases by advising the members of the Seventeenth Regiment of Virginia Infantry to accept John Langton as their captain. In his absence, his younger sister Jane becomes engaged to his friend Semmes, but the marriage never takes place because Jane is assaulted by her black half-brother Yellow Jim and is so traumatized that she enters a convent.

George returns home to confront the repercussions of the tragic incident, and when Semmes kills Yellow Jim for ruining his marriage plans, George in turn avenges his black half-brother's death by murdering Semmes. This string of violence continues when George joins the army as a private under the command of Captain Langton, who immediately insults him. Responding irrationally to this transgression, George shoots Langton in the face. He is ordered to surrender his weapon and leave the brigade, and he departs with the intention of going to Georgetown where he hopes to escape the havoc that has been caused by his violence.

Potter, Israel. *Israel Potter: His Fifty Years of Exile.* Herman Melville. 1854.

Israel Potter, a humble, earnest youth, leaves his home in the Berkshire Mountains of Massachusetts to fight in the Revolutionary War. Instead of bringing him glory and fame, his valiant efforts to serve his country result in exile, poverty, and misfortune.

Israel embarks on his first voyage as a sailor at the age of eighteen. When he returns and discovers that his betrothed married another man in his absence, he enlists in the fight against the British. After being wounded at Bunker Hill, Israel volunteers aboard a brigantine engaged in cutting off aid to the British in Boston Harbor; the vessel is captured by enemy ships, and he soon finds himself en route to England.

Israel's imprisonment marks the first in a series of harrowing misadventures. He manages to escape after the ship has landed and makes his way to London, where he obtains employment as a grounds worker, first for a sympathetic nobleman and then for King George III. Israel is forced to go into hiding when his status as an escaped prisoner is discovered, and it is only through the efforts of sympathetic friends and strangers that he is able to elude capture. Just as he is contemplating turning himself in, he is approached by Squire John Woodcock, a powerful British nobleman and a secret supporter of the American struggle for independence, and entrusted with the perilous task of carrying a message to Dr. Benjamin Franklin in Paris.

Outfitted with a pair of hollow-heeled boots, Israel crosses the English Channel. He narrowly escapes having the boots stolen before reaching the home of Dr. Franklin, with whom he lodges for a time. During Israel's stay, he and Franklin are visited by the arrogant and fiery Captain John Paul Jones, who is waiting to commission a ship to fight the British at sea.

Back at Squire John's, Israel must conceal himself in a tiny windowless room no bigger than a coffin and is left there alone when Squire John unexpectedly dies. Clambering out of his hiding place, he makes another narrow escape by pretending to be Squire John's ghost. He is eventually apprehended by soldiers and impressed once again into service in the British navy.

Israel is not long on a British ship before it is captured by an American ship, commanded by none other than John Paul Jones. There follows a brief period of happiness as he becomes Paul's loyal follower and friend, and sails the Atlantic, seeking and attacking British ships. But Israel's apprenticeship to Paul is abruptly terminated when, in the midst of a battle, he follows orders to board the enemy ship. The ship pulls away and escapes with Israel stranded on board.

On the British ship, Israel manages to avoid ill treatment by pretending to be insane; when the ship finally docks at Falmouth, he takes advantage of a commotion in the town to elude the other members of the crew and makes his way to London. There he earns a subsistence wage, first as a bricklayer and then as a chair-bottomer. After the war ends, he tries to save money for a passage back to the United States but ends up spending his savings on his wedding—to a young woman who nurses him back to health after he is run over by a cart.

Fifty years later, in 1826, Israel, now slightly senile, returns to the United States with his son, the only one of his eleven children to have survived. He goes to the Berkshire Mountains but finds no trace of either his family or his former home. He dictates "a little book, a record of his fortunes," before dying penniless and obscure "on the same day that the oldest oak on his native hills was blown down."

Powers, Cleotha. "The Peach Stone." Paul Horgan. 1942.

Cleotha Powers, wife and mother, drives with her husband Jodey, her nine-year-old son Buddy, and Arlene Latcher, a schoolteacher, to the town of Weed, New Mexico. The four-hour trip is a solemn one. Weed is Cleotha's hometown, but she is not returning there for a happy reunion; instead, Cleotha, her family, and Arlene Latcher are traveling with a small wooden coffin that contains the corpse of Cleotha's two-year-old daughter who died the day before. The little girl perished in a fire when sparks from their chimney landed on dry tumbleweeds that had collected in their yard. Jodey had repeatedly promised Cleotha that he would clear out the tumbleweeds, but he failed to do so in time. Now, after this family tragedy, Cleotha and the others are deeply absorbed in their own thoughts and make most of the trip to Weed in total silence.

The previous night Cleotha had stopped weeping, and on this day something happens inside her. Overwhelmed by the depth of her grief, she finds a new resource within herself and for the first time in her life looks at the familiar sights on the road as if she were really seeing and not simply looking. Jodey, trying to think of something to say to her, drives on; Buddy, feeling the separateness of the three of them, silently wishes Cleotha would turn her face toward him. Cleotha is afraid to speak or look at them. As the car passes a peach orchard, she pictures the orchard from her childhood in Weed and remembers the old saying that if you held a peach stone in your hand long enough, it would sprout. Cleotha had believed this as a child. Looking at the orchard today, she rejoices in the sight of living, growing nature.

Cleotha knows that Buddy wants her to look at him,

but she is afraid to, lest she lose her serenity and be overcome again by grief. Content with glimpsing his look from the corner of her eye, she continues to watch the roadway. When they pass the home of old man Melendez, a well-known eccentric, Cleotha sees him sitting on a weathered bench beside his mongrel dog. She feels a new joy as she takes in the details of the old man from whom she had always turned her gaze in the past out of a sense of delicacy and disgust. Ahead, she sees a ball of blinding light, like a huge diamond, dancing in the middle of the road. She closes her eyes; when she opens them again, the road curves, and the light turns into the tin signs on the back of a huge oil truck.

A few minutes outside of Weed, the car passes more familiar sights, and Cleotha's heart begins to hurt again. Buddy whispers "Mumma?" to her; no longer able to look out the window, she winks both eyes at him. The sight of this simple affection between a mother and son makes Miss Latcher—a proper, clean-cut woman who secretly envies Cleotha and her family their suffering—begin to cry. Jodey scolds Miss Latcher, but Cleotha gently comforts her.

At the graveside, surrounded by the people of Weed, Cleotha has a sense of being in total communion with life. At the crest of the hill, a boy stops, looks down at the graveside gathering, and seems to wonder what the group is doing. Eager to know, he comes closer with respectful curiosity; then he walks away down the hill. This is the most beautiful, memorable sight Cleotha sees on this day. With renewed ability to rejoice in life and to "believe," as if holding a peach stone in her palm, Cleotha puts her face in her hands and weeps. The group moves closer to her, and Jodey feels his wife has returned to them at last.

Presley. *The Octopus.* Frank Norris. 1901.

As resident poet and artistic conscience of the ranch communities, Presley serves at times as the closest thing *The Octopus* has to a controlling consciousness. As the ranchers battle the constricting presence of the railroad, his introspective, brooding nature provides a meditative commentary on the fast-paced and sometimes violent action of the story.

Just over a bout of consumption, Presley has come to live on Rancho de los Muertos in order to recuperate. College educated, trained in the classics, Presley is the odd man among the ranchers, but he is by no means ostracized. His dream as the novel opens is to write the great epic of the American West, encompassing its grandeur, its beauty, and its people. But he detests the actual lives of the people, whom he finds "sordid" overall.

However, as one indignity after another is heaped upon the heads of his rancher friends, MAGNUS DERRICK, Harran Derrick, and Buck Annixter, Presley grows more and more outraged at the power that opposes them; he comes to see the railroad as "the leviathan, with tentacles of steel clutching into the soil." Encouraged by his mysterious vagabond-poet friend Vanamee, Presley composes a long, ardent poem called "The Toilers." Published in the daily newspapers, "The Toilers" causes a nationwide sensation. But Presley is frustrated; his poem has made nothing happen, has forced no one's hand.

In fact, Presley constantly finds himself a feckless power on the periphery of any action. Even when the ranchers engage in a climactic shoot-out with the hired deputies of the railroad, Presley must sit on the sidelines. Enraged by the ensuing slaughter, he delivers a vitriolic, socialistic address to a group of people gathered to hear about the problems between the ranchers and the railroad. The speech rouses people's hearts but fails to move their minds. Like his poem, Presley's political oratory has no effect.

Determined to make something happen, Presley obtains a pipe bomb from the revolutionary bartender Caraher and hurls it through the window of the railroad agent, S. BEHRMAN. But even his bomb proves ineffectual; Behrman emerges unharmed.

Turning from violence to compassion, Presley tries to help the destitute family of a farmer killed in the gunfight. Mrs. Hooven and her daughters have moved to San Francisco to find work, but unused to the ways of the city, they have ended up on the streets. Presley has good intentions, but he arrives too late to save the elder daughter from prostitution and the mother from death by exhaustion.

In the end, tired and despairing, Presley sails for India. He ponders the fact that although men had perished, the wheat, the tremendous "nourisher of nations," still "moved onward in its appointed grooves"; and he acknowledges that when the dust has settled, "all things . . . resistlessly work together for good."

Prewitt, Robert E. Lee "Prew." *From Here to Eternity.* James Jones. 1951.

Born a miner's son in Harlan County, Kentucky, Robert E. Lee Prewitt, or "Prew," left home in his early teens during a mining strike. After several hard years on the road, he enlisted in the army, and proclaiming himself a "thirty-year man," he embraced the army not only as his career but also as his home, his family, and his true love. However, Prew's background bred in him a fierce love of justice that equals his love of the army, and when these two loves collide, he is destroyed.

As the novel opens, justice and army politics have already clashed to the detriment of Prew, now thirty years old and still a low-ranking enlisted man. A talented welterweight boxer, Prew earlier refused to box for the Twenty-seventh Regiment because he had promised his mother never to hurt anyone unless absolutely necessary. Prew then transferred into the luxurious Bugle Corps, where his exceptional talent earned him the honor of playing "Taps" at Arlington Cemetery. But Prew's sense of justice is offended when a homosexual officer makes his lover First Bugler over him; as a result Prew transfers out of the Bugle Corps and renounces his beloved bugle forever.

Now stationed in a rifle corps in Hawaii, Prew is pressured by his company commander to join the company's boxing team. When Prew stubbornly resists this pressure, he is given "The Treatment," which consists of cruel and unusual labor assignments, excessive surveillance by superiors, and harsh physical punishments. Prew withstands "The Treatment" and finds occasional relief on furloughs in town, where he falls in love with a prostitute, Loren. He also derives comfort from writing "The Re-Enlistment Blues" with fellow guitar players on their off hours. When his pent-up frustrations erupt in a fight with another soldier, however, he is sentenced to three months at hard labor in the stockade.

Prew's toughness and fortitude win him the respect of the most hardened prisoners in the stockade, and sadistic Staff Sergeant Judso earns Prew's undying hatred. Shortly after his release, Prew murders Judso and hides out with Loren. Now a deserter, he feels a sense of betrayal of his revered army that tortures him to distraction, especially when he cannot join the action after the attack on Pearl Harbor. When all prisoners are released on Hawaii due to the national emergency, Prew decides to try sneaking back to his regiment. He is apprehended by a patrol, and when he makes a break to run, the patrol opens fire on him.

At this point Prew, who realizes that his love of the army and his love of justice can never be reconciled, drops his gun to his side and allows himself to be shot to death.

Pride, Lucy. *Boston Adventure*. Jean Stafford. 1944.

As the role model who inspires SONIE MARBURG's vision of a higher way of life, Lucy Pride embodies the virtues and foibles of Boston society in the 1930s. Intelligent, well educated, generous, and of an independent spirit, she is also imbued with a narrow-minded New England provincialism and the arrogance of the rich. It is only through her failure to mold Sonie into a martinet totally submissive to her will that she comes to acknowledge her need of the girl-become-woman as a friend and source of support.

Miss Pride, in her early sixties and still undiminished in energy and wit, first meets Sonie, a ten-year-old who works as a chambermaid, at a beach hotel where Miss Pride regularly summers. At first it is Sonie's father, a melancholic ne'er-do-well German shoemaker, who interests Miss Pride most because of his skills as a master craftsman. She is a reactionary critic of the machine age and its shoddy products; her idea of utopia is a republic of farmers and craftsmen governed by patricians.

For some years Miss Pride patronizes Herr Marburg's shop and takes only occasional notice of Sonie. When Sonie is fifteen, her father deserts his home, and she is left to support her mentally unstable mother and a baby brother. When the baby brother dies, she makes an appeal to Miss Pride for money to bury him. Miss Pride is intrigued by Sonie's oppressive circumstance and proposes that Sonie move in with her and attend business school and learn a secretarial trade.

Miss Pride isolates Sonie at first from the Boston society that frequents her house. Sonie submits to a harsh indoctrination of "do's" and "don'ts" and after some months makes her debut. She is a success; her reward is Miss Pride's approval. However, Miss Pride's relationship to Sonie is soon complicated by Hopestill Mather, Miss Pride's niece and former ward. Hopestill has dated Philip, a young doctor, off and on for some years, and Miss Pride is determined that they marry. But Hopestill is rebellious; she plays with Philip and runs with a wild crowd. Miss Pride is doubly irritated when Sonie falls in love with Philip, who flirts with Sonie in Hopestill's absence. At the same time Sonie is growing more sophisticated and less malleable to Miss Pride's will, and they drift further and further apart.

When Hopestill learns that she is pregnant by another man, she agrees to marry the unsuspecting Philip. When he learns the truth after the wedding, Philip goes into a rapid, drunken decline. Now rather less set on her own will, Miss Pride begins to see in Sonie a woman of spirit. She humbles herself to ask Sonie, whom she recognizes as her only true friend, to stand by her through old age.

Priest, Lucius. *The Reivers*. William Faulkner. 1962.

Lucius Priest is the eleven-year-old narrator who undergoes a wild series of adventures that help him discard his childhood innocence. Working Saturdays at his grandfather Lucius "Boss" Priest's livery stable, young Lucius becomes friends with the hulking BOON HOGGANBECK, a farmhand. When Boon steals the automobile belonging to Lucius's grandfather for a joyride to Memphis, Lucius sneaks away to accompany him.

The thieves end up at what Lucius gradually realizes is a Memphis brothel, where Boon visits his heartthrob, a prostitute named Miss Corrie. The eleven-year-old Lucius is paired off with Corrie's deviant, stunted nephew Otis on the assumption that the latter will learn a little decency from him. When Otis tells him how he spied on his aunt while she was "pugknuckling" and then sold peep shows at a nickel a viewing, Lucius defends her honor, getting cut across the fingers in the process. Touched, Corrie, whose real name Lucius now knows is Everbe, vows to renounce prostitution and take up an honorable profession.

When NED WILLIAM MCCASLIN, who was a stowaway in the car on the trip to Memphis, trades the car for a racehorse, the lightweight Lucius is drafted into service as the jockey. Everyone goes down to Parsham, Tennessee, for the race, and Ned and Lucius spend as much time as possible training the horse, Lightning. After losing the first heat, Lucius employs Ned's Ben Hur–like tactics to win the second, only to find Ned and Boon under arrest for horse stealing. While the men are held by the sheriff, the boy is housed at the home of Parsham Hood, an acquaintance of Ned's.

Finally, Lucius and Lightning (under Ned's direction) win the third heat, and they lose one more that the owners had insisted on staging. When Lucius returns home to Jefferson, Mississippi, after what has been a remarkably eventful trip for an eleven-year-old, his grandfather tells him the lesson to be learned from his adventures: "A gentleman accepts the responsibility of his actions and bears the burden of their consequences." Lucius also learns from Ned a little about the hidden gentlemanliness within the relations between some southern black men and some southern white men. And he learns that he has himself taught Boon and Everbe something about honor: They get married and name their first child after him.

The Princess. "The Lady, or the Tiger?" Frank R. Stockton. 1953.

The unnamed princess, who in this story must decide the fate of her lover, is the hot-blooded daughter of a semi-barbaric king. The king has devised a novel method of dispensing justice: The accused is placed in a public arena and given the choice between two doors. Behind one door lies a vicious, man-eating tiger, and behind the other is a maiden to whom the vindicated subject is then married, regardless of his wishes.

The princess, an imperious, beautiful young woman, is adored by her father and has inherited his exuberant and slightly barbarous nature. She has taken as her lover a courtier who, although low in station, is the handsomest and bravest youth in the realm. The ardent affair lasts for many months before the king discovers it and casts the young man in prison to await his trial in the arena. Never in the history of the kingdom had a subject dared to become the lover of a princess, and so the public anticipates the trial with great enthusiasm.

On the appointed day, the princess sits next to her father in the arena. She has thought of nothing else since her lover was arrested. Due to her power, influence, and force of character, she has managed to discover behind which doors the lady and the tiger will be. The princess also knows the identity of the lady; she is one of the most beautiful ladies of the court, who on more than one occasion has made the king's daughter jealous because of her admiration for the handsome young courtier. Since discovering the secret of the doors, the princess has tortured herself night after night with thoughts of the two possible outcomes. She is horrified by visions of her lover being torn to pieces by the tiger but feels violent jealousy

and agony at the thought of the courtier and the lady becoming man and wife.

The princess makes eye contact with her lover when he enters the arena; they are able to communicate intuitively, and he realizes that she knows the secret of the doors. With a glance he asks her which door he should open. The princess responds without hesitation, gesturing toward the door on the right, behind which awaits either the lady or the tiger. The courtier's fate remains unknown as the story concludes.

Pritchett, Muriel. *The Accidental Tourist.* Anne Tyler. 1985.

Only in her mid-twenties, Muriel Pritchett has already led a tough life, and she is quite capable of taking care of herself. A tall, very thin woman, Muriel is given to wearing thrift shop clothes, which, combined with her frizzy hairstyle, give her a bizarre appearance. She is working as a dog trainer at the Meow-Bow Animal Hospital when she meets MACON LEARY, a travel book writer, who has brought in his dog Edward. When Macon returns to pick up Edward, she gives him her card and asks him to call her "just to talk." But the recently separated Macon isn't interested.

Macon is soon in need of Muriel's services, however. He goes to live with his sister and two brothers after breaking his leg, and Edward gets increasingly cantankerous. Muriel is excited when Macon calls asking her to train Edward, and she charges him only half-price for Edward's lessons.

As Muriel trains Edward she tells Macon the story of her life. She became pregnant at seventeen and married the baby's father, Norman, but the marriage didn't last long. Their son Alexander was born with multiple allergies and was in the hospital for a long time. After Norman's mother hinted to him that Alexander might not be his baby, he left her. She has raised Alexander, now seven, by holding a variety of odd jobs. Macon is amazed at her spirit. One day after Muriel told him about the breakup of her marriage, he suddenly kisses her. He apologizes immediately, but Muriel seizes the opportunity and invites him to dinner. He accepts, but she later finds him trying to put under her door a note canceling the dinner. Hesitatingly, he tells Muriel that his son was murdered the year before, and his loss makes it impossible for Macon to go to dinner with people and their little boys. Muriel listens, then wordlessly leads Macon upstairs, where she puts him to bed.

Macon moves in with Muriel and Alexander. Muriel relaxes, and Macon sees that she does have faults: She is sometimes bad tempered, and her treatment of Alexander varies from inattention to overprotectiveness. Yet Muriel has many good qualities. Macon is drawn to her determination and zest for life. She does not criticize him, and her house is lively and warm. They are very content together.

Muriel finds a threat to their cozy existence in Sarah, Macon's estranged wife, whom she sees at the wedding of Macon's sister. The normally brash, self-assured Muriel begins to worry, and asks Macon repeatedly if he is going to leave her. Their conversations increasingly touch on the subject of marriage, from which Macon shies away. She gets angry when he tells her that he may never marry again.

Muriel's worst fears are confirmed when Macon returns from a business trip and moves back in with Sarah. Yet Muriel is a determined woman. Macon is astounded to find her on the plane as he is taking off on a business trip to Paris. She has brought along his travel guide and follows him to his hotel. Muriel is not discouraged by Macon's rebuffs, and gradually his resolve is worn down by her spirit. They eat dinner together a few times and, emboldened, Muriel asks him if she can come in one night to watch television. Macon refuses, telling her that he has been married to Sarah for a long time and can't change his life now.

For a while Macon refuses to answer when Muriel knocks on his door. Muriel does not know that he has hurt his back and is lying in his room ignoring her presence. Muriel becomes discouraged when Sarah arrives to see Macon. As she is juggling packages on her way to the airport, however, a cab stops to pick her up. Macon is in it.

Profane, Benny. *V.* Thomas Pynchon. 1961.

The son of a Jewish mother and Catholic father, Benny Profane considers himself an irrecoverable "schlemiehl." Although he is overweight and straightforward about his irresponsible attitude, women seem to "happen like accidents" to him. As soon as he leaves the navy in 1954, Profane gets a job as assistant salad man at a restaurant in New York. He meets Rachel Owlglass, who practically runs him over in the sporty MG given to her by her father. They date for the summer before Rachel returns to her senior year at Bennington College. Despite Profane's reluctance to acknowledge his feelings, he finds himself in love with her. His feelings change, however, when he accidentally observes Rachel making love overtures to her car. Profane despises inanimate objects, and this ridiculous display of materialism causes him to leave her.

While unemployed, which is most of the time, Profane spends his days "yo-yoing," or drifting aimlessly. He wanders up and down the East Coast until a fight at a 1955 New Year's Eve party changes his fate. Escaping from a massive brawl at the Sailor's Grave Bar in Norfolk, Virginia, Profane finds himself with a dependent, Paola Maijstral, who has fled with him. Paola is a teen bride from Malta who abandoned her navy husband, Pappy Hod, soon after she reached the United States. The last thing Profane wants is a dependent, so he buys two tickets to New York City, where he plans to dump Paola with Rachel Owlglass. In New York, Rachel does take Paola in and finds her a job, and Profane, who wishes to rid himself of the situation, takes to yo-yoing on subway lines.

After days of underground yo-yoing, Profane is befriended by Puerto Rican brothers, who take him into their home and set him up with a job hunting alligators in the sewers of New York. Pleased to be working with animate objects, Profane works until he is laid off, and lives with the family until their sister, Josephine Mendoza, makes a pass at him. On the streets again with no money, Profane randomly visits an employment agency where, coincidentally, Rachel Owlglass works.

Rachel allows Profane to stay at her apartment. She finds him a job as a security guard at the Anthro-Research Associates laboratory where experiments are performed on synthetic humans. Profane finds this job very unsettling because the experimental subjects, made of both animate and inanimate parts, propose an existential dilemma for him. One day Profane's alarm clock fails to sound, and he is late for work. As luck would have it, the lab malfunctions, and Profane is fired. Taking this as a sign, Profane considers accepting an offer to go to Malta with Paola and an adventurer named Herbert Stencil. Even though he knows this will hurt Rachel, who pressures him to grow up, Profane continues to act the schlemiehl.

Herbert Stencil's overriding goal is the discovery of the enigmatic "V." Obsessed with a journal entry that his father made in 1899 referring to V., Stencil has been traveling the world following leads. His latest clue involves Paola's father back in Malta, but Paola refuses to leave the country without Profane. She claims that she is in love with Profane and tries to seduce him. When he spurns her advances because he still wants no dependents, Paola points out that Profane has dependents whether or not he acknowledges them. Realizing that Paola is right to some degree, Profane decides that he would not mind a free trip to Malta. Stencil briefs him on the mysterious cabal that is V.

Once in Malta, Profane awaits his next accident of fate as he finds himself abandoned by both Stencil, who is off to Stockholm to pursue another clue, and by Paola, who reunites with her husband once again. Letting fate dictate his actions, Benny Profane ends his story by adjusting to life in Malta, looking for temporary jobs and transitional women.

Prosser, Gabriel. *Black Thunder.* Arna Bontemps. 1936.

Gabriel Prosser is a fictional version of the slave whose courageous and practical leadership of the slave uprising near Richmond, Virginia, in 1800 inspired this novel. The story begins with the death of a slave, Bundy, who on his deathbed urges his old friend Ben to join the Masons. It is soon revealed that Gabriel, under the guise of the Masons, has organized slaves from his own and surrounding plantations into a resistance movement.

Under cover of Bundy's funeral, the slaves make plans to attack the arsenal and other strongholds at Richmond. Once the revolt is under way, Ben and another old slave, Gen'l John, are to journey to other counties to spread the news. After the plans are made, the makeshift army awaits September 1.

Once the day arrives, Gabriel leads his contingent toward town, expecting to rendezvous there with several other columns of the resistance. Meanwhile, a horrible storm has blown up. Neither Ben nor Gen'l John is able to make the journey to herald the uprising. Despite the news that several groups of slaves from outlying plantations cannot proceed because of the storm, Gabriel decides to continue with his troops. They come to a raging stream, and the turbulent, high waters and his men's superstition that the storm is a bad omen force Gabriel to postpone the revolt. They decide to attempt the attack again in two days. The slaves disperse and return to their homes.

The next day Old Ben and a younger slave, Pharoah, separately betray the rebellion. Ben identifies the leaders, the plan to revolt is abandoned, and the participants flee to the hills. Many are captured and killed, but Gabriel eludes capture for several weeks. Finally, declaring to himself that a general must not be taken in an undignified manner, Gabriel surrenders on a boat dock in Norfolk. Identifying himself as the general and mastermind behind the slave revolt, Gabriel is hanged.

Protagonist. *Beach Red.* Peter Bowman. 1945.

The unnamed protagonist is one of several soldiers facing heavy combat on an island under attack on the Pacific Front close to the end of the World War II. As the novel opens, the platoon is about to disembark from their transport ship onto a beach where they will become immediate targets for Japanese soldiers who are hidden in the hills above the shore. While they near the beachhead, the men's fear mounts steadily, but they are both goaded on and calmed by Captain MacDonald, who offers them a "countdown to hell," that time when they will have to dash through the surf hoping to make it to the beach alive.

Throughout the novel, which is told in the form of a lyric poem, the action focuses on the events following their landing. The craft of the protagonist is the third to approach Beach Red, the U.S. Army's designation, and it lands while there is still action going on ahead. As he wades through the swirling surf, trying to keep his weapon dry and his feet from slipping out from under him, the young soldier must also be mindful of sniper action ahead. Although the beach and its surrounding hills have been shelled in preparation for the landing, there is no assurance that the enemy presence has been eradicated. Throughout the account mortal danger is imminent, a fact concretely

demonstrated by the bullets shooting past the soldiers as they approach the beach.

After the beachhead is established, it is the soldiers' duty to push onward to the terrain behind the beach, which is likely to be filled with enemy strongholds. Here, during the slow hours of uncertainty, the soldiers find themselves regaling one another with thoughts, feelings, and evidence of Japanese inferiority. As the novel continues, the focus narrows to the protagonist and three other soldiers, who are sent ahead of the rest of the troops to scout the area, to determine Japanese strength and positioning before further U.S. advances can be made. Along the way, a short stretch of several hundred yards, danger lurks with every step. The soldiers witness artful deceptions that hide the presence of snipers, and they note traps and hidden dangers left by their enemy. As they begin to realize that a strong enemy presence is in the area, disaster befalls their group.

First, in an effort to ambush an unwitting Japanese sentry, Sergeant Lindstrom is bayoneted in the stomach. Although he is not in immediate danger of dying, he must be removed from further harm or capture, so Private Whitney assists Lindstrom back for medical attention. In the meantime, the protagonist, in radio contact with the captain, receives orders that he is to lead Private Egan onward to continue their probe. He does this although gripped by mortal fear and doubt. As they continue deeper into the jungle, they eventually come upon an enemy stronghold, and despite their best efforts, they are attacked when in a very vulnerable position. Egan is shot, and the protagonist is forced to hide behind Egan's body to protect himself. He tries to radio back, to warn the others, but his contact was broken just after he told the captain of the large numbers of Japanese soldiers they found. Ultimately, the protagonist, too, is shot, and as his mind spirals backward to the girl he left behind, he slowly dies. The novel ends with his body being discovered by another soldier who tells the captain that the only thing moving now is the hand on the protagonist's watch.

Protagonist. "The Grey Champion." Nathaniel Hawthorne. 1837.

The Grey Champion is a venerable patriarch who defends the American people against British tyranny. He appears in the streets of Boston one afternoon in April 1689. The governor of the colony, Sir Edmund Andros, has amassed his councillors and the Governor's Guard and begun a march through the city; the townspeople have assembled in King-Street and are preparing themselves for a possibly violent confrontation with the troops of the Crown. As the soldiers draw near, an ancient man steps into the middle of the street between the two factions.

The old man has a long gray beard and wears the dress that was the fashion among the Puritans at least fifty years previously. He carries a heavy sword and walks at first with the help of a staff. The man proceeds down the street toward the troops, turning at one point to the crowd of colonials with a gesture of both encouragement and warning. He walks with such dignity and authority that the townspeople excitedly speculate on his identity and wonder why they do not recognize him. As he draws closer to the soldiers, he appears to gain strength and begins to march with the step of a younger man.

When he is twenty yards from the governor's troops, the Gray Champion pauses, holds his staff in front of him, and orders the soldiers to stand. The old man's commanding presence causes the Guard to stop short; the governor and his councillors ride forward to discover the reason for the halt and, still mounted on their horses, surround the gray-bearded figure. He stands thoroughly unintimidated and unmoved as the governor's men alternately threaten and laughingly insult him. Sir Edmund Andros then asks him if he is mad, to interfere thus with the progress of King James's governor. The old man calmly answers that in the past he has stayed the march of a king himself, and explains that he has appeared once again on earth in response to the cry of an oppressed people. He then announces that James, unbeknownst to the colonials, has been deposed and that by the next day the governor himself will be in prison.

The townspeople, thrilled by the words of their champion, confront the soldiers without fear. Andros, cowed either by the mien of the venerable old man or by the attitude of the crowd, orders a retreat. The Gray Champion disappears in the excitement that follows this victory of the colonials over their oppressors, and a few individuals claim to have seen his spectral figure fade before their eyes. The men of that generation watch for his reappearance in vain, although it is rumored that he walks again in King-Street eighty years later.

Protagonist. "King of the Bingo Game." Ralph Ellison. 1944.

The anonymous protagonist is a black man from Rocky Mount, North Carolina, who tries to survive a destitute life in a northern metropolis. He is in a theater watching a movie he has already seen three times, waiting for the start of the local bingo game, on which he is pinning all his hopes for the future. He is famished and unemployed. Laura, the woman he loves, is going to die because they have no money for a doctor.

One of the scenes in the movie consists of the hero rescuing a woman who is tied to a bed; the protagonist imagines what the reaction of the audience would be if the script were rewritten and the hero did not release her but started to undress her instead. Tired of watching the picture, the hungry, worried man drifts off to sleep and has a nightmare set in the South of his boyhood; he is awakened by a man who tells him to stop yelling and then offers him a swig of whiskey to calm him down.

Finally the bingo game begins. The protagonist has managed to obtain five bingo cards and hits the number that allows him to go up on stage and spin the wheel. If the wheel stops on the double zero, he will win $36.90. Even though he knows the routine quite well by this time, he begins to panic, feeling the effects of the whiskey and confused by the noise and the bright lights. He stands trembling before the wheel, then presses the button that controls its motion. As he stands with the button in his palm, he becomes obsessed with the speed of the wheel and begins to think that it will repay him for all the suffering he has experienced in his life.

Refusing to release the button despite the protests of the emcee and the audience, the protagonist is convinced that he holds the secret not only to winning the game but to life itself; he announces to the yelling crowd, "This is God!" He desperately maintains control, thinking that Laura will be all right as long as he is connected to the wheel. Suddenly, he realizes with shock and a sense of sadness that he cannot remember his own name. He then decides that he does not need to remember because as long as he holds the button he will be reborn as "The-man-who-pressed-the-button-who-held-the-prize-who-was-the-King-of-Bingo."

He thinks of Laura and screams for her to live because he has no one else. He then becomes aware that the audience is applauding the arrival of two policemen on the stage. He attempts to elude them while keeping hold of the button, which they eventually manage to wrest from his hand. He watches without surprise as the wheel finally spins to a stop at the double zero, the winning number. Happy with his good fortune, he fails to notice the man standing behind him, who brutally hits him on the head as the curtain descends. Before losing consciousness, the King of the Bingo Game recognizes that his luck has run out.

Protagonist. "The Man in the Brooks Brothers Shirt." Mary McCarthy. 1941.

The story's unnamed protagonist is a young woman who engages in a short sexual affair in a train en route from New York City to Portland, Oregon, to inform her family of her intention to get married for the second time. A twenty-four-year-old writer whose primary source of publication is a Left-wing magazine called the *Liberal*, she left home to attend college on the East Coast and became engaged to a painter. Prior to her first marriage, she remained relatively inexperienced in the collegiate dating game that surrounded her. Subsequent to her divorce, however, she has made up for lost time by embarking on a series of unsatisfactory affairs that culminate in this brief and bizarre encounter with BILL BREEN, a middle-aged man who sports a green Brooks Brothers shirt.

When Breen first enters her car, she silently deprecates his appearance and decides that he looks like a pig with unpleasant pink skin; he is not to be considered for the purpose of whiling away the hours practicing the art of flirtation. Resuming her conversation with the woman sitting next to her, the protagonist notices out of the corner of her eye that the green-shirted man has begun a conversation in a relatively loud tone of voice, an indication that he is trying to impress her with his intelligence. When her conversation partner abandons her to go to the dining car, she buries her nose in a book and wonders scornfully what corny opening line the man will use when he gets up the nerve to approach her. When he finally makes his move, she is pleasantly surprised at his tactics and amazed that Bill is actually quite intelligent, witty, and likable. After exchanging a few preliminary comments which divulge that he is a married executive in the steel industry in Cleveland, he invites her to his compartment to drink highballs, promising to leave the door open in order to allay her suspicions. Almost despite herself, the protagonist begins enjoying herself and agrees to remain in the compartment to share a lunch.

As the day progresses and their consumption of cocktails loosens their tongues, their conversation becomes increasingly intimate. The protagonist even supplies a litany of her various lovers and explains the reasons she left her first husband, who she claims was too kind and good for her. Although she feels that Bill is physically unattractive and resents his conservative political views, she continues to like him for some inexplicable reason, and as the evening progresses she agrees to have dinner with him. Her memory and volition soon begin to abandon her, and the next morning she finds herself naked in his bed with no recollection of what transpired during the night. Mortified, she pieces together parts of the evening, which included singing ribald songs and engaging in a peculiar kind of lovemaking highlighted by dirty language and physical blows that she fears may have left bruises. Intending to sneak out of the compartment before Bill awakens, she is foiled when he rolls over and professes his intention to marry her. Genuinely upset by her behavior of the previous night, she begins to cry and vomits into the toilet, whereupon he insists on plying her with a hair-of-the-dog drink to calm her stomach. This done, the process begins all over again, and she eventually agrees to make love out of what she considers the only genuine act of self-sacrifice and charity she has ever performed in her life. Although she refuses to accept Breen's proposal and follows through on her intention of visiting her family in Portland, her strange experience in the Pullman car makes her decide against a second marriage.

Protagonist. "A Reasonable Man." Ann Beattie. 1976.
The protagonist of this short story is an unnamed woman who suffers from inertia and depression. Her husband, a seemingly reasonable, logical man, has not made love to her since a disagreement arose between them over

the care of their young son Robby. Presumably because of the woman's depression, the husband decided months ago that Robby should live with his paternal grandmother instead of with his mother and himself. The woman, who took good care of Robby, did not want her son to leave, and now she misses him. She is allowed to see him only on Sundays when she and her husband go to the grandmother's house for the day. During the rest of the week, the woman attends craft classes, cooks delicious, nutritious meals for her husband, occasionally goes outside to shop or to the cleaner's, and sits around the house staring at the walls, obsessively wondering when the telephone will ring.

One day on her way home from the cleaner's, the woman tries to remember the last telephone conversation she had. She cannot, and it occurs to her that if she kept a journal, she would be able to recall her daily activities. With this in mind, she enters a drugstore and buys a theme book, a fountain pen, and a bottle of ink. At home she grows frustrated when she has difficulty filling the pen. She begins to wonder what she should write in her journal; what would be the point, she asks, of writing things that would later embarrass her? She is already embarrassed when she sees her pottery bowls around the house, even though her husband likes them. He tells her she should dust them and take pride in them because there is no such thing as "perfection." Thinking about him, she wonders if he has had the phone disconnected, but she is afraid to ask.

The woman spends a lot of time every week attending craft classes, but she does not feel totally comfortable with craft-making. She believes she is too old, lacks imagination, and does not have a delicate touch; her teacher, a sympathetic man, tells her that she is wrong. He has bought a ring from her and wears it to every class, and although she is flattered, she does not know if he wears it outside class. The teacher gives her a book of poems to read—*Winter Trees* by Sylvia Plath. She takes it home and reads it, and it depresses her.

One night her instructor asks to speak to her after class. When all the other students have left, he opens the door to a small bedroom at the back of the classroom. The instructor asks her what she thought of the Sylvia Plath book, and she tells him it depressed her. He nods in agreement and lends her two more books. She knows that the instructor talked with her mother-in-law, who came to register her for the classes; now she wonders what her mother-in-law told him about her, but she decides not to ask. He boils water for tea, and she chats briefly about the weather. Encouraging her to write and express herself, he tells her she should not feel obliged to act nicely or feel happy.

The woman tells her instructor about something that happened during a summer vacation at the beach with her husband and son. Racing with her son at the edge of the shore, she was suddenly overcome with a burst of energy. She kept running until she came to the end of the beach. Afterward she spent hours trying to find her son and husband; she could barely remember what they looked like. Her husband finally found her, and he was furious. Now, still with her kind, attentive crafts instructor, the woman is not sure how to connect this story to what she really wants to talk about: the inexplicably silent telephone.

Protagonist. *The Room.* Hubert Selby, Jr. 1971.

The unnamed protagonist of this novel is incarcerated in an excruciatingly small cell after having been arrested for the alleged attempted robbery of a jewelry store. For much of the novel the prisoner anxiously awaits his court date. In order to keep himself occupied, he spends a good deal of time obsessing over a facial pimple, and periodically he casts his mind back over his earlier life. It is clear that the prisoner's life has been characterized by loneliness and unhappiness, and that even the one relationship he can recall only highlights his loneliness and isolation. As he remembers his relationship with Mary, the prisoner focuses only on the personal and sexual dissatisfactions he experienced. He views his former lover chiefly as lacking any understanding of him and as having only selfish motives in her demands of him. After recalling his unhappy past, the prisoner turns his thoughts slowly toward revenge fantasies, through which he will redeem his shattered life.

The most detailed sequence of the prisoner's revenge fantasy involves an elaborate scheme to kidnap the two policemen who initially arrested him. He imagines that once he has them under his control, he will systematically strip them of their authority and dignity. He imagines holding them captive and naked, with wires around various parts of their anatomies through which he is able to control the administration of pain and gradually recondition them as guard dogs. This fantasy culminates in the prisoner's display of his well-trained dogs before the frightened and disgusted eyes of the officers' families and colleagues. Here the prisoner imagines that his dogs demonstrate their hunting skills by fighting and eventually killing a thirsty and starving rat. The display concludes when the "dogs" are forced to have sexual intercourse in front of the same audience. While this fantasy cools his anxiety to a degree, the prisoner soon recalls his situation, and reacting to the cramped space, once again pays inordinate attention to his pimple.

Another reverie takes over as the prisoner decides that he can show the officers up during court proceedings. He imagines that he can cleverly manipulate direct-and cross-examinations in order to show that the officers have no accurate memory of what they did. This part of the novel focuses on the contradictory and confusing nature of the officers' claims, and the prisoner decides that his method

of questioning would undoubtedly lead to his exoneration. Once this fantasy begins to break down, the prisoner again imagines that he could physically overcome the officers even if it meant attacking them in the courtroom itself. As he sees it, the battle would be brief because of his brute strength and innate superiority. This fantasy ends as the prisoner is jolted back to reality by a prison guard who opens his cell door and tosses a blue uniform at him. It seems, at last, that the actual court date has arrived. As the novel ends, the prisoner awaits the trial, as he had at the beginning.

Protagonist. "Tennessee's Partner." Bret Harte. 1870.

This title character is not known by any other name to the inhabitants of Sandy Bar, California. Short and stout, Tennessee's Partner is an unimposing man with a simple and serious mien. A gold miner, he exhibits a single-minded practicality and an unwavering loyalty to his partner.

In 1853, Tennessee's Partner leaves Poker Flat to find a wife in San Francisco. He travels as far as Stockton, where he becomes enamored of the waitress who serves him in the hotel. He marries her a week later. The couple returns to Poker Flat, where the groom lives with his partner Tennessee. Some time later, the bride and Tennessee become lovers and move to Marysville; Tennessee's Partner accepts his loss simply and seriously, and much to everyone's surprise, he greets Tennessee with affectionate warmth when the man eventually returns without the woman.

The reputation of Tennessee's Partner among the people of Sandy Bar is damaged somewhat by his friend's shady character and criminal doings. Tennessee is eventually caught red-handed after robbing a stranger en route to Red Dog and is brought before a judge and jury who are already convinced of his guilt. In the middle of the trial, Tennessee's Partner appears and asks to speak on behalf of the prisoner. He enters looking disheveled, carrying a heavy carpetbag. He addresses the court gravely and politely, explaining that he was just passing by and wanted to see how things were going for his partner. In a very dilatory manner, he talks about his friend's actions and suggests that the $1,700 worth of gold he has brought with him in the carpetbag would be a fair price to pay for the man's offense. Before anyone can stop him, he empties the contents of the bag out on the floor of the courtroom, causing an uproar among the spectators.

When order is restored in the court, Tennessee's Partner is told that his friend's freedom cannot be bought. He slowly puts the gold back in the bag with a serious, perplexed face, shakes Tennessee's hand in farewell, and withdraws from the room. The prisoner's fate is sealed in the judge's mind by the bribe, and he is hanged the next morning; Tennessee's Partner does not attend but appears afterward with his donkey cart and asks permission to take the body and bury it. The townspeople accompany the man back to his desolate cabin on the outskirts of Sandy Bar. They stand silently while he says a few words about his partner and, unaided, fills in the grave he has dug.

Tennessee's Partner is later cleared of any complicity in his friend's doings, and the citizens of Sandy Bar treat him with kindness. But from the day of the hanging his health begins to fail, and he takes to his bed. He expires one rainy night after having a vision that he is going in his donkey cart to meet his partner, Tennessee.

Protagonist. "To Build a Fire." Jack London. 1908.

The unnamed male protagonist of this short story is weathering his first winter in the extreme climate of the Klondike. He has split from his group of friends and business associates in order to explore the possibility of procuring logs from the islands of the remote region when the cold weather breaks in the spring. An old-timer had warned him never to travel alone in the Klondike when the temperature dips down to fifty degrees or more below zero, but he ignores this advice, and his life is endangered by the bitter cold.

Traveling through the spruce timberland with a large husky dog as his only companion and with lunch as his only baggage, the protagonist faces temperatures dipping to seventy-five below zero. His beard is caked with ice, and his mouth is frozen into one position. Because it is winter, the sun is not shining, and the cold is so extreme that the protagonist's spittle makes a crackling sound when it hits the ground. His dog, who is equipped with the instinctual knowledge that it is in fact too cold to be traveling safely, is anxious and longs to burrow in the snow to escape the raw air or take refuge around the warmth of the fire he knows his master is capable of building. But the protagonist is sure of his ability to take care of himself in the wilderness no matter how extreme the weather and is confident that by six o'clock that evening he will reach his destination, a camp at an old mining claim on the left fork of Henderson.

The protagonist's confidence is tested when he nearly breaks through the ice covering a bubbling spring. Wetting his feet in this climate could be life-threatening and, at the very least, would cause the man to lose time because he would be forced to build a fire and dry off his feet, socks, and boots. But for the moment the man eludes this danger and continues to choose his route carefully along the streambed.

At twelve-thirty in the afternoon, the protagonist stops at a fork in the creek he is following, builds a fire to thaw out his mouth, and enjoys his lunch and a leisurely pipe of tobacco. He then forces his unwilling husky to abandon the fire, and together they continue walking toward the camp.

Despite the man's careful surveillance of the landscape,

he fails to detect a spring beneath the snow, and he falls through the thin ice, wetting his feet and legs halfway up to his knees. Cursing his bad luck, he hurriedly begins to make a fire, for he is well aware that he has very little time before frostbite attacks his wet limbs. His extremities are very quickly becoming numb, but he successfully builds a fire and smugly congratulates himself on his prowess in the wilderness. But his complacence is short-lived because he has made the mistake of building the fire under a spruce tree whose branches are laden with heavy snow. The tree is disturbed when he plucks twigs from its branches, and it dumps a large quantity of snow onto the fire, instantly extinguishing it. The increasingly panicky man attempts to build another fire, but by now his hands are so frozen that he cannot manipulate his fingers to perform the necessary tasks. Becoming wild with fear, he begins to run in order to attempt to regain body heat, but he eventually realizes the futility of this endeavor and sits down quietly to face an inevitable death by freezing.

Protagonist. "A Tree * A Rock * A Cloud." Carson McCullers. 1943.

The eccentric unnamed transient who buttonholes a young newspaper boy in a streetcar café and proceeds to tell him his life story is a man who claims to have developed a "science" that enables him to love everything in the world.

One rainy morning, an older man drinking beer at the counter of a café catches the attention of a boy who is on his way out the door. The twelve-year-old paper boy walks over to the man and asks him what he wants. The man places one hand on the boy's shoulders, grabs his chin with the other, and, after examining the youthful face, tells him that he loves him. The other men in the café laugh and the child shrinks away, but the man assures him that he is not teasing and says that he will explain what he means if the boy will sit and have a drink with him. The boy agrees and has another cup of coffee. The man pulls out two extremely blurry photographs of a woman and asks the youth if he has ever seen her before. The nervous boy says no, and the transient, after a sip of beer, begins to tell him about his life.

Twelve years before, the man had married the woman in the photograph, whom he called "Dodo." They had met at a filling station and were married three days later; he was fifty-one years old at the time, and she was thirty. He loved her and believed himself to be loved in return. For the first time in his life, he felt that all the "loose pieces" of his soul became complete through his love for the woman. Employed as a railroad engineer, he provided her with comforts and luxuries, but one night when he came home, he found that she had run off with another man.

For the next two years the former railroad engineer traveled around the country searching for his wife and her lover. He tracked down every man she had known and went to every town she had ever mentioned, including Tulsa, Atlanta, Chicago, Cheehaw, and Memphis. Then, in the third year, he realized that he had no control over his memories and emotions; at times he would forget what she looked like, and at other moments the pain of his loss would come so suddenly that he ceased to function. He felt that she was chasing him around in his soul. During the next couple of years he drank and fornicated, indulging in any vices that appealed to him.

In the fifth year after his wife left him, however, he found a sense of peace and began to develop his "science." He reasoned that the problem with men is that the first time they fall in love it is with a woman, an event he considers the dangerous and sacred climax of love. Instead, he decided, love should begin with such things as a tree, a rock, a cloud. He built his "science" slowly, picking up odd objects in the street and concentrating on loving them. For the next six years he wandered around the country perfecting his technique to the point where he could love anything and anybody.

When the transient finishes his odd narrative, the newspaper boy asks him whether he has ever fallen in love with a woman again. The fervency with which the man told his story drains away. For the first time his eyes look vague and scattered as he admits that he is not quite ready for that last step in his science. On his way out of the café, he stands briefly in the doorway and tells the boy to remember that he loves him. The door closes softly behind him, leaving the perplexed youth to wonder whether the man was crazy or not.

Protagonist. "The Way We Live Now." Susan Sontag. 1987.

The unnamed protagonist of this story is slowly dying of an unnamed disease whose symptoms make it clear that he is suffering from AIDS. Although he is a wealthy collector who lives in an urban penthouse, his money and intelligence cannot protect him from this grave illness and the alienation of his wide circle of friends when they are confronted by his condition.

A thirty-eight-year-old bisexual man, once extremely sexually active, the protagonist has never suffered from a serious illness, and he attempts to repress the fact that he is losing weight and beginning to feel a general decline in his health. Although his friends had warned him that his promiscuity was dangerous and had begged him to practice "safe sex," he refused to heed their advice, claiming that sex was of such importance to him that he could not possibly change his life-style despite the risks. When he contracts pneumonia and is hospitalized, his hospital room becomes crowded with flowers and gifts, and his friends visit him frequently and jealously vie for his attention and intimacy. Having recovered from his bout of pneumonia, the patient is treated with a new experimental

drug and is attended to by a specialist in the field of AIDS research.

He is eventually allowed to return to his apartment to convalesce under the supervision of an ex-lover, Quentin. Dividing his time between entertaining a stream of visitors and writing in a diary for the first time in his life, the protagonist hopes that he will survive and someday reread this chronicle of the darkest days of his existence. But for all his wishful thinking and despite his specialized treatment, the protagonist's health falters, and he is once again hospitalized.

As the protagonist's condition steadily declines, fear of watching a friend die and previously buried personality conflicts cause his friends to begin visiting him less. In order to assure that the patient does not have to face the horrors of AIDS without the benefit of a support system, Quentin devises the method of keeping a visiting book to ensure a steady stream of callers.

The protagonist begins to unnerve his friends with the air of detachment he adopts to cope with his terror and pain. Although his fears threaten at times to drive him mad, he admits that a certain euphoria sometimes accompanies his terror, arousing within him a kind of high that causes him, paradoxically, to feel powerful, even invincible. The severity of his illness prompts his mother to fly in from Mississippi, but his condition improves to the extent that she returns home, and the doctors are convinced that he will be discharged within a couple of weeks. But his friends are horrified by the telling deterioration of his handwriting, which is becoming increasingly illegible and faint. Although the protagonist is still alive at the end of the story, an atmosphere of doom pervades.

Prothero, Mary "Pokey." *The Group.* Mary McCarthy. 1954.

Mary Prothero, whose college buddies nickname her "Pokey," is the richest and least well behaved of a clique of eight Vassar students. Very active in New York society life, she claims to have her pick of the crop of prospective husbands, thanks to her yachtsman father's wealth and influence. Although she has to be tutored to get through her college courses, she loves animals and aspires to become a veterinarian, a goal that is announced in the Vassar yearbook. Despite her lazy disposition and relatively unpromising undergraduate career, Pokey does manage to live a very interesting and successful life after graduating from Vassar, class of 1933.

The seven other members of Pokey's group band together to try to help their fair, plump friend to blunder her way through college. When she oversleeps and threatens to miss mandatory assemblies, they awaken her by throwing stones at her windows and, having hurriedly dressed her, chaperone her to functions. Rather lacking in morality, Pokey steals library books, cheats on exams, and sneaks off the campus on the weekends. But Pokey is plucky to the extent that she defied her parents, who are against higher education, by slipping out of the house to take college entrance examinations. She applied secretly to Vassar and even forged her parents' signatures on her application. Not believing, as her family does, that ignorance is a sign of high-class breeding, Pokey pursues her own eccentric but laudable ambitions.

Given the nature of her upbringing, Pokey's desire to break with family tradition to establish herself in a scientific career is a feat of considerable courage and foresight. As far back as anyone in the family can remember, none of the Protheros achieved a higher degree, and her little sister Phyllis drops out of high school at the age of sixteen, much to her mother's relief. According to Mrs. Prothero, Phyllis surpasses her sister by marrying at nineteen instead of entertaining silly notions of becoming a horse doctor. At home, Pokey is pampered by a number of servants, including a very distinguished British butler who resembles Henry James and virtually runs the household. Thanks to the shallow sensibilities of her parents, Pokey inherits an obnoxious, affected high-society tone of voice, but her Prothero crassness is muted by a more substantial and interesting drive to be different.

Having prepared herself for veterinary school by majoring in zoology at Vassar, Pokey subsequently attends Cornell Agricultural School. She eventually marries a poet named Beauchamp, a distant cousin and a graduate student at Princeton, where they reside luxuriously with servants, their own stables, and hunting facilities. Pokey is able to continue her studies in Ithaca by commuting in an airplane that she herself pilots, and at home she assumes the responsibility for the twins she has borne. When last seen in the novel, she very generously donates a space in her family's cemetery plot to KAY LEILAND STRONG, the first member of the Vassar group to die, having lived a life far less successful than that of the slow-starting but bold and original "Pokey" Prothero Beauchamp.

Prouder, Usury "Zury." *Zury: The Meanest Man in Spring County.* Joseph Kirkland. 1887.

Originally from Pennsylvania, Usury "Zury" Prouder moves west with his parents and young sister in the early 1800s. Extremely clever and hardworking, he is determined to make his family's farm a success. But during their first winter on the frontier, Zury's sister dies because the family lacks enough money for medicine and basic necessities. Zury adopts the attitude that money is the essential ingredient for life and happiness, and dedicates himself to the accumulation of a fortune.

Zury's success grows over the years. Through many shrewd business deals he not only pays off his family's debts but also holds mortgages on several other farms in Spring County. He has earned a reputation as "the Meanest Man in Spring County"; his fellow frontiersmen even believe him to be the most frugal man in the world. But

although he is a sharp businessman and a penny pincher, he is neither cruel nor heartless. Zury would always prefer to do a good deed for another man than do him harm, and he is in favor of charity as long as he is spared donating too large a portion of his wealth.

Zury eventually weds Mary Peddicomb. The couple has two children right away, but both boys die while very young. The large Prouder estate seems quiet and lifeless to Zury. Soon a new schoolteacher from Boston arrives. Anne Sparrow, a fair-skinned redhead, is afraid that she will spend her life as an old maid. As soon as she meets Zury, a mutual attraction develops between them. Their friendship survives a number of trials over the next several years.

When Mary succumbs to a long illness, Zury is left a bachelor again. Anne entertains the hope that he might propose to her, but an embarrassing public incident leads to a falling out between them. Zury therefore decides to propose to his late wife's sister, Flora Peddicomb. In response to Zury's engagement, Anne finally accepts the advances of John McVey, a persistent man who has been devotedly pursuing Anne for years. Anne moves to the town of Springville and has two children, Philip and Margaret. John dies a few years later.

Meanwhile, Zury has been campaigning for the Illinois state legislature. Anne returns to Spring County to help Zury run. Benefiting from both her speech-writing skills and his own oratory abilities, Zury is elected to the House of Representatives. He serves two relatively quiet terms. While Zury is in office, Flora dies, leaving him alone again.

Zury then tries to use his money to convince Anne to marry him. She refuses, and Zury is crushed. He is determined, however, to be patient and win her over slowly. Over the next few years Zury carefully reestablishes his relationship with Anne. He gets to know Philip and Margaret, and even helps to set Philip up in a mining enterprise. The mutual affection between Zury and Anne gradually grows, and Anne accepts Zury's second proposal. At the close of the novel, Zury and Anne have moved back to the Prouder farm in Spring County where they live together in comfort and raise their new son.

Proudhammer, Caleb. *Tell Me How Long the Train's Been Gone.* James Baldwin. 1968.

At seventeen, Caleb Proudhammer is too old to be corrected by his Barbadian father and American-born mother—or at least too old for the punishment to do any good—so that it has become their habit to trust Caleb unless he is blatantly guilty. This situation allows Caleb the freedom for such mischief as leaving their Harlem home to take his brother LEO (PROUDHAMMER) to the movies and then abandoning him there.

This behavior is more a sign of Caleb's teenage selfishness than of sibling resentment, for he clearly loves and respects his little brother. Caleb begins associating with a crowd of juvenile delinquents. One falsely indicts Caleb as an accomplice in his own thievery, and three white police officers come to arrest him. When Leo grabs the leg of the officer carrying Caleb away, he is brutally kicked to the side.

Caleb returns four years later, thinner, tougher, and more prone to weeping. One night he wakes sobbing in the bed he shares with the now fourteen-year-old Leo. Leo begins comforting Caleb, but this surprisingly becomes a sexual act. The brothers seem closer after sex. In the middle of another weeping night, Caleb reveals to Leo the physical, psychological, and sexual abuse he suffered in prison at the hands of white guards. The next day Caleb follows through on his promise to seek work at the garment center where his father has worked for many years. Humiliated by the way his father is treated, Caleb cannot stay; Leo comes home to find Caleb packing to go to California, where he hopes to find work in a shipyard. When this does not work out, he joins the army.

The brothers are separated for years, and Leo pursues an acting career. One evening Caleb pays a surprise visit to the restaurant where Leo works as a singing waiter. Now a preacher with a wife and children, Caleb seems a bit judgmental about Leo's chosen career, which has thus far left the younger man, now in his mid-twenties, little to show for his dedication. Caleb reveals to Leo the story of the last man he wanted to kill before turning his life over to God—a fellow soldier, a white man, who bragged about all the women he had had. Resentful of the fact that the Europeans treated U.S. soldiers equally, white soldiers began spreading rumors about the black soldiers. Caleb's "friend" Frederick, jealous that Caleb and a white woman had fallen in love and planned to marry, sabotaged Caleb's plans by trying to "steal" her for himself; instead she rejected them both. Trying to shoot Frederick, Caleb aimed, but the man was felled by another sniper, and within minutes Caleb was hit with the wound that resulted in his discharge.

Caleb's next and last appearance in the novel is a nonappearance: Worried about Leo after a heart attack, he is also concerned about abandoning his parish to go to see his brother. Leo's friend, who speaks with Caleb over the phone, interrupts Caleb's guilty reply. As though he were a distant relative, Caleb asks to be kept posted in case there is a need for him to come.

Proudhammer, Leo. *Tell Me How Long the Train's Been Gone.* James Baldwin. 1968.

The novel opens with the heart attack of protagonist Leo Proudhammer. This monumental event finally forces him to cease his perennial push to attain his goals and to reflect on the forty years that it has taken him to become the most successful African-American actor in history.

As a child in 1920s and 1930s Harlem, Leo recalls the rats and lack of heat in his family's apartment, the cruelty

of its landlord, the nationalist ravings of his Barbadian father, the pride and support of his fair-skinned African-American mother, and the mischief of his teenage brother CALEB (PROUDHAMMER). At seventeen, Caleb is falsely accused of stealing. Three white police officers find Caleb at a friend's home and physically brutalize both Caleb and Leo, who had attempted to protect his big brother.

When Caleb returns from prison four years later, it is important to fourteen-year-old Leo to impress upon his big brother that he has matured. One night Caleb wakes crying in the bed he shares with Leo, and Leo comforts him. Their passions are soon aroused and Leo initiates sex with Caleb, who complies. Shortly thereafter, Leo discovers the source of Caleb's agony: the profound physical, sexual, and psychological abuse inflicted on African-American prisoners by white guards.

As a nineteen-year-old living in Greenwich Village, Leo befriends Barbara King, a white Kentuckian with thespian aspirations, and her Italian boyfriend Jerry, who live in the same rundown apartment complex known as Paradise Alley. In Jerry's absence Leo accompanies Barbara to a party, where they meet Lola and Saul San-Marquand, an older white couple who are respected in the theatrical world. Seeing the potential in the two young actors, the San-Marquands write to invite them to attend one of their famous workshops the following summer.

When the time comes, Leo, Barbara, and Jerry share a place in the small New Jersey town, with Leo and Barbara running errands for the workshop and rehearsing their scene. While out for pizza one night, Madeleine, the lead in the current workshop production, joins the three of them. Leo also invites the two other African-American men to join them. The group ends up going to a bar on the African-American side of town. The evening closes with a night of sex for Leo and Madeleine at her place. The next day she leaves earlier than he, and his leaving alone brings inquiries from a couple of white neighbors, whom Leo answers with uninhibited sarcasm. Leo is later arrested, and the San-Marquands must bail him out. They subtly chastise him for his indiscreet behavior and caution him for the future.

The next day Barbara informs Leo that she is in love with him. Having angered Jerry with this news, Barbara must walk through town with Leo. After being threatened with dirty looks and racial slurs, they arrive safely at the theater. But Saul criticizes Barbara's performance and attitude, and tells Leo that he has absolutely no talent.

When fall comes, Leo makes a living as a singing waiter in a restaurant owned by a Jamaican woman. There he meets Greek director Konstantine Rafaeleto and is cast in his production of *The Corn Is Green.* This is Leo's first real role, but he has already been through the African-American actor routine of playing walk-on waiters many times.

Leo rises quickly to stardom. Neither he nor Barbara

marries, and she continues to love him unrequitedly. She even goes as far as making love to Christopher, his lover, in order to get closer to Leo. It is this young man who finally brings meaning into Leo's life after his years of success and loneliness. With his lifelong friend Barbara at his side, Leo waits for Christopher to accompany him to the south of France for a lengthy rest.

Prynne, Hester. *The Scarlet Letter.* Nathaniel Hawthorne. 1850.

Hester Prynne is one of American literature's most resilient figures. As the tragic victim of the Puritan obsession with sin, she endures her penance for adultery—the embroidered letter *A* that she must wear on her bosom—with unfailing faith and nobility.

Hawthorne's narrative opens in seventeenth-century Boston with a choruslike condemnation of the young heroine by the town gossips. Hester, married to an elderly, dispassionate English scholar who has not been heard from in two years, emerges from the jail carrying her illegitimate infant. Placed on the town pillory, she is exhorted to divulge the name of the child's father. She refuses and accepts her sentence.

Hester recognizes in the crowd a deformed little man, a stranger to the villagers. It is Hester's husband, who had been captured by Indians and has made his way to Boston to find his young wife on trial for adultery. Later, when Hester and her child require a physician to visit their jail cell, the man, posing as a doctor named ROGER CHILLINGWORTH, examines them. In his interview with Hester, Chillingworth vows to discover the identity of Hester's fellow sinner. Before leaving, he convinces Hester to swear that she will not reveal Chillingworth's true identity.

Hester leaves prison and establishes herself in an abandoned cottage on the outskirts of town, providing for herself and her daughter, strange young PEARL PRYNNE, through the skillful work of her needle. In her penitence she becomes a friend to the sick and the poor, and the *A* comes to signify "Able" among many of the villagers.

Hester's partner in sin, the minister ARTHUR DIMMESDALE, has meanwhile been declining. Tormented by his secret guilt, he grows sickly and pale, and accepts the proffered medical aid of Chillingworth. The two become regular companions. One night in May, the minister meets Hester and Pearl, who have been watching at the deathbed of Governor Winthrop in the center of town. As he stands with them on the town pillory, an immense letter *A* lights up the sky.

Soon after, Hester, disturbed by Dimmesdale's failing health, resolves to reveal Chillingworth's identity and to warn the minister of his evil intentions. On a cold afternoon she and Pearl meet the minister in the woods. She insists that their passion had a consecration of its own and convinces Dimmesdale that they must escape the community and take passage to England. She flings away the

scarlet letter, but Pearl, who has been playing nearby, refuses to join her mother until she replaces it on her breast.

On the eve of their departure, Dimmesdale delivers the election sermon for the new governor. The sermon seems to have drained his last resources of strength. With help from Hester and Pearl, he ascends the pillory and with his last breath declares before the townspeople that his is a polluted soul. Bearing his breast, he reveals what some spectators claim is a scarlet letter engraved on his skin. He acknowledges Pearl and Hester, then dies.

The novel closes some years later when Hester, after some absence, returns to Boston to live out her life and her penance in her cottage at the edge of the woods. When she dies, she is buried next to Dimmesdale, under a tombstone serving both graves that reads, "On a field, sable, the letter A, gules."

Prynne, Pearl. *The Scarlet Letter.* Nathaniel Hawthorne. 1850.

Pearl is the elfin child of HESTER PRYNNE and her lover, the Puritan minister ARTHUR DIMMESDALE. As the child of an illicit love affair, Pearl is the manifestation for her Puritan community of the ends of sin.

Pearl first appears in the narrative as an infant in the arms of Hester, who slowly ascends the steps of the town pillory to receive her sentence for committing adultery. Hester refuses to reveal the identity of Pearl's father and humbly accepts her punishment: She is to wear a scarlet letter *A* on her bosom for the rest of her life. Before she steps down from the pillory, Hester recognizes in the crowd her husband, an unfeeling old scholar who has been missing and presumed dead for the several years since Hester arrived in the Puritan community of Boston. Later, the man, ROGER CHILLINGWORTH, visits Hester and Pearl in jail under the guise of a physician. With a demonic look on his face, he vows he will discover the identity of Pearl's father.

Released from jail, Hester establishes herself and her daughter in an abandoned cottage on the edge of town. She provides for Pearl with her beautiful needlework and becomes a friend to the sick and the poor. Years pass, and for some of the villagers the *A* comes to stand more for "Able" than for "Adulteress."

Pearl, meanwhile, has become an exquisite but strange little child. Strong-willed and precocious, she seems to have an intuitive understanding of all that goes on in the adult world. One night when they are returning from sitting at the deathbed of the governor, she and her mother meet Arthur Dimmesdale at the town pillory. Pearl asks the minister if he will stand on the pillory with her and her mother the following day. He replies that he will stand with them on judgment day. Pearl breaks into laughter, just as a huge letter *A* seems to light up the night sky above them. On another occasion, while she is playing by the shore, Pearl fashions a letter *A* out of green eelgrass and attaches it to her breast. When she begs her mother to tell her what the letter stands for, Hester brushes her questions off uneasily.

Hester becomes concerned that Chillingworth, who has been attending the ailing Dimmesdale, has evil intentions. She resolves to warn Dimmesdale and arranges to meet him in the woods outside the town. The two lovers decide to leave Boston together and sail with Pearl on the next ship for England. Hester tears the scarlet letter from her bosom and flings it away, but Pearl, who has been playing nearby, refuses to come near her mother until the letter is replaced.

Before their departure, Dimmesdale delivers his final sermon. While he is speaking, Pearl charms the captain of the ship the three are to sail on. He tells her to give her mother the message that Chillingworth has arranged to take passage on the same ship. Chillingworth's scheming is all for nought, however, for the sermon seems to have robbed Dimmesdale of his last bit of strength. Supported by Pearl and Hester, the minister mounts the pillory and confesses his sins to the villagers. Then, dramatically pulling his vestments away, he reveals what appears to be a scarlet letter A engraved on his chest. After acknowledging his daughter and her mother, Dimmesdale dies.

The novel concludes with an epilogue. Hester, after some absence, has returned to Boston to reestablish herself in her cottage at the edge of town. Pearl, it is said, inherited a fortune from Roger Chillingworth and married in England. Little else is known about the child who caused such a stir in Puritan Boston, but some of the villagers claim to have seen Hester embroidering an elaborate baby garment for shipment to England, presumably for Pearl's child.

Puttermesser. *Levitation.* Cynthia Ozick. 1982.
The only child of doting parents, Puttermesser grew up in a Jewish neighborhood in the Bronx. As a response to her parents' repeated attempts to pass their Jewish heritage on to her, she became an overachiever who, after graduating at the top of her college class, attended Yale Law School.

Puttermesser begins practicing law at a small but prestigious firm in Manhattan, where she is one of three Jews employed there and, much to her discomfort, the only woman. During this time her parents finally leave their tenement in the Bronx and move to Florida. Puttermesser is more affected by their departure than she had anticipated and begins taking Hebrew lessons from her uncle Zindel.

Shortly after a fire ravages the Bronx building where she continues to live, Puttermesser changes her residence and employment and begins working for the city. While pleased to be free of the male-dominated atmosphere of the firm she left, she now finds herself buried in the endless red tape of the city bureaucracy.

Through her new job Puttermesser meets a businessman named Rappaport, with whom she has a brief affair. At this point she is well into her thirties and quite content to spend most of her free time reading—a habit that soon begins to irk her new lover. He accuses her of being cold and indifferent, and leaves her after a brief period of cohabitation. Not long afterward she is demoted from her city job and replaced by a political crony.

At this point Puttermesser experiences an astonishing event: the magical appearance of a golem, created from the earth of the plants with which she adorns her apartment. Puttermesser recovers sufficiently from the shock of beholding this lifelike monster to assign it to light household chores, such as cooking and cleaning. But the golem, who gives her name as Xanthippe, soon aspires to more important responsibilities.

Although reluctant at first, Puttermesser succumbs to Xanthippe's urging and allows the golem to accompany her to work. At the office Xanthippe, the "new secretary," types hundreds of pages of notes, detailing the ways in which living conditions in the city could be improved. Before long, Puttermesser, armed with these notes, is running for mayor and with the help of Xanthippe completely changing the face of New York City. Crime ceases; the garbage disappears; the economy booms. All goes well until Rappaport reappears. He wants Puttermesser back; she refuses, and so he runs off with Xanthippe.

In no time at all the city returns to its degenerate, crime-ridden former state. By bribing Rappaport with a new job, Mayor Puttermesser is able to lure Xanthippe back to her employ, whereupon she quickly decapitates the golem and returns her to the potted earth from whence she came.

Puyat, Pauline (Sister Leopolda). *Love Medicine; Tracks.* Louise Erdrich. 1984; 1988.
Pauline Puyat notes that the Puyats, with the exception of herself, are quiet; others say that she talks too much and is given to improving on the truth. The unlovable Pauline is, nonetheless, one of the two first-person narrators in *Tracks*, the third published volume of this loosely connected Chippewa trilogy. At the end of that novel, she takes the name Leopolda with her vows. Throughout *Love Medicine* she is known only as the violent and masochistic Sister Leopolda.

Born one-quarter white and three-quarters Chippewa, Pauline struggles to identify and be identified as white. Tall, skinny, hunched over, and with a large nose, she knows that her looks are so plain that men especially cannot see her; she uses this invisibility to watch and learn more about others. In particular, while living and working with her aunt south of the reservation, at Kozka Meats in Argus, North Dakota, this invisibility allows her to watch the effect that the mysterious Chippewa woman FLEUR PILLAGER has on men. It is Pauline who pushes the bolt behind the three men who have taken refuge in an ice-filled meat locker after having raped Fleur, effectively trapping them during a tornado. In the aftermath of the storm and the deaths of the three men, only Pauline knows that Fleur, with her mysterious powers, caused the storm in retaliation.

When Pauline returns to the reservation, she lives with Bernadette Morrissey and helps with her work among the dying and the dead. But Fleur continues to fascinate her. However, this time Pauline falls in love with Fleur's lover, Eli Kashpaw. When Eli refuses her, she purchases love medicine from Old Man Pillager and has Bernadette's beautiful and sensuous young daughter Sophie seduce him. As she had earlier done with Fleur and Eli, Pauline vicariously enjoys the passion between Sophie and Eli. Although Fleur knows the role that Pauline has played in Eli's infidelity, she punishes the unwitting puppet and not Pauline, the puppeteer. Pauline finally becomes the lover of the indifferent Napolean Morrissey.

Pauline commits herself to taking the vows of a nun when she discovers her pregnancy. Bernadette, who puts a halt to Pauline's inept attempts at aborting Napolean's seed, agrees to help hide the pregnancy and then to take the unwanted child. Pauline considers the baby Satan and will not even nurse the girl when she finally fights her way out of her mother's resisting body. It is Bernadette, then, who names the child MARIE (LAZARRE KASHPAW).

At the convent, Pauline takes on penance so that by her pain she can prove her worthiness. She wears her shoes on the wrong feet; starves herself; wears harsh, painful clothing beneath her habit; will allow herself to go to the bathroom only twice a day; and takes insufficient precautions against the cold northern winters. She hallucinates that God comes and tells her that she is not Indian but wholly white (Indian women were not permitted to join the convent). She also believes that Jesus intends her to exorcise the pagan gods from among the Indians. But when she foolishly plunges her hands into a pot of boiling water that Nanapush and Old Man Pillager had prepared as part of a cleansing ceremony for Fleur, Pauline concludes that Christ, who she thought would preserve the flesh on her hands and arms, is weak and does not know how to combat Indian gods. She does.

Pauline takes Leopolda as her name when she marries Christ as a nun. Believing that her special task is to find all the places in which Satan lurks, Leopolda brutally drives the devil from the lives of the girls who attend the convent school. In particular, Leopolda finds Satan lodged deeply in the heart of Marie, an adolescent Indian girl. Ostensibly to purify the girl, Leopolda pours boiling water over Marie's back. But after she has also pierced the girl's palm with a cooking fork and knocked her unconscious with a poker, Leopolda tells the other nuns that Marie fainted when the Lord implanted the stigmata on her hand. The nuns' subsequent devotion to Marie is almost more

than Leopolda can handle. Fortunately for Leopolda, Marie leaves the convent.

When Leopolda is visited on her deathbed years later by Marie, the decrepit and emaciated nun's hate is still so powerful that it raises her up out of bed and gives her the strength to try to strike the younger woman.

Pym, Arthur Gordon. *Narrative of Arthur Gordon Pym*. Edgar Allan Poe. 1838.

A young man looking for adventure on the seas, Arthur Gordon Pym faces more danger than he bargained for. While plunging himself into situations from which he must make desperate and daring escapes, Arthur's thirst for adventure seems unabated even though he has more than one brush with death.

A resident of New Bedford, Massachusetts, Arthur is fascinated by the sea. On one occasion he and his friend Augustus, on Augustus's suggestion, go out sailing one stormy night in Arthur's sailboat. The two young men, both drunk, are almost killed in the process. Unwilling to heed this lesson and stop trusting Augustus's suggestions, Arthur agrees to engage in an adventure with his rash friend that proves to be terrifying.

Arthur, whose grandfather has forbidden his pursuing a life at sea, stows away on a ship captained by Augustus's father. Hidden away in the hold of the ship and well stocked with books and provisions, Arthur plans to keep himself concealed until the ship is well out to sea. His prospects of a pleasant journey are disturbed, however. His food runs out after a few days, and Augustus does not come to replenish them. When Augustus finally rescues Arthur, he reveals that some crew members have mutinied and set the captain and other sailors afloat. Eventually Arthur and Augustus, in league with Peters, a sailor who has a change of heart, kill all but one of the mutinous sailors, regaining control of the ship.

The ship has become dangerous through storm damage and neglect. One day another ship appears on the horizon, but when it finally comes in sight, Augustus and the others see that everyone on board is dead and decaying. Despairing of rescue, the four must also contend with starvation because the ship's food supplies are locked in a flooded cabin. They must resort to cannibalism, determining the victim by drawing lots held by Arthur. The man who had survived the retaking of the ship dies to save Arthur and his friends.

Four days after the man is sacrificed, Arthur manages to break into the storeroom and retrieve some food. Fortified by the olives and turtle that they eat, Arthur feels his strength returning in some measure. Augustus is sinking fast, however, and finally dies when a wound turns gangrenous. Not long after his friend's death, Arthur is rescued, along with Peters, by a passing ship.

The vessel that rescues them is heading south, toward Antarctica. Arthur enthusiastically encourages the captain to push onward to unexplored regions. After sailing through icy regions they arrive in a warm climate and land near a small island. Trade relations are established with the natives, and when a party is organized to farm crustaceans, Arthur and Peters are among their number.

The seemingly friendly natives cause a landslide and kill everyone in the party except Arthur and Peters. As the two watch from their hiding place on the island, the crew is murdered and the ship looted and then blown up by the crafty natives. Arthur and Peters are forced to hide for a few days until they manage to kill some of the natives, taking one of them hostage, and steal a boat. At sea they drift farther south, through a region where the air is white and misty and the sea almost boiling hot. Pym's narrative ends abruptly; and although he makes his way back to tell his story, there is no indication at the end of the tale as to how he did it.

Pyncheon, Hepzibah. *The House of the Seven Gables.* Nathaniel Hawthorne. 1851.

Caught in the conflict between her former life as a genteel, aristocratic lady and the present demand to be a modern, capitalistic woman, creaky jointed, scowling old Hepzibah Pyncheon longs for the dingy elegance of yesteryear. Hepzibah's Puritan ancestor, Colonel Pyncheon, wrangled the land for his many-gabled house from Matthew Maule, whom Pyncheon had tried and executed for witchcraft. On the scaffold Maule issued a curse on the family and house of his powerful accuser. The house, built by Maule's son, rises in grotesque Gothic luxuriance and stands as a testament to Pyncheon's un-Puritan lust for pride. Soon thereafter the Colonel died mysteriously— perhaps, as many suspect, of Maule's curse. Although the next generation of Pyncheons inherit the house and the attendant guilt of their fathers, they do not—in a newly democratic society—inherit the grandeur of aristocratic entitlement.

Profoundly mortified at the affront to her old family gentility, Hepzibah is forced to open a one-cent shop in a front room of the house in order to make ends meet.

Each ring of the store's doorbell rankles her nerve endings. Her ugly temper and equally ugly disposition provoke a laugh or sneer from potential customers, and consequently business suffers. The guilt-ridden Hepzibah equally laments both slights to and acknowledgments of her former nobility.

Soon after opening the shop, Hepzibah receives several visitors. The first is her cousin, Judge Jaffrey Pyncheon, a hateful, land-hungry politician. Next to arrive is Hepzibah's lovely young country cousin, Phoebe Pyncheon. Practical, cheerful, and efficient, the fresh-faced Phoebe makes a striking contrast to the morose and sluggish Hepzibah. With a mixture of love and jealousy the elder Pyncheon acknowledges that her young cousin is a vastly superior shopkeeper but certainly not a proper aristocratic lady.

Hepzibah is next visited by Clifford, her brother, who thirty years earlier was imprisoned by Judge Pyncheon for the alleged murder of his uncle. Old, white-haired, and helpless, Clifford takes a childish delight in all things sensual; he is completely unrefined and oblivious to intellectual values. Hepzibah adopts as her mission the care and protection of her compassionless brother. The judge returns to the house to harass Clifford with threats of commitment to an insane asylum. He also threatens to take the house away from Hepzibah. But he dies mysteriously as Clifford and Hepzibah flee the burden of their house and history.

Enjoying what they think is the heady air of freedom, Hepzibah and her brother take a giddy train ride to celebrate their release from domestic prison. Upon returning from their romp, the siblings discover that Phoebe is engaged to marry HOLGRAVE, a young daguerreotypist who is a boarder at the house. In a series of happy endings, it is disclosed that Holgrave is actually a member of the Maule family. As such, he reveals the hidden location of the deed to the house, transfers legal ownership to Hepzibah, and removes the curse of guilt. Clifford and Hepzibah leave the house of seven gables and move to the elegant country estate of the recently deceased judge to live out their lives happily.

Q

Queeg, Lieutenant Commander Philip Francis. The Caine Mutiny. Herman Wouk. 1951.

This tale of naval adventure during World War II centers on the mutiny aboard the destroyer *Caine* against

Lieutenant Commander Philip Francis Queeg. The fate of the psychologically disturbed Queeg raises subtle questions about the justifiability of mutiny.

Toward the end of the war, Queeg is assigned to the

Caine, a destroyer-minesweeper operating in the Pacific. He quickly reveals himself to be a poor ship handler, on several occasions directing the *Caine*'s movements in a shockingly incorrect manner and then attempting to conceal his errors from command headquarters. Whenever he is criticized by his superiors, he lays the blame on various members of his crew, and he blackmails his officers into supporting his lies by threatening to give them low marks on their fitness reports.

Recognizing his own incompetence, Queeg attempts to compensate by adhering with absurd strictness to naval rules and regulations, employing extraordinarily harsh measures to punish the crew for infractions. As alarm and discontent mount among the officers and crew, Queeg reveals himself to be a coward. On one occasion he hurries the *Caine* away from a battle on shore before the ship has adequately completed its mission, and on another occasion he refuses to take advantage of an opportunity to open fire on the enemy. In addition, he goes to great lengths to position himself on the side of the *Caine* facing away from battle.

Queeg spends most of his time cloistered in his cabin devising complex punishments for crew members who are out of favor with him and perpetually rolling two steel balls between his fingers. When Queeg conducts an extraordinarily time-consuming and obviously fruitless search for some strawberries stolen from the ship's kitchen, Executive Officer Stephen Maryk becomes convinced that Communications Officer Tom Keefer is correct in having diagnosed Queeg as a paranoid schizophrenic. A few days later when the ship is caught in a typhoon and Queeg handles the ship in a manner Maryk considers dangerous, Maryk takes over command of the *Caine*.

In the ensuing court-martial, it initially appears that Maryk had been in the wrong. Accounts of Queeg's transgressions raise eyebrows among the officers of the court, but these transgressions do not appear as serious on land as they had appeared at sea. In fact, it is later revealed that Maryk's lawyer, Greenwald, felt that his client was indeed in the wrong, although Greenwald blames Tom Keefer more than Maryk since the former incited the latter to his mutinous action. Despite his misgivings, however, Greenwald manages to get Maryk acquitted. Although Queeg seemed in full possession of his faculties throughout the court proceedings, when Greenwald puts the commander on the stand and leads him into a lengthy, incoherent, and clearly paranoid account of his tribulations and mistreatment aboard the *Caine*, Queeg's mental instability becomes apparent. The charges against Maryk are dropped, and Queeg is relieved of command due to "illness."

Queequeg. *Moby Dick*; or, *The Whale*. Herman Melville. 1851.

Queequeg, a native of the mythical island Kokovoko, becomes the faithful companion of ISHMAEL, the narrator of this epic novel of American whaling. Although he lives among Westerners and Christians, Queequeg refuses to adopt their ways completely. After only a short period in the company of whalers, he has become convinced that they are "miserable and wicked," and so he decides to remain faithful to his own customs and beliefs.

Queequeg was born to a noble family of Kokovoko; his father was a High Chief, his uncle a High Priest. Although destined to inherit his father's title, he became curious about what lay beyond the island and determined to make a passage to "Christian lands." Having failed in his first attempt to gain a place as a sailor on board, Queequeg paddled his canoe to meet the ship as it sailed out, climbed onto the deck, and refused to move until the captain consented to take him. He then became a harpooner, a position that requires considerable stamina, agility, and courage.

To earn money between cruises, Queequeg walks through the port town of New Bedford hawking embalmed heads. One night he returns to his inn to find a stranger in his bed. The terrified young man, Ishmael, shrieks for the landlord's protection when he first sees Queequeg, whose dark skin is covered with purplish tattoos. When Ishmael is made to understand that Queequeg is interested in hunting whales, not men, they lie down comfortably together and sleep. Queequeg's command of English is not perfect, but with some effort the two strike up a friendship. By the end of the following evening, Queequeg performs a traditional ritual, pronouncing them "bosom friends."

Because they are now bound to each other, Queequeg vows to share Ishmael's fate by sailing on the same whaling ship with him. Once Ishmael has signed onto the *Pequod*, Queequeg visits its owners to demonstrate his expertise with the harpoon and is immediately chosen by STARBUCK, the first mate, as his harpooner. Once the voyage is under way, Queequeg must also assist with preparing the whale for boiling by inserting a great hook into its back in order to remove the blubber. To accomplish this task, Queequeg is attached to a "monkey-rope," the other end of which is held by Ishmael. Should one of them slip, both would fall into the jaws of the sharks that are milling hungrily about the underbelly of the whale.

Queequeg stands out for his bravery even among the hardy crew of the *Pequod*. At one point another harpooner, Tashtego, falls into the severed head of the whale while he is working to extract its precious spermaceti oil. The paralyzed crew stands watching while Queequeg dives in and surfaces several minutes later with Tashtego in tow. In another instance Queequeg falls ill with a fever, and on the verge of death he requests that a coffin be made. With stoic calm he tries out the coffin to make sure it is comfortable. When he magically recovers, the coffin is sealed and used as the *Pequod*'s life buoy.

Along with the other sailors on the *Pequod*, Queequeg has pledged to assist CAPTAIN AHAB in wreaking vengeance on the fabled white whale, Moby Dick; his whale boat is destroyed, along with the ship itself, in their final battle. However, Queequeg's coffin, which he had covered with hieroglyphics similar to those tattooed on his body, shoots out of the water and keeps Ishmael, the wreck's sole survivor, afloat until he is rescued by a passing ship.

Quesadilla, Hector "Little Cheese." "The Hector Quesadilla Story." T. Coraghessan Boyle. 1985.

Hector Quesadilla, a veteran baseball player, has not played regularly on a starting lineup for over ten years. As his physical condition continues to deteriorate, he promises his wife that he will retire at the end of the season. But at his birthday party on the morning of a home game, he foresees that he will save the game with some feat worthy of his past glory and redeem himself in the eyes of his family and fans.

Hector remembers the old days, before he met his wife Asuncion, when he was a rookie on a Mexican team. At that time his hearing had been so keen that he could judge a pitch by the sound the ball made in the pitcher's hand. In contrast, he now suffers a number of middle-aged ailments: muscle ache, hemorrhoids, and corns. After a long career, playing on five teams in the United States alone, Hector finds that he can barely drag himself to breakfast in time to revive for practice with the Los Angeles Dodgers.

One morning in the kitchen Hector realizes that he has reached yet another birthday in his fourth decade. His children and grandchildren arrive and shower him with gifts, which only make him more depressed. When he finds out they will be at the afternoon game, however, he has a premonition that, even though he rarely plays at all anymore, he will score the deciding hit in this important game.

At the park, the manager sends Hector to bat with the score tied at five at the bottom of the ninth inning. The old player struts out and waves to his family, only to be replaced at the last minute by another Dodger. After screaming at the manager for embarrassing him, Hector waits through more and more tied innings for a chance to clinch the winning run. Night falls on the park. The vendors run out of snacks. By the twenty-second tied inning, the game becomes the longest in American history. Hector wants to become the man who won the longest game in history, but the manager continues to pass him by in the batting order.

By the thirty-first inning, fans and players alike are dropping from exhaustion. Even though Hector is twice as old as most of the other players, he wills himself to go on as the game turns surreal. Hector hits a line drive, but with his limbs beginning to fail him, he gets tagged at third base. He redeems himself in the next inning, however, by pitching cleverly enough to keep his team in the game.

The story closes with the image of Hector at bat with the bases loaded, in a game that will never end, the ball hanging in front of him like a birthday piñata.

Quickskill, Raven. *Flight to Canada.* Ishmael Reed. 1976.

Raven Quickskill, the novel's central character, is a poet and slave who escapes from the Virginia plantation where he was raised. Despite his ostensible privileges as a slave—he eats in the main house and is Master Swill's trusted bookkeeper—Quickskill is one of the first slaves on the plantation to escape. He flees to a haven called Emancipation City and spends his time writing poetry and giving antislavery lectures. He composes a poem entitled "Flight to Canada" in which he sharply criticizes his ex-master and his notoriously corrupt plantation. The poem is published in a small literary magazine, *The Beulahland Review*.

Using clues gleaned from the publication of "Flight to Canada," two of Master Swill's agents trace Raven Quickskill to his hideout in Emancipation City. They pay Quickskill a polite visit, claiming they have orders to repossess him. Quickskill receives them but, using a simple ploy, manages to climb out a back window and escape.

Quickskill then goes for assistance to his friend Stray Leechfield who lives in an old warehouse district. Leechfield runs a business making pornographic daguerreotypes with himself as a model. Leechfield and Quickskill get into an argument over the implications of freedom. Leechfield suggests that Quickskill "buy himself" from Swill and offers to lend him the money to do so. But Quickskill declines, claiming proudly that he isn't anybody's property to begin with.

Disappointed, Quickskill seeks out another friend named 40s, who lives in a boathouse by the river. He tries to persuade 40s to join him and Leechfield in a resistance against Swill, but 40s only answers that he is "not going to put in with no chump." 40s claims he can hide out in the mountains with his trusted rifle for twenty years but doesn't think Quickskill is capable. Quickskill, for his part, doesn't want to hide—he wants to face up to Swill.

In recognition of his poem "Flight to Canada," Raven unexpectedly receives an invitation to the White House from Abraham Lincoln, who is holding a reception in honor of "the leading scribes of America." At the reception, Quickskill reflects on the fact that his writing poetry has resulted in so much: money to live on, a chance to mingle with the great celebrities of the country at the White House, and, less happily, being tracked down by Swill's agents.

Still on the run, Quickskill bumps into an old acquaintance of his, Princess Quaw Quaw Tralaralara. They reminisce and discuss what course of action Quickskill should take next. He decides to leave Emancipation City and flee to Canada with Quaw Quaw. Unfortunately, the yacht they hire to transport them across the river is owned and operated by Yankee Jack, Quaw Quaw's estranged husband. Quaw Quaw and Yankee Jack argue, and Quaw Quaw becomes so upset that she jumps from the boat and is lost in the rapids near Niagara Falls. Thinking he has lost her forever, Quickskill continues his trip into Canada. A few days later, as he is taking in the view of the falls, Quickskill is surprised by Quaw Quaw's reappearance. She is walking a tightrope across the river toward him, carrying a banner that proclaims her love for him.

Eventually Master Swill dies, leaving his estate to one of his slaves, and as the novel closes, Quickskill returns to Virginia.

Quinn, James. *The Sporting Club.* Thomas McGuane. 1969.

James Quinn, the protagonist in this surrealistic novel of male bonding and aggression, is the son of a prominent Michigan family, the owner of a prosperous tool and die business in Detroit, and a life member of the Centennial Club, a sporting club in the Michigan wilderness.

Bored with his business, Quinn escapes to his seven-room cabin at the club to rest and fish. Immediately upon arriving he is drawn toward a childhood acquaintance, VERNOR STANTON, a rich and erratic man who is living there permanently with his beautiful mistress Janey. Quinn, as always, finds himself intrigued and repelled by Stanton's eccentric behavior.

Stanton, Quinn, and Janey go to the Mackinac Bridge dedication, where Stanton steals a bus, embarrasses state legislators, and then sails away on his powerful yacht. The three go together to a party at the "Bug House," where the club's elite gather. Quinn is anxious to avoid Stanton but inwardly admires his audacity when Stanton humiliates pompous members. He becomes sentimental about their youthful pranks and awkward attempts to define their manhood.

Gradually, however, Quinn begins to believe his trip to the Sporting Club was a mistake. Stanton orchestrates a coup by replacing the club manager, a competent man, with a lout named Earl Olive. As always, Quinn finds himself pulled into Stanton's wild schemes. He joins Earl's party of bikers and misfits and is seduced by a young girl. Attempting to restore himself to normalcy, he goes fishing at night and is nearly drowned when Olive dynamites the dam, sending the lake's water down the river.

Although Quinn soon realizes that his stay is no longer pleasurable, he can't seem to leave the club as Stanton's psychotic scheme begins to unfold. Club members gather in a large carnival tent after many of their buildings are blown up. They swiftly regress toward primitive behavior. Detroit seems increasingly remote as Quinn attempts to make sense of the terrible nightmare occurring in the wilderness around him. He is convinced that Stanton is crazy.

On the Fourth of July, the members, who have suffered a rapid moral deterioration, dig up a time capsule that has been buried for a century. Only the club and its history stands between them and chaos as they copulate openly and hunt Olive and his gang of thugs. Even Quinn finds himself caught up in the antic behavior of the night.

When Quinn and Stanton dig up the time capsule, they discover it contains nothing but a photograph of their forefathers, the club members of the past, engaged in a wild sex circus. The secret of the club has been discovered, and the current members are prompted into an even wilder frenzy of activity. Quinn, alone and desperate, finds the fireworks and shoots them off one by one over the desolate landscape while an insane Stanton holds the entire club at bay as he fires his machine guns wildly into the night.

When order is restored, Quinn alone is rational enough to report on the strange proceedings. He returns to Detroit scarred by his wild summer adventures. Stanton, who has now bought the club and installed himself as sole occupant, still exercises an odd hold over Quinn. He visits and finds his friend in the company of Janey and two aides, dueling with plywood guns, talking in memorized conversations, and acting as lord over the club he destroyed.

R

Rae Ann. "A Girl's Story." Toni Cade Bambara. 1977.

As the story opens, Rae Ann, a pubescent African-American girl, is lying on her bed, afraid to look at herself, afraid of the blood that is issuing from between her legs. Her condition is a frightening mystery, and she tries to stop it the only way she can think of: by lying down and stuffing toilet paper into her vagina. One of Rae Ann's principal fears, however, is that her grandmother, M'Dear, will discover that she has ruined one of her towels.

Staring at a map of Mozambique as she lies there, Rae Ann's thoughts drift to Dada Bibi, a strong, proud African-American woman who counsels young women at the community center. Rae Ann feels certain that Dada Bibi would offer reassurance and help, but she dares not go to the center for fear of bleeding to death on the way.

Rae Ann remembers Dada Bibi's story of an African queen who refused to marry until she had expelled the intruding, enslaving Europeans from her country. Savoring the part of the story where the gallant suitors kept proposing to the queen, Rae Ann regrets that she knows no such gallant young men. The boys of her acquaintance just stand on the corner and scream for her to "get her ass outside."

As her elevated legs begin to fatigue, Rae Ann remembers that Dada Bibi has been telling her lately that she is becoming a young woman now and that they should talk. But Rae Ann, anticipating a sermon about not letting boys touch her breasts, has been avoiding the proposed tête-à-tête.

Oozing blood, Rae Ann eventually creeps to the bathroom, where she sits on the toilet and worries that she has left the smell of death everywhere. Her brother Horace bangs on the door and bellows at her to get out of the bathroom, but he begins to grow concerned when she doesn't comply. He asks if she's okay; Rae Ann responds hysterically, "Go away!"

Horace does go away, only to return with their grandmother, M'Dear. Assuming and implying that she's suffering from a botched abortion, Horace begins to taunt Rae Ann through the door. M'Dear eventually coerces her out of the bathroom, and Rae Ann confesses that she is bleeding. M'Dear immediately begins screaming that Rae Ann has let some filthy man go up her with a coat hanger and that she is going to wind up just like her mother. But Rae Ann protests so passionately and sincerely that M'Dear soon realizes she is mistaken. Her granddaughter is menstruating. Without a word of explanation or reassurance, M'Dear runs off to the drugstore.

While M'Dear is gone, Rae Ann realizes she is not dying, but she feels she is being punished for something. To atone, she wants to make a promise to her people. But she cannot vow to die for them, for it would make her feel scared and cheated, and she cannot vow to live for them, for it would make her feel confused and inadequate. Finally, Rae Ann decides to find out what she has done wrong and then take her whipping. As she makes this decision, M'Dear returns and, tossing her a mysterious package from the drugstore, leaves Rae Ann to open it by herself.

Raffine, Andy. *Her.* Lawrence Ferlinghetti. 1960.

Andy Raffine, the narrator, explains that he is writing in the "fourth-person singular," the tense that most accurately relates his surreal experiences. Raffine is seeking a physical madonna to fulfill his need for spiritual love, and his emotional despair distorts his perception of the real as well as the lucidity of his narrative. Continually confusing the real and the illusory, the past and the present, Raffine attempts to come to terms with his overwhelming sense of alienation.

An expatriate from Brooklyn, Raffine lives in Paris in the 1950s and spends most of his time on Rue du Cherche Midi trying to meet the woman of his dreams. This unnamed woman is a sculptor who sculpts what she perceives to be her own image. In dreamlike sequences, Raffine describes making love to her but then goes to a café with the hope that the waiter there will introduce him to this woman.

Images and events from Raffine's past recur in his perceptions and descriptions of the present. For instance, Raffine collected string as a child, and string images, both real and imaginary, haunt him in Paris: A man is selling shoelaces, birds bring him string, and the lover he eventually meets uses string as a bookmark that gets soiled. Other recurring images are those of birds and pigeons, music on phonographs, Piblokto (Eskimo winter madness), abstract painting, body parts, roots, and primordial sexuality. Raffine often imagines himself trying to paint a scene, capturing its essence through the use of color, and the language he uses to describe painting is blatantly sexual. He often compares life to art either by evoking images that artists such as Giotto or Van Gogh have made famous or by making literary references. Beginning in Paris, Raffine would have the Poetry Police transform civilization by making love possible and popular.

Awkward and fat, Raffine unexpectedly meets a girl in a pensione in Rome. Obsessed with his weight and how his body moves and occupies space, he constantly derides his own physicality. The girl he meets is shy, sullen, and dark, and they maintain a friendship for several weeks that centers around books. He believes that the characters in the books she gives him to read are meant to be representative of her own personality, which she is too timid to reveal. They make love one night, and Raffine wakens to find her gone and a note that says she will never return. Overwhelmed with feelings of frustration, he realizes that the act of making love is only a poor attempt at trying to prove spiritual love exists. As the novel closes, Raffine, who feels he will not be able to overcome the void with love, desires to fade into nothing. Although he finds God a confusing and somewhat foreign concept, his thoughts turn to death and being rescued by God.

Ragged Dick. *Ragged Dick.* Horatio Alger, Jr. 1868.

Ragged Dick is Horatio Alger, Jr.'s perfect American boy, who appears (in much less ragged attire) in a few of Alger's early works and was cloned by Alger to create the upwardly struggling heroes of over a hundred additional rags-to-riches novels for boys. An orphan at three, a bootblack at seven, and an unrepentant hedonist at fourteen, Ragged Dick lives hand-to-mouth on the streets of New York City. He jokes a lot, smokes some, gambles a bit, and heads to the theater when he can scrape together enough pennies. Thus, decadent and poor, dirty and droll, Ragged Dick would be ever outcast by fortune and society were it not for his singular advantages. "Our hero," as he is dubbed, is bright, honest, good-looking, and unimaginably lucky.

In a single remarkable day Ragged Dick is launched on his path to success. He shines the shoes of a Mr. Greyson, who later, impressed with Dick's honesty, will invite him to attend Sunday school at a Fifth Avenue church. Dick offers to show a young, affluent visitor around the city and is immediately reimbursed with his first real friend, a new set of clothes, five dollars, and the inspiration to save money and get an education. With these assets Dick abandons his life on the streets, rents a room on Mott Street, and takes under his wing a less aggressive shoeshine boy named Fosdick, who agrees to teach him to read in exchange for a place in the relative luxury of Dick's room and Dick's bed.

From then on the two boys spend their evenings studying. Dick is an attentive student, so he quickly adds literacy, penmanship, and mathematics to the skills he has learned on the street: ingenuity, self-defense, and an uncanny ability to see through confidence games. In nine months Fosdick has helped deliver a new, Protestant, and unragged Dick: Richard Hunter. Dick now has a real name, a real savings account, and a real correspondence with his out-of-town friend. Sunday school goes well, too, and after church on Sundays, Mr. Greyson's daughter Ida flirts with Dick.

Dick's gradual ascendance is greatly accelerated by an-

other stroke of luck. When Dick courageously saves a drowning boy from the depths of the East River, the boy's father, Mr. Rockwell, in a frenzy of gratitude, gives Dick a brand-new suit and the next day hires him for the counting room of his trading company at the exorbitant salary of ten dollars a week. Well on the road to realizing the American dream, Dick and Fosdick, who now works in a hat shop, move to more spacious rooms on St. Mark's Place.

Dick's philanthropy does not end with helping Fosdick out with rent money, though. In a subsequent novel, *Mark the Match Boy*, it is Dick who helps Fosdick recover a sizable fortune from his late father's embezzling broker. Similarly, it is Dick who befriends the sickly Match Boy of the novel's title, and Dick who reunites the Match Boy with his grandfather, the very broker who made Fosdick rich. From here, "Ragged" Dick Hunter continues on into Alger's world, a patron to street boys and a totemic version of success in the unlikely America where bootblacks make good, where virtue is rewarded and snobbery scourged, and where you can really tell how honest a man is by staring him in the eye.

Railroad Shorty. *The Neon Wilderness.* Nelson Algren. 1960.

Despite the railroad accident that robbed him of both legs at a very early age, Railroad Shorty is a man of endless versatility and unfailing resources. Among his many talents are a proficiency at cards, the ability to overhaul a car in a matter of minutes, and a talent for mixing drinks that can either knock a man off his feet or have no visible effect for five hours. He can guess a man's weight within two pounds, and although he has never carried a watch, he can guess the correct time within two minutes, day or night. Shorty earns twenty dollars a day selling perfumed water, which he bottles himself. He spends money so freely that on those rare occasions when he runs short, the other regulars at the dingy Chicago tavern he frequents think he is holding out on them.

Shorty takes an odd kind of pleasure whenever a crippled man walks past him. With the upper torso of a bodybuilder, he is constantly warning the regulars at the tavern, Brother B.'s, that he can outdrink and outfight any of them. His cronies know that Shorty's worst fear is to be considered handicapped.

When Shorty hears that young Fancy, the bartender at Brother B.'s, has been making derogatory comments about him to a local prostitute named Venus, Shorty comes rolling in that very afternoon. He shouts insults at the young bartender and is egged on by the other regulars, who love nothing better than a good fight. Brother B., the owner of the bar, pulls down the shades and locks the front door, the custom when a fight is about to break out. Although doing his best to avoid a confrontation, Fancy realizes that a fight with Shorty is unavoidable.

Following prefight etiquette, the two shake hands while the men around them clear away furniture to give them room. Fancy immediately grabs a spittoon and thrusts it into Shorty's torso. While evading the oncoming spittoon, Shorty loses his balance sufficiently for Fancy to kick him between the eyes. The onlookers urge Fancy to get Shorty while he is still stunned, but the young bartender experiences a moment of compassion for the legless Shorty.

He soon pays for his mistake when Shorty, having quickly recovered, hurls a table at him. Infuriated at being treated mercifully because he is handicapped, Shorty swiftly rolls over to the prostrate Fancy and pummels him repeatedly with his enormous arms. The cheers of the onlookers gradually turn to pleas for Shorty to stop, but he continues to beat the unconscious Fancy.

Shorty is finally restrained by the nauseated onlookers. Without saying a word, he leaves the bloodied mess that had been Fancy lying in the middle of the floor and rolls out of Brother B.'s.

Ralph. "The Doctor's Wife." John Updike. 1961.

Ralph and his wife Eve are two white Americans vacationing on a remote island in the Caribbean. They picked the most obscure island they could find, one next to St. Martin, because it is cheap and rarely frequented by tourists.

At the start of the story, the couple is enjoying a day at the beach with the wife of the local doctor, "the only fully white woman resident." The doctor's wife is a sort of "queen" on this island where she has been living for the past ten years. She plays hostess to the rare British official or royalty who comes to visit, and she has deigned to pay Ralph and his wife a call to welcome them.

At the beach, the doctor's wife describes the island's former Anglican vicar, an old white man named Vic Johnson who, she claims, "loved the people." Eve quickly hears the prejudice beneath the words of the doctor's wife and asserts her own appreciation for the native people, particularly Hannah, the domestic whose services came with the house they have rented. Ralph, noticing the tension between the two women, tries to mediate, but the doctor's wife seems unable to let the subject drop. She asks how black people are "cared for" in America. Eve, whom Ralph thinks of as a liberal, again becomes defensive, and the conversation turns tense, with the doctor's wife pressing them to tell her if blacks are well off and where they are allowed to go to school. She asks if they would want their children to go to school with black children. Ralph attempts in vain to end the conversation, but the doctor's wife forges on, saying "the blacks are pouring into London." Eve, disgusted, retreats farther down on the beach.

Looking after her, the doctor's wife comments that Eve is quite tan. Ralph relaxes somewhat, suddenly understanding that the doctor's wife is threatened by having another white woman on her territory, but the task of interceding between them has taxed him. He is uncomfortable with the connection between his family and the doctor's that this visit has created, fearing that it will somehow be held against them. The doctor's wife asks him if he knows what the islanders are saying about Eve. Because of her dark tan, she says, the people are insinuating that Eve is part black and that this is what prevents them from going to the better islands, not finances. She looks at Ralph both curiously and maliciously, seeming to expect that Ralph will corroborate her accusations. Ralph insists that they chose this island because it was inexpensive, and when the doctor's wife maintains that the natives believe all Americans are rich, he is certain that this is what she believes also.

Ralph goes down to the water alone. He feels that Eve would have wanted him to reply that his wife was indeed part black and that in America such things are not cause for any gossip. But at the same time he understands that for such a response to be funny it would depend on a "vast unconscious pride of race." His association with the doctor's wife leaves him filled with guilt; he thrashes about in the water, torn between his fear of sharks and his fear of the doctor's wife.

Ramos, Connie Comacho. *Woman on the Edge of Time.* Marge Piercy. 1976.

Connie Comacho Ramos is an impoverished and victimized woman whose life is destroyed by financial instability and by a heartless family that incarcerates her in mismanaged mental institutions. At the outset, Connie is determined to maintain a positive and productive life-style in spite of her tragic history of familial strife and romantic disappointments.

Born in Texas to a poor Mexican-American couple, Connie moves to Chicago at the age of seven. She works hard throughout her years in secondary school and eventually earns a scholarship to a community college. After two years, however, she is forced to leave college because of an unwanted pregnancy that she terminates with an abortion. Thrown out of her house by her enraged parents and threatened by a man who clearly intends to rape her, Connie flees to New York where she marries a man named Martin Alvarez. Their happiness is cut short when Martin is stabbed to death at the age of twenty-one. She then marries Eddie Ramos, and they have a daughter, Angelina. But Eddie subsequently walks out, leaving Connie with the task of raising her child alone. For a time she manages to eke out a living by working at low-paying jobs.

Connie's happiness is reinstated when she begins dating a blind black saxophone player named Claud, with whom she makes a living as a pickpocket before they are both arrested. He is sent to jail, and she is put on probation. Her luck continues to fail her: Claud dies in prison after participating in a medical experiment in which he was injected with a hepatitis virus. Following this devastating event, Connie descends into a drugged, alcoholic stupor and physically abuses Angelina, whereupon she is institutionalized and Angelina is put up for adoption and taken in by a family in Scarsdale.

After eight months of criminally incompetent treatment, Connie is released, only to be recommitted when she attacks Geraldo, the pimp of her favorite niece, Dolly, in an attempt to stop him from beating her. Geraldo and her niece lie, claiming that Connie attacked them, and they commit her to Bellevue, a public psychiatric hospital. There, in an attempt to survive, she has bizarre, futuristic fantasies in which the strong and sympathetic woman LUCIENTE attempts to understand Connie's dilemma and provide her with advice and solace.

It is not long before Connie herself becomes a subject for medical research. Terrified of the results of this experiment, which involves planting electrodes under the skulls of patients in order to monitor their pathological mood swings, Connie steals some poison while on a furlough for Thanksgiving and proceeds to poison the coffee of the doctors in charge of the experiment. Although she escapes being made into a mindless guinea pig, she is nevertheless unable to convince the authorities to release her. The novel concludes with a synopsis of her supposed psychological maladies, evidence that she will continue in her miserable state as an institutionalized, wrecked woman.

Ramsey, Nat. "The Old Forest." Peter Taylor. 1979.

This is the story of Nat Ramsey, a man in his mid-sixties, who remembers an incident from his youth, which he sees as one of the decisive experiences of his life.

Nat is twenty-three years old and a week away from his marriage to Caroline Braxley when, on a cold December day, he takes a drive by the old forest outside Memphis with a woman named Lee Ann Deehart. They get into a minor collision, which leaves Nat momentarily unconscious. When he comes to, he finds that Lee Ann has run off into the forest. Nat is taken to the hospital for stitches and then sent home. He is worried and mystified by what Lee Ann has done. He is worried, too, that Caroline will learn he was out riding with Lee Ann.

Lee Ann is not a part of the wealthy well-ordered Memphis world to which Nat and Caroline belong. Her family background is mysterious, but she is at home in Memphis among a group of girls similar to herself—young working girls living alone or in boardinghouses, vulnerable and independent and oddly out of place for Memphis in 1931. Nat has known Lee Ann for two years. He and his friends have spent time with these vaguely bohemian girls in a playful, romantic way. The girls enjoy teasing Nat and his friends about how old-fashioned and dependent they are—Nat's ambition is to go into business with his father. Although Lee Ann and her friends sometimes sleep with men, their interest in Nat's crowd rarely goes that far.

Nat has dinner at Caroline's house and learns, to his surprise, that she and her parents already know about Lee Ann running off. Caroline is surprisingly practical: She offers to help Nat find her. Lee Ann is gone all night. The next day, Sunday, it snows, and Nat thinks of the pioneer women who felt so shackled by frontier life that they disappeared into the forest. On Monday, Nat goes with the police to make the rounds of Lee Ann's friends. They all say they haven't seen her. Nat is struck by how protective the policemen are toward the young girls. While he is at his father's office, he receives a phone call from a girl saying that Lee Ann wants the search called off. Nat asks to speak to Lee Ann. The girl hangs up. That night another girl calls. She says Lee Ann has kept one house ahead of the search party all day. Nat asks why Lee Ann is doing this and why she ran away at all. The girl says Lee Ann was feeling depressed. "About what?" Nat asks. "About life in general, you bastard," the girl says, "isn't that enough?" Looking back after forty years, Nat understands very well what the girl means. At the time all he knew was that if he didn't find Lee Ann, Caroline might break off their engagement. He had a strange and fleeting thought that maybe Lee Ann was the girl he should have been marrying.

After another futile day, Caroline insists on joining the search. She and Nat make the rounds together, finally visiting a girl named Fern Morris, with whom Nat actually had an affair. Fern realizes that Caroline won't marry Nat until Lee Ann is found, and although she won't tell them where Lee Ann is, she gives them enough information for them to find out. They learn that Lee Ann has gone to her grandmother, who owns a bar in Memphis. Lee Ann does have a family, after all.

Nat and Caroline drive over to the bar, and Nat thinks he sees Lee Ann's face in a room upstairs. Caroline insists that she go in alone. Nat protests, but Caroline says he must never see Lee Ann again. He waits outside for nearly an hour. Looking back, he realizes that this was his last chance to reach out beyond the narrow circumstances of his life into something more vital. Years later Nat will have his own crisis. When he is thirty-seven, he will rebel against his settled life in Memphis and drift into the world of academia, in search of the thing that was irrevocably lost when he decided to stay in the car that afternoon.

When Caroline comes out of the house, she wants to drive faster and faster, outside Memphis, as if she could drive away from this day, for now all her fear about Nat's infidelity has risen to the surface. As they drive along, with Caroline crying and talking wildly, it is as if they are trying to drive away from themselves and the limited lives they will inevitably lead. Like Nat, Caroline has been shaken by the possibility of freedom expressed in Lee Ann's brief flight, by Lee Ann's bravery and sadness. Caroline realizes she could not live a life like that. She says it is somehow too late for her, and therefore it was necessary for her to find Lee Ann in order to save herself and to be certain that she and Nat could marry. Nat remains silent while Caroline speaks, and she seems grateful for his silence. Looking back, he believes that Caroline thought he understood more than he could have at the time. But he connects her gratitude with the great support she gave him when, in his late thirties, he attempted his own limited flight to freedom.

Randall, Rebecca. *Rebecca of Sunnybrook Farm.* Kate Douglas Wiggin. 1903.

At the age of ten, Rebecca Randall, the novel's adolescent heroine, leaves her large family and moves to Riverboro to live with her two maiden aunts, Miranda and Jane, who have promised to give her a proper education. Rebecca takes after her dead father, an artist who was considered an irresponsible dreamer by the aunts and who failed to support his family. Because Rebecca has inherited her father's intelligence, creativity, and fascination with life, her aunts suspect her of having his character flaws as well; consequently, they see her only as an undisciplined and troublesome child.

Although Rebecca's imagination is constantly getting her into trouble, her loving personality, clever sense of humor, and sincere desire to better herself help her to win the hearts of the Riverboro community. Among the friends she develops are Mr. and Mrs. Cobbs, to whom she turns when escapades get her in too much trouble to go straight home to Aunt Miranda; Emma Jane, her dull-witted but adoring schoolmate; Miss Maxwell, her teacher at boarding school who recognizes Rebecca's creative and literary promise; and Adam Ladd, who was first charmed by Rebecca when she sold him soap to raise money for some poor friends of hers and who continues to look out for her interests.

Rebecca lives her life with a sense of the dramatic. She writes little poems about her daily experiences and invents theatrical events during playtime. Her efforts to improve her character are also undertaken with dramatic zeal, but the results are often unexpected. One day, deciding she is vain, she resolves to throw her most precious possession, her pink parasol, into a well. Her plan to keep her punishment secret backfires when the well plugs up and she is ridiculed by Aunt Miranda for her endeavor. On another occasion she decides that she can no longer live with her aunt and runs away to Mr. Cobbs', but she returns after he helps her visualize the dreadful consequences of her disappearance.

Aunt Miranda is not the only cause of difficulty in Rebecca's life. Her family is poor, and she feels guilty about having the privilege of an education while her brothers and sisters work diligently on the farm. Various crises happen to her family members. Her mother has a serious accident, and Rebecca has to return home to care for her. Then the life savings of Miranda and Jane are threatened, and they have to cut their needs to the bare minimum in order to keep Rebecca in school. Consequently, she rarely has new clothes, and any money she does acquire, such as the fifty-dollar scholarship for the school's best essay, she immediately sends home.

At seventeen, Rebecca graduates from boarding school with honors and awards, but instead of accepting any of the jobs Miss Maxwell has investigated for her, she returns to Riverboro to nurse Miranda, who sadly dies before Rebecca arrives. However, Miranda has bequeathed to Rebecca her house and savings, revealing her affection for her niece and leaving Rebecca independent. At the novel's close, Miss Maxwell and Adam Ladd long to discover what Rebecca will become.

Ransom, Basil. *The Bostonians.* Henry James. 1886.

Basil Ransom, a once wealthy Southern gentleman, represents the unbroken spirit of the conservative, chivalrous South, set in opposition to the Northern feminist spirit of the novel's two female protagonists. He is the romantic reactionary who rescues a weak-minded young girl from the clutches of the Feminist movement and reestablishes the status quo.

Ransom has just arrived in New York to establish himself as a lawyer. On a trip to Boston he is brought by his cousin OLIVE CHANCELLOR to a meeting of suffragettes, and here he encounters the young and beautiful VERENA TARRANT. He listens as Verena orates, and although he dismisses her ideals as rhetoric, he finds her style and manner charming.

Because he scorns feminism, Ransom soon incurs Olive's hatred. He returns to New York, and after a string of bad luck in his legal practice, he reappraises his situation. He decides that his ambition is to be an illustrious shaper of opinions, specifically, a political essayist. As his legal clientele thins, he begins writing in earnest.

Months later, with his practice on the edge of ruin, Ransom faces his greatest crisis when he is also rejected by a large number of publishers. He visits the wealthy Mrs. Luna, a conservative but very bold woman who has clear marital designs on him. He is on the verge of asking Mrs. Luna for her hand when the topic of Verena comes up. He realizes he does not love Mrs. Luna and decides to visit Verena in Boston.

This visit is a success, and Verena sends Ransom an invitation to a small speech she is giving in New York. Before she returns to Boston with Olive, her self-appointed guardian, he takes her on a walk through Central Park, where Verena draws out his views and helps him reveal his inner self.

The nature of Ransom's conservatism springs from his view of the Civil War and the abolitionists. Ransom, as Verena notes, is filled with bitterness from the losses his family incurred in the war, losses he blames on the Northern crusade for equality. Similarly, he considers the women's movement a mere sophistic patina of slogans covering a voracious totalitarian impulse.

This bitterness is not reflected in his own behavior, however; Ransom is a sympathetic character and has the opportunity to practice his Southern charm and chivalry without acting on his seventeenth-century ideals. Only in discussion is it clear that he feels women ought not to rebel against their own enslavement. He has no opportunity or capacity to see the restrictions of real injustice and has little understanding of the issue of women's oppression.

After her tour of the park with Ransom, Verena, afraid of betraying Olive by falling in love with him, flees to Boston. Some time later, one of Ransom's essays is accepted by a journal, and his self-esteem is instantly restored. Ransom's goal now is to lure Verena away from Olive. To that end he becomes the uninvited guest at their retreat on Cape Cod, where, over Olive's strenuous objections, he insists on taking long walks with Verena to talk her into marrying him. Just as he seems about to succeed, Verena again flees to Boston and disappears.

Weeks later, when Ransom learns that Verena's oratorical career will be launched before a huge crowd in Boston, he sets out to win her once and for all. He shows up at the theater and insists that Verena renounce her career. Despite her pleadings, he refuses to allow her debut, exercising his male prerogative to set the terms of their relationship: She is to perform only for him, perhaps before small, select audiences in their home. He cannot have her pursue her career in the women's movement. After some pleading, Verena agrees not to speak and runs away with him, and in the end Olive is humiliated before all Boston society.

Ransom, Minnie. *The Salt Eaters.* Toni Cade Bambara. 1980.

Minnie Ransom is the legendary faith healer of Claybourne, Georgia. Even the skeptical teenager Nadine, who scoffs at the occult, acknowledges Minnie as the "real thing." When nothing else helps VELMA HENRY, a remarkable political activist, Minnie Ransom is summoned to perform a healing.

A trip to New York leaves the once healthy Minnie drastically changed, and she astonishes people in town with her extravagant madness. She is found on her hands and knees eating dirt, then seen dashing madly from the porch to the table to the woods, listening to inaudible voices. Her period of madness comes to an end one day when, kneeling in the dirt at the top of a cliff, she suddenly understands her gift.

Minnie has an ability to concentrate her energy in such a way that she can heal all types of illness, even fatal ones like cancer. She perceives the world with a psychic's acuity, sensing the significance of apparently ordinary events. She sees the auras around trees and stones, and is able to detect the hidden sources of people's troubles. For healings, Minnie calls on the help of a group of twelve students, called The Master's Mind. All of the members are "psychically adept," but they rely on Minnie for guidance.

Claybourne's center for spiritual and political instruction is called The Academy of the 7 Arts, which "encompasses the performing arts, the martial arts, the medical arts, the scientific arts, and the arts and humanities." The school body is divided into two factions: One, led by Minnie, believes that social change will come about through spiritual teaching; the other rejects anything that smacks of religion and takes a strictly political approach, addressing issues of "race, class, and struggle." Tensions between the factions are high; Minnie's patient, Velma Henry, breaks down and attempts suicide when she can no longer negotiate between the two groups, both of which she sees as essential to the community.

Velma is taken to the Southwest Community Infirmary but remains sick until Minnie arrives for a public healing session. The Master's Mind and the audience become concerned as the session drags on, and Minnie appears to be making no progress. Her usual method, involving placing her hands on the patient's body, is not working. Minnie asks Velma repeatedly if she wants the responsibilities that accompany "wholeness." Minnie's patience eventually allows Velma to think through her difficult past; she decides to continue with her struggle for justice within the community and beyond, and is successfully healed.

Raphael, Queenie. *Queenie.* Hortense Calisher. 1971.

Queenie Raphael narrates her story in the form of tape recordings she addresses to various interlocutors: a college admissions officer, a priest, a monsignor, a college professor, the President of the United States, and finally herself. All these narratives concern her happy childhood with her aunt Aurine, an elegant and wealthy prostitute, and the other "ladies," and her struggle to leave this childhood behind as she matures sexually.

Queenie grows up in a New York City penthouse with Aurine and an adoptive father, Aurine's lover Oscar. In her first tape, Queenie explains that having a happy childhood makes it hard to leave home for college. Queenie and her best friend Giorgio, the son of a prostitute, discuss the differences between men and women, and speak obscenely in order to break with their old-fashioned parents, who are polite and refined. In this tape Queenie also explains her "time lag": Although she describes having her first orgasm at age fifteen while on her rooftop with a male guest, she is now almost seventeen years old and still a virgin.

After she has been accepted, Queenie argues that girls need to go to college to find the answers to questions about sexuality. She describes three going-away parties that represent saying good-bye to her background. The first is a stag party at Oscar's; the second is for the ladies at the restaurant her aunt owns, where an angry maître d' spikes all the food with his own urine and where, for the first time, Queenie thinks of her gender as a "prison" as she meditates on the notion of penis envy. At the third and final party, Queenie's guest, Schubert Fish, exposes himself to her after boasting that he is uncircumcised. Fish doesn't realize that several of the prostitutes are watching, and their burst of laughter humiliates him. After this incident, Queenie, who had been wondering whether God was "queer for men," decides that God favors women's anatomy, not men's.

In her third tape, Queenie is at college and living with two friends. She feels old-fashioned because she is a virgin in a sexually active environment. Although Queenie still hasn't confessed her virginity, her friends decide to attend a "grieve-in" (a political orgy), where Queenie discovers she is "frigid in groups" as well. She decides that she wants to have intercourse for personal pleasure, not as a political statement.

Having run out of interlocutors, Queenie addresses her next tape to the President. On Easter vacation she visits Giorgio on a South American island and begins to travel back and forth from Europe with him as his lover. She learns that Giorgio, now a "revolutionary," is hijacking planes and counterfeiting money, which he spends lavishly. But he finally admits that he really wants to be a bourgeois poet. When Giorgio wants to quit his hijacking career with a bang, they decide to have Queenie address her last tape to the President. Queenie records an imaginary scenario in which they kidnap the President aboard a plane, play all her tapes to him—as well as the current one that tells him it's his turn to be a victim of their backgrounds—and leave him stranded on the plane to fend for himself.

In the final tape Queenie addresses herself. She and Giorgio have had to escape from their island and are now producing a musical based on her tapes, which will explain youth to the world. American sales of their presidential tape are already bringing in money, and they will soon produce the show in New York. Queenie informs Aurine and Oscar that she is pregnant but then discovers she was mistaken. The tape ends as Queenie and Giorgio share a moment of happy intimacy, during which she says *ciao* to her childhood, wondering whether she means hello or good-bye.

Rappaccini, Beatrice. "Rappaccini's Daughter." Nathaniel Hawthorne. 1844.

Beatrice Rappaccini is the beautiful daughter of a well-known, somewhat notorious doctor living in Padua, Italy. She seems not to have a job but instead spends her time in her father's walled-in garden, tending to the splendid array of flowers and herbs her father has cultivated. Beatrice's father specializes in poisonous plants and is reviled by many for his callous attitude toward his patients and

his tendency to experiment on them. One particular plant has large blossoms that exude a powerful poison; this is Beatrice's favorite, and she spends so much time caring for the plant, touching its deadly skin and breathing in its poisonous fragrance, that she becomes inured to its toxins. In fact, she becomes poisonous herself.

Although Beatrice is admired by all the men in the village, she keeps to herself and seems to have no friends. When Giovanni Guasconti, a handsome young student, moves into a room overlooking the garden, he soon becomes enamored of Beatrice. Beatrice sees him looking down from his window at her and, despite her shyness, is able to speak with him on a daily basis. She accepts the bouquet he drops to her and is pleased when he finds his way into the garden, having been shown an entrance by his landlady. Beatrice does not notice Giovanni's trepidation when the flowers he holds wilt in a moment or when the insects she breathes on fall out of the air, dead. But she will not let him touch her, for fear that he may be adversely affected.

The two young people fail to realize that their incipient romance is being witnessed by Dr. Rappaccini. He allows them to visit and seems pleased and interested in their union. They visit every day, and soon they fall in love. Giovanni seems troubled, however. He angrily confronts Beatrice about her love for the flowered plant and about her father's activities. It turns out that Giovanni has begun to exude poison as well. Dr. Rappaccini has known all along that Giovanni would undergo a process of immunization, developing a tolerance for the poisons in the garden, and eventually become the perfect mate for his daughter.

Beatrice is unhappy because Giovanni is unhappy. He has brought with him a vial containing a universal antidote, given to him by Professor Baglioni, one of Dr. Rappaccini's jealous peers. Beatrice knows intuitively that the antidote will destroy her; because her physiology is almost entirely toxic, it will have the reverse effect on her from what is intended. Professor Baglioni has convinced Giovanni that this is the only way out of his predicament. Beatrice is too much in love to resist the idea, and perhaps too weak-willed. At Giovanni's insistence, she swallows the contents of the vial and dies before her father's eyes and before the eyes of her lover. Seeing this, Professor Baglioni yells triumphantly from his second-story vantage point: "Rappaccini! and is *this* the upshot of your experiment!"

Ratliff, Vladimir Kyrilytch. *The Hamlet; The Town; The Mansion.* William Faulkner. 1931; 1957; 1959.

A shrewd and inscrutable salesman, Vladimir Kyrilytch Ratliff leads a nomadic existence, traveling through Yoknapatawpha County selling sewing machines and making other business deals. He knows the names and faces of everyone on his route and carries information about them throughout the county. He has known the Snopeses, for example, since childhood and relates the first stories of their legendary malevolence.

Although he rarely misjudges people, Ratliff is fooled twice by the Snopeses. Shortly after a serious illness and operation, Ratliff has the opportunity to buy a herd of fifty goats belonging to Ben Quick and sell them for a profit. FLEM SNOPES, the most powerful member of the Snopes clan, beats him to the purchase of Quick's goats, and even after negotiations, he still comes out behind. Ratliff tries to comfort himself with the thought that his recent illness has dulled his awareness. But then Flem fools Ratliff a second time by tricking him and two friends into buying the Old Frenchman's Mansion with the false promise of hidden treasure on the grounds. From that point on Ratliff thinks of Flem as a formidable con man.

By the second volume of the trilogy, Ratliff has formed an alliance with GAVIN STEVENS, the county attorney. Although Gavin is much more educated, he often appears naive and vulnerable in comparison to the more experienced Ratliff, especially when it comes to "Snopes-dodging." When Gavin departs Jefferson to study in Heidelberg, he solemnly leaves the town and the surveillance of the Snopeses in Ratliff's hands. Ratliff dutifully corresponds with him during the five-year absence. When Gavin returns and resumes protecting Jefferson from the Snopeses, Ratliff grows concerned over his friend's romantic life. Ratliff tries but fails to prevent the attorney from falling in love, first with EULA VARNER SNOPES, Flem's wife, and later with Flem's legal daughter LINDA (SNOPES KOHL).

Another notable intrigue between Ratliff and Flem concerns the freeing of MINK SNOPES. Ratliff and Gavin help Linda Kohl obtain a pardon for this relative, who has been unfairly imprisoned as a result of Flem's trickery. Gavin arranges for a sum of money to be given to Mink in exchange for a promise that he will leave Mississippi before sundown on the day of his release, to ensure that he will not murder Flem Snopes in revenge. On that day Ratliff calls Gavin from the prison to warn him that Mink has left without the money. Within a matter of days Mink has murdered Flem. In this final crisis, Ratliff proves that he has developed a superior power of prediction about the next deadly move of a Snopes.

However, the peculiar circumstances of Flem's death lead Ratliff to adopt a new perspective on Flem. The Snopes patriarch, it appears, could have escaped between the first blank shot that Mink fired and the second one that killed him. Ratliff believes that his old rival had a fair chance to defeat Mink and Linda, and in this final moment gave them an equal chance to defeat him. Ratliff wants to find a moral in the Snopes tale, but Gavin denies that ethics have played any role at all. They finally agree that

the "pore sons of bitches," as they think of people in general, just do the best they can.

Ravenal, Gaylord. *Show Boat.* Edna Ferber. 1926.

A handsome and dashing gambler, Gaylord Ravenal steals the heart of the novel's heroine just as easily as he wins money at cards on a good day. Gaylord meets, charms, marries, and finally deserts MAGNOLIA HAWKS RAVENAL, leaving her heartbroken but stronger, wiser, and more mature.

The black sheep of an old, aristocratic family, Gaylord joins the company of the Cotton Blossom Floating Palace Theatre after his luck turns bad. As he stands on a dock contemplating his uncertain future, Gaylord is offered a chance to replace the company's departing male lead. Although not an actor by trade, Gaylord decides to join, swayed by the prospect of earning steady money and the chance to woo Magnolia, whom he spies standing on board the show boat. Magnolia is the company's fetching female ingenue and daughter of Andy and Parthenia Hawks, the owners of the Cotton Blossom.

Gaylord and Magnolia take an instant liking to each other, but Parthenia Hawks is not so easily won. She does everything she can to keep her daughter away from Gaylord when they are not onstage together. Unable to sway Parthenia with his considerable charm, Gaylord turns to Magnolia's father, who sees the young man as a basically decent fellow who obviously loves his daughter. After Gaylord and Magnolia marry secretly, Andy Hawks not only accepts the fact but gives the two his blessing. When Andy is killed years later, Gaylord is truly grieved.

Although Gaylord works hard to win Parthenia's approval, the woman constantly berates him as a gambler, murderer (he had killed a man in self-defense), and skirt chaser. Unable to take this abuse anymore, Gaylord convinces Magnolia that they and their young daughter Kim should leave the Cotton Blossom and settle in Chicago. Once in Chicago, Gaylord shows his family the pleasures of city life but also the uncertainty that being dependent on a professional gambler entails. Gaylord often has a run of good luck, and the family is well dressed, eats at the finest restaurants, and rides around the city in style. At other times Gaylord's luck turns, and the glittery belongings must be sold or pawned to pay his debts.

Gaylord fancies himself a gentleman gambler, and although his fortunes may fail, appearances must always be kept up. He must smoke the best cigars. He must wear suits of the finest cut and cloth even after they grow shabby. And above all he must not ask his fellow gamblers for money. After a particularly long string of bad luck, when it seems Gaylord can fall no further, he sets out one evening determined to pull his family out of the poverty into which he plunged them. After many hours away he returns with liquor on his breath and $2,000 in his pocket.

He admits to Magnolia that half was borrowed from a fancy Chicago madam and the other half won at roulette. Gaylord passes out, and in the morning Magnolia, not willing to be indebted to a woman of shady morals, returns the money to the madam. When she comes home she finds $600 and a note from Gaylord saying that he will be away for a few weeks. Gaylord's wife and child never see him again.

Ravenal, Magnolia Hawks. *Show Boat.* Edna Ferber. 1926.

The daughter of the owners of the Cotton Blossom Floating Palace Theatre, Magnolia Hawks Ravenal is destined for the stage. Magnolia's life is as turbulent as the Mississippi, the river that is her first home and enduring love.

Although dominated by her bossy mother Parthenia, Magnolia is a spirited child. She befriends the show boat's crew and the blacks who work along the Mississippi, but her closest companion is the slightly faded but still beautiful actress Julie Dozier. Magnolia sees Julie as a languidly mysterious woman, and the actress, for her part, takes a liking to the wide-eyed child. When the show boat is docked at the small towns where the company performs, Magnolia and Julie spend hours wandering together in the countryside. Julie finds Magnolia a welcome contrast to the strict and joyless Parthenia. Their friendship is abruptly terminated, however, when it is revealed that Julie is part black and that her marriage to a white man violates anti-miscegenation laws. Julie and her husband must leave the show boat and Magnolia forever.

As Magnolia blossoms into young womanhood on board the show boat, the opportunity opens for her to become an actress. The regular female ingenue leaves the company, and Magnolia becomes first her substitute and then her permanent replacement. Parthenia's initial objections are overcome as Magnolia becomes an integral part of the company and an audience favorite.

Magnolia soon catches the eye of GAYLORD RAVENAL, a charming professional gambler who is down on his luck. Gaylord joins the show boat troupe as male lead, and the two quickly fall in love. Once again Magnolia faces her mother's objections, but she marries Gaylord and gives birth to a daughter, Kim. When Kim is a toddler, the Ravenal family leaves the show boat life to settle in Chicago.

It is in Chicago that Magnolia realizes just what type of man she has married. Gaylord is loving but unreliable. His gambling fortunes fluctuate; the family lives at one time in opulence and at the next in poverty.

One evening, after a long stretch of bad luck, Gaylord returns with $2,000, half the proceeds of gambling and half lent to him by a madam. Because it makes her uncomfortable, Magnolia returns the madam's money the next morning. While in the whorehouse, Magnolia sees a

woman who looks like Julie, but the mysterious figure flees before Magnolia can speak to her. When Magnolia returns home, she finds $600 and a note from Gaylord that he will be away for a few weeks. He never returns.

To support herself and her daughter, Magnolia goes to work on the Chicago vaudeville stage. She becomes successful, and when Kim grows up, she follows in her mother's footsteps, pursuing a career in the legitimate theater. After Parthenia Hawks dies, Magnolia rejoins the show boat as its owner and director.

Raymond. *Home to Harlem.* Claude McKay. 1973.

Raymond, an intellectual born in Haiti, is eventually thrown into the chaos of Harlem when he meets JACOB BROWN, known as "Jake," the novel's protagonist, on a train that runs along the East Coast. Jake is working as a cook, while Ray holds the more prestigious job of waiter. However, this relatively comfortable position falls severely short of the life Ray might have had.

The friendship between the two men begins when Ray lends Jake two dollars for gambling. When Jake repays Ray, he casually asks what he is reading. Ray explains that he is reading Sappho, and they are led into a discussion about Ray's origins and his native language, French. Upon learning that Jake has been inspired by stories of Toussiant L'Ouverture, the black leader of the Haitian revolution, Ray relates the history of his own family's struggle against American imperialism. His father had been an official in Haiti when the country was seized by the United States during World War I. Ray's father was subsequently thrown in jail for his opposition to the American occupation, and his brother was murdered in the street by American Marines. Ray, who was studying at Howard University in Washington, could no longer pay his tuition and was forced to leave school.

Ray is obviously out of place among the train staff, which caters to whites. The cooks and other waiters scornfully call him "professor" and tell Jake to stay away. On the overnights in various East Coast cities, Ray prefers to read a book while the others go to cabarets, bars, and parties. He still has dreams, not only of returning to college but of writing great books. One night in Pittsburgh the bunks are so bug-infested that he finds he cannot sleep. He accompanies Jake to a speakeasy, where Jake flirts and drinks until Ray, uneasy and impatient, insists that they return to their quarters. Jake falls asleep instantly, but Ray remains awake, thinking tortured thoughts about "race and nation," loathing everyone around him except Jake. Finally, Ray takes a drug that Jake had brought home from the speakeasy and sinks into colorful, reminiscent dreams. The next day, however, he is unable to rise and must be taken to the hospital.

Ray recovers and continues to work on the train. Jake, who seems indestructible, also becomes ill. While he is confined to bed in Harlem, Ray sends his girlfriend Agatha to visit him. Jake is impressed with Agatha's quiet sophistication and hopes that his sister, whom he has not seen in many years, might resemble her. When Jake has a relapse, Ray becomes concerned about his living conditions and arranges for him to move into an apartment in his building. Ray has grown tired of Harlem, however. Once Jake is well again, they have a celebration dinner, and Ray leaves on a freighter, after signing on as a mess boy.

Redburn, Wellingborough. *Redburn: His First Voyage.* Herman Melville. 1849.

With his shooting jacket and his brother's gun, Wellingborough Redburn boards a steamer bound for New York City from his Hudson Valley home. The raw youth equips himself poorly for the subsequent voyage to Liverpool and has difficulty earning the respect of his fellow sailors, but by the time they return to port, he has acquitted himself ably and has come of age.

The story opens with a young Redburn avidly reading over ship advertisements and remembering his deceased father's stories about business travel. Seeking adventure on the seas and in Liverpool, England, Redburn departs for New York with only his brother's "fowling piece," or gun, a bundle of clothes, his fancy gray shooting jacket, and only half of the steamer's two-dollar fare. The captain's clerk asks for his ticket; Redburn gives him his last dollar and spends the rest of the trip menacing his fellow passengers with the gun.

In New York City he looks up Mr. Jones, a friend of his brother, who takes the lad to the docks to ship on the *Highlander*. Exaggerating Redburn's family wealth, Mr. Jones procures from a seemingly benevolent Captain Riga poor wages and the requirement that Redburn pay for his own clothing. After pawning the gun and throwing his last penny in the water, Redburn boards the boat, where he is quickly humiliated.

Calling him "Buttons" after the ornaments on his shooting jacket, the various able seamen educate Redburn—by cursing and drinking, choosing him last for the night watch, and ridiculing his seasickness, but also by showing him how to wash the decks, eat the food, climb the riggings, and adjust the sails. At first he is clumsy, dropping several hammers overboard in the process of cleaning the anchor, but before long he is comfortable in the riggings, actually preferring to be aloft during a storm when the tossing of the waves makes stairs of the ropes.

When the ship arrives in Liverpool, Redburn passes a few sordid evenings ashore in the company of his fellow sailors and then proceeds to tour the city with the aid of his father's guidebook. His wanderings quickly prove the fifty-year-old guide ineffective, and his dreams of following in his father's footsteps are abandoned. He walks along the docks, admiring the boats of many nations, and is on his way to his boardinghouse when he comes across a

woman and her daughters in a cellar fifteen feet below the street. He asks several policemen and tavernkeepers for some welfare for the doomed family, but when he is rebuffed, he can only steal some bread and cheese, and carry as much water as will fit in his hat. He encounters more poverty by the docks and resolves to strike out for the country. After being threatened by various mantraps and dogs, Redburn happens upon the home of "three young charmers" and their parents, the father inviting him in and the mother hurrying him back out.

Back in Liverpool, Redburn meets Harry Bolton, a mysterious youth who may be a luckless gambler, a disenfranchised lord, or a former midshipman in India. The secretive Harry agrees to ship to America, but before the friends are able to board, he takes Redburn on an errand to London. Although Redburn is thrilled with the prospect of visiting the capital, he never sees the city: Harry takes him to a mysterious brothel-like apartment and disappears. At the night's end, Harry turns up, manic and penniless, and they return to Liverpool.

The *Highlander* soon sails, and before long it becomes clear that Harry has never sailed before. After Harry comes down off the riggings with bad nerves, Redburn marvels that Harry failed where he succeeded. The return voyage lasts longer than the trip out, but Redburn has significantly less trouble. Illness breaks out among the immigrant passengers, and many are buried at sea, but the ship arrives in New York without serious incident for Redburn. The friends, departing the ship, attempt to receive their wages from Captain Riga, who at first denies they have been on board. He pays Harry, though, and then deducts $12.00 from Redburn's pay for running away and $7.75 for misplaced hammers.

Redburn and Harry part ways in New York, and Redburn goes on to later sea voyages on board a whaler. The novel closes with Redburn hearing of Harry's death in a whaling accident: He was crushed between a whale and the side of the boat.

Reddick, Max. *The Man Who Cried I Am.* John A. Williams. 1967.

Max Reddick, a black novelist and reporter, attempts to assert himself in a society that limits, humiliates, and finally kills him.

As a reporter on the *Democrat*, a Harlem newspaper, Max confronts the difficulty of being a black man in America on a daily basis. When he is assigned to cover the story of Moses Boatwright, a black Harvard graduate who cannibalized a white man, Max is haunted by the case. His initial horror turns to a kind of understanding of the anguish that drove Boatwright to his insane act.

Max has his own demons to confront. He is frustrated that his first novel has not attracted the attention given the works of his black novelist friend HARRY AMES. Max's sense of rivalry only grows when Harry's white wife

Charlotte convinces Max to sleep with her. He feels that he has betrayed Harry and that perhaps he has given in to the stereotypical image of black men desiring white women.

After a stint in Italy in the segregated United States Army in World War II, Max receives a discharge when he suffers from jaundice and severe hemorrhoids. Returning home, he meets and falls in love with Lillian, a schoolteacher who dreams of a middle-class life. Max looks for work but, turned down by the downtown magazines and newspapers, despairs of ever making Lillian happy and begins to resent her desire that he "settle down." When Lillian dies from a back alley abortion, Max's anger at the white world can barely be contained.

Max eventually wins a job on a new liberal magazine, *Pace*, and begins making a name for himself with his reporting. Coming to the attention of Washington, he is recruited by the President as a speech writer, but when he finds that the administration's commitment to civil rights is hollow, Max returns to *Pace*.

In Europe to visit the now expatriated Harry Ames, Max travels to Amsterdam where he meets Magrit, who reminds him of Lillian. His series of unsatisfying, meaningless relationships comes to an end when he falls in love with and eventually marries this Dutch woman. Their marriage is not a successful one, however. Harry discovers he has colon cancer and does his best to push Magrit away for fear of showing weakness. After living briefly with him in the United States, Magrit returns to Europe.

Years later Max travels to Europe for Harry's funeral and is told by Michelle, Harry's longtime lover, that Harry left a package for him. The package contains documents attesting to the United States' participation in Alliance Blanc, a coalition of nations devoted to suppressing black liberation. Harry was killed for his knowledge of the Alliance and of the plans of the United States to intern and then deport black Americans should black protest become widespread.

Not afraid of being murdered, since his cancer has doomed him anyway, Max relates the information to Minister Q, an American Black Muslim who he is sure will publicize it. While driving to Amsterdam to see Magrit, Max is pursued by Roger Wilkinson and Alphonse Edwards, two black expatriates who, unbeknownst to Max, have been in the employ of the U.S. government. Max is only able to fire two shots before Edwards subdues him and administers a fatal dose of the morphine he had been using to soothe the pain of his cancer.

Redfield, Irene. *Passing*. Nella Larsen. 1929.

As a member of the black bourgeoisie, Irene Redfield believes that she has every reason to be happy: Her husband is a successful doctor, she has two children and a fashionable Harlem home, and she has earned the respect of her 1920s Harlem society. But when CLARE KENDRY BELLEW, a woman whom Irene knew as a child, reappears and asks to renew their friendship, discord and confusion enter Irene's otherwise orderly life.

Irene is startled one day to receive a note from Clare in the morning mail. Her mind returns to her childhood memories of Clare, the beautiful, light-skinned, "catlike" daughter of a white alcoholic father. Irene had seen Clare only once since the death of the latter's father, and Irene's memory of that chance meeting is as vivid as her memory of Clare's unhappy childhood and subsequent removal by distant relatives from the Chicago community where she grew up.

Two summers before receiving Clare's note, Irene had been visiting her family in Chicago for a few weeks. On an unbearably hot day she took refuge in the cool dining room of one of the city's best hotels to enjoy a glass of iced tea. Shown to a table next to hers was a stylish woman who began to stare unashamedly at Irene. At first afraid that the woman knew and would inform the waiter that she was black—and not Spanish, as her lightly bronzed skin tone seemed to suggest—Irene suddenly realized, with great surprise, that the woman was Clare Kendry.

Clare confirmed the rumors which circulated soon after her father's death that she had decided to "pass for white," and she told Irene that she was married to a white man who suspected nothing. Torn between repulsion at Clare's opportunistic abandonment of her race and an uncomfortable, almost sexual attraction for the beautiful woman, Irene rebuffed Clare's requests to pay a visit to her home. A few days later, however, she agreed to call on Clare and her husband, John Bellew, a decision she swiftly regretted when John made clear his hatred of blacks. Irene then vowed to have nothing to do with Clare again.

Two years later, when Irene receives Clare's note, her husband Brian advises her not to respond to Clare's request for a renewal of their friendship. Brian's advice is offered casually, an attitude that has characterized all his relations with his wife since the time, after the birth of their second child, she had hinted at divorce in order to dissuade him from his plan of moving the family to South America, a plan he believed would enable them to escape from the rampant prejudice in the United States.

Clare, claiming that only with other blacks does she have the freedom to act naturally, soon forces her way into Irene's circle of friends—and her consciousness. Irene tolerates the intrusion but suspects that Clare has also forced herself on Brian and that he has accepted her sexual advances.

One day while shopping downtown with a friend who is obviously black, Irene literally runs into John Bellew. He tries to shake her hand, but Irene turns from him; his face clouds as he sees Irene's friend and realizes that Irene herself is black. Irene tells no one about this encounter but knows that doubts have surely arisen in John's mind over his wife's true race. Irene is not concerned about Clare's being protected from her husband's anger but that she not be given the chance to establish a stronger relationship with Brian, a chance that a divorce from John would allow.

Weeks later Clare and the Redfields are attending a small party on the sixth floor of a Harlem brownstone when the gathering is interrupted by the uninvited John Bellew. The guests are stunned when John reveals that he knows his wife is black, but Clare, smiling slightly, says nothing. Irene angrily rushes to her, believing that Clare's enigmatic grin may express the relief that she feels, knowing that John will now divorce her. Just as Irene lays a hand on Clare's arm, the latter falls out the open window to the snow-covered ground below. Irene is amazed and relieved that the woman who had disrupted her life could be removed from it so quickly, but doubts linger—in her mind and in the minds of the other guests—as to whether Clare threw herself out of the window or Irene pushed her.

Reed, Mary Jane "the Monkey." *Portnoy's Complaint.* Philip Roth. 1967.

Mary Jane Reed, or "the Monkey," is an ex-model who befriends ALEXANDER PORTNOY. A onetime poser for underwear ads, the Monkey leads a life of stupidity and indulgence that mirrors and contrasts with Alex's life.

The Monkey was born in Moundsville, West Virginia, the daughter of a miner who was "little more than first cousin to a mule" and a woman who also lacked intelligence. At the age of eighteen the Monkey moves to New York City, where she acquires a job as a model. While on an assignment in Florence, Italy, she meets a wealthy French industrialist whom she later marries. Their short marriage fails, and at the age of twenty-five the Monkey tries unsuccessfully to kill herself.

On a street corner in New York City one night, a well-dressed stranger, Alexander Portnoy, proposes oral sex. The Monkey, half-scornful, complies. Monkey's therapist, "Harpo" Frankel, contends that this involvement constitutes a breakthrough. Henceforth the Monkey and "Breakie," as she now calls Portnoy, engage in a furiously sexual relationship that Portnoy attempts to refine by educating the Monkey with various books and ideas. The Monkey has a high opinion of the intelligent, successful Portnoy but also a low opinion of his sexual fanaticism. Nevertheless, they do enjoy each other, particularly on a trip to Vermont where both glimpse a peaceful life-style that is alien to them.

The Monkey decides to apply to Hunter College to refine herself. At thirty now, she hopes to settle down in marriage. However, her relationship with Portnoy is still characterized by sex above all else. On a trip to Europe she and "Breakie" have a falling out in Rome over the

question of who is the more perverted. When they move on to Athens, the Monkey threatens to jump off their hotel balcony if Portnoy refuses to marry her. Portnoy leaves her to fly off to Israel, and the Monkey's fate remains unknown.

Reifsneider, Henry. "The Lost Phoebe." Theodore Dreiser. 1918.

Henry Reifsneider, a thin, crotchety old man, has lived in the same house since his childhood. He married Phoebe Ann forty-eight years ago, and the two stayed in the half-log, half-frame house bringing up their children and tending to their garden and livestock. Over the years Henry and Phoebe remained a loving couple until finally the children left home and the only animals remaining were a pig and one sleepy horse.

In their old age, Henry and Phoebe were partners who had attached themselves to each other to weather out their final days. Sometimes, when Henry misplaced his corn knife and asked Phoebe for it, she would teasingly threaten to leave him for good if he did not hush. Henry knew she would never willfully abandon him, but one day she does leave. Phoebe dies when Henry is seventy years old, leaving him sorrowful and uncertain as to whether he can face the world without her.

For five months after Phoebe's death the old man lives from day to day. He has little appetite, and he thinks constantly of her and of his own impending death. Then late one night he sees an exact representation of Phoebe in his living room. The figure does not answer his calls and soon vanishes, but Henry is sure he will see the figure again. After a few more sightings he makes the subtle transition from illusion to hallucination and arrives at the conclusion that Phoebe left him after a senseless quarrel about the whereabouts of his pipe. Believing that his wife is still alive and means to come home, he decides to search for her.

Henry visits his neighbors and friends and asks them if they have seen Phoebe. At first they are amazed by his confusion, but over time, after the authorities deem it inadvisable to take him into custody, Henry becomes a known character. For several years he walks and walks, not eating much, calling and looking for his lost Phoebe. The longer he roams, the more he hallucinates. Eventually, he begins to carry a few utensils with him—a knife and fork, and a coffee pot—for use on his expeditions. His clothes fade, his hair grows, and his body becomes thin and worn.

Henry starts to camp among a patch of trees at the top of Red Cliff, a wall of red sandstone about one hundred feet high. One night during his seventh year of wandering, he stops at these trees and falls asleep. When he wakes up in the middle of the night, he sees, moving in the distance along a path, a figure that he is sure is Phoebe herself. As the figure passes near him, he sees it is the younger, sweeter, gayer Phoebe whom he knew years ago. Overcome, Henry calls out to her as he watches her move happily about. He gets up and tries to hurry toward her. Feeling the lure of a past world where love was young and Phoebe lived as this vision presents her, Henry calls out again and leaps toward her.

A group of farmer boys first discover some tin utensils beneath a tree and, later, at the bottom of Red Cliff, the broken body of old Henry, with a peaceful, delighted smile on his lips.

Reilly, Ignatius Jacques. *A Confederacy of Dunces.* John Kennedy Toole. 1980.

Ignatius Jacques Reilly regards the twentieth century as monstrously lacking in proper "theology and geometry." Offended by most of what is forced upon him in the chaotic streets of New Orleans, Ignatius prefers to remain in his room where he is working on a historical study, documenting the steady decline of Western culture. Although Ignatius is thirty years old and has a master's degree, he views work as a perversity and resists any type of employment until a small tragedy thrusts him into the working world.

When Ignatius's drunken mother, IRENE (REILLY), smashes her car into a building, she begs him to go to work and help pay for the damages. Ignatius finally relents and comforts himself with the thought that working within the system will sharpen his critique of it. Ignatius's first job is in the office of Levy Pants, a failing organization that produces clothes which are consistently out of fashion. Mr. Gonzalez, the office manager, is desperate for help and hires Ignatius as a file clerk. Ignatius proceeds to discard most of what is to be filed and instead spends his time decorating the office.

In addition to working on a fictionalized journal, chronicling his experiences as a "working boy," Ignatius carries on a correspondence with Myrna Minkoff. A friend from college who now lives in New York City, Myrna is a folk singer and political activist. In order to impress Myrna, who has decided his passivity is a form of mental illness, he organizes a revolt of the underpaid black factory workers. Ignatius leads the Crusade for Moorish Dignity into the Levy Pants office and orders the workers to attack Mr. Gonzalez. Already skeptical, the assembly balks at this command and returns grumbling to the factory. The only result of the Crusade is Ignatius's dismissal by Mr. Levy.

While searching for a new job, Ignatius pauses at the garage of Paradise Vendors for a hotdog. After consuming more of these delicacies than he can pay for, he is pressed into service as a vendor. He eats more hotdogs than he sells, thereby increasing his already enormous weight. When his employer, Mr. Clyde, receives a complaint from the Board of Health about him, Ignatius is condemned to wheel his cart in the French Quarter, a "sinkhole of vice."

At the outset of his venture, Ignatius discovers a way of escaping from several hours of work. He agrees to hide some pornographic pictures in his cart for a young dealer named George. Because George is afraid that Ignatius will expose him to the police, he consents to watch the cart while Ignatius sees a movie. Ignatius tears open one of the packages and sees the photographs of a naked woman posed as a teacher, her face hidden behind one of Ignatius's favorite books: Boethius's *The Consolation of Philosophy.* Convinced that she is a brilliant but destitute woman, he becomes determined to find her. The address on the package leads him to the Night of Joy bar, where Ignatius reads the advertisement for a performance by "Harlett O' Hara, Virgin-ny Belle." He plans to attend opening night.

Several days later, while pushing his cart, Ignatius encounters Dorian Greene, a young dandy. Dorian is fascinated by Ignatius's original costume, which includes a plastic saber and a large gold novelty earring. During their somewhat hostile exchange, Ignatius plans to impress Myrna Minkoff by organizing a political party for world peace. Since Dorian has hosted several embarrassingly dull gatherings, he invites Ignatius to make a speech before a group of his friends in the hope that this will liven up the festivities. The following week Ignatius arrives at Dorian's apartment, but instead of amusing the guests as Dorian had hoped, he infuriates them. Ignatius is chased from the house by three irate lesbians, who warn him not to remain within the boundaries of the Quarter.

Ignatius goes to the Night of Joy bar and finds a seat from which to watch "Harlett O' Hara." He requests a Dr. Nut, and the waitress brings him a bottle of champagne, for which she demands twenty-four dollars. While the waitress is loudly insisting that Ignatius pay, Harlett O' Hara begins her atrocious act, which involves a parrot. The parrot spies Ignatius's gold earring, dashes for it, and sends Ignatius barreling toward the street. He narrowly escapes being hit by a bus, falls into a faint, and wakes up in a hospital bed.

After this incident, Mrs. Reilly decides that her son has given her enough trouble and for his own good must be locked away. There is a possibility he will be involved in the lawsuit as a result of a letter he wrote while at Levy Pants. Although Mrs. Reilly does not tell Ignatius of her decision to call the Charity Hospital, her unusually affectionate manner arouses his suspicion. When Myrna Minkoff arrives unexpectedly, Ignatius hurriedly packs his bags, telling her that he is ready to "flower" in Manhattan. As they drive away, Ignatius sees the Charity Hospital ambulance speeding toward his house. He gratefully kisses Myrna's long pigtail.

Reilly, Irene. *A Confederacy of Dunces.* John Kennedy Toole. 1980.

Irene Reilly struggles bravely to remain patient with her dictatorial, petulant son IGNATIUS JACQUES REILLY. Even though Ignatius is thirty years old and has a master's degree, Irene allows him to live in her ramshackle house in New Orleans. When a car accident puts Irene into debt, she begs her son to help her pay for the damages.

The event is typical of a series of miserable accidents in Irene's life. Ignatius's father had taken Irene to a movie and grew amorous afterward. Before Irene was able to come to any decisions, she was pregnant and married to him. Ignatius is a difficult child, and his father dies young, leaving Irene with all the responsibilities of raising him. She works hard to put him through college and graduate school, but after earning his master's degree, Ignatius makes only a few feeble attempts to find a job. After Ignatius is fired from a teaching job, he is content to remain sequestered in his room, writing a historical study. Irene cooks his meals, buys him the enormous quantities of cake and doughnuts he regularly consumes, and withstands his perpetual tirades and insults. On the day of her accident, Irene is purchasing wine cakes for Ignatius at the D. H. Holmes department store while he waits outside for her.

When Irene emerges from the store, a crowd has formed around Ignatius, who is bellowing at a policeman. Officer ANGELO MANCUSO had tried to arrest Ignatius as a "suspicious character." Ignatius hustles his mother off while Officer Mancuso consoles himself by arresting Mr. Robichaux, an old man who was defending Ignatius. After walking a few blocks toward the car, Ignatius is panting hard and threatens to collapse if they do not rest. Irene, remembering that he had carried out similar threats, pushes him through the door of the Night of Joy bar. Irene—a heavy drinker—has several beers while Ignatius tells Darlene, the "B-girl," about a bus ride he took to Baton Rouge. Irene and Ignatius are eventually chased from the bar by the proprietress, Lana Lee.

After leaving the Night of Joy, Irene tries for some time to maneuver her old Plymouth out of its parking space. It suddenly leaps out of the space, skids across the street, and smashes into a building. Officer Mancuso is just rounding the corner. He later visits Irene and informs her sadly that the owner of the building demands a thousand dollars for damages. Irene begs Ignatius to go to work, and after a certain amount of goading, he gets a job as a file clerk for Levy Pants.

Once her son is occupied for a significant portion of the day, Irene's life changes dramatically. She becomes friends with Officer Mancuso and with his elderly aunt, Santa Battaglia. They have an informal bowling club and meet regularly at one another's homes. Santa introduces Irene to Claude Robichaux, the old man who was arrested in Ignatius's place, and a romance flowers between them. Claude and Santa are extremely sympathetic to Irene's complaints about Ignatius. When Ignatius loses his job at Levy Pants and is hired as a hotdog vendor, Irene considers his job shameful. Mother and son become increasingly suspicious of each other's activities. Mr. Levy of Levy

Pants appears at the house one day with a letter Ignatius had written, criticizing a client. As a result of this letter, Mr. Levy is being sued for $500,000.

Santa convinces Irene to have Ignatius committed to the Charity Hospital before they become involved in the lawsuit. While her friend calls the hospital, Irene hastily says good-bye to Ignatius and leaves the house. Irene's unusually affectionate manner arouses Ignatius's suspicion, and he escapes to New York with a friend just before the ambulance arrives at the house.

Rejnev, Domna. *The Groves of Academe.* Mary McCarthy. 1952.

Domna Rejnev, an idealistic young woman who teaches Russian and French literature, becomes entangled in the complex politics of Jocelyn College during her first year there as an instructor. Domna becomes a crusader for HENRY MULCAHY, an instructor who seems to have been unjustly fired. Without ever compromising her strict morals, Domna is implicated in the ugly consequences of Henry's trickery.

Like her friend Henry who is an anomaly at the small Pennsylvania college, Domna stands out not only because of her unusual background but also because of her beauty and integrity. Domna's family emigrated from Russia to France, where her grandfather was a famous radical and her father became a jewelry salesman. When Domna was fifteen, she witnessed her mother's death of typhoid on a ship en route from Lisbon to Buenos Aires. It was at Domna's insistence that the family fled Nazi-occupied Paris, and her relatives held her responsible for her mother's death. Domna became a serious and severe young woman with an incorruptible air.

At twenty-three, Domna has come to Jocelyn with a B.A. from Radcliffe. Henry, who perceives that Domna is the sort of woman who "could very easily throw herself away," singles her out for friendship shortly after her arrival. Counting on various favors to create a sense of obligation in Domna, he rushes immediately to her office when he receives notice of his dismissal and relates the astounding circumstances. Not only had the president, Maynard Hoar, made a verbal contract with Henry to keep him on for another year, but he was also aware of his wife's severe illness; the shock of such an event could easily kill her, and it therefore must be kept secret. Henry indicates further that the dismissal must have something to do with his Communist Party affiliation. Domna is shocked, outraged, and extremely concerned about Henry's wife, Cathy, who is also a friend. She organizes a group of supporters from among the other faculty members and acts as a delegate, confronting Maynard Hoar to demand that Henry's contract be renewed.

That evening, Henry invites Domna to his home for a dinner in order to celebrate the successful meeting with Maynard. Domna goes reluctantly because Maynard was able to produce evidence that much of Henry's alleged claims were false. Before their dinner begins, Cathy slips in conversation, revealing that she and Henry are accomplices in the plot. Domna leaves their house as quickly as politeness allows and later that evening, goes to the home of her colleague, John Bentkoop, to pour out her despair over Henry's deception. John, who has already seen through Henry's facade, is very sympathetic but not at all surprised.

During the months following, Domna studiously avoids Mulcahy and becomes passionately involved in teaching. She is almost always seen on campus with John Bentkoop and Milton Kantarowitz, a painter. Alma Fortune, an older woman who also teaches literature, becomes Domna's friend and mentor. The two women initiate a protest when Henry and his disciple Ellison organize a Leftist poetry conference. They succeed in arranging a more balanced program, and the conference runs smoothly until a "proletarian poet," Vincent Keogh, approaches Henry with reminiscences of their days in the John Reed club.

When Keogh is hustled to the president's office, at Domna's suggestion, he reveals that he was assigned to recruit Henry for the Communist Party but had no success. Domna laughs at this conclusive evidence of Henry's deception; it is the perfect touch of comic irony. She leaves the meeting as usual, in subdued conference with John Bentkoop, who later learns that Maynard has been forced by Henry to resign. Along with Maynard and the other well-intentioned characters in this bleak tale, Domna emerges defeated and disillusioned.

Renfrew, Dottie. *The Group.* Mary McCarthy. 1954.

Dottie Renfrew is an attractive young woman from Boston whose apparent staidness and appreciation of traditional decorum contrasts sharply with her extremely sensual nature. Because her failing health as a child kept her out of school at various intervals, Dottie, who is almost twenty-three, is the eldest of her eight-member clique who attended Vassar College, class of 1933. Although Dottie suspects that she will eventually develop into a sensual woman, she is a virgin and is frightened by the thought of defloration.

While visiting New York City to attend the wedding of one of the members of the Vassar group, KAY LEILAND STRONG, Dottie meets Dick Brown, and he begins to flirt with her. Listening to Dick's account of how he and his ex-wife recently celebrated their divorce by having sex and to his bold assessment of the body of the bride, Dottie is attracted by his racy conversation. She begins to reciprocate his attentions despite her sneaking suspicion that he thinks of her as a stereotypical old maid. A proud and bitter young painter, Dick informs her that he lives in a very modest furnished room, has never attended college, and is definitely not in the same class as Dottie, whose family is relatively well off, thanks to her father's import

business. Far from being put off, Dottie is intrigued by this flirtatious man. Dick manages to entice her to his apartment after an acquaintance of only two days. When they engage in mutually satisfying sex, Dottie discovers that she is indeed a sensual woman. As she leaves his apartment after this, their first encounter, Dick suggests to Dottie that she go to a doctor to get a contraceptive diaphragm so they can enjoy future romps. He then forbids her to fall in love with him, cautioning her that their relationship is to remain strictly physical. Dottie agrees so as not to lose Dick.

Having performed the nerve-racking legwork necessary to purchase a birth control mechanism, Dottie calls Dick, who has promised to house the device in his attic room. But Dick is not home. As the night wears on, Dottie begins to feel nervously conspicuous while she waits on a bench in Washington Square. Finally, convinced that he is out carousing and does not care enough to be available on such a momentous occasion, she hides the contraceptive equipment beneath the bench on which she is seated. Sobbing, she returns to her room at the Vassar Club. The following day she returns heartbroken to Boston without even trying to visit her callous first lover.

Although ignorant of the exact cause of her malaise, Dottie's mother senses that she is not feeling well and decides to send her to Arizona to convalesce. During her stay there, Dottie meets a wealthy mining tycoon and widower named Brook Latham, whom she decides to marry. While tending to the wedding preparations back in Boston, Dottie breaks down in front of her mother and admits that she is still in love with Dick. Even so, she refuses to heed her mother's suggestion that she should postpone her wedding and locate Dick in order to test her troubled emotions. Following through on her original plan, Dottie marries and settles down to her new life with the assumption that she will learn to love her husband.

Renfro, Gloria Short. *Losing Battles.* Eudora Welty. 1970.

Gloria Short Renfro is married to JACK JORDAN RENFRO, the best loved of the huge Renfro-Beecham clan, and lives with his family on their farm in Banner, Mississippi. Gloria has earned her in-laws' contempt as well as their respect: They see her as an orphan of unknown parentage who rose to become the town's schoolteacher, but they resent her ambition and her haughty airs as she flaunts her store-bought wedding dress and flowing red hair.

On the occasion of Granny Beecham's eightieth birthday party and the Renfro-Beecham family reunion, Gloria waits along with the whole of Jack's family for her husband's return from prison. While waiting, several of his relatives remember that, before marrying Jack, Gloria had taught school in Banner. In fact, it was on Gloria's first day of teaching that Jack, who was then only her student, had the fight with his rival, Curly Stovall, that landed him in prison.

Between the time of this fight and Jack's consequent incarceration at Parchman County Prison, Gloria and Jack began and consummated their courtship. They were married the day before Jack's arraignment by Judge Moody, but Curly Stovall, acting as Justice of the Peace, brought Jack to the courthouse before Gloria and Jack could share their nuptial bed. While Jack served his eighteen-month sentence, however, Gloria gave birth to their child, Lady May.

On the day of Jack's return, Gloria insists that only she and Lady May accompany him to Banner Top, where he aims to gain his revenge on Judge Moody. Alone with Jack, Gloria attempts to dissuade him from forcing the Moodys' car into a ditch. Lady May thwarts Jack's plans by running into the road, with Gloria close behind her. When Judge Moody swerves around the two and almost off the edge of Banner Top, Jack changes his mind about his feelings for the judge and invites the stranded Moody to his family's reunion.

It is revealed at the reunion that it was Julia Mortimer, the former Banner teacher and bane of the childhoods of many generations of Banner residents, who took Gloria from her orphanage and instilled in her the ambition to be a teacher. With Miss Mortimer guiding her life, Gloria excelled. She graduated from high school and went on to receive a two-year teaching certificate. She took her first job at Banner in order to gain experience and earn the money needed to complete her degree. Gloria and Miss Mortimer initially perceived her stint in Banner as temporary. Gloria's decision to marry Jack came as a shock and grave disappointment to Miss Mortimer.

The after-dinner conversation at the reunion turns to Gloria's relationship with Miss Mortimer and the mystery of Gloria's parentage. Granny breaks into the talk and declares that Gloria's mother was Rachel Sojourner, a woman from Banner who lived as an adolescent with the Beechams for several years. Although Gloria has lived in the Beecham-Renfro house since she came to teach in Banner, no one there had thought she could be related to them, least of all Gloria. When the other members of the reunion add the bits and pieces of Gloria's story that they know, they decide that her father must be Jack's uncle, Sam Dale Beecham, who died in World War I. Gloria, upset that her parents were not of a higher social status, vehemently denies that Rachel and Sam Dale could have been her parents. The implication of the revelation is that Jack and Gloria are cousins, and their marriage is illegal in Mississippi. Gloria and Jack nevertheless agree to love each other and remain married even if they are blood relatives.

Renfro, Jack Jordan. *Losing Battles.* Eudora Welty. 1970.

All the characters in this mock-heroic tale are waiting for Jack Renfro. At nineteen, Jack is the oldest and most beloved child of Beulah Beecham and Ralph Renfro. On the occasion of his great-grandmother's eightieth birthday, his parents, sisters, brother, wife, and the whole of his extended family gather in the rural Mississippi town of Banner for a family reunion. None doubt that Jack will arrive, although eighteen months earlier, on Jack's wedding day, Judge Moody made a "living example" of him by sending him to the Parchman County Prison for fighting with Curly Stovall, his lifelong rival and the town's current Justice of the Peace.

Good-natured if bumbling, Jack arrives at the family's drought-stricken farm in a fury of dust and barking dogs. His family bursts with uncontainable happiness and delight at the return of the son they still perceive as their savior. Jack finds his aloof former schoolteacher, GLORIA SHORT (RENFRO)—now his wife, but they were not able to spend their wedding night together—in her wedding dress awaiting his return. Gloria proudly presents Jack with the child born in his absence. The baby, Lady May, unceremoniously sticks her sharp heel in his eye.

To get there in time for the reunion, Jack and his accomplice, Aycock Comfort, escaped from Parchman. Together they ran, rode horseback, and hitched rides across several counties. Unknown to Jack, his last surreptitious ride—the one that brought him all the way into Banner—was on the bumper of a car belonging to none other than Judge Moody. When the judge swerved into a ditch at the side of the road, Jack graciously presented himself to his nemesis and, unwittingly, helped extract the vehicle.

When Jack later learns the identity of the recipient of his largesse, he sheepishly endures the ridicule of his relatives. To save face he sets off for Banner Top, accompanied by his wife and daughter, with the aim of forcing Judge Moody into another ditch. This time Jack intends to leave the judge stuck. As usual, however, nothing goes as he plans. Just as the car nears, Lady May, followed by Gloria, runs into the middle of the road; the judge steers around them, nearly off the edge of Banner Top, and saves their lives.

Jack, overcome with gratitude, insists that he alone will help Judge Moody and Mrs. Moody recover their car, which now sits precariously balanced at the cliff's edge. While Jack considers how best to extract the car from its dangerous resting place, he learns that during his stay in prison, his adversary, Curly Stovall, has took Renfro's horse and truck in lieu of debts owed his store by the Renfros. When Curly refuses to use his truck to help the Moodys until the following morning, Jack graciously invites the stranded judge and his wife to join the Renfro-Beecham family at their reunion dinner.

The conversation at the table that evening turns to the parentage of Gloria, who is an orphan. Each of the older members of the family offers a half-remembered bit of her story, whatever can be recalled. They finally conclude that

Gloria and Jack are cousins. Although this knowledge would make their marriage illegal in the state of Mississippi, Jack and Gloria vow to love each other in defiance of the law.

The following morning, when he finally has the aid of Curly's truck as well as the assistance of his family, the Moodys, and others, Jack can succeed only in slowly dropping the judge's car from Banner Top. Although he always inspires confidence, he nonetheless loses all battles.

Reynolds (Mrs.). *Mrs. Reynolds.* Gertrude Stein. 1952.

Mrs. Reynolds, whose first name is never divulged in the novel, resides in the French countryside with her husband William. Their pleasant life is disrupted by the outbreak of World War II, and Mrs. Reynolds becomes increasingly nervous about the threat posed by Angel Harper (a caricature of Adolph Hitler). Although her daily routine is not drastically altered by the ominous presence of Angel Harper, the tranquility she had enjoyed before the war is replaced by a lurking fear so intense as to render her susceptible to bouts of hysteria. Day after torturous day Mrs. Reynolds prays for Joseph Lane (a character based on Joseph Stalin), an adversary of Angel Harper.

When not oppressed by the anxiety of living in an area that is threatened by occupation by enemy troops, Mrs. Reynolds is a contented woman with a penchant for gossip, gardening, cooking, and playing with her dogs. The militaristic climate notwithstanding, she still engages in these hobbies with the exception of cooking, which is hindered by food shortages resulting from the war.

Mrs. Reynolds misses the freedom to travel and is particularly lonesome for an urban environment. But these personal frustrations are trivial in comparison with the horrors perpetrated by an all-too-proximate war. Her paranoia eventually becomes so intense that she stops reading the newspapers and listening to the radio in order to avoid confrontations with the war's abominations. Mr. Reynolds, whose Rock of Gibraltar personality precludes nervous excitation and even fear, comforts Mrs. Reynolds, and when she is feeling particularly frightened or depressed, he recommends what he considers a cure-all—sleep, the one realm to which Angel Harper cannot gain access.

Because a series of people once predicted accurately that Mrs. Reynolds would marry someone so named at the age of twenty-three, she is an avid believer in prognostications. She keeps lists of saints and believes that they and Jewish people are particularly gifted in envisioning the future. Saint Odile foretells a devastating worldwide war that will end in the defeat of the horrible perpetrator. According to Mrs. Reynolds's reading of Saint Odile's writings, Angel Harper will die before he reaches the age of fifty-five.

As the end of the war approaches, Mrs. Reynolds becomes increasingly impatient and finds that her fears are only assuaged when she contemplates Saint Odile's forecasts. Her faith in the validity of prognostications is ultimately justified with the death of Angel Harper at the age of fifty-four.

Richards, Edward. "The Man That Corrupted Hadleyburg." Samuel L. Clemens (Mark Twain). 1900.

Edward Richards and his wife Mary are prominent citizens of Hadleyburg, a community well known for its honest and upright populace. Along with the rest of the town's upstanding citizens, the elderly couple falls victim to the ploy of a disgruntled visitor who is determined to cure the haughty community of its lofty self-righteousness.

One evening a stranger visits the Richards home and leaves a heavy sack accompanied by a cryptic note which explains that the contents of the sack, $40,000 in gold pieces, should go to the citizen of Hadleyburg who had years before befriended the then-penniless author with a gift of $20. The rightful owner of the fortune must provide proof of his identity by offering the phrase he spoke when he gave the gift, a phrase that the author says changed his life. If the candidate's remark matches the one in a sealed envelope in the sack, the fortune is rightfully his.

After delivering the note to the newspaper to be published, in accordance with the stranger's instructions, the Richardses begin speculating about who the do-gooder might have been. They agree that only the late Barclay Goodson, a curmudgeon who often criticized the high-and-mighty citizenry of the town, could have been generous enough to give the gift.

During the course of their conversation, Mr. Richards confesses to his wife that he alone had information that would have saved the minister, Reverend Burgess, from scandal, but that he withheld it for fear of the town's scorn. He did warn Burgess to leave town when the citizens' wrath was at its peak, however, and for that small kindness he earned Burgess's eternal gratitude. Mr. Richards spends a sleepless night trying to guess the secret phrase. The next morning, after the stranger's note is made public, his fellow townspeople begin to do the same.

One week before the official opening of the sack, Mr. and Mrs. Richards receive another letter, this one signed by a stranger named Stephenson. He writes that the benefactor was indeed Goodson and that Goodson disclosed to him the secret phrase. He goes on to say that Goodson once told him that a citizen of Hadleyburg did him a great service which he wanted to repay with a fortune. Stephenson says he believes, although he is not positive, that citizen was Edward Richards. Writing that he is confident Mr. Richards will not claim the money if he is not the right man, he discloses the secret phrase: "You are far from being a bad man: go, and reform."

Although Mr. Richards cannot remember ever doing Goodson such a great favor, he and his wife prepare to enjoy their wealth. Meanwhile, in the other prominent households, there is a similar celebratory atmosphere, for a letter was delivered to each that was similar in every way except one: in place of Edward Richards's name, each prominent citizen found his own.

Predictably, the official opening of the sack is chaotic. With Reverend Burgess officiating, each candidate's entry is read, and all are shown to be liars because they could not furnish the second half of the phrase in the sack, which reads "or, mark my words—someday, you will die and go to hell or Hadleyburg—TRY AND MAKE IT THE FORMER." Only Richards is spared, for Burgess, desiring to repay his debt of gratitude, withholds the old man's entry. The sack proves to be full of worthless gilded lead disks, and another note reveals that there was no do-gooder and no secret phrase; the stranger had in fact been dishonored in Hadleyburg and had wished to punish the town by destroying its sterling reputation. The Richardses uneasily receive the congratulations of all present for being the only members of town who did not stoop to dishonesty.

Soon after, a stranger, whom Mrs. Richards recognizes as the man who delivered the sack, delivers another package to the Richards home. Along with a letter commending the Richardses for their honesty, the package contains bank notes totaling nearly $40,000. The Richardses struggle with their guilt but eventually reconcile themselves with their sin of dishonesty; however, they soon become preoccupied with worries that they will be found out. Convinced that Burgess has betrayed him to the rest of the town, Richards becomes ill, and Mrs. Richards's health also begins to fail. Richards destroys the bank notes, but his health continues to deteriorate, and in his delirium he reveals to nurses that he also was a false claimant for the sack of money.

When Mr. and Mrs. Richards are on their deathbeds, Mr. Richards calls for Burgess. He publicly admits his wrongdoing and forgives Burgess, whom he believes has exposed him. But he fails before dying to provide the testimony that would have cleared Burgess's name. His wife dies soon after, and the town is stripped, once and for all, of its former glory.

Rink, Jett. *Giant.* Edna Ferber. 1952.

The truculent Jett Rink occupies a place of some distinction as a ranch hand on Reata, the three-million-acre Benedict cattle ranch in south Texas. His relationship with JORDAN "BICK" BENEDICT, the owner of the ranch, turns sour, however, when Jett takes a liking to Bick's Virginia-bred wife LESLIE LYNNTON BENEDICT. At first Jett is cast by Bick as Leslie's protector; he takes her on a tour of the area, but it soon becomes obvious to Leslie that his interest in her goes beyond being merely a tour guide. She finds his insolent and swaggering manner unattractive and dislikes the superior attitude he displays toward the Mexicans who work on the ranch. Although Jett tells Leslie he likes her because she is different and "afraid of nothing," he

warns her not to get him sore or there will be trouble. He leaves the young wife a bit afraid of what he is capable of doing.

Her opinion is confirmed when Jett dares Luz Benedict, Bick's spinster sister, to ride his newly acquired racehorse, My Mistake—not only to ride her but to do so in a hoop skirt while roping a steer. Luz is thrown from My Mistake and dies, causing Bick to force Jett to leave the ranch. Following the incident, Jett forms a lifelong grudge against the Benedicts.

Years go by in which Jett Rink is only a name, said with disfavor on and near Reata. A rumor persists that he has acquired land and is drilling for oil, an abhorrence to the cattle ranchers. One day Leslie meets him in Viento, and he tells her he is "the works, the driller, tool dresser, and grease monkey all in one." Again she finds his presence threatening and disquieting, but Jett goes away, causing her no harm.

A few years later he reappears at Reata during a family dinner. Filthy and drunk, he bursts into the Big House and tells Bick that his well has come in, and he is now rich—richer than the Benedicts—and that the day will come when he will be able to buy Reata from under them. He annoys Leslie, and soon he and Bick are engaged in a fistfight that ends with Bick injured and Jett once more unwelcome at the ranch.

Rumors of Jett Rink abound as he gradually amasses an enormous fortune, spends lavishly, and makes his way through four or five marriages. Years later his path crosses the Benedicts' again when he accosts Leslie and her grown daughter Luz in Hermosa. Forcing them into his chauffeur-driven car, he tells Leslie that he has been crazy about her for years and that he will never let up on them. Leslie and Luz escape, shaken but unhurt, and Luz comments that Rink is "a modern version of a buccaneer."

Whatever the case, Jett Rink becomes the fashion in Texas, a fabulously wealthy, incredibly uncouth, bigoted Texas billionaire whose fortune is not based on cattle but on oil. He becomes chic, keeping company with movie stars, rising politicians, the governor of Texas, and European socialites. The ranchers who once disdained him as a hired hand find themselves eager to attend the opening of the new Jett Rink Airport, his gift to the city of Hermosa. The man who says he was "weaned on loco weed as a baby" has, in typical Texas fashion, built a huge and ostentatious monument to himself.

Rittenmeyer, Charlotte. *The Wild Palms.* William Faulkner. 1939.

Charlotte Rittenmeyer is a fairly successful sculptor. Her pieces are elegant, bizarre, fantastic, and perverse, and she is much like her work. Wife of an upper-middle-class businessman and mother of two little girls, there is something wild about her that makes her restless, willful, and savagely passionate. She leaves her family to embark

on a life of passion with a penniless doctor, HARRY WIL-
BOURNE, whom she seduces and who loves her with the
ardor of one who has never known love before. The story
of their flight and passion makes up "The Wild Palms,"
one of the novel's two separate but thematically interre-
lated story lines.

Charlotte loves her husband, "Rat" Rittenmeyer, in her
fashion, but something is missing, and Rat, because he
loves her, cannot deny her her chance to find happiness.
So when Harry finds $1,275 in a wallet in a trash bin,
Charlotte tells Harry that it will allow them to start a life
together. After telling Rat that she is leaving him for Harry,
she and Harry move to Chicago where Harry works in a
clinic while Charlotte sculpts. Harry soon loses his job,
but through a friend Charlotte has made, they are allowed
use of a cabin in the Wisconsin woods where they live
rent free. When their food runs out, Charlotte accepts a
job in Chicago, and they are happy again for a while.
When Harry realizes that they have become enmeshed in
the comforts of middle-class life, he decides to accept a
job as a doctor in a Utah mining camp.

While there, coerced by Charlotte and the mine's caretaker, Harry performs a successful abortion on the caretaker's wife. Shortly thereafter, Charlotte becomes
pregnant and begs Harry to perform an abortion on her,
but Harry cannot because he loves her. They move to New
Orleans in the hope of either locating an abortionist or
finding a job for Harry that will support a family. When
his job-hunting efforts fail, Harry agrees to perform the
abortion, but by now it is very late in Charlotte's first
trimester.

On a visit to Rat, Charlotte tells her husband that Harry
has performed the abortion. Harry suspects toxemia when
Charlotte continues to lose blood for a while, but she
refuses to see a doctor. Charlotte tells Rat that no matter
what happens now, he is to stand by Harry. She and Harry
then rent a ramshackle cabin on the coast and wait.

The cottage they rent is owned by an old doctor and
his wife who live in the cottage next door. As soon as the
doctor sees Charlotte, he knows that she is gravely ill.
Four nights later, when Charlotte begins bleeding again,
Harry summons the doctor. The doctor immediately divines the problem, and he summons an ambulance and
the police, holding Harry away from Charlotte at gunpoint. Charlotte dies in the hospital before Harry is allowed to see her.

Rivers, Clementine "Tish." *If Beale Street Could Talk.*
James Baldwin. 1974.

Clementine "Tish" Rivers, the nineteen-year-old narrator, is the youngest daughter of Joseph and Sharon Rivers. She lives in Harlem with her family, which includes
her older sister Ernestine. Ever since childhood Tish has
been in love with Alonzo Hunt, who, now twenty-two,
has been arrested on a false charge of rape.

Most of Tish's life has been devoted to her relationship
with Alonzo, nicknamed "Fonny," and by the time she is
eighteen, they have decided to marry. Fonny is a sculptor,
and the two find a loft to rent after they are married. In
the meantime, they consummate their relationship, and
Tish becomes pregnant. Because Fonny is in jail awaiting
trial, Tish must tell him of the pregnancy under the harsh
visiting conditions. She manages to tell him, and the couple draws strength from this sign of the vitality of their
relationship.

When she returns home, she informs her mother about
the pregnancy; in turn, Sharon Rivers relays the news to
the other family members, and all resoundingly support
Tish. At the same time they decide to redouble the efforts
under way to secure Fonny's release. Their next step is to
inform the Hunt family of the news. Only Frank Hunt,
Fonny's father, is pleased. Mrs. Hunt and her two haughty
daughters rely on invective to accuse Tish of whoring
around and Fonny of his typical uselessness. These women
are convinced that Fonny is guilty and vow to have nothing
to do with him.

Tish continues to work in an otherwise all-white department store, where she sells perfume, and she regularly
visits Fonny in the Tombs, New York City's short-term
jail. During her pregnancy, attempts to move Fonny's trial
date up are stymied, despite the efforts of their attorney,
Arnold Hayward. Although Fonny is innocent, a street
cop, Officer Bell, has encouraged Mrs. Rogers, née San-
chez, to identify Fonny as the assailant. This pressure on
the witness results in her flight to Puerto Rico.

The Rivers family, along with Frank Hunt, all work
extra hours, and the men engage in extra-legal activities
to earn the money for Fonny's bail. However, shortly after
Tish quits working because her father insists that she protect herself, the unborn child, and Fonny's sanity, Frank
Hunt is caught stealing on the job and is fired. In response,
Frank commits suicide. On the morning of Frank's death,
Tish goes into labor. The novel ends with the birth of the
child and the hope that, now that the bail money has been
raised and the state's case has been eroded by the alleged
victim's breakdown, Fonny can be reunited with Tish and
their child and resume his career as a sculptor.

Roane, Gloria "Glory." *Country Place.* Ann Petry.
1947.

Gloria Roane, better known as "Glory," is a self-
centered and ambitious young woman whose husband has
just returned from World War II. During the war, Glory
had written dutifully to her husband Johnnie, concealing
her true feelings. She is no longer interested in her husband, and despite his complete love for her, she spurns
his attentions on the first night he returns. Although she
is shocked and frightened when he nearly strangles her in
response to her cold rejection of him, she pretends to enjoy
his attentions the next night. Soon after Johnnie's return,

Glory begins an affair with Ed Barrell, who has had brief flings with many of the women in the small Connecticut town, including Glory's mother. Although Glory has a distant relationship with her mother, LILLIAN GRAMBY, the women share a desire for social prominence.

Johnnie is saddened when he learns of Glory's affair from the town's gossipers. Glory's brazen response is to take off for a tryst in Ed's cabin in the woods, but Johnnie follows the pair. During a powerful storm, Johnnie follows the lovers, beats Ed, then attacks Glory, slapping her as she taunts him with his inadequacies. Finally, Glory admits to having slept with Ed and informs her husband that she would always take Ed over him.

Glory resolves that she will leave Johnnie regardless of what else happens. She has no desire to accompany her husband to New York where he wants to study art, or live with him anywhere else. When Glory attempts to confide in her mother about her marital problems, Lillian rebuffs her, complaining that Glory has to learn to live her own life.

Glory has always planned to move someday into the Gramby mansion, the home of her mother's husband, but this plan deteriorates when Lillian tries to poison old Mrs. Gramby. Glory herself soon becomes persona non grata as she publicly humiliates a returning war hero, thereby revealing herself to be a selfish and amoral individual. Ironically, just as she plans to move into her own home with Ed, he falls down the stairs of the local courthouse and dies.

Roark, Howard. *The Fountainhead.* Ayn Rand. 1952.

Howard Roark is a brilliant architect who struggles to assert his high standards of personal and artistic integrity. He becomes an inspiration to those who can respond positively to the beauty of his character, and a serious threat to those who find comfort and power in purposeful mediocrity. Expelled from the Stanton Institute of Architecture for his refusal to adapt his ingenious style to the popular aesthetic guidelines of the school, Roark goes to work for a failing architect named Henry Cameron, whose work he appreciates. Through Cameron's guidance, Roark's genius is refined and perfected. When Cameron's business is forced to close due to lack of commissions, Roark goes to work for his former classmate, Peter Keating, a mediocre architect who is moving up in the field through social manipulation. Because Roark cannot stand to see a building badly designed, he helps Peter on many of his projects, until he is fired for his "insolence" to the firm's president. From there his work is rejected by many firms. Finally, he is recognized by Roger Enright, who commissions him to build a house and pays him enough to open an office. He receives a few commissions following this project, but his work is unpopular and he is closed down.

Unable to pursue architecture, Roark goes to work in a Connecticut granite quarry owned by architect Guy Françon. While there he meets Françon's daughter, DOMINIQUE FRANÇON. They are captivated by each other, but while Dominique becomes obsessed, Roark remains independent. Shortly after a passionate, violent act of love between them, Roark receives a commission and leaves the quarry suddenly. They meet again in the architectural social circle, where Dominique realizes that he is the architect whose brilliance she had recognized from drawings and buildings. Although in love with him, she seeks to destroy his career with the help of journalist Ellsworth Toohey; Roark suffers but enjoys the challenge to survive her efforts. Unafraid of a world that terrifies her, he fills Dominique with fear and hope. He is commissioned to build a temple by a man named Stoddard, but once the building is complete, Stoddard sues him for malpractice, claiming the building is not a temple. Dominique defends Roark in court and is devastated when he loses. Roark is hurt when she then marries Peter Keating, but he lets her go, knowing he must wait until she overcomes her fear of the evil in people and the world.

Roark sees little of Dominique during the next seven years. He continues to get small commissions until he is discovered by Gail Wynand, whom Dominique has married in the meantime. Not revealing that Dominique is his former lover, Roark agrees to build a house for him. He recognizes Gail's integrity, and the two become close friends. When Roark becomes involved in another lawsuit after destroying a building he designed for Peter Keating, Gail is forced to denounce him publicly. But Gail lets Dominique marry Roark, who is eventually acquitted. In tribute to Roark's integrity, Gail commissions him to build the Wynand Building.

Roberts, Humphrey. "Do You Like It Here?" John O'Hara. 1953.

Humphrey Roberts, the story's central character, was born at West Point, New York, the son of an army officer. As a child he lived in many different places because his father was often transferred. Humphrey did not go to a regular school until he was ten, when his mother divorced his father and moved to San Francisco, where they lived for one year. His mother remarried and after a couple of years in Chicago, they settled on the East Coast. However, Humphrey's stepfather, a certified public accountant, also required the family to move frequently, and the boy was again shifted from school to school.

At the story's beginning, Humphrey is in the second form at a new boarding school. He is sitting in his room during study period when Hughes, a boy he particularly dislikes, enters without knocking and announces that Humphrey is wanted in the office of the headmaster, a strict disciplinarian named Van Ness. Wondering why he is in trouble, Humphrey proceeds to Van Ness's suite. He has been at enough schools to know the difference between hearing that a headmaster wants to see you and being told that the man is waiting for you in his office. The situation is serious, Humphrey thinks, but he cannot imagine what he could have done to warrant the summons.

When Humphrey enters the office, Van Ness cruelly makes the boy stand for a while before speaking to him and allowing him to take a seat. The man then asks Humphrey to tell him where he comes from, why he went to so many schools, and so forth. Humphrey, extremely discomfited by the sarcasm of the headmaster when he is asking his questions, relates the story of his young life. Van Ness then asks him if he likes his current school; when the boy unenthusiastically answers in the affirmative, he asks if he would want to change anything about the school. Humphrey responds quite honestly that, while some schools are better than others, there are things that could be changed at any school.

Van Ness sits quietly for a moment, then suddenly yells at Humphrey and holds out a wristwatch in his fist. Did the boy ever see it before? Humphrey quite truthfully says no. The watch had been stolen from the headmaster's desk, then returned when a search was instituted. Van Ness apparently does not believe Humphrey's declaration of innocence; he repeatedly tells the boy that there is no room for a thief at the school and that the culprit will assuredly be caught. Humphrey begins to give his word of honor that he is not responsible, but is dismissed from the office without being allowed to complete a sentence. The schoolboy returns to his room and, sitting on his bed, curses the headmaster over and over again.

Robinson, Hyacinth. *The Princess Casamassima.* Henry James. 1886.

Although Hyacinth Robinson grows up in the London slums, he feels in his heart that he is of the upper class. He receives the first clue of his real identity as a child when Pinnie, the hat maker who raises him, takes him to prison to see a dying woman. Pinnie does not tell him that the woman is his mother or that she is in prison for killing his father, an English lord who had deserted her after she became pregnant. Instead, Hyacinth is made to believe that the woman is in prison for stealing, and he is ashamed to see her. When, as a young man, Hyacinth confronts Pinnie again, she finally tells him the truth.

After learning about his illegitimate heritage, Hyacinth becomes at once fascinated and repulsed by the lives of the wealthy. He wanders the streets of London; although obsessed with the world of refined excess from which he is barred, he does not want to partake in the pleasures of the upper classes but only wants to know what they are. He learns the trade of bookbinding, and in his shop falls under the influence of Paul Muniment, a young revolutionist. Soon he is attending meetings of a society of blow-

hards called the Sun and Moon, who meet and plot ineffectual acts of terrorism against the class system.

One day at a performance of *The Pearl of Paraguay*, which he attends with Millicent Henning, a haberdasher with a lusty appetite for buns, beer, and life, Hyacinth makes the acquaintance of Captain Sholto, an idle gentleman who knows him from the Sun and Moon. The captain and he switch places for the second act, and while Captain Sholto talks to Millicent Henning, Hyacinth meets and becomes enraptured with Princess Casamassima. Wealthy and beautiful, and estranged from her husband, an Italian prince, the Princess claims to be committed to the revolution and to learning about slums, poverty, and the darker side of life. She adopts Hyacinth as her pet revolutionist.

When Hyacinth announces at the Sun and Moon that he would risk his life for the revolution, Paul Muniment brings him to see the revolutionist Hoffendahl, and Hyacinth takes an oath of unquestioning obedience to the revolution. At this time he also commits himself to future acts of terrorism for the revolution. When Princess Casamassima invites him to Medley, her country estate, Hyacinth is dazzled by the opulent surroundings, and despite the warnings of Muniment, Sholto, and Madame Grandoni, the Princess's chaperone, he neglects his bookbinding work in order to remain with the Princess for a week.

After his experience of aristocratic life at Medley, Hyacinth begins to lose his sympathy for the revolution. Pinnie dies, and he spends his inheritance on a trip to Paris and Italy. When he returns, he finds out that the Princess has lost her enthusiasm for him and has started associating with Paul Muniment. She has moved into a lower-middle-class neighborhood and is supporting the revolutionary organization with her husband's money.

Because he has given his word of honor, Hyacinth must remain committed to the cause despite his changed views. Upon receiving his instructions to assassinate a duke at a party, he visits the Princess one last time. She does not know that he has already been informed of his mission and callously accuses him of refusing to honor his agreement. Hyacinth considers fleeing with Millicent Henning but learns that she has become Captain Sholto's mistress. Reflecting that he does not want to bring more shame to his mother's memory, he takes the pistol and shoots himself, leaving the Princess to discover his body.

Rodgers, James "Sandy." *Not Without Laughter.* Langston Hughes. 1963.

A quietly observant youth, James "Sandy" Rodgers awakens to the stark reality of being "colored" in a world dominated by "white folks" as he witnesses the various effects of racial prejudice on the daily lives of his relatives and acquaintances.

As the novel commences, Sandy and AUNT HAGER WILLIAMS, his grandmother, watch as one of the sudden cyclones typical of the Midwest overtakes their small hometown. A similar metaphorical storm dominates the lives of Sandy, his family, and the other blacks of Stanton. Racism—capricious, destructive, and sudden as a twister—limits and controls Sandy and all those around him. Aunt Hager, an ex-slave, takes in wash, converting her home into a laundry six days a week in order to care for herself and Sandy. Jimboy Rodgers, Sandy's father, leaves home for months at a time seeking more dignified employment and forcing Sandy's mother Annjee to work long hours as a domestic in the home of a rich white family. Sandy's aunt, sixteen-year-old Harriett, has grown bitter, refuses to return to school after the summer, and eventually runs away with a traveling carnival rather than work at a humiliating job at the all-white Stanton Country Club. Faced with these obstacles, Sandy watches his family disintegrate.

The winter following the storm is a harsh one for the family. With Annjee sick and unable to work and Hager forced to take in washing, the family is so poor that Sandy must wear his mother's shoes to school. Christmas Day proves to be a dismal affair as Sandy attempts to appear pleased by the crude homemade sled that Annjee and Hager present in place of the Golden Flyer sled that they cannot afford. As the winter passes, Annjee regains her health and returns to service, and Harriett returns home.

By the anniversary of the storm that opened the novel, Sandy and his grandmother are the only remaining members of the family. Harriett has become a prostitute living in the disreputable Bottoms, and Annjee has followed Jimboy to Detroit. All her children gone, Hager clings to her grandson, admonishing him to be a credit to her and the race like Booker T. Washington and Frederick Douglass. Sandy enters the working world, attempting to assert his manhood even as he experiences the full impact of racism.

When Hager collapses and dies several days later, Sandy is sent to live with his aunt Tempy, a woman with bourgeois pretensions. Sandy struggles with his desire to be with "regular" black folk such as the teenage boys who frequent the pool hall, and with Tempy's determination that he keep company with the "nice" people who attend the Episcopal church and do not act "niggerish."

This contest of wills is abruptly interrupted when Annjee, whose husband has gone off to fight in World War I, writes from Chicago that she wants the son she has not seen in five years to join her. He gains employment as an elevator operator and quickly realizes that his mother intends for him to support them both rather than allow him to return to school in the fall. The endless monotony of his job and his desire to live up to his grandmother's expectations for him inspire Sandy to return to school in spite of his mother's objections. Harriett, now a successful blues singer, helps to convince Annjee to allow Sandy to attend school and thereby fulfill the promise his grandmother had recognized in him.

Rogers, Ellen. *Ellen Rogers*. James T. Farrell. 1941.

Ellen Rogers is a young woman adrift within the narrow confines of lower-middle-class life on the south side of Chicago during the 1920s. She amuses herself by manipulating the men in her life—her widowed father and various boyfriends—until she meets Ed Lanson, with whom she falls desperately in love. Awed by his articulate and often violent defiance of the banal and the conventional, Ellen absorbs Ed's self-serving Nietzschean philosophizing, little suspecting what results its narcissistic elements will have for her.

The novel opens with Ellen making a fool of her lover, Bill. She bullies him into proposing marriage with threats of pregnancy and suicide, then jilts him. She is already a year out of high school, jobless, and still living with her father.

At a dance a few nights later she meets Ed Lanson. Besides being good-looking, he is a glib talker. With amusing irony Ed tells her that he is smitten and that they are destined to be together. On their first date he quotes Kipling and Nietzsche before confessing that he quit school after the eighth grade. He proclaims an ambition "to write about the unattainable dreams of men." He has also just quit his sales job—one in a succession—because of the fine spring weather.

On a second date he presents her with an imitation diamond for their engagement. Ellen, surprised by the depth and force of her infatuation, accepts it without knowing that Ed has bilked his other unsuspecting girlfriend out of the cash to buy it. Indeed, Ed has never repaid any of his numerous debts, and when not living at his mother's, he runs up hotel bills and then walks out without paying. He rationalizes his rapaciousness by quoting Nietzsche: transvalue values; move beyond good and evil; eschew all "Babbitry."

Ellen and Ed become lovers, but after a passionate few months together, Ed tells her that they must separate; Chicago is too small for his ambitions. He will make big money in New York in advertising, begin his book, and then send for Ellen. Instead, he goes to Washington to become a lobbyist and sends letters to Ellen requesting funds. When Ed returns to Chicago for a few weeks, Ellen discovers a letter from Ed's Washington lover. Badly disillusioned, she abandons him, only to return when he threatens suicide.

Ed decides to leave Ellen because, he claims, he needs a less passionate woman. But Ellen refuses to be so blithely abandoned. She tracks him down, haunts him at his job, and sleeps with his boss. Finally, she catches him with another woman and in a frenzied outburst humiliates him with the truth: He is a liar, a con man, and a fleecer of women. Ellen then tries to make amends, but Ed runs from her. In total despair, she drowns herself in Lake Michigan.

Rogers, Major Robert. *Northwest Passage.* Kenneth Roberts. 1936.

Major Robert Rogers is a charismatic leader in this historical novel that takes place in the mid-eighteenth century. Rogers is big, brave, and, in a certain way, boyish. Thirsty for glory rather than status, hard-drinking and hardworking, he is an adventurer and a schemer who will beg, borrow, swindle, and seduce in order to finance his next adventure.

Rogers is a soldier by profession and leader of the famous Rogers' Rangers during the French and Indian Wars. His Rangers, fighting on the side of the British, are skilled hunters, emphatically more successful in the New England woods than stiff British redcoats or clumsy provincial regulars. The Rangers' last campaign, against the St. Francis Indians, involves a rugged expedition through swamp and forest, a climactic massacre of Indians, and a wretched, cold, and hungry retreat. All of this is Rogers's specialty; he moves his men along as if by will alone. When they are weak with hunger and exhaustion, Rogers, though emaciated and unsteady himself, personally sets out on a makeshift raft to find supplies downriver.

After the French and Indian Wars, Rogers marries Elizabeth Browne, the daughter of a New Hampshire minister. But Reverend Browne is something of a prig—and so greedy that he charges Major and Mrs. Rogers rent when they stay with him. Elizabeth is dazzled by status and ultimately reveals herself to be quite a shrew. In the face of these terrors, Rogers escapes to London where he makes a sensation in high society while writing accounts of his adventures with the assistance of a besotted secretary. Eventually, he starts scheming his next exploit: the discovery of the Northwest Passage.

Through patronage at court, Rogers returns to the colonies as governor of Michilimackinac, a fort and trading post on the Great Lakes, which are the gateway, he supposes, to the Northwest Passage. But glory and patronage have made enemies for Rogers as well as friends; his career on the Great Lakes is marked by great popularity among Indians and traders, but extreme unpopularity among his superiors. He is nagged by his wife, denied needed gifts for the Indians, and refused permission to go westward. Done in by jealous superiors, he is arrested, nearly killed in captivity, and dragged off to Montreal for a trumped-up court-martial. He is thrown in a London debtors' prison, where he drinks to forget his bitterness.

The rest of Rogers's life is the life of a phantom. The novel's narrator, LANGDON TOWNE, occasionally hears rumors of Rogers working for the Dey of Algiers or Rogers's return to America during the revolution or Rogers' Rang-

ers resurrected to fight George Washington at White Plains. Appearing in Albany, Concord, New Jersey, Philadelphia, and Connecticut, this mysterious, charismatic, captivating major lingers on.

Rogers, Marie. *Daughter of Earth.* Agnes Smedley. 1923.

Marie Rogers wrestles throughout her life with desperate unhappiness, self-hatred, and a bitterness toward the social conditions and political institutions that control her existence. The novel chronicles the working-class woman's painful struggle to educate herself, to establish for herself a meaningful role in society, and to come to grips with the terror she perpetually feels with regard to society's treatment of her sex.

Born in the mid-1890s, Marie is raised in severe poverty in the Southwest by a mother who physically abuses her and a father who repeatedly deserts his family. She hates her parents bitterly, and early in life develops a loathing for the institution of marriage in general and for women who are wives in particular. Marie is bright, but her education is erratic; while still a girl, she is forced to help support her family by working at such jobs as kitchen helper, babysitter, washerwoman, tobacco stripper, store clerk, and waitress. When she is fifteen, a twenty-eight-year-old cowboy named Jim Watson proposes to her; she agrees at first but rejects him with horror when the "duties" of marriage are explained to her.

One year later Marie becomes a schoolteacher in New Mexico even though she never graduated from grammar school. She lies about her age and despite low marks on the placement examination is given a job teaching for a time in a remote cattle frontier camp. Marie makes her way to Denver, works briefly as a typist in the office of a magazine editor, and goes on the road selling subscriptions, but she almost starves and is sexually harassed. With the financial help of a friend she attends a school for teachers in Phoenix where she studies hard, eventually becoming the editor of the school's weekly newspaper. She is befriended by brother and sister Karin and Knut Larson. When Marie is eighteen, she agrees to marry Knut despite her fear of sex, and they go to San Francisco. She works as a stenographer, begins to write, and is introduced to socialist political thought. Marie and Knut love each other, but their marriage is doomed. She tries to kill herself the first time she gets pregnant; after her second illegal abortion, the couple divorces.

Marie goes to New York, where she works as a journalist, attends night school, and becomes involved with a nationalist revolutionary group struggling for the liberation of India. She is raped by one of the group's members, a vicious man named Juan Diaz, and she tries to kill herself when she realizes that she desired him. She is arrested for shielding one of her comrades and spends six months in prison without the benefit of a trial; she writes about the experience and is hired by a socialist daily newspaper. During this time she has various brief affairs but keeps them secret out of shame and fear. Marie then meets and falls in love with Anand Manvekar, a gentle, intellectual Indian revolutionary. She marries him and for the first time in her life feels the beauty of love, and her bitterness and loathing of sex are swept away. She is extremely happy for a while but becomes fearful when her husband begins to express jealousy about her past sex life.

Then, at a meeting of the revolutionary group, Anand finds out about the rape. Diaz blackmails him, threatening to make the deed public, which would jeopardize Anand's position among his comrades who do not readily include women in their liberationist ideology. Marie loves her husband, but their relationship suffers badly; in the end she decides to leave him in order to prevent his political and personal ruin. Filled with despair and grief, Marie leaves Anand and goes to stay with her friend Karin in Denmark where, at age thirty, she begins to write the painful story of her life.

Rojack, Stephen. *An American Dream.* Norman Mailer. 1965.

This startling vision of the underside of the American dream explores the subterranean impulses of Stephen Rojack, an upstanding citizen turned murderer. When the novel opens, Rojack is forty-three years old. A Harvard graduate, he earned a Distinguished Service Medal in his youth for slaying four German soldiers in a significant World War II battle. He went on to become a Democratic congressman at the age of twenty-six. However, Rojack's exposure to violent death aroused in him a mystical superstition at odds with his public persona. As a result he abandoned politics, earned his Ph.D., and became a professor of existential psychology at a New York university. In his classes, his controversial talk show, and his popular book, *The Psychology of the Hangman*, Rojack promulgates his thesis that magic, dread, and the perception of death are the sole motivating forces for human beings.

Similar forces apparently had propelled Rojack into marrying Deborah, a wealthy heiress and devout Catholic who, like Rojack, is preoccupied by the forces of good and evil and who also vividly embodies both forces in a way that simultaneously fascinates and repulses her husband. When the novel opens, Rojack and Deborah are separated, but Rojack feels compelled to pay her a visit. During the visit, Deborah viciously attacks Rojack's masculinity and then attacks him physically. In the ensuing fight, Rojack strangles her.

Rojack enters a state that he describes as hallucinogenic. Over the course of the next day and a half he feels a new power within himself that alerts him to unseen vibrations and mysterious signs. These sensations control his behavior throughout subsequent events.

After killing his wife, Rojack engages in intercourse with her maid, then pushes Deborah's body out of a window and calls the police. While being questioned he meets blonde and beautiful Cherry, a singer whom he follows to a seamy after-hours nightclub where he confronts her former boyfriend. Cherry and Rojack feel that together they are experiencing love for the first time; Rojack wants to love Cherry as he was unable to love Deborah and also to have children with her, which he was unable to do with Deborah.

Many people, including the detectives and Deborah's family, suspect Rojack of the murder. Rojack's father-in-law, Kelly, a powerful international businessman, finally demands a meeting. Despite an intuition that he should not keep the appointment, Rojack leaves Cherry alone to meet Kelly. Although he manages to appease his father-in-law, Rojack returns to Cherry's apartment to find her murdered.

Cleared of his wife's murder by lack of evidence, Rojack leaves New York for Las Vegas, makes a great deal of money gambling, and, as the novel closes, heads south to Mexico and South America.

Romano, Nick. *Knock on Any Door.* Willard Motley. 1947.

Nick Romano's motto is "Live fast, die young, and leave a good-looking corpse." His story begins in Denver, Colorado, where at the age of twelve he is a regular churchgoer and an altar boy. The Romano family's fortune changes, however, when Mr. Romano loses his shop to creditors, and the family is forced to relocate to the slums of west Denver.

Almost immediately after their move, Nick's outlook on life is radically transformed by the new group of youngsters he meets at school. He soon develops behavioral problems at home and at the various schools he attends, and serves several months in reform school. There, the brutal and humiliating treatment the boys face only helps to make a career criminal out of Nick, who vows to remain on the outside of the law. After his release from the school, he returns to his family in Chicago, where Aunt Rosa has been helping his parents reestablish themselves. Nick likes the idea of living in the same city as the legendary mobster Al Capone.

Nick joins a regular gang of youths who haunt the bars and who encourage him to become a jack roller, someone who lures men into alleys in order to rob them. During the next few years Nick sometimes works as a male prostitute and has a series of confrontations with Officer Riley, a sadistic policeman who notches his belt each time he kills a man and who arrests Nick and beats him nearly unconscious on general suspicion.

For a brief time Nick attempts to normalize his life. He marries Emma Schultz, a friend of his sister, and the two establish a home together. Marriage, working, and domesticity prove too much for him, however, and he soon returns to petty crimes. Emma, realizing that her marriage has failed and assuming responsibility for this outcome, commits suicide. Shortly after this, in guilt and despair, Nick returns to Owen, a man who has loved him and who has given him money and emotional support at intervals following his release from reform school.

One night Nick robs a bar, using a gun he has long kept hidden at home, and in the course of his flight from the scene of the crime, he encounters Officer Riley. A fight ensues, and because of his accumulated rage, Nick kills the policeman, shooting him in the face repeatedly until the officer is no longer recognizable.

After a lengthy search Nick is captured by the police, who beat him mercilessly before accusing him of Riley's murder. Despite the intervention of Grant Holloway, a socially conscious journalist who has followed the fortunes of Nick and his family since Nick's reform school days, the prosecutor, Mr. Kerman, succeeds in getting a conviction against Nick for first-degree murder. No pleas for mercy are accepted, and Nick is sentenced to die in the electric chair. The novel concludes with a horrifying and moving depiction of his last days and of the execution itself.

Rooth, Miriam. *The Tragic Muse.* Henry James. 1890.

Miriam Rooth transforms herself from an awkward, embarrassing "tea-party ranter" into an actress of arresting brilliance and sensitivity. She effects the metamorphosis with the help of a renowned elderly actress, Madame Carre, whose demanding and harsh method of teaching would discourage anyone who did not have Miriam's fierce determination. An unwavering focus on her work carries the young actress from mediocrity and obscurity to a promising career in London, where she becomes a sensation.

Miriam has an unusual and difficult childhood, marked by the death of her father, Rudolf Rooth, a German Jewish stockbroker and a "dealer in curiosities." Mrs. Rooth supports her daughter and herself by selling off her husband's peculiar antiques piece by piece as they wander from one European city to the next. Miriam becomes fluent in several languages and familiar with each national culture, but she learns to love the dramatic literature of France and England in particular. When Miriam first appears in the novel, she and her mother are living in Paris, meeting with their old friend Gabriel Nash and hoping to find someone to help Miriam with her dream of becoming an actress.

Although Nash doubts Miriam has any talent and is generally discouraging, he does her the favor of introducing her to Madame Carre, the preeminent actress, who agrees to evaluate the young woman. At their first meeting Miriam is so terrified that she begins to weep and then performs her two pieces clumsily, in a monotonous, dragging voice. When PETER SHERRINGHAM, another friend of Madame Carre's who is present, takes her aside to ask the great actress's opinion, she replies that Miriam is "loud and coarse." Although she admits the young woman is beautiful, she can see no artistic promise in her.

If Miriam senses Madame Carre's lack of interest, it does not prevent her from appearing uninvited at the actress's house and demanding her help. The older woman submits unwillingly to her requests for instruction. When Miriam withstands her cutting criticisms and continues to return for more work, Madame Carre begins to respect her. For several months Miriam suffers and struggles under the instruction of Madame Carre, who grows genuinely fond of her. While this is going on, Peter Sherringham often takes Miriam out, and he is there to witness a decisive change in her abilities. Miriam's transformation into an actress of genius is sudden and miraculous. With Peter's help she auditions for and wins a part in a London production, and travels there to begin her career.

Miriam achieves instant success with her first small production, called *Yolande.* She is clearly magnificent on stage and cannot be induced to leave it, even to marry Peter Sherringham, now a rising diplomat. She continues to have certain doubts, however, and discusses her worries with NICHOLAS DORMER, a young man who recently gave up a career in Parliament in order to paint. During one of the sessions when Miriam is sitting for her portrait, she confesses to feeling guilty about her "successful crudities" and accuses herself of being a "humbug." In spite of this, her fame increases steadily, and her performance of Juliet in Shakespeare's play is said to mark an "era in contemporary art."

Eventually Miriam marries her innocuous colleague Basil Dashwood, who buys a theater so that they can perform whatever they choose. The marriage is not one of romantic love but rather an alliance between two intimate friends with common goals. Her performance of Juliet shows again that Miriam's passion is for her work and that the world of the stage is the realm in which her real life will unfold.

Rosa. "The Shawl." Cynthia Ozick. 1980.

Rosa, the story's central character, marches for miles toward a concentration camp with Stella, her cold-hearted fourteen-year-old daughter, and Magda, her infant, who is hidden under Rosa's shawl. Rosa, Stella, and Magda are starving; Rosa has no more milk to nurse her infant, Stella's limbs are grotesquely thin, and Magda, trying to keep herself alive, relinquishes her mother's dry breasts to suck relentlessly on her shawl.

Rosa does not feel hungry; she feels light, as if in a trance. Looking into Magda's tiny face, she dreams of giving the child away to one of the women who are standing on the road and watching the lines of marching victims. But if she moves out of line, the soldiers might shoot; or she might accidentally drop Magda and the shawl, and Magda would fall out, strike her head, and die.

Miraculously, Magda survives and learns to walk, although her belly is "fat with air" and her legs are like wooden spindles. Rosa gives almost all her food to Magda, but Stella gives nothing; Rosa looks at Stella's bones without pity because she suspects that Stella is waiting for Magda to die in order to eat her corpse. In the concentration camp, Rosa hides Magda in her barracks, but she is afraid that someone will inform or that someone besides Stella will steal Magda to eat her. Since Magda learned to walk, Rosa feels certain that her daughter will soon die.

Indeed, Magda does die. One day, because she is cold, Stella takes Magda's shawl. When she discovers the shawl is missing, Magda leaves the barracks and searches frantically for it. Rosa tries to stop her, but she sees that Magda has already walked into the roll-call arena outside the barracks. Although she has been mute ever since her last drink of milk on the road, Magda, desperate to find her shawl, suddenly cries out "Maaaa!"

Rosa sees that Magda is about to die. Her mind races; she does not know whether to go after the shawl or run to Magda. She enters the barracks and tears the shawl away from Stella, who is sleeping beneath it. Back outside, she stands on the margin of the arena. She sees Magda far away, riding high on the shoulders of a soldier. Rosa unfurls the shawl and waves it in the air, and Magda reaches up with her tiny arms. But Rosa sees that Magda is heading away from her and the shawl. She watches as the soldier hurls her daughter through the air into the electric fence.

The electric fence hums and buzzes loudly in Rosa's ears, and she hears voices telling her to run to the spot where Magda has fallen. But she does not obey the voices. She stands still, knowing that if she tries to pick up Magda's body, the soldiers will shoot her. Rosa stuffs Magda's shawl into her own mouth so that she can taste her daughter's saliva, and then she sucks the shawl dry.

Rosedale, Simon. *The House of Mirth.* Edith Wharton. 1905.

Simon Rosedale is one of the richest but least attractive of LILY BART's many suitors in this comedy of manners. Symbolic of the nouveau riche at the turn of the century, Rosedale pursues the beautiful and well-connected Lily until she falls from the graces of fashionable society.

Jeered at by the anti-Semitic members of the New York social world as "the little Jew who has bought the Greiner house," Rosedale has coarse manners and an uncertain grasp of the subtle and complicated ways of upper-class social interaction. It is nonetheless his most ardent desire to be accepted by New York's upper crust, and he sees marriage to a beautiful, fashionable lady like Lily Bart as the surest way to gain entry.

When he initially approaches her, Lily longs to dismiss Rosedale haughtily. But she must balance disdain with politeness because Rosedale knows about her secret and potentially scandalous private meetings with a young man named Lawrence Selden. Rosedale also knows that Lily has borrowed money from Gus Trenor, her best friend's husband. Thus, although Rosedale annoys her, Lily courts his favor, an act that results in more proposals.

Ultimately, because of her gambling and other acts of impropriety, Lily loses face in her society. But while her fortunes spiral downward, Rosedale's rise. His business acumen enables him to profit even during a stock market recession. Rosedale never has great success impressing society women, but he does get closer to the men, who respect his financial savvy. Gus Trenor, for example, pressures his wife, a mogul of upper-class social affairs, into inviting Rosedale into their set.

By this time Lily, who has been banished from the upper social realm, needs Rosedale's money more than he needs her sponsorship. At one point Lily informs Rosedale that she is ready to accept him as her husband. While he finds her as beautiful and fascinating as ever, indeed more so, he also realizes that she has become something of a social liability. Learning that Lily has it in her power to blackmail Bertha Dorset, the woman primarily responsible for her ostracism, Rosedale all but pledges that he will marry Lily and end her problems.

Although she refuses him, Rosedale does not completely abandon Lily. Even after she becomes an unemployed wanderer of the streets, he offers to relieve her of her debts and even visits her in her miserable boardinghouse. He wants, as he says, to "put you where you could wipe your feet on 'em." But Lily knows that Rosedale still finds her attractive, and she shudders to think what repayment would entail. She chooses to remain in poverty and soon takes her own life.

Rosewater, Eliot. *God Bless You, Mr. Rosewater (or Pearls Before Swine).* Kurt Vonnegut, Jr. 1965.

Eliot Rosewater, one of the central characters of this satirical novel, is the son of a United States senator, Lister Ames Rosewater, and president of a "foundation" founded in 1947 by his father to protect the enormous Rosewater family fortune. As a generous young man, Eliot appears to have a promising life ahead of him, but he later takes to drink, becomes mentally unstable, and faces the loss of his fortune.

The Rosewater legacy began in Indiana, but Eliot is raised on the East Coast, where he learns to sail on Cape Cod and attends an Ivy League college and Harvard Law School. In his initial years as president of the family foundation, he devotes his time and the foundation's money to philanthropic pursuits such as cancer and sociological research. Soon, however, he begins to drink more and more, and one day he disappears from the New York City home he shares with his beautiful French wife, SYLVIA DuVRAIS ZETTERLING ROSEWATER. Eliot roams the country, carousing with volunteer firemen and attending lectures on science fiction.

Eliot enters psychoanalysis upon returning to New York, but after a year his doctor gives up and drops the case. Eliot soon suffers a second breakdown, this time wandering back to Rosewater County, Indiana. Sylvia decides to join him; they move into the Rosewater family mansion and associate only with the poor and deranged townspeople.

Five years later Sylvia herself has a breakdown and eventually initiates divorce proceedings against Eliot at the behest of her physician. In her absence, Eliot abandons the ostentatious family home and sets up an office over a lunchroom and liquor store, trying to live by the motto "You've got to be kind." The people of the town come to him for money, medicine, love, and understanding, which Eliot administers indiscriminately.

Eliot and Sylvia decide to meet one last time in Indianapolis before the divorce is final. As he is preparing to leave, his father arrives to inform him that Norman Mushari, a greedy lawyer who used to work for the firm that represents the Rosewater Foundation, will be bringing Eliot to trial to prove he is insane. If the lawyer is successful, the fortune will be transferred to a distant relative, FRED ROSEWATER, and the lawyer will be able to keep some of the money for himself. On his way to meet Sylvia, Eliot suffers his most devastating breakdown. He appears to function "sanely" for a full year but has no memory of anything that has happened when he ultimately "awakens" on the eve of his trial. To escape the trial, Eliot writes a conciliatory check to Fred Rosewater and declares all newborn babies in Rosewater County to be his—thus providing himself with an heir to the Rosewater fortune.

Rosewater, Fred. *God Bless You, Mr. Rosewater (or Pearls Before Swine)*. Kurt Vonnegut, Jr. 1965.

Fred Rosewater is a distant relative of ELIOT ROSEWATER, the central character and president of a fabulously wealthy family foundation. Fred is an insurance salesman in Pisquontuit, Rhode Island, where a Princeton degree and a talent for sailing allow him to socialize with the rich, although he is very poor himself and sells insurance only to other poor people in the town. Fred is driven to the brink of suicide by poverty and despair, but he is saved by a scheming lawyer who tells him about his wealthy relatives.

Fred's family is descended from George Rosewater, brother of the man who established the wealthy Indiana Rosewaters. Fred is unaware of this potentially lucrative connection, however. Fred's father killed himself, and Fred's only way to better his social ranking is to rub elbows with the rich while selling life insurance to his fellow downtrodden Pisquontuiters. His self-disgust is exacerbated by his Kansas-born wife Caroline, who is perpetually disappointed because, contrary to her pretentious

hopes, Fred's Princeton degree has not provided her with a big bankroll.

Fred becomes overwrought with the boredom and futility of his life and decides to kill himself, following in his father's footsteps. Wandering into the basement of his home, he discovers a fictitious family history written by his father before his violent suicide. The account claims a connection between the Rhode Island Rosewaters and British royalty. Newly inspired, Fred hurries to Caroline downstairs to prove to her that they no longer have to feel ashamed of who they are. Ready to learn more about the wonderful lives of his ancestors, Fred turns the page of the manuscript to find that the remaining pages have been destroyed by maggots.

Demoralized, Fred readies a noose in the basement to hang himself. Suddenly, Norman Mushari, a young and greedy lawyer formerly employed by the firm that represents the Indiana Rosewaters, steps in to inform Fred of his connection to Eliot Rosewater. Mushari hopes to bring Eliot to trial on the grounds of insanity, which would automatically transfer the fortune to Fred, with a fee paid to Mushari himself.

But in the end Eliot claims to have heirs in his hometown of Rosewater, Indiana, and Fred is paid off with a check for $100,000.

Rosewater, Sylvia DuVrais Zetterling. *God Bless You, Mr. Rosewater (or Pearls Before Swine)*. Kurt Vonnegut, Jr. 1965.

Sylvia DuVrais Zetterling is the unfortunate wife of ELIOT ROSEWATER, the novel's uncertifiably crazy hero. Sylvia, a Parisian haute-bourgeois beauty, suffers through her husband's self-destruction and her own mental breakdowns and eventually retreats from the world in a nunnery. She met Eliot during World War II when her father organized chamber music to be played for the patients of the Paris hospital where Eliot was recovering from combat fatigue. Eliot was later invited to the Zetterling home for dinner, and Sylvia fell in love with him immediately.

After their marriage, Sylvia dutifully and heroically withstands Eliot's disappearances, alcoholism, and mental breakdowns. Despite her own upper-class background, she follows him to Rosewater, Indiana, to set up housekeeping in the family mansion and entertain the poor and underprivileged of the county. After five years, however, she also suffers a nervous collapse.

In a mental hospital in Indianapolis, Sylvia is diagnosed by Dr. Ed Brown as having "samaritrophia," a new term denoting indifference to the problems of less-privileged people on the part of someone who is inherently loving and generous. The doctor administers chemotherapy and electric shock to release Sylvia's conscience, which has been suppressed by the rest of her mind. Now considered cured, she returns to Paris and becomes a member of the international jet set.

Sylvia embraces her new life-style, refusing to accept Eliot's letters and phone calls. But she remains happy only for a short time and soon breaks down again. Obsessing about Eliot and the sad people of Rosewater County, she goes to Switzerland for six months of treatment. Her doctor convinces her to divorce Eliot and remain in Europe. She agrees and flies to America for a final meeting with Eliot's father, Senator Rosewater, and the lawyers.

Sylvia tries to defend Eliot and his unconditional love for the people of Rosewater against his father's condemnation, although she knows that she must preserve her own sanity and stay away from the town. She maintains that Eliot's care for those people is beautiful and charitable because he recognizes that they are human. The senator complains that Eliot and Sylvia should be more concerned about their lack of children; a child would provide an heir to the vast Rosewater fortune. While in Rosewater, Sylvia calls Eliot, and they decide to meet one last time in Indianapolis. Both are terribly sad before the planned meeting. Eliot still loves her, and Sylvia is ashamed and miserable because she knows she isn't strong enough to join him. On the bus to Indianapolis, Eliot is struck by his most severe breakdown yet, a year-long blackout. He discovers, upon regaining consciousness, that Sylvia has entered a Belgian nunnery and taken a vow of silence.

Rosicky, Anton. "Neighbour Rosicky." Willa Cather. 1932.

The robust Anton Rosicky is in his mid-sixties and slowly coming to grips with the fact that he is aging. As the story opens, Anton is warned by his doctor that, due to a heart condition, he must abandon most of the strenuous activities he is accustomed to doing on his large farm. The doctor, a family friend, points out that Anton has a large family with five strong sons, all of whom could help with the chores. But Anton is proud, and although he cuts back on his chores to a degree, he remains fairly active. As the story continues, Anton has occasion to reminisce on his life, which witnessed poverty and despair, city and rural living, loneliness and companionship.

Anton was born in Bohemia, a section of Czechoslovakia, but when still quite young he was sent to London to live with a cousin in order to escape the poverty of his homeland. Upon his arrival in London, the young boy, who spoke no English, was shocked to learn that his cousin had moved to the United States. After several days of loneliness and hunger, Anton was taken in by a poor German tailor who spoke a little Czech and who made Anton a part of his family. Eventually, with the help of benefactors, Anton was able to leave London and sail to the United States where for several years he led a satisfying and active life in Manhattan. Within a few years, Anton, nearing his mid-thirties, began to long for his own piece of land. After consulting various Bohemian papers, he realized that by moving west he stood a chance of at least working on someone else's farm. To his surprise, upon his arrival in the West he is actually able to purchase a good-sized farm.

Many happy years follow as Anton marries Mary, who, although fifteen years his junior, is endlessly loving and devoted, and the two produce a large and happy family. Despite some years of sheer despair due to climate and crop conditions, the Rosickys soon become widely known and respected for their kindness, their dignity, and their good farming practices. However, the community does not fully appreciate the fact that Anton and Mary had consciously decided to devote their energies to family rather than to establishing financial security or expanding their land holdings, as most others in their area did. Eventually, Rudolph, the eldest son, marries, and the family is faced with an outsider, for the new bride, Polly, is an American. Despite Polly's non-Bohemian background and his reservations about the marriage, Anton assiduously works to include her in the family, and he goes out of his way to see that the struggling young couple is not destroyed by economic and social pressures.

As the story draws to its close, Anton decides that some farm work needs to be done at Rudolph's farm. While working, severe chest pains strike, and Polly rushes to his rescue. She gets him into her home and sits with him as he recovers. During this time she acknowledges her probable pregnancy and realizes how much she loves this unique man. Anton passes a peaceful evening, but the next morning, while doing some mending, he suffers another heart attack, which ends his life.

Roxana. *The Tragedy of Pudd'nhead Wilson.* Samuel L. Clemens (Mark Twain). 1894.

Only one-sixteenth black, Roxana is considered black according to the racial codes of mid-nineteenth-century Missouri. Despite being a slave for much of the novel, she is as proud of her aristocratic Virginian ancestry as she is of her descent from African nobility.

Early on she watches as three of her fellow slaves are sold by their master for petty theft. Unwilling to see her own child grow up to face that kind of treatment, she switches the nursing infant, THOMAS À BECKET DRISCOLL, child of her master, for her own baby, Valet de Chambre. No one notices, and as the children grow up they behave in the manner their new identities demand. The only person Roxy fears is DAVID "PUDD'NHEAD" WILSON, who she believes is a necromancer because of his interest in people's fingerprints.

Freed by her master on his deathbed, Roxy spends several years on a Mississippi riverboat until the bank in which she has been placing her savings goes bankrupt and leaves her penniless. She returns to her home, Dawson's Landing, Missouri, to beg help from her son, now regarded as the ward and heir of the eminent Judge Driscoll.

Tom reviles her, disdaining to be sentimental over a former slave. Wounded by his rejection, Roxy tells him that she knows a secret about him which, if she communicated it to Judge Driscoll, would lead to his disinheritance. Tom is afraid that Roxy is aware of his gambling debts and therefore agrees to pay her part of his monthly stipend. He is appalled and astonished when she reveals to him the secret of his ancestry.

In spite of his treatment of her, Roxy still loves her son. When he is desperate for money to pay off gambling debts, she volunteers to have herself sold back into slavery, providing that her owner is decent and lives nearby. Instead, Tom sells her down the river, into an Arkansas farm where the wife of the relatively decent farmer despises her and heaps abuse on her.

After several months of indignity and suffering, Roxy escapes by hitting her overseer on the head and returns to confront Tom. She insists that he confess his gambling to Judge Driscoll, knowing that this will cause him to be disinherited once and for all. Instead, Tom steals money from his uncle and kills the old man in the process.

Tom buys Roxy back but does not tell her that it was he and not the visiting Italian twins, Luigi and Angelo, who killed Judge Driscoll. When David Wilson, after examining his fingerprint records, names Tom as the Judge's assassin and Roxy's child, Roxy is heartbroken. Her son is sold down the river, the very event that Roxy had hoped to prevent by switching the identities of the children so many years before.

Royall (Mr.). *Summer*. Edith Wharton. 1917.

Mr. Royall is a temperamental but kind lawyer, and the guardian of CHARITY ROYALL. Although he is intelligent and talented, Royall never accomplishes the great things that had once seemed possible for him. He leaves the tiny town of North Dormer and becomes a successful lawyer, but some years later he returns, much to the surprise of its many townspeople. He is revered in North Dormer as the most educated man around, but with little to keep him occupied, he grows embittered and temperamental.

Royall's change in personality makes life difficult for his foster daughter, Charity. Mr. Royall and his wife brought Charity down from her mountain home, at the request of a man whom Mr. Royall had sent to prison, in order to give her a better chance in life. When Mrs. Royall dies during Charity's adolescence, there is talk of sending the girl away to school. Charity chooses to stay with the lonely Mr. Royall, however, and he is grateful for her company. One night, when Charity is seventeen, a lonely and drunk Mr. Royall makes sexual advances toward her; she refuses him angrily. Tormented by guilt, Royall asks Charity to marry him the next day. She dismisses him and soon after takes a job at the local library. Royall begins to retreat to his offices at home and at the town hall. Mr. Royall's business occupies him for only a few hours a day, and he spends much of his time sitting around the general store and talking to his male friends.

Charity shows little respect for Royall. He nevertheless remains devoted to her and feels he must protect her whenever possible. When there are complaints about Charity's work at the library, he tries to help, but she ignores him and angrily quits her job. She is then dissuaded from such action by LUCIUS HARNEY, a young architect studying the area.

Royall rents a buggy for Lucius to allow him to do his research and invites Lucius to take meals with his family while Lucius's hostess is away. Royall watches the friendship between Charity and Lucius with wary eyes. When the relationship between them becomes more serious, Royall tells Lucius that he needs the buggy back and that the cook is too overworked to feed him anymore.

Royall then becomes worried by a neighbor's report that Charity has spent several hours alone with Lucius in the house where he is now staying. He confronts her, points out that she is in danger of losing her good reputation, and proposes marriage to her. When she refuses, he claims that he will force Lucius to marry her instead. Proud and angry, Charity rebukes him.

On the Fourth of July, Royall runs into Lucius and Charity together as they are returning to North Dormer. Royall is drunk and furious at Charity for lying about where she was going and creates a scene by swearing at her loudly. Following this episode, he and Charity rarely speak again. Charity begins seeing Lucius secretly, and Royall loses himself in planning the speech he is supposed to give at a town celebration.

Finally, Royall, intent on protecting his foster daughter, demands to know whether Lucius plans to marry her. Soon afterward he reluctantly agrees to an engagement, but Charity herself breaks off their relationship when she finds he has been involved with another woman. She later discovers she is pregnant and runs away, but Royall finds her and once again asks her to marry him. Realizing how much Royall cares for her, Charity finally agrees, and as the novel closes, the couple begins their life together.

Royall, Charity. *Summer*. Edith Wharton. 1917.

Charity Royall, a young woman coming of age, struggles to come to terms with her own sexuality. Brought from a poor mountain community when she was five, Charity has been in the foster care of MR. ROYALL. At seventeen, some years after Mr. Royall's wife has died, Mr. Royall returns home drunk one evening and makes sexual advances toward her. He repents afterward and begs her to marry him, but she refuses. Charity becomes established in her job at the town library and begins saving money so that she can leave the little village of North Dormer as soon as possible.

Charity's life changes when LUCIUS HARNEY, a young architect, moves to North Dormer to study the historical buildings of the town. She helps Lucius with his research, finding him books and showing him some of the older homes. A friendship blossoms, and soon Charity finds herself falling in love with the young man. One day, obsessed with learning more about him, she stands outside his room and watches him work for several hours.

When she returns home, Mr. Royall accuses her of having been alone in the house with Lucius and says he is concerned about her morals and her honor. Charity is outraged at his accusations, but when she convinces him of the truth, he reminds her that such activities will cause rumors which will put her reputation in jeopardy. He offers once again to marry her or to force Lucius to marry her, but she angrily refuses both offers.

One evening, after a Fourth of July celebration, Charity and Lucius are confronted by an angry and intoxicated Mr. Royall, who swears derisively at the young woman. Charity is shaken and becomes more determined in her resolve to leave town. She and Lucius continue their relationship, however, meeting secretly in a deserted cabin in the mountains.

At a community celebration at which Mr. Royall is scheduled to speak, Charity sees Lucius whispering intimately to a wealthy young woman from a neighboring town. Later, at the deserted cabin, she and Lucius receive a surprise visit from Mr. Royall, who demands to know whether Lucius and Charity plan to wed. Lucius, obviously intimidated and with some reluctance, promises that they will marry. Soon after this meeting, however, Charity hears a rumor that he is actually engaged to another woman, and she breaks off the relationship.

Charity then discovers, to her dismay, that she is pregnant. Determined to start her life over again, she departs for the mountains in search of her biological mother; she finds her shortly after the woman's death. Despondent over her mother's death and shocked at the poverty of the people who live in the mountain community, Charity starts to return to the village.

Mr. Royall finds Charity as she is making her way down the mountain, and she begins to see that his concern for her is not as patronizing as she had formerly believed. Touched by his love and dedication to her, Charity agrees to marry him. On their wedding night, in a gesture meant to show that he means her no harm, Mr. Royall sleeps in an easy chair and leaves the bed to his bride. Now at peace with Mr. Royall and with herself, Charity settles into a new life.

Rubinov, Ezekiel. *By the Waters of Manhattan.* Charles Reznikoff. 1930.

Ezekiel Rubinov, the prodigal son of SARAH YETTA VOLSKY and Saul Rubinov, is sullen and despondent as a youth, keenly aware that he is a disappointment to his Russian Jewish parents who immigrated to America to find a better life for themselves and their progeny. Coming of age in New York City during the early twentieth century, Ezekiel passes his time at the Forty-second Street library, where he dreams of an improved station in life while his parents and siblings toil for their survival. Eventually, however, he vows that he is finished working for other people and realizes his dream of becoming an entrepreneur.

Looking for space in which to open a bookshop, Ezekiel negotiates with the owner of an empty grocery store in Greenwich Village. Although he wants two months' rent in advance, Ezekiel convinces the grocer to give him a chance. On learning Ezekiel's name, the grocer is momentarily surprised that his new tenant is a Jew, but he does not cancel their deal. When Ezekiel tells Sarah about the project, she is no more excited than she was at his last hopeful venture.

While he cleans the store, Ezekiel invites people to come in and chat or hear him read poetry. The store is finally prepared, and he sets out to get books to stock it. He goes from publisher to publisher, asking for books on consignment. Twice rebuffed, Ezekiel walks across the Brooklyn Bridge and considers simply walking into Brooklyn and giving up his plans. On the way home, however, he visits a publisher in financial trouble who agrees to consign to Ezekiel twenty-five copies each of forty books.

Books soon arrive at the store, and the first day of business is a success. As days pass, he becomes more and more secure. He gets a lease from the grocer and pays off the publisher. One night Ezekiel spies his father, Saul, staring in the bookshop window. He invites him to enter, but Saul refuses.

Winter comes, and Ezekiel grows more prosperous. A woman with blond hair and black eyes enters the shop one day. He offers to deliver the books she has purchased, but when he goes to her home after work, he is met by the maid, not the blond-haired Miss Dauthendey. The next time she comes by, he asks her how she liked the books, then launches into an attack of them. She only half-listens.

On the day Miss Dauthendey returns an umbrella that she had borrowed from Ezekiel on a previous visit, a cloudburst begins, setting her laughing. He walks her home and, after a hint, invites her to walk across the Brooklyn Bridge. Although Ezekiel has ambivalent feelings about this woman, the two begin to spend a lot of time together. At dinner he quotes Rilke and talks about his family; she tells him her grandmother was a "Jewess." Ezekiel realizes he is drawn to her beauty and sensuality but repelled by her intellect, and this concerns him. He stops seeing her, but only temporarily; he cannot get her out of his mind, and they are reunited. At the book's close, the successful young shopkeeper remains in this dissatisfying and troubling relationship.

Rudkus, Jurgis. *The Jungle.* Upton Sinclair. 1905.

Jurgis Rudkus is a quiet, broad-shouldered Lithuanian who immigrates to America with the woman he hopes to marry, ONA LUKOSZAITE, his father Dede Antanas, and several of Ona's relatives. Together they share a vision of America as a Promised Land of wealth and opportunity. Jurgis, strong, naive, and eager to create enough savings to marry Ona, has faith that the answers to his problems lie in Chicago where an earlier immigrant from their village has reportedly met with great success. By the end of the novel, however, the immigrant's faith and optimism are severely challenged by his experiences in the New World.

When Jurgis sees the poverty and filth of Chicago's stockyard district, Packingtown, where he aims to earn his living, his dreams of great wealth instantly evaporate. For the time being it is most important simply to get work so that he and the others can survive and afford their own lodgings. Jurgis is hired at one of the mammoth meat-packing plants because of his youth and brawn, and Ona's brother Jonas and cousin Marija Berczynskas also succeed in getting work.

Jurgis's job at the plant is dirty and strenuous, but with his as yet undiminished Old World work ethic he sees the complaints of his fellow workers as unjustified. Nevertheless, when he learns how his father has to pay a bribe to get employment, Jurgis has his first misgivings about the justice of this huge jungle. Jurgis also encounters corruption in the plant inspection system and in the real estate market, where he and his household face a series of disillusioning hidden costs. Increasingly cynical, Jurgis now joins the union he once scorned as ungrateful.

Jurgis and Ona must borrow and scrimp to have their *veselija*, or wedding feast, and Ona herself must now work to pay for it and for their "new" house. Jurgis occasionally becomes hysterical with rage at his situation, but Ona and their new baby Antanas, with whom Jurgis is charmingly enamored, combine to keep his emotions under control.

One day Jurgis injures his ankle when a steer rampages across the plant's killing floor, and he must settle for less arduous work in the plant's putrid fertilizer mill since to his former boss he is now just a worn-out industrial tool. Things get even worse for him when he discovers that Ona has been coerced into prostitution by her foreman, Phil Connor. Jurgis attacks Connor and ends up in jail, too poor to make bail or pay the fine. When he gets out a month later, the members of his household have moved back to a cheap flat because they were unable to make the house payments. Jurgis goes on a drinking binge and comes home to see both Ona and her second baby die in childbirth.

After being laid off at a number of other jobs, Jurgis jumps a train and tramps through the countryside, stealing, drinking, whoring, and working odd jobs. Back in Chicago, he runs with Jack Duane, a career thief he met in prison. Before long, Jurgis is part of Chicago's criminal-political machine, selling votes and participating in other confidence schemes.

While working as a union infiltrator during a stockyard strike, Jurgis sees Connor and attacks him. Since Connor is part of the machine, Jurgis is denied the help he ordinarily would have received. Once again without a job, Jurgis wanders the streets begging and drinking.

One night Jurgis goes into a political meeting to rest and begins to listen to the orator. He finds to his astonishment that the speaker, a Socialist, articulates everything he had realized about the economic, political, and social organization of the country. Jurgis later meets Comrade Ostrinski, who gives him shelter and gets him work at a hotel owned by a humane Socialist, where Jurgis enjoys warm camaraderie and vigorous discussion. As the novel closes, he is at last able to see his own horrifying experiences in a clearer light.

Rufe, Hamm. *Capital City.* Mari Sandoz. 1939.
Born into the wealthy Hammond family in Franklin, the capital city of the fictitious state of Kanewa, Hamm Rufe rejects his roots and embraces the cause of labor. In the extremely conservative city of Kanewa, steeped in southern tradition, Hamm becomes ostracized from both his peers and his family. When he begins to support an attempt to unionize the labor of the town of Franklin, the animosity between him and the other members of his family increases. His activities attract the attention of "Gold Shirts," a local secret society akin to the Ku Klux Klan, and his living at home becomes impossible. At the age of fifteen, Hamm is forced to run away from home.

He spends a good part of his youth wandering in the South and Midwest, working in various social services. During a fight to help win rights for coal miners, Hamm meets a young woman named Stephani, with whom he falls in love. While the two maintain a close relationship during their labor battle in Alabama, Stephani confides to Hamm that she has given her life to the cause of helping others and, consequently, must move on as soon as her work there is completed. When the struggle in Alabama is over, the two separate, with Hamm keeping a small photo of Stephani to remember her.

A despondent Hamm returns to Franklin. He lives in a shack in a small settlement known by the disapproving townspeople as "Herb's Addition," on a hill overlooking the town. There he befriends an author named ABIGAIL ALLERTON, whose recent book chronicling life in Franklin, while critically acclaimed, has caused her ostracization from her community.

Abigail and Hamm become involved with a truck driver's strike that takes place in Franklin and neighboring towns. Despite an impressive show of solidarity among the local and out-of-state drivers, who have rerouted to avoid using highways near the area of the capital city, strong-arm tactics are employed by management and the town of Franklin, who look upon the striking drivers as "Reds" and "communist agitators." The press feeds anti-labor propaganda to the populace, and "Gold Shirts" step in as strikebreakers, beating and terrorizing the union leaders.

Hamm begins to campaign for a liberal and union sympathizer, a Senate candidate named Carl Halzer. Although Hamm thinks Halzer has no chance at victory, he believes that the candidate might succeed in calling attention to the injustices of management if he can win enough of a protest vote. In the middle of the mud-slinging campaign that ensues, Stephani returns to Hamm. Always seeking a cause to fight for, she agrees to aid Halzer in his bid for the Senate.

Halzer wins a substantial portion of the statewide vote, thanks to the efforts of Hamm, Abigail, and Stephani. Much to Hamm's disappointment, Halzer has developed an attraction for Stephani during the course of the campaign. He decides that he wants her to be happy, so he eventually gives the couple his blessing. Stephani and Halzer leave the capital city together, and Hamm must content himself with the small photo of her that he keeps in his shack.

Rumfoord, Beatrice. *The Sirens of Titan.* Kurt Vonnegut, Jr. 1959.

Beatrice Rumfoord, wife of the famous entrepreneur WINSTON NILES RUMFOORD, is an attractive combination of "dignity, suffering, intelligence, and a piquant dash of bitchiness." Her estrangement from her husband begins when he purchases his own spaceship against her wishes and is temporally and spatially spread across the unifiverse from his encounter with the cosmic phenomenon known as the "chrono-synclastic infundibula." He visits Beatrice infrequently, materializing at their mansion from time to time.

But Beatrice refuses to see her husband after the first materialization when he tries to tell her that it is her destiny to go to Mars and bear a child for West Coast billionaire MALACHI CONSTANT. She locks herself up in her mansion with her fortune and becomes a recluse, avoiding all contact with the outside world in an effort to thwart her husband's prophecy.

Beatrice loses her entire fortune in a stock market crash. Furious at her husband for not warning her, she tries to make money by charging three dollars a person for a tour of her mansion. She is eventually kidnapped by her husband and put on a spaceship to Mars. Kept in a small room on the ship, she has no contact with any of the other passengers. One night a strange man sneaks into her room and rapes her; in the morning she sees that it is Malachi Constant.

As her husband predicted, Beatrice gives birth to a boy named Chrono when they arrive on Mars. Her memory removed, she works as a respiratory instructor for other brainwashed recruits and lives with her son in Mars's only city, Phoebe, for eight years. When Malachi appears one day, AWOL from the army of Mars, she is unable to remember him.

Beatrice and her son are the last to leave Mars during the great invasion of Earth. When the automatic pilot in their spaceship malfunctions and the craft crash-lands in the Amazon rain forest, Beatrice and Chrono are the only survivors. They are adopted by a Gumbo tribe, from whom they learn to drink water from condensation and eat the roots of the salpa salpa, an Amazonian blue poplar tree. A year later they are rescued by Rumfoord, who sets Beatrice up with a lucrative concession stand, where she and Chrono sell religious paraphernalia for the Church of God the Utterly Indifferent. Rumfoord returns to them one day and introduces them to the cosmic Space Wanderer, the supposed martyr for his new religion. To Rumfoord's dismay, the Space Wanderer is Malachi Constant.

Bolstered by his throngs of religious zealots, Rumfoord banishes Malachi, Beatrice, and their son Chrono to Titan, a moon of Saturn, where Rumfoord lives with his dog in an isolated palace. Beatrice lives out the rest of her days on Titan, enjoying the love and companionship of her husband and Malachi, and writing a book called *The True Purpose of Life in the Solar System.*

Rumfoord, Winston Niles. *The Sirens of Titan.* Kurt Vonnegut, Jr. 1959.

Winston Niles Rumfoord is an affluent entrepreneur with a sense of adventure. When the government announces the discontinuation of its space program due to the appearance of a "chrono-synclastic infundibula," a strange phenomenon occurring between the Earth and Mars, Rumfoord buys his own spaceship and becomes the first man to have a privately owned space vehicle. With his enormous dog Kazak as a companion, the eccentric Rumfoord leaves his Newport, Rhode Island, mansion and directs his spaceship straight into the mysterious chrono-synclastic infundibula.

The experience leaves him a changed man. He becomes omniscient, aware of past and future events, and is able to read other people's thoughts. There are negative side effects, however: His journey has left him impotent. He and his dog are never present in one place for any period of time; rather, they "materialize" in different places around the galaxy.

With the aid of Salo, a shipwrecked messenger from the planet Tralfamador, Rumfoord establishes a military training facility on the planet Mars. Recruits are taken from Earth, promised untold fortunes, and then transported. They arrive at Mars only to have their memory removed and a small antenna implanted at the base of their skulls. Through this antenna, spasms of pain are inflicted by remote control on those who behave improperly. Rumfoord creates a super-army of soldiers who would rather strangle their best friends than suffer the pain from the antenna.

Rumfoord also has his wife BEATRICE (RUMFOORD), who is still a virgin after several years of marriage, brought to Mars. On the trip he arranges for her to be raped and impregnated by a recruit named MALACHI CONSTANT because he believes these events to be her destiny.

With the aid of Salo, Rumfoord initiates a series of attacks on the Earth's moon as the first move in his grand scheme, the conquest of the Earth. But Rumfoord's war lasts only sixty-seven days. The Martians, equipped with only knives, handguns, and an occasional rifle, are no match for the Earth's nuclear weaponry. By the time Mars itself is destroyed, not a single living creature is left on it.

Yet this mass suicide is what Rumfoord had been planning all along. His real motivation in the ill-fated war was to lay the groundwork for the new religion he hopes to invent: the Church of God the Utterly Indifferent. The invaders from Mars, he tells the people of Earth, were themselves earthlings who died for the single purpose of finally creating a Brotherhood of Man. Their dying wish was a world united under the God of the Utterly Indifferent.

Rumfoord's new religion spreads like wildfire, but the constant materializations around the solar system begin to take their toll on Rumfoord. Racked by sickness, he retires to a palace on Titan, a moon of Saturn, where he lives with Kazak. Beatrice, Malachi, and their son Chrono also live on the planet and are present when he confesses on his deathbed that he wishes to be remembered "as a gentleman of Newport, Earth, and the Solar System."

Ryder, Amelia de Grier. *Ryder.* Djuna Barnes. 1929.

Amelia Ryder, née de Grier, is the abused and unhappy wife of the bizarre and promiscuous philanderer WENDELL RYDER. Born in Tittencote, a tiny British country seat, Amelia makes the horrendous mistake of agreeing to marry Ryder and accompanying him home to his farm, "Bulls'-Ease," in New York State. Although life on the farm is utterly miserable, she does not flee from Ryder because she fears that he will neglect their children. Powerless to improve her sad plight, she endures countless personal injuries and the public scorn that results from her husband's immoral activities.

When the twenty-four-year-old Amelia first meets Ryder and his manipulative mother Sophia in London, she is studying voice and violin at the Conservatory of Music with the intention of pursuing a career as a performer. Although she realizes that Ryder is a free thinker and a believer in polygamy, she convinces herself that he will not subject her to the actual enactment of his unconventional beliefs. Amelia is also cognizant of the fact that if she marries Ryder, the burden of supporting him and his mother will fall on her because Ryder is supposedly too

ill with stomach problems to hold a job. Nevertheless, despite her sister Ann's frantic warnings, she agrees to become Ryder's wife, and they journey across the Atlantic to "Bulls'-Ease," her new inhospitable home.

It soon becomes apparent that Ryder expects Amelia to act as a baby machine in order to cater to his megalomaniacal desire to populate the globe with the products of his loins. Agonized by fears of death during childbirth and disgusted by Ryder's proclivities, which include not only extramarital affairs but acts of bestiality, Amelia must also support her family by hiring herself out to Ryder's rich brother as a charwoman. But the crowning act of humiliation comes when, after ten years of marriage, Ryder invites a crass, fat contralto named Kate-Careless to live with them in their tiny log cabin. While Amelia gives birth to her third of five children, Kate is pregnant by Ryder with her first of three. Amelia grimly assesses her situation with the distinction, "To man is the vision, to his wife the droppings!"

This domestic fiasco explodes when Kate's son Elisha pummels Amelia's youngest boy Hannel on the head, and a furious Amelia whacks Elisha in retaliation. When the matter is presented to Ryder for arbitration, Kate lies and pretends that Hannel actually provoked the attack. Ryder concludes that Amelia's son is culpable because he inherited a vindictive and volatile temper from his mother. Mutually infuriated, Amelia and Kate vow to quit the farm forever; Amelia rides off on a horse, while Kate follows suit on a cow. They meet by chance and engage in bloody fisticuffs, which Amelia eventually wins. They suddenly realize, however, that they have abandoned their children, and both decide to return to "Bulls' Ease."

Reunited, this bizarre family carries on as before until local authorities finally intimidate Ryder into sending one of his women away. He chooses to keep Kate, and the piteous Amelia, entrusted to the care of Sophia's brother, is completely divested of her conjugal rights.

Ryder, Japheth "Japhy." *The Dharma Bums.* Jack Kerouac. 1958.

Japhy Ryder, a charismatic young Buddhist scholar, attempts to live a simple monastic life in the midst of Berkeley's bohemian underworld. RAYMOND SMITH, a student of Buddhism recently arrived from New York, believes Japhy possesses a deep wisdom. He spends the year carefully observing Japhy's decadent and ascetic way of life.

Japhy grew up in eastern Oregon, where his parents owned a log cabin in the woods. Before his life as a student, Japhy was a logger and learned to exist with only the barest necessities. When Ray meets him, Japhy lives in a small shack near the Berkeley campus; the hut does not even contain a chair but is decorated with straw mats and crates neatly stacked with Japhy's books of Oriental philosophy and literature, many in the original languages. When Ray visits him, Japhy is often sitting cross-legged on the floor, reading and drinking tea.

When Japhy is not studying, however, his habits are not so monastic. He is a great favorite with women; there are always several in love with him, but he never becomes particularly attached to any of them. Japhy invites them to his hut to play "yabyum," a sort of nude staring contest that frequently turns into an orgy. Although Japhy worries about Ray's heavy drinking habits, he is nevertheless an enthusiastic participant in the wild parties organized by their circle of unconventional friends.

The decadent life of Berkeley sometimes becomes too much for Japhy, and he packs a rucksack to go hiking. Japhy takes Ray and their friend Morley on the strenuous climb up Mount Matterhorn. As they approach the peak, Morley sits down patiently by a lake to wait, but Ray becomes terrified by the height and stops. Japhy bounds up the mountain alone, yodeling when he reaches the top, and leaps back down again. Ray feels exhilarated by the sight of Japhy's impressive jumps down the steep incline.

Ray leaves during the winter months, and when he returns, Japhy has moved into a new hut built by Sean Monahan, a close friend of theirs who is a carpenter. When Ray moves in with Japhy, he seems to have changed into a sadder man, but Japhy's pessimism wears off as the spring progresses. Because lodging in the hut is free, they need very little money and earn it all by logging. At the end of spring there is a massive party for Japhy who has received a scholarship to study for a year in Japan. The party is still going on after three days when Japhy and Ray leave to go on a hike up Mount Tamalpais. The hike is as satisfying as their first one, and Japhy relishes it more since he must leave.

Japhy is to leave for Japan on a ship early in the summer. His girlfriend Psyche, who fought with Japhy at the farewell party, has relented. She writes him a note and then appears in his cabin just before the ship is to depart. Psyche refuses to leave when the last warning in given, and Japhy picks her up and throws her onto the dock as the boat pulls away.

Ryder, Wendell. *Ryder*. Djuna Barnes. 1929.

Wendell Ryder is the eccentric protagonist whose proclivities destroy all semblance of normalcy for his bizarre family. Driven by lust, Ryder indulges in both polygamy and acts of bestiality; his dream is to have access to thirty women simultaneously. Although authorities in the neighborhood of his farm, suggestively called "Bulls'-Ease," complain about the reprehensible manner in which he conducts the affairs of his family, Ryder successfully counters their intervention and maintains his exploitative and outrageous life-style, to the chagrin of the female members of his household.

In addition to championing the institution of polygamy, Ryder sports a number of other sexist notions, including the idea that a woman in labor is at the pinnacle of her potential and that the most saintly women are those who die in childbirth since their continued existence would constitute a diminishment of their stature as females. Ryder also believes that all women are morally corrupt and that the most desirable partners are those whose extreme fertility is available to men through a submissiveness and powerlessness that complements the superiority of the male sex. Claiming to be incapacitated by a bad stomach and therefore unable to work, Ryder relies on funds provided by his wife Amelia's labors as a charwoman and by money his doting mother Sophia manages to raise by begging through the mail. Although unemployed, Ryder is a busy man whose energies are monopolized in the sexual pursuit of his wife, his live-in mistress Kate-Careless, and scores of prostitutes and other willing partners.

Ryder's neighbors are so scandalized by his behavior that many of them speed up their buggies when they pass his property. Concern over the fact that Ryder's children do not attend school causes the community to call a meeting to which they invite Ryder so that he can attempt to explain this situation. A smooth-talking Ryder enters the crowded schoolhouse and proceeds to criticize the Board of Education, claiming that he does a better job of educating his children himself. He delivers his coup de grace when he escorts the assembled crowd to the school's well, which is polluted with the carcasses of three rats and a cat; this turns public opinion against public education. Ryder thereby wins the day and henceforth remains unmolested by educational authorities.

On another occasion, a delegation led by a social worker visits Ryder to demand an account of the parentage of the eight children on his farm and to justify the presence of Kate-Careless. Once again Ryder displays his rhetorical prowess and hoodwinks his gullible visitors by claiming that a traveling salesman who visits punctually once a year fathered Kate-Careless's three children. Ryder says he has assumed their care in the absence of their real father. An extremely slippery character, Ryder continues to flout both public authority and personal decency as he sexually exploits as many beasts and women as possible in his attempt to single-handedly populate the globe.

S

St. Clare, Evangeline "Eva." *Uncle Tom's Cabin, or Life Among the Lowly.* Harriet Beecher Stowe. 1852.

Although she dies at an early age, Evangeline St. Clare lives long enough to bring joy to the lives of those around her. Her kindness and Christian spirit are redemptive, and after her death it is partly her father's remembrance of her that persuades him to embrace a Christian life and resolve to free his many slaves.

Eva, as she is known, is the only child of a prosperous New Orleans couple. As she, her father Augustine, and her aunt Ophelia are traveling on a boat bound for home, Eva meets and befriends UNCLE TOM, a slave on his way to New Orleans to be sold. Their shared love of the Bible unites the two, and they spend many hours together talking and reading. When Eva accidentally falls overboard, Tom dives into the river and saves her life. She asks her father to buy Tom and take him to live with them in their house in the city.

Once back in the family's home, Eva resumes what is her accustomed place as the darling of the household. She is adored by all the slaves, especially Mammy, who, separated from her own children, is more affectionate toward Eva than the child's own mother. Her father regards her as a rare jewel, and Aunt Ophelia, although critical of the child's familiarity with the slaves, loves Eva for her Christian spirit and generous nature. Tom, in addition to his other duties, becomes Eva's companion as they play and read the Bible together. Only Eva's pampered and self-centered mother Marie is unaffected by the light the child brings to the home.

One day while Tom and Eva are sitting in the garden reading, Eva confesses to Tom that she thinks she will soon die and go to heaven. Saddened as he is by this revelation, Tom cannot dispute it; in the past several months he has noticed that Eva has been growing thin and pale, and is sometimes short of breath or feverish.

During a period of Eva's remission from her illness, the St. Clare family is visited by Augustine's brother Alfred and his son Henrique. Although Eva is charmed by her young cousin's gallant behavior toward her, the manner in which he treats his slave Dodo disturbs her. Because she is so gentle, Eva cannot understand people who abuse their servants. Dodo accepts the small coin that Henrique offers him to compensate for his poor treatment of the slave, but Dodo finds the smile and kind words that Eva bestows a far more precious gift.

Despite occasional improvements, Eva becomes weaker. Even through her sickness, however, she bears her suffering with dignity, thinking more of those around her, especially her father and the slaves, than of herself. The only worry she expresses about death is that it will take her away, if only temporarily, from the people she loves. She implores them to love Jesus and to pray that they will all be united in heaven, but she asks her father to act in a way that will affect the slaves' lives on earth: She asks him to free them all. Eva dies embracing God as well as the hope that all the people who love her will act on her words.

St. Clair, Ying-Ying. *The Joy Luck Club.* Amy Tan. 1989.

Ying-Ying St. Clair, one of the four mothers in this novel of two Chinese-American generations, possesses the two distinguishing characteristics of those born in the year of the Tiger. A Tiger can leap forward with fierce determination or stand very still, waiting for something to come along. When Ying-Ying arrives in America, she loses her Tiger qualities and can only chastise herself for not protecting her family from tragedy.

Ying-Ying's story begins in China in 1918 when she is four. It is the day of the Moon Festival on which, her Amah tells her, she can tell her secret wish to the Moon Lady. Although the weather is hot, Ying-Ying's Amah dresses her in a heavy embroidered silk jacket and pants. The day's celebration takes place on a boat in Tai Lake. During the hottest hours of the day, everyone lies down on mats to sleep, but Ying-Ying is restless and wanders toward the back of the boat. She is transfixed by the spectacle of fish being caught. She notices too late that her new clothes are covered with scales and spots of blood. Thinking that she can hide the spots by painting her clothes red, Ying-Ying smears herself with turtle's blood.

Her Amah is furious when she sees Ying-Ying and strips off all her clothing, leaving only her undergarments and slippers. She stands quietly watching the fireworks, and in the excitement nobody notices when Ying-Ying falls overboard. After a few moments of panic, she is hoisted out of the water in a fishing net by some peasants, then left on shore. Ying-Ying wanders toward a crowd of people and with them watches enthralled as a troupe of elaborately costumed actors enact the tragedy of the Moon Lady. She creeps backstage to whisper her wish to the Moon Lady, who, beneath the costume, is a man. Ying-Ying's wish—to be found—is fulfilled.

Ying-Ying grows into a beautiful and extremely arrogant adolescent. Girls around her express their hopes to be married, while Ying-Ying sees no one she considers good enough. A marriage is nevertheless arranged for her, and all her efforts to evade it are unsuccessful. Strangely, she falls desperately in love with the man she is made to marry and does everything in her power to be desirable to him. During her first pregnancy, however, Ying-Ying's husband leaves her for an opera singer. Ying-Ying gives herself an abortion and sequesters herself for ten years in the house of her poor cousins near Shanghai. At the end of this time she feels ready to emerge from hiding. Ying-Ying goes to Shanghai and becomes a salesperson in a clothing store.

Clifford St. Clair, an American businessman, meets Ying-Ying in the shop in Shanghai and courts her for four years, until her first husband dies. Then, although she has little feeling for him, she allows him to marry her and moves to California. In California, Ying-Ying relinquishes her Tiger strength, slowly giving way to insanity, and the miscarriage of a son pushes her into madness. She feels a frenzy of guilt about the abortion she performed on herself years before and about the death of this infant. Ying-Ying frantically rearranges the furniture in her apartment, trying to chase away the evil spirits, then gives up and lies motionless for hours. Her husband, who speaks little Chinese, and her thoroughly American daughter Lena offer her no comfort.

After her husband dies, Ying-Ying decides to try to reach Lena, who seems so distant, with the story of her life in China. Once she tells this story, Ying-Ying believes, her fierceness will return, and she will be able to help Lena repair her failing marriage.

St. George, Henry. "The Lesson of the Master." Henry James. 1888.

After a long and prolific career as England's most widely read and highly respected writer, Henry St. George finds he is unable to equal his earlier success. Indeed, his latest novels have a "queerness" about them, a kind of lackluster that is noticed both by critics and by the author himself. Still financially well off, and with a wife and three sons, St. George begins to write less and less. After writing a very personal manuscript that his wife burns because she dislikes it so much, St. George and his wife go to the country to spend a week with the family of their friend, the retired General Fancourt.

At the Fancourt country home, Henry St. George is very much taken by the General's beautiful young daughter Marian. The two take long walks in the country together, much to the disapproval of Mrs. St. George, who is unable to accompany them because of her failing health. While the renowned writer spends his time discussing literature and his career with the young Miss Fancourt, his wife is left with another novelist, PAUL OVERT, who is much younger than St. George but already the author of three promising novels.

St. George finally meets the young writer after reading the first twenty pages of one of his novels, given to him by Marian Fancourt. The two of them talk briefly, with St. George telling the pleased Overt of his great respect for his work. The subject of Marian Fancourt comes up, and Overt confesses a great affection for her. After lavishing praise on the free-thinking, independent young woman, St. George lightly adds that the General's daughter is "not for me," and then they make plans for Overt to visit the St. George country house.

St. George, himself enraptured by Marian Fancourt, attends an art gallery opening the next week in London with her, and by chance they meet Paul Overt once again. Marian invites Overt to a gathering of friends at her father's house in London the following week, which St. George has also promised to attend, but St. George sends his apologies to the Fancourts that he will be unable to attend. Yet when Overt is leaving the party, he sees St. George arriving at their London mansion.

Some time later St. George finally invites Overt to his summer cottage, and the two have a long and candid discussion about the hardships a writer must endure for the sake of his art. The writer, St. George explains, must forsake a wife, children, and virtually all material comforts so that he may fully appreciate the full spectrum of the human experience. Overt points out that St. George himself has a wife, three sons, and lives in comfort and luxury. St. George confides to the young Overt that the material pleasures which surround him are the cause of the deterioration of the quality of his latest works.

During the next two years Overt stays in seclusion abroad to finish a novel, while St. George's wife passes away. St. George, still unable to recapture his earlier passion for writing and still very much in love with Marian Fancourt, decides to forsake his career as a novelist once and for all, and he marries the young Miss Fancourt.

St. Peter, Godfrey. *The Professor's House.* Willa Cather. 1925.

Professor Godfrey St. Peter holds the Chair in European History at Hamilton University in a small town on Lake Michigan during the post–World War I years. He has just recently completed an eight-volume work called *Spanish Adventurers in North America,* which took him fifteen years to write and earned him an Oxford prize of nearly $20,000. The money from the prize allows him to buy a new house for his wife Lillian. The Professor is deeply attached to the old house, however, especially the attic sewing room where he writes and studies at night; it had been the scene of the domestic drama of his wife and two daughters, who are now both married.

Although at the height of success, St. Peter is increasingly introverted and depressed. Part of his depression arises from the growing distance he feels from his family's material and social concerns. Godfrey met his wife when he was in his early twenties and living in France. Because he wanted to get married, he accepted a position in European History at Hamilton. He and his wife had been quite happy together until the death of Tom Outland, a close friend of the professor and the only first-rate mind that ever came into his classes. Tom had been engaged to Godfrey's oldest daughter Rosamund. When he died in the war, Tom left to Rosamund the patent for engines he had been working on while studying with the Professor. Rosamund has now married an ambitious man with sharp business acumen who has made a fortune out of the patent and, to the Professor's dismay, named their estate Outland after Tom. When Kathleen, the Professor's younger daughter, comes to complain to him about Rosamund and her husband's ostentation and superior attitude, Godfrey cannot help but feel the irony of the greed and pettiness that Tom's noble and innocent researches have wrought. His wife Lillian basks in the attentions of their two sons-in-law and wishes that Godfrey would take more pleasure in life and their new house.

When Rosamund and her husband plan a summer trip to Paris with the Professor and Lillian, the Professor refuses to go, preferring to stay on at the old house and edit the diary Tom wrote about his six months exploring an old cliff dwellers' city on an unclimbed mesa. During this time he reflects on how Tom's experiences in the Southwest and his energetic pursuit of his studies had brought him relief from the dullness of habit. The Professor resumes his lectures as the autumn term begins, but he sincerely believes his life is going to end and dreads the return of his family. His doctor tells him there is absolutely nothing wrong with him, so he retreats to the comfort of the old house. While he is sleeping, a storm blows out the fire in the old gas stove and slams the window shut. The Professor awakens in a daze with the realization that the stove will asphyxiate him, but he doesn't care enough to open the window. Augusta, the seamstress who used to share his study space with him, comes to get the keys for the new house from him and winds up saving his life. During his recovery Godfrey experiences a spiritual awakening that leads to an overall sense of resolve. He no longer anticipates his family's return with characteristic dread.

Salzman, Pinye. "The Magic Barrel." Bernard Malamud. 1958.

Pinye Salzman is a shabby but effective veteran Jewish matchmaker. Salzman's store of prospective brides and grooms, whose vital statistics he records on individual note cards, is so large that the drawers of his Bronx apartment are overflowing with them. His skills are tested to the utmost when he is confronted by the protagonist of the story, a young, immature rabbinical student named LEO FINKLE who seeks a bride because married rabbis stand the best chance of securing a congregation.

Salzman is an aging, rather shabby but dignified man whose animated carriage contrasts curiously with his mild, mournful blue eyes. He advertises his craft in the Yiddish newspaper, *The Jewish Daily Forward*, and,

armed with his parcel of cards representing prospective marriage candidates, spends his days roaming the city in order to present his wares to his clients. Salzman visits Leo Finkle, a soon-to-be-ordained sixth-year rabbinical student at Yeshiva University, and gives him a few frequently handled cards bearing the personality credentials of six unmarried women. The candidates include a twenty-four-year-old widow with a dowry of $8,000, a high school teacher of thirty-two, and a nineteen-year-old whose only defect is a limp that is the result of injuries sustained in an automobile accident. Salzman responds to Finkle's despair that he is being offered only six marital candidates by assuring him that very few women are worthy of becoming the wife of a rabbi. After a return visit the following night, the marriage broker finally convinces Finkle to meet the high school teacher, but the interview proves unsuccessful and the rabbinical student vows never again to consult a matchmaker.

Apparently undaunted by Finkle's curt dismissal of his services, Salzman waits a couple of weeks before visiting the future rabbi and is horrified by his insistence that he will not consider marriage until he has experienced premarital love. Ignoring Finkle's protestations that he is no longer interested in the marriage broker's assistance, Salzman leaves behind a packet of photographs of yet another group of unmarried women. Weeks later a now enthusiastic Finkle informs Salzman of his choice. Salzman groans and insists that the photograph was mistakenly included in the packet and proclaims that the woman is wild, shameless, and certainly not worthy of being the wife of a rabbi. But Finkle will not be dissuaded, and the matchmaker finally consents to introduce him to the young woman in question: Salzman's own daughter. The short story ends abruptly with the amicable meeting of the prospective bride and groom, the latter wondering if Pinye Salzman had not craftily orchestrated his emotions.

Sammler, Artur. *Mr. Sammler's Planet.* Saul Bellow. 1970.

Artur Sammler is a septuagenarian Polish refugee living in Manhattan with his German niece, Margotte Arkin. Sammler is a striking gentleman, over six feet tall and with shaggy white hair and dark glasses that he wears to protect his partial vision. He is financially supported by his nephew Arnold Gruner, a wealthy physician, and spends most of his time reading at the library and reflecting on his turbulent life and the equally unstable nature of the present day.

The details of Sammler's long life are revealed through his memories. As a young man he had lived with his wife in London, serving as a foreign correspondent for Polish newspapers. It was in London that Sammler befriended H. G. Wells. He began a biography of the man, which was later lost in the war. Sammler was blinded in one eye by the butt of a soldier's gun during World War II; moments later his wife Antonina was among those killed in a Nazi massacre. Sammler himself narrowly escaped being shot but fell into the mass grave alongside the bodies of his dead compatriots. He crawled naked through the woods to take shelter in a mausoleum and was kept alive by a friend who brought him food. Raids into German territory led Sammler to disarm a Nazi, steal his clothing, and shoot him, a fact that figures largely in his later thoughts on the meaning of life. Sammler leaves America only once after arriving there, to witness firsthand the six-day Arab-Israeli war.

Sammler's wise and philosophical contemplations of life are thrown into relief by the antics of those around him. At the start of the novel, he suspects he has been spotted by a black pickpocket he sees in action on the bus. Later the same day, the thief follows Sammler home, corners him in the lobby, and obscenely exposes himself. A shocked Sammler retreats to his apartment, only to find that his eccentric daughter Shula has brought him a manuscript by a prominent Hindu scientist, V. Govinda Lal, concerning potential colonization of the moon.

Sammler takes the manuscript with him to the hospital where his nephew Gruner is recovering from surgery for a brain aneurysm. On the way home he runs into his friend Lionel Feffer, who informs him that the manuscript was stolen from Dr. Lal and not borrowed. Once at home again, Sammler asks Margotte to take a letter to Dr. Lal, explaining the confusion about the manuscript. He then returns to the hospital.

Gruner is close to dying, and his two grown children, the promiscuous Angela and the scatterbrained Wallace, are both there waiting. Margotte telephones Sammler at the hospital to say that she and Dr. Lal have returned to the apartment and that the manuscript is nowhere to be found. Frantic to locate Shula, Sammler decides to accompany Wallace to the family home in New Rochelle, where the young Gruner insists his father has hidden a large cache of money. Shula is indeed at New Rochelle but tells Sammler that the manuscript is in a locker at the Grand Central train station. Wallace tears the wheels off a plane he is flying in a reckless stunt. Sammler learns this over the phone and offends Angela by telling her she should ask her father's forgiveness for her promiscuity.

The next morning Sammler wakes up to find that Dr. Lal and Margotte have returned to the city to find the manuscript. He is taken back to the hospital by the Gruner chauffeur. When he finally arrives, he learns that Gruner is undergoing some tests; while waiting, he implores Angela to reconcile with her father before it is too late. But soon after, the doctor informs them that Gruner has died. Sammler goes to view the body, and while standing above his nephew, he realizes that the meaning of life must be that every person inherently understands the terms of his or her "personal contract" and that he, Sammler, has met his.

Sammy. "A & P." John Updike. 1961.

Sammy, the story's narrator, is a nineteen-year-old cashier at the local supermarket in a small New England town. He is totaling a customer's groceries when three bikini-clad teenage girls walk in, and their appearance startles him so much that he rings up the same item twice. He is particularly struck by the girl he silently names "Queenie," the apparent ringleader of the group, whose bikini straps have slipped alluringly off her shoulders. Sammy jokes about the women with Stokesie, a fellow cashier, then watches as the girls walk around the store.

Although her two friends seem to be self-conscious, "Queenie" walks with firm assurance through the store's aisles. Sammy watches as the other shoppers, housewives in pin curls, become flustered at seeing them. A few shoppers turn and stare after pushing their carts past the girls to be sure their eyes didn't deceive them.

When the three girls eventually approach Sammy's check-out counter, "Queenie" is holding a small jar of herring. She hands it to him and then, to his surprise and delight, pulls a bill from the top of her bikini to pay for it. But then, says Sammy, "everybody's luck begins to run out." The store manager, Lengel, tells the girls they are indecently dressed. "Queenie" blushingly protests, but Lengel insists that they are violating store policy.

The girls, embarrassed and in a hurry to leave, quickly take their change and start to exit the store. Hoping they will hear him and be impressed, Sammy tells Lengel he quits. The girls go out the door without turning around, but Sammy continues to untie his apron, determined to follow through with his symbolic gesture.

When Lengel protests, Sammy tells him it wasn't necessary to humiliate the girls, who by now have disappeared from the parking lot. As he saunters out the store's automatic door, Sammy looks in vain for the girls, then looks over his shoulder through the windows of the store. He sees Lengel at his counter checking out the faceless shoppers as if nothing has happened. Realizing that his gesture has had no meaning, Sammy sadly reflects "how hard the world was going to be."

Sandoz, Jules. *Old Jules.* Mari Sandoz. 1935.

Jules Sandoz, an archetypal frontiersman, acquires the nickname "Old Jules" while he is still young because it reflects his status as one of the earliest settlers of Nebraska. Passionate and violent, he manages to make his living from the inhospitable land.

Jules's story begins in Nebraska, where he has settled. He becomes friendly with some Oglala Sioux Indians and builds a dugout. But he finds ground breaking to be back breaking; rather than trying to work the land himself, Jules begins charging new settlers for relocating on his land. One day when two of his rowdy friends help him dig a well, they play a practical joke on him. The two men pull him up and down in the bucket inside the well until the frayed rope breaks. He is eventually found and taken to a fort to recover. His ankle is broken, and complications ensue. Refusing to allow his foot to be amputated, Jules recovers very slowly. He is partially crippled for the rest of his life.

Jules becomes a leader of the farming community and is able to mobilize people to help him fight the injustices of rich cattlemen who repeatedly try to drive the farmers out. He goes to jail for threatening people with guns, but he never stays for long. Meanwhile, he works his way through a series of wives. The first, Henriette, is a friend of his sister whom Jules convinces to come west to marry him. Henriette is unprepared for the wildness of the land and her husband's demanding nature. They divorce but remain friends.

Shortly after his divorce, Jules convinces another young woman, Emelia, to come to America to marry him. He watches her carefully, but after two weeks she sneaks away to a nearby town with another man. Jules eventually gets married again, this time to Mary. She had come from Switzerland to live with her brother, but he failed to meet her at the station. Jules met her instead and later convinced her to marry him.

Mary stays with Jules through all the feuds, droughts, fires, and brutal winters. Finally married to a woman willing to work as hard as he, Jules is able to acquire more land. They ultimately have to rent out some of their land because they have too much to take care of themselves. Mary and Jules have six children with whom Jules has a turbulent relationship. He makes them work hard and sometimes forbids them to go to school. For a while two of the children are sent to live on some land that Jules bought on the condition that it be occupied, and they must fend for themselves.

Mary bears the brunt of the fighting between her children and her husband, and after the birth of her sixth child, she refuses to sleep with him anymore. As Jules gets older, he starts to slow down a little, although he still has grand plans, including moving to Mexico or Canada to start a new settlement, but he never does. Jules's health grows poor, and he suffers from diabetes and arthritis. He dies in bed of old age, still planning for the future.

Sanford, Major Peter. *The Coquette*; or, *The Life and Letters of Eliza Wharton*. Hannah Foster. 1866.

Major Peter Sanford, a scheming seducer living in New England in the late eighteenth century, is the villain in this sentimental novel. It is Sanford who brings about the moral downfall of the novel's heroine, ELIZA WHARTON.

When Sanford meets pretty, vivacious Eliza, he has squandered his fortune and fallen into bankruptcy. His financial situation is not known in the community, but he has a reputation as a rake and a seducer, and Eliza's friends warn her that he is disreputable. Vexed by the cold reception he receives from her friends when he visits her,

and excited by the challenge presented by the respected cleric J. BOYER, a competing suitor, Sanford determines to win the woman's love.

Sanford proceeds to charm Eliza. He has no intention of marrying her because she lacks the fortune he desires. He is taken by her beauty and vitality, however, and makes every effort to be near her at all times and to keep the equally persistent Boyer from her side. For her part, Eliza is caught in a dilemma: She is hesitant to enter into the stultifying life of a cleric's wife but knows that her friends and family disapprove of the more attractive Sanford.

Finally, pressed to make a decision, Eliza follows her friends' advice and decides to marry Boyer. But just as she is about to tell Sanford of her decision, Boyer discovers the two in close conference and becomes convinced that Eliza has betrayed him. He refuses to listen to her explanation and storms away angrily. Sanford soon leaves on a trip of some years, during which time he has no contact with Eliza.

When he returns, Sanford, now married to an heiress, finds Eliza despondent and in failing health. She has already discovered, through a self-righteous letter from Boyer, that the cleric is engaged to be married, and when she finds that Sanford, too, has forsaken her for another woman, she is crushed. Sanford is still drawn to Eliza, however, and has no intention of abandoning his pursuit. He charms her into a seemingly innocent friendship, then begins to contrive to be alone with her. With her moral resolve weakened by her despondency and her illness, Eliza eventually enters into a secret affair with Sanford.

When it becomes clear that she is carrying his child, Sanford arranges for Eliza to take up residence in another town. She does so, repentant and awaiting certain death. Indeed, after granting Sanford the forgiveness he begs for, she has a stillborn child and dies. It is only at the news of her death that Sanford becomes contrite. Deserted by his wife, shunned by the community, penniless, and lonely, he feels tortured by guilt and warns a friend, in his final letter in the novel, "to shun the dangerous paths which I have trodden."

Santiago. *The Old Man and the Sea*. Ernest Hemingway. 1952.

Santiago is an old Cuban fisherman who, in doing battle with a giant marlin far out at sea, pushes himself to the limits of his physical and mental endurance.

As a young man Santiago had an exciting life. A job on a ship once took him to Africa, where he saw lions on the beaches in the evening; all of his subsequent life he dreams about the lions playing like young cats in the dusk. Now Santiago is very poor; he has gone eighty-four days without catching a fish. For the first forty days he was accompanied by Manolin, a boy very dear to him, but after so many days of bad luck, his parents forbade their partnership. The boy is still close to Santiago, however, and keeps the old man alive by providing both food and companionship.

Early one September morning, Santiago hooks a huge marlin, and it tows him straight out to sea for a journey that lasts three days. The second day, the fish jumps and Santiago sees it for the first time; it is eighteen feet long and weighs more than a thousand pounds. Santiago realizes that the people who will eventually eat the fish will not be worthy of it. Even so, Santiago never doubts the rectitude of his killing it since humans are the more intelligent of the two species.

As the journey continues, Santiago becomes increasingly weak from the lack of food, water, and sleep. His hands are a bloody mess from holding the line, and he is light-headed and muddled. He begins to identify increasingly with the fish and feels a blood brotherhood with it: "You are killing me, fish . . . but you have a right to. Never have I seen a greater, or more beautiful, or a calmer or more noble thing than you, brother. Come on and kill me. I do not care who kills who."

Eventually, despite his weakened state, Santiago kills the fish by driving a harpoon into its heart. He attaches the fish to the bow and stern of his boat and heads toward home. But as he does so, a shark appears and takes a forty-pound bite out of the marlin, causing it to bleed further and attract more sharks. Santiago kills many sharks that night but eventually there are too many, and they pick the carcass clean. Ill and weak, Santiago manages to make his way home where he falls asleep and dreams once again about the lions on the beach.

Sanutee. *The Yemassee: A Romance of Carolina.* William Gilmore Simms. 1835.

Sanutee is the most influential chief of a Native American nation known as the Yemassee. The chief has spent the majority of his life as a friend and ally of the British colonists who settled the Atlantic coast frontier district known as Beaufort in the province of Carolina. Sanutee's loyalties change, however, when the settlers encroach too aggressively on the territory of the Yemassee. Using arms and ammunition supplied by the Spanish settlement of St. Augustine, Sanutee organizes an insurrection that unites Native American nations from Georgia, Florida, and Carolina.

Virtually every aspect of Sanutee's life has been tainted or destroyed by contact with the European colonists. His son Occonestoga, who was once a noble and respected warrior, has degenerated into a sloppy alcoholic who tracks down the settlers' slaves in exchange for liquor. Disgusted with his behavior, the chief banishes his son, who is then bribed with alcohol by the governor of Carolina to spy on his own father's preparations for war. When Occonestoga is found hiding in Sanutee's house, Sanutee condemns him to be executed.

A philosophical man with pragmatic foresight, Sanutee

realizes that his nation is doomed to be sacrificed to the advance of European civilization, but he refuses to be passive in the face of this inevitability. In order to assess the strength of the colonists' defense capabilities, Sanutee inspects the blockhouse that acts as a fortress for his enemies and decides that a surprise attack is essential. Returning to his capital city of Pocota-ligo after this excursion, he attends a council meeting with his fellow chieftains and a deputation from the Carolinian government in an attempt to procure more land from the Yemassee.

When Sanutee discovers that some of the chiefs, motivated by greed, have agreed to bargain with the colonists, he retaliates by reminding the people that the land is not theirs to sell because it is a gift from their ancestors which must be reserved for subsequent generations. Their ire aroused, several Yemassee warriors round up these errant chiefs, shear off the sacred tattoo that signifies their membership in the Yemassee tribe, and banish them to the forests.

Sanutee then appeals to the chiefs of neighboring tribes to join the Yemassee in their insurrection against the British colonists. These nations agree unanimously to support the war efforts, and an army of six thousand warriors gathers at Pocota-ligo to participate in the traditional precombat rituals. Sanutee also enlists the support of the twenty pirates who were responsible for transporting the arms from St. Augustine to Pocota-ligo.

Sanutee's desire to take the settlers by surprise is foiled by the governor of Carolina, CHARLES CRAVEN, who warns the community that the Yemassee are on the war path. As a result, although Sanutee's troops do manage to burn down the blockhouse, a group of settlers drive the Yemassee back into the forest. In areas outside the Beaufort region that do not have the governor's leadership, Sanutee's campaign is much more successful. Charleston, the most important town in all of Carolina, is surrounded by the Native American armies, and its inhabitants are threatened with starvation.

Although his confidence is bolstered by these victories, Sanutee pauses in his campaign to wait for additional recruits that have been promised by the Spanish in St. Augustine. In the middle of the night Sanutee leads his troops to the governor's camp. Craven has anticipated this strategy, however, and turns the tables on Sanutee by ambushing the Yemassee in a surprise attack. Sanutee and his troops fight bravely, but they are nevertheless massacred. The brutal battle is the death knell of the Yemassee nation. Sanutee, proud to the end, expires on the battlefield with a war song on his lips.

Sartoris, Bayard. *Sartoris;* "An Odor of Verbena." William Faulkner. 1929; 1938.

Bayard Sartoris, a young man in the post-Reconstruction South, has grappled all his life with the conflict between violence and renewed peace. Violence rules his culture through a seemingly endless cycle of vendettas originating from the war, then passed on through father and son.

As "An Odor of Verbena" opens, twenty-four-year-old Bayard has entered his fourth year of college at Oxford, Mississippi, where he studies law. His black servant Ringo has ridden from nearby Jefferson to tell Bayard that his father, Colonel John Sartoris, has been killed in a shootout with his former partner in the railroad business, a lawyer named Redmond. Four years earlier, Sartoris beat Redmond in a race for the state legislature. It is also revealed that Sartoris and his men had killed numerous carpetbaggers after the war and that when Bayard was sixteen, he and Ringo had also killed a man. This deed had turned Bayard against bloodshed, and thus he disapproved of Sartoris's senseless vendetta against Redmond. On the election night, Bayard had discussed this issue with his father's young wife, DRUSILLA HAWK SARTORIS, who had seduced Bayard into kissing her and then urged him to tell Colonel Sartoris about their attraction to each other. Bayard had not been able to bring himself to do so, however, just as, after his father's death, he cannot bring himself to kill Redmond.

Everyone except his father's sister Jenny expects Bayard to seek revenge: Ringo, his father's men, and especially Drusilla, who immediately hands him a pair of dueling pistols and takes a sprig of verbena from her hair and puts it into his lapel, as she had done on the night they kissed. Drusilla intuits that Bayard will not kill Redmond, and so she only laughs when Bayard comes to her room before heading into town the next morning, having spent the night grieving for his father. When Bayard arrives in town, his father's men, led by Wyatt, are waiting in front of Redmond's office. Wyatt offers Bayard a pistol, but he also senses that Bayard will not kill Redmond and turns away from him in disgust.

Bayard finds Redmond waiting for him with a pistol. As Bayard approaches, Redmond fires twice but deliberately misses Bayard, thus giving Bayard the chance to kill him. Bayard just stands there, so Redmond leaves, and when Wyatt enters the room, he realizes what has happened and that Bayard entered Redmond's office unarmed. Wyatt expresses respect for the youth's courage and says that perhaps Bayard is right, perhaps there has been enough killing. Wyatt sends word to Bayard's family about what has happened, and although by the time Bayard returns home Drusilla has gone to her family in Montgomery, she has left a sprig of verbena on Bayard's pillow.

Many years later, Bayard dies of a heart attack when his reckless grandson, the young BAYARD SARTORIS, gets them involved in an automobile accident.

Sartoris, Bayard. *Sartoris.* William Faulkner. 1929.

Bayard Sartoris, a veteran of World War I and the grandson of the BAYARD SARTORIS seen in "An Odor of

Verbena," carries on the family tradition of swaggering vainglorious violence. He and his twin brother John join the war effort in 1916 as Air Force pilots in the same squadron. But John is shot down while on a suicidally dangerous mission, and Bayard returns home alone. The loss of his brother, coupled with his anachronistic loyalty to the romantic and ultimately self-destructive traditions of the Old South, undermines Bayard's ability to function in an environment that does not provide outlets for his melodramatic personality.

In his absence, Bayard's wife bore a son named for him, but both mother and child died before his return from Europe. When he arrives in his hometown of Jefferson, Mississippi, a small town in Faulkner's fictional Yoknapatawpha County, Bayard lives with his grandfather and his great-great-aunt.

Although these relatives attempt to convince Bayard to contain his "leashed cold violence," he terrorizes the community with his daredevil feats. When a horse trader brings a dangerous wild stallion to town, Bayard insists on riding the animal. After a harrowing ride, the stallion slips and falls, and horse and rider crash to the ground. Although Bayard's head is seriously injured, he immediately proceeds to pursue more trouble by embarking on an unruly drunken spree. The binge includes a tour of Jefferson with a group of black men who join him in serenading various young women in the town, and the wild day terminates with Bayard being incarcerated in the local jail.

When he is released, Bayard buys an automobile and begins to take reckless joy rides around the county, frightening fellow travelers with the breakneck speeds he insists on maintaining. This maniacal driving culminates in an accident that Bayard survives only because a witness pulls his body out of the car that has careened into a river. Despite this calamity, Bayard does not learn caution. His grandfather, Bayard Sartoris, begins riding with him in an attempt to make him drive more sanely, but after a particularly dangerous motoring feat, the unfortunate man dies of fright.

While bedridden due to injuries incurred while performing one of his less successful automobile stunts, he begins courting Narcissa Benbow, a neighbor. Their courtship is characterized by the same cold violence that permeates Bayard's personality. At first Narcissa resists his rough advances, but she gradually begins to transfer her love for Bayard's dead brother to his surviving twin. They first kiss in a distinctly unromantic setting: Bayard has just frightened Narcissa by trying to duplicate the stunt in his car that had ended with the nearly fatal crash into the river. In part because she pities him, Narcissa eventually marries Bayard despite her clear perception of the futility that dominates his troubled existence.

Marriage temporarily assuages Bayard's despair, but he cannot shake off his own sense of doom. In an effort to elude his depression, he leaves Jefferson and begins to roam around Mexico, Brazil, and California, periodically wiring for money. Bayard's suicidal tendencies ultimately triumph over his will to live, and he is killed while test-piloting an experimental plane that no other pilot would agree to fly.

Sartoris, Drusilla Hawk. "An Odor of Verbena." William Faulkner. 1929.

Drusilla Hawk Sartoris is a woman with a strong desire for vengeance. Men like her husband, Colonel John Sartoris, see it as their duty to protect the South from carpetbaggers, scalawags, and politically inclined blacks.

Drusilla's fiancé Gavin Breckbridge was killed at the beginning of the Civil War, and thereafter she rides with Sartoris's troops, wearing men's clothes and with her black hair cut short. Riding across Georgia and both Carolinas in front of Sherman's army, she wears verbena in her hair, explaining that its scent is the only one that can be smelled above the odor of horses and courage, and thus the only one worth wearing.

After the war Drusilla marries Sartoris. Although her husband insists that she wear a dress rather than pants, she keeps her hair short, and her body stays hard and agile, like a boy's. Drusilla is proud of her husband's acts of violence during Reconstruction, and one night she defends Sartoris to her stepson BAYARD SARTORIS, saying that Sartoris's dream of rebuilding the South was worth killing for. On that night Drusilla seduces Bayard into kissing her and urges him to tell Sartoris immediately about their attraction for each other. She then pulls a sprig of verbena from her hair and places it in Bayard's lapel. Bayard decides not to tell his father about the episode with Drusilla, however, and several years later, when Colonel Sartoris is killed by a man named Redmond, Bayard once again fails to fulfill Drusilla's wishes.

When Bayard arrives home after his father's death, Drusilla is standing on the porch waiting for him, feverish and exalted. Leading Bayard into the room where Sartoris's body is laid out, she hands him a pair of dueling pistols with which she expects him to kill Redmond. She takes two sprigs of verbena from her hair, places one in Bayard's lapel and crushes the other, saying that she will now abjure verbena forever, for she no longer needs its scent to rise above the odor of horses and courage. Assuming that Bayard will kill Redmond with his right hand, she lifts his hand and kisses it; at that moment she suddenly intuits that Bayard has no intention of avenging his father's death. With this shock, she becomes hysterical, begins laughing uncontrollably, and is led away to her room.

The next morning Bayard goes to her room before leaving to confront Redmond, but again Drusilla only laughs hysterically. Later that day she learns that Bayard went to Redmond's office unarmed and stood bravely as Redmond fired two shots at him. By the time Bayard returns home late in the afternoon, Drusilla has fled to her family in Montgomery, but she has left a sprig of verbena on Bayard's pillow.

Sassafrass. *Sassafrass, Cypress & Indigo*. Ntozake Shange. 1982.

Sassafrass, the eldest daughter of Hilda Effrania, was educated at a fine private and mostly white high school because her mother's employer, the wealthy Mrs. Fitzhugh, offered to pay her expenses. Upon her graduation, though, Sassafrass decided not to continue with her education, preferring to practice the craft of weaving that she had first learned under her mother's tutelage.

Sassafrass packs up her weaving equipment, including the loom which the women of her family had used since slavery, and relocates to Los Angeles, where she lives with her lover Mitch, an indigent junkie who is also a painter and a musician. For a time the relationship is a good one, but when Mitch twice strikes Sassafrass after she grows angry at being insulted by some of his friends, she leaves him. Sassafrass travels to San Francisco to join her sister CYPRESS in her communelike home.

After a period of living with her dancer-sister and her artist friends, Sassafrass begins to forget Mitch and soon has an affair with Leroy McCullough. She also starts to focus on becoming a writer. Her affair with Leroy is barely off the ground when she receives a message from Mitch via Cypress that he wants her to come back to him immediately. Although wary of being hit again, she does love Mitch and decides to return to Los Angeles, where she finds a newly loving and caring man. Mitch's band is performing at below-union wages in a blues club. Cypress, who had given Sassafrass some cocaine to sell to finance her and Mitch's relocation to a new African community outside New Orleans, disapproves of Sassafrass's return but wishes her sister well. Mitch appropriates the cocaine, with Sassafrass's consent, in order to pay off an old debt.

Sassafrass and her lover are eventually able to move to the spiritually based commune. It becomes Sassafrass's ambition to become a priestess, but she is repeatedly told that in order for her to attain that rank, she will have to give up Mitch. She turns her attention to weaving special fabrics for various rites, and she also weaves cloth that is made into clothes for visiting tourists to buy.

Because Mitch isn't satisfied with their new life and because Sassafrass is confused about what to do once she becomes pregnant, she writes to her mother. Hilda Effrania has corresponded with Sassafrass frequently, offering love, support, and advice. She agrees to Sassafrass's request to return home, and the novel ends with Sassafrass in labor, attended by her mother and her sisters, Cypress and INDIGO.

Saunders, Jr., Solomon "Solly." *And Then We Heard the Thunder*. John Oliver Killens. 1962.

Solomon "Solly" Saunders, Jr., is a young black law student with an ambitious wife. Despite his own intelligence and a general desire to get ahead, Solly is troubled by Milly's aspirations; but his domestic concerns must be put on hold when he enlists in the military at the outbreak of World War II. Even here, however, Milly argues that he should strive to get ahead and enter Officer's Training School. Despite his misgivings about his future, Solly becomes part of the Fifty-fifth Quartermaster regiment and in due time is sent to Fort Dix to complete his training. With the exception of its commanding officers, this regiment is composed entirely of black soldiers. Most of Solly's new companions bitterly resent having to fight for a system that has systematically excluded them from the privileges of a democratic society.

As Solly's longing for Milly increases, he is urged by his friends to join them on excursions into town and to the canteen, where he eventually meets Fannie Mae Banton, a young woman with whom he soon becomes romantically and sexually involved. This affair is interrupted, though, when Solly is brutally beaten by local police and a white army officer, who catch him off base without a pass.

This event leads Solly to a reappraisal of the racism inherent in the U.S. military and society. He drafts a letter to several black newspapers and to Eleanor Roosevelt detailing the black soldier's plight and complaints. This in turn earns the entire company the wrath of the white and higher-ranking officers, who cope with the "problem" by shipping them off to California in preparation for duty in the Pacific Theater. Solly informs Fannie of his departure and tells her that he is married; despite her sorrow and anger, she vows to always love him. In the meantime, Milly has informed him that she is pregnant and that she will meet him in California.

Milly arrives soon after Solly gets to California, and they enjoy passionate lovemaking. However, Milly, who had sensed that Solly was drifting away from her, confesses that she lied about the pregnancy. Despite this problem, the couple manages to reaffirm their love, and when Milly returns to New York, she learns that she is in fact pregnant. Solly, whose political consciousness continues to be raised by his fellow soldiers, is delighted by this news, and it comforts him as he grapples with the horrors of warfare in the Pacific. Eventually, in the midst of heavy fighting, Solly is seriously wounded and is shipped to Australia for a long recuperation. Here he learns that his son has been born but that Milly died as a result of the strenuous birth.

This news throws Solly into a deep depression, which is gradually eased by his nurse Celia, who falls in love with him and seduces him. But their fledgling relationship is threatened by Solly's furious insistence that because she is white, she cannot really love him. This tension is un-

derscored by a violent outburst between U.S. soldiers, who erupt into racially divided combat, with blacks killing whites and vice versa. Solly joins the battle that rages throughout the Australian city. As the novel ends, with the fighting quieted down, Solly looks forward to meeting his son and to marrying Fannie, who breaks her engagement to another man when Solly proposes.

Savaard, Lydia. *Bridgeport Bus*. Maureen Howard. 1965.

Prim Lydia Savaard is the roommate of the beguiling MARY AGNES KEELY. Raised in a proper midwestern family, trusting young Lydia married Henry Savaard, an easterner from a highly respected family whose vast wealth had all but disappeared. Lydia had felt intoxicated by Henry's charm and privileged to be an honorary member of such a blue-blooded family. But shortly after their marriage, her husband had a breakdown and was confined to a mental hospital. With scars both psychological and physical—one of her husband's tirades left her with a deep cut across her chest—Lydia tries to begin life anew.

In a woman's hotel in Manhattan, Lydia meets Mary Agnes, who has recently moved to New York to escape her overbearing mother. Although she is at first put off by the lively, eccentric woman, Lydia soon finds herself agreeing to share an apartment with her. In spite of their vastly different personalities, they are relatively compatible. They find it easy to divide household chores: Agnes, intoxicated by her newfound freedom, cooks exotic gourmet dinners, while Lydia cleans obsessively, taking her frustrations out on the kitchen floors and counters.

In Manhattan, Lydia resumes a job editing children's books that she had held before her marriage. At the same time she sets about trying to divorce her husband. Her lawyer suggests that an annulment might be easier to get; she only needs evidence that Henry was ill even before the marriage and that she entered into the relationship with no knowledge of his history. Lydia knows Henry had been away for some time before they were married, and she suspects he was hospitalized.

In order to procure the annulment, Lydia and her lawyer go to Long Island to visit Henry's mother, a domineering woman who proudly maintains the last vestiges of the family's wealth and fiercely protects her son. Lydia soon sees that even her lawyer is cowed by the sneering Mrs. Savaard, who refuses to sign any papers recognizing a previous illness in her son. She won't allow an annulment or a divorce, and, what's more, she insists that Lydia begin paying her son's medical bills on her meager salary. She also insists that Lydia begin visiting Henry at the institution.

Crushed, Lydia returns to New York and starts visiting her husband every weekend. He shows some progress by Christmas and is even allowed to take Lydia on a short skiing excursion. Nevertheless, she panics when his doctor tells her that he may be released.

Some time later, Henry is indeed released, and he and Lydia begin living in the guest cottage of his mother's huge house on Long Island. The two treat each other gingerly, as if their lives might crumble into dust at any moment. Henry's mother dominates, planning their lives and intruding on their quiet existence. Lydia dreams of being back in her Manhattan apartment, and she sometimes believes that Henry was happier in the institution.

When Mary Agnes comes to visit, she reveals that she is pregnant with her young lover's child. Henry and Lydia are sincere in their offer to take care of the unwed mother until her baby is born, but Mary Agnes declines their hospitality. Soon after, Mary Agnes receives a call from Lydia, who tells her that Henry has been killed in a boating accident. As the novel closes, it is clear that Lydia must begin her life once again.

Savage, Richard Ellsworth. *U.S.A. (Nineteen Nineteen; The Big Money).* John Dos Passos. 1932; 1936.

Essentially fatherless, Richard Ellsworth Savage, a hard-bitten opportunist, comes of age in Trenton, New Jersey, where he excels in school as a child and wins a scholarship to Kent. In the summers, Dick works at a seaside hotel where he is befriended by the minister, Edwin Thurlow, and, more particularly, by his wife; Hilda Thurlow, bored and romantic, seduces Dick and teaches him to adopt the postures of an aesthete. After a wealthy benefactor has sent him to Harvard, Dick and a fashionably aesthetic friend, Blake Wigglesworth, play at being poets. They get invited to dinner by the famous Amy Lowell, and Dick avidly supports President Wilson's antiwar platform.

At the first opportunity Dick joins the volunteer ambulance service. He sees his share of combat in France and Italy, but spends as much of this period in the bedroom as on the battlefield. Dick remains strongly antiwar and talks a lot about the imminent revolution of the workers; when Italian censors intercept some apparently seditious letters he has sent from Rome, he loses his position in the ambulance corps and returns to Paris to be sent home.

Although he returns home in military disgrace, Dick still receives the support of the wealthy benefactor who had sent him to Harvard. Since Dick's grandfather had been a Civil War general, he gets commissioned as a second lieutenant and returns to France. He ingratiates himself with a colonel, and his rank is soon upped to captain. When the armistice comes, he attends the peace conference, where he meets the public relations giant JOHN WARD MOOREHOUSE and ELEANOR STODDARD. Dick's ardent political dissidence has subsided by this time.

During his final year in Europe he meets the vivacious and somewhat reckless southern belle ANNE ELIZABETH "DAUGHTER" TRENT, who is immediately charmed by

him. He is genuinely fond of her and seduces her, but when she becomes pregnant and wants to get married, he withdraws and she kills herself.

Back in New York, Dick goes to work for Ward Moorehouse's public relations firm. He finds himself scrambling to land lucrative accounts and competing for the boss's esteem. During a weekend at Moorehouse's Long Island mansion, he becomes his boss's closest confidant. He entertains an eccentric purveyor of home remedies whose business the agency covets, and when Moorehouse goes to Washington, D.C., to battle legislation that would make such home remedies illegal, Dick goes along. On the trip Moorehouse suffers a heart attack and leaves his assistant in charge of his affairs.

Throughout, Dick has been drinking enormous amounts of prohibition gin. After one evening spent careening around Harlem clubs, he wakes to find he has been robbed by a transvestite named Gloria Swanson. Feeling he needs to get his life in order, he buckles down to work; he is last seen preparing to court the daughter of the home remedy magnate.

Sawyer, Miranda. *Rebecca of Sunnybrook Farm.* Kate Douglas Wiggin. 1903.

Miranda Sawyer is the sour-tempered maiden aunt of REBECCA RANDALL. When her younger sister, Aurelia, marries a man of whom Miranda strongly disapproves, communication between the two stops. Years later, however, when Aurelia is a widow with seven children, Miranda offers to take over the care of the girl and to see that she is properly educated.

Living alone in a house with only her mild-tempered sister Jane for company, Miranda sees very little of society. When Rebecca arrives, she takes an immediate dislike to the child, whose youthfulness and energy intrude upon her simple and organized life-style. She has a nasty tongue and a quick temper, and unmercifully criticizes Rebecca. The relationship between them is strained as Rebecca strives to please Miranda, and Miranda always fails to be pleased. Miranda is incapable of appreciating Rebecca's creativity and her enthusiasm for a multitude of projects, which often land her in peculiar situations; she considers only the aggravations the child causes her.

As time passes, Rebecca gains a favorable reputation in the Riverboro community, and Miranda's opinion begins to soften. When Rebecca is thirteen, Miranda's failing health keeps her from her longtime family duty of attending visiting missionaries. She commissions Rebecca to represent the Sawyer clan. Rebecca, trying to be responsible, extends her hospitality, along with Miranda's and Jane's, to the missionary family and invites them to stay at her aunts' house, although this tradition had ended years ago with the death of Miranda's father. Miranda, although distressed at the sudden arrival of guests, is secretly pleased that Rebecca's act has brought respect to her household. She is also surprised to find herself enjoying the commotion. Through this and other examples, Rebecca adds pleasure to her aunt's life and works her way into her heart. Miranda continues to voice nothing but criticism, but her feelings change, and she becomes privately proud of Rebecca.

Over the years Miranda finds herself struggling with real financial burdens, but she is determined to keep her promise to Aurelia and stoically tightens her own budget to a bare minimum in order to keep Rebecca in school. Her pride in the child steadily increases, but she stubbornly continues to hide it. She is unable to attend Rebecca's graduation from boarding school but refuses to let Rebecca know how sick she is until the festivities are over. As a result, she dies before Rebecca can see her. In her will she leaves Rebecca her house, her land, and all her small savings. Although she never told Rebecca of the pride and affection she developed for her, this act reveals her love more clearly than any words.

Sawyer, Tom. *The Adventures of Tom Sawyer; The Adventures of Huckleberry Finn.* Samuel L. Clemens (Mark Twain). 1875.

Tom Sawyer is the quintessential American boy: enterprising, mischievous, curious, a troublemaker with a good heart. Despite the grief he willfully causes his caretaker, Aunt Polly, he has an intuitive sense of justice and an intolerance for any kind of hypocrisy. He also has a fertile imagination, both for problem-solving in unusual ways and for dreaming up worlds outside his own experience.

Tom undergoes a series of trials and exercises in ingenuity that episodically form the story of his moral development. For example, when made to whitewash a fence as punishment for playing hooky and lying, Tom turns whitewashing into a desirable activity by creating a competitive sense of importance about it. He persuades the boys of St. Petersburg that they should pay him for the privilege of doing the job.

Tom and his friend HUCKLEBERRY "HUCK" FINN, a vagabond youth of the town, go to the cemetery one night to get rid of warts by using a dead cat (one of many elaborate superstitions in the book). While there, they inadvertently witness Dr. Robinson, Muff Potter, and the villainous Injun Joe in an encounter. Injun Joe murders Dr. Robinson but persuades Muff that he was the one who did it, in drunken confusion. Tom and Huck know the truth but vow to tell no one of what they've seen. When Muff Potter is wrongly accused of the murder, Tom and Huck are too scared to come to his defense. Potter is jailed until a trial can take place, while Injun Joe remains on the loose.

In another adventure, Tom, Huck, and Joe Harper run away to nearby Jackson's Island, where they plan to be pirates. When they are gone for more than a day, the town thinks they have drowned and begins mourning them. The boys return triumphantly a few days later, in time for Tom to burst into church right after he's heard his own eulogy.

At Dr. Robinson's murder trial a few weeks later, Tom breaks his vow of secrecy and tells how Injun Joe was the real murderer and how he framed Muff Potter. Injun Joe breaks away and escapes from the courthouse. Later, in an expedition to a haunted house in search of buried treasure, Tom and Huck overhear Injun Joe and a comrade talking about more murders they are planning. They discover that the criminals are there to dig up a box of money, which they will transfer to a new hiding place.

Tom goes off to a picnic on Jackson's Island with his sweetheart, Becky Thatcher. When everyone else goes home, Tom and Becky find themselves lost in the elaborate underground cave there. Meanwhile, back in town, Huck Finn has tracked down the criminals and thwarts their plan to harm the innocent Widow Douglas.

Lost for days in the cold dark cave, Tom and Becky are about to give up hope. The town realizes they are lost, but rescue parties fail to reach them. At the same time, Injun Joe has come to the cave to hide out there and bury his chest of money. Tom manages to find a way out of the cave through a small opening, and he and Becky escape. Unbeknownst to Tom, Judge Thatcher has the entrance to the cave sealed. When Tom reveals that Injun Joe is inside, the whole town runs over, only to find Injun Joe's corpse; he had been struggling hopelessly to escape.

When the commotion has died down, Tom and Huck sneak back into the cave and find the lost treasure. They return to discover the Widow Douglas giving a party in their honor and declaring her intention to be guardian to Huck Finn. When the boys reveal their treasure, a considerable sum in silver, they astonish the town once again.

Some time later, Tom goes to Huck's aid by concocting a plan to free Huck's friend JIM, an escaped slave who has been imprisoned on the farm of Tom's Aunt Sally. The escape backfires, and Tom ends up being shot and wounded. After he has recovered, he attaches the bullet that wounded him to a watch-guard around his neck so that he can look at it whenever he tells the time.

Scarecrow. *The Wonderful Wizard of Oz.* L. Frank Baum. 1900.

Despite his desire to ask the WIZARD OF OZ for some brains, the Scarecrow is the thinker of DOROTHY's traveling party. The Scarecrow was created by a Munchkin to guard his cornfields; a day later Dorothy, a Kansas lass blown to the Land of Oz by a cyclone, finds him hanging on a pole and unable to scare away the crows. She lets him down, and he decides to go with her to the Emerald City with the hope that the Wizard who lives there will replace the straw in his head with a brain.

Being made of straw, the Scarecrow never needs to sleep, so he watches over Dorothy that night. The next day they rescue a TIN WOODMAN from the perils of rust and head into the dark forest, where the COWARDLY LION joins their party. The Scarecrow falls into a hole once, not knowing enough to walk around it, but he learns from his mistake and warns the group to stop when they come to a huge trench. He also helps formulate a plan to get across it. He later has the Tin Woodman build a raft to get them across a river that cuts across their path, the yellow brick road. Halfway across the river, however, the Scarecrow pushes his makeshift oar too far into the riverbed. Before he can let go, the raft is swept downstream, and he is left clinging to the pole. To Dorothy's great relief, he is rescued by a Stork and rejoins the travelers.

When they finally arrive in the Emerald City, each of the travelers is granted a separate audience with Oz, the Great and Terrible. To the Scarecrow, Oz appears as a lovely lady who tells him that she will not grant his wish until one of them kills the Wicked Witch of the West. As each member of the group is told to meet the same requirement, they set out to complete this mission.

On their way to the land of the Winkies, where the Witch resides, the Scarecrow is torn apart by the Winged Monkeys. The Monkeys act on orders of the Witch, who has seen the party approaching. Dorothy is able to kill the Witch by melting her with water, and she reunites the party. The Scarecrow is restuffed and restitched so that he is as good as new.

They return to the Emerald City to claim their reward. They soon discover, however, that the Wizard is, as the Scarecrow puts it, nothing but a "humbug" who has no magical powers. Nonetheless, he wants to be of help and grants the party's requests in imaginative ways. Instead of using a real brain, he replaces the straw in the Scarecrow's head with bran and pins and needles—to make him "sharp." The Wizard tries to take Dorothy back to Kansas in a hot-air balloon and appoints the Scarecrow to take his place as ruler of the Emerald City. Dorothy misses the balloon, and the party must go on one final adventure, to the Good Witch of the South, in order to ensure her return to her home. Once Dorothy is whisked back to Kansas, the Scarecrow returns to the Emerald City, where he remains as a well-loved ruler.

Schearl, David. *Call It Sleep*. Henry Roth. 1934.

When David Schearl and his mother Genya arrive on Ellis Island in 1907, they are greeted by David's father Albert, a Polish Jewish immigrant who has been living in America for several years. On this occasion David is frightened into tears by Albert's surly, even hostile greeting, and his fear on this occasion sets the tone for his first years in America.

The Schearls live in Brownsville, where Albert works as a printer at a series of shops. Irascible, paranoid, and violent, Albert is unable to keep a job or to control his temper at home. David's affectionate, refined, and protective mother shields him from his father's wrath, how-

ever, and from the fear of darkness he acquired from looking at the cellar door in their tenement building and from an episode in a closet in which an older girl made sexual advances toward him.

David clings to his mother, preferring her soothing presence to the noisy, vulgar children in his neighborhood. Thus he is deeply disturbed when he intuits that a co-worker of his father's is attempting to seduce her and is relieved when the family moves to the Lower East Side. David's situation improves in their new home. Their new tenement has no cellar door, and Albert is able to keep his new job as milkman and to be more civil at home.

At the age of seven David enters Hebrew school, where he proves to be a brilliant student and exhibits genuine interest in the study of Scripture. Through his studies he comes to associate light with godliness and safety and becomes obsessed with light: the light shining off the East River, the light emitted by the dangerous third rail of the train tracks, and the light at the end of a mysterious flight of stairs leading up to his roof. Venturing timidly to the rooftop, David meets his first friend, Leo, a Christian boy who shows him a picture of a haloed Christ and tells him that Christian relics will protect him from all harm.

David reluctantly agrees to help Leo seduce a cousin of his in return for a rosary. His father learns of this incident while embroiled in a quarrel with Genya in which he falsely accuses her of having had David by a Christian man in Poland. When Albert vents his wrath on David, Genya protectively thrusts him from their home. David wanders, delirious, through the city toward the train track and deliberately makes contact with the deadly third rail, whose light, he confusedly believes, will cause him to be reborn. Ironically, his intuition is in a sense correct. David recovers from the shock, and his experience of electrical power has somehow healed him of his fear. When he comes to, he feels his first sensation of power over his father, and as the novel closes, David has finally discovered a sensation that is "not pain, not terror, but strangest triumph, strangest acquiescence."

Schofield, Penrod. *Penrod; Penrod and Sam; Penrod Jashber*. Booth Tarkington. 1913; 1916; 1929.

Penrod Schofield is the irrepressible, all-American twelve-year-old boy whose adventures comprise these episodic novels. Penrod is part of an upstanding middle-class family in a typical small town during that era when, as the author states, "the stable was empty, but not yet rebuilt into a garage." He shares his home with his father and mother; Margaret, his older sister; Duke, his small, wistful, and much harassed dog; and Della, the family cook.

Mrs. Schofield tries to mold her son into a respectable young citizen, but it is a monumental task. Although Penrod makes some attempts to comply, his mischievous nature usually wins out. When he is sent to Sunday school by his mother, he uses his collection money to attend a motion picture show instead. Rather than go to elementary school, Penrod feigns a headache until he is allowed to stay home, where he can make a quick recovery and continue enjoying himself.

Penrod somehow manages to do harm both inside and outside school. Inspired by a motion picture on the evils of drink, he explains a late homework assignment by informing his teacher that he had been forced to stay up all night comforting his aunt whose husband—in truth a sober Baptist minister—had taken to the bottle.

Another day and another botched homework assignment call for more of Penrod's impromptu ingenuity. Asked to write a friendly letter to be read in front of the class, he uses one of Margaret's love letters. His poor sister, who only wants to find a suitable husband, is frequently victimized by Penrod's pranks. When one of her suitors makes the mistake of referring to Penrod as a "little gentleman," Penrod puts tar in the man's hat, thereby ensuring that he will never return.

With the help of his friend SAM WILLIAMS and some vials of old medicine, Penrod plays "drugstore" with his dog Duke as an unwilling customer. When Sam and Penrod meet two children and discover that one is missing a finger and the other can't speak, they make them the starring attraction of a backyard show. Later, they terrify the neighborhood with a huge snake, actually one of Margaret's stockings stuffed with—among other things— Sam's pet cat.

Penrod also loves pulp novels that tell stories of detectives and violent criminals. He becomes so enamored of one of these characters that he takes the man's name and becomes "George B. Jashber, Detective No. 103." Having assumed the guise of a detective, "Penrod Jashber" must find a criminal to pursue. He promptly proceeds to ruin the reputation of a perfectly respectable young man— another of Margaret's suitors—by fabricating and spreading rumors about his criminal activities. The young man leaves town of his own will, but Penrod's mischief is nevertheless discovered by the adults. When asked why he chose this particular young man as a victim, Penrod wins back his ever-tenuous popularity by saying that there must be something wrong with a man who could like his sister Margaret so much.

Schuman, Paul August Heinrich. *Never Call Retreat.* Joseph Freeman. 1943.

In 1942, Paul August Heinrich Schuman, a Viennese professor of the history of Western civilization, goes to a psychiatrist in New York because he is tortured by terrible dreams and is completely unable to function in society. Paul is a man whose hope and ardent belief in the historical progress of man has been shattered by his experience of being incarcerated in a Nazi concentration camp for three years, the greatest horror of which was the self-destructive hatred of the victims for one another.

Paul was born on January 1, 1901, to a middle-class Austrian family. As a child, he is loved but neglected; his father is a socialist drama critic, and his mother, a former opera singer. Schuman enters the university during the fourth year of World War I, but when he turns eighteen he enlists in the army, is captured by the enemy, and spends one year in a prisoner-of-war camp. Following the armistice, he studies for three years in war-torn Vienna, then goes to Paris to finish his doctoral thesis on the French Revolution. Paul returns to Vienna, begins to teach, and for a number of years pursues his private intellectual ambitions without becoming particularly involved in the developing conflict between socialists and fascists.

When Paul is thirty-three years old, his father dies fighting the fascists in the streets. He meets, falls in love with, and eventually marries Margaret "Peggy" Bishop, a British journalist sent to cover the riots. As the Nazis solidify their power, Paul and his wife become increasingly involved in anti-fascist political activity. Soon after the couple finds out that they cannot have children, Peggy leaves Paul behind in Vienna and goes to help the orphans of the Spanish Civil War, where she is killed. KURT HERTZFELD, a German socialist poet who had been a friend of Paul's father, is also arrested and sent to a concentration camp. Filled with grief, Paul works feverishly on a book about the history of human freedom and becomes obsessed with researching a fourth-century Umbrian manuscript.

When the Nazis take over Austria, Paul is arrested; his notebook on human freedom is destroyed because it is "incriminating," while the Umbrian manuscript, thought to be written in code, is sent to Berlin. Paul is sent to a concentration camp, where he manages to survive with difficulty for the next three years. Various former acquaintances are there as well, including Kurt Hertzfeld and Hans Bayer, a militant socialist leader. As time passes, Paul is particularly distressed by the suspicion and hatred of the prisoners for one another. He avoids becoming involved in the strife between political factions among the inmates until Hans, fearing for his own authority, has a falling out with Kurt. An attempted escape plan is revealed to the Nazis, and, later, both Kurt and Hans are executed. Paul himself is led to the scaffold to be killed, but he faints and his life is spared. He wakes up in the prison hospital, suffering from nervous shock and total amnesia. In June 1941, after six months in isolation, Paul's escape is arranged by one of his father's former associates, and he makes his way first to Switzerland then to New York.

Paul is treated with kindness in New York; he is hired as a translator for a newspaper and befriended by coworker Michael Gordon and his sister Joan. He is given U.S. citizenship in December 1941. He is still haunted by his experiences, however; he feels despair, cannot do his job, spends all his time in movie houses, suffers from terrifying dreams, and begins to alienate Michael and Joan with his strange aloofness and inability to interact socially. Finally, in desperation, he contacts a psychiatrist. After seven months of treatment, he is healed, marries Joan, and decides to enlist in the U.S. military.

Scott, Ida. *Another Country.* James Baldwin. 1962.

Raised as the youngest child of a religious family in the Harlem, New York, Ida Scott is a young black woman who ultimately aspires to be a professional singer. She begins painfully to discover the world beyond that of her childhood following the suicide of her older brother RUFUS (SCOTT). Following the discovery of Rufus's body in the Hudson River, Ida becomes more personally involved with Richard Silenski, Rufus's high school English teacher; Cass Silenski, Richard's wife; Eric Jones, Rufus's former lover; and VIVALDO MOORE, Rufus's best friend.

In particular, Ida begins a stormy and intense relationship with Vivaldo, who is white. Although Ida moves from Harlem to Greenwich Village to live with Vivaldo, their relationship is punctuated by the frequent intrusions of racism from their neighbors, who react angrily to Ida's presence. Ida also accuses Vivaldo of innate racism. Her feeling is that Vivaldo, despite his dramatic protestations to the contrary, could not have loved Rufus since he could never know or understand a black person's reality. She also exhibits raw anger toward Leona, Rufus's former girlfriend, whom Ida blames for Rufus's violent end, and her anger at Leona spills over toward Vivaldo.

As her relationship intensifies, Ida begins to develop herself professionally. Her career starts off slowly and includes occasional sessions with her brother's former band members. Gradually, Ida begins to travel for out-of-town performances and starts making a name for herself. She meets Steve Ellis, a married white man who is also a prominent television producer. He is captivated by Ida's beauty and talent, and promises to accelerate the pace of her career. But, however unwillingly, Ida must pay for this assistance: She becomes his part-time mistress.

While Ida is pleased with the success of her professional life, beginning to take their toll are the pressures of her personal life: tensions in her relationship with Vivaldo; confrontations with racism and sexual politics; her reconstruction of Rufus's life, of which she had been largely ignorant and which repulses her; and her affair with Stanley. The major victim of Ida's unrest is Vivaldo, who bears the brunt of her frustration, anger, and guilt. Vivaldo ultimately turns to Eric Jones, and the two men share an evening of conversation and lovemaking. Vivaldo keeps this to himself until Ida tells him of her affair with the producer. After a harrowing scene between them, they recommit themselves to each other.

By the novel's conclusion, Ida's anger and self-doubts have been exposed, and she and Vivaldo (along with Eric and his recently arrived French lover Yves) survive intact despite the complicated sexual, political, and racial entanglements that were encountered.

Scott, Rufus. *Another Country.* James Baldwin. 1962.

Rufus Scott, a young black jazz musician who was born and raised in Harlem, reappears in New York City following an absence of several months. Broke, hungry, and cold, he solicits a stranger for food and drink in exchange for money and sex. Suddenly repulsed by his own behavior, however, Rufus does not go through with the transaction and finally ends up at a jazz club, where he meets Leona, a young white woman from Georgia. He invites Leona to a party uptown in Harlem, and they begin what will be a tempestuous relationship. Leona moves in with Rufus, and for a time the couple enjoys their newfound intimacy.

Rufus and Leona have had troubled pasts, and they soon begin to avenge their torment on each other. The relationship suffers from mutual charges of racism, and before long Rufus begins to physically abuse Leona. In addition to suspecting Leona of racism, Rufus experiences the aftermath of an affair he once had with the young white actor Eric Jones, who also hails from the deep South. The tensions caused by Rufus's sexual confusion also contribute to the violence in his relationship with Leona.

Leona, whose husband had repeatedly beaten her and had legally deprived her of their child, is no stranger to the emotional and physical consequences of a strained relationship. Rufus, for his part, has been unable to trust women, especially white women, and has rarely ever had a long-term relationship. As Leona and Rufus's relationship breaks down, VIVALDO MOORE, Rufus's Irish-Italian best friend and a novelist, must step in to prevent severe harm to Leona. This intervention enrages Rufus even more.

Eventually, though, Rufus's pent-up anger, violence, and sexual frustration culminate in a ferocious assault on Leona, which leads to her hospitalization in Bellevue. She is placed under the care of her brother, who returns her to the South where she is permanently institutionalized. This pushes Rufus to the limits of his endurance, and despite Vivaldo's efforts and those of Richard Silenski, a novelist and Rufus's high school English teacher, and Richard's wife Cass Silenski, Rufus climbs onto the George Washington Bridge and leaps to his death in the Hudson River.

Although Rufus's death takes place relatively early in the novel, it serves as a catalyst for his survivors and their confrontations with their psychological, sexual, and social identities. The remainder of the story follows the interactions of Vivaldo Moore, Rufus's younger sister IDA SCOTT, Eric Jones, and the Silenskis as they work through their own pasts and the ways in which Rufus both brought them together and held them apart.

Scott, Samuel. *Dark Princess: A Romance.* W. E. B. Du Bois. 1928.

The Honorable Samuel Scott, known to his friends as "Sammy," is a black Chicago lawyer who becomes involved in the underground association of corrupt businessmen, city officials, and thieves known as the "machine." Born in Mississippi, he has received little education but hides this deficiency with charm and excessive confidence. As an alderman, Sammy is able to manipulate the system, intended to benefit "black Chicago," for his own profit.

In 1910, Sammy begins his political career as a protector of gambling enterprises, houses of prostitution, and petty thieves. With the cash paid to him by these customers, he bribes police and city officials into leaving them alone. In exchange, Sammy pays a "little army" of henchmen to ensure that black voters elect the officials he bribes. Although this system is already in place before his arrival, he manages to improve it and becomes an indispensable figure in the "machine."

Sammy's ambition is to organize a "political machine to run all black Chicago." With the increasing migration of African Americans to the city, however, he begins to have trouble managing the business. Hordes of other "bosses," both black and white, share his dream, and their interests inevitably conflict. When the amount of work becomes overwhelming, he hires a secretary, SARA ANDREWS.

Although Sara is not exactly beautiful, she radiates intelligence, efficiency, and good taste. On the second day she spends in his isolated little office, Sammy kisses her, and when she responds unfavorably, he decides to move her to a less important position. He fears that her prudery indicates the kind of conscience that has no place in his line of work. Fortunately, he soon discovers that although she objects to promiscuity, she accepts lying and stealing without question. They work closely together for four years, and Sara proves to be an extremely shrewd politician herself. After his initial disappointment, Sammy continues to think of marrying Sara, but he insists to inquiring friends that he is "not a marrying man."

When the business is running quite well, Sara suggests hiring Matthew Towns, an educated young man who has been unjustly imprisoned. They soon succeed in getting Matthew released, and Sammy is astonished at how much his "machine" improves with his help. A split occurs, however, when Matthew and Sara are married, and she manages to send him to the legislature in Sammy's stead. Sara incurs even worse trouble when she decides to get Matthew nominated to Congress.

For years Sara has helped Sammy plan his own nomination. Because of Matthew's success in the state legislature and the change in Sara's allegiance, Sammy knows he cannot beat the younger man. Instead, he accepts a $25,000 bribe to support the renomination of the white incumbent Doolittle, with the hope that he can defeat Matthew. The infuriated Sara, claiming he had promised to refuse Doolittle another term, announces her break with Sammy's machine. She then turns the story of the bribe over to the newspapers, and the city breaks into an uproar against him.

Still refusing to give up, Sammy does his best to dig up information incriminating or shaming Matthew, but is unsuccessful. Doolittle dies suddenly, however, and when Sara appeals to Sammy to join forces with her and Matthew, he agrees. He uses his own expertise to help Sara's husband secure the nomination. Suddenly, on the triumphant day the announcement is to be made, Matthew declines the offer and walks away from the party with a strange woman. Sara leaves town, and while she is away, Sammy has a windfall. He has been left in charge of some of Sara's belongings, among them a bag of priceless jewels belonging to Matthew's companion, who happens to be an Indian princess. When one of her subjects comes to fetch the bag, Sammy is allowed to keep one of the jewels as a reward for his cooperation.

With the money from this single jewel, worth thousands of dollars, and other assets he has "salted away," Sammy purchases an elegant home and a new car. When Sara returns from her trip, he promptly asks her to marry him, and she accepts. Sammy is enormously proud of his future bride and of his wealth, and as the novel closes, he feels confident that he and Sara will be able to bring about his own nomination to Congress.

Seagraves, Harry. *Paris Trout.* Pete Dexter. 1988.

A prominent lawyer in Cotton Point, Georgia, in the early 1950s, Harry Seagraves reluctantly agrees to defend a man he has represented on several instances in the past, the child-killer PARIS TROUT. Unfortunately, Seagraves underestimates the extent of his client's brutality and the power of his own conscience.

Shortly after accepting Trout's case, Seagraves visits the Cornell clinic, where he is confronted with the disturbing sight of the mortally wounded Rosie Sayers, Trout's young victim. Although he is unable to erase her image from his mind, Seagraves is nonetheless unwilling to conclude that he should drop Trout's case. A crafty and successful attorney, he doggedly attempts to compile a case for the defense. This work leads him to the defendant's abused wife, HANNA (TROUT), who, Seagraves believes, can help her husband immeasurably by agreeing to appear at the trial. Hanna has been deeply affected by her husband's brutal act, however, and refuses to assist Trout in any way. Despite her obstinacy, Seagraves is powerfully attracted to Hanna and enters into an affair with her. Yet Hanna's questioning of Seagraves's involvement in the case on moral grounds continues to unsettle him.

Seagraves's confidence in his ability to win Trout's acquittal reaches a low point immediately preceding the trial when, in a criminal breach of ethics, he bribes Trout's partner in crime, Buster Devonne, to testify on Trout's behalf. Although both Devonne and Trout perjure themselves before the court, Seagraves is unable to present a compelling case because of overwhelming evidence to the contrary. Trout is convicted for second-degree murder. While the decision is a professional setback, the guilt-ridden Seagraves cannot help but acknowledge that justice has been done.

The logical next step would be to appeal the conviction as far as the court will allow. However, Seagraves finally refuses to represent Trout any longer and hands over the case file to his furious client, who vows to carry on the fight alone. Meanwhile, Seagraves continues his affair with Hanna, who will not let him forget that he has not fully grasped the moral implications of his previous involvement in the case. For his part, Seagraves is more than willing to wash his hands of the whole dirty business and get on with his life. For a time he does succeed to some extent in holding the Trout affair at arm's length, but his belief that he can put the Trout affair behind him is tragically shortsighted: Seagraves, along with two others, is shot to death by Trout in a showdown at the Cotton Point courtroom.

Sears, Lemuel. *Oh What a Paradise It Seems.* John Cheever. 1982.

Lemuel Sears views himself as an aging man in a world that is growing less beautiful. Involvement in two odd love affairs with younger people does little to stall Sears's sense of his own mortality, but through the fight to save a pond from destruction, he is able to preserve a small corner of the world's beauty.

One pleasant winter day Sears goes skating on Beasley's Pond. Speeding across the ice, he thinks of scenes from Brueghel and wonders whether prehistoric peoples skated. When he returns to the pond a few weeks later, he finds that it has been turned into a dump. Outraged, he asks his law firm to investigate.

Back in New York City, Sears becomes fascinated by an attractive woman on line at the bank. When the woman, Renee Herndon, proves to be a real estate agent, he pursues a relationship with her under the guise of looking for an apartment. Their relationship quickly moves from one of business to pleasure as they proceed to have an affair.

Sears is delighted by his and Renee's sexual compatibility, but she is an enigmatic woman. She tells him often that he has no understanding of women, and in her case he must admit this is true. Renee has Sears pick her up after meetings at churches and community centers, but she will never reveal to him the nature of the meetings. In fact, she demands that he never ask her what she is doing with her time. More frustrating for Sears is Renee's moodiness. Although she is generally demonstrative,

Renee is often cold and distant just when Sears needs her affection.

One evening after Renee brushes him off, a dejected Sears stands outside the door of her apartment. The elevator door opens to reveal Eduardo, the elevator man. He embraces Sears, then takes him downstairs to a room where the two make love. Puzzled by this encounter since he had always considered himself heterosexual, Sears begins to see an unsympathetic psychiatrist. He eventually grows more comfortable with the relationship and even takes a trip with Eduardo, although he is still infatuated with the moody Renee.

Meanwhile, Sears hears news about Beasley's Pond. The lawyer who had been sent to investigate the dumping is murdered, and an environmentalist, Horace Chisholm, has arranged a town meeting to fight the destruction of the pond. Chisholm is murdered after the meeting, and it seems that the end of the pond is near. Only the intervention of Betsy Logan, who anonymously threatens to poison food in the local supermarket if the pond is filled in, saves Beasley's Pond.

With the pond abandoned by speculators, Sears arranges for the creation of a charitable organization that will oversee its restoration to its natural state. The world, or at least one small section of it, seems like paradise again.

Seeger, Norman. "An Act of Faith." Irwin Shaw. 1950.

At the beginning of this story set at the end of World War II, Norman Seeger, a cheerful, dependable young Jewish man, walks with his friend Olson to the tent of their commanding officer, Captain Taney. Seeger, Olson, and their comrade Welch are all noncommissioned officers waiting with increasing impatience to be shipped home from their camp on the Rheims plain in France. The three men have received passes to take a trip to Paris, but they do not have enough money to make the journey. Seeger, elected to ask Taney to lend them money, enters Taney's tent to explain the situation.

Sympathetic but also low on money, Taney can only give Seeger two hundred francs. Returning to their tent, Seeger and Olson greet Welch, who has an idea. Welch figures that Seeger, who owns a Luger pistol, can sell it and buy another one for a low price, clearing at least twenty-five dollars for the trip. Seeger is reluctant to sell his prized weapon, which he had taken from a German soldier whom he killed. Welch asks Seeger to consider the deal carefully, then hands him a letter from home.

Seeger's letter is an unprecedented plea for help from his father. Seeger's brother Jacob, as the letter describes, has been discharged from the army and is at home, suffering from combat fatigue, depression, and hallucinations. Seeger's father describes Jacob's behavior in great detail, revealing that Jacob's hallucinations and moments of madness express a deeply felt fear for the survival of the Jewish people. His father confides that, much to his own horror, he finds himself believing that Jacob's behavior is really not neurotic. In the anti-Semitic atmosphere of the United States, he has begun to hate seeing Jewish names on committees or reading about Jews fighting poverty. The enemy has won a subtle victory over him: It has made him disassociate himself from honest causes by calling them foreign or communist and by using Jewish names connected with them as ammunition. For these and other reasons, he believes that Jacob is sane and that he himself is mad. He asks for his son's help in explaining what he cannot comprehend.

Seeger walks out into a field. He is angry at his father for forcing him to consider ideas that the conditions of wartime had allowed him to forget for three years. When he returns to Olson and Welch, they sense that something is bothering him and tell him that if he doesn't want to sell the Luger pistol, it's okay with them. Seeger remembers incidents during the war in which Olson, Welch, and Taney had saved his life. Suddenly he asks them what they think of the Jews. They are puzzled, but Olson finally answers, "The Jews? What are they? Welch, you ever hear of the Jews?"

Looking at their faces, Seeger realizes that later on, out of uniform, he will have to rely on them even more than he has during the war. He agrees to sell the Luger pistol. Responding to their protests, Seeger tells them that he would have no use for the weapon in America.

Selbst, Woody. "A Silver Dish." Saul Bellow. 1974.

Sixty-six-year old Woody Selbst, the story's narrator, is having difficulty coping with the death of his octogenarian father, Morris. A "modern" man and owner of the Selbst Tile Company of south Chicago, Woody finds himself alone and depressed the first Sunday after Morris's death. They usually spent the day together, and waves of nostalgia come over Woody as the church bells of the town begin ringing. Woody himself dressed his deceased father in a Hawaiian shirt and buried him among Jews, per his request, although the only outward sign of Morris's faith was that he read a Yiddish newspaper. When Woody was a child, his relatives would tell him that he was a little thief just like Morris—but this was far from the truth.

Woody studied to enter the ministry during the Depression but could not afford to complete more than two years of college. Although his religious upbringing was somewhat tumultuous, he personally believed that God's ideal for the world was one of pure love. Unlike Morris, Woody is very responsible and cares for his two spinster sisters, his wife from whom he has been separated for fifteen years, and his mistress. He not only helps them financially but takes them on errands and sends them on vacations. Woody himself enjoys exotic vacations and has traveled the world extensively. Morris, on the other hand, squandered and gambled and had to borrow from Woody to

repay the bookies. As long as Woody can remember, his father turned to him for money.

When Woody was a youth, his father asked for and received Woody's entire savings so that he could abandon the family. A few years later Morris asked Woody to accompany him to visit Mrs. Sklogund, a wealthy, widowed Swede who was hoping to hurry the second coming, in order to borrow money. Woody was a favorite of the widow's because he would stand up in church to relate the joy of being converted to Christianity—his aunt paid him to do this. Woody and Morris braved a terrible blizzard to call on Mrs. Sklogund, who first had to pray to God for guidance before deciding to write Morris a check. While they waited in the parlor for her to pray, Morris broke into a cabinet and stole a silver dish. Although outraged, Woody could not persuade his father to return the dish, and a physical battle ensued. Morris took the dish anyway, and several days later Woody was made to face the consequences: He was suspended from the seminary where he had been working and was shamed for associating with his father. Morris's attitude toward his son's predicament was as nonchalant as ever, and Woody could not understand why he consistently allowed his father to scam him.

When Morris died, Woody learned that his respect for his father was based on the fact that Morris always did things on his own terms. Even as he was dying, he would not lie in the hospital bed with needles and machines attached to him. Woody had to subdue Morris by climbing into bed to restrain him, and he remained there even after his father was calmed. This physical contest reminded Woody of the fight they had had in Mrs. Sklogund's parlor; even when Woody thought he had him pinned down, Morris called the shots. This time, however, Morris escaped from Woody forever.

Selden, Lawrence. *The House of Mirth.* Edith Wharton. 1905.

Lawrence Selden, an attorney, maintains a safe distance between his private ambitions and those of the New York aristocratic society to which he belongs. In many ways he is the perfect companion for the novel's heroine, LILY BART: He embodies decorousness without hypocrisy, tastefulness without snobbery, and romance without excessive passion. Selden seems to exemplify all the best and none of the worst of high society's values. Ironically, however, this very idealism is what eventually serves to hasten Lily's demise.

Selden's passion is to appreciate Lily from a position of detachment. As the novel opens, he is regarding her in Grand Central Station, admiring her as an exemplar of fashionable beauty. After they adjourn for tea in his apartment unchaperoned—an act that would have scandalized their turn-of-the-century contemporaries—his admiration for Lily increases. He follows her to the mansion of her

friend Judy Trenor, where they spend an afternoon together in the woods. He explains to her that what he prizes
most is "personal freedom," exemption from "all the material accidents," and claims membership in what he calls
a "republic of the spirit."

It ultimately becomes clear that this republic, in freeing
one from material accidents, also frees one from responsibility. Twice Selden verges on proposing marriage to
Lily; both times nothing comes of the idea, partly because
they agree that Selden is not rich enough to afford her
expensive tastes but primarily because Selden contrives to
make his offers sound not entirely earnest. Proposals, to
Selden, are essentially aesthetic experiences; he loves the
transcendent moment of mutual adoration but will not
acknowledge the material responsibilities that these moments entail.

Physically, morally, and emotionally, Selden manages
to preserve an ironic distance in his dealings with Lily. In
one exemplary scene, Lily enacts *en tableau vivant* a character from a painting by Joshua Reynolds, and Selden sees
her transcending "her little world," catching "that eternal
harmony of which her beauty was a part." But whenever
she descends from that eternal harmony back into her
world, Selden feels she has been vulgarized. Thus,
when he subsequently sees her late at night with the salacious Gus Trenor, he vows to renounce his own attraction
to her.

Selden once had an affair with Lily's enemy, Bertha
Dorset, presumably because he enjoyed the freedom of
loving a married woman. Lily acquires some incriminating
love letters from Bertha to Selden, and as potential blackmail the letters serve throughout the novel as the "material
accidents" around which Lily's world revolves. Selden
never learns that Lily has the letters; because of her admiration for him, she continually refuses to use them to
attain her former place in society after gambling and impropriety compromised her position there.

When she falls indebted to her best friend's husband
and is thoroughly ostracized from society, Lily becomes
deeply depressed and begins contemplating suicide. In
their last meeting before her death, Lily postpones her
mission to blackmail Bertha in order to pay Selden a visit.
Before renouncing the project, she half-confesses what she
is doing by suggesting that she is leaving her idealistic side,
the side he helped bring into being, with him. Although
he still feels himself drawn to her—indeed, they take leave
of each other in enraptured silence—Selden cannot bring
himself to act and thus fails to change Lily's circumstances
in any way.

The following morning Selden, a changed man, walks
toward Lily's shabby boardinghouse. He has decided to
risk loving her. But when he reaches her room he finds
Lily lying dead from an overdose of chloral. His old doubts
about Lily resurface when he finds a note to Gus Trenor
on her bureau, but gazing at her beautiful, unresponsive

form, he realizes at last that he truly loved her, and she
him. The novel closes with Selden leaning over Lily's dead
body, "draining their last moment to its lees" and exchanging with her, in this new and permanent silence, "the
word which made all clear."

Seldon, Hari. *Foundation.* Isaac Asimov. 1951.

Hari Seldon, the father of the science of psychohistory
in this science fiction novel, was born to middle-class parents on Helicon, in the Arcturus sector, in the 11,988th
year of the Galactic Era, or seventy-nine years before the
beginning of the Foundational Era he was to orchestrate.
From early on he showed a tremendous aptitude for mathematics.

The narrative opens just two years before Seldon's
death. The field of psychohistory, which Seldon founded
as a collection of vague theorems, has been turned, under
his guidance, into a statistical science, charting and pre-
dicting the reactions of human social groups to fixed social
and economic stimuli. Through this science Seldon is able
to foresee the death of the beneficent Empire and a return
to feudalism across the galaxy for thirty thousand years,
before galactic civilization can build itself up again. The
Empirical government, aware that it is vulnerable, attempts to persecute Seldon for treason. He convinces them
that, although the fall of the Empire is unavoidable, the
following Dark Ages may be reduced to a relatively short
one thousand years.

Seldon proposes to do this by saving the knowledge of
the entire human race in his project, the Encyclopedia
Galactica, with a total staff of one hundred thousand.
Although he is safe from persecution because of the tenuous state of the Empire, he nevertheless remains an annoyance to the aristocratic governing body. The solution,
which Seldon had anticipated two and a half years earlier,
is to exile the entire project to Terminus, a planet on the
edge of the galaxy.

With a scientific refuge at Terminus and another at the
other end of the galaxy, Seldon's plan is to be set in motion.
His project includes planning for his successor to foment
the fall at the right time and in the right manner. Furthermore, while those exiled to Terminus know they are
working on the Encyclopedia Galactica, they do not know
that their mission was created to speed the rebirth of
civilization. Seldon himself will die before the exile
is complete. There are to be no psychohistorians or
psychohistorical texts on the planet since the knowledge of psychohistorical analysis would alter the
randomness of their future actions, thus ruining all of
Seldon's calculations.

So closely has Seldon charted the future of the group
that he is able to make a series of holographic messages
to be played automatically at the height of each historical
crisis. Those present are thus given assurance that there
is one—and only one—way out of each crisis. That way

is not revealed, nor is psychohistory, but the real mission is; there is no reason not to reveal it since at that point Seldon's plans will have progressed too far to be changed. The successive "Seldon Cries," episodic tales of the galaxy's journey back toward civilization, form the rest of the novel.

Semple, Jesse B. "Simple." *Simple Speaks His Mind; Simple Takes a Wife; The Best of Simple.* Langston Hughes. 1950; 1953; 1961.

Jesse B. Semple, created by Langston Hughes as the persona of his column in the *Chicago Defender* during the 1940s, is a black Everyman who is always conscious of the race problem in America. Semple's view of black and white America is comic, wise, and insightful. Nicknamed "Simple" by friends and listeners, he is in and of the urban ghetto, yet he suffers from none of the psychological inhibitions of a ghetto dweller. Simple's perspective combines humor, cynicism, down-home simplicity, and naiveté. He frequents Paddy's Bar, where he debates the race problem with "I," an educated black man who functions as Simple's straight man.

Hughes brought Simple and his profound logic to the American public from the postwar years through the early 1960s in order to discuss age-old issues that blacks have faced as well as issues of topical interest.

In "There Ought to Be a Law," Simple learns that the government is setting up game preserves all over the country. Recalling the fate of blacks who were beaten and lynched across the nation, he declares that there ought to be a law that sets aside land on which blacks can live unmolested, free from harm. "Spring Time" finds Simple praising the South, where spring is glorious and where it comes earlier than in New York. But he will not return to the South's springtime because life for blacks there is so horrible. Still, says Simple, if he were there, he would fish and dream.

When he hears of the filibuster by white southerners in Congress, Simple evinces the bitterness that occasionally overshadows his cool humor in "For the Sake of Argument." In a bitter tirade against the southern filibusters, he declares that were he in Congress, he would go on a one-man filibuster for his people. Allowing his imagination to run free in "Fancy Free," Simple imagines becoming a bird and flying over the world, going to baseball games, to the South, everywhere with a bird's-eye view; but in the end he would come back to earth because he would miss his wife and friends. "That Word *Black*" shows Simple delving into the world of language. He wonders why *black* always means bad, and he promises to create a new language in which *white* carries negative connotations. Over the years Simple pontificates on the income tax, lynching, voting rights, American democracy, funerals, and the world.

Servosse, Colonel Comfort. *A Fool's Errand.* Albion W. Tourgée. 1880.

The "fool" of this semi-autobiographical novel is Comfort Servosse, a Union colonel during the Civil War. His "errand" begins when, just after the war, he buys a ruined plantation in the South and moves there with his wife and young daughter. An ultra-liberal in race relations and a well-connected Republican, he hopes he can help bring harmony to two still unreconciled cultures.

Servosse's efforts begin badly. Selling off some of his land to be worked by newly freed slaves and speaking freely in public for their exercise of full civil rights, he is ostracized by his neighbors. Over the next few years Colonel Servosse's career follows the course of the Reconstruction period. Threats by recalcitrant Southerners force the "fool" to turn his house into a garrison as he watches with horror the rising power of carpetbaggers and the Ku Klux Klan. An enlightened Southerner attempts to school the Colonel in the reasons for the South's continued resistance, but the Colonel remains unmoved—truly foolhardy in the face of the reality of bodily harm.

Meanwhile, his daughter Lily has grown to womanhood and has attracted the love of a noble young Southerner, Melville Gurney, son of a former Confederate general. Warned by an anonymous letter that her father will be killed in a raid by the Klan, Lily, after a wild horseback ride, manages to foil the plot. Melville reveals his love for Lily to the Colonel, who reluctantly gives consent; Lily will not wed him, however, unless General Gurney also agrees.

The romance remains a stalemate until late in the book when Colonel Servosse, disillusioned by such acts in Washington as the pardoning of members of the disbanded Klan, admits that, after twelve years, Reconstruction, has been a failure. His has truly been "a fool's errand." He takes his family to the North for what is planned to be a year's stay, but he is hired by some entrepreneurs there to work for them in a Central American republic. On his way back from abroad to reopen his plantation home, he contracts yellow fever and dies in his house before his family—alerted by a telegram from General Gurney—can reach him. This personal message confirms Lily's suspicion that it was the General who had sent her the message that allowed her to save her father from the Klan; the lovers can finally be united.

Seth. "Blackberry Winter." Robert Penn Warren. 1946.

In 1910, Seth, the story's narrator, was a nine-year-old boy on his parents' farm in Tennessee. Now forty-four, Seth looks back to the June his mother called "blackberry winter" and an incident that he has remembered all these years.

On this morning in his childhood, Seth wants to go outside to investigate the damage of a summer storm that has flooded the nearby river. His mother insists that he put on shoes because of the blackberry winter that brings unusual cold despite the time of year. As Seth stands before the hearth wondering how he can persuade his mother to let him go outside barefoot, he looks out the window to see a tramp approaching their farm from the woods. Seth's mother gives the tramp a few chores, mostly cleaning up the storm's damage.

While his mother prepares something for the tramp to eat, Seth waits outside by the chicken coop to show him where to clean up the chicks that drowned in the flood. Then, forgotten momentarily by his mother, Seth steals away, barefoot, to the creek, where people from the county are judging the water level and assessing the damage. Seth's father is there and pulls Seth onto his horse to sit with him.

When Seth and his father return home, Seth runs down to see Dellie, their cook, in her cabin. He is cold and knows she will have a fire and won't make him put shoes on. But Dellie is ill and bedridden; Seth plays for a bit with Dellie's boy Jebb, but when their games become too loud, Dellie gets mad and slaps Jebb. Seth runs out of the cabin and retreats into the barn where Old Jebb, Dellie's companion of twenty-five years, is shelling corn.

Seth loves Jebb, who is in his seventies, almost as much as his own parents. Shivering with cold, he watches Jebb's powerful hands handling the ears of corn. Jebb notices him shaking, but when Seth says he is cold because of the blackberry winter, Jebb insists that it is too late for that. He begins to preach to Seth about how the earth is tired and can't produce anymore, that the earth told God it just couldn't do any more and God allowed it to take a rest. He says that people only think about their stomachs and exploit the earth for food and that, in the end, the earth and everyone on it will die.

Seth is confused by Jebb's words and runs out of the barn, repeating that his mother must be right about the blackberry winter. Outside he finds his father telling the tramp that he has no more work for him and gives him a half-day's pay. When the tramp cusses back at him, Seth's father tells him to get off the farm. The tramp spits on the ground in front of Seth's father and slowly moves out of the yard.

Seth follows along a few feet after him, wanting to know where he came from and where he is going. The tramp hears the questions, turns on him, and tells him to go away, threatening to cut his throat if he doesn't obey.

The memory of the tramp stays with Seth over the next thirty-five years as the event that interrupted the normal routine of his life and differentiated that blackberry winter from all the rest.

Sethe. *Beloved.* Toni Morrison. 1987.

Sethe is the fugitive slave whose overwhelming love for her children and indelible terror of slavery stun both the black and white populations of Cincinnati. Born on a rice plantation in Carolina during the mid-1830s, she learns that her mother kept only her and not the children fathered by her white rapists.

When she is fourteen, Sethe's owner sells her to Sweet Home, a small plantation in Kentucky. Mr. and Mrs. Garner, the owners of Sweet Home, buy Sethe as a house servant to replace the aging BABY SUGGS, whose freedom has been worked off by her son Halle. After a year at Sweet Home, Sethe marries Halle and, although she knows nothing of raising children and has no means of learning, Sethe begins to have babies. When the relatively benevolent Mr. Garner has a stroke and dies, Mrs. Garner's brother-in-law, known only as Schoolteacher, takes over the running of the plantation. Along with the other Sweet Home slaves, Sethe laughs at Schoolteacher's interest in the circumference of their skulls, the number of their teeth, their height, and their other physical attributes until she overhears Schoolteacher instructing his nephews on the correct classification of her animal and human attributes.

Although Sethe is heavy with her fourth child, she and Halle join the other blacks in their plan to escape to Ohio. On the day set for their break, Schoolteacher and his nephews hold down the lactating Sethe and force milk from her breasts for their study. When Sethe tells the ailing Mrs. Garner of this, one of the nephews whips Sethe's back until the open wounds look as though an entire tree has been etched into her flesh. Sethe cannot find Halle, and Schoolteacher captures the other men when they try to leave. Sethe sends her children ahead of her and waits for her husband; when he does not arrive, she escapes alone. Companionless and nearly nine months pregnant, with festering wounds on her back, Sethe collapses near the Ohio River. A young indentured white girl rescues her and helps deliver the baby in an abandoned canoe. Stamp Paid, of the underground railroad, helps Sethe to her mother-in-law's house outside Cincinnati, where Sethe's children await her.

A month after her arrival at 124 Bluestone Road, Sethe, Baby Suggs, and Stamp Paid cook a dinner that escalates into a party for over ninety people. Instead of feeling grateful, the neighbors who receive Sethe's and Baby Suggs's largesse are offended by this excess of generosity. When Schoolteacher, the sheriff, and a slave-catcher come the day after the party to find Sethe and her children, none of the neighbors sends a warning. Sethe sees the white men approaching and gathers her four children into a woodshed behind the house. Then she rips a saw across the throats of her two sons and her younger daughter. As Sethe swings the head of her month-old daughter Denver toward the wall, the white men stand numbed by the clarity of her passion, and Stamp Paid catches the baby's head. She also kills her older daughter before being restrained.

The two boys live and the infant Denver joins Sethe in prison. The magistrate allows Sethe to leave jail and attend the burial of her daughter. At the cemetery, Sethe only hears the minister say the two words *Dearly Beloved.* When her jailers release her, Sethe prostitutes herself for a rose-colored headstone inscribed with one word: BELOVED.

From that day on, the residence is haunted by Sethe's dead daughter. Sethe's two sons, who live with the fear that whatever made her try to kill them once may return, run away. Ostracized by her community, Sethe lives quietly and works in the kitchen of Sawyer's restaurant. Almost nine years after Baby Suggs dies, PAUL D GARNER, one of the men from Sweet Home, moves in as Sethe's lover and confidant. He succeeds in chasing the spirit of Sethe's daughter from the house but, like Sethe herself, fails to recognize the strange woman calling herself BELOVED who suddenly and mysteriously arrives at their home.

In time Sethe learns the identity of her guest and feels compelled to justify herself to Beloved. She stops going to work and caters to Beloved's every whim until the two become obsessed with each other. When a white man drives up in a carriage, Sethe imagines that he has come to once again take her daughter from her and tries to kill him with an ice pick. Beloved disappears, and Paul D remains to help Sethe recover.

Settlers of the New Farm. "A Pretty Story." Frances Hopkinson. 1744.

In this unfinished allegorical short story, the Settlers of the New Farm are the first Americans, the men and women who settled in the New World as subjects of England and eventually rebelled against the government of their mother country. The settlers' story is recounted from the founding of the "New Farm" (America) to the prewar uprisings sparked by the unjust economic policies imposed by the "Old Farm" (England).

In addition to the settlers of the New Farm, the principal characters of the story are the nobleman (King George III); the nobleman's wife (Parliament); the nobleman's steward (Lord North, the prime minister); and Jack (a settler, the state of Massachusetts). The nobleman and his subjects are bound together in an agreement called the Great Paper (the Magna Carta), which clearly states that the nobleman will impose no hardships on his children without the consent of their elected mother.

The nobleman, whose very valuable farm yields large annual profits, obtains a distant piece of land and gives some of his children permission to leave the Old Farm and establish a new settlement. These children encounter great difficulties on the new land—wild beasts, overgrown and inaccessible foliage, stagnant waters—but gradually, through perseverance and ingenuity, they manage to settle comfortably and to reap abundant harvests.

The settlers' correspondence with the nobleman continues, but soon, because she sees an opportunity to accumulate more wealth, the nobleman's greedy wife begins to issue edicts controlling the earnings of the settlers on the New Farm. She gradually imposes more and more taxes until the settlers, objecting to the wife's unjust policies, begin to defy her. The nobleman grows old and infirm, and the steward, who has debauched the nobleman's wife, takes responsibility for dealing with the New Farm. The settlers soon see that the steward is their enemy and that their elected mother is base and avaricious. They write letters to the nobleman and plead for fair economic policies, but to no avail.

The settlers' grievances with the Old Farm culminate in an episode involving "water gruel" (tea), a fashionable substance that the settlers have grown accustomed to consuming. When the steward imposes a tax on water gruel and arranges the shipment of vast quantities of this substance to the New Farm, the settlers know that if they buy it, they will be giving the nobleman and his wife the right to break the tenor of the Great Paper. Accordingly, the settlers refuse to buy water gruel when it appears on their land. One of the settlers, Jack, demolishes the entire cargo. The nobleman and his wife are furious, and they proceed to make an example of Jack by padlocking his gate and refusing to open it until he has paid for the gruel he destroyed.

The settlers are at a loss as to what to do, and they begin to meet secretly to discuss matters. In support of Jack, they raise generous contributions and pass this bounty secretly over his garden wall. The nobleman sends a mean-spirited overseer, who issues an edict prohibiting the settlers from meeting and declaring such meetings traitorous, treasonable, and rebellious. The settlers are thoroughly irritated by these harsh and unconstitutional proceedings.

And here, Hopkinson's allegory abruptly ends.

Severance, Alan. *Recovery.* John Berryman. 1973.

This unfinished novel takes place within a rehabilitation center for chronic alcoholism where Alan Severance, a successful scientist, professor, and Pulitzer Prize winner, has returned for his third attempt at recovery. Severance has ruined two marriages through "liquor and bad sex," and is in the process of ruining the third. He knows that he will die if he doesn't stop drinking but does not understand where he went wrong in his previous treatments. Through the course of the book he struggles desperately to confront his problem honestly and without delusion.

Severance is a proud, tough man, even a bit abrasive. In the group sessions that make up part of the treatment, he is berated by the staff and other patients for acting superior and defensive. However, he judges himself at least as harshly as he does the others. The confrontations in the group form part of a larger philosophy in the treatment.

The doctors and staff do not treat the patients gently. They see brutal honesty as the only hope for recovery, for delusions lead to drinking, and drinking leads to certain death. Severance embraces this idea and strives for honesty with others and himself. In his journals, which punctuate the narrative, he reaches back into his past to examine the fear and loneliness he has felt throughout his life. He focuses particularly on his wives and children, his uneasy possession of money and fame, and his feelings about his father's suicide. All the while he readies himself for the commitment of the "Twelve Steps" toward recovery set up by Alcoholics Anonymous. He attributes his earlier failures to dishonesty in taking these steps.

The novel carefully tracks Severance's emotional highs and lows. It is a painstaking record of his emotional battle. After some time Severance makes several important self-discoveries. First, he begins to recognize his attraction to Judaism. He recalls his attempt to learn Hebrew and his fascination with the Book of Job, and comes to see conversion as a way of coping with a life without drinking.

Then Severance remembers a drunken episode years before when he made an incomplete pass at his aunt. He confesses this in the group but feels humiliated afterward. However, his confession marks a turning point in his recovery. Finally, Severance comes to some terms with his guilt and anger over his father's death. He sees how these feelings correspond to his guilt over neglecting his own children.

The rest of the novel is composed of outlines and notes anticipating Severance's triumph over alcoholism.

Seymour, John. *Pink and White Tyranny.* Harriet Beecher Stowe. 1871.

John Seymour is the idealistic husband of the pampered LILLIE ELLIS. Having fallen in love with a romanticized vision of a woman who reminds him of his mother, John finds his moral and prudent life turned upside down by his extravagant and spoiled wife.

John is a rich businessman from the old New England aristocracy. He lives peacefully with his temperate sister until he falls in love with and marries the charming and lovely Lillie, and takes her back to his home in Springdale. Lillie not only destroys the intimacy of his relationship with his sister but slowly becomes a financial and emotional burden to the patient John.

John completely submits to his "pink and white empress," and indulges her extravagant desires. Ordinarily a man who detests deception, he forgives Lillie for having lied to him during their courtship about her age. He allows her to adorn his once comfortable old home with silky French furniture, to socialize with undesirable people, to spend on clothes and jewels money he would normally give to charity, and to travel alone to Newport and New York. He sacrifices his ethical and social standards and his financial stability in order to keep his insatiable wife happy. His romantic adoration of women convinces him

to trust Lillie and to believe that she will eventually model her behavior after his own example.

When Lillie finally becomes a mother, John adores her even more. But Lillie treats her little daughter as a rival and then as a toy. John gradually comes to recognize that his vision of Lillie is false, that she will always be a moral and emotional hindrance to him. When he informs her that business failures will require them to radically cut expenses, her selfish reaction convinces him that he can no longer love or respect her. He condemns her to his sister, who urges him to persevere in his husbandly Christian duty. Having learned to expect little from his wife, John takes increasing pleasure in raising his little daughter.

When, at the novel's end, Lillie falls fatally ill, she confesses her love for John and expresses regret at the trials he has undergone for her. After she dies, John's only memories of her are those of his ideal first love; his angelic daughter, also named Lillie, becomes the reward for his constancy and goodness.

Shackford, Richard. *The Stillwater Tragedy.* Thomas Bailey Aldrich. 1880.

Richard Shackford is a heroic figure, a man who seems to have everything in life by dint of his birth but who has decided to take a more difficult route that eventually leads him to material success. When the treacherous act of a childhood friend threatens to destroy his honor and all that he has worked for, he manages to emerge triumphant through the strength of his wit and character.

Born to a mother who dies while he is young, Richard is adopted by his wealthy and miserly cousin, Lemuel Shackford. He grows up emotionally and materially neglected, with little to occupy him but his clay carvings. Miraculously, however, he develops into a young man of a genuinely pleasant and sympathetic disposition with a strong sense of his own self-worth.

When he reaches manhood, Richard learns of his cousin's intentions to send him to school to be a lawyer and place him at a firm notorious for its lack of ethics. He decides to flee his home and seek adventure as a sailor. After years of seasickness, he returns home penniless and must stay with his cousins until he finds a job as an artisan at a large yard. Unfortunately, the yard's owner, Rowland Slocum, has been involved in a longstanding feud with Lemuel.

Taking on the job with Mr. Slocum drives an even greater wedge between Richard and his cousin; they soon find it hard even to exchange pleasantries. Meanwhile, Richard becomes increasingly popular for his friendliness and good spirits. After winning the admiration of both his superior and the men working at the factory, Richard falls in love with Slocum's daughter Margaret, and with Slocum's blessing, the two are engaged to be married.

As Slocum's right-hand man, Richard takes on the responsibility of transforming the yard. He convinces his boss not to give in to the demands of the yard's union leaders for raises and to challenge the union's tradition of keeping out new apprentices. Although Richard is generally well liked at the yard, one man is filled with bitterness about his presence: Durgin, a childhood friend and now a workman at the yard. Durgin becomes obsessively jealous of Richard, who has been appointed to a superior position at the company with very little training.

As fate would have it, Richard's life is cruelly interrupted by the sudden murder of his cousin. Although on bad terms with Lemuel at the time of his death, he feels great remorse at the occurrence and dutifully cooperates in the full-scale investigation that follows. He even offers a reward to anyone who can assist in bringing the offender to justice.

The inspector assigned to the case comes to the conclusion, however, that Richard has played a major role in his cousin's death. Although devastated, Richard remembers certain incidents that would implicate Durgin. Believing that he has been framed, Richard states his case to the inspector and eventually clears his name.

During the confusion of the investigation, Durgin has conveniently left town. Richard is greatly relieved but derives his greatest satisfaction from learning that Margaret never doubted his innocence. The story ends happily, as Richard marries Margaret and becomes a co-partner in her father's business.

Shadrack. *Sula.* Toni Morrison. 1973.

Shadrack is a well-known character in the small town of Medallion, Ohio. As a late teen he fights in World War I, and the insanity he experiences lands him insensate in a hospital for a year. When he regains consciousness, he is terrified of his hands, which appear to be growing to monstrous sizes. His panic causes him to be violent with the nurses, thereby speeding his release. He wanders the streets in a daze and, thought to be drunk, is jailed.

Once released, Shadrack returns to Medallion, determined to institutionalize and thereby control insanity. He establishes National Suicide Day on January 3, during which he walks through town ringing a cowbell, offering anyone who wants to kill themselves or another person a legitimate opportunity to do so. At first the community responds with fear, hiding behind locked doors. Shadrack's march becomes a tradition, however, and people eventually respond with acceptance.

The rest of the year Shadrack supports himself by catching and selling fish. Living alone outside of town, he elicits disgust and suspicion by his foul language, heavy drinking, and open hostility.

The only person with whom Shadrack is friendly is the title character of the novel, SULA MAY PEACE. He sees her for the first time after she has accidentally caused a little boy to drown. Fearing that Shadrack witnessed the incident, she runs to his house and is shocked to observe the military neatness and order of his humble place. Assured that her tadpole-shaped birthmark means they are kindred souls, he says enigmatically, "Always." As Sula runs away, her belt falls off, and Shadrack hangs it on a nail as a memento of his one guest and friend. Years later when he sees her on the street and recognizes her by her birthmark, he tips his hat to her. By this time Sula has the reputation of being a witch, and Shadrack's politeness to her, contrasted with his obscenity to everyone else, confirms the townspeople's suspicion of them both.

Although Shadrack never communicates further with Sula, he is strangely affected by her early death. He goes out for his annual suicide march, but something seems wrong. For the first time the whole town follows him, creating a jovial parade, laughing and dancing through the white part of town, all the way to the new bridge that the black community had wanted but had not been allowed to help build. There their jubilation turns to rage, and they try to destroy the bridge. The bridge collapses, and many are crushed or drowned as Shadrack's National Suicide Day comes morbidly true.

Shane. *Shane.* Jack Schaefer. 1949.

The title character of this classic tale of the American West is Shane, a mysterious stranger who rides into a Wyoming valley in the summer of 1889. Bob Starrett, the young narrator, first sees Shane from a distance and notices two cowhands stop and stare after him with intense curiosity. The dark-clad horseman presents an unusual figure: He carries neither gun nor holster, and his once-fine clothes are worn, stained, and patched. The horseman's expression is fixed and habitually alert, and there is in his easy-seeming manner a tension—the tension "of a coiled spring, of a set trap."

Bob's father and mother, Joe and Marian, befriend Shane. Early on they seem to understand what the man's personal history has been, but they know instinctively that they need not fear him. A bond is soon forged among the three adults, and the boy begins to look upon the former gunman with an admiration akin to hero worship. Although he is a loner by nature, Shane remains with the family and eventually agrees to stay on with the homesteaders as a hired hand when he learns of the strong-arm tactics of the local rancher, Luke Fletcher.

The summer passes without incident. Shane gradually loses the wary, haunted look in his eyes and becomes more and more at ease with the simple life of the farmer. In the fall, however, tensions erupt on the range as Fletcher once again pressures the local homesteaders to give up their land. Fletcher is wary of Shane's presence at the Starretts'. Chris, a cowhand in Fletcher's employ, accosts Shane in a local saloon, but Shane refuses to react to his taunts. The homesteaders, who had been tacitly relying on Shane for protection, do not admire him for his reluctance to fight the young man. Shane remains indifferent to their disapproval until he realizes that public opinion of Joe Starrett is being adversely affected. He goes back into town and, much to his own disgust, systematically beats Chris and breaks his arm. From that moment on, Shane acts like a different man. His carefree good humor, developed gradually under the attentions of the Starrett family, disappears, and the hurt, desperate look returns to his eyes.

Another period of inactivity ensues. Later in the fall, Shane is attacked once again, this time by five of Fletcher's men; Shane, although greatly outnumbered, puts up an impressive fight and, with Joe's help at the end, emerges battered but victorious. Fletcher then hires a professional gunman named Stark Wilson, who kills one of the other homesteaders and attempts to intimidate Shane and the Starretts. Joe, upset by the pain he thinks he is causing Shane by drawing him back into the habits of his violent past, announces that he intends to face Wilson himself and goes so far as to suggest that if he were killed, Marian might be better off under Shane's protection anyway.

Starrett's comments galvanize Shane: He retrieves the gun he has hidden in his pack since his arrival, knocks Joe unconscious to prevent him from carrying out his intentions, and rides into town for the final showdown with Wilson and Fletcher. In a dramatic fight in the saloon, he kills the rancher and his hired gunslinger.

As the novel closes, Shane, having finally accepted the truth of his own violent nature, bids farewell to Bob and rides out of the valley.

Shaper, Dan. "Love and Like." Herbert Gold. 1960.

Dan Shaper is a troubled thirty-two-year-old man who, having divorced his wife of ten years and left his two daughters and their home in Cleveland, moves to New York in the hope of building a new, more successful life. But the agony caused by his dissolved marriage and his longing for the company of his children haunt the young divorcé and taint his efforts to reestablish a happy and meaningful existence.

Although for many years the Shapers enjoyed a healthy relationship, several problems developed that progressively alienated the couple, until their communication was fraught with verbal and physical abuse. Desperately wanting to have a son, Dan's wife tried various regimes designed to determine the sex of an embryo. Dan was especially annoyed by her special diets and her efforts to time their intercourse according to astrological and alchemical considerations. She in turn grew increasingly jealous of his attentions to other women, to the point where she became hysterical in her accusations. On his part, Dan grew so disgusted with his wife's expensive psychological therapy and her manias and tantrums that he finally fulfilled her expectations by having an affair with a young student at the Institute of Music. After almost a year his wife discovered his infidelity, and they

contacted their lawyers, who negotiated a painful and difficult divorce.

Taking a vacation from his job writing technical manuals for General Electric's New York office, Dan visits his daughters in Cleveland and is forced to come into contact with his former wife. Four-year-old Cynthia and six-year-old Paula ask him painfully direct questions about whether or not he is still in love with their mother and when he will return home to the family. He forces himself to explain to them that although he does not love their mother anymore, they still like each other, and they both love their children as much as they ever did. Pulling her thumb out of her mouth, the brutally honest Paula informs her father that she is sick and tired of the words "love" and "like."

Although his former wife is initially civil to her ex-husband and they both apologize for their mutual responsibility for the dissolution of the marriage, their relationship becomes increasingly strained as the days of the visit progress. Although Dan refrains from flaunting his ongoing relationship with a beautiful blonde named Sally, his wife makes sure he is aware that she is having an affair. Despite their desire to maintain a mature relationship characterized by mutual respect and practical friendliness, they replicate the pattern of hateful fighting that had destroyed their conjugal compatibility.

On the final day of his visit, Dan brings their friend Pete along as a chaperon with the hope that his presence will prevent him and his wife from fighting. Having regretfully said good-bye to his children, he climbs into the car with Pete. But before he can leave, his wife runs out of the house and tries to force him to agree to pay the bill for Paula's expensive private school, despite his remonstrations that they cannot afford the tuition. A terrible argument ensues wherein his enraged wife declares that he is an inept lover and that she has finally found another man who knows how to satisfy her sexual desires. When Dan Shaper visits his lover Sally before returning to New York, he admits to himself that he does not love her and, given the ultimate agony of his experience of love, wonders if he will ever be capable of that emotion again.

Shaw, Steven. *Afterlife.* Paul Monette. 1990.

Steven Shaw, fortyish and growing somewhat pudgy, has mourned the death of his lover Victor Diamond for a year. Steven shares his longings and anger with the other "widows," SONNY CEVATHAS and LORENZO DELGADO "DELL" ESPINOZA. For Steven and Dell the grief is particularly horrifying as they are both aware that they have tested positive for exposure to the AIDS virus. Sonny has so far refused to take the test, but he shares their dread of the disease, a dread heightened by the chillingly varied and gruesome physical problems and failures faced by AIDS patients. As the novel begins, Steven has decided that it is time to end their weekly gatherings and that each man must somehow begin anew. Accordingly, he determines to put his eight years with Victor behind him and to move on with his life. Almost immediately he encounters Mark Inman, a man whom he knew briefly before and who had a brief relationship with Victor in the past.

Like Steven, Mark has tested HIV positive, and he convinces Steven to attend a group rap session for people in similar circumstances. Once Steven attends, he gradually realizes that his burden can be shared, and he feels himself coming alive again. He rediscovers an interest in sex and starts a relationship with Mark, but since the sex isn't particularly good, they agree to be buddies instead. Steven has abandoned control of his travel agency, Shaw Travel, to his best friend, Margaret Kirkham, through whom he learns that one of their employees, Ray Lee, is sick. It turns out that Ray has AIDS, and in his case the symptoms include severe neurological impairment. Despite his reluctance to deal with illness and death, Steven immediately agrees to help Margaret help Ray. As Thanksgiving approaches, Steven's house begins to fill with refugees of various kinds. Sonny moves in while in pursuit of a new lover; Dell moves in while being pursued by the police; and Steven picks up a new boyfriend, Andy Larkin, at the Thursday night rap group, who also moves in for a time. Given the crowd around him, Steven decides to host a Thanksgiving dinner even though that had been Victor's province.

Other friends join Steven at Thanksgiving: Mark returns from Florida, dismayed to find Andy on the scene. Ray Lee, although extremely ill, manages to attend; other women from work and the support groups make up the rest of the guest list. Even though the shadow of AIDS lurks over the gathering, the day is a good one, and all are glad that Ray has been able to contribute to and enjoy the celebration. Only a few days later, Ray has a final crisis bout with fever and dies in a state of delirium. Together Steven, Margaret, and Mark dispose of Ray's possessions and close his apartment. Ray's death seems to spur Steven to accept, however cautiously, the love that Mark has offered. Both men know that they may be living on "borrowed time," but they are eager not to give up on their lives and love. At the conclusion of the novel, Steven and Mark are spending almost all their time together, and Mark has moved into Steven's house almost completely. They vow to travel and enjoy life as much as possible.

Shawmut, Herschel "Harry." "Him with His Foot in His Mouth." Saul Bellow. 1984.

This short story takes the form of a letter of apology from Dr. Herschel Shawmut, called "Harry," to a woman whom the narrator had inadvertently snubbed thirty-five years earlier. Shawmut is a widower who lives in exile in Vancouver, British Columbia. He has fled the United States because of legal entanglements following his brother Philip's death: The brothers had engaged in a business venture together, and Philip stealthily milked the profits by hiding

them under the names of his wife and children. After Philip's death, creditors descend in droves, and Shawmut is forced to flee. As he writes to Miss Rose, now a retired librarian living in Florida, he knows it is quite likely that a federal marshal will arrive soon to escort him back to the States where he will be forced to deal with his creditors.

Shawmut's letter is inspired by another letter sent to Shawmut by Edward Ballard Walish, a former colleague. The two men had met when Shawmut accepted a teaching post in New England. Here Shawmut quickly demonstrated his lifelong penchant for saying the wrong thing at the wrong time. When Miss Rose innocently remarked that he looked like an archeologist, Shawmut tactlessly replied that she looked like something he dug up. According to Walish, who castigates Shawmut for virtually every aspect of his behavior, Miss Rose was permanently devastated by this remark, which accounts for the fact that she never married.

Shawmut also describes the talks he has with Mrs. Gracewell, an elderly and religious woman, who seems to encourage his speculative turn. He reveals his sorrow that his mother, his only surviving family member, doesn't recall having had a son other than Philip. Now in his sixties, Shawmut persists in desiring some sign of approval from his mother, but it is not forthcoming. As he explains himself to Miss Rose, Shawmut also mentions that he had lost a lawyer after insulting his office, and a set of friends after insulting them over dinner; he had also jeopardized his brother-in-law Hansl's relations with a prospective bride.

Throughout his letter Shawmut relies on his appreciation of the arts to convey his feelings about himself, his dead siblings, his dead wife, and his forthcoming bankruptcy. He focuses on political issues raised by the poet Allen Ginsberg, whom he singles out as the voice of democracy. Shawmut seems to find in Ginsberg's poetry the ability to transcend the self that he has so pointedly lacked in his own endeavors. As one note of apology, Shawmut muses that his surname was probably derived from a Yiddish term indicating social lowliness within the hierarchy of a synagogue community. Extrapolating from this, he reckons that his brother's attitude toward him was derived in part from Shawmut's refusal to ignore their Jewish background, which had been attempted by Philip and his wife. As the letter ends, Shawmut ruefully notes that he will miss Mrs. Gracewell, and he knows that he will be extradited soon.

Shawnessy, Esther Root. *Raintree County.* Ross Lockridge, Jr. 1948.

Esther Root, an Indiana farm girl turned schoolteacher, is the second wife of JOHN WICKLIFF SHAWNESSY, the principal character of this epic novel of life in America in the nineteenth century. The daughter of a stern religious fundamentalist, Esther has grown up in a restrictive environment. Nevertheless, she is the most intelligent of the many children in her family, and her father's favorite. But Esther's devotion to her father begins to waver when, as a small girl, she develops a love for her schoolteacher, the ill-fated John, who, having married a woman who went insane, now lives alone in his hometown in Raintree County. John becomes Esther's hero and the romantic center of her life.

John leaves Esther's school while she is still young, and years pass before she sees him again. She goes to the county seat to take the examination to become a teacher and finds that John is proctoring the exam. Although few words pass between them, he once again fills her dreams and takes her mind off her darkly possessive father.

Having heard that John has moved to New York City, Esther is surprised when she sees him for a second time at a Teacher's Institute held at Paradise Lake. The site is aptly named for Esther and John, who fall deeply in love. Nearly twenty years her senior, John is, for Esther, a "poet, priest, prophet . . . god." She declares her love for him, but her devotion is sorely tested by the knowledge that his wife Susannah is still alive, although institutionalized in New Orleans. Knowing that her father would not approve, Esther continues her love affair in secret. She senses that other women love and admire John, and she is torn by the pull of the two men in her life. John means everything to her, but she perceives her love for her father as "the most ancient part of herself" and realizes that she has not fully detached herself from her earliest family ties.

Inevitably, Esther's father learns of the secret trysts and letters, and in a rage threatens to kill John. At the same time John's wife is discovered missing and presumed dead, leaving John free for a second marriage. When Esther's father refuses him, John proposes to her through an open letter in the paper; her father, enraged by her now public romance, demands that Esther leave with him for the West. Esther acquiesces at first, then changes her mind and marries John.

The day during which the novel takes place, July 4, 1892, finds Esther devoted both to John, who is now the principal of the local school, and to their three young children. She still thinks her husband is perfect, and her love for him is as absolute as it was when she was a small dark-haired student and he was her favorite teacher. She is blissfully ignorant of a secret truth about John—that his first wife, SUSANNAH DRAKE SHAWNESSY, was not yet dead when they married—but she is aware of rumors linking her husband and Evalina Brown in romantic gossip.

During the patriotic festivities occurring throughout the day, Esther sees her father talking to the local evangelist; the sight makes her nervous, although she cannot guess that they are planning to accuse John openly of adultery that evening. The accusation ensues. Esther stands by her husband and watches as the ire of the towns-

people turns from John to the preacher, whose amorous conquests of the townswomen is well known. The day's end finds Esther returning home, a loving and contented woman, with her husband by her side.

Shawnessy, John Wickliff. *Raintree County.* Ross Lockridge, Jr. 1948.

Although the action of this epic novel covers the events of a single day, it tells the life story of the central character, John Wickliff Shawnessy, a nineteenth-century Indiana man who describes himself as "a seeker after knowledge, scholar, poet, teacher, preacher, and lover of beauty."

Born in 1839 to prairie settlers of staunch Scottish-Irish heritage, John is a childhood dreamer fascinated by history and words. As a teenager he writes a column for the local paper, studies the classics under the tutelage of Professor JERUSALEM WEBSTER STILES, becomes a teacher himself, and falls in love with a beautiful girl named Nell Gaither, who is convinced that he will someday be a great man.

Although he loves Nell, the twenty-year-old John is seduced by SUSANNAH DRAKE (SHAWNESSY), a lovely but strange Southern belle who has a tragic past and an odd fascination with dolls. When Susannah informs John that she is pregnant, he marries her, only to learn that the pregnancy is a ruse. Soon after, John becomes aware that Susannah is half-mad, a condition that worsens steadily after the birth of their son. One day he returns home to find that Susannah has taken the child and fled. He searches desperately for them, and Susannah eventually returns home but then sets fire to the house, killing the child.

After Susannah is institutionalized by her family, John returns to his parents' home to live and teach school. The Civil War breaks out, however, and he finds himself serving with General Sherman's army, taking part in the battles at Chickamauga Creek, Lookout Mountain, and Missionary Ridge, and the Burning of Atlanta and the March to the Sea. During the long years of the war, he "learns to curse, smoke, drink, and whore." He is reported dead and returns home after the war to see his own tombstone in the tiny cemetery at Danwebster.

Feeling lonely, John goes to New York City and becomes reacquainted with his old friend and mentor Professor Stiles. Indiana once again stirs his blood, and he returns home, vowing to "live in his hick town forever." His married status makes romance impossible, but then he meets ESTHER ROOT (SHAWNESSY), who had been a small child in his first school and has become a schoolteacher in her own right. Esther falls in love with John in spite of the vehement objections of her father. When Susannah is reported missing and presumed dead in New Orleans, Esther and John marry, although John later discovers he had married Esther before Susannah died.

John, Esther, and their three children live quietly and

happily in the small town of Waycross, where he is principal of the school and a writer. On the day the novel takes place, July 4, 1882, he attends the Grand Patriotic Program at Waycross in the company of Professor Stiles and his old political rival, Senator Garwood Jones. John takes part in the patriotic festivities, watches a bull impregnate a heifer, and attends a tent meeting held by Preacher Jarvey, an abrasive opportunist. John stands firm when the preacher falsely accuses him of adultery. The novel closes with John, a dignified and highly respected member of the community, returning home with Esther to retire for the night.

Shawnessy, Susannah Drake. *Raintree County*. Ross Lockridge, Jr. 1948.

Susannah Drake is the ill-starred and mysterious first wife of JOHN WICKLIFF SHAWNESSY. Although she grew up as the privileged daughter of a wealthy New Orleans gentleman, Susannah's life has been marred by tragedy. The woman whom she believes to be her mother and whom she dislikes intensely becomes insane, and her father enters into an adulterous relationship with an African-American slave. This African-American woman, Henrietta, is Susannah's beloved nurse and childhood companion. When Susannah's mother sets fire to the house in a fit of jealous rage, all three adults are killed, Susannah's doll is half-burned, and she herself is hurt. Her physical wounds heal, but the trauma of the event stays with her.

Years later, while she is living for the summer in Indiana, Susannah meets and seduces John, a young schoolteacher who is captivated by her wanton but compelling manner, a mixture of sensuous abandon and Southern charm. She returns to New Orleans and sends a letter informing him that she is pregnant. The two are married, although John has deep misgivings about her erratic behavior, especially regarding her obsessive attachment to the childhood relic, the half-burned doll, and to the hundreds of dolls she insists on taking with her wherever they go. He also finds it curious that so beautiful and wealthy a girl has never had a serious suitor.

Even though the pregnancy was a ruse, the two lovers are content at first, and Susannah soon gives birth to a son, James—an event that sets in motion her downward spiral into madness. One day while John is away, she takes the baby and leaves town. Attempting to follow her, John encounters a photographer who took daguerreotypes of a woman calling herself Henrietta Drake who had with her small boy and a burned doll, but John is unable to locate her. Susannah soon returns, however, and sets fire to their home, with suicide the possible motive. She is pulled out by a townsman, but the baby perishes.

Returning to New Orleans, her hometown, Susannah is institutionalized by her family. She writes half-mad let-

ters to John, and from the stories he hears from her as well as those of her family members, he begins to reconstruct her mysterious past. John becomes convinced that Susannah, through maliciousness or misinformed jealousy, caused the fire that destroyed her parents and Henrietta. He also becomes convinced that the madwoman who was kept in the upstairs bedroom of Susannah's family home was not her mother but her nurse, Henrietta.

The rest of Susannah's life remains clouded in mystery. At one point she is reported missing from the hospital in which she had been incarcerated. A few years after John has remarried, the body of a woman is discovered in the Mississippi River: the burn scars are unmistakably Susannah's.

Sherringham, Peter. *The Tragic Muse*. Henry James. 1890.

Peter Sherringham, an ambitious English diplomat, finds his life complicated by a passionate interest in the theater. When he falls desperately in love with MIRIAM ROOTH, a gifted actress, he must endure a painful confrontation with his inner conflicts. Peter finally becomes determined to cross over into Miriam's world, but the decision comes too late to save his relationship with her.

Peter grows up on his parents' estate, Windrush, and attends Eton and Cambridge. After passing the required exam, he is appointed to a subordinate diplomatic post in Germany. Peter later obtains a position as a secretary of the embassy in Paris and seems content to remain there in a post of modest importance rather than go as a "principal" to another city. He attends the theater religiously, believes passionately in its value, and even makes the acquaintance of certain members of its elite circles, among them the preeminent Madame Carre, who invites him one afternoon to hear Miriam, an aspiring English actress, recite. The performance is essentially a failure, but Peter finds himself interested in Miriam in spite of her meager talents, and she later gives a recital at his home.

Peter comes to play a pedagogical, almost fatherly role in the life of Miriam, who lives alone in relative poverty with her mother. He takes her to plays and ends up enjoying her enthusiasm more than the production itself. As the months go by and Miriam's talents unfold under the instruction of Madame Carre, Peter falls under her spell. Eventually, Peter feels he has lost all control over his life, so complete is Miriam's power over him. He nevertheless clings to his profession, which forbids him to marry an actress.

Peter follows Miriam to London where she achieves instant success on the stage. After watching her stunning performance one evening, Peter proposes to her, pleading with her to leave the theater in order to become his wife. Miriam refuses, pointing out that he expects her to make enormous sacrifices while he is willing to make none. If

Peter renounces his profession and goes on the stage himself, Miriam says, she will marry him. By saying this she hopes to force him to face the consequences of the theory he has long defended, that the theater is "important" to the human spirit. Miriam believes he should devote himself fully to the art he cares about so deeply and cease trying to serve God and mammon at once.

After Miriam refuses his proposal, Peter leaves London to take up a new post in Central America where he hopes to forget his love for her. Only a little time passes, however, before Peter returns to see her, ready to agree to her terms for marriage. He arrives on the day of her first remarkable performance as Juliet, only to find out that she was married a few days before to Basil Dashwood, a colleague in the theater. He is unable to sit through the performance and spends the time walking the streets. Avoiding all his friends and relatives in London, he leaves immediately for Paris.

By the time Peter returns to London, he is sufficiently reconciled to the fact that Miriam has married and begins courting someone else. He pays several visits to Bridget Dormer, his charming young cousin. Having admired Peter for years, Biddy turned down another proposal from a very eligible man in order to wait for him. She and Peter marry, and spend a short period at his post in Central America before he is assigned to a better position. Peter's marriage and promotion at the book's end suggest that he chooses, in Miriam's terms, not God but mammon—favoring his career over his unsettling desires and over his belief in the spiritual value of art.

Sherwood, Helen. *The Gentleman from Indiana.* Booth Tarkington. 1899.

The third-person narrative voice of this novel shifts perspective when Helen Sherwood becomes its focal character. In the opening pages, the mysterious JOHN HARKLESS carries the tale. Harkless, who arrives in Plattville, Indiana, at the turn of the century to revive the failing town newspaper he has just purchased, leads a reclusive private life despite the public and political influence he maintains through his newspaper. His romantic interest in Helen eventually colors his every action, but after he reveals his chauvinism and thereby damages their blossoming romance, it is Helen who dominates the narrative. She angrily spurns him and inadvertently causes him to be injured; Harkless goes out of town to recover, and while he is away, she works hard to prove not only that she respects him but that gender is no measure of a person's capabilities.

Helen attended an eastern school with the beautiful, stylish Minnie Briscoe, and she stays with the Briscoe family while visiting Plattville from her hometown of Rouen. Her presence in Plattville instigates much gossip. When she attends a public lecture, the citizens of Plattville

cannot help but notice the impression she leaves on Mr. Fisbee. Formerly a town drunk and object of ridicule, Mr. Fisbee, who was once a respectable archaeology professor, is given a second chance when Harkless hires him as a reporter for the *Herald.* The townspeople are surprised at Mr. Fisbee's interest in Helen because he is old enough to be her father.

Fisbee visits Helen at the Briscoes' residence, but he also encourages Harkless to call on her. When Harkless finally does, he realizes that she is the girl who has haunted his dreams and instantly falls in love with her. Her singing voice reminds him that they have met before; she is the younger sister of his dearest college friend. After a day together at the carnival, Helen tells Harkless that she would rather stay in Plattville as an employee for the *Herald* than return to Rouen.

Harkless, however, laughs at the idea of her earning a living, and refuses. Enraged, she believes that her small stature prevents him from taking her seriously. Certain that this is their last good-bye, Helen anticipates Harkless's sentiments and says without explanation, "No, I— I do not love you." Distraught, Harkless runs off into a summer storm and is abducted by his political enemies, who beat him and leave him for dead. Helen, feeling responsible for allowing the editor to be endangered, goes to the authorities to aid in locating him.

Harkless is found in critical condition but has little will to live because of his rejection by Helen. Fisbee's "nephew" is reportedly called into town to help run the *Herald,* and all but Harkless are aware that the new editor, H. Fisbee, is actually Helen Sherwood. Helen is Fisbee's daughter; she was reared by her aunt and uncle when her father fell to financial ruin, although his trouble was never revealed to her. Helen learns that Harkless is responsible for her father's recovery. She has not allowed herself to feel romantically for Harkless because she believes that would be brazen, in light of the gratitude she owes him.

Helen proves to be extraordinarily capable of running the *Herald.* She increases its circulation from thrice weekly to daily. She creates new columns, one especially for women and another with financial information; she writes powerful editorials; and she breaks the story that oil has been discovered in Plattville. The town booms; Harkless, in the meantime, is pleased with his new editor whose writing he finds strong and masculine. Harkless plans to give the paper to H. Fisbee, to whom he grants unconditional control, until he becomes suspicious that H. Fisbee is in cahoots with the corrupt politician responsible for his beating.

The still-ailing Harkless garners new strength and returns to Plattville, only to find that H. Fisbee has nominated Harkless himself as the town's congressional candidate. Helen then reveals her true identity to him and explains why she felt it impossible to reciprocate his love.

Pragmatic and ambitious, she has proven her capabilities to herself and to Harkless. Her debt of gratitude has been paid, and romance between them is now inevitable.

Shevek. *The Dispossessed.* Ursula K. Le Guin. 1974.

Shevek, born on Anarres, a utopian moon colony, longs to experience life on Urras, the capitalist mother planet of his civilization. As an extremely inquisitive child, Shevek becomes quietly critical of Anarresti society, which he sees as stifling to creativity and virtually all individual pursuits. When he grows up to be a brilliant physicist and forms a theory that could make space travel dramatically faster, he finds that few of his fellow citizens will even consider the implications of his scientific breakthrough. In search of a forum for his ideas, Shevek begins sending his papers to scientists on Urras, although contact with such "counterrevolutionaries" is anathema to the Anarresti.

One hundred and fifty years before the opening of the novel, Odo, a Urrasti woman, led a revolution in protest of the violent and decadent conditions on her planet. She persuaded thousands of workers to strike against the ruling class and put an end to the inequities of capitalism. Although the Odonian Revolution ultimately failed on Urras, the government decided to allow the dissenters to form their own society on Anarres, a largely barren moon.

Shevek grows up in a world based on the utopian vision of Odo. To maintain the revolution's goal of complete equality among citizens, money and property do not exist on Anarres, and government, seen as a tool of ruling-class power, has been replaced by the Production and Distribution Coordination (PDC), a computerized system that regulates work and resources without personal bias. Shevek recognizes the positive aspects of his culture. Unlike patriarchal Urras, men and women work side by side on Anarres, live for free in dormitories, and couple with whichever sex they prefer. The only sin on Anarres is to "egoize," to pursue personal goals at the expense of communal works.

Shevek cannot convince his community that he works in the public interest. No one on Anarres can understand his main interest—called Simultaneity, which promises to revolutionize travel in space and time—so Shevek soon gains a reputation as an "egoizer." Alarmed at this perception, Shevek tries to convince the officials of the PDC that he does important work, but he finds they are hardly open to new ideas. In his passion that his work be communicated at all costs, Shevek begins sending data secretly to scientists on Urras. The Urrasti scientists award Shevek their highest honor and ask him to visit A-IO, one of the most powerful nations, ostensibly on a mission of brotherhood.

At first Shevek enjoys Urras. Unlike bleak Anarres, it has a lush and varied landscape, and its cities are filled with countless amusements. The amount of attention paid to Shevek surprises him. The people on the streets recognize him as the brilliant man from the moon, and scientists flock to his quarters to keep abreast of his latest work. But after a few months Shevek begins to see a dark side to all this attention: He receives an anonymous note reminding him that the immense wealth of A-IO masks a reality of poverty for the majority of its citizens, and representatives of other nations warn him that the A-IO government plans to use his theory to consolidate power against the other governments on the planet.

As Shevek finalizes his theory and sees even more clearly how it could be applied for military gains, he realizes that he cannot let his idea become the property of the A-IO state. One night he flees his university room for the poor section of the city and joins with a revolutionary group that has modeled itself on Odonian principles. Sickened by the squalor outside the showcase cities, Shevek gives an impassioned speech on justice during a labor rally. When the police descend upon the crowd and kill at random, he decides that he can do no more in A-IO. He makes his way to the embassy of the most peaceable Urrasti nation and obtains a promise of safe passage back to Annares.

Shevek broadcasts his theory to all nations simultaneously so that no one nation can use it to gain advantage of another, and then he returns to his planet as he had left—"with empty hands."

Shimerda, Antonia. *My Ántonia.* Willa Cather. 1918.

With her indomitable spirit and zest for life, Antonia Shimerda epitomizes the sturdy, heroic immigrant pioneer woman, arriving at her Nebraska homestead in the back of a hay wagon. Her Bohemian family then struggles to survive with little knowledge of farming and still less of American customs or language. The fifteen-year-old Antonia soon begins English lessons with young JIMMY BURDEN, the story's narrator and neighbor to the Shimerdas. Jimmy and Antonia quickly become friends and enjoy the freedom of their youth, listening to the stories of other immigrants and exploring the countryside when not attending to their chores. Charmed by her liveliness and spirit, Jimmy develops a deep and abiding love for Antonia.

Because Antonia's family is poor, Jimmy's grandparents, who are successful Midwest farmers, assist them with everything from food to farming equipment. During their first Nebraska winter, Antonia's father, a former musician and European urbanite, commits suicide because he has been unable to adapt to the harsh life of a farmer and the close quarters of the family house. Her father's favorite, Antonia bears his death with a certain stoicism but is influenced throughout her life by his memory. She must now work in the fields helping her sullen brother Ambrosch. Proud of her strength and endurance, Antonia boasts that she works as hard as any of her male counterparts.

When the Burdens move into Black Hawk, the nearby town, they soon lure Antonia from the farm by finding her a job as the housekeeper for the neighboring Harling family. The Burdens hope that contact with the rich Harlings will refine Antonia's coarse, unfeminine manner. Intelligent and hardworking, Antonia learns her job quickly and becomes invaluable to Mrs. Harling and her children, whom Antonia adores. Yet when the dancing tent becomes the center of town social life, Antonia and the Harlings, who disapprove of her wild manner of dancing, must part company. Antonia goes to work for the disreputable Wick Cutter. One of the most popular of the "hired girls" and certainly the best dancer, Antonia is never at a loss for partners and soon realizes that this is her one opportunity to be carefree.

Over the years Jim and Antonia spend less and less time together as he studies for college and she consorts with the local men and women. Nevertheless, she continues to exert a protective influence over Jim's life by shielding him from what she perceives to be feminine deception. However, when the Cutters leave on a short trip, Antonia is curiously wary and turns to Jim for protection. That night Wick Cutter mistakes Jim for the sleeping Antonia and pounces on him. No longer able to bear Wick's loathsome advances, Antonia leaves the Cutters and returns to her family farm.

Antonia then shocks the small town when she goes to Denver to marry an unscrupulous railroad conductor, but she returns unmarried and pregnant. With her trousseau in hand, she reappears on the Shimerda farm and takes her place in the fields with her brother until the day she gives birth. Antonia refuses to speak about her problem and loves her little girl without reservation. Although always a favorite with the more established town families, Antonia is perceived as less successful than her former friend LENA LINGARD, who has since left Black Hawk and become a successful dress merchant.

Antonia appears for the last time twenty years after she and Jimmy Burden have last spoken. Married now to another Bohemian immigrant, Anton Cuzak, Antonia has built a farm and given birth to nine more children. She herself ensures the success of the farm, for although her husband is hardworking, he is a city man with no knowledge of the land. Surrounded by her adoring children, Antonia inspires people with her vitality and good nature, and she tells Jimmy that she could never leave the farm—her identity and lifeblood.

Shipley, Andrew. *The Catherine Wheel.* Jean Stafford. 1951.

Andrew Shipley, a melancholy twelve-year-old, becomes obsessed with murderous thoughts during a lonely summer. Andrew leads a double life: He spends dreary,

formal winters in his parents' house and is set free during the summer, which he spends with his cousin KATHARINE CONGREVE in Hawthorne. At Congreve House, he enjoys the uninterrupted companionship of Victor Smithwick, a peculiar and adventurous boy whose mother is rumored to be a witch.

Andrew despises the school he attends in Boston. It is dominated by young athletes who sneer at Andrew for his weakness and by devoted students with whom Andrew is unable to compete. Although intelligent, he is too dreamy to concentrate on his schoolwork. He spends the year longing for the summer months, which he spends on the beach in Hawthorne, clamming and fishing, or exploring the town with Victor, who accepts him unconditionally. Andrew is particularly eager to leave for Congreve House. His parents have been acting more inattentive than usual, and there seems no relief from the anxiety of school.

This year, however, when Victor's companionship would be so welcome, Andrew is disappointed. Victor's older brother Charles, a sailor, has contracted an illness and is home in Hawthorne convalescing. Victor, who worships his brother, refuses to leave his side to see Andrew. Andrew waits day after day, lounging miserably in a hammock and only catching glimpses of Victor as he runs to town to get something to amuse Charles. His older sisters, twins Honor and Harriet, cannot comprehend Andrew's lazy hostility and offer no sympathy. Cousin Katharine, who is usually Andrew's greatest comfort, is absorbed this summer in her own problems and makes little effort to cure Andrew of his depression.

Finding no help from his family, Andrew continues to mourn for the loss of Victor's friendship, wishing desperately that Charles would go back to sea or, preferably, die. This wish becomes an inner voice that hounds Andrew perpetually. Guilt over his murderous desires begins to poison his relationship with Cousin Katharine; he interprets her unusual behavior as an indication that she suspects him. Andrew begins to detect an ominous significance in certain events. When Cousin Katharine orders an elaborate tombstone for herself, he regards this as a sign that something terrible is going to happen to Charles, himself, or both.

The threatening atmosphere of the summer finally erupts in tragedy on the last night when Cousin Katharine throws an elaborate party. After a disagreement between them, Katharine mollifies Andrew by allowing him to help set off fireworks, the main attraction of the party. Also appointed to this position are Adam, Katharine's coachman, and Charles Smithwick. The fireworks display goes smoothly until the final one, a Catherine wheel. It is apparently a dud, but in his determination to make it go off, Charles lights his hair on fire. Katharine runs toward him in a panic, and Andrew shrieks: "Now do you hear it, Cousin Katharine? You hear the voice in my head, don't you?" Trying to save Charles, Katharine allows her own dress to catch fire. Charles's hair is singed, but he is otherwise unhurt, while Katharine is seriously burned. Andrew looks into her face, now unrecognizable, and realizes that her love had always meant more to him than Victor's friendship. As she dies, Andrew desperately tells Katharine that she is the only person he ever loved.

Sieppe, Trina. *McTeague.* Frank Norris. 1899.

Trina Sieppe's diminutive size and childlike charm make her an odd companion for the lumbering "Mac" McTeague. Initially an amiable person, Trina is transformed by her relationship with Mac into a neurotic woman whose self-loathing eventually leads to lunacy and death.

When Trina bravely sits under Mac's drill during their first meeting in his dental parlors, she has little thought of marrying him; she thinks of herself as more or less betrothed to her cousin Marcus Schouler. But when Marcus magnanimously gives her up to his friend, she reluctantly yields herself to Mac's will to conquer and subdue her.

Winning $5,000 in a lottery shortly before her wedding stimulates rather than allays Trina's latent miserliness. She insists that they live on Mac's dental practice income and the small amount she makes carving Noah's ark animals for her uncle, the wealthy proprietor of a toy store. With $5,000 in the bank and another $200 of hidden savings, she finds herself unable to send her desperately poor family $50 or even the $12 she had decided would be sufficient.

Even when their own fortunes take a turn for the worse, as Mac loses his dental practice through the machinations of the envious Marcus, she refuses to break into her lottery horde or her cache of secret savings. Although she had succeeded in upgrading McTeague's tastes and personal habits, her parsimony causes him to revert to his former habits.

One day Mac loses a job and comes home in the middle of the day. Trina sends the exhausted man back out into the rain without carfare to find another job. Her wounded and resentful husband comes home drunk, for the first time, and tortures her. Trina conceives a strange passion for her husband's tortures, which include pinching and gnawing on her fingers; her pain makes her feel more and more reliant on him, and she even boasts to her friend Maria Macapa, another battered wife, that her husband is the more brutal. When she walks in one day to find that Maria has been murdered by her husband, who was convinced that she had gold hidden somewhere, Trina fails to realize her own husband's potential for violence.

Mac finally steals her savings and leaves her. After having two fingers amputated because of his gnawing, she goes to work as a scrubwoman, resolving never to let him come back. She replenishes her supply of money by drawing her lottery winnings from the bank and converting the sum into gold pieces. She conceives a highly erotic passion for them; she shines them to sunlike brightness, spreads them out on her bed, and rolls naked in them all night.

When Mac does come home, bedraggled and starving, she sends him away without a dime. She instantly regrets her harshness, but before she has a chance to rectify it, he returns in a rage, beats her to death, and steals the $5,000 for himself.

Silver, Mattie. *Ethan Frome.* Edith Wharton. 1911.

Prior to her tragic accident, Mattie Silver is the sole bright spot in the life of the hero, Ethan Frome, who lives with his hypochondriac wife in the austere town of Starkfield, Massachusetts.

Mattie, a twenty-year-old relative of Ethan's wife Zenobia Pierce "Zeena" Frome, comes to the Frome farm from a resented and recently impoverished branch of the family to help her ailing cousin with housework. Zeena dislikes Mattie from the moment of her arrival and masks her resentment behind complaints about the young woman's inexperience as a housekeeper. Perhaps jealous of the attention Mattie receives from Ethan, Zeena soon begins seeking excuses to remove her pretty cousin from the household.

However, Ethan has evidently loved Mattie since shortly after her arrival because as her liveliness and curiosity waken in him an aesthetic sensibility that he thought had vanished into the hard Massachusetts soil. Courted by the young bucks of Starkfield, Mattie nevertheless nurses her admiration for the unavailable Ethan.

When Zeena goes away overnight for medical care, Mattie prepares Ethan an unusually pleasant meal using Zeena's prized pickle dish. In a scene that prefigures Mattie's own ultimate destruction, the pretty dish shatters: Mattie's effort to bring beauty into Ethan's life rebounds upon her own unfortunate head and ensures her banishment.

When Zeena returns to announce that Mattie must be replaced by a more competent caretaker, Mattie is heartbroken and desperate. With no one to turn to and no way to support herself, she begins preparing for a life of penury. Ethan takes her on a winter night to the train station but along the way convinces her to go sledding with him. The experience brings them a brief moment of elation and pure exhilaration. They allow themselves a few desperate kisses, and seeing that they must now never be parted, they agree to destroy themselves in this moment of exaltation by steering toward the big elm tree at the bottom of the hill.

But the lovers are not destroyed. Instead, Mattie becomes paralyzed and must now be nursed by Zeena in the Frome house. Ultimately the situation transforms her into a demanding, complaining invalid. Her liveliness and sensibility now dead, she becomes as brittle as her cousin Zeena.

Simpson, Homer. *The Day of the Locust.* Nathanael West. 1939.

Homer Simpson, a highly agitated and socially maladroit middle-aged man from Wayneville, Iowa, migrates to California after suffering a severe case of pneumonia. Simpson's relatively stable life-style in California is interrupted when he meets Faye Greener, a seventeen-year-old aspiring actress who lives with her father Harry Greener, a veteran of vaudeville and burlesque circuits. When Harry dies, Faye convinces Homer to let her live with him platonically with the understanding that she will pay him back for his hospitality when she has achieved stardom. Faye rewards his generosity with malicious abuse and eventually abandons Homer without letting him know that she plans to move out. Devastated by her cruelty, Homer loses his tenuous grasp on sanity and becomes mad and murderously violent.

Prior to moving to California, Homer worked for twenty years as a bookkeeper in a Wayneville hotel. Homer's life in Wayneville was mostly routine, and the only event that interrupted his mundane schedule continues to haunt him. One day his boss asked him to deliver a bill to Miss Martin, an alcoholic guest at the hotel, whose payment was delinquent. In the course of carrying out his mission, Homer became uncharacteristically aggressive and forced himself on Miss Martin, who at first resisted and then acquiesced to his advances. The following day Miss Martin disappeared, and although Homer attempted to locate her, he was unsuccessful. Since this was Homer's only experience with women, Faye Greener can easily hoodwink him with her charms.

Homer's personality is extremely eccentric, and his hands seem to have a will of their own. He is often embarrassed when they become agitated at inopportune moments. When not obsessing about his wayward hands, Homer amuses himself by sitting on his patio watching an ongoing battle between flies and a lizard who stalks them. Homer, who sides with the insects, often prays that the flies will succeed in avoiding the predatory jaws of the lizard.

When Faye moves in, Homer busies himself with cooking for her and catering to her every whim. Faye eventually convinces Homer to allow two of her friends, Earle Shoop and Miguel, to move into his garage. Both men manifest undisguised designs on Faye. As time passes, Faye becomes more and more insensitive to Homer's feelings, and her residency terminates when Homer catches her in bed with Miguel in his own house. The morning after this incident, Faye disappears.

Despite the fact that Faye treated him so cruelly, Homer is devastated by her departure. Deranged by his grief, he begins wandering the streets of Hollywood, suitcases in hand, with the intention of returning home to Wayneville. When he wanders into an unruly crowd gathered in front of Kahn's Persian Palace Theatre in the hopes of seeing celebrities who are attending a film premiere, calamity ensues. A young boy named Adore Loomis throws a rock at Homer's face, and his sanity snaps completely. Adore tries to run away but trips and falls, and Homer begins jumping up and down on the boy's back with all the force of his large muscular body. Tod Hackett, the novel's narrator, tries to pull him off the boy but fails and is himself dragged into the crowd.

Singer, John. *The Heart Is a Lonely Hunter.* Carson McCullers. 1940.

John Singer, a deaf mute from birth who now works for a jeweler, lives with Spiros Antonapoulos, a mentally retarded mute. John talks to Spiros in sign language; Spiros doesn't sign much himself, but his unresponsiveness has never bothered John, who imagines that his friend responds on some deeper level with total understanding.

After they have lived together for ten years, Spiros begins to show signs of instability; he steals, causes public disruptions, and assaults people. John attempts to cover up his friend's increasingly bizarre behavior, but Spiros's cousin and employer succeeds in having him committed to an asylum. In his loneliness John moves into a boardinghouse in another part of town and at night walks aimlessly through the streets. He thinks constantly of Spiros. Gradually, though not purposely, he begins to attract the attention of others.

John eats all his meals at the New York Café, whose owner, Biff Brannon, takes an immediate interest in him because of his handicap. One evening John meets Jake Blount, a stranger in town who has been frequenting the café. Blount, who is often drunk, talks for hours to John without noticing that he never answers and that he is deaf. He discusses his political beliefs, vents his frustration at the workers' resignation to injustice, and is generally relieved to have found someone who seems to understand him.

One night Blount brings Dr. Copeland, a black physician who is frustrated in his desire to better his race, into the New York Café. Dr. Copeland, finding himself in a white restaurant, assumes Blount is trying to make a fool of him. Later, on the street, John offers the doctor a light. Copeland is dumbfounded to find a white man who treats him as an equal, and he soon begins to visit John regularly. In the meantime, John acquires his fourth confiding friend: MICK KELLY, the daughter of the couple that owns the boardinghouse where John lodges. Mick longs to learn about music—she even attempts to write it herself—but is thwarted by her family's financial problems. Believing that John understands something about music, she tells him her hopes and dreams.

John is bemused by these people who never seem to stop talking. He continues to long for Spiros. Spiros is even less communicative now, but John faithfully writes letters, which he knows his friend can't read, and occasionally visits him in the asylum. Like his own visitors, John remains oblivious to Spiros's lack of response.

One day John arranges for his visitors to meet. To his dismay, they have nothing to say to one another, and their encounter is quite strained. Copeland, whose political beliefs are similar to Blount's, still resents this white liberal; Blount reacts against the black doctor's hatred. Biff, who has a guilt-ridden crush on Mick, tries to cover it up with gruffness but succeeds only in infuriating her. Each resents the presence of the others, for each assumes exclusive rights to John.

John begins to feel trapped and smothered. Once again he plans a trip to visit his friend. When he arrives at the hospital, however, he discovers that Spiros is dead. Wandering the streets before his train leaves, he passes a pool hall where he sees three mutes signing to each other. He greets them, and they welcome him. But John is so paralyzed with grief that he can think of nothing to say, and eventually the mutes leave him. Singer returns to his room and shoots himself. To the four who are left behind, his death remains a mystery.

Sister. "Why I Live at the P.O." Eudora Welty. 1941.

Sister, the story's narrator and central figure, finds herself in conflict with her eccentric southern family on one particular Fourth of July. It is their lack of understanding, she claims, that drives her to leave home and take up residence at the town post office.

Sister is the postmistress in the tiny town of China Grove, Mississippi, where she lives peaceably with her mother, her uncle Rondo, and her grandfather, known as Papa-Daddy. Her problems begin when her sister, Stella-Rondo, separates from her husband and moves back to the house with a two-year-old daughter whom she tells everyone is adopted. Sister comments on the likeness of the girl, Shirley-T., to both Papa-Daddy and Stella-Rondo's ex-husband, and in so doing earns Stella-Rondo's wrath.

To get back at her, Stella-Rondo turns Papa-Daddy against Sister by implying that Sister doesn't like her grandfather's beard, his pride and joy. The outraged Papa-Daddy then refuses to listen to Sister's protests. Sister suggests to her mother that perhaps there is something wrong with the two-year-old, who hasn't uttered a word since her arrival. Mama asks Stella-Rondo if the child is normal, and she responds by having the girl demonstrate her singing and dancing abilities. Satisfied, Mama insists that Sister apologize to both mother and child.

Next, Stella-Rondo makes an ally of Uncle Rondo, a pharmacist who gets high on prescription medicines every Fourth of July. She tells Uncle Rondo that Sister thought he looked ridiculous when he was wearing Stella-Rondo's flesh-colored kimono. Offended, Uncle Rondo throws a string of lit firecrackers into Sister's room the next morning. Claiming that the whole family has turned against her, Sister informs them that she will move into the P.O.

Sister takes much care in packing for her move, claiming as her own the fern she alone watered, the preserves she put up, and the sewing machine engine she paid the most for when the family gave it as a Christmas gift to Mama. After a final confrontation in which Stella-Rondo bursts into tears and the rest of the family members vow never to set foot in the post office again, Sister makes her dramatic exit.

When the story closes, Sister has been living in the P.O. for five days and nights, and has not seen any member of her family since then. Her abode, she says, is ideal, with butter beans planted outside and peace inside. She admits that there is little mail, as her family members are the main people in China Grove; but in any case, she insists, she is there to stay.

Skeffington, Frank. *The Last Hurrah.* Edwin O'Connor. 1956.

Septuagenarian mayor Frank Skeffington announces his bid for reelection with an energy that belies his age and surprises his political enemies. The hard-bitten Irish-American politician claims that he is running for office because he does not want to leave his beloved city in the hands of any of the other candidates for mayor. But as he admits to his nephew, ADAM CAULFIELD, he is also running for another term because he enjoys the power and responsibility of being mayor.

Skeffington invites his orphaned nephew, a comic strip writer, to accompany him on the coming campaign, insisting that this will probably be Adam's last chance to see an election campaign run in the "old style." More than this, however, the mayor wants a companion for the hard weeks ahead. With his loving wife dead and his only son a disappointing, weak-charactered man, Skeffington feels that he has no equals or confidants, and he hopes that Adam will be a comfort during the trials of campaigning.

After making the offer to his nephew, Skeffington does not see the young man again for some time because he is kept busy with the duties of running the city and planning a campaign. Upon arriving at his office in his siren-topped limousine each day, Skeffington wades through a crowd of staff and supporters to meet with his two most trusted advisors: his personal advisor Sam Weinberg and the powerful ward boss John Gorman.

While his opponents see Skeffington as an outright crook and a detriment to the city, his supporters see him as an able rogue with a good heart. His loyal supporters believe that although Skeffington's methods of operation are not always honorable, he has done good things for the city. For instance, Skeffington manipulates and threatens to blackmail a prominent banker, but he does so in order to get a loan for a much-needed housing project.

For his reelection campaign Skeffington uses television and radio, but still relies heavily on the traditional tactics of appearing at nearly every public gathering in the city. Himself an Irishman for whom politics was a way out of poverty, Skeffington appeals to the Irish, Italians, and Poles in the city. He negotiates with the representatives of special-interest groups, unions, and the various city wards for the votes of their members.

With the momentum of the campaign culminating on election night, Skeffington's faithful gather to await the election results and celebrate their victory. The mayor confidently watches the returns and sees, before his supporters and advisors, that he is losing the election. Shaken by the unexpected defeat, Skeffington goes home. Soon afterward he suffers a heart attack. A few days of recovery give him a chance to review his life, his happy marriage, and his long political career. He realizes suddenly that he has never had time to reflect. This time is especially important to him after he suffers another heart attack and comes to the realization that he will soon die.

When Skeffington is receiving the last rites, one of the people present, a strong critic of the mayor, exclaims that Skeffington would surely live his life differently if given the chance to repeat it. "The hell I would!" Skeffington replies. At this the venerable old politician dies, fully content with his unorthodox life and career.

Skelton, Thomas. *Ninety-two in the Shade.* Thomas McGuane. 1972.

Thomas Skelton returns home to Key West from the university where he has been studying biology. At school he gradually lost the sense that his studies had any connection with the natural world, which has deep religious significance for him. Skelton now feels that being out on the ocean where he can see the expanse of sky and water is a matter of "simple survival": His sanity depends on it.

Skelton's father and grandfather both live in Key West, and, like him, they were drawn to the sea when they were young. The grandfather, Goldsboro Skelton, went to sea before he was twenty and once headed a mutiny on a freighter whose captain was mistreating him and several friends. Later in life Goldsboro owned a cruiser, which he frequently sailed to Cuba for mysterious reasons. Skelton's father owned a fishing boat, once the property of a rum-runner, from which he flew a black anarchist flag. Neither man offers Skelton great hope for his own future; Goldsboro becomes a corrupt politician and a womanizer, and Skelton's father, who hates Goldsboro, has no career of any kind and eventually loses his mind. Judging from the lives of his forebears, Skelton feels he can look forward to one of two possibilities: "universal consciousness or early death."

Skelton seems to have opted for the latter. As soon as he makes known his intention to be a sea guide to NICHOL DANCE, an older guide whose performance is irregular, Skelton feels he must defend his position. Dance warns

him to stay off the water and then plays a frightening trick on the young man to prove his seriousness. When Dance attacks a man and gets himself put in jail, he lends his skiff to Skelton, ostensibly for the period of his incarceration. Skelton takes a couple, the Rudleighs, fishing, and while he is out of the boat netting a fish, Dance and his friend Carter evacuate them. Skelton is terrified that the Rudleighs were lost or drowned, but later that day he sees them in a bar and realizes the whole affair was staged. In revenge, he throws a burning rag into Dance's boat and destroys it. When Dance threatens to kill him if he attempts to guide, Skelton is not shocked and gives no indication of changing his plans.

Instead of preventing Skelton from guiding, Dance's threat encourages him. He explains to his frustrated and frightened girlfriend Miranda that he admires Dance. Because he knows his time is limited, Skelton is living intensely and loving Miranda passionately. He experiences moments of terror and even imagines the path of a bullet through his chest, but he does not stop; exhilarated by the confrontation and excited by the building and outfitting of his new skiff, Skelton proceeds toward certain death.

On the morning of his first day as a guide, the euphoric Skelton takes his client, a Montana miner named Olie Slatt, to look for bonefish at Snipe Point. Dance's skiff approaches; he enters Skelton's boat with a pistol and asks him where he would like to be shot. Skelton points to the place on his chest where he had earlier imagined the bullet entering. In the moment before Dance shoots him, he makes a great discovery: He has courage.

Skipper Edward. *Second Skin.* John Hawkes. 1963.

This novel concerns the ways in which Skipper Edward, the narrator and a latter-day quest figure, attempts to escape the confines of cultural expectation by establishing a new life for himself and joining a new community on a remote desert island. The story, much of it filled with allusions to classical literature, is told mainly in flashbacks.

Edward—usually called Skipper or "Skip" because of his position aboard a ship—is an innocent, a "lover of the hummingbird," who maintains his gentle nature despite the horrors and betrayals he has experienced. As a child he was literally surrounded by death: His youth was spent in a funeral home under the constant shadow of the hearse outside, which functioned as the family car on weekends. His father, a mortician with "white boneless mortician's hands," committed suicide in the lavatory while Edward stood outside the door and played the cello. After hearing the fatal gunshot, his mother filled her ears with hot candle wax and fled to her brother's house twenty miles away.

Edward survived and became an officer on a ship. He and Sonny, his black companion and solitary confidant, traveled to many ports together. Sonny, loyal and trustworthy, managed to save Edward from many unfortunate experiences, including a mutiny attempt by a man named Tremlow. Sonny is present throughout the narrative as the one solid entity that is a constant life force amid the "seeds of death" that surround Edward.

Edward's "naked history" is shaped by "victims, courageous victims" who exist as vampiric forces, intent on draining him and themselves of life. On the ship Edward's wife Gertrude, his daughter Cassandra, her husband Fernandez, and Tremlow, a trusted sailing mate, all succumb to their own self-destructive drive: killing themselves or being killed by another. Like all the characters in the narrative who succumb to their melancholia, these figures are products of the mainland. Weakened and corrupted, they are ultimately unable to move beyond the constraints imposed on them by civilization.

Despite his encounters with this desperate landscape, Edward remains the bearer of life. He settles on an island with Sonny and becomes an artificial inseminator of cows. On the island he and Sonny enter into the dual fatherhood of a child with an island woman named Catalina Kate. As Edward discovers, only the island people—Sonny, Catalina Kate, and others—are able to live freely. Edward finds solace in their ability to look into the face of death without fear, and through them he finds the reflection of his love.

Slade, Alida. "Roman Fever." Edith Wharton. 1911.

Alida Slade, the widow of a famous corporation lawyer, is flooded with memories while sitting on a terrace in Rome with her companion, Grace Ansley. Mrs. Slade and Mrs. Ansley are elite New Yorkers who ran into each other while vacationing in Rome.

When the story opens, the ladies' two daughters, Jenny Slade and the magnificent, vivacious Barbara "Babs" Ansley, are just leaving to enjoy the sights, sounds, and young men of the city. After they leave, Mrs. Slade and Mrs. Ansley decide to linger on the restaurant terrace as the afternoon fades. Mrs. Slade stares at the view—the ruins of the Palace of the Caesars, the Forum, and the Colosseum—while Mrs. Ansley, who is quieter, smaller, and paler than her companion, knits thoughtfully without looking up. Mrs. Slade thinks about Mrs. Ansley, whom she realizes she does not know very well even after all these years. She considers Mrs. Ansley an old-fashioned, predictable neighbor but remembers how beautiful she was when they were young. Still, she wonders how the Ansleys, both "museum specimens" of old New York, could have produced their dynamic daughter Babs. Mrs. Slade is somewhat bored with her own daughter, who is angelic but not exciting and who has never been in love.

Mrs. Slade recalls to Mrs. Ansley how their mothers and grandmothers instructed them to guard against Roman fever, the sickness caused by exposure to sudden changes in temperature. A person caught outside during the cool hours of the Roman sunset was almost certain to catch this often serious malady. Mrs. Ansley, Mrs. Slade remembers, had once become quite ill when they were visiting Rome as young women; everyone had assumed it was because she went out one night and caught the fever. Mrs. Slade then says she knew that when they were young and unmarried, Mrs. Ansley had been in love with Delphin Slade, the man who was then Mrs. Slade's fiancé. No longer able to conceal her dark secret, Mrs. Slade confesses that she had written a letter telling Mrs. Ansley to go to the Colosseum at sunset, and she had signed Delphin's name to it. She intended, she now admits, for her rival in love to catch Roman fever.

When Mrs. Ansley says she did meet Delphin that night at the Colosseum, Mrs. Slade at first does not believe her. But Mrs. Ansley tells Mrs. Slade that she had answered the letter, and Delphin came accordingly. Mrs. Slade realizes her plan had backfired. After the initial shock, she tells Mrs. Ansley she won't begrudge her that one evening with Delphin. After all, she says, "I had everything; I had him for twenty-five years." But the final, ironic blow comes to Mrs. Slade when Mrs. Ansley responds, after a pause, "I had Barbara."

Slade, Simon. *Ten Nights in a Bar-Room, and What I Saw There.* Timothy Shay Arthur. 1854.

Simon Slade, proprietor of the Sickle and Sheaf Tavern, is at the center of one town's ten-year conflict with alcohol. What starts innocently enough when Slade reinvests the earnings gained from the sale of his successful milling operation in a new tavern, finishes with his brutal death at the hands of his son; for, as is the case with everything in the small town of Cedarville, what touches alcohol must come to an evil end.

An industrious family man, Slade had earned an honest living as the owner and operator of the local mill. As the novel opens, Slade has sold the mill over the objections of his wife and has purchased the Sickle and Sheaf Tavern. Slade's business venture finds wide support in the town of Cedarville, especially among the property owners nearby, and the tavern attracts a prosperous, hardworking, and hard-drinking crowd. Yet from the outset the tavern, and the insidious effect of alcohol, weakens the Slade family structure and its owner's own good nature.

Slade's new callousness shows itself in his treatment of his former mill partner, Joe Morgan. Joe, a longtime alcoholic, lost his job when Slade sold the mill and has taken to drinking his money away at the tavern. Slade sees Joe's drunkenness and his sometimes resentful defiance as a threat to his business, and one night he throws an empty glass at him. The glass misses Morgan and instead strikes his young daughter Mary, who had always followed him to the tavern in an effort to save him from alcohol. Mortally wounded, Mary elicits a pledge from Joe never to return to the tavern again.

Having escaped the ensuing murder indictment through his connections with a judge, Slade begins to offer his tavern as a haven to professional gambler Harvey Green. As the years pass, Green and Slade become partners in a gambling ring that entwines the young Willy Hammond, son of a town judge. One night young Willy is shot dead by Green in a card fight at the tavern. The town erupts in violence, and Green himself becomes the victim of the mob's bullets; Slade escapes only by hiding out.

Eight years later we see how the Sickle and Sheaf has devastated the Slade family. Mrs. Slade has been committed to an insane asylum after losing herself to remorse over the death of Mary Morgan. Frank, Simon Slade's only son, has become increasingly vulgar and has begun to have bitter fights with his father. Flora Slade, his only daughter, is imprisoned in the grimy world of the tavern and subject to the crude propositions of its increasingly rowdy patrons. One day during a fight over Frank's excessive drinking, Frank strikes his father in the head with a whiskey bottle, and Slade dies as a result.

Slade's fall from prosperous merchant to patricide victim parallels Cedarville's ten-year descent into the grip of alcohol. At the close of the novel, the citizens of Cedarville decide to prohibit the consumption and purchase of alcohol in their town. The Sickle and Sheaf, symbol of Slade's own state of affairs, has in ten short years fallen into shambles and is closed.

Slaughter, Nathan. *Nick of the Woods, or The Jibbenainosay: A Tale of Kentucky.* Robert Bird. 1928.

Nathan Slaughter lives with a terrible paradox. Publicly, he is a pacifist Quaker who refuses to fight, but privately, he is the "Jibbenainosay," a mysterious figure who secretly kills Indians to avenge the murder of his family. A tall, gaunt, middle-aged man with piercing black eyes and a little dog named Peter, Nathan has a meek, passive disposition that has earned him the seemingly mocking nickname "Bloody Nathan." But when he helps two friends escape from the Indians, Nathan is forced to fight openly and finally achieves his revenge.

In 1782, Roland and Edith Forrester, two cousins emigrating from Virginia to Ohio, arrive at a Kentucky station where they first encounter Nathan, who is also known as "Wandering Nathan," an outcast who has no permanent home. Because of his reputation as the only man in Kentucky who won't fight, Nathan is constantly persecuted, but he must frequent the station in order to trade skins for hunting supplies. In general, though, he stays in the woods, and when Roland, Edith, and their companions are lost there during an all-out war between Indians and Kentuckians, they meet him for a second time. At first Nathan declines to guide the lost party to the lower ford of the river because he fears that Roland will force him to fight. Having secured Roland's oath to the contrary, he and Peter skillfully and prudently guide the company away

from the Indians who are tracking them. Although Roland questions this quiet stranger about his past, Nathan will not discuss his life before he came to the Kentucky wilderness.

Nathan leads the party to an abandoned cabin but soon realizes with fear that he has brought them to an Indian hiding place. When the Indians attack, Nathan fights in self-defense and assists Roland. He continually expresses his guilt and justifies shooting the Indians by citing his obligation to save the innocent women. When fighting, Nathan's ferocity is even greater than Roland's, but he begs Roland to acknowledge that he shed blood only to save the innocent.

Nathan escapes from the cabin and attempts to bring back help. During his absence, the party leaves the house and is ambushed and captured by Indians. Nathan, having followed the tracks of his friends, later rescues Roland from three Indians by killing them in their sleep. He asks Roland not to betray the secret of his bloody deed.

Edith remains a hostage at the Shawnee village headed by an aging chief named Wenonga. Provoked by Roland's despair over Edith's capture, Nathan finally tells his own tragic story. Originally from Pennsylvania, he lived with his mother, wife, and five children. When Shawnees attacked, he gave them his weapons as a gesture of peace, and they used his own knife and gun to murder his entire family. Nathan frantically recounts his tale until he falls into an epileptic fit. Having recovered his senses, he plans a cunning rescue of Edith and no longer attempts to justify his own violence.

Nathan arrives at the Indian village disguised as an Indian and directs Roland to wait in the forest for his return. Passing through the town's drunken and sleeping Indians, he makes his way to Wenonga's cabin where he discovers Edith and steals her away, only to be surrounded and captured by the Shawnees. When Nathan falls into another epileptic fit, Wenonga believes he is a medicine man who can reveal the secret of how to kill the Jibbenainosay.

Nathan is tied up and brought to Wenonga's cabin. Wenonga asks him to bring him the Jibbenainosay; in the Shawnee tongue, Nathan accuses the chief of lying. Stunned, Wenonga boasts of his fearless conquests, including the peaceful Quaker family who were his friends and whose scalps hang in his cabin. Overcome with rage, Nathan taunts Wenonga into cutting him free and immediately kills him in his violent ritualistic style.

Upon discovering their dead chief, the Shawnees begin to take revenge on the prisoners. But unbeknownst to the Indians, Nathan has directed a large force of men from the Kentucky station to the village. They arrive, save the prisoners, and destroy the village. Nathan, virtually possessed, kills many Indians and zealously ignites the wigwams. Afterward, Nathan refuses Roland's offers of money and asks only that he not say anything to disparage the Quaker faith. Wishing to avoid the militant Kentuckians who exalt him for his prowess, Nathan stalks off into the woods with Peter and eventually leaves the area altogether.

Slocum, Bob. *Something Happened.* Joseph Heller. 1974.

Bob Slocum, a minor executive in a large corporation, has an odd neurosis about closed doors. He anxiously dwells on the details of his past and present relationships with family members, coworkers, and lovers, and is convinced that "something happened" to make him and those around him into pathetic and miserable creatures. The first-person narrative of Slocum's obsessions, often interspersed with his nervous, sardonic laughter, describes every aspect of the office in which he works and of his home life in Connecticut.

According to Slocum, the office is a place where everyone is afraid of someone else. Andy Kagle, his boss, is a gauche, self-made man who walks with a limp and does not carry his position well. Although Slocum tries to protect him and tells him to improve his image, when Kagle fails to change, Slocum often has a perverse desire to kick him in the leg. Later, Arthur Baron, head of the division, secretly offers Slocum a promotion to Kagle's position, but Slocum has a crisis of conscience; although the promotion would mean the end of Kagle and other colleagues, including Martha, the department's typist who is slowly going crazy, he hesitates to accept it.

Slocum hates his wooden colonial house on a choice country acre on Peapod Lane in Connecticut, and his attractive, well-dressed wife is equally unhappy. Bored and lonely, she has begun drinking during the day and flirting at parties. Slocum resents her and refuses to tell her that he loves her; in fact, he wants to divorce her but worries about the repercussions. He has many affairs with lonely younger women, but he even finds this irritating.

In his reveries Slocum compulsively returns to the time when he was seventeen years old and working as a clerk in an automobile casualty insurance company. At that time he was infatuated with Virginia Markowitz, a twenty-one-year-old buxom blonde with whom he traded dirty jokes. Several times each working day he and the free-spirited Virginia met in the storeroom or on a staircase landing, where they hurriedly kissed and petted and clutched for a few seconds until Virginia panicked and bolted away. Slocum never worked up the courage to press Virginia for more. Her experience intimidated him: At Duke University five football players forced her to have sex with them, and she told Slocum that although she resisted at first, she actually enjoyed it. When Slocum looks her up years later, he learns that she has committed suicide.

Slocum's children are also a source of anguish for him. His fifteen-year-old daughter, who was playful and responsive as a baby, has become overweight, lonely, depressed, and malicious. She seeks her father's attention by baiting him, and Slocum responds with a compulsive need to outfox her in every conversation. He is very attached to his nine-year-old son, who is not named and who is the person he loves most in the world. He suffers because his little boy is sensitive and timid, and so generous that he gives his money away to friends. The boy lacks a competitive spirit, and Slocum feels a desperate need to protect him. Slocum claims that he does not love his youngest child, Derek, who is mentally retarded. He feels the unspoken desire of everyone in his family to send Derek away.

Slocum agonizes over what could have caused everyone around him to become so unhappy. He wonders why his nine-year-old son has stopped talking to him. One day while walking on the street, he hears a teenager calling to his friend: "Something happened!" Slocum follows the crowd and sees that his favorite son has been run over. Terror-stricken, he runs over and hugs the bleeding boy on the ground, squeezing him tightly. The doctor later tells Slocum that the boy's wounds were superficial and that his son died of asphyxiation. No one else knows what Slocum has done.

After this incident Slocum appears to have been transformed. He impresses everyone by artfully maneuvering into Kagle's position and then firing him. He tells his wife that he loves her and buys his daughter a car. When Martha, the typist, finally loses her sanity, Slocum steps in, calls the ambulance, and arranges to have her taken away. "Everyone seems pleased," he remarks, "with the way I've taken command."

Sloper, Catherine. *Washington Square.* Henry James. 1880.

Catherine Sloper is an unextraordinary twenty-year-old woman whose best attribute, according to her father, is the fact that she is an heiress. Catherine's character and her father's judgment are put to the test when a young man begins courting her, apparently out of love.

Although Catherine adores her father, the wealthy Dr. Sloper of New York, and desires only to please him, she always falls short of his glorious image of her mother, a woman of great beauty and intelligence who died soon after Catherine's birth. Catherine is painfully aware of her plain face and lack of wit; she is also painfully shy. The promise of her money has brought several suitors to her door, but she has been content to remain in her father's house in Washington Square. Her attitude changes, however, when she goes to a party and meets a young man named Morris Townsend who has just returned from the Continent.

Catherine decides at first glance that Morris is the most beautiful young man she has ever seen, and she is not surprised to find that he has social graces to complement his looks. But she is amazed when Morris begins turning all of his attention toward her. Morris seems undaunted by Catherine's lack of beauty. He seems charmed, even humbled, by her presence. Catherine's aunt Lavinia, a widow and a busybody, sees the attention Morris is paying to Catherine. She invites Morris to the house and tells Catherine that Morris "is coming a-courting!"

Catherine sees Morris as a young knight in a poem. She falls completely in love with him after only a few days. Inside of two months she agrees to marry him. But Dr. Sloper is suspicious. Rumor has it that Morris has been wild, that he has squandered what little money he had, lives off his widowed sister, and has no prospects for the future. It seems to Dr. Sloper that Morris is after one thing only: Catherine's money. Dr. Sloper does not hesitate to make his suspicions known to Catherine, and she is confused by her father's callousness. She confronts Morris, who assures her that he loves her beyond any concern for wealth. However, his request that she speak to her father on his behalf only increases Dr. Sloper's suspicion. Catherine is already worth $10,000 a year from an inheritance from her mother. Upon Dr. Sloper's death, she will be worth an additional $20,000. Dr. Sloper believes Morris is angling for this additional income.

Catherine is plunged into a crisis. She trusts her father and wants to be a good daughter, yet Morris's love seems true. Her aunt suggests that she and Morris elope. Morris urges her to speak once more to her father. Dr. Sloper tells her that if she marries Morris, she won't receive a farthing from him. Catherine decides to marry Morris anyway and throw the $20,000 to the winds.

Then Dr. Sloper asks Catherine to go to Europe with him for six months. Morris approves of the idea: It will show her father that they can wait. Although she would rather elope, Catherine agrees to the trip. Again, Morris tells her to try to change her father's mind. She is unable to do so during the six months abroad; when Dr. Sloper suggests they stay on for another six months, she reluctantly agrees. After a year, Dr. Sloper asks if she has forgotten Morris. Catherine says no. Dr. Sloper is disgusted, and his disgust manifests itself in a terrible coldness toward her, which has an unexpected effect. Finally fathoming her father's dislike of her, Catherine's heart freezes. She feels separated from her father for the first time and for all time. She will not try to please him again.

When Catherine returns to America, it is with the intention of marrying Morris and living happily on $10,000 a year. When she tells Morris, however, the young man acts strangely toward her. He does nothing overt, but in a thousand little ways Catherine senses that something is very wrong. Morris leaves, saying he will see her again in a week. "Why not tomorrow?" Catherine asks. Morris says he may have to go away. Catherine panics. He assures her there is nothing the matter and manages to get out the door. When she is left alone, Catherine flings herself on the sofa and weeps. She does not even know what has happened. She knows only that Morris seems to have left forever.

It is some twenty years before Catherine sees Morris again. She languishes in Washington Square, knitting tapestries and nursing her broken heart. When Dr. Sloper asks her before he dies to assure him she will never marry Morris, Catherine refuses to do so even though she knows very well what Morris is worth. Dr. Sloper disinherits Catherine. He dies without realizing that she did not want his money anyway. Then, on a warm summer night, Morris returns. Life has not been good to him. His looks have faded, and he has not made his fortune. Now, it seems, he will gladly settle for $10,000 a year. Catherine's response is brief. She is not angry, but she cannot forget what has happened and asks him to leave forever. Then she returns to her knitting, "for life, as it were."

Slothrop, Tyrone. *Gravity's Rainbow.* Thomas Pynchon. 1973.

The paranoid and unpredictable Tyrone Slothrop was born in the early 1920s in the town of Mingeborough, Massachusetts, where his family has lived since before the American Revolution. As an infant Tyrone was the subject of the Pavlovian Laszlo Jamf's experiments. Jamf conditioned Slothrop's reflexive sexual response to loud noise. Jamf, however, failed to properly extinguish Slothrop's conditioned response. As a result, when the Germans begin to fire their new, supersonic rockets at England during the later years of World War II, Lieutenant Slothrop unwittingly senses their approach before firing: He becomes sexually aroused when he nears a point where a rocket will strike.

While stationed in England, Slothrop works for ACHTUNG (Allied Clearing House, Technical Units, Northern Germany). He shares an office with the British Lieutenant Oliver "Tantivy" Mucker-Maffick. Slothrop tells Tantivy of his sexual experiences with women; he even hangs a map of London with dated markers indicating the names of the women and the sections of the city in which he had his encounters. In his paranoia, Slothrop begins to believe that one of the German rockets will kill him. Nevertheless, it is Tantivy's friend, Teddy Bloat, an employee of PISCES (Psychological Intelligence Schemes for Expediting Surrender), who first notices the undeviating correlation between Slothrop's encounters with women and the Germans' rocket bombardment of London.

Pointsman, an agent working on a subgroup of PISCES, Operation Black Wing, headquartered at an insane asylum called The White Visitation, attempts to force Slothrop to go ultraparadoxical. He wants Slothrop to become so paranoid and focused on rockets that all his other thoughts and behavior will be inhibited. Pointsman sends Slothrop, with Tantivy and Bloat as ostensible companions, to Casino Hermann Goering on the Mediterranean coast. While sleeping with Katje (another PISCES employee), Slothrop's clothes and all of his forms of identification are stolen. Unaware of Pointsman's plan, Slothrop begins to focus most of his attention on the technical development of rockets. He escapes from Hermann Goering with a counterfeit passport and borrowed clothes, although PISCES may have arranged his escape.

Following various leads on the Germans' new V-5 rocket and the people constructing it, as well as trying to hide from the various people he thinks may be following him, Slothrop crisscrosses much of Europe. In his travels he falls in with several bizarre underground organizations, including one that gives him a superhero costume (complete with cape) and sends him into the Russian-occupied section of Berlin to rescue a stash of hashish. In time Slothrop comes to suspect that everyone and everything is part of an elaborate international network, and he is probably right.

Slovoda, Sam. "The Man Who Studied Yoga." Norman Mailer. 1956.

The story takes place on one Sunday in the life of Sam Slovoda, a mild, frustrated man of forty who once flirted with radical politics and bohemia, but now spends his time writing copy for comic books and arguing with his wife Eleanor.

Sam gets up, hung over from a night at a party, and he and Eleanor, who have been married for ten years, gossip somewhat viciously about the guests at the party, particularly a girl with whom Sam was flirting. They speak in language laced with jargon. Sam is in the process of being psychoanalyzed, and his mind is filled with phrases from psychoanalytic textbooks. He hates the fact that he speaks in jargon, but he can't help himself. One of the things Sam's analyst, Dr. Sergius, has done for him is highlight his weaknesses and limitations without giving him the ability to change them.

Sam has vague plans of someday writing a great novel, and he hopes to make some notes on it today. But he picks up the Sunday paper, grows angry at the inane headlines and foolish articles, and finally drifts off into half-formed thoughts about the hopelessness of world conditions, the danger of the media, and the like. The image of Sergius occasionally rises up in his mind and chases some of his grander thoughts away.

Then Marvin Rossman telephones Sam and Eleanor with an unusual request. Marvin and his wife have gotten hold of a pornographic movie and want to use Sam's projector. Sam invites them over, to Eleanor's annoyance. He then becomes quite anxious about the condition of the projector. Will the bulb burn out? Does the motor need oil? He realizes that he is trying to keep out of his mind the reactions Sergius will certainly have when Sam tells him he watched a dirty movie.

The Rossmans arrive with another couple, the Sperbers. Sam listens to the nervous general talk that precedes the screening and contributes to it as well, but all the while he is feeling superior to the two couples. They are contented petite bourgeoisie, while he, Sam Slovoda, is a rebel in his heart.

The pornographic movie is entitled *The Evil Act*. By a strange coincidence one of the characters in the film is named Eleanor, and this gets a big laugh from the small audience. The ludicrous opening moments of the film contribute to everyone's giddiness, but the film becomes more explicit and the crowd silences. In spite of themselves, they are transported by the erotic images on the screen, and when the film ends, they cannot look at one another. They watch the film again. Sam thinks of the Deer Park of Louis XV where young maidens were brought and ravished for the pleasures of the king. Sam wonders if it is possible that when the film is over, he and his friends will take off their clothes and perform the orgy that is on all their minds. He knows they will not. They will drink, make jokes, and gorge themselves on food. He will be the first to make the jokes.

This is indeed what happens. They talk and talk, and succeed in driving the film out of their minds. Other topics are brought up. Marvin mentions an old friend, an ex-Party member whom he and Sam used to know. The old friend is now a drunken bum. Sam reflects on the failure of revolutionary idealism in the present day. "Modern life is schizoid," he says.

The guests leave, and Eleanor remarks on what a waste the day has been. Sam agrees. He is now thinking about having sex with Eleanor, an act that was once wondrous but now seems as entangled with complexities and annoyances as anything else. The couple watches the film again, and as the projector rolls they make love. Sam is by turns passionate and unbelievably self-conscious, but Eleanor is happy and mentions that she may have seen the film once before. It was at a small orgy, maybe ten years ago, before she and Sam were married. Sam already knows the story of Eleanor's little affair, but he still feels jealous. Yet as he falls asleep next to Eleanor, the pain of jealousy mixes with the pleasure of being near her, and he begins to drift off to sleep.

Then he remembers his novel. He knows he will never finish it. He can't even find a hero for it—there are none today. He realizes he lacks the energy and belief to become a novelist. He wishes he could fall asleep. Then he remembers a woman he and Eleanor had known in their bohemian days, a woman who ended up in a mental hospital and who said she was sexually violated there. Sam realizes he knows nothing of madness or religion. The mental hospital was like a concentration camp. And the world itself? He hears the voice of Dr. Sergius saying, "Do not try to solve the problems of the world." Sam thinks again of his novel. Then he begins playing the game of putting himself to sleep. "I do not feel my toes, my toes are asleep." A thought comes to him, he grapples with it for a moment, and then goes back to thinking about his toes. Finally, sleep overtakes him.

Small, Lennie. *Of Mice and Men.* John Steinbeck. 1937.

Lennie Small is a huge, bearlike man, immensely strong but with the mind of a child. He is incapable of caring for himself and is reliant on his guardian GEORGE MILTON. Lennie and George are migrant workers in California during the Depression. The precise circumstances of their upbringing are not revealed although Lennie has vague memories of an aunt who cared for him as a child.

As the novel opens, Lennie and George are camping by a pond a few miles from a ranch where they are planning to ask for a job. Lennie's excessive strength, although an asset on any work crew, has cost them their previous employment in a town called Weed. Lennie has a childlike love for soft, warm things; he is continually adopting mice and other small animals to carry in his pockets to pet. Inevitably he crushes them and is filled with remorse. In Weed he was attracted by a woman's red velvet dress. His attempt to "pet" the dress was seen as an assault, and the two were forced to leave town.

Because the two look after each other and are not alone, George says, they have a future. Sitting by the pond, Lennie makes George recite for the thousandth time the dream of the future that makes their migrant life bearable. Someday, George promises, they will have a place of their own with a cow and some pigs, where they will (as Lennie interjects) "live off the fatta the lan'." Lennie's most cherished dream is that when the time comes, he will be able to tend the rabbits. Before they leave, Lennie promises George that he will stay quiet at the ranch and let George do the talking. And he understands that if there is any trouble, he is to meet George again at the pond.

At the ranch, the two are no sooner shown their sleeping quarters than Lennie's silence arouses the wrath of Curley, the boss's son. Curley, a lightweight boxer, is insecure because of both his small stature and his inability to keep his new wife from fraternizing with the hired men. As a result he is constantly spoiling for a fight. Although Lennie would be more than a match for Curley, he is frightened by the smaller man's rage and gives him no provocation.

The incident is soon forgotten. With the exception of Curley, Lennie and George get along well with most of the hands. They go as far as letting Candy, the old crippled sweeper, in on their plans for the farm. In his childlike innocence, Lennie even manages to befriend Crooks, the black "stable buck." And Slim, the foreman, promises Lennie one of the pups from his dog's litter. Even Curley (it seems) ceases to be a threat, for when he picks a second fight with Lennie, he quickly has his hand broken, a fate too humiliating to be used as a pretext for firing the newcomers.

Although George, Lennie, and Candy have almost enough money among them to make a down payment on a small farm, their plans are doomed to failure. Attracted by Lennie's thrashing of her quick-tempered husband, Curley's wife approaches him in the barn while all the other hands are playing horseshoes. After talking to him for a while, she encourages him to stroke her hair. He strokes too roughly, and she panics. She screams, and he becomes anxious, thinking George will be mad and won't let him tend the rabbits (a frequent threat). While trying to stifle her cries, he accidentally breaks her neck.

Realizing he has "done a bad thing," Lennie flees to the pond where he hides and waits for George. Knowing where Lennie will be, George slips away from the posse (led by Curley) hunting for his friend. He meets Lennie and quietly tells him the story of the farm and the rabbits for the last time, insisting that he was never mad at him. As the others approach, George shoots Lennie in the back of the head, knowing it is better to do this than have him taken alive by the mob.

Smiley, Jim. "The Celebrated Jumping Frog of Calaveras County." Samuel L. Clemens (Mark Twain). 1867.

Jim Smiley is an incurable and infamous gambling man, willing to lay a bet on anything from horse races, to dog fights, to the particular path a wandering bug might take. Fortunately for Jim, he nearly always comes up on the winning side of his contests. His ungainly old mare seems always to be afflicted with some debilitating illness, and yet it somehow wins nearly all the races Jim arranges for it. Jim's bulldog doesn't look like much of a fighter, but by biting his opponents' hind legs, it always seems to come out of a dogfight the champion. The dog loses a match only when it is pitted against a dog who lost both hind legs in an accident. Indeed, Jim's wagers are on a variety of animals—terriers, chicken cocks, and tomcats—and most are winners.

One day Jim catches a frog and determines to train it for competition. Naming the frog Dan'l Webster, he sets to work teaching it to jump and perform stunts in midair. In the three-month training period Dan'l shows remarkable talent, and most agree that he jumps farther than any frog they have ever seen.

Jim wastes no time laying bets. When a stranger comes to town, Jim offers him the chance to lay a wager of forty dollars against Dan'l's expert jumping. The stranger shows interest but declines because he doesn't have a frog of his own to pit against Jim's. Eager to prove his own frog's superiority, Jim volunteers to procure a frog for the stranger and sets off to find one.

While Jim is gone, the stranger pries open Dan'l's mouth and fills it with quail shot. When Jim returns with a frog and starts the contest, he is stunned to see that while the competitor is a lively jumper, his own frog seems unable to move. As the stranger leaves with his winnings, a dumbfounded Jim watches as Dan'l Webster belches out a double handful of shot.

Smith, Joseph. *Children of God.* Vardis Fisher. 1939.

This historical novel depicts the life and struggles of Joseph Smith, one of the founders of the Church of Latter-Day Saints.

Despite the best efforts of his mother, who brought him and his brothers to hear every evangelist who passed through their small town in western New York State, Joseph was not initially religious. He followed in the footsteps of his father, who generally viewed with skepticism the many different hybrids of Christianity that competed for followers among the townspeople. Joseph's life is changed forever, however, when he experiences a revelation at the age of fourteen.

In his vision an angel of God speaks to Joseph, describing to him four golden plates that he has hidden in the countryside, containing his laws that Joseph must transcribe in the following years. Joseph immediately declares himself a prophet to his incredulous family and neighbors, and goes off to seek the golden plates.

Although Joseph is able to win a few followers, most of the townspeople regard him as little more than a freak, and he and his family quickly become the object of scorn and derision. Many believe that the golden plates Joseph seeks are some kind of buried treasure, and they try to force him and his family to reveal its whereabouts. To bring himself closer to God as well as to protect his family, Joseph runs off into the forest for the next few years to lead a life of quiet prayer and solitary meditation.

While Joseph is living in the forest, God speaks to him again, this time delivering to him the golden plates, which he then begins to transcribe. Joseph starts to roam around the countryside of New York State, where, despite the resistance he encounters, he manages to gain an increasingly large number of converts, due in no small part to the miracles he performs in the course of his travels. One of his followers, a young man named BRIGHAM YOUNG, becomes Joseph's most trusted assistant, handling most of the earthly matters while Joseph tends to the spiritual ones.

Joseph takes the Mormons, as his followers are now called, to Ohio where they establish a small socialist religious community. It is in Ohio that Joseph, who throughout his life had had a wandering eye for many of his female converts, develops his theory of "celestial marriage." After taking a number of attractive young female Mormons to live with him in his house (much to the disapproval of his wife Emma), Joseph finally reveals to Brigham Young and a few of his other close advisors that the more wives and offspring a man has in this world, the more power and glory he will receive in the next. In short, as Joseph reveals to his incredulous Council of Twelve, God sanctions plural marriage for high-ranking church officials such as themselves.

While Joseph and the church elders do their best to keep the "celestial marriage" tenet of their church a secret from their thousands of followers, not to mention the outside world, they are unable to keep the rumors from spreading. When word leaks out, the outraged citizens of Ohio begin terrorizing the Mormon settlement. Joseph has no choice but to move his people westward, to the still untamed country of Missouri.

As the Mormons build another community in the woods and swamplands of Missouri, Joseph continues to take wives. By the time he has forty wives (and over a hundred sons and daughters), the Mormons have become infamous. Forces determined to drive them off the continent have reached their settlement. While at first Joseph takes the advice of Brigham and flees westward, he finds himself unable to abandon his people and returns to be arrested. In jail awaiting his trial, he is shot by an angry mob and becomes a martyr to the religion he founded.

Smith, Joseph Fielding "Seldom Seen." *The Monkey Wrench Gang.* Edward Abbey. 1975.

Joseph Fielding Smith, commonly known as "Seldom Seen," is determined to save the environment he has grown to revere from the destructive effects of industrialization. To do so, he forms a four-member gang of terrorists whose mission is to throw a monkey wrench into the works of the great machine threatening the land.

Lanky and rough-hewn, Seldom Seen makes the perfect professional guide; he is the operator of a river-running outfit named Back of Beyond Expeditions. He longs for the good old days before the river was ruined by the building of the Glen Canyon Dam. While this manmade obstruction created a lake—Lake Powell, or "the blue death," as it is otherwise nicknamed—it also destroyed the river that once flowed effortlessly to the sea. Seldom fondly remembers the canyons, the roaring rapids, and the "great amphitheaters" that once were naturally fed by the river's flow. He notes how industrialization is marring both the facade of the landscape and the security of his own business.

One day Seldom sets off on a routine river trip with George Washington Hayduke serving as his assistant boatman. Among the clients are a middle-aged man named Doc Sarvis and his companion Bonnie Abbzug. On the first night Seldom, Hayduke, and Doc make a blood pact to thwart the various industrialization projects spreading over the area, "to slow the growth of Growth," and ultimately to destroy the Glen Canyon Dam. Once they are joined by Bonnie, the Monkey Wrench Gang is formed.

The group's first project is to raid Comb Wash where a large number of bulldozers and other heavy machinery are being used in the construction of a highway. The gang cuts the power lines, dumps sand and corn syrup in the fuel lines, and drains the oil out of all the machines. After the raid, Bonnie and Doc return to Albuquerque, and Hayduke and Seldom go to Lake Powell to survey the next target, the White Canyon Bridge. They notice a smell of decay, and Seldom comments that the river is now a stagnant "garbage dispose-all, a 180-mile-long incipient sewage lagoon." They also notice that the Hite Marina Airstrip is undergoing expansion, and they drive the bulldozer being used there into the lake. This operation was observed, however, by a Mormon bishop named Love and his Search and Rescue Team, and Love becomes as determined to put a stop to the terrorism as the Monkey Wrench Gang is to halt the attack on the environment. Love pursues Smith and Hayduke, but the two escape by dropping a boulder on Love's truck.

In the ensuing weeks Smith and Hayduke continue their acts of sabotage, wreaking havoc on bulldozers, geophones, oil rigs, and fences until they rejoin Bonnie and Doc. With rallied spirits the gang plans its next project: to blow up the strip-mining operation of the Peabody Coal Company. The four members dynamite a bridge as a coal-laden train is passing over it.

Raised a Mormon, Seldom's only remaining fidelity to his religion is his practice of polygamy, and he interrupts his terrorist acts to visit all three of his wives. He later rejoins the gang for an attempt at destroying the bridge over White Canyon Gorge. They hope to ruin the highway suspended above Lake Powell. They set high-temperature thermite flares on the bridge, but the white light these create attracts Bishop Love. Once again the gang is chased into the arid canyon country northwest of Lake Powell. Pursued for several days, they grow more and more dehydrated. Finally, Bishop Love is stricken with a heart attack, and Doc and Bonnie surrender in order to help him.

Hayduke and Seldom attempt to hold out, but they grow very hungry and thirsty. Seldom begins missing one of his wives, Susan, and intimates to Hayduke that he, too, might be willing to return to civilization and accept punishment; soon after, while Seldom is sleeping, Hayduke leaves him. Still, Seldom would have escaped punishment for his terrorist acts were he not caught stealing meat from a group of picnickers.

Thanks to a combination of plea bargaining and expert legal aid, Seldom, Bonnie, and Doc's trial results in a jail term of only six months, with four and a half years of probation. Two of Seldom's three wives sue him for divorce, but Susan remains loyal. The couple settles near the Green River in a house next door to Bonnie and Doc's, at whose wedding Seldom was best man. Seldom has accepted a quieter life-style, and when he is visited by his old friend Hayduke, the only member of the group to uphold its terrorist mission, the two find they have grown far apart.

Smith, Perry Edward. *In Cold Blood.* Truman Capote. 1966.

Perry Smith, the soft-spoken killer of this novel based on a true account of a multiple murder, is one of the most disturbing characters in American literature. A refined, sensitive, and poetic soul, Perry lives in an imagined world of richly textured dreams and ambitions in which the brutal vagaries of his own childhood, his years as a drifter in and out of jobs and penitentiaries, and his robberies and murders do not exist.

As the narrative begins, Perry is in a coffee shop in Olathe, Kansas, a few hours before the murder. He is lost in reveries of fame and fortune. He imagines himself singing at a famous nightclub in Las Vegas and diving for sunken treasure off the coast of Mexico. While awaiting the arrival of his former cellmate, DICK HICKOCK, he takes three aspirins, for he suffers from chronic pain in his stunted legs, broken in a motorcycle accident some years back. Perry is startled from his dreams by the blaring of a horn outside: It is Dick, arriving late, and armed with a twelve-gauge shotgun.

As they drive toward Holcomb, Kansas, Dick reveals his plan to Perry. While in prison Dick heard about a wealthy farmer, Herbert Clutter, who keeps a safe full of cash in his home. Dick has a map of the house; they will steal everything and leave no witnesses.

All is quiet and dark on the Clutter farm. The robbers search the house but find nothing. Together they ascend the stairs to rouse Herbert Clutter from his bed. They lock Herbert Clutter in the upstairs bathroom, along with his wife Bonnie, his sixteen-year-old daughter Nancy, and his fifteen-year-old son Kenyon. One by one the family members are taken out, tied up, and shot.

A few days later Dick and Perry meet in Kansas City where Dick cashes enough phony checks to get them to Mexico. Perry has brought his guitar, a box of books and memorabilia, and his maps of sunken treasures. No sooner do they reach Mexico City than Perry's sense of adventure begins to wane. He envies Dick his confidence, his muscular body, his all-American grin. But he considers Dick crass and uneducated, and is disgusted by his proclivities for drink and prostitutes.

Perry and Dick soon run out of money. Perry reluctantly agrees to return to Kansas City, where Dick cashes more phony checks, before going on to Miami Beach, Texas, and Las Vegas. The ruthless pragmatism Perry once admired in Dick seems to have dissolved into empty arrogance, but when Perry contemplates leaving Dick, he grows afraid. So confident are they of their success that they do not notice the police when they pull up alongside the stolen car in which they are sitting, parked on the street.

On the way with the police to Garden City, Kansas, Perry breaks down and confesses to the Clutter family murder. He wanted to teach Dick a lesson, he tells the detectives. In a soft, whispery voice he describes the killings: first, how he slit Herbert Clutter's throat, then shot him as he struggled to break free of the ropes; and how he shot Kenyon, whom they had left tied up on the couch (Perry had earlier seen the boy's discomfort and carefully placed a pillow under his head). Dick killed the women, Perry claims.

Awaiting his trial in the Garden City jail, Perry spends his days writing in a diary and playing with a squirrel he has tamed and christened Big Red. Out of consideration for Dick's parents, he changes his story and takes responsibility for all four killings. He apologizes shyly for his deeds before stepping up to the gallows on April 14, 1965.

Smith, Raymond. *The Dharma Bums.* Jack Kerouac. 1958.

Raymond Smith wanders back and forth across America, finding inspiration in the landscape for his meditations on Buddhist philosophy. For several months Ray remains in Berkeley, where he finds others exploring Eastern religious thought and rejecting, as he does, the values of modern American life. JAPHETH "JAPHY" RYDER, who becomes his closest friend, is among the leaders of this group and the most devoted Buddhist scholar.

When the two first meet, Ray is completing the final leg of his customary route across the country from New York to San Francisco via Mexico City. Japhy Ryder is also hitchhiking, swinging along a San Francisco street with an enormous rucksack. They meet again at a poetry reading given by Berkeley's "intellectual hepcats." After a great deal of wine drinking and poetry, Ray leaves with a group of people who accompany Japhy to his favorite Chinese restaurant. Ray and Japhy begin discussing Buddhism, reciting tales of their favorite "Zen lunatics." Ray becomes convinced of Japhy's wisdom.

Ray moves in with Alvah Bookbinder, who is also a poet but is very skeptical of Buddhism and spirituality in general. Preferring Japhy's enthusiasm and earnestness to Alvah's cynicism, Ray begins spending more time in Japhy's tiny shack. Their friendship flourishes despite two conflicts between them: Japhy disapproves of Ray's heavy drinking, and Ray feels uncomfortable with Japhy's sexual promiscuity, especially when it involves Princess, a woman with whom Ray had been in love.

Japhy, who grew up in the woods of Oregon, teaches Ray about the environment by taking him hiking. With their friend Morley, they make the challenging climb up Mount Matterhorn. Although Ray does not quite reach the peak, he feels purified by the experience. He comes away with the knowledge that "it's impossible to fall off mountains."

At Christmas time Ray hitchhikes back across the country via Mexico to North Carolina, where his mother, sister, and brother-in-law live. He remains there through the winter months, spending most of his time meditating in the woods. Ray prefers to meditate during the middle of the night even though it is bitterly cold. When spring arrives, he hitchhikes back to San Francisco and moves into a shack that he shares with Japhy. They both chop wood to earn money, but they need very little. The spring ends with an enormous party for Japhy who is leaving for a year's study in Japan. As the party is winding down, Ray and Japhy leave together and hike alone up Mount Tamalpais.

After Japhy's departure, Ray hikes north to Shagit Valley in Washington State where he has a job as a fire lookout. He spends July and August alone in a hut atop Desolation Peak, a station Japhy had occupied before him. Ray is lonely at first but comes to feel a strange ecstasy, a love for the mountains that surround him. Before leaving the lookout at the end of August, he kneels down and says a little prayer of gratitude to the shack as he had seen Japhy do when they left a campsite.

Smith, Valentine Michael. *Stranger in a Strange Land.* Robert A. Heinlein. 1961.

Born of human parents on the first human expedition to Mars and raised by Martians after their death, Valentine Michael Smith finally journeys to Earth as an adult. After his arrival and a time of blind confusion, Michael attunes his Martian thought patterns to a careful and objective look at twenty-first-century America. His interest is very Martian, however. He observes, waiting and knowing that in due time he will "grok," or understand, this new thing in all its material and spiritual significance.

Unbeknownst to Michael, his life—or at least his freedom—is directly threatened by the Federation government, whose laws could make him an instant multimillionaire and Martian world leader. Michael literally owns Mars, having been the sole resident there since the colonists left; technically, other citizens are merely immigrants unless he grants them citizenship. Federation administrators attempt to control him by interning him in a hospital ward. Michael is rescued from the hospital by Gillian Boardman, his nurse. Gillian, treating Michael as her patient, innocently offers him water. Since Martians live on a planet with little water, they made the offering of this precious liquid the highest sacred ritual, conferring on the individual "water brothers" all the responsibilities and assurances of total commitment.

Gillian then transports Michael to Jubal Harshaw's guarded estate in the Poconos. There Michael begins to learn about Earth, and a handful of people learn about Michael, his extraordinary powers, and his startling way of looking at life. Michael feels especially close to Jubal because Jubal's intelligent cynicism is closer to objectivity than the self-interest of the other humans with whom he has come in contact. Jubal teaches Michael to control his powers and arranges for him to be a free and very rich person by relinquishing his potential ability to upset the political balance.

A Martian by acculturation, Michael does not think in the same way as other humans. To him, one dies when one has fully "grokked" that it is the right time to "discorporate." Michael is truly bewildered by the religion of Earth and formulates his own translation of human beliefs: "Thou art God."

Soon he and Gillian go underground and live as circus people. They become much closer while he slowly teaches her his Martian control over matter and she teaches him what it means to desire, to laugh, to be human. When he realizes the irony of human existence, he also sees the tragedy of an unfulfilled race and sets out to do something about it. After unsuccessful stints at a seminary and in the armed forces, he gets himself ordained through a diploma mill as the "Founder and Pastor of the Church of All Worlds." His church works as a "holy roller" setup to interest people, but the upper levels of ritual teach the initiates the Martian control and patience needed to see how humans can live together in total harmony. Michael constructs his own Utopian community, characterized by free love, free money, and water-brotherhood.

It is not long before Michael is persecuted by other religions. His church is burned down, and he is arrested. Jubal goes to help him but finds that the fire was expected. Although Michael has freed himself, the end is near.

Michael finishes dictating a Martian dictionary, his philosophical legacy, to his inner circle. He is troubled and asks Jubal if he is doing right in trying to show people how to live. Jubal can see nothing wrong with his ideas—they are merely foreign.

Michael has founded a religion based on a fierce sense of individual responsibility and on the removal of jealousy. Most humans are not ready for this, and when he greets an angry crowd outside his hotel, they tear him apart. This only fulfills his potential, however; he has now entered into an afterlife where his powers seem truly boundless and his ideas clearly focused.

Smith, Will. *Contending Forces.* Pauline E. Hopkins. 1900.

Will Smith, a young, aspiring black man, lives with his sister Dora in the boardinghouse run by their widowed mother in Boston. Most of his time is spent in study, for he hopes to do graduate work in philosophy at Harvard, but he makes time to enjoy amusements with his sister and her fiancé JOHN P. LANGLEY, a lawyer whose influence in the black community is growing. Into the Smiths' domestic scene is introduced a new boarder, the lovely SAPPHO CLARK. Will is immediately charmed by Sappho's beauty and gentle, almost saintly manner.

After meeting Sappho, study is much more difficult. Will's mind wanders from the scholarly books and papers before him to contemplate her delightful form. Determined to marry her, he begins to set about making his interest known to Sappho. He even goes so far as to clean the heating stove in her room each morning. One day Sappho finds him there, and he banters with her awkwardly, asking her to think of him as her sweetheart. She blushes but does not agree.

A benefit fair held soon afterward gives Will another opportunity to approach Sappho. He draws her into a secluded area to speak privately to her. They are interrupted, however, first by Dora and then by John P. Langley, who bears a message that Will's mother wants to see him. Will goes, leaving Sappho alone with his friend.

At a sadder occasion, a meeting held to decide how Boston's black community should respond to the news of another lynching, Will makes an impressive appearance. Speaking after some conciliatory blacks, and directly following another man's tale of a black teenager raped by a white man who was never punished, Will is reasoned but rousing. He argues that only through agitation and liberal education will the condition of blacks be elevated. Decrying violence, Will also decries inaction. The crowd is moved and impressed, but one person does not hear the speech: Sappho had been carried out after fainting on hearing the previous speaker's story. Later, at a men's club dinner where Will is one of three black guests, Will again bears himself admirably, winning the respect of all present and in particular an Englishman, Charles Withington.

Once more Will presses his suit to Sappho. He meets her in a park on Easter Sunday and confesses his love for her. Sappho hesitates but returns his love, and agrees to marriage. They plan to tell Dora and Mrs. Smith of the engagement the next day. Will rises early to relay the happy news, but Sappho has vanished, taking her jewelry and some clothes with her. A letter arrives later from Sappho that reveals she had been the teenager who had been raped by a white man in the story told at the meeting. John P. Langley, who learned of her past, was able to convince her that Will would never have her. Fearing the loss of Will's love and unwilling to consent to being the lustful John's mistress, she fled.

Heartbroken and angry, Will resolves to confront John. Only the timely intervention of Arthur Lewis, a Negro-school president who is in love with Dora, saves both men from committing rash actions. Will hires detectives to search for Sappho, but they find no trace of her. Now education becomes the only occupation for the despairing Will. He receives his Harvard degree and plans to do more graduate study in Germany.

An unexpected visit from Charles Withington alters the family's fortunes. After hearing Mrs. Smith's story of her family background, Charles reveals that his family and hers are related and that a legacy of $150,000 is due her. The money speeds Will's study abroad, and after earning his degree and traveling, he returns to the United States to visit Dora and her husband, Dr. Lewis. Visiting a Catholic church, Will is astonished to see Sappho. His love undiminished, he asks her again to marry him, and the two are wed. Their happiness is only increased by the presence of Alphonse, Sappho's child by the man who raped her so many years ago, whom Will accepts as his own son.

Smolinsky, Sara. *Bread Givers.* Anzia Yezierska. 1925.

Sara Smolinsky, the heroine of this autobiographical novel depicting immigrant life in the Lower East Side at the turn of the century, reconstructs her experiences as a Jewish-American woman struggling against her culture's Old World mores. In her patriarchal household Sara is the youngest of four sisters born to a rabbi and his submissive wife. Nicknamed "Blut und Eisen" ("blood and iron") for her hardheaded stubbornness, Sara watches in dismay as her sisters are married off one by one by their father to men they do not love. Reb Smolinsky is a learned man who considers it appropriate for his family to work so that he can spend time with his holy books; he is thoroughly impractical when he turns his attention to anything else. When he is swindled in an improbable business venture, seventeen-year-old Sara resolves to "make herself for a person": She rents a hall bedroom in a tenement, supports herself by factory work, and attends night school.

The price Sara must pay for her independence is severe loneliness and a feeling of rootlessness. In her desire to make herself over as an American, Sara finds she has little in common with her beaten-down sisters; the one man who courts her gives up in frustration at her eagerness for learning. Sara, in turn, knows that "to him, a wife would only be another piece of property." In her college courses, she feels set apart from the other students because of her drab pushcart wardrobe and her overemotional ways, but she manages to graduate, even winning an important prize.

As a public school teacher Sara rents a spare, clean, bright room and marvels at her distance from her childhood tenement existence. When her mother dies, however, Sara is once again thrown into combat with her father, who takes as a second wife a woman who makes him miserable.

Hugo Seelig, the principal of Sara's school, tries to help Sara with her domestic difficulties. He, too, is an immigrant, from a Polish village not far from the Smolinskys'. Seelig is drawn to Sara's resilience and inner strength, and reminds her that "it's from [your father] you got the iron for the fight you had to make to be what you are now." He understands Reb Smolinsky; when he and Sara decide to marry, he wants to bring the old man into their household. Although Seelig has helped Sara to a new awareness of the importance of her ancestry, her father's tyrannical teachings, based on the most patriarchal interpretation of Judaism, make true reconciliation with him impossible. As the novel closes, Sara Smolinsky feels herself caught between two cultures, the Old World and the New, and it seems clear that she will never find peace.

Snell, Balso. *The Dream Life of Balso Snell.* Nathanael West. 1931.

Balso Snell is a picaresque hero on a surrealistic dream journey in this burlesque of the epics of Dante and Homer. Aspects of the modern spirit such as science and scholarship, religion, romance, and, most forcibly, art are personified and satirized with black scatological humor.

Balso, identified as a poet, begins his bizarre journey on the plains of Troy where he sights Homer's wooden horse. He enters it through the *Anus Mirabilis* and meets a guide in the large intestine. When the man attempts discussions on art, however, Balso deserts him, explaining that "art is not nature, but rather nature digested. Art is a sublime excrement." Further along the intestine he meets a Catholic mystic, Maloney the Areopagite, who is attempting to crucify himself with thumbtacks. Maloney relates the tale of Saint Puce, a flea who lived on the body of Christ. Maloney is reduced to devotional weeping, and Balso advises him, "Take your eyes off your navel.... Stop sniffing mortality. Play games... eat more meat."

Next, Balso finds a secret crime journal signed "John Gilson, Class 8B, P.S. 186, Miss McGeeney, teacher." In it a super-sensitive library worker murders a man for his peculiar laugh. As Balso finishes reading, the twelve-year-old author appears and explains that he writes only in order to impress and seduce women. He sells Balso a pamphlet that describes a love affair. The hero of the story was at first convinced that he was a rare spirit and expressed his innermost self to the girl; then, to avoid sameness, he employed art in his confessions; finally, fevered by his overwrought imagination, he began to beat her. The author calls this a parable of the artist and his audience. He envisions the day when his drama will enthrall the most discriminating audience and "the ceiling of the theater will be made to open and cover the occupants with tons of loose excrement." Balso travels on and meets Miss McGeeney, who is writing the biography of the biographer of the biographer of Boswell.

Wearied, Balso takes a nap and dreams. He is in Carnegie Hall surrounded by disabled girls who sublimate their needs through art. He tries to seduce a beautiful hunchback. She shows him two letters from the man who jilted her, Beagle Darwin. The letters are scenarios of what might have been had he taken her with him. She, pregnant and unmarried, commits suicide. After her death Balso turns his remorse into art by composing a tragedy with himself as hero.

Balso awakes from his nap. Miss McGeeney is there, and she says she is the author of what he has dreamed. Suddenly they recognize each other as long lost sweethearts. He seduces her by arguing that pleasure is good for its own sake and that writers have to experience it to write. In the final scene Balso's orgasm is likened to death: "His body broke free from the bard."

Snopes, Abner. "Barn Burning"; *The Hamlet.* William Faulkner. 1939; 1940.

Abner Snopes, father of Colonel Sartoris "Sarty" Snopes and Flem Snopes, is a lawless and fiercely independent man. He enlists during the Civil War, not in order to fight but to have access to booty on both sides. He later travels with his young family from farm to farm. They work in one location for a short time, then move on. Ab moves through life with no regard for his fellow humans and with no respect for their right to material possessions. He burns barns out of hatred toward others, to show that he is totally beyond the law.

After being acquitted of one barn burning due to a lack of hard evidence, Ab, who wears a black coat and walks with a limp because he was once shot for stealing a horse, travels with his family to the property of Major de Spain. Ordering his family to unload the wagon, he takes young Colonel Sartoris with him to the de Spain house where he intends to have a word with the man he thinks will own him "body and soul" for the next eight months. Stepping deliberately in a pile of horse manure, Snopes pushes his way past de Spain's dignified black servant and walks into the house, spreading manure all over the entrance hall rug.

Furious, Major de Spain orders Snopes to clean the rug. Snopes's daughters scrub it with homemade lye soap; when they are finished, the soiled spots have been bleached, and the rug is ruined. Snopes rolls up the rug, tosses it over the back of his mule, rides back to de Spain's house, throws the rug disrespectfully on the front porch, and leaves. The Major fines Snopes twenty bushels of corn for the damage.

In the Justice of the Peace's court, Sartoris, who does not know they have come to discuss the rug question, starts to defend his father by saying "he ain't done it! He ain't burnt . . ." Snopes, already sensing that his son has conflicting feelings toward him, abruptly orders the boy to wait for him in the wagon. The judge reduces Snopes's fine to ten bushels, but Snopes tells his sons he will not pay anything.

That night Snopes pours kerosene into a five-gallon can in ritualistic preparation for his next act of arson. He shoves his wife away when she tugs at his arm and tries to restrain him. Intending to guard against Sartoris's betrayal, he picks up his son by the back of the shirt and hands him to his wife. He orders her to hold on to him and not let him run away. After Snopes leaves the house with his older son and the can of kerosene, Sartoris escapes from his mother and runs to the house of Major de Spain. The Major, informed by Sartoris of the danger, finds Snopes and his other son and shoots them before they can burn his barn.

Snopes, Colonel Sartoris "Sarty." "Barn Burning"; *The Hamlet.* William Faulkner. 1939; 1940.

Colonel Sartoris Snopes, usually referred to as "Sarty" or "the boy," is the younger son of the amoral ABNER "AB" SNOPES. Caught between his role as an obedient, loyal son and his sense of right and wrong, Sarty silently stands by while his father burns the barns of landowners—until one day his instincts propel him to act, and he makes a bold decision to uphold justice and free himself from the tyranny of his father.

Sarty crouches on a keg in the back of a country store where a Justice of the Peace's court is held and listens as his father is accused of burning the barn of a local man named Harris. Feeling a desperate but fierce loyalty, he forces himself to think of Harris as his own enemy as well as his father's. When Harris and the judge consider calling him to the witness stand, Sarty, terrified and speechless, knows his father expects him to lie. But the boy is not called, and because Harris can produce only circumstantial evidence, Snopes is acquitted. The judge orders him to leave town and never return again.

The Snopes family moves on in its covered wagon, and Sarty tries to stop himself from thinking bad thoughts about his father. That night when the family stops to camp out, Abner Snopes aggressively asks Sarty if he intended to tell the judge the truth. Sarty doesn't answer, and his father hits him, saying he must learn to stick by his own blood.

In the morning they arrive at a two-room house on the property of Major de Spain. Planning to harvest the Major's corn to earn some money, they unload their belongings, and Sarty goes with his father to the Major's house. When he sees the house, Sarty is awed. Its grandeur makes him forget about his father and the terror and despair he constantly feels, and he idealistically believes that people whose lives are part of such peace and dignity must be beyond his father's destructive touch. But he watches a few minutes later as his father deliberately steps in horse manure and forces his way into the de Spain house, spreading manure all over the entrance hall rug.

Following the Major's orders, Sarty's two sisters scrub the soiled rug, but when they finish, the washed areas have bleached, and the rug is ruined. Furious, the Major demands twenty bushels of corn to pay for the damage. Sarty, still trying hard to remain loyal, feels hopeful that his father will change and that the grief he feels from being pulled in two directions will end.

Snopes's fine is reduced to ten bushels, but he declares to his sons that the Major won't get even one bushel. At sunset Sarty sees his father pouring kerosene into a five-gallon can and knows he is about to commit another barn burning. Abner Snopes, who no longer trusts his younger son, tells his wife to hold on to Sarty and not let him escape. After Abner leaves the house, Sarty manages to get free and runs to Major de Spain's house, yelling "Barn! Barn!" to warn them. As he runs away Sarty hears one gunshot, then two. He cries out to his father but continues to flee. At midnight he rests on the crest of a hill and thinks of his father, whispering that he was a brave man.

As a chorus of whippoorwills sings in the forest below him, he walks down the hill toward the dark woods without looking back.

Snopes, Eula Varner. *The Hamlet; The Town; The Mansion.* William Faulkner. 1940; 1957; 1959.

Eula Varner Snopes, the daughter of Mississippi landowner WILL VARNER, possesses a beauty so ravishing that it transforms her into a mythical being comparable to Helen of Troy. Even as a child in the hamlet of Frenchman's Bend, Mississippi, Eula exerts a strange power over people and effortlessly becomes the town's "centrice." But her influence over men never extends to her impotent husband FLEM SNOPES, the most successful member of a greedy and malevolent clan of country people. It is with Flem and her only child LINDA (SNOPES KOHL) that Eula lives her adult life as a doomed but masked woman whose inner state remains mysterious to those around her.

Like her father, Eula is incurably lazy; she spends her first eight years simply sitting. When she is eight, her brother Jody insists that she attend school. Eula refuses to go unless she does not have to walk, so Jody transports her on horseback. Jody, convinced that the eyes of men are always on Eula, grows increasingly jealous and suspicious as she matures. The young schoolteacher, Labove, becomes obsessed with her and stays in town several years longer than he intended because he is mad with desire for her. One day after school Labove tries to seduce Eula but fails. Afterward he spends several hours in terror, thinking Jody will pursue him with a gun. When he learns later that Eula has not even mentioned the incident to Jody, he leaves Frenchman's Bend without giving any notice, and the school abruptly shuts down.

Eula is fourteen years old at the time, the serene center of a group of noisy, pushy admirers. A few years later her serious suitors have narrowed themselves down to three young men who take turns visiting her. One of them, Hoake McCarron, slowly evolves into Eula's favorite. The young men of the town, believing that Eula's innocence and good reputation must be protected, attack McCarron while he and Eula are driving together in a buggy. Eula takes McCarron to her home; after Varner sets McCarron's broken arm and goes to bed, Eula and McCarron go out to the veranda and make love.

Eula conceives a child, but by the time her pregnancy is discovered, all three of her suitors have left town. To save her honor, Will Varner buys a marriage certificate for Eula and the cold and ambitious Flem Snopes, who has been clerking in Varner's store since Eula was twelve and living in the Varner house almost as long. The Snopeses have their honeymoon in Texas and return home after a year with their daughter Linda.

Eula and Flem take up residence in Jefferson, a small town near Frenchman's Bend, where Flem owns a small restaurant. While Flem, who is impotent, rises from power plant supervisor to bank vice president, Eula carries on an affair with Manfred de Spain, former mayor and now bank president. GAVIN STEVENS, the county attorney, comes forward as a rival for Eula's affection, but he eventually refuses her because he believes she acts only out of pity.

When Linda reaches adolescence, Gavin turns his attention to her and away from her mother. He visits Eula and threatens to reveal to Linda that she is McCarron's illegitimate child if Eula does not consent to send Linda away from Jefferson to college. Eula insists that it is Flem's decision to keep Linda in Jefferson. Seeing no other solution, Eula urges Gavin to marry her daughter, but Gavin views this as a way of entrapping rather than liberating Linda. Eventually, Flem changes his mind and allows Linda to attend college in Oxford, Mississippi.

One day when Linda is away at school, Flem secretly visits Will Varner, who holds the controlling portion of stock in the bank where Flem is vice president. Flem uses the fact of Eula's affair with de Spain and a will Linda had drawn up leaving her portion of Varner's inheritance to Flem as a means to convince Varner to oust de Spain and make Flem president. Outraged, Varner storms into Eula's home the following morning. Later that day Eula visits Gavin Stevens, tells him that she will leave Jefferson with de Spain, and demands a promise that he will take care of Linda and marry her if necessary for her happiness. He agrees. But at nine that evening, Eula commits suicide. Gavin, in anguished disbelief after her death, meditates on the reason. In a sense, he thinks, she was bored; she had love to give but had tried and failed twice to find a man who fully deserved or could accept it.

Snopes, Flem. *The Hamlet; The Town; The Mansion.* William Faulkner. 1940; 1957; 1959.

Flem Snopes's cold, persistent rapacity enables him to rise from dirt farmer to bank president within the span of forty years. Once Flem comes to understand the sacredness of money, he disregards all human values in order to obtain it. He eliminates all who stand in his way until he has firmly established himself as the most powerful man in Jefferson, Mississippi. Flem's ruthless quest for power, influence, and respectability leaves behind many victims—including those responsible for his final destruction.

Flem first arrives in Yoknapatawpha County to farm on the plot his father, barn burner ABNER "AB" SNOPES, rents from WILL VARNER, the big landowner in the hamlet of Frenchman's Bend. Varner's son Jody agrees to hire Flem to work in their general store, with the agreement that Ab will refrain from arson as long as his son can wear a white shirt and a tie to work. Before long, Flem has replaced Jody as Varner's right-hand man. Flem moves into the Varner house, and when Varner's daughter EULA VARNER (SNOPES) becomes pregnant by another man, Flem agrees to marry her. For saving her honor he receives as dowry Varner's crumbling mansion, the Old Frenchman's place. Flem plants a fake "treasure" on the property and promptly tricks three men into buying the worthless land.

When a relative, MINK SNOPES, is convicted of murder, Flem deliberately fails to put up the bond, wanting to banish Mink from his society. Mink is sentenced to life in Parchman prison.

Flem and Eula return from a year-long honeymoon in Texas with their daughter LINDA (SNOPES KOHL) and move to Jefferson, a neighboring town, where Flem co-owns a small restaurant. Soon the ambitious Flem is appointed superintendent of the power plant. Two years later he takes another step up when Manfred de Spain resigns from his position as mayor of Jefferson and becomes president of the only other bank in town. Because Will Varner controls most of the stock at the bank, de Spain makes Flem vice president.

In the meantime, everyone in town knows that de Spain is having an affair with Flem's wife Eula. The more acute observers know that Linda was conceived before their marriage and guess correctly that Flem is impotent. Flem remains silent and passive about Eula's affair; he appears to be holding on to his knowledge for some special purpose.

In contrast to the peculiar freedom he allows his wife, Flem controls his daughter with an iron hand. Because of the terms of Varner's will, Flem can obtain no inheritance from him if Linda marries. When Linda approaches high school graduation, a battle erupts over whether or not she will be allowed to go away to college. Flem resists for over a year and then suddenly allows her to attend college in Oxford, Mississippi. Soon afterward Flem receives another will, from Linda in Oxford, in which she relinquishes her inheritance to him. Flem takes this will to Varner's home and informs Varner that Eula is having an affair with de Spain. Varner storms into their house the following morning, and Eula commits suicide that evening. De Spain leaves town after the funeral, and Flem replaces him as bank president and eventually moves into de Spain's mansion.

Having achieved his desired financial position, Flem concentrates on attaining social respectability. He begins ridding the town of his numerous disreputable or unseemly relatives. When Montgomery Ward Snopes sets up a pornographic night show in Jefferson, Flem underhandedly causes him to be arrested, and he is sentenced to two years in Parchman prison. For a price, Flem then uses Montgomery Ward to trick MINK SNOPES into attempting escape, which adds another twenty years to Mink's sentence. Flem drives out another relative—I. O. Snopes, who is under suspicion for arson—by paying him to move back to Frenchman's Bend. WALLSTREET PANIC SNOPES, who runs a reputable wholesale business, is the only Snopes allowed by Flem to remain.

Linda enables Mink, by far the most dangerous Snopes, to return to Jefferson. With the help of her friend, the county attorney GAVIN STEVENS, she obtains a pardon for Mink, and he is released from Parchman. A few days after his release Mink stands before Flem in Flem's house and shoots him. Flem might have escaped between the first blank shot and the second, live one, but instead he sits motionless and allows himself to be killed. A friend tells the incredulous Gavin Stevens that perhaps Flem had a certain sense of fairness after all; in accepting his fate, he may have been giving Linda and Mink a chance to avenge themselves on him.

Snopes, Mink. *The Hamlet; The Town; The Mansion.* William Faulkner. 1940; 1957; 1959.

When he is arrested for shooting a man, Mink Snopes, a stubborn, proud, belligerent farmer, expects his wealthier cousin FLEM SNOPES to post bail. But Flem is glad to be rid of Mink, whom he considers a nuisance. Nearly forty years later, Mink leaves prison and takes revenge on his sneaky relative.

Mink arrives in Frenchman's Bend, Mississippi, with the first wave of the Snopes invasion. He brings his wife and two daughters, rents a ramshackle house and a small farm from WILL VARNER, and almost immediately becomes entangled in a feud with the ever-conspiring Flem. It begins when Mink pays VLADIMIR KYRILYTCH RATLIFF, the sewing-machine agent, with an IOU for ten dollars, to be paid by Flem, an act that implies a wealthy man should be more generous with his poor relatives.

While Flem is away in Texas on his honeymoon, Mink becomes involved in another disagreement with Jack Houston, his comparatively wealthy neighbor, who is almost as irascible as Mink himself. Mink allows his dry and emaciated cow to wander onto Houston's property, and when Houston orders him to remove it, Mink claims that he sold it to someone else. The cow spends the winter among Houston's fat, healthy cows, eating the quality feed he provides for them. Mink then brings a rope to collect the cow, telling him that the cow was his again, but Houston refuses to let Mink take her since she is now worth much more than the few dollars he offers to pay.

To settle the argument, Will Varner, the justice of the peace, the town constable, and two professional cattle buyers are called in. They decide Mink must pay Houston $18.75 for the cow, and Houston hires him at fifty cents a day to fence in a new pasture so that he can work it off. Mink works almost uninterruptedly between Houston's pasture and his own farm until the cow is paid off. Houston then claims he owed another dollar "pound fee" since the cow remained on his property for an extra day. It is for this extra dollar, and not for the thirty-seven days he worked on Houston's property, that Mink shoots Houston. Mink is arrested and taken to Jefferson, and while awaiting trial, he calls out to passers-by on the street, telling them to contact Flem Snopes for him. Even in the courtroom Mink remains convinced that Flem will appear to rescue him, and he keeps his eyes on the door.

Mink is sentenced to life in Parchman prison. He learns from his lawyer that if he behaves well and does not try to escape, he will be eligible for parole in twenty years. After fifteen years, Flem manages to send another relative, Montgomery Ward Snopes, to Parchman in order to trick Mink into attempting escape. Mink is easily caught, and another twenty years are added to his sentence. Mink is on his best behavior after this and once even risks his own life to prevent an escape attempt.

After thirty-eight years in prison, Flem's legal daughter, LINDA SNOPES KOHL, obtains a pardon for Mink. In exchange for the pardon and an impressive sum of money, Mink must agree to leave Mississippi before sundown and never return. Mink agrees but hands the money to the trustee before leaving and therefore considers himself free to stay. He hitchhikes to Memphis where he buys a rusty pistol in a pawnshop and then makes his way to Jefferson. He finds Flem in his mansion, sitting in a chair. Mink confronts him, fires one blank shot, then a real bullet, killing Flem.

Two men, friends of Linda Kohl's, find Mink later in a temporary roadside hiding place and again offer him money on condition that he leave the state. Mink accepts. Linda is probably happy to be rid of Flem, who was preventing her from marrying.

As the book ends, Mink lies down facing east and waits for sleep to overtake him; he is rejoicing in his newfound freedom and in the thought that when dawn comes, he will move on.

Snopes, Wallstreet Panic. *The Hamlet; The Town; The Mansion.* William Faulkner. 1940; 1957; 1959.

Wallstreet Panic Snopes is the representative member of an unusual branch of the Snopes family. Wallstreet's more typical relative, Montgomery Ward Snopes, observes that the Snopeses are a "species of pure sons of bitches." He also believes, however, that Wallstreet's father, Eck, was an illegitimate child, and although he is a true "son of a bitch," he is not a true Snopes. Eck and his sons, Wallstreet Panic and Admiral Dewey, are honest and compassionate people, and, according to Montgomery, cannot be considered members of the Snopes clan.

Eck is sixteen when his son is born. His wife dies shortly afterward, so the child is left with his grandmother until Eck has settled in Frenchman's Bend with work as a blacksmith. Up to this point the boy has been called by his grandfather's name, but when he arrives in Frenchman's Bend, Eck names him Wallstreet Panic. He hopes that his

son might get rich like "the folks that run that Wallstreet panic."

After Eck breaks his neck in a strange accident, the family moves to Jefferson, a larger town nearby, where Eck eventually works as a night watchman for an oil tank. When Wallstreet finds out about the school in town, he insists on entering kindergarten even though he is already twelve. By Christmas of the first term, Wallstreet has moved up to the second grade where he receives special help from Vaiden Wyott, the second-grade teacher. Miss Wyott explains to him the meaning of "Wallstreet panic" and suggests he call himself just "Wall" because that was a good family name in Mississippi.

While making up two grades, Wall has a job in a little back-alley grocery store as a part-time clerk and errand boy. The following summer, while Miss Wyott is helping him pass the third grade, Wall gets a delivery route for a Memphis paper, and in the fall, for a Jackson paper. After this, anyone who wants handbills passed out goes to Wall Snopes, who already has several boys working for him.

When Wall is sixteen, his father dies in an oil tank explosion. With the $2,000 she receives as compensation, Mrs. Snopes buys a half-interest in the store where Wall works and makes him a partner. When he is nineteen, the owner sells Mrs. Snopes the other half of the store and retires. Although Wall is only nineteen and the store is not yet in his name, he is clearly the person in charge.

On the last day of school, while they are standing in the schoolyard, Wall asks Vaiden Wyott to marry him. She bursts into tears, explaining that she is already engaged; however, within the week she introduces him to the small, fierce woman whom Wall eventually marries. The new Mrs. Snopes has a violent hatred for FLEM SNOPES, Wall's powerful uncle, and disdain for all the Snopeses outside Wall's immediate family. She feels a calling to live down the Snopes reputation and "purify" its name.

When, some time later, Wall overbuys his stock and urgently needs financial help, he considers taking a personal loan from Flem. Mrs. Snopes insists that he refuse, and fortunately a salesman named VLADIMIR KYRILYTCH RATLIFF comes forward with enough money to save the business. Wallstreet makes Ratliff a partner, and they expand the shop into a wholesale company. While the other Snopeses continue to exist by cheating and manipulating others, Wallstreet thrives on "simple honesty and industry."

Snow White. *Snow White.* Donald Barthelme. 1965.

Snow White is the title character of this modern-day satire of the classic fairy tale. A twenty-two-year-old beauty with jet black hair and ivory skin, Snow White is well versed in subjects such as psychology, the modern woman, poetry, painting, and Italian novels. At the novel's opening, she has been discovered wandering lost and hungry in the woods by the seven "dwarves": Bill, Dan, Henry, Hubert, Edward, Kevin, and Clem. They take her to live with them as a "housekeeper," although she is also sexually involved with each of them. Snow White worries about her reputation, believing their neighbors will not be fooled by their ruse.

Snow White is racked with boredom, dissatisfaction, and longing. She loves the "dwarves" but feels incomplete. She waits desperately for a "prince" to appear and provide her life with the meaning she feels it has been lacking. Snow White soon finds her escape in a family friend, Paul. When Paul enters a monastery, she is unable to deal with her pain and ennui. She positions herself in a window of the dwarves' house and dangles her four-foot-long black hair out of the window in order to attract attention. For days she remains this way, refusing to cook, clean, or sleep with the men.

At last Snow White is visited by Jane, the evil stepmother figure. Jane's personality is dominated by malice, and when she learns that her lover fancies Snow White, Jane decides to take out her frustration on the raven-haired beauty. She offers Snow White a poisoned vodka Gibson; but at the last minute Paul, on leave from the monastery, grabs the drink from Snow White's hand. The book leaves Snow White placing chrysanthemums on his grave while the seven men "depart in search of a new principle."

Soames, Henry. *Nickel Mountain: A Pastoral Novel.* John Gardner. 1963.

Henry Soames is the aging proprietor of the Stop-off diner in the farming community centered around a town named Slater in upstate New York. At the novel's beginning in 1954, Henry is in his fifties. He has a weak heart and thinks about death while biding his time anxiously in the diner. But Henry's life is changed when he hires Calliope Wells, a local girl, as a waitress.

Henry is given to late-night bouts of nonstop talking, raving about the human condition and his love for it, and people have begun to wonder about his stability. Alone most of the time, he preserves a fierce attachment to the truckers and farmers who come into the diner. He contemplates the truck drivers he has known who have jackknifed on the highway nearby. He thinks about his father, now dead of a heart attack, who would read poetry to himself and weep. Henry has a similar sensibility but no comparable outlet.

Callie is the daughter of Henry's first love, Eleanor, and a country girl of Welsh stock. He hires her out of sentimentality. She dates a local boy, Willard Freund, the son of the wealthiest merchant in Slater. As Willard is about to leave to go to Cornell, Callie learns she is pregnant. Willard leaves nonetheless. Henry attempts to marry Callie off to a friend named George Loomis, but in his muddled pleas to George he reveals his own love for her. Callie agrees to marry Henry.

The child, James Soames, is born after three days of labor. In the interim Henry is tormented by Callie's hysterical screams of pain. He feels that she does not love him. The physician, Doc Cathey, is disgusted at Henry's tenderness—"You'd think it was the first brat born on earth"—and George, also on hand, is likewise uneasy with Henry's devotion. The reader learns that George's emotional detachment arises from his Korean War trauma as well as from a farming accident that took off his right arm. George has become a collector of things—*National Geographic*s, paperweights, spinning wheels, items from country auctions—and repeatedly attempts to explain to Henry the nature of value. Henry, who is not a materialist, maintains a faith in his new family.

When a hotel clerk from town, Simon Bale, is burned out of his house and loses his wife, Henry takes him in, although the two men hardly know each other. Simon, a badly groomed, obnoxious Jehovah's Witness, harasses Henry's customers with pamphlets and argues with George over the existence of God. But two-year-old Jimmy takes to him, and Simon begins to proselytize to the child about repentance. Henry is kind to Simon; he pays for the funeral of Simon's wife and defends him in front of the sheriff against charges of arson. Simon, essentially a lunatic, is unmoved. One day Henry finds Jimmy cowering in his room, and when Simon approaches, Jimmy screams, "It's the devil!" Simon flees, and in his retreat he falls down the stairs and is killed. Henry, plagued by guilt, eats constantly; he is attempting slow suicide by gaining excessive weight, which will strain his heart.

Willard Freund returns from college. He is ashamed of his poor treatment of Callie and, seeing her and Henry in the general store, runs off down the highway. Henry follows him and betrays no anger, only good-natured forgiveness. When Henry takes Jimmy with him on errands a few days later, they meet an old couple at the cemetery exhuming their son's body; their rage and grief, many years after the death, tires Henry, but he is as patient with their hysteria as he had been with Willard. He reflects that "a bad heart is the beginning of wisdom." Hoping for a chance to rest, Henry leads Jimmy home.

Son. *Tar Baby.* Toni Morrison. 1981.

Son flouts his rebellious attitudes toward American society and its capitalist ideals. Born and raised in Eloe, a tiny town in southern Florida, Son values the fraternity that he felt among its black inhabitants and that he alone, of all the American blacks in the novel, finds present among the islanders in the Caribbean. A veteran of the Vietnam War, Son believes that money-hungry American society destroys the sense of community with which he was raised and, with it, the integrity of all who participate.

As a result, when Son is charged with murder, he simply leaves the country to spend eight years in exile. His "crime" was a crime of passion: Finding his wife Cheyenne in bed with a teenage boy, Son drove his car through the tiny house, setting it on fire. He managed to rescue his wife's lover, but Cheyenne died of her burns. Soon afterward Son boarded a ship and fled the country.

For eight years Son works as a hand on ships, reads about the United States in foreign papers, and feels lucky to have escaped the blood-thirsty country. Eventually he leaves the ship and inadvertently finds himself on a private island called the Isle des Chevaliers. Starving, he sneaks into a mansion and takes food from the kitchen after the occupants have retired. When he finally ventures to look into the other rooms, Son, a one-time jazz pianist, discovers the piano and decides to stay. He also finds the bedroom of the Streets' part-time social secretary, JADINE CHILDS, an extremely beautiful young black American. For many nights he crouches in the darkness of Jadine's room, watching her sleep and turning her dreams toward himself. He slips out just before dawn. One day, however, he remains during the daylight hours and is caught hiding in a closet.

Son expects to be turned over to the police. Instead, the cordial white aristocratic master of the house, Valerian Street, offers him a drink and invites him to stay for dinner. Although still caked with dirt, Son spends the night in the Streets' elegant guest room and wears a pair of Valerian's silk pajamas to bed. The following morning he goes to Jadine's room, but because he has watched her for so long, he already knows that he cannot afford to frighten her away. During their first conversation, in order to arouse an emotional response from her, he deliberately insults her until she is infuriated and leaves the room.

The following day Son invites Jadine for a picnic on the beach, and the hostile but erotic banter between them continues. Soon afterward, during Christmas dinner, Son impresses Jadine by standing up to Valerian in a family argument; they then become accomplices. Son borrows a passport and flies to New York City, where he waits in a hotel for Jadine. They spend several blissful months together, so engrossed in each other that they barely notice anyone else.

The harmony between them is destroyed when they visit Eloe, where their opposing values and backgrounds clash. Son is welcomed back by his circle of friends and family, while Jadine, feeling alone, sees only poverty and ignorance in the town. When Jadine goes back to New York to work as a model, Son remains behind several days longer than he had promised.

Finally returning to New York, Son continues to insist on the importance of Eloe and the ideas it symbolizes for him. Jadine argues that Son's sentimentality about his hometown is naive and narrow-minded. He should prepare himself for work outside Eloe, she says, in a city where she can also find jobs. Their arguments escalate into physical violence, and Jadine disappears.

Alone in the apartment, waiting for her return, Son can only sit very still while looking at the photographs Jadine took of Eloe. Closely examining the pictures, he slowly begins to see Eloe through Jadine's eyes, and he decides to seek her out. Returning to the islands, he is told by his Caribbean friends Gideon and Thérèse that Jadine has left. "Forget her," Thérèse advises. "She has forgotten her ancient properties." Urged to seek the mythical men who are "waiting in the hills" for him, Son disembarks from Thérèse's launch on the private Isle des Chevaliers and crawls, then runs, across the rocks and into the woods.

Sonny. "Sonny's Blues." James Baldwin. 1957.

As Sonny's story opens, the narrator, who is his older brother and a schoolteacher, reads of Sonny's arrest in a newspaper. He is immediately shocked and angry, and he feels guilty for the turn of events in Sonny's life. Sonny, a jazz musician and heroin addict, has been arrested on charges related to his addiction. As the narrator continues, it becomes clear that he is trying in some way to piece together and understand the causes and consequences of his brother's drug use.

The brothers, seven years apart in age, grew up in Harlem, facing poverty and racism. Their paternal uncle, as they learned well after the fact, was run down and killed by a carload of drunken white men. Although the older brother eventually becomes a teacher, he was faced after their mother's death with the task of attempting to finish Sonny's upbringing. But while he was in the army, he had to leave Sonny in the care of his wife Isabel and her family.

Sonny's interest in music is at first encouraged by the family, but his obsession with music eventually leads him to hours of repetitive and loud playing, and to drop out of high school. His family tries to discourage him, and in response Sonny flees the house, taking all his records. He moves to Greenwich Village, where he has been "sitting in" with bands instead of going to school, and then abruptly joins the Navy.

Following his hitch in the Navy, Sonny returns to Greenwich Village to resume his career as a musician. The brothers have one awkward encounter that leads to an abrupt severing of communication, and the two do not meet again until Sonny's release from jail. By this time his brother has written to him to inform him of the death by polio of Sonny's young niece, his brother's daughter Grace. Sorrow draws the brothers together, but the relationship is still tenuous when Sonny goes to live with the narrator and Isabel and their two surviving children.

After his release Sonny gradually begins to "sit in with a few guys." However, the issue of heroin, especially given its popularity among musicians, continues to trouble both Sonny and his brother. Sonny describes how heroin made him feel and why he thinks people use it: "to keep from shaking to pieces." He does not assert that he is completely cured, but during the time of the story at least, he seems to have kicked the habit.

The story concludes with Sonny's invitation to his brother to hear him play in the Village. The narrator does go to the Village, and despite an initial lack of understanding, he begins to empathize with his brother's plight and to respect Sonny's genius as he hears and feels the strength in Sonny's performance. During the final scene, the narrator describes Sonny's tremendous and exciting grappling with the intricacies of his improvisational rendition of the blues classic "Am I Blue?"

Sowerby, Dickon. *The Secret Garden.* Frances Hodgson Burnett. 1911.

Dickon Sowerby, a gentle Yorkshire boy, has the power to charm animals and people. He spends his days on the Yorkshire moor where he makes friends with sick and injured animals and tends his mother's garden. When a frail and "contrary" child brought up in India, MARY LENNOX, is brought to Misselthwaite Manor, the nearby estate where his sister works as a maid, Dickon finds an unusual companion and pupil.

Dickon is first introduced to Mary by his sister Martha, who brings the child her meals. Mary is used to being waited on and is too lazy to go outside even though there is nothing for her to do in the house. After Martha persuades Mary to explore the grounds around the house, Dickon receives a letter from the little girl asking him to bring his tools to a secret garden she has found. When Dickon arrives with the tools and his two tame squirrels, he escorts Mary through the garden and instructs her on how to tend the plants.

Dickon and Mary meet daily in the garden and work hard so that all the flowers will have room to grow. Mary discovers another secret in Misselthwaite Manor: Colin Craven, the young son of Mr. Craven, master of the house. Colin has been confined to bed since infancy, when his mother died. Colin, although usually as sour as Mary once was, is also enchanted by stories of Dickon and wants to meet him.

The doctor gives permission for Dickon to wheel Colin in his chair out to the park, where they safely disappear into the secret garden. Besides instructing them in gardening, Dickon teaches his friends some exercises he learned from a boxer. Dickon's mother, Susan Sowerby, gives him eggs, potatoes, and fresh rolls to bring to the garden. Because of these gifts, Colin can continue to refuse the meals made for him at the mansion and keeps his recovery secret until Mr. Craven returns from his trip.

Dickon provides inspiration for both Mary and Colin as they grow stronger. They regard him as possessing a kind of "magic" that enables Colin to walk a little farther every day and eventually to become as strong as Dickon himself. When Mr. Craven returns, they reveal the secret of his recovery and welcome him into the garden, which they have brought back to life with Dickon's help.

Spade, Sam. *The Maltese Falcon.* Dashiell Hammett. 1930.

The quintessential hard-boiled detective, Sam Spade, a private investigator in San Francisco in the 1920s, becomes caught in a web of intrigue following the murder of his partner, Miles Archer. At times wildly hot-tempered and at others cold and calculating, Sam ultimately reveals a practical code of justice that underlies his bitter cynicism about human nature.

The trouble begins when a beautiful woman who calls herself Miss Wonderly hires the partners to follow a man named Floyd Thursby. Miles takes the job and is found murdered later that night in Chinatown; Thursby's body is discovered thirty-five minutes later. Sam, who has no alibi for either crime, not only intensely disliked his late partner but was having an affair with Archer's wife, Iva. The police suspect him of one or both of the murders. Miss Wonderly, whose real name is Brigid O'Shaughnessy, contacts Sam again, and he agrees to help her even though he knows that she tells him nothing but lies. They soon become lovers.

Before long the detective enters into conflict with various shady characters involved in the case, including a devious Greek named Joel Cairo, a vicious young gunman named Wilmer Cook, and his obese employer, Casper Gutman, who is obsessed with "recovering" the statuette of a falcon, a priceless medieval artifact from Malta. With the help of his trustworthy secretary Effie Perine, Sam unscrupulously uses his wits to sort through the tangled history of his adversaries, often playing one partner in crime against another. He also manages to fend off the police, the local district attorney, and Miles's widow, all of whom he sees as threats to his freedom.

Sam gains possession of the statuette when the sea captain who had been hired by Brigid to transport it from Hong Kong shows up at the detective's office and falls dead on the spot, clutching the artifact. Brigid, motivated by greed and forced by circumstances to join forces with Gutman, Cairo, and Wilmer, attempts to lure Sam away from the falcon. She phones and pretends to be in mortal danger, leading the detective on a futile chase, but not before he deposits the treasure in a local station's parcel room and mails the check stub to his postal box. Brigid is waiting tearfully for Sam when he finally arrives home, but the others are waiting for him inside as well.

Sam bargains with Gutman for the price of the Maltese falcon, insisting as part of the deal that a fall guy be found to take the heat from the police. He suggests Wilmer as the logical candidate since he actually murdered Thursby and the sea captain. Gutman and Cairo eventually agree, albeit reluctantly, and the group waits until morning when Effie retrieves the falcon and delivers it to Sam. However, the statuette proves to be a worthless piece of lead. Sam returns all but $1,000 of the money Gutman had given him. Wilmer escapes, and Gutman and Cairo leave together to continue their quest for the authentic artifact. After calling the police to arrange for the arrest of the three departing cohorts, Sam must deal with his beautiful but treacherous lover.

The detective knows by now that Brigid shot Miles in order to frame her former partner Thursby for the murder, not aware at the time that Gutman had ordered Wilmer to shoot Thursby. Sam informs her that he intends to turn her over to the police, but she refuses to believe him at first because they are in love with each other. He acknowledges their mutual passion but brutally declares it irrelevant considering her history of betrayal. Sam's principles dictate that he do something about the murder of his partner even though he disliked the man. Wilmer, Cairo, and Brigid are arrested, but not before Wilmer kills Gutman for his treachery. Sam gives the money he had taken from Gutman to the police in order to avoid being implicated in the conspiracy.

The detective expresses absolutely no remorse for his actions at the conclusion of the case, but he turns pale when his secretary Effie, upset at what he did to Brigid, refuses to let him touch her. Iva, Miles's widow, arrives moments later, and Sam shivers as he tells Effie to send her in.

Spangler, Joseph. *The Human Comedy.* William Saroyan. 1943.

Joseph Spangler, manager of the telegraph office in the small town of Ithaca, California, carries a hard-boiled egg with him for good luck. The bemused way Spangler contemplates and cradles the simple egg is characteristic of the way he looks at the world. Gentle, kind, and generous, Spangler is a comforter and a protector of his fellow man.

Instructing HOMER MACAULEY, the new messenger, on how he should perform his job, Spangler tells the boy to be kind and polite, not to be afraid of people, and to be efficient. The instructions reflect Spangler's own ideas on how one should work and live. For instance, when a poor young man wants to send a telegram to his mother, Spangler instantly lends him the money to do so.

While running to pick up a telegram, Spangler sees a girl standing on the corner who seems to embody all the loneliness in the world. He stops for a moment to kiss her on the cheek, then goes on his way, feeling good about life and all the good people he meets. He later goes out for dinner and to a movie with his girlfriend Diana Steed and is pleased when she declares that she is certain he really loves her even though he has never said so.

Spangler is in a good mood at the office that night when the young man to whom he had lent the money comes in with a gun to rob the office. But when Spangler offers to give the boy all the money in the telegraph office, the robber explains that he does not really want it. He had come instead to see how Spangler would react to his threatening demand. Disgusted with the fear, anger, and

corruption that he saw in everyone he met, the man had been skeptical when Spangler first acted kindly toward him. He came back to be sure that Spangler was a good man. Seeing that Spangler is truly kindhearted makes the robber decide that he, too, can be an good member of society.

Driving in the country with Diana, who has become his fiancée, Spangler expresses his love for all things, including her. They pass by picnickers of different nationalities. Spangler describes each group flatteringly but calls the Americans the best because they mix all the separate nationalities together.

When he returns from his drive in the country, Spangler learns that the telegraph operator, William Grogan, has died of a heart attack. William died while typing a telegram announcing the death of a soldier, the brother of young Homer. Spangler goes for a walk with Homer. He eats the hard-boiled egg that he had carried as a good luck charm and listens to Homer's questions about the meaning of his brother's death. He tells Homer that he cannot comfort him but can only assure him that a good man like his brother lives on wherever there is love.

Spenser, Roderick. *Susan Lenox: Her Fall and Rise.* David Graham Phillips. 1917.

A kindhearted young journalist from a small Ohio town, Roderick Spenser meets and befriends SUSAN LENOX.

Spenser and Susan meet in the rustic setting of the Ohio River, where Susan is in hiding after fleeing a forced marriage. He is whistling "La Donna é Mobile," the Duke's song from *Rigoletto* on woman's fickle nature. Sizing up Susan's circumstances, he offers to help her by bringing her food and sneaking her into a hotel as his sister. He lends her money and then leaves for a few days, but he is eventually prevented from returning.

Years later when Susan has accumulated the money to repay him, she and Spenser are reunited at his Cincinnati newspaper office. Within hours they are in love. Spenser reveals his plan to move to New York to begin his career as a playwright and begs Susan to accompany him. They dwell in charmed quarters in New York for several weeks until the money runs out, Spenser cannot get his plays performed, and his cruel gibes about Susan's infidelity escalate. Before becoming Spenser's lover, Susan had once resorted to prostitution when her resources were exhausted and she wanted to pay a friend's medical bills. Spenser's knowledge of this episode embitters him and perverts his already archaic view of women's virtues. A libertine depressed by his lack of talent, he nonetheless holds Susan to higher standards, and when he drinks—which is regularly when his debts accumulate—he berates her for her past and accuses her of still being a prostitute.

Susan finally leaves Spenser. Unwilling to become a rich man's mistress—one of the few options available to her professionally—her own career languishes, and she ends up a prostitute and opium user in the Lower East Side tenements. Her determination to succeed is frustrated by the cycle of poverty, but when she finds Spenser passed out in a tavern, diseased, and filthy, her willingness to help him is a moral catalyst for her rise. Robert Brent, a successful playwright, selects her as the leading actress for his plays, and for her sake helps Spenser as well. Brent's attitude toward Susan contrasts sharply with Spenser's: He respects Susan's professionalism and has no interest in deriding her for her descent into poverty. Susan moves in with Spenser again, out of kindness rather than love, and this time their relationship is characterized by her autonomy rather than her submissiveness. Offered success by mysterious means, Spenser becomes profligate again.

Susan ultimately achieves economic independence through Brent, as the only heir to his fortune, and Spenser enjoys scattered theatrical successes. The novel concludes with a firm view of Susan's moral rise and a fading glance at Spenser on his way to a tavern.

Spotswood, Glenn. *Adventures of a Young Man.* John Dos Passos. 1939.

Glenn Spotswood lives a life completely centered around radical Left-wing politics. His political bent begins in his teenage years when, after his mother's tragic death, he gets a job as a camp counselor. He engages the youngsters in a game of Russian Revolution, Reds versus Whites, and is eventually fired from that job. He enters college and spends his summers as a migrant farm worker, hopping freight trains between jobs and staying in bedbug-ridden flophouses.

When invited by Mike Gulick, his sociology professor, to move to New York and enroll at Columbia University, Glenn accepts. He moves in with Gulick and his wife, for whom Glenn develops a great fondness. When he discovers she is having an affair, however, the disillusioned Glenn leaves and moves in with his Columbia friend, Boris Springarn, and his wife Gladys, an ardent communist.

Glenn then has an affair with the capricious Gladys and is crushed when she returns to her husband. Still suffering from the rejection, he vows that "the new Glenn Spotswood . . . [is] going on, without any private life, renouncing the capitalist world and its pomps." From that moment on he offers himself to the revolutionary working class.

Yet upon his graduation from college Glenn allows his family to arrange a comfortable job for him in a Texas bank. There he becomes involved with striking Mexican pecan shellers, loses his job, and is virtually run out of town. His efforts capture the interest of two Communist Party members who convince him to organize the illiterate coal miners of Slade County.

After an important meeting with the miners there, the local sheriffs appear with arrest warrants and announce that two local deputies have been killed in gunfire with miners. Glenn attempts to testify on behalf of the accused murderers, but they are convicted and one is later killed in a jail break attempt. Now considered a failure, Glenn is expelled from the Party.

Feeling almost totally isolated, he goes to fight in Spain. He cannot escape his past, however, and is accused of representing the Trotsky counterrevolution in America and aiding the Barcelona uprising. Faced with the prospect of imminent execution, Glenn confronts his life for the first time. Up until then he had thought that he didn't care about living, but now he realizes that he does not want to die. He wants instead to be free, "to go home." He languishes in jail and listens to the enemy's approach.

While heavy fighting is going on, Glenn is finally released, with the proviso that he carry water to the front lines. On the way he is hit by enemy fire and dies.

Spragg, Undine. *The Custom of the Country.* Edith Wharton. 1908.

Beautiful, petulant, and selfish, Undine Spragg is hopelessly spoiled by her parents and dreams only of furthering her social position. Considering herself buried in the isolated Midwest town of Apex, she bullies her wealthy parents into moving to New York City, whose social world she has read about all her life.

After two years in New York, Undine has made little headway into the social realms for which she yearns. But her fortunes change when she meets Ralph Marvell of the very old and prestigious Dagonet family in the city. Within weeks Undine has married Marvell and sailed for a honeymoon in Europe. Undine soon learns that the Dagonet name carries clout but not the finances she desires and needs in order to "go with" the country-hopping, party-going heavyweights of her circle.

Four years and an unwanted baby boy later, Undine, now possessed of an excellent pedigree but an insufficient cash flow, is determined to obtain the funds necessary to satisfy her needs. Attempting to cash in on a longtime flirtation with the wealthy Peter Van Degen, Undine files divorce proceedings against Ralph from Europe. Only after she divorces Ralph does Undine realize her mistake. Not only has Van Degen no intention of marrying her, but her status as a divorced woman has ostracized her from the New York social scene. She flees to Paris where she spends two years in isolation.

When she attracts the attention of Raymond de Chelles, a French nobleman, Undine is rescued from social exile. Determined to regain her lost prominence, she plots to marry the Marquis de Chelles. This time, however, she finds her way barred by the Catholic Church, which does not recognize divorce. Discovering that with enough money she can obtain an annulment of her marriage to Ralph, Undine schemes, because she is penniless herself, to extort the money from her former husband.

Although at the time of her divorce Undine was awarded custody of her son Paul, she has shown no interest in the child. Driven by greed, she threatens to take custody unless Ralph pays her $100,000. When he cannot raise the sum, Ralph kills himself. Undine receives custody of Paul along with control of his inheritance. Six months later she is the Marquise de Chelles.

Once again the socialite from Apex discovers she has married well socially but not financially. To her utter chagrin she sees the de Chelles capital being spent on the upkeep of the chateau and farmlands that she found so charming prior to her marriage. She is further frustrated when the Hôtel de Chelles, the fashionable Paris residence around which she planned to build her social empire, is turned over to the younger brother of the Marquis.

Not yet defeated, Undine turns to Elmer Moffatt, an old acquaintance from her Apex days. While at one time she would have avoided Moffatt at all costs, Undine now regrets her former harshness toward him. Moffatt has amassed a large fortune and gained a certain degree of social standing.

Several years later Undine has managed to disentangle herself from de Chelles in order to marry Moffatt. She appears to have "arrived," yet she remains dissatisfied with her status; she criticizes her husband for not obtaining an ambassadorship. The novel closes with Moffatt's brutally honest reply: The diplomatic service does not appoint "divorced ambassadresses."

Stahr, Monroe. *The Last Tycoon.* F. Scott Fitzgerald. 1941.

Monroe Stahr, the main character of this unfinished novel, is a young Jewish producer who initially is the epitome of success in Hollywood in the 1930s. Like JAY GATSBY of *The Great Gatsby*, Stahr is a romantic individualist, an innocent idealist surrounded by the corrupt pragmatists of Hollywood.

Unlike those around him, including his partner Brady, Stahr's concern is not for money, fame, or sensation but for the art of making movies. First and foremost, Stahr is an artist, and a brilliant one. He has risen to the top in Hollywood, not by blind ambition or shady deals but by the time-honored American qualities of hard work, integrity, and ingenuity.

A few years prior to the opening of the novel, Stahr's actress wife died, and since that time Stahr has been literally working himself to death. As a result of his grueling schedule, he has developed a heart condition and is expected to die within six months. Remaining aloof from personal attachments, Stahr fails to respond to the eager overtures of Cecilia Brady, his partner's daughter and the novel's narrator. He then meets Kathleen, who bears an uncanny resemblance to his dead wife. He and Kathleen fall instantly and passionately in love. However, when her fiancé arrives in Hollywood earlier than expected and in-

stantly marries her, Kathleen and Stahr must carry on their affair clandestinely.

At this point Fitzgerald's draft of the novel stops, but his notes and letters reveal his plans for the remainder of the novel. Stahr was to become disenchanted with Kathleen. Although his genuine love for her would eventually bring him back to her, he first rejects Kathleen largely because her lower-class background renders her unsuitable for his life-style but perhaps also because her husband was to be part of a plot against him organized by Brady.

Stahr and his partner, the unscrupulous Brady, have long been at cross-purposes, and their antagonism was to reach a climax toward the end of the novel. In order to defend his position in the industry and his ideals about how business should be conducted, Stahr would have supported the movement toward unionization brewing within the industry even though he is fundamentally opposed to the ideology of unionization that is gaining ground throughout the country. Stahr typifies the benevolent capitalist, the kindly but paternalistic employer who maintains that success is to be attained as he has attained it—by individual industry, ability, and inventiveness.

But Stahr's ideals would have been defeated in this novel. Intending to end the book with Stahr's death in a plane crash, Fitzgerald meant to indicate that the future of the motion picture industry would thereafter be dictated by men like Fleishacker, the ambitious, unscrupulous, and entirely uncreative company lawyer. The death of Stahr would symbolize the defeat of the artist and individualist by the corporate businessman.

Stais. "Gunner's Passage." Irwin Shaw. 1966.

Stais, a nineteen-year-old soldier, listens to his companions with the patience and wisdom of a much older man. Having just returned from a nearly fatal mission in Greece, he is too weak to move. With deep compassion Stais hears the stories of two other soldiers, one strangely altered by his experiences in the Air Force, the other waiting anxiously to be sent on his first mission.

Stais has already been sent on twenty-one missions before his plane is shot down in Greece. Out of seven men, Stais is one of three remaining soldiers who survived with injuries. The soldiers spend fourteen days in the Greek hills before they are discovered by a group of farmers who call for help. Three days later the rescue plane finally appears. It has rained so heavily, however, that the plane is bogged down in mud and cannot take off. The only solution is to hide the plane with branches and wait for the rain to stop. The farmers and the soldiers, who are so weak they can hardly stand, help to break off branches to hide the huge plane. The rain finally ceases, and the Greek farmers stand waving as the plane takes off. Only ten miles away the plane is fired on from a German camp but escapes harm.

After he recovers in a Cairo hospital, Stais is moved to

a base in Africa and then scheduled to fly home. In the intervals between Stais's dream-filled naps, he listens to Whitejack, a gunner and aerial photographer in a mapping and survey squadron. Whitejack talks of his mother's cooking, the Blue Ridge Mountains where he was in the forestry service, and his friends. When Whitejack describes it, America seems reassuringly near, although Stais has not been there for nineteen months. Whitejack seems astonishingly cheerful and at ease despite the fact that he has recently seen a plane carrying a close friend shot down and that Johnny Moffat, an airman who is to be his brother-in-law, is missing. Stais becomes very concerned about Moffat, although he does not speak to him.

Novak, a younger soldier who looks up to Stais as having "been through it," tells him the story of a relationship with a woman in Flushing, Long Island, which lasted the few weeks of his training course in aerial cameras. Novak seems to recognize the poignancy of the fact that this interval represents the high point of his experience with women. He continues to write to the woman, although she is now seeing a technical sergeant who is posted in Flushing. After interviewing Stais extensively on his mission in Greece, Novak shyly asks him and Whitejack if they have been afraid. Whitejack is scornful of the question, but Stais responds candidly.

Later that night Stais is told he will be leaving for home. Whitejack escorts Stais to the plane, gives him a slip of paper with his name written on it, and invites him to visit in North Carolina for a hunting trip. As Stais's plane begins its departure, another plane is landing: the missing plane from Whitejack's squadron, carrying Johnny Moffat. Stais sees the plane pull to a stop and momentarily is relieved of the guilt he feels for going home.

Stamper, Hank. *Sometimes a Great Notion.* Ken Kesey. 1964.

Hank Stamper is a logger known for his inhuman strength and impersonal relations with the people of his small Oregon town. He is the protector of the Stamper clan's logging business and the focus of his younger brother LEE STAMPER's hatred. Despite the changes that occur around him, Hank retains his detached stolidity.

Hank's feelings of isolation go back to his childhood when, despite his local fame as a great football player, he was without real friends. During his teenage years he began sleeping with his stepmother, Lee's mother. The affair ended when he joined the army. After serving in Korea he made a cross-country trip back to Oregon by motorcycle, and on the way he met his future wife Viv, a farmer's daughter from Colorado.

Upon returning to Oregon, Hank goes to work for his father's timber-cutting operation. He does so with cool determination and fierce independence. Although outwardly polite and friendly to the townspeople, he is indifferent to the interests of those around him. He mistrusts

those who are educated and liberal, although he acknowledges that he is not bright or learned enough to defend his knee-jerk conservatism.

When the workers of the local lumber mill go on strike, Hank further isolates himself by committing the Stampers to providing the mill with timber. As the people of the town turn against him, he becomes even more stubborn in his individualism. He handles the conflict with the community without showing any concern for the workers and families who have been hurt by the Stamper operation. At the same time he becomes estranged from Viv, who comes to realize through her brother-in-law Lee that staying with Hank has limited her experiences.

Throughout the ordeal, Hank remains in control, cunningly manipulating events to suit his own needs and remaining unmoved in his determination to succeed. When saboteurs wreck the saws at the mill the Stampers are using, Hank resourcefully uses the breakdown as an excuse to get the mill workers to help fell trees. When a local mountain of a man put out of his job by the Stamper operation picks a fight with Hank, he calmly accepts the challenge and fells the challenger. When he is jumped by hired thugs on a dark night, he is not dispirited by the beating but sticks to his resolve to meet the family's contract with the mill.

Eventually, though, Hank loses control. Many of the Stamper workers, influenced by Hank's lack of sympathy, give in to pressure from the community to quit. Thus the Stampers must try to meet their deadline with an undersized crew, and this causes an accident that leaves Hank's father's arm crushed and his uncle, Joe Ben, dead. Shortly afterward Hank discovers that Lee has had an affair with Viv. He responds by attacking Lee and further isolating himself from Viv.

The loss of Joe Ben at first leads Hank to concede that he will not be able to meet the mill contract. But seeing the union leader, a longtime rival, gloat over his victory drives Hank to continue working with an almost superhuman effort. He gathers his skeleton crew, rents a tugboat, and in the novel's last scene is joined by Lee in a last-ditch effort to take their logs down the rain-swelled river to the mill.

Stamper, Lee. *Sometimes a Great Notion.* Ken Kesey. 1964.

Lee Stamper is the weak, suicidal, pill-popping Yale student who returns to his native Oregon to seek vengeance on his half-brother HANK STAMPER. Lee is the youngest son of Henry Stamper, a sinewy old man whose motto is "Never give an inch!" But Lee is of a slightly different blood than the rest of the Stampers, for his mother, Henry Stamper's second wife, was a delicate easterner with social credentials. Hank, who is twelve years older, sparked Lee's rage at a young age when he began sleeping with Lee's mother. But Lee was sent off to school in the East before he could unleash his anger.

Lee's decision to return to Oregon comes after his failure as a student. Having adopted the pose of a self-destructive, suicidal intellectual, he is driven to Oregon not by his rage but by the fear that he will be arrested if he stays in New Haven. While he journeys westward, he fantasizes about destroying his older brother in a climactic conflict. As his bus reaches the Stamper house, he feels a deep-seated disgust for his heritage.

After years on the East Coast, the sight of the Stamper house is even more startling than Lee had expected. The house itself is beautiful, sitting on the other side of a rugged river like a white fortress. Yet the Stamper clan does not possess the majesty their house suggests. Lee finds his father's and older brother's brutal, primitive values contemptible but still watches in awe as his brother swims the powerful river current to meet him. Lee attempts to steer a boat across the river to the Stamper house and nearly proves too meek and incompetent for the task. When the brothers first meet, Lee eyes Hank menacingly, although he is hardly a match for the older Hank who is unimpressed by his brother's return from college.

Lee does not resign himself to being dominated by his overpowering brother but chooses instead to wait for an ideal time to strike. Submitting to the Stamper way of life, he goes to work on the family timber operation. The Stampers need his assistance because they are struggling to meet a contract with the local mill whose workers are on strike. Because of this, the family has become the object of scorn in the community. Lee does not sympathize with the union families who suffer as a result of the Stamper operation; instead, he shows the same ruthless pride and determination as his father and brother.

As he absorbs the Stamper chauvinism, Lee loses his pretentious self-image but still romanticizes his desire to destroy Hank. He also comes to see Hank as more complex than he had first believed. Hank is not a mere brute who can be subdued by blows; despite his outward machismo, he is a vulnerable man who loves his wife Viv deeply. Hoping to get Viv to leave Hank for him, Lee begins to woo her and eventually convinces himself that he is in love with her.

As Lee plans his conquest, the Stamper household is struck a serious blow. Working without Lee, the undermanned logging crew loses control of a huge log. The log crushes Henry's arm, and Joe Ben, the uncle of Hank and Lee, is pinned under the log and drowned. Yet Lee carries out his careful plan, and through the same peephole Lee had used to watch the young Hank having sex with his mother, Hank now observes the affair of his brother and his wife.

This incites Hank to attack Lee, and Lee hopes the attack will win him Viv's sympathy. Viv, however, spurns Lee. Undaunted, he decides to stay with the family rather than return to the East, and he joins Hank and the few remaining Stamper loggers in a daring attempt to take their logs down a rain-swelled river in order to meet their contract with the mill.

Stant, Charlotte. *The Golden Bowl.* Henry James. 1904.

Charlotte Stant, a handsome and independent young American woman, travels to London to attend the wedding of her former lover, PRINCE AMERIGO, to her old school friend, MAGGIE VERVER. Without close family or a permanent home, Charlotte has freely roamed Europe and America. Shortly before the Prince's wedding, she arrives at the house of a mutual friend, FANNY ASSINGHAM, and with her assistance proceeds to carve out a place for herself in his life.

Like the Prince's relatives, who are from Rome, Charlotte's family consists of corrupt and impoverished aristocrats. Her parents are American, but Charlotte was born and raised in Florence, educated at a Tuscan convent, and later at a Parisian boarding school. In Paris she became acquainted with Maggie Verver, the daughter of an American millionaire. Although Maggie remains in contact with Charlotte over the years, she knows nothing of Charlotte's affair with the Prince. Because they are both too poor to marry each other, Charlotte has no choice but to break off the affair with the Prince, after which she leaves for America.

Charlotte has no "interests" in America and finds no attractive prospects for marriage. News of the Prince's marriage to Maggie provides her with an excuse to return to London. When she encounters the Prince at Fanny's home, Charlotte exacts a promise that he will help her choose a wedding present for Maggie. They meet secretly, and Charlotte confesses that she returned to London for this hour alone with him. In a small antique shop in Bloomsbury, Charlotte and the Prince discuss the possibility of exchanging gifts as mementos of their time together. They are shocked when the shop owner intrudes upon their conversation and erroneously addresses Charlotte as "Signora Principessa" in Italian, the language in which they had been conversing in order to ensure a modicum of privacy. Having captured Charlotte's attention, he takes the opportunity to show her the Golden Bowl, an elegant object of crystal overlaid with gold. Despite the high price, Charlotte is tempted to purchase the Bowl, but the Prince insists that it is flawed. It would be, he claims, a bad omen for his marriage if she were to buy him a flawed piece as a wedding gift.

Maggie, the Prince's new wife, has a deep admiration for Charlotte, and now that she is among them again, she wants to help her. Maggie fears Charlotte's magnificence will be wasted without a home or husband. She encourages her father, ADAM VERVER, to invite the young woman to his home at Portland Place. While Maggie and the Prince are vacationing in Paris, Charlotte maintains a perfect balance of familiarity and respect with Mr. Verver and finds various ways of pleasing him, such as playing the piano. After several idyllic days in the country, Mr. Verver asks Charlotte to marry him. Charlotte refuses to answer until she receives the Prince's approval. She believes the marriage will allow for a certain freedom between herself and the Prince.

In spite of the claustrophobic intimacy between the two newly married couples, Charlotte and her lover are able to spend time alone. Absolutely secure in their secret, Charlotte and the Prince take some surprising liberties, including spending a day alone together at Matcham where the four have been vacationing. After this, however, Maggie happens upon the Golden Bowl herself, and the shopkeeper relates Charlotte's revealing conversation with the Prince.

If Charlotte knows that Maggie has discovered their secret, she never acknowledges it. Her performance once the affair is over is no less magnificent than when it was at its height. When questioned about her peculiar reserve, Maggie reassures Charlotte that nothing at all is wrong. The two women are seen embracing after this exchange, and the household is convinced they have reconciled their differences. Mr. Verver seems to understand the awkwardness of their situation, however, and arranges to move with Charlotte to America.

During their final meeting, Charlotte accuses Maggie of "loathing" her marriage with Mr. Verver and attempting to ruin it. She tells Maggie that the move to America was her own design, an attempt to save her marriage. Maggie bravely affirms this bit of sophistry and accepts Charlotte's accusation. Charlotte's exit from the novel is characteristically triumphant and proud, and the Prince later assures his concerned wife that Charlotte is not unhappy.

Stanton, Vernor. *The Sporting Club.* Thomas McGuane. 1969.

Vernor Stanton, the son of rich alcoholic parents, a Harvard graduate, and a wildly eccentric man, lives in his family's lavish cottage at the Centennial Club, a Sporting Club in the Michigan wilderness. With him is Janey, a beautiful southern woman who seems to exercise a strange hold over her dangerous lover. In describing Stanton to JAMES QUINN, a childhood friend who is visiting, Janey says, "Inactivity makes his mind run wild." One sign of this wildness is the dueling gallery he has created in his basement and the duels with wax bullets that he forces on Quinn.

Stanton has always lived a life of lawless and erratic pranks, and in isolation, his behavior veers quickly from boisterous fun to eccentricity and, finally, to the brink of lunacy. When he, Janey, and Quinn attend the dedication of the Mackinac Bridge, he commandeers a bus, embarrasses legislators and their wives, and finally sails away in his enormous yacht. When the three go to a formal party at the "Bug House," a club meeting ground, he humiliates pompous club members, embarrasses Quinn, and vilifies Janey but remains unperturbed himself.

Quinn fears for Janey's safety but also for Stanton, who seems more and more obsessed with his gun collection. When the club's competent manager crosses him, Stanton sees to it that he is replaced by Earl Olive, a loutish biker who holds wild parties with his friends on the club's grounds. Stanton and the new manager soon have a misunderstanding, however, and in a wax-bullet duel, Stanton hurts Olive. Olive in turn blows up the dam, flooding the river and drying up the club's lake. Quinn, who initially feels a loyalty to Stanton because of their adolescent friendship, finds himself drawn into the other man's increasingly bizarre behavior while at the same time being repelled by it. He hears from Janey of the paranoia Stanton exhibited while the two traveled together through Europe and the Caribbean.

As the summer progresses, members of the club deteriorate rapidly into a primitive state. They live together in a huge carnival tent that becomes increasingly rank as the members grow dirty and promiscuous. Their goal is to find and destroy Earl Olive. A second goal is to dig up the time capsule that has been buried for a century and learn something about their families, the founders of the club. At a Fourth of July celebration, Stanton and Quinn aid in unearthing the capsule and open it, only to discover that all it contains is a lewd photograph showing their ancestors engaged in a sexual circus.

Inspired by the photo, the club deteriorates even further. Only Quinn and Stanton remain apart from the activities, but while Quinn tries to establish a hold on himself, Stanton slips into complete psychosis. He lures Olive into a duel, this time with real bullets, and becomes wild when the other man won't shoot him. Finally he holds the entire club at bay with his machine gun as he methodically shoots into the night.

Once the fiasco has ended and all the members have left, Stanton buys the land the club was on and lives on in the wilderness, shooting duels with toy guns and holding imaginary conversations with Janey and two aides.

Stapleton, Iris Joplin. *Sissie.* John A. Williams. 1963.

While preparing to visit for the last time the mother she has not seen in years, Iris Joplin Stapleton lets her mind wander through her accumulated store of memories. Now a successful jazz singer living in Europe, she has mixed feelings about being in the United States and seeing her dying mother, whom Iris felt never really loved her.

From the time she was very young Iris has felt that her mother, SISSIE PETERSON JOPLIN DUNCAN, behaved strangely toward her. Although Sissie was strict with Iris's brother RALPH JOPLIN, she was always detached from her daughter. After Big Ralph, Iris, and Ralph's father abandoned the family during the Great Depression, Iris found herself even more set apart. She had never been close to her mother, and when Sissie began to take on lovers, Iris's response was to withdraw into her own world and to start wetting her bed.

Iris did make some connection with her brother Ralph. Ralph had always had a special relationship with their sister Mary Ellen, and her death affected him deeply. When Ralph took Iris roller-skating and led her to Mary Ellen's grave, the brother and sister finally established a bond that would last throughout their lives, even when they were thousands of miles apart.

Eventually Iris outgrew her bed-wetting and matured into an attractive young woman. She met Harry Stapleton, a lieutenant who was soon to travel to Europe with the Army of Occupation. In Germany, Iris quickly grew bored with her life as an army wife and was unsatisfied with Harry's clumsy lovemaking. She longed to go back on the stage and sing, as she had done back home. One day she impulsively joined in as an American jazz combo was practicing in a local bar. They urged her to look them up if she ever needed a job. When she fell completely out of love with her husband, she traveled to Munich and joined the combo.

As they traveled around Europe, Iris found that she was developing an attraction for Time, the combo's pianist and business manager. After a few years of flirting between the two, with the group becoming more and more successful, Time and Iris finally became a couple. Real fame soon followed, first for the group as a whole and then for Iris alone.

When Iris receives word of her mother's illness, she has not been to the United States for more than ten years. She has also been without Time, having grown impatient with their erratic relationship. A feeling of loyalty—but not exactly love—forces her to return to the United States and see her dying mother. Once in New York she stays with her brother Ralph and his wife Eve while bad weather clears enough for them to continue on to California. Ralph, now a successful playwright, tells Iris how, years before, he had read some old letters between Sissie and Big Ralph, and Sissie and another man, Arthur. One letter explained, Ralph tells her, that Sissie let Big Ralph believe Iris was not his but was Arthur's daughter. Suddenly Iris understands the distance that Sissie put between herself and her daughter.

The bad weather clears, and Ralph and Iris are finally able to fly west. They arrive in the hospital just in time to hear Sissie's impassioned last words. She tells Iris that she is indeed Big Ralph's child and begs her daughter to tell her she loves her. Iris remains silent. Sissie dies, and although Iris is sad, she is also free: free of her mother and, she believes, free of lies.

Starbuck. *Moby Dick*; or, *The Whale*. Herman Melville. 1851.

Starbuck, the first mate of the whaling vessel *Pequod*, is the only man on board to openly challenge CAPTAIN AHAB, the ship's monomaniacal captain. An able and judicious seaman, Starbuck refuses to share the other sailors' enthusiasm for the hunt for Moby Dick, the fabled white whale. His powers of resistance are not strong enough to overcome Ahab, however, and in the end he, too, perishes in the terrible outcome of the mad captain's quest for vengeance.

A Quaker by descent, born in the famous American port of Nantucket, Starbuck was destined to become a whaler. He has earned himself a reputation for being a cautious and sober sailor, not given to taking risks for the sake of adventure. This caution is due partly to his devotion to the young wife and child he has left ashore, and partly to his sensitivity to "outward portents and inward presentiments." Starbuck possesses a sort of practiced superstition that warns him when the risks of a whaling chase are too high. This intuition, as well as the conviction that seeking vengeance on an animal is blasphemous, causes Starbuck to protest when Ahab announces his intention to hunt Moby Dick, to whom he has lost a leg. Although Ahab succeeds in exacting pledges from the others to hunt the whale to the death, Starbuck remains silent.

Starbuck's relationship with Ahab changes when he dares to engage in an argument with him over some leaking casks of oil in the ship's hold. Starbuck boldly tells Ahab that the casks must be hauled out, examined, and repaired, or they will risk wasting more oil in a day than they can collect in a year. When Ahab angrily dismisses him, Starbuck warns him gravely to "beware of thyself." After reflecting later on this exhortation, Ahab gives the order to repair the casks.

When a typhoon in the sea off Japan threatens the *Pequod*, Starbuck sees this as a sign. He points out that if the *Pequod* continues on the course plotted by Ahab, she will head into the heart of the storm, whereas if she were to turn toward Nantucket, the wind would carry her safely home. Knowing that Ahab's vengeful quest is endangering the lives of all the sailors, Starbuck is tempted to murder him for the good of the crew. One night he goes to Ahab's cabin with a loaded musket, but after staring at the captain, who yet raves as he sleeps, he relinquishes the idea. He is incapable of the sin of murder.

On a calm day shortly before encountering Moby Dick, Ahab turns to Starbuck and in a rare moment of compassion proclaims that he is grateful to look at a human countenance rather than at the sea. Seeing in Starbuck's eyes the memory of his own wife and child, Ahab is almost moved to turn back. But the moment passes as abruptly as it had arrived; instead of abandoning the chase, Ahab instructs Starbuck to stay behind on the *Pequod* when the whaleboats are lowered for the chase of Moby Dick.

When Moby Dick is finally sighted, Starbuck stays behind to command the *Pequod* in Ahab's absence. From the relatively safe deck of the ship he witnesses the first two days of the chase. After Ahab's whaleboat is split in two and the old man himself is almost killed, Starbuck insists that it would be "impiety and blasphemy" to continue the chase. His warning goes unheeded; on the third day Moby Dick destroys the three remaining whaleboats and heads for the *Pequod*. Knowing that he has disobeyed his God in obeying Ahab, and praying for deliverance, Starbuck perishes with the rest of the crew.

Stark, Mary "Molly." *The Virginian: A Horseman of the Plains.* Owen Wister. 1902.

Mary "Molly" Stark is the heroine of this romance of the American West. Hailing from Bennington, Vermont, Molly can claim descent from a grandfather who fought the British at Saratoga and a determined grandmother, her namesake, who stood beside the patriot even in battle. Imbued with the same indomitable courage that characterized her grandmother, Molly faces the hardship and the mystery of the Great Plains in her long search for identity.

Molly leaves the tradition, security, and pride of her Vermont family in order to become the schoolteacher in a one-room schoolhouse in the tiny settlement of Bear Creek, Wyoming. Although the first letter of solicitation that Molly sends the Bear Creek parents is signed "Your very sincere spinster," Molly is hardly that. She is twenty-three years old and is being courted by Sam Bannett, a particularly eligible suitor, in Bennington. But to her genuine dismay Molly cannot return Sam's affections for her, and she secretly fears that she cannot love at all. Wyoming is her solution to these problems.

The trip out to the plains is not uneventful. Molly's growing loneliness is exacerbated by the discomfort of stagecoach travel, frequent proposals of marriage proffered by complete strangers, and finally a drunken stage driver who gets her stuck in the rushing water of a ford. Luckily a mysterious "tall rider" whisks her to the riverbank. Thus Molly first encounters THE VIRGINIAN, a perfect specimen of the cowboy: handsome, honest, manly, and resourceful. After her timely rescue from the river, Molly notices that her flowered handkerchief is missing, and it is clear that the gallant Virginian has taken it as a memento of their first brief meeting. Molly, in her confused way, feels "maidenly resentment toward her rescuer" at the same time that she entertains a "maidenly hope" of seeing him again.

When Molly reaches Bear Creek, she finds a newly constructed cabin waiting for her, an ever-growing number of pupils, and the eager eyes of every unmarried man in the territory. She sees the Virginian again at a barbecue,

and for the next two years Molly is reluctantly wooed by the Virginian whenever his cow punching takes him to the area. She rides with him, discusses literature with him (after he reads what she wants him to), and eventually falls in love with him, although she is too scared and too proud to admit this even to herself. On a brief visit to Vermont, Molly does disclose her feelings to her aged and sympathetic aunt. When she returns to Wyoming, however, her already tumultuous emotions are further confused when she hears that the Virginian has participated in the "law" of the plains, the hanging of a cattle thief. She packs to leave the West for good.

This time Molly cannot run away from herself. She takes a last Wyoming ride and by chance discovers the Virginian lying by a stream badly wounded by an Indian's bullet. She gets him back to her cabin, now stacked with packing boxes, and abandons her departure to nurse him back to health. By the time he recovers, she has accepted his proposal of marriage. Molly is pained when her mother disapproves, but nothing can make her abandon her love now, not even the horror she feels when the Virginian is forced into a shootout on the eve of their wedding. They are married, spend a brief honeymoon in the mountains, and visit Vermont in order to show off their happiness and prove to New England that its patriotic past and the gallantry of old Virginia are well suited to each other in America's beckoning future, the West.

Stark, Willie. *All the King's Men.* Robert Penn Warren. 1946.

Willie Stark is the hard-driving, populist governor of a Depression-era southern state. Known as "the Boss," he remains a man who believes that his ultimately good ends will always justify his unsavory means. Stark grows up in the red hills of impoverished Mason County. His humble circumstances restrict his opportunities, but he is bright and driven and educates himself in history, literature, and finally, law. After World War I he marries a schoolteacher, and they have a son. Willie is ambitious enough to get elected Mason County treasurer with the aid of the courthouse ring, but he is public-minded enough to balk when the county commissioners, ignoring a lower bid, award the contract for a new schoolhouse to a firm with financial connections to one of their own. The ring turns Willie out of office, but he is vindicated several years later when a fire escape at the poorly built school collapses, killing several children.

In 1926, Willie's sense of duty and of his own destiny lead him to agree to run for governor. He is terrible on the stump, where he earnestly drones on about the state's needs. But when he learns from one of his handlers, Sadie Burke, and a newspaperman, JACK BURDEN, that his candidacy has been covertly promoted by incumbent governor Joe Harrison with the hope of splitting the rural constituency of Harrison's chief rival, Sam MacMurfee, he decides to take action. Shocked out of his naiveté but not out of his ambition or his principles, Willie drops out of the race and makes fiery speeches against Harrison. He demands that his "hick" audiences "nail up" anybody who stands in their way.

Four years later Willie campaigns against Governor MacMurfee and conquers the state in the name of the people. The Stark administration raises state fees for corporate use of its coal and oil lands, institutes income taxes, builds roads on a massive scale, and provides a number of free public services. Yet Willie is no gentleman reformer; he bullies and blackmails, bringing into his organization old machine politicians such as Tiny Duffy. When in 1933 the state auditor is found to be lining his pockets, Willie tries to scare the legislature off the case—not to save the auditor's hide but to keep MacMurfee's faction from using the scandal to undermine his program. His enemies begin impeachment proceedings against Willie on charges of coercing the legislature, ut by stump speaking and digging up "dirt" on unfriendly legislators, he saves himself and is overwhelmingly reelected the following year.

Although unscrupulous, Willie is no hypocrite. He articulately defends his strong-arm methods. Only force, he suggests, can loosen the grip that oligarchs and special interests continue to hold on the state. Given the pervasive evil and corruption of the world, Willie believes one must use evil men and methods to do whatever one chooses to define as good. Yet Jack Burden, now Willie's aide, recognizes that "the Boss" is not completely comfortable with his own moral relativism. As his methods grow more unsavory, he becomes more committed to building a fine, free public hospital. This project, he swears, will be untainted by graft.

As Willie's power grows, his personal life becomes increasingly tangled. He is involved in extramarital affairs, most prominently with Sadie Burke and Anne Stanton, the blue-blooded daughter of a former governor and Burden's childhood friend. Willie and his wife Lucy become estranged, not because of his affairs but because Lucy disapproves of Willie's politics and of his indulgence of their son Tom, who has grown into a handsome, athletic lout.

By the middle of his second term, Willie's methods and habits seem to have edged him over a moral divide. Corrupt means advance his public goals and clearly begin to serve private ends. His efforts to shield Tom from a paternity suit and to guarantee his own victory in the 1938 senatorial campaign ultimately bring him down. MacMurfee threatens to expose Tom's sexual indiscretion if Willie does not renounce his senatorial ambitions. Unable to deal with MacMurfee through his ally, Judge Montague Irwin, who commits suicide when he is blackmailed, Willie is forced to buy off a MacMurfee lieutenant by granting him the general contract for his beloved hospital.

After Tom is crippled during a college football game, Willie Stark struggles to redeem himself. He cancels the corrupt hospital deal, infuriating Tiny Duffy who had acted as a go-between. He also returns to Lucy, infuriating Sadie. She has Duffy tell Adam Stanton, a noted surgeon who accepted the directorship of the hospital despite his patrician disdain for Stark's grubby politics, that he has been appointed only because his sister Anne is Willie's mistress. Enraged, Stanton guns Willie down in the state capitol and is killed himself by a guard.

Even in his last moments Willie reveals his desire to right the wrongs of his career. As he is dying, he insists to Burden, "It might have been different. . . . If it hadn't happened, it might—have been different—even yet."

Starks, Joe "Jody." *Their Eyes Were Watching God.* Zora Neale Hurston. 1937.

Urbane and stylish, Joe "Jody" Starks is the man who rescues JANIE MAE CRAWFORD from her unhappy marriage to an aging farmer. But the role he offers her—wife of the mayor of an all-black township—is ultimately no more satisfying than the drudgery Janie had experienced on the farm. Jody's ambition and jealousy eventually come into conflict with Janie's independent spirit, and their marriage founders.

Jody first sees Janie when he is passing by the farm owned by her husband. He asks her for a drink of water and is immediately taken by her youthful beauty. He tells her that he is on his way to a town settled by blacks and that he has saved up enough money to establish himself so that he will never have to work for whites again. Drawn to his promise of a new life, and tired of work on the farm and her loveless marriage, Janie agrees to run away with him. After they are married, they depart for Eatonville, Florida.

When the couple arrives in newly founded Eatonville, Jody immediately impresses the townspeople by buying a parcel of land and building a much-needed store. In gratitude the citizens of the town vote Jody their mayor. Jody takes his authoritative position to heart, building a great white house that among the poorer homes of Eatonville looks like a mansion surrounded by servants' quarters. He acts as judge and jury to any wrongdoers in town and uses grandiose language to humiliate and manipulate the townspeople. He becomes jealous and possessive of Janie. He keeps her working in the store and refuses to allow her to participate in the spirited tale-telling sessions that are the chief entertainment in Eatonville. When the townspeople put on a humorous mock funeral for a dead horse, Jody refuses to let Janie attend, telling her that a mayor's wife is above such shenanigans. He also forces her to hide her beautiful long hair beneath a kerchief so that she will be less appealing to other men.

Stifled by Jody's overpowering demeanor, Janie at first accepts her public role as submissive "Mrs. Mayor," but when he publicly insults her in the store, Janie lashes out, humiliating him with a loud reference to his impotence. Jody beats her for her insubordination, but it soon becomes clear that his grip on her is weakening. His loss of psychological power over Janie becomes manifested in his physical deterioration: He becomes flabby and worn-looking, and his health begins to fail. He refuses to allow Janie to nurse him, preferring the care of neighbors and the town conjurer to that of Janie and the medical doctor she hires.

Although Jody insists he is not dying, Janie knows he is deteriorating quickly. Finally, when he is on his deathbed, Janie confronts Jody. She tells him he is going to die, and then, although she pities him, she forces him to hear her speak of the sins he has committed against her. After he dies, Jody is given an elaborate funeral, and Janie plays the public role of the grieving wife. Privately, however, she rejoices at her freedom from the tyrant who had selfishly ruled over her.

Stein, Gertrude. *The Autobiography of Alice B*. Toklas. Gertrude Stein. 1933.

In this book Gertrude Stein describes her pivotal position in the modernist art scene in Paris during the first third of the twentieth century. Adopting the point of view of her lover, ALICE TOKLAS, Stein attests to her own artistic genius and to her central role as friend and patron of such artists as Pablo Picasso, Henri Matisse, and Paul Cézanne. The vitality of Stein's ego is exemplified by her co-option of Toklas's voice, a ruse that the reader discovers in the final paragraph of the work. On the other hand, the book is a tribute to the exceptional relationship between Gertrude Stein and Alice Toklas.

Gertrude Stein was born in Allegheny, Pennsylvania, and was raised in Europe and California. After attending Radcliffe College and enrolling in medical school at Johns Hopkins, she moves to Paris in 1903 and begins investing in the paintings of Picasso and other modernist painters whose reputations have not yet been established. In fact, she even becomes the subject of one of Picasso's most famous paintings, which now hangs at the Metropolitan Museum of Art in New York City. Stein poses for him in a broken armchair in his atelier some eighty or ninety times.

With the help of Alice Toklas, Stein maintains a salon in the rue de Fleurus; its popularity hinges both on her formidable charisma and on the notoriety of Picasso's portraits of her, which shock the general public. Stein's skill as an entertainer is demonstrated repeatedly. For example, when a number of artists lunch with Stein and Toklas, the hostesses arrange the seating so that each artist eats facing his own paintings, thus appealing to the egotism of the guests.

Stein's hospitality extends to American soldiers during World War I. Having purchased a Ford truck from the United States, Gertrude and Alice join the ranks of the American Fund for French Wounded and distribute medical supplies to various military hospitals. When they meet soldiers on the road, they give them rides, meals, and encouragement. Having made a soldier's acquaintance, they then correspond with him and send him "comfort packages" filled with dainties. Many of these military godsons remain friends for life.

Stein repeatedly refers to herself as a genius whose work is superior to any other living writer. She acknowledges that she was influential in the careers of many young writers, including Ernest Hemingway and Sherwood Anderson. Nevertheless, she voices some frustration at the fact that many of her works remain unpublished due to the experimental quality of her writing. When Stein approaches the Grafton Press in New York to print her first published work, *Three Lives*, the press, assuming she is French, sends an editor to Paris to investigate her proficiency in English. She assures the editor that everything in her writing style is deliberate and that stylistic aberrations are absolutely intentional. Toklas, who types Stein's manuscripts, eventually begins acting as her publicist and publisher.

As Gertrude Stein's literary reputation becomes more established, she is asked to give lecture tours on the subject of her writing. *The Autobiography* describes the responses of Alice and Gertrude to enthusiastic audiences at Oxford and Cambridge universities and throughout the United States. Stein's legendary public and artistic stature was galvanized with the publication of *The Autobiography of Alice B. Toklas*, which became a best-seller.

Steiner, Judah "Judd." *Compulsion*. Meyer Levin. 1956.

Judah Steiner, who is known as "Judd," is the fictional stand-in for Nathan Leopold, Jr., in this novel depicting the infamous 1924 murder of Robert Franks, which is known as the Leopold-Loeb murder. In the novel, Judd is a brilliant teenager who has become deeply enamored of the concept of an *Ubermensch*, or superman, one who by virtue of superior intellect is placed above common morality and law. He and his friend ARTHUR STRAUS spend a good deal of time discussing this and similar theories, and gradually they determine that each of them is above the law. To prove their invulnerability, the boys enter a pact to commit the so-called perfect crime. This desire leads to the killing of Paulie Kessler, the novel's Robert Franks figure. Judd and Artie kill Paul and conceal his body. Following the murder they attempt to extort $10,000 from the victim's father but are thwarted in their efforts when the boy's body is discovered, and the police investigation steadily closes in on them.

In the course of the investigation and in the ensuing trial, Judd's family background and psychological profile slowly emerge. It is revealed that the boys had made an arrangement whereby Judd would agree to a crime selected by Artie, and Artie must return the favor by having sex with Judd. Prior to his arrest, however, Judd begins a brief affair with a young girl who suspects that he is tormented but who has no idea of his involvement in the murder. Judd, the son of an enormously wealthy family, has long held an idealized vision of his mother, who died following a lengthy illness triggered by his birth. Her death when he was quite young led him to visualize her as a veritable saint; at the same time, his father and much older brother were remote figures, which gave him ample time for fantasy. While Judd attempts to rape Ruth, the girl he is beginning to fall in love with, he is unable to complete the act; his contrition, coupled with his confusion, lead Ruth to continue seeing him in the brief span of time between the attack and his arrest.

Once the boys are arrested, a prominent attorney, Jonathan Wilks, Levin's fictionalized Clarence Darrow, is hired to defend them. Because they ultimately confess to the crime, Wilks's goal is to prevent their execution, and he argues vehemently for a life sentence. Psychiatrists are called in for both the defense and the state, and it is determined that each boy suffers to some degree from mental incompetence. In Judd's case, his attitudes, sexual fantasies, relationship to Artie, and idealization of his mother lead the specialists to determine that he is quite childish and prone to "magical thinking." In addition, physical examinations are conducted, and it is revealed that he suffered from a prematurely calcified bone that had stunted his pineal gland and gave rise to a delusional approach to life. These findings, coupled with Wilks's impassioned defense, lead to a sentence of life in prison despite Judd's marked lack of contrition. As of the writing of the novel, the narrator notes that more than thirty years had passed since he had covered the investigation and trial, and that Judd remained, at fifty years of age, in prison.

Stenham, John. *The Spider's House.* Paul Bowles. 1955.

John Stenham is an American writer living and working in Fez, Morocco, during its 1954 war with the French. As Fez finally erupts into fighting, John finds he can no longer ignore the tensions that are threatening to change a city he would prefer to see as static and medieval.

Having lived in Morocco for several years and able to speak Arabic, John considers himself something of an expert on Moslem culture and religion. He takes a condescending delight in analyzing the mysterious behavior of a people he deems charming but mentally undeveloped, and he prides himself on knowing more about them than other foreigners. He also refuses to acknowledge that a year of French interference has irrevocably changed the city he has come to love.

John wants Fez to remain the same because its ancient culture is to his aesthetic and philosophical taste. He resents claims that the Moroccan people must advance. He

hates the French for destroying the unique rituals of Moroccan life, and he hates the Moroccan nationalists for trying to modernize their country. John sympathizes only with the poor people who would suffer under either regime. He is convinced that wisdom consists not in striving for change but in passively obeying natural laws, which he believes to be hierarchical: Equality is a fiction, and to struggle for it a mistake.

As the novel progresses, John's values are elicited and challenged by intriguing new acquaintances. He first meets POLLY LEE BURROUGHS, an American woman who believes that Morocco's poor, diseased peasants would welcome modern European technology. Despite his anger at her agenda, John becomes increasingly involved with Lee. He takes her on a long carriage ride around the city, followed by tea in a café. When they become trapped in the café during a violent skirmish between Moslem nationalists and French police, John makes the acquaintance of AMAR, a Moslem boy. Lee insists that they shield Amar from the French police outside, who would probably arrest him, and they take the appreciative boy to their hotel under the guise of a servant. Although Amar feels that John's attempts to understand the Moslems are inadequate, he finds him a sincere and reliable friend.

The next morning John and Polly are forced to leave their hotel because of the escalating war. John decides to go to the mountains to observe an annual Moslem feast; Lee and Amar accompany him. Continuing to question Amar about his political and religious beliefs, John finds his fidelity to the precepts and practice of Islam astonishing. For the first time he doubts his facile generalizations about the Moslems: They are not the predictable and homogeneous people he thought they were. The depth of the boy's faith convinces John that his whole theory about the Moslems is wrong. John and Lee argue continuously about what to do with Amar and about their own needs, but they develop an affection for each other by the time they are ready to return to Fez, where Amar has preceded them. Perhaps because both become aware of their own shortcomings, they suddenly seem to need each other, and they become lovers.

John and Lee return to Fez and prepare to leave for Casablanca. At their hotel they encounter Amar for the last time. Although Amar sees John as his only remaining friend and protector, John, now romantically involved with Lee, seems to have no further interest in the boy and uncaringly abandons him. Amar wants to travel with them to Meknès, but John, acting like a true outsider, fails to understand his needs; he insists that he can't take him any farther in their cab and leaves him alone on the empty road.

Step. *Let Me Breathe Thunder.* William Attaway. 1939.

Step, a strong, volatile, charismatic young man, and his friend Ed, the soft-hearted, more practical narrator, are migrants looking for work and adventure during the Great Depression. Ed tries to steer Step clear of entanglements with women and fighting with local thugs, but to no avail. Step sees no future beyond the next stop on the freight line.

As the novel opens, Step and Ed have jumped a boxcar to Seattle with a nine-year-old Mexican child, called "Hi Boy," one of the few English phrases he knows. In Seattle, on the way to a long-awaited meal, Step stops at a saloon for one whiskey but ends up drinking several. After the bouncer harasses a Mexican prostitute, Step nearly beats him to death. Ed manages to pull his friend away, and the next morning they flee the city by passenger train.

Still hungry, they eat in the dining car but find that they can't pay the bill. As they plan their escape at the next stop, Sampson, a distinguished man sitting across from them, overhears and offers to pay. He has taken a liking to Hi Boy and offers Step and Ed work at his sheep farm near Yakima.

At first they refuse the job, but tired of being exposed at night to the elements, they soon catch a freight to Yakima. Step had been to this town before. He knows Mag, a black ex-prostitute who has invested her earnings in real estate. She now lives with Cooper, her old pimp.

During a big meal at Mag's place, Hi Boy becomes jealous of the others. He depends on the constant attention and approval of Step. When Step calls him "yellow," Hi Boy stabs a fork into his own hand to prove he is not scared. Mag dresses the wound and later gives the boy a shotgun to distract him from the pain. Hi Boy turns out to be a masterful shot.

When they reach Sampson's farm, Ed notices the attraction between Step and Anna, Sampson's teenage daughter. Sampson, a widower, seems undisturbed by their flirting; Step and Ed remind him of his own sons who died in World War I. But Ed knows that Step thinks of all women as prostitutes and makes him promise not to pursue Anna. Ed likes the farm and tries to convince Step that they would have a much better life if they stayed there permanently. While they work the land with Sampson, Hi Boy spends his days tracking small animals and pests with his gun. The boy is very happy on the farm but never manages to keep his wounded hand clean. When it swells with infection, Sampson has to have him treated by a doctor in town.

One night Step, Anna, Ed, and a local girl have a party, and they end up at Mag's place where they get drunk on rice wine. While Ed necks with his partner, Step and Anna sneak off to a room in another part of the house. After Step takes her virginity, Anna is terrified and bleeding, but now hopelessly in love. Mag helps Anna clean herself up, and the group attributes their late return to a broken wheel. Sampson doesn't protest.

Life settles back to normal at the farm, although Step and Anna continue to rendezvous in the woods and oc-casionally at Mag's place. Soon Step tires of Anna's attentions and tells Ed that they will leave after payment for a month's work. After much discussion, Step agrees to let Hi Boy stay with Sampson. Hi Boy follows them to Yakima. Word of their departure devastates Anna. At the last minute she runs off to Mag's for a final encounter. When Step learns that she is waiting there, he and Ed run to get her out of Mag's before Sampson arrives in town to pick up Hi Boy. On the way an angry crowd reveals that Anna has accidentally been shot in the arm at Mag's. Thinking they will be held responsible, Step, Ed, and Hi Boy escape on the next freight.

That night, which is bitter cold, the three head east over the Rocky Mountains. Hi Boy's hand grows worse, and he develops a high fever. In the morning they are surprised to find a terrified Cooper in the same car. He tells them of his disastrous misjudgment at Mag's. Apparently Cooper had been looking for a way out of his long involvement with Mag, and knowing she was in the next room, he pretended to force himself on the defenseless Anna, who was forlorn over Step's abandonment. But instead of kicking him out, Mag shot at the pair. He fled Yakima to avoid hanging at the hands of the mob.

Alarmed at Hi Boy's condition, the three turn back, but it is too late. High Boy dies in a boxcar, and Step and Ed realize that they can never return to Sampson's farm. They hop another car, this one heading for Kansas.

Sterling, David. *Work.* Louisa May Alcott. 1873.

David Sterling was thrust into the role as head of his family by his father's premature death, and he was forced at a very early age to take odd jobs to support his mother and sister RACHEL (STERLING). Despite his lack of schooling, David reads voraciously and struggles to better himself because of the conditions of extreme poverty in which he and his family live.

David thus feels responsible when Rachel, tired of their poverty, longs to leave the family to see if she can make a life of her own. She runs away, leaving David to care for their mother, who nearly suffers a stroke at the shock of losing her only daughter. The economic burden is now eased with one less mouth to feed, but David develops an intense resentment toward his sister. A year later he receives a letter from her describing the difficult life that she now leads, and she asks to be taken back into the family. Still seething with anger, David replies that she has nearly killed their mother, brought disgrace to the family, and is never welcome home again.

David immediately regrets his cruelty to his sister, however, and sets out to find her. He learns that she is planning to leave on a ship bound for Europe. David arrives minutes late, and the ship on which she was booked leaves before he can apologize to her. His disappointment turns to horror when he learns a few months later that the ship was lost at sea; Rachel's name is listed among the victims.

Guilt-stricken, David spends the next few years as a recluse, living with his mother and spending most of his time working in their garden. To compensate for the cruelty inflicted on his sister, he begins to aid the local pastor, Mr. Power, in the rehabilitation of wayward young ladies. Despite his best efforts, he begins to develop an affection for one of these ladies, CHRISTIE DEVON.

One day in town David is shocked to run into Rachel on the street. His sister tells him how her ship left for Europe without her and how the past years were spent working at various jobs. Overjoyed, he apologizes profusely for his past cruelty to her and begs her forgiveness. His heart and conscience freed at last, David brings Rachel back to the family and marries Christie, who, unbeknownst to David, had become close friends with Rachel while they were working together as seamstresses.

His happiness is short-lived, however, because the Civil War soon breaks out. He enlists, and Christie follows him, working as a nurse in a nearby hospital. David's courage soon wins him a promotion to major. On a mission in the last months of the war, David comes across a number of women and children slaves massacred by Confederate soldiers. Unable to let such cruelty go unpunished, David leads the counterattack, where he is critically wounded. The grief-stricken Christie arrives at his side in the hospital, and David dies in her arms.

Sterling, Philip. *The Gilded Age.* Samuel L. Clemens (Mark Twain). 1873.

Philip Sterling is the sole representative of levelheadedness, integrity, and dignity in this novel's late-nineteenth-century sociopolitical milieu dominated by speculators and con men. While others brew farfetched schemes for immediate gain, Philip doggedly studies engineering because he realizes that hard work and determination are the most valuable resources for a prosperous future.

Philip enters the speculative scene with his more visionary and voluble friend Henry Brierly, not yet aware that "he wanted several other things quite as much as he wanted wealth." He takes part in a scheme with Henry and Colonel Beriah Sellers to develop the imaginary railway town of Napoleon, Missouri. But as funds dwindle, his own and the project's, and as Henry goes to Washington, D.C., to exercise his promotional talents, Philip drifts toward sounder speculations, studying the science and engineering behind the schemes.

While Henry hopes his persuasive speeches will help him succeed in Washington, Philip strives to succeed by his toil. When Henry is promoting gaudy land deals in the capital, Philip works on the land itself, trying to quarry anthracite from the inner veins of the Pennsylvania hills. Unlike Henry, who falls in love with every attractive young woman he meets, Philip remains loyal to the aspiring doctor Ruth Bolton.

Philip's romance with Ruth proceeds according to a conventional formula. First she affects to disdain him, but when he is injured while protecting her from stampeding theatergoers, she nurses him back to health. Finally, he saves her family from financial ruin. Returning to bring them the good news, he finds her in a state of poor health but revives her by the mere force of his presence. They vow in the end to marry.

In order to save Ruth's family, Philip must rely on his stalwart and at times relentless faith in his skills as a geological engineer. He has involved her father in a coal speculation that he is scientifically assured will pay off. Even when the father's money runs out and the coal miners must take other jobs, Philip keeps drilling by himself until he strikes the vein of anthracite. Obsessed with the promise of success, he becomes the epitome of single-minded determination.

Sterling, Rachel. *Work.* Louisa May Alcott. 1873.

Rachel Sterling's father died when she was very young, and she lived with her mother and brother DAVID (STERLING) in extreme poverty in a small New England town. Despite her brother's best efforts to make a good life for the family, Rachel longs for the privilege and refinement that she knows is beyond her reach. Much to the sadness and despair of her family, she decides to leave home and try to earn her own way in the world.

Possessing no particular skills or training, Rachel is unable to find work. On the point of starvation, she is forced to turn to prostitution to survive. She writes a letter to her family a year later asking them to take her back; David writes back that she has disgraced them and that they never want to see her again.

Rachel plans to leave the country but at the last minute is unable to raise enough money for passage. When the ship is lost at sea and her name is listed among the missing, she does nothing to correct the error, preferring to be assumed dead now that she has been cast out by her family.

Rachel is eventually able to gain employment as a seamstress, but at work she is melancholy and withdrawn. One morning she finds a dozen yellow roses on her work table and discovers they had been left for her by a new seamstress, CHRISTIE DEVON. Christie's friendliness and warmth gradually melt Rachel's cold exterior, and the two become close friends.

Rachel's past catches up with her once again, however, when the head seamstress, the shrewish Miss Cotton, discovers her disreputable employment record. Rachel is immediately dismissed and must keep Christie from quitting out of loyalty to her friend. After a brief stay with Christie, she sets out to find a new job. The toughness Rachel has developed from her previous experience sees her through the hard months that follow. She is finally able to gain employment as a nurse in a small-town hospital. When she sees the face of her long-lost brother David on the street one day, she resists the urge to duck away and calls out to him. Much to her surprise, David is overjoyed at the sight of his sister, whom he had presumed dead. He tells Rachel that the letter he sent her had been written in a moment of anger and that he had suffered all these years for the cruelty he had inflicted on her.

Rachel is then reunited with her family. Much to her delight, she finds her old friend Christie among them as well, preparing to marry her brother David. They all live together in happiness for a short period of time until the outbreak of the Civil War. When David enlists and Christie follows him to war, Rachel is finally able to make up for the injustices she had inflicted on her mother by caring for her while the others are away.

When Rachel's mother passes away and David is killed in the last months of the war, Christie returns home to Rachel, and the two of them find solace once again in their work.

Stern. *Stern*. Bruce Jay Friedman. 1962.

Stern is a middle-aged Jewish man who writes copy for product labels in an unidentified New York firm. At the start of the book Stern moves into the suburbs with his wife and young son Donald. This move, from Stern's middle-class background and city apartment into a multi-roomed house, represents a leap of many rungs on the social ladder for Stern. Delirious with the grandeur of his new life, he has the garden redone by Italian landscapers and fantasizes about entertaining the many friends he really does not have.

Things begin to go wrong when caterpillars destroy half of every tree and shrub in the yard, turning it into a miserable "cancer garden," and the newly laid tile floor begins to buckle. Stern then discovers that in order to reach the train station he must trek across a deserted estate down the road; he is escorted home nightly by two vicious dogs. Come winter, Stern finds that his house is barren and forlorn, and his wife and son are lonely and without friends. Life takes a turn for the better when spring arrives; he discovers a shortcut through the estate, and his trees begin to blossom. But one day after work his wife informs him that a neighbor down the street pushed her to the ground and called her a "kike."

It is this incident that engenders Stern's agonizing battle with fear, anxiety, and self-hatred. Each day he engages in a tortured debate with himself about how to avoid passing the man's house on his way home from the train station. He obsesses over his Jewishness and wishes for ways to convince the man that he is really not so different. The worst of it is his unbearable shame at not having confronted the man upon learning of the rude remark. He remembers other instances in his life when he felt inadequate and peripheral. Eventually, Stern's constant worrying brings on an acute ulcer, and he is forced into a rest home to recuperate.

Stern spends five weeks in the home. He continues to obsess over his wicked neighbor and hopes that the man will somehow learn of his sickness and stop "tormenting" him. His agony is exacerbated by suspicions that his wife is being unfaithful to him while he is away. Gradually, however, the ulcer begins to heal, and he makes a few friends and achieves a popularity and position previously unknown to him.

On returning home, however, Stern's distrust of his wife increases, and although desperate for relaxation, he is forced to confront the fact that in his absence a neighborhood boy cut his son and called him "Matzoh." Stern begins to experience a trembling sensation that leads to a nervous breakdown, where he is overcome with fear, paranoia, and shaking. It is only when he finally recovers that Stern realizes his mind is free of thoughts of his neighbor, whom he has come to think of as the "kike man." To rid himself completely of the legacy of that incident, Stern goes to the neighbor's house and, reminding him of the slur that occurred over a year ago, challenges him to a fistfight. The man punches Stern in the ear, but Stern's ability to remain standing gives him the courage to reprimand the neighbor.

At home again, Stern is surprised to find he feels afraid of the neighbor; still, he experiences a moment of calm and wholeness when he goes to his son's room to tuck him in and is joined by his wife, who gives him a tender hug.

Steuben, Max'l. *The Foundry*. Albert Halper. 1934.

Max'l Steuben, an enormous man in his early forties who suffers from a weak heart, is the senior partner and driving force behind the successful Fort Dearborn Electrotype Foundry. He began working at the foundry as an errand boy at the age of fourteen and made his way up through the ranks to become boss. Extremely competent in business matters, he is at times mean-tempered and treats his less knowledgeable partners with contempt. He often makes them do unpleasant things such as firing workers when he himself wishes to avoid a scene. The foundry men respect Max'l and think of him as the "real boss" while considering the other partners, JACK DUFFY and Ezekiel Cranly, to be no more than clerks.

Steuben's main passion is the day-to-day business of the foundry, and he spends much of his time working in secret on a model of a new labor-saving machine he has designed. He also regularly attends meetings of the Midwest Electrotypers Employers Association, a group of bosses whose purpose is to devise ways to outwit the union. He is concerned when, in the fall of 1928, the union sends as a replacement finisher the most radical electrotyper in Chicago, a man named Karl Heitman. Suffering from heart trouble and worried about the amount of money he has invested in the stock market, Max'l becomes increasingly short-tempered; when he catches a worker against whom he has held a grudge eating a sandwich, he makes Duffy fire him. However, the workers begin to produce an extraordinary number of defective plates, and Steuben, angry but helpless, is forced to rehire the man in order to stop the sabotage.

On Christmas day Max'l suffers his first heart attack but continues to work as hard as ever throughout the spring of 1929 without telling anyone about the incident. In the summer he is almost killed by a worker after accusing the man of laziness, and he has another heart attack. While recovering, Steuben arranges for the new machinery to be installed at the foundry. The shop erupts in an uproar when the workers discover that the machine will replace jobs; after another batch of defective plates, the furious Max'l is forced to promise the union that he will not fire any workers on account of the machine.

In the fall Max'l's health continues to fail, and he becomes depressed as he becomes increasingly aware of the emptiness of his life. He is worried about the amount of money he has invested in the market but is swayed by the greedy optimism of his business associates and decides to hold on to his stocks a little longer. After being robbed of the foundry's payroll, Max'l suffers more palpitations and is forced to stay in bed for a time; he returns to the foundry subdued and depressed. The market then begins to slip. Steuben suffers yet another heart attack after reading the financial news. He is still sick in bed, reduced to tears, when Tuesday, October 29, arrives; his wife refuses to show him the newspapers of that historic day.

Stevenson, Charles. *The Messenger.* Charles Wright. 1963.

The novel's first-person narrator, Charlie Stevenson, a light-skinned African American, works as a messenger in New York City. Twenty-nine years old and a failed writer, Charlie has no direction and is deeply unhappy. He drinks heavily and is caught up in a deadening routine of homosexual prostitution, which continues not because he desires it but because he seeks to make social connections and supplement his small income. It is the summer of 1962, and from his apartment on West Forty-ninth Street, where he lives illegally in a neighborhood of gypsies, prostitutes, con artists, and transvestites, Charlie struggles with his loneliness and searches desperately for an excitement that never comes.

Although Charlie is constantly surrounded by various friends and sexual partners, he is always aware of his loneliness, which began when he was a boy in Missouri. His father lived away from home; his mother died when he was four, and his grandfather when he was fourteen. Charlie lived with his grandmother, whom he loved very much but who could not erase his sense of isolation. In order to dispel the loneliness of small-town life, Charlie traveled every weekend into St. Louis or Kansas City

where he had sex with men and women for excitement and money. At this time he felt he was "searching for something," although he did not know what it was. Later he joined the army and fought in the Korean War. Korea did not make him a hero, nor was it the glorious adventure he had thought it would be, but it taught him about the range of human suffering.

Charlie also suffers from the repercussions of racism. As a boy, white employers would not hire him, the police harassed him for walking in a white neighborhood, and black children hated him for being light-skinned. Now, as an adult, he faces discriminatory hiring, and both his male and female tricks eroticize his skin color.

The summer is almost over, and Charlie, who drinks now more than ever, wonders why he lives in New York City. He originally intended only to visit, but the city's exciting pace and the anonymity it offers compelled him to stay for five years. Still, New York is corrupt and stifling, and Charlie wonders if he really belongs here. Remembering the peace of his last visit to his grandmother, just before she died, he is burdened by a profound sense of loss and of the futility of his life.

When Charlie learns that he is being evicted, he takes stock of his situation and admits that he lacks direction and is rapidly aging. He decides to sell his possessions and move to Mexico. At his going-away party, which degenerates into a drunken escape from fear and pain, Charlie quarrels with his ex-girlfriend as he hears a transvestite friend screaming obscenities from upstairs.

Stevens, F. Hilary. *Mrs. Stevens Hears the Mermaids Singing.* May Sarton. 1965.

F. Hilary Stevens, a prominent poet and novelist, lives alone in her home on Cape Ann, Massachusetts. Much of the novel is concerned with Hilary's preparation for and handling of an interview conducted by two young, awestruck journalists. She has rarely given such interviews, but the unexpected success of her most recent collection of poems has renewed the reading public's interest in her. Now seventy, she has published several volumes of poetry, yet she still feels drawn to writing as though there was still some problem for her to solve. It is during the interview that her development as a person and a writer is revealed, along with her deep-rooted and lifelong commitment to understanding women's roles and lives.

Born into an upper-middle-class Boston family, Hilary, an only child, received a great deal of attention and encouragement; however, her parents, while not scornful, fail to understand her vocation as a writer. While still young, Hilary relocates to Europe, where she lives until her parents' deaths some years later. She earns fame and notoriety in England with her first novel, which describes a love affair between two women. At this time Hilary marries Adrian Stevens, a veteran of World War I. The marriage is a happy one until he is killed in a riding accident after only three years. Devastated by her loss, Hilary suffers a nervous collapse and is hospitalized for the better part of a year. During this time, and with the encouragement of her doctor, she composes her first volume of poetry. Upon her release she returns to the literary and intellectual circles that had previously interested her and becomes enamored of her landlady, Willa MacPherson, with whom she has a brief affair and for whom she composes a sonnet sequence. When the relationship ends, Hilary returns to the United States. After a time she becomes involved with another woman and again composes a volume of poetry and a second novel.

During her interview, as she recalls the joyous, tragic, and inspirational events of her past, Hilary is also aware of Mer Hemmer, the young man who has helped her with her garden during the recent summer. This young man, whom she has inspired to begin writing poetry, is torn by his awakening homosexual desire and the memory of his one and only affair, which ended badly and with great emotional pain. Hilary, who feels that Mer has heard "the mermaids singing," that is he has whatever it takes to write poetry and to live as a writer, finds herself grappling with the reemergence of that singing in her own consciousness.

As the interview comes to a close, Hilary recalls her remote and troubled relationship with her mother, and she begins to realize that it is probably there that her next subject, and possibly her last, resides. Following a brief scene with Mer, whom she confronts directly about his writing, Hilary can hardly wait to resume writing—the process of wonder and discovery that has preoccupied her throughout her life.

Stevens, Gavin. *Intruder in the Dust; Requiem for a Nun; The Town; The Mansion.* William Faulkner. 1948; 1951; 1957; 1959.

The most ubiquitous of Faulkner characters, lawyer Gavin Stevens spends most of his life fighting for justice. He is involved in some of the most celebrated trials in Jefferson, Mississippi, and, more covertly, seeks to counter the plague of "Snopesism" that threatens Yoknapatawpha County.

Gavin has clearly been chosen by "Old Moster," as Jeffersonians call God, to lead a singular life. After childhood in an exceedingly isolated town, he finds his way to New York City, then to Harvard for a master's degree, and eventually to Heidelberg, Germany, where he earns a doctorate. Back in Mississippi, Gavin passes the bar and is elected to the position his father once held, county attorney.

As county attorney, Gavin defends a proud black man, LUCAS BEAUCHAMP, who has been wrongly accused of murder; he also convinces the perjuring TEMPLE DRAKE

to offer the real evidence that explains why a black nursemaid would have murdered Temple's infant daughter.

In a less official capacity, Gavin is perpetually engaged in countering the forces of his archrival, the powerful FLEM SNOPES. Gavin enlists the help of Maggie Mallison, his sister, and VLADIMIR KYRILYTCH RATLIFF, the local sewing machine salesman and grass-roots philosopher, in his crusade against the malevolent Snopes brood.

In 1908, Flem returns to Jefferson with his wife, EULA VARNER (SNOPES) and her baby daughter LINDA (SNOPES KOHL), who has been fathered by another man. Along with the rest of the town, Gavin watches indignantly while the mayor, Manfred de Spain, carries on an affair with Eula. After Gavin hits de Spain at a dance, the townspeople begin to regard their attorney as the third contender for Eula's affections. Gavin attempts to destroy both Flem and de Spain by filing a suit in which he holds them responsible for some valuable brass that had been stolen from a power plant which the two men once supervised. The plan backfires. De Spain resigns gracefully as mayor, only to be appointed president of the town bank. Then WILL VARNER, Eula's powerful father, sees to it that Flem becomes vice president of the bank.

As time passes, Gavin begins inviting the adolescent Linda to the drugstore twice a week. He buys her ice cream and tries to foster in her a sense of the possibilities beyond Jefferson. He urges her to attend school away from home. After much tension Flem allows Linda to leave for the university in Oxford, Mississippi. She eventually travels to New York and marries a sculptor there, Barton Kohl, who dies fighting in the Spanish Civil War.

Although a bomb explosion during the war has left her deaf, Linda returns to Jefferson and takes up social causes. She and Gavin meet regularly. He helps her improve her voice and suggests suitable employment. He confesses his affection for her, but she persuades him to marry Melisandre Backus, a wealthy widow with two grown children.

Gavin also helps Linda secure the release of MINK SNOPES, a relative of Flem's who has been unjustly imprisoned for nearly forty years. Gavin knows that Mink holds a grudge against Flem, and he arranges the release on the condition that Mink take $250 and leave Jefferson forever.

Gavin is horrified to learn that Mink has sacrificed the money to avenge himself by killing Flem. Although he considers himself an accessory to the murder, he does not want to attribute any evil intent to Linda, even though the circumstances indicate that Linda might well have intended her father's murder.

In their final meeting, Linda tells Gavin that she has never truly loved anyone but him. Gavin and Ratliff perform a final service for Linda by tracking down Mink and securing his departure with another offer of cash. Gavin feels that not only has he failed to rescue Eula and Linda from "Snopesism" but he might have caught the disease himself.

Stevens, Gowan. *Sanctuary; Requiem for a Nun; The Town.* William Faulkner. 1931; 1951; 1957.

A graduate of the University of Virginia (the institution where he learns to "drink like a gentleman"), Gowan Stevens is a flirtatious, self-assured young man whose pretensions conceal an essentially cowardly, irresponsible character. One of his girlfriends, TEMPLE DRAKE, is a seventeen-year-old student at the University of Mississippi at Oxford who is on academic probation for sneaking out of her dormitory room at night in order to date noncollegiate men. When Gowan arrives drunk to pick up Temple for their scheduled date to attend a baseball game in Starkville, she is disgusted; nevertheless, she climbs into his car, thereby beginning a journey that drastically alters her life.

Although Gowan is already drunk, he insists on making a detour to Lee Goodwin's bootlegger establishment at the Old Frenchman's Place in order to purchase more alcohol. Near their destination, Gowan runs into a tree. Gowan goes inside, and instead of trying to secure another ride, he proceeds to drink more. He passes out twice, and when he finally regains consciousness, he is so embarrassed by his sloppy behavior that he sneaks away without even saying good-bye to Temple, who meanwhile has been threatened with sexual assault by the various men who inhabit Old Frenchman's Place. Gowan does pay a man with a car to pick up Temple and deliver her to her dormitory, but this hired driver pockets the money without carrying out the assigned task.

Eight years pass before Gowan finds out what has happened to Temple since his cowardly exit. He discovers that she has been raped with a corn cob and forced into prostitution by a perverted thug named POPEYE VITELLI. Gowan decides to make what reparations he can by marrying Temple.

The Stevenses settle down to a superficially respectable life in Jefferson, Mississippi; they have a son, Bucky, and a daughter who is not named. Gowan and Temple cannot escape tragedy, however. Their domestic life is shattered when their nanny, a reformed prostitute and drug addict named Nancy Mannigoe, smothers their infant daughter in the cradle.

Nancy is tried and sentenced to death by hanging, but the night before her execution, her lawyer, GAVIN STEVENS, who is Gowan's uncle, attempts to persuade the governor to reduce the sentence. In the company of the governor and the lawyer, Temple admits that Nancy murdered their child in a desperate, deluded attempt to stop Temple from running away with one of the men who had formerly held her in sexual bondage. After Temple has finished her story, Gavin Stevens reveals that Gowan has been hiding in the room to hear Temple's confession. Nan-

cy's sentence is not commuted, but the confession forces both Gowan and Temple to confront the evil they have experienced and to realize that its repercussions cannot be avoided through hypocrisy.

Stiles, Jerusalem Webster. *Raintree County.* Ross Lockridge, Jr. 1947.

Professor Jerusalem Webster Stiles is the lifelong mentor and cynical friend of JOHN WICKLIFF SHAWNESSY,, the main character of this epic novel of life in Indiana in the nineteenth century.

A native of Raintree County, Stiles was considered a child prodigy. When his mother, a Bible-thumping evangelical woman whom he dearly loves, dies, leaving him orphaned at ten, he discovers that "the secret of life is death." He studies the classics and goes on to become the schoolmaster of the Pedee Academy near Waycross. At the academy he meets John Shawnessy, an enthusiastic student who becomes his protégé, confidant, and friend.

Indiana soon proves too narrow a domain for Stiles, and he leaves the academy. He and John meet again and again as their lives unfold in different directions, John's toward an early marriage and Stiles's, toward loose women and a fulfillment of his "pagan spirit." When the Civil War comes, he serves as a war correspondent and listens to Lincoln at Gettysburg. At the war's end he becomes something of a wanderer before eventually settling down in New York City where he pursues fine women with teeth that can "leave a mark of senile passion on the shoulders of the most beautiful." He attracts argumentative, intellectual friends and perfects his philosophical approach to America.

Stiles argues that America has been hurt by its own greatness and that in many ways it is yet to be discovered, and he calls the vast country through which he has traveled "the love child of history." Intrigued by Marxism, he is busy writing a history of mankind. He believes that America stands on the threshold of immense change, that the old America of the forefathers has been killed by the Civil War, and that the Constitution never anticipated the modern city. If Thomas Jefferson were to come back, Stiles claims, he would be astonished at what has happened to his republic.

On July 4, 1892, Stiles returns to his hometown of Waycross, Indiana, in Raintree County for the Grand Patriotic Program. He reacquaints himself with John Shawnessy, now the school principal, and with Evalina Brown, the president of the Women's Christian Temperance Union, an ardent feminist and a beautiful woman with whom he is half in love. Yet he tells John that he considers marriage "a kind of funeral" and thus has not and will never marry.

On the day on which the novel takes place, Stiles, in the company of John and Senator Garwood Jones, attends the patriotic entertainment, goes to a neighborhood farm to watch an enormous bull impregnate a heifer, and attends a meeting of the literary society, where he leads a discussion on "The Golden Bough."

Although John Shawnessy is content in this small midwestern town, Stiles finds it stifling, a place to visit and enjoy spirited conversation but not to live. After the last fireworks explode across the sky of Raintree County, he boards the midnight train and begins his journey back to New York City. As a parting flourish he lifts his cane and scrawls his initials in huge letters across the sky.

Stingo. *Sophie's Choice.* William Styron. 1976.

Stingo, the twenty-two-year-old narrator of this novel set in the late 1940s, was born and educated in the South but moves to Manhattan to become a writer, hoping that in this very literary milieu he will be able to indulge his almost erotic affinity for the written word. He gets a job at McGraw-Hill but soon becomes disillusioned with the world of publishing and, penniless but defiant, leaves the company. Alone in New York, Stingo soon grows depressed both at his inability to write more than the first paragraph of his novel and at his failure to find an outlet for his constant state of sexual, as well as creative, arousal. Some solace arrives with an inheritance, money that had been earned years before by the sale of one of his grandmother's slaves. Liberated by the money, yet burdened by the way in which it implicates him in the South's guilty history, Stingo, feeling very much "a Southerner living in the kingdom of the Jews," moves to Brooklyn.

This move provides the necessary release for Stingo's frustrated creative energies and a rite of passage from innocent Southerner to worldly adult, for it is in Brooklyn that he meets Sophie and Nathan. His first encounter with this couple is characteristically a sexual one. As he lies in bed one night, Stingo becomes at once aroused and annoyed by the noisy and enthusiastic lovemaking in the room above his own. When he finally meets Sophie and Nathan, Stingo's annoyance suddenly turns to fascination. Nathan is intelligent and articulate; Sophie is beautiful and haunted by a past visible only in the numbers tattooed on her wrist. Stingo is instantly drawn into their lives.

In spite of a sense of foreboding about his involvement with them, Stingo finds his admiration for Nathan increasing and his feeling for Sophie developing into love. This initiation into the world of more adult relationships sparks a sudden creative release. His father writes to him, telling him about the suicide of Maria Hunt, an old girlfriend of Stingo's; inspired by a story that seems typically Southern to Stingo, his novel quickly develops. Stingo's fascination with Nathan is tempered by Nathan's vicious outbursts against the South and against Stingo as a representative Southerner. The violence of Nathan's words stun him, and he finds himself defending a heritage that he actually feels is a burden. Yet in spite of Nathan's unpredictability, and the frustration of his feelings for

Sophie, Stingo generally finds their friendship liberating and embraces the freedom that Nathan and Sophie appear to offer him.

Yet Stingo's foreboding finally proves founded, and his relationship with Nathan and Sophie disintegrates as the lies and secrets he had only guessed at become clearer. The past that Sophie has gradually narrated to Stingo turns out to be a construction of half-truths. When she finally reveals her own and her family's involvement in Poland's fascist past, and tells him of the choice she was forced to make between her two children at a concentration camp, Stingo realizes the insurmountable distance between them.

Stingo also discovers that Nathan is secretly mentally ill and that he ruthlessly destroys those closest to him. When Nathan finally turns on both Stingo and Sophie, Stingo sees the chance to build a life with Sophie and protect her from the horrors of her past in Poland and her life with Nathan. He tries, absurdly, to take Sophie to a peanut farm inherited by his father, but only as they travel there does he realize the truth that Sophie has tried to conceal. After Sophie's most honest revelation, she and Stingo make love. When he wakes up, she has gone; he hurries back to Brooklyn, only to find that she and Nathan have committed suicide. As the book draws to its apocalyptic close, Stingo discovers his own resilience in the face of death and finds himself resurrected.

Stoddard, Eleanor. *U.S.A. (The 42nd Parallel; Nineteen Nineteen; The Big Money).* John Dos Passos. 1930; 1932; 1936.

Growing up near the Chicago stockyards and having her father come home every evening with the stockyard stench on him, Eleanor Stoddard learns to despise everything unclean and sordid. She develops a taste for art and spends all her time at the Chicago Art Institute. At eighteen she leaves home to live in a boardinghouse.

One day at the Art Institute she meets a young woman named EVELINE HUTCHINS, and the two become fast friends. Through Eveline she meets various artsy Chicagoans who teach her to despise the Art Institute for being ignorant of futurism and cubism.

Eleanor earns more money working at Marshall Field's, where her interest in decoration is fostered. When she fails to inherit the dreamed-of millions of an aged spinster she has befriended, she and Eveline become interior decorators; soon, through an admirer of Eveline, they get an opportunity to do the sets and costumes for a New York stage production.

The show flops, but Eleanor remains in New York. Decorating the house of the Moorehouses of Great Neck, she meets JOHN WARD MOOREHOUSE and develops an apparently platonic attachment to him. They begin to spend a great deal of time together; this arouses the suspicions of his wife and her wealthy relatives, but Ward insists that Eleanor is exclusively a spiritual inspiration to him. When the war breaks out and Ward volunteers his public relations expertise in the service of the country, Eleanor resolves to join the Red Cross.

From the time she arrives in Paris, Eleanor's personality takes on the same crisp, icy veneer as her exquisite wardrobe, and, as with Ward, one sees little more of her inner life. When Eveline barges into Eleanor's Paris apartment to find Ward in the bedroom and discreetly shuts the bedroom door, Eleanor icily thanks her; the door to her personal life shuts as well. She serves as Ward's companion and amanuensis throughout the war. Eleanor is responsible for hiring Ward's new assistant, RICHARD ELLSWORTH SAVAGE and saving Richard from what she deems an unwise marriage, but she appears only in other people's stories; little is revealed of her own.

When Eleanor is last seen, several years after the war, she is back in New York and has apparently abandoned Moorehouse to marry Prince Mingraziali, a deposed Russian nobleman.

Stokes, Justin. *The Finishing School.* Gail Godwin. 1985.

Justin Stokes, a fourteen-year-old girl, lives in the town of Clove in rural upstate New York. She spent the first decade of her life in Fredericksburg, Virginia, where she enjoyed an idyllic life with her brother Jem, her mother Louise, her father River, and her extended southern aristocratic family. Justin's happiness collapsed during a relatively short period in which her beloved grandparents died and her father was killed in a car crash. Rather than face a cruel world on her own, a world that might not continue to provide her with the comforts she had grown used to, Justin's mother decided to move in with her sister-in-law Mona.

Justin feels uncomfortable with the transformation her life has undergone. She must now make do with a small one-level house in a development called Lucas Meadows, situated near the local IBM plant. Her mother no longer carries herself with the grace and dignity of the southern gentry; instead she seems apologetic and obsequious in the presence of Aunt Mona. With Aunt Mona's teenage daughter Becky she is positively doting. Justin feels completely alienated by her circumstances—right down to the color of the wallpaper in her room, which she laments is named Raspberry Ice. To escape these surroundings, which she fears will turn her into a boring, complacent person, Justin goes on long bike rides by herself.

One summer day Justin happens upon a middle-aged woman sunbathing by a small pond and shack. Ursula DeVane, a retired actress, lives in a house nearby with her brother Julian, who gives piano lessons to the local children. Ursula is friendly, intelligent, and, above all, mysterious; Justin is overcome with admiration and in subsequent visits to the DeVane house seems to draw from the couple a sustaining antidote to her dreary life at home.

To the consternation of her family, who regard the DeVanes as eccentric and potentially dangerous snobs, Justin cultivates a close relationship with Ursula, who takes her on as the daughter she never had. She attempts to mold Justin into a bold, creative, and independent person, one who will never "congeal" or stop changing. As their relationship develops and Justin's "crush" on Ursula intensifies, Justin is privy to increasingly sensitive secrets about the DeVanes. One of these is that Ursula's mother had an affair with a young German whom the family had taken in as a tutor to Julian. Ursula discovered her mother and Karl making love in the shack by the pond, which Ursula has now dubbed her "finishing school."

As Justin and Ursula's relationship reaches a pinnacle of intimacy, ambiguities begin to multiply. Justin wonders if their relationship is an echo of an earlier one Ursula had experienced while teaching, when her favorite female student appeared naked in her bed one night, only to have Ursula caress her hair apologetically until morning. Is Ursula trying to shape Justin to fit the projection of her own ambitions? Is Justin a lesbian, like the protégés of Sappho on the Isle of Lesbos? Justin promises herself that she won't see Ursula for a week.

Before the week is up, however, Justin finds herself bicycling over at night to Ursula's pond. No one is there. Justin sits for a while; then, hearing something in the shack, she moves to look inside, just as Ursula had moved to spy on her mother many years before. What Justin sees topples her idol from the pedestal: Ursula *in flagrante delicto* with a local farmer.

Fate takes over. Justin's uncle has come to the DeVanes' to look for her. When he hears Justin scream, a sound that is followed by a splash, he runs with his flashlight to the little pond. There he sees Ursula, naked, pulling Justin to the shore while his neighbor, Mr. Christiana, wearing only pants, looks on. Ursula's brother rushes up and is even more shocked than Justin's uncle. Justin is taken home and learns the next day that Julian has hanged himself and that news of Mr. Christiana's infidelity is all over town, thus threatening his marriage and rendering Ursula a permanent outcast.

Years later, Justin looks back on this summer from the perspective of a successful New York theater actress. She absolves herself and her former friend of any guilt with regard to Julian's suicide—he had always been morbid and unstable—and decides that, despite her faults, she is exceedingly glad to have known Ursula.

Stoneman, Austin. *The Clansman: A Historical Romance of the Ku Klux Klan.* Thomas Dixon, Jr. 1905.

In this historical romance, the author praises the Ku Klux Klan and denigrates liberal reformers during the Reconstruction period. Congressman Austin Stoneman, a character loosely based on the historical figure Thaddeus Stevens, is one of those reformers. A hideous and unpleasant man in his seventies, Stoneman is the most powerful person in Washington, D.C., after President Lincoln. He lives in a small house next to the Capitol with a beautiful, "animal-like," mulatto housekeeper who seems to have an evil influence over him.

Stoneman goes to see President Lincoln immediately following the end of the Civil War. He berates the President for his plan to allow the Southern states back into the Union without insisting either on black suffrage or on punishment and exile for the white rebels. Stoneman tells the President that his ameliorative plan will never be allowed and that black suffrage will become a reality.

Soon after this encounter, Lincoln is assassinated. Stoneman holds a party at his house at which he tells his friends and followers that his plan for the South includes confiscating land from white Southerners and dividing it among the freed blacks. He sends two men to the South to set up his Union League and begin this secret plan.

Meanwhile, he proceeds to push Congress to adopt his agenda. He calls for a Committee on Reconstruction to be formed. Once this is done, Stoneman is elected the head of the committee. In addition, through intimidation, he is able to get the Reconstruction Act passed, giving blacks the right to vote. He also introduces impeachment proceedings against President Johnson. The impeachment does not pass, and during the proceedings Stoneman collapses. His doctor orders him to rest and recuperate in a warmer climate. Stoneman agrees to move but only because it will position him better to secretly direct his Union League and the redistribution of land and power.

Stoneman's children, Phil and ELSIE (STONEMAN), make arrangements to bring their father to Piedmont, South Carolina. Although Stoneman does not know it, Piedmont is the hometown of Phil's girlfriend Margaret and her brother BEN CAMERON, who is romantically involved with Elsie. Soon after arriving in South Carolina, Stoneman suffers a paralyzing stroke. It takes him months to recover.

Chaos reigns in Piedmont as Stoneman's Reconstruction plans are put into place. Stoneman's children become more and more sympathetic to the plight of the white Southerners. Dr. Cameron, the father of Margaret and Ben and a prominent Piedmont citizen, visits Stoneman and explains the devastation being caused by the "Negro" takeover. But Stoneman is unswerving in his beliefs. The tension between Stoneman and the white Southerners—Elsie's and Phil's new friends—increases.

The old man receives a threatening note from the Ku Klux Klan. He also learns that Ben is the leader of the North Carolina branch of the organization. Ben is sent to jail for murdering a black man, and Stoneman sets about to have him executed for the crime. Unbeknownst to him, however, his son Phil (the actual murderer) switches places with Ben in jail. Ben's sister Margaret searches for Stoneman to tell him about the switch, but in the meantime preparations are under way for the execution. By the time

Stoneman finds out that it is Phil who is about to be executed, he fears it is too late to have the execution stopped. As he begins to mourn his loss, Phil walks in, escorted by Ben and Elsie in Klan uniforms. Ironically, Stoneman's son has been saved by his enemies—Ben and the Ku Klux Klan.

Stoneman, Elsie. *The Clansman: A Historical Romance of the Ku Klux Klan.* Thomas Dixon, Jr. 1905.

Elsie Stoneman, a Union sympathizer at the end of the Civil War, is the daughter of AUSTIN STONEMAN, a radical Republican and powerful congressman. While volunteering at a makeshift hospital for wounded soldiers, Elsie meets BEN CAMERON, a young Confederate soldier. Although he is supposedly an enemy, she finds herself falling in love with him. Elsie befriends Ben's mother and uses her influence to arrange a meeting between Mrs. Cameron and President Lincoln. Mrs. Cameron pleads with Lincoln to pardon her son, who faces a death sentence for violating rules of war. Thanks to Elsie's intervention, Ben is saved.

Elsie is confused by her growing love for Ben and by her shifting loyalties, away from her father's radical views and toward the plight of her new Southern friends. She decides that her background and her father, whom she loves dearly, make it impossible to start a life in the South with Ben. She tells Ben she will be moving to New York. The night before she is scheduled to leave, however, Ben convinces her to go on a boat ride with him. Here, they profess their love for each other, and the differences in their politics and backgrounds no longer seem important to Elsie.

Elsie's father becomes very ill, and his doctor orders him to go to the South for warmth and relaxation. Elsie and her brother, who has fallen in love with Ben's sister Margaret, make arrangements to take their father to Piedmont, South Carolina—the hometown of Ben and Margaret. Once settled in Piedmont, the sympathy that Elsie and her brother feel for the white Southerners continues to grow. Elsie sees that her new friends are being threatened, victimized, and ruined by the new "Negro" Reconstruction governments; Elsie's father is the force behind these new governments. She worries about how to tell her sick father that she wants to marry one of his enemies. She finally tells him, and he consents to the union.

However, before long the tensions in Piedmont intensify. Elsie's father receives a threatening note from the Ku Klux Klan. It becomes clear that Ben plays an important role in the Klan; in fact, he is the highest-ranking Klan officer in South Carolina. Elsie tells Ben they can no longer see each other unless he gives up his Klan involvement. Ben refuses, and they part for a time.

When Elsie learns that Ben has been jailed and sentenced to death for murdering a black man, she is moved to profess her devotion to him once more. Ben gets out of jail when Elsie's brother Phil decides to secretly switch places with him; in doing so, Phil assumes that his father will get him released. But it is finally the Klan and not Elsie's father that saves Phil from execution with no time to spare. When Elsie last appears in the novel, she is standing by Ben's side, wearing a Klan uniform.

Storyteller. "The Big Bear of Arkansas." T. B. Thorpe. 1845.

The vivacious storyteller, a stranger who joins a heterogeneous group of passengers aboard a steamship on the Mississippi River, narrates a tale within a tale in this nineteenth-century short story. When he tells of hunting a monstrous bear in Arkansas, the storyteller reveals his own superstitious awe of the animal that nearly outwitted him.

In his home state of Arkansas, the storyteller earned a reputation as the best bear-hunter in his district. One fall day he saw fresh marks on a sassafras tree and knew they were put there by the biggest bear that ever lived. He resolved either to find and kill this bear or give up the hunting business altogether. His first chase lasted eighteen long miles, at the end of which his hunting dogs collapsed, his horse gave out, and he was totally exhausted. Unaccustomed to being seriously challenged by a bear, the storyteller began to waste away as the bear "took hold of his vitals" and became an obsession.

The storyteller's second hunting effort started one morning at sunrise. He found the bear's trail and followed it to open country, where he saw the bear leisurely ascending a hill with the hunting dogs close at his heels. The storyteller tells his steamboat audience that the bear was a real beauty and that he loved him like a brother. After the bear climbed a tree, the storyteller's hunting companion aimed and fired a bullet at the bear's head. The bear shook his head, climbed gently and gracefully down the tree, and lost his temper over the bullet wound. The storyteller reprimanded his friend for shooting the bear and causing this unnecessary wrath.

On an island across a lake, the hunting dogs cornered the bear in a thicket. The storyteller paddled toward the bear. When he saw him, he shot and was certain that he had finally killed the bear, but when he pulled the bear out of the water with a rope, the storyteller was astounded to see that this was not the great bear he had been hunting but an ordinary female bear. Judging from the evidence, he was even more convinced that he was hunting the devil himself.

After the storyteller's second failure, his neighbors began to doubt his word, and they wondered if the legendary bear existed at all. The storyteller was still determined to find the bear, and one day in the woods he finally saw him. He aimed, shot, and fired. The bear wheeled around, yelled out, walked directly through a log fence, and died in a nearby thicket. It took five people plus the storyteller to hoist the bear onto a mule's back, and the mule nearly collapsed under the bear's weight.

At the end of the storyteller's tale, the steamboat audience is quiet. The storyteller finally breaks the silence and invites everyone to drink with him before going to bed.

Strange, Laurentine. *The Chinaberry Tree.* Jessie Redmon Fauset. 1931.

Laurentine Strange is the illegitimate daughter of an African-American woman, SARAH "AUNT SAL" STRANGE, and Colonel Frank Halloway, a member of the town's most prominent white family. By nature Laurentine is intelligent, beautiful, and circumspect, but the circumstances of her birth deny her access to the respectable world she envies. Her consummate modesty cannot compensate, she feels, for her mother's past actions; she is not close to her mother and regards her present life as a tangle of passions and duties from which the future will rescue her.

This future seems to arrive in the form of the educated and wealthy Phil Hackett. As she discovers his feelings for her, Laurentine believes that she has really fallen in love with this man who she thinks can offer her a respectable means of escape from her solitary existence. Yet these hopes are shattered with the arrival of MELISSA PAUL, Laurentine's cousin, whose vivacity soon causes a scandal that scares Phil Hackett away from the Strange women. Laurentine is devastated by this betrayal and begins to lose hope that she will ever recover from the taint of illegitimacy.

Yet Laurentine finds other ways to make her own way and begins to realize that marriage is not the only option. She begins a dressmaking business that is soon successful and strikes up a friendship with Mrs. Ismay, a black woman who provides for Laurentine a model of education, independence, and ambition. As she discovers her own circle of friends, Laurentine begins to place more hope in the life she is able to create for herself. When she meets Stephen Denleigh, a black doctor, she is wary of falling in love. She slowly comes to realize, however, that he is a man who would make her happy, and she is able to believe in the sincerity of his feelings for her.

Even as Laurentine finally seems assured of the life she wants, the past intrudes, this time in the person of Melissa who is about to marry a man she does not realize is her brother. When Stephen tries to warn her, Laurentine blames her mother's past once again. This time, however, she comes to recognize that Stephen's concern does not result from a desire to flee but from the degree to which he feels a part of her family. As the novel ends, Laurentine looks to a future that promises not an escape but rather a wholehearted acceptance of the life her mother has given her.

Strange, Sarah "Aunt Sal." *The Chinaberry Tree.* Jessie Redmon Fauset. 1931.

A somewhat mysterious figure, Sarah Strange, known as Aunt Sal, is characterized by a serenity that is rarely ruptured and a sense of calm that she draws from her constant reflection on her past. However, this past overshadows the life of her daughter Laurentine, and Sal's unrepentant nonconformity breeds in her daughter an overwhelming desire to conform. As past and present and mother and daughter encounter each other through the course of the novel, Sal comes to stand as an emblem of the power of the past and the legacy of the older generation.

Aunt Sal's haunting past begins when, as the daughter of a poor Alabama family, she is working as a maid for the white Halloway family. She is intelligent, loyal, and perceptive, and is tied to such menial work by her gender, color, and class. She falls in love with Frank Halloway, the family's son; they have an affair that lasts until Halloway's death and persists in spite of the town's outrage, his family's protestations, and, later, his wife's disgust. Their notoriety increases when their daughter Laurentine is born; yet they remain loyal to each other throughout.

After Halloway dies, Sal retreats into their shared past, living on the memories contained in the house he has given her and sheltering under the chinaberry tree that he brought her from Alabama. Sal is content with total solitude, which is partly enforced and partly of her own making since she finds the present less engaging than the past. Laurentine is frustrated by this solitary existence, however, and Sal finds her daughter growing further away from her without being able to explain why. Yet Sal is soon forced to realize that her past is intruding on her daughter's present—that in fact it is the cause of Laurentine's unhappiness. When the wealthy and respectable Phil Hackett expresses an interest in Laurentine, Sal fervently hopes that this marriage will give Laurentine the respectability she wants.

However, Laurentine's tenuous happiness is shattered by the arrival of MELISSA PAUL, the daughter of Sal's sister Judy who years before had fled the town under mysterious circumstances. Melissa has inherited her mother's vivacity and reputation, and Laurentine's suitor is scared away by suggestions of impropriety in the Strange household. Sal is powerless to do anything and cannot even comfort Laurentine, who blames her for this destruction of her hopes. Sal sees the past being relived before her eyes as Laurentine retreats further and further into herself. The sight of this loneliness without any of the consolations that she herself had experienced finally ruptures Sal's habitual calm. The tears she cries at this point are the only ones she has shed in front of Laurentine, but mother and daughter are by this point too estranged for the tears to bring them closer.

With the arrival of the affectionate Melissa, Sal begins to feel that she has found another daughter. Yet this relationship is also haunted by past indiscretions, and Sal again has to watch a young woman she loves become frustrated by her mother's past. Finally, though, Laurentine and Melissa overcome such legacies and achieve the comforts they have so ardently desired. As the novel ends, Sal is free to sink back into her past with Frank Halloway, a past that she can now openly dwell on with no regrets. Faced with the hard-won respectability of her daughter and niece, Sal resists respectability in favor of a passionate happiness.

Strasser-Mendana, Grace Tabor. *A Book of Common Prayer.* Joan Didion. 1977.

Grace Tabor Strasser-Mendana attempts to understand the elusive and self-destructive character of her American friend CHARLOTTE AMELIA HAVEMEYER BOGART DOUGLAS by carefully analyzing what she learns about Charlotte during their approximately year-long acquaintance. Born in Denver, Colorado, Grace is an inhabitant of the capital city of the volatile state of Boca Grande in Central America. Her family by marriage is prominent in the city because of its wealth and its involvement in the intrigue that periodically explodes into revolution. A former anthropologist whose interests have since moved into the field of biochemistry, Grace takes on another hobby when she becomes intrigued with Charlotte and determines to make sense of her friend's odd, often irrational and dangerous, behavior.

Orphaned at the age of ten after her father died of gunshot wounds, Grace lived alone until the age of sixteen in the suite her family had taken at the Brown Palace Hotel in Denver. Having studied anthropology with the famous scientists Kroeber and Lévi-Strauss, Grace conducts experiments and catalogs the rites and ethics of several societal systems. Eventually she loses her faith in the validity of anthropological speculations, retires from the field, and marries Edgar Strasser-Mendana, a rich planter of coconut palms who makes his home in Boca Grande. Once she is installed in her new country and life, Grace turns her scientific energies to biochemistry, conducting experiments on such subjects as the synthesis of the molecular properties of the protein that causes human beings to experience fear. Despite her scientific training, she finds that she is unable to analyze the chemical or emotional properties that motivate Charlotte Douglas.

Although she is dying of cancer by the time she meets Charlotte, Grace remains mobile enough to continue her research and her social life, which is active even though she is a widow. Grace's relationship with Charlotte is intensified when the latter becomes involved in a sexual relationship with Grace's son Gerardo, who is involved in plans to forcibly overthrow the existing government. Grace is fascinated by Charlotte's eccentric behavior, which includes frequenting airports for no apparent reason, attempting to publish letters that inaccurately describe the history and social climate of Boca Grande, and coming up with a plan to improve the country's economic status by attracting tourists with an annual film festival. But the aspect of Charlotte that most intrigues Grace is the history of Charlotte's missing daughter as a terrorist revolutionary in the United States. When the planned coup in Boca Grande threatens to explode into the civil war that will eventually be referred to as the October Violence, Grace unsuccessfully insists that Charlotte join her in fleeing from the besieged country. However, Charlotte is shot, and her body is thrown onto the lawn of the American embassy.

Perplexed by Charlotte's inexplicable refusal to save her own life, Grace sees to it that her dead friend's body is sent to California to be buried. After she locates Charlotte's fugitive daughter in Buffalo, New York, Grace visits her to tell her of her mother's death. She tries to glean additional information that might explain the mysterious behavior of her assassinated friend, but this effort, like all the others, leaves Grace at a loss to understand the complex and compelling life of the woman who continues to fascinate and bewilder her even in death.

Straus, Arthur. *Compulsion.* Meyer Levin. 1956.

Arthur Straus is the stand-in for Richard Loeb in this fictionalized account of the 1924 Leopold-Loeb murder. In the novel, Artie Straus and his best friend JUDAH "JUDD" STEINER are arrested and tried for the murder of a young boy, here called Paulie Kessler. The two wealthy young men, believing in their moral and intellectual superiority, had determined that they could enact the perfect crime.

While Artie at first desires to murder his younger and much-pampered brother, Judd persuades him to select another victim, and more or less at random they choose Paulie Kessler, whom they kill and hide in a nearby wooded area. Following the murder, the two try to extort $10,000 from the victim's father, but their plan is disrupted by the early discovery of the boy's body. During the following investigation, Judd is detained first, and he sticks to an alibi on which they had earlier agreed; however, Artie decides that the alibi is no longer valid since he and Judd had agreed to use it only within a week of the crime. Eventually, under persistent questioning, the youths' alibis coincide, and they are about to be released when a letter from Judd to Artie is made public. This piece of evidence reveals both their twisted relationship and their involvement in a number of crimes. At this point they confess, and Artie blames the killing on Judd, although according to the novel it was Artie who committed the actual murder.

The families of the two confessed murderers hire defense attorney Jonathan Wilks—a fictionalized Clarence Darrow. During the trial and a seemingly endless series of tests and personality profiles, Artie is revealed as an exceptionally bright young man who suffered from faulty sexual development perhaps due to a deficient metabolism. The emotional coldness exhibited by his parents and his jealousy of his younger brother's place in his mother's affections are also implicated in Artie's development into a sociopathic killer. Although the boys had a sexual relationship, it is made clear that Artie had sex with Judd in compliance with their pact. It was Artie who desired to commit the crimes, and he "earned" Judd's compliance by agreeing to have sex with his friend. At the same time Artie had a reputation as a ladies' man, but more important, he was seriously implicated in a number of other crimes including the murder and castration of a taxi driver and the disappearance of two male students.

These crimes are not at issue in the novel, and Artie's involvement is not proven by a confession, although he alludes to such crimes while being interviewed. The defense is able to persuade the judge to render a life sentence on their guilty plea rather than the death penalty sought by the state. Both Artie and Judd are sentenced to life in prison where, twelve years after the end of the trial, Artie is killed during a fight with a jealous inmate.

Street, Margaret. *Tar Baby.* Toni Morrison. 1981.

Margaret Street, now fifty years old and a fading beauty, is angry at her husband Valerian who insists on spending his retirement at their house on a private island in the Caribbean. Specifically, as the Christmas holidays approach, Margaret fears that her thirty-year-old son Michael, the only person whose love she wants, will not make the trip from California to visit them.

When Margaret was a child in the small town of South Suzanne, Maine, her astonishing beauty, her flaming red hair, and her brilliant blue eyes greatly affected the ways others interacted with her. In particular, her parents, who regarded her as having great advantages, not only neglected to impart to her the wisdom they felt their other children needed, but they also doubted her parentage. This special, though not preferential, treatment led to Margaret's emotional instability and acute craving for familial warmth.

After being named the "Principal Beauty of Maine" at the age of seventeen, Margaret marries Valerian, the hereditary owner of a flourishing, family-run candy business, and his disapproving female relatives advise her to create a family of her own as soon as possible. Margaret moves with Valerian to his mansion in Philadelphia. Feeling overwhelmed by Philadelphia society, she befriends the cook, a young black woman named Ondine who is the aunt of the bold and independent JADINE CHILDS. When Valerian comes home, Margaret and Ondine are often giggling in the kitchen, and even during parties the hostess escapes to chat with her only friend. Valerian chastises Margaret and orders her not to fraternize with the hired help; their argument leads to a rift in the marriage.

The eventual birth of their son Michael does not ease Margaret's loneliness. Emotionally frail, she begins to abuse her child by burning him and sticking him with sharp objects until Ondine discovers her. Ondine keeps her mistress's secret; nevertheless, the distance between Margaret and her husband grows. Margaret, now quite unstable, becomes disoriented and cannot remember the uses of familiar objects; Valerian assumes she is secretly drinking. When he retires to the Caribbean, Margaret refuses to make her permanent home with him and instead divides her time between America, where Michael lives, and the island.

As a Christmas gift to Michael, Margaret invites his favorite poet to come to their Caribbean house. Her spirits are high, but Valerian, because of past experiences, doubts Michael's arrival. When the guests fail to arrive, Margaret and Valerian sit down to Christmas dinner with Ondine and her husband Sydney. The tension in the house finally erupts when Ondine finds out that her kitchen help has been fired over a trifle, and without her knowledge. She slaps Margaret's face and, shouting, tells Valerian about the injuries his wife inflicted on their now absent son.

Following this incident, the relationships in the house are drastically altered. Margaret is relieved that Ondine has unmasked her, and she begins to free herself from her neuroses. Valerian is too shocked to hear any details, but Margaret, wanting to experience the punishment she feels she deserves, tells him anyway, little by little. Valerian never chastises her, however. He ages rapidly and becomes helpless, and Margaret learns to be his nurse. Although Valerian remains the center of attention in the household, Margaret begins to have a sense of her own importance there, and she gradually relinquishes her dream of recovering Michael's childhood.

Strether, Lambert. *The Ambassadors.* Henry James. 1903.

The ineffectual Lambert Strether, unsuccessfully attempting to be zealous and curious, remains detached and indifferent to life. His wife and son died long ago, a tragedy that left him permanently insulated against experiencing life to its fullest.

When the novel opens, Strether is sent to France by his fiancée, Mrs. Newsome, who instructs him to retrieve Chad Newsome, her wayward son. Mrs. Newsome wants Strether to bring Chad back to America and to his family obligations, and she stipulates that their marriage is contingent upon her success as his ambassador. En route to France, Strether befriends Maria Gostrey, who henceforth serves as his advisor and confidante.

Arriving in Paris, Strether is shocked to learn that Chad is involved with a woman, but he is also pleasantly surprised by Chad's newfound self-assurance and sophisti-

cation. Although secretly envious of what he considers Chad's hedonistic life-style, Strether informs Chad that he must return to America immediately. Later, when Chad introduces Strether to Madame de Vionnet and her daughter, Strether is convinced that the woman who binds Chad to Paris is the beautiful daughter herself.

Seeing the fullness of Chad's life, Strether realizes that he has let so much of life pass him by since the death of his wife and son, leading him to declare emotionally that it is always a mistake to avoid experiencing life completely. Immediately after this declaration, Strether sees Chad with Madame he Vionnet and has a revelation: Chad loves Madame de Vionnet, not her young daughter.

Intrigued, Strether gets to know Madame de Vionnet, who is ten years Chad's senior, and she entreats him to give a favorable report of her to Mrs. Newsome. Strether promises to try to save her; he then realizes that she is the savior because she has so greatly enriched Chad's character. Growing increasingly unenthusiastic about his mission, Strether writes a glowing but vague report to Mrs. Newsome. Mrs. Newsome, who has been dogging Strether with insistent letters, now decides he is not performing his mission to her satisfaction and dispatches more ambassadors, including her daughter Sarah and Sarah's husband. In addition, Mrs. Newsome issues an ultimatum: If he cannot retrieve Chad, Strether must return to America immediately.

But Strether does not want to return. Annoyed by Mrs. Newsome's blind obstinacy and her refusal to see Madame de Vionnet as anything but horrible, Strether now feels he is experiencing the youth he missed. Chad, in the meantime, intuitively recognizes that Strether, like himself, has succumbed to the charms of Parisian life. Sarah and her husband, disgusted by Strether's failure to complete his mission, return home at the summons of Mrs. Newsome.

Strether escapes to the French countryside where he witnesses a rendezvous between Chad and Madame de Vionnet. In a flash he realizes that not only are they in love, but they are intimately involved. Strether now sees so much of life and, at the same time, how much he has denied himself. Painfully aware of his position as an outsider to life itself, Strether returns to Paris.

Strether knows he is too changed to return to Mrs. Newsome and that she will never take him back anyway. He bids good-bye to his confidante Maria Gostrey; she comes close to declaring her love for him, but he is not attuned to her intimations. Strether remains detached and dispassionate, destined to spend the rest of his life a lonely widower.

Stringham, Susan Shepherd. *The Wings of the Dove.* Henry James. 1902.

Susan Shepherd Stringham becomes the companion and confidante of a twenty-two-year-old heiress from New York City, MILDRED THEALE. A widow, Susan abandons her life as a writer in Boston in order to accompany Milly on a journey to Europe. Susan regards herself as making a complete commitment to Milly, and she remains with her faithfully until her death.

Susan thinks of Milly as a "princess" but characterizes herself proudly as a "woman of the world." Susan was a young girl when her father died, and her brave mother brought Susan and her sister from Vermont to Europe with no assistance. She gave them five years in Switzerland and Germany, and Susan has wonderful memories of her school days there. Many years later, after the death of her own husband, Susan courageously begins a career as a writer in Boston. She becomes a regular contributor of short stories to the "best" magazines and conceives as her literary mission the portrayal of that neglected New England which is not quaint and domestic. Susan meets Milly in Boston and immediately senses that Boston is not "seeing" the profundity of this New York character. She instantly renounces her old life to meet Milly in New York. In accompanying the heiress to Europe, Susan expects to receive a thorough education in "life."

Before they depart for Europe, Susan secretly meets with Milly's doctor and learns that an illness, now in its earliest stages, threatens to prevent them from carrying out their plans. In spite of their concerns, they sail for Italy and are later received at Lancaster Gate, the London estate of Susan's old friend Maud Lowder. While Milly is pronounced a brilliant success in London society, Susan finds that she herself is regarded as a rather uninteresting figure. She accepts this position without resentment, considering it her first duty to support Milly. Susan tells the young woman sincerely that she would die for her and feels rewarded by Milly's confidence and openness.

As Milly's illness progresses, however, she becomes unwilling to confide in anyone. After several weeks in London, Milly decides to visit Sir Luke Strett, a famous doctor, and Susan knows from her cheerfully evasive response that her health is worse. Susan escapes from their hotel to Maud's home so that Milly does not see her weep. Sir Luke Strett has prescribed "happiness" for Milly, which Susan and Maud take to mean that Milly must fall in love. They have both detected a change in Milly since the arrival of Merton Densher, a young journalist who is secretly engaged to Maud's niece Kate Croy but whom Maud forbids her to marry. They assume that by putting Densher "in the way of it," they can force him to care for Milly instead. Susan and Maud agree to deny that Kate feels anything for Densher so that Milly will feel free to fall in love with him herself. Susan is surprised to find how willing she is to work against Kate for Milly's sake.

The plan unfolds smoothly since Kate, who is aware that Milly is dying, demands that her lover court the young heiress. If he can inherit Milly's fortune, they can then marry in spite of Maud's disapproval. The party moves in August from London to Venice where Milly has rented

a palace. After Maud Lowder and Kate Croy return to London, Densher remains behind and visits the palace daily. When the most severe phase of the illness strikes Milly, Susan becomes desperate. The romantic remedy becomes poisonous when Lord Mark, a rejected suitor, informs Milly that Kate and Densher have been engaged while he has been courting her. The news eventually kills Milly; after hearing it, she simply "turns her face to the wall." Susan visits Densher, who has been waiting for some sign from the palace, hoping that he will come to Milly with a life-saving denial. Densher visits the palace but only to say goodbye. Susan remains alone with Milly in Venice until her death several weeks later.

Strong, Joseph. *Marching! Marching!* Clara Weatherwax. 1935.

One of a long line of lumberjacks, Joe Strong works at the mill owned by GEORGE BAYLISS. Joe and his wife Mary, who works in the local bar, live relatively happily in the shadow of the Bayliss mill despite the financial hardships and dangerous working conditions imposed by its owner. There are occasional attempts at unionization of all local working-class laborers, but in the tradition of his family, Joe dismisses such activities as "communist." His attitudes change, however, when Bayliss's utter lack of concern for the welfare of his workers leads to a tragic accident in which his brother Tim is killed.

Joe does his best to help his sister-in-law Annie with the meager funds he can save from the mill and the little that Mary makes. He fully expects the mill to pay compensation to his brother's widow, but Bayliss refuses to give any financial assistance to Annie, claiming that his mill is in no way responsible for the accident that resulted in Tim's death. In a fit of rage, Joe fights back at the enormous lumber company in the only way he can. With the aid of an immigrant union organizer named Mario, Joe organizes a meeting of all the local unions to discuss the possibility of a general strike.

Joe and Mary make extensive preparations for the meeting, taking pains to serve a wide array of refreshments and even hiring a piano player to provide entertainment to attract a large cross-section of the local working class. Much to Joe's horror, however, Mario, his co-organizer and catalyst for the lumberman's union, is beaten to death by Bayliss and his thugs a few days before the meeting. Joe is worried that the union solidarity they seek will be destroyed before it begins, but Mario's death has the opposite effect. Joe makes the immigrant worker a kind of martyr to the labor movement, and in a rush of emotion, the assembled workers agree to go on strike.

But Joe and the rest of the striking workers are unprepared for the resistance their fledgling strike meets. After employing police officers and thug strikebreakers to subdue the picketing lumbermen, Bayliss pays off the local media, who denounce the workers as subversive "communists" and "reds." When these efforts are not enough to quell the laborers' movement, Bayliss has Joe and another labor organizer arrested for attempted murder, claiming they tried to push him down the stairs during a demonstration.

Joe is imprisoned without bail and is forced to stand trial on bogus charges. Through the window of his prison cell he sees the parading laborers showing their support for the strike, marching past the jail in solidarity.

Strong, Kay Leiland. *The Group.* Mary McCarthy. 1954.

Kay Leiland Strong was raised in Salt Lake City, Utah, and is the first of her clique of Vassar graduates, class of 1933, to marry. A theater major in college, Kay marries a would-be playwright named Harald Petersen from Boise, Idaho. Petersen graduated from Reed College and spent a year at the Yale Drama School before the Depression forced him to move to New York City. There he supports himself working sporadically as a stage manager while Kay supplements their income by becoming a sales clerk at Macy's department store. At their highly unconventional wedding, to which none of the newlyweds' relatives are invited, Kay's seven best friends—the "group"—are concerned that their friend is marrying because of her ambition to be affiliated with theater people. Furthermore, they are not convinced by the groom's behavior that he is sincerely in love with her. Even so, the wedding takes place, and the couple settles down in the same apartment in the East Fifties they had shared before becoming wife and husband.

After Kay gives up her own aspirations to become a director, she settles into her routine at Macy's and devotes her energies to contributing both financially and emotionally to Harald's career. Kay is convinced that Harald is a genius and is sure that he will be extraordinarily successful. Despite her support, his career fails to gel. He is frequently unemployed and does not manage to get his plays produced, in part because of the shaky foundation of the theater in New York during the Great Depression. Frustrated by his lack of success, Harald begins drinking excessively and engages in sexual liaisons behind Kay's back. Kay becomes increasingly jealous, and their marriage flounders. Finally a drunken Harald, countering Kay's own rage that causes her to threaten his life with a knife, physically abuses her and then commits her to the Payne Whitney Clinic, claiming she is both suicidal and dangerously aggressive toward him. Harald eventually regrets his rash behavior; he goes to the mental institution, apologizes to his wife, and assures her that she is free to leave the premises at will. Together they decide that she could in fact use a rest, and she decides to stay on at the hospital, where she experiences a genuine nervous breakdown in reaction to the disintegration of her marriage. After she recovers from her bout of debilitating anxiety,

she moves back home with her parents in Salt Lake City.

Kay's return to her childhood home proves unsuccessful because her parents are unsympathetic to the vagaries of her life. After she recovers her equilibrium sufficiently, she returns to New York City with the hope that she will be able to land a sales position at Saks Fifth Avenue. Shortly after her return, however, she falls twenty stories to her death from a window of the Vassar Club where she had been living temporarily. Her friends are shocked when they hear the news, and opinions differ as to whether or not Kay committed suicide. Since the official report claims that her death was accidental, she is granted a Christian burial. The group tends to Kay's funeral arrangements, and they try to come to terms with the tragedy of their friend's ill-fated life.

Stroud, George. *The Big Clock.* Kenneth Fearing. 1946.

George Stroud, the central character and occasional narrator, is executive editor of *Crimeways*, an affiliate of the mass-market magazine syndicate Janoth Enterprises. Having worked in the past as a timekeeper on a construction gang, a racetrack operator, a tavern proprietor, a newspaperman, and an advertising consultant, George is restless in his current job at the publishing conglomerate. He sees himself as an imaginative man—a rebel in the organization—but is perceived by his coworkers as aloof, arrogant, and ambitious.

Despite an apparently happy home life with his wife Georgette (nicknamed "George") and young daughter Georgia (also called "George"), George enters into a brief affair with the sensual and mysterious Pauline Delos, who happens to be the mistress of his boss, Earl Janoth. While taking leave of her half a block from her apartment after a romantic weekend, George witnesses Janoth arriving and then entering the building with Pauline. Janoth notices but does not recognize George.

The next day George reads in his morning paper that Pauline has been murdered, apparently minutes after he had last seen her with Janoth. The paper reports that Janoth claimed he had not seen the woman for several days. George is emotionally shaken, primarily because he is uncertain as to whether or not Janoth recognized him. He is displeased at finding himself in the position of having to choose between going to the police and thereby ruining his marriage or somehow trying to extricate himself from his difficulties on his own. Throughout the novel George perceives his predicament (and indeed his life as a whole) in terms of the naturalistic imagery of a big clock whose intricate mechanisms determine what has been and what will be. He therefore decides not to go to the police but to wait and see if he can outwit both Janoth and the clock in the process.

George soon discovers that the situation is even more complicated than he thought: Janoth, advised by his ruthless majordomo Steve Hagen, launches an investigation—

purportedly to track down a figure in a business and political conspiracy, but in reality to find the unidentified man who could place the corporate leader at the scene of the crime. George himself, as head of *Crimeways*, is put in charge of the investigation and is given carte blanche with the company's resources and manpower. George feels somewhat relieved at this point, counting on the fact that he may be able to point his subordinates in false directions and impede the inquiry in other subtle ways. He underestimates the staff's ability, however; it is soon discovered that the mystery man works in the Janoth building. Witnesses are brought on the scene to identify him, and an office-to-office search commences, ostensibly directed by George himself. Just as the net begins to close around him, he is called to an executive meeting in which a business merger is announced, and Janoth is forced to step down from the helm of the corporation by the company's controlling board.

George takes advantage of the upheaval and orders that the search for the culprit be suspended, thereby narrowly escaping capture. As the novel concludes, George is riding in a taxi, musing that the big clock had forgotten about him, at least for the moment, when his eye catches a newspaper headline announcing Janoth's suicide.

Sue. "Bright and Morning Star." Richard Wright. 1947.

Battered but not beaten by poverty and prejudice, Sue feels that she achieves a limited but real victory over oppression when she sacrifices her life to protect the members of a fledgling communist group in a small southern town.

Sue has long struggled to maintain her dignity and keep her family strong in the face of ugly racial prejudice. In a world where just having enough food to eat is a challenge, Sue has managed to imbue her sons Johnny-Boy and Sug with a sense of their own self-worth. When her boys joined the Communist Party, hoping to secure equal rights for blacks, she supported them. Now that Sug has been arrested and murdered by the sheriff's men because of his activities, Sue is left with only one son, and his life is also in danger.

One night in a howling storm Sue sings a spiritual while doing her housework. Somehow the words comfort her despite her communist sympathies. Sue has need of comfort on this cheerless night because Johnny-Boy has not yet come home. Her fears that he may have been captured by the sheriff's men on the evening before an important Party meeting seem confirmed when she hears a knock on the door. Sue senses danger, but the visitor is Reva, a white Party member who has come to tell Sue that the next night's meeting has been canceled because the sheriff has learned about it. Reva repeatedly assures Sue that nothing has happened to Johnny-Boy as far as she knows but that someone must tell all the comrades not to come to the meeting. Against Reva's objections—for she loves Johnny-

Boy and is fearful for his safety—Sue promises to send Johnny-Boy with the warning.

When Johnny-Boy finally gets home, Sue gives him dinner and debates telling him about the canceled meeting because she has already sacrificed one son. But reasoning that only Johnny-Boy can warn the other comrades and despite the danger of the mission, Sue reveals to Johnny-Boy that someone has told the sheriff of the meeting. She blames one of the new, white members of the Party for the leak.

Hours after Johnny-Boy has left the house to communicate the news of the canceled meeting, Sue is awakened by strange voices: The sheriff's posse has come to question her about Johnny-Boy's whereabouts. Sue will not answer their questions and, feeling a desperate kind of strength, goes so far as to challenge the white men. Even after they beat her mercilessly, she feels triumphant over them.

Coming out of unconsciousness, Sue finds herself staring up at the face of Booker, a white man who is a new recruit to the Party. Her resolve considerably weakened by the beating, she tells him the names of the Party members when he says he will warn them that the meeting has been canceled. When Reva once again comes to her house, Sue is appalled to learn that Booker is suspected of being the one who told the sheriff of the meeting. Now Sue must act to save the Party.

Taking a gun, Sue wraps it in a sheet and ventures out into the night. Finally coming upon the sheriff and his men, she tells them that she has brought the sheet as a shroud for Johnny-Boy. Sue is then taken to where her son lies, beaten but still alive. The sheriff's men try to convince Sue to tell her son to reveal the names of his comrades, but she will not bow to their pressure. Still clutching the gun, she watches as they break his kneecaps and burst his eardrums.

When Booker arrives, boasting that he has the names of the communists, Sue removes the gun from its coverings and shoots Booker in the head as Johnny-Boy watches confusedly. Sue is wrestled to the ground and made to watch as her son is murdered. When she is shot through the chest, she knows before she dies that her death is not her defeat.

Sullivan, Paco. *Paco's Story.* Larry Heinemann. 1979.

The lone survivor of a horrific firefight that decimated Alpha Company at Fire Base Hariette in Vietnam, Paco Sullivan drifts across America, the scarred outcast of a society incapable of comprehending the depths of emotional and physical trauma inflicted on the war's veterans. The narrator of his tale is a ghost, or perhaps a collective of ghosts, of those killed on that fateful day at Fire Base Hariette. This voice, not sympathetic to Paco's condition, haunts his life and represents the feelings of guilt with which he is burdened.

After a description of the aftermath of the firefight during which Paco is treated for his wounds by a medic whose life is forever altered as a result, Paco arrives in Boone, Texas, with nothing more than a duffel bag and a walking cane. He is driven into town by a mechanic who rekindles both his memory of being near death and his willful determination to survive despite the almost unbearable pain. Paco recalls the carnage of the massacre and his long convalescence in graphic detail.

Once in town Paco makes a concerted effort to find gainful employment, only to suffer the frustrations of being repeatedly rebuffed by any number of townsfolk. Eventually, however, he is hired as a dishwasher by Ernest Monroe, a sympathetic World War II veteran and owner of the Texas Lunch, a small diner. Paco establishes residency at the Geronimo Hotel across the street from the diner and immediately begins a routine of working long days, earning just enough to make ends meet, and whiling away nights by consuming alcohol, antidepressants, and muscle relaxants in an attempt to numb his pain. But try as he may, Paco is unable to escape such memories of war's brutality as his slaughter of a Vietcong soldier or his participation in the rape and murder of a teenage Vietnamese girl. Further, Paco consistently suffers from nightmares springing out of his experiences.

One day a Vietnam veteran by the name of Jesse arrives at the diner and discusses with Paco his own experiences of the war. Paco admits he has grown embittered but that, all else being equal, he is glad to be alive. Indeed, Paco is determined to live without either self-pity or self-destructive anger in the face of his memory of unspeakable horrors. Later, after returning to the hotel, Paco decides to break into a room adjacent to his own, which is occupied by an attractive young woman named Cathy who has on several occasions teased and aroused Paco by strutting around her apartment in various states of undress. Paco ultimately discovers her diary and learns that she is repulsed by the sight of his scarred body. Accepting the fact that he is unlikely to ever be accepted by the population at large, Paco pens a parting note for Ernest and boards a westbound bus, unsure of his destination.

Summerlad, Elvira. *Jeremy's Version.* James Purdy. 1970.

Matt Lacey dictates the story of Elvira Summerlad and her family, once intimate friends of his, to Jeremy Cready, a fifteen-year-old paper boy who has recently befriended him. The story begins as Elvira, living in poverty and disgrace with her sons for ten years, is about to divorce her husband Wilders. She finds herself in an emotional crisis as her own desires for freedom conflict with the demands and needs of her two sons.

As a wealthy and beautiful young woman, Elvira led a charmed life in her small Ohio town, whose residents respected and idealized her. When her dream of becoming an actress is thwarted by her father, Elvira marries the prosperous and striking young financier Wilders Fergus, who soon loses all their money and her family's money. Wilders eventually leaves Elvira, and she ends up running a boardinghouse in order to support her sons.

When her husband returns after a ten-year absence, Elvira decides to divorce him even though he claims he is returning for good. She has spent these years in poverty and shame, maintaining various lovers and saddled with a reputation for running a "disorderly house." She is extremely possessive of her sons, whose affection she has won by saying that she would die before leaving them and by reiterating that their father abandoned them. But she is losing control over them. Her son Rick has sex with the town's cultured men and women in order to make connections, and he wants to leave her to become an actor in New York. Her middle son, Jethro, who never knew his father, had a near-fatal accident at age six and has been morose, resentful, and distant ever since.

When Rick inherits $6,000 from an aunt and informs her that he is going to New York with Matt, Elvira panics. She asks him to stay only until she has dealt with Wilders; she, too, wants her freedom. Elvira gives Wilders a cold reception upon his return, but two days later she asks Rick to concede to his father's request that the boy "lend" him his inheritance money for a business deal. Incredibly, Elvira has faith that Wilders will not lose the money this time. When Rick resentfully gives up the money, Elvira realizes her folly; three weeks later his savings have been lost. Elvira, grieved at Rick's long absence from home, informs Wilders that she is initiating divorce procedures and finds that even her demanding chores can't distract her from her sorrows.

Wilders's sister Winifred, who always hated Elvira, tries to intimidate her into dropping the divorce. But when Winifred arrives at her house to ask the boys to live with Wilders, Elvira thrashes her and drives her away. Elvira hesitates to pursue the divorce, which will expose her to public scrutiny and to Winifred's continued threats, but she decides that she can never again be tied to Wilders. She discovers, however, that her mother and sons are not nearly as eager for the divorce as she is, and she must pressure Rick into testifying against his father. At the trial Rick makes an absurdly dramatic speech in which he denounces Wilders not only for losing his money but for leaving him for years in the clutches of his controlling mother.

The judge grants the divorce after Rick and Jethro send him letters praising their mother's virtue. But while Rick has complied in order to secure his own freedom to go to New York, Jethro, who sees Rick and Elvira as "lovers" conspiring against him, has decided that he must kill Elvira. Jethro wants Elvira to give him all the love he lacked as a child; if she retains her various lovers now that she is free from Wilders, she must be punished. Jethro writes her a scathing letter accusing her of being a whore, and he attempts to shoot her at a picnic celebrating her divorce.

Jethro goes to live at Aunt Winifred's house, where Elvira visits him one night to forgive his behavior and declare her love for him. She explains that with the boardinghouse up for sale and with Rick in New York, she must marry again for money; Jethro can no longer live with her. Jeremy's version of Elvira's story ends at this tragic moment, for Matt Lacey dies the next morning.

Sutpen, Judith. *Absalom, Absalom!* William Faulkner. 1936.

Continually beset by misfortune, the enigmatic Judith Sutpen maintains her strength in the face of great personal adversity. More than twenty-five years after her death, her story still haunts the imagination of her aunt Rosa Coldfield, QUENTIN COMPSON, and his Harvard roommate Shreve McCannon. They attempt to reconstruct her life based on fragments of fact. But the portrait that emerges is based on a great deal of speculation.

Judith is the daughter of Ellen Coldfield Sutpen and THOMAS SUTPEN, a ruthlessly ambitious Mississippi planter of mysterious origin. Growing up with her brother Henry and her black half-sister Clytemnestra, or "Clytie," Judith does not seem disturbed by the violence on Sutpen's Hundred, her father's plantation. When her father stages bare-knuckle boxing matches for the men of Jefferson, she watches impassively, while Henry vomits at the bloody sight. On Sundays she orders the family driver to race the twelve miles between Sutpen's Hundred and the town church.

Henry brings home a college friend, CHARLES BON, when Judith is eighteen. Ellen sees a possible match for her daughter. Judith and Charles start a relationship that Henry characterizes as curiously passionless. When Sutpen realizes that Charles is his son from a previous marriage, he informs Henry that Charles is his half-brother but does not admit that Charles has partial black ancestry. Henry does not believe his father and leaves with Charles to fight in the Civil War.

Sutpen also fights in the Civil War. While he is away, Ellen dies, the slaves run off, and Judith and Clytie subsist with the help of Wash Jones, a squatter on their land. During the war Judith receives a few letters from Charles promising that he will return. Judith and Clytie fashion a wedding dress from scraps of fabric left in the house.

One day Judith and Clytie hear a commotion as they are working on the dress. Henry bursts into their room and deposits Charles's lifeless body at Judith's feet. Although he killed Charles to prevent her from marrying someone with mixed blood, Henry does not explain his motive and flees the farm.

Judith learns that Charles had a son by his octoroon mistress. Without comment and seemingly numb to Henry's violence, she oversees Charles's funeral. When her father finally returns from the war, she allows herself one moment of tears and sadness, but quickly regains the composure that she will not lose for the rest of her life.

Unable to retain all of Sutpen's Hundred, Sutpen opens a country store, but before he can rebuild his fortune, he is killed by Wash Jones for impregnating and then abandoning Jones's teenage daughter. Judith asks a family friend, Quentin Compson's grandfather, to sell the store. With the proceeds she purchases tombstones for her father, her fiancé, and herself. Once the stones are placed, Charles's grieving mistress arrives with her son to visit the grave. After they return to New Orleans, Judith sends for the child, Charles Etienne de Saint Valery Bon.

Judith raises the young Charles, treating him with a strange mixture of ferocity and love. But the young man's confusion about his race—his skin is white, but he is considered black by the standards of the day—lead to uncontrollable behavior. Judith frequently bails him out of jail for fighting and later rents land to him when he returns with a black wife after a long absence. When yellow fever breaks out, Judith nurses him. But she soon falls to the epidemic as well, and they both die.

Sutpen, Thomas. *Absalom, Absalom!* William Faulkner. 1936.

Born into poverty in early nineteenth-century West Virginia, Thomas Sutpen becomes one of the richest men in Jefferson, Mississippi. During his lifetime, his blighted past remains largely shrouded. But fifty years later QUENTIN COMPSON and his Harvard roommate, Shreve McCannon, manage to piece together the story of a misguided man who ruthlessly sacrifices his family for an ideal of southern gentility, wealth, and power.

After his mother's death, the young Sutpen leaves West Virginia with his father and family to work on a large plantation in the Tidewater region. One day he is sent to deliver a message to the wealthy planter. Naive concerning the complicated social hierarchy of a plantation, he calls at the front door. When a slave tells him he must use the back entrance, he feels greatly slighted. Instead of rejecting the arbitrariness of an unfair social order, he decides that he must become a rich planter himself. He leaves home the next morning and never sees his family again.

In the West Indies, Sutpen increases his wealth and marries the daughter of a sugar planter. She bears him a son, but Sutpen abandons them both when he learns of his wife's mixed heritage. He knows that no matter how rich he might become, he will never be accepted among the southern elites if he has any black blood in his family.

Sutpen arrives in Jefferson, Mississippi, with a wagonload of slaves and a French architect. They proceed to build a mansion on the hundred square miles of land that he has purchased from an Indian tribe. While the house is under construction, he hosts hunting parties for the men in town, but they remain wary of this stranger. Only Mr.Compson, Quentin's grandfather, becomes friendly enough to learn part of Sutpen's history, which Mr. Compson passes on to his own family.

Sutpen marries Ellen Coldfield, the daughter of a local merchant, and she bears him two children, Henry and JUDITH (SUTPEN). Over the years Sutpen becomes the richest man in the county. His composure is tested, however, when Henry returns from college with a friend, CHARLES BON. Sutpen immediately recognizes his abandoned son and tries to put a stop to a romance between Charles and Judith. Sutpen tells Henry that Charles is his half-brother, but Henry does not want to believe it. He and Charles join a regiment to fight in the Civil War. Later Sutpen enters the conflict as an officer.

According to Quentin and Shreve, Sutpen encounters Henry during the war and decides to tell him that Charles has black ancestry. When Sutpen returns to Jefferson, he learns that Ellen has died and that Henry has shot Charles to death on the plantation, then fled.

Sutpen remains determined to create a dynasty. He suggests to Rosa Coldfield, his sister-in-law, that they copulate and then marry only if she bears a son. She refuses, and out of desperation he forms a liaison with the teenage daughter of Wash Jones, a squatter on his land. When the girl has a daughter, Sutpen spurns both of them. Outraged at this treatment of his daughter, Wash Jones kills Sutpen with a rusty scythe.

The Swede. "The Blue Hotel." Stephen Crane. 1898.

The Swede, the story's protagonist, is a mentally imbalanced man who is referred to only by his supposed nationality. Arriving on the train in Fort Romper, Nebraska, during a particularly intense blizzard, the Swede is met at the station by Patrick Scully, the Irish proprietor of the local Palace Hotel, who convinces him to take a room at his establishment along with two fellow travelers, a cowboy named Bill and an unnamed easterner. The relative calm of this sleepy small town is disrupted when the fates of these three travelers collide with those of a local professional gambler, Scully, and his hot-headed son Johnnie.

Having led his customers through the raging storm to the hotel, which is painted bright blue, Pat Scully escorts them to the front room and invites them to warm themselves around the stove. Everyone present immediately perceives that there is something very strange about the Swede who, although silent, is behaving as if he were extremely afraid of some threat that is not apparent. When he finally breaks his silence, he makes the odd observation that western towns can be dangerous and then laughs in a weird, loud manner. According to the easterner's analysis, which he delivers when the Swede leaves the room, the deranged

man has read one too many dime novels that portray the Wild Wild West as a lawless, perilous world. After dinner the men return to the front room and start playing a card game called High-Five, which the Swede remembers having played in the past when he had adopted an alias. Approaching the makeshift card table as if he expects someone to attack him, he eventually voices his fears: Someone in the room intends to murder him. Becoming increasingly agitated, he continues to shock the company with his paranoid accusations until he can no longer endure the fear that being with these men stirs in him and proposes to leave the hotel. Determined not to lose a customer, Scully follows the Swede to his room, offers him a drink, and finally convinces his guest to change his mind and spend the night there.

When Patrick and the Swede rejoin the men in the front room, the Swede's demeanor changes drastically, and he is contemptuous and disdainful of the company. He demands that they play another game of High-Five, which he then interrupts by accusing Johnnie of cheating. Johnnie becomes belligerent, and after exchanging a volley of insults, the two go out into the inclement weather to fight it out. After a long, bloody brawl, the burly Swede emerges the battered but proud champion, and, hurling a few more insults at his adversaries, leaves the saloon.

Groping his way through the blizzard, the Swede stumbles on another saloon, where he begins to drink heavily in celebration of his victory. When a group of men who are acquainted with his victim refuse to drink to his success, he seizes one of the men by the throat and begins to drag him across the room. After a brief scuffle, the man, a gambler by trade, pulls out a knife and stabs the amazed Swede, who does not survive his wound. Despite the severity of the crime, the gambler receives only a three-year sentence, for he is highly respected and the mad Swede had made a singularly negative impression on the small midwestern town.

Swift, Kate. *Winesburg, Ohio* ("The Strength of God"; "The Teacher"). Sherwood Anderson. 1919.

Kate Swift, who appears in both "The Strength of God" and "The Teacher," is a thirty-year-old schoolteacher whose private life is inundated with repressed passions that occasionally explode, sometimes shocking the relatively staid members of the midwestern community whose lives are chronicled in *Winesburg, Ohio*. Having passed through an adventurous period of her life during which she traveled in Europe and lived in New York City for two years, Kate decides to return to Winesburg, a small town inhabited by solitary and inhibited individuals whose limited imaginative horizons fail to provide her with sufficient emotional and intellectual stimulation. Despite the mundane and stifling nature of her environment,

Kate's imagination seethes with passions and aspirations that belie the superficial sangfroid that causes her neighbors to erroneously consider her an old maid.

Although Kate's appearance and manner are not without their charms, the inhabitants of Winesburg are critical of her looks, especially the blotches that mar her complexion and exemplify the fact that she suffers from medical problems. Her doctor has warned her that she must be careful to tend to her health or risk the loss of her hearing. Kate's image as an undesirable old maid is exacerbated by the fact that she has chosen to live with her widowed mother, thus forgoing the privacy and freedom that living alone would allow.

With very few friends and limited entertainment at her disposal, Kate spends the majority of her evenings at home with a book, smoking and reading in bed, where she unwittingly provides vicarious sensual entertainment for her guilt-ridden neighbor, the Reverend Curtis Hartman, who spies on her from the height of the bell tower of his church in "The Strength of God." When Kate's loneliness overwhelms her, she throws herself onto her bed. Indulging her volatile emotions by weeping and pounding her fists on her pillow, she tries to dispel the emotional demons that haunt her in her isolation. She also takes long walks in the middle of the night in order to work through the desires and fears that rage in her mind and threaten to overthrow the balance of her embattled emotional temperament.

As "The Teacher," Kate is known to be stern and distant, but despite her austerity she is a favorite among her pupils. When she deviates from her habitually reserved and solemn demeanor, the students regard her with a kind of awe and bask in the ambiance of her happiness. When a particularly communicative mood overtakes her, she begins to pace rapidly and to tell amusing and fantastic anecdotes about the lives of the notable individuals the class is studying. Kate takes a particular interest in GEORGE WILLARD, a former student whose writing impressed her as having a sort of genius, which she sought to cultivate by encouraging him to become a professional writer.

One night when she is particularly obsessed with thoughts about him, Kate ventures out into a storm with the intention of visiting George, who works at the local newspaper office on Main Street. For an impassioned hour she raves at the young man, admonishing him to discover the essence of people rather than accepting their superficial qualities. Her intellectual excitement intensifies until it explodes into a physical craving that manifests itself in a desire to kiss George, and she allows him to hold her in his arms for a moment. But her confused emotions betray her, and she suddenly begins to beat her fists against his face, before fleeing from both the office and her fears of a passion for a man so many years her junior and clearly incapable of satisfying the fervid longing that grips her heart.

Swift, Tom. *Tom Swift and His Electric Runabout,* or *The Speediest Car on the Road.* Victor Appleton. 1910.

In this tale, one of a series of twenty-nine adventures, Tom Swift, the young inventor-genius from Shopton, New York, surpasses the limits of twentieth-century technology and vanquishes a number of vengeful bullies and vicious gangsters.

Tom is the son of Barton Swift, now a widower, who is also a noted inventor. Tinkering and mechanical expertise come naturally to the lad, and his early triumphs involve a speedy motorcycle and motorboat, a fancifully designed airship, and a harrowing escapade in his father's submarine. On, in, and with these vehicles, Tom and his associates have sent the dastardly Happy Harry Gang to prison, foiled more than one band of robbers, and recovered sunken treasure off the South American coast.

Tom's next challenge is a contest to design and race the best electric car. The Touring Club of America is offering a $3,000 prize. Winning would also give Tom an opportunity to get the best of his rival Andy Foger, Shopton's red-haired bully. An oxide of nickel battery with steel and oxide of iron electrodes in a lithium hydrate solution are Tom's innovative measures for ensuring an electric car that is fast and requires infrequent recharging. Producing enough of these batteries and the car to go with them takes time, however, and Tom faces a few unexpected impediments. Andy Foger and his rough friends continually taunt Tom and one night succeed in kidnapping him. At first it looks as if Tom Swift, tied to a tree in a remote area of the woods, is going to be tarred and feathered by these young hoodlums, but he is much too quick for his opponents. He manages to throw a chemical powder into their bonfire and causes a blinding blue flash followed by their panicked retreat.

Meanwhile, Andy Foger's father, who is not any more virtuous than his son, is hatching a scheme to ruin the bank in which Tom and Barton Swift have a vested interest; it is there that the Swifts have deposited the bulk of their South American treasure trove. The electric roundabout is everything but painted (it will eventually resemble a gigantic purple bullet) when Tom must take it on a breakneck test ride to a nearby city in order to retrieve cash to meet a run on the foundering bank. The outbound forty miles are filled with potholes and anxieties, and the return trip is interrupted by escaped convicts. The stickup is handily foiled by a trio of farmers who come to the rescue with two pitchforks and a whip. Tom races back to Shopton just in time to save his father's bank.

The day of the race finally arrives. Tom's purple car is only seriously challenged by two entrants, a green one and a red one. In the stands is Tom's sweetheart, Mary Nestor. The five-hundred-mile race (around a spiffy new five-mile track on Long Island) is hours long. An early tire blowout puts Tom behind the red and green competitors, but the race evens out after four hundred miles when all three cars require recharging. Tom has invented a new process of recharging and is able to make up lost time. He wins the race in a last minute spurt of "juice." Then he nonchalantly collects his $3,000 and the congratulations of Miss Nestor, as he clasps her white gloves in his oily, dusty hands.

T

Talcott, Ray. *Bitter Creek.* James Boyd. 1938.

Thirteen-year-old Ray Talcott lives in Twin Forks, Illinois, with his prosperous but unloving father and his gentle, affectionate mother. When Ray's mother runs away with another man, Ray's father takes his bitterness out on Ray, regularly and viciously beating the boy. Ray runs away, headed for cowboy country. In his travels he receives aid from several people who are drawn by his unusual refinement, sensitivity, and strength of character. The most important of these figures are Nolly and Nancy Greevy—a retarded boy and his younger sister—and Springtime, a cowboy who takes Ray on as his partner on a large cattle ranch on the Great Plains.

Ray tries to get in touch with his mother but fails, and after a period of intense grief, he dismisses her from his mind and becomes a cowboy whose only loves are of wide-open spaces, hard work, and the excellent conversation of his colorful cohorts. In his mid-twenties, however, in order to help out his old friends Nolly and Nancy, Ray gets Mr. Greevy a job as foreman on the ranch where he works. When the Greevys come West, it becomes clear that Ray has awaited Nancy's arrival with more than friendly interest, for he has cherished her image throughout the years.

Ray is disappointed to discover, however, that Nancy has not grown up to be a pretty woman; specifically, her hair does not look like his mother's beautiful hair. Nancy is also no longer a defenseless little girl; she has become a woman, and Ray does not trust women. He therefore ignores her overtures of friendship and is glad when the Greevys leave to start their own ranch on Bitter Creek, enabling Ray to become foreman of the ranch.

When Nancy is abducted by Indians, Ray realizes that he truly loves her; after rescuing her from the Indians, he proposes to her, and they marry. But Ray still cannot trust Nancy, nor can he give himself to her completely, although he longs to do so. Soon after their marriage, Ray becomes unwarrantedly jealous of another cowboy, quits his job, and abandons Nancy.

In the nearby town of Greasewood, Ray turns to alcohol and prostitutes in an unsuccessful effort to alleviate his sorrow and despair. He eventually learns that his mother, who has recently died, had been looking for him ever since he ran away from home. This discovery precipitates an emotional crisis for Ray, and he returns to Nancy. She agrees to live with Ray again but refuses to have conjugal relations with him. Ray realizes that Nancy has been too deeply hurt by him to ever fully recover, and although at the novel's close he is trying hard to create a loving relationship with her, the reader is left in doubt as to how successful he will be.

Tall Convict. *The Wild Palms.* William Faulkner. 1939.

The Tall Convict is a lean, impassive, quiet man who has spent the past seven years in the State Penitentiary. Sentenced to fifteen years for a train robbery he attempted at nineteen, he has adjusted well to prison life and finds working on the prison's cotton plantation satisfying. He knows that the Mississippi River, the "Old Man," is just beyond the levee, although he has never seen it. But when heavy rains cause the river to flood, Tall Convict at last gets a look at the river, and his life is changed by the events that follow.

When the great river floods, Tall Convict is sent with other inmates to help in the rescue effort. He and another prisoner take a rowboat and attempt to save a man stranded on a roof, but as they near him, the skiff turns over. The other inmate reaches shore, but Tall Convict, clinging to the overturned boat, is swept downstream, and the overseers of the prison crew assume he has drowned.

In fact, Tall Convict manages to right the boat. Drifting, he finds himself under a tree in which a pregnant woman sits. He helps her into the skiff and sets about looking for his fellow convict, but he becomes disoriented and paddles all day in the wrong direction. That night, the flood waters carry the two even farther away.

Determined to get back to the prison authorities and to get the pregnant woman off his hands, Tall Convict appeals to a group of fugitives. But they are put off when they learn that he is trying to return to prison. He and the woman eventually come upon an Indian burial mound covered with water moccasins stranded by the flood; it is here that the woman gives birth to her baby.

When they are driven away by the snakes, they again take to the water. In time they come upon a steamboat full of flood victims and are taken aboard. The convict tells his rescuers he only wants to get back to the safety of prison authority. He and the woman are put ashore on a levee, and they trek inland through a swamp, reaching a house on stilts where a reclusive alligator hunter takes them in. The Tall Convict hunts with the man and becomes adept at wrestling and killing gators, and for a time he feels the same satisfaction he had working on the prison's plantation. Within weeks, however, the group learns that in order to ease the still-flooding river waters, the levee protecting the house must be dynamited.

Although the house is in imminent danger of being washed away, the convict and the woman remain there. A sheriff evacuating the area finds the two, and when the convict tells his story, he is immediately taken into custody. In his absence, however, he had been declared a hero who gave his life rescuing flood victims. The authorities, who have posthumously paroled him, are in a quandary when they discover that he is alive. To resolve the problem, they reason that he had actually attempted to escape; to the Tall Convict's joy, they add ten years to his former sentence.

Tarnopol, Peter. *My Life as a Man.* Philip Roth. 1970.

Peter Tarnopol, a young writer driven to collapse by his disastrous personal relationships, attempts desperately to find meaning and sanity in his life through his writing, describing himself through alter egos in two short stories. Increasingly frustrated with the inability of these fictional creations to capture the horror of his life, he turns to an autobiographical novel that he identifies as his "true" life story.

Tarnopol presents two fictional versions of his youth. One short story focuses on his imagined teenage sexual escapades with a young woman eager to act out his fantasies; a second story describes his young adulthood as a composition professor and his relationship with a tortured, emotionally disturbed, rather sexless young woman.

Both of Tarnopol's short fictions highlight his characteristic addiction to suffering and his conviction that his development into manhood will be tempered by punishment. These themes of his life are the focus of his autobiographical novel. Writing in self-imposed exile at an artists' colony in Vermont, Tarnopol looks back at his adulthood in an attempt to understand the mounting turmoil that drove him into psychiatric care and to retreat from society. He remains obsessed with his late wife Maureen who tormented him throughout their marriage and separation. Suffering from artistic delusions of grandeur, she was violently jealous of Tarnopol's own success as a writer, and her skillful abuse succeeded in draining Tarnopol of his creative and intellectual energy. Yet, much as he grew to despise Maureen, he found himself incapable of severing the relationship.

Tarnopol underwent episodes of panic and paralysis, the most dramatic of which occurred before an audience at Brooklyn College. Having been invited to deliver a lecture on fiction writing, the young author/professor rose to the podium and found himself unable to speak or move. After collapsing at the New York airport on the way home to Maureen and his life as a professor in Wisconsin, Tarnopol was temporarily sequestered at the Manhattan home of his brother Moe who refused to accept Maureen's phone calls and encouraged Tarnopol not to return to her.

Maureen, who would not be scorned or escaped, flew to New York and took an apartment. She then began an elaborate series of punishments that played upon Tarnopol's guilt and his inability to separate himself from her insanity. She slandered Tarnopol's character, publicizing his love affair with a young student at the University of Wisconsin. Tarnopol was forced by the court to pay Maureen a large alimony settlement, which drove him to near bankruptcy; when Tarnopol commented on the unfairness of the situation, Maureen threatened suicide.

Tarnopol went around in a state of tearful rage, finally collapsing in the office of Dr. Otto Spielvogel, a New York psychiatrist. He reviewed the circumstances of his life and specifically examined his relationship with Maureen, which came increasingly to obsess him. Maureen had attempted to trick him into marriage by faking pregnancy; despite his knowledge of the deception, Tarnopol agreed to marry her anyway. The relationship was troubled thereafter by violence and bizarre behavior on both their parts.

When Maureen announced that she had no intention of ever "freeing" Tarnopol from her power, a violent battle ensued that ended with Tarnopol beating Maureen, who wailed and defecated all over his apartment. Several months later Tarnopol learned of Maureen's sudden death in a car accident. At first disbelieving, he still did not feel free even when he learned that the news was true; his obsession with Maureen continued, even intensified, after her death. He broke off a three-year relationship with Susan Seabury McCall, who was also neurotic and masochistic, yet attractive to Tarnopol by virtue of the quiet, kind nature of her insanity.

Tarnopol's relationship with Dr. Spielvogel, his psychiatrist, became greatly strained after the doctor fictionalized the case in an article for a psychoanalytic journal. Tarnopol found the article offensive on moral as well as aesthetic grounds. Soon after, Tarnopol withdrew from the doctor's care and retreated to the colony in Vermont, where he attempts to understand and exorcise his obsession with Maureen by writing about it.

Tarrant, Verena. *The Bostonians.* Henry James. 1886.

Verena Tarrant is a malleable young woman who becomes the center of a contest of wills and ideologies when a dashing young Southern reactionary tries to woo her away from her feminist companions.

The daughter of an upper-class mother and a father who practices mesmerist displays and quack healings, Verena has spent her childhood among the intellectual riffraff of the carpetbagging circuit. This upbringing makes her vulnerable to the strong-willed OLIVE CHANCELLOR, whom she meets at a suffragette meeting. She is easily persuaded to devote her life to the cause, and under Olive's tutoring learns to be a master orator. The two women plan their illustrious future as leaders of the suffragette movement, but love intervenes: BASIL RANSOM, Olive's charming Southern cousin, falls in love with Verena and begins competing with Olive for Verena's loyalty and affection.

At first Verena deceives herself and does not accept that Ransom has fallen in love with her. Once he declares his feelings, however, and impresses her as a sincere, strong-willed, and honest fellow, she begins to care for him. Worried that she might betray Olive, Verena decides to avoid Ransom and continue her intellectual apprenticeship to Olive. But when Ransom follows her to the retreat on Cape Cod where she is preparing for her speaking debut, Verena begins to weaken. Against Olive's wishes, she takes long walks with him, and as Ransom's romancing slowly creeps over her will, she begins to embrace his repressive view of social relations.

Verena finally feels so guilty about betraying Olive's affections that she flees once more to Boston. On the night of her speaking debut before the intellectual elite of Boston, a lavish affair organized by Olive, Ransom makes an appearance. Verena is flustered by his presence in the theater and cannot go on stage.

Ransom finally gains admittance to her dressing room, and while the crowd impatiently waits for her, Verena pleads with him to leave and allow her to speak. Ransom refuses, insisting that she submit to him and leave immediately for New York. She flees with Ransom, humiliating Olive before all of Boston.

Tarwater, Francis Marion. *The Violent Bear It Away.* Flannery O'Connor. 1955.

Francis Marion Tarwater is a fourteen-year-old orphan raised in the woods of Tennessee by a religious old man who claims to be his great-uncle. The great-uncle dies at breakfast one day, and Tarwater leaves him sitting at the kitchen table. While he is digging the old man's grave, Tarwater hears a voice telling him he can choose between Jesus and himself. Tarwater gets drunk on the old man's liquor supply and passes out. Unbeknownst to him, a neighboring black man, Buford Munson, buries his great-uncle.

Awaking at night with the belief that the old man is still inside, Tarwater sets the house on fire. He then catches a ride to the city, reflecting along the way on his own convoluted family history. His great-uncle's sister had been a prostitute who had two children, Rayber and Tarwater's mother. The great-uncle then gave up on his sister but resolved to save her son. When Rayber was seven, his uncle kidnapped him for four days, during which time he baptized him and preached to him. Later Rayber, having rejected the old man's teachings, encouraged his sister's illicit affair with a friend. She was pregnant with Tarwater when she and her parents were killed in a car accident. Tarwater was born at the crash site, and Rayber took him in. Rayber reluctantly allowed the old man to live with them but refused to let him ruin Tarwater with his teachings; however, the old man baptized Tarwater against Rayber's wishes. When his nephew wrote an article stating that his religion arose from insecurity, the great-uncle stole Tarwater and took him back to his farm, Powderhead. Rayber later married and had a dimwitted child, Bishop.

Having mulled this over, Tarwater arrives in the city where Rayber now lives to see if what the old man taught him was right. He goes to see Rayber and tells him about the burning of his great-uncle. Rayber thinks that he might be able to help Tarwater be a useful person, but Tarwater realizes his uncle is just a decoy set up by the old man to lure him to the city. When his cousin Bishop appears, Tarwater knows he was sent there to baptize him. He angrily avoids the child as much as possible.

Tarwater remains in the city for the next few days. When he leaves the house in the middle of the night, Rayber follows him to a tabernacle where a family of missionaries is preaching. Confronted by an angry Rayber, Tarwater is suddenly submissive and claims that he only went to the tabernacle "to spit on it."

The next day Tarwater is again aloof. On their way to a museum, Bishop climbs into a fountain. When Tarwater starts to follow him, Rayber assumes that he intends to baptize the little boy and pulls him out first. What he doesn't know is that Tarwater's voice told him not to baptize Bishop but to drown him.

Rayber decides to take Tarwater back to Powderhead in order to get him to open up. While they are fishing, Rayber tells Tarwater about once trying to drown Bishop. Tarwater says that Rayber is all words and no action, and that when Tarwater gets ready to do something, he'll do it without words. After throwing up his lunch, Tarwater jumps in and swims for shore.

That night at dinner Rayber confronts Tarwater openly about the old man's teachings. The only way to be born again, he tells him, is through your own efforts to know yourself. Rayber gives Tarwater a glass of water with which to baptize Bishop, but he pushes it away. Tarwater leaves the table, and with Bishop following him, heads out to the water. There, Tarwater drowns the boy.

As Tarwater is heading back to Powderhead, he feels he has proved that he is not a prophet. He accidentally baptized Bishop as he was drowning him, but he feels that the act doesn't mean anything, for Bishop can't be born again. The next day Tarwater hitches a ride with a stranger in a lavender car. He drinks the stranger's whiskey and falls asleep. When Tarwater awakes, he discovers that he is in the woods naked. He sets fire to the ground and bushes around him. At this moment he experiences a profound change.

Tarwater reaches Powderhead later in the day, and the voice tells him he will never be alone again. He sets fire to the bushes where he feels the voice's presence. Afterward he sees Buford, who reveals that he had buried the old man the fateful day when Tarwater had gotten drunk. Looking at the field, Tarwater sees that it is crowded with people, all eating from one basket. He sees his great-uncle and realizes his hunger is the same as the old man's. Hearing a voice that tells him to "warn the children of God of the terrible speed of Mercy," Tarwater sets out for the city.

Tarzan. *Tarzan of the Apes.* Edgar Rice Burroughs. 1912.

In this novel and its twenty-five sequels, as well as comic books and Hollywood films, Tarzan—the jungle barbarian who is really an English lord—comes to personify adventure and exoticism.

When Tarzan's parents, John and Alice Clayton, Lord and Lady Greystoke, are marooned by mutineers on a torrid African coast, they have little chance of survival. Still less has their infant son who is born in their lonely jungle cabin. When little Lord Greystoke is a year old, both of his parents die. Miraculously, the baby is seized by an ape, Kala, who, crazed with grief at the death of her own offspring, immediately adopts him. She calls him Tarzan, which means, in her language, "white skin."

Under the tutelage and the protection of the gentle Kala, Tarzan grows and becomes part of a roving band of apes, a tribe of hunter-gatherers led by the fierce Kerchak. Although slow to develop, compared to his ape brothers, Tarzan, the "white ape," becomes inhumanly strong and, despite the influence of his simian companions, humanly resourceful. He even teaches himself to read in the deserted Greystoke cabin, to which he feels irresistibly drawn.

Years later when an American professor and his beautiful daughter JANE PORTER are marooned with their small party at the old Greystoke site, Tarzan, sensing some kinship with these helpless white visitors, becomes their protector. He saves the professor from the jaws of death; he saves William Clayton, who is really Tarzan's cousin, the present Lord Greystoke, although neither know it; and he saves Jane. Swinging through the trees with Jane in his arms, Tarzan knows he loves her, and Jane, for her part, is fairly sure she loves this primitive wild man who rescues her but cannot speak English.

Clayton and the Porters are rescued by the French navy, and while Tarzan is absent saving yet another white man, Lieutenant D'Arnot, they sail for home. Heartbroken, Tarzan nurses the French lieutenant back to health and is himself introduced to civilization through the lieutenant's kind attentions. The long-forgotten diary of Tarzan's father, Lord John, gives both men an inkling of Tarzan's true identity.

Tarzan searches for Jane and finds her in Wisconsin, where she is being forced into an unhappy marriage. Although his loincloth has been replaced by a Parisian suit, Tarzan still acts as Jane's protector, rescuing her from an American forest fire and playing a large role in repulsing her unwanted suitor. But Jane does not like this tame jungle man quite as much as the original Tarzan of the apes. When given the choice between two adoring gentlemen, she opts to marry Clayton. Tarzan, who likes Clayton and is feeling the call of the jungle, decides not to reveal that he is in fact Lord Greystoke. The book leaves both Tarzan and Jane uncertain as to whether they have done the right thing and wondering what the future holds.

Tate, Brother. *Sent for You Yesterday.* John Edgar Wideman. 1983.

Brother Tate is frequently found with his best friend CARL FRENCH and his sister LUCY (TATE). Brother and Lucy are not actual siblings but are among the many orphans who had been unofficially adopted by a childless couple, the Tates. Lucy, who is younger than Brother, arrived at the Tates' first; therefore, she regards Brother as a younger sibling. Additionally, because he is an albino, Lucy considers him in need of special attention; for example, she wheels him in a dilapidated carriage, keeping a floppy hat on his head to prevent exposure to the sun. Once he matures, though, Brother becomes the buddy of Carl French, and he spends most of his time at the French house. For the most part Brother is extremely quiet and rarely speaks. He and Carl participate in an array of games, including daring each other to brave the danger of a speeding train by standing as close to the tracks as possible while the train passes. This becomes the substance of an alluring yet frightening nightmare that plagues the young man.

When Brother is in his early twenties, he forms a liaison with Samantha, one of the darkest of the residents of Cassina Way, the street in Homewood on which they live. Samantha has already had several children and takes great pride in them and in her unspoiled beauty. At first she is actually frightened of Brother's color, but after traveling to the library to research albinism, she feels assured that there's nothing inherently wrong with him.

The couple eventually has a son named Junebug, but the little boy is scorned and rejected by his siblings who mock his lightness—he inherited his father's pigmentation—and torment him whenever possible. Brother watches from a distance, after becoming aware that his visits spur Samantha's many other children into greater acts of violence against his son. Despite the problems, Brother loves Junebug, and when the boy is accidentally burned to death on the Fourth of July, 1946, Brother ceases to speak for the rest of his life. The only utterances he makes are be-bop phrases.

Prior to Junebug's death Brother had demonstrated great skill as a pianist, but he also abandoned this after his son's death. Carl, who returns from World War II and begins to study art, introduces his friend to drawing, and Brother takes this to heart, becoming a skillful artist. Neither his talent as an artist nor his abandoned music suffice to fill the void in his life, however, and in 1962, while still quite young, Brother commits suicide on the railroad tracks. His memory, kept alive in Carl and Lucy's conversation and in his sketches, is of central concern to Carl's nephew, Doot French, who was named for a scat sound sung to him by Brother. His image as a role model and as a good friend attracts the young narrator to Brother's story, thus keeping him alive in Homewood for at least one more generation.

Tate, Lucy. *Sent for You Yesterday*. John Edgar Wideman. 1983.

Lucy Tate, one of the adopted children of the elderly and kindhearted Tates, is one of many residents of Cassina Way in Homewood. From the beginning of her life on Cassina Way, Lucy is a devoted daughter, and when BROTHER TATE, an older boy and an albino, arrives to live with the Tates, Lucy assumes his care as a personal project. Although he is older, Lucy reasons that he is her younger brother since she was with the Tates longer. She wheels him about in a dilapidated carriage and covers his head with her hat to protect him from the sun. Lucy eventually befriends CARL FRENCH, a young boy who has become Brother's best friend.

By the time Lucy is thirteen, she already has a reputation as a fast girl and works part-time at a local bar, the Bucket of Blood, where she cleans up. One day she is required to clean up the mess following the assassination of Albert Wilkes, the best friend of Carl's father, who has been killed to settle an old grudge. While mopping up the blood, Lucy finds a piece of Albert's skull; she keeps it and soon shows it to Carl. With this grisly token of a historic event in Homewood, Lucy assumes the role of a preserver of local lore and legend.

On the same day Lucy finds and decides to keep the piece of bone, she and Carl make love for the first time. For Carl, who isn't exactly sure of what's happening to him physically, the experience is amazing; for Lucy it confirms a bond between her and Carl that will be lifelong, although three more years will pass before she allows him to have sex with her again. Eventually Lucy, along with Carl and Brother, explores various drugs and finally ends up addicted to heroin, which Brother forces her to quit by locking her in her room to undergo withdrawal cold turkey.

The three friends survive the trial of their addictions, but Lucy is powerless to prevent Brother's agony when his only child is burned to death in an accident. Following the boy's death, Brother retreats into a form of speechlessness, emitting only scat syllables instead of speech. Since there is nothing she can do for Brother, she and Carl encourage him to draw, a hobby Carl introduces him to after the war.

When Carl returns after World War II, haunted by vivid memories, Lucy becomes his full-time lover and confidante. Finally, although he never asked her about it, Lucy tells Carl that while she loves him more than anyone alive, especially after Brother's suicide in 1962, she could never marry him. Physical fidelity is hard enough, she explains, but her real stumbling block is an inability to remain emotionally or mentally faithful. Carl seems to have no need to marry her, however, and the relationship continues undamaged. Both Lucy and Carl, in an effort to preserve Brother's memory and to make sense of their and Homewood's past, teach Carl's nephew, Doot French, about the neighborhood, its people, and their stories. In this way they sense that the next generation will be made aware of its roots in a loving, though threatened and at times dangerous, community.

Tateh. *Ragtime*. E. L. Doctorow. 1974.

Tateh, an Eastern European immigrant, works his way from rags on the Lower East Side of New York City to riches in California.

When Tateh, his young wife Mameh, and their child first arrive in New York, all three must work to maintain their one-room apartment on the Lower East Side. Because Tateh is singularly unsuccessful as a pushcart peddler, his wife and daughter sew from dawn to dusk, making knee pants for the small sum of seventy cents a dozen. Calamity strikes the family when they receive a letter stating that by law their daughter is obliged to attend school. With the loss of her deft hands in the marketplace, Tateh and Mameh find it impossible to keep up with the bills and rent. Mameh has been fondled repeatedly by her boss for the price of a dollar for food; when she succumbs further to her employer's lust, Tateh expels her from the household and undertakes the task of raising his daughter alone.

Following his wife's departure, Tateh begins bringing his exceedingly beautiful daughter along with him as he peddles his artistic wares. He creates silhouette portraits from crepe paper for fifteen cents a portrait. To protect her from being kidnapped into the sexual slave trade, Tateh secures his daughter to his body with a clothes line. Although he is only thirty-two years old, Tateh's beard is gray, and he is weak from the breakup of his marriage. When life in New York City becomes intolerable, he and his daughter abandon the squalor of their apartment and venture out into the world.

Tateh's next home proves no more amenable than the one he just left. Working as a loom operator in a factory in Lawrence, Massachusetts, he is forced to leave his daughter unattended at home during the day because he is afraid she will be damaged by the frightening conditions in the schools available to children of the labor force. But for once Tateh gets lucky: He discovers that the "movie books" he has been making to amuse his daughter are marketable. These books depict a moving scene when the pages are flipped rapidly one after the other. His contract with the Franklin Novelty Company marks the beginning of an extremely successful artistic career.

Tateh subsequently masters the art of filmmaking and establishes himself as a rich man with his own company. He dyes his hair and beard black, regains his vigorous character, and changes his name to Baron Ashkenazy. While working on a fifteen-reel photoplay in Atlantic City, he meets a married woman whose comely towheaded son, THE LITTLE BOY, becomes his daughter's constant companion. When this unnamed woman's husband is killed, Tateh confesses to the falsity of his title, proposes marriage to her, and is accepted. In order to be nearer the film industry, the new family moves to California where Tateh enjoys his well-earned happiness.

Taylor, Felicitas Maria. *The Company of Women.* Mary Gordon. 1980.

Felicitas Maria Taylor, a feisty young girl from Brooklyn, is raised by her dynamic widowed mother Charlotte and a group of single women whose loving indulgence help form her precocious and headstrong personality. This intimate community first bonded at religious retreats for working women conducted by Father Cyprian, an eccentric Catholic priest who provides the only formidable male influence during Felicitas's formative years. She returns Cyprian's dedication with equal intensity and is equally devoted to her mother's friends. She prefers adult company to that of children her own age, whom she considers trivial and boring.

This cohesive extended family is disrupted when Felicitas enrolls in Columbia University's Division of General Studies. Exposed to the collegiate environment, she develops a bitter disdain for the older women she had previously cherished. In particular, she resents having been denied the opportunity to date and socialize, both of which seem to come so naturally to her peers. Determined to change her life-style, she becomes enmeshed in the rebellious spirit of the late 1960s, heedless of the fact that she alienates Father Cyprian and wounds her mother and the women who attended so assiduously to her youthful needs.

Felicitas takes up with an older man, Robert Cavendish, the professor of her modern political theory class. From the first meeting of class she has been spellbound by his magnificent body and breathtaking countenance. The attraction proves mutual, and she accepts Robert's recommendation that she drop his class so that they can become lovers without having to face the potential awkwardness resulting from academic affiliation. Although she feels guilty, Felicitas longs to fit in with Robert's "hip" crowd. At the same time she feels increasingly claustrophobic because Cyprian and her mother's friends continue to assert their own thwarted hopes and desires, as if she were capable of achieving the worldly distinction and the personal satisfaction that they failed to attain. Justifying her decision to move by condemning their emotional dependence on her, Felicitas leaves Brooklyn to join Robert's communal household, which includes two women, Iris and Sally, and the latter's son, Mao. Felicitas's excellent academic record begins to plummet drastically, but she revels in her newfound, independent, hipster life, and basks in the erotic radiance of her former professor.

Felicitas's bliss proves short-lived. Robert insists that she has been irrevocably steeped in bourgeois values such as monogamy, which he finds despicable. Exercising his free-love ethic, he successfully convinces her to sleep with their neighbor Richard. Amid these sexual and social upheavals, Felicitas discovers that she is pregnant. Although she visits a doctor with the intention of obtaining an illegal abortion, she changes her mind at the last minute and decides to return home to her mother's to bear the child.

Charlotte decides that they should move to the small town of Orano, New York, where Cyprian lives on a large piece of land. Felicitas, her mother, and the entire group of old friends eventually settle there, establishing an even more cohesive and supportive community. After a period of denial when she scorns her infant daughter Linda, Felicitas develops an intense love for the child. Eventually she marries an extremely conventional man—the owner of the local hardware store—in order to provide her daughter with domestic and social security.

Felicitas works as an assistant librarian and takes courses at the local Hiram Wallace College to finish her B.A. degree so that she can take over when the aging librarian retires. Although she fears that she will lose the idiosyncratic and vibrant personality traits of which she has always been proud, she is confident that she has built a solid and productive life, based not so much on personal choice as on the powerful and positive legacy of Cyprian and "the company of women" who raised her.

Taylor, Raymond. *Infants of the Spring.* Wallace Thurman. 1932.

Together with a group of friends and acquaintances, Raymond Taylor, a young would-be novelist, attempts to establish a haven for African-American intellectuals in the midst of the Harlem Renaissance. After arriving from the South and having her hopes of being a race leader dashed,

Euphoria Blake decided that only money and art would free the American Negro. Consequently, she bought a house in Harlem and opened it to Negro intellectuals and artists.

The coterie of Niggeratti Manor include its inhabitants, Raymond, Pelham, and Eustace, and its frequent visitors, Samuel, Paul, Aline, and Janet. As the novel opens, the clique of the Manor gather in Eustace's basement apartment for one of their frequent gin-drinking parties. Ray becomes acquainted with Stephen Jorgenson, a young Nordic who is studying at Columbia University, and the two become fast friends. One day Steve surprises Ray by announcing he has become so enchanted with Harlem that he wants to become his roommate. The Nordic moves into the Manor, and the residents continue their routine of gin parties, giving short shrift to their various artistic pursuits. As the weeks go by, life at Niggeratti Manor begins to disintegrate.

The first sign of dissipation comes when Pelham is arrested for rape. It seems that after painting the portrait of the underage daughter of a woman who lives upstairs in the Manor, Pelham began an affair with the young girl. While the inhabitants of the Manor await Pelham's trial, Ray enlists Samuel to get a downtown audition for Eustace. Samuel succeeds in getting the appearance, but both he and Ray are stymied when Eustace refuses to take it if he is asked to sing Negro spirituals instead of the classical music he prefers. Ray eventually talks Eustace into learning several spirituals. In the meantime, Ray, Paul, Steve, Eustace, and Euphoria are present in the Washington Heights court when Pelham is tried, convicted, and sentenced to the maximum prison term.

As these situations have been developing, Janet and Aline have begun a battle over Steve, who is the first white man either young woman has ever wanted. Steve, unaware of the mystique surrounding him, begins an alliance with Aline, to Janet's chagrin. By the time Pelham's trial takes place, the two women are barely speaking. As the struggle between Aline and Janet intensifies, Ray notices a change in Steve's demeanor that cannot be attributed to this romantic tug-of-war.

The turning point for the residents of Niggeratti Manor occurs when Eustace and Paul throw a grocery party that operates on the same basis as the Harlem rent party: Rather than money, partygoers bring groceries. The party is a wild success, so wild, in fact, that the African-American presses reprimand the young intellectuals for their drunkenness and sensuality.

After this negative publicity, life at the Manor goes into rapid decline. First, Steve disappears during the grocery party and does not return. He writes Ray a letter in which he states that he has suddenly acquired an aversion to Negroes so intense that he feels tainted. Next, Eustace returns devastated from a series of unsuccessful auditions downtown. As the household crumbles, Euphoria calls the group together to tell them that in the face of the publicity generated by Pelham's case and the lack of productive activity in Niggeratti Manor, she has decided they must move because she intends to turn the place into a dormitory for single women.

With Steve gone, Aline crossing the "color line" in order to "pass" for white, Janet living in New Jersey, Pelham in jail, Paul residing in the Village, and Eustace a walking shell, Ray feels utterly alone. He makes plans to move in with a girl with whom he has been engaged off and on. Finally, on his last night in the Manor, he receives a call from Paul's roommate in the Village. Paul dressed himself in a crimson mandarin robe, carpeted the bathroom floor with pages from his novel, and committed suicide by slitting his wrists.

Taylor, Reverend Dan. "Fire and Cloud." Richard Wright. 1936.

A leader of his community, Reverend Dan Taylor is called upon to make some difficult decisions that in turn alter his understanding of his role in life. When the black community in a southern city, plagued by hunger in the midst of the Great Depression, have to decide whether to join a communist-sponsored protest, Reverend Taylor must find within himself the strength to demand justice in the face of prejudice. A belief in the unity of his people rather than faith in God gives him that strength.

Before he felt the call to preach, Dan Taylor had worked hard to make his living on the land. Becoming a preacher meant assuming other duties as well—taking on the responsibility of the spiritual well-being of his congregation. He has performed this job well, earning the respect of his flock and a position of authority in the black community as a whole. Taylor also functions as a liaison between his people and the white community.

When people begin to go hungry, however, Taylor feels the burden of his role. The woman at the relief office claims she can do nothing; his son Jimmy itches to engage in some brash, youthful action; a member of his church, Deacon Smith, urges caution and conciliation; and his wife May is simply afraid. When Taylor comes home from his fruitless visit to the relief office, Jimmy tells him that members of his congregation are in the church, the mayor and the chief of police are in the parlor, and two communists are in the Bible Room.

Meeting with his parishioners, Taylor is indecisive. He gives the last of his money to them and urges calm. His meeting with the communists, Hadley and Green, is scarcely better. They ask permission to put his name on the handbills announcing the next day's march, but Taylor is afraid to give such overt support. Hadley and Green try to convince him that the march—which will have the participation of poor whites—will not be successful unless blacks show up in force as well. In his meeting with the mayor and the chief of police, Taylor is spoken to smilingly by the one and insulted by the other. Despite their different tactics, the two white men share the same message: Don't march.

In consultation with the deacons of his church, support for the march is voiced, although Deacon Smith is violently opposed to the measure. Taylor himself is inclined to lead his people in the march, but before he can state his opinion fully, his son interrupts with the message that some white men in a car outside want to see him. Excusing himself, Taylor goes to the men, who administer a swift beating and haul him into their car. They take Taylor to the woods where they force him to recite the Lord's Prayer while they whip him mercilessly.

After making his way back home, Taylor is told by his son that after he had disappeared the night before, Deacon Smith convinced the other deacons to vote Taylor out of his position, claiming that Taylor had abandoned them. He also learns that many of the city's blacks have been beaten. They gather in his home, bruised, bloody, and wrapped in bandages, wondering what to do. After his lonely ordeal in the woods he is now aware that only when people stand together are they strong, Taylor urges his former congregation to act as one. Taylor marches with them, not at the head of the group but as one of its members. Together they merge with the white marchers and make their way past the massed police force to city hall.

Tayo. *Ceremony.* Leslie Marmon Silko. 1977.

Tayo, a young man with a Native American mother and a white father, has just returned from serving in World War II. As he tries to recover from his experiences of battle, he realizes that he must reconcile the opposing ways and beliefs of the two cultures that shaped him or succumb to futility and despair.

Tayo suffers constant hallucinations of his experiences in the war. He cannot sleep at night because he is afraid of what he will see. Recalling his part in a firing squad, he imagines that he has killed his uncle and not a Japanese soldier. He relives the death of his cousin Rocky. He remembers cursing the rain of the land that was so different from the arid climate of his native Arizona, and then imagines that his curse was the cause of the drought that currently plagues the Lagunas.

Tayo's aunt, who believes in modern ways, urges him to seek help from the army doctors, while his Native American counterparts counsel him to rely on the old traditions and visit the medicine man. Tayo believes that neither the doctors nor the medicine men will be able to cure his hallucinations because they cannot understand the internal struggles that plague him.

Tayo turns to alcohol to alleviate his distress and spends time with his buddies reliving their glory days as American soldiers. He soon realizes, however, that he and his friends are living in a dream. As a Native American he knows that people respected him only for the uniform he was wearing. He senses that alcohol, although a pleasant diversion, is causing him to slide further and further away from his Native American heritage.

Finally, Tayo visits Betonie, a medicine man who has been exposed to white culture and who is willing to offer those who have come in contact with it a more liberal form of counsel. Betonie helps Tayo understand that the traditional ways of healing are still important, while conceding that as times have changed, so, too, the old ceremonies have to be changed.

Under Betonie's direction Tayo starts to perform the ceremonies and rituals of his tribe. They dance to purge the evil of killing Japanese soldiers from Tayo's heart. They converse at length, and Tayo comes to understand that the prejudice he experienced from white people because of his dark skin is no different from the treatment he received at the hands of certain Native Americans who knew that his father was white. As the novel closes, Tayo is determined to return to the mountains where he will plant herbs and remove the curse he had invoked while fighting in the South Pacific. The last lines are an invocation of a Native American prayer, signaling the end of the drought and a promise, for Tayo, of healing: "Sunrise, accept this offering, sunrise."

Tease, Jack. *The Enemy Gods.* Oliver LaFarge. 1937.

Taken from the reservation where he lived with his family and sent to a strict boarding school run by priests, "Jack Tease," as he is called by the administrators, takes an instant dislike to his new surroundings. Unlike many other young Native American boys who, having been taken from their reservation, submit to having their culture stripped from them, Jack is rebellious toward his teachers and refuses to shed his Navajo identity.

Jack's best friend at boarding school is almost the complete opposite of him. Bright and articulate, "Myron" has been almost completely assimilated into the white man's world. A model student, his work is proudly exhibited by all the priests at the school to any visitors as "proof" of the success of their program to Americanize the Indians. Jack attempts to convert Myron to a rediscovery of the culture that the administrators at their school are trying to bury. He brings Myron to a "medicine man" on a reservation nearby, and the two begin to spend an increasingly large amount of time there. The medicine man keeps them entertained with stories about ancient Navajo warriors and begins to kindle an interest for both boys in their all but forgotten Navajo culture.

Word gets back to the school officials that the two boys are seeing the aged medicine man. Thinking Jack Tease a "bad influence" on their stellar student Myron, they separate the two. Jack, embittered by his forced estrangement from Myron, becomes even more of a rebel at the school and is constantly in trouble with the authorities.

Jack is on the verge of expulsion when his life changes.

He meets a young Native American called "Ethel" by the nuns who instruct her at school. Jack immediately falls deeply in love and makes her a bracelet in one of his crafts classes. Soon, however, despite his affection for Ethel, Jack becomes aware of a certain detachment on the part of the young woman. While he at first ignores the subtle signs of indifference she begins to show toward him, he is later horrified to learn that she has become attracted to Myron. Overcome with feelings of anger and remorse, Jack watches as Ethel leaves for Myron, preferring the refined and "Americanized" ways of his best friend to his own Navajo culture.

Jack turns to a gypsy life and spends the next few months roaming the countryside on his horse, living in the way of his forefathers. He eventually returns to his reservation and finds Ethel waiting. She has decided to return to her Navajo ways and to Jack Tease.

Temple, Charlotte. *Charlotte Temple.* Susanna Rowson. 1791.

Caught in the conflict between the licentiousness and luxuriance of Old World Europe and the chastity and honest decency of Jeffersonian America, Charlotte Temple suffers the whims of a dual fortune: her lack of money and her ill-fated destiny.

Charlotte, innocent, artless, and perpetually blushing, is the fifteen-year-old daughter of the youngest son of an English nobleman, a man whose reputation far exceeds his financial means. Charlotte attends boarding school in England and is under the tutelage of the envious, evil-spirited, lascivious Mademoiselle La Rue, who is determined to bring any manifestation of innocence down to her own sinful level. To this end La Rue invites Charlotte to meet Montraville, a dashing young British lieutenant of fashionable elegance who has previously set his designs on the lovely young girl.

Montraville plots to seduce Charlotte with his plan to elope with her to America. Charlotte, forgetful of her obligations to family and God, succumbs to Montraville's sweet talk and sets sail with him to New York. While there, however, Montraville woos and marries the wealthy Julie Franklin, goes off to fight in the Revolutionary War, and all but abandons Charlotte, who is now pregnant with his child. Disowned by her family, abandoned by her lover, wretched and alone in a strange country, Charlotte sets out to find Mademoiselle La Rue, who is also in New York. La Rue, now married to a British colonel, denies ever having known her former student. It is her butler who takes in the destitute waif and helps her give birth to a baby girl.

Soon afterward Charlotte's father arrives from England in search of his wayward daughter. He finds Charlotte near death; with her eyes toward heaven, she conveys her illegitimate baby into his arms and dies. But the tale does not end without poetic justice. The evil Mademoiselle La Rue, the architect of Charlotte's destruction, also dies; and the roguish Montraville lives out his life battling severe fits of melancholy. In this fashion the natural innocence of America wins the day over the seductive luxury of Europe.

Ten Eyck, Guert. *Satanstoe.* James Fenimore Cooper. 1845.

The eldest son of an affluent family of immigrants from Holland, Guert Ten Eyck's position of privilege and class among the residents of the small Connecticut town make him a somewhat arrogant and self-centered youth. Although a young man when introduced in the story, Guert never rids himself of his boyhood concerns and spends most of his adult life wasting his time on childish pursuits. To get away from his disapproving, hardworking parents, Guert takes frequent trips to New York City, where he stays with distant relatives, the Mordaunts.

It is on one of these trips that Guert meets a young man named CORNELIUS "CORNY" LITTLEPAGE. Although possessed of sterner temperament, Littlepage soon comes to enjoy Guert's boyish enthusiasms, while Guert, despite the mild contempt with which most New Englanders view native New Yorkers, takes a similar liking to "Corny." The two become fast friends. Guert introduces Corny to his beautiful cousin Anneke, with whom Corny immediately falls in love. Meanwhile, Guert himself is enamored of Anneke's friend, Mary Wallace.

Despite repeated warnings that the river ice is unsafe because of the increasingly springlike weather, Guert takes the other three on a sleigh ride on the Hudson River. They soon pay the price for Guert's arrogance: The sheet of ice covering the Hudson begins to break into chunks when they are only halfway across. After quickly abandoning their sleigh, Guert, separated from Corny and Anneke, is able to lead Mary to safety by climbing across cakes of ice toward shore.

Confident after valiantly saving Mary's life, Guert works up enough courage to propose to her. He is crushed when Mary, despite her affection for the young man, deems him irresponsible and gently declines. The inconsolable Guert, wanting to find out if there is any hope of winning Mary over, journeys with Corny to a fortune teller; after paying her a large sum, Guert learns that he will win Mary only after proving his worthiness to her.

Soon afterward Corny and Guert, accompanied by Anneke and Mary, escort the Mordaunts up to their summer house in Albany. They encounter a company of militia heading north to fight the approaching French army. Stirred with patriotism, Corny decides to join the company after delivering the Mordaunts safely to their summer house. While possessing no desire whatsoever to risk his life, Guert, seeing this as his opportunity to prove himself to Mary, agrees to accompany him.

Guert and Corny fight valiantly against the French but

are attacked by Indians on the way back. Guert is injured and captured, and is about to be scalped when he is rescued by Corny and a band of militia. However, on the verge of escape, Guert is shot and killed.

Tertan, Ferdinand R. *Of This Time, of That Place.* Lionel Trilling. 1943.

Ferdinand R. Tertan, a gawky, verbose student, first appears in the freshman writing seminar of the young professor JOSEPH HOWE. Howe's new pupil is extremely awkward and uses speech that is rambling and overly descriptive. When Tertan discovers that Howe's poetry has come under attack by a famous critic, he promptly glorifies Howe as an intellectual paragon in the same class as Kant or Nietzsche. One habit of Tertan's that the educator notes is extremely odd is the freshman's almost anachronistic sense of formality. Tertan stands when he speaks, and he bows to Howe when he is about to depart.

Tertan's writing is no less florid than his speech. Howe finds Tertan's essays impossible to criticize since each sentence seems to consist of nothing more than tangential point after tangential point. Tertan's first paper asks, "Who am I? Tertan I am, but what is Tertan? Of this time, of that place, of some parentage, what does it matter?" After one particularly exasperating class, Howe decides to discover just exactly who Tertan is.

Howe's inquiry leaves him frustrated. Tertan's files reveal that he is highly intelligent, a scholarship student, and the son of a Hungarian-born engineer (now unemployed) and an English housewife. Nonetheless, Howe reports to the dean that he believes Tertan is insane. The dean promises to look into the situation.

Tertan then requests that Howe recommend him for a position in Dwight College's literary society. Howe agrees, but that does not halt the investigation concerning Tertan's mental stability. Blackburn claims that Tertan caused a ruckus at the meeting for the society.

After the dean reads the doctor's report on Tertan, he decides to allow the young man to stay at Dwight College for the rest of the year. Tertan will receive treatment at the conclusion of the term. As the story closes, Tertan is present at the school's convocation ceremonies. He sits apart from everyone, dressed in a Panama hat and a silk suit. His last words to Howe are "instruments of precision," spoken as he stares off into the sky.

Tetley (Major). *The Ox-bow Incident.* Walter Van Tilburg Clark. 1940.

With brutal and cold-blooded efficiency, Major Tetley tracks down and kills a group of men suspected of cattle rustling in this novel of the American West.

The novel begins with the murder of Larry Kinkaid, a rancher living near the small western town of Bridger's Wells. Rustlers are suspected since news of cattle being stolen from his ranch comes with the news of his death.

The killing incites the citizens of Bridger's Wells to form a search party that will find and kill the criminals; Tetley, who had been a Confederate officer during the Civil War, is an ideal candidate for leadership of the group.

With the help of ARTHUR DAVIES, a store owner in town, the local judge speaks to the vigilantes and almost dissuades them from their mission. Tetley encourages the men, however, by restoring their anger and desire for revenge. The judge relents under the insistence of the posse but orders that the rustlers be returned to town and jailed after they are captured. After swearing a brief oath, the posse departs.

Tetley uses his knowledge of military campaigns to guide his men through a snowstorm, which impedes them from the beginning of their journey. He determines a stopping place at each day's end, finds locations that provide the most shelter from the elements, and discovers the easiest, shortest paths through the wilderness.

The posse eventually encounters a stagecoach whose passengers report a sighting of campers a few miles off. Tetley divides his men into four groups, intending for them to spread out and then converge when they reach the rustlers' campsite. The hunters wait in a forest near the campsite until all the rustlers are asleep, and then, led by Tetley, the posse moves in. The three men—a Mexican named Juan Martinez, a mildly insane older man named Alva Hardwick, and a younger man named Donald Martin—awaken, only to be disarmed by Tetley and his son Gerald.

Tetley conducts a mock interrogation and then informs the men of their approaching execution. The three individuals protest that they are innocent, and Davies supports their claim, demanding a fair trial. Tetley does not believe the men, nor do his followers. Because of continued protest from Davies, however, the execution is postponed until the following day. Martin is given paper on which to write a letter to his wife, and Martinez is granted a confession.

At the time of the hanging, Tetley orders the three men to be seated on horses beneath the branches of a tall tree and their heads placed carefully in nooses. Tetley orders his son to slap Martin's horse, but because Gerald does not slap Martin's horse hard enough, the condemned man squirms slightly in the noose. Tetley then orders his men to shoot Martin during his strangulation. After all three men are executed, the posse returns to Bridger's Falls.

Gerald Tetley, sick with guilt, hangs himself upon returning home. His father impales himself on his sword when he hears the news.

Thatcher, Ellen. *Manhattan Transfer.* John Dos Passos. 1925.

The beautiful and beloved daughter of an overworked accountant and his neurasthenic wife, Ellen Thatcher grows up reading Tennyson and romantic novels, and dreaming of knights and ladies. As a child she insists on being called "Elaine the lily maid of Astolat," and she retains the name Elaine when she grows up and aspires to a career on the stage.

At sixteen she elopes with an aesthetic, poetic young man named John Oglethorpe. They end up living in moderately bohemian circumstances in upper Manhattan, in an apartment full of artists and actors. Although the couple is still on good terms, the marriage has not been entirely successful; they live in separate rooms, and John is evidently having an affair with a dancer named Tony Hunter.

Ellen, meanwhile, is trying to advance her career and to rise in New York social life generally. She flirts with the lawyer George Baldwin, and through him she meets Stan Emery, the son of George's boss. Stan is a charming, reckless, dissipated college dropout, cynical about everything in the world except his automobile. Unwilling to enter the financial world of his relatives and unable to separate himself from them altogether, he contents himself with exhausting as much of their money as he can. Ellen adores him as a tragically transported Adonis.

Nevertheless, she remains serious about her career. She accepts the advances of salacious casting directors, and she continues to flirt with George because he takes her out to fashionable restaurants where she will be seen. One night the two are at a popular restaurant in Canarsie owned by a bootlegger named Congo Jake. When George has too much to drink and pulls a gun on her, Ellen relies on her friend JIMMY HERF to take her away from the ensuing brouhaha. She subsequently relies on Jimmy's friendship and tact to conceal her relationship with Stan, mindless of the fact that Jimmy has obviously fallen in love with her himself.

Stan gets drunk one night, marries a chorus girl, and burns himself up in an apartment fire. Ellen is devastated, especially since she finds herself pregnant. But unwilling as always to let emotion interfere with ambition, she has an abortion and returns to her theatrical work.

During the war Ellen serves in the Red Cross. When she returns, she has married Jimmy Herf, borne a son, and begun calling herself Helena. Jimmy has trouble finding a job, so Ellen goes to work as an editor and does quite well. Through all events, Ellen is unflappable and not easily deterred. At one point she stops a police raid on a bohemian party she is attending by coolly calling a friend of George's. When her dressmaker's shop catches fire and a young worker is maimed, Ellen calms the other customers and prevents a panic.

Even after Jimmy finds employment with *The New York Times*, Ellen is impatient with his lack of ambition, and finally she leaves him. She prefers strong, ambitious men who share her hunger for success. In her last appearance in the novel she consents to marry George Baldwin, who has become a candidate for public office.

Thayer, Deborah. *Pembroke.* Mary Wilkins Freeman. 1893.

Deborah Thayer, the stern wife of Caleb Thayer, is the mother of one of the town's most eligible young men, Barnabas Thayer. In addition, Deborah has a daughter Rebecca and a younger son Ephraim, who has suffered from apparent heart disease all his life.

As the novel begins Deborah is happily preparing for her elder son's wedding. Barnabas is to marry the attractive and dutiful CHARLOTTE BARNARD. For much of her life Deborah has rigorously adhered to strict religious principles and a staunch moral sensibility. Due to Ephraim's illness, Deborah has not allowed him to go to school but makes him do daily do reading exercises drawn from the Bible. In addition to making him read, Deborah quizzes him, while dodging his chronic requests for forbidden sweets or other foods. Deborah's attention shifts when she is confronted by the sudden and hot-headed action of Barnabas. Following a disagreement about politics with his father-in-law Cephas, Barnabas vows never to set foot in the Barnard house again, thereby breaking off his engagement to Charlotte.

Deborah, furious at all parties involved, makes a brief attempt to reconcile the warring factions; when this fails she banishes her beloved son from her house over the feeble protests of her increasingly decrepit husband Caleb. Although it pains her greatly, Barnabas's lack of filial respect and his unwillingness to amend the disgrace he has caused the innocent Charlotte has put him beyond Deborah's moral bounds. As if this were not enough, as the community watches, Rebecca Thayer undertakes a relationship with William Berry, first cousin to Charlotte Barnard, although her mother has forbidden her to see him. Nonetheless, the clandestine relationship continues until one day, while fitting a dress for the pale and sickly girl, Deborah discovers that her unwed daughter is pregnant. With the determination of an ancient prophet, Deborah instantly casts her daughter out of the home into a fierce blizzard. Caleb fetches Barnabas, who tracks William down, and together they find the girl. The guilty couple is hastily wed. This makes no difference at all to Deborah, who now feels that she has but one child left in the world.

Although she continues in her routines about the house, Deborah's real emphasis is placed on the improvement of Ephraim's soul. She becomes stricter and stricter with him in order to compensate for her losses. Ephraim chafes under this attention and longs for the freedom apparent in other boys' lives. One night, not long after Rebecca gives birth to a child, Ephraim commits the one great sin of his life: He sneaks out near midnight and sleds for more than an hour, and then upon returning home, snitches half of a mince pie and devours it. The boy goes to sleep vastly pleased with his evening, but he is deathly ill the next day. Later that day Deborah decides, against a lifelong medical ban, that the boy has to be whipped for failing to follow the instructions that were given him. Once again Caleb protests, but to no avail. As Deborah is set to deliver her second blow, Ephraim falls to the floor; he dies soon after.

Now bereft of her family, Deborah prays constantly, veering between recrimination and remorse, but speaks to no one. Finally, after months of grief, it is revealed to her that Ephraim had sneaked out the night before his death and that he had eaten the forbidden food. In a tremendous surge of relief at this news, Deborah's body shakes violently, and she collapses. Astonishingly, at the reprieve of guilt over her son's death, Deborah is released from the chains that bound her to life, and within a few hours she, too, dies.

Theale, Mildred. *The Wings of the Dove.* Henry James. 1902.

Mildred Theale, a twenty-two-year-old heiress from New York City, departs for Europe with an immense fortune after the death of her last family members. Knowing it is likely that she, too, has a fatal disease, Milly is determined to live as intensely as possible. Charmingly eccentric and possessing an ethereal beauty, Milly captivates all of London—with the exception of Merton Densher, with whom she is thoroughly in love.

Utterly alone and with no obligations, she promptly invites Susan Stringham, a widow who earns her living as a writer, to accompany her on a trip to Europe. As the two friends envision it, the journey has neither a specific plan nor any limitations; the goal is simply to give Milly opportunities to "live." Fortunately, Susan is connected to London society through an old friendship with Mrs. Maud Lowder, the mistress of Lancaster Gate, and as a result, Milly and Susan are received there with great enthusiasm. Milly suddenly finds herself "the talk of the town" and feels as if she is in love with everyone "within range."

Milly befriends Kate Croy, Mrs. Lowder's perceptive but mercenary niece. Kate and Lord Mark, an English nobleman, are among the most intimate members of the Lancaster Gate circle. Kate is the "wondrous London girl" whom Milly has already grown to admire from reading current English fiction; the only difference is that Kate is also "nice." Kate, in return, regards Milly as extraordinary, and the two become inseparable during the early days of Milly's London success. But an unstated conflict emerges between them when Merton Densher, an Englishman whom Milly met in New York shortly before her departure, returns to London from his journalistic assignment in America. Although Milly remains characteristically silent on the subject, she obviously has a romantic interest in Densher. It is widely understood in Mrs. Lowder's circle, however, that the young man is in love with Kate Croy.

Kate accompanies Milly to visit Sir Luke Strett, a famous physician, who confirms Milly's fears that she has a fatal illness. Strett's advice to Milly indicates his hopelessness about curing her: He offers no medication or treatment but simply prescribes that Milly "live"—which her friends take to mean that she must fall in love. A conspiracy develops at Lancaster Gate to foster a romance, perhaps even a marriage, between Milly and Merton Densher. Kate Croy, who is herself in love with Densher and secretly engaged to him, requires of her fiancé that he play along. According to her plan, Milly will leave Densher her fortune, which he can then use to marry Kate. Without the money, Kate is unwilling to marry Densher because both are poor and she cannot secure her wealthy aunt's support or approval. Milly, purposefully given the impression that Densher cares for Kate but that Kate does not return the affection, has a clear conscience when she allows herself to fall in love with him.

The entire party moves in August from London to Venice where Milly has rented a dreamlike "palace" called the Palazzo Leporelli. With its elaborately painted ceilings and marble floors, the palace strikes Milly as the ideal place to die. The signs of her illness are concealed even at this late stage, and no one ever mentions her condition. Lord Mark awkwardly proposes marriage to her but retreats back to London when she rejects him. Sir Luke arrives; shortly afterward Kate and Maud Lowder also return to England, the only sign that Milly is worse. At Kate's insistence Densher remains in Venice, where he halfheartedly but quite effectively courts Milly.

The vengeful, inscrutable Lord Mark returns to Venice, determined that Milly should know the truth. Milly is utterly devastated when he tells her the news that ultimately hastens her death: that Kate Croy and Merton Densher have been engaged during the time Densher has been courting her. Hoping that Densher will deny this fact, Milly invites him to the palace one final time before dismissing him from Venice. Although this hope is unfulfilled, Milly leaves Densher her fortune so that he may marry Kate. As Kate tells Densher, this act is proof of the purity and generosity of her love for him.

Thomas, Bigger. *Native Son.* Richard Wright. 1940.

Bigger Thomas is a Mississippi-born twenty-year-old black youth with an eighth-grade education. From the start of his story, when he battles a huge rat that has invaded the one-room apartment he shares with his mother, brother, and sister, Bigger is preyed upon by squalor, hatred, and deprivation—the forces conditioning life for blacks in the 1930s Chicago slums.

A sullen youth filled with inarticulate hate, Bigger spends his time smoking cigarettes, playing pool, and robbing an occasional store. His mother presses him to accept a position as chauffeur for the Daltons, a wealthy white family that contributes millions of dollars to organizations for the advancement of blacks. On the first day of his new job, Bigger is told to take the Daltons' daughter Mary to a lecture. Once they are in the car, however, Mary tells Bigger that she actually plans to spend the evening with her lover Jan Erlone, a communist of whom her parents strongly disapprove. After Jan arrives, their conversation turns to racial matters, and Mary earnestly asks Bigger how his "people" live. The couple asks to be driven to a restaurant in the ghetto. This treatment angers and disturbs Bigger, who is unable to determine if Mary and Jan are crazy, sincere, or patronizing. Nonetheless, he joins them at their insistence and then drives through a park for a few hours while they kiss in the backseat. Finally, late in the night, Bigger drops Jan off at the train and drives the intoxicated Mary home.

When they reach the Dalton residence, it is apparent that Bigger will have to bring Mary, who is too drunk to stand up, to her bedroom. Once there, Bigger is overcome with fear, which accelerates as Mrs. Dalton approaches and enters the room. Even though Bigger knows Mrs. Dalton is blind, he is gripped with terror. He places his hand and then a pillow over Mary's face to keep her from talking. When Mrs. Dalton smells the liquor emanating from Mary's bed, she leaves in disgust, but by then, as Bigger discovers, Mary is dead of suffocation.

Because Mary had been planning a short trip the next morning, her trunk is sitting half-packed in the bedroom; desperately trying to conceal the murder, Bigger packs her body into the trunk and brings it downstairs. He decides to burn the body in the furnace, the care of which is one of his duties. He decapitates the body when it proves to be too large, then covers it with coals to facilitate the cremation. Over the course of the next two days, as the Daltons realize something awful has happened, Bigger concocts a plan to extort $10,000 from them by faking a kidnapping. At the same time he attempts to point suspicion in the direction of Jan, the despised communist.

In order to work out his ransom demand he enlists the aid of his girlfriend Bessie Mears. Although she suspects he has killed Mary, she agrees to help him. His ransom plot almost works—until Mary's bones are discovered by a group of newspaper men who are interviewing Bigger in the basement. Bigger escapes the Dalton house and, after finding Bessie, takes refuge in an abandoned building. Later that night, however, he decides that Bessie is too much of a liability, and after brutally raping her, he dumps her body down an air shaft. Ultimately it is revealed that Bessie did not die from the head injuries or her fall but instead froze to death as she tried to crawl out of the alleyway.

Bigger flees but is captured by the police a few days later. Soaking wet and half-frozen to death, he is dragged by his feet down several flights of stairs, beaten unconscious, and thrown in prison. At Jan's request a communist lawyer, Mr. Max, is enlisted for Bigger's defense. Despite an impassioned argument concerning the detrimental effects of environment and the workings of racial prejudice,

Mr. Max is unable to prevent Bigger from being sentenced to death. As the novel closes, Bigger, facing electrocution within hours, has reconciled himself to being punished for his crime, but it is clear that he would do it again if he had to. As he tells his attorney, he could give voice to his feelings only by killing; only then could he feel, for the first and last time in his life, creative and free.

Thompson, Royal Earle. "Noon Wine." Katherine Anne Porter. 1936.

Royal Earle Thompson is a decent, sometimes temperamental Texas dairy farmer whose life has not quite met his own expectations. His wife Ellie was lovely as a young woman, but she has turned out to be weak and sickly. Now Thompson's farm is not profitable, his property is slowly falling apart, and his extra money goes into paying for Ellie's doctors. But thanks to the hard work of a stranger, Thompson's situation improves—until one day he is provoked into committing a violent, life-changing deed.

The story begins when Olaf Helton, a reticent Swedish man from North Dakota who has arrived in Texas needing work, asks Thompson for a job on the farm. Thompson agrees to hire him for seven dollars a day plus meals, which he wants Helton to eat with him and his family. At the first family meal, Thompson tries unsuccessfully to make conversation with Helton. But although the stranger is uncommunicative, he does know how to work; indeed, because of Helton's thorough, consistent efforts, Thompson's farm begins to make a profit.

In his second year in Thompson's employ, Helton suggests that Thompson buy a cheese press. He does, and they sell the cheese that Helton makes along with the extra butter and eggs he produces. In the third and fourth years, Thompson gives Helton a raise. Helton still does not talk much, but Thompson, impressed by his dedication to the farm, grows very fond of him. As time passes, Thompson's two sons, who were criticized by their father for being wild when they were young, grow up with solid characters and hearts of gold. Thompson recognizes their merits and is relieved.

One day while chopping firewood, Thompson is visited by a stranger, Homer T. Hatch. Thompson feels an instinctual dislike for this man, who is slow and indirect about stating the nature of his visit. Finally, Hatch tells Thompson he is looking for Olaf Helton. He reveals that Helton escaped from an asylum and is wanted by the authorities; Hatch, who will receive a reward for finding and returning Helton, has brought handcuffs with him and asks for Thompson's help in capturing the escapee. Thompson, growing more and more angry, refuses to cooperate; when Hatch goads him by saying it won't look good if he harbors escaped lunatics on his property, Thompson explodes and tells him to leave. At this moment Helton runs toward them, and Thompson sees Hatch pull out a knife. Helton is stabbed, and in a moment of passion, Thompson brings his axe down on Hatch's head.

Captured and imprisoned, Helton dies in his cell. Thompson goes to trial for the murder of Homer Hatch, and although he is acquitted, he can tell that the neighbors do not believe he is innocent. His wife begins to dread life and falls into a deep despair. Lying in bed one night, Thompson relives the event in his mind, trying to figure out if he had to kill Hatch or if he could have done something else. When his memories become unbearable, he jumps out of bed; Mrs. Thompson, who is lying next to him, cries out in agony as if she were having a nightmare. Their two sons hear the commotion and enter the room. Thinking that their father has done something terrible to their mother, they threaten to hurt Thompson if he ever touches her again.

Thompson, realizing that his credibility is gone forever and that no one believes he is not a murderer, leaves the house with a lantern, a shotgun, paper and pencil. In a field away from his house, he writes a note swearing that he did not take Homer Hatch's life on purpose and aims the shotgun at his own head.

Tiflin, Jody. *The Red Pony.* John Steinbeck. 1945.

Jody Tiflin, an ingenuous, sensitive young boy, lives with his parents and a ranch hand in the beautiful, fertile Salinas Valley in California. Despite his youth, Jody must perform several chores on the ranch, which he dispatches with a cunning akin to that of Tom Sawyer. In order to make filling the stove's woodbox a less arduous chore, he carefully stacks each piece in such a way that the box appears to be full after only two armloads but is really filled predominantly with air. This ingenious means of shirking responsibility is brave on Jody's part because he has much to fear if caught in the act of misbehaving by his parents, especially from his father Carl Tiflin, whose moodiness and temper tantrums often frighten and depress the boy. Neither parent is sufficiently sympathetic to the emotional needs of their son, whose progress toward adulthood they satirize by calling him Big Britches when he does something that a more supportive adult might call precocious.

Jody is struck to solemn shyness when his father returns from Salinas with a red pony as a gift for him. He works hard to keep his pony Galiban clean, fed, and watered. Contrary to the promise of the stable man, BILLY BUCK, when Galiban gets caught out in a rainstorm, he becomes terribly sick. Although Jody and Billy nurse the pony around the clock, the pony escapes one night while Jody is asleep in the stall. Jody wakes and rushes up the mountain to find Galiban almost dead, surrounded by buzzards.

Later, the family mare Nellie becomes pregnant, and Jody anxiously awaits the new foal to replace his lost pony. Just before the birth, Billy Buck realizes that the foal is turned inside Nellie and may not live. Billy kills Nellie and delivers the newborn in order to present Jody with the living colt.

One windy summer Saturday afternoon, as Jody anticipates taking his dogs on a mouse hunt, he spots his father returning from the range on his horse and spies an envelope in his hand. Jody races back to the house with the hope that the letter will be read aloud. His excitement is squelched when the contents of the letter are divulged by his mother, who informs her family that her father is to be expected that very afternoon. Carl, whose mood was not sunny when he arrived, becomes increasingly morose as the news that his tedious father-in-law is on his way sinks in, and he finally becomes so annoyed that he vents his anger on his son and fiercely orders him to leave the house. Jody is delighted by the news and rushes down to the road to meet his grandfather, who very shortly approaches the ranch in a cart drawn by a bay horse. Gussied up in a black broadcloth suit and spats with a close-cut, combed white beard, Jody's grandfather is the picture of old-fashioned formal dignity. Chatting amiably, they make their way to the farmhouse where dinner awaits them.

Midway through the meal the amicable atmosphere at the table begins to deteriorate when Carl is noticeably bothered by his father-in-law's inclination to dwell on the past, endlessly repeating stories of his escapades as the leader of a wagon train that traversed the plains and did not stop moving in a westerly direction until they confronted the Pacific Ocean in California. Jody's father attempts to interrupt the grandfather's stories, much to the resentment of the boy's mother. After dinner Carl is so rude that Jody begins to empathize with his grandfather, understanding how empty his father's cruelty left the victim of his wrath. When Jody goes to bed, he fantasizes about life on the frontier, the romantic world of buffaloes, Indians, and fearless men of gargantuan stature. The boy wishes he had had the opportunity to live during that heroic frontier era but agrees with his grandfather that he and his contemporaries probably do not possess the courageous mettle which characterized the pioneer spirit in America.

The following morning, as the family awaits Jody's grandfather at the breakfast table, Carl starts ranting about how he can no longer countenance listening to the tedious stories of a doddering old fool who can think of nothing but the past. When the grandfather walks into the room, it is apparent to everyone that he overheard this monologue. Carl apologizes, but the grandfather, although deeply wounded, ponders the criticism and sadly concurs that it is time to let go of the past. Sensing his grandfather's melancholy mood, Jody postpones his beloved mouse hunt and offers to make the elderly pioneer a lemonade. His grandfather accepts the offer when he sees that the boy is trying to share in his grief over the loss of the true frontier spirit in America.

Till, Nancy. *Sapphira and the Slave Girl.* Willa Cather. 1940.

Nancy Till is the young and highly attractive slave girl of the novel's title. Nancy's early years are spent in the good favor of SAPPHIRA COLBERT, her mistress, who also holds Nancy's mother, the slave Till, in high regard. But as the novel begins, Nancy, who has among her tasks the maintenance of cleanliness and order in Henry Colbert's quarters at the Colbert Mill, has unaccountably fallen out of favor with her mistress. Although she and her mother cannot account for the change in attitude, the other slaves, particularly the jealous and lazy Bluebell, and her mother, the fat and bitter cook Lizzie, conjecture that Mr. Colbert's affections may be the issue, and they even tell Nancy that she had better be careful of the white man.

But Henry Colbert sees the young girl as little more than a worker; while he certainly feels affection for her, he mainly notices her if her tasks are left undone for some reason. Nonetheless, Sapphira's jealously mounts and takes its toll on Nancy's composure. Eventually, Sapphira decides to take Nancy along with her on her annual Easter visit to her sisters in Winchester, Virginia. The prospect terrifies the young girl, who has not been to a city before and who will be expected to execute duties for which she is not yet fully prepared. Trying to allay Nancy's fears, Till instructs her as best she can. The trip to Winchester goes well, but upon their return to the mill and the arrival of Martin Colbert, the son of one of Henry's brothers, Nancy's life takes a dramatic turn.

It seems that Sapphira, who had in mind a plan to possibly sell Nancy, decided to undermine the girl in another way, and motivated by her ill-founded jealousy, she invites the young man into her home, hoping that Martin will take advantage of Nancy. After weeks of enduring his verbal and then physical advances, the distraught Nancy turns to RACHEL COLBERT BLAKE, Sapphira's daughter, who has a reputation for being helpful to everyone. After a few attempts at running interference for Nancy, Rachel finally decides that her only recourse is the extreme step of sending Nancy away via the Underground Railroad. With money provided in secret by her father, Rachel escorts the frightened but determined Nancy across the river and into the hands of the first of a chain of strangers who will help her make it to Montreal.

Nothing more is heard from Nancy for several years, and then she begins writing to Till and sending her fifty dollars each Christmas. Finally, twenty-five years after her flight, Nancy returns for a six-week visit. She finds her mother aged but enormously proud of her daughter, who speaks eloquently, has a very good position with a wealthy family in Montreal, and now, at forty-four, is herself a mother of three children and has a loving husband. She regales the gathering, comprised mainly of Rachel and Till, with accounts of her life over the last quarter-century and demonstrates that Sapphira's first estimation of her had

been correct: She was indeed a worthy person, and had led a just life as a free woman.

Tin Woodman. *The Wonderful Wizard of Oz.* L. Frank Baum. 1900.

Once a regular man, the Tin Woodman became tin at the hands of the Wicked Witch of the East. As a man of flesh, he was in love with a girl and intended to marry her as soon as he could build her a bigger house. Her mother was selfish, however, and relied on the girl to do all her cooking and cleaning. To prevent her daughter from leaving, the woman asked the Wicked Witch for help. The Witch enchanted the Woodman's axe, and it cut him apart limb by limb. Each time he lost a limb, he simply went to the local tinsmith for a replacement, which worked fine until the axe cut off his head and chopped his body in two. The tin replacements lacked a brain and, most important, a heart. Without a heart, the Tin Woodman no longer loved the girl and did not care if he ever married her. He joins DOROTHY and the SCARECROW on their pilgrimage to the Emerald City in order to ask the WIZARD OF OZ for a heart, for without one, he says, he can never be happy.

Dorothy and the Scarecrow find the Tin Woodman immobilized by rust, frozen in the midst of chopping down a tree. They oil his joints, and soon he is as good as new. As the trio follows the yellow brick road, the forest becomes very thick, and he chops away the branches that impede them. They then meet the COWARDLY LION, who joins them. As they proceed, the Tin Woodman accidentally steps on and kills a beetle. The death makes him so sad that he cries, rusting his jaw shut. Thereafter, the Tin Woodman is careful to step over every ant that crosses his path.

Several adventures later the party arrives in the Emerald City where each member is given a separate audience with the Wizard. To the Tin Woodman, Oz appears as a terrible beast with the head of a rhinoceros, a woolly body, and five legs. Oz tells the Tin Woodman what he told the others: No wishes will be granted until they kill the Wicked Witch of the West. They set off for her home in the country of the Winkies, but the witch sees them coming and sends the Winged Monkies to stop them. They drop the Tin Woodman onto some sharp rocks, leaving him a veritable heap of scrap metal until Dorothy, having killed the Wicked Witch with a bucket of water, returns to rescue him. Several Winkie tinsmiths repair him, and when all the members of the party are back in shape, they return to the Emerald City to claim their reward.

There they soon discover that Oz is a fraud; he is a man, not a wizard. Nonetheless, they still want their wishes granted, and Oz agrees. For the Tin Woodman, Oz provides a silk heart stuffed with sawdust, which makes the Woodman very content. The Wizard is also successful at granting the wish of the Lion, for courage, and the wish of the Scarecrow, a brain. When it comes to Dorothy, however, he botches his attempt to get her back to her home in Kansas.

Determined to help her, the Tin Woodman, the Scarecrow, and the Lion take her to Glenda, the Good Witch of the South, who not only helps Dorothy get home but also places each of her former companions in his own kingdom. The Tin Woodman returns to the land of the Winkies, who lack a ruler because of the death of the Wicked Witch. There he rules, it is safe to assume, with kindness.

Tobin, Wiltshire "Wilt." *Monday Night.* Kay Boyle. 1938.

Wiltshire Tobin is a forty-three-year-old American writer living in Paris where he has spent twenty years mostly in brothels and bars, buying love and drinks. When sober, "Wilt" dwells on the failure of his life as both writer and lover; when drunk, he hopes for love, has ideas for novels, and argues that Shakespeare and Milton produced nothing until they reached middle age. Yet in spite of a life fraught with failure and an appearance on which years of drink and despair have left their mark, he retains a certain dignity and a notable capacity for compassion.

As the novel opens, Wilt has met up with Bernie Lord, a young American doctor who has come to Paris in search of Monsieur Sylvestre, an eminent toxicologist whose scientific evidence has convicted a series of murderers. As they follow the trail of Sylvestre from his pharmacy in Paris to his house in Malmaison, Wilt constantly battles against the suspicion and distaste aroused by Bernie's disreputable appearance: His ear has been mutilated after a night spent in prison, his clothes are dirty and worn, and his face speaks of a man who long ago stopped thinking of his appearance. For Wilt, though, it is only his ear that distinguishes him, and this shameful injury comes to symbolize the world's disdainful treatment of him and the pathetic nobility of his life. The tale of this injury becomes, in his telling of it, the book he never wrote, an epic story of his struggles against the nameless forces that silence and oppress every man who will not submit to their law.

Yet as the novel progresses, Wilt becomes involved in a greater epic: the search for the mysterious Sylvestre. This search leads Wilt and Bernie to Sylvestre's house in Malmaison where the devoted butler sings the praises of his absent master. Wilt begins to piece together the man behind the public front, sensing that Sylvestre, whose science exposes other men's secrets, is himself hiding something. Wilt stands drunkenly in Sylvestre's study, listening to the voices he hears there, and realizes that the doctor is a criminal. Soon, against Bernie's wishes, Wilt embarks on his own quest to rectify the injustice done by Sylvestre and denounce him in the book he feels he is destined to write.

Suddenly everything Wilt had dreamed of seems to be within his grasp. He sets out to establish the proof necessary to accuse Sylvestre, and he meets and falls in love with the wife of one of the men condemned to death by Sylvestre's evidence. Yet just as his hopes are about to be realized, Wilt is thwarted by a newspaper article that uncovers the injustice he had suspected. Sylvestre is publicly denounced, his evidence revealed as false, and Wilt is deprived of both his book and the woman he loved. But even now Wilt is rescued from despair by his resolute compassion. His first thought is not that he has been deprived of his book but that he must find Bernie and gently explain to him that his idol has fallen.

Todd. "Flying Home." Ralph Ellison. 1944.

Todd dreamed of flying planes when he was a boy and became an air force pilot. One day, flying his plane too high and too fast, he was startled when a buzzard crossed his path. He panicked, lost control of the plane, and crashed. Now, lying in a field and feeling the tremendous pain in his ankle, he is gripped by an old fear of being touched by white people. The sound of a black man's voice relieves him, and memories of the crash flash into his mind. Immobilized, helpless, and upset, he must now accept the help of the kind old black man and boy who are standing over him.

When the boy suggests that they take Todd into town on their mule, Todd refuses, telling them he has orders not to leave his plane. In truth, the thought of being carried on a mule past the white townspeople humiliates him deeply, and he knows this is one humiliation he can spare himself. Jefferson tells the boy to fetch Mr. Graves; Todd, thinking Graves might be white, asks them to send word to the base instead.

While they are waiting for the boy to return, Jefferson asks Todd why he wants to fly. Todd thinks to himself that flying is a meaningful act, and it makes him less like the old man standing over him. But when Jefferson asks when Todd's superiors will actually let him fight, Todd tenses; this is the question that all his fellow blacks ask him, and he cannot answer it. Jefferson proceeds to tell a story about the time he died and went to heaven and was banished by Saint Peter for flying too fast. Jefferson amuses himself with his story, but Todd bursts out, "Why do you laugh at me this way?" Exhausted and pained, he says he cannot help it if they won't let the black pilots fly. Jefferson, who has been misunderstood, apologizes.

Todd remembers being a boy and asking his mother for a model airplane. His mother repeatedly said no, so one day, overcome by his desire for the plane, he devised a plan: e would stand on the roof and catch a white boy's plane as it flew by. When the plane appeared, Todd reached for it, lost his balance, and fell off the roof. The doctor was called, and Todd was put to bed for a week. In his dreams, hearing his grandmother warning "Yo' arms too short to box with God," he would reach out to grab the plane and miss it.

Jefferson tells Todd that Graves, who owns the land, once killed five black men and cares only for himself. Todd feels uneasy. When the boy returns with Graves and two other white men wearing hospital uniforms, the whites put Todd in a straitjacket, and Graves insultingly says that "nigger brains" are not meant for high altitudes. When they are about to carry him away on the stretcher, Todd surprises everyone by telling the white men not to touch him. Graves kicks him in the chest, and Todd responds by laughing hysterically, unable to control himself. Jefferson speaks up, informing Graves that Todd has orders not to leave his plane. Graves wants Todd off his land, so Jefferson and the boy carry him themselves. As Todd is being transported, he feels lifted out of his dreamlike isolation and back into the world of men. A new current of communication flows between Jefferson, the boy, and him.

Todd, Joanna. *The Country of the Pointed Firs.* Sarah Orne Jewett. 1896.

The sad story of Joanna Todd, who has been dead for twenty-two years, is the most important of many for the residents of Dunnet Landing, Maine. The collective memory of Joanna's plight is one of the means by which the town is kept a community as its residents die and its importance as a fishing village diminishes. The pleasure taken by Mrs. ALMIRY TODD, a cousin of Joanna's by marriage, in telling the tale to the visiting NARRATOR seems to arise in part from the fact that the narrator can help keep the story alive as the townspeople do.

Joanna's story is told to the narrator by Mrs. Todd and her friend Mrs. Fosdick one chilly evening as all three women are gathered around the Franklin stove in the narrator's room. When Mrs. Todd mentions Shell-heap Island, a small rocky island eight miles off the coast of Dunnet Landing, Mrs. Fosdick tells the narrator that a woman—Joanna—went to live there alone.

Rejected by the man she had expected to marry, Joanna decides that she cannot face the pitying gazes of the Dunnet Landing townspeople. She turns over her half of the family farm to her brother, gathers some provisions, and sets out for the island in a small boat. Although the island is small and rocky, Joanna lives there with only a few chickens for company for the rest of her life. At first the curious townspeople gaze at the island, looking for smoke from her chimney and other signs of Joanna's well-being, but eventually Joanna's self-imposed exile becomes a familiar part of their lives. Sometimes the town's fishermen leave small packages on the island, packed with things she would need for the cold winters. One man, an admirer of Joanna's whom Mrs. Fosdick is sure wanted to marry the lonely woman, even brings her a chicken coop.

The only people to visit Joanna are the town's minister, Mr. Dimmick, and Mrs. Todd. On their one trip to the island Mr. Dimmick offers Joanna a prayer as he and Mrs. Todd sit in her tiny house. When the minister goes out to explore the island, Mrs. Todd begs Joanna to return with them to the mainland, but the woman declines. Explaining that when her lover jilted her she all but cursed God in her anger, Joanna judges herself unfit to live among other people. But she does ask Mrs. Todd to tell the townspeople who ask about her that she is well and only wants to be left to live alone.

Joanna spends the rest of her life in solitude. When she dies, most of the townspeople gather on Shell-heap Island to say farewell, and in subsequent years the novel's narrator is among those who visit the spot where this strong-willed woman chose to exile herself.

Todd, Almiry. *The Country of the Pointed Firs.* Sarah Orne Jewett. 1896.

As the resident herb expert of Dunnet Landing, Maine, Mrs. Almiry Todd plays an important role in her town. Supplying soothing medicines and sound advice, the elderly Mrs. Todd acts not only as an apothecary but as a repository for the community's news and stories. When she provides a room for the novel's NARRATOR one summer, Mrs. Todd helps the woman overcome her sense of rootless isolation and recruits another soul to perpetuate the stories that animate the community.

At first the narrator finds Mrs. Todd a bit obtrusive. The older woman is not at all reluctant to engage her tenant in conversation as she bustles about her small cottage, preparing syrups, powders, and poultices for her patients. The narrator, who has come to Dunnet Landing to write, enjoys the elderly woman's company but must leave the house in order to get any work done. Mrs. Todd's project of drawing the woman into her little community circle seems thwarted.

One day, however, when the narrator leaves her work to talk to Captain Littlepage, an eccentric town resident, Mrs. Todd realizes that the narrator will eventually respond to her offer of friendship. Mrs. Todd mentions that her brother William and Mrs. Blackett, her mother, live on nearby Green Island. The narrator jumps at the chance to meet Mrs. Todd's relatives, and Mrs. Todd promises a trip out. She even gives the narrator a glass of her special herb beer, a drink she doesn't share with just anyone. On the island Mrs. Todd takes the narrator herb gathering and shows her the family pictures she carries with her.

On another occasion an old friend, Mrs. Fosdick, pays a visit to Mrs. Todd. The two sit and talk together, with the narrator eagerly listening and urging the women to tell stories about the town and its residents, living and dead. The stories they share, especially that of JOANNA TODD, Mrs. Todd's relative who isolated herself on a remote island after a disappointment in love, attest to the rich history of the town and its inhabitants. More stories are revealed at a large family reunion the women attend.

When the summer draws to a close, the narrator must return to the city. Although she tries to hide her sadness at the narrator's parting by acting brusquely toward her, Mrs. Todd can conceal neither the love she feels nor her disappointment at the imminent departure of someone who has become, in a short space of time, a friend. Mrs. Todd never says good-bye to the narrator, but she does leave her a basket filled with food for her journey home, a bunch of southernwood and bayleaf, and a coral pin. And both women take away from the encounter the gift of friendship and fellowship.

Toklas, Alice. *The Autobiography of Alice B. Toklas.* Gertrude Stein. 1933.

Alice Toklas, the ostensible narrator of this "autobiography," describes her integral involvement in the modernist art movement in Paris during the first third of the twentieth century. Most of Toklas's reminiscences revolve around the activities of such artists as Pablo Picasso, Henri Matisse, Paul Cézanne, Henri Rousseau, Ernest Hemingway, Virgil Thomson, and her lover, Gertrude Stein. Although the story of Stein and Toklas's establishment of their famous salon on rue de Fleurus is recounted from Alice's point of view, the majority of the book is devoted to a celebration of Stein's art and life. In the last paragraph of the autobiography, the reader learns that the real author of the book is in fact Gertrude Stein.

After a brief account of her life in San Francisco before she met Stein, Alice Toklas describes her extraordinary reaction to being introduced to her. Toklas claims that during the course of her lifetime she became acquainted with three geniuses—Stein, Picasso, and Alfred Whitehead—and the first time she met each of these people, the sound of a bell ringing within her indicated their intellectual or artistic stature. Meeting Gertrude was a momentous occurrence in Alice's life, and their relationship became the central concern of her existence. Apparently Stein was equally impressed with Toklas because she immediately took her under her wing and introduced her to her bohemian life-style.

Not long after Alice arrived in Paris, she began living at 27 rue de Fleurus with Gertrude. She became intimately involved in every aspect of Gertrude's life. When the proofs of Stein's first published book, *Three Lives*, arrived from New York, Toklas helped to correct them. She also began typing Gertrude's handwritten manuscripts. When Gertrude agreed to deliver lectures at Cambridge and Oxford universities and in the United States, Alice accompanied her as a kind of manager. Eventually, Alice contributed to the success of Gertrude's career as a writer by acting as her publisher, publicist, and distributor. In *The Autobiography of Alice B. Toklas*, Alice expresses her pride in the fact that she was the mastermind behind putting what became Stein's signature quote, "A rose is a rose is a rose is a rose," on letter paper, table linen, or any suitable display media. This pride exemplifies Toklas's enthusiasm for her involvement in the making of the legendary Stein.

In the conclusion of the book, Alice admits to being a talented housekeeper, gardener, seamstress, secretary, editor, and veterinarian. Because Alice was so busy performing these various duties, Gertrude Stein volunteered to take on the task of writing Alice's autobiography. *The Autobiography*, which became a best-seller, is a tribute to the highly successful joint careers of these two extraordinary American expatriates.

Topouzoglou, Stavros. *America America.* Elia Kazan. 1962.

Stavros Topouzoglou, the eldest of eight children in an impoverished Greek family, lives his entire life with the goal of one day reaching America. From the beginning of the novel when Stavros's best friend, the Armenian Vartan Damadian, is killed trying to prevent a brutal Turkish attack on an Armenian church, Stavros realizes that he must escape his Turkish-dominated homeland. His plans are interrupted, however, when his father Isaac informs him that he has been selected to save his family's fortunes by investing their entire savings in a cousin's Constantinople rug business.

After he is robbed on his way to the city by a ferryman who threatens to drown both the boy and his heavily laden donkey, Stavros falls into the hands of an unscrupulous highwayman named Abdul. Before long, Stavros finds himself alone and penniless en route to Constantinople. When Abdul reappears, taunting Stavros with his easy victory, Stavros responds by killing the thief and recouping a small measure of his possessions. When he finally does arrive in the city, Stavros is shocked to learn that his cousin's establishment is rundown and far from profitable. Driven by shame and an ardent desire to get to America, Stavros works two jobs in order to save money for his passage.

After nearly a year of constant work, he is exhausted and has managed to save less than ten percent of the fare. One night, desperate for some human contact, he agrees to a liaison set up by his fellow worker Garabet. The man arranges for Stavros to spend the night with his prostitute daughter. After their sexual encounter, Stavros's first, the young prostitute robs the sleeping Stavros of all his money. He cannot recoup his losses entirely, and Stavros's anger leads him to become slowly involved in Garabet's underground anti-Turkish movement. This, too, is an ill-fated decision, as the police interrupt a meeting one night and kill most of the group. While the police throw the bodies into the ocean, Stavros manages to roll into a ditch and eventually makes his way back to Garabet's daughter, who provides him with food, shelter, and eventually a new suit.

Stavros returns to his cousin and agrees to a business marriage with the daughter of a wealthy carpet seller.

Although Thomna, the young girl, quickly falls for Stavros, he enters the agreement solely to get the money for passage to America. Through Thomna's father, Stavros encounters some wealthy visiting Americans and takes up with the wife of the American businessman. Serving as the steward/companion to the bored wife, he finally boards a ship heading for America.

Although Stavros is thrilled to be sailing for America, the fact remains that he has let his family down. He writes to them, promising that his new plan will work out soon. By the time the ship reaches New York Harbor, Stavros's patron has sickened of his wife's interest in the boy and threatens to have him arrested and shipped back to Turkey. Stavros assumes the name of a fellow would-be immigrant who committed suicide rather than risk deportation as a consumptive. Under his dead friend's name, Stavros eludes capture by the authorities and arrives at Ellis Island, where once again he gets a new name, Joe Arness, and is allowed into the country.

Once in America, he sends his family the fifty dollars given to him by the businessman's wife, hinting that soon there would be more money. As the novel ends, however, Stavros has yet to work off the two years of unpaid labor he has contracted for. He is surviving in his dreamland on tips he receives, while his eager family awaits its eventual deliverance.

Topsy. *Uncle Tom's Cabin,* or *Life Among the Lowly.* Harriet Beecher Stowe. 1852.

When she makes her first appearance in this classic abolitionist novel, Topsy, a young slave girl, is a half-naked, barely human victim of years of physical abuse. The influence of love and religion transform her, however, and by the end of her story she is about to be taken to the North and freed.

A wealthy New Orleans slave owner, Augustine St. Clare, purchases Topsy as a gift for his cousin Miss Ophelia, a New England woman who has come to live with the St. Clare family. Although Miss Ophelia's New England upbringing has made her critical of slavery, she remains prejudiced against blacks, whom she views as inferior. Topsy initially seems to confirm all of Miss Ophelia's suspicions about blacks. The girl is cunning and mischievous, an accomplished liar, and a compulsive thief. Most disturbing to Miss Ophelia is Topsy's ignorance of morality and religion.

Under Miss Ophelia's questioning, Topsy reveals what little she knows of her background. She was taken from her parents at such an early age that she doesn't know who they are or where she was born. Raised for market by speculators, Topsy was sold to innkeepers who taught her little more than how to clean and who beat her regularly and brutally.

By now unused to gentle treatment, Topsy understandably distrusts Miss Ophelia's kindness. While Miss Ophelia tries to teach the child how to make her bed, Topsy pretends to listen but devotes more attention to stealing ribbons and gloves from the woman. Confronted with the evidence against her, Topsy lies about the theft, but confesses to having stolen other things that she has not in fact taken because she thinks her lies will please Miss Ophelia and save her from a beating.

With Miss Ophelia's guidance Topsy learns that it is not unusual for people to treat one another with kindness and respect, and Miss Ophelia learns that her prejudices against blacks are unfounded. Even before Miss Ophelia can overcome her abhorrence of blacks and begin to love Topsy, however, EVANGELINE "EVA" ST. CLARE, Augustine St. Clare's pious young daughter, offers Topsy her unconditional love and respect.

Topsy, like all the slaves, is heartbroken when Eva begins to suffer from a mysterious illness. On her sickbed Eva gives Topsy a lock of her hair as a remembrance and pleads with her to be good and to trust the people who love her. Topsy's loving trust of Miss Ophelia is repaid, for after Eva's death the woman has her cousin give her legal ownership of Topsy so that she can take the child to the North and grant her freedom.

Tosamah, John "Big Bluff." *House Made of Dawn.* N. Scott Momaday. 1966.

The satirical yet insightful Right Reverend John "Big Bluff" Tosamah functions as a pivotal figure for the novel's hero, ABEL. The big, shaggy pastor of the Los Angeles Holiness Pan-Indian Rescue Mission, Tosamah preaches on two themes that situate him in opposition to Father Olguin, the Christianized spiritual leader of the fictional Tanoan reservation Walatowa Cañon de San Diego, on which Abel lives.

After serving a seven-year prison sentence for a murder he committed following his return from World War II, Abel is relocated to Los Angeles by a Bureau of Indian Affairs agent. At the urging of his Navajo roommate, Ben Benally, he attends the Mission, a dimly lit, ramshackle establishment in the basement of a two-story red-brick building. Here Tosamah, accompanied by his squat and perspiring disciple Cruz, draws from the Bible's book of John to assert that Anglo culture, with its commercialized proliferation of words, has diluted the potent, medicinal force—the sanctity—available in a Native American relation to language. This directly addresses Abel's own sense of cultural alienation and inarticulateness, his inability to step into the "old rhythm" of his people following his return from wartime duty. Furthermore, in differentiating the Native American and Anglo American attitudes toward language, Tosamah inadvertently causes Abel to reflect on how the Anglo jury that convicted him could not have been fully equipped for interpreting the rationale behind his act of murder. "Their language," as he calls it, with all its legal phrases, acted as a barrier to mutual understanding.

In the sermon that follows, Tosamah offers an account of the history of his people, the Kiowa, whose heritage he proudly upholds. While he celebrates his tribal identity, Tosamah also derides Abel for wearing his hair long and "being too damn dumb to be civilized." Abel responds to this remark with a vengeance. He physically assaults Tosamah and subsequently falls into a drinking binge that causes him to lose his job. Soon afterward he is beaten by a Chicano policeman and hospitalized. Following his internment, he returns to his reservation to carry on the tradition of his dying grandfather, as exemplified by his participation in a ceremonial race against evil. By returning to his homeland and reinscribing himself in the tradition of his people, Abel demonstrates a respect for the past that Tosamah at once denounces and upholds.

Towne, Langdon. *Northwest Passage.* Kenneth Roberts. 1936.

Langdon Towne is the narrator and the focal point of this historical novel that portrays Towne's maturation against a backdrop of colonial American upheavals. His story symbolizes the coming-of-age of an American consciousness and the birth of the American nation.

The son of a rope maker in Kittery, Maine, Langdon Towne has a family tree that includes Salem witches and New England yeoman farmers. Langdon is the first in the family to be sent to Harvard College, but his passion for drawing, his outspokenness, and his two rowdy woodsmen friends all combine to get him thrown out of college, out of his girlfriend's house, and into jail, all in quick succession. After escaping from jail Langdon must get out of reach of the law, so he joins the army.

The company Langdon joins is Rogers' Rangers, a band of woodsmen-soldiers who are bravely and effectively assisting the British in the French and Indian Wars. The Rangers are commanded by the charismatic MAJOR ROBERT ROGERS, and Langdon's story is largely the story of his own obsessive regard for Rogers and then his long, gradual disillusionment with the brash, ambitious leader. Langdon is just in time for the Rangers' last campaign, a reckless, cross-country march against the St. Francis Indians. They completely destroy the Indian village and all its adult males, and then endure an arduous retreat through the New England woods. Starving and freezing, Langdon and the other Rangers seem kept alive by Rogers's charisma alone.

Back in civilization, the uniformed Langdon swaggers about the town he had lately been forced to flee. He returns to his girlfriend, Eliza Brown, only to be beat out in his suit by Rogers himself. Brokenhearted, Langdon sails for England to study art in London after he is encouraged to do so by the young John Singleton Copley. Langdon manages to be moderately successful painting vivid Indians

and realistic frontier scenes for British aristocrats. When Rogers appears one day in London, Langdon is again caught up in the officer's infectious enthusiasm. Rogers is determined to find the Northwest Passage, and Langdon decides to go along to paint portraits of the Indians.

But the Northwest Passage expedition is nothing like the daring success of Rogers' Rangers against the St. Francis Indians. Rogers finds his hands tied by red tape and political infighting. Langdon, who nearly makes it to the Northwest Passage, returns to their base camp to find Rogers in irons, Mrs. Elizabeth Brown Rogers almost insane, and his new sweetheart, Ann, dragged off by her drunken father after Rogers had made advances on her.

Langdon finds Ann worth pursuing and catches up with her in London. They are married and live happily off Langdon's ethnographically accurate paintings of Indians. London is haunted by rumors of Rogers, however, and by news of the uprising in America. Ann and Langdon return to New England during the revolution. Although he is too modest to suggest it, Langdon is the forerunner of a new American school of art, a school inspired by the raw nature of America and unhindered by the divisive aesthetic conventions of Britain and the continent.

Towns, Matthew. *Dark Princess: A Romance.* W. E. B. Du Bois. 1928.

Matthew Towns, a brilliant young African-American medical student, was born in rural Virginia and raised by his devout, hardworking mother. He moved north to New York City to attend high school and afterward completed the pre-medical course at City College. Working with almost superhuman energy, Matthew was able to win prizes and fellowships, and enrolled in the prestigious medical school at the University of Manhattan. When he tried to take up his position as an intern in obstetrics, however, he was informed that the trustees had decided to exclude African Americans from the college. Enraged and despairing, Matthew sailed immediately for Europe.

In a Berlin café Matthew comes upon an aristocratic woman, impeccably dressed and exquisitely beautiful. When a vulgar American begins harassing her and follows her outside, Matthew knocks the man down and steps into a cab with her. During tea at the Tiergarten, he tells the enchanting woman his story, and she gives him her name and invites him to dinner. She is KAUTILYA, PRINCESS OF BWODPUR, India. The dinner is an occasion for a meeting of radical world leaders from many oppressed nations, including Japan, China, India, and Egypt, all of whom are in the process of forming an alliance against white imperialism. The others have been doubtful about including African Americans, whom they regard as unfit for the demands of the fight for liberation. Kautilya has argued for their inclusion and chooses Matthew as their representative.

Matthew is determined to serve Kautilya's cause, with

his life if necessary. Under orders from her, he returns to the United States to establish contact with underground radical leader Perigua. He also means to survey the general state of African Americans, to determine whether they are prepared to join the movement. In order to see black America, he takes a job as a pullman porter, a humiliating and difficult experience. When his letters to Kautilya are never answered, he gradually loses hope of ever seeing her again. His despair deepens when a close friend, Jimmie, is lynched on a train carrying Ku Klux Klan members. He attempts to organize a porters' strike in protest, but when his efforts fail, he agrees instead to go along with Perigua's revenge scheme. Perigua will bomb an overpass in order to wreck another "Klan special," and Matthew, who consents to die in the crash, carries placards explaining their motive.

Perigua bombs the bridge and is killed by the explosion, but the train is not wrecked. Kautilya, on her way to observe the Klan meeting, is also riding on it, and Matthew stops the train before it reaches the destroyed overpass. In spite of Perigua's death, Matthew assumes responsibility for the near-tragedy, and, refusing to name his friend, is sentenced to ten years in prison. A powerful black Chicago politician, SAMUEL SCOTT, gets Matthew released from prison in order to add him to his political "machine." Matthew eventually marries Sammy's assistant, an ambitious light-skinned African-American woman named SARA ANDREWS, who helps get him elected to the state legislature. He consciously sets aside all his old dreams of a just society and, with them, thoughts of Kautilya. On the eve of a grand dinner marking his nomination to Congress, Matthew suddenly realizes that he is selling his soul for power. Fortunately, Kautilya, who has been keeping watch over him, recognizes that he is becoming lost and goes to the party to rescue him. He declines the nomination and leaves both the astonished guests and his infuriated wife.

Matthew and Kautilya live together in blissful isolation for several months. Like Kautilya, who has spent years doing menial labor, he renounces all thoughts of wealth and prestige, and takes a job digging for the new Chicago subway. When Kautilya departs abruptly, Matthew is sure that the romance has ended, but after many anxious months, she summons him. She has been in Virginia, at the home of Matthew's mother. Their son has been born, and he is crowned Maharajah of Bwodpur. With his marriage to Kautilya, Matthew's patience and courage are rewarded and his hope renewed. He has faith that the child will carry on their fight for justice.

Tozer, Leora. *Arrowsmith*. Sinclair Lewis. 1925.

Leora Tozer is the long-suffering wife of scientist MARTIN ARROWSMITH. Her devotion to her husband, remarkable for its constancy and certainty, both overshadows

and complements Martin's wayward and zealous devotion to science.

Leora was born and raised in the hamlet of Wheatsylvania, North Dakota, where she was surrounded by a family that did not appreciate her independent spirit and enthusiastic acceptance of modern values. She grabs the chance for freedom offered by the prospect of caring for a bedridden aunt in Zenith, Winnemac, and leaves home to begin her training as a nurse. Leora first appears in the novel as she is bad-temperedly scrubbing the floor in Zenith General Hospital—her punishment for smoking a cigarette. Martin, with a characteristic feeling of superiority, comes across Leora as he is tramping through the hospital in quest of a strain of meningococcus from an interesting patient. He is both infuriated and attracted by Leora's "alert impudence." After a brief meeting, the two become engaged. But Martin has another fiancée, Madeline Fox. When the two women meet, Leora wins by demonstrating that fixity of purpose and loyalty which are to characterize her relationship with her future husband.

Throughout the story Leora remains the constant backdrop to Martin's whims and his faithful advocate as he is frequently misunderstood by those he clumsily tries to educate. As Martin moves from job to job, Leora follows him unquestioningly, always supportive of his most recent change of heart. Although she makes few demands on him, she is always firm when her sense of justice is affronted by his thoughtlessness or when he insults her unwavering fidelity with his interest in other women. As Martin noisily pursues his high-minded ideals, Leora quietly pursues her own, less ambitious, projects. After the miscarriage of their first child, she devotes herself to French lessons and dreams of going to France. These pursuits are always secondary to her love for Martin, and as the novel progresses, she retreats further and further into her own world, unable to handle the increasing demands made on her by Martin's profession. Leora is not unhappy or dissatisfied, however. Her strength is drawn from her faith in her own mind and her belief in the inherent rightness of her ideals. She continually acts as a restraining and rational influence on her husband by tempering his impulsive idealism with her innate and humorous pragmatism.

Ironically, it is this very unquestioning and singleminded devotion to her husband that is the cause of Leora's tragic death. She insists on accompanying Martin to the plague-stricken island of St. Hubert, where he is experimenting with a new cure. Always aware of the importance of her husband's work and unwilling to make demands that might threaten his career, Leora reluctantly agrees to stay in the main town as Martin travels around. Lonely and dependent on her husband to such an extent that she forgets to inject herself with an anti-plague toxin, Leora contracts the virus through an infected cigarette that Martin has left, only half-smoked, in his laboratory. She dies alone, longing for Martin—who at that moment is halfheartedly fighting his attraction to another woman—and sure that he will return to save her.

Throughout the novel Leora's devotion to Martin is the perfect realization of that single-minded devotion which Martin himself repeatedly fails to find in his scientific study. The completeness of her devotion is marked by the final sacrifice she makes. Yet, in spite of her willingness to efface herself in front of her husband's science, Leora emerges as a strong and independent idealist in her own right. Her enthusiastic, although uninformed, appreciation of Martin's work becomes the ideal of society's acceptance of the forms and forerunners of scientific progress.

Tralala. *Last Exit to Brooklyn.* Hubert Selby, Jr. 1963.

Tralala spends most of her time in a bewildering array of sexual and criminal activity. Still a young woman, Tralala began her career as a prostitute and petty criminal. Most of the time she robs the men she goes with after having sex with them or after they pass out from excessive drinking. Tralala's chief asset, as she herself sees it, are her breasts, which are prominent and—as she demonstrates when drunk—the biggest of any woman around her. She frequently flaunts this attribute and uses it as a means to procure male attention. However, after a stint with a drunken sailor, whom she robs, her association with her former comrades deteriorates when they realize she has lied about the amount of money she stole from the sailor. When he tearfully pleads for his identification back, the men beat him up, only to be joined by Tralala, who kicks him in the groin and then kicks his head until his eyes bleed. Scornful of the sailor's weakness and cast off as a liar, Tralala travels into Manhattan to make her own way.

Once in Manhattan, Tralala gravitates to Times Square, where she frequents bars commonly filled by servicemen. She encounters a series of men and abandons each one as soon as she finds another of a higher rank who is likely to have more money to spend on her or for her to steal. Eventually, and partly because she is too preoccupied to take care of herself, the young girl's appearance becomes increasingly seedy; she is ultimately thrown out of a flophouse as being too undesirable even for that low setting. Tralala returns to a bar where she has previously had some success, but this time she fails. While here and while she is being ignored, Tralala's anger mounts, and she wonders why the men around her can't appreciate her for her assets. She imagines that she would castrate them all if she only had a knife. Eventually, drunk and down on her luck, Tralala returns to Brooklyn and to the environment she had previously left. In the past she had been bilked out of a large share of the take from a robbery she had helped with there, and she remains angry about the episode; but she has nowhere else to go.

Here again she appears dirty and drunk, and swiftly and loudly begins to challenge the men in the bar to acknowledge her for her large breasts. While this angers the women, the men are at first amused, then piqued by her apparent aggression. In response they move Tralala outside to a vacant lot where they place her in an abandoned car and proceed to take turns raping her. Word spreads, and more and more men arrive; they send for beer and take turns with her, then get back in line for another turn. After a while Tralala, bleeding and unconscious, is moved out of the car, which the men now find offensive for its stench, but the rapes continue. Eventually the men are sated, and they leave; at their departure the teenage boys who have witnessed the attack further it with more abuse, including stubbing out cigarettes on her naked body. Finally even they grow bored and leave, abandoning Tralala altogether.

Trapp, Bill. *Beetlecreek.* William Demby. 1950.

Bill Trapp is an aging lonely white man who becomes friends with JOHNNY JOHNSON, a young black boy from Pittsburgh. Although neither is a native of Beetlecreek, West Virginia, they have been led here to "settle down." Prior to his arrival in Beetlecreek, Bill Trapp's life had been one of acute loneliness and estrangement from society punctuated only rarely by an interlude of friendship.

Following the death of their parents, Bill and his sister Hilda were adopted by Mrs. Haines. Although embarrassed by being adopted, Bill and Hilda find a measure of love and security in their new home. Following Mrs. Haines's death, the two live together for twenty years, working and saving money so that one day they will be the respectable people they know they are. Hilda works at a boardinghouse, where she eventually moves, and Bill works for Harry Simcoe's Continental Show, a traveling carnival complete with side shows. After Hilda's sudden death, Bill befriends a broken-down former trapeze artist who now works a dog act for Simcoe's show. This man, known as the Italian, is perennially drunk, and though he and Bill become friends, the relationship is terminated by the Italian's untimely death.

After the loss of his friend, Bill decides to leave the show, and he settles down in West Virginia on an old farm located between the black section of town, Beetlecreek, and the white section of town, Ridgeville. This action is followed by fifteen years of living in isolation. Bill neither seeks companionship nor is he sought out for it.

One day Bill finds a group of boys stealing apples from his property. He "catches" one of them, Johnny Johnson, and the two slowly become friends. Johnny's uncle, David Diggs, comes looking for the boy, and Bill and Diggs also develop a friendship. This latter relationship in particular arouses suspicion and scorn on both sides of town, but for a time Bill is awakened to the possibilities of friendship and community.

Buoyed by a new sense of belonging, Bill donates a wheelbarrow full of pumpkins to the black community's Fall Festival, and he achieves a measure of acceptance from the Beetlecreek community. This in turn encourages him to host a picnic for the town's children. Here Bill makes a near-fatal error, for he invites children of both races. While the picnic goes smoothly, its aftermath does not. During the party one of Bill's guests snoops through his house and tears a "dirty picture" out of an old encyclopedia. She brings the picture home, and with exaggeration and lies manages to create a furor in both parts of town over the fact that Bill Trapp is clearly a "sex fiend."

Before long the "Bill Trapp Committee on Decency" is formed to address this terrifying issue. Although both David Diggs and Johnny know that Bill is no sex fiend, for various and mostly selfish reasons they simply avoid him while he is tried and convicted by the town. The novel ends with Johnny setting fire to Bill's home in a misguided effort to become a member of a local gang. The fire trucks heading to the May Farm will not arrive in time to salvage the residence, nor will Bill be able to trust in others again.

Trask, Adam. *East of Eden.* John Steinbeck. 1952.

Adam Trask, wealthy and idealistic, is a veteran of post–Civil War anti–native American campaigns. The first son of Cyrus Trask, a Civil War veteran who lied about his actual combat service, Adam grows up feeling the taint of his mother's suicide. Mrs. Trask had killed herself when Adam was only weeks old. His father had quickly remarried; his new wife bore him a son named Charles, Adam's half-brother and rival.

As the boys approach their teens, they are torn apart by the obvious difference in their father's love. Adam, who Cyrus thinks needs improvement as a man, is goaded into military service. He is sworn in as a cavalryman while he is recuperating from a vicious beating he received from Charles, their father's apparent favorite.

Adam then spends several years fighting Native Americans on the western frontier. Although he deplores military service, he reenlists because he cannot face returning home to Connecticut where Charles maintains the family farm. After Adam's second term ends, he travels south, where he is twice arrested for vagrancy. With only three days left in his second sentence, Adam boldly escapes the chain gang and slowly makes his way north.

When he returns to Connecticut, he and Charles attempt to establish a joint household, but the brothers are incapable of sustaining an amicable relationship. This tense situation is further exacerbated when CATHERINE AMES (TRASK) appears on their doorstep after having been brutally beaten. They take the young woman in, against Charles's wishes, and as she heals, Adam falls in love with her. Even though Charles despises the woman, Adam marries her. But Catherine soon proves to be the bane of Adam's existence as well.

Against Charles's wishes, Adam takes his new wife and migrates to California where he buys a large, lush ranch and begins building a new home. Cathy is adamantly opposed, however, and despite her pregnancy, she plans to leave Adam as soon as it is feasible. She delivers twins, ARON (TRASK) and CALEB (TRASK), and within weeks leaves Adam and her children. When Adam resists her departure, she ruthlessly shoots him in the shoulder.

For the next eleven years Adam remains indifferent to his surroundings. As his ranch goes undeveloped and the half-built house rots, his sons are attended by LEE, their surrogate parent and friend. Eventually, Adam decides to take charge of his life and relocates the family to Salinas, where he buys an ice factory and plans to ship out-of-season fruits and vegetables back East. When this venture fails due to a series of misfortunes, his sons are as crushed as he is.

Caleb takes it upon himself to recoup his father's losses so that Aron can go to college. When Adam learns that Caleb has made his money through war profiteering, he rejects the money his son offers. Caleb angrily reveals to Aron that their mother is the most notorious madam in the city. Although Adam has long known of his wife's perfidy, the news virtually destroys Aron.

Aron enlists in the army and is killed in World War I. This news leads to the most severe in a series of strokes Adam has suffered. As the novel ends, with an apparent reconciliation between Caleb and Adam, it appears that the latter's death is imminent.

Trask, Aron. *East of Eden.* John Steinbeck. 1952.

Aron Trask is the overly sensitive and religious son of ADAM TRASK. At birth Aron and his twin brother CALEB (TRASK) become the unwitting victims of their parents' failed marriage. Their mother, the heartless CATHERINE AMES (TRASK), shoots her husband shortly after their sons' birth. After her departure, Aron and Caleb are left primarily in the care of LEE, a Chinese American who has been hired by Adam to serve as cook and housekeeper.

As the Trask boys mature, Aron finds comfort and security in the company of Caleb but is never quite able to measure up to Caleb's abilities as a hunter. Unlike his brother, Aron is gentle, incapable of intentionally harming anyone or anything. A telling instance occurs when he and Caleb first encounter Abra Bacon, a young girl whose parents have stopped at the Trask ranch seeking shelter from a storm. Aron, although quite young, immediately falls in love with Abra and offers her a rabbit he and his brother have just killed. He also includes a proposal of marriage in the box with the rabbit. Caleb convinces the young Abra that Aron is actually evil and plans to harm her. Abra discards the box; as she and her parents drive away, Aron is devastated.

While still a teenager, Aron receives his spiritual calling. After the Trask family has moved to Salinas, he begins an assiduous study of religion. Although he becomes involved with Abra, the relationship takes place on an idealistic plane as he grapples with the notion of lifetime celibacy. Abra's parents, aware of the notoriety of Aron's mother's as the town madam, heartily disapprove of the liaison. Nonetheless, the couple stays together during their high school years, even though Aron's studies lead him further away from the everyday world.

A turning point in the family occurs when the boys present special gifts to their father, and their world is subsequently shattered. Caleb's gift, $15,000, is rejected by Adam because the money was raised through trading beans in a market artificially inflated by World War I. Aron's gift—his early graduation and intention to pursue higher education—pleases Adam a great deal.

In a jealous fury, Caleb takes Aron to the downtown area of Salinas and brings him to their mother's bordello. Here Aron recoils in shock at his own connection with such sinfulness, and he immediately flees the city. His illusion destroyed, he enlists in the army and is sent overseas where he is killed in action during World War I.

Trask, Caleb. *East of Eden.* John Steinbeck. 1952.

The tough and volatile Caleb Trask and his twin brother ARON (TRASK) are abandoned by their mother CATHERINE AMES (TRASK) shortly after their birth. Because their father ADAM (TRASK) is incapable of overcoming his grief at Catherine's departure, Caleb and Aron are raised principally by LEE, a Chinese American who serves the family as cook, homemaker, confidant, and friend. Caleb prospers under Lee's guidance, but he possesses a mean streak that leads him, from an early age, to torment others—especially his brother.

When a girl named Abra Bacon arrives at the Trask ranch in Salinas with her parents, the young Caleb recognizes Aron's attraction to her. Caleb, who is jealous, manages to disrupt the budding romance by lying to Abra about Aron's evil character. While Caleb is usually ashamed after he mistreats Aron, he cannot get rid of this need to hurt his more gentle and favored brother. When the family moves to the city of Salinas, the difference in the boys' natures becomes even more apparent. Caleb tells his father that he wants nothing more than to return to the ranch someday so that he can farm it himself.

After Adam loses a great deal of money, Caleb resolves to help his father. He puts his knowledge of farming to use and with a local businessman develops a marketing scheme whereby they will profit on the sale of beans. Caleb buys beans at three cents over market value, then sells them in an artificially inflated market for much more. He earns $15,000, with which he intends to supplement his father's wealth, prove his capability to manage the ranch, and pay for Aron's college education. Adam scorns Caleb's gift, however, and denounces his efforts as evil.

Caleb has long known of his mother's past treatment of their father and of her flourishing career as a madam. Lee has always discouraged Caleb from believing that, like his mother, he is incapable of loving others. In his need to strike back against the pain he feels at being rejected by his father, Caleb brings Aron to their mother's whorehouse. The revelation about their mother's career prompts Aron to abandon Abra Bacon and enlist in the army.

Although he feels guilty about what he did to his brother, Caleb nevertheless develops a relationship with Abra, after they confesses to each other that they had difficulties coping with Aron's religiosity. They realize that they share a tainted heritage since Abra's father was exposed as an embezzler. Adam Trask, who has slowly declined in health, suffers a severe stroke when he learns of Aron's death in combat during World War I. He and Caleb learn that Cathy Trask has killed herself, and prompted by the ever-faithful Lee, Adam, near death, forgives Caleb for his role in Aron's tragic flight from his family.

Trask, Catherine Ames. *East of Eden.* John Steinbeck. 1952.

Catherine Ames is the only child of the Ames family, and while her mother dotes on her and is puzzled by her coolness, Cathy's father suspects his daughter of being essentially evil. It is not until after her death that Catherine's one ironic gesture toward goodness is revealed—a gesture that comes only when it is too late to be received.

When Cathy announces her intentions of completing high school and entering college, her parents are elated. Halfway through high school, however, she decides to relinquish her education and run away. Her father catches up with her, brings her home, and beats her for the first and only time. Cathy, sensing a weakness in her father that makes him suffer when he hurts her, exaggerates the pain she feels, thereby diminishing the force of his blows.

Her ability to manipulate her father's behavior gives Cathy a new lease on life, and she begins to plot carefully her escape from the family. Eventually she concocts a plan to burn the house, then make it appear that she has been abducted. She executes this plan, and her parents burn to death; Cathy makes her escape and arrives in another town where she assumes a new identity. Here she soon develops an emotional and sexual stranglehold over the cold and practical whoremaster Mr. Edwards. When he finally realizes the nature of her power over him, he brings her with him on a business trip, intending to kill her by forcing her to continuously prostitute herself. His rage gets the better of him, however, and he beats her nearly to death and abandons her on a deserted roadside.

When Cathy regains consciousness, she realizes she must seek help and painfully crawls to the nearest house. Here she encounters ADAM TRASK and his younger brother Charles. The two men assist her and call for a doctor. Adam falls in love with her almost immediately and asks her to marry him; although she intuitively senses a weakness in him and despises him, she marries him as soon as she is well enough. Eventually, against her wishes, Cathy and Adam leave Connecticut and move to California, where Cathy attempts to abort herself once she realizes she is pregnant. Adam fretfully cares for her and plans to build a fine house for their new family, even though Cathy tells him she has no desire either to live in California or to be with him.

After the birth of their twin sons, ARON (TRASK) and CALEB (TRASK), Cathy leaves Adam, whom she shoots in the shoulder when he tries to prevent her departure. She travels as far as Salinas, where she gets a job as a prostitute in a fairly respectable house run by a woman named Faye. Cathy, now calling herself Kate, dyes her hair and begins to befriend the older and childless Faye. Ultimately, Faye comes to regard Kate as her daughter; in due course she stipulates in her will that Kate should inherit the house and business. This prompts Cathy to plan a year-long poisoning that results in Faye's death.

Once Cathy owns the establishment, she reorients its business so that she can cater to the more exotic sexual tastes of sadists and masochists, thus enabling her to charge higher fees and reap greater profits. She successfully thwarts the efforts of an employee to blackmail her and gain control of the establishment.

When Adam reappears in Cathy's life, she is at first seductive, then abusive toward him. She still shows no interest in her sons and is astonished when they appear at her doorstep. Caleb has vengefully brought the naive Aron to see her in her sordid surroundings, and Cathy kills herself soon after their visit.

Cathy's will reveals that she left her estate to her son Aron, having learned from both Adam and Caleb that he was a gentle and religious young man. What she did not know at the time of her death was that Aron was also dead. In shock after learning about his mother's sinful life-style, he had gone to fight in World War I and died very soon thereafter.

The Traveler. *The Asiatics.* Frederic Prokosch. 1941.

The unnamed traveler, journeying across a landscape he calls Asia, is a Spenglerian poet engaged in a youthful quest for obscure truth. Like Odysseus, the traveler does not undergo any dramatic change or come to any transforming insights along his journey. He is without a homeland and looks ahead, never behind, never reflecting on past hardships or triumphs.

Though young, the traveler is neither impetuous nor bold. He has the knockabout bravery to keep going on his travels even after being imprisoned and nearly shot by a firing squad, and crashing in an aeroplane and being captured by bedouins who have a passion for torture. He remains undaunted only because, as he puts it, he possesses a youth's conviction of personal immortality and does not fear death.

As a result, although the traveler continually notes the ever-present tinge of death and sees it as a central component of the "Soul of the Asiatic," his own youth and inexperience prevent him from ever grappling with it in any but a falsely poetic sense. He is aware of this; he is unsure whether he has enough strength to peer into the "true nature of things."

Inconsequential details assume a strange significance for the traveler. A passing camel requires an attentive gaze; a cart stacked with dead bodies continually crosses his path. But the traveler remains unable to bring reason and meaning to these symbols and sights. An obscure metaphysics beckons to him—a mysterious, impenetrable metaphysics of the "Orient," which the traveler tries to unravel but cannot. This opaqueness is mutual: Many of the Asians he meets diagnose his spirit in ways that seem to be as obscure and indulgent as the traveler's own philosophizing.

The traveler gradually learns to refrain from judgment and to accept that life is cruel and unfeeling, a challenge for the honest and unsentimental. He comes to regard his own selfishness as a fact of life and ceases to confront or question it.

The companions to whom the traveler is drawn prove the validity of this philosophy; they are traitorous, attractive, corrupt, and sensual people who demand little of him. His friends, all males, steal from him or attempt to turn him in to the police. The women he meets are moved solely by their sexual impulses. They often betray husbands and companions for a quick experience with the exotic foreigner, although their taste for the exotic soon pales as they realize how selfish and incapable the foreigner is of loving them. There is, in fact, a remarkable absence of love altogether; in the traveler and in those he meets, the predominant emotion is one of distaste combined with a driving but distanced curiosity.

The traveler's world remains fatally divided because of the changes being wrought in the lands through which he drifts. Apathy has infected everything. When set against the tireless wandering spirit that propels him, this listlessness bespeaks the despoliation of Asia by the colonial Westerners. The book leaves the traveler on the outskirts of Hanoi; it remains unclear at the end whether he will overcome the surrounding malice and find a way of life that offers him happiness.

Trent, Anne Elizabeth "Daughter." *U.S.A. (Nineteen Nineteen).* John Dos Passos. 1932.

Anne Elizabeth Trent, or "Daughter," as she is known to her family, is an idealistic, honest, naive American who is destroyed by unscrupulous, ambitious people.

A tomboyish misfit whose father is a prominent Dallas lawyer, Daughter grows up riding horses and flirting with a young lawyer named Joe Washburn. One night she dives into a creek from the edge of a cliff, and Joe has to save her. As she convalesces, he reads Dickens to her, and she falls in love with him.

Her father sends her to boarding school in Pennsylvania, but after she runs away, he agrees to let her go to Columbia University. In New York she meets Edwin Vinal, a sociology student with ardent political commitments. He gets her involved in social work, and they make a loose agreement to marry in a few years.

Daughter remains torn between her socially committed life in New York and the security of her home in Texas. After seeing Joe again, she returns to New York and dumps Edwin for a waggish activist named Webb Cruthers. Webb takes her along to labor demonstrations where she meets a number of vibrant communists. At a mill strike in New Jersey, Daughter slugs a policeman and gets arrested.

Called home by her shocked family, she studies journalism until the war begins and then does Red Cross work in San Antonio. Deranged after her brother's death, she continues nevertheless with her humanitarian efforts and at the war's end goes to Europe to do relief work.

On her way to Rome, Daughter meets RICHARD ELLSWORTH SAVAGE. She thinks of him as a poet and is soon charmed into falling in love with him. She considers the two of them engaged once they are sexually involved but is worried when she discovers herself pregnant after he has returned to Paris—especially since he proves a sluggish correspondent. When he returns to Rome and urges her to have an abortion because he cannot support a child until he has "some definite career," she promises to try to end the pregnancy through reckless horseback riding.

The horseback riding fails her, and when she next sees Dick and finds him still reluctant to marry, she gives up on him. She then contemplates marrying the labor leader G. H. Barrow, but she can see that the vaguest hint of her condition makes him waver. One night she runs away from him and meets up with some buoyant French airmen. Dragging one of them, Pierre, away from the party, she pleads with him to take her up in his plane and "loop the loop." Pierre is quite drunk, but Daughter insists. Riding high above Paris, she hears a ripping sound, and her last vision is of one of the wings gliding by itself as the plane drops from the sky.

Trimpie, Nathaniel. "Caviar." T. Coraghessan Boyle. 1985.

Nathaniel Trimpie, a young commercial fisherman on the Hudson River, has a wife who desperately wants a baby. At first Nat resists the idea. He tells his wife Marie that they can't afford it. She knows, however, that the insurance payment from her mother's car accident would largely cover expenses, and to prove her determination, she buries her diaphragm in the backyard. After this, they attempt to conceive in earnest, often making love several times a day. When several months pass without success,

Marie brings Nat to a church called the Coptic Brotherhood of Ethiop, where Sister Eleazar, an African-American faith healer, paints an X on Marie's abdomen and tells Nat to use mustard as an aphrodisiac. The mustard proves ineffective, but it does not deter Marie from trying other quack remedies: One day Nat comes home from the docks to find her dancing nude around a rooster in the basement.

Nat sees an article in a science magazine about testtube babies, and soon the couple is at a fertility clinic having full examinations by Dr. Ziss, a flashy young doctor with a gunmetal gray Mercedes. He tells them that Marie suffers from Stein-Leventhal syndrome, an untreatable condition of the ovaries that makes it impossible for her to get pregnant. Indignant because almost everyone thus far has blamed him for their failure, Nat nevertheless feels sorry for Marie and recognizes at last his own overwhelming desire to have a child. When Dr. Ziss suggests the artificial insemination of a surrogate mother, they quickly agree, despite the fee of over $10,000. Dr. Ziss mentions that he has already contacted someone on their behalf.

A few days later the doctor arrives at the Trimpie household with Wendy, a first-year medical student in need of tuition money. At first Nat is disappointed by the skinny, orange-haired woman who has been sent to get to know them before the procedure. Despite the clinical nature of the eventual insemination, he nonetheless begins to feel a growing erotic and spiritual attachment. Strange examples of their bonding include Nat's nausea during Wendy's morning sickness, and the foods they both crave. One day, while Marie is at work, they finally sleep together.

When Wendy begins to show, she moves to a small apartment on the other side of town, and Marie begins to pad her body to make it look as if she is pregnant. Nat, deeply in love at this point, occasionally manages to meet with Wendy, but she seems to be growing increasingly distant from him. Sometimes on random drives through Wendy's neighborhood Nat sees Dr. Ziss's Mercedes. He finds this strange but not unjustified; after all, Dr. Ziss is the physician assigned to their case.

The birth of Nathaniel, Jr., thrills Marie, but Nat sees Wendy's appearance in every characteristic of the baby, and it infuriates him. A week after the birth, he drives over to Wendy's, only to find the Mercedes in front of the apartment again. He peers into the window and finally realizes that Wendy and Dr. Ziss have been carrying on an affair. Nat goes inside and confronts Wendy, who explains that a lasting relationship would be impossible between the two because they come from such different social backgrounds. This drives Nat into a rage, and he attacks Dr. Ziss in the backyard, pummeling him until the police drag him away. Since rumor travels fast in a small town, everyone soon knows about the Trimpies' surrogate mother and Nat's relations with her.

Marie pays for Nat's bail but keeps him locked out of the house. Having nowhere else to go, Nat takes his boat onto the river and goes fishing. He broods about Marie and Wendy until a giant sturgeon gets trapped in his net. The story closes with him cleaning the fish, watching as the countless eggs fall through his hands like a jackpot.

Trippe, Bobby. *Deliverance.* James Dickey. 1970.

Bobby Trippe is one of four men who take a nightmarish canoeing trip through a region in rural Georgia that will soon be flooded by a dam. A salesman by trade, Bobby is known to be affable and slightly cynical; he considers the excursion a crazy idea but agrees to go on the condition that he may bring liquor along. His companions are sportsman and survivalist LEWIS MEDLOCK, mild-mannered DREW BALLINGER, and ED GENTRY, who narrates the novel.

On the first day down the river Bobby demonstrates his complete incompetence in outdoor activities. On the second day he is ill-tempered, and it is clear that he already regrets his decision to take the trip. Later in the day Bobby and Ed pull over to the shore to rest; the second canoe has lagged far behind. Two vicious men appear unexpectedly out of the woods. Ed is lashed to a tree, then one man sodomizes Bobby while the other holds a gun to his head. They approach Ed and are about to assault him when Lewis, a champion archer, shoots one of the attackers in the back with an arrow. The other retreats into the forest.

Bobby, humiliated and in pain, closes himself off from his companions thereafter. He says nothing as they hotly debate whether to conceal the killing in order to avoid having homicide charges brought against them. When asked directly for his opinion, he responds by furiously kicking the corpse in the face. The four bury the body deep in the woods, reasoning that it will not be found before the area is flooded by the dam.

They continue downriver until they reach rough water, and then disaster strikes. Drew is shot in the head by a sniper on the cliffs, and both canoes capsize. Bobby is swept down a violent, rock-strewn stretch of the river. The three survivors manage to reach calm water and the shore just as darkness sets in, but Lewis has a severely broken leg. Ed determines that the only way to survive is to climb the cliffs and kill the man, who will probably try to ambush them come daylight. Bobby, pathetically fearful and helpless, has difficulty grasping the nature of their situation and half-believes that Ed plans to desert him.

Ed impatiently instructs Bobby to start down the river again as soon as there is just enough light to see the water; then he leaves him to tend the injured Lewis. Bobby does not start on time, and only because Ed guesses where their attacker is hiding and kills him is Bobby saved from being an easy target. They then tie heavy stones to the corpse and sink him in the river. They do the same thing later with Drew's body, planning to say that he was drowned when the canoe capsized.

Bobby is little help on the rest of the journey, but despite his fear and anger he manages to listen to Ed's instructions on what lies to tell the police. In fact, much to Ed's surprise, Bobby performs well when questioned by the authorities, who, although suspicious, eventually allow the survivors to leave town. Bobby does not keep in touch with his fellow adventurers after that. He quits his job, tries running a Chicken-in-a-Basket drive-in restaurant for a time, then finally moves to Hawaii.

Trout, Hanna. *Paris Trout.* Pete Dexter. 1988.

The forty-five-year-old wife of a child killer, Hanna Trout has tolerated her husband's eccentric, abusive behavior over the years because she cannot imagine leaving him. She had forfeited a career with the Georgia State Department of Schools to marry prominent businessman PARIS TROUT simply because he was present at a moment when she felt she needed to give "shape" to her life. Since then, he has isolated her from virtually all outside contact and made her a prisoner of his whims. However, when Paris is charged with the cold-blooded murder of fourteen-year-old Rosie Sayers, Hanna realizes that her life will never be the same.

Upon learning of Paris's crime, Hanna discovers that Rosie Sayers is the young girl she had rushed to the town clinic with a fox bite on her leg some time ago. Although she is immediately sickened, she is paralyzed with indecision as to what kind of action she should take, if any, against her husband. Paris himself forces the issue when he sexually assaults Hanna. This brutal act imbues Hanna with the strength to defy him. Playing on Paris's paranoia, she manages to convince him that she has been slowly poisoning him, and he flees their home.

Harry Seagraves, Paris's defense attorney, sees the advantage of persuading Hanna to support her husband by appearing at his upcoming murder trial. But she refuses to waver in this instance and tries to convince Seagraves to drop Paris as a client by appealing to his sense of moral decency. Although Seagraves refuses to drop Paris, Hanna enters into an affair with him. Meanwhile, Paris is freed by the court to pursue appeals against his conviction. Hanna, who steadfastly refused to show her husband any support whatsoever during his trial, is horrified by the town's equivocal behavior. She takes steps to secure a divorce and regain the $4,000 Paris had borrowed from her by hiring a young lawyer named Carl Bonner to press her case.

Paris kills his mother, Harry Seagraves, Carl Bonner, and, finally, himself in a shooting at the Cotton Point Courthouse. Sensing that she has become an embarrassment to the hypocritical town of Cotton Point, Hanna sells her house and moves to Savannah where she embarks on a career as a teacher.

Trout, Kilgore. *Breakfast of Champions.* Kurt Vonnegut, Jr. 1973.

For years Kilgore Trout, a science fiction writer, has sent his stories for publication to World Classics Library without self-addressed stamped envelopes or a return address. Occasionally he has discovered these stories published as filler in pornographic magazines, but he has received neither credit nor remuneration for them. A self-proclaimed failed artist, Kilgore Trout lives alone with his parakeet Bill in Cohoes, New York, where he installs aluminum screen doors and persists in his writing. Born in Bermuda, Trout spent a depressing childhood measuring the wing spans of now extinct Bermuda erns. His pessimism shriveled all three of his loving, beautiful wives and drove away his only son Leo.

Trout's first fan letter changes his life forever. Eliot Rosewater, a millionaire from Midland City, believes Trout is the greatest writer in the English language and arranges for him to speak at the Midland City Festival of the Arts. This invitation starts Kilgore Trout on the journey that culminates in his disastrous encounter with the insane DWAYNE HOOVER and the Creator of his Universe, the "author."

With $500 pinned to his underwear, Trout leaves for New York City so that he might arrive in Midland City as the very image of an unhappy failure. He spends the night in a porn theater on Forty-second Street, is mugged and beaten upon leaving, and wakes up under the Queensboro Bridge. He tells the police that, for all he knows, the muggers could have come from Pluto, and the next morning all of New York worries about the Pluto Gang. Next, he hitches a ride on an eighteen-wheeler hauling Spanish olives. Trout and the driver converse through their drive on topics such as Vietnam, friendship, sex, aluminum siding, strip mining, and advertising. Trout reflects on American culture and recalls some characters and plots from his science fiction stories.

When they are stopped in a traffic jam just outside Midland City, Trout takes off on foot for the Holiday Inn, the center of the Arts Festival. As he wades across the two-inch-deep Sugar Creek, his feet become encased in plastic waste from a local factory. When he reaches the festival, he is recognized by the hotel desk clerk and disconcerted by his own fame. He is also wary because he senses the presence of the author who plans to reveal himself to Trout and set him free. His feet sweating from the plastic coating, he enters the cocktail lounge where Dwayne Hoover, an insane Pontiac dealer, reads his short story and bites off Trout's fingertip.

Trout is taken to the hospital to have his injured finger inspected. After wandering back to the hotel, he is waylaid by the author, who explains that Trout is a character in a novel who is about to be set free. Transporting his character through time and space, the author proves his power to the mystified science fiction writer. When he finally sets Trout free, the author dematerializes, and Trout is heard crying "make me young." After the festival, Trout becomes world famous, wins the Nobel Prize in medicine for his work with the mentally ill, and ultimately publishes 209 novels.

Trout, Paris. *Paris Trout.* Pete Dexter. 1988.

Paris Trout is a wealthy and prominent citizen of Cotton Point, Georgia. He is also a blatant racist whose self-righteous rage and festering paranoia lead to brutal acts of violence that devastate his complacent community.

Trout, the proprietor of a small country store out of which he operates his own bank, lends a young black man, Henry Ray Boxer, enough money to purchase a car. The contract that Boxer signs includes a $227 insurance policy which the young man attempts to make good on after becoming involved in a highway accident. Trout reneges on his end of the bargain, however, and refuses to finance any repairs. In retaliation, Boxer returns the car, arguing that he is no longer obliged to make any payments on it. A livid Trout then appears at Boxer's home with a hired henchman, Buster Devonne, and attempts to collect his money. Rage quickly overcomes Trout. He pulls out a gun and shoots Boxer's mother, Mary McNutt, several times, and slaughters a fourteen-year-old named Rosie Sayers in cold blood.

Released on his own recognizance until the outcome of the trial, Trout is able to pursue his defense, including a strategy of cooperation with attorney Harry Seagraves, who has somewhat reluctantly agreed to take the case. Trout is unable to comprehend the depths of his depravity and feels that he has unjustly become a target himself. He covers his floor with panes of glass and lays a lead sheet beneath his bed in case someone shoots at him from below. His wife HANNA (TROUT) becomes thoroughly alienated from him because of the murder, and as her husband's paranoia grows, she becomes the victim of his harassments and a sexual assault. Hanna finally succeeds in chasing him out of the house by implying that she has been gradually poisoning him.

Trout complicates Seagraves's defense by refusing to adopt a contrite posture. Although he and Buster Devonne insist that they acted in self-defense when they shot Mary and Rosie, Trout is eventually found guilty of second-degree murder. Even so, his standing in the community leads to a decision that allows him to roam Cotton Point free pending his appeals to higher courts. His sense of persecution deepens when he learns that the IRS is investigating allegations that he has never filed an income tax return. Unable to convince Seagraves to press his case further, Trout undertakes the prodigious task of putting together his own defense. He works furiously in an effort to forge a convincing appeals case but is finally out of options when the U.S. Supreme Court upholds his conviction.

Soon after, Trout is arrested and transported to the state prison farm. When he reaches the penitentiary, his new attorney, the corrupt Rodney Dalmar, hires the equally corrupt Judge Raymond Mims to have him released on the basis of a writ of habeas corpus, citing perjured testimony at the trial. Meanwhile, Cotton Point has been preparing for its sesquicentennial gala, and the organizing committee has decreed that for the duration of the celebration all men must sport a beard. The punishment for those who break this law is a small fine or a short period in the specially built stocks.

Trout is apprehended and ordered to the stocks for remaining clean-shaven. But as he is approaching the stockade, he stops and refuses to be imprisoned. He then breaks the stocks in the process of fighting off his captors. Before Trout is able to do serious injury to anyone, Seagraves intervenes, and he is let go. This humiliating spectacle pushes him over the edge. Trout goes home, loads a rifle and a handgun with ammunition, and retrieves his mother from the nursing home before heading for the town courthouse, where he shoots his mother, a young lawyer, Seagraves, and himself.

Tull, Ezra. *Dinner at the Homesick Restaurant*. Anne Tyler. 1982.

Ezra Tull is the owner of the Homesick Restaurant, the homespun family restaurant that becomes his life's work. The third child and favorite son of PEARL TULL, the novel's central character, Ezra spends his life trying to administer to the needs of others. Over the years his restaurant is the sight of many tumultuous, sometimes unfinished meals for the Tull family, who struggle to piece together what has been lost in their lives and to maintain some measure of love among them.

Ezra is a sleepy, blond youth who likes to play odd sentimental tunes on his penny whistle. He is popular with everyone except his brother Cody, who is fiercely jealous of his good nature. When Ezra is nine years old, his father, Beck, deserts the family; Ezra, Cody, and their sister Jenny are reared from then on by their mother. Although hurt by the loss, Ezra finds ways to fill the gap in his life. Specifically, he becomes the protégé of Mrs. Scarlatti, owner of the only "nice" restaurant in his neighborhood.

As a young man Ezra is drafted into the army to serve in Korea. At first everyone is surprised by the idea of the quiet, tame youth being a soldier. He turns out to be a conscientious hardworking serviceman but is honorably discharged without ever seeing Korea for sleepwalking around the base.

Soon after Ezra returns home, Mrs. Scarlatti becomes bedridden with cancer. Suddenly inspired, Ezra rips down the restaurant curtains, walls, and partitions, turning the once formal establishment into a home-style restaurant with an open kitchen. His aim is to feed people what they need, not simply what they order; he fantasizes about providing his patrons with the right food to satisfy the deeper needs of body and soul.

Ezra manages unwittingly to attract the affections of every girl his brother Cody brings around. When Ezra falls in love with Ruth, a country girl who cooks her native dishes in his restaurant, Cody begins an unrelenting campaign to win Ruth away from him. At first, with his conventional sophistication and good looks, Cody is so foreign to Ruth that she believes he is making fun of her. Later, in an effort to be what she thinks Cody wants in a woman, Ruth—who is most comfortable in boots and cut-off dungarees—remakes herself in stiff ladylike dresses and high-heeled shoes. Ezra, trusting and unobservant, does not notice his brother's ploys. Although Ezra and Ruth are a perfect match, Cody ultimately wins. Witnessing their ensuing courtship, the devastated Ezra remains passive and does nothing to regain Ruth's affections.

After the marriage, Cody works hard to ensure that Ezra and Ruth never spend more than a few unsupervised minutes together. Ruth and Cody have a son, Luke, who—much to Cody's chagrin—strongly resembles Ezra, with his long locks of straw-colored hair and passive, easygoing nature. As a teenager Luke runs away to stay with his uncle Ezra. Ezra is deeply moved by the visit, which is cut short when Cody discovers where the boy has gone.

Because he never marries, Ezra remains Pearl's lifelong companion and lives with her in the Baltimore row house where he grew up. His life is spent running the Homesick Restaurant with the help of his best friend Josiah and an assortment of fringe characters, who pass on exotic, healing recipes as they come and go. He never tires of organizing special dinners to bring his family together. At his dying mother's request, Ezra invites Beck to her funeral; afterward, the final meal at the Homesick Restaurant includes Ezra's entire remaining family, including Beck, the father they haven't seen in forty years.

Tull, Pearl. *Dinner at the Homesick Restaurant*. Anne Tyler. 1982.

Pearl Tull is the matriarch of the beleaguered Tull family through whose memory the narrative unfolds. In the 1920s, thirty-year-old Pearl marries the handsome Beck Tull, a traveling salesman. Pearl and Beck have three children: Cody, Jenny, and EZRA (TULL). When the children are still young, Beck decides he no longer wants to be married; he leaves Pearl and his family, and does not return. Stubborn, proud, but also deeply humiliated, Pearl never explains to the three what has happened. She pretends that Beck is on an extended business trip and rears the children alone. Pearl's lifelong career as a mother is imperfect, to say the least, and when she dies, she leaves her offspring still struggling to find happiness amid the scattered wreckage of their childhood memories.

At the opening of the story, Pearl is in her eighties and dying of pneumonia. Wishing her children had an extra mother to take care of them now that she is going, she begins to look back on moments from her life. She remembers the reason she first wanted to have three children: Years ago, when Cody, the oldest, fell ill with a serious case of croup, she decided to have more babies as a kind of insurance against fate, in case Cody should die. After Jenny and Ezra were born, Pearl realized that her idea had been fundamentally flawed. Instead of insurance, she now had a triple threat, and the loss of any one child would be more than she could bear.

Pearl remembers a time, before Beck left them, when he returned home from a trip with one of his characteristically impractical presents: an archery set. With the aim of teaching Cody how to shoot, he drove the family on an outing to the country. There, Cody accidentally shot his mother in the chest. After Beck went off on another trip, Pearl's wound became dangerously infected, and she had to be hospitalized. Her anger at his foolish gifts, her nagging disapproval, and the overwhelming futility of trying to please his wife and the children—all these, Pearl reflects, combined to drive Beck away.

Life without Beck was full of tension. Terrified by the unending responsibility of having three children to feed and clothe, Pearl was forced to take a job at the local supermarket but was profoundly ashamed of her position and wanted it kept quiet. She counted on her children to help with the household chores; their lack of discipline and respect for household order incensed her, and she often blew up at them, tossing their belongings in heaps around their rooms and screaming at them over dinner. Cody later remembers Pearl angrily wishing they would all die. She was forever dissatisfied with her children. She wanted Cody to be more responsible; Jenny to pay more attention to her looks and dress; and Ezra to change in virtually every way.

Her youngest and favorite child, Ezra remains with Pearl in their bleak Baltimore row house throughout her life. He is her companion, and at the end of her life, when she is blind but refuses to admit it, Ezra becomes her eyes. Using the utmost tact to spare Pearl any embarrassment, he devises ingenious ways to let her know the simple things she can no longer see, such as the fine, inaudible rain that falls as they leave their house and the play-by-play action of a baseball game they attend.

Ezra also becomes the keeper of Pearl's touchstones. She periodically asks him to help her sort through her drawers full of mementos and diaries from her girlhood. One day Ezra helps her find what she has been looking for: He reads her a passage from an early diary in which she describes a moment of pure happiness experienced while digging in her garden on a bright clear day. With this bit of writing found and the tiny moment remembered, Pearl is satisfied; she knows that she once knew happiness, if only for a moment.

Before she dies, Pearl asks Ezra to invite Beck to her funeral. The novel ends as Cody and Jenny, their spouses and children, Ezra, and the long-lost Beck eat a typically tumultuous family dinner, for the first time in forty years, at Ezra's Homesick Restaurant.

Turner, Nat. *The Confessions of Nat Turner.* William Styron. 1966.

This novel is a fictionalized recreation of the life of Nat Turner, who led the only effective, sustained revolt in the annals of American slavery. Born in 1800 in southwestern Virginia, Nat is the son of a runaway father whom he never knew and the property of Benjamin Turner. Because his mother is Turner's cook, Nat is raised as a house servant and thus escapes the grinding labor required of the field slaves, over whom he comes to feel superior. His sense of superiority is fostered by Samuel Turner, who inherits Nat upon the death of his brother and who appreciates Nat's intelligence and desire to learn. The Turner women tutor Nat in reading, writing, arithmetic, and Episcopal catechism, and later, after apprenticing Nat to a carpenter, Samuel reveals to Nat that when he has thoroughly learned his trade, he will be granted his freedom.

Nat's sense that he is destined for a special fate is confirmed by a mystical vision he experiences in his mid-teens, which informs him of his vocation to be a preacher. Although the seeds of bitterness have been sown in Nat by his awareness of his enslaved condition and witnessing his mother's rape by a white overseer, he retains his goodwill and optimism.

When the Virginia tobacco crops fail, however, Samuel sells his property and moves farther south, leaving Nat in the care of Reverend Eppes, who has promised to carry out Nat's freedom plan but who instead sells Nat to Thomas More, a cruel man who whips, overworks, and underfeeds him. During the near decade of Nat's ownership by More, he develops a hatred of all whites, and his frustrated sexual desires become channeled into fantasies about brutally raping white women and mystical visions that direct him toward the mission of murdering whites.

As of 1829, Nat has formed definite plans for conducting his rebellion and has enlisted confederates from among his congregation. In the same year, More dies and his sister marries Joseph Travis, but the kindness of his new masters does not deter Nat from his bloody intentions.

On Independence Day, 1831, the rebellion begins. Nat finds himself incapable of murder, however, and as a result he begins to lose control of his confederates. Just when his followers' distrust of him reaches a crisis, Nat is confronted with the opportunity to murder Margaret Whitehead, a pretty sweet-natured young girl who has been especially kind to Nat and for whom Nat has developed a desire compounded of both love and hatred.

Nat kills Margaret, and after the uprising has been quelled and Nat is captured and imprisoned, he is tortured by his inability to communicate with God. When he realizes that he had loved Margaret and deeply repents her death, he feels she has shown him the way back to God and he can go in peace to his execution.

Tyndale, Mollie. *Capital City.* Mari Sandoz. 1939.

Possessing stunning beauty and a natural charm, Mollie Tyndale gains instant popularity among her classmates when her family moves to Franklin, capital city of the fictitious state of Kanewa. While Mollie is basically happy and contented, her father Samuel longs for his family to be accepted into the elite social circle of Franklin's ruling class. Earning a good income from the filling station he operates within Franklin, the Tyndales lack only the family legacy that third-and fourth-generation Franklin families can claim.

In high school Mollie begins to see a young man named Burt Parr whose honesty and sensitivity make him her choice over a number of other young men who court her. Despite Mollie's happiness, her parents look upon her new boyfriend, the son of poor German farmers, with extreme disapproval. They tell her she will never be accepted among the Franklin elite social circles with a boyfriend of such lowly birth.

Mollie learns that spring that she has been selected, along with a number of other favored young Franklin ladies, to represent the capital city as a "duchess" in the town's annual Labor Day pageant. The pageant, a kind of elaborate beauty contest from which one lucky young woman will be chosen as "empress," represents a pinnacle in the small community of Franklin's ruling class. While Mollie initially views the pageant with indifference, her parents are ecstatic and spare no expense in preparing for the Labor Day event.

As Labor Day approaches, Mollie finds herself increasingly caught up in the town's and her parents' anticipation of the annual pageant. While she continues to assure Burt, who is convinced that the social and economic gap between their two families will destroy their relationship, that she is participating only to please her family, Mollie finds herself spending more time with the society families that she had previously ignored.

When the day of the pageant arrives, Mollie, to the delight of her family, finds she is easily the most attractive of all the "duchesses." But the "empress" title goes, as all but the Tyndales had expected, to a fourth-generation Franklin girl. Furious at her daughter's failure, Samuel Tyndale blames Burt Parr and forbids her to see him in the future.

Although the reluctant Mollie has no choice but to obey her father, her disappointment is soon assuaged by an increased social status during her senior year. She begins to date a third-generation Franklin man while her parents are planning for an elaborate Presentation Party for her at graduation, after which she will travel to Europe. By the time graduation arrives, however, Mollie finds that she has grown weary of the social responsibility and constraints of her new position within the elite circle of Franklin's young ladies. She begins to miss Burt's wholesomeness and sincerity, and shares none of her parents' enthusiasm for her upcoming Presentation Party.

Much to her surprise, Burt visits her secretly the night before her Presentation Party and begs her to run away with him. Mollie is overwhelmed; she agrees, and the two are secretly married across the state line, to start a new life beyond the reach of the capital city.

Tyne, William. *A Walk in the Sun.* Harry Brown. 1944.

Corporal William Tyne of Providence, Rhode Island, is a World War II soldier who is forced by circumstance to become the leader of a platoon on a dangerous mission. Despite being ill-prepared for the role into which he is thrust, Tyne must, for better or worse, become a leader of men.

When the officer in charge of Tyne's outfit is mortally wounded by a mortar shell fragment shortly before he and his men are to land on an Italian beach, the next in command, Sergeant Halverson, is entrusted with the responsibility of leading the soldiers on a six-mile trek to an Italian farmhouse. Halverson is unsure of the mission's ultimate objective, however, and once they land, he temporarily turns over charge of the troops to Sergeant Eddie Porter and wanders off by himself in search of a clarification of orders. But Halverson does not return, and Porter opts to move his men away from the open space of the beach to a terrain providing more cover from German air attacks.

As the platoon marches off, Tyne agrees to remain near the beach and wait for the sergeant's expected return, a task rapidly concluded when Tyne learns of Halverson's death in a German machine-gun ambush. During Tyne's attempt to rejoin the others, enemy planes begin a strafing attack that kills several of the platoon's members. Porter, thoroughly rattled and now fearing the worst, finally decides to try to reach the farmhouse, the directions to which are on a map Tyne had procured earlier.

With the trek under way, Porter turns to Tyne for advice and guidance. Tyne says that the platoon's mission should be to secure the farmhouse, blow the bridge adjacent to it, and thus make a German counterattack impossible. Porter, while agreeing with him, nonetheless becomes unnerved by the prospect of combat. He becomes paralyzed by a crisis of confidence, and when more men die at the hands of a German air attack, he effectively relinquishes command to Tyne. As the platoon launches a successful attack on an armored car, Porter breaks down entirely and must be left behind.

Although the last miles of the march are marked by grave uncertainty, Tyne's confidence peaks and his fear of the unknown dissipates. When the decimated platoon finally reaches the farmhouse, it is a clear-headed Tyne who orders a four-man patrol to discover whether the house is occupied by Germans. Unfortunately, it is, and two members of the patrol are killed. Having surrendered the element of surprise, Tyne must make his most difficult decision of all: how to occupy the farmhouse in the face of assuredly high casualties. He devises a plan whereby two patrols follow each other around the perimeter of the farmhouse, destroying the bridge along the way and finally engaging the Germans. The remainder of the platoon, led by Tyne himself, is to give the patrols a half-hour head start and then head directly for the house, creating enough of a diversion to allow the patrols to surprise the Germans. The story concludes indecisively with the men, led by Tyne, charging through a torrent of German machine-gun fire.

U

Uncle Tom. *Uncle Tom's Cabin, or Life Among the Lowly.* Harriet Beecher Stowe. 1852.

Although a victim of American slavery, Uncle Tom feels blessed because he is a Christian. It is this Christian spirit that grants him the strength to withstand the degradations of the American slave system portrayed in this novel.

One night after the prayer meeting that Tom holds regularly for the slaves, Tom and his wife Chloe are startled by the appearance on their doorstep of the house servant Eliza and her child. Informing them that Mr. Shelby has sold her son and Tom to a slave trader, Eliza tells them of her plan to flee to the North with her child. Although Eliza advises Tom to escape, he declines, realizing that his sale will help pull his master out of debt. The next morning Tom is taken in chains to begin his journey away from his wife and children, and the home he loves.

While on a ship bound for Louisiana with a group of other slaves, Tom is horrified by the treatment received by the slaves, especially when one woman whose son is taken away throws herself overboard. He is cheered, however, by his friendship with a little girl named EVANGELINE "EVA" ST. CLARE, who is traveling with her father, Augustine St. Clare. After Tom saves Eva from drowning when she falls overboard, her father buys Tom and takes him to the St. Clare plantation to be a house servant and companion to the child.

Once on the plantation, Tom and Eva's friendship grows, as does her interest in religion, even as she becomes weak from a mysterious illness. Tom, partly to console St. Clare as Eva approaches death and partly to save the slave owner's soul, works to instill in St. Clare the same depth of religious feeling that he and Eva experience.

After Eva's death, St. Clare becomes more receptive to religion and resolves that because Christianity and slaveholding are incompatible, he will free his slaves. Tom's joy at the prospect of freedom and a return to his family is cut short, however, when St. Clare is accidentally stabbed to death. Because St. Clare left no will, his wife is free to sell Tom and the other slaves.

Tom's new master, SIMON LEGREE, is a cruel one. He beats the work out of his slaves, and Tom is no exception. Tom makes no physical resistance, but because the slave's spiritual resistance and refusal to become a brute even while he is treated like one provokes Legree's wrath, Tom is singled out for especially harsh treatment.

After one savage beating, a fellow slave, Cassy, comes to Tom's assistance. She tells him the story of her life in bondage and of her determination to kill Legree. Tom talks her out of committing this act, but the woman eventually decides to free herself from Legree's sexual exploitation by escaping with another slave, Emmeline, who is in danger of becoming Legree's next victim. When the two women escape, Tom refuses to join Legree's search or to betray his friends and thus endanger their lives by revealing their hiding place. Legree, enraged, beats him mercilessly.

Tom is killed by Legree's savage beating, but even in the midst of it, he never gives up his faith in God and heavenly salvation. Although Tom is dead, he is not defeated; his death allows Cassy and Emmeline to achieve a new life outside the grip of slavery, and it represents as well the triumph of a Christian spirit over evil.

Unger, John T. "The Diamond as Big as the Ritz." F. Scott Fitzgerald. 1922.

John T. Unger is invited by a prep school classmate,

Percy Washington, to visit his home. As they travel on the train to Montana, Percy tells John that his father owns a diamond as big as the Ritz Carlton Hotel. John thinks nothing of this seemingly hyperbolic statement, unaware that he is about to behold truly extraordinary opulence.

The Washingtons' magnificent chateau is situated on top of a mountain in a lovely, isolated valley. Percy explains that his grandfather and father have manipulated government affairs to prevent their land being surveyed because they do not want to be discovered. Once inside the chateau, John is overwhelmed by the beauty and sensuality of the interiors. He dines with the Washington family and falls asleep.

The next morning Percy tells John that in the 1860s, Percy's grandfather discovered a mountain that was a solid diamond. Fearing the measures the government might take if it was told of the diamond, he decided to mine the mountain in secret. In a short time he had accumulated a vast fortune. When Grandfather Washington died, his son Braddock (Percy's father) knew that enough wealth had been extracted from the mountain to support generations of Washingtons in unparalleled luxury, and he decided to seal the mine to protect the great family secret. The chateau sits on top of the sealed mountain, and Braddock maintains three antiaircraft guns that he is prepared to fire in the event of an air raid.

After listening to Percy's story, John takes a walk in the garden where he meets Percy's beautiful younger sister Kismine. The two flirt innocently, and John is flattered when Kismine says that she likes him and that no boy has ever been in love with her before. Soon after, Percy and Braddock give John a tour of the property. Braddock, a cold and arrogant man, shows John the slaves' quarters and points out "the cage," a cavity in the earth covered by a strong iron grating where dozens of aviators are being held captive because they discovered the Washington estate.

John and Kismine fall in love and plan to elope. One day, however, Kismine lets slip the fact that no guest of the Washingtons has ever left the estate alive. Furious, John immediately decides to run away, but he concedes when Kismine insists on joining him. His anger subsides, and his love for her returns.

That night an airplane attack begins. Kismine and John flee to a rooftop garden and watch as the slaves' quarters and one of the antiaircraft guns go up in flames. Fearing for their lives, they wake Jasmine, Kismine's older sister, and start to leave the house. Kismine is excited about being "free and poor," but John, saying he would rather be rich, has her grab the contents of her jewelry box on their way out.

At three in the morning John, Kismine, and Jasmine reach a concealed spot in the woods, far from the chateau, where they can safely watch the fight. After the last antiaircraft gun gives out and quiet fills the valley, Kismine and her sister fall asleep. John suddenly hears footsteps and follows them to a high boulder, where he sees Braddock Washington silhouetted against the sky with two slaves crouching at his feet. When Braddock signals, the slaves stand and lift a huge diamond toward the sky. Braddock calls out, "You there!" John, amazed, realizes that he is offering a bribe to God. The sky darkens, the birds grow quiet, and thunder sounds in the distance; Braddock, realizing he has been defeated, goes back to the diamond mountain.

John returns to his companions in time for all of them to see the Washingtons' mountain explode, killing everyone else. Heading back to civilization, the three young people walk until sunset before resting for a picnic. When John asks for the diamonds that Kismine has brought, he sees to his horror that they are rhinestones. Although Kismine is happy to be penniless, John is gloomy and says now they will have to live in Hades. Kismine marvels at the dreamlike quality of her life, but John says everyone's youth is a dream. He says everyone should experience love, a form of divine madness, and rejecting consciousness, he wraps himself in a blanket and falls asleep.

The Unhurried Waiter. "A Clean, Well-Lighted Place." Ernest Hemingway. 1927.

The unhurried waiter sits with his younger colleague while their last customer, a deaf old man, drinks on the terrace of a Spanish café. It is late, and the colleague, a younger man, is impatiently waiting to close the café so that he can return home to his wife. The unhurried waiter shares an understanding with the deaf old man, however, and is reluctant to make him leave.

As the two waiters watch the old man getting drunk, they discuss the suicide attempt he is said to have made recently out of despair. When their customer signals for another brandy, the impatient younger waiter says he wishes that the old man had succeeded. The other waiter is more understanding; he explains that the old man is lonely, that he has no wife to go home to, and that, in any case, he is a dignified drunk who sips his brandy without spilling it.

The younger waiter is not swayed by his colleague's sympathy. When the old man asks for yet another brandy, the younger waiter brusquely tells him that they must close and that he must go home. As the drunk walks away somewhat unsteadily but with his dignity intact, the unhurried waiter wonders aloud why his colleague was not more sympathetic. The older waiter tells the younger man that he understands the drunkard because he, too, likes to stay late in cafés. He does not have the confidence or the youth of his colleague, and he is often reluctant to return to his lonely room. The younger waiter reminds him that their customer is free to go to an all-night bodega; the older waiter insists that one needs a pleasant café, a clean, well-lighted place from which to face nightfall.

When his colleague leaves, the unhurried waiter contemplates his own fear of night and the awful nothingness he often feels. As he makes his way from the café he stops at a bar and orders coffee. He comments to the bartender that, while the light there is good, the bar is sadly unpolished. The bartender gives him a steely look, and willing himself to contemplate no further, the waiter leaves the bar. He walks toward his single room, knowing that he likely will not sleep until daylight.

Upshur, Mariah. *This Child's Gonna Live.* Sarah E. Wright. 1969.

Mariah Upshur, a young and extremely impoverished black woman who lives in the tiny village of Tangierneck, Maryland, in the late 1920s, must struggle against poverty and hunger to hold her family together. Mariah and her husband Jacob share the burden of eking out a living during one of the nation's worst economic periods. The Upshurs already have three children, all sons, and have lost an infant daughter to poor nutrition and bad luck.

When the novel begins, Mariah, now pregnant for the fifth time, vows that in spite of everything this child will live. She plans from the beginning to leave the stultifying poverty behind her, whether or not her husband complies. Mariah's desire to leave is reinforced by her continual praying to the Lord; both she and her husband, although no longer church members, rely heavily on daily conversations with God to preserve their sanity and to carry them through the habitual grind of hard work, low pay, and inadequate food.

Mariah is surrounded by a vigorous company of women, including her mother Mamma Effie, Jacob's adopted sister Vyella, and the local preacher. Another force in Mariah's life is the white Miss Bannie, who has managed to appropriate a large tract of land that properly belongs to Jacob's father and his family. Mariah struggles against Miss Bannie, the embodiment of ideological white supremacy and real economic strength. In the autumn of 1929, Mariah gives birth to a daughter, whom Jacob names Bardetta Tometta. The child's birth stirs rumors of Mariah's infidelity because the baby is nearly white in complexion. Since Jacob knows his family has white blood, he is not swayed by the rumors.

On the same day as Bardetta's birth there are a number of deaths in Tangierneck, among them Miss Bannie's. The day before, Mariah had found the woman lying alone and badly beaten. At first she intended to pass by, but then she decided to help her. When she assists the woman home, she is told that Miss Bannie will certainly find a way to make reparations for the land she has taken and will also provide the greatly needed milk for Mariah's children. Mariah's eldest child is sent for the promised milk the next day, only to discover that Miss Bannie has died.

The Upshurs soon relocate, following the available migrant work in the Bay area, including tomato canning and oyster shelling. During this period the last of Jacob's three brothers dies, as does their son Horace, also known as Rabbit. Shocked and numbed, they return home to bury their child in Cleveland Hills, the community cemetery. Then, despite the overwhelming presence of death in Tangierneck, Jacob and Mariah return with their three children and assume responsibility for several recently orphaned children, including Vyella's, one of which was fathered by Jacob. At the novel's conclusion, the relationship between the Upshurs has disintegrated. Indomitable to the last, Mariah longs for a new child to replace the son who died, even as she and her family face the prospect of continuing hardship.

Father Urban. *Morte D'Urban.* J. F. Powers. 1956.

Father Urban is one of the leading priests of the Order of Saint Clement. Because the order has fallen into mediocrity and obscurity, it is Father Urban's foremost aspiration to single-handedly carry the order to a more prominent status. Urban is in his mid-fifties, tall, handsome, well educated, and a gifted speaker, qualities that give him the charisma to attract a certain following among the Catholic audiences to whom he lectures or preaches.

After Mass on Sunday, on an auspicious day for the Order and for Father Urban, Billy Cosgrove, a wealthy businessman, enters the sacristy. Impressed by the sermon, Billy is eager to meet the charismatic Father Urban. A friendship slowly develops between the priest and the businessman, and as a result of Billy's donation, the Clementines move from their squalid offices in downtown Chicago to a prestigious address on the north side.

For several years Father Urban had been the order's "man in the field," traveling out of Chicago in order to preach to retreats and parish missions throughout the country. Suddenly, however, he receives a letter from the Father Provincial relieving him of his duties and requesting that he report to a new retreat house in rural Minnesota.

Arriving at the retreat house, Urban is dismayed to find that it is disorderly and shabby, and that the head priest requires him to do manual labor—which Urban considers an enormous waste of his talents. The house is a failure until Father Urban implements a grandiose scheme to bring in large numbers of retreatants of "a better class" and succeeds in securing the financial backing of his friend Billy Cosgrove. A neighboring farm is purchased, a nine-hole golf course is built, and the retreat house begins to flourish.

Still riding the crest of his great success, Father Urban is asked to accompany Billy on a fishing trip. After two days with no sign of fish, however, Billy becomes extremely frustrated and attempts to drown a deer. In a decisive moment Urban throws the boat into high gear, hurling Billy overboard and setting the deer free. Billy is furious; when back in the boat, he pushes Urban into the lake, leaving him to be rescued later by the lodgekeeper.

The incident permanently severs relations between the two men, forcing Urban to reflect ruefully about the course of his life. On his way back from the fishing trip, another painful event occurs that exacerbates his rapidly growing sense of failure and depression. Sally Hopwood, the daughter of a wealthy woman whose patronage Urban had been pursuing, lures him to a small island under a seemingly innocent pretext. After a few drinks she gives Urban some harsh insights about himself that appear to hit home. She tells him that he is a trained operator attempting to procure funds from the rich people he abhors and that he hasn't a real friend in the world. She then tries to persuade him to go for a swim and takes off all her clothes. Although taken with her loveliness, Urban nevertheless resists the temptation. Spurned, Sally leaves him stranded on the island, and he is forced to swim to the mainland.

Father Urban returns to the retreat house a broken man. On the strength of his administrative accomplishments he is elected Father Provincial for the order. Although numerous changes are expected by the parish, he makes none. Having lost all desire for worldly recognition, Father Urban begins to acquire an unsought but not unwarranted reputation for quiet piety.

Usher, Roderick. "The Fall of the House of Usher." Edgar Allan Poe. 1839.

Because Roderick Usher is the last surviving male member of his family, his case is a difficult one. The mentally and physically ill Usher has called on an old friend to pull him out of the doldrums into which he has fallen. However, even his friend's assistance cannot prevent Roderick's eventual death and the end of the Usher family line.

When the narrator, Roderick's friend, arrives at the stately Usher home, he is struck by its decayed aspect. The mansion overlooks a small, swampy lake, and the house is a crumbling, fungus-covered structure. Roderick himself is finely molded in appearance, with large, luminous eyes, yet he is pallid and deathlike. With difficulty he tries to conceal a certain nervous agitation that plagues him. To the narrator, who has not seen his friend in many years,

Roderick seems to display the characteristics of a habitual drunkard or opium abuser.

Roderick has reason to behave as if he is weighted down by troubles. His beloved sister—his only living relative—is wasting away from some mysterious illness. Additionally, Roderick's own nervous disease is a serious one. He has become overly sensitive to sound and averse to most tastes; even his skin is sensitive, to the degree that he cannot bear the pressure of most fabrics.

What troubles the narrator most about Roderick is the sick man's insistence on the sentience of vegetation. It is Roderick's belief that the very fungi that live in the swampy water in front of his mansion possess feeling. As evidence he cites the sharp decline of his family line caused, he believes, by the miasmic atmosphere emitted by the fungi. Consumed by these worries, Roderick has the awful presentiment that he will soon lose his grip on reality altogether and plunge into a life-and-death struggle with his own dark fears.

When Roderick's sister Madeline dies, he calls upon the narrator to help him carry the body to a vault in the house for her temporary entombment. Together they bear the coffin to the small dark room in the depths of the mansion. Roderick insists on opening the coffin for a final look at Madeline who, he reveals to the narrator, is his twin.

Days later Roderick, his emotions aroused by a wild storm, goes to the narrator's room. The narrator attempts to calm Roderick by reading him a romance, but each incident in the story that mentions a loud sound is accompanied by a similar sound somewhere in the house. Only when the shrieks, groans, and gratings come near the door is Roderick aroused from his trancelike state. Confessing that he has heard such sounds for days, he screams that his sister is alive, outside their chamber. The door flies open, and a bloodied, white-clad Madeline stands before them. When she falls dead into Roderick's arms, he dies as well. The narrator flees the cursed mansion just as the House of Usher crumbles into the fungus-choked waters of the lake.

V

V. *The Real Life of Sebastian Knight.* Vladimir Nabokov. 1941.

In this novel concerning the lives of aristocrats after the Bolshevik Revolution, the narrator, referred to only as

V., sets out to write a biography of his recently deceased half-brother, the moderately well-known writer Sebastian Knight. V. claims that the only extant biography of his brother is a farce. To prove that he alone has the background to understand his brother, he juxtaposes passages from Sebastian's novels with memories from their childhood. V. wants to show a great affinity for the man and work, but he only conveys his lifelong feelings of inferiority toward Sebastian. As V. describes his research, which is mainly a pursuit of someone he believes to have been Sebastian's secret mistress, his authority as a biographer—not to mention his general sanity—is constantly called into question.

The novel opens with V.'s diatribe on John Goodman, former assistant to Sebastian, who has written the first biography of the writer. The narrator claims that Goodman's wild speculations were calculated to appeal to vulgar commercial tastes. He also resents that Goodman did not even acknowledge his existence in the story of Sebastian's life. V. wants to write his own version because, he claims, it is the kind of book Sebastian would have written. The narrator initially says he discovered in his brother's flat an ad placed to find characters for a false biography. He infers that this would have been the writer's next book. Although always careful to contrast his middling talents with Sebastian's soaring genius, V. suggests that he will begin his literary career where his brother left off.

Such behavior is consistent with a childhood spent following after Sebastian but always failing to live up to the older brother's talents. Recalling their early years as part of the Russian aristocracy, V. tells of always trotting behind Sebastian, unable to keep up. In those days he would spit at his brother, not to annoy him but simply to make him acknowledge his existence. Having been forced into exile by the Russian Revolution, V. and Sebastian were later educated at the best schools in England and France. But even as an adult the narrator failed to gain Sebastian's confidence or interest. Especially after receiving some notice for his writing talent, Sebastian often cut their infrequent meetings short for other appointments. He found it a strain to carry on personal conversations with V.

V. promises great insight into Sebastian's life and work, but more often he reveals how his thwarted affection for his brother has turned him into a silhouette of a person; he never mentions other family, friends, or any activities that are not connected in some way to his obsession with his brother. The narrator apparently spends all his time interviewing the writer's former acquaintances, reading his personal letters, and getting sidetracked for weeks by his own hypotheses.

When he discovers that Sebastian had periodically visited the Beaumont Hotel in Blauberg, he assumes that he had a longtime lover. The narrator visits the resort to find information about the single women who had been there during Sebastian's longest stay, the summer of 1929. For no apparent reason he eventually limits his search to three women. The first two had nothing to do with Sebastian, but the third claims to know the mistress. She invites V.

to her home for the weekend, promising to invite the mistress as well. What follows is a game of seduction; V. begins to suspect that either woman might want to sleep with him because of his famous brother. He feels torn between asking pertinent questions for the biography and taking up where Sebastian left off with the mistress. V. does not reveal his choice.

The novel ends with V. remembering how he rushed to the hospital to comfort his dying brother. He arrived in the middle of the night, after visiting hours, and persuaded the nurse to let him stay and wait for any news on the writer's grave coronary condition. Outside a darkened hospital room, listening to the labored breathing, V. imagined that he had discovered a mystical connection not just to Sebastian but to all humanity. Looking back on this crucial moment, V. affirms that the soul is "not a constant state—that any soul may be yours, if you find and follow its undulations." Applying this theory to his own life, he concludes: "I am Sebastian, or Sebastian is I, or perhaps we both are someone whom neither of us knows."

Vaiden, Kate. *Kate Vaiden.* Reynolds Price. 1986.

Kate Vaiden is a feisty, independent spirit who seems to have a knack both for encountering horrifically tragic situations and for fleeing all responsibilities. She tells the story of her childhood and teen years from the vantage point of late middle age, when she decides to see again the son she abandoned forty years earlier and never knew.

Her parents, Frances and Dan, had a lovely courtship and apparently a beautiful marriage. At eleven, Kate returns to her hometown of Macon, North Carolina, for a cousin's funeral; her father suddenly shows up and kills his wife and himself. Kate is raised by her aunt Caroline and uncle Holt, and their black maid Noony.

As she matures, Kate discovers love and sex for the first time with Gaston Stegall, a kind and gentle local boy. They fall deeply in love over the course of a few years and plan to get married. Gaston joins the army to fight in World War II but dies at the training camp, an apparent suicide.

Kate appears remarkably level-headed in the face of these tragedies. However, when her cousin Swift tries to rape her, she decides to run away from Macon to live with her other cousin, Walter Porter, and his lover, Douglas Lee, who had been run out of Macon some years before because of a scandal over their homosexual relationship.

Kate is quite happy in Norfolk with Walter and Douglas. The trio makes a sort of family, and one happy Christmas Eve, Kate has a vision of the Virgin Mary giving birth to Jesus. She tells this to no one but takes comfort in it. She enrolls in a Catholic high school and appears frail but stable until she and Douglas have an affair behind Walter's back and Kate becomes pregnant. Although she feels some affection for Douglas, Kate doesn't really love him and doesn't want to marry him although she seriously considers the idea. Douglas is willing and able, but Kate runs away and hides out with Tim Slaugher, a taxi driver in his fifties whom she met when she first arrived in town. When Douglas finds her, they agree to take the train to Raleigh and live together there. The train stops in Macon, however, and while Douglas is in the bathroom, Kate slips away.

Back in Macon, Kate settles in with her old family until the baby is born. Her family, while unapproving, tries to be supportive. She has the baby and names him Daniel Lee Vaiden. Aunt Caroline helps her raise the child, but Kate is concerned because it appears that Douglas, who is now living in Raleigh, is in trouble. She leaves the child with her aunt and uncle and visits Douglas's employer, Whitfield Eller, a blind man who had enlisted Douglas as a driver and companion. Kate befriends Whitfield after learning that Douglas tried to rob him, and eventually she moves in with him. Having promised her aunt and uncle that she would come home, Kate bides her time until Douglas returns. He surprises her and Whitfield by committing suicide in their bathtub.

Attempting once more to absorb a tragedy too great to comprehend, Kate goes with Whitfield to the hills of North Carolina, near Asheville, where Whitfield proposes marriage. She says no and again sneaks off without a word.

Kate settles into a lonely and uneventful life in Greensboro. There she receives another proposal, but the fact that she has a son whom she abandoned scares away her potential husband. After a near-fatal struggle with cervical cancer and an inspirational trip to Rome, Kate decides to see her son before she dies. When she returns to Macon, her former servant Noony greets her coldly. Nobody has missed her, it seems. She finds her cousin Swift, the only surviving relative, in a nursing home. He tells her Lee's whereabouts: He has been in the navy for years and is now on a ship somewhere. He also tells her the reason her father killed himself and her mother: He was in a jealous fury because he thought she had been unfaithful to him with Swift.

As the novel ends, Kate calls her cousin Walter's number in Norfolk and hears Lee's voice on the answering machine. Instead of contacting him right way, she decides to write her autobiography—the book that is *Kate Vaiden*.

Vaillant, Father Joseph. *Death Comes for the Archbishop.* Willa Cather. 1927.

Father Joseph Vaillant, pioneer, devout priest, and bishop of Denver, is a character of immediate and widespread appeal. Modeled after Joseph P. Machebeuf, the first archbishop of Denver, he is a man of the people, tireless in his missionary efforts, impetuous, and spirited, a man "greater than the sum of his qualities."

Born in Auvergne, France, Joseph Vaillant is the son of a baker, descended from a people of "humble station."

He is a rather homely man, frail in body, undersized, and very pale, yet he possesses great energy and enthusiasm. As a young seminarian Vaillant makes the acquaintance of FATHER JEAN MARIE LATOUR, a man far superior to him in breeding, scholarship, and physical prowess. The two become instant and lasting friends. When the call is raised for missionaries to the New World, Fathers Vaillant and Latour go together, first to the parish on the shores of Lake Ontario and then, in 1851, to Santa Fe, seat of the new diocese created by the Mexican cession. They establish mission schools and after some time succeed in building a cathedral.

What Vaillant lacks in scholarship and physical ability, he more than makes up for in faith. He rigidly observes all church fasts and is impressed by the stories of faith his people tell him. One day soon after their arrival in Santa Fe, Vaillant brings Padre Escolastico Herrera to see Father Latour. The padre relates to the bishop a story of the Virgin Mary particularly precious to all Catholics in New Mexico. When the man leaves, Vaillant exclaims to a somewhat skeptical Latour, "Doctrine is well enough for the wise, but the miracle is something we can hold in our hands and love."

As a young man Father Vaillant has desired to live a solitary life of seclusion, but he cannot be happy for long without human contact. He likes nearly everyone, and what's more, nearly everyone likes him. Outgoing and jovial, he is able to move people with vitality rather than eloquence, humor rather than intelligence. On one of his missionary journeys, Vaillant stops at the ranch of Manuel Lujon, a rich Mexican landowner. The morning after the priest's arrival, Lujon takes Vaillant to his stable to show off his mules, Contento and Angelica. Vaillant, intent on having the mules for himself and Father Latour, talks of the need for such animals among missionaries and of the inadequacy of his own mare. Greatly moved by Vaillant, Lujon presents Contento and Angelica to him and will accept only the priest's prayers and gratitude in return.

Borrowing and begging is a way of life for Vaillant, who has few possessions of his own. When the gold rush hits Colorado, Vaillant packs his possessions into a custom-built wagon, bids his friend of twenty-five years farewell, and sets off for Camp Denver. There he continues to minister to the miners and other "lost sheep," often with even fewer comforts than those he enjoyed in Santa Fe. When Father Vaillant, consecrated bishop of Denver, dies, there is not a building in Denver—or all of the West, for that matter—large enough to hold the mourners.

Valmondé, Désirée. "Désirée's Baby." Kate Chopin. 1899.

Désirée Valmondé is the gentle gray-eyed protagonist of this tragic story. Abandoned as a toddler at the gateway to the Valmondé estate in Louisiana, she is adopted by the Valmondés who, childless, consider her a gift from some generous Providence.

Various theories as to Désirée Valmondé's parentage are offered by the community, including the notion that she was left behind on purpose by a group of pioneering Texans or that she had somehow wandered off on her own accord and became lost. But the Valmondés cease to speculate about her past and simply enjoy the fact that they finally have a loving and beautiful child to raise.

When Désirée is wooed by Armand Aubigny, a charming young man who had been raised in Paris until the death of his mother, her practical-minded stepfather warns her suitor to consider the fact that her origin is obscure and her real name unknown. But Armand claims that these facts are immaterial. Armand sends for a handsome *corbeille* from Paris, a sumptuous collection of gowns, laces, hats, and other elegant accessories, and the young couple marries and settles down on Armand's estate, L'Abri.

Marriage has a positive effect on the dark and handsome Armand who in the past had exhibited a stern dictatorial demeanor and an exacting strictness bordering on cruelty in his treatment of his slaves. The birth of their son, of whom Armand is extremely proud, further softens his nature, and Désirée shares both his pride and his happiness. But when their son is three months old, Désirée begins to be plagued by a subtle and mysterious foreboding. A strange aura surrounds the slave population, whom Armand begins to treat with unprecedented imperiousness. At the same time Désirée begins to receive unexplained visits from distant friends. Her husband also starts behaving in an odd manner. He becomes less attentive to his wife and son and takes trips without accounting for his absences. A miserable Désirée is mystified but does not receive an explanation for her husband's upsetting behavior.

One warm afternoon when she is sitting watching a young male quadroon slave fan her baby, Désirée suddenly gasps, horrified; she compares the two boys. When Armand enters the room, she staggers over to him and asks him vaguely, "Tell me what it means." Removing her hand from her arm, he brutally answers that their son is not a caucasian boy and that Désirée herself cannot therefore be white. Désirée denies the charge, pointing out her gray eyes and the fact that her husband's skin is darker than her own, but he holds his ground and insults her, likening her to one of their slaves named La Blanche. When she asks him if he would prefer if she and their son leave L'Abri, he callously replies in the affirmative.

Compliant with Armand's cruel wishes, Désirée ignores her mother's offer to take her in and disappears along the banks of the bayou, never to be seen again. Some time later, as her husband is rummaging through L'Abri in search of Désirée's possessions that he is burning in a bonfire, Armand Aubigny discovers a letter from his late mother to his father. The black blood exhibited in his son is actually inherited not from Désirée but from Armand himself.

Van Weyden, Humphrey. *The Sea Wolf.* Jack London. 1904.

Soon after writer Humphrey Van Weyden sets sail on a ferryboat bound for San Francisco, the ship collides with another and pitches him into the sea, where he all but loses consciousness before being rescued by the crew of the *Ghost*. A vessel bound for Alaska during seal hunting season, the *Ghost* is run by the dictatorial captain WOLF LARSEN. After an unsuccessful attempt to flag down a passing ship and thereby escape the clutches of the sadistic Larsen, Humphrey is forced to assume the duties of a cabin boy.

The journey is a harrowing one for Humphrey, who is derisively referred to as "Hump" by Larsen. Unused to manual labor, Humphrey is nonetheless forced to perform physical chores while being subjected to the abuse of Thomas "Cooky" Mugridge, the cowardly cook, who takes out his bitterness on the new crew member. Mugridge is a minor threat compared to Larsen, however, whose erudition fascinates Humphrey almost as much as his viciousness repels him. Sometimes, when feeling expansive, Larsen engages Humphrey in discussions on the meaning of human existence and reveals that he places little value on human life.

After Humphrey injures his knee during a storm, Larsen lavishes unexpected preferential treatment on him. This favoritism enrages Mugridge, who threatens Humphrey with a knife; Humphrey, newly emboldened, intimidates the cook into treating him with respect. But Humphrey's troubles are not over. After Larsen unmercifully beats several members of his crew, a full-fledged mutiny breaks out. Two of the attempted coup's leaders escape; Larsen orders the ship to pursue them, then allows the men to drown when their boat capsizes. While chasing the mutineers, the *Ghost* rescues five survivors of a shipwreck.

Larsen has designs on Maud Brewster, one of those rescued, but Humphrey, determined to protect her, stabs Larsen in the arm when he attacks the woman. The captain subsequently experiences a seizure and attendant blindness, both results of a brain tumor from which he is ailing. Humphrey and Maud take advantage of the situation by making their escape. After several days at sea they arrive at the deserted Endeavor Island, which becomes their temporary home. Here they fall deeply in love.

Their idyll is short-lived, however, for the *Ghost* is shipwrecked off shore. Humphrey boards and turns his rifle on the demented Larsen, but he cannot shoot. Realizing that the *Ghost* provides his and Maud's best means of escape, Humphrey sets about repairing the vessel, but not before Larsen makes an attempt on his life. Ultimately, Wolf Larsen dies, and Humphrey and Maud are rescued after they set sail.

Van Winkle, Rip. "Rip Van Winkle." Washington Irving. 1820.

Rip Van Winkle is perhaps the most well-known oversleeper in all of American literature. Set in the Kaatskill Mountains of pre–Revolutionary War New York, Irving's famous tale tells the story of this good-natured, lovable ne'er-do-well. Suffering from an intense aversion to profitable labor of all kinds, the henpecked Rip ignores the incessant nagging of his termagant wife Dame Van Winkle and favors the idle chitchat on current events that takes place daily outside Nicholas Vedder's village inn.

One day, to escape yet another tirade from Dame Van Winkle, Rip strolls through the woods of the Kaatskills with his faithful dog Wolf. Along the way he encounters a stranger who leads him to a band of odd-looking little men enjoying a game of ninepins in a clearing. Rip takes a sip from the stranger's flagon of strange brew and slips into his infamous nap.

Thinking he has slept for one night at most and not the twenty years he has in fact slumbered, Rip hurries down the mountain, afraid of the wrath he may encounter from his wife. As he enters the village, Rip notices that he now mysteriously sports a long gray beard. Moreover, he recognizes none of the once-familiar buildings or faces in the town, nor is he himself recognized. He returns to Nicholas Vedder's inn only to discover a strange red-white-and-blue banner fluttering in the wind. A portrait of George Washington has replaced that of King George III.

Perhaps even more disturbingly, Rip notices that the whole character of the village has been transformed from drowsy tranquility to one of hustle and bustle. He witnesses a boisterous political orator and soon realizes his own monarchial sympathies are no longer in vogue. With all his old cronies and ideals dead and gone, Rip finds himself alone in the world. His reawakening into unfamiliar cultural and political surroundings precipitates a profound crisis in self-confidence and identity.

In his rambles through the town, Rip runs into his daughter, now married with children. At first she does not recognize her own father, but she soon realizes what has happened. She informs him that Dame Van Winkle died in a fit of angry rage at a New England merchant. Although the townsfolk think Rip's story a bit farfetched, a local folklorist corroborates Rip's claims about the presence of fairy creatures in the woods. He soon resumes his place as Elder Gossip of the town inn. He learns of the events of the Revolutionary War but remains unimpressed. Rip, it would seem, is happier to have escaped the domestic tyranny of Dame Van Winkle than the political oppression of kindly King George.

Vance, Eleanor. *The Haunting of Hill House.* Shirley Jackson. 1959.

Invited by a man she doesn't know to visit a place she's never heard of, Eleanor Vance accepts an invitation to participate in an experiment in parapsychology. The week that the mousy Eleanor spends as Dr. John Montague's guest at Hill House is the most important and most tragic of her life.

Eleanor does not usually venture far from her family. Homeless after the death of the invalid mother she cared for over the course of eleven years, she lives with her married sister. The unexpected invitation to visit an eighty-year-old country mansion comes to Eleanor because she had been involved in a mysterious situation during her childhood. A shower of rocks had fallen on her family home, angering her mother, confusing their neighborhood, and pushing young Eleanor even further into a shell from which she only begins to emerge at Hill House.

Against her sister's will, Eleanor takes the car that they jointly own and drives to the secluded Hill House. It is an ugly, forbidding place, and she must muster up all her courage to enter it. Later Dr. Montague and his other guests arrive. Eleanor immediately takes a liking to Theodora, a beautiful, rather bohemian woman, and Luke, the nephew of the owner of Hill House. Eleanor finds that she is surprisingly comfortable with the other three temporary inhabitants of Hill House. The house itself, however, is scarcely welcoming. Doors won't stay open, light won't penetrate, and, as Dr. Montague explains, the many rooms were deliberately built at strange angles. The atmosphere of Hill House is almost suffocating, and as Eleanor broods on the two little girls who grew up there long ago, their father absent and their mother dead, she feels the weight of decades of discontent.

The house lives up to its haunted reputation. One night Eleanor joins a frightened Theodora in her bed as the room grows frigid and a wild thumping sounds in the hallway outside the locked door. On another occasion Theodora's clothes are found ripped and spotted with what looks like blood. On the wall above, written in the same red liquid, are the words HELP ELEANOR COME HOME. Hill House, for all its seeming unfriendliness, is calling her.

The other guests try to disguise their concern that Hill House is singling out Eleanor, but Eleanor herself knows that, for the first time in her life, something wants her. While the four sit together, the Dr. Montague and Luke playing chess, and Theodora turning over the pages of a book, Eleanor is often spoken to by voices no one else hears. She is afraid but excited.

Events come to a climax when Dr. Montague's pushy wife and her macho friend arrive at the house. Mrs. Montague's consultations with a Ouija board–like device reveal that something wants Eleanor. That night the house is rocked by spirits, and the other guests begin to speak of sending Eleanor home. When Eleanor frightens everyone the next evening by running through the house, pounding on bedroom doors, and finally ending up on the rickety library spiral staircase from which she must be rescued by Luke, Dr. Montague decides that it would be safest for her to leave.

Eleanor is stubborn but is finally all but forced into her car to make the trip back to her sister's home. Thinking as she drives away that she will fool them all and never leave Hill House, Eleanor accelerates the car and turns off the road. Her final thought before she crashes into a tree is to wonder why she is killing herself.

Vandover. *Vandover and the Brute.* Frank Norris. 1914.

An indulged and self-indulgent figure, Vandover struggles with the perverse, dark, and bestial aspects of human nature. Having traveled to turn-of-the-century San Francisco with his father after the death of his invalid mother, he goes unsupervised in childhood and eventually grows into an ill-disciplined but artistically minded youth.

Together with other young men returning to the city from Harvard, Vandover embarks on a life of dissipation. Although Vandover and his set flourish in "society," they frequent resorts, drink heavily, and fraternize with "fast girls and lost women." After several years of such activity, Vandover meets his life's calamity in the form of Ida Wade, one of the young women he enjoys "rushing" out of sight of society.

One night Vandover escorts Ida, who although "fast" is not yet fallen, to the Imperial, a resort that has private rooms for smoking and dining, and he seduces her. Several months later Ida commits suicide. Knowing that Ida may have been pregnant, Vandover confesses to his father, who is deeply shocked, and decides to renounce his life of debauchery and devote himself to his art. Following his father's advice, Vandover takes a cruise to San Diego and then plans to leave for Paris immediately upon his return. But he is destined never to reach that haven of artists: On the return trip from San Diego, the ship is wrecked, and Vandover is stranded at sea. He reaches San Francisco just minutes after his father dies of the grief and shock caused by news of the shipwreck.

Sobered by the suicide of Ida, the wreck, and his father's death, Vandover resolves to defeat the brute within him. But despite his determination to return to his art, he continues to lead a life of leisure and indulgence after settling his father's estate. Several months later he decides to venture out into society again. He is shocked when his former "set," including his girlfriend of several years, give him the cold shoulder at a dance. Only then does he learn that, although no one knows for certain, every one of his old friends holds him responsible for Ida's suicide. At first humiliated by his disgrace, Vandover eventually feels liberated by society's snub and spends a year consumed in "drunkenness, sensuality, and gambling."

At the end of that year the opera comes to San Francisco, and Vandover, mesmerized by the music, awakens to his better self. Seeking once more to conquer his darker side, he turns finally to his art—only to discover that his talent has deserted him. It is at this disastrous juncture that he learns Hiram Wade, Ida's father, is suing him for $25,000.

After a tortured night, Vandover decides to kill himself. He puts a revolver to his head and pulls the trigger; no explosion issues from the gun, however, and he faints. By morning he has become completely indifferent to his fate and decides that "his whole life had been one long suicide." In this state he confronts Charlie Geary, a lifelong friend who turns out to be the counsel for Wade and who plans to use the situation to swindle Vandover out of some valuable real estate. On the advice of Geary, Vandover settles out of court by selling the land he owns to Geary and paying the cash to Wade.

Vandover's demise follows rapidly. The brute that has threatened to overtake him all his life begins to prey on his mind. Increasingly, he imagines himself to have literally become a beast and suffers attacks during which he goes down on all fours and utters guttural noises resembling the growls of a dog or wolf. After depleting all his resources through gambling and extravagant living, he finally turns to Geary, who has parlayed the land into a block of lucrative rented cottages.

Oddly pleased that he has avoided the vices and pitfalls that lead one to such an end, Geary grudgingly hires Vandover to clean the cottages when they are vacated by renters. The novel closes as Vandover, dirty and exhausted, sits on the floor of a cottage looking into the eyes of the young son of the family waiting to inhabit the cottage he has just cleaned.

Vane, John. *Honest John Vane.* J. W. De Forest. 1875.

A manufacturer of refrigerators, John Vane is a self-made man who lives a simple but happy life in the small New England town of Slowburgh. A widower, he rooms with his two young children at the boardinghouse of Mrs. Rensellaer Smiles. But when Vane enters politics, in an attempt to woo the woman he loves, he undergoes a drastic change of life and character, and loses his honest, "country" ways.

Although Vane makes a good living selling refrigerators, he becomes lonely and develops an affection for Mrs. Smiles's eldest daughter Olympia. Despite her modest birth, Olympia has cultivated a taste for the finer things in life, and her considerable beauty enables her to attract men of extravagant means. She regards the simple Vane as a country bumpkin because of his unrefined manners and humble ways. When he finally musters up enough courage to ask her to marry him, she tells him in no uncertain terms that she will not, nor will she ever, consider such a proposition.

Devastated, Vane seeks the advice of an acquaintance, Darius Dorman, who tells him that he must impress Olympia with his independence by moving out of her mother's boardinghouse. Soon afterward Dorman suggests to Vane that a man of his simple beliefs and firm honesty might consider a career in politics, especially in the wake of the scandal caused by the latest representative. The idea appeals to Vane, and with the considerable political savvy of Dorman behind him, he runs as "Honest John Vane" and wins the nomination.

As the election approaches, Vane is thrilled to find that Olympia has taken a new interest in him. Olympia's affection for him increases in proportion to his political popularity. The day after he is elected representative, Vane proposes to Olympia, who accepts despite her previous vow. Very shortly thereafter the newlyweds, along with Vane's two children from his previous marriage, move to Washington, D.C.

Olympia soon finds that being a congressman does not necessarily entail all the luxuries she desires. She complains to Vane about the boardinghouse in which they live and longs for the luxury apartments held by some of the senior representatives. Vane, regarded as a rather plain dimwit by his colleagues because of his steadfast honesty, is far removed from the elite social circles that his wife so desperately covets.

Dorman, who follows Vane to Washington as a lobbyist, approaches Vane with a business offer concerning a House vote that could conceivably make them a great deal of money. Vane hesitates at first but eventually agrees to the shady transaction in order to appease his nagging wife. For the next few months he buys Olympia all the luxuries she desires. Once it becomes known that he is "approachable," however, he is beset by hundreds of other similarly dubious offers. Because of the way in which he changes with the political winds, Honest John Vane is now known as "Weathercock John."

When an investigation uncovers Vane's money-making scheme, he is able to save himself through deception and half-truths—means he had learned during his term in office. He easily wins the next election to the "den of thieves," the United States Congress.

Vansant, J. R. *J. R.* William Gaddis. 1975.

J. R. Vansant is the title character of this satirical novel. An eleven-year-old boy who wears an old sweater and dirty sneakers, J.R. attends sixth grade in a despicable Long Island school where drug use abounds, where teachers seem terminally burned out, and where witless administrators and the misuse of money have produced an educational setting that stifles creativity to the point of being utterly ridiculous.

J.R. is both cynical and naive, the product of one of the many dysfunctional and crumbling families in the novel. Yet his ambition is remarkable; given a social studies assignment on free enterprise, he turns his project into an enormous corporation. J.R. makes a deal to buy navy surplus picnic forks and from this beginning develops a family of business enterprises that becomes the J. R. Cor-

poration. He enlists the aid of a ruthless stock broker, Mr. Crawley, and a teacher at his school, the failing composer Edward Bast, to be the adult elements in his scheme. Throughout the growth phase of his corporation, J.R. remains the "boss," manipulating Bast, the lawyer Piscator, and a host of minor characters as he runs his enormous conglomerate from a small apartment on Ninety-sixth Street that is hopelessly cluttered with junk and noise. He makes his deals from the post office and from public phones, carefully placing a handkerchief over the mouthpiece to disguise his youthful voice.

What began with picnic forks soon becomes an empire of shaky schemes involving gas leases, green aspirin, pork bellies, matchbooks, legal marijuana, defense contracts, toilet paper, land deals, and a string of nursing homes that double as funeral parlors. Along the way, artists lose their will to create, honest people are compromised, and marriages crumble as everyone from congressmen to landless Indians get enveloped in the corporation's schemes. But through it all J.R. insists that he is only "trying to find out what I'm supposed to do." He is obsessed with money and the power it brings, but none of his ventures provides him with any material reward. At the end of the novel he is still wearing the same dirty sneakers.

As the novel closes, J.R. seems to be caught in the growing turmoil of his collapsing business empire and the collapsing world based on money and greed that the J. R. Corporation represents. His paper empire becomes worthless; in fact, money itself seems worthless. Bast and the others have succumbed to inertia or fallen victim to disease or insanity. Only J.R., who is at once the perpetrator, victim, and sole survivor of this debacle, seems able to see above his own calamitous enterprise and face the future with youthful optimism.

Varner, Will. *The Hamlet; The Town; The Mansion.* William Faulkner. 1940; 1957; 1959.

Will Varner, a lazy and mild-mannered old farmer, is among the most powerful men in Faulkner's fictional Yoknapatawpha County. In addition to being the largest landowner in the area surrounding his hometown of Frenchman's Bend, Mississippi, he is also the beat supervisor, the justice of the peace, and the election commissioner. Varner controls the politics and the economy of the county, a power that he extends into the personal lives of those who inhabit it.

Varner is married and the father of sixteen children, fourteen of whom have married and moved west or died before the story begins. His wife is still strong and active, and his daughter EULA (VARNER SNOPES), is indisputably the belle of the county. Varner leaves the management of the family business, which includes the store, the mill, and the cotton gin, to his thirty-year-old bachelor son Jody. Jody is not the most competent of managers, but fortunately things take care of themselves; townspeople continue to trade with them because it is considered "bad luck" to do business with anyone but Varner. As a result, Will Varner is free to spend his time energetically doing nothing. He rides around on his fat white horse and sometimes sits on the porch of his decrepit mansion, the Old Frenchman's Place—a crumbling monstrosity that he says is the only thing he cannot seem to sell.

Jody Varner makes a grave error when he rents one of his father's farms to ABNER SNOPES, whom he soon finds out is a "barn burner," an arsonist. As a "fire insurance policy," Jody agrees to hire Abner's son FLEM SNOPES to clerk in the store. Before long the determined Flem supplants Jody as Will Varner's closest associate. Varner rides in his carriage with Flem by his side, surveying his property, and when the year is over, Flem assists Varner in balancing the books, a ritual from which even Jody has always been excluded.

When Jody discovers that his younger sister Eula is pregnant, he becomes hysterical and wants to shoot someone to defend the Varner name. Varner is not the least bit ruffled by this turn of events, however; he even mocks Jody lightly for his old-fashioned attitude. He swiftly purchases a marriage certificate for Eula and Flem, turns the Old Frenchman's Place over to Flem as a dowry, and sends them to Texas for a year-long "honeymoon." When Flem cons three men into buying the mansion, which he says has a treasure on its land, Varner begins to resent Flem and his manipulative ways. Flem judiciously moves his wife and daughter to Jefferson, a town some distance away.

Varner continues to have a great deal of control over the Snopes family. He is the major stockholder in Colonel John Sartoris's bank in Jefferson, and when Sartoris dies, he is free to make any decision regarding the bank. When Flem's relative, Byron Snopes, runs off with a portion of the bank's money and the former mayor, Manfred de Spain, replaces it, Will Varner allows de Spain to become president of the bank. He also makes sure that Flem is made vice president—not as a favor to Flem but out of concern for his daughter. Finally, his most controlling act is to insert a clause into his will stating that if LINDA (SNOPES KOHL), who is Eula's daughter and Flem's stepdaughter, marries, Flem can obtain no part of the Varner inheritance.

Flem's chance to turn the tables on Varner comes when Linda is away at school and has her own will drawn up, which leaves her part of the inheritance to Flem. In order to oust de Spain and take over his position, Flem takes this will to the Varner house and informs Mrs. Varner that Eula and de Spain have been having an affair. Early the next morning, upon learning the news, Varner drives to Jefferson, enters the Snopes house screaming, and later informs de Spain that he must leave town. That evening Eula kills herself. Flem soon becomes bank president.

Neither Varner nor his small-town empire is deeply affected by these crises in Jefferson. He continues to flourish; he even provides support, when it seems useful, to the Snopes family. In his late seventies, twelve years a widower, Varner marries a young woman of twenty-five who was being courted by his own grandson. Varner remains a cheerful and virtually invulnerable character whose status in Yoknapatawpha County continues admirably into old age.

Veen, Van. *Ada.* Vladimir Nabokov. 1969.

Van Veen is an extremely intelligent and lusty man who, at the age of fourteen, falls passionately in love with his half-sister Ada, a coquettish twelve-year-old genius. He becomes enamored of her during a summer visit to Ardis, Ada's parents' country estate. At first Ada resists Van's amorous entreaties, preferring to bury herself in botany, but one night while everyone has left the house to watch a nearby fire, she succumbs to the incestuous temptation and the two youngsters initiate their affair.

Van and Ada's desire for each other is insatiable. They spend the remaining portion of Van's stay stealing away from the family for one tryst after another while Lucette, Ada's younger sister, tries her best to destroy the affair.

Van leaves Ardis to attend prep school, but his relationship with Ada continues through a series of coded letters. During the separation Van begins performing as Mascodagama, a circus character that stands on his head and walks on his hands. His act travels throughout the world to wide critical acclaim.

Van revisits Ardis, and the love between him and Ada is quickly rekindled despite the fact that both of them have had affairs during their separation. Lucette, who has begun to blossom into a beautiful girl, now poses a serious threat to the secrecy of Van and Ada's affair. They try to assuage her jealousy by allowing her to join in one of their meadowy romps. The girls' mother, Marina, suspects that Lucette has a crush on Van and warns him to be careful around her since she is vulnerable to the perils of love. Van, relieved that his affair with Ada has remained secret, promises that he will keep a mature distance from Lucette.

On his way back to school Van gets wounded in a gun duel. While recovering he has an affair with the flirtatious Cordula de Prey, a former schoolmate of Ada's. The affair leaves Van unfulfilled and only reminds him of his passion for Ada. In order to keep his mind off the difficulties of that affair, he develops an interest in philosophy. For several years he passes from one educational institute to another writing and developing his theories on place and time.

During this time Van is visited by Lucette, who declares her love for him. She also tells him of her own affair with

Ada during his absence. Despite his sexual appetite, Van declines her amorous offer, preferring not to complicate matters further. But some time later, after an evening of heavy drinking and against his better judgement, Van enjoys a brief night of passion with Ada and Lucette. This onetime frolic is rather distasteful to Van but leaves Lucette more obsessed with her cousin.

Finally, Van's affair with Ada is accidentally discovered by Demon, their father, when he visits Van's apartment unannounced. He forbids his son to continue the romance. Van has little choice but to return to his philosophical pursuits while Ada marries one of her many suitors, Andrey Vinelander, and becomes an actress.

Van manages to maintain a connection to Ada by becoming a screenwriter for the movies in which Ada now stars. At one point Van meets Lucette coincidentally, and she restates her desire for him. With some hesitation he reinforces his refusal. They meet a second time, again by chance, and Van remains firm. Lucette is devastated by the rejection and drowns herself.

No longer able to resist his one romantic compulsion, Van resolves to visit Ada. After a formal evening with her husband he steals a private moment with her, and they start their affair anew. For several years they continue to see each other in secrecy while Andrey grows ill. After Andrey dies, Van and Ada decide to spend the rest of their lives together.

Venner, Elsie. *Elsie Venner: A Romance of Destiny.* Oliver Wendell Holmes. 1892.

Elsie Venner is a mysterious and mesmerizing young woman whose bizarre behavior causes rumors that she is cursed with an unholy affiliation with evil. Elsie's mother, who had been bitten by a snake while pregnant, swooned when she first saw the birthmark that encircles the girl's neck, a physical omen bespeaking her unnerving strangeness. She eventually conceals this mark under a gold necklace that she never removes. Left motherless as an infant, Elsie is taken care of by her kindly father who is frankly terrified by her peculiar personality. The strength of her character is overpowering; he finds that although he can sometimes influence his daughter, she defies his efforts to govern her wild activities. Left to her own devices, Elsie displays her strong attraction to the wilderness, taking dangerous midnight rambles in such terrifying places as Dead Man's Hollow and Rattlesnake Ledge, where other people do not dare venture. Although her conduct is so deviant that many of the inhabitants of her hometown, Rockland, feel that she should be incarcerated in an asylum, she keeps to herself and harms no one so that she is allowed to indulge her strange personality without restraint.

Elsie's singular beauty causes her to be the object of considerable attention, but her cold, piercing eyes so frighten people that she is surrounded by an ominous circle of isolation. Dominated by animal instincts, she collects rare manifestations of nature such as crows' nests, the eggs of exotic birds, and unusual flowers and mosses from obscure locations known only to herself. Although many people think Elsie is incapable of falling in love, she develops an interest in one of her schoolteachers, Bernard Langdon, and attempts to express her affection by placing a rare wildflower in his copy of the *Aeneid*. Curious to discover where she could possibly have found such an uncommon species of flower, Bernard ventures onto Rattlesnake Ledge. Just as he confronts a viper that is on the verge of biting him with its deadly fangs, Elsie appears and causes the paralyzing charm of the snake's eyes to dissolve. Luckily for him, Elsie possesses strange powers that include the ability to enchant reptiles as well as people. But these uncanny powers preempt her natural affections so that she is more at home in the wilderness than in the company of those with whom she might share love.

As a child Elsie lashed out and bit her cousin, Dick Venner, when he made the mistake of provoking her. Realizing that he must separate the two to avoid further violence, Elsie's father sent Dick away, but he returns to Rockland as an adult and begins to entertain mercenary hopes of marrying her in order to seize her inheritance. But Dick makes the mistake of attempting to murder Bernard Langdon because of Elsie's interest in the schoolteacher; when his attempt is unsuccessful, he is again forced to leave Rockland.

Thus freed of her cousin's undesirable attentions, Elsie approaches Langdon and desperately requests that he devote his love to her, only to learn that although he cares for her as a brother, he cannot offer her romantic affection. Returning home, Elsie takes to her bed, begins to languish, and ultimately develops a fever. Growing weaker and weaker due to an illness that the doctor cannot identify, her personality begins to undergo changes and she begins to act more and more like her gentle, departed mother. When informed of this resemblance, Elsie weeps at the thought of the mother she never knew. Her father is convinced that these tears are a sign of redemption and exorcism of the spirit of evil that has possessed her. On her deathbed Elsie presents Langdon with a bracelet as a parting gift. When Elsie dies, the golden necklace is removed from her neck, and her loved ones discover that her ominous birthmark has miraculously disappeared.

Vere, Captain Edward Fairfax. *Billy Budd, Sailor (An Inside Narrative).* Herman Melville. 1924.

Captain Edward Fairfax Vere, the commander of the warship *Bellipotent*, is an honest, fair-minded, and disciplined officer with an impeccable record of service in the United States Navy. An unusually learned and aristocratic man, he is inclined at times to a certain dreaminess, which has earned him the name "Starry Vere" among his shipmates. Vere's military career has been enhanced by his moral sensibility; in 1797, a year of violence and unrest on English ships, he commands a singular respect and admiration from his subordinates. But when BILLY BUDD, a foretopman, unintentionally murders JOHN CLAGGART, the master-at-arms, in his presence, Vere exacts from the young sailor a justice that, while in keeping with military regulations, ill accords with his passion for virtue.

Because he has evolved a liking for Billy, whose cheerful manner and winsome good looks make him a favorite among the crew, Vere is taken aback when Claggart approaches him on the quarterdeck and accuses Billy of plotting a mutiny. Vere, an acute judge of character, is vaguely repelled by Claggart, who couches his complaint in silvery, obsequious tones. Recognizing immediately the gravity and delicacy of this situation, and sensing the other crewmen looking on, Vere sends for Billy Budd and retreats with Claggart to his cabin.

In their private meeting below, Billy, who stutters in moments of extreme emotion, is incensed by Claggart's accusations. Vere, registering the contrast between Billy's inarticulate outrage and Claggart's reptilian manipulations, commands Billy to defend himself, to speak. But he cannot. Instead, Billy fells the master-at-arms with a single blow to the head.

With Claggart dead, Vere realizes he will no longer be able to contain the incident. Rather than wait for the admiralty to decide this unprecedented case, he summons the other officers and arranges for Billy to be tried aboard ship. At this crucial moment he allows the paternal feelings he harbors for the young man to be superseded by his sense of duty and perhaps, the narrator intimates, by ambition. Nevertheless, when Billy testifies to his own innocence, Vere cannot refrain from exclaiming, "I believe you, my man!" As the court-martial proceeds, he gazes abstractedly out the porthole, weighing the expediencies of the case, knowing that Billy must die.

Vere himself brings the court's decision—death by hanging—to Billy. The actual content of their interview remains undisclosed, but the narrator speculates that Vere's demeanor would have been gentle, compassionate, and fatherly. When he leaves the stateroom, his expression betrays "the agony of the strong"—an agony unknown to innocents like Billy.

At Billy's hanging, Vere stands rigidly at attention. Billy's last words as he steps up to the scaffold are "God bless Captain Vere!"—a statement that receives a sympathetic echo from the men gathered on the deck below. During this extraordinary exchange, Vere's countenance remains dutifully fixed.

Vere's subsequent history is brief. On the return voyage, the *Bellipotent* does battle with the *Athée*, and he is fatally wounded by an enemy musket. His dying words—mur- mured, his attendant claims, without remorse—are "Billy Budd, Billy Budd."

Verver, Adam. *The Golden Bowl.* Henry James. 1909.

Adam Verver is an American collector of art and antiques who settles in Europe after the death of his wife. A quiet man given to introspection, Verver frequently finds himself wondering how different his existence might be if he had not been liberated by her death. While she was alive he restricted his purchases to the kind of frilly, decorative curiosities that pleased her most, and he is convinced that if she had lived, his own artistic sensibilities would never have had a chance to develop. He thinks of his married years as the era of darkness, which fortunately gave way to these last years of light.

Mr. Verver now cultivates a "passion for perfection" and selects art according to a strict ideal. As the crowning touch to a brilliant career, he plans to open a magnificent museum in America, a sort of temple for artistic treasures. Very little else concerns him outside his efforts to refine his collection. He only feels threatened by the "formidable" women who intrude on him, hoping for marriage proposals. Verver's sole concern outside of art is the happiness of his daughter MAGGIE. After his wife's death, Maggie, at only ten, becomes his European traveling companion and an enthusiastic confidante who delights in his fantastic plans.

Maggie eventually marries PRINCE AMERIGO, an elegant young Italian, who meets Verver's standards of aesthetic perfection. Verver is troubled by the thought that his own solitude may cause Maggie to worry now that they cannot be together as before. It is on Maggie's advice that he invites CHARLOTTE STANT, a school friend she deeply admires, to spend time at his London home, Portland Place. While Maggie and the Prince are away, Verver and Charlotte settle into a pleasant domestic existence together, with the common task of watching over Maggie's son, the Principino. Although Verver never claims to be in love with Charlotte, he asks her to marry him on the basis of their "beautiful days" together. Their decision to marry depends largely on the Prince's consent and on Maggie's encouragement.

Verver never succeeds in transferring his affection or his allegiance from Maggie to his young wife. Instead of bringing Maggie and her husband closer together, the Principino strengthens the bond between her and her father. Perhaps partly because of Verver's indifference to her, Charlotte continues an affair with the Prince that she had begun long before his marriage to Maggie. If Verver suspects anything, he permits the intrigue to continue without protest. His decision to return to America is apparently not caused by the suspicious relationship between Charlotte and the Prince but rather in response to a change in Maggie. She insists that she has sacrificed her father, that his marriage was a means of fulfilling her desires, not his. Verver assures her that if she has continued to believe in him, then he has not been sacrificed. In tears, Maggie tells her generous father that she believes in him more than in anyone else.

Charlotte later tells Maggie it is her desire to begin a new life in America that causes their move, but it is also an agreement between Maggie and her father. Maggie's happiness depends on Charlotte's departure. They close this era of their lives on a surprising note: on the assertion of Charlotte's value and the success of Verver's marriage. In speaking these words, Maggie and her father find the courage to part.

Verver, Maggie. *The Golden Bowl.* Henry James. 1909.

Maggie Verver, the pampered and isolated daughter of an American millionaire, confronts her husband's infidelity with profound dignity and patience. Maggie's close friend, FANNY ASSINGHAM, characterizes her as a being "outside of ugly things," a being whose innocence of evil is proof of her absolute purity. Faced with a grotesque and potentially explosive situation, Maggie acts with surprising tact and clarity of thought to alleviate a crisis in her own life and in the lives of her cultivated friends.

The motives for Maggie's heroic behavior are external: She acts out of love for her father, ADAM VERVER, and for her husband, PRINCE AMERIGO. Her mother died when she was only ten years old, and afterward an unusual camaraderie develops between her and her father.

The Ververs have left their home in America in order to travel throughout Europe together. Over late dinners in fine restaurants in France and Italy, they exchange plans and discoveries. Mr. Verver has made his fortune collecting art and antiques, and Maggie is therefore privileged to see Europe through the eyes of a connoisseur. In spite of his enormous professional and financial success, however, Maggie feels a desire to protect her father. She feels his generosity blinds him to the fact that others take advantage of him.

Maggie's adventurous, innocent years with her father are brought to an end when Fanny Assingham introduces her to Prince Amerigo. Normally cautious and reserved, Maggie allows herself to fall desperately in love with him. She is encouraged by her father's enthusiastic approval. To Adam Verver, the Prince is a rare and exquisite work of art. For the Prince, whose family has become impoverished in recent generations, the marriage with Maggie allows for a suitably refined and extravagant existence.

On the eve of their marriage, a beloved old school friend, CHARLOTTE STANT, appears in London. Concerned about Charlotte's unstable existence—for she is without family and a permanent home—Maggie asks her father to invite Charlotte into his house, Portland Place, for an extended visit. During a vacation in Paris with the Prince, Maggie receives a letter announcing her father's intention

to marry Charlotte; she promptly sends word of her approval.

The two married couples settle down to a life as neighbors in London. It is a situation of almost suffocating intimacy. Maggie is inexplicably alienated from her husband, and her strongest relationship is still with her father. Even the birth of her son, the Principino, seems to draw her closer to her father than to the Prince. Maggie lives in quiet torment, suspecting a terrible reason for the Prince's distance from her and for the odd configuration of relationships among the four.

As she observes Charlotte and the Prince together, it becomes apparent to Maggie that their friendship predated both marriages and shows signs of having been too intimate for any explanation to their current spouses. Her anxiety, which she has kept carefully under control, flares up after Charlotte and the Prince spend a day alone together at a friend's home in Matcham.

Maggie stumbles on evidence of their liaison while strolling through London in search of a birthday gift for her father. In a Bloomsbury antique shop she discovers a marvelous golden bowl, which she agrees to purchase for a high price. The shopkeeper's guilt for having overcharged her prompts him to visit Maggie, and at her home his attention is caught by pictures of Charlotte and the Prince. They had also been in his shop; the conversation that he recalls proves to Maggie that they were lovers. In desperation, Maggie summons Fanny to hear the story, and on an impulse Fanny smashes the bowl on the floor. The Prince appears at the instant she commits this violent act. Confronting the Prince with uncharacteristic directness, Maggie demands the truth about his affair.

Afterward, Maggie's pride and compassion tell her that, regardless of what she has done, Charlotte must continue to appear "magnificent" in her father's eyes and in her own. She accepts with dignity Charlotte's accusation that Maggie loathes her marriage to her father. According to an unspoken agreement with Maggie, Adam Verver decides to take his wife to America. When father and daughter part, it is with words of praise for Charlotte and the assertion that the marriage has been a success. In the final moment of the novel, Maggie embraces the Prince with a deep sense of joy and relief. She knows she has behaved nobly toward all the characters concerned, and in so doing has won the Prince's complete attention.

Vesey, Dred. *Dred, a Tale of the Great Dismal Swamp.* Harriet Beecher Stowe. 1856.

As a child Dred Vesey listened to the preaching of his father Denmark Vesey, a free black. After Denmark's arrest and execution for his part in an attempted rebellion, Dred kept his father's Bible and also kept alive his dream of freedom for all blacks. As he grew into a deeply religious and physically powerful young man, no master could control him or crush that dream. The only overseer who tried to discipline Dred was killed in one blow by the desperate slave. After committing this murder, Dred fled to the sanctuary of the Great Dismal Swamp.

Dred first lives alone in the swamp, with only his Bible and his God for company. Eventually, however, he is able to gather followers about him. An escaping slave he saves from the fugitive-tracking dogs becomes his wife. Other blacks, longing for freedom, join Dred in the cultivated area he has carved out in the midst of the dreary swamp. Blacks on surrounding plantations know about and assist this tiny community because they know that Dred would help them in their time of need.

One day Dred approaches HARRY GORDON on the outskirts of the swamp. Harry, the slave and half-brother of the lovely plantation owner NINA GORDON, is troubled because Nina's wastrel brother Tom has designs on Harry's wife Lisette. Dred advises Harry to flee Nina's plantation and the threat to his and Lisette's happiness that Tom represents. Loyal to his owner, Harry refuses. Dred can only pity him and warn him of the judgment that he believes will be rendered against the whites.

Later, Dred interrupts a well-attended camp meeting with his own preaching. After white ministers finish their attempts to find biblical justification for slavery, Dred offers his own interpretation. Keeping himself hidden but with his voice booming out into the wilderness, Dred damns them for their hypocrisy and perversion of the Gospel. His confused but captivated listeners hear his warning that God will no longer abide their buying and selling of human flesh, rape of black women, and destruction of black families.

When the threat to his own marriage becomes more than he can bear, Harry Gordon finally takes Dred's advice and flees into the swamp with Lisette. Dred welcomes Harry and Lisette, just as he welcomes all fugitives. His condemnation of whites is not indiscriminate; Dred even gives assistance to EDWARD CLAYTON, a planter whose growing anti-slavery sentiments have made him unpopular among the other whites. When Clayton is beaten senseless by Tom Gordon, Dred brings Clayton to his community and assists in his recovery. Clayton listens with interest to Dred's prophecy but advises him not to attempt God's work with human hands.

Despite this advice, Dred's resolve to lead a rebellion is unshaken. He holds secret meetings with the blacks in his community and in the surrounding plantations in order to plan a successful rebellion. A slave, Aunt Milly, is able to persuade Dred to postpone his uprising until he receives a clear sign from God, but it seems that the tide of rebellion cannot be stemmed. While attempting to save the life of another slave, Dred is mortally wounded by slave hunters. Before he can lead the rebellion he seemed destined to raise, Dred dies, surrounded by his followers, in the Great Dismal Swamp.

Vetch, Fleda. *The Spoils of Poynton.* Henry James. 1897.

Fleda Vetch is plain and penniless, but she has one great asset: her fine and discriminating mind. She is discreet and very sensitive, which endears her to those closest to her, but she is also highly ethical. Ironically, her high ethical standards keep Fleda from aggressively pursuing what she desires, thereby causing her to lose both the man she loves and the home she deserves to her less scrupulous rival.

Fleda has befriended the recently widowed ADELA GERETH, with whom she has many sympathies, the greatest of which is their mutually exquisite taste. In accordance with English law, Mrs. Gereth must now relinquish control of Poynton, her deceased husband's small but resplendent estate, to her son OWEN GERETH, leaving her to spend her final years at a modest dower house. But Mrs. Gereth is obstinate and will not surrender her home. Poynton is what Mrs. Gereth has made it, for she dedicated her entire married life, through judicious investment of her husband's income, to making Poynton a showcase of beauty and taste. Thus Poynton, thought a harmonious collection of the finest furniture, paintings, tapestries, and artifacts from around the world, is much more than an assemblage of "spoils"—it is the record and the emblem of Mrs. Gereth's entire life.

Mrs. Gereth reveres her home, and Fleda, with her innate sense of taste, shares Mrs. Gereth's devout appreciation of Poynton. Recognizing Fleda's appreciation, Mrs. Gereth resolves to orchestrate a marriage between the penniless Fleda and her son Owen, knowing that her fellow aesthete will allow her to retain at least nominal proprietorship of Poynton.

But Owen is captivated by the beautiful but philistine Mona Brigstock, to whom he soon becomes engaged. Mona does not appreciate Poynton, but she covets it because it will be hers by right as Owen's wife. Mrs. Gereth, knowing that this marriage will result in her banishment from Poynton, brusquely and openly expresses her loathing of Mona, while Fleda, who is secretly in love with the insipid but boyishly charming Owen, is crestfallen. Because Owen is bound by the honor of his pledge to Mona, the conscientious Fleda will not risk the compromise of his honor by making her feelings known to him, although she senses that he is drawn to her.

Owen is indeed drawn to Fleda, who is sympathetic to Owen's anguish over having to oust his mother from Poynton. Owen appeals to Fleda to arbitrate, recognizing that her tact and sensitivity can peaceably effect the removal of Mrs. Gereth from Poynton to Ricks, her dower house. Fleda, who is touched by Owen's anguish—and it is precisely for this anguish that she loves him—agrees to arbitrate.

Mrs. Gereth does relent and moves to Ricks, but she takes with her all the priceless artifacts of Poynton, much to the horror of Fleda. The avaricious Mona, realizing that Poynton has in effect been taken away from her, delays her marriage to Owen until he can muster the will to force his mother to restore the estate. Mrs. Gereth sees her chance: If she can withhold the "spoils" long enough, then Mona will cease to be a threat altogether. Owen grows more openly fond of Fleda, the sole person sympathetic to his quandary. He confesses to Fleda that his feelings for Mona have changed, and he cryptically entreats Fleda to "save" him. In the meantime, the shrewd Mrs. Gereth recognizes Fleda's secret love for Owen, and she implores Fleda to reveal this love to him, knowing that her insipid son will be utterly captivated by her sensitive charm. But Fleda, ever honor-bound, will not consent to marry him, nor will she openly declare her affection for him until he has officially broken his engagement to Mona. And although her secret love has been discovered by Mrs. Gereth, Fleda continues to guard a more precious secret—that of Owen's changed feelings for Mona—because she knows that, in the hands of the ruthless Mrs. Gereth, this secret will wreak havoc on his life and honor.

As time passes it becomes increasingly apparent that Owen's marriage to Mona will not occur, so Mrs. Gereth, sure that her son will soon turn to Fleda, returns the "spoils" to Poynton. Sure of Owen's feelings for her, Fleda finally gives Owen a glimpse of her feelings for him, and, at Fleda's behest, Owen goes off to officially terminate his engagement to Mona. But Mona, who has learned of Poynton's restoration, seduces Owen into marrying her.

Thus defeated, Fleda and Mrs. Gereth resign themselves to living together at Ricks, which, although meager, possesses a simple charm. Fleda senses a poignancy about this charm, and she suggests to Mrs. Gereth that perhaps they will be quietly happy together at Ricks. Fleda receives a letter from Owen that, as an oblique apology for his failure of nerve in their relationship, fervently asks her to select one treasure from Poynton as a token of his esteem. So while Owen and Mona are on an extended vacation, Fleda journeys to Poynton to collect her treasure. Upon arrival, however, Fleda's anguish is renewed as she witnesses Poynton, struck by an accidental fire, burn to the ground.

Victor, Inez Christian. *Democracy.* Joan Didion. 1984.

Inez Christian Victor, the beautiful and enigmatic subject of this novel, is a remote but compelling figure whose life has been shaped by constant media exposure. After growing up in a wealthy family in Hawaii, Inez marries Senator Harry Victor and has twins, a son and daughter, Adlai and Jessie. To all outward appearances she leads a storybook existence. As the novel unfolds it becomes clear, however, that her happiness has been irrevocably marred not only by family tragedy but by the obliteration of self that results from living too long in the public eye.

The novel's narrator, a journalist named Joan Didion, tries to piece together Inez's history from newspaper clip-

pings, old film reels, and remembered conversations. Inez's mother leaves the family when Inez is young and boards an ocean liner bound for the American continent. At her seventeenth birthday party, Inez meets Jack Lovett, an older married man. She is wearing a white dress and dark glasses because she has spent the day crying in her room. She seems about to remove her sunglasses but runs a hand through her hair instead, loosening a gardenia that has been pinned there. Inez smiles at Jack; the flower falls to the ground.

Inez continues to meet Jack clandestinely for several months, without any notion of commitment, before attending college on the East Coast. There she meets Harry Victor, an ambitious young activist and politician, becomes pregnant, and walks out of her dance class to marry him one Tuesday afternoon. Two months later she miscarries.

As Inez follows Harry in his rise to power, she acquires all the habits and accoutrements of a conventional politician's wife. She collects recipes, attends luncheons for charity, and is shown bathing the children or playing with the family dog in photographs for glossy magazines. Yet she also maintains a certain aloofness, an apparent indifference, which seems to separate her from these images.

Inez runs into Jack now and then, at airports and in hotels all over the world. She never expects to see him and never spends a moment alone with him but takes a keen pleasure in secretly thinking about him and in knowing that he will occasionally appear. For instance, when Inez, the children, Harry, and his entourage—all oblivious of the explosive political situation—arrive in Jakarta, Indonesia, in 1969, Jack meets them at the airport and arranges for them to be evacuated to a bungalow in the country. In one of the few moments that Inez is able to remember, she and Jack are standing together watching the mists waft down from the hills.

Jack appears again at the Honolulu airport in 1975 as Inez is disembarking from her plane. She has received news that her sister Janet has been shot by their deranged father, Paul Christian. As the narrator looks on, Inez— now forty, an age "when it is still possible to look very good at certain times of the day"—crushes her lei on the tarmac in the rain.

As her sister lies dying, Inez recalls that Janet had telephoned to ask whether or not she remembered their mother crying at Janet's wedding. Inez thinks of how she had said she did not when in fact she did. When Jack walks into the living room of the family house and asks her to leave with him, she wordlessly complies.

Inez and Jack spend a few months together traveling until he dies suddenly in the swimming pool at a Jakarta hotel. She flies with the body back to Honolulu and insists that he be buried in a little military graveyard near a jacaranda tree whose blossoms will just reach the headstone when they fall. When the narrator last sees her, Inez has settled in Kuala Lumpur, Malaysia, to work in the administration of the surrounding refugee camps. She claims that she will not return to the United States until the last refugee has been dispatched. Asked by one of Harry's friends why she chose this particular job in this particular place, Inez replies simply, "Colors, moisture, heat, enough blue in the air."

Viner, Sophy. *The Reef.* Edith Wharton. 1912.

Sophy Viner relinquishes an extraordinary chance for a secure life when a past lover reappears to thwart her upcoming marriage. The novel opens with a chance meeting between Sophy, who is alone and without much money, and GEORGE DARROW, a slight acquaintance who is kind enough to accompany her to Paris. Sophy pays dearly for this brief interlude of happiness when Darrow arrives later at the home where she is employed as a governess.

As a child Sophy is pushed aside by those who are supposed to care for her, and she learns very early to take care of herself. After the death of both parents, Sophy's overworked guardian places her in a New York boarding school. Her older sister Laura is too occupied with marrying and remarrying to be concerned with Sophy. When the guardian has a sudden illness and his personal life collapses, Sophy's small inheritance is lost in the confusion. She regards this as liberating, however, and immediately sets off to find work. She leaves her first position as a governess because of the family valet's relentless advances. She is then invited by a school friend, Mamie Hoke, to accompany her and her parents to Europe. The tour is cut short when Mamie elopes with a matinee idol, and Sophy retreats to the home of some American friends in Paris, the Farlows.

Unaware of the disservice they are doing her, the Farlows have Sophy placed as a secretary in the Chelsea home of the infamous Mrs. Murrett. Mrs. Murrett has a salon of sorts, and Sophy is able to tolerate the position by observing the parade of figures through the house. Although Sophy endures Mrs. Murrett's tirades for five years, longer than any of her other employees, her appointment there inevitably ends in an argument. Mrs. Murrett withholds Sophy's salary for the final month, and the young woman departs with only the one trunk containing all her possessions. Then, while she is waiting in the pouring rain for the boat that is to take her to Paris, Sophy discovers her trunk has been lost.

At this moment George Darrow, whom Sophy recognizes from Mrs. Murrett's, sees her standing helplessly with an inside-out umbrella and guides her to a sheltered corner. Because of the storm, the boat is delayed for two hours, and Sophy has time to explain her circumstances to Darrow. She is going to Paris to become an actress, she says, and she plans to contact her friends the Farlows as soon as she arrives. Out of concern for her, Darrow agrees to escort Sophy to Paris. When they arrive at the Farlows' door, they find that her friends moved out of Paris the week before and their letter had not yet reached Mrs. Murrett's.

Because Sophy appears to be stranded, Darrow offers to amuse her for a day until the Farlows can be contacted. He takes her to the theater, and she can hardly believe her good fortune. The trip to the Farlows' is repeatedly deferred, and Darrow accompanies Sophy to other theater performances, dinner, and museums. They return to adjoining hotel rooms. When Darrow kisses her, Sophy returns his passion although she senses that his thoughts are with someone else. The innocent holiday becomes an affair, and Sophy is convinced she has fallen in love with Darrow.

When they part and Sophy finally contacts the Farlows, they offer her a new position as a governess for nine-year-old Effie Leath who resides with her widowed mother and stepbrother in an elegant French country home called Givre. After working there for five months, Sophy becomes involved with Owen, Effie's stepbrother, who, like Sophy, is in his early twenties. His offer of marriage is a great promise for a secure life. Shortly before the marriage is announced, however, George Darrow arrives at Givre to visit the widow ANNA SUMMERS LEATH, to whom he is engaged.

Darrow, whose security is also threatened, tries to persuade Sophy that the marriage would be unwise. Sophy is extremely distraught and, after several conversations with Darrow, concludes that she still loves him and therefore cannot marry Owen. Her sudden decision to leave arouses Anna's suspicions, and she questions Sophy, who dissolves into tears and confesses. When the fact of their affair is revealed, Darrow is dismissed from Givre. Several days later, in Paris, Sophy visits Anna and tries to persuade her to accept Darrow. When Anna later goes to the apartment of Sophy's sister to tell Sophy that she will not accept him, the young woman has already left Paris, accompanying Mrs. Murrett to India.

The Virginian. *The Virginian: A Horseman of the Plains.* Owen Wister. 1902.

The Virginian personifies the innate nobility of the rare, honest man who shines in rough surroundings and brings the spirit of the first Virginia settlers westward to the cattle ranches of Wyoming and the empty reaches of the Great Plains.

The Virginian left his family and his home state when he was fourteen. For ten years he "had a look at the country," visiting the South, the Southwest, the Far West, and the Plains. At twenty-four he is a cowboy on Judge Henry's Sunk Creek Ranch and is sent on a four-day ride to Medicine Bow, Wyoming, to pick up an eastern visitor at the nearest train station. Beyond offering the usual diverting flirtations and practical jokes, his trip is eventful in three respects. First, Judge Henry's eastern visitor, a young "tenderfoot," glimpses the Virginian roping a horse as his train pulls in and is hooked himself, becoming the novel's narrator and the Virginian's devout admirer. Second, the sore loser whom the Virginian beats at cards, a murderous cattle thief named Trampas, becomes his sworn enemy, a formidable antagonist in the future. And third, the schoolmarm whom the Virginian hears Bear Creek is "taking steps" to acquire and who is introduced to his kin, MARY "MOLLY" STARK of Bennington, Vermont, is the woman he will later love and marry.

The hero periodically plays "nurse" to the tenderfoot narrator by teaching him the roving ways of the West. The Virginian naturally excels in all things. He shows his excellence, for example, when he rescues the arriving Molly Stark from a runaway stagecoach. He is smitten at once. Through the long years of courtship that follow, the Virginian tries to appease the independent-minded schoolteacher by educating himself as he takes care of Judge Henry's far-flung cattle interests. He alternately courts high culture, devouring her collection of literary greats, and low culture, impressing the cowboys under him with his resourcefulness and his knack for tall tales.

When the Virginian, deserted by a sadistic companion, is wounded by Indians, Molly Stark finds him and nurses him to health, and she finally accepts his marriage proposal. During their engagement he suffers still further trials. After chasing a gang of cattle thieves, Trampas included, one of the apprehended rustlers whom he must hang (according to the unwritten code of the West) turns out to be an old friend lately gone astray. The Virginian does his duty, although his role as hangman unsettles Molly who is already at odds with her proper New England family. Trampas remains at large, and it is not until the eve of the Virginian's wedding in Medicine Bow that things come to a crisis. The Virginian is goaded into a shootout with Trampas, and Molly breaks their engagement. But when the Virginian kills Trampas, Molly, even in her horror, cannot resist him, and the two are married. Ahead lies an edenic mountain honeymoon and a palliative trip to Vermont to meet the Starks. As always, the Virginian excels: The Starks see that he is handsome, polite, manly, and sensible enough to possess coal-rich property back home in Wyoming and provide for his family's future.

Vitelli, Popeye. *Sanctuary; Requiem for a Nun.* William Faulkner. 1931; 1951.

The son of a professional strikebreaker and a department store clerk, Popeye Vitelli, hindered by congenital syphilis, is a sickly problem child who does not begin walking and talking until the age of four. While still a child he almost burns to death after his demented grandmother sets fire to their house. Later he cuts up two love-birds with scissors and runs away from home. For this cruel act he spends five years in a correctional facility for children. Such sadistic behavior foreshadows Popeye's capacity for violence.

As an adult Popeye supports his deviant life-style by participating in a bootlegging ring. The ring operates out of a dilapidated mansion called Old Frenchman's Place, near the town of Jefferson, Mississippi. When GOWAN STEVENS, a drunken young graduate of the University of Virginia, brings the seventeen-year-old University of Mississippi student TEMPLE DRAKE to Old Frenchman's Place to purchase alcohol, Popeye becomes sexually interested in the young woman. Eventually, Popeye discovers Temple hiding in a corn crib to avoid the bootleggers' sexual advances. In order to gain access to her, he attacks the dimwitted man named Tommy who has taken it upon himself to guard Temple, and kills him. Popeye then proceeds to brutally rape Temple with a corn cob, a prop that he must wield because he has an underdeveloped penis. He then transports Temple to a Memphis whorehouse, run by Reba Rivers, where he locks her in a room as if she were chattel.

In order to spice up his sex life, Popeye brings a young man named Alabama Red to Reba's house of prostitution. Popeye takes voyeuristic pleasure in watching Alabama Red ravish Temple, and makes whinnying noises that signal his arousal. When he finds out that Temple has taken the initiative to rent a hotel room so that she and Red can have sex alone without being subjected to Popeye's agitated gaze, he murders Red for his audacity.

Popeye then flees, and en route to Pensacola, Florida, for his annual visit to his mother (who thinks he is a night clerk in a Memphis hotel), he is unjustly arrested in Birmingham for the murder of a policeman in a small Alabama town. Meanwhile, his fellow bootlegger Lee Goodwin is tried and convicted for the murder of Tommy. When Temple Drake lies in court in order to suppress the fact that she has not only been raped but has also been a prostitute, Lee is lynched for the crimes Popeye committed. Having been tried and sentenced to death by hanging for the murder of the policeman, an indifferent Popeye refuses the representation of a Memphis lawyer who wants to appeal the case. His last request before execution is that the sheriff fix his hair.

Vogel, Jesse. *Wonderland.* Joyce Carol Oates. 1971.

This novel tells the bizarre life story of Dr. Jesse Vogel, a successful surgeon. Jesse's life changes forever when his father, a poor garage owner with the last name Harte, kills Jesse's brother, sisters, and pregnant mother, and then shoots the escaping Jesse in the shoulder before turning the gun on himself. At fourteen Jesse Harte finds himself an orphan, the only survivor of a brutal massacre. Throughout the rest of his life he wanders away from this tragedy and into a macabre, modern-day "wonderland."

After a stay in the hospital, Jesse is shuttled from the farm of his cold-hearted grandfather, to the home of well-meaning relatives, to the Niagara County Home for Boys. Finally, he is adopted by the enormous DR. KARL PEDERSEN, a famous physician who is fascinated by the tragedy of the boy's life, and taken to live at the beautiful Pedersen home in Lockport, New York.

In Lockport, Jesse Pedersen does his best to fit into his new family and to live up to the great expectations of Dr. Pedersen. Like Pedersen's other children, the musically gifted Frederich and the mathematically prodigious Hilda, Jesse must report each evening at dinner on the progress he has made in his quest for perfection. Destined to be a great doctor, according to Dr. Pedersen, Jesse is required to recite pages from the science books he studies. Mealtimes are central to the Pedersen household, and the family consumes vast amounts of food. All the Pedersens are obese, and before long Jesse also begins to put on weight.

Jesse idolizes the great Dr. Pedersen, whose diagnostic clinic has gained him worldwide respect, and he feels lucky to be part of such a remarkable family. But in the years that follow, the doctor's maniacal desire for absolute control over those around him begins to have a devastating effect on the members of the family. Grossly obese Hilda suffers a breakdown at a demonstration of her mathematical ability when she is unable to compete with an idiot savant. And one day Mrs. Pedersen locks herself in the bathroom and passes out in an alcoholic stupor. As Jesse witnesses these events and tries to help his sister and mother, he begins to wonder if all the Pedersens are "freaks." Finally, when a pathetically neurotic Mrs. Pedersen decides to leave her husband, Jesse is enlisted to help her. He checks her into a hotel, and together they eat and eat. But while Jesse is out getting more food, Dr. Pedersen finds his wife, forces her to return home with him, and leaves a note disowning Jesse.

Orphaned once again, Jesse begins school at the University of Michigan and changes his last name to Vogel, after Mrs. Pedersen's kindly father. After several years of poverty and self-sacrifice, he finds himself a bleary-eyed medical student, one whose seriousness and intelligence have gained him recognition. He is befriended by Talbot "Trick" Monk, a popular young doctor with an unsettling sense of humor. When Jesse becomes engaged to Helene Cady, the daughter of a brilliant neurochemist, Trick insists he is happy for the couple, but later he confesses his love for Helene. When he takes them out to dinner, Trick reveals his frighteningly pathological nature with his story of cooking and eating part of a female cadaver. Soon after, Trick vanishes.

In the years following, Jesse's life changes dramatically. Outwardly he appears to have achieved enviable success.

After the birth of his second daughter, Jesse inherits a small fortune from his adopted grandfather Vogel, and his dedication gains him great respect in the medical world. But Jesse is not happy; his marriage is crumbling, and he has fallen obsessively in love with a mysterious woman who shuttles between lovers and once asks Jesse to perform an abortion on her.

Jesse's obsession for the woman, Reva Denk, ends only when he turns his attention to the search for his runaway teenage daughter Shelly. Jesse tracks Shelly through the enigmatic letters she sends him and at one point discovers that she has met Monk, now a drug-addicted radical poet. Finally, Jesse finds Shelley, nearly dead from drug abuse and possibly hepatitis, in a house in Toronto. Jesse gives her addict boyfriend money to allow him to take her away. Crazed with grief, he leads her to a waterfront and takes her aboard a small boat. The novel ends as a police marine cruiser picks up the boat near dawn.

Volkbein, Felix. *Nightwood.* Djuna Barnes. 1936.

Felix Volkbein is a wealthy Austrian Jewish man with a mysteriously vague background who succeeds in permanently disrupting the emotional equilibrium of his life by marrying a bizarre and destructive woman. Having inherited a baronage that he does not realize is bogus because it originated in the imagination and cunning artifice of his father, Baron Volkbein increases his fortune in the banking business thanks to his facility with numbers and his mastery of seven languages. Despite his many achievements, Felix is prone to an excruciating tendency toward self-effacing embarrassment, which he attempts to overcome by immersing himself in the close study and emulation of European aristocracy and nobility. He harbors a particularly high regard for historical figures whose magnificence he energetically romanticizes. Disqualified from military service during World War I because he is blind in one eye, Felix resides in Paris where he meets ROBIN VOTE, a strange and sensuous woman who captivates his romantic attentions and ultimately undermines his psychic well-being.

When Felix first meets Robin in the Hôtel Récamier, she is reclining luxuriantly on a bed and surrounded by myriad exotic plants that enhance her animal-like sensuality. After a brief courtship, Felix proposes marriage, and the couple embarks on a tempestuous honeymoon before eventually settling down in Paris. Early on in the marriage Felix realizes that his oddly silent and frighteningly sensual wife will not conform as he had hoped to his conception of the behavior befitting a baroness, but he persists in trying to mold her personality, much to the detriment of his peace of mind. When Robin eventually submits to Felix's desire to have a child and becomes pregnant, she becomes even more eccentric and terrifies Felix by wandering through the countryside and to other cities for as many as three days in a row. Robin finally delivers her baby in a drunken stupor, and Felix is horrified by her subsequent behavior, which includes further wandering, boozing, and even physical violence. Despite her atrocious behavior, Felix is upset when she expresses her hostility toward their young son. She deserts her family, and Felix is left to raise their child as a single parent.

Single-handedly tending to his son Guido's welfare, Baron Felix relinquishes his position at the bank. In his spare time he continues his research on noble families and begins to study religion when his son expresses a desire to pursue a religious vocation. Although Felix is very fond of Guido, he cannot help admitting that the boy is odd: At the age of ten Guido is only as tall as a normal six-year-old and is similarly intellectually impaired. Felix also notices that his son's emotional reactions are excessive and that he exhibits a penchant for ecstasy that contributes to his interest in spiritual life. Felix becomes so worried about his son's strange personality that he consults a physician, DR. MATTHEW O'CONNOR, and asks him to determine whether Guido is not in fact insane. The doctor denies this claim and attempts to assuage Felix's fears by averring that Guido's singularly eccentric character is a product of heightened rather than deficient sensibilities. Drinking heavily while being concerned about Guido, Felix conscientiously continues to raise his bizarre son as he attempts to maintain his own shaky emotional health.

Volsky, Sarah Yetta. *By the Waters of Manhattan.* Charles Reznikoff. 1930.

Sarah Yetta Volsky is born in poverty and grows up in various villages in Czarist Russia where her father moves the family around in order to find work. A peculiar girl with a desire to educate herself and all the boys, Sarah Yetta longs to improve her lot in life.

Sarah Yetta is no stranger to hardship. By the time she is twelve, she has watched her brother being beaten by a teacher until blood ran from his ear; she has seen neighbors conscripted for military service and soldiers quartered in her own home; she has nursed her father and practically run the house. Through it all her family discourages her reading, citing her bad eyes and a belief that women will neglect their housework if they read. Sarah Yetta does not listen.

Meanwhile, there is talk that the family will move to America. Although her mother is against the plan, the idea attracts Sarah Yetta and remains a remote but enticing dream, undimmed by all the hard work she invests in her family's various business enterprises. She becomes reacquainted with Saul Rubinov, a childhood neighbor, whose mother presses for a quick marriage. Sarah Yetta's father refuses to consent to the proposed matrimony, then leaves for a job away from home. Not long after his departure, Sarah Yetta has a dream of a red cloud in the shape of a lion; she is told it means that her father is dead. Her father

has indeed been struck down by influenza. More than a year after his death, Sarah Yetta leaves for America.

She arrives in New York without money but meets her father's friend. The plan is for Sarah Yetta to work in New Haven as a tailor even though she has never before worked at this trade. She eventually settles in New York, where she earns more and more money and again renews her friendship with Saul Rubinov. After a confusing conversation with Saul, which she thinks is in reference to another woman Saul is courting, Sarah Yetta discovers that Saul was actually referring to an engagement to her. This time she agrees to the marriage.

Sarah Yetta finally achieves security when she joins a clothing manufacturing firm. Although they had vowed to employ no more Jews, the firm hires Sarah Yetta when she makes improvements in their dresses. Saul soon joins the firm as well. Married at last, the two settle down in Manhattan with their newborn son EZEKIEL (RUBINOV), whom they name after Sarah Yetta's father. Thinking of the opportunities for her son, she wistfully concludes, "We are a lost generation. It is for our children to do what they can."

Von Humboldt, Fleisher. *Humboldt's Gift.* Saul Bellow. 1973.

In the 1930s, Fleisher Von Humboldt publishes his book of poetry, *Harlequin Ballads*, and gains instant fame. His success lasts only about ten years, however, due to his increasing bouts of insanity. Humboldt grows paranoid and dies in lonely poverty. Assessing his career at a later date, his "blood brother" CHARLES CITRINE concludes that Humboldt's failure was the failure America demanded of its poets. Indeed, Humboldt's inability to resist the debilitating effects of American society on the artist directly causes his downfall.

Humboldt is living in Greenwich Village when he receives a fan letter from a Fuller Brush salesman, Charlie Citrine, who is fresh from Madison, Wisconsin, and full of enthusiasm for literature. Humboldt invites him over, and they drink coffee and gin and become good friends. Later on, Humboldt marries and moves to a "country house," a weed-ridden place in "Nowhere, New Jersey." He and Charlie continue their friendship there, staying up and talking into the early hours of the morning. Humboldt gets year-long appointments for himself and Charlie at Princeton.

In their year of teaching, the two enjoy themselves talking about life and literature, and gain a reputation for their eccentric activities, such as composing a prospectus for a screenplay about an Italian cannibal named Caldofreddo. Humboldt also exerts his influence to get Charlie's play, *Von Trenck*, produced, and the play becomes a huge success. As symbols of their blood brotherhood and mutual trust, the two friends exchange blank checks made out to each other.

Unfortunately, however, as Charlie's career begins its ascent, Humboldt's begins its decline. He grows very suspicious of his wife and beats her, forcing her to abandon him. His jealousy and anger at his own lack of success cause him to become increasingly irrational, and eventually he has to be restrained and taken to a mental hospital, where he convalesces ever resentful of what he sees as his betrayal and abandonment. After his release he begins picketing outside the theater where Charlie's play is running, holding a sign that read THE AUTHOR OF THE PLAY IS A TRAITOR. He also cashes his blood brother's check for almost $7,000 and buys a car; due to his poor mental health, however, he forgets where it is parked and has to abandon it.

Humboldt never regains his full power and never fulfills what he and Charlie saw as his promise to be a great American poet. Shortly before his death, however, he writes a lucid letter to Charlie in which he apologizes for his injustice in accusing his friend and violating their blood brotherhood. And he leaves Charlie a bequest: the outline for a movie and documented proof that he and Charlie had written the story of Caldofreddo the Italian cannibal. At the time, Humboldt is living in a New York flophouse; Charlie sees him and feels that "he had death all over him." The playwright's intuition proves correct when, shortly afterward, Humboldt dies of a heart attack while he is taking out the garbage.

Von Vampton, Hinckle. *Mumbo Jumbo.* Ishmael Reed. 1972.

An ideological descendant of the Crusaders, Hinckle Von Vampton is one of the leading forces against African-American cultural expression. At the outset of the novel, panic spreads among white political and military circles over a virus called Jes Grew that is spreading throughout the United States. This "germ" causes people, especially African Americans, to revel in dance and movement, and reject their tranquil subservience to the social order.

As he notices this development, Von Vampton, an employee of the *New York Sun*, allows a banner headline to reveal that "Voodoo Generals" had surrounded U.S. Marines sent into Haiti to quell a rebellion. This headline is traced to Von Vampton who is forced to resign his post. When called in by the authorities, at the office of Hierophant 1, Von Vampton agrees to do all he can to suppress Jes Grew. He agrees to a deal that he will either rid the United States of Jes Grew in six months or kill himself.

With the aid of Black Herman, his assistant, Hinckle Von Vampton establishes a tabloid newspaper, *The Benign Monster.* The newspaper's aim is to stop, with the aid of pornography, the spread of Jes Grew, which is moving closer to Manhattan from its origin in New Orleans. After the tabloid gains strategic national publicity by being banned in Boston, Von Vampton hires the young and not-too-bright Woodrow Wilson Jefferson, a would-be poet, to write the column expressing the "Negro Point of View." Von Vampton tells Jefferson both what to think and what to write. Even so, Von Vampton alone is not very successful in suppressing Jes Grew, which spreads rapidly as his six months dwindle away.

By the terms of his deal with the anti–Jes Grew Wallflower Order, Von Vampton is responsible for the development of a Talking Android. This black figurehead will enable the whites who are in power to control the black population while ostensibly remaining at a distance. Von Vampton's sense of urgency, since his own life is at stake, is exacerbated when, after a nightmare-ridden night, he awakens to find that the Jes Grew forces have reached political strength. During a Cotton Club performance, Cab Calloway has announced his intention to run for President on the Jes Grew ticket. Not surprisingly, Von Vampton's Talking Android project is even less successful than is his house organ.

Eventually PAPA LABAS, the voodoo priest of the Mumbo Jumbo Kathedral, learns that the Jes Grew phenomenon is tied to the existence of the ancient text, the *Book of Thoth.* When it develops that this text has been destroyed, Jes Grew loses its momentum. Ironically, through none of his own efforts, Von Vampton is able to give the appearance of having forestalled Jes Grew at New York City's gates and even to have dispelled its force nationwide.

Vote, Robin. *Nightwood.* Djuna Barnes. 1937.

Robin Vote is a disturbed young woman who succeeds in destroying the lives of a series of lovers who are attracted to her primitive, almost animalistic charms. Seemingly more at home in a jungle atmosphere than in a drawing room, Robin is nevertheless able to attract the attention of relatively sophisticated suitors of both sexes. Physically, Robin sports a very tall, boylike body that betrays a smoldering sensuality of sometimes frightening intensity. A somnambulist who is also a raging alcoholic, Robin is a woman so bizarre that she defies the boundaries of eccentricity.

When Robin is about twenty years old, she meets and marries FELIX VOLKBEIN, an Austrian who has inherited a fake claim to a baronage, and they set up housekeeping in Paris. Robin's sexual drive is so overpowering that the baron soon realizes his mistake in assuming he could change her to suit his conception of how a baroness should conduct herself. When Robin gratifies her husband's desire to have children and gets pregnant, she begins to take aimless walks and sometimes disappears for several days at a time. In addition, she inexplicably converts to Catholicism, as if she knew that her monstrous, bestial soul was in need of spiritual elevation and salvation. When the drunken Robin delivers a son amid hysterical swearing and crying, she becomes even less capable of functioning normally in the world. She dislikes the role of motherhood and threatens to dash her sad little boy against the ground. Her unhappiness peaks when she slaps Felix and shouts at him that she had never wanted a child. Having made her disinclination to marriage and motherhood perfectly clear, she deserts her family and moves to the United States.

In America, Robin begins an affair with a woman named NORA FLOOD, who is notorious for having the weirdest salon in the nation. Nora entertains a variety of eccentric people, including artists, radicals, paupers, and black magic devotées. When they eventually relocate to Paris, Nora purchases the apartment of Robin's choosing, and they settle down to a tempestuous relationship characterized once again by Robin's tendency to wander from café to café, as well as her indulgence in alcoholic binges and lesbian affairs. Although Robin knows that she is endangering herself and that her strange personality acts as a magnet for catastrophe, she persists in this behavior and continues to rely on the tolerant support of Nora, who is both repulsed and fascinated by her degraded lifestyle. Robin finally breaks Nora's heart and leaves in order to commence a relationship with a petite but ferociously aggressive middle-aged widow named Jenny Petherbridge, a "squatter" by nature, who delights in stealing other people's lovers.

Less tolerant of Robin's amoral and flirtatious personality, Jenny physically abuses her when seized by fits of jealous rage. They move to New York City and take up residence in a hotel. For the first few weeks Robin is uncharacteristically listless. Eventually she begins to wander again and often visits churches, where she kneels in a thoughtless stupor. She begins sleeping in the woods and wanders closer and closer to where Nora has taken up residence, until one evening she encounters her ex-lover's dog in an abandoned chapel. She throws herself down on all fours and begins to make advances at the frightened animal, as if to engage in sexual intercourse. At the book's end, Robin has come to feel more at home with beasts than with the higher order of human beings.

Vrunsky, Sonya. *Salome of the Tenements.* Anzia Yezierska. 1923.

Raised in the poverty and squalor of a Lower East Side tenement in New York City, Sonya Vrunsky becomes a woman driven to find beauty and freedom. Sonya envisions herself leading the good life of the wealthy, free of ignoble cares. Filled with intense desire and armed with a strong will and the capacity to bewitch men, she rises from the ghetto to the home of an uptown millionaire and beyond.

Sonya is the daughter of two Russian Jewish immigrants who live on Delancey Street in the Lower East Side ghetto. As a child she is so willful and assertive that her father, a religious fanatic, regards her as a changeling and a pun-

ishment for his sins. Both of her overworked parents die young, leaving Sonya to fend for herself. She works in a factory, then as a secretary, and eventually becomes a journalist for the *Ghetto News*. This job provides her with an opportunity to pursue John Manning, a millionaire and noted philanthropist whose special interest is helping Russian Jews in Sonya's ghetto. Intent on getting an interview for the *Ghetto News* and unable to reach Manning through his secretary, she boldly stops him on the street to make an appointment. He is so taken with her after their first meeting that they plan to meet again.

In triumphant euphoria, Sonya feels capable of overcoming all obstacles to make herself appealing to Manning and "catch onto" him. When she finds herself dissatisfied with the gaudy clothing at her usual Essex Street shops, Sonya goes instead to a renowned Fifth Avenue designer, Jacques Hollins, and forces her way in to see him. Hollins, himself a Russian Jew who rose from poverty, is stunned by Sonya's charisma and her longing for beauty. He designs an exquisite dress for her free of charge. She wears the dress to her second meeting with John Manning, and it works its magic on him. A third appointment is made, this time at Sonya's home.

During the two weeks before her date, Sonya is able to transform her rundown tenement apartment into a charming little den, perfectly suited to Manning's refined tastes. In order to decorate her apartment to her satisfaction, she must borrow money from Honest Abe, a money lender notorious for his heartlessness and greed. With the hundred dollars she borrows, Sonya decorates her apartment, and Manning is deeply appreciative when he sees it. Convinced now of Sonya's taste and understanding, he invites her to become his secretary.

Sonya spends a tense and unpleasant stretch of weeks as Manning's secretary. Her moods alternate as she tries desperately to decipher her reserved employer and determine whether he is attracted to her. Without giving her any prior clues about his feelings, he embraces her in the hallway one day and then whisks her off to Greenwold, his family estate in the country. They are married shortly afterward, and Sonya spends their month-long honeymoon at Greenwold in complete happiness.

Almost as soon as they return to Manning's New York City town house, however, Sonya begins to sense his usual coldness returning. After Sonya demonstrates her lack of "society" manners at a party held at their home, he becomes openly disdainful toward her. Meanwhile, Sonya's anxiety is increasing as she receives a series of letters from Honest Abe, each one demanding more money. Although Sonya gets a small monthly allowance, she has nowhere near enough to pay off the moneylender. When she finally tells Manning of the problem, he informs her that they are "through." Taking neither money nor possessions, and determined to prove her independence, Sonya leaves him.

She longs to run to her friend Hollins, the dress designer, but would be ashamed for him to see her in this poor state. She decides instead to learn the art of designing herself. After working as a waitress for some time, she is hired as a machine hand in a dress shop where she devotes herself to observing the designers and cutters. When an idea for a dress occurs to her, she spends the night in the shop making the garment. The owner and designers are stunned by the simple, elegant dress and decide to call it the "Sonya model." It is displayed in all the expensive department stores. The Sonya model even attracts the attention of Hollins, who comes to the shop to bring Sonya to his Fifth Avenue business. They become partners in

design and are eventually engaged to be married. Sonya feels a strange uneasiness, which she is unable to explain until Manning appears at her home one day and declares his passion for her. They experience a moment of "absolute revelation" and are suddenly filled with compassion for each other.

After he leaves, Sonya struggles with the question of which man she really loves: Manning, who provokes such powerful emotions, or Hollins, who understands her. Although she is now pledged to Hollins, the novel closes with her meditation on Manning's "fineness" and the transformative quality of their romance.

W

Wakefield. "Wakefield." Nathaniel Hawthorne. 1837.

For reasons unknown even to himself, Wakefield leaves his London home one morning and does not return for twenty years. The night before his departure, he informs his good wife that he is going on a business trip and that she should not expect his return before Friday. Mrs. Wakefield is saddened, but she has no reason to suspect anything untoward because of her husband's impending absence. After all, Wakefield is an intelligent, if dull and unimaginative, man. His mind seldom troubles itself with difficult or original thoughts. The only real fire in his character comes from his peculiar secretiveness about inconsequential things.

After gathering his belongings together, Wakefield kisses his wife good-bye and steps out the door. In a moment the door opens again, and he pokes his head back into the house to give his wife an enigmatic smile. The next moment he is gone. A circuitous route through the city takes him to a lodging in the street next to his own. Wakefield had feared someone would detect his escape, but no one in the vast city notices it.

Lying in bed later, Wakefield muses that he will not spend another night alone; he will return home the next day. He rises early, wondering what sort of changes his day-long absence has wrought upon his wife and whether she feels any sense of loss. His thoughts thus occupied, Wakefield goes out into the streets. Almost automatically his steps turn to the door of his home, but his foot has only to touch the doorstep for him to be awakened from his reverie. He darts away, fearing that he has been detected.

As days become weeks, Wakefield often sees his wife

from a distance. Each time she is more haggard and wan. Eventually an apothecary, then a doctor, and finally a minister visit the Wakefield home. Wakefield, concerned but not overly so, does not return home. After Mrs. Wakefield apparently recovers, he guesses that she would not welcome him anyway.

Years later Wakefield is making his way through the London throng when the crowd pushes him against a matronly woman. As their eyes meet, he realizes it is Mrs. Wakefield, older and broader but still familiar. He rushes to his lodgings, throws himself on his bed, and calls himself mad. As he has been saying for twenty years, Wakefield tells himself he will go back. A sudden rain shower that leaves the unprotected Wakefield wet and cold finally leads him home. He knocks, and the door opens. As he steps over the threshold, that sly smile, seen by his wife so many years ago, raises the corners of his lips.

Walden, Ty-Ty. *God's Little Acre.* Erskine Caldwell. 1933.

Ty-Ty Walden, the half-comic, half-tragic protagonist of this novel about poor southern whites during the Depression, exemplifies the beauty and the absurdity of idealism. Both fool and hero, the engaging but maddening Ty-Ty transcends and falls victim to the hardships of his era.

As the narrative opens, the reader learns that rumors of gold on his property have motivated Ty-Ty and his three sons to spend fifteen years fruitlessly digging for gold rather than raising crops on the family farm. The Waldens have transformed the farm into an eerie landscape of dirt piles, leaving only a small amount of land to be farmed by the two black sharecroppers and setting aside one acre—"God's little acre"—to remain untouched.

Fifteen years of profitless labor have failed to dim Ty-Ty's enthusiasm; although he has had to move God's little acre all over the farm in order to dig new ground and although the lack of crops has resulted in near starvation for the sharecroppers and impending starvation for his family, Ty-Ty remains convinced that he will strike gold any day. As a result he remains oblivious to the trouble brewing around him—to the privation of his dependents, to the rivalry among two of his sons and his son-in-law over his beautiful daughter-in-law Griselda, and to the violence and despair slowly rising to the surface in the nearby mill town where the workers have gone on strike to protest the lowering of wages.

While these dangerous forces build around him, Ty-Ty is busy trying to enlist new diggers, borrowing money from his one wealthy son to get the family through a winter of digging and even capturing an albino man and bringing him to the farm because, although Ty-Ty swears he is a strictly scientific miner, he has heard that albinos can divine gold.

For all his wasteful foolishness, however, Ty-Ty proves admirable in some respects. He is more cheerful, sure of himself, and forward-looking than the other characters. His dreams keep alive in him a youthful idealism, while his many years of experience have given him a certain wisdom. He is capable of astute insights into the personalities and motives of his children and their spouses, and he works hard to keep peace in his family and God in his heart. A particular wisdom of Ty-Ty's, which Griselda recognizes at the end of the novel and which Ty-Ty tries to share with his sons, is his understanding that sex is a beautiful, necessary, even spiritual element of human life and that sexual jealousy and sexual possessiveness are ungodly and destructive.

Ty-Ty's dreams are illusions, but his optimism and his humor are real. The novel closes with three of his four sons having been killed and Ty-Ty beginning to dig again for gold, wondering when his only living son, who had rejected his family and become wealthy, will come join him in the effort.

Wales, Charlie. "Babylon Revisited." F. Scott Fitzgerald. 1931.

Charlie Wales, who lived the wild high life of Paris in the 1920s, returns to the city in the autumn of 1931 after the stock market has crashed and his own life has fallen to pieces. Charlie is hoping to regain custody of his daughter Honoria, a little girl whom he now sees as the only thing of real value left in his life.

At age thirty-five, Charlie looks back on his life a few years before with a mixture of wonder and terror. Paris has changed. The drunken party that seemed as if it would last forever collapsed with the stock market, and the rich young Americans who danced in the fountains have scattered. Some, now merely destitute, are trying to live humble, working lives somewhere else. Others have gone to asylums or to their graves. Charlie, who had a nervous breakdown and was hospitalized for alcoholism, has managed to get back on his feet. But his wife Helen died of heart failure after a long bout with pneumonia, and Charlie feels at least partially culpable: Helen first became ill when Charlie locked her out of their apartment after a drunken fight on a freezing night in the winter of 1929.

Charlie's daughter is now in the custody of Helen's sister Marion and her husband Lincoln Peters. Marion was always cold to Charlie, and she has grown to hate him. She blames him for Helen's death. Lincoln, however, is more sympathetic. Charlie hopes that by proving himself sober and responsible, he can persuade them to let him have Honoria back. When he visits them and sees the home they have built for their children, his desire for Honoria intensifies. The little girl clearly loves him and wants to be with him. Charlie feels a desperate need to put something of himself in her before she crystallizes completely into her own person.

After a difficult talk with Marion and Lincoln in which he tentatively presents the idea of taking Honoria away, Charlie takes his daughter out to lunch in a hotel. As they leave the restaurant, they run into Duncan Shaeffer and Lorraine Quarrles, two friends from the lavish times of a few years back. Charlie still feels an attraction for Lorraine, of whom Helen had been jealous, but he quickly dismisses her and Duncan. They seem to be wanting to prey on him now that he is strong and able to function again. He vows to steer clear of them and move toward the world of Honoria and a home of his own.

Charlie lunches with Lincoln, who tells him that Marion is slowly coming around to the idea of letting Charlie have Honoria. Lincoln tells Charlie to come over that evening at six to settle the details. When Charlie gets back to his hotel, he finds a letter from Lorraine, asking why he brushed her off so quickly and suggesting they meet for old times' sake for a drink at five o'clock at the Ritz. Charlie thinks again of the nightmarish days of his recent past. There is no question of his accepting Lorraine's invitation. Instead, he goes to buy presents for Marion, Lincoln, and their children.

That evening Charlie senses that he has won. Marion will never like him, but she understands his love for Honoria and seems to see his improvement. But as they finalize their plans, the doorbell rings, and two drunken people—Lorraine and Duncan—come in looking for Charlie. They are loud and playfully drunk, but when Charlie orders them out of the house, they get ugly. "I remember once you hammered on my door at 4 AM," Lorraine says. "I was good enough to give you a drink." Charlie ushers them out and apologizes profusely for their intrusion, saying he has no idea how they found out where he was. But the damage has been done. This clear reminder of the wild years that destroyed her sister sends Marion into a fit of anger. Lincoln tells Charlie that the best thing to do is leave until she cools off.

Charlie goes to the Ritz bar; he tries to figure out how Lorraine and Duncan got his brother-in-law's address. He does not even remember that it was he who gave it to the bartender at the Ritz several days before, with orders to send Duncan Schaeffer there, should he show up. While it is not clear that Charlie wanted Lorraine and Duncan to sabotage his plans to regain Honoria, it is certain that Charlie is not quite ready to give up the wild years of the late 1920s. His horror at the past is mixed with a nostalgia for the grandeur that has disappeared from his life, and for Helen, whom he loved so bitterly yet so much. Charlie is not surprised when he calls Lincoln and learns that he and Marion have decided to keep Honoria for the time being. But Charlie vows to return someday to claim his child. He is no longer young and no longer full of hopes and dreams. And he is absolutely sure that Helen would not have wanted him to be so alone.

Walker, Jr., Coalhouse. *Ragtime*. E. L. Doctorow. 1974.

Coalhouse Walker, Jr., is a respectable and talented professional ragtime pianist whose successful life is disrupted by racism in the first decades of the twentieth century. An extremely proud and confident man, Walker is intolerant of the bigotry that makes most American blacks defer to whites out of self-defense. His pride in his own considerable capabilities gives him the impetus to excel in both work and love, but his pride is also detrimental in this hostile environment. In order to defend his dignity, Coalhouse Walker, Jr., changes almost overnight from an upstanding groom-to-be to a terrorist guilty of murder and arson.

Walker's debut in *Ragtime* finds him driving a brand-new Model T Ford, a rare and elaborate possession at the time. In a white middle-class neighborhood in New Rochelle, New York, he pulls up to the home of the LITTLE BOY and his family—Mother, FATHER, and MOTHER'S YOUNGER BROTHER—and asks to be presented to Sarah, a black woman who lives there with her son. But Sarah, who is almost overwhelmed by grief, initially refuses to entertain her caller, who then makes weekly appearances at the house despite her persistent rebuffs. Her newborn infant, Coalhouse's son, had been discovered by her host family in their garden, almost completely buried in dirt and nearly dead. The mother of the family decided to take in both mother and child in order to save them from charity wards and possible murder charges. When Sarah finally agrees to grant Coalhouse an audience, he conducts a courtship that is heavily laced with repentance. Sarah's spirits and health begin to improve, and finally, convinced that Walker is both penitent and reliable, she agrees to marry him.

On his return to Manhattan one Sunday after visiting Sarah, a group of volunteer firemen, under the supervision of Fire Chief Will Conklin, stop Walker and vandalize his car. His demands for reparation are met with laughter by the firemen and indifference by police authorities. Upon learning that he intends to postpone the wedding until justice is served, Sarah attends a political rally where she hopes to find a politician who will intercede on her fiancé's behalf. As she pushes through a police line in an effort to approach the politician, she is delivered a lethal blow by a gun butt. In reaction, Walker assembles a small group of willing accomplices—among them Mother's Younger Brother—that detonates bombs in manned fire stations and announces they will continue to do so until his Model T Ford is restored to mint condition and Fire Chief Will Conklin is delivered up to his vigilante justice.

Calling themselves the Provisional American Government, Walker's group finally takes over the priceless library of J. Pierpont Morgan, which they threaten to blow up if their demands are not honored. With the help of such mediators as Booker T. Washington, Coalhouse is finally convinced to back down on his demands and accept reparation in the form of a public display: Conklin repairing the Model T in front of the library. Walker agrees to this form of reparation on the condition that his accomplices be allowed to escape. When the car has been restored and his supporters have fled to safety, Coalhouse Walker, Jr., surrenders himself to the authorities who, claiming later that he bolted for freedom, shoot him down in the street as he descends the library steps.

Wallach, Gabriel. *Letting Go*. Philip Roth. 1962.

Narrator Gabe Wallach is a graduate student at the University of Iowa. He is in the midst of writing his dissertation on Henry James when his mother dies. After a brief visit to the Jewish neighborhood in Brooklyn where he was raised, during which his overbearing father once again makes him feel guilty for moving so far away, Gabe befriends another graduate student, PAUL HERZ, and feels a strange attraction to Paul's frail wife Libby.

Gabe lends Paul a Henry James novel that contains a letter from his mother. When he visits the Herz house to retrieve it, Gabe finds Libby home by herself. After a long conversation on the subject of Henry James, Libby returns the letter to Paul and confesses that she has read it. Irritated at first, Gabe finds himself drawn to Libby; he kisses her before forcing himself to leave.

Gabe separates himself from the Herzes as much as possible after this ambiguous encounter. After graduating from the University, he moves to Chicago, where he is offered a position teaching freshman composition at the University of Chicago. There, he meets a young woman named Martha Reganhart whose husband has abandoned her and two young children. After Gabe spends a week in bed with a bad case of the flu, Martha asks him to move in with her and her children. Gabe agrees but keeps his old apartment.

Gabe's new living arrangement soon deteriorates, however, when Martha, who is forced to support her children by herself, accuses Gabe of not paying his own way. Gabe also has trouble getting along with her daughter Cynthia, who resents his presence in the apartment. To make matters worse, Martha's husband returns to Chicago. He is about to remarry and wants his children back. Knowing she will be looked upon by the court as a bad influence on her children because she is "living in sin" with Gabe, and not wanting to subject her children to a long court battle, Martha surrenders them to her husband. Unable to live with Martha any longer, Gabe travels to New York to visit his father and then returns to his old apartment in Chicago.

During this time the Herzes have moved to Chicago because of a teaching position Gabe secured for Paul at the university. The relationship between Paul and Libby is deteriorating. During a vicious argument between the two, Gabe suggests that they have a child, and then he is ashamed when Paul informs him that Libby is unable to bear children. When Gabe learns of a pregnant student who wants to put her baby up for adoption, he helps Paul arrange the adoption.

While their new child rejuvenates his friends' dysfunctional marriage, Gabe feels a new emptiness in his own life and, enamored with the Herzes' new daughter, whom they have named Rachel, he decides to try secretly to gain legal custody of her. After paying the real father an advance of $500, Gabe, who is the child's babysitter for the evening, kidnaps Rachel and takes her to the house of her rightful parents. Her father, fearing repercussions for any legal wrongdoing, refuses at the last minute to sign any papers. The humiliated Gabe returns Rachel to the Herzes, and unable to face his old friends, he soon flees to Europe.

Years later Gabe receives an invitation to Rachel's fifth birthday party. He replies that he will be unable to accept their token of forgiveness until he can forgive himself.

Walsh, Monte. *Monte Walsh*. Jack Schaeffer. 1963.

Monte Walsh is sixteen years old and living with his mother and stepfather in Colorado in 1872. When Monte busts his first bronco, a horse belonging to his stepfather that he was told not to touch, he decides to run away rather than take a beating. Monte spends the next few years riding with various outfits, driving herds of cattle from Texas up through the Plains states. Along the way Monte meets his best friend, Chet Rollins, in Dodge City. The two are inseparable for the next twenty-five years, during which time they witness the transformation of the American West.

In 1881, Monte joins the Slash Y cattle outfit, a ranch just outside Harmony, New Mexico, headed by Cal Brennan. By now Monte has acquired the reputation as the best bronco buster in the West. No horse, it seems, is too wild for Monte to ride. In Antelope Junction he rides a horse so explosive that it would rather kill itself by running into a fencepost than be busted.

In the same town he meets a man who offers him fifty dollars a week plus expenses to perform in a Wild West show. He accepts, mostly because he fancies a woman in the show, but he quickly realizes he would rather be a real cowboy and rides back to the Slash Y.

There is no test of courage that Monte will not accept. In order to impress a certain woman named Miss Hazel, he agrees to try to last two minutes in a boxing ring with a grizzly bear. It takes the bear only a minute and fifty seconds to knock Monte unconscious, but this is still a new record for Monte.

In 1888 a couple of cattle rustlers set fire to some land on the Slash Y and murder one of its top hands, Powder Kent. Despite the overwhelming smoke and heat, Monte heroically puts out the fire, saving the ranch's land from destruction. Monte is nearly killed in the attempt, and it leaves him with two blackened, barely functioning lungs.

The years continue to pass, and by 1894 the old gang at the Slash Y has broken up. Monte returns to Harmony for Chet Rollins's wedding. Finding that he objects to the "quiet and dignified" atmosphere of the wedding and wishing to create a celebration of his own, Monte runs into the plaza and fires his gun in the air. It doesn't take long for a violent frenzy to erupt as the other former members of the Slash Y join him. Monte makes Chet's wedding a day to remember, and the town is very nearly destroyed.

Monte spends the next ten years drifting from town to town, taking whatever jobs he can. He often finds himself unable to keep pace with the rapidly modernizing world around him. When he is past fifty, he settles in a small New Mexico town. Although the age of the automobile has arrived, Monte still continues to make do with his faithful dun-colored horse. He makes his living by running cattle for a wealthy businessman and keeps himself busy by taking whatever odd jobs come his way.

Monte has just delivered the mail to a small ranch in the valley when the only bridge leading to town is destroyed by flood waters. At the same time there is a slide at a nearby mine, and three men are badly hurt. The mine is on the same side of the river, and there is no way to get to town for help. Monte volunteers to make the treacherous journey. After his horse is killed falling down a flooded embankment, he must go the rest of the way on foot and is barely alive by the time he reaches the town. A fever takes hold of him, and he slips into a coma. Chet Rollins comes to his bedside, but Monte dies within a few days. His epitaph reads: MONTE WALSH, 1856–1913. A GOOD MAN WITH A HORSE.

Wandrous, Gloria. *Butterfield 8*. John O'Hara. 1935.

The beautiful and defiant Gloria Wandrous lives among the speakeasies of the Depression era, moving from one casual affair to another, faithful to one man only as long as she wants to be. Her determined resistance to the respectability and stability of her conventional background propels her through an underworld existence in New York. Gloria struggles to harden herself against her increasing feelings of despair, refusing to admit any remorse for her actions or dissatisfaction with her life.

The primary cause of Gloria's recurring mood of despair is an event that occurred during her childhood: She was sexually abused by a man old enough to be her father. Brought up by a devoted uncle and a widowed mother, Gloria led a stable life until the arrival of Major Boam, who quickly realized that he adored this small, beautiful twelve-year-old with the eyes of a woman. Finding himself alone with Gloria, Boam sexually maltreated her in a flurry of desire, panic, and haste, and then disappeared. A year later, after finally telling her mother and her uncle about the incident, Gloria was sent to a school in New York where, it was hoped, she would forget. After three years and another change of school, Gloria seems to have forgotten the incident; in fact, she is left with a heightened curiosity about her own sexuality and a knowledge of sexual experience that belies her age and appearance. One summer Gloria meets an older man on a train, and she responds to his interest. A month later she has her first affair.

Gloria moves to New York with her mother and uncle, and drifts into a life of sexual encounters and drinking in the numerous speakeasies. Her only friend is EDDIE BRUNNER, the one man Gloria can depend on and with whom she can have a nonsexual relationship. Yet as Gloria increasingly begins to despise her promiscuity and then desperately attempts to justify it, she interprets Eddie's resistance to her charms as criticism and disgust. Her failure to seduce Eddie is at once the foundation for their friendship and the cause of their growing distance.

WESTON LIGGETT is one of the many men Gloria has had affairs with but believes she doesn't want to keep. Wealthy and married, Liggett seems to Gloria the ideal one-night stand. But as she gradually yearns for stability and respectability, Gloria finds herself being drawn to Liggett and everything he can offer her. Torn between her unwillingness to commit herself and her increasing attraction to Liggett, Gloria is forced to admit, for the first time, that she has become vulnerable. She determines to free herself from the hurt that Liggett's apparent detachment is causing her and decides to leave New York, for a short while, on a boating trip.

Yet Liggett has finally decided to leave his wife and family to marry Gloria. He follows her to the *City of Essex*, which is just embarking, and unknown to Gloria, he joins her on the boat. When Gloria, isolated and unsure as to what she has done, finally sees Liggett, she decides that she will accept the life he is offering her and sees herself becoming the good wife her mother was. She goes with Liggett to his cabin but suddenly realizes that she cannot sleep with him in the cold, damp room. At this moment Gloria has discovered the self-respect she has so long discounted. But Liggett misinterprets her silent leave-taking. He follows her to apologize, and when she catches sight of him, Gloria slips and falls screaming off the deck into the boat's side wheel. In the end, Gloria Wandrous becomes the property of unscrupulous journalists, all determined to prove that her tragic death is a fitting emblem for the immorality of the age.

Wang Lung. *The Good Earth*. Pearl S. Buck. 1931.

Wang Lung, an illiterate Chinese peasant in the second half of the nineteenth century, works with his father and makes a meager living off the land. When it comes time to marry, Wang Lung seeks a plain wife to ensure she is a virgin. The chosen bride, O-LAN, has been a slave in the richest household in the nearby town. O-lan works by her husband's side in his fields and, to his great joy, quickly bears him a son. Another son follows, and then a girl who cannot speak and appears retarded; after each birth O-lan rejoins her husband in the fields on the same day. With his wife's help, Wang Lung prospers and saves enough to buy a parcel of land from O-lan's former household, which has, through neglect and dissipation, fallen on lean times.

But Wang Lung's luck does not hold. A devastating famine strikes the region; Wang Lung and his family are driven to eat their ox and then, in desperation, the grass and the earth itself. O-lan miscarries. On the brink of starvation, the family heads for a southern city. There Wang Lung rents a rickshaw, and with the money his wife and children earn by begging, they slowly regain their health. When an insurgent mob storms the doors of a rich citizen's palace, Wang Lung and O-lan join them. Wang Lung carries off a small mountain of gold.

The family returns to its land. With his newfound gold, Wang Lung buys large parcels of land from O-lan's former household. Determined to see his sons educated, he hires workers to help with the farming. O-lan delivers male and female twins. Although he is prosperous, Wang Lung grows restless with increasing age. He begins to frequent a teahouse in the town, where he falls in love with a prostitute named Lotus. He installs her in his household, along with the "madam" of the teahouse, Cuckoo, who had once been a fellow servant in O-lan's former household. Wang Lung is happy for a time, but as his children grow up and make it plain that they do not wish to work the land as their father did, he is faced with new trials. When O-lan falls ill with a "fire in her vitals," he comes to realize her true worth and honors her every dying wish.

Wang Lung's children marry and procreate. His sons' families coexist uneasily in the extended family, which now includes not only Lotus and Cuckoo but Wang Lung's demanding uncle and his family. Wang Lung's wealth grows, and he moves into the now-vacant courts of the palace from which he had once taken O-lan. In his late years he chooses a new companion, a young girl named Pear Blossom. who cares for him tenderly. When his death is imminent, he takes Pear Blossom and his retarded daughter back to his farm. He arranges for Pear Blossom to poison his "poor fool" of a daughter after his death, for he is sure that no one will care for her as he has. In his final days he hears his sons make plans for the future of the land. Although they reassure him that they do not mean to sell any land, Wang Lung knows that they have no idea of the worth or the meaning of the land he has fought so hard to keep.

Wapshot, Coverly. *The Wapshot Chronicle; The Wapshot Scandal.* John Cheever. 1957; 1959.

During his childhood, Coverly Wapshot, the younger of LEANDER WAPSHOT's two sons, is likened to Icarus because he fails the expectations of his father. When Coverly's brother MOSES WAPSHOT is made to leave their home in St. Botolphs, Massachusetts, to take work in Washington D. C., Coverly leaves for New York of his own accord. He plans to work at a cousin's carpet factory but is disappointed when he cannot pass an interview with a psychologist before being hired. Honest, stable, and hardworking, Coverly takes a job as a stock clerk and enrolls in civil service night school. He plans to become a taper, to translate physics experiments into code for computers.

He begins dating Betsey, a diner waitress from Georgia, and soon moves in with her. They marry when Coverly passes his civil service exam but are separated immediately as Coverly is assigned a nine-month position at a Pacific Island rocket-launching base. He and Betsey eventually settle in army housing at a new station in Remsen Park, and Betsey gets pregnant. Betsey's days are terribly lonely and boring, and she spends her time trying to turn neighbors into friends; her ennui causes continual marital tension. When Betsey finally befriends a married couple, the man makes a pass at her, Coverly decks him, and Betsey miscarries. After spending weeks in bed, she leaves Coverly, who has been overly patient, attentive, and understanding.

Homesick for St. Botolphs and for the comfort of his marriage, Coverly becomes friendly with Pancras, a successful homosexual coworker. Coverly suppresses his homosexual longings after writing to his father for advice. Betsey returns home, and they resume their marriage and have a son, thereby receiving financial support from Coverly's wealthy great-aunt Honora.

Coverly visits Honora at his childhood home and finds that it is haunted by his deceased father's ghost. Continuing to blame Coverly for her unhappiness, Betsey denies him sex and companionship and has a breakdown. Cov-

erly spends his nights secretly coding the poetry of Keats into the base computer and is discovered by Cameron, the melancholy and eccentric site director. Cameron, whose sanity is under congressional investigation, is impressed by Coverly's "block-headedness" and makes him his lackey. While he is returning from a conference that Cameron makes him attend, Coverly's plane is robbed in flight by air pirates. He returns to work only to find that his security clearance at the site has been suspended because his cousin Honora, who is wanted for tax evasion, skipped the country. As a result of further bureaucratic confusion, Coverly and Betsey are evicted from their home. While planning his next move, Coverly receives an urgent telegram from Honora, who is back in St. Botolphs. He goes to visit her and finds the formerly feisty and leonine great-aunt frail and dying; she refuses to eat and is drinking herself to death. Filled with nostalgia, Coverly honors Honora's dying wishes, one of which is for him to eat Christmas dinner in her home after her death with guests she has already invited.

Wapshot, Honora. *The Wapshot Chronicle; The Wapshot Scandal.* John Cheever. 1957; 1959.

Honora Wapshot's commanding presence pervades the thoughts and actions of the entire Wapshot family in this first novel. Described by the third-person narrator as a typically eccentric old lady of any New England town, Honora is stubborn and feisty. Her wealth also renders her extremely influential.

Honora prides herself on the prestigious Wapshot heritage and the fact that she was born in Polynesia, although her parents died there soon after her birth. Honora was raised by her wealthy uncle, Lorenzo Wapshot, in St. Botolphs, Massachusetts. A tomboy in her youth, Honora attended St. Wilbur's Academy and worked in social services until Lorenzo's death. Having inherited an extremely large trust fund from him, she married a man she thought was a marquis who owned a castle in Spain. Their marriage lasted less than eight months, however, and after discovering that her husband had neither wealth nor title, she returned to Lorenzo's house, reassumed her maiden name, and became the benefactor of LEANDER WAPSHOT's family.

Honora lives alone except for the company of her housekeeper Maggie, who finds her ornery and unpredictable. As the childless matriarch of the Wapshot family, she considers herself the guardian of morals as well as the main source of income for Leander and his two spoiled sons, MOSES (WAPSHOT) and COVERLY (WAPSHOT). Moses and Coverly are to be the inheritors of her entire estate, provided they marry and produce male heirs. When Honora accidentally overhears Moses making love to a girl who is staying at his parents' home, she abruptly cuts support to the entire family. Without revealing her secret knowledge, Honora sends Moses into the world to prove his worth.

When she is subsequently investigated for income tax evasion, Honora, who has given away her money all her life and never bothered to file taxes, fears she will go to the poorhouse. At the advice of the local judge, she leaves the country to settle in Italy. She travels by ship and befriends a swindling stowaway, only to feel spurned when she realizes that she is not the sole object of his attentions or the only one to know his secret. Little is heard of Honora until the end of the novel when a very pleasant government agent locates her in Italy and brings her back to the United States. Just prior to leaving, Honora hands out hundreds of lira notes to everyone she sees in the Piazza di Spagna in order to cleanse herself of the filth of money.

Back in St. Botolphs, knowing that she will soon die, Honora sends for Coverly. She has begun drinking herself to death with whiskey and refuses to eat. Upon seeing her, Coverly is shocked at Honora's appearance; once robust and leonine, she is now thin and frail. Knowing that it would be useless to confront her, Coverly gives in to her dying wishes: that she will die at home and that Coverly and his family will have Christmas in her house with the guests she has already invited. Honora passes away that night, and Coverly is the only member of the family able to attend her funeral. On Christmas day he is not surprised to learn that, in Honora's usual Christmas tradition, she has invited people to dinner who have no other place to go. On this, the last Christmas of her generosity, she has invited the Hutchins Institute for the Blind.

Wapshot, Leander. *The Wapshot Chronicle; The Wapshot Scandal.* John Cheever. 1957; 1959.

Leander Wapshot is the father of MOSES (WAPSHOT) and COVERLY (WAPSHOT) and cousin of the childless matriarch HONORA WAPSHOT. Married to Sarah Coverly, he lives in the house of his youth in St. Botolphs, Massachusetts. A simple man, Leander has never held a job for long and lives off the generosity of wealthy Honora. Acting as captain of cousin Honora's boat, the *Topaze*, Leander gives his days purpose by ferrying commuters across the bay. He hopes that his sons will imitate the manly ceremoniousness of his life, which demonstrates his appreciation of the "excellence and continuousness of things." As his sons separately discover, even Leander's fishing trips are filled with mysterious ritual. Thoroughly romantic, Leander's memories are filled with sensual nostalgia for the long summer days of his youth and the girls at the seaside. When Honora threatens to sell the *Topaze*, Leander feels his very existence threatened and is ashamed of his financial dependence on her. Realizing that Honora must have her reasons, he attempts to make peace by agreeing to send his eldest son out into the world to prove the worth of the Wapshot blood.

The narration alternates between third-person and first-person points of view when Leander begins writing his autobiography. In fragmented sentences he describes the various people and events of his past in dramatic detail. He held his first job as a lackey for J. B. Whittier, a shoe manufacturer, and was eventually pressured into marrying a girl whom his married boss impregnated. Leander fell in love with the pregnant Clarissa, but when her newborn was forcibly taken from her, she drowned herself. No one in Leander's family knows this secret, nor do they meet Helen Rutherford, Clarissa's grown daughter, when she comes to St. Botolphs to accuse Leander of immorality and neglect.

More troubling for Leander is the sinking of the *Topaze* in a storm. Although he is not able to raise funds to repair it, his wife is able to secure a loan to turn it into a floating gift shop. His self-esteem is ruined, and he takes work again in a table-silver factory to fill his days. He continues his autobiography, and a letter to his son Coverly reveals Leander's youthful experimentation with homosexuality. Leander quits his factory job as soon as he learns of his son's plan to buy him a boat, but these plans are never fulfilled because Leander goes for a swim in the sea and is never seen again. Leander's funeral is well attended and, in accordance with his wishes, Coverly reads Shakespeare at the service. As Coverly is reading, a note to his sons falls from the book; it contains eclectic advice on women, whiskey, and life's pleasures.

Later on, Leander appears briefly as a ghost. He believed that one's payment for life's pleasures lingers on after death, and his presence is so strong at his now empty home in St. Botolphs that no one will rent it. Honora finds and reads a small portion of Leander's autobiography in the attic; Leander's words about the enduring and immortal soul of man end *The Wapshot Scandal*.

Wapshot, Melissa Scaddon. *The Wapshot Chronicle; The Wapshot Scandal.* John Cheever. 1957; 1959.

Melissa Scaddon is the beautiful twenty-eight-year-old adopted daughter of the wealthy, miserly, and priggish Justina Scaddon of Clear Haven. Melissa's parents died when she was seven, and the Scaddons adopted her because of her sweet nature, although none of the Scaddons' fortune will be left to her. Little of Melissa's dark past is divulged except that when MOSES WAPSHOT asks Justina's permission to marry Melissa, he is warned that Melissa is unstable, moody, and has been married before. This does not daunt Moses, who spends the summer before their marriage at Clear Haven Castle getting to know Melissa and hopping the rooftops to spend secret, passionate nights with her.

Melissa has not left Clear Haven since her divorce. Although she does not make use of Justina's wedding gift of twin beds to her and Moses, the extent of Justina's power over her soon becomes clear. When Justina interferes with a dinner party that Melissa and Moses throw for some friends, Melissa suffers a personality change: She becomes frigid, withdrawn, and austere, and refuses all contact with Moses. Although chaste with Moses, Melissa flirts with the gardener and her ex-husband when he comes to visit. Melissa recovers her personality instantly when Justina plans to throw a large party, but when the castle catches fire during the party and burns to the ground, Justina moves to Athens, and Melissa and Moses relocate in New York.

Melissa and Moses settle in Proxine Manor, a suburb filled with bored and unfaithful housewives. Melissa is soon hospitalized with pains and fever. During her recovery, she becomes painfully aware of the monotony of her life; she and Moses have little in common except sex, and he has taken to heavy drinking. Emile, a nineteen-year-old grocery boy, becomes Melissa's sexual obsession. She takes him on trips and buys him expensive gifts, all the while trying to rationalize her needs.

Although they have both tried to end the relationship, it is Emile's mother who eventually separates the couple by telling Moses of the affair. When Moses, now a habitual drinker, leaves Melissa, she moves to Italy. Emile takes a job on a trading ship and, quite coincidentally, jumps ship on the same island where Melissa now lives. After winning a body-building contest, Emile finds himself on a human auction block and is reunited with Melissa, who has purchased him. They renew their affair, this time with more dedication, and move to Rome to live together. The last mention of Melissa occurs in the final pages of the novel when the narrator describes her food shopping in Rome. Melissa's manner is girlish, a result of having a much younger lover, but her heart is filled with sorrow. Tearful and alienated, she is a figure of dignified grief.

Wapshot, Moses. *The Wapshot Chronicle; The Wapshot Scandal.* John Cheever. 1957; 1959.

Moses Wapshot is a strong, gentle, bright, and lustful young man. After an unexceptional college education he chooses to return to his parents' home in St. Botolphs, Massachusetts, to continue his life of leisure. Moses's days of fishing and amorous pursuits come to an end one summer day when his advances to a woman staying with his parents are overheard accidentally by his great-aunt HONORA WAPSHOT. Honora, the wealthy, childless matriarch who supports the entire Wapshot family financially, is offended by Moses's actions. Without revealing her secret knowledge, Honora insists that Moses leave St. Botolphs to prove his worth in the world.

Although his departure is filled with nostalgia for the past, Moses is excited to begin working at the top secret job in Washington, D.C., that Honora has arranged for him. He is soon promoted and moves from a boardinghouse to an apartment. Moses begins dating a married woman, Beatrice, whom he meets in a bar. Beatrice gets into trouble with the police and wrongfully implicates Moses in a crime; now considered a security risk, Moses loses his government job. Needing time to think, Moses takes a hunting trip and helps save the life of a woman who was thrown from a horse in the woods. This woman's married, wealthy lover offers Moses a lucrative banking job.

Working again and going to bond school, Moses attends a dance and meets MELISSA SCADDON (WAPSHOT), his future wife. Melissa was raised by a guardian, Justina, who is an extremely wealthy, stingy, and stubborn prude and an ancient cousin of Honora's. Moses spends the summer in Justina's Clear Haven castle in the wing farthest from Melissa's, crossing the rooftops to spend nights secretly in Melissa's room. He is a demanding but patient lover and cannot understand why Melissa turns frigid soon after their marriage. Believing that personality changes in women are common, he ignores Melissa's flirtations with her ex-husband who comes to visit at Clear Haven. To Moses's mostly physical relief, Melissa recovers her normal personality when Justina arranges to throw an extravagant party. However, when he goes to fix a blown fuse during the party, he discovers that the house is on fire; the guests manage to escape, but the house burns to the ground. Moses finally moves to New York with his wife and leaves his banking job to work at a shady brokerage house. Melissa gives birth to a son, thereby fulfilling Honora's stipulations for resuming financial support of Moses.

Moses and Melissa settle in suburban Proxine Manor, a town of bored housewives and marital infidelities. Although he is very attentive to Melissa sexually, they agree on little else but sex. In this volume, the narrative emphasis shifts from Moses's to Melissa's affairs; he does not question Melissa's behavior and takes to drinking heavily. When he finally confronts Melissa, he starts to strangle her but drops her before hurting her. Moses visits his brother COVERLY (WAPSHOT) but does not tell him of his marital problems and stays drunk for the entire visit. Moses surfaces again later, at Christmas time, drunk in a boardinghouse in his hometown of St. Botolphs. The owner of the house phones Coverly, who picks up his alcoholic brother so he can spend Christmas with the family.

Ward, Elizabeth. *The Turn of the Balance.* Brand Whitlock. 1907.

The daughter of the wealthy and well-respected broker Stephen Ward, Elizabeth Ward was brought up surrounded by wealth and privilege in a mansion in New York City. After graduating from boarding school, Elizabeth returns home. Much to her mother's consternation, however, she takes little interest in fulfilling the various social duties to which young women of her class are bound, and spends most of her free time socializing with the housemaid Gusta, a German girl her own age.

Elizabeth is very disheartened when Gusta leaves the Ward home after her father is crippled in a work-related accident. A few days later she pays a visit to the grieving Gusta, who must care for her father in the tiny flat shared by her extended family. Realizing that Gusta's father will need a lawyer to fight for the reparation he deserves, Elizabeth enlists the aid of Gordon Marriott, a family friend and successful attorney.

At a party at the Wards' mansion a few weeks later, Elizabeth is introduced to another lawyer named Eades, a prosecutor for the district attorney's office. An old adversary of Marriott, the ambitious Eades is soon captivated by Elizabeth, who finds his profession of sending people to jail decidedly unattractive. Eades continues to call on Elizabeth, however, and she sees him out of respect for her mother. By this time Elizabeth is well into her twenties, and her mother is anxious to for her to be married. After several weeks Eades finally proposes to Elizabeth. Against her mother's wishes, and despite the bright future of the rising young lawyer, Elizabeth politely rejects him.

To clear her mind of the troubles weighing on her and at the same time to escape the wrath of her furious mother, Elizabeth takes a vacation in Europe. But she finds that she is unable to enjoy herself and soon returns home. No sooner does she return than Gusta pays her a visit and tearfully relates how her brother Archie has been falsely accused of murder. Elizabeth once again pays a visit to Marriott, who, although still battling the railroad company for reparations for Gusta's injured father, agrees to help her brother as well. Elizabeth attends the trial in person, only to see Marriott lose his case to the state-appointed prosecutor Eades. The horrified Elizabeth is later informed that Archie has been sentenced to death in the electric chair.

That night Elizabeth's brother Dick enters her bedroom and tearfully confesses that he has embezzled over $20,000 from the bank where he is employed. After consulting Marriott, who tells her that the decision whether or not to prosecute rests in the hands of Eades, Elizabeth pays a visit to the district attorney's office and begs Eades not to press charges against her brother.

But Eades ignores Elizabeth's pleas. Returning home, she finds that her father has paid off the bank, with interest, and that the complainant has taken an extended vacation in order to thwart the prosecution. Thoroughly disgusted with the criminal justice system, Elizabeth is then visited by Marriott, who confesses his love to her. Despite the weight of the misfortunes of those around her, Elizabeth is able to find personal happiness in her new relationship with Marriott.

Ward, Mira. *The Women's Room.* Marilyn French. 1977.

Mira Ward is an oppressed housewife who, through her experiences with the feminist movement, develops into an enlightened professor of English. Although her increased understanding of feminism cannot bring her happiness in a male-dominated world, the sense of personal worth and self-reliance she gains does provide a small compensation for the loneliness and bitterness she feels.

Born around 1930, Mira has a "correct" upbringing and is trained in the social niceties of middle-class America. She reads Nietzsche at fourteen and speculates about God and injustice. She also thinks about boys and envies and resents their freedom. A relationship at nineteen with Lanny, a college friend, falls apart because she refuses to have sexual relations with him. One night he abandons her at a bar, and she is nearly gang-raped.

Feeling a need for protection from the hostile and aggressive world of men, she marries a safe but dispassionate medical student, Norm. Their sexual life is not fulfilling for Mira, but Norm actually seems glad about this. Mira bears two children, Normie and Clark, and begins living a life of self-sacrifice for her family. She loves them, but she takes pleasure in their lives at the expense of her own self-fulfillment.

In 1955 the family moves from their cramped and confining apartment to a small suburban home in Meyersville. Mira becomes friends with a group of housewives, all of whom suffer from the implicit assumption that they are worth less than their husbands, that their work is less relevant, their minds less interesting, and their sexual needs less important. One by one the women's lives fall apart. Lily has nervous breakdowns; Martha attempts suicide after an unsuccessful affair; Samantha is abandoned and resorts to welfare. Mira is a model housewife and feels a smug pride at her ability to keep her life and marriage together. She is shattered when Norm sues for divorce, and she bitterly demands compensation for her unpaid years of housework. Norm is deeply hurt that she views their marriage in monetary terms.

Mira begins studying for a doctorate in English literature at Harvard University. While there she becomes involved with a group of women, among whom are a strident feminist, Val, her sixteen-year-old daughter Chris, and the warm and charismatic lesbian Isolde. These women discuss feminism and support one another during their academic and personal crises and experiences. Despite their friendship, though, each one is in some way defeated by the masculine institutions of academia, marriage, politics, and business. Chris is raped and then humiliated in court; Val is killed during a militant feminist attempt to free an innocent female prisoner; and two other women leave their husbands for Isolde, who feels unable to commit herself to either one.

Meanwhile, Mira becomes involved in a very strong and positive relationship with Ben, an expert on African. They love each other, but when he receives an appointment in Africa, he assumes that she will accompany him there and support his life and career at the expense of her own.

They part, and he marries a more traditional woman in Africa.

Mira remains in the United States but can find employment only at a small community college in Maine. She teaches courses on fairy tales and walks the beaches, full of disillusionment and sorrow, still confused about the seeming impossibility of love and equality between men and women.

Warden, Milton Anthony. *From Here to Eternity.* James Jones. 1951.

First Sergeant Milton Anthony Warden—"the Warden"—is the highest ranking hero in this novel of life in the armed forces in Hawaii on the eve of World War II. The thirty-four-year-old Warden has become head of the Orderly Room of G Company in Schofield Barracks. Exceptionally intelligent and hardworking, Warden has brought greater order to the company than it has ever seen; manipulating his less experienced and knowledgeable superiors with the wily cunning of a practiced soldier, he in fact virtually runs the company. Big, muscular, tough, and gruff, Warden is hard on his underlings but retains their respect by treating them fairly and by excelling in all soldierly duties.

Warden hates all commissioned officers, especially his decadent, politicking superior Captain Holmes. To avenge himself against Holmes, Warden seduces the captain's wife, Karen. Karen has a reputation for promiscuity, and Warden initially intends simply to use her for his own purposes of vengeance and sexual relief. However, he is immediately taken aback by Karen's strong, individualistic personality and marked intelligence, and soon he and Karen fall deeply in love with each other and make plans to marry.

Their affair is a dangerous one, for Warden's career would be over if they were discovered. To protect him, Karen insists that Warden apply for an officer's commission because as a commissioned officer he cannot be prosecuted for their affair. Further, his commissioned status would enable Karen to keep custody of her son after divorcing Holmes and marrying Warden.

Warden agrees to the plan, but during their ecstatic first months together, he lies about having applied for the commission. The lie is eventually exposed, but Karen—urging him not to make the application—explains that she understands his dislike of becoming an officer. Eager to remain with Karen, however, Warden does make the application and shortly thereafter sails through the qualifying examination. At this point the lovers' relationship begins to falter; although they try desperately to regain their earlier enthusiasm and continue to love each other to distraction, nothing goes well with Karen and Warden after he applies to become an officer.

Shortly after the attack on Pearl Harbor, Warden receives his appointment as second lieutenant, but after he

and his cook Maylon Stark go on a drunken spree together, he tears his commission papers in two and goes to say farewell to Karen, who is being shipped stateside and whom he knows he will never see again. Warden recognizes that Karen is the one great love of his life, but he also recognizes that he cannot love her, or anyone, as an officer.

Ware, Theron. *The Damnation of Theron Ware; or Illumination.* Harold Frederic. 1896.

When he first appears, the Reverend Theron Ware has delivered a spectacular sermon at a Methodist conference in which a number of communities are choosing a new minister. He is eager to be awarded a comfortable, remunerative post where his talents will be appreciated. Instead, the bishop appoints him to direct the congregation at Octavius, a smaller and substantially more conservative community. During his first meeting with his new trustees, he is informed that he is to preach "the plain, old-fashioned Word of God, without any palaver." Although he doesn't know it, the moment initiates the process of his "illumination," a religious skepticism that changes his life.

Chafing under the restrictions imposed by the trustees, which extend even to the flowers in his wife's bonnet, Theron takes long walks. One day he encounters members of the town's Irish community carrying an injured workman. Going with the group to the man's house, Theron gets his first exposure to the Catholic sacraments. First the beautiful Celia Madden enters the house to tend to the family's needs (the man had been mortally injured while working for her father), and then the parish priest, Father Forbes, comes to administer extreme unction. Theron is transported by the beauty, sensuousness, and solemnity of the Catholic ceremony.

Through Father Forbes, Theron—barely swallowing his alarm at the priest's reference to "this Christ-myth of ours"—learns of higher criticism and becomes acquainted with Dr. Ledsmar, a misanthropic scientist who conducts strange experiments in evolution. These late-nineteenth-century intellectual crises provide the spark that ignites Theron's "Illumination."

But the women Theron encounters have an even greater effect on the state of his soul. An evangelist named Sister Soulsby, who comes to Octavius to conduct a "debt-raiser," teaches him the value of pragmatic expedience, informing him that "you simply can't get along without some of the wisdom of the serpent." She not only fertilizes his growing contempt for his religion but also encourages him to begin seeing the serpent in everyone.

It is Celia Madden, however, who approaches Theron where he is most vulnerable to seduction. Pre-Raphaelite in creed and appearance, Celia has liberal views about art and morals. She invites Theron into her parlor where she plays Chopin; then, during a walk in the woods, she encourages his worship of "the maternal ideal," the primal veneration for fertility at the center of her "religion."

All these ideas, taken together, unhinge Theron's moral compass. He finds lewdness under every rock. Conceiving the outrageous notion that his wife Alice is having an affair, he insults her and her only friend, the lawyer Levi Gorringe. He then becomes obsessed with the idea that there is a similar liaison taking place between Celia and Father Forbes. Theron exhausts first Dr. Ledsmar's and then Father Forbes's waning patience with him through his circuitous references to their supposed affiliation.

When Theron learns that Celia and Father Forbes are going to New York on the same train, he follows, with vague notions of heroically preserving her honor. He bursts into her room, and, cornered, she quietly informs him that she, Father Forbes, and Dr. Ledsmar have all along been bored and disgusted by him, that they had liked only his innocence, an innocence he had long abandoned.

Theron goes on a deranged drinking binge until he is saved by Sister Soulsby, who rescues him and returns him to his wife. A year later, after a kind of moral convalescence, Theron is preparing to take up a new life in the West as superintendent of a real estate company that is developing the Washington Territory, and he is planning to enter politics.

Warland, Owen. "The Artist of the Beautiful." Nathaniel Hawthorne. 1846.

A strange passion drives Owen Warland, the title character of Nathaniel Hawthorne's story. A watchmaker who interacts with the mundane world only reluctantly, Owen creates a thing of beauty that brings joy, but only briefly.

Even as a child Owen was fascinated by things mechanical. His parents tried to encourage the interest by taking the child to see engines and motors, but Owen was always repulsed by large machinery. Only the small, the delicate, the intricately wrought was of interest to him. In recognition of this fact, Owen's parents apprenticed him to the watchmaker Peter Hovendon. Owen learned watchmaking from Hovendon and took over the shop when his master's eyesight became too poor for him to work. Still, he is not devoted to his trade.

Owen is more concerned with creating something beautiful and delicate than repairing mere timepieces. No one in his practical town, least of all his former master, Hovendon, can appreciate his more philosophical bent. Hovendon and the local blacksmith Robert Danforth recognize Owen's skill but feel he is wasting it on baseless enterprises. Only Annie, Hovendon's beautiful young daughter, seems ethereal enough to Owen to share his interest in the beautiful. Owen harbors a secret passion for her.

One day Hovendon pays Owen a visit. The old man mocks the young dreamer and thoughtlessly destroys one of his delicate creations. The destruction of his art plunges Owen into a depression whose depths match the heights of his previous elation. This cycle of euphoria and despair is repeated on other occasions. Even Annie, whom Owen had thought could share his love for the beautiful, destroys one of his creations with her earthly touch, smashing not only Owen's dreams of beauty but his fantasy of making Annie his life companion.

For a time Owen seems to abandon his desire to create, and he gains a respect from the townspeople he had never expected or perhaps even desired. However, a subsequent bout of his characteristic despair, in which he uncharacteristically begins drinking, reduces him to his former status as a useless dreamer. The entry of a beautiful butterfly into the grog shop where he is drowning his sorrows ends Owen's depression. The news that Annie is to marry the brawny Robert Danforth is a blow, one that causes him to break one of his creations himself, but he never seems to hit the psychological bottom he did before.

Five years after Annie's marriage, Owen pays her and Danforth an unexpected visit, bearing a belated wedding present. When Annie opens the intricately carved box, out flies what appears to be a butterfly. Annie, Danforth, Peter Hovendon, and Annie's young son are amazed by the creature, which comes to rest on Annie's finger. Annie is convinced it is mechanical, and Danforth seems persuaded as well. Hovendon is skeptical, however, and when the butterfly rests on his finger, its glorious colors fade—the result, Owen says, of Hovendon's doubt. Finally it alights on the child's finger, blazing up again, and then takes flight around the room. As a look somewhat like his doubting grandfather's comes across Owen's face, Annie and Danforth's son grabs the creature, crushing it. Rather than being saddened by the destruction, Owen is placid, for now he knows that beauty cannot last and that few can appreciate it as he does.

Washington, John. *The Chaneysville Incident.* David Bradley. 1981.

John Washington, a thirty-one-year-old black man, is a brilliant historian who lives and works in Philadelphia with his white lover Judith. They have lived together for several years, and despite some turbulence in their relationship, have established a stable and satisfying life together. However, after John receives a call informing him that Jack Crawley is dying in John's hometown just north of the Mason-Dixon line, John's history, and the history of African Americans, begin to emerge from the shadowy background to which John has consigned them and to threaten his hard-won peace of mind.

John's father died when John was a teenager, and Jack Crawley had become like a father to him, teaching him how to hunt and how to drink liquor and endlessly telling him stories of the past. John returns home to nurse Jack through his last days, and after Jack dies, John stays on to study his father's numerous but mysterious notes and records, using his coldly dispassionate historical research techniques to piece together the histories of his father, Moses, and his grandfather, C. K., both of whom had fought in surreptitious but heroic and effective ways for their people.

As John delves into the history of his family, the history of African Americans from colonial days onward unfolds in a taut and carefully wrought narrative that is propelled forward by two primary questions: What happened to C. K., and how and why did Moses die?

John addresses these questions with an unemotional, coldly observational attitude. He starts to need more and more liquor to dissolve the iciness forming within him, and his controlled anger begins to reveal itself in his ruthless, vengeful treatment of his mother, the white townsmen of his community, and even Judith. It becomes clear that John is deeply disturbed, consumed with love and hatred for his father, bitterness against his mother for sending his brother off to the Vietnam War to be killed, and rage at all whites everywhere—a rage that had once caused him to rape a white woman and that prevents him from trusting Judith.

As his fury, and his fear, simmer beneath the surface of a too-controlled, too-analytic exterior, John begins to appear dangerous to himself and others, especially after it is revealed that his father had committed suicide at a graveyard in Chaneysville.

Eventually Judith joins John for the last days of his "investigation." Together they visit the Chaneysville graveyard, where the last pieces of the puzzle come together in such a way that John finally can imagine the endings of his father's and grandfather's stories. Then Judith and John prepare to leave Jack's shack, but John sends Judith ahead of him into town, and as he piles his research notes and papers onto a bonfire to destroy them, the reader is given reason to believe that John, trapped by history, will destroy himself as well.

Waugh, J. Henry. *The Universal Baseball Association, Inc.* Robert Coover. 1968.

J. Henry Waugh is the driving force behind a league of eight baseball teams embroiled in a fierce pennant race. Henry has an encyclopedic knowledge of the UBA's history, knows each player intimately, and energetically follows team standings, league politics, and the many scandals involving players and managers. But the UBA is no ordinary baseball league. A product of a lonely man's energetic imagination, it is a complicated dice game governed by an intricate system of charts and rules, and it is J. Henry Waugh's religion and obsession.

By devoting all of his free time to the Association, often playing several dozen games in a night on his kitchen table, Henry has logged fifty-six seasons. He has compiled volumes of statistics and player histories, and has seen the

sons and grandsons of the UBA's early players take the field. Damon Rutherford, son of the legendary pitcher Brock Rutherford, is the most shining of these descendants, and as the novel opens he is in the process of pitching a perfect game for the Pioneers, who are two games behind the Knickerbockers in the pennant race. Henry is buoyed by Damon's no-hitter, accomplished by a final toss of the dice. At a local bar and then at his apartment, he shares his celebration with Hettie, a B-girl who is entertained, if confused, by Henry's references to perfect games, shining rookies, and statistics.

Unfortunately, reality encroaches on Henry's baseball universe. Hungover and still giddy over Damon's rare achievement, he appears at his accounting job several hours late. In spite of a reprimand from his boss, Mr. Zifferblatt, he leaves ten minutes early to return to his game. Lou, Henry's clumsy but well-meaning colleague, expresses concern, but Henry brushes him off.

At home, Henry plays several games and then, anxious to see Damon pitch again, he begins a contest between the Pioneers and Knickerbockers, pitting Rutherford against another bright rookie, Jock Casey. But in the third inning, with Damon batting against the menacing Casey, three dice throws of triple ones necessitates referral to Henry's Extraordinary Occurence chart. According to the chart, such a toss means that the batter is struck fatally by a wild pitch; that Damon Rutherford is dead.

Henry is devastated by the tragedy. Skipping work, he goes on a bender at the local bar, imagining himself a participant in a raucous wake thrown by the ballplayers for Rutherford. Returning in the early hours, exhausted, he reluctantly finishes the game he had started. As if to mock him, the Knickerbockers score run after run, and Henry leaves for work on Friday with the score eighteen-to-one. Mr. Zifferblatt, who has been told there was a death in Henry's family, is somewhat understanding, but sends Henry home with the warning that if he is late or falls asleep at his desk again he will be fired immediately.

But Henry's mind is on the Association. His determination that the Pioneers should win the pennant drives him to play relentlessly, and in twenty-four hours he pushes himself through sixty games, nearly a quarter of the season. When he breaks to have dinner with Lou, however, the Pioneers have fallen far behind in the standings, and the Knickerbockers remain in first place. Fearing that the Association has become too much for him, Henry invites Lou to join him in a game the following evening.

By the time Lou arrives on Sunday, Henry has played forty-eight games; the Knickerbockers have dropped out of first, but the Pioneers have fallen to last place. With a twinge of guilt, he gives Lou charge of the Knicks, while he takes the dice for the Pioneers. Lou's ineptitude is frustrating, but when he ignorantly replaces his veteran pitcher with Casey, Henry becomes excited. With Henry's roll of 6-6-6 against pitcher Casey causing a referal to the Extraordinary Occurrences chart, Lou leaves, reminding Henry that they are expected at the office the next day.

Alone, Henry rolls again, hoping for a second set of sixes, and then another, knowing that such rolls are the only way to return the league to equilibrium. Instead, he rolls 2-6-6, but carefully tips the two over to a third six. Then, just as carefully, after apologizing to Casey, he takes up the dice and sets them down so that they show a third roll of triple six, indicating, according to the chart, "Pitcher struck fatally by linedrive through box."

The novel closes some twenty seasons later on "Damonsday," the annual ceremonial game marking the young rookie's death. Donning the uniforms of two decades ago, the players take the roles of Damon, his teammates, and the opposition, and prepare to reenact, with a sense of resignation and an odd comfort in the inevitable, the fateful game.

Webber, George. *You Can't Go Home Again.* Thomas Wolfe. 1934.

George Webber, a naive young writer, finds fame and love, and learns from painful experience that they are not enough to make him happy. Always styling himself an outsider, George discovers, in the wake of his hometown's rejection of him, that his spirit will know no rest.

Raised by an aunt after his divorced mother dies, George grows up in the southern city of Libya Hill with an ambition to write. At the opening of the narrative, his first book has just been accepted for publication by the well-known editor FOXHALL "FOX" EDWARDS. George's joy over the novel's impending release and his budding friendship with Fox is interrupted by the news that his aunt Maw has died. On the southbound train that bears him home for the funeral, he meets many residents of Libya Hill. One traveler, the blind and sinister Judge Bland, warns George that he can't ever return home.

The Judge's pronouncement seems true. George is treated as a stranger by all but his friends Randy and Margaret Shepperton. The townspeople's treatment of him, as well as the mad real estate speculation in which they are engaged, alienate George. Even articles that appear in the local newspaper about his upcoming book leave him cold, for they misrepresent the novel. When the book is released after George's return to New York, the citizens of Libya Hill send him tons of hate mail because of his autobiographical work.

Back in New York, George wonders how to proceed with his affair with ESTHER JACK, a wealthy theater designer whose husband is a stockbroker. While attending a party she is throwing in her luxurious apartment, George finally realizes that, as a writer, he has no place in the whirl of wealthy society. He resolves to leave her, although he loves her.

For years George practices his craft in a cramped apartment in a working-class area in Brooklyn. He observes how the Great Depression has burst the bubble of easy money in New York and also learns that speculation has ruined his hometown. Fearing that there is something ugly in the spirit of America, George goes to England for a while to write. There he meets Lloyd McHarg, a famous writer who is even more restless than George. If fame cannot satisfy one's soul, George wonders, what will?

A visit to Germany, a country he has always loved, does little to soothe George. His second novel has just been published to acclaim, so he is treated with respect, even adulation, but Germany has changed. The rise of Nazism has darkened the German spirit, he finds, and his visit is marred by ugly incidents of fear, anti-Semitism, and bigotry. In a letter he writes to Fox after he returns home, George expresses sadness over the death of his innocence, but refuses to give up hope that hatred and fear will ultimately be defeated. Knowing that Fox, who is essentially a fatalist, cannot share this dream, George parts with him professionally, but expresses in his letter to him the hope that they will always remain friends.

Webster, Daniel "Dan'l." "The Devil and Daniel Webster." Stephen Vincent Benét. 1937.

Daniel "Dan'l" Webster is consulted by his fellow New Hampshireman Jabez Stone and finds himself involved in the most difficult legal case of his life. Frustrated by his life, which has been one long string of bad luck, Jabez Stone bargains with the devil for prosperity. After almost a decade of prosperous living, Stone, now known and respected around the state, must fulfill his part in the bargain with the devil, who appears as a stranger. When the stranger will not allow Stone to renege on their agreement, the desperate man travels to Marshfield to enlist the help of the great and legendary Webster.

The two return to Stone's home to await the arrival of the devil. The great lawyer and the devil, Scratch, are introduced and begin to argue over Stone's contract. Webster uses every legal ploy that he knows, but in the end the devil remains unshaken. Frustrated, Webster declares that Stone is an American citizen and cannot be forced into service by a foreign prince. Scratch is unfazed and claims to be an American and entitled to Stone. Webster pounces on this declaration and requests a trial for Stone, complete with an American judge and jury.

Instantly, Stone's kitchen door opens to admit twelve jurors from the nether world, each of whom played an evil part in the formation of the United States from the colonial period through Webster's day. The judge is one of the Salem witch trial justices who never repented of those doings. The case is presented to the jury and Webster is treated unfairly throughout. Infuriated by this treatment, Webster plans to assault the judge and jury with a wily trick of law he knows. He is stopped, however, by the white fury that he reads in the jury's eyes as he approaches them. He suddenly realizes that they and Scratch intend to acquire his soul as well as Stone's and that he has been about to play into their hands.

Instead of the violent attack he originally planned, he resorts to a patriotic oration about the formation of the Union. He recalls incidents of childhood days and reminds his audience of the frailness of humanity. The jurors from hell are so moved that they find in Webster's favor, and Stone is freed of his contract with Mr. Scratch.

The jury and judge depart, leaving the three to conclude the matter. Realizing that the devil, once defeated, no longer has any power, Webster grabs him and forces him to write a contract liberating Stone and all his descendants. Additionally, he forces Mr. Scratch to leave New Hampshire and never to bother any of its inhabitants again.

Webster, John. *Many Marriages.* Sherwood Anderson. 1923.

As a young man of twenty, John Webster has a strange encounter with Mary, the girl who will become his wife. Because John's parents are away, he is invited to spend the Christmas holidays at the home of a friend and his sister, with whom John is also friendly. Mary comes to the house as a guest of the sister, but there are unspoken hopes that John and Mary might like one another. Before John even knows she has arrived, he enters his room after a bath and finds her asleep in the bed. Both are naked and, John never having seen a naked woman before, stands entranced until the girl awakes. Later he hears her crying from shame, but instead of apologizing, he rushes into the room and embraces her. Mary looks up at him, longingly he thinks, as if she were coming up "out of a deep buried place." John regards this moment as a spiritual union, a "marriage," and he later sends her long love letters, asking her to marry him.

After the marriage takes place, John and Mary Webster travel on their wedding journey to Kentucky, to honeymoon at a farmhouse. They remain in awkward, watchful silence, in which John becomes painfully conscious of his desire for her. On the afternoon of their arrival in Kentucky, the pair take a long walk, and stop to rest on a hilltop, where John meditates on the beauty of the scene and his love of life. At the height of his ecstatic, almost hallucinatory reflections, he approaches Mary, and, taking her into his arms, does not stop his advances, in spite of her cries and protests. That night, she explains how deeply ashamed she felt after he saw her naked on that first day, and that she afterwards had become a devoted churchgoer. Their marriage, Mary now feels, should be a "pure thing, based on comradeship." They should make love only for the purpose of bringing children into the world. Realizing that Mary is merely a child frightened by passion, John resolves to subdue his desires, to "make everything all right."

The couple takes up residence in the small Wisconsin town where John's father owns a washing-machine fac-

tory, which he eventually inherits. After the birth of their daughter, Jane, John moves into a private room, and satisfies his sexual needs by travelling to Chicago and finding a prostitute. He manages to dull his feelings so that the failure of his marriage causes him little pain, and seventeen years go by before he experiences his erotic awakening. This transformation takes place when he initiates a love affair with Natalie Swartz, the young woman who has been his secretary for three years. After several weeks of passionate intimacy with Nancy, John confronts his wife and daughter and tells them that he is going away to live with Natalie. Before leaving, he tells his daughter Jane the story of his marriage and is convinced she sympathizes with him. He gives Jane a small stone he found, which he calls the "Jewel of Life," for her to hold in moments of doubt.

John meets Natalie near daybreak, and they walk to the train station. They are planning to go to Chicago, but are uncertain about what they will do there. As they walk, John, questioning his behavior, wonders if he is not just using Natalie to escape from his marriage. But he dismisses these thoughts; he is taking a worthwhile risk, he decides, and even if he cannot live happily with Natalie, he is still taking a chance on life.

Weisnix, Ilka. *Her First American.* Lore Segal. 1985.

Ilka Weisnix, a Jewish refugee from Vienna after World War II, is initiated into American culture by the aging, worldly black writer CARTER BAYOUX. Ilka is proof that sympathy and affection between people can endure the pressures of racism.

Upon her arrival in America, Ilka moves in with her cousin Fishgoppel on the Upper West Side of New York City. The building is full of first-generation immigrants. When a woman at the employment agency advises her to practice English, Ilka complains that the only people she knows are "outlanders," foreigners who know only other foreigners and who can speak even less English than she. Fishgoppel sends her on a train trip to the Midwest to find the "real" America. When Ilka meets Carter in a bar in Nevada, she decides this handsome figure must be the "first American" she was seeking.

Carter, who lives in New York City, introduces Ilka to his circle of friends, including writers, singers, painters, actresses, and diplomats of all ages, religions, and races. On their first disastrous outing in New York, Carter brings Ilka to the wedding reception of an old girlfriend, but he creates a scene when he begins shouting drunkenly at the bridegroom. Carter later takes Ilka "uptown" to see his ex-wife Ebony perform a skit. One of three whites there, Ilka fixes a false smile on her face for the duration of the skit, which mocks white stereotypes of blacks.

Although Carter is widely respected, Ilka becomes increasingly aware that he is also an outsider. They spend the summer in a house in Connecticut, which they share with other interracial couples. Ilka is delighted by the country landscape and the small varied community. But tensions within the group over a white couple's crusade to adopt a black baby end the vacation prematurely, and Ilka returns to New York to care for her ailing mother, who has arrived from Austria.

Ilka is often bewildered and always understands less than the reader. She relies on Carter for explanations and bitterly humorous stories that reveal the intricacies of the culture. These stories, along with "protocol," are the outsiders' keys to survival. Ilka remains half-convinced that Carter himself created this mysterious and fascinating place.

Carter also relies on Ilka's patience to pull him through his bouts of heavy drinking, which often land him in the hospital. During his binges he withdraws from his usually active social life. Carter becomes unable to leave his room and calls Ilka at work to ask her for the time of day or to beg her to bring him something to eat. Toward the end of the novel, Ilka makes the surprisingly independent and sober decision to leave Carter. At the time of Carter's death, not long after their separation, Ilka is already happily married to a young man named Carl and has a child.

Welland, May. *The Age of Innocence.* Edith Wharton. 1920.

May Welland, fiancée and later wife of NEWLAND ARCHER, is a beautiful, elite young woman without the imagination or desire to question or contradict the social conventions she has grown up in. She plans her life to follow a preordained pattern, a pattern into which her engagement to Newland fits perfectly.

May sits at the opera with her mother, grandmother, and black-sheep cousin COUNTESS ELLEN OLENSKA. When they leave the opera to attend a ball, May is happy to announce publicly her engagement to Newland. Not wanting Ellen to think that Newland is available, she asks Newland to tell Ellen about their plans to marry, believing he is the right person to do so. May is protective of her cousin, whose reputation has been damaged by a recent marital scandal.

Later, at a dinner party, May—resembling the goddess Diana—enters the room surrounded by admirers while Newland is talking with Ellen. May is considered by all to be the most beautiful young woman in the room, but she is unaware of her fiancée's growing unspoken criticisms of her values and conventional ways, and she does not know that he has become obsessed with Ellen. When Newland asks her to elope and urges that they strike out for themselves and take life as more of an adventure, May, although thrilled by what she takes as evidence of his love for her, resists his suggestion. She perceives elopement as vulgar and tells him that they can't behave like people in novels.

May decides to take a trip to Florida. While she is there, Newland visits her and says he wants them to marry sooner than planned. May, sensing that Newland has feelings for another woman, tells him he must take all the time he needs to decide if she is the right bride for him. Not wanting Newland to abandon the woman he loves, she selflessly and tearfully insists that he should not sacrifice anything for her if another woman exists. Newland, surprised by her intuition, tells her she is wrong. After he leaves, May changes her mind and sends him a telegram, saying she will marry him immediately.

Now married, May, continuing to abide by the social codes, joins her family in opposing Ellen's decision not to return to her husband. Newland is the only one who supports Ellen, and this difference of opinion causes tension between him and May. May eventually realizes that Newland is in love with Ellen. She visits Ellen and talks to her at length, and while their conversation is never directly related in the novel, we understand that through it May somehow conveys to Ellen her deep need for Newland and their marriage. When Ellen subsequently decides to move to Paris, May, who sincerely loves her cousin but is relieved that she is going, announces Ellen's decision to Newland and arranges a huge farewell dinner for her.

May dies years later of pneumonia, leaving behind Newland and three happy children. Newland learns after her death that May, on her deathbed, privately told their oldest son that he and his siblings would always be safe with their father, who had given up "the thing he most wanted" when she asked it of him

Wells, Calliope "Callie." *Nickel Mountain: A Pastoral Novel.* John Gardner. 1973.

Sixteen-year-old Calliope "Callie" Wells starts to work in 1954 as a waitress in the Stop-off Diner, owned by HENRY SOAMES. She is the daughter of Henry's first love, Eleanor, and although he cannot afford extra help, Henry has hired her due to sentimental regard for the memory of that relationship. In the small community of Slater in upstate New York, such ties are constantly evoked, and although Callie intends to move to New York City, she is drawn into the preexisting connections of family and friendship.

During that first summer at the diner, Callie is seduced by Willard Freund, the son of Slater's wealthiest merchant, and becomes pregnant. Henry offers to marry her, and because Willard has left to attend Cornell, she agrees. Her wedding takes place in the midst of small-town anxiety over illegitimate children; but the Slater community shows its willingness to ignore such circumstances by sending her lavish wedding gifts. She and Henry build an annex to the diner as their home.

James "Jimmy" Soames is born after three days of labor. Callie, hysterical from the pain, tells Henry that she does not love him. But the marriage is stabilized by their mutual amnesia on this point; Callie accommodates herself to a life as Henry's wife even when it means accepting his bad heart and fat body. Settling into a domestic routine, Callie cleans up the diner and makes plans for a bigger restaurant. When Henry permits Simon Bale, a Jehovah's Witness who does not bathe, to stay with them after his house burns down, Callie is outraged but silent. George Loomis, a neighbor, voices his objections to Simon's insanity and sanctimoniousness, but Callie is more concerned about two-year-old Jimmy, who is now friends with Simon and has been having frequent nightmares. When Simon is killed falling down a flight of stairs, his ghost haunts Callie in the garden, where he used to sit with the newspaper.

Henry's response to Simon's death—he blames himself for the accident—is to eat gluttonously, to strain his heart and make it stop. A drought plagues the region, and the farmers gather in the diner to discuss their debts. The atmosphere is tense with these personal and financial crises. Nick Blue, a Native American and something of a prophet, predicts rain, which does not come on the appointed day; but Callie consoles the farmers with the suggestion that they keep the faith, and eventually the rain does come.

When Willard Freund returns to Slater, he meets Callie and Jimmy, who is now four years old, in the general store and is sheepish and mortified at the sight of his child. Callie is tight-lipped and unresponsive, but Henry is all friendliness and forgiveness. The Soameses open a new restaurant, the Maples, where Callie, newly capable and mature, presides like a monarch. She reflects on her feelings for Henry, and both partners realize that not only have their lives changes, but they have changed chiefly through the force of her love for him.

Weltstein, Gabriel. *Caesar's Column: A Story of the Twentieth Century.* Ignatius Donnelly. 1890.

The New York visited by Gabriel Weltstein in this futuristic novel is a city of contrasts. Gabriel is fascinated with the technological developments evident in the wealthy part of the city but is soon introduced to the squalid lives of most of New York's inhabitants, and he becomes a reluctant participant in their bloody revolution.

Gabriel, a rancher of Swiss descent living with his family in a remote area of Uganda, travels to New York planning to find a market for his wool. One day while admiring the city's splendors he sees a coachman beating a beggar. As the two women in the coach look on, Gabriel rescues the ragged beggar, who warns him that his good deed may land him in jail. They flee the scene together as the beggar explains that the coach belongs to the powerful Prince Cabano, one of the handful of businessmen who rule the entire country.

The beggar takes Gabriel to a stately home where he reveals that he is really MAXIMILIAN PETION, a wealthy attorney who is one of the leaders of the Brotherhood of Destruction, a 100-million-member workers' organization committed to overthrowing the world domination of the business oligarchy. With the assistance of the Brotherhood's network of spies and information gatherers, Gabriel and Maximilian learn that one of the women in Prince Cabano's coach, Estella Washington, has been sold to the Prince by her aunt and will soon be forced to become one of the Prince's mistresses. Gabriel, captivated by the woman's innocent expression, vows to save her from this fate.

While hiding in the Prince's mansion, Gabriel witnesses a meeting of the de facto rulers of the country. The businessmen are aware of the Brotherhood's plans for revolution, and they formulate a scheme that will ruthlessly crush any rebellion and result in the deaths of millions of poor, innocent people as well as the destruction of the Brotherhood. Unable to hear of this horrible possibility without trying to stop it, Gabriel springs from his hiding place and begs the men to reconsider their bloody program. Fleeing from the unmoved businessmen before the Prince's guards arrive, Gabriel is able to rescue Estella and take her to Maximilian's house.

Later, at a meeting of the Brotherhood, Gabriel informs the members of the group of the Prince's plan. He counsels them to begin the work of rebuilding the world rather than destroying it, but the Brotherhood has been patient long enough and has suffered too much to be reasonable or constructive.

Fearing the cataclysm that will surely come, Gabriel dreams of taking Estella with him to Uganda. Although he loves the young woman, he does not want to take advantage of her friendlessness and vulnerability. He discovers his concerns are groundless, however, when Estella confesses her love for him. They are married in a double wedding with Maximilian and his fiancée Christina.

Their honeymoon is barely over when the revolution begins. The workers triumph as they kill Prince Cabano, his colleagues, and others who have oppressed the people. As Gabriel foretold, victory leads to a reign of terror as the people, loosed from the bounds that had held them so long, go on a rampage of murder, pillage, and arson. Caesar, one of the Brotherhood's leaders, constructs a huge obelisk, filled with the bodies of dead capitalists, to stand in monument to the destruction. Gabriel supplies the inscription at the base of the column—a lament for the end of civilization. As Gabriel and his friends escape New York in an airship, Caesar's column is one of the few structures standing in the rubble of a once-great civilization. Europe, they discover as they fly over it, is also in ruins.

Once in Uganda, Gabriel is able to convince his fellow settlers to construct a government that is strong enough to protect the rights of its citizens from the abuses that destroyed the rest of the world. There he and Estella, together with Maximilian and his family, live in peace.

Wendall, Jules. *Them.* Joyce Carol Oates. 1970.

Jules Wendall is the firstborn of the Wendall family chronicled in this novel of the 1950s and 1960s. Working-class Catholics unappreciative of Jules's precocity and intelligence, his mother LORETTA (WENDALL) and the other members of his family drive him out at an early age to a life of violence and rage.

Jules's first excursion from Loretta's authority takes place in the country outside Detroit, where at age four he witnesses a particularly grisly auto accident. He is irrevocably affected by the scene and becomes numb to other episodes of violence. Jules stays with his family in Detroit until he is fourteen, when his father dies. Jules, who cannot remember his father's face on the day of the funeral, detaches himself from Loretta. His sisters, Betty and MAUREEN (WENDALL), see him in zoot suits, smoking, and seducing girls, but they cannot induce him to return home or to finish school.

As a teenager Jules selects only "significant" lovers. He undergoes a series of earnest crushes in Catholic school, including one on a nun. Then he meets wealthy Faye, who puts him to work chauffeuring for a man named Bernie who promises to send Jules to college. But Bernie is murdered before he can do so. Jules then pursues Bernie's niece Nadine, whom he is unable to seduce, on an absurd road trip to Texas, where she abandons him. His obsession with Nadine persists, and when he returns to Detroit they reunite and declare their love. After a protracted day of lovemaking, she walks with him to his car and shoots him twice, injuring him.

By 1967, when Detroit is in flames, Jules has fallen in with a radical sociology professor named Mort, who advocates symbolic assassination although he can't decide between Lyndon Johnson and Martin Luther King as the target, nor Vietnam and Black Power as the issue. Jules is indifferent to such nuances and seduces Mort's student Vera, a mousy would-be radical, while still sleeping with Marcia, a sturdy teamster with a young son. After the riots Mort is a television celebrity for his sociological analysis of urban malaise, and he takes Jules as part of his entourage to California. The astonished Loretta sees Jules on television, a mouthpiece for Mort and an apologist for violence. Jules visits his sister Maureen, who is now married. She tells him that they must separate not only from each other but from "them"—their family and their class.

Wendall, Loretta. *Them.* Joyce Carol Oates. 1970.

Loretta Wendall, matriarch of the Wendall family, spends her days in undignified rage at the case workers who want to cut her off welfare. At home she deals un-

comprehendingly with her three children and her declining Detroit neighborhood.

As the novel opens, sixteen-year-old Loretta is preening at her mirror on a Saturday night. Before the night is over, her Bernie is shot by her brother, and Loretta flees to Howard, a police officer, who rescues her from the murder charges. She marries Howard and has three children. When Howard is disgraced and dropped from the police force for taking bribes from a brothel owner, he and Loretta go to live in the country with his parents. Howard goes to war in Germany, and Loretta wars with her mother-in-law over dominion of the home. Frustrated, Loretta takes the children back to Detroit, and on her first day while attempting to raise money, she is arrested for solicitation.

The Wendall house is always filled with conflict, drinking, and beatings. Howard returns from the war and retreats into silence until one day he is crushed by a machine at work and dies. Loretta then marries Pat Furlong, an alcoholic, and continues her manic scolding of her children. Her son JULES (WENDALL), meanwhile, has left home; her daughter Betty begin to rebel; and her other daughter, MAUREEN (WENDALL), who is left to clean the house and soothe Loretta's nerves, slowly begins to lose her sanity. Through all the family's crises—Howard's death, Maureen's madness, Betty's arrests, and so on—Loretta persists in her complaint against the sheer unfairness of her life and occasionally alludes to the shooting of her lover as the catalyst for all her troubles.

When all her children have left home and history comes to life in the streets in the form of the 1967 Detroit riots, Loretta is burned out of her house. Taken in by the Red Cross, she watches a television program about the riots and sees her son Jules, now a member of a radical leftist organization, who advocates burning down American cities in order to build a new society. Loretta weeps because she has raised a murderer. The novel concludes with all the characters, but particularly Loretta, individually condemning "them"—the family and class they come from—for holding them back.

Wendall, Maureen. *Them.* Joyce Carol Oates. 1970.

Born into a working-class Catholic family in Detroit in the late 1940s, Maureen Wendall is pretty and fond of books. While attending a Catholic school, she is appointed secretary to her homeroom and meticulously maintains the minutes until one day when the record book is lost. The missing record book and the nuns' disapproval haunts her for years; her obsession with the incident reveals her to be predisposed toward madness and compulsion. Maureen's older brother JULES (WENDALL) and her younger sister Betty both run with wilder crowds, while she looks after the house, retrieves her drunken stepfather from his friends, and spends her few free hours in the public library.

Notwithstanding Maureen's exemplary life, her mother

LORETTA (WENDALL) is convinced that she is the troublemaker of the family and about to bring shame on them at any moment. Loretta's harsh treatment of Maureen is based on this assumption of sin, and Maureen finally does transgress quite significantly: She starts to have sex for money. She hopes to earn enough money to be able to leave home. When her stepfather learns what she is doing, he tries to beat her to death. The trauma renders her insane, and for over a year she is unable to leave her bed.

As part of her therapy Maureen enrolls in two English composition courses—the author Joyce Carol Oates's own course and another with a man named Kovack. When she writes in letters to Oates that she will marry Kovack, the reader takes this to be the fanciful conclusion of a lonely young woman who has scarcely recovered from madness. But she does marry Kovack: He leaves his wife within weeks. In the novel's final days, when the Detroit riots of 1967 burn Loretta out of her house, Maureen has moved away from her family to a suburb with Kovack, repudiating "them," the underclass she comes from and the family whose violent ways have brought her misery.

West, Julian. *Looking Backward: 2000–1887; Equality.* Edward Bellamy. 1888; 1897.

Cast into the future, time-traveler Julian West divides his attention between learning about the new world in which he finds himself and "looking backward" on his own nineteenth-century America.

The novel begins as Julian is preparing to wed Edith Bartlett. As members of Boston's late-nineteenth-century patrician class, they cannot marry until they have a proper home, and because of strikes in the building industries, construction of their house has been indefinitely postponed. Thus Julian remains in a once prosperous but now rundown section of the city in his ancestral home, a mansion surrounded by sprawling proletarian destitution.

As if in subconscious alarm at his society's economic condition, Julian develops insomnia. In order to sleep, he must seal himself away nightly in a soundproof basement chamber and be lulled into slumber by a mysterious "Professor of Animal Magnetism." One night after the professor has administered his hypnotic treatment and left, Julian's house burns down. The fire kills a servant, the only other person who knows of the secret chamber. Thus Julian is presumed dead and is left in a state of suspended animation for 113 years.

In the year 2000, Julian is discovered and reawakened by Dr. Leete, a retired physician, and his wife and daughter. Once Julian has overcome his disorientation at being disjoined from his native epoch, he settles into a lengthy conversation with Dr. Leete about the differences between nineteenth-and twentieth-century economies.

Within fifty years of Julian's slumber, he finds, the social body was reorganized on a military model, with all persons serving in a great "industrial army." Largely through the elimination of wages and the centralization of all industry, social imbalances and ills have been eliminated. Each person receives an education, then serves a time as general laborer before settling into the profession that suits his or her capabilities. Women are included in the industrial army although their spheres of activity are largely kept separate from those of men. Other subjects that Julian and Dr. Leete discuss include education, religion, politics, law, international affairs, social classes, and universal brotherhood.

Dr. Leete's daughter Edith is actually the great-granddaughter of Julian's fiancée Edith Bartlett. Julian, struck by her likeness to his former love, soon succumbs to her charms and looks forward to a purposeful and illuminating life with her in the twenty-first century.

Westcott, Irene. "The Enormous Radio." John Cheever. 1953.

An enormous radio, designed to entertain, brings great discord to the life of Irene Westcott. The naive Irene discovers the extent of the ugliness in the lives of her neighbors and in her marriage.

Irene's comfortable, upper-middle-class existence is filled with such activities as lunching with friends, supervising her maid, caring for her children, and making sure that her husband Jim has a peaceful place to come home to after a hard day. When the family's radio breaks, Jim has an expensive new one delivered to their apartment, and the couple's troubles begin.

The large, ugly radio clashes with Irene's carefully chosen decor, but the way the machine works is even more of an annoyance. Initially it only blares static. Jim has the radio repaired. That evening Irene notices that the sounds coming through the receiver are not the usual waltzes, commercials, and news broadcasts of a radio station but the private conversations of her neighbors. Somehow this enormous radio allows them to tune into the lives of the people who live in their Sutton Place apartment building.

The radio's bizarre powers turn Irene into an eavesdropper. On the first evening that she and Jim discover its magical ability, they are amused by the petty concerns they hear expressed. Irene takes to listening to the radio more often, however, and discovers that in her building there are adulterous affairs, demanding parents, victims of disease, families facing bankruptcy, and even a call girl. Jim reassures Irene that their lives are not as sordid as their neighbors'.

Jim comes home one evening to find Irene crying. She has listened to the radio and overheard a man beating his wife. Jim refuses to interfere and has the radio fixed once again. Although they can no longer hear the disputes of others, Irene and Jim quickly begin to quarrel over their own problems. One day Jim accuses Irene of not appreciating the $400 he spent on the radio. When Jim's comments turn ugly, Irene locks herself in another room. She listens to Jim calling out their secrets near the front door while an announcer on the radio coolly recounts the day's disasters.

Wharton, Eliza. *The Coquette; or, The Life and Letters of Eliza Wharton.* Hannah Foster. 1797.

Eliza Wharton's story is told in epistolary form. Courted simultaneously by a respectable but stuffy cleric and a roguish flatterer, Eliza finds herself torn between social respectability and sexual desire. Her dilemma causes hesitation, and hesitation causes her downfall as she loses the respect of one suitor and succumbs to the seduction of the other. By her society's standards, she dies a ruined woman.

When the novel opens, vivacious young Eliza has narrowly escaped the fate of a miserable marriage; the stodgy clergyman to whom she was engaged in accordance with her family's wishes has fallen ill and died. Feeling elated in her sudden freedom, Eliza resolves to participate unfettered in "those pleasures which youth and innocence afford." She departs for an extended visit with her cousin Mrs. Richman. It is at the Richman residence that Eliza is introduced to the serious cleric J. BOYER. In spite of the young woman's insistence on remaining unattached for the time being, Boyer pursues her doggedly.

Boyer is rivaled in his suit by MAJOR PETER SANFORD, a charming aristocrat with a reputation as a rake. Unbeknownst to the community, Sanford, having squandered his fortune, is in dire financial straits. He is intrigued by Eliza and writes in a letter to a friend that he would marry her immediately if only she were an heiress. Still, excited by the challenge presented by a rival suitor, he resolves to pursue her even while he courts wealthier women.

Eliza soon becomes torn between what seem to be two equally unsatisfactory options. She knows that if she marries Boyer she will live the stultifying life of a clergyman's wife. But her friends and family discourage her from associating with the more attractive Major Sanford. Finally, pressed to make her decision, she resolves to follow her friends' advice and accept Boyer's proposal. But when she meets with Sanford to inform him of her choice, the two are discovered by Boyer, who assumes they are having a clandestine affair. Insisting in a letter to Eliza that he has been betrayed, Boyer ends their relationship. Soon afterward Sanford leaves town and is not heard from for some time.

Lonely and despondent, Eliza gives up her society life to become a recluse in her mother's house. Some months later, her health failing, she writes to Boyer and begs his forgiveness. He responds with a cruelly condescending letter that informs her of his engagement to another woman. Shortly thereafter Sanford returns to town with a new wife, a wealthy young woman, and Eliza is further demoralized.

Sanford has not lost his interest in seducing Eliza, however, and she is so despondent and morally weakened that she surrenders, entering into a secret affair with him. Meanwhile, her health continues to decline. By the time it becomes clear that she is carrying Sanford's child, Eliza is seriously ill. She writes final letters to her mother and her close friend Julia, apologizing for her conduct, then disappears.

When it is discovered that Eliza is missing, Julia confronts Sanford and demands to know her friend's whereabouts. Sanford, now somewhat contrite, informs her that Eliza is well taken care of but has asked him not to tell her friends or family where she is. He has, in fact, established her in Danvers, Massachusetts where she lives alone, awaiting certain death.

In her final days Eliza becomes spiritually awakened, forgiving Sanford and hoping for pardon for her own sins. Her child is stillborn, and she dies soon after. Eliza's friends visit her grave in Danvers, erecting a stone that reads in part: LET CANDOR THROW A VEIL OVER HER FRAILTIES FOR GREAT WAS HER CHARITY.

Wheeler, April Johnson. *Revolutionary Road.* Richard Yates. 1961.

April Johnson Wheeler is a young suburban housewife who longs for a more meaningful and stimulating life. April was the only child of a wealthy playboy and a flapper, who were divorced within a year of April's birth and who both died when April was still quite young. Most of her childhood was spent in the care of various aunts in a tedium relieved only by the infrequent and separate visits of one of her parents. Eventually April was sent to a sheltered boarding school where she finished out her teens. Upon graduation April left for New York City, where she briefly enrolled in drama school; but when she met FRANKLIN H. WHEELER, she soon found herself married and living a pleasantly exciting bohemian life in Greenwich Village. Things soured for her when she realized, not long after her marriage, that she was already pregnant. Frustrated and angered by what seemed a hindrance to the grand plans she and Frank had concocted, April decides to take a friend's advice and abort herself at the end of her first trimester. When she informs Frank of her plan, he refuses to condone it and eventually persuades her to have the child.

After their daughter's birth Frank moves the family to a suburb north of the city, and they buy a house on Revolutionary Road. Here April spends most of her time caring for the child and socializing with neighbors whom she doesn't really like. Because she also knows that Frank hates his job, April decides that they should abandon their stultifying life and take a chance on a new life in Paris, especially since they are only now turning thirty. Before long, April manages to convince Frank that her plan is a good one, and she convinces him that she can support them while he takes the time to "find himself." Accordingly, April researches travel arrangements, sorts out clothes, and begins to prepare to move to Paris. These plans are thwarted, however, when April realizes that she is pregnant again. As with her first pregnancy, April decides that she should abort herself. Once again, although armed this time with analytical arguments based on April's past and her lack of a normal family, Frank manages to convince her that they can simply postpone the move to Europe until the new baby is a few years old. April finally agrees, and as her first trimester ends, she prepares herself to complete the pregnancy.

One night soon after this, the Wheelers go to a nightclub with their friends and neighbors, the Campbells. After a while Frank is called upon to drive Milly Campbell home because she is quite drunk, and Shep and April stay behind to wait until Shep's car is unblocked. After a few more dances and some drinks, April and Shep make love in the back of his car. For Shep this is the fulfillment of a fantasy, for he has found April nearly irresistible; on April's part it is a meaningless, if not stupid, one-night stand. Soon after this, however, April asks Frank to let her sleep alone; the request prompts an argument, and April informs Frank that she has recently realized that she does not and probably never did love him. The next day, after making breakfast for Frank, April carefully cleans the house and then performs a late abortion on herself. Despite calling for assistance after the fetus appeared, April dies later that night of massive hemorrhaging, leaving a note for Frank in which she urges him not to blame himself, regardless of what happens.

Wheeler, Claude. *One of Ours.* Willa Cather. 1922.

Claude Wheeler, a young Nebraska farm boy, spends most of his youth in a fruitless search for meaning and excitement. During his late teens he and his best friend Ernest Havel spend hours in daring philosophical speculation. The boys yearn to expand their horizons. For Claude, though, the situation is one of restraint as he is forced to attend a conservative Christian college nearby, rather than the state university in Lincoln. He eventually manages to attend some courses in Lincoln, and he befriends a large and boisterous family, the Erlichs, who spur his desire for more knowledge.

However, while Claude decides to attend the university full-time, his father has determined another course for him. The elder Wheeler, a wealthy and conservative farmer, has taken advantage of a good financial deal and purchased a large ranch in Colorado. He decides that his youngest son, Ralph, should manage the ranch and that the family farm should be placed under Claude's care. The other Wheeler son, the dour Bayliss, has already established himself as a businessman in their hometown of Frankfort. Although disappointed, Claude complies with his father's wishes, remains on the farm, and begins to

court Enid Royce, the youngest daughter of the town miller.

The courtship culminates in a proposal that is at first rejected, then later accepted by Enid, who finds many things that concern her about their differences. Claude is not especially religious, while Enid is a zealous Christian. Nonetheless, Claude and Enid are married and in due course build a house. As might be expected, the marriage is weak from the start. Enid is a dutiful wife, but she does not like sex and devotes most of her energies to promoting the temperance movement, along with Bayliss Wheeler who also disapproves of drinking. By the time the first year of marriage is over, Ernest Havel is no longer welcome at Claude's home because Enid abhors his "freethinking" ways. The marriage shows no signs of improvement, and Claude gradually sinks into depression. He offers only a token opposition when Enid decides to travel to China to tend her ill sister, a missionary. Because she will be gone for a year, Claude closes their house and returns to his parents' homestead. There he enjoys the attentions of his mother and Mahailey, the family's maid, and all are preoccupied by the developments abroad.

National sentiment slowly builds and culminates in the entry of the United States into World War I; Claude is one of the first and most willing of the volunteers. After his training he is sent abroad on a troopship and endures a horrendous outbreak of influenza in which twenty-five men perish during the crossing. But for Claude the experience is exhilarating, and once in France he finds himself excited all the more by the new language and culture. He befriends another officer, David Gerhardt, and the two share military duties and leisure-time activities.

Eventually, Claude sees action and is lightly wounded in a shell barrage; but this does not dampen his enthusiasm, and he greets his next military assignment with fervent excitement. During this engagement—a trench-to-trench bombardment followed by the German troops' attack—David is killed by an exploding shell. Claude remains ignorant of this and bravely leads his troops in the defense of their position until he himself is killed, days after his twenty-fifth birthday.

Wheeler, Franklin H. *Revolutionary Road.* Richard Yates. 1961.

Franklin H. Wheeler, a thirty-year-old World War II veteran, lives with his wife APRIL (JOHNSON WHEELER) and their two children on Revolutionary Road north of New York City. Frank is the youngest son of middle-aged parents, who had already raised two sons by the time of his birth. As a result, Frank was left on his own from a young age and soon learned to develop somewhat romantic assumptions about his future. When he was eighteen he joined the army and was sent to Germany where he fought in the final campaigns of the war, and then he spent a year traveling through postwar Europe. Following this he returned to the United States and entered Columbia University; he did well academically and earned a reputation among his peers as a deep thinker and one who would have future success. He and two of his friends jointly rented an apartment in Greenwich Village; by the time they graduated, Frank had met April, and they had married and decided to use the apartment as their first home.

Although Frank despised his father's profession as a mediocre salesman for an office machine corporation, he soon takes a job with the same firm in order to support April and their family. April becomes pregnant with their first child and plans a self-induced abortion in order to allow Frank the time to explore his options for the successful future they envisioned, but Frank talks her out it. Eventually, stuck in a boring and meaningless job, Frank relocates his young family to the suburbs, and they purchase a house on Revolutionary Road. Here the young couple and their two children join the routine of suburbia, but April eventually comes up with a plan to move to Paris "for good" so that their early promise can be fulfilled. They announce these plans to their stunned and jealous neighbors, and begin preparations to move to Europe. At the same time, having just turned thirty, Frank finds himself restless and turns to a trivial affair with a coworker, twenty-two-year-old Maureen Grube from upstate New York. Although Frank isn't emotionally involved with Maureen, he sees her fairly frequently, especially since April announces, in a state of depression, that she is once again pregnant. April again plans an abortion and Frank works assiduously to talk her out of it.

Frank is able to convince April that they can go to Europe later, after the baby is a few years old, and in the meantime he has had a promising development on the job that seems to point in the direction of a better career. When April's pregnancy has passed the first trimester, Frank decides that he should break things off with Maureen, a decision prompted in part by the fact that April has asked him to move out of their bedroom. Finally, after ending his affair, Frank tells April about it in a moment of anger. He is deeply shocked when she tells him that she doesn't care and that she has only recently realized that she doesn't love him anyway and probably never has. Frank insists that she does love him, and the couple has a lengthy fight that results in a stalemate. During the night Frank tosses restlessly, imagining that he and April will patch things up, and the next morning he awakens to a hearty breakfast that April has prepared to fortify him for the business meeting which will determine his future career path. That day Frank is summoned to the hospital because April, now nearly in her fifth month, induced an abortion. She dies later that night. As the novel ends, Frank is once again living in New York City; his children are settled with an older brother, and Frank visits them on weekends.

Wheeler, Jason. *Union Square.* Albert Halper. 1933.

Jason Wheeler is a cynical, embittered writer living in New York in the early 1930s who manages to survive each successive day despite a broken heart, ill health, substance addiction, and a severe loss of faith and purpose. He describes himself as an ex-communist and ex-poet, but does not hesitate to criticize the political and literary practices of others.

Jason had been a prize-winning economics student at a midwestern university and at one time was celebrated as an extremely promising young poet. Before arriving in New York City, he traveled the country for three years, working as a dishwasher in Seattle, a steward on a Great Lakes excursion liner, a pipe-layer in Texas, a road worker in Iowa, and a busboy in Chicago. Once a belligerently active communist, Jason quit the Party in 1930 and now takes great pleasure in arguing with his only friend, LEON FISHER, a politically dedicated artist who makes posters for public demonstrations. He stopped writing poetry at the same time, became an alcoholic, and began to earn his living as a hack for cheap sex-story magazines. Until a few months before the beginning of the novel, Jason had been living with a woman named Sylvia, but she left him after trying unsuccessfully to rid him of his drinking habit.

One day in October 1931, Jason goes for a walk and on impulse walks into a hospital and says there is something wrong with his chest or lungs; there is no doctor available until the next morning, but the nurse, Miss Allen, takes pity on him and gives him some medicine, which he promptly throws away when he leaves. Some time later Miss Allen gets in touch with him, and they begin to take regular walks together. Jason is still obsessed with Sylvia, however, and spends much of that fall writing letters to her in Philadelphia without receiving a response. On Christmas Day, Leon arrives excitedly with a letter from Philadelphia in his hand; Jason is severely disappointed when he learns it is an announcement that one of Leon's paintings has been accepted in an exhibition in that city. Later that day he finds Miss Allen and tells her not to waste her time on a drunk like him.

After New Year's, Jason decides to go to Philadelphia to get Sylvia back; he returns the next day and almost overdoses on dope, which apparently he has been taking for some time. A few days later Leon, worried about his friend, badgers him into attending a political meeting followed by a proletarian poetry reading. The once-celebrated poet's presence causes a stir, and his opinion is solicited after the reading; he angers the group by saying that the poems were neither good nor proletarian and, further, that what the revolution needs is workers, not parasite artists. After the meeting Jason takes the opportunity to talk to Helen Jackson, a tough Party member from New Orleans who happens to live in his building. The mild-mannered and virginal Leon is in love with Helen and is completely unaware that she is another man's mistress. Jason threatens to break every bone in her body if she ever hurts Leon.

Jason continues to write to Philadelphia without success, but he quits taking dope. Miss Allen visits one day, and he warns her off again but makes love to her when she breaks down crying. Later that afternoon he goes out, after carelessly dropping a cigarette butt in the basement. A letter from Sylvia is in his mailbox, but he tears it up without even reading it as he makes his way to Union Square where a big demonstration is being held. Meanwhile, Leon arrives at Jason and Helen's building, discovers that it is on fire, goes upstairs to give the alarm, and sees Helen and her lover naked together. Devastated, he leaves by another exit so as not to face the woman again. Jason returns to find his building in flames, and Helen tells him that Leon is still inside. He punches her and kicks her when he understands what has happened, and then he finds out that the fire was caused by his cigarette butt. As the novel concludes, Jason, believing that Leon is dead, makes his way to the hospital to ask Miss Allen for money to pay for a room.

Whipple, Judge Silas. *The Crisis.* Winston Churchill. 1901.

Silas Whipple, the fanatical abolitionist in this novel, holds the position of judge in St. Louis, Missouri. He oversees STEPHEN BRICE's transformation from conservative New England aristocrat to supporter of President Abraham Lincoln and proponent of the anti-slavery movement.

Stephen's father, now dead, was an old friend of the Judge's. Whipple agrees to assist Stephen, who is well bred but poor, in furthering his legal education. The first meeting between the two men is tense, however. They have radically opposing ideas about the nature of slavery. Whipple believes that those who are held in bondage have souls. According to the Judge, any system that perpetuates the belief that material possessions are more important than the spiritual and physical state of individuals is morally bankrupt. Stephen argues that property is the most important condition to ensure that liberty for America's citizens is maintained. To deny one form of property means that any form of property can be denied, and soon all liberties and freedoms will be lost.

Despite their opposing views, Whipple likes Stephen and can easily detect his natural virtues. Whipple is open-minded enough to count among his friends COLONEL COMYN CARVEL, the prominent local slave owner whose daughter gradually falls in love with Stephen. Whipple and Carvel often argue over the morality of slavery. Whipple usually takes the unbending moral position that has gained him the reputation as a good man, but a man quite radical and eccentric for the St. Louis community. He eventually succeeds in winning Stephen over to the anti-slavery cause. After meeting with Abraham Lincoln, Stephen tells the Judge that he feels he has been born again in the West.

When the elderly Whipple becomes ill, the Colonel's daughter Virginia insists that the Judge seek the advice of a doctor and get some rest. His health steadily worsens as the Civil War rages. Stephen, now a major in the Union Army, visits his mentor and pleases the Judge by his new insights into the issues that are tearing the nation apart. Even Colonel Carvel risks charges of spying behind enemy lines to see his old friend before he dies. Whipple dies before the end of the war, but his work will be capably carried on by Stephen and his new bride, Virginia.

Whitacre, Michael. *The Young Lions.* Irwin Shaw. 1958.

Michael Whitacre, a Broadway stage manager, has recently married Hollywood starlet Laura Harrington. But Michael feels a nagging emptiness in his life that his personal and professional success cannot fill. At a party in his wife's honor he listens to the tales of an Irish mercenary and yearns for the thrill and adventure that is missing from his life.

As Michael listens on the radio to the series of events in Europe leading up to World War II, the deteriorating world political climate reminds him of his own crumbling marriage. His wife grows increasingly distant, and Michael begins to suspect that she is having an affair with another actor. Michael, meanwhile, develops an interest in a young woman named Margaret Freemantle, the girlfriend of one of his wife's producer friends. He and Margaret become sexually involved. When Laura confesses to him that she, too, has been maintaining an outside relationship, the two decide to separate.

When the United States enters the war after the Japanese attack on Pearl Harbor, Michael delays enlistment only long enough to finish the Broadway show he is working on. Despite various offers from influential friends, and much to the horror of his girlfriend Margaret, Michael insists on starting at the bottom of the military ladder as a private in the infantry. He is barely able to survive the intensive training or to endure the other members of his company, whom he considers ignorant farmhands. When the brutal prejudice displayed by the other men in his barracks causes a Jewish soldier named NOAH ACKERMAN to go AWOL, Michael makes a phone call to an influential friend to secure a clerical post overseas.

Stationed in an army headquarters in London, Michael immediately despises his office job and hates himself even more for not having the courage to remain with his old company. When he befriends a captain in a London pub, the captain is able to arrange for him to become his driver. One day on a tour of one of the American hospitals, Michael runs into Private Ackerman, recovering from a leg injury. When Ackerman confides to him that he is going to try to make it back to his old company, Michael sees his last opportunity for combat before the end of the war. He goes AWOL and returns with Ackerman.

With the Nazis in retreat, Michael sees very little combat after arriving with Ackerman back at his old company. But when they come across a deserted concentration camp, Ackerman is killed by a sniper, CHRISTIAN DIESTL, while talking to Michael. The horrified Michael finally has his opportunity for combat as he clumsily hunts the German in the nearby woods. With more than a little luck, Michael is able to kill the German soldier. Changed and bitter from his first real war experience, he returns to the camp with Ackerman's corpse in his arms.

White, Carrie. *Carrie.* Stephen King. 1974.

Carrie White is a tortured, lonely adolescent with telekinetic powers. Pimpled, dumpy, and shy, she has always been the scapegoat of her classmates and subject to the distorted religious beliefs of her mother Margaret. Although Margaret struggles to keep Carrie outside the secular world, she sometimes relents because she knows Carrie can use her powers to wreak great physical destruction. Carrie's classmates are unaware of her supernatural abilities, however.

While showering at the high school after gym class, Carrie, sixteen, gets her period for the first time. Chris Hargensen, a cruel popular girl, notices the blood and shouts "Period, period" at her. Carrie, terrified, thinks that she is bleeding to death. The other girls in the locker room join the torment; they throw tampons and sanitary napkins at her and chant "Plug it up" until they're halted by the arrival of the gym teacher, Miss Desjardin.

Disgusted by her students' heartlessness, Miss Desjardin angrily sends them away and helps Carrie clean up. Sensing the girl's bafflement, Miss Desjardin briefly explains menstruation and sends her home to recuperate. But home is no refuge for Carrie. Margaret has purposely never told her daughter about reproduction. To Margaret, anything connected with reproduction is the devil's work. She banishes Carrie to the closet to pray away the lustful thoughts that, according to her twisted beliefs, must have brought on the period. The closet, with its harrowing depiction of Jonathan Edwards's "Sinners in the Hands of an Angry God," terrifies Carrie. She begs not to be locked in, but Margaret is unrelenting in her fury.

Carrie has the power, through telekinesis, to subdue her mother, but she usually hesitates to use it. It's difficult for her to challenge the authority of the only person who has ever loved her. Above all, Carrie wants to be normal. She daydreams about wearing fashionable clothes like the popular girls, rather than the dumpy, outmoded styles insisted on by her mother. To release the frustration she feels, Carrie practices moving the objects in her room by mind power.

Miss Desjardin disciplines the girls involved in the locker room incident. They must submit to grueling detention in the gym or forfeit their prom tickets. Chris Hargensen loses her tickets and promises revenge on those who give in to Miss Desjardin. But most of the others, including Susan Snell, who feels horrible about having participated in the sadistic treatment of Carrie, gladly submit to the punishment. To further appease her guilt, Susan convinces her boyfriend, the handsome Tommie Ross, to invite Carrie to the prom. Hearing of this, Chris plots a horrible humiliation for Carrie's first dance.

Dumbstruck and wary of the invitation, Carrie nevertheless sews herself a beautiful velvet dress. She resists her mother's warnings and threats about the sinfulness of such an event. Margaret protests until the very day of the dance, but she realizes that locking up Carrie again might prove disastrous. Years earlier, after being punished for looking at a neighbor in a bikini, Carrie called down a rain of rocks on their house. Margaret fears another display of powers that she believes come from the devil.

Tommie is impressed by Carrie when he picks her up. Although shy with each other, they realize they have a chance for a nice time, despite the oddness of the situation. At the prom, those who once called her names greet her with surprising kindness. Miss Desjardin expresses her delight at Carrie's looking so pretty and happy, and wishes her a magical evening.

Chris has had the voting rigged to ensure that Carrie and Tommie become king and queen of the prom. Carrie stands on the stage beaming with undreamed of happiness, unaware that Chris and her hoodlum boyfriend are perched in the rafters with a bucket of pig's blood. When the cheer goes up for the new king and queen, Carrie finds herself suddenly drenched in red liquid. Little by little the prom-goers begin to laugh, and Carrie stumbles out in shame.

A few minutes later Carrie returns to take her revenge. Imagining a large-scale plot behind her ultimate humiliation, she uses telekinesis to bolt the gymnasium doors and turn on the sprinklers. At first she only means to frighten everyone inside, but the past cruelties begin to fill her mind. As the students begin screaming for help, a spark from the sound equipment electrocutes a band member, and the fire that ensues turns the locked gym into an inferno. Carrie wanders through the town and knocks the tops off every fireplug, which renders the rest of the townspeople helpless.

At home Margaret has been plotting to kill the child that she couldn't save from the devil. She manages to stab Carrie through the shoulder with a huge knife before faltering under her daughter's powers. Carrie uses her mind to slowly stop Margaret's heart. Carrie then staggers back into town, where she dies from her wound on the town common. She leaves behind over four hundred dead. The few survivors write books, grant interviews, and bicker about the mysterious Carrie White who leveled their town.

White Fang. *White Fang.* Jack London. 1928.

This tale traces the transformation of the wild wolf cub White Fang to a domesticated but vicious dog and then to a devoted and trusted pet. As a pup, White Fang, born in a carefully selected lair, imagines that the walls of his cave encompass the entire world. Of five cubs, he alone survives to stumble out into the world beyond the lair. White Fang soon learns to abide by the credo "eat or be eaten," and he comes to display a true knack for survival.

When still a young cub, White Fang is caught by the Indian tribe from which his mother Kiche had escaped. The Indians recapture his mother, and she and White Fang become the property of Gray Beaver. The wolves display an instinctive desire to obey people, or "gods," as White Fang imagines them. Although White Fang attempts to escape once after his mother is sold, he returns and becomes indispensable as a protector of Gray Beaver and his family. Meanwhile, his relationship with the camp's other dogs is one of total mutual antagonism: They hate and fear him, and he will kill any dog who attempts to interfere with him or his master.

At Fort Yukon with Gray Beaver on a trading expedition, White Fang spends his time killing the unsuspecting dogs newly arrived at the northern land. Gray Beaver is eventually forced to sell his dog to Beauty Smith, a merciless coward who turns White Fang into a professional fighter. Smith exacerbates White Fang's natural ruthlessness by treating the dog with abject cruelty, and the dog becomes legendary for his prowess as a killer. White Fang finally meets his match in a bulldog, an unfamiliar breed impervious to his slashing techniques. In the death clutches of this dog, White Fang is saved by Weedon Scott, who becomes his new master.

For the first time in his life White Fang is treated with kindness. Scott patiently endures White Fang's hostility while offering him soft words and loving caresses. In turn, White Fang grows to worship his new master, and this limitless affection governs all his actions. He refuses to allow his master out of his sight and lives for the sound of his voice. So devoted is he that Scott decides to take White Fang back with him to California.

White Fang is forever haunted by streetcars, his first taste of civilization. On the Scott ranch he must learn to coexist peacefully with the other dogs and animals as well as the master's family. For the love of his master, he subdues his natural aggression. White Fang grows in the estimation of the skeptical family when he saves Scott after he is thrown from a horse. He earns the name Blessed Wolf when he kills a convict who attempts to murder Judge Scott, Weedon's father. After surviving nearly fatal wounds inflicted by the convict, White Fang unequivocally becomes one of the family. He hobbles down to the barn on weak legs to nuzzle the puppies he has sired.

White-Jacket. *White-Jacket; or The World in a Man-of-War.* Herman Melville. 1850.

In this semi-autobiographical account, the author relates through the narrator, White-Jacket, his experiences aboard a United States frigate. The character White-Jacket—whose name derives from his homemade coat—is often subsumed by Melville the polemicist. The plot consists of a loosely assembled series of anecdotes and observations made on the homeward-bound voyage of the United States frigate *Neversink.*

White-Jacket views his ship as a microcosmic allegory for American democracy. As such, he attempts to expose the arbitrary fictions and pretensions that underlie military authority and, by extension, all social hierarchies. The extreme cleanliness of the ship, which is maintained only by rigid discipline, symbolizes the use of arbitrary power to maintain a system so neat it seems natural, and so natural that the sailors never think life can be otherwise. The crew is allowed occasional release from oppression in the carefully ordered disorder of theatricals and "sky-larkings." But these events and onshore "liberties" only create the illusion of freedom.

White-Jacket's most vivid commentary can be found in his descriptions of flogging. The naval authorities justify these institutionalized beatings by calling them an appeal to order and discipline. The crew, and indeed the United States Congress, allows the practice to continue because their moral sense has been dulled by the monotony of tradition. Evil customs have become so habitual that they no longer seem cruel. White-Jacket engages in a minute examination of the "self-evident" Articles of War and concludes that these blatantly immoral, violent acts threaten to turn the Declaration of Independence into a vain lie.

Although White-Jacket exposes the hypocrisies of a democratic system, he also exuberantly hopes that past history will be wiped out to enable the limitless potential of the future to be realized. He maintains an idealistic belief in progress as the foundation of his desire for institutional reform. At times his visionary optimism lapses into an almost jingoistic nationalism: America was, is, and will be the vanguard of the free world. And yet beneath this impulse to reform lies a desperate suspicion that evil is innate, corruption is organic, and change is impossible.

White-Jacket's individual identity in this system is made manifest by the odd-looking jacket itself. Since it is different from standard navy issue, the jacket becomes the source of his identity, indeed his very name. And yet the jacket also weighs heavily as a burden; it singles him out, makes him the object of prejudice and ridicule, and almost causes his death. While aloft in the rigging, White-Jacket is blinded by the voluminous material of the coat and falls overboard. In a scene symbolic of baptism and rebirth, he cuts himself loose from the jacket, thus saving himself from drowning.

White-Jacket ends his account in a summarily equivocal fashion: He still believes it is important to expose the ills of society, but he has come to the intensely bitter realization that it is we ourselves who impose these evils on one another. Perhaps the only tentative solution he can offer is the ritualistic hope for self-renewal and rebirth.

Wieland, Clara. *Wieland; or the Transformation: An American Tale.* Charles Brockden Brown. 1798.

Clara Wieland is the only daughter of the wealthy and nobly descended Theodore Wieland, Sr. After the deaths of their parents, Clara and her brother THEODORE (WIE-LAND, Jr.) divide the family estate; Clara takes up residence in a small house set off from the nearby main house, which is occupied by her brother, his wife, and their children. Their tranquility is disrupted when Clara, along with the rest of her family, is drawn into a welter of mysterious and frightening events initiated by the arrival of an intelligent but odd stranger, FRANCIS CARWIN.

The strange events begin as Theodore and his childhood friend PLEYEL walk the grounds of his estate. They are talking about the chances of going to Europe, where Pleyel has fallen in love with Theresa, Baroness de Stolberg, whom he wishes to marry. Their conversation is interrupted, however, when they seem to hear Catharine, Theodore's wife, saying that the baroness has died. They cannot account for this voice because they know that Catharine is with Clara. This odd circumstance is further complicated when Clara overhears what appears to be a plot to take her life. In her fear over such a plan, Clara rushes to Theodore's home but faints when she reaches the door.

As time passes, Carwin becomes a regular guest of Clara and of Theodore. During this period Clara begins to fall in love with Pleyel, and she hopes that before long he will propose to her. On one particular occasion Clara, having dreamed that her brother was trying to kill her, is paralyzed with fear; when Carwin arrives, her anxiety is exacerbated as she contemplates his odd background and manners. Pleyel arrives the next morning, but Clara had expected him the night before; he denounces her bitterly for her fall from grace. As it turns out, as he tells Theodore, Pleyel had overheard Carwin and Clara in a "profligate" conversation, and he therefore can no longer feel affection or respect for the genteel woman to whom he was about to propose. The perplexed Clara maintains her innocence, but Pleyel remains unmoved. Relying on a news item to persuade Clara of the dangers of her association, Pleyel exposes Carwin as a convicted and escaped murderer.

Angered and humiliated, Clara agrees to see Carwin late at night in order to stop him from interfering with her life any further. Events take an even more bizarre turn when Clara discovers the body of her dead sister-in-law.

In shock, Clara immediately falls ill, and her situation worsens when she learns that Theodore's entire family has been murdered. Clara remains ill for a long time.

While the despairing Clara languishes, longing for her own death, she learns that Pleyel has returned and that he attended her faithfully during her illness despite the fact that his baroness was alive. In order to escape the horrible memories facing her in America, Clara agrees to travel to Europe with her uncle; before leaving she returns to her house to destroy her diary. Here she meets Carwin, who explains that his abilities as a mimic and ventriloquist have inadvertently led to the dire events in the Wieland family. As he explains this to an angry Clara, Theodore—the true killer—escapes from jail and attempts to continue what he thinks of as his divine mission by killing Clara. Theodore ultimately fails, because Carwin uses ventriloquism to convince him that the sacrifice of Clara is unnecessary, and commits suicide. The novel ends with a postscript explaining that the baroness died during childbirth, Clara is now reunited with Pleyel, and the couple resides in Europe with Clara's maternal uncle, Thomas Cambridge.

Wieland, Theodore. *Wieland; or The Transformation: An American Tale.* Charles Brockden Brown. 1798.

Theodore Wieland is a well-educated classical scholar and the respected brother of CLARA (WIELAND). The Wieland estate has been divided between them. The family's history has been besmirched by a series of untoward and mysterious events, including the spontaneous combustion of Theodore Wieland, Sr., who died after a strange occurrence at his temple, located on the grounds of the Wieland estate. The family, in particular its men, has had a long preoccupation with religious and spiritual matters, and Wieland, Jr., is no exception. He and his closest friend PLEYEL engage in frequent disputations about such matters. In addition, Wieland is married to Catharine Pleyel, his friend's sister, and the couple has four young children.

As the novel progresses, a new series of strange events begin to take place in and around the grounds of the estate. Voices are heard and recognized, but cannot be accounted for. Wieland is convinced he has heard his wife calling out to him, even though he is told that she remained in the house with Clara and Pleyel; more frighteningly, Clara believes she has overheard a plot to kill her. Voices continue to plague the Wielands, and both siblings are increasingly on edge. A newcomer, FRANCIS CARWIN, appears. Pleyel met him when he traveled in Spain. Carwin, although odd-looking and unusually dressed, is accepted into the circle of friends and family, and he becomes a regular guest of both Wieland and Clara.

Carwin becomes a participant in the Wielands' intellectual conversations, but things take a turn for the worse when Pleyel, who had decided to marry Clara, overhears a conversation between Clara and Carwin. Shocked by the details he hears, Pleyel scornfully rejects Clara and explains to Wieland that the things he heard were degrading and shocking, and they precluded any further attentions on his part. Clara is unable to convince Pleyel of her innocence, but Wieland appears to believe her account of the previous evening when she did not see Carwin at all. While Clara attempts one more time to dissuade Pleyel from his conviction of her sinfulness, Wieland's life takes a dramatic turn. When Clara returns home with the hope of having it out with Carwin, she discovers her sister-in-law's dead body. This discovery, coupled with news of the death of Wieland's entire family, causes Clara to become very ill, and she is too sick to follow the events in the aftermath of the killings. As it turns out, Wieland, in a religious frenzy augmented by the continuation of the strange voices, became convinced that God wanted him to kill his wife and children in order to assure his salvation and theirs.

Wieland is arrested, tried, and convicted after his confession reveals him to be mentally unbalanced. He escapes twice after his incarceration, and each time he is recaptured during an effort to locate and kill Clara and Pleyel. He eventually escapes and travels to Clara's house, where he finds her with Carwin who has just explained his role in the events leading to the murders. When Wieland realizes that the voices he suspected of divinity were in fact produced by Carwin, a mimic and ventriloquist, he understands that he lost his senses and combined the results of Carwin's ventriloquism with his own need for communication with God. As Carwin once more uses ventriloquism to prevent Clara's death, Wieland, realizing his folly, seizes Clara's knife and kills himself.

Wilbourne, Harry. *The Wild Palms.* William Faulkner. 1939.

Raised in an orphanage and later by an older half-sister, Harry must use almost all the money he earns to pay for medical school. His life becomes totally devoid of sensation of any kind, including love, so that at twenty-seven, when he meets CHARLOTTE RITTENMEYER, he succumbs easily to her charms. Charlotte is a sculptor married to "Rat" Rittenmeyer. She is domineering and viciously passionate (when she wants his attention, she grabs him; when she wants to kiss him, she jerks him by the hair). Harry is hopelessly in love with her, but she soon decides to terminate their affair since he has no money. Then he finds $1,275 in a wallet in a trash bin; Charlotte leaves Rat, who loves her, and she and Harry escape to a life of passion.

The couple travels to Chicago and work there for a while, but Harry loses his job. A friend of Charlotte's allows them to use a cabin in the Wisconsin woods, but when their food runs out, they must return to Chicago. Charlotte gets a job dressing windows, and Harry writes true confession stories.

As their life together is supposed to be about passion

and not middle-class safety, Harry decides they have to leave Chicago. He accepts a job as a doctor in a Utah mining camp. He and Charlotte arrive, only to find that they must share a two-room house with the caretaker and his wife and that no one has been paid in more than a year. The caretaker and his wife are waiting for the spring when they will take the train out; but the wife becomes pregnant, and their meager savings will not support them and a child. The caretaker and Charlotte convince Harry to abort the fetus. He does, and the caretaker couple leaves, as do the rest of the miners. Harry and Charlotte are alone for the first time since they arrived. They make passionate love, but without, as Harry finds out later, Charlotte's usual anti-pregnancy precautions. She soon discovers she is pregnant and wants Harry to perform an abortion, but he refuses. They travel to New Orleans to try to find some other method of terminating the pregnancy, to no avail.

Eventually, Harry agrees to perform the abortion very late in Charlotte's trimester. Something goes wrong: Charlotte is not healing, but she refuses to see a doctor. Harry suspects that Charlotte will die, and they go to the seaside cottage they have rented to wait. The cottage is owned by an old doctor and his wife who live next door. The old couple watches Harry and Charlotte move in and quickly realizes that Charlotte is ill. When the old doctor guesses the cause of Charlotte's illness, he calls the police and an ambulance, and holds Harry at gunpoint. Charlotte dies in the hospital, and Harry is arrested. Rittenmeyer visits him, pays his bail, and gives him money to flee, but Harry cannot. At the trial, Harry is sentenced to fifty years of hard labor in the state penitentiary at Parchman. After Harry is sentenced, Rittenmeyer visits him again and offers him a cyanide capsule. Harry cannot take that escape, either; he realizes that the reason he cannot accept escape from punishment is that running away or dying would diminish the passion of the memory of the only love he has ever known.

Wilbur, Ross. *Moran of the Lady Letty.* Frank Norris. 1898.

A Yale graduate and turn-of-the-century San Francisco club man, Ross Wilbur is one of the most popular young men in society. One day, as he is strolling down to the waterfront to await the arrival of a friend, he is shanghaied aboard the schooner *Bertha Millner* and thrown into the greatest adventure of his life. He is immediately pressed into service by the sea-hardened skipper, Captain Kitchell, and the Chinese crew, and within hours of his capture he finds himself sailing out into the Pacific.

Wilbur quickly adapts to his new environment, for Captain Kitchell has promised to make a seafaring man of him or throw him to the sharks. Within weeks Captain Kitchell and his crew come upon an apparently abandoned ship. Kitchell and Wilbur board the ship, which has been disabled by an explosion, and discover a lone survivor. When Wilbur returns to the *Bertha Millner* with the wounded sailor, Kitchell remains behind; minutes later the ship, the *Lady Letty*, sinks, taking the captain to a watery grave. Wilbur is shocked to realize that the sailor he has rescued is a woman named Moran Sternersen. Moran turns out to be a seaworthy sailor; she had captained the *Lady Letty* with her father who died in the explosion.

With Moran as captain, the crew continues its shark-fishing trip down the California coast. Once they reach Magdalena Bay, Wilbur and Moran are abandoned by the rest of the crew when a mysterious entity causes the ship to rise and list on the ocean. Then as Moran and Wilbur prepare to sail the ship back to San Francisco alone, they are approached by a beachcombers' junk whose crew convinces the two seafarers to help them hoist a whale and gather its oil. The beachcombers divide their take with Moran and Wilbur and are heading out to sea when Moran discovers a huge deposit of ambergris in the whale's carcass. Knowing that the fragrant secretion will result in a fortune, Moran attempts to gather the substance aboard without attracting the attention of the departing sailors, but she is unsuccessful. After their valuable cargo is stolen and their ship is damaged, the companions race for the beach.

After camping on the beach and repairing their ship, the couple is reunited with their AWOL crew, whose leader informs them that the junk has been wrecked offshore and the beachcombers have come ashore with designs on the *Bertha Millner*. Determined to retrieve the ambergris, Moran recruits the *Bertha Millner*'s crew to help her and Wilbur ambush the beachcombers. During the fight Wilbur kills another human being for the first time. The taking of a life awakens some primeval strength in him that impels him to perform magnificently during the battle. As the battle rages, he engages in a deadly contest with Moran who attacks him in a blind frenzy. When he outmaneuvers her, she submits to him and offers the declaration of love that she withheld when earlier Wilbur had revealed his amorous feelings for her.

When the *Bertha Millner* sails out of Magdalena Bay the next day, a new captain commands her. Moran has become a woman in love, desiring the protection of her man. The crew finally sails into the waters off San Diego, and Wilbur receives a hero's welcome when he appears unexpectedly at a cotillion being given by some of his set from San Francisco. Wilbur informs his friends that he can never return to his former meaningless life of leisure and instead plans to sail with Moran to Cuba. He and Moran sail the *Bertha Millner* on to San Francisco where Wilbur goes ashore.

Later, Wilbur walks along the shore toward the Golden Gate Bridge, attempting to decide whether he wants to sail with Moran into the open seas or return to his life as a dandy. His musings are interrupted by the captain of the Lifeboat Station, who runs him down to tell him that Moran has been murdered by one of the beachcombers and that the *Bertha Millner* is heading unmanned out to open sea. Wilbur watches from the shore as Moran's body is taken out to sea by the drifting ship.

Wilhelm, Tommy. *Seize the Day.* Saul Bellow. 1956.

When Tommy Wilhelm (originally "Wilky Adler") is in college, an alleged talent scout, Maurice Venice, spots his handsome face in the college paper and invites him to his New York office for an interview, claiming to have placed several well-known personages in show business. Since Tommy is drifting in college, he agrees to take a screen test. Following his newfound "ambition" or "delusion" to be an actor, Tommy moves to Los Angeles. With the exception of a couple of roles as an extra, his career goes nowhere for seven years.

Upon returning to his native New York, Tommy marries a woman named Margaret. He and Margaret, whose college education he pays for, have two boys. Having gone to work as a salesman for the Rojax Corporation, Tommy eventually has the responsibility of the entire New England region. Because of his new position, Tommy moves to an apartment in Roxbury, Massachusetts, and there he becomes close to a woman named Olive.

When Tommy asks Margaret for a divorce, she refuses, and shortly afterward he is fired from the Rojax Corporation. Viewing his life as one series of wrong decisions, he finds himself confused about the direction in which he has gone and is going.

Tommy now lives on upper Broadway in New York at the Hotel Gloriana, predominantly occupied by the elderly, of whose ranks his widowed father, Dr. Adler, is a member. Dr. Adler, concerned solely with his own approaching death, is openly indifferent to Tommy's litany of emotional and financial difficulties. Dr. Adler criticizes him for his sloppiness and his uncertain position in life, and tells him over and over to return to his wife.

Also residing at the hotel is Dr. Tamkin, an alleged doctor and expert in psychological matters who is an advocate of playing the stock market. Tamkin looks upon Tommy as a patient and espouses his various interpretations of man's condition. Tommy can't decide whether Dr. Tamkin is a sage or a confidence man. Tamkin advises Tommy to forget about the past and future, for these can only be a source of pain and anxiety, and to "seize the day" instead. He convinces Tommy to collaborate on an investment in lard futures. But to his chagrin, Tommy sees that Tamkin contributes only $300 to Tommy's thousand.

En route to the local branch stockbroker office, Tommy and Tamkin encounter a blind man, whom Tommy ushers across the street. Tamkin meanwhile goes into the office. When Tommy returns, Tamkin is gone, and so is Tommy's investment. After a useless talk with his father and then with his wife, Tommy searches the streets for Tamkin. He finds himself swept by a crowd into a funeral procession, where he breaks down and cries with deep spiritual pain next to the open casket of a stranger.

Wilkerson, Thomas. *The Lynchers.* John Edgar Wideman. 1973.

Thomas Wilkerson is one of a group of four young black men whose anger at racism leads them to formulate a violent plan of revenge. Thomas was raised by his hard-working mother and his philandering father in a ghetto area. Despite the family's efforts, they gained little economic advancement, partly due to Mr. Wilkerson's propensity for liquor and other women. At the time of the novel, Thomas is a struggling schoolteacher and his parents' marriage is seemingly ending. However, Thomas tries to maintain his sense of purpose in his chaotic world.

Only gradually does he become involved in the plan to lynch a white police officer, under the supervision of his friend WILLIE "LITTLEMAN" HALL. Thomas is drawn to the plan both because of its revolutionary nature and his own unexplored need for revenge against the system. His anger is only deepened when his parents cause a scene as he is presenting his girlfriend Tanya to them. On the night of their scheduled dinner, his father arrives home after a two-day absence, and he and Thomas's mother fall into a vicious argument that results in Thomas's departure with Tanya.

Thomas increasingly turns his attention to the proposed lynching, especially after Littleman is incapacitated and the men must proceed without his physical presence. As the preliminary stages of the plan evolve into action, Thomas begins to feel a gnawing doubt about its efficacy and morality. Nonetheless, he continues to conspire with his friends, and the day of the first stage of the plan swiftly approaches.

The hesitation that Thomas experiences gradually leads him to think that he should not participate in the plan. The movement of his resolve away from the proposed violence is exacerbated by the sudden arrest of his father, who is imprisoned after inadvertently murdering his best friend in a drunken knife fight. Thomas's mother is devastated. When she is unable to see her husband in jail, the task devolves to Thomas. This visit with his incarcerated father further augments Thomas's abhorrence of violence.

As he begins planning his father's defense, Thomas comes to see that the violence his father committed is directly related to what he and his friends were planning. In the few days following his father's arrest, Thomas's mother is eventually able to visit her husband, and the two seem to connect through the medium of their sorrow. This in turn prompts Thomas to draw closer to Tanya, and he suddenly appears in her apartment with a rambling explanation of his actions. Thomas eventually expresses his desire to thwart the lynching, and by the end of the novel he has, along with another of the planners, managed to prevent the successful implementation of the plot. The novel ends on an optimistic note, with Thomas hoping that he will be able to achieve a sense of peace and dignity.

Wilkes, Ashley. *Gone with the Wind.* Margaret Mitchell. 1936.

Ashley Wilkes is the well-educated and philosophical scion of the wealthy Wilkes family of Georgia. Although Ashley marries his cousin MELANIE HAMILTON (WILKES) soon after the outbreak of the Civil War, he is beset with doubts when the passionate SCARLETT O'HARA, fiery daughter of Gerald and Ellen O'Hara from the neighboring plantation of Tara, repeatedly declares her love for him.

Despite his revulsion for war, Ashley enlists in the Confederate Army. He endures much hardship and understands that the way of life to which he was born cannot exist again. On leave in Atlanta, Ashley stays with Melanie and Scarlett at the home of Melanie's aunt. Before he returns to battle, he begs Scarlett to watch over the pregnant Melanie. After being incarcerated in a northern prison camp, Ashley returns to find Twelve Oaks, the Wilkeses' plantation, burned to the ground. His family and its fortune have been devastated by war.

Although fiercely proud, Ashley is forced to stay at Tara with Melanie and his new child simply because of the scarcity of food and shelter. The close proximity to Scarlett rekindles his old confusion, and the two nearly elope before reason and duty prevail. Following a tearful scene with Scarlett, Melanie persuades Ashley to relocate the family to Atlanta where he can help Scarlett run the lumber shop and mill that she and her new husband Frank Kennedy own.

In Atlanta, the tensions grow. Scarlett defies convention by running her business even while pregnant. Ashley, along with Frank Kennedy, becomes involved in a Ku Klux Klan raid on a shantytown following an attack on Scarlett. The two men fare poorly in this attack; Frank is killed and Ashley is wounded. It is only through a ruse on the part of RHETT BUTLER that the men are saved from arrest by the Yankee occupation forces.

After Frank's death, Scarlett relies more heavily on Ashley's help, although he disapproves of her practice of hiring convicts as cheaper labor than freed blacks. Despite their business disagreements, Ashley continues to work for Scarlett after her marriage to Rhett Butler. As Reconstruction continues, the Wilkeses' fortunes continue to improve, and Ashley eventually acquires the business from Scarlett, thus enabling him to institute his own reforms.

Tragedy strikes once again when Melanie, against medical advice, becomes pregnant a second time. She eventually loses the baby and then dies as a result of her miscarriage. After Melanie's death, Ashley reveals to Scarlett that Melanie was the only woman he ever loved.

Wilkes, Melanie Hamilton. *Gone with the Wind.* Margaret Mitchell. 1936.

Melanie Hamilton Wilkes is the compassionate and loving wife of ASHLEY WILKES, her cousin. Soft-spoken and well educated, Melanie epitomizes the elegant, aristocratic lady of the antebellum South. Melanie's stability and gentleness stand in counterpoint to the haughty demeanor of her sister-in-law SCARLETT O'HARA. The two become in-laws when Scarlett marries Charles Hamilton in outrage after Melanie's engagement to Ashley is announced.

Melanie's child, conceived while Ashley was on leave from the Civil War, is born during the final siege of Atlanta. The two are brought at great risk to the O'Hara plantation by a frightened but determined Scarlett. Here, as she recovers from the birth, Melanie begins to help Scarlett with her plans to revitalize Tara, the O'Hara plantation. The two women supervise the household, and Melanie particularly devotes herself to caring for the worn-out and injured Confederate soldiers who are returning to their devastated homelands. Melanie reasons that some Northern woman may help Ashley on his way home, so she assists all strangers, despite Tara's acute food shortage.

Eventually Ashley does return, and after Scarlett's sudden marriage to Frank Kennedy, the Wilkeses relocate to Atlanta to assist Scarlett in the management of Frank's lumber shop and the mill that Scarlett acquires. Although Melanie has long been aware of Scarlett's love for Ashley, she is steadfast in her loyalty to her "sister." Even such gossipmongers as her cousin India Wilkes cannot deter Melanie's affection.

As tensions in Atlanta grow among Yankees, white Southerners, and freed blacks, the Ku Klux Klan is formed. Ashley and Frank Kennedy join its ranks. Finally, to avenge an attack upon Scarlett, Ashley is injured and Frank is killed in a raid on a black-occupied shantytown. Once again Melanie comes to the fore, defending Scarlett against her accusers and praising RHETT BUTLER for his ingenious rescue—an effort that undoubtedly saved Ashley's life. Melanie is one of the few who recognize Rhett's love for Scarlett, and she is delighted when the two marry and establish the wealthiest household in Atlanta. She cares for Scarlett during her confinement and during Scarlett's illness following a miscarriage.

Scarlett and Rhett's marriage falls apart, however, just as Melanie, against medical advice, has become pregnant again. This pregnancy, resulting in a miscarriage, kills Melanie. On her deathbed Melanie urges Scarlett to look after Ashley and their son Beauregard; she also tells Scarlett how much Rhett loves her.

Willard, George. *Winesburg, Ohio.* Sherwood Anderson. 1919.

George Willard, the central character of Sherwood Anderson's short story cycle *Winesburg, Ohio*, is seen by many of Winesburg's inhabitants as the one person to whom they can relate their stories of isolation, desire, and disappointment. A cub reporter for the *Winesburg Eagle*, he is also seen as the one person capable of articulating what they cannot. Before George can assume his role as a writer, however, he must acquire maturity and an understanding of himself, and this development occurs in the several stories in which Anderson casts him as the main character.

George is the son of Elizabeth and Tom Willard, proprietors of the New Willard House in Winesburg. Elizabeth Willard spends most of her time in bed, sick and broken from an unfulfilled life with her husband Tom. A beautiful, adventurous woman in her youth, she bases her bond with George, her only son, on the dreams of her girlhood, believing that she let those dreams be killed. Against his mother's hopes that George will live out those dreams, Tom Willard tells his son that he's got to "wake up." Ambitious for the young Willard, Tom advises him that in order to be a successful man he must not be a dreamer.

Wing Biddlebaum, a fat, silent, little man, "who for twenty years had been the town mystery," encourages George to ignore his father's advice, to live for the dreams Tom would extinguish. George is the one person with whom Wing loses his timidity and breaks his silence. Wing speaks to George with his fluttering hands and long, expressive fingers, and George restrains himself from asking about them. Pleading with George that he "must become a dreamer," Wing realizes with horror that his hands have strayed to the boy's shoulders. Abruptly, he stops speaking and leaves.

One day George receives a note from Louise Trunnion that says, "I'm yours if you want me." George feels no sympathy for Louise, and as she draws close to him physically, he responds with a flood of words, becoming "wholly the male, bold and aggressive." George dismisses their rendezvous, a joining of parts devoid of communication, by reassuring himself that "nobody knows."

Nevertheless, Winesburg's inhabitants look upon George as one who will one day tell their stories. Dr. Parcival, who has a dirty office and few patients, beseeches George to listen to him: "You must pay attention to me. . . . Perhaps you will be able to write the book that I may never get written." Kate Swift is also attracted to George, her former student, and advises him "not to become a mere peddler of words." Her desire to have George Willard understand the importance of his role as a writer becomes confused with physical desire, and Kate Swift eventually flees from him.

George walks about at night with Belle Carpenter; he swaggers along, full of big words, sure of his masculine power over her: "Lust and night and women," he whispers as they embrace. Later he cannot understand what has happened when Ed Handby, Belle's true lover, wordlessly flings George aside and walks away with her.

Many other characters reveal their dreams and secrets, some only partially and cryptically, and it is clear that despite their belief in George's superior powers of expression, his understanding of them is limited. George's mother dies just as he turns eighteen, and he assumes a more mature relationship with Helen White, the banker's daughter, to whom he remarks that perhaps he "had better stop talking" and from whom he must depart for the city on an April morning. He sits dreaming on the train, and when he looks out the window, "the town of Winesburg had disappeared and his life there had become but a background on which to paint the dreams of his manhood."

Willard, Jim. *The City and the Pillar.* Gore Vidal. 1948.

Jim Willard is a young man in love with his tennis partner and best friend Bob Ford. After Bob's graduation from high school, they play one last game of tennis. Before Bob leaves Virginia to become a seaman, they spend a weekend together making love. Jim spends the next seven years trying to recapture this experience.

When he graduates, Jim, hoping to find Bob at sea, becomes a cabin boy on a freighter. In Seattle he and his friend Collins spend an evening with two women, but Jim cannot have sex with his date because he compares her unfavorably to Bob. Collins accuses him of being a homosexual, and Jim abandons ship and heads to California.

In Hollywood, Jim works as a tennis instructor at a hotel and becomes friendly with the bellboys, most of whom are gay. Jim likes the fact that they are attracted to him, but their femininity repulses him and makes him fear that he himself is not thoroughly masculine. He dates and eventually moves in with Ronald Shaw, a handsome, popular actor. Jim learns many social skills from Shaw but dislikes Shaw's circle of gay friends. He continues to think of Shaw as a temporary lover, an interlude in his journey back to Bob.

At a party Jim meets Paul Sullivan, a writer whose boyish laugh reminds him of Bob. They become lovers, although Paul's feelings are stronger than Jim's. Jim decides to keep secret his desire to find Bob.

In New Orleans, Jim and Paul meet Maria Verlaine, an old friend of Paul's, who invites them to drift with her to Mexico. Although Jim is attracted to Maria, he cannot perform sexually with her. When news of the entry of the United States into World War II interrupts their journey, Jim is excited. He looks forward to escaping from Paul and Maria and going into action.

Jim longs to be sent overseas, believing that there he will finally find Bob. He falls in love with fellow soldier Ken Woodrow—again because the young man reminds him of his lost love. One night Jim gets Ken drunk and tries to make love to him; Ken repels Jim's advances, and their friendship ends. Soon afterward Jim contracts rheumatoid arthritis and waits to be discharged. Brooding, he considers his childhood and his homosexuality. He reasons that he is homosexual because his father was emotionally distant and his mother overbearing.

Upon being discharged, Jim returns to New York City and works as a tennis instructor. There he is reunited with Shaw, who by now has himself joined the army. But Jim's brief reentry into the gay social life frustrates him because while he wants to be able to like openly gay people, he prefers more masculine, closeted bisexuals. He and Sullivan briefly resume their affair, but they split up when Sullivan accepts an offer to write a book in Africa and Jim hears that Bob (now married with a child) has returned home to Virginia. Returning to Virginia himself, Jim hopes to take a job in the local high school and resume his affair with Bob.

The two eventually meet again. At dinner with Bob and his wife Sally, Jim feels assured that Bob also wants to resume their affair. Bob expresses a desire to remain at sea, which Jim interprets as a signal that Bob still loves him. During a weekend in New York City, however, Bob exhibits clear signs of homophobia. Jim remains hopeful: In their hotel room, when Bob is very drunk and nearly asleep, he touches Bob's body. Bob reacts with anger and punches Jim. But Jim is the stronger of the two; he subdues Bob on his bed and penetrates him. He then leaves in triumph.

At a bar Jim harshly rebuffs a mild-mannered man from Detroit who makes sexual advances toward him. He then goes to the docks and contemplates starting his life afresh—perhaps by going back to sea or by traveling in the West.

Williams, Aunt Hager. *Not Without Laughter.* Langston Hughes. 1963.

Aunt Hager Williams, an ex-slave and a washerwoman, is the novel's guiding spirit. Reared in slavery, she witnesses the deterioration of her family in the face of racial prejudice. Although the old woman escapes the debilitating effects of despair and bitterness through her deep religious faith, her children are unable to gain solace from the same source.

Set in pre–World War I Stanton, Kansas, the novel opens just as a twister blows through the town, causing death and property damage. It becomes apparent that racism functions in Stanton in much the same manner as the storm—capriciously, suddenly, and destructively. Hager's young grandson Sandy is compelled to sit at the back of the classroom behind the white students. The beautiful, fun-loving Harriett, Hager's sixteen-year-old daughter, bitterly hates white people, views completing high school as futile, and escapes to the blues and jazz. Annjelica, Sandy's mother, works long hours in the home of a white family. Her husband, Jimboy Rodgers, unable to accept the menial jobs that are the only employment open to blacks in Stanton, leaves home for months at a time in search of more dignified work. Tempy, Hager's oldest child, copes by moving into the black petite bourgeoisie and attempting to prove her worth to the white world.

Controlled by forces she cannot withstand, Hager struggles unsuccessfully to keep her family intact. Her first defeat comes when Harriett, unable to abide a difficult and humiliating summer job at the Stanton Country Club, runs away with a traveling carnival. Next, wanderlust strikes Jimboy, and he leaves the family. When school begins for Sandy, he, his mother, and his grandmother begin the harshest winter they have ever experienced. Hager attempts to provide for the three of them by taking in wash, but the family is so poor that Sandy must wear his mother's shoes to school.

An already dismal period is made worse when Harriett writes requesting money so that she can come home; the family can send only three dollars. Christmas Day brings little comfort—Tempy's store-bought gifts contrast sharply with the shoddy, homemade ones Aunt Hager and the rest of the near-destitute family can afford.

The anniversary of the storm that opens the novel finds Hager and Sandy alone, the remaining fragments of the family. With all her children gone, Hager clings to her grandson. It is Hager's dream that Sandy "be somebody." She admonishes him to finish school and to be a credit to the black race. Describing her last days in slavery and the years immediately following, she warns Sandy against becoming bitter and hateful.

After this night of reminiscing, Hager collapses at her washpot and dies several days later. Yet her spirit hovers over the closing chapters of the novel. Her charge to Sandy to be a credit to the race provides the crucial inspiration he needs to defy his mother when she wants him to quit school and go to work. As the novel closes, it is agreed that Sandy will return to his senior year of high school in the fall with the support of his mother and aunt.

Williams, Blake. *Who Walk in Darkness.* Chandler Brossard. 1952.

Blake Williams is an unemployed man living in New York in the 1950s. Blake wastes his time drinking and dating until he begins to develop a meaningful relationship with Grace, the girlfriend of his best friend and rival, Henry Porter. Through his affection for Grace and his knowledge of the suffering of his friend Harry Lees, Blake is forced to grapple with strong emotions that he has previously tried to deny.

Although Blake narrates the novel, he has a very reticent personality. He tries to separate himself from his friends and is embarrassed by the obligations involved in being complimented or bought a drink. He describes himself as

feeling "empty all the time" and refuses to share any thoughts that will reveal the sentimental aspect of his personality. When asked if he has a religion, Blake replies that he believes in eating, sleeping, and himself. He does not believe in others because he thinks that people are only out for themselves.

Consequently, Blake is embarrassed by his own kindness when he helps Porter's girlfriend Grace obtain an abortion. He finds a doctor for her and escorts her to Brooklyn for the operation; he also honors his promise to keep the abortion a secret. Nursing her back to health, Blake admits to himself how much he enjoys having her in the apartment with him, and wonders to himself what she sees in Porter. When Grace decides to move back home, Blake regrets that she is leaving but refuses to try to persuade her to stay. He feels sorry for himself for being lonely but tells himself that everyone is really alone and that the only way to survive is to overcome the sadness of the fact and to convince others of your self-sufficiency. If others mark you as a lonely person, he reasons, they will want nothing to do with you.

The demands of emotional commitment are put on Blake not only by Grace but by his friend Harry Lees. Harry tells Blake that he is his only friend. Although Blake does not want this responsibility, Harry goes on to confess his most private secret: He fears he may be homosexual. Blake does not want to be the recipient of such a confession, not because he now feels differently about Harry but because he had to witness Harry's pain and confusion in telling it. Despite his nonchalance, Blake is more affected by the revelation than he admits, for it comes back to haunt him. Typically, when Harry later apologizes for having burdened him with his secret, Blake claims he has already forgotten about it.

Following a quarrel, Grace finally breaks up with Porter, and she and Blake become lovers. They are very happy and begin to speculate on their future together. But the peace of their first night in bed is broken by the news that Harry is in the hospital dying of injuries sustained in a beating from local hoods. As Grace voices her fear and expresses a desire to leave New York, Blake, in a rare moment of vulnerability and honesty, admits that he, too, is scared.

Williams, L. G. "Ellgee." *Reflections in a Golden Eye.* Carson McCullers. 1941.

Private L. G. "Ellgee" Williams is a strange, slow-witted soldier stationed at an army post in the South between the two world wars. He keeps to himself in the barracks and is something of a mystery to the other men. He has never been known to laugh or become angry, nor does he willingly participate in any activity or enter into conversation with his bunkmates. His unformed mind has never taken stock of his own actions, past or present. Five years before the novel begins, Williams killed a black man in an argument over a wheelbarrow of manure, a crime that has never been discovered.

Williams's most distinctive characteristics are his amber-brown eyes, with their mute, emotionless expression, and his ability to move with the agility of a wild animal. During his years at the military post Williams has developed the habit of taking his horse into the secluded woods, stripping, and lying naked in the sun.

One day, after two years of being assigned to permanent stable fatigue, the soldier is sent to the quarters of CAPTAIN WELDON PENDERTON to help clear a small section of woods behind the man's house. Williams incurs the captain's wrath when he misunderstands his instructions and mutilates the officer's favorite oak tree. Penderton already holds a grudge against Williams, both because the private is in charge of his wife's horse and because Williams spilled coffee on an expensive suit a year and a half before. Later in the day Williams witnesses the captain's wife LEONORA (PENDERTON) taunt her effeminate husband during an argument by undressing in the living room and walking naked through the house. He becomes obsessed with Leonora, the first naked woman he has ever seen. Every evening for the next two weeks the soldier slips into the woods after his duties are completed and watches the Penderton household through the windows. Then one evening he enters the house, climbs the stairs to Leonora's bedroom, and watches her as she sleeps until dawn.

One day at the Penderton orders Williams to saddle Leonora's horse, an unusual request. Penderton beats the animal after a wild ride in the woods, loses consciousness, then wakes to find the completely naked Williams watching him. The soldier steps over the officer's body, takes the abused horse by the reins, and leads it back to the stables, acknowledging Penderton's presence. From that time on, Penderton becomes obsessed with the young soldier and starts showing up in the stables and outside the barracks where the enlisted men are quartered in the hope of coming in contact with him. Williams knows that the captain is following him but accepts it without thinking too much about it.

Unbeknownst to Penderton, Williams continues to visit Leonora's bedroom at night. One evening, however, he is seen entering the house by Alison Langdon, a neighbor whose husband, Major Morris Langdon, is having an affair with Leonora. Alison, thinking to catch the lovers in the act, follows the unidentified figure, only to come face-to-face with Williams; she tries to tell Captain Penderton what has happened, but he assumes that she is referring to her husband and pretends not to believe her because he wants to avoid a scene.

After being confronted by Mrs. Langdon, Williams stays away from the Penderton house for a full two weeks, during which time his behavior begins to change. He becomes both more sociable and more aggressive, provokes fights with other soldiers, and ceases his solitary excursions into the woods. Then one night he returns. Penderton is awake and sees a shadowy figure enter his wife's bedroom. The officer collects his pistol, enters the room, and fatally shoots Private Williams as he squats by the sleeping woman's bed.

Williams, Lincoln "Link." *The Narrows.* Ann Petry. 1953.

Lincoln "Link" Williams, an African-American college-educated Navy veteran, is twenty-six years old at the time this novel takes place. The novel is largely set in Link's home community, called the Narrows, which is the black section of the Connecticut town of Monmouth. Link was adopted as a young boy by ABBIE CRUNCH and her husband, The Major. Link's misfortunes began when The Major died; he was eight years old, and in her grief Abbie literally forgot his existence for three full months until reminded of him by her closest friend, FRANCES F. K. JACKSON. During this time the boy took refuge in a local saloon, the Last Chance, which was owned and operated by the mysterious Bill Hod, who ran most of the community's bars and brothels. Link swiftly became attached to the older man, a father figure who periodically provided a home and jobs for him.

One night on a fog-enshrouded dock, Link rescues a young woman from the pursuit of a hideously disfigured and mutilated man known as Cat Jimmie. At first he does not realize that the woman, Camilo Williams, is not only white but also married and extraordinarily wealthy. The two soon become lovers. Link's relations with Camilo are seriously disrupted, however, when Abbie discovers the couple in bed and throws Camilo out of the house. On Bill Hod's advice, Link, who has been deeply affected by their subsequent breakup, takes a two-week skiing trip to Canada. While he is gone, Camilo frequents the Last Chance, waiting for him to appear. Their affair resumes upon his return. All goes smoothly until one day Link discovers that Camilo is heiress to the immense Treadway fortune. This revelation infuriates Link, who now feels that he has been just a gigolo for a spoiled rich white girl.

When Link confronts her with his knowledge of her true identity, Camilo insists that she withheld the information in order to ensure that his attraction for her was not based on her wealth, but Link is not persuaded. Camilo, who begins to drink heavily, pursues him, and one night when he rebuffs her, she has him arrested for attempted rape.

Bill Hod bails Link out of jail, and the scandal is suppressed in the local papers through Mrs. Treadway's influence. Camilo's behavior becomes increasingly erratic, however, and she receives more publicity when she hits a young girl in the Narrows. This event prompts Mrs. Treadway and Captain Bunny Sheffield, Camilo's husband, to hire some men to force a confession from Link. Link grimly maintains his innocence in the face of Mrs. Treadway's questioning until she threatens him with a gun. Before Link has the opportunity to sign the confession, Bunny grabs the gun and shoots him dead at point-blank range.

Williams, Roy. "Home." Langston Hughes. 1934.

Roy Williams is a successful young African-American violinist. He has just returned to the United States after several years as a musician in Europe. His career has taken him throughout the depression-torn continent, and although he loved the opportunity to play both classical and jazz music, he has been profoundly disturbed by the rampant poverty and despair he witnessed. At one point he muses that the poverty and hunger he sees is even worse than that faced by his people back in the United States.

Roy has become seriously ill, apparently with tuberculosis, and has decided to return home in order to see his mother, for he knows that his death is imminent. After leaving Europe, he arrives in the United States on the same day President Hoover forcefully removes protesting war veterans from Washington, D.C. Roy spends some time in Harlem but is anxious to return to his small hometown, Hopkinsville, so he soon boards a Pullman and heads south.

Roy disembarks from the train in Hopkinsville, much to the discomfort of the community's white folks who are disgruntled by his obvious success. He is greeted coolly by a former childhood playmate, but when he makes his way to his mother's house, he is welcomed as a returning hero. Soon afterward he gives a concert at his mother's church, to the applause of both white and black members of the audience. At the performance Roy notices one woman in particular, an older white woman, who seems to both know and take pleasure in the assorted classical pieces he performs. After the performance Roy's mother introduces the woman as Miss Reese, the "old maid" music teacher at the white high school. Soon after this Roy receives an invitation to play in her class with her accompaniment. Although the two musicians enjoy themselves, the white students report back to their parents that a black musician was in their class and played music that none of them liked. Meanwhile, Roy's illness worsens steadily, and he begins to develop insomnia.

One night, unable to sleep, Roy dresses in his fancy clothes and goes out for a walk. He travels downtown, where he encounters Miss Reese, and the two shake hands. Unfortunately, a group of young white men see the encounter, and Roy is immediately attacked. Miss Reese screams out; her scream is taken as proof that she is being raped, and the young men redouble their assault. Finally, surrounded by a dozen or so angry and murderous attackers, including his former playmate, Roy realizes that the end is near. The attack ends with Roy's dead and naked body suspended from a tree, left to turn in the wind all night.

Williams, Sam. *Penrod; Penrod and Sam; Penrod Jashber.* Booth Tarkington. 1913; 1916; 1929.

Eleven-year-old Sam Williams is partner-in-mischief to PENROD SCHOFIELD, the young hero of these three episodic novels. Like Penrod, Sam comes from a white, middle-class home in turn-of-the-century America and, like Penrod, has an underdeveloped sense of responsibility and an overdeveloped imagination. These attributes quickly lead to trouble and eventually to punishment, meted out in the upstairs bedroom by an exasperated Mr. Williams. Although Sam is always interested in any new experiences the world has to offer, in his own estimation he has seen a lot and has "known grasshoppers chewed tobacco since I was five years old."

To further experience the world, Sam and Penrod mount a backyard "Big Show" starring two smaller children they have discovered, one missing a finger and the other "tongue-tied," or practically mute. Both are featured in the show, not only because of their peculiarities, which Sam finds exceedingly interesting, but because their father is serving time in prison on a felony charge. The fun really begins, however, when a well-behaved boy named Georgie Bassett asks to join their "Backyard Club," an organization headquartered in an old piano crate in Sam's backyard. As an initiation rite, Sam and Penrod frighten and thrash George to such an extent that he ends up crying and calling attention to the club's activities. Sam is severely chastised for his part in the ugliness.

One day the boys decide to play "Drug Store" with Penrod's unfortunate dog Duke and a neighborhood boy they dislike. They brew a vile concoction, composed of household condiments, old medicine, arsenic, and licorice water. Although both subjects become ill, they do survive the incident, and Sam and Penrod go unpunished.

On another occasion they discover a stray horse and chase it until, by chance, it runs into the Schofields' stable. In the hope of receiving a reward, they advertise the discovery and a description of the horse. The boys wind up being praised by the Humane Society and by their parents for rescuing and feeding the horse when in fact their motives had been to derive pleasure from frightening the old animal and to profit from its capture.

In the last book of the trilogy, a complete stranger is subject to town scrutiny and suspicion, and almost suffers legal proceedings because Penrod and Sam decide to play detective and to treat him as their suspect. Sam is encouraged in this endeavor by his older brother Robert, to the tune of fifty cents, and proceeds to help ruin the reputation of a perfectly respectable young man—who happens to be a suitor of Penrod's sister Margaret—by spreading rumors of criminal activity. When the culprits are interrogated by their parents, it becomes apparent that Robert paid the boys in order to further his own interests in Margaret, and Sam is once again miraculously off the hook.

Wilner, Mitch. *The Old Bunch.* Meyer Levin. 1937.

In this account of a group of Jewish youths growing up in Chicago in the 1920s and 1930s, Mitch Wilner, unlike his friends, remains removed from social and political movements. He single-mindedly pursues the most cherished dream of his own and his friends' immigrant forefathers: to become a respected and successful professional man.

With his close friend Rudy Stone, Mitch enters the University of Chicago to study medicine. He quickly becomes fascinated by the study of the bloodstream, especially the phenomenon of blood shock, or anaphylaxis. After publishing a paper on this topic, he is elected to Sigma Xi, an honorary science society. This early success earns him a fellowship from a large medical research company that enables him to conduct intensive research on anaphylaxis. It also earns him the love of Sylvia Abramsonn, who has dated Mitch's friend JOE FREEDMAN for several years but is now single. However, Mitch insists on delaying their marriage until he has become established.

After two years of research, Mitch achieves significant results that are well received by the medical community. He hopes that his success will enable him to realize his long-held dream of conducting further research at the Mayo Clinic, but his application for a research position at Rochester is turned down on what he feels certain are anti-Semitic grounds. Soon afterward Mitch is further disillusioned when he discovers the medical company that had funded his research now owns the results he achieved and that it is using medical students to conduct the further research Mitch himself wanted to conduct at the Mayo Clinic.

At this point Sylvia's parents, who have made their fortune as slumlords and manufacturers, set Mitch up in general practice. He and Sylvia finally marry, although Mitch insists that they cannot yet afford to have a child.

Mitch and Rudy now have offices in the same building. By this time the Depression has hit, and both doctors fall idle due to lack of patients. Rudy becomes involved in a revolutionary plan to open a medical clinic that will give patients better health care at lower cost, and he urges Mitch to join the idealistic but unpopular venture. Fearing reprisals from the medical community, Mitch refuses to become involved. When Rudy discovers that there is an opening at a prestigious Chicago hospital, he urges Mitch to apply for the position and to overcome his diffidence in pursuing the job.

Mitch receives the appointment and soon thereafter begins teaching. As his career takes off, his friendship with

Rudy fades away and relations with Sylvia's family become increasingly strained. At the novel's end, Sylvia is spending most of her time with their newborn baby while Mitch pursues his only true love: the study of medicine.

Wilson, David "Pudd'nhead." *Pudd'nhead Wilson.* Samuel L. Clemens (Mark Twain). 1894.

David Wilson gains his nickname "Pudd'nhead" the first day he moves to Dawson's Landing, Missouri, by surprising the residents with a witty response to a barking dog. The name, as well as the reputation, sticks; and being a pudd'nhead, David is unable to get any customers in his professional capacity as a lawyer. Only the eminent Judge Driscoll has any respect for David, and the two become good friends.

For the next twenty-three years David supports himself by doing accounting work, and he amuses himself by taking periodic sets of fingerprints of everyone in the town. Two of his earliest impressions are those of the infants THOMAS À BECKET DRISCOLL, Judge Driscoll's charge, and Valet de Chambre, the ninety-seven percent white son of the slave ROXANA. When Roxana switches the two nearly identical infants in order to prevent her child from ever being sold, she fears the possibility of detection only by David, who she suspects is a witch.

Along with fingerprinting, David engages in the equally eccentric hobby of palmistry, a pursuit that sets off the climactic events of the novel. He divines that Luigi, an Italian nobleman visiting Dawson's Landing with his twin brother Angelo, has at some time killed someone—in self-defense, he is assured. The instrument the Italian used was an exotic Indian dagger that Tom Driscoll, now grown and burdened by gambling debt, has stolen. Rumors of the murder circulate (unleashed by Judge Driscoll for political reasons), causing the twins to fall out of public favor.

When Tom, driven by his need for money, kills his guardian with the stolen dagger, suspicion falls on Luigi. The twins, in fact, are discovered standing over the bleeding corpse, and David Wilson has the unenviable assignment of proving their innocence in his first full-scale trial defense.

Tom tricks David for a time because he committed this and earlier crimes disguised as a woman, prompting David to attempt to match the fingerprints on the dagger with those of the town's women. But finally Tom himself inadvertently reveals his incriminating prints, and David has his day in court. Demonstrating to the stunned gallery that everyone has identifying marks on his or her fingers and that the marks never change, he proves that Tom's prints are on the dagger and that he is the murderer. Furthermore, by comparing Tom's infantile prints with his adult prints, David reveals that Tom is in fact the slave Valet de Chambre.

Wilson, Scratchy. "The Bride Comes to Yellow Sky."
Stephen Crane. 1898.

Scratchy Wilson, one of the first denizens of the small
turn-of-the-century town called Yellow Sky, has been
toughened by years of survival in the rugged and untamed
land of early America. Widely known as a crack shot, he
carries two six-guns in holsters at his side. For the most
part he is harmless and amicable, but every few weeks he
drunkenly "goes on a tear" and reignites a rivalry with
the town marshal, Jack Potter. Potter, the only person
brave enough to stop these rampages, once shot Scratchy
in the leg. But on the day of this story, the marshal is out
of town.

Several people are drinking in the Yellow Sky bar in
the afternoon, but Scratchy is not one of them. When
someone reports that he is "drunk and has turned loose
both hands," the group discusses the marshal's absence
nervously. No one knows why the sheriff has gone to San
Antonio, but they all regret his absence intensely. They
know that, after searching the suddenly empty town for
some target for his intoxicated rage, Scratchy will make
his way to the bar. Those in the bar slide a wooden dead-
bolt across the heavy wooden door and hope for the best.
Scratchy has tried to shoot his way into the bar three times
in the past, but each time he has failed. The bartender
hides behind the counter just in case, making sure to align
himself with the structure's metal portions for extra protection.

At 3:25 P.M., Marshal Potter steps off the train from
San Antonio, completely ignorant of the situation in town.
His mind is on his new bride and on the embarrassment
he feels for having brought home a woman without having
made any announcements or having obtained his friends'
approval. The couple happily and abashedly walks
through the quiet town with their luggage. Meanwhile,
Scratchy has already shot up the saloon door and moved
on in search of new quarry. After terrorizing the town
dog, he decides to go to Potter's house and challenge him
to a final shooting contest.

When Scratchy yells at the marshal's house, there is no
response. Convinced that the man is in there and that he
has grown just as cowardly as the rest of the town,
Scratchy commences shooting. After emptying his guns,
he reloads. Potter and his new bride turn the last corner
to the house just as Scratchy puts the last bullet in his
second gun.

The last thing the couple expects to see is Scratchy
Wilson waving a revolver in front of them. Scratchy demands to have a showdown with the marshal and smirks
when Potter says he is unarmed. Potter mentions his
marriage as the reason for his unpreparedness. Dumbfounded, Scratchy exclaims, "Married? No!" Potter confirms that the woman by his side is his wife. Scratchy is
so taken aback that, much to the couple's relief, he lets
them go. "A simple child of the earlier plains," Scratchy

does not adapt well to change. He holsters his revolver
and shuffles off.

Wilson, William. "William Wilson." Edgar Allan Poe.
1839.

The narrator of this story of doppelgangers admits that
he is no hero and that William Wilson isn't even his real
name. Because of the worldwide scorn to which he has
been subject because of his lifetime of debauchery, he
would rather not reveal his actual name.

Wilson, the child of a wealthy but common English
family, has always been a willful pleasure-seeker. As a child
he rejected any guidance his weak and all-too-indulgent
parents may have offered him, and followed his own childish whims. By the time he attends boarding school he is
manipulative and tyrannical.

But he is also charming, and he easily wins over most
of the boys who live in the rambling, mazelike Elizabethan
building that houses the school. The only dissenting voice
among his schoolmates is a boy who arrived at the school
the same day Wilson did. Coincidentally, the boy has the
same birthday, general build, and appearance, and even
the same name as the narrator. Unlike the narrator, however, this Wilson has a soft, barely audible voice, and
strong moral principles.

Wilson is enraged over the existence at such close proximity of this "twin." He plays practical jokes on the gentle-
voiced child in an attempt to humiliate him and distance
him from himself. For his part, the second Wilson somehow detects Wilson-the-narrator's well-concealed discomfort over his existence. The second Wilson, much to the
narrator's chagrin, exacts his revenge by mimicking the
clothing, carriage, and speech of his more popular but
dissolute namesake. Only the narrator notices this attempt
at duplication. One night when Wilson observes his sleeping rival, he is so disturbed by the uncanny resemblance
that he runs away from school, never to return.

Eventually he enrolls at Eton, where he continues his
carousing. Late one night Wilson is called away from a
drinking and gambling party by the arrival of a visitor. A
figure, dressed much as Wilson himself, approaches, grabs
his arm, and whispers, "William Wilson," then disappears. Wilson tries to shrug off this incident, but it
haunts him.

Years later, while in the process of cheating at cards,
the figure returns, and Wilson recognizes him as his namesake. The visitor reveals to the gamblers that Wilson has
been cheating, disgracing him. What follows for Wilson
are years of debauchery in the pleasure capitals of Europe,
his nemesis dogging him all the while.

Finally Wilson resolves to act. At a costume party he
confronts his pursuer, who is clothed in an identical costume. He engages him in a dagger fight, mortally wounding the man. As the second Wilson dies, he tells his

murderer that he has killed not his enemy but the best part of himself.

Wing, Isadora Zelda White Stollerman. *Fear of Flying*. Erica Jong. 1973.

Isadora Zelda White Stollerman Wing, disillusioned with her second husband after five years of marriage, attempts to cure her boredom and malaise by having an affair with a British psychoanalyst whom she meets while at a convention in Germany with her husband. This extramarital fling fails to satisfy her contradictory cravings that continue to haunt her as she explores the opportunities and inhibitions confronting modern American women.

Born and raised in New York City, Isadora has an imagination imbued with wild fantasies worthy of the most liberal and decadent of the Big Apple's myriad subcultures. She searches for a true "zipless fuck," her term for perfect sexual intercourse wherein zippers miraculously disappear to allow access to a passion that is not encumbered with emotional baggage and romantic responsibility. Isadora's hyperactive sexual imagination is thwarted by the traditional morality of a puritanical society, but she finds an outlet through writing and becomes a published author known for her erotic poetry. Words alone do not satisfy her physical drives, though, and her sexuality comes to disrupt what little order and tranquility she establishes in her life.

Isadora met her first husband Brian Stollerman in her first year at Barnard College and dated him for four years before agreeing to marry him. Although Brian is a genius with an IQ over two hundred, his brain is ill equipped for everyday human existence, and Isadora is forced to divorce him after he attempts to strangle her during one of his psychotic episodes. After obtaining a master's degree in English literature from Columbia University, Isadora decides to abandon her graduate studies upon marrying her second husband, Bennett Wing, a Chinese-American psychoanalyst whose meticulous demeanor and emotional stability contrast sharply with her own tempestuous personality. Despite Bennett's relative perfection, Isadora cannot resist having an affair with another analyst, Adrian Goodlove, at a psychoanalytical convention in Vienna. At the climax of this messy triangular romantic configuration, Bennett bursts into the room where Isadora and Adrian are sleeping together and engages in violent sexual intercourse with his wife in front of her lover. After Bennett climaxes, Isadora, Bennett, and Adrian fall asleep together and subsequently pretend that absolutely nothing unusual has happened.

Isadora becomes increasingly upset with Adrian's self-serving manipulation of their relationship, but she remains with him because she cannot face making the decision to return to Bennett and is terrified of the thought of life without a man by her side and in her bed. Finally, Adrian shocks Isadora by committing the ultimate betrayal of his own *carpe diem* ethics by dumping Isadora in Paris in order to meet his wife and children for a short vacation in Brittany. Unable to conceive of an independent existence, Isadora tracks down her husband in London. The novel concludes as she is soaking in his hotel bathtub, knowing she will survive despite the uncertainty of her nebulous future and renewing her commitment to a life-saving career as a writer.

Winner, Arthur. *By Love Possessed*. James Gould Cozzens. 1957.

Quiet and thoughtful, Arthur Winner followed in his father's footsteps by going to law school and then taking a job in his father's firm. When his father passes away relatively early in his career, Arthur is left with the aging Noah Tuttle, the firm's other senior partner, to handle their considerable case load. It is during this time that his wife Hope, with whom he has had three children, also dies. Trying to drown his grief over his deceased wife, Arthur becomes consumed with his work at the law firm and is soon the most respected lawyer in Brocton, the town in which he lives. Years later he marries a young woman named Constance.

At the opening of the novel, Winner is facing a new crisis. The brother of his faithful and longtime secretary Helen, an irresponsible young man named Ralph, is accused of rape. Unable to afford counsel of her own, Helen asks Arthur for help. In spite of the fact that he has never cared for Ralph, Arthur, who has been vacationing at his summer house with Constance and their children, returns to Brocton to come to her aid.

After a careful examination of Ralph's story and the claims of his accuser, a woman with a bad reputation, Arthur decides that Ralph did receive consent and therefore is not guilty of the crime of rape. After intense questioning by Arthur, Ralph reveals the fact that he had been having a fight with his fiancée, who refused to have sex with him until they were married. Ralph then paid an angry visit to the rape victim, who was known around town as sexually active.

As Arthur prepares his case for Ralph, he must deal with the behavior of his increasingly senile partner Noah Tuttle. Because he believes Ralph is lazy and no good, Noah suggests that they decline to defend him. But Arthur, ever loyal to Helen, goes ahead with the case.

Arthur soon learns that Ralph, who posted bail with the mortgage on Helen's house, has fled to New York. Arthur is told that the charges have been dropped, but he is duty-bound to inform the district attorney that Ralph has skipped bail. The town sheriff sends out a dispatch to have the fugitive Ralph picked up. Despite Ralph's flight, the district attorney decides not to prosecute him. Arthur then learns to his horror that Helen committed suicide by swallowing a bottle of disinfectant when she learned that Ralph had run away.

Winslow, Rachel. *In His Steps.* Charles M. Sheldon. 1897.

Rachel Winslow, a beautiful church soloist with a heavenly voice, seems destined for a grand career in opera until the REVEREND HENRY MAXWELL makes a proposal in a sermon that changes her life irrevocably. Rachel's first appearance in the book highlights the most enduring aspect of her singing: its calming effect on Reverend Maxwell and other parishioners. Her solo is met with muted applause, extraordinary for the normally austere congregation.

When an impoverished man dies soon after plaintively interrupting the service in which Rachel sang, Rachel's minister is inspired to make a unique proposition. The minister proposes that members of the congregation take a pledge to enter a new discipleship, constantly asking themselves "What would Jesus do?" in daily situations. Rachel is one of the first parishioners to make the pledge in the back of the church. Although she is initially unsure of how to apply Jesus' teachings to her life, the soprano undergoes a transformation so great that her solos are no longer objects of worldly admiration but divine sacraments.

One of the first actions of Rachel's new discipleship is to persuade Virginia Page, a wealthy young heiress, to pledge her riches to doing God's work in their city, Raymond. The soprano also decides, to the amazement of all, to refuse an offer from a comic opera company that would have brought her fame and a fine salary. She feels that Jesus would not use his voice for such material gain. This surprising decision brings stinging criticism from Virginia's brother Rollin and her grandmother, Madam Page, both wealthy pillars of society.

As Rachel leaves the Page mansion, she is followed by the handsome young Rollin, who proposes marriage to her. The soloist refuses, repulsed by the society gentleman's frivolous life-style. At home she has a fierce argument with her mother before heading to the Rectangle, a notorious slum and the site of a revivalist's tent meetings. Rachel offers her voice, and her singing calms the rowdy crowd in her first Rectangle service.

Rachel's romantic entanglements grow as she witnesses Rollin undergo a spiritual transformation at the Rectangle. She also refuses another wedding proposal, this time from Jasper Chase, a popular novelist who insincerely took the "What would Jesus do?" pledge and whom Rachel had previously loved. But romance is eclipsed by more spiritual pursuits as Virginia inspires Rachel to found a singing school for poor young women of the Rectangle.

Weeks later it becomes apparent to Rachel that Rollin has undergone a complete transformation and is now preaching to his high-society friends. The icy barrier between the two disciples finally melts, and they are able to proclaim their mutual love, a sanctified love that was previously foreign to them.

The soloist eventually finds herself taking care of the young Rose Sterling of Chicago, whose seemingly wealthy father kills himself because of poor finances. The suicide takes place just after the new discipleship movement reaches Chicago. The novel ends as the soprano, along with other original members of the movement, tours Chicago churches and is received enthusiastically. Rachel's voice soothes her audiences once again and makes them receptive to Reverend Maxwell's now nationally known call to act according to the question, "What would Jesus do?"

Winterbourne, Frederick. *Daisy Miller.* Henry James. 1878.

Frederick Winterbourne, a sober, well-mannered young American, has been living in the society of high-class American expatriates in Europe. His principal residence is Geneva, but he travels to the fashionable spots of Europe to keep company with his fellow expatriates, all of whom subscribe to their own hyperorthodox version of an aristocratic life-style.

While vacationing in Vevey, Switzerland, Winterbourne meets DAISY MILLER, a young American touring Europe with her apathetic and unsophisticated mother and her impish young brother. Daisy, who hails from Schenectady, New York, is far more provincial than the urbane Winterbourne, but she enters the polite society of Winterbourne and his compatriots with enthusiasm. Without any apparent coyness or reservation, Daisy asks Winterbourne to escort her to the Chateau de Chillon without a chaperone. Winterbourne, although captivated by her beauty and charm, is shocked by her forthrightness and seeming lack of propriety. Is Daisy Miller a sophisticated coquette or a naive but plucky flirt? Winterbourne's reason cannot help him decide this question and his instinct fails him, but he finally gives her the benefit of the doubt: Her flirtation is innocent, he concludes.

However, Winterbourne's aunt, Mrs. Costello, the grande dame of their American expatriate society, tries to dissuade him from consorting with Daisy Miller. It is his social duty, she explains, to avoid uncultivated Americans like the Millers. He has been away too long from such Americans; if he becomes involved with Daisy Miller, she warns him, he will undoubtedly make a great mistake. Mrs. Costello's advice notwithstanding, Winterbourne decides to spend what turns out to be a delightful afternoon with Daisy Miller at the Chateau de Chillon. Shortly thereafter the Millers journey to Rome, where Winterbourne will also be going to join his aunt.

In Rome, Daisy and Winterbourne meet once more at the home of their mutual acquaintance, Mrs. Walker. They are delighted to see each other again, and Daisy playfully chides Winterbourne for not coming to see her earlier. But Daisy is going off to meet Mr. Giovanelli, a handsome but obsequious Italian gentleman who is, she declares without guile or shame, an intimate friend of hers. Both Mrs. Walker and Winterbourne insist upon escorting her to her rendezvous. Mrs. Walker follows in her carriage, and she insists that Daisy cease this blatant indiscretion and leave with her immediately, but Daisy refuses. Mrs. Walker and Winterbourne depart together, leaving Daisy and Giovanelli unchaperoned.

Unable to countenance Daisy Miller's continual and blatant impropriety, Mrs. Walker shuns her publicly. Winterbourne tries to reason with Daisy about her indiscreet behavior, but she dismisses his advice as tedious preaching. Winterbourne is once again in a quandary over Daisy Miller: Is she too naive and too uncultivated to even perceive, much less understand, her social ostracism, or are her actions a guileful bid for attention? To assuage his misgivings, Winterbourne rationalizes that the only thing to expect from Daisy Miller is the unexpected.

Late one evening, however, as Winterbourne is strolling about the streets of Rome, he chances upon Daisy and Giovanelli in the shadows of the Colosseum. He is stunned at her audacious impropriety. Furthermore, not only is her behavior deadly for her already damaged reputation, it is deadly for her health, for the Colosseum is infested with malaria. But Daisy simply had to see the Colosseum by moonlight. Winterbourne entreats Daisy to leave for the sake of her health, and he condemns her subtly but unequivocally as not worthy of his respect. Daisy understands this subtle rejection, to which she responds defiantly that she does not care.

Daisy Miller has in fact caught a severe case of malaria, and she dies swiftly—but not before she gets a message to Winterbourne. The essence of Daisy's message is that her trysts with Giovanelli were innocent and that she would have appreciated Winterbourne's esteem. Winterbourne does not at first understand this message, but while visiting her grave he is joined by Giovanelli, who affirms that Daisy was the most innocent of young women.

Later, Winterbourne rues the fact that his inflexible morality precluded his acceptance of the naive but irrepressible Daisy, and he recalls with irony his aunt's earlier admonition that in involving himself with Daisy he would surely make some great mistake. Nevertheless, he does not abandon the genteel life-style of his fellow expatriates. He returns to Geneva, where doubtless he will soon be in pursuit of some clever European lady.

Wirz, Henry. *Andersonville.* McKinley Kantor. 1955.

Captain Henry Wirz, a zealous Swiss immigrant and Confederate soldier, is the commander of the Confederate prison camp at Anderson, Georgia.

Wirz, a thin-faced, dyspeptic man past forty who still speaks English poorly, is a staunch Confederate wounded in the arm in an early campaign of the war. The wound, which continually reinfects and drains, causes him constant pain. He is reduced to taking morphia and acting as his own surgeon in unsuccessful attempts to relieve his suffering. This injury has bred in him a terrible hatred of all Yankee soldiers. Selected to run the hastily constructed prison camp because he is a surgeon, Wirz fulfills expectations that he will be brutal to the prisoners.

Andersonville is an appalling tragedy. Since it is nothing more than a large stockade, prisoners construct their own shelters, called "she-bangs," out of any available material. Those with nothing to trade are given a diet of cornpone. A creek, ironically called the Sweetwater, runs through the camp, providing the only drinking water, but since it is also used for sanitation, it soon becomes a swamp of human excrement.

A bitter man who dislikes everyone except his wife and small daughter, Wirz enjoys tormenting the prisoners. He is particular in his attempts to devise cruel punishments for minute infractions, frequently by withholding the meager rations for days at a time. When he enters the stockade, he sees the prisoners as animals who scramble for chunks of the carrots he deigns to throw to them.

Even Wirz realizes the camp has become a horror when over thirty thousand soldiers, most with malaria, scurvy, and dysentery, are crowded into the open stockade. He begs the Confederate command not to send more men to Andersonville and reluctantly allows a makeshift hospital to be created outside the stockade. Still, he does nothing to alleviate the misery of the prisoners. When soldiers form themselves into renegade gangs, called Raiders, to prey on new prisoners, he arms other prisoners, the Regulators, who attempt to keep some semblance of order within the camp.

After the burning of Atlanta, with the Confederate cause in collapse and with no supplies being sent to the camp, Wirz lives in fear of a prison break. At the request of his sadistic commander, General Winder, he tells fifteen thousand still ambulatory soldiers that they are being exchanged. Full of hope, they board trains only to be sent to another stockade farther north. As the war draws to a close, Wirz is presiding over a fetid swamp that houses fifteen thousand starving and dying men. Food and supplies for the hospital have become nonexistent. Finally, with the surrender, Union troops liberate the prisoners and come to arrest Wirz. He is taken north to be tried for his inhumanity. Jeered at along the way and still in agony from his festering arm, Wirz feels he has merely obeyed the orders he was given.

Withersteen, Jane. *Riders of the Purple Sage.* Zane Grey. 1912.

Jane Withersteen, the proud and pious daughter of the late founder of Cottonwoods, a Mormon villa in Utah, struggles with the conflict between her training as an obedient Mormon woman and her perception of the cruelty and injustices committed in the name of her religion.

The year is 1871. The brutish Elder Tull wishes to make Jane one of his wives, and he arrives at her ranch, accompanied by churchmen, with the intention of driving away Bern Venters, a Gentile rider who has been befriended by the woman. As the men prepare to whip Venters, with Jane standing helplessly by, a mysterious gunman rides onto the scene. He saves Venters and reveals himself to be LASSITER, the notorious gunslinger who has reputedly terrorized much of Utah.

Although intimidated by the gunman, Jane invites him to supper for Venters's sake and asks him why he has ridden to her ranch. She learns that Lassiter has come to Cottonwoods in order to discover the identity of the Mormon proselytizer who years before stole a woman named Milly Erne from her home and husband. Jane, who apparently knows the identity of the man, agrees to show Milly's unmarked grave to Lassiter but vows never to speak the name of the man in question. She decides that she could serve her religion best by exerting her feminine charms to stay Lassiter's hand against her people, so she convinces the gunman to remain and help her look after the ranch.

However, Jane underestimates the implacable determination of Elder Tull and his cronies. She soon must deal with a gradually escalating series of disasters orchestrated by the invisible hand of the Church, including the loss of her cattle and most of her riders. Venters leaves for Deception Pass to trace the destination of the herd that had been stolen in a drive led by the infamous Masked Rider. When she learns that the women of her household have been acting as spies against her, Jane finds much to her own consternation that Lassiter is the only one who stands between her and total ruin.

Throughout all this adversity, Jane refuses to reject completely the authority of her churchmen. Even after she becomes aware that Lassiter has fallen in love with her, she keeps secret the identity of the man he is hunting and tries to convince him to stop carrying his gun. The worst blow for Jane occurs when her prize possessions, her horses, are stolen; it finally becomes clear to her that the churchmen mean to break her will as well as leave her penniless and powerless. As armed men are seen lurking in the vicinity of the ranch, Jane and Lassiter mount two swift horses and ride toward the secret canyon in Deception Pass where Venters has been hiding with his newfound love Bess, an innocent young woman who had been disguised as the notorious Masked Rider. The four meet, and it is revealed that Bess is actually Elizabeth Erne, Milly's daughter. Lassiter explains that he is Elizabeth's uncle Jim, and Jane, upon hearing this revelation, breaks her vow of silence and identifies her own father as the man responsible for Milly's ruin.

Venters and Elizabeth take the horses so that they may safely escape Mormon territory while Jane and Lassiter, pursued by Tull and his men, make their way to Surprise Valley, the secluded hideaway Venters had discovered. Barely reaching the spot ahead of their pursuers, Jane and Lassiter must decide whether to await certain capture or push the great stone that hovers above the entrance of the valley, thereby starting an avalanche that would forever shut them off from the rest of the world. Lassiter, thinking of Jane's virtue, is unable to take such an irreversible step, but Jane, telling the gunman that she loves him, makes the decision and instructs him to roll the rock.

Witla, Eugene. "The Genius." Theodore Dreiser. 1915.

Eugene Witla is the ambitious son of a sewing machine agent in Alexandria, Illinois, in the 1880s. Although reserved in outward appearance, Eugene is emotional, sensitive, and artistically inclined.

As a teenager Witla takes a job at the local newspaper working as a typesetter. But he soon tires of it and of life in Alexandria in general. When one of his coworkers suggests that he try Chicago, he moves and rents a room. While working at a series of odd jobs, Eugene is amazed and a bit awed by the large city, and he also makes the acquaintance of several accommodating women.

Eugene undergoes several changes in Chicago that help shape the course of his life. He develops an interest in and an aptitude for art; he decides to take night classes at the Art Institute. As his artistic sensibilities begin to emerge, Eugene begins to resent what he sees as the narrow perspective of life in a small town. During these years Eugene also meets Angela Blue, a friend of his sister from a small town in Wisconsin who is pretty and passionate despite her conventional exterior. To the sensitive Eugene, Angela comes to represent a purer beauty and a higher sensibility. He eventually proposes marriage and Angela accepts, although the two have to wait to marry until Eugene's finances improve. By this time Eugene is working as an illustrator for a Chicago newspaper, but he informs Angela that he is going to move to New York and try to find more newspaper art work. While Angela waits back in Wisconsin, Eugene begins an upward struggle in an indifferent but fascinating metropolis. He gets some commissions to draw for smaller magazines, but his big break comes when a well-known journal reproduces one of his city sketches of New York life. Eugene gets increasing recognition, which culminates in a successful exhibition that brings him international attention.

Meanwhile, Eugene is forced to marry Angela when, after nearly two years, she threatens suicide. Eugene now regrets his proposal: He sees in other women a level of refinement and intellectual development far above that of the girl from Blackwood, Wisconsin. After Angela joins him in New York, however, he begins to appreciate her domestic abilities and slavish solicitude.

Eugene's artistic career is then jeopardized when he

experiences a severe nervous breakdown precipitated, he thinks, by too much sex. Finding himself unable to paint or draw, he takes a job working for a railroad as a way of regaining his health. When Angela goes back to Wisconsin for a visit, Eugene befriends Carlotta Wilson, with whom he has a passionate affair. Angela discovers this upon her return, so Eugene decides to be more circumspect for the time being.

With his health regained and with the help of a friend, Eugene goes into publishing and after a few years finds himself at the peak of his profession. Nevertheless, his success is eventually endangered by a relationship with eighteen-year-old Suzanne Dale. Suzanne's mother learns of their plan to run off together, and she engineers the dismissal of Eugene from his prominent position. When Angela dies in childbirth soon afterward, Eugene finds himself alone in the universe and resigned to the depths of its mysteries.

Wizard of Oz. *The Wonderful Wizard of Oz.* L. Frank Baum. 1900.

The title character is not a wizard at all. He is an ordinary man from Omaha, Nebraska, who was carried to the magical Land of Oz in a balloon intended to lure people to a circus. When he landed in Oz the people, seeing him arrive from the clouds, assumed he must have magical powers. The Wizard allowed them to believe this and had the Emerald City built as his capital. In order for the city to appear much more lush and green than it really was, he had green spectacles affixed to the eyes of everyone who entered the walled city. His only concern is the two wicked witches who live in the land and, unlike him, really do have magical powers.

One day a little girl from Kansas named DOROTHY, her dog Toto, a COWARDLY LION, a SCARECROW, and a TIN WOODMAN arrive in the Emerald City. The Wizard soon learns that Dorothy (or at least Dorothy's house, which was blown to the Land of Oz in a cyclone) has killed the Wicked Witch of the East. He is so relieved that one of the witches is dead that he grants each of the travelers a separate audience. To Dorothy he appears as a great head (really papier-mâché) and promises to return her to Kansas if she will kill the Wicked Witch of the West. He makes similar deals with each of the others, promising a heart to the Scarecrow (to whom Oz appears as a beautiful lady), a brain to the Tin Woodman (to whom he appears as a terrible beast), and courage to the Cowardly Lion (to whom he appears as a ball of fire).

Dorothy does eventually kill the Wicked Witch of the West, but when she and her friends return to the Wizard with the good news, they discover the truth: He is a very kindhearted man, but he hasn't a magical bone in his body. They still want his help, however, and he easily formulates a plan to grant the wishes of Dorothy's three friends, who already have the attributes they are seeking but simply do not know it. Oz gives each a sort of placebo. He fills the Scarecrow's head with some bran and some pins and needles, making him believe he is sharp. Then the Wizard places a silk heart stuffed with sawdust in the Tin Woodman's breast, convincing him that he is kind. Finally, Oz gives the Lion a strong drink, which makes him feel bolder and more courageous. Dorothy's problem, however, seems to lack such a simple remedy.

The Wizard decides that the only way he can get Dorothy back to Kansas is to take her there himself via his hot-air balloon. Leaving the Scarecrow in charge of the Emerald City, Oz sets off in the balloon, but Dorothy, who runs after Toto when he chases a cat, misses her ride. That is the last that is seen of the Wonderful Wizard. Dorothy does eventually get back to Kansas through the help of a good witch, and the people of the Emerald City grieve for their ruler and remember him fondly.

Wolfe, Hugh. "Life in the Iron Mills." Rebecca Harding Davis. 1861.

This grimly realistic story focuses on the daily life and work of Hugh Wolfe, a furnace stoker at one of the Kirby & John's rolling mills. Though strong and not yet twenty years old, Hugh is already daunted by years of work as the story opens. Like most young men in his community, he has been working in various capacities in the mill since the age of nine or ten. His efforts and their meager recompense contribute to the support of an ailing father, a young girl Janey, who clings to Hugh as to an adored older brother, and his cousin Deborah, who works long hours in the local cotton mills.

Despite the unending drudgery and back-breaking work, Hugh aspires to more than his current lot. He frequently spends hours carving rough but beautiful sculptures out of korl, a substance that is left over from the iron-making process. Quite often, even if he has spent a great deal of time on a particular effort, Hugh smashes the statue when it is finished because it does not meet his artistic expectations.

One of these statues becomes an issue when the mill is visited during Hugh's shift. The visitors—which include Mr. Kirby, one of the owners' sons, Dr. May, and Mr. Mitchell—are engaged in a conversation on the nature of society and political control through economics. When they near Hugh, Kirby sees one of Hugh's creations illustrated by the furnace. Mitchell identifies the stoker as the sculptor, and the visitors begin to cross-examine Hugh on his artistic intents and explain his failings to him. Dr. May remains somewhat aloof from the conversation, then finally informs Hugh that he can be whatever he wants to be, by right. When Hugh replies that he needs his help, the doctor's kindliness vanishes into an inability to assist Hugh. The visitors all agree that if Hugh had money, he could probably become a fine sculptor.

Later, in a dismal confrontation with Deborah, the

young man pours out his grief and frustration, only to be met by her misguided sympathy. In an effort to help her cousin, Deborah has stolen money from Mr. Mitchell. The money she took with the intent of allowing Hugh to become whatever he wants to be is not a large sum but is enough to produce a moral crisis in the young stoker.

That night Hugh wrestles with himself over whether or not to turn the money over to the police. He finally decides to do so, it seems, but is arrested anyway. After a speedy trial Hugh is sentenced to nineteen years of hard labor, a sentence he is already familiar with, and Deborah is sentenced to three years. Incarceration proves too much for Hugh, who tries desperately to escape. Chained to his bed to prevent future attempts, Hugh finds another way out, as he weakens steadily due to consumption. Finally, after a passionate visit from Deborah, Hugh apparently manages to take his own life, thus living a long life behind bars.

Wolfe, Nero. *Fer-de-Lance.* Rex Stout. 1934.

In this, the first of a series of novels that feature him, Nero Wolfe, a famous sleuth who solves all his cases from a chair with a bottle of beer, sends his young assistant through the city searching for clues to solve the murder of two men, Carlo Maffei and Peter Oliver Barstow.

The story begins in New York City in 1933 with Carlo Maffei's disappearance. His sister Maria asks Nero Wolfe, an overweight genius, to take the case. He is reluctant at first but decides to take it after reviewing his financial situation. He searches Carlo Maffei's room and talks with a young girl named Anna Fiore, who lives at the same boardinghouse as Carlo, and concludes that Carlo was commissioned by someone to make a golf club that could hold a poisonous dart.

Wolfe also concludes that Carlo's disappearance was in fact a murder linked with the death of a prominent upstate professor, Peter Oliver Barstow. Wolfe sends his assistant, Archie Goodwin, to White Plains, New York, to speak with Mr. Anderson, a lawyer who is working on the case, about placing a $10,000 wager based on Wolfe's certainty that if Peter's body were lifted from the grave, they would find a poison dart in it. After reading several newspaper clippings, Wolfe comes to the conclusion that Peter Barstow was poisoned by a dart inserted in his golf club (which is now lying on the bottom of the Hudson). When the body is finally lifted from the grave and an autopsy is performed, Wolfe's suspicions are confirmed.

Soon afterward Archie reads in the newspapers an advertisement from Peter Barstow's wife Ellen saying that she will pay $50,000 to any person who finds the murderer of her husband. Wolfe is soon paid a visit by Sara Barstow, Ellen's daughter. She tells Wolfe that she and her brother Larry disapprove of the reward on moral grounds. They declare that they know of no one who had a serious grievance against their father.

Wolfe invites Dr. Bradford, the family physician, to his home. They discuss why he diagnosed Peter with heart failure when he knew that he had been murdered. Dr. Bradford admits, like Sara and Larry Barstow, that he was trying to save Ellen Barstow because they feared she might have killed her husband.

Wolfe puts the family's mind at ease when he learns that Peter actually used a club from the bag of E. D. Kimball, a longtime friend and neighbor. Wolfe begins to suspect that someone was trying to kill Kimball and that Peter Barstow was the unfortunate victim. After a visit with him, Wolfe discovers that E. D. Kimball has a shady past and instantly begins to suspect his son Manuel of the murder of Peter Barstow and Carlo Maffei, and the attempted murder of his father E. D. Kimball. Manuel Kimball pays an angry visit to Wolfe and threatens to contact the police if he pursues his family any further.

Days later Wolfe receives a fake bomb and a letter, and finds a poisonous snake—a Fer-de-lance—in his desk drawer. His suspicions are confirmed. Wolfe organizes an ambush on Manuel Kimball. Archie, Mr. Anderson, and their support go to Manuel's only to discover that he is flying his plane with his father. Manuel Kimball sends Archie the missing club by messenger, along with a letter stating that he is the murderer, and then his plane crashes, killing both him and his father.

Woo, Jing-Mei. *The Joy Luck Club.* Amy Tan. 1989.

Jing-Mei Woo cannot live up to her mother's outrageous expectations. Her mother Suyuan, a refugee from China, believes that anything is possible in America and is convinced that Jing-Mei can be a prodigy of some kind. Although Jing-Mei does not prove to be a genius, her gentle, unassuming voice cleverly relates her mother's story.

Jing-Mei was born in California in 1951, with the official American name "June May." From a very early age she is engaged in a struggle with Suyuan, who insists that she can be outstanding at something; Suyuan's close friend Lindo has a daughter, Waverly Jong, who is a chess prodigy. Jing-Mei's hair is permed, and she is encouraged to develop her potential as a Shirley Temple–style actress. Later, her mother invents a series of tests to determine whether she can perform such feats as remembering the names of every national capital or memorizing at a glance an entire page of text. Suyuan arranges for Jing-Mei to take piano lessons from an aged, deaf music teacher, Mr. Chong. Jing-Mei discovers that she can make any number of mistakes, provided she maintains a precise rhythm, and Mr. Chong will never notice.

After a disastrous performance in a church talent show, Jing-Mei refuses to practice the piano anymore. This assertion of her will infuriates Suyuan. When Jing-Mei shrieks, "I wish I'd never been born!", her mother gives up and in the ensuing years gradually relaxes her efforts to transform her daughter. They never discuss the awful recital or the events that led up to it, so Jing-Mei never asks her mother "why she had hoped for something so large that failure was inevitable."

Suyuan's accusation that Jing-Mei is too flexible and "flows in too many directions" haunts her adult life. Jing-Mei begins a college degree in biology, then a degree in art, but finishes neither. She takes a job as a secretary in a small advertising agency, eventually moving up to the position of copywriter. She writes an advertisement for the law firm where Waverly Jong works, and when the firm is late in paying her, she confronts Waverly at the family New Year's party. Waverly hedges and finally admits that she was unwilling to tell Jing-Mei that the company found her work unacceptable and couldn't use it. After the party Jing-Mei expects to hear Suyuan's reprimand, but instead her mother gives her a jade pendant, calling it her "life's importance." Although Jing-Mei is never quite certain of the significance of the piece, she wears it constantly, musing over possible meanings.

Jing-Mei is thirty-six when her mother dies, and she is asked to replace her in the Joy-Luck Club, which Suyuan initiated. Suyuan invented the club in Kweilin, China, during wartime when the city was being destroyed and she felt hopeless. She invited three other young women like herself to have weekly celebrations, playing mah-jongg, eating, telling stories, and trying to think only of their happiness. The club forms again when Suyuan immigrates, and the three other couples are like Jing-Mei's family. She hesitates to join the group, however, knowing it is impossible to replace her mother. At the first Joy Luck meeting she attends, the other members announce to Jing-Mei that they have bought her and her father tickets to China. Jing-Mei is to meet her twin half-sisters, left behind when her mother was fleeing the Japanese in Kweilin.

As soon as Jing-Mei reaches China, she feels that she "becomes Chinese." Her father's family welcomes them warmly, and they celebrate in a Western-style hotel with American food. Jing-Mei's father tells her in detail the story of her mother's first marriage to an army officer, his death, and her escape to Chungking. On the way to Chungking, Suyuan left the babies by the road, hoping someone would care for them since she was convinced they would all die if she tried to carry them farther. The babies were saved by a pious Muslim family. Suyuan continued to send letters to China to try to establish contact, but the connection was not made until after Suyuan's death.

The sisters meet in Shanghai, laughing and weeping with joy at having found one another. Looking at a Polaroid photo of themselves, the three are astonished at the resemblance they all bear to their mother.

Woods, Vergible ''Tea Cake.'' *Their Eyes Were Watching God.* Zora Neale Hurston. 1937.

Vergible "Tea Cake" Woods is the third of JANIE MAE CRAWFORD's husbands. He shares with her a love more pure than any she has known before and, more important, leads her toward her own self-discovery.

Tea Cake meets Janie some months after the death of Mayor JOE "JODY" STARKS, the self-important second husband who had ruled over her for several years. Her first marriage, to a hard-driving farmer, was no more successful, and Janie is in no hurry to give up her newfound freedom for marriage with any of the several suitors who pursue her. Tea Cake is different from the others, however. A good deal younger than Janie, he encourages her to enjoy life to the fullest, teaching her to play checkers and fish, and promises that as his wife she will have "de keys to de kingdom." They fall deeply in love and create a scandal in town when they elope.

Their marriage has a rocky beginning as Tea Cake disappears on a gambling spree the morning after the wedding night. But the two soon learn to trust each other, and their relationship gains strength. Together they move to "de Muck," as the Florida Everglades is known, so that Tea Cake can pick vegetables as an itinerant worker. Hating to be separated from Tea Cake even for a day, Janie dons overalls and joins him in the fields. They work side by side and are so congenial that they attract the friendship of many of the other workers. The porch of their shack soon becomes the regular gathering place for the field hands at day's end.

Although their marriage is passionate, it is not always peaceable. In a moment of jealousy Janie physically attacks Tea Cake in the field; soon after, Tea Cake becomes so possessive of Janie's love that he beats her to show she belongs to him alone. On the whole, however, their relationship is one of undying mutual love and respect. Their love for each other even survives the harrowing hurricane that pummels the swampy Everglades. Forced out into the storm across the flooding fields, Janie and Tea Cake cling to each other for moral support. At one point Tea Cake risks his life to save Janie from drowning and is bitten by a rabid dog in the process. They eventually reach higher ground and safety.

The floods subside, and Tea Cake's wound heals. A troop of white men force him at gunpoint to assist in burying the dead left behind by the storm, but Tea Cake is so worried about Janie that he again risks his life by breaking away and rushing to her side. Soon afterward he develops a raging fever. Janie tries desperately to care for him, but she feels helpless and his delirium frightens her. She leaves to try to procure medicine, and when she returns, Tea Cake rashly accuses her of infidelity. Out of his mind with sickness, he aims a pistol at her, but Janie, who has anticipated and feared such a moment, shoots first. Tea Cake falls to the ground, and Janie runs to him and cradles his head in her arms as his life ebbs away.

Woolston, Mark. *The Crater; or, Vulcan's Peak.* James Fenimore Cooper. 1848.

Born the son of a Buck's County physician, Mark Woolston is the personification of American nobility. He has the advantages of a comfortable upbringing and at least part of a Princeton education before he drops out of school to go to sea.

By the time he is nineteen Mark has made two trading voyages to China and is promoted to first officer on the *Rancocus.* Before his third, eventful voyage, he secretly marries the daughter of his father's arch-rival. But Mark and Bridget (née Yardley) are found out by their two irate fathers and must separate before their union is consummated. Mark is off again to the Pacific, unhappily overseen by an alcoholic captain who gets the *Rancocus* into deep trouble. The ship strikes an uncharted reef. A drunken Captain Crutchley is washed overboard, and most of the panicky crew is swirled away in the ship's one lifeboat, leaving Mark and his close friend Bob Betts alone on the seemingly doomed wreck.

Daylight reveals a tiny volcanic island where Mark and Bob must make their home. The *Rancocus* is safe but entirely stuck within the confines of the reef. Mark and Bob quickly populate the island with the *Rancocus's* small store of domestic animals: pigs, poultry, and a goat. The ship's Quaker owner has providentially stored some seeds aboard, and the two castaways expend much energy manufacturing a suitable mixture of guano, volcanic ash, and seaweed mulch in order to plant their garden in the island's quiescent crater.

The two build a small sailing craft with the thought of escaping, but unhappily Bob Betts is swept away in the pinnace during a terrible storm. Mark is entirely alone. He suffers loneliness, sickness, and finally complete disorientation when, while he is asleep one night, the dormant volcano comes to life in a violent eruption. Mark awakes to find a much bigger island. The reef has risen from the sea, the *Rancocus* is comfortably protected by a bay, and a large land mass, Vulcan's Peak, is visible to the south. Mark visits the Peak and from its summit sees an approaching sail. It is Bob Betts, returning from America with a party of colonists, including Mark's sister, brother-in-law, and lovely wife Bridget.

Mark is quickly elected governor, a semi-autocratic office. He is, in addition, the growing colony's wealthiest member and, very soon, a proud father. Mark sails to America on a profitable trading voyage and returns to the colony with needed supplies and more personnel. Despite two attacks by bloodthirsty Pacific islanders and one encounter with pirates, the young colony thrives. Its degree of "culture" increases with its population, however, and soon Mark's little Eden is convulsed with civil strife, popular discontent, and religious sectarianism. A lawyer and a newspaper editor seem to seal the fate of the colony:

Mark is deposed as governor in a general upswell of ignorant dissatisfaction.

The Woolstons sail to America for a vacation. When Mark returns to the Pacific many months later, he is unable to locate the colony. Crossing and recrossing the area, he finally discerns a minuscule island with a single tree. It is the very tip of Vulcan's Peak, which has apparently disappeared with the colony's evolving divisiveness, the victim of another volcanic convulsion.

Wright, Cabot. *Cabot Wright Begins.* James Purdy. 1964.

Cabot Wright has just been released from prison where he has been serving time for the rapes of over three hundred women. He is hiding out in Brooklyn, at the See-River Manor, trying to escape publicity and the hordes of writers seeking to get his life story. Aspiring novelist Bernie Gladhart finds Cabot Wright in his hotel. Cabot is deaf and has suffered partial memory loss. He cannot remember any of the rapes, but he can tell whether accounts in the popular press are true or false.

Zoe Bickley, who has been assigned by editor Princeton Keith to rewrite Bernie's manuscript, sets out to learn the truth. In Bernie's account, Cabot begins as what his parents call a "suppositious" child; Cabot takes this to mean he is adopted and believes it is a clue to his character. Yale-educated, Cabot lands a job with a Wall Street firm, and Mr. Warburton is his boss. He marries Cynthia Adams, a dress designer, and they move into an apartment in Brooklyn Heights.

The only sign that anything is amiss with Cabot is his insistence on walking to work over the Brooklyn Bridge. No one is surprised when he announces he is suffering from fatigue. He begins to take treatments from a mysterious Dr. Bigelow-Martin. The doctor's unorthodox methods may or may not be effecting a change in Cabot. Reading a technical description of the botanical reproduction of tropical plants in a Brooklyn branch library, Cabot begins to sweat copiously. Before he knows it he has coaxed a young woman into a dark room to commit his first "rape." Several more follow, including an episode with Warburton's wife. In every case the woman is willing; newspapers speculate that the rapist is a hypnotist. Cynthia, meanwhile, mystified over the change in Cabot, has a dramatic fit in a supermarket and is hospitalized as insane. Warburton, tormented by his inability to believe or disbelieve his wife's story, kills himself, leaving Cabot heir to his fortune.

With his new wealth, Cabot opens his brownstone to friends and strangers who need a place to live. When a social worker investigates a neighbor's complaint, Cabot seduces her as well. He is now cured, he tells Zoe, except for his bad memory and the fact that he can only giggle, not laugh.

Cabot Wright disappears, but not without writing to Zoe that he will stay in touch. The novel that Princeton Keith concocts out of Bernie and Zoe's efforts, called *Indelible Smudge*, cannot be published because it is "dirty and well written." Cabot surfaces again in a long letter to Zoe, saying that he has returned to Brooklyn to sell his property and retire forever, and that he is now cured completely and able to laugh. People may never know what makes him tick, he writes, but he wants Zoe to know he is ticking away.

Wright, Nel. *Sula.* Toni Morrison. 1973.

Nel Wright is the best friend of the title character, SULA MAY PEACE, in this novel about the black community of Medallion, Ohio. When they learn that Nel's great-grandmother is dying, Nel and her mother take a trip to New Orleans to see her. The first and only time Nel travels from Medallion, this experience changes her life. She hears her proud mother called "gal" by the white train conductor and sees her smile at him in return. Nel is humiliated and vows that she will never need anybody from that point on.

Nel's house is always immaculate, and she squirms under the restrictions of her mother's social snobbery, resenting the control that extends as far as forcing Nel to wear a clothespin on her nose every night in the hope of making it less flat. When Nel meets Sula, suddenly all the unpleasant practicality of her life seems to fall away. They spend their whole day together, complementing each other perfectly, able to communicate without talking. They walk downtown, braving the stares and comments of the men they pass, delighting in the compliments. One day Nel is physically harassed by a group of Irish schoolboys, causing her to change her daily path home from school until Sula insists on a confrontation during which she cuts off part of her finger, successfully terrifying the boys.

On another occasion Nel and Sula are playing by the river with a small boy, Chicken Little. Nel watches Sula swing the boy around and let go of his hands so that he sails into the water. The boy drowns. Nel is surprised at how calm and practical she feels compared to the panicked Sula. She becomes Sula's support during the ordeal of the funeral.

When Nel gets married to a handsome and relatively successful man, Jude, Sula is loving and helpful. But directly after the wedding, Sula disappears for ten years. When she returns, Nel has three children and a happy marriage. They rekindle their friendship, and Nel realizes how much she has missed Sula and her way of looking at the world. Through Sula she learns how to laugh again. One day she returns home to find Sula and Jude having sex, and she is shocked when Jude leaves her for Sula, then leaves Medallion for good when Sula rejects him. Nel is devastated by loneliness, missing both Jude and the closeness of her friendship with Sula. In her unhappiness she begins to smother her children with love.

When Nel hears that Sula, who lives alone, has fallen ill, she brings her friend medicine. They have a painful argument about the breach of their friendship. Although Sula dies that night, something about their meeting heals Nel. Still loyal to her childhood friend, she is the only black person to attend Sula's funeral. Years later Nel visits Sula's grandmother, EVA PEACE, in a nursing home. The visit sparks her memory; she recalls Sula's funeral, when she finally understood that all the years she thought she was missing Jude, she was actually missing Sula.

Wright, Richard. *Black Boy.* Richard Wright. 1937.

In this autobiographical novel, Richard Wright struggles in a world that seeks to suppress his fierce pride, intelligence, and honesty. An impoverished black child in the deep South of the 1920s, Richard confronts daily the shameless, astonishing racism of white southerners. His genius and his passion for literature also isolate him from the black community, and in solitude he seeks paths out of his desperate situation.

Richard's childhood is perpetually interrupted by moves and by the arrivals and departures of adults. In the first scenes, four-year-old Richard, looking for an amusing game, sets fire to the living room curtains and burns down the house. Richard's mother beats him severely, and he remains ill for some time. Not long afterward they move to Memphis, where Richard's father works as a night porter. Because Richard and his brother are punished if they are not absolutely silent while their father sleeps during the day, he becomes a source of terror to him. Richard has no emotional response when his father leaves.

While Richard's mother takes a job as a cook for white people, Richard himself is tormented by perpetual, violent hunger. He wanders the streets begging drinks at a saloon until his mother finds someone to watch him. When she can no longer pay the rent, she sends him and his brother to an orphanage, where they remain hungry, frightened, and miserable.

Richard's mother eventually retrieves her sons and takes them to her mother's home in Jackson and then to her sister's house in Arkansas, where they live in relative luxury. Richard hoards bread in his pockets, unable to believe that there will still be enough to eat the next day. It is at his aunt Maggie's house, however, that he has his first shocking view of racist violence. His uncle Hoskins is unexpectedly shot in the successful saloon he owns, and the family must flee. With the family on its own again, Richard's mother becomes ill from overwork and has a stroke. Richard is sent away to his uncle's house to live but is unable to conform to the strict code of behavior and is sent back to Granny's house, where his mother is recovering.

While living at Granny's, Richard is able to get four years of consistent schooling, up through the ninth grade. Although he does well in school, his behavior with his classmates is confrontational and often violent. At home he does constant battle with his grandmother and aunt Addie, who view his aggression as evil and want to convert him to docile Christianity. Richard will not convert and refuses to counterfeit religious faith. In the same independent spirit, when he is made valedictorian, he insists upon reading his own speech, although reading the one supplied by the principal would get him a teaching job.

In addition to going to school, Richard works mornings, evenings, and weekends doing chores for white families, who routinely insult him. In order to collect enough money to move away from home, he needs a way to save more quickly. He resorts to taking a job at a movie theater where the employees have set up a scam to resell tickets and make a profit for themselves. As soon as he has enough money for a train ticket, Richard quits the job and moves to Memphis.

In Memphis, Richard takes a room in a boardinghouse and gets a job running errands and washing lenses at an optical company. By this time he has mastered perfectly the obsequious manners that are crucial to his survival. Reading a newspaper one day, he notices some harsh criticism of H. L. Mencken and determines to read Mencken's work. An Irish employee of the optical company, Mr. Falk, allows him to use his library card and forge notes so it appears that Falk is sending him for books. Richard begins reading Mencken and continues reading novels obsessively, sensing that his world is being altered and enlarged by each book. Although he feels that reading alone sustains him, his rapid intellectual growth puts an increasing distance between him and everyone around him. When he has finally earned enough to send for his mother and brother, they leave Memphis for Chicago. As they ride north, Richard hopes that he will one day live in a world free of fear, where people can treat one another with dignity.

Wursup, Frederick. *Natural Shocks.* Richard Stern. 1978.

Fred Wursup, internationally celebrated journalist and cult personality, is a tough but philosophical man. Wursup spent his professional career and personal life distancing those people, ideas, and situations closest to him with his sharp cynicism. Now middle-aged, he is assigned to write an article about death and dying, and finds himself questioning mortality in a personal way, instead of as a removed, objective journalist. He uncovers the truth not only of his profession but also of his own "story," his behavior and motivation in romantic relationships, friendships, and family relations.

Divorced from his first wife Susannah, a practical, un-sentimental woman who writes for a small but growing political magazine, Wursup lives comfortably with his girlfriend Sookie in New York City in the 1970s. Wursup feels "passionate affection" for Sookie because she is beautiful, intelligent, and understanding. But Sookie, who is a geologist, does not share Wursup's fascination with mortality and human struggle; in her mind both life and death can be reduced to "a little carbon zone dangled between ice ages."

Their apartment is right across the street from the apartment where Susannah and his sons live, and from his roof Wursup can spy directly into Susannah's apartment. He watches through binoculars, as Susannah reads the paper, talks with their children, and meets with her lover Kevin, who is the editor and publisher of the magazine for which she works. Through his voyeurism Wursup learns how Susannah is changing and developing her life apart from him. Her movements and activities become increasingly foreign to him, suggesting that she is becoming a different person.

To research his article on death and dying, Wursup goes to a hospital to visit with terminally ill patients. There he meets Francesca "Cicia" Buell, a fragile but sparkling beauty who is dying of cancer. Instead of distancing himself as a journalist, Wursup is intensely drawn to her. He wants to bring Cicia into his world, to show her the places he has seen while he covered news in the Middle East, Europe, and the Orient. In an effort to do so, he gives Cicia his collection of postcards, which depict points of interest in cities around the world.

Wursup visits Cicia frequently at first, in the hospital and at her home in Manhattan, but then, confused by his complex feelings for her and unable to confront her illness, he retreats into self-examination and escapes by traveling. He goes to Brooklyn to talk with his old friend Will Eddy, who gives him peace of mind and solid advice; he flies to Rome to see Jim Doyle, a friend and competitor about whom Wursup wrote in his best-seller *Down the American Drain*; he spends the night in Bruges with his sometime lover Gretchen. It is while Wursup is in Bruges that Sookie calls to tell him his father and stepmother have committed suicide.

Wursup flies back to the States to settle his father's estate. In Chicago, where his father lived and where Wursup grew up, Wursup finds a suicide note revealing his father's macho feelings that turned into tender affection for him. The novel ends cathartically. As Wursup ponders his father's life as a meter-reader for People's Gas and as a closet poet, and his own double life as a famous journalist, divorced man, and father, Cicia slips into unconsciousness and dies at the hospital, and Susannah, now married to Kevin, moves out of her apartment. The novel closes with Wursup entering a new phase in his life, leaving the old in print.

Wyeth, Maria. *Play It As It Lays.* Joan Didion. 1970.

Maria Wyeth is a beautiful, troubled woman who spirals downward into quiet despair. A successful actress who has stopped working, Maria lives a life that sometimes seems pointless to her. She narrates her story from a mental hospital, where she has been taken after being found asleep with her friend BZ, who is dead from an overdose of sleeping pills.

Maria, born in Nevada, grows up there with her parents, who are always involved in wild schemes to turn profits on cattle ranches or obscure ski resorts. After graduating from high school, Maria goes to New York City to take acting lessons. Finding success as a model, she begins to win roles in the movies and live the fast-paced, stimulating life of an up-and-coming actress. Her mother dies in Nevada during this time, and she becomes obsessed with wondering what she was doing at the moment her mother died. She has a few rocky love affairs that threaten to spoil her ability to act, and then she marries director Carter Lang.

She and Carter move to California, where Carter puts Maria in a couple of movies. The two spend time at all sorts of show-business parties and with their friends BZ and Helene. The two couples are always fighting and making up, and the relationship between Maria and Carter is rocky as well. Some time after the birth of their daughter Kate, who is retarded, Carter moves out of their home in Beverly Hills.

Haunted by her child's illness and the failure of her marriage, Maria tries to stop thinking and having nightmares. She tries driving, drinking—anything to escape her pain. When she discovers that she is pregnant, Carter pressures her into having an abortion. After the abortion is botched, Maria grows more and more disconnected. She sleeps at strange hours, stops answering the phone, and begins calling her friends at strange hours.

Maria tries to work again and lands a few cameo roles on television, but she is not sought after as she used to be because she has acquired a reputation for being difficult to work with. One night she brings home a man for sex. When he proves abusive and rude, she takes his car and drives to Nevada. She is eventually arrested for stealing the man's car, but her manager manages to get the charges dropped.

Maria tries to shut down her brain entirely and live only from moment to moment, becoming aimless. Carter tries to help her by taking her out to the desert with him, Helene, and BZ. Like Maria, BZ is tired of life. One night he goes to Maria's hotel room where she is sleeping alone. The two of them talk a little about life, nothingness, and suicide. BZ takes an overdose of sleeping pills; aware of what is happening, Maria falls asleep holding his hand. She is awakened a few hours later when Helene and Carter return to find BZ dead next to her. They take Maria to a private mental hospital, where she dreams only of a quiet settled life with her daughter Kate.

Wynne, Arthur. *Hugh Wynne: Free Quaker.* S. Weir Mitchell. 1897.

Arthur Wynne is an ambitious and villainous Tory and a captain in Great Britain's Revolutionary War army. A Welshman who aspires to the title of a large family estate called Wyncote in Wales, Captain Wynne unscrupulously attempts to wrest claim to the estate from his American cousin HUGH WYNNE, whose Quaker grandfather and father relinquished their claim to their rightful inheritance and moved to the United States to conduct a lucrative shipping business. Adept at assuming a noble and virtuous facade, Arthur Wynne schemes his way through the Revolution, creating havoc in the lives of innocent people as he steadily approaches the realization of his insidious and materialistic designs.

Having been sent to the United States prior to the war as a representative of the British army, the virile and swarthy Arthur Wynne meets his cousin Hugh for the first time at a drunken gambling party. The party is interrupted when Hugh's concerned mother arrives to fetch her errant son, whose religion forbids such carousing. The tipsy Captain Wynne, unaware that the woman at the door is his aunt, advances toward her and puts his arm around her waist in a lascivious manner, whereupon Hugh defends his mother's honor by knocking Arthur over with a blow to the face. Arthur eventually apologizes for his affront and the incident is forgotten, but this initial strife between the cousins, who fight in enemy armies, characterizes their relationship throughout the war.

The tension is exacerbated by the fact that Captain Wynne woos and becomes engaged to Darthea Peniston, a perky young woman who had already inspired Hugh's affections. In addition, Arthur takes advantage of Hugh's estrangement from his father, who is seriously displeased with his son's Whig sentiments. Arthur manages to make the old man feel that his nephew is more of a son to him than his actual offspring. Arthur's cultivation of his relationship with Mr. Wynne is far from sincere; it is motivated purely by the captain's determination to convince his uncle to transfer the official deed of Wyncote into his name.

Arthur's ill will toward his cousin becomes so pronounced that when he finds his cousin delirious in a rat-infested British prison after having been captured during a military foray, he pretends not to recognize him and leaves him there with the hope that he will perish. Their next encounter takes place when Arthur recognizes a disguised Hugh, who is on a spying mission in Philadelphia. Arthur is prevented from seizing and arresting his cousin only by the timely interruption of Darthea, who suffers a fainting spell that requires Arthur's immediate attention.

His treachery is once again manifested when he recommends to his superiors that Hugh be hoodwinked into delivering a treasonous dispatch from Benedict Arnold. Despite this litany of treachery, Captain Wynne's facade remains intact and his reputation unblemished.

Arthur's conflict with his cousin culminates when they meet by chance on a battlefield and fight a grim duel. Hugh is the better swordsman, but he is tripped up by a dying soldier; Arthur is prevented from slaying him only because another American soldier intrudes and manages to wound him. He does not see Hugh again until after the war when, because Hugh has informed Darthea of the dishonesty that stains Arthur's character, he finds that he must relinquish his claim to her. Defeated in love and in war, Arthur returns to Wales to take up residence at Wyncote. He is unofficial heir to the estate because his American cousin has no desire to claim his old-world inheritance.

Wynne, Hugh. *Hugh Wynne: Free Quaker.* S. Weir Mitchell. 1897.

Hugh Wynne, a dashing young Revolutionary War hero, is the legal heir to Wyncote, a vast estate in Wales. His grandfather abandoned his legacy when his Quaker ethics collided with the political and economic expectations of church officials and public magistrates. Wynne's father's strict adherence to the Quaker faith and to the Tory party ultimately causes him to become estranged from his son when Hugh embraces the Whig party's opposition to Britain's control of the American colonies. Having relinquished his position in his father's shipping business, Hugh sneaks out of occupied Philadelphia and joins troops under the command of General Washington and Colonel Hamilton. Shortly after his enlistment he is

wounded in battle and taken prisoner by British troops, who convey him to an abominable prison where typhus and dysentery run rampant. The prison food supply is so inadequate that the men are driven to eat rats, which they manage to capture and cook when the prison authorities deign to supply fuel in the midst of a bitterly cold winter. One of only six prisoners of his company to survive this incarceration, Hugh escapes with the help of a Catholic nun who contacts Darthea Peniston, who in turn succeeds in smuggling him out of the prison.

During the course of the war, Hugh repeatedly declares his love for the charming Darthea, but she rebuffs his advances because she has promised her hand to his cousin ARTHUR WYNNE. Arthur, a captain in the British army, stands to inherit Wyncote if Hugh decides he does not wish to reclaim the title to his family's Welsh estate. A bitter rivalry develops between the two cousins. Still estranged from his father, Hugh is unable to undermine Arthur's burgeoning relationship with him. The feud between the cousins culminates in a duel on the battlefield. Although Hugh is clearly the better swordsman, his superior skill is rendered useless when a wounded soldier grabs his leg and pulls him to the ground just as he is about to claim his victory. Hugh's life is saved by his best friend Jack Warder, who intervenes and manages to wound Arthur Wynne.

Darthea's eyes are finally opened to Arthur's treachery against his cousin, and she agrees to marry Hugh after the war is over. The young lovers decide that Hugh should allow his cousin to inherit Wyncote, and after his youthful escapades as a brave and adventurous Revolutionary War soldier, Hugh settles down to a peaceful and contented life as husband and father.

X, Sergeant. "For Esmé—with Love and Squalor." J. D. Salinger. 1953.

In April 1944, Sergeant X is one of sixty men taking a pre-invasion training course directed by British Intelligence in Devon, England. Like most of the other men, he is not much of a mixer; rather, he writes letters to his wife, reads books, and goes for walks. On a rainy Saturday, the day on which his group will entrain for London, Sergeant X takes a walk into the little town and enters a church where some children are practicing for the choir.

The unaccompanied and melodious voices temporarily lift the lonely young man out of the reality of the war. He notices one girl in particular who has the sweetest-sounding and surest voice of the group.

When, a little while later, Sergeant X is sitting in the civilian tearoom, this girl walks in with her five-year-old brother and their governess. Self-consciously hiding the black filling between his two front teeth, Sergeant X returns her smile and invites her to join him for tea. Although he is delighted at her presence, he can think of nothing to talk about but the weather. Esmé, however, dispenses with small talk and engages him in an earnest discussion of their respective lives. Sergeant X reacts honestly to each new subject and is clearly moved by Esmé's precociousness and frankness, and even her snobbery. Suddenly their conversation is interrupted by little Charles, who asks why people in films always kiss sideways. Familiar with this baffling problem from his own childhood, Sergeant X replies that it must be because actors' noses are too big to kiss head-on.

Sergeant X tells Esmé that he would like to think of himself as a professional short-story writer. Esmé tells him that she would be extremely flattered if he would write her a story one day—not something silly and childish but a sensuous story about "squalor." She offers to write to him and makes him promise not to forget to write the story for her.

Several weeks after V-E day and a year after meeting Esmé, Sergeant X has taken a room in a civilian home in Gaufurt, Bavaria. Having suffered a nervous breakdown, he chain-smokes and is weak-headed, and his hands and face shake involuntary. Inspired by the sad inscription, "Dear God, life is hell," that a young Nazi girl had written in a Goebbels book, he tries to respond in English but realizes that his writing is illegible.

Suddenly the door bangs open and Corporal Z, known as Clay, tries to revive Sergeant X by talking and joking with him. Z's uneducated manner allows him to tell X unselfconsciously that he looked like a corpse while he was in the hospital. X changes the subject to Z's girlfriend Loretta, for X was the one who composed most of the love letters sent to her by Z. When Clay subsequently brings up the subject of a cat he had killed during a shelling, X has had enough. He turns to the wastebasket and throws up. Heeding X's plea to leave him alone, Clay leaves.

Thinking it might be therapeutic for him to write a letter, X tries to roll the paper into his typewriter but fails on account of his shaking hands. With his head on the desk in despair and in pain, X notices a small package for him that has had several forwarding addresses. Inside is a letter from Esmé written almost a year ago. She expresses her excitement over the D-Day operations and her concern for his safety. Charles, whom she is teaching to read and write, adds many hellos in the P.S. of the letter. Esme explains that she has enclosed her father's chronographic-looking wristwatch, which X had admired; it is a lucky talisman for him during these difficult days.

The crystal on the watch has been broken in transit, but Sergeant X sits with it in his hand for a long while. The memory of Esmé and her fresh presence break the spell of misery for Sergeant X, and he feels sleepy for the first time in months. At the end of the story, he addresses Esmé directly, telling her in his own aloof way that she helped bring his faculties back. Although Esmé has married another man, Sergeant X keeps his promise and writes a story for her—with love and squalor.

Yossarian, John. *Catch-22.* Joseph Heller. 1961.

John Yossarian is a bombardier captain in the Fighting 256th Squadron on the island of Pianosa, off Italy, eight miles south of Elba, in the final years of World War II. Yossarian's job involves sitting in the Plexiglas nose of a B-25 bomber (separated from the rest of the plane by a tight crawlway) and radioing instructions to the pilot regarding which way to turn to avoid flak and the most opportune moment to begin dropping bombs. Yossarian does not like his work and insists that everyone around him is trying to kill him. Not only is it abundantly clear that the entire German army wants him dead, but his own countrymen are little better, for they persist in sending him on bombing missions in areas they know full well are infested with enemy troops. He is also frustrated by his commanding officer Colonel Cathcart, who persists in raising the number of missions required for a tour of duty. While men in other units of the Air Force go home after flying forty missions, the men of the Fighting 256th are required to fly over eighty. This, Yossarian feels, is clearly unfair.

Yossarian's main goal is to stay alive, and thus he attempts to avoid flying missions in various clever and devious ways. In the opening pages of the novel he is in a hospital, feigning illness, but the combination of the hideous "soldier in white," who is nothing but a body cast with fluid dripping in one tube and out another, and a hideously affable Texan, who is universally despised, drive him back to active duty. He attempts to have himself declared insane and thereby be excused from combat, but there is a catch: Catch-22. Catch-22 stipulates that any man who is certifiably insane will automatically be released from active duty, but it also specifies that anyone who expresses a desire to be released from active duty is rational enough to fly.

Because of the novel's fragmented style, it is difficult to establish a precise chronology of events in his life. It is grimly apparent, however, that as Yossarian's friends are all killed or lost in action, his superiors remain utterly callous and removed from the realities of combat. He is most horrified by the death of Snowden, a young gunner in his plane who is killed in a mission over Avignon. Seeing a huge gash "the size of a football" in Snowden's thigh, Yossarian works frantically to dress the wound, only to discover that flak has penetrated Snowden's flying jacket, and his stomach has been blown to pieces. The stark horror of Snowden's death, contrasted with the callous stupidity and surreal triviality of events at Headquarters (where, among other things, all combat operations are accidentally placed under the supervision of the USO), leads to Yossarian's refusal to fly any more missions.

Ultimately, Yossarian is confronted by his superiors, who have decided that his protest is damaging morale, and the best way to quiet him would be to give him a medal, a promotion, and an honorable discharge. Despite his hatred for the men who offer him the deal, Yossarian initially accepts. Memories of Snowden make him change his mind. If he refuses the deal, he will be court-martialed, a possibility he accepts stoically.

Just as he finally resolves to defy the authorities, Yossarian receives miraculous news. His friend Orr, shot down over the Mediterranean, has washed ashore safe and sound in neutral Sweden. Amazing as it seems, he rowed there on a small emergency raft after his plane went down. Orr had a habit of being shot down, and for this reason Yossarian refused his frequent offers to fly with him. Suddenly Yossarian realizes this was all part of a coherent plan; Orr was practicing his escape. Following his friend's example, Yossarian grabs a raft, some provisions, and an oar, and loudly shouting that Colonel Cathcart and the rest can go to hell, sets off on his journey.

Young, Brigham. *Children of God.* Vardis Fisher. 1939.

A young, spirited drifter in the backwoods of New York in the early 1800s, Brigham Young led a wild and irreligious life until he met a traveling evangelist by the name of JOSEPH SMITH. Impressed with the vision and faith of the young prophet, Brigham decides to follow Smith and his growing band of Mormons, as they call themselves, to Ohio, where they intend to build a religious community based on the gospel that God reveals through the prophet Joseph.

Brigham quickly becomes an integral part in the successful running of the Mormon community in Ohio. When a number of the Mormons are terrorized by neighboring gentiles, Brigham, who had always believed in Joseph's powers as a prophet but often questioned his judgment in earthly matters, leads secret raids against the offending townsmen. Continuing to rise in power in the void left by an increasingly detached Joseph, Brigham does his best to hold together the fragmented Mormon community through both force and diplomacy.

When Joseph begins to fear his own position of leadership in the Mormon church, he sends Brigham, along with various other Mormon leaders known as the Council of Twelve, out across the United States to gather converts. While fully aware of the prophet's motivation in sending him away from the community, Brigham, still loyal to the man who brought religion to his life, accedes to Joseph's wishes.

After several months and making hundreds of converts, Brigham is recalled to Ohio, where he finds Joseph has called an emergency meeting for the high-ranking church officials. Joseph tells them of a new commandment to their faith that God recently told him about, known as "celestial marriage." By this tenet, high-ranking church officials such as themselves, in order to secure a more powerful position in the next world, may take as many wives as they please. Joseph then proceeds to instruct the horrified Council of Twelve to keep "celestial marriage" a secret from the rest of the Mormons until God deems the time appropriate to reveal it to the masses.

Despite their best efforts, however, word of rampant polygamy among the Mormons spreads throughout Ohio, and they are forced to move westward to Missouri, where they once again struggle to build a new community. In addition, the church leadership becomes more fragmented than ever, with most of the high-ranking church officials believing that Joseph's steadfast insistence on "celestial marriage" will bring about the end of their church. As rumors and exaggerations of ungodliness in the Mormon community continue to spread, President Martin Van Buren finally sends federal troops out to arrest the Mormon leaders. Joseph and the rest of the church officials are captured, but the wily Brigham Young escapes and goes into hiding.

Very shortly afterward Brigham Young receives word that Joseph has been killed by an angry lynch mob. He immediately returns to the rapidly deteriorating settlement in Missouri, where he is able to seize power from the other church leaders. Realizing that his people must find a home away from the persecution of the U.S. government, he leads several expeditions of Mormons to Utah, near the great Salt Lake, where he tells them they will build a city out of the untamed wilderness and barren desert.

After a brutal first winter and various other hardships, Brigham's dream comes true as the Mormons establish a blossoming city outside the reach of the government's rule. Brigham lives out the rest of his days in their new city, where the Mormon religion founded by Joseph would continue to thrive.

Young, Della Dillingham. "The Gift of the Magi." O. Henry. 1906.

As this bittersweet story opens, Della Dillingham Young is sitting on the shabby little couch of the Youngs' shabby $8 flat, weeping. She has spent all year scrimping and saving pennies to buy her husband Jim a Christmas present, whiling away many happy hours planning to buy something nice, something fine and rare that will be worthy of "the honor of being owned by him." But Jim's income has recently shrunk from $30 a week to $20, and thus she has managed to save only a pitiful $1.87.

The Dillinghams have two possessions in which they take tremendous pride: the gold watch that had been Jim's father's and grandfather's, and Della's long brown hair, which reaches below her knees. Looking at her hair in the pier glass that serves as her mirror, Della makes a decision to go to a hair goods store and sell her tresses for twenty dollars. She spends the next two hours in the stores looking for a suitable present, finally finding the perfect gift: a platinum fob chain for Jim's watch, simple and chaste in design, possessing quietness and value, like her Jim. Returning home, Della sobers somewhat. Getting out her curling iron, she goes to work on her hair, covering her head with tiny, close-lying curls. As she hears Jim's steps on the stairs, she prays he will still consider her pretty.

When Jim opens the door, she sees how very thin and serious he looks and notes that he needs a new overcoat and some gloves. When Jim stares blankly at her hair, she rushes to him, explaining what she has done and that her hair will grow back quickly. Urging him to be merry with her on this Christmas Eve, she says that the hairs on her head were numbered, but nobody could ever count her love for him.

Jim snaps out of his stunned trance and assures Della that nothing she could do to her hair would make him love her less, but the package he has brought her will explain his stunned reaction. Eagerly she tears open the package and screams with joy when she sees that he bought her some beautiful combs that she has admired for a long time in a Broadway window—pure tortoiseshell combs with jewelled rims that are just the right shade for her hair. Tears come to Della's eyes as she realizes what has happened, but she quickly recovers and, hugging her gift to her bosom, urges Jim to open his present. He does so, and when she asks him to put the chain on his watch, Jim smiles lovingly at her and explains that he sold the watch to buy the combs.

Young, Eugenia. *The Europeans.* Henry James. 1878.

European-born Eugenia Camilla Dolores Young, the Baroness Munster of Silberstadt-Schreckenstein, is not pretty in the conventional sense, but she is a cultured and refined woman with a flair for the exotic. She wears her hair in braids that give her an "Oriental or exotic aspect" and speaks in a melodramatic manner using French epithets for effect. Eugenia is wed to the German Prince of Silberstadt-Schreckenstein, but because she is a commoner, her husband has the right to dissolve the marriage with her consent. Her husband has requested a separation, and she holds the "renunciation" papers. Before signing the papers, however, Eugenia decides to go to America to seek her fortune amid her wealthy American relatives, the Wentworths.

Eugenia arrives in Boston with her brother FELIX (YOUNG), a bohemian artist who seeks adventure and good fortune in America. She is struck by the provinciality and barrenness of New England. She and Felix move into a house adjacent to the Wentworths'. Eugenia decorates the modest house to give it an exotic flair, adding "India shawls and pink silk blinds in the windows" and a band of velvet along the chimney. She has brought a French servant with her from Europe and is charmed by the idea of having an old black woman in a yellow turban as a cook. Although her puritanical uncle, Mr. Wentworth, and her cousin Charlotte are put off by Eugenia's decadent manner, her younger cousin Gertrude Wentworth is quite taken with her exotic airs.

Eugenia spends evenings at the main house and receives frequent visits from her uncle and a neighboring cousin, Robert Acton. Acton is considered the most worldly of the American cousins and the prize of the Wentworth family. He graduated from Harvard and is now a successful businessman. Recently returned from a trip to China, Acton delights in his European cousin's company, but although he is attracted to Eugenia, he fears he cannot trust her. She tells him about her marriage "renunciation" papers and hopes he will profess his affections for her.

While Acton is away on a business trip, Eugenia becomes increasingly depressed. She spends evenings trying to reform Clifford, the youngest of the Wentworth cousins, who was suspended from Harvard for having a drinking problem. When Acton returns, Eugenia visits his ailing mother, Mrs. Acton, to tell her that she plans to return soon to Europe. Eugenia runs into Robert, and he asks whether she has signed her renunciation. She says she has, but he rightly doubts her word.

Disappointed at the outcome of her relationship with Robert, Eugenia decides to return to Europe before the wedding of her brother Felix to Gertrude Wentworth. Eugenia admits to Felix that she has not signed the renunciation and presumably returns to be with her husband. Felix and Gertrude are happily wed, Clifford and Acton's younger sister Lizzie marry soon after, and, after the death of his mother, Robert Acton marries "a particularly nice young girl."

Young, Felix. *The Europeans.* Henry James. 1878.

Felix Young is a carefree European-born young man who arrives in America, along with his sister EUGENIA (YOUNG), to seek his fortune with their wealthy, puritanical cousins, the Wentworths of Boston. Felix is "bright and gay and fond of amusement," as the name Felix, meaning "happy," implies. A self-described bohemian and amateur artist, he has painted his way through France and Italy, played violin with a band of musicians, and joined a troupe of strolling Shakespearean actors throughout Europe. At length, however, he admits he is a "terrible philistine" who wishes only to make a living and have a family.

Upon arriving in Boston, Felix is charmed by the beauty of the country, in particular the American sunsets. His openness and enthusiasm directly contrast the superior stance of his Europeanized sister Eugenia, who finds New England life provincial. Felix calls on his American cousins on a Sunday afternoon and finds all of them at church except his youngest cousin Gertrude, who is alone reading *Arabian Nights.* Felix is immediately charmed by this carefree young lady, and she is enthralled by the tales of his adventures in foreign lands.

Felix and Eugenia soon take up residence in a small house adjacent to the Wentworths' main house, but Felix spends afternoons painting and evenings dining with his cousins. Gertrude asks Felix to paint her portrait, and with her father's consent they agree to begin work. Felix and Gertrude become increasingly fond of each other, but Felix does not want to disrupt his cousin's courtship with an ecclesiastical minister, Mr. Brand, who has been enlisted by Gertrude's father to try to discipline the young lady. Gertrude rejects Brand's affections, but Brand, encouraged by Wentworth, persists. Felix, meanwhile, notices a growing mutual interest between Brand and Charlotte, Gertrude's older and more conventional sister.

Eventually Felix can no longer deny his affections for Gertrude and decides to confront Brand about his feelings for Charlotte. Brand, realizing that he and Charlotte would make a better match, recommends to Wentworth that he give his consent to the marriage of Felix and Gertrude. Urged by Brand and Charlotte, Wentworth finally consents, and Felix and Gertrude arrange to be married. Eugenia returns to Europe before the wedding, Felix and Gertrude are happily married and move "far away," and Charlotte and Brand are wed soon after.

Young Boy. "Chickamauga." Ambrose Bierce. 1898.

This grim, horrifying story focuses on a traumatic day in the life of its protagonist, a six-year-old boy, who has wandered away from his family's home to play in the nearby woods. As the son of a southerner who once fought against Native Americans, the boy came to love soldiers and soldiering and made a small sword for himself, which he brandishes as he goes farther away from his home. While he plays alone, he imagines himself beating back the enemy and surviving as the unvanquished hero of the war. However, when he comes upon a rabbit, which he startles, the boy is suddenly deeply frightened, and he turns, running and calling out inarticulate cries designed to bring his mother to his aid. Unfortunately, his flight takes him even farther from his home, and eventually, still sobbing, he falls asleep.

When the boy awakens several hours later, it is nearly nighttime, and he is unaware of the distant sounds of thunder. He begins to wander again, crawling through the underbrush until he nearly reaches a creek and more open ground. Suddenly he sees something moving but cannot tell what it is. He imagines that it is a bear, for he has seen pictures of them and has thought he'd like to see one. He soon realizes that the creature does not have the frightful ears he saw on the rabbit earlier; thus comforted, the boy does not move as the creature advances toward him. In fact, there are many more such creatures approaching him, apparently headed for the creek. As it turns out, these are men who were among the thirty-four thousand casualties of one of the Civil War's most fearsome engagements, the battle at Chickamauga on September 19–20, 1863. The boy, who is fascinated by the odd and various gaits he sees, investigates the matter more closely. He notices that some of the men stop abruptly and move no more, while others change their positions and seem to be adjusting themselves in an attitude of prayer. He notices one man crawling on all fours. The boy recalls pretending that he was on horseback by riding the backs of his father's slaves. With this in mind, the boy clambers on the crawling man, who dashes the boy to the ground and, rising to his knees, waves his fist. The young boy also jumps up, only to see that the man's entire lower jaw was blown away. This terrifies him and he flees.

From a new vantage point he begins to realize the enormity of the scene in front of him; simultaneously, he becomes aware of a reddish glow lighting the now-darkened sky. The men continue to make their way toward the creek, where many, after slaking their thirst, lie still, too weak to even pull their heads from the water, and drown. As he begins to wander again, the boy notices many artifacts left behind and imagines them as spoils of battle, but eventually he comes upon some buildings that look familiar. As it turns out, they are his father's outbuildings, which are now on fire. More frightened than ever, the boy runs toward his home, where he is shocked to find the body of a woman, his mother. The boy immediately sees that she is dead, with the top of her head blown off by a shell. He stands there, gesturing with his hands and making more inarticulate sounds. Only then is it revealed that the boy had slept through the battle and was inarticulate because he was both deaf and mute.

The Young Man. "An Experiment in Misery." Stephen Crane. 1893.

The story's protagonist is an apparently homeless and nameless young man. Huddled in his tattered coat against the cold, he is wandering through downtown New York City. He notices with discomfort the well-dressed people around him as they make their way toward the Brooklyn Bridge. The crowd begins to change as the young man continues down Park Row, where he sees other men as shabbily dressed as he. He is beginning to be preoccupied with the problem of procuring a night's sleep. After a little more wandering, the young man encounters two men, one of whom is characterized as an assassin.

Fortunately for these cold and hungry men, there is a nearby saloon that offers free hot soup, and they hasten inside to eat. This accomplished, there remains the problem of a place to sleep. The young man asks a stranger where he sleeps, and it turns out that the ten cents a night the man spends is literally too much for the young man. The assassin knows of a place, though, and with no further delays the two men make their way to the flophouse. When they get there, they pay their few cents for a cot, are taken through dark and nauseatingly foul-smelling rooms, and deposited on cots that have closets standing over them like tombstones.

While the assassin seems to fall asleep relatively quickly, the young man does not. He is acutely aware of the sights and sounds around him, even though the room is poorly lit by the hazy light from a gas jet. After silently cataloging the sleeping men, many of whom seem to be cadavers, the young man snuggles under his coat and blanket on the cold leathery cot and finally falls asleep.

In the morning the confusion of many strange men waking and dressing offsets the meager beauty of the sunrise. The young man sees that there is a wide variety of men in the flophouse. He hears much cursing and shouting as the men wake, and he is eager to get away. He leaves with the assassin, who mumbles incoherently about the sights he has seen. The young man is hungry; the assassin, who would rather have a drink, agrees to the young man's offer of a loan of three cents for breakfast; but the young man tells him that he will have to hustle, that he is in no position to support his new friend.

Over a breakfast of coffee and a roll, the two men talk, particularly the assassin, who regales the young man with tales of various jobs he has had and various places he has worked. The young man listens, apparently attentively, but the assassin's account of himself is rambling and hard to follow. After breakfast the two men take a walk together before settling down on a bench. Here they sit for hours, watching the crowds pass. At the story's end, they continue to sit there, and the young man gradually comes to see how far he has fallen from what he once valued. With furtive and guilty eyes, he sits and watches the life of the unconcerned city pass him by once more.

Young Writer. *The Daring Young Man on the Flying Trapeze.* William Saroyan. 1934.

The unnamed young writer lives his last poignant day mimicking the actions of a living human being. Having survived on coffee, bread, and cigarettes, the young man, nearly starved, has only coffee remaining. Still, he dresses himself and goes out to seek employment. As he walks the path to various employment agencies, he dreams of the food he would buy if he had the money—"untasted delicacies from Norway, Italy, and France."

Sensing his approaching death, the young man of twenty-two accepts it without pity for himself, thinking only that he must write an "Application for Permission to Live" sometime soon. "A living young man who was in need of money with which to go on being one," he acquiesces to the lack of work and carries his ailing body to the YMCA. There he begins to compose his application. Suddenly becoming faint, he leaves the YMCA and goes to the public library, where he reads Proust. Acute physical suffering drives him back to his room. Once there he inventories its contents and feels ashamed at the absence of his books, which he has been forced to sell.

Finally, polishing a penny he found earlier in the day so that he can read the Latin phrases imprinted on it, he takes leave of his body. Dying "with the grace of the young man on the trapeze," he is "for an eternal moment . . . all things at once: the bird, the fish, the rodent, the reptile, and man."

Youngblood, Joseph. *Youngblood.* John Oliver Killens. 1954.

Joseph Youngblood is a physically imposing, hardworking, and dauntless African-American laborer and deacon. From the outset Joe's life has been difficult. Born on April Fool's Day, 1898, in rural Georgia, he lost his father at the age of six and his mother at nine. When he was eleven, his "uncle" Rob, with whom he lived, informed Joe that he would have to leave school and go to work as a field hand. Determined not to perform such work or to work for the white man he despises, Joe steals away in the night and begins his life as an itinerant worker.

He eventually settles down in the town of Waycross, Georgia. While living in Waycross, Joe develops into a determined and steady worker with an amazing physical strength, but it is his dream of success in the North that truly keeps him going. He decides to travel to Chicago, where he has heard repeatedly of the opportunities available even to black men. Disaster strikes, however, when white men board his northbound train and force the black men into slavery for the Buck Plantation. Joe escapes the brutality of the plantation after nearly two full weeks of captivity.

His faith shattered, Joe resolves to return to Georgia, where he settles in the small town of Crossroads. Once again he enters a life of constant work and struggle, which eases only when he meets LAURIE LEE BARKSDALE (YOUNGBLOOD). He and "Little Bits," as he calls Laurie Lee, marry and have two children, Jenny Lee and ROBERT (YOUNGBLOOD).

Joe works as a deacon for his local church but spends most of his time toting heavy barrels at a local plant. It is a matter of routine that he and the other black workers are cheated on payday by the white cashier who keeps up to a dollar of their nine-dollar salary. Joe finally challenges the cashier, who has insulted him one time too often, and forces him to acknowledge his "counting error." However, his assertion of his rights lead to further troubles. Although there is no immediate problem, Joe feels threatened enough to inform Laurie that he may have endangered them all. Although frightened, Laurie is proud that Joe does not let himself be demeaned. Gradually, realizing that he has been too involved in his growing exhaustion at work and rage at his own humiliation, he begins to help the children with their homework and to perform household chores.

As the years pass, Joe, with the encouragement of Rob's high school teacher, Richard Wendell Myles, begins to reassess how the ways of white and black folks could be changed. Even though the Great Depression hits and he injures his back, he continues to try to find work, but finally he returns to his old job. Here, at the end of his first week, Joe is cheated once again, and in a rage he assaults the aggressively arrogant cashier. This time, though, he is shot several times, and despite his friends' efforts, he dies. During his funeral the white members of town sense that the town's black population will no longer remain still under the oppressive "traditions" of their community, state, and nation.

Youngblood, Laurie Lee Barksdale. *Youngblood.* John Oliver Killens. 1954.

Laurie Lee Barksdale Youngblood endures a life of hardship leavened only by her love for her family and her fierce pride in her African-American heritage. Laurie spends her first twelve years enjoying the love and approval she receives from her doting parents and her grandmother, Big Mama, whose wisdom sustains Laurie and her adoring brother Tim throughout the years to come. Things begin to change by 1912, however.

First, Laurie is sexually assaulted by a white man. Then she is fired when she punches her employer for scolding her harshly. Following this, her mother's untimely death shocks the household, which is further dismayed by Big Mama's death four months later. After Big Mama's death, Tim Barksdale is sent to a reformatory for having fought with white boys. Despite these hardships, Laurie Lee graduates at the head of her high school class and plans to attend college.

Since it is not economically feasible for her to go to college, Laurie Lee becomes a schoolteacher. When she meets JOSEPH YOUNGBLOOD, the two are instantly attracted to each other, and marriage soon follows. Joe works hard, and Laurie takes in laundry to augment their income. Within a few years the Youngbloods are the proud parents of Jenny Lee and ROBERT (YOUNGBLOOD).

As the children mature, Laurie Lee inculcates them with a strong sense of their value as human beings. It is not until the children are older that she must put her lessons to the test. On one occasion, after Rob attacked some white boys who were accosting Jenny Lee, he is arrested and taken to jail. The white sheriff summons Laurie Lee and threatens her with a reformatory sentence for her son. She is mindful of the outcome of her brother's term in the reformatory and ends up beating the boy until he is bruised, swollen, and bloody, while the white policeman crudely goads her on.

The family develops a close bond with Richard Wendell Myles, who is Rob's high school teacher. Laurie Lee responds to his talk of struggle against racial discrimination and prejudice, and his timely assistance over the years. Meanwhile, the Great Depression arrives, throwing Joe out of work. Laurie Lee redoubles her efforts, taking in more and more laundry. At the same time their son lands a job, which leads to trouble. Rob and his employer's daughter are discovered about to make love. In order to avoid public scandal, Mrs. Cross, the girl's mother, goes to Laurie Lee. Despite the threat of reform school again, Laurie Lee stands her ground and accuses the white woman of covering up for her daughter's sexual desire. Laurie Lee's stand shocks and gladdens her family but devastates Mrs. Cross, who faints at Laurie Lee's feet.

The final test of Laurie Lee's strength occurs when her husband is brutally murdered simply for asking for his correct pay. Although he lingers for a while, his death comes soon after he has been shot. Laurie Lee, despite the enormity of her grief and rage, turns her thoughts to the future, even as her husband's funeral takes place. She resolves that neither she nor her fellow African Americans will ever again accept a position of inferiority.

Youngblood, Robert. *Youngblood.* John Oliver Killens. 1954.

Robert Youngblood, the son of LAURIE LEE BARKSDALE YOUNGBLOOD and JOE YOUNGBLOOD, matures during a period of severe social, racial, and economic strife. Although he learns early in life that he should never view himself as inferior to anyone, the lessons he receives from the outside world are in opposition to those his parents offer. This is apparent when a young Robby is dragged home by a black woman who is outraged at having seen him fight with a white boy near the white section of Crossroads, Georgia. Robby's mother, although not as shocked as her neighbor, does attempt to explain the odd codes of behavior by which African Americans and Caucasians coexist in the Deep South. Robby's lessons in the vagaries of racism escalate as he matures.

Robby eventually becomes more involved with schoolwork, after Richard Wendell Myles moves from New York City to teach in Crossroads. Richard attempts to comfort the Youngblood family after Laurie Lee is forced to whip Robby at the police station where he has been brought for having attacked some white boys, who were in fact assaulting his sister. When Robby runs away, he goes to Richard's house. The kindly teacher gently leads the confused and saddened youth back home.

Laurie Lee's steadfastness saves Robby from danger when his white employer discovers her daughter and Robby together, about to make love. After this controversy and Robby's graduation from high school, he journeys to New York City. He does not find the liberation he expected, but he does observe that the workers in the North seem to have successfully integrated. With this knowledge at hand, Robby resolves to return to the South and seriously attempt to organize a union. The Youngbloods are caught in the grip of the Great Depression, but Robby eventually lands a job as a bellboy at a local hotel. There

he is once again subjected to a series of racially motivated humiliations, including sexual propositions from drunken and half-naked white women who attempt to lure him into their rooms. Under Richard's tutelage he becomes interested in the labor movement, thus earning the disdain of the hotel owner and the other whites.

As his efforts to unionize the hotel progress, Robby continues to court Ida Mae Raglin, a schoolteacher. Again with the assistance of Richard Myles, Robby turns to other workers, including whites and women, in order to broaden the power base of the emerging union. One of these whites, Oscar Jefferson, has always seemed to be on the side of the blacks in their struggle for equality. When Joe Youngblood lies dying, shot by a cashier who was cheating him of his pay, Oscar is the only white person who donates blood to the ailing man. Although stunned by his father's shooting, Robby is amazed at Jefferson's show of support.

A few days later, at Joe Youngblood's funeral, Robby feels confident that this death will not be in vain and that he will become a strong force in the movement for both unionization and social and racial equality.

Z

Zawistowska, Sophie. *Sophie's Choice.* William Styron. 1976.

Sophie Zawistowska relates her past to her neighbor STINGO, yet reveals at first only a construction of half-truths, concealing the realities of her life in Poland before the war and her experience as a gentile in Auschwitz. But as Stingo and Sophie grow closer, the truth of her past emerges through a series of confessions that continually redefine her character. Her present is revealed to be as fraught with lies as her past.

Sophie lives in Brooklyn with NATHAN LANDAU, a handsome and brilliant scientific researcher. Sophie tells Stingo of her happy childhood in Cracow, her father and husband (both professors at the university), and the roundup by Nazis that took both men away from her. She can hardly speak of her horrific experience at Auschwitz and tells Stingo only sketchily of the events leading up to the day she fainted in Brooklyn and was rescued by Nathan. What is clear is her rebirth through Nathan. Their relationship is passionate and exciting, and provides Sophie with a barrier against the past. Nathan indulges her love of music, a love she was deprived of for

years, and has helped her discover a new and exultant sexuality.

Yet Nathan does not prove the ideal partner for Sophie. He is a diagnosed schizophrenic who is at once Sophie's savior and her cruelest and most ruthless enemy, accusing her of infidelity and taunting her with her survival in the face of the destruction of millions of Polish Jews. Sophie loves Nathan in spite of these cruel attacks and is both unable and unwilling to tear herself away from him. Although he can open her old wounds, he is also the only person who is truly capable of making her forget her past—at least temporarily.

As Sophie and Stingo grow closer, she reveals more of the truth about her past, telling Stingo of her father's involvement in Poland's anti-Semitism, his pro-German feelings, and her hatred of both him and her husband. When Nathan's moods grow more extreme, Sophie turns more frequently to Stingo and, in describing Nathan's cruel taunts, reveals more of her experiences in Auschwitz. She talks of the guilt she feels, a guilt that stems from the children she only briefly mentions, and from a choice she was forced to make. As Sophie confesses more and more to Stingo, he falls deeper and deeper in love. Yet Sophie is still obsessed with Nathan and cannot tear herself away from the support which she knows is killing her.

It is only after Nathan begins to humiliate Sophie physically and threaten her with death that she reveals the whole truth to Stingo. Just as her other revelations have been prompted by Nathan's cruelty, so this greatest revelation follows the climax of Nathan's violence: the death threat he makes to Sophie and Stingo. The two of them run away, and Stingo asks Sophie to live with him on a peanut farm inherited by his father, where he can finally protect her from Nathan.

It is now that Sophie reveals to Stingo the choice she had to make between her two children at Auschwitz, consigning her daughter to death in the hope of saving the son she never saw again. After this final revelation, Sophie and Stingo make love; while he is still sleeping, she leaves to join Nathan in a suicide pact. Stingo realizes that Sophie's lies were a necessary attempt to retain her composure and sanity. In finally freeing herself of these lies, Sophie prepared herself for the death that life with Nathan demanded.

Zenobia. *The Blithedale Romance.* Nathaniel Hawthorne. 1852.

Long a champion of women's rights, the beautiful Zenobia finds it difficult to maintain her stance that women are the equal of men when she falls in love. In fact, Zenobia would rather embrace death than face the prospect of life without the man for whom she holds an unrequited love.

Zenobia is one of the first to settle in the utopian community of Blithedale, a farm in the suburbs of Boston. She is on hand to welcome MILES COVERDALE, an observant poet, and HOLLINGSWORTH, a burly, single-minded prison reformer, to the cooperative settlement. Zenobia is amused but somewhat annoyed to find that Hollingsworth has brought with him a young woman, Priscilla, whom a strange little man had urged him to take to Blithedale. On meeting Zenobia, the frail Priscilla immediately falls at her feet in an attitude of worship that continues while they live at Blithedale.

With Priscilla often at her heels, and Miles Coverdale not far behind, Zenobia takes to strolling about the grounds with Hollingsworth when the day's work is done. Rumors fly that Hollingsworth and Zenobia will marry and build their own cottage on one of the rolling hills in the area. After an afternoon at a site known as Eliot's pulpit, the futures of Zenobia and Hollingsworth seem even more linked. Zenobia, blinded by love, abandons her feminism to defend Hollingsworth's reactionary position on the question of woman's role in society.

A few days later Zenobia holds an animated conversation, seen by Coverdale, with a stranger to Blithedale, the mysterious Professor Westervelt. Coverdale sees Zenobia and Westervelt together again in Boston, once more holding a heated discussion. When Zenobia spots Coverdale observing them from the window of his hotel room, she makes a dismissive gesture, barely able to conceal her contempt for him, then draws the shade. Coverdale has the audacity to call on her the next day, and Zenobia treats him with cold civility.

Zenobia's next appearance before Coverdale is not so haughty. Like a dethroned queen she lies at Hollingsworth's feet, near Eliot's pulpit, crushed after the man she loves reveals that he will marry Priscilla. Zenobia feels that Hollingsworth led her on and that now, since it has been revealed that Priscilla is her half-sister and entitled to all Zenobia's riches, he is being opportunistic and cruel. She castigates him for loving the pale and girlish Priscilla rather than her, a woman with experience in the world.

Hollingsworth and Priscilla depart, leaving the grieving Zenobia alone with Coverdale. The poet tries to comfort her but seems more interested in learning what Zenobia's exact connection to Professor Westervelt is. Zenobia will not reveal the nature of their relationship, but Coverdale suspects the two are married. Charging Coverdale to carry a message to Hollingsworth—that he has caused her death—Zenobia leaves Coverdale alone in the woods. Later that night, acting on his suspicions, Coverdale awakens Hollingsworth, and they find the beautiful Zenobia's lifeless body in a nearby lake.

Zizendorf. *The Cannibal.* John Hawkes. 1949.

Zizendorf, the narrator of this novel of post–World War II Germany, is either a sane man in an insane world or just the opposite. Beginning with a fantastical description of a town named Spitzen-on-the-Dein and all the characters who live there, Zizendorf eventually unveils his plan to capture the belongings of an American soldier, Leevey, who is an "observer" responsible for the region. This and other violent acts will enable him to affirm his leadership over the town and to issue a proclamation to all "English-speaking peoples" indicting the "Allied Antagonists" and heralding "German Liberation."

The population of the town has been recently liberated from what sounds suspiciously like an asylum. Madame Stella Snow, who had presided over the town before World War II, has now fallen out of power. The other officials—the Mayor, the Duke, and the Census-Taker—do not carry out their duties, if there are any left to perform after the devastation of war. To make the government even more unstable, it turns out that the Duke is a deranged killer, the cannibal of the novel's title. He eats the son of Zizendorf's mistress, a woman named Jutta, who is also Madame Snow's sister.

Zizendorf describes all "his people" as weak, struggling, defeated, and easily led. Alluding to both literary texts and historical data, Zizendorf tells the story of Germany's rise, beginning with the assassination of Archduke Franz Ferdinand in 1914. This narrative is interwoven with the story of the town and of Madame Snow who, with her husband Ernst and sister Jutta, dominated the social and political life of Spitzen-on-the-Dein. Zizendorf's narration continues through the advent of World War II and to its culmination, when the fortunes of the nation and of the Snow oligarchy decline to ruin.

In the novel's final section, Zizendorf—with the help of his two assistants, Stumpfegel and Fegelein—is able to kill the American soldier. Having confiscated Leevey's possessions, the trio returns to town to meet at the offices of a local newspaper called the *Crooked Zeitung*, once owned by Jutta's ex-husband. Here they print a manifesto calling for the emancipation of Germany and a new political order. Having asserted that he is a "natural leader," Zizendorf sets about proving it. He kills a musician named Stintz, who had lecherously pursued Jutta's daughter Selvaggia, and then murders the town's Mayor. Zizendorf appoints the cannibalistic Duke as the new Chancellor, and the novel ends on the eve of a new era for Zizendorf's Germany, its "natural" leadership fully restored.

Zora. *The Quest of the Silver Fleece.* W. E. B. Du Bois. 1911.

At once impish and mature, Zora is the wildly independent daughter of Elspeth, a conjure woman who lives in the swamp on the outskirts of Tooms County, Alabama. She has spent her childhood playing in the swamp and is little more than an innocent child of nature when Bles Alwyn comes to Tooms to attend Miss Sarah Smith's School for Blacks. Zora and Bles are immediately deeply attracted to each other, and within a couple of years Bles has convinced Zora to attend Miss Sarah's school. When Bles tells Zora the legend of Jason and the Golden Fleece, which he heard from his teacher, MARY TAYLOR CRESSWELL, the two decide to plant cotton in the middle of the swamp and sell it at harvest time. Thus begins the couple's quest for the Silver Fleece.

Long after Zora and Bles have toiled to clear the swamp, obtain magic cotton seeds from Elspeth, and watch them blossom into magnificent plants, their happy spell is broken. Miss Taylor, a Wellesley graduate who has been dispatched to the South by her ambitious brother, warns Bles that Zora is far from a pure maiden. Bles confronts Zora, who is too distracted to explain that she has been taken advantage of by Harry Cresswell, the son of the wealthiest cotton planter in Tooms. Shocked and appalled, Bles leaves the county, and the distraught Zora eventually finds work as the maid of Mrs. Vanderpool, a wealthy northern woman.

Zora travels with Mrs. Vanderpool to New York City and then to Washington, D. C., where she discovers that Bles has unwittingly become involved in politics. From behind the scenes and through Mrs. Vanderpool she attempts to help Bles's political career. However, when Mrs. Vanderpool fails to fulfil her promises to ensure Bles's

advancement without Bles having to compromise his integrity, Zora leaves her and returns to Tooms.

Once back in Tooms, Zora decides that her great calling is to help her people gain freedom from the oppressive force of tenant farming and sharecropping. To that end she joins with Miss Sarah, giving the woman the $10,000 that Mrs. Vanderpool presented to her upon her departure. She buys a two-hundred-acre section of the swamp from Colonel Cresswell and convinces a number of local blacks to become tenants and a great many others to help turn the swamp into an independently run community center. In the midst of Zora's industry, Bles returns from the North. He begins to work with Zora and at one point tells her that they must get married. Zora is unwilling to take Bles on his terms now, however, and turns him down, telling herself that she must have his complete love and respect.

Meanwhile, the arrival of a cotton mill in town together with mill workers from the North has brought change to the social, political, and economic makeup of Tooms. The political power has shifted from the hands of old Southern gentlemen such as Colonel Cresswell to those of the mill owners.

Just after the cotton crop is harvested, Colonel Cresswell decides that the time is ripe for him to reclaim the land he supposedly sold to Zora. When he attempts to cheat her by saying that he only meant to rent the land rather than sell it, Zora challenges him in court. Supported by the new judge, who is not part of the Colonel's old political machine, Zora wins her case.

Soon afterward a mob attempts to destroy Zora's compound but is thwarted by the tenants. In the confusion of their retreat, the members of the mob kill and wound several of their number. The next morning they spread the tale that the black tenants committed the crime and return as a sanctioned posse; two black men are captured and lynched. Three months later Colonel Cresswell dies guilt-ridden, leaving his house and plantation to Miss Sarah's School. As the novel closes, Bles declares his love for Zora, who, now confident of his absolute respect, accepts.

Zoraïde. "La Belle Zoraïde." Kate Chopin. 1894.

The story begins one stifling summer night near the Bayou St. John as Manna-Loulou, a black servant to Madame Delisle, overhears an old song of Creole romance, reminding her of a long-forgotten tale. In her Creole patois, Manna-Loulou begins to tell Madame Delisle the story of La Belle Zoraïde: Zoraïde was beautiful and graceful, with skin the color of café-au-lait. As a slave she held the then-privileged position of personal maid to her mistress, Madame Delarivière. Often urging her to marry, and promising her a church wedding befitting a slave of her status, Mme. Delarivière reminded Zoraïde that Ambroise, body servant to Dr. Langlé, would marry her whenever she was ready. Zoraïde was secretly disdainful of

Ambroise, however; she considered him a cruel, detestable little mulatto, so she told Mme. Delarivière she could not possibly consent to marriage yet, so happy was she with her mistress.

Zoraïde could never consent to marry Ambroise since she had seen Mézor dance the Bamboula in Congo Square. She had been entranced by the powerful movements of his glistening ebony body and, after the dance, by the sweetness in his eyes and the gentleness in his voice. One day Zoraïde finally mustered the courage to tell her mistress that it was Mézor she wanted to marry. Outraged, Mme. Delarivière forbade Zoraïde to marry "that Negro." Zoraïde gently protested that she was not white either, but to no avail. Like Ambroise, Mézor was owned by Dr. Langlé, but he was only a lowly field hand and therefore unsuitable for the refined Zoraïde, according to Mme. Delarivière. Zoraïde was forbidden to speak to Mézor, but she was soon meeting him clandestinely.

Although she loved Mézor, Zoraïde was nevertheless troubled by her own duplicity, so she bravely confessed to her mistress, telling her of their deep, abiding love. Mme. Delarivière, although momentarily pained by Zoraïde's anguish, responded by prevailing upon Dr. Langlé to sell Mézor in Georgia or South Carolina. Zoraïde was heartbroken but took some comfort in knowing that she would soon be having Mézor's baby.

Attended by her mistress and a nurse, Zoraïde gave birth a few months later, but when she asked for her baby, they lied and told her it had died. Hoping to rid her of reminders of Mézor and thus return Zoraïde to her former lively self, Mme. Delarivière sent the newborn to her family plantation. Thus deprived, Zoraïde grew listless and sorrowful, and her descent into madness began.

Zoraïde soon made herself a surrogate child out of old rags, which she coddled and nurtured as her own baby. Stung with remorse over the affliction she caused, Mme. Delarivière brought the infant back, presenting her to Zoraïde with the assurance that the child would never be taken away again. But Zoraïde reacted only with sullen suspicion, and she rejected the child while fiercely guarding her rag bundle. Never to know the love of mother or father, the child was sent back to the plantation. No longer beautiful, Zoraïde was shunned by all, and cared for the rag doll for the rest of her long life.

Her story finished, Manna-Loulou softly asks Mme. Delisle if she is asleep yet, but she has been too moved to sleep. Whispering in Creole patois, Mme. Delisle emotionally declares it would have been better if the poor little one had died.

Zuckerman, Nathan. *The Ghost Writer; Zuckerman Unbound; The Anatomy Lesson.* Philip Roth. 1979; 1981; 1983.

Writer Nathan Zuckerman appears in three novels where he confronts his ambivalent feelings about his writing, his Jewish heritage, and sex. As he is beginning his career as a writer, Nathan spends the night at the home of renowned reclusive author, EMANUEL ISIDORE "E.I." LONOFF. Nathan is fascinated by Lonoff's work because they share an obsession: the status of the Jews. At Lonoff's house, Nathan meets Lonoff's assistant, the enigmatic Amy Ballette, and his wife, the long-suffering Hope Lonoff. Nathan spends part of the night penning drafts of a letter to his father, who fears from Nathan's fiction that his son is an anti-Semite, a self-hating Jew. Nathan is frustrated by his failure to express his feelings about his Jewish identity, both in his fiction and in his life. He is fascinated with Amy, who reminds him of Anne Frank, a figure who is meaningful to him throughout the trilogy.

Nathan becomes rich and famous but remains terrified and guilty about his success. His novel *Carnovsky* is received as sexually irresponsible and anti-Semitic, which brings him scorn and rebuke from both feminists and Zionists. His novel seriously affects his parents, who are plagued by reporters and privately distressed by its nature.

Separated from his third wife, the WASP do-gooder Laura, Nathan becomes involved with sexy Irish actress Caesara O'Shea, who shares his conflicted feelings about fame and identity. She leaves him after a brief but passionate relationship to renew an ongoing affair with Fidel Castro.

Meanwhile, Nathan has met the bizarre Alvin Pepler, who shares Nathan's heritage as a native Newarker but believes he is famous for being "Alvin the Jewish Marine" or "Pepler the Man of the People" after winning on a game show in the fifties. Pepler is a would-be writer obsessed with having lost to Hewlett Lincoln, a New England WASP, on a question about Americana. Paranoid and mentally unstable, Pepler is convinced that the game show was fixed and that no Jew on a game show was allowed to win more than $100,000, an act of anti-Semitism propagated by the very Jews who ran the program. During the novel Pepler haunts and harasses Nathan, who begins to fear that Pepler is the man who has been anonymously threatening to kidnap his mother, and accusing Nathan of stealing his identity and life story in the novel *Carnovsky.*

Hearing that his father is on his deathbed, Nathan flies to Florida and learns through a confrontation with his younger brother Henry that Nathan's offensive novel led to his father's heart attack and death. Confused, guilty, and unhappy, Nathan goes to Newark on his way home in search of his Jewish origins but is disappointed to find that all his memories are gone.

Some time later Nathan is plagued by a severe pain of unknown origin in the neck and shoulder. Unable to be cured by a variety of medical practitioners, Nathan prescribes for himself a treatment of vodka, painkillers, sex, self-pity, and intense introspection. Still ambivalent about his Jewish heritage, he becomes obsessed with critic Milton Appel, a Zionist who has trashed his work as anti-Semitic and now suggests that he write an op-ed piece on behalf of Israel for the *New York Times*.

Unable to write and consumed with pain, Nathan decides to become a doctor. He is drawn to the idea of a stable structured life where one is respected and appreciated by patients and family. High on painkillers, he flies to Chicago to interview with Bobby Fretag, an anesthesiologist and former college roommate, for medical school. He introduces himself to strangers as Milton Appel, pretending to be a pornographer. He phones Appel, and they argue violently but with no resolution. Now nearly deranged with pain and delirious from the drugs, Nathan offers to take Bobby's grieving father to the cemetery to visit the grave of his recently deceased wife. There he assaults the old man for his reverence of the Jewish heritage, then passes out and smashes his face on the headstone. Nathan spends the ensuing time recovering, still dreaming of being a doctor who can heal pain and be loved by all.

List of Authors

Abbey, Edward	Smith, Joseph Fielding "Seldom Seen"	*The Monkey Wrench Gang*
Adams, Henry	Dudley, Esther	*Esther*
Adams, Henry	Lee, Madeleine	*Democracy*
Agee, James	Follet, Jay	*A Death in the Family*
Agee, James	Follet, Mary	*A Death in the Family*
Agee, James	Follet, Rufus	*A Death in the Family*
Aiken, Conrad	Hasleman, Paul	"Silent Snow, Secret Snow"
Alcott, Louisa May	Blake, Nathaniel	*Little Men*
Alcott, Louisa May	Brooke, John "Demi"	*Little Men*
Alcott, Louisa May	Dan	*Little Men*
Alcott, Louisa May	Devon, Christie	*Work*
Alcott, Louisa May	Fletcher, Phillip	*Work*
Alcott, Louisa May	Harding, Nancy	*Little Men*
Alcott, Louisa May	Laurence, Theodore "Laurie"	*Little Women*
Alcott, Louisa May	March, Amy	*Little Women*
Alcott, Louisa May	March, Beth	*Little Women*
Alcott, Louisa May	March, Josephine "Jo"	*Little Women*
Alcott, Louisa May	March, Margaret "Meg"	*Little Women*
Alcott, Louisa May	Sterling, David	*Work*
Alcott, Louisa May	Sterling, Rachel	*Work*
Aldrich, Thomas Bailey	Bailey, Tom	*Story of a Bad Boy*
Aldrich, Thomas Bailey	Shackford, Richard	*The Stillwater Tragedy*
Alger, Horatio, Jr.	Ragged Dick	*Ragged Dick*
Algren, Nelson	Bicek, Bruno "Lefty"	*Never Come Morning*
Algren, Nelson	Linkhorn, Dove	*A Walk on the Wild Side*
Algren, Nelson	Machine, Frankie	*The Man with the Golden Arm*
Algren, Nelson	Orlov, Roman	*The Neon Wilderness*
Algren, Nelson	Railroad Shorty	*The Neon Wilderness*
Allen, Hervey	Adverse, Anthony	*Anthony Adverse*
Allen, Paula Gunn	Atencio, Ephanie	*The Woman Who Owned the Shadows*
Allen, Woody	Kugelmass, Sidney	"The Kugelmass Episode"
Anderson, Edward	Bowers, Bowie A.	*Thieves Like Us*
Anderson, Sherwood	Dudley, Bruce	*Dark Laughter*
Anderson, Sherwood	Grey, Aline Aldridge	*Dark Laughter*
Anderson, Sherwood	Grey, Fred	*Dark Laughter*
Anderson, Sherwood	Hartman, Reverend Curtis	"The Strength of God," *Winesburg, Ohio*
Anderson, Sherwood	Long, Ethel	*Beyond Desire*
Anderson, Sherwood	McGregor, Norman "Beaut"	*Marching Men*
Anderson, Sherwood	McVey, Hugh	*Poor White*
Anderson, Sherwood	Mathers, Walter	"I'm a Fool"
Anderson, Sherwood	Moorehead, Edgar "Tar"	*Tar: A Midwest Childhood*
Anderson, Sherwood	Narrator	"The Egg"
Anderson, Sherwood	Narrator	"I Want to Know Why"
Anderson, Sherwood	Narrator	"The Man Who Became a Woman"
Anderson, Sherwood	Oliver, Red	*Beyond Desire*
Anderson, Sherwood	Swift, Kate	"The Strength of God"; "The Teacher," *Winesburg, Ohio*
Anderson, Sherwood	Webster, John	*Many Marriages*
Anderson, Sherwood	Willard, George	*Winesburg, Ohio*

Andrews, Raymond	Appalachee Red	*Appalachee Red*
Appleton, Victor	Swift, Tom	*Tom Swift and His Electric Runabout,* or, *The Speediest Car on the Road*
Arnow, Harriet	Nevels, Gertie	*The Dollmaker*
Arthur, Timothy Shay	Slade, Simon	*Ten Nights in a Bar-Room, and What I Saw There*
Asimov, Isaac	Calvin, Dr. Susan	*I, Robot*
Asimov, Isaac	Seldon, Hari	*Foundation*
Atherton, Gertrude	Clavering, Lee	*Black Oxen*
Atherton, Gertrude	De la Vega y Arillaga, Don Vincente	"The Pearls of Loreto"
Atherton, Gertrude	Ogden, Mary	*Black Oxen*
Attaway, William	Moss, Big Mat	*Blood on the Forge*
Attaway, William	Moss, Melody	*Blood on the Forge*
Attaway, William	Step	*Let Me Breathe Thunder*
Austin, Mary	Escobar, Isidro	*Isidro*
Baldwin, James	David	*Giovanni's Room*
Baldwin, James	Grimes, Elizabeth	*Go Tell It on the Mountain*
Baldwin, James	Grimes, Gabriel	*Go Tell It on the Mountain*
Baldwin, James	Grimes, John	*Go Tell It on the Mountain*
Baldwin, James	Miller, Julia	*Just Above My Head*
Baldwin, James	Montana, Arthur	*Just Above My Head*
Baldwin, James	Montana, Hall	*Just Above My Head*
Baldwin, James	Moore, Vivaldo	*Another Country*
Baldwin, James	Narrator	"This Morning, This Evening, So Soon"
Baldwin, James	Proudhammer, Caleb	*Tell Me How Long the Train's Been Gone*
Baldwin, James	Proudhammer, Leo	*Tell Me How Long the Train's Been Gone*
Baldwin, James	Rivers, Clementine "Tish"	*If Beale Street Could Talk*
Baldwin, James	Scott, Ida	*Another Country*
Baldwin, James	Scott, Rufus	*Another Country*
Baldwin, James	Sonny	"Sonny's Blues"
Bambara, Toni Cade	Hazel	"Gorilla, My Love"
Bambara, Toni Cade	Henry, Velma	*The Salt Eaters*
Bambara, Toni Cade	Rae Ann	"A Girl's Story"
Bambara, Toni Cade	Ransom, Minnie	*The Salt Eaters*
Banks, Russell	Dorsinville, Vanise	*Continental Drift*
Banks, Russell	Dubois, Robert Raymond	*Continental Drift*
Baraka, Amiri	Johns, Ray	"Mondongo"
Baraka, Amiri	Jones, LeRoi	*The System of Dante's Hell*
Baraka, Imamu Amiri	Laffawiss, Irv	"Mondongo"
Barnes, Djuna	Flood, Nora	*Nightwood*
Barnes, Djuna	O'Connor, Dr. Matthew	*Nightwood*
Barnes, Djuna	Ryder, Amelia de Grier	*Ryder*
Barnes, Djuna	Ryder, Wendell	*Ryder*
Barnes, Djuna	Volkbein, Felix	*Nightwood*
Barnes, Djuna	Vote, Robin	*Nightwood*
Barth, John	Andrews, Todd	*The Floating Opera*
Barth, John	Bellerophon	*Chimera*
Barth, John	Cooke, Ebenezer "Eben"	*The Sot-Weed Factor*
Barth, John	Dunyazade	*Chimera*
Barth, John	Giles	*Giles Goat-Boy*
Barth, John	Horner, Jacob	*The End of the Road*
Barth, John	M____, Ambrose	"Lost in the Funhouse"

Barth, John	Perseus	*Chimera*
Barthelme, Donald	Narrator	"Views of My Father Weeping"
Barthelme, Donald	Snow White	*Snow White*
Baum, L. Frank	Cowardly Lion	*The Wonderful Wizard of Oz*
Baum, L. Frank	Dorothy	*The Wonderful Wizard of Oz*
Baum, L. Frank	Scarecrow	*The Wonderful Wizard of Oz*
Baum, L. Frank	Tin Woodman	*The Wonderful Wizard of Oz*
Baum, L. Frank	Wizard of Oz	*The Wonderful Wizard of Oz*
Beattie, Ann	Charles	*Chilly Scenes of Winter*
Beattie, Ann	McGuire, Sam	*Chilly Scenes of Winter*
Beattie, Ann	Protagonist	"A Reasonable Man"
Bell, Thomas	Dobrejcak, John "Dobie"	*Out of This Furnace*
Bell, Thomas	Dobrejcak, Mike	*Out of This Furnace*
Bell, Thomas	Kracha, George Dzedo	*Out of This Furnace*
Bellamy, Edward	West, Julian	*Looking Backward: 2000–1887; Equality*
Bellow, Saul	Citrine, Charles	*Humboldt's Gift*
Bellow, Saul	Corde, Albert	*The Dean's December*
Bellow, Saul	Feiler, Clarence	"The Gonzaga Manuscripts"
Bellow, Saul	Grebe, George	"Looking for Mr. Green"
Bellow, Saul	Henderson, Eugene	*Henderson the Rain King*
Bellow, Saul	Herzog, Moses Elkanah	*Herzog*
Bellow, Saul	Joseph	*The Dangling Man*
Bellow, Saul	Leventhal, Asa	*The Victim*
Bellow, Saul	March, Augie	*The Adventures of Augie March*
Bellow, Saul	Mosby, Willis	*Mosby's Memoirs*
Bellow, Saul	Sammler, Artur	*Mr. Sammler's Planet*
Bellow, Saul	Selbst, Woody	*A Silver Dish*
Bellow, Saul	Shawmut, Herschel "Harry"	"Him with His Foot in His Mouth"
Bellow, Saul	Von Humboldt, Fleisher	*Humboldt's Gift*
Bellow, Saul	Wilhelm, Tommy	*Seize the Day*
Bemelmans, Ludwig	Cassard, Maurice	*Dirty Eddie*
Benét, Stephen Vincent	Butterwick, Lige	"A Tooth for Paul Revere"
Benét, Stephen Vincent	John	"By the Waters of Babylon"
Benét, Stephen Vincent	Webster, Daniel "Dan'l"	"The Devil and Daniel Webster"
Berger, Thomas	Crabb, Jack	*Little Big Man*
Berger, Thomas	Old Lodge Skins	*Little Big Man*
Berry, Wendell	Coulter, Nathan	*Nathan Coulter*
Berryman, John	Severance, Alan	*Recovery*
Bierce, Ambrose	Farquhar, Peyton	"An Occurrence at Owl Creek Bridge"
Bierce, Ambrose	Young Boy	"Chickamauga"
Bird, Robert	Slaughter, Nathan	*Nick of the Woods, or the Jibbenainosay: A Tale of Kentucky*
Black, David	Gottenberg, Abraham	*Minds*
Bodenheim, Maxwell	May, Georgie	*Georgie May*
Bontemps, Arna	Madison, Little Augie	*God Sends Sunday*
Bontemps, Arna	Prosser, Gabriel	*Black Thunder*
Bourjaily, Vance	Beniger, Thomas	*The Violated*
Bourjaily, Vance	Bissle, Edward	*The Violated*
Bourjaily, Vance	Galt, Thomas Skinner	*The End of My Life*
Bowles, Jane	Goering, Christina	*Two Serious Ladies*
Bowles, Paul	Amar	*The Spider's House*
Bowles, Paul	Burroughs, Polly "Lee"	*The Spider's House*
Bowles, Paul	Moseby, Kit	*The Sheltering Sky*
Bowles, Paul	Stenham, John	*The Spider's House*

Bowman, Peter	Protagonist	*Beach Red*
Boyd, James	Talcott, Ray	*Bitter Creek*
Boyeson, Hjalmar H.	Larkin, Horace	*The Mammon of Unrighteousness*
Boyle, Kay	The Bus Driver	"Defeat"
Boyle, Kay	The Doctor	"The White Horses of Vienna"
Boyle, Kay	Tobin, Wiltshire "Wilt"	*Monday Night*
Boyle, T. Coraghessan	Quesadilla, Hector "Little Cheese"	"The Hector Quesadilla Story"
Boyle, T. Coraghessan	Trimpie, Nathaniel "Nat"	"Caviar"
Brackenridge, H. H.	Farrago, Captain John	*Modern Chivalry*
Brackenridge, H. H.	O'Regan, Teague	*Modern Chivalry*
Bradbury, Ray	Halloway, Charles	*Something Wicked This Way Comes*
Bradbury, Ray	Halloway, Will	*Something Wicked This Way Comes*
Bradbury, Ray	Montag, Guy	*Farenheit 451*
Bradbury, Ray	Nightshade, Jim	*Something Wicked This Way Comes*
Bradley, David	Washington, John	*The Chaneysville Incident*
Brautigan, Richard	inBOIL	*In Watermelon Sugar*
Brautigan, Richard	Narrator	*Trout Fishing in America*
Brautigan, Richard	Narrator	*In Watermelon Sugar*
Brodkey, Harold	Narrator	"First Love and Other Sorrows"
Bromfield, Louis	Pentland, Olivia	*Early Autumn*
Brooks, Gwendolyn	Phillips, Maud Martha	*Maud Martha*
Brossard, Chandler	Williams, Blake	*Who Walk in Darkness*
Brown, Charles Brockden	Carwin, Francis	*Wieland, or The Transformation: An American Tale*
Brown, Charles Brockden	Dudley, Constantia	*Ormond*
Brown, Charles Brockden	Edny, Clithero	*Edgar Huntly; or, Memoirs of a Sleepwalker*
Brown, Charles Brockden	Huntly, Edgar	*Edgar Huntly; or, Memoirs of a Sleepwalker*
Brown, Charles Brockden	Pleyel	*Wieland; or The Transformation: An American Tale*
Brown, Charles Brockden	Wieland, Clara	*Wieland; or The Transformation: An American Tale*
Brown, Charles Brockden	Wieland, Theodore	*Wieland, or The Transformation: An American Tale*
Brown, Charles Brockton	Mervyn, Arthur	*Arthur Mervyn*
Brown, Harry	Tyne, William	*A Walk in the Sun*
Brown, Rita Mae	Banastre, Hortensia Reedmuller	*Southern Discomfort*
Brown, Rita Mae	Bolt, Molly	*Rubyfruit Jungle*
Brown, William Hill	Harrington	*The Power of Sympathy; or, The Triumph of Nature*
Brown, William Wells	Linwood, Clotelle	*Clotelle; or, The Colored Heroine*
Buck, Pearl S.	O-lan	*The Good Earth*
Buck, Pearl S.	Wang Lung	*The Good Earth*
Buechner, Frederick	Bone, Tristram	*A Long Day's Dying*
Bukowski, Charles	Chinaski, Henry "Hank"	*Ham on Rye*
Burnett, Frances Hodgson	Craven, Colin	*The Secret Garden*
Burnett, Frances Hodgson	Crewe, Sara	*A Little Princess*
Burnett, Frances Hodgson	The Earl of Dorincourt	*Little Lord Fauntleroy*
Burnett, Frances Hodgson	Errol, Cedric "Ceddie"	*Little Lord Fauntleroy*

List of Authors

Burnett, Frances Hodgson	Lennox, Mary	*The Secret Garden*
Burnett, Frances Hodgson	Sowerby, Dickon	*The Secret Garden*
Burnett, W. R.	Bandello, Cesare Rico	*Little Caesar*
Burroughs, Edgar Rice	Porter, Jane	*Tarzan of the Apes*
Burroughs, Edgar Rice	Tarzan	*Tarzan of the Apes*
Burroughs, William Seward	Benway (Dr.)	*Naked Lunch*
Burroughs, William Seward	Lee, William	*Junky; Queer; Naked Lunch*
Busch, Niven	Chavez, Pearl	*Duel in the Sun*
Cabell, James Branch	Jurgen	*Jurgen: A Comedy of Justice*
Cable, George Washington	Bras-Coupé	*The Grandissimes*
Cable, George Washington	Frowenfeld, Joseph	*The Grandissimes*
Cable, George Washington	Grandissime, Honoré	*The Grandissimes*
Cable, George Washington	Grandissime, Honoré f.m.c.	*The Grandissimes*
Cahan, Abraham	Levinsky, David	*The Rise of David Levinsky*
Cahan, Abraham	Podkovnik, Yekl "Jake"	*Yekl*
Cain, George	Cain, Georgie	*Blueschild Baby*
Cain, James M.	Beragon, Montgomery "Monty"	*Mildred Pierce*
Cain, James M.	Chambers, Frank	*The Postman Always Rings Twice*
Cain, James M.	Huff, Walter	*Double Indemnity*
Cain, James M.	Nirdlinger, Phyllis	*Double Indemnity*
Cain, James M.	Papadakis, Cora	*The Postman Always Rings Twice*
Cain, James M.	Pierce, Mildred	*Mildred Pierce*
Cain, James M.	Pierce, Veda	*Mildred Pierce*
Caldwell, Erskine	Carlisle, Jim	"Daughter"
Caldwell, Erskine	Lester, Jeeter	*Tobacco Road*
Caldwell, Erskine	McCurtain, Jeff	*Trouble in July*
Caldwell, Erskine	Miller, Cora	"Masses of Men"
Caldwell, Erskine	Newsome, Lonnie	"Kneel to the Rising Sun"
Caldwell, Erskine	Walden, Ty-Ty	*God's Little Acre*
Calisher, Hortense	Halescy, Edwin	*The New Yorkers*
Calisher, Hortense	Mannix, David	*The New Yorkers*
Calisher, Hortense	Mannix, Ruth	*The New Yorkers*
Calisher, Hortense	Mannix, Simon	*The New Yorkers*
Calisher, Hortense	Raphael, Queenie	*Queenie*
Capote, Truman	Bobbit, Miss Lily Jane	"Children on Their Birthdays"
Capote, Truman	Buddy	"A Christmas Memory"
Capote, Truman	Golightly, Holly	*Breakfast at Tiffany's*
Capote, Truman	Hickock, Dick	*In Cold Blood*
Capote, Truman	Knox, Joel Harrison	*Other Voices, Other Rooms*
Capote, Truman	Smith, Perry Edward	*In Cold Blood*
Carver, Raymond	Carlyle	"Fever"
Carver, Raymond	McGinnis, Mel	"What We Talk About When We Talk About Love"
Carver, Raymond	Narrator	"Where I'm Calling From"
Cassill, R. V.	Anderson, Clem	*Clem Anderson*
Cather, Willa	Archie, Howard	*The Song of the Lark*

List of Authors

Churchill, Winston	Whipple, Judge Silas	*The Crisis*
Clark, Walter Van Tilburg	Bridges, Harold "Hal"	*The Track of the Cat*
Clark, Walter Van Tilburg	Davies, Arthur	*The Ox-bow Incident*
Clark, Walter Van Tilburg	Jenkins (Dr.)	"The Portable Phonograph"
Clark, Walter Van Tilburg	Tetley (Major)	*The Ox-bow Incident*
Clemens, Samuel (Mark Twain)	Driscoll, Thomas à Beckett	*The Tragedy of Pudd'nhead Wilson*
Clemens, Samuel (Mark Twain)	Finn, Huckleberry "Huck"	*The Adventures of Tom Sawyer; The Adventures of Huckleberry Finn*
Clemens, Samuel (Mark Twain)	Jim	*The Adventures of Huckleberry Finn*
Clemens, Samuel (Mark Twain)	Morgan, Hank	*A Connecticut Yankee in King Arthur's Court*
Clemens, Samuel (Mark Twain)	Richards, Edward	"The Man That Corrupted Hadleyburg"
Clemens, Samuel (Mark Twain)	Roxana	*The Tragedy of Pudd'nhead Wilson*
Clemens, Samuel (Mark Twain)	Sawyer, Tom	*The Adventures of Tom Sawyer; The Adventures of Huckleberry Finn*
Clemens, Samuel (Mark Twain)	Smiley, Jim	"The Celebrated Jumping Frog of Calaveras County"
Clemens, Samuel (Mark Twain)	Sterling, Philip	*The Gilded Age*
Clemens, Samuel (Mark Twain)	Wilson, David "Pudd'nhead"	*The Tragedy of Pudd'nhead Wilson*
Clemens, Samuel (Mark Twain); Warner, Charles Dudley	Hawkins, Laura	*The Gilded Age*
Connell, Evan S., Jr.	Bridge, India	*Mr. Bridge; Mrs. Bridge*
Connell, Evan S., Jr.	Bridge, Walter	*Mr. Bridge; Mrs. Bridge*
Conroy, Frank	Conroy, Frank	*Stop-Time*
Cooper, James Fenimore	Bumppo, Nathaniel "Natty"	*The Leatherstocking Tales*
Cooper, James Fenimore	Chingachgook	*The Leather Stocking Tales (The Pioneers; The Last of the Mohicans; The Prairie; The Deerslayer; The Pathfinder)*
Cooper, James Fenimore	Effingham, Edward	*Home as Found*
Cooper, James Fenimore	Effingham, Eve	*Home as Found*
Cooper, James Fenimore	Effingham, John	*Home as Found*
Cooper, James Fenimore	Littlepage, Cornelius "Corny"	*Satanstoe*
Cooper, James Fenimore	Ten Eyck, Guert	*Satanstoe*
Cooper, James Fenimore	Woolston, Mark	*The Crater; or, Vulcan's Peak*
Coover, Robert	Bruno, Giovanni	*The Origin of the Brunists*
Coover, Robert	Miller, Justin "Tiger"	*The Origin of the Brunists*
Coover, Robert	Nixon, Dick	*The Public Burning*
Coover, Robert	Waugh, J. Henry	*The Universal Baseball Association, Inc.*
Cozzens, James Gould	Beal, General Ira "Bus"	*Guard of Honor*
Cozzens, James Gould	Carricker, Lieutenant Colonel Benny	*Guard of Honor*
Cozzens, James Gould	Coates, Abner	*The Just and the Unjust*
Cozzens, James Gould	Cudlipp, Ernest	*Men and Brethren*

Dixon, Melvin	McPhee, Ruella	*Vanishing Rooms*
Dixon, Thomas Jr.	Cameron, Ben	*The Clansman: A Historical Romance of the Ku Klux Klan*
Dixon, Thomas Jr.	Stoneman, Austin	*The Clansman: A Historical Romance of the Ku Klux Klan*
Dixon, Thomas Jr.	Stoneman, Elsie	*The Clansman: A Historical Romance of the Ku Klux Klan*
Doctorow, E. L.	Altschuler, Edgar	*World's Fair*
Doctorow, E. L.	Billy	*Billy Bathgate*
Doctorow, E. L.	Father	*Ragtime*
Doctorow, E. L.	Isaacson, Daniel (Daniel Lewin)	*The Book of Daniel*
Doctorow, E. L.	Isaacson, Paul	*The Book of Daniel*
Doctorow, E. L.	Isaacson, Rochelle	*The Book of Daniel*
Doctorow, E. L.	Isaacson, Susan (Susan Lewin)	*The Book of Daniel*
Doctorow, E. L.	Mother's Younger Brother	*Ragtime*
Doctorow, E. L.	Tateh	*Ragtime*
Doctorow, E. L.	The Little Boy	*Ragtime*
Doctorow, E. L.	Walker, Coalhouse, Jr.	*Ragtime*
Doig, Ivan	McCaskill, Angus Alexander	*Dancing at the Rascal Fair*
Doig, Ivan	McCaskill, John Angus "Jick"	*English Creek; Ride with Me, Mariah Montana*
Donnelly, Ignatius	Petion, Maximilian	*Caesar's Column: A Story of the Twentieth Century*
Donnelly, Ignatius	Weltstein, Gabriel	*Caesar's Column: A Story of the Twentieth Century*
Dos Passos, John	Anderson, Charley	*U.S.A. (The 42nd Parallel; Nineteen Nineteen; The Big Money)*
Dos Passos, John	Andrews, John	*Three Soldiers*
Dos Passos, John	Chrisfield, Chris	*Three Soldiers*
Dos Passos, John	Dowling, Margo	*U.S.A. (The 42nd Parallel; Nineteen Nineteen; The Big Money)*
Dos Passos, John	French, Mary	*U.S.A. (The 42nd Parallel; Nineteen Nineteen; The Big Money)*
Dos Passos, John	Fuselli, Dan	*Three Soldiers*
Dos Passos, John	Herf, Jimmy	*Manhattan Transfer*
Dos Passos, John	Hutchins, Eveline	*U.S.A. (The 42nd Parallel; Nineteen Nineteen; The Big Money)*
Dos Passos, John	McCreary, Fenian "Mac"	*U.S.A. (The 42nd Parallel; Nineteen Nineteen; The Big Money)*
Dos Passos, John	Moorehouse, John Ward	*U.S.A. (The 42nd Parallel; Nineteen Nineteen; The Big Money)*
Dos Passos, John	Savage, Richard Ellsworth "Dick"	*U.S.A. (The 42nd Parallel; Nineteen Nineteen; The Big Money)*
Dos Passos, John	Spotswood, Glenn	*Adventures of a Young Man*
Dos Passos, John	Stoddard, Eleanor	*U.S.A. (The 42nd Parallel; Nineteen Nineteen; The Big Money)*
Dos Passos, John	Thatcher, Ellen	*Manhattan Transfer*
Dos Passos, John	Trent, Anne Elizabeth "Daughter"	*U.S.A. (The 42nd Parallel; Nineteen Nineteen; The Big Money)*
Douglas, Lloyd C.	Ashford, Nancy	*Magnificent Obsession*
Douglas, Lloyd C.	Demetrius	*The Robe*
Douglas, Lloyd C.	Gallio, Marcellus	*The Robe*
Douglas, Lloyd C.	Hudson, Dr. Wayne	*Magnificent Obsession*
Douglas, Lloyd C.	Hudson, Helen Brent	*Magnificent Obsession*

Douglas, Lloyd C.	Merrick, Robert "Bobby"	*Magnificent Obsession*
Dreiser, Theodore	Alden, Roberta	*An American Tragedy*
Dreiser, Theodore	Barnes, Solon	*The Bulwark*
Dreiser, Theodore	Blue, Angela	*"The Genius"*
Dreiser, Theodore	Butler, Aileen	*The Financier; The Titan; The Stoic*
Dreiser, Theodore	Cowperwood, Frank	*The Financier; The Titan; The Stoic*
Dreiser, Theodore	Davies, Elmer	*"Nigger Jeff"*
Dreiser, Theodore	Drouet, Charles	*Sister Carrie*
Dreiser, Theodore	Finchley, Sondra	*An American Tragedy*
Dreiser, Theodore	Gerhardt, Jennie	*Jennie Gerhardt*
Dreiser, Theodore	Griffiths, Clyde	*An American Tragedy*
Dreiser, Theodore	Hurstwood, George W.	*Sister Carrie*
Dreiser, Theodore	Kane, Lester	*Jennie Gerhardt*
Dreiser, Theodore	Meeber, Caroline "Carrie"	*Sister Carrie*
Dreiser, Theodore	Reifsneider, Henry	*"The Lost Phoebe"*
Dreiser, Theodore	Witla, Eugene	*"The Genius"*
Du Bois, W.E.B.	Andrews, Sara	*Dark Princess, A Romance*
Du Bois, W.E.B.	Cresswell, Mary Taylor	*The Quest of the Silver Fleece*
Du Bois, W.E.B.	Jones, John	*"Of the Coming of John"*
Du Bois, W.E.B.	Kautilya, Princess of Bwodpur	*Dark Princess, A Romance*
Du Bois, W.E.B.	Scott, Samuel "Sammy"	*Dark Princess, A Romance*
Du Bois, W.E.B.	Towns, Matthew	*Dark Princess, A Romance*
Du Bois, W.E.B.	Zora	*The Quest of the Silver Fleece*
Dunbar, Paul Laurence	Hamilton, Berry	*The Sport of the Gods*
Eastlake, William	Mike	*"The Biggest Thing Since Custer"*
Edmonds, Walter D.	Martin, Gilbert	*Drums Along the Mohawk*
Edmonds, Walter D.	Martin, Magdelana "Lana" Borst	*Drums Along the Mohawk*
Edwards, Junius	Bradley, James "Brad"	*"Duel with the Clock"*
Edwards, Junius	Harris, Will	*If We Must Die*
Eggleston, Edward	Goodwin, Morton "Mort"	*The Circuit Rider*
Elkin, Stanley	Gibson, Dick	*The Dick Gibson Show*
Ellis, Bret Easton	Clay	*Less Than Zero*
Ellis, Edward S.	Jones, Seth	*Seth Jones of New Hampshire*
Ellison, Ralph	Narrator	*Invisible Man*
Ellison, Ralph	Protagonist	*"King of the Bingo Game"*
Ellison, Ralph	Todd	*"Flying Home"*
Erdrich, Louise	Adare, Karl	*The Beet Queen*
Erdrich, Louise	Adare, Mary	*The Beet Queen*
Erdrich, Louise	Adare, Wallacette Darlene "Dot"	*Love Medicine; The Beet Queen*
Erdrich, Louise	James, Celestine	*The Beet Queen*
Erdrich, Louise	Kashpaw, Marie Lazarre	*Love Medicine; Tracks*
Erdrich, Louise	Kashpaw, Nector	*Love Medicine; Tracks*
Erdrich, Louise	Lamartine, Lulu Nanapush	*Love Medicine; Tracks*
Erdrich, Louise	Nanapush	*Tracks*
Erdrich, Louise	Pillager, Fleur	*Tracks*
Erdrich, Louise	Puyat, Pauline (Sister Leopolda)	*Love Medicine; Tracks*
Exely, Frederick	Exely, Frederick	*A Fan's Notes*
Fante, John	Bandini, Arturo	*Ask the Dust*
Farrell, James T.	Clare, Bernard	*Bernard Clare*
Farrell, James T.	Dan	*"Helen, I Love You"*
Farrell, James T.	Gallagher, Tommy	*Tommy Gallagher's Crusade*
Farrell, James T.	George	*"Spring Evening"*

Faulkner, William	Sutpen, Judith	*Absalom, Absalom!*
Faulkner, William	Sutpen, Thomas	*Absalom, Absalom!*
Faulkner, William	Tall Convict	*The Wild Palms*
Faulkner, William	Varner, Will	*The Hamlet; The Town; The Mansion*
Faulkner, William	Vitelli, Popeye	*Sanctuary; Requiem for a Nun*
Faulkner, William	Wilbourne, Harry	*The Wild Palms*
Fauset, Jessie Redmon	Cary, Oliver	*Comedy: American Style*
Fauset, Jessie Redmon	Cary, Olivia Blanchard	*Comedy: American Style*
Fauset, Jessie Redmon	Cary, Teresa	*Comedy: American Style*
Fauset, Jessie Redmon	Grant, Phebe	*Comedy: American Style*
Fauset, Jessie Redmon	Marshall, Joanna	*There Is Confusion*
Fauset, Jessie Redmon	Murray, Angela	*Plum Bun*
Fauset, Jessie Redmon	Paul, Melissa	*The Chinaberry Tree*
Fauset, Jessie Redmon	Strange, Laurentine	*The Chinaberry Tree*
Fauset, Jessie Redmon	Strange, Sarah "Aunt Sal"	*The Chinaberry Tree*
Fearing, Kenneth	Stroud, George	*The Big Clock*
Ferber, Edna	Benedict, Jordan "Bick"	*Giant*
Ferber, Edna	Benedict, Leslie Lynnton	*Giant*
Ferber, Edna	Cravat, Sabra Venable	*Cimarron*
Ferber, Edna	Cravat, Yancey	*Cimarron*
Ferber, Edna	Ravenal, Gaylord	*Show Boat*
Ferber, Edna	Ravenal, Magnolia Hawks	*Show Boat*
Ferber, Edna	Rink, Jett	*Giant*
Ferlinghetti, Lawrence	Raffine, Andy	*Her*
Fern, Fannie	Hall, Ruth	*Ruth Hall*
Field, Ben	Cow	"Cow"
Finley, Martha	Dinsmore, Elsie	*Elsie Dinsmore*
Fisher, Rudolph	Cynthie (Miss)	"Miss Cynthie"
Fisher, Rudolph	Jones, Joshua "Shine"	*The Walls of Jericho*
Fisher, Rudolph	Patmore, Henry	*The Walls of Jericho*
Fisher, Vardis	Smith, Joseph	*Children of God*
Fisher, Vardis	Young, Brigham	*Children of God*
Fitzgerald, F. Scott	Bernice	"Bernice Bobs Her Hair"
Fitzgerald, F. Scott	Blaine, Amory	*This Side of Paradise*
Fitzgerald, F. Scott	Buchanan, Daisy	*The Great Gatsby*
Fitzgerald, F. Scott	Carraway, Nick	*The Great Gatsby*
Fitzgerald, F. Scott	Diver, Dr. Richard "Dick"	*Tender Is the Night*
Fitzgerald, F. Scott	Diver, Nicole Warren	*Tender Is the Night*
Fitzgerald, F. Scott	Gatsby, Jay	*The Great Gatsby*
Fitzgerald, F. Scott	Green, Dexter	"Winter Dreams"
Fitzgerald, F. Scott	Hoyt, Rosemary	*Tender Is the Night*
Fitzgerald, F. Scott	Hunter, Anson	"The Rich Boy"
Fitzgerald, F. Scott	Jones, Judy	"Winter Dreams"
Fitzgerald, F. Scott	Miller, Rudolph	"Absolution"
Fitzgerald, F. Scott	Patch, Anthony	*The Beautiful and Damned*
Fitzgerald, F. Scott	Patch, Gloria Gilbert	*The Beautiful and Damned*
Fitzgerald, F. Scott	Stahr, Monroe	*The Last Tycoon*
Fitzgerald, F. Scott	Unger, John T.	"The Diamond as Big as the Ritz"
Fitzgerald, F. Scott	Wales, Charlie	"Babylon Revisited"
Fitzgerald, Zelda	Knight, Alabama Beggs	*Save Me the Waltz*
Ford, Richard	Bascombe, Frank	*The Sportswriter*
Foster, Hannah	Boyer, J.	*The Coquette; or, The Life and Letters of Eliza Wharton*
Foster, Hannah	Sanford, Major Peter	*The Coquette; or, The Life and Letters of Eliza Wharton*

List of Authors

Foster, Hannah	Wharton, Eliza	*The Coquette; or, The Life and Letters of Eliza Wharton*
Frederic, Harold	Ware, Theron	*The Damnation of Theron Ware; or, Illumination*
Freeman, Joseph	Hertzfeld, Kurt	*Never Call Retreat*
Freeman, Joseph	Schuman, Paul August Heinrich	*Never Call Retreat*
Freeman, Mary Wilkins	Barnard, Charlotte	*Pembroke*
Freeman, Mary Wilkins	Ellis, Louisa	"A New England Nun"
Freeman, Mary Wilkins	Thayer, Deborah	*Pembroke*
French, Marilyn	Ward, Mira	*The Women's Room*
Friedman, Bruce Jay	Stern	*Stern*
Fuchs, Daniel	Hayman, Philip	*Summer in Williamsburg*
Fuchs, Daniel	Papravel, Nicholas	*Summer in Williamsburg*
Fuller, Henry B.	Brainard, Erastus	*The Cliff-Dwellers*
Fuller, Henry B.	Marshall, Jane	*With the Procession*
Fuller, Henry B.	Marshall, Richard Truesdale	*With the Procession*
Fuller, Henry B.	Ogden, George	*The Cliff-Dwellers*
Gaddis, William	Vansant, J. R.	*J.R.*
Gaines, Ernest J.	Pittman, Jane	*The Autobiography of Miss Jane Pittman*
Gardner, Erle Stanley	Mason, Perry	*The Case of the Velvet Claws*
Gardner, John	Grendel	*Grendel*
Gardner, John	Soames, Henry	*Nickel Mountain: A Pastoral Novel*
Gardner, John	Wells, Calliope "Callie"	*Nickel Mountain: A Pastoral Novel*
Garland, Hamlin	Haskins, Timothy	"Under the Lion's Paw"
Garris, George W.	Lovingood, Sut	*Sut Lovingood's Yarns*
Gass, William H.	Jorge	"The Pedersen Kid"
Gass, William H.	Narrator	"In the Heart of the Heart of the Country"
Gilman, Charlotte Perkins	Jennings, Vandyck	*Herland, and with Her in Ourland*
Gilman, Charlotte Perkins	Narrator	"The Yellow Wallpaper"
Glasgow, Ellen	Archbald, Jenny Blair	*The Sheltered Life*
Glasgow, Ellen	Birdsong, George	*The Sheltered Life*
Glasgow, Ellen	Pedlar, Dorinda Oakley	*Barren Ground*
Glasgow, Ellen	Pedlar, Nathan	*Barren Ground*
Godwin, Gail	Bolt, Cameron	*Glass People*
Godwin, Gail	Bolt, Francesca	*Glass People*
Godwin, Gail	Stokes, Justin	*The Finishing School*
Gold, Herbert	Berman, Daniel	*Therefore Be Bold*
Gold, Herbert	Shaper, Dan	"Love and Like"
Gold, Michael	Gold, Herman	*Jews Without Money*
Gold, Michael	Gold, Katie	*Jews Without Money*
Gold, Michael	Gold, Michael	*Jews Without Money*
Gordon, Caroline	Chapman, Catherine Lewis	*The Women on the Porch*
Gordon, Mary	Taylor, Felicitas Maria	*The Company of Women*
Grau, Shirley Ann	Carmichael, Margaret	*The Keepers of the House*
Grau, Shirley Ann	Howland, William	*The Keepers of the House*
Grau, Shirley Ann	Mason, Abigail Howland	*The Keepers of the House*
Grey, Zane	Lassiter	*Riders of the Purple Sage*
Grey, Zane	Withersteen, Jane	*Riders of the Purple Sage*
Guthrie, A. B.	Caudill, Boone	*The Big Sky*
H.D. (Hilda Doolittle)	Ashton, Julia	*Bid Me to Live*
Hale, Edward Everett	Nolan, Philip	"The Man Without a Country"

Hemingway, Ernest	Frazer (Mr.)	"The Gambler, the Nun, and the Radio"
Hemingway, Ernest	George	"The Killers"
Hemingway, Ernest	Harry	"The Snows of Kilimanjaro"
Hemingway, Ernest	Henry, Frederic	*A Farewell to Arms*
Hemingway, Ernest	Jordan, Robert	*For Whom the Bell Tolls*
Hemingway, Ernest	Macomber, Francis	"The Short Happy Life of Francis Macomber"
Hemingway, Ernest	Pilar	*For Whom the Bell Tolls*
Hemingway, Ernest	Santiago	*The Old Man and the Sea*
Hemingway, Ernest	The Unhurried Waiter	"A Clean, Well-Lighted Place"
Henderson, George	Ollie Miss	*Ollie Miss*
Henry, O.	Driscoll, Bill	"The Ransom of Red Chief"
Henry, O.	Young, Della Dillingham	"The Gift of the Magi"
Hentz, Caroline Lee	Moreland, Eulalia Hastings "Eula"	*The Planter's Northern Bride*
Hentz, Caroline Lee	Moreland, Russell	*The Planter's Northern Bride*
Herbert, Frank	Atreides, Paul	*Dune*
Hersey, John	Joppolo, Major Victor	*A Bell for Adano*
Heyward, DuBose	Bess	*Porgy*
Heyward, DuBose	Porgy	*Porgy*
Hijuelos, Oscar	Castillo, Cesar	*The Mambo Kings Play Songs of Love*
Hildreth, Richard	Moore, Archy	*The Slave; or, Memoirs of Archy Moore*
Hilton, James	Chipping (Mr.)	*Goodbye, Mr. Chips; To You, Mr. Chips*
Hilton, James	Conway, Hugh	*Lost Horizon*
Himes, Chester	Black Boy	"The Night's for Cryin' "
Himes, Chester	Gordon, Lee	*Lonely Crusade*
Himes, Chester	Johnson, Coffin Ed	*The Real Cool Killers; The Heat's On; Cotton Comes to Harlem*
Himes, Chester	Jones, Grave Digger	*The Real Cool Killers; Cotton Comes to Harlem; The Heat's On*
Himes, Chester	Jones, Robert Bob	*If He Hollers Let Him Go*
Himes, Chester	Mason, Mamie	*Pinktoes*
Himes, Chester	Monroe, James Buchannan "Jimmy"	*Cast the First Stone*
Hobson, Laura Z.	Green, Philip	*Gentleman's Agreement*
Holmes, John Clellon	Hobbes, Paul	*Go*
Holmes, Oliver Wendell	Venner, Elsie	*Elsie Venner: A Romance of Destiny*
Hopkins, Pauline E.	Clark, Sappho	*Contending Forces*
Hopkins, Pauline E.	Langley, John P.	*Contending Forces*
Hopkins, Pauline E.	Smith, Will	*Contending Forces*
Hopkinson, Frances	Settlers of the New Farm	"A Pretty Story"
Horgan, Paul	Powers, Cleotha	"The Peach Stone"
Howard, Maureen	Keely, Mary Agnes	*Bridgeport Bus*
Howard, Maureen	Savaard, Lydia	*Bridgeport Bus*
Howells, William Dean	Arbuton, Miles	*A Chance Acquaintance*
Howells, William Dean	Balcom, Editha	"Editha"
Howells, William Dean	Bowen, Lina	*Indian Summer*
Howells, William Dean	Colville, Theodore	*Indian Summer*
Howells, William Dean	Durgin, Thomas Jefferson	*The Landlord at Lion's Head*
Howells, William Dean	Ellison, Kitty	*A Chance Acquaintance*
Howells, William Dean	Gaylord, Marcia	*A Modern Instance*
Howells, William Dean	Homos, Aristides	*A Traveler from Altruria; Through the Eye of the Needle*
Howells, William Dean	Hubbard, Bartley	*A Modern Instance*
Howells, William Dean	Kilburn, Annie	*Annie Kilburn*
Howells, William Dean	Lapham, Silas	*The Rise of Silas Lapham*

Howells, William Dean	March, Basil	*Their Wedding Journey; A Hazard of New Fortunes*
Howells, William Dean	March, Isabel	*Their Wedding Journey; A Hazard of New Fortunes*
Hughes, Langston	Lesche, Eugene	"Rejuvenation Through Joy"
Hughes, Langston	Rodgers, James Sandy	*Not Without Laughter*
Hughes, Langston	Semple, Jesse B. "Simple"	*Simple Speaks His Mind; Simple Takes a Wife; The Best of Simple*
Hughes, Langston	Williams, Aunt Hager	*Not Without Laughter*
Hughes, Langston	Williams, Roy	"Home"
Humphrey, William	Hunnicutt, Hannah	*Home from the Hill*
Humphrey, William	Hunnicutt, Theron	*Home from the Hill*
Humphrey, William	Ordway, Sam	*The Ordways*
Hunter, Evan	Dadier, Rick	*The Blackboard Jungle*
Hunter, Evan	Miller, Gregory	*The Blackboard Jungle*
Hurston, Zora Neale	Crawford, Janie Mae	*Their Eyes Were Watching God*
Hurston, Zora Neale	Meserve, Arvay Henson	*Seraph on the Suwanee*
Hurston, Zora Neale	Meserve, Jim	*Seraph on the Suwanee*
Hurston, Zora Neale	Starks, Joe "Jody"	*Their Eyes Were Watching God*
Hurston, Zora Neale	Woods, Vergible "Tea Cake"	*Their Eyes Were Watching God*
Irving, John	Berry, Winslow	*The Hotel New Hampshire*
Irving, John	Garp, T. S.	*The World According to Garp*
Irving, Washington	Crane, Ichabod	*The Legend of Sleepy Hollow*
Irving, Washington	Van Winkle, Rip	"Rip Van Winkle"
Jackson, Charles	Birnam, Don	*The Lost Weekend*
Jackson, Helen Hunt	Ortegna, Ramona	*Ramona*
Jackson, Shirley	Blackwood, Mary Katherine "Merri-cat"	*We Have Always Lived in the Castle*
Jackson, Shirley	Hutchinson, Tess	"The Lottery"
Jackson, Shirley	Vance, Eleanor	*The Haunting of Hill House*
James, Henry	Alden, Bessie	*An International Episode*
James, Henry	Archer, Isabel	*The Portrait of a Lady*
James, Henry	Assingham, Fanny	*The Golden Bowl*
James, Henry	Brydon, Spencer	"The Jolly Corner"
James, Henry	Chancellor, Olive	*The Bostonians*
James, Henry	Croy, Kate	*The Wings of the Dove*
James, Henry	de Bellegarde, Valentin	*The American*
James, Henry	de Cintré, Claire	*The American*
James, Henry	Densher, Merton	*The Wings of the Dove*
James, Henry	Dormer, Nicholas	*The Tragic Muse*
James, Henry	Farange, Maisie	*What Maisie Knew*
James, Henry	Gereth, Adela	*The Spoils of Poynton*
James, Henry	Gereth, Owen	*The Spoils of Poynton*
James, Henry	Goodwood, Caspar	*The Portrait of a Lady*
James, Henry	The Governess	*The Turn of the Screw*
James, Henry	Lambert, Nora	*Watch and Ward*
James, Henry	Lawrence, Roger	*Watch and Ward*
James, Henry	The Literary Critic	"The Figure in the Carpet"
James, Henry	Marcher, John	"The Beast in the Jungle"
James, Henry	Merle, Madame Serena	*The Portrait of a Lady*
James, Henry	Miller, Daisy	*Daisy Miller*
James, Henry	Moreen, Morgan	"The Pupil"
James, Henry	Narrator	"The Author of Beltraffio"

Lewis, Sinclair	Cornplow, Sara	*The Prodigal Parents*
Lewis, Sinclair	Cornplow, William Fred	*The Prodigal Parents*
Lewis, Sinclair	Dodsworth, Samuel	*Dodsworth*
Lewis, Sinclair	Gantry, Elmer	*Elmer Gantry*
Lewis, Sinclair	Gottlieb, Max	*Arrowsmith*
Lewis, Sinclair	Kennicott, Carol Milford	*Main Street*
Lewis, Sinclair	Kennicott, Dr. Will	*Main Street*
Lewis, Sinclair	Kingsblood, Neil	*Kingsblood Royal*
Lewis, Sinclair	Tozer, Leora	*Arrowsmith*
Lewisohn, Ludwig	Levy, Arthur	*The Island Within*
Lewisohn, Ludwig	Levy, Jacob	*The Island Within*
Lippard, George	Devil-Bug	*The Quaker City; or, The Monks of Monk-Hall*
Lockridge, Ross, Jr.	Shawnessy, Esther Root	*Raintree County*
Lockridge, Ross, Jr.	Shawnessy, John Wickliff	*Raintree County*
Lockridge, Ross, Jr.	Shawnessy, Susannah Drake	*Raintree County*
Lockridge, Ross, Jr.	Stiles, Jerusalem Webster	*Raintree County*
London, Jack	Buck	*The Call of the Wild*
London, Jack	Eden, Martin	*Martin Eden*
London, Jack	Everhard, Avis	*The Iron Heel*
London, Jack	Everhard, Ernest	*The Iron Heel*
London, Jack	Koskoosh	"The Law of Life"
London, Jack	Larsen, Wolf	*The Sea Wolf*
London, Jack	Morse, Ruth	*Martin Eden*
London, Jack	Protagonist	"To Build a Fire"
London, Jack	Van Weyden, Humphrey	*The Sea Wolf*
London, Jack	White Fang	*White Fang*
Lumpkin, Grace	Denis	*A Sign for Cain*
Lumpkin, Grace	Duncan, Bill	*A Sign for Cain*
Lumpkin, Grace	Gault, Caroline	*A Sign for Cain*
Lumpkin, Grace	Gault, Jim	*A Sign for Cain*
Lumpkin, Grace	Kirkland, John	*To Make My Bread*
Lytle, Andrew	Cree, Lucius	*The Velvet Horn*
McBain, Ed	Carella, Stephen	*Cop Hater*
McCarthy, Mary	Andrews, Polly	*The Group*
McCarthy, Mary	Breen, Bill	"The Man in the Brooks Brothers Shirt"
McCarthy, Mary	Davison, Helena	*The Group*
McCarthy, Mary	Eastlake, Elinor "Lakey"	*The Group*
McCarthy, Mary	Furness, Howard	*The Groves of Academe*
McCarthy, Mary	Hartshorn, Priss	*The Group*
McCarthy, Mary	MacAusland, Elizabeth "Libby"	*The Group*
McCarthy, Mary	Mulcahy, Henry	*The Groves of Academe*
McCarthy, Mary	Protagonist	"The Man in the Brooks Brothers Shirt"
McCarthy, Mary	Prothero, Mary "Pokey"	*The Group*
McCarthy, Mary	Rejnev, Domna	*The Groves of Academe*
McCarthy, Mary	Renfrew, Dottie	*The Group*
McCarthy, Mary	Strong, Kay Leiland	*The Group*
McCullers, Carson	Addams, Frankie	*The Member of the Wedding*
McCullers, Carson	Evans, Miss Amelia	*Ballad of the Sad Café*
McCullers, Carson	Frances	*Wunderkind*
McCullers, Carson	Kelly, Mick	*The Heart Is a Lonely Hunter*
McCullers, Carson	Penderton, Captain Weldon	*Reflections in a Golden Eye*
McCullers, Carson	Penderton, Leonora	*Reflections in a Golden Eye*
McCullers, Carson	Protagonist	"A Tree * A Rock * A Cloud"

Morris, Wright	Horter, Earl	*Love Among the Cannibals*
Morris, Wright	Oelsligle, Kermit Boy	*Fire Sermon*
Morrison, Toni	Baby Suggs	*Beloved*
Morrison, Toni	Beloved	*Beloved*
Morrison, Toni	Breedlove, Cholly	*The Bluest Eye*
Morrison, Toni	Breedlove, Pauline Williams	*The Bluest Eye*
Morrison, Toni	Breedlove, Pecola	*The Bluest Eye*
Morrison, Toni	Childs, Jadine	*Tar Baby*
Morrison, Toni	Dead, Macon "Milkman"	*Song of Solomon*
Morrison, Toni	Garner, Paul D.	*Beloved*
Morrison, Toni	Peace, Eva	*Sula*
Morrison, Toni	Peace, Sula May	*Sula*
Morrison, Toni	Sethe	*Beloved*
Morrison, Toni	Shadrack	*Sula*
Morrison, Toni	Son	*Tar Baby*
Morrison, Toni	Street, Margaret	*Tar Baby*
Morrison, Toni	Wright, Nel	*Sula*
Motley, Willard	Romano, Nick	*Knock on Any Door*
Nabokov, Vladimir	Pnin, Timofrey Pavlovich	*Pnin*
Nabokov, Vladimir	Haze, Charlotte Becker	*Lolita*
Nabokov, Vladimir	Haze, Dolores "Lolita"	*Lolita*
Nabokov, Vladimir	Humbert, Humbert	*Lolita*
Nabokov, Vladimir	Kinbote, Charles	*Pale Fire*
Nabokov, Vladimir	Peters, Margot	*Laughter in the Dark*
Nabokov, Vladimir	Veen, Van	*Ada*
Nabokov, Vladimir	V.	*The Real Life of Sebastian Knight*
Naylor, Gloria	Andrews, George	*Mama Day*
Naylor, Gloria	Day, Miranda "Mama Day"	*Mama Day*
Naylor, Gloria	Day, Ophelia "Cocoa"	*Mama Day*
Naylor, Gloria	Mason, Willie "White"	*Linden Hills*
Naylor, Gloria	Michael, Mattie	*The Women of Brewster Place*
Naylor, Gloria	Nedeed, Luther	*Linden Hills*
Norris, Frank	Behrman, S.	*The Octopus*
Norris, Frank	Derrick, Magnus	*The Octopus*
Norris, Frank	Jadwin, Curtis	*The Pit*
Norris, Frank	Jadwin, Laura Dearborn	*The Pit*
Norris, Frank	McTeague, Mac	*McTeague*
Norris, Frank	Presley	*The Octopus*
Norris, Frank	Sieppe, Trina	*McTeague*
Norris, Frank	Vandover	*Vandover and the Brute*
Norris, Frank	Wilbur, Ross	*Moran of the Lady Letty*
Oates, Joyce Carol	Bellefleur, Germaine	*Bellefleur*
Oates, Joyce Carol	Bellefleur, Gideon	*Bellefleur*
Oates, Joyce Carol	Bellefleur, Leah	*Bellefleur*
Oates, Joyce Carol	Bonham, Daisy	"Daisy"
Oates, Joyce Carol	Connie	"Where Are You Going, Where Have You Been?"
Oates, Joyce Carol	Courtney, Iris	*Because It is Bitter, And Because It Is My Heart*
Oates, Joyce Carol	Fairchild, Verlyn Rayburn "Jinx"	*Because It Is Bitter, And Because It Is My Heart*
Oates, Joyce Carol	Howe, Elena Ross	*Do with Me What You Will*
Oates, Joyce Carol	Howe, Marvin	*Do with Me What You Will*

Rechy, John	Narrator	*City of Night*
Reed, Ishmael	Jones, Reverend Clement	*The Terrible Threes*
Reed, Ishmael	LaBas, PaPa	*Mumbo Jumbo*
Reed, Ishmael	Quickskill, Raven	*Flight to Canada*
Reed, Ishmael	Von Vampton, Hinckle	*Mumbo Jumbo*
Reznikoff, Charles	Rubinov, Ezekiel	*By the Waters of Manhattan*
Reznikoff, Charles	Volsky, Sarah Yetta	*By the Waters of Manhattan*
Rice, Elmer	Coleman, Gaillard "Gay"	*Imperial City*
Richter, Conrad	Brewton, James Colonel	*The Sea of Grass*
Richter, Conrad	Brewton, Lutie Cameron	*The Sea of Grass*
Richter, Conrad	Hal	*The Sea of Grass*
Rivera, Edward	Malánguez, Santos	*Family Installments: Memories of Growing Up Hispanic*
Robbins, Tom	Hankshaw, Sissy	*Even Cowgirls Get the Blues*
Roberts, Elizabeth Madox	Chesser, Ellen	*The Time of Man*
Roberts, Kenneth	Rogers, Major Robert	*Northwest Passage*
Roberts, Kenneth	Towne, Langdon	*Northwest Passage*
Rolvaag, O. E.	Hansa, Beret	*Giants in the Earth*
Rolvaag, O. E.	Hansa, Per	*Giants in the Earth*
Ross, Leonard Q.	Kaplan, Hyman	*The Education of Hyman Kaplan*
Ross, Leonard Q.	Parkhill (Mr.)	*The Education of Hyman Kaplan*
Rossner, Judith	Dunn, Theresa	*Looking for Mr. Goodbar*
Roth, Henry	Schearl, David	*Call It Sleep*
Roth, Philip	Freedman, Oscar	"The Conversion of the Jews"
Roth, Philip	Herz, Paul	*Letting Go*
Roth, Philip	Kepesh, David	*The Professor of Desire*
Roth, Philip	Klugman, Neil	*Goodbye, Columbus*
Roth, Philip	Lonoff, Emanuel Isidore "E.I."	*The Ghost Writer*
Roth, Philip	Marx, Nathan	"Defender of the Faith"
Roth, Philip	Patimkin, Brenda	*Goodbye, Columbus*
Roth, Philip	Peck, Eli	"Eli, the Fanatic"
Roth, Philip	Portnoy, Alexander	*Portnoy's Complaint*
Roth, Philip	Reed, Mary Jane "the Monkey"	*Portnoy's Complaint*
Roth, Philip	Tarnopol, Peter	*My Life as a Man*
Roth, Philip	Wallach, Gabriel	*Letting Go*
Roth, Philip	Zuckerman, Nathan	*The Ghost Writer; Zuckerman Unbound; The Anatomy Lesson*
Rowson, Susanna	Temple, Charlotte	*Charlotte Temple*
Runyon, Damon	Marker, Little Miss "Marky"	"Little Miss Marker"
Salinger, J. D.	Caulfield, Holden	*The Catcher in the Rye*
Salinger, J. D.	Caulfield, Phoebe	*The Catcher in the Rye*
Salinger, J. D.	Esmé	"For Esmé—with Love and Squalor"
Salinger, J. D.	Glass, Buddy	*Raise High the Roof Beam, Carpenters; Seymour: An Introduction*
Salinger, J. D.	Glass, Francis "Franny"	*Franny and Zooey*
Salinger, J. D.	Glass, Seymour	"A Perfect Day for Bananafish"; *Raise High the Roof Beam, Carpenters; Seymour: An Introduction*
Salinger, J. D.	Glass, Zachery Martin "Zooey"	*Franny and Zooey*
Salinger, J. D.	X, Sergeant	"For Esmé—with Love and Squalor"
Sandoz, Mari	Allerton, Abigail	*Capital City*
Sandoz, Mari	Rufe, Hamm	*Capital City*
Sandoz, Mari	Sandoz, Jules	*Old Jules*

Stowe, Harriet Beecher	Gordon, Harry	*Dred, a Tale of the Great Dismal Swamp*
Stowe, Harriet Beecher	Gordon, Nina	*Dred, a Tale of the Great Dismal Swamp*
Stowe, Harriet Beecher	Holyoke, Horace	*Oldtown Folks*
Stowe, Harriet Beecher	Legree, Simon	*Uncle Tom's Cabin* or, *Life among the Lowly*
Stowe, Harriet Beecher	Seymour, John	*Pink and White Tyranny*
Stowe, Harriet Beecher	St. Clare, Evangeline "Eva"	*Uncle Tom's Cabin* or, *Life Among the Lowly*
Stowe, Harriet Beecher	Topsy	*Uncle Tom's Cabin* or, *Life Among the Lowly*
Stowe, Harriet Beecher	Uncle Tom	*Uncle Tom's Cabin* or, *Life Among the Lowly*
Stowe, Harriet Beecher	Vesey, Dred	*Dred, a Tale of the Great Dismal Swamp*
Styron, William	Culver, Jack	*The Long March*
Styron, William	Flagg, Mason	*Set This House on Fire*
Styron, William	Landau, Nathan	*Sophie's Choice*
Styron, William	Leverett, Peter	*Set This House on Fire*
Styron, William	Loftis, Helen	*Lie Down in Darkness*
Styron, William	Loftis, Milton	*Lie Down in Darkness*
Styron, William	Loftis, Peyton	*Lie Down in Darkness*
Styron, William	Stingo	*Sophie's Choice*
Styron, William	Turner, Nat	*The Confessions of Nat Turner*
Styron, William	Zawistowska, Sophie	*Sophie's Choice*
Suckow, Ruth	Kaetterhenry, August	*Country People*
Suckow, Ruth	Kaetterhenry, Emma Stille	*Country People*
Swados, Harvey	Metzger, Irwin	*Standing Fast*
Swados, Harvey	Norman "Norm"	*Standing Fast*
Tan, Amy	Hsu, An-Mei	*The Joy Luck Club*
Tan, Amy	Jong, Lindo	*The Joy Luck Club*
Tan, Amy	St. Clair, Ying-Ying	*The Joy Luck Club*
Tan, Amy	Woo, Jing-Mei	*The Joy Luck Club*
Tarkington, Booth	Adams, Alice	*Alice Adams*
Tarkington, Booth	Beaucaire, Monsieur	*Monsieur Beaucaire*
Tarkington, Booth	Harkless, John	*The Gentleman from Indiana*
Tarkington, Booth	Minivar, George Amberson	*The Magnificent Ambersons*
Tarkington, Booth	Minivar, Isabel Amberson	*The Magnificent Ambersons*
Tarkington, Booth	Schofield, Penrod	*Penrod; Penrod and Sam; Penrod Jashber*
Tarkington, Booth	Sherwood, Helen	*The Gentleman from Indiana*
Tarkington, Booth	Williams, Sam	*Penrod; Penrod and Sam; Penrod Jashber*
Tate, Allen	Buchan, Lacy	*The Fathers*
Tate, Allen	Posey, George	*The Fathers*
Taylor, Peter	Carver, Betsy	*A Summons to Memphis*
Taylor, Peter	Dorset, Louisa	"Venus, Cupid, Folly and Time"
Taylor, Peter	Dudley, Quintus Cincinnatus Lovell	*A Woman of Means*
Taylor, Peter	Elizabeth	"A Spinster's Tale"
Taylor, Peter	Narrator	"Dean of Men"
Taylor, Peter	Ramsey, Nat	"The Old Forest"
Thorpe, T. B.	Storyteller	"The Big Bear of Arkansas"
Thurber, James	Martin, Erwin	"The Catbird Seat"
Thurber, James	Mitty, Walter	"The Secret Life of Walter Mitty"
Thurman, Wallace	Morgan, Emma Lou	*The Blacker the Berry . . .*
Thurman, Wallace	Taylor, Raymond	*Infants of the Spring*
Toole, John Kennedy	Mancuso, Angelo	*A Confederacy of Dunces*
Toole, John Kennedy	Reilly, Ignatius Jacques	*A Confederacy of Dunces*

List of Authors

Toole, John Kennedy	Reilly, Irene	*A Confederacy of Dunces*
Tourgée, Albion W.	Servosse, Colonel Comfort	*A Fool's Errand*
Trilling, Lionel	Blackburn, Theodore	"Of This Time, of That Place"
Trilling, Lionel	Howe, Joseph	"Of This Time, of That Place"
Trilling, Lionel	Tertan, Ferdinand R.	"Of This Time, of That Place"
Trumbo, Dalton	Bonham, Joe	*Johnny Got His Gun*
Tyler, Anne	Leary, Macon	*The Accidental Tourist*
Tyler, Anne	Moran, Maggie	*Breathing Lessons*
Tyler, Anne	Pritchett, Muriel	*The Accidental Tourist*
Tyler, Anne	Tull, Ezra	*Dinner at the Homesick Restaurant*
Tyler, Anne	Tull, Pearl	*Dinner at the Homesick Restaurant*
Updike, John	Angstrom, Harry "Rabbit"	*Rabbit, Run; Rabbit Redux; Rabbit Is Rich; Rabbit at Rest*
Updike, John	Angstrom, Janice Springer	*Rabbit, Run; Rabbit Redux; Rabbit Is Rich; Rabbit at Rest*
Updike, John	Bech, Henry	*Bech: A Book; Bech Is Back*
Updike, John	Kern, David	"Pigeon's Feathers"
Updike, John	Kohler, Dale	*Roger's Version*
Updike, John	Lambert, Roger	*Roger's Version*
Updike, John	Narrator	"Deaths of Distant Friends"
Updike, John	Nordholm, John	"The Happiest I've Been"
Updike, John	Ralph	"The Doctor's Wife"
Updike, John	Sammy	"A & P"
Uris, Leon	Canaan, Ari Ben	*Exodus*
Uris, Leon	Clement, Karen Hansen	*Exodus*
Uris, Leon	Fremont, Kitty	*Exodus*
Van Vechten, Carl	Kasson, Byron	*Nigger Heaven*
Van Vechten, Carl	Love, Mary	*Nigger Heaven*
Vidal, Gore	Breckinridge, Myra	*Myra Breckinridge*
Vidal, Gore	Willard, Jim	*The City and the Pillar*
Vonnegut, Kurt, Jr.	Bokonon	*Cat's Cradle*
Vonnegut, Kurt, Jr.	Constant, Malachi	*The Sirens of Titan*
Vonnegut, Kurt, Jr.	Hoover, Dwayne	*Breakfast of Champions*
Vonnegut, Kurt, Jr.	John	*Cat's Cradle*
Vonnegut, Kurt, Jr.	McLuhan, Nancy	"Welcome to the Monkey House"
Vonnegut, Kurt, Jr.	Pilgrim, Billy	*Slaughter-House Five*
Vonnegut, Kurt, Jr.	Rosewater, Eliot	*God Bless You, Mr. Rosewater (or Pearls Before Swine)*
Vonnegut, Kurt, Jr.	Rosewater, Fred	*God Bless You, Mr. Rosewater (or Pearls Before Swine)*
Vonnegut, Kurt, Jr.	Rosewater, Sylvia DuVrais Zetterling	*God Bless You, Mr. Rosewater (or Pearls Before Swine)*
Vonnegut, Kurt, Jr.	Rumfoord, Beatrice	*The Sirens of Titan*
Vonnegut, Kurt, Jr.	Rumfoord, Winston Niles	*The Sirens of Titan*
Vonnegut, Kurt, Jr.	Trout, Kilgore	*Breakfast of Champions*
Vorse, Mary Heaton	Deane, Ferdinand	*Strike!*
Walker, Alice	Albert "Mister"	*The Color Purple*
Walker, Alice	Avery, Shug	*The Color Purple*
Walker, Alice	Celie	*The Color Purple*
Walker, Alice	Copeland, Brownfield	*The Third Life of Grange Copeland*
Walker, Alice	Copeland, Grange	*The Third Life of Grange Copeland*
Walker, Alice	Copeland, Mem	*The Third Life of Grange Copeland*

List of Titles

"A & P"	Sammy	John Updike
Absalom, Absalom!	Bon, Charles	William Faulkner
Absalom, Absalom!	Sutpen, Judith	William Faulkner
Absalom, Absalom!	Sutpen, Thomas	William Faulkner
"Absolution"	Miller, Rudolph	F. Scott Fitzgerald
The Accidental Tourist	Leary, Macon	Anne Tyler
The Accidental Tourist	Pritchett, Muriel	Anne Tyler
"An Act of Faith"	Seeger, Norman	Irwin Shaw
Ada	Veen, Van	Vladimir Nabokov
The Adventures of Augie March	March, Augie	Saul Bellow
Adventures of a Young Man	Spotswood, Glenn	John Dos Passos
The Adventures of Huckleberry Finn	Jim	Samuel Clemens (Mark Twain)
The Adventures of Tom Sawyer; The Adventures of Huckleberry Finn	Finn, Huckleberry "Huck"	Samuel Clemens (Mark Twain)
The Adventures of Tom Sawyer; The Adventures of Huckleberry Finn	Sawyer, Tom	Samuel Clemens (Mark Twain)
Afterlife	Cevathas, Sonny	Paul Monette
Afterlife	Espinoza, Lorenzo Delgado "Dell"	Paul Monette
Afterlife	Shaw, Steven	Paul Monette
The Age of Innocence	Archer, Newland	Edith Wharton
The Age of Innocence	Olenska, Countess Ellen	Edith Wharton
The Age of Innocence	Welland, May	Edith Wharton
Alice Adams	Adams, Alice	Booth Tarkington
All the King's Men	Burden, Jack	Robert Penn Warren
All the King's Men	Stark, Willie	Robert Penn Warren
The Ambassadors	Strether, Lambert	Henry James
America America	Topouzoglou, Stavros	Elia Kazan
The American	de Bellegarde, Valentin	Henry James
The American	Cintré, Claire	Henry James
The American	Newman, Christopher	Henry James
An American Dream	Rojack, Stephen	Norman Mailer
An American Tragedy	Alden, Roberta	Theodore Dreiser
An American Tragedy	Finchley, Sondra	Theodore Dreiser
An American Tragedy	Griffiths, Clyde	Theodore Dreiser
Andersonville	Claffey, Ira	McKinley Kantor
Andersonville	Claffey, Lucy	McKinley Kantor
Andersonville	Elkins, Harrell "Harry"	McKinley Kantor
Andersonville	Wirz, Henry	McKinley Kantor
And Then We Heard the Thunder	Saunders, Solomon "Solly," Jr.	John Oliver Killens
"Angel Levine"	Manischevitz	Bernard Malamud
Annie Kilburn	Kilburn, Annie	William Dean Howells

Another Country	Moore, Vivaldo	James Baldwin
Another Country	Scott, Ida	James Baldwin
Another Country	Scott, Rufus	James Baldwin
Anthony Adverse	Adverse, Anthony	Hervey Allen
Appalachee Red	Appalachee Red	Raymond Andrews
Appointment in Samarra	English, Julian	John O'Hara
Arrowsmith	Arrowsmith, Martin	Sinclair Lewis
Arrowsmith	Gottlieb, Max	Sinclair Lewis
Arrowsmith	Tozer, Leora	Sinclair Lewis
Arthur Mervyn	Mervyn, Arthur	Charles Brockton Brown
"The Artificial Nigger"	Head (Mr.)	Flannery O'Connor
"The Artificial Nigger"	Nelson	Flannery O'Connor
"The Artist of the Beau-tiful"	Warland, Owen	Nathaniel Hawthorne
As I Lay Dying	Bundren, Addie	William Faulkner
As I Lay Dying	Bundren, Anse	William Faulkner
As I Lay Dying	Bundren, Jewel	William Faulkner
As I Lay Dying; The Sound and the Fury	Bundren, Dewey "Dell"	William Faulkner
As I Lay Dying; "Uncle Willy"	Bundren, Darl	William Faulkner
The Asiatics	The Traveler	Frederic Prokosch
Ask the Dust	Bandini, Arturo	John Fante
The Assistant	Alpine, Frank	Bernard Malamud
The Assistant	Bober, Helen	Bernard Malamud
The Assistant	Bober, Morris	Bernard Malamud
"Athénaïse"	Athénaïse	Kate Chopin
"At the 'Cadian Ball"; "The Storm"	Calixta	Kate Chopin
"At the 'Cadian Ball"; "The Storm"	Laballière, Alcée	Kate Chopin
"The Author of Beltraf-fio"	Narrator	Henry James
The Autobiography of Alice B. Toklas	Stein, Gertrude	Gertrude Stein
The Autobiography of Alice B. Toklas	Toklas, Alice	Gertrude Stein
Autobiography of an Ex-Colored Man	Narrator	James Weldon Johnson
The Autobiography of Miss Jane Pittman	Pittman, Jane	Ernest J. Gaines
The Awakening	Pontellier, Edna	Kate Chopin
Babbitt	Babbitt, George Follansbee	Sinclair Lewis
Babylon Revisited	Wales, Charlie	F. Scott Fitzgerald
The Bad Seed	Penmark, Rhoda	William March
Ballad of the Sad Cafe	Evans, Miss Amelia	Carson McCullers
Banana Bottom	Plant, Bita	Claude McKay
Banjo: A Story Without a Plot	Daily, Lincoln Agrippa "Banjo"	Claude McKay
"Barn Burning"; *The Hamlet*	Snopes, Abner Ab	William Faulkner
"Barn Burning"; *The Hamlet*	Snopes, Colonel Sartoris "Sarty"	William Faulkner
Barren Ground	Pedlar, Dorinda Oakley	Ellen Glasgow

List of Titles

List of Titles

List of Titles

Do Androids Dream of Electric Sheep?	Deckard, Richard "Rick"	Philip K. Dick
"The Doctors Wife"	Ralph	John Updike
Dodsworth	Dodsworth, Samuel	Sinclair Lewis
Dog Soldiers	Converse, John	Robert Stone
Dog Soldiers	Hicks, Ray	Robert Stone
The Dollmaker	Nevels, Gertie	Harriet Arnow
"Double Birthday"	Engelhardt, Albert	Willa Cather
"Double Birthday"	Engelhardt, Dr. Albert	Willa Cather
Double Indemnity	Huff, Walter	James M. Cain
Double Indemnity	Nirdlinger, Phyllis	James M. Cain
Do with Me What You Will	Howe, Elena Ross	Joyce Carol Oates
Do with Me What You Will	Howe, Marvin	Joyce Carol Oates
Do with Me What You Will	Morrissey, Jack	Joyce Carol Oates
Do You Like It Here?	Roberts, Humphrey	John O'Hara
The Dream Life of Balso Snell	Snell, Balso	Nathanael West
Dred, a Tale of the Great Dismal Swamp	Clayton, Edward	Harriet Beecher Stowe
Dred, a Tale of the Great Dismal Swamp	Gordon, Harry	Harriet Beecher Stowe
Dred, a Tale of the Great Dismal Swamp	Gordon, Nina	Harriet Beecher Stowe
Dred, a Tale of the Great Dismal Swamp	Vesey, Dred	Harriet Beecher Stowe
Drums Along the Mohawk	Martin, Gilbert	Walter D. Edmonds
Drums Along the Mohawk	Martin, Magdelana "Lana" Borst	Walter D. Edmonds
"Dry September"	Cooper, Minnie	William Faulkner
Dubin's Lives	Dubin, William	Bernard Malamud
Duel in the Sun	Chavez, Pearl	Niven Busch
"Duel with the Clock"	Bradley, James "Brad"	Junius Edwards
Dune	Atreides, Paul	Frank Herbert
Early Autumn	Pentland, Olivia	Louis Bromfield
East of Eden	Lee	John Steinbeck
East of Eden	Trask, Adam	John Steinbeck
East of Eden	Trask, Aron	John Steinbeck
East of Eden	Trask, Caleb	John Steinbeck
East of Eden	Trask, Catherine Ames	John Steinbeck
Edgar Huntly; or, Memoirs of a Sleepwalker	Edny, Clithero	Charles Brockden Brown
Edgar Huntly; or, Memoirs of a Sleepwalker	Huntly, Edgar	Charles Brockden Brown
"Editha"	Balcom, Editha	William Dean Howells
The Education of Hyman Kaplan	Kaplan, Hyman	Leonard Q. Ross
The Education of Hyman Kaplan	Parkhill (Mr.)	Leonard Q. Ross
"The Egg"	Narrator	Sherwood Anderson

List of Titles

List of Titles

Gentleman's Agreement	Green, Philip	Laura Z. Hobson
Georgie May	May, Georgie	Maxwell Bodenheim
The Ghost Writer	Lonoff, Emanuel Isidore "E.I."	Philip Roth
The Ghost Writer; Zuck-erman Unbound; The Anatomy Lesson	Zuckerman, Nathan	Philip Roth
Giant	Benedict, Jordan "Bick"	Edna Ferber
Giant	Benedict, Leslie Lynnton	Edna Ferber
Giant	Rink, Jett	Edna Ferber
Giants in the Earth	Hansa, Beret	O. E. Rolvaag
Giants in the Earth	Hansa, Per	O. E. Rolvaag
"The Gift of the Magi"	Young, Della Dillingham	O. Henry
The Gilded Age	Hawkins, Laura	Samuel Clemens (Mark Twain); Charles Dudley Warner
The Gilded Age	Sterling, Philip	Samuel Clemens (Mark Twain)
Giles Goat-Boy	Giles	John Barth
Giovanni's Room	David	James Baldwin
The Girl	The Girl	Meridel LeSueur
"The Girls in Their Sum-mer Dresses"	Frances	Irwin Shaw
A Girls Story	Rae Ann	Toni Cade Bambara
Glass People	Bolt, Cameron	Gail Godwin
Glass People	Bolt, Francesca	Gail Godwin
Go	Hobbes, Paul	John Clellon Holmes
God Bless You, Mr. Rose-water (or Pearls Before Swine)	Rosewater, Eliot	Kurt Vonnegut, Jr.
God Bless You, Mr. Rose-water (or Pearls Before Swine)	Rosewater, Fred	Kurt Vonnegut, Jr.
God Bless You, Mr. Rose-water (or Pearls Before Swine)	Rosewater, Sylvia DuVrais Zetterling	Kurt Vonnegut, Jr.
The Godfather	Corleone, Don Vito	Mario Puzo
The Godfather	Corleone, Michael	Mario Puzo
God Sends Sunday	Madison, Little Augie	Arna Bontemps
God's Little Acre	Walden, Ty-Ty	Erskine Caldwell
Going After Cacciato	Berlin, Paul	Tim O'Brien
The Golden Bowl	Assingham, Fanny	Henry James
The Golden Bowl	Prince Amerigo	Henry James
The Golden Bowl	Stant, Charlotte	Henry James
The Golden Bowl	Verver, Adam	Henry James
The Golden Bowl	Verver, Maggie	Henry James
Gone with the Wind	Butler, Rhett	Margaret Mitchell
Gone with the Wind	Mammy	Margaret Mitchell
Gone with the Wind	O'Hara, Scarlett	Margaret Mitchell
Gone with the Wind	Wilkes, Ashley	Margaret Mitchell
Gone with the Wind	Wilkes, Melanie Hamilton	Margaret Mitchell
"The Gonzaga Manu-scripts"	Feiler, Clarence	Saul Bellow
Good as Gold	Gold, Bruce	Joseph Heller
Goodbye, Columbus	Klugman, Neil	Philip Roth
Goodbye, Columbus	Patimkin, Brenda	Philip Roth
Goodbye, Mr. Chips; To You, Mr. Chips	Chipping (Mr.)	James Hilton

"Good Country People"	Hopewell, Hulga	Flannery O'Connor
The Good Earth	O-lan	Pearl S. Buck
The Good Earth	Wang Lung	Pearl S. Buck
"A Good Man Is Hard to Find"	The Grandmother	Flannery O'Connor
Good Times/Bad Times	Hoyt, Franklyn	James Kirkwood
Good Times/Bad Times	Kilburn, Peter	James Kirkwood
"Gorilla, My Love"	Hazel	Toni Cade Bambara
Go Tell It on the Mountain	Grimes, Elizabeth	James Baldwin
Go Tell It on the Mountain	Grimes, Gabriel	James Baldwin
Go Tell It on the Mountain	Grimes, John	James Baldwin
The Grandissimes	Bras-Coupé	George Washington Cable
The Grandissimes	Frowenfeld, Joseph	George Washington Cable
The Grandissimes	Grandissime, Honoré	George Washington Cable
The Grandissimes	Grandissime, Honoré f.m.c.	George Washington Cable
The Grapes of Wrath	Casy, Jim	John Steinbeck
The Grapes of Wrath	Joad, Ma	John Steinbeck
The Grapes of Wrath	Joad, Rose of Sharon	John Steinbeck
The Grapes of Wrath	Joad, Tom	John Steinbeck
Gravity's Rainbow	Slothrop, Tyrone	Thomas Pynchon
The Gray Champion	The Gray Champion	Nathaniel Hawthorne
The Gray Champion	Protagonist	Nathaniel Hawthorne
The Great Gatsby	Buchanan, Daisy	F. Scott Fitzgerald
The Great Gatsby	Carraway, Nick	F. Scott Fitzgerald
The Great Gatsby	Gatsby, Jay	F. Scott Fitzgerald
Grendel	Grendel	Gardner, John
The Group	Andrews, Polly	Mary McCarthy
The Group	Davison, Helena	Mary McCarthy
The Group	Eastlake, Elinor "Lakey"	Mary McCarthy
The Group	Hartshorn, Priss	Mary McCarthy
The Group	MacAusland, Elizabeth "Libby"	Mary McCarthy
The Group	Prothero, Mary "Pokey"	Mary McCarthy
The Group	Renfrew, Dottie	Mary McCarthy
The Group	Strong, Kay Leiland	Mary McCarthy
The Groves of Academe	Furness, Howard	Mary McCarthy
The Groves of Academe	Mulcahy, Henry	Mary McCarthy
The Groves of Academe	Rejnev, Domna	Mary McCarthy
Guard of Honor	Beal, General Ira "Bus"	James Gould Cozzens
Guard of Honor	Carricker, Lieutenant Colonel Benny	James Gould Cozzens
Guard of Honor	Hicks, Captain Nathaniel	James Gould Cozzens
"Gunner's Passage"	Stais	Irwin Shaw
The Hamlet; The Town; The Mansion	Kohl, Linda Snopes	William Faulkner
The Hamlet; The Town; The Mansion	Ratliff, Vladimir Kyrilytch	William Faulkner
The Hamlet; The Town; The Mansion	Snopes, Eula Varner	William Faulkner
The Hamlet; The Town; The Mansion	Snopes, Flem	William Faulkner
The Hamlet; The Town; The Mansion	Snopes, Wallstreet Panic	William Faulkner

List of Titles

List of Titles

Light in August	Hightower, Gail	William Faulkner
The Light in the Piazza	Johnson, Margaret	Elizabeth Spencer
"Like a Winding Sheet"	Johnson	Ann Petry
The Lime Twig	Banks, Margaret	John Hawkes
The Lime Twig	Banks, Michael	John Hawkes
Linden Hills	Mason, Willie "White"	Gloria Naylor
Linden Hills	Nedeed, Luther	Gloria Naylor
"Lions, Harts, Leaping Does"	Didymus (Father)	J. F. Powers
Little Big Man	Crabb, Jack	Thomas Berger
Little Big Man	Old Lodge Skins	Thomas Berger
Little Caesar	Bandello, Cesare Rico	W. R. Burnett
Little Lord Fauntleroy	The Earl of Dorincourt	Frances Hodgson Burnett
Little Lord Fauntleroy	Errol, Cedric Ceddie	Frances Hodgson Burnett
Little Men	Blake, Nathaniel	Louisa May Alcott
Little Men	Brooke, John Demi	Louisa May Alcott
Little Men	Dan	Louisa May Alcott
Little Men	Harding, Nancy	Louisa May Alcott
Little Miss Marker	Marker, Little Miss "Marky"	Damon Runyon
A Little Princess	Crewe, Sara	Frances Hodgson Burnett
"The Little Wife"	Hinckley, Joe	William March
Little Women	Laurence, Theodore "Laurie"	Louisa May Alcott
Little Women	March, Amy	Louisa May Alcott
Little Women	March, Beth	Louisa May Alcott
Little Women	March, Josephine "Jo"	Louisa May Alcott
Little Women	March, Margaret "Meg"	Louisa May Alcott
The Living Is Easy	Judson, Bart	Dorothy West
The Living Is Easy	Judson, Cleo Jericho	Dorothy West
"Livvie"	Livvie	Eudora Welty
Lolita	Haze, Charlotte Becker	Vladimir Nabokov
Lolita	Haze, Dolores "Lolita"	Vladimir Nabokov
Lolita	Humbert, Humbert	Vladimir Nabokov
Lonely Crusade	Gordon, Lee	Chester Himes
Lonesome Dove: A Novel	McCrae, Augustus	Larry McMurtry
A Long Day's Dying	Bone, Tristram	Frederick Buechner
"The Long-Distance Runner"	Faith	Grace Paley
The Long March	Culver, Jack	William Styron
Look Homeward, Angel	Gant, Benjamin Harrison	Thomas Wolfe
Look Homeward, Angel	Gant, Eliza Pentland	Thomas Wolfe
Look Homeward, Angel	Gant, Eugene	Thomas Wolfe
Look Homeward, Angel	Gant, W. O.	Thomas Wolfe
Looking Backward: 2000–1887; Equality	West, Julian	Edward Bellamy
Looking for Mr. Goodbar	Dunn, Theresa	Judith Rossner
"Looking for Mr. Green"	Grebe, George	Saul Bellow
Losing Battles	Renfro, Gloria Short	Eudora Welty
Losing Battles	Renfro, Jack Jordan	Eudora Welty
Lost Horizon	Conway, Hugh	James Hilton
"Lost in the Funhouse"	M——, Ambrose	John Barth
A Lost Lady	Forrester, Marian	Willa Cather
A Lost Lady	Herbert, Niel	Willa Cather
"The Lost Phoebe"	Reifsneider, Henry	Theodore Dreiser

Moby Dick; or, The Whale	Ishmael	Herman Melville
Moby Dick; or, The Whale	Queequeg	Herman Melville
Moby Dick; or, The Whale	Starbuck	Herman Melville
Modern Chivalry	Farrago, Captain John	H. H. Brackenridge
Modern Chivalry	O'Regan, Teague	H. H. Brackenridge
A Modern Instance	Gaylord, Marcia	William Dean Howells
A Modern Instance	Hubbard, Bartley	William Dean Howells
Monday Night	Tobin, Wiltshire "Wilt"	Kay Boyle
"Mondongo"	Johns, Ray	Amiri Baraka
"Mondongo"	Laffawiss, Irv	Imamu Amiri Baraka
The Monkey Wrench Gang	Smith, Joseph Fielding "Seldom Seen"	Edward Abbey
Monsieur Beaucaire	Beaucaire, Monsieur	Booth Tarkington
The Monster	Johnson, Henry	Stephen Crane
Monte Walsh	Walsh, Monte	Jack Schaefer
Moon-Calf	Fay, Felix	Floyd Dell
The Moon Is Down	Orden, Mayor	John Steinbeck
Moran of the Lady Letty	Wilbur, Ross	Frank Norris
Morte D'Urban	Father Urban	J. F. Powers
Mosby's Memoirs	Mosby, Willis	Saul Bellow
The Mountain Lion	Fawcett, Ralph	Jean Stafford
The Moviegoer	Bolling, John Bickerson "Binx"	Walker Percy
The Moviegoer	Cutrer, Kate	Walker Percy
The Moving Target	Archer, Lew	Ross MacDonald
Mr. Bridge; Mrs. Bridge	Bridge, India	Evan S. Connell, Jr.
Mr. Bridge; Mrs. Bridge	Bridge, Walter	Evan S. Connell, Jr.
Mr. Sammler's Planet	Sammler, Artur	Saul Bellow
Mrs. Reynolds	Reynolds (Mrs)	Gertrude Stein
Mrs. Stevens Hears the Mermaids Singing	Stevens, F. Hilary	May Sarton
Mumbo Jumbo	LaBas, PaPa	Ishmael Reed
Mumbo Jumbo	Von Vampton, Hinckle	Ishmael Reed
"The Murders in the Rue Morgue"; "The Mystery of Marie Rogêt"; "The Purloined Letter"	Dupin, C. Auguste	Edgar Allan Poe
My Ántonia	Burden, Jimmy	Willa Cather
My Ántonia	Lingard, Lena	Willa Cather
My Ántonia	Shimerda, Ántonia	Willa Cather
"My Kinsman, Major Molineux"	Molineux, Robin	Nathaniel Hawthorne
My Life as a Man	Tarnopol, Peter	Philip Roth
My Mortal Enemy	Henshawe, Myra	Willa Cather
"My Old Man"	Butler, Joe	Ernest Hemingway
Myra Breckinridge	Breckinridge, Myra	Gore Vidal
My Sister Eileen	McKenney, Ruth	Ruth McKenney
The Mystery at the Moss-Covered Mansion	Drew, Nancy	Carolyn Keene
The Naked and the Dead	Croft, Sergeant Sam	Norman Mailer
The Naked and the Dead	Cummings, General Edward	Norman Mailer

List of Titles

The Outsider	Cross, Damon	Richard Wright
The Ox-bow Incident	Davies, Arthur	Walter Van Tilburg Clark
The Ox-bow Incident	Tetley (Major)	Walter Van Tilburg Clark
"O Yes"	Carol	Tillie Olsen
Paco's Story	Sullivan, Paco	Larry Heinemann
"The Pagan Rabbi"	Kornfeld, Rabbi Isaac	Cynthia Ozick
"The Pagan Rabbi"	Narrator	Cynthia Ozick
The Painted Bird	Narrator	Jerzy Kosinski
Pale Fire	Kinbote, Charles	Vladimir Nabokov
Pal Joey	Pal Joey	John O'Hara
Paris Trout	Seagraves, Harry	Pete Dexter
Paris Trout	Trout, Hanna	Pete Dexter
Paris Trout	Trout, Paris	Pete Dexter
Passing	Bellew, Clare Kendry	Nella Larsen
Passing	Redfield, Irene	Nella Larsen
"The Patterns of Love"	Arnold	William Maxwell
"Paul's Case"	Paul	Willa Cather
The Pawnbroker	Nazerman, Sol	Edward Lewis Wallant
"The Peach Stone"	Powers, Cleotha	Paul Horgan
The Pearl	Kino	John Steinbeck
"The Pearls of Loreto"	De la Vega y Arillaga, Don Vincente	Gertrude Atherton
"The Pedersen Kid"	Jorge	William H. Gass
Pembroke	Barnard, Charlotte	Mary Wilkins Freeman
Pembroke	Thayer, Deborah	Mary Wilkins Freeman
Penrod; Penrod and Sam; Penrod Jashber	Schofield, Penrod	Booth Tarkington
Penrod; Penrod and Sam; Penrod Jashber	Williams, Sam	Booth Tarkington
"A Perfect Day for Bananafish"; *Raise High the Roof Beam, Carpenters; Seymour: An Introduction*	Glass, Seymour	J. D. Salinger
Peyton Place	Cross, Selena	Grace Metalious
Peyton Place	MacKenzie, Allison	Grace Metalious
Pictures from an Institution	Johnson, Gertrude	Randall Jarrell
Pictures from an Institution	Morgan, Constance	Randall Jarrell
Pictures of Fidelman: An Exhibition	Fidelman, Arthur	Bernard Malamud
Pierre; or, The Ambiguities	Glendinning, Pierre	Herman Melville
"Pigeon Feathers"	Kern, David	John Updike
Pink and White Tyranny	Ellis, Lillie	Harriet Beecher Stowe
Pink and White Tyranny	Seymour, John	Harriet Beecher Stowe
Pinktoes	Mason, Mamie	Chester Himes
The Pistol	Mast, Richard	James Jones
The Pit	Jadwin, Curtis	Frank Norris
The Pit	Jadwin, Laura Dearborn	Frank Norris
Plains Song: For Female Voices	Atkins, Cora	Wright Morris
Plains Song: For Female Voices	Atkins, Sharon Rose	Wright Morris

The Planter's Northern Bride	Moreland, Eulalia Hastings "Eula"	Caroline Lee Hentz
The Planter's Northern Bride	Moreland, Russell	Caroline Lee Hentz
Play It as It Lays	Wyeth, Maria	Joan Didion
Plum Bun	Murray, Angela	Jessie Redmon Fauset
Pnin	Pnin, Timofrey Pavlovich	Vladimir Nabokov
Poor White	McVey, Hugh	Sherwood Anderson
Porgy	Bess	DuBose Heyward
Porgy	Porgy	DuBose Heyward
"The Portable Phonograph"	Jenkins (Dr.)	Walter Van Tilburg Clark
Portnoy's Complaint	Portnoy, Alexander	Philip Roth
Portnoy's Complaint	Reed, Mary Jane "the Monkey"	Philip Roth
The Portrait of a Lady	Archer, Isabel	Henry James
The Portrait of a Lady	Goodwood, Caspar	Henry James
The Portrait of a Lady	Merle, Madame Serena	Henry James
The Portrait of a Lady	Osmond, Gilbert	Henry James
The Postman Always Rings Twice	Chambers, Frank	James M. Cain
The Postman Always Rings Twice	Papadakis, Cora	James M. Cain
The Power of Sympathy; or, The Triumph of Nature	Harrington	William Hill Brown
Praisesong for the Widow	Johnson, Avatara Avey	Paule Marshall
Praisesong for the Widow	Johnson, Jerome	Paule Marshall
"A Pretty Story"	Settlers of the New Farm	Frances Hopkinson
The Princess Casamassima	Robinson, Hyacinth	Henry James
"The Prison"	Castelli, Tommy	Bernard Malamud
The Prodigal Parents	Cornplow, Hazel	Sinclair Lewis
The Prodigal Parents	Cornplow, Howard	Sinclair Lewis
The Prodigal Parents	Cornplow, Sara	Sinclair Lewis
The Prodigal Parents	Cornplow, William Fred	Sinclair Lewis
The Professor of Desire	Kepesh, David	Philip Roth
The Professor's House	St. Peter, Godfrey	Willa Cather
The Public Burning	Nixon, Dick	Robert Coover
Pudd'nhead Wilson	Driscoll, Thomas á Beckett	Samuel Clemens (Mark Twain)
Pudd'nhead Wilson	Wilson, David Pudd'nhead	Samuel Clemens (Mark Twain)
"The Pupil"	Moreen, Morgan	Henry James
"The Pupil"	Pemberton	Henry James
The Quaker City; or, The Monks of Monk-Hall	Devil-Bug	George Lippard
Queenie	Raphael, Queenie	Hortense Calisher
The Quest of the Silver Fleece	Cresswell, Mary Taylor	W.E.B. Du Bois
The Quest of the Silver Fleece	Zora	W.E.B. Du Bois
Quicksand	Crane, Helga	Nella Larsen

List of Titles

Rabbit, Run; Rabbit Redux; Rabbit Is Rich; Rabbit at Rest	Angstrom, Harry "Rabbit"	John Updike
Rabbit, Run; Rabbit Redux; Rabbit Is Rich; Rabbit at Rest	Angstrom, Janice Springer	John Updike
Ragged Dick	Ragged Dick	Horatio Alger, Jr.
Ragtime	Father	E. L. Doctorow
Ragtime	The Little Boy	E. L. Doctorow
Ragtime	Mother's Younger Brother	E. L. Doctorow
Ragtime	Tateh	E. L. Doctorow
Ragtime	Walker, Coalhouse, Jr.	E. L. Doctorow
Raintree County	Shawnessy, Esther Root	Ross Lockridge, Jr.
Raintree County	Shawnessy, John Wickliff	Ross Lockridge, Jr.
Raintree County	Shawnessy, Susannah Drake	Ross Lockridge, Jr.
Raintree County	Stiles, Jerusalem Webster	Ross Lockridge, Jr.
Raise High the Roof Beam, Carpenters; Seymour: An Introduction	Glass, Buddy	J. D. Salinger
Ramona	Ortegna, Ramona	Helen Hunt Jackson
"The Ransom of Red Chief"	Driscoll, Bill	O. Henry
"Rappaccini's Daughter"	Rappaccini, Beatrice	Nathaniel Hawthorne
The Real Cool Killers; Cotton Comes to Harlem; The Heat's On	Johnson, Coffin Ed	Chester Himes
The Real Cool Killers; The Heat's On; Cotton Comes to Harlem	Jones, Grave Digger	Chester Himes
The Real Life of Sebastian Knight	V.	Vladimir Nabokov
"The Real Thing"	Narrator	Henry James
"A Reasonable Man"	Protagonist	Ann Beattie
Rebecca of Sunnybrook Farm	Ladd, Adam	Kate Douglas Wiggin
Rebecca of Sunnybrook Farm	Randall, Rebecca	Kate Douglas Wiggin
Rebecca of Sunnybrook Farm	Sawyer, Miranda	Kate Douglas Wiggin
Recovery	Severance, Alan	John Berryman
The Red Badge of Courage	Fleming, Henry	Stephen Crane
Redburn; His First Voyage	Redburn, Wellingborough	Herman Melville
"Red Leaves"	The Negro	William Faulkner
The Red Pony	Buck, Billy	John Steinbeck
The Red Pony	Tiflin, Jody	John Steinbeck
The Reef	Darrow, George	Edith Wharton
The Reef	Leath, Anna Summers	Edith Wharton
The Reef	Viner, Sophy	Edith Wharton
Reflections in a Golden Eye	Penderton, Captain Weldon	Carson McCullers
Reflections in a Golden Eye	Penderton, Leonora	Carson McCullers

Reflections in a Golden Eye	Williams, L. G. "Ellgee"	Carson McCullers
Reflex and Bone Structure	Hull, Cora	Clarence Major
The Reivers	McCaslin, Ned William	William Faulkner
The Reivers	Priest, Lucius	William Faulkner
The Reivers; The Bear	Hogganbeck, Boon	William Faulkner
"Rejuvenation Through Joy"	Lesche, Eugene	Langston Hughes
Revolutionary Road	Wheeler, April Johnson	Richard Yates
Revolutionary Road	Wheeler, Franklin H.	Richard Yates
Richard Carvel	Carvel, Richard	Winston Churchill
"The Rich Boy"	Hunter, Anson	F. Scott Fitzgerald
Riders of the Purple Sage	Lassiter	Zane Grey
Riders of the Purple Sage	Withersteen, Jane	Zane Grey
"Rip Van Winkle"	Van Winkle, Rip	Washington Irving
The Rise of David Levinsky	Levinsky, David	Abraham Cahan
The Rise of Silas Lapham	Lapham, Silas	William Dean Howells
The Robe	Demetrius	Lloyd C. Douglas
The Robe	Gallio, Marcellus	Lloyd C. Douglas
Roger's Version	Kohler, Dale	John Updike
Roger's Version	Lambert, Roger	John Updike
"Roman Fever"	Slade, Alida	Edith Wharton
The Room	Protagonist	Hubert Selby, Jr.
"A Rose for Emily"	Grierson, Emily	William Faulkner
Rubyfruit Jungle	Bolt, Molly	Rita Mae Brown
Run River	McClellan, Everett	Joan Didion
Run River	McClellan, Lily Knight	Joan Didion
Ruth Hall	Hall, Ruth	Fannie Fern
Ryder	Ryder, Amelia de Grier	Djuna Barnes
Ryder	Ryder, Wendell	Djuna Barnes
Salome of the Tenements	Vrunsky, Sonya	Anzia Yezierska
The Salt Eaters	Ransom, Minnie	Toni Cade Bambara
The Salt Eaters	Henry, Velma	Toni Cade Bambara
Sanctuary; Requiem for a Nun	Vitelli, Popeye	William Faulkner
Sanctuary; Requiem for a Nun; The Town	Drake, Temple	William Faulkner
Sanctuary; Requiem for a Nun; The Town	Stevens, Gowan	William Faulkner
Sapphira and the Slave Girl	Blake, Rachel Colbert	Willa Cather
Sapphira and the Slave Girl	Colbert, Sapphira Dodderidge	Willa Cather
Sapphira and the Slave Girl	Till, Nancy	Willa Cather
Sartoris	Sartoris, Bayard	William Faulkner
Sassafrass Cypress & Indigo	Cypress	Ntozake Shange
Sassafrass Cypress & Indigo	Indigo	Ntozake Shange
Sassafrass Cypress & Indigo	Sassafrass	Ntozake Shange

List of Titles

Satanstoe	Littlepage, Cornelius "Corny"	James Fenimore Cooper
Satanstoe	Ten Eyck, Guert	James Fenimore Cooper
Save Me the Waltz	Knight, Alabama Beggs	Zelda Fitzgerald
The Scarlett Letter	Chillingworth, Roger	Nathaniel Hawthorne
The Scarlett Letter	Dimmesdale, Arthur	Nathaniel Hawthorne
The Scarlet Letter	Prynne, Pearl	Nathaniel Hawthorne
The Scarlet Letter	Prynne, Hester	Nathaniel Hawthorne
"Scylla, the Sea Robber"	Carter, Nick	Frederick Van Rensellaer Dey
The Sea of Grass	Brewton, James Colonel	Conrad Richter
The Sea of Grass	Brewton, Lutie Cameron	Conrad Richter
The Sea of Grass	Hal	Conrad Richter
The Sea Wolf	Larsen, Wolf	Jack London
The Sea Wolf	Van Weyden, Humphrey	Jack London
Second Skin	Skipper Edward	John Hawkes
The Secret Garden	Craven, Colin	Frances Hodgson Burnett
The Secret Garden	Lennox, Mary	Frances Hodgson Burnett
The Secret Garden	Sowerby, Dickon	Frances Hodgson Burnett
"The Secret Life of Walter Mitty"	Mitty, Walter	James Thurber
Seize the Day	Wilhelm, Tommy	Saul Bellow
Sent for You Yesterday	French, Carl	John Edgar Wideman
Sent for You Yesterday	Tate, Brother	John Edgar Wideman
Sent for You Yesterday	Tate, Lucy	John Edgar Wideman
A Separate Peace	Forrester, Gene	John Knowles
A Separate Peace	Phineas "Finny"	John Knowles
Seraph on the Suwanee	Meserve, Arvay Henson	Zora Neale Hurston
Seraph on the Suwanee	Meserve, Jim	Zora Neale Hurston
Seth Jones of New Hampshire	Jones, Seth	Edward S. Ellis
Set This House on Fire	Flagg, Mason	William Styron
Set This House on Fire	Leverett, Peter	William Styron
Shane	Shane	Jack Schaefer
"The Shawl"	Rosa	Cynthia Ozick
The Sheltered Life	Archbald, Jenny Blair	Ellen Glasgow
The Sheltered Life	Birdsong, George	Ellen Glasgow
The Sheltering Sky	Moseby, Kit	Paul Bowles
"The Sheriff's Children"	Sheriff Campbell	Charles W. Chesnutt
"Shiloh"	Moffitt, Leroy	Bobbie Ann Mason
"The Short Happy Life of Francis Macomber"	Macomber, Francis	Ernest Hemingway
Show Boat	Ravenal, Gaylord	Edna Ferber
Show Boat	Ravenal, Magnolia Hawks	Edna Ferber
A Sign for Cain	Denis	Grace Lumpkin
A Sign for Cain	Duncan, Bill	Grace Lumpkin
A Sign for Cain	Gault, Caroline	Grace Lumpkin
A Sign for Cain	Gault, Jim	Grace Lumpkin
The Silent Partner	Garth, Priscilla "Sip"	Elizabeth Stuart Phelps
The Silent Partner	Kelso, Perley	Elizabeth Stuart Phelps
"Silent Snow, Secret Snow"	Hasleman, Paul	Conrad Aiken
A Silver Dish	Selbst, Woody	Saul Bellow
Simple Speaks His Mind; Simple Takes a Wife; The Best of Simple	Semple, Jesse B. "Simple"	Langston Hughes
The Sirens of Titan	Constant, Malachi	Kurt Vonnegut, Jr.

The Sirens of Titan	Rumfoord, Beatrice	Kurt Vonnegut, Jr.
The Sirens of Titan	Rumfoord, Winston Niles	Kurt Vonnegut, Jr.
Sissie	Duncan, Sissie Peterson Joplin	John A. Williams
Sissie	Joplin, Ralph	John A. Williams
Sissie	Stapleton, Iris Joplin	John A. Williams
Sister Carrie	Drouet, Charles	Theodore Dreiser
Sister Carrie	Hurstwood, George W.	Theodore Dreiser
Sister Carrie	Meeber, Caroline "Carrie"	Theodore Dreiser
Slaughter-House Five	Pilgrim, Billy	Kurt Vonnegut, Jr.
The Slave; or, Memoirs of Archy Moore	Moore, Archy	Richard Hildreth
"The Snows of Kiliman-jaro"	Harry	Ernest Hemingway
Snow White	Snow White	Donald Barthelme
Soldiers of Fortune	Clay, Robert	Richard Harding Davis
Something Happened	Slocum, Bob	Joseph Heller
Something Wicked This Way Comes	Halloway, Charles	Ray Bradbury
Something Wicked This Way Comes	Halloway, Will	Ray Bradbury
Something Wicked This Way Comes	Nightshade, Jim	Ray Bradbury
Sometimes a Great Notion	Stamper, Hank	Ken Kesey
Sometimes a Great Notion	Stamper, Lee	Ken Kesey
Song of Solomon	Dead, Macon "Milkman"	Toni Morrison
The Song of the Lark	Archie, Howard	Willa Cather
The Song of the Lark	Kronborg, Thea	Willa Cather
The Song of the Lark	Ottenburg, Fred	Willa Cather
"Sonny's Blues"	Sonny	James Baldwin
Sophie's Choice	Landau, Nathan	William Styron
Sophie's Choice	Stingo	William Styron
Sophie's Choice	Zawistowska, Sophie	William Styron
So Red the Rose	Bedford, Sarah Tait "Aunt Sal"	Stark Young
So Red the Rose	McGehee, Hugh	Stark Young
The Sot-Weed Factor	Cooke, Ebenezer "Eben"	John Barth
The Sound and the Fury; Absalom, Absalom!	Compson, Quentin	William Faulkner
The Sound and the Fury; The Mansion	Compson, Benjamin "Benjy"	William Faulkner
The Sound and the Fury; The Mansion	Compson, Candace "Caddy"	William Faulkner
The Sound and the Fury; The Mansion	Compson, Jason	William Faulkner
The Sound and the Fury; "That Evening Sun"	Gibson, Dilsey	William Faulkner
Southern Discomfort	Banastre, Hortensia Reedmuller	Rita Mae Brown
The Spider's House	Amar	Paul Bowles
The Spider's House	Burroughs, Polly "Lee"	Paul Bowles
The Spider's House	Stenham, John	Paul Bowles
"A Spinster's Tale"	Elizabeth	Peter Taylor
The Spoils of Poynton	Gereth, Adela	Henry James
The Spoils of Poynton	Gereth, Owen	Henry James
The Spoils of Poynton	Vetch, Fleda	Henry James

List of Titles

The Sporting Club	Quinn, James	Thomas McGuane
The Sporting Club	Stanton, Vernor	Thomas McGuane
The Sport of the Gods	Hamilton, Berry	Paul Laurence Dunbar
The Sportswriter	Bascombe, Frank	Richard Ford
"Spring Evening"	George	James T. Farrell
Standing Fast	Metzger, Irwin	Harvey Swados
Standing Fast	Norman "Norm"	Harvey Swados
Steps	Narrator	Jerzy Kosinski
Stern	Stern	Bruce Jay Friedman
The Stillwater Tragedy	Shackford, Richard	Thomas Bailey Aldrich
Stop-Time	Conroy, Frank	Frank Conroy
Story of a Bad Boy	Bailey, Tom	Thomas Bailey Aldrich
The Story of Avis	Ostrander, Avis Dobell	Elizabeth Stuart Phelps
The Story of Avis	Ostrander, Philip	Elizabeth Stuart Phelps
Strange Fruit	Anderson, Nonnie	Lillian Smith
Strange Fruit	Deen, Tracy	Lillian Smith
Stranger in a Strange Land	Smith, Valentine Michael	Robert A. Heinlein
The Street	Johnson, Lutie	Ann Petry
"The Strength of God" (*Winesburg, Ohio*)	Hartman, Reverend Curtis	Sherwood Anderson
"The Strength of God"; "The Teacher" (*Winesburg, Ohio*)	Swift, Kate	Sherwood Anderson
Strike!	Deane, Ferdinand	Mary Heaton Vorse
The Subterraneans	Fox, Mardou	Jack Kerouac
The Subterraneans	Percepied, Leo	Jack Kerouac
Such Was the Season	Hicks, Annie Eliza	Clarence Major
Such Was the Season	North, Adam Juneboy	Clarence Major
Sula	Peace, Eva	Toni Morrison
Sula	Peace, Sula May	Toni Morrison
Sula	Shadrack	Toni Morrison
Sula	Wright, Nel	Toni Morrison
Summer	Harney, Lucius	Edith Wharton
Summer	Royall (Mr.)	Edith Wharton
Summer	Royall, Charity	Edith Wharton
Summer in Williamsburg	Hayman, Philip	Daniel Fuchs
Summer in Williamsburg	Papravel, Nicholas	Daniel Fuchs
A Summons to Memphis	Carver, Betsy	Peter Taylor
The Sun Also Rises	Ashley, Brett	Ernest Hemingway
The Sun Also Rises	Barnes, Jake	Ernest Hemingway
The Sun Also Rises	Cohn, Robert	Ernest Hemingway
Susan Lenox: Her Fall and Rise	Brent, Robert	David Graham Phillips
Susan Lenox: Her Fall and Rise	Lenox, Susan	David Graham Phillips
Susan Lenox: Her Fall and Rise	Spenser, Roderick	David Graham Phillips
Sut Lovingood's Yarns	Lovingood, Sut	George W. Garris
"The Swimmer"	Merrill, Ned	John Cheever
The System of Dante's Hell	Jones, LeRoi	Amiri Baraka
Tales of the South Pacific	Fry, Tony	James A. Michener
Tar: A Midwest Childhood	Moorehead, Edgar "Tar"	Sherwood Anderson

Tar Baby	Childs, Jadine	Toni Morrison
Tar Baby	Son	Toni Morrison
Tar Baby	Street, Margaret	Toni Morrison
Tarzan of the Apes	Porter, Jane	Edgar Rice Burroughs
Tarzan of the Apes	Tarzan	Edgar Rice Burroughs
"Tell Me a Riddle"	David	Tillie Olsen
"Tell Me a Riddle"	Eva	Tillie Olsen
Tell Me How Long the Train's Been Gone	Proudhammer, Caleb	James Baldwin
Tell Me How Long the Train's Been Gone	Proudhammer, Leo	James Baldwin
"The Tell-Tale Heart"	Narrator	Edgar Allan Poe
The Tenants	Lesser, Harry	Bernard Malamud
The Tenants of Moonbloom	Moonbloom, Norman	Edward Lewis Wallant
Tender Is the Night	Diver, Dr. Richard "Dick"	F. Scott Fitzgerald
Tender Is the Night	Diver, Nicole Warren	F. Scott Fitzgerald
Tender Is the Night	Hoyt, Rosemary	F. Scott Fitzgerald
"Tennessee's Partner"	Protagonist	Bret Harte
Ten Nights in a Bar-Room, and What I Saw There	Slade, Simon	Timothy Shay Arthur
The Terrible Threes	Jones, Reverend Clement	Ishmael Reed
"That Evening Sun"	Nancy	William Faulkner
Their Eyes Were Watching God	Crawford, Janie Mae	Zora Neale Hurston
Their Eyes Were Watching God	Starks, Joe "Jody"	Zora Neale Hurston
Their Eyes Were Watching God	Woods, Vergible "Tea Cake"	Zora Neale Hurston
Their Wedding Journey; A Hazard of New Fortunes	March, Basil	William Dean Howells
Their Wedding Journey; A Hazard of New Fortunes	March, Isabel	William Dean Howells
Them	Wendall, Jules	Joyce Carol Oates
Them	Wendall, Loretta	Joyce Carol Oates
Them	Wendall, Maureen	Joyce Carol Oates
Theophilus North	North, Theophilus	Thornton Wilder
Therefore Be Bold	Berman, Daniel	Herbert Gold
There Is Confusion	Marshall, Joanna	Jessie Redmon Fauset
They Came Like Swallows	Morison, Peter "Bunny"	William Maxwell
Thieves Like Us	Bowers, Bowie A.	Edward Anderson
The Things They Carried	O'Brien, Tim	Tim O'Brien
The Thin Man	Charles, Nick	Dashiell Hammett
The Thin Man	Charles, Nora	Dashiell Hammett
The Third Life of Grange Copeland	Copeland, Brownfield	Alice Walker
The Third Life of Grange Copeland	Copeland, Grange	Alice Walker
The Third Life of Grange Copeland	Copeland, Mem	Alice Walker
This Child's Gonna Live	Upshur, Mariah	Sarah E. Wright

List of Titles

"This Morning, This Evening, So Soon"	Narrator	James Baldwin
This Side of Paradise	Blaine, Amory	F. Scott Fitzgerald
Three Lives	Federner, Anna	Gertrude Stein
Three Lives	Herbert, Melanctha	Gertrude Stein
Three Lives	Mainz, Lena	Gertrude Stein
Three Soldiers	Andrews, John	John Dos Passos
Three Soldiers	Chrisfield, Chris	John Dos Passos
Three Soldiers	Fuselli, Dan	John Dos Passos
The Time of Man	Chesser, Ellen	Elizabeth Madox Roberts
Tobacco Road	Lester, Jeeter	Erskine Caldwell
"To Build a Fire"	Protagonist	Jack London
To Kill a Mockingbird	Finch, Atticus	Harper Lee
To Kill a Mockingbird	Finch, Jean Louise "Scout"	Harper Lee
To Kill a Mockingbird	Finch, Jem	Harper Lee
To Make My Bread	Kirkland, John	Grace Lumpkin
Tommy Gallagher's Crusade	Gallagher, Tommy	James T. Farrell
Tom Swift and His Electric Runabout, or, The Speediest Car on the Road	Swift, Tom	Victor Appleton
"A Tooth for Paul Revere"	Butterwick, Lige	Stephen Vincent Benét
"Torch Song"	Harris, Joan	John Cheever
The Tower Treasure	Hardy, Frank and Joe	Franklin W. Dixon
The Town and the City	Martin, George	Jack Kerouac
The Town and the City	Martin, Peter	Jack Kerouac
The Track of the Cat	Bridges, Harold "Hal"	Walter Van Tilburg Clark
Tracks	Nanapush	Louise Erdrich
Tracks	Pillager, Fleur	Louise Erdrich
The Tragedy of Pudd'nhead Wilson	Roxana	Samuel Clemens (Mark Twain)
The Tragic Muse	Dormer, Nicholas	Henry James
The Tragic Muse	Rooth, Miriam	Henry James
The Tragic Muse	Sherringham, Peter	Henry James
A Traveler from Altruria; Through the Eye of the Needle	Homos, Aristides	William Dean Howells
"A Tree * A Rock * A Cloud"	Protagonist	Carson McCullers
A Tree Grows in Brooklyn	Nolan, Frances "Francie"	Betty Smith
Tripmaster Monkey: His Fake Book	Ah Sing, Wittman	Maxine Hong Kingston
Tropic of Cancer	Miller, Henry	Henry Miller
Trouble in July	McCurtain, Jeff	Erskine Caldwell
Trout Fishing in America	Narrator	Richard Brautigan
The Turn of the Balance	Marriott, Gordon	Brand Whitlock
The Turn of the Balance	Ward, Elizabeth	Brand Whitlock
The Turn of the Screw	The Governess	Henry James
Two Serious Ladies	Goering, Christina	Jane Bowles

Typee; A Peep at Polynesian Life; Omoo; A Narrative of Adventure in the South Seas	Narrator	Herman Melville
U.S.A. (The 42nd Parallel; Nineteen Nineteen; The Big Money)	Anderson, Charley	John Dos Passos
U.S.A. (The 42nd Parallel; Nineteen Nineteen; The Big Money)	Dowling, Margo	John Dos Passos
U.S.A. (The 42nd Parallel; Nineteen Nineteen; The Big Money)	French, Mary	John Dos Passos
U.S.A. (The 42nd Parallel; Nineteen Nineteen; The Big Money)	Hutchins, Eveline	John Dos Passos
U.S.A. (The 42nd Parallel; Nineteen Nineteen; The Big Money)	McCreary, Fenian "Mac"	John Dos Passos
U.S.A. (The 42nd Parallel; Nineteen Nineteen; The Big Money)	Moorehouse, John Ward	John Dos Passos
U.S.A. (The 42nd Parallel; Nineteen Nineteen; The Big Money)	Savage, Richard Ellsworth "Dick"	John Dos Passos
U.S.A. (The 42nd Parallel; Nineteen Nineteen; The Big Money)	Stoddard, Eleanor	John Dos Passos
U.S.A. (The 42nd Parallel; Nineteen Nineteen; The Big Money)	Trent, Anne Elizabeth "Daughter"	John Dos Passos
Uncle Remus	Uncle Remus	Joel Chandler Harris
Uncle Tom's Cabin or, *Life Among the Lowly*	Legree, Simon	Harriet Beecher Stowe
Uncle Tom's Cabin or, *Life Among the Lowly*	St. Clare, Evangeline "Eva"	Harriet Beecher Stowe
Uncle Tom's Cabin or, *Life Among the Lowly*	Topsy	Harriet Beecher Stowe
Uncle Tom's Cabin or, *Life Among the Lowly*	Uncle Tom	Harriet Beecher Stowe
"Under the Lions Paw"	Haskins, Timothy	Hamlin Garland
Union Square	Fisher, Leon	Albert Halper
Union Square	Wheeler, Jason	Albert Halper
The Universal Baseball Association, Inc.	Waugh, J. Henry	Robert Coover
The Unpossessed	Flinders, Margaret "Maggie"	Tess Slesinger
The Unpossessed	Leonard, Bruno	Tess Slesinger
"The Use of Force"	Narrator	William Carlos Williams
V	Profane, Benny	Thomas Pynchon
"The Valiant Woman"	Firman, Father John	J. F. Powers
Vandover and the Brute	Vandover	Frank Norris
Vanishing Rooms	Durand, Jesse	Melvin Dixon

List of Titles

Vanishing Rooms	McPhee, Ruella	Melvin Dixon
The Velvet Horn	Cree, Lucius	Andrew Lytle
"Venus, Cupid, Folly and Time"	Dorset, Louisa	Peter Taylor
The Victim	Leventhal, Asa	Saul Bellow
"Views of My Father Weeping"	Narrator	Donald Barthelme
Vineland	Chastain, DL	Thomas Pynchon
Vineland	Gates, Frenesi	Thomas Pynchon
The Violated	Beniger, Thomas	Vance Bourjaily
The Violated	Bissle, Edward	Vance Bourjaily
The Violent Bear It Away	Tarwater, Francis Marion	Flannery O'Connor
The Virginian; A Horseman of the Plains	Stark, Mary Molly	Owen Wister
The Virginian; A Horseman of the Plains	The Virginian	Owen Wister
"A Visit from the Footbinder"	Pleasure Mouse	Emily Prager
The Voice at the Back Door	Harper, Duncan	Elizabeth Spencer
Waiting for Nothing	Kromer, Thomas	Tom Kromer
"Wakefield"	Wakefield	Nathaniel Hawthorne
A Walk in the Sun	Tyne, William	Harry Brown
A Walk on the Wild Side	Linkhorn, Dove	Nelson Algren
The Walls of Jericho	Jones, Joshua Shine	Rudolph Fisher
The Walls of Jericho	Patmore, Henry	Rudolph Fisher
The Wapshot Chronicle; The Wapshot Scandal	Wapshot, Coverly	John Cheever
The Wapshot Chronicle; The Wapshot Scandal	Wapshot, Honora	John Cheever
The Wapshot Chronicle; The Wapshot Scandal	Scaddon, Leander	John Cheever
The Wapshot Chronicle; The Wapshot Scandal	Wapshot, Melissa Scanlon	John Cheever
The Wapshot Chronicle; The Wapshot Scandal	Wapshot, Moses	John Cheever
The Warriors	Hector	Sol Yurick
Washington Square	Sloper, Catherine	Henry James
Watch and Ward	Lambert, Nora	Henry James
Watch and Ward	Lawrence, Roger	Henry James
The Wayward Bus	Chicoy, Juan	John Steinbeck
The Wayward Bus	Carson, Edward "Pimples"	John Steinbeck
The Way We Live Now	Protagonist	Susan Sontag
"The Web of Circumstance"	Davis, Ben	Charles W. Chesnutt
"The Wedding: Beacon Hill"	Hopestill	Jean Stafford
Weeds	Blackford, Judith	Edith Summers Kelley
We Have Always Lived in the Castle	Blackwood, Mary Katherine "Merricat"	Shirley Jackson
Welcome to the Monkey House	McLuhan, Nancy	Kurt Vonnegut, Jr.
"What Every Boy Should Know"	Gellert, Edward	William Maxwell

Woman on the Edge of Time	Luciente	Marge Piercy
Woman on the Edge of Time	Ramos, Connie Comacho	Marge Piercy
The Woman Warrior: Memoirs of a Girlhood Among Ghosts	Brave Orchid	Maxine Hong Kingston
The Woman Who Owned the Shadows	Atencio, Ephanie	Paula Gunn Allen
The Women of Brewster Place	Michael, Mattie	Gloria Naylor
The Women on the Porch	Chapman, Catherine Lewis	Caroline Gordon
The Women's Room	Ward, Mira	Marilyn French
The Wonderful Wizard of Oz	Cowardly Lion	L. Frank Baum
The Wonderful Wizard of Oz	Dorothy	L. Frank Baum
The Wonderful Wizard of Oz	Scarecrow	L. Frank Baum
The Wonderful Wizard of Oz	Tin Woodman	L. Frank Baum
The Wonderful Wizard of Oz	Wizard of Oz	L. Frank Baum
Wonderland	Monk, Talbot Waller "Trick"	Joyce Carol Oates
Wonderland	Pedersen, Dr. Karl	Joyce Carol Oates
Wonderland	Vogel, Jesse	Joyce Carol Oates
Woodcraft	Porgy, Captain	William Gilmore Simms
"Woolen Drawers"	Ochs, Alice	William March
Work	Devon, Christie	Louisa May Alcott
Work	Fletcher, Phillip	Louisa May Alcott
Work	Sterling, David	Louisa May Alcott
Work	Sterling, Rachel	Louisa May Alcott
The World According to Garp	Garp, T. S.	John Irving
A World I Never Made; No Star Is Lost; Father and Son; My Days of Anger; The Face of Time	O'Neill, Danny	James T. Farrell
"The World of Apples"	Bascomb, Asa	John Cheever
World's Fair	Altschuler, Edgar	E. L. Doctorow
"A Worn Path"	Jackson, Phoenix	Eudora Welty
A Wrinkle in Time; A Wind in the Door; A Swiftly Tilting Planet	Murry, Meg	Madeleine L'Engle
Wunderkind	Baxter, Jody	Carson McCullers
The Yearling	Baxter, Ora	Marjorie Kinnan Rawlings
The Yearling	Baxter, Penny	Marjorie Kinnan Rawlings
The Yearling	Frances	Marjorie Kinnan Rawlings
Yekl	Podkovnik, Yekl "Jake"	Abraham Cahan
"The Yellow Wallpaper"	Narrator	Charlotte Perkins Gilman
"Yellow Woman"	Narrator	Leslie Marmon Silko
The Yemassee: A Romance of Carolina	Craven, Charles	William Gilmore Simms

The Yemassee: A Romance of Carolina	Sanutee	William Gilmore Simms
Yonnondio: From the Thirties	Holbrook, Anna	Tillie Olsen
You Can't Go Home Again	Edwards, Foxhall "Fox"	Thomas Wolfe
You Can't Go Home Again	Jack, Esther	Thomas Wolfe
You Can't Go Home Again	Webber, George	Thomas Wolfe
You Know Me Al: A Busher's Letters	Keefe, John Jack	Ring Lardner
Youngblood	Youngblood, Joseph	John Oliver Killens
Youngblood	Youngblood, Laurie Lee Barksdale	John Oliver Killens
Youngblood	Youngblood, Robert "Robby"	John Oliver Killens
"Young Goodman Brown"	Brown, Young Goodman	Nathaniel Hawthorne
The Young Lions	Ackerman, Noah	Irwin Shaw
The Young Lions	Diestl, Christian	Irwin Shaw
The Young Lions	Whitacre, Michael	Irwin Shaw
Young Lonigan: A Boyhood in Chicago Streets; The Young Manhood of Studs Lonigan; Judgment Day	Lonigan, William "Studs"	James T. Farrell
"You Were Perfectly Fine"	Peter	Dorothy Parker
Zury: The Meanest Man in Spring County	Prouder, Usury "Zury"	Joseph Kirkland

List of Characters' Alternate Names

Ab	Snopes, Abner	"Barn Burning"; *The Hamlet*
Aunt Sal	Strange, Sarah	*The Chinaberry Tree*
Avey	Johnson, Avatara	*Praisesong for the Widow*
Banjo	Daily, Lincoln Agrippa	*Banjo: A Story Without a Plot*
Beaut	McGregor, Norman	*Marching Men*
Benjy	Compson, Benjamin	*The Sound and the Fury; The Mansion*
Bick	Benedict, Jordan	*Giant*
Big Bluff	Tosamah, John	*House Made of Dawn*
Binx	Bolling, John Bickerson	*The Moviegoer*
Bo	Mason, Harry	*The Big Rock Candy Mountain*
Bobby	Merrick, Robert	*Magnificent Obsession*
Bocksfuss, Billy	Giles	*Giles Goat-Boy*
Boy	Oelsligle, Kermit	*Fire Sermon*
Brad	Bradley, James	"Duel with the Clock"
Bunny	Morison, Peter	*They Came Like Swallows*
Bus	Beal, General Ira	*Guard of Honor*
Caddy	Compson, Candace	*The Sound and the Fury; The Mansion*
Callie	Wells, Calliope	*Nickel Mountain*
Cap	Le Noir, Capitola	*The Hidden Hand: Or, Capitola the Madcap*
Carrie	Meeber, Caroline	*Sister Carrie*
Ceddie	Errol, Cedric	*Little Lord Fauntleroy*
Cocoa	Day, Ophelia	*Mama Day*
Corny	Littlepage, Cornelius	*Satanstoe*
Dan'l	Webster, Daniel	"The Devil and Daniel Webster"
Daughter	Trent, Anne Elizabeth	*U.S.A. (Nineteen Nineteen)*
Deerslayer	Bumppo, Nathaniel	*The Leatherstocking Tales*
Dell	Espinoza, Lorenzo Delgado	*Afterlife*
Demi	Brooke, John	*Little Men*
Dick	Diver, Dr. Richard	*Tender Is the Night*
Diddy	Harron, Dalton	*Death Kit*
Disher, Max	Fisher, Matthew	*Black No More*
Dobie	Dobrejcak	*Out of This Furnace*
Dot	Adare, Wallacette Darlene	*Love Medicine; The Beet Queen*
Eben	Cooke, Ebenezer	*The Sot-Weed Factor*
E.I.	Lonoff, Emanuel Isidore	*The Ghost Writer*
Ellgee	Williams, L. G.	*Reflections in a Golden Eye*
Eula	Moreland, Eulalia Hastings	*The Planter's Northern Bride*
Eva	St. Clare, Evangeline	*Uncle Tom's Cabin*
Ex	Exely, Frederick	*A Fan's Notes*
Fer	Deane, Ferdinand	*Strike!*
Finny	Phineas	*A Separate Peace*
F.K.	Jackson, Frances	*The Narrows*
Fox	Edwards, Foxhall	*You Can't Go Home Again*
Francie	Nolan, Frances	*A Tree Grows in Brooklyn*
Franny	Glass, Frances	*Franny and Zooey*

Fred	Cornplow, William	*The Prodigal Parents*
Gay	Coleman, Gaillard	*Imperial City*
Glory	Roane, Gloria	*Country Place*
Hal	Bridges, Harold	*The Track of the Cat*
Hank	Chinaski, Henry	*Ham on Rye*
Harry	Bogen, Heshalle	*I Can Get It for You Wholesale*
Harry	Elkins, Harrell	*Andersonville*
Harry	Shawmut, Herschel	*"Him with His Foot in His Mouth"*
Hawkeye	Bumppo, Nathaniel	*The Leatherstocking Tales*
Haze	Motes, Hazel	*Wise Blood*
Ike	McCaslin, Isaac	*"The Bear"; "Delta Autumn"*
Indian John	Chingachgook	*The Leatherstocking Tales*
Jack	Keefe, John	*You Know Me, Al: A Busher's Letters*
Jake	Brown, Jacob	*Home to Harlem*
Jake	Podkovnik, Yekl	*Yekl*
Japhy	Ryder, Japheth	*The Dharma Bums*
Jay	Johnson, Jerome	*Praisesong for the Widow*
Jeff	Durgin, Thomas Jefferson	*The Landlord at Lion's Head*
Jick	McCaskill, John Angus	*English Creek; Ride with Me, Mariah Montana*
Jimmy	Monroe, James Buchannan	*Cast the First Stone*
Jinx	Fairchild, Verlyn Rayburn	*Because It Is Bitter, and Because It Is My Heart*
Jo	March, Josephine	*Little Women*
Jody	Starks, Joe	*Their Eyes Were Watching God*
Judd	Steiner, Judah	*Compulsion*
Juneboy	North, Adam	*Such Was the Season*
Lakey	Eastlake, Elinor	*The Group*
La Longue Carabine	Bumppo, Nathaniel	*The Leatherstocking Tales*
Lana	Martin, Magdelana Borst	*Drums Along the Mohawk*
Laurie	Laurence, Theodore	*Little Women*
Lee	Burroughs, Polly	*The Spider's House*
Lefty	Bicek, Bruno	*Never Come Morning*
Le Gros Serpent	Chingachgook	*The Leatherstocking Tales*
Lewin, Daniel	Isaacson, Daniel	*The Book of Daniel*
Lewin, Susan	Isaacson, Susan	*The Book of Daniel*
Libby	MacAusland, Elizabeth	*The Group*
Lieutenant	Duffy, Jack	*The Foundry*
Link	Williams, Lincoln	*The Narrows*
Little Cheese	Quesadilla, Hector	*"The Hector Quesadilla Story"*
Littleman	Hall, Willie	*The Lynchers*
Lolita	Haze, Delores	*Lolita*
Mac	MacLeod	*In Dubious Battle*
Mac	McCreary, Fenian	*U.S.A. (The 42nd Parallel)*
Maggie	Flinders, Margaret	*The Unpossessed*
Mama Day	Day, Miranda	*Mama Day*
Marky	Marker, Little Miss	*"Little Miss Marker"*
Meg	March, Margaret	*Little Women*
Merricat	Blackwood, Mary Katherine	*We Have Always Lived in the Castle*
Milkman	Dead, Macon	*Song of Solomon*
Mister	Albert	*The Color Purple*
Molly	Stakr, Mary	*The Virginian: A Horseman of the Plains*

List of Characters' Alternate Names

Monty	Beragon, Montgomery	*Mildred Pierce*
Nan	Harding, Anne	*Little Men*
Nat	Black, Nathaniel	*Little Men*
Natty	Bumppo, Nathaniel	*The Leatherstocking Tales*
Norm	Norman	*Standing Fast*
Ozzie	Freedman, Oscar	"The Conversion of the Jews"
Pathfinder	Bumppo, Nathaniel	*The Leatherstocking Tales*
Pimples	Carson, Edward	*The Wayward Bus*
Pokey	Prothero, Mary	*The Group*
Prew	Prewitt, Robert E. Lee	*From Here to Eternity*
Pudd'nhead	Wilson, David	*Pudd'nhead Wilson*
Rabbit	Angstrom, Harry	*Rabbit, Run;* and other works
Rick	Deckard, Richard	*Do Androids Dream of Electric Sheep?*
Sagamore	Chingachgook	*The Leatherstocking Tales*
Sallie	Bedford, Sarah Tait	*So Red the Rose*
Sam	Hughes, Samantha	*In Country*
Sammy	Scott, Samuel	*Dark Princess: A Romance*
Sandy	Rodgers, James	*Not Without Laughter*
Sarty	Snopes, Colonel Sartoris	"Barn Burning"; *The Hamlet*
Scout	Finch, Jean Louise	*To Kill a Mockingbird*
Seldom Seen	Smith, Joseph Fielding	*The Monkey Wrench Gang*
Shine	Jones, Joshua	*The Walls of Jericho*
Simple	Semple, Jesse B.	*Simple Speaks His Mind;* and other works
Sip	Garth, Priscilla	*The Silent Partner*
Sister Leopolda	Puyat, Pauline	*Love Medicine; Tracks*
Skinner	Galt, Thomas	*The End of My Life*
Solly	Saunders, Solomon, Jr.	*And Then We Heard the Thunder*
Studs	Lonigan, William	*Young Lonigan;* and other works
Tar	Moorehead, Edgar	*Tar: A Midwest Childhood*
Tea Cake	Woods, Vergible	*Their Eyes Were Watching God*
Tiger	Miller, Justin	*The Origin of the Brunists*
Tish	Rivers, Clementine	*If Beale Street Could Talk*
Trick	Monk, Talbot Waller	*Wonderland*
Van	Jennings, Vandyk	*Herland, and with Her in Ourland*
Vyry	Brown, Elvira Dutton	*Jubilee*
White	Mason, Willie	*Linden Hills*
White Man's Dog	Fools Crow	*Fools Crow*
Wilt	Tobin, Wiltshire	*Monday Night*
Win	Berry, Winslow	*The Hotel New Hampshire*
Win	Everett, Walter, Jr.	*Libra*
Zenna	Frome, Zenobia Pierce	*Ethan Frome*
Zooey	Glass, Zachery Martin	*Franny and Zooey*
Zury	Prouder, Usury	*Zury: The Meanest Man in Spring County*